Geometry

Timothy D. Kanold

Edward B. Burger

Juli K. Dixon

Matthew R. Larson

Steven J. Leinwand

Printed in the U.S.A.

ISBN 978-1-328-90003-6

3 4 5 6 7 8 9 10 0868 26 25 24 23 22 21 20 19 18

4500712737 A B C D E F G H

Authors

Timothy D. Kanold, Ph.D., is an award-winning international educator, author, and consultant. He is a former superintendent and director of mathematics and science at Adlai E. Stevenson High School District 125 in Lincolnshire, Illinois. He is a past president of the National Council of Supervisors of Mathematics (NCSM) and the Council for the Presidential Awardees of Mathematics (CPAM). He has served on several writing and leadership commissions for NCTM during the past decade. He presents motivational professional development seminars with a focus on developing professional learning communities (PLC's) to improve the teaching, assessing, and learning of students. He has recently authored nationally recognized articles, books, and textbooks for mathematics education and school leadership, including *What Every Principal Needs to Know about the Teaching and Learning of Mathematics*.

Edward B. Burger, Ph.D., is the President of Southwestern University, a former Francis Christopher Oakley Third Century Professor of Mathematics at Williams College, and a former vice provost at Baylor University. He has authored or coauthored more than sixty-five articles, books, and video series; delivered over five hundred addresses and workshops throughout the world; and made more than fifty radio and television appearances. He is a Fellow of the American Mathematical Society as well as having earned many national honors, including the Robert Foster Cherry Award for Great Teaching in 2010. In 2012, Microsoft Education named him a "Global Hero in Education."

Juli K. Dixon, Ph.D., is a Professor of Mathematics Education at the University of Central Florida. She has taught mathematics in urban schools at the elementary, middle, secondary, and post-secondary levels. She is an active researcher and speaker with numerous publications and conference presentations. Key areas of focus are deepening teachers' content knowledge and communicating and justifying mathematical ideas. She is a past chair of the NCTM Student Explorations in Mathematics Editorial Panel and member of the Board of Directors for the Association of Mathematics Teacher Educators.

Matthew R. Larson, Ph.D., is the K-12 mathematics curriculum specialist for the Lincoln Public Schools and served on the Board of Directors for the National Council of Teachers of Mathematics from 2010 to 2013. He is a past chair of NCTM's Research Committee and was a member of NCTM's Task Force on Linking Research and Practice. He is the author of several books on implementing the Common Core Standards for Mathematics. He has taught mathematics at the secondary and college levels and held an appointment as an honorary visiting associate professor at Teachers College, Columbia University.

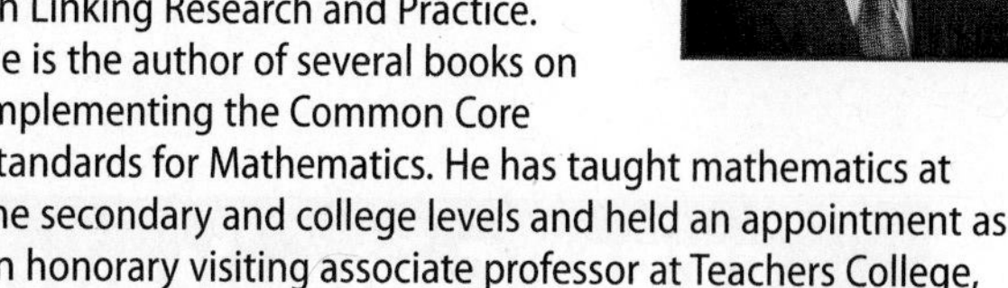

Steven J. Leinwand is a Principal Research Analyst at the American Institutes for Research (AIR) in Washington, D.C., and has over 30 years in leadership positions in mathematics education. He is past president of the National Council of Supervisors of Mathematics and served on the NCTM Board of Directors. He is the author of numerous articles, books, and textbooks and has made countless presentations with topics including student achievement, reasoning, effective assessment, and successful implementation of standards.

Performance Task Consultant

Robert Kaplinsky
Teacher Specialist, Mathematics
Downey Unified School District
Downey, California

STEM Consultants

Science, Technology, Engineering, and Mathematics

Michael A. DiSpezio
Global Educator
North Falmouth, Massachusetts

Michael R. Heithaus
Executive Director, School of Environment, Arts, and Society
Professor, Department of Biological Sciences
Florida International University
North Miami, Florida

Reviewers

Mindy Eden
Richwoods High School
Peoria School District
Peoria, IL

Dustin Johnson
Badger High School Math Teacher
Department Chair
Lake Geneva-Genoa City Union High School District
Lake Geneva, WI

Ashley D. McSwain
Murray High School
Murray City School District
Salt Lake City, UT

Rebecca Quinn
Doherty Memorial High School
Worcester Public Schools District
Worcester, MA

Ted Ryan
Madison LaFollette High School
Madison Metropolitan School District
Madison, WI

Tony Scoles
Fort Zumwalt School District
O'Fallon, MO

Cynthia L. Smith
Higley Unified School District
Gilbert, AZ

Phillip E. Spellane
Doherty Memorial High School
Worcester Public Schools District
Worcester, MA

Mona Toncheff
Math Content Specialist
Phoenix Union High School District
Phoenix, AZ

Transformations and Congruence

MODULE 1 Tools of Geometry

MODULE 2 Transformations and Symmetry

Congruent Figures

Lines, Angles, and Triangles

UNIT 2

MODULE 4 Lines and Angles

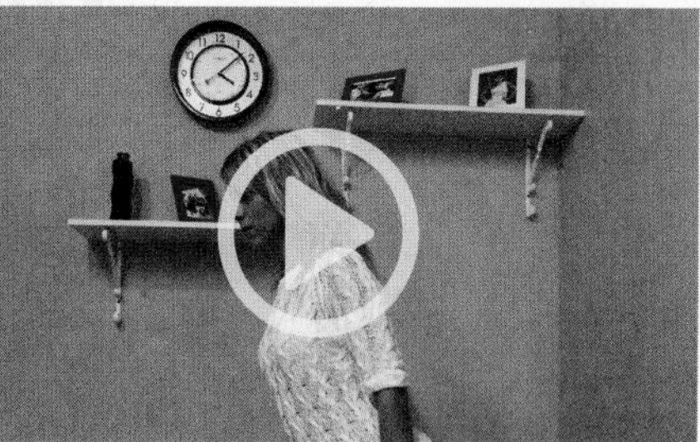

MODULE 5 Triangle Congruence Criteria

Applications of Triangle Congruence

Properties of Triangles

Special Segments in Triangles

UNIT 3 Quadrilaterals and Coordinate Proof

MODULE 9 Properties of Quadrilaterals

MODULE 10 Coordinate Proof Using Slope and Distance

Similarity

UNIT 4

Similarity and Transformations

Using Similar Triangles

Trigonometry

Trigonometry with Right Triangles

Trigonometry with All Triangles

Properties of Circles

MODULE 15 Angles and Segments in Circles

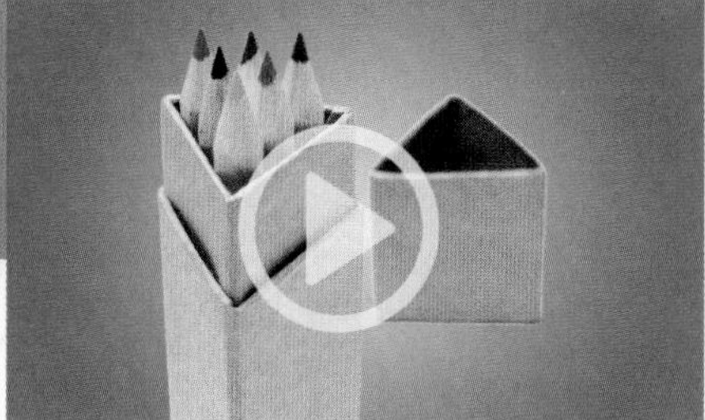

MODULE 16 Arc Length and Sector Area

MODULE 17 Equations of Circles and Parabolas

Measurement and Modeling in Two and Three Dimensions

MODULE 18 Volume Formulas

MODULE 19 Visualizing Solids

Modeling and Problem Solving

Probability

Introduction to Probability

Conditional Probability and Independence of Events

Probability and Decision Making

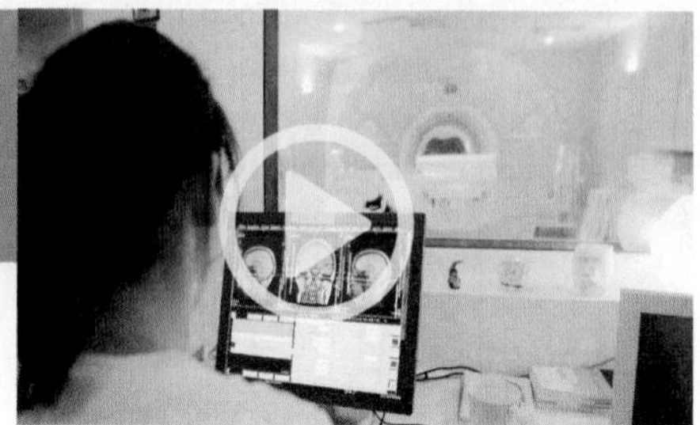

Contents of Student Edition Resources

UNIT 1

Transformations and Congruence

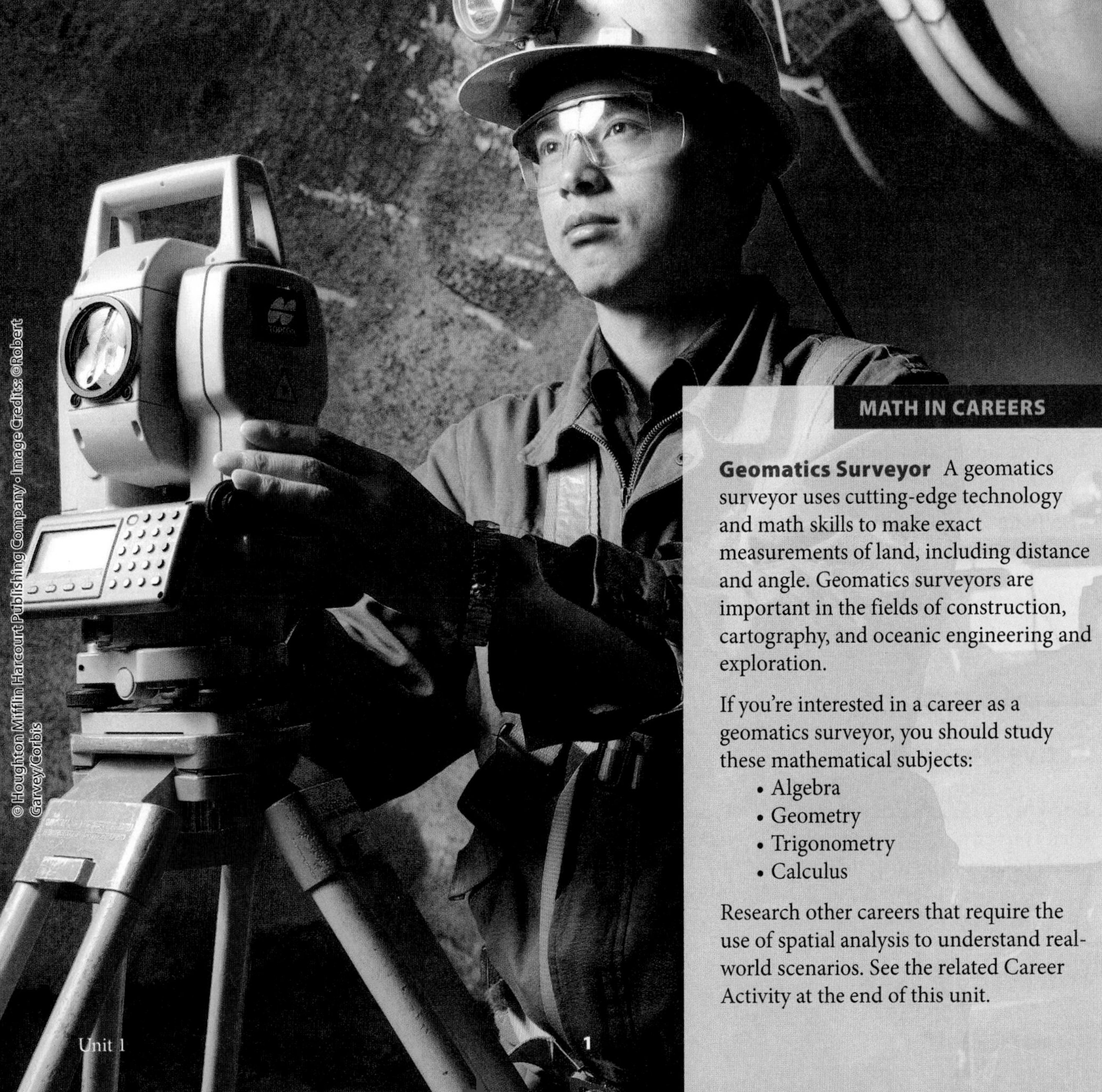

MATH IN CAREERS

Geomatics Surveyor A geomatics surveyor uses cutting-edge technology and math skills to make exact measurements of land, including distance and angle. Geomatics surveyors are important in the fields of construction, cartography, and oceanic engineering and exploration.

If you're interested in a career as a geomatics surveyor, you should study these mathematical subjects:

- Algebra
- Geometry
- Trigonometry
- Calculus

Research other careers that require the use of spatial analysis to understand real-world scenarios. See the related Career Activity at the end of this unit.

Vocabulary

Review Words

✔ midpoint *(punto medio)*
✔ angle *(ángulo)*
✔ transformation *(transformación)*
✔ complementary angle *(ángulo complementario)*
✔ supplementary angle *(ángulo suplementario)*
✔ acute angle *(ángulo agudo)*
✔ obtuse angle *(ángulo obtuso)*

Preview Words

angle bisector *(bisectriz de un ángulo)*
vertex *(vértice)*
collinear *(colineales)*
postulate *(postulado)*

Visualize Vocabulary

Copy the chart and use the ✔ words to complete it. You may put more than one word in each box.

Angle	Description	Example	?	?
?	Angle whose measure is less than 90°	40°	50°	140°
?	Angle whose measure is greater than 90°	110°	None	70°

Understand Vocabulary

Complete the sentences using the preview words.

1. A(n) __?__ is a ray that divides an angle into two angles that both have the same measure.

2. The common endpoint of two rays that form an angle is the __?__ of the angle.

3. Points that lie on the same line are __?__ .

Active Reading

Booklet Before beginning each module, create a booklet to help you organize what you learn. As you study each lesson, draw the different graphical concepts that you learn and write their definitions.

Tools of Geometry

MODULE 1

Essential Question: How can you use the tools of geometry to solve real-world problems?

REAL WORLD VIDEO
Check out how the tools of geometry can be used to solve real-world problems, like planning a park fountain's location to be the same distance from the park's three entrances.

MODULE PERFORMANCE TASK PREVIEW

How Far Is It?

How does your cellphone know how far away the nearest restaurant is? In this module, you'll explore how apps and search engines use GPS coordinates to calculate distances. So enter your present location and let's find out!

Are YOU Ready?

Complete these exercises to review skills you will need for this module.

Personal Math Trainer

- Online Homework
- Hints and Help
- Extra Practice

Algebraic Representations of Transformations

Example 1 Shift $y = \sqrt{x}$ horizontally 2 units to the right.

$(0, 0)$ to $(2, 0)$ Write the starting point and its transformation.

$y - 0 = \sqrt{x - 2}$ Use the transformed point to write the equation.

$y = \sqrt{x - 2}$ Simplify.

Transform the equations.

1. Shift $y = 5x$ 3 units up.

2. Stretch $y = 5x$ vertically about the fixed x-axis by a factor of 2.

3. Shift $y = 5\sqrt{x} + 3$ horizontally 2 units to the right and stretch by a factor of 3. (Stretch vertically about the fixed $y = 3$ line.)

Angle Relationships

Example 2 Find the angle complementary to the given angle, 75°.

$x + 75° = 90°$ Write as an equation.

$x = 90° - 75°$ Solve for x.

$x = 15°$

Find the complementary angle.

4. 20°

5. 35°

6. 67°

Find the supplementary angle.

7. 80°

8. 65°

9. 34°

Distance and Midpoint Formulas

Example 3 Find the distance between $(2, 3)$ and $(5, 7)$.

$\sqrt{(5-2)^2 + (7-3)^2}$ Apply the distance formula.

$= \sqrt{9 + 16}$ Simplify each square.

$= 5$ Add and find the square root.

Find the distance and midpoint for each pair of given points.

10. The points $(6, 14)$ and $(1, 2)$

11. The points $(4, 6)$ and $(19, 14)$

1.1 Segment Length and Midpoints

Essential Question: How do you draw a segment and measure its length?

Resource Locker

Explore — Exploring Basic Geometric Terms

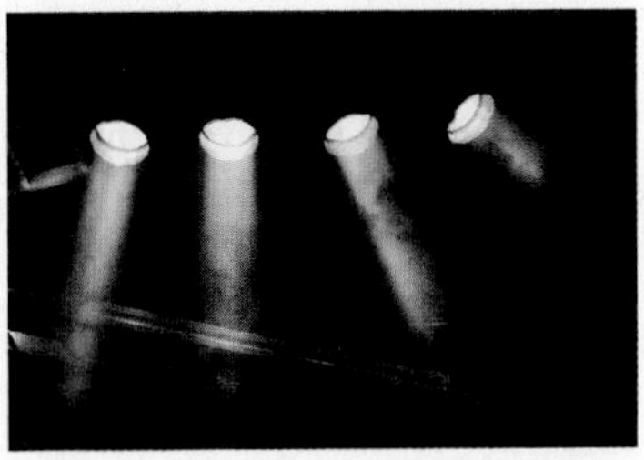

In geometry, some of the names of figures and other terms will already be familiar from everyday life. For example, a *ray* like a beam of light from a spotlight is both a familiar word and a geometric figure with a mathematical definition.

The most basic figures in geometry are *undefined terms*, which cannot be defined using other figures. The terms *point*, *line*, and *plane* are undefined terms. Although they do not have formal definitions, they can be described as shown in the table.

Undefined Terms

Term	Geometric Figure	Ways to Name the Figure
A **point** is a specific location. It has no dimension and is represented by a dot.	• *P*	point *P*
A **line** is a connected straight path. It has no thickness and it continues forever in both directions.	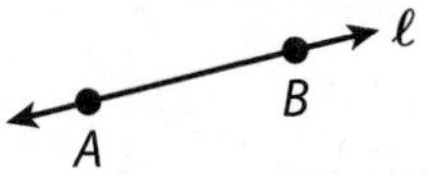	line ℓ, line *AB*, line *BA*, $\overleftrightarrow{AB}$, or $\overleftrightarrow{BA}$
A **plane** is a flat surface. It has no thickness and it extends forever in all directions.	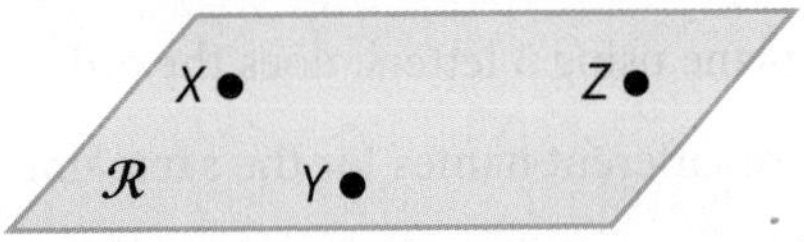	plane ℛ or plane *XYZ*

In geometry, the word *between* is another undefined term, but its meaning is understood from its use in everyday language. You can use undefined terms as building blocks to write definitions for defined terms, as shown in the table.

Defined Terms

Term	Geometric Figure	Ways to Name the Figure
A **line segment** (or *segment*) is a portion of a line consisting of two points (called **endpoints**) and all points between them.		segment *CD*, segment *DC*, $\overline{CD}$, or $\overline{DC}$
A **ray** is a portion of a line that starts at a point (the *endpoint*) and continues forever in one direction.	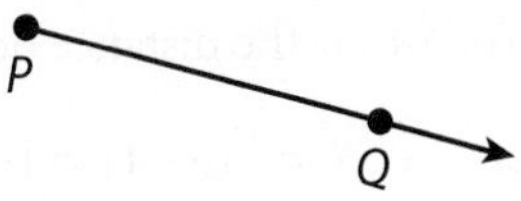	ray *PQ* or $\overrightarrow{PQ}$

You can use points to sketch lines, segments, rays, and planes.

(A) Draw two points J and K. Then draw a line through them. (Remember that a line shows arrows at both ends.)

(B) Draw two points J and K again. This time, draw the line segment with endpoints J and K.

(C) Draw a point K again and draw a ray from endpoint K. Plot a point J along the ray.

(D) Draw three points J, K, and M so that they are not all on the same line. Then draw the plane that contains the three points. (You might also put a script letter such as $\mathcal{B}$ on your plane.)

(E) Give a name for each of the figures you drew. Then state whether the type of figure is an undefined term or a defined term.

Point	?
Line	?
Segment	?
Ray	?
Plane	?

Reflect

1. In Step C, would $\overrightarrow{JK}$ be the same ray as $\overrightarrow{KJ}$? Why or why not?
2. In Step D, when you name a plane using 3 letters, does the order of the letters matter?
3. **Discussion** If $\overleftrightarrow{PQ}$ and $\overleftrightarrow{RS}$ are different names for the same line, what must be true about points P, Q, R, and S?

Explain 1 Constructing a Copy of a Line Segment

The distance along a line is undefined until a unit distance, such as 1 inch or 1 centimeter, is chosen. You can use a ruler to find the distance between two points on a line. The distance is the absolute value of the difference of the numbers on the ruler that correspond to the two points. This distance is the length of the segment determined by the points.

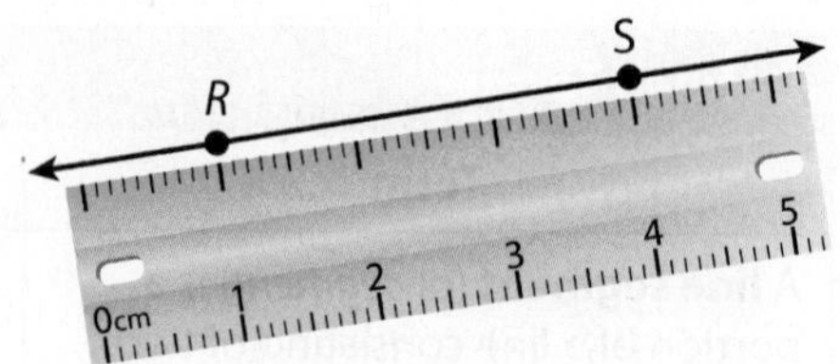

In the figure, the length of $\overline{RS}$, written RS (or SR), is the distance between R and S.

$RS = |4 - 1| = |3| = 3$ cm   or $SR = |1 - 4| = |-3| = 3$ cm

Points that lie in the same plane are **coplanar**. Lines that lie in the same plane but do not intersect are **parallel**. Points that lie on the same line are **collinear**. The *Segment Addition Postulate* is a statement about collinear points. A **postulate** is a statement that is accepted as true without proof. Like undefined terms, postulates are building blocks of geometry.

Postulate 1: Segment Addition Postulate

Let *A*, *B*, and *C* be collinear points. If *B* is between *A* and *C*, then $AB + BC = AC$.

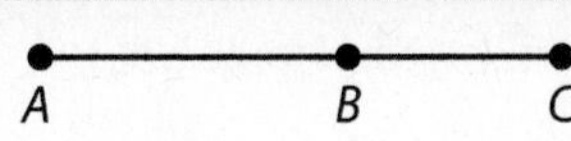

A *construction* is a geometric drawing that produces an accurate representation without using numbers or measures. One type of construction uses only a compass and straightedge. You can construct a line segment whose length is equal to that of a given segment using these tools along with the Segment Addition Postulate.

Example 1 **Use a compass and straightedge to construct a segment whose length is $AB + CD$.**

(A)

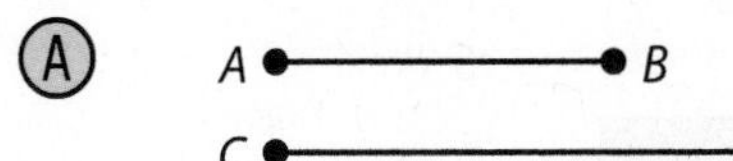

Step 1 Use the straightedge to draw a long line segment. Label an endpoint *X*. (See the art drawn in Step 4.)

Step 2 To copy segment *AB*, open the compass to the distance *AB*.

Step 3 Place the compass point on *X*, and draw an arc. Label the point *Y* where the arc and the segment intersect.

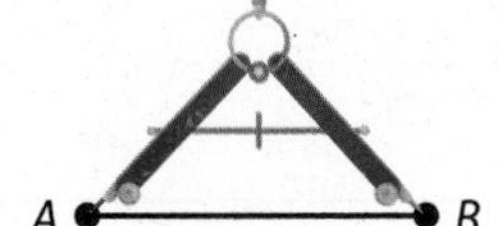

Step 4 To copy segment *CD*, open the compass to the distance *CD*. Place the compass point on *Y*, and draw an arc. Label the point *Z* where this second arc and the segment intersect. $\overline{XZ}$ is the required segment.

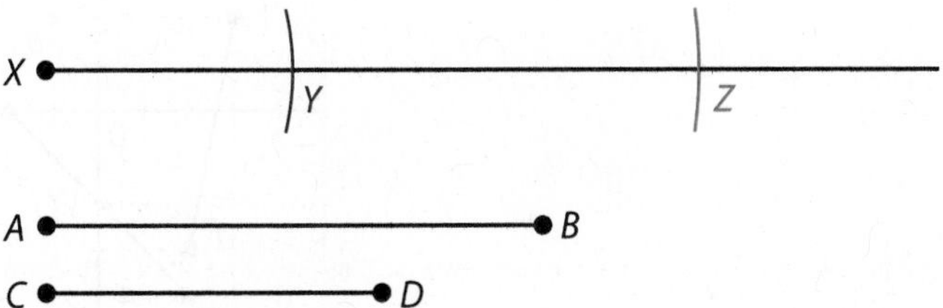

Step 1 Use the straightedge to draw a long line segment. Label an endpoint *X*.

Step 2 To copy segment *AB*, open the compass to the distance *AB*.

Step 3 Place the compass point on *X*, and draw an arc. Label the point *Y* where the arc and the segment intersect.

Step 4 To copy segment *CD*, open the compass to the distance *CD*. Place the compass point on *Y*, and draw an arc. Label the point *Z* where this second arc and the segment intersect. $\overline{XZ}$ is the required segment.

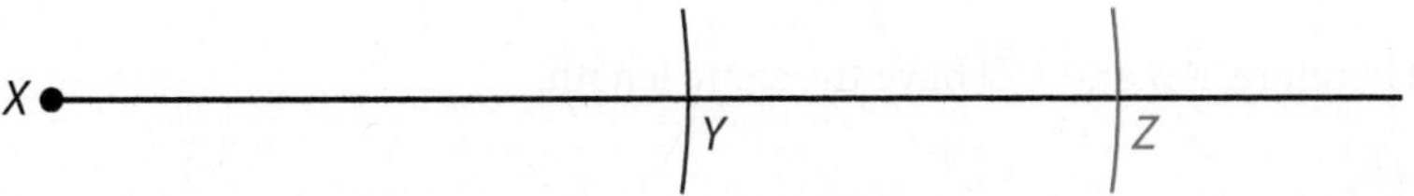

Reflect

4. **Discussion** Look at the line and ruler above Example 1. Why does it not matter whether you find the distance from R to S or the distance from S to R?

5. In Part B, how can you check that the length of $\overline{YZ}$ is the same as the length of $\overline{CD}$?

Your Turn

6. Use a ruler to draw a segment PQ that is 2 inches long. Then use your compass and straightedge to construct a segment MN with the same length as $\overline{PQ}$.

Explain 2 Using the Distance Formula on the Coordinate Plane

The Pythagorean Theorem states that $a^2 + b^2 = c^2$, where a and b are the lengths of the legs of a right triangle and c is the length of the hypotenuse. You can use the Distance Formula to apply the Pythagorean Theorem to find the distance between points on the coordinate plane.

The Distance Formula

The distance between two points (x_1, y_1) and (x_2, y_2) on the coordinate plane is $\sqrt{(x_2 - x_1)^2 + (y_2 - y_1)^2}$.

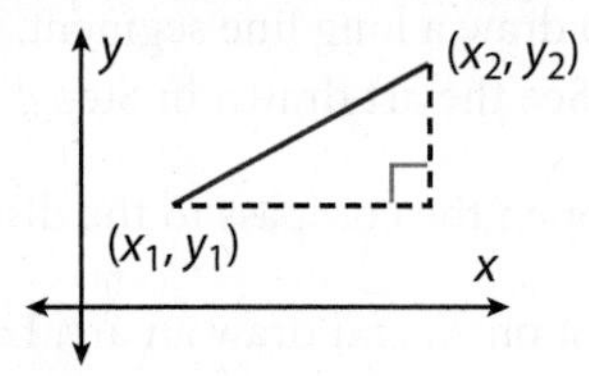

Example 2 **Determine whether the given segments have the same length. Justify your answer.**

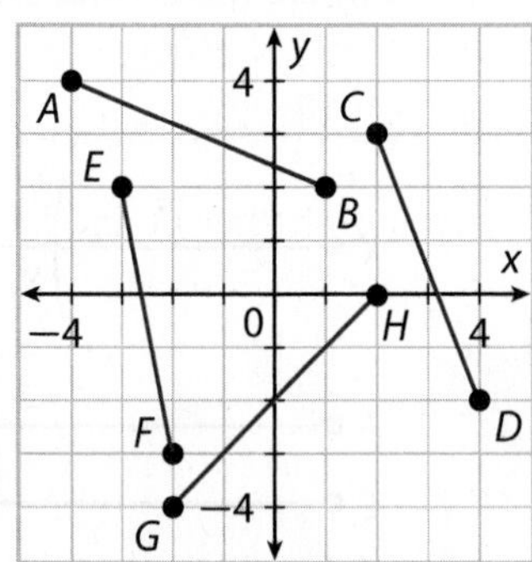

Ⓐ $\overline{AB}$ and $\overline{CD}$

Write the coordinates of the endpoints. $A(-4, 4)$, $B(1, 2)$, $C(2, 3)$, $D(4, -2)$

Find the length of $\overline{AB}$. $AB = \sqrt{(1 - (-4))^2 + (2 - 4)^2}$

Simplify the expression. $= \sqrt{5^2 + (-2)^2} = \sqrt{29}$

Find the length of $\overline{CD}$. $CD = \sqrt{(4 - 2)^2 + (-2 - 3)^2}$

Simplify the expression. $= \sqrt{2^2 + (-5)^2} = \sqrt{29}$

So, $AB = CD = \sqrt{29}$. Therefore, $\overline{AB}$ and $\overline{CD}$ have the same length.

(B) $\overline{EF}$ and $\overline{GH}$

Write the coordinates of the endpoints. $E(-3, 2), F(-2, -3), G(-2, -4), H(2, 0)$

Find the length of $\overline{EF}$. $EF = \sqrt{\left(-2 - (-3)\right)^2 + \left(-3 - 2\right)^2}$

Simplify the expression. $= \sqrt{\left(1\right)^2 + \left(-5\right)^2} = \sqrt{26}$

Find the length of $\overline{GH}$. $GH = \sqrt{\left(2 - (-2)\right)^2 + \left(0 - (-4)\right)^2}$

Simplify the expression. $= \sqrt{\left(4\right)^2 + \left(4\right)^2} = \sqrt{32}$

So, $EF \neq GH$. Therefore, $\overline{EF}$ and $\overline{GH}$ do not have the same length.

Reflect

7. Consider how the Distance Formula is related to the Pythagorean Theorem. To use the Distance Formula to find the distance from $U(-3, -1)$ to $V(3, 4)$, you write $UV = \sqrt{\left(3 - (-3)\right)^2 + \left(4 - (-1)\right)^2}$. Explain how $\left(3 - (-3)\right)$ in the Distance Formula is related to a in the Pythagorean Theorem and how $\left(4 - (-1)\right)$ in the Distance Formula is related to b in the Pythagorean Theorem.

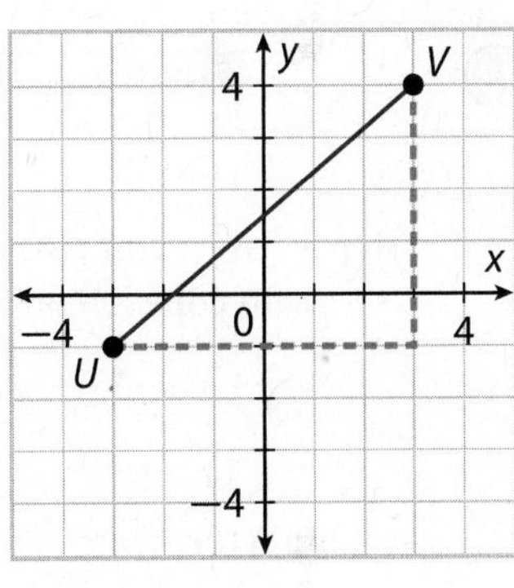

Your Turn

8. Determine whether $\overline{JK}$ and $\overline{LM}$ have the same length. Justify your answer.

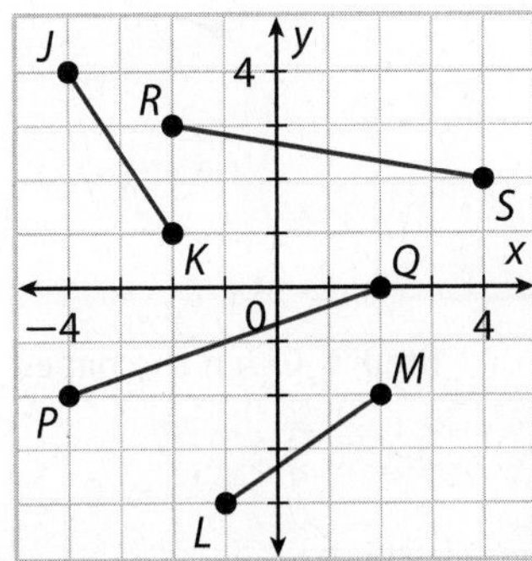

Explain 3 Finding a Midpoint

The **midpoint** of a line segment is the point that divides the segment into two segments that have the same length. A line, ray, or other figure that passes through the midpoint of a segment is a **segment bisector**.

In the figure, the tick marks show that $PM = MQ$. Therefore, M is the midpoint of $\overline{PQ}$ and line ℓ bisects $\overline{PQ}$.

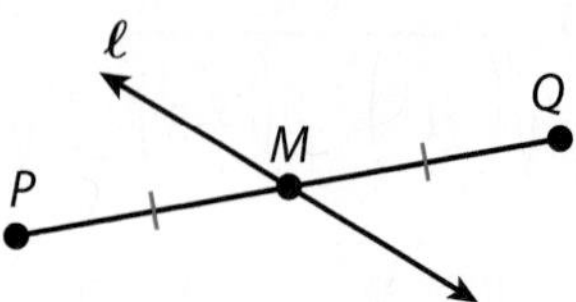

You can use paper folding as a method to construct a bisector of a given segment and locate the midpoint of the segment.

Example 3 **Use paper folding to construct a bisector of each segment.**

Step 1 Use a compass and straightedge to copy $\overline{AB}$ on a piece of paper.

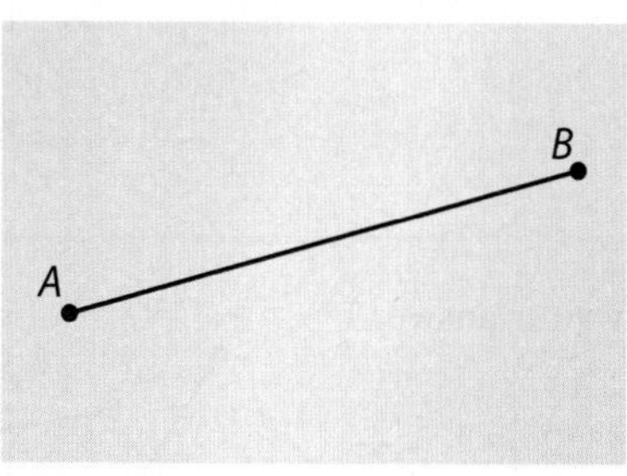

Step 2 Fold the paper so that point B is on top of point A.

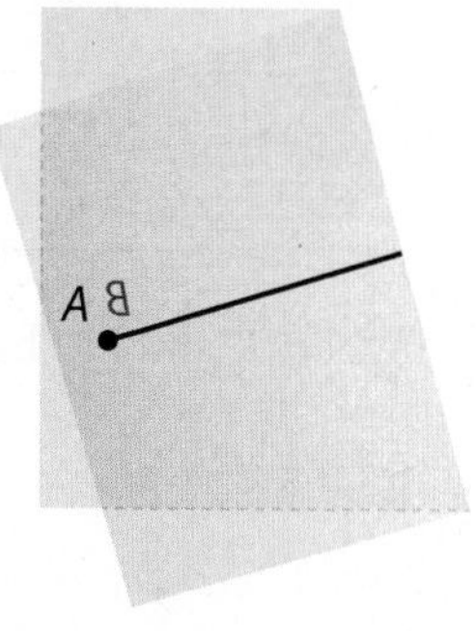

Step 3 Open the paper. Label the point where the crease intersects the segment as point M.

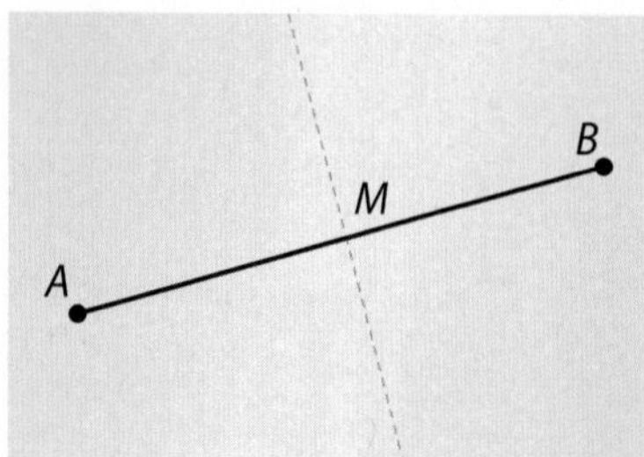

Point M is the midpoint of $\overline{AB}$ and the crease is a bisector of $\overline{AB}$.

Ⓑ **Step 1** Use a compass and straightedge to copy $\overline{JK}$ on a piece of paper.

Step 2 Fold the paper so that point K is on top of point J.

Step 3 Open the paper. Label the point where the crease intersects the segment as point N.

J
N
K

Point N is the midpoint of $\overline{JK}$ and the crease is a bisector of $\overline{JK}$.

Step 4 Make a sketch of your paper folding construction or attach your folded piece of paper.

Reflect

9. Explain how you could use paper folding to divide a line segment into four segments of equal length.

Your Turn

10. Explain how to use a ruler to check your construction in Part B.

Explain 4 Finding Midpoints on the Coordinate Plane

You can use the *Midpoint Formula* to find the midpoint of a segment on the coordinate plane.

The Midpoint Formula

The midpoint M of $\overline{AB}$ with endpoints $A(x_1, y_1)$ and $B(x_2, y_2)$ is given by $M\left(\frac{x_1 + x_2}{2}, \frac{y_1 + y_2}{2}\right)$.

y
$B(x_2, y_2)$
$M\left(\frac{x_1 + x_2}{2}, \frac{y_1 + y_2}{2}\right)$
$A(x_1, y_1)$
x

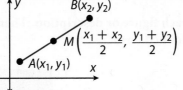

Example 4 **Show that each statement is true.**

Ⓐ If $\overline{PQ}$ has endpoints $P(-4, 1)$ and $Q(2, -3)$, then the midpoint M of $\overline{PQ}$ lies in Quadrant III.

Use the Midpoint Formula to find the midpoint of $\overline{PQ}$. Substitute the coordinates, then simplify.

$$M\left(\frac{-4 + 2}{2}, \frac{1 + (-3)}{2}\right) = M(-1, -1)$$

So M lies in Quadrant III, since the x- and y-coordinates are both negative.

Ⓑ If $\overline{RS}$ has endpoints $R(3, 5)$ and $S(-3, -1)$, then the midpoint M of $\overline{RS}$ lies on the y-axis.

Use the Midpoint Formula to find the midpoint of $\overline{RS}$. Substitute the coordinates, then simplify.

$$M\left(\frac{3 + \boxed{-3}}{2}, \frac{5 + \boxed{-1}}{2}\right) = M\left(\boxed{0}, \boxed{2}\right)$$

So M lies on the y-axis, since the x-coordinate is 0.

Your Turn

Show that each statement is true.

11. If $\overline{AB}$ has endpoints $A(6, -3)$ and $B(-6, 3)$, then the midpoint M of $\overline{AB}$ is the origin.

12. If $\overline{JK}$ has endpoints $J(7, 0)$ and $K(-5, -4)$, then the midpoint M of $\overline{JK}$ lies in Quadrant IV.

Elaborate

13. Explain why the Distance Formula is not needed to find the distance between two points that lie on a horizontal or vertical line.

14. When you use the Distance Formula, does the order in which you subtract the x- and y-coordinates matter? Explain.

15. When you use the Midpoint Formula, can you take either point as (x_1, y_1) or (x_2, y_2)? Why or why not?

16. **Essential Question Check-In** What is the difference between finding the length of a segment that is drawn on a sheet of blank paper and a segment that is drawn on a coordinate plane?

Evaluate: Homework and Practice

- Online Homework
- Hints and Help
- Extra Practice

Write the term that is suggested by each figure or description. Then state whether the term is an undefined term or a defined term.

1. 

2. 

3. 

4. 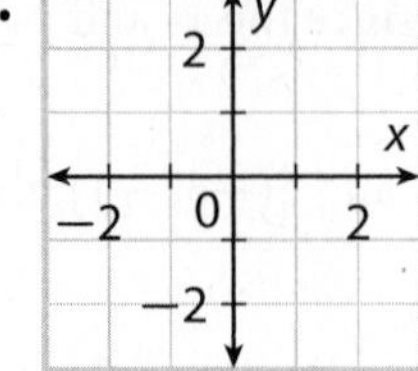

Copy each pair of segments onto a sheet of paper. Then use a compass and straightedge to construct a segment whose length is $AB + CD$.

5. A ——— B
C ——— D

6. A ——— B
C ——— D

Copy each segment onto a sheet of paper. Then use paper folding to construct a bisector of the segment.

7. A ——— B

8. L
K

Determine whether the given segments have the same length. Justify your answer.

9. $\overline{AB}$ and $\overline{BC}$

10. $\overline{EF}$ and $\overline{GH}$

11. $\overline{AB}$ and $\overline{CD}$

12. $\overline{BC}$ and $\overline{EF}$

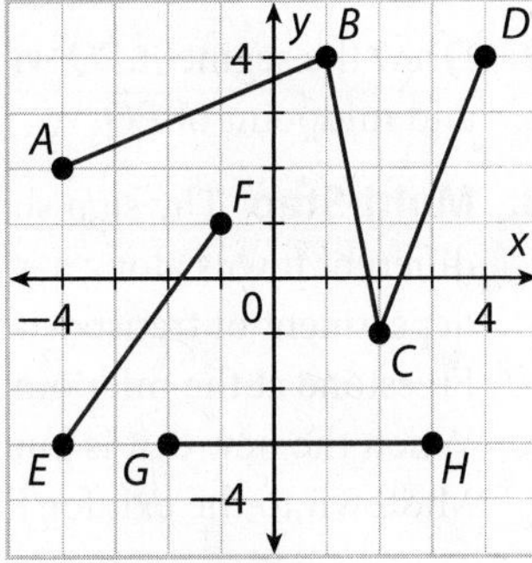

Show that each statement is true.

13. If $\overline{DE}$ has endpoints $D(-1, 6)$ and $E(3, -2)$, then the midpoint M of $\overline{DE}$ lies in Quadrant I.

14. If $\overline{ST}$ has endpoints $S(-6, -1)$ and $T(0, 1)$, then the midpoint M of $\overline{ST}$ lies in on the x-axis.

15. If $\overline{JK}$ has endpoints $J(-2, 3)$ and $K(6, 5)$, and $\overline{LN}$ has endpoints $L(0, 7)$ and $N(4, 1)$, then $\overline{JK}$ and $\overline{LN}$ have the same midpoint.

16. If $\overline{GH}$ has endpoints $G(-8, 1)$ and $H(4, 5)$, then the midpoint M of $\overline{GH}$ lies on the line $y = -x + 1$.

Use the figure for Exercises 17 and 18.

17. Name two different rays in the figure.

18. Name three different segments in the figure.

Sketch each figure.

19. two rays that form a straight line and that intersect at point P

20. two line segments that both have a midpoint at point M

21. Draw and label a line segment, $\overline{JK}$, that is 3 inches long. Use a ruler to draw and label the midpoint M of the segment.

22. Draw the segment PQ with endpoints $P(-2, -1)$ and $Q(2, 4)$ on the coordinate plane. Then find the length and midpoint of $\overline{PQ}$.

23. Multi-Step The sign shows distances from a rest stop to the exits for different towns along a straight section of highway. The state department of transportation is planning to build a new exit to Freestone at the midpoint of the exits for Roseville and Edgewood. When the new exit is built, what will be the distance from the exit for Midtown to the exit for Freestone?

24. On a town map, each unit of the coordinate plane represents 1 mile. Three branches of a bank are located at $A(-3, 1)$, $B(2, 3)$, and $C(4, -1)$. A bank employee drives from Branch A to Branch B and then drives halfway to Branch C before getting stuck in traffic. What is the minimum total distance the employee may have driven before getting stuck in traffic? Round to the nearest tenth of a mile.

25. A city planner designs a park that is a quadrilateral with vertices at $J(-3, 1)$, $K(1, 3)$, $L(5, -1)$, and $M(-1, -3)$. There is an entrance to the park at the midpoint of each side of the park. A straight path connects each entrance to the entrance on the opposite side. Assuming each unit of the coordinate plane represents 10 meters, what is the total length of the paths to the nearest meter?

26. Communicate Mathematical Ideas A video game designer places an anthill at the origin of a coordinate plane. A red ant leaves the anthill and moves along a straight line to $(1, 1)$, while a black ant leaves the anthill and moves along a straight line to $(-1, -1)$. Next, the red ant moves to $(2, 2)$, while the black ant moves to $(-2, -2)$. Then the red ant moves to $(3, 3)$, while the black ant moves to $(-3, -3)$, and so on. Explain why the red ant and the black ant are always the same distance from the anthill.

27. Which of the following points are more than 5 units from the point $P(-2, -2)$? Select all that apply.

A. $A(1, 2)$

B. $B(3, -1)$

C. $C(2, -4)$

D. $D(-6, -6)$

E. $E(-5, 1)$

H.O.T. Focus on Higher Order Thinking

28. Analyze Relationships Use a compass and straightedge to construct a segment whose length is $AB - CD$. Use a ruler to check your construction.

29. Critical Thinking Point M is the midpoint of $\overline{AB}$. The coordinates of point A are $(-8, 3)$ and the coordinates of M are $(-2, 1)$. What are the coordinates of point B?

30. Make a Conjecture Use a compass and straightedge to copy $\overline{AB}$ so that one endpoint of the copy is at point X. Then repeat the process three more times, making three different copies of $\overline{AB}$ that have an endpoint at point X. Make a conjecture about the set of all possible copies of $\overline{AB}$ that have an endpoint at point X.

X

Lesson Performance Task

A carnival ride consists of four circular cars—*A*, *B*, *C*, and *D*—each of which spins about a point at its center. The center points of cars *A* and *B* are attached by a straight beam, as are the center points of cars *C* and *D*. The two beams are attached at their midpoints by a rotating arm. The figure shows how the beams and arm can rotate.

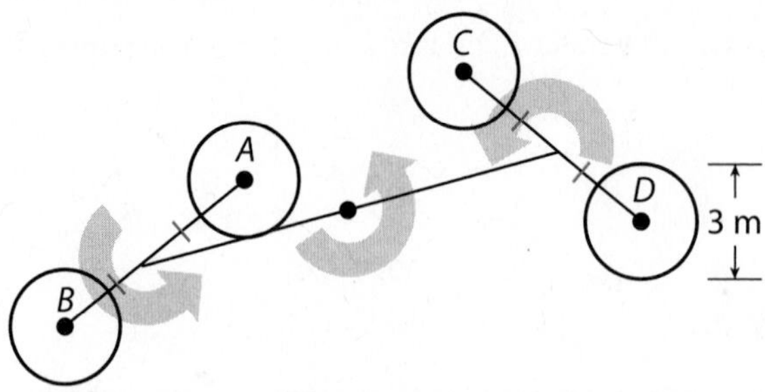

A plan for the ride uses a coordinate plane in which each unit represents one meter. In the plan, the center of car *A* is $(-6, -1)$, the center of car *B* is $(-2, -3)$, the center of car *C* is $(3, 4)$, and the center of car *D* is $(5, 0)$. Each car has a diameter of 3 meters.

The manager of the carnival wants to place a fence around the ride. Describe the shape and dimensions of a fence that will be appropriate to enclose the ride. Justify your answer.

1.2 Angle Measures and Angle Bisectors

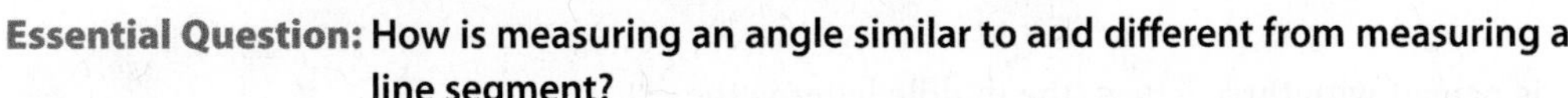

Essential Question: **How is measuring an angle similar to and different from measuring a line segment?**

Explore — Constructing a Copy of an Angle

Start with a point X and use a compass and straightedge to construct a copy of $\angle S$.

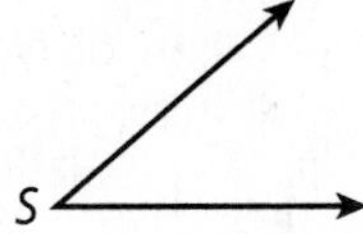

X

(A) Use a straightedge to draw a ray with endpoint X.

(B) Place the point of your compass on S and draw an arc that intersects both sides of the angle. Label the points of intersection T and U.

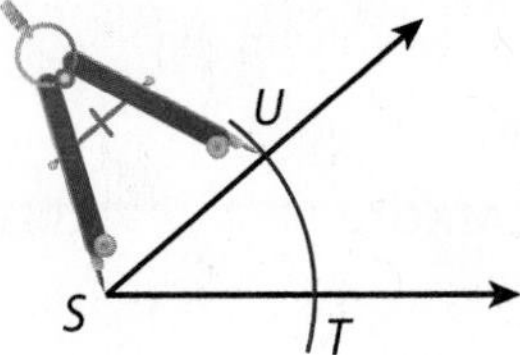

(C) Without adjusting the compass, place the point of the compass on X and draw an arc that intersects the ray. Label the intersection Y.

(D) Place the point of the compass on T and open it to the distance TU.

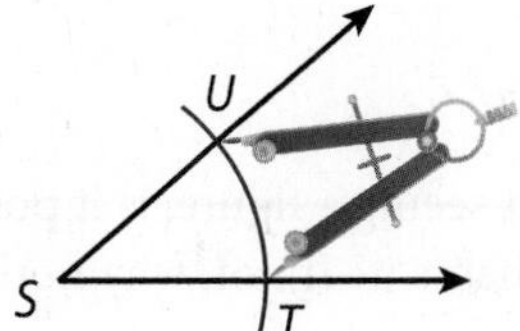

(E) Without adjusting the compass, place the point of the compass on Y and draw an arc. Label the intersection with the first arc Z.

(F) Use a straightedge to draw $\overrightarrow{XZ}$. $\angle X$ is a copy of $\angle S$.

Reflect

1. If you could place the angle you constructed on top of $\angle S$ so that $\overrightarrow{XY}$ coincides with $\overrightarrow{ST}$, what would be true about $\overrightarrow{XZ}$? Explain.

2. **Discussion** Is it possible to do the construction with a compass that is stuck open to a fixed distance? Why or why not?

Explain 1 Naming Angles and Parts of an Angle

An **angle** is a figure formed by two rays with the same endpoint. The common endpoint is the **vertex** of the angle. The rays are the **sides** of the angle.

Example 1 **Draw or name the given angle.**

(A) $\angle PQR$

When an angle is named with three letters, the middle letter is the vertex. So, the vertex of angle $\angle PQR$ is point Q.

The sides of the angle are two rays with common endpoint Q. So, the sides of the angle are $\overrightarrow{QP}$ and $\overrightarrow{QR}$.

Draw and label the angle as shown.

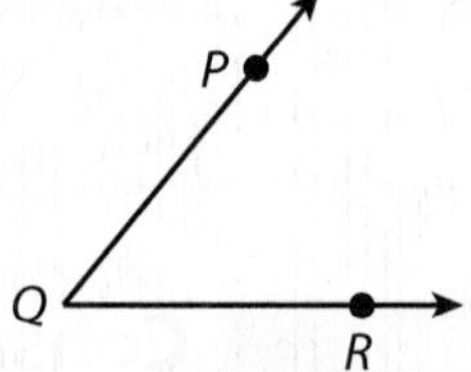

(B)

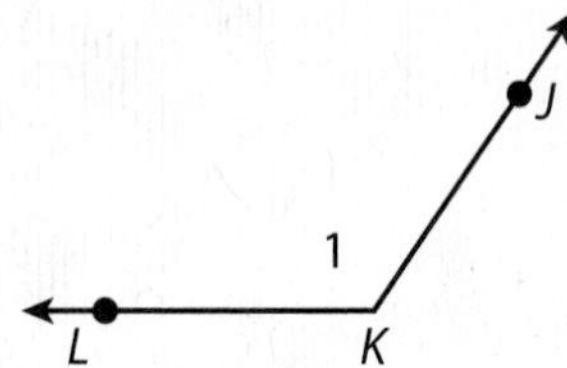

The vertex of the angle shown is point K. A name for the angle is $\angle$ K.

The vertex must be in the middle, so two more names for the angle are $\angle$ J K L and $\angle$ L K J.

The angle is numbered, so another name is $\angle$ 1.

Reflect

3. Without seeing a figure, is it possible to give another name for $\angle MKG$? If so, what is it? If not, why not?

Your Turn

Use the figure for 4–5.

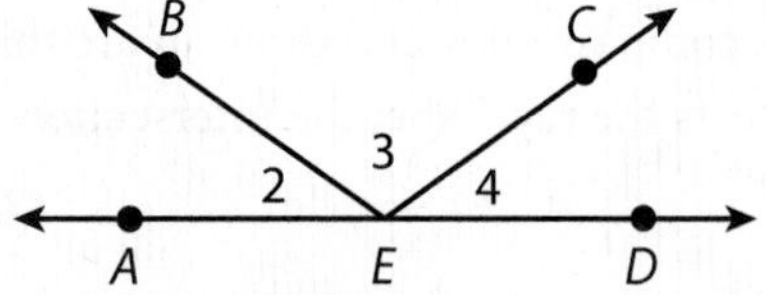

4. Name $\angle 2$ in as many different ways as possible.

5. Use a compass and straightedge to copy $\angle BEC$.

Explain 2 Measuring Angles

The distance around a circular arc is undefined until a measurement unit is chosen. **Degrees** (°) are a common measurement unit for circular arcs. There are 360° in a circle, so an angle that measures 1° is $\frac{1}{360}$ of a circle. The measure of an angle is written $m\angle A$ or $m\angle PQR$.

You can classify angles by their measures.

Classifying Angles			
Acute Angle	**Right Angle**	**Obtuse Angle**	**Straight Angle**
$0° < m\angle A < 90°$	$m\angle A = 90°$	$90° < m\angle A < 180°$	$m\angle A = 180°$

Example 2 **Use a protractor to draw an angle with the given measure.**

(A) 53°

Step 1 Use a straightedge to draw a ray, $\overrightarrow{XY}$.

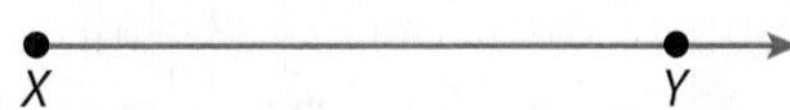

Step 2 Place your protractor on point X as shown. Locate the point along the edge of the protractor that corresponds to 53°. Make a mark at this location and label it point Z.

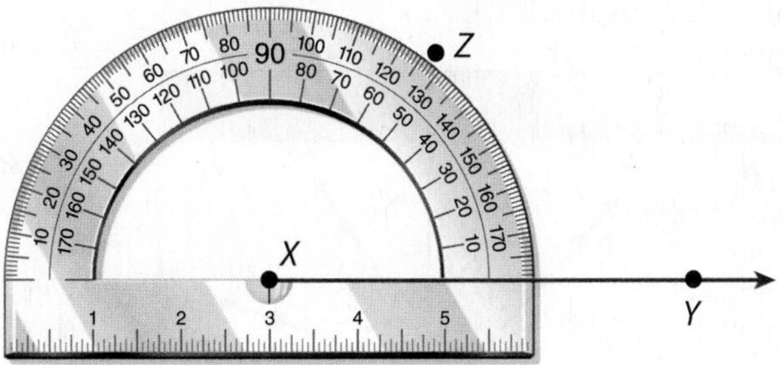

Step 3 Draw $\overrightarrow{XZ}$. $m\angle ZXY = 53°$.

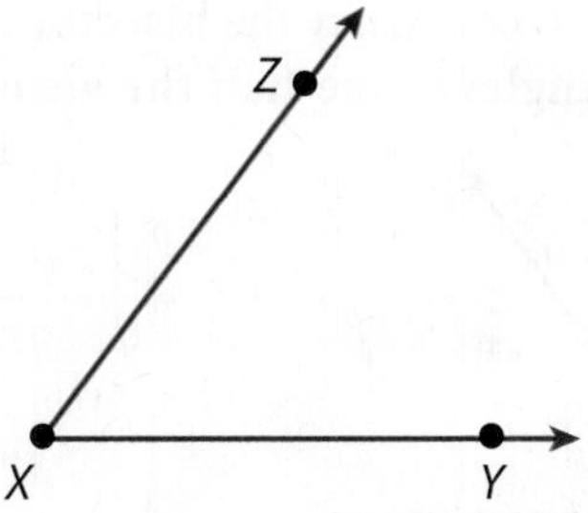

(B) 138°

Step 1 Use a straightedge to draw a ray, $\overrightarrow{AB}$.

Step 2 Place your protractor on point A so that $\overrightarrow{AB}$ is at zero.

Step 3 Locate the point along the edge of the protractor that corresponds to 138°. Make a mark at this location and label it point C.

Step 4 Draw $\overrightarrow{AC}$. $m\angle CAB = 138°$.

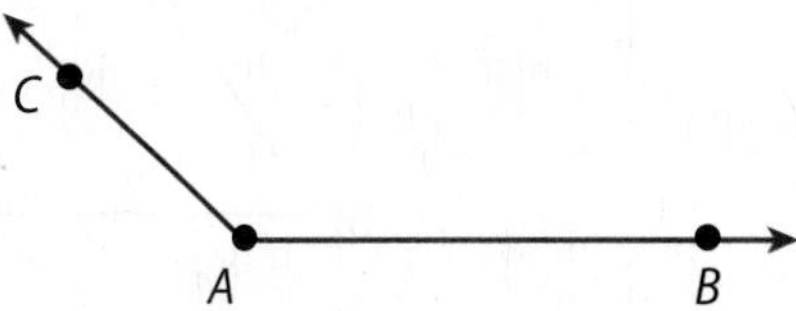

Reflect

6. Explain how you can use a protractor to check that the angle you constructed in the Explore is a copy of the given angle.

Your Turn

Each angle can be found in the rigid frame of the bicycle. Use a protractor to find each measure.

7.

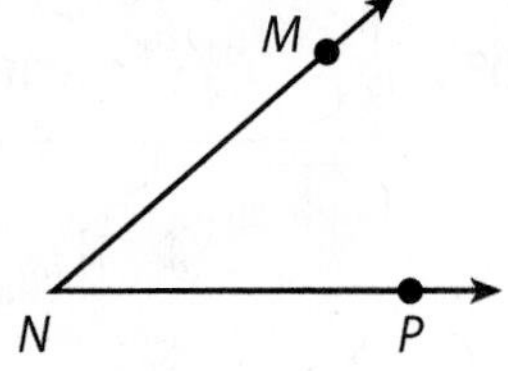

8.

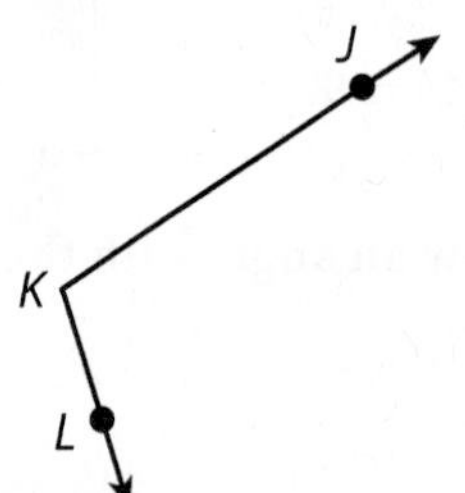

Explain 3 Constructing an Angle Bisector

An **angle bisector** is a ray that divides an angle into two angles that both have the same measure. In the figure, $\overrightarrow{BD}$ bisects $\angle ABC$, so $m\angle ABD = m\angle CBD$. The arcs in the figure show equal angle measures.

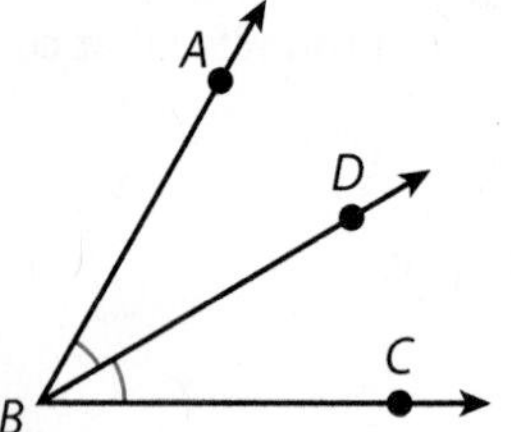

Postulate 2: Angle Addition Postulate

If S is in the interior of $\angle PQR$, then $m\angle PQR = m\angle PQS + m\angle SQR$.

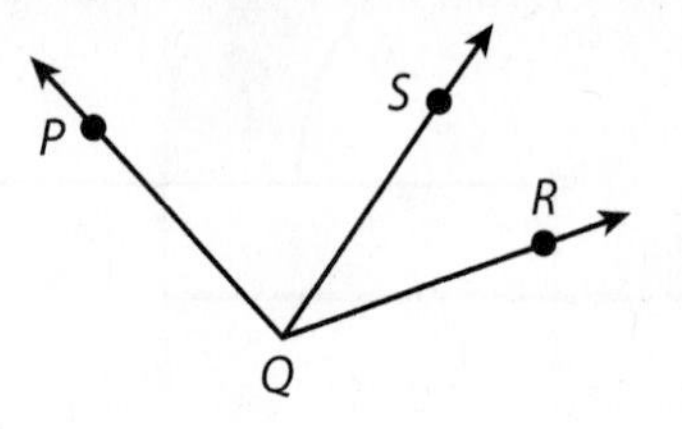

Example 3 **Use a compass and straightedge to construct the bisector of the given angle. Check that the measure of each of the new angles is one-half the measure of the given angle.**

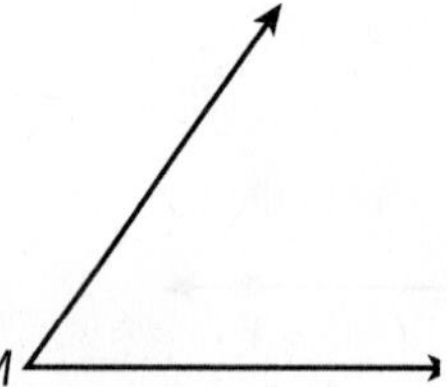

Step 1 Place the point of your compass on point M. Draw an arc that intersects both sides of the angle. Label the points of intersection P and Q.

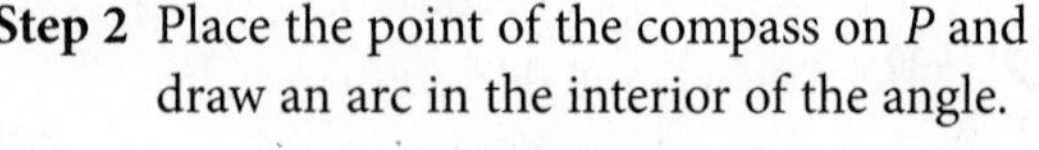

Step 2 Place the point of the compass on P and draw an arc in the interior of the angle.

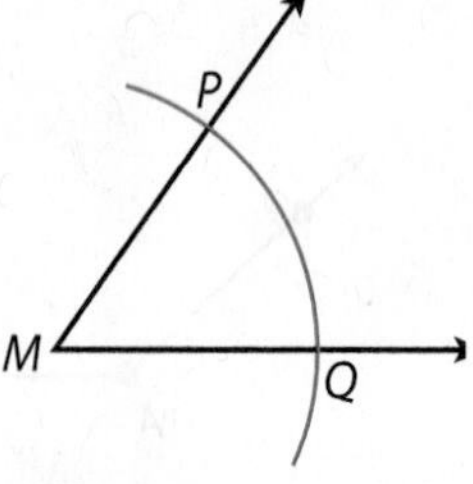

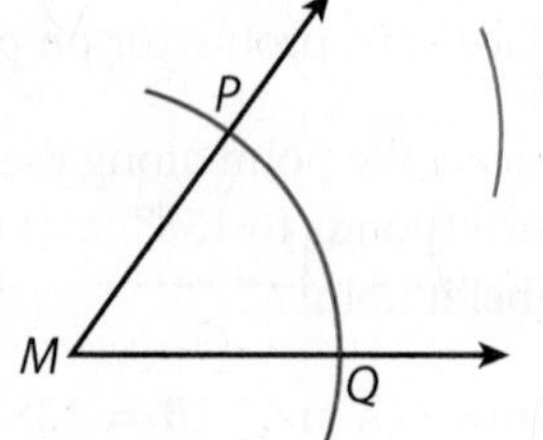

Step 3 Without adjusting the compass, place the point of the compass on Q and draw an arc that intersects the last arc you drew. Label the intersection of the arcs *R*.

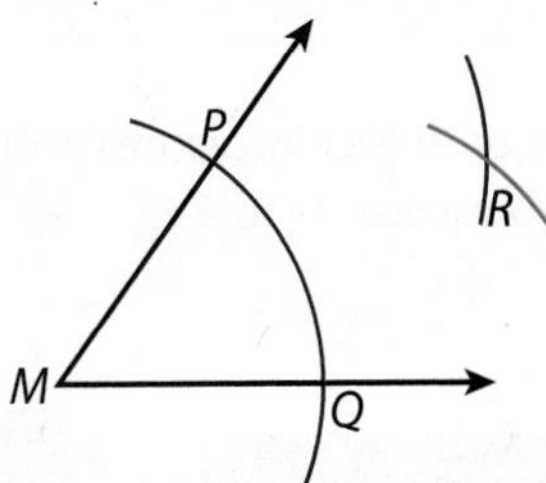

Step 4 Use a straightedge to draw $\overrightarrow{MR}$.

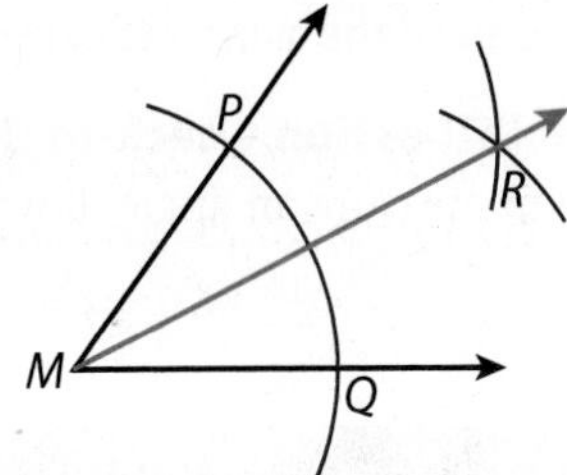

Step 5 Measure with a protractor to confirm that $m\angle PMR = m\angle QMR = \frac{1}{2}m\angle PMQ$.
$27° = 27° = \frac{1}{2}(54°)$✓

Ⓑ

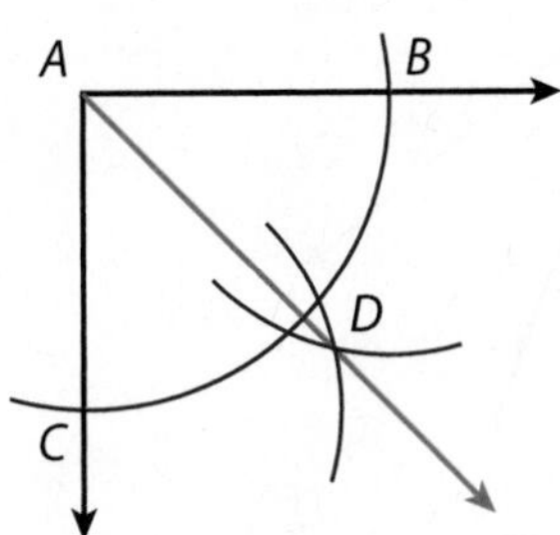

Step 1 Draw an arc centered at *A* that intersects both sides of the angle. Label the points of intersection *B* and *C*.

Step 2 Draw an arc centered at *B* in the interior of the angle.

Step 3 Without adjusting the compass, draw an arc centered at *C* that intersects the last arc you drew. Label the intersection of the arcs *D*.

Step 4 Draw $\overrightarrow{AD}$.

Step 5 Check that $m\angle BAD = m\angle CAD = \frac{1}{2}m\angle BAC$.

$45° = 45° = \frac{1}{2}(90°)$✓

Reflect

9. Discussion Explain how you could use paper folding to construct the bisector of an angle.

Your Turn

Copy the angle. Use a compass and straightedge to construct the bisector of the angle. Check that the measure of each of the new angles is one-half the measure of the given angle.

10.

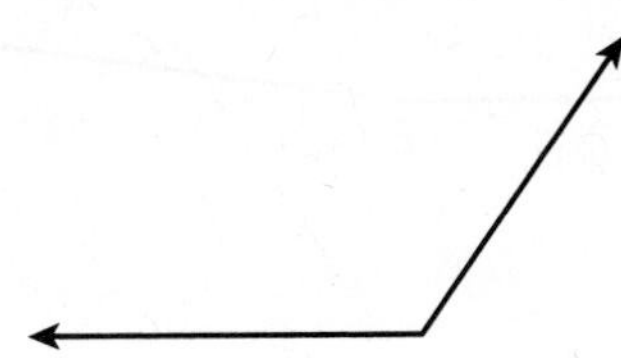

11.

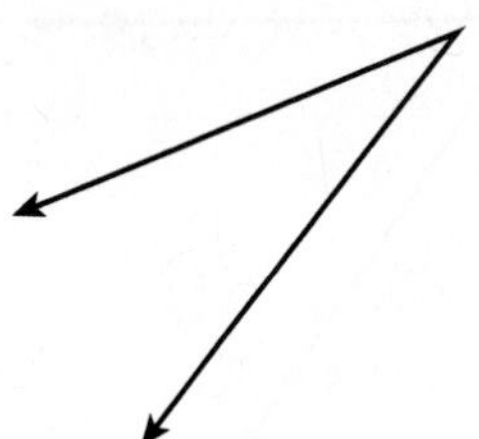

Elaborate

12. What is the relationship between a segment bisector and an angle bisector?

13. When you copy an angle, do the lengths of the segments you draw to represent the two rays affect whether the angles have the same measure? Explain.

14. **Essential Question Check-In** Many protractors have two sets of degree measures around the edge. When you measure an angle, how do you know which of the two measures to use?

Evaluate: Homework and Practice

- Online Homework
- Hints and Help
- Extra Practice

Use a compass and straightedge to construct a copy of each angle.

1. 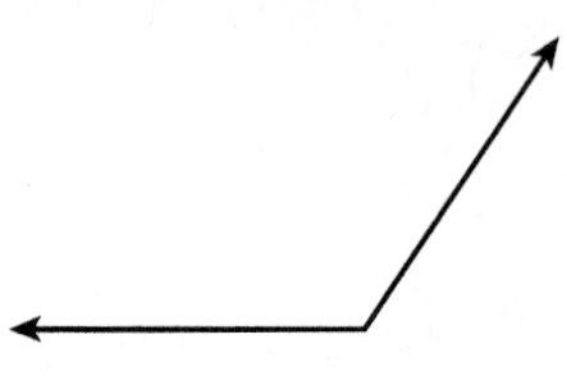

2. 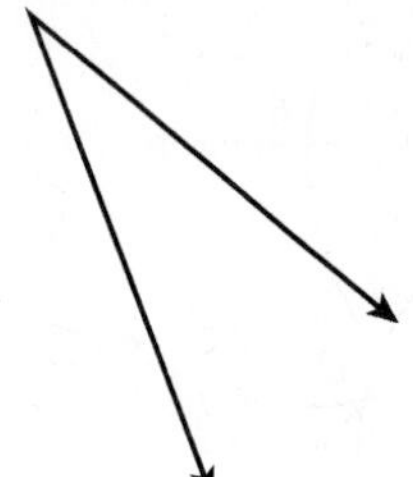

3. 

Draw an angle with the given name.

4. $\angle JWT$

5. $\angle NBQ$

Name each angle in as many different ways as possible.

6. 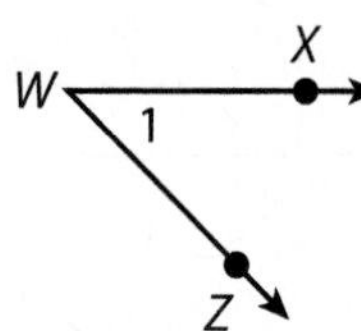

7. 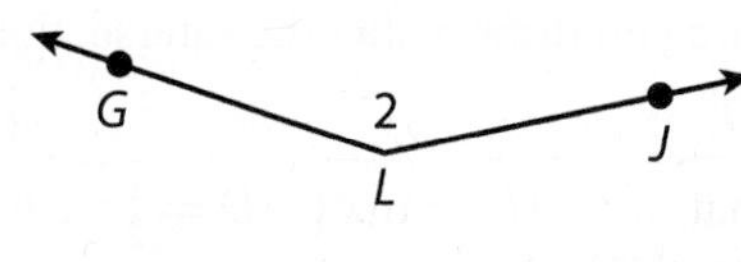

Use a protractor to draw an angle with the given measure.

8. 19°

9. 100°

Use a protractor to find the measure of each angle.

10. 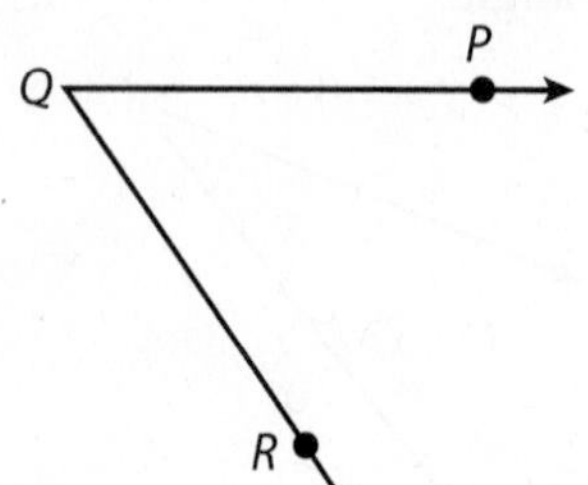

11. 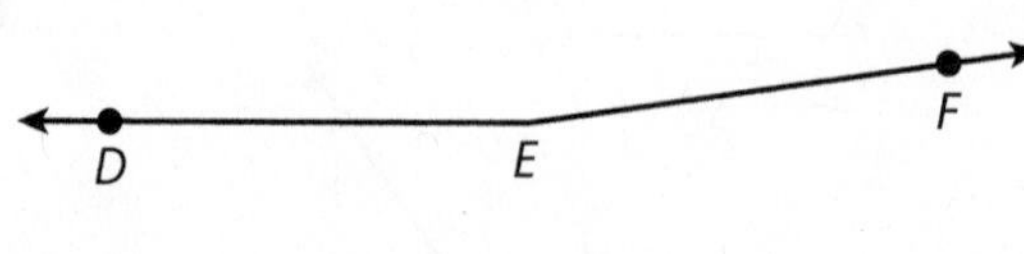

Copy the angle. Then use a compass and straightedge to construct the bisector of the angle. Check that the measure of each of the new angles is one-half the measure of the given angle.

12. **13.** **14.**

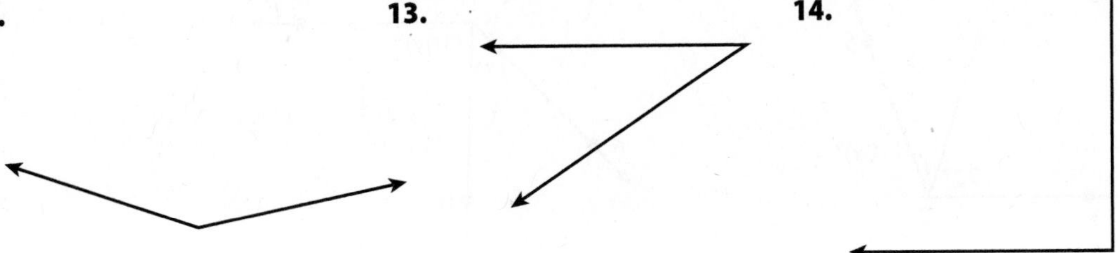

Use the Angle Addition Postulate to find the measure of each angle.

15. $\angle BXC$

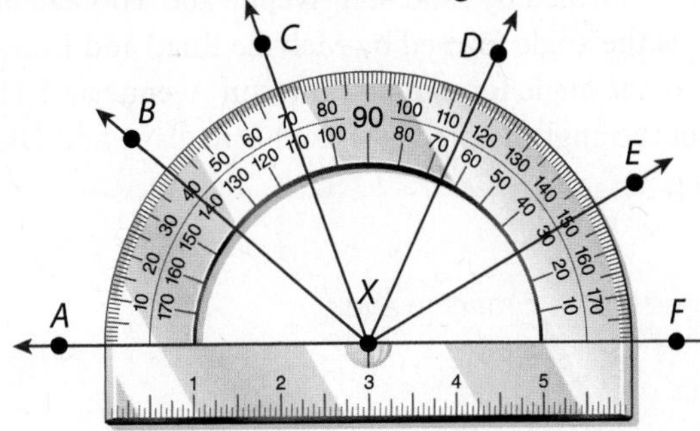

16. $\angle BXE$

Use a compass and straightedge to copy each angle onto a separate piece of paper. Then use paper folding to construct the angle bisector.

17. **18.**

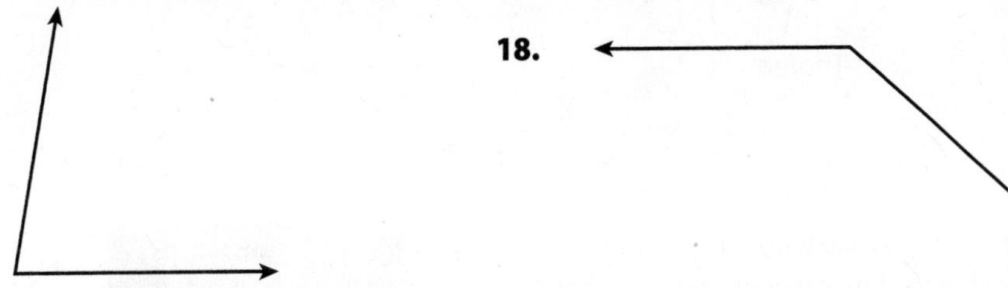

19. Use a compass and straightedge to construct an angle whose measure is $m\angle A + m\angle B$. Use a protractor to check your construction.

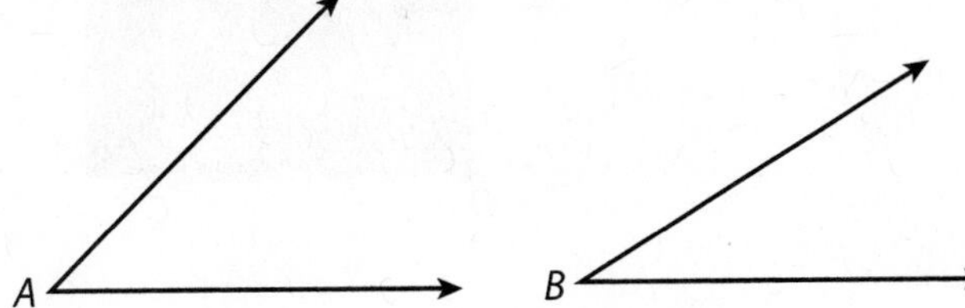

20. Find the value of x, given that $m\angle PQS = 112°$.

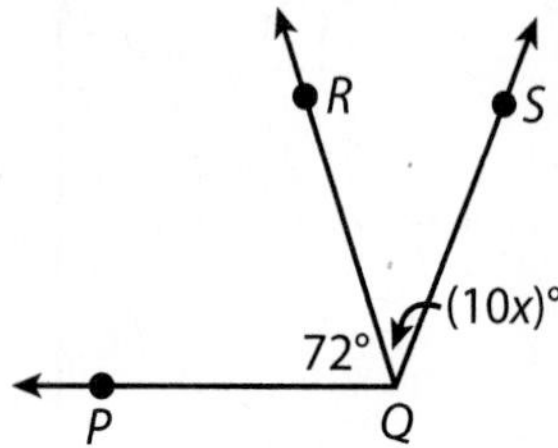

21. Find the value of y, given that $m\angle KLM = 135°$.

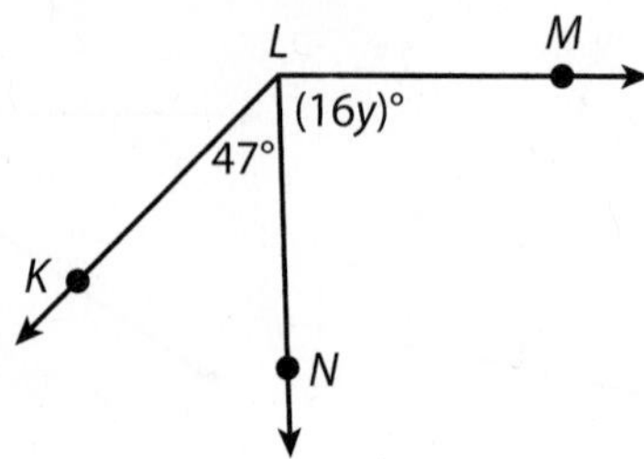

22. **Multi-Step** The figure shows a map of five streets that meet at Concord Circle. The measure of the angle formed by Melville Road and Emerson Avenue is 118°. The measure of the angle formed by Emerson Avenue and Thoreau Street is 134°. Hawthorne Lane bisects the angle formed by Melville Road and Emerson Avenue. Dickinson Drive bisects the angle formed by Emerson Avenue and Thoreau Street. What is the measure of the angle formed by Hawthorne Lane and Dickinson Drive? Explain your reasoning.

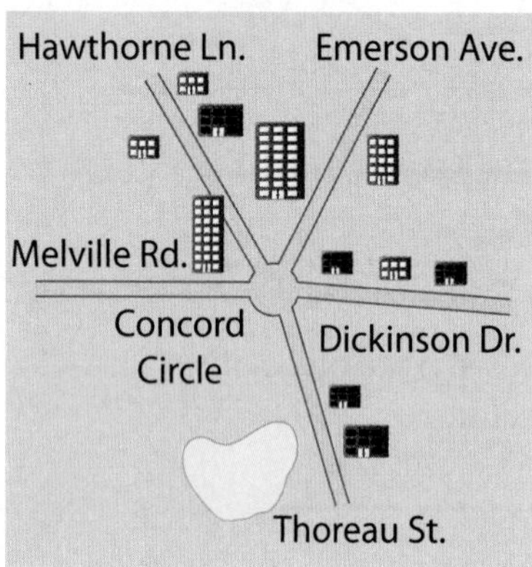

23. **Represent Real-World Problems** A carpenter is building a rectangular bookcase with diagonal braces across the back, as shown. The carpenter knows that $\angle ADC$ is a right angle and that $m\angle BDC$ is 32° greater than $m\angle ADB$. Write and solve an equation to find $m\angle BDC$ and $m\angle ADB$.

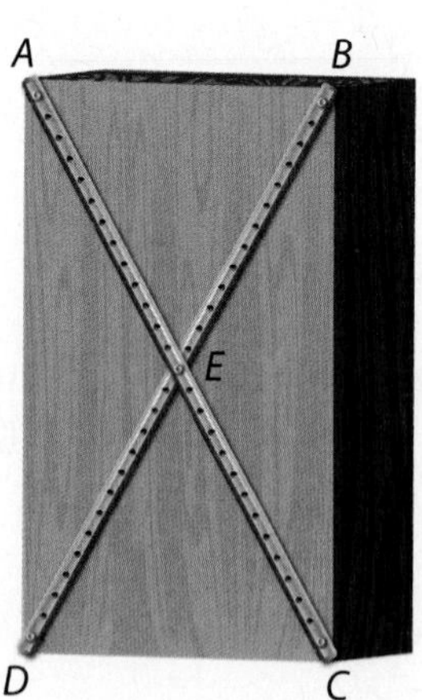

24. Describe the relationships among the four terms.

Angle bisector
Angle
Ray
Defined terms
Line
Undefined term

25. Determine whether each of the following pairs of angles have equal measures. Write Yes or No for each pair.

A. $\angle KJL$ and $\angle LJM$

B. $\angle MJP$ and $\angle PJR$

C. $\angle LJP$ and $\angle NJR$

D. $\angle MJK$ and $\angle PJR$

E. $\angle KJR$ and $\angle MJP$

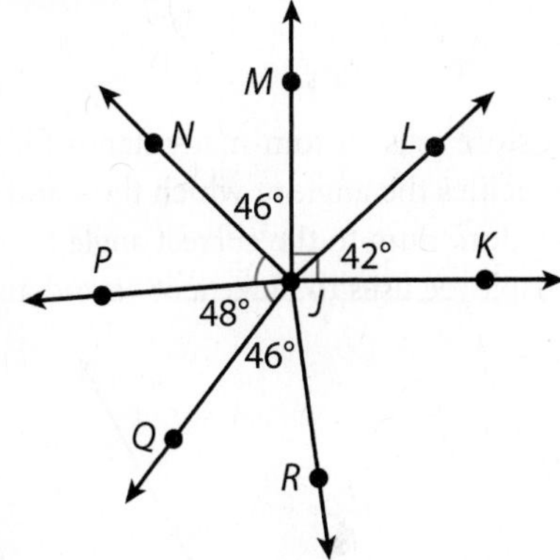

26. Make a Conjecture A rhombus is a quadrilateral with four sides of equal length. Copy each of the rhombuses shown. Then use a compass and straightedge to bisect one of the angles in each rhombus. Use your results to state a conjecture.

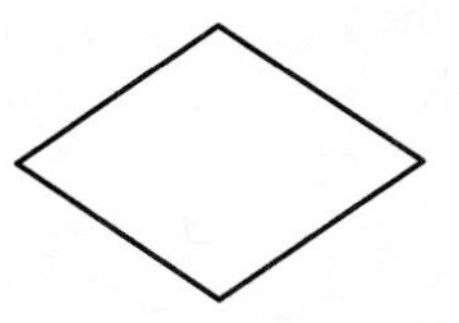

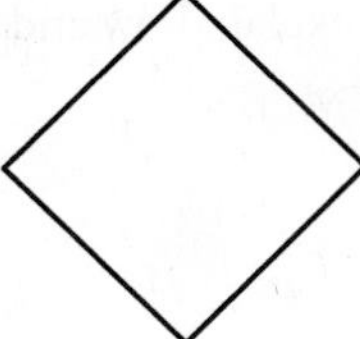

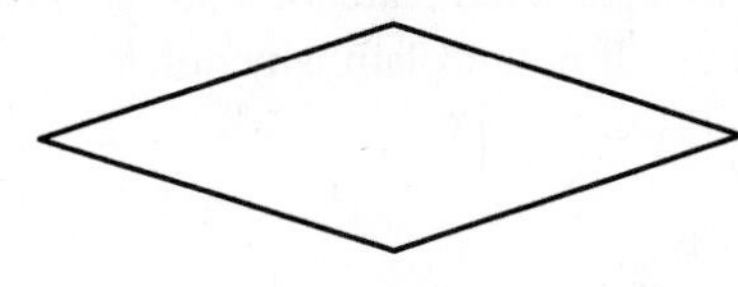

H.O.T. Focus on Higher Order Thinking

27. What If? What happens if you perform the steps for constructing an angle bisector when the given angle is a straight angle? Does the construction still work? If so, explain why and show a sample construction. If not, explain why not.

28. Critical Thinking Use a compass and straightedge to construct an angle whose measure is $m\angle A - m\angle B$. Use a protractor to check your construction.

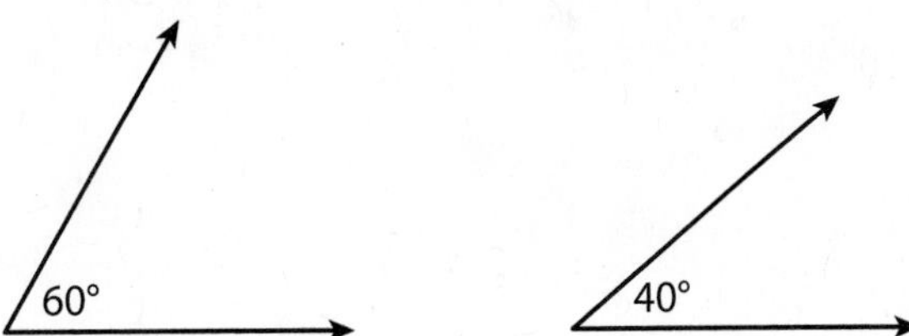

29. Communicate Mathematical Ideas Explain the steps for using a compass and straightedge to construct an angle with $\frac{1}{4}$ the measure of a given angle. Then draw an angle and show the construction.

Lesson Performance Task

A store sells custom-made stands for tablet computers. When an order comes in, the customer specifies the angle at which the stand should hold the tablet. Then an employee bends a piece of aluminum to the correct angle to make the stand. The figure shows the templates that the employee uses to make a 60° stand and a 40° stand.

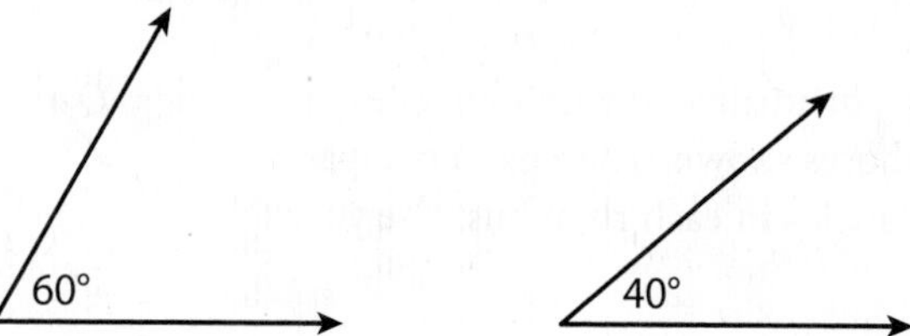

The store receives an order for a 50° stand. The employee does not have a template for a 50° stand and does not have a protractor. Can the employee use the existing templates and a compass and straightedge to make a template for a 50° stand? If so, explain how and show the steps the employee should use. If not, explain why not.

1.3 Representing and Describing Transformations

Resource Locker

Essential Question: How can you describe transformations in the coordinate plane using algebraic representations and using words?

Explore — Performing Transformations Using Coordinate Notation

A **transformation** is a function that changes the position, shape, and/or size of a figure. The inputs of the function are points in the plane; the outputs are other points in the plane. A figure that is used as the input of a transformation is the **preimage**. The output is the **image**. Translations, reflections, and rotations are three types of transformations. The decorative tiles shown illustrate all three types of transformations.

You can use *prime notation* to name the image of a point. In the diagram, the transformation T moves point A to point A' (read "A prime"). You can use function notation to write $T(A) = A'$. Note that a transformation is sometimes called a *mapping*. Transformation T *maps* A to A'.

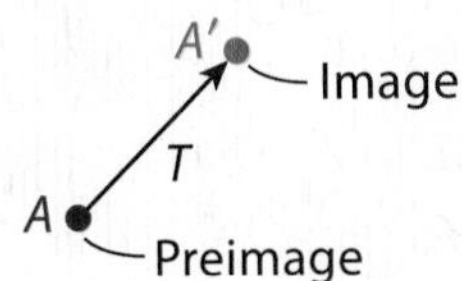

Coordinate notation is one way to write a rule for a transformation on a coordinate plane. The notation uses an arrow to show how the transformation changes the coordinates of a general point, (x, y).

Find the unknown coordinates for each transformation and draw the image. Then complete the description of the transformation and compare the image to its preimage.

Ⓐ $(x, y) \rightarrow (x - 4, y - 3)$

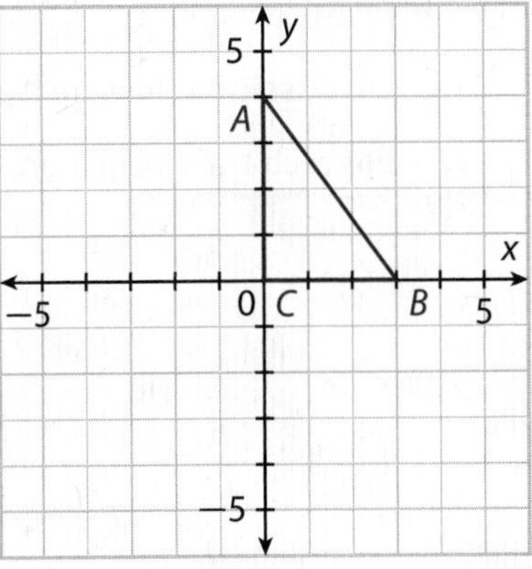

Preimage (x, y)		Rule $(x, y) \rightarrow (x - 4, y - 3)$		Image $(x - 4, y - 3)$
$A(0, 4)$	→	$A'(0 - 4, 4 - 3)$	=	$A'(-4, 1)$
$B(3, 0)$	→	$B'(3 - 4, 0 - 3)$	=	B'(? , ?)
$C(0, 0)$	→	$C'(0 - 4, 0 - 3)$	=	C'(? , ?)

The transformation is a translation 4 units ? and 3 ? .

A comparison of the image to its preimage shows that ?

Ⓑ $(x, y) \rightarrow (-x, y)$

Preimage (x, y)		Rule $(x, y) \rightarrow (-x, y)$		Image $(-x, y)$
$R(-4, 3)$	$\rightarrow$	$R'(-(-4), 3)$	$=$	$R'(?, ?)$
$S(-1, 3)$	$\rightarrow$	$S'(-(-1), 3)$	$=$	$S'(?, ?)$
$T(-4, 1)$	$\rightarrow$	$T'(-(-4), 1)$	$=$	$T'(?, ?)$

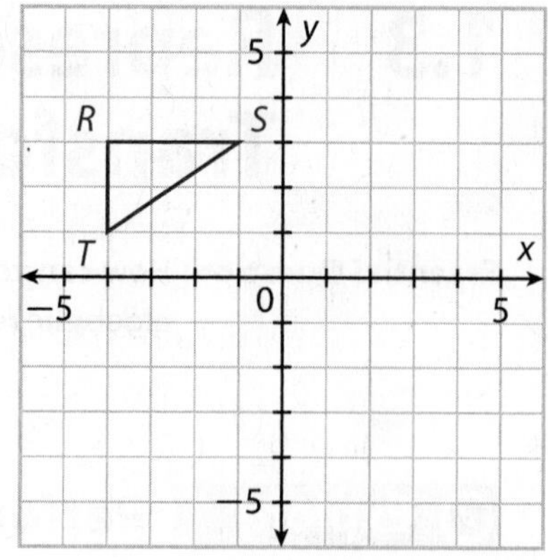

The transformation is a reflection across the ? axis.

A comparison of the image to its preimage shows that ?

Ⓒ $(x, y) \rightarrow (2x, y)$

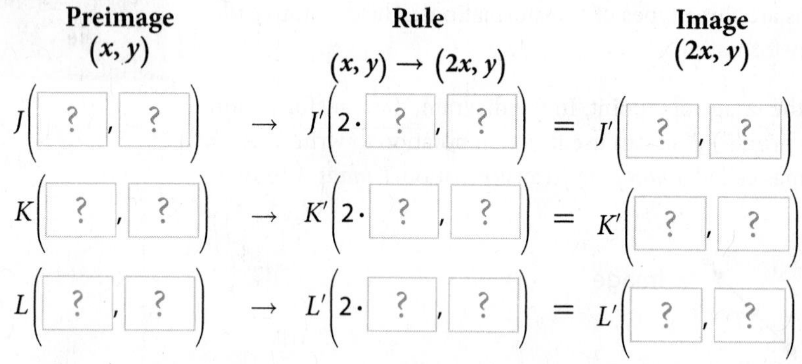

Preimage (x, y)		Rule $(x, y) \rightarrow (2x, y)$		Image $(2x, y)$
$J(?, ?)$	$\rightarrow$	$J'(2 \cdot ?, ?)$	$=$	$J'(?, ?)$
$K(?, ?)$	$\rightarrow$	$K'(2 \cdot ?, ?)$	$=$	$K'(?, ?)$
$L(?, ?)$	$\rightarrow$	$L'(2 \cdot ?, ?)$	$=$	$L'(?, ?)$

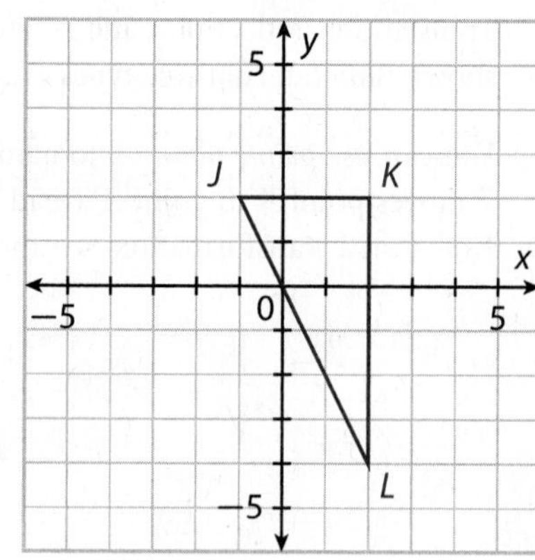

The transformation is a (horizontal/vertical) stretch by a factor of ?.

A comparison of the image to its preimage shows that ?

Reflect

1. **Discussion** How are the transformations in Steps A and B different from the transformation in Step C?
2. For each transformation, what rule could you use to map the image back to the preimage?

 Explain 1

Describing Rigid Motions Using Coordinate Notation

Some transformations preserve length and angle measure, and some do not. A **rigid motion** (or *isometry*) is a transformation that changes the position of a figure without changing the size or shape of the figure. Translations, reflections, and rotations are rigid motions.

Properties of Rigid Motions	
• Rigid motions preserve distance. • Rigid motions preserve angle measure. • Rigid motions preserve betweenness.	• Rigid motions preserve collinearity. • Rigid motions preserve parallelism.

If a figure is determined by certain points, then its image after a rigid motion is determined by the images of those points. This is true because of the betweenness and collinearity properties of rigid motions. Rotations and translations also preserve *orientation*. This means that the order of the vertices of the preimage and image are the same, either clockwise or counterclockwise. Reflections do not preserve orientation.

Example 1 **Use coordinate notation to write the rule that maps each preimage to its image. Then identify the transformation and confirm that it preserves length and angle measure.**

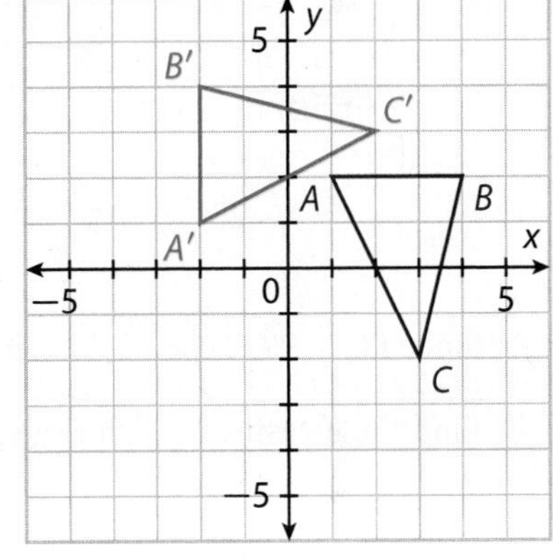

Ⓐ

Preimage		**Image**
$A(1, 2)$	$\rightarrow$	$A'(-2, 1)$
$B(4, 2)$	$\rightarrow$	$B'(-2, 4)$
$C(3, -2)$	$\rightarrow$	$C'(2, 3)$

Look for a pattern in the coordinates.

The x-coordinate of each image point is the opposite of the y-coordinate of its preimage.

The y-coordinate of each image point equals the x-coordinate of its preimage.

The transformation is a rotation of 90° counterclockwise around the origin given by the rule $(x, y) \rightarrow (-y, x)$.

Find the length of each side of $\triangle ABC$ and $\triangle A'B'C'$. Use the Distance Formula as needed.

$AB = 3$ $\qquad$ $A'B' = 3$

$BC = \sqrt{(3-4)^2 + (-2-2)^2}$ $\qquad$ $B'C' = \sqrt{(2-(-2))^2 + (3-4)^2}$

$= \sqrt{17}$ $\qquad$ $= \sqrt{17}$

$AC = \sqrt{(3-1)^2 + (-2-2)^2}$ $\qquad$ $A'C' = \sqrt{(2-(-2))^2 + (3-1)^2}$

$= \sqrt{20}$ $\qquad$ $= \sqrt{20}$

Since $AB = A'B'$, $BC = B'C'$, and $AC = A'C'$, the transformation preserves length.

Find the measure of each angle of $\triangle ABC$ and $\triangle A'B'C'$. Use a protractor.

$m\angle A = 63°$, $m\angle B = 76°$, $m\angle C = 41°$ $\qquad$ $m\angle A' = 63°$, $m\angle B' = 76°$, $m\angle C' = 41°$

Since $m\angle A = m\angle A'$, $m\angle B = m\angle B'$, and $m\angle C = m\angle C'$, the transformation preserves angle measure.

(B) **Preimage** → **Image**

$P(-3, -1) \rightarrow P'(-3, 1)$
$Q(3, -1) \rightarrow Q'(3, 1)$
$R(1, -4) \rightarrow R'(1, 4)$

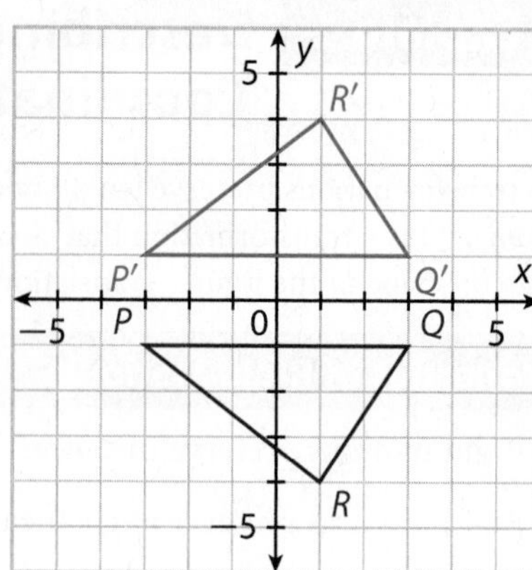

Look for a pattern in the coordinates.

The x-coordinate of each image point equals the x-coordinate of its preimage.

The y-coordinate of each image point is the opposite of the y-coordinate of its preimage.

The transformation is a reflection across the x-axis given by the rule $(x, y) \rightarrow (x, -y)$.

Find the length of each side of $\triangle PQR$ and $\triangle P'Q'R'$.

$PQ = 6$ $\qquad$ $P'Q' = 6$

$QR = \sqrt{(1 - 3)^2 + (-4 - (-1))^2} = \sqrt{13}$ $\qquad$ $Q'R' = \sqrt{(1 - 3)^2 + (4 - 1)^2} = \sqrt{13}$

$PR = \sqrt{(1 - (-3))^2 + (-4 - (-1))^2} = \sqrt{25} = 5$ $\qquad$ $P'R' = \sqrt{(1 - (-3))^2 + (4 - 1)^2} = \sqrt{25} = 5$

Since $PQ = P'Q'$, $QR = Q'R'$, and $PR = P'R'$, the transformation preserves length.

Find the measure of each angle of $\triangle PQR$ and $\triangle P'Q'R'$. Use a protractor.

$m\angle P = 37°$, $m\angle Q = 56°$, $m\angle R = 87°$ $\qquad$ $m\angle P' = 37°$, $m\angle Q' = 56°$, $m\angle R' = 87°$

Since $m\angle P = m\angle P'$, $m\angle Q = m\angle Q'$, and $m\angle R = m\angle R'$, the transformation preserves angle measure.

Reflect

3. How could you use a compass to test whether corresponding lengths in a preimage and image are the same?

4. Look back at the transformations in the Explore. Classify each transformation as a rigid motion or not a rigid motion.

Your Turn

Use coordinate notation to write the rule that maps each preimage to its image. Then identify the transformation and confirm that it preserves length and angle measure.

5.

Preimage		Image
$D(-4, 4)$	$\rightarrow$	$D'(4, -4)$
$E(2, 4)$	$\rightarrow$	$E'(-2, -4)$
$F(-4, 1)$	$\rightarrow$	$F'(4, -1)$

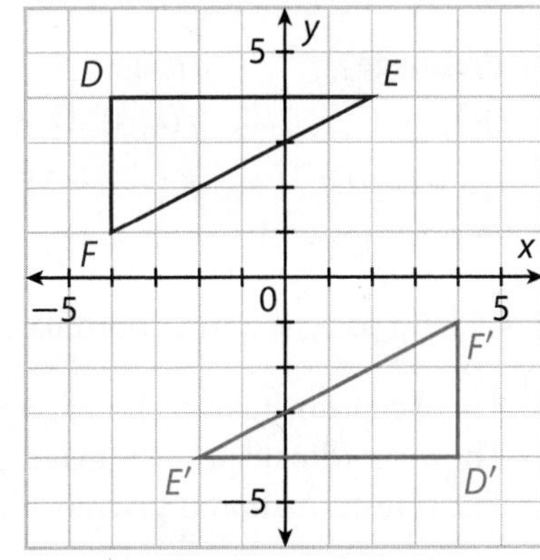

6.

Preimage		Image
$S(-3, 4)$	$\rightarrow$	$S'(-2, 2)$
$T(2, 4)$	$\rightarrow$	$T'(3, 2)$
$U(-2, 0)$	$\rightarrow$	$U'(-1, -2)$

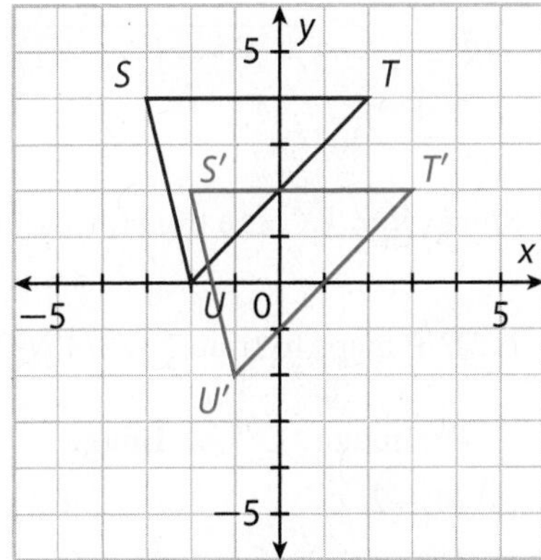

Explain 2 Describing Nonrigid Motions Using Coordinate Notation

Transformations that stretch or compress figures are not rigid motions because they do not preserve distance.

The view in the fun house mirror is an example of a vertical stretch.

Example 2 **Use coordinate notation to write the rule that maps each preimage to its image. Then confirm that the transformation is not a rigid motion.**

(A) $\triangle JKL$ maps to triangle $\triangle J'K'L'$.

Preimage		Image
$J(4, 1)$	$\rightarrow$	$J'(4, 3)$
$K(-2, -1)$	$\rightarrow$	$K'(-2, -3)$
$L(0, -3)$	$\rightarrow$	$L'(0, -9)$

Look for a pattern in the coordinates.

The x-coordinate of each image point equals the x-coordinate of its preimage.
The y-coordinate of each image point is 3 times the y-coordinate of its preimage.
The transformation is given by the rule $(x, y) \rightarrow (x, 3y)$.

Compare the length of a segment of the preimage to the length of the corresponding segment of the image.

$$JK = \sqrt{(-2-4)^2 + (-1-1)^2} = \sqrt{40}$$

$$J'K' = \sqrt{(-2-4)^2 + (-3-3)^2} = \sqrt{72}$$

Since $JK \neq J'K'$, the transformation is not a rigid motion.

(B) $\triangle MNP$ maps to triangle $\triangle M'N'P'$.

Preimage		Image
$M(-2, 2)$	$\rightarrow$	$M'(-4, 1)$
$N(4, 0)$	$\rightarrow$	$N'(8, 0)$
$P(-2, -2)$	$\rightarrow$	$P'(-4, -1)$

The x-coordinate of each image point is twice the x-coordinate of its preimage.

The y-coordinate of each image point is half the y-coordinate of its preimage.

The transformation is given by the rule $(x, y) \rightarrow \left(2x, \frac{1}{2}y\right)$.

Compare the length of a segment of the preimage to the length of the corresponding segment of the image.

$$MN = \sqrt{(x_2 - x_1)^2 + (y_2 - y_1)^2} = \sqrt{\left(4 - \boxed{-2}\right)^2 + \left(0 - \boxed{2}\right)^2} = \sqrt{\boxed{6}^2 + \boxed{-2}^2} = \sqrt{\boxed{40}}$$

$$M'N' = \sqrt{(x_2 - x_1)^2 + (y_2 - y_1)^2} = \sqrt{\left(\boxed{8} - \boxed{-4}\right)^2 + \left(\boxed{0} - \boxed{1}\right)^2} = \sqrt{\boxed{12}^2 + \boxed{-1}^2} = \sqrt{\boxed{145}}$$

Since $MN \neq M'N'$, the transformation is not a rigid motion.

Reflect

7. How could you confirm that a transformation is not a rigid motion by using a protractor?

Your Turn

Use coordinate notation to write the rule that maps each preimage to its image. Then confirm that the transformation is not a rigid motion.

8. $\triangle ABC$ maps to triangle $\triangle A'B'C'$.

Preimage		Image
$A(2, 2)$	$\rightarrow$	$A'(3, 3)$
$B(4, 2)$	$\rightarrow$	$B'(6, 3)$
$C(2, -4)$	$\rightarrow$	$C'(3, -6)$

9. $\triangle RST$ maps to triangle $\triangle R'S'T'$.

Preimage		Image
$R(-2, 1)$	$\rightarrow$	$R'(-1, 3)$
$S(4, 2)$	$\rightarrow$	$S'(2, 6)$
$T(2, -2)$	$\rightarrow$	$T'(1, -6)$

Elaborate

10. Critical Thinking To confirm that a transformation is not a rigid motion, do you have to check the length of every segment of the preimage and the length of every segment of the image? Why or why not?

11. Make a Conjecture A polygon is transformed by a rigid motion. How are the perimeters of the preimage polygon and the image polygon related? Explain.

12. Essential Question Check-In How is coordinate notation for a transformation, such as $(x, y) \rightarrow (x + 1, y - 1)$, similar to and different from algebraic function notation, such as $f(x) = 2x + 1$?

Evaluate: Homework and Practice

- Online Homework
- Hints and Help
- Extra Practice

On a coordinate grid, draw each figure and its image under the given transformation. Then describe the transformation in words.

1. $(x, y) \rightarrow (-x, -y)$

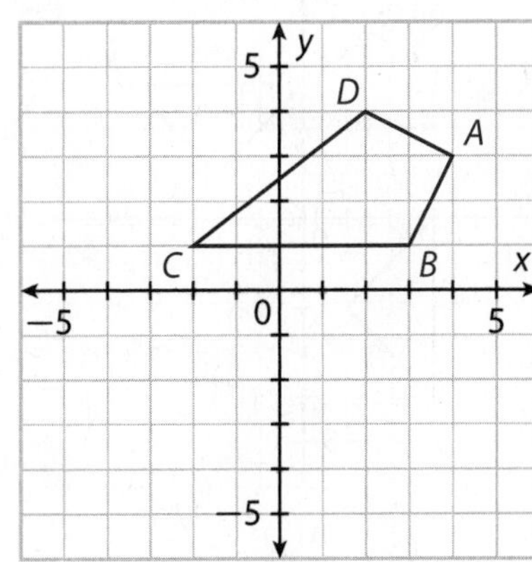

2. $(x, y) \rightarrow (x + 5, y)$

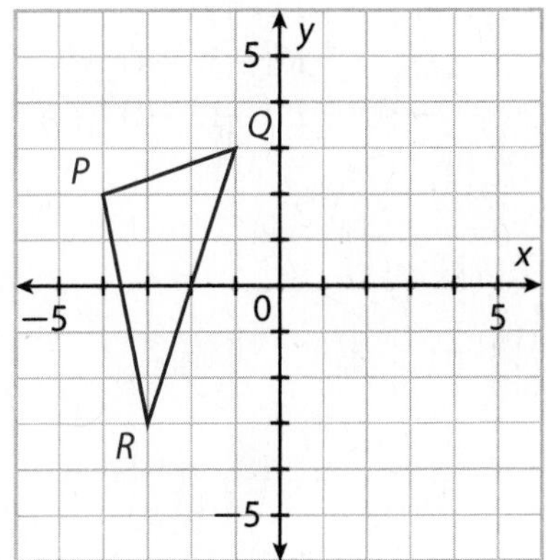

3. $(x, y) \rightarrow \left(x, \frac{1}{3}y\right)$

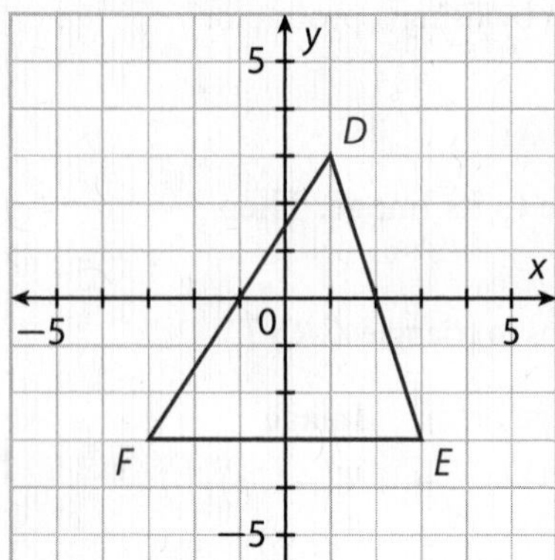

4. $(x, y) \rightarrow (y, x)$

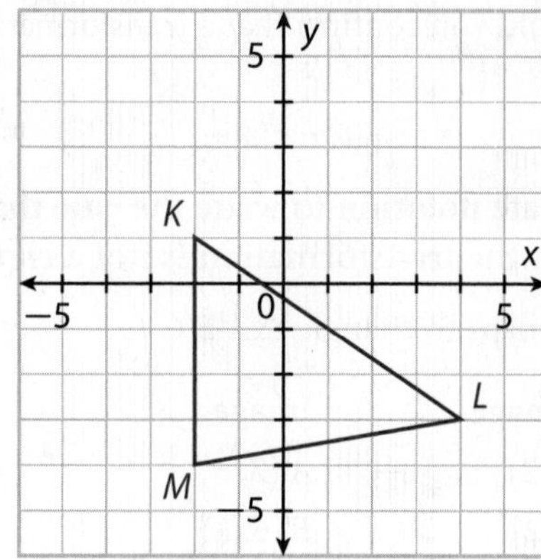

Use coordinate notation to write the rule that maps each preimage to its image. Then identify the transformation and confirm that it preserves length and angle measure.

5.

Preimage		**Image**
$A(-4, 4)$	$\rightarrow$	$A'(4, 4)$
$B(-1, 2)$	$\rightarrow$	$B'(2, 1)$
$C(-4, 1)$	$\rightarrow$	$C'(1, 4)$

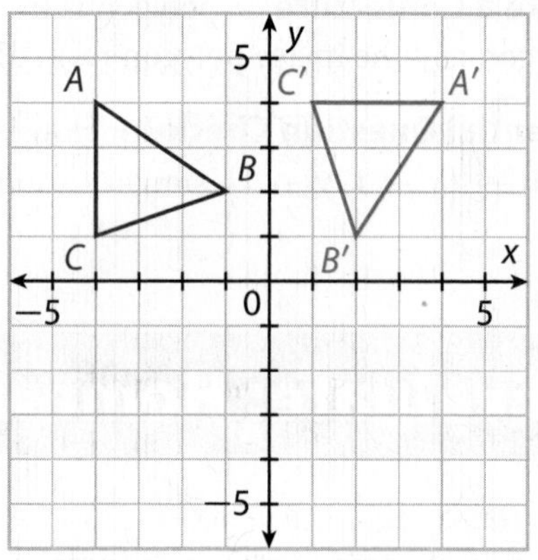

6.

Preimage		**Image**
$J(0, 3)$	$\rightarrow$	$J'(-3, 0)$
$K(4, 3)$	$\rightarrow$	$K'(-3, -4)$
$L(2, 1)$	$\rightarrow$	$L'(-1, -2)$

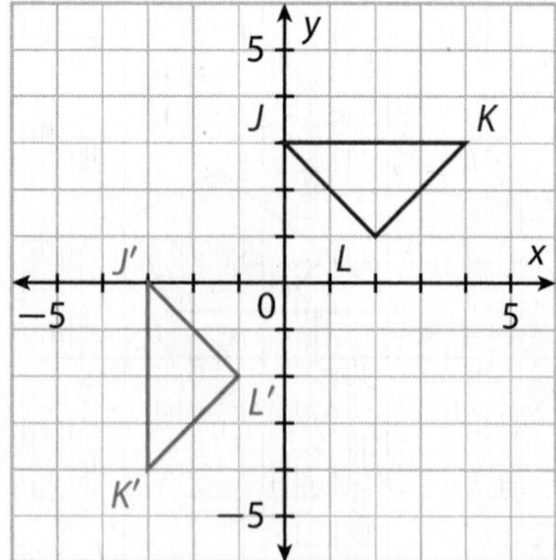

Use coordinate notation to write the rule that maps each preimage to its image. Then confirm that the transformation is not a rigid motion.

7. $\triangle ABC$ maps to triangle $\triangle A'B'C'$.

Preimage		Image
$A(6, 6)$	$\rightarrow$	$A'(3, 3)$
$B(4, -2)$	$\rightarrow$	$B'(2, -1)$
$C(0, 0)$	$\rightarrow$	$C'(0, 0)$

8. $\triangle FGH$ maps to triangle $\triangle F'G'H'$.

Preimage		Image
$F(-1, 1)$	$\rightarrow$	$F'(-2, 1)$
$G(1, -1)$	$\rightarrow$	$G'(2, -1)$
$H(-2, -2)$	$\rightarrow$	$H'(-4, -2)$

9. **Analyze Relationships** A mineralogist is studying a quartz crystal. She uses a computer program to draw a side view of the crystal, as shown. She decides to make the drawing 50% wider, but to keep the same height. Draw the transformed view of the crystal. Then write a rule for the transformation using coordinate notation. Check your rule using the original coordinates.

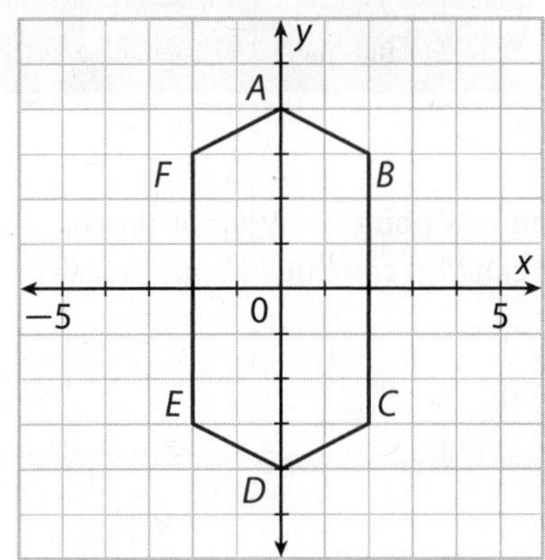

10. Use the points $A(2, 3)$ and $B(2, -3)$.

a. Describe segment AB and find its length.

b. Describe the image of segment AB under the transformation $(x, y) \rightarrow (x, 2y)$.

c. Describe the image of segment AB under the transformation $(x, y) \rightarrow (x + 2, y)$.

d. Compare the two transformations.

11. Use the points $H(-4, 1)$ and $K(4, 1)$.

a. Describe segment HK and find its length.

b. Describe the image of segment HK under the transformation $(x, y) \rightarrow (-y, x)$.

c. Describe the image of segment HK under the transformation $(x, y) \rightarrow (2x, y)$.

d. Compare the two transformations.

12. Make a Prediction A landscape architect designs a flower bed that is a quadrilateral, as shown in the figure. The plans call for a light to be placed at the midpoint of the longest side of the flower bed. The architect decides to change the location of the flower bed using the transformation $(x, y) \rightarrow (x, -y)$. Describe the location of the light in the transformed flower bed. Then make the required calculations to show that your prediction is correct.

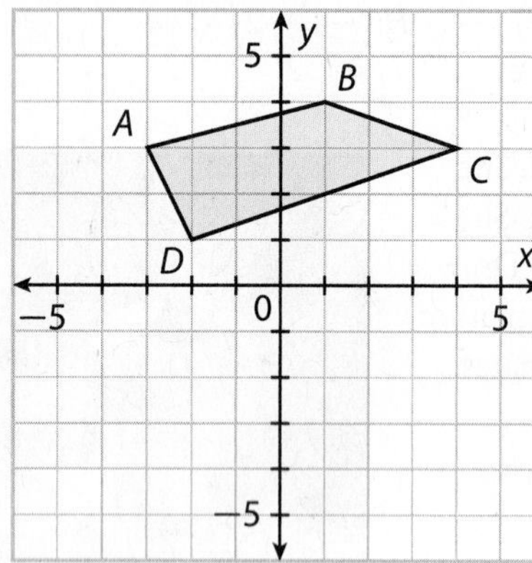

13. Multiple Representations If a transformation moves points only up or down, how do the coordinates of the point change? What can you conclude about the coordinate notation for the transformation?

14. Match each transformation with the correct description.

A. $(x, y) \rightarrow (3x, y)$	**a.** ___?___ dilation with scale factor 3
B. $(x, y) \rightarrow (x + 3, y)$	**b.** ___?___ translation 3 units up
C. $(x, y) \rightarrow (x, 3y)$	**c.** ___?___ translation 3 units right
D. $(x, y) \rightarrow (x, y + 3)$	**d.** ___?___ horizontal stretch by a factor of 3
E. $(x, y) \rightarrow (3x, 3y)$	**e.** ___?___ vertical stretch by a factor of 3

On a coordinate grid, draw each figure and its image under the given transformation. Then describe the transformation as a rigid motion or not a rigid motion. Justify your answer.

15. $(x, y) \rightarrow (2x + 4, y)$

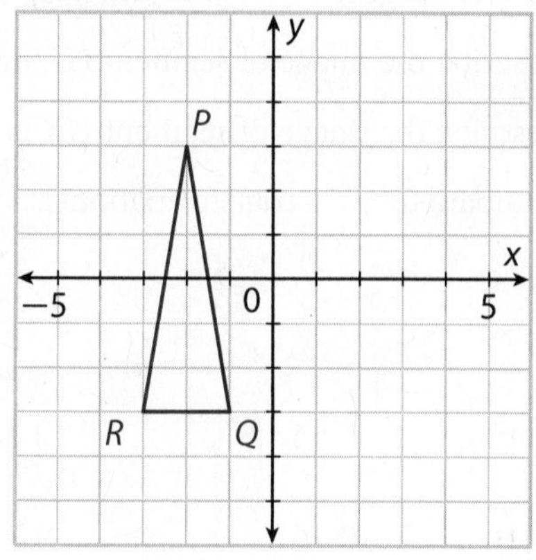

16. $(x, y) \rightarrow (0.5x, y - 4)$

H.O.T. Focus on Higher Order Thinking

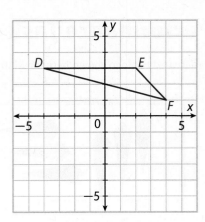

17. Explain the Error A student claimed that the transformation $(x, y) \rightarrow (3x, y)$ is a rigid motion because the segment joining $(5, 0)$ to $(5, 2)$ is transformed to the segment joining $(15, 0)$ to $(15, 2)$, and both of these segments have the same length. Explain the student's error.

18. Critical Thinking Write a rule for a transformation that maps $\triangle STU$ to $\triangle S'T'U'$.

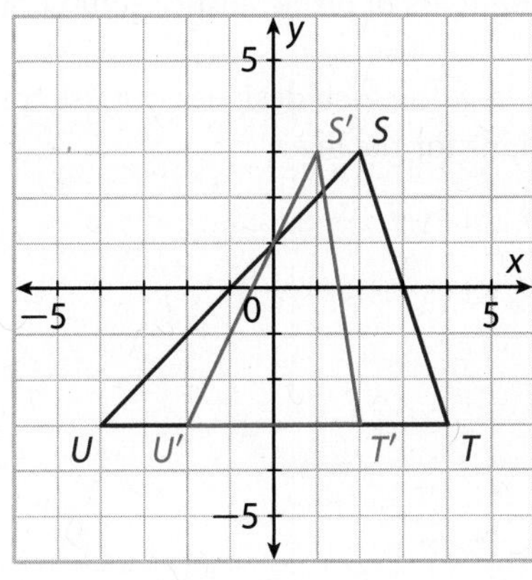

19. Justify Reasoning Consider the transformation given by the rule $(x, y) \rightarrow (0, 0)$. Describe the transformation in words. Then explain whether or not the transformation is a rigid motion and justify your reasoning.

20. Communicate Mathematical Ideas One of the properties of rigid motions states that rigid motions preserve parallelism. Explain what this means, and give an example using a specific figure and a specific rigid motion. Include a graph of the preimage and image.

Lesson Performance Task

A Web designer has created the logo shown here for Matrix Engineers.

The logo is 100 pixels wide and 24 pixels high. Images placed in Web pages can be stretched horizontally and vertically by changing the dimensions in the code for the Web page.

The Web designer would like to change the dimensions of the logo so that lengths are increased or decreased but angle measures are preserved.

a. Find three different possible sets of dimensions for the width and height so that lengths are changed but angle measures are preserved. The dimensions must be whole numbers of pixels. Justify your choices.

b. Explain how the Web designer can use transformations to find additional possible dimensions for the logo.

1.4 Reasoning and Proof

Essential Question: How do you go about proving a statement?

Resource Locker

Explore — Exploring Inductive and Deductive Reasoning

A **conjecture** is a statement that is believed to be true. You can use reasoning to investigate whether a conjecture is true. **Inductive reasoning** is the process of reasoning that a rule or statement may be true by looking at specific cases. **Deductive reasoning** is the process of using logic to *prove* whether all cases are true.

Complete the steps to make a conjecture about the sum of three consecutive counting numbers.

(A) Write a sum to represent the first three consecutive counting numbers, starting with 1.

(B) Is the sum divisible by 3?

(C) Write the sum of the next three consecutive counting numbers, starting with 2.

(D) Is the sum divisible by 3?

(E) Complete the conjecture:

The ? of three consecutive counting numbers is divisible by ? .

Recall that postulates are statements you accept are true. A **theorem** is a statement that you can prove is true using a series of logical steps. The steps of deductive reasoning involve using appropriate undefined words, defined words, mathematical relationships, postulates, or other previously-proven theorems to prove that the theorem is true.

Use deductive reasoning to prove that the sum of three consecutive counting numbers is divisible by 3.

(F) Let the three consecutive counting numbers be represented by n, $n + 1$, and ? .

(G) The sum of the three consecutive counting numbers can be written as $3n +$? .

(H) The expression $3n + 3$ can be factored as $3($? $)$.

(I) The expression $3(n + 1)$ is divisible by ? for all values of n.

Ⓙ Recall the conjecture in Step E: The sum of three consecutive counting numbers is divisible by 3.

Look at the steps in your deductive reasoning. Is the conjecture true or false?

Reflect

1. **Discussion** A **counterexample** is an example that shows a conjecture to be false. Do you think that counterexamples are used mainly in inductive reasoning or in deductive reasoning?

2. Suppose you use deductive reasoning to show that an angle is not acute. Can you conclude that the angle is obtuse? Explain.

Explain 1 Introducing Proofs

A **conditional statement** is a statement that can be written in the form "If p, then q" where p is the *hypothesis* and q is the *conclusion*. For example, in the conditional statement "If $3x - 5 = 13$, then $x = 6$," the hypothesis is "$3x - 5 = 13$" and the conclusion is "$x = 6$."

Most of the Properties of Equality can be written as conditional statements. You can use these properties to solve an equation like "$3x - 5 = 13$" to prove that "$x = 6$."

Properties of Equality	
Addition Property of Equality	If $a = b$, then $a + c = b + c$.
Subtraction Property of Equality	If $a = b$, then $a - c = b - c$.
Multiplication Property of Equality	If $a = b$, then $ac = bc$.
Division Property of Equality	If $a = b$ and $c \neq 0$, then $\frac{a}{c} = \frac{b}{c}$.
Reflexive Property of Equality	$a = a$
Symmetric Property of Equality	If $a = b$, then $b = a$.
Transitive Property of Equality	If $a = b$ and $b = c$, then $a = c$.
Substitution Property of Equality	If $a = b$, then b can be substituted for a in any expression.

Example 1 **Use deductive reasoning to solve the equation. Use the Properties of Equality to justify each step.**

Ⓐ $14 = 3x - 4$

$14 = 3x - 4$

$18 = 3x$ Addition Property of Equality

$6 = x$ Division Property of Equality

$x = 6$ Symmetric Property of Equality

(B) $9 = 17 - 4x$

$9 = 17 - 4x$		
$9 - 17$	$= -4x$	Subtraction Property of Equality
-8	$= -4x$	
2	$= x$	Division Property of Equality
$x =$	2	Symmetric Property of Equality

Your Turn

Write each statement as a conditional statement.

3. All zebras belong to the genus *Equus*.

4. The bill will pass if it gets two-thirds of the vote in the Senate.

5. Use deductive reasoning to solve the equation $3 - 4x = -5$.

6. Identify the Property of Equality that is used in each statement.

If $x = 2$, then $2x = 4$.	?
$5 = 3a$; therefore, $3a = 5$.	?
If $T = 4$, then $5T + 7$ equals 27.	?
If $9 = 4x$ and $4x = m$, then $9 = m$.	?

Explain 2 Using Postulates about Segments and Angles

Recall that two angles whose measures add up to 180° are called *supplementary angles*. The following theorem shows one type of supplementary angle pair, called a *linear pair*. A **linear pair** is a pair of adjacent angles whose non-common sides are opposite rays. You will prove this theorem in an exercise in this lesson.

The Linear Pair Theorem

If two angles form a linear pair, then they are supplementary.

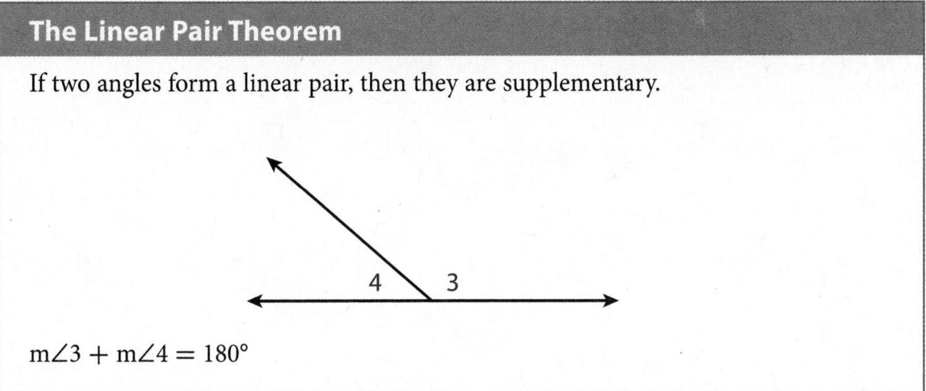

$m\angle 3 + m\angle 4 = 180°$

You can use the Linear Pair Theorem, as well as the Segment Addition Postulate and Angle Addition Postulate, to find missing values in expressions for segment lengths and angle measures.

Example 2 **Use a postulate or theorem to find the value of x in each figure.**

(A) Given: $RT = 5x - 12$

$x + 2$ $3x - 8$

R S T

$5x - 12$

Use the Segment Addition Postulate.

$$RS + ST = RT$$

$$(x + 2) + (3x - 8) = 5x - 12$$

$$4x - 6 = 5x - 12$$

$$6 = x$$

$$x = 6$$

(B) Given: $m\angle RST = (15x - 10)°$

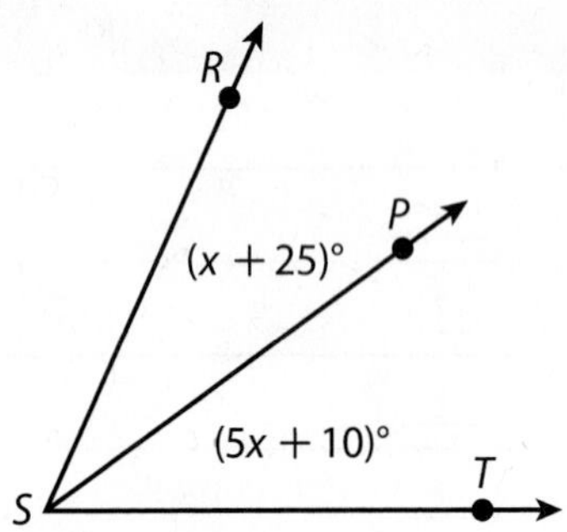

Use the Angle Addition Postulate.

$m\angle RST = m\angle$ [RSP] $+ m\angle$ [PST]

$(15x - 10)° =$ [$(x + 25)$]$° +$ [$(5x + 10)$]$°$

$15x - 10 =$ [$(6x + 35)$]

[9] $x =$ [45]

$x =$ [5]

Reflect

7. **Discussion** The Linear Pair Theorem uses the terms *opposite rays* as well as *adjacent angles*. Write a definition for each of these terms. Compare your definitions with your classmates.

Your Turn

8. Two angles *LMN* and *NMP* form a linear pair. The measure of $\angle LMN$ is twice the measure of $\angle NMP$. Find $m\angle LMN$.

Explain 3 Using Postulates about Lines and Planes

Postulates about points, lines, and planes help describe geometric figures.

Postulates about Points, Lines, and Planes

Through any two points, there is exactly one line.

Through any three noncollinear points, there is exactly one plane containing them.

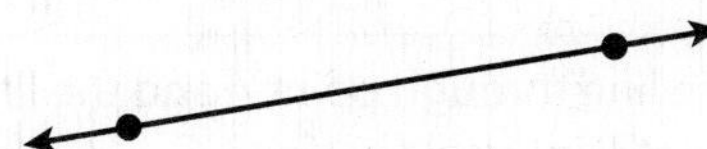

If two points lie in a plane, then the line containing those points lies in the plane.

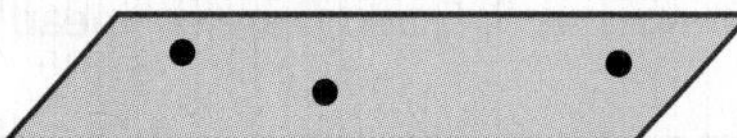

If two lines intersect, then they intersect in exactly one point.

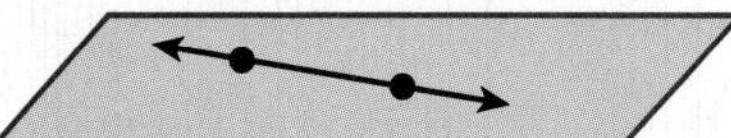

If two planes intersect, then they intersect in exactly one line.

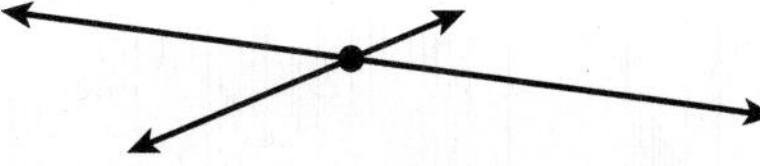

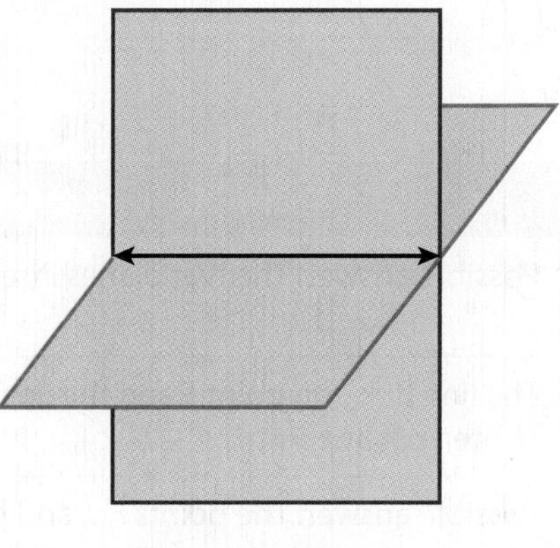

Example 3 **Use each figure to name the results described.**

Ⓐ

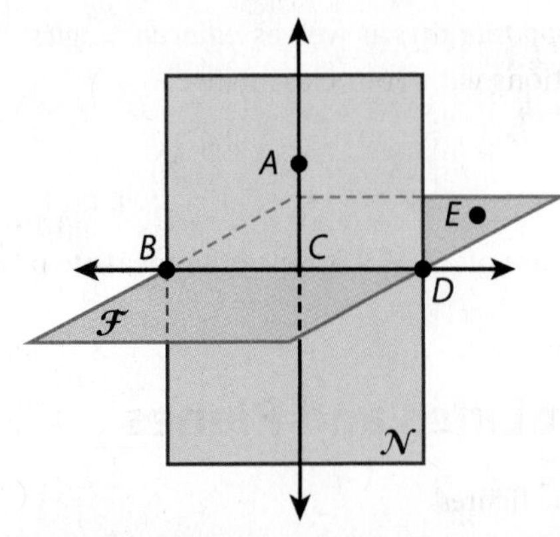

Description	Example from the figure
the line of intersection of two planes	Possible answer: The two planes intersect in line *BD*.
the point of intersection of two lines	The line through point *A* and the line through point *B* intersect at point *C*.
three coplanar points	Possible answer: The points *B*, *D*, and *E* are coplanar.
three collinear points	The points *B*, *C*, and *D* are collinear.

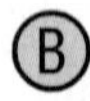

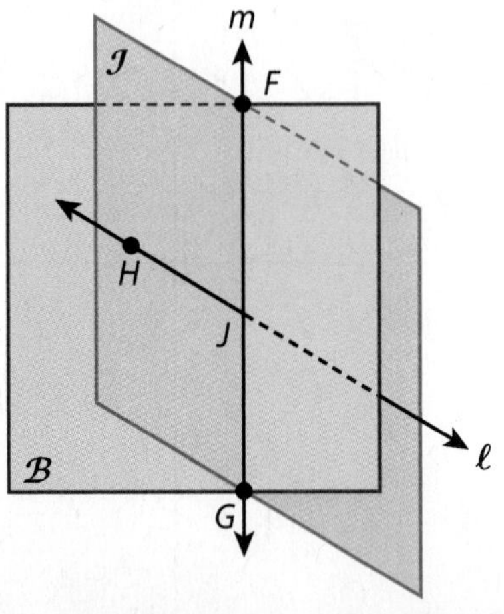

Description	Example from the figure
the line of intersection of two planes	Possible answer: The two planes intersect in line *JF*.
the point of intersection of two lines	The line through point *F* and the line through point *H* intersect at point *J*.
three coplanar points	Possible answer: The points *F*, *J*, and *H* are coplanar.
three collinear points	The points *F*, *J*, and *G* are collinear.

Reflect

9. Find examples in your classroom that illustrate the postulates of lines, planes, and points.

10. Draw a diagram of a plane with three collinear points and three points that are noncollinear.

Elaborate

11. What is the difference between a postulate and a definition? Give an example of each.

12. Give an example of a diagram illustrating the Segment Addition Postulate. Write the Segment Addition Postulate as a conditional statement.

13. Explain why photographers often use a tripod when taking pictures.

14. **Essential Question Check-In** What are some of the reasons you can give in proving a statement using deductive reasoning?

Evaluate: Homework and Practice

- Online Homework
- Hints and Help
- Extra Practice

Explain why the given conclusion uses inductive reasoning.

1. Find the next term in the pattern: 3, 6, 9. The next term is 12 because the previous terms are multiples of 3.

2. $3 + 5 = 8$ and $13 + 5 = 18$, therefore the sum of two odd numbers is an even number.

3. My neighbor has two cats and both cats have yellow eyes. Therefore when two cats live together, they will both have yellow eyes.

4. It always seems to rain the day after July 4th.

Give a counterexample for each conclusion.

5. If x is a prime number, then $x + 1$ is not a prime number.

6. The difference between two even numbers is positive.

7. Points A, B, and C are noncollinear, so therefore they are noncoplanar.

8. The square of a number is always greater than the number.

In Exercises 9–12 use deductive reasoning to write a conclusion.

9. If a number is divisible by 2, then it is even.
The number 14 is divisible by 2.

10. If two planes intersect, then they intersect in exactly one line.
Planes $\mathfrak{R}$ and $\mathfrak{I}$ intersect.

11. Through any three noncollinear points, there is exactly one plane containing them.
Points W, X, and Y are noncollinear.

12. If the sum of the digits of an integer is divisible by 3, then the number is divisible by 3.
The sum of the digits of 46,125 is 18, which is divisible by 3.

Identify the hypothesis and conclusion of each statement.

13. If the ball is red, then it will bounce higher.

14. If a plane contains two lines, then they are coplanar.

15. If the light does not come on, then the circuit is broken.

16. You must wear your jacket if it is cold outside.

Use a definition, postulate, or theorem to find the value of x in the figure described.

17. Point E is between points D and F. If $DE = x - 4$, $EF = 2x + 5$, and $DF = 4x - 8$, find x.

18. Y is the midpoint of $\overline{XZ}$. If $XZ = 8x - 2$ and $YZ = 2x + 1$, find x.

19. $\overrightarrow{SV}$ is an angle bisector of $\angle RST$. If $m\angle RSV = (3x + 5)°$ and $m\angle RST = (8x - 14)°$, find x.

20. $\angle ABC$ and $\angle CBD$ are a linear pair. If $m\angle ABC = m\angle CBD = 3x - 6$, find x.

Use the figure for Exercises 21 and 22.

21. Name three collinear points.

22. Name two linear pairs.

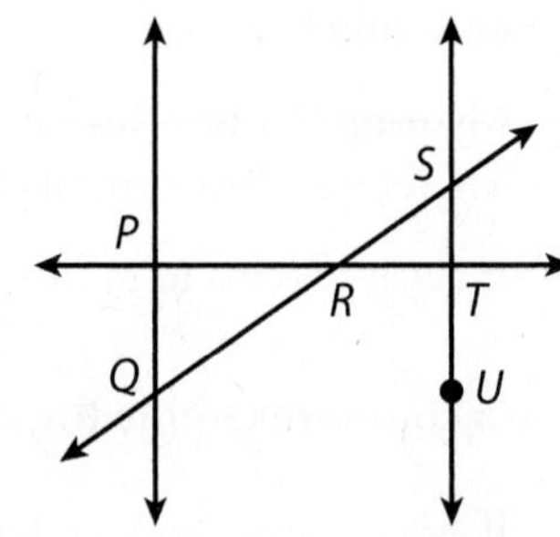

Explain the error in each statement.

23. Two planes can intersect in a single point.

24. Three points have to be collinear.

25. A line is contained in exactly one plane

26. If $x^2 = 25$, then $x = 5$.

H.O.T. Focus on Higher Order Thinking

27. Analyze Relationships What is the greatest number of intersection points 4 coplanar lines can have? What is the greatest number of planes determined by 4 noncollinear points? Draw diagrams to illustrate your answers.

28. Justify Reasoning Prove the Linear Pair Theorem.
Given: $\angle MJK$ and $\angle MJL$ are a linear pair of angles.
Prove: $\angle MJK$ and $\angle MJL$ are supplementary.

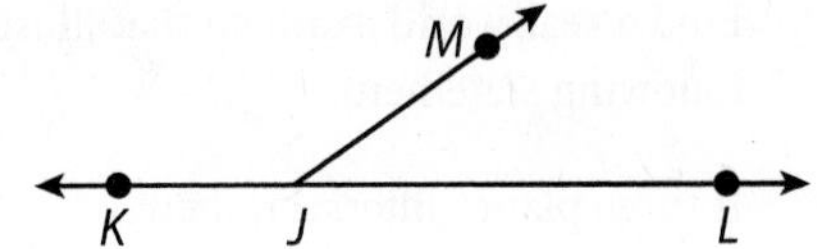

Complete the proof by writing the missing reasons. Choose from the following reasons.

Angle Addition Postulate

Definition of linear pair

Substitution Property of Equality

Given

Statements	Reasons
1. $\angle MJK$ and $\angle MJL$ are a linear pair.	1. ?
2. $\overrightarrow{JL}$ and $\overrightarrow{JK}$ are opposite rays.	2. ?
3. $\overrightarrow{JL}$ and $\overrightarrow{JK}$ form a straight line.	3. Definition of opposite rays
4. $m\angle LJK = 180°$	4. Definition of straight angle
5. $m\angle MJK + m\angle MJL = m\angle LJK$	5. ?
6. $m\angle MJK + m\angle MJL = 180°$	6. ?
7. $\angle MJK$ and $\angle MJL$ are supplementary.	7. Definition of supplementary angles

Lesson Performance Task

If two planes intersect, then they intersect in exactly one line.

Find a real-world example that illustrates the postulate above. Then formulate a conjecture by completing the following statement:

If three planes intersect, then ______________________________.

Justify your conjecture with real-world examples or a drawing.

Tools of Geometry

Essential Question: How can you use tools of geometry to solve real-world problems?

KEY EXAMPLE *(Lesson 1.1)*

Find the midpoint of (5, 6) and (1, 3).

$\left(\frac{5+1}{2}, \frac{6+3}{2}\right)$ Apply the midpoint formula.

$= \left(\frac{6}{2}, \frac{9}{2}\right)$ Simplify the numerators.

$= \left(3, \frac{9}{2}\right)$ Simplify.

KEY EXAMPLE *(Lesson 1.2)*

The ray $\overrightarrow{BD}$ is the angle bisector of $\angle ABC$ and $m\angle ABC = 40°$. Find $m\angle ABD$.

$\overrightarrow{BD}$ is the angle bisector of $\angle ABC$ so it divides the angle into two angles of equal measure.

Then $m\angle ABD + m\angle DBC = m\angle ABC$ and $m\angle ABD = m\angle DBC$.

So, $2 \cdot m\angle ABD = m\angle ABC$.

$m\angle ABD = 20°$ Substitute the angles and simplify.

KEY EXAMPLE *(Lesson 1.3)*

Use the rule $(x, y) \rightarrow (x + 1, 2y)$ and the points of a triangle, $A(1, 2)$, $B(2, 4)$, and $C(2, 2)$ to draw the image. Determine whether this is a rigid motion.

$A'(1 + 1, 2(2)), B'(2 + 1, 2(4)), C'(2 + 1, 2(2))$ Use the transformation rule.

$A'(2, 4), B'(3, 8), C'(3, 4)$ Simplify.

$A'B' = \sqrt{(3-2)^2 + (8-4)^2}$ Use the distance formula to find the distance between A' and B'.

$= \sqrt{17} \approx 4.1$ Simplify.

$AB = \sqrt{(2-1)^2 + (4-2)^2}$ Use the distance formula to find the distance between A and B.

$= \sqrt{5} \approx 2.2$ Simplify.

The image is not a rigid motion because the side lengths are not equal.

Key Vocabulary

point *(punto)*
line *(línea)*
plane *(plano)*
line segment *(segmento de línea)*
endpoints *(punto final)*
ray *(rayo)*
coplanar *(coplanares)*
parallel *(paralelo)*
collinear *(colineales)*
postulate *(postulado)*
midpoint *(punto medio)*
segment bisector *(segmento bisectriz)*
angle *(ángulo)*
vertex *(vértice)*
side *(lado)*
degrees *(grados)*
angle bisector *(bisectriz de un ángulo)*
transformation *(transformación)*
preimage *(preimagen)*
image *(imagen)*
rigid motion *(movimiento rígido)*
conjecture *(conjetura)*
inductive reasoning *(razonamiento inductivo)*
deductive reasoning *(razonamiento deductivo)*
theorem *(teorema)*
counterexample *(contraejemplo)*
conditional statement *(sentencia condicional)*
linear pair *(par lineal)*

EXERCISES

Find the midpoint of the pairs of points. (Lesson 1.1)

1. $(4, 7)$ and $(2, 9)$

2. $(5, 5)$ and $(-1, 3)$

Find the measure of the angle formed by the angle bisector. (Lesson 1.2)

3. The ray $\overrightarrow{BD}$ is the angle bisector of $\angle ABC$ and $m\angle ABC = 110°$. Find $m\angle ABD$.

Use the rule $(x, y) \rightarrow (3x, 2y)$ to find the image for the preimage defined by the points. Determine whether the transformation is a rigid motion. (Lesson 1.3)

4. $A(3, 5)$, $B(5, 3)$, $C(2, 2)$

Determine whether the conjecture uses inductive or deductive reasoning. (Lesson1.4)

5. The child chose Rock in all four games of Rock-Paper-Scissors. The child always chooses Rock.

MODULE PERFORMANCE TASK

How Far Is It?

Many smartphone apps and online search engines will tell you the distances to nearby restaurants from your current location. How do they do that? Basically, they use latitude and longitude coordinates from GPS to calculate the distances. Let's explore how that works for some longer distances.

The table lists latitude and longitude for four state capitals. Use an app or search engine to find the latitude and longitude for your current location, then complete the table.

City	Latitude	Longitude
Austin, TX	30.31° N	97.76° W
Columbus, OH	39.98° N	82.99° W
Nashville, TN	36.17° N	86.78 ° W
Sacramento, CA	38.57° N	121.5° W
Your Location	?	?

- Which of the state capitals do you think is nearest to you? Which is farthest away? Use the distance formula to calculate your distance from each of the cities in degrees. Then convert each distance to miles.

- Use an app or search engine to find the distance between your location and each of the capital cities. How do these distances compare with the ones you calculated? How might you account for any differences?

Ready to Go On?

1.1–1.4 Tools of Geometry

- Online Homework
- Hints and Help
- Extra Practice

Use a definition, postulate, or theorem to find the value desired.

1. Point M is the midpoint between points $A(-5, 4)$ and $B(-1, -6)$. Find the location of M. *(Lesson 1.1)*

Draw triangle *EFG* on a coordinate grid. Then graph its image *E′F′G′* and confirm that the transformation preserves length and angle measure. *(Lesson 1.1)*

2. $(x, y) \rightarrow (x - 1, y + 5)$

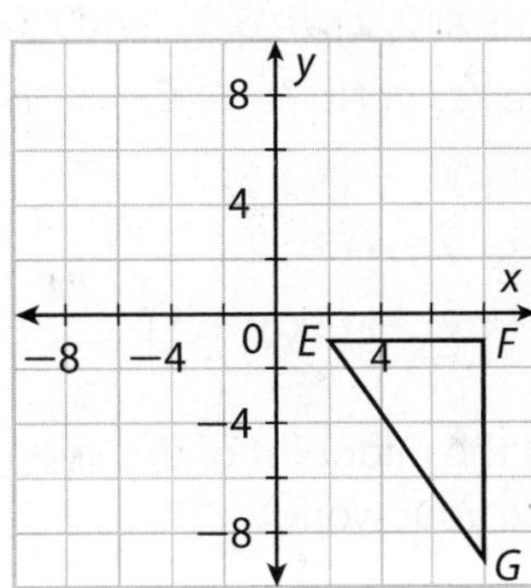

Find the measure of the angle formed by the angle bisector. *(Lesson 1.2)*

3. The ray $\overrightarrow{GJ}$ is the angle bisector of $\angle FGH$ and $m\angle FGH = 75°$. Find $m\angle FGJ$.

4. The ray $\overrightarrow{XZ}$ is the angle bisector of $\angle WXY$ and $m\angle WXY = 155°$. Find $m\angle YXZ$.

ESSENTIAL QUESTION

5. When is a protractor preferred to a ruler when finding a measurement?

MODULE 1
MIXED REVIEW

Assessment Readiness

1. For two angles, $\angle ABC$ and $\angle DBC$, $m\angle ABC = 30°$ and $\angle DBC$ is its complement. Ray $\overrightarrow{BE}$ is the angle bisector of $\angle ABD$. Consider each angle. Does the angle have a measure of 45°?

Write Yes or No for A–C.

A. $\angle DBC$

B. $\angle ABE$

C. $\angle DBE$

2. Consider the effect of the transformation $(x, y) \longrightarrow (x, 2y)$ on the parallelogram *ABCD* with vertices $A(0, 0)$, $B(1, 1)$, $C(3, 1)$, and $D(2, 0)$.

A. The transformation preserves parallelism.

B. The transformation preserves distance.

C. The transformation preserves angle measure.

3. Triangle *ABC* is given by the points $A(1, 1)$, $B(3, 2)$, and $C(2, 3)$. Consider each rule of transformation. Does the rule result in an image with points $A'(2, 2)$, $B'(6, 3)$, and $C'(4, 4)$?

Write Yes or No for A–C.

A. $(x, y) \rightarrow (x, y + 1)$

B. $(x, y) \rightarrow (2x, 2y)$

C. $(x, y) \rightarrow (2x, y + 1)$

4. Find the midpoint of the line segment with endpoints (4, 5) and (–2, 12). Show your work.

Transformations and Symmetry

MODULE 2

Essential Question: How can you use transformations to solve real-world problems?

REAL WORLD VIDEO
Check out how transformations can be used to cut patterns out of fabric as efficiently as possible.

MODULE PERFORMANCE TASK PREVIEW

Animating Digital Images

In this module, you will use transformations to create a simple animation of a bird in flight. How do computer animators use translations, rotations, and reflections? Let's find out.

Are YOU Ready?

Complete these exercises to review the skills you will need for this module.

- Online Homework
- Hints and Help
- Extra Practice

Properties of Reflections

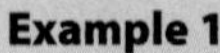

Example 1 A figure in the first quadrant is reflected over the x-axis. What quadrant is the image in?

The image is in the fourth quadrant. A figure drawn on tracing paper can be reflected across the x-axis by folding the paper along the axis.

Find the quadrant of each image.

1. The image from reflecting a figure in the first quadrant over the y-axis

2. The image from reflecting a figure in the second quadrant over the x-axis

Properties of Rotations

Example 2 A figure in the first quadrant is rotated 90° counterclockwise around the origin. What quadrant is the image in?

The image is in the second quadrant. In the second quadrant, each point of the figure forms a clockwise 90° angle around the origin with its corresponding point in the original figure.

Find the quadrant of each image.

3. The image from rotating a figure in the third quadrant 180° clockwise

4. The image from rotating a figure in the first quadrant 360° clockwise

Properties of Translations

Example 3 A figure in the first quadrant is translated up 3 units and to the right 1 unit. What quadrant is the image in?

The image is in the first quadrant. A translation only moves the image in a direction; the image is not reflected or rotated.

Answer each question.

5. A figure in the first quadrant is translated down and to the right. Is it known what quadrant the image is in?

6. A figure is translated 3 units up and 2 units left. How large is the image in comparison to the figure?

2.1 Translations

Resource Locker

Essential Question: How do you draw the image of a figure under a translation?

Explore — Exploring Translations

A translation slides all points of a figure the same distance in the same direction.

You can use tracing paper to model translating a triangle.

(A) First, draw a triangle on lined paper. Label the vertices *A*, *B*, and *C*. Then draw a line segment *XY*. An example of what your drawing may look like is shown.

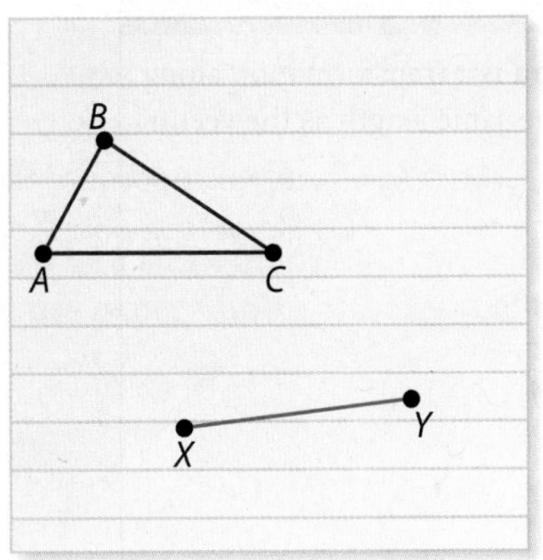

(B) Use tracing paper to draw a copy of triangle *ABC*. Then copy $\overline{XY}$ so that the point *X* is on top of point *A*. Label the point made from *Y* as *A*′.

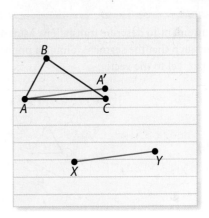

(C) Using the same piece of tracing paper, place *A*' on *A* and draw a copy of $\triangle ABC$. Label the corresponding vertices *B*′ and *C*′. An example of what your drawing may look like is shown.

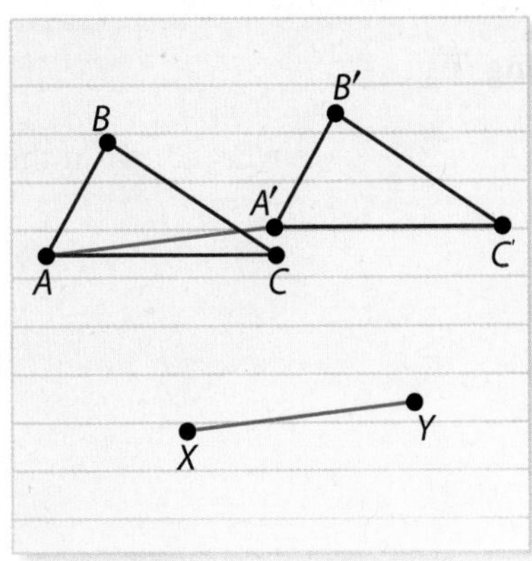

(D) Use a ruler to draw line segments from each vertex of the preimage to the corresponding vertex on the new image.

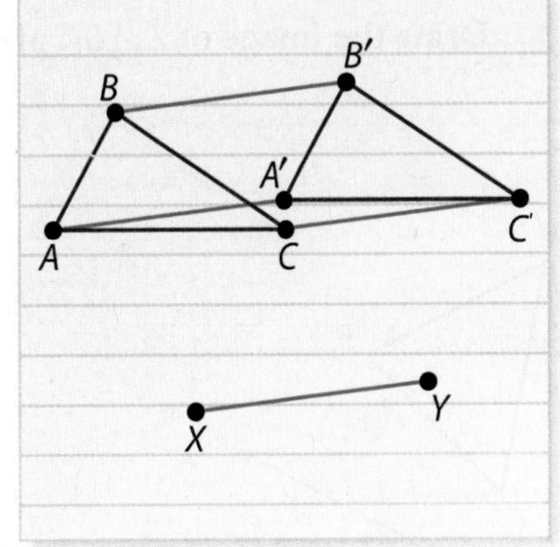

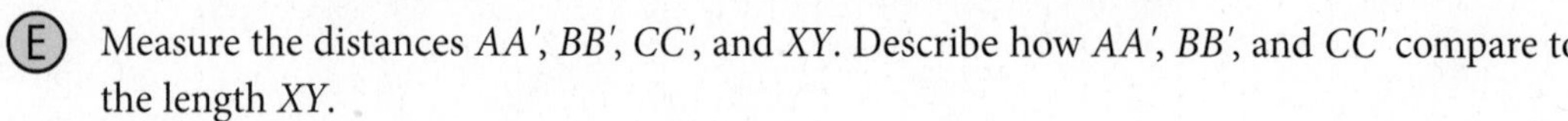

(E) Measure the distances AA', BB', CC', and XY. Describe how AA', BB', and CC' compare to the length XY.

Reflect

1. Are BB', AA', and CC' parallel, perpendicular, or neither? Describe how you can check that your answer is reasonable.

2. How does the angle BAC relate to the angle $B'A'C'$? Explain.

Explain 1 Translating Figures Using Vectors

A **vector** is a quantity that has both direction and magnitude. The **initial point** of a vector is the starting point. The **terminal point** of a vector is the ending point. The vector shown may be named $\overrightarrow{EF}$ or $\vec{v}$.

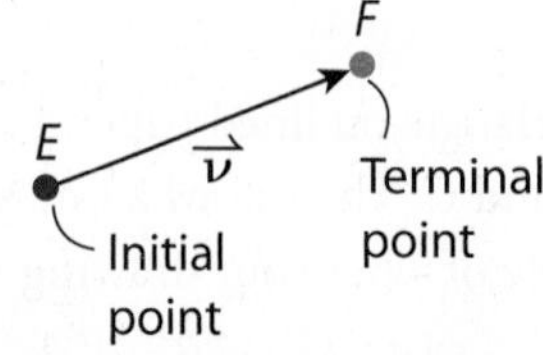

Translation

It is convenient to describe translations using vectors. A **translation** is a transformation along a vector such that the segment joining a point and its image has the same length as the vector and is parallel to the vector.

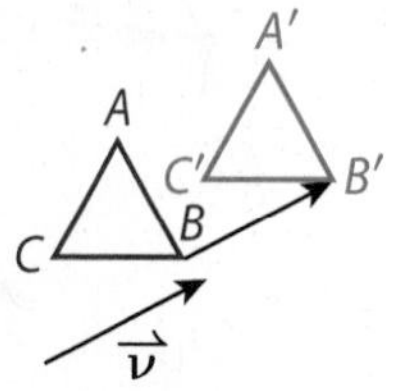

For example, BB' is a line segment that is the same length as and is parallel to vector $\vec{v}$.

You can use these facts about parallel lines to draw translations.

- Parallel lines are always the same distance apart and never intersect.
- Parallel lines have the same slope.

Example 1 **Draw the image of $\triangle ABC$ after a translation along $\vec{v}$.**

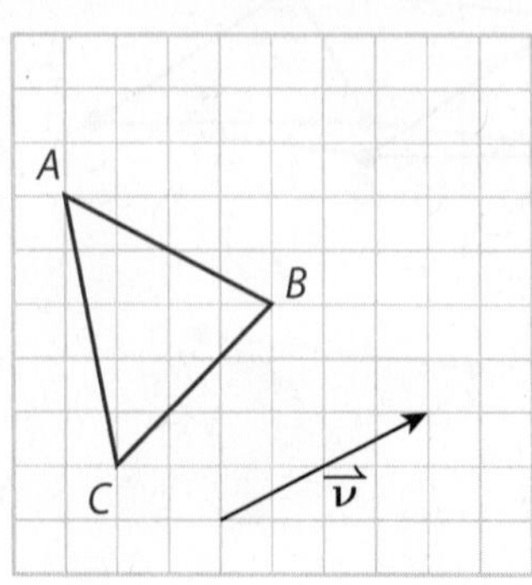

Draw a copy of $\vec{v}$ with its initial point at vertex A of $\triangle ABC$. The copy must be the same length as $\vec{v}$, and it must be parallel to $\vec{v}$. Repeat this process at vertices B and C.

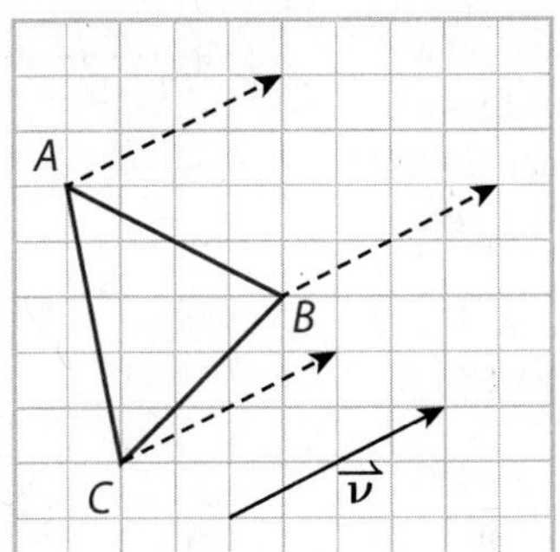

Draw segments to connect the terminal points of the vectors. Label the points A', B', and C'. $\triangle A'B'C'$ is the image of $\triangle ABC$.

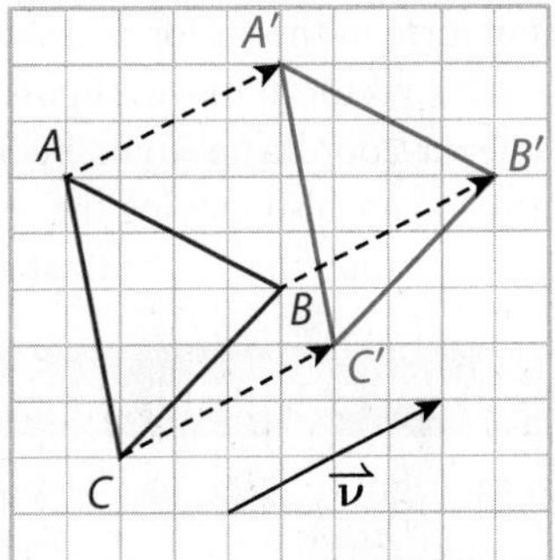

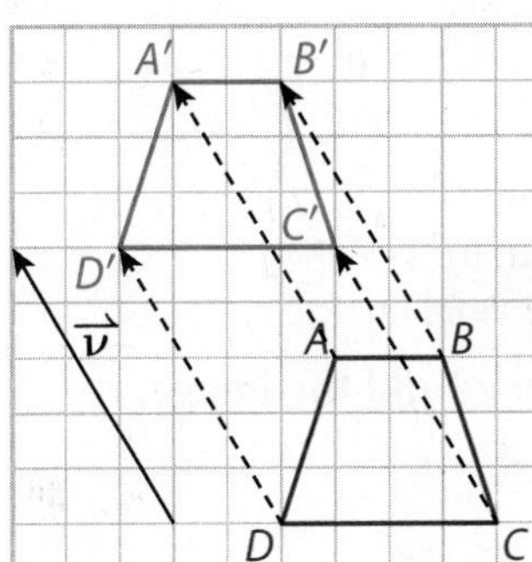

Draw a vector from the vertex A that is the same length as and parallel to vector $\vec{v}$. The terminal point A' will be 5 units up and 3 units left.

Draw three more vectors that are parallel from B, C, and D with terminal points B', C', and D'.

Draw segments connecting A', B', C', and D' to form quadrilateral $A'B'C'D'$.

Reflect

3. How is drawing an image of quadrilateral $ABCD$ like drawing an image of $\triangle ABC$? How is it different?

Your Turn

4. Copy $\triangle ABC$ and vector $\vec{v}$ on a coordinate grid. Then draw the image of $\triangle ABC$ after a translation along $\vec{v}$.

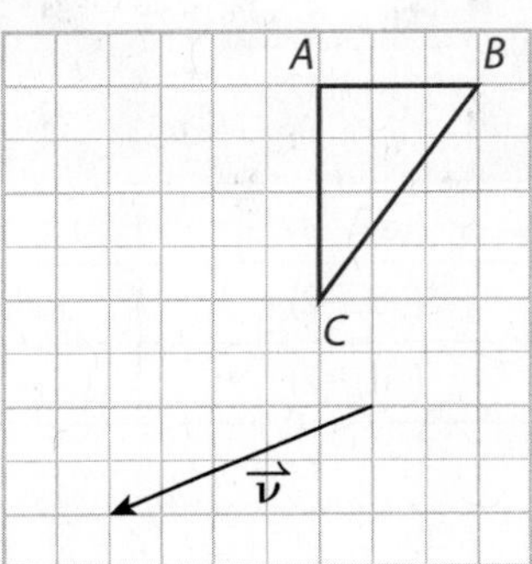

Explain 2 Drawing Translations on a Coordinate Plane

A vector can also be named using component form, $\langle a, b\rangle$, which specifies the horizontal change a and the vertical change b from the initial point to the terminal point. The component form for $\overline{PQ}$ is $\langle 5, 3\rangle$.

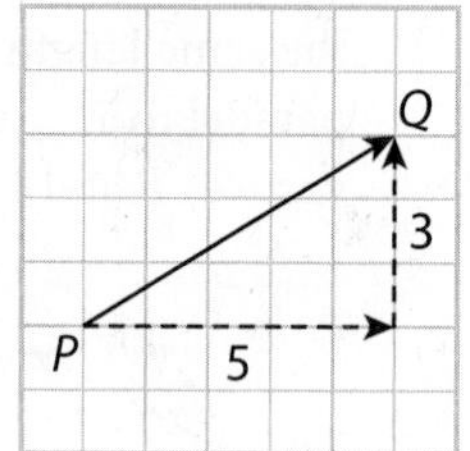

You can use the component form of the vector to draw coordinates for a new image on a coordinate plane. By using this vector to move a figure, you are moving the x-coordinate 5 units to the right. So, the new x-coordinate would be 5 greater than the x-coordinate in the preimage. Using this vector you are also moving the y-coordinate up 3 units. So, the new y-coordinate would be 3 greater than the y-coordinate in the preimage.

Rules for Translations on a Coordinate Plane	
Translation a units to the right	$(x, y) \rightarrow (x + a, y)$
Translation a units to the left	$(x, y) \rightarrow (x - a, y)$
Translation b units up	$(x, y) \rightarrow (x, y + b)$
Translation b units down	$(x, y) \rightarrow (x, y - b)$

So, when you move an image to the right a units and up b units, you use the rule $(x, y) \rightarrow (x + a, y + b)$ which is the same as moving the image along vector $\langle a, b\rangle$.

Example 2 **Calculate the vertices of the image figure. Graph the preimage and the image.**

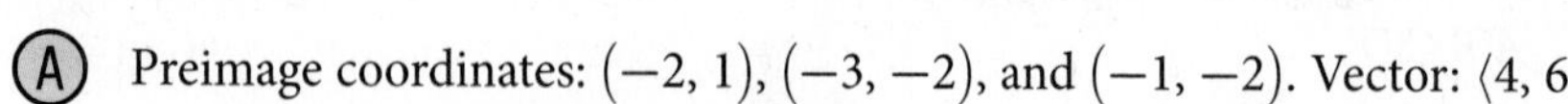

Ⓐ Preimage coordinates: $(-2, 1)$, $(-3, -2)$, and $(-1, -2)$. Vector: $\langle 4, 6\rangle$

Predict which quadrant the new image will be drawn in: 1st quadrant.

Use a table to record the new coordinates. Use vector components to write the transformation rule.

Preimage coordinates (x, y)	Image $(x + 4, y + 6)$
(−2, 1)	(2, 7)
(−3, −2)	(1, 4)
(−1, −2)	(3, 4)

Then use the preimage coordinates to draw the preimage, and use the image coordinates to draw the new image.

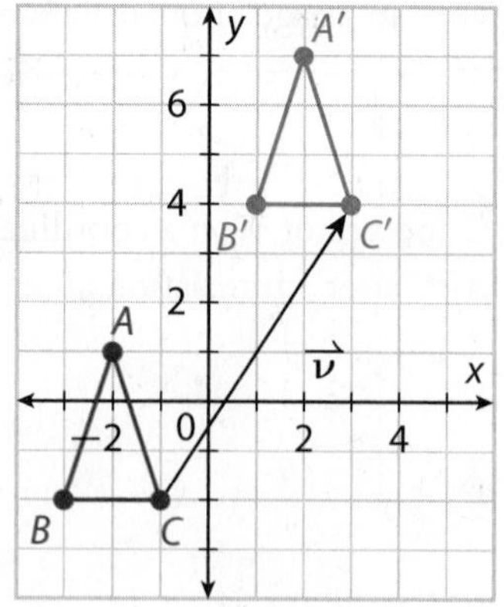

Ⓑ Preimage coordinates: $A(3, 0)$, $B(2, -2)$, and $C(4, -2)$. Vector $\langle -2, 3 \rangle$

Prediction: The image will be in Quadrant 1.

Preimage coordinates (x, y)	Image $(x - \boxed{2}, y + \boxed{3})$
(3, 0)	$(\boxed{1}, \boxed{3})$
(2, −2)	$(\boxed{0}, \boxed{1})$
(4, −2)	$(\boxed{2}, \boxed{1})$

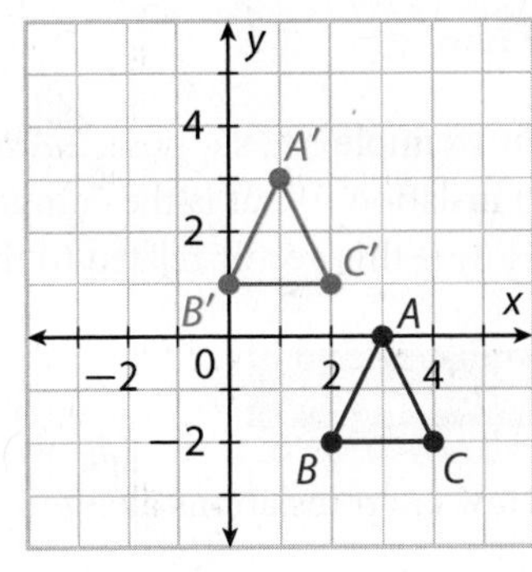

Your Turn

Draw the preimage and image of each triangle under a translation along $\langle -4, 1 \rangle$.

5. Triangle with coordinates: $A(2, 4)$, $B(1, 2)$, $C(4, 2)$.

6. Triangle with coordinates: $P(2, -1)$, $Q(2, -3)$, $R(4, -3)$.

Explain 3 Specifying Translation Vectors

You may be asked to specify a translation that carries a given figure onto another figure. You can do this by drawing the translation vector and then writing it in component form.

Example 3 **Specify the component form of the vector that maps $\triangle ABC$ to $\triangle A'B'C'$.**

Ⓐ

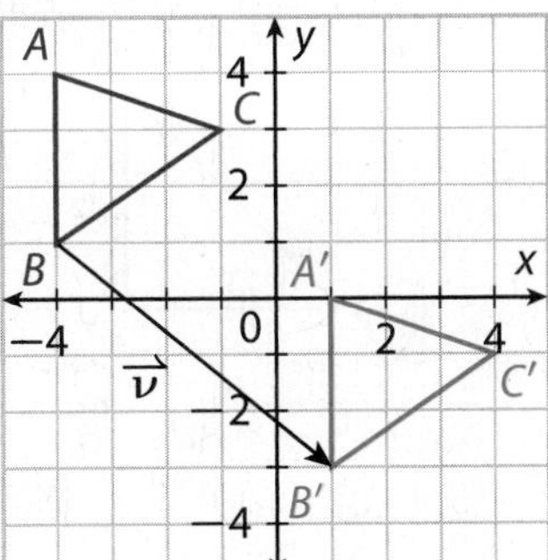

Determine the components of $\vec{v}$.

The horizontal change from the initial point (−4, 1) to the terminal point (1, −3) is $1 - (-4) = 5$.

The vertical change from the initial point (−4, 1) to the terminal point (1, −3) is $-3 - 1 = -4$

Write the vector in component form.

$$\vec{v} = \langle 5, -4 \rangle$$

Ⓑ

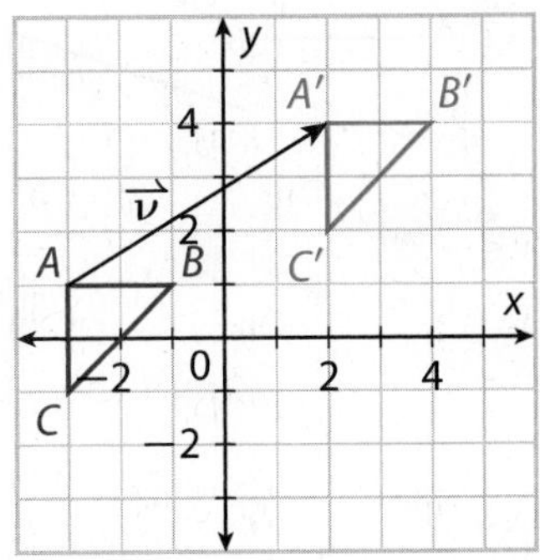

Draw the vector $\vec{v}$ from a vertex of $\triangle ABC$ to its image in $\triangle A'B'C'$.

Determine the components of $\vec{v}$.

The horizontal change from the initial point $(-3, 1)$ to the terminal point $(2, 4)$ is $2 - (-3) = 5$.

The vertical change from the initial point to the terminal point is $4 - 1 = 3$

Write the vector in component form. $\vec{v} = \langle \boxed{5}, \boxed{3} \rangle$

Reflect

7. What is the component form of a vector that translates figures horizontally? Explain.

Your Turn

8. In Example 3A, suppose $\triangle A'B'C'$ is the preimage and $\triangle ABC$ is the image after translation. What is the component form of the translation vector in this case? How is this vector related to the vector you wrote in Example 3A?

Elaborate

9. How are translations along the vectors $\langle a, -b \rangle$ and $\langle -a, b \rangle$ similar and how are they different?

10. A translation along the vector $\langle -2, 7 \rangle$ maps point P to point Q. The coordinates of point Q are $(4, -1)$. What are the coordinates of point P? Explain your reasoning.

11. A translation along the vector $\langle a, b \rangle$ maps points in Quadrant I to points in Quadrant III. What can you conclude about a and b? Justify your response.

12. **Essential Question Check-In** How does translating a figure using the formal definition of a translation compare to the previous method of translating a figure?

Evaluate: Homework and Practice

- Online Homework
- Hints and Help
- Extra Practice

Copy $\triangle ABC$ and vector $\vec{v}$ on a coordinate grid. Then draw the image of $\triangle ABC$ after a translation along $\vec{v}$.

1.

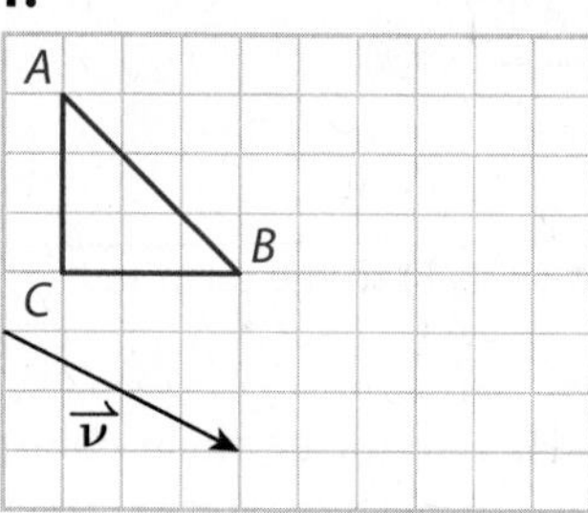

2.

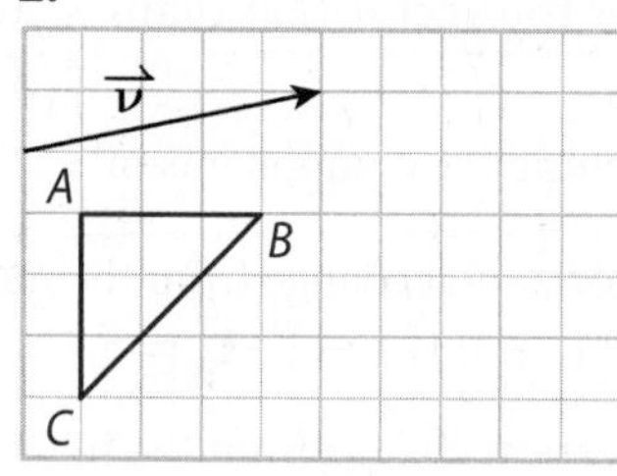

3.

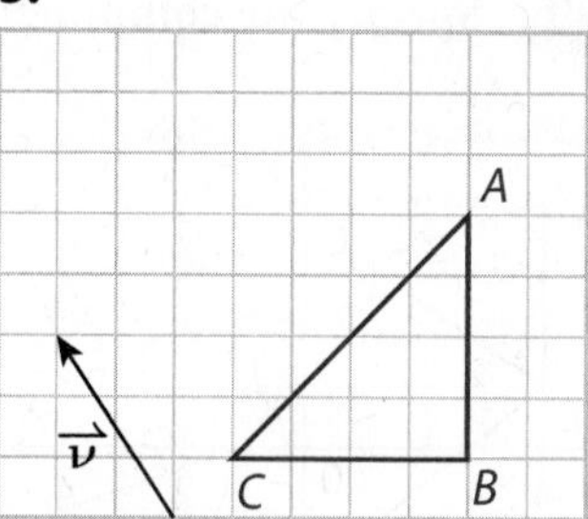

4. Line segment $\overline{XY}$ was used to draw a copy of $\triangle ABC$. $\overline{XY}$ is 3.5 centimeters long. What is the length $AA' + BB' + CC'$?

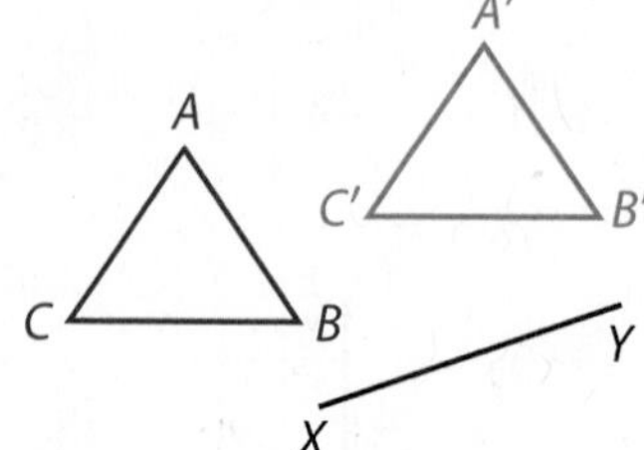

Draw the preimage and image of each triangle under the given translation.

5. Triangle: $A(-3, -1)$; $B(-2, 2)$; $C(0, -1)$; Vector: $\langle 3, 2 \rangle$

6. Triangle: $P(1, -3)$; $Q(3, -1)$; $R(4, -3)$; Vector: $\langle -1, 3 \rangle$

7. Triangle: $X(0, 3)$; $Y(-1, 1)$; $Z(-3, 4)$; Vector: $\langle 4, -2 \rangle$

8. Find the coordinates of the image under the transformation $\langle 6, -11 \rangle$.

$(x, y) \rightarrow$ __?__ $(2, -3) \rightarrow$ __?__

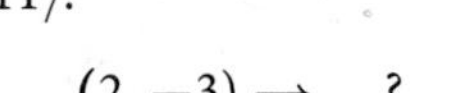

$(3, 1) \rightarrow$ __?__ $(4, -3) \rightarrow$ __?__

9. Name the vector. Write it in component form.

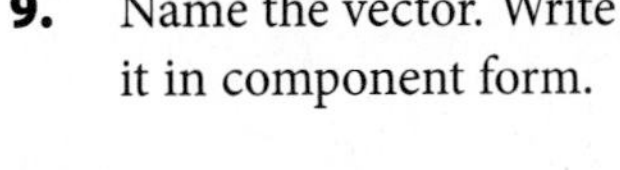

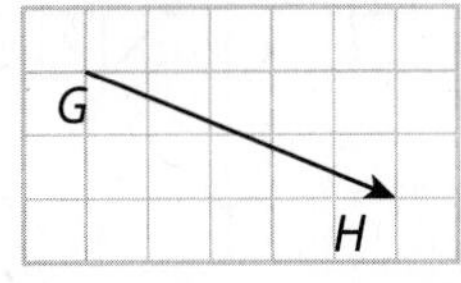

10. Match each set of coordinates for a preimage with the coordinates of its image after applying the vector $\langle 3, -8 \rangle$.

A. $(1, 1)$; $(10, 1)$; $(6, 5)$ **a.** __?__ $(6, -10)$; $(6, -4)$; $(9, -3)$

B. $(0, 0)$; $(3, 8)$; $(4, 0)$; $(7, 8)$ **b.** __?__ $(1, -6)$; $(5, -6)$; $(-1, -8)$; $(7, -8)$

C. $(3, -2)$; $(3, 4)$; $(6, 5)$ **c.** __?__ $(4, -7)$; $(13, -7)$; $(9, -3)$

D. $(-2, 2)$; $(2, 2)$; $(-4, 0)$; $(4, 0)$ **d.** __?__ $(3, -8)$; $(6, 0)$; $(7, -8)$; $(10, 0)$

11. Persevere in Problem Solving Emma and Tony are playing a game. Each draws a triangle on a coordinate grid. For each turn, Emma chooses either the horizontal or vertical value for a vector in component form. Tony chooses the other value, alternating each turn. They each have to draw a new image of their triangle using the vector with the components they chose and using the image from the prior turn as the preimage. Whoever has drawn an image in each of the four quadrants first wins the game.

Emma's initial triangle has the coordinates $(-3, 0)$, $(-4, -2)$, $(-2, -2)$ and Tony's initial triangle has the coordinates $(2, 4)$, $(2, 2)$, $(4, 3)$. On the first turn the vector $\langle 6, -5 \rangle$ is used and on the second turn the vector $\langle -10, 8 \rangle$ is used. What quadrant does Emma need to translate her triangle to in order to win? What quadrant does Tony need to translate his triangle to in order to win?

Specify the component form of the vector that maps each figure to its image.

12.

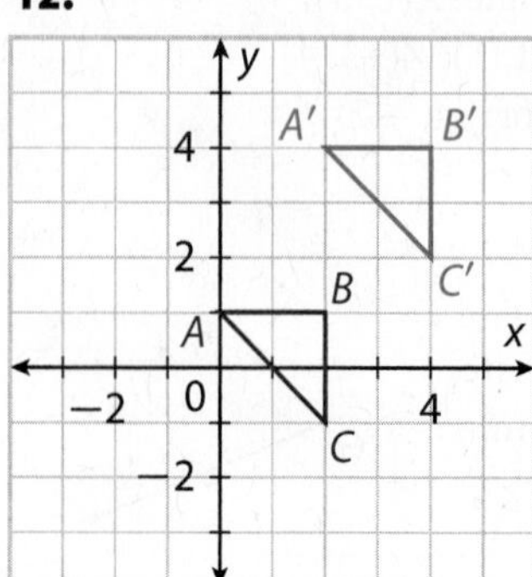

13.

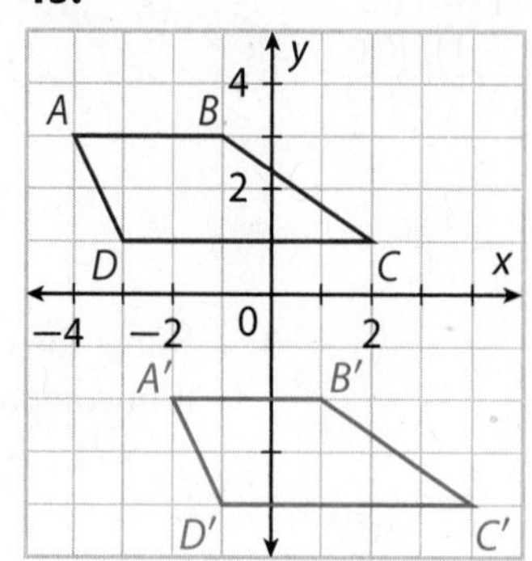

14.

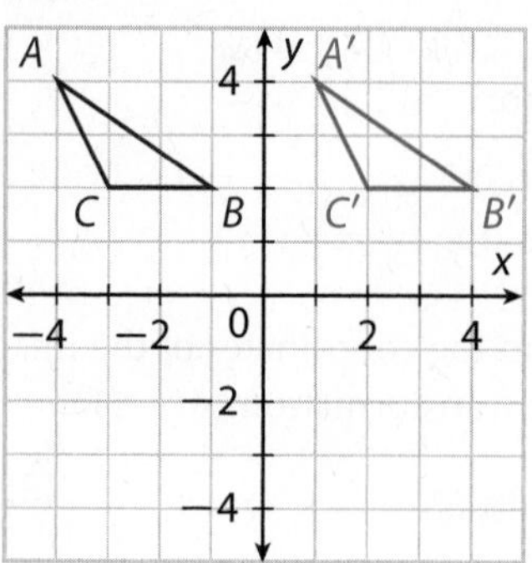

15. Explain the Error Andrew is using vector $\vec{v}$ to draw a copy of $\triangle ABC$. Explain his error.

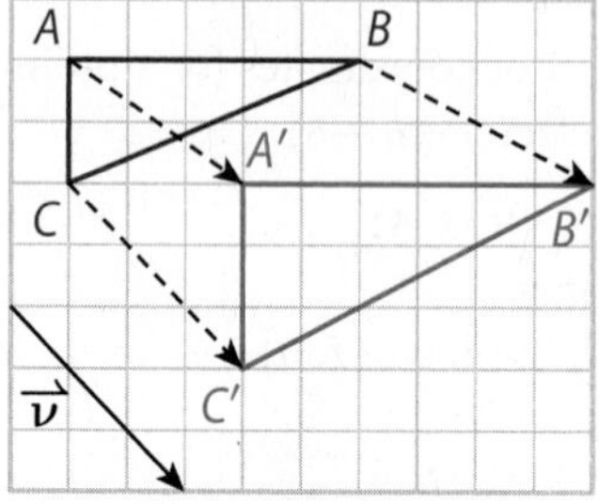

16. Explain the Error Marcus was asked to identify the vector that maps $\triangle DEF$ to $\triangle D'E'F'$. He drew a vector as shown and determined that the component form of the vector is $\langle 3, 1 \rangle$. Explain his error.

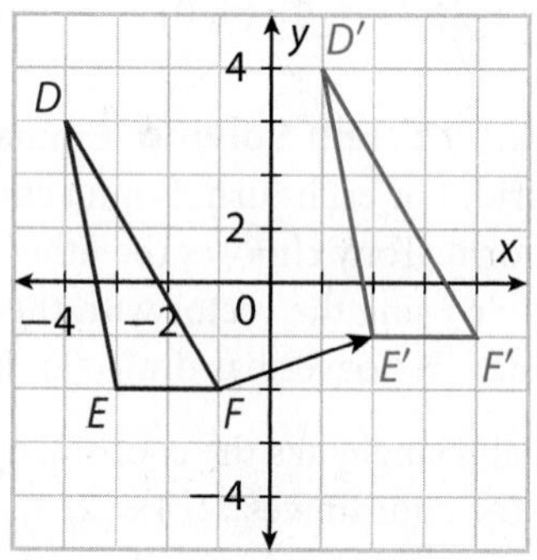

17. Algebra A cartographer is making a city map. Line m represents Murphy Street. The cartographer translates points on line m along the vector $\langle 2, -2 \rangle$ to draw Nolan Street. Copy the graph. Draw the line for Nolan Street on the coordinate plane and write its equation. What is the image of the point $(0, 3)$ in this situation?

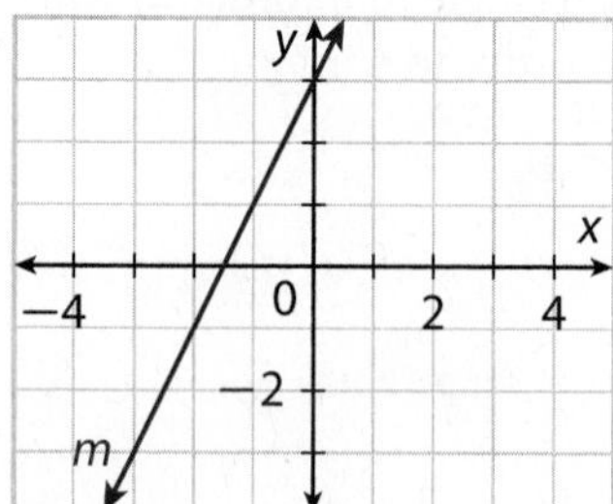

H.O.T. Focus on Higher Order Thinking

18. Represent Real-World Problems A builder is trying to level out some ground with a front-end loader. He picks up some excess dirt at (9, 16) and then maneuvers through the job site along the vectors $\langle -6, 0\rangle$, $\langle 2, 5\rangle$, $\langle 8, 10\rangle$ to get to the spot to unload the dirt. Find the coordinates of the unloading point. Find a single vector from the loading point to the unloading point.

19. Look for a Pattern A checker player's piece begins at *K* and, through a series of moves, lands on *L*. What translation vector represents the path from *K* to *L*?

20. Represent Real-World Problems A group of hikers walks 2 miles east and then 1 mile north. After taking a break, they then hike 4 miles east to their final destination. What vector describes their hike from their starting position to their final destination? Let 1 unit represent 1 mile.

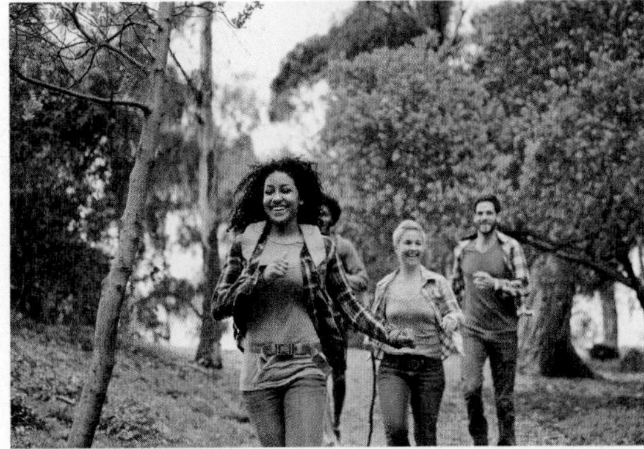

21. Communicate Mathematical Ideas In a quilt pattern, a polygon with vertices $(-4, -2)$, $(-3, -1)$, $(-2, -2)$, and $(-3, -3)$ is translated repeatedly along the vector $\langle 2, 2\rangle$. What are the coordinates of the third polygon in the pattern? Explain how you solved the problem.

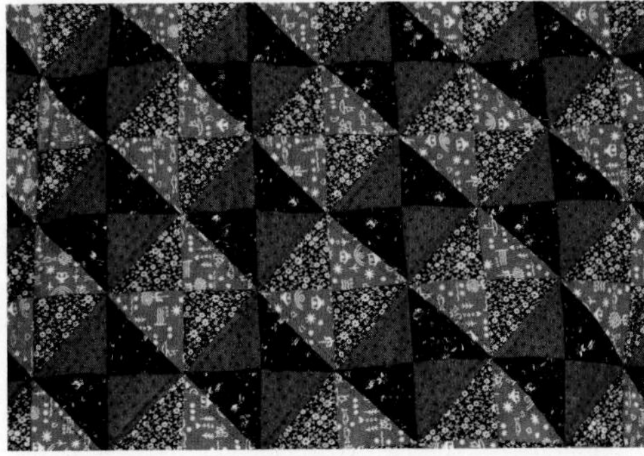

Lesson Performance Task

A contractor is designing a pattern for tiles in an entryway, using a sun design called Image *A* for the center of the space. The contractor wants to duplicate this design three times, labeled Image *B*, Image *C*, and Image *D*, above Image *A* so that they do not overlap. Identify the three vectors, labeled $\overrightarrow{m}$, $\overrightarrow{n}$, and $\overrightarrow{p}$ that could be used to draw the design, and write them in component form. Draw the images on grid paper using the vectors you wrote.

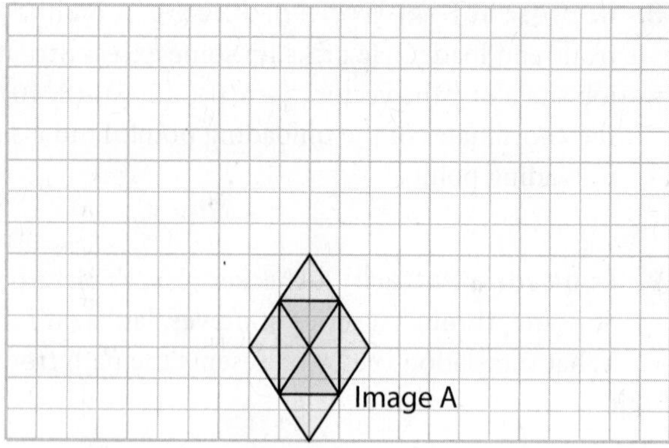

2.2 Reflections

Essential Question: How do you draw the image of a figure under a reflection?

Explore Exploring Reflections

Use tracing paper to explore reflections.

(A) Draw and label a line ℓ on tracing paper. Then draw and label a quadrilateral *ABCD* with vertex *C* on line ℓ.

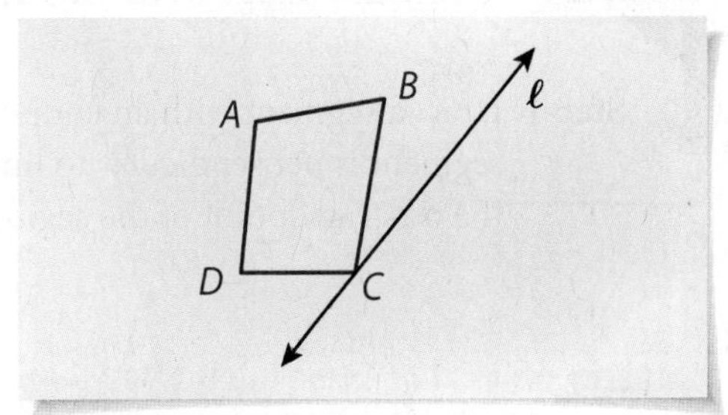

(B) Fold the tracing paper along line ℓ. Trace the quadrilateral. Then unfold the paper and draw the image of the quadrilateral. Label it A' B' C' D'.

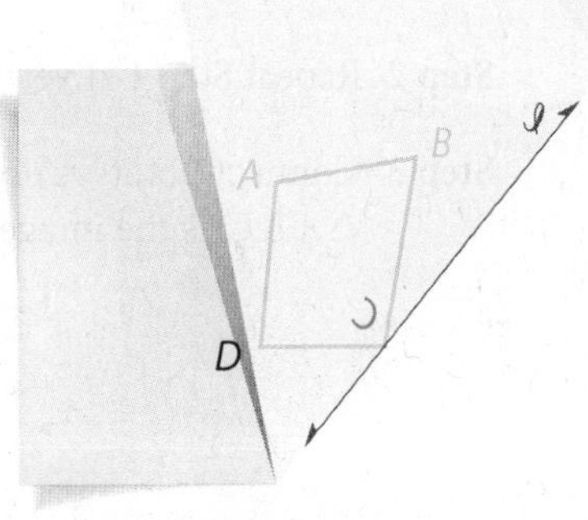

(C) Draw segments to connect each vertex of quadrilateral *ABCD* with its image. Use a protractor to measure the angle formed by each segment and line ℓ. What do you notice?

(D) Use a ruler to measure each segment and the two shorter segments formed by its intersection with line ℓ. What do you notice?

Reflect

1. In this activity, the fold line (line ℓ) is the line of reflection. What happens when a point is located on the line of reflection?

2. **Discussion** A student claims that a figure and its reflected image always lie on opposite sides of the line of reflection. Do you agree? Why or why not?

Explain 1 Reflecting Figures Using Graph Paper

Perpendicular lines are lines that intersect at right angles. In the figure, line ℓ is perpendicular to line m. The right angle mark in the figure indicates that the lines are perpendicular.

The **perpendicular bisector** of a line segment is a line perpendicular to the segment at the segment's midpoint. In the figure, line n is the perpendicular bisector of $\overline{AB}$.

A **reflection** across line ℓ maps a point P to its image P'.

- If P is not on line ℓ, then line ℓ is the perpendicular bisector of $\overline{PP'}$.
- If P is on line ℓ, then $P = P'$.

Example 1 **Draw the image of $\triangle ABC$ after a reflection across line ℓ.**

Ⓐ **Step 1** Draw a segment with an endpoint at vertex A so that the segment is perpendicular to line ℓ and is bisected by line ℓ. Label the other endpoint of the segment A'.

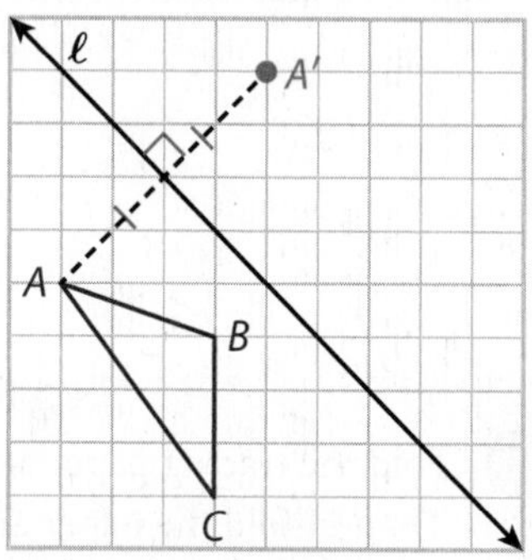

Step 2 Repeat Step 1 at vertices B and C.

Step 3 Connect points A', B', and C'.
$\triangle A'B'C'$ is the image of $\triangle ABC$.

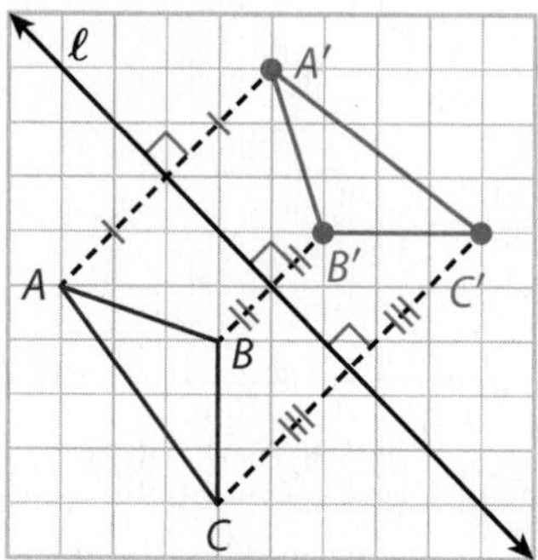

Ⓑ Copy $\triangle ABC$ and line ℓ on a coordinate grid. Then draw the image of $\triangle ABC$ after a reflection across line ℓ.

Step 1 Draw a segment with an endpoint at vertex A so that the segment is perpendicular to line ℓ and is bisected by line ℓ. Label the other endpoint of the segment A'.

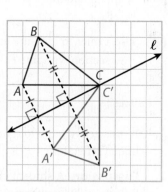

Step 2 Repeat Step 1 at vertex B.
Notice that C and C' are the same point because C is on the line of reflection.

Step 3 Connect points A', B', and C'. $\triangle A'B'C'$ is the image of $\triangle ABC$.

Reflect

3. How can you check that you drew the image of the triangle correctly?

4. In Part A, how can you tell that $\overline{AA'}$ is perpendicular to line ℓ?

Your Turn

Copy $\triangle ABC$ and line ℓ on a coordinate grid. Then draw the image of $\triangle ABC$ after a reflection across line ℓ.

5.

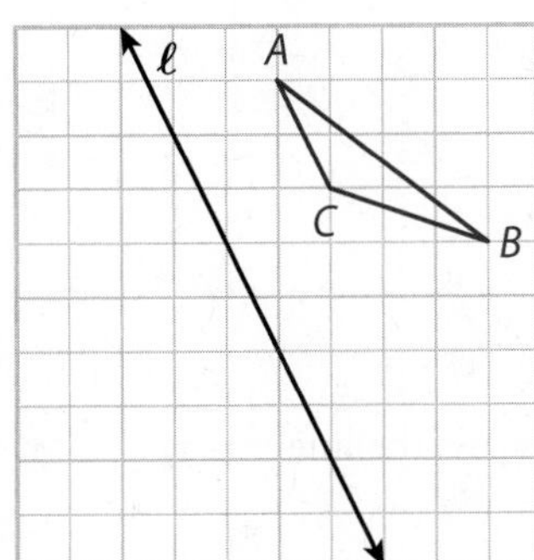

6.

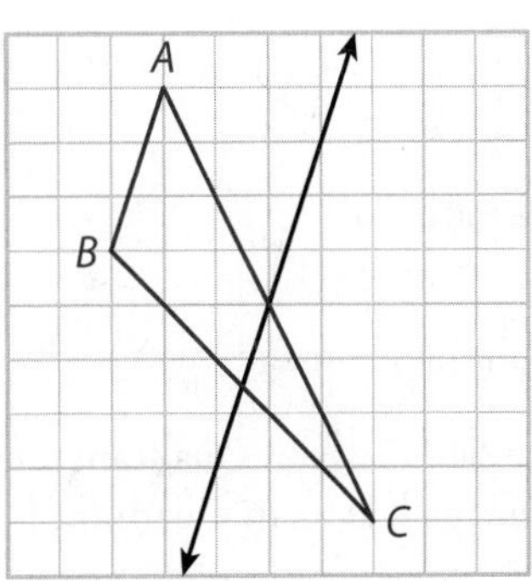

Explain 2 Drawing Reflections on a Coordinate Plane

The table summarizes coordinate notation for reflections on a coordinate plane.

Rules for Reflections on a Coordinate Plane	
Reflection across the x-axis	$(x, y) \rightarrow (x, -y)$
Reflection across the y-axis	$(x, y) \rightarrow (-x, y)$
Reflection across the line $y = x$	$(x, y) \rightarrow (y, x)$
Reflection across the line $y = -x$	$(x, y) \rightarrow (-y, -x)$

Example 2 **Reflect the figure with the given vertices across the given line.**

(A) $M(1, 2)$, $N(1, 4)$, $P(3, 3)$; y-axis

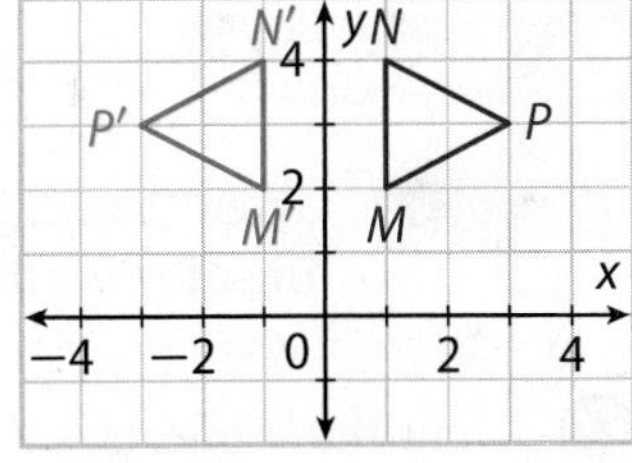

Step 1 Find the coordinates of the vertices of the image.

$A(x, y) \rightarrow A'(-x, y)$.

$M(1, 2) \rightarrow M'(-1, 2)$

$N(1, 4) \rightarrow N'(-1, 4)$

$P(3, 3) \rightarrow P'(-3, 3)$

Step 2 Graph the preimage.

Step 3 Predict the quadrant in which the image will lie. Since $\triangle MNP$ lies in Quadrant I and the triangle is reflected across the y-axis, the image will lie in Quadrant II.

Graph the image.

(B) $D(2, 0), E(2, 2), F(5, 2), G(5, 1); y = x$

Step 1 Find the coordinates of the vertices of the image.

$A(x, y) \rightarrow A'(\boxed{y}, \boxed{x})$

$D(2, 0) \rightarrow D'(\boxed{0}, \boxed{2})$

$E(2, 2) \rightarrow E'(\boxed{2}, \boxed{2})$

$F(5, 2) \rightarrow F'(\boxed{2}, \boxed{5})$

$G(5, 1) \rightarrow G'(\boxed{1}, \boxed{5})$

Step 2 Graph the preimage.

Step 3 Since $DEFG$ lies in Quadrant I and the quadrilateral is reflected across the line $y = x$, the image will lie in Quadrant I.

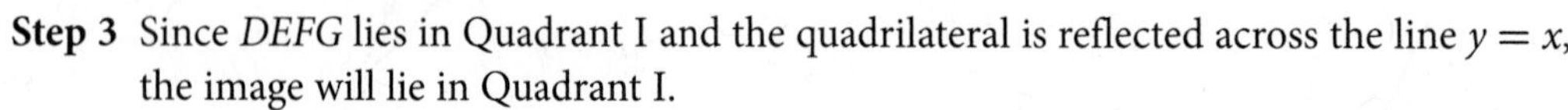

Graph the image.

Reflect

7. How would the image of ΔMNP be similar to and different from the one you drew in Part A if the triangle were reflected across the x-axis?

8. A classmate claims that the rule $(x, y) \rightarrow (-x, y)$ for reflecting a figure across the y-axis only works if all the vertices are in the first quadrant because the values of x and y must be positive. Explain why this reasoning is not correct.

Your Turn

Reflect the figure with the given vertices across the given line.

9. $S(3, 4), T(3, 1), U(-2, 1), V(-2, 4)$; x-axis

10. $A(-4, -2), B(-1, -1), C(-1, -4); y = -x$

Explain 3 Specifying Lines of Reflection

Example 3 **Given that $\Delta A'B'C'$ is the image of ΔABC under a reflection, draw the line of reflection.**

(A) Draw the segments $\overline{AA'}$, $\overline{BB'}$, and $\overline{CC'}$.

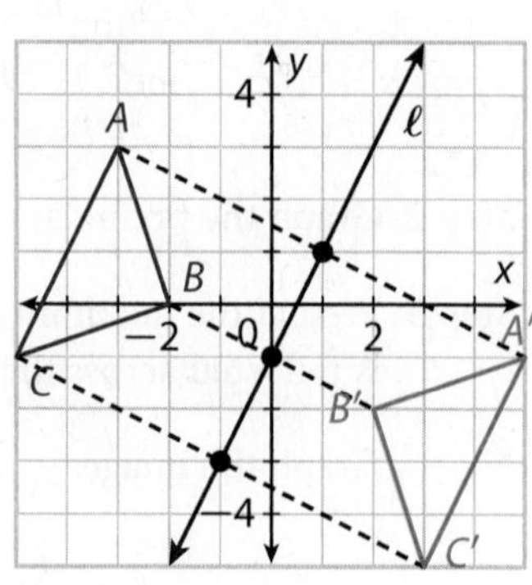

Find the midpoint of each segment.

The midpoint of $\overline{AA'}$ is $\left(\frac{-3 + 5}{2}, \frac{3 + (-1)}{2}\right) = (1, 1)$.

The midpoint of $\overline{BB'}$ is $\left(\frac{-2 + 2}{2}, \frac{0 + (-2)}{2}\right) = (0, -1)$.

The midpoint of $\overline{CC'}$ is $\left(\frac{-5 + 3}{2}, \frac{-1 + (-5)}{2}\right) = (-1, -3)$.

Plot the midpoints. Draw line ℓ through the midpoints.

Line ℓ is the line of reflection.

(B) Draw $\overline{AA'}$, $\overline{BB'}$, and $\overline{CC'}$. Find the midpoint of each segment.

The midpoint of $\overline{AA'}$ is $\left(\dfrac{-3 + -5}{2}, \dfrac{3 + -1}{2}\right) = (-4, 1)$.

The midpoint of $\overline{BB'}$ is $\left(\dfrac{2 + -2}{2}, \dfrac{3 + -5}{2}\right) = (0, -1)$.

The midpoint of $\overline{CC'}$ is $\left(\dfrac{5 + 3}{2}, \dfrac{-1 + -5}{2}\right) = (4, -3)$.

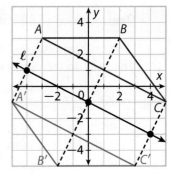

Plot the midpoints. Draw line ℓ through the midpoints. Line ℓ is the line of reflection.

Reflect

11. How can you use a ruler and protractor to check that line ℓ is the line of reflection?

Your Turn

$\triangle A'B'C'$ is the image of $\triangle ABC$ under a reflection. On a coordinate grid, draw $\triangle ABC$, $\triangle A'B'C$, and the line of reflection.

12.

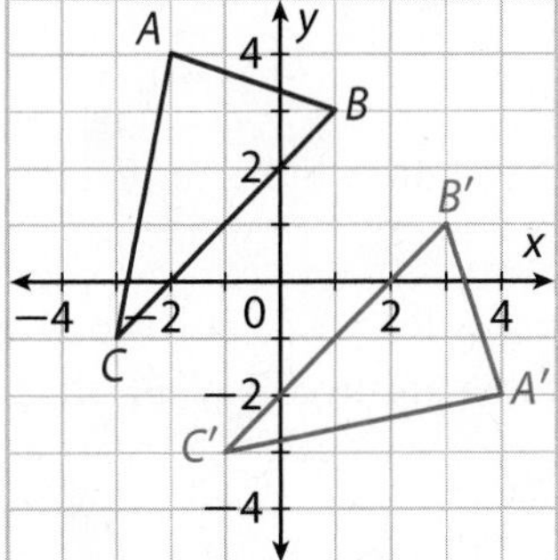

13.

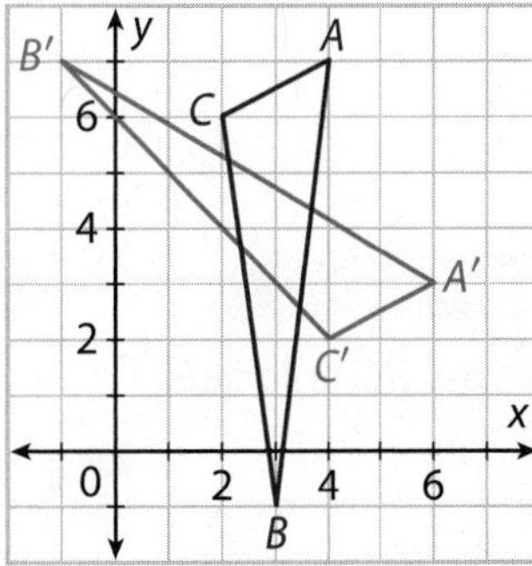

Explain 4 Applying Reflections

Example 4

The figure shows one hole of a miniature golf course. It is not possible to hit the ball in a straight line from the tee T to the hole H. At what point should a player aim in order to make a hole in one?

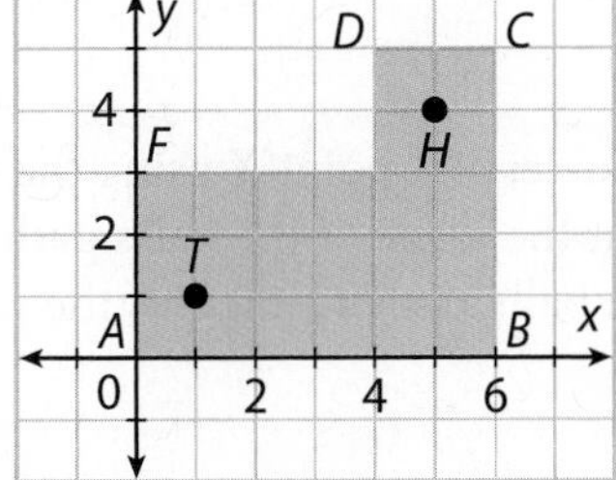

Understand the Problem

The problem asks you to locate point X on the wall of the miniature golf hole so that the ball can travel in a straight line from T to X and from X to H.

Make a Plan

In order for the ball to travel directly from T to X to H, the angle of the ball's path as it hits the wall must equal the angle of the ball's path as it leaves the wall. In the figure, $m\angle 1$ must equal $m\angle 2$.

Let H' be the reflection of point H across $\overline{BC}$.

Reflections preserve angle measure, so $m\angle 2 = m\angle$ [3]. Therefore, $m\angle 1$ is equal to $m\angle 2$ when $m\angle 1$ is equal to $m\angle 3$. This occurs when T, [X], and H' are collinear.

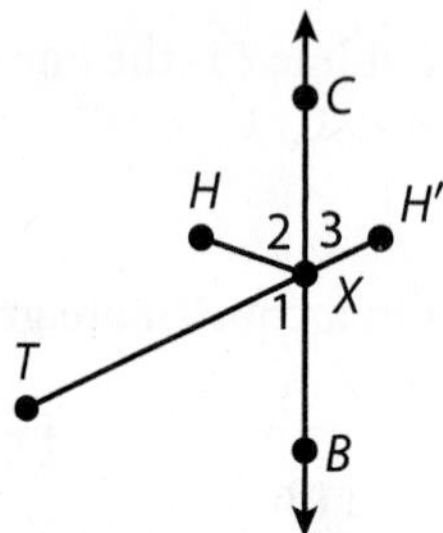

Solve

Reflect H across $\overline{BC}$ to locate H'.

The coordinates of H' are ([7], [4]).

Draw $\overline{TH'}$ and locate point X where $\overline{TH'}$ intersects $\overline{BC}$.

The coordinates of point X are ([6], [3.5]).

The player should aim at this point.

Look Back

To check that the answer is reasonable, plot point X using the coordinates you found. Then use a protractor to check that the angle of the ball's path as it hits the wall at point X is equal to the angle of the ball's path as it leaves the wall from point X.

Reflect

14. Is there another path the ball can take to hit a wall and then travel directly to the hole? Explain.

Your Turn

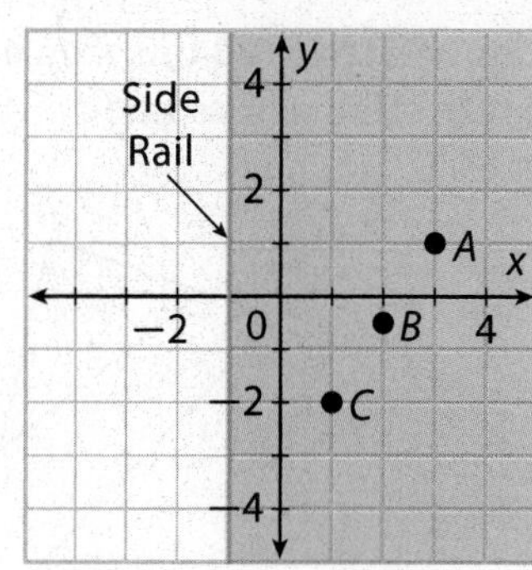

15. Cara is playing pool. She wants to use the cue ball C to hit the ball at point A without hitting the ball at point B. To do so, she has to bounce the cue ball off the side rail and into the ball at point A. Find the coordinates of the exact point along the side rail that Cara should aim for.

Elaborate

16. Do any points in the plane have themselves as images under a reflection? Explain.

17. If you are given a figure and its image under a reflection, how can you use paper folding to find the line of reflection?

18. **Essential Question Check-In** How do you draw the image of a figure under a reflection across the x-axis?

Evaluate: Homework and Practice

- Online Homework
- Hints and Help
- Extra Practice

Use tracing paper to copy each figure and line ℓ. Then fold the paper to draw and label the image of the figure after a reflection across line ℓ.

1.

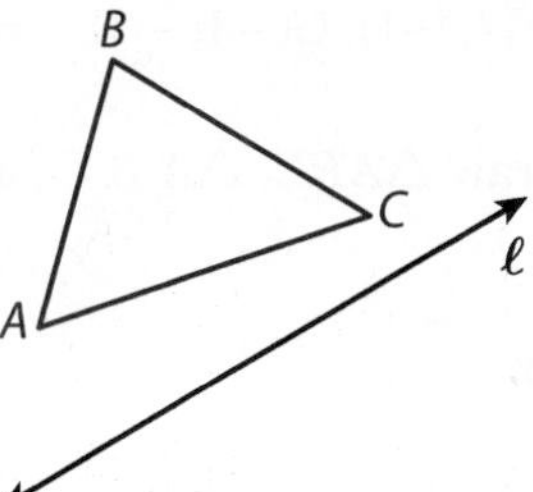

2.

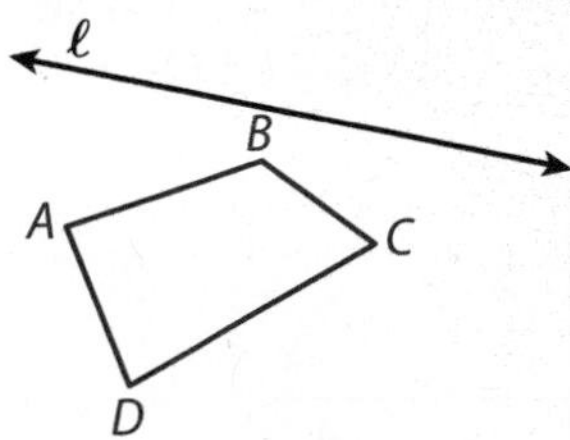

3.

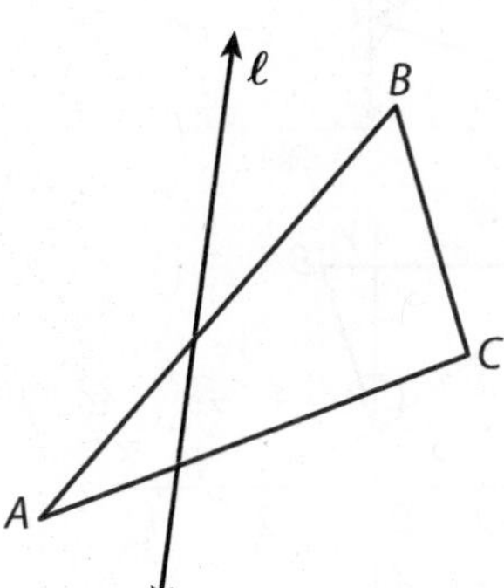

4.

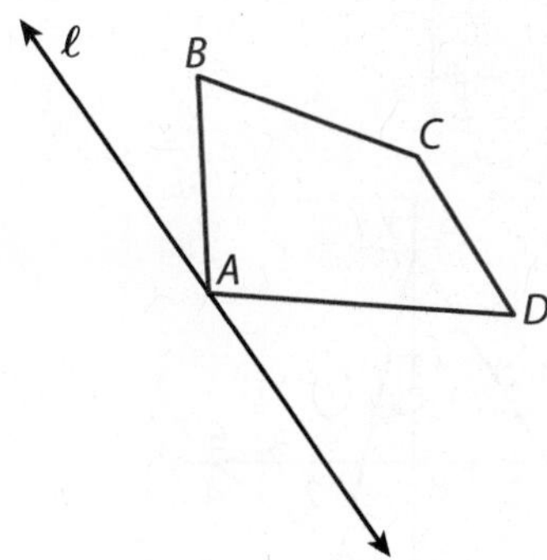

Copy $\triangle ABC$ and line ℓ on a coordinate grid. Then draw the image of $\triangle ABC$ after a reflection across line ℓ.

5.

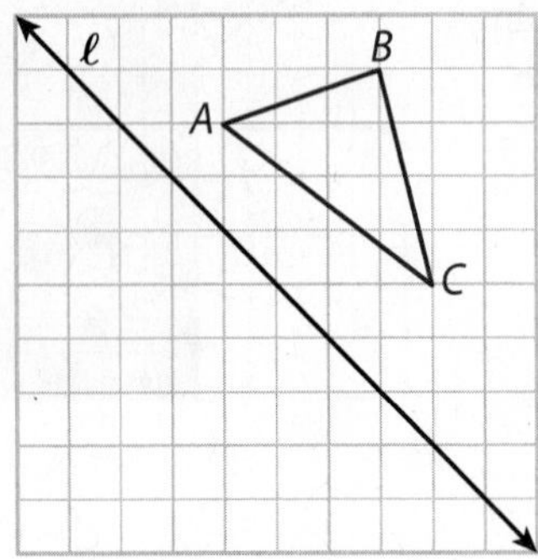

6.

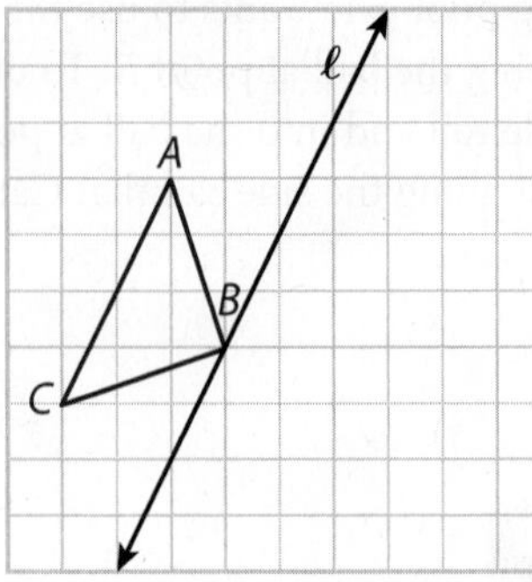

7.

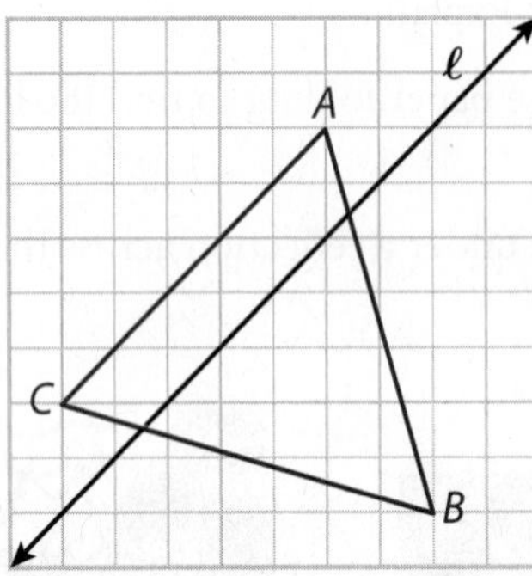

8.

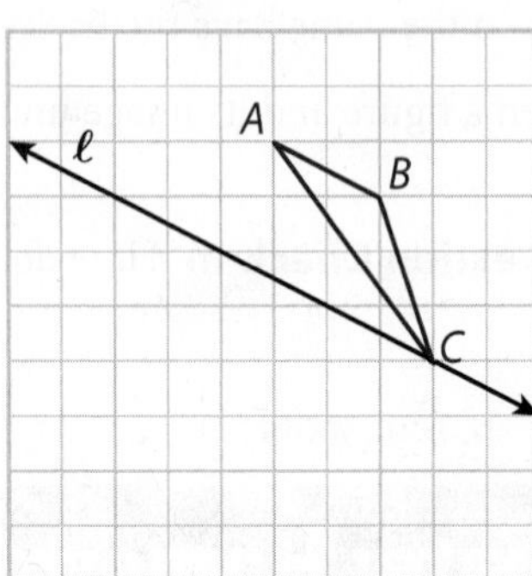

Reflect the figure with the given vertices across the given line.

9. $P(-2, 3)$, $Q(4, 3)$, $R(-1, 0)$, $S(-4, 1)$; x-axis

10. $A(-3, -3)$, $B(1, 3)$, $C(3, -1)$; y-axis

11. $J(-1, 2)$, $K(2, 4)$, $L(4, -1)$; $y = -x$

12. $D(-1, 1)$, $E(3, 2)$, $F(4, -1)$, $G(-1, -3)$; $y = x$

$\triangle A'B'C'$ is the image of $\triangle ABC$ under a reflection. On a coordinate grid, draw $\triangle ABC$, $\triangle A'B'C'$, and the line of reflection.

13.

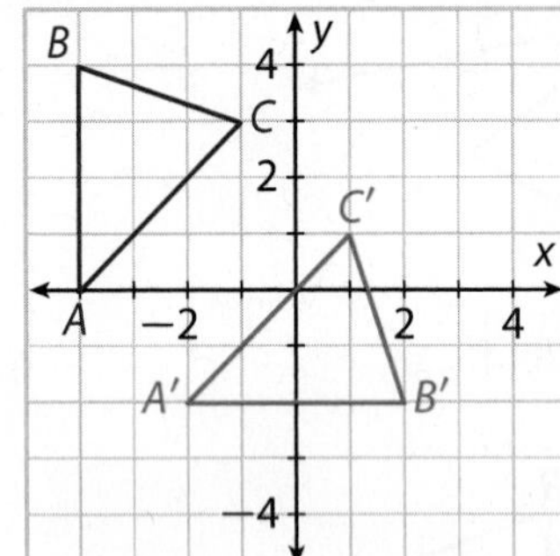

14.

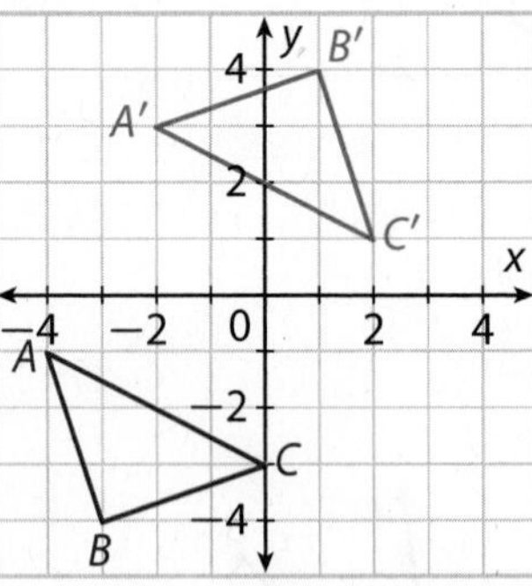

15.

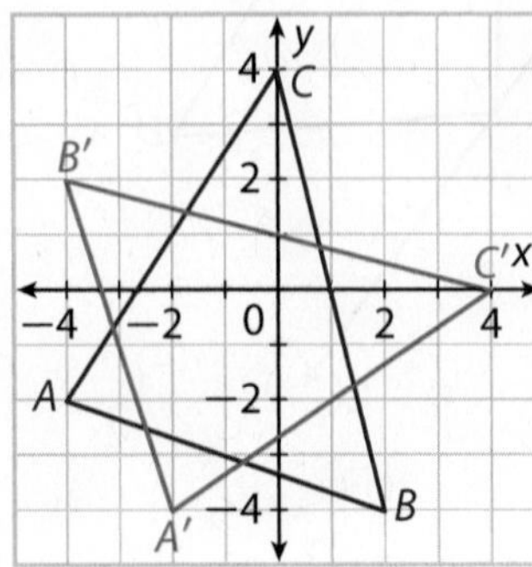

16.

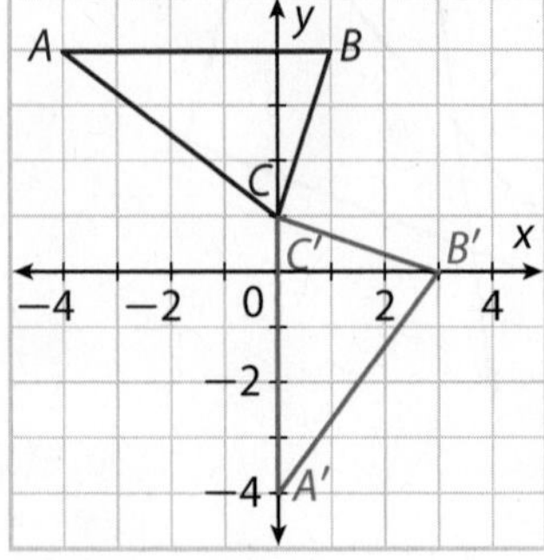

17. Jamar is playing a video game. The object of the game is to roll a marble into a target. In the figure, the shaded rectangular area represents the video screen and the striped rectangle is a barrier. Because of the barrier, it is not possible to roll the marble M directly into the target T. At what point should Jamar aim the marble so that it will bounce off a wall and roll into the target?

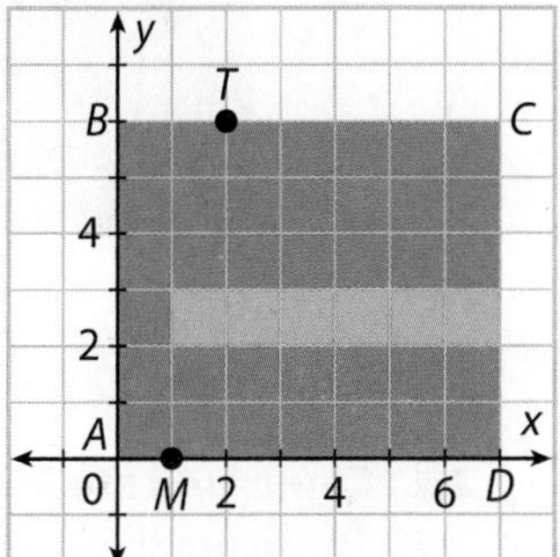

18. A trail designer is planning two trails that connect campsites A and B to a point on the river, line ℓ. She wants the total length of the trails to be as short as possible. At what point should the trails meet the river?

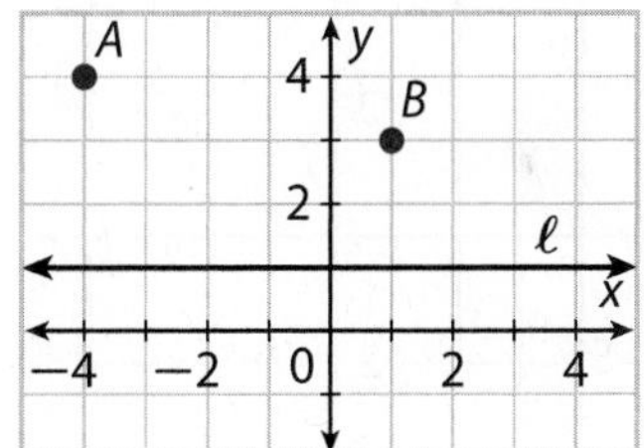

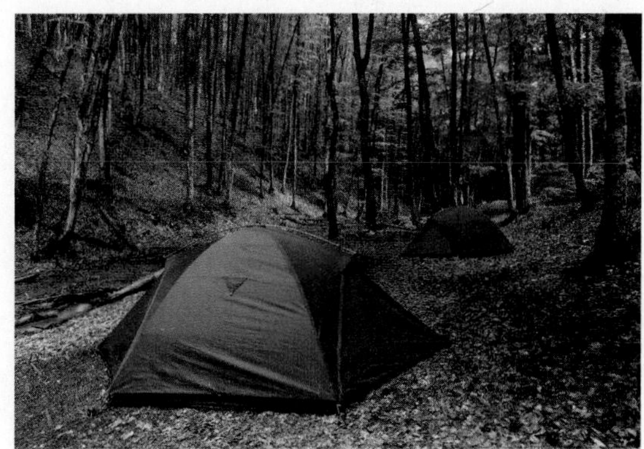

Algebra **In the figure, point K is the image of point J under a reflection across line ℓ. Find each of the following.**

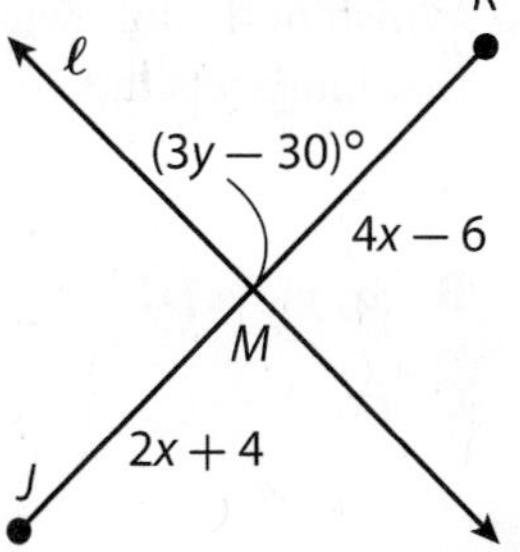

19. JM

20. y

21. **Make a Prediction**
Each time Jenny presses the tab key on her keyboard, the software reflects the logo she is designing across the x-axis. Jenny's cat steps on the keyboard and presses the tab key 25 times. In which quadrant does the logo end up? Explain.

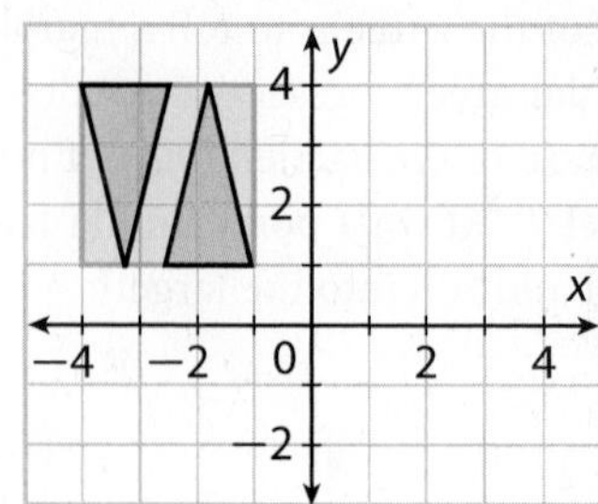

22. **Multi-Step** Write the equation of the line of reflection.

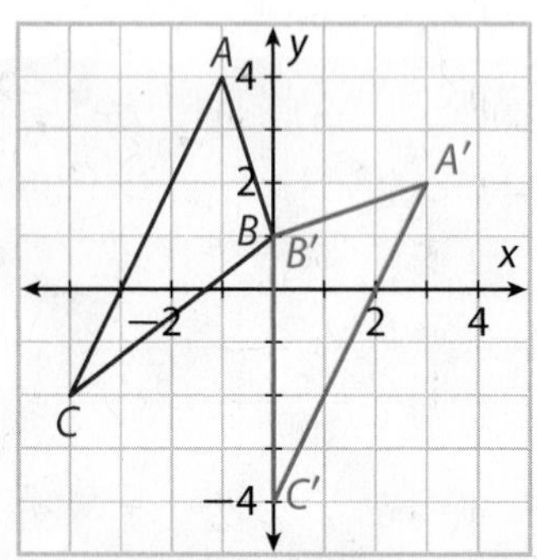

23. **Communicate Mathematical Ideas**
The figure shows rectangle $PQRS$ and its image after a reflection across the y-axis. A student said that $PQRS$ could also be mapped to its image using the translation $(x, y) \rightarrow (x + 6, y)$. Do you agree? Explain why or why not.

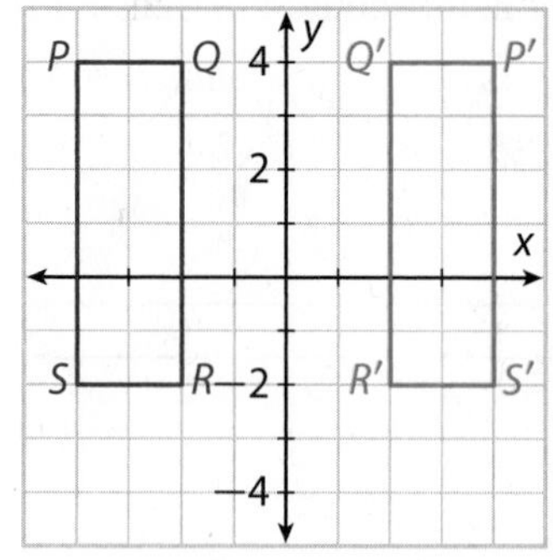

24. Which of the following transformations map $\triangle ABC$ to a triangle that intersects the x-axis? Write all that apply.

A. $(x, y) \rightarrow (-x, y)$

B. $(x, y) \rightarrow (x, -y)$

C. $(x, y) \rightarrow (y, x)$

D. $(x, y) \rightarrow (-y, -x)$

E. $(x, y) \rightarrow (x, y + 1)$

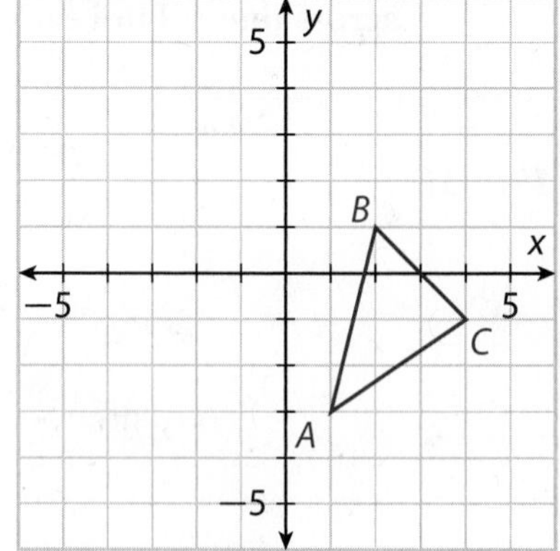

H.O.T. **Focus on Higher Order Thinking**

25. Explain the Error $\triangle M'N'P'$ is the image of $\triangle MNP$. Casey draws $\overline{MM'}$, $\overline{NN'}$, and $\overline{PP'}$. Then she finds the midpoint of each segment and draws line ℓ through the midpoints. She claims that line ℓ is the line of reflection. Do you agree? Explain.

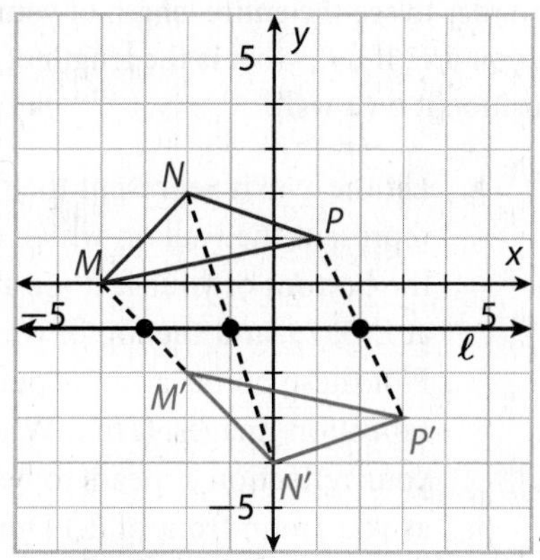

26. Draw Conclusions On a coordinate grid, plot the images of points D, E, F, and G after a reflection across the line $y = 2$. Then write an algebraic rule for the reflection.

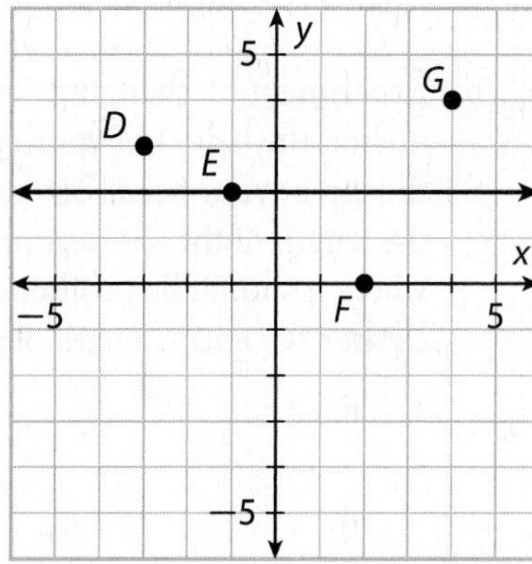

27. Critique Reasoning Mayumi wants to draw the line of reflection for the reflection that maps $\triangle ABC$ to $\triangle A'B'C'$. She claims that she just needs to draw the line through the points X and Y. Do you agree? Explain.

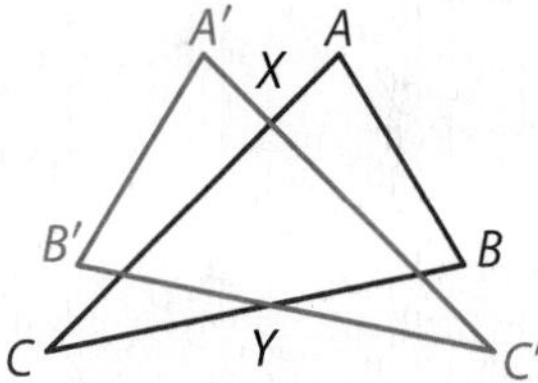

28. Justify Reasoning Point Q is the image of point P under a reflection across line ℓ. Point R lies on line ℓ. What type of triangle is $\triangle PQR$? Justify your answer.

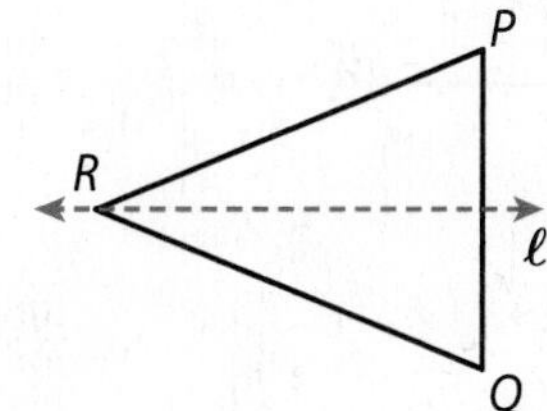

Lesson Performance Task

In order to see the entire length of your body in a mirror, do you need a mirror that is as tall as you are? If not, what is the length of the shortest mirror you can use, and how should you position it on a wall?

a. Let the x-axis represent the floor and let the y-axis represent the wall on which the mirror hangs. Suppose the bottom of your feet are at $F(3, 0)$, your eyes are at $E(3, 7)$, and the top of your head is at $H(3, 8)$. Plot these points and the points that represent their reflection images. (*Hint:* When you look in a mirror, your reflection appears to be as far behind the mirror as you are in front of it.) Draw the lines of sight from your eyes to the reflection of the top of your head and to the reflection of the bottom of your feet. Determine where these lines of sight intersect the mirror.

b. Experiment by changing your distance from the mirror, the height of your eyes, and/or the height of the top of your head. Use your results to determine the length of the shortest mirror you can use and where it should be positioned on the wall so that you can see the entire length of your body in the mirror.

2.3 Rotations

Resource Locker

Essential Question: How do you draw the image of a figure under a rotation?

Explore Exploring Rotations

You can use geometry software or an online tool to explore rotations.

(A) Draw a triangle and label the vertices A, B, and C. Then draw a point P. Mark P as a center. This will allow you to rotate figures around point P.

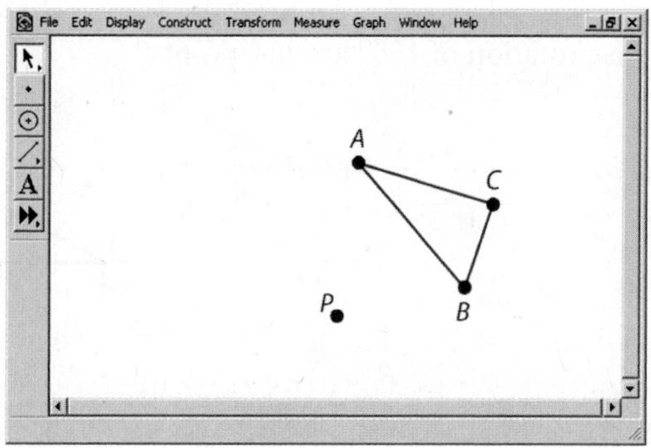

(B) Select $\triangle ABC$ and rotate it 90° around point P. Label the image of $\triangle ABC$ as $\triangle A'B'C'$. Change the shape, size, or location of $\triangle ABC$ and notice how $\triangle A'B'C'$ changes.

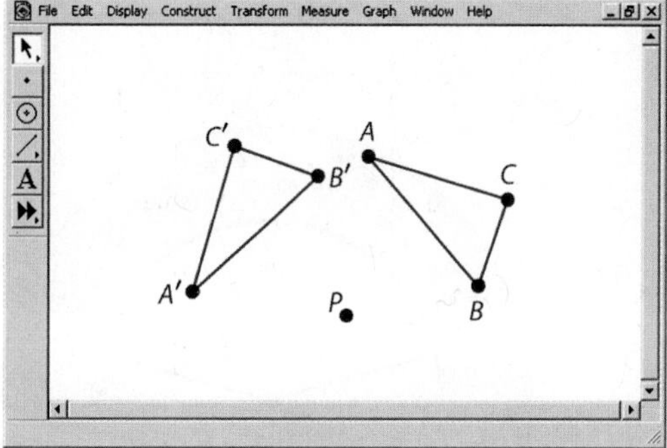

(C) Draw $\angle APA'$, $\angle BPB'$, and $\angle CPC'$. Measure these angles. What do you notice? Does this relationship remain true as you move point P? What happens if you change the size and shape of $\triangle ABC$?

(D) Measure the distance from A to P and the distance from A' to P. What do you notice? Does this relationship remain true as you move point P? What happens if you change the size and shape of $\triangle ABC$?

Reflect

1. What can you conclude about the distance of a point and its image from the center of rotation?

2. What are the advantages of using geometry software or an online tool rather than tracing paper or a protractor and ruler to investigate rotations?

Explain 1 Rotating Figures Using a Ruler and Protractor

A **rotation** is a transformation around point P, the **center of rotation**, such that the following is true.

- Every point and its image are the same distance from P.
- All angles with vertex P formed by a point and its image have the same measure. This angle measure is the **angle of rotation**.

In the figure, the center of rotation is point P and the angle of rotation is 110°.

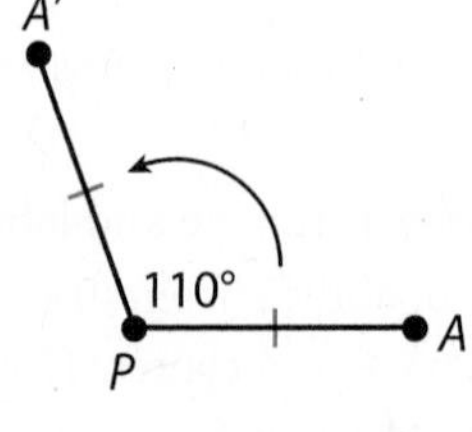

Example 1 **Draw the image of the triangle after the given rotation.**

(A) Counterclockwise rotation of 150° around point P

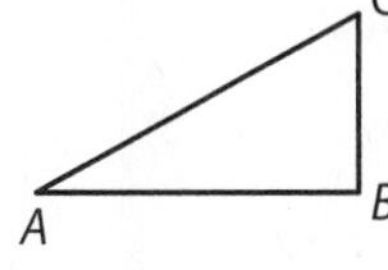

Step 1 Draw $\overline{PA}$. Then use a protractor to draw a ray that forms a 150° angle with $\overline{PA}$.

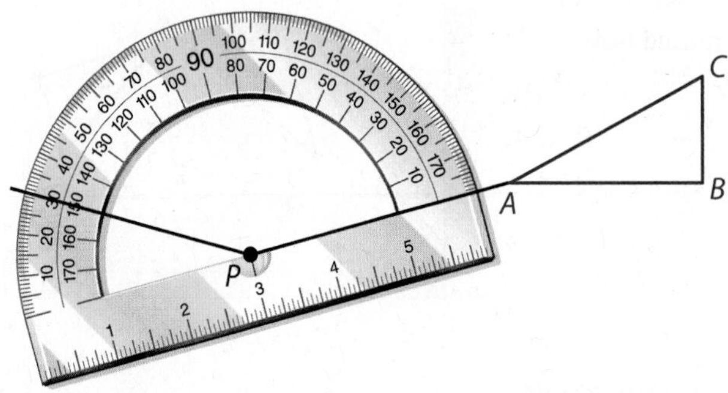

Step 2 Use a ruler to mark point A' along the ray so that $PA' = PA$.

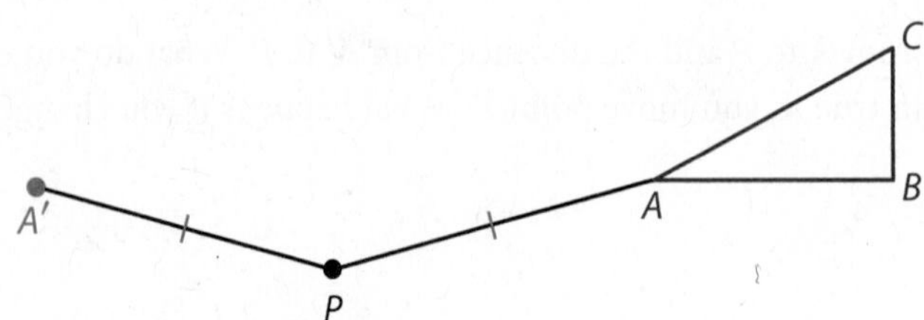

Step 3 Repeat Steps 1 and 2 for points B and C to locate points B' and C'. Connect points A', B', and C' to draw $\triangle A'B'C'$.

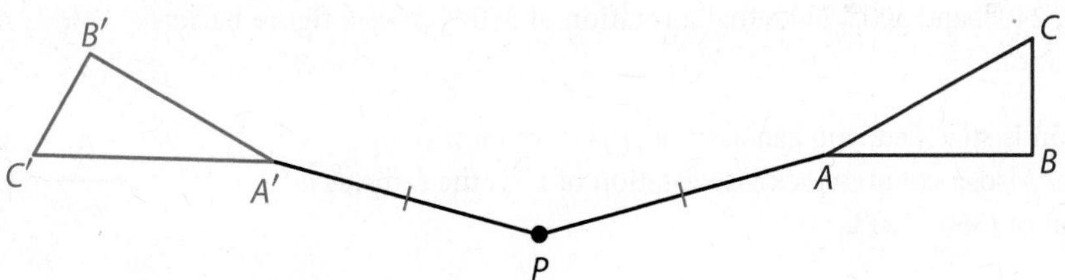

(B) Clockwise rotation of 75° around point Q

Step 1 Draw $\overline{QD}$. Use a protractor to draw a ray forming a clockwise 75° angle with $\overline{QD}$.

Step 2 Use a ruler to mark point D' along the ray so that $QD' = QD$.

Step 3 Repeat Steps1 and 2 for points E and F to locate points E' and F'. Connect points D', E', and F' to draw $\triangle D'E'F'$.

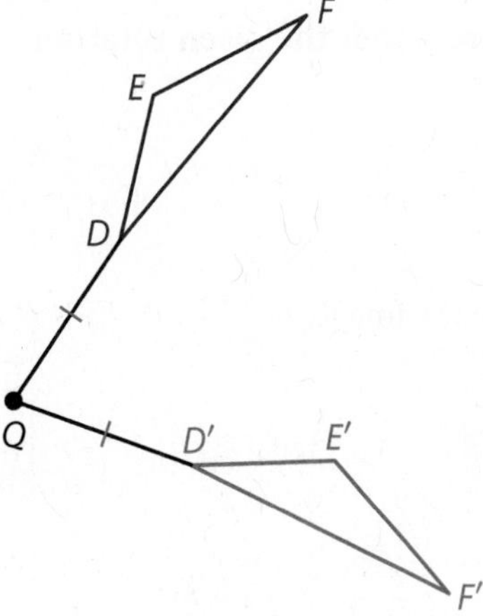

Reflect

3. How could you use tracing paper to draw the image of $\triangle ABC$ in Part A?

Your Turn

Copy the triangle. Then draw its image after the given rotation.

4. Counterclockwise rotation of 40° around point P

5. Clockwise rotation of 125° around point Q

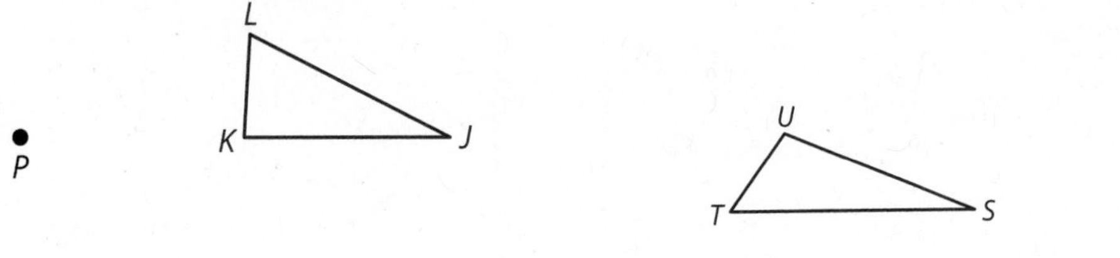

Explain 2 Drawing Rotations on a Coordinate Plane

You can rotate a figure by more than 180°. The diagram shows counterclockwise rotations of 120°, 240°, and 300°. Note that a rotation of 360° brings a figure back to its starting location.

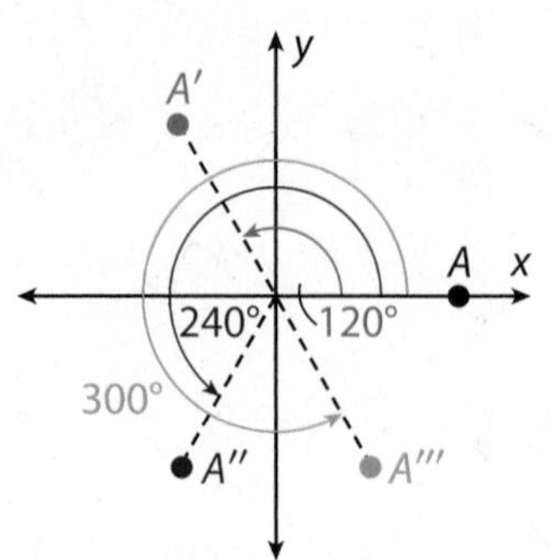

When no direction is specified, you can assume that a rotation is counterclockwise. Also, a counterclockwise rotation of $x°$ is the same as a clockwise rotation of $(360 - x)°$.

The table summarizes rules for rotations on a coordinate plane.

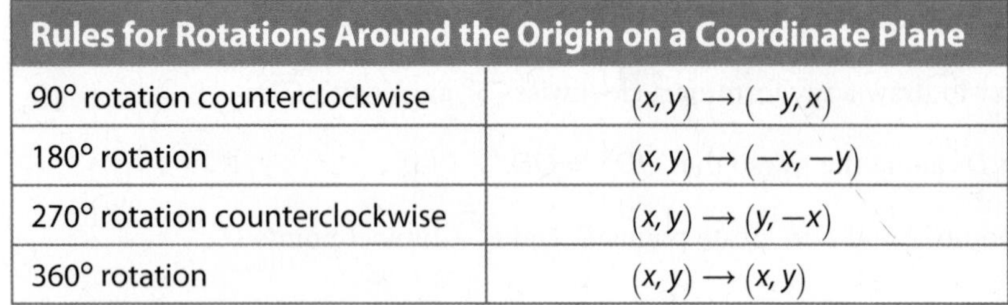

Rules for Rotations Around the Origin on a Coordinate Plane	
90° rotation counterclockwise	$(x, y) \rightarrow (-y, x)$
180° rotation	$(x, y) \rightarrow (-x, -y)$
270° rotation counterclockwise	$(x, y) \rightarrow (y, -x)$
360° rotation	$(x, y) \rightarrow (x, y)$

Example 2 **Draw the image of the figure under the given rotation.**

(A) Quadrilateral $ABCD$; 270°

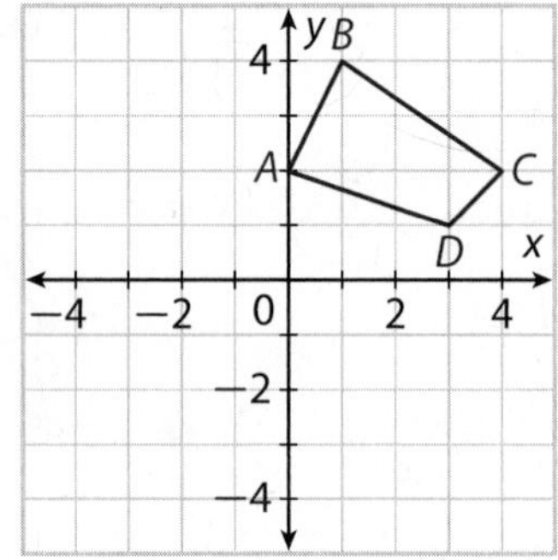

The rotation image of (x, y) is $(y, -x)$.

Find the coordinates of the vertices of the image.

$A(0, 2) \rightarrow A'(2, 0)$

$B(1, 4) \rightarrow B'(4, -1)$

$C(4, 2) \rightarrow C'(2, -4)$

$D(3, 1) \rightarrow D'(1, -3)$

Predict the quadrant in which the image will lie. Since quadrilateral $ABCD$ lies in Quadrant I and the quadrilateral is rotated counterclockwise by 270°, the image will lie in Quadrant IV.

Plot A', B', C', and D' to graph the image.

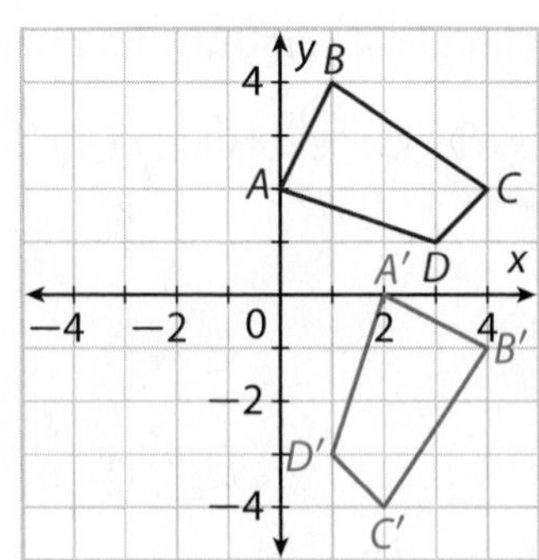

Ⓑ $\triangle KLM$; 180°

The rotation image of (x, y) is $(-x, -y)$.

Find the coordinates of the vertices of the image.

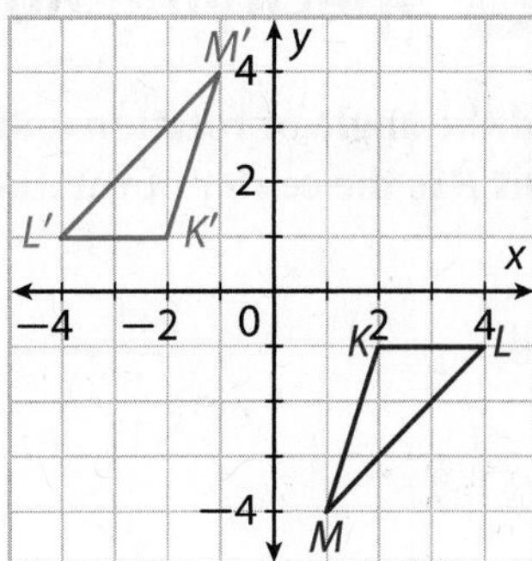

$K(2, -1) \rightarrow K'(-2, 1)$

$L(4, -1) \rightarrow L'(-4, 1)$

$M(1, -4) \rightarrow M'(-1, 4)$

Predict the quadrant in which the image will lie. Since $\triangle KLM$ lies in Quadrant IV and the triangle is rotated by 180°, the image will lie in Quadrant II.

Plot K', L', and M' to graph the image.

Reflect

6. **Discussion** Suppose you rotate quadrilateral *ABCD* in Part A by 810°. In which quadrant will the image lie? Explain.

Your Turn

On a coordinate grid, draw the image of the figure under the given rotation.

7. $\triangle PQR$; 90°

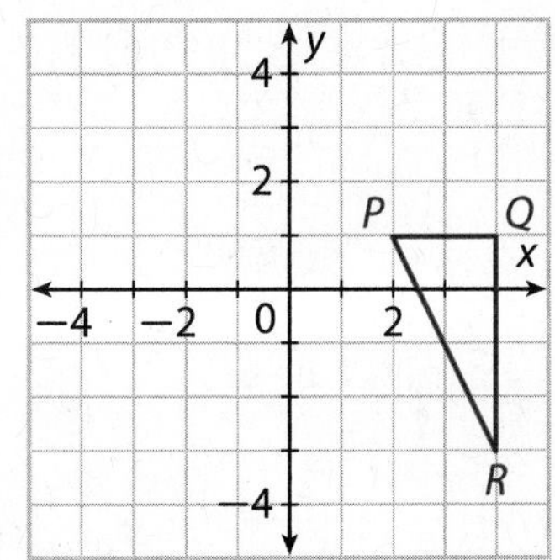

8. Quadrilateral *DEFG*; 270°

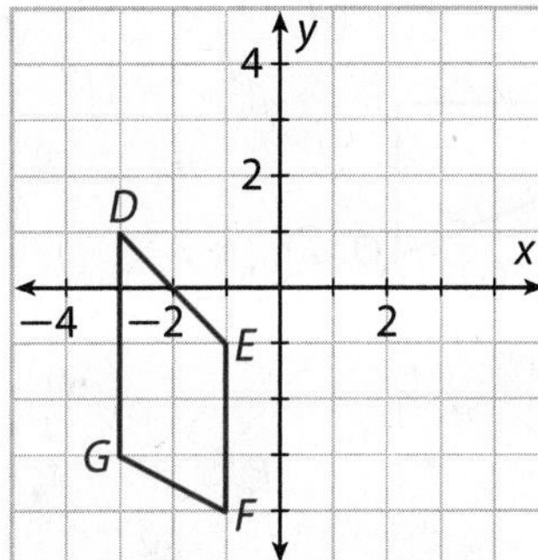

 Explain 3

Specifying Rotation Angles

Example 3 **Find the angle of rotation and direction of rotation in the given figure. Point *P* is the center of rotation.**

(A)

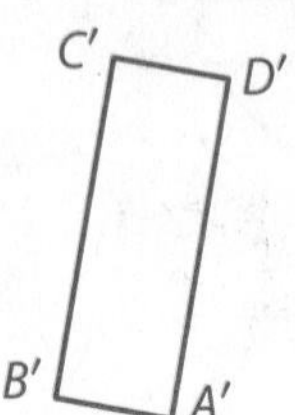

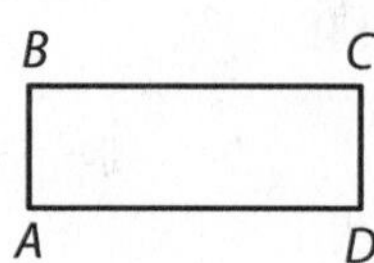

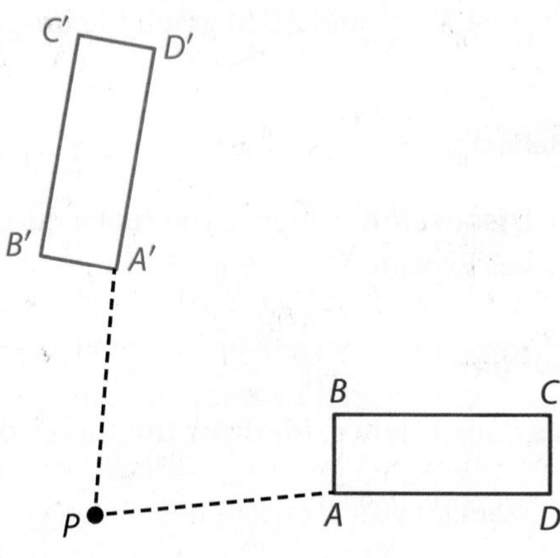

Draw segments from the center of rotation to a vertex and to the image of the vertex.

Measure the angle formed by the segments. The angle measure is 80°.

Compare the locations of the preimage and image to find the direction of the rotation.

The rotation is 80° counterclockwise.

(B)

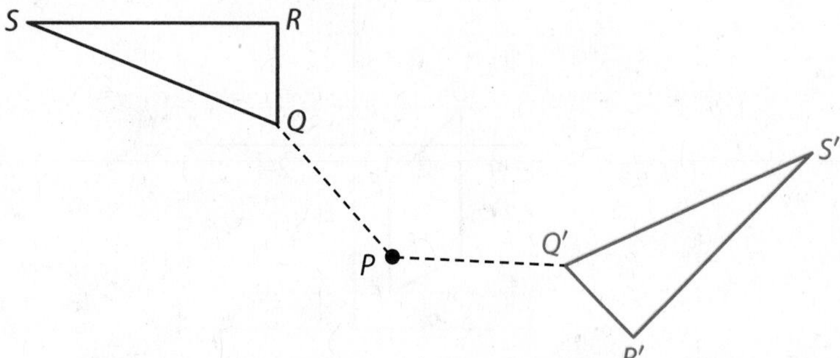

Draw segments from the center of rotation to a vertex and to the image of the vertex.

Measure the angle formed by the segments.

The angle measure is 135 °.

The rotation is 135 ° clockwise.

Reflect

9. **Discussion** Does it matter which points you choose when you draw segments from the center of rotation to points of the preimage and image? Explain.

10. In Part A, is a different angle of rotation and direction possible? Explain.

Your Turn

Copy the diagram. Then find the angle of rotation and direction of rotation in the given figure. Point P is the center of rotation.

11.

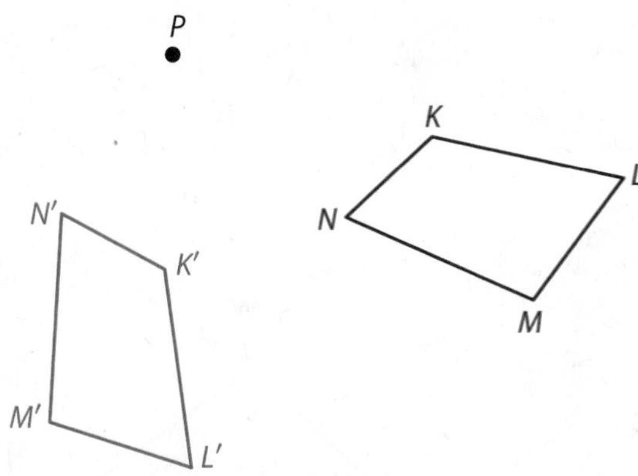

Elaborate

12. If you are given a figure, a center of rotation, and an angle of rotation, what steps can you use to draw the image of the figure under the rotation?

13. Suppose you are given $\triangle DEF$, $\triangle D'E'F'$, and point P. What are two different ways to prove that a rotation around point P cannot be used to map $\triangle DEF$ to $\triangle D'E'F'$?

14. **Essential Question Check-In** How do you draw the image of a figure under a counterclockwise rotation of 90° around the origin?

Evaluate: Homework and Practice

- Online Homework
- Hints and Help
- Extra Practice

1. Alberto uses geometry software to draw $\triangle STU$ and point P, as shown. He marks P as a center and uses the software to rotate $\triangle STU$ 115° around point P. He labels the image of $\triangle STU$ as $\triangle S'T'U'$.

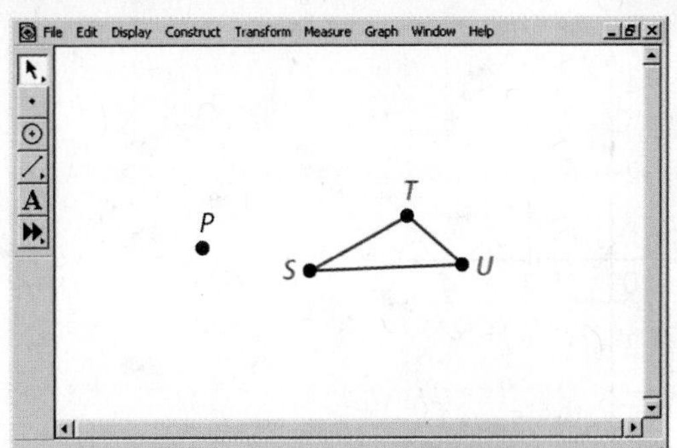

Which three angles must have the same measure? What is the measure of these angles?

Copy the triangle and the given point. Then draw the image of the triangle after the given rotation.

2. Counterclockwise rotation of 30° around point P

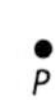

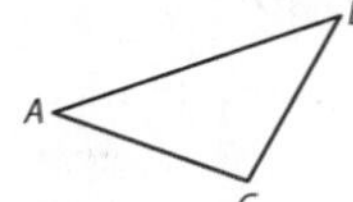

3. Clockwise rotation of 55° around point J

J

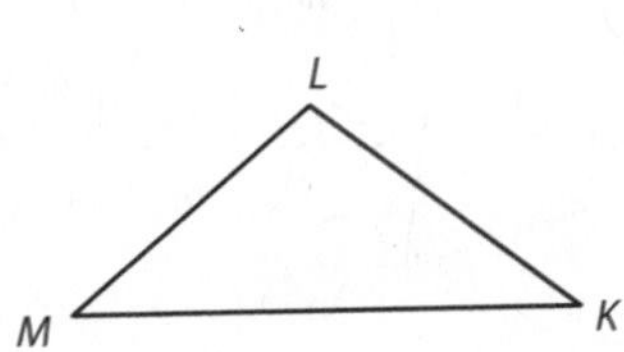

4. Counterclockwise rotation of 90° around point P

P

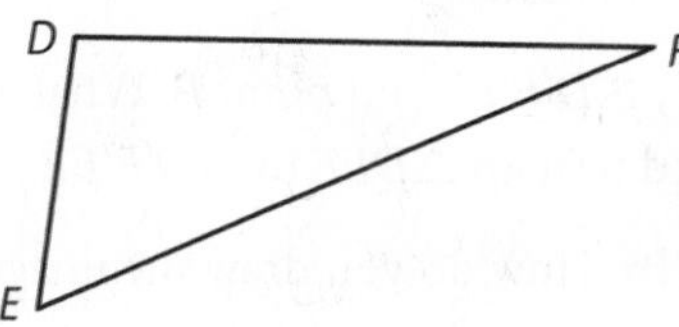

On a coordinate grid, draw the image of the figure under the given rotation.

5. $\triangle ABC$; 270°

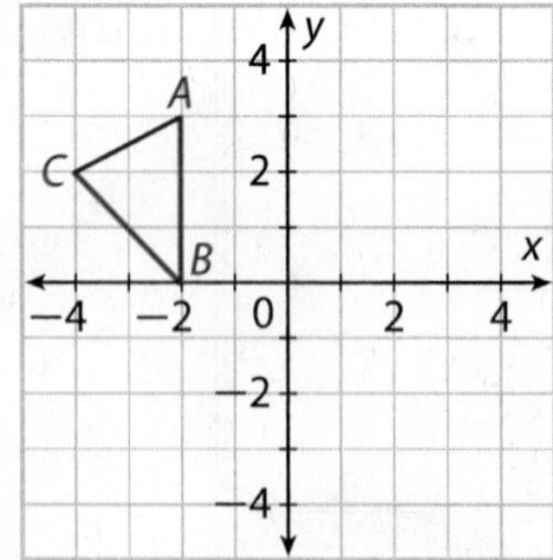

6. $\triangle RST$; 90°

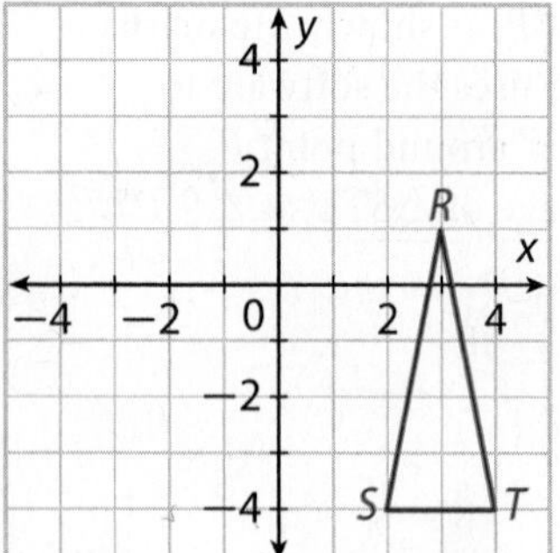

7. Quadrilateral *EFGH*; 180°

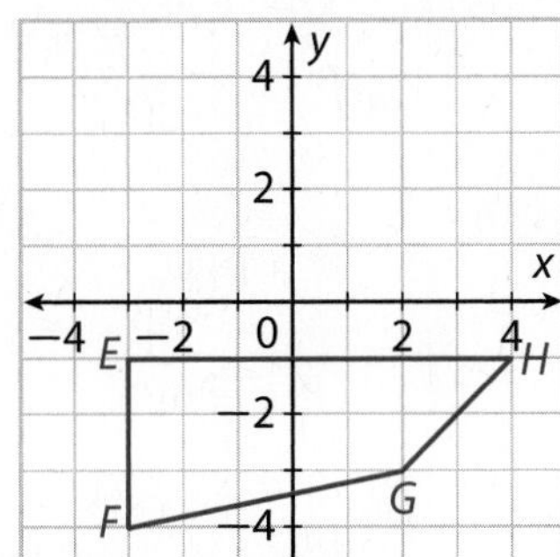

8. Quadrilateral *PQRS*; 270°

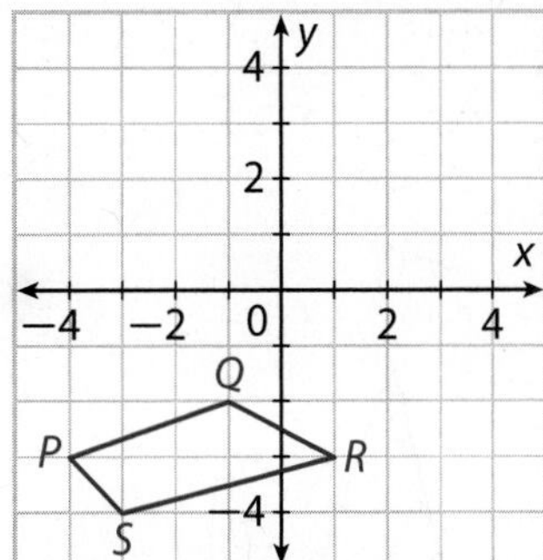

Find the angle of rotation and direction of rotation in the given figure. Point *P* is the center of rotation.

9.

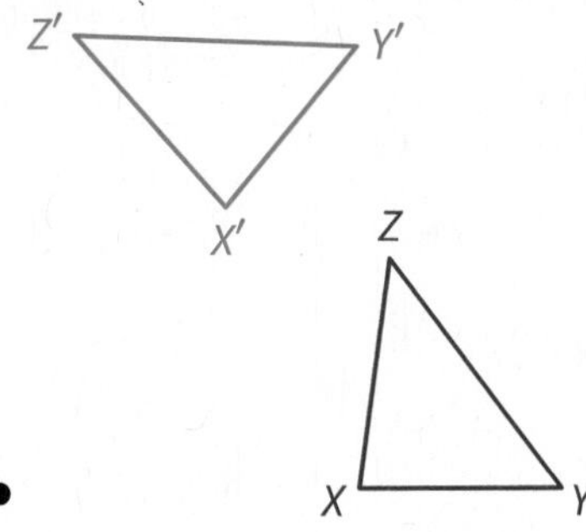

10.

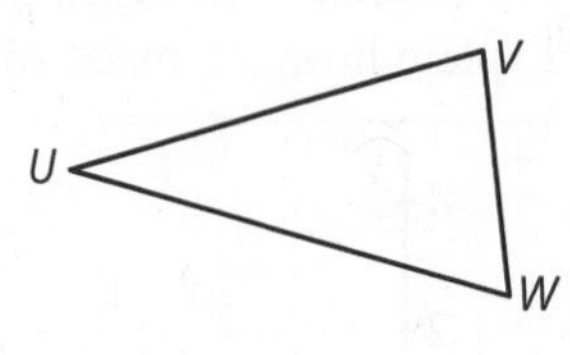

P

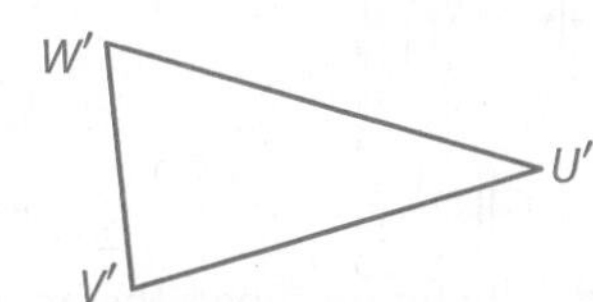

Write an algebraic rule for the rotation shown. Then describe the transformation in words.

11.

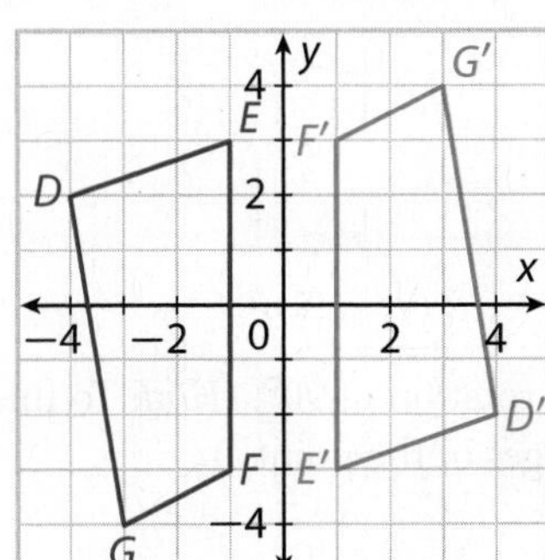

12.

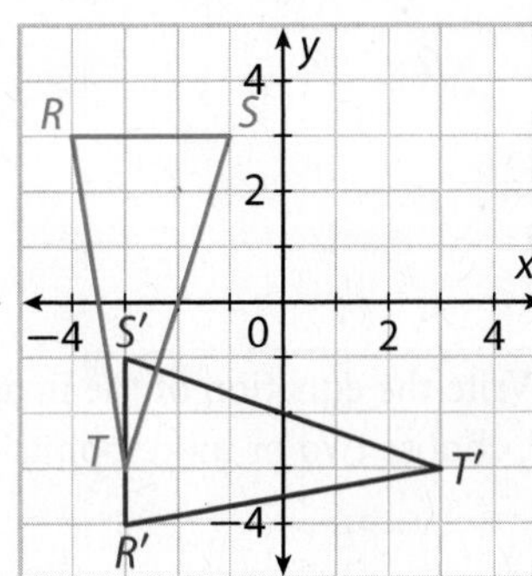

13. Vanessa used geometry software to apply a transformation to $\triangle ABC$, as shown. According to the software, $m\angle APA' = m\angle BPB' = m\angle CPC'$. Vanessa said this means the transformation must be a rotation. Do you agree? Explain.

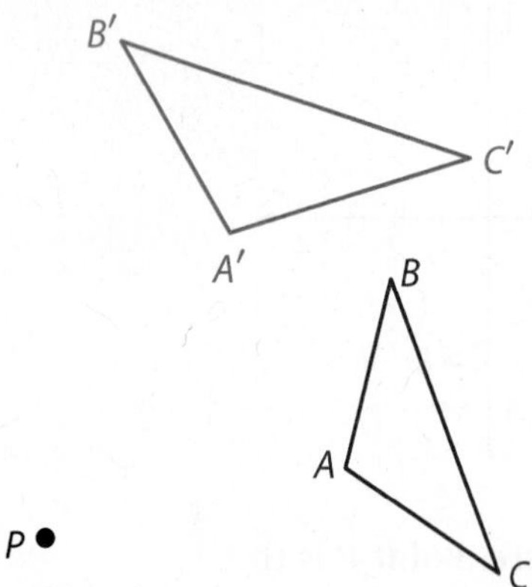

14. Make a Prediction In which quadrant will the image of $\triangle FGH$ lie after a counterclockwise rotation of 1980°? Explain how you made your prediction.

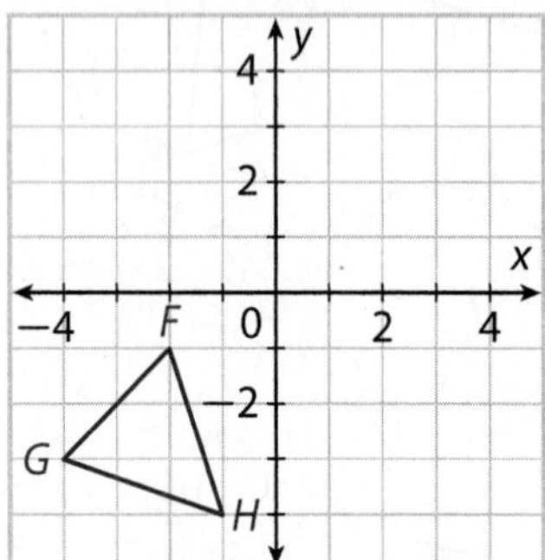

15. Critical Thinking The figure shows the image of $\triangle MNP$ after a counterclockwise rotation of 270°. On a coordinate grid, draw and label $\triangle MNP$.

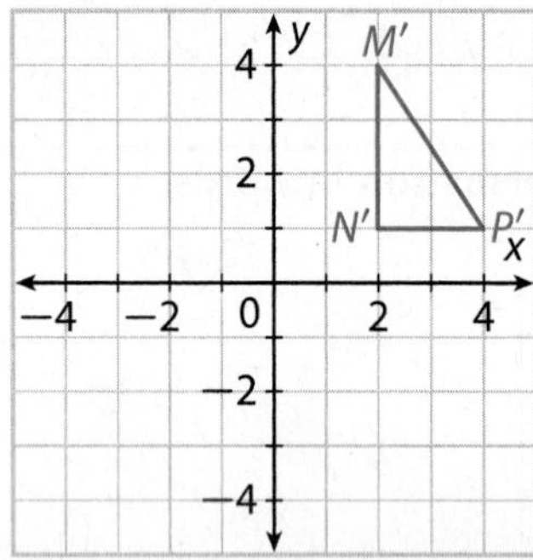

16. Multi-Step Write the equation of the image of line ℓ after a clockwise rotation of 90°. (*Hint*: To find the image of line ℓ, choose two or more points on the line and find the images of the points.)

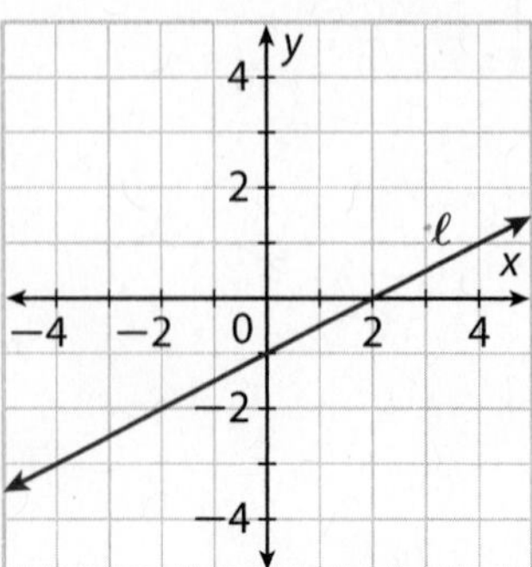

17. A Ferris wheel has 20 cars that are equally spaced around the circumference of the wheel. The wheel rotates so that the car at the bottom of the ride is replaced by the next car. By how many degrees does the wheel rotate?

18. The Skylon Tower, in Niagara Falls, Canada, has a revolving restaurant 775 feet above the falls. The restaurant makes a complete revolution once every hour. While a visitor was at the tower, the restaurant rotated through 135°. How long was the visitor at the tower?

19. Amani plans to use drawing software to make the design shown here. She starts by drawing Triangle 1. Explain how she can finish the design using rotations.

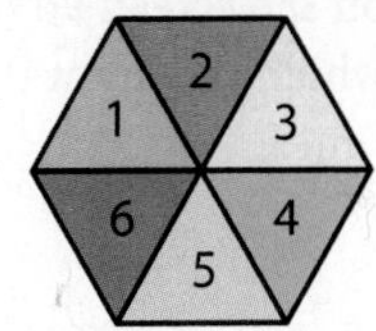

20. An animator is drawing a scene in which a ladybug moves around three mushrooms. The figure shows the starting position of the ladybug. The animator rotates the ladybug 180° around mushroom A, then 180° around mushroom B, and finally 180° around mushroom C. What are the final coordinates of the ladybug?

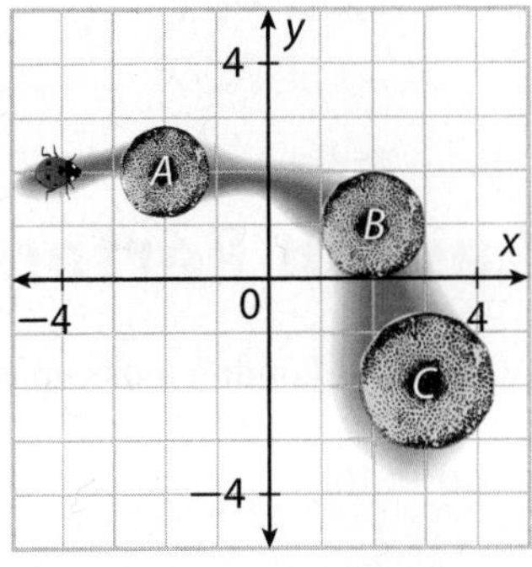

21. Determine whether each statement about the rotation $(x, y) \to (y, -x)$ is true or false.

a. Every point in Quadrant I is mapped to a point in Quadrant II.

b. Points on the x-axis are mapped to points on the y-axis.

c. The origin is a fixed point under the rotation.

d. The rotation has the same effect as a 90° clockwise rotation.

e. The angle of rotation is 180°.

f. A point on the line $y = x$ is mapped to another point on the line $y = x$.

H.O.T. Focus on Higher Order Thinking

22. Communicate Mathematical Ideas Suppose you are given a figure and a center of rotation P. Describe two different ways you can use a ruler and protractor to draw the image of the figure after a 210° counterclockwise rotation around P.

23. Explain the Error Kevin drew the image of $\triangle ABC$ after a rotation of 85° around point P. Explain how you can tell from the figure that he made an error. Describe the error.

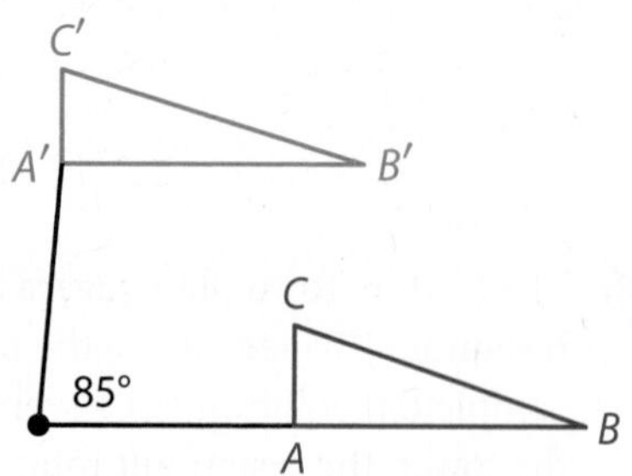

24. Critique Reasoning Isabella said that all points turn around the center of rotation by the same angle, so all points move the same distance under a rotation. Do you agree with Isabella's statement? Explain.

25. Look for a Pattern Isaiah uses software to draw $\triangle DEF$ as shown. Each time he presses the left arrow key, the software rotates the figure on the screen 90° counterclockwise. Explain how Isaiah can determine which quadrant the triangle will lie in if he presses the left arrow key n times.

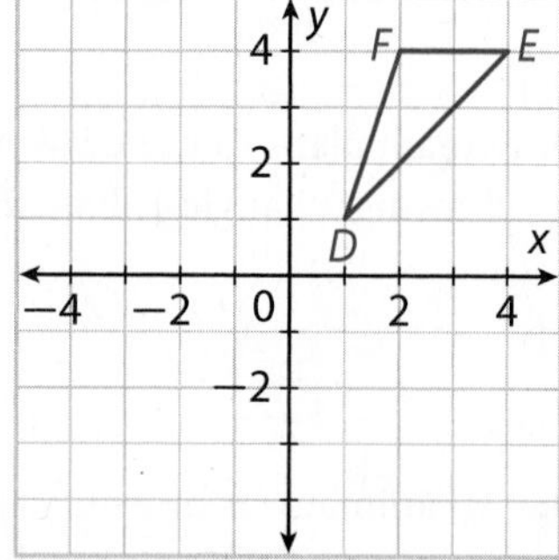

Lesson Performance Task

A tourist in London looks up at the clock in Big Ben tower and finds that it is exactly 8:00. When she looks up at the clock later, it is exactly 8:10.

a. Through what angle of rotation did the minute hand turn? Through what angle of rotation did the hour hand turn?

b. Make a table that shows different amounts of time, from 5 minutes to 60 minutes, in 5-minute increments. For each number of minutes, provide the angle of rotation for the minute hand of a clock and the angle of rotation for the hour hand of a clock.

2.4 Investigating Symmetry

Essential Question: How do you determine whether a figure has line symmetry or rotational symmetry?

Resource Locker

Explore 1 Identifying Line Symmetry

A figure has **symmetry** if a rigid motion exists that maps the figure onto itself. A figure has **line symmetry** (or *reflectional symmetry*) if a reflection maps the figure onto itself. Each of these lines of reflection is called a **line of symmetry**.

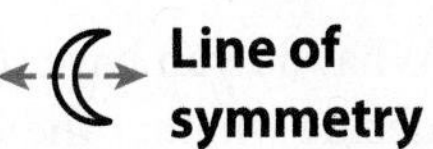

You can use paper folding to determine whether a figure has line symmetry.

(A) Trace the figure on a piece of tracing paper.

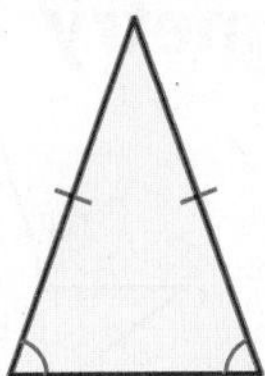

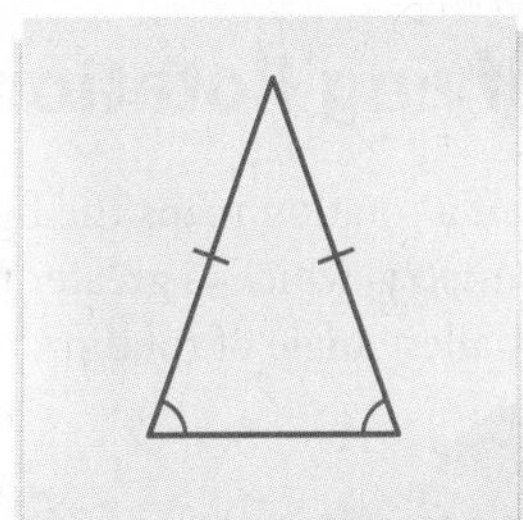

(B) If the figure can be folded along a straight line so that one half of the figure exactly matches the other half, the figure has line symmetry. The crease is the line of symmetry. Place your shape against the original figure to check that each crease is a line of symmetry.

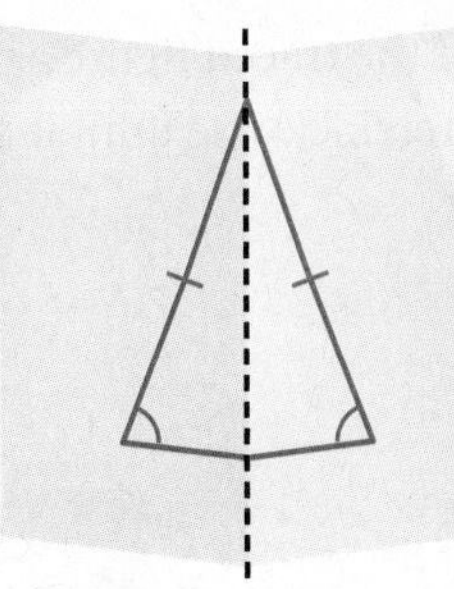

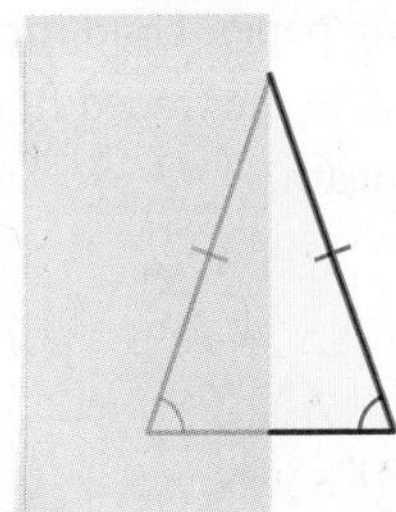

(C) Sketch any lines of symmetry on the figure.

The figure has [?] line of symmetry.

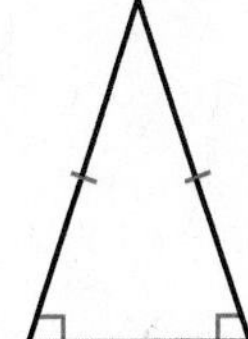

Ⓓ Copy each figure and draw any lines of symmetry. Tell the total number of lines of symmetry each figure has.

Figure	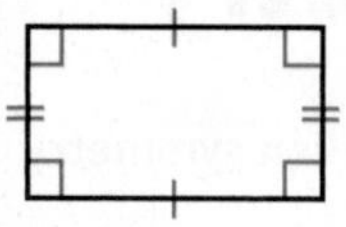	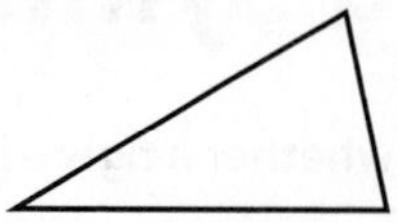	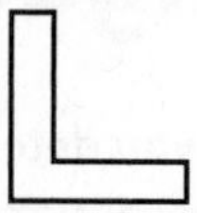
How many lines of symmetry?	?	?	?

Reflect

1. What do you have to know about any segments and angles in a figure to decide whether the figure has line symmetry?
2. What figure has an infinite number of lines of symmetry?
3. **Discussion** A figure undergoes a rigid motion, such as a rotation. If the figure has line symmetry, does the image of the figure have line symmetry as well? Give an example.

Explore 2 Identifying Rotational Symmetry

A figure has **rotational symmetry** if a rotation maps the figure onto itself. The **angle of rotational symmetry**, which is greater than 0° but less than or equal to 180°, is the smallest angle of rotation that maps a figure onto itself.

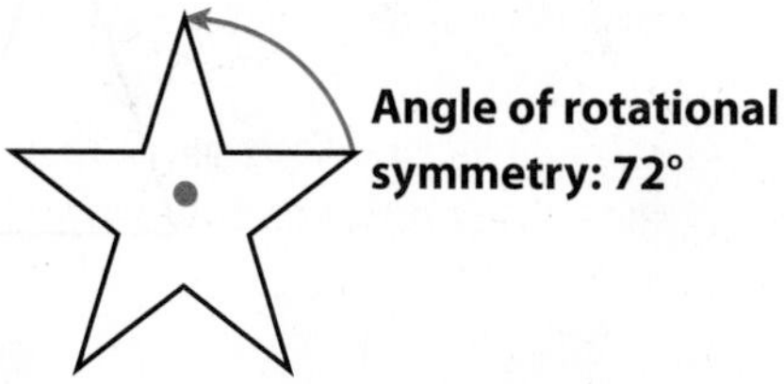

An angle of rotational symmetry is a fractional part of 360°. Notice that every time the 5-pointed star rotates $\frac{360°}{5} = 72°$, the star coincides with itself. The angles of rotation for the star are 72°, 144°, 216°, and 288°. If a copy of the figure rotates to exactly match the original, the figure has rotational symmetry.

Ⓐ Trace the figure onto tracing paper. Hold the center of the traced figure against the original figure with your pencil. Rotate the traced figure counterclockwise until it coincides again with the original figure beneath.

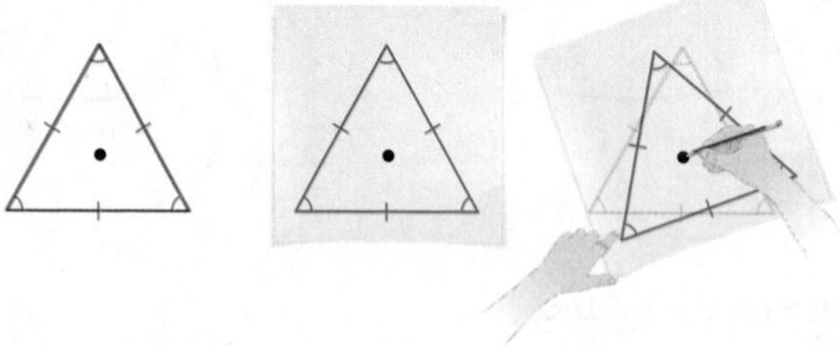

By how many degrees did you rotate the figure?

What are all the angles of rotation?

(B) Determine whether each figure has rotational symmetry. If so, identify all the angles of rotation less than 360°.

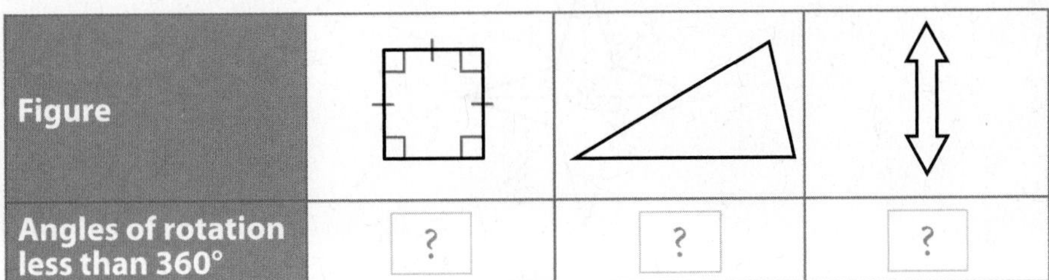

Figure	[square]	[triangle]	[double arrow]
Angles of rotation less than 360°	?	?	?

Reflect

4. What figure is mapped onto itself by a rotation of any angle?

5. **Discussion** A figure is formed by line l and line m, which intersect at an angle of 60°. Does the figure have an angle of rotational symmetry of 60°? If not, what is the angle of rotational symmetry?

Explain 1 Describing Symmetries

A figure may have line symmetry, rotational symmetry, both types of symmetry, or no symmetry.

Example 1 **Describe the symmetry of each figure. Draw the lines of symmetry, name the angles of rotation, or both if the figure has both.**

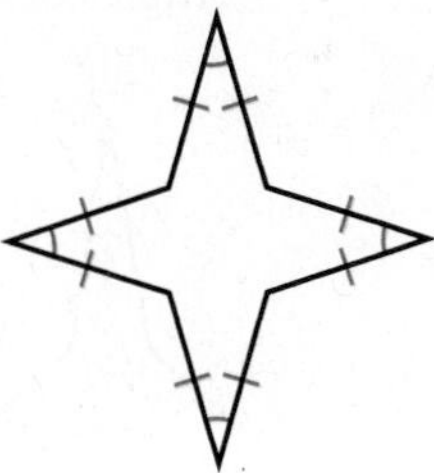

Step 1 Begin by finding the line symmetry of the figure. Look for matching halves of the figure. For example, you could fold the left half over the right half, and fold the top half over the bottom half. Draw one line of symmetry for each fold. Notice that the lines intersect at the center of the figure.

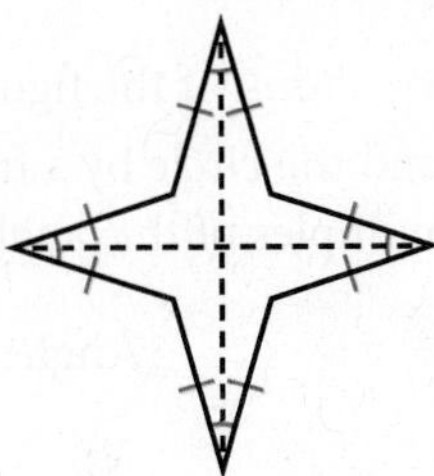

Step 2 Now look for other lines of symmetry. The two diagonals also describe matching halves. The figure has a total of 4 lines of symmetry.

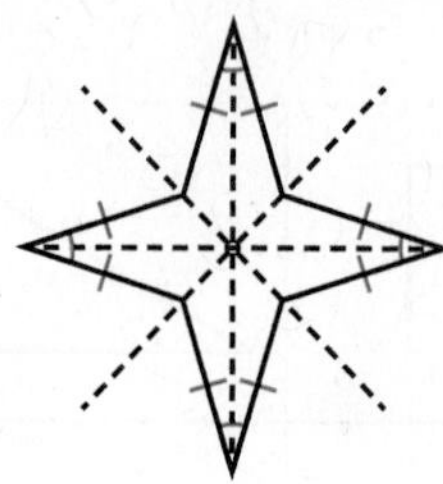

Step 3 Next, look for rotational symmetry. Think of the figure rotated about its center until it matches its original position. The angle of rotational symmetry of this figure is $\frac{1}{4}$ of 360°, or 90°.

The other angles of rotation for the figure are the multiples of 90° that are less than 360°. So the angles of rotation are 90°, 180°, and 270°.

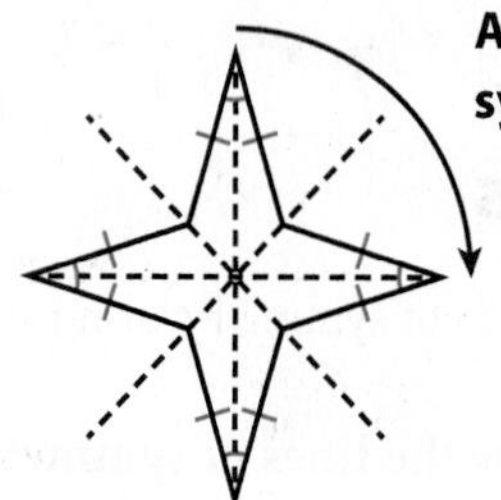

Angle of rotational symmetry: 90°

Number of lines of symmetry: 4 Angles of rotation: 90°, 180°, 270°

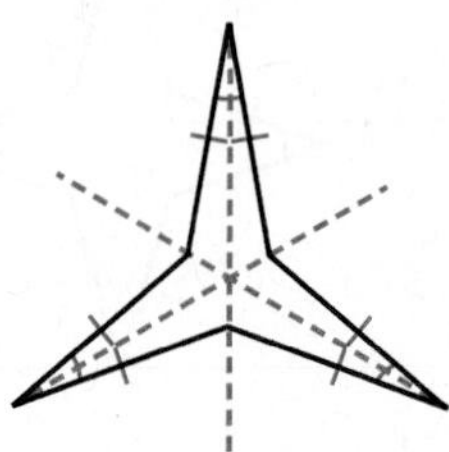

Step 1 Look for lines of symmetry. One line divides the figure into left and right halves. Draw this line on the figure. Then draw similar lines that begin at the other vertices of the figure.

Step 2 Now look for rotational symmetry. Think of the figure rotating about its center until it matches the original figure. It rotates around the circle by a fraction of $\frac{1}{3}$. Multiply by 360° to find the angle of rotation, which is 120°. Find multiples of this angle to find other angles of rotation.

Number of lines of symmetry: 3 Angles of rotation: 120°, 240°

Your Turn

Describe the type of symmetry for each figure. Copy the figure. Draw the lines of symmetry, name the angles of rotation, or both if the figure has both.

6. Figure *ABCD*

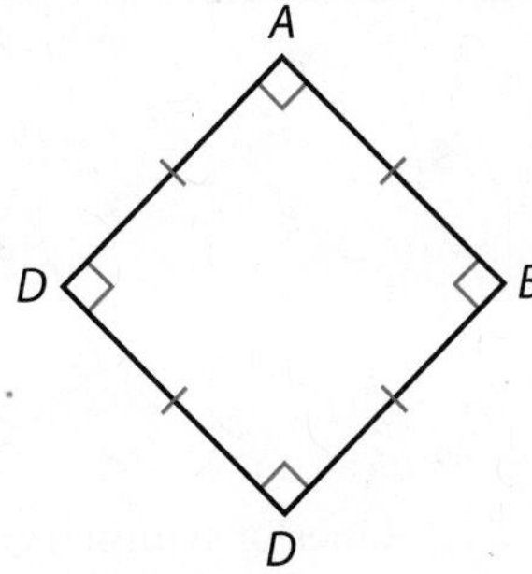

Types of symmetry:

Number of lines of symmetry:

Angles of rotation:

7. Figure *EFGHI*

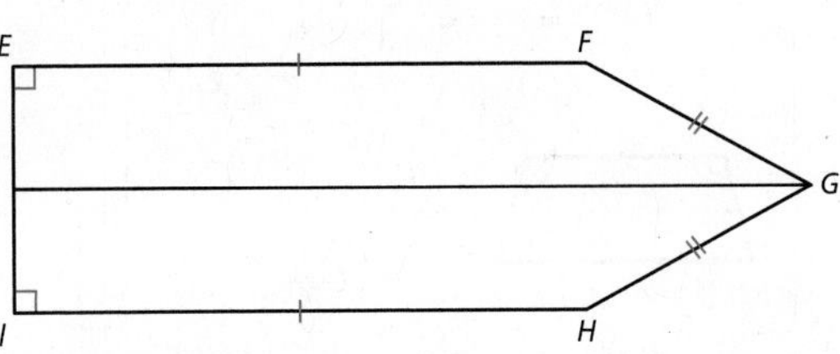

Types of symmetry:

Number of lines of symmetry:

Angles of rotation:

8. Figure *KLNPR*

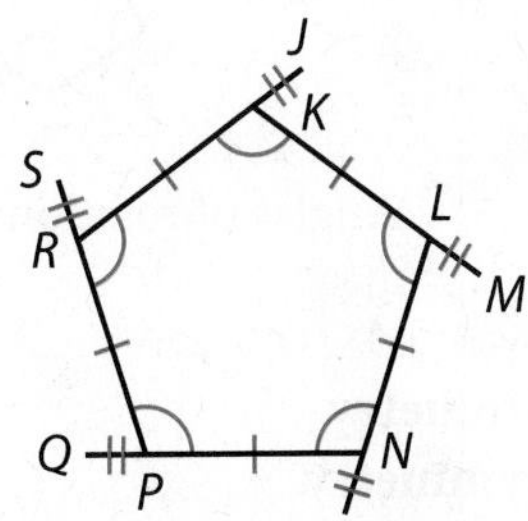

Types of symmetry:

Number of lines of symmetry:

Angles of rotation:

9. Figure *TUVW*

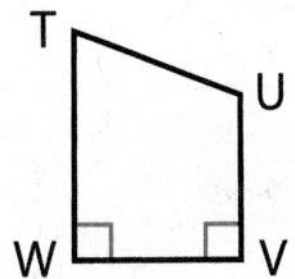

Types of symmetry:

Number of lines of symmetry:

Angles of rotation:

Elaborate

10. How are the two types of symmetry alike? How are they different?

11. Essential Question Check-In How do you determine whether a figure has line symmetry or rotational symmetry?

Evaluate: Homework and Practice

- Online Homework
- Hints and Help
- Extra Practice

Copy the figure. Draw all the lines of symmetry for the figure, and give the number of lines of symmetry. If the figure has no line symmetry, write zero.

1.

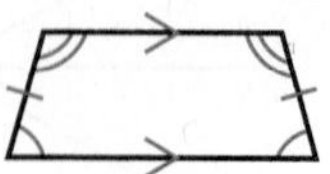

Lines of symmetry: ?

2.

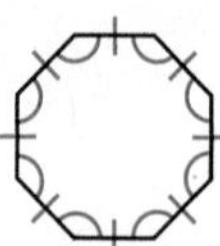

Lines of symmetry: ?

3.

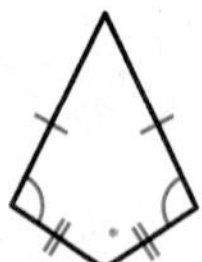

Lines of symmetry: ?

For the figures that have rotational symmetry, list the angles of rotation less than 360°. For figures without rotational symmetry, write "no rotational symmetry."

4.

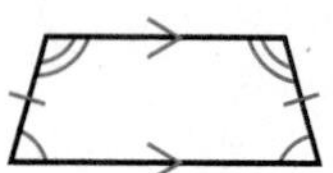

Angles of rotation: ?

5.

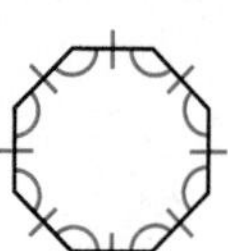

Angles of rotation: ?

6.

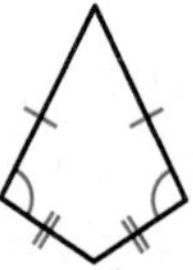

Angles of rotation: ?

In the tile design shown, identify whether the pattern has line symmetry, rotational symmetry, both line and rotational symmetry, or no symmetry.

7.

8.

For figure *ABCDEF* shown here, identify the image after each transformation described. For example, a reflection across $\overline{AD}$ has an image of figure *AFEDCB*. In the figure, all the sides are the same length and all the angles are the same measure.

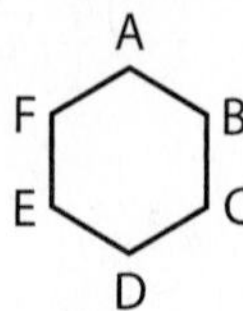

9. reflection across $\overline{CF}$

Figure ?

10. rotation of 240° clockwise, or 120° counterclockwise

Figure ?

11. reflection across the line that connects the midpoint of $\overline{BC}$ and the midpoint of $\overline{EF}$

Figure ?

Sketch an example of a figure with the given characteristics.

12. no line symmetry; angle of rotational symmetry: 180°

13. one line of symmetry; no rotational symmetry

14. Describe the line and rotational symmetry in this figure.

H.O.T. Focus on Higher Order Thinking

15. Communicate Mathematical Ideas How is a rectangle similar to an ellipse? Use concepts of symmetry in your answer.

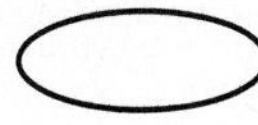

16. Explain the Error A student was asked to draw all of the lines of symmetry on each figure shown. Identify the student's work as correct or incorrect. If incorrect, explain why.

a. 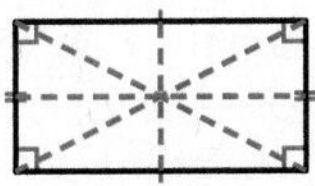

b. 

c. 

Lesson Performance Task

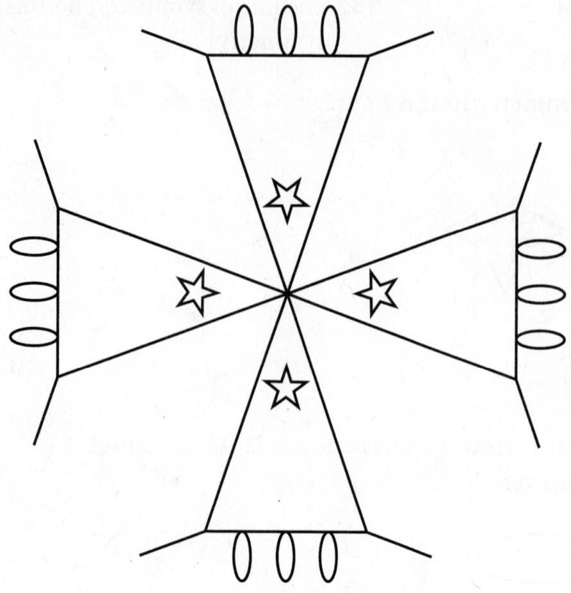

Use symmetry to design a work of art. Begin by drawing one simple geometric figure, such as a triangle, square, or rectangle, on a piece of construction paper. Then add other lines or two-dimensional shapes to the figure. Next, make identical copies of the figure, and then arrange them in a symmetric pattern.

Evaluate the symmetry of the work of art you created. Rotate it to identify an angle of rotational symmetry. Compare the line symmetry of the original figure with the line symmetry of the finished work.

STUDY GUIDE REVIEW

Transformations and Symmetry

MODULE 2

Essential Question: How can you use transformations to solve real-world problems?

Key Vocabulary

vector (*vector*)
initial point (*punto inicial*)
terminal point (*punto terminal*)
translation (*translación*)
perpendicular lines (*líneas perpendiculares*)
perpendicular bisector (*mediatriz*)
reflection (*reflexión*)
rotation (*rotación*)
center of rotation (*centro de rotación*)
angle of rotation (*ángulo de rotación*)
symmetry (*simetría*)
line symmetry (*simetría de línea*)
line of symmetry (*línea de simetría*)
rotational symmetry (*simetría rotacional*)
angle of rotational symmetry (*ángulo de simetría rotacional*)

KEY EXAMPLE (Lesson 2.1)

Translate the square $ABCD$ along the vector $\langle 2, 1 \rangle$.

$A(1, 2), B(3, 2), C(1, 4), D(3, 4)$.

$(x, y) \rightarrow (x + a, y + b)$ — Write the rule for translation along the vector $\langle a, b \rangle$.

$A(1, 2) \rightarrow A'(1 + 2, 2 + 1)$ — Apply the rule to each point.

$B(3, 2) \rightarrow B'(3 + 2, 2 + 1)$

$C(1, 4) \rightarrow C'(1 + 2, 4 + 1)$

$D(3, 4) \rightarrow D'(3 + 2, 4 + 1)$

$A'(3, 3), B'(5, 3),$
$C'(3, 5), D'(5, 5)$ — Now simplify.

KEY EXAMPLE (Lesson 2.2)

Determine the vertices of the image of $\triangle ABC$.

$A(2, 3), B(3, 4)$, and $C(3, 1)$ reflected across the line $y = x$.

$(x, y) \rightarrow (y, x)$ — Write the rule for reflection across the line $y = x$.

$A(2, 3), A'(3, 2)$ — Apply the rule to each point.

$B(3, 4), B'(4, 3)$

$C(3, 1), C'(1, 3)$

KEY EXAMPLE (Lesson 2.3)

Determine the vertices of the image of $\triangle DFE$.

$D(1, 2), F(2, 2)$, and $E(2, 0)$, rotated 270° counterclockwise about the origin.

$(x, y) \rightarrow (y, -x)$ — Write the rule for a rotation 270° counterclockwise.

$D(1, 2), \rightarrow D'(2, -1)$ — Apply the rule to each point.

$F(2, 2), \rightarrow F'(2, -2)$

$E(2, 0), \rightarrow E'(0, -2)$

EXERCISES

Translate each figure along each vector. *(Lesson 2.1)*

1. The line segment determined by $A(4, 7)$ and $B(2, 9)$ along $\langle 0, -2 \rangle$.

   The endpoints of the image are __?__.

2. The triangle determined by $A(-3, 2)$, $B(4, 4)$, and $C(1, 1)$ along $\langle -1, -3 \rangle$.

   The vertices of the image are __?__.

Determine the vertices of each image. *(Lesson 2.2)*

3. The image of the rectangle $ABCD$ reflected across the line $y = -x$.

   $A(-3, 2)$, $B(3, 2)$, $C(-3, -3)$, $D(3, -3)$

   The vertices of the image are __?__.

4. The image of the polygon $ABCDE$ reflected across the x-axis.

   $A(-1, -1)$, $B(0, 1)$, $C(4, 2)$, $D(6, 0)$, $E(3, -3)$

   The vertices of the image are __?__.

Determine the vertices of the image. *(Lesson 2.3)*

5. The figure defined by $A(3, 5)$, $B(5, 3)$, $C(2, 2)$ rotated 180° counterclockwise about the origin.

   The vertices of the image are __?__.

MODULE PERFORMANCE TASK

Animating Digital Images

A computer animator is designing an animation in which a bird flies off its perch, swoops down and to the right, and then flies off the right side of the screen. The graph shows the designer's preliminary sketch, using a triangle to represent the bird in its initial position (top) and one intermediate position.

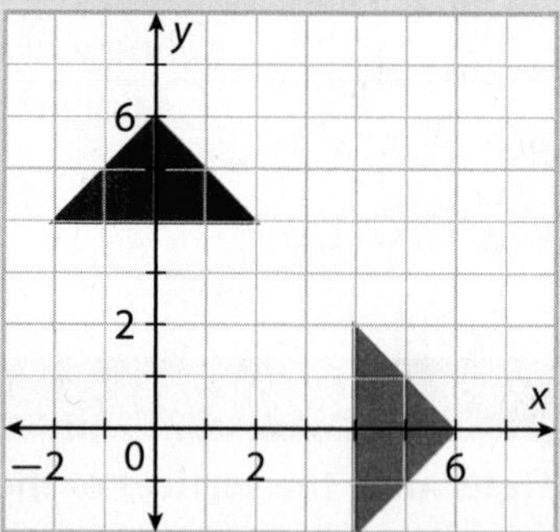

Plan a series of rotations and translations to animate the flight of the bird. Sketch each rotation and translation on a graph and label the coordinates of the triangle's vertices at each position. If you wish, you can test out how well your animation works by making a flipbook of your graphs.

Ready to Go On?

2.1–2.4 Transformations and Symmetry

- Online Homework
- Hints and Help
- Extra Practice

1. Line segment $\overline{YZ}$ was used to translate *ABCDE*. $\overline{YZ}$ is 6.2 inches long. What is the length of $AA' + BB' + CC' + DD' + EE'$? (Lesson 2.1)

Given figure *FGHI* and its image *F'G'H'I'*, answer the following. (Lesson 2.2, 2.3)

2a. Write an algebraic rule for the rotation shown and then describe the rotation in words.

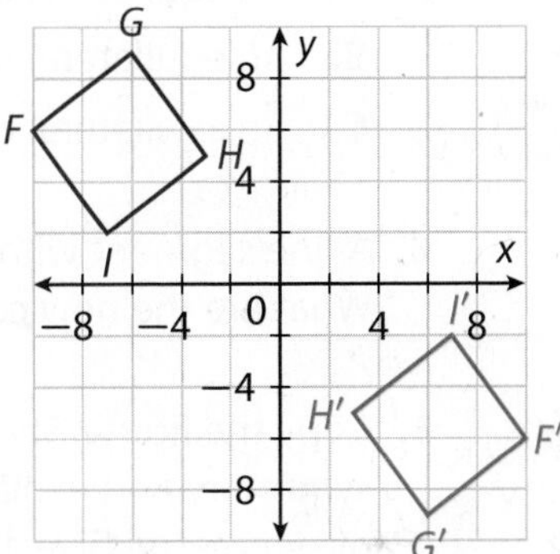

2b. Tell whether the figure *FGHI* has line symmetry, rotational symmetry, both types of symmetry, or no symmetry. If the figure has line symmetry, record the number. If the figure has rotational symmetry, list the angles of rotation that are less than 360°. (Lesson 17.3)

Types of symmetry	Number of lines of symmetry	Angles of rotation
?	?	?

3. Given triangle *ABC* with $A(-2, 4)$, $B(-2, 1)$, and $C(-4, 0)$, and its image $A'B'C'$ with $A'(2, 0)$, $B'(-1, 0)$, and $C'(-2, -2)$, find the line of reflection. (Lesson 2.2)

Essential Question

4. In which situations are translations useful for transformations? Reflections? Rotations?

MODULE 2
MIXED REVIEW

Assessment Readiness

1. Triangle ABC is given by the points $A(-1, 5)$, $B(0, 3)$, and $C(2, 4)$. It is reflected over the line $y = -2x - 2$. Tell whether the image contains the given point.

A. $A'(-5, 3)$

B. $B'(-4, 6)$

C. $C'(-6, 0)$

2. A triangle, $\triangle ABC$, is rotated 90° counterclockwise, reflected across the x-axis, and then reflected across the y-axis. Determine if each statement is True or False.

A. Rotating $\triangle ABC$ 180° clockwise is an equivalent transformation.

B. Rotating $\triangle ABC$ 270° counterclockwise is an equivalent transformation.

C. Reflecting $\triangle ABC$ across the y-axis is an equivalent transformation.

3. Determine if each statement about equilateral triangles is True or False.

A. An equilateral triangle has 3 equal angle measures.

B. An equilateral triangle has 3 equal side measures.

C. An equilateral triangle has 3 lines of symmetry.

4. A line segment with points $P(1, 2)$ and $Q(4, 3)$ is reflected across the line $y = x$. What are the new coordinates of the points of the line segment?

5. Copy the figure. Then draw on the figure all lines of symmetry and explain why those lines are the lines of symmetry. Give all angles of rotational symmetry less than 360°.

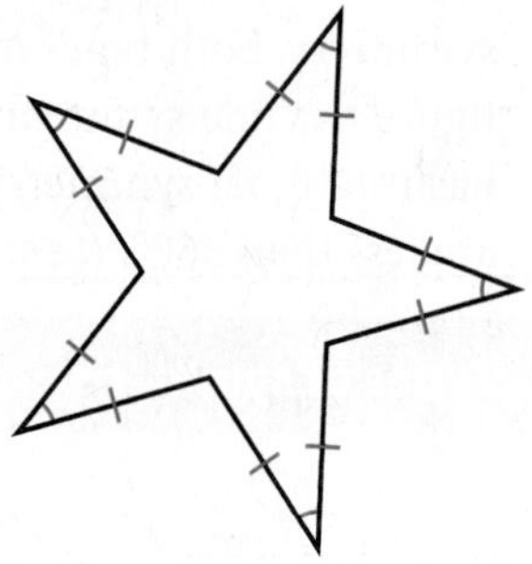

Congruent Figures

MODULE 3

Essential Question: How can you use congruency to solve real-world problems?

REAL WORLD VIDEO
Check out how landscape architects use transformations of geometric shapes to design green space for parks and homes.

MODULE PERFORMANCE TASK PREVIEW

Jigsaw Puzzle

In this module, you will use congruency and a series of transformations to solve a portion of a jigsaw puzzle. What is some of the basic geometry behind a jigsaw puzzle? Let's get started on finding out how all the pieces fit together!

Are YOU Ready?

Complete these exercises to review skills you will need for this module.

- Online Homework
- Hints and Help
- Extra Practice

Properties of Reflections

Example 1 Find the points that define the reflection of the figure given by $A(1, 1)$, $B(2, 3)$, and $C(3, 1)$ across the y-axis.

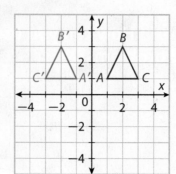

Use the rules for reflections on a coordinate plane. For a reflection across the y-axis:

$(x, y) \rightarrow (-x, y)$

$A(1, 1) \rightarrow A'(-1, 1)$, $B(2, 3) \rightarrow B'(-2, 3)$,
$C(3, 1) \rightarrow C'(-3, 1)$

Find the vertices of the reflected figure.

1. $\triangle ABC$ reflected across the x-axis

2. $\triangle ABC$ reflected across $y = x$

Properties of Rotations

Example 2 Find the vertices of $\triangle ABC$ rotated 90° counterclockwise around the origin.

$(x, y) \rightarrow (-y, x)$ Write the rule for rotation.

$A(1, 1) \rightarrow A'(-1, 1)$, $B(2, 3) \rightarrow B'(-3, 2)$,

$C(3, 1) \rightarrow C'(-1, 3)$ Apply the rule.

Find the vertices of the rotated figure.

3. $\triangle ABC$ rotated 180° around the origin

Properties of Translations

Example 3 Calculate the vertices of the image of $\triangle ABC$ translated using the rule $(x, y) \rightarrow (x + 2, y + 1)$.

$A(1, 1) \rightarrow A'(3, 2)$, $B(2, 3) \rightarrow B'(4, 4)$,

$C(3, 1) \rightarrow C'(5, 2)$ Apply the rule.

Calculate the vertices of the image.

4. $\triangle ABC$ translated using the rule $(x, y) \rightarrow (x - 2, y + 2)$

3.1 Sequences of Transformations

Resource Locker

Essential Question: What happens when you apply more than one transformation to a figure?

Explore Combining Rotations or Reflections

A transformation is a function that takes points on the plane and maps them to other points on the plane. Transformations can be applied one after the other in a sequence where you use the image of the first transformation as the preimage for the next transformation.

Find the image for each sequence of transformations.

(A) Using geometry software, draw a triangle and label the vertices A, B, and C. Then draw a point outside the triangle and label it P.

Rotate $\triangle ABC$ 30° around point P and label the image as $\triangle A'B'C'$. Then rotate $\triangle A'B'C'$ 45° around point P and label the image as $\triangle A''B''C''$. Sketch your result.

(B) Make a conjecture regarding a single rotation that will map $\triangle ABC$ to $\triangle A''B''C''$. Check your conjecture, and describe what you did.

(C) Using geometry software, draw a triangle and label the vertices D, E, and F. Then draw two intersecting lines and label them j and k.

Reflect $\triangle DEF$ across line j and label the image as $\triangle D'E'F'$. Then reflect $\triangle D'E'F'$ across line k and label the image as $\triangle D''E''F''$. Sketch your result.

(D) Consider the relationship between $\triangle DEF$ and $\triangle D''E''F''$. Describe the single transformation that maps $\triangle DEF$ to $\triangle D''E''F''$. How can you check that you are correct?

Reflect

1. Repeat Step A using other angle measures. Make a conjecture about what single transformation will describe a sequence of two rotations about the same center.

2. Make a conjecture about what single transformation will describe a sequence of three rotations about the same center.

3. **Discussion** Repeat Step C, but make lines j and k parallel instead of intersecting. Make a conjecture about what single transformation will now map $\triangle DEF$ to $\triangle D''E''F''$. Check your conjecture and describe what you did.

Explain 1 Combining Rigid Transformations

In the Explore, you saw that sometimes you can use a single transformation to describe the result of applying a sequence of two transformations. Now you will apply sequences of rigid transformations that cannot be described by a single transformation.

Example 1 **Draw the image of $\triangle ABC$ after the given combination of transformations.**

(A) Reflection over line ℓ then translation along $\vec{v}$

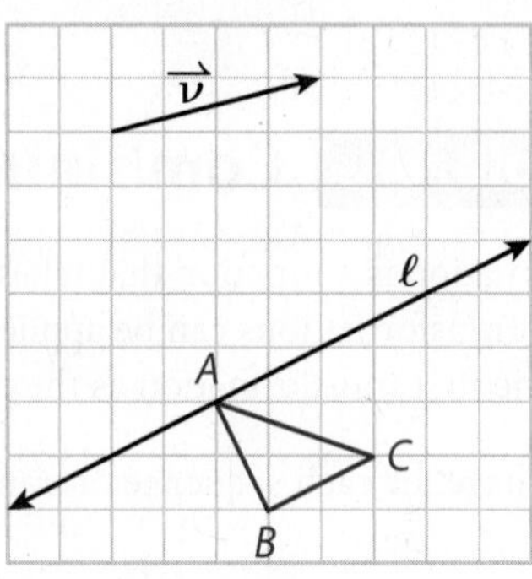

Step 1 Draw the image of $\triangle ABC$ after a reflection across line ℓ. Label the image $\triangle A'B'C'$.

Step 2 Translate $\triangle A'B'C'$ along $\vec{v}$. Label this image $\triangle A''B''C''$.

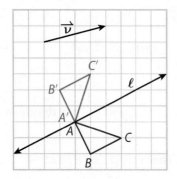

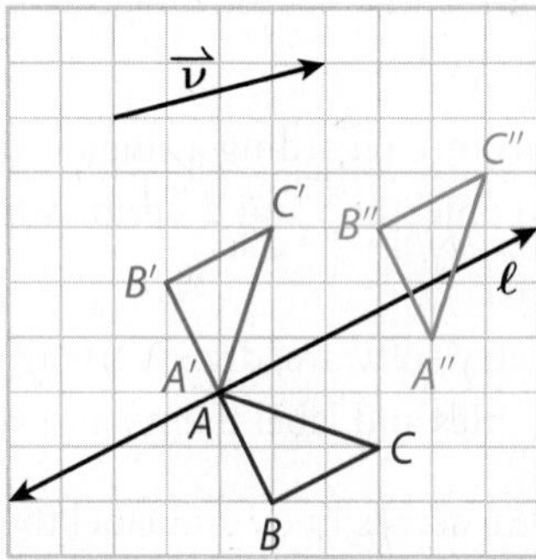

(B) 180° rotation around point P, then translation along $\vec{v}$, then reflection across line ℓ

Apply the rotation. Label the image $\triangle A'B'C'$.

Apply the translation to $\triangle A'B'C'$. Label the image $\triangle A''B''C''$.

Apply the reflection to $\triangle A''B''C''$. Label the image $\triangle A'''B'''C'''$.

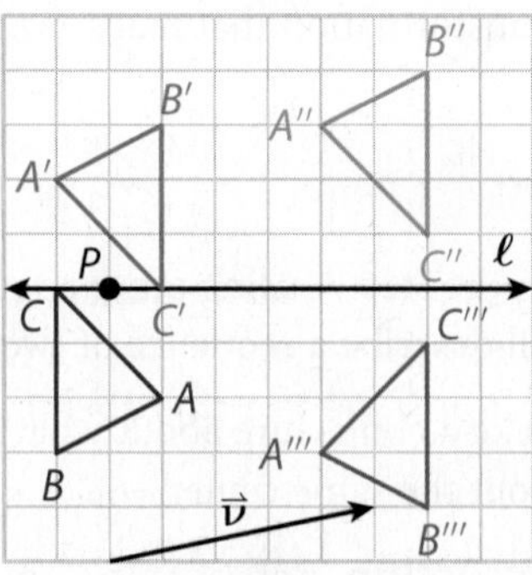

Reflect

4. Are the images you drew for each example the same size and shape as the given preimage? In what ways do rigid transformations change the preimage?

5. Does the order in which you apply the transformations make a difference? Test your conjecture by performing the transformations in Part B in a different order.

6. For Part B, describe a sequence of transformations that will take $\triangle A''B''C''$ back to the preimage.

Your Turn

Copy ΔABC on grid paper. Then draw the image of the triangle after the given combination of transformations.

7. Reflection across ℓ then 90° rotation around point P

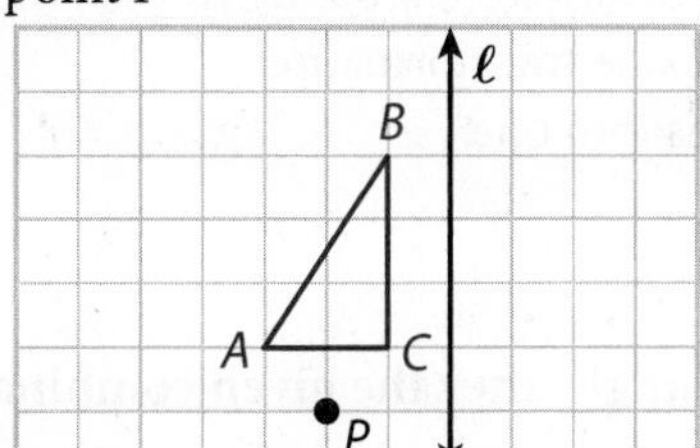

8. Translation along $\vec{v}$ then 180° rotation around point P then translation along $\vec{u}$

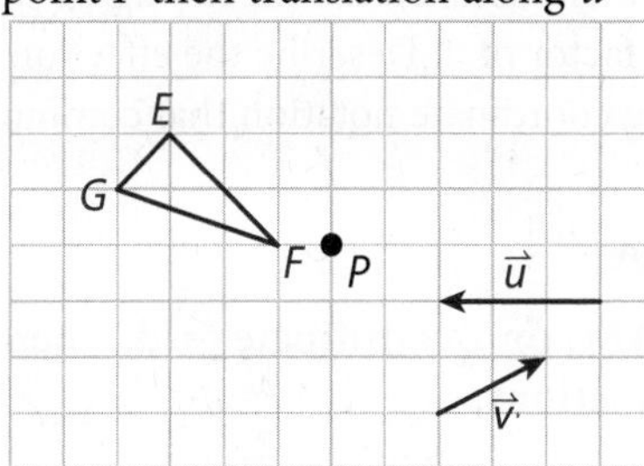

Explain 2 Combining Nonrigid Transformations

Example 2 **Draw the image of the figure in the plane after the given combination of transformations.**

Ⓐ $(x, y) \rightarrow \left(\frac{3}{2}x, \frac{3}{2}y\right) \rightarrow (-x, y) \rightarrow (x + 1, y - 2)$

1. The first transformation is a dilation by a factor of $\frac{3}{2}$. Apply the dilation. Label the image $A'B'C'D'$.
2. Apply the reflection of $A'B'C'D'$ across the y-axis. Label this image $A''B''C''D''$.
3. Apply the translation of $A''B''C''D''$. Label this image $A'''B'''C'''D'''$.

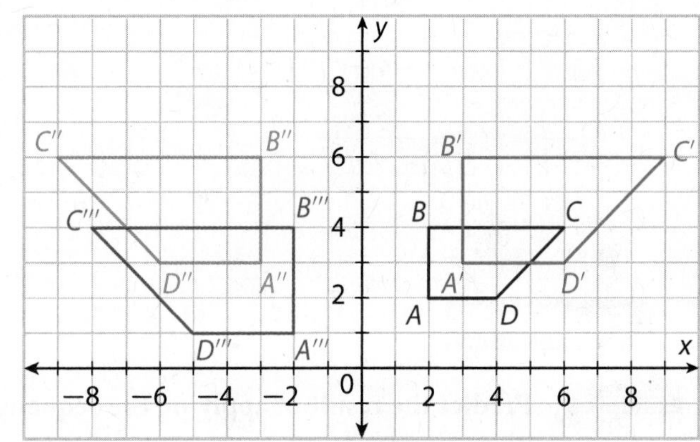

Ⓑ $(x, y) \rightarrow (3x, y) \rightarrow \left(\frac{1}{2}x, -\frac{1}{2}y\right)$

1. The first transformation is a horizontal stretch by a factor of 3. Apply the stretch. Label the image $\Delta A'B'C'$.
2. The second transformation is a dilation by a factor of $\frac{1}{2}$ combined with a reflection.
3. Apply the transformation to $\Delta A'B'C'$. Label the image $\Delta A''B''C''$.

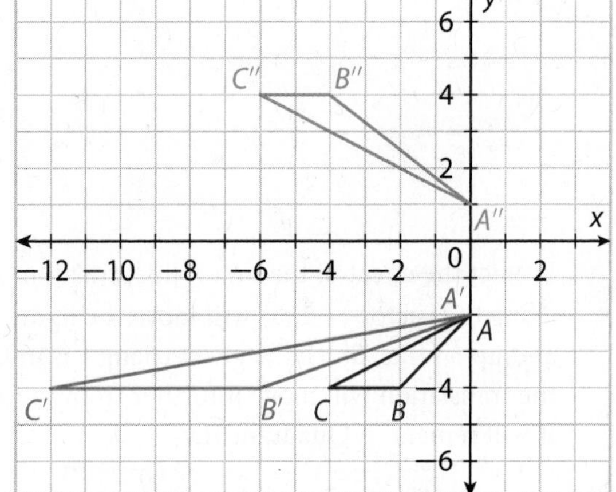

Reflect

9. If you dilated a figure by a factor of 2, what transformation could you use to return the figure back to its preimage? If you dilated a figure by a factor of 2 and then translated it right 2 units, write a sequence of transformations to return the figure back to its preimage.

10. A student is asked to reflect a figure across the y-axis and then vertically stretch the figure by a factor of 2. Describe the effect on the coordinates. Then write one transformation using coordinate notation that combines these two transformations into one.

Your Turn

Draw ΔABC on a coordinate grid. Then draw the image of the triangle after the given combination of transformations.

11. $(x, y) \rightarrow (x - 1, y - 1) \rightarrow (3x, y) \rightarrow (-x, -y)$

12. 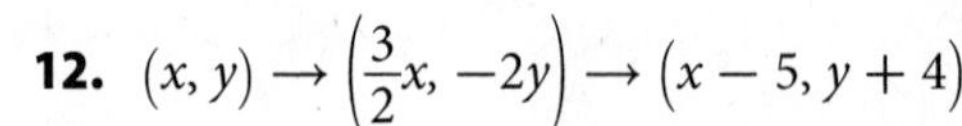
$(x, y) \rightarrow \left(\frac{3}{2}x, -2y\right) \rightarrow (x - 5, y + 4)$

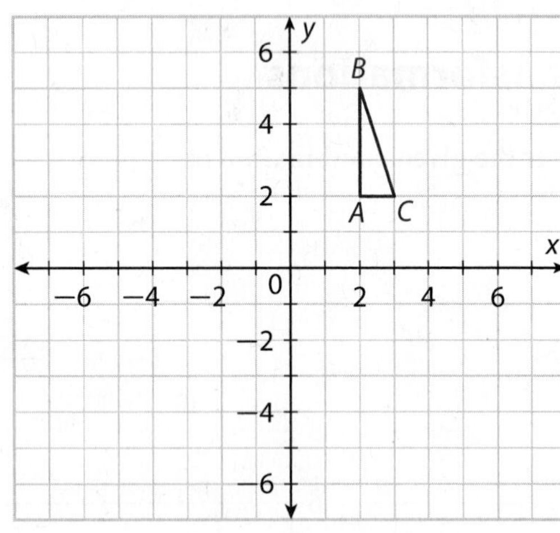

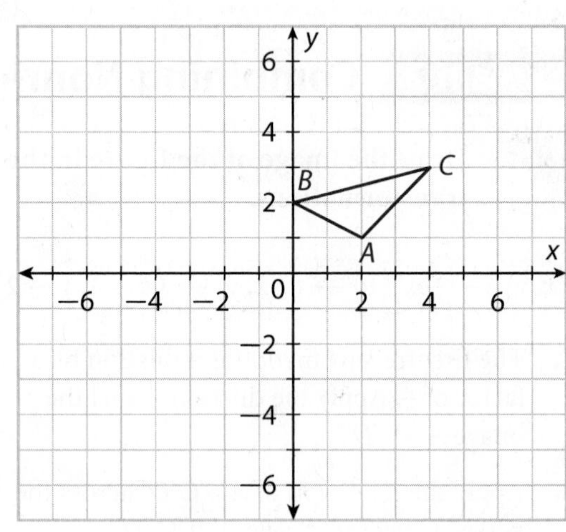

Explain 3 Predicting the Effect of Transformations

Example 3 **Predict the result of applying the sequence of transformations to the given figure.**

(A) $\triangle LMN$ is translated along the vector $\langle -2, 3 \rangle$, reflected across the y-axis, and then reflected across the x-axis.

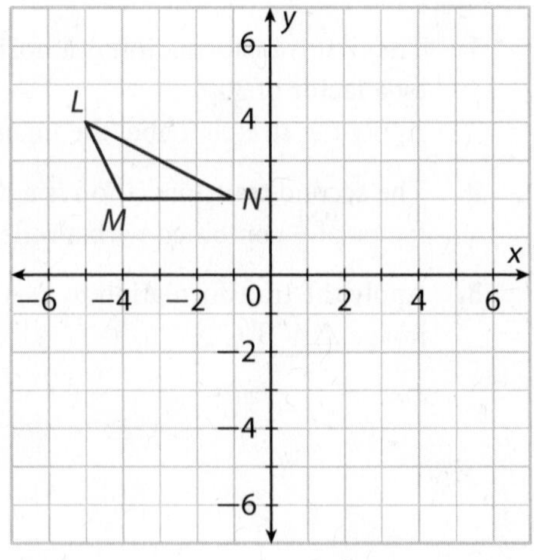

Predict the effect of the first transformation: A translation along the vector $\langle -2, 3 \rangle$ will move the figure left 2 units and up 3 units. Since the given triangle is in Quadrant II, the translation will move it further from the x- and y-axes. It will remain in Quadrant II.

Predict the effect of the second transformation: Since the triangle is in Quadrant II, a reflection across the y-axis will change the orientation and move the triangle into Quadrant I.

Predict the effect of the third transformation: A reflection across the x-axis will again change the orientation and move the triangle into Quadrant IV. The two reflections are the equivalent of rotating the figure 180° about the origin.

The final result will be a triangle the same shape and size as $\triangle LMN$ in Quadrant IV. It has been rotated 180° about the origin and is farther from the axes than the preimage.

(B) Square $HIJK$ is rotated 90° clockwise about the origin and then dilated by a factor of 2, which maps $(x, y) \rightarrow (2x, 2y)$.

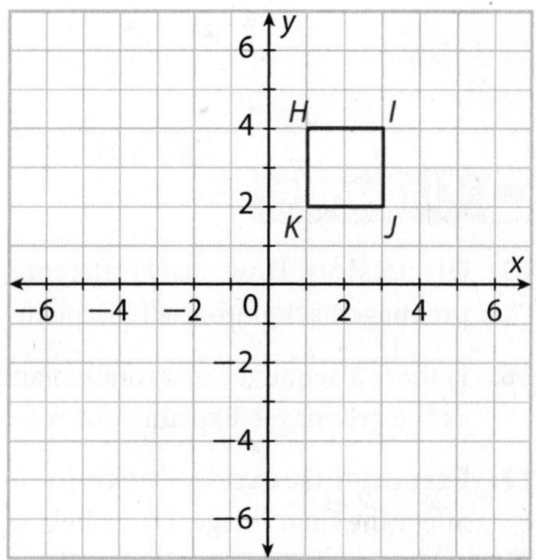

Predict the effect of the first transformation: A 90° clockwise rotation will map it to Quadrant IV. Due to its symmetry, it will appear to have been translated, but will be closer to the x-axis than it is to the y-axis.

Predict the effect of the second transformation: A dilation by a factor of 2 will double the side lengths of the square. It will also be further from the origin than the preimage.

The final result will be a square in Quadrant 4 with side lengths twice as long as the side lengths of the original. The image is further from the origin than the preimage.

Your Turn

Predict the result of applying the sequence of transformations to the given figure.

13. Rectangle $GHJK$ is reflected across the y-axis and translated along the vector $\langle 5, 4 \rangle$.

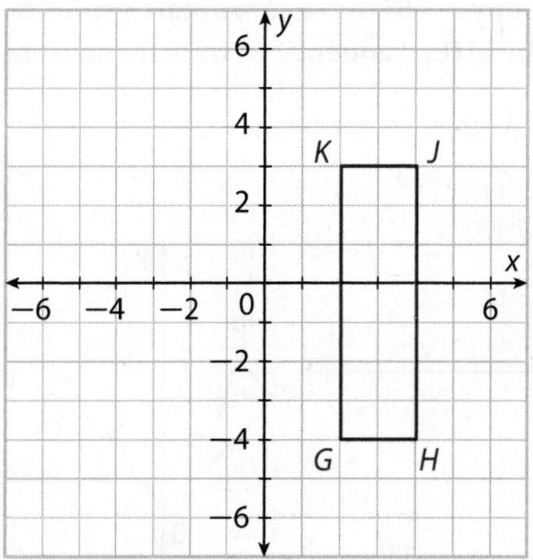

14. $\triangle TUV$ is horizontally stretched by a factor of $\frac{3}{2}$, which maps $(x, y) \rightarrow \left(\frac{3}{2}x, y\right)$, and then translated along the vector $\langle 2, 1 \rangle$.

Elaborate

15. **Discussion** How many different sequences of rigid transformations do you think you can find to take a preimage back onto itself? Explain your reasoning.

16. Is there a sequence of a rotation and a dilation that will result in an image that is the same size and position as the preimage? Explain your reasoning.

17. **Essential Question Check-In** In a sequence of transformations, the order of the transformations can affect the final image. Describe a sequence of transformations where the order does not matter. Describe a sequence of transformations where the order does matter.

Evaluate: Homework and Practice

- Online Homework
- Hints and Help
- Extra Practice

Copy $\triangle ABC$ on a coordinate grid. Then draw and label the final image of $\triangle ABC$ after the given sequence of transformations.

1. Reflect $\triangle ABC$ over the y-axis and then translate by $\langle 2, -3 \rangle$.

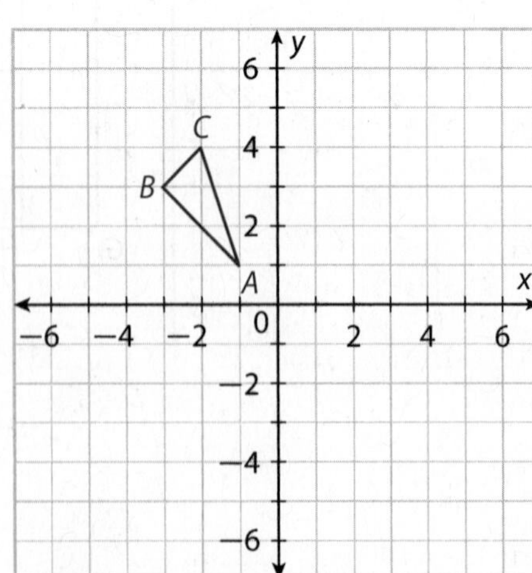

2. Rotate $\triangle ABC$ 90 degrees clockwise about the origin and then reflect over the x-axis.

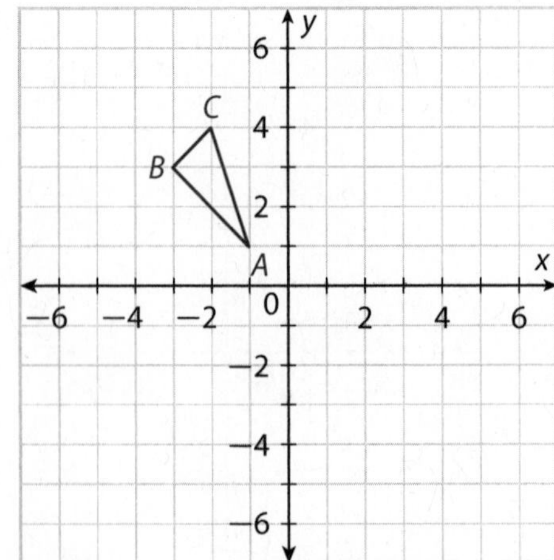

3. Translate $\triangle ABC$ by $\langle 4, 4 \rangle$, rotate 90 degrees counterclockwise around A, and reflect over the y-axis.

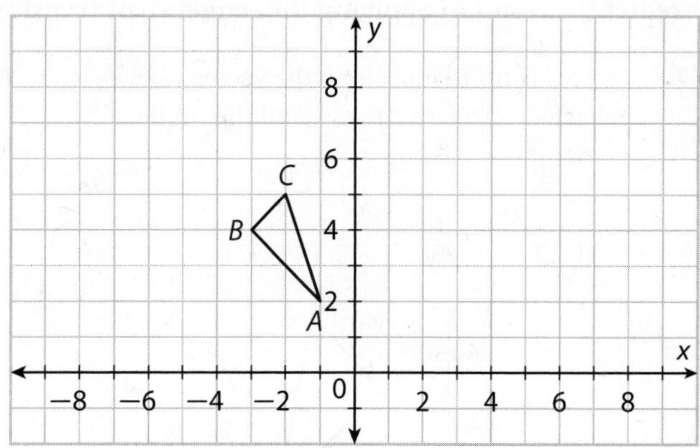

4. Reflect $\triangle ABC$ over the x-axis, translate by $\langle -3, -1 \rangle$, and rotate 180 degrees around the origin.

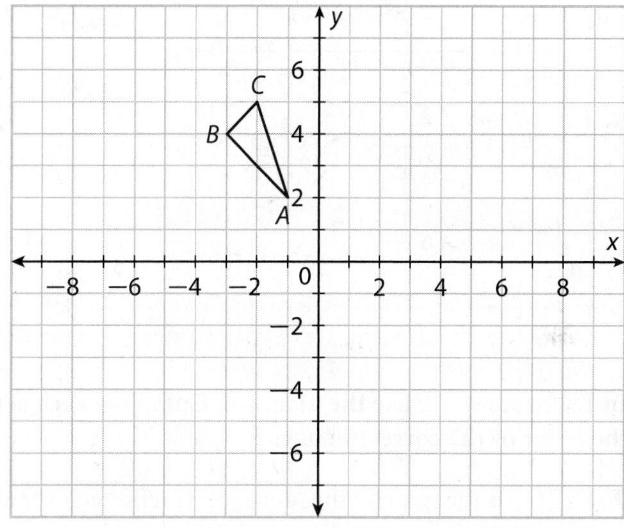

Copy ΔABC on a coordinate grid. Then draw and label the final image of $\triangle ABC$ after the given sequence of transformations.

5. $(x, y) \rightarrow \left(x, \frac{1}{3}y\right) \rightarrow (-2x, -2y)$

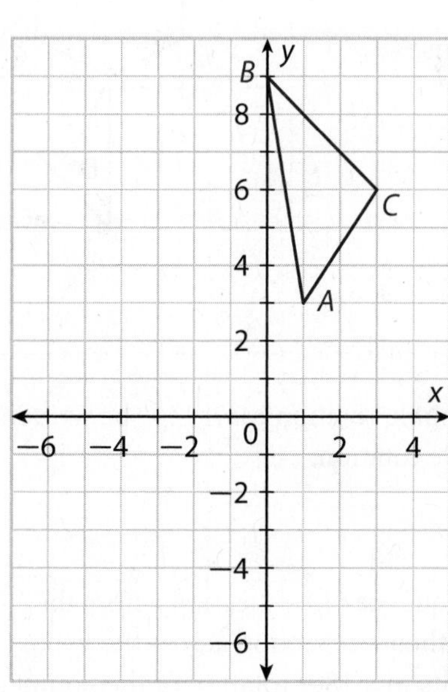

6. $(x, y) \rightarrow \left(-\frac{3}{2}x, \frac{2}{3}y\right) \rightarrow (x + 6, y - 4) \rightarrow \left(\frac{2}{3}x, -\frac{3}{2}y\right)$

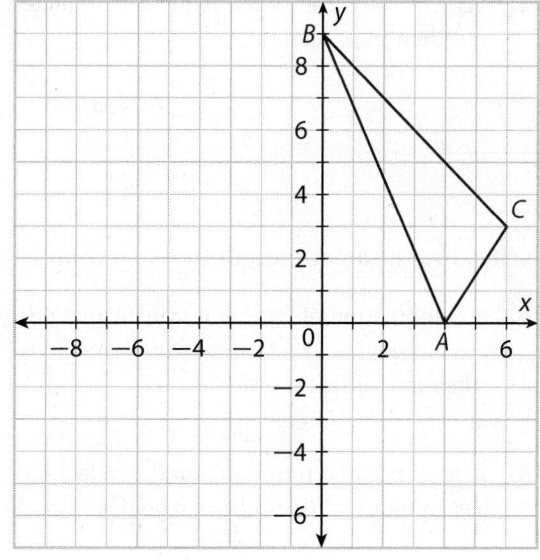

Predict the result of applying the sequence of transformations to the given figure.

7. $\triangle ABC$ is translated along the vector $\langle -3, -1 \rangle$, reflected across the x-axis, and then reflected across the y-axis.

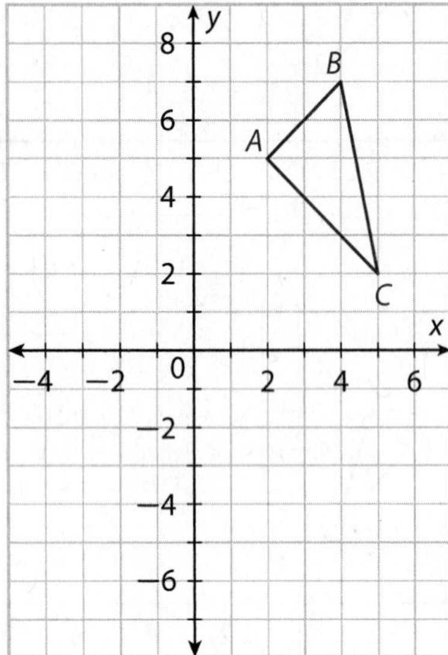

8. $\triangle ABC$ is translated along the vector $\langle -1, -3 \rangle$, rotated 180° about the origin, and then dilated by a factor of 2.

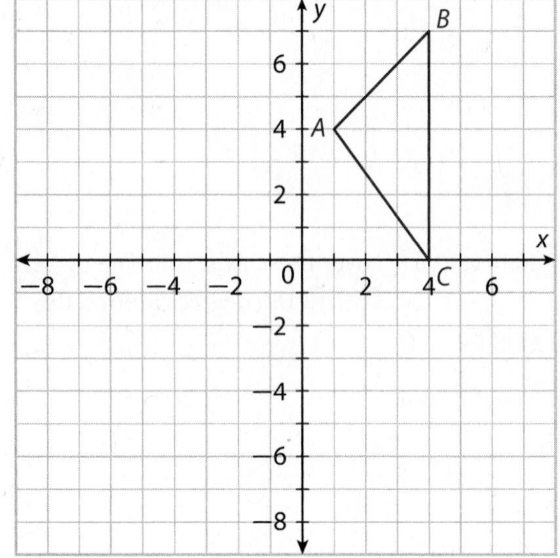

In Exercises 9–12, use the diagram. Complete each sentence with the letter of the correct image.

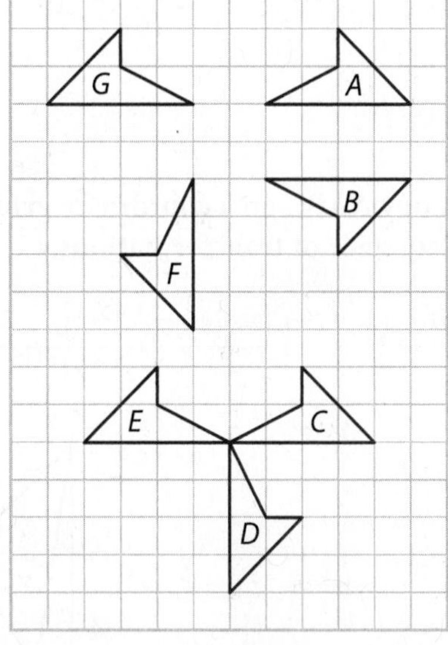

9. __?__ is the result of the sequence: G reflected over a vertical line and then a horizontal line.

10. __?__ is the result of the sequence: D rotated 90° clockwise around one of its vertices and then reflected over a horizontal line.

11. __?__ is the result of the sequence: E translated and then rotated 90° counterclockwise.

12. __?__ is the result of the sequence: D rotated 90° counterclockwise and then translated.

Write always, sometimes, or never to complete a true statement.

13. A combination of two rigid transformations on a preimage will __?__ produce the same image when taken in a different order.

14. A double rotation can __?__ be written as a single rotation.

15. A sequence of a translation and a reflection __?__ has a point that does not change position.

16. A sequence of a reflection across the x-axis and then a reflection across the y-axis __?__ results in a 180° rotation of the preimage.

17. A sequence of rigid transformations will __?__ result in an image that is the same size and orientation as the preimage.

18. A sequence of a rotation and a dilation will __?__ result in an image that is the same size and orientation as the preimage.

19. $\triangle QRS$ is the image of $\triangle LMN$ under a sequence of transformations. Tell whether each of the following sequences can be used to create the image, $\triangle QRS$, from the preimage, $\triangle LMN$.

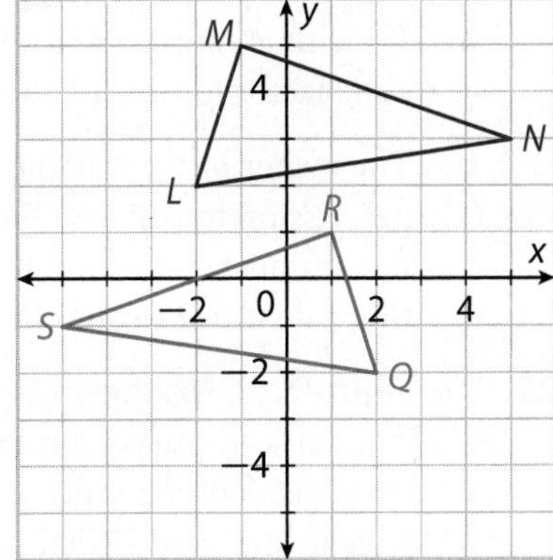

a. Reflect across the y-axis and then translate along the vector $\langle 0, -4 \rangle$.

b. Translate along the vector $\langle 0, -4 \rangle$ and then reflect across the y-axis.

c. Rotate 90° clockwise about the origin, reflect across the x-axis, and then rotate 90° counterclockwise about the origin.

d. Rotate 180° about the origin, reflect across the x-axis, and then translate along the vector $\langle 0, -4 \rangle$.

20. A teacher gave students this puzzle: "I had a triangle with vertex A at (1, 4) and vertex B at (3, 2). After two rigid transformations, I had the image shown. Describe and show a sequence of transformations that will give this image from the preimage."

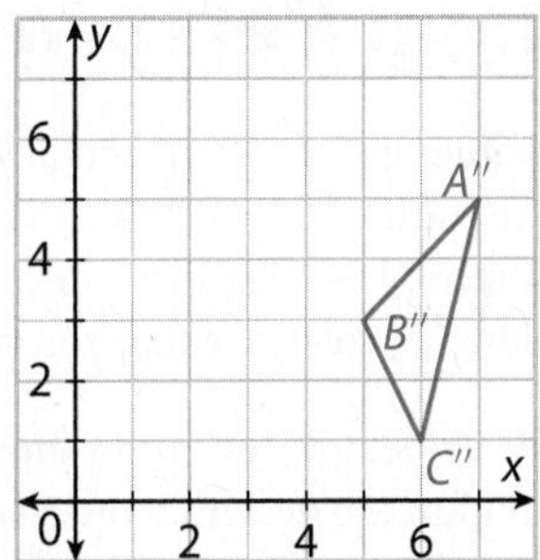

H.O.T. Focus on Higher Order Thinking

21. Analyze Relationships What two transformations would you apply to $\triangle ABC$ to get $\triangle DEF$? How could you express these transformations with a single mapping rule in the form of $(x, y) \rightarrow (?, ?)$?

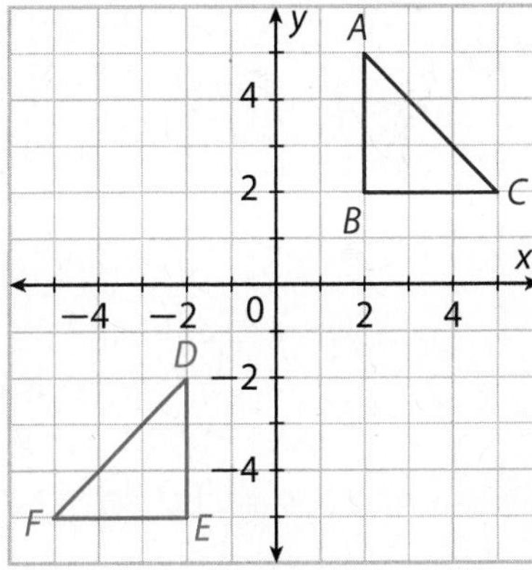

22. Multi-Step Muralists will often make a scale drawing of an art piece before creating the large finished version. A muralist has sketched an art piece on a sheet of paper that is 3 feet by 4 feet.

a. If the final mural will be 39 feet by 52 feet, what is the scale factor for this dilation?

b. The owner of the wall has decided to only give permission to paint on the lower half of the wall. Can the muralist simply use the transformation $(x, y) \rightarrow \left(x, \frac{1}{2}y\right)$ in addition to the scale factor to alter the sketch for use in the allowed space? Explain.

23. Communicate Mathematical Ideas As a graded class activity, your teacher asks your class to reflect a triangle across the y-axis and then across the x-axis. Your classmate gets upset because he reversed the order of these reflections and thinks he will have to start over. What can you say to your classmate to help him?

Lesson Performance Task

The photograph shows an actual snowflake. Draw a detailed sketch of the "arm" of the snowflake located at the top left of the photo (10:00 on a clock face). Describe in as much detail as you can any translations, reflections, or rotations that you see.

Then describe how the entire snowflake is constructed, based on what you found in the design of one arm.

3.2 Proving Figures are Congruent Using Rigid Motions

Essential Question: How can you determine whether two figures are congruent?

Resource Locker

Explore Confirming Congruence

Two plane figures are congruent if and only if one can be obtained from the other by a sequence of rigid motions (that is, by a sequence of reflections, translations, and/or rotations).

A landscape architect uses a grid to design the landscape around a mall. Use tracing paper to confirm that the landscape elements are congruent.

(A) Trace planter *ABCD*. Describe a transformation you can use to move the tracing paper so that planter *ABCD* is mapped onto planter *EFGH*. What does this confirm about the planters?

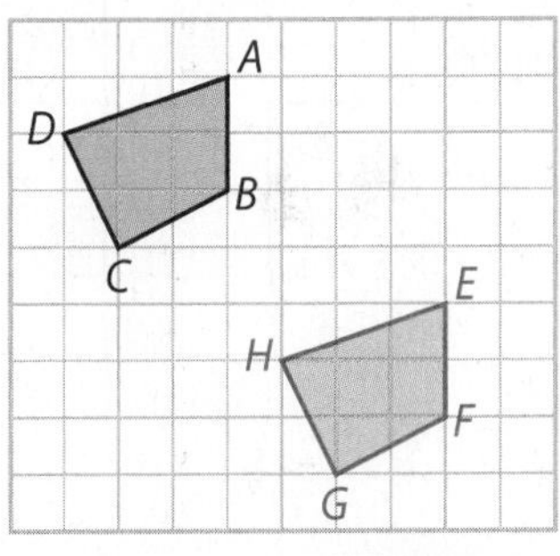

(B) Trace pools *JKLM* and *NPQR*. Fold the paper so that pool *JKLM* is mapped onto pool *NPQR*. Describe the transformation. What does this confirm about the pools?

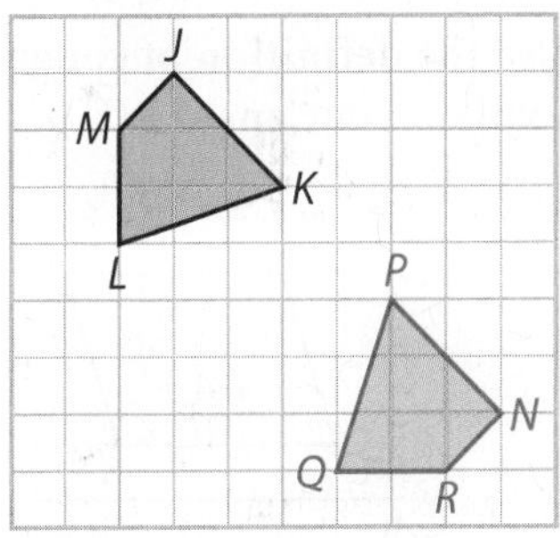

(C) Determine whether the lawns are congruent. Is there a rigid transformation that maps $\triangle LMN$ to $\triangle DEF$? What does this confirm about the lawns?

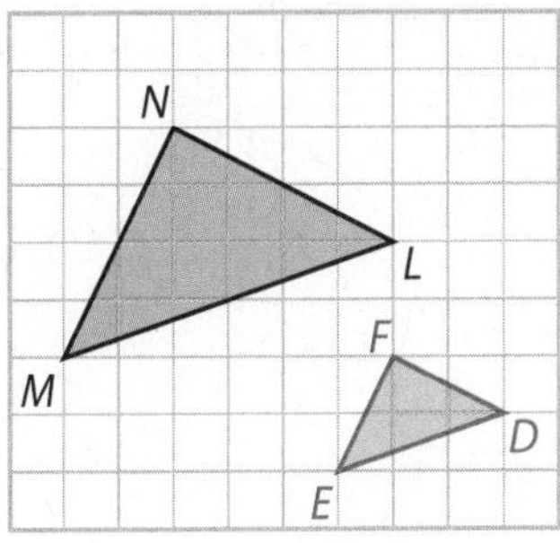

Reflect

1. How do the sizes of the pairs of figures help determine if they are congruent?

Explain 1 Determining if Figures are Congruent

Example 1 **Use the definition of congruence to decide whether the two figures are congruent. Explain your answer.**

Ⓐ

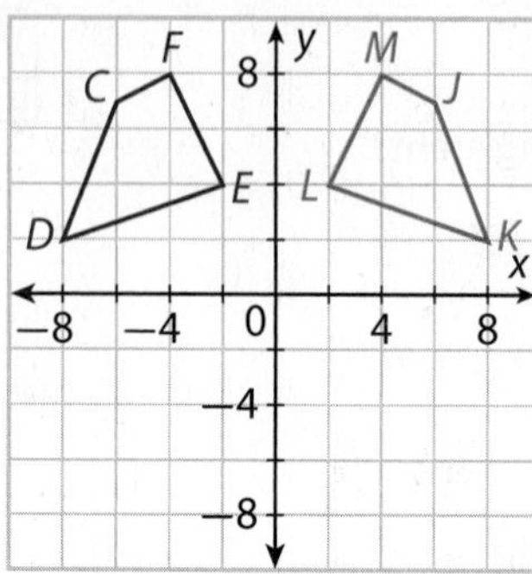

The two figures appear to be the same size and shape, so look for a rigid transformation that will map one to the other.

You can map *CDEF* onto *JKLM* by reflecting *CDEF* over the *y*-axis. This reflection is a rigid motion that maps *CDEF* to *JKLM*, so the two figures are congruent.

The coordinate notation for the reflection is $(x, y) \rightarrow (-x, y)$.

Ⓑ

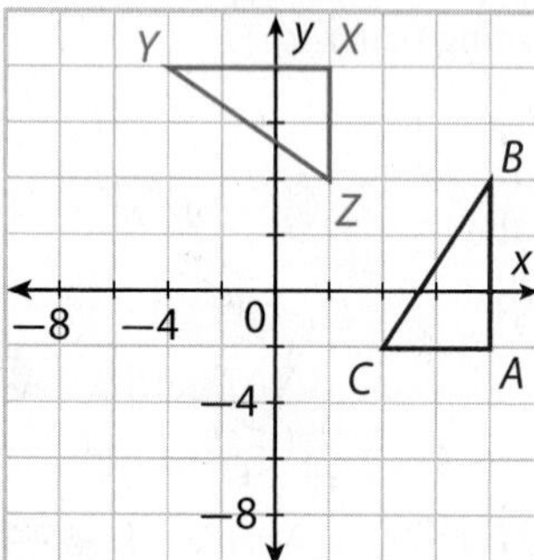

The two figures appear to be the same.

You can map $\triangle ABC$ to $\triangle XYZ$ by a counter-clockwise rotation of 90° around the origin.

This is a rigid motion that maps $\triangle ABC$ to $\triangle XYZ$, so

the two figures are congruent.

The coordinate notation for the rotation is $(x, y) \rightarrow (-y, x)$.

Your Turn

Use the definition of congruence to decide whether the two figures are congruent. Explain your answer.

2.

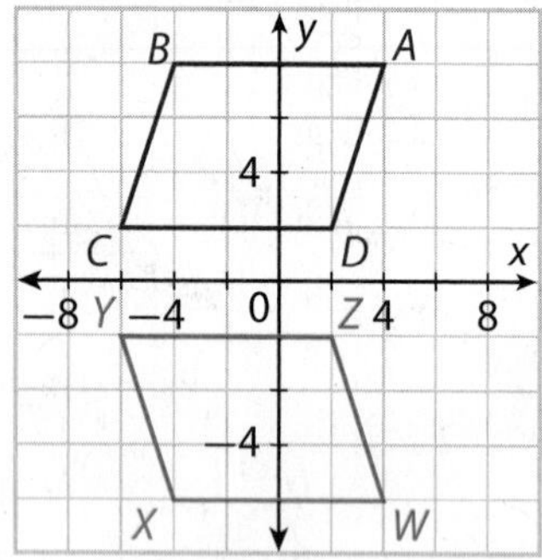

3.

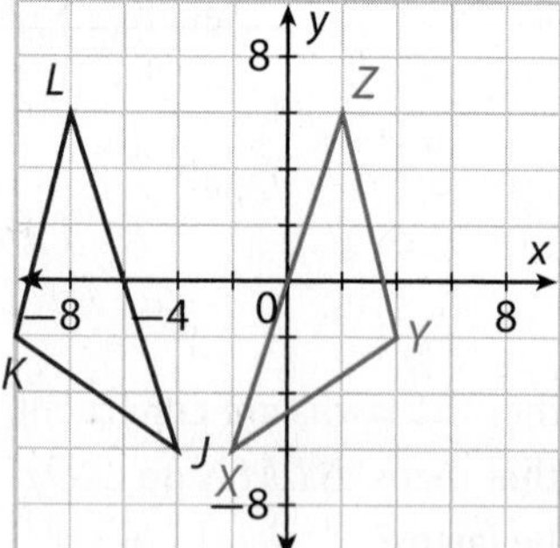

Explain 2 Finding a Sequence of Rigid Motions

The definition of congruence tells you that when two figures are known to be congruent, there must be some sequence of rigid motions that maps one to the other.

Example 2 **The figures shown are congruent. Find a sequence of rigid motions that maps one figure to the other. Give coordinate notation for the transformations you use.**

(A) $\triangle ABC \cong \triangle PQR$

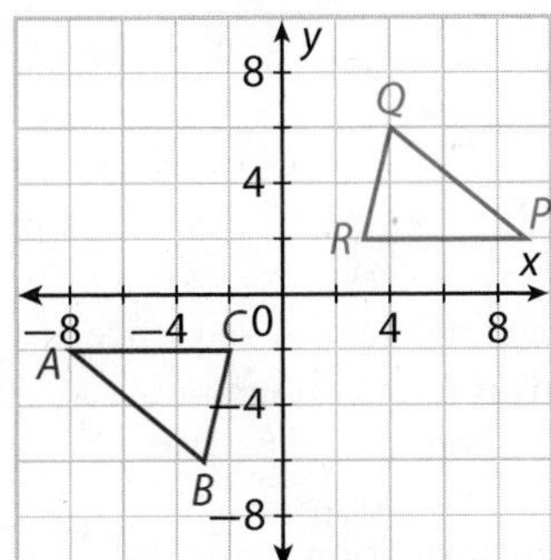

Map $\triangle ABC$ to $\triangle PQR$ with a rotation of 180° around the origin, followed by a horizontal translation.

Rotation: $(x, y) \rightarrow (-x, -y)$

Translation: $(x, y) \rightarrow (x + 1, y)$

(B) $ABCD \cong JKLM$

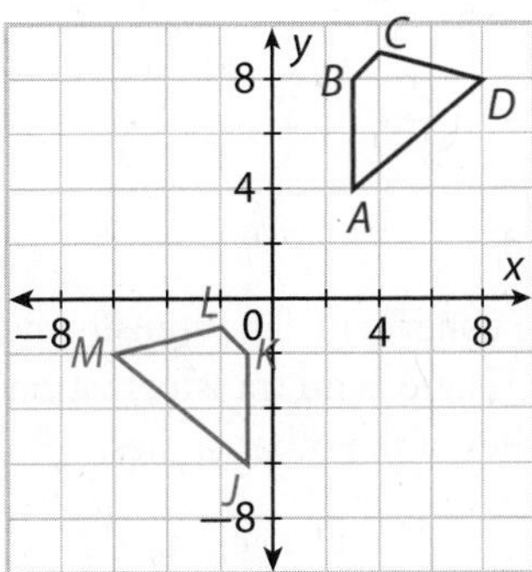

Map $ABCD$ to $JKLM$ with a reflection across the y-axis, followed by a translation.

Reflection: $(x, y) \rightarrow (-x, y)$

Translation: $(x, y) \rightarrow (x + 2, y - 10)$

Reflect

4. How is the orientation of the figure affected by a sequence of transformations?

Your Turn

The figures shown are congruent. Find a sequence of rigid motions that maps one figure to the other. Give coordinate notation for the transformations you use.

5. $JKLM \cong WXYZ$

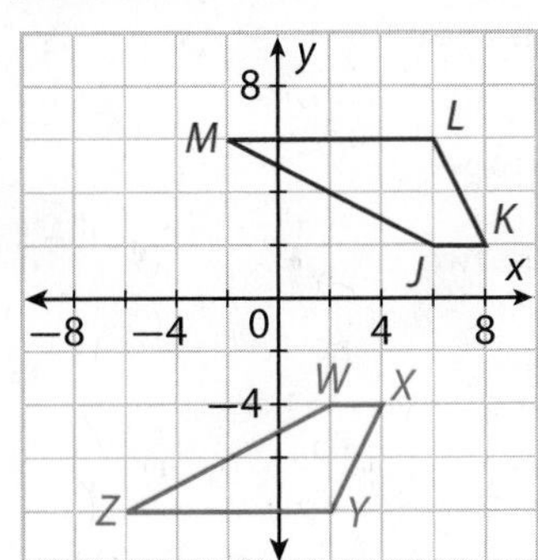

6. $ABCDE \cong PQRST$

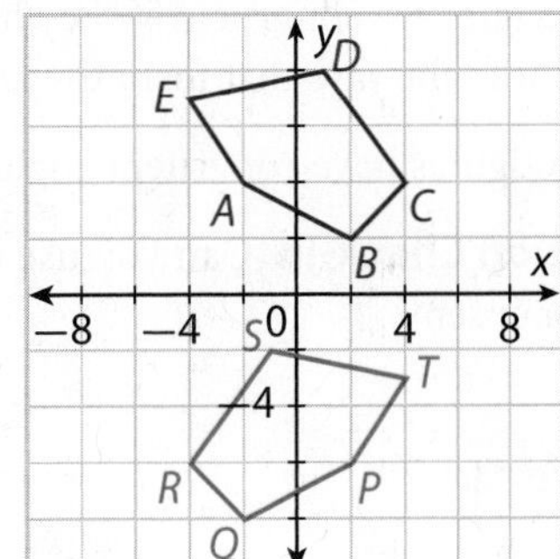

Explain 3 Investigating Congruent Segments and Angles

Congruence can refer to parts of figures as well as whole figures. Two angles are congruent if and only if one can be obtained from the other by rigid motions (that is, by a sequence of reflections, translations, and/or rotations.) The same conditions are required for two segments to be congruent to each other.

Example 3 **Determine which angles or segments are congruent. Describe transformations that can be used to verify congruence.**

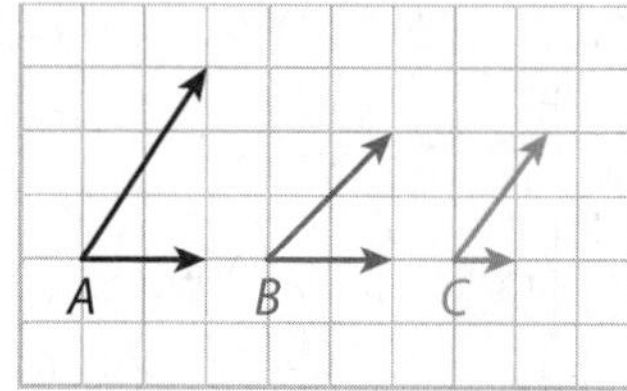

$\angle A$ and $\angle C$ are congruent. The transformation is a translation. There is no transformation that maps $\angle B$ to either of the other angles.

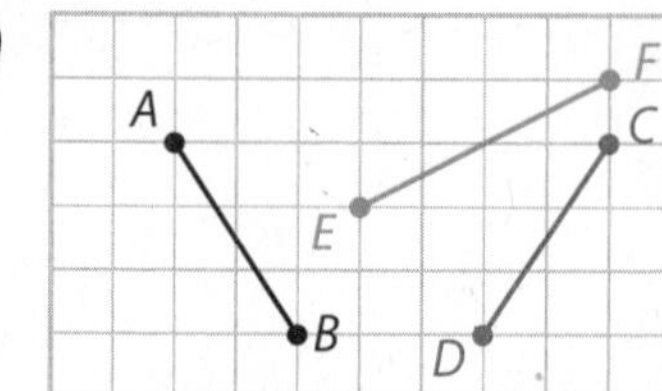

$\overline{AB}$ and $\overline{CD}$ are congruent. A sequence of transformations is a reflection and a translation.

There is no transformation that maps $\overline{EF}$ to either of the other segments.

Your Turn

7. Determine which segments and which angles are congruent. Describe transformations that can be used to show the congruence.

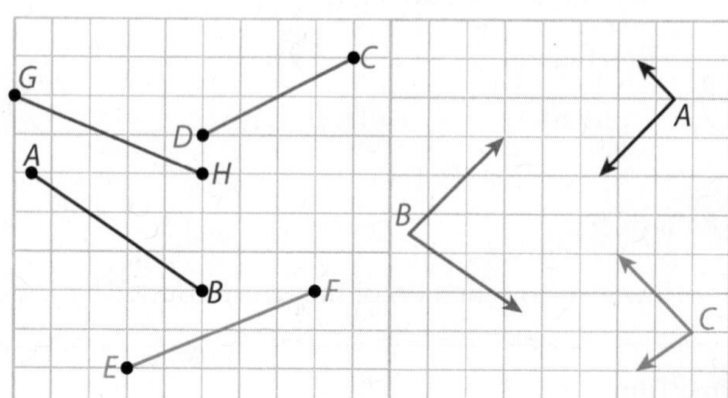

Elaborate

8. Can you say two angles are congruent if they have the same measure but the segments that identify the rays that form the angle are different lengths?

9. **Discussion** Can figures have congruent angles but not be congruent figures?

10. **Essential Question Check-In** Can you use transformations to prove that two figures are not congruent?

Evaluate: Homework and Practice

- Online Homework
- Hints and Help
- Extra Practice

Use the definition of congruence to decide whether the two figures are congruent. Explain your answer. Give coordinate notation for the transformations you use.

1.

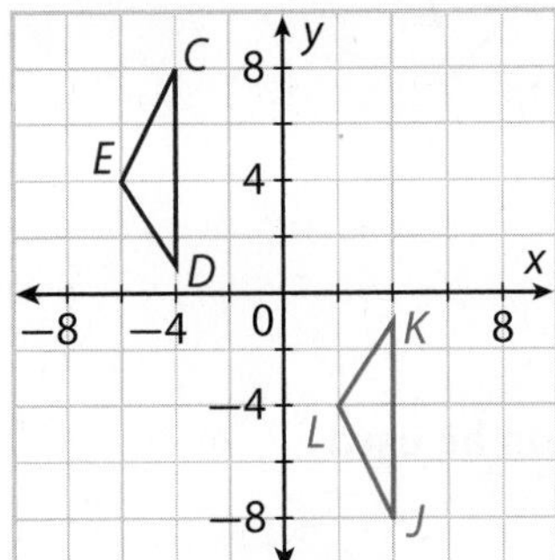

2.

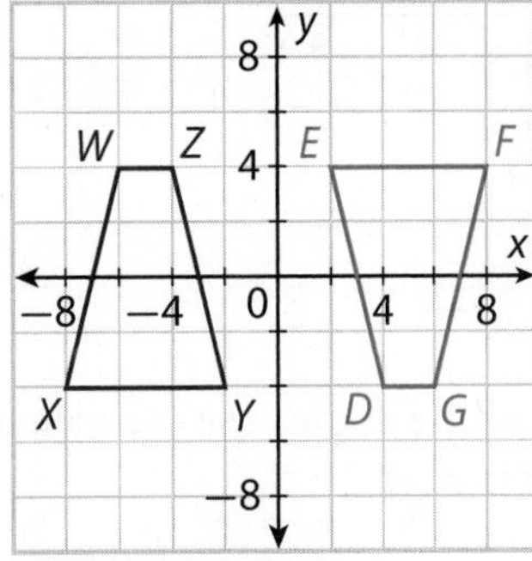

3.

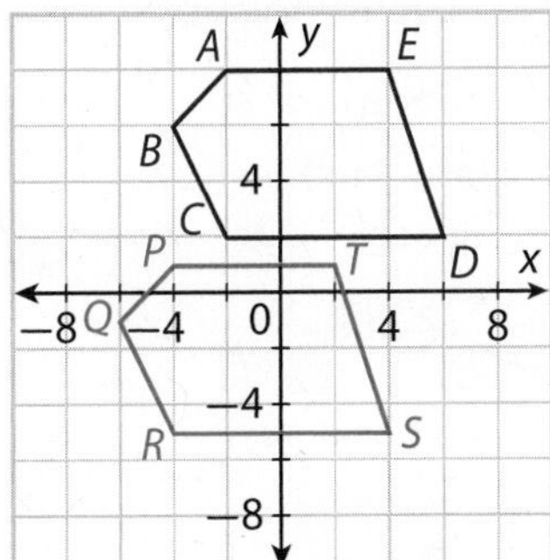

4.

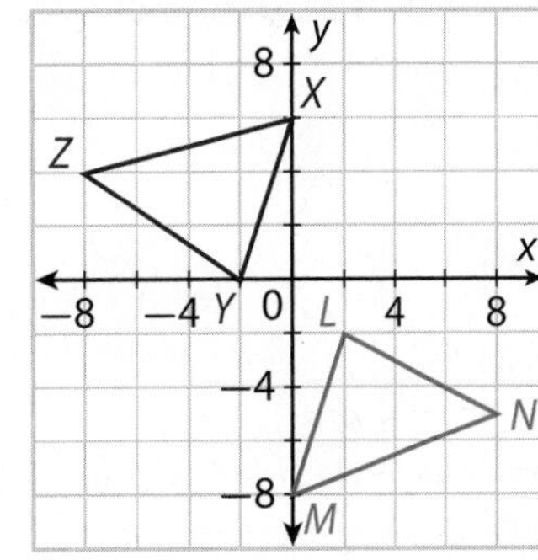

5.

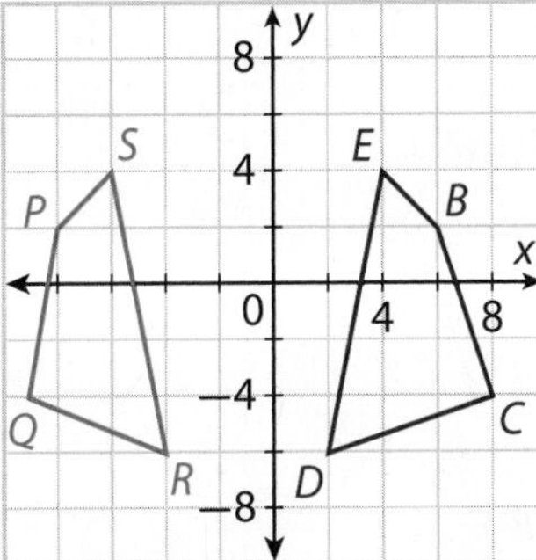

The figures shown are congruent. Find a sequence of rigid motions that maps one figure to the other. Give coordinate notation for the transformations you use.

6. $RSTU \cong WXYZ$

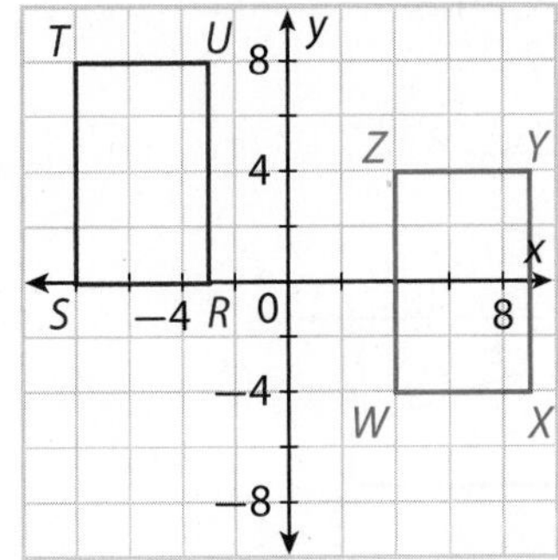

7. $\triangle ABC \cong \triangle DEF$

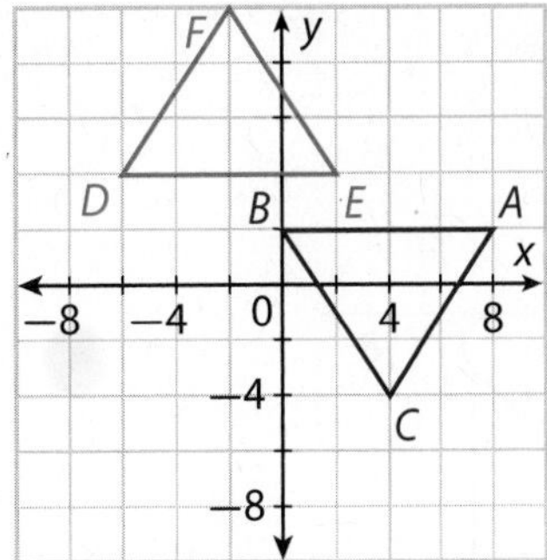

8. $DEFGH \cong PQRST$

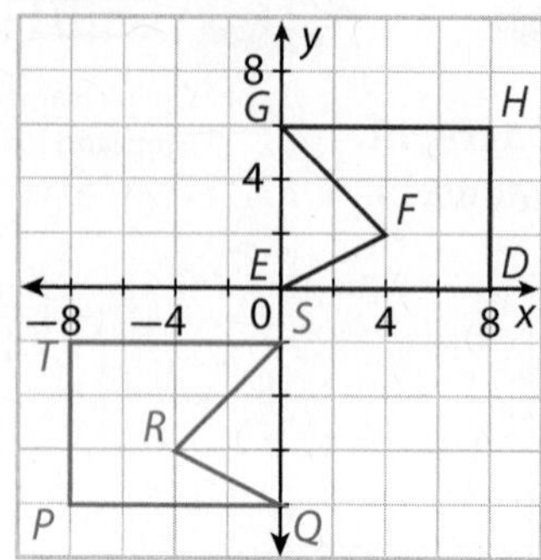

9. $\triangle CDE \cong \triangle WXY$

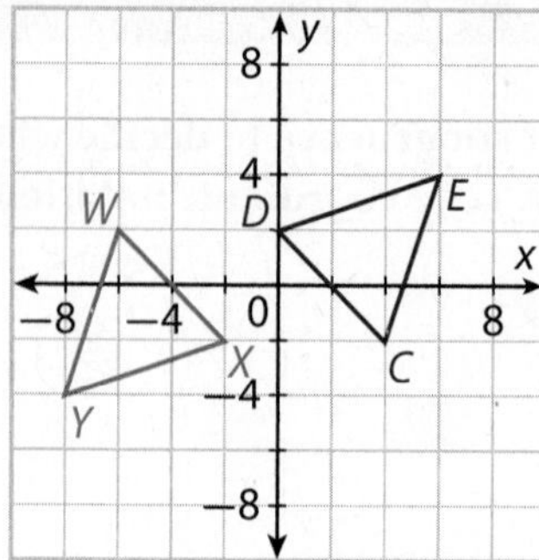

Determine which of the angles are congruent. Which transformations can be used to verify the congruence?

10.

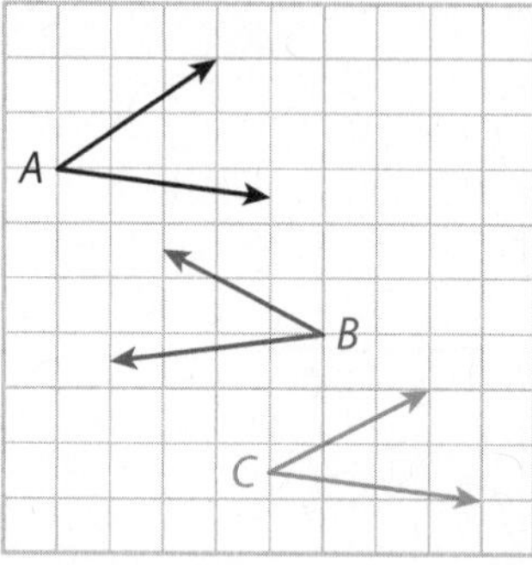

11.

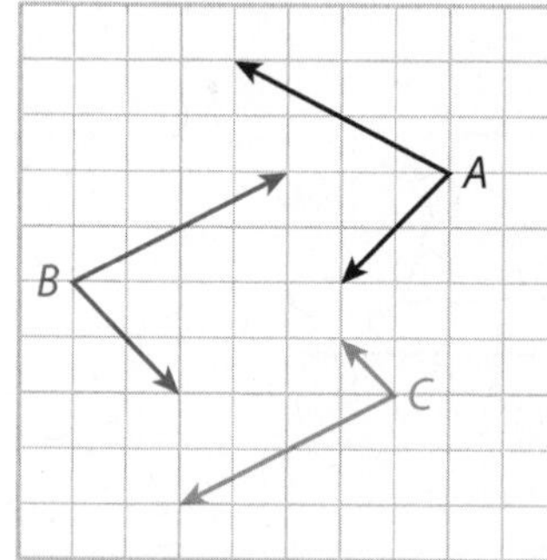

Determine which of the segments are congruent. Which transformations can be used to verify the congruence?

12.

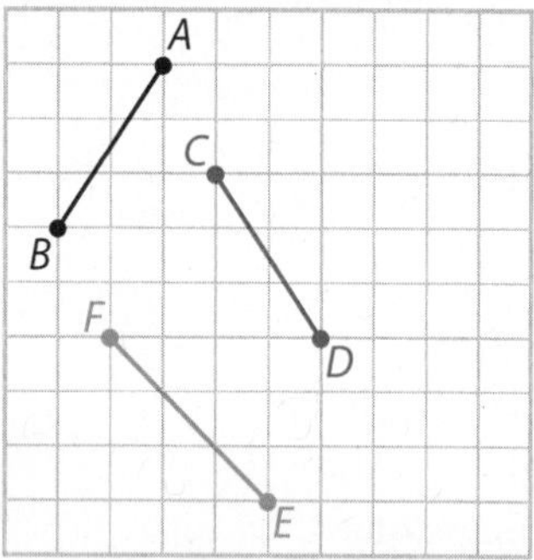

13.

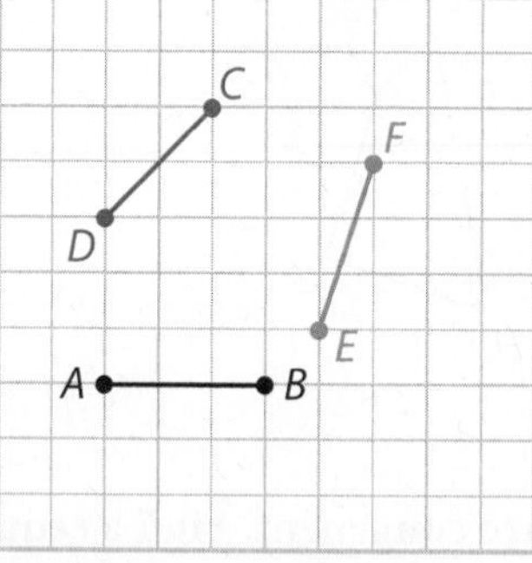

For 14-17, use the definition of congruence to decide whether the two figures are congruent. Explain your answer. Give coordinate notation for the transformations you use.

14.

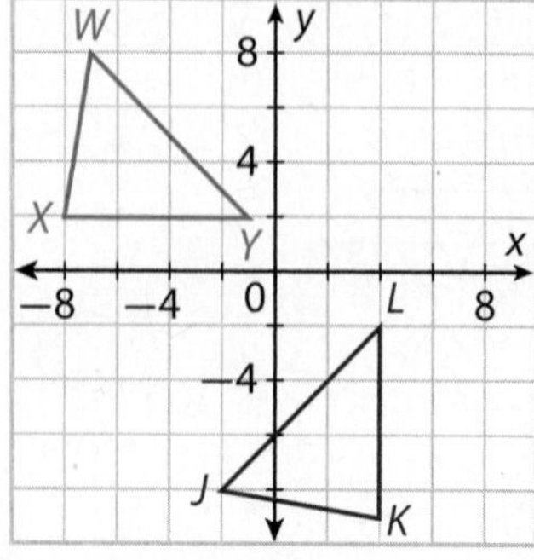

15.

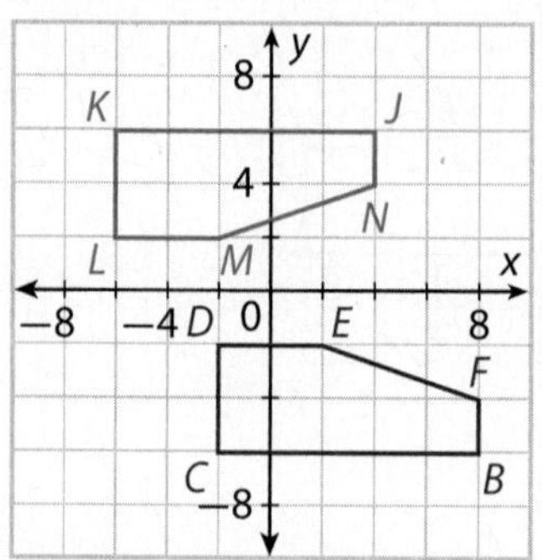

16. 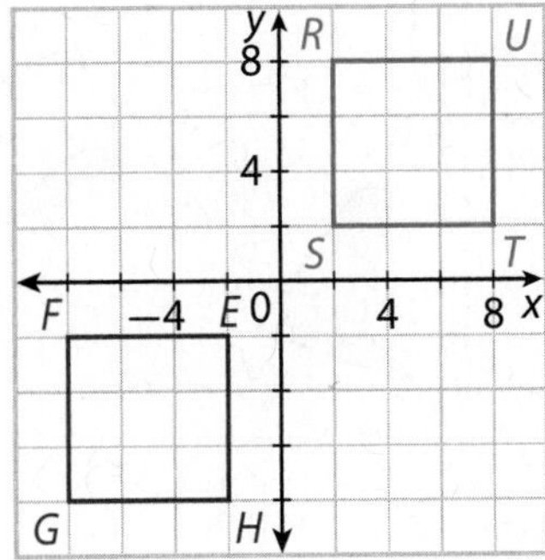

17. 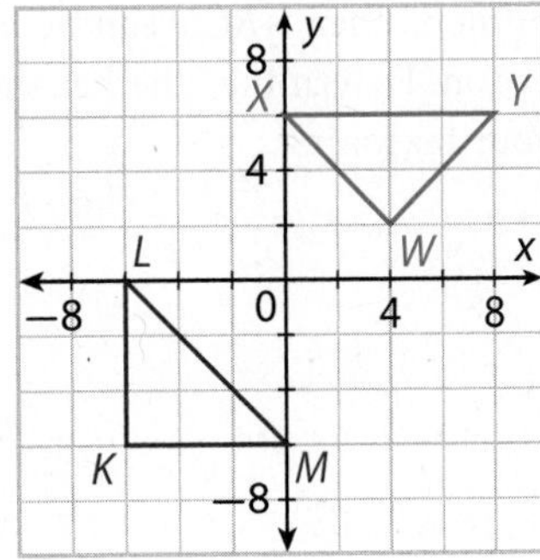

The figures shown are congruent. Find a sequence of transformations for the indicated mapping. Give coordinate notation for the transformations you use.

18. Map *PQRST* to *DEFGH*.

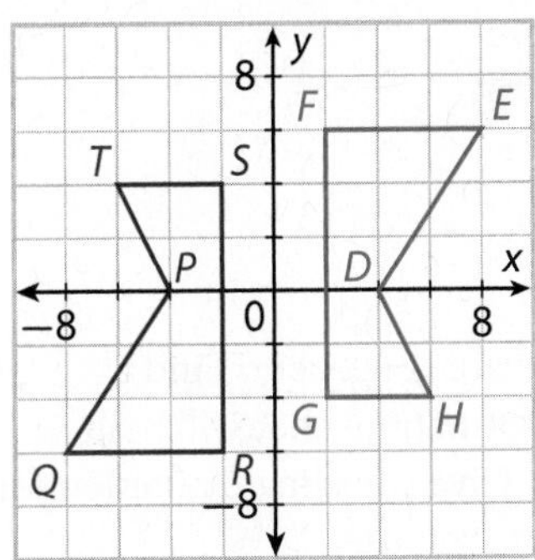

19. Map *WXYZ* to *JKLM*.

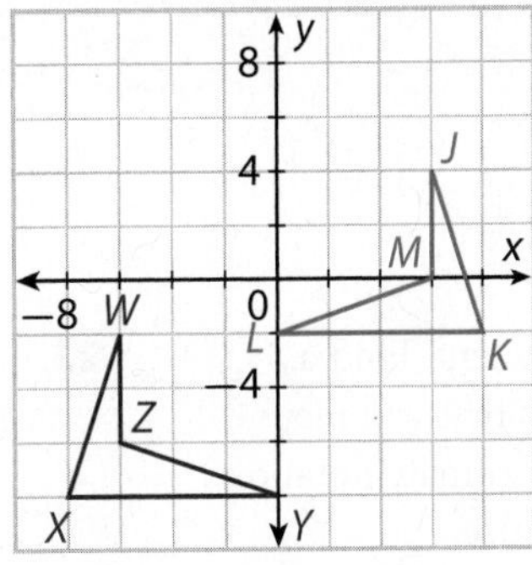

20. Map *PQRSTU* to *ABCDEF*.

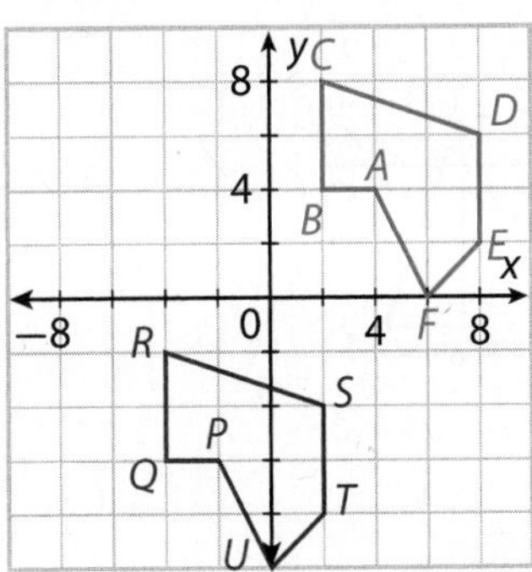

21. Map △*DEF* to △*KLM*.

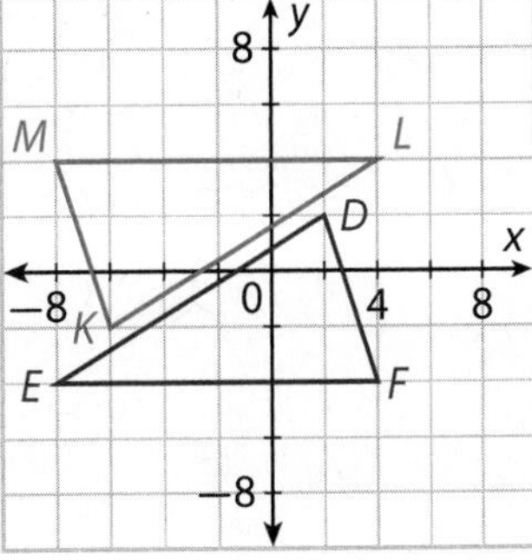

22. Determine whether each pair of angles is congruent or not congruent.

a. ∠*A* and ∠*B*

b. ∠*A* and ∠*C*

c. ∠*B* and ∠*C*

d. ∠*B* and ∠*D*

e. ∠*C* and ∠*D*

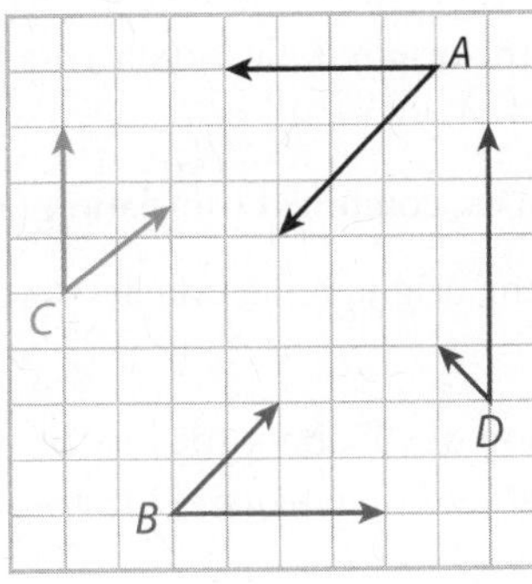

23. If *ABCD* and *WXYZ* are congruent, then *ABCD* can be mapped to *WXYZ* using a rotation and a translation. Determine whether the statement is true or false. Then explain your reasoning.

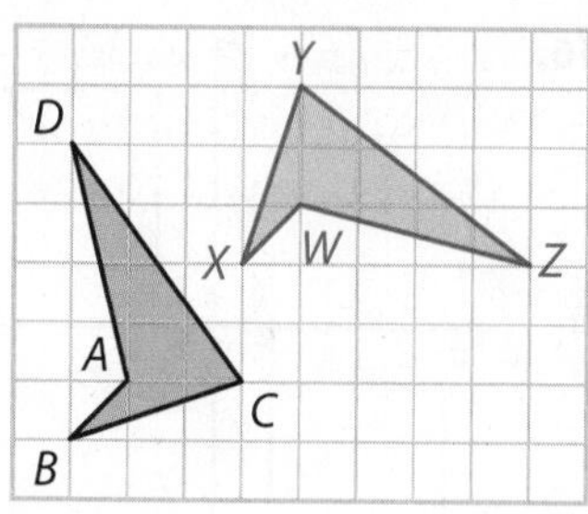

24. Which segments are congruent? Which are not congruent? Explain.

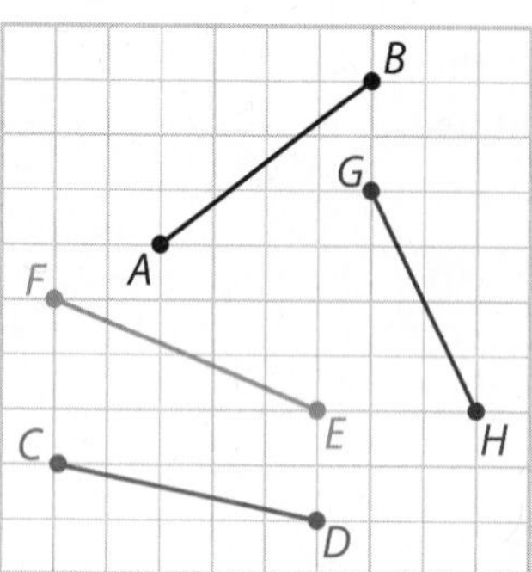

25. Which angles are congruent? Which are not congruent? Explain.

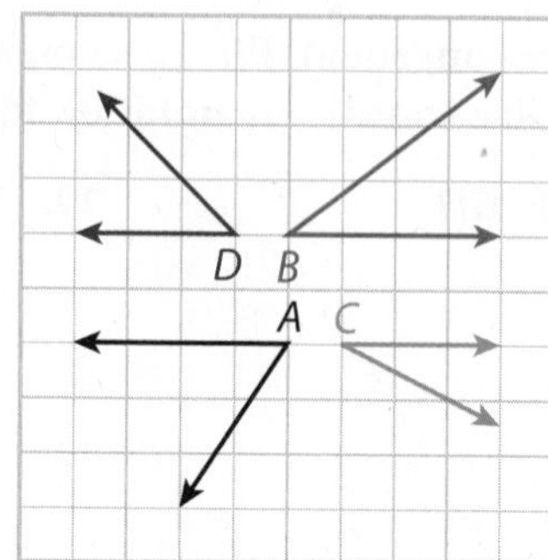

26. The figures shown are congruent. Find a sequence of transformations that will map *CDEFG* to *QRSTU*. Give coordinate notation for the transformations you use.

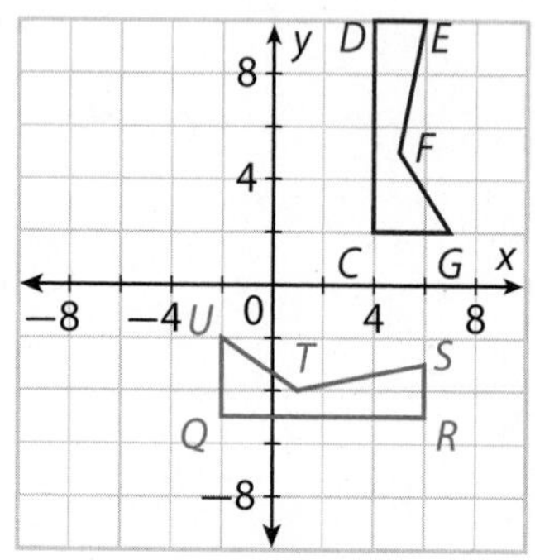

27. The figures shown are congruent. Find a sequence of transformations that will map $\triangle LMN$ to $\triangle XYZ$. Give coordinate notation for the transformations you use.

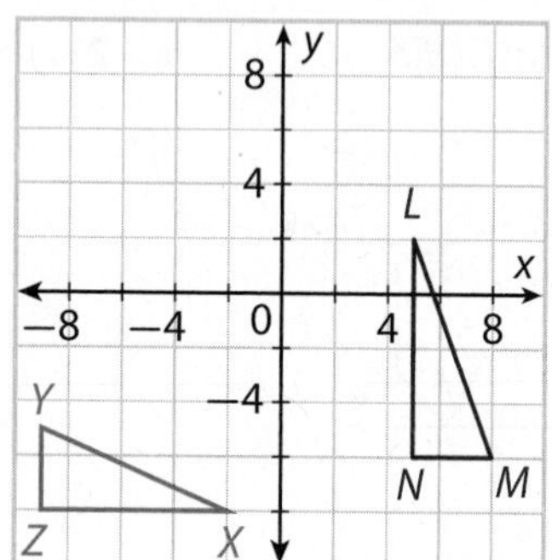

28. Which sequence of transformations does not map a figure onto a congruent figure? Explain.

A. Rotation of 180° about the origin, reflection across the *x*-axis, horizontal translation $(x, y) \rightarrow (x + 4, y)$

B. Reflection across the *y*-axis, combined translation $(x, y) \rightarrow (x - 5, y + 2)$

C. Rotation of 180° about the origin, reflection across the *y*-axis, dilation $(x, y) \rightarrow (2x, 2y)$

D. Counterclockwise rotation of 90° about the origin, reflection across the *y*-axis, combined translation $(x, y) \rightarrow (x - 11, y - 12)$

29. The figures shown are congruent. Find a sequence of transformations that will map *DEFGH* to *VWXYZ*. Give coordinate notation for the transformations you use.

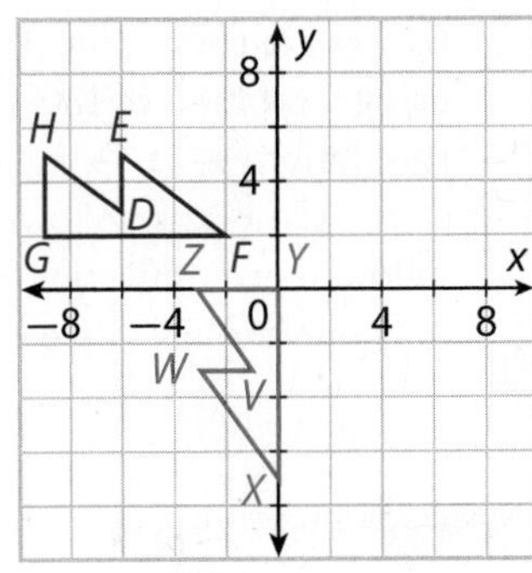

30. How can you prove that two arrows in the recycling symbol are congruent to each other?

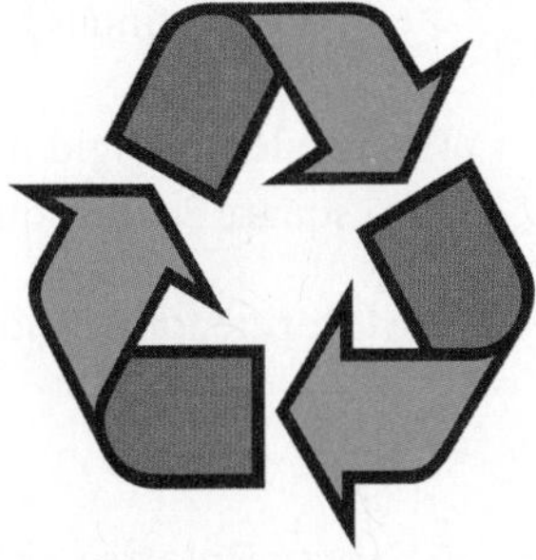

31. The city of St. Louis was settled by the French in the mid 1700s and joined the United States in 1803 as part of the Louisiana Purchase. The city flag reflects its French history by featuring the fleur-de-lis. How can you prove that the left and right petals are congruent to each other?

32. Draw Conclusions Two students are trying to show that the two figures are congruent. The first student decides to map *CDEFG* to *PQRST* using a rotation of 180° around the origin, followed by the translation $(x, y) \rightarrow (x, y + 6)$. The second student believes the correct transformations are a reflection across the *y*-axis, followed by the vertical translation $(x, y) \rightarrow (x, y - 2)$. Are both students correct, is only one student correct, or is neither student correct?

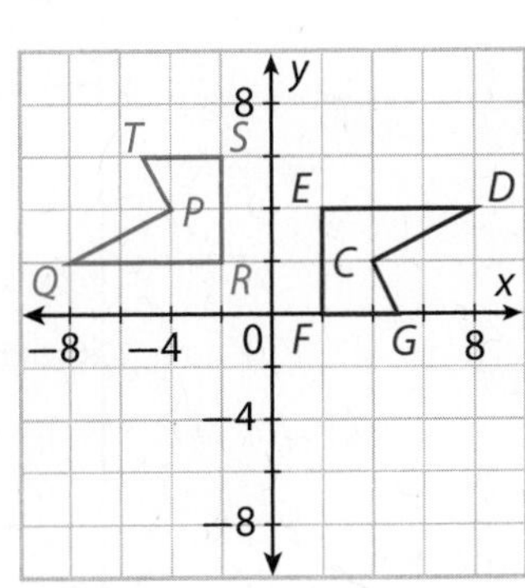

33. Justify Reasoning Two students are trying to show that the two figures are congruent. The first student decides to map *DEFG* to *RSTU* using a rotation of 180° about the origin, followed by the vertical translation $(x, y) \rightarrow (x, y + 4)$. The second student uses a reflection across the *x*-axis, followed by the vertical translation $(x, y) \rightarrow (x, y + 4)$, followed by a reflection across the *y*-axis. Are both students correct, is only one student correct, or is neither student correct?

H.O.T. Focus on Higher Order Thinking

34. Look for a Pattern Assume the pattern of congruent squares shown in the figure continues forever.

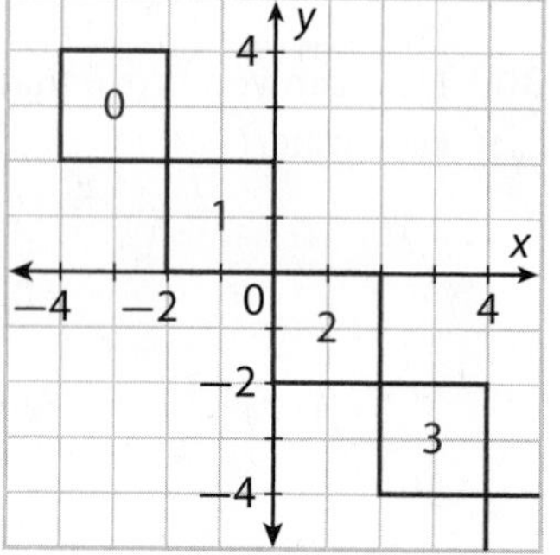

Write rules for rigid motions that map square 0 onto square 1, square 0 onto square 2, and square 0 onto square 3.

Write a rule for a rigid motion that maps square 0 onto square *n*.

35. Analyze Relationships Suppose you know that $\triangle ABC$ is congruent to $\triangle DEF$ and that $\triangle DEF$ is congruent to $\triangle GHJ$. Can you conclude that $\triangle ABC$ is congruent to $\triangle GHJ$? Explain.

36. Communicate Mathematical Ideas Ella plotted the points $A(0, 0)$, $B(4, 0)$, and $C(0, 4)$. Then she drew $\overline{AB}$ and $\overline{AC}$. Give two different arguments to explain why the segments are congruent.

Lesson Performance Task

The illustration shows how nine congruent shapes can be fitted together to form a larger shape. Each of the shapes can be formed from Shape #1 through a combination of translations, reflections, and/or rotations.

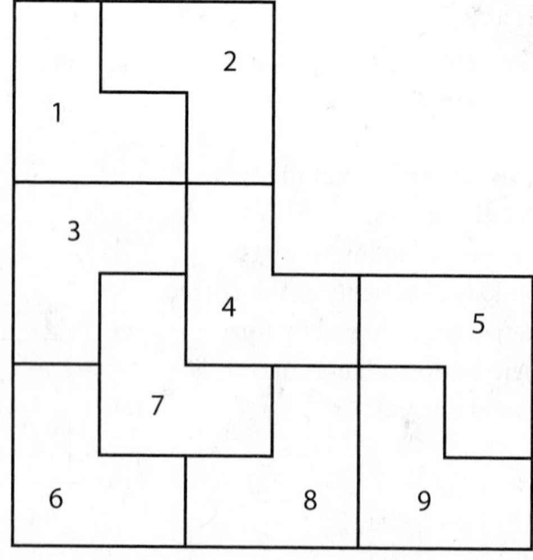

Describe how each of Shapes 2–9 can be formed from Shape #1 through a combination of translations, reflections, and/or rotations. Then design a figure like this one, using at least eight congruent shapes. Number the shapes. Then describe how each of them can be formed from Shape #1 through a combination of translations, reflections, and/or rotations.

3.3 Corresponding Parts of Congruent Figures Are Congruent

Resource Locker

Essential Question: What can you conclude about two figures that are congruent?

Explore Exploring Congruence of Parts of Transformed Figures

You will investigate some conclusions you can make when you know that two figures are congruent.

(A) Fold a sheet of paper in half. Use a straightedge to draw a triangle on the folded sheet. Then cut out the triangle, cutting through both layers of paper to produce two congruent triangles. Label them $\triangle ABC$ and $\triangle DEF$, as shown.

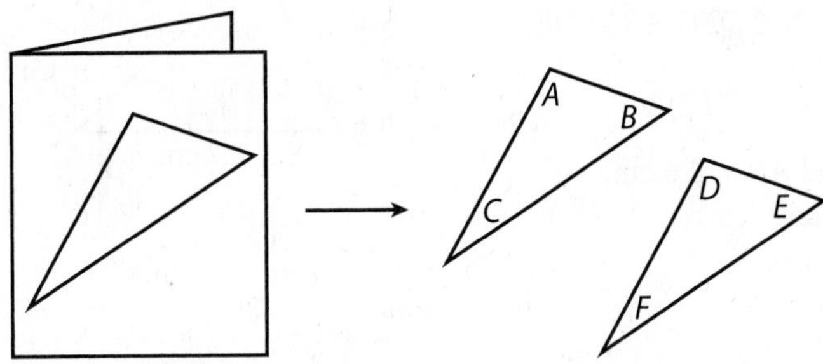

(B) Place the triangles next to each other on a desktop. Since the triangles are congruent, there must be a sequence of rigid motions that maps $\triangle ABC$ to $\triangle DEF$. Describe the sequence of rigid motions.

(C) The same sequence of rigid motions that maps $\triangle ABC$ to $\triangle DEF$ maps parts of $\triangle ABC$ to parts of $\triangle DEF$. Complete the following.

$\overline{AB} \rightarrow$? $\quad \overline{BC} \rightarrow$? $\quad \overline{AC} \rightarrow$?

$A \rightarrow$? $\quad B \rightarrow$? $\quad C \rightarrow$?

(D) What does Step C tell you about the corresponding parts of the two triangles? Why?

Reflect

1. If you know that $\triangle ABC \cong \triangle DEF$, what six congruence statements about segments and angles can you write? Why?

2. Do your findings in this Explore apply to figures other than triangles? For instance, if you know that quadrilaterals *JKLM* and *PQRS* are congruent, can you make any conclusions about corresponding parts? Why or why not?

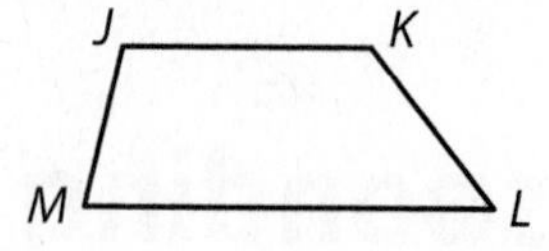

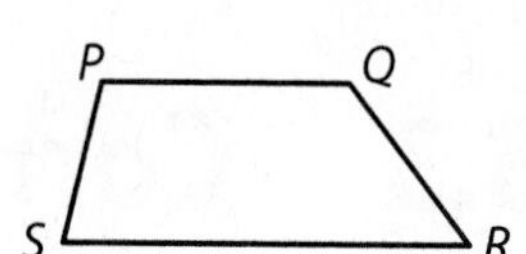

Explain 1 Corresponding Parts of Congruent Figures Are Congruent

The following true statement summarizes what you discovered in the Explore.

Corresponding Parts of Congruent Figures Are Congruent

If two figures are congruent, then corresponding sides are congruent and corresponding angles are congruent.

Example 1 $\triangle ABC \cong \triangle DEF$. **Find the given side length or angle measure.**

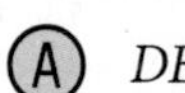

(A) *DE*

Step 1 Find the side that corresponds to $\overline{DE}$.

Since $\triangle ABC \cong \triangle DEF$, $\overline{AB} \cong \overline{DE}$.

Step 2 Find the unknown length.

$DE = AB$, and $AB = 2.6$ cm, so $DE = 2.6$ cm.

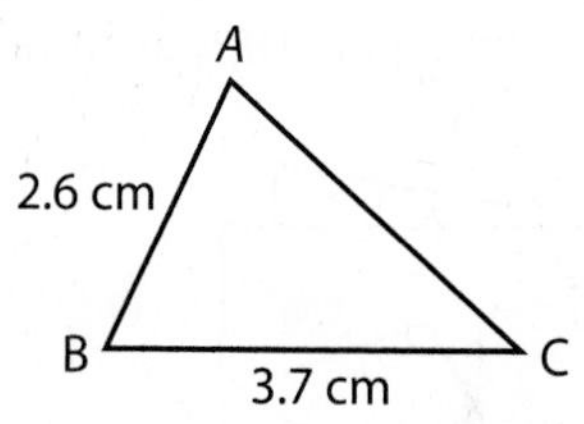

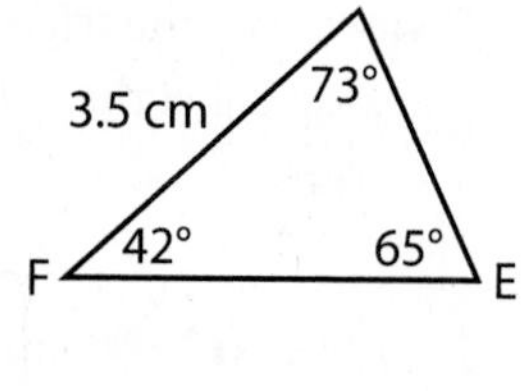

(B) $m\angle B$

Step 1 Find the angle that corresponds to $\angle B$.

Since $\triangle ABC \cong \triangle DEF$, $\angle B \cong \angle$ E.

Step 2 Find the unknown angle measure.

$m\angle B = m\angle$ E, and $m\angle$ E $=$ 65°, so $m\angle B =$ 65°.

Reflect

3. Discussion The triangles shown in the figure are congruent. Can you conclude that $\overline{JK} \cong \overline{QR}$? Explain.

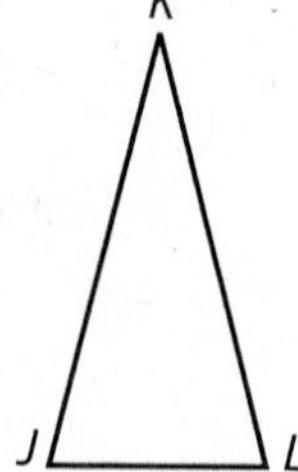

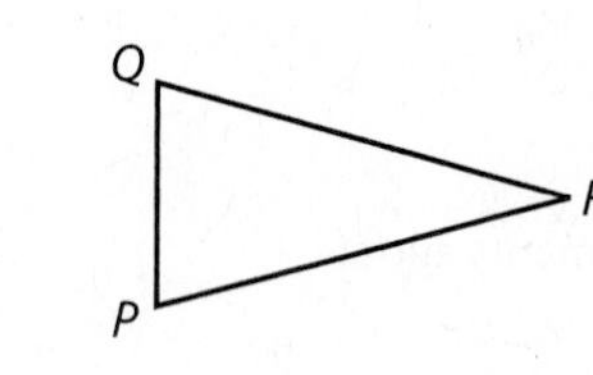

Your Turn

$\triangle STU \cong \triangle VWX$. Find the given side length or angle measure.

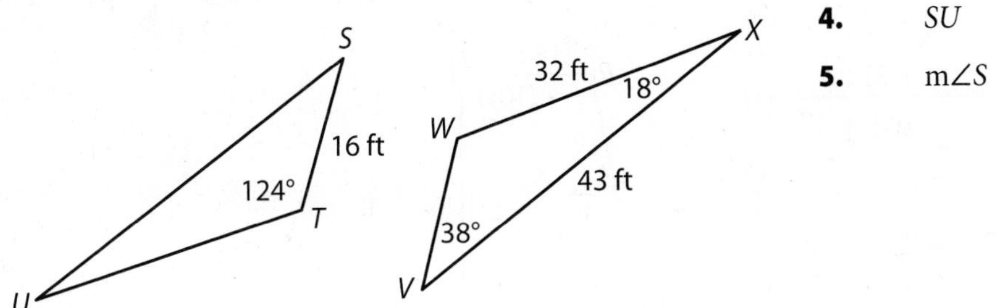

4. SU

5. $m\angle S$

Explain 2 Applying the Properties of Congruence

Rigid motions preserve length and angle measure. This means that congruent segments have the same length, so $\overline{UV} \cong \overline{XY}$ implies $UV = XY$ and vice versa. In the same way, congruent angles have the same measure, so $\angle J \cong \angle K$ implies $m\angle J = m\angle K$ and vice versa.

Properties of Congruence	
Reflexive Property of Congruence	$\overline{AB} \cong \overline{AB}$
Symmetric Property of Congruence	If $\overline{AB} \cong \overline{CD}$, then $\overline{CD} \cong \overline{AB}$.
Transitive Property of Congruence	If $\overline{AB} \cong \overline{CD}$ and $\overline{CD} \cong \overline{EF}$, then $\overline{AB} \cong \overline{EF}$.

Example 2 **$\triangle ABC \cong \triangle DEF$. Find the given side length or angle measure.**

(A) AB

Since $\triangle ABC \cong \triangle DEF$, $\overline{AB} \cong \overline{DE}$.
Therefore, $AB = DE$.

Write an equation. $3x + 8 = 5x$

Subtract $3x$ from each side. $8 = 2x$

Divide each side by 2. $4 = x$

So, $AB = 3x + 8 = 3(4) + 8 = 12 + 8 = 20$ in.

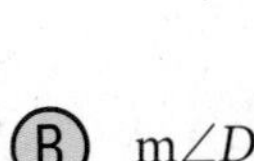

(B) $m\angle D$

Since $\triangle ABC \cong \triangle DEF$, $\angle$ A $\cong \angle D$. Therefore, $m\angle$ A $= m\angle D$.

Write an equation. $5y +$ 11 $=$ $6y$ $+ 2$

Subtract $5y$ from each side. $11 =$ y $+ 2$

Subtract 2 from each side. 9 $=$ y

So, $m\angle D = (6y + 2)^\circ = (6 \cdot$ 9 $+ 2)^\circ =$ 56 $^\circ$.

Your Turn

Quadrilateral $GHJK \cong$ quadrilateral $LMNP$. Find the given side length or angle measure.

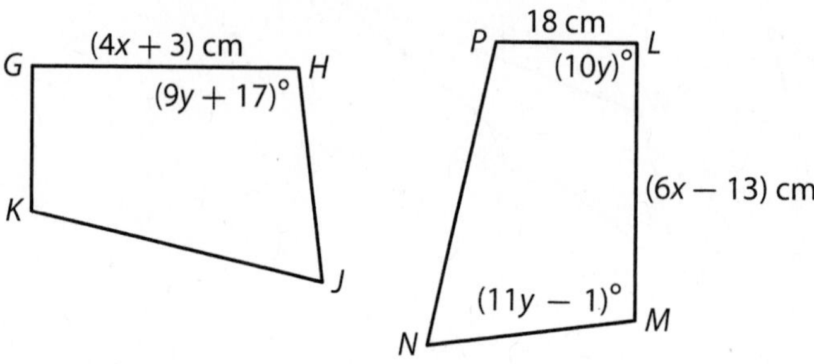

6. LM

7. $m\angle H$

Explain 3 Using Congruent Corresponding Parts in a Proof

Example 3 Write each proof.

(A) Given: $\triangle ABD \cong \triangle ACD$

Prove: D is the midpoint of $\overline{BC}$.

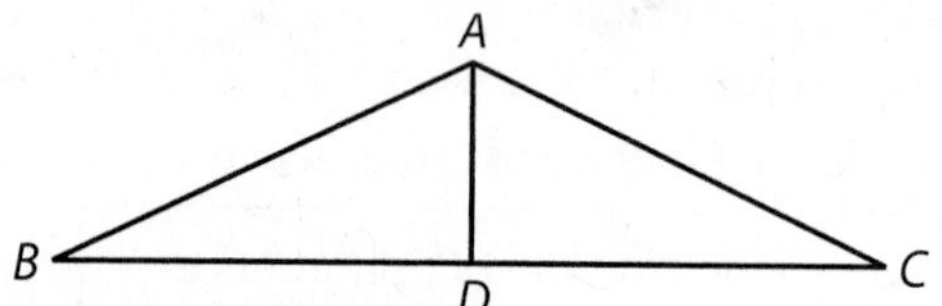

Statements	Reasons
1. $\triangle ABD \cong \triangle ACD$	**1.** Given
2. $\overline{BD} \cong \overline{CD}$	**2.** Corresponding parts of congruent figures are congruent.
3. D is the midpoint of $\overline{BC}$.	**3.** Definition of midpoint.

(B) Given: Quadrilateral $JKLM \cong$ quadrilateral $NPQR$; $\angle J \cong \angle K$

Prove: $\angle J \cong \angle P$

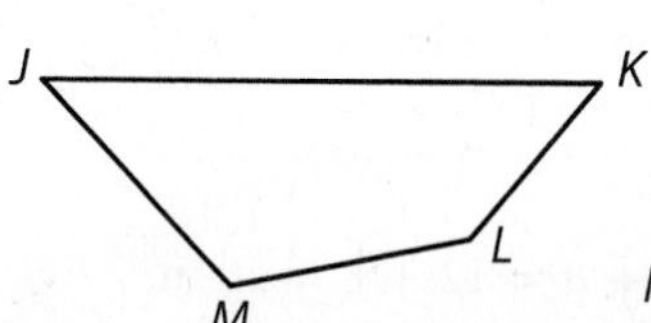

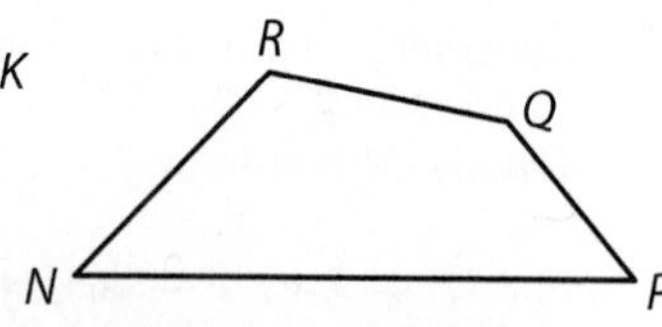

Statements	Reasons
1. Quadrilateral $JKLM \cong$ quadrilateral $NPQR$	**1.** Given
2. $\angle J \cong \angle K$	**2.** Given
3. $\angle K \cong \angle P$	**3.** Corresponding parts of congruent figures are congruent.
4. $\angle J \cong \angle P$	**4.** Transitive Property of Congruence

Your Turn

Write each proof.

8. Given: $\triangle SVT \cong \triangle SWT$

Prove: $\overline{ST}$ bisects $\angle VSW$.

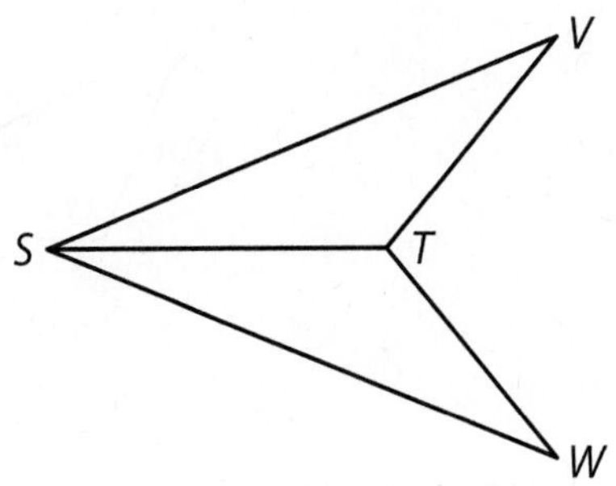

9. Given: Quadrilateral $ABCD \cong$ quadrilateral $EFGH$; $\overline{AD} \cong \overline{CD}$

Prove: $\overline{AD} \cong \overline{GH}$

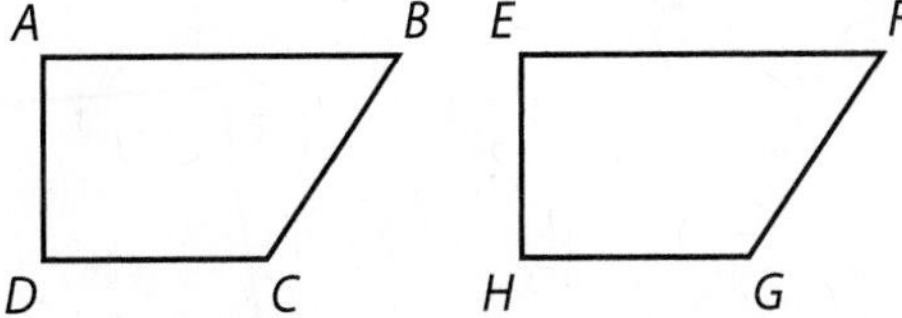

Elaborate

10. A student claims that any two congruent triangles must have the same perimeter. Do you agree? Explain.

11. If $\triangle PQR$ is a right triangle and $\triangle PQR \cong \triangle XYZ$, does $\triangle XYZ$ have to be a right triangle? Why or why not?

12. **Essential Question Check-In** Suppose you know that pentagon *ABCDE* is congruent to pentagon *FGHJK*. How many additional congruence statements can you write using corresponding parts of the pentagons? Explain.

Evaluate: Homework and Practice

- Online Homework
- Hints and Help
- Extra Practice

1. Danielle finds that she can use a translation and a reflection to make quadrilateral *ABCD* fit perfectly on top of quadrilateral *WXYZ*. What congruence statements can Danielle write using the sides and angles of the quadrilaterals? Why?

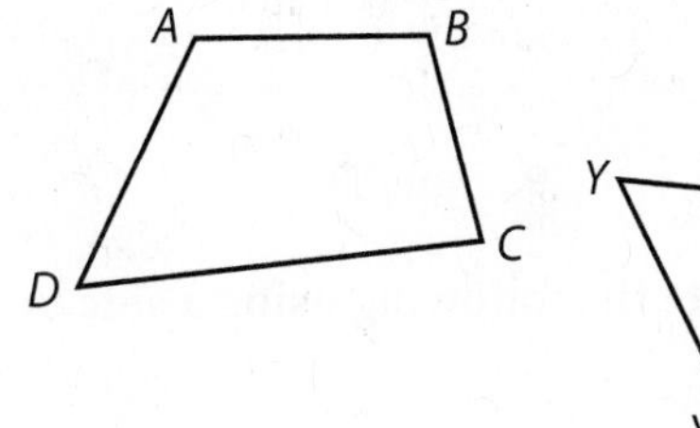

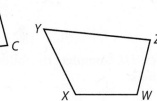

$\triangle DEF \cong \triangle GHJ$. **Find the given side length or angle measure.**

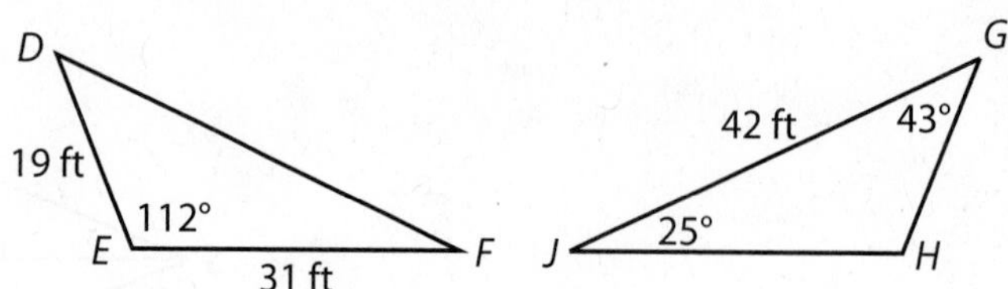

2. JH

3. $m\angle D$

$KLMN \cong PQRS$. **Find the given side length or angle measure.**

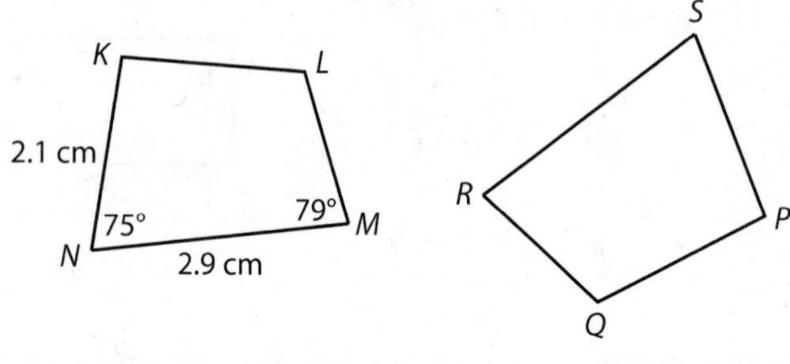

4. $m\angle R$

5. PS

$\triangle ABC \cong \triangle TUV$. **Find the given side length or angle measure.**

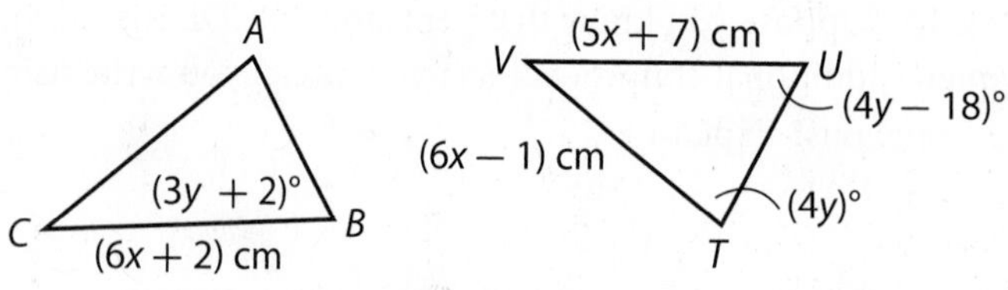

6. BC

7. $m\angle U$

$DEFG \cong KLMN$. **Find the given side length or angle measure.**

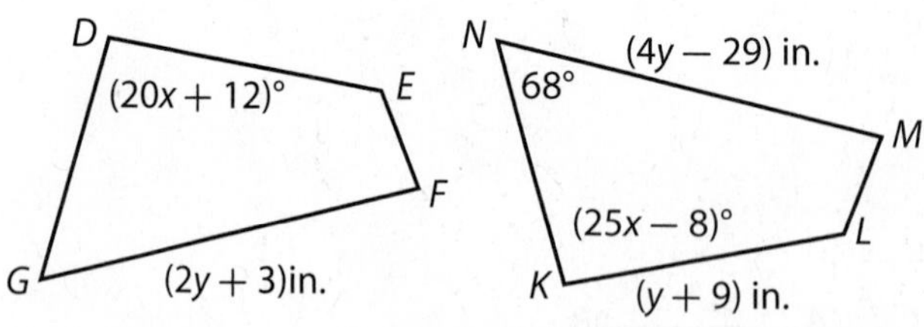

8. FG

9. $m\angle D$

$\triangle GHJ \cong \triangle PQR$ **and** $\triangle PQR \cong \triangle STU$. **Complete the following using a side or angle of** $\triangle STU$. **Justify your answers.**

10. $\overline{GH} \cong$ __?__

11. $\angle J \cong$ __?__

12. $GJ =$ __?__

13. $m\angle G =$ __?__

Write each proof.

14. Given: Quadrilateral $PQTU \cong$ quadrilateral $QRST$
Prove: $\overline{QT}$ bisects $\overline{PR}$.

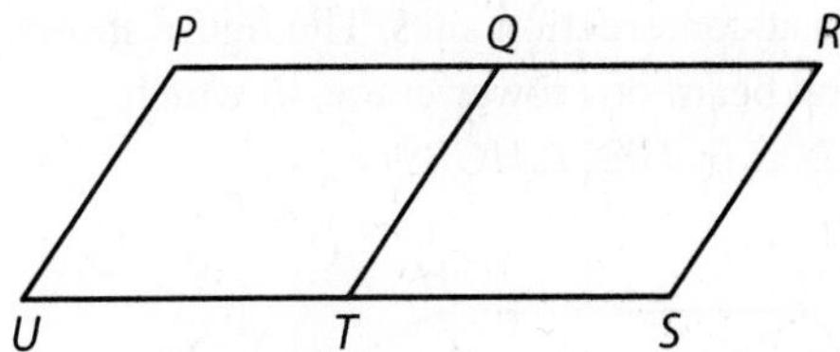

15. Given: $\triangle ABC \cong \triangle ADC$

Prove: $\overline{AC}$ bisects $\angle BAD$ and $\overline{AC}$ bisects $\angle BCD$.

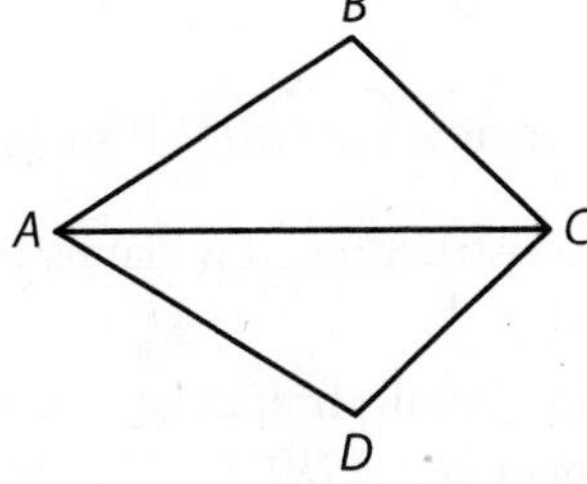

16. Given: Pentagon $ABCDE \cong$ pentagon $FGHJK$; $\angle D \cong \angle E$
Prove: $\angle D \cong \angle K$

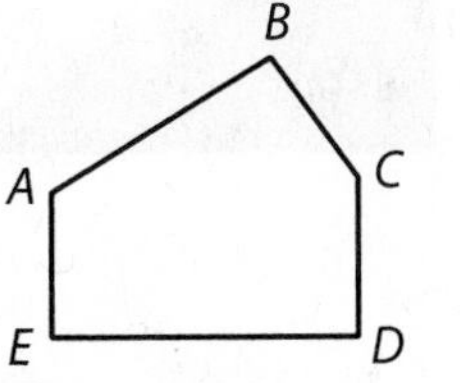

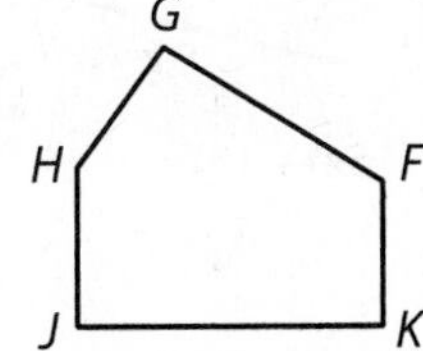

$\triangle ABC \cong \triangle DEF$. Find the given side length or angle measure.

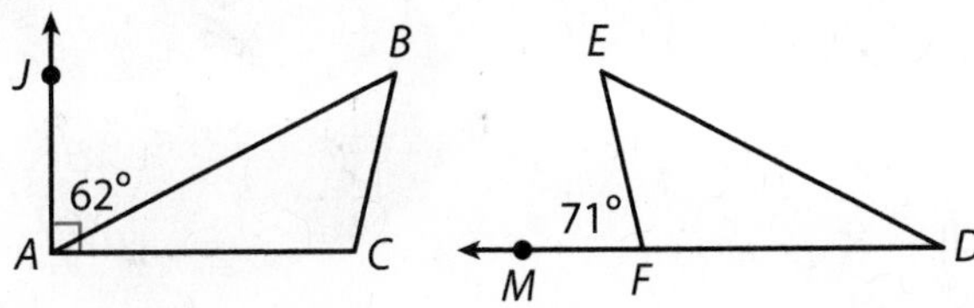

17. $m\angle D$

18. $m\angle C$

19. The figure shows the dimensions of two city parks, where $\triangle RST \cong \triangle XYZ$ and $\overline{YX} \cong \overline{YZ}$. A city employee wants to order new fences to surround both parks. What is the total length of the fences required to surround the parks?

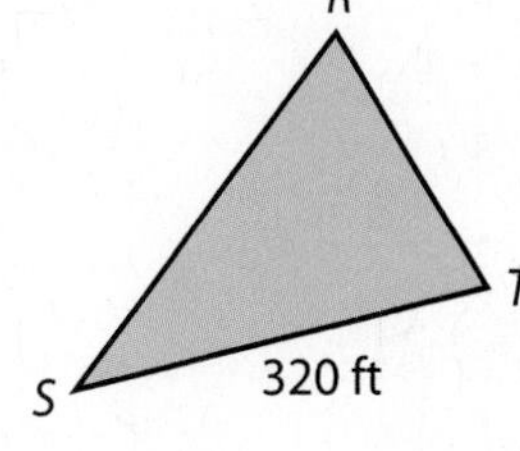

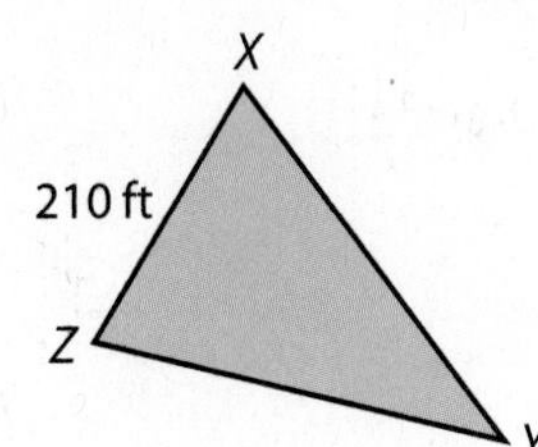

20. A tower crane is used to lift steel, concrete, and building materials at construction sites. The figure shows part of the horizontal beam of a tower crane, in which $\triangle ABG \cong \triangle BCH \cong \triangle HGB$.

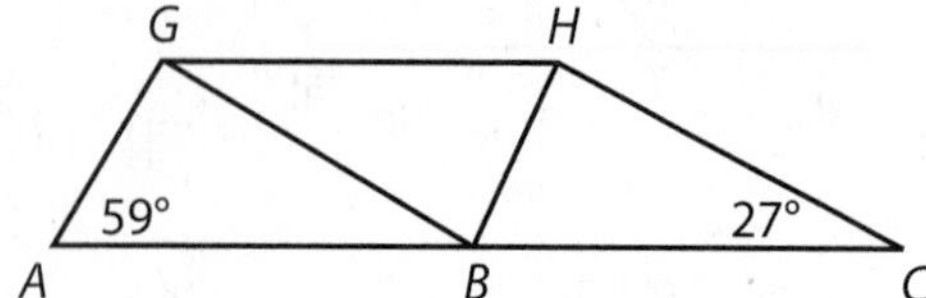

a. Is it possible to determine $m\angle GBH$? If so, how? If not, why not?

b. A member of the construction crew claims that $\overline{AC}$ is twice as long as $\overline{AB}$. Do you agree? Explain.

21. Multi-Step A company installs triangular pools at hotels. All of the pools are congruent and $\triangle JKL \cong \triangle MNP$ in the figure. What is the perimeter of each pool?

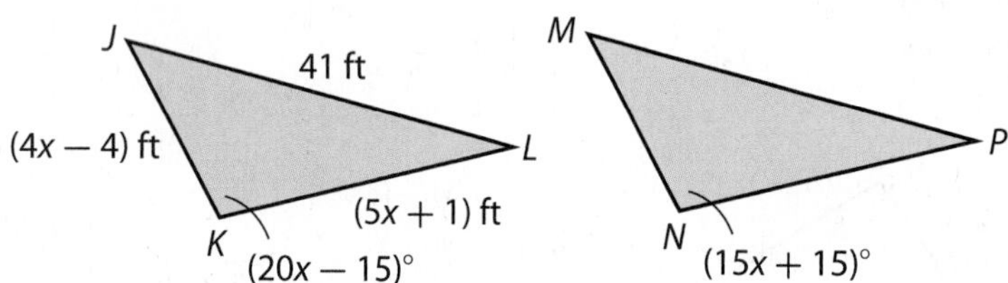

22. Kendall and Ava lay out the course shown below for their radio-controlled trucks. In the figure, $\triangle ABD \cong \triangle CBD$. The trucks travel at a constant speed of 15 feet per second. How long does it take a truck to travel on the course from A to B to C to D? Round to the nearest tenth of a second.

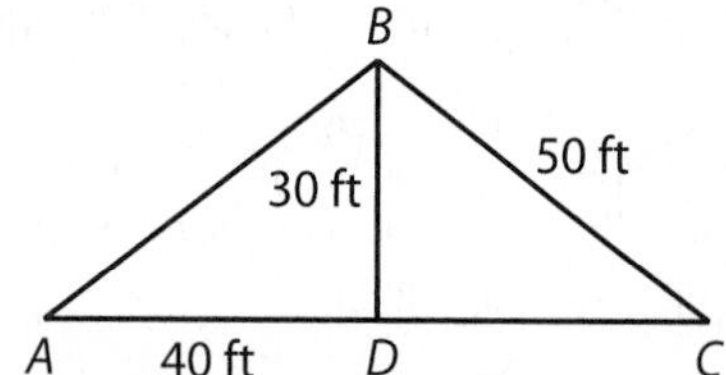

23. $\triangle MNP \cong \triangle QRS$. Determine whether each statement about the triangles is true or false.

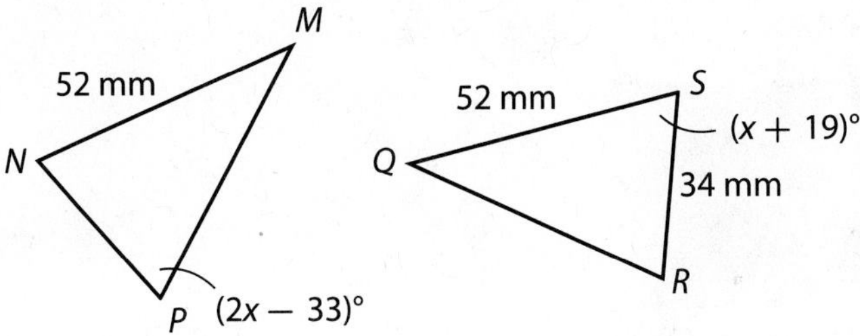

a. $\triangle QRS$ is isosceles.

b. $\overline{MP}$ is longer than $\overline{MN}$.

c. $m\angle P = 52°$

d. The perimeter of $\triangle QRS$ is 120 mm.

e. $\angle M \cong \angle Q$

H.O.T. Focus on Higher Order Thinking

24. Justify Reasoning Given that $\triangle ABC \cong \triangle DEF$, $AB = 2.7$ ft, and $AC = 3.4$ ft, is it possible to determine the length of $\overline{EF}$? If so, find the length and justify your steps. If not, explain why not.

25. Explain the Error A student was told that $\triangle GHJ \cong \triangle RST$ and was asked to find GH. The student's work is shown below. Explain the error and find the correct answer.

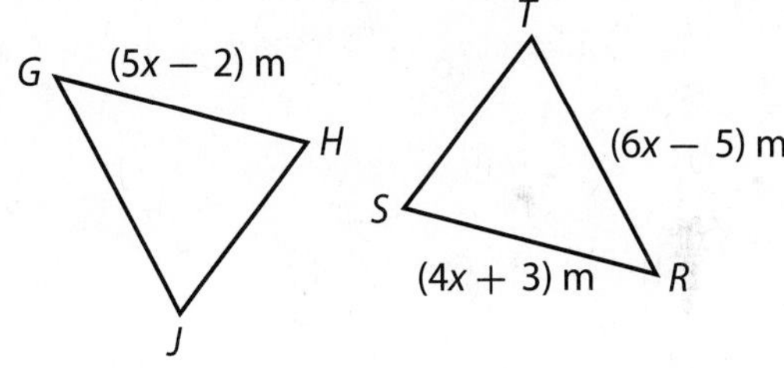

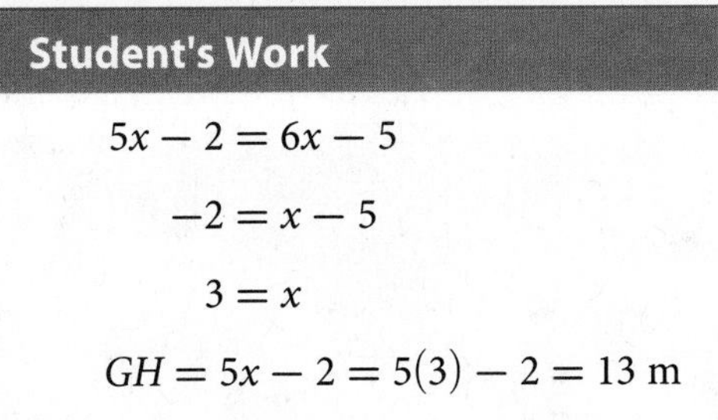

Student's Work

$$5x - 2 = 6x - 5$$
$$-2 = x - 5$$
$$3 = x$$
$$GH = 5x - 2 = 5(3) - 2 = 13 \text{ m}$$

26. Critical Thinking In $\triangle ABC$, $m\angle A = 55°$, $m\angle B = 50°$, and $m\angle C = 75°$. In $\triangle DEF$, $m\angle E = 50°$, and $m\angle F = 65°$. Is it possible for the triangles to be congruent? Explain.

27. Analyze Relationships $\triangle PQR \cong \triangle SQR$ and $\overline{RS} \cong \overline{RT}$. A student said that point R appears to be the midpoint of $\overline{PT}$. Is it possible to prove this? If so, write the proof. If not, explain why not.

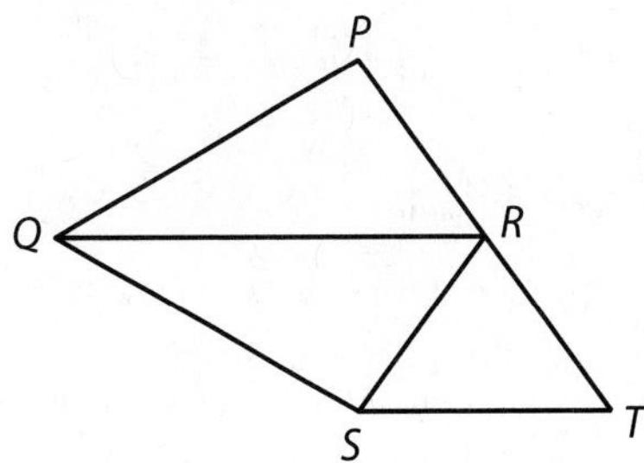

Lesson Performance Task

The illustration shows a "Yankee Puzzle" quilt.

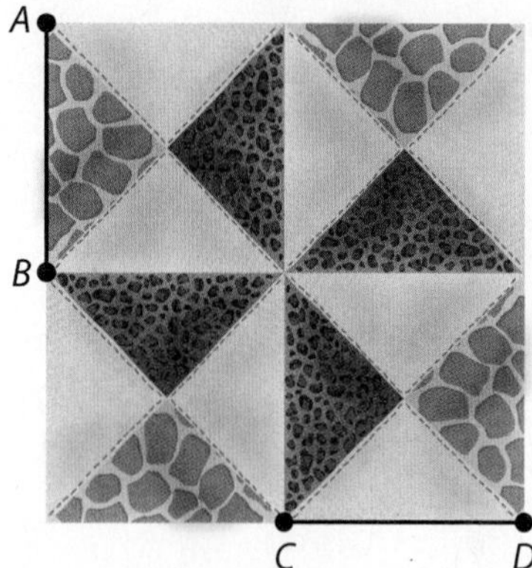

a. Use the idea of congruent shapes to describe the design of the quilt.

b. Explain how the triangle with base $\overline{AB}$ can be transformed to the position of the triangle with base $\overline{CD}$.

c. Explain how you know that $CD = AB$.

Congruent Figures

Essential Question: How can you use congruency to solve real-world problems?

KEY EXAMPLE (Lesson 3.1)

Write the vertices of the image of the figure given by $A\,(2, 1)$, $B\,(3, 3)$, $C\,(2, 4)$ after the transformations.

$(x, y) \rightarrow (x + 1, y + 2) \rightarrow (3x, y)$

$A\ (2, 1) \rightarrow A'\ (3, 3)$

$B\ (3, 3) \rightarrow B'\ (4, 5)$

$C\ (2, 4) \rightarrow C'\ (3, 6)$

Apply the transformations in order to each point. Apply the first transformation.

$A'\ (3, 3) \rightarrow A''\ (9, 3)$

$B'\ (4, 5) \rightarrow B''\ (12, 5)$

$C'\ (3, 6) \rightarrow C''\ (9, 6)$

Apply the second transformation.

The image of the transformed figure is determined by the points $A''\ (9, 3)$, $B''\ (12, 5)$, $C''\ (9, 6)$.

KEY EXAMPLE (Lesson 3.2)

Determine whether a triangle $\triangle ABC$ is congruent to its image after the transformations $(x, y) \rightarrow (x + 1, y + 2) \rightarrow (2x, y)$.

The transformation $(x, y) \rightarrow (x + 1, y + 2)$ is a translation, which is a rigid motion, so after this transformation the image is congruent. The transformation $(x, y) \rightarrow (2x, y)$ is a dilation, which is not a rigid motion, so the image from this transformation is not congruent.

After the transformations, the image is not congruent to $\triangle ABC$ because one of the transformations is not a rigid motion.

KEY EXAMPLE (Lesson 3.3)

Find the angle in $\triangle DFE$ congruent to $\angle A$ and the side congruent to $\overline{BC}$ when $\triangle ABC \cong \triangle DFE$.

Since $\triangle ABC \cong \triangle DFE$, and corresponding parts of congruent figures are congruent, $\angle A \cong \angle D$ and $\overline{BC} \cong \overline{FE}$.

EXERCISES

Write the vertices of the image of the figure after the transformations. *(Lesson 3.1)*

1. The figure given by $A(1, -2)$, $B(2, 5)$, $C(-3, 7)$, and the transformations

$(x, y) \rightarrow (x, y - 1) \rightarrow (-y, 2x)$

Find the rigid motions to transform one figure into its congruent figure. *(Lesson 3.2)*

2. In the figure, $\triangle ABC \cong \triangle DEF$.

The rigid motions to transform from $\triangle ABC$ to $\triangle DEF$ are

___?___.

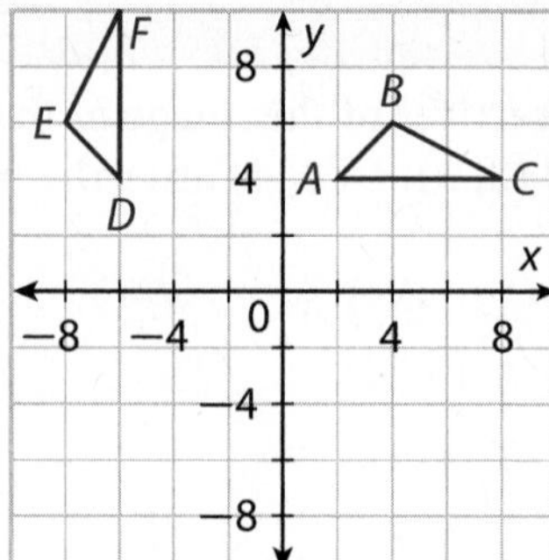

Find the congruent parts. *(Lesson 3.3)*

3. Given $\triangle ABC \cong \triangle DEF$, $\angle A \cong$ ___?___.

4. Given $\triangle ABC \cong \triangle DEF$, $\overline{CA} \cong$ ___?___.

MODULE PERFORMANCE TASK

Jigsaw Puzzle

A popular pastime, jigsaw puzzles are analogous to the series of transformations that can be performed to move one figure onto another congruent figure.

In the photo, identify at least three pieces that would likely fit into one of the empty spaces in the puzzle. Describe the rotations and translations necessary to move the piece to its correct position in the puzzle.

Ready to Go On?

3.1–3.3 Congruent Figures

- Online Homework
- Hints and Help
- Extra Practice

Predict the results of the transformations. *(Lesson 3.1)*

1. Triangle $\triangle ABC$ is in the first quadrant and translated along $\langle 2, 1 \rangle$ and reflected across the x-axis.
Which quadrant will the triangle be in after the first transformation?
Which quadrant will the triangle be in after the second transformation?

Determine whether the triangles are congruent using rigid motions. *(Lesson 3.2)*

2. Using the graph with $\triangle ABC$, $\triangle DEF$, and $\triangle PQR$:

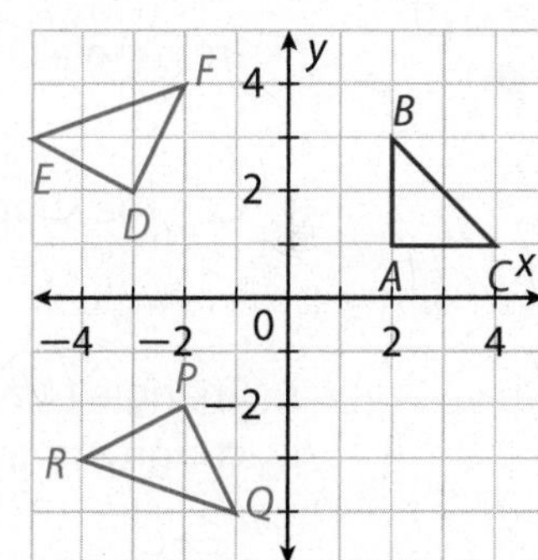

A. Determine whether $\triangle ABC$ is congruent to $\triangle DEF$.

B. Determine whether $\triangle DEF$ is congruent to $\triangle PQR$.

Find the congruent parts of the triangles. *(Lesson 3.3)*

3. List all of the pairs of congruent sides for two congruent triangles $\triangle ABC$ and $\triangle DEF$.

ESSENTIAL QUESTION

4. How can you determine whether a figure is congruent to another figure?

MODULE 3
MIXED REVIEW

Assessment Readiness

1. A line segment with points $R(3, 5)$ and $S(5, 5)$ is reflected across the line $y = -x$ and translated 2 units down. Determine whether each choice is a coordinate of the image of the line segment.

   A. $R'(-5, -3)$

   B. $R'(-5, -5)$

   C. $S'(-5, -7)$

2. The polygon *ABCD* is congruent to *PQRS*. The measure of angle *B* is equal to 65°. Determine if each statement is True or False.

   A. The supplement of angle *Q* measures 115°.

   B. Angle *Q* measures 115°.

   C. The supplement of angle *B* measures 115°.

3. Triangle *LMN* is a right triangle. The measure of angle *L* is equal to 35°. Triangle *LMN* is congruent to $\triangle PRQ$ with right angle *R*. Determine if each statement is True or False.

   A. The measure of angle *Q* is 55°.

   B. The measure of angle *R* is 90°.

   C. The measure of angle *P* is 35°.

4. The two triangles, $\triangle ABC$ and $\triangle DEF$, are congruent. Which side is congruent to $\overline{CA}$? Which side is congruent to $\overline{BA}$?

UNIT 1 MIXED REVIEW

Assessment Readiness

- Online Homework
- Hints and Help
- Extra Practice

1. Consider each expression. if $x = -2$, is the value of the expression a positive number?

A. $-2(x - 2)^2$

B. $-3x(5 - 4x)$

C. $x^3 + 6x$

2. A bedroom is shaped like a rectangular prism. The floor has a length of 4.57 meters and a width of 4.04 meters. The height of the room is 2.3 meters. Determine if each statement is True or False.

A. The perimeter of the floor with the correct number of significant digits is 17.22 meters.

B. The area of the floor with the correct number of significant digits is 18.46 square meters.

C. The volume of the room with the correct number of significant digits is 42 cubic meters.

3. Determine whether the ray *BD* bisects $\angle ABC$.

A. $m\angle ABC = 60°$, $m\angle ABD = 30°$

B. $m\angle ABC = 96°$, $m\angle ABD = 47°$

C. $m\angle ABC = 124°$, $m\angle ABD = 62°$

4. Is the point *C* the midpoint of the line $\overline{AB}$?

Write Yes or No for each set of points.

A. $A(1, 2)$, $B(3, 4)$, and $C(2, 3)$

B. $A(-1, 2)$, $B(3, -1)$, and $C(1, 0)$

C. $A(-3, 0)$, $B(-1, 5)$, and $C(-2, 2)$

5. Is $\overline{RS}$ a translation of $\overline{DF}$?

Write Yes or No for each set of endpoints.

A. $R(2, 2)$, $S(5, 2)$, and $D(3, 3)$, $F(5, 3)$

B. $R(-1, 3)$, $S(2, -2)$, and $D(-4, 2)$, $F(-1, -3)$

C. $R(5, -3)$, $S(2, 2)$, and $D(1, -4)$, $F(-1, -3)$

6. Does the shape have rotational symmetry?

Write Yes or No for each shape.

A. A square

B. A trapezoid

C. A right triangle

7. Determine whether each image of $\triangle ABC$, with $A(1, 3)$, $B(2, 3)$, $C(4, 5)$, can be formed with only the given transformation. Determine if each statement is True or False.

A. $A'(2, 4)$, $B'(3, 4)$, $C'(5, 6)$ is formed by translation.

B. $A'(-1, 3)$, $B'(-2, 3)$, $C'(-4, 5)$ is formed by rotation.

C. $A'(1, -5)$, $B'(2, -3)$, $C'(4, -1)$ is formed by reflection.

8. For $\triangle DEF$, with $D(2, 2)$, $E(3, 5)$, $F(4, 3)$, and $\triangle D'E'F'$, with $D'(4, 2)$, $E'(3, 5)$, $F'(2, 3)$, determine whether the image can be formed with the sequence of transformations. Write True or False for each statement.

A. The image is formed by a reflection followed by a translation.

B. The image is formed by a rotation followed by a reflection.

C. The image is formed by two consecutive reflections.

9. Use the figure to answer the questions below.

A. What is a specific series of rigid transformations that maps $\triangle ABC$ to $\triangle DEF$?

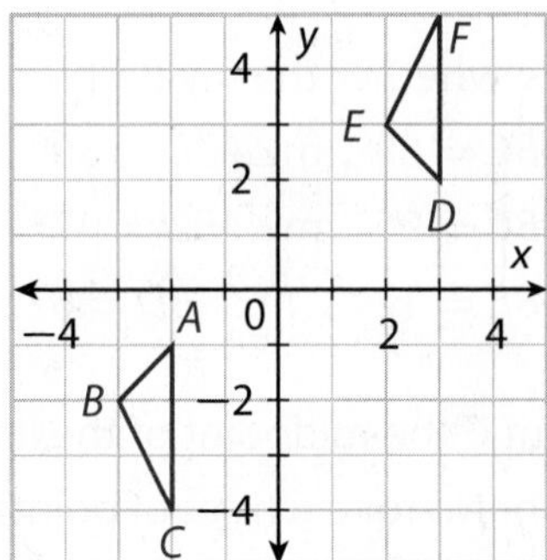

B. List all congruent pairs of angles and sides for the two figures.

Performance Tasks

★**10.** A student has drawn a figure of a square *PQRS* with points $P(-5, 5)$, $Q(1, 5)$, $R(1, -1)$, and $S(-5, -1)$. For the next assignment, the teacher wants students to inscribe another square, but with sides of length $\sqrt{18}$, inside the first square. How would a student find the correct square? What are the vertices of the inscribed square?

★★**11.** A square table is set with four identical place settings, one on each side of the table. Each setting consists of a plate and spoon. Choose one as the original place setting. What transformation describes the location of each of the other three? Express your answer in terms of degrees, lines of reflection, or directions from the original place setting.

★★★**12.** In spherical geometry, the plane is replaced by the surface of a sphere. In this context, straight lines are defined as great circles, which are circles that have the same center as the sphere. They are the largest possible circles on the surface of the sphere.

A. On a globe, lines of longitude run north and south. In spherical geometry, are lines of longitude straight lines? Are any lines of longitude parallel (nonintersecting)?

B. Lines of latitude run east and west. In spherical geometry, are lines of latitude straight lines? Are any lines of latitude parallel (nonintersecting)?

C. In general, in how many places does a pair of straight lines intersect in spherical geometry?

MATH IN CAREERS

Geomatics Surveyor A geomatics surveyor is surveying a piece of land of length 400 feet and width 300 feet. Standing at one corner, he finds that the elevation of the opposite corner is 50 feet greater than his elevation. Find the distance between the surveyor and the middlemost point of the piece of land (ignoring elevation), the elevation of the middlemost point in comparison to his location (assuming that the elevation increases at a constant rate), and distance between the surveyor and the middlemost point of the piece of land considering its elevation.

UNIT 2

Lines, Angles, and Triangles

MATH IN CAREERS

Architect An architect is responsible for designing spaces where people work and live. In addition to a keen eye for detail and strong artistic skills, architects use mathematics to create spaces that are both functional and aesthetically pleasing.

If you're interested in a career as an architect, you should study these mathematical subjects:

- Algebra
- Geometry
- Trigonometry

Research other careers that require the use of spatial analysis to understand real-world scenarios. See the related Career Activity at the end of this unit.

Reading Start-Up

Visualize Vocabulary

Use the ✔ words to complete the case diagram. Write the review words in the bubbles and draw a picture to illustrate each case.

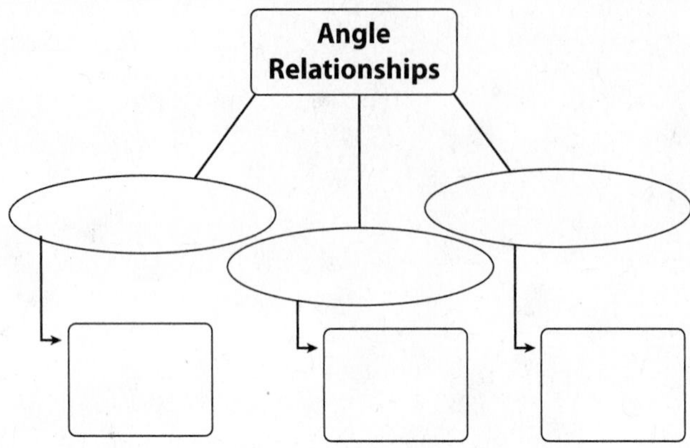

Understand Vocabulary

Complete the sentences using the preview words.

1. A(n) __?__ has three sides with the same length.

2. A circle is __?__ in a polygon if each side of the polygon is tangent to the circle.

3. The __?__ of a right triangle is the longest side of the triangle.

Active Reading

Key-Term Fold While reading each module, create a Key-Term Fold to help you organize vocabulary words. Write vocabulary terms on one side and definitions on the other side. Place a special emphasis on learning and speaking the English word while discussing the unit.

Vocabulary

Review Words

- ✔ adjacent angles *(ángulos adyacentes)*
- ✔ parallel lines *(líneas paralelas)*
- ✔ congruence *(congruencia)*
- ✔ vertical angles *(ángulos verticales)*
- ✔ complementary angles *(ángulos complementarios)*
- ✔ supplementary angles *(ángulos suplementarios)*
- ✔ transversal *(transversal)*

Preview Words

indirect proof *(demostración indirecta)*
hypotenuse *(hipotenusa)*
legs *(catetos)*
interior angle *(ángulo interior)*
exterior angle *(ángulo exterior)*
isosceles triangle *(triángulo isósceles)*
equilateral triangle *(triángulo equilátero)*
circumscribe *(circunscrito)*
inscribed *(apuntado)*

Lines and Angles

MODULE 4

Essential Question: How can you use parallel and perpendicular lines to solve real-world problems?

REAL WORLD VIDEO
Check out how properties of parallel and perpendicular lines and angles can be used to create real-world illusions in a mystery spot building.

MODULE PERFORMANCE TASK PREVIEW

Mystery Spot Building

In this module, you will use properties of parallel lines and angles to analyze the strange happenings in a mystery spot building. With a little bit of geometry, you'll be able to figure out whether mystery spot buildings are "on the up-and-up!"

Are YOU Ready?

Complete these exercises to review skills you will need for this module.

Personal Math Trainer

- Online Homework
- Hints and Help
- Extra Practice

Angle Relationships

Example 1

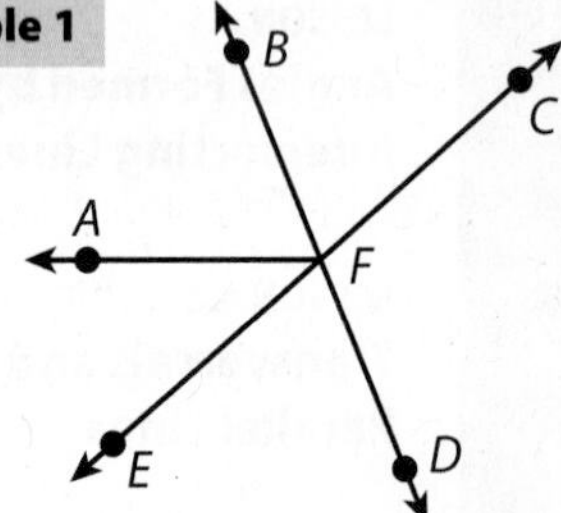

The measure of $\angle AFB$ is 70° and the measure of $\angle AFE$ is 40°. Find the measure of angle $\angle BFE$.

$m\angle BFE = m\angle AFB + m\angle AFE$ Angle Addition Postulate

$m\angle BFE = 70° + 40°$ Substitute.

$m\angle BFE = 110°$ Solve for $m\angle BFE$.

Find the measure of the angle in the image from the example.

1. The measure of $\angle BFE$ is 110°. Find $m\angle EFD$.

$m\angle EFD =$ ___?___

2. The measure of $\angle BFE$ is 110°. Find $m\angle BFC$.

$m\angle BFC =$ ___?___

Parallel Lines Cut by a Transversal

Example 2 The measure of $\angle 7$ is 110°. Find $m\angle 3$. Assume $p \parallel q$.

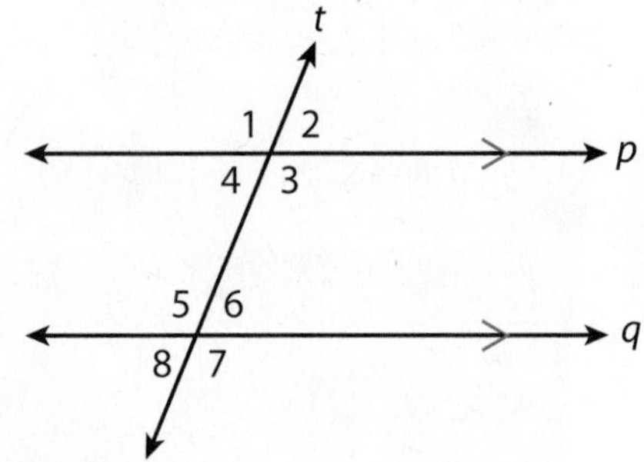

$m\angle 3 = m\angle 7$ Corresponding Angles Theorem

$m\angle 3 = 110°$ Substitute.

Find the measure of the angle in the image from the example. Assume $p \parallel q$.

3. The measure of $\angle 3$ is 110°. Find $m\angle 1$. $m\angle 1 =$ ___?___

4. The measure of $\angle 3$ is 110°. Find $m\angle 6$. $m\angle 6 =$ ___?___

Writing Equations of Parallel, Perpendicular, Vertical, and Horizontal Lines

Example 3 Find the line parallel to $y = 2x + 7$ that passes through the point $(3, 6)$.

$(y - y_1) = m(x - x_1)$ Use point-slope form.

$(y - 6) = 2(x - 3)$ Substitute for m, x_1, y_1. Parallel lines have the same slope, so $m = 2$.

$y - 6 = 2x - 6$ Simplify.

$y = 2x$ Solve for y.

Find the equation of the line described.

5. Perpendicular to $y = 3x + 5$; passing through the point $(-6, -4)$

6. Parallel to the x-axis; passing through the point $(4, 1)$

4.1 Angles Formed by Intersecting Lines

Resource Locker

Essential Question: How can you find the measures of angles formed by intersecting lines?

Explore 1 Exploring Angle Pairs Formed by Intersecting Lines

When two lines intersect, like the blades of a pair of scissors, a number of angle pairs are formed. You can find relationships between the measures of the angles in each pair.

(A) Using a straightedge, draw a pair of intersecting lines like the open scissors. Label the angles formed as 1, 2, 3, and 4.

(B) Use a protractor to find each measure.

Angle	Measure of Angle
m∠1	?
m∠2	?
m∠3	?
m∠4	?
m∠1 + m∠2	?
m∠2 + m∠3	?
m∠3 + m∠4	?
m∠1 + m∠4	?

You have been measuring *vertical angles* and *linear pairs* of angles. When two lines intersect, the angles that are opposite each other are **vertical angles**. Recall that a *linear pair* is a pair of adjacent angles whose non-common sides are opposite rays. So, when two lines intersect, the angles that are on the same side of a line form a linear pair.

Reflect

1. Name a pair of vertical angles and a linear pair of angles in your diagram in Step A.
2. Make a conjecture about the measures of a pair of vertical angles.
3. Use the Linear Pair Theorem to tell what you know about the measures of angles that form a linear pair.

Explore 2 Proving the Vertical Angles Theorem

The conjecture from the Explore about vertical angles can be proven so it can be stated as a theorem.

The Vertical Angles Theorem

If two angles are vertical angles, then the angles are congruent.

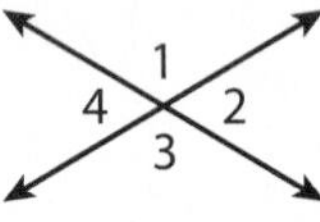

$\angle 1 \cong \angle 3$ and $\angle 2 \cong \angle 4$

You have written proofs in two-column and paragraph proof formats. Another type of proof is called a *flow proof*. A **flow proof** uses boxes and arrows to show the structure of the proof. The steps in a flow proof move from left to right or from top to bottom, shown by the arrows connecting each box. The justification for each step is written below the box. You can use a flow proof to prove the Vertical Angles Theorem.

Follow the steps to write a Plan for Proof and a flow proof to prove the Vertical Angles Theorem.

Given: $\angle 1$ and $\angle 3$ are vertical angles.

Prove: $\angle 1 \cong \angle 3$

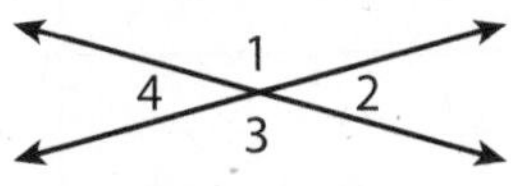

 Write the final steps of a Plan for Proof:

Because $\angle 1$ and $\angle 2$ are a linear pair and $\angle 2$ and $\angle 3$ are a linear pair, these pairs of angles are supplementary. This means that $m\angle 1 + m\angle 2 = 180°$ and $m\angle 2 + m\angle 3 = 180°$. By the Transitive Property, $m\angle 1 + m\angle 2 = m\angle 2 + m\angle 3$.

Next: ? .

(B) Use the Plan for Proof to complete the flow proof. Begin with what you know is true from the Given or the diagram. Use arrows to show the path of the reasoning.

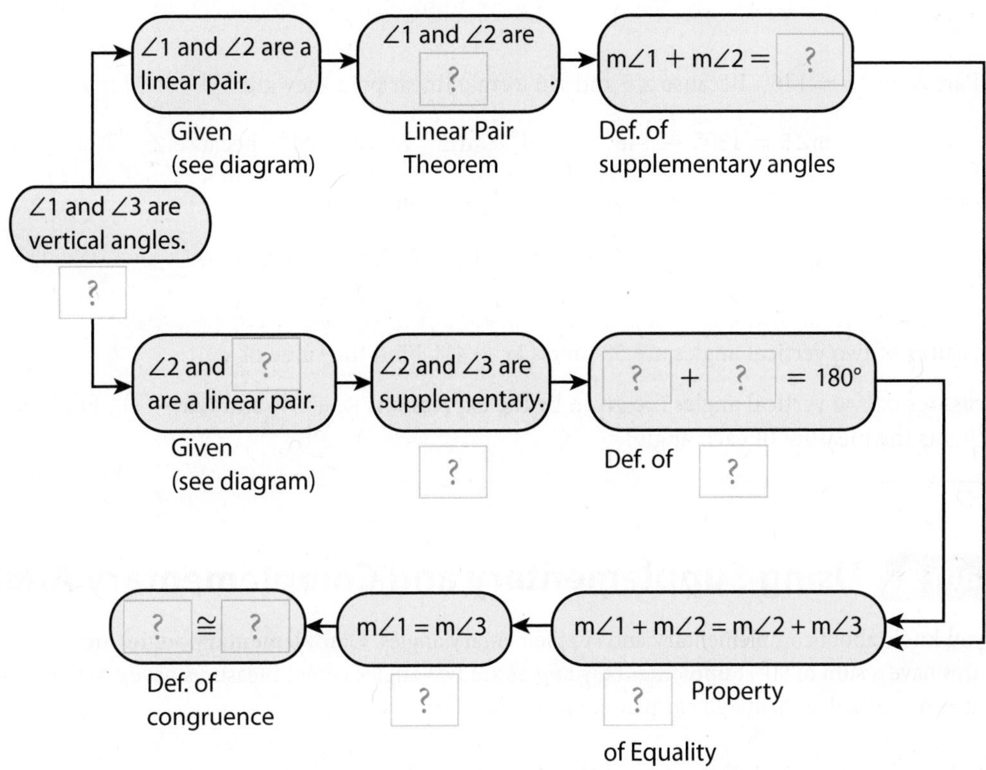

Reflect

4. **Discussion** Using the other pair of angles in the diagram, ∠2 and ∠4, would a proof that ∠2 ≅ ∠4 also show that the Vertical Angles Theorem is true? Explain why or why not.

5. Draw two intersecting lines to form vertical angles. Label your lines and tell which angles are congruent. Measure the angles to check that they are congruent.

Explain 1 Using Vertical Angles

You can use the Vertical Angles Theorem to find missing angle measures in situations involving intersecting lines.

Example 1 **Cross braces help keep the deck posts straight. Find the measure of each angle.**

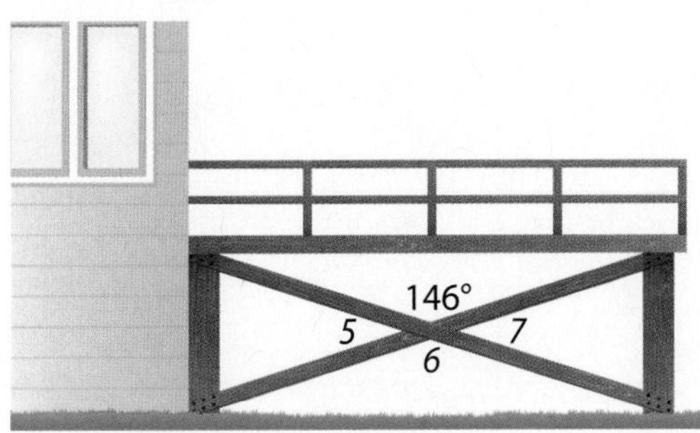

(A) $\angle 6$

Because vertical angles are congruent, $m\angle 6 = 146°$.

(B) $\angle 5$ and $\angle 7$

From Part A, $m\angle 6 = 146°$. Because $\angle 5$ and $\angle 6$ form a linear pair, they are supplementary and $m\angle 5 = 180° - 146° =$ 34° . $m\angle$ 7 = 34° because $\angle$ 7 also forms a linear pair with $\angle 6$, or because it is a vertical angle with $\angle 5$.

Your Turn

6. The measures of two vertical angles are 58° and $(3x + 4)°$. Find the value of x.

7. The measures of two vertical angles are given by the expressions $(x + 3)°$ and $(2x - 7)°$. Find the value of x. What is the measure of each angle?

Explain 2 Using Supplementary and Complementary Angles

Recall what you know about complementary and supplementary angles. **Complementary angles** are two angles whose measures have a sum of 90°. **Supplementary angles** are two angles whose measures have a sum of 180°. You have seen that two angles that form a linear pair are supplementary.

Example 2 **Use the diagram below to find the missing angle measures. Explain your reasoning.**

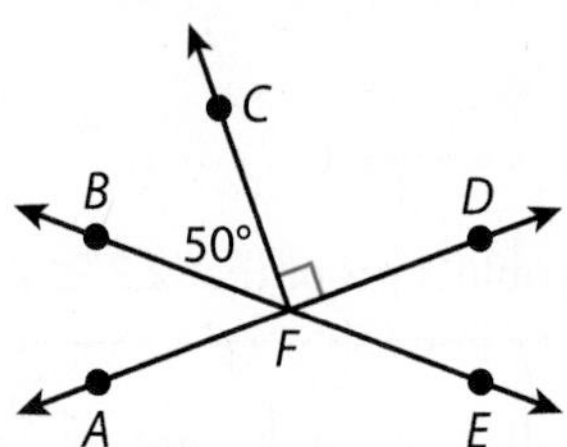

(A) Find the measures of $\angle AFC$ and $\angle AFB$.

$\angle AFC$ and $\angle CFD$ are a linear pair formed by an intersecting line and ray, $\overleftrightarrow{AD}$ and $\overrightarrow{FC}$, so they are supplementary and the sum of their measures is 180°. By the diagram, $m\angle CFD = 90°$, so $m\angle AFC = 180° - 90° = 90°$ and $\angle AFC$ is also a right angle.

Because together they form the right angle $\angle AFC$, $\angle AFB$ and $\angle BFC$ are complementary and the sum of their measures is 90°. So, $m\angle AFB = 90° - m\angle BFC = 90° - 50° = 40°$.

(B) Find the measures of $\angle DFE$ and $\angle AFE$.

$\angle BFA$ and $\angle DFE$ are formed by two intersecting lines and are opposite each other, so the angles are vertical angles. So, the angles are congruent. From Part A

$m\angle AFB = 40°$, so $m\angle DFE =$ 40° also.

Because $\angle BFA$ and $\angle AFE$ form a linear pair, the angles are supplementary and the sum of their measures is 180°. So, $m\angle AFE =$ 180° $- m\angle BFA =$ 180° $-$ 40° $=$ 140°.

Reflect

8. In Part A, what do you notice about right angles $\angle AFC$ and $\angle CFD$? Make a conjecture about right angles.

Your Turn

You can represent the measures of an angle and its complement as $x°$ and $(90 - x)°$. Similarly, you can represent the measures of an angle and its supplement as $x°$ and $(180 - x)°$. Use these expressions to find the measures of the angles described.

9. The measure of an angle is equal to the measure of its complement.

10. The measure of an angle is twice the measure of its supplement.

Elaborate

11. Describe how proving a theorem is different than solving a problem and describe how they are the same.

12. Discussion The proof of the Vertical Angles Theorem in the lesson includes a Plan for Proof. How are a Plan for Proof and the proof itself the same and how are they different?

13. Draw two intersecting lines. Label points on the lines and tell what angles you know are congruent and which are supplementary.

14. Essential Question Check-In If you know that the measure of one angle in a linear pair is 75°, how can you find the measure of the other angle?

Evaluate: Homework and Practice

• Online Homework
• Hints and Help
• Extra Practice

Use this diagram and information for Exercises 1–4.

Given: $m\angle AFB = m\angle EFD = 50°$

Points *B*, *F*, *D* and points *E*, *F*, *C* are collinear.

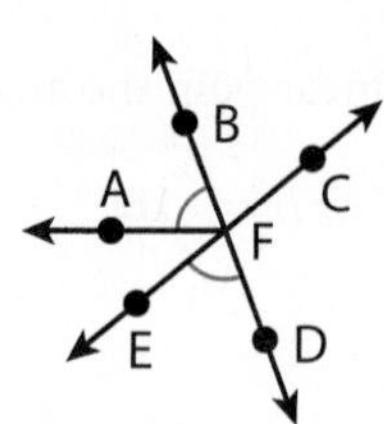

1. State whether each pair of angles is a pair of vertical angles, a linear pair of angles, or neither.

A. $\angle BFC$ and $\angle DFE$

B. $\angle BFA$ and $\angle DFE$

C. $\angle BFC$ and $\angle CFD$

D. $\angle AFE$ and $\angle AFC$

E. $\angle BFE$ and $\angle CFD$

F. $\angle AFE$ and $\angle BFC$

2. Find $m\angle AFE$.

3. Find $m\angle DFC$.

4. Find $m\angle BFC$.

5. **Represent Real-World Problems** A sprinkler swings back and forth between *A* and *B* in such a way that $\angle 1 \cong \angle 2$, $\angle 1$ and $\angle 3$ are complementary, and $\angle 2$ and $\angle 4$ are complementary. If $m\angle 1 = 47.5°$, find $m\angle 2$, $m\angle 3$, and $m\angle 4$.

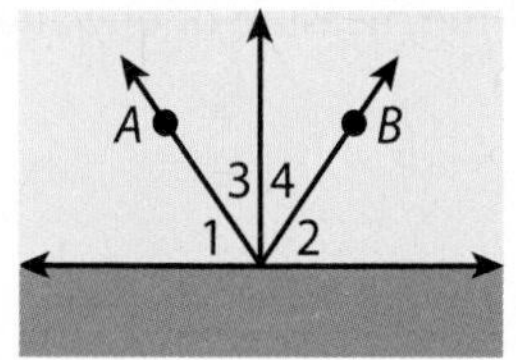

Determine whether each statement is true or false. If false, explain why.

6. If an angle is acute, then the measure of its complement must be greater than the measure of its supplement.

7. A pair of vertical angles may also form a linear pair.

8. If two angles are supplementary and congruent, the measure of each angle is 90°.

9. If a ray divides an angle into two complementary angles, then the original angle is a right angle.

You can represent the measures of an angle and its complement as $x°$ and $(90 - x)°$. Similarly, you can represent the measures of an angle and its supplement as $x°$ and $(180 - x)°$. Use these expressions to find the measures of the angles described.

10. The measure of an angle is three times the measure of its supplement.

11. The measure of the supplement of an angle is three times the measure of its complement.

12. The measure of an angle increased by 20° is equal to the measure of its complement.

Write a plan for a proof for each theorem.

13. If two angles are congruent, then their complements are congruent.

Given: $\angle ABC \cong \angle DEF$

Prove: The complement of $\angle ABC \cong$ the complement of $\angle DEF$.

14. If two angles are congruent, then their supplements are congruent.

Given: $\angle ABC \cong \angle DEF$

Prove: The supplement of $\angle ABC \cong$ the supplement of $\angle DEF$.

15. Justify Reasoning Complete the two-column proof for the theorem "If two angles are congruent, then their supplements are congruent."

Statements	Reasons
1. $\angle ABC \cong \angle DEF$	1. Given
2. The measure of the supplement of $\angle ABC = 180° - m\angle ABC$.	2. Definition of the __?__ of an angle
3. The measure of the supplement of $\angle DEF = 180° - m\angle DEF$.	3. __?__
4. __?__	4. If two angles are congruent, their measures are equal.
5. The measure of the supplement of $\angle DEF = 180° - m\angle ABC$.	5. Substitution Property of __?__
6. The measure of the supplement of $\angle ABC$ = the measure of the supplement of $\angle DEF$.	6. __?__
7. The supplement of $\angle ABC \cong$ the supplement of __?__.	7. If the measures of the supplements of two angles are equal, then supplements of the angles are congruent.

16. Probability The probability P of choosing an object at random from a group of objects is found by the fraction $P(\text{event}) = \frac{\text{Number of favorable outcomes}}{\text{Total number of outcomes}}$. Suppose the angle measures 30°, 60°, 120°, and 150° are written on slips of paper. You choose two slips of paper at random.

a. What is the probability that the measures you choose are complementary?

b. What is the probability that the measures you choose are supplementary?

H.O.T. Focus on Higher Order Thinking

17. Communicate Mathematical Ideas Write a proof of the Vertical Angles Theorem in paragraph proof form.

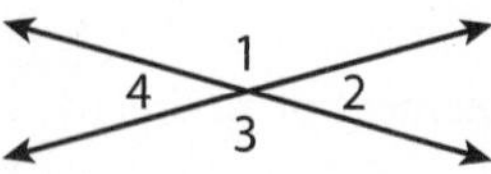

Given: ∠2 and ∠4 are vertical angles.

Prove: ∠2 ≅ ∠4

18. Analyze Relationships If one angle of a linear pair is acute, then the other angle must be obtuse. Explain why.

19. Critique Reasoning Your friend says that there is an angle whose measure is the same as the measure of the sum of its supplement and its complement. Is your friend correct? What is the measure of the angle? Explain your friend's reasoning.

20. Critical Thinking Two statements in a proof are:

$$m\angle A = m\angle B$$

$$m\angle B = m\angle C$$

What reason could you give for the statement $m\angle A = m\angle C$? Explain your reasoning.

Lesson Performance Task

The image shows the angles formed by a pair of scissors. When the scissors are closed, $m\angle 1 = 0°$. As the scissors are opened, the measures of all four angles change in relation to each other. Describe how the measures change as $m\angle 1$ increases from 0° to 180°.

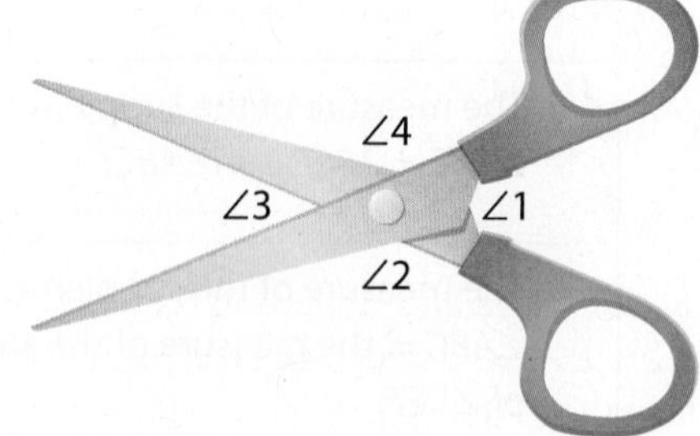

4.2 Transversals and Parallel Lines

Resource Locker

Essential Question: How can you prove and use theorems about angles formed by transversals that intersect parallel lines?

Explore — Exploring Parallel Lines and Transversals

A **transversal** is a line that intersects two coplanar lines at two different points. In the figure, line t is a transversal. The table summarizes the names of angle pairs formed by a transversal.

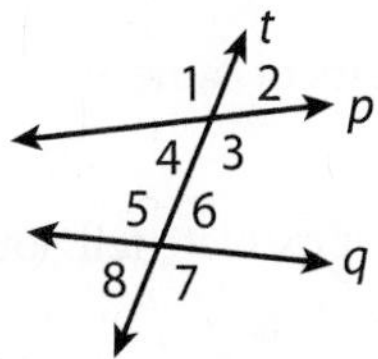

Angle Pair	Example
Corresponding angles lie on the same side of the transversal and on the same sides of the intersected lines.	$\angle 1$ and $\angle 5$
Same-side interior angles lie on the same side of the transversal and between the intersected lines.	$\angle 3$ and $\angle 6$
Alternate interior angles are nonadjacent angles that lie on opposite sides of the transversal between the intersected lines.	$\angle 3$ and $\angle 5$
Alternate exterior angles lie on opposite sides of the transversal and outside the intersected lines.	$\angle 1$ and $\angle 7$

Recall that parallel lines lie in the same plane and never intersect. In the figure, line ℓ is parallel to line m, written $\ell \parallel m$. The arrows on the lines also indicate that they are parallel.

ℓ

m

$\ell \parallel m$

When parallel lines are cut by a transversal, the angle pairs formed are either congruent or supplementary. The following postulate is the starting point for proving theorems about parallel lines that are intersected by a transversal.

Same-Side Interior Angles Postulate

If two parallel lines are cut by a transversal, then the pairs of same-side interior angles are supplementary.

Follow the steps to illustrate the postulate and use it to find angle measures.

(A) Draw two parallel lines and a transversal, and number the angles formed from 1 to 8.

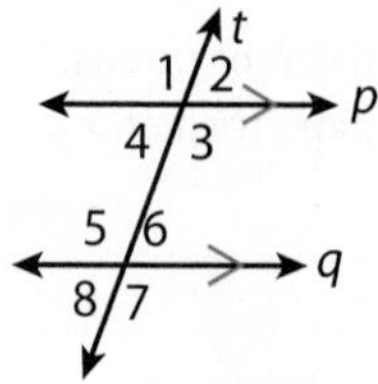

(B) Identify the pairs of same-side interior angles.

(C) What does the postulate tell you about these same-side interior angle pairs?

(D) If $m\angle 4 = 70°$, what is $m\angle 5$? Explain.

Reflect

1. Explain how you can find $m\angle 3$ in the diagram if $p \parallel q$ and $m\angle 6 = 61°$.
2. **What If?** If $m \parallel n$, how many pairs of same-side interior angles are shown in the figure? What are the pairs?

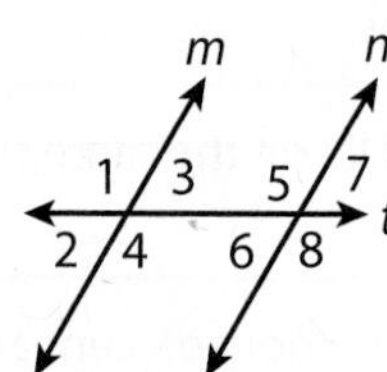

Explain 1 Proving that Alternate Interior Angles are Congruent

Other pairs of angles formed by parallel lines cut by a transversal are alternate interior angles.

Alternate Interior Angles Theorem

If two parallel lines are cut by a transversal, then the pairs of alternate interior angles have the same measure.

To prove something to be true, you use definitions, properties, postulates, and theorems that you already know.

Example 1 **Prove the Alternate Interior Angles Theorem.**

Given: $p \parallel q$

Prove: $m\angle 3 = m\angle 5$

Complete the proof by writing the missing reasons. Choose from the following reasons. You may use a reason more than once.

- Same-Side Interior Angles Postulate
- Given
- Definition of supplementary angles
- Subtraction Property of Equality
- Substitution Property of Equality
- Linear Pair Theorem

Statements	Reasons
1. $p \parallel q$	**1.** Given
2. $\angle 3$ and $\angle 6$ are supplementary.	**2.** Same-Side Interior Angles Postulate
3. $m\angle 3 + m\angle 6 = 180°$	**3.** Definition of supplementary angles
4. $\angle 5$ and $\angle 6$ are a linear pair.	**4.** Given
5. $\angle 5$ and $\angle 6$ are supplementary.	**5.** Linear Pair Theorem
6. $m\angle 5 + m\angle 6 = 180°$	**6.** Definition of supplementary angles
7. $m\angle 3 + m\angle 6 = m\angle 5 + m\angle 6$	**7.** Substitution Property of Equality
8. $m\angle 3 = m\angle 5$	**8.** Subtraction Property of Equality

Reflect

3. In the figure, explain why $\angle 1$, $\angle 3$, $\angle 5$, and $\angle 7$ all have the same measure.

4. Suppose $m\angle 4 = 57°$ in the figure shown. Describe two different ways to determine $m\angle 6$.

Explain 2 Proving that Corresponding Angles are Congruent

Two parallel lines cut by a transversal also form angle pairs called corresponding angles.

Corresponding Angles Theorem

If two parallel lines are cut by a transversal, then the pairs of corresponding angles have the same measure.

Example 2 Complete a proof in paragraph form for the Corresponding Angles Theorem.

Given: $p \| q$

Prove: $m\angle 4 = m\angle 8$

By the given statement, $p \| q$. $\angle 4$ and $\angle 6$ form a pair of alternate interior angles.

So, using the Alternate Interior Angles Theorem, $m\angle 4 = m\angle 6$.

$\angle 6$ and $\angle 8$ form a pair of vertical angles. So, using the Vertical Angles Theorem, $m\angle 6 = m\angle 8$. Using the Substitution Property of Equality in $m\angle 4 = m\angle 6$, substitute $m\angle 4$ for $m\angle 6$. The result is $m\angle 4 = m\angle 8$.

Reflect

5. Use the diagram in Example 2 to explain how you can prove the Corresponding Angles Theorem using the Same-Side Interior Angles Postulate and a linear pair of angles.

6. Suppose $m\angle 4 = 36°$. Find $m\angle 5$. Explain.

Explain 3 Using Parallel Lines to Find Angle Pair Relationships

You can apply the theorems and postulates about parallel lines cut by a transversal to solve problems.

Example 3 **Find each value. Explain how to find the values using postulates, theorems, and algebraic reasoning.**

(A) In the diagram, roads a and b are parallel. Explain how to find the measure of $\angle VTU$.

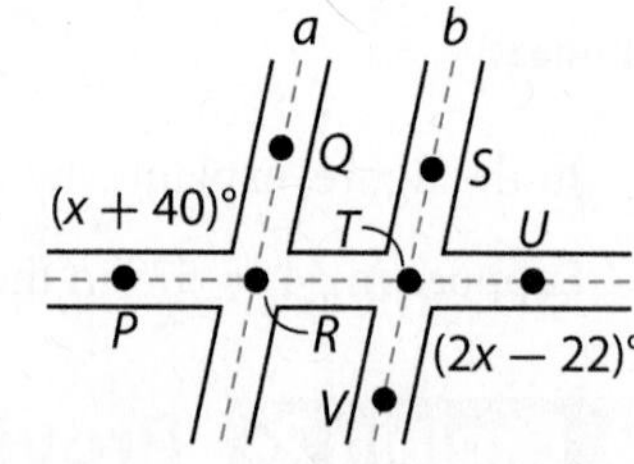

It is given that $m\angle PRQ = (x + 40)°$ and $m\angle VTU = (2x - 22)°$. $m\angle PRQ = m\angle RTS$ by the Corresponding Angles Theorem and $m\angle RTS = m\angle VTU$ by the Vertical Angles Theorem. So, $m\angle PRQ = m\angle VTU$, and $x + 40 = 2x - 22$. Solving for x, $x + 62 = 2x$, and $x = 62$. Substitute the value of x to find $m\angle VTU$: $m\angle VTU = \left(2(62) - 22\right)° = 102°$.

(B) In the diagram, roads a and b are parallel. Explain how to find the measure of $m\angle WUV$.

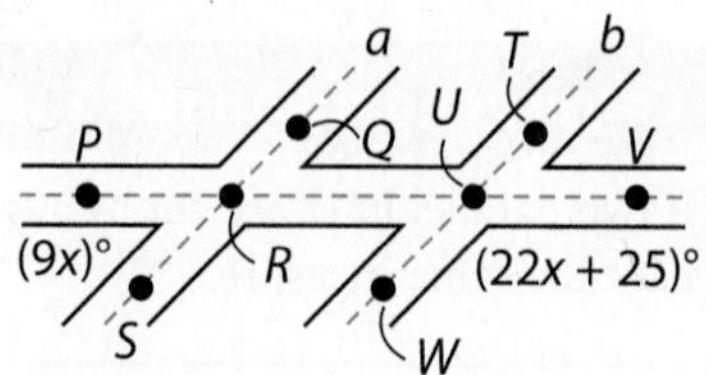

It is given that $m\angle PRS = (9x)°$ and $m\angle WUV = (22x + 25)°$. $m\angle PRS = m\angle RUW$ by the Corresponding Angles Theorem. $\angle RUW$ and $\angle WUV$ are supplementary angles. So, $m\angle RUW + m\angle WUV = 180°$. Solving for x, $31x + 25 = 180$, and $x = 5$. Substitute the value of x to find $m\angle WUV$; $m\angle WUV = \left(22(5) + 25\right)° = 135°$.

Your Turn

7. In the diagram of a gate, the horizontal bars are parallel and the vertical bars are parallel. Find x and y. Name the postulates and/or theorems that you used to find the values.

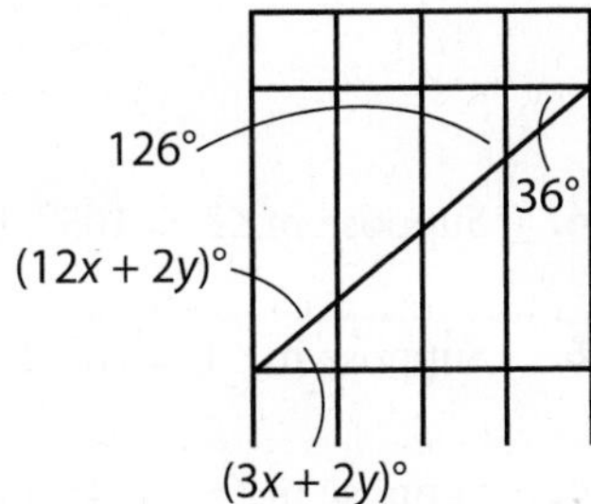

Elaborate

8. How is the Same-Side Interior Angles Postulate different from the two theorems in the lesson (Alternate Interior Angles Theorem and Corresponding Angles Theorem)?

9. **Discussion** Look at the figure below. If you know that p and q are parallel, and are given one angle measure, can you find all the other angle measures? Explain.

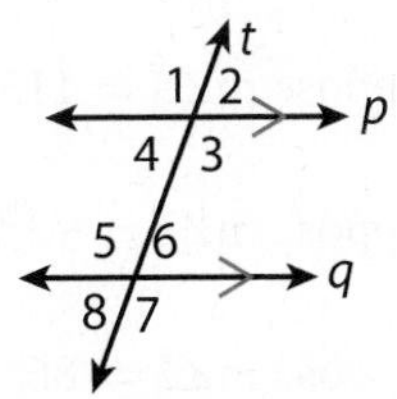

10. **Essential Question Check-In** Why is it important to establish the Same-Side Interior Angles Postulate before proving the other theorems?

Evaluate: Homework and Practice

Personal Math Trainer

- Online Homework
- Hints and Help
- Extra Practice

1. In the figure below, $m \| n$. Match the angle pairs with the correct label for the pairs.

A. $\angle 4$ and $\angle 6$ **a.** ___?___ Corresponding Angles

B. $\angle 5$ and $\angle 8$ **b.** ___?___ Same-Side Interior Angles

C. $\angle 2$ and $\angle 6$ **c.** ___?___ Alternate Interior Angles

D. $\angle 4$ and $\angle 5$ **d.** ___?___ Vertical Angles

2. Complete the definition: A __?__ is a line that intersects two coplanar lines at two different points.

Use the figure to find angle measures. In the figure, $p \parallel q$.

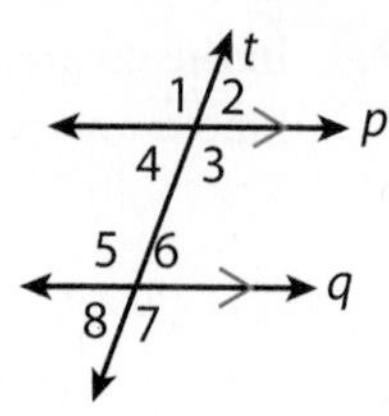

3. Suppose $m\angle 4 = 82°$. Find $m\angle 5$.

4. Suppose $m\angle 3 = 105°$. Find $m\angle 6$.

5. Suppose $m\angle 3 = 122°$. Find $m\angle 5$.

6. Suppose $m\angle 4 = 76°$. Find $m\angle 6$.

7. Suppose $m\angle 5 = 109°$. Find $m\angle 1$.

8. Suppose $m\angle 6 = 74°$. Find $m\angle 2$.

Use the figure to find angle measures. In the figure, $m \parallel n$ and $x \parallel y$.

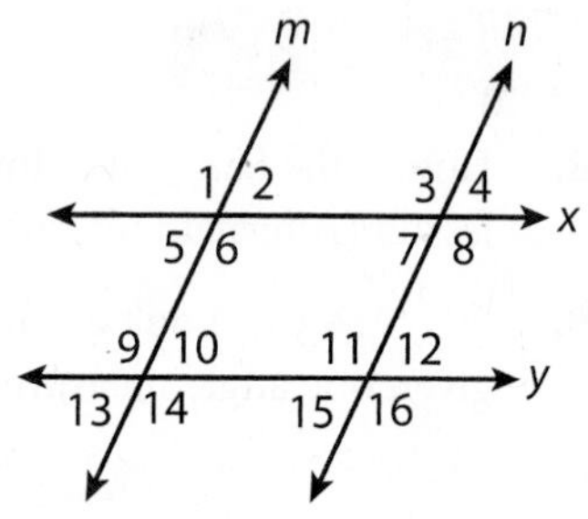

9. Suppose $m\angle 5 = 69°$. Find $m\angle 10$.

10. Suppose $m\angle 9 = 115°$. Find $m\angle 6$.

11. Suppose $m\angle 12 = 118°$. Find $m\angle 7$.

12. Suppose $m\angle 4 = 72°$. Find $m\angle 11$.

13. Suppose $m\angle 4 = 114°$. Find $m\angle 14$.

14. Suppose $m\angle 5 = 86°$. Find $m\angle 12$.

15. Ocean waves move in parallel lines toward the shore. The figure shows the path that a windsurfer takes across several waves. For this exercise, think of the windsurfer's wake as a line. If $m\angle 1 = (2x + 2y)°$ and $m\angle 2 = (2x + y)°$, find x and y. Explain your reasoning.

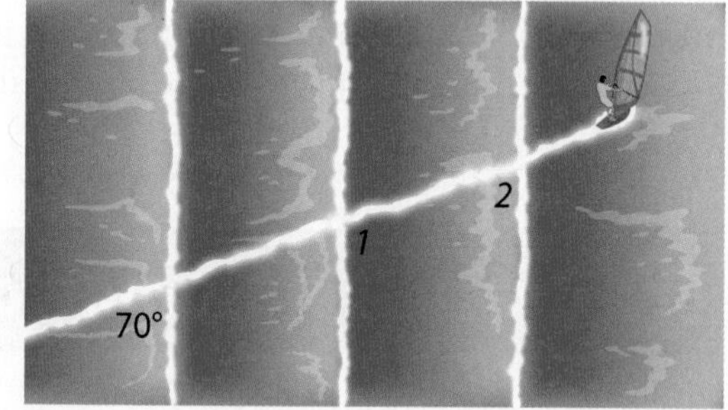

In the diagram of movie theater seats, the incline of the floor, f, is parallel to the seats, s.

16. If $m\angle 1 = 60°$, what is x?

17. If $m\angle 1 = 68°$, what is y?

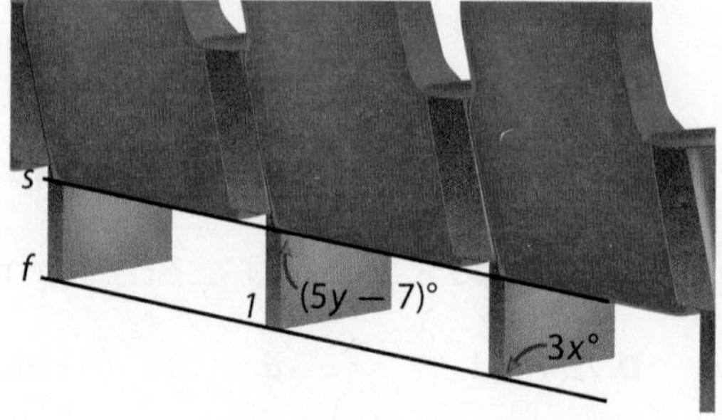

18. Complete a proof in paragraph form for the Alternate Interior Angles Theorem.

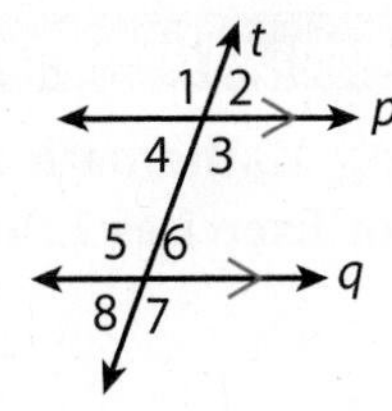

Given: $p \parallel q$

Prove: $m\angle 3 = m\angle 5$

It is given that $p \parallel q$, so using the Same-Side Interior Angles Postulate, $\angle 3$ and $\angle 6$ are ___?___. So, the sum of their measures is ___?___ and $m\angle 3 + m\angle 6 = 180°$. You can see from the diagram that $\angle 5$ and $\angle 6$ form a line, so they are a ___?___, which makes them ___?___. Then $m\angle 5 + m\angle 6 = 180°$. Using the Substitution Property of Equality, you can substitute ___?___ in $m\angle 3 + m\angle 6 = 180°$ with $m\angle 5 + m\angle 6$. This results in $m\angle 3 + m\angle 6 = m\angle 5 + m\angle 6$. Using the Subtraction Property vof Equality, you can subtract ___?___ from both sides. So, ___?___ .

19. Write a proof in two-column form for the Corresponding Angles Theorem.

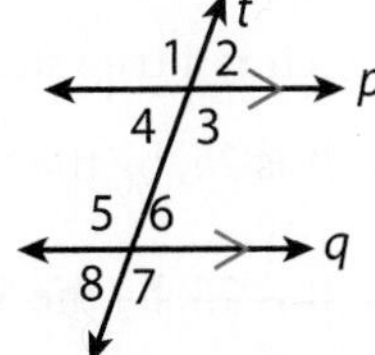

Given: $p \parallel q$

Prove: $m\angle 1 = m\angle 5$

20. Explain the Error Angelina wrote a proof in paragraph form to prove that the measures of corresponding angles are congruent. Identify her error, and describe how to fix the error.

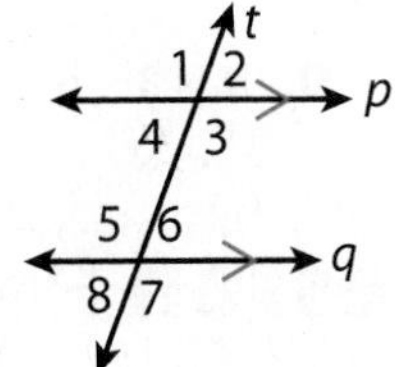

Angelina's proof:

I am given that $p \parallel q$. $\angle 1$ and $\angle 4$ are supplementary angles because they form a linear pair, so $m\angle 1 + m\angle 4 = 180°$. $\angle 4$ and $\angle 8$ are also supplementary because of the Same-Side Interior Angles Postulate, so $m\angle 4 + m\angle 8 = 180°$. You can substitute $m\angle 4 + m\angle 8$ for $180°$ in the first equation above. The result is $m\angle 1 + m\angle 4 = m\angle 4 + m\angle 8$. After subtracting $m\angle 4$ from each side, I see that $\angle 1$ and $\angle 8$ are corresponding angles and $m\angle 1 = m\angle 8$.

21. Counterexample Ellen thinks that when two lines that are not parallel are cut by a transversal, the measures of the alternate interior angles are the same. Write a proof to show that she is correct or use a counterexample to show that she is incorrect.

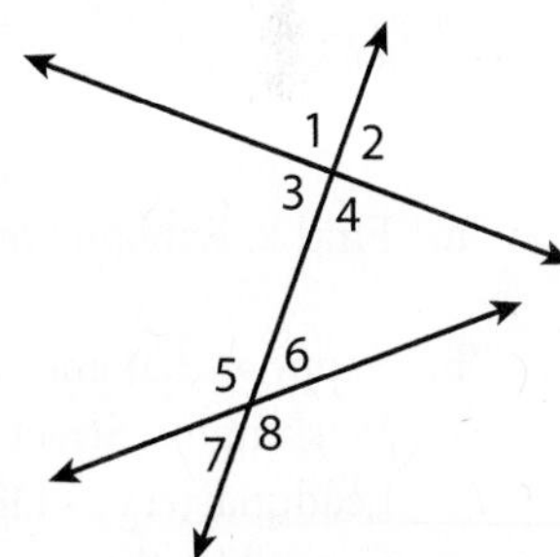

H.O.T. Focus on Higher Order Thinking

Analyzing Mathematical Relationships **Use the diagram of a staircase railing for Exercises 22 and 23. $\overline{AG} \parallel \overline{CJ}$ and $\overline{AD} \parallel \overline{FJ}$. Choose the best answer.**

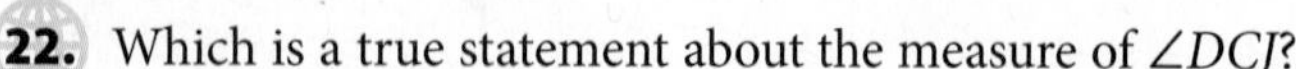

22. Which is a true statement about the measure of $\angle DCJ$?

A. It is 30°, by the Alternate Interior Angles Theorem.

B. It is 30°, by the Corresponding Angles Theorem.

C. It is 50°, by the Alternate Interior Angles Theorem.

D. It is 50°, by the Corresponding Angles Theorem.

23. Which is a true statement about the value of n?

A. It is 25, by the Alternate Interior Angles Theorem.

B. It is 25, by the Same-Side Interior Angles Postulate.

C. It is 35, by Alternate Interior Angles Theorem.

D. It is 35, by the Corresponding Angles Theorem.

Lesson Performance Task

Washington Street is parallel to Lincoln Street. The Apex Company's headquarters is located between the streets. From headquarters, a straight road leads to Washington Street, intersecting it at a 51° angle. Another straight road leads to Lincoln Street, intersecting it at a 37° angle.

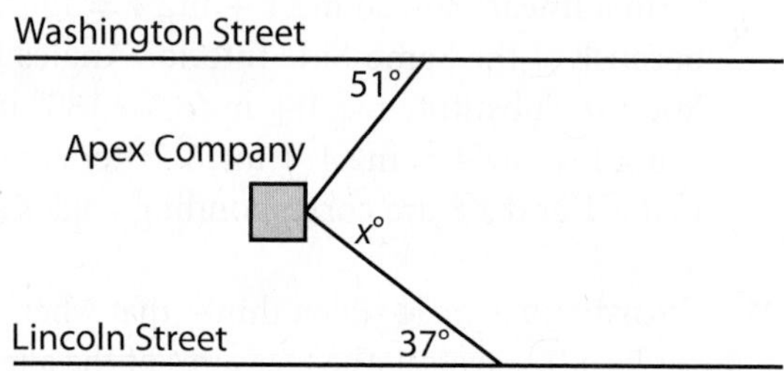

a. Find x. Explain your method.

b. Suppose that another straight road leads from the opposite side of headquarters to Washington Street, intersecting it at a $y°$ angle, and another straight road leads from headquarters to Lincoln Street, intersecting it at a $z°$ angle. Find w, the measure of the angle formed by the two roads. Explain how you found w.

4.3 Proving Lines are Parallel

Essential Question: How can you prove that two lines are parallel?

Resource Locker

Explore Writing Converses of Parallel Line Theorems

You form the **converse** of and if-then statement "if p, then q" by swapping p and q. The converses of the postulate and theorems you have learned about lines cut by a transversal are true statements. In the Explore, you will write specific cases of each of these converses.

The diagram shows two lines cut by a transversal t. Use the diagram and the given statements in Steps A–D. You will complete the statements based on your work in Steps A–D.

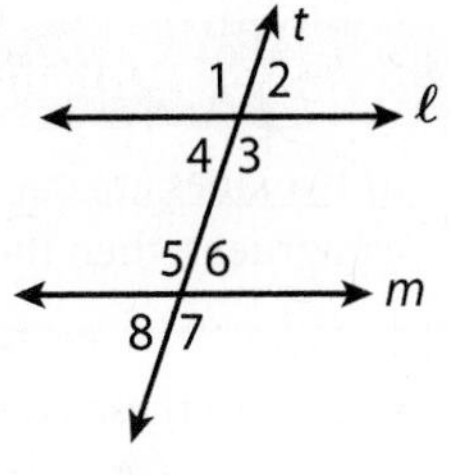

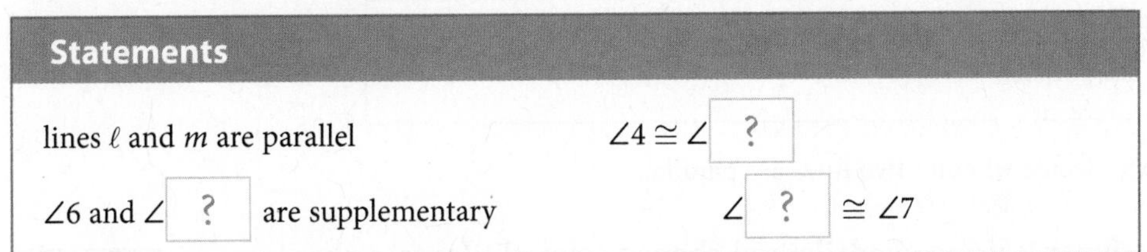

Statements	
lines ℓ and m are parallel	$\angle 4 \cong \angle$?
$\angle 6$ and $\angle$? are supplementary	$\angle$? $\cong \angle 7$

Ⓐ Use two of the given statements together to complete a statement about the diagram using the Same-Side Interior Angles Postulate.

By the postulate: If ? , then $\angle 6$ and $\angle$? are supplementary.

Ⓑ Now write the converse of the Same-Side Interior Angles Postulate using the diagram and your statement in Step A.

By its converse: If ? , then ? .

Ⓒ Repeat to illustrate the Alternate Interior Angles Theorem and its converse using the diagram and the given statements.

By the theorem: If ? , then $\angle 4 \cong \angle$? .

By its converse: If ? , then ? .

Ⓓ Use the diagram and the given statements to illustrate the Corresponding Angles Theorem and its converse.

By the theorem: If ? , then $\angle$? $\cong \angle 7$.

By its converse: ? .

Reflect

1. How do you form the converse of a statement?
2. What kind of angles are $\angle 4$ and $\angle 6$ in Step C? What does the converse you wrote in Step C mean?

Explain 1 Proving that Two Lines are Parallel

The converses from the Explore can be stated formally as a postulate and two theorems. (You will prove the converses of the theorems in the exercises.)

Converse of the Same-Side Interior Angles Postulate

If two lines are cut by a transversal so that a pair of same-side interior angles are supplementary, then the lines are parallel.

Converse of the Alternate Interior Angles Theorem

If two lines are cut by a transversal so that any pair of alternate interior angles are congruent, then the lines are parallel.

Converse of the Corresponding Angles Theorem

If two lines are cut by a transversal so that any pair of corresponding angles are congruent, then the lines are parallel.

You can use these converses to decide whether two lines are parallel.

Example 1 **A mosaic designer is using quadrilateral-shaped colored tiles to make an ornamental design. Each tile is congruent to the one shown here.**

The designer uses the colored tiles to create the pattern shown here.

(A) Use the values of the marked angles to show that the two lines ℓ_1 and ℓ_2 are parallel.

Measure of $\angle 1$: 120° Measure of $\angle 2$: 60°

Relationship between the two angles: They are supplementary.

Conclusion: $\ell_1 \parallel \ell_2$ by the Converse of the Same-Side Interior Angles Postulate.

(B) Now look at this situation. Use the values of the marked angles to show that the two lines are parallel.

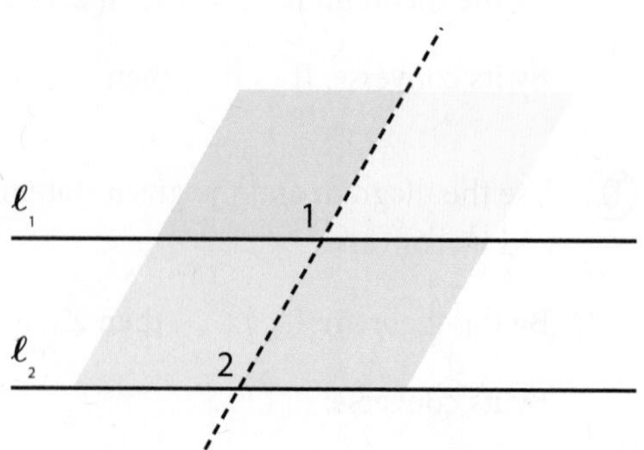

Measure of $\angle 1$: 120° Measure of $\angle 2$: 120°

Relationship between the two angles: They are congruent corresponding angles.

Conclusion:

$\ell_1 \parallel \ell_2$ by the Converse of the Corresponding Angles Theorem.

Reflect

3. **What If?** Suppose the designer had been working with this basic shape instead. Do you think the conclusions in Parts A and B would have been different? Why or why not?

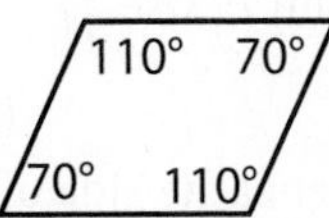

Your Turn

Explain why the lines are parallel given the angles shown. Assume that all tile patterns use this basic shape.

4.

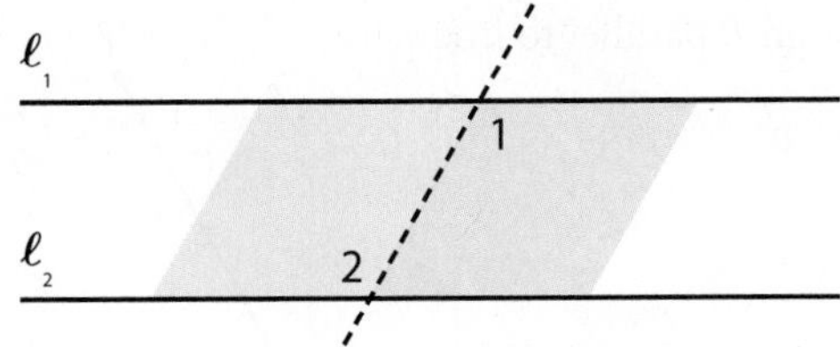

5.

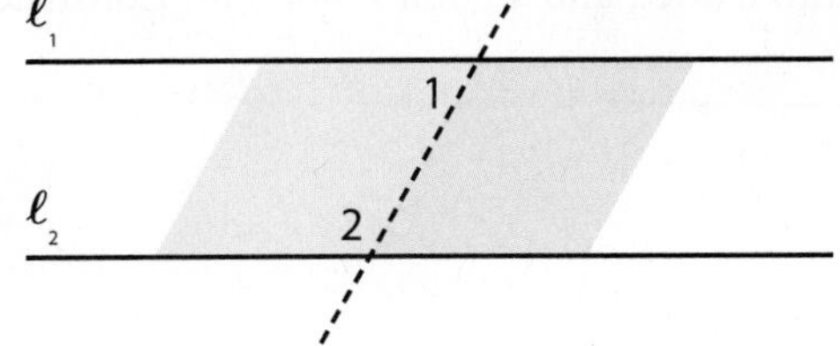

Explain 2 Constructing Parallel Lines

The Parallel Postulate guarantees that for any line ℓ, you can always construct a parallel line through a point that is not on ℓ.

The Parallel Postulate

Through a point P not on line ℓ, there is exactly one line parallel to ℓ.

Example 2 **Use a compass and straightedge to construct parallel lines.**

(A) Construct a line m through a point P not on a line ℓ so that m is parallel to ℓ.

Step 1 Draw a line ℓ and a point P not on ℓ.

Step 2 Choose two points on ℓ and label them Q and R. Use a straightedge to draw $\overleftrightarrow{PQ}$.

Step 3 Use a compass to copy $\angle PQR$ at point P, as shown, to construct line m. Line $m \parallel$ line ℓ.

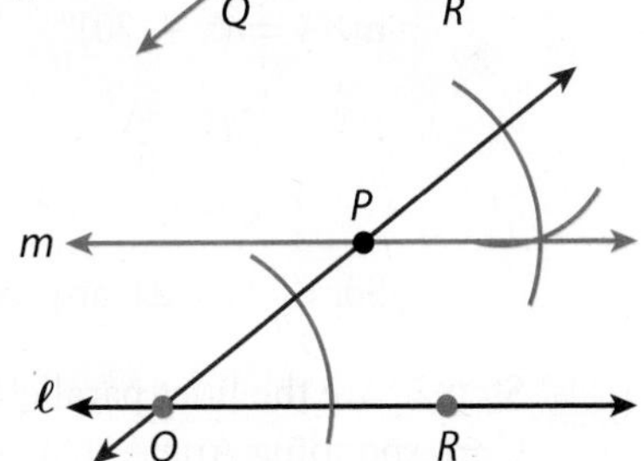

(B) Use a separate sheet of paper. Follow the steps to construct a line r through a point G not on a line s so that r is parallel to s.

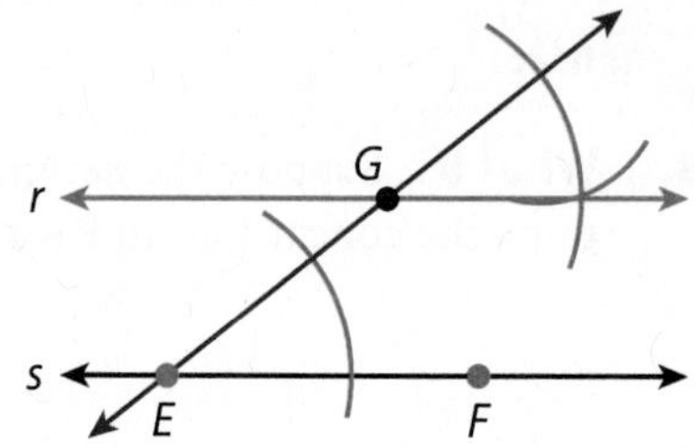

Step 1 Draw a line s and a point G not on s.

Step 2 Choose two points on s and label them E and F. Use a straightedge to draw $\overleftrightarrow{GE}$.

Step 3 Use a compass to copy $\angle GEF$ at point G. Label the side of the angle as line r. Line $r \parallel$ line s.

Reflect

6. **Discussion** Explain how you know that the construction in Part A or Part B produces a line passing through the given point that is parallel to the given line.

Your Turn

7. Draw a line ℓ and a point P not on ℓ. Construct a line m through P parallel to line ℓ.

Explain 3 Using Angle Pair Relationships to Verify Lines are Parallel

When two lines are cut by a transversal, you can use relationships of pairs of angles to decide if the lines are parallel.

Example 3 **Use the given angle relationships to decide whether the lines are parallel. Explain your reasoning.**

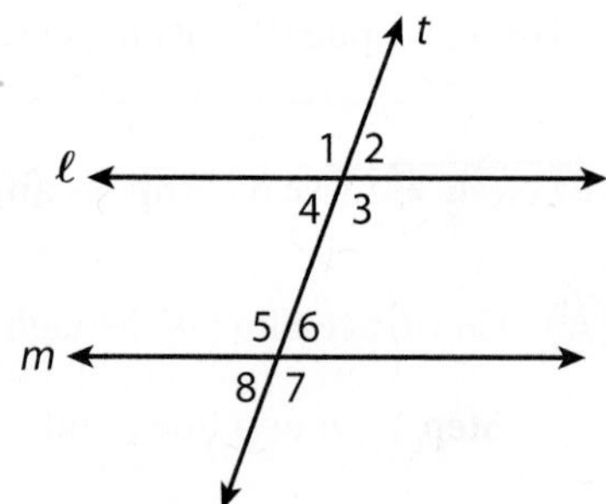

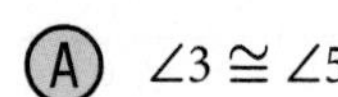

(A) $\angle 3 \cong \angle 5$

Step 1 Identify the relationship between the two angles.
$\angle 3$ and $\angle 5$ are congruent alternate interior angles.

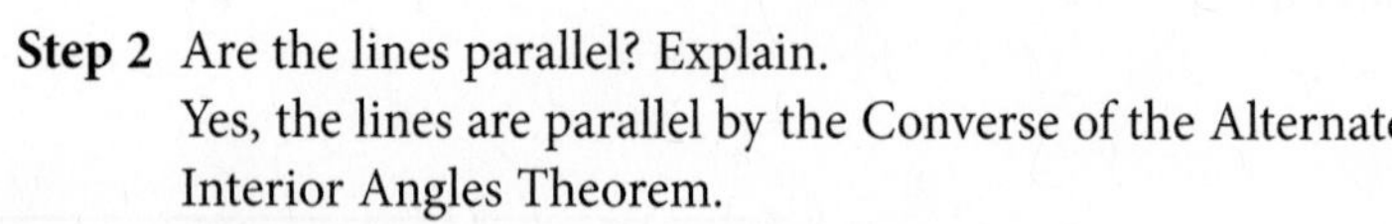

Step 2 Are the lines parallel? Explain.
Yes, the lines are parallel by the Converse of the Alternate Interior Angles Theorem.

(B) $m\angle 4 = (x + 20)°$, $m\angle 8 = (2x + 5)°$, and $x = 15$.

Step 1 Identify the relationship between the two angles.

$m\angle 4 = (x + 20)°$ $= \left(\boxed{15} + 20 \right)° = \boxed{35°}$

$m\angle 8 = (2x + 5)°$ $= \left(2 \cdot \boxed{15} + 5 \right)° = \boxed{35°}$

So, $\angle 4$ and $\angle 8$ are congruent corresponding angles.

Step 2 Are the lines parallel? Explain. Yes, the lines are parallel by the Converse of the Corresponding Angles Theorem.

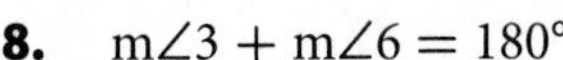

Your Turn

Identify the type of angle pair described in the given condition. How do you know that lines ℓ and m are parallel?

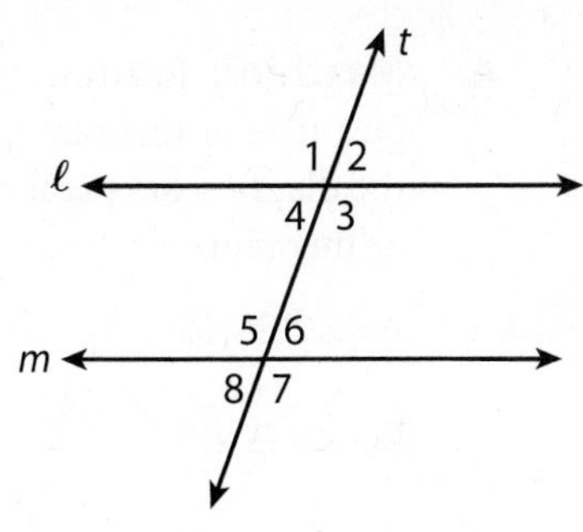

8. $m\angle 3 + m\angle 6 = 180°$

9. $\angle 2 \cong \angle 6$

Elaborate

10. How are the converses in this lesson different from the postulate/theorems in the previous lesson?

11. **What If?** Suppose two lines are cut by a transversal such that alternate interior angles are both congruent and supplementary. Describe the lines.

12. **Essential Question Check-In** Name two ways to test if a pair of lines is parallel, using the interior angles formed by a transversal crossing the two lines.

Evaluate: Homework and Practice

- Online Homework
- Hints and Help
- Extra Practice

Complete the statements below. Then use the statements and the diagram in Exercises 1–3.

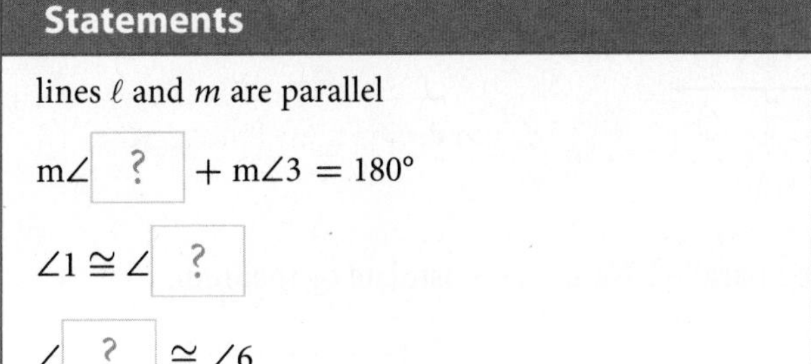

Statements
lines ℓ and m are parallel
$m\angle$? $+ m\angle 3 = 180°$
$\angle 1 \cong \angle$?
$\angle$? $\cong \angle 6$

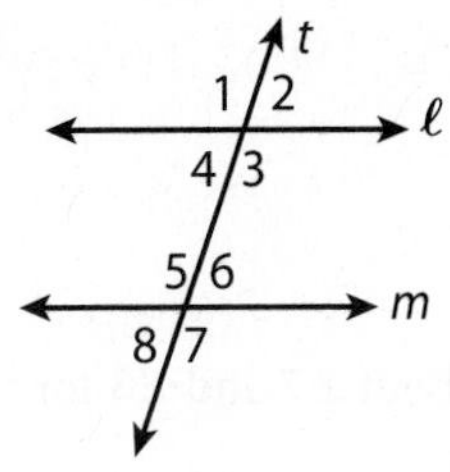

1. Use two of the given statements together to complete statements about the diagram to illustrate the Corresponding Angles Theorem. Then write its converse.

By the theorem: If ? , then $\angle 1 \cong \angle$? .

By its converse: ?

2. Use two of the given statements together to complete statements about the diagram to illustrate the Same-Side Interior Angles Postulate. Then write its converse.

By the postulate: If ? , then $m\angle$? $+ m\angle 3 = 180°$.

By its converse: ?

3. Use two of the given statements together to complete statements about the diagram to illustrate the Alternate Interior Angles Theorem. Then write its converse.

By the theorem: If ? , then $\angle$? $\cong \angle 6$.

By its converse: ?

4. **Matching** Justify each angle pair relationship with the name of a postulate or theorem that you could use to prove that lines ℓ and m in the diagram are parallel. Several angle pairs may use the same postulate or theorem.

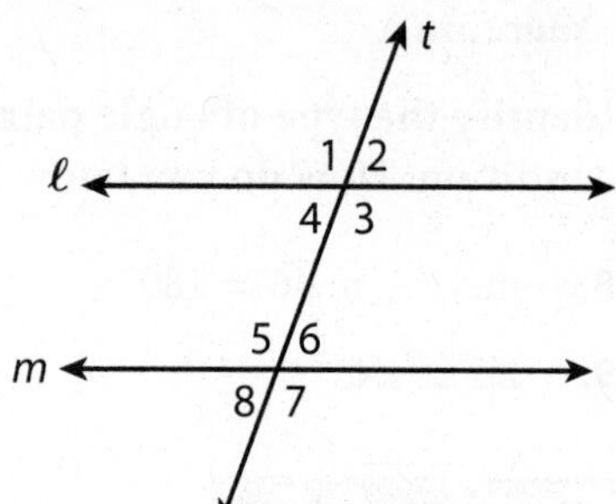

A. $\angle 2 \cong \angle 6$

B. $\angle 3 \cong \angle 5$

C. $\angle 4$ and $\angle 5$ are supplementary.

D. $\angle 4 \cong \angle 8$

E. $m\angle 3 + m\angle 6 = 180°$

F. $\angle 4 \cong \angle 6$

a. ___?___ Converse of the Corresponding Angles Theorem

b. ___?___ Converse of the Same-Side Interior Angles Postulate

c. ___?___ Converse of the Alternate Interior Angles Theorem

Use the diagram for Exercises 5–8.

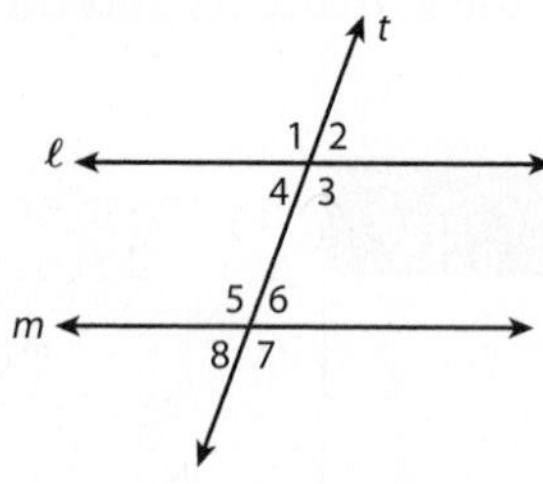

5. What must be true about $\angle 7$ and $\angle 3$ for the lines to be parallel? Name the postulate or theorem.

6. What must be true about $\angle 6$ and $\angle 3$ for the lines to be parallel? Name the postulate or theorem.

7. Suppose $m\angle 4 = (3x + 5)°$ and $m\angle 5 = (x + 95)°$, where $x = 20$. Are the lines parallel? Explain.

8. Suppose $m\angle 3 = (4x + 12)°$ and $m\angle 7 = (80 - x)°$, where $x = 15$. Are the lines parallel? Explain.

Use a converse to answer each question.

9. What value of x makes the horizontal parts of the letter Z parallel?

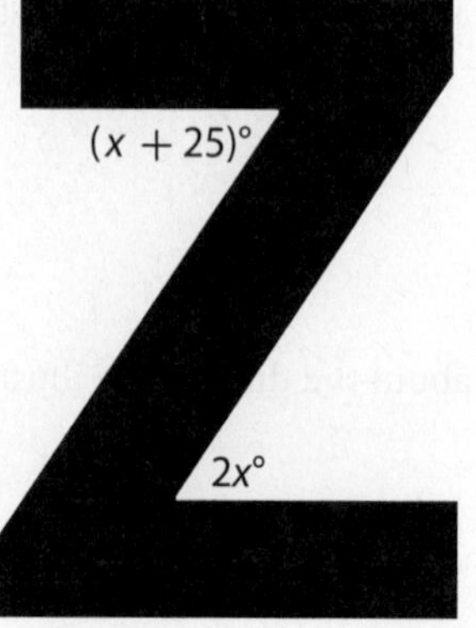

10. What value of x makes the vertical parts of the letter N parallel?

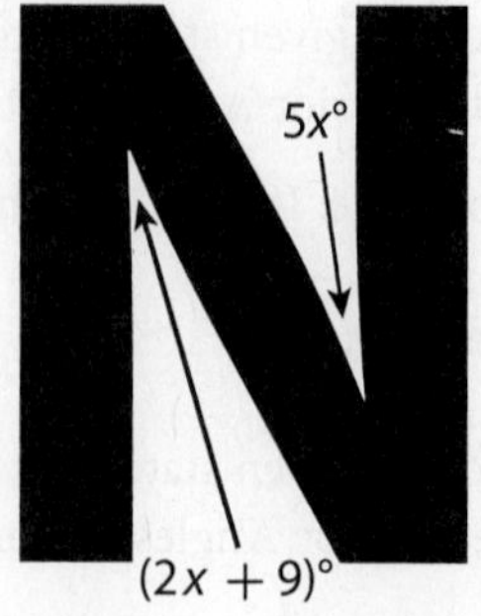

11. Engineering An overpass intersects two lanes of a highway. What must the value of x be to ensure the two lanes are parallel?

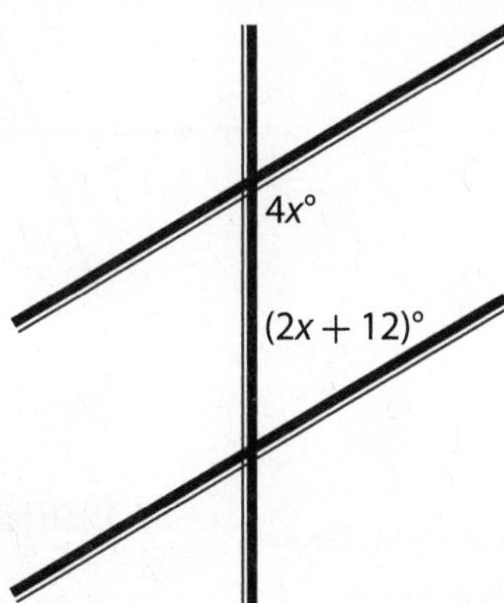

12. A trellis consists of overlapping wooden slats. What must the value of x be in order for the two slats to be parallel?

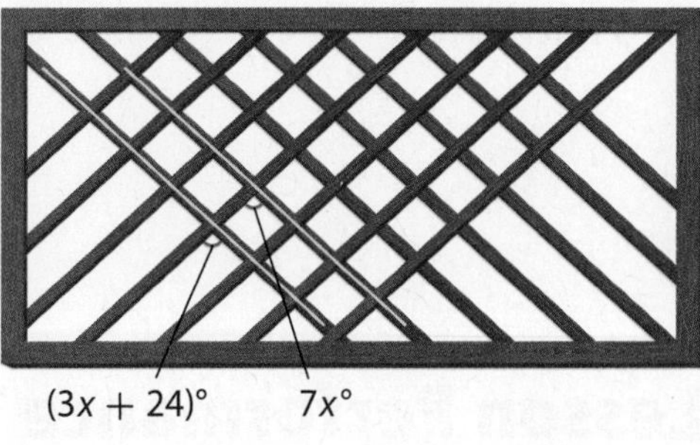

13. Draw a line ℓ and a point P not on ℓ. line parallel to ℓ that passes through P.

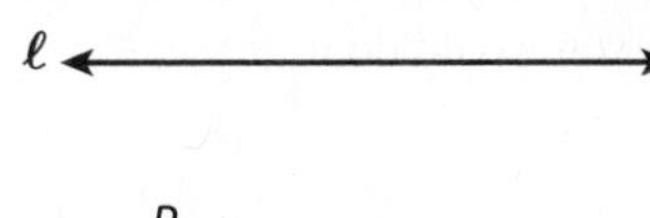

14. Communicate Mathematical Ideas In Exercise 13, how many parallel lines can you draw through P that are parallel to ℓ? Explain.

H.O.T. Focus on Higher Order Thinking

15. Justify Reasoning Write a two-column proof of the Converse of the Alternate Interior Angles Theorem.

Given: lines ℓ and m are cut by a transversal t; $\angle 1 \cong \angle 2$

Prove: $\ell \parallel m$

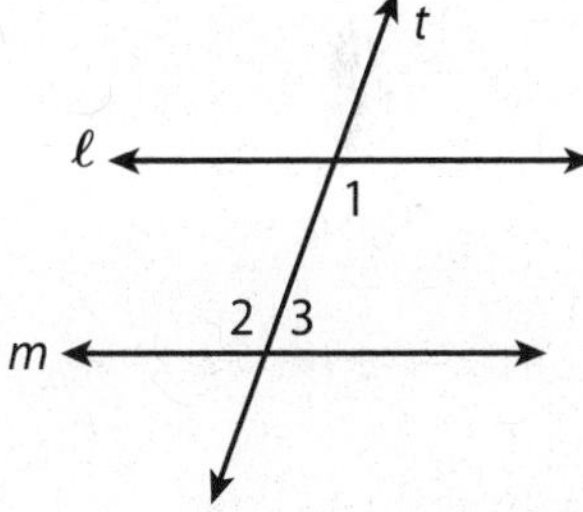

16. Justify Reasoning Write a two-column proof of the Converse of the Corresponding Angles Theorem.

Given: lines ℓ and m are cut by a transversal t; $\angle 1 \cong \angle 2$

Prove: $\ell \parallel m$

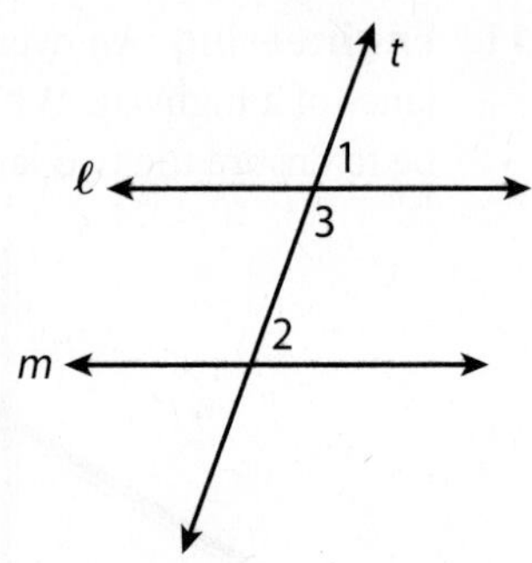

Lesson Performance Task

A simplified street map of a section of Harlem in New York City is shown at right. Draw a sketch of the rectangle bounded by West 110th Street and West 121st Street in one direction and Eighth Avenue and Lenox Avenue in the other. Include all the streets and avenues that run between sides of the rectangle. Show St. Nicholas Avenue as a diagonal of the rectangle.

Now imagine that you have been given the job of laying out these streets and avenues on a bare plot of land. Explain in detail how you would do it.

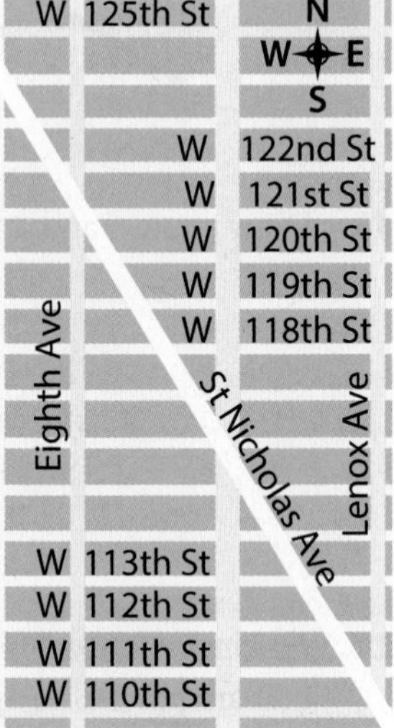

4.4 Perpendicular Lines

Essential Question: What are the key ideas about perpendicular bisectors of a segment?

Resource Locker

Explore Constructing Perpendicular Bisectors and Perpendicular Lines

You can construct geometric figures without using measurement tools like a ruler or a protractor. By using geometric relationships and a compass and a straightedge, you can construct geometric figures with greater precision than figures drawn with standard measurement tools.

In Steps A–C, construct the perpendicular bisector of $\overline{AB}$.

(A) Place the point of the compass at point A. Using a compass setting that is greater than half the length of $\overline{AB}$, draw an arc.

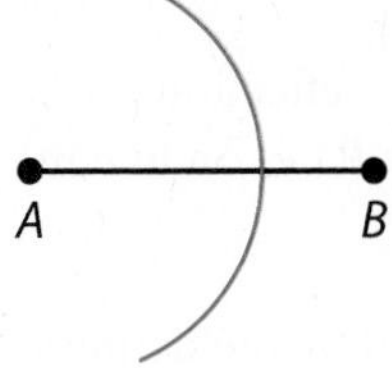

(B) Without adjusting the compass, place the point of the compass at point B and draw an arc intersecting the first arc in two places. Label the points of intersection C and D.

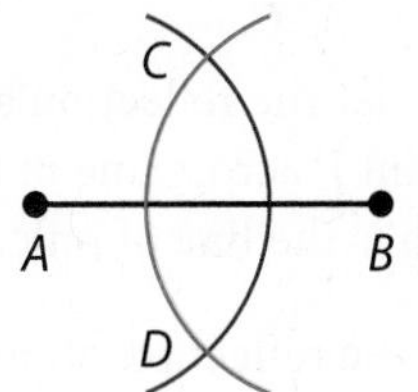

(C) Use a straightedge to draw $\overline{CD}$, which is the perpendicular bisector of $\overline{AB}$.

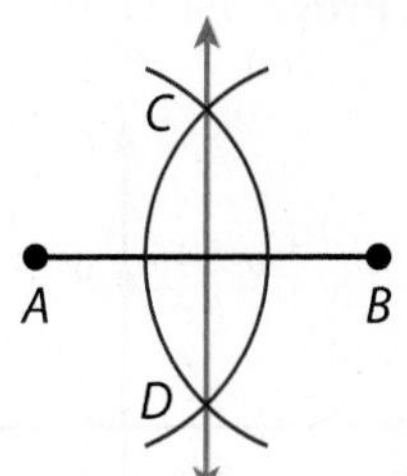

In Steps D–E, construct a line perpendicular to a line ℓ that passes through some point P that is not on ℓ.

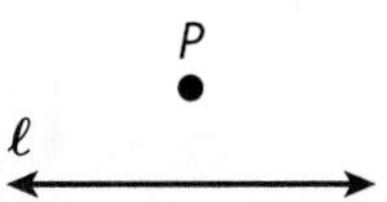

(D) Place the point of the compass at P. Draw an arc that intersects line ℓ at two points, A and B.

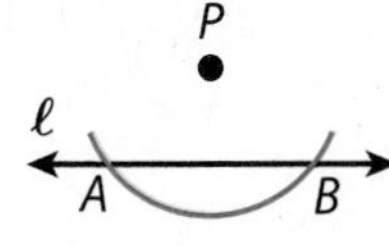

(E) Use the methods in Steps A–C to construct the perpendicular bisector of $\overline{AB}$.

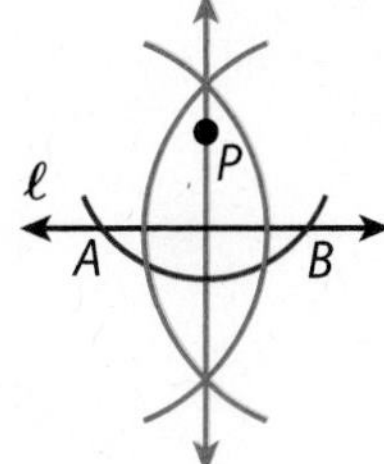

Because it is the perpendicular bisector of $\overline{AB}$, then the constructed line through P is perpendicular to line ℓ.

Reflect

1. In Step A of the first construction, why do you open the compass to a setting that is greater than half the length of $\overline{AB}$?

2. **What If?** Suppose Q is a point *on* line ℓ. Is the construction of a line perpendicular to ℓ through Q any different than constructing a perpendicular line through a point P *not* on the line, as in Steps D and E?

Explain 1 Proving the Perpendicular Bisector Theorem Using Reflections

You can use reflections and their properties to prove a theorem about perpendicular bisectors. These theorems will be useful in proofs later on.

Perpendicular Bisector Theorem

If a point is on the perpendicular bisector of a segment, then it is equidistant from the endpoints of the segment.

Example 1 **Prove the Perpendicular Bisector Theorem.**

Given: P is on the perpendicular bisector m of $\overline{AB}$.

Prove: $PA = PB$

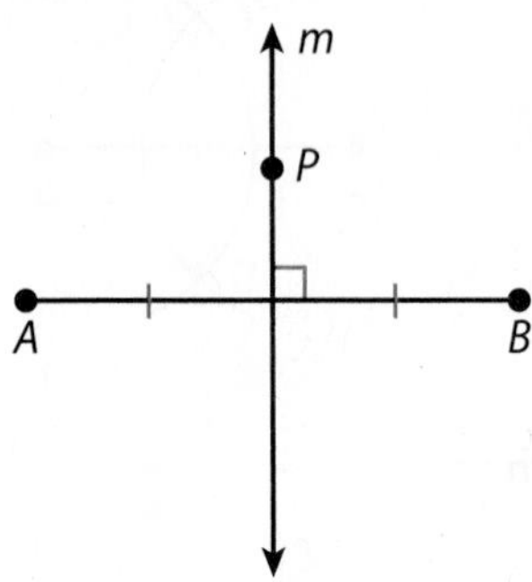

Consider the reflection across line m. Then the reflection of point P across line m is also P because point P lies on line m, which is the line of reflection.

Also, the reflection of point A across line m is B by the definition of reflection.

Therefore, $PA = PB$ because reflection preserves distance.

Reflect

3. **Discussion** What conclusion can you make about $\triangle KLJ$ in the diagram using the Perpendicular Bisector Theorem?

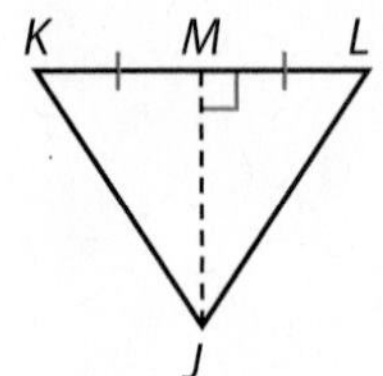

Your Turn

Use the diagram shown. $\overline{BD}$ is the perpendicular bisector of $\overline{AC}$.

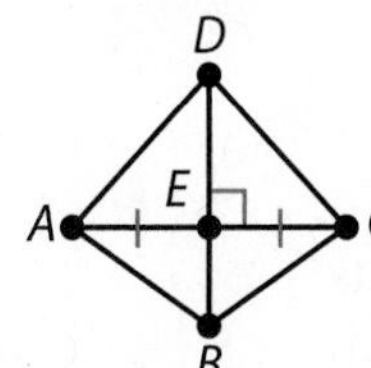

4. Suppose $ED = 16$ cm and $DA = 20$ cm. Find DC.

5. Suppose $EC = 15$ cm and $BA = 25$ cm. Find BC.

Explain 2 Proving the Converse of the Perpendicular Bisector Theorem

The converse of the Perpendicular Bisector Theorem is also true. In order to prove the converse, you will use an *indirect proof* and the *Pythagorean Theorem.*

In an **indirect proof**, you assume that the statement you are trying to prove is false. Then you use logic to lead to a contradiction of given information, a definition, a postulate, or a previously proven theorem. You can then conclude that the assumption was false and the original statement is true.

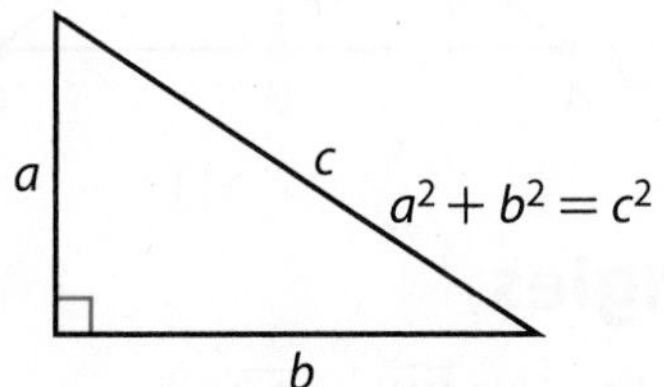

Recall that the Pythagorean Theorem states that for a right triangle with legs of length a and b and a hypotenuse of length c, $a^2 + b^2 = c^2$.

Converse of the Perpendicular Bisector Theorem

If a point is equidistant from the endpoints of a segment, then it lies on the perpendicular bisector of the segment.

Example 2 **Prove the Converse of the Perpendicular Bisector Theorem**

Given: $PA = PB$

Prove: P is on the perpendicular bisector m of $\overline{AB}$.

Step A: Assume what you are trying to prove is false.

Assume that P is *not* on the perpendicular bisector m of $\overline{AB}$. Then, when you draw a perpendicular line from P to the line containing A and B, it intersects $\overline{AB}$ at point Q, which is not the midpoint of $\overline{AB}$.

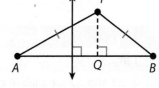

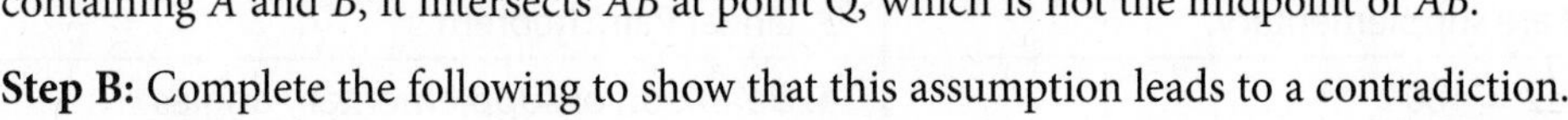

Step B: Complete the following to show that this assumption leads to a contradiction.

$\overline{PQ}$ forms two right triangles, $\triangle AQP$ and $\triangle BQP$.

So, $AQ^2 + QP^2 = PA^2$ and $BQ^2 + QP^2 =$ PB^2 by the Pythagorean Theorem.

Subtract these equations:

$AQ^2 + QP^2 = PA^2$

$BQ^2 + QP^2 = PB^2$

$AQ^2 - BQ^2 = PA^2 - PB^2$

However, $PA^2 - PB^2 = 0$ because $PA = PB$.

Therefore, $AQ^2 - BQ^2 = 0$. This means that $AQ^2 = BQ^2$ and $AQ = BQ$. This contradicts the fact that Q is not the midpoint of $\overline{AB}$. Thus, the initial assumption must be incorrect, and P must lie on the perpendicular bisector of $\overline{AB}$.

Reflect

6. In the proof, once you know $AQ^2 = BQ^2$, why can you conclude that $AQ = BQ$?

Your Turn

7. $\overline{AD}$ is 10 inches long. $\overline{BD}$ is 6 inches long. Find the length of $\overline{AC}$.

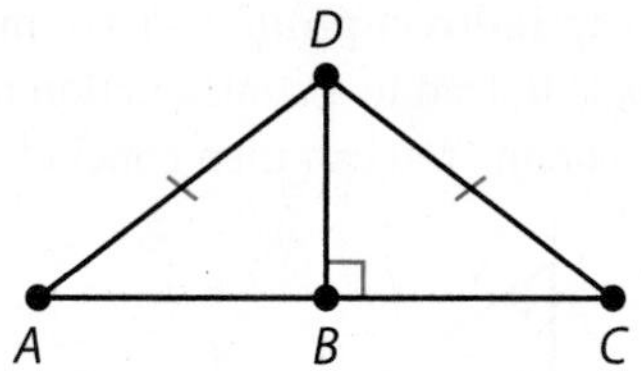

Explain 3 Proving Theorems about Right Angles

The symbol ⊥ means that two figures are perpendicular. For example, $\ell \perp m$ or $\overleftrightarrow{XY} \perp \overline{AB}$.

Example 3 **Prove each theorem about right angles.**

(A) If two lines intersect to form one right angle, then they are perpendicular and they intersect to form four right angles.

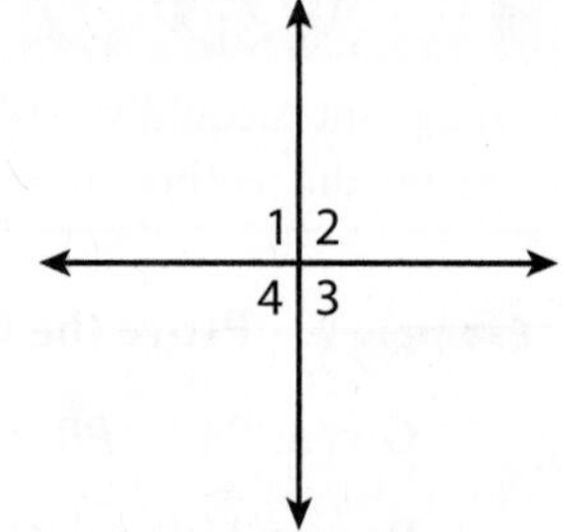

Given: m∠1 = 90° **Prove:** m∠2 = 90°, m∠3 = 90°, m∠4 = 90°

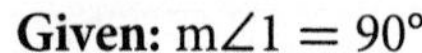

Statement	Reason
1. m∠1 = 90°	**1.** Given
2. ∠1 and ∠2 are a linear pair.	**2.** Given
3. ∠1 and ∠2 are supplementary.	**3.** Linear Pair Theorem
4. m∠1 + m∠2 = 180°	**4.** Definition of supplementary angles
5. 90° + m∠2 = 180°	**5.** Substitution Property of Equality
6. m∠2 = 90°	**6.** Subtraction Property of Equality
7. m∠2 = m∠4	**7.** Vertical Angles Theorem
8. m∠4 = 90°	**8.** Substitution Property of Equality
9. m∠1 = m∠3	**9.** Vertical Angles Theorem
10. m∠3 = 90°	**10.** Substitution Property of Equality

(B) If two intersecting lines form a linear pair of angles with equal measures, then the lines are perpendicular.

Given: $m\angle 1 = m\angle 2$ **Prove:** $\ell \perp m$

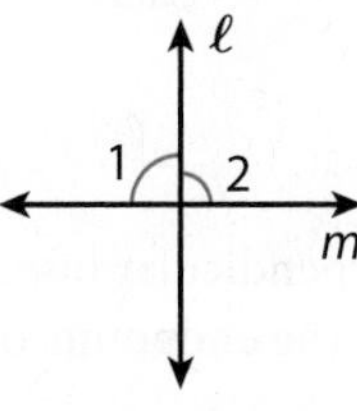

By the diagram, $\angle 1$ and $\angle 2$ form a linear pair so $\angle 1$ and $\angle 2$ are supplementary by the Linear Pair Theorem. By the definition of supplementary angles, $m\angle 1 + m\angle 2 = 180°$. It is also given that $m\angle 1 = m\angle 2$, so $m\angle 1 + m\angle 1 = 180°$ by the Substitution Property of Equality. Adding gives $2 \cdot m\angle 1 = 180°$, and $m\angle 1 = 90°$ by the Division Property of Equality. Therefore, $\angle 1$ is a right angle and $\ell \perp m$ by the definition of perpendicular lines.

Reflect

8. State the converse of the theorem in Part B. Is the converse true?

Your Turn

9. Given: $b \parallel d$, $c \parallel e$, $m\angle 1 = 50°$, and $m\angle 5 = 90°$. Use the diagram to find $m\angle 4$.

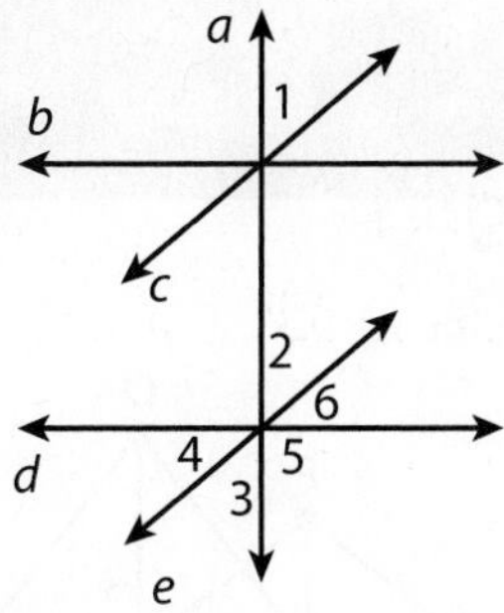

Elaborate

10. Discussion Explain how the converse of the Perpendicular Bisector Theorem justifies the compass-and-straightedge construction of the perpendicular bisector of a segment.

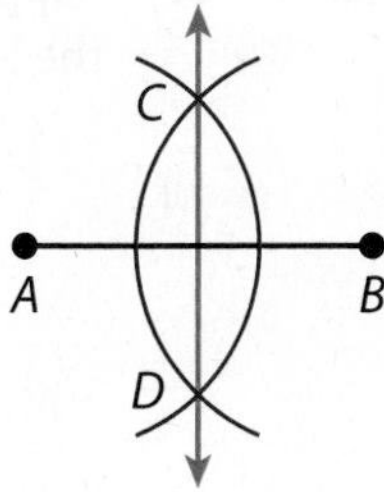

11. Essential Question Check-In How can you construct perpendicular lines and prove theorems about perpendicular bisectors?

Evaluate: Homework and Practice

- Online Homework
- Hints and Help
- Extra Practice

1. How can you construct a line perpendicular to line ℓ that passes through point P using paper folding?

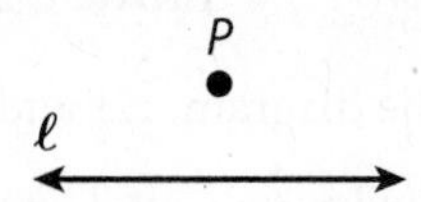

2. **Check for Reasonableness** How can you use a ruler and a protractor to check the construction in Elaborate Exercise 10?

3. Describe the point on the perpendicular bisector of a segment that is closest to the endpoints of the segment.

4. **Represent Real-World Problems** A field of soybeans is watered by a rotating irrigation system. The watering arm, $\overline{CD}$, rotates around its center point. To show the area of the crop of soybeans that will be watered, construct a circle with diameter CD.

Use the diagram to find the lengths. $\overline{BP}$ is the perpendicular bisector of $\overline{AC}$. $\overline{CQ}$ is the perpendicular bisector of $\overline{BD}$. $AB = BC = CD$.

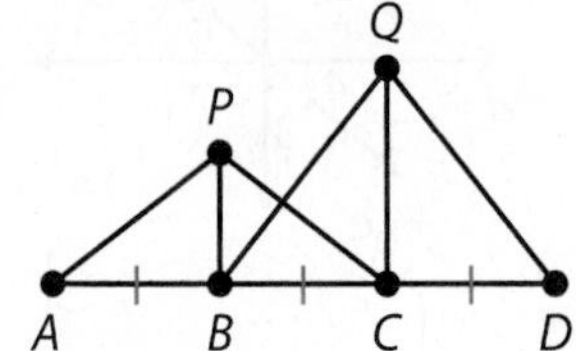

5. Suppose $AP = 5$ cm. What is the length of $\overline{PC}$?

6. Suppose $AP = 5$ cm and $BQ = 8$ cm. What is the length of $\overline{QD}$?

7. Suppose $AC = 12$ cm and $QD = 10$ cm. What is the length of $\overline{QC}$?

8. Suppose $PB = 3$ cm and $AD = 12$ cm . What is the length of $\overline{PC}$?

Given: $PA = PC$ and $BA = BC$. Use the diagram to find the lengths or angle measures described.

9. Suppose $m\angle 2 = 38°$. Find $m\angle 1$.

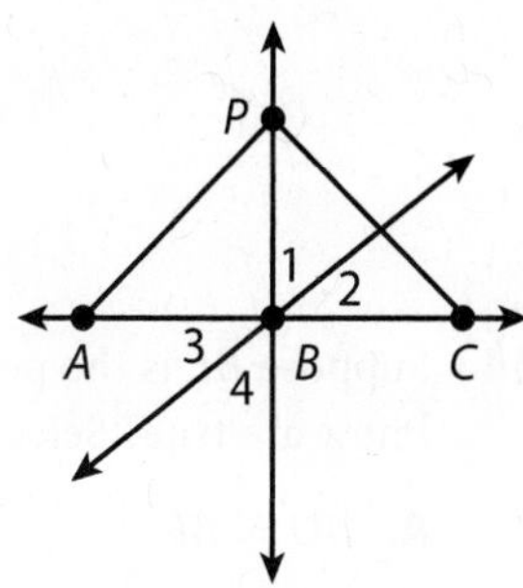

10. Suppose $PA = 10$ cm and $PB = 6$ cm. What is the length of $\overline{AC}$?

11. Find $m\angle 3 + m\angle 4$.

Given: $m \parallel n$, $x \parallel y$, and $y \perp m$. Use the diagram to find the angle measures.

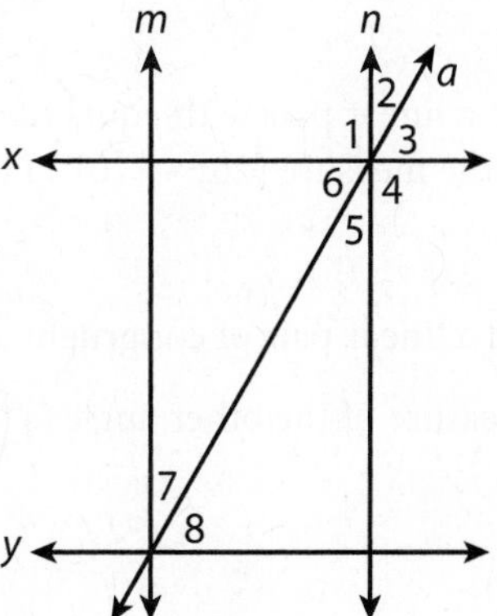

12. Suppose $m\angle 7 = 30°$. Find $m\angle 3$.

13. Suppose $m\angle 1 = 90°$. What is $m\angle 2 + m\angle 3 + m\angle 5 + m\angle 6$?

Use this diagram of trusses for a railroad bridge in Exercise 14.

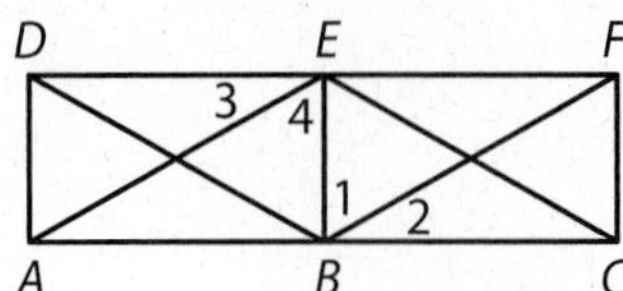

14. Suppose $\overline{BE}$ is the perpendicular bisector of $\overline{DF}$. Which of the following statements do you know are true? Select all that apply. Explain your reasoning.

A. $BD = BF$

B. $m\angle 1 + m\angle 2 = 90°$

C. E is the midpoint of $\overline{DF}$.

D. $m\angle 3 + m\angle 4 = 90°$

E. $\overline{DA} \perp \overline{AC}$

15. Algebra Two lines intersect to form a linear pair with equal measures. One angle has the measure $2x°$ and the other angle has the measure $(20y - 10)°$. Find the values of x and y. Explain your reasoning.

16. Algebra Two lines intersect to form a linear pair of congruent angles. The measure of one angle is $(8x + 10)°$ and the measure of the other angle is $\left(\frac{15y}{2}\right)°$. Find the values of x and y. Explain your reasoning.

H.O.T. Focus on Higher Order Thinking

17. Communicate Mathematical Ideas The valve pistons on a trumpet are all perpendicular to the lead pipe. Explain why the valve pistons must be parallel to each other.

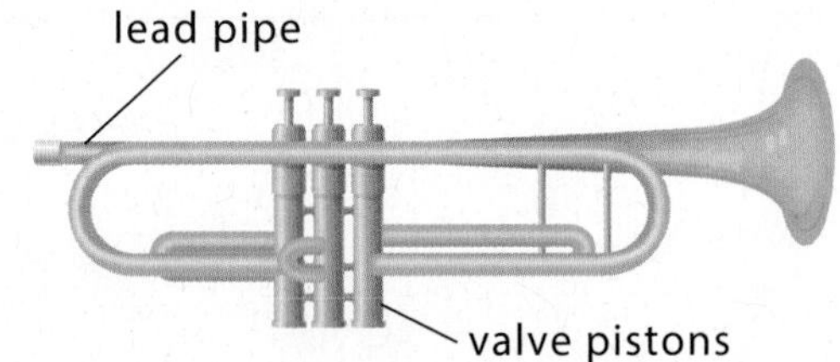

18. Justify Reasoning Prove the theorem: In a plane, if a transversal is perpendicular to one of two parallel lines, then it is perpendicular to the other.

Given: $\overline{RS} \perp \overline{CD}$ and $\overline{AB} \parallel \overline{CD}$ Prove: $\overline{RS} \perp \overline{AB}$

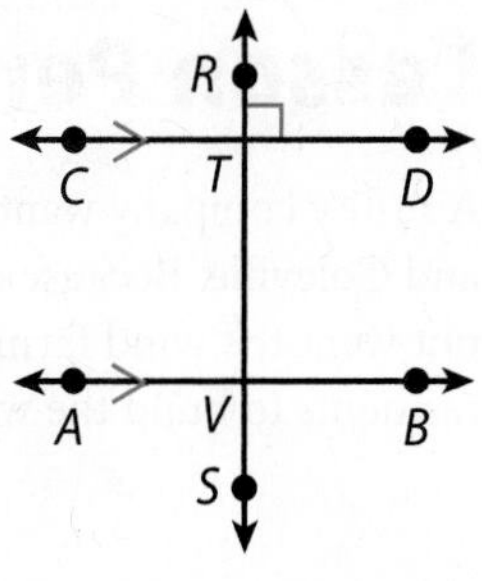

19. Analyze Mathematical Relationships Complete the indirect proof to show that two supplementary angles cannot both be obtuse angles.

Given: $\angle 1$ and $\angle 2$ are supplementary.

Prove: $\angle 1$ and $\angle 2$ cannot both be obtuse.

Assume that two supplementary angles *can* both be obtuse angles. So, assume that

$\angle 1$ and $\angle 2$ __?__. Then $m\angle 1 > 90°$ and $m\angle 2 >$ [?]

by __?__. Adding the two inequalities,

$m\angle 1 + m\angle 2 >$ [?]. However, by the definition of supplementary angles,

__?__. So $m\angle 1 + m\angle 2 > 180°$ contradicts the given information.

This means the assumption is __?__, and therefore __?__.

Lesson Performance Task

A utility company wants to build a wind farm to provide electricity to the towns of Acton, Baxter, and Coleville. Because of concerns about noise from the turbines, the residents of all three towns do not want the wind farm built close to where they live. The company comes to an agreement with the residents to build the wind farm at a location that is equally distant from all three towns.

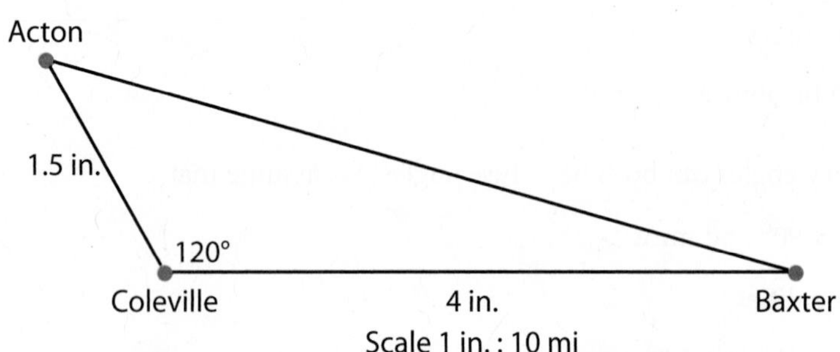

a. Use the drawing to draw a diagram of the locations of the towns using a scale of 1 in. : 10 mi. Draw the 4-inch and 1.5-inch lines with a 120° angle between them. Write the actual distances between the towns on your diagram.

b. Estimate where you think the wind farm will be located.

c. Use what you have learned in this lesson to find the exact location of the wind farm. What is the approximate distance from the wind farm to each of the three towns?

4.5 Equations of Parallel and Perpendicular Lines

Essential Question: How can you find the equation of a line that is parallel or perpendicular to a given line?

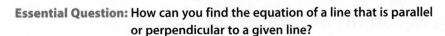

Explore Exploring Slopes of Lines

Recall that the *slope* of a straight line in a coordinate plane is the ratio of the *rise* to the *run*. In the figure, the slope of $\overline{AB}$ is $\frac{\text{rise}}{\text{run}} = \frac{4}{8} = \frac{1}{2}$.

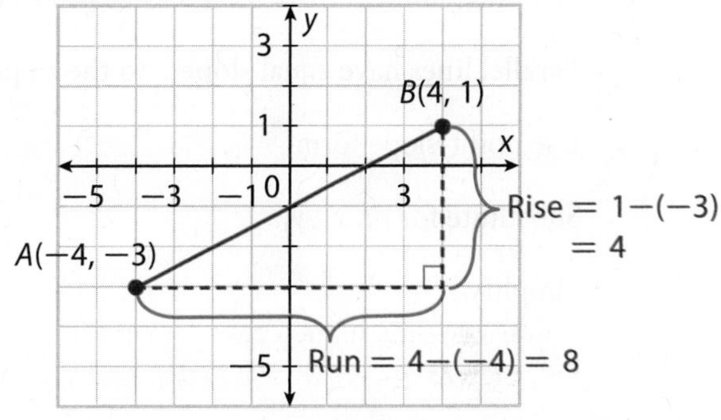

(A) Graph the equations $y = 2(x + 1)$ and $y = 2x - 3$.

(B) What do you notice about the graphs of the two lines? About the slopes of the lines?

(C) The graphs of $x + 3y = 22$ and $y = 3x - 14$ are shown. Use a protractor. What is the measure of the angle formed by the intersection of the lines. What does that tell you about the lines?

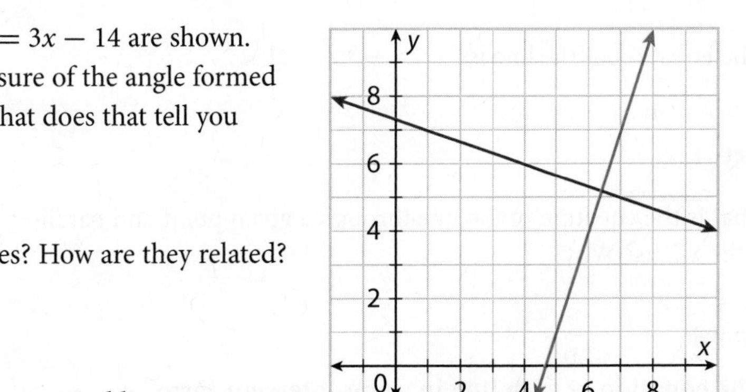

(D) What are the slopes of the two lines? How are they related?

(E) Complete the statements: If two nonvertical lines

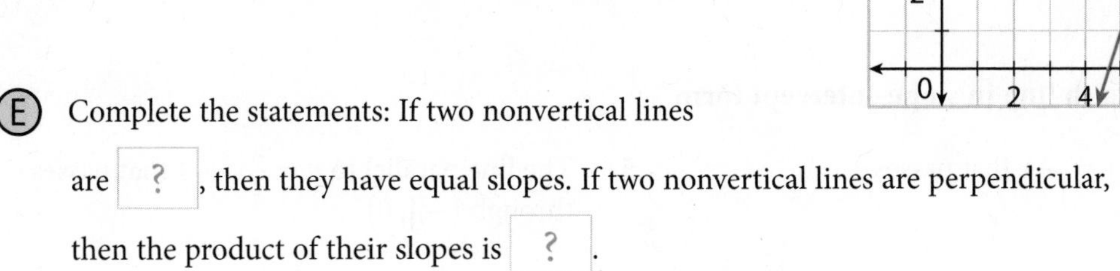

are ? , then they have equal slopes. If two nonvertical lines are perpendicular, then the product of their slopes is ? .

Reflect

1. Your friend says that if two lines have opposite slopes, they are perpendicular. He uses the slopes 1 and –1 as examples. Do you agree with your friend? Explain.

2. The frets on a guitar are all perpendicular to one of the strings. Explain why the frets must be parallel to each other.

Explain 1 Writing Equations of Parallel Lines

You can use slope relationships to write an equation of a line parallel to a given line.

Example 1 **Write the equation of each line in slope-intercept form.**

(A) The line parallel to $y = 5x + 1$ that passes through $(-1, 2)$

Parallel lines have equal slopes. So the slope of the required line is 5.

Use point-slope form. $y - y_1 = m(x - x_1)$

Substitute for m, x_1, y_1. $y - 2 = 5(x - (-1))$

Simplify. $y - 2 = 5x + 5$

Solve for y. $y = 5x + 7$

The equation of the line is $y = 5x + 7$.

(B) The line parallel to $y = -3x + 4$ that passes through $(9, -6)$

Parallel lines have equal slopes. So the slope of the required line is -3.

Use point-slope form. $y - y_1 = m(x - x_1)$

Substitute for m, x_1, y_1. $y - (-6) = -3(x - 9)$

Simplify. $y + 6 = -3x + 27$

Solve for y. $y = -3x + 21$

The equation of the line is $y = -3x + 21$.

Reflect

3. What is the equation of the line through a given point and parallel to the x-axis? Why?

Your Turn

Write the equation of each line in slope-intercept form.

4. The line parallel to $y = -x$ that passes through $(5, 2.5)$

5. The line parallel to $y = \frac{3}{2}x + 4$ that passes through $(-4, 0)$

Explain 2 Writing Equations of Perpendicular Lines

You can use slope relationships to write an equation of a line perpendicular to a given line.

Example 2 **Write the equation of each line in slope-intercept form.**

(A) The line perpendicular to $y = 4x - 2$ that passes through $(3, -1)$

Perpendicular lines have slopes that are opposite reciprocals, which means that the product of the slopes will be -1. So the slope of the required line is $-\frac{1}{4}$.

$y - y_1 = m(x - x_1)$	Use point-slope form.
$y - (-1) = -\frac{1}{4}(x - 3)$	Substitute for m, x_1, y_1.
$y + 1 = -\frac{1}{4}x + \frac{3}{4}$	Simplify.
$y = -\frac{1}{4}x - \frac{1}{4}$	Solve for y.

The equation of the line is $y = -\frac{1}{4}x - \frac{1}{4}$.

(B) The line perpendicular to $y = -\frac{2}{5}x + 12$ that passes through $(-6, -8)$

The product of the slopes of perpendicular lines is -1. So the slope of the required line is $\frac{5}{2}$.

$y - y_1 = m(x - x_1)$	Use point-slope form.
$y - -8 = \frac{5}{2}\left(x - -6\right)$	Substitute for m, x_1, y_1.
$y + 8 = \frac{5}{2}x + 15$	Simplify.
$y = \frac{5}{2}x + 7$	Solve for y.

The equation of the line is $y = \frac{5}{2}x + 7$.

Reflect

6. A carpenter's square forms a right angle. A carpenter places the square so that one side is parallel to an edge of a board, and then draws a line along the other side of the square. Then he slides the square to the right and draws a second line. Why must the two lines be parallel?

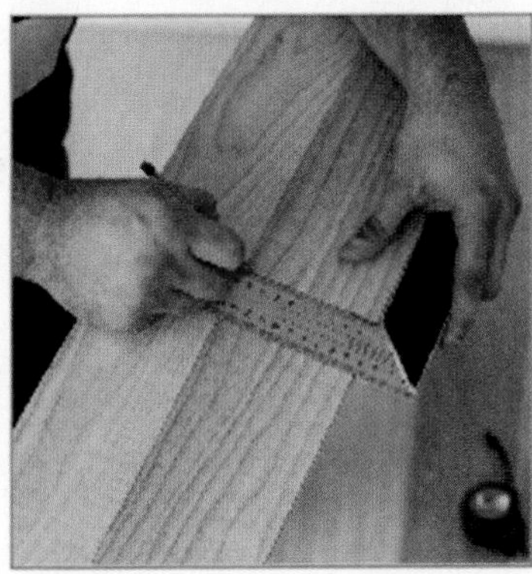

Your Turn

Write the equation of each line in slope-intercept form.

7. The line perpendicular to $y = \frac{3}{2}x + 2$ that passes through $(3, -1)$

8. The line perpendicular to $y = -4x$ that passes through $(0, 0)$

Elaborate

9. **Discussion** Would it make sense to find the equation of a line parallel to a given line, and through a point on the given line? Explain.

10. Would it make sense to find the equation of a line perpendicular to a given line, and through a point on the given line? Explain.

11. **Essential Question Check-In** How are the slopes of parallel lines and perpendicular lines related? Assume the lines are not vertical.

Evaluate: Homework and Practice

- Online Homework
- Hints and Help
- Extra Practice

Use the graph for Exercises 1–4.

1. A line with a positive slope is parallel to one of the lines shown. What is its slope?

2. A line with a negative slope is perpendicular to one of the lines shown. What is its slope?

3. A line with a positive slope is perpendicular to one of the lines shown. What is its slope?

4. A line with a negative slope is parallel to one of the lines shown. What is its slope?

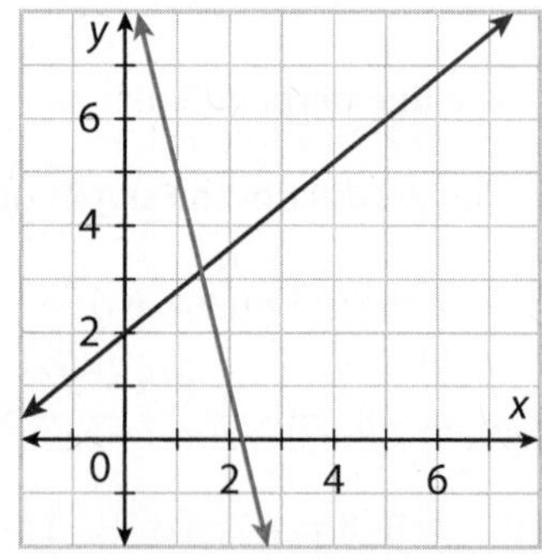

Find the equation of the line that is parallel to the given line and passes through the given point.

5. $y = -3x + 1$; $(9, 0)$

6. $y = 0.6x - 3$; $(-2, 2)$

7. $y = 5(x + 1)$; $\left(\frac{1}{2}, -\frac{1}{2}\right)$

Find the equation of the line that is perpendicular to the given line and passes through the given point.

8. $y = 10x$; $(1, -3)$

9. $y = -\frac{1}{3}x - 5$; $(12, 0)$

10. $y = \frac{5x + 1}{3}$; $(1, 1)$

11. Determine whether the lines are parallel. Use slope to explain your answer.

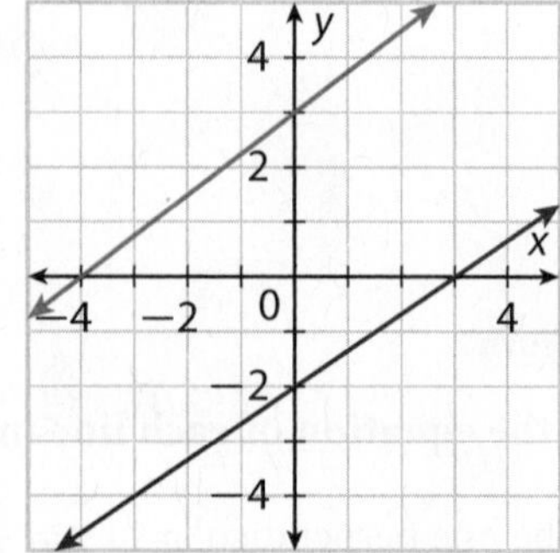

The endpoints of a side of rectangle *ABCD* in the coordinate plane are at $A(1, 5)$ and $B(3, 1)$. Find the equation of the line that contains the given segment.

12. $\overline{AB}$

13. $\overline{BC}$

14. $\overline{AD}$

15. $\overline{CD}$ if point C is at $(7, 3)$

16. A well is to be dug at the location shown in the diagram. Use the diagram for parts (a–c).

a. Find the equation that represents the road.

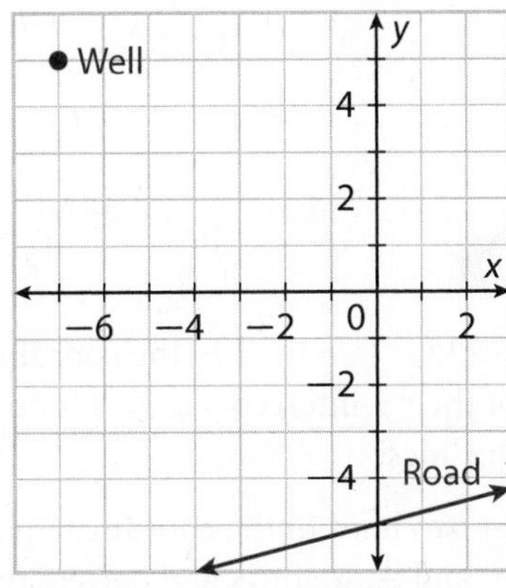

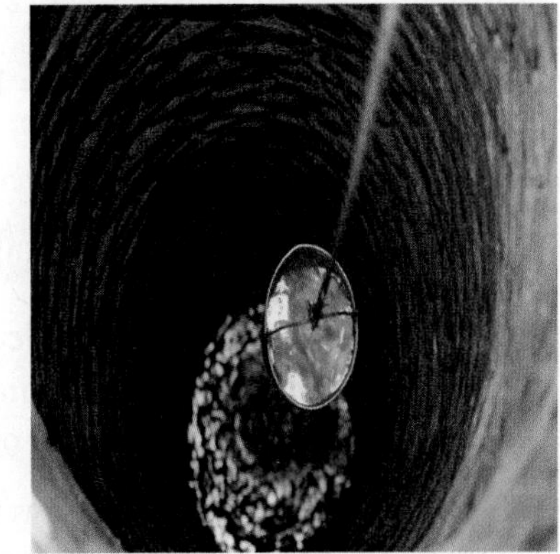

b. A path is to be made from the road to the well. Describe how this should be done to minimize the length of the path.

c. Find the equation of the line that contains the path.

17. Use the graph for parts a–c.

a. Find the equation of the perpendicular bisector of the segment. Explain your method.

b. Find the equation of the line that is parallel to the segment, but has the same *y*-intercept as the equation you found in part **a**.

c. What is the relationship between the two lines you found in parts (a) and (b)?

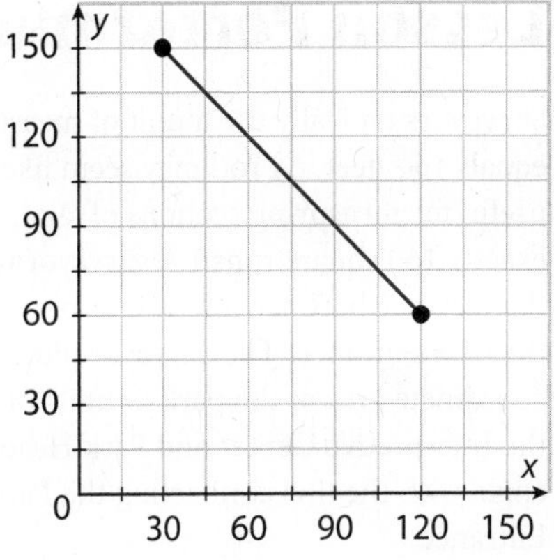

18. Line *m* is perpendicular to $x - 3y = -1$ and passes through $(1, 5)$. What is the slope of line *m*?

A. -3

B. $\frac{1}{3}$

C. 3

D. 5

19. State whether each pair of lines is parallel, perpendicular, or neither.

a. $x - 2y = 12; y = x + 5$

b. $\frac{1}{5}x + y = 8; y = 5x$

c. $3x - 2y = 12; 3y = -2x + 5$

d. $y = 3x - 1; 15x - 5y = 10$

e. $7y = 4x + 1; 14x + 8y = 10$

H.O.T. Focus on Higher Order Thinking

20. Communicate Mathematical Ideas Two lines in the coordinate plane have opposite slopes, are parallel, and the sum of their y-intercepts is 10. If one of the lines passes through $(5, 4)$, what are the equations of the lines?

21. Explain the Error Alan says that two lines in the coordinate plane are perpendicular if and only if the slopes of the lines are m and $\frac{1}{m}$. Identify and correct two errors in Alan's statement.

22. Analyze Relationships Two perpendicular lines have opposite y-intercepts. The equation of one of these lines is $y = mx + b$. Express the x-coordinate of the intersection point of the lines in terms of m and b.

Lesson Performance Task

Surveyors typically use a unit of measure called a rod, which equals $16\frac{1}{2}$ feet. (A rod may seem like an odd unit, but it's very useful for measuring sections of land, because an acre equals exactly 160 square rods.) A surveyor was called upon to find the distance between a new interpretive center at a park and the park entrance. The surveyor plotted the points shown on a coordinate grid of the park in units of 1 rod. The line between the Interpretive Center and Park Headquarters forms a right angle with the line connecting the Park Headquarters and Park Entrance.

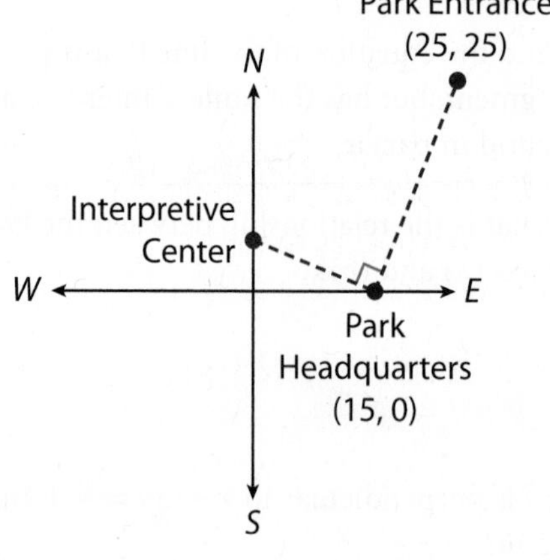

What is the distance, in feet, between the Interpretive Center and the park entrance? Explain the process you used to find the answer.

STUDY GUIDE REVIEW

Lines and Angles

MODULE 4

Essential Question: How can you use parallel and perpendicular lines to solve real-world problems?

Key Vocabulary
vertical angles (*ángulos verticales*)
complementary angles (*ángulos complementarios*)
supplementary angles (*ángulos suplementarios*)
transversal (*transversal*)
indirect proof (*prueba indirecta*)

KEY EXAMPLE (Lesson 4.1)

Find $m\angle ABD$ given that $m\angle CBE = 40°$ and the angles are formed by the intersection of the lines $\overleftrightarrow{AC}$ and $\overleftrightarrow{DE}$.

When two lines intersect, they form two pairs of vertical angles at their intersection. Note that $\angle ABD$ and $\angle CBE$ are vertical angles and $\angle DBC$ and $\angle ABE$ are vertical angles.

$\angle ABD \cong \angle CBE$ — Vertical Angles Theorem

$m\angle ABD = m\angle CBE = 40°$ — Definition of congruence of angles

KEY EXAMPLE (Lesson 4.2)

Find $m\angle APD$ given that $\overleftrightarrow{AB}$ intersects the parallel lines $\overleftrightarrow{DE}$ and $\overleftrightarrow{FG}$ at the points P and Q, respectively, and $m\angle AQF = 70°$.

When a transversal intersects two parallel lines, it forms a series of angle pairs. Note that $\angle APD$ and $\angle AQF$ are a pair of corresponding angles.

$m\angle APD = m\angle AQF$ — Corresponding Angles Theorem

$m\angle APD = 70°$ — Substitute the known angle measure.

KEY EXAMPLE (Lesson 4.3)

Determine whether the lines $\overleftrightarrow{DE}$ and $\overleftrightarrow{FG}$ are parallel given that $\overleftrightarrow{AB}$ intersects them at the points P and Q, respectively, $m\angle APE = 60°$, and $m\angle BQF = 60°$.

Lines $\overleftrightarrow{AB}$ and $\overleftrightarrow{DE}$ intersect, so they create two pairs of vertical angles. The angle which is the opposite of $\angle APE$ is $\angle DPB$, so they are called vertical angles.

$\angle APE \cong \angle DPB$ — Vertical Angles Theorem

$m\angle APE = m\angle DPB$ — Definition of congruence

$m\angle DPB = 60°$ — Substitute the known angle measure.

$m\angle BQF = m\angle DPB = 60°$

$\angle BQF \cong \angle DPB$ — Definition of congruence

Thus, the lines $\overleftrightarrow{DE}$ and $\overleftrightarrow{FG}$ are parallel by the converse of the Corresponding Angles Theorem because their corresponding angles are congruent.

EXERCISES

Find the angle measure.

1. $m\angle ABD$ given that $m\angle CBD = 40°$ and the angles are formed by the intersection of the lines $\overleftrightarrow{AC}$ and $\overleftrightarrow{DE}$. *(Lesson 4.1)*

2. $m\angle BPE$ given that $\overleftrightarrow{AB}$ intersects the parallel lines $\overleftrightarrow{DE}$ and $\overleftrightarrow{FG}$ at the points P and Q, respectively, and $m\angle AQF = 45°$. *(Lesson 4.2)*

Determine whether the lines are parallel. *(Lesson 4.3)*

3. $\overleftrightarrow{DE}$ and $\overleftrightarrow{FG}$, given that $\overleftrightarrow{AB}$ intersects them at the points P and Q, respectively, $m\angle APD = 60°$, and $m\angle BQG = 120°$.

Find the distance and angle formed from the perpendicular bisector. *(Lesson 4.4)*

4. Find the distance of point D from B given that D is the point at the perpendicular bisector of the line segment $\overline{AB}$, $\overleftrightarrow{DE}$ intersects $\overline{AB}$, and $AD = 3$. Find $m\angle ADE$.

Find the equation of the line. *(Lesson 4.5)*

5. Perpendicular to $y = \frac{2}{3}x + 2$ and passes through the point $(3, 4)$.

MODULE PERFORMANCE TASK

Mystery Spot Geometry

Inside mystery spot buildings, some odd things can appear to occur. Water can appear to flow uphill, and people can look as if they are standing at impossible angles. That is because there is no view of the outside, so the room appears to be normal.

The illustration shows a mystery spot building constructed so that the floor is at a 25° angle with the ground.

View from outside

View from inside

- A table is placed in the room with its legs perpendicular to the floor and the tabletop perpendicular to the legs. Sketch or describe the relationship of the tabletop to the floor, walls, and ceiling of the room. What would happen if a ball were placed on the table?
- A chandelier hangs from the ceiling of the room. How does it appear to someone inside? How does it appear to someone standing outside of the room?

Use your own paper to complete the task. Use sketches, words, or geometry to explain how you reached your conclusions.

Ready to Go On?

4.1–4.5 Lines and Angles

Personal Math Trainer
• Online Homework
• Hints and Help
• Extra Practice

Find the measure of each angle. Assume lines $\overleftrightarrow{GB}$ and $\overleftrightarrow{FC}$ are parallel. *(Lessons 4.1, 4.2)*

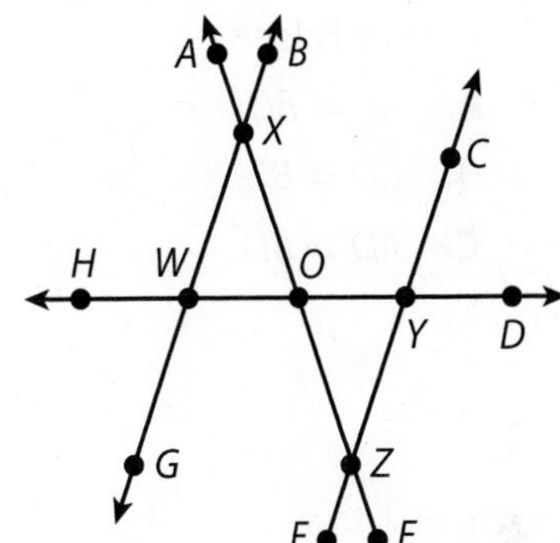

1. The measure of $\angle WOX$ is 70°. Find $m\angle YOZ$.

2. The measure of $\angle AXB$ is 40°. Find $m\angle FZE$.

3. The measure of $\angle XWO$ is 70°. Find $m\angle OYC$.

4. The measure of $\angle BXO$ is 110°. Find $m\angle OZF$.

Use the diagram to find lengths. $\overline{PB}$ is the perpendicular bisector of $\overline{AC}$. $\overline{QC}$ is the perpendicular bisector of $\overline{BD}$. $AB = BC = CD$. *(Lessons 4.3, 4.4)*

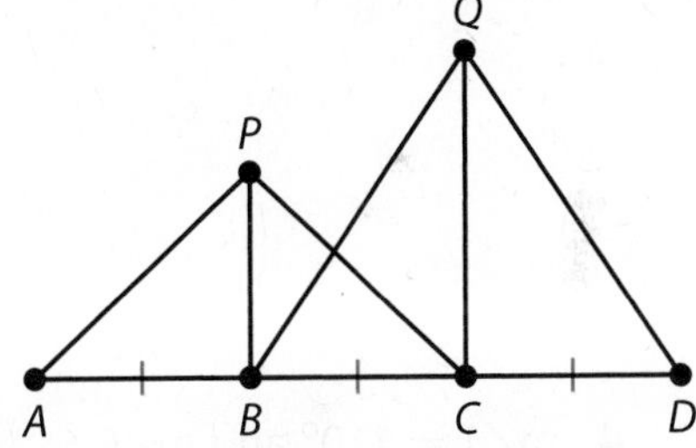

5. Given $BD = 24$ and $PC = 13$, find PB.

6. Given $QB = 23$ and $BC = 12$, find QD.

Find the equation of each line. *(Lessons 4.5)*

7. The line parallel to $y = -\frac{3}{7}x + 5$ and passing through the point $(-7, -1)$

8. The line perpendicular to $y = \frac{1}{5}x + 3$ and passing through the point $(2, 7)$

9. The perpendicular bisector to the line segment with endpoints $(-3, 8)$ and $(9, 4)$

ESSENTIAL QUESTION

10. Say you want to create a ladder. Which lines should be parallel or perpendicular to each other?

MODULE 4
MIXED REVIEW

Assessment Readiness

1. Consider each equation. Is it the equation of a line that is either parallel or perpendicular to $y = 3x + 2$?

A. $y = -\frac{1}{3}x - 8$

B. $y = 3x - 10$

C. $y = 2x + 4$

2. Consider the following statements about $\triangle ABC$. Determine if each statement is True or False.

A. $AC = BC$

B. $CD = BC$

C. $AD = BD$

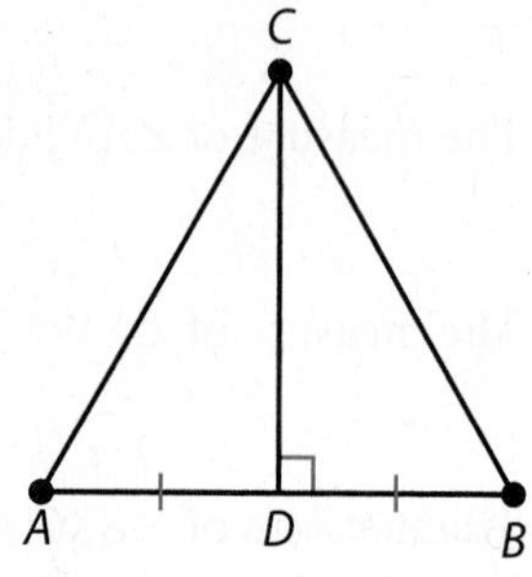

3. The measure of angle 3 is 130° and the measure of angle 4 is 50°. State two different relationships that can be used to prove m∠1 = 130°.

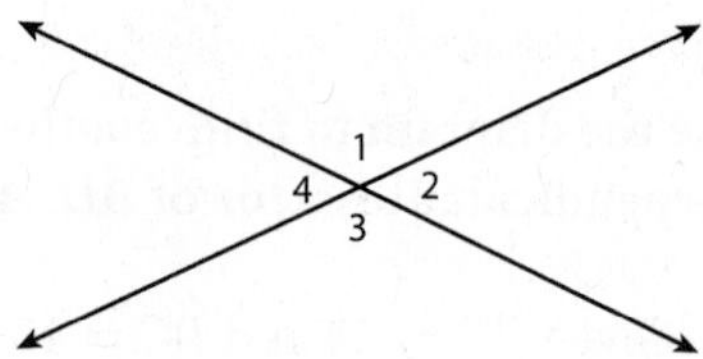

4. m∠1 = 110° and m∠6 = 70°. Use angle relationships to show that lines *m* and *n* are parallel.

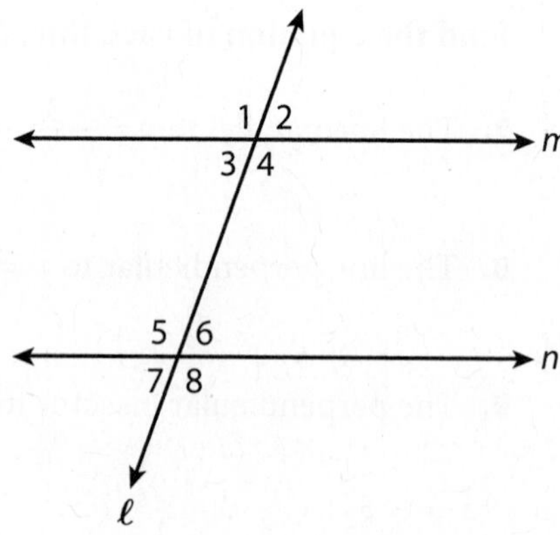

Triangle Congruence Criteria

MODULE 5

Essential Question: How can you use triangle congruence to solve real-world problems?

REAL WORLD VIDEO
Take a look at some of the geometry involved in the engineering marvels of the Golden Gate Bridge in San Francisco.

MODULE PERFORMANCE TASK PREVIEW

Golden Gate Triangles

In this module, you will explore congruent triangles in the trusses of the lower deck of the Golden Gate Bridge. How can you use congruency to help figure out how far apart the two towers of the bridge are? Let's find out.

Are YOU Ready?

Complete these exercises to review the skills you will need for this module.

- Online Homework
- Hints and Help
- Extra Practice

Angle Relationships

Example 1 Line segments *AB* and *DC* are parallel. Find the measure of angle $\angle CDE$.

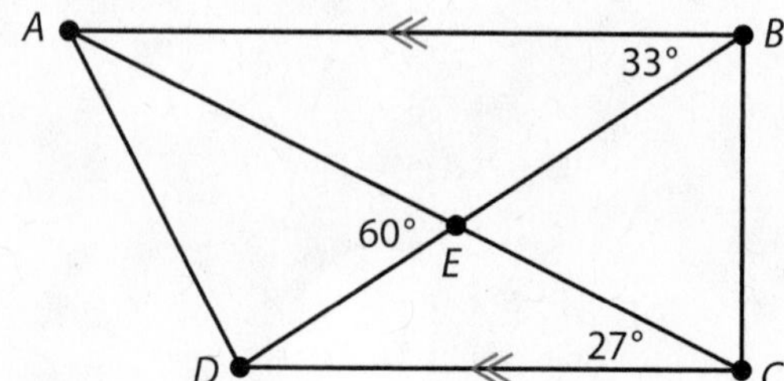

$m\angle CDE = m\angle ABE$ Equate alternate interior angles.

$m\angle CDE = 33°$ Substitute.

Find the measure of each angle in the image from the example.

1. $m\angle BEC$

2. $m\angle BAE$

Congruent Figures

Example 2 Find the length *DF*. Assume $\triangle DEF \cong \triangle GHJ$.

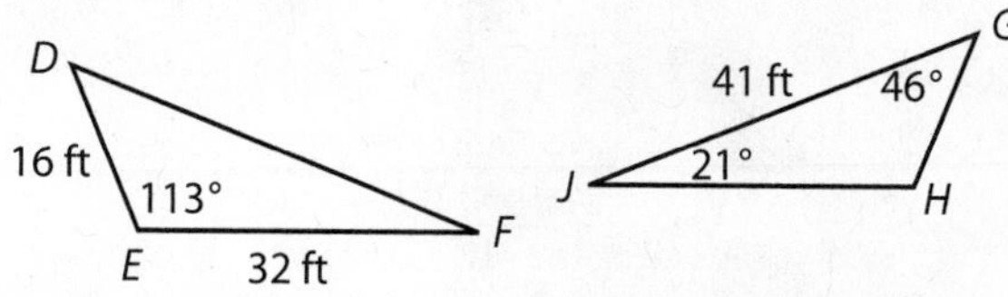

Since $\triangle DEF \cong \triangle GHJ$, the sides $\overline{DF}$ and $\overline{GJ}$ are congruent, or $\overline{DF} \cong \overline{GJ}$. Thus, $DF = GJ$. Since $GJ = 41$ ft, length *DF* must also be 41 ft.

Use the figure from the example to find the given side length or angle measure. Assume $\triangle DEF \cong \triangle GHJ$.

3. Find $m\angle GHJ$.

4. Find the length *GH*.

5. Find $m\angle FDE$.

6. Find the length *HJ*.

5.1 Exploring What Makes Triangles Congruent

Essential Question: How can you show that two triangles are congruent?

Explore Transforming Triangles with Congruent Corresponding Parts

You can apply what you've learned about corresponding parts of congruent figures to write the following true statement about triangles.

If two triangles are congruent, then the corresponding parts of the triangles are congruent.

The statement is sometimes referred to as *CPCTC*. The converse of CPCTC can be stated as follows.

If all corresponding parts of two triangles are congruent, then the triangles are congruent.

Use a straightedge and tracing paper to explore this converse statement.

(A) Trace the angles and segments shown to draw $\triangle ABC$. Repeat the process to draw $\triangle DEF$ on a separate piece of tracing paper. Label the triangles.

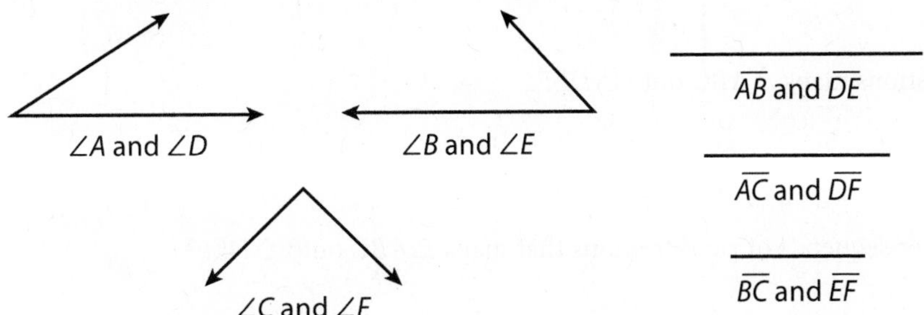

(B) What must you do to show that the triangles are congruent?

(C) Flip the piece of tracing paper with $\triangle ABC$ and arrange the two triangles on a desk as shown in the figure. Then move the tracing paper with $\triangle ABC$ so that point A maps to point D. Name the rigid motion that you used.

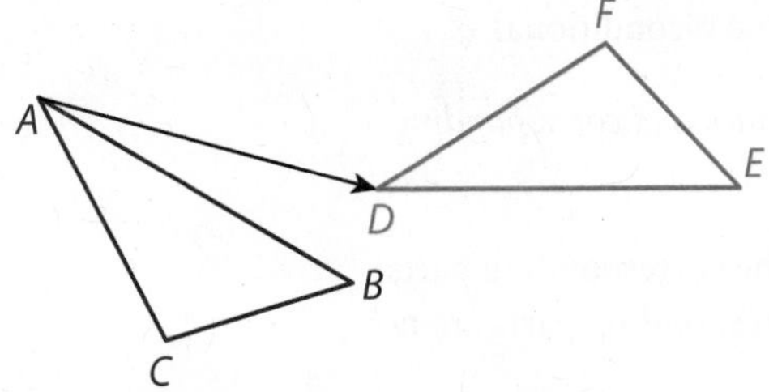

(D) Name a rigid motion you can use to map point B to point E. How can you be sure the image of B is E?

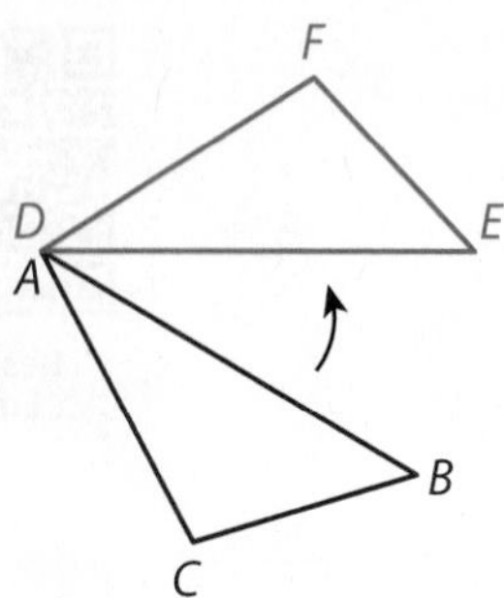

(E) Name a rigid motion you can use to map point C to point F.

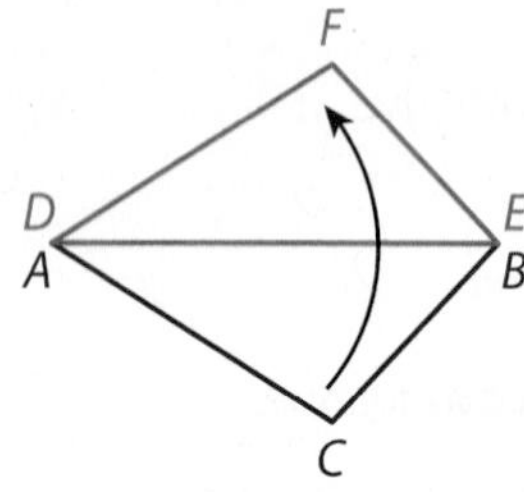

(F) To show that the image of point C is point F, complete the following.

$\angle A$ is reflected across $\overleftrightarrow{DE}$, so the measure of the angle is preserved. Since $\angle A \cong \angle D$, you can conclude that the image of $\overrightarrow{AC}$ lies on [?]. It is given that $\overline{AC} \cong$ [?], so the image of point C must be [?].

(G) What sequence of rigid motions maps $\triangle ABC$ onto $\triangle DEF$?

Reflect

1. **Discussion** Is there another sequence of rigid motions that maps $\triangle ABC$ onto $\triangle DEF$? Explain.

2. **Discussion** Is the converse of CPCTC always true when you apply it to triangles? Explain why or why not based on the results of the Explore.

Explain 1 Deciding If Triangles are Congruent by Comparing Corresponding Parts

A **biconditional** is a statement that can be written in the form "p if and only if q." You can combine what you learned in the Explore with the fact that corresponding parts of congruent triangles are congruent to write the following true biconditional.

Two triangles are congruent if and only if corresponding pairs of sides and corresponding pairs of angles are congruent.

To decide whether two triangles are congruent, you can compare the corresponding parts. If they are congruent, the triangles are congruent. If any of the corresponding parts are not congruent, then the triangles are not congruent.

Example 1 **Determine whether the given triangles are congruent. Explain.**

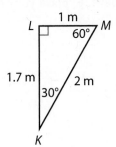

(A)

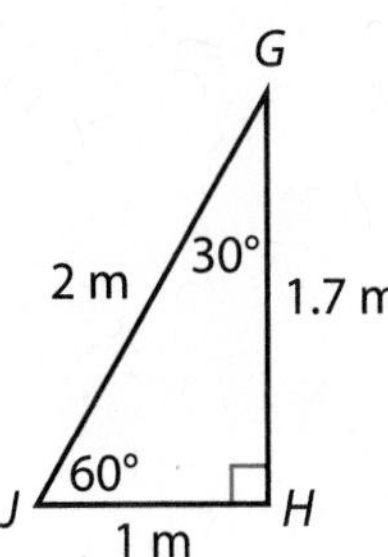

L 1 m M
60°
1.7 m
2 m
30°
K

Compare corresponding sides to decide if they are congruent.

$GH = KL = 1.7$ m, $HJ = LM = 1$ m, and $GJ = KM = 2$ m.

So, $\overline{GH} \cong \overline{KL}$, $\overline{HJ} \cong \overline{LM}$, and $\overline{GJ} \cong \overline{KM}$.

Compare corresponding angles to decide if they are congruent.

$m\angle G = m\angle K = 30°$, $m\angle H = m\angle L = 90°$, and $m\angle J = m\angle M = 60°$.

So, $\angle G \cong \angle K$, $\angle H \cong \angle L$, and $\angle J \cong \angle M$.

$\triangle GHJ \cong \triangle KLM$ because all pairs of corresponding parts are congruent.

(B)

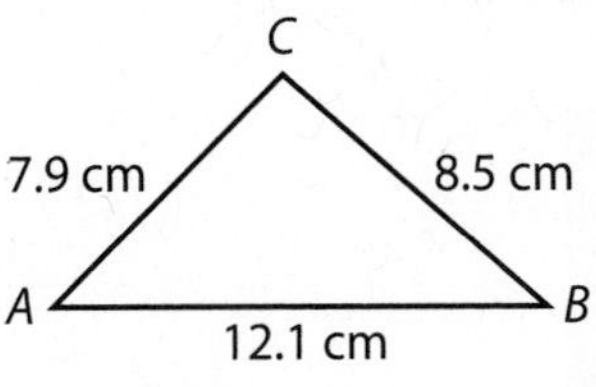

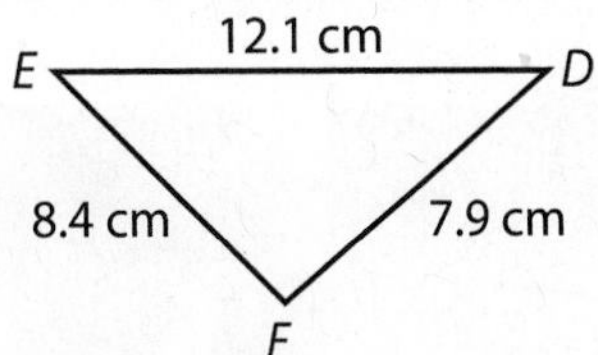

Compare corresponding sides to decide if they are congruent.

$AB =$ [DE] $=$ [12.1] cm, so $\overline{AB} \cong$ [$\overline{DE}$]. $AC =$ [DF] $=$ [7.9] cm, so $\overline{AC} \cong$ [$\overline{DF}$].

However, $BC \neq$ [EF], so $\overline{BC}$ is not congruent to [$\overline{EF}$].

The triangles are not congruent because there is a pair of corresponding sides that are not congruent.

Reflect

3. **Critique Reasoning** The **contrapositive** of a conditional statement "if p, then q" is the statement "If not q, then not p." The contrapositive of a true statement is always true. Janelle says that you can justify Part B using the contrapositive of CPCTC. Is this accurate? Explain your reasoning.

Your Turn

Determine whether the given triangles are congruent. Explain your reasoning.

4.

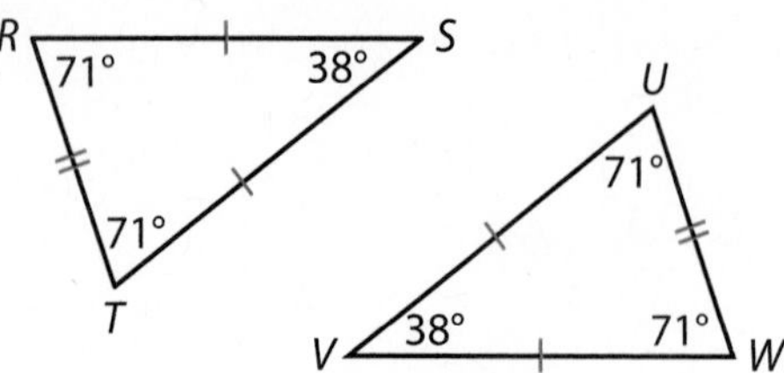

5.

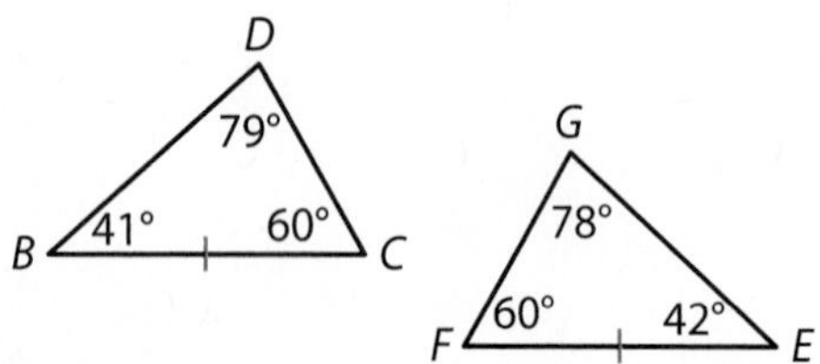

Explain 2 Applying Properties of Congruent Triangles

Triangles are part of many interesting designs. You can ensure that triangles are congruent by making corresponding sides congruent and corresponding angles congruent. To do this, you may have to use the Triangle Sum Theorem, which states that the sum of the measures of the angles of a triangle is 180°. You will explore this theorem in more detail later in this course.

Example 2 **Find the value of the variable that results in congruent triangles.**

(A)

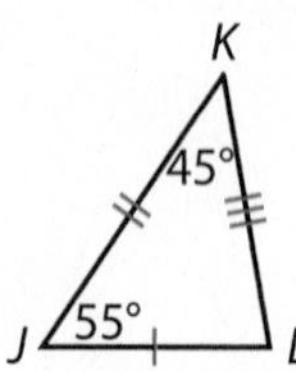

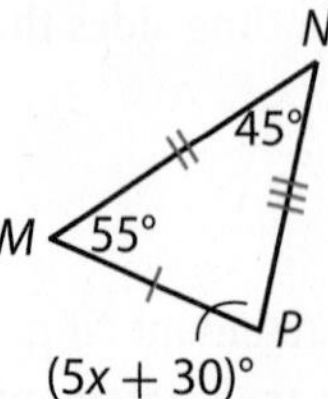

Step 1 Identify corresponding angles.

$\angle M$ corresponds to $\angle J$, because they have the same measure and they are formed by congruent corresponding sides. Similarly, $\angle N$ corresponds to $\angle K$. So, $\angle P$ corresponds to $\angle L$.

Step 2 Find $m\angle L$.

Triangle Sum Theorem	$m\angle J + m\angle K + m\angle L = 180°$
Substitute.	$55° + 45° + m\angle L = 180°$
Simplify.	$100° + m\angle L = 180°$
Subtract 100° from each side.	$m\angle L = 80°$

Step 3 Write an equation to find the value of x.

Set corresponding measures equal.	$m\angle P = m\angle L$
Substitute.	$5x + 30 = 80$
Subtract 30 from each side.	$5x = 50$
Divide each side by 5.	$x = 10$

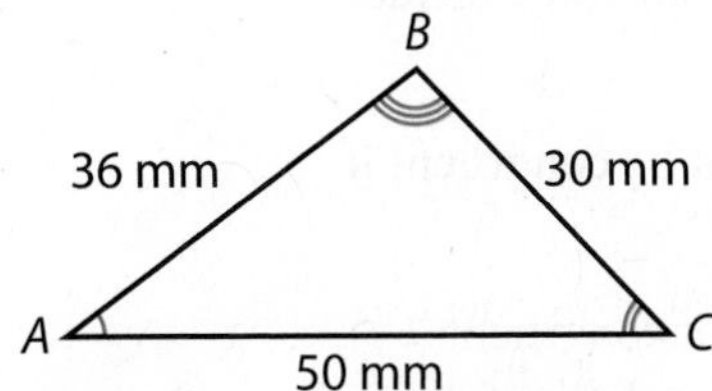

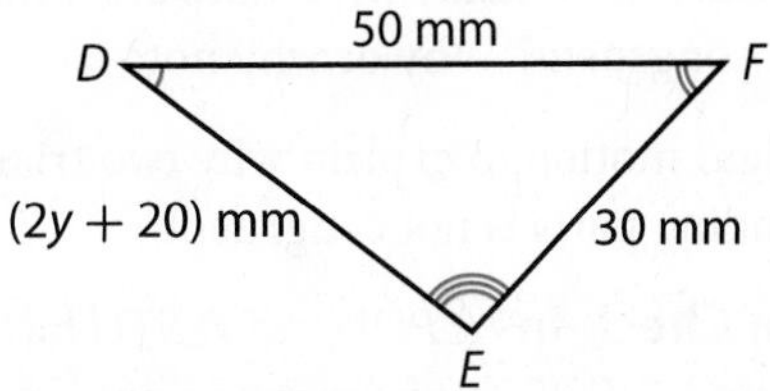

Step 1 Identify corresponding sides, beginning with side $\overline{DE}$.

$\angle A \cong \angle$ D, $\angle B \cong \angle$ E, and, $\angle C \cong \angle$ F, so $\overline{DE}$ corresponds to $\overline{AB}$.

Step 2 Write an equation to find the value of y.

Set corresponding measures equal.	$DE =$ 36 mm
Substitute.	$2y + 20 =$ 36
Subtract 20 from each side.	$2y =$ 16
Divide each side by 2.	$y =$ 8

Reflect

6. The measures of two angles of $\triangle QRS$ are 18° and 84°. The measures of two angles of $\triangle TUV$ are 18° and 76°. Is it possible for the triangles to be congruent? Explain.

Your Turn

Find the value of the variable that results in congruent triangles.

7.

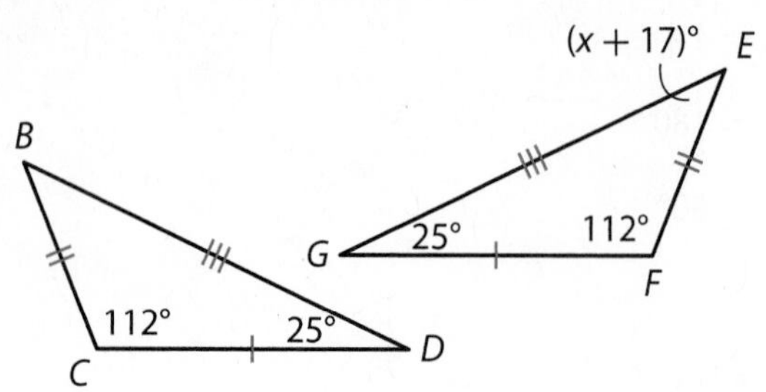

8.

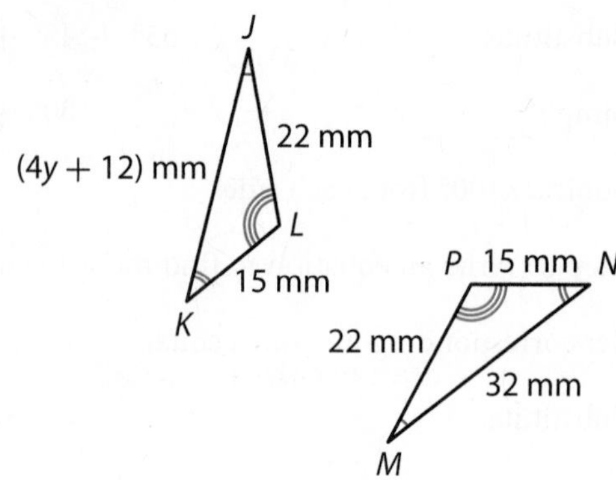

Elaborate

9. All three angles of $\triangle ABC$ measure 60° and all three sides are 4 inches long. All three angles of $\triangle PQR$ measure 60° and all three sides are 4 inches long. Can you conclude that the triangles are congruent? Why or why not?

10. Use the concept of rigid motion to explain why two triangles cannot be congruent if any pair of corresponding parts is not congruent.

11. **Essential Question Check-In** $\triangle PQR$ and $\triangle STU$ have six pairs of congruent corresponding parts and $\triangle PQR$ can be mapped onto $\triangle STU$ by a translation followed by a rotation. How are the triangles related? Explain your reasoning.

Evaluate: Homework and Practice

- Online Homework
- Hints and Help
- Extra Practice

1. Describe a sequence of rigid motions that maps $\triangle MNP$ onto $\triangle MQR$ to show that $\triangle MNP \cong \triangle MQR$.

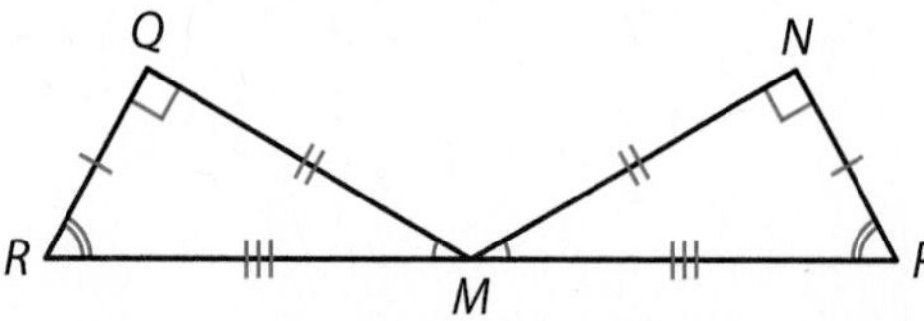

For 2-5, determine whether the given triangles are congruent. Explain your reasoning.

2.

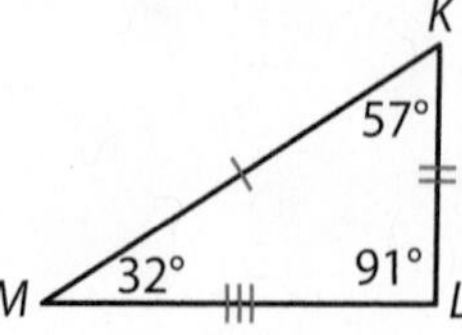

Q 57° R 91° 32° S

3.

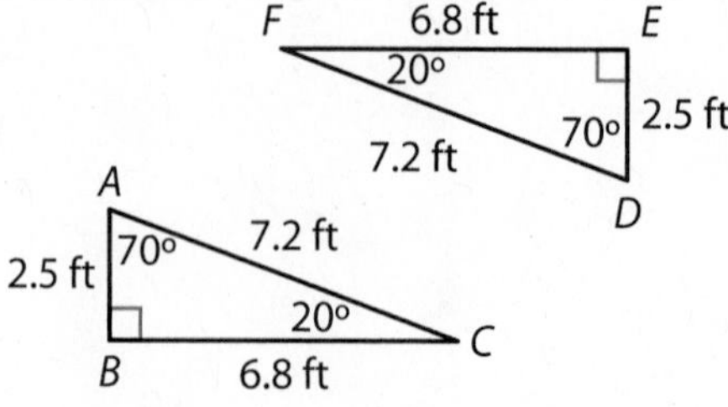

4.

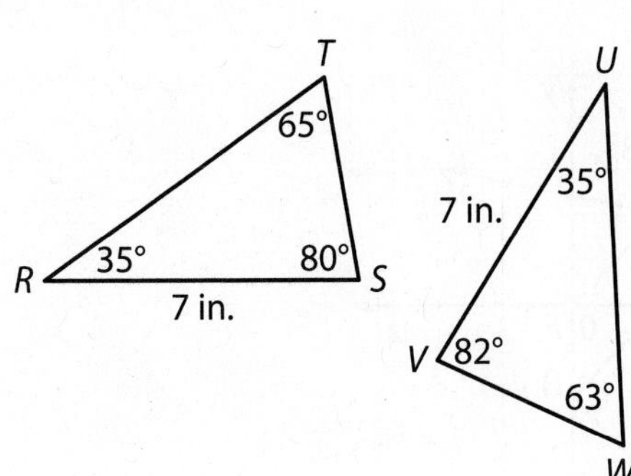

5.

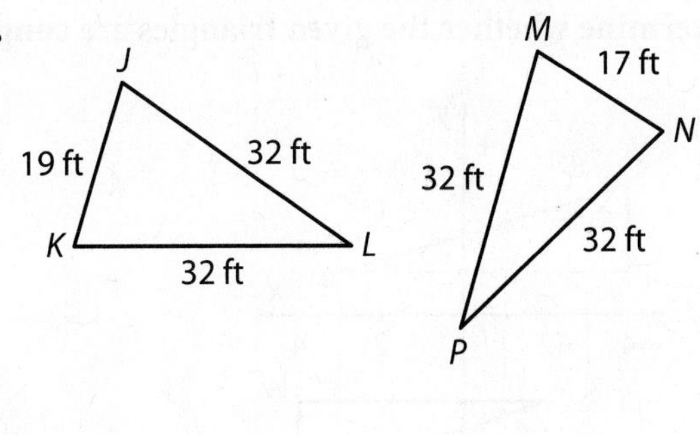

Find the value of the variable that results in congruent triangles.

6.

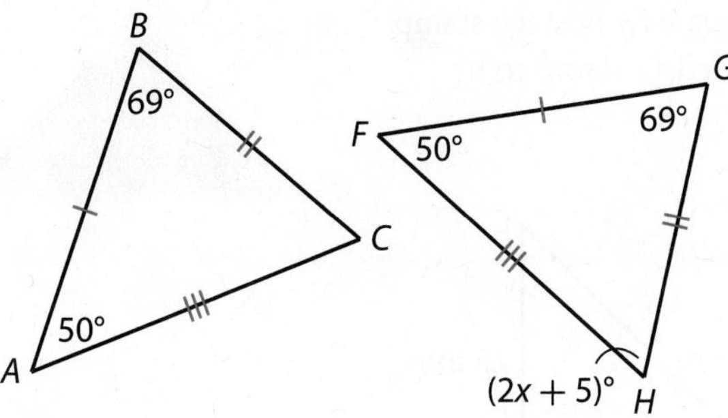

7.

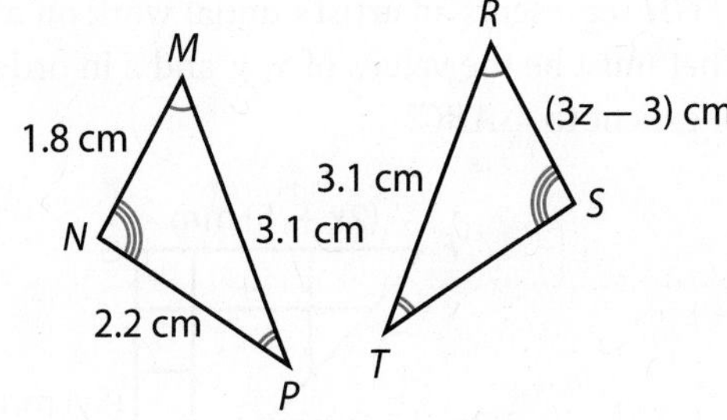

8.

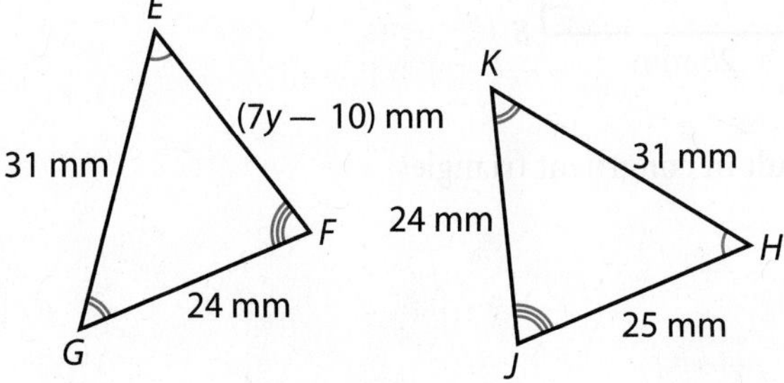

9.

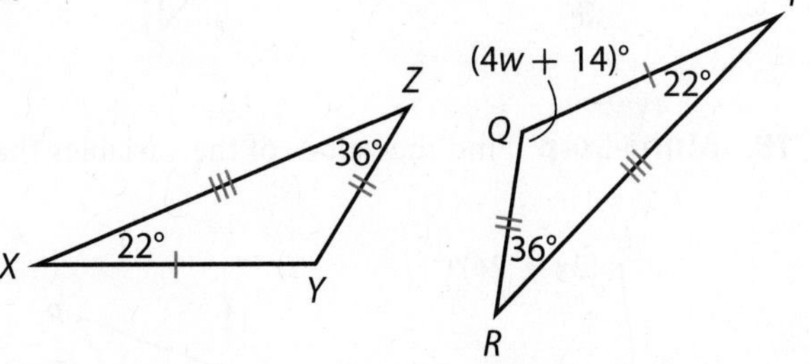

For 10-13, determine whether the given triangles are congruent. Explain.

10.

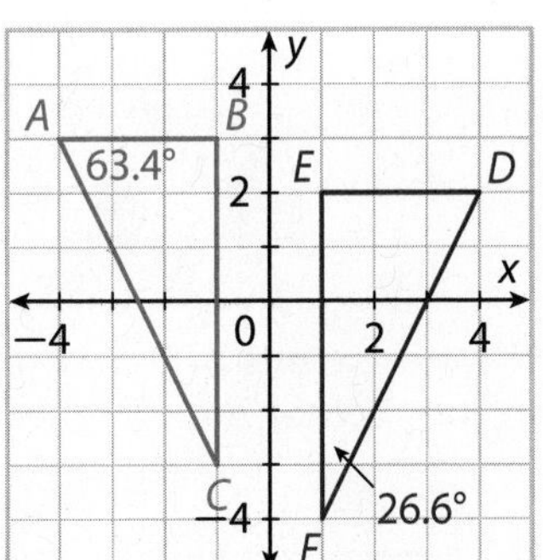

11.

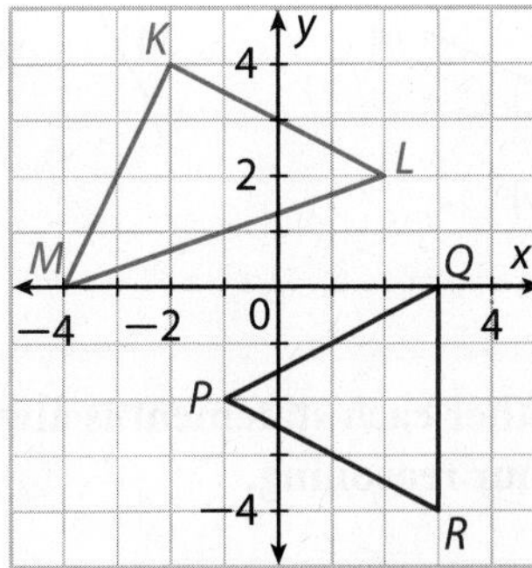

Determine whether the given triangles are congruent. Explain.

12.

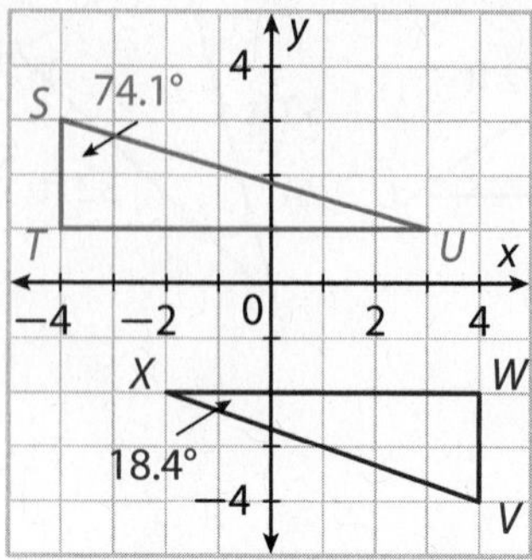

13.

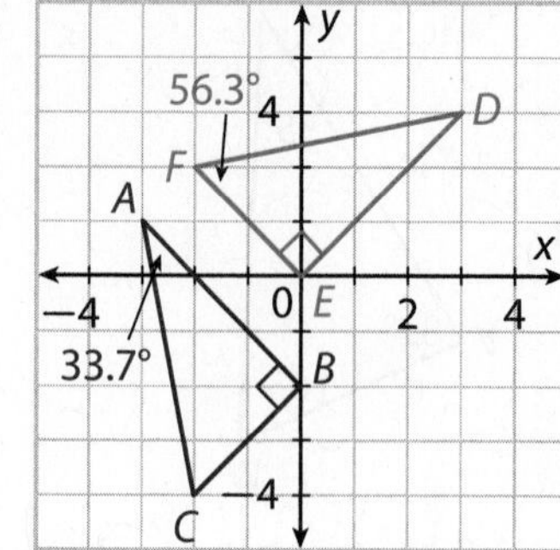

14. $\triangle FGH$ represents an artist's initial work on a design for a new postage stamp. What must be the values of x, y, and z in order for the artist's stamp to be congruent to $\triangle ABC$?

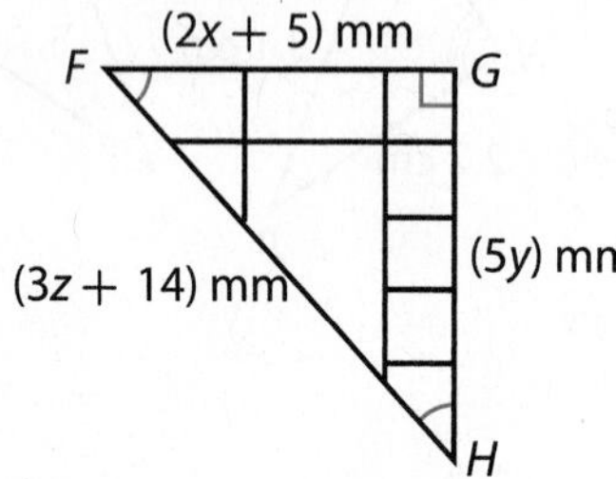

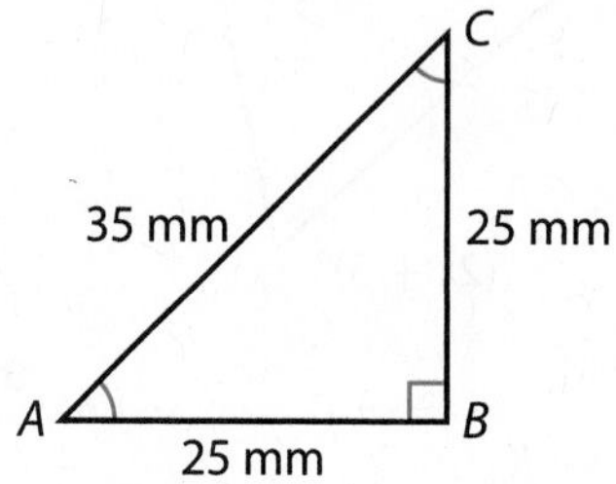

15. Multi-Step Find the values of the variables that result in congruent triangles.

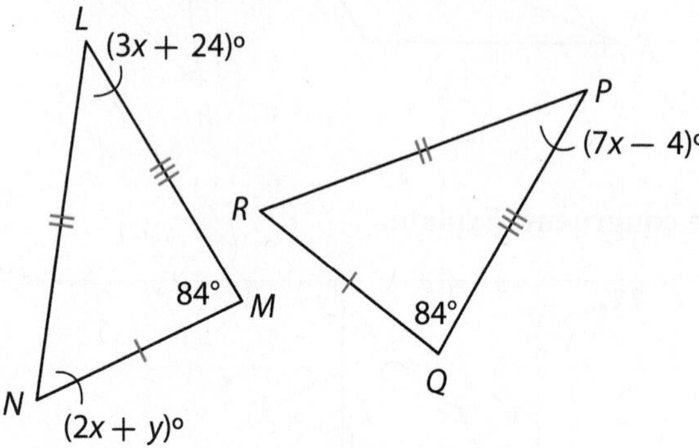

Determine whether each statement is always, sometimes, or never true. Explain your reasoning.

16. If $\triangle ABC$ has angles that measure 10° and 40°, and $\triangle DEF$ has angles that measure 40° and 120°, then $\triangle ABC \cong \triangle DEF$.

17. Two triangles with different perimeters are congruent.

18. If $\triangle JKL \cong \triangle MNP$, then $m\angle L = m\angle N$.

19. Two triangles that each contain a right angle are congruent.

20. Tenaya designed the earrings shown. She wants to be sure they are congruent. She knows that the three pairs of corresponding angles are congruent. What additional measurements should she make? Explain.

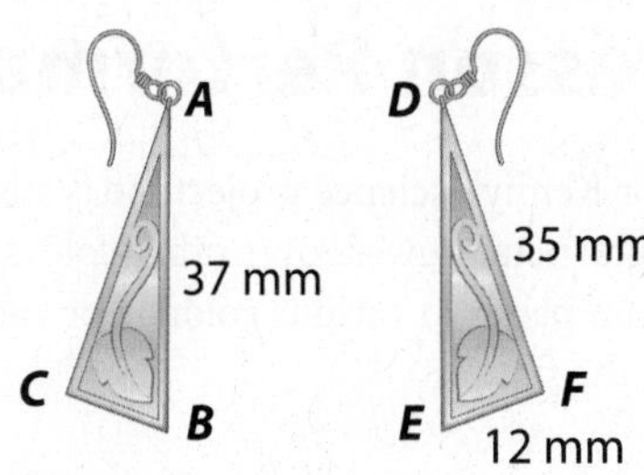

21. Determine whether $\triangle JKL$ and $\triangle PQR$ are congruent or not congruent based on the given information.

a. $m\angle J = m\angle K = m\angle L = 60°$, $m\angle P = m\angle Q = m\angle R = 60°$, $JK = KL = JL = 1.2$ cm, $PQ = QR = PR = 1.5$ cm

b. $m\angle J = 48°$, $m\angle K = 93°$, $m\angle P = 48°$, $m\angle R = 39°$, $\overline{JK} \cong \overline{PQ}$, $\overline{KL} \cong \overline{QR}$, $\overline{JL} \cong \overline{PR}$

c. $\angle J \cong \angle P$, $\angle K \cong \angle Q$, $\angle L \cong \angle R$, $JK = PQ = 22$ in., $KL = QR = 34$ in., $JL = PR = 28$ in.

d. $m\angle J = 51°$, $m\angle K = 77°$, $m\angle P = 51°$, $m\angle R = 53°$

e. $m\angle J = 45°$, $m\angle K = 80°$, $m\angle Q = 80°$, $m\angle R = 55°$, $JK = PQ = 1.5$ mm, $KL = QR = 1.3$ mm, $JL = PR = 1.8$ mm

H.O.T. Focus on Higher Order Thinking

22. **Counterexamples** Isaiah says it is not necessary to check all six pairs of congruent corresponding parts to decide whether two triangles are congruent. He says that it is enough to check that the corresponding angles are congruent. Sketch a counterexample. Explain your counterexample.

23. **Critique Reasoning** Kelly was asked to determine whether $\triangle KLN$ is congruent to $\triangle MNL$. She noted that $\overline{KL} \cong \overline{MN}$, $\overline{KN} \cong \overline{ML}$, and that the three pairs of corresponding angles are congruent. She said that this is only five pairs of congruent corresponding parts, so it is not possible to conclude that $\triangle KLN$ is congruent to $\triangle MNL$. Do you agree? Explain.

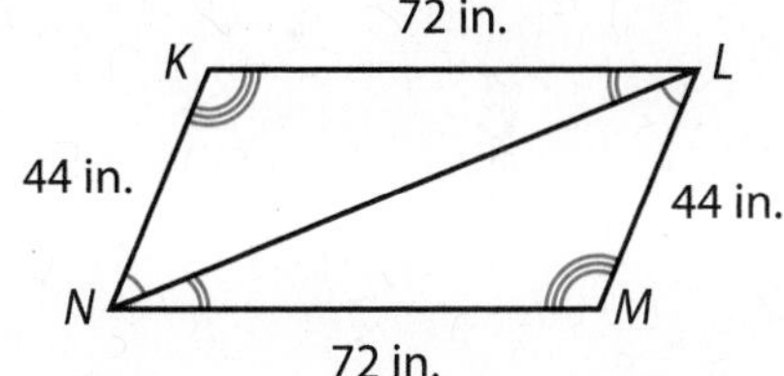

24. **Analyze Relationships** David uses software to draw two triangles. He finds that he can use a rotation and a reflection to map one triangle onto the other, and he finds that the image of vertex D is vertex L, the image of vertex V is vertex C, and the image of vertex W is vertex Y. In how many different ways can David write a congruence statement for the triangles? Explain.

Lesson Performance Task

For Kenny's science project, he is studying whether honeybees favor one color of eight-petal flowers over other colors. For his display, he is making eight-petal flowers from paper in various colors. For each flower, he'll cut out eight triangles like the one in the figure.

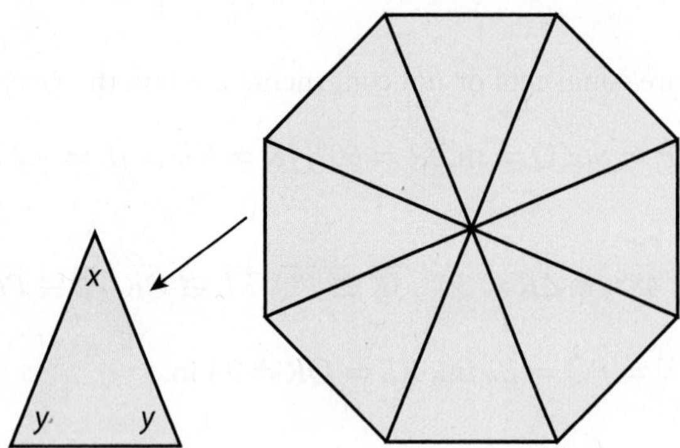

a. Find x, the measure in degrees of the top angle of each triangle. Explain how you found x.

b. Find y, the measure in degrees of the two base angles of each triangle. Explain how you found y.

c. Explain how Kenny could confirm that one of his triangles is congruent to the other seven.

5.2 ASA Triangle Congruence

Essential Question: What does the ASA Triangle Congruence Theorem tell you about triangles?

Explore 1 Drawing Triangles Given Two Angles and a Side

You have seen that two triangles are congruent if they have six pairs of congruent corresponding parts. However, it is not always possible to check all three pairs of corresponding sides and all three pairs of corresponding angles. Fortunately, there are shortcuts for determining whether two triangles are congruent.

(A) Draw a segment that is 4 inches long. Label the endpoints A and B.

(B) Use a protractor to draw a 30° angle so that one side is $\overline{AB}$ and its vertex is point A.

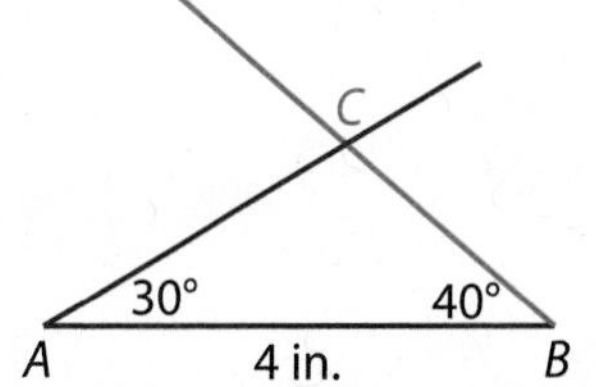

(C) Use a protractor to draw a 40° angle so that one side is $\overline{AB}$ and its vertex is point B. Label the point where the sides of the angles intersect as point C.

(D) Put your triangle and a classmate's triangle beside each other. Is there a sequence of rigid motions that maps one to the other? What does this tell you about the triangles?

Reflect

1. In a polygon, the side that connects two consecutive angles is the *included side* of those two angles. Describe the triangle you drew using the term *included side*. Be as precise as possible.

2. **Discussion** Based on your results, how can you decide whether two triangles are congruent without checking that all six pairs of corresponding sides and corresponding angles are congruent?

Explore 2 Justifying ASA Triangle Congruence

Explain the results of Explore 1 using transformations.

(A) Use tracing paper to make two copies of the triangle from Explore 1 as shown. Identify the corresponding parts you know to be congruent and mark these congruent parts on the figure.

$\angle A \cong$?

$\angle B \cong$?

$\overline{AB} \cong$?

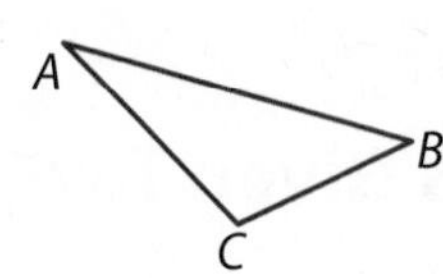

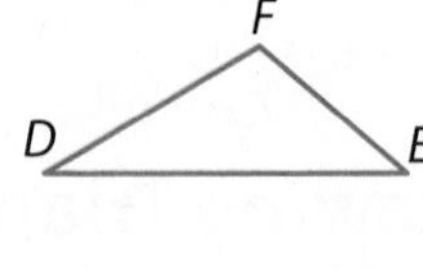

(B) What can you do to show that these triangles are congruent?

(C) Translate $\triangle ABC$ so that point A maps to point D. What translation vector did you use?

(D) Use a rotation to map point B to point E. What is the center of the rotation? What is the angle of the rotation?

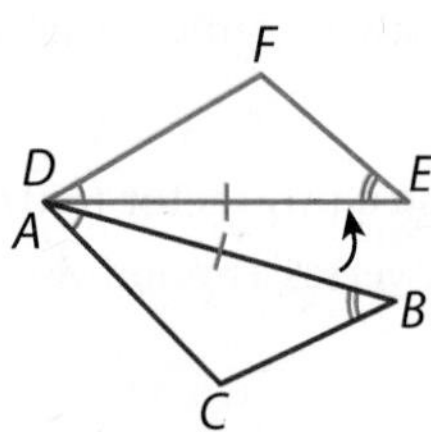

(E) How do you know the image of point B is point E?

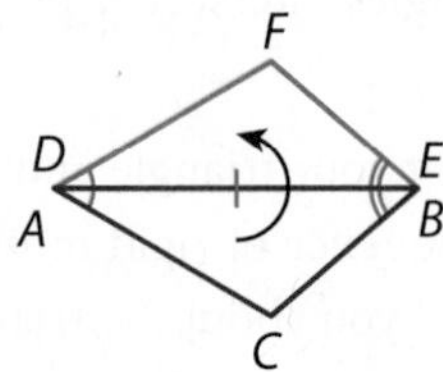

(F) What rigid motion do you think will map point C to point F?

(G) To show that the image of point C is point F, notice that $\angle A$ is reflected across $\overleftrightarrow{DE}$, so the measure of the angle is preserved. Since $\angle A \cong \angle D$ you can conclude that the image of $\overline{AC}$ lies on ? . In particular, the image of point C must lie on ? . By similar reasoning, the image of $\overline{BC}$ lies on ? and the image of point C must lie on ? . The only point that lies on both $\overline{DF}$ and $\overline{EF}$ is ? .

(H) Describe the sequence of rigid motions used to map $\triangle ABC$ to $\triangle DEF$.

Reflect

3. **Discussion** Arturo said the argument in the activity works for any triangles with two pairs of congruent corresponding angles, and it is not necessary for the included sides to be congruent. Do you agree? Explain.

Explain 1 Deciding Whether Triangles Are Congruent Using ASA Triangle Congruence

You can state your findings about triangle congruence as a theorem. This theorem can help you decide whether two triangles are congruent.

ASA Triangle Congruence Theorem

If two angles and the included side of one triangle are congruent to two angles and the included side of another triangle, then the triangles are congruent.

Example 1 **Determine whether the triangles are congruent. Explain your reasoning.**

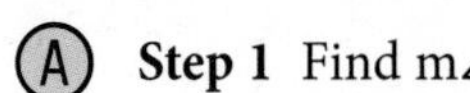

Ⓐ **Step 1** Find $m\angle D$.

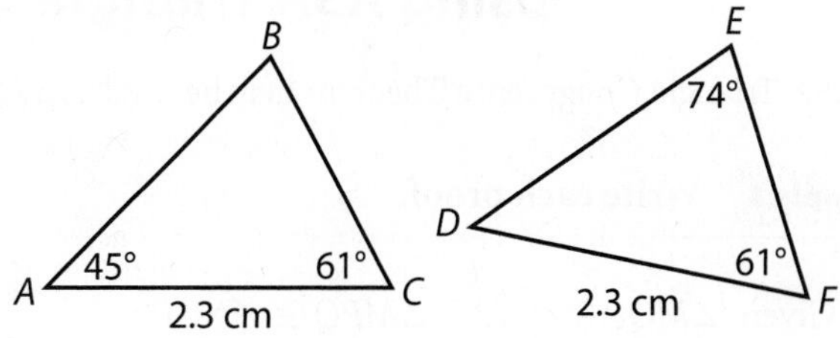

$$m\angle D + m\angle E + m\angle F = 180^\circ$$

$$m\angle D + 74^\circ + 61^\circ = 180^\circ$$

$$m\angle D + 135^\circ = 180^\circ$$

$$m\angle D = 45^\circ$$

Step 2 Compare the angle measures and side lengths.

$m\angle A = m\angle D = 45^\circ$, $AC = DF = 2.3$ cm, and $m\angle C = m\angle F = 61^\circ$

So, $\angle A \cong \angle D$, $\overline{AC} \cong \overline{DF}$, and $\angle C \cong \angle F$.

$\angle A$ and $\angle C$ include side $\overline{AC}$, and $\angle D$ and $\angle F$ include side $\overline{DF}$.

So, $\triangle ABC \cong \triangle DEF$ by the ASA Triangle Congruence Theorem.

Ⓑ **Step 1** Find $m\angle P$.

$$m\angle M + m\angle N + m\angle P = 180^\circ$$

$$\boxed{31}^\circ + \boxed{38}^\circ + m\angle P = 180^\circ$$

$$\boxed{69}^\circ + m\angle P = 180^\circ$$

$$m\angle P = \boxed{111}^\circ$$

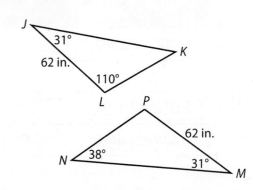

Step 2 Compare the angle measures and side lengths.

None of the angles in $\triangle MNP$ has a measure of $\boxed{110^\circ}$.

Therefore, there is not a sequence of rigid motions that maps $\triangle MNP$ onto $\triangle JKL$, and $\triangle MNP$ is not congruent to $\triangle JKL$.

J
31°
K
62 in.
110°
L
P
62 in.
N
38°
31°
M

Reflect

4. In Part B, do you need to find $m\angle K$? Why or why not?

Your Turn

Determine whether the triangles are congruent. Explain your reasoning.

5.

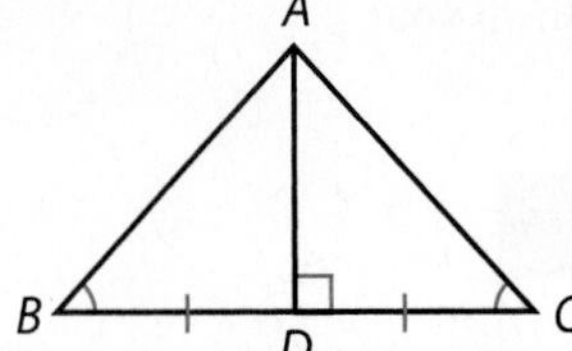

6.

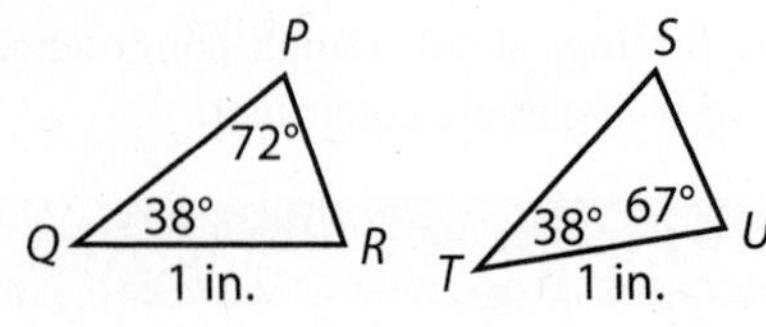

Explain 2 Proving Triangles Are Congruent Using ASA Triangle Congruence

The ASA Triangle Congruence Theorem may be used as a reason in a proof.

Example 2 Write each proof.

(A) Given: $\angle MQP \cong \angle NPQ$, $\angle MPQ \cong \angle NQP$

Prove: $\triangle MQP \cong \triangle NPQ$

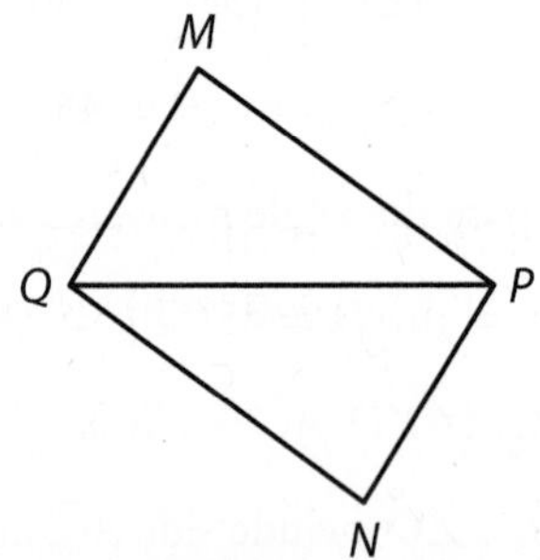

Statements	Reasons
1. $\angle MQP \cong \angle NPQ$	1. Given
2. $\angle MPQ \cong \angle NQP$	2. Given
3. $\overline{QP} \cong \overline{QP}$	3. Reflexive Property of Congruence
4. $\triangle MQP \cong \triangle NPQ$	4. ASA Triangle Congruence Theorem

(B) Given: $\angle A \cong \angle C$, E is the midpoint of $\overline{AC}$.

Prove: $\triangle AEB \cong \triangle CED$

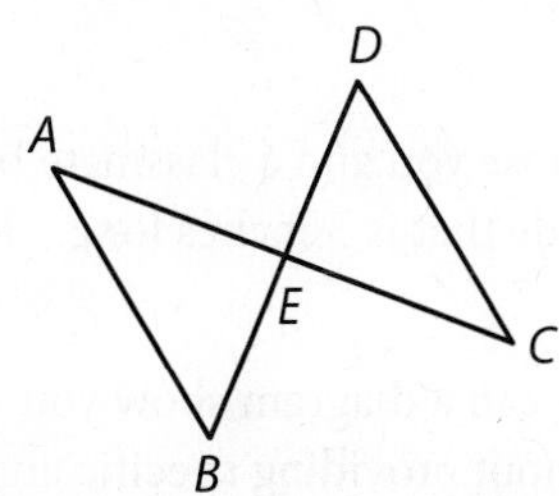

Statements	Reasons
1. $\angle A \cong \angle C$	1. Given
2. E is the midpoint of $\overline{AC}$.	2. Given
3. $\overline{AE} \cong \overline{CE}$	3. Definition of midpoint
4. $\angle AEB \cong \angle CED$	4. Vertical angles are congruent.
5. $\triangle AEB \cong \triangle CED$	5. ASA Triangle Congruence Theorem

Reflect

7. In Part B, suppose the length of $\overline{AB}$ is 8.2 centimeters. Can you determine the length of any other segments in the figure? Explain.

Your Turn

Write each proof.

8. Given: $\angle JLM \cong \angle KML$, $\angle JML \cong \angle KLM$

Prove: $\triangle JML \cong \triangle KLM$

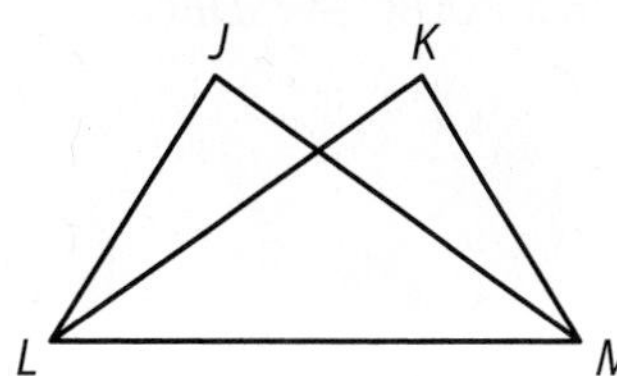

9. Given: $\angle S$ and $\angle U$ are right angles, $\overline{RV}$ bisects $\overline{SU}$.

Prove: $\triangle RST \cong \triangle VUT$

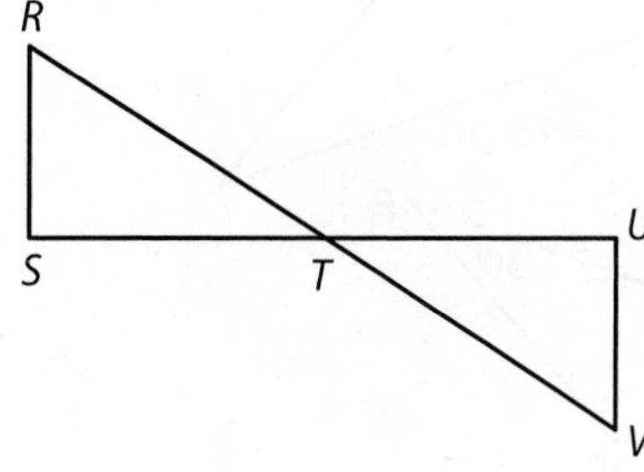

Elaborate

10. Discussion Suppose you and a classmate both draw triangles with a 30° angle, a 70° angle, and a side that is 3 inches long. How will they compare? Explain your reasoning.

11. Discussion How can a diagram show you that corresponding parts of two triangles are congruent without providing specific angle measures or side lengths?

12. Essential Question Check-In What must be true in order for you to use the ASA Triangle Congruence Theorem to prove that triangles are congruent?

Evaluate: Homework and Practice

Personal Math Trainer

- Online Homework
- Hints and Help
- Extra Practice

1. Natasha draws a segment $\overline{PQ}$ that is 6 centimeters long. She uses a protractor to draw a 60° angle so that one side is $\overline{PQ}$ and its vertex is point P. Then she uses a protractor to draw a 35° angle so that one side is $\overline{PQ}$ and its vertex is point Q.

a. Draw a triangle following the instructions that Natasha used. Label the vertices and the known side and angle measures.

b. Will there be a sequence of rigid motions that will map your triangle onto Natasha's triangle? Explain.

2. Tomas drew two triangles, as shown, so that $\angle B \cong \angle E$, $\overline{BC} \cong \overline{EC}$, and $\angle ACB \cong \angle DCE$. Describe a sequence of one or more rigid motions Tomas can use to show that $\triangle ABC \cong \triangle DEC$.

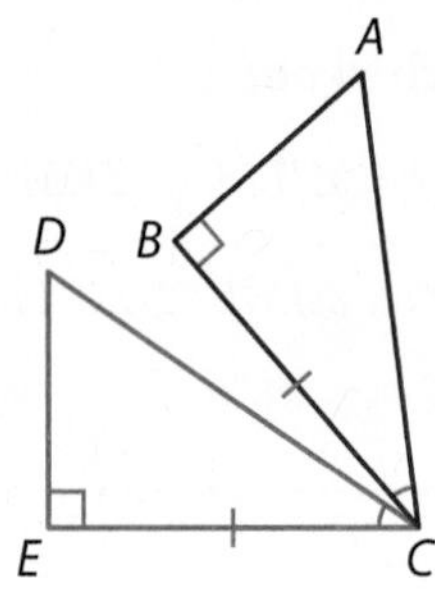

Determine whether the triangles are congruent. Explain your reasoning.

3.

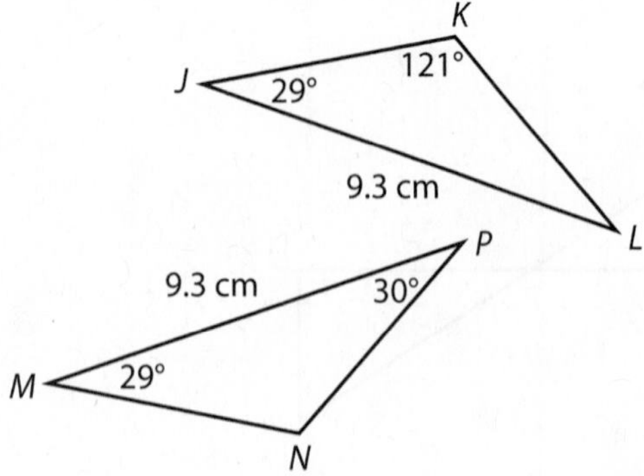

4.

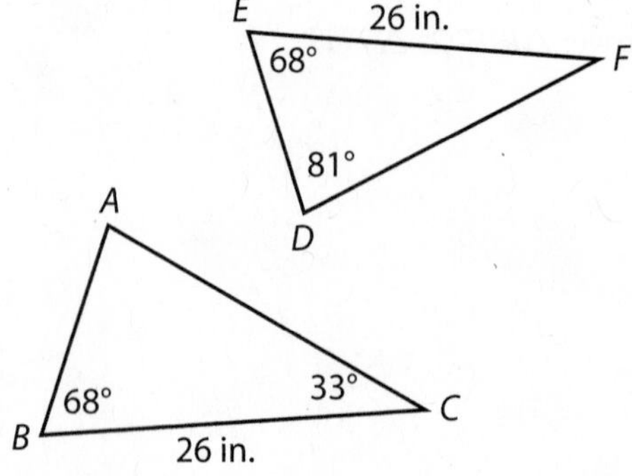

Determine whether the triangles are congruent. Explain your reasoning.

5.

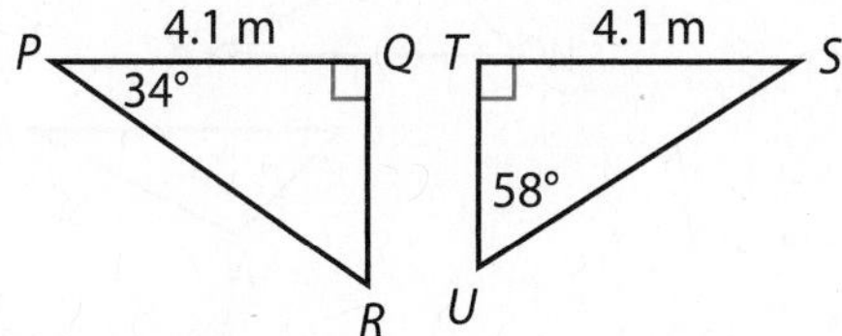

6.

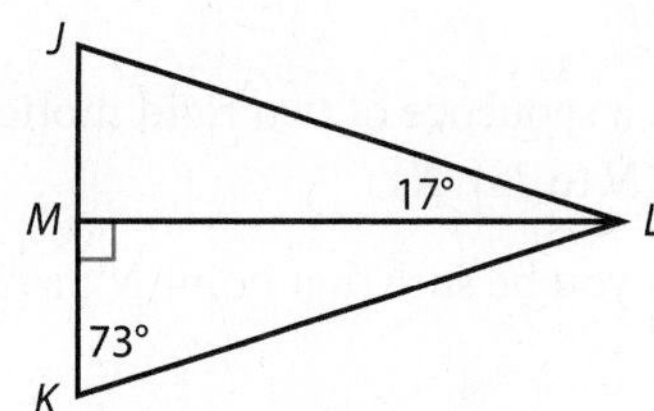

Write each proof.

7. **Given:** $\overline{AB}$ bisects $\angle CAD$ and $\angle CBD$.

Prove: $\triangle CAB \cong \triangle DAB$

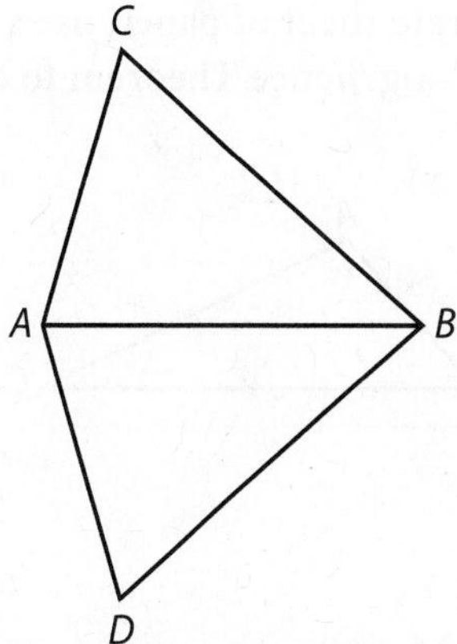

Statements	Reasons
1. $\overline{AB}$ bisects $\angle CAD$ and $\angle CBD$	1. ?
2. $\angle CAB \cong \angle DAB$	2. Definition of bisector
3. ?	3. Definition of bisector
4. ?	4. Reflexive Property of Congruence
5. $\triangle CAB \cong \triangle DAB$	5. ?

8. **Given:** $\overline{AB}$ is parallel to $\overline{CD}$, $\angle ACB \cong \angle CAD$.

Prove: $\triangle ABC \cong \triangle CDA$

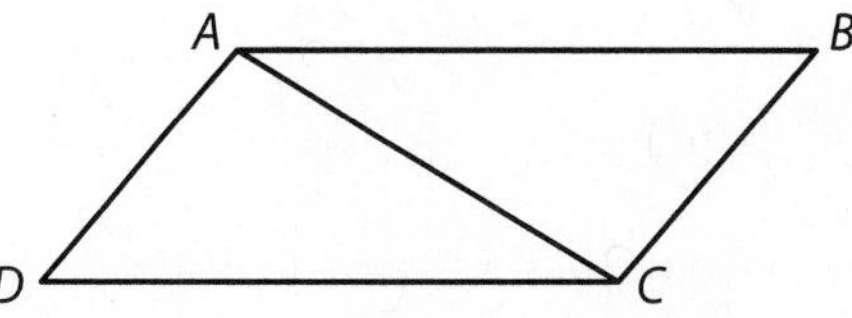

9. **Given:** $\angle H \cong \angle J$, G is the midpoint of $\overline{HJ}$, $\overline{FG}$ is perpendicular to $\overline{HJ}$.

Prove: $\triangle FGH \cong \triangle FGJ$

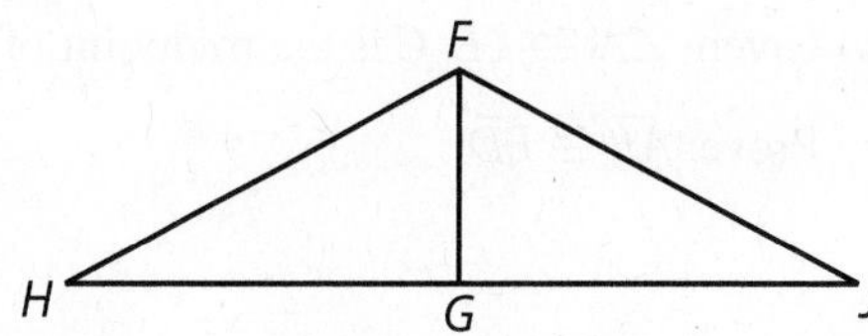

10. The figure shows quadrilateral $PQRS$. What additional information do you need in order to conclude that $\triangle SPR \cong \triangle QRP$ by the ASA Triangle Congruence Theorem? Explain.

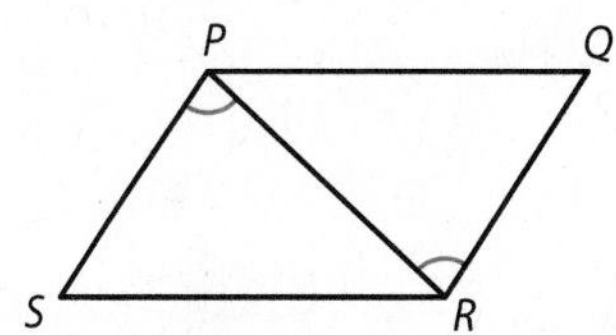

11. **Communicate Mathematical Ideas** In the figure, $\overline{WX}$ is parallel to $\overline{LM}$.

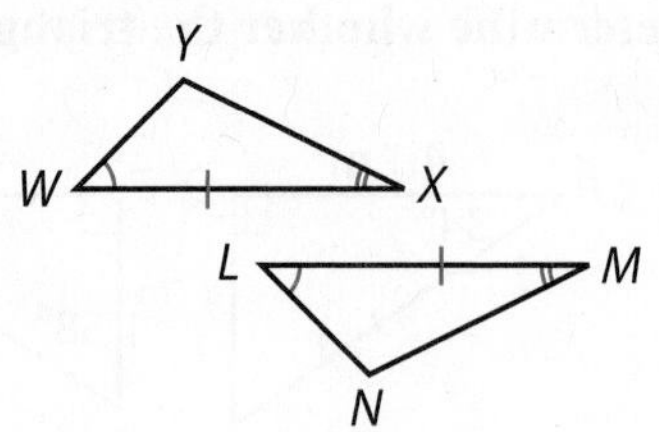

a. Describe a sequence of two rigid motions that maps $\triangle LMN$ to $\triangle WXY$.

b. How can you be sure that point N maps to point Y?

On a separate sheet of paper, use a compass and straightedge and the ASA Triangle Congruence Theorem to construct a triangle that is congruent to $\triangle ABC$.

12.

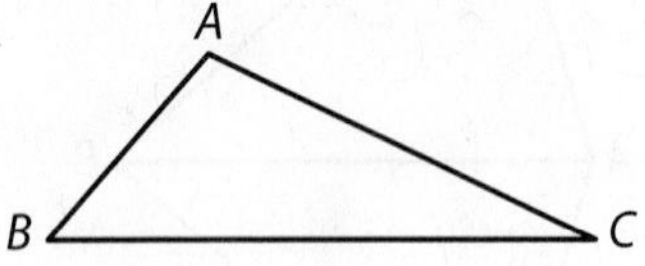

13.

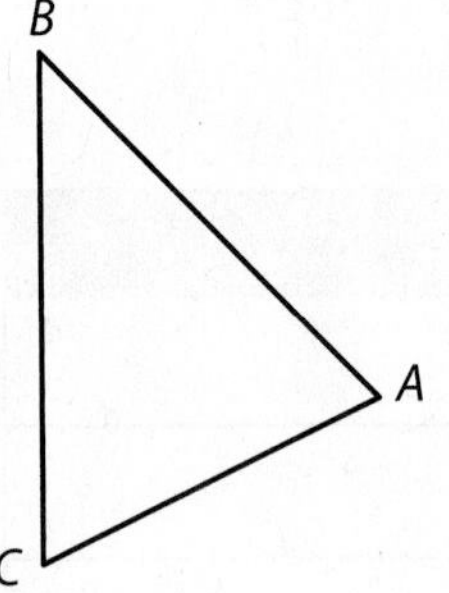

14. **Multi-Step** For what values of the variables is $\triangle QPR$ congruent to $\triangle SPR$? In this case, what is $m\angle Q$?

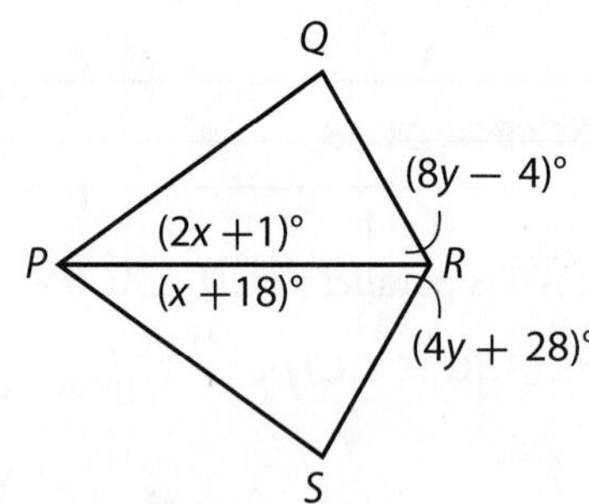

15. Given: $\angle A \cong \angle E$, C is the midpoint of $\overline{AE}$.

Prove: $\overline{AB} \cong \overline{ED}$

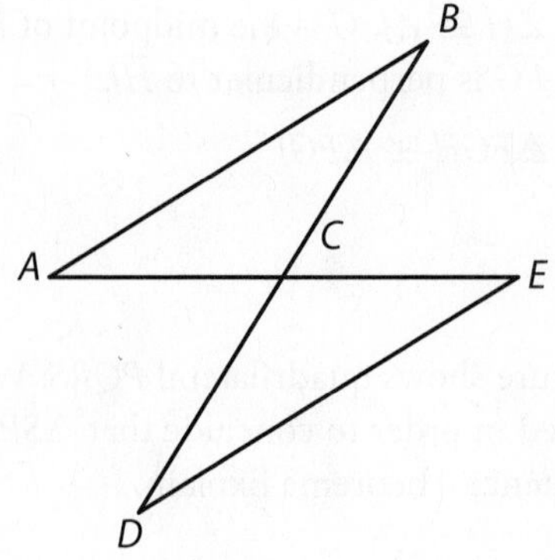

16. The figure shows $\triangle GHJ$ and $\triangle PQR$ on a coordinate plane.

a. Explain why the triangles are congruent using the ASA Triangle Congruence Theorem.

b. Explain why the triangles are congruent using rigid motions.

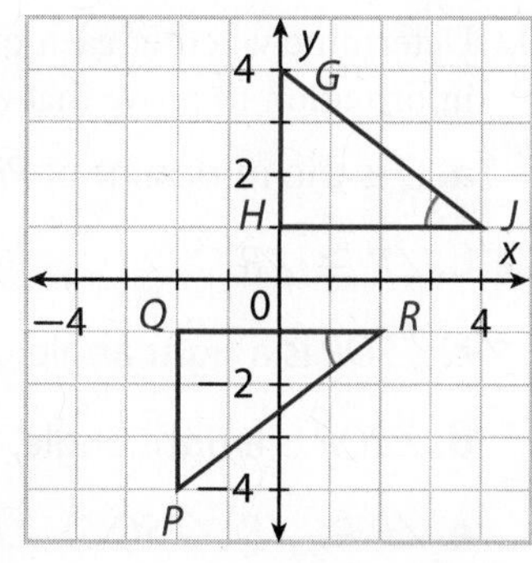

17. **Justify Reasoning** A factory makes triangular traffic signs. Each sign is an equilateral triangle with three 60° angles. Explain why two signs that each have a side 36 inches long must be congruent.

18. **Represent Real-World Problems** Rob is making the kite shown in the figure.

a. Can Rob conclude that $\triangle ABD \cong \triangle ACD$? Why or why not?

b. Rob says that $AB = AC$ and $BD = CD$. Do you agree? Explain.

c. Given that $BD = x + 15$ cm and $AB = x$ cm, write an expression for the distance around the kite in centimeters.

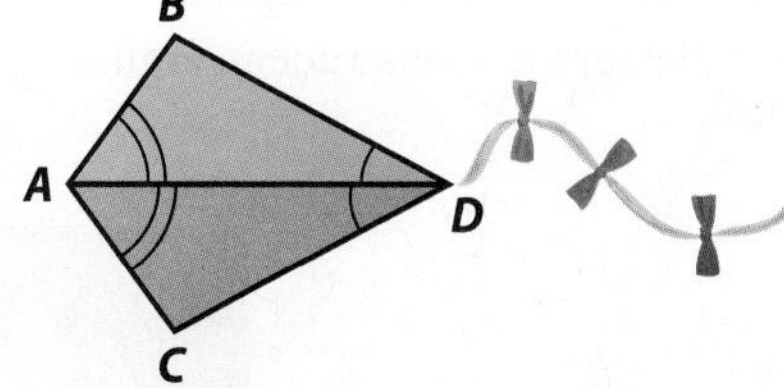

19. In order to find the distance across a canyon, Mariela sites a tree across the canyon (point A) and locates points on her side of the canyon as shown. Explain how she can use this information to find the distance AB across the canyon.

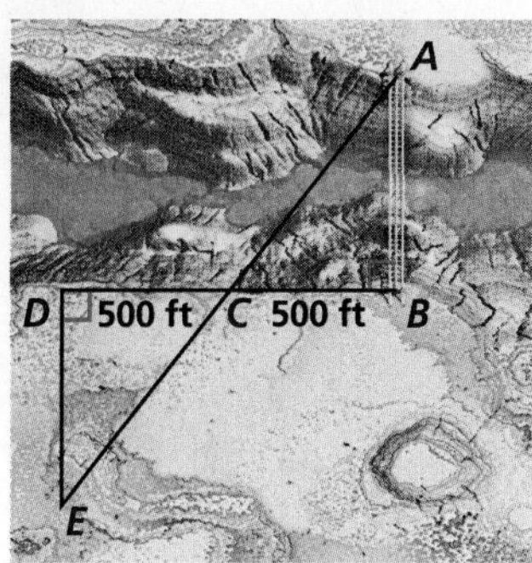

20. Determine whether each of the following provides enough information to prove that $\triangle SQP \cong \triangle SQR$.

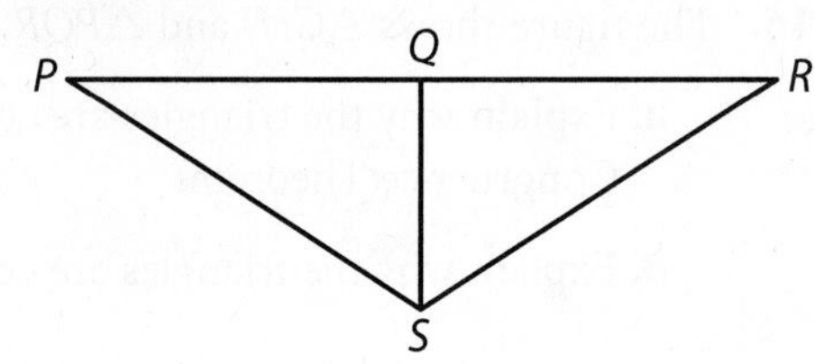

a. Q is the midpoint of $\overline{PR}$.

b. $\angle P \cong \angle R$

c. $\angle SQP$ is a right angle, $\angle PSQ \cong \angle RSQ$

d. $\angle SQP$ is a right angle, $m\angle P = 32°$, $m\angle RSQ = 58°$.

e. $\angle P \cong \angle R$, $\angle PSQ \cong \angle RSQ$

H.O.T. Focus on Higher Order Thinking

21. Counterexamples Jasmine said that the ASA Triangle Congruence Theorem works for quadrilaterals. That is, if two angles and the included side of one quadrilateral are congruent to two angles and the included side of another quadrilateral, then the quadrilaterals are congruent. Sketch and mark a figure of two quadrilaterals as a counterexample to show that Jasmine is incorrect.

22. Critique Reasoning $\triangle ABC$ and $\triangle DEF$ are both right triangles and both triangles contain a 30° angle. Both triangles have a side that is 9.5 mm long. Yoshio claims that he can use the ASA Triangle Congruence Theorem to show that the triangles are congruent. Do you agree? Explain.

23. Draw Conclusions Do you think there is an ASAS Congruence Theorem for quadrilaterals? Suppose two quadrilaterals have a pair of congruent consecutive angles with a pair of congruent included sides and an additional pair of congruent corresponding sides. Must the quadrilaterals be congruent? Justify your response.

Lesson Performance Task

The flag of the Congo Republic consists of green and red right triangles separated by a yellow parallelogram. Construct an argument to prove that $\triangle BAF \cong \triangle EDC$.

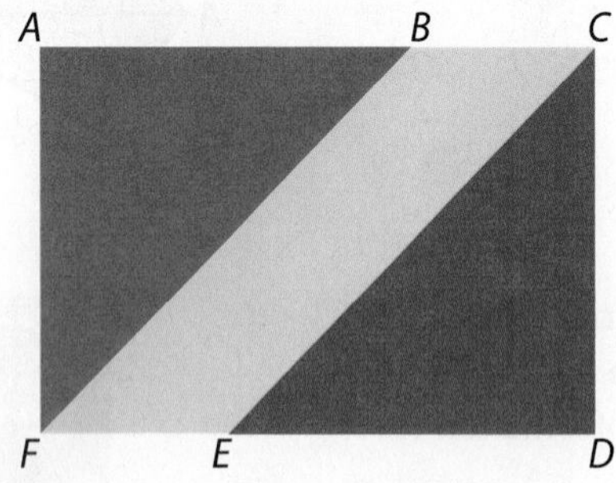

5.3 SAS Triangle Congruence

Resource Locker

Essential Question: What does the SAS Triangle Congruence Theorem tell you about triangles?

Explore 1 Drawing Triangles Given Two Sides and an Angle

You know that when all corresponding parts of two triangles are congruent, then the triangles are congruent. Sometimes you can determine that triangles are congruent based on less information.

For this activity, cut two thin strips of paper, one 3 in. long and the other 2.5 in. long.

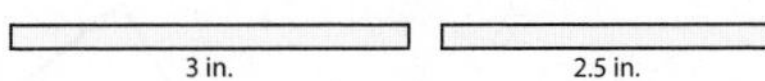

(A) On a sheet of paper use a straightedge to draw a horizontal line. Arrange the 3 in. strip to form a 45° angle, as shown. Next, arrange the 2.5 in. strip to complete the triangle. How many different triangles can you form? Support your answer with a diagram.

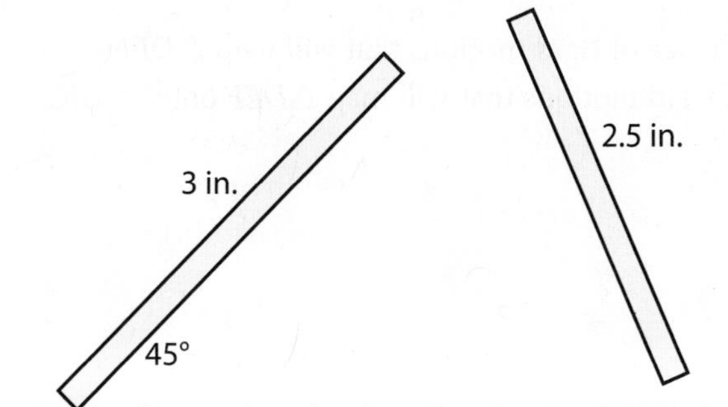

(B) Now arrange the two strips of paper to form a 45° angle so that the angle is *included* between the two consecutive sides, as shown. With this arrangement, can you construct more than one triangle? Why or why not?

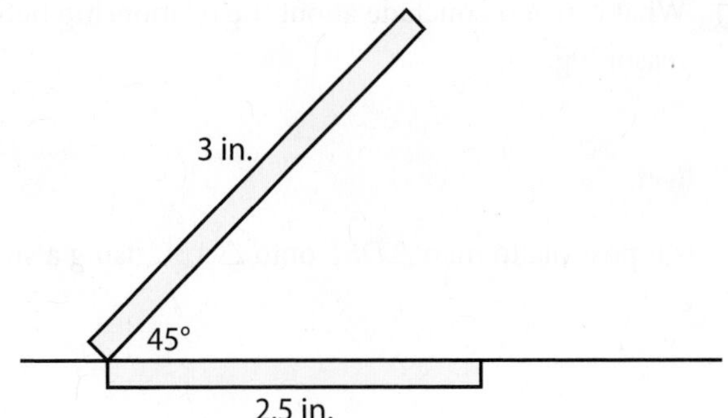

Reflect

1. **Discussion** If two triangles have two pairs of congruent corresponding sides and one pair of congruent corresponding angles, under what conditions can you conclude that the triangles must be congruent? Explain.

Explore 2 Justifying SAS Triangle Congruence

You can explain the results of Explore 1 using transformations.

(A) On a separate sheet of paper, construct $\triangle DEF$ by copying $\angle A$, side $\overline{AB}$, and side $\overline{AC}$. Let point D correspond to point A, point E correspond to point B, and point F correspond to point C, and place point E on the segment shown.

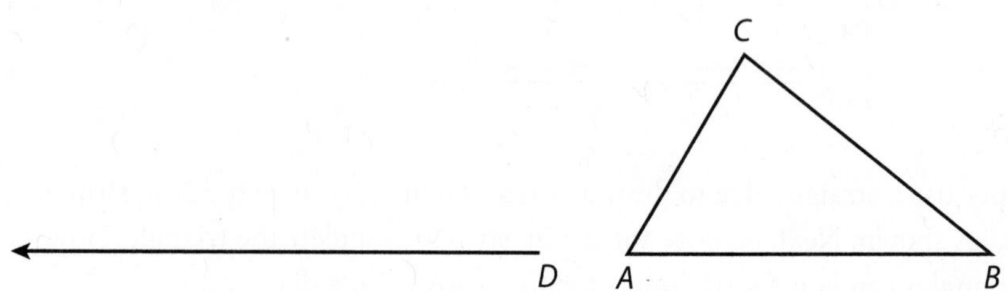

(B) The diagram illustrates one step in a sequence of rigid motions that will map $\triangle DEF$ onto $\triangle ABC$. Describe a complete sequence of rigid motions that will map $\triangle DEF$ onto $\triangle ABC$.

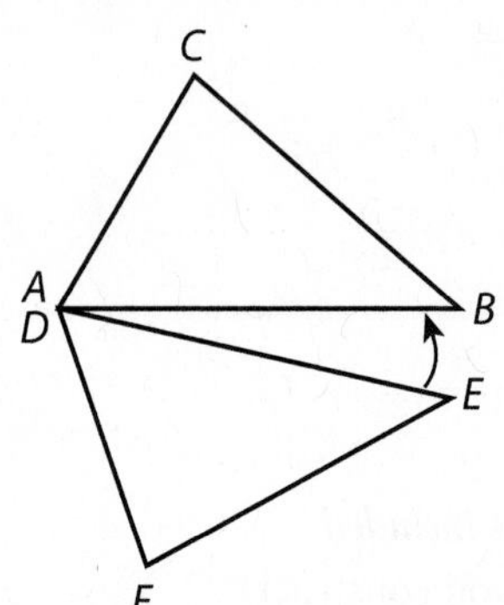

(C) What can you conclude about the relationship between $\triangle ABC$ and $\triangle DEF$? Explain your reasoning.

Reflect

2. Is it possible to map $\triangle DEF$ onto $\triangle ABC$ using a single rigid motion? If so, describe the rigid motion.

Explain 1 Deciding Whether Triangles are Congruent Using SAS Triangle Congruence

What you explored in the previous two activities can be summarized in a theorem. You can use this theorem and the definition of congruence in terms of rigid motions to determine whether two triangles are congruent.

SAS Triangle Congruence Theorem

If two sides and the included angle of one triangle are congruent to two sides and the included angle of another triangle, then the triangles are congruent.

Example 1 **Determine whether the triangles are congruent. Explain your reasoning.**

 Look for congruent corresponding parts.

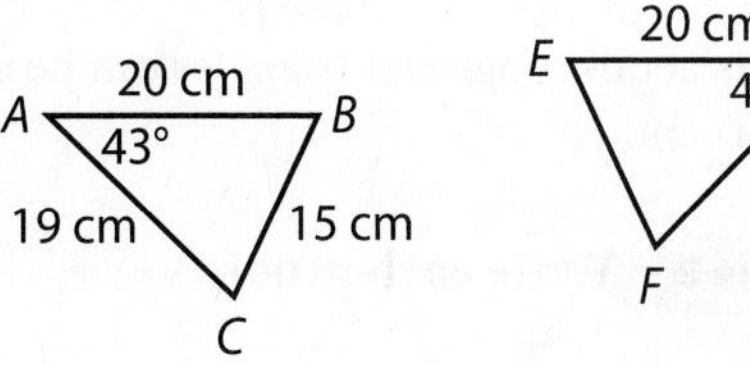

- Sides $\overline{DE}$ and $\overline{DF}$ do not correspond to side $\overline{BC}$, because they are not 15 cm long.
- $\overline{DE}$ corresponds to $\overline{AB}$, because $DE = AB = 20$ cm.
- $\overline{DF}$ corresponds to $\overline{AC}$, because $DF = AC = 19$ cm.
- $\angle A$ and $\angle D$ are be corresponding angles because they are included between pairs of corresponding sides, but they don't have the same measure.

The triangles are not congruent, because there is no sequence of rigid motions that maps $\triangle ABC$ onto $\triangle DEF$.

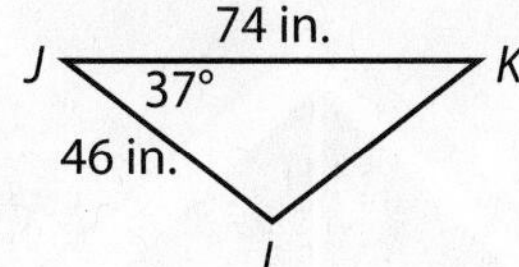

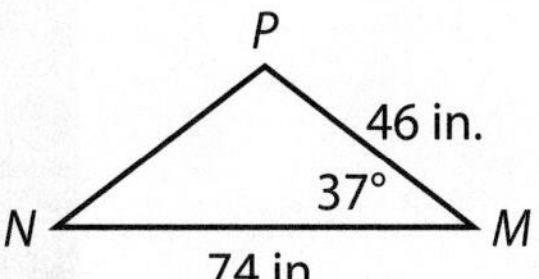

Look for congruent corresponding parts.

- $\overline{JL}$ corresponds to $\overline{MP}$, because $JL = MP = 46$ in.
- $\overline{JK}$ corresponds to MN, because $JK = MN = 74$ in.
- $\angle J$ corresponds to $\angle M$, because $m\angle J = m\angle M = 37°$.

Two sides and the included angle of $\triangle JKL$ are congruent to two sides and the included angle of $\triangle MNP$. $\triangle JKL \cong \triangle MNP$ by the SAS Triangle Congruence Theorem.

Your Turn

3. Determine whether the triangles are congruent. Explain your reasoning.

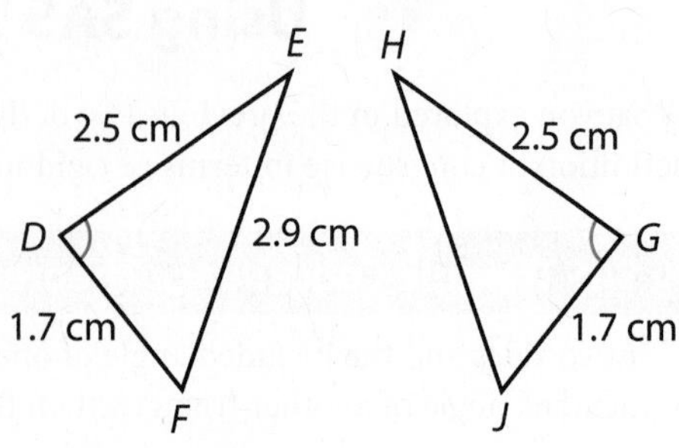

Explain 2 Proving Triangles Are Congruent Using SAS Triangle Congruence

Theorems about congruent triangles can be used to show that triangles in real-world objects are congruent.

Example 2 **Write each proof.**

Ⓐ Write a proof to show that the two halves of a triangular window are congruent if the vertical post is the perpendicular bisector of the base.

Given: $\overline{BD}$ is the perpendicular bisector of $\overline{AC}$.
Prove: $\triangle BDA \cong \triangle BDC$

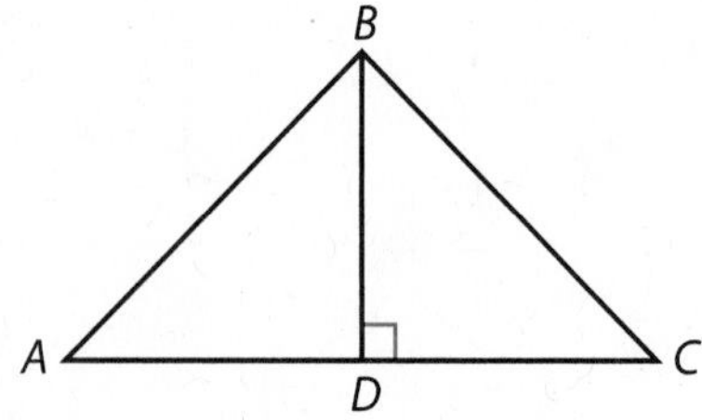

It is given that $\overline{BD}$ is the perpendicular bisector of $\overline{AC}$. By the definition of a perpendicular bisector, $AD = CD$, which means $\overline{AD} \cong \overline{CD}$, and $\overline{BD} \perp \overline{AC}$, which means $\angle BDA$ and $\angle BDC$ are congruent right angles. In addition, $\overline{BD} \cong \overline{BD}$ by the reflexive property of congruence. So two sides and the included angle of $\triangle BDA$ are congruent to two sides and the included angle of $\triangle BDC$. The triangles are congruent by the SAS Triangle Congruence Theorem.

Given: $\overline{CD}$ bisects $\overline{AE}$ and $\overline{AE}$ bisects $\overline{CD}$

Prove: $\triangle ABC \cong \triangle EBD$

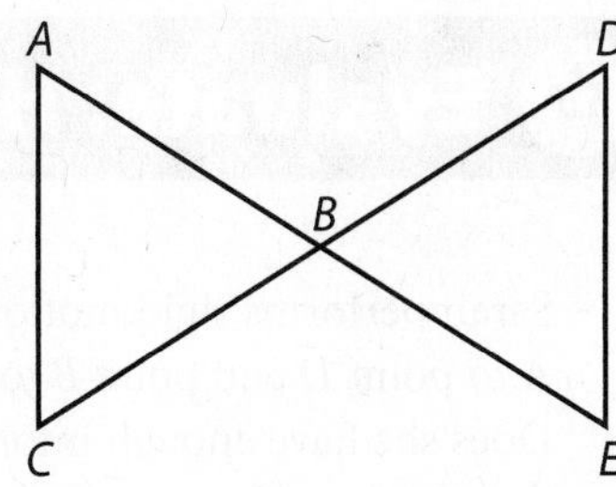

It is given that $\overline{CD}$ bisects $\overline{AE}$ and $\overline{AE}$ bisects $\overline{CD}$. So by the definition of a bisector, $AB = EB$ and $CB = DB$, which makes $\overline{AB} \cong \overline{EB}$ and $\overline{CB} \cong \overline{DB}$. $\angle ABC \cong \angle EBD$ because they are vertical angles. So two sides and the included angle of $\triangle ABC$ are congruent to two sides and the included angle of $\triangle EBD$. The triangles are congruent by the SAS Triangle Congruence Theorem.

Your Turn

4. Given: $\overline{AB} \cong \overline{AD}$ and $\angle 1 \cong \angle 2$

Prove: $\triangle BAC \cong \triangle DAC$

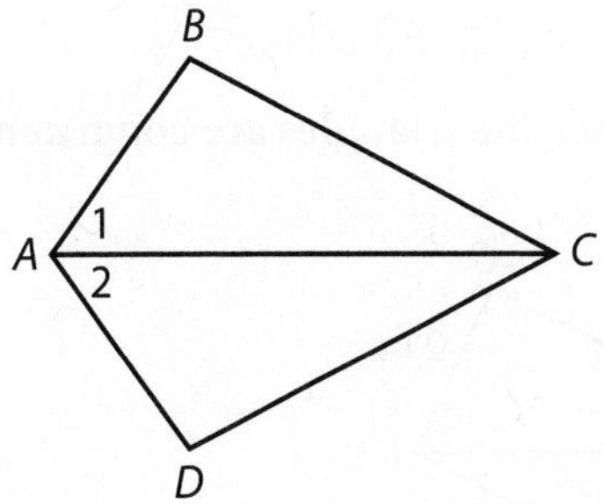

Elaborate

5. Explain why the corresponding angles must be *included* angles in order to use the SAS Triangle Congruence Theorem.

6. Jeffrey draws $\triangle PQR$ and $\triangle TUV$. He uses a translation to map point P to point T and point R to point V as shown. What should be his next step in showing the triangles are congruent? Why?

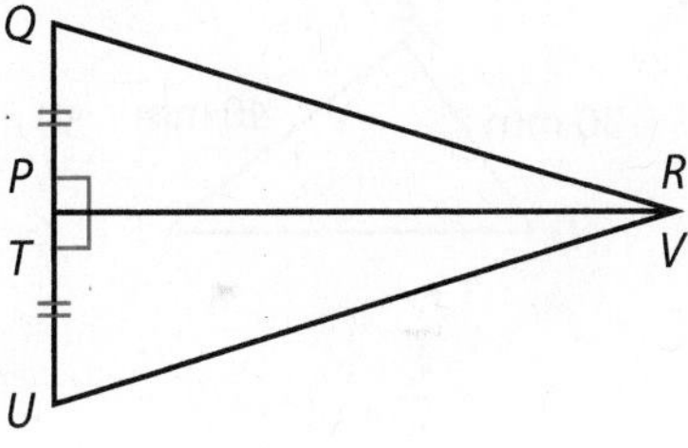

7. **Essential Question Check-In** If two triangles share a common side, what else must be true for the SAS Triangle Congruence Theorem to apply?

Evaluate: Homework and Practice

- Online Homework
- Hints and Help
- Extra Practice

1. Sarah performs rigid motions mapping point A to point D and point B to point E, as shown. Does she have enough information to confirm that the triangles are congruent? Explain your reasoning.

Determine whether the triangles are congruent. Explain your reasoning.

2.

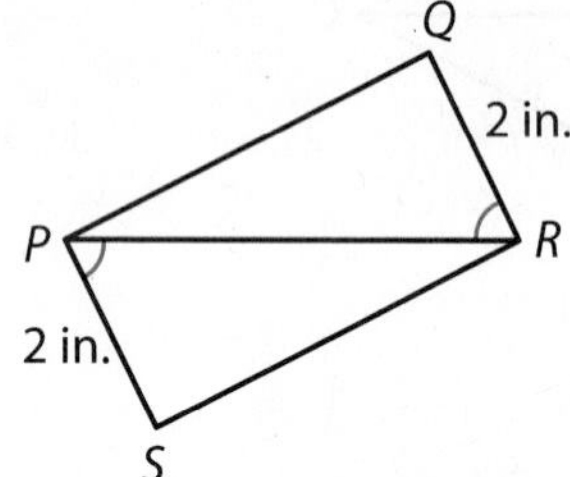

3.

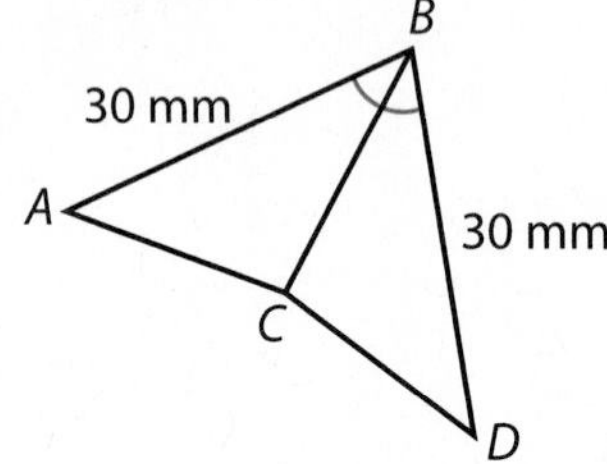

4.

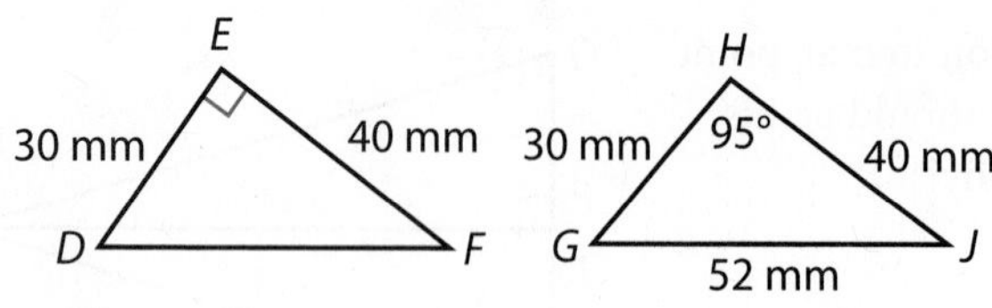

5.

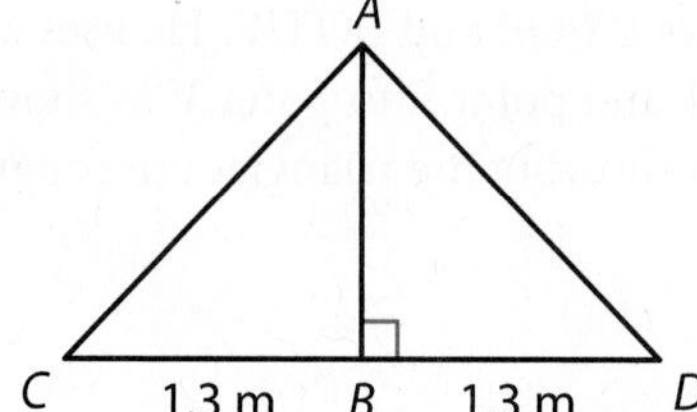

Find the value of the variable that results in congruent triangles. Explain.

6.

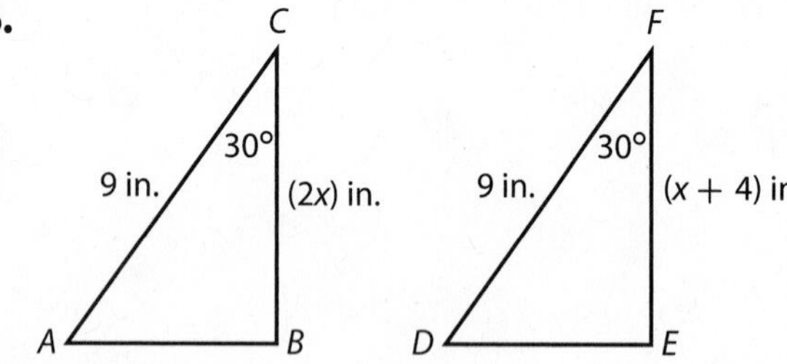

7.

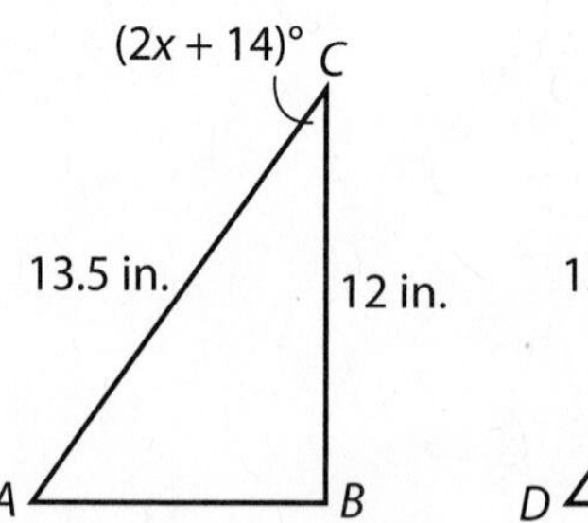

8. Given that polygon $ABCDEF$ is a regular hexagon, prove that $\overline{AC} \cong \overline{AE}$.

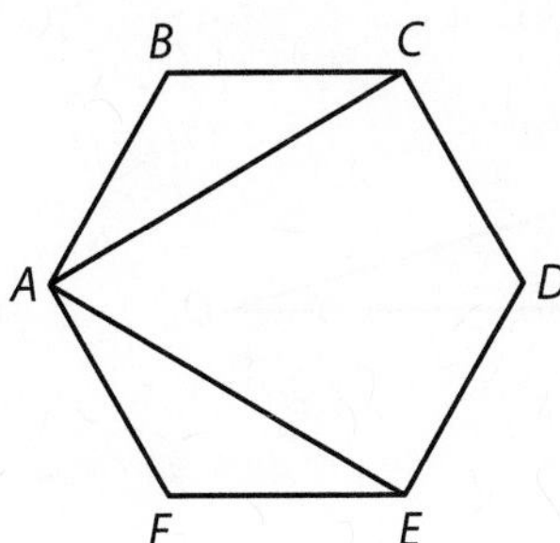

9. A product designer is designing an easel with extra braces as shown in the diagram. Prove that if $\overline{BD} \cong \overline{FD}$ and $\overline{CD} \cong \overline{ED}$, then the braces $\overline{BE}$ and $\overline{FC}$ are also congruent.

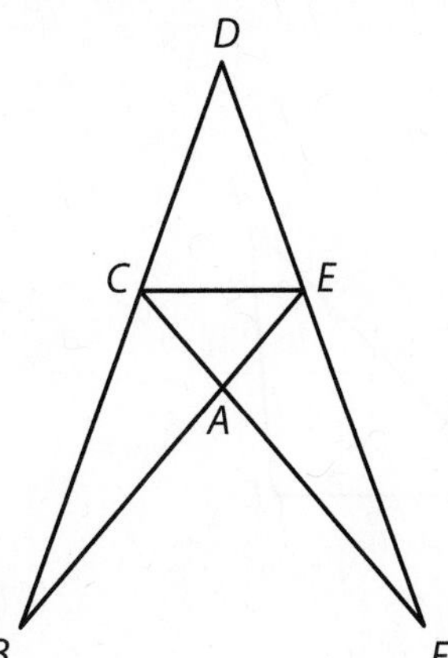

10. An artist is framing a large picture and wants to put metal poles across the back to strengthen the frame as shown in the diagram. If the metal poles are both the same length and they bisect each other, prove that $\overline{AB} \cong \overline{CD}$ and $\overline{AD} \cong \overline{CB}$.

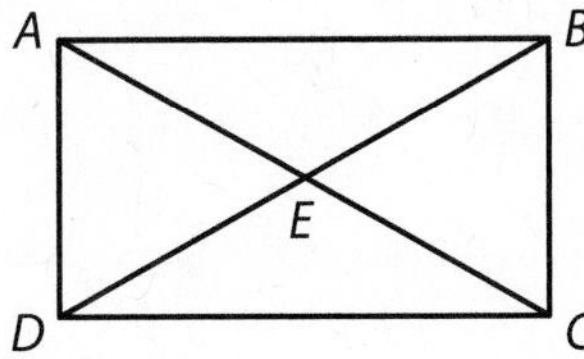

11. The figure shows a side panel of a skateboard ramp. Kalim wants to confirm that the right triangles in the panel are congruent.

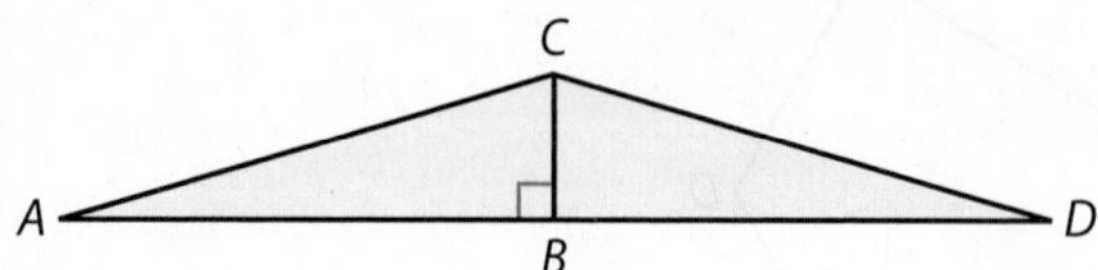

a. What measurements should Kalim take if he wants to confirm that the triangles are congruent by SAS? Explain.

b. What measurements should Kalim take if he wants to confirm that the triangles are congruent by ASA? Explain.

12. Which of the following are reasons that justify why the triangles are congruent? Select all that apply.

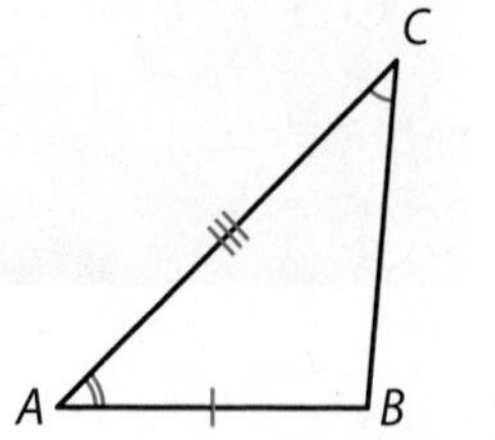

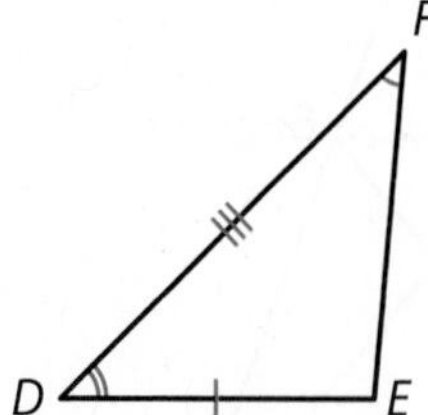

A. SSA Triangle Congruence Theorem

B. SAS Triangle Congruence Theorem

C. ASA Triangle Congruence Theorem

D. Converse of CPCTC

E. CPCTC

H.O.T. Focus on Higher Order Thinking

13. Multi-Step Refer to the following diagram to answer each question.

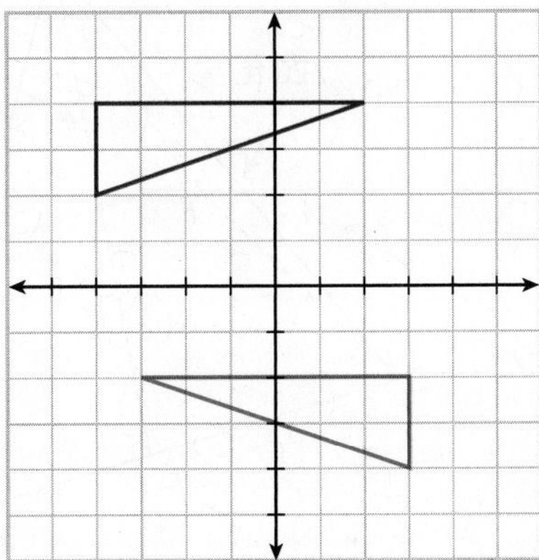

a. Use a triangle congruence theorem to explain why these triangles are congruent.

b. Describe a sequence of rigid motions to map the top triangle onto the bottom triangle to confirm that they are congruent.

14. Explain the Error Mark says that the diagram confirms that a given angle and two given side lengths determine a unique triangle even if the angle is not an included angle. Explain Mark's error.

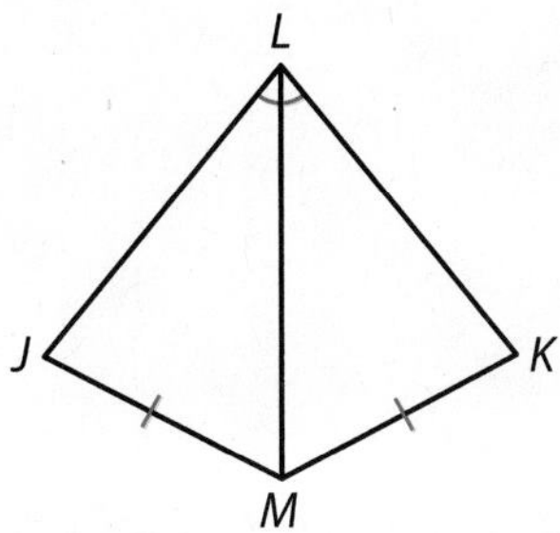

15. Justify Reasoning The opposite sides of a rectangle are congruent. Can you conclude that a diagonal of a rectangle divides the rectangle into two congruent triangles? Justify your response.

Lesson Performance Task

The diagram of the Great Pyramid at Giza gives the approximate lengths of edge $\overline{AB}$ and slant height $\overline{AC}$. The slant height is the perpendicular bisector of $\overline{BD}$. Find the perimeter of $\triangle ABD$. Explain how you found the answer.

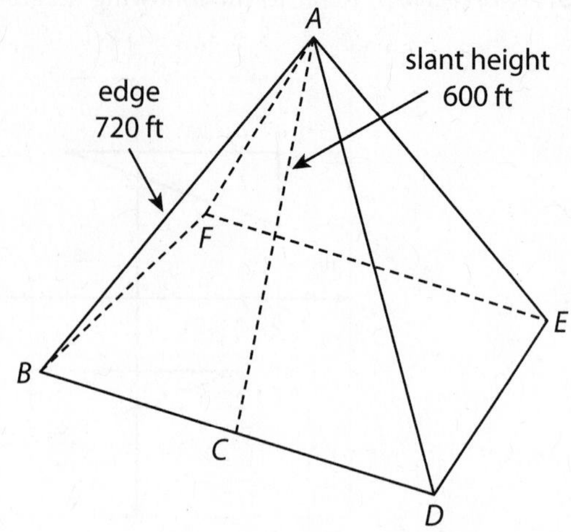

5.4 SSS Triangle Congruence

Essential Question: What does the SSS Triangle Congruence Theorem tell you about triangles?

Resource Locker

Explore Constructing Triangles Given Three Side Lengths

Two triangles are congruent if and only if a rigid motion transformation maps one triangle onto the other triangle. Many theorems can also be used to identify congruent triangles.

Follow these steps to construct a triangle with sides of length 5 in., 4 in., and 3 in. Use a ruler, compass, and either tracing paper or a transparency.

(A) Use a ruler to draw a line segment of length 5 inches. Label the endpoints A and B.

(B) Open a compass to 4 inches. Place the point of the compass on A, and draw an arc as shown.

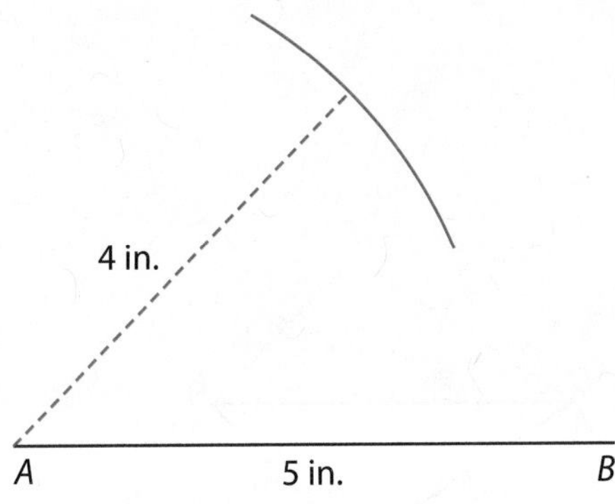

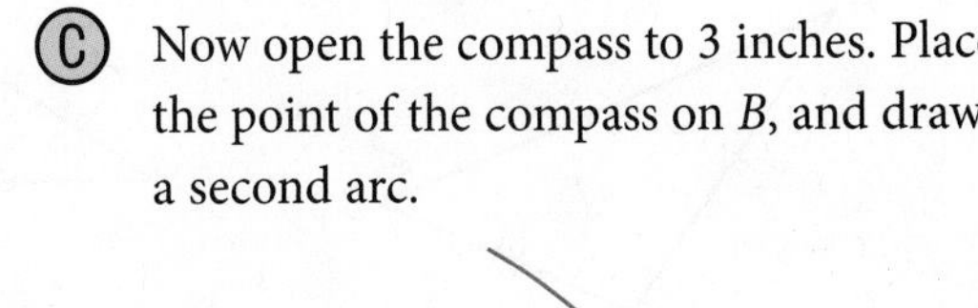
(C) Now open the compass to 3 inches. Place the point of the compass on B, and draw a second arc.

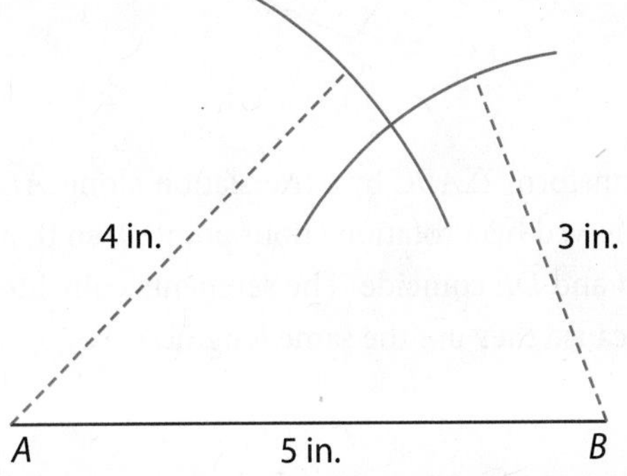

(D) Next, find the intersection of the two arcs. Label the intersection C. Draw $\overline{AC}$ and $\overline{BC}$. Label the side lengths on the figure.

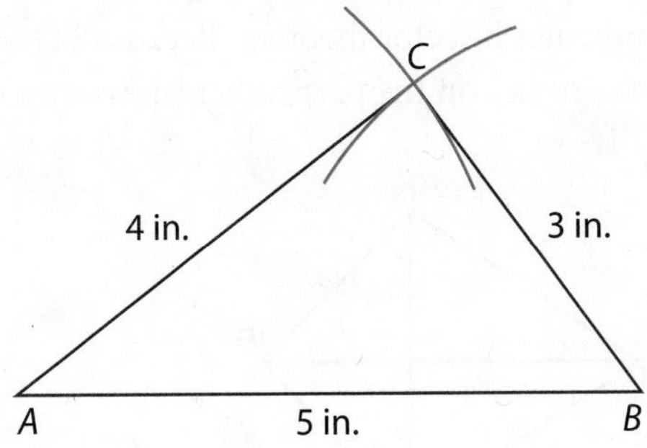

(E) Repeat steps A through D to draw $\triangle DEF$ on a separate piece of tracing paper. The triangle should have sides with the same lengths as $\triangle CAB$. Start with a segment that is 4 in. long. Label the endpoints D and E as shown.

(F) Compare $\triangle CAB$ and $\triangle DEF$. Are they congruent? How do you know?

Reflect

1. **Discussion** When you construct $\triangle CAB$, how do you know that the intersection of the two arcs is a distance of 4 inches from A and 3 inches from B?

2. Compare your triangles to those made by other students. Are they all congruent? Explain.

Explain 1 Justifying SSS Triangle Congruence

You can use rigid motions and the converse of the Perpendicular Bisector Theorem to justify this theorem.

SSS Triangle Congruence Theorem

If three sides of one triangle are congruent to three sides of another triangle, then the triangles are congruent.

Example 1 **In the triangles shown, let $\overline{AB} \cong \overline{DE}$, $\overline{AC} \cong \overline{DF}$, and $\overline{BC} \cong \overline{EF}$. Use rigid motions to show that $\triangle ABC \cong \triangle DEF$.**

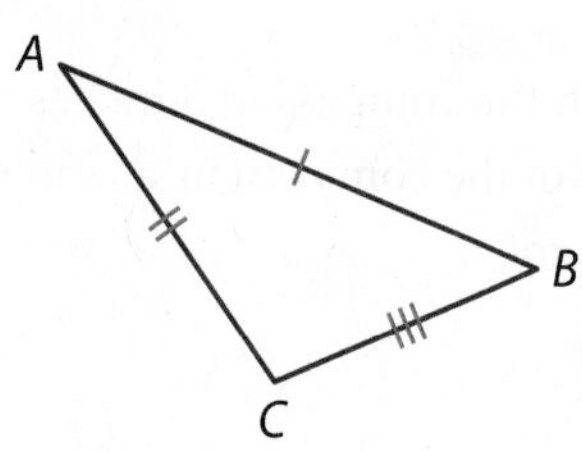

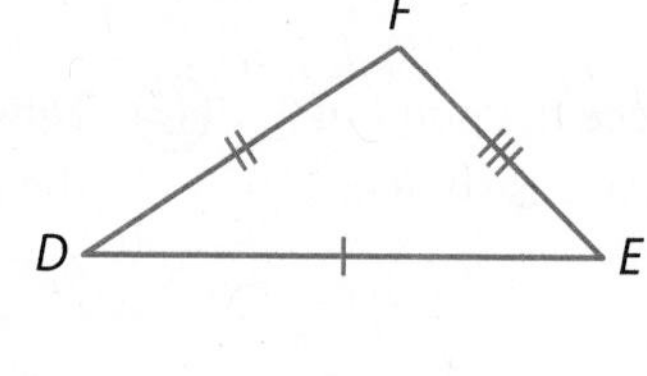

(A) Transform $\triangle ABC$ by a translation along $\overrightarrow{AD}$ followed by a rotation about point D, so that $\overline{AB}$ and $\overline{DE}$ coincide. The segments coincide because they are the same length.

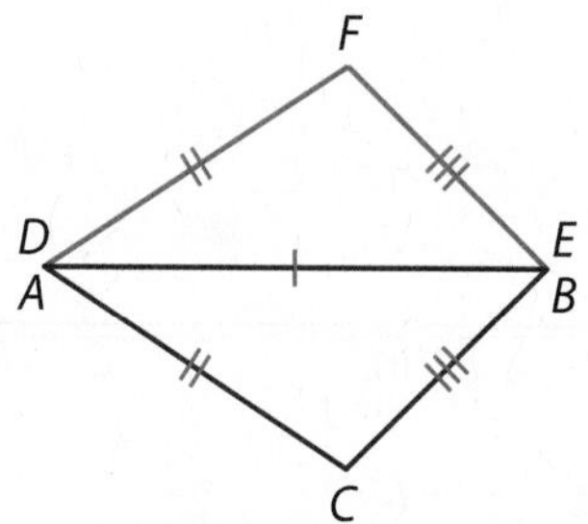

Does a reflection across $\overline{AB}$ map point C to point F? To show this, notice that $DC = DF$, which means that point D is equidistant from point C and point F.

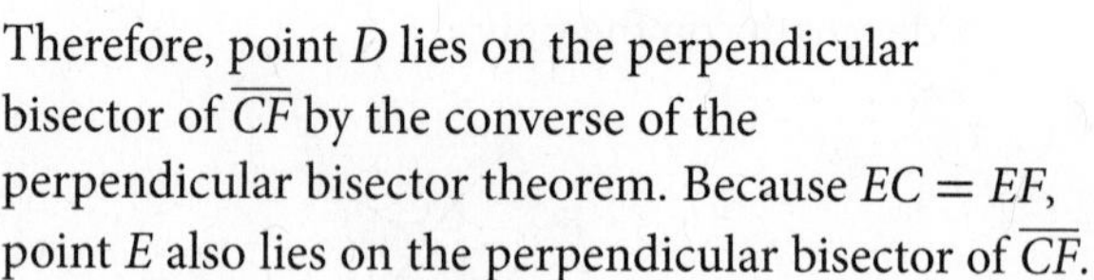
Therefore, point D lies on the perpendicular bisector of $\overline{CF}$ by the converse of the perpendicular bisector theorem. Because $EC = EF$, point E also lies on the perpendicular bisector of $\overline{CF}$.

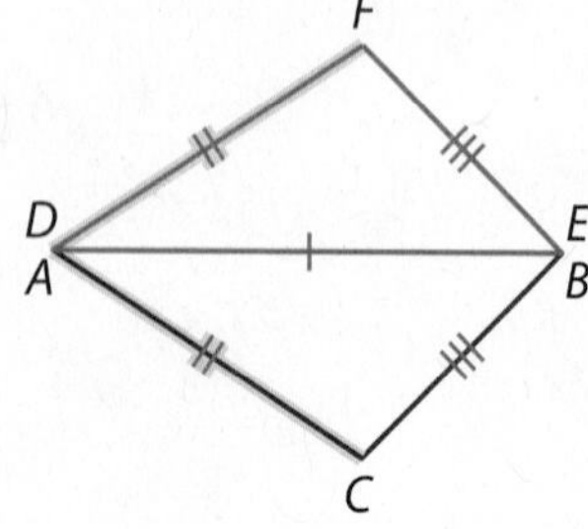

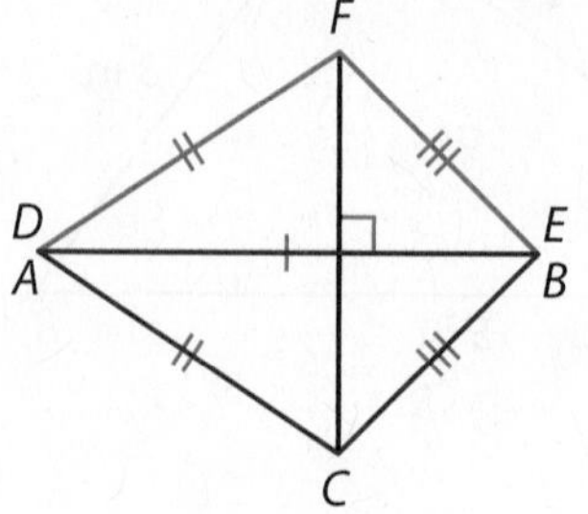

Since point D and point E both lie on the perpendicular bisector of $\overline{CF}$ and there is a unique line through any two points, $\overleftrightarrow{DE}$ is the perpendicular bisector of $\overline{CF}$. By the definition of reflection, the image of point C must be point F. Therefore, $\triangle ABC$ is mapped onto $\triangle DEF$ by a translation, followed by a rotation, followed by a reflection, and the two triangles are congruent.

(B) Show that $\triangle ABC \cong \triangle PQR$.

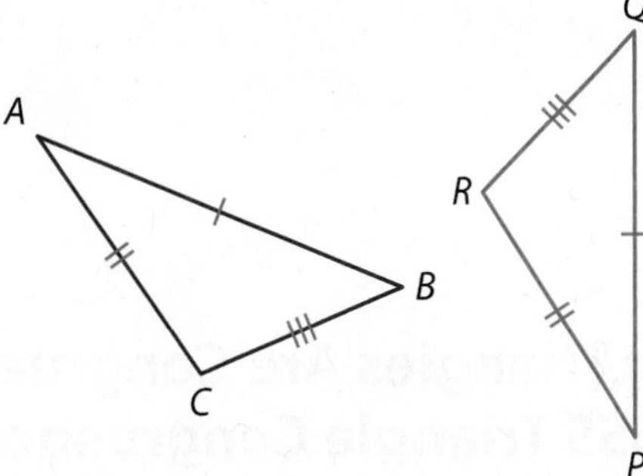

Triangle ABC is transformed by a sequence of rigid motions to form the figure shown below. Identify the sequence of rigid motions.

<table>
<tr>
<td>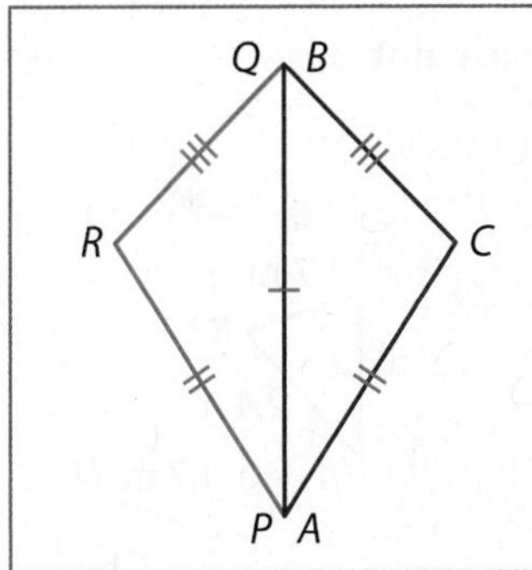</td>
<td>1. Translation along $\overrightarrow{AP}$
2. Rotation about P so that $\overline{PQ}$ and $\overline{AB}$ coincide.
3. Reflection across $\overline{PQ}$.</td>
</tr>
</table>

Because $\overline{QR} \cong \overline{QC}$, point Q is equidistant from R (or C) and C (or R). Therefore, by the converse of the Perpendicular Bisector Theorem, point Q lies on the perpendicular bisector of $\overline{RC}$. Similarly, $\overline{PR} \cong \overline{PC}$. So point P lies on the perpendicular bisector of $\overline{RC}$. Because two points determine a line, the line $\overleftrightarrow{PQ}$ is the perpendicular bisector of $\overline{RC}$. By the definition of reflection, the image of point C must be point R. Therefore, $\triangle ABC \cong \triangle PQR$ because $\triangle ABC$ is mapped to $\triangle PQR$ by a translation, a rotation, and a reflection.

Reflect

3. Can you conclude that two triangles are congruent if two pairs of corresponding sides are congruent? Explain your reasoning and include an example.

Your Turn

4. Use rigid motions and the converse of the perpendicular bisector theorem to explain why $\triangle ABC \cong \triangle ADC$.

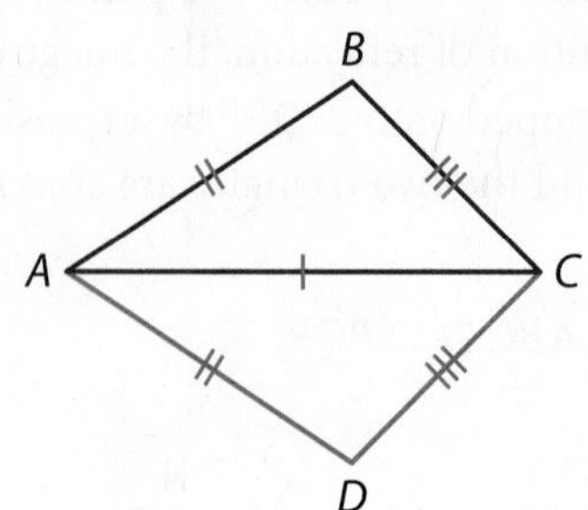

Explain 2 Proving Triangles Are Congruent Using SSS Triangle Congruence

You can apply the SSS Triangle Congruence Theorem to confirm that triangles are congruent. Remember, if any one pair of corresponding parts of two triangles is not congruent, then the triangles are not congruent.

Example 2 **Prove that the triangles are congruent or explain why they are not congruent.**

(A) $AB = DE = 1.7$ m, so $\overline{AB} \cong \overline{DE}$.

$BC = EF = 2.4$ m, so $\overline{BC} \cong \overline{EF}$.

$AC = DF = 2.3$ m, so $\overline{AC} \cong \overline{DF}$.

The three sides of $\triangle ABC$ are congruent to the three sides of $\triangle DEF$.

$\triangle ABC \cong \triangle DEF$ by the SSS Triangle Congruence Theorem.

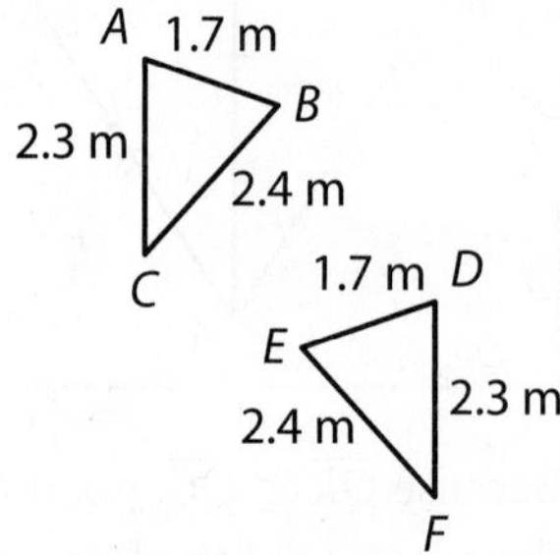

(B) $DE = FG = 20$ cm, so $\overline{DE} \cong \overline{FG}$.

$DH = FH = 12$ cm, so $\overline{DH} \cong \overline{FH}$.

$EH = GH = 24$ cm, so $\overline{EH} \cong \overline{GH}$.

The three sides of $\triangle DEH$ are congruent to the three sides of $\triangle FGH$, so the two triangles are congruent by the SSS Triangle Congruence Theorem.

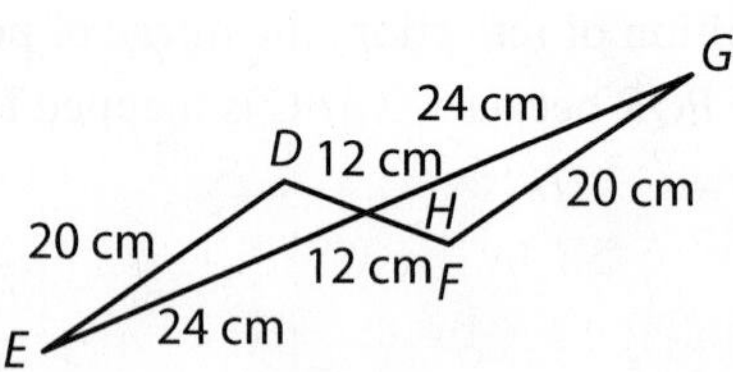

Your Turn

Prove that the triangles are congruent or explain why they are not congruent.

5.

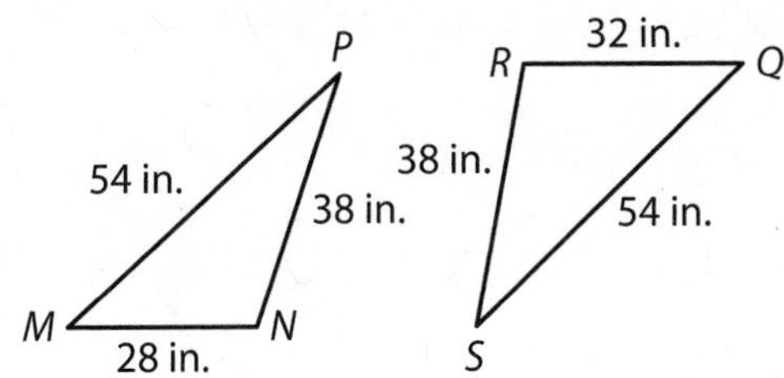

6.

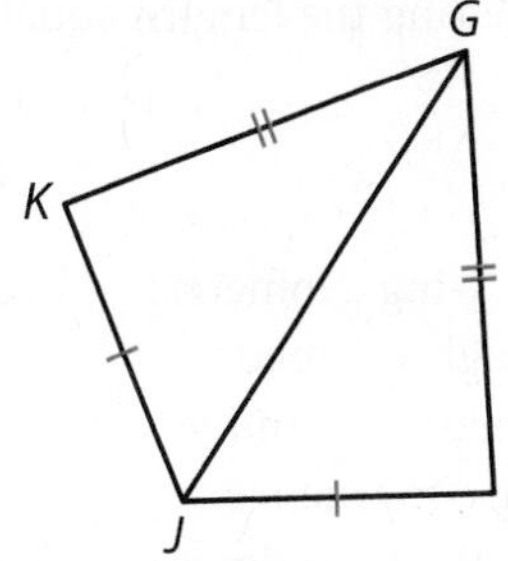

Explain 3 Applying Triangle Congruence

You can use the SSS Triangle Congruence Theorem and other triangle congruence theorems to solve many real-world problems that involve congruent triangles.

Example 3 **Find the value of x for which you can show the triangles are congruent.**

(A) Lexi bought matching triangular pendants for herself and her mom in the shapes shown. For what value of x can you use a triangle congruence theorem to show that the pendants are congruent? Which triangle congruence theorem can you use? Explain.

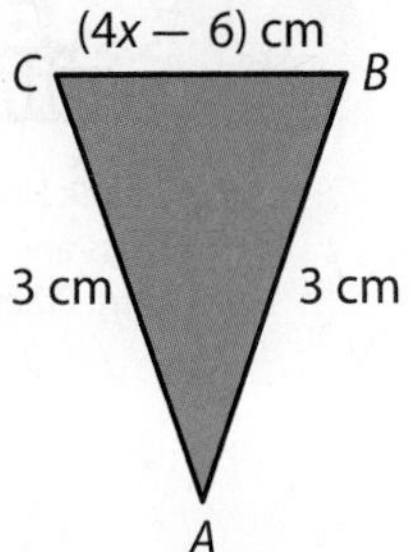

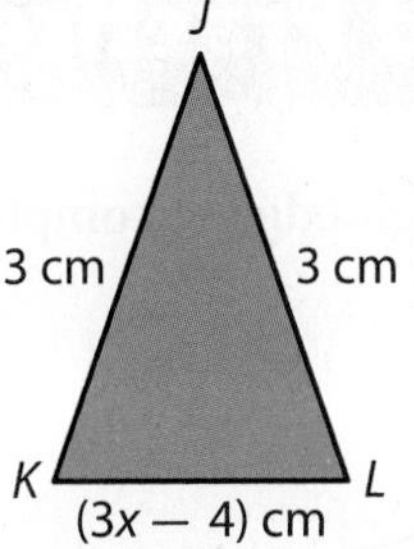

$\overline{AB} \cong \overline{JK}$ and $\overline{AC} \cong \overline{JL}$, because they have the same measure. So, if $\overline{BC} \cong \overline{KL}$, then $\triangle ABC \cong \triangle JKL$ by the SSS Triangle Congruence Theorem. Write an equation setting the lengths equal and solve for x. $4x - 6 = 3x - 4$; $x = 2$

(B) Adeline made a design using triangular tiles as shown. For what value of x can you use a triangle congruence theorem to show that the tiles are congruent? Which triangle congruence theorem can you use? Explain.

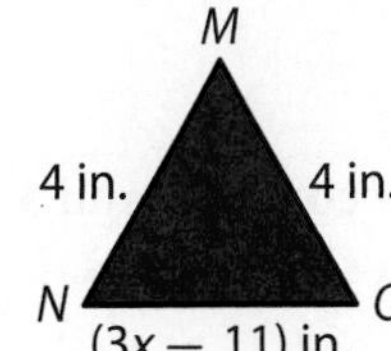

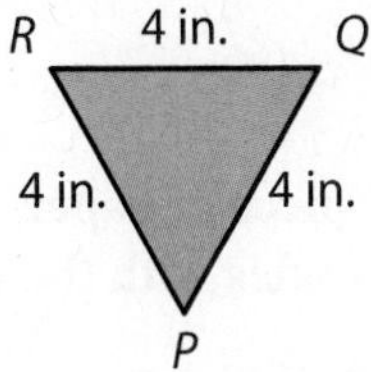

Notice that $\overline{PQ} \cong \overline{MN}$ and $\overline{PR} \cong \overline{MO}$, because they have the same measure.

If $\overline{NO} \cong \overline{QR}$, then $\triangle MNO \cong \triangle PQR$ by the SSS Triangle Congruence Theorem.

Write an equation setting the lengths equal and solve for x. $3x - 11 = 4$, $3x = 15$, $x = 5$

Your Turn

7. Craig made a mobile using geometric shapes including triangles shaped as shown. For what value of x and y can you use a triangle congruence theorem to show that the triangles are congruent? Which triangle congruence theorem can you use? Explain.

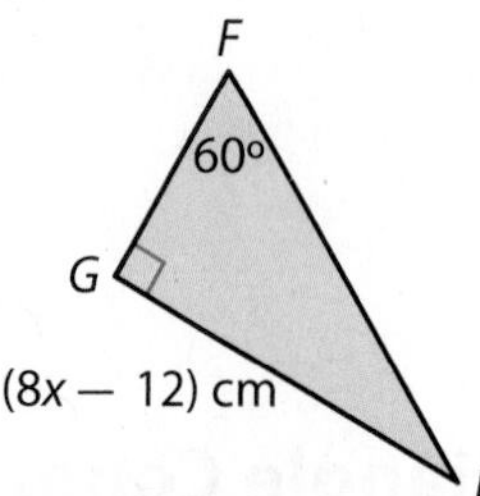

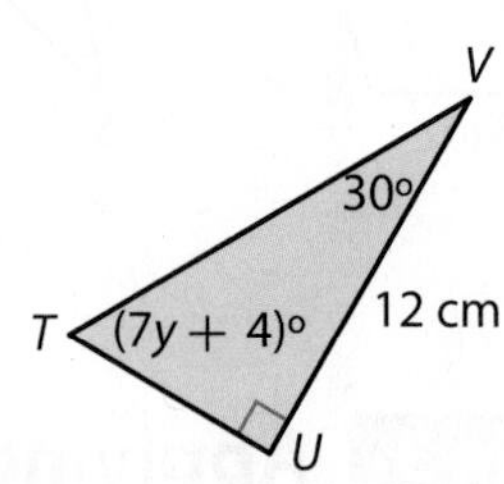

Elaborate

8. An isosceles triangle has two sides of equal length. If we ask everyone in class to construct an isosceles triangle that has one side of length 8 cm and another side of length 12 cm, how many sets of congruent triangles might the class make?

9. **Essential Question Check-In** How do you explain the SSS Triangle Congruence Theorem?

Evaluate: Homework and Practice

- Online Homework
- Hints and Help
- Extra Practice

On a separate piece of paper, use a compass and a straightedge to complete the drawing of $\triangle DEF$ so that it is congruent to $\triangle ABC$.

1.

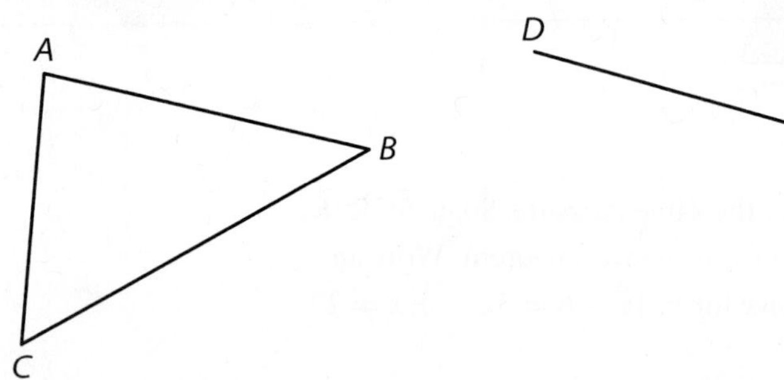

On a separate piece of paper, use a compass and a ruler to construct two congruent triangles with the given side lengths. Label the lengths of the sides.

2. 3 in., 3.5 in., 4 in.

3. 3 cm, 11 cm, 12 cm

Identify a sequence of rigid motions that maps one side of $\triangle ABC$ onto one side of $\triangle DEF$.

4.

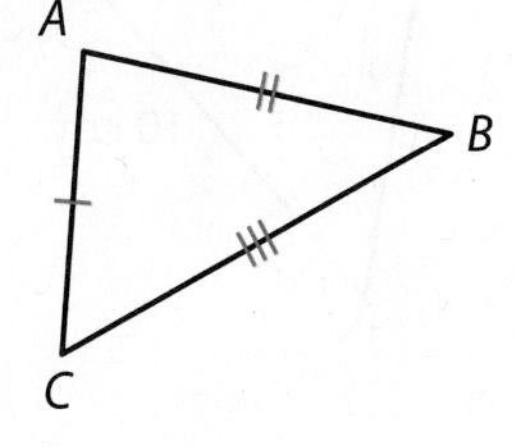

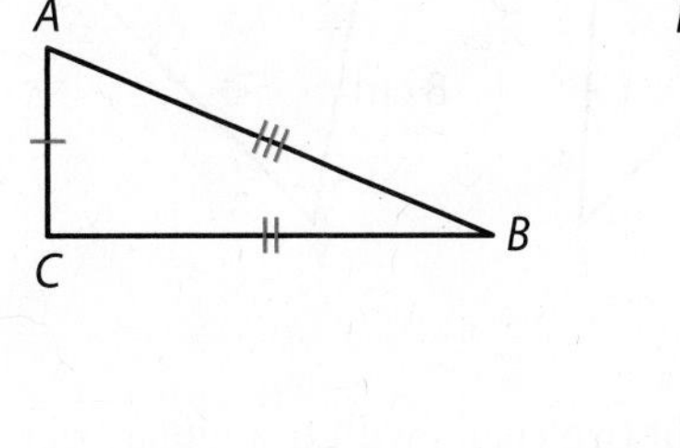

5.

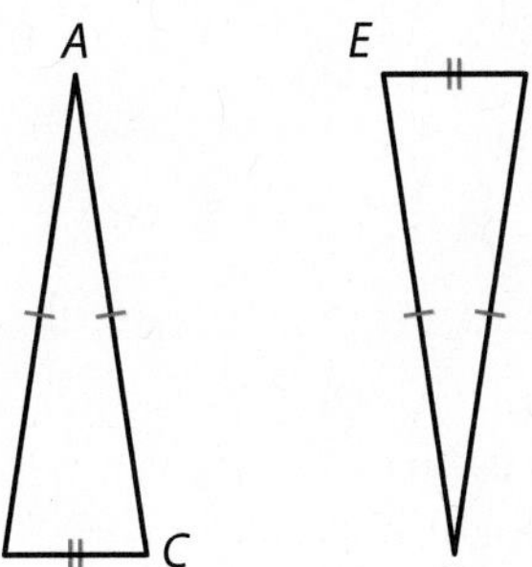

6.

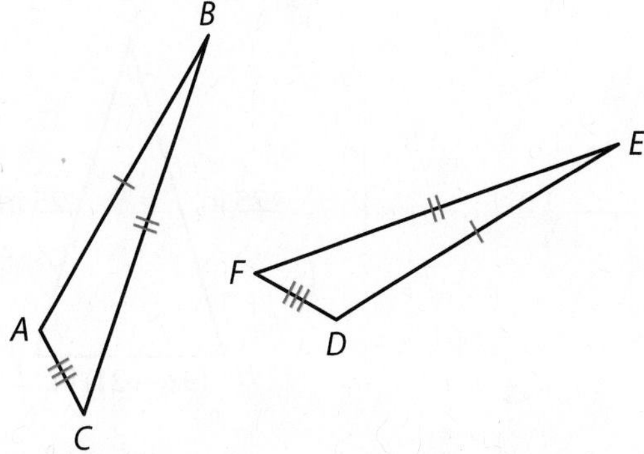

7.

In each figure, identify the perpendicular bisector and the line segment it bisects, and explain how to use the information to show that the two triangles are congruent.

8.

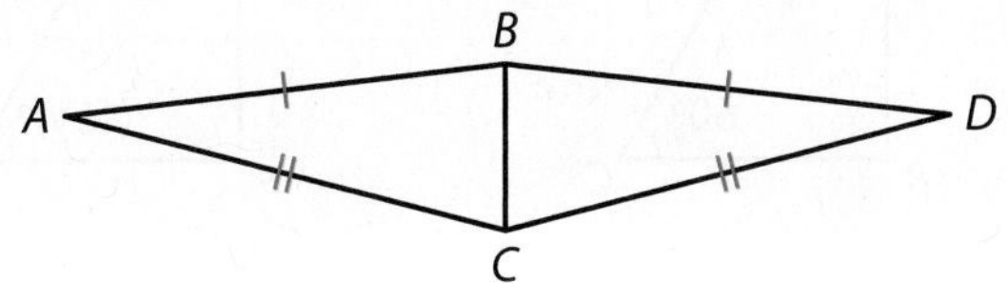

9.

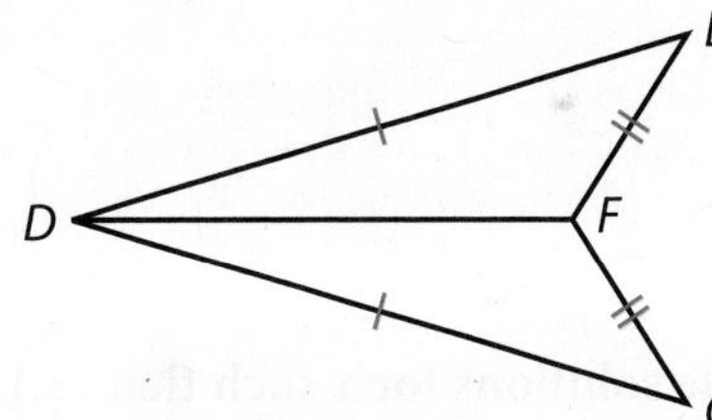

Prove that the triangles are congruent or explain why this is not possible.

10.

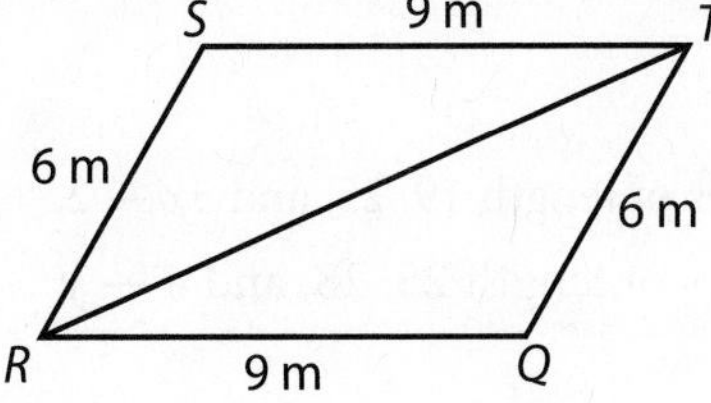

11.

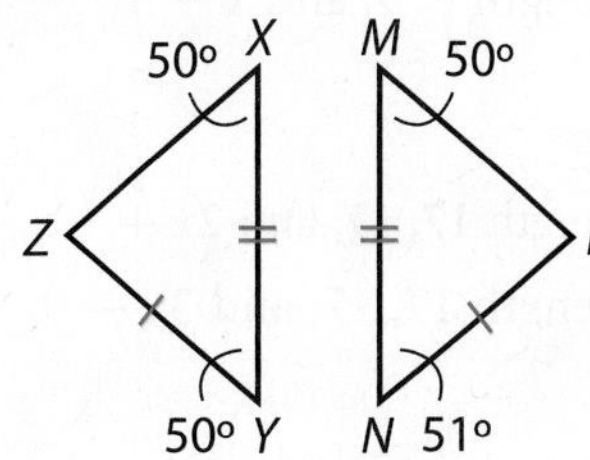

12.

J 8 cm K 12 cm L

W 10 cm X 8 cm Y

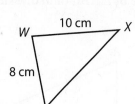

13.

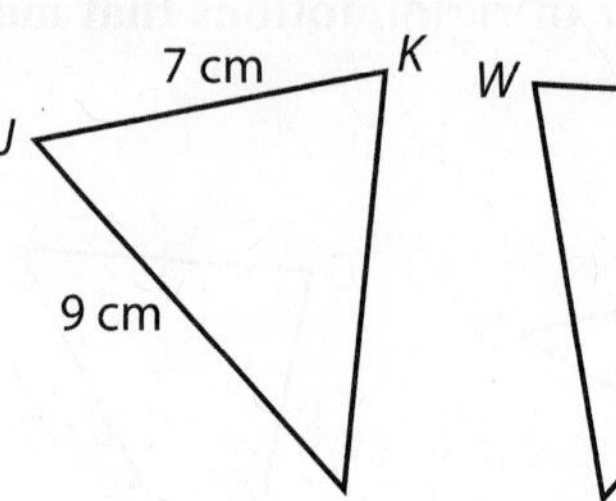

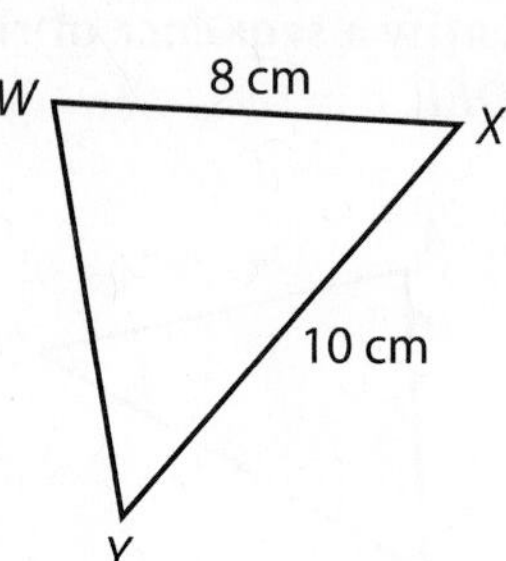

14. Carol bought two chairs with triangular backs. For what value of x can you use a triangle congruence theorem to show that the triangles are congruent? Which triangle congruence theorem can you use? Explain.

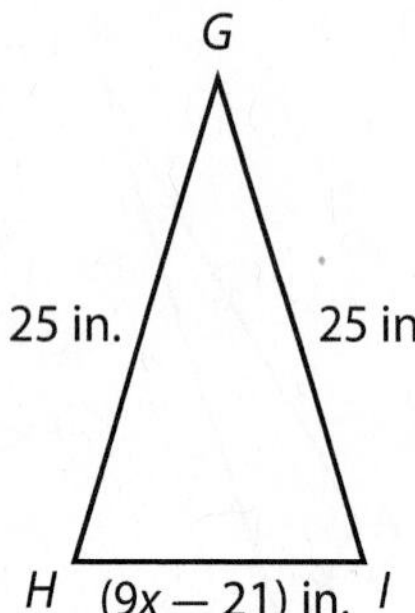

T 25 in. 25 in. U 15 in. V

15. For what values of x and y can you use a triangle congruence theorem to show that the triangles are congruent? Which triangle congruence theorem can you use? Explain.

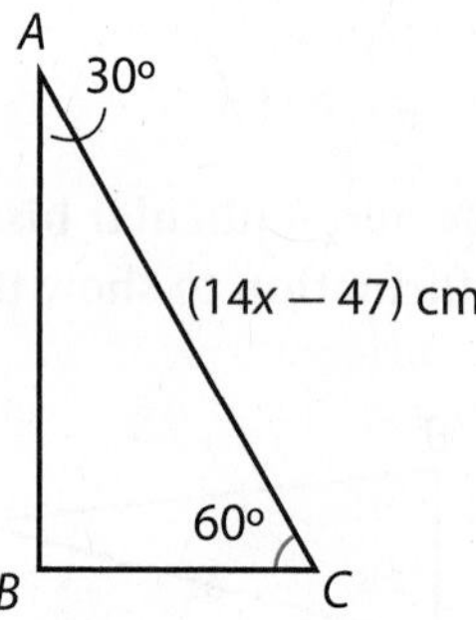

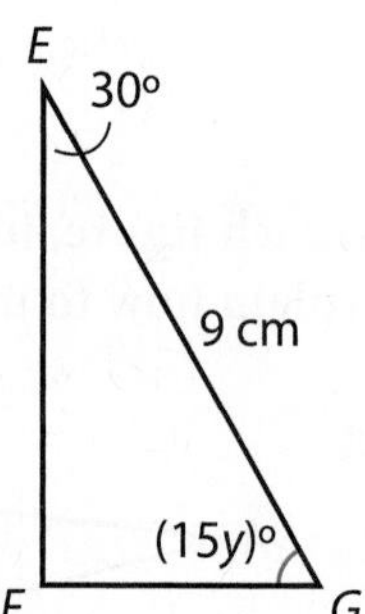

Find all possible solutions for x such that $\triangle ABC$ is congruent to $\triangle DEF$. One or more of the problems may have no solution.

16. $\triangle ABC$: sides of length 6, 8, and x.
$\triangle DEF$: sides of length 6, 9, and $x - 1$.

17. $\triangle ABC$: sides of length 3, $x + 1$, and 14.
$\triangle DEF$: sides of length 13, $x - 9$, and $2x - 6$

18. $\triangle ABC$: sides of length 17, 17, and $2x + 1$.
$\triangle DEF$: sides of length 17, 17, and $3x - 9$

19. $\triangle ABC$: sides of length 19, 25, and $5x - 2$.
$\triangle DEF$: sides of length 25, 28, and $4 - y$

20. $\triangle ABC$: sides of length 8, $x - y$, and $x + y$
$\triangle DEF$: sides of length 8, 15, and 17

21. $\triangle ABC$: sides of length 9, x, and $2x - y$
$\triangle DEF$: sides of length 8, 9, and $2y - x$

22. These statements are part of an explanation for the SSS Triangle Congruence Theorem. Write the statements in a logical order. The statements refer to triangles ABC and DEF shown here.

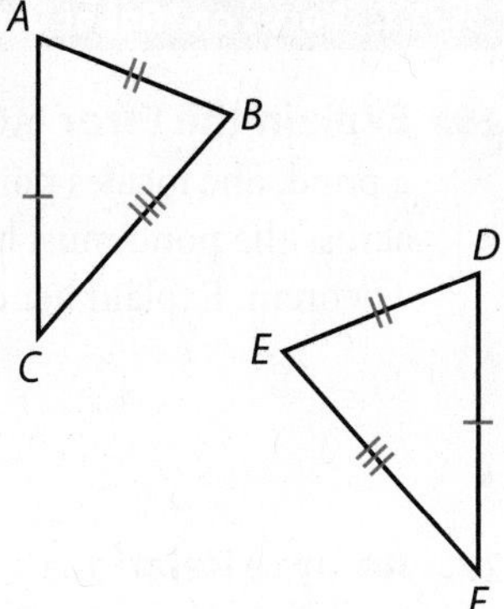

Rotate the image of $\triangle ABC$ about E, so that the image of $\overline{BC}$ coincides with $\overline{EF}$.

Apply the definition of reflection to show D is the reflection of A across $\overrightarrow{EF}$.

Conclude that $\triangle ABC \cong \triangle DEF$ because a sequence of rigid motions maps one triangle onto the other.

Translate $\triangle ABC$ along $\overrightarrow{BE}$.

Define $\overrightarrow{EF}$ as the perpendicular bisector of the line connecting D and the image of A.

Identify E, and then F, as equidistant from D and the image of A.

23. State whether the given information is sufficient or not sufficient to guarantee that two triangles are congruent.

A. The triangles have three pairs of congruent corresponding angles.

B. The triangles have three pairs of congruent corresponding sides.

C. The triangles have two pairs of congruent corresponding sides and one pair of congruent corresponding angles.

D. The triangles have two pairs of congruent corresponding angles and one pair of congruent corresponding sides.

E. Two angles and the included side of one triangle are congruent to two angles and the included side of the other triangle.

F. Two sides and the included angle of one triangle are congruent to two sides and the included angle of the other triangle.

24. **Make a Conjecture** Does a version of SSS congruence apply to quadrilaterals? Provide an example to support your answer.

25. Are two triangles congruent if all pairs of corresponding angles are congruent? Support your answer with an example.

H.O.T. Focus on Higher Order Thinking

26. Explain the Error Ava wants to know the distance JK across a pond. She locates points as shown. She says that the distance across the pond must be 160 ft by the SSS Triangle Congruence Theorem. Explain her error.

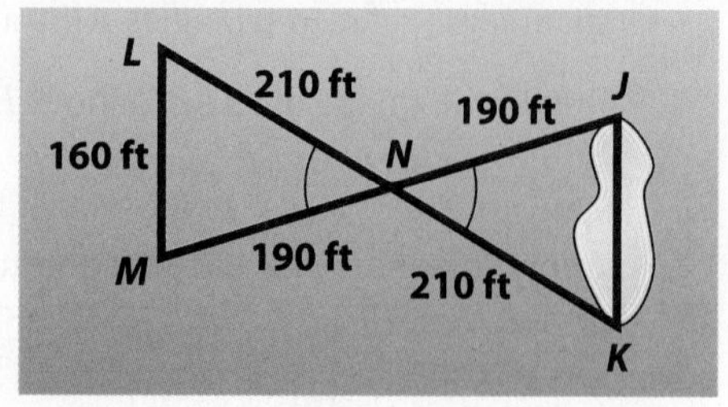

27. Analyze Relationships Write a proof.

Given: $\angle BFC \cong \angle ECF$, $\angle BCF \cong \angle EFC$

$\overline{AB} \cong \overline{DE}$, $\overline{AF} \cong \overline{DC}$

Prove: $\triangle ABF \cong \triangle DEC$

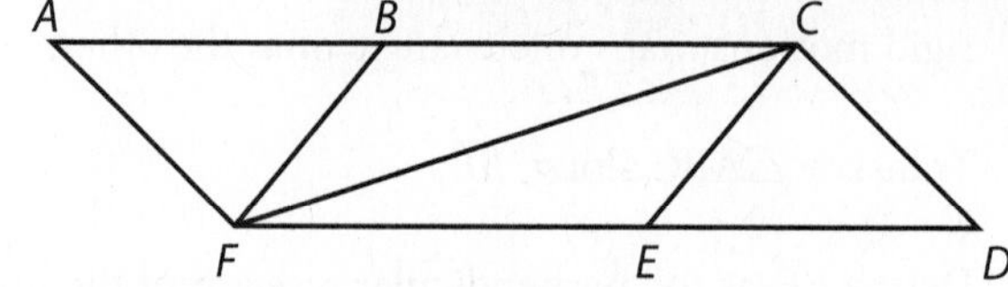

Lesson Performance Task

Mike and Michelle each hope to get a contract with the city to build benches for commuters to sit on while waiting for buses. The benches must be stable so that they don't collapse, and they must be attractive. Their designs are shown. Judge the two benches on stability and attractiveness. Explain your reasoning.

STUDY GUIDE REVIEW

Triangle Congruence Criteria

MODULE 5

Essential Question: How can you use triangle congruence criteria to solve real-world problems?

KEY EXAMPLE (Lesson 5.1)

Triangle $\triangle ABC$ is congruent to $\triangle DEF$. Given that $AB = 7$ and $DE = 5y - 3$, find y.

$\overline{AB} \cong \overline{DE}$	Corresponding parts of congruent triangles are congruent.
$AB = DE$	Definition of congruent sides
$5y - 3 = 7$	Write the equation.
$5y = 10$	Add 3 to each side.
$y = 2$	Divide each side by 5.

KEY EXAMPLE (Lesson 5.2)

Given: $\overline{AB} \cong \overline{BC} \cong \overline{CD} \cong \overline{DA}$

$m\angle DAB = m\angle ABC = m\angle BCD = m\angle ADC = 90°$

$\angle EDC \cong \angle ECD$

Prove: E is the midpoint of $\overline{AB}$.

$m\angle DAB = m\angle ABC$	Given.
$\angle DAB \cong \angle ABC$	Definition of congruent angles.
$\angle EDC \cong \angle ECD$	Given
$m\angle ADC = m\angle BCD$	Given
$m\angle ADC - m\angle EDC = m\angle BCD - m\angle ECD$	Subtraction property of equality.
$\angle ADE \cong \angle BCE$	
$\overline{AD} \cong \overline{BC}$	Given.
$\triangle ADE \cong \triangle BCE$	ASA Triangle Congruence Theorem.
$AE = EB$	CPCT

Therefore, E is the midpoint of $\overline{AB}$ by the definition of midpoint.

KEY EXAMPLE (Lesson 5.3)

Determine whether the triangles are congruent. Explain your reasoning.

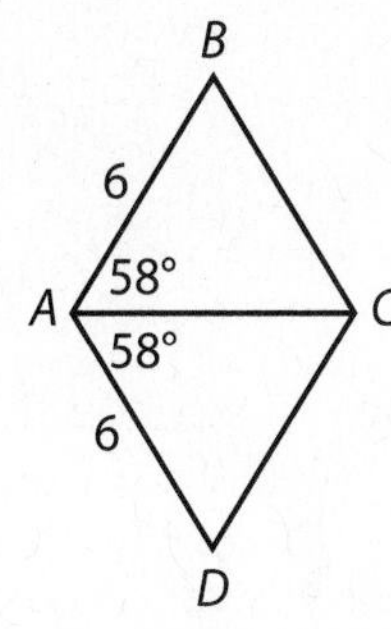

It is given that $\overline{AB} \cong \overline{AD}$ and $\angle BAC \cong \angle DAC$. By the reflexive property of congruence, $\overline{AC} \cong \overline{AC}$. Since two sides and an included angle of each triangle are congruent, $\triangle BAC \cong \triangle DAC$ by the SAS Triangle Congruence Theorem.

EXERCISES

Solve for y given each set of constraints. *(Lesson 5.1)*

1. Given $\triangle PQR \cong \triangle DEF$, $PQ = 15$, $QR = 10$, $RP = 8$, and $EF = 6y + 4$.

2. Given $\triangle PQR \cong \triangle ABC$, $m\angle P = 60°$, $m\angle Q = 40°$, and $m\angle C = (7y + 10)°$.

Determine whether the triangles are congruent.
Explain your reasoning. *(Lesson 5.3)*

3. 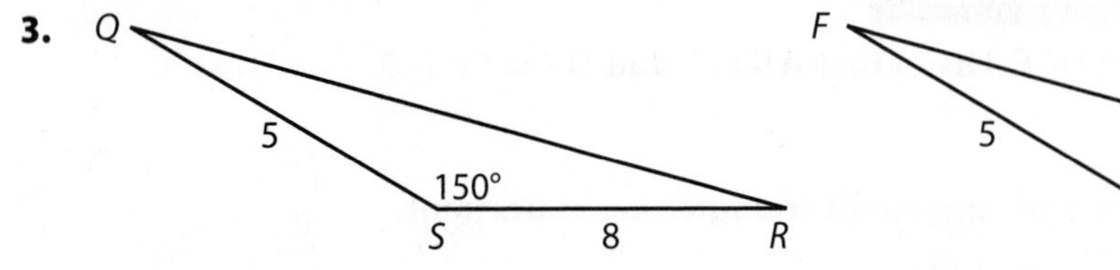

4. Barbara and Sherwin want to use the SSS Triangle Congruence Theorem to see if their triangular slices of watermelon are congruent. They each measure two sides of their slices. Barbara measures sides of lengths 7 inches and 6 inches, while Sherwin measures sides of lengths 8 inches and 5 inches. Do they need to measure the third sides of their slices to determine whether they are congruent? If so, what must the side lengths be for the slices to be congruent? Explain. *(Lesson 5.4)*

MODULE PERFORMANCE TASK

Golden Gate Triangles

The Golden Gate Bridge in San Francisco is famous worldwide. The suspension bridge spans the Golden Gate strait with suspension cables attached to two towers that are 4200 feet apart. The bridge also uses trusses, support structures formed by triangles, to help support the weight of the towers and the rest of the bridge.

Use visual evidence from the photo to estimate how many isosceles triangles can be found between the two towers.

Be sure to write down all your data and assumptions. Then use graphs, numbers, words, or algebra to explain how you reached your conclusion.

Ready to Go On?

5.1–5.4 Triangle Congruence Criteria

- Online Homework
- Hints and Help
- Extra Practice

1. $\triangle ABC \cong \triangle EDF$. Determine the value of x. *(Lesson 5.1)*

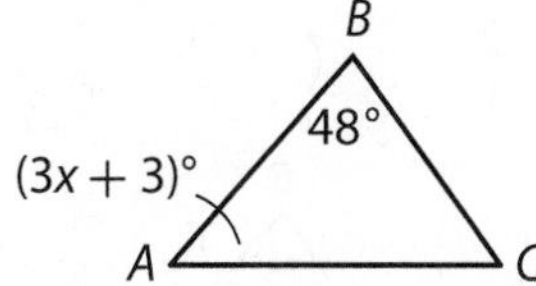

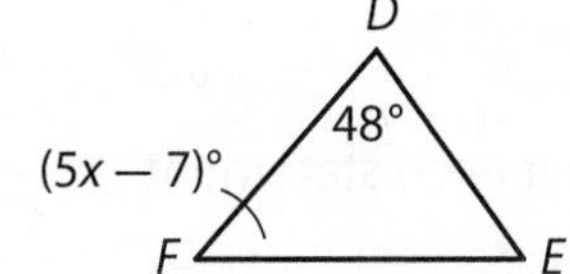

2. Find the coordinates of point F so that $\triangle ABC \cong \triangle FGH$. Identify a sequence of rigid motions that maps $\triangle ABC$ onto $\triangle FGH$ and use a theorem to explain why the triangles are congruent. *(Lessons 5.3, 5.4)*

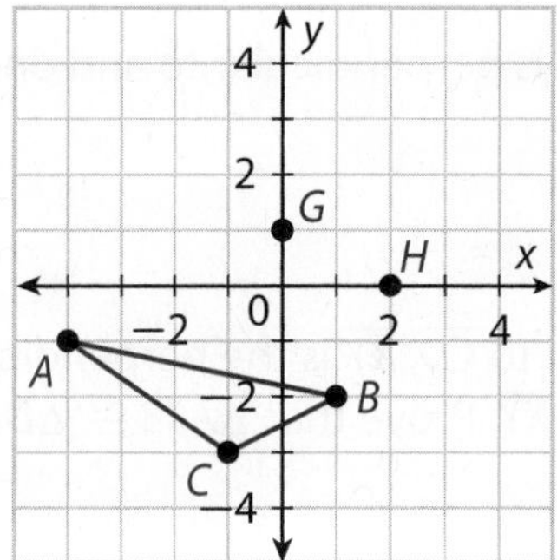

ESSENTIAL QUESTION

3. How can you tell that triangles are congruent without knowing the lengths of all sides and the measures of all angles?

MODULE 5
MIXED REVIEW

Assessment Readiness

1. Two triangles, $\triangle ABC$ and $\triangle XYZ$, are congruent. The measure of angle C, $m\angle C$, is equal to 81°. The measure of angle X, $m\angle X$, is equal to 56°.

A. Does $m\angle A = 99°$?

B. Does $m\angle B = 43°$?

C. Are $\angle A$ and $\angle Z$ congruent?

2. Look at the triangles to the right. Determine if each statement is True or False.

A. A value of $x = 16$ results in congruent triangles.

B. A value of $x = 27$ results in congruent triangles.

C. A value of $x = 31$ does not result in congruent triangles.

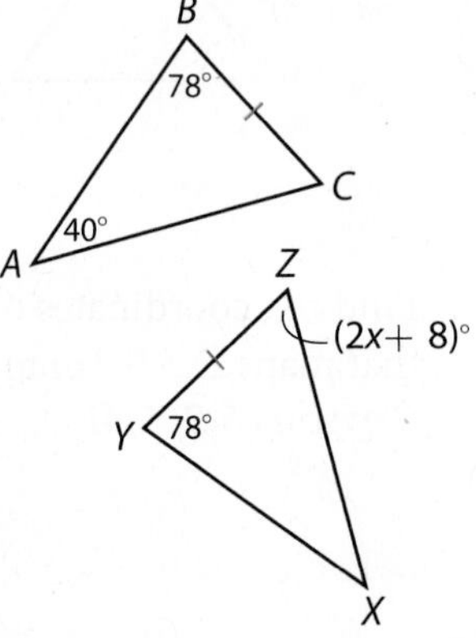

3. Write the equation of one line that is perpendicular to and one line that is parallel to $y = 7x + 9$.

4. In the figure, segment $\overline{AB}$ is parallel to $\overline{CD}$, $\overline{XY}$ is the perpendicular bisector of $\overline{AB}$, E is the midpoint of $\overline{XY}$. Prove that $\triangle AEB \cong \triangle DEC$.

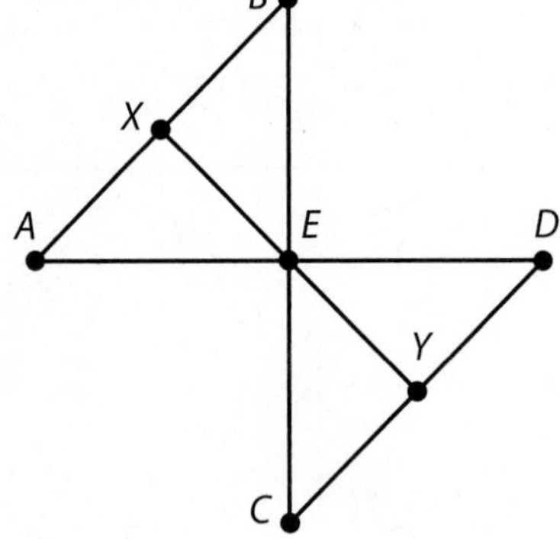

MODULE 6

Applications of Triangle Congruence

Essential Question: How can you use applications of triangle congruence to solve real-world problems?

REAL WORLD VIDEO
A geodesic dome encloses the greatest volume of space for a given surface area. Check out how applications of triangles are involved in the design of geodesic domes.

MODULE PERFORMANCE TASK PREVIEW

Geodesic Domes

In this module, you will use a three-dimensional shape called an icosahedron to explore the geometry of a geodesic dome. Let's dive in and find out what triangles have to do with icosahedrons and geodesic domes.

Are YOU Ready?

Complete these exercises to review the skills you will need for this chapter.

Personal Math Trainer

- Online Homework
- Hints and Help
- Extra Practice

Distance Formulas

Example 1 Find the distance between (1, –6) and (–1, –2).

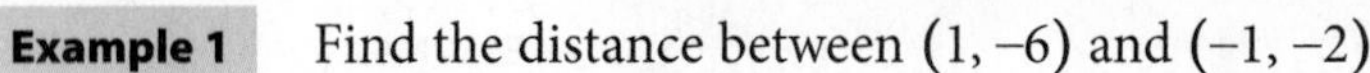

$\sqrt{(-1-1)^2 + (-2-(-6))^2}$ Apply the distance formula.

$= \sqrt{4 + 16}$ Simplify each square.

$= \sqrt{20}$ Simplify.

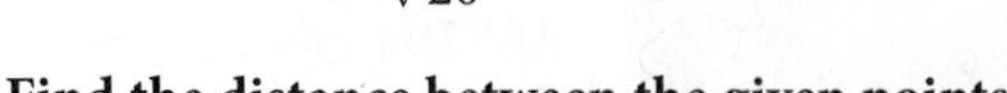

Find the distance between the given points.

1. The points (–1, 2) and (2, –2)

2. The points (–5, 21) and (0, 19)

Congruent Figures

Example 2 Determine whether the triangles are congruent. Explain your reasoning.

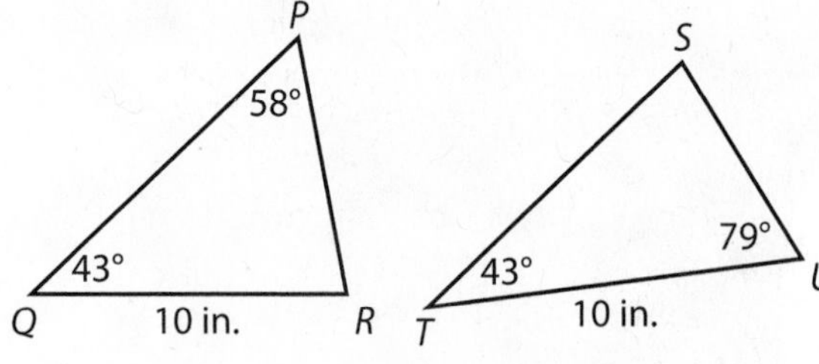

Step 1: Find $m\angle R$.

$m\angle R + m\angle P + m\angle Q = 180°$

$m\angle R + 58° + 43° = 180°$

$m\angle R = 79°$

So, $\triangle QPR \cong \triangle TSU$ by the ASA Triangle Congruence Theorem.

3. Determine whether the triangles are congruent. Explain your reasoning.

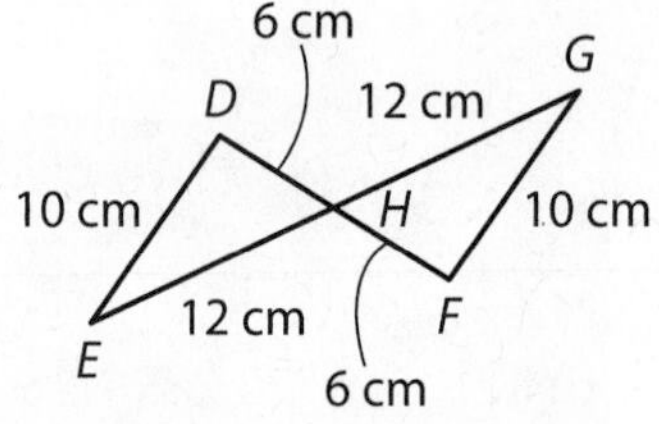

Angle Theorems for Triangles

Example 3 Given $a = 7$ cm and $b = 5$ cm, find the missing length.

$a^2 + b^2 = c^2$ Pythagorean Theorem

$(7)^2 + (5)^2 = c^2$ Substitute a = 7 and b = 5.

$c = \sqrt{49 + 25}$ Solve for c.

$c = \sqrt{74}$ cm Simplify.

Use the given values to find the missing lengths in the figure from the example.

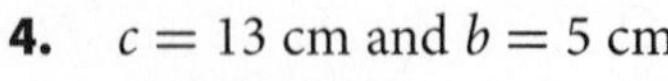

4. $c = 13$ cm and $b = 5$ cm

$a =$ ___?___

5. $c = 7$ cm and $a = 6$ cm

$b =$ ___?___

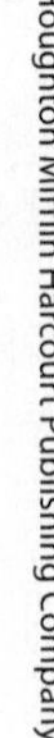

6.1 Justifying Constructions

Essential Question: How can you be sure that the result of a construction is valid?

Explore 1 Using a Reflective Device to Construct a Perpendicular Line

You have constructed a line perpendicular to a given line through a point not on the line using a compass and straightedge. You can also use a reflective device to construct perpendicular lines.

(A) **Step 1** On a separate sheet of paper, draw a line ℓ and point P approximately as they appear in the diagram. Place the reflective device along line ℓ. Look through the device to locate the image of point P on the opposite side of line ℓ. Draw the image of point P and label it P'.

Step 2 Use a straightedge to draw $\overleftrightarrow{PP'}$.

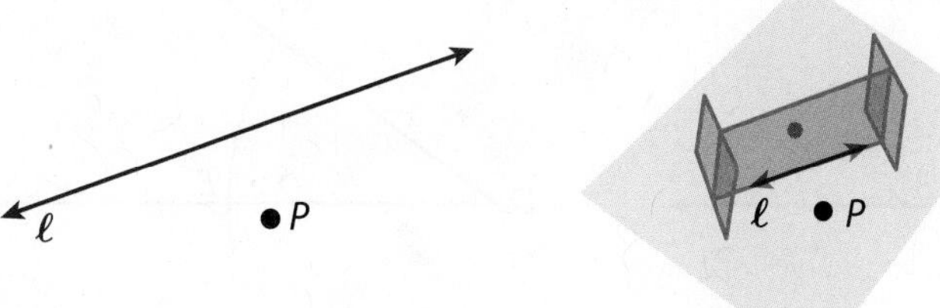

Explain why $\overleftrightarrow{PP'}$ is perpendicular to line ℓ.

(B) Draw a line m and point Q approximately as they appear in the diagram. Place the reflective device so that it passes through point Q and is approximately perpendicular to line m. Adjust the angle of the device until the image of line m coincides with line m. Draw a line along the reflective device and label it line n. Explain why line n is perpendicular to line m.

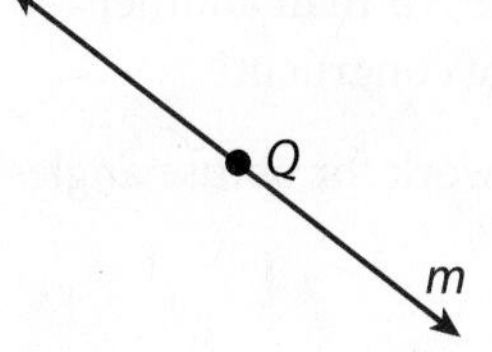

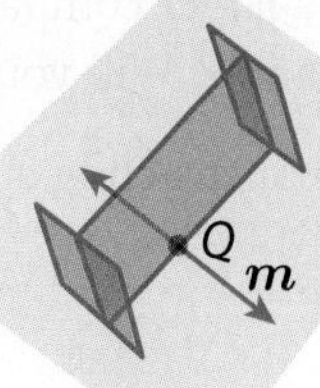

Reflect

1. How can you check that the lines you drew are perpendicular to lines ℓ and m?
2. Use the reflective device to draw two points on line ℓ that are reflections of each other. Label the points X and X'. What is true about PX and PX'? Why? Use a ruler to check your prediction.
3. Describe how to construct a perpendicular bisector of a line segment using paper folding. Use a rigid motion to explain why the result is a perpendicular bisector.

Explore 2 Justifying the Copy of an Angle Construction

You have seen how to construct a copy of an angle, but how do you know that the copy must be congruent to the original? Recall that to construct a copy of an angle A, you use these steps.

Step 1 Draw a ray with endpoint D.

Step 2 Draw an arc that intersects both rays of $\angle A$. Label the intersections B and C.

Step 3 Draw the same arc on the ray. Label the point of intersection E.

Step 4 Set the compass to the length BC.

Step 5 Place the compass at E and draw a new arc. Label the intersection of the new arc F. Draw $\overrightarrow{DF}$. $\angle D$ is congruent to $\angle A$.

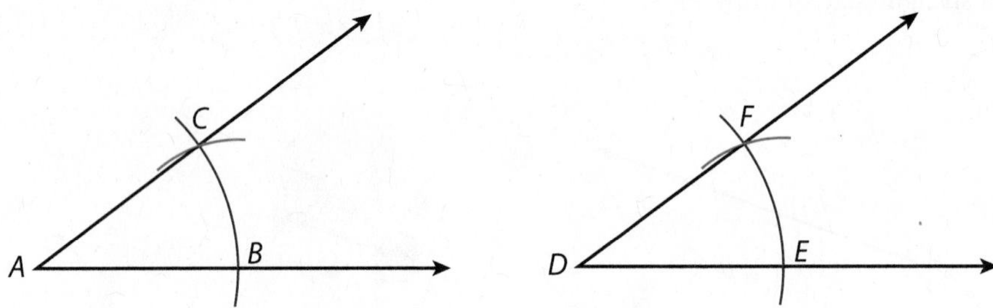

(A) Name the two triangles that are created.

(B) What segments do you know are congruent? Explain how you know.

(C) Are the triangles congruent? How do you know?

Reflect

4. **Discussion** Suppose you used a larger compass setting to create $\overline{AB}$ than another student when copying the same angle. Will your copied angles be congruent?
5. Does the justification above for constructing a copy of an angle work for obtuse angles?

Explain 1 Proving the Angle Bisector and Perpendicular Bisector Constructions

You have constructed angle bisectors and perpendicular bisectors. You now have the tools you need to prove that these compass and straightedge constructions result in the intended figures.

Example 1 **Prove two bisector constructions.**

 You have used the following steps to construct an angle bisector.

Step 1 Draw an arc intersecting the sides of the angle. Label the intersections B and C.

Step 2 Draw intersecting arcs from B and C. Label the intersection of the arcs as D.

Step 3 Use a straightedge to draw $\overline{AD}$.

Prove that the construction results in the angle bisector.

The construction results in the triangles ABD and ACD. Because the same compass setting was used to create them, $\overline{AB} \cong \overline{AC}$ and $\overline{BD} \cong \overline{CD}$. The segment $\overline{AD}$ is congruent to itself by the Reflexive Property of Congruence. So, by the SSS Triangle Congruence Theorem, $\triangle ABD \cong \triangle ACD$.

Corresponding parts of congruent figures are congruent, so $\angle BAD \cong \angle DAC$.

By the definition of angle bisector, $\overrightarrow{AD}$ is the angle bisector of $\angle A$.

 You have used the following steps to construct a perpendicular bisector.

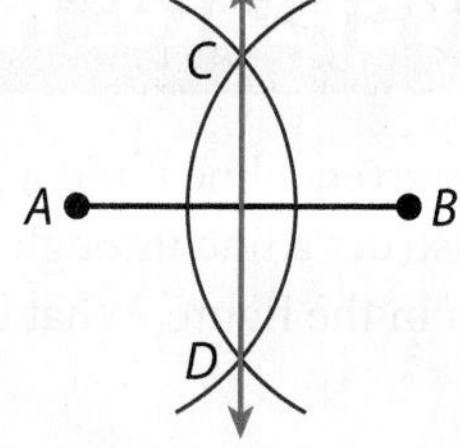

Step 1 Draw an arc centered at A.

Step 2 Draw an arc with the same diameter centered at B. Label the intersections C and D.

Step 3 Draw $\overline{CD}$.

Prove that the construction results in the perpendicular bisector.

The point C is equidistant from the endpoints of $\overline{AB}$, so by the Converse of the Perpendicular Bisector Theorem, it lies on the perpendicular bisector of $\overline{AB}$. The point D is also equidistant from the endpoints of $\overline{AB}$, so it also lies on the perpendicular bisector of $\overline{AB}$. Two points determine a line, so $\overleftrightarrow{CD}$ is the perpendicular bisector of $\overline{AB}$.

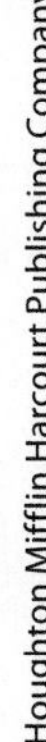

Reflect

6. In Part B, what can you conclude about the measures of the angles made by the intersection of $\overline{AB}$ and $\overline{CD}$?

7. **Discussion** A classmate claims that in the construction shown in Part B, $\overline{AB}$ is the perpendicular bisector of $\overline{CD}$. Is this true? Justify your answer.

Your Turn

8. The construction in Part B is also used to construct the midpoint R of $\overline{MN}$. How is the proof of this construction different from the proof of the perpendicular bisector construction in Part B?

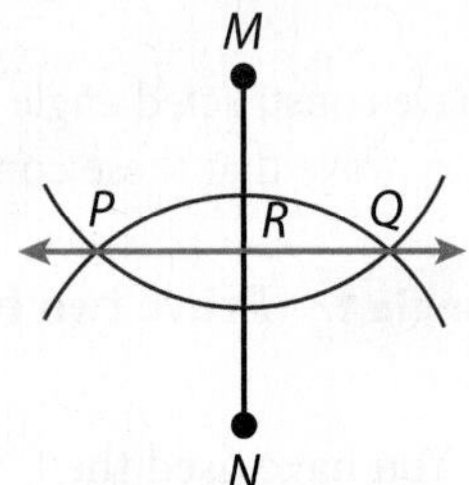

9. How could you combine the constructions in Example 1 to construct a 45° angle?

10. Describe how you can construct a line that is parallel to a given line using the construction of a perpendicular to a line.

11. Copy $\overline{AB}$ on a separate sheet of paper. Use a straightedge and a piece of string to construct an equilateral triangle that has AB as one of its sides. Then explain how you know your construction works. (*Hint*: Consider an arc centered at A with radius AB and an arc centered at B with radius AB.)

12. **Essential Question Check-In** Is a construction something that must be proven? Explain.

Evaluate: Homework and Practice

- Online Homework
- Hints and Help
- Extra Practice

1. Julia is given a line ℓ and a point P not on line ℓ. She is asked to use a reflective device to construct a line through P that is perpendicular to line ℓ. She places the device as shown in the figure. What should she do next to draw the required line?

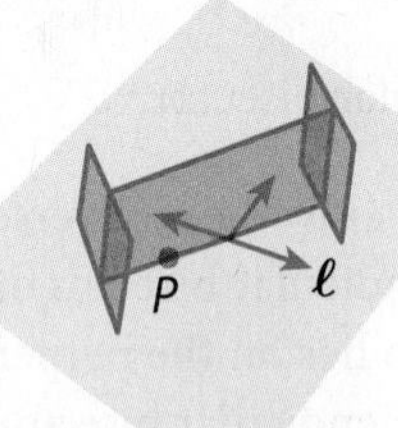

2. Describe how to construct a copy of a segment. Explain how you know that the segments are congruent.

For Exercises 3–4, copy and complete the table.

3. Complete the proof of the construction of a segment bisector.
Given: the construction of the segment bisector of $\overline{AB}$
Prove: $\overline{CD}$ bisects $\overline{AB}$

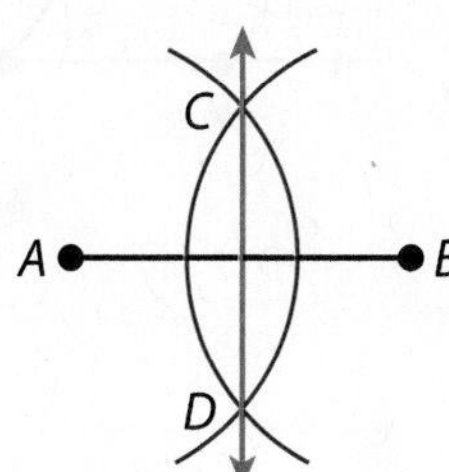

Statements	Reasons
1. $AC =$? and $AD =$? .	1. Same compass setting used
2. C is on the perpendicular bisector of $\overline{AB}$.	2. ?
3. D is on the perpendicular bisector of $\overline{AB}$.	3. ?
4. ? is the perpendicular bisector of $\overline{AB}$.	4. Through any two points, there is exactly one line.
5. ?	5. Definition of ?

4. Complete the proof of the construction of a congruent angle.
Given: the construction of $\angle CAB$ given $\angle HFG$
Prove: $\angle CAB \cong \angle HFG$

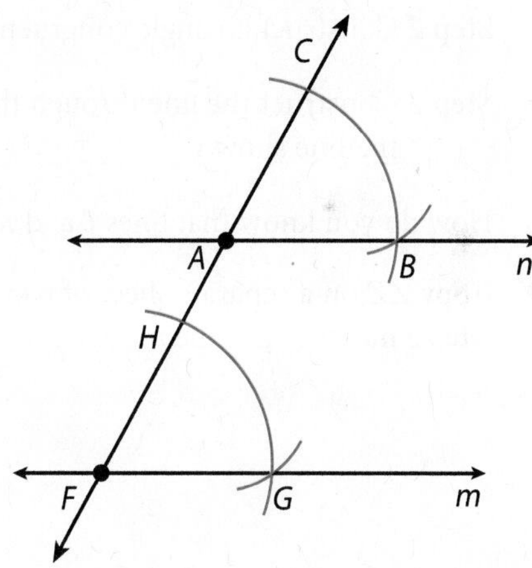

Statements	Reasons
1. $FG = FH =$? $= AC$	1. same compass setting
2. $GH = CB$	2. ?
3. $\triangle FGH \cong \triangle ABC$	3. ?
4. $\angle CAB \cong \angle HFG$	4. ?

To construct a line through the given point P, parallel to line ℓ, you use the following steps.

Step 1 Choose a point Q on line ℓ and draw $\overline{QP}$.

Step 2 Construct an angle congruent to $\angle 1$ at P.

Step 3 Construct the line through the given point, parallel to the line shown.

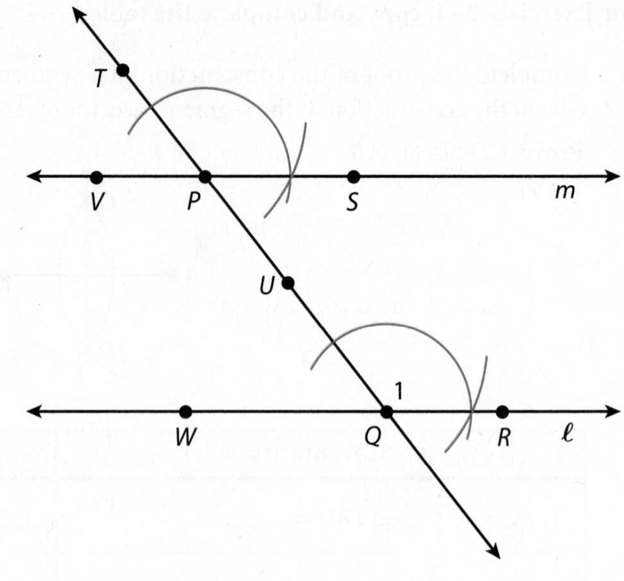

Describe the relationship between the given angles or segments. Justify your answer.

5. $\angle TPS$ and $\angle UQR$

6. $\angle SPU$ and $\angle RQU$

7. $\angle VPU$ and $\angle UQR$

8. $\angle TPS$ and $\angle WQU$

9. $\overline{QU}$ and $\overline{PS}$

10. $\overline{QU}$ and $\overline{PT}$

11. To construct a line through the given point P, parallel to line ℓ, you use the following steps.

Step 1 Draw line m through P and intersecting line ℓ.

Step 2 Construct an angle congruent to $\angle 1$ at P.

Step 3 Construct the line through the given point, parallel to the line shown.

How do you know that lines ℓ and n are parallel? Explain.

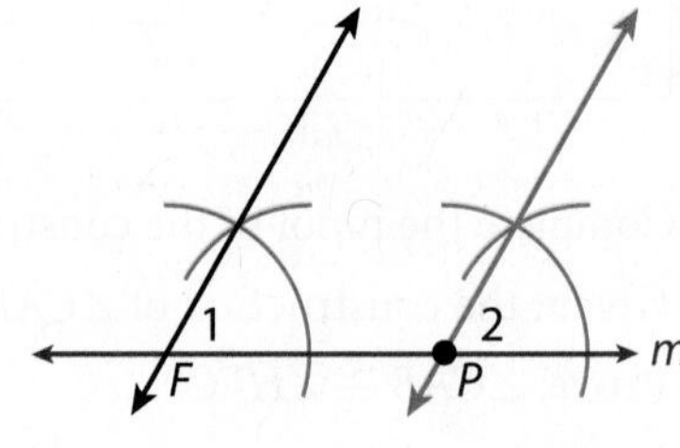

12. Copy $\angle Z$ on a separate sheet of paper. Then construct an angle whose measure is $\frac{1}{4}$ the measure of $\angle Z$. Justify the construction.

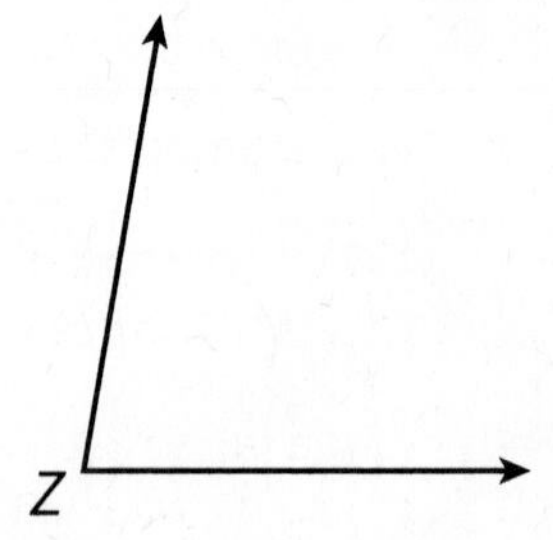

In Exercises 13 and 14, use the diagram shown. The diagram shows the result of constructing a copy of an angle adjacent to one of the rays of the original angle. Assume the pattern continues.

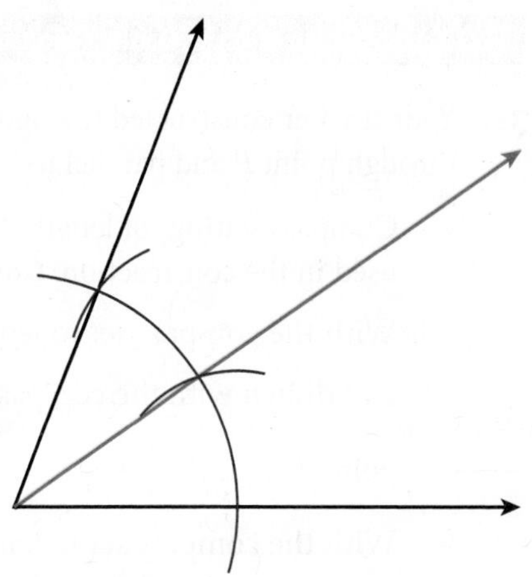

13. If it takes 10 more copies of the angle for the last angle to overlap the first ray (the horizontal ray), what is the measure of each angle?

14. If it takes 8 more copies of the angle for the last angle to overlap the first ray (the horizontal ray), what is the measure of each angle?

15. Sonia draws a segment on a piece of paper. She wants to find three points that are equidistant from the endpoints of the segment. Explain how she can use paper folding to help her locate the three points.

In Exercises 16–18, a polygon is inscribed in a circle if all of the polygon's vertices lie on the circle.

16. Follow the given steps to construct a square inscribed in a circle.

Use your compass to draw a circle. Mark the center.

Draw a diameter, $\overline{AB}$, using a straightedge.

Construct the perpendicular bisector of $\overline{AB}$. Label the points where the perpendicular bisector intersects the circle as C and D.

Use the straightedge to draw $\overline{AC}$, $\overline{CB}$, $\overline{BD}$, and $\overline{DA}$.

17. Suppose you are given a piece of tracing paper with a circle on it and you do not have a compass. How can you use paper folding to inscribe a square in the circle?

18. Follow the given steps to construct a regular hexagon inscribed in a circle.

Tie a pencil to one end of the string.

Mark a point O on your paper. Place the string on point O and hold it down with your finger. Pull the string taut and draw a circle. Mark and label a point A.

Hold the point on the string that you placed on point O, and move it to point A. Pull the string taut and draw an arc that intersects the circle. Label the point as B.

Hold the point on the string that you placed on point A, and move it to point B. Draw an arc to locate point C on the circle. Repeat to locate points D, E, and F. Use your straightedge to draw $ABCDEF$.

H.O.T. Focus on Higher Order Thinking

19. Your teacher constructed the figure shown. It shows the construction of line *PT* through point *P* and parallel to line *AB*.

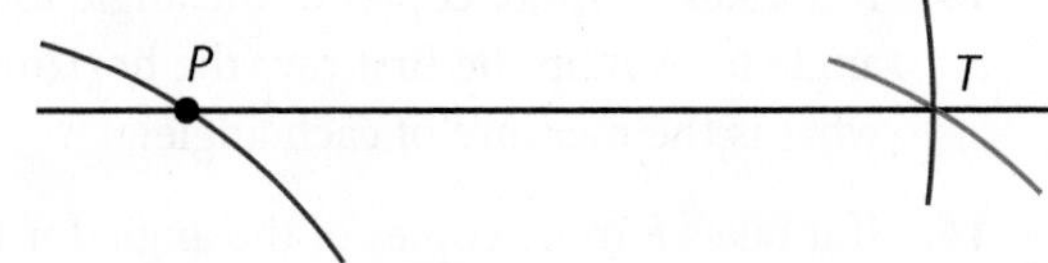

a. Compass settings of length *AB* and *AP* were used in the construction. Complete the statements:

With the compass set to length *AP*, an arc was drawn with the compass point at point ? .

With the compass set to length ? , an arc was drawn with the compass point at point ? .

The two arcs intersect at point ? .

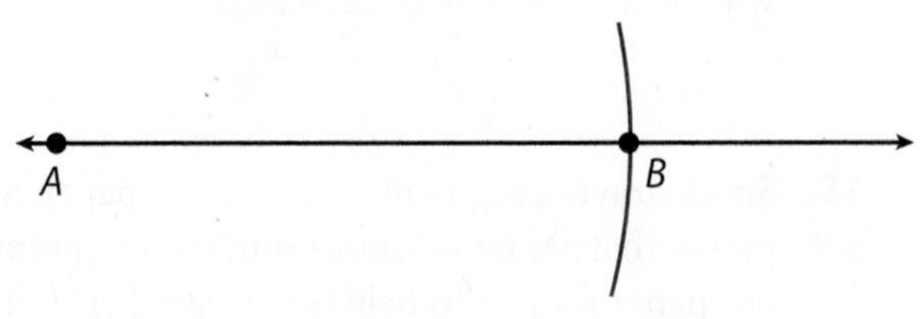

b. Write two congruence statements involving segments in the construction.

c. Write a proof that the construction is true. That is, given the construction, prove $\overline{PT} \parallel \overline{AB}$. (*Hint*: Draw segments to create two congruent triangles.)

20. Use the segments shown. Construct and label a segment, $\overline{XY}$, whose length is the average of the lengths of $\overline{AB}$ and $\overline{CD}$. Justify the method you used.

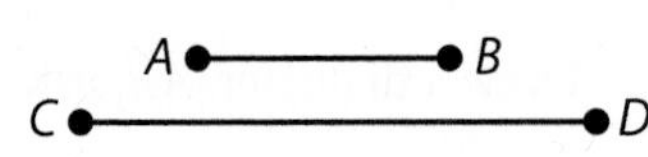

Lesson Performance Task

A plastic "mold" for copying a 30° angle is shown here.

a. If you drew a 30°—60°—90° triangle using the mold, how would you know that your triangle and the mold were congruent?

b. Explain how you know that any angle you would draw using the lower right corner of the mold would measure 30°.

c. Explain the meaning of "tolerance" in the context of drawing an angle using the mold.

6.2 AAS Triangle Congruence

Resource Locker

Essential Question: What does the AAS Triangle Congruence Theorem tell you about two triangles?

Explore Exploring Angle-Angle-Side Congruence

If two angles and a non-included side of one triangle are congruent to the corresponding angles and side of another triangle, are the triangles congruent?

In this activity you'll be copying a side and two angles from a triangle.

(A) Use a compass and straightedge to copy segment AC. Label it as segment EF.

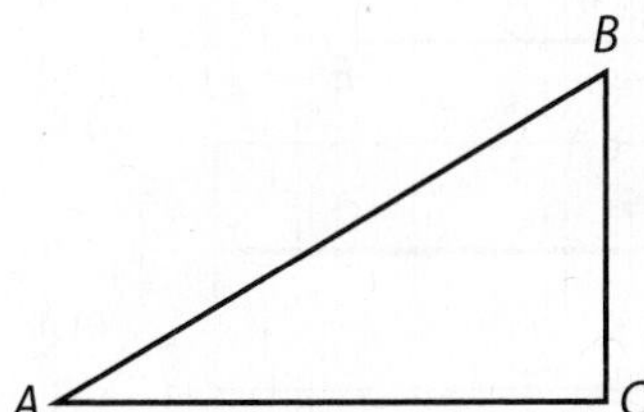

(B) Copy $\angle A$ using $\overline{EF}$ as a side of the angle.

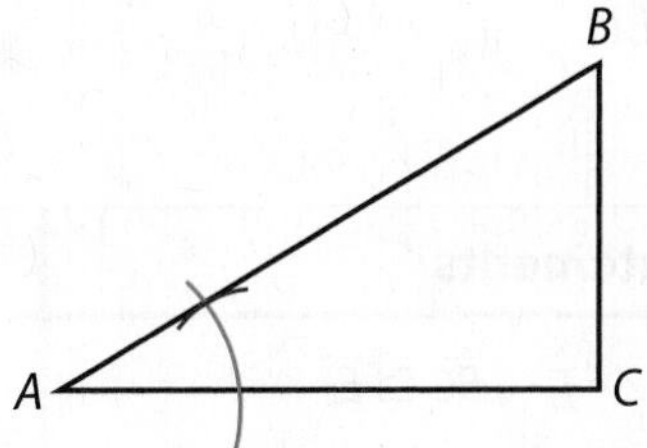

(C) On a transparent sheet or a sheet of tracing paper, copy $\angle B$. Label its vertex G. Make the rays defining $\angle G$ longer than their corresponding sides on $\triangle ABC$.

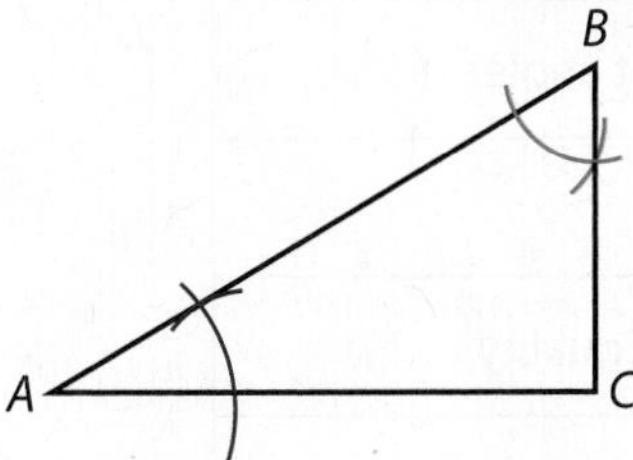

(D) Now overlay the ray from $\angle E$ with the ray from $\angle G$ to form a triangle. Make sure that side $\overline{EF}$ maintains the length you defined for it.

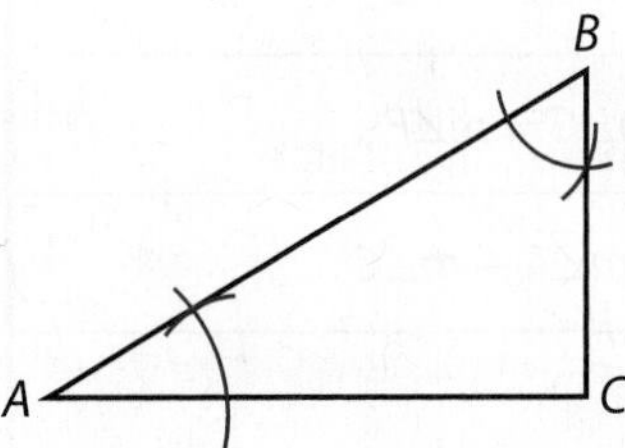

(E) How many triangles can you construct?

(F) Copy all of $\triangle EFG$ to the transparency. Then overlay it on $\triangle ABC$. Are the triangles congruent? How do you know?

Reflect

1. Suppose you had started this activity by copying segment BC and then angles A and C. Would your results have been the same? Why or why not?

2. Compare your results to those of your classmates. Does this procedure work with any triangle?

Explain 1 Justifying Angle-Angle-Side Congruence

The following theorem summarizes the previous activity.

Angle-Angle-Side (AAS) Congruence Theorem

If two angles and a non-included side of one triangle are congruent to the corresponding angles and non-included side of another triangle, then the triangles are congruent.

Prove the AAS Congruence Theorem.

Given: $\angle A \cong \angle D$, $\angle C \cong \angle F$, $\overline{BC} \cong \overline{EF}$

Prove: $\triangle ABC \cong \triangle DEF$

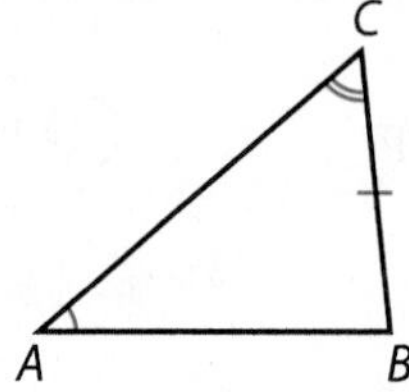

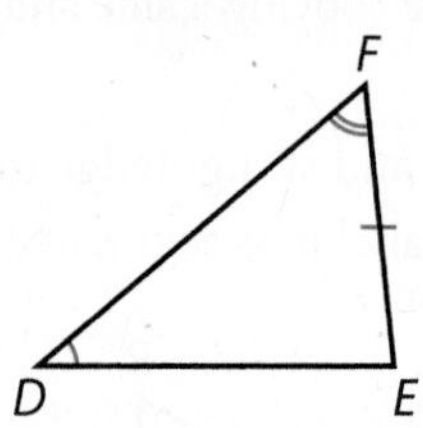

Statements	Reasons
1. $\angle A \cong \angle D$, $\angle C \cong \angle$ F , $\overline{BC} \cong \overline{EF}$	1. Given
2. $m\angle A + m\angle B + m\angle C = 180°$	2. Triangle Sum Theorem
3. $m\angle B = 180° - m\angle A - m\angle$ C	3. Subtraction Property of Equality
4. $m\angle$ D $+ m\angle E + m\angle F = 180°$	4. Triangle Sum Theorem
5. $m\angle E = 180° - m\angle D - m\angle$ F	5. Subtraction Property of Equality
6. $m\angle A = m\angle D$, $m\angle C = m\angle F$	6. Definition of congruent angles
7. $m\angle E = 180° - m\angle A - m\angle C$	7. Substitution
8. $m\angle$ E $= m\angle B$	8. Transitive Property of Equality
9. $\angle E \cong \angle B$	9. Definition of congruent angles
10. $\triangle ABC \cong \triangle DEF$	10. ASA Triangle Congruence Theorem

Reflect

3. **Discussion** The Third Angles Theorem says "If two angles of one triangle are congruent to two angles of another triangle, then the third pair of angles are congruent." How could using this theorem simplify the proof of the AAS Congruence Theorem?

4. Could the AAS Congruence Theorem be used in the proof? Explain.

Explain 2 Using Angle-Angle-Side Congruence

Example 2 Use the AAS Theorem to prove the given triangles are congruent.

(A) Given: $\overline{AC} \cong \overline{EC}$ and $m \| n$

Prove: $\triangle ABC \cong \triangle EDC$

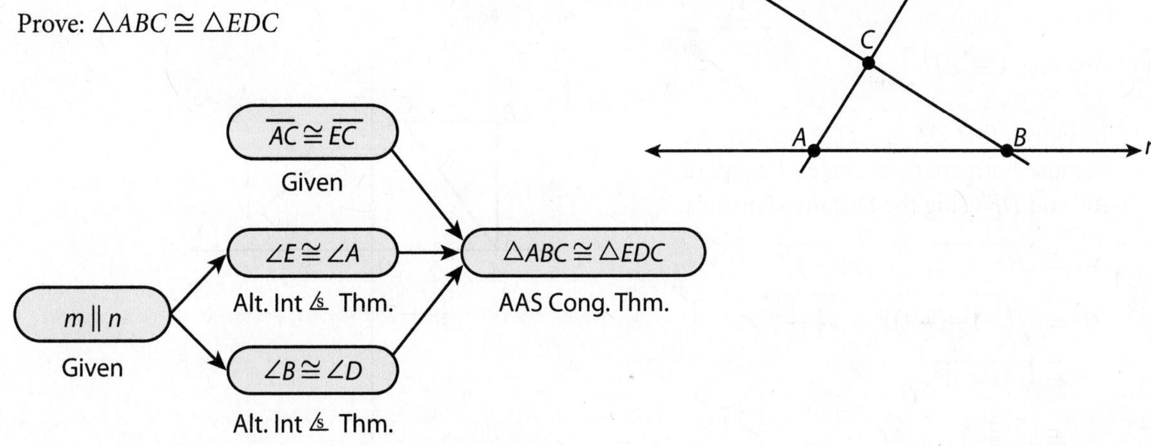

(B) Given: $\overline{CB} \parallel \overline{ED}$, $\overline{AB} \parallel \overline{CD}$, and $\overline{CB} \cong \overline{ED}$.

Prove: $\triangle ABC \cong \triangle CDE$

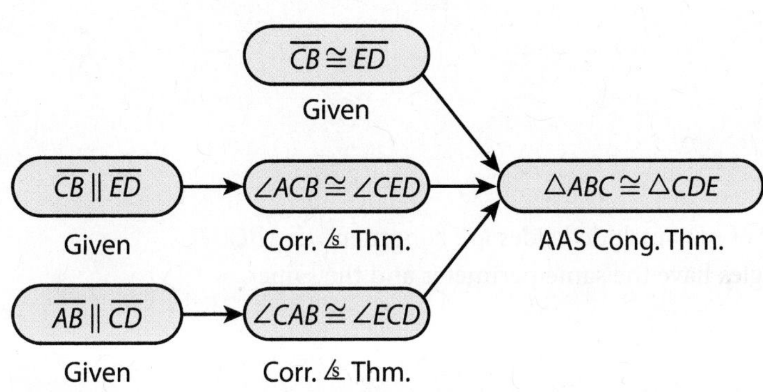

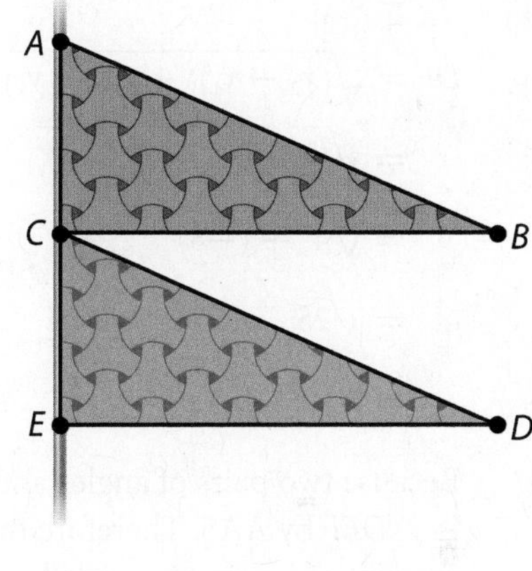

Your Turn

5. Given: $\angle ABC \cong \angle DEF$, $\overline{BC} \parallel \overline{EF}$, $\overline{AC} \cong \overline{DF}$. Use the AAS Theorem to prove the triangles are congruent.

Write a paragraph proof.

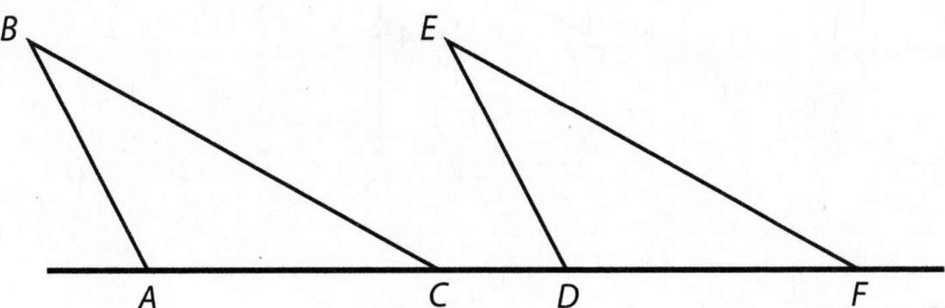

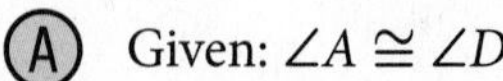

Explain 3 Applying Angle-Angle-Side Congruence

Example 3 **The triangular regions represent plots of land. Use the AAS Theorem to explain why the same amount of fencing will surround either plot.**

Ⓐ Given: $\angle A \cong \angle D$

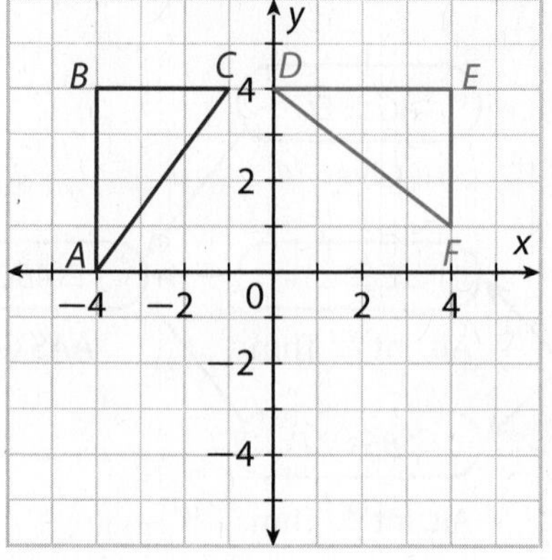

It is given that $\angle A \cong \angle D$. Also, $\angle B \cong \angle E$ because both are right angles. Compare AC and DF using the Distance Formula.

$$AC = \sqrt{(x_2 - x_1)^2 + (y_2 - y_1)^2}$$
$$= \sqrt{(-1-(-4))^2 + (4 - 0)^2}$$
$$= \sqrt{3^2 + 4^2}$$
$$= \sqrt{25}$$
$$= 5$$

$$DF = \sqrt{(x_2 - x_1)^2 + (y_2 - y_1)^2}$$
$$= \sqrt{(4 - 0)^2 + (1 - 4)^2}$$
$$= \sqrt{4^2 + (-3)^2}$$
$$= \sqrt{25}$$
$$= 5$$

Because two pairs of angles and a pair of non-included sides are congruent, $\triangle ABC \cong \triangle DEF$ by AAS. Therefore the triangles have the same perimeter and the same amount of fencing is needed.

Ⓑ Given: $\angle P \cong \angle Z$, $\angle Q \cong \angle X$

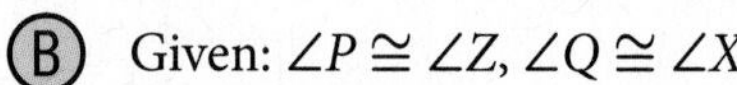

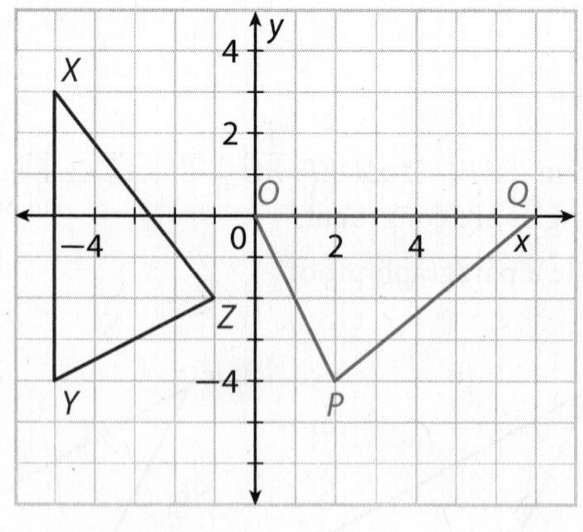

It is given that $\angle P \cong \angle Z$ and $\angle Q \cong \angle X$.

Compare YZ and OP using the distance formula.

$$YZ = \sqrt{(x_2 - x_1)^2 + (y_2 - y_1)^2}$$
$$= \sqrt{\left(\boxed{-1} - (-5)\right)^2 + \left(\boxed{-2} - (-4)\right)^2}$$
$$= \sqrt{\left(\boxed{4}\right)^2 + \left(\boxed{2}\right)^2}$$
$$= \sqrt{\boxed{16} + \boxed{4}}$$
$$= \sqrt{\boxed{20}}$$

$$OP = \sqrt{(x_2 - x_1)^2 + (y_2 - y_1)^2}$$

$$= \sqrt{\left(\boxed{2} - 0\right)^2 + \left(\boxed{-4} - 0\right)^2}$$

$$= \sqrt{\left(\boxed{2}\right)^2 + \left(\boxed{-4}\right)^2}$$

$$= \sqrt{\boxed{4} + \boxed{16}}$$

$$= \sqrt{\boxed{20}}$$

Because two pairs of angles and a pair of non-included sides are congruent, $\triangle XYZ \cong \triangle QOP$ by AAS. Therefore the triangles have the same perimeter and the same amount of fencing is needed.

Reflect

6. Explain how you could have avoided using the distance formula in Example 2B.

Your Turn

Refer to the diagram to answer the questions.

Given: $\angle A \cong \angle D$ and $\angle B \cong \angle E$

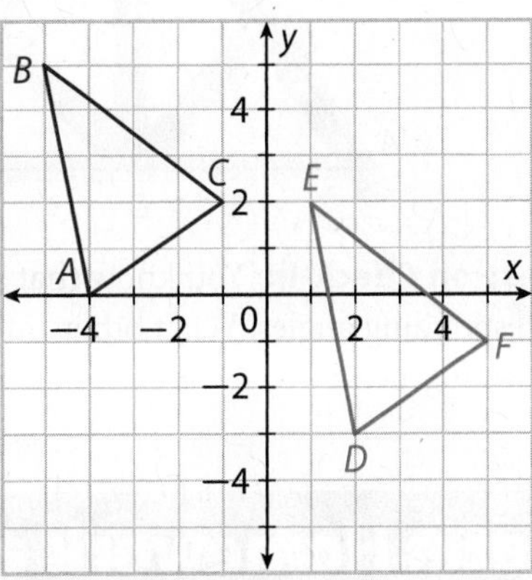

7. Show that the two triangles are congruent using the AAS Theorem. Use the distance formula to compare BC and EF.

8. Show that the two triangles are congruent using the AAS Theorem. Use the distance formula to compare AC and DF.

Elaborate

9. Two isosceles triangles share a side. With which diagram can the AAS Theorem be used to show the triangles are congruent? Explain.

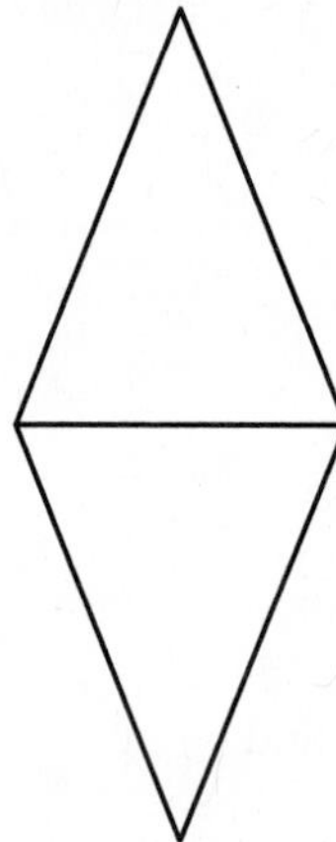

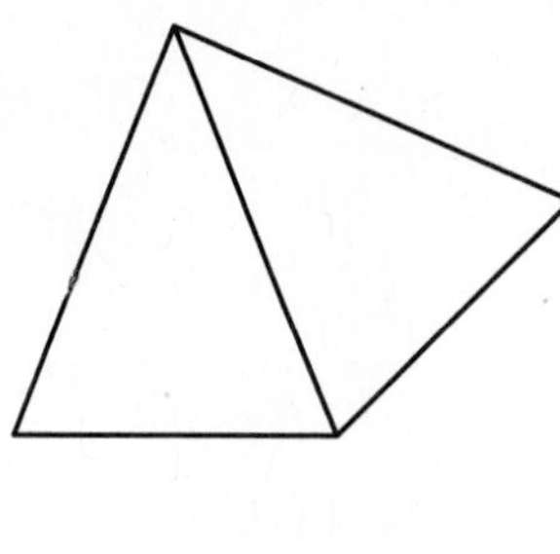

10. What must be true of the right triangles in the roof truss to use the AAS Congruence Theorem to prove the two triangles are congruent? Explain.

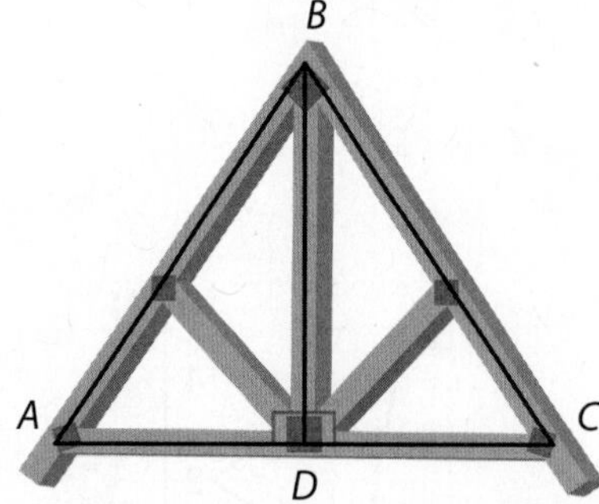

11. Essential Question Check-In You know that a pair of triangles has two pairs of congruent corresponding angles. What other information do you need to show that the triangles are congruent?

Evaluate: Homework and Practice

- Online Homework
- Hints and Help
- Extra Practice

For 1–6, decide whether you have enough information to determine that the triangles are congruent. If they are congruent, explain why.

1.

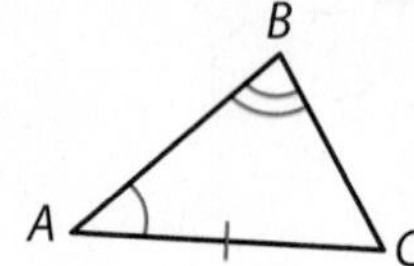

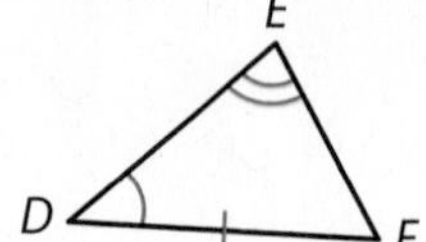

2.

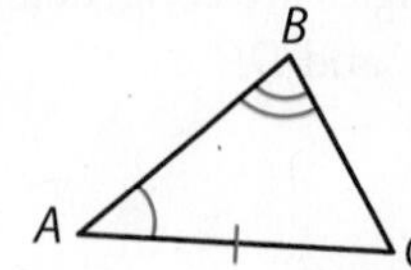

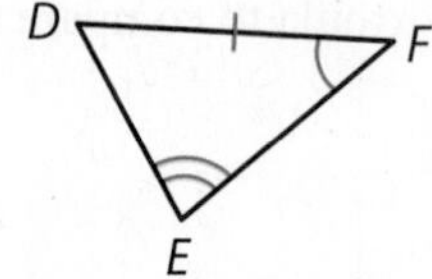

3.

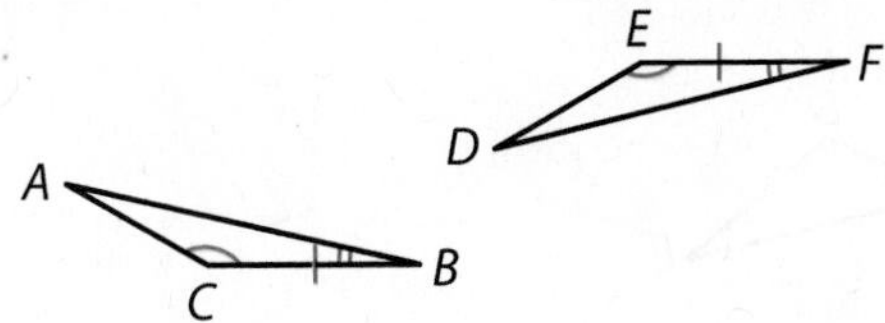

4.

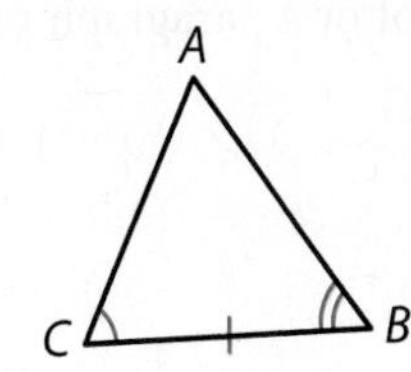

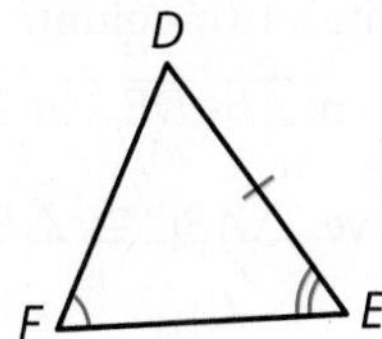

5.

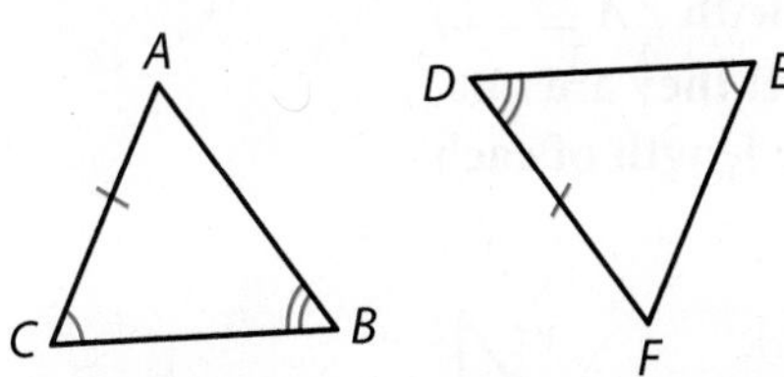

6.

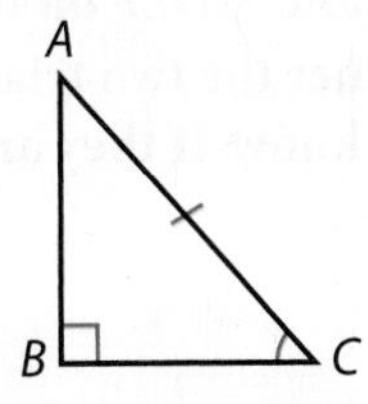

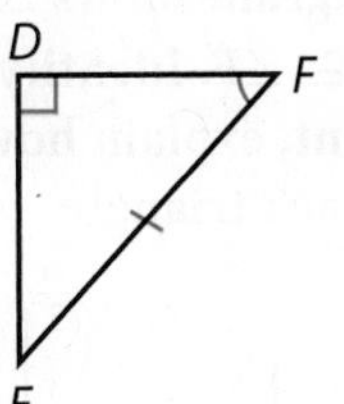

Each diagram shows two triangles with two congruent angles or sides. Identify one additional pair of corresponding angles or sides such that, if the pair were congruent, the two triangles could be proved congruent by AAS.

7.

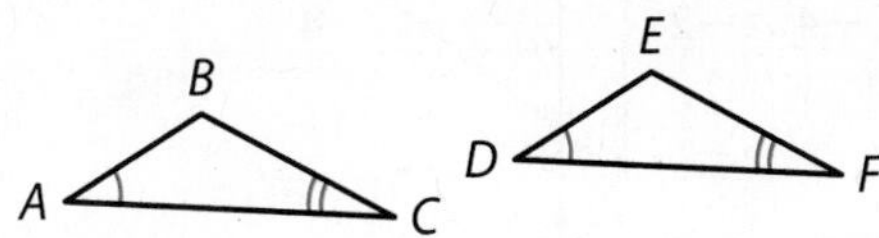

8.

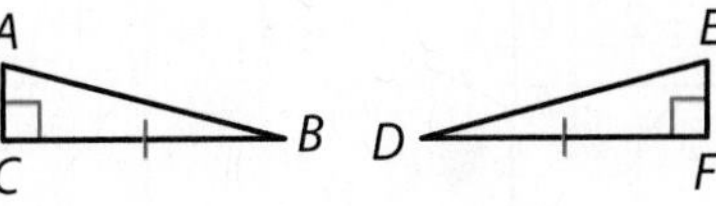

9.

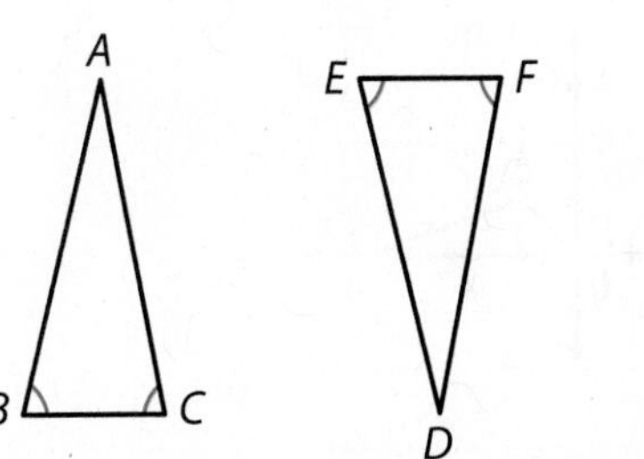

10.

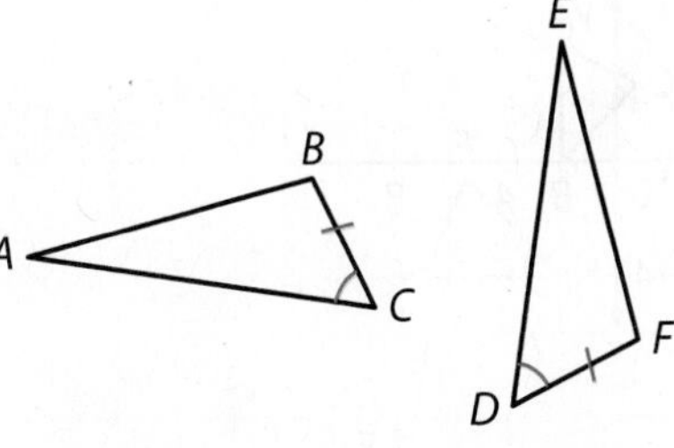

11.

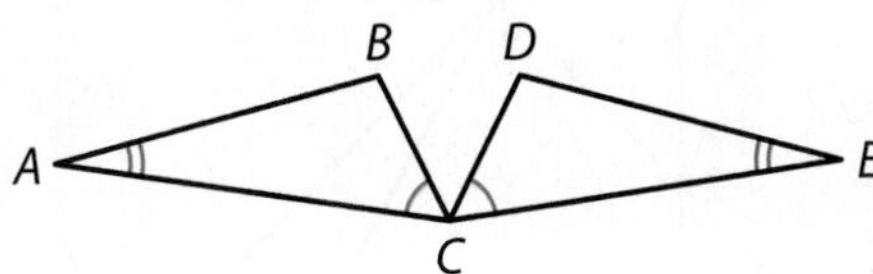

12.

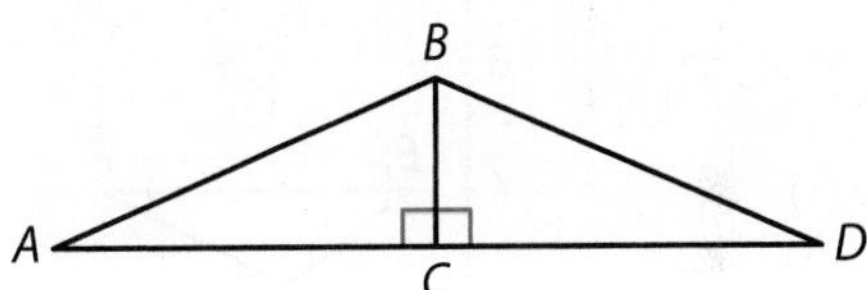

13. Copy the table and complete the proof.

Given: $\angle B \cong \angle D$, $\overleftrightarrow{AC}$ bisects $\angle BCD$.

Prove: $\triangle ABC \cong \triangle ADC$

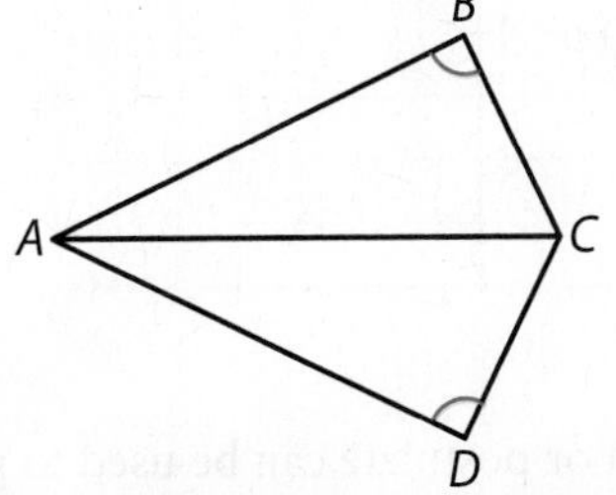

Statements	Reasons
1. $\overline{AC} \cong \overline{AC}$	1. ?
2. $\overleftrightarrow{AC}$ bisects $\angle BCD$.	2. Given
3. ?	3. Definition of angle bisector
4. ?	4. Given
5. $\triangle ABC \cong \triangle ADC$	5. ?

14. Write a two-column proof or a paragraph proof.

Given: $\overline{AB} \parallel \overline{DE}$, $\overline{CB} \cong \overline{CD}$.

Prove: $\triangle ABC \cong \triangle EDC$

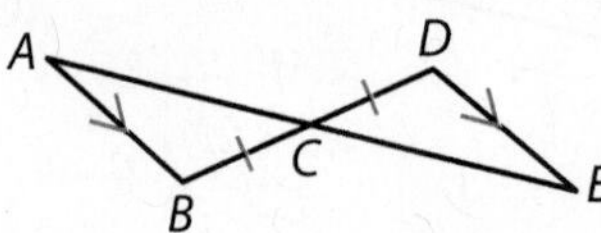

Each diagram shows $\triangle ABC$ and $\triangle DEF$ on the coordinate plane, with $\angle A \cong \angle E$, and $\angle C \cong \angle F$. Identify whether the two triangles are congruent. If they are not congruent, explain how you know. If they are congruent, find the length of each side of each triangle.

15.

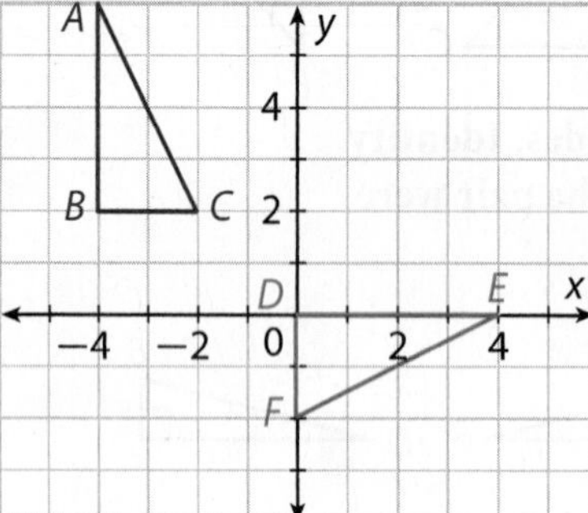

16.

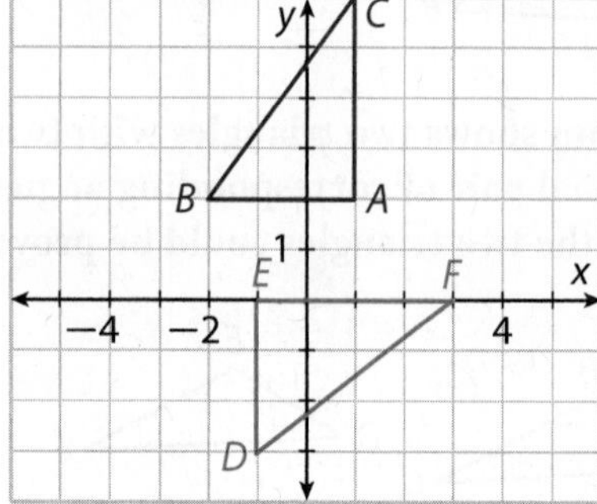

17.

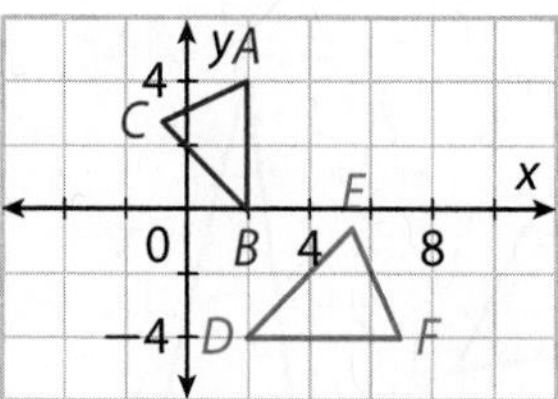

18.

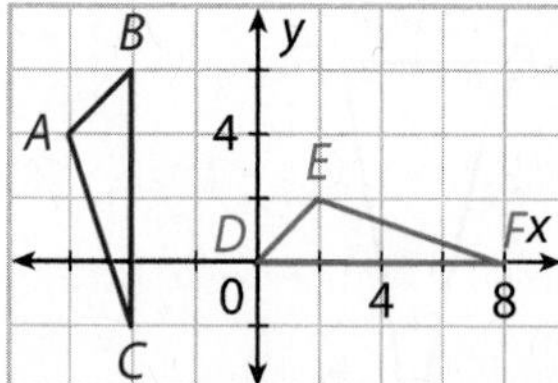

19.

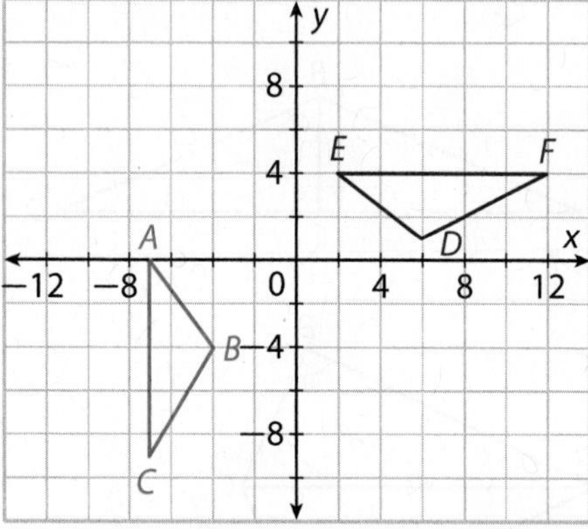

20.

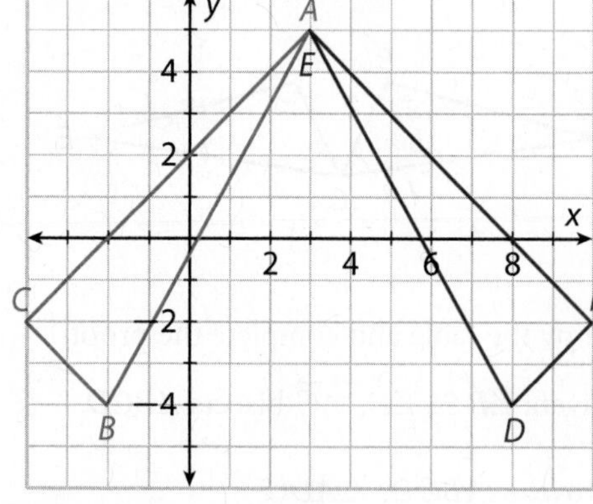

21. Which theorem or postulate can be used to prove that the triangles are congruent? Select all that apply.

A. ASA　　**B.** SAS　　**C.** SSS　　**D.** AAS

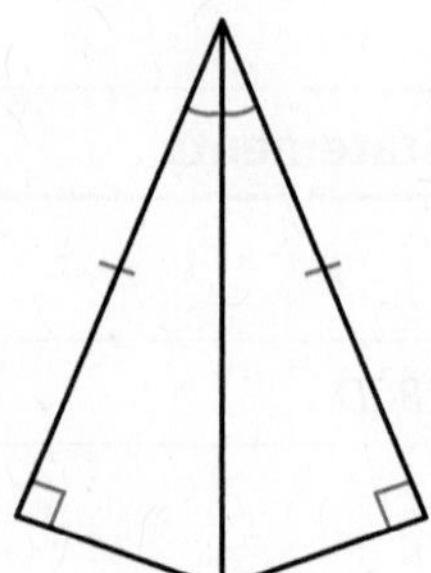

H.O.T. Focus on Higher Order Thinking

22. Analyze Relationships $\triangle XYZ$ and $\triangle KLM$ have two congruent angles: $\angle X \cong \angle K$ and $\angle Y \cong \angle L$. Can it be concluded that $\angle Z \cong \angle M$? Can it be concluded that the triangles are congruent? Explain.

23. Communicate Mathematical Ideas $\triangle GHJ$ and $\triangle PQR$ have two congruent angles: $\angle G \cong \angle P$ and $\angle H \cong \angle Q$. If $\overline{HJ}$ is congruent to one of the sides of $\triangle PQR$, are the two triangles congruent? Explain.

24. Make a Conjecture Combine the theorems of ASA Congruence and AAS Congruence into a single statement that describes a condition for congruency between triangles.

25. Justify Reasoning Triangles *ABC* and *DEF* are constructed with the following angles: $m\angle A = 35°$, $m\angle B = 45°$, $m\angle D = 65°$, $m\angle E = 45°$. Also, $AC = DF = 12$ units. Are the two triangles congruent? Explain.

26. Justify Reasoning Triangles *ABC* and *DEF* are constructed with the following angles: $m\angle A = 65°$, $m\angle B = 60°$, $m\angle D = 65°$, $m\angle F = 55°$. Also, $AB = DE = 7$ units. Are the two triangles congruent? Explain.

27. Algebra A bicycle frame includes $\triangle VSU$ and $\triangle VTU$, which lie in intersecting planes. From the given angle measures, can you conclude that $\triangle VSU \cong \triangle VTU$? Explain.

$m\angle VUS = (7y - 2)°$	$m\angle VUT = \left(5\frac{1}{2}x - \frac{1}{2}\right)°$
$m\angle USV = 5\frac{2}{3}y°$	$m\angle UTV = (4x + 8)°$
$m\angle SVU = (3y - 6)°$	$m\angle TVU = 2x°$

Lesson Performance Task

A mapmaker has successfully mapped Carlisle Street and River Avenue, as shown in the diagram. The last step is to map Beacon Street correctly. To save time, the mapmaker intends to measure just one more angle or side of the triangle.

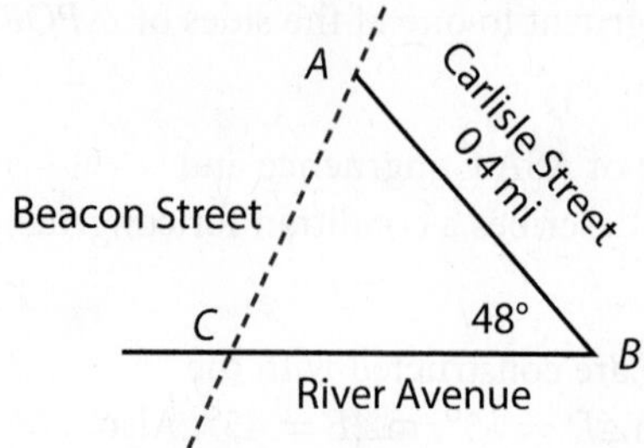

a. Which angle(s) or side(s) could the mapmaker measure to be sure that only one triangle is possible? For each angle or side that you name, justify your answer.

b. Suppose that instead of measuring the length of Carlisle Street, the mapmaker measured $\angle A$ and $\angle C$ along with $\angle B$. Would the measures of the three angles alone assure a unique triangle? Explain.

6.3 HL Triangle Congruence

Resource Locker

Essential Question: What does the HL Triangle Congruence Theorem tell you about two triangles?

Explore Is There a Side-Side-Angle Congruence Theorem?

You have already seen several theorems for proving that triangles are congruent. In this Explore, you will investigate whether there is a SSA Triangle Congruence Theorem.

Follow these steps to draw $\triangle ABC$ such that $m\angle A = 30°$, $AB = 6$ cm, and $BC = 4$ cm. The goal is to determine whether two side lengths and the measure of a non-included angle (SSA) determine a unique triangle.

(A) Use a protractor to draw a large 30° angle on a separate sheet of paper. Label it $\angle A$.

(B) Use a ruler to locate point B on one ray of $\angle A$ so that $AB = 6$ cm.

(C) Now draw $\overline{BC}$ so that $BC = 4$ cm. To do this, open a compass to a distance of 4 cm. Place the point of the compass on point B and draw an arc. Plot point C where the arc intersects the side of $\angle A$. Draw $\overline{BC}$ to complete $\triangle ABC$.

(D) What do you notice? Is it possible to draw only one $\triangle ABC$ with the given side length? Explain.

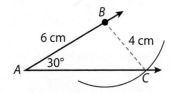

Reflect

1. Do you think that SSA is sufficient to prove congruence? Why or why not?

2. **Discussion** Your friend said that there is a special case where SSA can be used to prove congruence. Namely, when the non-included angle was a right angle. Is your friend right? Explain.

Explain 1 Justifying the Hypotenuse-Leg Congruence Theorem

In a right triangle, the side opposite the right angle is the **hypotenuse**. The two sides that form the sides of the right angle are the **legs**.

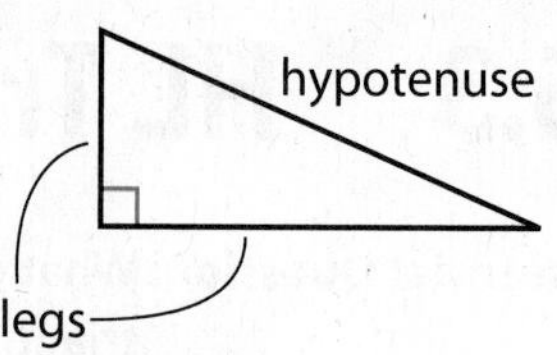

You have learned four ways to prove that triangles are congruent.

- Angle-Side-Angle (ASA) Congruence Theorem
- Side-Side-Side (SSS) Congruence Theorem
- Side-Angle-Side (SAS) Congruence Theorem
- Angle-Angle-Side (AAS) Congruence Theorem

The Hypotenuse-Leg (HL) Triangle Congruence Theorem is a special case that allows you to show that two right triangles are congruent.

Hypotenuse-Leg (HL) Triangle Congruence Theorem

If the hypotenuse and a leg of a right triangle are congruent to the hypotenuse and a leg of another right triangle, then the triangles are congruent.

Example 1 **Prove the HL Triangle Congruence Theorem.**

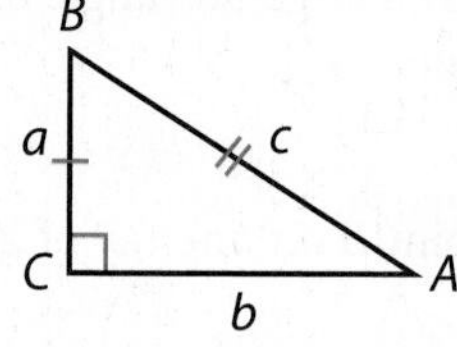

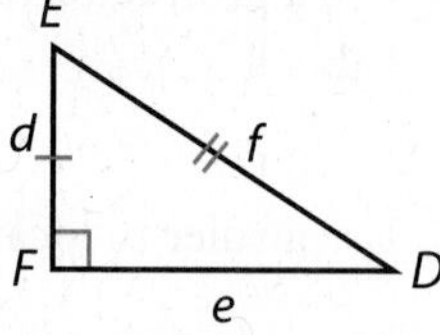

Given: $\triangle ABC$ and $\triangle DEF$ are right triangles; $\angle C$ and $\angle F$ are right angles.

$\overline{AB} \cong \overline{DE}$ and $\overline{BC} \cong \overline{EF}$

Prove: $\triangle ABC \cong \triangle DEF$

By the Pythagorean Theorem, $a^2 + b^2 = c^2$ and $d^2 + e^2 = f^2$. It is given that $\overline{AB} \cong \overline{DE}$, so $AB = DE$ and $c = f$. Therefore, $c^2 = f^2$ and $a^2 + b^2 = d^2 + e^2$. It is given that $\overline{BC} \cong \overline{EF}$, so $BC = EF$ and $a = d$. Substituting a for d in the above equation, $a^2 + b^2 = a^2 + e^2$.

Subtracting a^2 from each side shows that $b^2 = e^2$, and taking the square root of each side, $b = e$.

This shows that $\overline{AC} \cong \overline{DF}$.

Therefore, $\triangle ABC \cong \triangle DEF$ by the SSS Triangle Congruence Theorem.

Your Turn

3. Determine whether there is enough information to prove that triangles $\triangle VWX$ and $\triangle YXW$ are congruent. Explain.

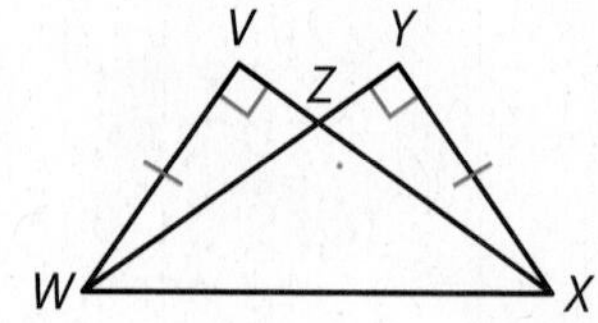

Explain 2 Applying the HL Triangle Congruence Theorem

Example 2 **Use the HL Congruence Theorem to prove that the triangles are congruent.**

(A) Given: $\angle P$ and $\angle R$ are right angles. $\overline{PS} \cong \overline{RQ}$
Prove: $\triangle PQS \cong \triangle RSQ$

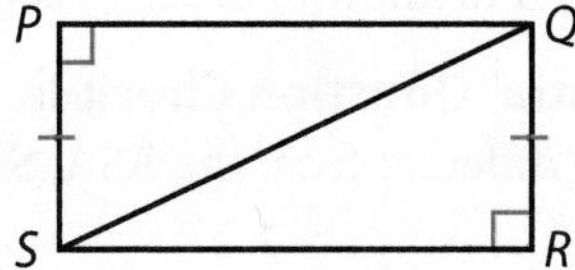

Statements	Reasons
1. $\angle P$ and $\angle R$ are right angles.	1. Given
2. $\overline{PS} \cong \overline{RQ}$	2. Given
3. $\overline{SQ} \cong \overline{SQ}$	3. Reflexive Property of Congruence
4. $\triangle PQS \cong \triangle RSQ$	4. HL Triangle Congruence Theorem

(B) Given: $\angle J$ and $\angle L$ are right angles. K is the midpoint of $\overline{JL}$ and $\overline{MN}$.
Prove: $\triangle JKN \cong \triangle LKM$

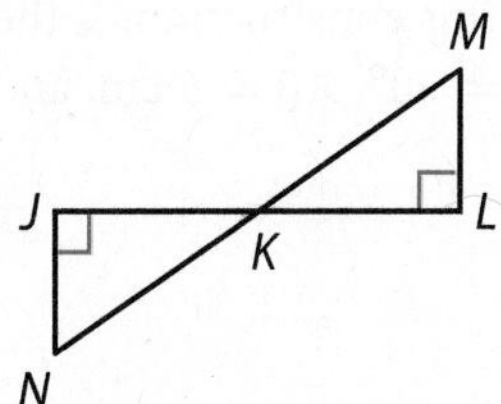

Statements	Reasons
1. $\angle J$ and $\angle L$ are right angles.	1. Given
2. K is the midpoint of $\overline{JL}$ and $\overline{MN}$.	2. Given
3. $\overline{JK} \cong \overline{LK}$ and $\overline{MK} \cong \overline{NK}$	3. Definition of midpoint
4. $\triangle JKN \cong \triangle LKM$	4. HL Triangle Congruence Theorem

Reflect

4. Is it possible to write the proof in Part B without using the HL Triangle Congruence Theorem? Explain.

Your Turn

Use the HL Congruence Theorem to prove that the triangles are congruent.

5. Given: $\angle CAB$ and $\angle DBA$ are right angles. $\overline{AD} \cong \overline{BC}$
Prove: $\triangle ABC \cong \triangle BAD$

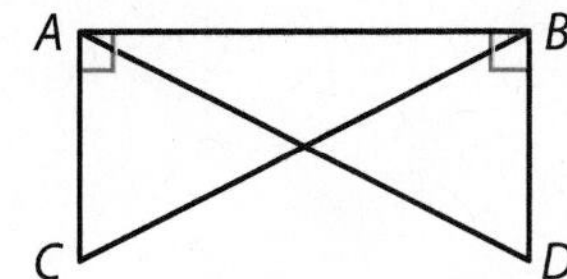

Elaborate

6. You draw a right triangle with a hypotenuse that is 5 inches long. A friend also draws a right triangle with a hypotenuse that is 5 inches long. Can you conclude that the triangles are congruent using the HL Congruence Theorem? If not, what else would you need to know in order to conclude that the triangles are congruent?

7. **Essential Question Check-In** How is the HL Triangle Congruence Theorem similar to and different from the ASA, SAS, SSS, and AAS Triangle Congruence Theorems?

Evaluate: Homework and Practice

- Online Homework
- Hints and Help
- Extra Practice

1. Tyrell used geometry software to construct $\angle ABC$ so that $m\angle ABC = 20°$. Then he dragged point A so that $AB = 6$ cm. He used the software's compass tool to construct a circle centered at point A with radius 3 cm. Based on this construction, is there a unique $\triangle ABC$ with $m\angle ABC = 20°$, $AB = 6$ cm, and $AC = 3$ cm? Explain.

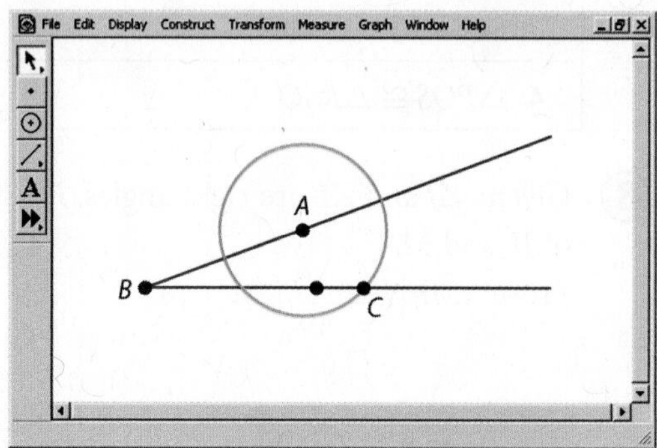

Determine whether enough information is given to prove that the triangles are congruent. Explain your answer.

2. $\triangle ABC$ and $\triangle DCB$

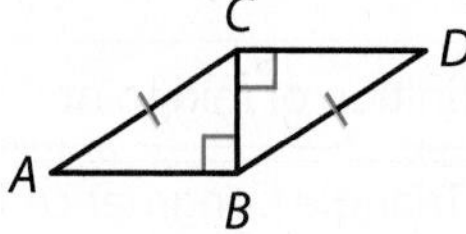

3. $\triangle PQR$ and $\triangle STU$

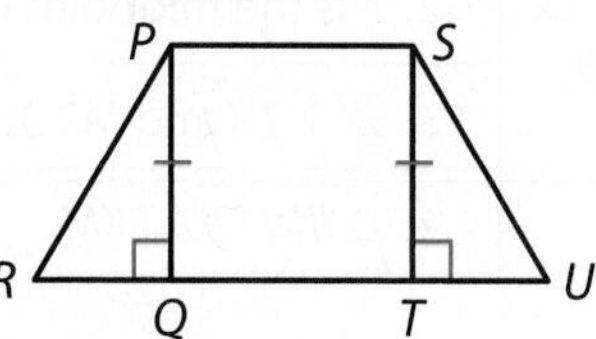

4. $\triangle GKJ$ and $\triangle JHG$

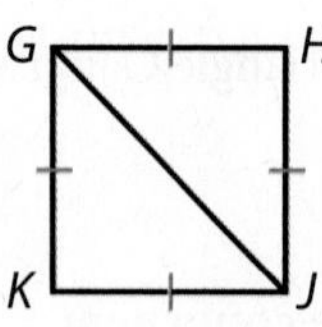

5. $\triangle EFG$ and $\triangle SQR$

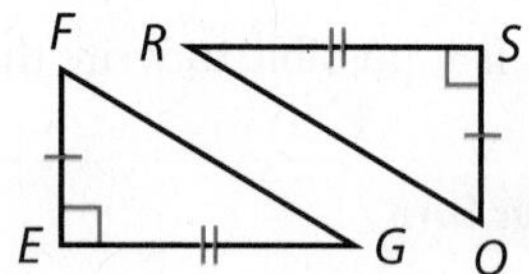

Write a two-column proof, using the HL Congruence Theorem, to prove that the triangles are congruent.

6. Given: $\angle A$ and $\angle D$ are right angles. $\overline{AB} \cong \overline{DC}$
Prove: $\triangle ABC \cong \triangle DCB$

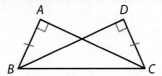

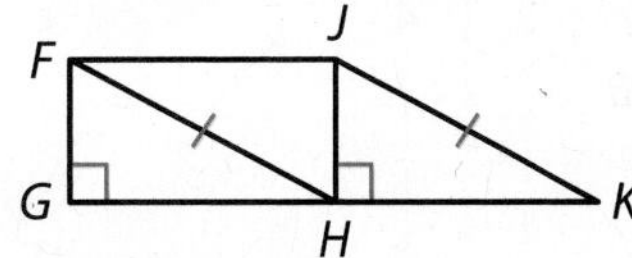

7. Given: $\angle FGH$ and $\angle JHK$ are right angles.
H is the midpoint of $\overline{GK}$. $\overline{FH} \cong \overline{JK}$
Prove: $\triangle FGH \cong \triangle JHK$

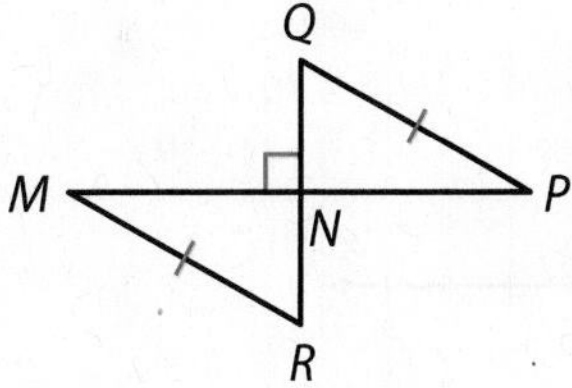

8. Given: $\overline{MP}$ is perpendicular to $\overline{QR}$.
N is the midpoint of $\overline{MP}$. $\overline{QP} \cong \overline{RM}$
Prove: $\triangle MNR \cong \triangle PNQ$

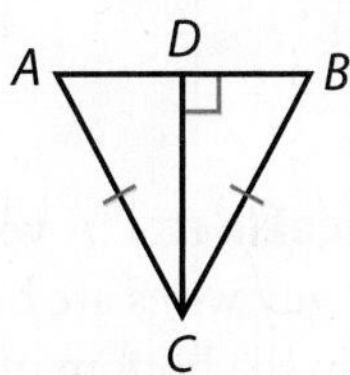

9. Given: $\angle ADC$ and $\angle BDC$ are right angles. $\overline{AC} \cong \overline{BC}$
Prove: $\overline{AD} \cong \overline{BD}$

Algebra What value of x will make the given triangles congruent? Explain.

10. $\triangle JKL$ and $\triangle JKM$

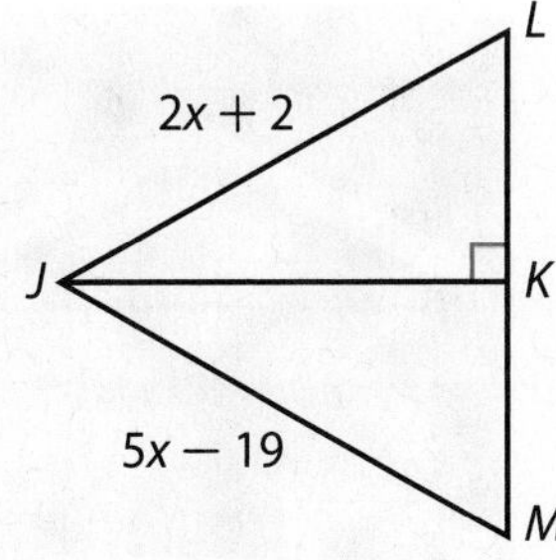

11. $\triangle ABC$ and $\triangle ABD$

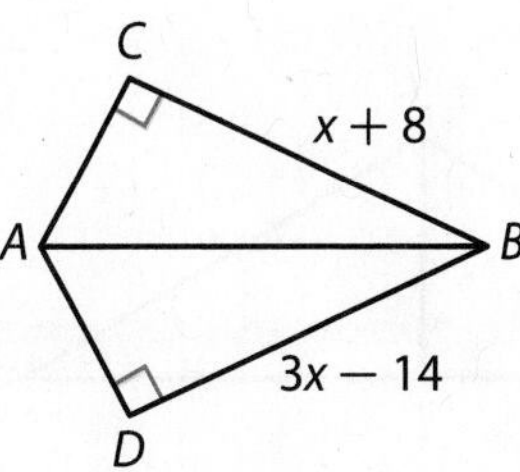

12. $\triangle STV$ and $\triangle UVT$

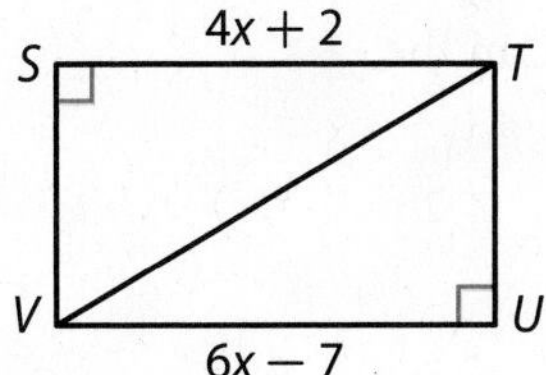

13. $\triangle MPQ$ and $\triangle PMN$

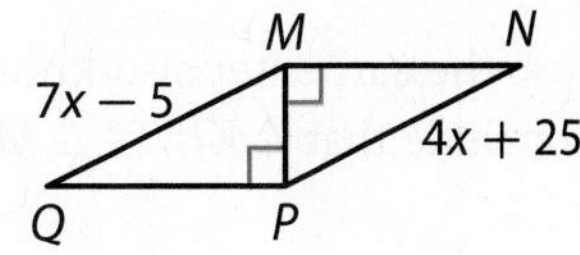

Algebra **Use the HL Triangle Congruence Theorem to show that $\triangle ABC \cong \triangle DEF$. (*Hint*: Use the Distance Formula to show that appropriate sides are congruent. Use the slope formula to show that appropriate angles are right angles.)**

14.

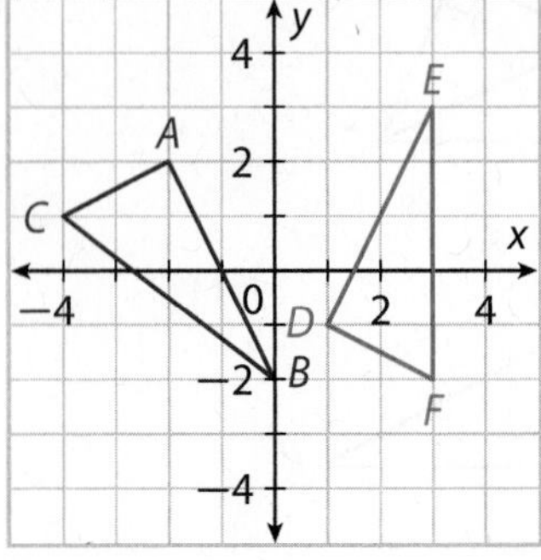

15.

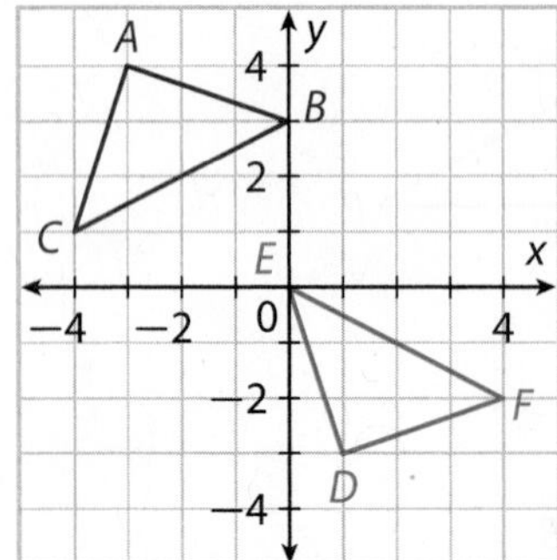

16. **Communicate Mathematical Ideas** A vertical tower is supported by two guy wires, as shown. The guy wires are both 58 feet long. Is it possible to determine the distance from the bottom of guy wire $\overline{AB}$ to the bottom of the tower? If so, find the distance. If not, explain why not.

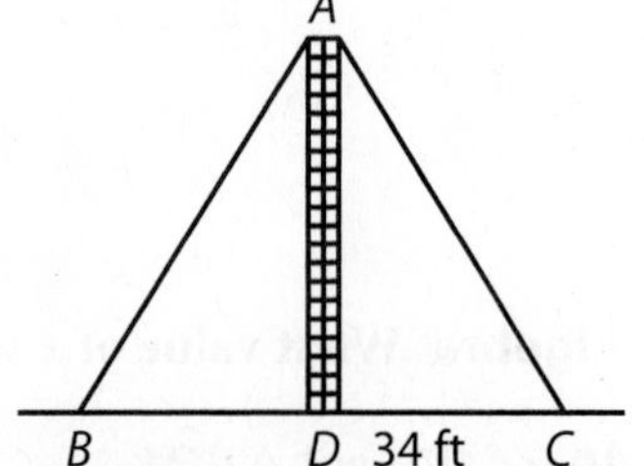

17. A carpenter built a truss, as shown, to support the roof of a doghouse.

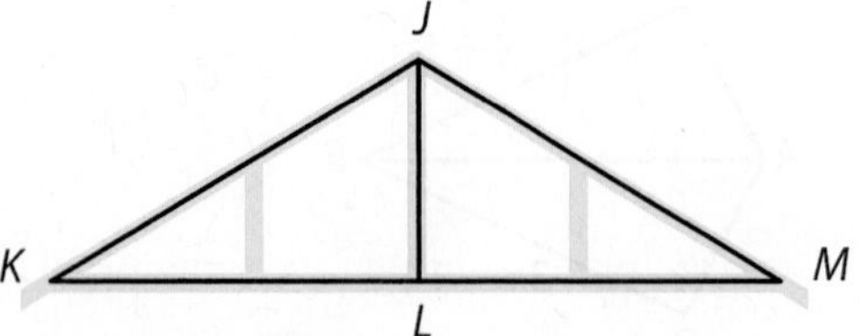

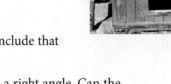

a. The carpenter knows that $\overline{KJ} \cong \overline{MJ}$. Can the carpenter conclude that $\triangle KJL \cong \triangle MJL$? Why or why not?

b. **What If?** Suppose the carpenter also knows that $\angle JLK$ is a right angle. Can the carpenter now conclude that $\triangle KJL \cong \triangle MJL$? Explain.

18. **Counterexamples** Denise said that if two right triangles share a common hypotenuse, then the triangles must be congruent. Sketch a figure that serves as a counterexample to show that Denise's statement is not true.

19. **Multi-Step** The front of a tent is covered by a triangular flap of material. The figure represents the front of the tent, with $\overline{PS} \perp \overline{QR}$ and $\overline{PQ} \cong \overline{PR}$. Jonah needs to determine the perimeter of $\triangle PQR$ so that he can replace the zipper on the tent. Find the perimeter. Explain your steps.

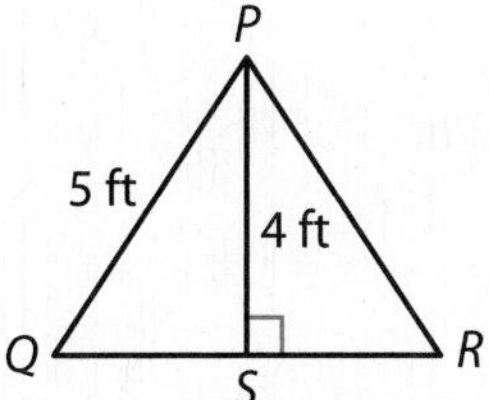

20. A student is asked to write a two-column proof for the following.

Given: $\angle ABC$ and $\angle DCB$ are right angles. $\overline{AC} \cong \overline{BD}$

Prove: $\overline{AB} \cong \overline{DC}$

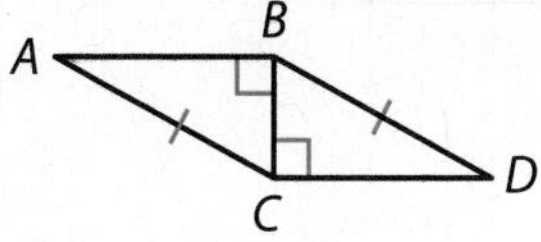

Assuming the student writes the proof correctly, which of the following will appear as a statement or reason in the proof? Select all that apply.

A. ASA Triangle Congruence Theorem

B. $\overline{BC} \cong \overline{BC}$

C. $\angle A \cong \angle D$

D. Reflexive Property of Congruence

E. CPCTC

F. HL Triangle Congruence Theorem

H.O.T. Focus on Higher Order Thinking

21. **Analyze Relationships** Is it possible for a right triangle with a leg that is 10 inches long and a hypotenuse that is 26 inches long to be congruent to a right triangle with a leg that is 24 inches long and a hypotenuse that is 26 inches long? Explain.

22. **Communicate Mathematical Ideas** In the figure, $\overline{JK} \cong \overline{LM}$, $\overline{JM} \cong \overline{LK}$, and $\angle J$ and $\angle L$ are right angles. Describe how you could use three different congruence theorems to prove that $\triangle JKM \cong \triangle LMK$.

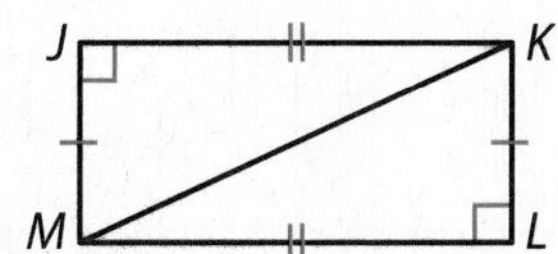

23. **Justify Reasoning** Do you think there is an LL Triangle Congruence Theorem? That is, if the legs of one right triangle are congruent to the legs of another right triangle, are the triangles necessarily congruent? If so, write a proof of the theorem. If not, provide a counterexample.

Lesson Performance Task

The figure shows kite *ABCD*.

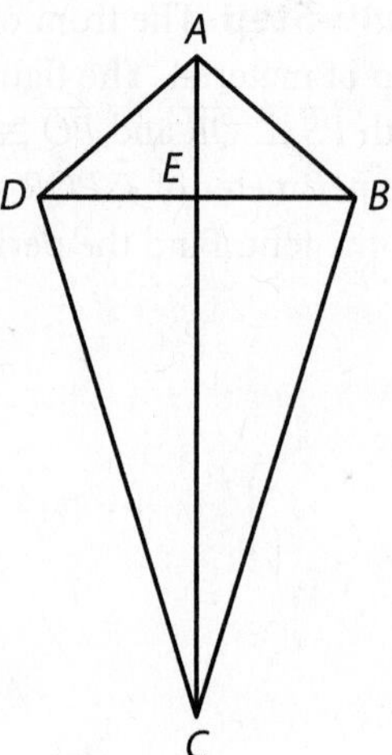

a. What would you need to know about the relationship between $\overline{AC}$ and $\overline{DB}$ in order to prove that $\triangle ADE \cong \triangle ABE$ and $\triangle CDE \cong \triangle CBE$ by the HL Triangle Congruence Theorem?

b. Can you prove that $\triangle ADC$ and $\triangle ABC$ are congruent using the HL Triangle Congruence Theorem? Explain why or why not.

c. How can you prove that the two triangles named in Part b are in fact congruent, even without the additional piece of information?

STUDY GUIDE REVIEW

Applications of Triangle Congruence

MODULE 6

Essential Question: How can you use triangle congruence to solve real-world problems?

Key Vocabulary
hypotenuse *(hipotenusa)*
legs *(catetos)*

KEY EXAMPLE *Lesson 6.1*

Construct the bisector of the angle shown.

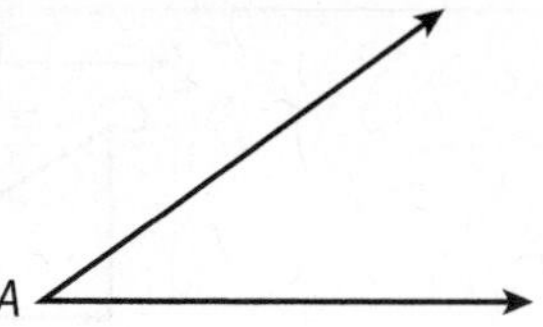

Place the point of the compass at A and draw an arc intersecting the sides of the angle. Label its points of intersection as B and C.

Use the same compass setting to draw intersecting arcs from B and C. Label the intersection of the arcs as point D.

Use a straight edge to draw $\overrightarrow{AD}$.

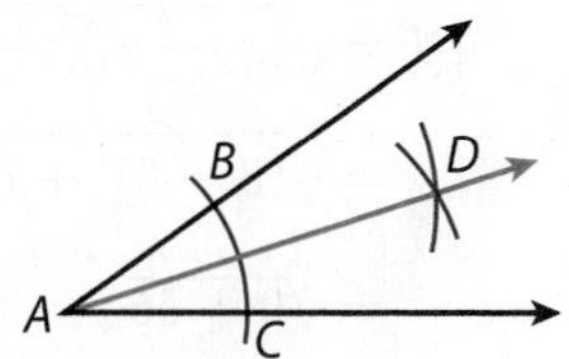

KEY EXAMPLE *(Lesson 6.2)*

Construct the line through the given point, parallel to the line shown.

Use a straightedge to draw $\overrightarrow{AC}$.

Copy $\angle CAB$. Start by constructing a pair of arcs.

Then construct the pair of arc intersections.

Draw line ℓ through C and the arc intersection. This line is parallel to m.

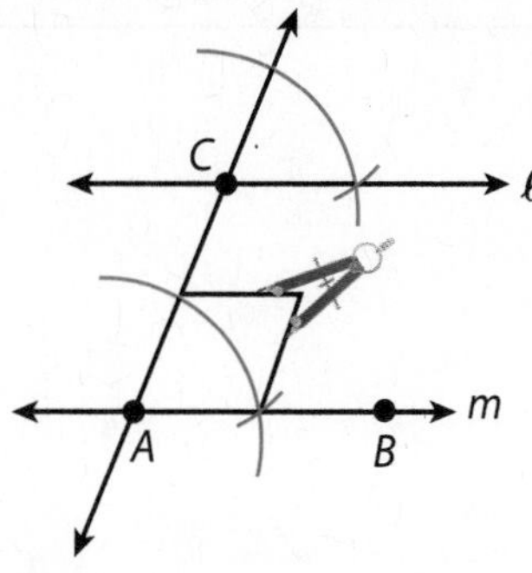

KEY EXAMPLE (Lesson 6.3)

The triangular regions represent plots of land. Use the AAS Theorem to explain why the same amount of fencing will surround either plot.

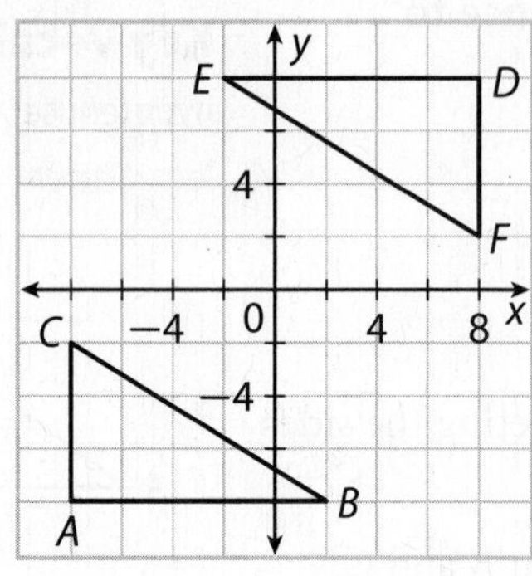

Given: $\angle B \cong \angle E$

$\angle A \cong \angle D$ Both are right angles.

Compare AC and DF using the Distance Formula.

$AC = \sqrt{(x_2 - x_1)^2 + (y_2 - y_1)^2}$ $DF = \sqrt{(x_2 - x_1)^2 + (y_2 - y_1)^2}$

$= \sqrt{(-8 - (-8))^2 + (-2 - (-8))^2}$ $= \sqrt{(8 - 8)^2 + (2 - 8)^2}$

$= \sqrt{0 + 36}$ $= \sqrt{0 + 36}$

$= 6$ $= 6$

Because two angles and a nonincluded side are congruent, $\triangle ABC \cong \triangle DEF$ by AAS. Therefore the triangles have the same perimeter by CPCTC and the same amount of fencing is needed.

KEY EXAMPLE (Lesson 6.3)

Write the proof.

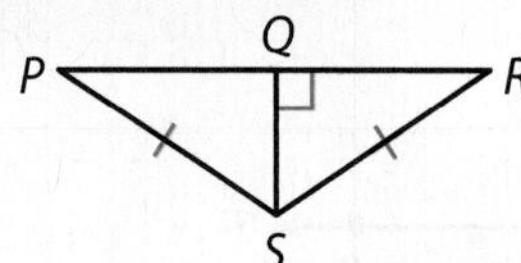

Given: $\overline{PS} \cong \overline{RS}$

Prove: $\triangle PQS \cong \triangle RSQ$

Statements	Reasons
1. $\angle PQS$ and $\angle RQS$ are right angles.	1. Given
2. $\overline{PS} \cong \overline{SR}$	2. Given
3. $\overline{SQ} \cong \overline{SQ}$	3. Reflexive Property of Congruence
4. $\triangle PQS \cong \triangle RQS$	4. HL Triangle Congruence Theorem

EXERCISES

Refer to the diagram, which shows isosceles triangle *ABC*, to find the measure of the angle. $\overline{AD}$ and $\overline{CD}$ are angle bisectors. *(Lesson 6.1)*

1. m∠*BAC*

2. m∠*ADC*

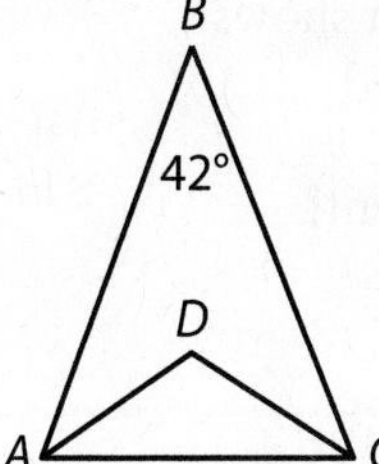

Identify the sides or angles that need to be congruent in order to make the given triangles congruent by AAS. *(Lesson 6.2)*

3.

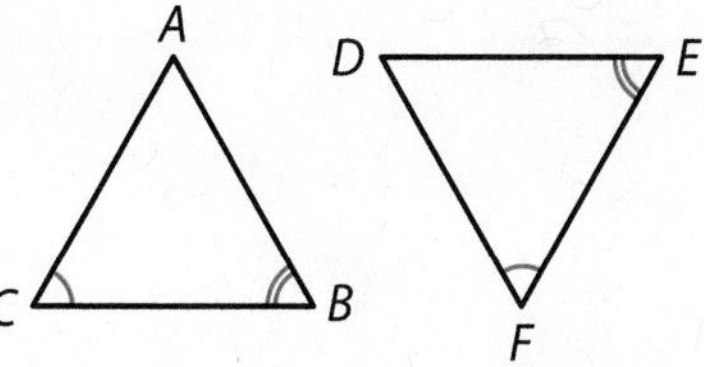

4.

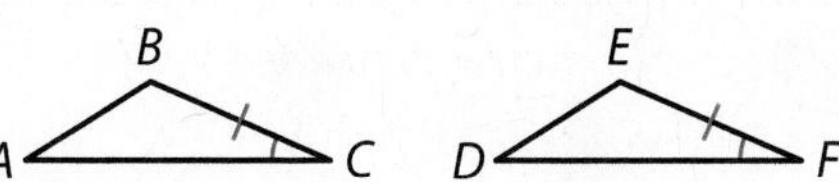

Determine whether the two triangles are congruent or not by the HL Theorem. Show all work. *(Lesson 6.3)*

5.

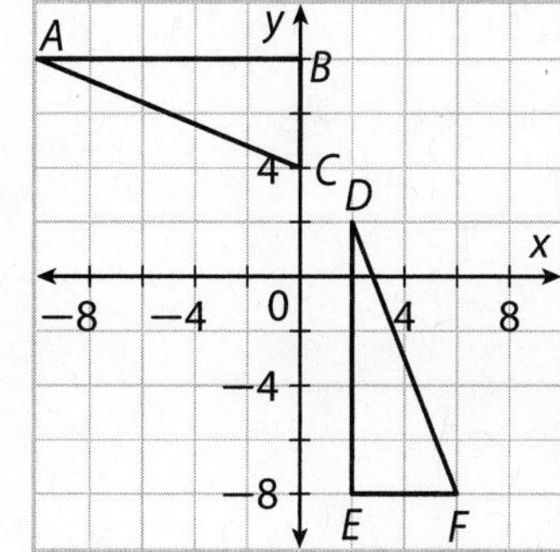

MODULE PERFORMANCE TASK

Geodesic Dome Design

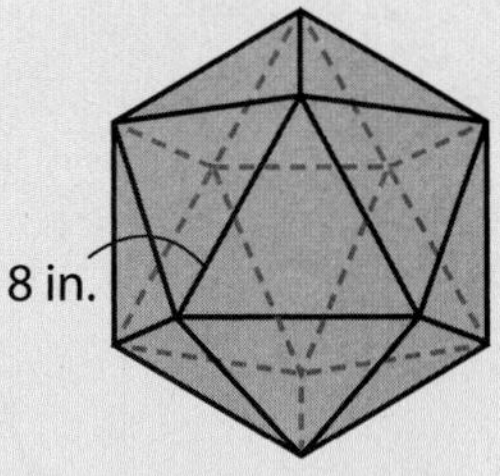

A geodesic dome is derived from a 20-sided structure called an icosahedron, made up of equilateral triangles. The illustration shows an icosahedron with the length of one side of a triangle labeled.

Are all of the triangles that make up the icosahedron congruent? How can you find the total surface area of the icosahedron?

Be sure to write down all your data and assumptions. Then use graphs, numbers, words, or algebra to explain how you reached your conclusion.

Ready to Go On?

6.1–6.3 Applications of Triangle Congruence

- Online Homework
- Hints and Help
- Extra Practice

Given the figure below, answer the following.

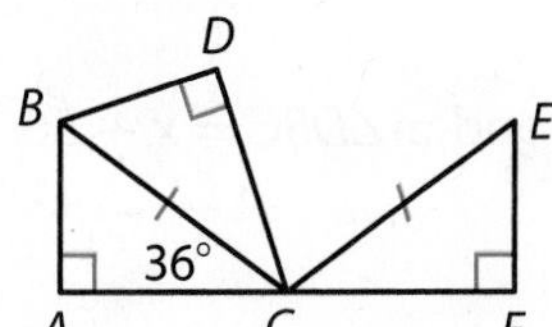

1. Given: $\angle A \cong \angle D$, $\overrightarrow{BC}$ bisects $\angle ACD$. Prove: $\triangle ABC \cong \triangle DBC$ *(Lessons 6.1, 6.3)*

2. Given: $\angle A$ and $\angle F$ are right angles, C is the midpoint of $\overline{AF}$, $\overline{BC} \cong \overline{EC}$. Prove: $\triangle ABC \cong \triangle FEC$ *(Lesson 6.3)*

3. Given: $\overrightarrow{BC}$ bisects $\angle ACD$ and m$\angle ACB$ is 36°. Find m$\angle BCD$. *(Lesson 6.1)*

ESSENTIAL QUESTION

4. When given two sides and an angle of two triangles are equal, when can it be proven and when can't it be proven that the two triangles are congruent?

MODULE 6
MIXED REVIEW

Assessment Readiness

1. Can the theorem be used to prove two triangles are congruent?
   A. SSA
   B. AAS
   C. SAS

2. Line *D* bisects $\angle ABC$, $m\angle ABD = 4x$, and $m\angle DBC = x + 36$. Determine if each statement is True or False.
   A. $m\angle ABC = 48°$
   B. $m\angle ABC = 96°$
   C. $m\angle DBC = 48°$

3. Given $\triangle GHI$ and $\triangle JKL$, $GI = 5$, $HI = 4$, $JK = 4$, and $JL = 5$, what else do you need to know to prove the two triangles are congruent using HL?

4. Given: $\overline{AB} \cong \overline{BC}$, $\overline{BD}$ is the perpendicular bisector of $\overline{AC}$
   Prove: $\triangle ABD \cong \triangle CBD$

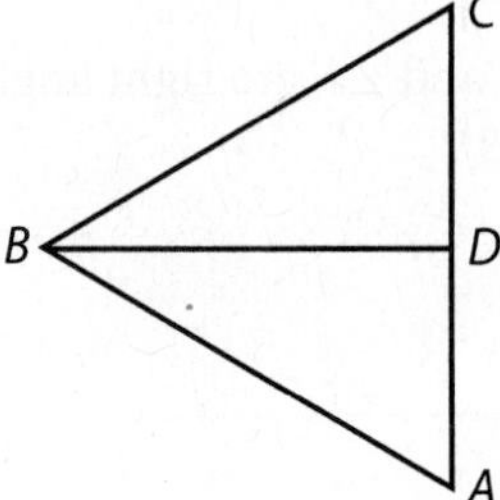

Properties of Triangles

MODULE 7

Essential Question: How can you use properties of triangles to solve real-world problems?

REAL WORLD VIDEO
Check out some of the famous buildings and landmarks in the Federal Triangle area of Washington, DC.

MODULE PERFORMANCE TASK PREVIEW

The Federal Triangle

Is the Federal Triangle really a triangle? In this module, you will use a map of the Federal Triangle to explore the geometric properties of the entire area. Time to "capitalize" on your geometry knowledge!

Are YOU Ready?

Complete these exercises to review the skills you will need for this module.

Personal Math Trainer

- Online Homework
- Hints and Help
- Extra Practice

Solving Inequalities

Example 1 What values of x make both inequalities true?

$x + 7 > 2$	$3 + x < 9$	Write the inequalities
$x > 2 - 7$	$x < 9 - 3$	Solve for x.
$x > -5$	$x < 6$	Simplify.
$-5 < x < 6$		Combine solved inequalities.

The solutions to the system are all values greater than –5 and less than 6.

What values of the variable make both inequalities true?

1. $\frac{d + 176}{3} < 116$
   $248 + d > 368$

2. $n + 14 > 16$
   $2(n + 68) < 148$

Angle Relationships

Example 2 Find the measure of $\angle x$.

$m\angle x + 72° = 180°$	Definition of supplementary angles
$m\angle x = 180° - 72°$	Solve for $m\angle x$.
$m\angle x = 108°$	Simplify.

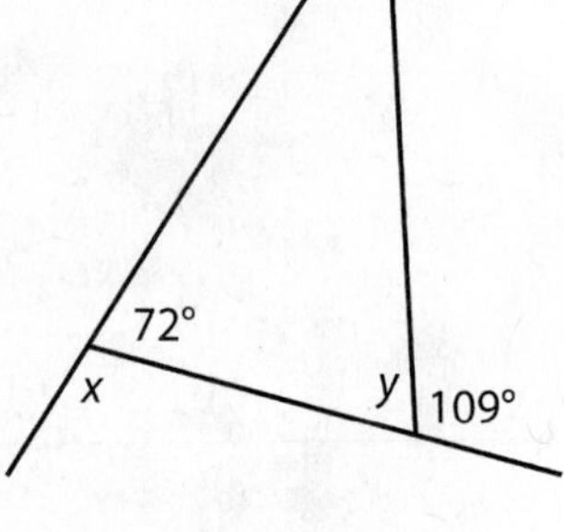

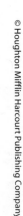

Find the measure of each angle in the image from the example.

3. $m\angle y =$ ___?___

4. $m\angle z =$ ___?___

Angle Theorems for Triangles

Example 3 Find the missing angle.

$62° + 62° + m\angle x = 180°$	Triangle Sum Theorem
$m\angle x = 180° - 62° - 62°$	Solve for $m\angle x$.
$m\angle x = 56°$	Simplify.

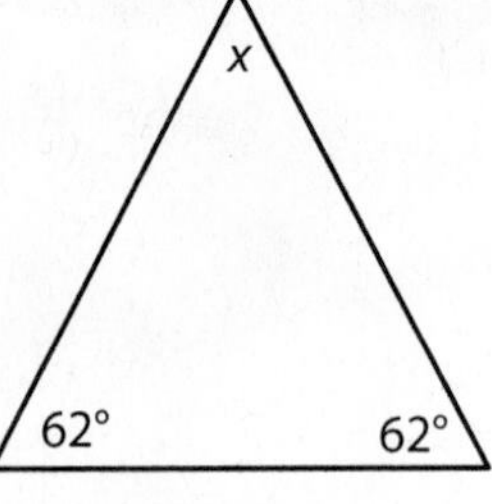

Find the missing angle measures in the given triangles.

5. 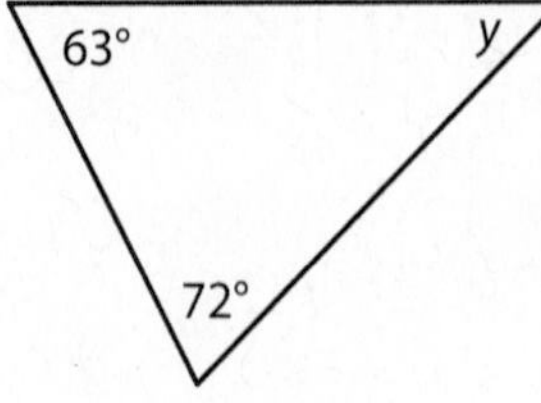

$y =$ ___?___

6. 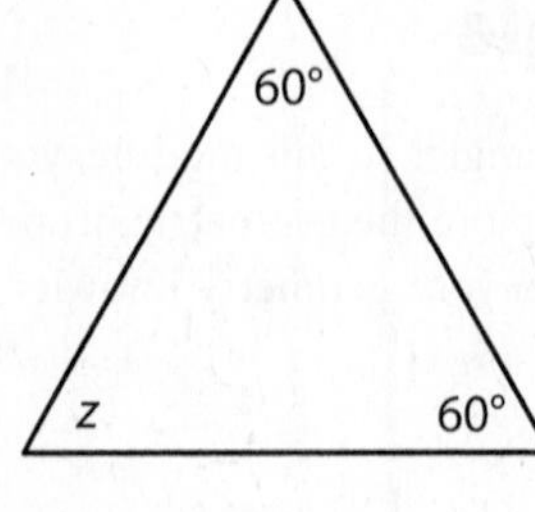

$z =$ ___?___

7.1 Interior and Exterior Angles

Essential Question: What can you say about the interior and exterior angles of a triangle and other polygons?

Resource Locker

Explore 1 Exploring Interior Angles in Triangles

You can find a relationship between the measures of the three angles of a triangle. An **interior angle** is an angle formed by two sides of a polygon with a common vertex. So, a triangle has three interior angles.

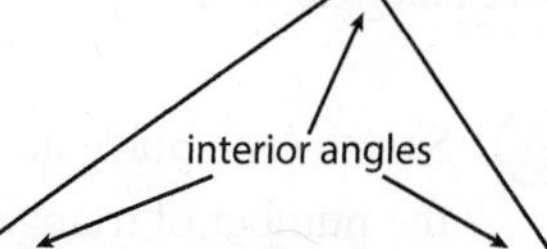

(A) Use a straightedge to draw a large triangle on a sheet of paper and cut it out. Tear off the three corners and rearrange the angles so their sides are adjacent and their vertices meet at a point.

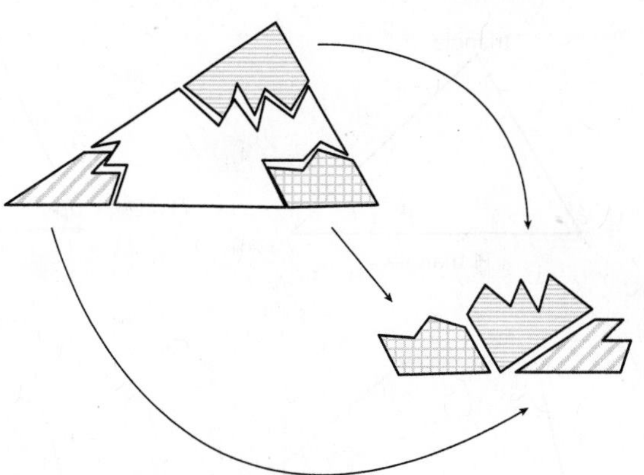

(B) What seems to be true about placing the three interior angles of a triangle together?

(C) Make a conjecture about the sum of the measures of the interior angles of a triangle.

The conjecture about the sum of the interior angles of a triangle can be proven so it can be stated as a theorem. In the proof, you will add an *auxiliary line* to the triangle figure. An **auxiliary line** is a line that is added to a figure to aid in a proof.

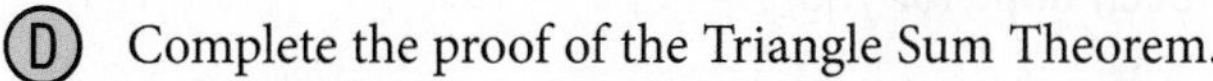

The Triangle Sum Theorem
The sum of the angle measures of a triangle is 180°.

(D) Complete the proof of the Triangle Sum Theorem.

Given: $\triangle ABC$

Prove: $m\angle 1 + m\angle 2 + m\angle 3 = 180°$

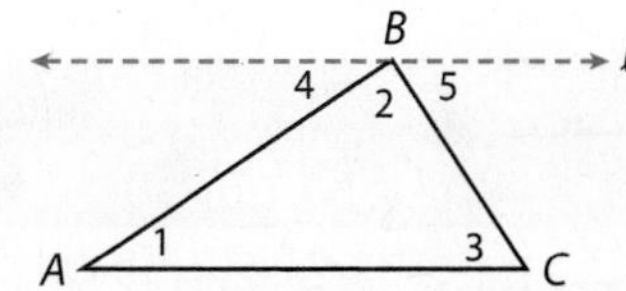

Statements	Reasons
1. Draw line ℓ through point B parallel to $\overline{AC}$.	1. Parallel Postulate
2. $m\angle 1 = m\angle$? and $m\angle 3 = m\angle$?	2. ?
3. $m\angle 4 + m\angle 2 + m\angle 5 = 180°$	3. Angle Addition Postulate and definition of straight angle
4. $m\angle$? $+ m\angle 2 + m\angle$? $=$ 180°	4. ?

Reflect

1. Explain how the Parallel Postulate allows you to add the auxiliary line into the triangle figure.
2. What does the Triangle Sum Theorem indicate about the angles of a triangle that has three angles of equal measure? How do you know?

Explore 2 Exploring Interior Angles in Polygons

To determine the sum of the interior angles for any polygon, you can use what you know about the Triangle Sum Theorem by considering how many triangles there are in other polygons. For example, by drawing the diagonal from a vertex of a quadrilateral, you can form two triangles. Since each triangle has an angle sum of 180°, the quadrilateral must have an angle sum of $180° + 180° = 360°$.

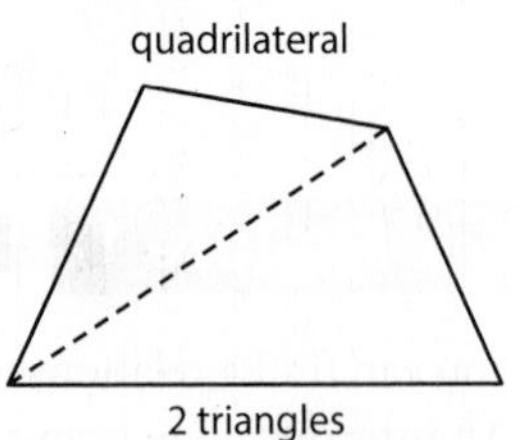

(A) Sketch each polygon. Draw the diagonals from any one vertex for each. Then state the number of triangles that are formed. The first two have already been completed.

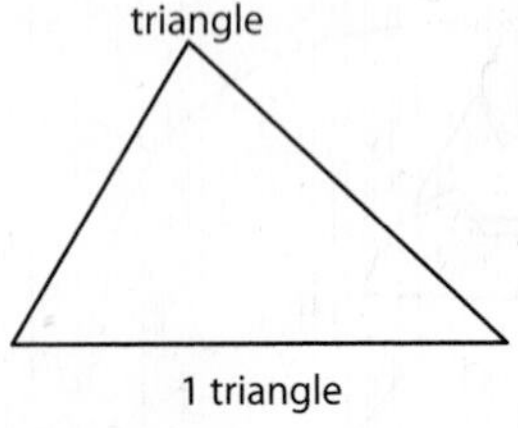

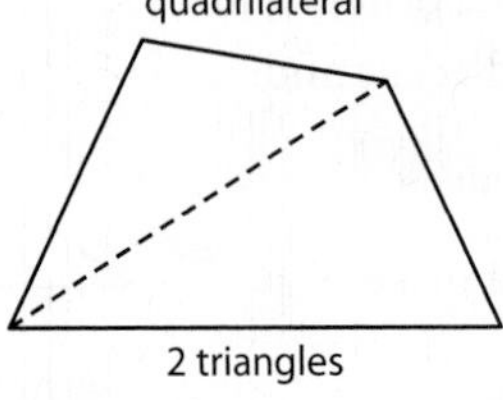

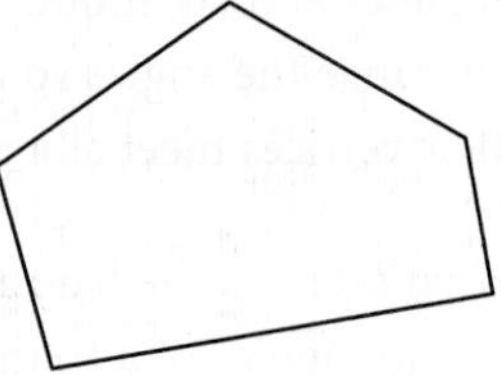

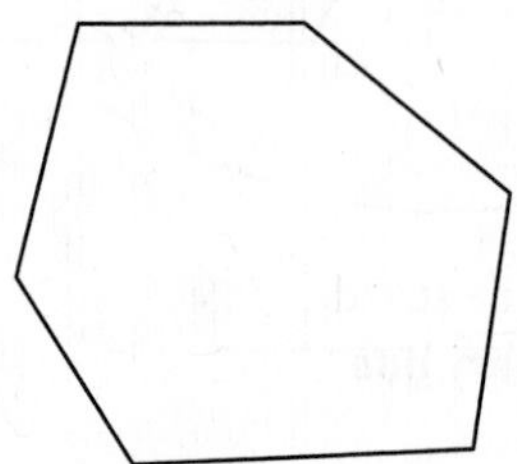

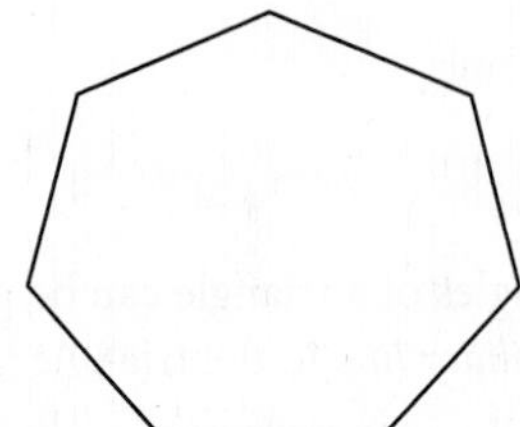

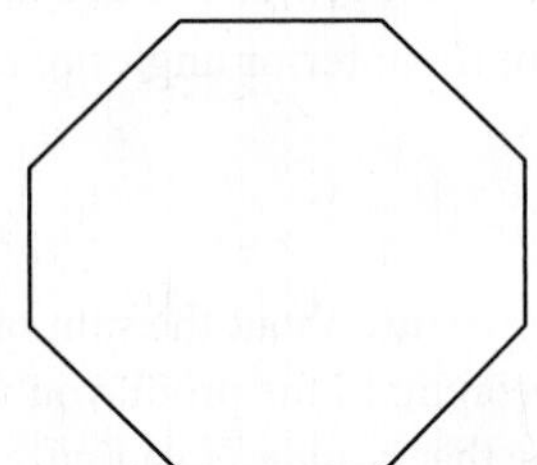

(B) For each polygon, identify the number of sides and triangles, and determine the angle sums. Then complete the chart. The first two have already been done for you.

Polygon	Number of Sides	Number of Triangles	Sum of Interior Angle Measures
Triangle	3	1	$(1)180° = 180°$
Quadrilateral	4	2	$(2)180° = 360°$
Pentagon	?	?	(?) 180° = ?
Hexagon	?	?	(?) 180° = ?
Decagon	?	?	(?) 180° = ?

(C) Do you notice a pattern between the number of sides and the number of triangles? If n represents the number of sides for any polygon, how can you represent the number of triangles?

(D) Make a conjecture for a rule that would give the sum of the interior angles for any n-gon.

Sum of interior angle measures = ?

Reflect

3. In a regular hexagon, how could you use the sum of the interior angles to determine the measure of each interior angle?

4. How might you determine the number of sides for a polygon whose interior angle sum is 3240°?

Explain 1 Using Interior Angles

You can use the angle sum to determine the unknown measure of an angle of a polygon when you know the measures of the other angles.

Polygon Angle Sum Theorem

The sum of the measures of the interior angles of a convex polygon with n sides is $(n - 2)180°$.

Example 1 **Determine the unknown angle measures.**

(A) For the nonagon shown, find the unknown angle measure $x°$.

First, use the Polygon Angle Sum Theorem to find the sum of the interior angles:

$n = 9$

$(n - 2)180° = (9 - 2)180° = (7)180° = 1260°$

Then solve for the unknown angle measure, $x°$:

$125 + 130 + 172 + 98 + 200 + 102 + 140 + 135 + x = 1260$

$x = 158$

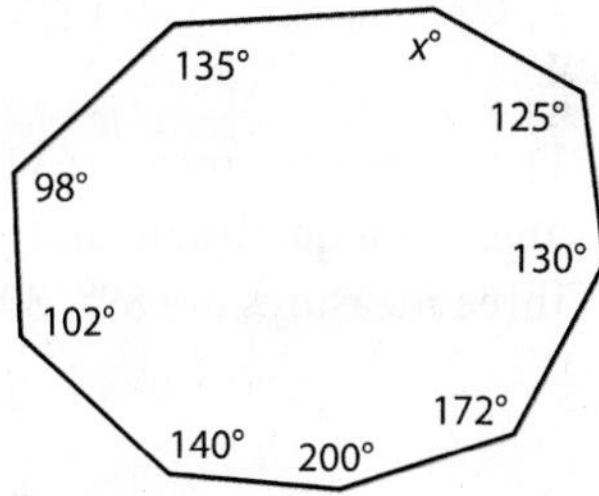

The unknown angle measure is 158°.

Ⓑ Determine the unknown interior angle measure of a convex octagon in which the measures of the seven other angles have a sum of 940°.

$n =$ 8

$\text{Sum} = (8 - 2)\,180° = (6)\,180° = 1080°$

$940 + x = 1080$

$x = 140$

The unknown angle measure is 140°.

Reflect

5. How might you use the Polygon Angle Sum Theorem to write a rule for determining the measure of each interior angle of any regular convex polygon with n sides?

Your Turn

6. Determine the unknown angle measures in this pentagon.

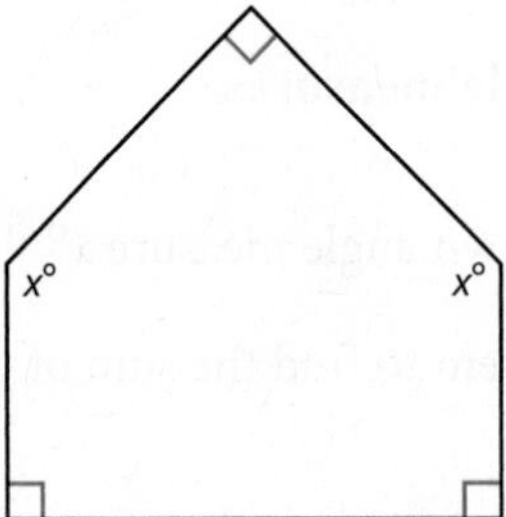

7. Determine the measure of the fourth interior angle of a quadrilateral if you know the other three measures are 89°, 80°, and 104°.

8. Determine the unknown angle measures in a hexagon whose six angles measure 69°, 108°, 135°, 204°, b°, and $2b$°.

Explain 2 Proving the Exterior Angle Theorem

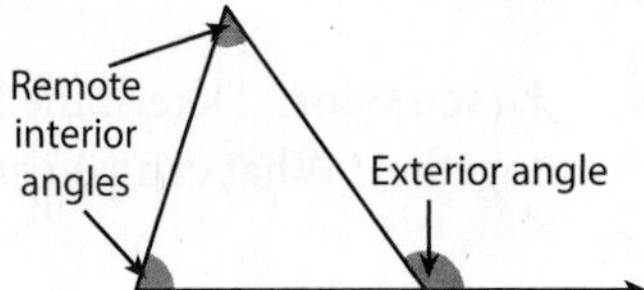

An **exterior angle** is an angle formed by one side of a polygon and the extension of an adjacent side. Exterior angles form linear pairs with the interior angles.

A **remote interior angle** is an interior angle that is not adjacent to the exterior angle.

Example 2 **Follow the steps to investigate the relationship between each exterior angle of a triangle and its remote interior angles.**

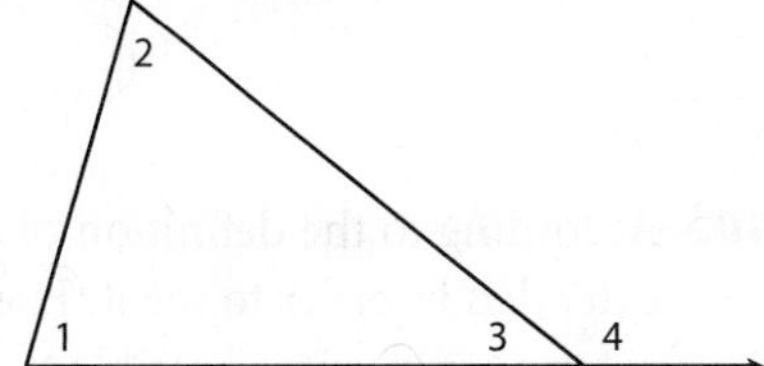

Step 1 Use a straightedge to draw a triangle with angles 1, 2, and 3. Line up your straightedge along the side opposite angle 2. Extend the side from the vertex at angle 3. You have just constructed an exterior angle. The exterior angle is drawn *supplementary* to its adjacent interior angle.

Step 2 You know the sum of the measures of the interior angles of a triangle.

$m\angle 1 + m\angle 2 + m\angle 3 = \boxed{180}\,°$

Since an exterior angle is supplementary to its adjacent interior angle, you also know:

$m\angle 3 + m\angle 4 = \boxed{180}\,°$

So, $m\angle 1 + m\angle 2 + m\angle 3 = m\angle 3 + m\angle 4$

$m\angle 1 + m\angle 2 = m\angle 4$

Make a conjecture: What can you say about the measure of the exterior angle and the measures of its remote interior angles?

Conjecture: The measure of the exterior angle is the same as the sum of the measures of its two remote interior angles.

The conjecture you made in Step 2 can be formally stated as a theorem.

Exterior Angle Theorem

The measure of an exterior angle of a triangle is equal to the sum of the measures of its remote interior angles.

Step 3 Complete the proof of the Exterior Angle Theorem.

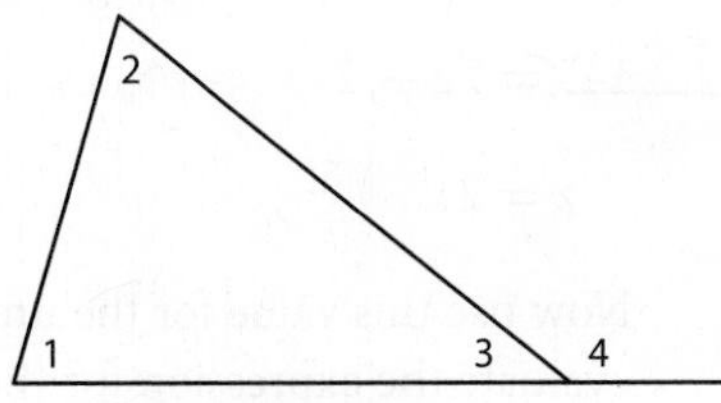

$\angle 4$ is an exterior angle. It forms a linear pair with interior angle $\angle 3$. Its remote interior angles are $\angle 1$ and $\angle 2$.

By the Triangle Sum Theorem, $m\angle 1 + m\angle 2 + m\angle 3 = 180°$.

Also, $m\angle 3 + m\angle 4 = 180°$ because they are supplementary and make a straight angle.

By the Substitution Property of Equality, then, $m\angle 1 + m\angle 2 + m\angle 3 = m\angle 3 + m\angle 4$.

Subtracting $m\angle 3$ from each side of this equation leaves $m\angle 1 + m\angle 2 = m\angle 4$.

This means that the measure of an exterior angle of a triangle is equal to the sum of the measures of the remote interior angles.

Reflect

9. **Discussion** Determine the measure of each exterior angle. Add them together. What can you say about their sum? Explain.

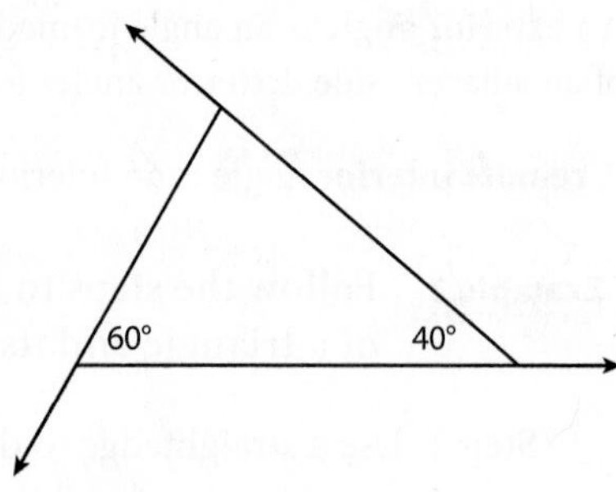

10. According to the definition of an exterior angle, one of the sides of the triangle must be extended in order to see it. How many ways can this be done for any vertex? How many exterior angles is it possible to draw for a triangle? for a hexagon?

Explain 3 Using Exterior Angles

You can apply the Exterior Angle Theorem to solve problems with unknown angle measures by writing and solving equations.

Example 3 **Determine the measure of the specified angle.**

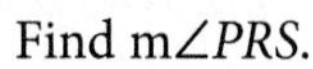

(A) Find $m\angle B$.

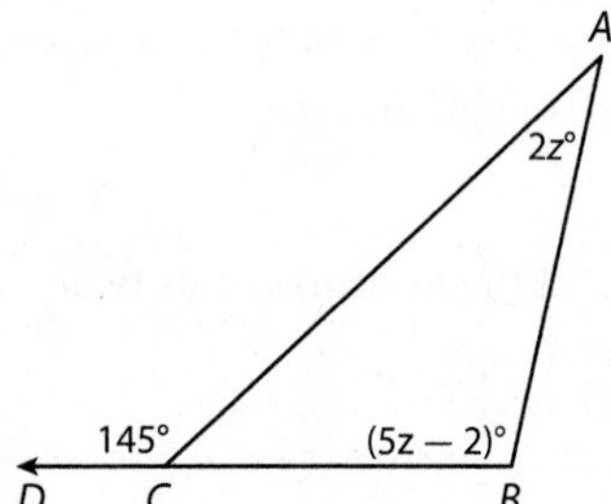

Write and solve an equation relating the exterior and remote interior angles.

$145 = 2z + 5z - 2$

$145 = 7z - 2$

$z = 21$

Now use this value for the unknown to evaluate the expression for the required angle.

$m\angle B = (5z - 2)° = (5(21) - 2)°$

$= (105 - 2)°$

$= 103°$

(B) Find $m\angle PRS$.

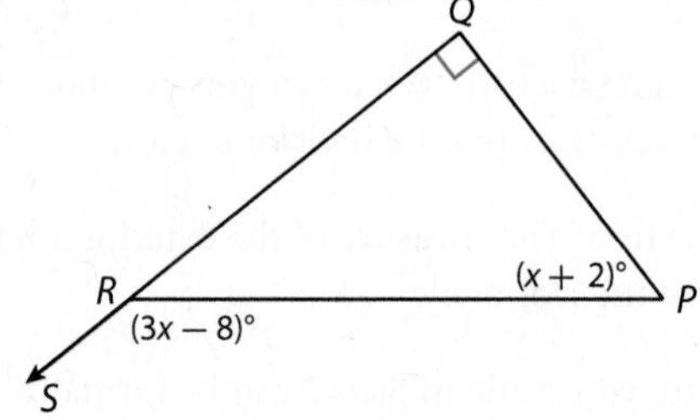

Write an equation relating the exterior and remote interior angles.

$3x - 8 = (x + 2) + 90$

Solve for the unknown. $3x - 8 = x + 92$

$2x = 100$

$x = 50$

Use the value for the unknown to evaluate the expression for the required angle.

$m\angle PRS = (3x - 8)° = \left(3(50) - 8\right)° = 142°$

Your Turn

Determine the measure of the specified angle.

11. Determine $m\angle N$ in $\triangle MNP$.

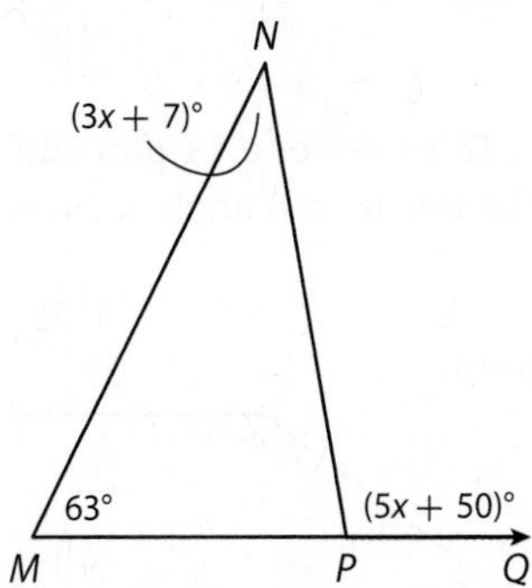

12. If the exterior angle drawn measures 150°, and the measure of $\angle D$ is twice that of $\angle E$, find the measure of the two remote interior angles.

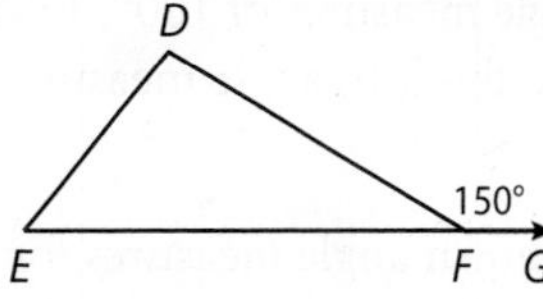

Elaborate

13. In your own words, state the Polygon Angle Sum Theorem. How does it help you find unknown angle measures in polygons?

14. When will an exterior angle be acute? Can a triangle have more than one acute exterior angle? Describe the triangle that tests this.

15. **Essential Question Check-In** Summarize the rules you have discovered about the interior and exterior angles of triangles and polygons.

Evaluate: Homework and Practice

Personal Math Trainer
- Online Homework
- Hints and Help
- Extra Practice

1. Consider the Triangle Sum Theorem in relation to a right triangle. What conjecture can you make about the two acute angles of a right triangle? Explain your reasoning.

2. Copy and complete the flow proof for the Triangle Sum Theorem.

Given $\triangle ABC$

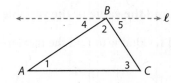

Prove $m\angle 1 + m\angle 2 + m\angle 3 = 180°$

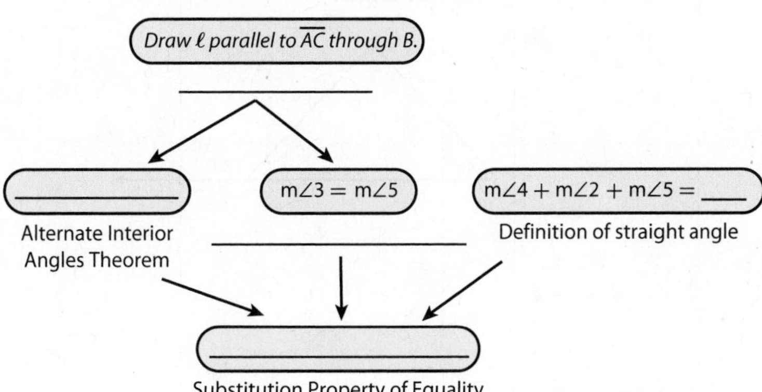

3. Given a polygon with 13 sides, find the sum of the measures of its interior angles.

4. A polygon has an interior angle sum of 3060°. How many sides must the polygon have?

5. Two of the angles in a triangle measure 50° and 27°. Find the measure of the third angle.

Solve for the unknown angle measures of the polygon.

6. A pentagon has angle measures of 100°, 105°, 110° and 115°. Find the fifth angle measure.

7. The measures of 13 angles of a 14-gon add up to 2014°. Find the fourteenth angle measure?

8. Determine the unknown angle measures for the quadrilateral in the diagram.

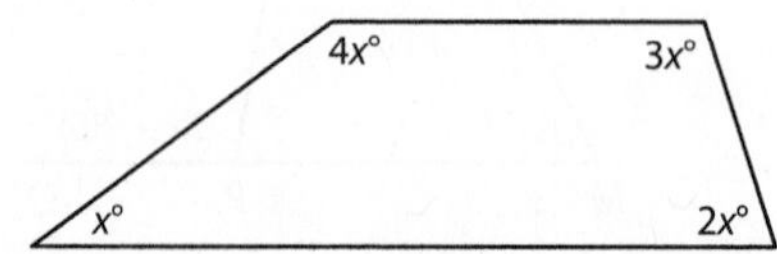

9. The cross-section of a beehive reveals it is made of regular hexagons. What is the measure of each angle in the regular hexagon?

10. Create a flow proof for the Exterior Angle Theorem.

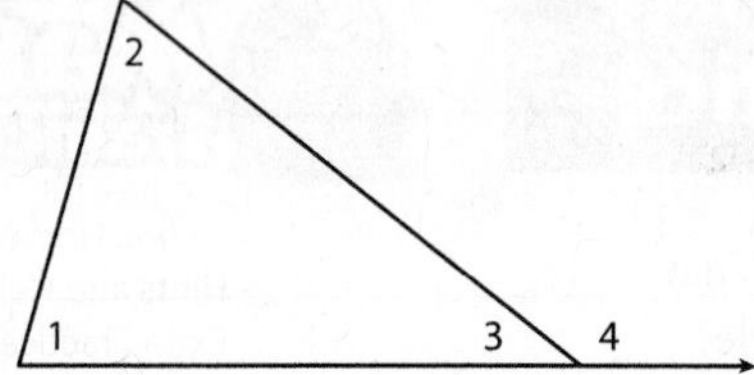

Find the value of the variable to find the unknown angle measure(s).

11. Find w to find the measure of the exterior angle.

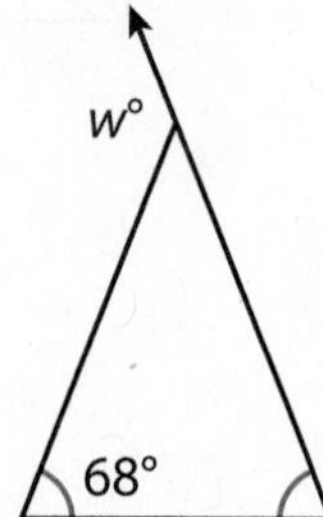

12. Find x to find the measure of the remote interior angle.

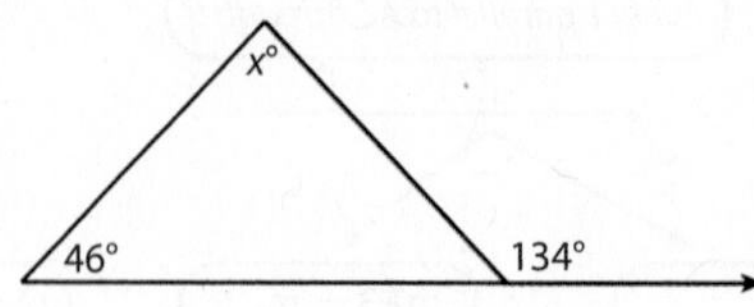

13. Find m∠H.

(6x − 1)°
H
126°
F G
J
(5x + 17)°

14. Determine the measure of the indicated exterior angle in the diagram.

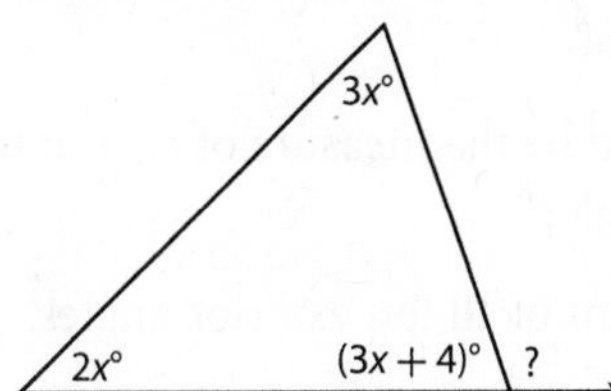

15. Match each angle with its corresponding measure, given $m\angle 1 = 130°$ and $m\angle 7 = 70°$.

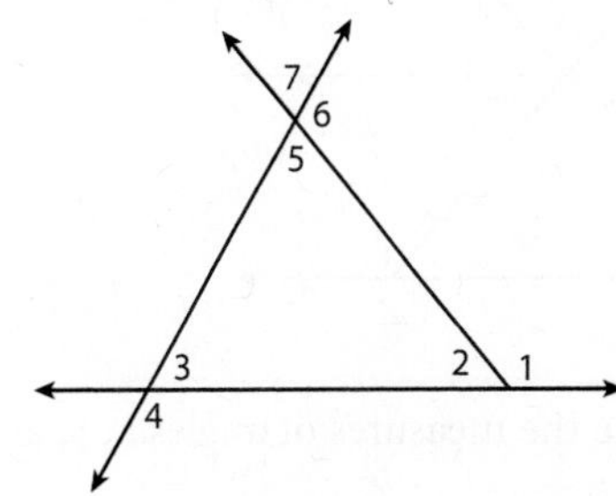

A. m∠2	**a.** ___?___	50°
B. m∠3	**b.** ___?___	60°
C. m∠4	**c.** ___?___	70°
D. m∠5	**d.** ___?___	110°
E. m∠6	**e.** ___?___	120°

16. The map of France commonly used in the 1600s was significantly revised as a result of a triangulation survey. The diagram shows part of the survey map. Use the diagram to find the measure of ∠KMJ. Note that ∠KMJ ≅ ∠NKM.

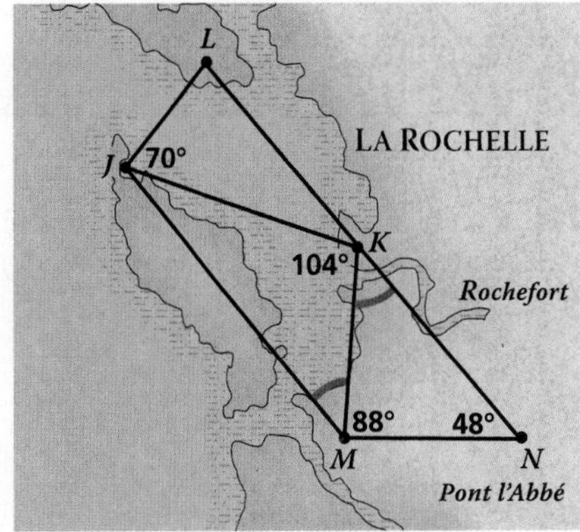

17. An artistic quilt is being designed using computer software. The designer wants to use regular octagons in her design. What interior angle measures should she set in the computer software to create a regular octagon?

18. A ladder propped up against a house makes a 20° angle with the wall. What would be the ladder's angle measure with the ground facing away from the house?

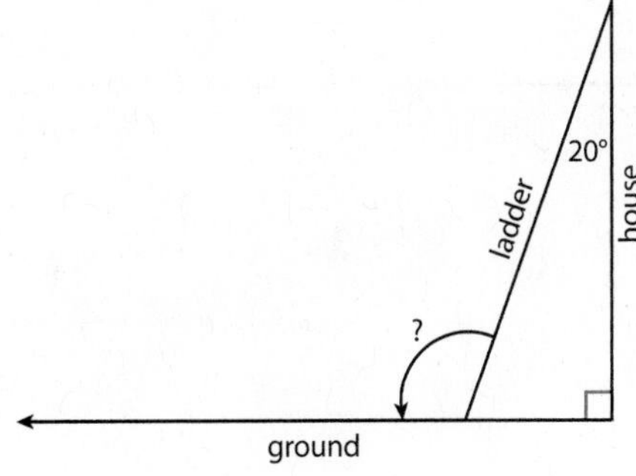

19. Photography The aperture of a camera is made by overlapping blades that form a regular decagon.

a. What is the sum of the measures of the interior angles of the decagon?

b. What would be the measure of each interior angle? each exterior angle?

c. Find the sum of all ten exterior angles.

20. Determine the measure of $\angle UXW$ in the diagram.

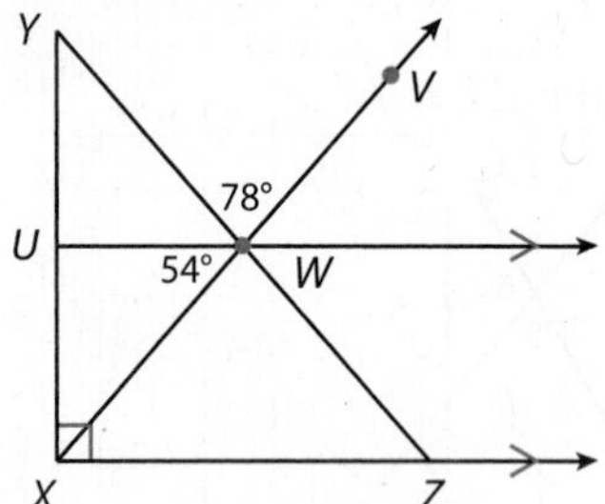

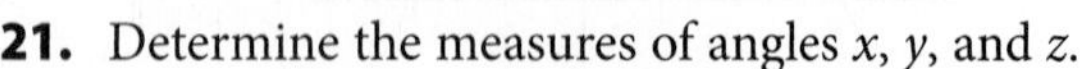

21. Determine the measures of angles x, y, and z.

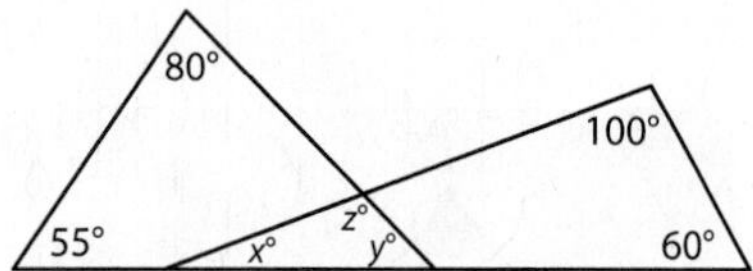

22. Given the diagram in which $\overrightarrow{BD}$ bisects $\angle ABC$ and $\overrightarrow{CD}$ bisects $\angle ACB$, what is $m\angle BDC$?

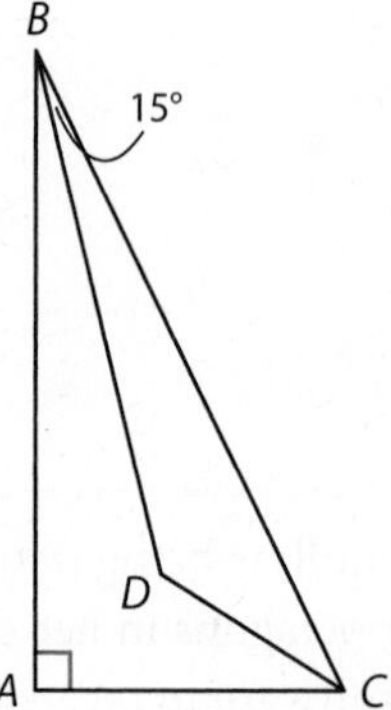

23. What If? Suppose you continue the congruent angle construction shown here. What polygon will you construct? Explain.

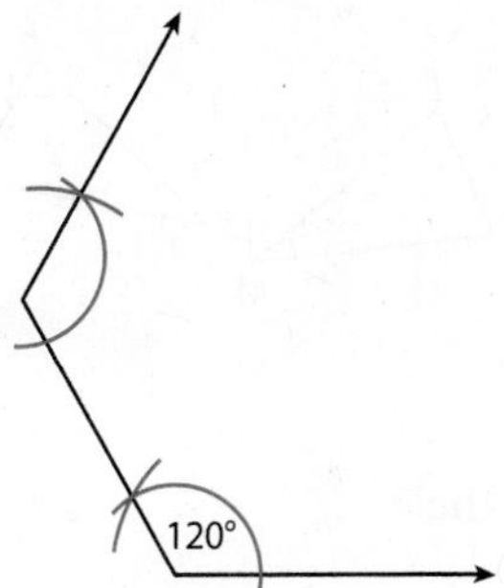

24. Algebra Draw a triangle ABC and label the measures of its angles $a°$, $b°$, and $c°$. Draw ray BD that bisects the exterior angle at vertex B. Write an expression for the measure of angle CBD.

25. Look for a Pattern Copy and complete the table. Find patterns within the table and extend the patterns to complete the table. What conjecture can you make about polygon exterior angles from Column 5?

Column 1 Number of Sides	Column 2 Sum of the Measures of the Interior Angles	Column 3 Average Measure of an Interior Angle	Column 4 Average Measure of an Exterior Angle	Column 5 Sum of the Measures of the Exterior Angles
3	180°	60°	120°	120°(3) = ?
4	360°	90°	90°	90°(4) = ?
5	540°	108°	?	?
6	?	120°	?	?

26. Explain the Error Find and explain what this student did incorrectly when solving the following problem.

What type of polygon would have an interior angle sum of 1260°?

$$1260 = (n - 2)180$$
$$7 = n - 2$$
$$5 = n$$

The polygon is a pentagon.

H.O.T. Focus on Higher Order Thinking

27. Communicate Mathematical Ideas Explain why if two angles of one triangle are congruent to two angles of another triangle, then the third pair of angles are also congruent.

Given: $\angle L \cong \angle R$, $\angle M \cong \angle S$

Prove: $\angle N \cong \angle T$

28. Analyze Relationships Consider a right triangle. How would you describe the measures of its exterior angles? Explain.

29. Look for a Pattern In investigating different polygons, diagonals were drawn from a vertex to break the polygon into triangles. Recall that the number of triangles is always two less than the number of sides. But diagonals can be drawn from all vertices. Make a table where you compare the number of sides of a polygon with how many diagonals can be drawn (from all the vertices). Can you find a pattern in this table?

Lesson Performance Task

You've been asked to design the board for a new game called Pentagons. The board consists of a repeating pattern of regular pentagons, a portion of which is shown in the illustration. When you write the specifications for the company that will make the board, you include the measurements of $\angle BAD$, $\angle ABC$, $\angle BCD$ and $\angle ADC$. Find the measures of those angles and explain how you found them.

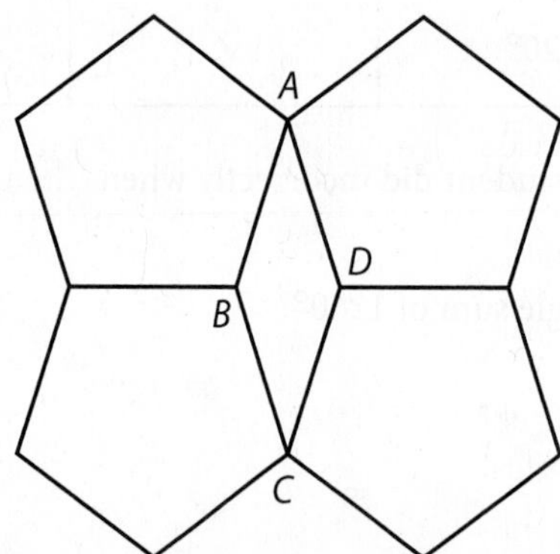

7.2 Isosceles and Equilateral Triangles

Resource Locker

Essential Question: What are the special relationships among angles and sides in isosceles and equilateral triangles?

Explore Investigating Isosceles Triangles

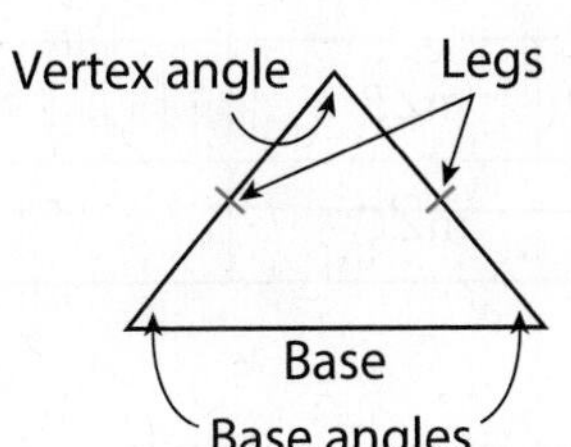

An **isosceles triangle** is a triangle with at least two congruent sides.

The congruent sides are called the **legs** of the triangle.

The angle formed by the legs is the **vertex angle**.

The side opposite the vertex angle is the **base**.

The angles that have the base as a side are the **base angles**.

In this activity, you will construct isosceles triangles and investigate other potential characteristics/properties of these special triangles.

(A) Use a straightedge to draw an angle. Label your angle $\angle A$, as shown in the figure.

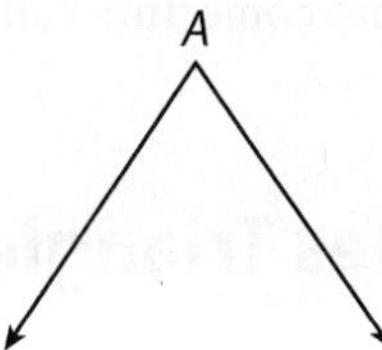

(B) Using a compass, place the point on the vertex and draw an arc that intersects the sides of the angle. Label the points B and C.

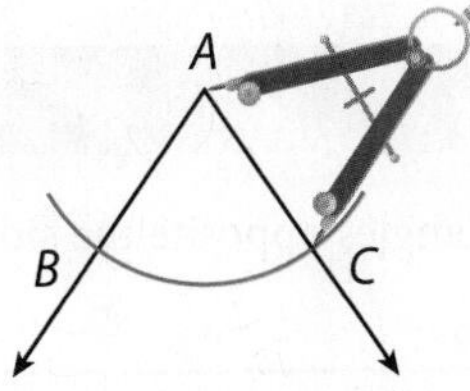

Ⓒ Use the straightedge to draw line segment $\overline{BC}$.

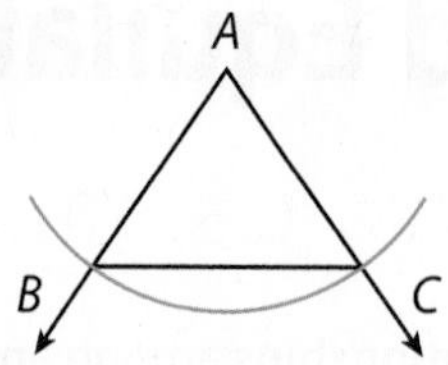

Ⓓ Use a protractor to measure each angle. Copy the table and record the measures in the column for Triangle 1.

	Triangle 1	Triangle 2	Triangle 3	Triangle 4
$m\angle A$	?	?	?	?
$m\angle B$	?	?	?	?
$m\angle C$	?	?	?	?

Ⓔ Repeat steps A–D at least two more times and record the results in the table. Make sure $\angle A$ is a different size each time.

Reflect

1. How do you know the triangles you constructed are isosceles triangles?
2. **Make a Conjecture** Looking at your results, what conjecture can be made about the base angles, $\angle B$ and $\angle C$?

Explain 1 Proving the Isosceles Triangle Theorem and Its Converse

In the Explore, you made a conjecture that the base angles of an isosceles triangle are congruent. This conjecture can be proven so it can be stated as a theorem.

Isosceles Triangle Theorem

If two sides of a triangle are congruent, then the two angles opposite the sides are congruent.

This theorem is sometimes called the Base Angles Theorem and can also be stated as "Base angles of an isosceles triangle are congruent."

Example 1 **Prove the Isosceles Triangle Theorem and its converse.**

Step 1 Complete the proof of the Isosceles Triangle Theorem.

Given: $\overline{AB} \cong \overline{AC}$

Prove: $\angle B \cong \angle C$

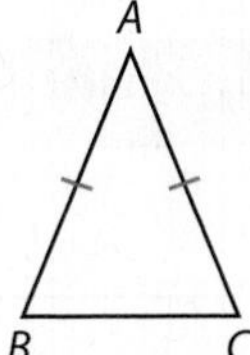

Statements	Reasons
1. $\overline{BA} \cong \overline{CA}$	1. Given
2. $\angle A \cong \angle A$	2. Reflexive Property of Congruence
3. $\overline{CA} \cong \overline{BA}$	3. Symmetric Property of Equality
4. $\triangle BAC \cong \triangle CAB$	4. SAS Triangle Congruence Theorem
5. $\angle B \cong \angle C$	5. CPCTC

Step 2 Complete the statement of the Converse of the Isosceles Triangle Theorem.

If two angles of a triangle are congruent, then the two sides opposite those angles are congruent.

Step 3 Complete the proof of the Converse of the Isosceles Triangle Theorem.

Given: $\angle B \cong \angle C$

Prove: $\overline{AB} \cong \overline{AC}$

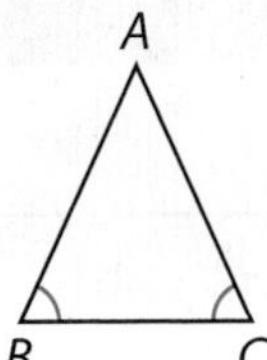

Statements	Reasons
1. $\angle ABC \cong \angle ACB$	1. Given
2. $\overline{BC} \cong \overline{CB}$	2. Reflexive Property of Congruence
3. $\angle ACB \cong \angle ABC$	3. Symmetric Property of Equality
4. $\triangle ABC \cong \triangle ACB$	4. ASA Triangle Congruence Theorem
5. $\overline{AB} \cong \overline{AC}$	5. CPCTC

Reflect

3. **Discussion** In the proofs of the Isosceles Triangle Theorem and its converse, how might it help to sketch a reflection of the given triangle next to the original triangle, so that vertex B is on the right?

Explain 2 Proving the Equilateral Triangle Theorem and Its Converse

An **equilateral triangle** is a triangle with three congruent sides.

An **equiangular triangle** is a triangle with three congruent angles.

Equilateral Triangle Theorem

If a triangle is equilateral, then it is equiangular.

Example 2 **Prove the Equilateral Triangle Theorem and its converse.**

Step 1 Complete the proof of the Equilateral Triangle Theorem.

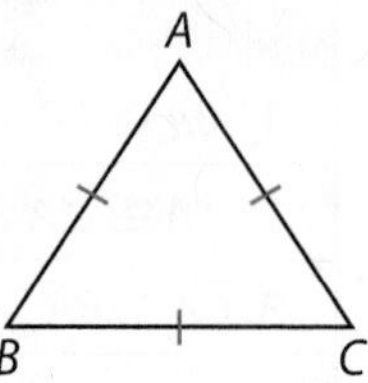

Given: $\overline{AB} \cong \overline{AC} \cong \overline{BC}$
Prove: $\angle A \cong \angle B \cong \angle C$

Given that $\overline{AB} \cong \overline{AC}$ we know that $\angle B \cong \angle C$ by the Isosceles Triangle Theorem.

It is also known that $\angle A \cong \angle B$ by the Isosceles Triangle Theorem, since $\overline{AC} \cong \overline{BC}$.

Therefore, $\angle A \cong \angle C$ by substitution.

Finally, $\angle A \cong \angle B \cong \angle C$ by the Transitive Property of Congruence.

The converse of the Equilateral Triangle Theorem is also true.

Converse of the Equilateral Triangle Theorem

If a triangle is equiangular, then it is equilateral.

Step 2 Complete the proof of the Converse of the Equilateral Triangle Theorem.

Given: $\angle A \cong \angle B \cong \angle C$

Prove: $\overline{AB} \cong \overline{AC} \cong \overline{BC}$

Because $\angle B \cong \angle C$, $\overline{AB} \cong$ $\overline{AC}$ by the Converse of the Isosceles Triangle Theorem.

$\overline{AC} \cong \overline{BC}$ by the Converse of the Isosceles Triangle Theorem because

$\angle A$ $\cong \angle B$.

Thus, by the Transitive Property of Congruence, $\overline{AB} \cong \overline{BC}$, and therefore, $\overline{AB} \cong \overline{AC} \cong \overline{BC}$.

Reflect

4. To prove the Equilateral Triangle Theorem, you applied the theorems of isosceles triangles. What can be concluded about the relationship between equilateral triangles and isosceles triangles?

Explain 3 Using Properties of Isosceles and Equilateral Triangles

You can use the properties of isosceles and equilateral triangles to solve problems involving these theorems.

Example 3 **Find the indicated measure.**

(A) Katie is stitching the center inlay onto a banner that she created to represent her new tutorial service. It is an equilateral triangle with the following dimensions in centimeters. What is the length of each side of the triangle?

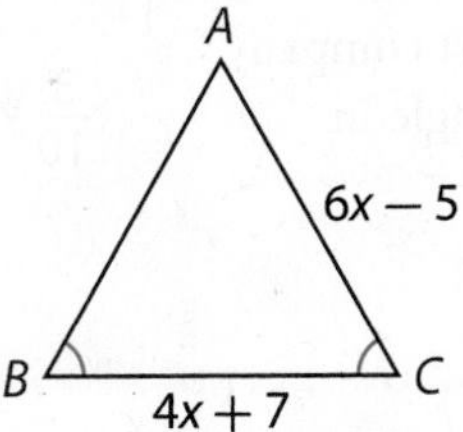

To find the length of each side of the triangle, first find the value of x.

$\overline{AC} \cong \overline{BC}$	Converse of the Equilateral Triangle Theorem
$AC = BC$	Definition of congruence
$6x - 5 = 4x + 7$	Substitution Property of Equality
$x = 6$	Solve for x.

Substitute 6 for x into either $6x - 5$ or $4x + 7$.

$6(6) - 5 = 36 - 5 = 31$ or $4(6) + 7 = 24 + 7 = 31$

So, the length of each side of the triangle is 31 cm.

(B) $m\angle T$

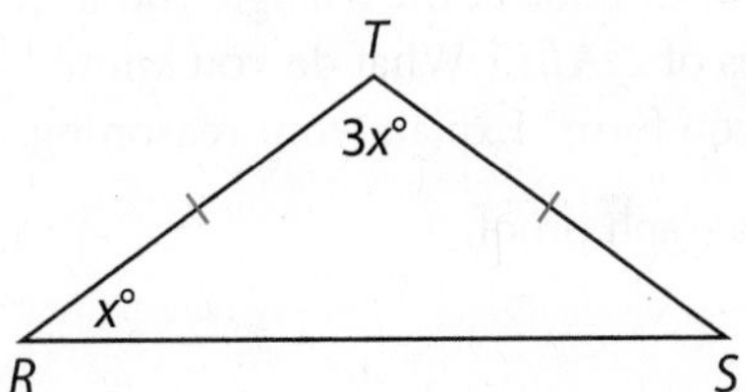

To find the measure of the vertex angle of the triangle, first find the value of x.

$m\angle R = m\angle S = x°$	Isosceles Triangle Theorem
$m\angle R + m\angle S + m\angle T = 180°$	Triangle Sum Theorem
$x + x + 3x = 180$	Substitution Property of Equality
$5x = 180$	Addition Property of Equality
$x = 36$	Division Property of Equality

So, $m\angle T = 3x° = 3(36)° = 108°$.

Your Turn

5. Find m$\angle P$.

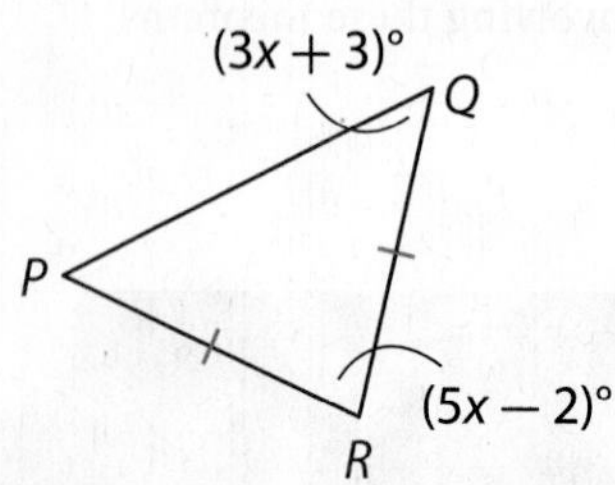

6. Katie's tutorial service is going so well that she is having shirts made with the equilateral triangle emblem. She has given the t-shirt company these dimensions. What is the length of each side of the triangle in centimeters?

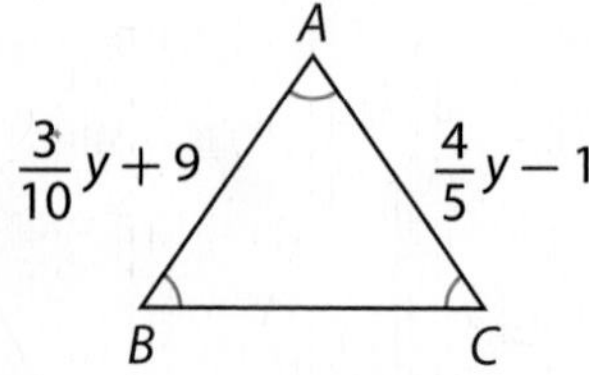

Elaborate

7. **Discussion** Consider the vertex and base angles of an isosceles triangle. Can they be right angles? Can they be obtuse? Explain.

8. **Essential Question Check-In** Discuss how the sides of an isosceles triangle relate to its angles.

Evaluate: Homework and Practice

- Online Homework
- Hints and Help
- Extra Practice

1. Use a straightedge. Draw a line. Draw an acute angle with vertex A along the line. Then use a compass to copy the angle. Place the compass point at another point B along the line and draw the copied angle so that the angle faces the original angle. Label the intersection of the angle sides as point C. Look at the triangle you have formed. What is true about the two base angles of $\triangle ABC$? What do you know about $\overline{CA}$ and $\overline{CB}$? What kind of triangle did you form? Explain your reasoning.

2. Prove the Isosceles Triangle Theorem as a paragraph proof.

Given: $\overline{AB} \cong \overline{AC}$

Prove: $\angle B \cong \angle C$

3. Copy and complete the flow proof of the Equilateral Triangle Theorem.

Given: $\overline{AB} \cong \overline{AC} \cong \overline{BC}$

Prove: $\angle A \cong \angle B \cong \angle C$

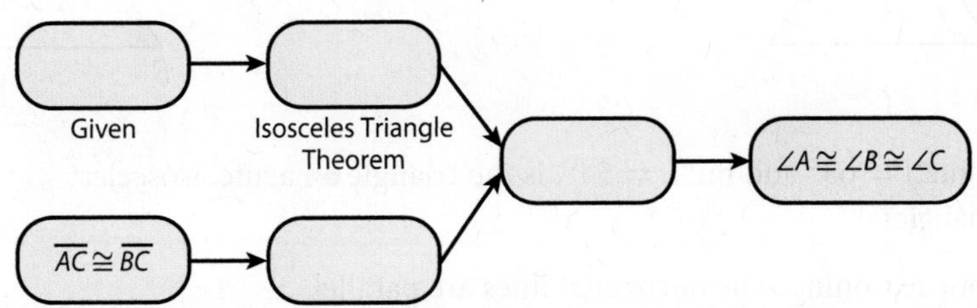

Find the measure of the indicated angle.

4. $m\angle A$

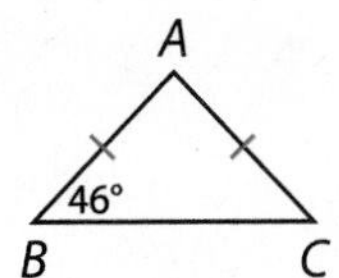

5. $m\angle R$

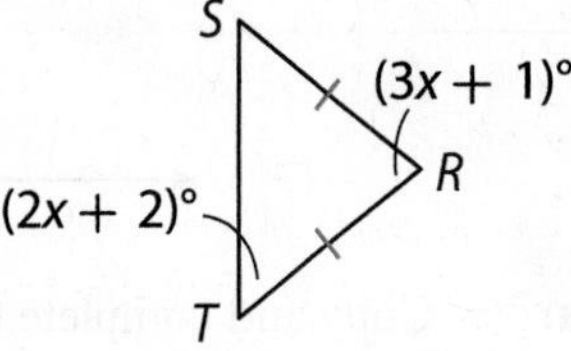

6. $m\angle O$

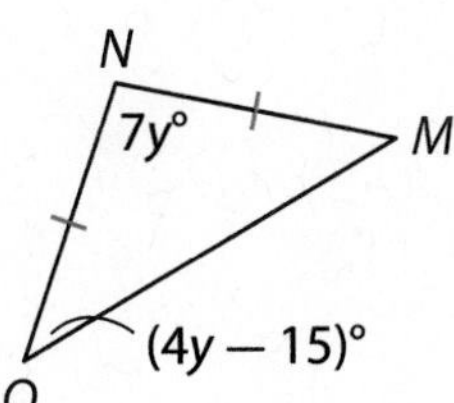

7. $m\angle E$

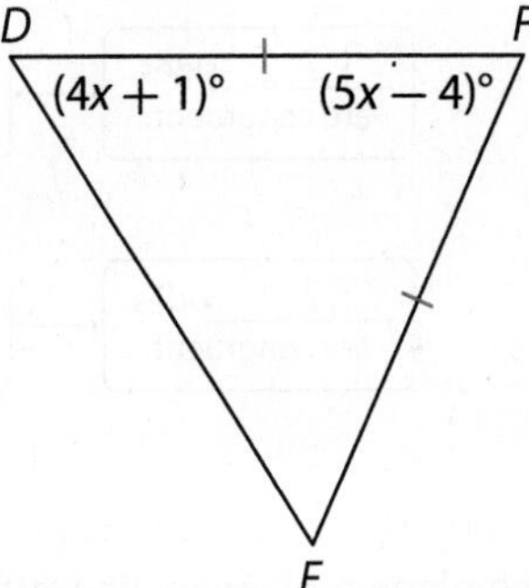

For 8–11, find the length of the indicated side.

8. $\overline{DE}$

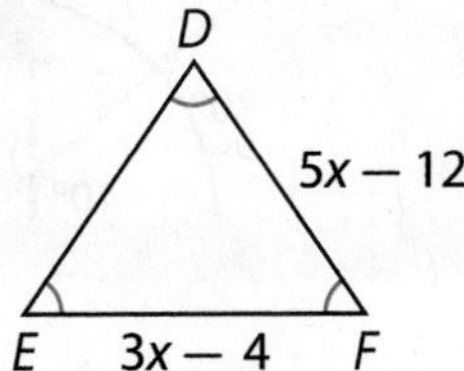

9. $\overline{KL}$

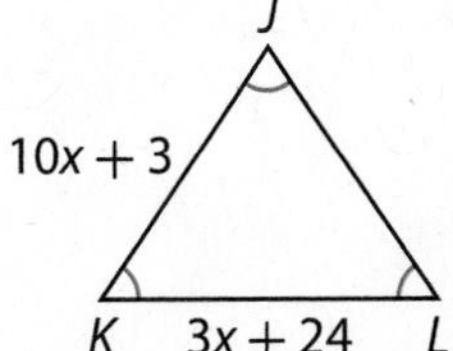

10. $\overline{AB}$

$\frac{3}{2}x+4$ $\frac{1}{5}x+9$

A B C

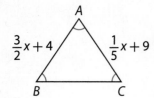

11. $\overline{BC}$

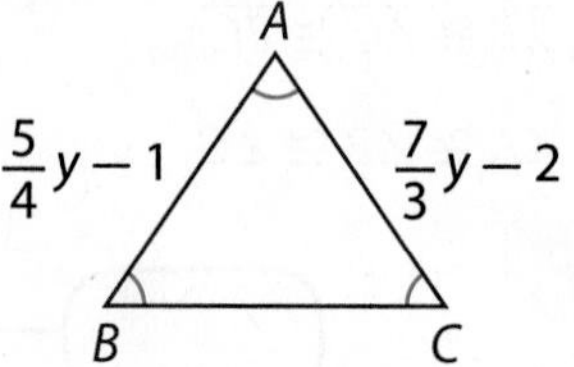

12. Given $\triangle JKL$ with $m\angle J = 63°$ and $m\angle L = 54°$, is the triangle an acute, isosceles, obtuse, or right triangle?

13. Find x. Explain your reasoning. The horizontal lines are parallel.

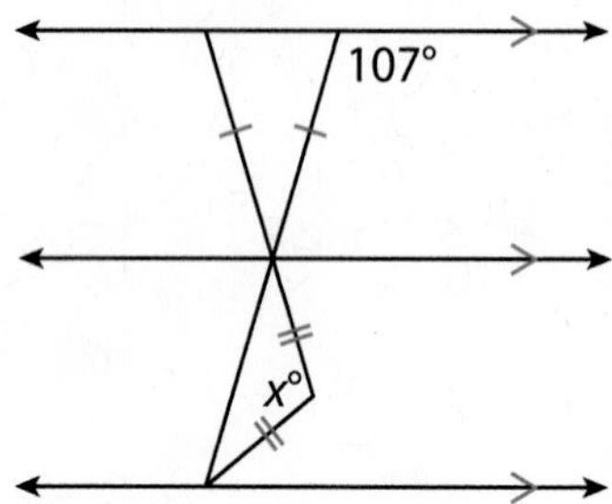

14. **Summarize** Copy and complete the diagram to show the cause and effect of the theorems covered in the lesson. Explain why the arrows show the direction going both ways.

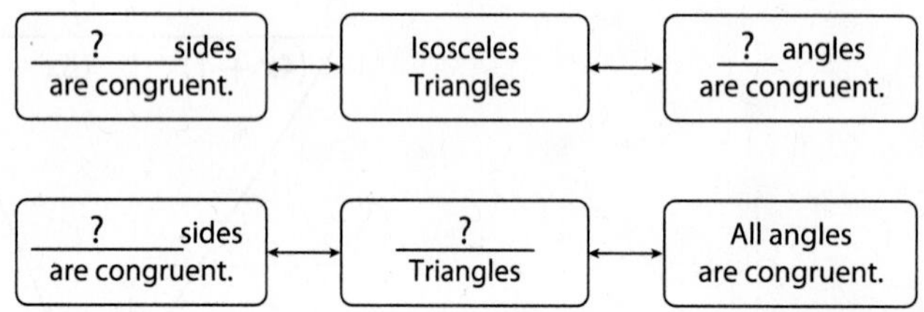

15. A plane is flying parallel to the ground along $\overrightarrow{AC}$. When the plane is at A, an air-traffic controller in tower T measures the angle to the plane as 40°. After the plane has traveled 2.4 miles to B, the angle to the plane is 80°. How can you find BT?

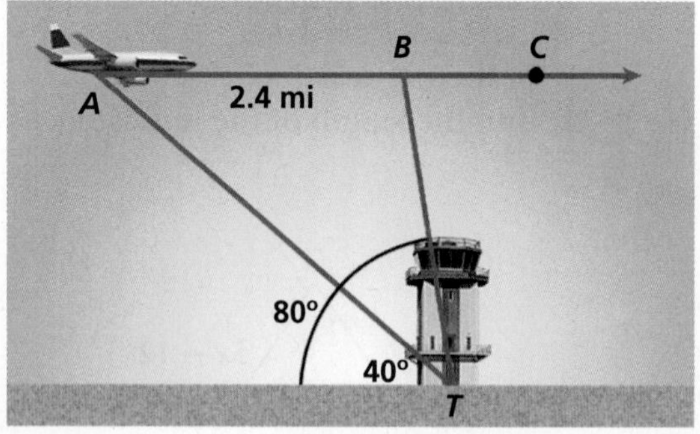

16. John is building a doghouse. He decides to use the roof truss design shown. If $m\angle DBF = 35°$, what is the measure of the vertex angle of the isosceles triangle?

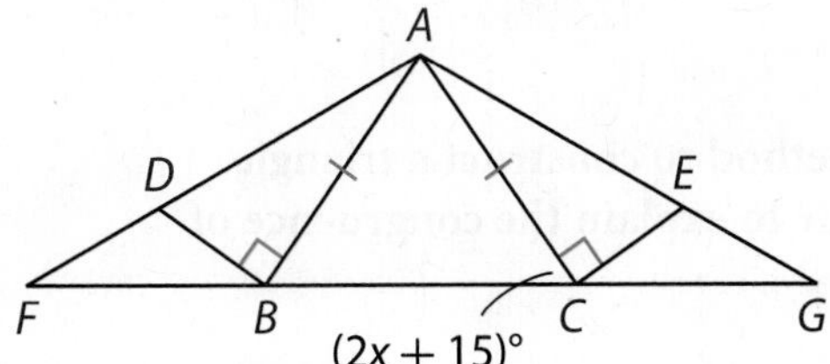

17. The measure of the vertex angle of an isosceles triangle is 12 more than 5 times the measure of a base angle. Determine the sum of the measures of the base angles.

18. **Justify Reasoning** Determine whether each of the following statements is true or false. Explain your reasoning.

  a. All isosceles triangles have at least two acute angles.

  b. If the perimeter of an equilateral triangle is P, then the length of each of its sides is $\frac{P}{3}$.

  c. All isosceles triangles are equilateral triangles.

  d. If you know the length of one of the legs of an isosceles triangle, you can determine its perimeter.

  e. The exterior angle of an equilateral triangle is obtuse.

19. **Critical Thinking** Prove $\angle B \cong \angle C$, given point M is the midpoint of $\overline{BC}$.

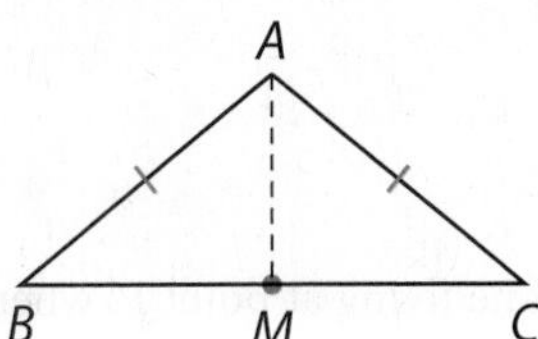

20. Given that $\triangle ABC$ is an isosceles triangle and $\overline{AD}$ and $\overline{CD}$ are angle bisectors, what is $m\angle ADC$?

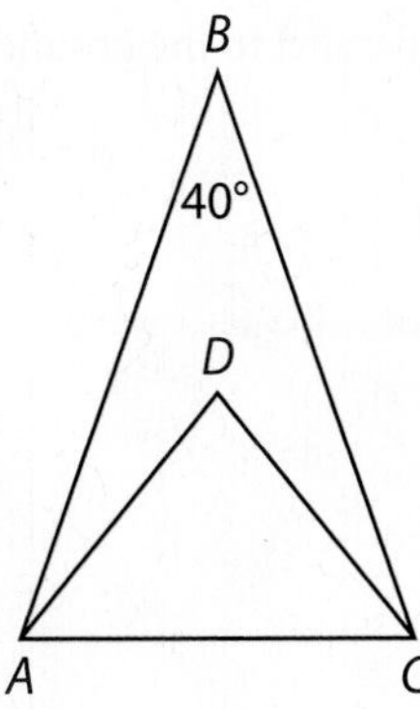

H.O.T. **Focus on Higher Order Thinking**

21. Analyze Relationships Isosceles right triangle *ABC* has a right angle at *B* and $\overline{AB} \cong \overline{CB}$. $\overline{BD}$ bisects angle *B*, and point *D* is on $\overline{AC}$. If $\overline{BD} \perp \overline{AC}$, describe triangles *ABD* and *CBD*. Explain. HINT: Draw a diagram.

Communicate Mathematical Ideas **Follow the method to construct a triangle. Then use what you know about the radius of a circle to explain the congruence of the sides.**

22. Construct an isosceles triangle. Explain how you know that two sides are congruent.

- Use a compass to draw a circle. Mark two different points on the circle.
- Use a straightedge to draw a line segment from the center of the circle to each of the two points on the circle (radii).
- Draw a line segment (chord) between the two points on the circle.

I know two sides are congruent because __?__

23. Construct an equilateral triangle. Explain how you know the three sides are congruent.

- Use a compass to draw a circle.
- Draw another circle of the same size that goes through the center of the first circle. (Both should have the same radius length.)
- Mark one point where the circles intersect.
- Use a straightedge to draw line segments connecting both centers to each other and to the intersection point.

I know the three sides are congruent because __?__

Lesson Performance Task

The control tower at airport *A* is in contact with an airplane flying at point *P*, when it is 5 miles from the airport, and 30 seconds later when it is at point *Q*, 4 miles from the airport. The diagram shows the angles the plane makes with the ground at both times. If the plane flies parallel to the ground from *P* to *Q* at constant speed, how fast is it traveling?

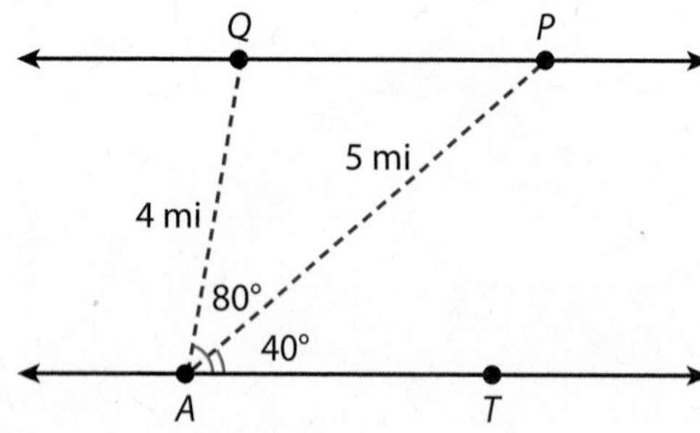

7.3 Triangle Inequalities

Essential Question: How can you use inequalities to describe the relationships among side lengths and angle measures in a triangle?

Explore Exploring Triangle Inequalities

A triangle can have sides of different lengths, but are there limits to the lengths of any of the sides?

(A) Consider a $\triangle ABC$ where you know two side lengths, $AB = 4$ inches and $BC = 2$ inches. On a separate piece of paper, draw $\overline{AB}$ so that it is 4 inches long.

(B) To determine all possible locations for C with $\overline{BC} = 2$ inches, set your compass to 2 inches. Draw a circle with center at B.

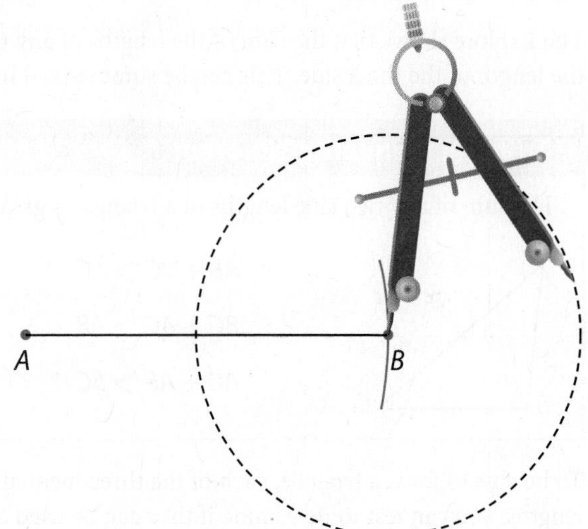

(C) Choose and label a final vertex point C so it is located on the circle. Using a straightedge, draw the segments to form a triangle.

Are there any places on the circle where point C cannot lie? Explain.

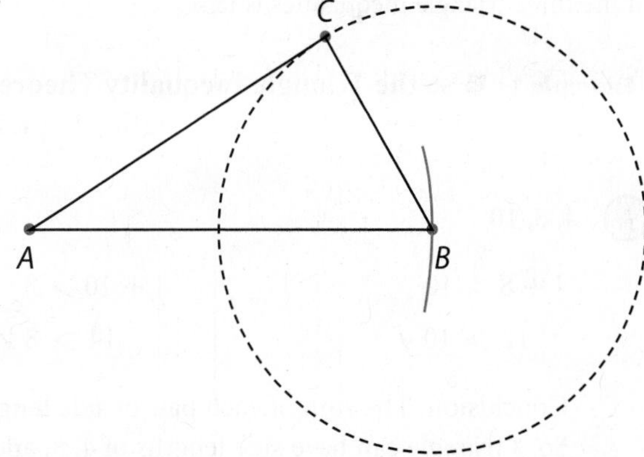

(D) Measure and record the lengths of the three sides of your triangle.

(E) The figures below show two other examples of $\triangle ABC$ that could have been formed. What are the values that AC approaches when point C approaches $\overline{AB}$?

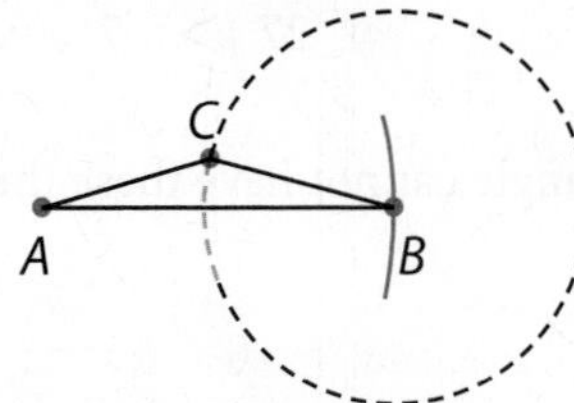

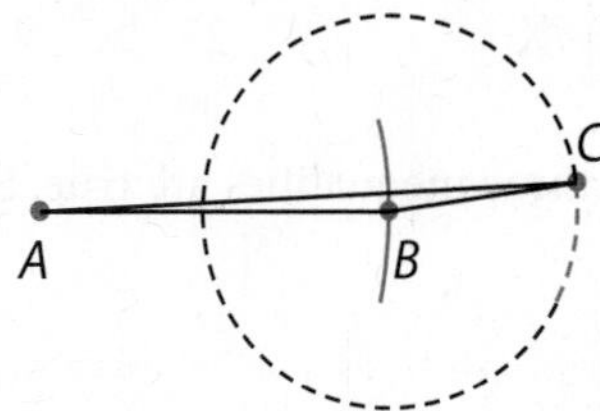

Reflect

1. Use the side lengths from your table to make the following comparisons. What do you notice?

$AB + BC \ ? \ AC$ $\qquad BC + AC \ ? \ AB$ $\qquad AC + AB \ ? \ BC$

2. Measure the angles of some triangles with a protractor. Where is the smallest angle in relation to the shortest side? Where is the largest angle in relation to the longest side?

3. **Discussion** How does your answer to the previous question relate to isosceles triangles or equilateral triangles?

Explain 1 Using the Triangle Inequality Theorem

The Explore shows that the sum of the lengths of any two sides of a triangle is greater than the length of the third side. This can be summarized in the following theorem.

Triangle Inequality Theorem

The sum of any two side lengths of a triangle is greater than the third side length.

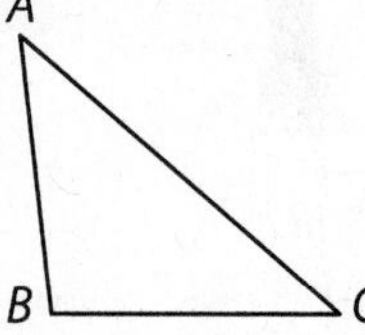

$$AB + BC > AC$$
$$BC + AC > AB$$
$$AC + AB > BC$$

To be able to form a triangle, each of the three inequalities must be true. So, given three side lengths, you can test to determine if they can be used as segments to form a triangle. To show that three lengths cannot be the side lengths of a triangle, you only need to show that one of the three triangle inequalities is false.

Example 1 **Use the Triangle Inequality Theorem to tell whether a triangle can have sides with the given lengths. Explain.**

(A) 4, 8, 10

$4 + 8 \overset{?}{>} 10$ $\qquad 4 + 10 \overset{?}{>} 8$ $\qquad 8 + 10 \overset{?}{>} 4$

$12 > 10$ ✓ $\qquad 14 > 8$ ✓ $\qquad 18 > 4$ ✓

Conclusion: The sum of each pair of side lengths is greater than the third length. So, a triangle can have side lengths of 4, 8, and 10.

(B) 7, 9, 18

$7 + 9 \overset{?}{>} 18$ $\qquad 7 + 18 \overset{?}{>} 9$ $\qquad 9 + 18 \overset{?}{>} 7$

$16 > 18$ X $\qquad 25 > 9$ ✓ $\qquad 27 > 7$ ✓

Conclusion: Not all three inequalities are true. So, a triangle cannot have these three side lengths.

Reflect

4. Can an isosceles triangle have these side lengths? Explain. 5, 5, 10

5. How do you know that the Triangle Inequality Theorem applies to all equilateral triangles?

Your Turn

Determine if a triangle can be formed with the given side lengths. Explain your reasoning.

6. 12 units, 4 units, 17 units

7. 24 cm, 8 cm, 30 cm

Explain 2 Finding Possible Side Lengths in a Triangle

From the Explore, you have seen that if given two side lengths for a triangle, there are an infinite number of side lengths available for the third side. But the third side is also restricted to values determined by the Triangle Inequality Theorem.

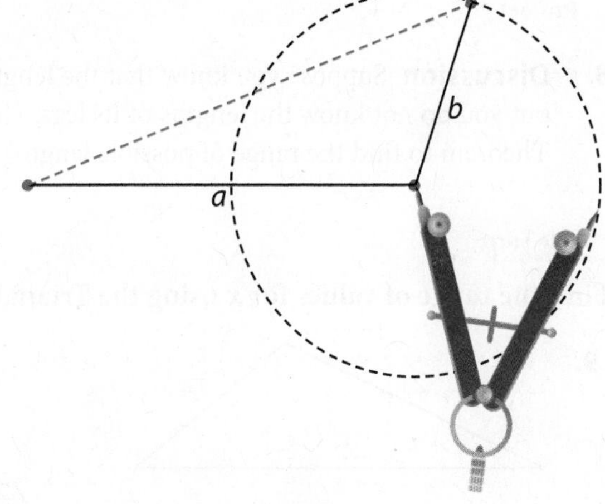

Example 2 **Find the range of values for x using the Triangle Inequality Theorem.**

(A) Find possible values for the length of the third side using the Triangle Inequality Theorem.

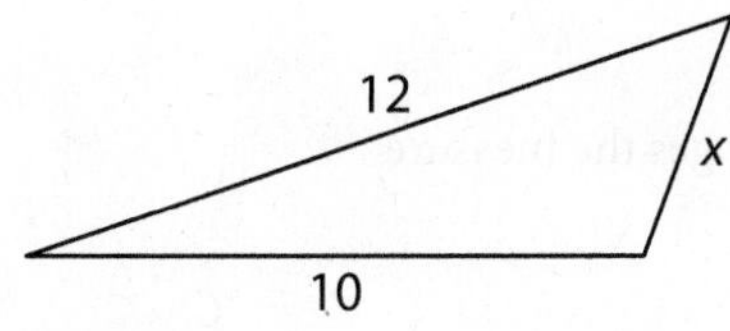

$x + 10 > 12$ $x + 12 > 10$ $10 + 12 > x$

$x > 2$ $x > -2$ $22 > x$

$2 < x < 22$

Ignore the inequality with a negative value, since a triangle cannot have a negative side length. Combine the other two inequalities to find the possible values for x.

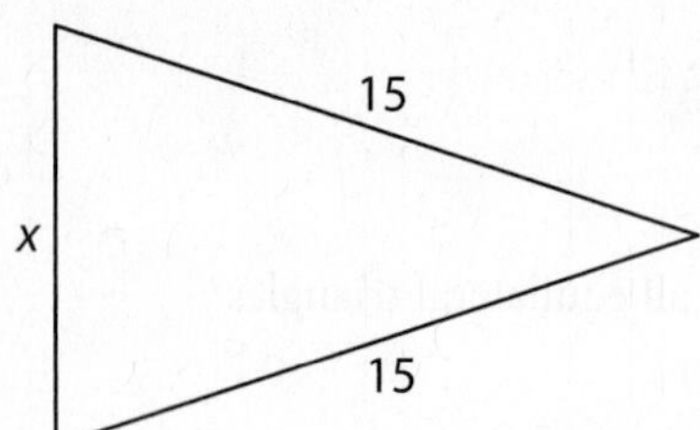

$x + 15 > 15$ $x + 15 > 15$ $15 + 15 > x$

$x > 0$ $x > 0$ $30 > x$

$0 < x < 30$

Reflect

8. **Discussion** Suppose you know that the length of the base of an isosceles triangle is 10, but you do not know the lengths of its legs. How could you use the Triangle Inequality Theorem to find the range of possible lengths for each leg? Explain.

Your Turn

Find the range of values for *x* using the Triangle Inequality Theorem.

9.

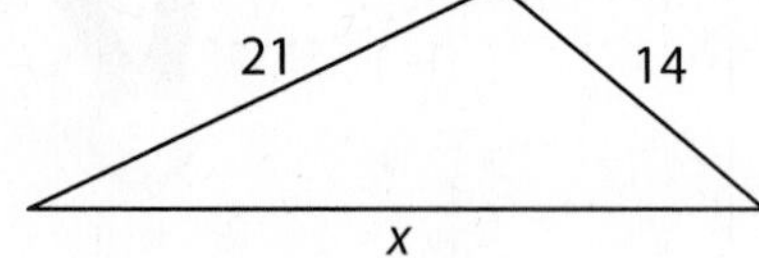

10.

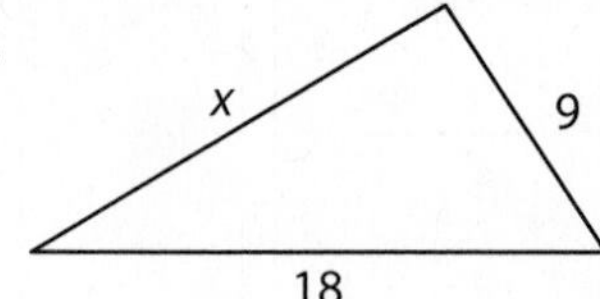

Explain 3 Ordering a Triangle's Angle Measures Given Its Side Lengths

From the Explore Step D, you can see that changing the length of $\overline{AC}$ also changes the measure of $\angle B$ in a predictable way.

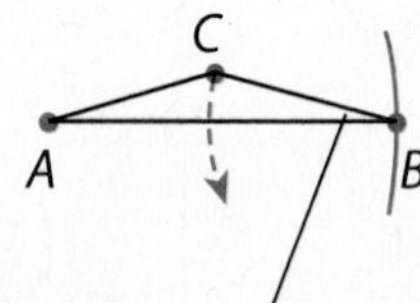

As side AC gets shorter, $m\angle B$ approaches 0°

As side AC gets longer, $m\angle B$ approaches 180°

Side-Angle Relationships in Triangles

If two sides of a triangle are not congruent, then the larger angle is opposite the longer side.

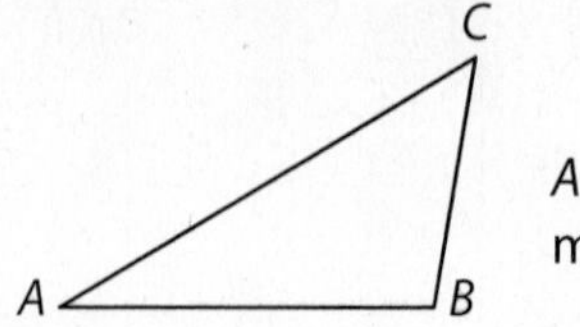

$AC > BC$
$m\angle B > m\angle A$

Example 3 **For each triangle, order its angle measures from least to greatest.**

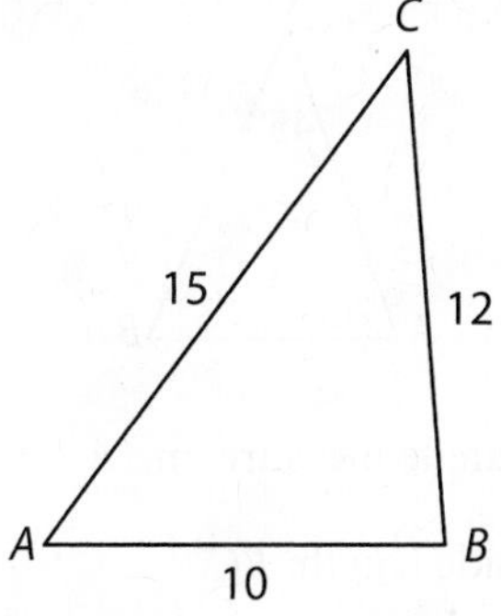

Longest side length: AC

Greatest angle measure: $m\angle B$

Shortest side length: AB

Least angle measure: $m\angle C$

Order of angle measures from least to greatest:
$m\angle C$, $m\angle A$, $m\angle B$

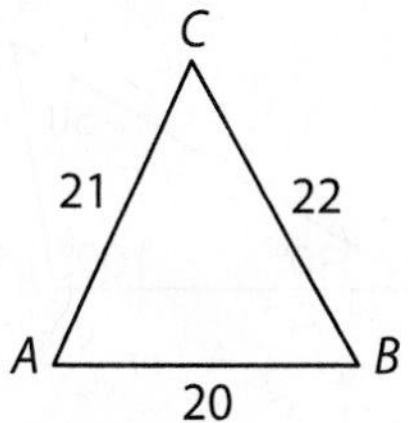

Longest side length: BC

Greatest angle measure: $m\angle A$

Shortest side length: AB

Least angle measure: $m\angle C$

Order of angle measures from least to greatest:
$m\angle C$, $m\angle B$, $m\angle A$

Your Turn

For each triangle, order its angle measures from least to greatest.

11.

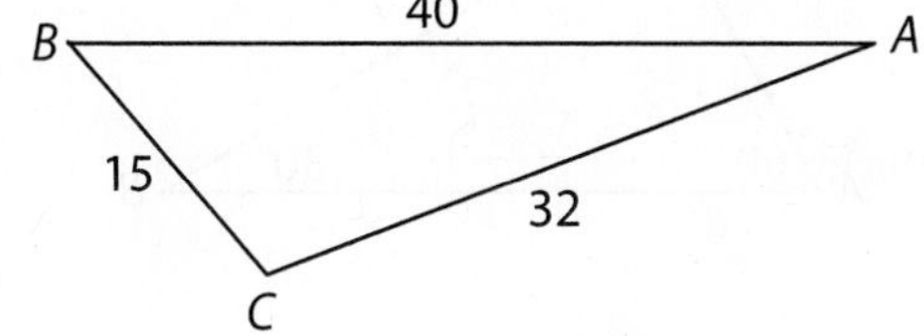

12.

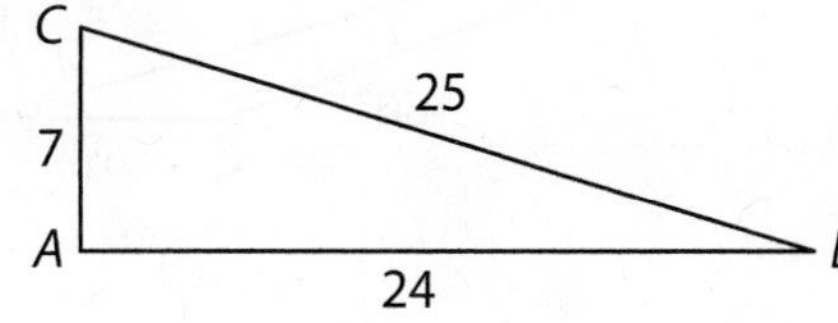

Explain 4 Ordering a Triangle's Side Lengths Given Its Angle Measures

From the Explore Step D, you can see that changing the the measure of $\angle B$ also changes length of $\overline{AC}$ in a predictable way.

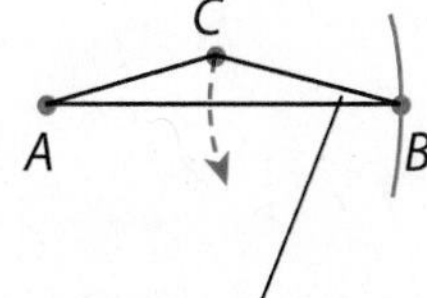

As $m\angle B$ approaches 0°, side AC gets shorter.

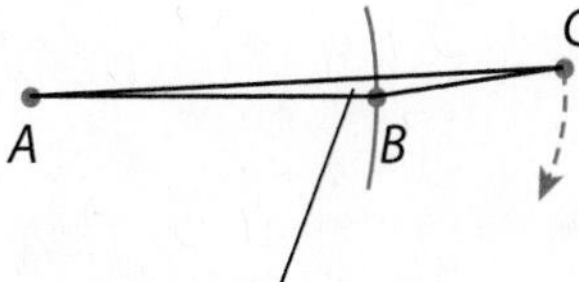

As $m\angle B$ approaches 180°, side AC gets longer.

Angle-Side Relationships in Triangles

If two angles of a triangle are not congruent, then the longer side is opposite the larger angle.

Example 4 **For each triangle, order the side lengths from least to greatest.**

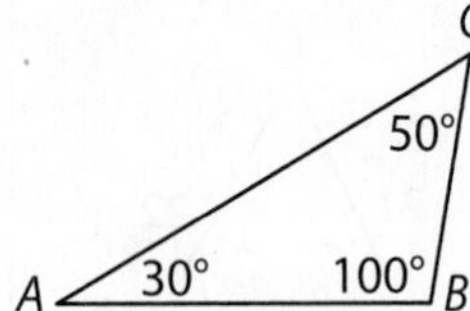

Greatest angle measure: m$\angle B$

Longest side length: AC

Least angle measure: m$\angle A$

Shortest side length: BC

Order of side lengths from least to greatest: BC, AB, AC

Ⓑ

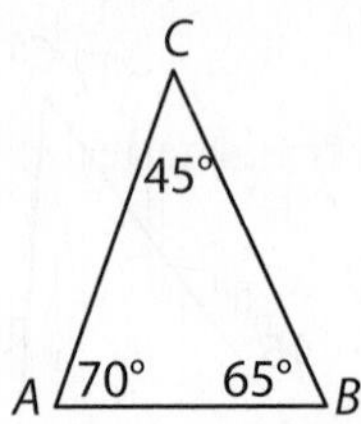

Greatest angle measure: m$\angle A$

Longest side length: BC

Least angle measure: m$\angle C$

Shortest side length: AB

Order of side lengths from least to great: AB, AC, BC

Your Turn

For each triangle, order the side lengths from least to greatest.

13.

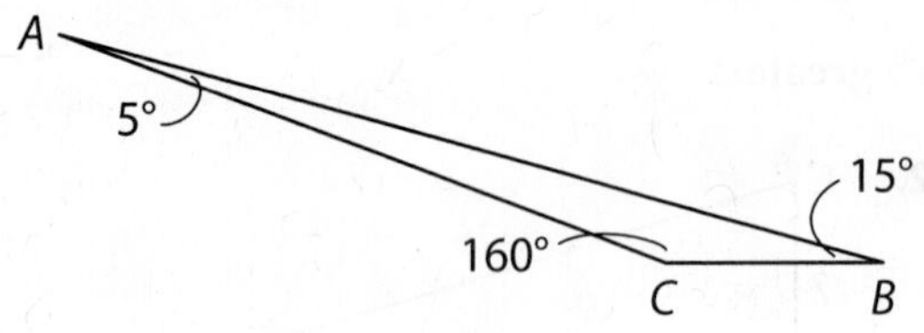

14.

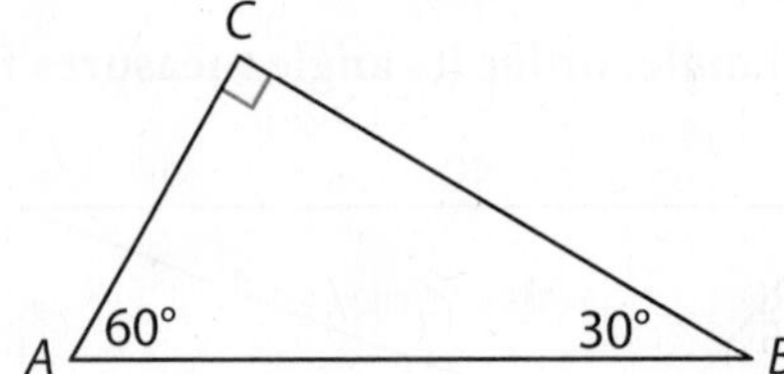

Elaborate

15. When two sides of a triangle are congruent, what can you conclude about the angles opposite those sides?

16. What can you conclude about the side opposite the obtuse angle in an obtuse triangle?

17. **Essential Question Check-In** Suppose you are given three values that could represent the side lengths of a triangle. How can you use one inequality to determine if the triangle exists?

Evaluate: Homework and Practice

- Online Homework
- Hints and Help
- Extra Practice

Use a compass and straightedge to decide whether each set of lengths can form a triangle.

1. 7 cm, 9 cm, 18 cm

2. 2 in., 4 in., 5 in.

3. 1 in., 2 in., 10 in.

4. 9 cm, 10 cm, 11 cm

Determine whether a triangle can be formed with the given side lengths.

5. 10 ft, 3 ft, 15 ft

6. 12 in., 4 in., 15 in.

7. 9 in., 12 in., and 18 in.

8. 29 m, 59 m, and 89 m

Find the range of possible values for *x* using the Triangle Inequality Theorem.

9.

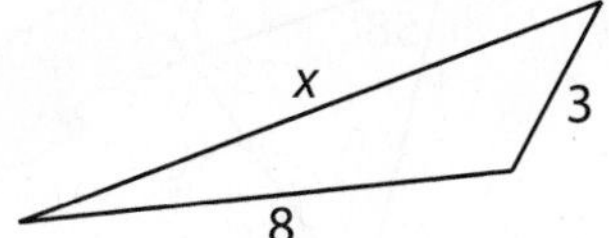

10.

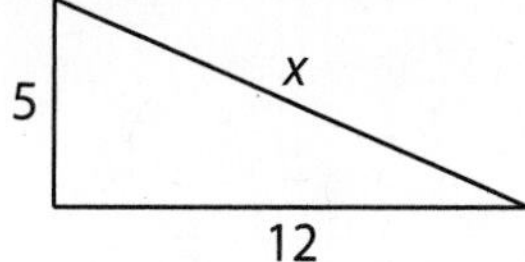

11. A triangle with side lengths 22.3, 27.6, and x

12. Analyze Relationships Suppose a triangle has side lengths AB, BC, and x, where $AB = 2 \cdot BC$. Find the possible range for x in terms of BC.

For each triangle, write the order of the angle measures from least to greatest.

13.

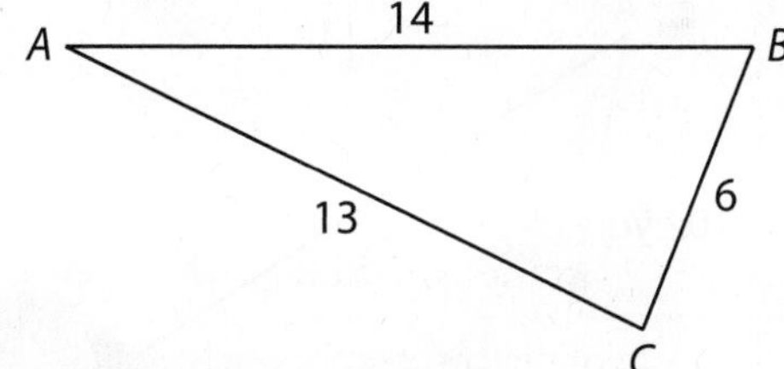

14.

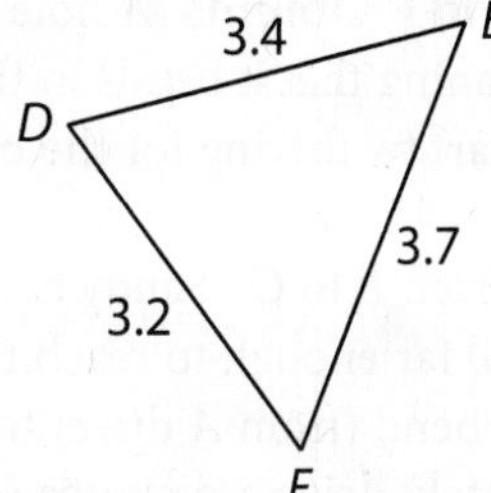

15. Analyze Relationships Suppose a triangle has side lengths PQ, QR, and PR, where $PR = 2PQ = 3QR$. Write the angle measures in order from least to greatest.

For each triangle, write the side lengths in order from least to greatest.

16.

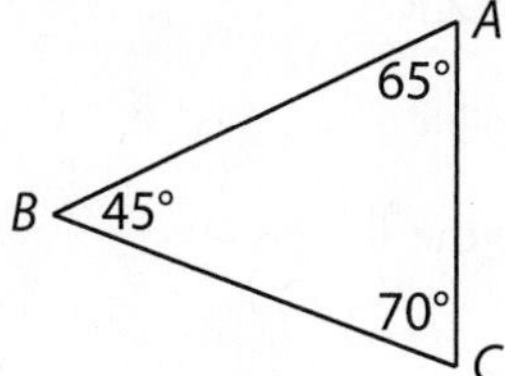

17.

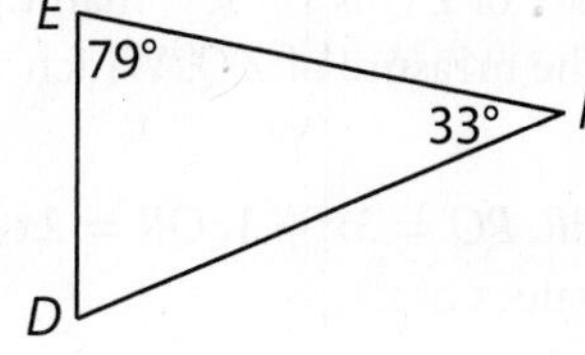

18. In $\triangle JKL$, $m\angle J = 53°$, $m\angle K = 68°$, and $m\angle L = 59°$.

19. In $\triangle PQR$, $m\angle P = 102°$ and $m\angle Q = 25°$.

20. Represent Real-World Problems Rhonda is traveling from New York City to Paris and is trying to decide whether to fly via Frankfurt or to get a more expensive direct flight. Given that it is 3,857 miles from New York City to Frankfurt and another 278 miles from Frankfurt to Paris, what is the range of possible values for the direct distance from New York City to Paris?

21. Represent Real-World Problems A large ship is sailing between three small islands. To do so, the ship must sail between two pairs of islands, avoiding sailing between a third pair. The safest route is to avoid the closest pair of islands. Which is the safest route for the ship?

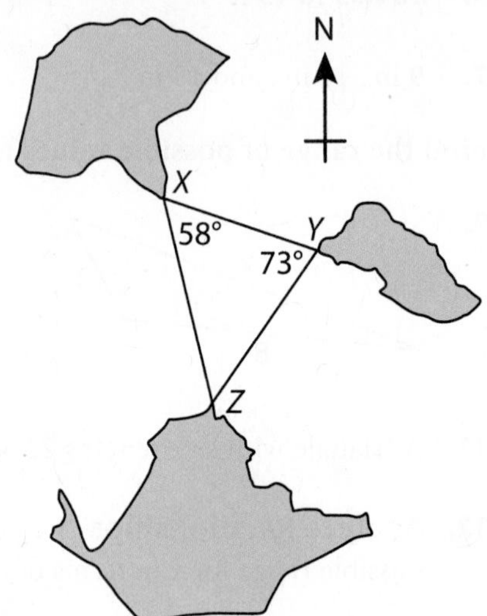

22. Represent Real-World Problems A hole on a golf course is a dogleg, meaning that it bends in the middle. A golfer will usually start by driving for the bend in the dogleg (from A to B), and then using a second shot to get the ball to the green (from B to C). Sandy believes she may be able to drive the ball far enough to reach the green in one shot, avoiding the bend (from A direct to C). Sandy knows she can accurately drive a distance of 250 yd. Should she attempt to drive for the green on her first shot? Explain.

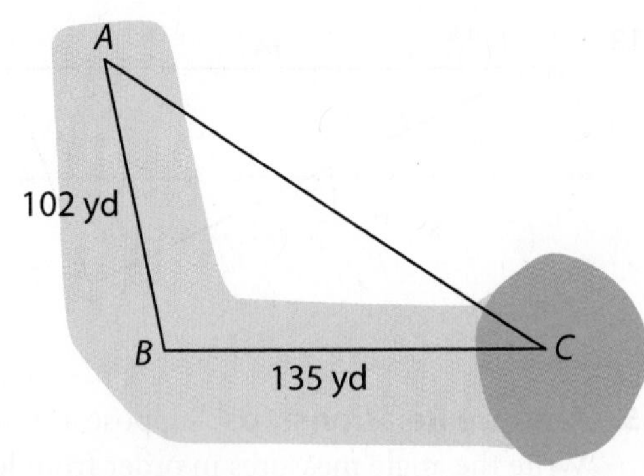

23. Represent Real-World Problems Three cell phone towers form a triangle, $\triangle PQR$. The measure of $\angle Q$ is 10° less than the measure of $\angle P$. The measure of $\angle R$ is 5° greater than the measure of $\angle Q$. Which two towers are closest together?

24. Algebra In $\triangle PQR$, $PQ = 3x + 1$, $QR = 2x - 2$, and $PR = x + 7$. Determine the range of possible values of x.

25. In any triangle ABC, suppose you know the lengths of $\overline{AB}$ and $\overline{BC}$, and suppose that $AB > BC$. If x is the length of the third side, $\overline{AC}$, use the Triangle Inequality Theorem to prove that $AB - BC < x < AB + BC$. That is, x must be between the difference and the sum of the other two side lengths. Explain why this result makes sense in terms of the constructions shown in the figure.

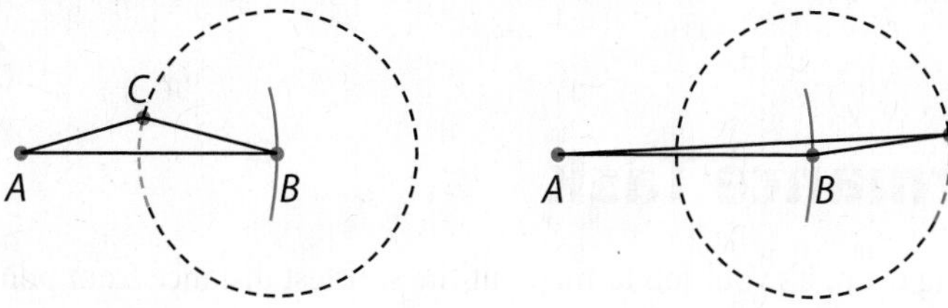

26. Given the information in the diagram, prove that $m\angle DEA < m\angle ABC$.

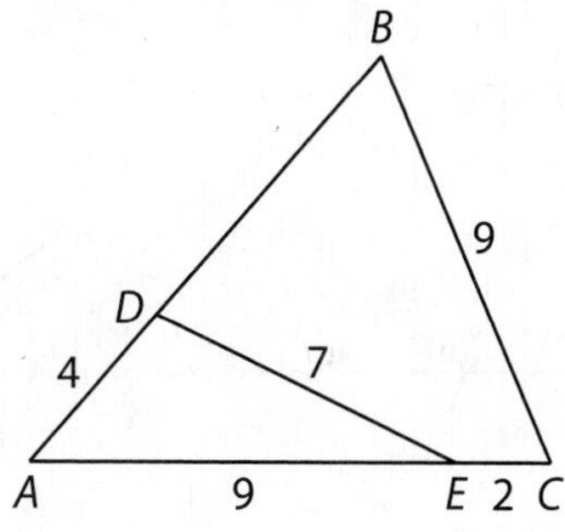

27. An isosceles triangle has legs with length 11 units. Which of the following could be the perimeter of the triangle? Choose all that apply. Explain your reasoning.

a. 22 units

b. 24 units

c. 34 units

d. 43 units

e. 44 units

H.O.T. Focus on Higher Order Thinking

28. Communicate Mathematical Ideas Given the information in the diagram, prove that $PQ < PS$.

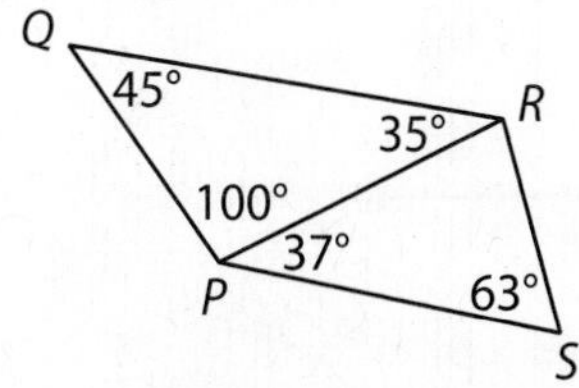

29. Justify Reasoning In obtuse $\triangle ABC$, $m\angle A < m\angle B$. The auxiliary line segment $\overline{CD}$ perpendicular to $\overrightarrow{AB}$ (extended beyond B) creates right triangles ADC and BDC. Describe how you could use the Pythagorean Theorem to prove that $BC < AC$.

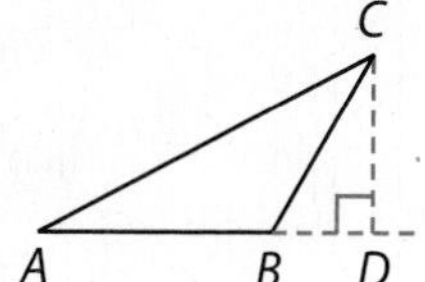

30. Make a Conjecture In acute $\triangle DEF$, $m\angle D < m\angle E$. The auxiliary line segment $\overline{FG}$ creates $\triangle EFG$, where $EF = FG$. What would you need to prove about the points D, G, and E to prove that $\angle DGF$ is obtuse, and therefore that $EF < DF$? Explain.

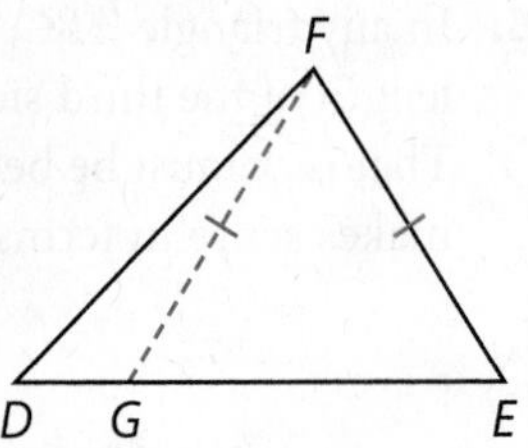

Lesson Performance Task

As captain of your orienteering team, it's your job to map out the shortest distance from point A to point H on the map. Justify each of your decisions.

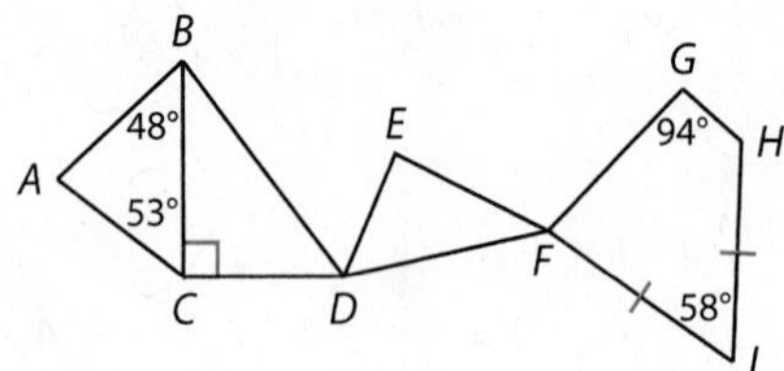

STUDY GUIDE REVIEW

Properties of Triangles

MODULE 7

Essential Question: How can you use the properties of triangles to solve real-world problems?

Key Vocabulary

interior angle *(ángulo interior)*
auxiliary line *(línea auxiliar)*
exterior angle *(ángulo exterior)*
remote interior angle *(ángulo interior remoto)*
isosceles triangle *(triángulo isósceles)*
legs *(catetos)*
vertex angle *(ángulo del vértice)*
base *(base)*
base angles *(ángulos de la base)*
equilateral triangle *(triángulo equilátero)*
equiangular triangle *(triángulo equiangular)*

KEY EXAMPLE *(Lesson 7.1)*

Determine the measure of the fifth interior angle of a pentagon if you know the other four measures are 100°, 50°, 158°, and 147°.

$\text{Sum} = (5 - 2)180° = 540°$	Apply the Polygon Angle Sum Theorem.
$100 + 50 + 158 + 147 + x = 540$	Set the sum of the angle measures equal to 540.
$455 + x = 540$	
$x = 85$	Solve for *x*.

KEY EXAMPLE *(Lesson 7.2)*

Given an isosceles triangle $\triangle ABC$ with $\overline{AB} \cong \overline{AC}$, $AB = 4x + 3$, and $AC = 8x - 13$, find AB.

$\overline{AB} \cong \overline{AC}$	Given
$4x + 3 = 8x - 13$	Substitution
$x = 4$	Solve for *x*.
$AB = 4(4) + 3$	Substitute the value of *x* into *AB*.
$AB = 19$	Simplify.

KEY EXAMPLE *(Lesson 7.3)*

Given a triangle with sides 7, 12, and *x*, find the range of values for *x*.

According to the Triangle Inequality Theorem, the sum of any two side lengths of a triangle is greater than the third side length.

$7 + 12 > x$	$7 + x > 12$	$x + 12 > 7$	Apply the Triangle Inequality Theorem.
$19 > x$	$x > 5$	$x > -5$	Simplify.
$5 < x < 19$			Combine the inequalities.

EXERCISES

Find how many sides a polygon has with the given interior angle sum. *(Lesson 7.1)*

1. 2700°

2. 1800°

Find the sum of interior angles a polygon has with the given number of sides. *(Lesson 7.1)*

3. 3

4. 19

Given an isosceles triangle $\triangle DEF$ with $\overline{DE} \cong \overline{DF}$, $DE = 26$, and $m\angle F = 45°$, find the desired measurements. *(Lesson 7.2)*

5. DF

6. $m\angle D$

Determine whether a triangle can have sides with the given lengths. *(Lesson 7.3)*

7. 5 mi, 19 mi, 15 mi

8. 4 ft, 3 ft, 10 ft

Find the range of the unknown side of a triangle with the given sides. *(Lesson 7.3)*

9. 5 mi, 19 mi, x mi

10. 4 ft, 3 ft, x ft

MODULE PERFORMANCE TASK

What's Up in the Federal Triangle?

The diagram shows a schematic of the Federal Triangle, an area located in Washington, DC. The area is bounded by Constitution Avenue on the south and Pennsylvania Avenue on the north and extends from 12th Street on the west to just past 6th Street on the east.

Is the shape of the Federal Triangle a triangle? How many sides does the Federal Triangle have? What is the actual shape of the Federal Triangle? What is the sum of the internal angles of the Federal Triangle? What portion of the area is actually a triangle?

Do some research and find the lengths of each side. Find the perimeter and area of the Federal Triangle. Find the area of the portion of the Federal Triangle that is a triangle.

Federal Triangle

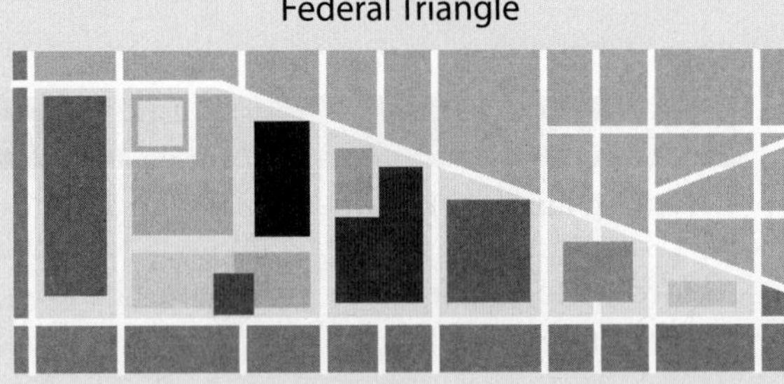

Ready to Go On?

7.1–7.3 Properties of Triangles

- Online Homework
- Hints and Help
- Extra Practice

Determine whether a triangle can be formed with the given side lengths. If the side lengths can form a triangle, determine if they will form an isosceles triangle, equilateral triangle, or neither. *(Lesson 7.1)*

1. 3 mi, 8 mi, 3 mi

2. 7 cm, 7cm, 7cm

3. 4 ft, 4 ft, 2 ft

4. 20 m, 30 m, 10 m

5. 3 m, 4 m, 5 m

6. 26 yd, 26 yd, 26 yd

Use the figure to answer the following. *(Lesson 7.2)*

7. Given $m\angle 2 = 76°$, $m\angle 1 = 3 \cdot m\angle 3$, and $\angle 4 \cong \angle 8$, find $m\angle 1$, $m\angle 3$, $m\angle 4$, $m\angle 5$, $m\angle 6$, $m\angle 7$, and $m\angle 8$.

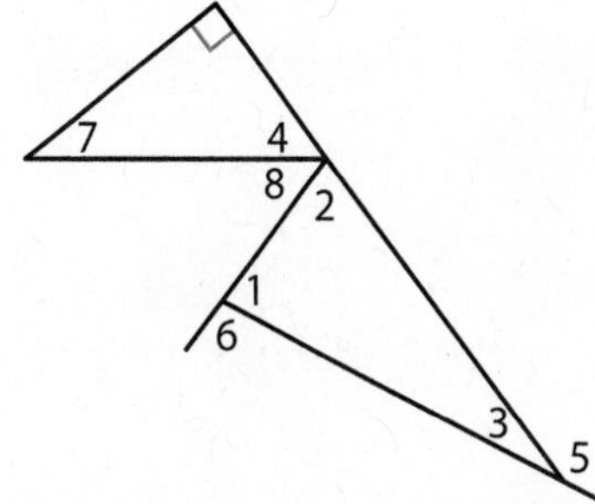

ESSENTIAL QUESTION

8. Is it possible for one angle of a triangle to be 180°? If so, demonstrate with an example. If not, explain why not.

MODULE 7
MIXED REVIEW

Assessment Readiness

1. Two angles in a triangle have measurements of 34° and 84°.

A. Does the third angle measure 62°?

B. Could a triangle congruent to this one contain an angle of 75°?

C. Is this triangle congruent to a right triangle?

2. Consider the following statements about a seven-sided polygon. Determine if each statement is True or False.

A. Each interior angle measures 135°.

B. The sum of the measures of the interior angles is 1260°.

C. The sum of the measures of the interior angles is 900°.

3. $\triangle ABC$ is an equilateral triangle, $AB = 4x + 45$, and $BC = 6x - 3$. Determine if each statement is True or False.

A. $x = 24$

B. The length of one side of the triangle is 141 units.

C. The distance from one vertex of the triangle to the midpoint of an adjacent side is 12 units.

4. Given a triangle with a side of length 6 and another side of length 13, find the range of possible values for the third side, x.

5. Given $\triangle DEF$, with $DE = 3EF$ and $DF = 4DE$, explain how to write the sides and angles in order of least to greatest.

Special Segments in Triangles

MODULE 8

Essential Question: How can you use special segments in triangles to solve real-world problems?

REAL WORLD VIDEO
Check out how the properties of triangles can be used by architects and urban planners to solve problems involving the positioning of landmarks.

MODULE PERFORMANCE TASK PREVIEW

Where Is the Heart of the Texas Triangle?

The Texas Triangle is a region with the cities of Dallas, Houston, and San Antonio as the vertices of the triangle. In this module, you will use theorems about triangles to explore the geometry of the region and locate its center. Are even triangles bigger in Texas?

Are YOU Ready?

Complete these exercises to review the skills you will need for this module.

- Online Homework
- Hints and Help
- Extra Practice

Distance and Midpoint Formulas

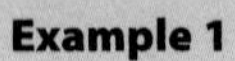

Example 1 Find the midpoint between (7, 1) and (–4, 8).

$\left(\frac{x_1 + x_2}{2}, \frac{y_1 + y_2}{2}\right)$ Midpoint Formula

$\left(\frac{7 - 4}{2}, \frac{1 + 8}{2}\right)$ Substitute.

$\left(\frac{3}{2}, \frac{9}{2}\right)$ Simplify.

Find each midpoint for the given points.

1. (2, 3) and (14, 9)

2. (–4, 7) and (–1, –11)

Angle Theorems for Triangles

Example 2 Given that $m\angle a = 72°$ and $m\angle c = 48°$, find the missing angle.

$m\angle a + m\angle b + m\angle c = 180°$ Triangle Sum Theorem

$72° + m\angle b + 48° = 180°$ Substitute.

$m\angle b + 120° = 180°$ Simplify.

$m\angle b = 60°$ Solve for $m\angle b$.

Find the missing angle in the figure from the example for the given values.

3. $m\angle b = 66°$ and $m\angle c = 75°$

4. $m\angle a = 103°$ and $m\angle c = 49°$

Geometric Drawings

Example 3 Use a compass and straightedge to construct the bisector of the given angle.

Angle with Bisector

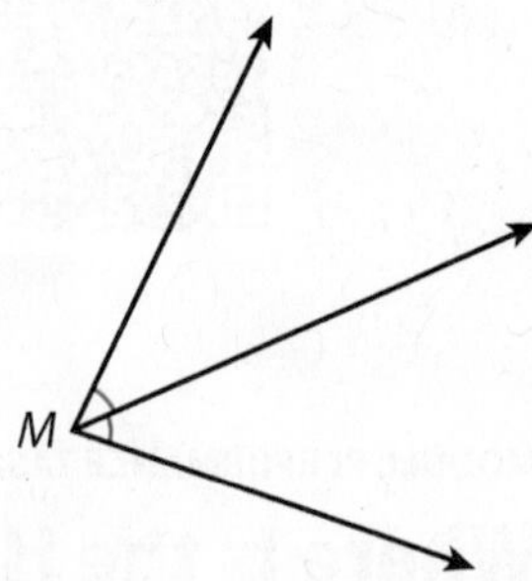

Copy the angle on a separate sheet of paper. Then use a compass and straightedge to construct the bisector of the angle.

5.

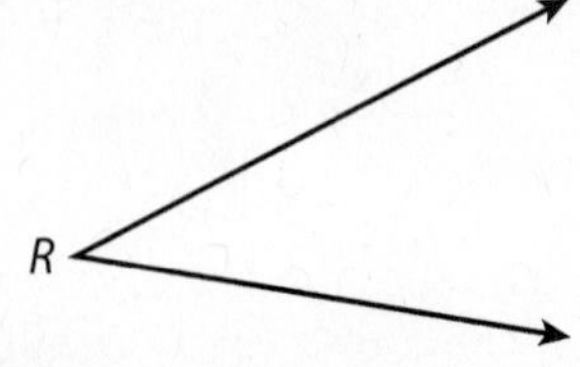

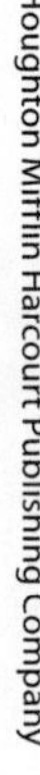

8.1 Perpendicular Bisectors of Triangles

Resource Locker

Essential Question: How can you use perpendicular bisectors to find the point that is equidistant from all the vertices of a triangle?

Explore Constructing a Circumscribed Circle

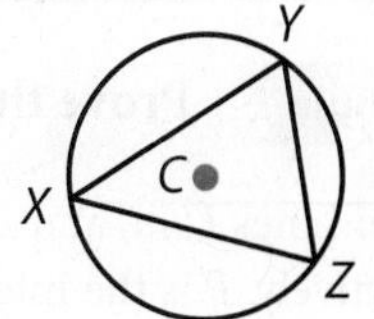

A circle that contains all the vertices of a polygon is **circumscribed** about the polygon. In the figure, circle C is circumscribed about $\triangle XYZ$, and circle C is called the **circumcircle** of $\triangle XYZ$. The center of the circumcircle is called the **circumcenter** of the triangle.

In the following activity, you will construct the circumcircle of $\triangle PQR$. Copy the triangle onto a separate piece of paper.

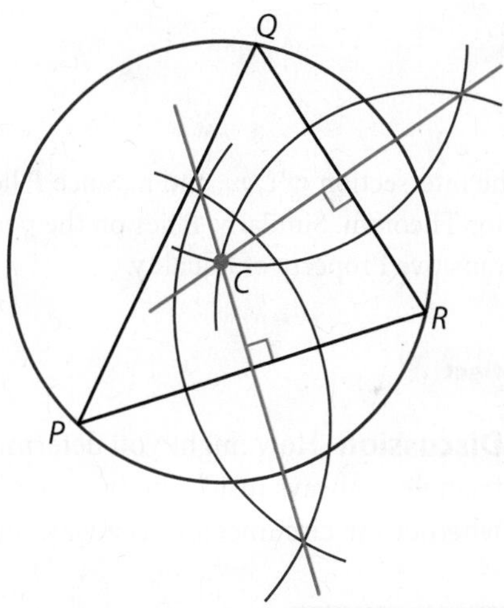

(A) The circumcircle will pass through P, Q, and R. So, the center of the circle must be equidistant from all three points. In particular, the center must be equidistant from Q and R.

The set of points that are equidistant from Q and R is called the [?] of $\overline{QR}$. Use a compass and straightedge to construct the set of points.

(B) The center must also be equidistant from P and R. The set of points that are equidistant from P and R is called the [?] of $\overline{PR}$. Use a compass and straightedge to construct the set of points.

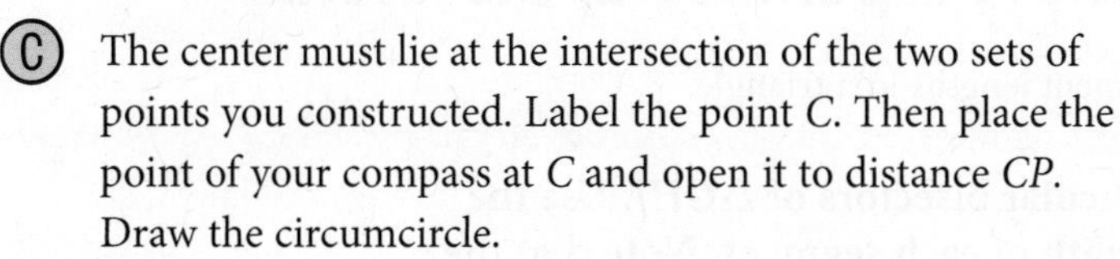

(C) The center must lie at the intersection of the two sets of points you constructed. Label the point C. Then place the point of your compass at C and open it to distance CP. Draw the circumcircle.

Reflect

1. **Make a Prediction** Suppose you started by constructing the set of points equidistant from P and Q and then constructed the set of points equidistant from Q and R. Would you have found the same center? Check by doing this construction.

2. Can you locate the circumcenter of a triangle without using a compass and straightedge? Explain.

Explain 1 Proving the Concurrency of a Triangle's Perpendicular Bisectors

Three or more lines are **concurrent** if they intersect at the same point. The point of intersection is called the **point of concurrency**. You saw in the Explore that the three perpendicular bisectors of a triangle are concurrent. Now you will prove that the point of concurrency is the circumcenter of the triangle. That is, the point of concurrency is equidistant from the vertices of the triangle.

Circumcenter Theorem

The perpendicular bisectors of the sides of a triangle intersect at a point that is equidistant from the vertices of the triangle.

$PA = PB = PC$

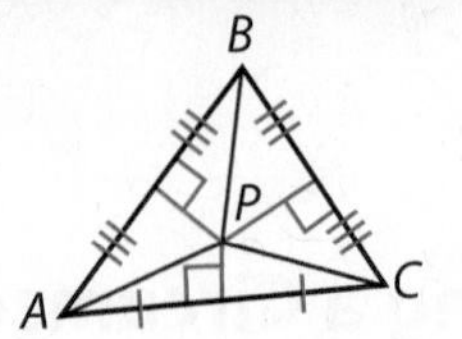

Example 1 **Prove the Circumcenter Theorem.**

Given: Lines ℓ, m, and n are the perpendicular bisectors of $\overline{AB}$, $\overline{BC}$, and $\overline{AC}$, respectively. P is the intersection of ℓ, m, and n.

Prove: $PA = PB = PC$

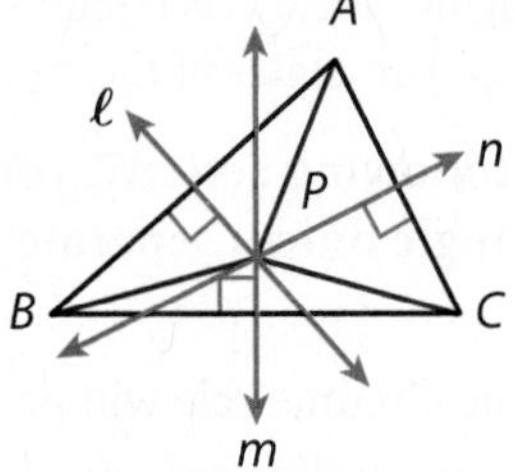

P is the intersection of ℓ, m, and n. Since P lies on the perpendicular bisector of $\overline{AB}$, $PA = PB$ by the Perpendicular Bisector Theorem. Similarly, P lies on the perpendicular bisector of $\overline{BC}$, so $PB = PC$. Therefore, $PA = PB = PC$ by the Transitive Property of Equality.

Reflect

3. **Discussion** How might you determine whether the circumcenter of a triangle is always inside the triangle? Make a plan and then determine whether the circumcenter is always inside the triangle.

Explain 2 Using Properties of Perpendicular Bisectors

You can use the Circumcenter Theorem to find segment lengths in a triangle.

Example 2 **$\overline{KZ}$, $\overline{LZ}$, and $\overline{MZ}$ are the perpendicular bisectors of $\triangle GHJ$. Use the given information to find the length of each segment. Note that the figure is not drawn to scale.**

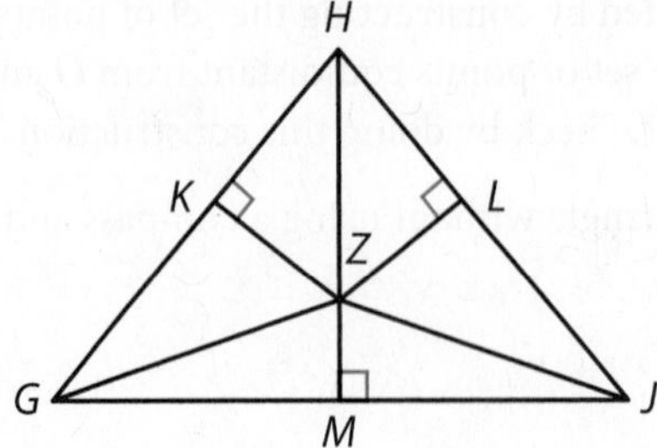

(A) Given: $ZM = 7$, $ZJ = 25$, $HK = 20$

Find: ZH and HG

Z is the circumcenter of $\triangle GHJ$, so $ZG = ZH = ZJ$.

$ZJ = 25$, so $ZH = 25$.

K is the midpoint of $\overline{GH}$, so $HG = 2 \cdot KH = 2 \cdot 20 = 40$.

(B) Given: $ZH = 85$, $MZ = 13$, $HG = 136$

Find: KG and ZJ

K is the midpoint of $\overline{HG}$, so $KG = \boxed{\frac{1}{2}}\ HG = \boxed{\frac{1}{2}} \cdot \boxed{136} = \boxed{68}$.

Z is the circumcenter of $\triangle GHJ$, so $ZG = ZH = ZJ$.

$ZH = 85$, so $ZJ = 85$.

Reflect

4. In $\triangle ABC$, $\angle ACB$ is a right angle and D is the circumcenter of the triangle. If $CD = 6.5$, what is AB? Explain your reasoning.

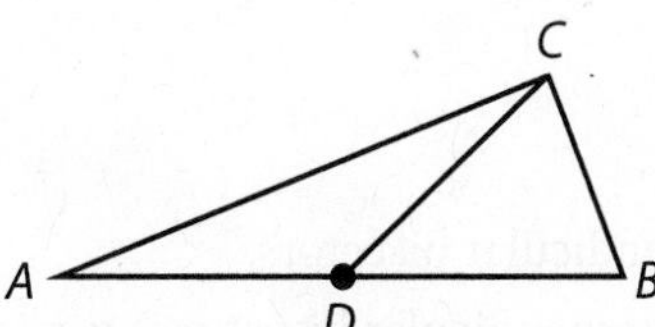

Your Turn

$\overline{KZ}$, $\overline{LZ}$, and $\overline{MZ}$ are the perpendicular bisectors of $\triangle GHJ$. Copy the sketch and label the given information. Use that information to find the length of each segment. Note that the figure is not drawn to scale.

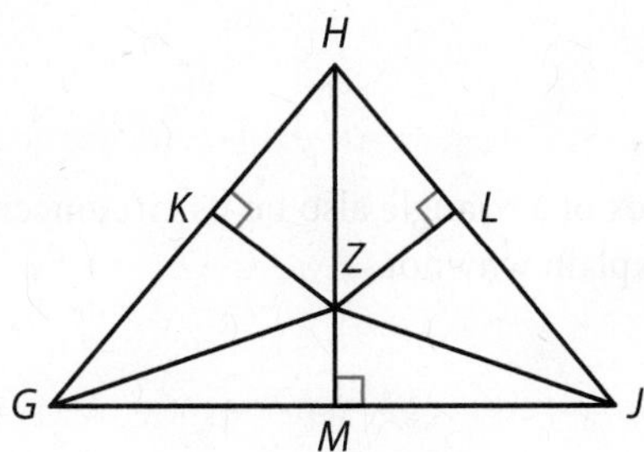

5. Given: $ZG = 65$, $HL = 63$, $ZL = 16$
Find: HJ and ZJ

6. Given: $ZM = 25$, $ZH = 65$, $GJ = 120$
Find: GM and ZG

Explain 3 Finding a Circumcenter on a Coordinate Plane

Given the vertices of a triangle, you can graph the triangle and use the graph to find the circumcenter of the triangle.

Example 3 **Graph the triangle with the given vertices and find the circumcenter of the triangle.**

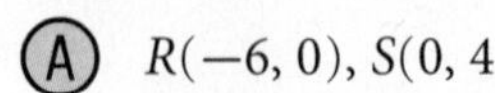

Ⓐ $R(-6, 0)$, $S(0, 4)$, $O(0, 0)$

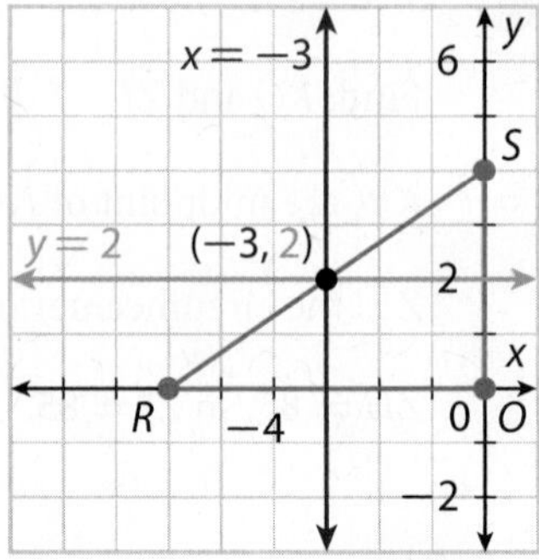

Step 1: Graph the triangle.

Step 2: Find equations for two perpendicular bisectors. Side $\overline{RO}$ is on the x-axis, so its perpendicular bisector is vertical: the line $x = -3$.

Side $\overline{SO}$ is on the y-axis, so its perpendicular bisector is horizontal: the line $y = 2$.

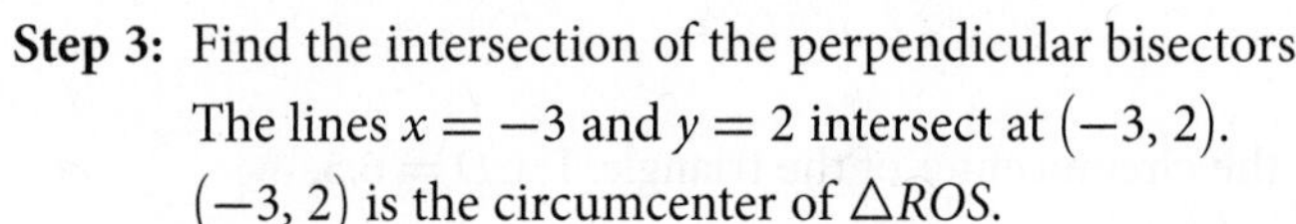

Step 3: Find the intersection of the perpendicular bisectors. The lines $x = -3$ and $y = 2$ intersect at $(-3, 2)$. $(-3, 2)$ is the circumcenter of $\triangle ROS$.

Ⓑ $A(-1, 5)$, $B(5, 5)$, $C(5, -1)$

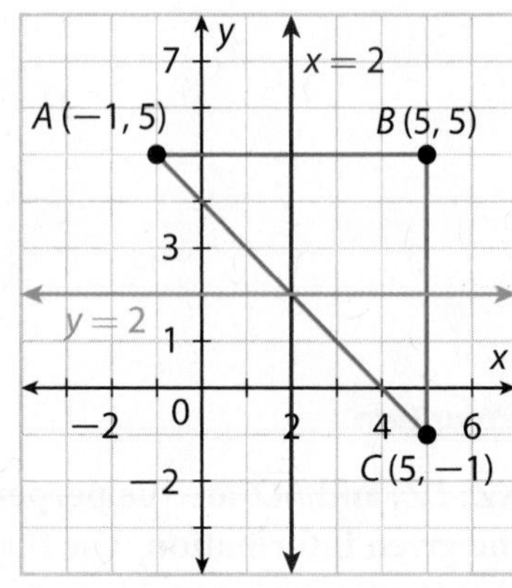

Step 1 Graph the triangle.

Step 2 Find equations for two perpendicular bisectors. Side $\overline{AB}$ is horizontal, so its perpendicular bisector is vertical. The perpendicular bisector of $\overline{AB}$ is the line $x = 2$. Side $\overline{BC}$ is vertical, so the perpendicular bisector of $\overline{BC}$ is the horizontal line $y = 2$.

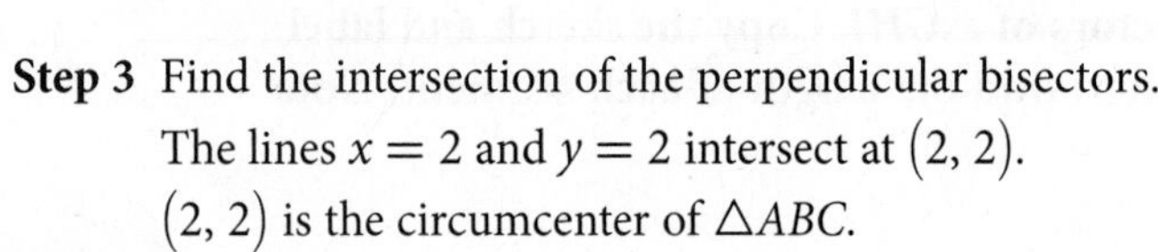

Step 3 Find the intersection of the perpendicular bisectors. The lines $x = 2$ and $y = 2$ intersect at $(2, 2)$. $(2, 2)$ is the circumcenter of $\triangle ABC$.

Reflect

7. **Draw Conclusions** Could a vertex of a triangle also be its circumcenter? If so, provide an example. If not, explain why not.

Your Turn

Graph the triangle with the given vertices and find the circumcenter of the triangle.

8. $Q(-4, 0)$, $R(0, 0)$, $S(0, 6)$

9. $K(1, 1)$, $L(1, 7)$, $M(6, 1)$

Elaborate

10. A company that makes and sells bicycles has its largest stores in three cities. The company wants to build a new factory that is equidistant from each of the stores. Given a map, how could you identify the location for the new factory?

11. A sculptor builds a mobile in which a triangle rotates around its circumcenter. Each vertex traces the shape of a circle as it rotates. What circle does it trace? Explain.

12. **What If?** Suppose you are given the vertices of a triangle *PQR*. You plot the points in a coordinate plane and notice that $\overline{PQ}$ is horizontal but neither of the other sides is vertical. How can you identify the circumcenter of the triangle? Justify your reasoning.

13. **Essential Question Check-In** How is the point that is equidistant from the three vertices of a triangle related to the circumcircle of the triangle?

Evaluate: Homework and Practice

- Online Homework
- Hints and Help
- Extra Practice

Copy each triangle and construct its circumcircle. Label the circumcenter *P*.

1.

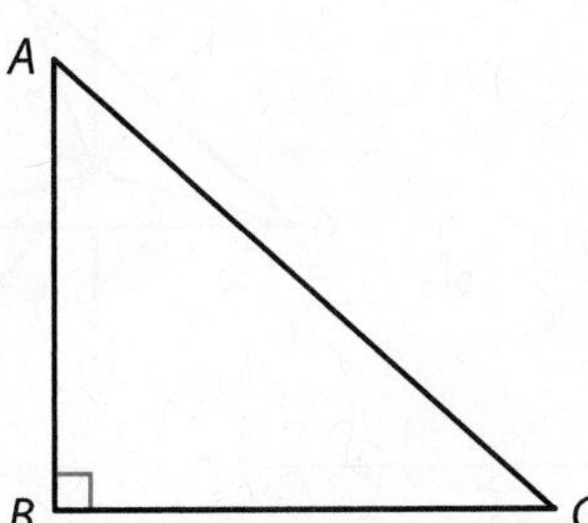

2.

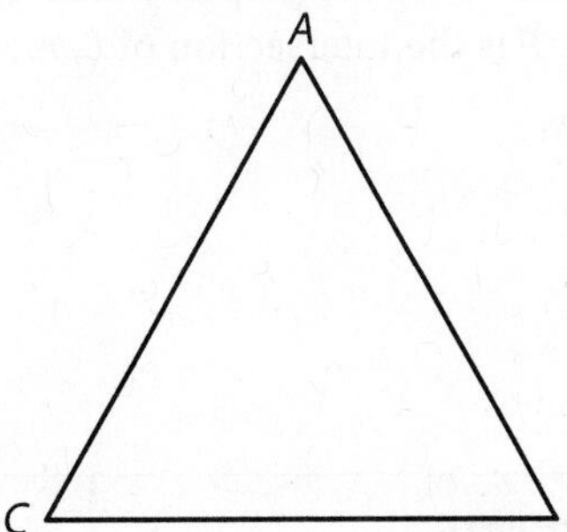

3.

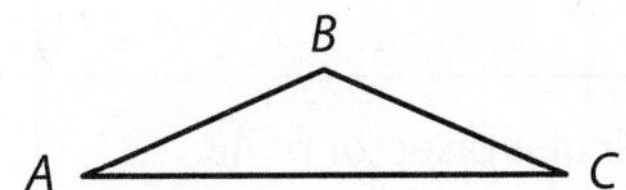

4.

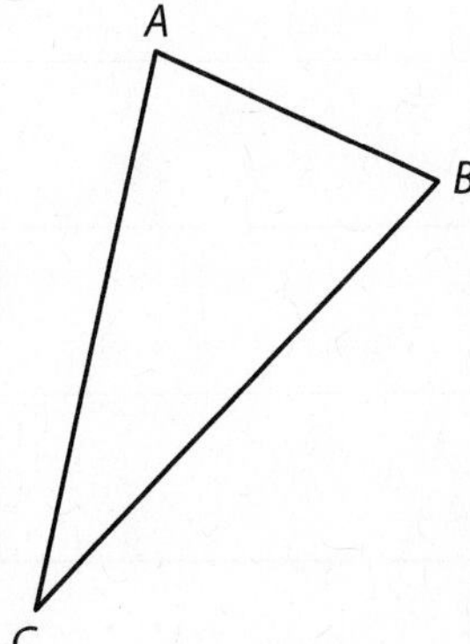

Use the diagram for Exercise 5–8. $\overline{ZD}$, $\overline{ZE}$, and $\overline{ZF}$ are the perpendicular bisectors of $\triangle ABC$. Use the given information to find the length of each segment. Note that the figure is not drawn to scale.

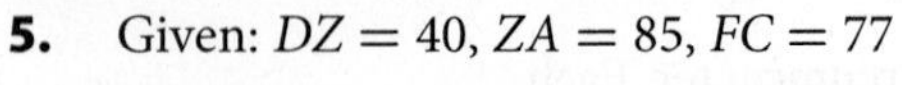

5. Given: $DZ = 40$, $ZA = 85$, $FC = 77$

Find: ZC and AC

6. Given: $FZ = 36$, $ZA = 85$, $AB = 150$

Find: AD and ZB

7. Given: $AZ = 85$, $ZE = 51$

Find: BC

(*Hint*: Use the Pythagorean Theorem.)

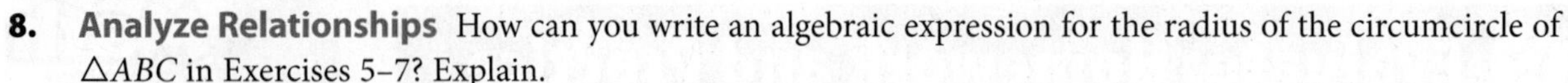

8. Analyze Relationships How can you write an algebraic expression for the radius of the circumcircle of $\triangle ABC$ in Exercises 5–7? Explain.

Copy and complete the table to prove the Circumcenter Theorem.

9. Given: Lines ℓ, m, and n are the perpendicular bisectors of $\overline{AB}$, $\overline{BC}$, and $\overline{AC}$, respectively. P is the intersection of ℓ, m, and n.

Prove: $PA = PB = PC$

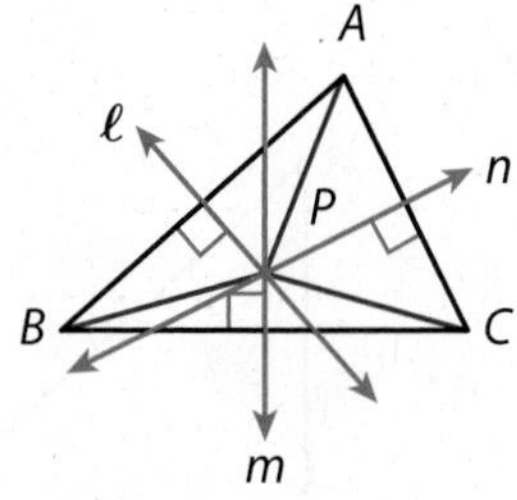

Statements	Reasons
1. Lines ℓ, m, and n are the perpendicular bisectors of $\overline{AB}$, $\overline{BC}$, and $\overline{AC}$.	1. ___?___
2. P is the intersection of ℓ, m, and n.	2. ___?___
3. $PA =$ ___?___	3. P lies on the perpendicular bisector of $\overline{AB}$.
4. ___?___ $= PC$	4. P lies on the perpendicular bisector of $\overline{BC}$.
5. $PA =$ ___?___ $=$ ___?___	5. ___?___

10. $\overline{PK}$, $\overline{PL}$, and $\overline{PM}$ are the perpendicular bisectors of sides $\overline{AB}$, $\overline{BC}$, and $\overline{AC}$. Tell whether the given statement is justified or not justified by the figure.

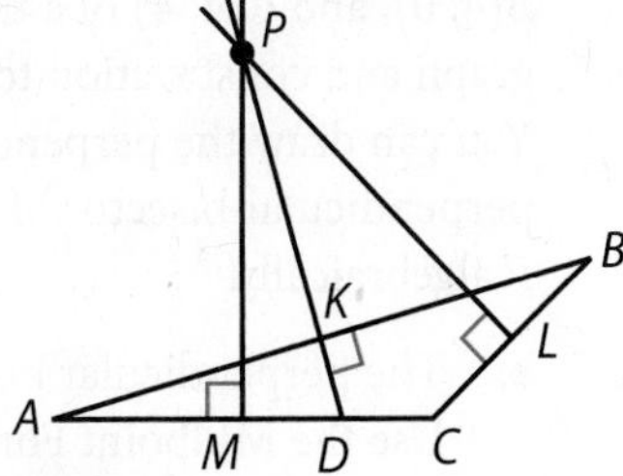

a. $AK = KB$

b. $PA = PB$

c. $PM = PL$

d. $BL = \frac{1}{2}BC$

e. $PK = KD$

Graph the triangle with the given vertices and find the circumcenter of the triangle.

11. $D(-5, 0)$, $E(0, 0)$, $F(0, 7)$

12. $Q(3, 4)$, $R(7, 4)$, $S(3, -2)$

13. **Represent Real-World Problems** For the next Fourth of July, the towns of Ashton, Bradford, and Clearview will launch a fireworks display from a boat in the lake. Draw a sketch to show where the boat should be positioned so that it is the same distance from all three towns. Justify your sketch.

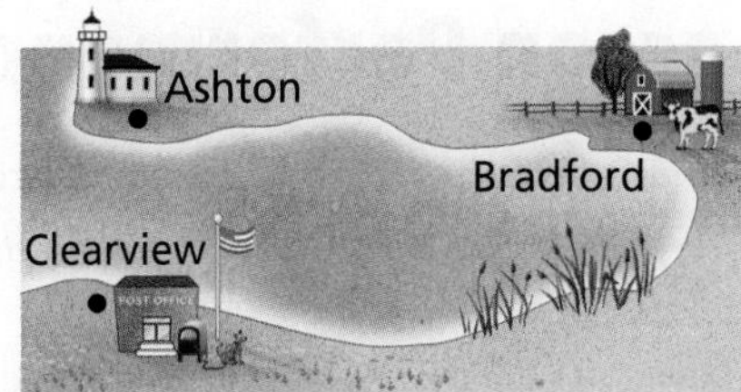

H.O.T. Focus on Higher Order Thinking

14. **Analyze Relationships** Explain how can you draw a triangle JKL whose circumcircle has a radius of 8 centimeters.

15. **Persevere in Problem Solving** $\overline{ZD}$, $\overline{ZE}$, and $\overline{ZF}$ are the perpendicular bisectors of $\triangle ABC$, which is not drawn to scale.

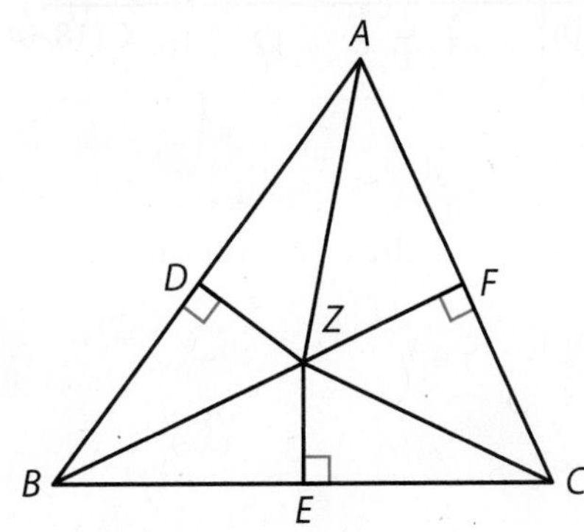

a. Suppose that $ZB = 145$, $ZD = 100$, and $ZF = 17$. How can you find AB and AC?

b. Find AB and AC.

c. Can you find BC? If so, explain how and find BC. If not, explain why not.

16. Multiple Representations Given the vertices $A(-2, -2)$, $B(4, 0)$, and $C(4, 4)$ of a triangle, the graph shows how you can use a graph and construction to locate the circumcenter P of the triangle. You can draw the perpendicular bisector of $\overline{CB}$ and construct the perpendicular bisector of $\overline{AB}$. Consider how you could identify P algebraically.

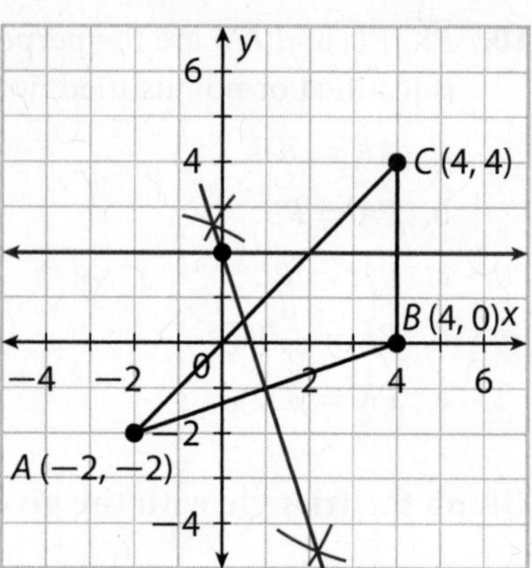

a. The perpendicular bisector of $\overline{AB}$ passes through its midpoint. Use the Midpoint Formula to find the midpoint of $\overline{AB}$.

b. What is the slope m of the perpendicular bisector of $\overline{AB}$? Explain how you found it.

c. Write an equation of the perpendicular bisector of $\overline{AB}$ and explain how you can use it find P.

Lesson Performance Task

A landscape architect wants to plant a circle of flowers around a triangular garden. She has sketched the triangle on a coordinate grid with vertices at $A(0, 0)$, $B(8, 12)$, and $C(18, 0)$.

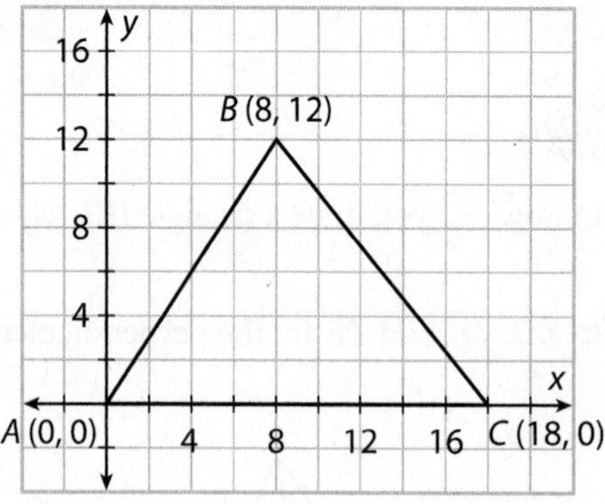

Explain how the architect can find the center of the circle that will circumscribe triangle ABC. Then find the radius of the circumscribed circle.

8.2 Angle Bisectors of Triangles

Resource Locker

Essential Question: How can you use angle bisectors to find the point that is equidistant from all the sides of a triangle?

Explore Investigating Distance from a Point to a Line

Use a ruler, a protractor, and a piece of tracing paper to investigate points on the bisector of an angle.

(A) Use the ruler to draw a large angle on tracing paper. Label it $\angle ABC$. Fold the paper so that $\overrightarrow{BC}$ coincides with $\overrightarrow{BA}$. Open the paper. The crease is the bisector of $\angle ABC$. Plot a point P on the bisector.

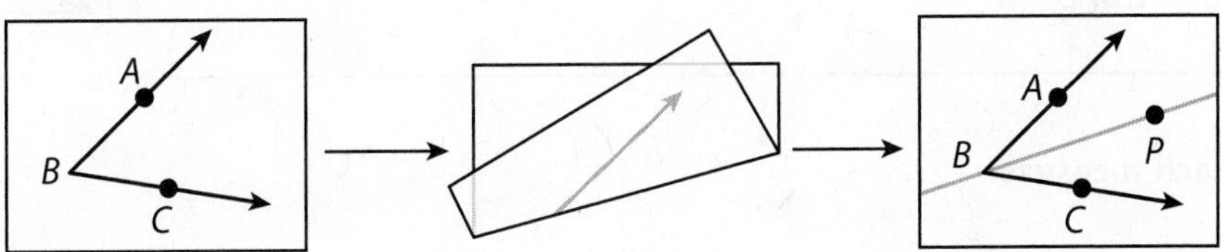

(B) Use the ruler to draw several different segments from point P to $\overrightarrow{BA}$. Measure the lengths of the segments. Then measure the angle each segment makes with $\overrightarrow{BA}$. What do you notice about the shortest segment you can draw from point P to $\overrightarrow{BA}$?

(C) Draw the shortest segment you can from point P to $\overrightarrow{BC}$. Measure its length. How does its length compare with the length of the shortest segment you drew from point P to $\overrightarrow{BA}$?

Reflect

1. Suppose you choose a point Q on the bisector of $\angle XYZ$ and you draw the perpendicular segment from Q to $\overrightarrow{YX}$ and the perpendicular segment from Q to $\overrightarrow{YZ}$. What do you think will be true about these segments?

2. **Discussion** What do you think is the best way to measure the distance from a point to a line? Why?

Explain 1 Applying the Angle Bisector Theorem and Its Converse

The **distance from a point to a line** is the length of the perpendicular segment from the point to the line. You will prove the following theorems about angle bisectors and the sides of the angle they bisect in Exercises 16 and 17.

Angle Bisector Theorem

If a point is on the bisector an of angle, then it is equidistant from the sides of the angle.

$\angle APC \cong \angle BPC$, so $AC = BC$.

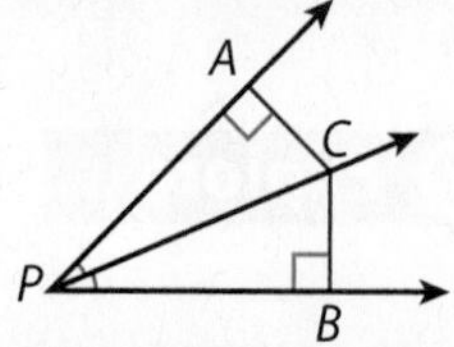

Converse of the Angle Bisector Theorem

If a point in the interior of an angle is equidistant from the sides of the angle, then it is on the bisector of the angle.

$AC = BC$, so $\angle APC \cong \angle BPC$

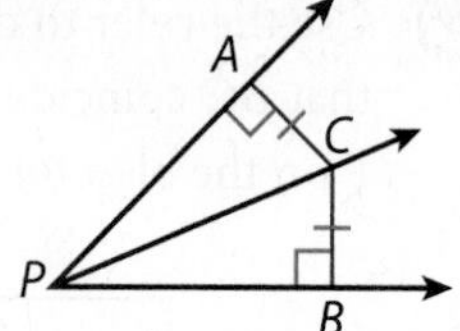

Example 1 **Find each measure.**

(A) LM

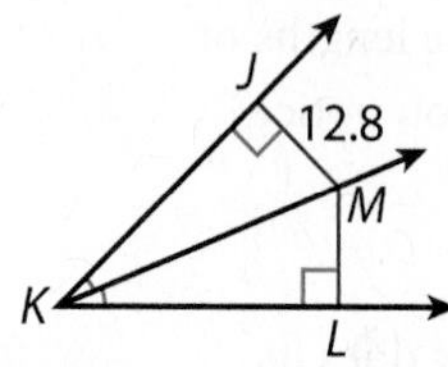

$\overrightarrow{KM}$ is the bisector of $\angle JKL$, so $LM = JM = 12.8$.

(B) $m\angle ABD$, given that $m\angle ABC = 112°$

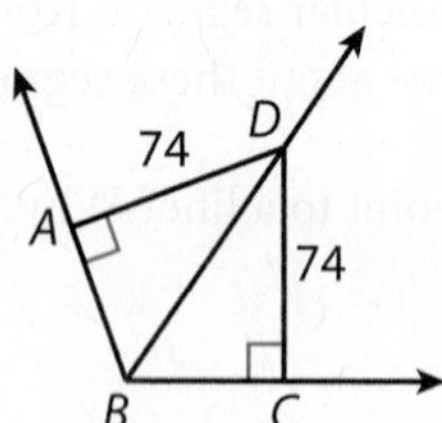

Since $AD = DC$, $\overline{AD} \perp \overrightarrow{BA}$, and $\overline{DC} \perp \overrightarrow{BC}$, you know that $\overrightarrow{BD}$ bisects $\angle ABC$ by the Converse of the Angle Bisector Theorem.

So, $m\angle ABD = \frac{1}{2}m\angle ABC =$ 56 °.

Reflect

3. In the Converse of the Angle Bisector Theorem, why is it important to say that the point must be in the *interior* of the angle?

Your Turn

Find each measure.

4. QS

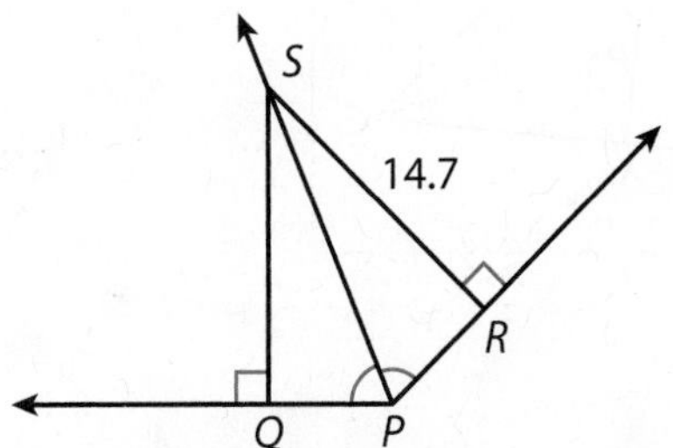

5. $m\angle LJM$, given that $m\angle KJM = 29°$

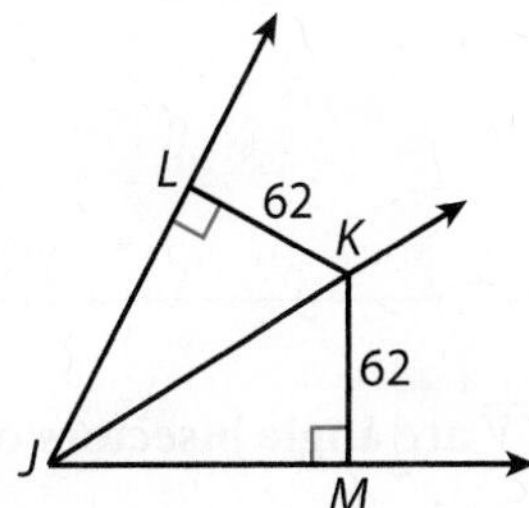

Explain 2 Constructing an Inscribed Circle

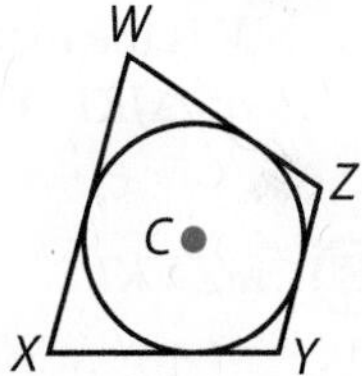

A circle is **inscribed** in a polygon if each side of the polygon is tangent to the circle. In the figure, circle C is inscribed in quadrilateral $WXYZ$ and this circle is called the **incircle (inscribed circle)** of the quadrilateral.

In order to construct the incircle of a triangle, you need to find the center of the circle. This point is called the **incenter** of the triangle.

Example 2 **Copy $\triangle PQR$. Then use a compass and straightedge to construct the inscribed circle of $\triangle PQR$.**

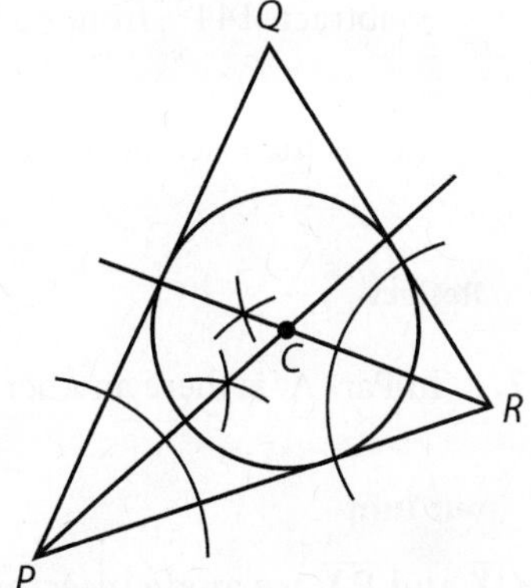

Step 1 The center of the inscribed circle must be equidistant from $\overline{PQ}$ and $\overline{PR}$. What is the set of points equidistant from $\overline{PQ}$ and $\overline{PR}$? the bisector of $\angle P$
Construct this set of points.

Step 2 The center must also be equidistant from $\overline{PR}$ and $\overline{QR}$. What is the set of points equidistant from $\overline{PR}$ and $\overline{QR}$? the bisector of $\angle R$
Construct this set of points.

Step 3 The center must lie at the intersection of the two sets of points you constructed. Label this point C.

Step 4 Place the point of your compass at C and open the compass until the pencil just touches a side of $\triangle PQR$. Then draw the inscribed circle.

Reflect

6. Suppose you started by constructing the set of points equidistant from $\overline{PR}$ and $\overline{QR}$, and then constructed the set of points equidistant from $\overline{QR}$ and $\overline{QP}$. Would you have found the same center point? Check by doing this construction.

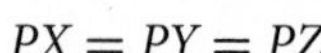 Explain 3 Using Properties of Angle Bisectors

As you have seen, the angle bisectors of a triangle are concurrent. The point of concurrency is the incenter of the triangle.

Incenter Theorem

The angle bisectors of a triangle intersect at a point that is equidistant from the sides of the triangle.

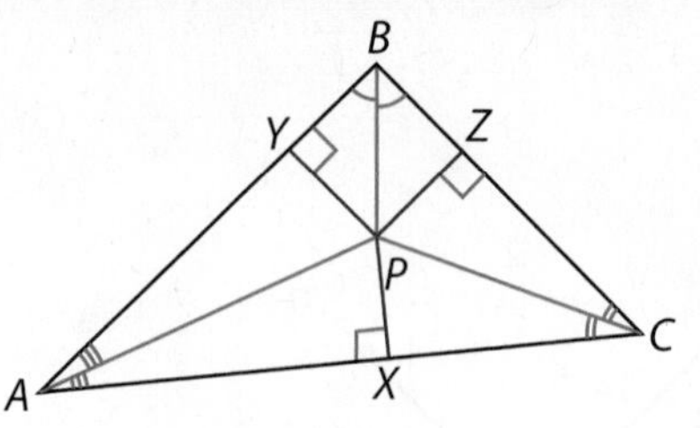

$PX = PY = PZ$

Example 3 $\overline{JV}$ **and** $\overline{KV}$ **are angle bisectors of** $\triangle JKL$**. Find each measure.**

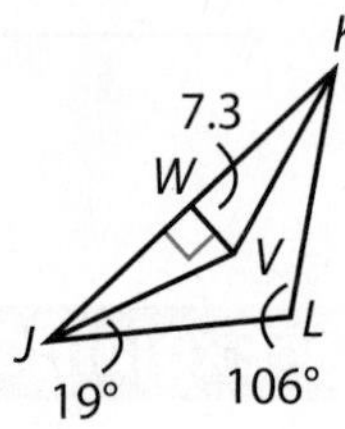

(A) the distance from V to $\overline{KL}$

V is the incenter of $\triangle JKL$. By the Incenter Theorem, V is equidistant from the sides of $\triangle JKL$. The distance from V to $\overline{JK}$ is 7.3. So the distance from V to $\overline{KL}$ is also 7.3.

(B) $m\angle VKL$

$\overline{JV}$ is the bisector of $\angle$ [KJL]. $m\angle KJL = 2([19°]) = [38°]$

Triangle Sum Theorem $[38°] + [106°] + m\angle JKL = 180°$

Subtract [144°] from each side. $m\angle JKL = [36°]$

$\overline{KV}$ is the bisector of $\angle JKL$. $m\angle VKL = \frac{1}{2}([36°]) = [18°]$

Reflect

7. In Part A, is there another distance you can determine? Explain.

Your Turn

$\overline{QX}$ **and** $\overline{RX}$ **are angle bisectors of** $\triangle PQR$**. Find each measure.**

8. the distance from X to $\overline{PQ}$

9. $m\angle PQX$

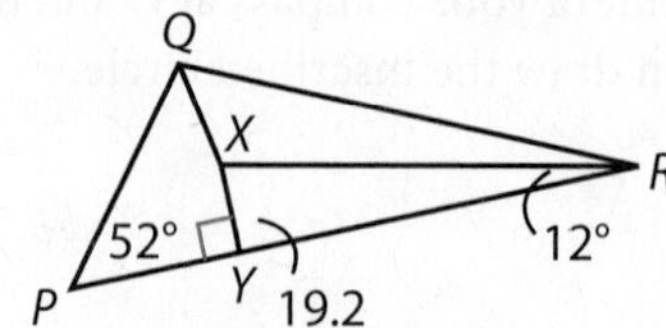

Elaborate

10. P and Q are the circumcenter and incenter of $\triangle RST$, but not necessarily in that order. Which point is the circumcenter? Which point is the incenter? Explain how you can tell without constructing any bisectors.

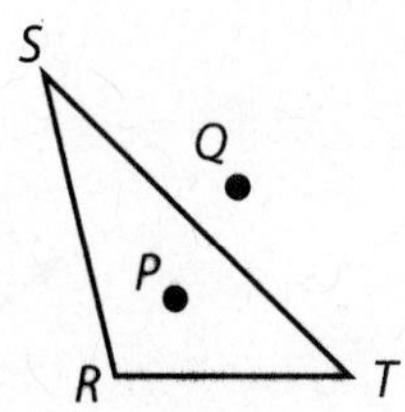

11. Copy and complete the table to make each statement true.

	Circumcenter	Incenter
Definition	The point of concurrency of the _?_	The point of concurrency of the _?_
Distance	Equidistant from the _?_	Equidistant from the _?_
Location (Inside, Outside, On)	Can be _?_ the triangle	Always _?_ the triangle

12. **Essential Question Check-In** How do you know that the intersection of the bisectors of the angles of a triangle is equidistant from the sides of the triangle?

Evaluate: Homework and Practice

- Online Homework
- Hints and Help
- Extra Practice

1. Use a compass and straightedge to investigate points on the bisector of an angle. On a separate piece of paper, draw a large angle A.

a. Construct the bisector of $\angle A$.

b. Choose a point on the angle bisector you constructed. Label it P. Construct a perpendicular through P to each side of $\angle A$.

c. Explain how to use a compass to show that P is equidistant from the sides of $\angle A$.

For 1–4, find each measure.

2. VP

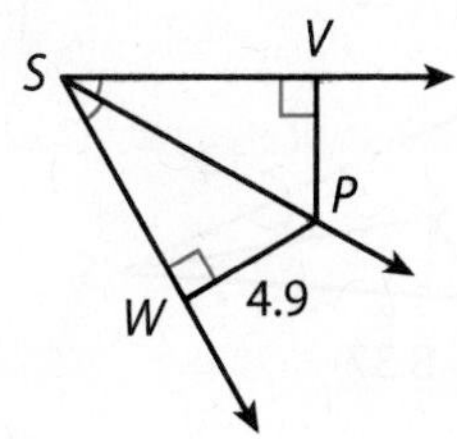

3. $m\angle LKM$, given that $m\angle JKL = 63°$

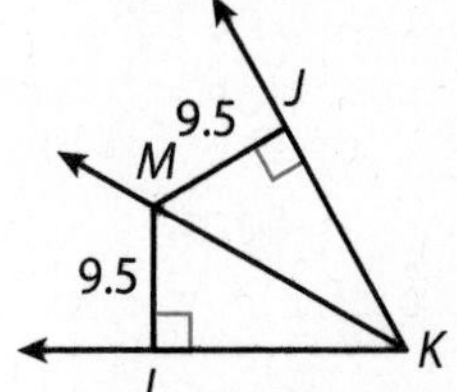

4. AD

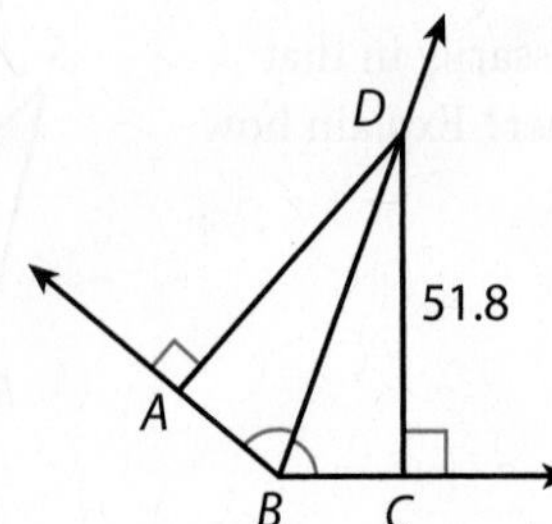

5. $m\angle HFJ$, given that $m\angle GFJ = 45°$

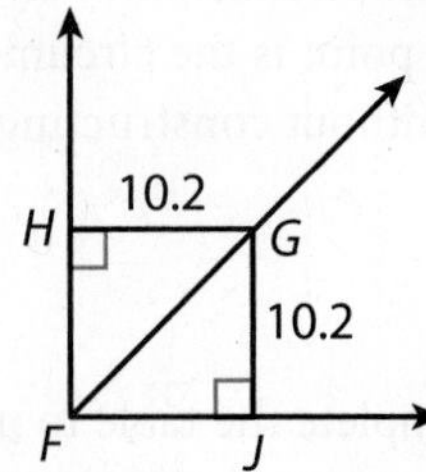

Copy each triangle. Then construct an inscribed circle for each triangle.

6.

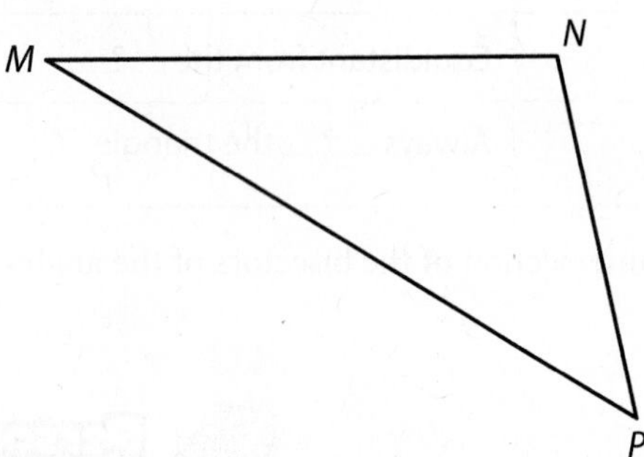

7.

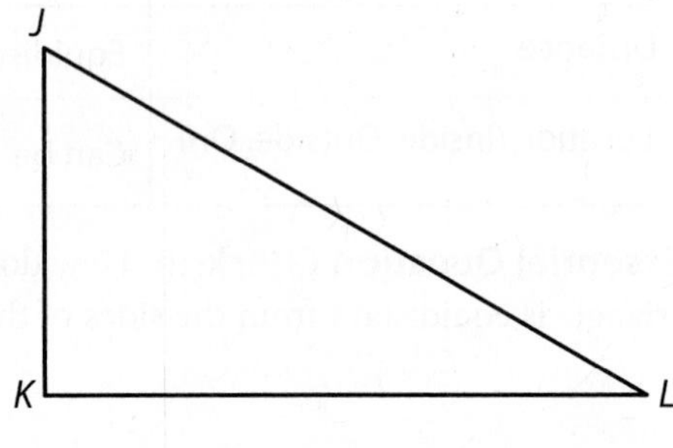

$\overline{CF}$ and $\overline{EF}$ are angle bisectors of $\triangle CDE$. Find each measure.

8. the distance from F to $\overline{CD}$

9. $m\angle FED$

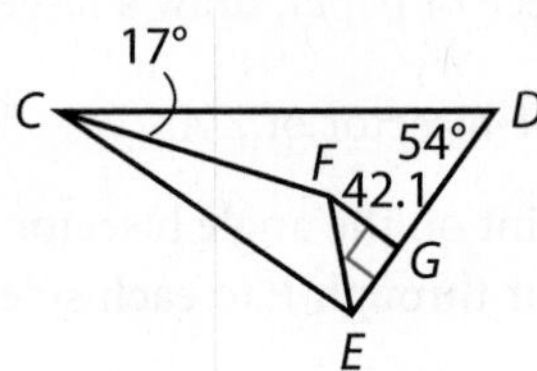

$\overline{TJ}$ and $\overline{SJ}$ are angle bisectors of $\triangle RST$. Find each measure.

10. the distance from J to $\overline{RS}$

11. $m\angle RTJ$

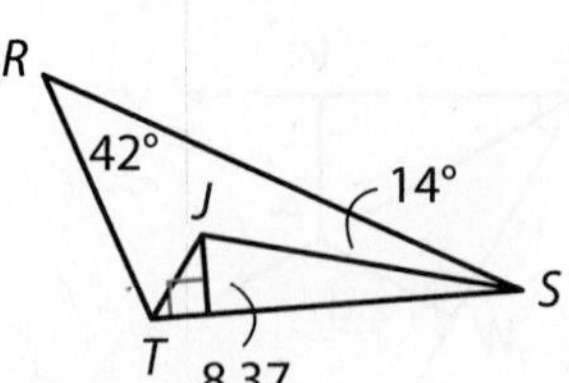

Find each measure.

12. BC

13. VY

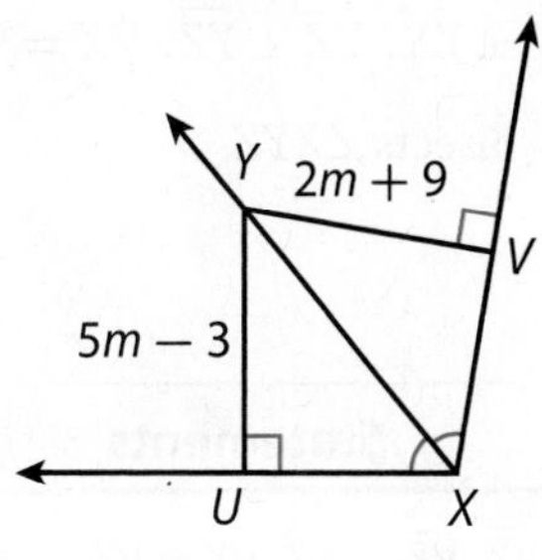

14. $m\angle JKL$

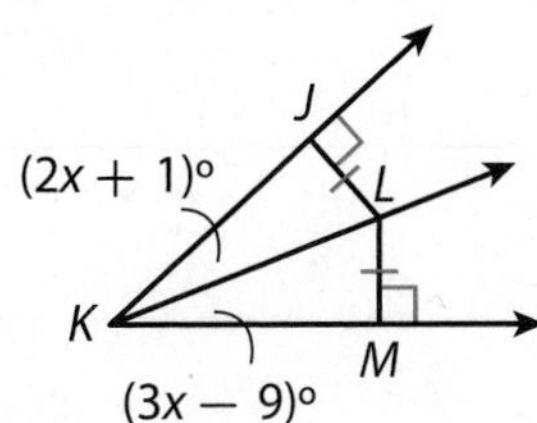

15. $m\angle GDF$

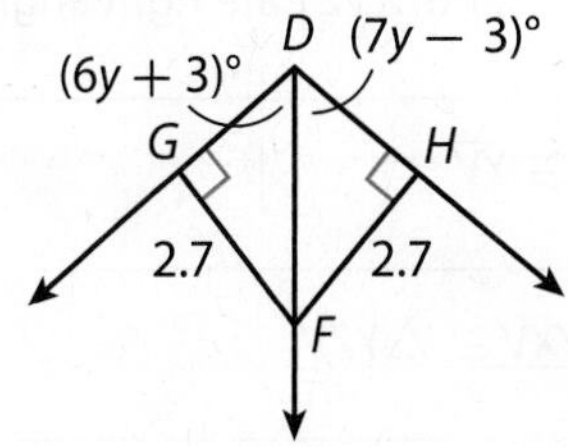

16. Copy and complete the following proof of the Angle Bisector Theorem.

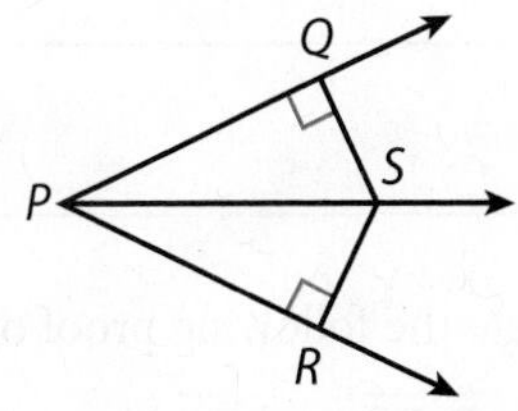

Given: $\overrightarrow{PS}$ bisects $\angle QPR$.

$\overline{SQ} \perp \overrightarrow{PQ}$, $\overline{SR} \perp \overrightarrow{PR}$

Prove: $SQ = SR$

Statements	Reasons
1. $\overrightarrow{PS}$ bisects $\angle QPR$. $\overline{SQ} \perp \overrightarrow{PQ}$, $\overline{SR} \perp \overrightarrow{PR}$	1. ?
2. $\angle QPS \cong \angle RPS$	2. ?
3. $\angle SQP$ and $\angle SRP$ are right angles.	3. Definition of perpendicular
4. $\angle SQP \cong \angle SRP$	4. All right angles are congruent.
5. ?	5. Reflexive Property of Congruence
6. ?	6. AAS Triangle Congruence Theorem
7. $\overline{SQ} \cong \overline{SR}$	7. ?
8. $SQ = SR$	8. Congruent segments have the same length.

17. Copy and complete the following proof of the Converse of the Angle Bisector Theorem.

Given: $\overline{VX} \perp \overrightarrow{YX}$, $\overline{VZ} \perp \overrightarrow{YZ}$, $VX = VZ$.

Prove: $\overrightarrow{YV}$ bisects $\angle XYZ$.

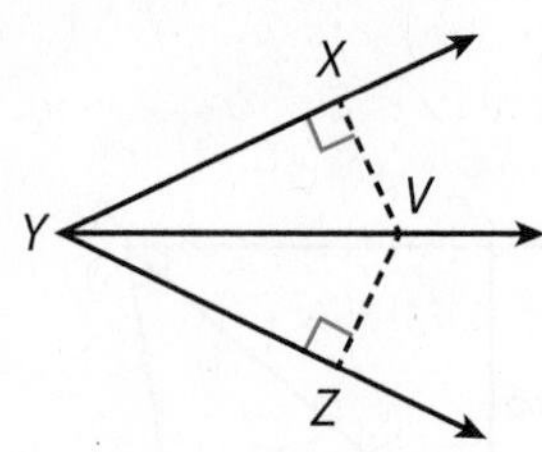

Statements	Reasons
1. $\overline{VX} \perp \overrightarrow{YX}$, $\overline{VZ} \perp \overrightarrow{YZ}$, $VX = VZ$	1. ?
2. $\angle VXY$ and $\angle VZY$ are right angles.	2. ?
3. $\overline{YV} \cong \overline{YV}$	3. ?
4. $\triangle YXV \cong \triangle YZV$	4. ?
5. $\angle XYV \cong \angle ZYV$	5. ?
6. ?	6. ?

18. Complete the following proof of the Incenter Theorem.

Given: $\overrightarrow{AP}$, $\overrightarrow{BP}$, and $\overrightarrow{CP}$ bisect $\angle A$, $\angle B$ and $\angle C$, respectively. $\overline{PX} \perp \overline{AC}$, $\overline{PY} \perp \overline{AB}$, $\overline{PZ} \perp \overline{BC}$

Prove: $PX = PY = PZ$

Let P be the incenter of $\triangle ABC$. Since P lies on the bisector of $\angle A$, $PX = PY$ by the ___?___ Theorem. Similarly, P also ___?___, so $PY = PZ$. Therefore, $PX = PY = PZ$, by the ___?___.

19. A city plans to build a firefighter's monument in a triangular park between three streets. Copy the figure. Then draw a sketch on the figure to show where the city should place the monument so that it is the same distance from all three streets. Justify your sketch.

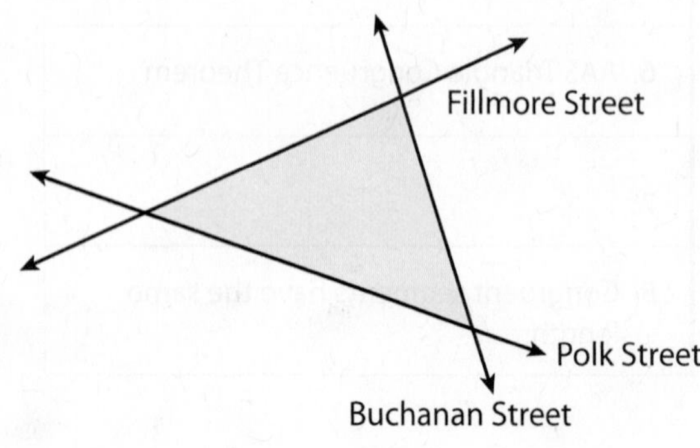

20. A school plans to place a flagpole on the lawn so that it is equidistant from Mercer Street and Houston Street. They also want the flagpole to be equidistant from a water fountain at W and a bench at B. Find the point F where the school should place the flagpole. Mark the point on the figure and explain your answer.

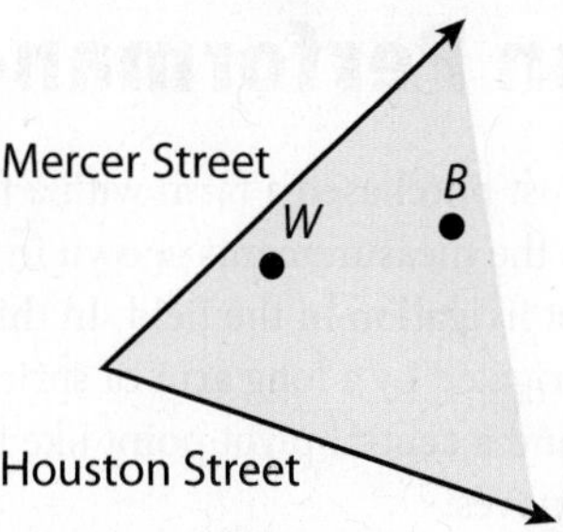

21. P is the incenter of $\triangle ABC$. Determine whether each statement is true or false.

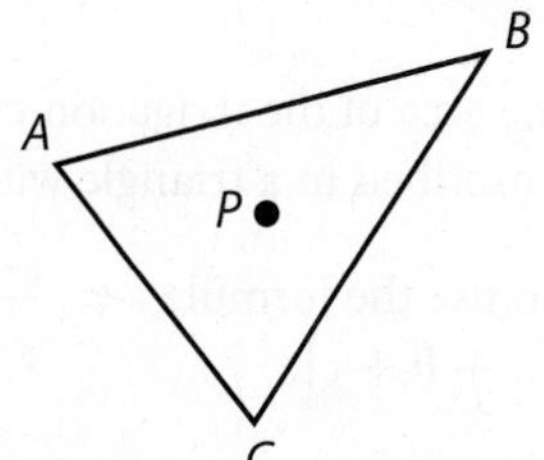

a. Point P must lie on the perpendicular bisector of $\overline{BC}$.

b. Point P must lie on the angle bisector of $\angle C$.

c. If AP is 23 mm long, then CP must be 23 mm long.

d. If the distance from point P to $\overline{AB}$ is x, then the distance from point P to $\overline{BC}$ must be x.

e. The perpendicular segment from point P to $\overline{AC}$ is longer than the perpendicular segment from point P to $\overline{BC}$.

H.O.T. Focus on Higher Order Thinking

22. What If? In the Explore, you constructed the angle bisector of acute $\angle ABC$ and found that if a point is on the bisector, then it is equidistant from the sides of the angle. Would you get the same results if $\angle ABC$ were a straight angle? Explain.

23. Explain the Error A student was asked to draw the incircle for $\triangle PQR$. He constructed angle bisectors as shown. Then he drew a circle through points J, K, and L. Describe the student's error.

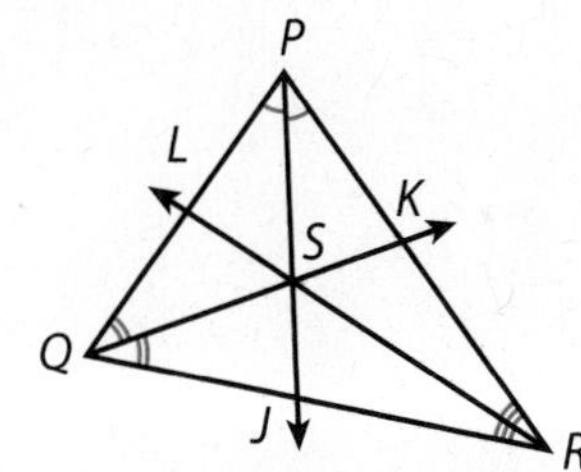

Lesson Performance Task

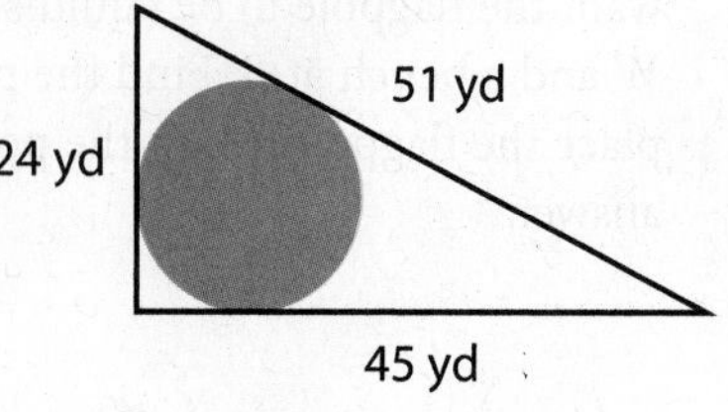

Teresa has just purchased a farm with a field shaped like a right triangle. The triangle has the measurements shown in the diagram. Teresa plans to install central pivot irrigation in the field. In this type of irrigation, a circular region of land is irrigated by a long arm of sprinklers—the radius of the circle—that rotates around a central pivot point like the hands of a clock, dispensing water as it moves.

a. Describe how she can find where to locate the pivot.

b. Find the area of the irrigation circle. To find the radius, r, of a circle inscribed in a triangle with sides of length a, b, and c, you can use the formula $r = \frac{\sqrt{k(k-a)(k-b)(k-c)}}{k}$, where $k = \frac{1}{2}(a+b+c)$.

c. About how much of the field will *not* be irrigated?

8.3 Medians and Altitudes of Triangles

Resource Locker

Essential Question: How can you find the balance point or *center of gravity* of a triangle?

Explore Finding the Balance Point of a Triangle

If a triangle were cut out of a sheet of wood or paper, the triangle could be balanced around exactly one point inside the triangle.

A **median** of a triangle is a segment whose endpoints are a vertex of a triangle and the midpoint of the opposite side.

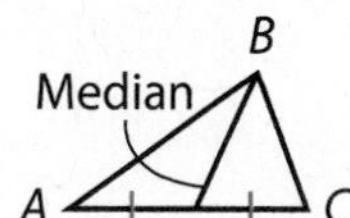

Every triangle has three distinct medians. You can use construction tools to show that the intersection of the three medians is the balance point of the triangle.

(A) Draw a large triangle on a sheet of construction paper. Label the vertices *A*, *B*, and *C*.

(B) Find the midpoint of the side opposite *A*, which is $\overline{BC}$. You may use a compass to find points equidistant to *B* and *C* and then draw the perpendicular bisector. Or you can use paper folding or a ruler. Write the label *X* for the midpoint.

(C) Draw a segment to connect *A* and *X*. The segment is one of the three medians of the triangle.

(D) Repeat Steps B and C, this time to draw the other two medians of the triangle. Write the label *Y* for the midpoint of the side opposite point *B*, and the label *Z* for the midpoint of the side opposite point *C*. Write the label *P* for the intersection of the three medians.

(E) Use a ruler to measure the lengths of each median and the subsegments defined by *P* in your triangle. Copy the table and record your measurements.

Median $\overline{AX}$:	$AX =$?	$AP =$?	$PX =$?
Median $\overline{BY}$:	$BY =$?	$BP =$?	$PY =$?
Median $\overline{CZ}$:	$CZ =$?	$CP =$?	$PZ =$?

Ⓕ What pattern do you observe in the measurements?

Ⓖ Let AX be the length of any median of a triangle from a vertex A, and let P be the intersection of the three medians. Write an equation to describe the relationship between AP and PX.

Ⓗ Let AX be the length of any median of a triangle from a vertex A, and let P be the intersection of the three medians. Write an equation to show the relationship between AX and AP.

Ⓘ Cut out the triangle, and then punch a very small hole through P. Stick a pencil point through the hole, and then try to spin the triangle around the pencil point. How easily does it spin? Repeat this step with another point in the triangle, and compare the results.

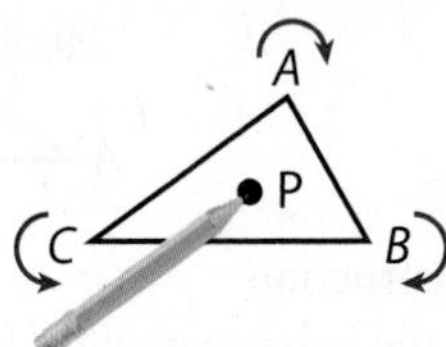

Reflect

1. Why is "balance point" a descriptive name for point P, the intersection of the three medians?
2. **Discussion** By definition, median $\overline{AX}$ intersects $\triangle ABC$ at points A and X. Could it intersect the triangle at a third point? Explain why or why not.

Explain 1 Using the Centroid Theorem

The intersection of the three medians of a triangle is the *centroid* of the triangle. The centroid is always inside the triangle and divides each median by the same ratio.

Centroid Theorem

The centroid theorem states that the **centroid** of a triangle is located $\frac{2}{3}$ of the distance from each vertex to the midpoint of the opposite side.

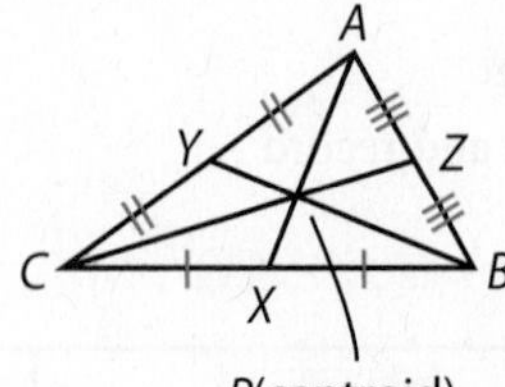

$AP = \frac{2}{3}AX$ $BP = \frac{2}{3}BY$ $CP = \frac{2}{3}CZ$

Example 1 **Use the Centroid Theorem to find the length.**

$AF = 9$, and $CE = 7.2$

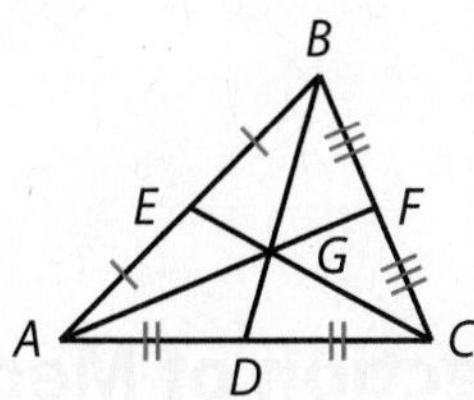

(A) AG

Centroid Theorem	$AG = \frac{2}{3}AF$
Substitute 9 for AF.	$AG = \frac{2}{3}(9)$
Simplify.	$AG = 6$

(B) GE

Centroid Theorem	$CG = \frac{2}{3}CE$
Substitute for the given value.	$CG = \frac{2}{3}(7.2)$
Simplify.	$CG = 4.8$
Segment Addition Postulate	$CG + GE = CE$
Subtraction Property of Equality	$GE = CE - CG$
Substitute for the value of CG.	$GE = 7.2 - 4.8$
Simplify.	$GE = 2.4$

Reflect

3. To find the centroid of a triangle, how many medians of the triangle must you construct?
4. Compare the lengths of $\overline{CG}$ and $\overline{GE}$ in Part B. What do you notice?
5. **Make a Conjecture** The three medians of $\triangle FGH$ divide the triangle into six smaller triangles. Is it possible for the six smaller triangles to be congruent to one another? If yes, under what conditions?

Your Turn

6. Vertex L is 8 units from the centroid of $\triangle LMN$. Find the length of the median that has one endpoint at L.
7. Let P be the centroid of $\triangle STU$, and let $\overline{SW}$ be a median of $\triangle STU$. If $SW = 18$, find SP and PW.

8. In $\triangle ABC$, the median $\overline{AD}$ is perpendicular to $\overline{BC}$. If $AD = 21$ feet, describe the position of the centroid of the triangle.

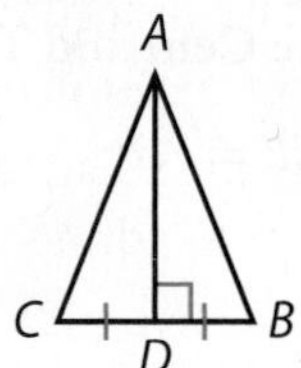

Explain 2 Finding the Intersection of Medians of a Triangle

When a triangle is plotted on the coordinate plane, the medians can be graphed and the location of the centroid can be identified.

Example 2 **Find the coordinates of the centroid of the triangle shown on the coordinate plane.**

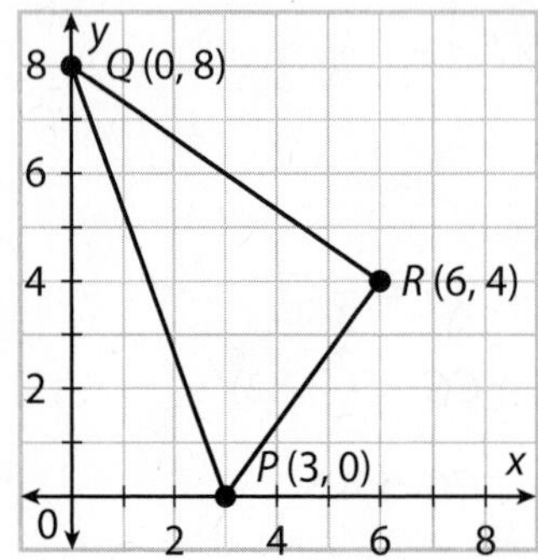

Analyze Information

What does the problem ask you to find? the centroid of the triangle
What information does the graph provide that will help you find the answer?
the coordinates of the three vertices of the triangle

Formulate a Plan

The centroid is the intersection of the medians of the triangle. Begin by calculating the midpoint of one side of the triangle. Then draw a line to connect that point to a vertex. You need to draw only two medians to find the centroid.

Solve

Find and plot midpoints.

Let M be the midpoint of $\overline{QR}$.

$$M = \left(\frac{0+6}{2}, \frac{8+4}{2}\right) = (3, 6)$$

Let N be the midpoint of $\overline{QP}$.

$$N = \left(\frac{0+3}{2}, \frac{8+0}{2}\right) = (1.5, 4)$$

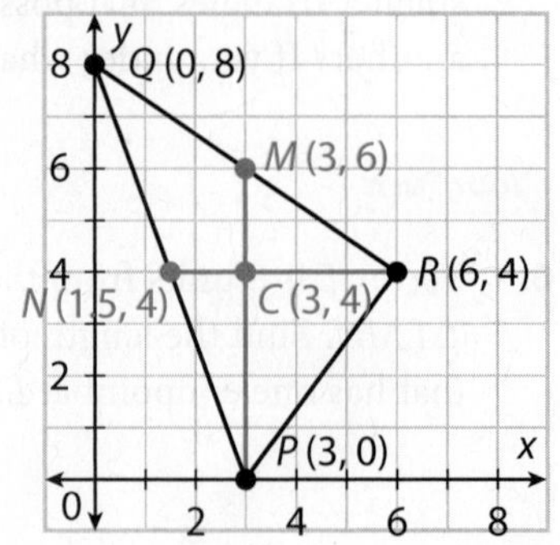

Draw the medians and identify equations.

Draw a segment to connect M and P.

The segment is a median and is described by the equation $x = 3$.

Draw a segment to connect N and R.

The segment is also a median and is described by the equation $y = 4$.

Find the centroid.

Identify the intersection of the two medians, which is (3, 4). Label it C.

Justify and Evaluate

The answer seems reasonable because it is positioned in the middle of the triangle. To check it, find the midpoint of $\overline{RP}$, which is (4.5, 2). Label the midpoint L, and draw the third median, which is $\overline{QL}$. The slope of the third median is $\frac{2-8}{4.5-0} = -\frac{4}{3}$, and the equation that describes it is $y = -\frac{4}{3}x + 8$. It intersects the other two medians at (3, 4), which confirms C as the centroid.

You can also apply the Centroid Theorem to check your answer.

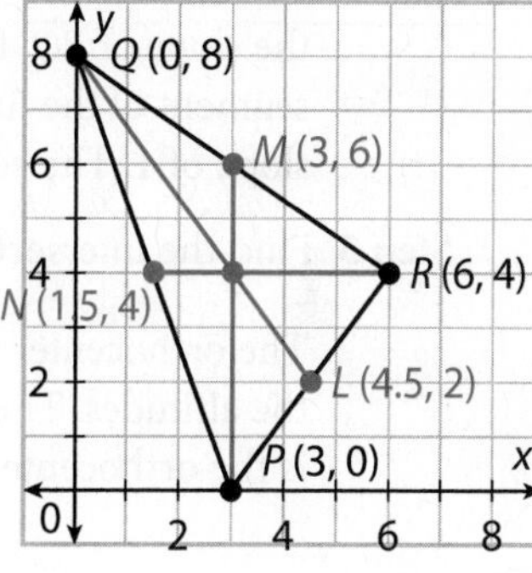

$RC = \frac{2}{3}RN$

$RN = 4.5$

$RC = 3$

Substitute values into the first equation:

$3 = \frac{2}{3}(4.5)$

The equality is true, which confirms the answer.

Your Turn

Find the centroid of the triangles with the given vertices. Show your work and check your answer.

9. $P(-1, 7), Q(9, 5), R(4, 3)$

10. $A(-6, 0), B(0, 12), C(6, 0)$

Explain 3 Finding the Orthocenter of a Triangle

Like the centroid, the *orthocenter* is a point that characterizes a triangle. This point involves the *altitudes* of the triangle rather than the medians.

An **altitude** of a triangle is a perpendicular segment from a vertex to the line containing the opposite side. Every triangle has three altitudes. An altitude can be inside, outside, or on the triangle.

In the diagram of $\triangle ABC$, the three altitudes are $\overline{AX}$, $\overline{BZ}$, and $\overline{CY}$. Notice that two of the altitudes are outside the triangle.

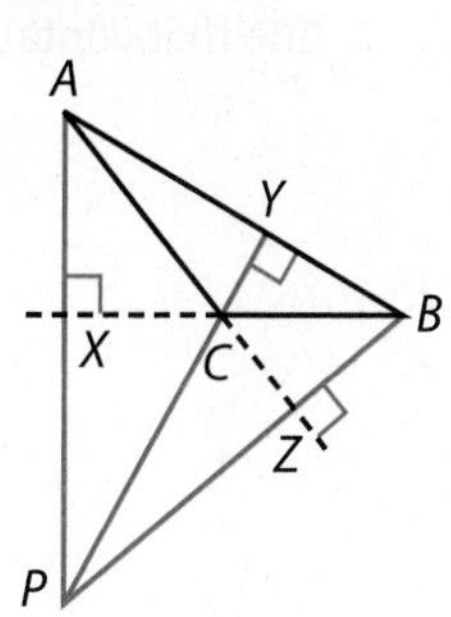

The length of an altitude is often called the height of a triangle.

The **orthocenter** of a triangle is the intersection (or point of concurrency) of the lines that contain the altitudes. Like the altitudes themselves, the orthocenter may be inside, outside, or on the triangle. Notice that the lines containing the altitudes are concurrent at P. The orthocenter of this triangle is P.

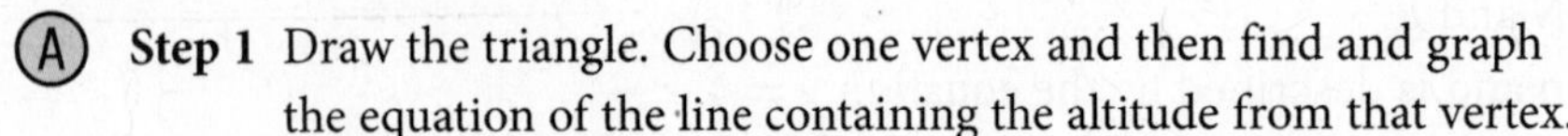

Example 3 **Find the orthocenter of the triangle by graphing the perpendicular lines to the sides of the triangle.**

Ⓐ **Step 1** Draw the triangle. Choose one vertex and then find and graph the equation of the line containing the altitude from that vertex.

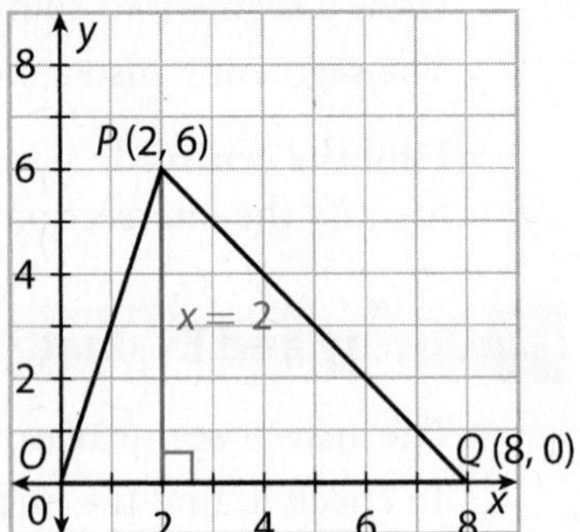

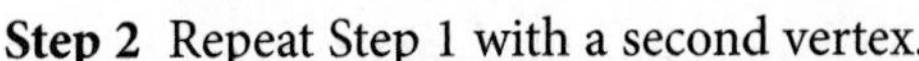

Triangle with vertices $O(0, 0)$, $P(2, 6)$, and $Q(8, 0)$

Choose P. The side opposite P is $\overline{OQ}$, which is horizontal, so the altitude is vertical. The altitude is a segment of the line $x = 2$.

Step 2 Repeat Step 1 with a second vertex.

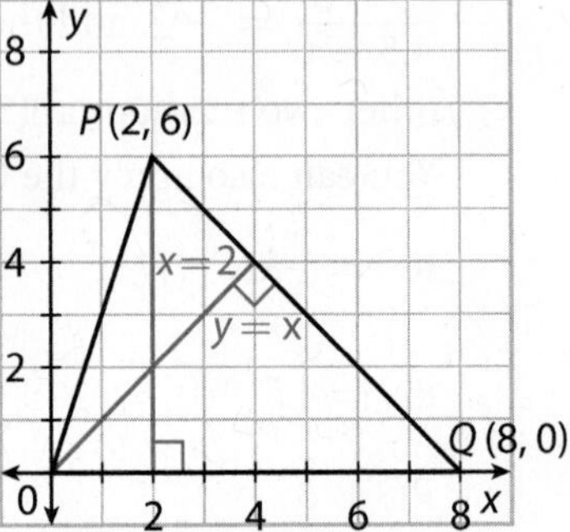

Choose O, the origin. The altitude that contains O is perpendicular to $\overline{PQ}$. Calculate the slope of $\overline{PQ}$ as $\frac{y_2 - y_1}{x_2 - x_1} = \frac{6 - 0}{2 - 8} = -1$.

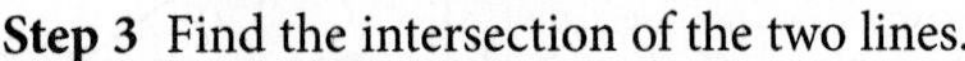

Since the slope of the altitude is the opposite reciprocal of the slope of $\overline{PQ}$, the slope of the altitude is 1. The altitude is a segment of the line that passes through the origin and has a slope of 1. The equation of the line is $y = x$.

Step 3 Find the intersection of the two lines.

The orthocenter is the intersection of the two lines that contain the altitudes. The lines $x = 2$ and $y = x$ intersect at $(2, 2)$, which is the orthocenter.

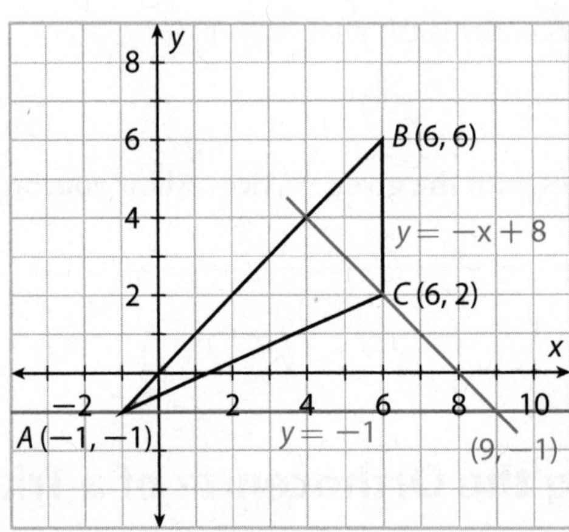

Step 1 Find the altitude that contains vertex A.

Because $\overline{BC}$ is vertical, the altitude through A is a horizontal segment. The equation of the line that contains the segment is $y = -1$. Draw this line.

Step 2 Find the altitude that contains vertex C.

First, calculate the slope of $\overline{AB}$. The slope is $\frac{6-(-1)}{6-(-1)}$, which equals 1.

The slope of the altitude to $\overline{AB}$ is the opposite reciprocal of 1, which is -1.

Use the point-slope form to find the equation of the line that has a slope of -1 and passes through C:
$y - 2 = -1(x - 6)$, which simplifies to $y = -x + 8$.

Draw this line.

Step 3 Find the intersection of the two lines.

$y = -1$

$y = -x + 8$

Substitute for y:

$-1 = -x + 8$

$x = 9$

The orthocenter is at $(9, -1)$.

Reflect

11. Could the orthocenter of a triangle be concurrent with one of its vertices? If yes, provide an example. If not, explain why not.

12. An altitude is defined to be a perpendicular segment from a vertex to the line containing the opposite side. Why are the words "the line containing" important in this definition?

Your Turn

Find the orthocenter for the triangles described by each set of vertices.

13. $Q(4, -3)$, $R(8, 5)$, $S(8, -8)$

14. $K(2, -2)$, $L(4, 6)$, $M(8, -2)$

Elaborate

15. Could the centroid of a triangle be coincident with the orthocenter? If so, give an example.

16. Describe or sketch an example in which the orthocenter P of $\triangle ABC$ is far away from the triangle. That is, PA, PB, and PC are each greater than the length of any side of the triangle.

17. A sculptor is assembling triangle-shaped pieces into a mobile. Describe circumstances when the sculptor would need to identify the centroid and orthocenter of each triangle.

18. **Essential Question Check-In** How can you find the centroid, or balance point, of a triangle?

Evaluate: Homework and Practice

- Online Homework
- Hints and Help
- Extra Practice

Use a compass and a straightedge to draw the medians and identify the centroid of the triangle. Label the centroid *P*.

1.

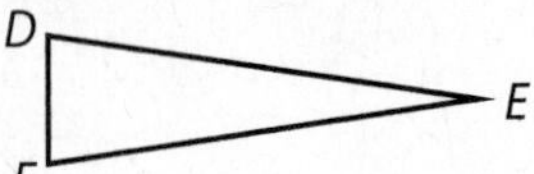

2.

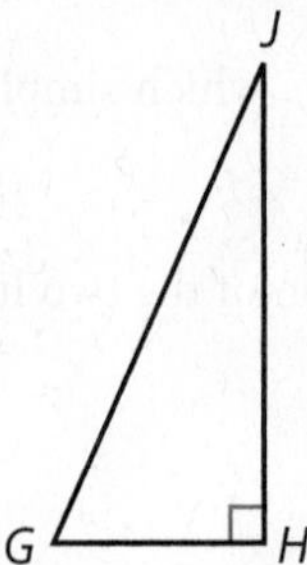

3. **Critique Reasoning** Paul draws $\triangle ABC$ and the medians from vertices A and B. He finds that the medians intersect at a point, and he labels this point X. Paul claims that point X lies outside $\triangle ABC$. Do you think this is possible? Explain.

4. For $\triangle ABC$ and its medians, match the segment on the left with its length.

A. $\overline{AM}$	a. ___?___ 1.5
B. $\overline{AP}$	b. ___?___ 2
C. $\overline{PM}$	c. ___?___ 2.5
D. $\overline{BK}$	d. ___?___ 3
E. $\overline{BP}$	e. ___?___ 4
F. $\overline{PK}$	f. ___?___ 4.5
G. $\overline{CL}$	g. ___?___ 5
H. $\overline{CP}$	h. ___?___ 6
I. $\overline{PL}$	i. ___?___ 7.5

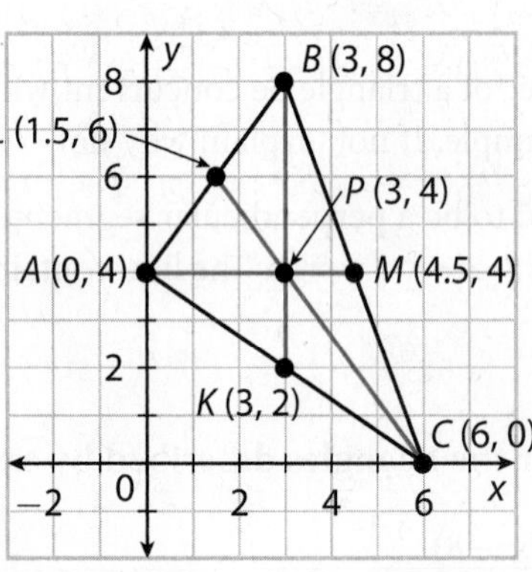

The diagram shows $\triangle FGH$, its medians, centroid P, and the lengths of some of the subsegments. Apply the Centroid Theorem to find other lengths.

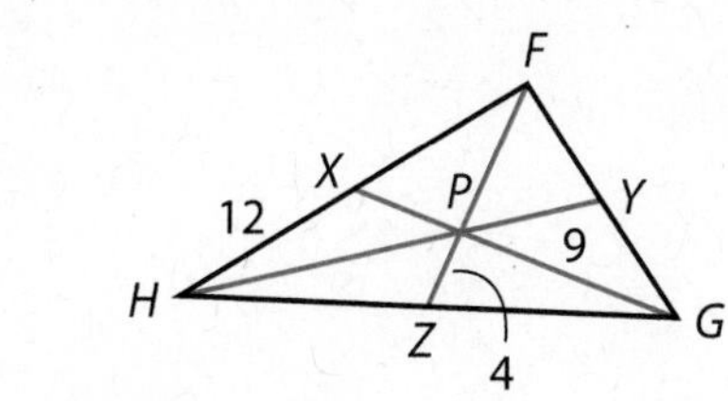

5. FH **6.** PF **7.** GX

The diagram shows $\triangle XYZ$, which has side lengths of 8 inches, 12 inches, and 15 inches. The diagram also shows the medians, centroid P, and the lengths of some of the subsegments. Apply the Centroid Theorem to find other lengths.

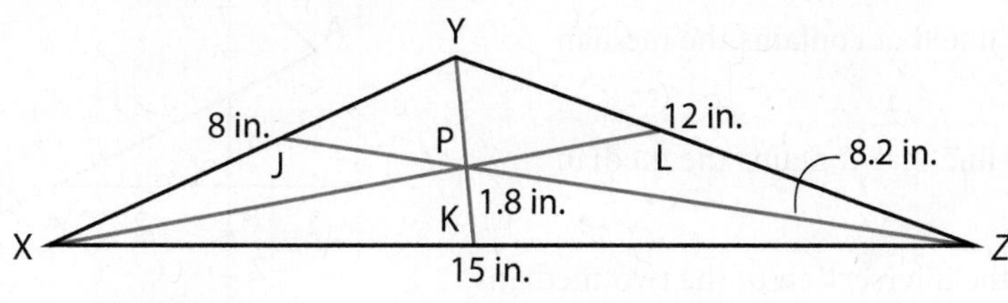

8. LY **9.** KY **10.** ZJ

11. The diagram shows $\triangle ABC$, its medians, centroid P, and the lengths of some of the subsegments as expressions of variables x and y. Apply the Centroid Theorem to solve for the variables and to find other lengths.

a. x

b. y

c. BP

d. BD

e. CP

f. PE

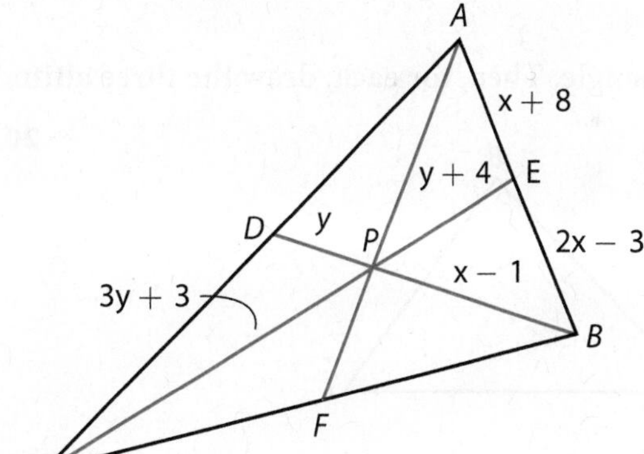

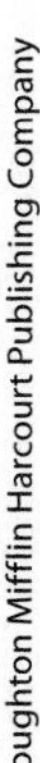

12. Copy $\triangle ABC$ on a coordinate grid. Then draw the medians from A to $\overline{BC}$ and from C to $\overline{AB}$.

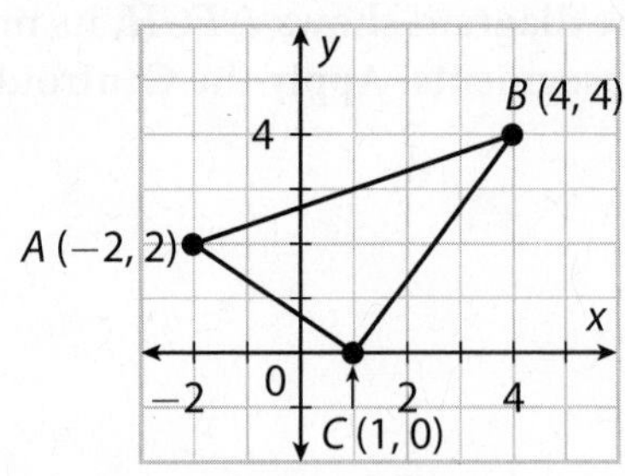

The vertices of a triangle are $A(-2, 3)$, $B(5, 10)$, and $C(12, -4)$. Find the coordinates or equations for each feature of the triangle.

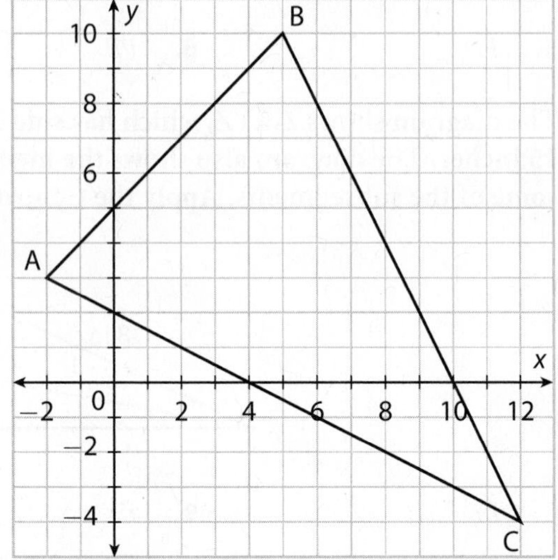

13. the coordinates of the midpoint of $\overline{AC}$

14. the coordinates of the midpoint of $\overline{BC}$

15. the equation of the line that contains the median through point B

16. the equation of the line that contains the median through point A

17. the coordinates of the intersection of the two medians

18. the coordinates of the center of balance of the triangle

Copy each triangle. Then, for each, draw the three altitudes and find the orthocenter. Label it P.

19.

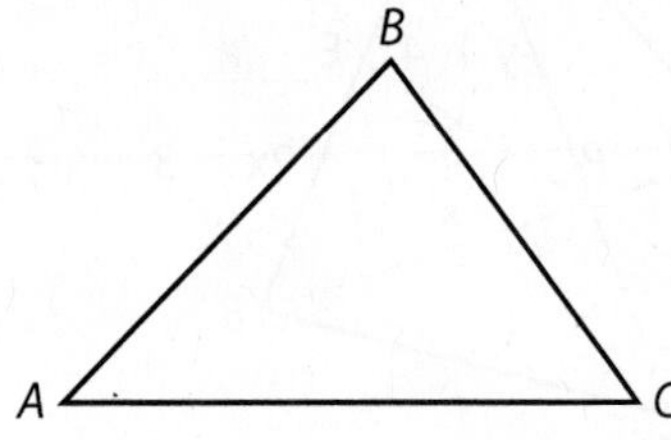

20.

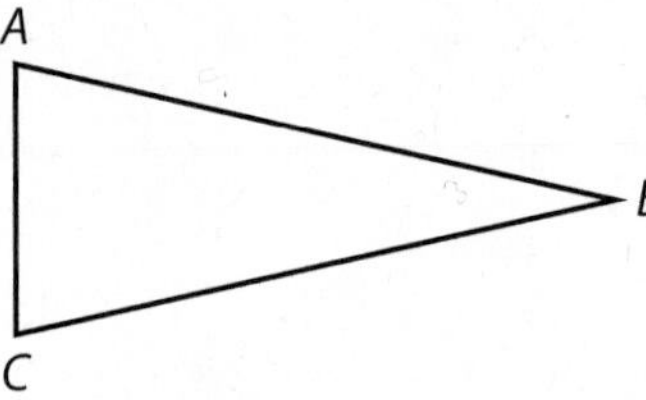

21.

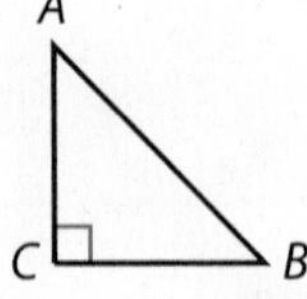

22.

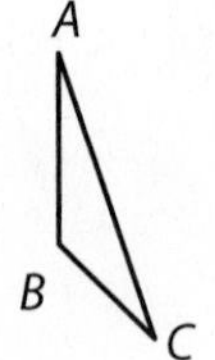

Find the orthocenter of each triangle with the given vertices.

23. $A(2, 2), B(2, 10), C(4, 2)$

24. $A(2, 5), B(10, -3), C(4, 5)$

25. $A(9, 3), B(9, -1), C(6, 0)$

H.O.T. Focus on Higher Order Thinking

26. **Draw Conclusions** Triangles *ABC*, *DBE*, and *FBG* are all symmetric about the *y*-axis. Show that all three triangles have the same centroid. What are the coordinates of the centroid?

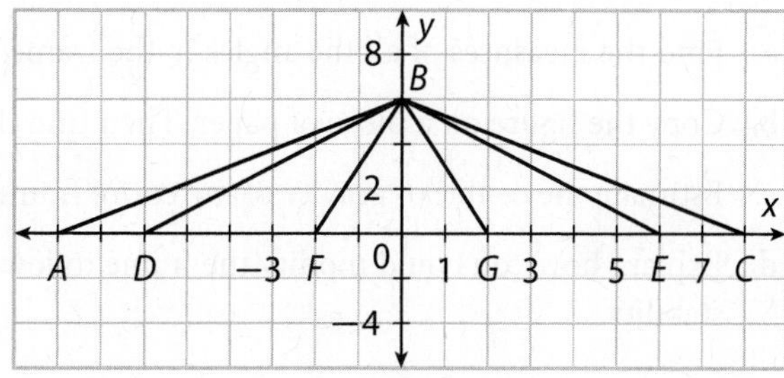

27. **Analyze Relationships** Triangle *ABC* is plotted on the coordinate plane. $\overline{AB}$ is horizontal, meaning it is parallel to the *x*-axis. $\overline{BC}$ is vertical, meaning it is parallel to the *y*-axis. Based on this information, can you determine the location of the orthocenter? Explain.

28. **What if?** The equilateral triangle shown here has its orthocenter and centroid on the *y*-axis. Suppose the triangle is stretched by moving *A* up the *y*-axis, while keeping *B* and *C* stationary. Describe and compare the changes to the centroid and the orthocenter of the triangle.

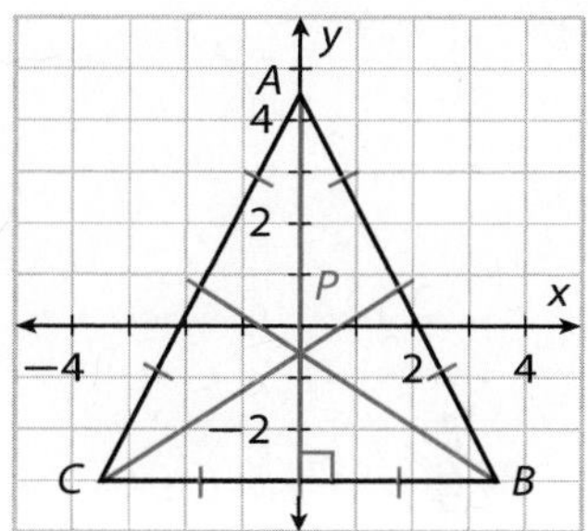

29. **What If?** The diagram shows right triangle *ABC* on the coordinate plane, and it shows the three medians and centroid *P*. How does the position of the centroid change when the triangle is stretched by moving *B* to the right along the *x*-axis, and keeping *A* and *C* stationary? How does the orthocenter change?

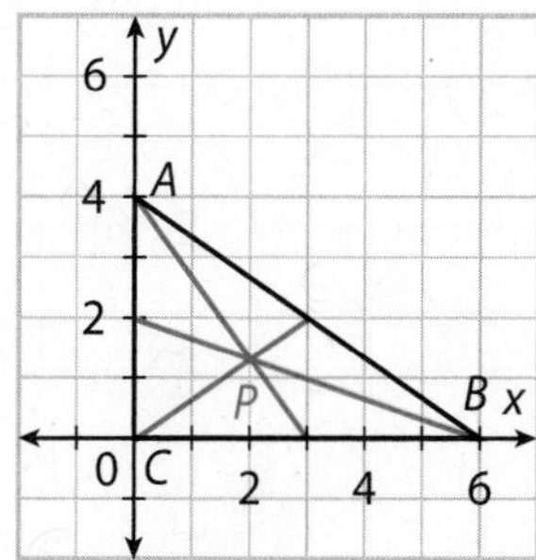

Lesson Performance Task

A bicycle frame consists of two adjacent triangles. The diagram shows the dimensions of the two triangles that make up the frame.

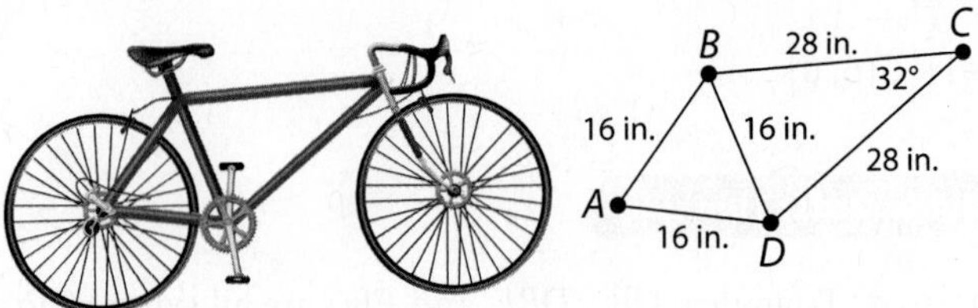

Answer these questions about the bicycle frame *ABCD*. Justify each of your answers.

a. Find the measures of all the angles in the frame.

b. Copy the figure on a piece of paper. Then find the center of gravity of each triangle.

c. Estimate the center of gravity of the entire frame and show it on your diagram.

d. Explain how you could modify the frame to lower its center of gravity and improve stability.

8.4 Midsegments of Triangles

Essential Question: How are the segments that join the midpoints of a triangle's sides related to the triangle's sides?

Resource Locker

Explore Investigating Midsegments of a Triangle

The **midsegment** of a triangle is a line segment that connects the midpoints of two sides of the triangle. Every triangle has three midsegments. Midsegments are often used to add rigidity to structures. In the support for the garden swing shown, the crossbar $\overline{DE}$ is a midsegment of $\triangle ABC$

You can use a compass and straightedge to construct the midsegments of a triangle.

(A) Sketch a scalene triangle and label the vertices A, B, and C.

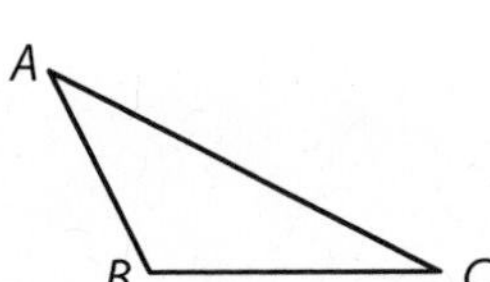

(B) Use a compass to find the midpoint of $\overline{AB}$. Label the midpoint D.

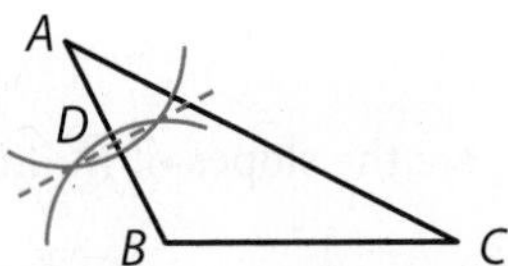

(C) Use a compass to find the midpoint of $\overline{AC}$. Label the midpoint E.

(D) Use a straightedge to draw $\overline{DE}$. $\overline{DE}$ is one of the midsegments of the triangle.

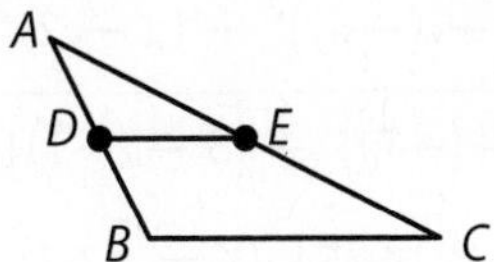

(E) Repeat the process to find the other two midsegments of $\triangle ABC$. You may want to label the midpoint of $\overline{BC}$ as F.

Reflect

1. Use a ruler to compare the length of $\overline{DE}$ to the length of $\overline{BC}$. What does this tell you about $\overline{DE}$ and $\overline{BC}$?

2. Use a protractor to compare $m\angle ADE$ and $m\angle ABC$. What does this tell you about $\overline{DE}$ and $\overline{BC}$? Explain.

3. Compare your results with your class. Then state a conjecture about a midsegment of a triangle.

Explain 1 Describing Midsegments on a Coordinate Grid

You can confirm your conjecture about midsegments using the formulas for the midpoint, slope, and distance.

Example 1 **Show that the given midsegment of the triangle is parallel to the third side of the triangle and is half as long as the third side.**

(A) The vertices of $\triangle GHI$ are $G(-7, -1)$, $H(-5, 5)$, and $I(1, 3)$. J is the midpoint of $\overline{GH}$, and K is the midpoint of $\overline{IH}$. Show that $\overline{JK} \parallel \overline{GI}$ and $JK = \frac{1}{2}GI$. Sketch $\overline{JK}$.

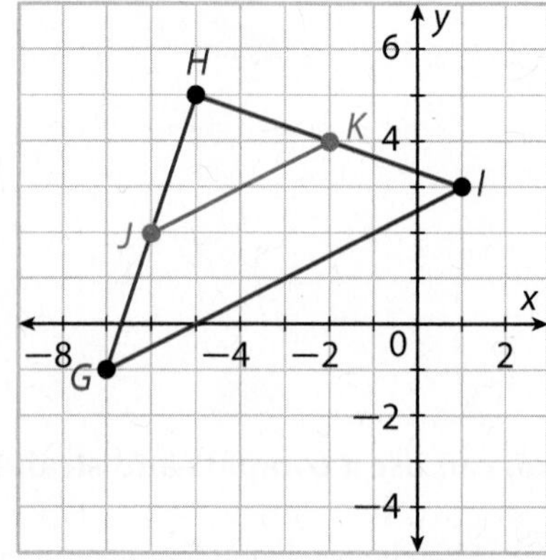

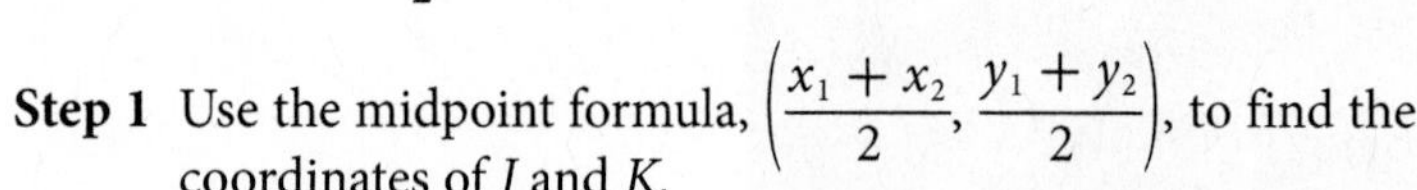

Step 1 Use the midpoint formula, $\left(\frac{x_1 + x_2}{2}, \frac{y_1 + y_2}{2}\right)$, to find the coordinates of J and K.

The midpoint of $\overline{GH}$ is $\left(\frac{-7-5}{2}, \frac{-1+5}{2}\right) = (-6, 2)$.

Graph and label this point J.

The midpoint of $\overline{IH}$ is $\left(\frac{-5+1}{2}, \frac{5+3}{2}\right) = (-2, 4)$. Graph and label this point K. Use a straightedge to draw $\overline{JK}$.

Step 2 Use $\left(\frac{y_2 - y_1}{x_2 - x_1}\right)$ to compare the slopes of $\overline{JK}$ and $\overline{GI}$.

Slope of $\overline{JK} = \frac{4-2}{-2-(-6)} = \frac{1}{2}$ Slope of $\overline{GI} = \frac{3-(-1)}{1-(-7)} = \frac{1}{2}$

Since the slopes are the same, $\overline{JK} \parallel \overline{GI}$.

Step 3 Use $\sqrt{(x_2 - x_1)^2 + (y_2 - y_1)^2}$ to compare the lengths of $\overline{JK}$ and $\overline{GI}$.

$JK = \sqrt{(-2-(-6))^2 + (4-2)^2} = \sqrt{20} = 2\sqrt{5}$

$GI = \sqrt{\left(1-(-7)\right)^2 + \left(3-(-1)\right)^2} = \sqrt{80} = 4\sqrt{5}$

Since $2\sqrt{5} = \frac{1}{2}\left(4\sqrt{5}\right)$, $JK = \frac{1}{2}GI$.

Ⓑ The vertices of $\triangle LMN$ are $L(2, 7)$, $M(10, 9)$, and $N(8, 1)$. P is the midpoint of $\overline{LM}$, and Q is the midpoint of $\overline{MN}$.

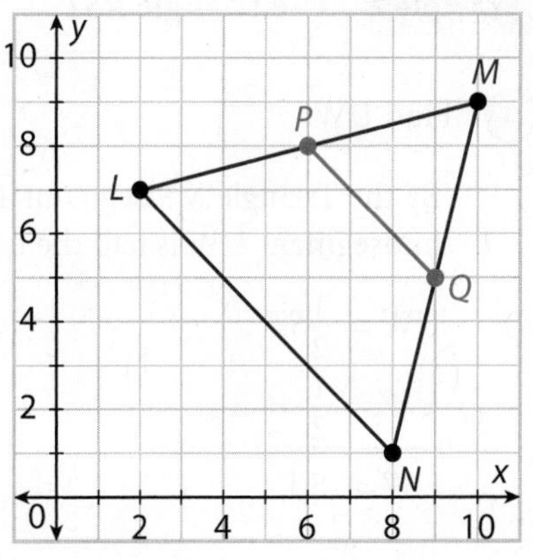

Show that $\overline{PQ} \parallel \overline{LN}$ and $PQ = \frac{1}{2}LN$. Sketch $\overline{PQ}$.

Step 1 The midpoint of $\overline{LM} = \left(\frac{2 + \boxed{10}}{2}, \frac{7 + \boxed{9}}{2}\right)$

$= \left(\boxed{6}, \boxed{8}\right)$. Graph and label this point P.

The midpoint of $\overline{NM} = \left(\frac{\boxed{8} + \boxed{10}}{2}, \frac{\boxed{1} + \boxed{9}}{2}\right)$

$= \left(\boxed{9}, \boxed{5}\right)$. Graph and label this point Q. Use a straightedge to draw $\overline{PQ}$.

Step 2 Slope of $\overline{PQ} = \frac{5 - 8}{9 - \boxed{6}} = \boxed{-1}$ Slope of $\overline{LN} = \frac{\boxed{1} - \boxed{7}}{\boxed{8} - \boxed{2}} = \boxed{-1}$

Since the slopes are the same, $\overline{PQ}$ and $\overline{LN}$ are parallel

Step 3 $PQ = \sqrt{\left(\boxed{9} - 6\right)^2 + (5 - 8)^2} = \sqrt{\boxed{9} + 9} = \sqrt{18} = 3\sqrt{2}$

$LN = \sqrt{\left(\boxed{8} - \boxed{2}\right)^2 + \left(\boxed{1} - \boxed{7}\right)^2} = \sqrt{\boxed{36} + \boxed{36}} = \sqrt{\boxed{72}} = 6\sqrt{\boxed{2}}$

Since $\boxed{3}\sqrt{\boxed{2}} = \frac{1}{2}\left(\boxed{6}\sqrt{\boxed{2}}\right)$, $\boxed{PQ} = \frac{1}{2}\boxed{LN}$.

The length of $\overline{PQ}$ is half the length of $\overline{LN}$.

Your Turn

4. The vertices of $\triangle XYZ$ are $X(3, 7)$, $Y(9, 11)$, and $Z(7, 1)$. U is the midpoint of $\overline{XY}$, and W is the midpoint of $\overline{XZ}$. Show that $\overline{UW} \parallel \overline{YZ}$ and $UW = \frac{1}{2}YZ$. Sketch $\triangle XYZ$ and $\overline{UW}$.

Explain 2 Using the Triangle Midsegment Theorem

The relationship you have been exploring is true for the three midsegments of every triangle.

Triangle Midsegment Theorem
The segment joining the midpoints of two sides of a triangle is parallel to the third side, and its length is half the length of that side.

You explored this theorem in Example 1 and will be proving it later in this course.

Example 2 Use triangle *RST*.

(A) Find *UW*.

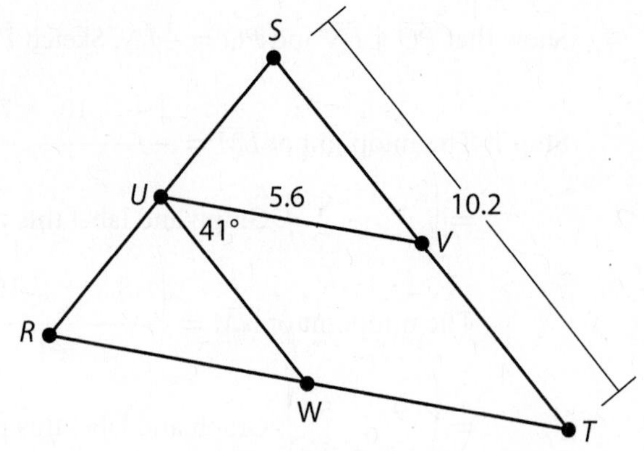

By the Triangle Midsegment Theorem, the length of midsegment $\overline{UW}$ is half the length of $\overline{ST}$.

$UW = \frac{1}{2}ST$

$UW = \frac{1}{2}(10.2)$

$UW = 5.1$

(B) Complete the reasoning to find m $\angle SVU$.

△Midsegment Thm.	$\overline{UW} \parallel \overline{ST}$
Alt. Int. Angles Thm.	m $\angle SVU$ = m $\angle VUW$
Substitute 41° for m$\angle VUW$	m $\angle SVU$ = 41°

Reflect

5. How do you know to which side of a triangle a midsegment is parallel?

Your Turn

6. Find *JL*, *PM*, and m $\angle MLK$.

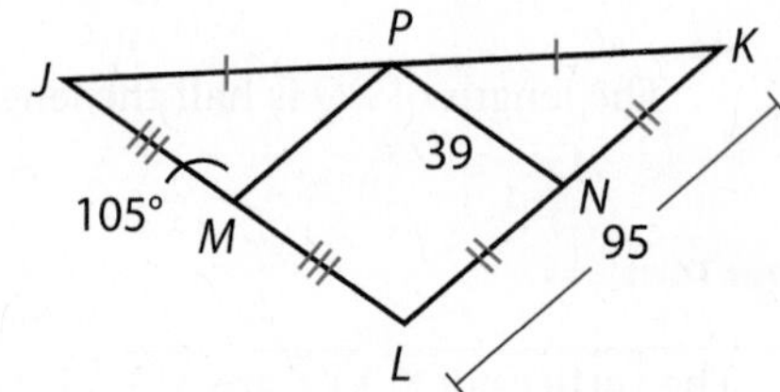

Elaborate

7. Discussion Explain why $\overline{XY}$ is NOT a midsegment of the triangle.

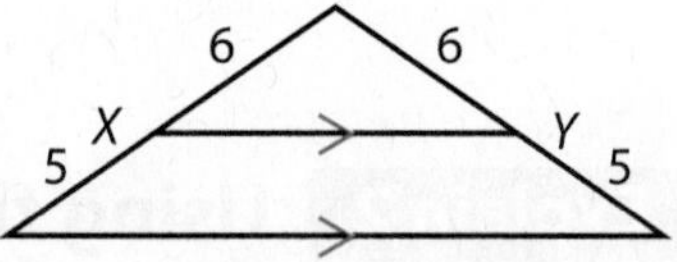

8. Essential Question Check-In Explain how the perimeter of △*DEF* compares to that of △*ABC*.

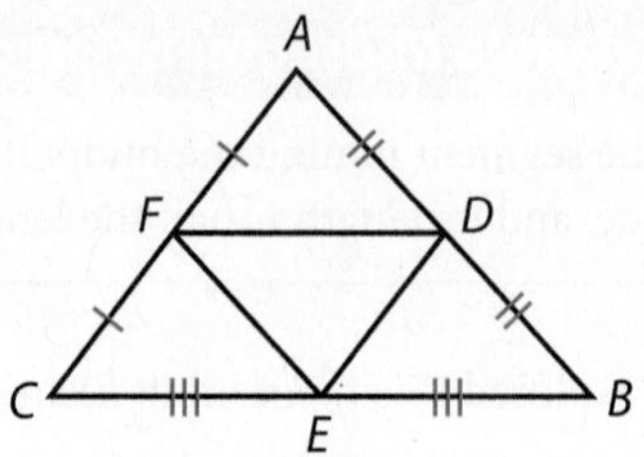

Evaluate: Homework and Practice

- Online Homework
- Hints and Help
- Extra Practice

1. Use a compass and a ruler or geometry software to construct an obtuse triangle. Label the vertices. Choose two sides and construct the midpoint of each side; then label and draw the midsegment. Describe the relationship between the length of the midsegment and the length of the third side.

2. The vertices of $\triangle WXY$ are $W(-4, 1)$, $X(0, -5)$, and $Y(4, -1)$. A is the midpoint of $\overline{WY}$, and B is the midpoint of $\overline{XY}$. Show that $\overline{AB} \parallel \overline{WX}$ and $AB = \frac{1}{2}WX$.

3. The vertices of $\triangle FGH$ are $F(-1, 1)$, $G(-5, 4)$, and $H(-5, -2)$. X is the midpoint of $\overline{FG}$, and Y is the midpoint of $\overline{FH}$. Show that $\overline{XY} \parallel \overline{GH}$ and $XY = \frac{1}{2}GH$.

4. One of the vertices of $\triangle PQR$ is $P(3, -2)$. The midpoint of $\overline{PQ}$ is $M(4, 0)$. The midpoint of $\overline{QR}$ is $N(7, 1)$. Show that $\overline{MN} \parallel \overline{PR}$ and $MN = \frac{1}{2}PR$.

5. One of the vertices of $\triangle ABC$ is $A(0, 0)$. The midpoint of $\overline{AC}$ is $J\left(\frac{3}{2}, 2\right)$. The midpoint of $\overline{BC}$ is $K(4, 2)$. Show that $\overline{JK} \parallel \overline{BA}$ and $JK = \frac{1}{2}BA$.

Find each measure.

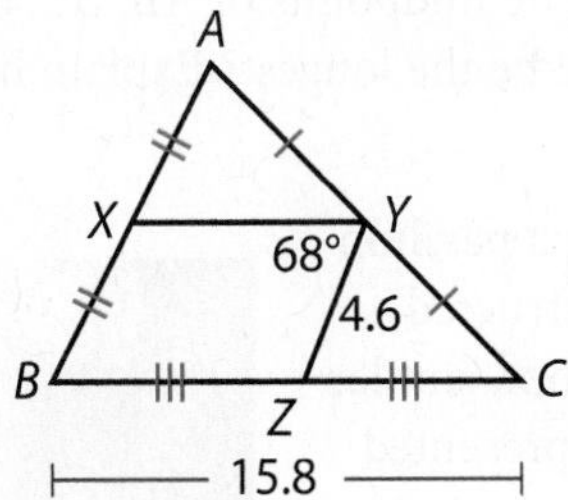

6. XY

7. BZ

8. AX

9. $m\angle YZC$

10. $m\angle BXY$

Algebra Find the value of n in each triangle.

11.

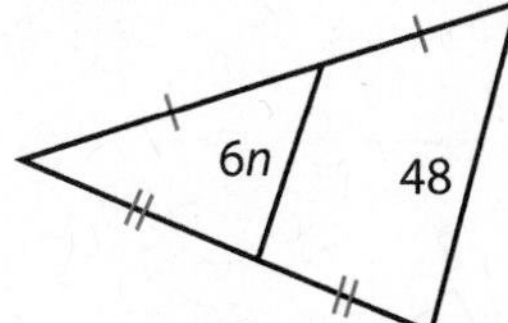

12.

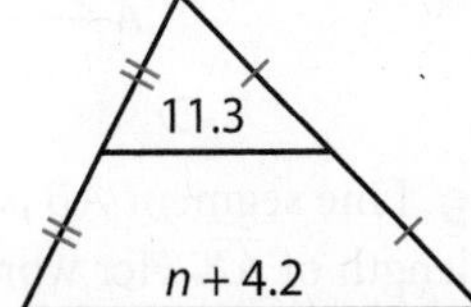

13.

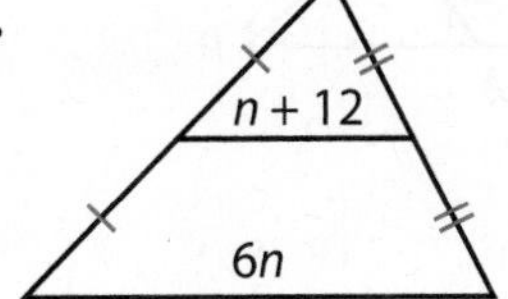

14.

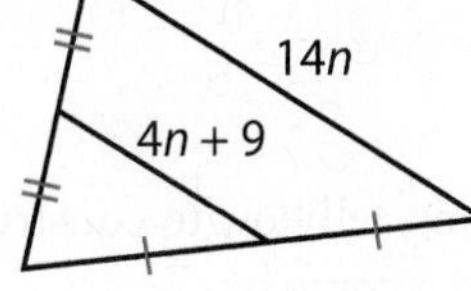

15. Line segment XY is a midsegment of $\triangle MNP$. Determine whether each of the following statements is true or false.

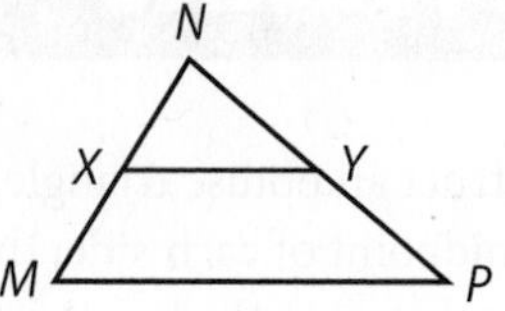

a. $MP = 2XY$

b. $MP = \frac{1}{2}XY$

c. $MX = XN$

d. $MX = \frac{1}{2}NX$

e. $NX = YN$

f. $XY = \frac{1}{2}MP$

16. What do you know about two of the midsegments in an isosceles triangle? Explain.

17. Suppose you know that the midsegments of a triangle are all 2 units long. What kind of triangle is it?

18. In $\triangle ABC$, $m\angle A = 80°$, $m\angle B = 60°$, $m\angle C = 40°$. The midpoints of $\overline{AB}$, $\overline{BC}$, and $\overline{AC}$ are D, E, and F, respectively. Which midsegment will be the longest? Explain how you know.

19. Draw Conclusions Carl's Construction is building a pavilion with an A-frame roof at the local park. Carl has constructed two triangular frames for the front and back of the roof, similar to $\triangle ABC$ in the diagram. The base of each frame, represented by $\overline{AC}$, is 36 feet long. He needs to insert a crossbar connecting the midpoints of $\overline{AB}$ and $\overline{BC}$, for each frame. He has 32 feet of timber left after constructing the front and back triangles. Is this enough to construct the crossbar for both the front and back frame? Explain.

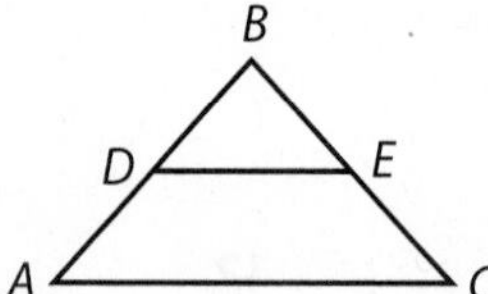

20. Critique Reasoning Line segment AB is a midsegment in $\triangle PQR$. Kayla calculated the length of $\overline{AB}$. Her work is shown below. Is her answer correct? If not, explain her error.

$$2(QR) = AB$$
$$2(25) = AB$$
$$50 = AB$$

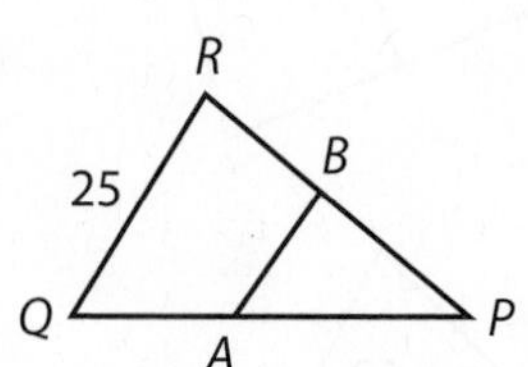

21. Using words or diagrams, tell how to construct a midsegment using only a straightedge and a compass.

H.O.T. Focus on Higher Order Thinking

22. Multi-Step A city park will be shaped like a right triangle, and there will be two pathways for pedestrians, shown by $\overline{VT}$ and $\overline{VW}$ in the diagram. The park planner only wrote two lengths on his sketch as shown. Based on the diagram, what will be the lengths of the two pathways?

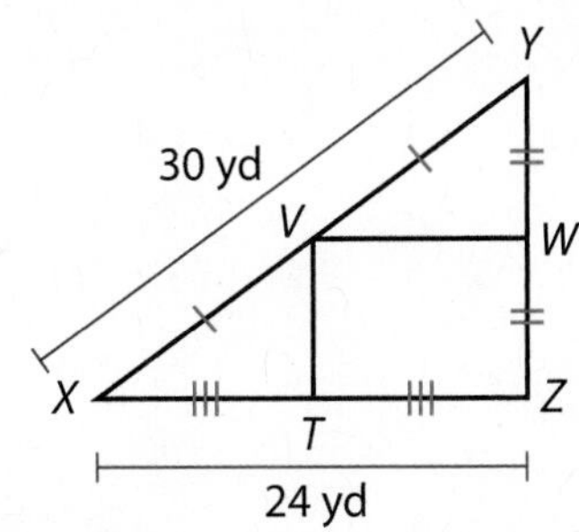

23. Communicate Mathematical Ideas $\triangle XYZ$ is the midsegment of $\triangle PQR$. Write a congruence statement involving all four of the smaller triangles. What is the relationship between the area of $\triangle XYZ$ and $\triangle PQR$?

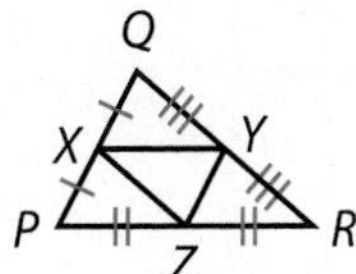

24. Copy the diagram shown. $\overline{AB}$ is a midsegment of $\triangle XYZ$. $\overline{CD}$ is a midsegment of $\triangle ABZ$.

a. What is the length of $\overline{AB}$? What is the ratio of AB to XY?

b. What is the length of $\overline{CD}$? What is the ratio of CD to XY?

c. Draw $\overline{EF}$ such that points E and F are $\frac{3}{4}$ the distance from point Z to points X and Y. What is the ratio of EF to XY? What is the length of $\overline{EF}$?

d. Make a conjecture about the length of non-midsegments when compared to the length of the third side.

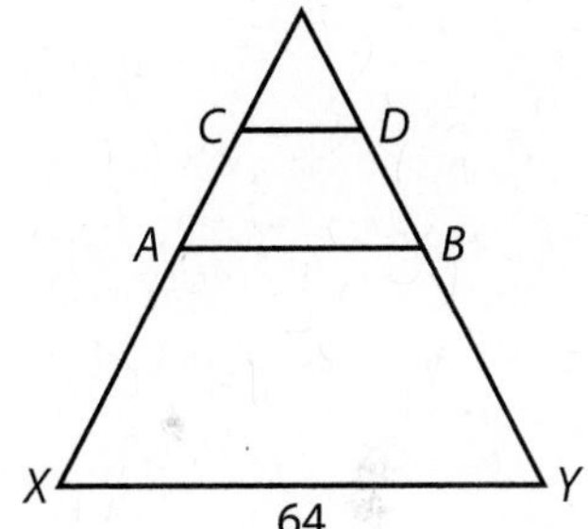

Lesson Performance Task

The figure shows part of a common roof design using very strong and stable triangular *trusses*. Points B, C, D, F, G, I, and J are midpoints of $\overline{AC}$, $\overline{AE}$, $\overline{CE}$, $\overline{GE}$, $\overline{HE}$, $\overline{AH}$, and $\overline{AI}$ respectively. What is the total length of all the stabilizing bars inside $\triangle AEH$? Explain how you found the answer.

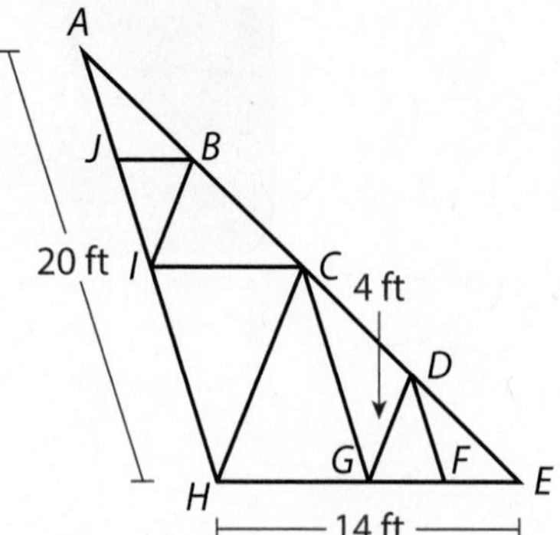

STUDY GUIDE REVIEW

Special Segments in Triangles

MODULE 8

Essential Question: How can you use special segments in triangles to solve real-world problems?

Key Vocabulary

altitude of a triangle *(altura de un triángulo)*
centroid of a triangle *(centroide de un triángulo)*
circumcenter of a triangle *(circuncentro de un triángulo)*
circumscribed circle *(círculo circunscrito)*
concurrent *(concurrente)*
distance from a point to a line *(distancia desde un punto hasta una línea)*
equidistant *(equidistante)*
incenter of a triangle *(incentro de un triángulo)*
inscribed circle *(círculo inscrito)*
median of a triangle *(mediana de un triángulo)*
midsegment of a triangle *(segment medio de un triángulo)*
orthocenter of a triangle *(ortocentro de un triángulo)*
point of concurrency *(punto de concurrencia)*

KEY EXAMPLE (Lesson 8.1)

Find the coordinates of the circumcenter of the triangle.

Coordinates: $A(-2, -2)$, $B(2, 3)$, $C(2, -2)$

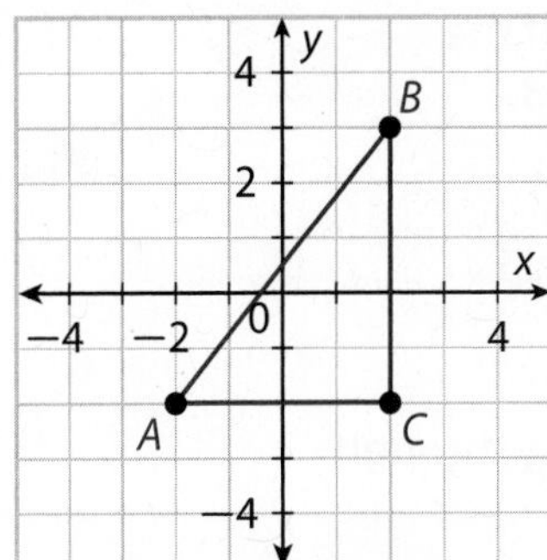

$M_{\overline{AC}} = \left(\frac{-2+2}{2}, \frac{-2+(-2)}{2}\right) = (0, -2)$ Midpoint of $\overline{AC}$

$\overline{AC}$ is horizontal, so the line perpendicular to it is vertical and passes through the midpoint. The equation is $x = 0$. Find the equation of the line perpendicular to $\overline{AC}$.

$M_{\overline{BC}} = \left(\frac{2+2}{2}, \frac{3+(-2)}{2}\right) = \left(2, \frac{1}{2}\right)$ Midpoint of $\overline{BC}$

$\overline{BC}$ is vertical, so the line perpendicular to it is horizontal and passes through the midpoint. The equation is $y = \frac{1}{2}$. Find the equation of the line perpendicular to $\overline{BC}$.

The coordinates of the circumcenter are $\left(0, \frac{1}{2}\right)$.

KEY EXAMPLE (Lesson 8.2)

$\overline{AP}$ and $\overline{CP}$ are angle bisectors of $\triangle ABC$, where P is the incenter of the triangle. The measure of $\angle BAC$ is 56°. The measure of $\angle BCA$ is 42°.

Find the measures of $\angle PAC$ and $\angle PCB$.

Since $\overline{AP}$ is an angle bisector of $\angle BAC$, the measures of $\angle PAC$ and $\angle PAB$ are equal. Since the measure of $\angle BAC$ is 56°, the measure of $\angle PAC$ is 28°.

Since $\overline{CP}$ is an angle bisector of $\angle BCA$, the measures of $\angle PCB$ and $\angle PCA$ are equal. Since the measure of $\angle BCA$ is 42°, the measure of $\angle PCB$ is 21°.

KEY EXAMPLE *(Lesson 8.3)*

Find the coordinates of the centroid of the triangle.

Coordinates: $A(-1, 2)$, $B(3, 6)$, $C(4, 2)$

Centroid:

$M_{\overline{AB}} = \left(\frac{-1+3}{2}, \frac{2+6}{2}\right) = (1, 4)$ — Midpoint of $\overline{AB}$

$m_{\overline{MC}} = \frac{2-4}{4-1} = -\frac{2}{3}$ — Slope of line passing through midpoint and C

$y - 4 = -\frac{2}{3}(x - 1)$

$y = -\frac{2}{3}x + \frac{14}{3}$ — Find the equation of the median from C to $\overline{AB}$.

$M_{\overline{AC}} = \left(\frac{-1+4}{2}, \frac{2+2}{2}\right) = \left(\frac{3}{2}, 2\right)$ — Midpoint of $\overline{AC}$

$m_{\overline{MB}} = \frac{6-2}{3-\frac{3}{2}} = \frac{8}{3}$ — Slope of line passing through midpoint and B

$y - 6 = \frac{8}{3}(x - 3)$

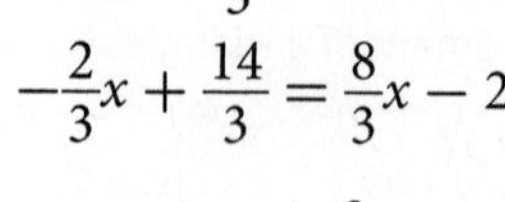

$y = \frac{8}{3}x - 2$ — Find the equation of the median $\overline{AC}$.

$-\frac{2}{3}x + \frac{14}{3} = \frac{8}{3}x - 2$ — Set the equations equal to each other to find the intersection.

$x = 2$

$y = \frac{8}{3}(2) - 2 = \frac{10}{3}$

The coordinates of the centroid are $\left(2, \frac{10}{3}\right)$.

KEY EXAMPLE *(Lesson 8.4)*

$\overline{DE}$ is a midsegment of $\triangle ABC$, and it is parallel to $\overline{AC}$. If the length of $\overline{BD}$ is 5 and the length of $\overline{EC}$ is 3, find the lengths of $\overline{DA}$ and $\overline{BE}$.

$\overline{DE}$ is a midsegment of $\triangle ABC$, so $\overline{BD}$ is half of $\overline{BA}$. $\overline{DA}$ is the other half of $\overline{BA}$. So, $DA = BD = 5$.

$\overline{DE}$ is a midsegment of $\triangle ABC$, so $\overline{EC}$ is half of $\overline{BC}$. $\overline{BE}$ is the other half of $\overline{BC}$. So, $EC = BE = 3$.

EXERCISES

Find the coordinates of the points. *(Lesson 8.1)*

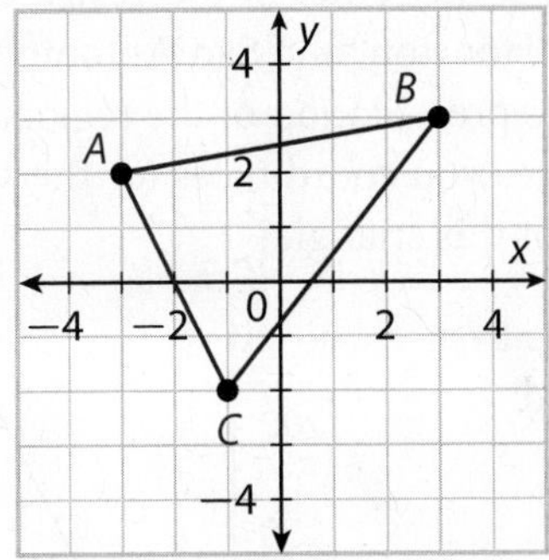

1. Circumcenter

$\overline{AP}$, $\overline{BP}$, and $\overline{CP}$ are angle bisectors of $\triangle ABC$, where P is the incenter of the triangle. The measure of $\angle BAC$ is 24°. The measure of $\angle BCA$ is 91°. Find the measures of the angles. *(Lesson 8.2)*

2. $\angle BAP$

3. $\angle ABP$

4. $\angle BCP$

Find the coordinates of the points. *(Lesson 8.3)*

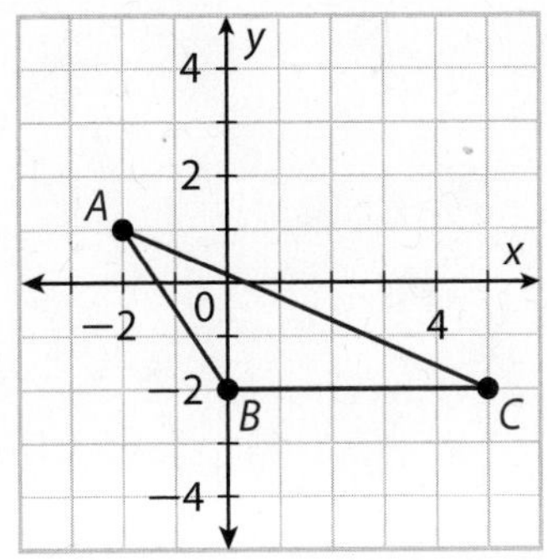

5. Centroid

6. Orthocenter

$\overline{DE}$, $\overline{DF}$, and $\overline{EF}$ are midsegments of $\triangle ABC$. Find the lengths of the segments. *(Lesson 8.4)*

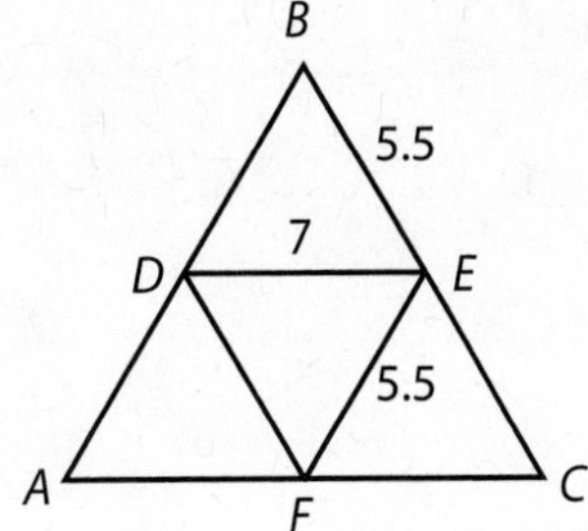

7. $\overline{BD}$

8. $\overline{EC}$

9. $\overline{AF}$

MODULE PERFORMANCE TASK

What's the Center of the Triangle?

The Texas Triangle Park in Bryan, Texas bills itself as being at the center of the Texas Triangle region. That is the region with the cities of Dallas, Houston, and San Antonio at the vertices of the triangle. The diagram shows a simple representation of the region with San Antonio located at the origin. The point B also gives you coordinates for the location of Bryan. So just how close is Bryan to the center of this triangle?

Before you tackle this problem, decide what you think is the best measure of the triangle's center in this context—the centroid, circumcenter, or orthocenter? Be prepared to support your decision.

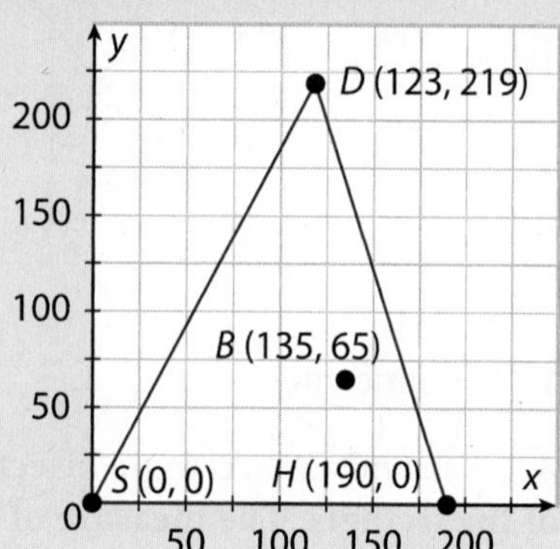

Start by listing the information you will need to solve the problem. Then complete the task. Be sure to write down all your data and assumptions. Then use graphs, numbers, words, or algebra to explain how you reached your conclusion.

Ready to Go On?

8.1–8.4 Special Segments in Triangles

- Online Homework
- Hints and Help
- Extra Practice

Segments $\overline{DE}$, $\overline{EF}$, and $\overline{DF}$ are midsegments of $\triangle ABC$ Find the lengths of the indicated segments. *(Lesson 8.1)*

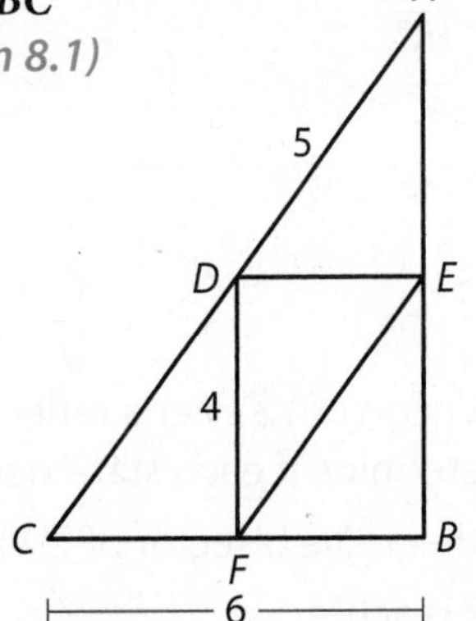

1. $\overline{AC}$

2. $\overline{CF}$

3. $\overline{DE}$

4. $\overline{AE}$

5. $\overline{AB}$

6. $\overline{EF}$

Locate centroids, circumcenters, and incenters. *(Lesson 8.2)*

7. Find the points of concurrency of $\triangle ABC$.

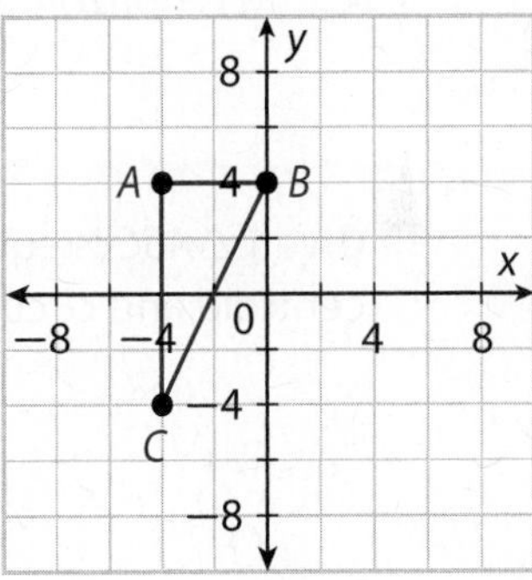

a. Determine the coordinates of the centroid of $\triangle ABC$.

b. Determine the coordinates of the circumcenter of $\triangle ABC$.

c. In what quadrant or on what axis does the incenter of $\triangle ABC$ lie?

ESSENTIAL QUESTION

8. Describe a triangle for which the centroid, circumcenter, incenter, and orthocenter are the same point. What features of this triangle cause these points to be concurrent and why?

MODULE 8
MIXED REVIEW

Assessment Readiness

1. Given $\triangle ABC$ and altitude $\overline{AH}$, decide whether each statement is necessarily true about $\triangle AHC$.

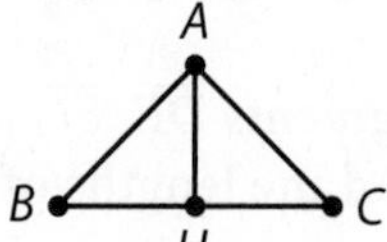

A. $\overline{AH} < \overline{HC}$

B. $\overline{AH} < \overline{AC}$

C. $\triangle AHC \cong \triangle AHB$

2. $\overline{YZ}$ is the image of $\overline{YX}$ after a reflection across line M. Determine if each statement is True or False.

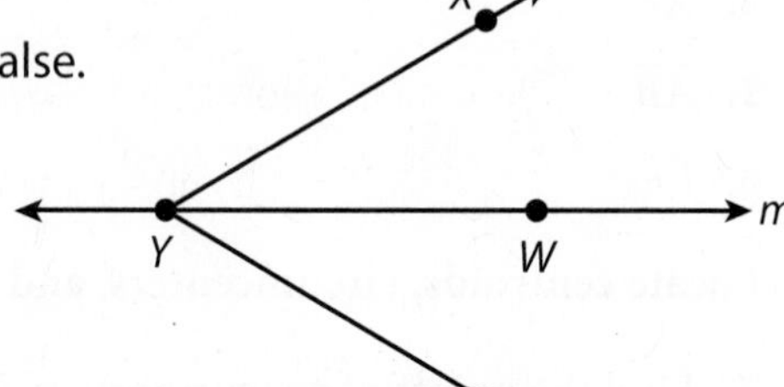

A. M is the angle bisector of $\angle XYZ$.

B. $\angle XYZ$ is acute.

C. M is horizontal.

3. Given $\triangle ABC$ is equilateral, what can be determined about its centroid and circumcenter?

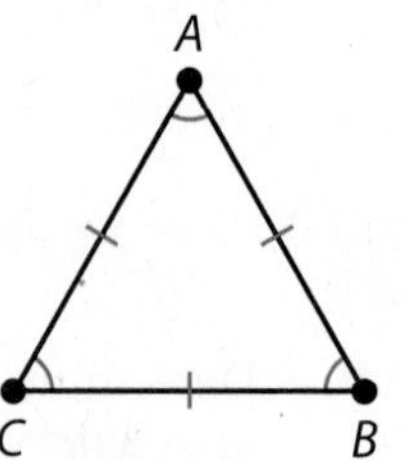

4. $\overline{DE}$, $\overline{EF}$, and $\overline{DF}$ are the midsegments of $\triangle ABC$. How does the perimeter of $\triangle DEF$ compare to the perimeter of $\triangle ABC$? Explain.

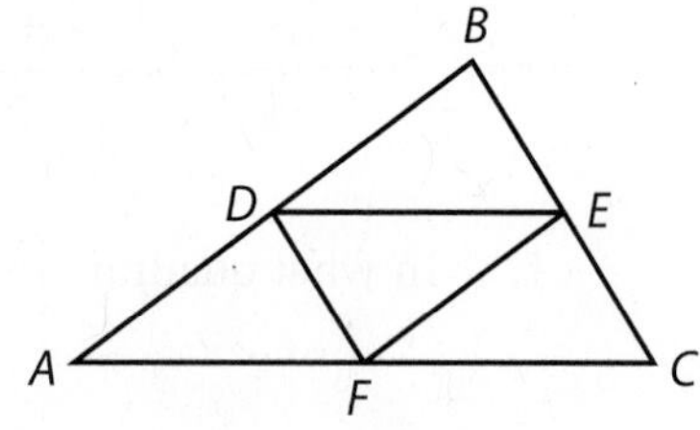

Personal Math Trainer

- Online Homework
- Hints and Help
- Extra Practice

1. Determine whether each pair of angles is a pair of vertical angles, a linear pair of angles, or neither.

   A. $\angle AFC$ and $\angle CFD$

   B. $\angle AFB$ and $\angle CFD$

   C. $\angle BFD$ and $\angle AFE$

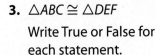

2. Does each transformation map a triangle in Quadrant II to Quadrant I?

   Write Yes or No for A–C.

   A. A rotation of 270°

   B. A translation along the vector $\langle -2, -2 \rangle$

   C. A reflection across the *y*-axis

3. 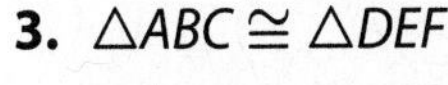

   $\triangle ABC \cong \triangle DEF$

   Write True or False for each statement.

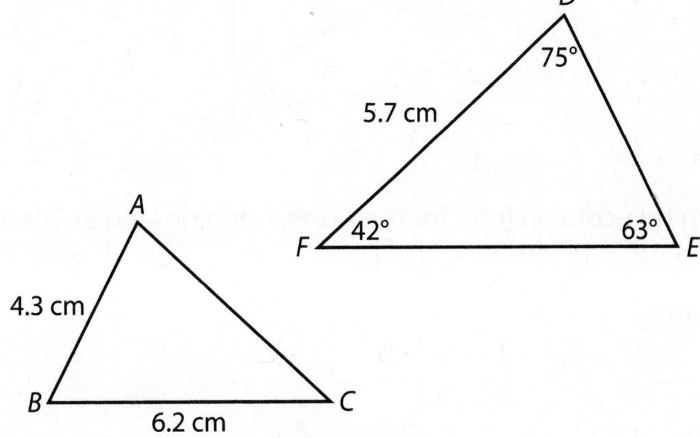

   A. $AC = 5.7$ cm

   B. $m\angle BAC = 75°$, $m\angle ABC = 63°$, and $DE = 4.3$ cm

   C. $m\angle ACB = 42°$, $m\angle ABC = 63°$, and $FE = 8.2$ cm

4. Triangle $\triangle ABC$ is in the second quadrant and translated along $(-3, 2)$ and reflected across the *y*-axis. Determine if the translation will be in the given quadrant. Write Yes or No for each statement.

   A. In the first quadrant after the first transformation

   B. In the second quadrant after the first transformation

   C. In the third quadrant after the second transformation

5. Given $\triangle ABC$ where $A(2, 3)$, $B(5, 8)$, $C(8, 3)$, $\overline{RS}$ is the midsegment parallel to $\overline{AC}$, $\overline{ST}$ is the midsegment parallel to $\overline{AB}$, and $\overline{RT}$ is the midsegment parallel to $\overline{BC}$. Determine if each statement is True or False.

   A. $\overline{ST} = 4$

   B. $\overline{RT} = 5$

   C. $\overline{RS} = 3$

6. Find each angle measure.

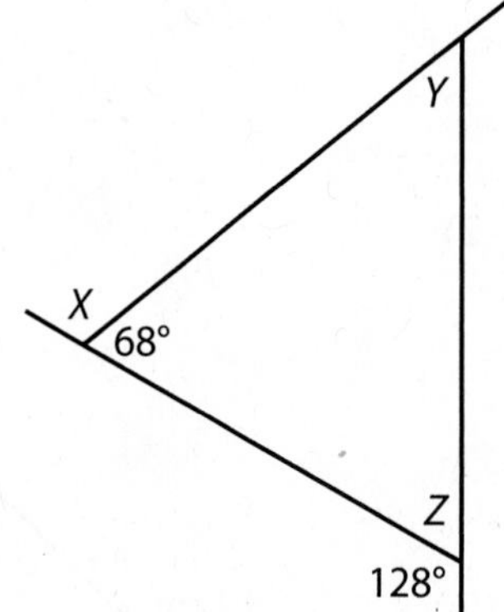

7. Write a proof in two-column form for the Corresponding Angles Theorem.

   Given: $\ell \parallel m$

   Prove: $m\angle 3 = m\angle 7$

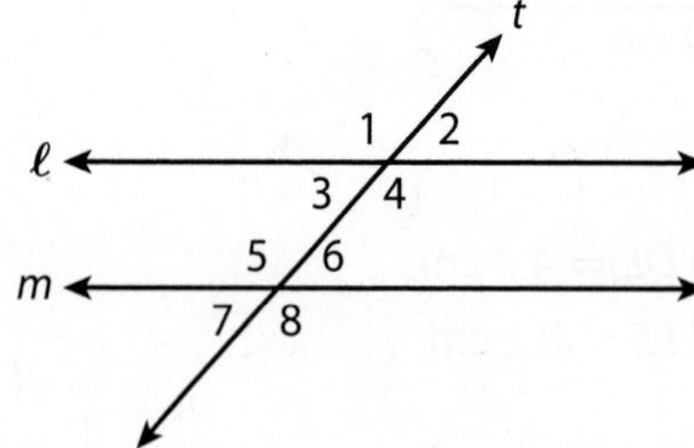

Performance Tasks

★ **8.** An employee is walking home from work and wants to take the long way to get more exercise. The diagram represents the two different routes, where A is the employee's work and B is the employee's home. Which route is longer and by how much? Show your work.

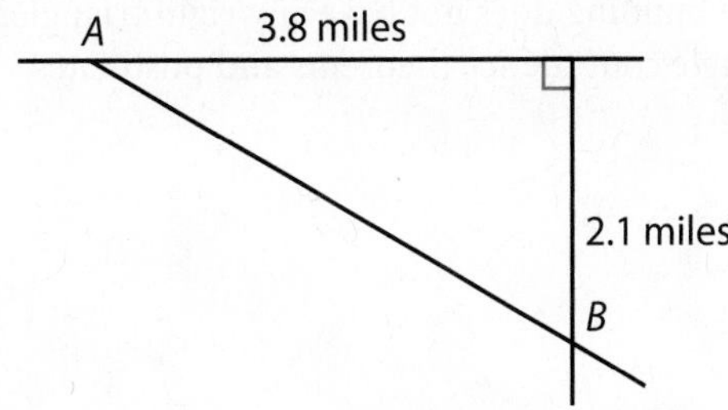

★★ **9.** A student was given the following triangle and asked to find the circumcenter. Find the point and explain the steps for finding it.

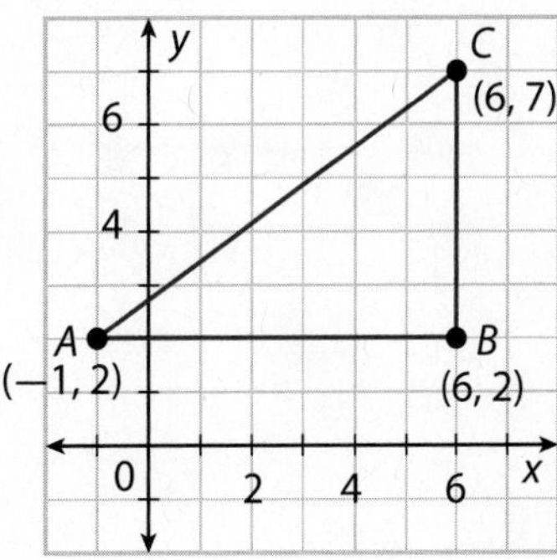

★★★**10.** While constructing a roof, a construction company built a triangle frame with a base 25 feet long. A cross bar needs to be inserted that connects the midpoints of both sides of the frame. Draw an image to represent the situation and then describe how much wood is needed for the crossbar. Assume the triangle is isosceles. Explain your answer.

MATH IN CAREERS

Architect An architect is writing the blueprints for a large triangular building to go in the middle of a city. The building needs to be congruent to a building that is already made, but the blueprints for the previous building were lost. What information will need to be known about each triangular face of the building in order to make sure all faces are congruent, knowing the building does not have any right triangles? Explain each possibility using known triangle congruence theorems and postulates.

UNIT 3

Quadrilaterals and Coordinate Proof

MODULE 9

Properties of Quadrilaterals

MODULE 10

Coordinate Proof Using Slope and Distance

MATH IN CAREERS

Urban Planners Urban planners design the way a city looks and functions. Urban planners use math to determine the size and placement of crucial elements in cities, based on factors such as population, industry, and transportation.

If you're interested in a career as an urban planner, you should study these mathematical subjects:

- Algebra
- Geometry
- Calculus
- Statistics
- Linear Algebra

Research other careers that require the use of spatial analysis and statistics to understand real-world scenarios. See the related Career Activity at the end of this unit.

Visualize Vocabulary

Copy and complete the chart with the correct review words.

?	A formula that finds the distance between two points, written as $(x_2 - x_1)^2 + (y_2 - y_1)^2 = d^2$.
?	Two lines that lie in the same plane and never intersect.
?	A formula that finds the midpoint of a line segment, written as $M = \left(\frac{x_1 + x_2}{2}, \frac{y_1 + y_2}{2}\right)$.
?	A ratio that is used to determine how steep a line is.
?	When two lines intersect, four angles result. This refers to either pair of angles that are not adjacent to each other.

Review Words

✔ distance formula *(fórmula de la distancia)*

✔ midpoint formula *(fórmula de punto medio)*

✔ opposite angles *(ángulos opuestos)*

✔ parallel *(paralelo)*

✔ slope *(pendiente)*

Preview Words

composite figure *(figura compuesta)*

coordinate proof *(demostración coordenado)*

parallelogram *(paralelogramo)*

quadrilateral *(cuadrilátero)*

rhombus *(rombo)*

Understand Vocabulary

To become familiar with some of the vocabulary terms in the unit, consider the following. You may refer to the module, the glossary, or a dictionary.

1. A __?__ is a quadrilateral with four congruent sides.

2. A __?__ is made up of simple shapes, such as triangles and quadrilaterals.

3. A __?__ is any quadrilateral whose opposite sides are parallel.

Active Reading

Before beginning the unit, create a booklet to help you organize what you learn. Write a main topic from each module on each page of the booklet. Write details of each main topic on the appropriate page to create an outline of the module. The ability to reword and retell the details of a module will help in understanding complex materials.

Properties of Quadrilaterals

MODULE 9

Essential Question: How can you use properties of quadrilaterals to solve real-world problems?

REAL WORLD VIDEO
Check out how architects use properties of quadrilaterals to design unusual buildings, such as the National Gallery of Art in Washington, D.C., or the Seattle Central Library.

MODULE PERFORMANCE TASK PREVIEW

How Big Is That Face?

In this module, you will use the geometry of trapezoids and other quadrilaterals to solve a problem related to the external dimensions of the Seattle Central Library. Let's get started and explore this interesting "slant" on architecture!

Are YOU Ready?

Complete these exercises to review the skills you will need for this module.

Personal Math Trainer

- Online Homework
- Hints and Help
- Extra Practice

Congruent Figures

Example 1

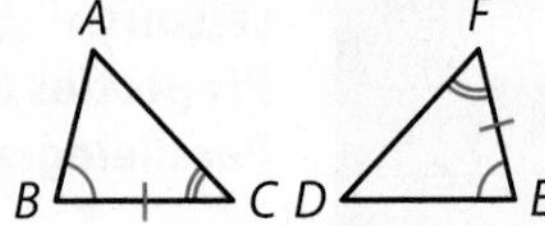

Determine if the pairs of figures are congruent and state the appropriate congruence theorem if applicable.

$\triangle ABC$ is congruent to $\triangle DEF$ via the ASA Congruence Theorem.

1. Determine if the figures are congruent and state the appropriate congruence theorem if applicable.

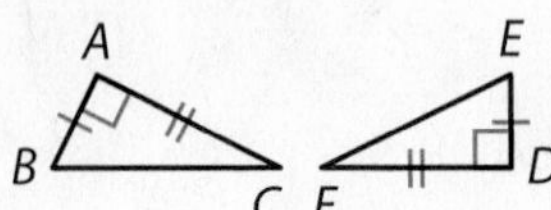

Example 2

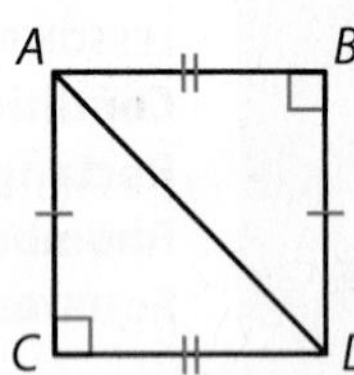

Determine whether the figure contains a pair of congruent triangles and state the appropriate congruence theorem if applicable.

Since $\overline{AD}$ is congruent to $\overline{DA}$ via the Reflexive Property of Congruence, $\triangle ABD$ is congruent to $\triangle DCA$ because of the SSS Congruence Theorem.

2. Determine whether the figure contains a pair of congruent triangles and state the appropriate congruence theorem if applicable.

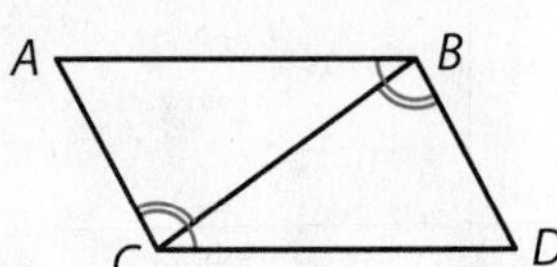

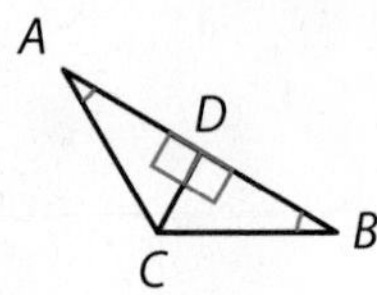

Parallelograms

Example 3

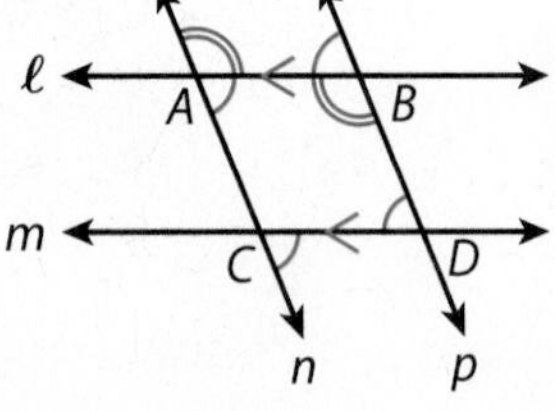

Determine if the figure is a parallelogram.

It is given that lines ℓ and m are parallel. Lines n and p are also parallel because of the Converse of the Corresponding Angles Theorem. Therefore, ABCD is a parallelogram.

3. Determine if the figure is a parallelogram.

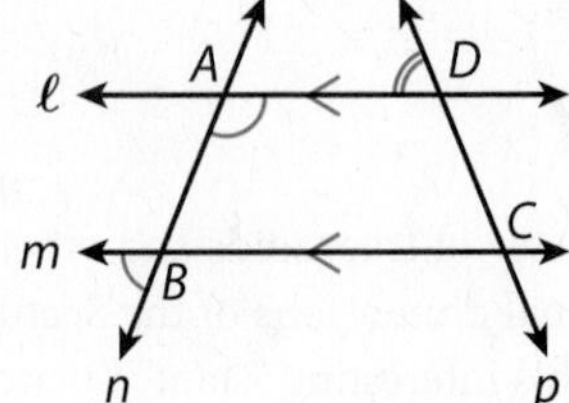

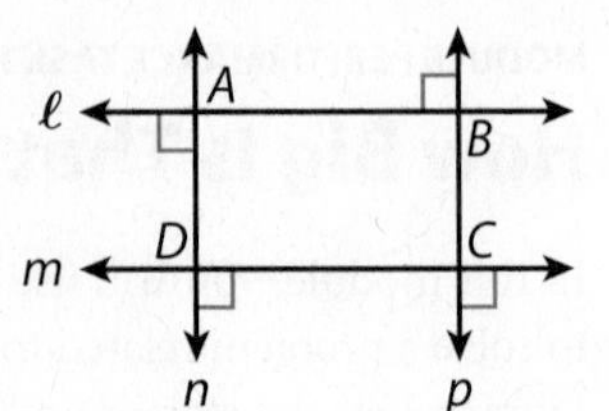

9.1 Properties of Parallelograms

Resource Locker

Essential Question: What can you conclude about the sides, angles, and diagonals of a parallelogram?

Explore Investigating Parallelograms

A **quadrilateral** is a polygon with four sides. A **parallelogram** is a quadrilateral that has two pairs of parallel sides. You can use geometry software to investigate properties of parallelograms.

(A) Draw a straight line. Then plot a point that is not on the line. Construct a line through the point that is parallel to the line. This gives you a pair of parallel lines.

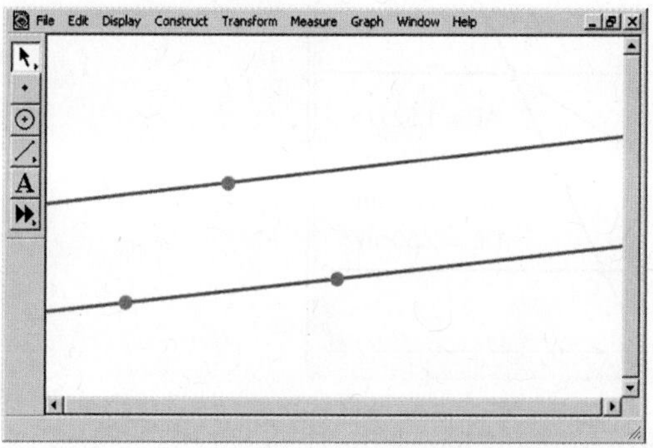

(B) Repeat Step A to construct a second pair of parallel lines that intersect those from Step A.

(C) The intersections of the parallel lines create a parallelogram. Plot points at these intersections. Label the points A, B, C, and D.

Identify the *opposite sides* and *opposite angles* of the parallelogram.

Opposite sides: ?

Opposite angles: ?

(D) Measure each angle of the parallelogram.

Measure the length of each side of the parallelogram. You can do this by measuring the distance between consecutive vertices.

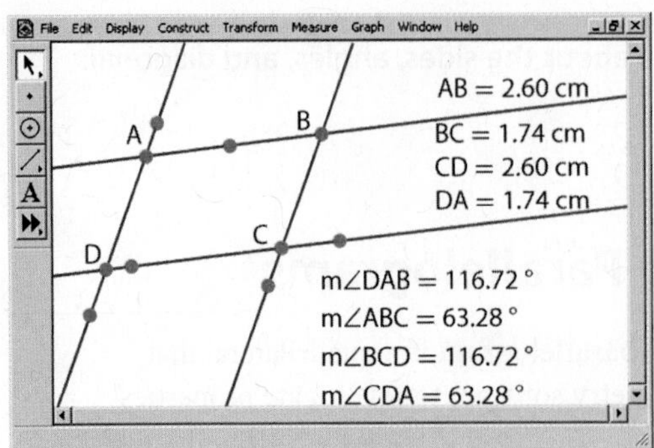

(E) Then drag the points and lines in your construction to change the shape of the parallelogram. As you do so, look for relationships in the measurements. Make a conjecture about the sides and angles of a parallelogram.

Conjecture: ?

(F) A segment that connects two nonconsecutive vertices of a polygon is a **diagonal**. Construct diagonals $\overline{AC}$ and $\overline{BD}$. Plot a point at the intersection of the diagonals and label it E.

(G) Measure the length of $\overline{AE}$, $\overline{BE}$, $\overline{CE}$, and $\overline{DE}$.

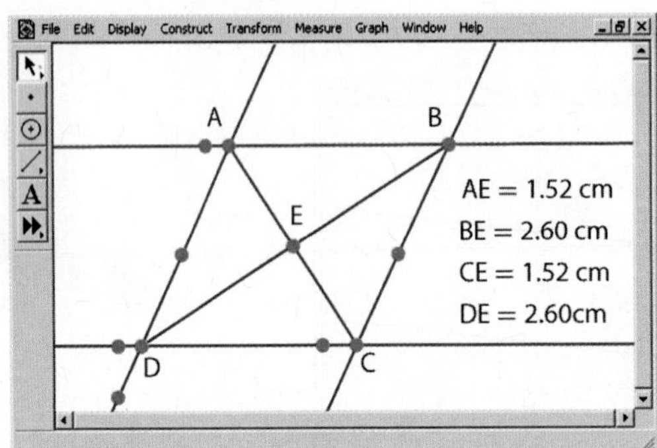

(H) Drag the points and lines in your construction to change the shape of the parallelogram. As you do so, look for relationships in the measurements in Step G. Make a conjecture about the diagonals of a parallelogram.

Conjecture: ?

Reflect

1. *Consecutive angles* are the angles at consecutive vertices, such as $\angle A$ and $\angle B$, or $\angle A$ and $\angle D$. Use your construction to make a conjecture about consecutive angles of a parallelogram.

Conjecture: ?

2. **Critique Reasoning** A student claims that the perimeter of $\triangle AEB$ in the construction is always equal to the perimeter of $\triangle CED$. Without doing any further measurements in your construction, explain whether or not you agree with the student's statement.

Explain 1 Proving Opposite Sides Are Congruent

The conjecture you made in the Explore about opposite sides of a parallelogram can be stated as a theorem. The proof involves drawing an *auxiliary line* in the figure.

Theorem
If a quadrilateral is a parallelogram, then its opposite sides are congruent.

Example 1 **Prove that the opposite sides of a parallelogram are congruent.**

Given: *ABCD* is a parallelogram.

Prove: $\overline{AB} \cong \overline{CD}$ and $\overline{AD} \cong \overline{CB}$

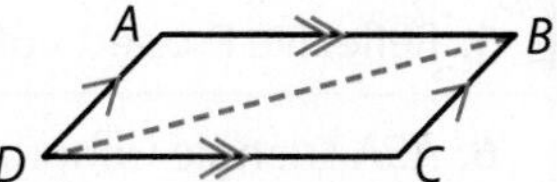

Statements	Reasons
1. *ABCD* is a parallelogram.	1. Given
2. Draw $\overline{DB}$.	2. Through any two points, there is exactly one line.
3. $\overline{AB} \parallel \overline{DC}$, $\overline{AD} \parallel \overline{BC}$	3. Definition of parallelogram
4. $\angle ADB \cong \angle CBD$ $\angle ABD \cong \angle CDB$	4. Alternate Interior Angles Theorem
5. $\overline{DB} \cong \overline{DB}$	5. Reflexive Property of Congruence
6. $\triangle ABD \cong \triangle CDB$	6. ASA Triangle Congruence Theorem
7. $\overline{AB} \cong \overline{CD}$ and $\overline{AD} \cong \overline{CB}$	7. CPCTC

Reflect

3. Explain how you can use the rotational symmetry of a parallelogram to give an argument that supports the above theorem.

Explain 2 Proving Opposite Angles Are Congruent

The conjecture from the Explore about opposite angles of a parallelogram can also be proven and stated as a theorem.

Theorem
If a quadrilateral is a parallelogram, then its opposite angles are congruent.

Example 2 **Prove that the opposite angles of a parallelogram are congruent.**

Given: *ABCD* is a parallelogram.

Prove: $\angle A \cong \angle C$ (A similar proof shows that $\angle B \cong \angle D$.)

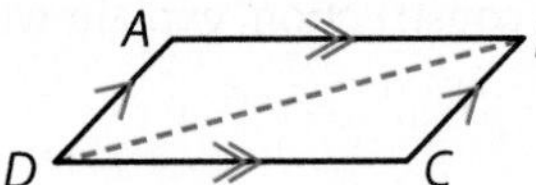

Statements	Reasons
1. *ABCD* is a parallelogram.	1. Given
2. Draw $\overline{DB}$.	2. Through any two points, there is exactly one line.
3. $\overline{AB} \parallel \overline{DC}$, $\overline{AD} \parallel \overline{BC}$	3. Definition of parallelogram
4. $\angle ADB \cong \angle CBD$, $\angle ABD \cong \angle CDB$	4. Alternate Interior Angles Theorem
5. $\overline{DB} \cong \overline{DB}$	5. Reflexive Property of Congruence
6. $\triangle ABD \cong \triangle CDB$	6. ASA Triangle Congruence Theorem
7. $\angle A \cong \angle C$	7. CPCTC

Reflect

4. Explain how the proof would change in order to prove $\angle B \cong \angle D$.

5. In Reflect 1, you noticed that the consecutive angles of a parallelogram are supplementary. This can be stated as the theorem, *If a quadrilateral is a parallelogram, then its consecutive angles are supplementary.*

Explain why this theorem is true.

Explain 3 Proving Diagonals Bisect Each Other

The conjecture from the Explore about diagonals of a parallelogram can also be proven and stated as a theorem. One proof is shown on the facing page.

Theorem

If a quadrilateral is a parallelogram, then its diagonals bisect each other.

Example 3 **Copy the diagram and complete the flow proof that the diagonals of a parallelogram bisect each other.**

Given: *ABCD* is a parallelogram.

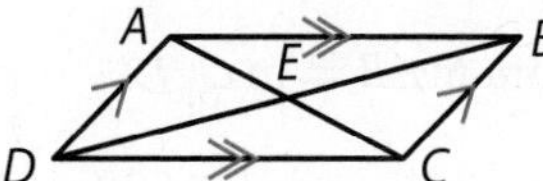

Prove: $\overline{AE} \cong \overline{CE}$ and $\overline{BE} \cong \overline{DE}$

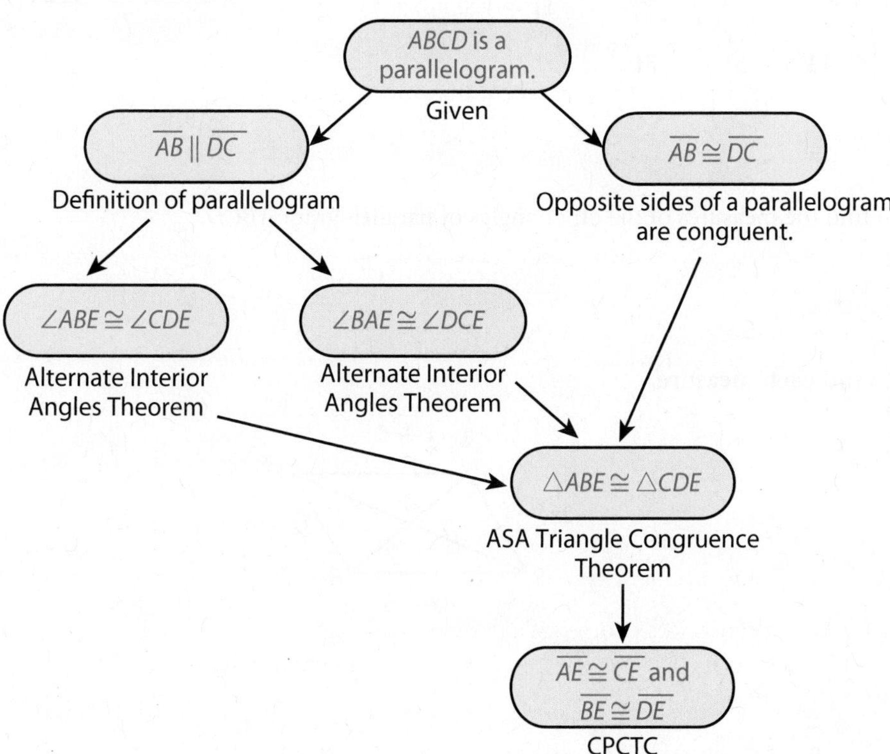

Reflect

6. **Discussion** Is it possible to prove the theorem using a different triangle congruence theorem? Explain.

Explain 4 Using Properties of Parallelograms

You can use the properties of parallelograms to find unknown lengths or angle measures in a figure.

Example 4 ***ABCD* is a parallelogram. Find each measure.**

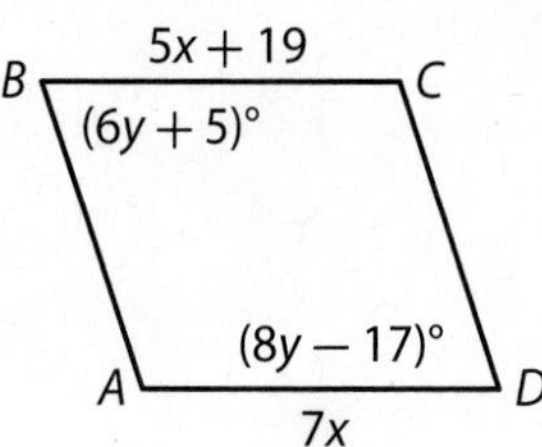

(A) *AD*

Use the fact that opposite sides of a parallelogram are congruent, so $\overline{AD} \cong \overline{CB}$ and therefore $AD = CB$.

Write an equation. $7x = 5x + 19$

Solve for *x*. $x = 9.5$

$AD = 7x = 7(9.5) = 66.5$

(B) m∠B

Use the fact that opposite angles of a parallelogram are congruent,

so $\angle B \cong \angle$ D and therefore $m\angle B = m\angle$ D .

Write an equation. $6y + 5 = 8y - 17$

Solve for y. $11 = y$

$m\angle B = (6y + 5)^\circ = \left(6(11) + 5\right)^\circ = 71^\circ$

B, C, A, D, 5x + 19, (6y + 5)°, (8y − 17)°, 7x

Reflect

7. Suppose you wanted to find the measures of the other angles of parallelogram *ABCD*. Explain your steps.

Your Turn

***PQRS* is a parallelogram. Find each measure.**

8. *QR*

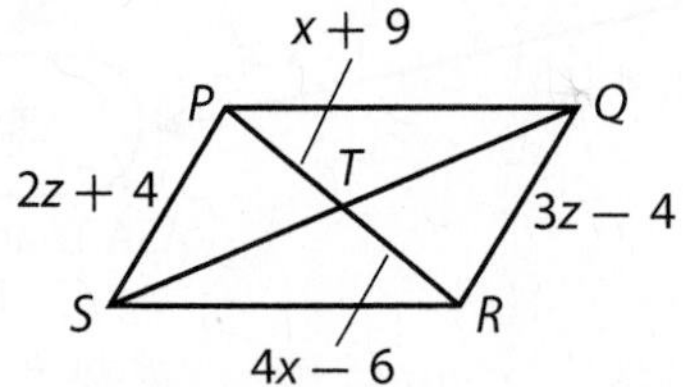

9. *PR*

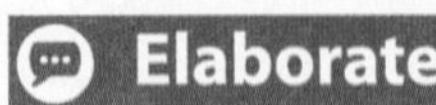

10. What do you need to know first in order to apply any of the theorems of this lesson?

11. In parallelogram *ABCD*, point *P* lies on $\overline{DC}$, as shown in the figure. Explain why it must be the case that $DC = 2AD$. Use what you know about base angles of an isosceles triangle.

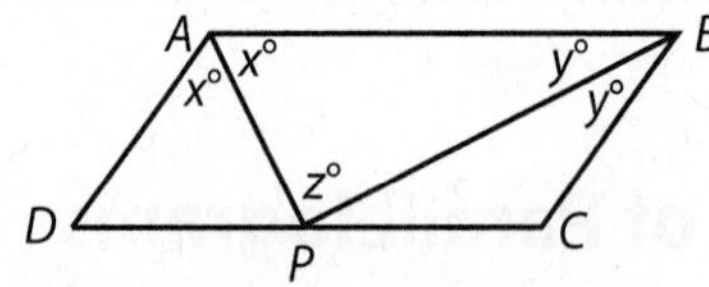

12. Essential Question Check-In *JKLM* is a parallelogram. Name all of the congruent segments and angles in the figure.

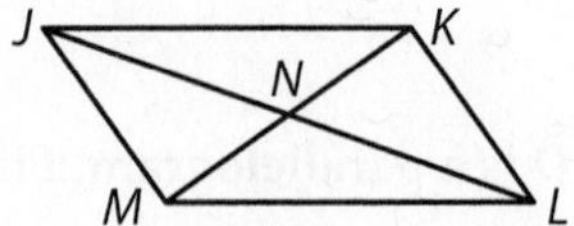

Evaluate: Homework and Practice

- Online Homework
- Hints and Help
- Extra Practice

1. Pablo traced along both edges of a ruler to draw two pairs of parallel lines, as shown. Explain the next steps he could take in order to make a conjecture about the diagonals of a parallelogram.

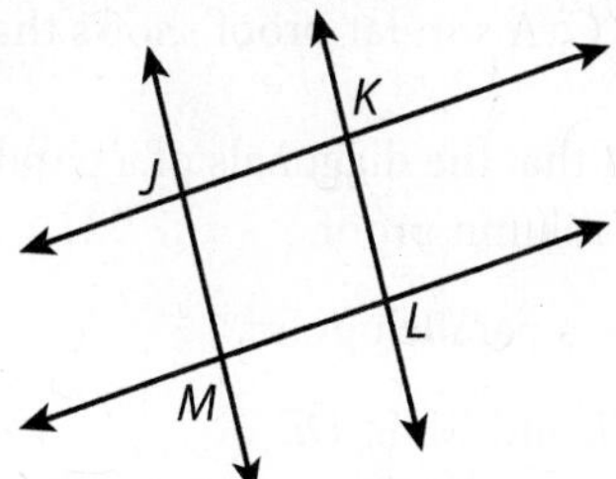

2. Sabina has tiles in the shape of a parallelogram. She labels the angles of each tile as $\angle A$, $\angle B$, $\angle C$, and $\angle D$. Then she arranges the tiles to make the pattern shown here and uses the pattern to make a conjecture about opposite angles of a parallelogram. What conjecture does she make? How does the pattern help her make the conjecture?

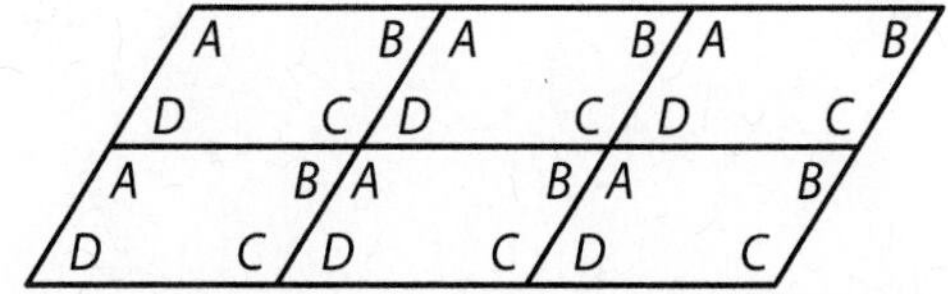

3. Copy the diagram. Then complete the flow proof that the opposite sides of a parallelogram are congruent.
Given: $ABCD$ is a parallelogram.
Prove: $\overline{AB} \cong \overline{CD}$ and $\overline{AD} \cong \overline{CB}$

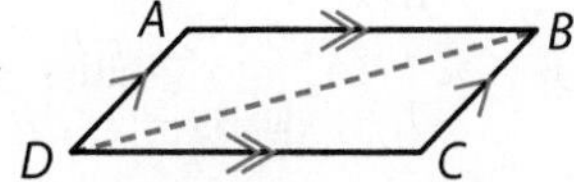

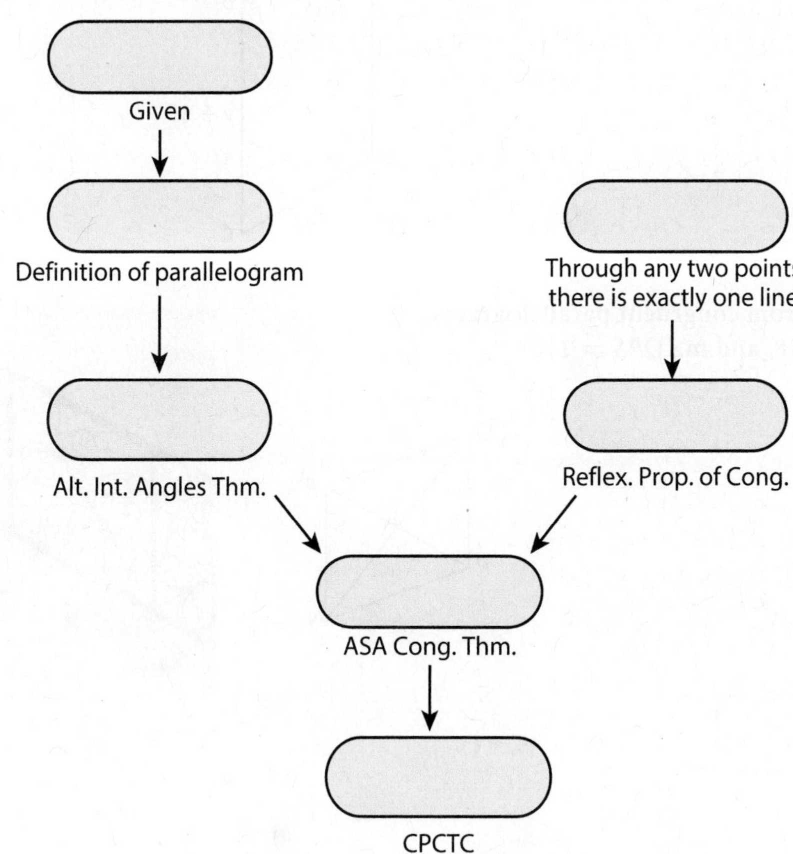

4. Write the proof that the opposite angles of a parallelogram are congruent as a paragraph proof.

Given: *ABCD* is a parallelogram.

Prove: $\angle A \cong \angle C$ (A similar proof shows that $\angle B \cong \angle D$.)

5. Write the proof that the diagonals of a parallelogram bisect each other as a two-column proof.

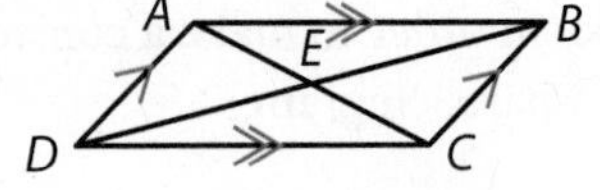

Given: *ABCD* is a parallelogram.

Prove: $\overline{AE} \cong \overline{CE}$ and $\overline{BE} \cong \overline{DE}$

***EFGH* is a parallelogram. Find each measure.**

6. *FG*

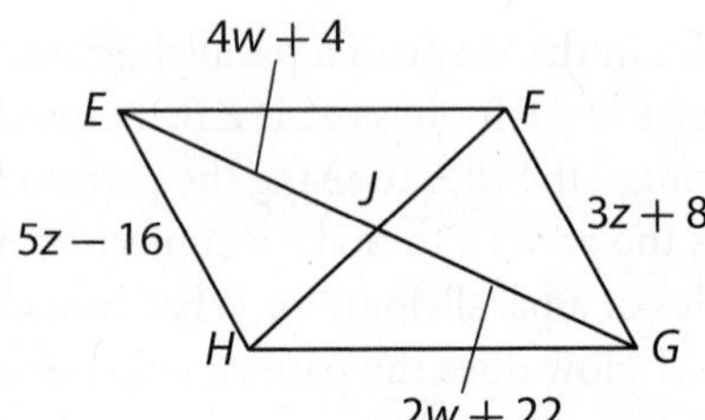

7. *EG*

***ABCD* is a parallelogram. Find each measure.**

8. $m\angle B$

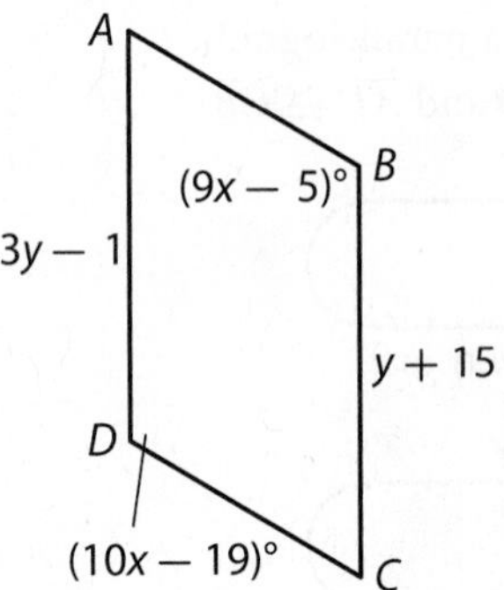

9. *AD*

A staircase handrail is made from congruent parallelograms. In ▱*PQRS*, $PQ = 17.5$, $ST = 18$, and $m\angle QRS = 110°$. Find each measure. Explain.

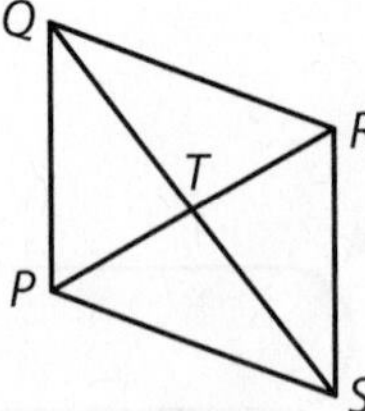

10. *RS*

11. *QT*

12. $m\angle PQR$

13. $m\angle SPQ$

Write each proof as a two-column proof.

14. Given: $GHJN$ and $JKLM$ are parallelograms.
Prove: $\angle G \cong \angle L$

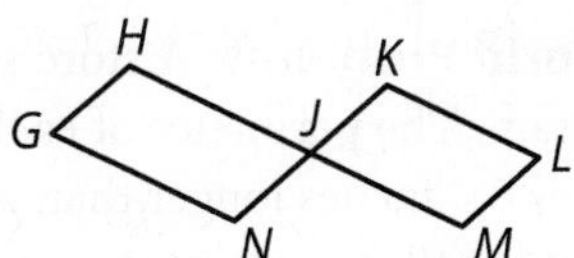

15. Given: $PSTV$ is a parallelogram. $\overline{PQ} \cong \overline{RQ}$
Prove: $\angle STV \cong \angle R$

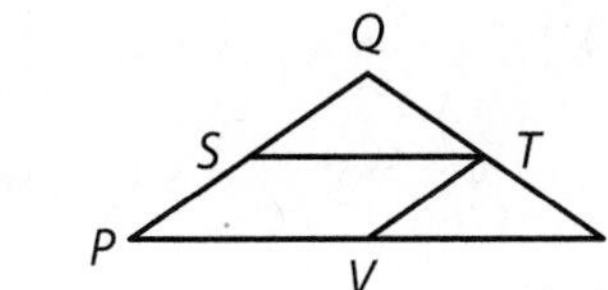

16. Given: $ABCD$ and $AFGH$ are parallelograms.
Prove: $\angle C \cong \angle G$

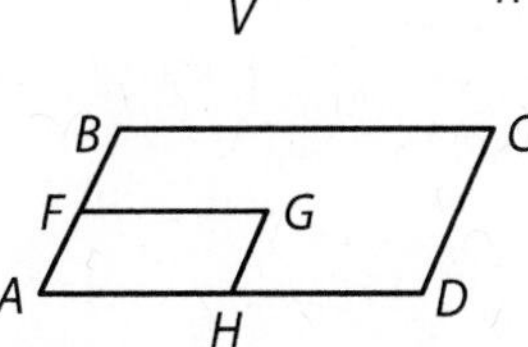

Justify Reasoning **Determine whether each statement is always, sometimes, or never true. Explain your reasoning.**

17. If quadrilateral $RSTU$ is a parallelogram, then $\overline{RS} \cong \overline{ST}$.

18. If a parallelogram has a 30° angle, then it also has a 150° angle.

19. If quadrilateral $GHJK$ is a parallelogram, then $\overline{GH}$ is congruent to $\overline{JK}$.

20. In parallelogram $ABCD$, $\angle A$ is acute and $\angle C$ is obtuse.

21. In parallelogram $MNPQ$, the diagonals $\overline{MP}$ and $\overline{NQ}$ meet at R with $MR = 7$ cm and $RP = 5$ cm.

22. **Communicate Mathematical Ideas** Explain how you can use the rotational symmetry of a parallelogram to give an argument that supports the fact that opposite angles of a parallelogram are congruent.

23. To repair a large truck or bus, a mechanic might use a parallelogram lift. The figure shows a side view of the lift. $FGKL$, $GHJK$, and $FHJL$ are parallelograms.

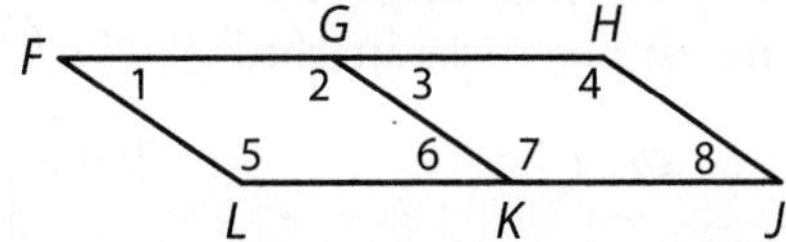

a. Which angles are congruent to $\angle 1$? Explain.

b. What is the relationship between $\angle 1$ and each of the remaining labeled angles? Explain.

24. **Justify Reasoning** $ABCD$ is a parallelogram. Determine whether each statement must be true. Write Yes or No. Explain your reasoning.

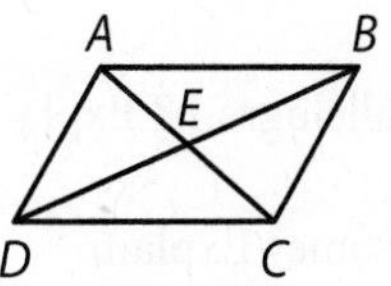

A. The perimeter of $ABCD$ is $2AB + 2BC$.

B. $DE = \frac{1}{2}DB$

C. $\overline{BC} \cong \overline{DC}$

D. $\angle DAC \cong \angle BCA$

E. $\triangle AED \cong \triangle CEB$

F. $\angle DAC \cong \angle BAC$

H.O.T. Focus on Higher Order Thinking

25. Represent Real-World Problems A store sells tiles in the shape of a parallelogram. The perimeter of each tile is 29 inches. One side of each tile is 2.5 inches longer than another side. What are the side lengths of the tile? Explain your steps.

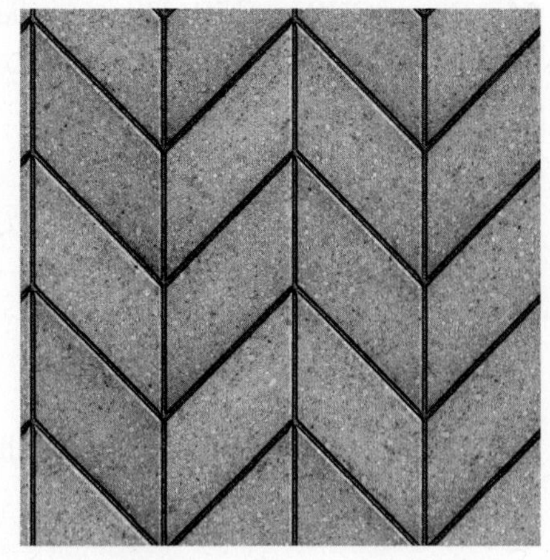

26. Critique Reasoning A student claims that there is an SSSS congruence criterion for parallelograms. That is, if all four sides of one parallelogram are congruent to the four sides of another parallelogram, then the parallelograms are congruent. Do you agree? If so, explain why. If not, give a counterexample. Hint: Draw a picture.

27. Analyze Relationships The figure shows two congruent parallelograms. How are x and y related? Write an equation that expresses the relationship. Explain your reasoning.

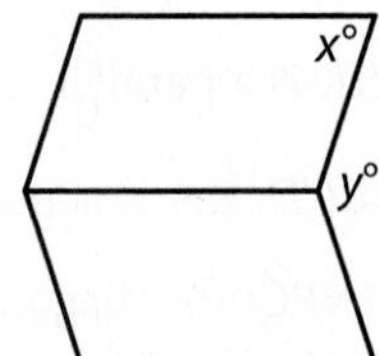

Lesson Performance Task

The principle that allows a scissor lift to raise the platform on top of it to a considerable height can be illustrated with four freezer pop sticks attached at the corners.

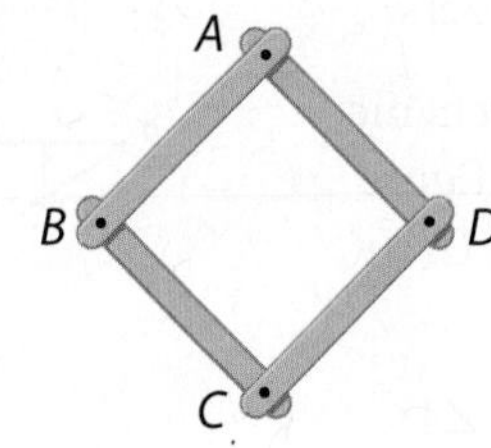

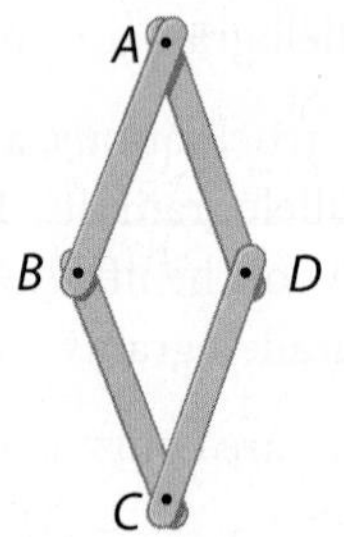

Answer these questions about what happens to parallelogram $ABCD$ when you change its shape as in the illustration.

a. Is it still a parallelogram? Explain.

b. Is its area the same? Explain.

c. Compare the lengths of the diagonals in the two figures as you change them.

d. Describe a process that might be used to raise the platform on a scissor lift.

9.2 Conditions for Parallelograms

Essential Question: What criteria can you use to prove that a quadrilateral is a parallelogram?

Resource Locker

Explore Proving the Opposite Sides Criterion for a Parallelogram

You can prove that a quadrilateral is a parallelogram by using the definition of a parallelogram. That is, you can show that both pairs of opposite sides are parallel. However, there are other conditions that also guarantee that a quadrilateral is a parallelogram.

Theorem

If both pairs of opposite sides of a quadrilateral are congruent, then the quadrilateral is a parallelogram.

Complete the proof of the theorem.

Given: $\overline{AB} \cong \overline{CD}$ and $\overline{AD} \cong \overline{CB}$

Prove: $ABCD$ is a parallelogram.

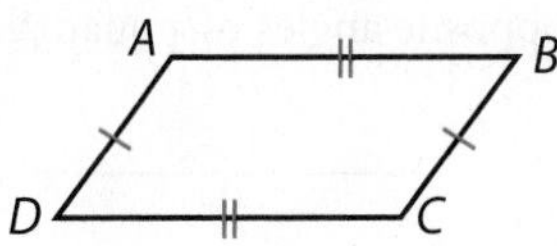

(A) Draw diagonal $\overline{DB}$.

Why is it helpful to draw this diagonal?

(B) Use triangle congruence theorems and corresponding parts to complete the proof that the opposite sides are parallel so the quadrilateral is a parallelogram.

Statements	Reasons
1. Draw $\overline{DB}$.	1. Through any two points, there is exactly one line.
2. $\overline{DB} \cong \overline{DB}$	2. ?
3. $\overline{AB} \cong \overline{CD}$; $\overline{AD} \cong \overline{CB}$	3. ?
4. $\triangle ABD \cong \triangle CDB$	4. ?
5. $\angle ABD \cong \angle CDB$; $\angle ADB \cong \angle CBD$	5. ?
6. $\overline{AB} \parallel \overline{DC}$; $\overline{AD} \parallel \overline{BC}$	6. ?
7. $ABCD$ is a parallelogram.	7. ?

It is possible to combine the theorem from the Explore and the definition of a parallelogram to state the following condition for proving a quadrilateral is a parallelogram. You will prove this in the exercises.

Theorem
If one pair of opposite sides of a quadrilateral are parallel and congruent, then the quadrilateral is a parallelogram.

Reflect

1. **Discussion** A quadrilateral has two sides that are 3 cm long and two sides that are 5 cm long. A student states that the quadrilateral must be a parallelogram. Do you agree? Explain.

Explain 1 Proving the Opposite Angles Criterion for a Parallelogram

You can use relationships between angles to prove that a quadrilateral is a parallelogram.

Theorem
If both pairs of opposite angles of a quadrilateral are congruent, then the quadrilateral is a parallelogram.

Example 1 **Prove that a quadrilateral is a parallelogram if its opposite angles are congruent.**

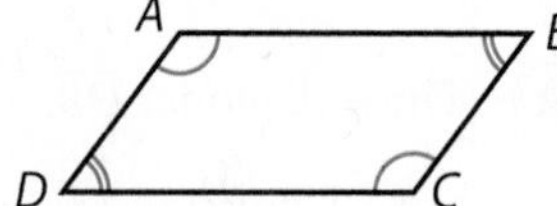

Given: $\angle A \cong \angle C$ and $\angle B \cong \angle D$ Prove: $ABCD$ is a parallelogram.

$m\angle A + m\angle B + m\angle C + m\angle D = 360°$ by the Polygon Angle Sum Theorem.

From the given information, $m\angle A = m\angle$ C and $m\angle B = m\angle$ D . By substitution,

$m\angle A + m\angle D + m\angle A + m\angle D = 360°$ or $2m\angle$ A $+ 2m\angle$ D $= 360°$. Dividing both sides by 2 gives $m\angle A + m\angle D = 180°$. Therefore, $\angle A$ and $\angle D$ are supplementary and so $\overline{AB} \parallel \overline{DC}$ by the Converse of the Same-Side Interior Angles Postulate.

A similar argument shows that $\overline{AD} \parallel \overline{BC}$, so $ABCD$ is a parallelogram by the definition of parallelogram.

Reflect

2. What property or theorem justifies dividing both sides of the equation by 2 in the above proof?

Explain 2 Proving the Bisecting Diagonals Criterion for a Parallelogram

You can use information about the diagonals in a given figure to show that the figure is a parallelogram.

Theorem
If the diagonals of a quadrilateral bisect each other, then the quadrilateral is a parallelogram.

Example 2 **Prove that a quadrilateral whose diagonals bisect each other is a parallelogram.**

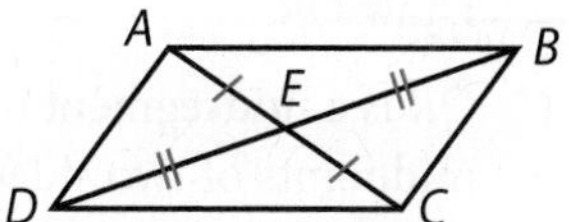

Given: $\overline{AE} \cong \overline{CE}$ and $\overline{DE} \cong \overline{BE}$

Prove: $ABCD$ is a parallelogram.

Statements	Reasons
1. $\overline{AE} \cong \overline{CE}$, $\overline{DE} \cong \overline{BE}$	1. Given
2. $\angle AEB \cong \angle CED$, $\angle AED \cong \angle CEB$	2. Vertical angles are congruent.
3. $\triangle AEB \cong \triangle CED$, $\triangle AED \cong \triangle CEB$	3. SAS Triangle Congruence Theorem
4. $\overline{AB} \cong \overline{CD}$, $\overline{AD} \cong \overline{CB}$	4. CPCTC
5. $ABCD$ is a parallelogram.	5. If both pairs of opposite sides of a quadrilateral are congruent, then it is a parallelogram.

Reflect

3. **Critique Reasoning** A student claimed that you can also write the proof using the SSS Triangle Congruence Theorem since $\overline{AB} \cong \overline{CD}$ and $\overline{AD} \cong \overline{CB}$. Do you agree? Justify your response.

Explain 3 Using a Parallelogram to Prove the Concurrency of the Medians of a Triangle

Sometimes properties of one type of geometric figure can be used to recognize properties of another geometric figure. Recall that you explored triangles and found that the medians of a triangle are concurrent at a point that is $\frac{2}{3}$ of the distance from each vertex to the midpoint of the opposite side. You can prove this theorem using one of the conditions for a parallelogram from this lesson.

Example 3 **Complete the proof of the Concurrency of Medians of a Triangle Theorem.**

Given: $\triangle ABC$

Prove: The medians of $\triangle ABC$ are concurrent at a point that is $\frac{2}{3}$ of the distance from each vertex to the midpoint of the opposite side.

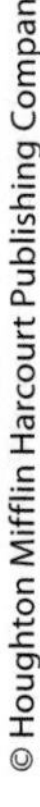

Let $\triangle ABC$ be a triangle such that M is the midpoint of $\overline{AB}$ and N is the midpoint of $\overline{BC}$. Label the point where the two medians intersect as P. Draw $\overline{MN}$.

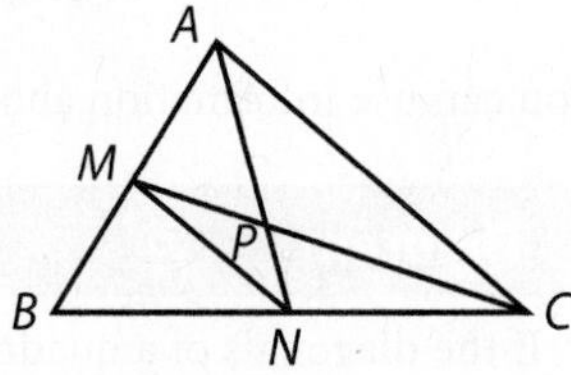

$\overline{MN}$ is a midsegment of $\triangle ABC$ because it connects the midpoints of two sides of the triangle.

$\overline{MN}$ is parallel to $\overline{AC}$ and $MN = \frac{1}{2}AC$ by the Triangle Midsegment Theorem.

Let Q be the midpoint of $\overline{PA}$ and let R be the midpoint of $\overline{PC}$.

Draw $\overline{QR}$.

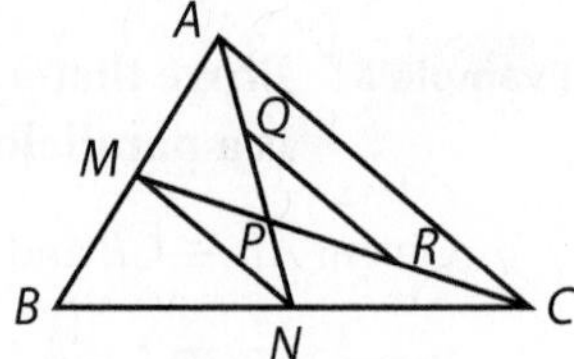

$\overline{QR}$ is a midsegment of $\triangle APC$ because it connects the midpoints of two sides of the triangle.

$\overline{QR}$ is parallel to $\overline{AC}$ and $QR = \frac{1}{2}AC$ by the Triangle Midsegment Theorem.

So, you can conclude that $MN = QR$ by substitution and that

$\overline{MN} \parallel \overline{QR}$ because both segments are parallel to the same segment.

Now draw $\overline{MQ}$ and $\overline{NR}$ and consider quadrilateral $MQRN$.

Quadrilateral $MQRN$ is a parallelogram because a pair of opposite sides are congruent and parallel.

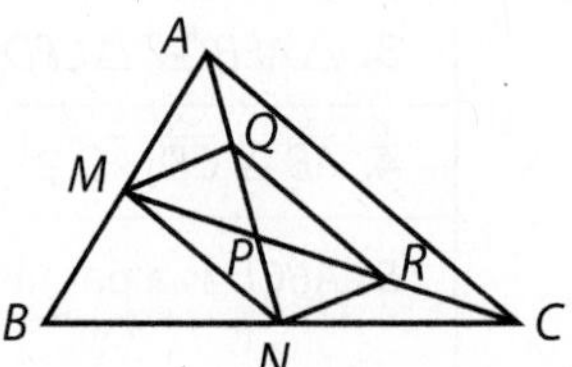

Since the diagonals of a parallelogram bisect each other, then $QP = NP$. Also, $AQ = QP$ since Q is the midpoint of $\overline{PA}$.

Therefore, $AQ = QP = NP$. This shows that point P is located on $\overline{AN}$ at a point that is $\frac{2}{3}$ of the distance from A to N.

By similar reasoning, the diagonals of a parallelogram bisect each other, so $RP = MP$.

Also, $CR = RP$ since R is the midpoint of $\overline{PC}$.

Therefore, $CR = RP = MP$. This shows that point P is located on $\overline{CM}$ at a point that is $\frac{2}{3}$ of the distance from C to M.

You can repeat the proof using any two medians of $\triangle ABC$. The same reasoning shows that the medians from vertices B and C intersect at a point that is also $\frac{2}{3}$ of the distance from C to M, so this point must also be point P. This shows that the three medians intersect at a unique point P and that the point is $\frac{2}{3}$ of the distance from each vertex to the midpoint of the opposite side.

Reflect

4. In the proof, how do you know that point P is located on $\overline{AN}$ at a point that is $\frac{2}{3}$ of the distance from A to N?

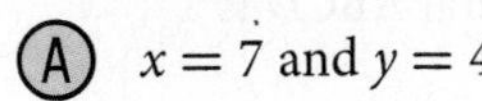

Explain 4 Verifying Figures Are Parallelograms

You can use information about sides, angles, and diagonals in a given figure to show that the figure is a parallelogram.

Example 4 **Show that each quadrilateral is a parallelogram for the given values of the variables.**

(A) $x = 7$ and $y = 4$

Step 1 Find BC and DA.

$BC = x + 14 = 7 + 14 = 21$

$DA = 3x = 3(7) = 21$

Step 2 Find AB and CD.

$AB = 5y - 4 = 5(4) - 4 = 16$

$CD = 2y + 8 = 2(4) + 8 = 16$

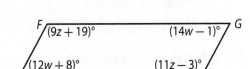

So, $BC = DA$ and $AB = CD$. $ABCD$ is a parallelogram since both pairs of opposite sides are congruent.

(B) $z = 11$ and $w = 4.5$

F (9z + 19)° (14w − 1)° G
E (12w + 8)° (11z − 3)° H

Step 1 Find m∠F and m∠H.

$m\angle F = (9z + 19)° = \big(9(11) + 19\big)° = 118°$

$m\angle H = (11z - 3)° = \big(11(11) - 3\big)° = 118°$

Step 2 Find m∠E and m∠G.

$m\angle E = (12w + 8)° = \big(12(4.5) + 8\big)° = 62°$

$m\angle G = (14w - 1)° = \big(14(4.5) - 1\big)° = 62°$

So, $m\angle F = m\angle$ H and $m\angle E = m\angle$ G . $EFGH$ is a parallelogram since both pairs of opposite angles are congruent.

Reflect

5. What conclusions can you make about $\overline{FG}$ and $\overline{EH}$ in Part B? Explain.

Your Turn

Show that each quadrilateral is a parallelogram for the given values of the variables.

6. $a = 2.4$ and $b = 9$

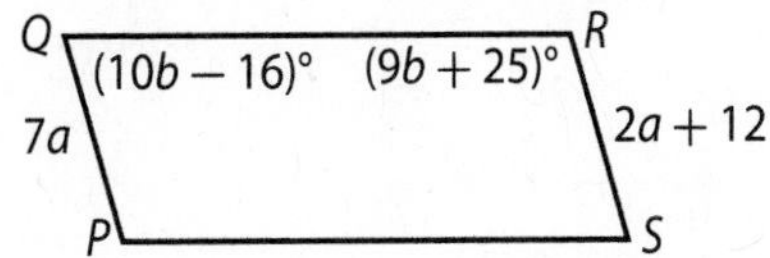

7. $x = 6$ and $y = 3.5$

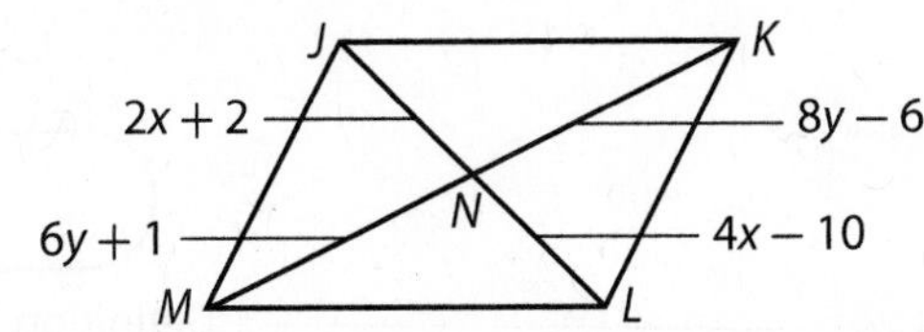

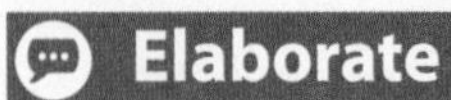

8. How are the theorems in this lesson different from the theorems in the previous lesson, Properties of Parallelograms?

9. Why is the proof of the Concurrency of the Medians of a Triangle Theorem in this lesson and not in the earlier module when the theorem was first introduced?

10. **Essential Question Check-In** Describe three different ways to show that quadrilateral *ABCD* is a parallelogram.

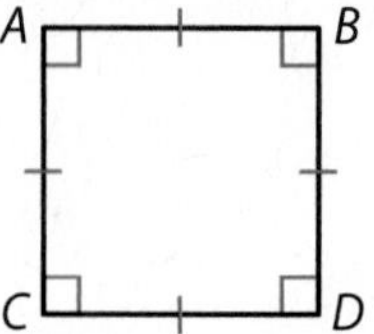

Evaluate: Homework and Practice

- Online Homework
- Hints and Help
- Extra Practice

1. You have seen a proof that if both pairs of opposite sides of a quadrilateral are congruent, then the quadrilateral is a parallelogram. Copy the diagram. Then write the proof as a flow proof.

Given: $\overline{AB} \cong \overline{CD}$ and $\overline{AD} \cong \overline{CB}$

Prove: *ABCD* is a parallelogram.

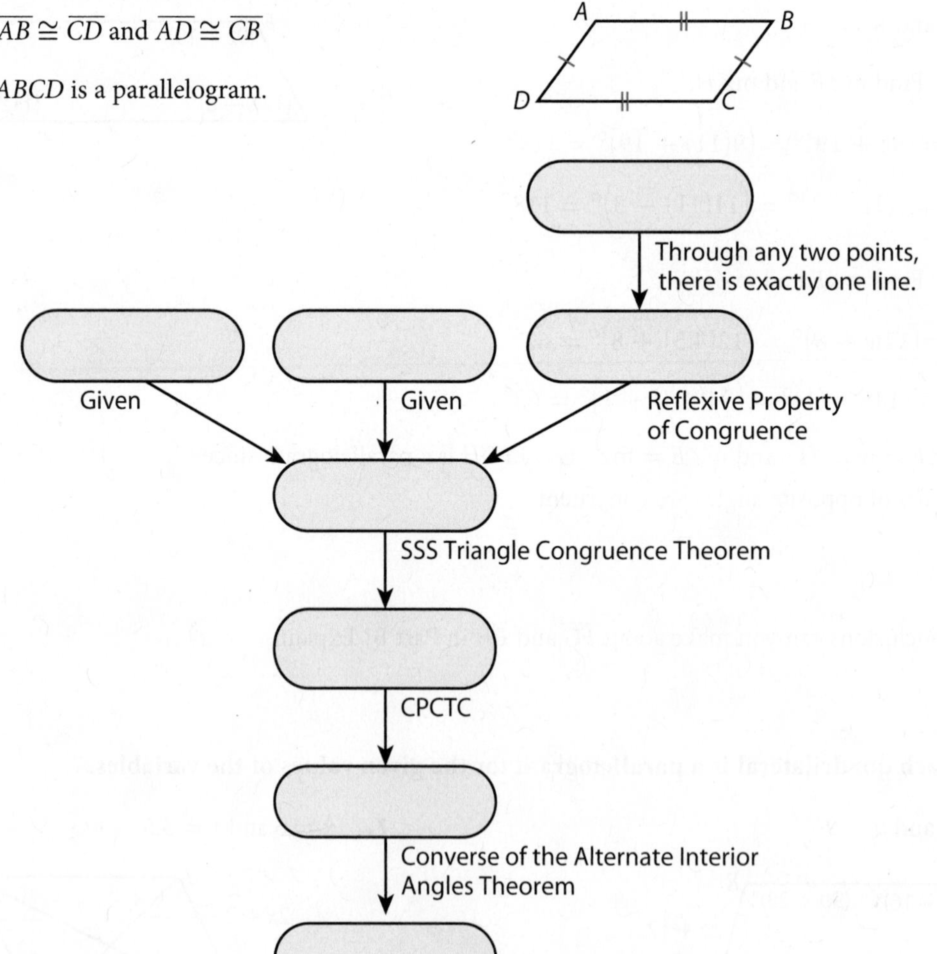

2. You have seen a proof that if both pairs of opposite angles of a quadrilateral are congruent, then the quadrilateral is a parallelogram. Write the proof as a two-column proof.

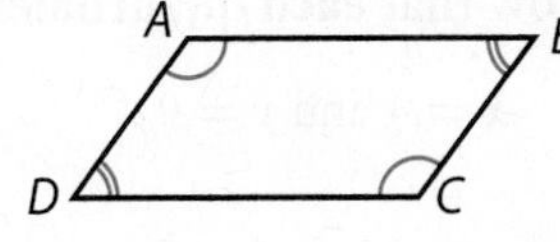

Given: $\angle A \cong \angle C$ and $\angle B \cong \angle D$

Prove: $ABCD$ is a parallelogram.

3. You have seen a proof that if the diagonals of a quadrilateral bisect each other, then the quadrilateral is a parallelogram. Write the proof as a paragraph proof.

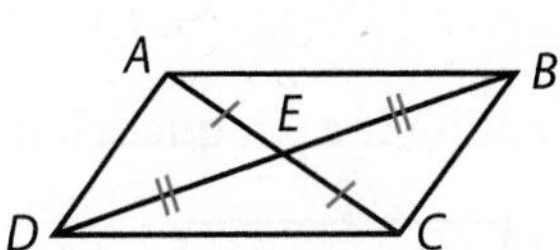

Given: $\overline{AE} \cong \overline{CE}$ and $\overline{DE} \cong \overline{BE}$

Prove: $ABCD$ is a parallelogram.

4. Complete the following proof of the Triangle Midsegment Theorem.

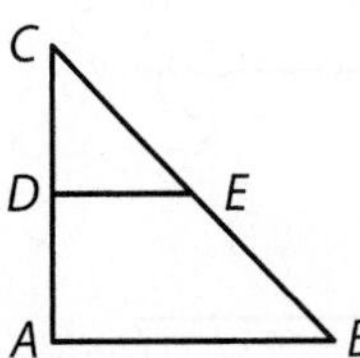

Given: D is the midpoint of $\overline{AC}$, and E is the midpoint of $\overline{BC}$.

Prove: $\overline{DE} \parallel \overline{AB}$, $DE = \frac{1}{2}AB$

Extend $\overline{DE}$ to form $\overline{DF}$ such that $\overline{DE} \cong \overline{FE}$. Then draw $\overline{BF}$, as shown.

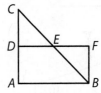

It is given that E is the midpoint of $\overline{CB}$, so $\overline{CE} \cong$ __?__.

By the Vertical Angles Theorem, $\angle CED \cong$ __?__.

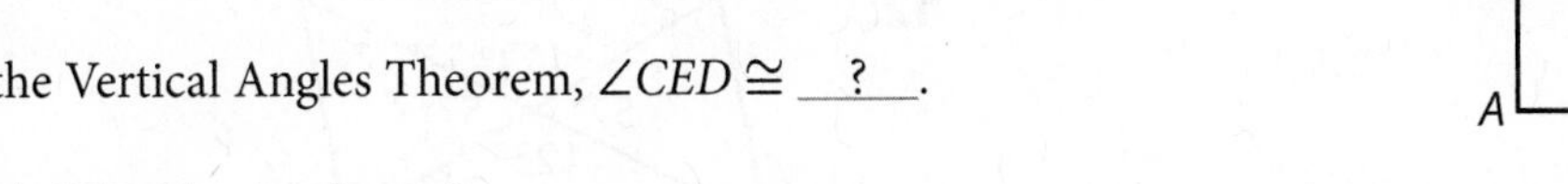

So, $\triangle CED \cong$ __?__ by __?__.

Since corresponding parts of congruent triangles are congruent, $\overline{CD} \cong$ __?__.

D is the midpoint of $\overline{AC}$, so $\overline{CD} \cong$ __?__.

By the Transitive Property of Congruence, $\overline{AD} \cong$ __?__.

Also, since corresponding parts of congruent triangles are congruent, $\angle CDE \cong$ __?__.

So, $\overline{AC} \parallel \overline{FB}$ by __?__.

This shows that $DFBA$ is a parallelogram because __?__.

By the definition of parallelogram, $\overline{DE}$ is parallel to __?__.

Since opposite sides of a parallelogram are congruent, $AB =$ __?__.

$\overline{DE} \cong \overline{FE}$, so $DE = \frac{1}{2}$ __?__ and by substitution, $DE = \frac{1}{2}$ __?__.

Show that each quadrilateral is a parallelogram for the given values of the variables.

5. $x = 4$ and $y = 9$

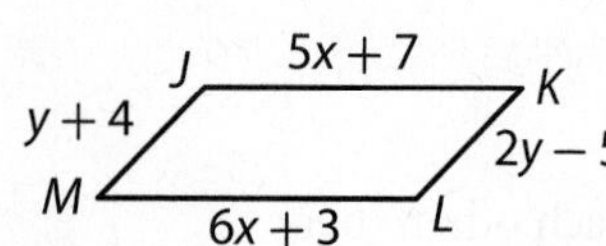

6. $u = 8$ and $v = 3.5$

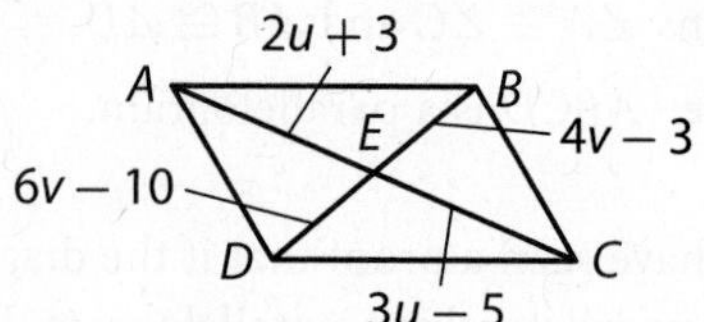

Determine if each quadrilateral must be a parallelogram. Justify your answer.

7.

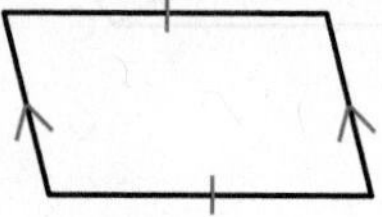

8.

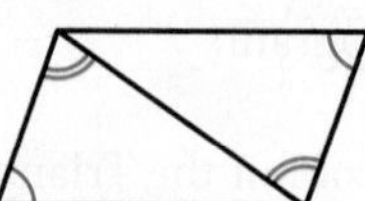

9.

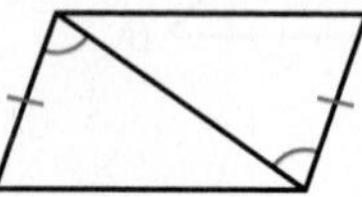

10.

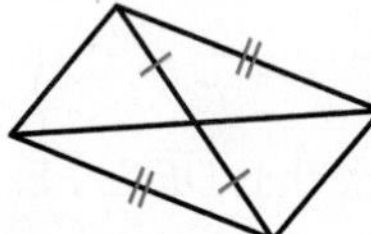

11.

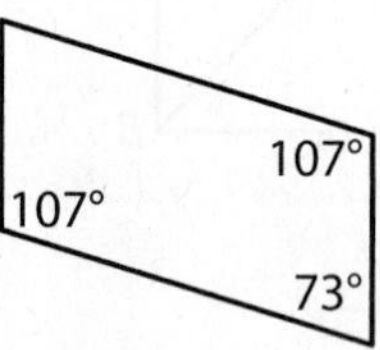

12.

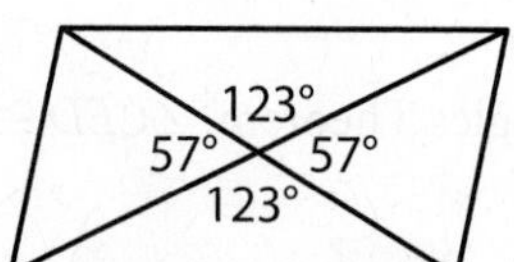

13. Communicate Mathematical Ideas Kalil wants to write the proof that the medians of a triangle are concurrent at a point that is $\frac{2}{3}$ of the distance from each vertex to the midpoint of the opposite side. He starts by drawing $\triangle PQR$ and two medians, $\overline{PK}$ and $\overline{QL}$. He labels the point of intersection as point J, as shown. What segment should Kalil draw next? What conclusions can he make about this segment? Explain.

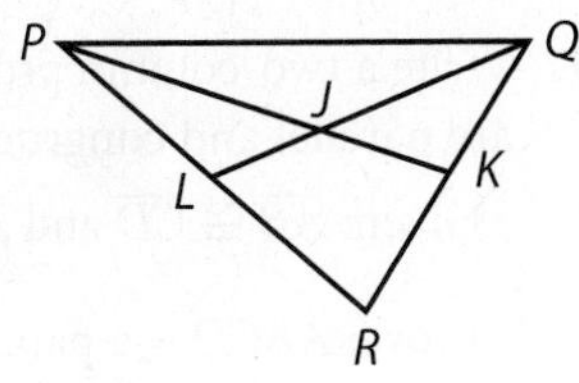

14. Critical Thinking Jasmina said that you can draw a parallelogram using the following steps.

1. Draw a point P.
2. Use a ruler to draw a segment that is 1 inch long with its midpoint at P.
3. Use the ruler to draw a segment that is 2 inches long with its midpoint at P.
4. Use the ruler to connect the endpoints of the segments to form a parallelogram.

Does Jasmina's method always work? Is there ever a time when it would not produce a parallelogram? Explain.

15. Critique Reasoning Matthew said that there is another condition for parallelograms. He said that if a quadrilateral has two congruent diagonals, then the quadrilateral is a parallelogram. Do you agree? If so, explain why. If not, give a counterexample to show why the condition does not work.

16. A parallel rule can be used to plot a course on a navigation chart. The tool is made of two rulers connected at hinges to two congruent crossbars, $\overline{AD}$ and $\overline{BC}$. You place the edge of one ruler on your desired course and then move the second ruler over the compass rose on the chart to read the bearing for your course. If $\overline{AD} \parallel \overline{BC}$, why is $\overline{AB}$ always parallel to $\overline{CD}$?

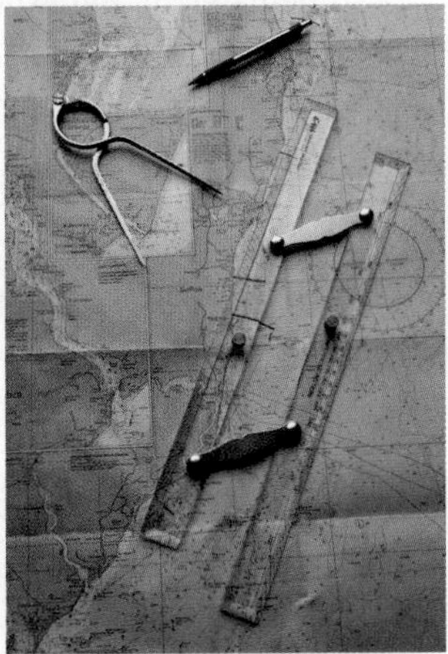

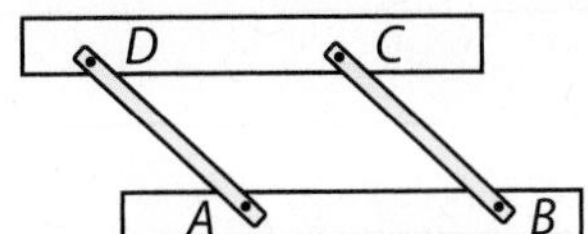

17. Write a two-column proof to prove that a quadrilateral with a pair of opposite sides that are parallel and congruent is a parallelogram.

Given: $\overline{AB} \cong \overline{CD}$ and $\overline{AB} \parallel \overline{CD}$

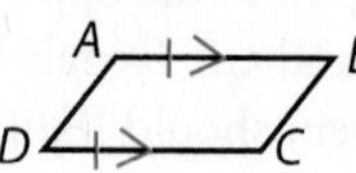

Prove: $ABCD$ is a parallelogram. (*Hint*: Draw $\overline{DB}$.)

18. Does each set of given information guarantee that quadrilateral $JKLM$ is a parallelogram? Write Yes or No for each lettered part.

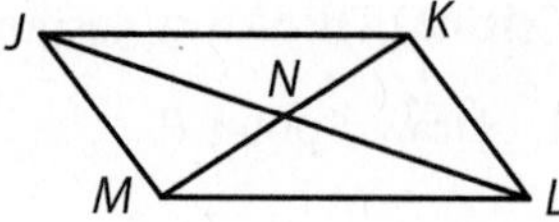

A. $JN = 25$ cm, $JL = 50$ cm, $KN = 13$ cm, $KM = 26$ cm

B. $\angle MJL \cong \angle KLJ$, $\overline{JM} \cong \overline{LK}$

C. $\overline{JM} \cong \overline{JK}$, $\overline{KL} \cong \overline{LM}$

D. $\angle MJL \cong \angle MLJ$, $\angle KJL \cong \angle KLJ$

E. $\triangle JKN \cong \triangle LMN$

H.O.T. Focus on Higher Order Thinking

19. **Explain the Error** A student wrote the two-column proof below. Explain the student's error and explain how to write the proof correctly.

Given: $\angle 1 \cong \angle 2$, E is the midpoint of $\overline{AC}$.

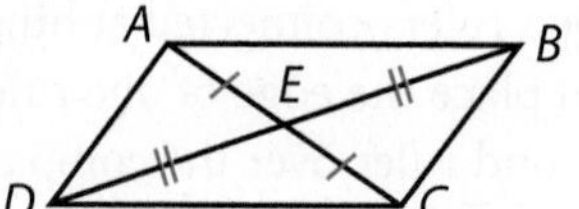

Prove: $ABCD$ is a parallelogram.

Statements	Reasons
1. $\angle 1 \cong \angle 2$	1. Given
2. E is the midpoint of $\overline{AC}$.	2. Given
3. $\overline{AE} \cong \overline{CE}$	3. Definition of midpoint
4. $\angle AED \cong \angle CEB$	4. Vertical angles are congruent.
5. $\triangle AED \cong \triangle CEB$	5. ASA Triangle Congruence Theorem
6. $\overline{AD} \cong \overline{CB}$	6. Corresponding parts of congruent triangles are congruent
7. $ABCD$ is a parallelogram.	7. If a pair of opposite sides of a quadrillateral are congruent, then the quadrillateral is a parallelogram.

20. Persevere in Problem Solving The plan for a city park shows that the park is a quadrilateral with straight paths along the diagonals. For what values of the variables is the park a parallelogram? In this case, what are the lengths of the paths?

$(5x + 2y)$ m

R S

$(12y + 50)$ m

V

U T

$(16y - 10)$ m

$(2x + 4y)$ m

21. Analyze Relationships When you connect the midpoints of the consecutive sides of any quadrilateral, the resulting quadrilateral is a parallelogram. Use the figure below to explain why this is true. (*Hint:* Draw a diagonal of *ABCD*.)

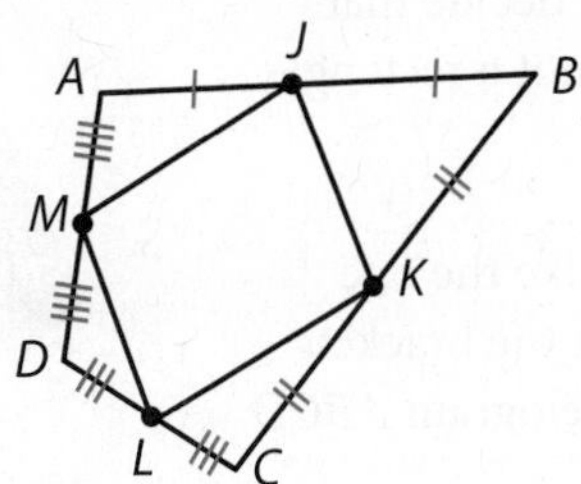

Lesson Performance Task

In this lesson you've learned three theorems for confirming that a figure is a parallelogram.

- If both pairs of opposite sides of a quadrilateral are congruent, then the quadrilateral is a parallelogram.
- If both pairs of opposite angles of a quadrilateral are congruent, then the quadrilateral is a parallelogram.
- If the diagonals of a quadrilateral bisect each other, then the quadrilateral is a parallelogram.

For each of the following situations, choose one of the three theorems and use it in your explanation. You should choose a different theorem for each explanation.

a. You're an amateur astronomer, and one night you see what appears to be a parallelogram in the constellation of Lyra. Explain how you could verify that the figure is a parallelogram.

b. You have a frame shop and you want to make an interesting frame for an advertisement for your store. You decide that you'd like the frame to be a parallelogram but not a rectangle. Explain how you could construct the frame.

c. You're using a toolbox with cantilever shelves like the one shown here. Explain how you can confirm that the brackets that attach the shelves to the box form a parallelogram *ABCD*.

9.3 Properties of Rectangles, Rhombuses, and Squares

Essential Question: What are the properties of rectangles, rhombuses, and squares?

Resource Locker

Explore Exploring Sides, Angles, and Diagonals of a Rectangle

A **rectangle** is a quadrilateral with four right angles. The figure shows rectangle *ABCD*.

Investigate properties of rectangles.

(A) Use a tile or pattern block and the following method to draw three different rectangles on a separate sheet of paper.

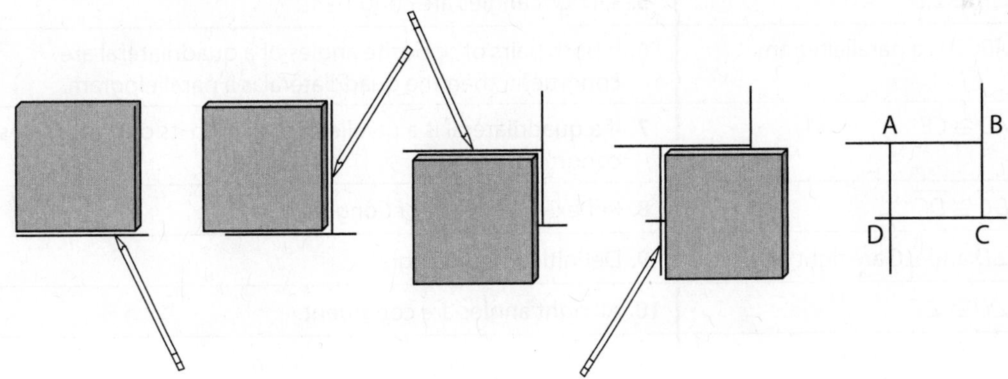

(B) Use a ruler to measure the sides and diagonals of each rectangle. Keep track of the measurements and compare your results to other students.

Reflect

1. Why does this method produce a rectangle? What must you assume about the tile?
2. **Discussion** Is every rectangle also a parallelogram? Make a conjecture based upon your measurements and explain your thinking.
3. Use your measurements to make two conjectures about the diagonals of a rectangle.

Explain 1 Proving Diagonals of a Rectangle are Congruent

You can use the definition of a rectangle to prove the following theorems.

Properties of Rectangles

If a quadrilateral is a rectangle, then it is a parallelogram.
If a parallelogram is a rectangle, then its diagonals are congruent.

Example 1 **Use a rectangle to prove the Properties of Rectangles Theorems.**

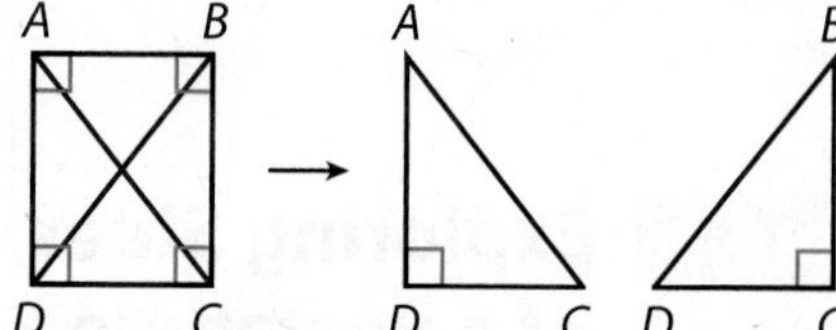

Given: *ABCD* is a rectangle.

Prove: *ABCD* is a parallelogram; $\overline{AC} \cong \overline{BD}$.

Statements	Reasons
1. *ABCD* is a rectangle.	1. Given
2. $\angle A$ and $\angle C$ are right angles.	2. Definition of rectangle
3. $\angle A \cong \angle C$	3. All right angles are congruent.
4. $\angle B$ and $\angle D$ are right angles.	4. Definition of rectangle
5. $\angle B \cong \angle D$	5. All right angles are congruent.
6. *ABCD* is a parallelogram.	6. If both pairs of opposite angles of a quadrilateral are congruent, then the quadrilateral is a parallelogram.
7. $\overline{AD} \cong \overline{CB}$	7. If a quadrilateral is a parallelogram, then its opposite sides are congruent.
8. $\overline{DC} \cong \overline{DC}$	8. Reflexive Property of Congruence
9. $\angle D$ and $\angle C$ are right angles.	9. Definition of rectangle
10. $\angle D \cong \angle C$	10. All right angles are congruent.
11. $\triangle ADC \cong \triangle BCD$	11. SAS Triangle Congruence Theorem
12. $\overline{AC} \cong \overline{BD}$	12. CPCTC

Reflect

4. **Discussion** A student says you can also prove the diagonals are congruent in Example 1 by using the SSS Triangle Congruence Theorem to show that $\triangle ADC \cong \triangle BCD$. Do you agree? Explain.

Your Turn

Find each measure.

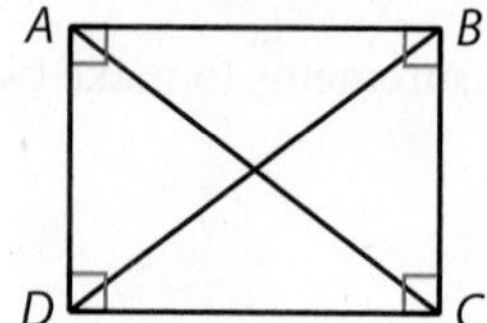

5. $AD = 7.5$ cm and $DC = 10$ cm. Find *DB*.

6. $AB = 17$ cm and $BC = 12.75$ cm. Find *DB*.

Explain 2 Proving Diagonals of a Rhombus are Perpendicular

A **rhombus** is a quadrilateral with four congruent sides.
The figure shows rhombus *JKLM*.

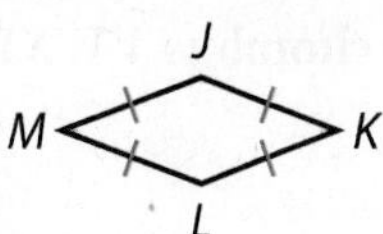

Properties of Rhombuses

If a quadrilateral is a rhombus, then it is a parallelogram.
If a parallelogram is a rhombus, then its diagonals are perpendicular.
If a parallelogram is a rhombus, then each diagonal bisects a pair of opposite angles.

Example 2 **Prove that the diagonals of a rhombus are perpendicular.**

Given: *JKLM* is a rhombus.

Prove: $\overline{JL} \perp \overline{MK}$

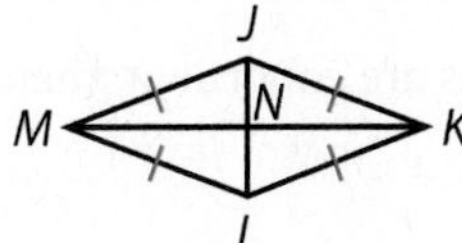

Since *JKLM* is a rhombus, $\overline{JM} \cong$ $\overline{JK}$. Because *JKLM* is also a parallelogram, $\overline{MN} \cong \overline{KN}$ because diagonals of a parallelogram bisect each other. By the Reflexive Property of Congruence, $\overline{JN} \cong \overline{JN}$, so $\triangle JNM \cong \triangle JNK$ by the SSS Triangle Congruence Theorem. So, $\angle JNM \cong \angle JNK$ by CPCTC.

By the Linear Pair Theorem, $\angle JNM$ and $\angle JNK$ are supplementary. This means that $m\angle JNM + m\angle JNK =$ $180°$.

Since the angles are congruent, $m\angle JNM = m\angle JNK$ so by substitution, $m\angle JNK + m\angle JNK = 180°$ or $2m\angle JNK = 180°$. Therefore, $m\angle JNK =$ $90°$ and $\overline{JL}$ $\perp \overline{MK}$.

Reflect

7. What can you say about the image of *J* in the proof after a reflection across $\overline{MK}$? Why?

8. What property about the diagonals of a rhombus is the same as a property of all parallelograms? What special property do the diagonals of a rhombus have?

Your Turn

9. Prove that if a parallelogram is a rhombus, then each diagonal bisects a pair of opposite angles.

Given: *JKLM* is a rhombus.

Prove: $\overline{MK}$ bisects $\angle JML$ and $\angle JKL$;
$\overline{JL}$ bisects $\angle MJK$ and $\angle MLK$.

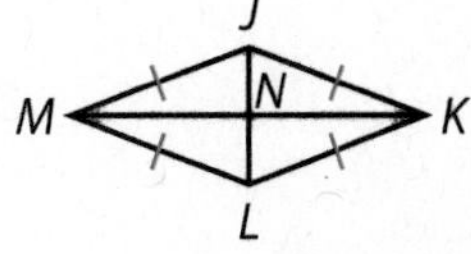

Explain 3 Using Properties of Rhombuses to Find Measures

Example 3 **Use rhombus $VWXY$ to find each measure.**

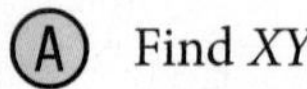

Ⓐ Find XY.

All sides of a rhombus are congruent, so $\overline{VW} \cong \overline{WX}$ and $VW = WX$.

Substitute values for VW and WX. $6m - 12 = 4m + 4$

Solve for m. $m = 8$

Sustitute the value of m to find VW. $VW = 6(8) - 12 = 36$

Because all sides of the rhombus are congruent, then $\overline{VW} \cong \overline{XY}$, and $XY = 36$.

Ⓑ Find $\angle YVW$.

The diagonals of a rhombus are perpendicular, so $\angle WZX$ is a right angle and

$m\angle WZX =$ 90° .

Since $m\angle WZX = (3n^2 - 0.75)°$, then $(3n^2 - 0.75°) = 90°$.

Solve for n. $3n^2 - 0.75 = 90$

$n =$ 5.5

Substitute the value of n to find $m\angle WVZ$.

$m\angle WVZ =$ 53.5°

Since $\overline{VX}$ bisects $\angle YVW$, then $\angle YVZ \cong \angle WVZ$

Substitute 53.5° for $m\angle WVZ$. $m\angle YVW = 2(53.5°) = 107°$

Your Turn

Use the rhombus $VWXY$ from Example 3 to find each measure.

10. Find $m\angle VYX$.

11. Find $m\angle XYZ$.

Explain 4 Investigating the Properties of a Square

A **square** is a quadrilateral with four sides congruent and four right angles.

Example 4 **Explain why each conditional statement is true.**

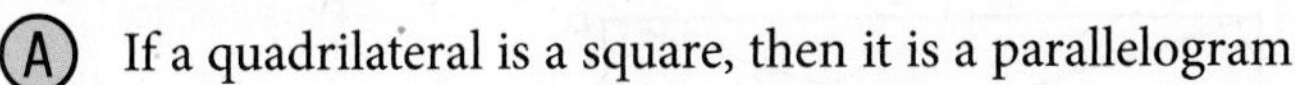

(A) If a quadrilateral is a square, then it is a parallelogram.

By definition, a square is a quadrilateral with four congruent sides.
Any quadrilateral with both pairs of opposite sides congruent is a parallelogram, so a square is a parallelogram.

(B) If a quadrilateral is a square, then it is a rectangle.

By definition, a square is a quadrilateral with four right angles.

By definition, a rectangle is also a quadrilateral with four right angles.
Therefore, a square is a rectangle.

Your Turn

12. Explain why this conditional statement is true: If a quadrilateral is a square, then it is a rhombus.

13. Look at Part A. Use a different way to explain why this conditional statement is true: If a quadrilateral is a square, then it is a parallelogram.

Elaborate

14. Discussion The Venn diagram shows how quadrilaterals, parallelograms, rectangles, rhombuses, and squares are related to each other. From this lesson, what do you notice about the definitions and theorems regarding these figures?

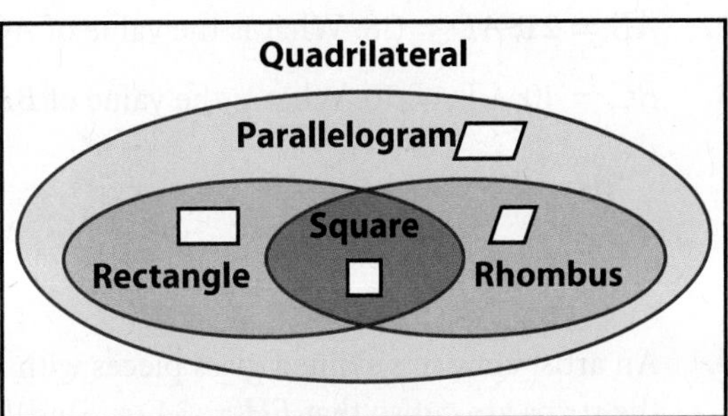

15. Essential Question Check-In What are the properties of rectangles and rhombuses? How does a square relate to rectangles and rhombuses?

Evaluate: Homework and Practice

Personal Math Trainer

- Online Homework
- Hints and Help
- Extra Practice

1. Complete the paragraph proof of the Properties of Rectangles Theorems.
   Given: *ABCD* is a rectangle.
   Prove: *ABCD* is a parallelogram; $\overline{AC} \cong \overline{BD}$.

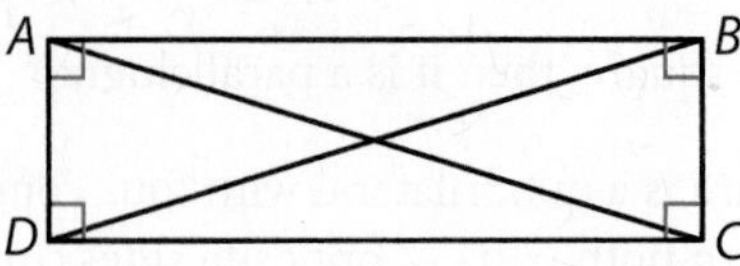

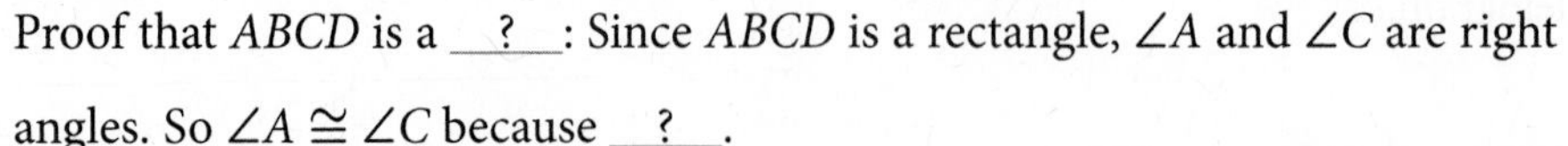

Proof that *ABCD* is a __?__: Since *ABCD* is a rectangle, $\angle A$ and $\angle C$ are right angles. So $\angle A \cong \angle C$ because __?__.

By similar reasoning, $\angle B \cong \angle D$. Therefore, *ABCD* is a parallelogram because __?__

Proof that the diagonals are congruent: Since *ABCD* is a parallelogram, $\overline{AD} \cong \overline{BC}$ because __?__.

Also, __?__ by the Reflexive Property of Congruence. By the definition of a rectangle, $\angle D$ and $\angle C$ are right angles, and so __?__ because all right angles are __?__. Therefore, $\triangle ADC \cong \triangle BCD$ by the __?__ and __?__ $\cong$ __?__ by CPCTC.

Find the lengths using rectangle *ABCD*.

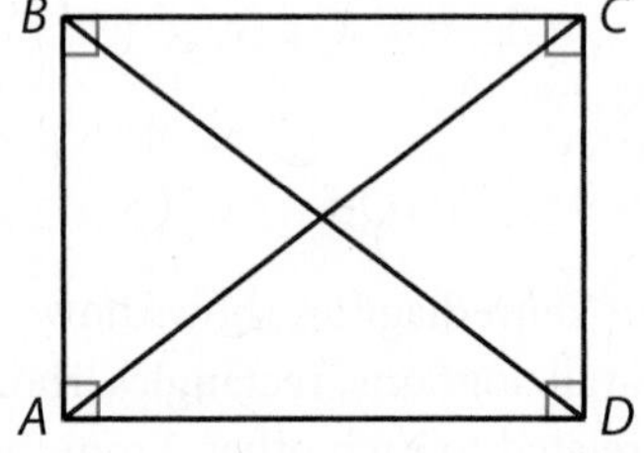

2. $AB = 21$; $AD = 28$. What is the value of $AC + BD$?
3. $BC = 40$; $CD = 30$. What is the value of $BD - AC$?

4. An artist connects stained glass pieces with lead strips. In this rectangular window, the strips are cut so that $FH = 34$ in. Find *JG*. Explain.

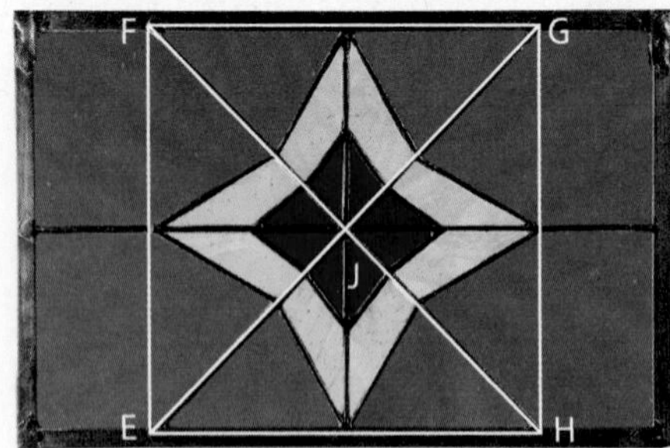

The rectangular gate has diagonal braces. Find each length.

5. Find HJ.

6. Find HK.

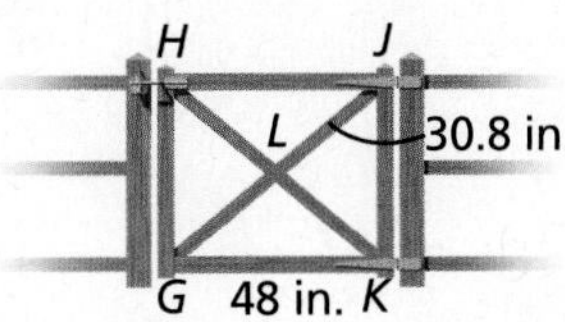

7. Find the measure of each numbered angle in the rectangle.

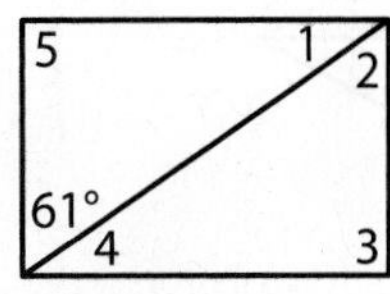

8. Complete the two-column proof that the diagonals of a rhombus are perpendicular.

Given: $JKLM$ is a rhombus.

Prove: $\overline{JL} \perp \overline{MK}$

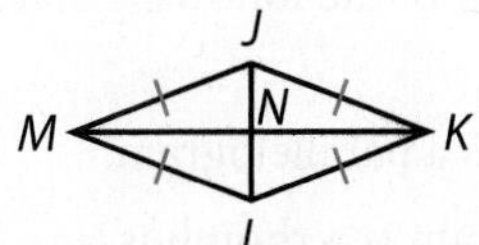

Statements	Reasons
1. $\overline{JM} \cong \overline{JK}$	1. Definition of rhombus
2. $\overline{MN} \cong \overline{KN}$	2. ___?___
3. $\overline{JN} \cong \overline{JN}$	3. Reflexive Property of Congruence
4. ___?___	4. SSS Triangle Congruence Theorem
5. $\angle JNM \cong \angle JNK$	5. ___?___
6. $\angle JNM$ and $\angle JNK$ are supplementary.	6. ___?___
7. ___?___	7. Definition of supplementary
8. $\angle JNM = \angle JNK$	8. Definition of congruence
9. ___?___ $+ \angle JNK = 180°$	9. Substitution Property of Equality
10. $2m\angle JNK = 180°$	10. Addition
11. $m\angle JNK = 90°$	11. Division Property of Equality
12. ___?___	12. Definition of perpendicular lines

ABCD is a rhombus. Find each measure.

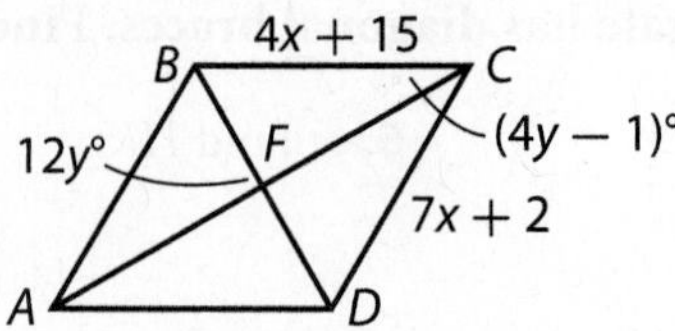

9. Find AB.

10. Find $m\angle ABC$.

Find the measure of each numbered angle in the rhombus.

11.

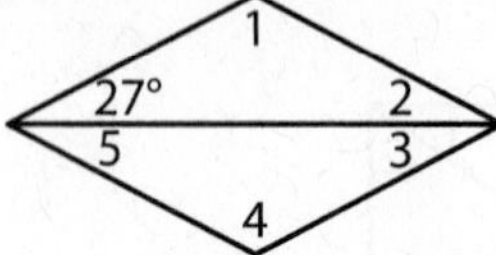

12.

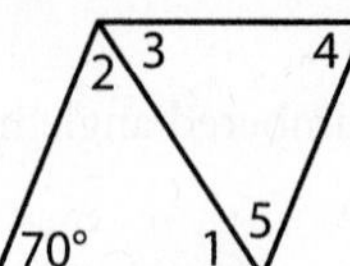

13. Tell whether each of the following statements is always true, sometimes true, or never true.

A. A rectangle is a parallelogram.

B. A parallelogram is a rhombus.

C. A square is a rhombus.

D. A rhombus is a square.

E. A rhombus is a rectangle.

14. Use properties of special parallelograms to complete the proof.
Given: $EFGH$ is a rectangle. J is the midpoint of $\overline{EH}$.
Prove: $\triangle FJG$ is isosceles.

Statements	Reasons
1. $EFGH$ is a rectangle. J is the midpoint of $\overline{EH}$.	1. Given
2. $\angle E$ and $\angle H$ are right angles.	2. Definition of rectangle
3. $\angle E \cong \angle H$	3. ?
4. $EFGH$ is a parallelogram.	4. ?
5. ?	5. ?
6. ?	6. ?
7. ?	7. ?
8. ?	8. ?
9. ?	9. ?

15. **Explain the Error** Find and explain the error in this paragraph proof. Then describe a way to correct the proof.

Given: *JKLM* is a rhombus.

Prove: *JKLM* is a parallelogram.

Proof: It is given that *JLKM* is a rhombus. So, by the definition of a rhombus, $\overline{JK} \cong \overline{LM}$, and $\overline{KL} \cong \overline{MJ}$. If a quadrilateral is a parallelogram, then its opposite sides are congruent. So *JKLM* is a parallelogram.

The opening of a soccer goal is shaped like a rectangle.

16. Draw a rectangle to represent a soccer goal. Label the rectangle *ABCD* to show that the distance between the goalposts, $\overline{BC}$, is three times the distance from the top of the goalpost to the ground. If the perimeter of *ABCD* is 64 feet, what is the length of $\overline{BC}$?

17. In your rectangle from Evaluate 16, suppose the distance from *B* to *D* is $(y + 10)$ feet, and the distance from *A* to *C* is $(2y - 5.3)$ feet. What is the approximate length of $\overline{AC}$?

18. *PQRS* is a rhombus, with $PQ = (7b - 5)$ meters and $QR = (2b - 0.5)$ meters. If *S* is the midpoint of $\overline{RT}$, what is the length of $\overline{RT}$?

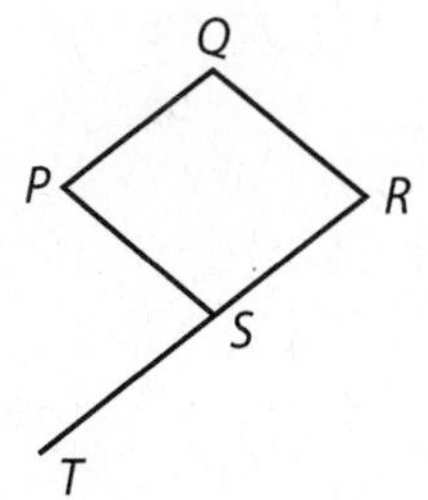

19. **Communicate Mathematical Ideas** List the properties that a square "inherits" because it is each of the following quadrilaterals.

a. a parallelogram

b. a rectangle

c. a rhombus

H.O.T. Focus on Higher Order Thinking

Justify Reasoning **For the given figure, describe any rotations or reflections that would carry the figure onto itself. Explain.**

20. A rhombus that is not a square

21. A rectangle that is not a square

22. A square

23. **Analyze Relationships** Look at your answers for Exercises 20–22. How does your answer to Exercise 22 relate to your answers to Exercises 20 and 21? Explain.

Lesson Performance Task

The portion of the Arkansas state flag that is not red is a rhombus. On one flag, the diagonals of the rhombus measure 24 inches and 36 inches. Find the area of the rhombus. Justify your reasoning.

9.4 Conditions for Rectangles, Rhombuses, and Squares

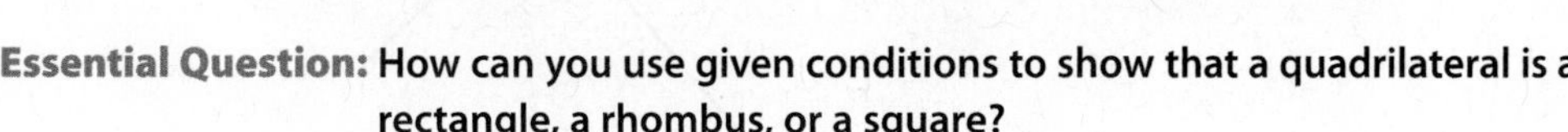

Essential Question: How can you use given conditions to show that a quadrilateral is a rectangle, a rhombus, or a square?

Explore Properties of Rectangles, Rhombuses, and Squares

In this lesson we will start with given properties and use them to prove which special parallelogram it could be.

(A) Start by drawing two line segments of the same length that bisect each other but are not perpendicular. They will form an X shape, as shown.

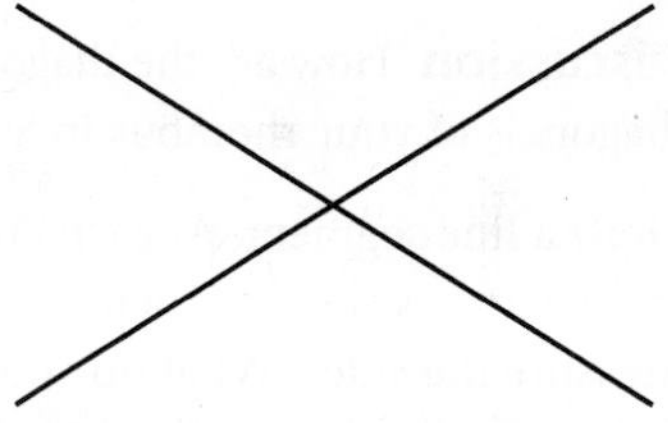

(B) Connect the ends of the line segments to form a quadrilateral.

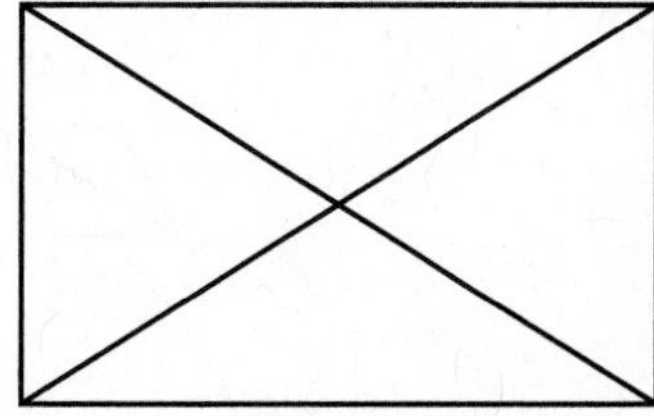

(C) Measure each of the four angles of the quadrilateral, and use those measurements to name the shape.

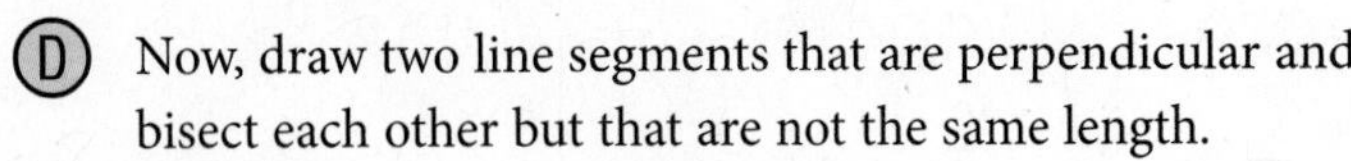

(D) Now, draw two line segments that are perpendicular and bisect each other but that are not the same length.

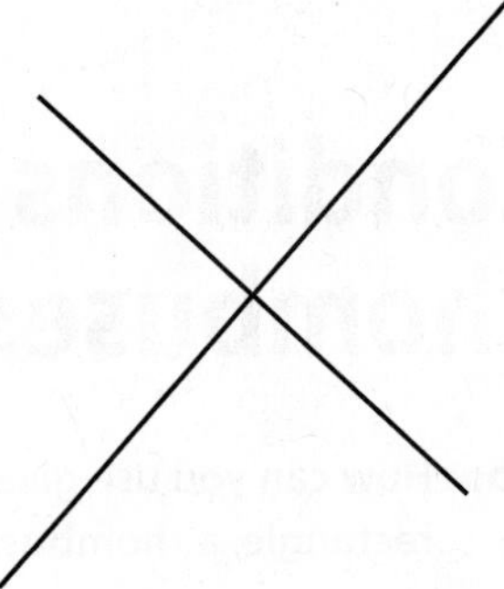

(E) Connect the ends of the line segments to form a quadrilateral.

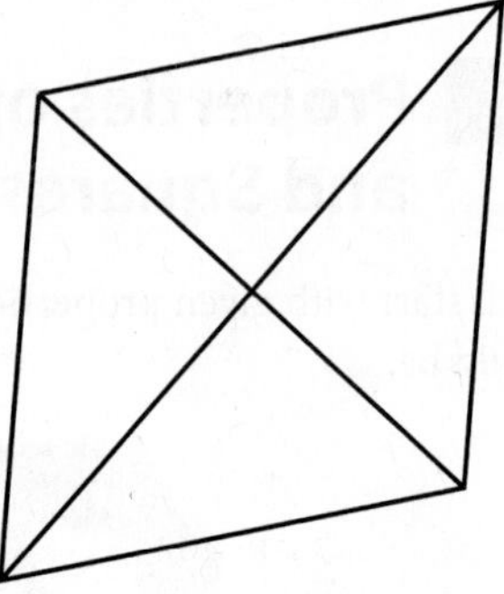

(F) Measure each side length of the quadrilateral. Then use those measurements to name the shape.

Reflect

1. **Discussion** How are the diagonals of your rectangle in Step B different from the diagonals of your rhombus in Step E?

2. Draw a line segment. At each endpoint draw line segments so that four congruent angles are formed as shown. Then extend the segments so that they intersect to form a quadrilateral. Measure the sides. What do you notice? What kind of quadrilateral is it? How does the line segment relate to the angles drawn on either end of it?

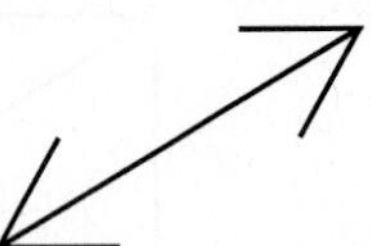

Explain 1 Proving that Congruent Diagonals Is a Condition for Rectangles

When you are given a parallelogram with certain properties, you can use the properties to determine whether the parallelogram is a rectangle.

Theorems: Conditions for Rectangles	
If one angle of a parallelogram is a right angle, then the parallelogram is a rectangle.	B C A D
If the diagonals of a parallelogram are congruent, then the parallelogram is a rectangle.	B C A D $\overline{AC} \cong \overline{BD}$

Example 1 **Prove that if the diagonals of a parallelogram are congruent, then the parallelogram is a rectangle.**

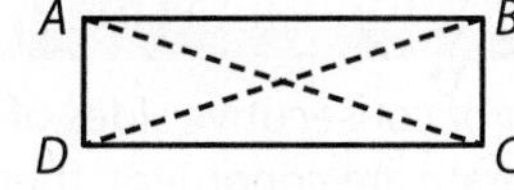

Given: $ABCD$ is a parallelogram; $\overline{AC} \cong \overline{BD}$.

Prove: $ABCD$ is a rectangle.

Because opposite sides of a parallelogram are congruent, $\overline{AB} \cong \overline{CD}$.

It is given that $\overline{AC} \cong \overline{BD}$, and $\overline{AD} \cong \overline{AD}$ by the Reflexive Property of Congruence.

So, $\triangle ABD \cong \triangle DCA$ by the SSS Triangle Congruence Theorem,

and $\angle BAD \cong \angle CDA$ by CPCTC. But these angles are supplementary

since $\overline{AB} \parallel \overline{DC}$. Therefore, $m\angle BAD + m\angle CDA = 180°$. So

$m\angle BAD + m\angle BAD = 180°$ by substitution, $2 \cdot m\angle BAD = 180°$,

and $m\angle BAD = 90°$. A similar argument shows that the other angles of $ABCD$ are

also right angles, so $ABCD$ is a rectangle.

Reflect

3. **Discussion** Explain why this is a true condition for rectangles: *If one angle of a parallelogram is a right angle, then the parallelogram is a rectangle.*

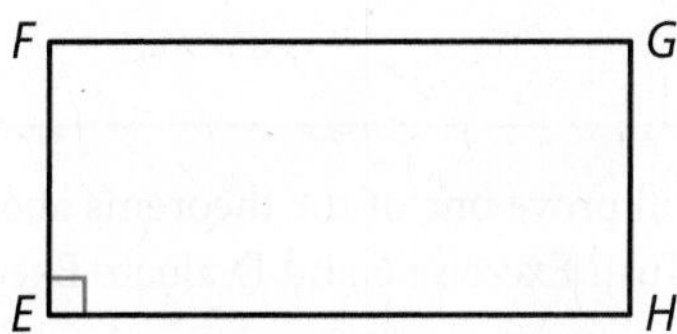

Your Turn

Use the given information to determine whether the quadrilateral is necessarily a rectangle. Explain your reasoning.

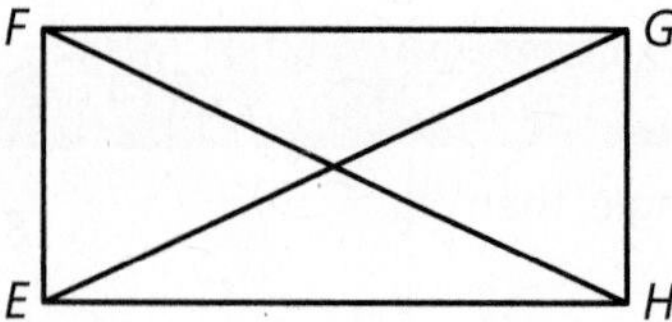

4. Given: $\overline{EF} \cong \overline{GF}$, $\overline{FG} \cong \overline{HE}$, $\overline{FH} \cong \overline{GE}$

5. Given: $m\angle FEG = 45°$, $m\angle GEH = 50°$

Explain 2 Proving Conditions for Rhombuses

You can also use given properties of a parallelogram to determine whether the parallelogram is a rhombus.

Theorems: Conditions for Rhombuses	
If one pair of consecutive sides of a parallelogram are congruent, then the parallelogram is a rhombus.	
If the diagonals of a parallelogram are perpendicular, then the parallelogram is a rhombus.	
If one diagonal of a parallelogram bisects a pair of opposite angles, then the parallelogram is a rhombus.	

You will prove one of the theorems about rhombuses in Example 2 and the other theorems in Your Turn Exercise 6 and Evaluate Exercise 22.

Example 2 **Complete the flow proof that if one diagonal of a parallelogram bisects a pair of opposite angles, then the parallelogram is a rhombus.**

Given: $ABCD$ is a parallelogram; $\angle BCA \cong \angle DCA$; $\angle BAC \cong \angle DAC$

Prove: $ABCD$ is a rhombus.

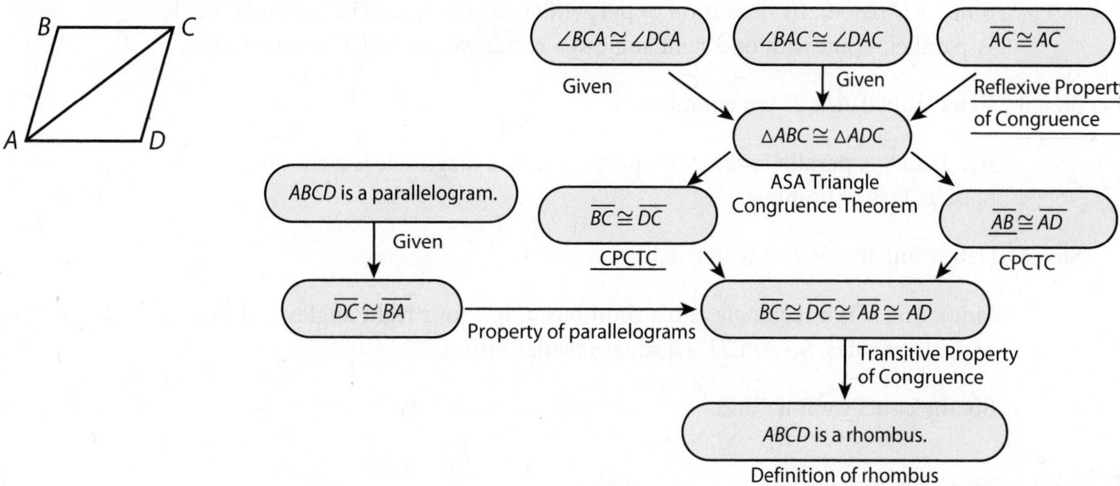

Your Turn

6. Prove that If one pair of consecutive sides of a parallelogram are congruent, then it is a rhombus.

Given: $JKLM$ is a parallelogram. $\overline{JK} \cong \overline{KL}$

Prove: $JKLM$ is a rhombus.

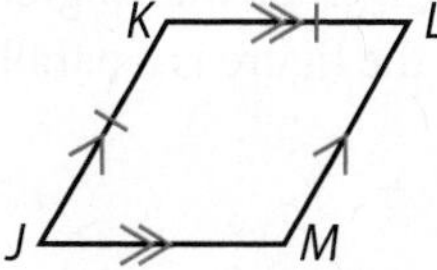

Explain 3 Applying Conditions for Special Parallelograms

In Example 3, you will decide whether you are given enough information to conclude that a figure is a particular type of special parallelogram.

Example 3 **Determine if the conclusion is valid. If not, tell what additional information is needed to make it valid.**

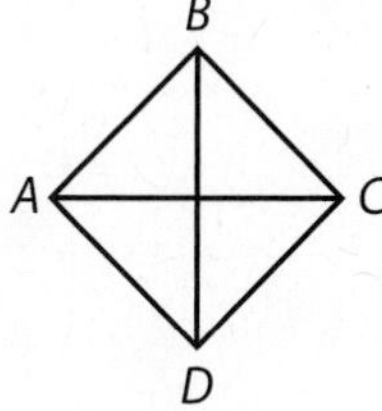

(A) **Given:** $\overline{AB} \cong \overline{CD}$; $\overline{BC} \cong \overline{DA}$; $\overline{AD} \perp \overline{DC}$; $\overline{AC} \perp \overline{BD}$

Conclusion: $ABCD$ is a square.

To prove that a given quadrilateral is a square, it is sufficient to show that the figure is both a rectangle and a rhombus.

Step 1: Determine if *ABCD* is a parallelogram.

$\overline{AB} \cong \overline{CD}$ and $\overline{BC} \cong \overline{DA}$ are given. Since a quadrilateral with opposite sides congruent is a parallelogram, we know that *ABCD* is a parallelogram.

Step 2: Determine if *ABCD* is a rectangle.

Since $\overline{AD} \perp \overline{DC}$, by definition of perpendicular lines, $\angle ADC$ is a right angle. A parallelogram with one right angle is a rectangle, so *ABCD* is a rectangle.

Step 3: Determine if *ABCD* is a rhombus.

$\overline{AC} \perp \overline{BD}$. A parallelogram with perpendicular diagonals is a rhombus. So *ABCD* is a rhombus.

Step 4: Determine if *ABCD* is a square.

Since *ABCD* is a rectangle and a rhombus, it has four right angles and four congruent sides. So *ABCD* is a square by definition.

So, the conclusion is valid.

(B) **Given:** $\overline{AB} \cong \overline{BC}$

Conclusion: *ABCD* is a rhombus.

The conclusion is not valid. It is true that if two consecutive sides of a parallelogram are congruent, then the parallelogram is a rhombus. To apply this theorem, however, you need to know that *ABCD* is a parallelogram. The given information is not sufficient to conclude that the figure is a parallelogram.

Reflect

7. Draw a figure that shows why this statement is not necessarily true: If one angle of a quadrilateral is a right angle, then the quadrilateral is a rectangle.

Your Turn

Determine if the conclusion is valid. If not, tell what additional information is needed to make it valid.

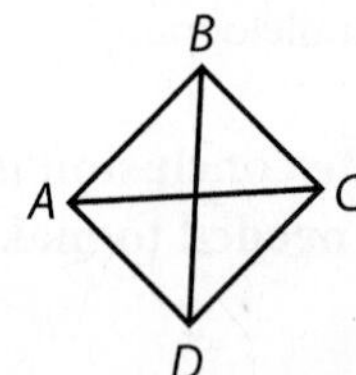

8. **Given:** $\angle ABC$ is a right angle.
Conclusion: *ABCD* is a rectangle.

Elaborate

9. Look at the theorem boxes in Example 1 and Example 2. How do the diagrams help you remember the conditions for proving a quadrilateral is a special parallelogram?

10. *EFGH* is a parallelogram. In *EFGH*, $\overline{EG} \cong \overline{FH}$. Which conclusion is incorrect?

A. *EFGH* is a rectangle.

B. *EFGH* is a square.

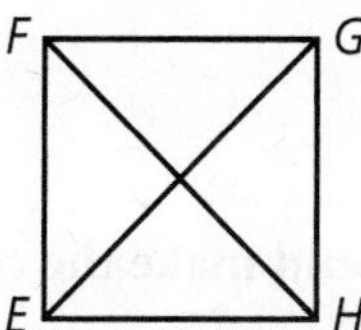

11. Essential Question Check-In How are theorems about conditions for parallelograms different from the theorems regarding parallelograms used in the previous lesson?

Evaluate: Homework and Practice

- Online Homework
- Hints and Help
- Extra Practice

1. Suppose Anna draws two line segments, $\overline{AB}$ and $\overline{CD}$ that intersect at point *E*. She draws them in such a way that $\overline{AB} \cong \overline{CD}$, $\overline{AB} \perp \overline{CD}$, and $\overline{AB}$ and $\overline{CD}$ bisect each other. What is the best name to describe *ACBD*? Explain.

2. Write a two-column proof that if the diagonals of a parallelogram are congruent, then the parallelogram is a rectangle.

Given: *EFGH* is a parallelogram; $\overline{EG} \cong \overline{HF}$.

Prove: *EFGH* is a rectangle.

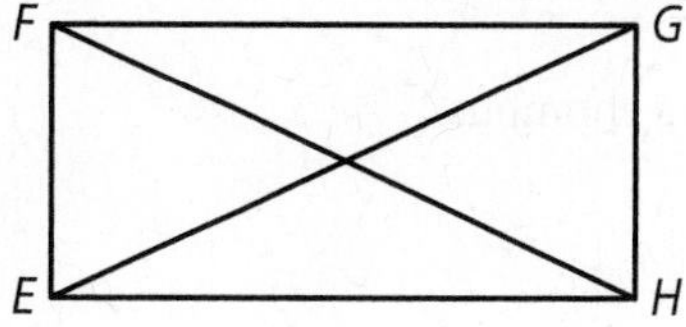

Determine whether each quadrilateral must be a rectangle. Explain.

3.

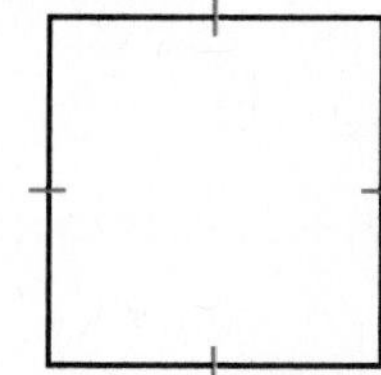

Given: $BD = AC$

4.

Each quadrilateral is a parallelogram. Determine whether each parallelogram is a rhombus or not.

5.

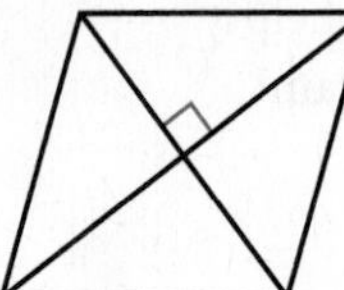

6.

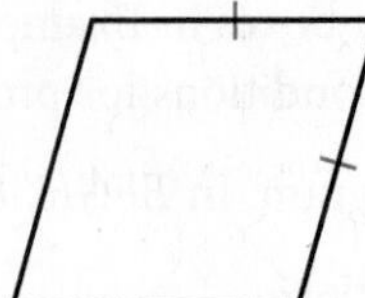

Give one characteristic about each figure that would make the conclusion valid.

7. Conclusion: *JKLM* is a rhombus.

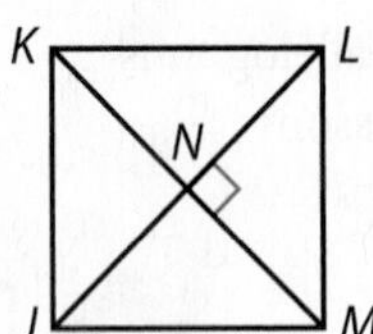

8. Conclusion: *PQRS* is a square.

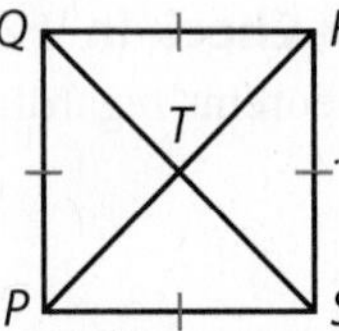

Determine if the conclusion is valid. If not, tell what additional information is needed to make it valid.

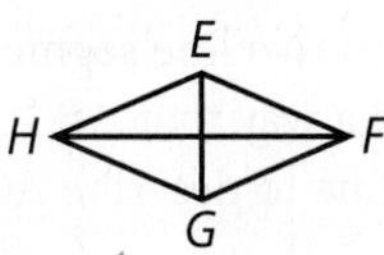

9. Given: $\overline{EG}$ and $\overline{FH}$ bisect each other. $\overline{EG} \perp \overline{FH}$

Conclusion: *EFGH* is a rhombus.

10. $\overline{FH}$ bisects $\angle EFG$ and $\angle EHG$.

Conclusion: *EFGH* is a rhombus.

Find the value of *x* that makes each parallelogram the given type.

11. square

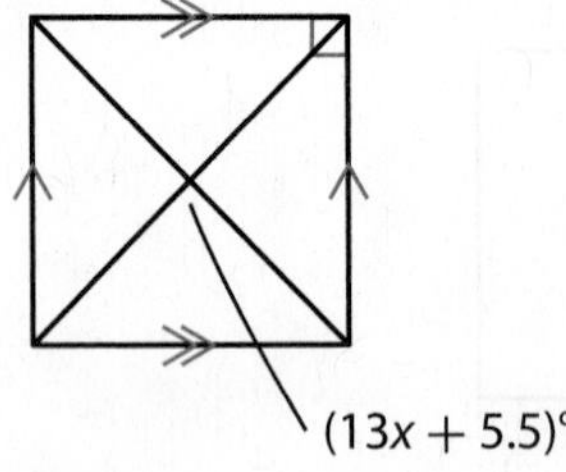

12. rhombus

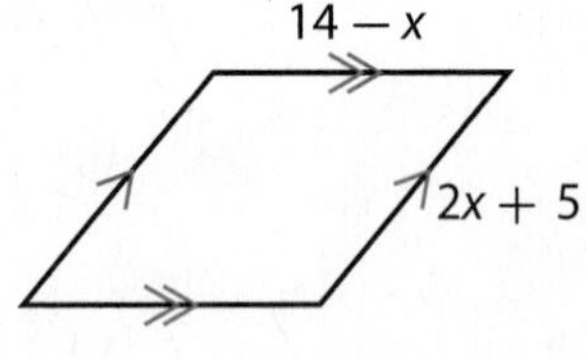

In Exercises 13–16, Determine which quadrilaterals match the figure: parallelogram, rhombus, rectangle, or square? List all that apply.

13. Given: $\overline{XY} \cong \overline{ZW}$, $\overline{XY} \parallel \overline{ZW}$, $\overline{WY} \cong \overline{XZ}$, $\overline{WY} \perp \overline{XZ}$

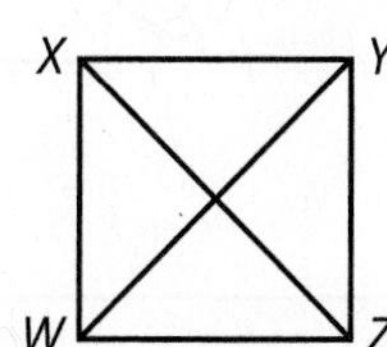

14. Given: $\overline{XY} \cong \overline{ZW}$, $\overline{XW} \cong \overline{ZY}$, $\overline{WY} \cong \overline{ZX}$

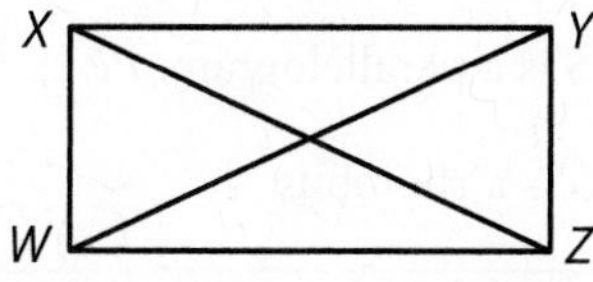

15. Given: $\angle WXY \cong \angle YZW$, $\angle XWZ \cong \angle ZYX$, $\angle XWY \cong \angle YWZ$, $\angle XYW \cong \angle ZYW$

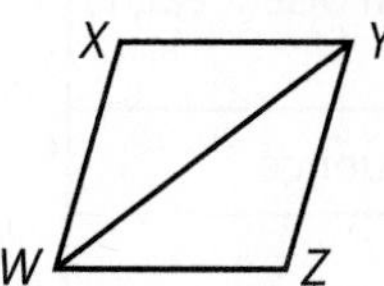

16. Given: $m\angle WXY = 130°$, $m\angle XWZ = 50°$, $m\angle WZY = 130°$

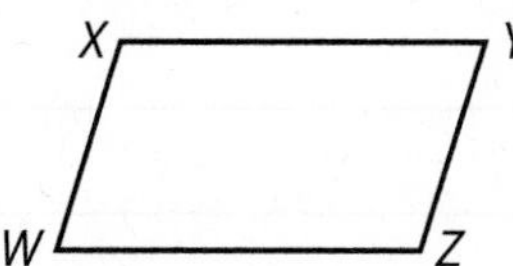

17. Represent Real-World Problems A framer uses a clamp to hold together pieces of a picture frame. The pieces are cut so that $\overline{PQ} \cong \overline{RS}$ and $\overline{QR} \cong \overline{SP}$. The clamp is adjusted so that PZ, QZ, RZ, and SZ are all equal lengths. Why must the frame be a rectangle?

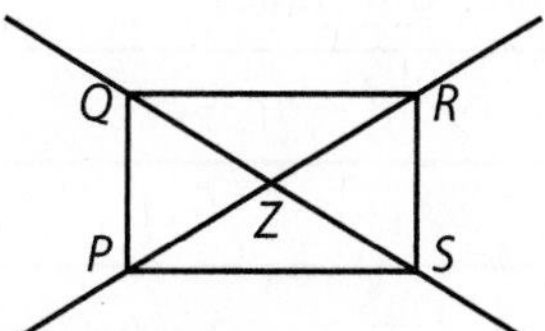

18. Represent Real-World Problems A city garden club is planting a square garden. They drive pegs into the ground at each corner and tie strings between each pair. The pegs are spaced so that $\overline{WX} \cong \overline{XY} \cong \overline{YZ} \cong \overline{ZW}$. How can the garden club use the diagonal strings to verify that the garden is a square?

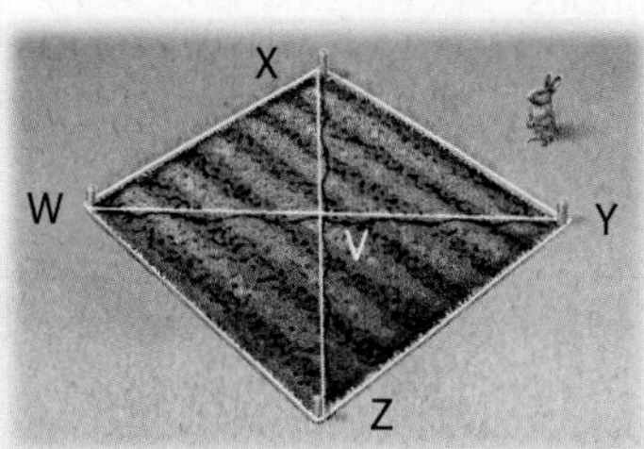

19. A quadrilateral is formed by connecting the midpoints of a rectangle. Which of the following could be the resulting figure? Select all that apply.

parallelogram	rectangle
rhombus	square

H.O.T. Focus on Higher Order Thinking

20. Critical Thinking The diagonals of a quadrilateral are perpendicular bisectors of each other. What is the best name for this quadrilateral? Explain your answer.

21. Draw Conclusions Think about the relationships between angles and sides in this triangular prism to decide if the given face is a rectangle.

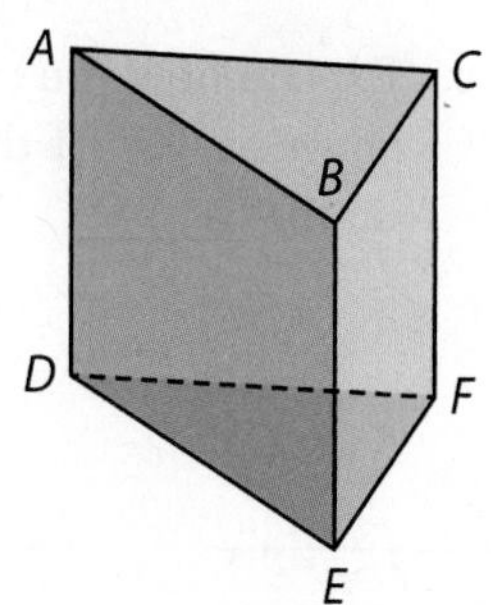

Given: $\overline{AC} \cong \overline{DF}$, $\overline{AB} \cong \overline{DE}$, $\overline{AB} \perp \overline{BC}$, $\overline{DE} \perp \overline{EF}$, $\overline{BE} \perp \overline{EF}$, $\overline{BC} \parallel \overline{EF}$

Prove: $EBCF$ is a rectangle.

22. Justify Reasoning Use one of the other rhombus theorems to prove that if the diagonals of a parallelogram are perpendicular, then the parallelogram is a rhombus.

Given: *PQRS* is a parallelogram. $\overline{PR} \perp \overline{QS}$

Prove: *PQRS* is a rhombus.

Statements	Reasons
1. *PQRS* is a parallelogram.	**1.** Given
2. $\overline{PT} \cong$ ___?___	**2.** Diagonals of a parallelogram bisect each other.
3. $\overline{QT} \cong$ ___?___	**3.** Reflexive Property of Congruence
4. $\overline{PR} \perp \overline{QS}$	**4.** Given
5. $\angle QTP$ and $\angle QTR$ are right angles.	**5.** ___?___
6. $\angle QTP \cong \angle QTR$	**6.** ___?___
7. $\triangle QTP \cong \triangle QTR$	**7.** ___?___
8. $\overline{QP} \cong$ ___?___	**8.** CPCTC
9. *PQRS* is a rhombus.	**9.** ___?___

Lesson Performance Task

The diagram shows the organizational ladder of groups to which tigers belong.

a. Use the terms below to create a similar ladder in which each term is a subset of the term above it.

Parallelogram	Geometric figures	Squares
Quadrilaterals	Figures	Rhombuses

b. Decide which of the following statements is true. Then write three more statements like it, using terms from the list in part (a).

If a figure is a rhombus, then it is a parallelogram.

If a figure is a parallelogram, then it is a rhombus.

c. Explain how you can use the ladder you created above to write if-then statements involving the terms on the list.

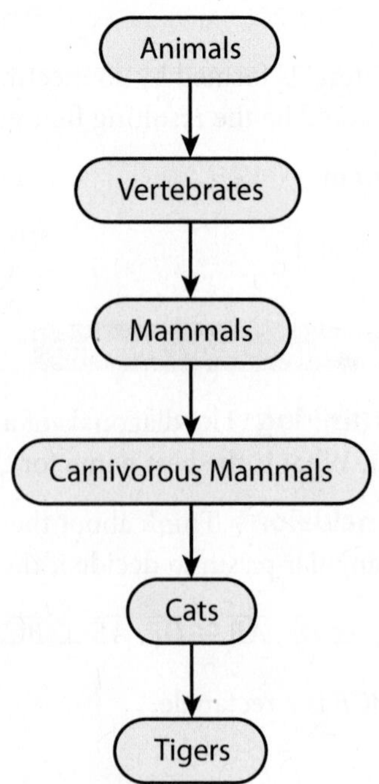

9.5 Properties and Conditions for Kites and Trapezoids

Essential Question: What are the properties of kites and trapezoids?

Resource Locker

Explore — Exploring Properties of Kites

A **kite** is a quadrilateral with two distinct pairs of congruent consecutive sides. In the figure, $\overline{PQ} \cong \overline{PS}$, and $\overline{QR} \cong \overline{SR}$, but $\overline{QR} \ncong \overline{QP}$.

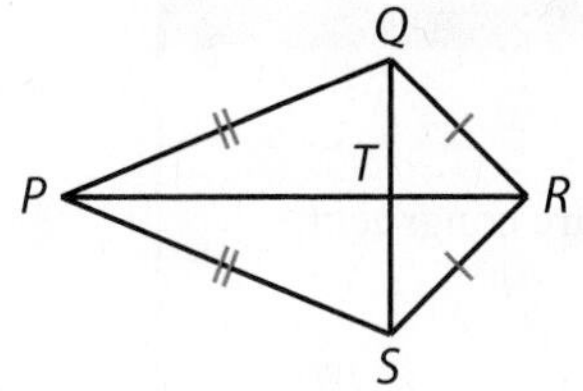

Measure the angles made by the sides and diagonals of a kite, noticing any relationships.

(A) Use a protractor to measure $\angle PTQ$ and $\angle QTR$ in the figure. What do your results tell you about the kite's diagonals, $\overline{PR}$ and $\overline{QS}$?

(B) Use a protractor to measure $\angle PQR$ and $\angle PSR$ in the figure. How are these opposite angles related?

(C) Measure $\angle QPS$ and $\angle QRS$ in the figure. What do you notice?

(D) Use a compass to construct your own kite figure on a separate sheet of paper. Begin by choosing a point *B*. Then use your compass to choose points *A* and *C* so that $AB = BC$.

(E) Now change the compass length and draw arcs from both points *A* and *C*. Label the intersection of the arcs as point D.

(F) Finally, draw the sides and diagonals of the kite.

Mark the intersection of the diagonals as point *E*.

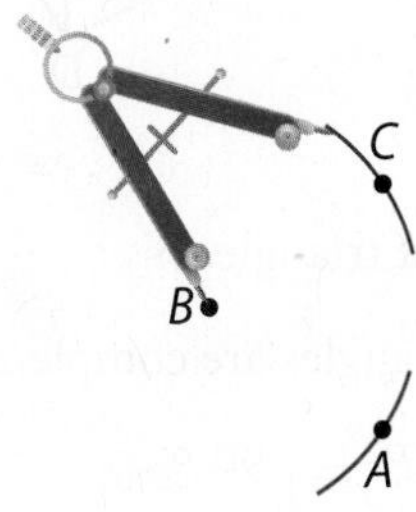

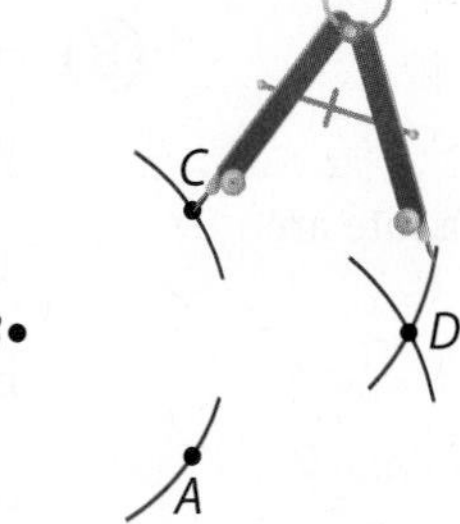

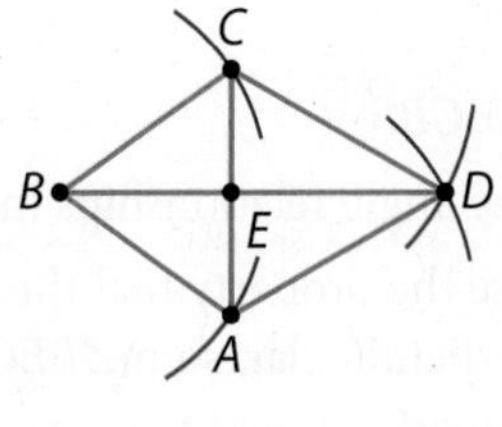

(G) Measure the angles of the kite *ABCD* you constructed in Steps D–F and the measure of the angles formed by the diagonals. Are your results the same as for the kite *PQRS* you used in Steps A–C?

Reflect

1. In the kite *ABCD* you constructed in Steps D–F, look at $\angle CDE$ and $\angle ADE$. What do you notice? Is this true for $\angle CBE$ and $\angle ABE$ as well? How can you state this in terms of diagonal $\overline{AC}$ and the pair of non-congruent opposite angles $\angle CBA$ and $\angle CDA$?

2. In the kite *ABCD* you constructed in Steps D–F, look at $\overline{EC}$ and $\overline{EA}$. What do you notice? Is this true for $\overline{EB}$ and $\overline{ED}$ as well? Which diagonal is a perpendicular bisector?

Explain 1 Using Relationships in Kites

The results of the Explore can be stated as theorems.

Four Kite Theorems

If a quadrilateral is a kite, then its diagonals are perpendicular.

If a quadrilateral is a kite, then exactly one pair of opposite angles are congruent.

If a quadrilateral is a kite, then one of the diagonals bisects the pair of non-congruent angles.

If a quadrilateral is a kite, then exactly one diagonal bisects the other.

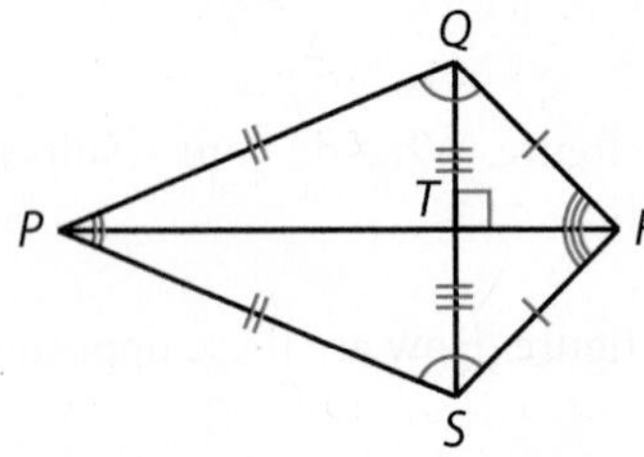

You can use the properties of kites to find unknown angle measures.

Example 1 **In kite *ABCD*, $m\angle BAE = 32°$ and $m\angle BCE = 62°$. Find each measure.**

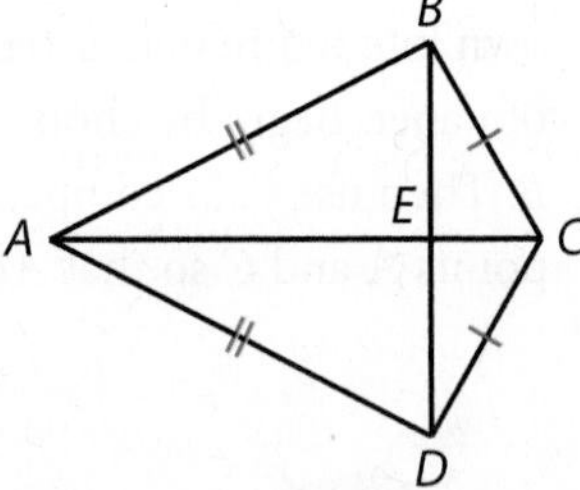

Ⓐ $m\angle CBE$

Use angle relationships in $\triangle BCE$.

Use the property that the diagonals of a kite are perpendicular, so $m\angle BEC = 90°$.

$\triangle BCE$ is a right triangle.

Therefore, its acute angles are complementary.

$m\angle BCE + m\angle CBE = 90°$

Substitute 62° for $m\angle BCE$, then solve for $m\angle CBE$.

$62° + m\angle CBE = 90°$

$m\angle CBE = 28°$

Ⓑ $m\angle ABE$

$\triangle ABE$ is also a right triangle.

Therefore, its acute angles are complementary.

$m\angle ABE + m\angle$ BAE $=$ 90 °

Substitute 32° for $m\angle$ BAE , then solve for $m\angle ABE$.

$m\angle ABE +$ 32 ° $=$ 90 °

$m\angle ABE =$ 58 °

Reflect

3. From Part A and Part B, what strategy could you use to determine m$\angle ADC$?

Your Turn

4. Determine m$\angle ADC$ in kite $ABCD$.

Explain 2 Proving that Base Angles of Isosceles Trapezoids are Congruent

A **trapezoid** is a quadrilateral with at least one pair of parallel sides.

The pair of parallel sides of the trapezoid (or either pair of parallel sides if the trapezoid is a parallelogram) are called the *bases* of the trapezoid.

The other two sides are called the *legs* of the trapezoid.

A trapezoid has two pairs of *base angles*: each pair consists of the two angles adjacent to one of the bases. An **isosceles trapezoid** is one in which the legs are congruent but not parallel.

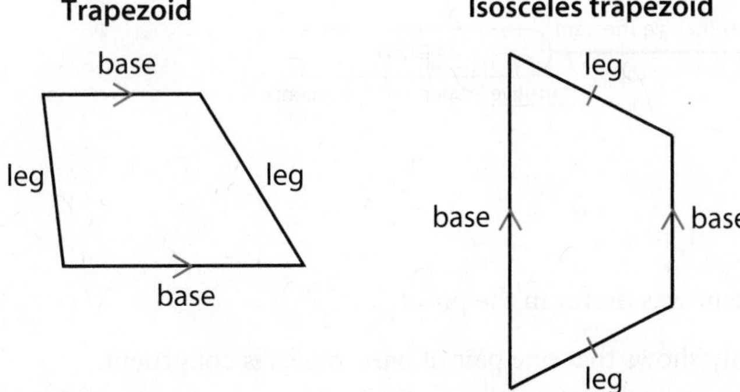

Three Isosceles Trapezoid Theorems
If a quadrilateral is an isosceles trapezoid, then each pair of base angles are congruent.
If a trapezoid has one pair of congruent base angles, then the trapezoid is isosceles.
A trapezoid is isosceles if and only if its diagonals are congruent.

You can use auxiliary segments to prove these theorems.

Example 2 Complete the flow proof of the first Isosceles Trapezoid Theorem.

Given: $ABCD$ is an isosceles trapezoid with $\overline{BC} \parallel \overline{AD}$, $\overline{AB} \cong \overline{DC}$.

Prove: $\angle A \cong \angle D$

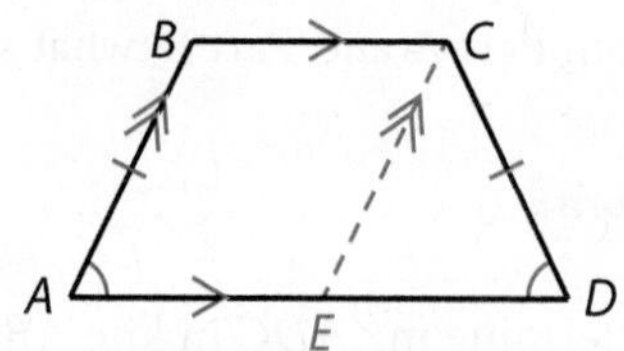

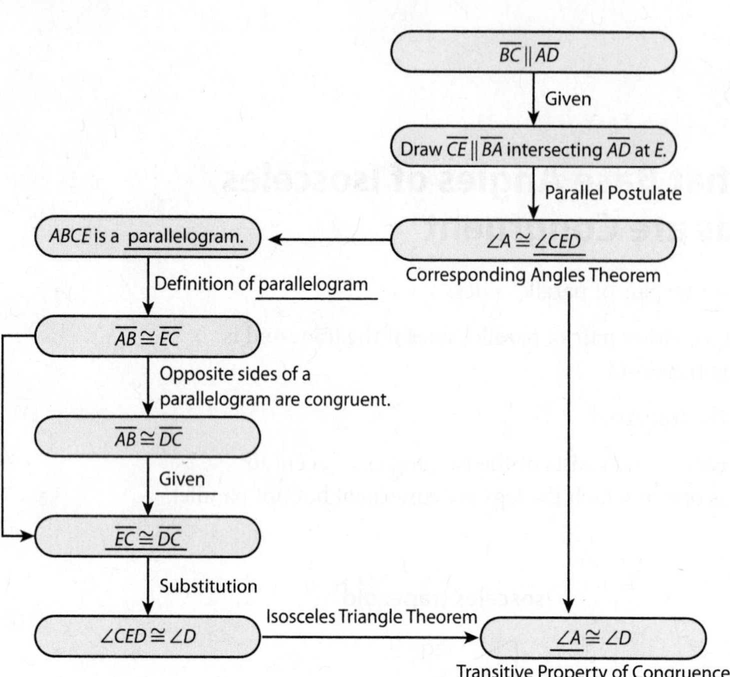

Reflect

5. Explain how the auxiliary segment was useful in the proof.

6. The flow proof in Example 2 only shows that one pair of base angles is congruent. Write a plan for proof for using parallel lines to show that the other pair of base angles $(\angle B$ and $\angle C)$ are also congruent.

Your Turn

7. Complete the proof of the second Isosceles Trapezoid Theorem: If a trapezoid has one pair of base angles congruent, then the trapezoid is isosceles.

Given: $ABCD$ is a trapezoid with $\overline{BC} \parallel \overline{AD}$, $\angle A \cong \angle D$.

Prove: $ABCD$ is an isosceles trapezoid.

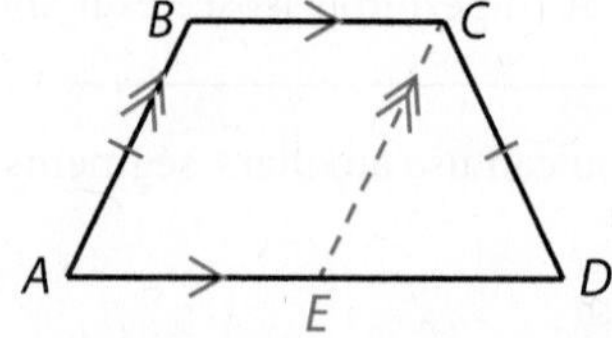

It is given that ? . By the ? , $\overline{CE}$ can be drawn parallel to ? so that ? intersects $\overline{AD}$ at E. By the Corresponding Angles Theorem, $\angle A \cong$? . It is given that $\angle A \cong$? , so by substitution, ? . By the Converse of the Isosceles Triangle Theorem, $\overline{CE} \cong$? . By definition, ? is a parallelogram. In a parallelogram, ? are congruent, so $\overline{AB} \cong$? . By the Transitive Property. of Congruence, $\overline{AB} \cong$? . Therefore, by definition, ? is an ? .

Explain 3 Using Theorems about Isosceles Trapezoids

You can use properties of isosceles trapezoids to find unknown values.

Example 3 **Find each measure or value.**

(A) A railroad bridge has side sections that show isosceles trapezoids. The figure *ABCD* represents one of these sections. $AC = 13.2$ m and $BE = 8.4$ m. Find *DE*.

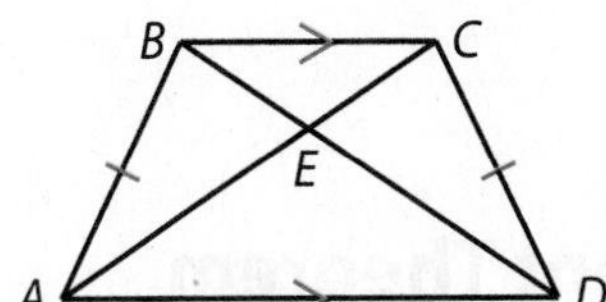

Use the property that the diagonals are congruent.	$\overline{AC} \cong \overline{BD}$
Use the definition of congruent segments.	$AC = BD$
Substitute 13.2 for *AC*.	$13.2 = BD$
Use the Segment Addition Postulate.	$BE + DE = BD$
Substitute 8.4 for *BE* and 13.2 for *BD*.	$8.4 + DE = 13.2$
Subtract 8.4 from both sides.	$DE = 4.8$

(B) Find the value of *x* so that trapezoid *EFGH* is isosceles.

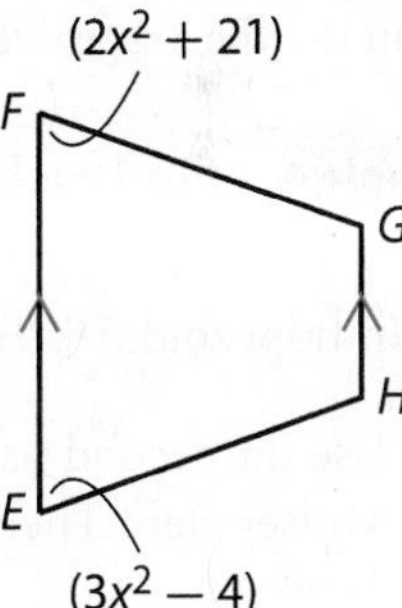

For *EFGH* to be isosceles, each pair of base angles are congruent.

In particular, the pair at *E* and *F* are congruent.	$\angle E \cong \angle F$
Use the definition of congruent angles.	$m\angle E = m\angle F$.
Substitute $3x^2 - 4$ for $m\angle E$ and $2x^2 + 21$ for $m\angle F$.	$3x^2 - 4 = 2x^2 + 21$
Substract $2x^2$ from both sides and add 4 to both sides.	$x^2 = 25$
Take the square root of both sides.	$x = 5$ or $x = -5$

Your Turn

8. In isosceles trapezoid $PQRS$, use the Same-Side Interior Angles Postulate to find $m\angle R$.

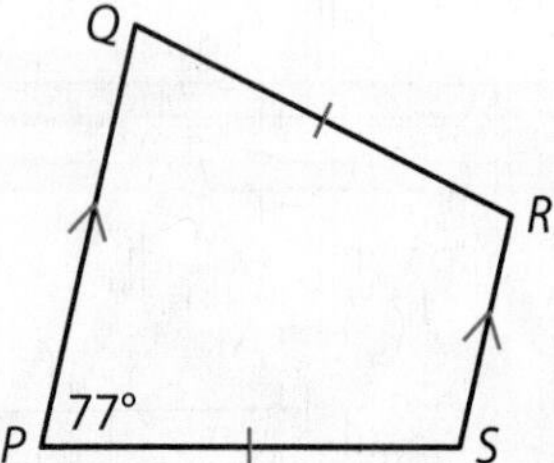

9. $JL = 3y + 6$ and $KM = 22 - y$. Determine the value of y so that trapezoid $JKLM$ is isosceles.

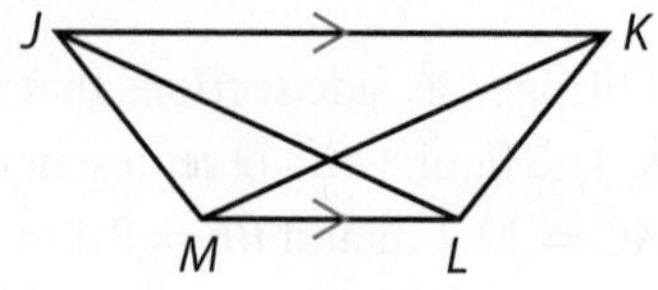

Explain 4 Using the Trapezoid Midsegment Theorem

The **midsegment of a trapezoid** is the segment whose endpoints are the midpoints of the legs.

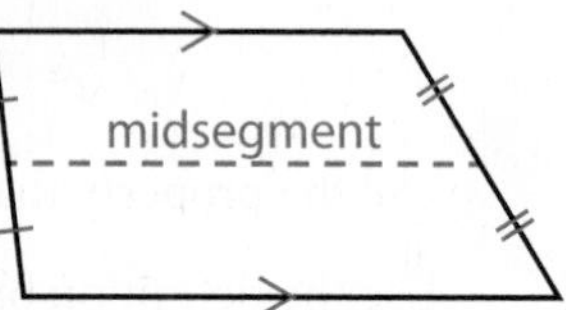

Trapezoid Midsegment Theorem

The midsegment of a trapezoid is parallel to each base, and its length is one half the sum of the lengths of the bases.

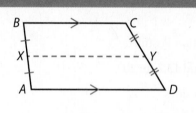

$\overline{XY} \parallel \overline{BC}$, $\overline{XY} \parallel \overline{AD}$

$XY = \frac{1}{2}(BC + AD)$

You can use the Trapezoid Midsegment Theorem to find the length of the midsegment or a base of a trapezoid.

Example 4 **Find each length.**

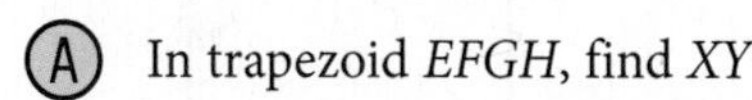

(A) In trapezoid $EFGH$, find XY.

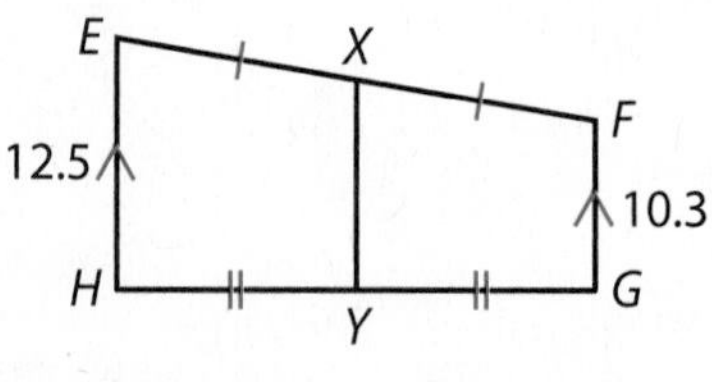

Use the second part of the Trapezoid Midsegment Theorem. $XY = \frac{1}{2}(EH + FG)$

Substitute 12.5 for EH and 10.3 for FG. $= \frac{1}{2}(12.5 + 10.3)$

Simplify. $= 11.4$

(B) In trapezoid $JKLM$, find JM.

Use the second part of the Trapezoid Midsegment Theorem. $PQ = \frac{1}{2}(KL + JM)$

Substitute 9.8 for PQ and 8.3 for KL. $9.8 = \frac{1}{2}(8.3 + JM)$

Multiply both sides by 2. $19.6 = 8.3 + JM$

Subtract 8.3 from both sides. $11.3 = JM$

Your Turn

10. In trapezoid $PQRS$, $PQ = 2RS$. Find XY.

Elaborate

11. Use the information in the graphic organizer to complete the Venn diagram.

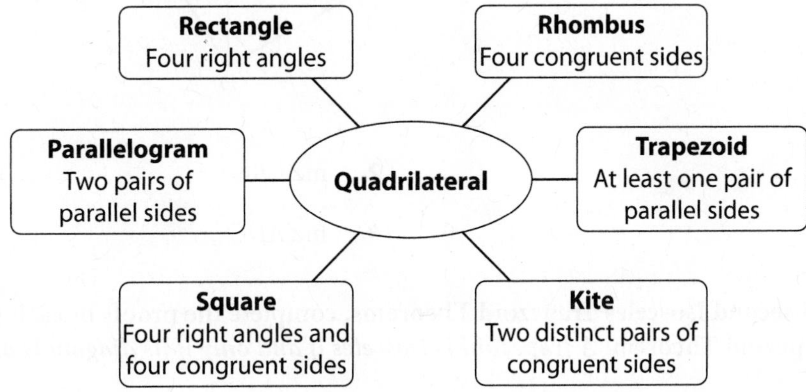

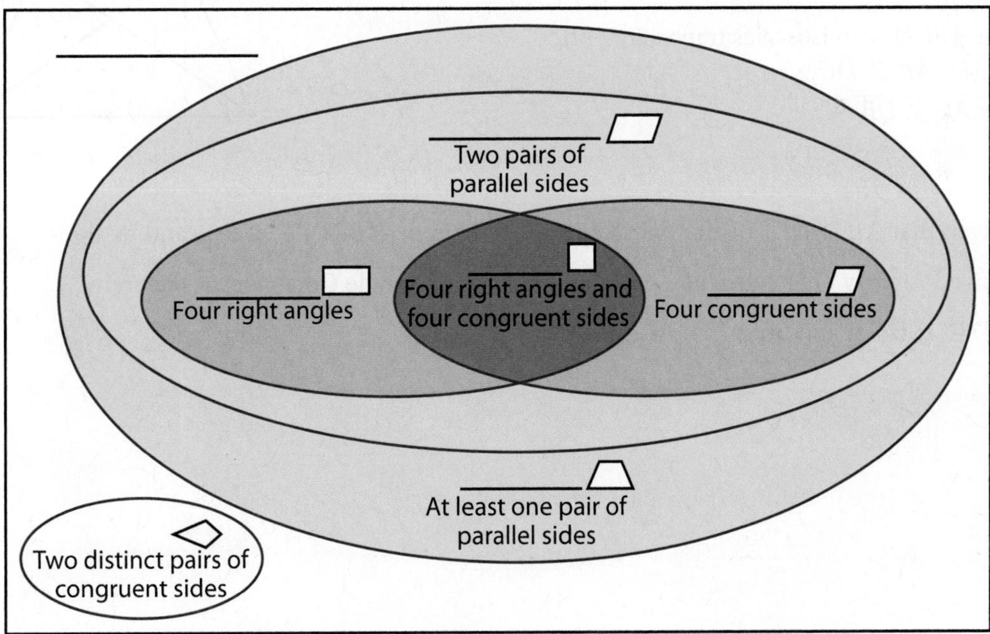

What can you conclude about all parallelograms?

12. **Discussion** The Isosceles Trapezoid Theorem about congruent diagonals is in the form of a biconditional statement. Is it possible to state the two isosceles trapezoid theorems about base angles as a biconditional statement? Explain.

13. **Essential Question Check-In** Do kites and trapezoids have properties that are related to their diagonals? Explain.

Evaluate: Homework and Practice

- Online Homework
- Hints and Help
- Extra Practice

In kite $ABCD$, $m\angle BAE = 28°$ and $m\angle BCE = 57°$. Find each measure.

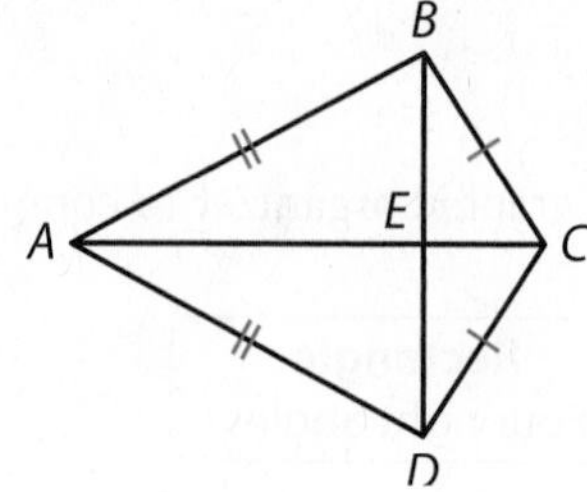

1. $m\angle ABE$

2. $m\angle CBE$

3. $m\angle ABC$

4. $m\angle ADC$

Using the first and second Isosceles Trapezoid Theorems, complete the proofs of each part of the third Isosceles Trapezoid Theorem: ***A trapezoid is isosceles if and only if its diagonals are congruent.***

5. Prove part 1: If a trapezoid is isosceles, then its diagonals are congruent.

Given: $ABCD$ is an isosceles trapezoid with $\overline{BC} \parallel \overline{AD}$, $\overline{AB} \cong \overline{DC}$.

Prove: $\overline{AC} \cong \overline{DB}$

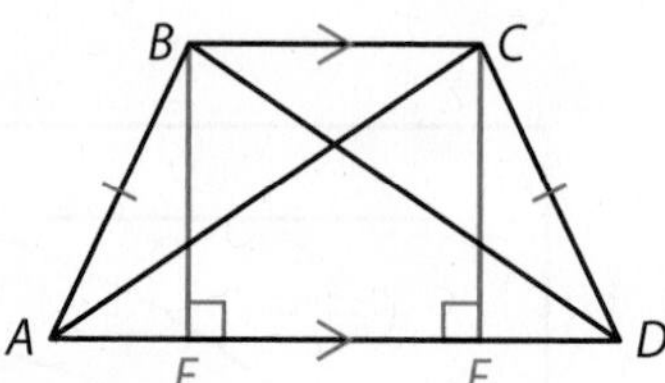

It is given that $\overline{AB} \cong \overline{DC}$. By the first Trapezoid Theorem, $\angle BAD \cong$? , and by the Reflexive Property of Congruence, ? . By the SAS Triangle Congruence Theorem, $\triangle ABD \cong \triangle DCA$, and by ? , $\overline{AC} \cong \overline{DB}$.

6. Prove part 2: If the diagonals of a trapezoid are congruent, then the trapezoid is isosceles.
Given: $ABCD$ is a trapezoid with $\overline{BC} \parallel \overline{AD}$ and diagonals $\overline{AC} \cong \overline{DB}$.
Prove: $ABCD$ is an isosceles trapezoid.

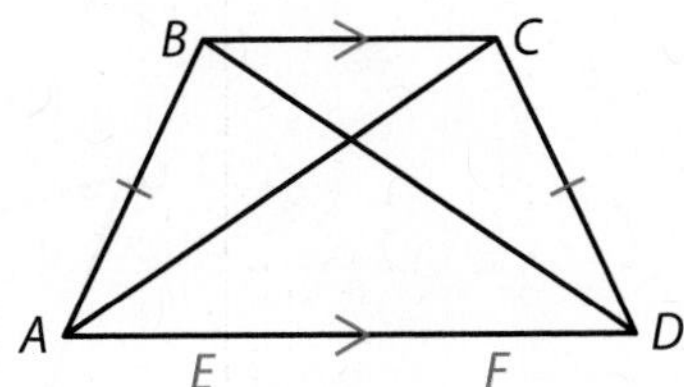

Statements	Reasons
1. Draw $\overline{BE} \perp \overline{AD}$ and $\overline{CF} \perp \overline{AD}$.	1. There is only one line through a given point perpendicular to a given line, so each auxiliary line can be drawn.
2. $\overline{BE} \parallel \overline{CF}$	2. Two lines perpendicular to the same line are parallel.
3. ?	3. Given
4. $BCFE$ is a parallelogram.	4. ? *(Steps 2, 3)*
5. $\overline{BE} \cong$?	5. If a quadrilateral is a parallelogram, then its opposite sides are congruent.
6. $\overline{AC} \cong \overline{DB}$	6. ?
7. ?	7. Definition of perpendicular lines
8. $\triangle BED \cong \triangle CFA$	8. HL Triangle Congruence Theorem *(Steps 5–7)*
9. $\angle BDE \cong \angle CAF$	9. ?
10. $\angle CBD \cong$? , ? $\cong \angle CAF$	10. Alternate Interior Angles Theorem
11. $\angle CBD \cong$?	11. Transitive Property of Congruence *(Steps 9, 10)*
12. ?	12. Given
13. $\overline{BC} \cong \overline{BC}$	13. ?
14. $\triangle ABC \cong \triangle DCB$	14. ? *(Steps 12, 13)*
15. $\angle BAC \cong \angle CDB$	15. CPCTC
16. $\angle BAD \cong$?	16. Angle Addition Postulate
17. $ABCD$ is isosceles.	17. If a trapezoid has one pair of base angles congruent, then the trapezoid is isosceles.

Use the isosceles trapezoid to find each measure or value.

7. $LJ = 19.3$ and $KN = 8.1$. Determine MN.

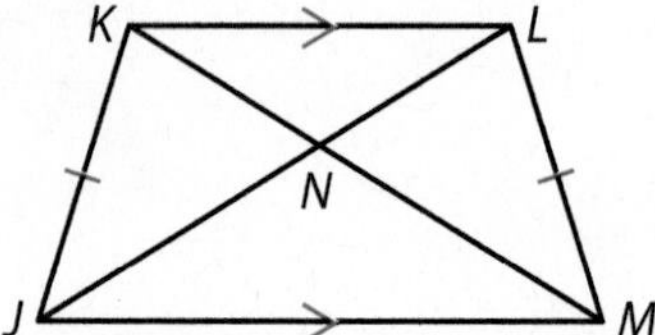

8. Find the positive value of x so that trapezoid $PQRS$ is isosceles.

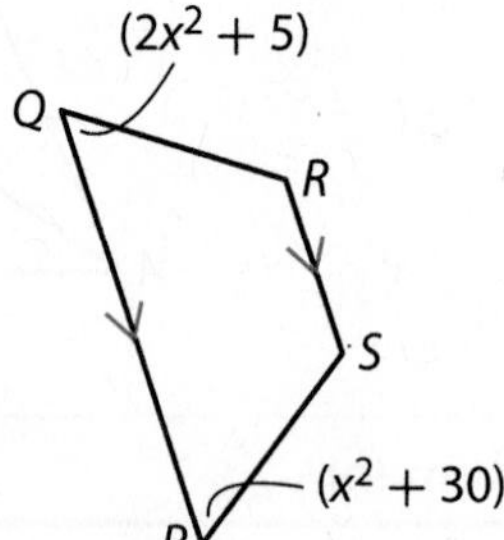

9. In isosceles trapezoid $EFGH$, use the Same-Side Interior Angles Postulate to determine $m\angle E$.

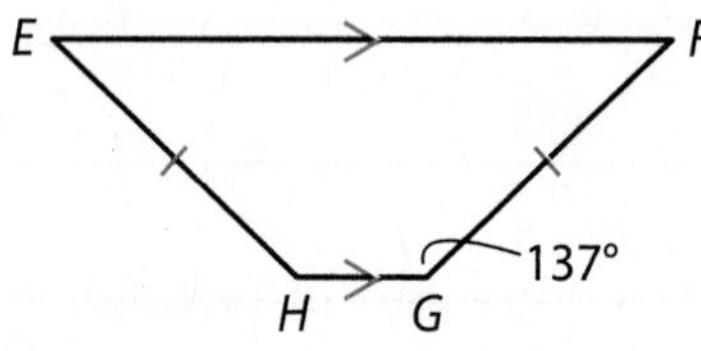

10. $AC = 3y + 12$ and $BD = 27 - 2y$. Determine the value of y so that trapezoid $ABCD$ is isosceles.

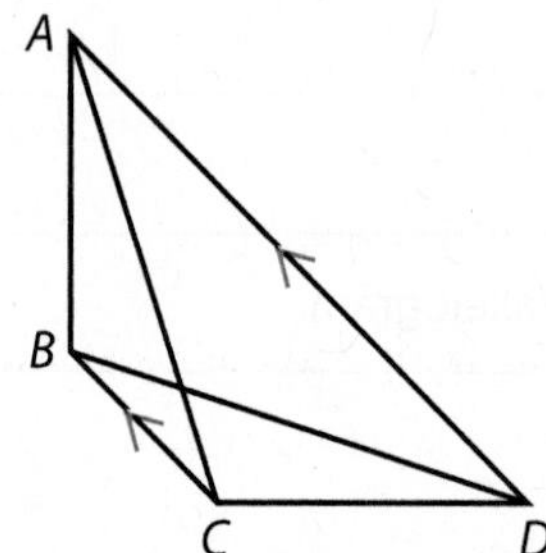

Find the unknown segment lengths in each trapezoid.

11. In trapezoid $ABCD$, find XY.

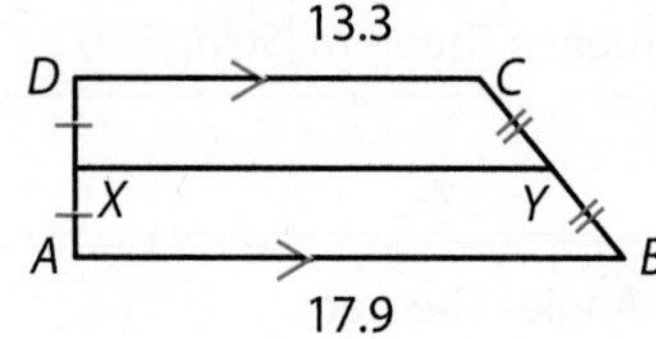

12. In trapezoid $EFGH$, find FG.

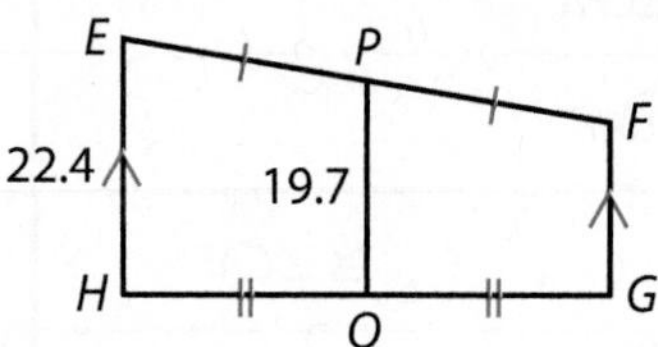

13. In trapezoid *PQRS*, $PQ = 4RS$. Determine *XY*.

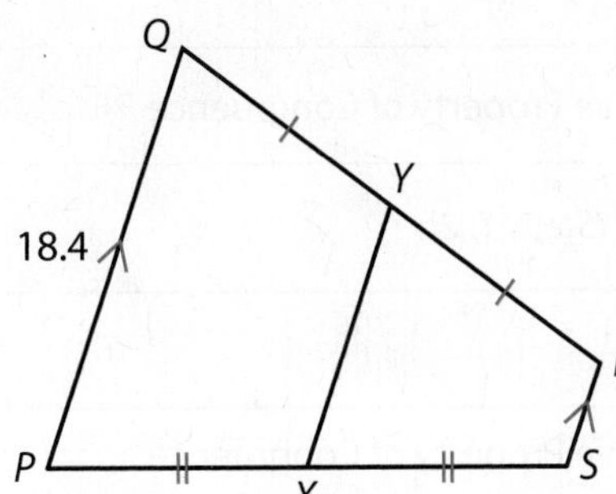

14. In trapezoid *JKLM*, $PQ = 2JK$. Determine *LM*.

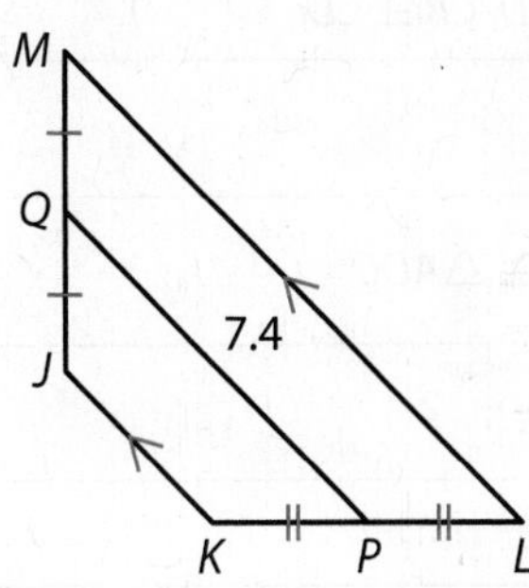

15. Determine whether each of the following describes a kite or a trapezoid.

A. Has two distinct pairs of congruent consecutive sides

B. Has diagonals that are perpendicular

C. Has at least one pair of parallel sides

D. Has exactly one pair of opposite angles that are congruent

E. Has two pairs of base angles

16. Multi-Step Complete the proof of each of the four Kite Theorems. The proof of each of the four theorems relies on the same initial reasoning, so they are presented here in a single two-column proof.

Given: *ABCD* is a kite, with $\overline{AB} \cong \overline{AD}$ and $\overline{CB} \cong \overline{CD}$.

Prove: (i) $\overline{AC} \perp \overline{BD}$;

(ii) $\angle ABC \cong \angle ADC$;

(iii) $\overline{AC}$ bisects $\angle BAD$ and $\angle BCD$;

(iv) $\overline{AC}$ bisects $\overline{BD}$.

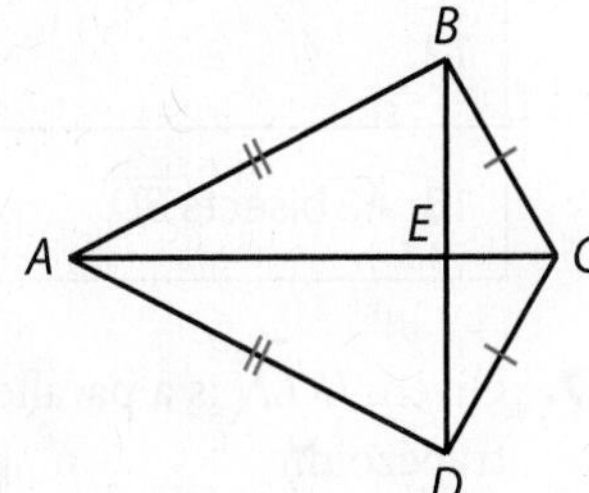

Statements	Reasons
1. $\overline{AB} \cong \overline{AD}$, $\overline{CB} \cong \overline{CD}$	1. Given
2. $\overline{AC} \cong$?	2. Reflexive Property of Congruence
3. $\triangle ABC \cong \triangle ADC$	3. ? *(Steps 1, 2)*
4. $\angle BAE \cong$?	4. CPCTC
5. $\overline{AE} \cong \overline{AE}$	5. Reflexive Property of Congruence
6. ?	6. SAS Triangle Congruence Theorem *(Steps 1, 4, 5)*
7. $\angle AEB \cong \angle AED$	7. ?
8. $\overline{AC} \perp \overline{BD}$	8. If two lines intersect to form a linear pair of congruent angles, then the lines are perpendicular.
9. $\angle ABC \cong$?	9. ? *(Step 3)*
10. $\angle BAC \cong$? and ? $\cong \angle DCA$	10. ? *(Step 3)*
11. $\overline{AC}$ bisects $\angle BAD$ and $\angle BCD$.	11. Definition of ?
12. ? $\cong$?	12. CPCTC *(Step 6)*
13. $\overline{AC}$ bisects $\overline{BD}$.	13. ?

17. Given: *JKLN* is a parallelogram. *JKMN* is an isosceles trapezoid.

Prove: $\triangle KLM$ is an isosceles triangle.

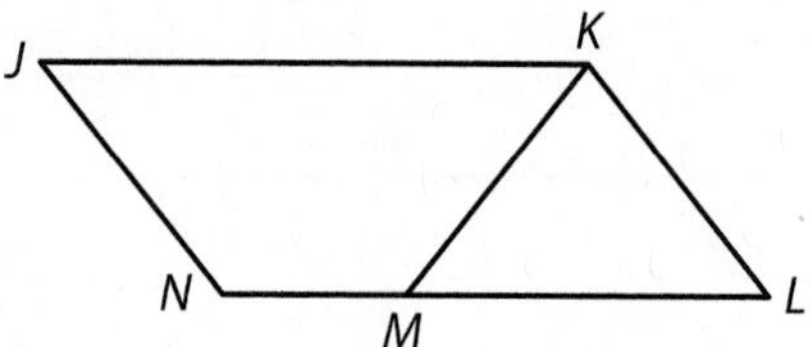

Algebra Find the length of the midsegment of each trapezoid.

18.

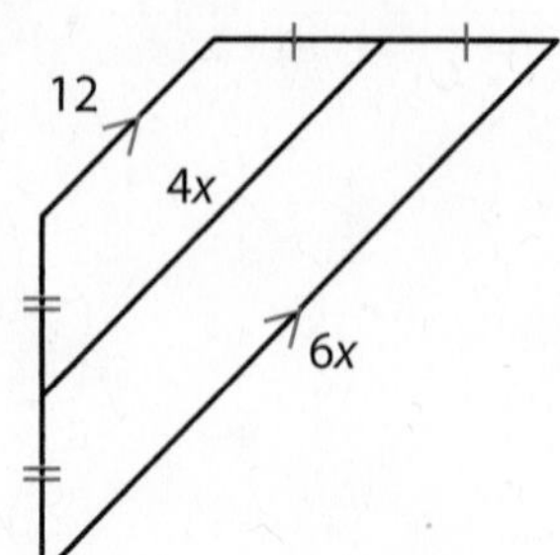

19.

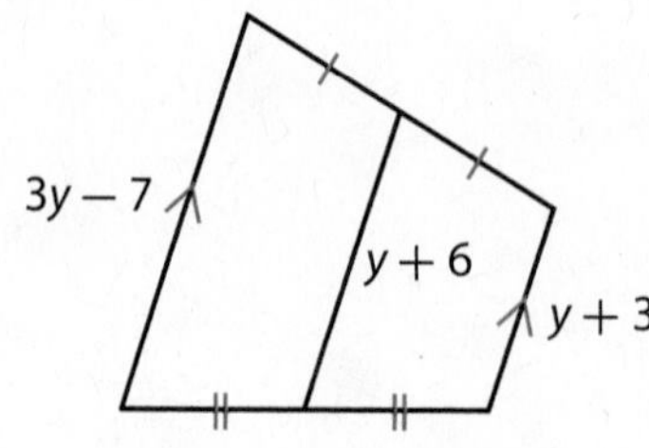

20. Represent Real-World Problems A set of shelves fits an attic room with one sloping wall. The left edges of the shelves line up vertically, and the right edges line up along the sloping wall. The shortest shelf is 32 in. long, and the longest is 40 in. long. Given that the three shelves are equally spaced vertically, what total length of shelving is needed?

21. Represent Real-World Problems A common early stage in making an origami model is known as the kite. The figure shows a paper model at this stage unfolded.

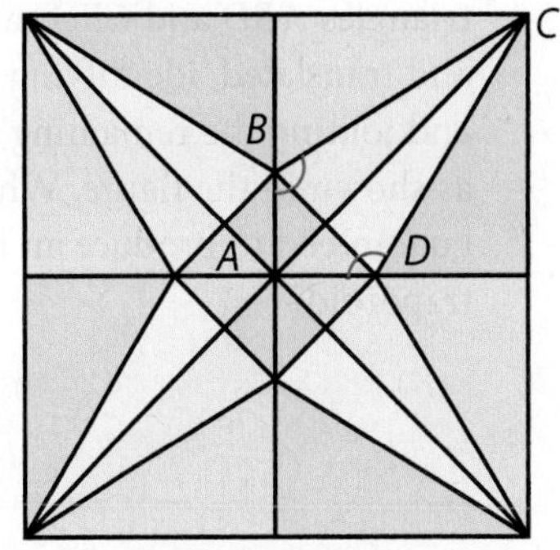

The folds create four geometric kites. Also, the 16 right triangles adjacent to the corners of the paper are all congruent, as are the 8 right triangles adjacent to the center of the paper. Find the measures of all four angles of the kite labeled *ABCD* (the point A is the center point of the diagram). Use the facts that $\angle B \cong \angle D$ and that the interior angle sum of a quadrilateral is 360°.

22. Analyze Relationships The window frame is a regular octagon. It is made from eight pieces of wood shaped like congruent isosceles trapezoids. What are $m\angle A$, $m\angle B$, $m\angle C$, and $m\angle D$ in trapezoid *ABCD*?

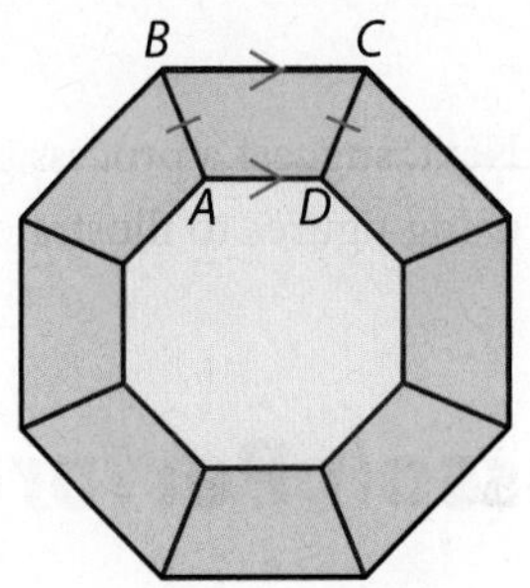

23. Explain the Error In kite *ABCD*, $m\angle BAE = 66°$ and $m\angle ADE = 59°$. Terrence is trying to find $m\angle ABC$. He knows that $\overline{BD}$ bisects $\overline{AC}$, and that therefore $\triangle AED \cong \triangle CED$. He reasons that $\angle ADE \cong \angle CDE$, so that $m\angle ADC = 2(59°) = 118°$, and that $\angle ABC \cong \angle ADC$ because they are opposite angles in the kite, so that $m\angle ABC = 118°$. Explain Terrence's error and describe how to find $m\angle ABC$.

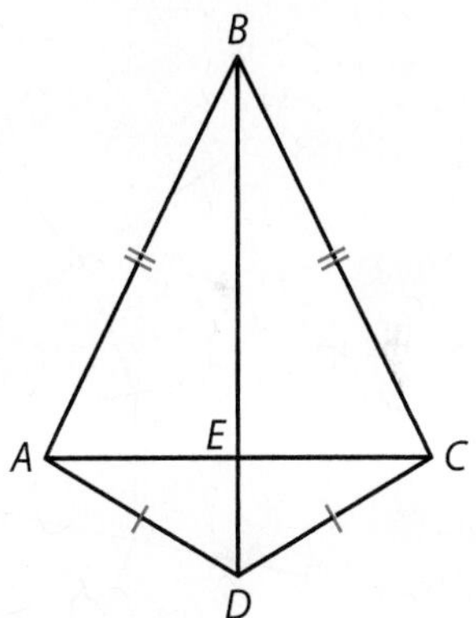

24. Copy and complete the table to classify all quadrilateral types by the rotational symmetries and line symmetries they must have. Identify any patterns that you see and explain what these patterns indicate.

Quadrilateral	Angle of Rotational Symmetry	Number of Line Symmetries
kite	?	1
non-isosceles trapezoid	none	?
isosceles trapezoid	?	?
parallelogram	180°	?
rectangle	?	?
rhombus	?	?
square	?	?

H.O.T. Focus on Higher Order Thinking

25. **Communicate Mathematical Ideas** Describe the properties that rhombuses and kites have in common, and the properties that are different.

26. **Analyze Relationships** In kite $ABCD$, triangles ABD and CBD can be rotated and translated, identifying $\overline{AD}$ with $\overline{CD}$ and joining the remaining pair of vertices, as shown in the figure. Why is this process guaranteed to produce an isosceles trapezoid?

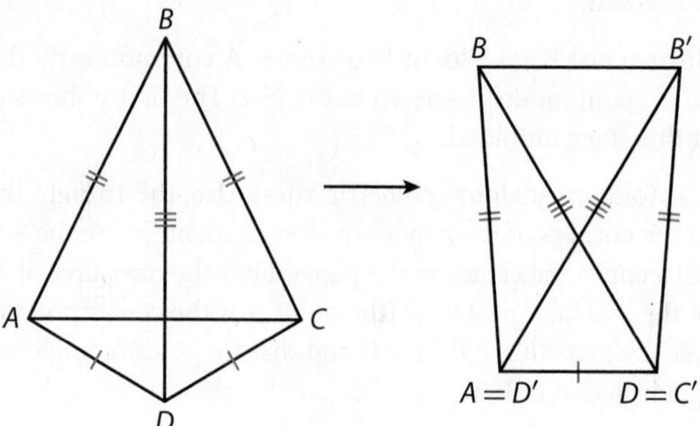

Next, suggest a process guaranteed to produce a kite from an isosceles trapezoid, using figures to illustrate your process.

Lesson Performance Task

This model of a spider web is made using only isosceles triangles and isosceles trapezoids.

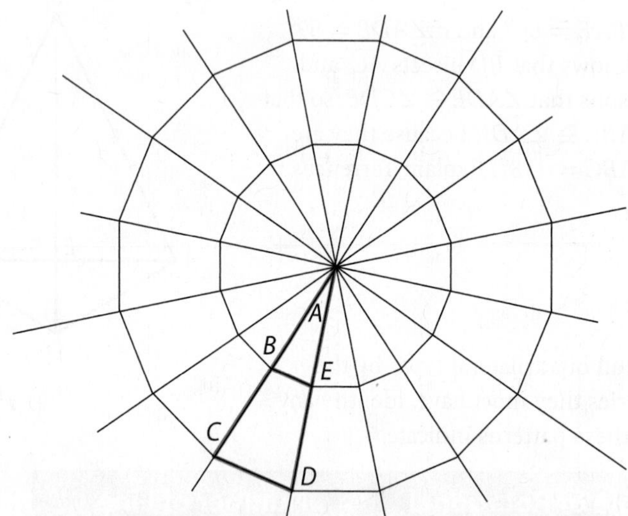

a. All of the figures surrounding the center of the web are congruent to figure $ABCDE$. Find $m\angle A$. Explain how you found your answer.

b. Find $m\angle ABE$ and $m\angle AEB$.

c. Find $m\angle CBE$ and $m\angle DEB$.

d. Find $m\angle C$ and $m\angle D$.

STUDY GUIDE REVIEW

Properties of Quadrilaterals

MODULE 9

Essential Question: How can you use properties of quadrilaterals to solve real-world problems?

Key Vocabulary

diagonal *(diagonal)*
isosceles trapezoid *(trapecio isósceles)*
kite *(el deltoide)*
midsegment of a trapezoid *(segmento medio de un trapecio)*
parallelogram *(paralelogramo)*
quadrilateral *(cuadrilátero)*
rectangle *(rectángulo)*
rhombus *(rombo)*
square *(cuadrado)*
trapezoid *(trapecio)*

KEY EXAMPLE (Lesson 9.1)

Given: *ABCD* and *EDGF* are parallelograms.

Prove: $\angle A \cong \angle G$

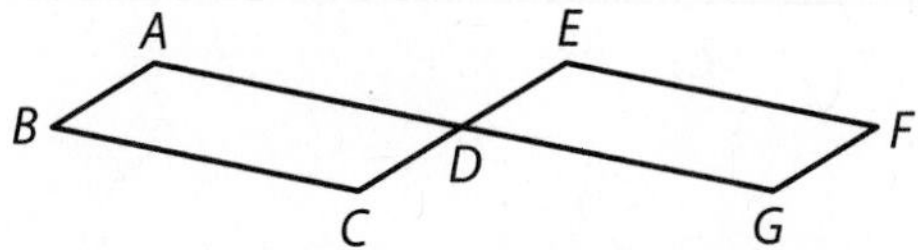

Statements	Reasons
ABCD and *EDGF* are parallelograms.	Given
$\angle A \cong \angle C$	Opposite angles of a parallelogram are congruent.
$\overline{BC} \parallel \overline{AG}$	Definition of a parallelogram
$\angle C \cong \angle CDG$	Alt. interior angles theorem
$\angle CDG \cong \angle ADE$	Vertical angles theorem
$\overline{CE} \parallel \overline{FG}$	Definition of a parallelogram
$\angle ADE \cong \angle G$	Corres. angles theorem
$\angle A \cong \angle G$	Transitive property of congruence

KEY EXAMPLE (Lesson 9.2)

Find the angle and side lengths when *t* is 19 to see if the figure is a parallelogram.

$2t + 13$

$(7t + 5)°$

$(3t - 15)°$

$3t - 6$

$2(19) + 13 = 51$

$3(19) - 6 = 51$

$3(19) - 15 = 42$

$7(19) + 5 = 138$

The top side is equivalent to the bottom. Also, the top side is parallel to the bottom because the same-side interior angles are supplementary. Therefore, this figure is a parallelogram because a pair of opposite sides are parallel and congruent.

KEY EXAMPLE (Lesson 9.3)

Prove that $\triangle ABE \cong \triangle ADE$ given that $ABCD$ is a rhombus.

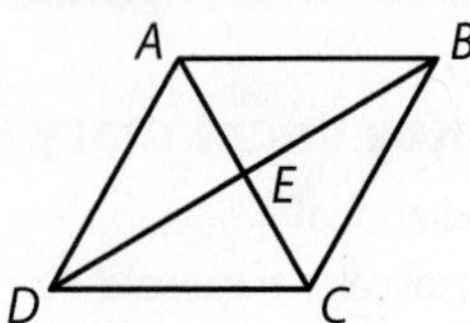

$\overline{AE} \cong \overline{AE}$ by the Reflexive Property.
Since $ABCD$ is a rhombus, $\overline{AB} \cong \overline{AD}$. Since a rhombus is also a parallelogram, $\overline{BE} \cong \overline{DE}$. Therefore, $\triangle ABE \cong \triangle ADE$ via the SSS Congruence Theorem.

KEY EXAMPLE (Lesson 9.4)

Determine which quadrilaterals match the figure: parallelogram, rhombus, rectangle, or square.

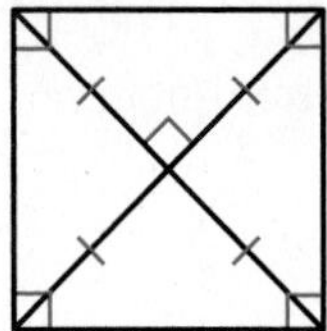

Since the figure has four 90° angles and the diagonals are perpendicular bisectors of each other, then the figure is a square. Since the figure is a square, then it is also a rectangle, rhombus, and parallelogram.

KEY EXAMPLE (Lesson 9.5)

Prove that $\triangle ADC \cong \triangle BCD$ given that $ABCD$ is an isosceles trapezoid.

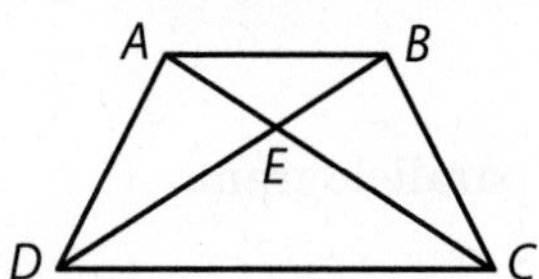

Statements	Reasons
$\overline{AD} \cong \overline{BC}$	Definition of an isosceles trapezoid
$\overline{AC} \cong \overline{BD}$	Diagonals of an isosceles trapezoid are congruent
$\overline{DC} \cong \overline{CD}$	Reflexive Property of Congruence
$\triangle ADC \cong \triangle BCD$	SSS Congruence Theorem

EXERCISES

***EFGH* is a parallelogram. Find the given side length.** *(Lesson 9.1)*

1. EF

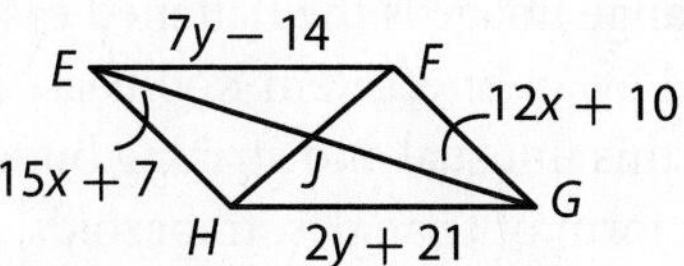

2. EG

Determine if each quadrilateral is a parallelogram. Justify your answer. *(Lesson 9.2)*

3.

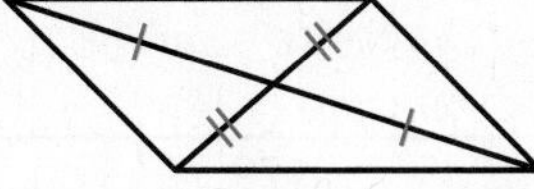

4.

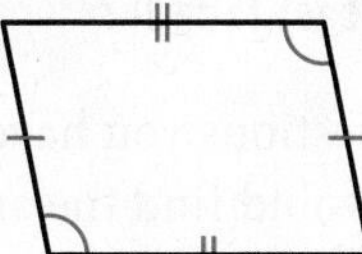

Find the measures of the numbered angles in each rhombus. *(Lesson 9.3)*

5.

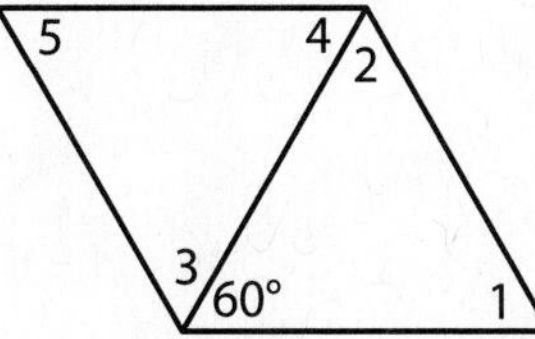

6.

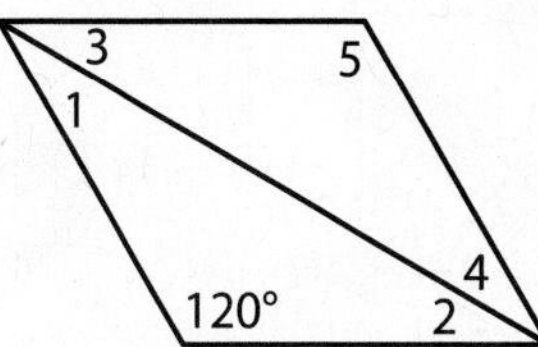

Find the value of *x* that makes each parallelogram the given type. *(Lesson 9.4)*

7. Rectangle

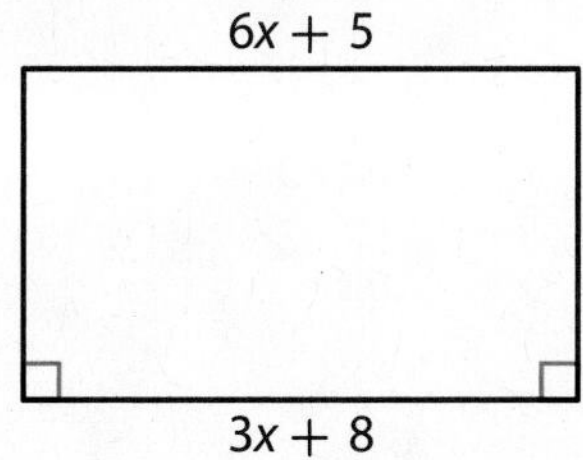

8. Square

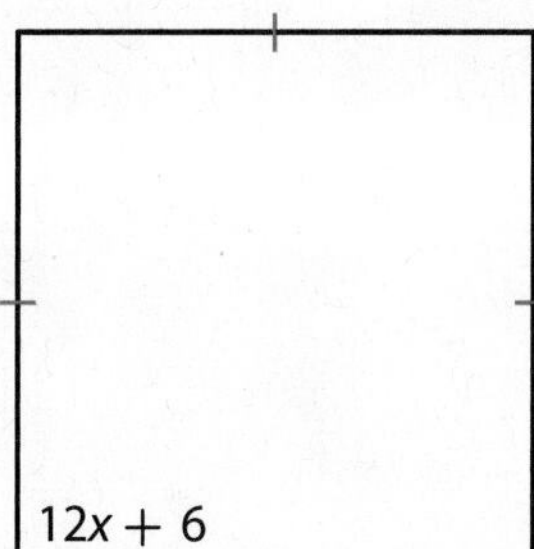

9. **A farm, in the shape of an isosceles trapezoid, is putting up fences on its diagonals. If one fence has sixteen 9-foot segments, how many 8-foot segments will the other fence have?** *(Lesson 9.5)*

MODULE PERFORMANCE TASK

How Big Is That Face?

This strange image is the flattened east façade of the central library in Seattle, WA, designed by architect Rem Koolhaas. The faces of this unusual and striking building take the form of triangles, trapezoids, and other quadrilaterals.

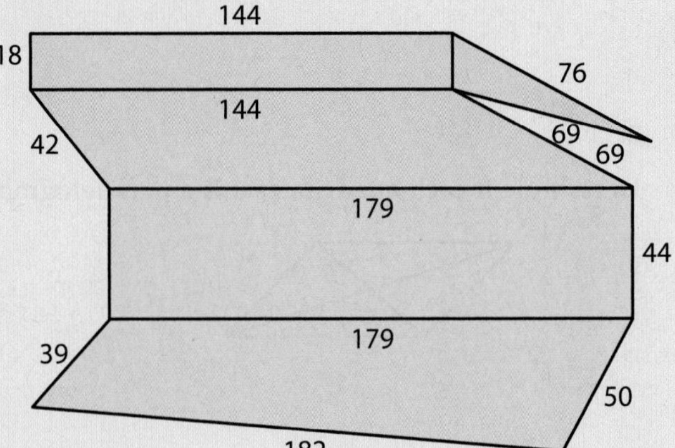

The diagram shows the dimensions of the faces labeled in feet. What is the total surface area of the east façade?

Write down any questions you have and describe how you would find the area. Be sure to write down all your data and assumptions. Then use numbers, words, or algebra to explain how you reached your conclusion.

Ready to Go On?

9.1–9.5 Properties of Quadrilaterals

- Online Homework
- Hints and Help
- Extra Practice

Find angle measure *x* on each given figure. *(Lessons 9.2, 9.4, 9.5)*

1.

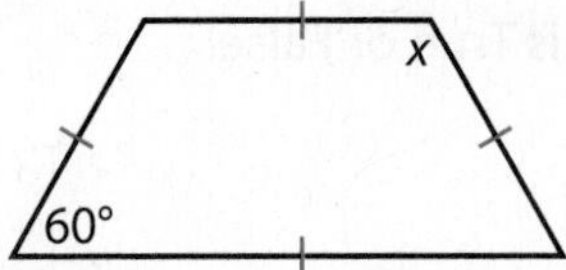

2.

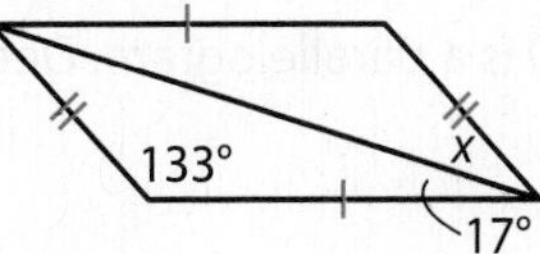

3.

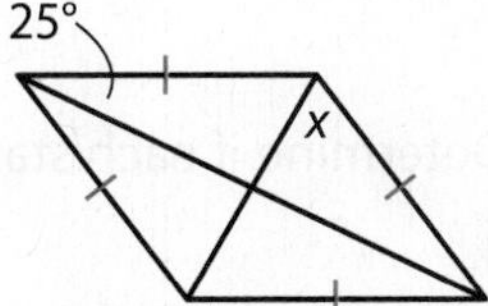

4.

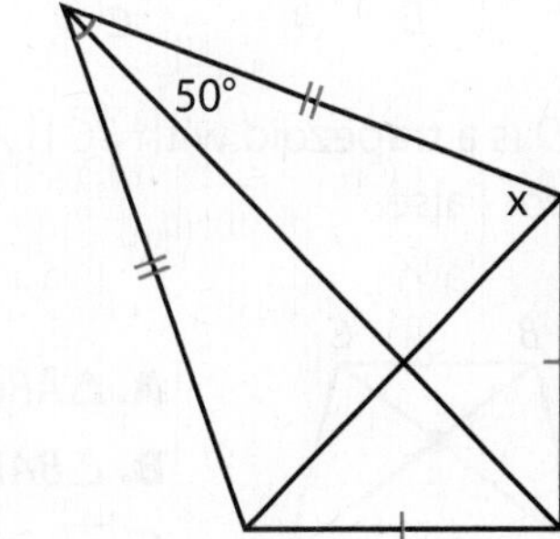

5. Determine whether the trapezoids are congruent. *(Lesson 9.5)*

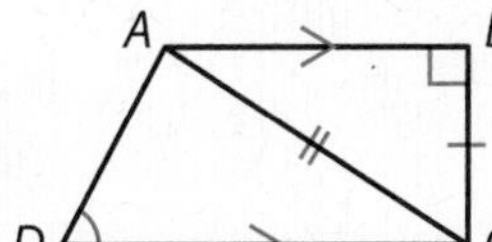

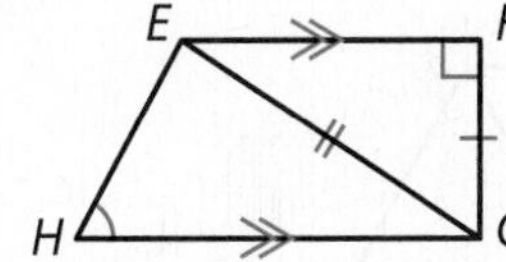

ESSENTIAL QUESTION

6. Name a time when it would be useful to know whether a shape is a rectangle or a trapezoid.

Assessment Readiness

1. Consider each of the following quadrilaterals. Decide whether each is also necessarily a parallelogram. Select Yes or No for A–C.
   A. Trapezoid
   B. Rhombus
   C. Square

2. *ABCD* is a parallelogram. Determine if each statement is True or False.

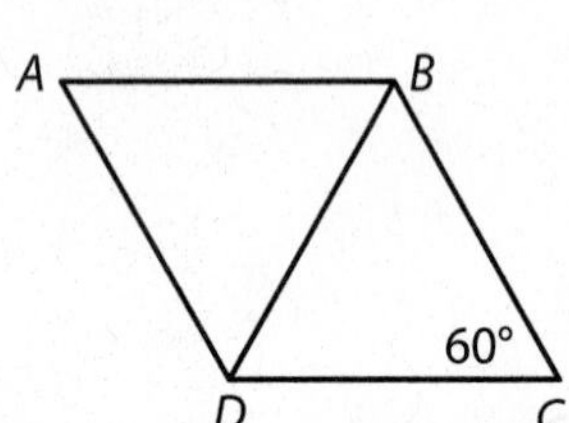

   A. $\angle A \cong \angle C$
   B. $\angle A$ and $\angle B$ are complementary.
   C. $\overline{AD} \parallel \overline{BC}$

3. *ABCD* is a trapezoid with $\overline{BC} \parallel \overline{AD}$ and $\angle BAD \cong \angle CDA$. Determine if each statement is True or False.

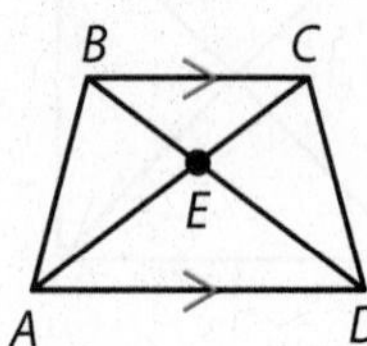

   A. $\triangle ABC \cong \triangle DCA$
   B. $\triangle BAD \cong \triangle CDA$
   C. $\overline{AB} \cong \overline{BC}$

4. Given that *ABCD* is a rhombus, prove that $\triangle ABD \cong \triangle CDB$ and that both triangles are equilateral.

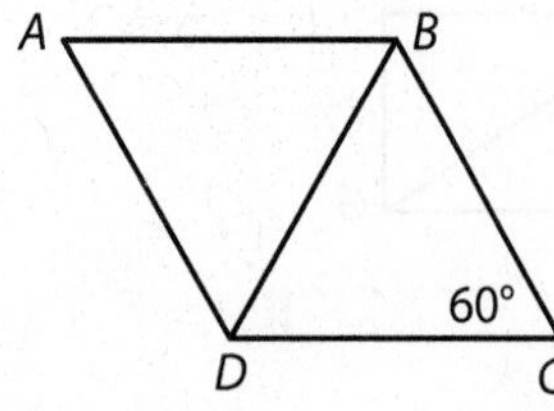

Coordinate Proof Using Slope and Distance

MODULE 10

Essential Question: How can you use coordinate proofs using slope and distance to solve real-world problems?

REAL WORLD VIDEO
Check out how workers use surveying tools and coordinate geometry to measure real-world distances and areas for the construction of roads and bridges.

MODULE PERFORMANCE TASK PREVIEW

How Do You Calculate the Containment of a Fire?

In this module, you will use concepts of perimeter and area to determine the percentage containment of a wildfire. To successfully complete this task, you'll need to master the skills of finding area and perimeter on the coordinate plane. So put on your safety gear and let's get started!

Are YOU Ready?

Complete these exercises to review the skills you will need for this module.

Personal Math Trainer

- Online Homework
- Hints and Help
- Extra Practice

Area of Composite Figures

Example 1

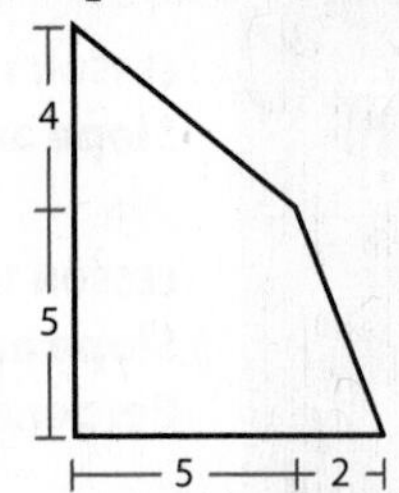

Find the area of the given figure.

Think of the shape as a square and two triangles. The square has sides of length 5 and an area of 25. The top triangle has a height of 4 and a base of 5, so its area is 10. The triangle on the right has a base of 2 and a height of 5, so its area will be 5. Altogether, the area will be 40.

Find the area of the given figure to the nearest hundredth as needed. Use 3.14 for π.

1.

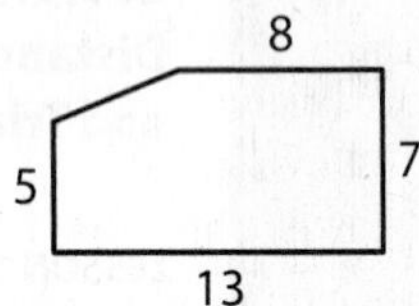

2.

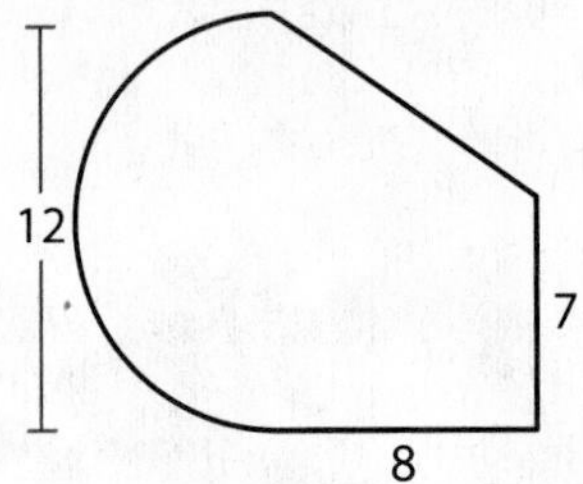

Distance and Midpoint Formula

Example 2 (3, 3) (5, 6)

Find the distance and midpoint for each set of ordered pairs.

$\sqrt{(5-3)^2 + (6-3)^2} = d$ Set up points in the distance formula.

$d = \sqrt{13}$ Simplify.

$M = \left(\frac{3+5}{2}, \frac{3+6}{2}\right)$ Set up points in the midpoint formula.

$M = (4, 4.5)$ Simplify.

Find the distance and midpoint for each set of ordered pairs, rounded to the nearest hundredth as needed.

3. (0, 9) (2, 5)

4. (2, 7) (4, 9)

5. (1, 8) (3, 8)

Writing Equations of Parallel, Perpendicular, Vertical, and Horizontal Lines

Example 3 Using the given xy-graph, find the equation of line C in slope-intercept form. The equation for this line is $y = 2$.

Using the given *xy*—graph, find the equation of the given line in slope-intercept form.

6. E

7. B

8. A

9. D

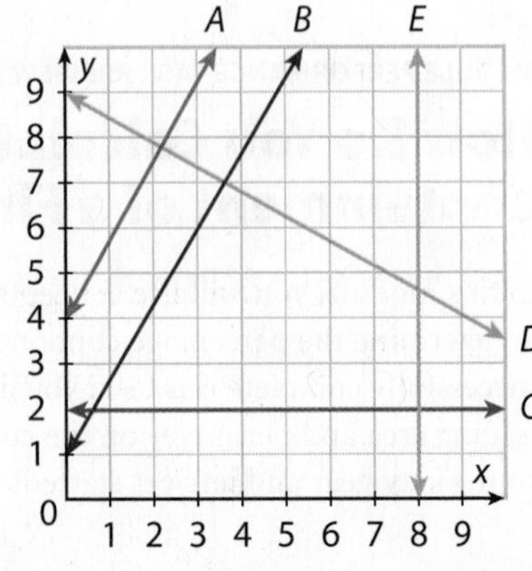

10.1 Slope and Parallel Lines

Essential Question: How can you use slope to solve problems involving parallel lines?

Proving the Slope Criteria for Parallel Lines

The following theorem states an important connection between slope and parallel lines.

Theorem: Slope Criteria for Parallel Lines
Two nonvertical lines are parallel if and only if they have the same slope.

Follow these steps to prove the slope criteria for parallel lines.

A First prove that if two lines are parallel, then they have the same slope.

Copy the figure below. Suppose lines m and n are parallel lines that are neither vertical nor horizontal.

Let A and B be two points on line m, as shown. You can draw a horizontal line through A and a vertical line through B to create the "slope triangle," $\triangle ABC$.

You can extend $\overline{AC}$ to intersect line n at point D and then extend it to point F so that $AC = DF$. Finally, you can draw a vertical line through F intersecting line n at point E.

Mark the figure to show parallel lines, right angles, and congruent segments.

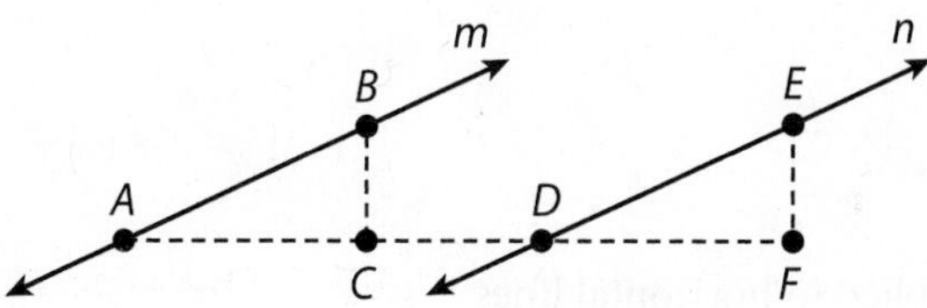

B When parallel lines are cut by a transversal, corresponding angles are congruent, so

$\angle BAC \cong$? .

$\triangle BAC \cong$? by the ? Triangle Congruence Theorem.

By CPCTC, $\overline{BC} \cong$? and $BC =$? .

The slope of line $m = \frac{?}{AC}$, and the slope of line $n = \frac{?}{DF}$.

The slopes of the lines are equal because ?

(C) Now prove that if two lines have the same slope, then they are parallel.

Suppose lines m and n are two lines with the same nonzero slope. You can set up a figure in the same way as before.

Let A and B be two points on line m, as shown. You can draw a horizontal line through A and a vertical line through B to create the "slope triangle," $\triangle ABC$.

You can extend $\overline{AC}$ to intersect line n at point D and then extend it to point F so that $AC = DF$. Finally, you can draw a vertical line through F intersecting line n at point E.

Mark the figure to show right angles and congruent segments.

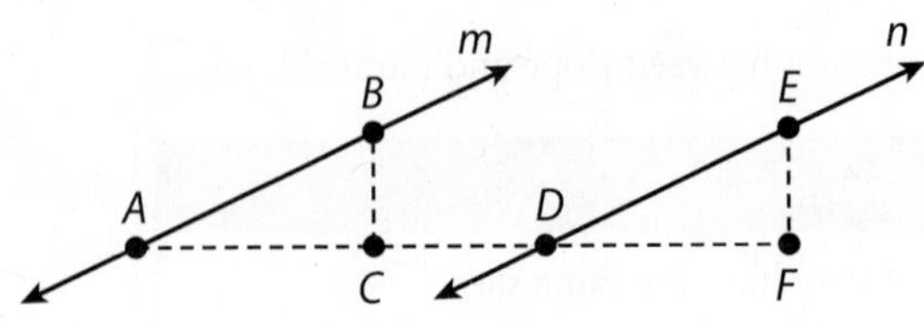

(D) Since line m and line n have the same slope, $\frac{?}{AC} = \frac{?}{DF}$.

But $DF = AC$, so by substitution, $\frac{?}{AC} = \frac{?}{AC}$.

Multiplying both sides by AC shows that $BC =$? .

Now you can conclude that $\triangle BAC \cong$? by the ? Triangle Congruence Theorem.

By CPCTC, $\angle BAC \cong$? .

Line m and line n are two lines that are cut by a transversal so that a pair of corresponding angles are congruent.

You can conclude that ? .

Reflect

1. Explain why the slope criteria can be applied to horizontal lines.
2. Explain why the slope criteria cannot be applied to vertical lines even though all vertical lines are parallel.

Explain 1 Using Slopes to Classify Quadrilaterals by Sides

You can use the slope criteria for parallel lines to analyze figures in the coordinate plane.

Example 1 **Show that each figure is the given type of quadrilateral.**

Ⓐ Show that $ABCD$ is a trapezoid.

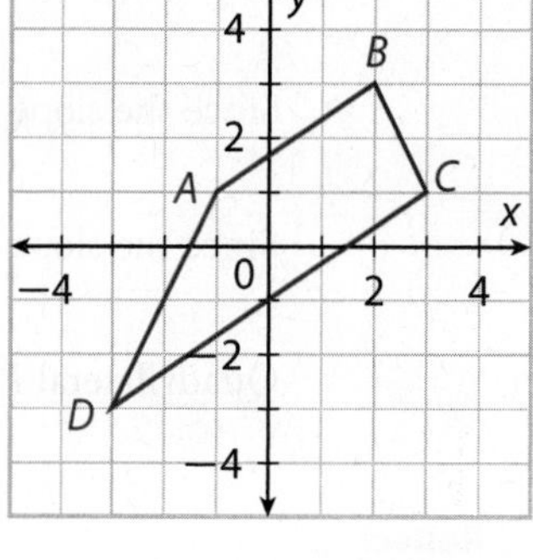

Step 1 Find the coordinates of the vertices of quadrilateral $ABCD$.

$A(-1, 1)$, $B(2, 3)$, $C(3, 1)$, $D(-3, -3)$

Step 2 Use the slope formula to find the slope of $\overline{AB}$ and the slope of $\overline{DC}$.

$$\text{slope of } \overline{AB} = \frac{y_2 - y_1}{x_2 - x_1} = \frac{3 - 1}{2 - (-1)} = \frac{2}{3}$$

$$\text{slope of } \overline{DC} = \frac{y_2 - y_1}{x_2 - x_1} = \frac{1 - (-3)}{3 - (-3)} = \frac{4}{6} = \frac{2}{3}$$

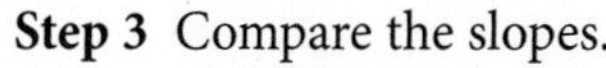

Step 3 Compare the slopes.

Since the slopes are the same, $\overline{AB}$ is parallel to $\overline{DC}$.

Quadrilateral $ABCD$ is a trapezoid because it is a quadrilateral with at least one pair of parallel sides.

Ⓑ Show that $PQRS$ is a parallelogram.

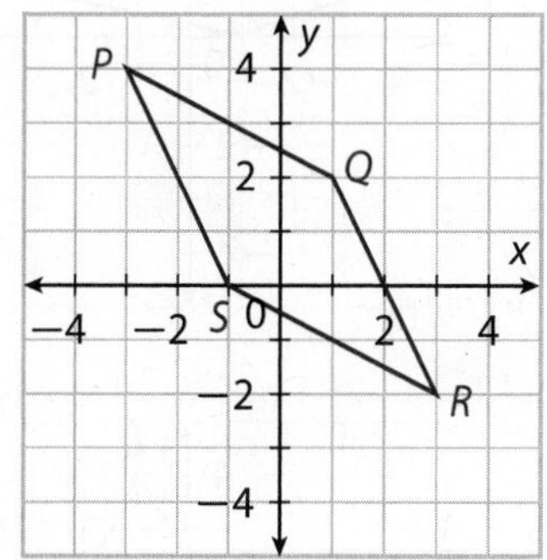

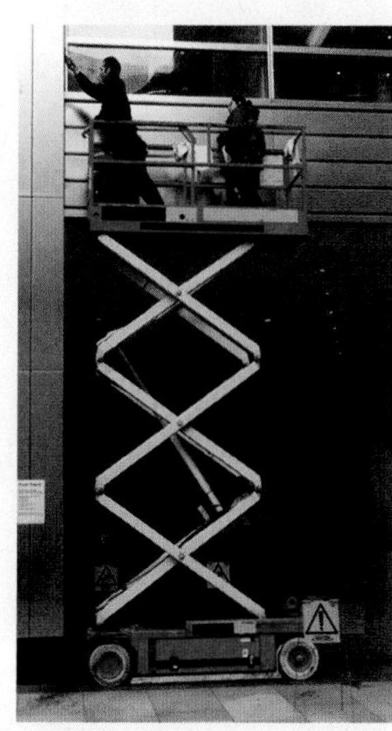

Step 1 Find the coordinates of the vertices of quadrilateral $PQRS$.

$P(-3, 4)$, $Q(1, 2)$, $R(\boxed{3}, \boxed{-2})$, $S(\boxed{-1}, \boxed{0})$

Step 2 Use the slope formula to find the slope of each side.

$$\overline{PQ}: \frac{y_2 - y_1}{x_2 - x_1} = \frac{2 - 4}{1 - (-3)} = \frac{-2}{4} = -\frac{1}{2}$$

$$\overline{QR}: \frac{y_2 - y_1}{x_2 - x_1} = \frac{\boxed{-2} - 2}{\boxed{3} - 1} = \frac{\boxed{-4}}{\boxed{2}} = \boxed{-2}$$

$$\overline{RS}: \frac{y_2 - y_1}{x_2 - x_1} = \frac{\boxed{0} - \boxed{-2}}{\boxed{-1} - \boxed{3}} = \frac{\boxed{2}}{\boxed{-4}} = -\frac{\boxed{1}}{\boxed{2}}$$

$$\overline{SP}: \frac{y_2 - y_1}{x_2 - x_1} = \frac{4 - \boxed{0}}{-3 - \boxed{-1}} = \frac{\boxed{4}}{\boxed{-2}} = \boxed{-2}$$

Step 3 Compare the slopes.

Since the slope of $\overline{PQ}$ is the same as the slope of $\overline{RS}$, $\overline{PQ}$ is parallel to $\overline{RS}$.

Since the slope of $\overline{QR}$ is the same as the slope of $\overline{SP}$, $\overline{QR}$ is parallel to $\overline{SP}$.

Quadrilateral *PQRS* is a parallelogram because both pairs of opposite sides are parallel.

Reflect

3. **What If?** Suppose you know that the lengths of $\overline{PQ}$ and $\overline{QR}$ in the figure in Example 1B are each $\sqrt{20}$. What type of parallelogram is quadrilateral *PQRS*? Explain.

Your Turn

Show that each figure is the given type of quadrilateral.

4. Show that *JKLM* is a trapezoid.

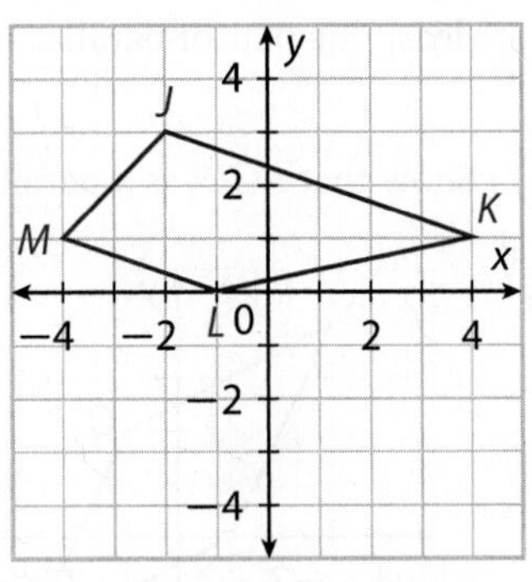

5. Show that *ABCD* is a parallelogram.

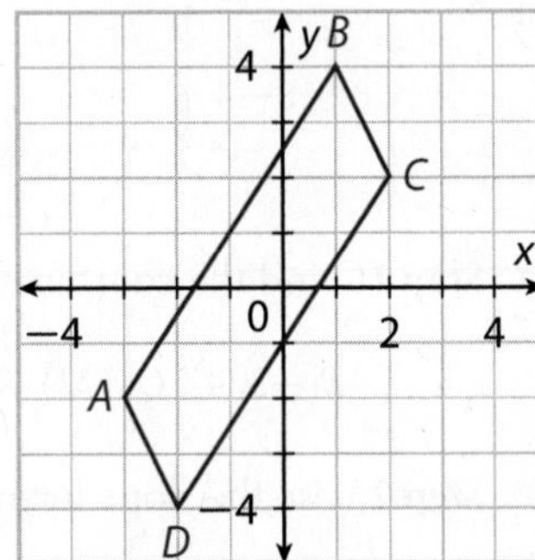

 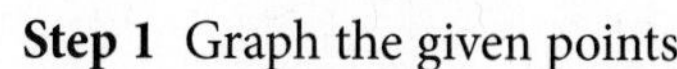

Explain 2 Using Slopes to Find Missing Vertices

Example 2 **Find the coordinates of the missing vertex in each parallelogram.**

(A) ▱$ABCD$ with vertices $A(1, -2)$, $B(-2, 3)$, and $D(5, -1)$

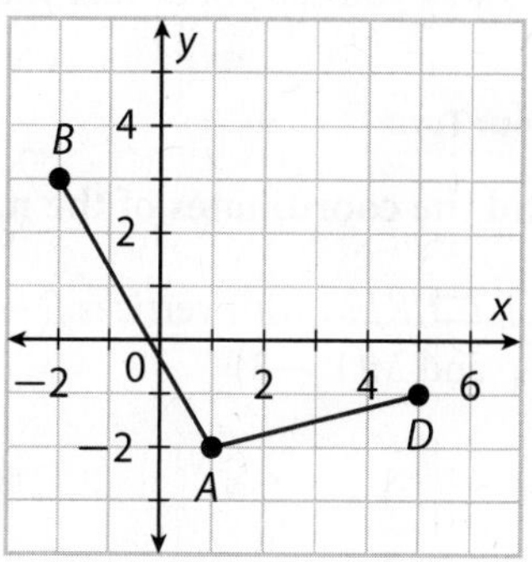

Step 1 Graph the given points.

Step 2 Find the slope of $\overline{AB}$ by counting units from A to B.

The rise from −2 to 3 is 5. The run from 1 to −2 is −3.

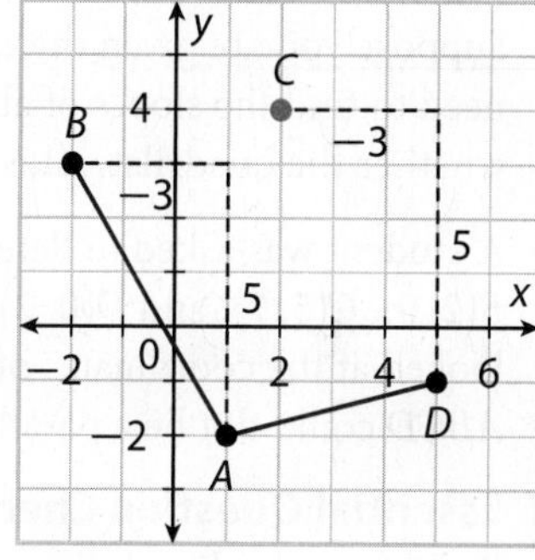

Step 3 Start at D and count the same number of units.

A rise of 5 from −1 is 4. A run of −3 from 5 is 2.

Label $(2, 4)$ as vertex C.

Step 4 Use the slope formula to verify that $\overline{BC} \parallel \overline{AD}$.

$$\text{slope of } \overline{BC} = \frac{4 - 3}{2 - (-2)} = \frac{1}{4}$$

$$\text{slope of } \overline{AD} = \frac{-1 - (-2)}{5 - 1} = \frac{1}{4}$$

The coordinates of vertex C are (2, 4).

(B) ▱$PQRS$ with vertices $P(-3, 0)$, $Q(-2, 4)$, and $R(2, 2)$

Step 1 Graph the given points.

Step 2 Find the slope of $\overline{PQ}$ by counting units from Q to P.

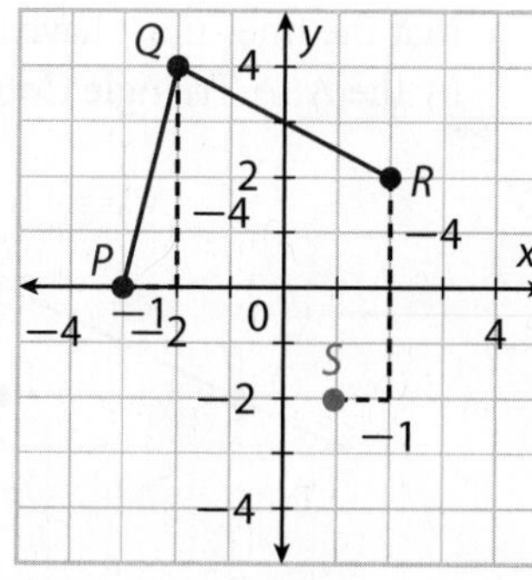

The rise from 4 to 0 is [−4]. The run from −2 to −3 is [−1].

Step 3 Start at R and count the same number of units.

A rise of [−4] from 2 is [−2]. A run of [−1] from 2 is [1].

Label ([1], [−2]) as vertex S.

Step 4 Use the slope formula to verify that $\overline{QR} \parallel \overline{PS}$.

$$\text{slope of } \overline{QR} = \frac{\boxed{2} - \boxed{4}}{\boxed{2} - \boxed{-2}} = -\frac{\boxed{1}}{\boxed{2}} \qquad \text{slope of } \overline{PS} = \frac{\boxed{-2} - \boxed{0}}{\boxed{1} - \boxed{-3}} = -\frac{\boxed{1}}{\boxed{2}}$$

The coordinates of vertex S are ([1], [−2]).

Reflect

6. **Discussion** In Part A, you used the slope formula to verify that $\overline{BC} \parallel \overline{AD}$. Describe another way you can check that you found the correct coordinates of vertex C.

Your Turn

Find the coordinates of the missing vertex in each parallelogram.

7. $\square JKLM$ with vertices $J(-3, -2)$, $K(0, 1)$, and $M(1, -3)$

8. $\square DEFG$ with vertices $E(-2, 2)$, $F(4, 1)$, and $G(3, -2)$

Elaborate

9. Suppose you are given the coordinates of the vertices of a quadrilateral. Do you always need to find the slopes of all four sides of the quadrilateral in order to determine whether the quadrilateral is a trapezoid? Explain.

10. A student was asked to determine whether quadrilateral $ABCD$ with vertices $A(0, 0)$, $B(2, 0)$, $C(5, 7)$, and $D(0, 2)$ was a parallelogram. Without plotting points, the student looked at the coordinates of the vertices and quickly determined that quadrilateral $ABCD$ could not be a parallelogram. How do you think the student solved the problem?

11. **Essential Question Check-In** What steps can you use to determine whether two given lines on a coordinate plane are parallel?

Evaluate: Homework and Practice

• Online Homework
• Hints and Help
• Extra Practice

1. Jodie draws parallel lines p and q. She sets up a figure as shown to prove that the lines must have the same slope. First she proves that $\triangle JKL \cong \triangle RST$ by the ASA Triangle Congruence Theorem. What should she do to complete the proof?

Show that each figure is the given type of quadrilateral.

2. Show that $ABCD$ is a trapezoid.

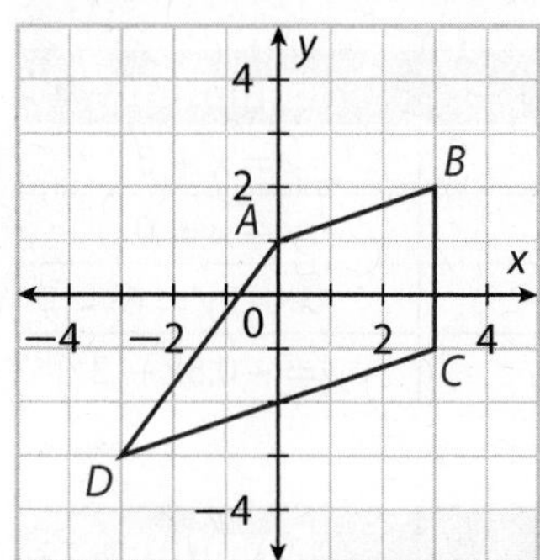

3. Show that $KLMN$ is a parallelogram.

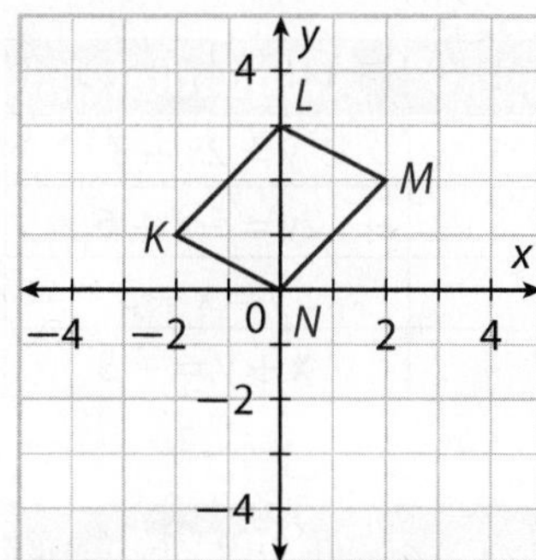

Find the coordinates of the missing vertex in each parallelogram. Use slopes to check your answer.

4. ▱$ABCD$ with vertices $A(3, -3)$, $B(-1, -2)$, and $D(5, -1)$

5. ▱$STUV$ with vertices $S(-3, -1)$, $T(-1, 1)$ and $V(0, 0)$

6. Show that quadrilateral $ABCD$ is *not* a trapezoid.

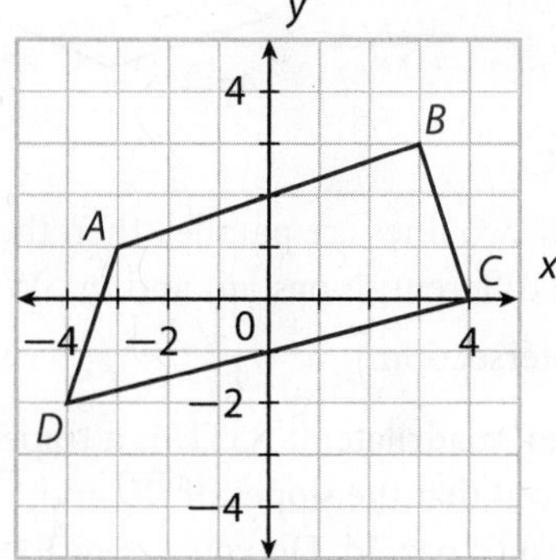

7. Show that quadrilateral $FGHJ$ is a trapezoid, but is not a parallelogram.

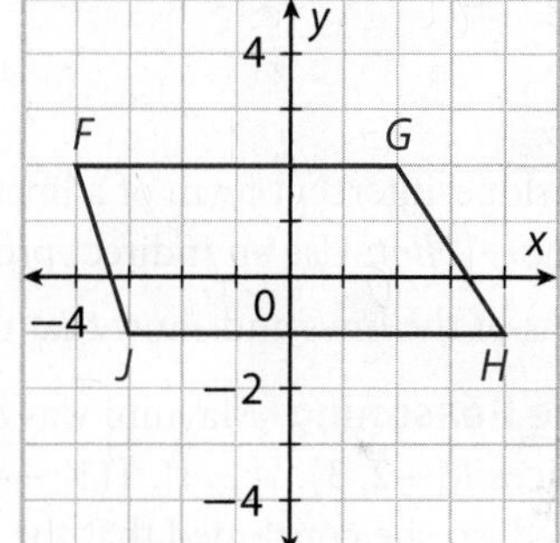

Determine whether each statement is always, sometimes, or never true. Explain your reasoning.

8. If quadrilateral $ABCD$ is a trapezoid and the slope of $\overline{AB}$ is 3, then the slope of $\overline{CD}$ is 3.

9. A parallelogram has vertices at $(0, 0)$, $(2, 0)$, $(0, 2)$, and at a point on the line $y = x$.

10. If the slope of $\overline{PQ}$ is $\frac{1}{3}$ and the slope of $\overline{RS}$ is $-\frac{1}{3}$, the quadrilateral $PQRS$ is a parallelogram.

11. If line m is parallel to line n and the slope of line m is greater than 1, then the slope of line n is greater than 1.

12. If trapezoid $JKLM$ has vertices $J(-4, 1)$, $K(-3, 3)$, and $L(-1, 4)$, then the coordinates of vertex M are $(2, 4)$

Explain whether the quadrilateral determined by the intersections of the given lines is a trapezoid, a parallelogram, both, or neither.

13.

Line	Equation
Line ℓ	$y = 2x + 3$
Line m	$2y = -x + 6$
Line n	$y = x - 3$
Line p	$x + y = -3$

14.

Line	Equation
Line ℓ	$y = x + 3$
Line m	$y - x = 0$
Line n	$x + 2y = 6$
Line p	$y = -0.5x - 3$

15.

Line	Equation
Line ℓ	$2y = x + 4$
Line m	$y + 5 = 2x$
Line n	$-2x + y = 2$
Line p	$x + 2y = -6$

16.

Line	Equation
Line ℓ	$3x + y = 4$
Line m	$y + 3 = 0$
Line n	$y = 3x + 5$
Line p	$y = 3$

Algebra Find the value of each variable in the parallelogram.

17.

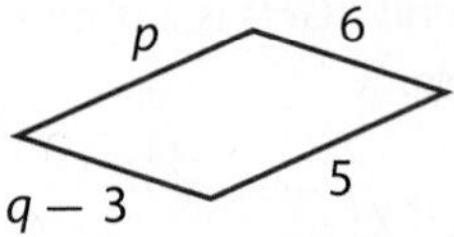

18.

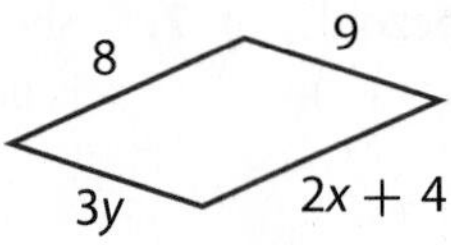

19.

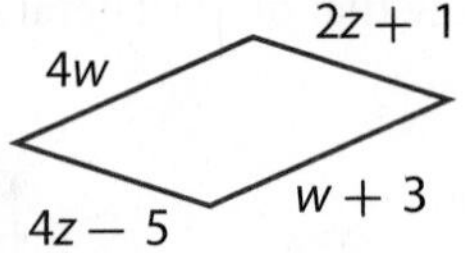

20. Use the slope-intercept form of a linear equation to prove that if two lines are parallel, then they have the same slope. (*Hint:* Use an indirect proof. Assume the lines have different slopes, m_1 and m_2. Write the equations of the lines and show that there must be a point of intersection.)

21. Critique Reasoning Mayumi was asked to determine whether quadrilateral $RSTU$ is a trapezoid given the vertices $R(-2, 3)$, $S(1, 4)$, $T(1, -4)$, and $U(-2, 1)$. She noticed that the slopes of $\overline{RU}$ and $\overline{ST}$ are undefined, so she concluded that the quadrilateral could not be a trapezoid. Do you agree? Explain.

22. Kaitlyn is planning the diagonal spaces for the parking lot at a mall. Each space is a parallelogram. Kaitlyn has already planned the spaces shown in the figure and wants to continue the pattern to draw the next space to the right. What are the endpoints of the next line segment she should draw? Explain your reasoning.

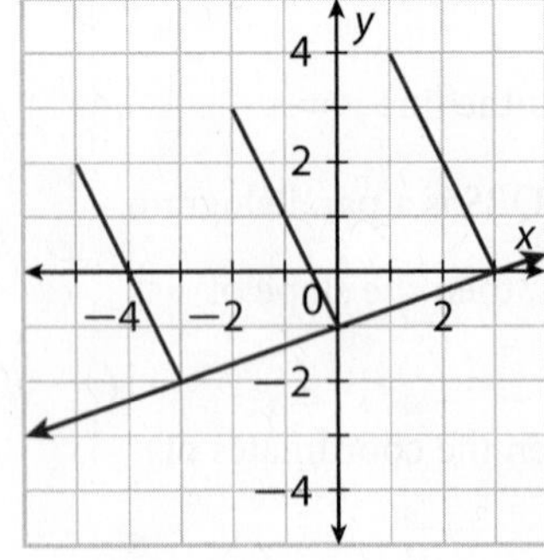

23. Multi-Step Two carpenters are using a coordinate plane to design a tabletop in the shape of a trapezoid. They have already drawn the two sides of the tabletop shown in the figure. They want side $\overline{AD}$ to lie on the line $x = -2$. What is the equation of the line on which side $\overline{CD}$ will lie? Explain your reasoning.

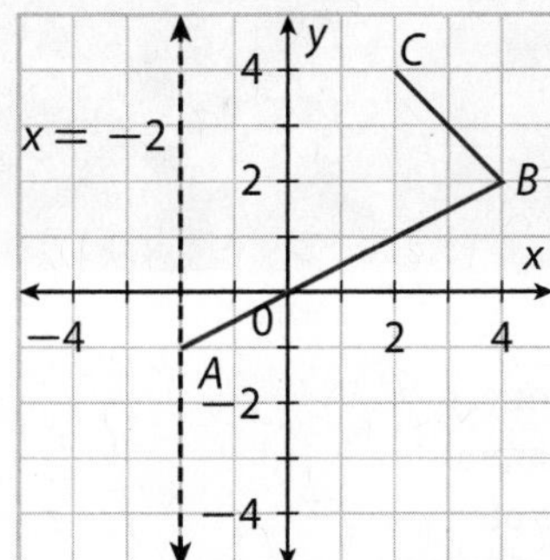

24. Quadrilateral $PQRS$ has vertices $P(-3, 2)$, $Q(-1, 4)$, and $R(5, 0)$. For each of the given coordinates of vertex S, determine whether the quadrilateral is a parallelogram, a trapezoid that is not a parallelogram, or neither.

a. $S(0, 0)$

b. $S(3, -2)$

c. $S(2, -1)$

d. $S(6, -4)$

e. $S(5, -3)$

H.O.T. Focus on Higher Order Thinking

25. Explain the Error Tariq was given the points $P(0, 3)$, $Q(3, -3)$, $R(0, -4)$, and $S(-2, -1)$ and was asked to decide whether quadrilateral $PQRS$ is a trapezoid. Explain his error.

$$\text{slope of } \overline{SP} = \frac{3-(-1)}{0-(-2)} = \frac{4}{2} = 2$$

$$\text{slope of } \overline{QP} = \frac{3-(-3)}{3-0} = \frac{6}{3} = 2$$

Since at least two sides are parallel, the quadrilateral is a trapezoid.

26. **Analyze Relationships** Four members of a marching band are arranged to form the vertices of a parallelogram. The coordinates of three band members are $M(-3, 1)$, $G(1, 3)$, and $Q(2, -1)$. Find all possible coordinates for the fourth band member.

27. **Make a Conjecture** Plot any four points on the coordinate plane and connect them to form a quadrilateral. Find the midpoint of each side of the quadrilateral and connect consecutive midpoints to form a new quadrilateral. What type of quadrilateral is formed? Repeat the process by starting with a different set of four points. Do you get the same result? State a conjecture about your findings.

Lesson Performance Task

Suppose archeologists uncover an ancient city with the foundations of 16 houses. The locations of the houses are as follows:

$(2, 2)$ $(-5, 6)$ $(3, -6)$ $(-1, 0)$ $(5, -8)$ $(3, 5)$ $(-3, 3)$ $(0, 5)$

$(-8, 1)$ $(4, -1)$ $(1, -3)$ $(-4, -3)$ $(8, -7)$ $(-5, -4)$ $(-2, 8)$ $(6, -4)$

a. How could you show that the streets are parallel? Explain.

b. Are the streets parallel?

10.2 Slope and Perpendicular Lines

Essential Question: How can you use slope to solve problems involving perpendicular lines?

Resource Locker

Explore Proving the Slope Criteria for Perpendicular Lines

The following theorem states an important connection between slope and perpendicular lines.

Theorem: Slope Criteria for Perpendicular Lines
Two nonvertical lines are perpendicular if and only if the product of their slopes is -1.

Follow these steps to prove the slope criteria for perpendicular lines.

(A) First prove that if two lines are perpendicular, then the product of their slopes is -1.

Suppose lines m and n are perpendicular lines that intersect at point P, and that neither line is vertical. Assume the slope of line m is positive. (You can write a similar proof if the slope of line m is negative.)

Copy the figure on a separate piece of paper. Mark your figure to show the perpendicular lines.

(B) Let Q be a point on line m, and draw a right triangle, $\triangle PQR$, as shown. Which line is this a "slope triangle" for?

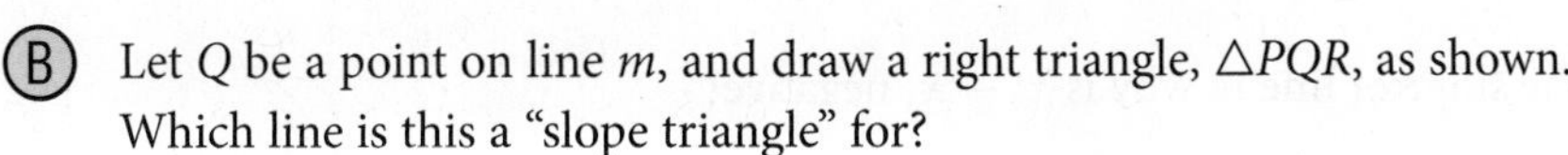

Mark the figure to show the perpendicular segments.

(C) Assume that a and b are both positive. The slope of line m is $\frac{?}{?}$.

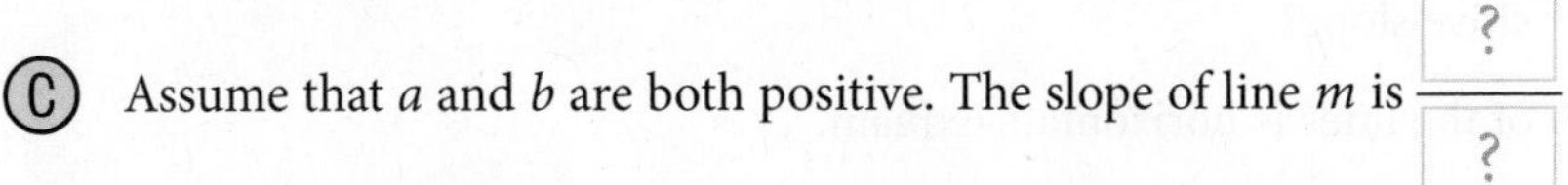

(D) Rotate $\triangle PQR$ 90° around point P. The image is $\triangle PQ'R'$, as shown.

Which line is $\triangle PQ'R'$ a slope triangle for?

Let the coordinates of P be (x_1, y_1) and let the coordinates of Q' be (x_2, y_2).

Then the slope of line n is $\frac{y_2 - y_1}{x_2 - x_1} = \frac{b}{?} = -\frac{?}{?}$.

(E) Now find the product of the slopes.

(slope of line m) $\cdot$ (slope of line n) $= \frac{?}{?} \cdot \left(-\frac{?}{?}\right) = ?$

Now prove that if the product of the slopes of two lines is -1, then the lines are perpendicular.

Let the slope of line m be $\frac{a}{b}$, where a and b are both positive. Let line n have slope z. It is given that $z \cdot \frac{a}{b} = -1$. Solving for z gives the slope of line n.

$z = -\frac{?}{?}$

Assume the lines intersect at P. Since the slope of m is positive and the slope of n is negative, you can set up slope triangles.

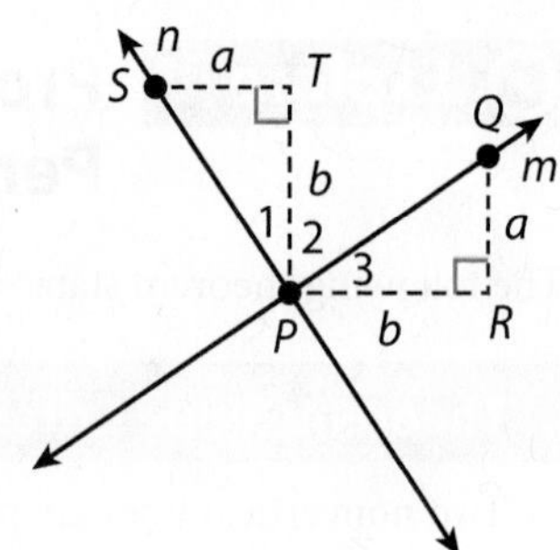

Based on the figure, $\overline{ST} \cong$? and $\overline{PT} \cong$? .

Also, $\angle T \cong$? because all right angles are congruent.

Therefore, ? $\cong$? by the SAS Triangle Congruence Theorem.

By CPCTC, $\angle 1 \cong$? .

Since $\overline{TP}$ is vertical and $\overline{PR}$ is horizontal, $\angle TPR$ is a right angle.

So $\angle 2$ and ? are complementary angles. You can conclude by substitution that

$\angle 2$ and ? are complementary angles.

By the Angle Addition Postulate, $m\angle 1 + m\angle 2 = m\angle SPQ$, so $\angle SPQ$ must measure ? , and therefore line m is perpendicular to line n.

Reflect

1. In Step D, when you calculate the slope of line n, why is $x_2 - x_1$ negative?
2. The second half of the proof begins in Step F by assuming that line m has a positive slope. If the product of the slopes of two lines is -1, how do you know that one of the lines must have a positive slope?
3. Does this theorem apply when one of the lines is horizontal? Explain.

Explain 1 Using Slopes to Classify Figures by Right Angles

You can use the slope criteria for perpendicular lines to analyze figures in the coordinate plane.

Example 1 **Show that each figure is the given type of quadrilateral.**

(A) Show that $ABCD$ is a rectangle.

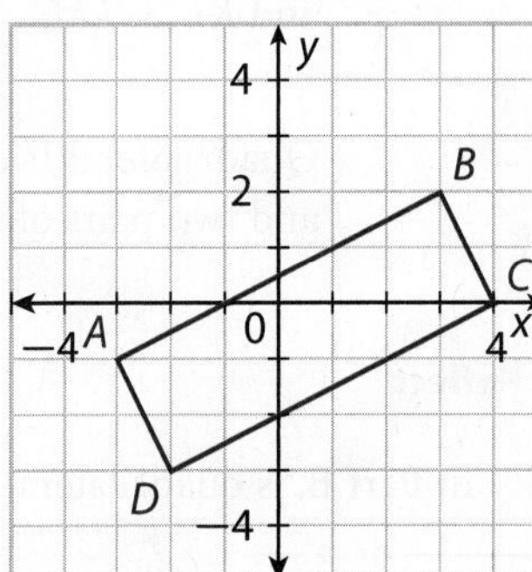

Step 1 Find the coordinates of the vertices of quadrilateral $ABCD$.

$A(-3, -1), B(3, 2), C(4, 0), D(-2, -3)$

Step 2 Use the slope formula to find the slope of each side.

$\overline{AB}: \frac{2-(-1)}{3-(-3)} = \frac{1}{2}$ $\overline{BC}: \frac{0-2}{4-3} = -2$

$\overline{CD}: \frac{-3-0}{-2-4} = \frac{1}{2}$ $\overline{DA}: \frac{-1-(-3)}{-3-(-2)} = -2$

Step 3 Compare the slopes.

$$\left(\text{slope of } \overline{AB}\right) \cdot \left(\text{slope of } \overline{BC}\right) = \frac{1}{2} \cdot (-2) = -1$$

$$\left(\text{slope of } \overline{BC}\right) \cdot \left(\text{slope of } \overline{CD}\right) = -2 \cdot \frac{1}{2} = -1$$

$$\left(\text{slope of } \overline{CD}\right) \cdot \left(\text{slope of } \overline{DA}\right) = \frac{1}{2} \cdot (-2) = -1$$

$$\left(\text{slope of } \overline{DA}\right) \cdot \left(\text{slope of } \overline{AB}\right) = -2 \cdot \frac{1}{2} = -1$$

Consecutive sides are perpendicular since the product of the slopes is −1.

Quadrilateral $ABCD$ is a rectangle because it is a quadrilateral with four right angles.

(B) Show that $JKLM$ is a trapezoid with two right angles.

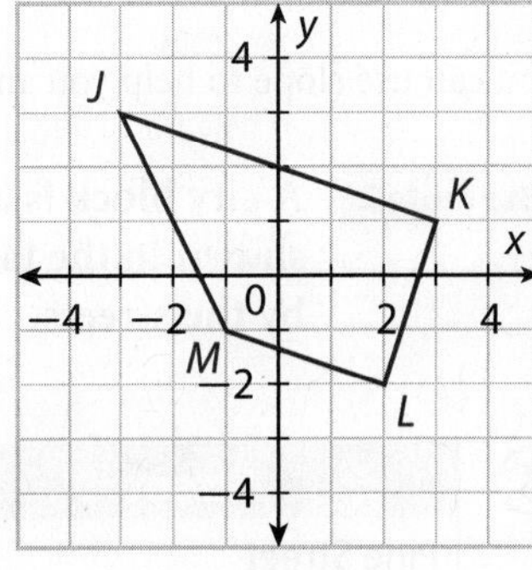

Step 1 Find the coordinates of the vertices of quadrilateral $JKLM$.

$J(-3, 3), K(3, 1), L\left(\boxed{2}, \boxed{-2}\right), M\left(\boxed{-1}, \boxed{-1}\right)$

Step 2 Use the slope formula to find the slope of each side.

$\overline{JK}: \frac{1-3}{3-(-3)} = \frac{-2}{6} = -\frac{1}{3}$

$\overline{KL}: \frac{\boxed{-2} - \boxed{1}}{\boxed{2} - \boxed{3}} = \frac{\boxed{-3}}{\boxed{-1}} = \boxed{3}$

$\overline{LM}: \frac{\boxed{-1} - \boxed{-2}}{\boxed{-1} - \boxed{2}} = \frac{\boxed{1}}{\boxed{-3}} = -\frac{\boxed{1}}{\boxed{3}}$

$\overline{MJ}: \frac{3 - \boxed{-1}}{-3 - \boxed{-1}} = \frac{\boxed{4}}{\boxed{-2}} = \boxed{-2}$

Step 3 Compare the slopes.

Since the slope of $\overline{JK}$ is the same as the slope of $\overline{LM}$, $\overline{JK}$ is parallel to $\overline{LM}$.

Since the $\left(\text{slope of } \overline{JK}\right) \cdot \left(\text{slope of } \overline{KL}\right) = -\frac{1}{3} \cdot \boxed{3} = \boxed{-1}$ and

$\left(\text{slope of } \overline{KL}\right) . \left(\text{slope of } \overline{LM}\right) = \boxed{3} \cdot \left(-\frac{\boxed{1}}{\boxed{3}}\right) = \boxed{-1}$, $\overline{JK} \perp \overline{KL}$

and $\overline{KL} \perp \overline{LM}$.

Quadrilateral *JKLM* is a trapezoid with two right angles because a pair of opposite sides are parallel and two pairs of consecutive sides are perpendicular.

Reflect

4. In Part B, is quadrilateral *JKLM* a parallelogram? Why or why not?

Your Turn

5. Show that *DEFG* is a rectangle.

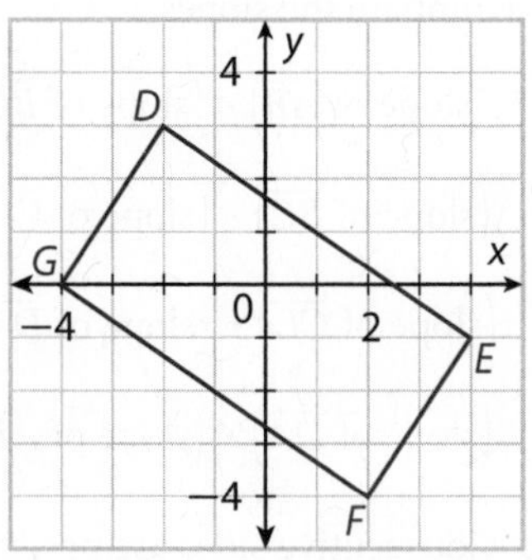

Explain 2 Using Slopes and Systems of Equations to Classify Figures

You can use slope to help you analyze a system of equations.

Example 2 **A city block is a quadrilateral bounded by four streets shown in the table. Classify the quadrilateral bounded by the streets.**

(A)

Street	Equation
Pine Street	$-x + 2y = 4$
Elm Road	$2x + y = 7$
Chestnut Street	$2y = x - 6$
Cedar Road	$y + 8 = -2x$

Step 1 Write each equation in slope-intercept form, $y = mx + b$.

Pine Street equation: $y = \frac{1}{2}x + 2$ Elm Road equation: $y = -2x + 7$

Chestnut Street equation: $y = \frac{1}{2}x - 3$ Cedar Road equation: $y = -2x - 8$

Step 2 Use the equations to determine the slope of each street.

Pine Street: $y = \frac{1}{2}x + 2$, so the slope is $\frac{1}{2}$.

Elm Road: $y = -2x + 7$, so the slope is -2.

Chestnut Street: $y = \frac{1}{2}x - 3$, so the slope is $\frac{1}{2}$.

Cedar Road: $y = -2x - 8$, so the slope is -2.

Step 3 Determine the type of quadrilateral bounded by the streets.

The product of the slopes of consecutive sides is -1.

So, the quadrilateral is a rectangle since it has four right angles.

Step 4 Check by graphing the equations.

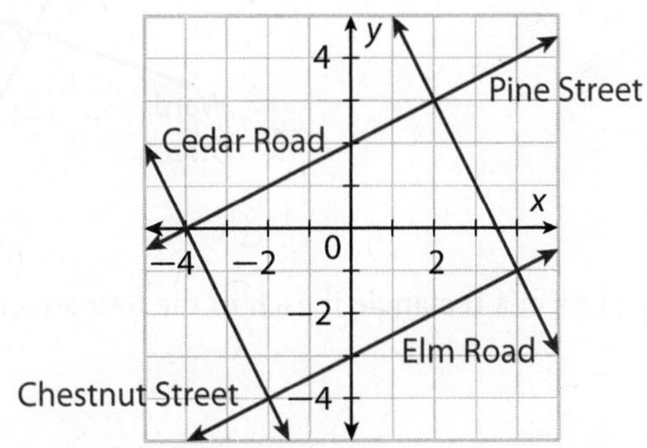

(B)

Street	Equation
Clay Avenue	$3y - 9 = x$
Fresno Road	$2x + y = 3$
Ward Street	$3y = x - 5$
Oakland Lane	$y + 4 = -2x$

Step 1 Write each equation in slope-intercept form, $y = mx + b$.

Clay Avenue equation: $y = \frac{1}{3}x + 3$

Fresno Road equation: $y = -2x + 3$

Ward Street equation: $y = \frac{1}{3}x - \frac{5}{3}$

Oakland Lane equation: $y = -2x - 4$

Step 2 Use the equations to determine the slope of each street.

Clay Avenue: $y = \frac{1}{3}x + 3$, so the slope is $\frac{1}{3}$.

Fresno Road $y = -2x + 3$, so the slope is -2.

Ward Street $y = \frac{1}{3}x + -\frac{5}{3}$, so the slope is $\frac{1}{3}$.

Oakland Lane: $y = -2x - 4$, so the slope is -2.

Step 3 Determine the type of quadrilateral bounded by the streets.

The slopes of opposite sides of the quadrilateral are equal.

So, the quadrilateral is a parallelogram since both pairs of opposite sides are parallel.

Step 4 Check by graphing the equations.

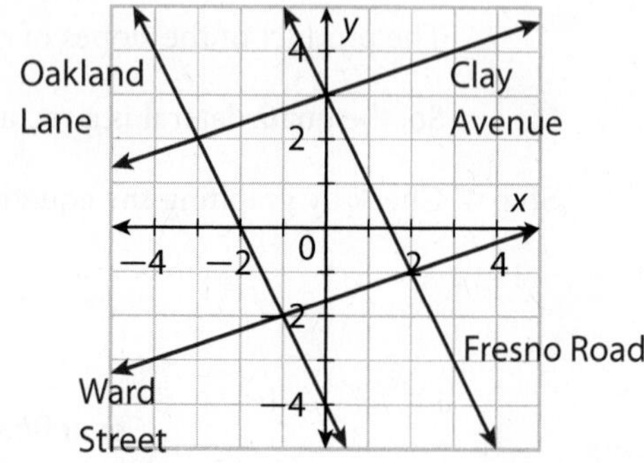

Reflect

6. **Discussion** Is it possible for four streets to form a rectangle if each of the four streets has a positive slope? Explain.

Your Turn

7. A farmers market is set up as a quadrilateral bounded by four streets shown in the table. Classify the quadrilateral bounded by the streets.

Street	Equation
Taft Road	$-2x + 3y = 13$
Harding Lane	$\frac{1}{3}y = -x - 1$
Wilson Avenue	$3y = 2x + 2$
Hoover Street	$3x + y = -14$

Elaborate

8. Suppose line ℓ has slope $\frac{a}{b}$ where $a \neq 0$ and $b \neq 0$, and suppose lines m and n are both perpendicular to line ℓ. Explain how you can use the slope criteria to show that line m must be parallel to line n.

9. **Essential Question Check-In** What steps can you use to determine whether two given lines on a coordinate plane are perpendicular?

Evaluate: Homework and Practice

- Online Homework
- Hints and Help
- Extra Practice

1. In the Explore, you proved that if two lines are perpendicular, then the product of their slopes is -1. You assumed that the slope of line m was positive. Follow these steps to complete the proof assuming that the slope of line m is negative.

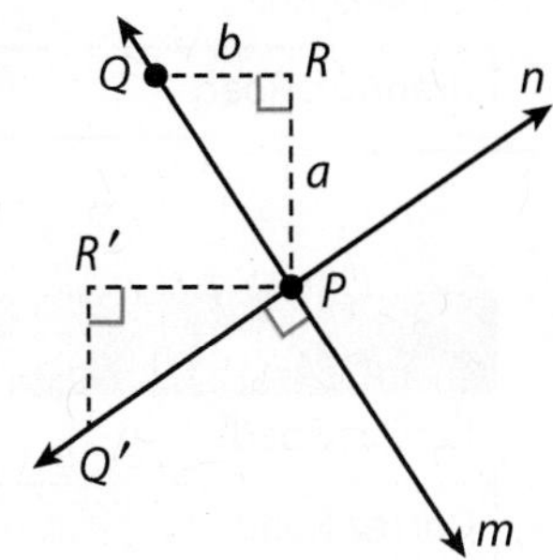

   a. Suppose lines m and n are nonvertical perpendicular lines that intersect at point P. Let Q be a point on line m and draw a slope triangle, $\triangle PQR$, as shown. Write the slope of line m in terms of a and b, where a and b are both positive.

   b. Rotate $\triangle PQR$ 90° around point P. The image is $\triangle PQ'R'$, as shown in the figure. Using $\triangle PQ'R'$, write the slope of line n in terms of a and b.

   c. Explain how to complete the proof.

Show that each figure is the given type of quadrilateral.

2. Show that $QRST$ is a rectangle.

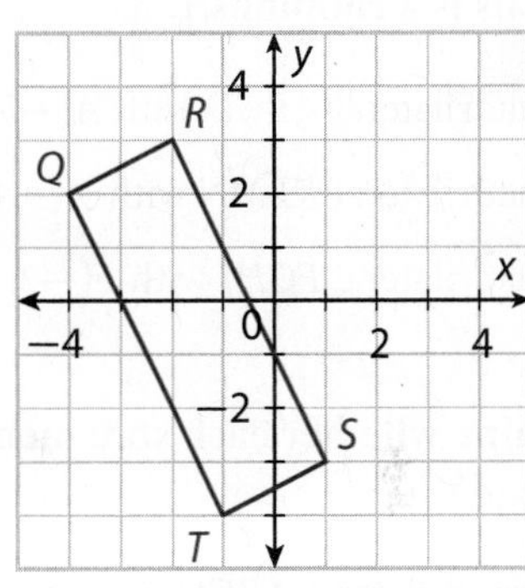

3. Show that $KLMN$ is a trapezoid with two right angles.

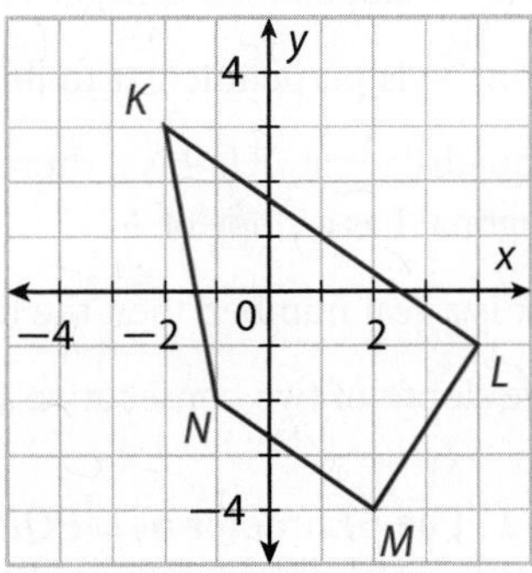

The boundary of a farm consists of four straight roads. Classify the quadrilateral bounded by the roads in each table.

4.

Road	Equation
Lewiston Road	$y - 8 = 2x$
Johnson Road	$2y = -x + 1$
Chavez Road	$-2x + y = -2$
Brannon Road	$x + 2y = -4$

5.

Road	Equation
Larson Road	$y + 1 = 2x$
Cortez Road	$2x + y = 3$
Madison Road	$2x = y + 5$
Jackson Road	$2x + y = -5$

Multi-Step Determine whether the quadrilateral with the given vertices is a parallelogram. If so, determine whether it is a rhombus, a rectangle, or neither. Justify your conclusions. (*Hint*: Recall that a parallelogram with perpendicular diagonals is a rhombus.)

6. Quadrilateral $ABCD$ with $A(-3, 0)$, $B(1, 2)$, $C(2, 0)$, and $D(-2, -2)$
7. Quadrilateral $KLMN$ with $K(-4, 2)$, $L(-1, 4)$, $M(3, 3)$, and $N(-3, -1)$
8. Quadrilateral $FGHJ$ with $F(-2, 3)$, $G(1, 2)$, $H(2, -1)$, and $J(-1, 0)$

Determine whether each statement is always, sometimes, or never true. Explain.

9. If quadrilateral $ABCD$ is a rectangle and the slope of $\overline{AB}$ is positive, then the slope of $\overline{BC}$ is negative.
10. If line m is perpendicular to line n, then the slope of line n is 0.
11. If quadrilateral $JKLM$ is a rhombus and one diagonal has a slope of 3, then the other diagonal has a slope of $\frac{1}{3}$.
12. If k is a real number, then the line $y = x + k$ is perpendicular to the line $y = -x + k$.
13. The slopes of two consecutive sides of a rectangle are $\frac{2}{3}$ and $\frac{3}{2}$.

Algebra The perimeter of ▱$PQRS$ is 84. Find the length of each side of ▱$PQRS$ under the given conditions.

14. $PQ = QR$
15. $QR = 3(RS)$
16. $RS = SP - 7$
17. $SP = RS^2$

18. Multiple Representations Line m has the equation $2x + 3y = 6$, line n passes through the points in the table, and line p contains the segment shown in the figure. Which of these lines, if any, are perpendicular? Explain.

Line *n*	
x	***y***
4	5
6	8
8	11

19. Three subway lines run along straight tracks in the city. The equation for each subway line is given. City planners want to add a fourth subway line and want the tracks for the four lines to form a rectangle. What is a possible equation for the fourth subway line? Justify your answer.

Subway Line	Equation
B	$-2x + y = 4$
N	$2y = -x + 8$
S	$y + 11 = 2x$

20. Quadrilateral *JKLM* is a rectangle. One side of the rectangle is shown in the figure. Which of the following are possible coordinates for vertices *L* and *M*? Select all that apply.

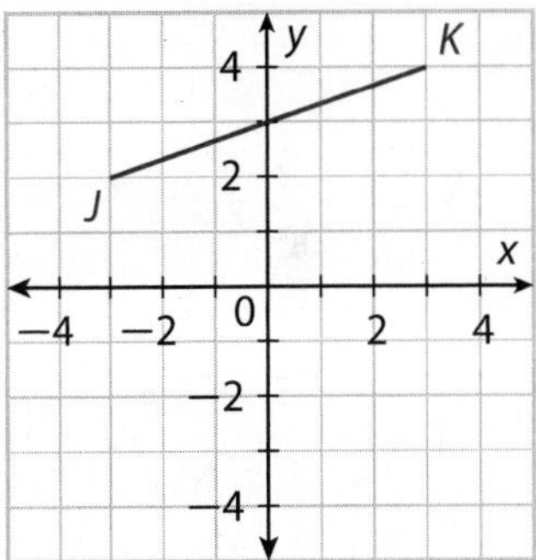

A. $L(4, 1)$ and $M(-2, -1)$

B. $L(5, -2)$ and $M(-1, -3)$

C. $L(4, 7)$ and $M(-2, 5)$

D. $L(5, -2)$ and $M(-1, -4)$

E. $L(3, 0)$ and $M(-3, 0)$

H.O.T. Focus on Higher Order Thinking

21. Analyze Relationships Quadrilateral $ABCD$ is a rectangle. The coordinates of vertices A and B are $A(-2, 2)$ and $B(2, 0)$. Vertex C lies on the y-axis. What are the coordinates of vertices C and D? Explain.

22. Counterexamples A student said that any three noncollinear points can be three of the vertices of a rectangle because it is always possible to choose a fourth vertex that completes the rectangle. Give a counterexample to show that the student's statement is false and explain the counterexample.

Lesson Performance Task

Each unit on the grid represents 1 mile. A ship is in distress at the point shown. The navigator knows that the shortest distance from a point to a line is on a perpendicular to the line. So, the navigator directs the captain to head the ship on a perpendicular course toward the shoreline.

If the ship succeeds in staying on course, where will it hit land? Explain your method.

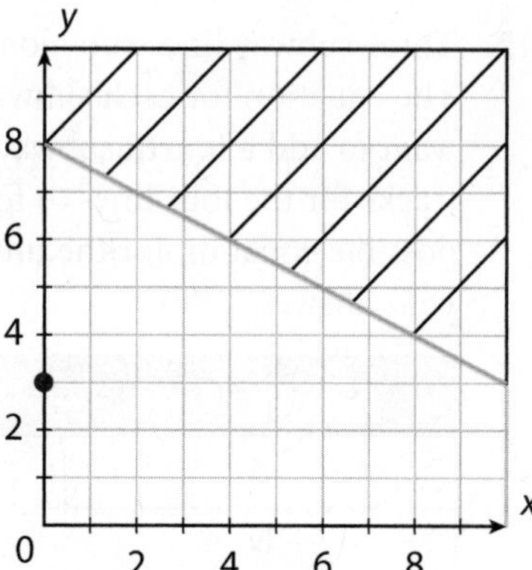

10.3 Coordinate Proof Using Distance with Segments and Triangles

Resource Locker

Essential Question: How do you write a coordinate proof?

Explore Deriving the Distance Formula and the Midpoint Formula

Complete the following steps to derive the Distance Formula and the Midpoint Formula.

Ⓐ To derive the Distance Formula, start with points J and K as shown in the figure.

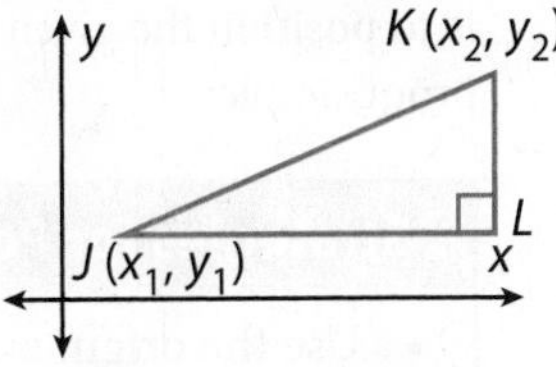

Given: $J(x_1, y_1)$ and $K(x_2, y_2)$ with $x_1 \neq x_2$ and $y_1 \neq y_2$

Prove: $JK = \sqrt{(x_2 - x_1)^2 + (y_2 - y_1)^2}$

Locate point L so that $\overline{JK}$ is the hypotenuse of right triangle JKL. What are the coordinates of L?

Ⓑ Find JL and LK.

Ⓒ By the Pythagorean Theorem, $JK^2 = JL^2 + LK^2$. Use this to find JK. Explain your steps.

Ⓓ To derive the Midpoint Formula, start with points A and B as shown in the figure.

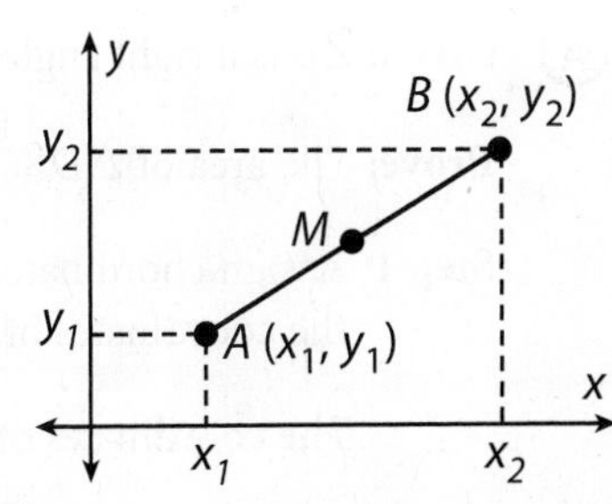

Given: $A(x_1, y_1)$ and $B(x_2, y_2)$

Prove: The midpoint of $\overline{AB}$ is $M\left(\frac{x_1 + x_2}{2}, \frac{y_1 + y_2}{2}\right)$.

What is the horizontal distance from point A to point B? What is the vertical distance from point A to point B?

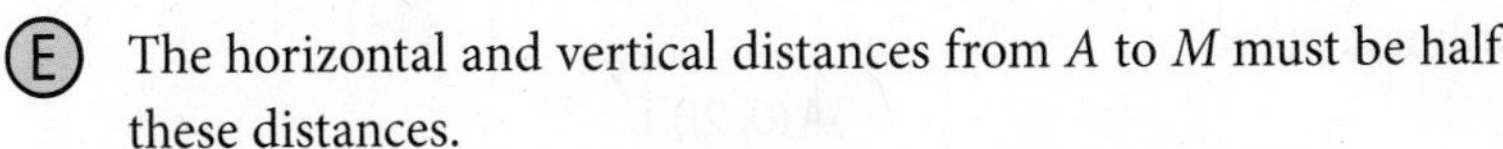

Ⓔ The horizontal and vertical distances from A to M must be half these distances.

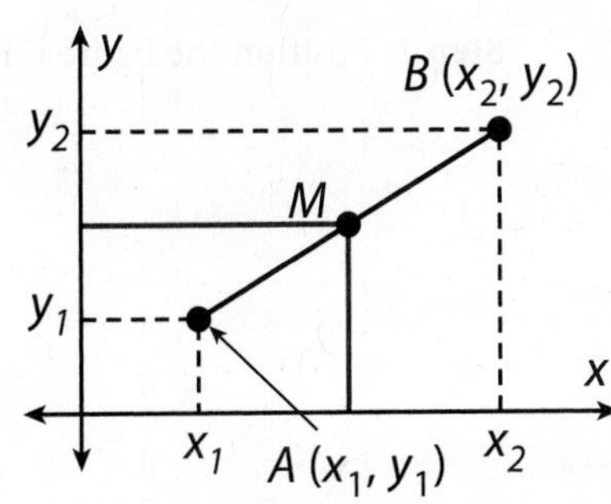

What is the horizontal distance from point A to point M?

What is the vertical distance from point A to point M?

Ⓕ To find the coordinates of point M, add the distances from Step E to the x- and y-coordinates of point A and simplify.

x-coordinate of point M: $x_1 + \frac{x_2 - x_1}{2} = \frac{2x_1}{2} + \frac{x_2 - x_1}{2} = \frac{2x_1 + x_2 - x_1}{2} = \frac{x_1 + x_2}{2}$

y-coordinate of point M: ?

Reflect

1. In the proof of the Distance Formula, why do you assume that $x_1 \neq x_2$ and $y_1 \neq y_2$?
2. Does the Distance Formula still apply if $x_1 = x_2$ or $y_1 = y_2$? Explain.
3. Does the Midpoint Formula still apply if $x_1 = x_2$ or $y_1 = y_2$? Explain.

Explain 1 Positioning a Triangle on the Coordinate Plane

A **coordinate proof** is a style of proof that uses coordinate geometry and algebra. The first step of a coordinate proof is to position the given figure in the plane. You can use any position, but some strategies can make the steps of the proof simpler.

Strategies for Positioning Figures in the Coordinate Plane

- Use the origin as a vertex, keeping the figure in Quadrant I.
- Center the figure at the origin.
- Center a side of the figure at the origin.
- Use one or both axes as sides of the figure.

Example 1 **Write each coordinate proof.**

Ⓐ **Given:** $\angle B$ is a right angle in $\triangle ABC$. D is the midpoint of $\overline{AC}$.

Prove: The area of $\triangle DBC$ is one half the area of $\triangle ABC$.

Step 1 Assign coordinates to each vertex. Since you will use the Midpoint Formula to find the coordinates of D, use multiples of 2 for the leg lengths.

The coordinates of A are $(0, 2j)$.

The coordinates of B are $(0, 0)$.

The coordinates of C are $(2n, 0)$.

Step 2 Position the figure on the coordinate plane.

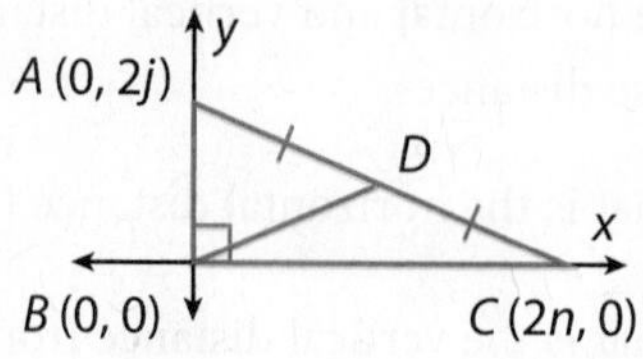

Step 3 Write a coordinate proof.

$\triangle ABC$ is a right triangle with height $2j$ and base $2n$.

$$\text{area of } \triangle ABC = \tfrac{1}{2}bh$$
$$= \tfrac{1}{2}(2n)(2j)$$
$$= 2nj \text{ square units}$$

By the Midpoint Formula, the coordinates of $D = \left(\frac{0 + 2n}{2}, \frac{2j + 0}{2}\right) = (n, j)$.

The height of $\triangle DBC$ is j units, and the base is $2n$ units.

$$\text{area of } \triangle DBC = \tfrac{1}{2}bh$$
$$= \tfrac{1}{2}(2n)(j)$$
$$= nj \text{ square units}$$

Since $nj = \frac{1}{2}(2nj)$, the area of $\triangle DBC$ is one half the area of $\triangle ABC$.

(B) **Given:** $\angle B$ is a right angle in $\triangle ABC$. D is the midpoint of $\overline{AC}$.

Prove: The area of $\triangle ADB$ is one half the area of $\triangle ABC$.

Assign coordinates and position the figure as in Example 1A.

A (0, 2j)
D
B (0, 0)
C (2n, 0)
x
y

$\triangle ABC$ is a right triangle with height $2j$ and base $2n$.

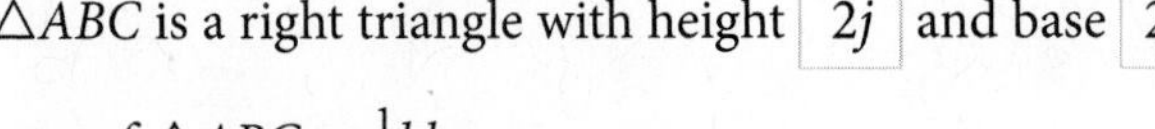

area of $\triangle ABC = \frac{1}{2}bh$

$= \frac{1}{2}\ 2n \cdot 2j$

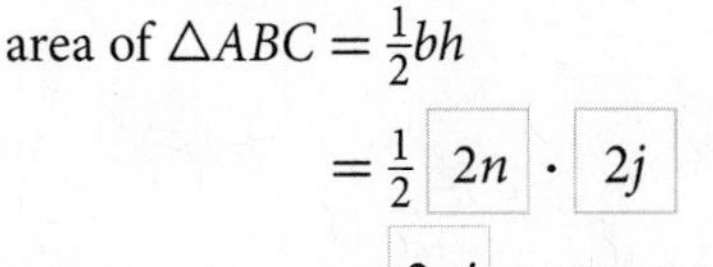

$= 2nj$ square units

By the Midpoint Formula, the coordinates of $D = \left(\frac{0 + 2n}{2}, \frac{2j + 0}{2}\right) = (n, j)$.

The height of $\triangle ADB$ is n units, and the base is $2j$ units.

area of $\triangle ADB = \frac{1}{2}bh = \frac{1}{2}\ 2j \cdot n = jn$ square units

Since $jn = \frac{1}{2}(2nj)$, the area of $\triangle ADB$ is one half the area of $\triangle ABC$.

Reflect

4. Why is it possible to position $\triangle ABC$ so that two of its sides lie on the axes of the coordinate plane?

Your Turn

Position the given triangle on the coordinate plane. Then show that the result about areas from Example 1 holds for the triangle.

5. A right triangle, $\triangle ABC$, with legs of length 2 units and 4 units

6. A right triangle, $\triangle ABC$, with both legs of length 8 units

Explain 2 Proving the Triangle Midsegment Theorem

In Module 8, you learned that the Triangle Midsegment Theorem states that a midsegment of a triangle is parallel to the third side of the triangle and is half as long as the third side. You can now use a coordinate proof to show that the theorem is true.

Example 2 **Prove the Triangle Midsegment Theorem.**

Given: $\overline{XY}$ is a midsegment of $\triangle PQR$.

Prove: $\overline{XY} \parallel \overline{PQ}$ and $XY = \frac{1}{2}PQ$

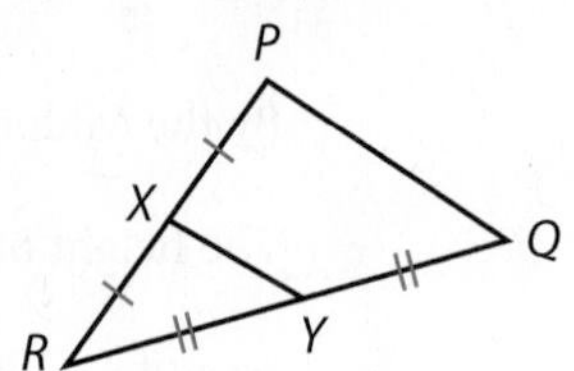

Place $\triangle PQR$ so that one vertex is at the origin. For convenience, assign vertex P the coordinates $(2a, 2b)$ and assign vertex Q the vertices $(2c, 2d)$.

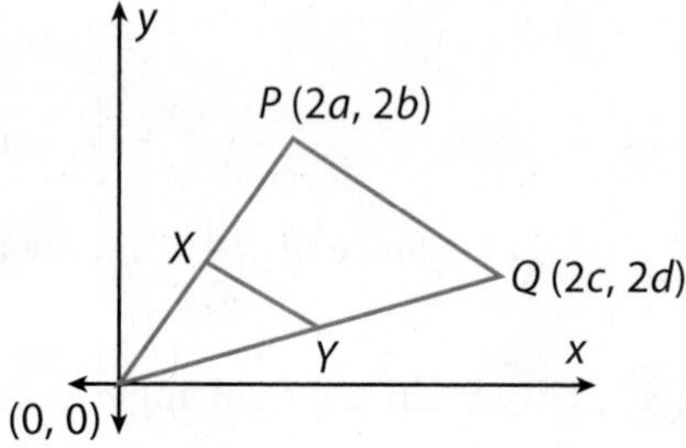

Use the Midpoint Formula to find the coordinates of X and Y.

The coordinates of X are $X\left(\frac{0+2a}{2}, \frac{0+2b}{2}\right) = X(a,b)$.

The coordinates of Y are $Y\left(\frac{0+2c}{2}, \frac{0+2d}{2}\right) = Y(c, d)$.

Find the slope of $\overline{PQ}$ and $\overline{XY}$.

slope of $\overline{PQ} = \frac{y_2 - y_1}{x_2 - x_1} = \frac{2d-2b}{2c-2a} = \frac{d-b}{c-a}$; slope of $\overline{XY} = \frac{y_2 - y_1}{x_2 - x_1} = \frac{d-b}{c-a}$

Therefore, $\overline{PQ} \parallel \overline{XY}$ since the slopes are the same.

Use the Distance Formula to find PQ and XY.

$$PQ = \sqrt{(x_2 - x_1)^2 + (y_2 - y_1)^2} = \sqrt{(2c-2a)^2 + (2d-2b)^2}$$

$$= \sqrt{4 \cdot (c-a)^2 + 4 \cdot (d-b)^2} = \sqrt{4 \cdot [(c-a)^2 + (d-b)^2]}$$

$$= \sqrt{4} \cdot \sqrt{(c-a)^2 + (d-b)^2} = 2\sqrt{(c-a)^2 + (d-b)^2}$$

$$XY = \sqrt{(x_2 - x_1)^2 + (y_2 - y_1)^2} = \sqrt{(c-a)^2 + (d-b)^2}$$

This shows that $XY = \frac{1}{2}PQ$.

Reflect

7. **Discussion** Why is it more convenient to assign vertex P the coordinates $(2a, 2b)$ and vertex Q the coordinates $(2c, 2d)$ rather than using the coordinates (a, b) and (c, d)?

Explain 3 Proving the Concurrency of Medians Theorem

You used the Concurrency of Medians Theorem in Module 8 and proved it in Module 9. Now you will prove the theorem again, this time using coordinate methods.

Example 3 **Prove the Concurrency of Medians Theorem.**

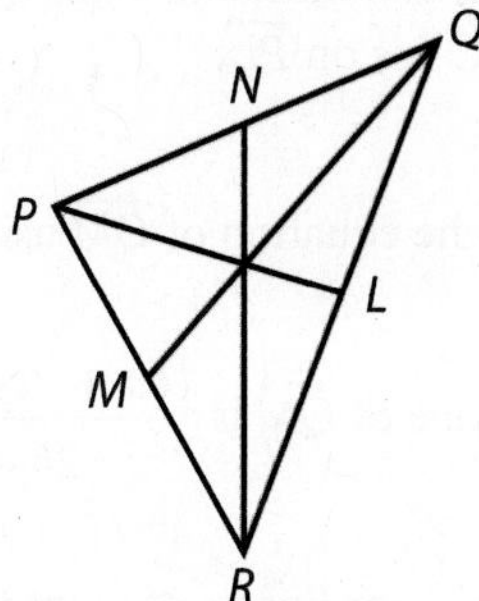

Given: $\triangle PQR$ with medians $\overline{PL}$, $\overline{QM}$, and $\overline{RN}$

Prove: $\overline{PL}$, $\overline{QM}$, and $\overline{RN}$ are concurrent.

Place $\triangle PQR$ so that vertex R is at the origin. Also, place the triangle so that point N lies on the y-axis. For convenience, assign point N the vertices $(0, 6a)$. (The factor of 6 will result in easier calculations later.)

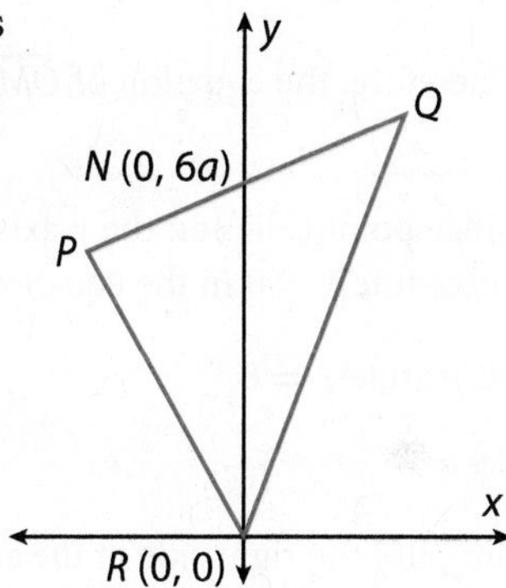

Since N is the midpoint of $\overline{PQ}$, assign coordinates to P and Q as follows.

The horizontal distance from N to P must be the same as the horizontal distance from N to Q. Let this distance be $2b$.

Then the x-coordinate of point P is $-2b$ and the x-coordinate of point Q is $2b$.

The vertical distance from N to P must be the same as the vertical distance from N to Q. Let this distance be $2c$.

Then the y-coordinate of point P is $6a - 2c$ and the y-coordinate of point Q is $6a + 2c$.

Complete the figure by writing the coordinates of points P and Q.

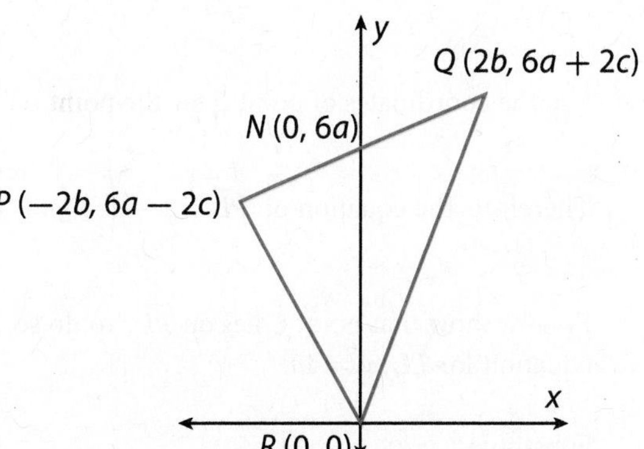

Now use the Midpoint Formula to find the coordinates of L and M.

The midpoint of $\overline{RQ}$ is $L\left(\dfrac{0 + 2b}{2}, \dfrac{0 + 6a + 2c}{2}\right) = L\left(b, 3a + c\right)$.

The midpoint of $\overline{RP}$ is $M\left(\dfrac{0 + -2b}{2}, \dfrac{0 + 6a - 2c}{2}\right) = M\left(-b, 3a - c\right)$.

Complete the figure by writing the coordinates of points L and M.

To complete the proof, write the equation of $\overleftrightarrow{QM}$ and use the equation to find the coordinates of point C, which is the intersection of the medians $\overline{QM}$ and $\overline{RN}$. Then show that point C lies on $\overleftrightarrow{PL}$.

Write the equation of $\overleftrightarrow{QM}$ using point-slope form.

The slope of $\overleftrightarrow{QM}$ is $\dfrac{(6a + 2c) - (3a - c)}{2b - (-b)} = \dfrac{3a + 3c}{3b} = \dfrac{a + c}{b}$.

Use the coordinates of point Q for the point on $\overleftrightarrow{QM}$.

Therefore, the equation of $\overleftrightarrow{QM}$ is $y - (6a + 2c) = \dfrac{a + c}{b} \cdot (x - 2b)$.

Since point C lies on the y-axis, the x-coordinate of point C is 0. To find the y-coordinate of C, substitute $x = 0$ in the equation of $\overleftrightarrow{QM}$ and solve for y.

Substitute $x = 0$. $\quad y - (6a + 2c) = \dfrac{a + c}{b} \cdot (0 - 2b)$

Simplify the right side of the equation. $\quad y - (6a + 2c) = -2(a + c)$

Distributive property $\quad y - (6a + 2c) = -2a - 2c$

Add $6a + 2c$ to each side and simplify. $\quad y = 4a$

So, the coordinates of point C are $C(0, 4a)$.

Now write the equation of $\overleftrightarrow{PL}$ using point-slope form.

The slope of $\overleftrightarrow{PL}$ is $\dfrac{(6a - 2c) - (3a + c)}{-2b - b} = \dfrac{3a - 3c}{-3b} = \dfrac{a - c}{-b}$.

Use the coordinates of point P for the point on $\overleftrightarrow{PL}$.

Therefore, the equation of $\overleftrightarrow{PL}$ is $y - (6a - 2c) = \dfrac{a - c}{-b} \cdot (x + 2b)$.

Finally, show that point C lies on $\overleftrightarrow{PL}$. To do so, show that when $x = 0$ in the equation for $\overleftrightarrow{PL}$, $y = 4a$.

Substitute $x = 0$. $\quad y - (6a - 2c) = \dfrac{a - c}{-b} \cdot (0 + 2b)$

Simplify right side of equation. $\quad y - (6a - 2c) = -2a + 2c$

Add $6a - 2c$ to each side and simplify. $\quad y = 4a$

Reflect

8. A student claims that the averages of the x-coordinates and of the y-coordinates of the vertices of the triangle are x- and y-coordinates of the point of concurrency, C. Does the coordinate proof of the Concurrency of Medians Theorem support the claim? Explain.

Explain 4 Using Triangles on the Coordinate Plane

Example 4 Write each proof.

Ⓐ **Given:** $A(2, 3)$, $B(5, -1)$, $C(1, 0)$, $D(-4, -1)$, $E(0, 2)$, $F(-1, -2)$

Prove: $\angle ABC \cong \angle DEF$

Step 1 Plot the points on a coordinate plane.

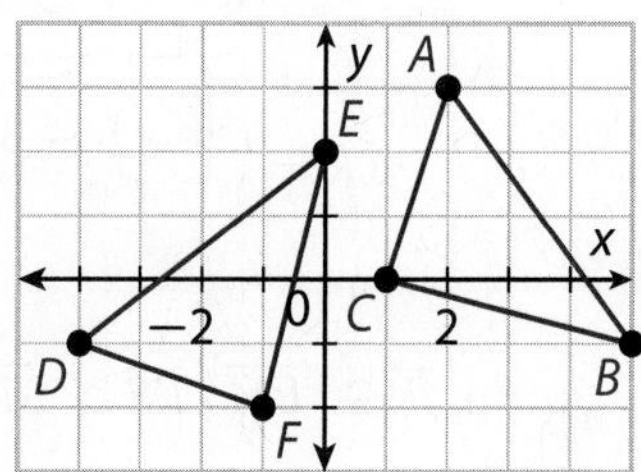

Step 2 Use the Distance Formula to find the length of each side of each triangle.

$AB = \sqrt{(5-2)^2 + (-1-3)^2} = \sqrt{25} = 5$; $BC = \sqrt{(1-5)^2 + 0 - (-1)^2} = \sqrt{17}$;

$AC = \sqrt{(1-2)^2 + (0-3)^2} = \sqrt{10}$; $DE = \sqrt{\left(0-(-4)\right)^2 + \left(2-(-1)\right)^2} = \sqrt{25} = 5$;

$EF = \sqrt{(-1-0)^2 + (-2-2)^2} = \sqrt{1+16} = \sqrt{17}$; $DF = \sqrt{\left(-1-(-4)\right)^2 + \left(-2-(-1)\right)^2}$

$= \sqrt{9+1} = \sqrt{10}$

So, $\overline{AB} \cong \overline{DE}$, $\overline{BC} \cong \overline{EF}$, and $\overline{AC} \cong \overline{DF}$. Therefore, $\triangle ABC \cong \triangle DEF$ by the SSS Triangle Congruence Theorem and $\angle ABC \cong \angle DEF$ by CPCTC.

Ⓑ **Given:** $J(-4, 1)$, $K(0, 5)$, $L(3, 1)$, $M(-1, -3)$, R is the midpoint of $\overline{JK}$, S is the midpoint of $\overline{LM}$.

Prove: $\angle JSK \cong \angle LRM$

Step 1 Plot the points on a coordinate plane.

Step 2 Use the Midpoint Formula to find the coordinates of R and S.

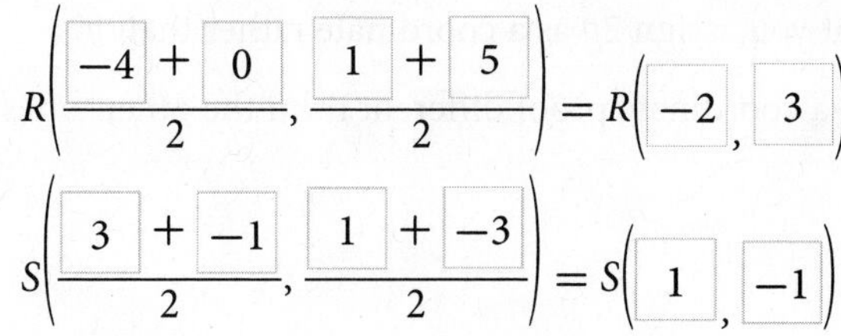

$R\left(\dfrac{-4 + 0}{2}, \dfrac{1 + 5}{2}\right) = R(-2, 3)$

$S\left(\dfrac{3 + -1}{2}, \dfrac{1 + -3}{2}\right) = S(1, -1)$

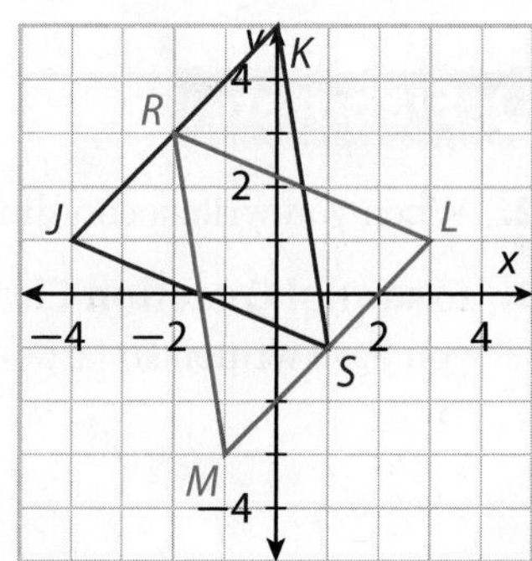

Step 3 Use the Distance Formula to find the length of each side of each triangle.

$$JK = \sqrt{(0-(-4))^2 + (5-1)^2} = \sqrt{16+16} = \sqrt{32}$$

$$KS = \sqrt{\left(\boxed{1} - 0\right)^2 + \left(\boxed{-1} - 5\right)^2} = \sqrt{\boxed{1} + \boxed{36}} = \sqrt{\boxed{37}}$$

$$JS = \sqrt{\left(\boxed{1} - (-4)\right)^2 + \left(\boxed{-1} - 1\right)^2} = \sqrt{\boxed{25} + \boxed{4}} = \sqrt{\boxed{29}}$$

$$LM = \sqrt{(-1-3)^2 + (-3-1)^2} = \sqrt{16+16} = \sqrt{32}$$

$$MR = \sqrt{\left(\boxed{-2} - (-1)\right)^2 + \left(\boxed{3} - (-3)\right)^2} = \sqrt{\boxed{1} + \boxed{36}} = \sqrt{\boxed{37}}$$

$$LR = \sqrt{\left(\boxed{-2} - 3\right)^2 + \left(\boxed{3} - 1\right)^2} = \sqrt{\boxed{25} + \boxed{4}} = \sqrt{\boxed{29}}$$

So, $\overline{JK} \cong \boxed{\overline{LM}}$, $\overline{KS} \cong \boxed{\overline{MR}}$, and $\overline{JS} \cong \boxed{\overline{LR}}$. Therefore, $\triangle JKS \cong \boxed{\triangle LMR}$ by the SSS Triangle Congruence Theorem and $\angle JSK \cong \angle LRM$ since corresponding parts of congruent triangles are congruent.

Reflect

9. In Part B, what other pairs of angles can you prove to be congruent? Why?

Your Turn

Write each proof.

10. **Given:** $A(-4, -2)$, $B(-3, 2)$, $C(-1, 3)$, $D(-5, 0)$, $E(-1, -1)$, $F(0, -3)$
Prove: $\angle BCA \cong \angle EFD$

11. **Given:** $P(-3, 5)$, $Q(-1, -1)$, $R(4, 5)$, $S(2, -1)$, M is the midpoint of $\overline{PQ}$, N is the midpoint of $\overline{RS}$.
Prove: $\angle PQN \cong \angle RSM$

Elaborate

12. When you write a coordinate proof, why might you assign $2p$ as a coordinate rather than p?

13. **Essential Question Check-In** What makes a coordinate proof different from the other types of proofs you have written so far?

Evaluate: Homework and Practice

- Online Homework
- Hints and Help
- Extra Practice

1. Explain how to derive the Distance Formula using $\triangle PQR$.

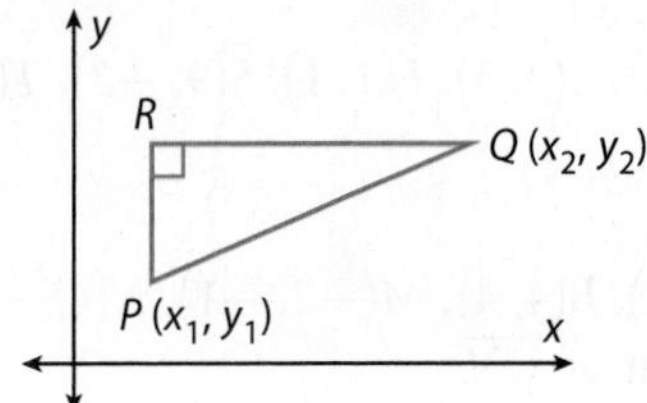

Write each coordinate proof.

2. **Given:** $\angle B$ is a right angle in $\triangle ABC$. M is the midpoint of $\overline{AC}$.

   Prove: M is equidistant from all three vertices of $\triangle ABC$.

   Use the coordinates that have been assigned in the figure.

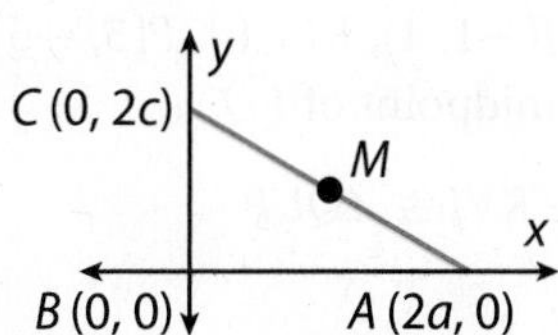

3. **Given:** $\triangle ABC$ is isosceles. X is the midpoint of $\overline{AB}$, Y is the midpoint of $\overline{AC}$, Z is the midpoint of $\overline{BC}$.

   Prove: $\triangle XYZ$ is isosceles.

   Use the coordinates that have been assigned in the figure.

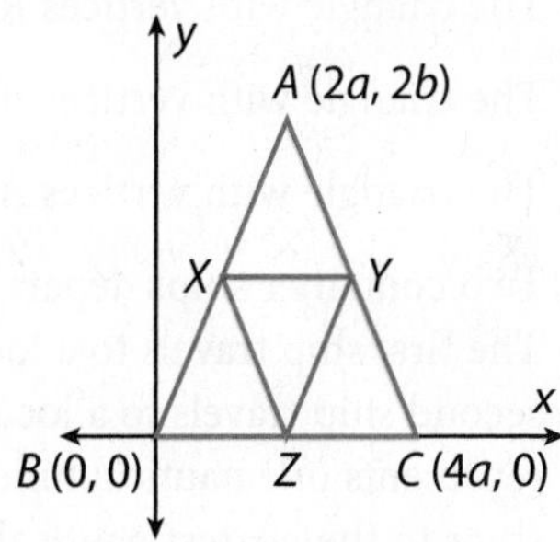

4. **Given:** $\angle R$ is a right angle in $\triangle PQR$. A is the midpoint of $\overline{PR}$. B is the midpoint of $\overline{QR}$.

   Prove: $\overline{AB}$ is parallel to $\overline{PQ}$.

5. **Given:** $\triangle ABC$ is isosceles. M is the midpoint of $\overline{AB}$. N is the midpoint of $\overline{AC}$. $\overline{AB} \cong \overline{AC}$

   Prove: $\overline{MC} \cong \overline{NB}$

6. Prove the Triangle Midsegment Theorem using the figure shown here.

   Given: $\overline{DE}$ is a midsegment of $\triangle ABC$.

   Prove: $\overline{DE} \parallel \overline{BC}$ and $DE = \frac{1}{2}BC$

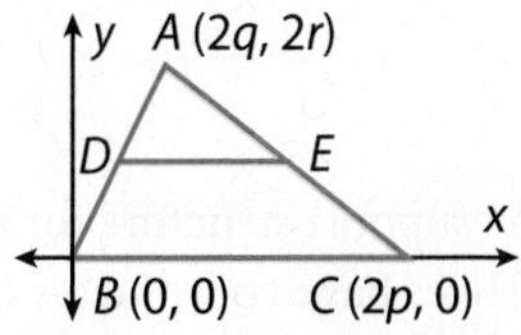

7. **Critique Reasoning** A student proves the Concurrency of Medians Theorem by first assigning coordinates to the vertices of $\triangle PQR$ as $P(0, 0)$, $Q(2a, 0)$, and $R(2a, 2c)$. The student says that this choice of coordinates makes the algebra in the proof a bit easier. Do you agree with the student's choice of coordinates? Explain.

Write each proof.

8. **Given:** $J(-2, 2)$, $K(0, 1)$, $L(-3, -1)$, $P(4, -2)$, $Q(3, -4)$, $R(1, -1)$

Prove: $\angle JKL \cong \angle PQR$

9. **Given:** $D(-3, 2)$, $E(3, 3)$, $F(1, 1)$, $S(9, -2)$, $T(3, -1)$, $U(5, -3)$

Prove: $\angle FDE \cong \angle UST$

10. **Given:** $A(-2, 2)$, $B(4, 4)$, $M(-2, -1)$, $N(4, -3)$, X is the midpoint of $\overline{AB}$, Y is the midpoint of $\overline{MN}$.

Prove: $\angle ABY \cong \angle MNX$

11. **Given:** $J(-1, 4)$, $K(3, 0)$, $P(3, -6)$, $Q(-1, -2)$, U is the midpoint of $\overline{JK}$, V is the midpoint of $\overline{PQ}$.

Prove: $\angle KVJ \cong \angle QUP$

Prove or disprove each statement.

12. The triangle with vertices $R(-2, -2)$, $S(1, 4)$, and $T(4, -5)$ is an equilateral triangle.

13. The triangle with vertices $J(-2, 2)$, $K(2, 3)$, and $L(-1, -2)$ is an isosceles triangle.

14. The triangle with vertices $A(-1, 3)$, $B(2, 1)$, and $C(0, -2)$ is a scalene triangle.

15. Two container ships depart from a port at $P(20, 10)$. The first ship travels to a location at $A(-30, 50)$, and the second ship travels to a location at $B(70, -30)$. Each unit represents one nautical mile. Find the distance between the ships to the nearest nautical mile. Verify that the port is the midpoint between the two ships.

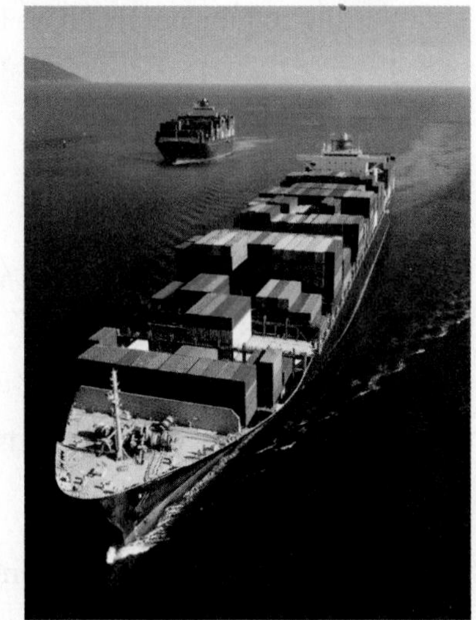

16. The support structure for a hammock includes a triangle whose vertices have coordinates $G(-1, 3)$, $H(-3, -2)$, and $J(1, -2)$.

a. Classify the triangle and justify your answer.

b. **Algebra** Each unit of the coordinate plane represents one foot. To the nearest tenth of a foot, how much metal is needed to make one of the triangular parts for the support structure?

17. **Communicate Mathematical Ideas** Explain how the perimeter of $\triangle JKL$ compares to the perimeter of $\triangle MNP$.

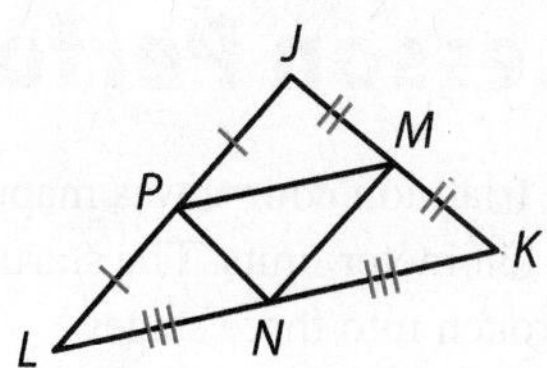

18. The coordinates of the vertices of $\triangle LMN$ are shown in the figure. Determine whether each statement is true or false.

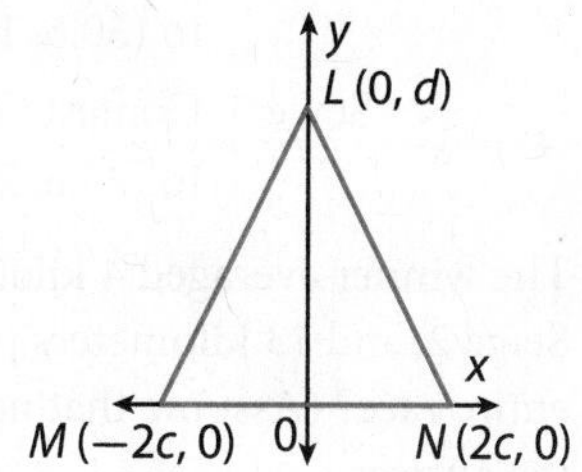

  a. $\triangle LMN$ is isosceles.
  b. One side of $\triangle LMN$ has a length of $2c$ units.
  c. If P is the midpoint of $\overline{LN}$, then $\overline{OP}$ is parallel to $\overline{LM}$.
  d. The area of $\triangle LMN$ is $4cd$ square units.
  e. The midpoint of $\overline{MN}$ is the origin.

H.O.T. Focus on Higher Order Thinking

19. **Explain the Error** A student assigns coordinates to a right triangle as shown in the figure. Then he uses the Distance Formula to show that $PQ = a$ and $RQ = a$. Since $PQ = RQ$, the student says he has proved that every right triangle is isosceles. Explain the error in the student's proof.

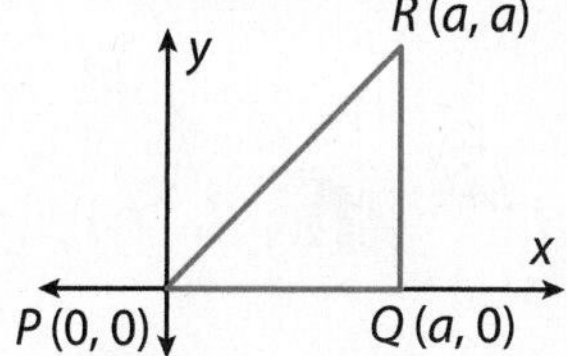

20. A carpenter wants to make a triangular bracket to hold up a bookshelf. The plan for the bracket shows that the vertices of the triangle are $R(-2, 2)$, $S(1, 4)$, and $T(1, -2)$. Can the carpenter conclude that the bracket is a right triangle? Explain.

21. **Analyze Relationships** The vertices chosen to represent an isosceles right triangle for a coordinate proof are at $(-2s, 2s)$, $(0, 2s)$, and $(0, 0)$. What other coordinates could be used so that the coordinate proof would be easier to complete? Explain.

Lesson Performance Task

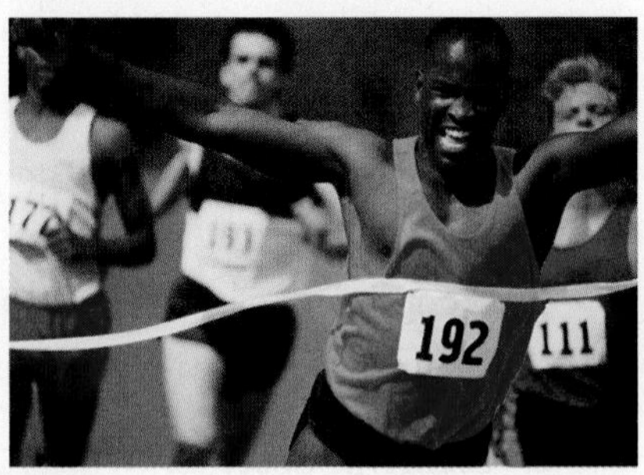

A triathlon course was mapped on a coordinate grid marked in 1-kilometer units. The starting point was (0, 0). The triathlon was broken into three stages:

- Stage 1: Contestants swim from (0, 0) to (0.6, 0.8).
- Stage 2: Contestants bicycle from the previous stopping point to (30.6, 16.8).
- Stage 3: Contestants run from the previous stopping point to (25.6, 28.8).

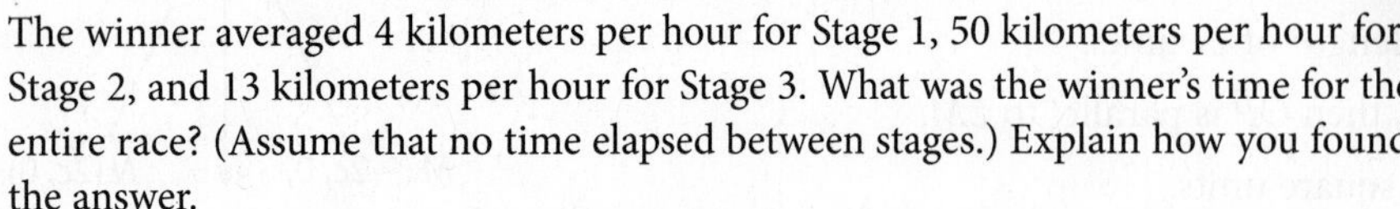

The winner averaged 4 kilometers per hour for Stage 1, 50 kilometers per hour for Stage 2, and 13 kilometers per hour for Stage 3. What was the winner's time for the entire race? (Assume that no time elapsed between stages.) Explain how you found the answer.

10.4 Coordinate Proof Using Distance with Quadrilaterals

Essential Question: How can you use slope and the distance formula in coordinate proofs?

Resource Locker

Explore Positioning a Quadrilateral on the Coordinate Plane

You have used coordinate geometry to find the midpoint of a line segment and to find the distance between two points. Coordinate geometry can also be used to prove conjectures.

Remember that in Lesson 10.3 you learned several strategies that make using a coordinate proof simpler. They are:

- Use the origin as a vertex, keeping the figure in Quadrant I.
- Center the figure at the origin.
- Center a side of the figure at the origin.
- Use one or both axes as sides of the figure.

Position a rectangle with a length of 8 units and a width of 3 units in the coordinate plane as described.

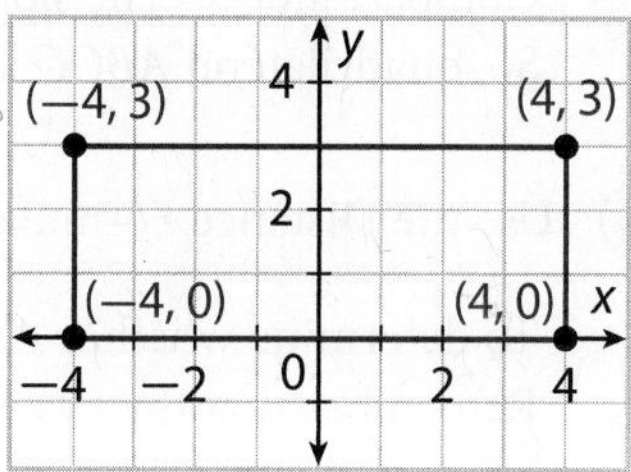

(A) **Method 1** Center the longer side of the rectangle at the origin.

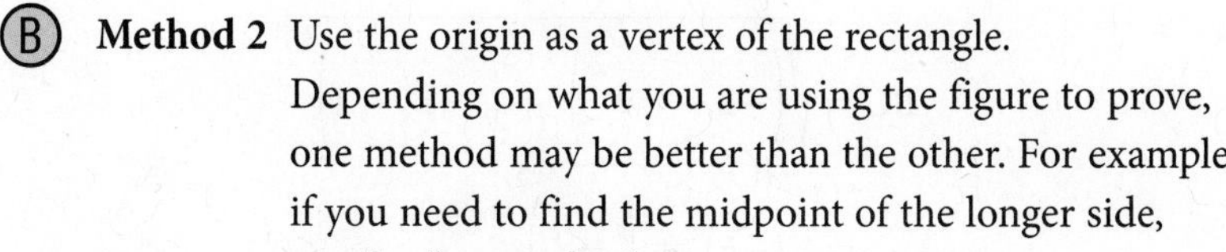

(B) **Method 2** Use the origin as a vertex of the rectangle.
Depending on what you are using the figure to prove, one method may be better than the other. For example, if you need to find the midpoint of the longer side, use the first method.

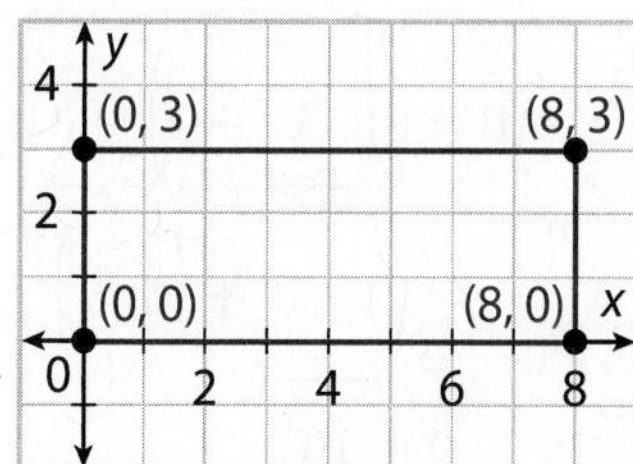

A coordinate proof can also be used to prove that a certain relationship is always true. You can prove that a statement is true for all right triangles without knowing the side lengths. To do this, assign variables as the coordinates of the vertices.

Position a square, with one vertex at the origin and side lengths $2a$, on a coordinate plane and give the coordinates of each vertex.

(C) Sketch the square. Label the side lengths.

(D) What are the coordinates of each vertex?

Reflect

1. **Discussion** Describe another way you could have positioned the square and give the coordinates of its vertices.

2. When writing a coordinate proof why are variables used instead of numbers as coordinates for the vertices of a figure?

Explain 1 Proving Conditions for a Parallelogram

You have already used the Distance Formula and the Midpoint Formula in coordinate proofs. As you will see, slope is useful in coordinate proofs whenever you need to show that lines are parallel or perpendicular.

Example 1 **Prove or disprove that the quadrilateral determined by the points $A(4, 4)$, $B(3, 1)$, $C(-2, -1)$, and $D(-1, 2)$ is a parallelogram.**

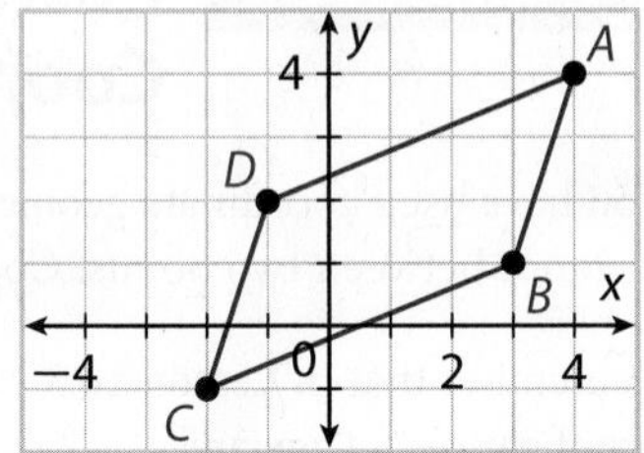

(A) Use slopes to write the coordinate proof.

To determine whether $ABCD$ is a parallelogram, find the slope of each side of the quadrilateral.

Slope of $\overline{AB} = \frac{y_2 - y_1}{x_2 - x_1} = \frac{1-4}{3-4} = \frac{-3}{-1} = 3$; Slope of $\overline{BC} = \frac{y_2 - y_1}{x_2 - x_1} = \frac{-1-1}{-2-3} = \frac{-2}{-5} = \frac{2}{5}$;

Slope of $\overline{CD} = \frac{y_2 - y_1}{x_2 - x_1} = \frac{2-(-1)}{-1-(-2)} = \frac{3}{1} = 3$; Slope of $\overline{DA} = \frac{y_2 - y_1}{x_2 - x_1} = \frac{4-2}{4-(-1)} = \frac{2}{5}$

Compare slopes. The slopes of opposite sides are equal. This means opposite sides are parallel. So, quadrilateral $ABCD$ is a parallelogram.

(B) Use the Distance Formula to write the coordinate proof.

To determine whether $ABCD$ is a parallelogram, find the length of each side of the quadrilateral. Remember that the Distance Formula is length $= \sqrt{(x_2 - x_1)^2 + (y_2 - y_1)^2}$.

$AB = \sqrt{\left(\boxed{3} - 4\right)^2 + (1-4)^2}$
$= \sqrt{(-1)^2 + \left(\boxed{-3}\right)^2}$
$= \sqrt{\boxed{10}}$

$BC = \sqrt{\left(-2 - \boxed{3}\right)^2 + \left(\boxed{-1} - 1\right)^2}$
$= \sqrt{(-5)^2 + \left(\boxed{-2}\right)^2}$
$= \sqrt{\boxed{29}}$

$CD = \sqrt{\left(-1 - \boxed{-2}\right)^2 + \left(\boxed{2} - (-1)\right)^2}$
$= \sqrt{(1)^2 + \left(\boxed{3}\right)^2}$
$= \sqrt{\boxed{10}}$

$DA = \sqrt{\left(4 - \boxed{-1}\right)^2 + \left(4 - \boxed{2}\right)^2}$
$= \sqrt{\left(\boxed{5}\right)^2 + \left(\boxed{2}\right)^2}$
$= \sqrt{\boxed{29}}$

Compare the side lengths. The lengths of the opposite sides are equal By the Opposites Sides Criterion for a Parallelogram, we can conclude that $ABCD$ is a parallelogram.

Reflect

3. Suppose you want to prove that a general parallelogram $WXYZ$ has diagonals that bisect each other. Why is it convenient to use general vertex coefficients, such as $2a$ and $2b$?

Your Turn

Write a coordinate proof given quadrilateral $ABCD$ with vertices $A(3, 2)$, $B(8, 2)$, $C(5, 0)$, and $D(0, 0)$.

4. Prove that $ABCD$ is a parallelogram.
5. Prove that the diagonals of $ABCD$ bisect each other.

Explain 2 Proving Conditions for Special Parallelograms

Example 2 **Prove or disprove each statement about the quadrilateral determined by the points $Q(2, -3)$, $R(-4, 0)$, $S(-2, 4)$, and $T(4, 1)$.**

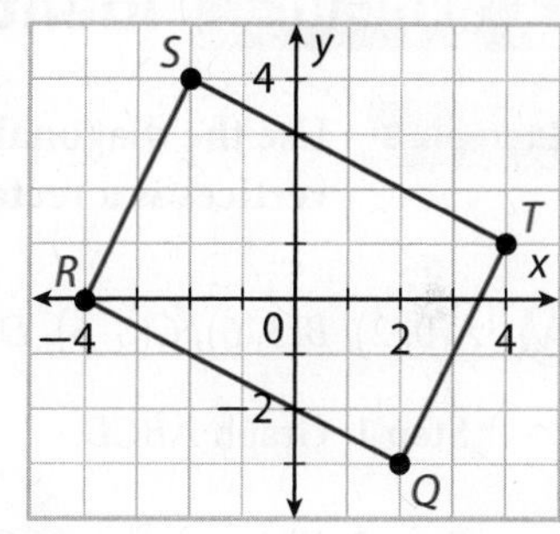

(A) The diagonals of $QRST$ are congruent.

The length of $\overline{SQ} = \sqrt{(2-(-2))^2 + (-3-4)^2} = \sqrt{65}$.

The length of $\overline{RT} = \sqrt{(-4-4)^2 + (0-1)^2} = \sqrt{65}$.

So, the diagonals of $QRST$ are congruent.

(B) $QRST$ is a rectangle.

Find the slope of each side of the quadrilateral.

Slope of $\overline{QR} = \frac{y_2 - y_1}{x_2 - x_1} = \frac{0-(-3)}{-4-2} = \frac{3}{-6} = -\frac{1}{2}$; Slope of $\overline{RS} = \frac{y_2 - y_1}{x_2 - x_1} = \frac{4 - 0}{-2 - -4} = \frac{4}{2} = 2$;

Slope of $\overline{ST} = \frac{y_2 - y_1}{x_2 - x_1} = \frac{1 - 4}{4 - -2} = \frac{-3}{6} = -\frac{1}{2}$;

Slope of $\overline{TQ} = \frac{y_2 - y_1}{x_2 - x_1} = \frac{-3 - 1}{2 - 4} = \frac{-4}{-2} = 2$

Find the products of the slopes of adjacent sides.

$(\text{slope of } \overline{QR})(\text{slope of } \overline{RS}) = -\frac{1}{2} \cdot 2 = -1$; $(\text{slope of } \overline{RS})(\text{slope of } \overline{ST}) = 2 \cdot -\frac{1}{2} = -1$;

$(\text{slope of } \overline{ST})(\text{slope of } \overline{TQ}) = -\frac{1}{2} \cdot 2 = -1$; $(\text{slope of } \overline{TQ})(\text{slope of } \overline{QR}) = 2 \cdot -\frac{1}{2} = -1$

You can conclude that adjacent sides are perpendicular. So, quadrilateral $QRST$ is a rectangle.

Reflect

6. Explain how to prove that *QRST* is not a square.

Your Turn

Prove or disprove each statement about quadrilateral *WXYZ* determined by the points $W(0, 0)$, $X(4, 3)$, $Y(9, 3)$, and $Z(5, 0)$.

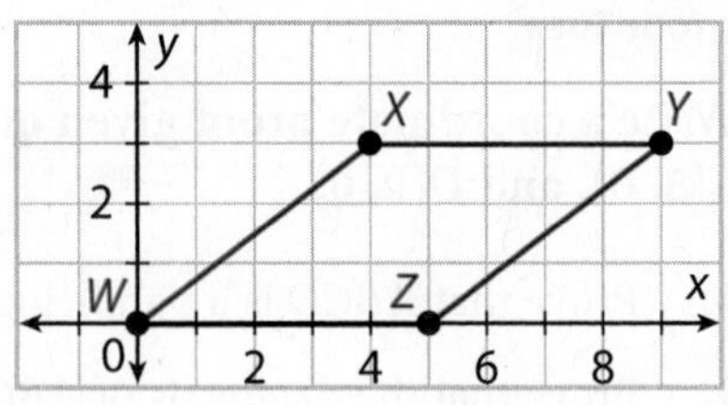

7. *WXYZ* is a rhombus.

8. The diagonals of *WXYZ* are perpendicular.

Explain 3 Identifying Figures on the Coordinate Plane

Example 3 **Use the diagonals to determine whether a parallelogram with the given vertices is a rectangle, rhombus, or square. Give all the names that apply.**

(A) $A(0, 2)$, $B(3, 6)$, $C(8, 6)$, $D(5, 2)$

Step 1 Graph *ABCD*.

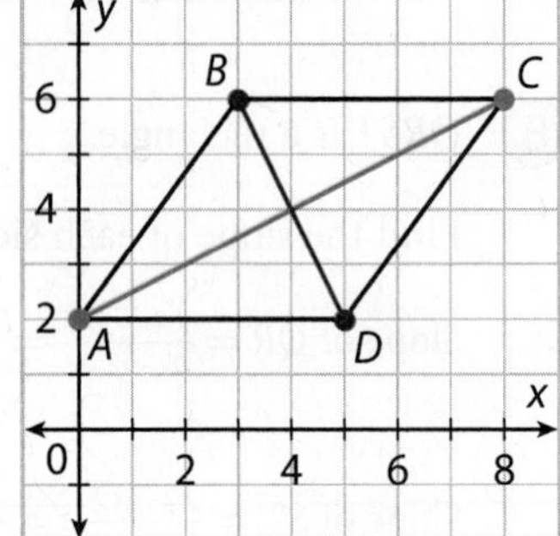

Step 2 Determine if *ABCD* is a rectangle.

$AC = \sqrt{(8-0)^2 + (6-2)^2} = \sqrt{80} = 4\sqrt{5}$

$BD = \sqrt{(5-3)^2 + (2-6)^2} = \sqrt{20} = 2\sqrt{5}$

Since $4\sqrt{5} \neq 2\sqrt{5}$, *ABCD* is not a rectangle. Thus, *ABCD* is not a square.

Step 3 Determine if *ABCD* is a rhombus.

Slope of $\overline{AC} = \dfrac{6-2}{8-0} = \dfrac{1}{2}$

Slope of $\overline{BD} = \dfrac{2-6}{5-3} = -2$

Since $\left(\dfrac{1}{2}\right)(-2) = -1$, $\overline{AC} \perp \overline{BD}$. *ABCD* is a rhombus.

(B) $E(-4, -1), F(-3, 2), G(3, 0), H(2, -3)$

Step 1 Graph *EFGH*.

Step 2 Determine if *EFGH* is a rectangle.

$$EG = \sqrt{\left(3 - \boxed{-4}\right)^2 + \left(0 - \boxed{-1}\right)^2} = \sqrt{\boxed{50}} = \boxed{5\sqrt{2}}$$

$$FH = \sqrt{\left(\boxed{2} - (-3)\right)^2 + \left(\boxed{-3} - 2\right)^2} = \sqrt{\boxed{50}} = 5\sqrt{\boxed{2}}$$

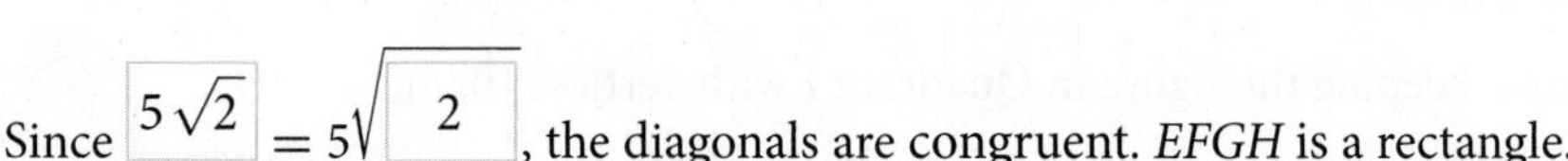

Since $\boxed{5\sqrt{2}} = 5\sqrt{\boxed{2}}$, the diagonals are congruent. *EFGH* is a rectangle.

Step 3 Determine if *EFGH* is a rhombus.

Slope of $\overline{EG} = \frac{0-(-1)}{3-(-4)} = \frac{1}{7}$; Slope of $\overline{FH} = \frac{-3-2}{2-(-3)} = \frac{-5}{5} = -1$

Since $\left(\frac{1}{7}\right)(-1) \neq -1$, $\overline{EG}$ is not perpendicular to $\overline{FH}$. So, *EFGH* is not a rhombus and cannot be a square.

Your Turn

Use the diagonals to determine whether a parallelogram with the given vertices is a rectangle, rhombus, or square. Give all the names that apply.

9. $K(-5, -1), L(-2, 4), M(3, 1), N(0, -4)$

10. $P(-4, 6), Q(2, 5), R(3, -1), S(-3, 0)$

Elaborate

11. How can you use slopes to show that two line segments are parallel? Perpendicular?

12. When you use the distance formula, you find the square root of a value. When finding the square root of a value, you must consider both the positive and negative outcomes. Explain why the negative outcome is not used in the coordinate proofs in the lesson.

13. **Essential Question Check-In** How can you use slope in coordinate proofs?

Evaluate: Homework and Practice

- Online Homework
- Hints and Help
- Extra Practice

1. Suppose you have a right triangle. If you want to write a proof about the midpoints of the legs of the triangle, which placement of the triangle would be most helpful? Explain.

A. Use the origin as a vertex, keeping the figure in Quadrant I with vertices $(0, 2b)$, $(2a, 0)$, and $(0, 0)$.

B. Center the triangle at the origin.

C. Use the origin as a vertex, keeping the figure in Quadrant I with vertices $(0, b)$, $(a, 0)$, and $(0, 0)$.

D. Center one leg of the triangle on the *y*-axis with vertices $(0, a)$, $(0, -a)$, and $(b, -a)$.

E. Use the *x*-axis as one leg of the triangle with vertices $(a, 0)$, (a, b), and $(a + c, 0)$.

2. Describe the position of a general isosceles trapezoid $WXYZ$ determined by the points $W(0, 0)$, $X(a, 0)$, $Y(a - c, b)$, and $Z(c, b)$. Then sketch the trapezoid.

Write a coordinate proof for the quadrilateral determined by the points $A(2, 4)$, $B(4, -1)$, $C(-1, -3)$, and $D(-3, 2)$.

3. Prove that $ABCD$ is a parallelogram.

4. Prove that $ABCD$ is a rectangle.

5. Prove that $ABCD$ is a rhombus.

6. Prove that $ABCD$ is a square.

Prove or disprove each statement about the quadrilateral determined by the points $W(-2, 5)$, $X(5, 5)$, $Y(5, 0)$, and $Z(-2, 0)$.

7. Prove that the diagonals are congruent.

8. Prove that the diagonals are perpendicular.

9. Prove that the diagonals bisect each other.

10. Prove that $WXYZ$ is a square.

Algebra Use the diagonals to determine whether a parallelogram with the given vertices is a rectangle, rhombus, or square. Give all the names that apply.

11. $A(-10, 4)$, $B(-2, 10)$, $C(4, 2)$, $D(-4, -4)$

12. $J(-9, -7)$, $K(-4, -2)$, $L(3, -3)$, $M(-2, -8)$

Analyze Relationships The coordinates of three vertices of parallelogram $ABCD$ are given. Find the coordinates of the fourth point so that the given type of figure is formed.

13. $A(4, -2)$, $B(-5, -2)$, $D(4, 4)$, rectangle

14. $A(-5, 5)$, $B(0, 0)$, $C(7, 1)$, rhombus

15. $A(0, 2)$, $B(4, -2)$, $C(0, -6)$, square

16. $A(2, 1)$, $B(-1, 5)$, $C(-5, 2)$, square

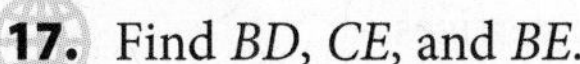

Paul designed a doghouse to fit against the side of his house. His plan consisted of a right triangle on top of a rectangle. Use the drawing for Exercises 17–18.

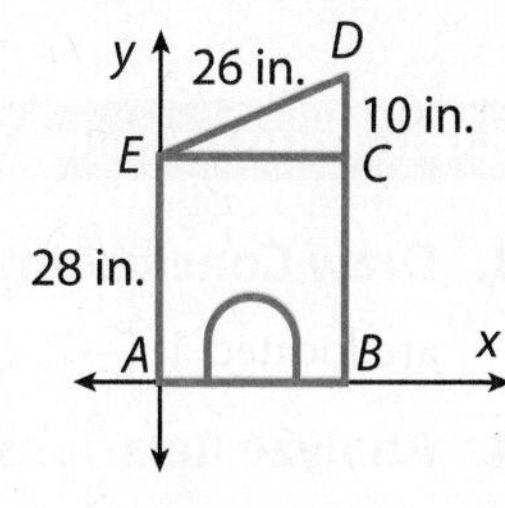

17. Find *BD*, *CE*, and *BE*.

18. Before building the doghouse, Paul sketched his plan on a coordinate plane. He placed *A* at the origin and $\overline{AB}$ on the x-axis. Find the coordinates of *B*, *C*, *D*, and *E*, assuming that each unit of the coordinate plane represents one inch.

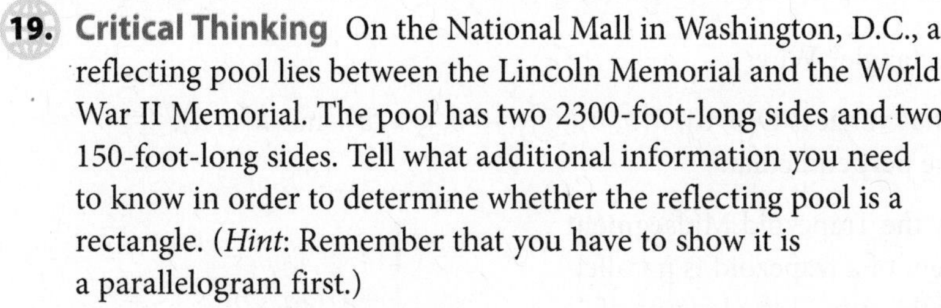

19. Critical Thinking On the National Mall in Washington, D.C., a reflecting pool lies between the Lincoln Memorial and the World War II Memorial. The pool has two 2300-foot-long sides and two 150-foot-long sides. Tell what additional information you need to know in order to determine whether the reflecting pool is a rectangle. (*Hint*: Remember that you have to show it is a parallelogram first.)

Algebra Write a coordinate proof.

20. The Bushmen in South Africa use the Global Positioning System to transmit data about endangered animals to conservationists. The Bushmen have sighted animals at the following coordinates: $(-25, 31.5)$, $(-23.2, 31.4)$, and $(-24, 31.1)$. Prove that the distance between two of these locations is approximately twice the distance between two other locations.

21. Two cruise ships leave a port located at $P(10, 50)$. One ship sails to an island located at $A(-40, -10)$, and the other sails to an island located at $B(60, 110)$. Suppose that each unit represents one nautical mile. Find the midpoint of the line segment connecting the two cruise ships. Verify that the port and the two cruise ships are in a line.

22. A parallelogram has vertices at $(0, 0)$, $(5, 6)$, and $(10, 0)$. Which could be the fourth vertex of the parallelogram? Choose all that apply.

A. $(5, -6)$

B. $(15, 6)$

C. $(0, -6)$

D. $(10, 6)$

E. $(-5, 6)$

H.O.T. Focus on Higher Order Thinking

23. Draw Conclusions The diagonals of a parallelogram intersect at $(-2, 1.5)$. Two vertices are located at $(-7, 2)$ and $(2, 6.5)$. Find the coordinates of the other two vertices.

24. Analyze Relationships Consider points $L(3, -4)$, $M(1, -2)$, and $N(5, 2)$.

a. Find coordinates for point P so that the quadrilateral determined by points L, M, N, and P is a parallelogram. Is there more than one possibility? Explain.

b. Are any of the parallelograms a rectangle? Why?

25. Critical Thinking Rhombus $OPQR$ has vertices $O(0, 0)$, $P(a, b)$, $Q(a + b, a + b)$, and $R(b, a)$. Prove the diagonals of the rhombus are perpendicular.

26. Multi-Step Use coordinates to verify the Trapezoid Midsegment Theorem which states "The midsegment of a trapezoid is parallel to each base, and its length is one half the sum of the lengths of the bases."

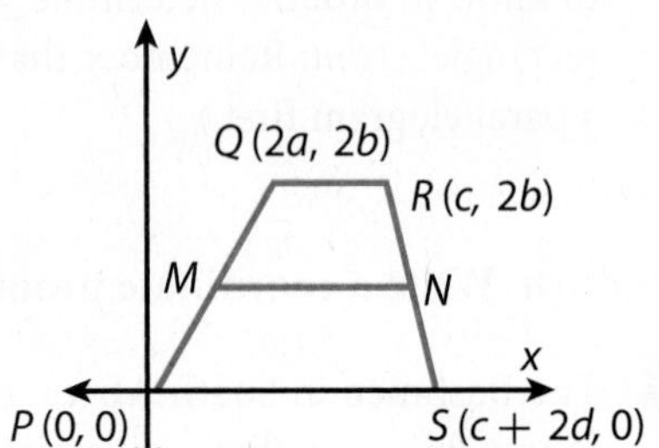

a. M is the midpoint of $\overline{QP}$. What are its coordinates?

b. N is the midpoint of $\overline{RS}$. What are its coordinates?

c. Find the slopes of $\overline{QR}$, $\overline{PS}$, $\overline{MN}$. What can you conclude?

d. Find QR, PS, MN. Show that $MN = \frac{1}{2}(PS + QR)$.

Lesson Performance Task

According to the new mayor, the shape of City Park is downright ugly. While the parks in all of the other towns in the vicinity have nice, regular polygonal shapes, City Park is the shape of an irregular quadrilateral. On a coordinate map of the park, the four corners are located at $(-3, 4)$, $(5, 2)$, $(1, -2)$, and $(-5, -4)$. The mayor's chief assistant knows a little mathematics and proposes that a special "inner park" be created by joining the midpoints of the sides of City Park. The assistant claims that the boundaries of the inner park will create a nice, regular polygonal shape, just like the parks in all the other towns. The mayor thinks the idea is ridiculous, saying, "You can't create order out of chaos."

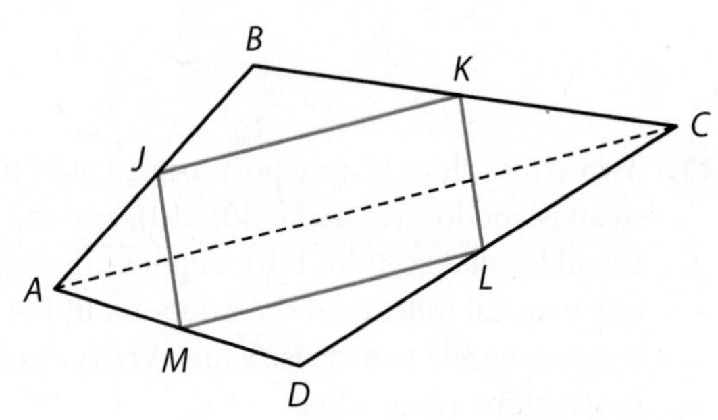

1. Who was right? Explain your reasoning in detail.
2. Irregular quadrilateral $ABCD$ is shown here. Points J, K, L, and M are midpoints.

   a. What must you show to prove that quadrilateral $JKLM$ is a parallelogram?

   b. How can you show this?

   c. If the adjacent sides of $JKLM$ are perpendicular, what type of figure does that make $JKLM$?

10.5 Perimeter and Area on the Coordinate Plane

Resource Locker

Essential Question: How do you find the perimeter and area of polygons in the coordinate plane?

Explore Finding Perimeters of Figures on the Coordinate Plane

Recall that the perimeter of a polygon is the sum of the lengths of the polygon's sides. You can use the Distance Formula to find perimeters of polygons in a coordinate plane.

Follow these steps to find the perimeter of a pentagon with vertices $A(-1, 4)$, $B(4, 4)$, $C(3, -2)$, $D(-1, -4)$, and $E(-4, 1)$. Round to the nearest tenth.

(A) Plot the points. Then use a straightedge to draw the pentagon that is determined by the points.

(B) Are there any sides for which you do not need to use the Distance Formula? Explain, and give their length(s).

(C) Use the Distance Formula to find the remaining side lengths.

(D) Find the sum of the side lengths.

Reflect

1. Explain how you can find the perimeter of a rectangle to check that your answer is reasonable.

Explain 1 Finding Areas of Figures on the Coordinate Plane

You can use area formulas together with the Distance Formula to determine areas of figures such as triangles, rectangles and parallelograms.

triangle	rectangle	parallelogram
$A = \frac{1}{2}bh$	$A = bh$	$A = bh$
rhombus	**kite**	**trapezoid**
$A = \frac{1}{2}d_1 d_2$	$A = \frac{1}{2}d_1 d_2$	$A = \frac{1}{2}(b_1 + b_2)h$

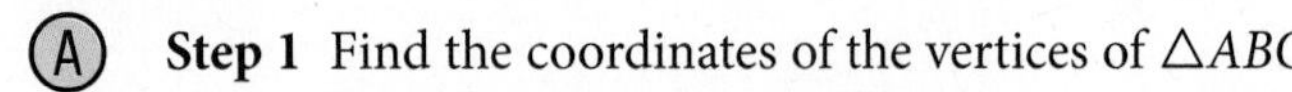

Example 1 **Find the area of each figure.**

(A) **Step 1** Find the coordinates of the vertices of $\triangle ABC$.

$A(-4, -2)$, $B(-2, 2)$, $C(5, 1)$

Step 2 Choose a base for which you can easily find the height of the triangle.

Use $\overline{AC}$ as the base. A segment from the opposite vertex, B, to point $D(-1, -1)$ appears to be perpendicular to the base $\overline{AC}$. Use slopes to check.

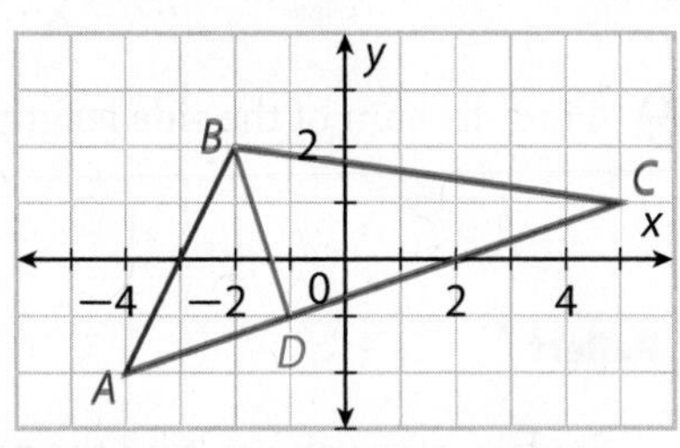

slope of $\overline{AC} = \dfrac{1 - (-2)}{5 - (-4)} = \dfrac{1}{3}$;

slope of $\overline{BD} = \dfrac{-1 - 2}{-1 - (-2)} = -3$

The product of the slopes is $\frac{1}{3} \cdot (-3) = -1$. $\overline{BD}$ is perpendicular to $\overline{AC}$, so $\overline{BD}$ is the height for the base $\overline{AC}$.

Find the length of the base and the height.

$$AC = \sqrt{(5 - (-4))^2 + (1 - (-2))^2} = \sqrt{90} = 3\sqrt{10};$$

$$BD = \sqrt{(-1 - (-2))^2 + (-1 - 2)^2} = \sqrt{10}$$

Step 3 Determine the area of $\triangle ABC$.

$$\text{Area} = \frac{1}{2}bh = \frac{1}{2}(AC)(BD) = \frac{1}{2} \cdot (3\sqrt{10})(\sqrt{10}) = \frac{1}{2} \cdot 30 = 15 \text{ square units}$$

(B) **Step 1** Find the coordinates of the vertices of *DEFG*.

$D(-2, 6), E(4, 3), F(2, -1), G(-4, 2)$

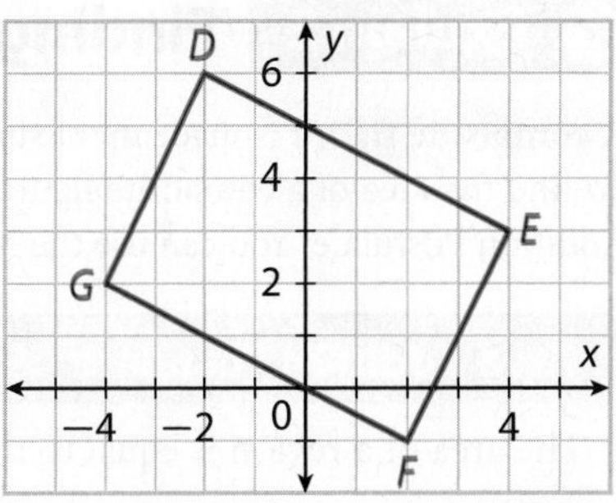

Step 2 *DEFG* appears to be a rectangle. Use slopes to check that adjacent sides are perpendicular.

slope of $\overline{DE}$: $\dfrac{3 - 6}{4 - (-2)} = \dfrac{-3}{6} = -\dfrac{1}{2}$; slope of $\overline{EF}$: $\dfrac{-1 - 3}{2 - 4} = \dfrac{-4}{-2} = 2$

slope of $\overline{FG}$: $\dfrac{2 - -1}{-4 - 2} = \dfrac{3}{-6} = -\dfrac{1}{2}$; slope of $\overline{DG}$: $\dfrac{2 - 6}{-4 - -2} = \dfrac{-4}{-2} = 2$

so *DEFG* is a rectangle.

Step 3 Find the area of *DEFG*.

$b = FG = \sqrt{\left(2 - -4\right)^2 + \left(-1 - 2\right)^2} = \sqrt{45} = 3\sqrt{5}$

$h = GD = \sqrt{\left(-2 - (-4)\right)^2 + \left(6 - 2\right)^2} = \sqrt{20} = 2\sqrt{5}$

Area of *DEFG*: $A = bh = \left(3\sqrt{5}\right)\left(2\sqrt{5}\right) = 30$ square units

Reflect

2. In Part A, is it possible to use another side of $\triangle ABC$ as the base? If so, what length represents the height of the triangle?

3. **Discussion** In Part B, why was it necessary to find the slopes of the sides?

Your Turn

4. Find the area of quadrilateral *JKLM* with vertices $J(-4, -2)$, $K(2, 1)$, $L(3, 4)$, $M(-3, 1)$.

Explain 2 Finding Areas of Composite Figures

A **composite figure** is made up of simple shapes, such as triangles, rectangles, and parallelograms. To find the area of a composite figure, find the areas of the simple shapes and then use the Area Addition Postulate. You can use the Area Addition Postulate to find the area of a composite figure.

Area Addition Postulate

The area of a region is equal to the sum of the areas of its nonoverlapping parts.

Example 2 Find the area of each figure.

(A) Possible solution: *ABCDE* can be divided up into a rectangle and two triangles, each with horizontal bases.

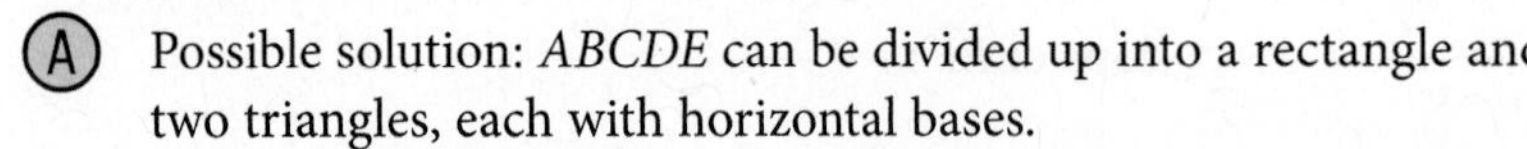

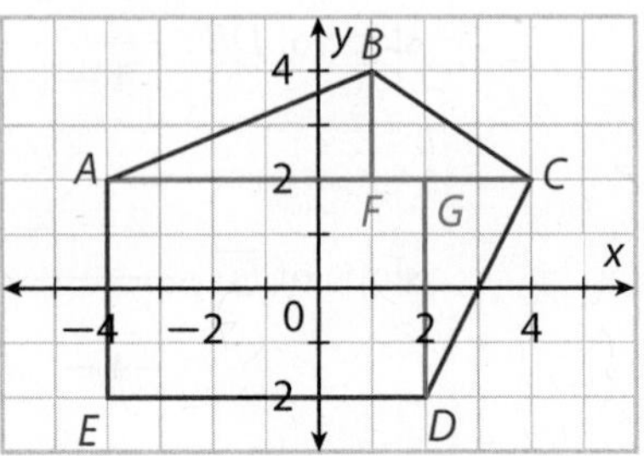

area of rectangle *AGDE*: $A = bh = (DE)(AE) = (6)(4) = 24$

area of $\triangle ABC$: $A = \frac{1}{2}bh = \frac{1}{2}(AC)(BF) = \frac{1}{2}(8)(2) = 8$

area of $\triangle CDG$: $A = \frac{1}{2}bh = \frac{1}{2}(CG)(DG) = \frac{1}{2}(2)(4) = 4$

area of *ABCDE*: $A = 24 + 8 + 4 = 36$ square units

(B) *PQRST* can be divided into a parallelogram and a triangle.

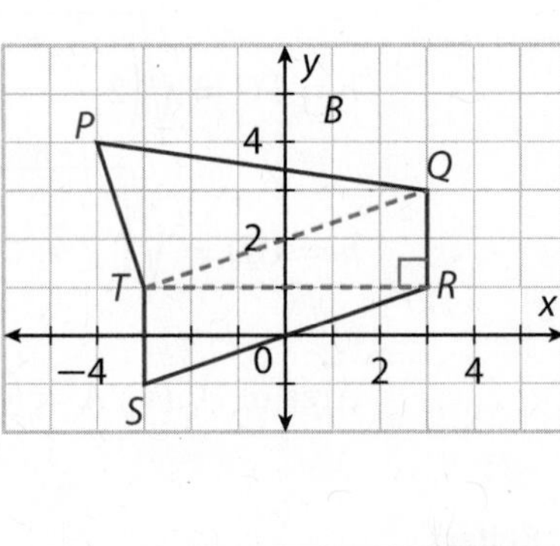

$\triangle PQT$ appears to be a right triangle. Check that $\overline{PT}$ and $\overline{QT}$ are perpendicular:

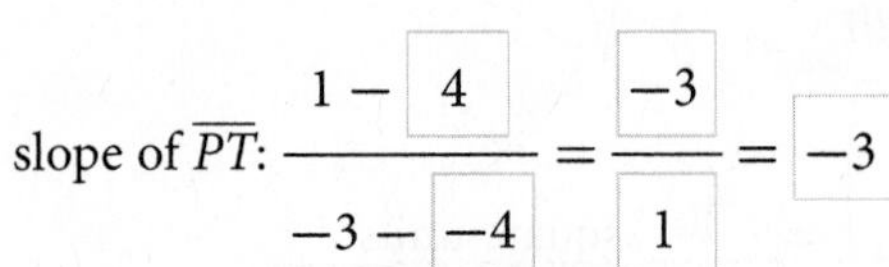

slope of $\overline{PT}$: $\frac{1 - 4}{-3 - (-4)} = \frac{-3}{1} = -3$

slope of $\overline{QT}$: $\frac{1 - 3}{-3 - 3} = \frac{-2}{-6} = \frac{1}{3}$

$\triangle PQT$ is a right triangle with base $\overline{PT}$ and height $\overline{QT}$.

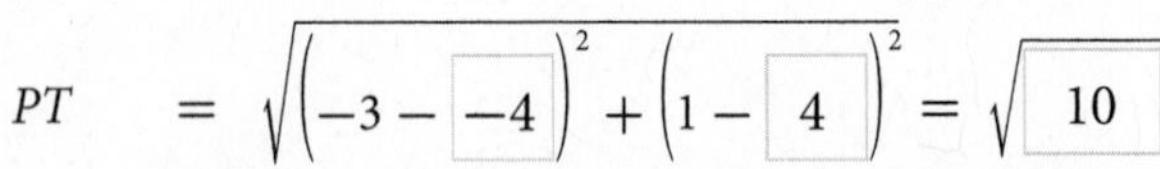

$PT = \sqrt{\left(-3 - (-4)\right)^2 + \left(1 - 4\right)^2} = \sqrt{10}$

$QT = \sqrt{\left(-3 - 3\right)^2 + \left(1 - 3\right)^2} = \sqrt{40} = 2\sqrt{10}$

area of $\triangle PQT$: $A = \frac{1}{2}bh = \frac{1}{2}\left(\sqrt{10}\right)\left(2\sqrt{10}\right) = 10$

$\overline{QR} \parallel \overline{TS}$ since both sides are vertical.

slope of $\overline{RS} = \frac{-1 - 1}{-3 - 3} = \frac{-2}{-6} = \frac{1}{3}$, so $\overline{QT} \parallel \overline{RS}$. Therefore, *QRST* is a parallelogram.

$\overline{RT}$ is a diagonal of $\triangle QRST$ and is horizontal. Because $\overline{RT} \perp \overline{RQ}$, $\triangle QRT$ is a right triangle with base $\boxed{\overline{RT}}$ and height $\boxed{\overline{QT}}$. Therefore, the area of $\triangle QRST = 2 \cdot (\text{area of } \triangle QRT)$.

$RT = \boxed{6}$, $QR = \boxed{2}$, so the area of $\triangle QRT = \frac{1}{2}\left(\boxed{6}\right)\left(\boxed{2}\right) = 6$.

$\triangle QRST = 2 \cdot (\text{area of } QRT) = 2 \cdot \boxed{6} = 12$

area of $PQRST$: $A = \boxed{10} + \boxed{12} = \boxed{22}$ square units

Reflect

5. Discussion How could you use subtraction to find the area of a figure on the coordinate plane?

Your Turn

6. Find the area of the polygon by addition.

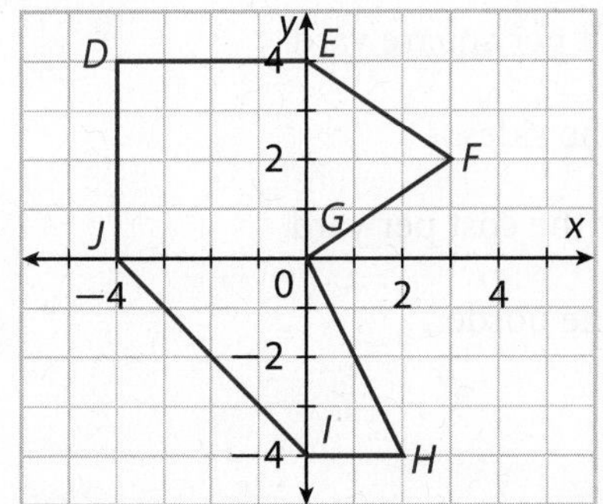

7. Find the area of polygon by subtraction.

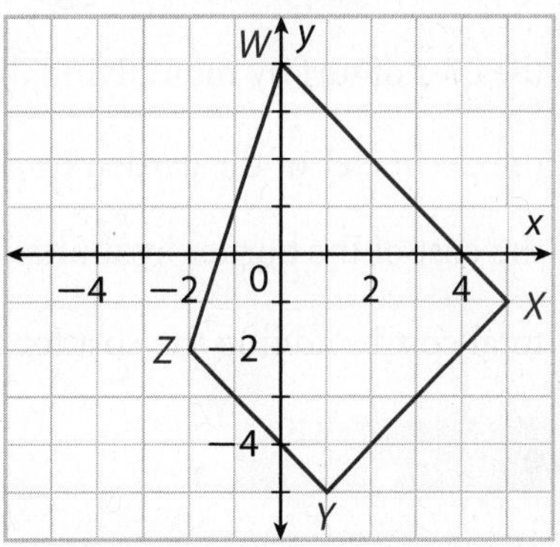

Explain 3 Using Perimeter and Area in Problem Solving

You can use perimeter and area techniques to solve problems.

Example 3 **Miguel is planning and costing an ornamental garden in the a shape of an irregular octagon. Each unit on the coordinate grid represents one yard. He wants to lay the whole garden with turf, which costs \$3.25 per square yard, and surround it with a border of decorative stones, which cost \$7.95 per yard. What is the total cost of the turf and stones?**

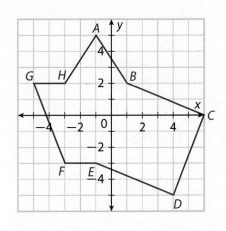

Analyze Information

Identify the important information.

- The vertices are $A(-1, 5)$, $B(1, 2)$, $C(6, 0)$, $D(4, -5)$, $E(-1, -3)$, $F(-3, -3)$, $G(-5, 2)$, and $H(-3, 2)$.
- The cost of turf is \$ 3.25 per square yard.
- The cost of the ornamental stones is \$ 7.95 per yard.

Formulate a Plan

- Divide the garden up into smaller figures.
- Add up the areas of the smaller figures.
- Find the cost of turf by multiplying the total area by the cost per square yard.
- Find the perimeter of the garden by adding the lengths of the sides.
- Find the cost of the border by multiplying the perimeter by the cost per yard.
- Find total cost by adding the cost for the turf and cost for the border.

Solve

Divide the garden into smaller figures.
The garden can be divided into square *BCDE*, kite *ABEH*, and parallelogram *EFGH*.

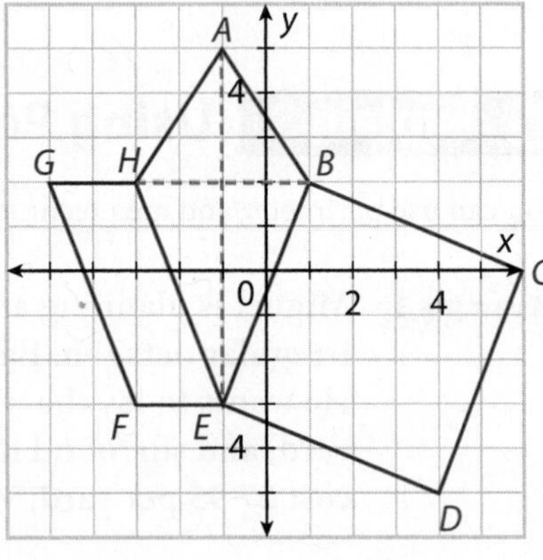

Find the area of each smaller figure.

area of *BCDE*:

slope of $\overline{BC}$: $\dfrac{0-2}{6-1} = -\dfrac{2}{5}$

slope of $\overline{CD}$: $\dfrac{-5-0}{4-6} = \dfrac{5}{2}$

Also, $BC = \sqrt{(6-1)^2 + (0-2)^2} = \sqrt{29}$ and

$CD = \sqrt{(4-6)^2 + (-5-0)^2} = \sqrt{29}$.

So *BCDE* is a square, with area $A = s^2 = \left(\sqrt{29}\ \text{yd}\right)^2 = 29\ \text{yd}^2$.

area of kite $ABEH$:

$HA = \sqrt{\left(-1 - \left(\boxed{-3}\right)\right)^2 + \left(\boxed{5} - 2\right)^2} = \sqrt{4 + \boxed{9}} = \sqrt{\boxed{13}}$;

$AB = \sqrt{\left(\boxed{1} - (-1)\right)^2 + \left(2 - \boxed{5}\right)^2} = \sqrt{\boxed{4} + 9} = \sqrt{\boxed{13}}$;

$HE = \sqrt{\left(-1 - \left(\boxed{-3}\right)\right)^2 + \left(\boxed{-3} - 2\right)^2} = \sqrt{\boxed{4} + 25} = \sqrt{\boxed{29}}$;

$BE = \sqrt{\left(\boxed{-1} - 1\right)^2 + \left(-3 - \boxed{2}\right)^2} = \sqrt{4 + \boxed{25}} = \sqrt{\boxed{29}}$

So, $\boxed{\overline{HA}} \cong \boxed{\overline{AB}}$ and $\boxed{\overline{HE}} \cong \boxed{\overline{BE}}$. Therefore $ABEH$ is a kite.

$b = d_1 = 8, h = d_2 = 4$

$vA = \frac{1}{2}d_1 d_2 = \frac{1}{2}\left(\boxed{8}\right)\left(\boxed{4}\right) = \boxed{16}\ \text{yd}^2$

area of parallelogram $EFGH$:

$\boxed{\overline{EF}}$ and $\overline{GH}$ are both horizontal, so are parallel;

slope of $\overline{EH}$: $\dfrac{2 - \boxed{-3}}{-3 - \boxed{-1}} = \dfrac{\boxed{5}}{\boxed{-2}} = -\frac{5}{2}$; slope of $\boxed{\overline{FG}}$: $\dfrac{2 - \boxed{-3}}{\boxed{-5} - \boxed{-3}} = \dfrac{\boxed{5}}{\boxed{-2}} = \boxed{-\frac{5}{2}}$

So $EFGH$ is a parallelogram, with base $\boxed{EF} = \boxed{2}$ and height. $FH = \boxed{5}$.

area of $EFGH$: $A = bh = \left(\boxed{2}\ \text{yd}\right)\left(\boxed{5}\ \text{yd}\right) = \boxed{10}\ \text{yd}^2$

Find the total area of the garden and the cost of turf.

area of garden: $A = \boxed{29}\ \text{yd}^2 + \boxed{16}\ \text{yd}^2 + \boxed{10}\ \text{yd}^2 = \boxed{55}\ \text{yd}^2$

cost of turf: $\left(\boxed{55}\ \text{yd}^2\right)\left(\$\ \boxed{3.25}\ /\text{yd}^2\right) = \$\ \boxed{178.75}$

Find the perimeter of the garden.

$EF = 2$ yd, $GH = 2$ yd

From area calculations, $BC = CD = DE = \sqrt{\boxed{29}}$ yd, and $AB = AH = \sqrt{\boxed{13}}$ yd

$FG = \sqrt{\left(\boxed{-5} - \boxed{-3}\right)^2 + \left(\boxed{2} - (-3)\right)^2} = \sqrt{\boxed{29}}$,

perimeter of garden $= GH + HA + AB + BC + CD + DE + EF + FG$

$= \boxed{2} + \boxed{\sqrt{13}} + \boxed{\sqrt{13}} + \boxed{\sqrt{29}} + \boxed{\sqrt{29}} + \boxed{\sqrt{29}} + \boxed{2} + \boxed{\sqrt{29}}$

Find the cost of the stones for the border.

cost of stones: $\left(\boxed{4} + 2\boxed{\sqrt{13}} + 4\boxed{\sqrt{29}}\ \text{yd}\right)\left(\$\ \boxed{7.95}\ \text{per yd}\right) \approx \$\ \boxed{260.38}$

Find the total cost.

total cost: \$ 178.75 + \$ 260.38 = \$ 439.13

Justify and Evaluate

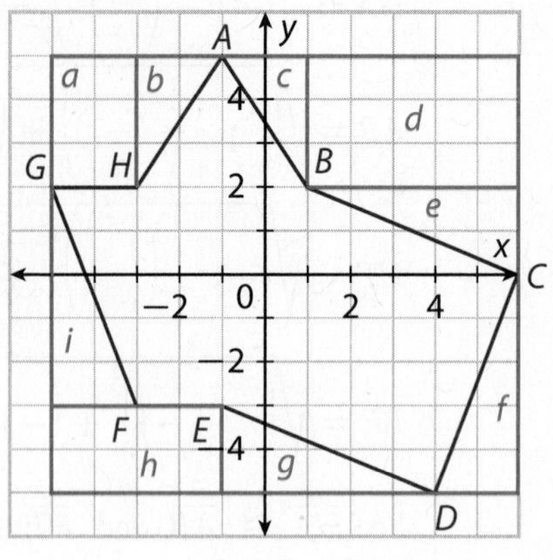

The area can be checked by subtraction:

area of large rectangle $= (11)(10) = 110$ square units

$$\text{area} = (11)(10) - (2)(3) - \frac{1}{2}(2)(3) - \frac{1}{2}(2)(3)$$

$$- (5)(3) - \frac{1}{2}(5)(2) - \frac{1}{2}(2)(5)$$

$$- \frac{1}{2}(5)(2) - (4)(2) - \frac{1}{2}(2)(5)$$

$$= 110 - 6 - 3 - 3 - 15 - 5 - 5 - 5 - 8 - 5 = 55$$

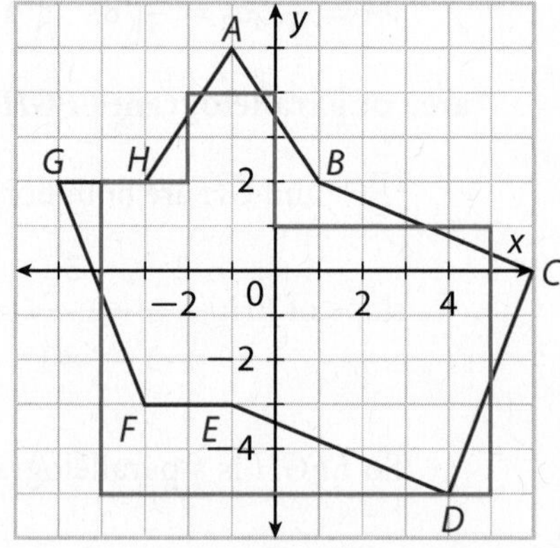

The perimeter is approximately the perimeter of the polygon shown:

The perimeter of the polygon shown is 36,

so the answer is reasonable.

Your Turn

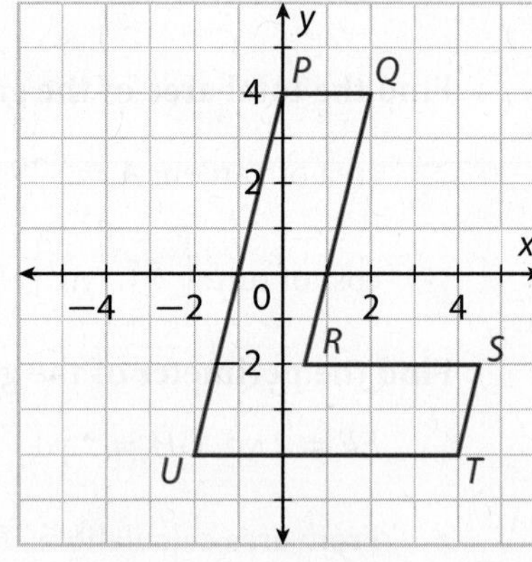

8. A designer is making a medallion in the shape of the letter "L." Each unit on the coordinate grid represents an eighth of an inch, and the medallion is to be cut from a 1-in. square of metal. How much metal is wasted to make each medallion? Write your answer as a decimal.

Elaborate

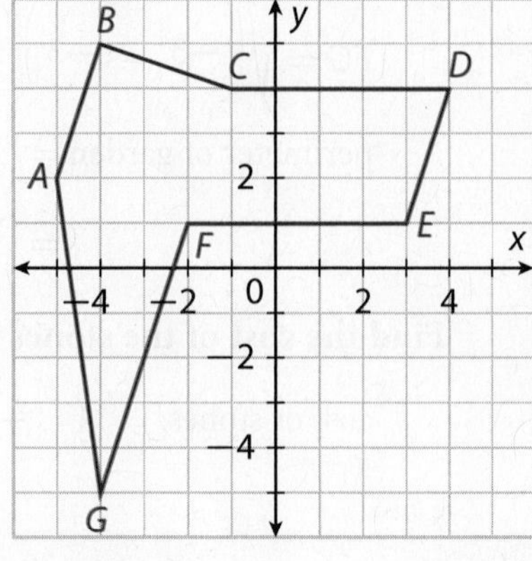

9. Create a flowchart for the process of finding the area of the polygon *ABCDEFG*. Your flowchart should show when, and why, the Slope and Distance Formulas are used.

10. Discussion If two polygons have approximately the same area, do they have approximately the same perimeter? Draw a picture to justify your answer.

11. Essential Question Check-In What formulas might you need to solve problems involving the perimeter and area of triangles and quadrilaterals in the coordinate plane?

Evaluate: Homework and Practice

- Online Homework
- Hints and Help
- Extra Practice

Find the perimeter of the figure with the given vertices. Round to the nearest tenth.

1. $D(0, 1)$, $E(5, 4)$, and $F(2, 6)$

2. $P(2, 5)$, $Q(-3, 0)$, $R(2, -5)$, and $S(6, 0)$

3. $M(-3, 4)$, $N(1, 4)$, $P(4, 2)$, $Q(4, -1)$, and $R(2, 2)$

4. $A(-5, 1)$, $B(0, 3)$, $C(5, 1)$, $D(4, -2)$, $E(0, -4)$, and $F(-2, -4)$

Find the area of each figure.

5.

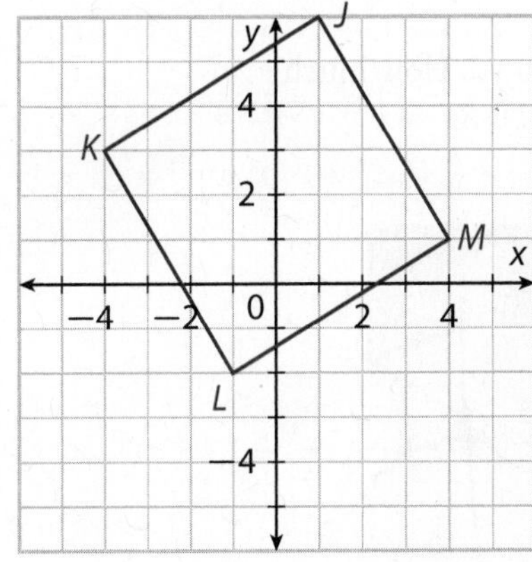

6.

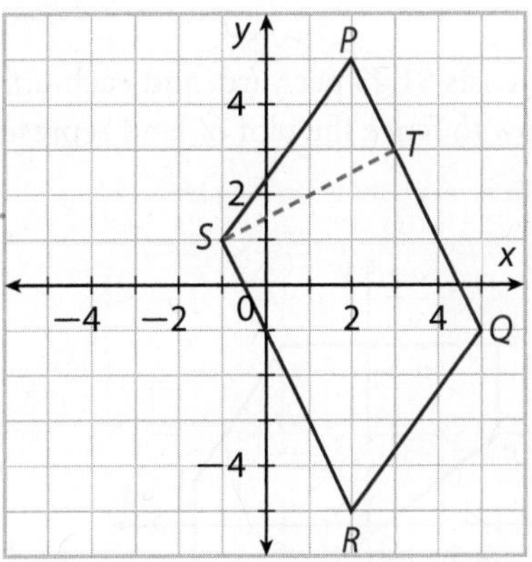

Find the area of each figure by addition.

7.

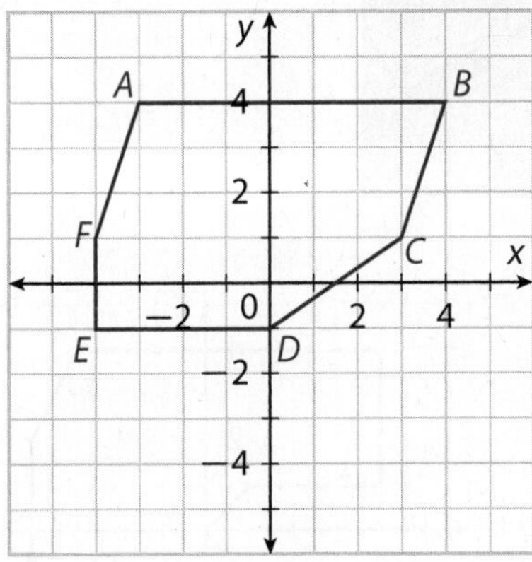

8.

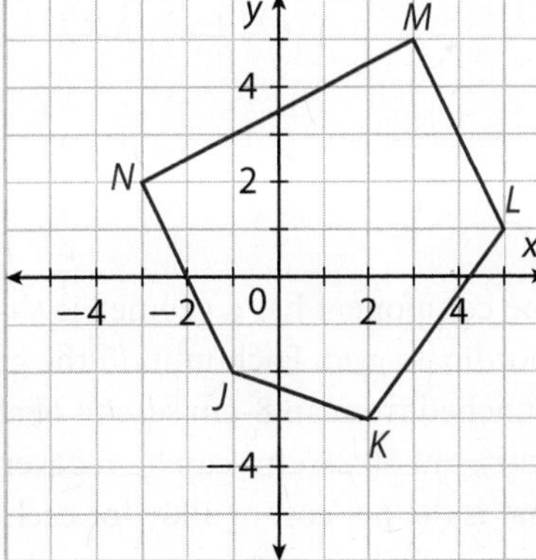

Find the area of each figure by subtraction.

9.

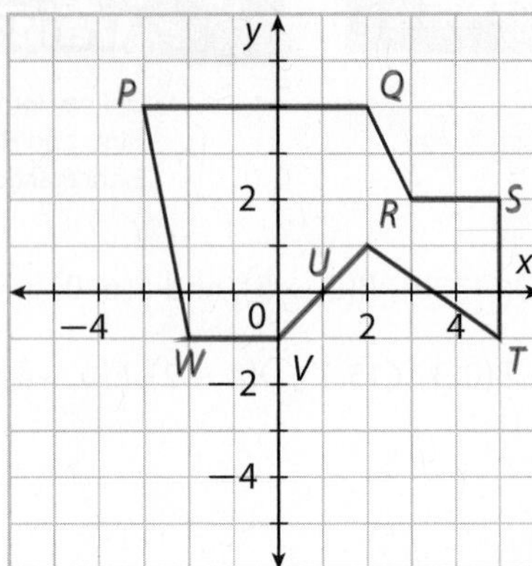

10.

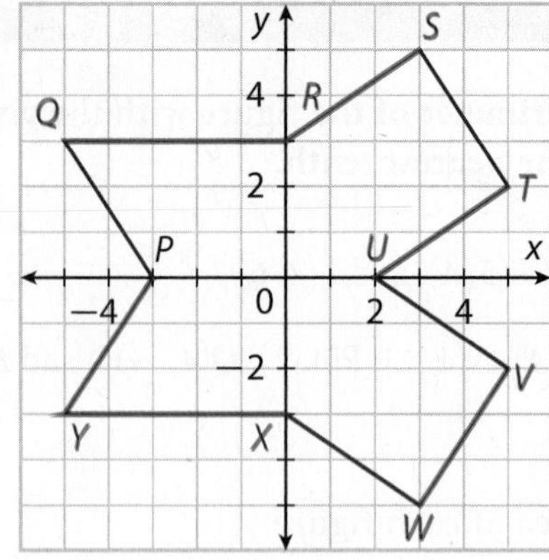

11. Fencing costs \$1.45 per yard, and each unit on the grid represents 50 yd. How much will it cost to fence the plot of land represented by the polygon *ABCDEF*?

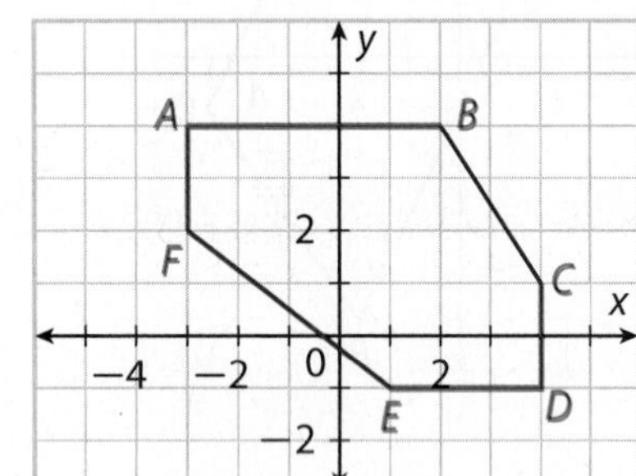

12. A machine component has a geometric shaped plate, represented on the coordinate grid. Each unit on the grid represents 1 cm. Each plate is punched from an 8-cm square of alloy. The cost of the alloy is \$0.43/cm^2, but \$0.28/cm^2 can be recovered on wasted scraps of alloy. What is the net cost of alloy for each component?

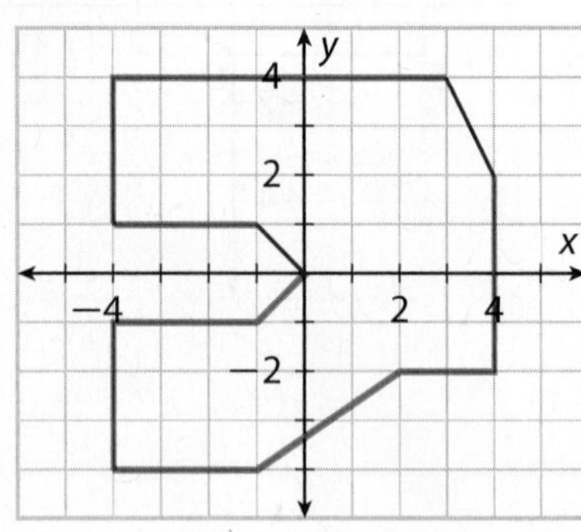

13. $\triangle ABC$ with vertices $A(1, 1)$ and $B(3, 5)$ has an area of 10 units^2. What is the location of the third vertex? Select all that apply.

A. $C(-5, 5)$

B. $C(3, -5)$

C. $C(-2, 5)$

D. $C(6, 1)$

E. $C(3, -3)$

14. Pentagon $ABCDE$ shows the path of an obstacle course, where each unit of the coordinate plane represents 10 meters. Find the length of the course to the nearest meter.

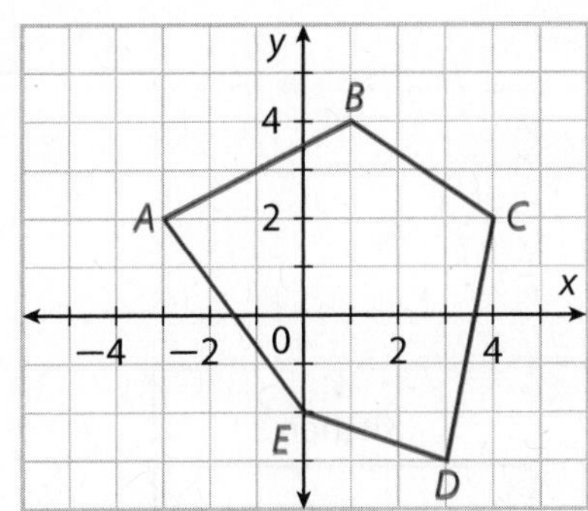

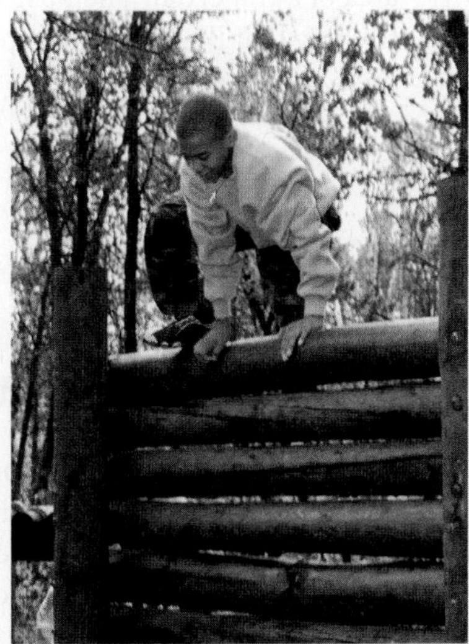

Algebra Graph each set of lines to form a triangle. Find the area and perimeter.

15. $y = 2$, $x = 5$, and $y = x$

16. $y = -5$, $x = 2$, and $y = -2x + 7$

17. Prove that quadrilateral $JKLM$ with vertices $J(1, 5)$, $K(4, 2)$, $L(1, -4)$, and $M(-2, 2)$ is a kite, and find its area.

H.O.T. Focus on Higher Order Thinking

18. Explain the Error Wendell is trying to prove that $ABCD$ is a rhombus and to find its area. Identify and correct his error. (*Hint:* A rhombus is a quadrilateral with four congruent sides.)

$AB = \sqrt{(2 - (-2))^2 + (5 - 2)^2} = \sqrt{25} = 5,$

$BC = \sqrt{(6 - 2)^2 + (2 - 5)^2} = \sqrt{25} = 5$

$CD = \sqrt{(2 - 6)^2 + (-1 - 2)^2} = \sqrt{25} = 5,$

$AD = \sqrt{(2 - (-2))^2 + (-1 - (2))^2} = \sqrt{25} = 5$

So $\overline{AB} \cong \overline{BC} \cong \overline{CD} \cong \overline{AD}$, and therefore $ABCD$ is a rhombus.

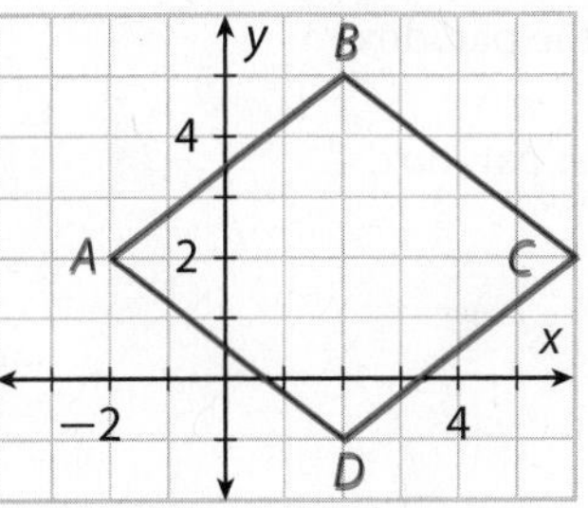

area of $ABCD$: $b = AB = 5$ and $h = BC = 5$, so $A = bh = (5)(5) = 25$

19. **Communicate Mathematical Ideas** Using the figure, prove that the area of a kite is half the product of its diagonals. (Do not make numerical calculations.)

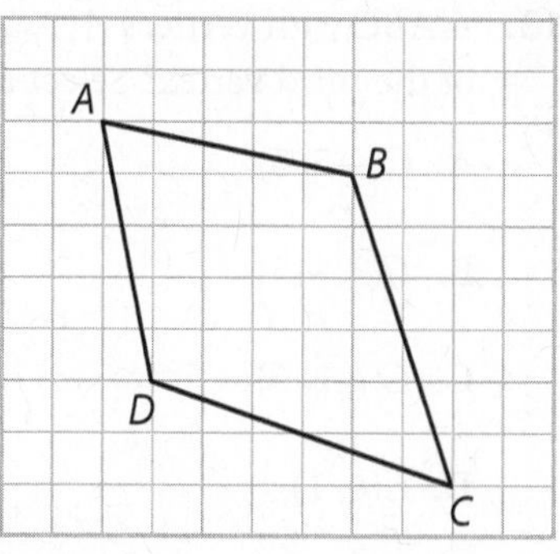

20. **Justify Reasoning** Use the figure to derive the formula for the area of a trapezoid. Then use the Trapezoid Midsegment Theorem to show that the area of a trapezoid is the product of the length of its midsegment and its height.

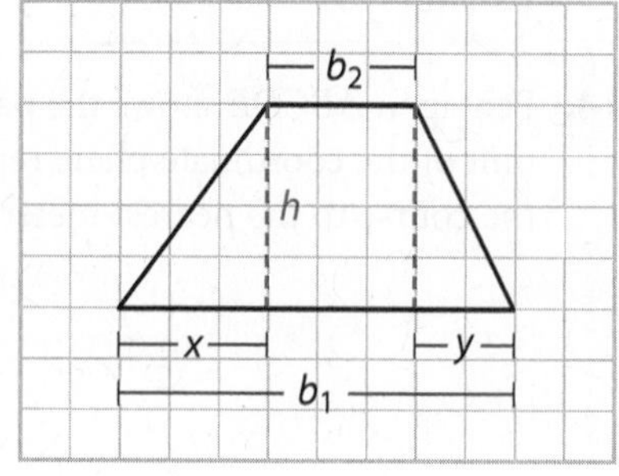

Lesson Performance Task

The coordinate plane shows the floor plan of two rooms in Fritz's house. Because he enjoys paradoxes, Fritz has decided to entertain his friends with one by drawing lines on the floor of his tiled kitchen, on the left, and his tiled recreation room, on the right. The four sections in the kitchen are congruent to the four sections in the recreation room. Each square on the floor plan measures 1 yard on a side.

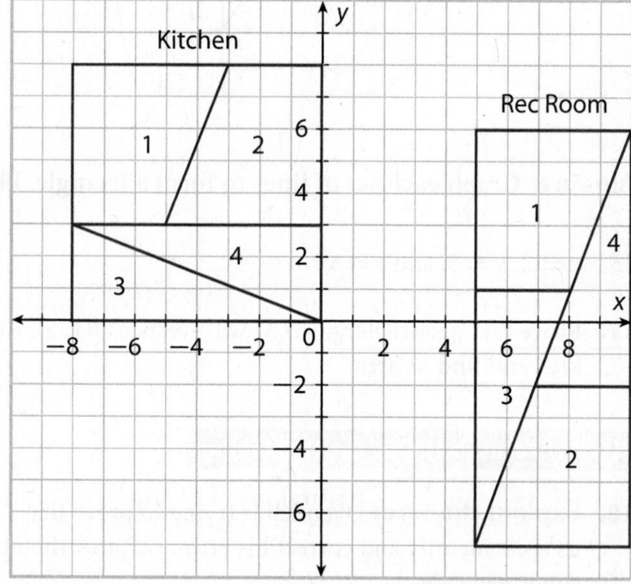

1. Find the area of each of the four sections of the kitchen. Add the four areas to find the total area of the kitchen.

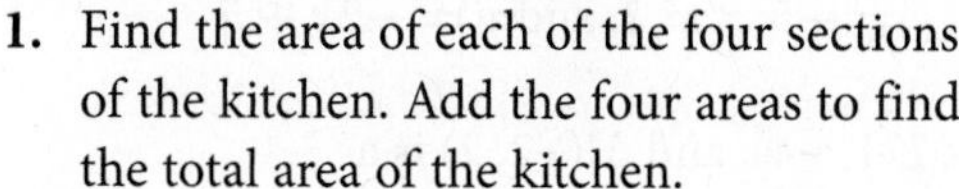

2. Find the area of the kitchen by finding the product of the length and the width.
3. Find the area of the recreation room by finding the product of the length and the width.
4. Describe the paradox.
5. Explain the paradox.

STUDY GUIDE REVIEW

Coordinate Proof Using Slope and Distance

MODULE 10

Essential Question: How can you use coordinate proofs using slope and distance to solve real-world problems?

Key Vocabulary
coordinate proof
(prueba coordenada)
composite figure
(figura compuesta)

KEY EXAMPLE *(Lesson 10.1)*

Show that the figure given by the points $A(2, 4)$, $B(3, 2)$, $C(2, 1)$, and $D(0, 5)$ is a trapezoid.

Determine whether the slopes of $\overline{AB}$ and $\overline{CD}$ are equal to determine whether they are parallel, and whether the figure is a trapezoid.

slope of $\overline{AB} = \frac{4-2}{2-3} = \frac{2}{-1} = -2$

slope of $\overline{CD} = \frac{5-1}{0-2} = \frac{4}{-2} = -2$

Thus, the figure *ABCD* is a trapezoid.

KEY EXAMPLE *(Lesson 10.2)*

Show that $\triangle ABC$ with points $A(-2, 1)$, $B(-3, 3)$, and $C(2, 3)$ is a right triangle.

A right triangle should have a pair of sides that are perpendicular.

slope of $\overline{AB} = \frac{1-3}{-2-(-3)} = \frac{-2}{1} = -2$

slope of $\overline{BC} = \frac{3-3}{-3-2} = \frac{0}{-5} = 0$

slope of $\overline{CA} = \frac{3-1}{2-(-2)} = \frac{2}{4} = \frac{1}{2}$

One pair of slopes has a product of -1, so the triangle is a right triangle.

KEY EXAMPLE *(Lesson 10.3)*

Prove the triangles $\triangle ABC$ and $\triangle DCB$ are congruent given $A(1, 1)$, $B(3, 1)$, $C(1, 4)$, and $D(3, 4)$.

Note that the triangles share a side. Find the length of each other side.

$AC = \sqrt{(1-1)^2 + (4-1)^2} = \sqrt{0+9} = 3$

$AB = \sqrt{(3-1)^2 + (1-1)^2} = \sqrt{4+0} = 2$

$DC = \sqrt{(3-1)^2 + (4-4)^2} = \sqrt{4+0} = 2$

$DB = \sqrt{(3-3)^2 + (4-1)^2} = \sqrt{0+9} = 3$

$AC = DB$, so $\overline{AC} \cong \overline{DB}$, and $AB = DC$, so $\overline{AB} \cong \overline{DC}$. Additionally, *CB* is congruent to itself by the Reflexive Property.

The triangles have three congruent sides, so are congruent by SSS.

EXERCISES

Determine whether the statement is True or False. *(Lesson 10.1)*

1. The figure given by the points $A(0, -1)$, $B(3, -2)$, $C(5, -4)$, and $D(-1, -2)$ is a trapezoid.
2. The figure given by the points $A(0, 3)$, $B(5, 3)$, and $C(2, 0)$ is a right triangle.

Prove or disprove the statement.

3. $\triangle ABC$ and $\triangle DEF$ are congruent, given $A(-4, 4)$, $B(-2, 5)$, $C(-3, 1)$, $D(-2, -1)$, $E(-1, -3)$, and $F(-5, -2)$. *(Lesson 10.2)*

Find the area of the polygon. *(Lesson 10.3)*

4. $ABCDE$ defined by the points $A(-3, 4)$, $B(-1, 4)$, $C(1, 1)$, $D(-1, 1)$, and $E(-4, -1)$

MODULE PERFORMANCE TASK

How Do You Calculate the Containment of a Fire?

Most news stories about large wildfires report some level of "containment" reached by firefighters. To prevent a blaze from spreading, firefighters dig a "fire line" around its perimeter. For example, if 3 miles of fire line have been dug around a fire that is 10 miles in perimeter, then the fire is said to be 30 percent contained.

The image shows a forest fire, the forest is shown by the shaded square while the fire is shown by the irregular pentagon. The darker lines show where fire lines have been dug. What is the percentage containment of the fire as well as the total area that has been burned?

Be sure to write down all your data and assumptions. Then use graphs, numbers, words, or algebra to explain how you reached your conclusions.

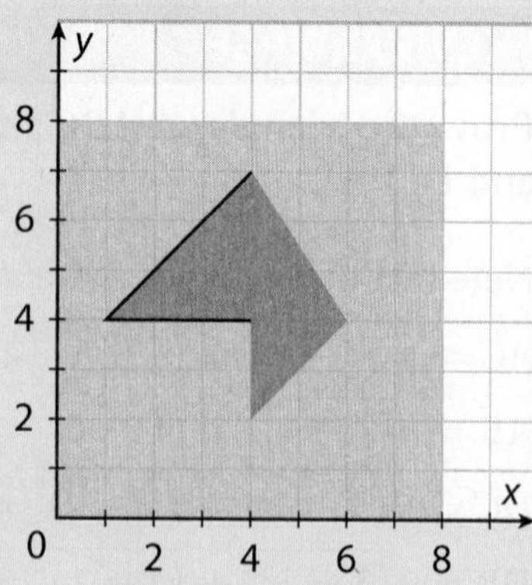

Ready to Go On?

10.1–10.5 Coordinate Proof Using Slope and Distance

- Online Homework
- Hints and Help
- Extra Practice

Determine and prove what shape is formed for the given coordinates for *ABCD*, and then find the perimeter and area as an exact value and rounded to the nearest tenth. *(Lessons 10.1, 10.2)*

1. $A(-10, 6), B(-7, 2), C(1, 8), D(-6, 9)$

2. $A(10, -6), B(6, -9), C(3, -5), D(7, -2)$

ESSENTIAL QUESTION

3. When is a quadrilateral both a trapezoid and a parallelogram? Is a quadrilateral ever a parallelogram but not a trapezoid?

MODULE 10
MIXED REVIEW

Assessment Readiness

1. Does the name correctly describe the shape given by the points $A(2, 2)$, $B(3, 4)$, $C(6, 4)$, and $D(5, 2)$? Answer Yes or No for each shape.
   A. Rectangle
   B. Parallelogram
   C. Square

2. Triangle ABC is given by the points $A(3, 2)$, $B(4, 4)$, and $C(5, 1)$. Determine if each statement is True or False.
   A. The perimeter of $\triangle ABC$ is 9.9 units.
   B. $\triangle ABC$ is an equilateral triangle.
   C. The perimeter of $\triangle ABC$ is 7.6 units.

3. Triangle DEF is given by the points $D(1, 1)$, $E(3, 8)$, and $F(8, 0)$. Determine if each statement is True or False.
   A. The area of $\triangle DEF$ is 25.5 square units.
   B. $\triangle DEF$ is a scalene triangle.
   C. The area of $\triangle DEF$ is 30 square units.

4. What type of triangle is given by the points $D(1, 1)$, $E(3, 8)$, and $F(5, 1)$? Explain how you could find the perimeter of the triangle.

5. For the polygon shown, specify how to find its area using triangles, parallelograms, and rectangles.

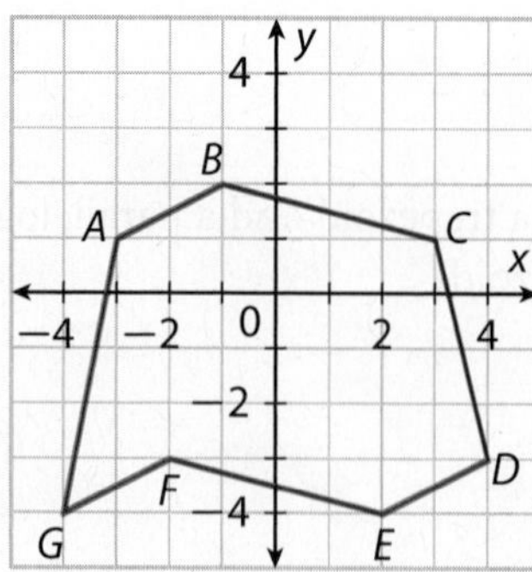

- Online Homework
- Hints and Help
- Extra Practice

1. Using known properties, determine if the statements are true or not.

A. If one pair of consecutive sides of a parallelogram is congruent, then the parallelogram is a rectangle.

B. If one pair of consecutive sides of a rhombus is perpendicular then the rhombus is a square.

C. If a quadrilateral has four right angles then it is a square.

2. Given the line $y = -\frac{2}{5}x + 3$, determine if the given line is parallel, perpendicular, or neither.

A. $y = \frac{2}{5}x + 7$

B. $5y + 2x = -10$

C. $-5x + 2y = 4$

3. Is $\overline{AB}$ parallel to $\overline{CD}$?

State Yes or No for each statement.

A. $A(-5, 12)$, $B(7, 18)$, $C(0, -4)$, and $D(-8, 0)$

B. $A(-6, 2)$, $B(4, 6)$, $C(7, -4)$, and $D(-3, -8)$

C. $A(-6, 2)$, $B(4, 6)$, $C(7, -4)$, and $D(-4, -8)$

4. Is $\overline{RS}$ perpendicular to $\overline{DF}$?

State Yes or No for each statement.

A. $R(6, -2)$ $S(-1, 8)$ and $D(-1, 11)$ $F(11, 4)$

B. $R(1, 3)$ $S(4, 7)$ and $D(3, 9)$ $F(15, 0)$

C. $R(-5, -5)$ $S(0, 2)$ and $D(8, 3)$ $F(1, 8)$

5. Use the distance formula to determine if $\angle ABC \cong \angle DEF$.

State Yes or No for each statement.

A. $A(-5, -7)$, $B(0, 0)$, $C(4, -7)$, $D(-6, -6)$, $E(-1, 1)$, $F(5, -8)$

B. $A(-3, 1)$, $B(1, 1)$, $C(-4, -8)$, $D(1, 1)$, $E(-3, 1)$, $F(4, 8)$

C. $A(-8, 8)$, $B(-4, 6)$, $C(-10, 2)$, $D(4, -4)$, $E(8, -2)$, $F(2, 2)$

6. Is Point M the midpoint of $\overline{AB}$? State Yes or No for each statement.

   A. $A(1, 2), B(3,4), M(2, 3)$

   B. $A(0, 8), B(10,-1), M(5, 3.5)$

   C. $A(-7, -5), B(6, 4), M(-1, -1)$

   D. $A(4, -2), B(6, -8), M(5, -5)$

7. Determine whether each statement about $QRST$ is true or false using the given image.

   A. The diagonals of $QRST$ are congruent.

   B. $QRST$ is a square.

   C. $QRST$ is a rectangle.

   D. The diagonals of $QRST$ are perpendicular.

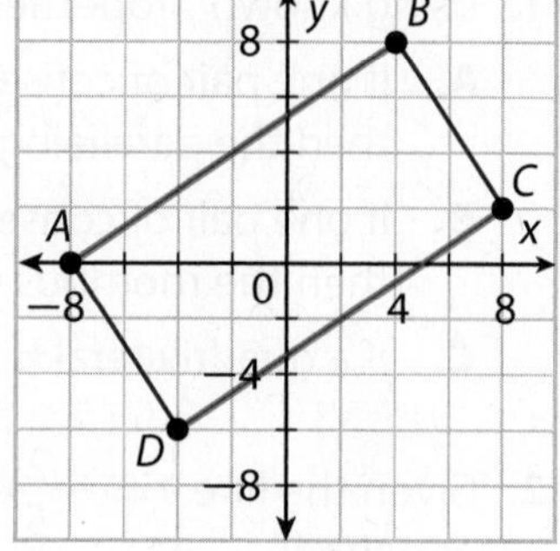

8. In trapezoid $JKLM$, determine LM.

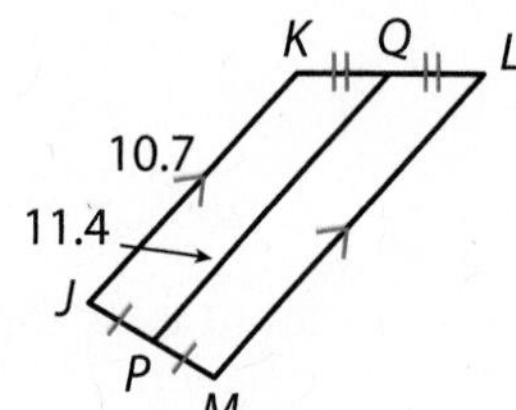

9. The midpoints of an irregular quadrilateral $ABCD$ are connected to form another quadrilateral inside $ABCD$. Explain why the quadrilateral is a parallelogram.

Performance Tasks

★**10.** Streets of a city can be represented by the equations in the given table. Use the equations to find the type of quadrilateral that the streets form. Justify your answer.

Street	Equation
Pine Street	$3x - y = -4$
Danis Road	$3y - x = 4$
Granite Park	$3y = x + 12$
Jason Drive	$y = 3x - 4$

★★**11.** The composite figure shown below represents the design for a new logo. Determine the area of a logo that has twice the area of the image provided. Allow 1 unit to represent two inches. Show your work.

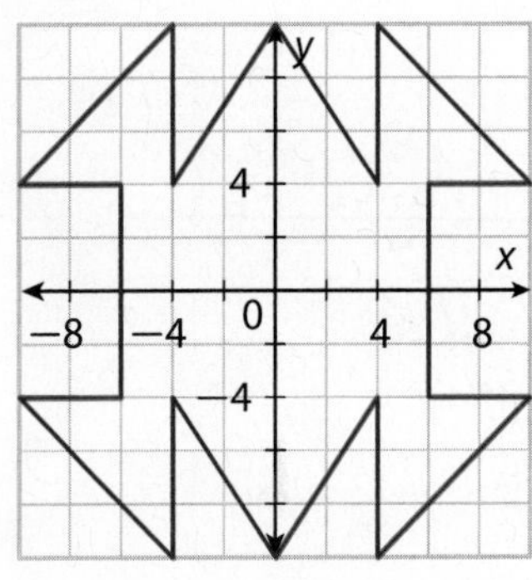

★★★**12.** Each square section in an iron railing contains four small kites. The figure shows the dimensions of one kite. What length of iron is needed to outline one small kite? How much iron is needed to outline one complete section, including the square? Explain how each answer was found.

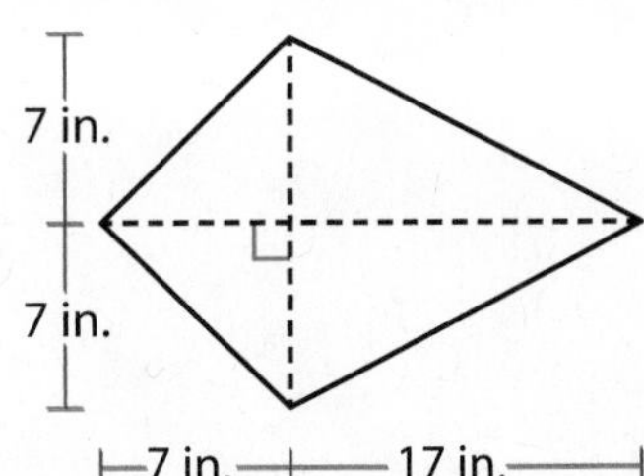

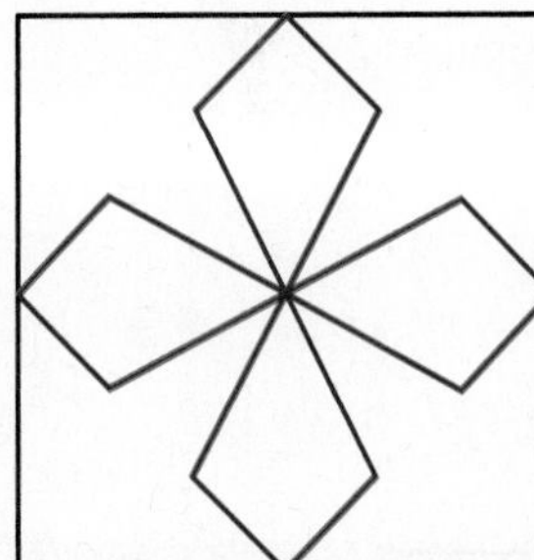

MATH IN CAREERS

Urban planners A city planner is working to add a new street for the purpose of easing traffic congestion. The current streets can be represented by the image given. Where could the planner add the new street so that the streets form a square? Give the equation and sketch the four streets on a coordinate grid.

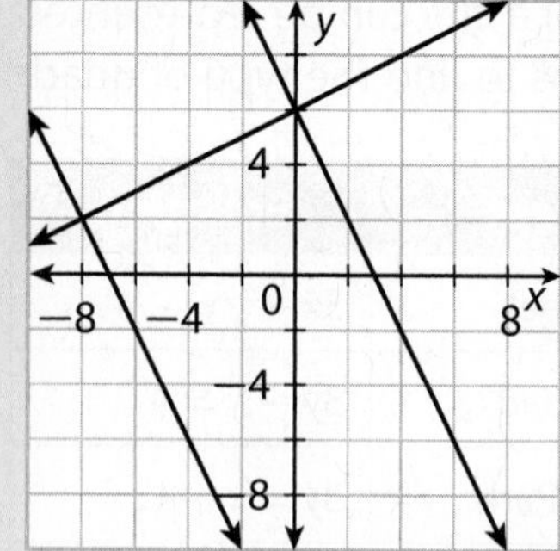

UNIT 4

Similarity

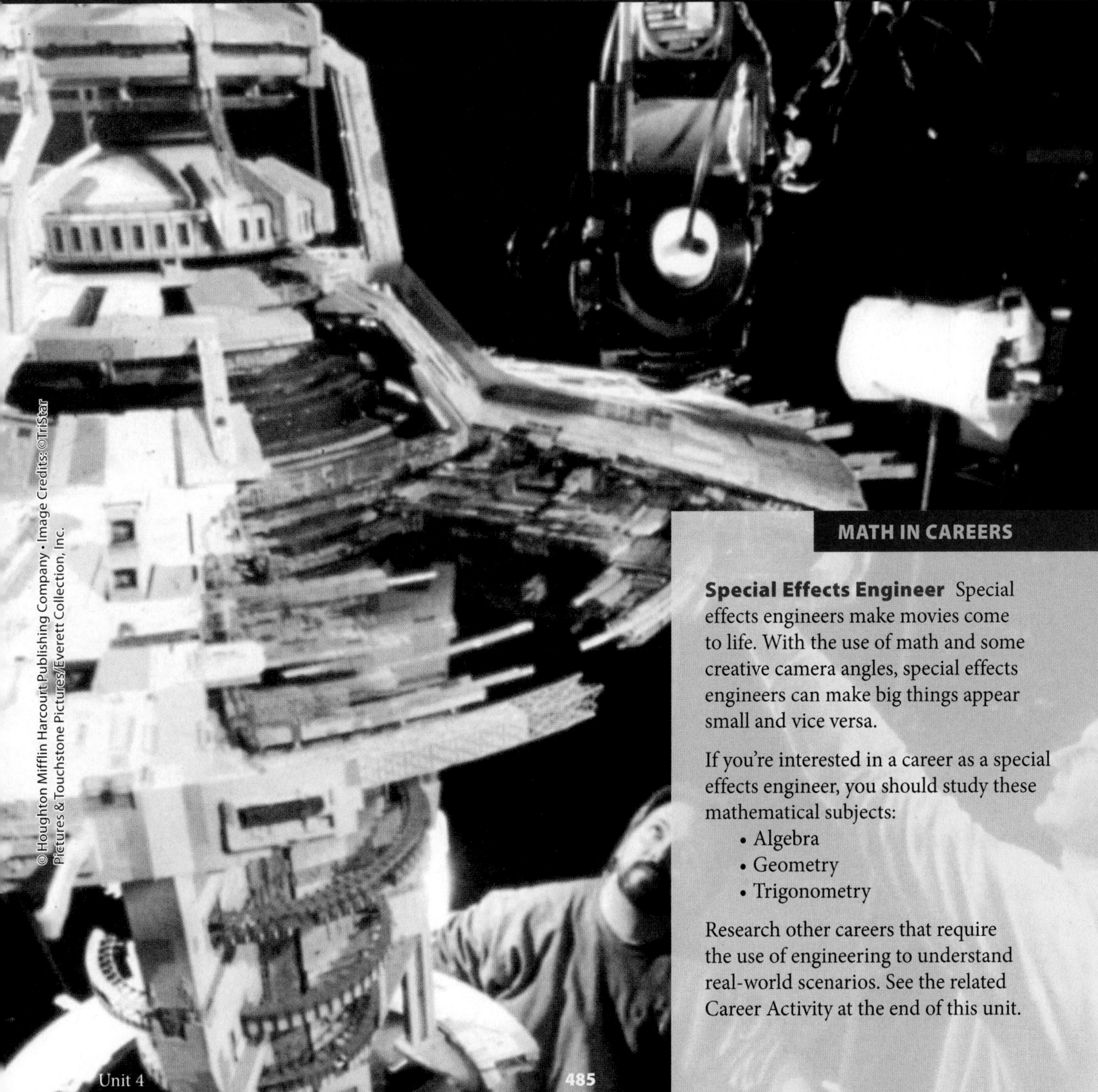

MATH IN CAREERS

Special Effects Engineer Special effects engineers make movies come to life. With the use of math and some creative camera angles, special effects engineers can make big things appear small and vice versa.

If you're interested in a career as a special effects engineer, you should study these mathematical subjects:

- Algebra
- Geometry
- Trigonometry

Research other careers that require the use of engineering to understand real-world scenarios. See the related Career Activity at the end of this unit.

Visualize Vocabulary

Copy the main-idea web. Use the ✔ words to complete it. Write the review words in the squares and include definitions.

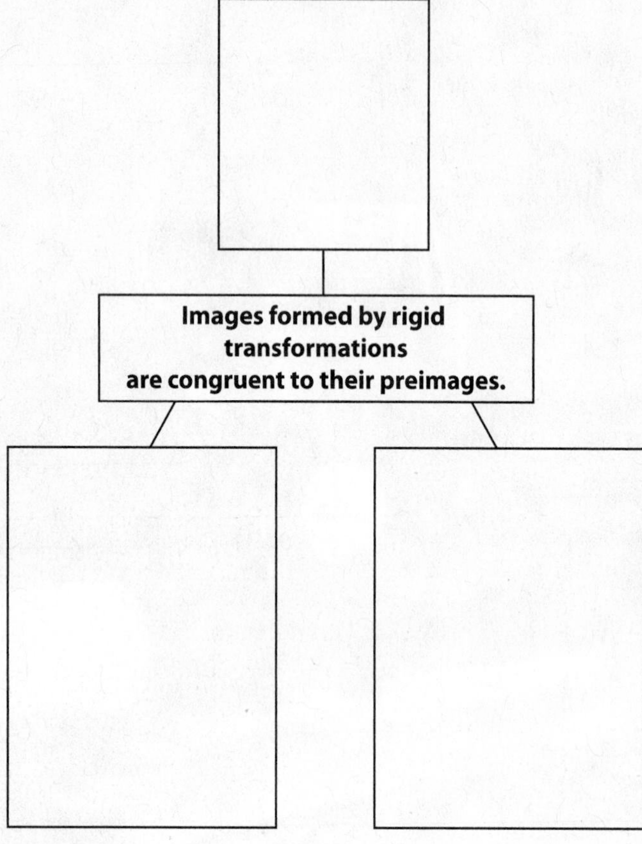
Images formed by rigid transformations are congruent to their preimages.

Review Words

✔ betweenness (*intermediación*)
✔ collinearity (*colinealidad*)
✔ congruent (*congruente*)
✔ orientation (*orientación*)
✔ parallel (*paralelo*)
✔ reflection (*reflejo*)
✔ rotation (*rotación*)
✔ transformation (*transformación*)
✔ translation (*traslación*)

Preview Words

center of dilation (*centro de la dilatación*)
dilation (*dilatación*)
geometric mean (*media geométrica*)
indirect measurement (*medición indirecta*)
scale factor (*factor de escala*)
similar (*similar*)
similarity transformation (*transformación de semejanza*)

Understand Vocabulary

Complete the sentences using the preview words.

1. The image formed by a(n) __?__ has the same shape as its pre-image.
2. The __?__ indicates the ratio of the lengths of corresponding sides of two similar figures.
3. In the proportion $\frac{a}{x} = \frac{x}{b}$, x is called the __?__.

Active Reading

Double-Door Fold Create a Double-Door Fold prior to starting the unit. Write characteristics of congruency under one flap. Fill out the other flap with corresponding characteristics of similarity so that the two topics can be compared more easily.

Similarity and Transformations

MODULE 11

Essential Question: How can you use similarity and transformations to solve real-world problems?

REAL WORLD VIDEO
Check out how properties of similarity and transformations can be used to create scale models of large, real-world structures like monuments.

MODULE PERFORMANCE TASK PREVIEW

Modeling the Washington Monument

In this module, you will be challenged to create a plan for a scale model of the Washington Monument. How can you use similarity and dilations to help you produce an accurate model? Let's find out.

Are YOU Ready?

Complete these exercises to review skills you will need for this module.

Personal Math Trainer

- Online Homework
- Hints and Help
- Extra Practice

Properties of Dilations

Example 1 Stretch $\triangle ABC$ with points $A(1, 2)$, $B(3, 2)$, and $C(3, -1)$ horizontally and vertically by a factor of 4.

$(x, y) \rightarrow (4x, 4y)$ Write the transformation rule.

$A'(4, 8)$, $B'(12, 8)$, $C'(12, -4)$ Use the transformation to write each transformed point.

Describe the transformation.

1. Stretch $\triangle DEF$ with points $D(-2, 1)$, $E(-1, -1)$, and $F(-2, -2)$ horizontally and vertically by a factor of -3.

2. Is the stretch a rigid motion?

3. Is it true that $\triangle DEF \cong \triangle D'E'F'$?

Similar Figures

Example 2 Transform $\triangle ABC$ with points $A(3, 4)$, $B(-1, 6)$, and $C(0, 1)$ by shifting it 2 units to the right and 1 unit up.

$(x, y) \rightarrow (x + 2, y + 1)$ Write the transformation rule.

$A'(5, 5)$, $B'(1, 7)$, $C'(2, 2)$ Write each transformed point.

Describe the transformation shown in the graph.

4. Write the rule used to transform $\triangle ABC$.

5. Describe in words the transformation shown in the figure.

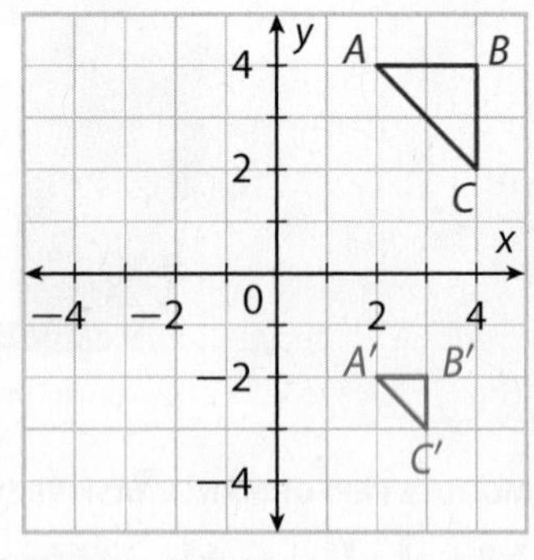

11.1 Dilations

Essential Question: How does a dilation transform a figure?

Resource Locker

Explore 1 Investigating Properties of Dilations

A **dilation** is a transformation that can change the size of a polygon but leaves the shape unchanged. A dilation has a *center of dilation* and a *scale factor* which together determine the position and size of the image of a figure after the dilation.

Use $\triangle ABC$ and its image $\triangle A'B'C'$ after a dilation to answer the following questions.

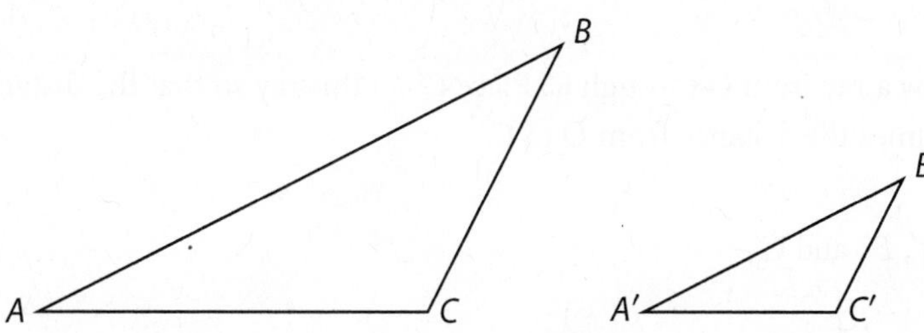

(A) Use a ruler to measure the following lengths. Measure to the nearest tenth of a centimeter.

$AB =$? cm $A'B' =$? cm

$AC =$? cm $A'C' =$? cm

$BC =$? cm $B'C' =$? cm

(B) Use a protractor to measure the corresponding angles.

$m\angle A =$? $m\angle A' =$?

$m\angle B =$? $m\angle B' =$?

$m\angle C =$? $m\angle C' =$?

(C) Complete the following ratios

$\frac{A'B'}{AB} = \frac{?}{?} = ?$ $\frac{A'C'}{AC} = \frac{?}{?} = ?$ $\frac{B'C'}{BC} = \frac{?}{?} = ?$

Reflect

1. What do you notice about the corresponding sides of the figures? What do you notice about the corresponding angles?

2. **Discussion** What similarities are there between reflections, translations, rotations, and dilations? What is the difference?

Explore 2 Dilating a Line Segment

The dilation of a line segment (the pre-image) is a line segment whose length is the product of the scale factor and the length of the pre-image.

Copy and label point O and $\overline{AC}$ on a separate sheet of paper. Use the following steps to apply a dilation by a factor of 3, with center at the point O, to $\overleftrightarrow{AC}$.

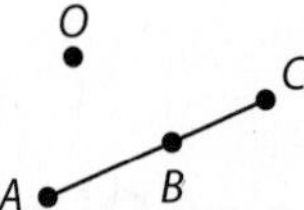

(A) To locate the point A', draw a ray from O through A. Place A' on this ray so that the distance from O to A' is three times the distance from O to A.

(B) To locate point B', draw a ray from O through B. Place B' on this ray so that the distance from O to B' is three times the distance from O to B.

(C) To locate point C', draw a ray from O through C. Place C' on this ray so that the distance from O to C' is three times the distance from O to C.

(D) Draw a line through A', B', and C'.

(E) Measure $\overline{AB}$, $\overline{AC}$, and $\overline{BC}$. Measure $\overline{A'B'}$, $\overline{A'C'}$, and $\overline{B'C'}$. Make a conjecture about the lengths of segments that have been dilated.

Reflect

3. Make a conjecture about the length of the image of a 4 cm segment after a dilation with scale factor k. Can the image ever be shorter than the preimage?

4. What can you say about the image of a segment under a dilation? Does your answer depend upon the location of the segment? Explain

Explain 1 Applying Properties of Dilations

The **center of dilation** is the fixed point about which all other points are transformed by a dilation. The ratio of the lengths of corresponding sides in the image and the preimage is called the **scale factor**.

Properties of Dilations

- Dilations preserve angle measure.
- Dilations preserve betweenness.
- Dilations preserve collinearity.
- Dilations preserve orientation.
- Dilations map a line segment (the pre-image) to another line segment whose length is the product of the scale factor and the length of the pre-image.
- Dilations map a line not passing through the center of dilation to a parallel line and leave a line passing through the center unchanged.

Example 1 **Determine if the transformation on the coordinate plane is a dilation. If it is, give the scale factor.**

(A) Preserves angle measure: yes

Preserves betweenness: yes

Preserves collinearity: yes

Preserves orientation: no

Ratio of corresponding sides: 1 : 1

Is this transformation a dilation? No, it does not preserve orientation.

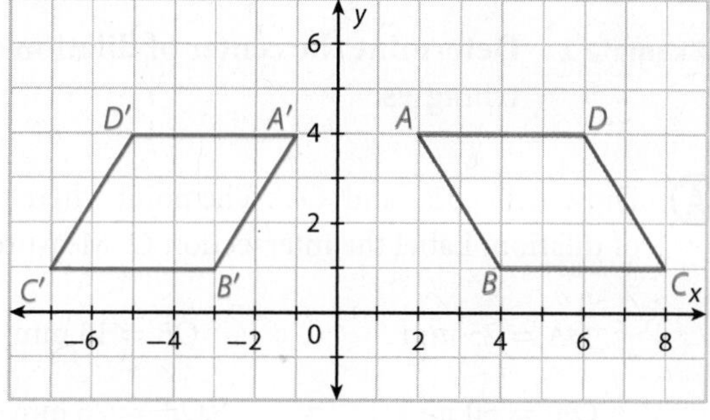

(B) Preserves angle measure: yes

Preserves betweenness: yes

Preserves collinearity: yes

Preserves orientation: yes

Scale Factor: 2

Is this transformation a dilation? yes

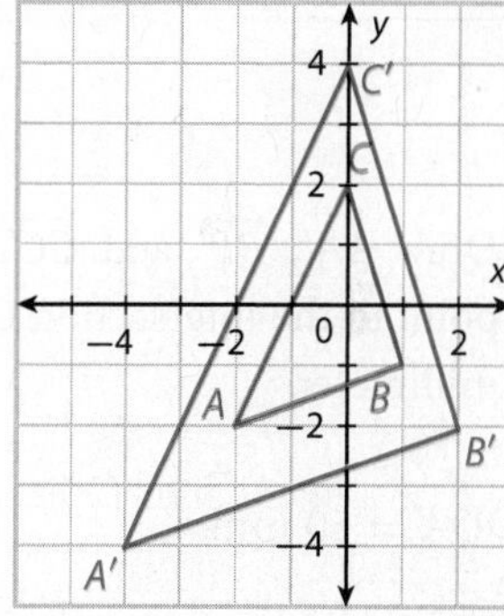

Your Turn

Determine if the transformations are dilations.

5.

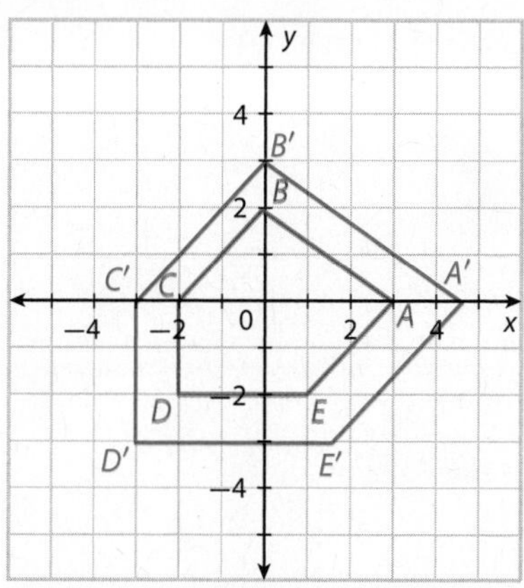

6.

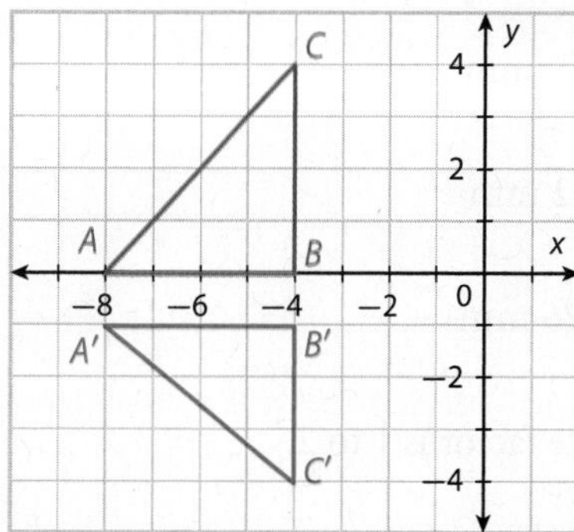

Explain 2 Determining the Center and Scale of a Dilation

When you have a figure and its image after dilation, you can find the center of dilation by drawing lines that connect corresponding vertices. These lines will intersect at the center of dilation.

Example 2 **Determine the center of dilation and the scale factor of the dilation of the triangles.**

(A) Draw $\overleftrightarrow{AA'}$, $\overleftrightarrow{BB'}$, and $\overleftrightarrow{CC'}$. The point where the lines cross is the center of dilation. Label the intersection O. Measure to find the scale factor.

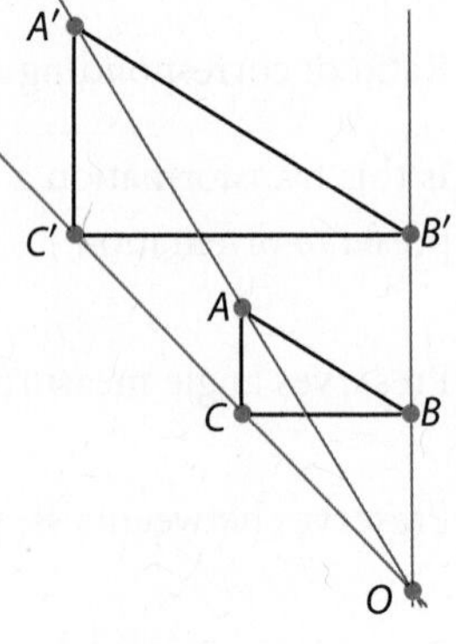

$OA = 25$ mm $\quad OB = 13$ mm $\quad OC = 19$ mm

$OA' = 50$ mm $\quad OB' = 26$ mm $\quad OC' = 38$ mm

The scale factor is 2 to 1.

(B) Draw $\overleftrightarrow{AA'}$, $\overleftrightarrow{BB'}$, and $\overleftrightarrow{CC'}$. Measure from each point to the intersection O to the nearest millimeter.

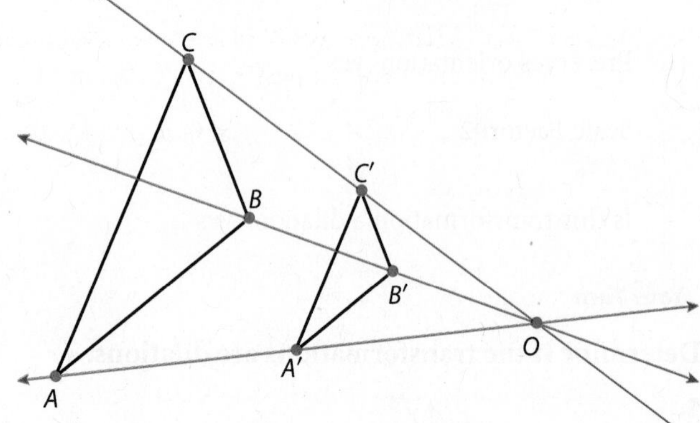

$OA = 60$ mm

$OA' = 30$ mm

$OB = 38$ mm

$OB' = 19$ mm

$OC = 52$ mm

$OC' = 26$ mm

The scale factor is 1 to 2.

Reflect

7. For the dilation in Your Turn 5, what is the center of dilation? Explain how you can tell without drawing lines.

Your Turn

8. Copy the triangles on a sheet of paper. Then find the center of dilation O, the scale factor of the dilation, OA', and OA.

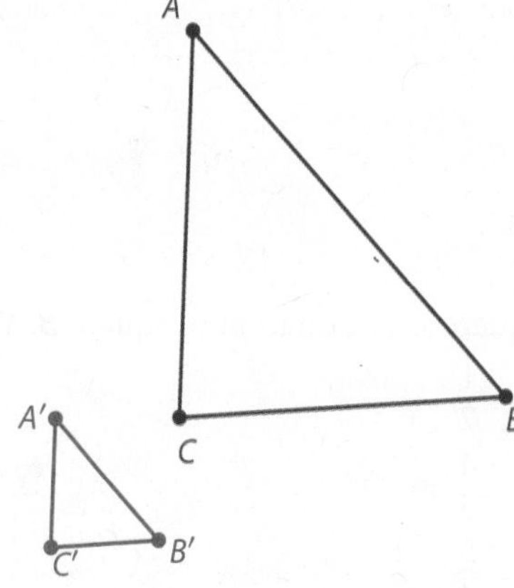

$OA' =$? , $OA =$?

The scale factor of the dilation is ? .

Elaborate

9. How is the length of the image of a line segment under a dilation related to the length of its preimage?

10. **Discussion** What is the result of dilating a figure using a scale factor of 1? For this dilation, does the center of dilation affect the position of the image relative to the preimage? Explain.

11. **Essential Question Check-In** In general how does a dilation transform a figure?

Evaluate: Homework and Practice

• Online Homework
• Hints and Help
• Extra Practice

1. Consider the definition of a dilation. A dilation is a transformation that can change the size of a polygon but leaves the shape unchanged. In a dilation, how are the ratios of the measures of the corresponding sides related?

Tell whether one figure appears to be a dilation of the other figure Explain.

2. 

3. 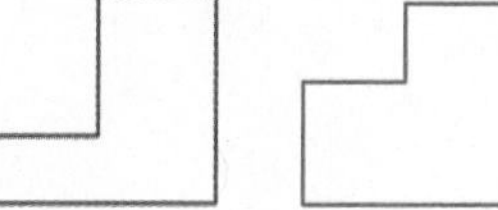

4. Is the scale factor of the dilation of $\triangle ABC$ equal to $\frac{1}{2}$? Explain.

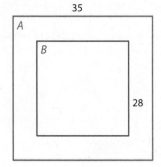

5. Square A is a dilation of square B. What is the scale factor?

a. $\frac{1}{7}$

b. $\frac{4}{5}$

c. $\frac{5}{4}$

d. 7

e. $\frac{25}{16}$

35

A

B

28

6. Copy each figure. Then apply a dilation to $\overline{AC}$ with a scale factor of 2 and center at the point O.

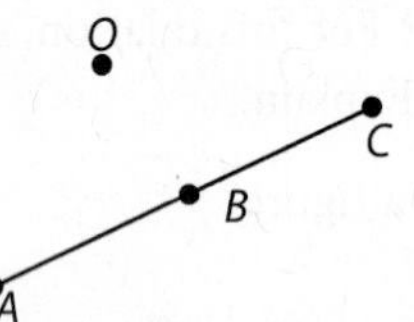

7. Copy each figure. Then apply a dilation to $\overline{AC}$ with a scale factor of $\frac{1}{3}$ and center at the point O.

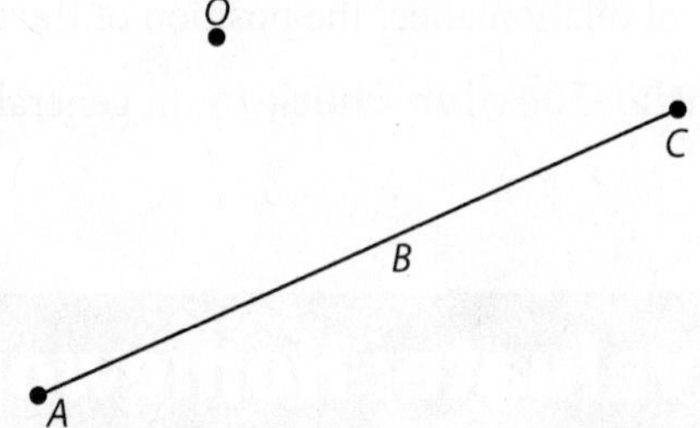

8. What happens when a triangle is dilated using one of the vertices as the center of dilation?

9. Draw $WXYZ$ and its image under a dilation. The center of the dilation is O, and the scale factor is 2.

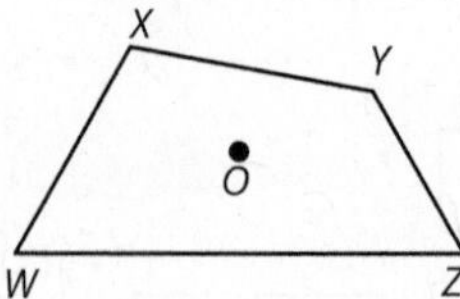

10. Draw $\triangle ABC$ and its image under a dilation. The center of dilation is C, and the scale factor is 1.5.

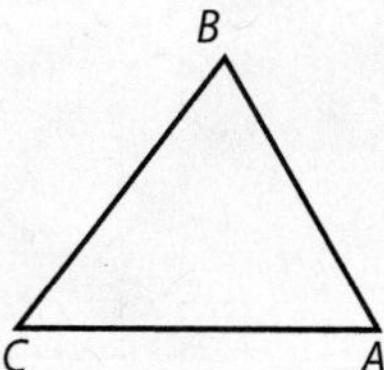

11. Compare dilations to rigid motions. How are they the same? How are they different?

Determine if the transformation of figure *A* to figure *B* on the coordinate plane is a dilation. Verify ratios of corresponding side lengths for a dilation.

12.

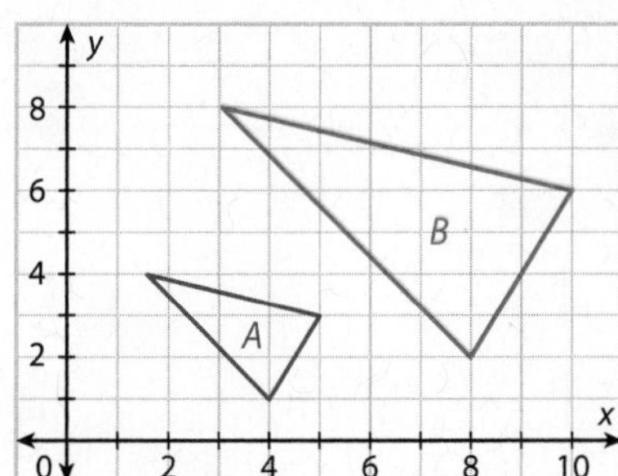

13.

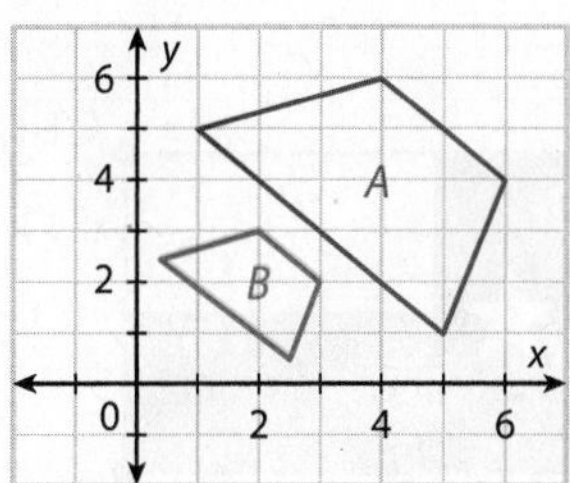

Determine the center of dilation and the scale factor of the dilation.

14.

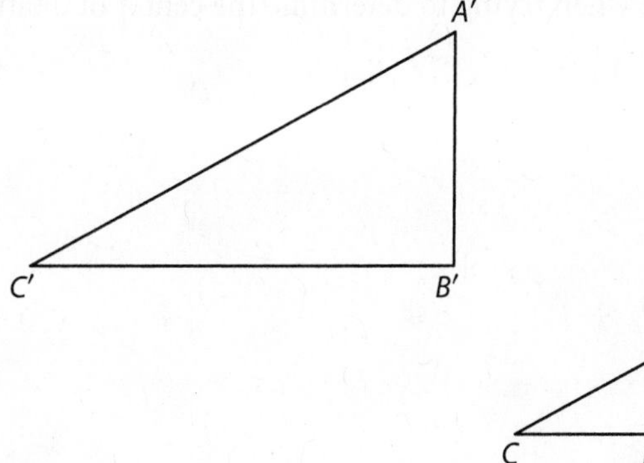

15.

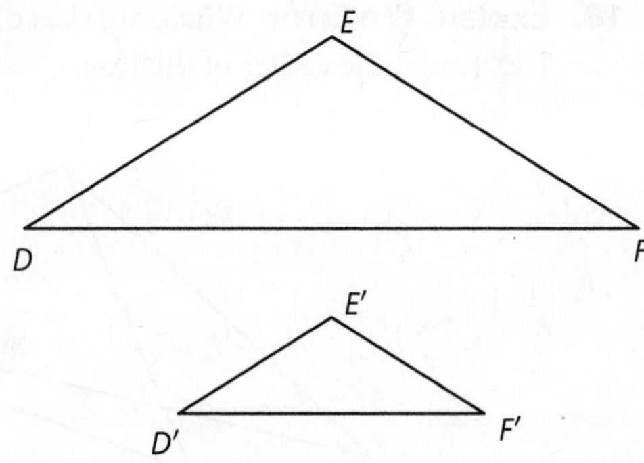

16. You work at a photography store. A customer has a picture that is 4.5 inches tall. The customer wants a reduced copy of the picture to fit a space of 1.8 inches tall on a postcard. What scale factor should you use to reduce the picture to the correct size?

17. **Computer Graphics** An artist uses a computer program to enlarge a design, as shown. What is the scale factor of the dilation?

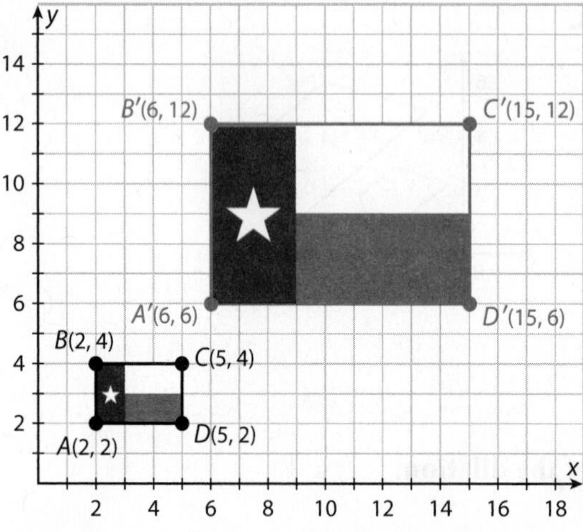

18. **Explain the Error** What mistakes did the student make when trying to determine the center of dilation? Determine the center of dilation.

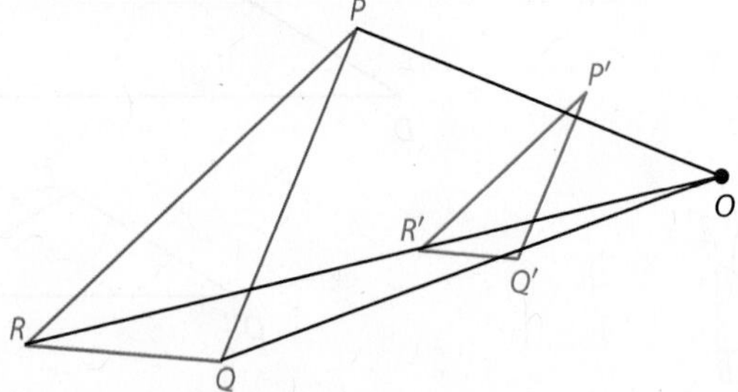

H.O.T. Focus on Higher Order Thinking

19. Draw $\triangle DEF$ with vertices D $(3, 1)$ E $(3, 5)$ F $(0, 5)$.

a. Determine the perimeter and the area of $\triangle DEF$.

b. Draw an image of $\triangle DEF$ after a dilation having a scale factor of 3, with the center of dilation at the origin $(0, 0)$. Determine the perimeter and area of the image.

c. How is the scale factor related to the ratios $\frac{\text{perimeter } \triangle D'E'F'}{\text{perimeter } \triangle DEF}$ and $\frac{\text{area } \triangle D'E'F'}{\text{area } \triangle DEF}$?

20. Draw $\triangle WXY$ with vertices $(4, 0)$, $(4, 8)$, and $(-2, 8)$.

a. Dilate $\triangle WXY$ using a factor of $\frac{1}{4}$ and the origin as the center. Then dilate its image using a scale factor of 2 and the origin as the center. Draw the final image.

b. Use the scale factors given in part (a) to determine the scale factor you could use to dilate $\triangle WXY$ with the origin as the center to the final image in one step.

c. Do you get the same final image if you switch the order of the dilations in part (a)? Explain your reasoning.

Lesson Performance Task

You've hung a sheet on a wall and lit a candle. Now you move your hands into position between the candle and the sheet and, to the great amusement of your audience, create an image of an animal on the sheet.

Compare and contrast what you're doing with what happens when you draw a dilation of a triangle on a coordinate plane. Point out ways that dilations and hand puppets are alike and ways they are different. Discuss measures that are preserved in hand-puppet projections and those that are not. Some terms you might like to discuss:

- pre-image
- image
- center of dilation
- scale factor
- transformation
- input
- output

11.2 Proving Figures are Similar Using Transformations

Essential Question: How can similarity transformations be used to show two figures are similar?

Explore Confirming Similarity

A **similarity transformation** is a transformation in which an image has the same shape as its pre-image. Similarity transformations include reflections, translations, rotations, and dilations. Two plane figures are **similar** if and only if one figure can be mapped to the other through one or more similarity transformations.

A grid shows a map of the city park. Use tracing paper to confirm that the park elements are similar.

(A) Trace patio *EFHG*. Turn the paper so that patio *EFHG* is mapped onto patio *LMON*. Describe the transformation. What does this confirm about the patios?

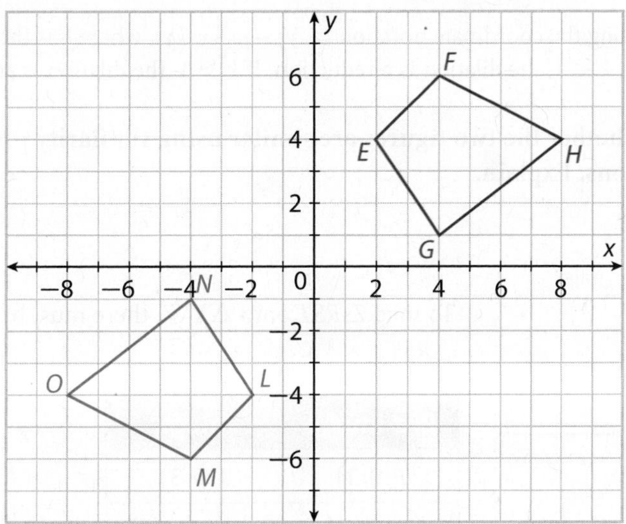

(B) Trace statues *ABCDEF* and *JKLMNO*. Fold the paper so that statue *ABCDEF* is mapped onto statue *JKLMNO*. Describe the transformation. What does this confirm about the statues?

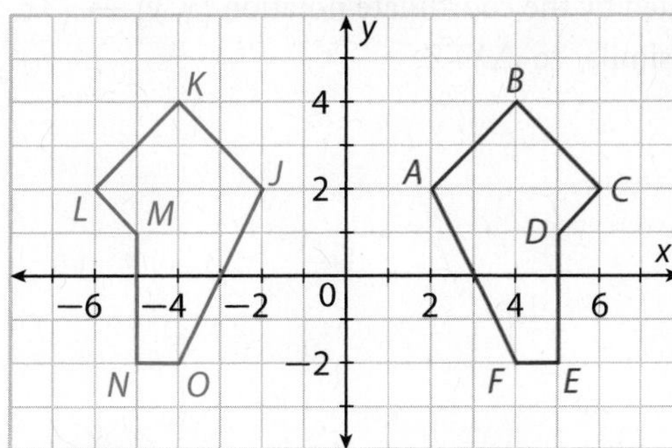

Ⓒ Describe the transformation you can use to map vertices of garden *RST* to corresponding vertices of garden *DEF*. What does this confirm about the gardens?

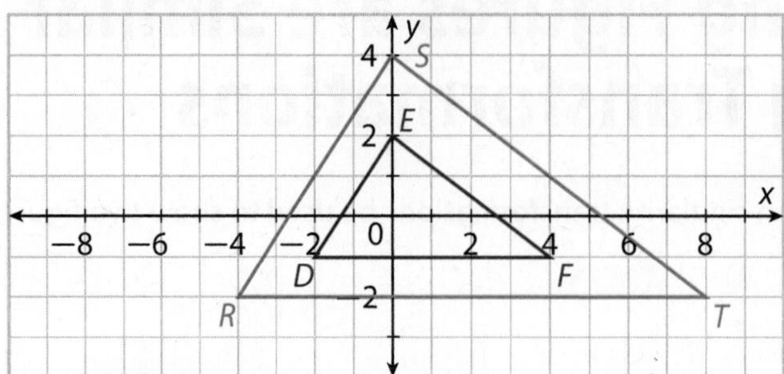

Reflect

1. Look back at all the steps. Were any of the images congruent to the pre-images? If so, what types of similarity transformations were performed with these figures? What does this tell you about the relationship between similar and congruent figures?

2. If two figures are similar, can you conclude that corresponding angles are congruent? Why or why not?

Explain 1 Determining If Figures are Similar

You can represent dilations using the coordinate notation $(x, y) \to (kx, ky)$, where k is the scale factor and the center of dilation is the origin. If $0 < k < 1$, the dilation is a reduction. If $k > 1$, the dilation is an enlargement.

Example 1 **Determine whether the two figures are similar using similarity transformations. Explain.**

Ⓐ $\triangle RST$ and $\triangle XYZ$

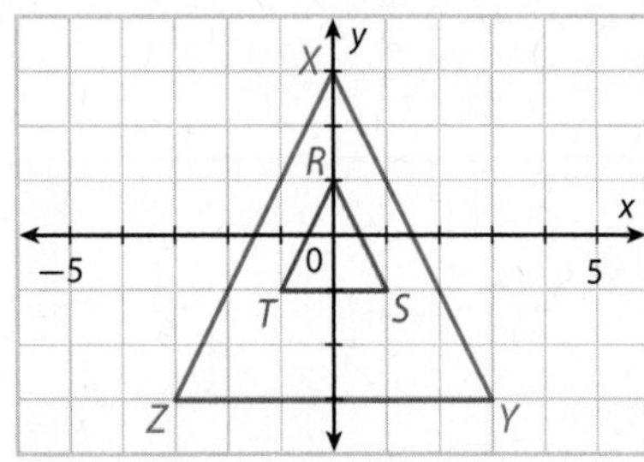

To map $\triangle RST$ onto $\triangle XYZ$, there must be some factor k that dilates $\triangle RST$.

Pre-image	Image
$R(0, 1)$	$X(0, 3)$
$S(1, -1)$	$Y(3, -3)$
$T(-1, -1)$	$Z(-3, -3)$

You can see that each coordinate of the pre-image is multiplied by 3 to get the image, so this is a dilation with scale factor 3. Therefore, $\triangle RST$ can be mapped onto $\triangle XYZ$ by a dilation with center at the origin, which is represented by the coordinate notation $(x, y) \to (3x, 3y)$. A dilation is a similarity transformation, so $\triangle RST$ is similar to $\triangle XYZ$.

Ⓑ *PQRS* and *WXYZ*

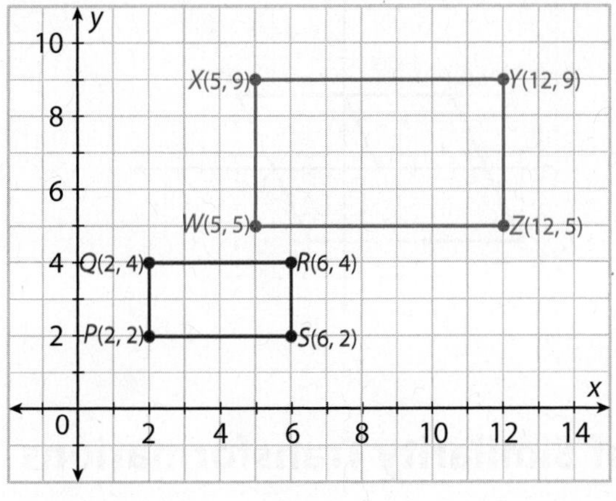

To map *PQRS* onto *WXYZ*, there must be some factor *k* that enlarges *PQRS*.

Pre-image	Image
$P(2, 2)$	$W(5, 5)$
$Q(2, 4)$	$X(5, 9)$
$R(6, 4)$	$Y(12, 9)$
$S(6, 2)$	$Z(12, 5)$

Find each distance: $PQ = 2$, $QR =$ 4 , $WX =$ 4 , and $XY = 7$

If $kPQ = WX$, then $k = 2$. However. $2QR \neq XY$.

No value of *k* can be determined that will map *PQRS* to *WXYZ*.

So, the figures are not similar.

Your Turn

Determine whether the two figures are similar using similarity transformations. Explain.

3. *LMNO* and *GHJK*

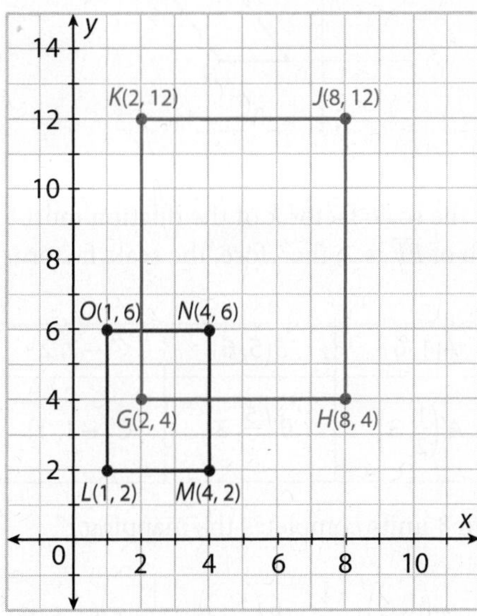

4. $\triangle JKL$ and $\triangle MNP$

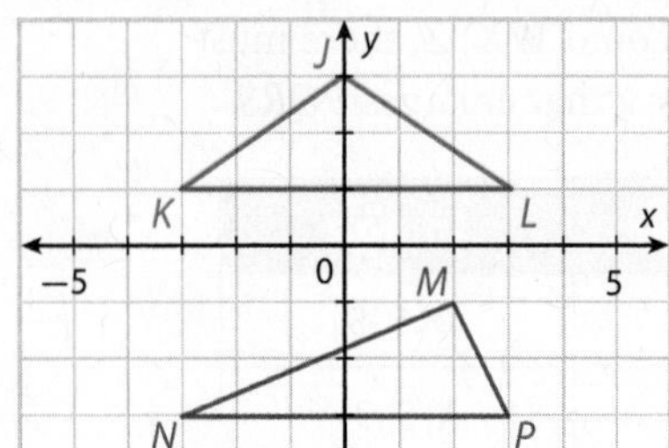

5. *CDEF* and *TUVF*

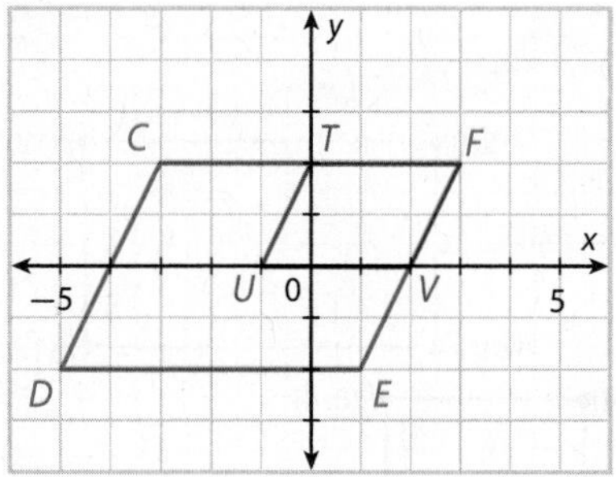

Explain 2 Finding a Sequence of Similarity Transformations

In order for two figures to be similar, there has to be some sequence of similarity transformations that maps one figure to the other. Sometimes there will be a single similarity transformation in the sequence. Sometimes you must identify more than one transformation to describe a mapping.

Example 2 **Find a sequence of similarity transformations that maps the first figure to the second figure. Write the coordinate notation for each transformation.**

(A) *ABDC* to *EFHG*

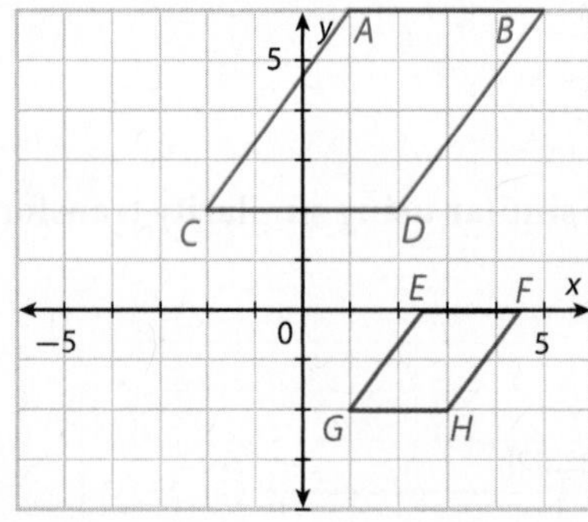

Since *EFHG* is smaller than *ABDC*, the scale factor k of the dilation must be between 0 and 1. The length of $\overline{AB}$ is 4 and the length of $\overline{EF}$ is 2; therefore, the scale factor is $\frac{1}{2}$. Write the new coordinates after the dilation:

Original Coordinates	$A(1, 6)$	$B(5, 6)$	$C(-2, 2)$	$D(2, 2)$
Coordinates after dilation $k = \frac{1}{2}$	$A'\left(\frac{1}{2}, 3\right)$	$B'\left(\frac{5}{2}, 3\right)$	$C'(-1, 1)$	$D'(1, 1)$

A translation right 2 units and down 3 units completes the mapping.

Coordinates after dilation	$A'\left(\frac{1}{2}, 3\right)$	$B'\left(\frac{5}{2}, 3\right)$	$C'(-1, 1)$	$D'(1, 1)$
Coordinates after translation $(x + 2, y - 3)$	$E\left(\frac{5}{2}, 0\right)$	$F\left(\frac{9}{2}, 0\right)$	$G(1, -2)$	$H(3, -2)$

The coordinates after translation are the same as the coordinates of *EFGH*, so you can map *ABDC* to *EFHG* by the dilation $(x, y) \to \left(\frac{1}{2}x, \frac{1}{2}y\right)$ followed by a translation $(x, y) \to (x + 2, y - 3)$.

Ⓑ $\triangle JKL$ to $\triangle PQR$

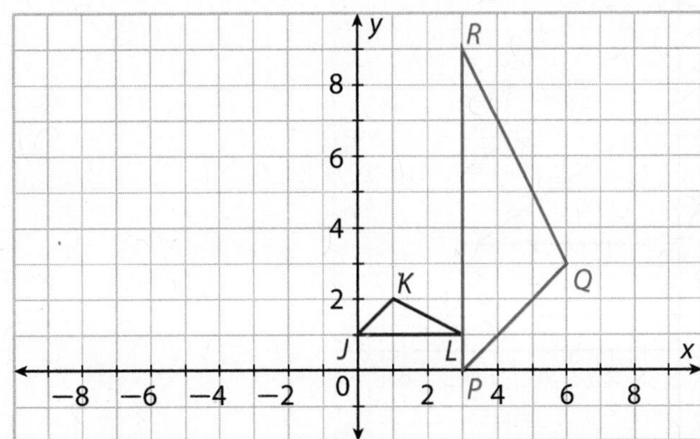

You can map $\triangle JKL$ to $\triangle PQR$ with a reflection across the x-axis followed by a dilation followed by a

90 ° counterclockwise rotation about the origin.

Reflection: $(x, y) \rightarrow (x, -y)$ Dilation: $(x, y) \rightarrow (3x, 3y)$

90 ° counterclockwise rotation: $(x, y) \rightarrow (-y, x)$

Reflect

6. Using the figure in Example 3A, describe a single dilation that maps *ABDC* to *EFHG*.

7. Using the figure in Example 3B, describe a different sequence of transformations that will map $\triangle JKL$ to $\triangle PQR$.

Your Turn

For each pair of similar figures, find a sequence of similarity transformations that maps one figure to the other. Use coordinate notation to describe the transformations.

8. *PQRS* to *TUVW*

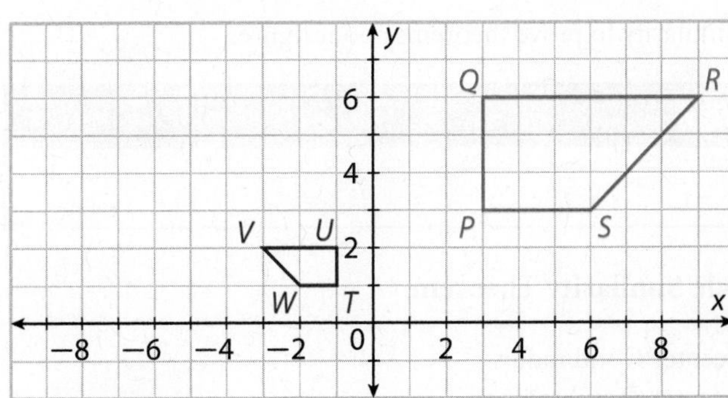

9. $\triangle ABC$ to $\triangle DEF$

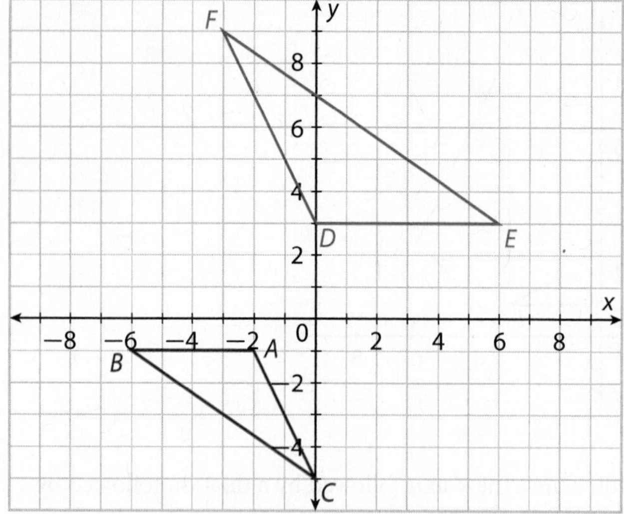

10. Describe a sequence of similarity transformations that maps *JKLMN* to *VWXYZ*.

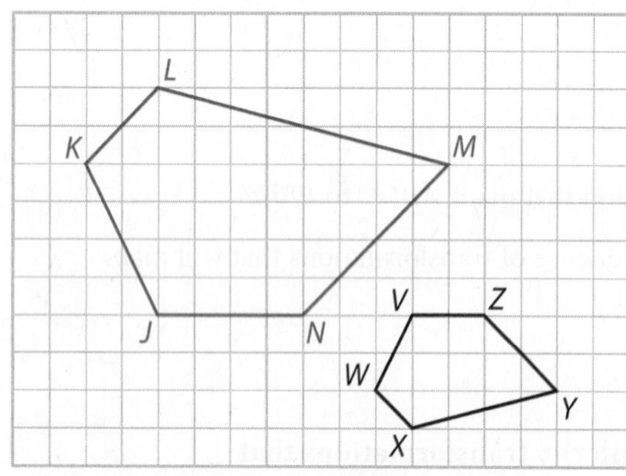

Explain 3 Proving All Circles Are Similar

You can use the definition of similarity to prove theorems about figures.

Circle Similarity Theorem

All circles are similar.

Example 3 **Prove the Circle Similarity Theorem.**

Given: Circle *C* with center *C* and radius *r*.
Circle *D* with center *D* and radius *s*.

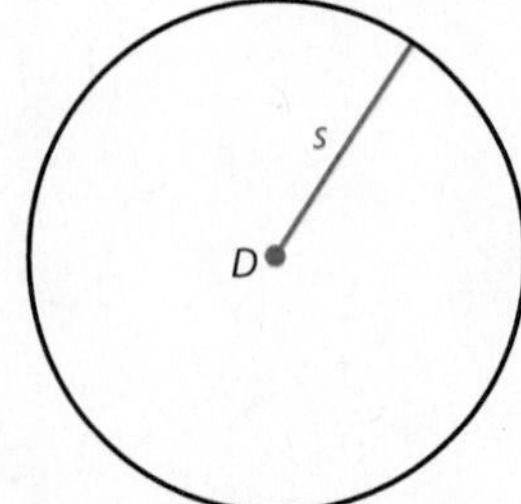

Prove: Circle *C* is similar to circle *D*.

To prove similarity, you must show that there is a sequence of similarity transformations that maps circle *C* to circle *D*.

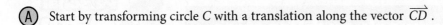

(A) Start by transforming circle C with a translation along the vector $\overrightarrow{CD}$.

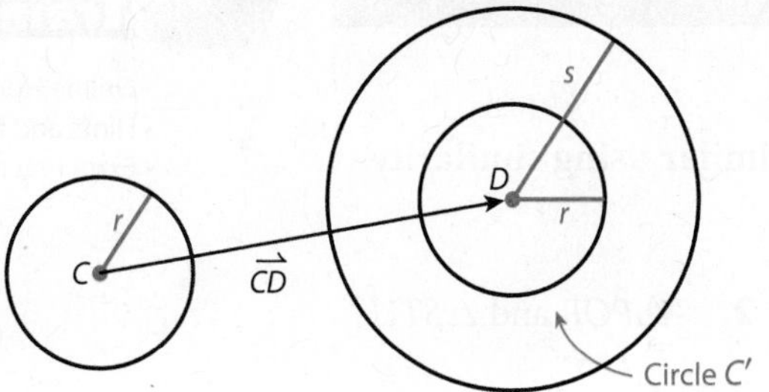

Through this translation, the image of point C is point D.
Let the image of circle C be circle C'. The center of circle C' coincides with point D.

(B) Transform circle C' with the dilation with center of dilation D and scale factor $\frac{s}{r}$.

Circle C' is made up of all the points at distance r from point D.

After the dilation, the image of circle C' will consist of all the points at distance $\frac{s}{r} \times r = s$ from point D.

These are the same points that form circle D. Therefore, the translation followed by the dilation maps circle C to circle D. Because translations and dilations are similarity transformations, you can conclude that circle C is similar to circle D.

Reflect

11. Can you show that circle C and circle D are similar through another sequence of similarity transformations? Explain.

12. Discussion Is it possible that circle C and circle D are congruent? If so, does the proof of the similarity of the circles still work? Explain.

Elaborate

13. Translations, reflections, and rotations are rigid motions. What unique characteristic keeps dilations from being considered a rigid motion?

14. Essential Question Check-In Two squares in the coordinate plane have horizontal and vertical sides. Explain how they are similar using similarity transformations.

Evaluate: Homework and Practice

- Online Homework
- Hints and Help
- Extra Practice

In Exercises 1–4, determine if the two figures are similar using similarity transformations. Explain.

1. *EFGH* and *ABCD*

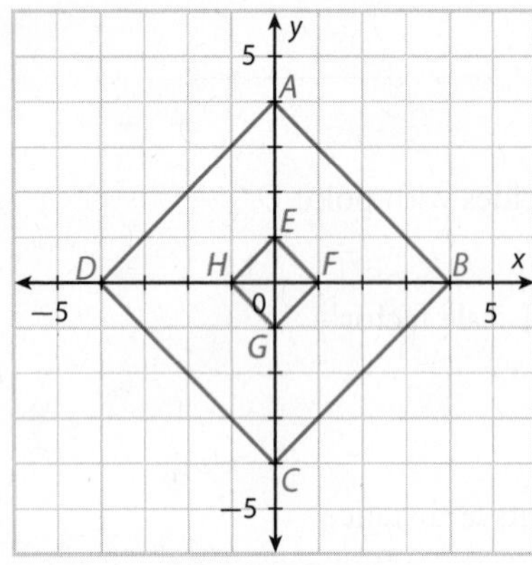

2. $\triangle PQR$ and $\triangle STU$

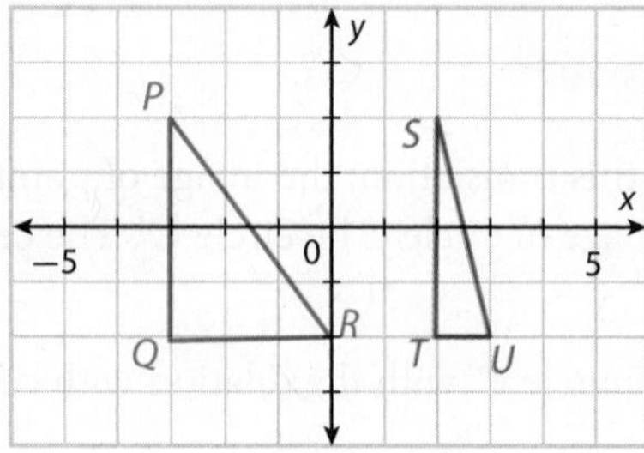

3. *JKLMN* and *JPQRS*

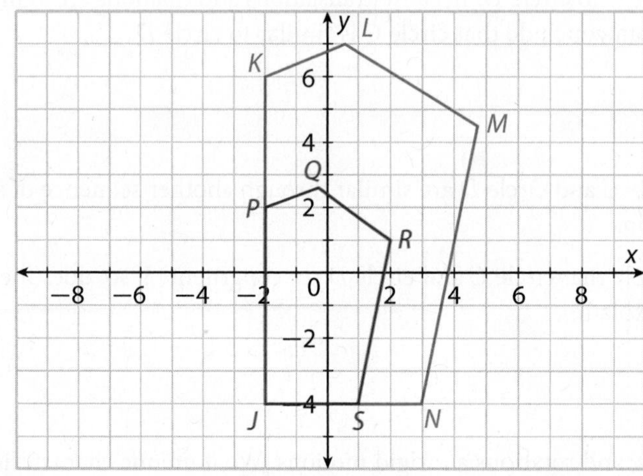

4. $\triangle UVW$ and $\triangle GHI$

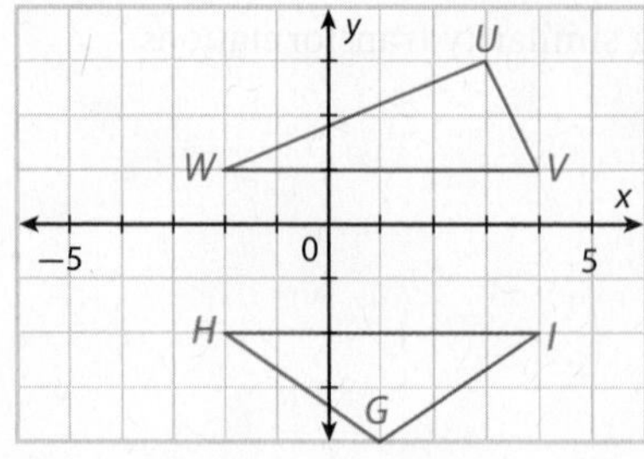

For the pair of similar figures in each of Exercises 5–10, find a sequence of similarity transformations that maps one figure to the other. Provide the coordinate notation for each transformation.

5. Map $\triangle ABC$ to $\triangle PQR$.

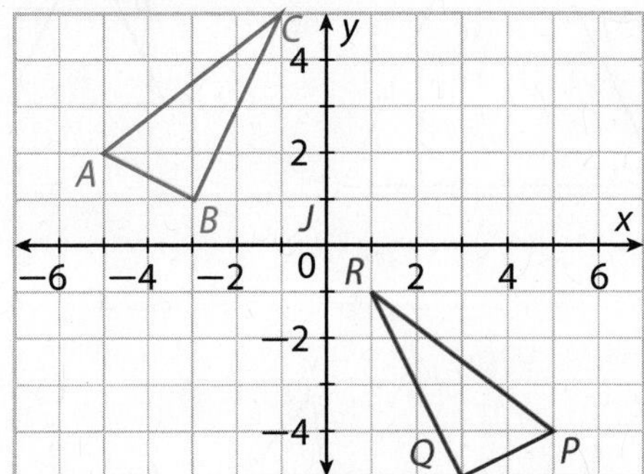

6. Map $ABCD$ to $EFGH$.

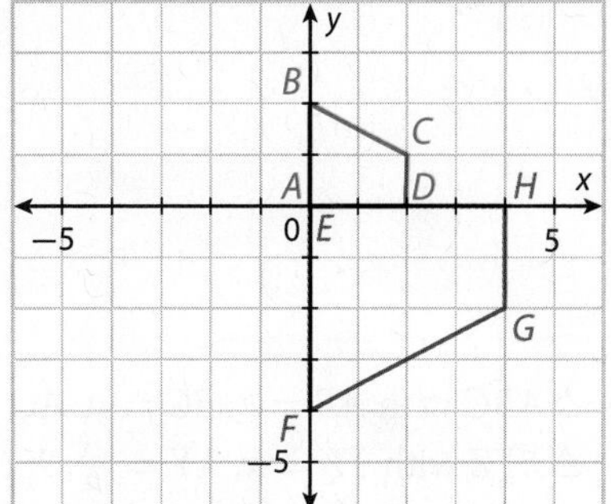

7. Map $\triangle CED$ to $\triangle CBA$.

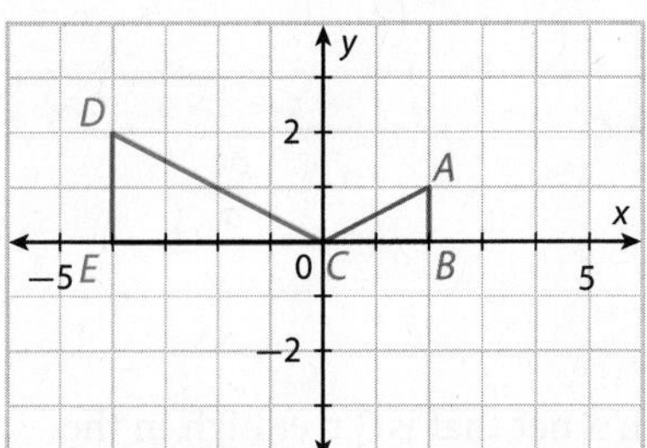

8. Map $ABCDE$ to $JKLMN$.

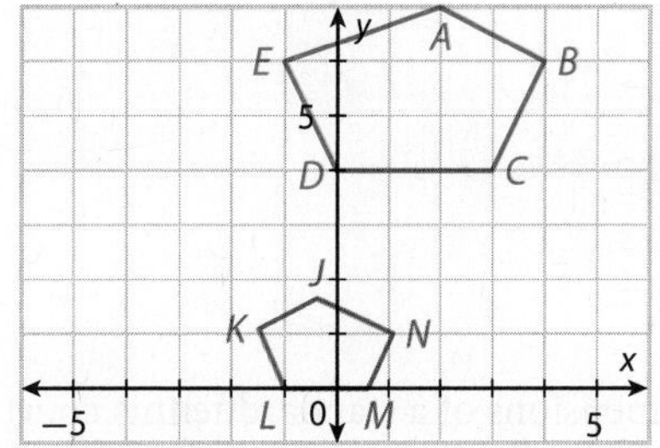

9. Map $ABCD$ to $JKLM$.

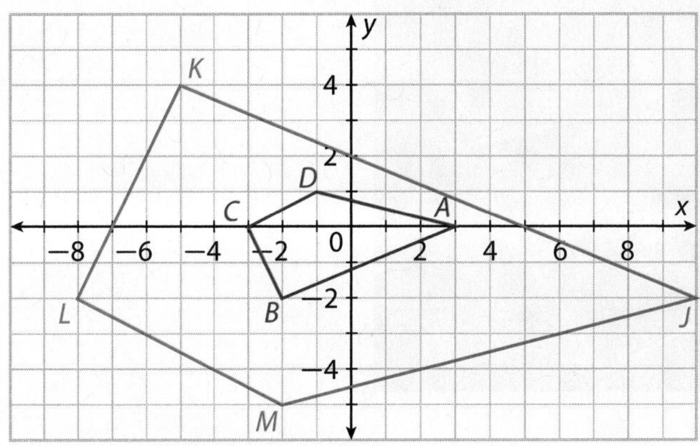

10. Map $\triangle JKL$ to $\triangle PQR$

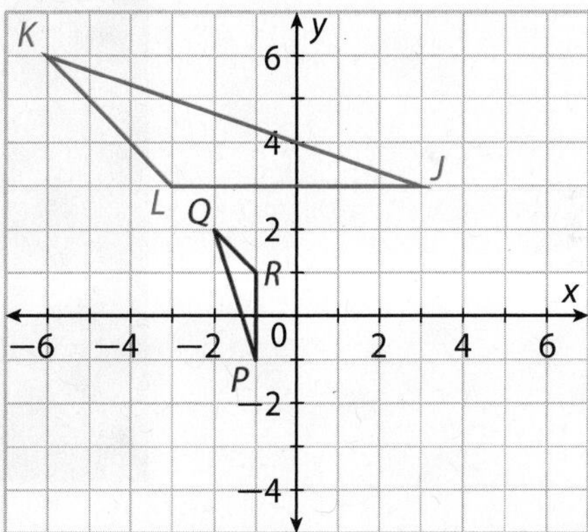

Complete the proof.

11. Given: Square $ABCD$ with side length x. Square $EFGH$ with side length y.

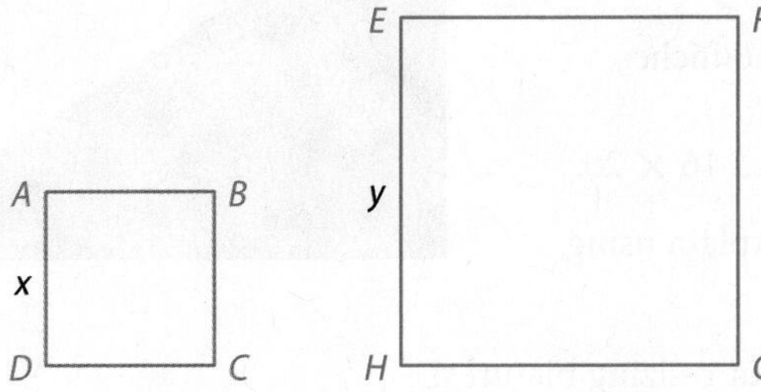

Prove: Square $ABCD$ is similar to square $EFGH$.

12. Given: Equilateral $\triangle JKL$ with side length j.
Equilateral $\triangle PQR$ with side length p

Prove: $\triangle JKL$ is similar to $\triangle PQR$.

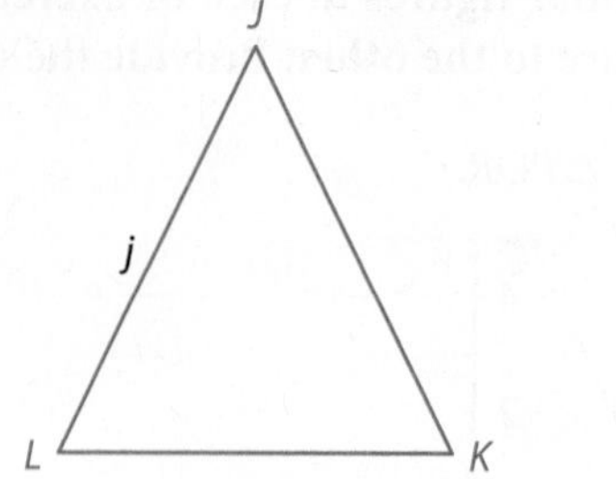

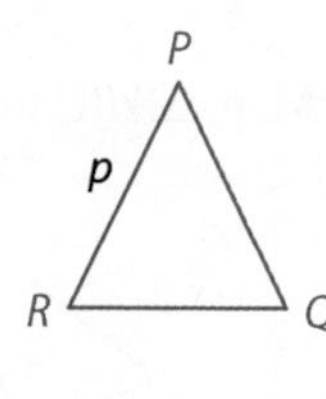

13. Given: $\triangle ABC$ with $AB = c$, $BC = a$, $AC = b$
$\triangle XYZ$ with $YZ = x$, $XY = \frac{cx}{a}$, $XZ = \frac{bx}{a}$

Prove: $\triangle ABC$ is similar to $\triangle XYZ$.

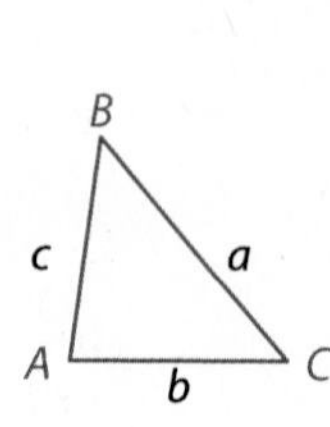

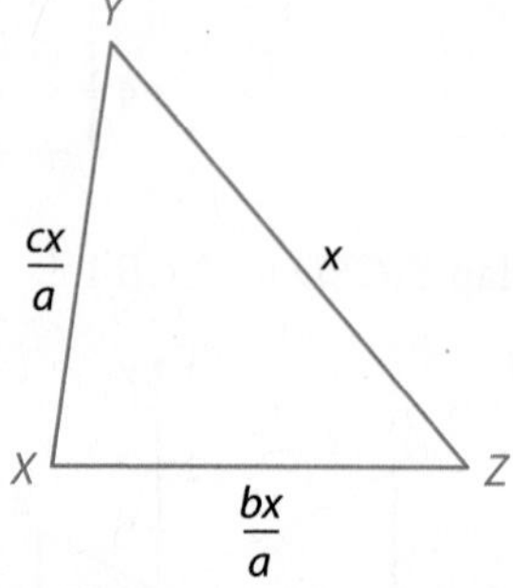

14. The dimensions of a standard tennis court are 36 feet × 78 feet with a net that is 3 feet high in the center. The court is modified for players aged 10 and under such that the dimensions are 27 feet × 60 feet, and the same net is used. Use similarity to determine if the modified court is similar to the standard court.

15. Represent Real-World Problems A scuba flag is used to indicate there is a diver below. In North America, scuba flags are red with a white stripe from the upper left corner to the lower right corner. Justify the triangles formed on the scuba flag are similar triangles.

16. The most common picture size is 4 inches ×6 inches. Other common pictures sizes (in inches) are 5 × 7, 8 × 10, 9 × 12, 11 × 14, 14 × 18, and 16 × 20.

a. Are any of these picture sizes similar? Explain using similarity transformations.

b. What does your conclusion indicate about resizing pictures?

17. Nicole wants to know the height of the snow sculpture but it is too tall to measure. Nicole measured the shadow of the snow sculpture's highest point to be 10 feet long. At the same time of day Nicole's shadow was 40 inches long. If Nicole is 5 feet tall, what is the height of the snow sculpture?

18. Which of the following is a dilation?

A. $(x, y) \rightarrow (x, 3y)$

B. $(x, y) \rightarrow (3x, -y)$

C. $(x, y) \rightarrow (3x, 3y)$

D. $(x, y) \rightarrow (x, y - 3)$

E. $(x, y) \rightarrow (x - 3, y - 3)$

19. What is not preserved under dilation? Select all that apply.

A. Angle measure

B. Betweenness

C. Collinearity

D. Distance

E. Proportionality

H.O.T. Focus on Higher Order Thinking

20. Analyze Relationships Consider the transformations below.

I. Translation **II.** Reflection **III.** Rotation **IV.** Dilation

a. Which transformations preserve distance?

b. Which transformations preserve angle measure?

c. Use your knowledge of rigid transformations to compare and contrast congruency and similarity.

Justify Reasoning For Exercises 21–23, use the figure shown. Determine whether the given assumptions are enough to prove that the two triangles are similar. Write the correct correspondence of the vertices. If the two triangles must be similar, describe a sequence of similarity transformations that maps one triangle to the other. If the triangles are not necessarily similar, explain why.

21. The lengths AX, BX, CX, and DX satisfy the equation $\frac{AX}{BX} = \frac{DX}{CX}$.

22. Lines AB and CD are parallel.

23. $\angle XAB$ is congruent to $\angle XCD$.

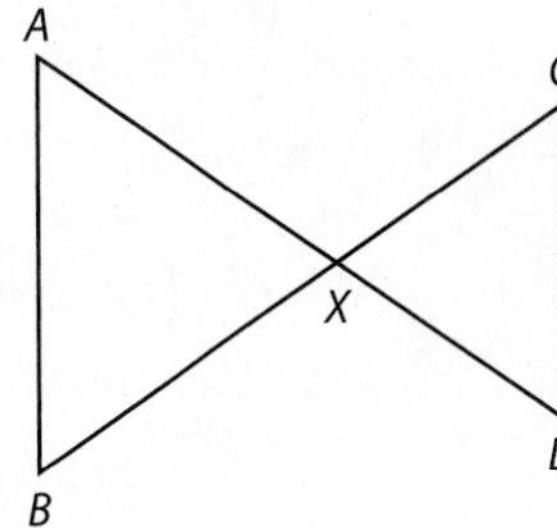

Lesson Performance Task

Answer the following questions about the dartboard pictured here.

1. Are the circles similar? Explain, using the concept of a dilation in your explanation.
2. You throw a dart and it sticks in a random location on the board. What is the probability that it sticks in Circle A? Circle B? Circle C? Circle D? Explain how you found your answers.

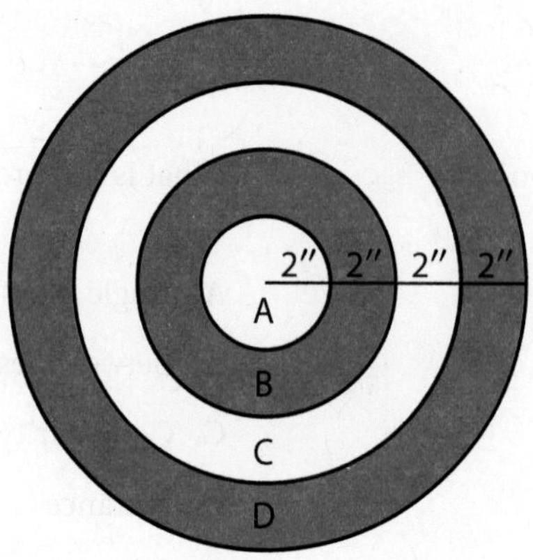

11.3 Corresponding Parts of Similar Figures

Essential Question: **If you know two figures are similar, what can you determine about measures of corresponding angles and lengths?**

Resource Locker

Explore Connecting Angles and Sides of Figures

You know that if figures are similar, the side lengths are proportional and the angle measures are equal. If you have two figures with proportional side lengths and congruent angles, can you conclude that they are similar?

Ⓐ Consider the graph of *ABCD* and *KLMN*.

Are corresponding angles congruent? ?

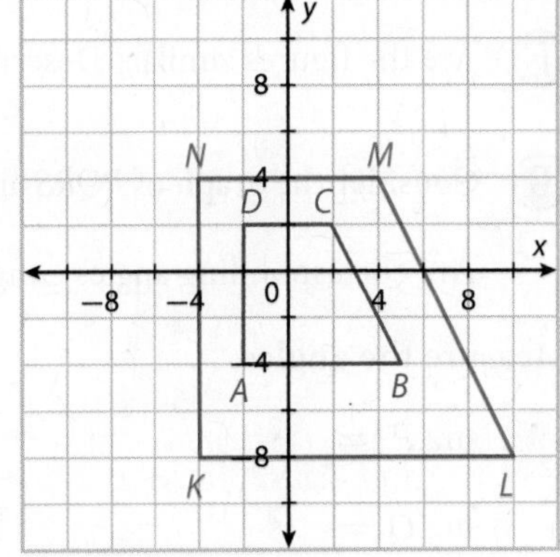

Measure the angles.

$m\angle A =$? $m\angle K =$?

$m\angle B =$? $m\angle L =$?

$m\angle C =$? $m\angle M =$?

$m\angle D =$? $m\angle N =$?

Ⓑ Are the ratios of corresponding side lengths equal? ?

$\frac{AB}{KL} = \frac{?}{?}$ $\frac{BC}{LM} = \frac{?}{?}$ $\frac{CD}{MN} = \frac{?}{?}$ $\frac{AD}{KN} = \frac{?}{?}$

Ⓒ Are the figures similar? Describe how you know using similarity transformations.

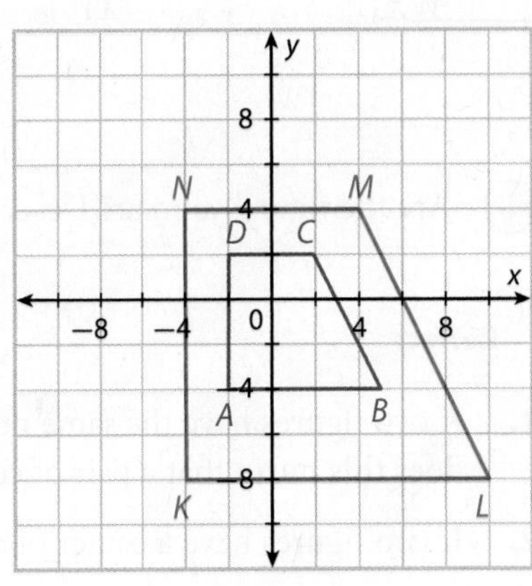

Ⓓ Consider the graph of *ABCD* and *EFGH*.

Are corresponding angles congruent? Explain.

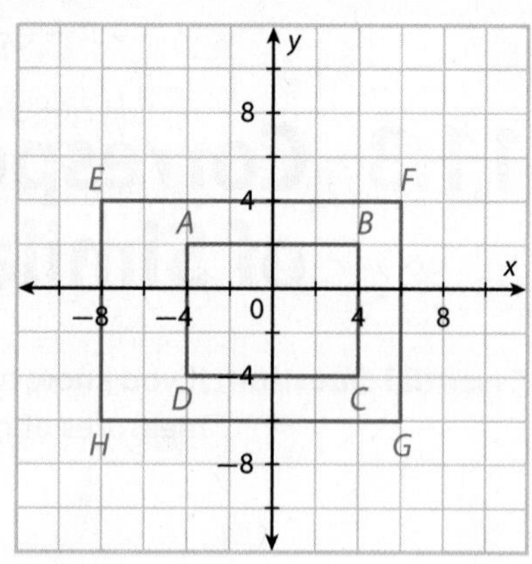

Ⓔ Are the ratios of corresponding side lengths equal?

$\frac{AB}{EF} = \frac{?}{?}$ $\frac{BC}{FG} = \frac{?}{?}$ $\frac{CD}{GH} = \frac{?}{?}$ $\frac{AD}{EH} = \frac{?}{?}$

Ⓕ Are the figures similar? Describe how you know using similarity transformations.

Ⓖ Consider the graph of *PQRS* and *WXYZ*.

Are corresponding angles congruent?

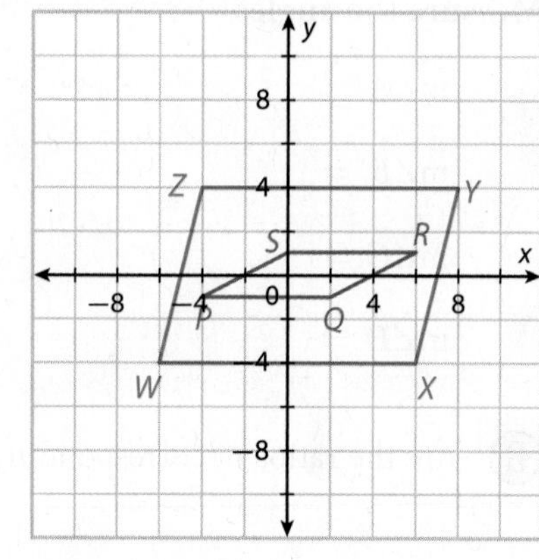

Measure the angles.

$m\angle P =$? $m\angle W =$?

$m\angle Q =$? $m\angle X =$?

$m\angle R =$? $m\angle Y =$?

$m\angle S =$? $m\angle Z =$?

Ⓗ Are the ratios of corresponding side lengths equal?

$\frac{PQ}{WX} = \frac{?}{?}$ $\frac{QR}{XY} = \frac{?}{?}$ $\frac{RS}{YZ} = \frac{?}{?}$ $\frac{PS}{WZ} = \frac{?}{?}$

Ⓘ Are the figures similar? Describe how you know using similarity transformations.

Reflect

1. If two figures have the same number of sides and the corresponding angles are congruent, does this mean that a pair of corresponding sides are either congruent or proportional?
2. If two figures have a center of dilation, is a corresponding pair of sides necessarily proportional?
3. If two figures have a correspondence of proportional sides, do the figures necessarily have a center of dilation?

Explain 1 Justifying Properties of Similar Figures Using Transformations

Two figures that can be mapped to each other by similarity transformations (dilations and rigid motions) are similar. Similar figures have certain properties.

Properties of Similar Figures

Corresponding angles of similar figures are congruent.

Corresponding sides of similar figures are proportional.

If $\triangle ABC \sim \triangle XYZ$, then

$\angle A \cong \angle X \quad \angle B \cong \angle Y \quad \angle C \cong \angle Z$

$\frac{AB}{XY} = \frac{BC}{YZ} = \frac{AC}{XZ}$

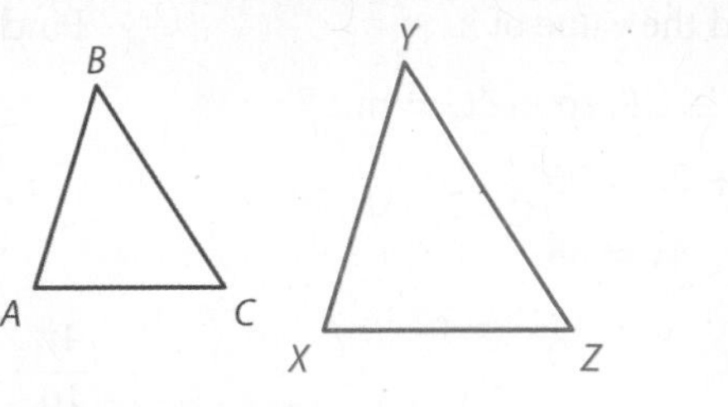

To show that two figures with all pairs of corresponding sides having equal ratio k and all pairs of corresponding angles congruent are similar, you can use similarity transformations.

Dilate one figure using k. The dilated figure is congruent to the second figure by the definition of congruence. So, there is a sequence of rigid motions (which are also similarity transformations) that maps one to the other.

Example 1 **Identify properties of similar figures.**

(A) Figure $EFGH$ maps to figure $RSTU$ by a similarity transformation. Write a proportion that contains EF and RU. List any angles that must be congruent to $\angle G$ or congruent to $\angle U$.

$\frac{EF}{RS} = \frac{EH}{RU}$ $\quad$ $\angle T$ is congruent to $\angle G$, and $\angle H$ is congruent to $\angle U$.

(B) Figure $JKLMN$ maps to figure $TUVWX$ by a similarity transformation. Write a proportion that contains TX and LM. List any angles that must be congruent to $\angle V$ or congruent to $\angle K$.

$\frac{\boxed{JN}}{TX} = \frac{LM}{\boxed{VW}}$ $\quad$ $\angle L$ is congruent to $\angle V$, and $\angle U$ is congruent to $\angle K$.

Reflect

4. If you know two figures are similar, what angle or side measurements must you know to find the dilation used in the transformations mapping one figure to another?

Your Turn

5. Triangles $\triangle PQR$ and $\triangle LMN$ are similar. If $QR = 6$ and $MN = 9$, what similarity transformation (in coordinate notation) maps $\triangle PQR$ to $\triangle LMN$?

6. **Error Analysis** Triangles $\triangle DEF$ and $\triangle UVW$ are similar. $\frac{DE}{UV} = \frac{VW}{EF}$ Is the statement true?

Explain 2 Applying Properties of Similar Figures

The properties of similar figures can be used to find the measures of corresponding parts.

Example 2 **Given that the figures are similar, find the values of x and y.**

(A)

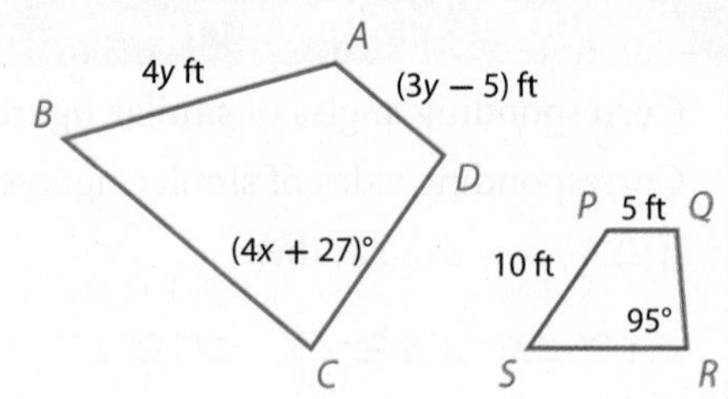

Find the value of x.

$\angle C \cong \angle R$, so $m\angle C = m\angle R$

$4x + 27 = 95$

$4x = 68$

$x = 17$

Find the value of y.

$$\frac{AB}{PS} = \frac{AD}{PQ}$$

$$\frac{4y}{10} = \frac{3y - 5}{5}$$

$$\frac{4y}{10} \cdot 10 = \frac{3y - 5}{5} \cdot 10$$

$$4y = 6y - 10$$

$$y = 5$$

(B)

K
(2y – 8) cm
L
M
5(x – 5)°
1.5 cm
J
N
Z
1 cm
4x°
Y
X
V
4 cm
W

Find the value of x.

$m\angle LMN = m\angle XYZ$

$5(x - 5) = 4x$

$5x - 25 = 4x$

$x = 25$

Find the value of y.

$$\frac{JK}{VW} = \frac{MN}{YZ}$$

$$\frac{2x - 8}{4} = \frac{1.5}{1}$$

$$2x - 8 = 1.5(4)$$

$$2x - 8 = 6$$

$$2x = 14$$

$$x = 7$$

Reflect

7. **Discussion** What are some things you need to be careful about when solving problems involving finding the values of variables in similar figures?

Your Turn

Use the diagram, in which $\triangle ABE \sim \triangle ACD$.

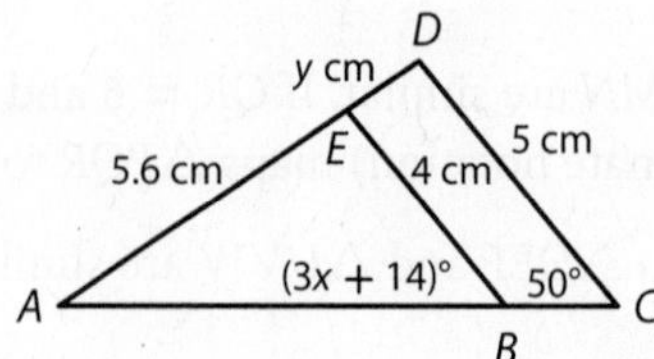

8. Find the value of x.

9. Find the value of y.

Elaborate

10. Consider two similar triangles $\triangle ABC$ and $\triangle A'B'C'$. If both $m\angle A' = m\angle C$ and $m\angle B' = m\angle A$, what can you conclude about triangle $\triangle ABC$? Explain your reasoning.

11. Rectangle $JKLM$ maps to rectangle $RSTU$ by the transformation $(x, y) \rightarrow (4x, 4y)$. If the perimeter of $RSTU$ is x, what is the perimeter of $JKLM$ in terms of x?

12. **Essential Question Check-In** If two figures are similar, what can we conclude about their corresponding parts?

Evaluate: Homework and Practice

- Online Homework
- Hints and Help
- Extra Practice

In the figures, are corresponding angles congruent? Are corresponding sides proportional? Are the figures similar? Describe how you know using similarity transformations.

1.

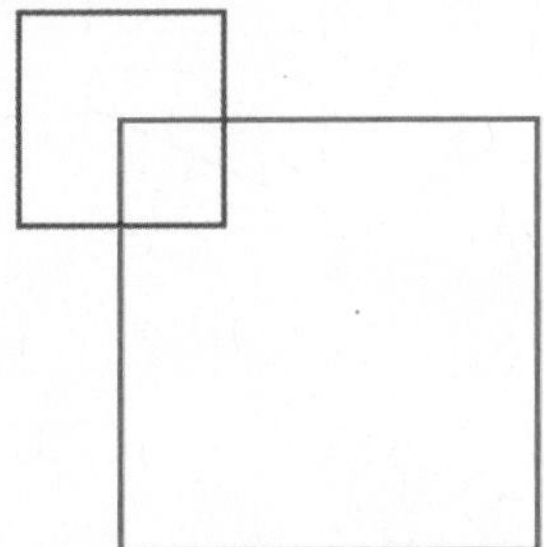

2.

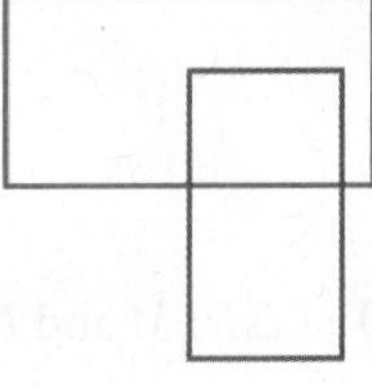

3.

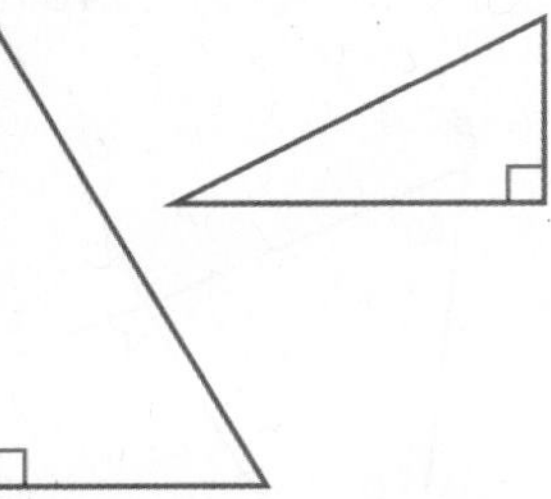

4.

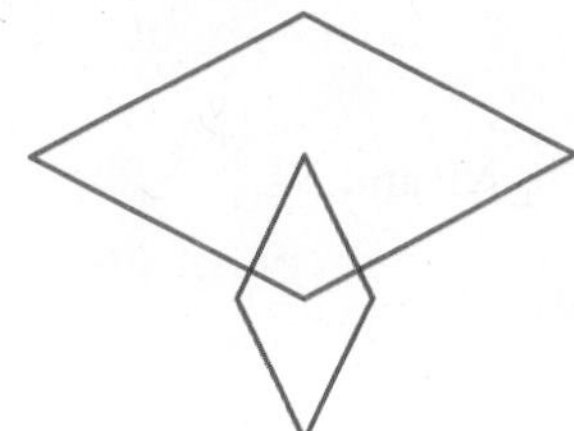

5. Figure $ABCD$ is similar to figure $MNKL$. Write a proportion that contains BC and KL.

6. $\triangle DEF$ is similar to $\triangle STU$. Write a proportion that contains ST and SU.

7. $\triangle XYZ$ is similar to $\triangle XVW$. Write the congruence statements that must be true.

8. $\triangle MNP$ is similar to $\triangle HJK$, and both triangles are isosceles. If $m\angle P > 90°$, name all angles that are congruent to $\angle H$.

9. $CDEF$ maps to $JKLM$ with the transformations $(x, y) \rightarrow (5x, 5y) \rightarrow (x - 4, y - 4)$. What is the value of $\frac{EF}{LM}$?

10. $\triangle PQR$ maps to $\triangle VWX$ with the transformation $(x, y) \rightarrow (x + 3, y - 1) \rightarrow (2x, 2y)$. If $WX = 12$, what does QR equal?

11. $\triangle QRS$ maps to $\triangle XYZ$ with the transformation $(x, y) \rightarrow (6x, 6y)$. If $QS = 7$, what is the length of XZ?

12. **Algebra** Two similar figures are similar based on the transformation $(x, y) \rightarrow (12x, 3a^2y)$. What is/are the value(s) of a?

13. **Algebra** $\triangle PQR$ is similar to $\triangle XYZ$. If $PQ = n + 2$, $QR = n - 2$, and $XY = n^2 - 4$, what is the value of YZ, in terms of n?

14. Which transformations will not produce similar figures? Select all that apply and explain your choices.

A. $(x, y) \rightarrow (x - 4, y) \rightarrow (-x, -y) \rightarrow (8x, 8y)$

B. $(x, y) \rightarrow (x + 1, y + 1) \rightarrow (3x, 2y) \rightarrow (-x, -y)$

C. $(x, y) \rightarrow (5x, 5y) \rightarrow (x, -y) \rightarrow (x + 3, y - 3)$

D. $(x, y) \rightarrow (x, 2y) \rightarrow (x + 6, y - 2) \rightarrow (2x, y)$

E. $(x, y) \rightarrow (x, 3y) \rightarrow (2x, y) \rightarrow (x - 3, y - 2)$

15. The figures in the picture are similar to each other. Find the value of x.

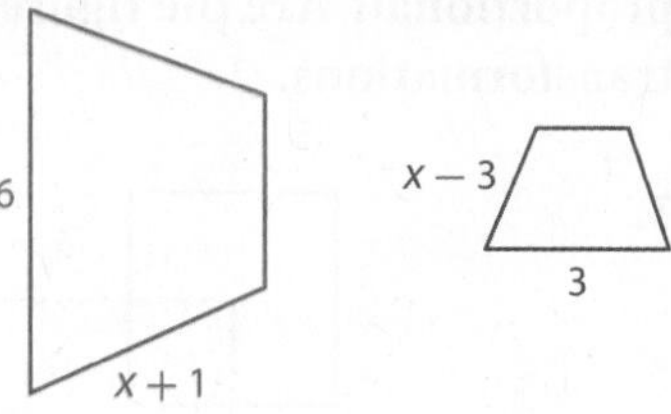

16. In the diagram, $\triangle NPQ \sim \triangle NLM$ and $PL = 5$.

a. Find the value of x.

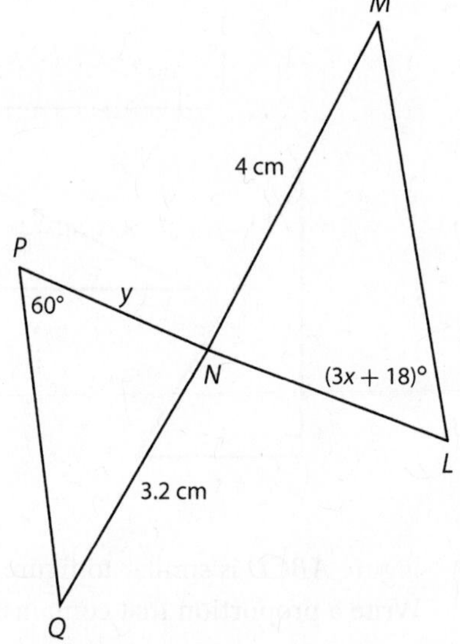

b. Find the lengths NP and NL.

17. $\triangle CDE$ maps to $\triangle STU$ with the transformations $(x, y) \rightarrow (x - 2, y - 2) \rightarrow (3x, 3y) \rightarrow (x, -y)$.
If $CD = a + 1$, $DE = 2a - 1$, $ST = 2b + 3$, and $TU = b + 6$, find the values of a and b.

18. If a sequence of transformations contains the transformation (ax, by), with $a \neq b$, could the pre-image and image represent congruent figures? Could they represent similar, non-congruent figures? Justify your answers with examples.

19. Is any pair of equilateral triangles similar to each other? Why or why not?

20. Figure *CDEF* is similar to figure *KLMN*. Which statements are false? Select all that apply and explain why.

A. $\frac{CD}{KL} = \frac{EF}{MN}$ B. $\frac{CF}{KN} = \frac{EF}{MN}$ C. $\frac{DE}{LM} = \frac{CF}{KN}$ D. $\frac{LM}{DE} = \frac{KL}{CD}$ E. $\frac{LM}{DE} = \frac{KN}{CD}$

Consider this model of a train locomotive when answering the next two questions.

21. If the model is 18 inches long and the actual locomotive is 72 feet long, what is the similarity transformation to map from the model to the actual locomotive? Express the answer using the notation $x \longrightarrow ax$, where x is a measurement on the model and ax is the corresponding measurement on the actual locomotive.

22. If the diameter of the front wheels on the locomotive is 4 feet, what is the diameter of the front wheels on the model? Express the answer in inches.

Use the following graph to answer the next two problems.

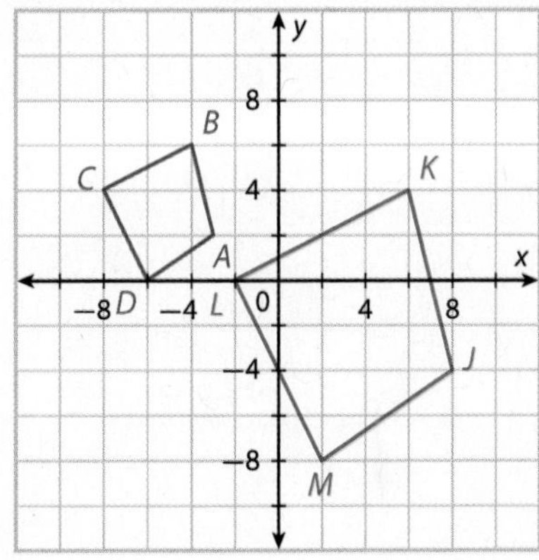

23. Specify a sequence of two transformations that will map *ABCD* onto *JKLM*.

24. Find the value of $\frac{AC + BD}{JL + KM}$.

H.O.T. Focus on Higher Order Thinking

25. **Counterexamples** Consider the statement "All rectangles are similar." Is this statement true or false? If true, explain why. If false, provide a counterexample.

26. **Justify Reasoning** If *ABCD* is similar to *KLMN* and *MNKL*, what special type of quadrilateral is *KLMN*? Justify your reasoning.

27. **Critique Reasoning** Consider the statement "If $\triangle PQR$ is similar to $\triangle QPR$, then $\triangle PQR$ is similar to $\triangle RPQ$." Explain whether or not this statement is true.

Lesson Performance Task

You've hired an architect to design your dream house and now the house has been built. Before moving in, you've decided to wander through the house with a tape measure to see how well the builders have followed the architect's floor plan. Describe in as much detail as you can how you could accomplish your goal. Then discuss how you can decide whether the room shapes and other features of the house are similar to the corresponding shapes on the floor plan.

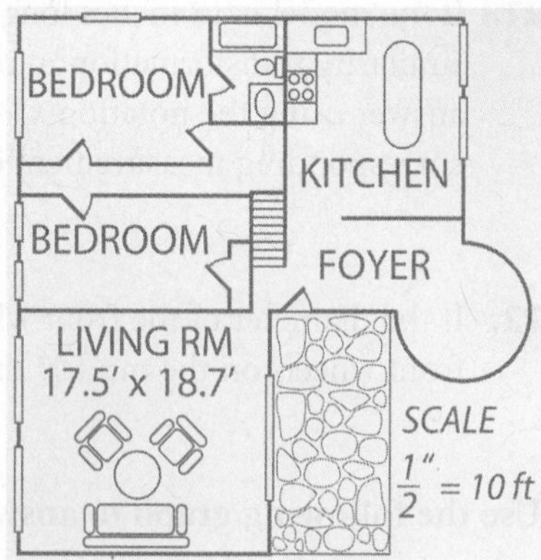

11.4 AA Similarity of Triangles

Essential Question: How can you show that two triangles are similar?

Resource Locker

Explore Exploring Angle-Angle Similarity for Triangles

Two triangles are similar when their corresponding sides are proportional and their corresponding angles are congruent. There are several shortcuts for proving triangles are similar.

(A) Draw a triangle and label it $\triangle ABC$. Elsewhere on your page, draw a segment longer than $\overline{AB}$ and label the endpoints D and E.

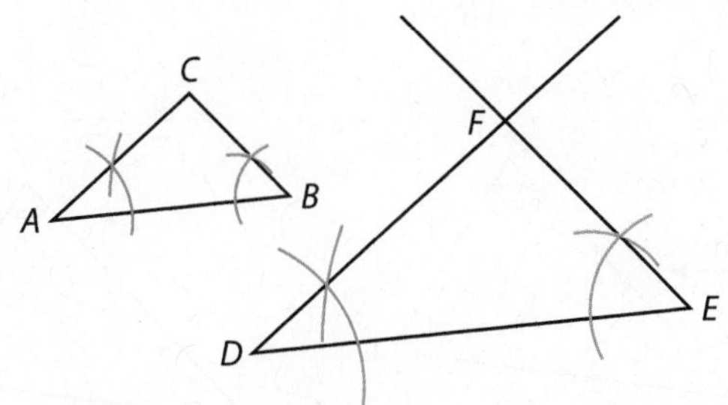

(B) Copy $\angle CAB$ and $\angle ABC$ to points D and E, respectively. Extend the rays of your copied angles, if necessary, and label their intersection point F. You have constructed $\triangle DEF$.

(C) You constructed angles D and E to be congruent to angles A and B, respectively. Therefore, angles C and F must also be [?] because of the [?] Theorem.

(D) Check the proportionality of the corresponding sides.

$$\frac{AB}{DE} = \frac{?}{?} = ? \qquad \frac{AC}{DF} = \frac{?}{?} = ? \qquad \frac{BC}{EF} = \frac{?}{?} = ?$$

Since the ratios are [?] the sides of the triangles are [?].

Reflect

1. **Discussion** Compare your results with your classmates. What conjecture can you make about two triangles that have two corresponding congruent angles?

Explain 1 Proving Angle-Angle Triangle Similarity

The Explore suggests the following theorem for determining whether two triangles are similar.

Angle-Angle (AA) Triangle Similarity Theorem

If two angles of one triangle are congruent to two angles of another triangle, then the two triangles are similar.

Example 1 **Prove the Angle-Angle Triangle Similarity Theorem.**

Given: $\angle A \cong \angle X$ and $\angle B \cong \angle Y$

Prove: $\triangle ABC \sim \triangle XYZ$

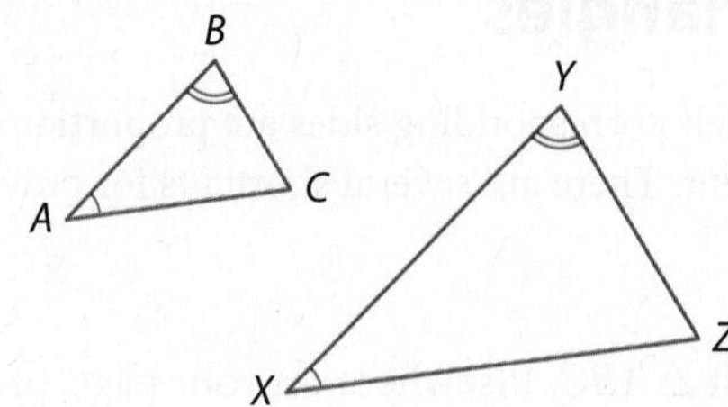

(1) Apply a dilation to $\triangle ABC$ with scale factor $k = \frac{XY}{AB}$. Let the image of $\triangle ABC$ be $\triangle A'B'C$.

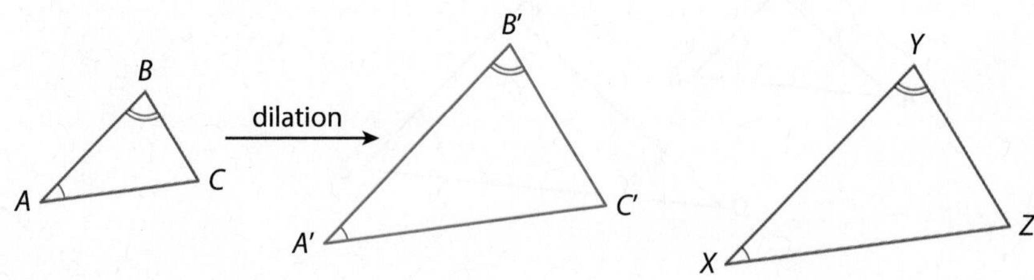

$\triangle A'B'C$ is similar to $\triangle ABC$, and $\angle A' \cong \angle A$ and $\angle B' \cong \angle B$ because corresponding angles of similar triangles are congruent.

Also, $A'B' = k \cdot AB = \frac{XY}{AB} \cdot AB = XY$.

(2) It is given that $\angle A \cong \angle X$ and $\angle B \cong \angle Y$

By the Transitive Property of Congruence, $\angle A' \cong \angle X$ and $\angle B' \cong \angle Y$.

So, $\triangle A'B'C' \cong \triangle XYZ$ by the ASA Triangle Congruence Theorem.

This means there is a sequence of rigid motions that maps $\triangle A'B'C'$ *to* $\triangle YYZ$.

The dilation followed by this sequence of rigid motions shows that there is a sequence of similarity transformations that maps $\triangle ABC$ to $\triangle XYZ$. Therefore, $\triangle ABC \sim \triangle XYZ$.

Reflect

2. **Discussion** Compare and contrast the AA Similarity Theorem with the ASA Congruence Theorem.

3. In $\triangle JKL$, $m\angle J = 40°$ and $m\angle K = 55°$. In $\triangle MNP$, $m\angle M = 40°$ and $m\angle P = 85°$. A student concludes that the triangles are not similar. Do you agree or disagree? Why?

Explain 2 Applying Angle-Angle Similarity

Architects and contractors use the properties of similar figures to find any unknown dimensions, like the proper height of a triangular roof. They can use a bevel angle tool to check that the angles of construction are congruent to the angles in their plans.

Example 2 **Find the indicated length, if possible.**

(A) BE

First, determine whether $\triangle ABC \sim \triangle DBE$.

By the Alternate Interior Angles Theorem, $\angle A \cong \angle D$ and $\angle C \cong \angle E$, so $\triangle ABC \sim \triangle DBE$ by the AA Triangle Similarity Theorem.

Find BE by solving a proportion.

$$\frac{BD}{BA} = \frac{BE}{BC}$$

$$\frac{54}{36} = \frac{BE}{54}$$

$$\frac{54}{36} \cdot 54 = \frac{BE}{54} \cdot 54$$

$$BE = 81$$

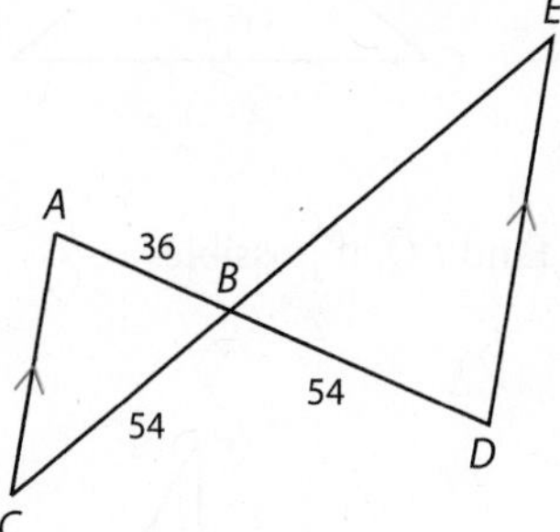

(B) RT

Check whether $\triangle RSV \sim \triangle RTU$:

It is given in the diagram that $\angle RSV \cong \angle T$. $\angle R$ is shared by both triangles,

so $\angle R \cong \angle R$ by the Reflexive Property of Congruence.

So, by the AA Triangle Similarity Theorem, $\triangle RST \sim \triangle RTU$.

Find RT by solving a proportion.

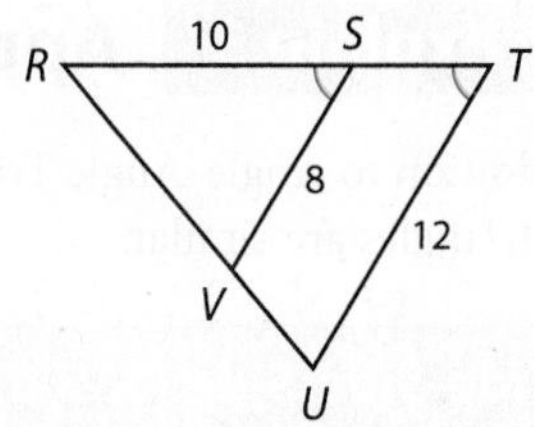

$$\frac{RT}{RS} = \frac{TU}{SV}$$

$$\frac{RT}{10} = \frac{12}{8}$$

$RT = 15$

Reflect

4. In Example 2A, is there another way you can set up the proportion to solve for BE?

5. Discussion When asked to solve for y, a student sets up the proportion as shown. Explain why the proportion is wrong. How should you adjust the proportion so that it will give the correct result?

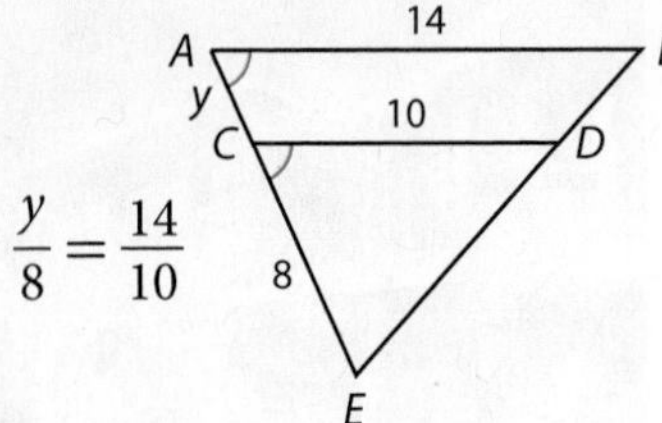

$$\frac{y}{8} = \frac{14}{10}$$

Your Turn

6. A builder was given a design plan for a triangular roof as shown. Explain how he knows that $\triangle AED \sim \triangle ACB$. Then find AB.

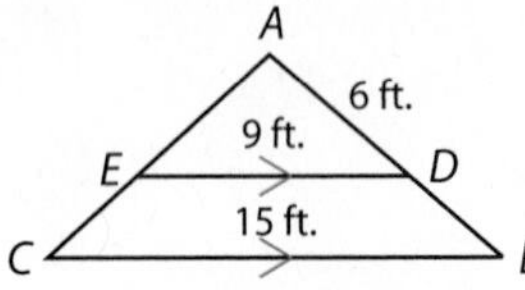

7. Find PQ, if possible.

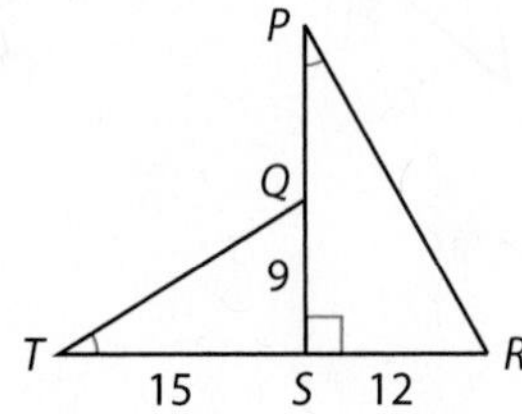

Explain 3 Applying SSS and SAS Triangle Similarity

In addition to Angle-Angle Triangle Similarity, there are two additional shortcuts for proving two triangles are similar.

Side-Side-Side (SSS) Triangle Similarity Theorem

If the three sides of one triangle are proportional to the corresponding sides of another triangle, then the triangles are similar.

Side-Angle-Side (SAS) Triangle Similarity Theorem

If two sides of one triangle are proportional to the corresponding sides of another triangle and their included angles are congruent, then the triangles are similar.

Example 3 **Determine whether the given triangles are similar. Justify your answer.**

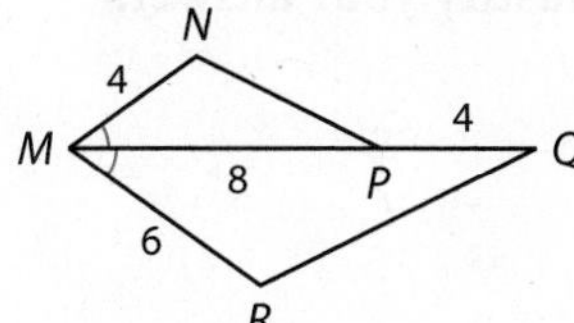

You are given two pairs of corresponding side lengths and one pair of congruent corresponding angles, so try using SAS.

Check that the ratios of corresponding sides are equal.

$\frac{MN}{MR} = \frac{4}{6} = \frac{2}{3}$ $\qquad \frac{MP}{MQ} = \frac{8}{8 + 4} = \frac{8}{12} = \frac{2}{3}$

Check that the included angles are congruent: $\angle NMP \cong \angle QMR$ is given in the diagram.

Therefore $\triangle NMP \sim \triangle RMQ$ by the SAS Triangle Similarity Theorem.

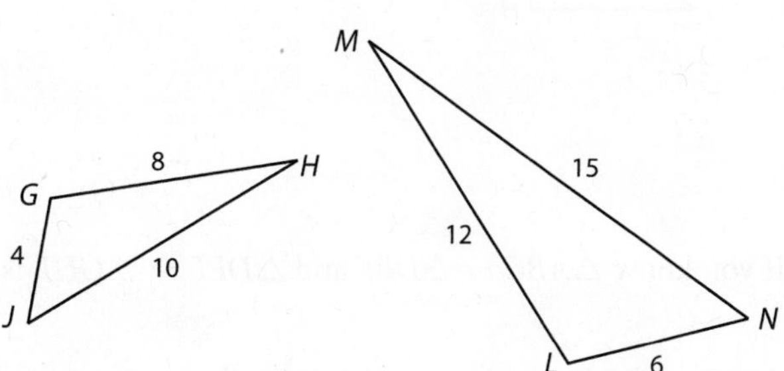

You are given three pairs of corresponding side lengths and zero congruent corresponding angles, so try using the SSS Triangle Similarity Theorem.

Check that the ratios of corresponding sides are equal.

$\frac{LM}{GH} = \frac{12}{8} = \frac{3}{2}$ $\qquad \frac{MN}{HJ} = \frac{15}{10} = \frac{3}{2}$ $\qquad \frac{GJ}{LN} = \frac{6}{4} = \frac{3}{2}$

Therefore $\triangle$ GHJ $\sim \triangle$ LMN by the SSS Triangle Similarity Theorem.

Since you are given all three pairs of sides, you don't need to check for congruent angles.

Reflect

8. Are all isosceles right triangles similar? Explain why or why not.

9. Why isn't Angle-Side-Angle (ASA) used to prove two triangles similar?

Your Turn

If possible, determine whether the given triangles are similar. Justify your answer.

10.

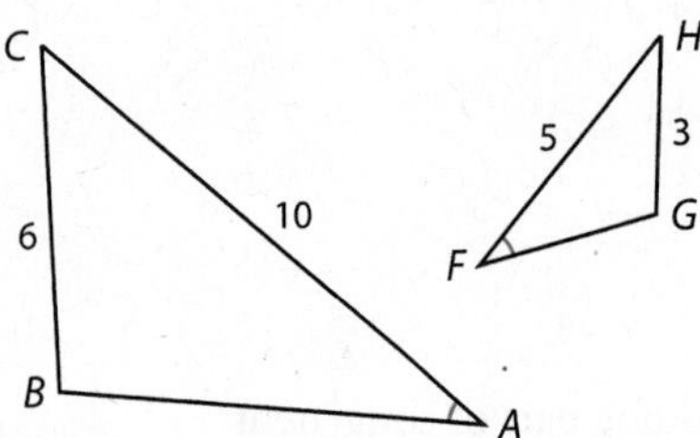

11.

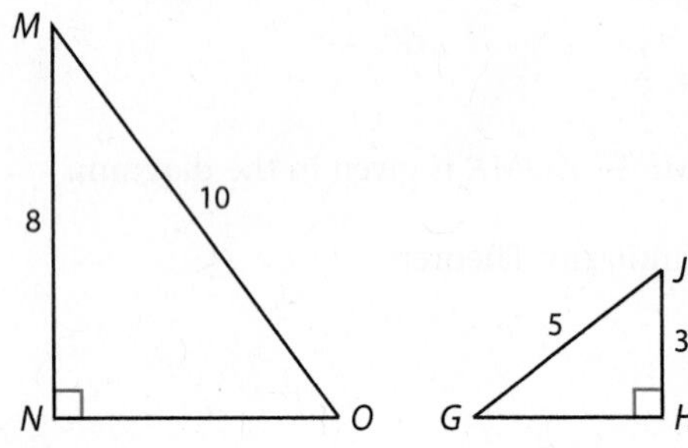

Elaborate

12. Is triangle similarity transitive? If you know $\triangle ABC \sim \triangle DEF$ and $\triangle DEF \sim \triangle GHJ$, is $\triangle ABC \sim \triangle GHJ$? Explain.

13. The AA Similarity Theorem applies to triangles. Is there an AAA Similarity Theorem for quadrilaterals? Use your geometry software to test your conjecture or create a counterexample.

14. **Essential Question Check-In** How can you prove triangles are similar?

Evaluate: Homework and Practice

- Online Homework
- Hints and Help
- Extra Practice

Show that the triangles are similar by measuring the lengths of their sides and comparing the ratios of the corresponding sides.

1.

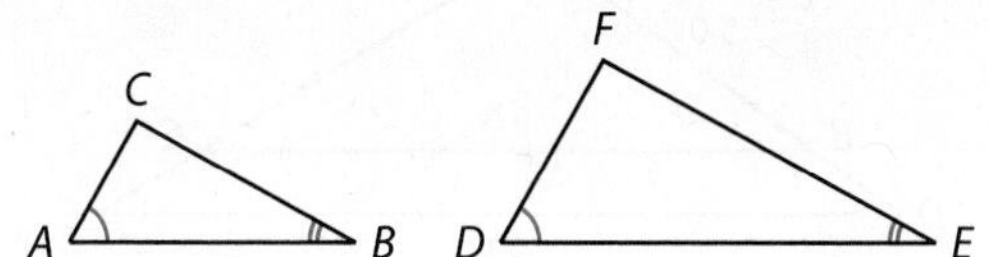

$\frac{DE}{AB} = \frac{?}{?} = ?$

$\frac{DF}{AC} = \frac{?}{?} = ?$

$\frac{EF}{BC} = \frac{?}{?} = ?$

2.

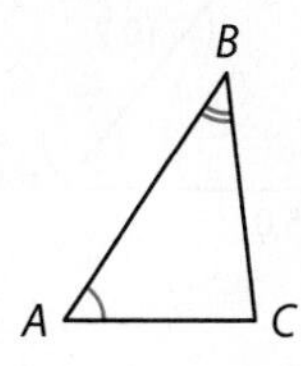

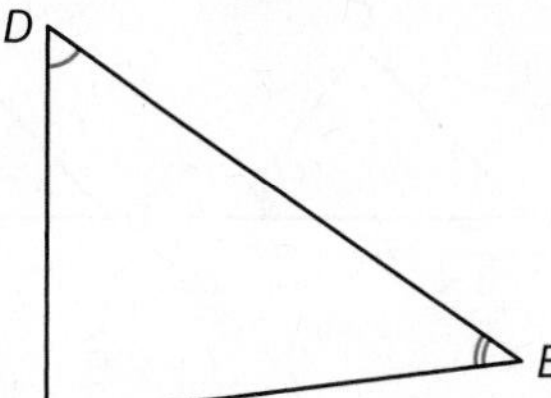

$\frac{AB}{DE} = \frac{?}{?} = ?$

$\frac{AC}{DF} = \frac{?}{?} = ?$

$\frac{BC}{EF} = \frac{?}{?} = ?$

Determine whether the two triangles are similar. If they are similar, write the similarity statement.

3.

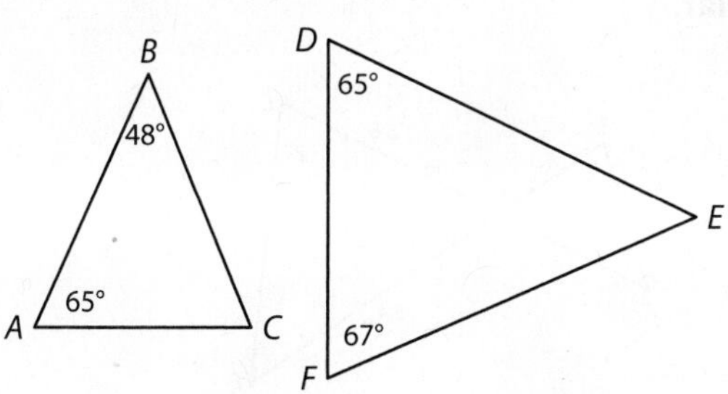

4.

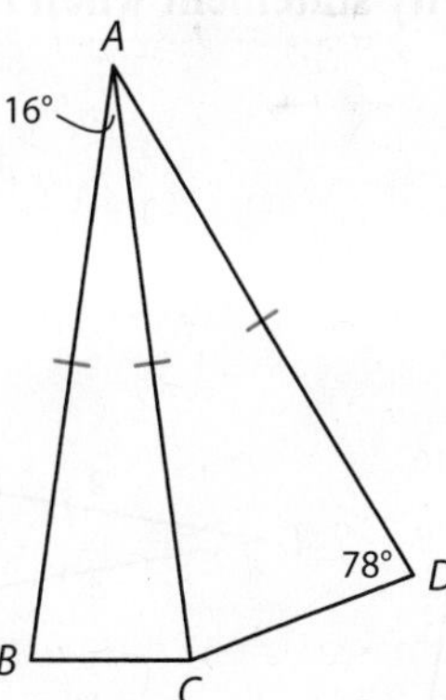

Determine whether the two triangles are similar. If they are similar, write the similarity statement.

5.

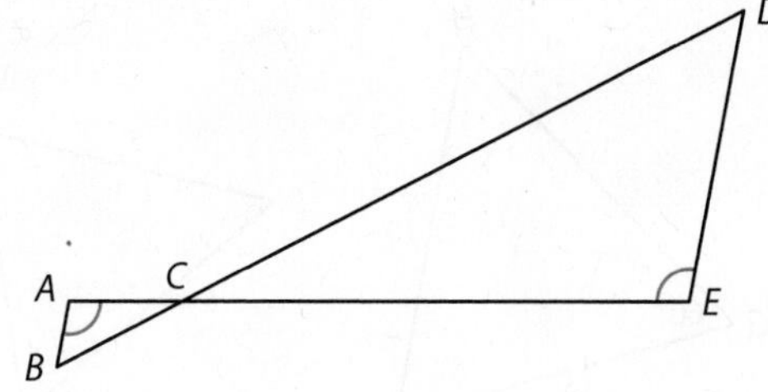

6.

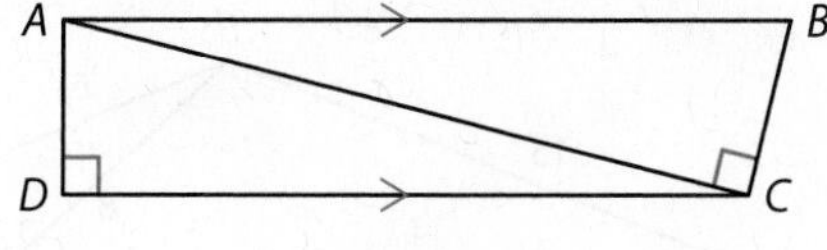

Explain how you know whether the triangles are similar. If possible, find the indicated length.

7. AC

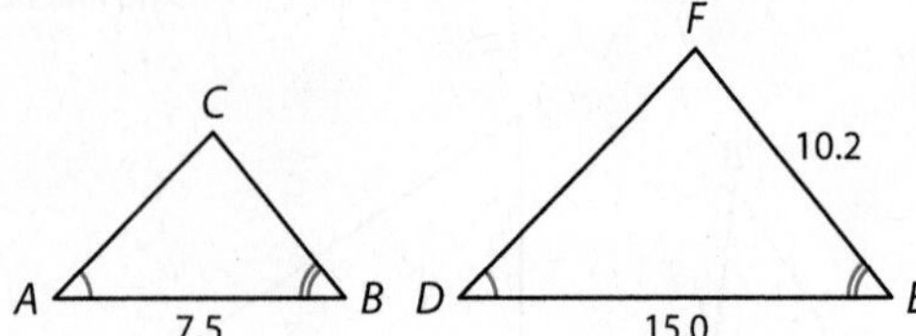

8. AD

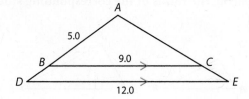

9. QR

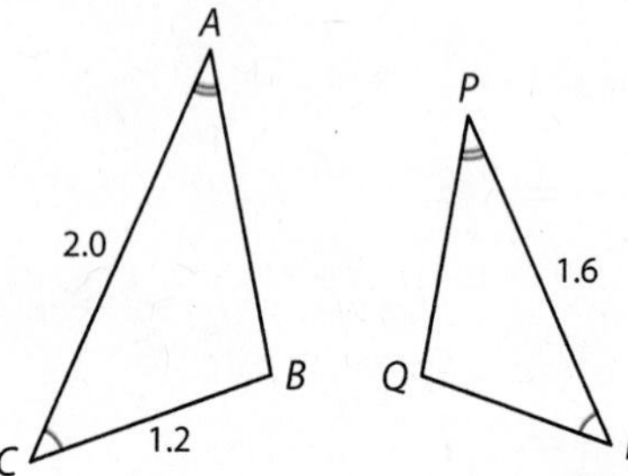

10. Find BD.

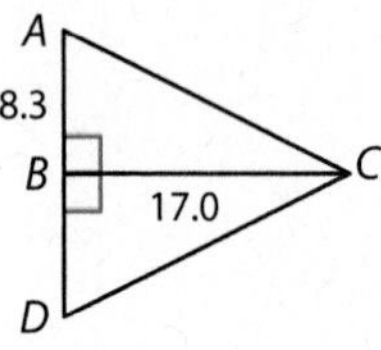

Show whether or not each pair of triangles are similar, if possible. Justify your answer, and write a similarity statement when the triangles are similar.

11.

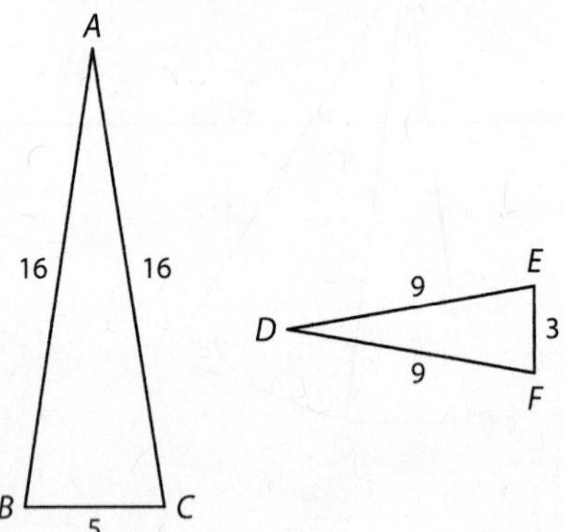

12.

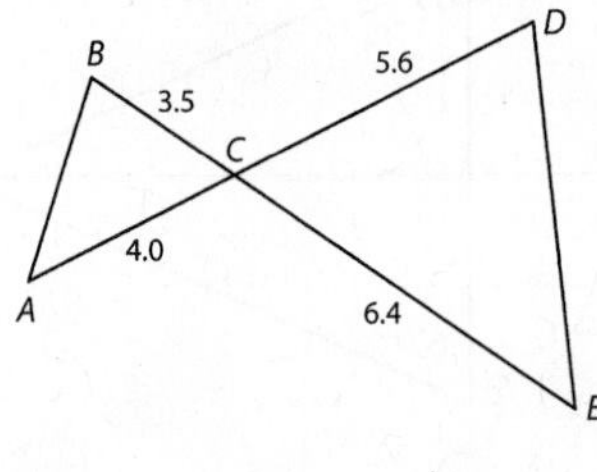

13.

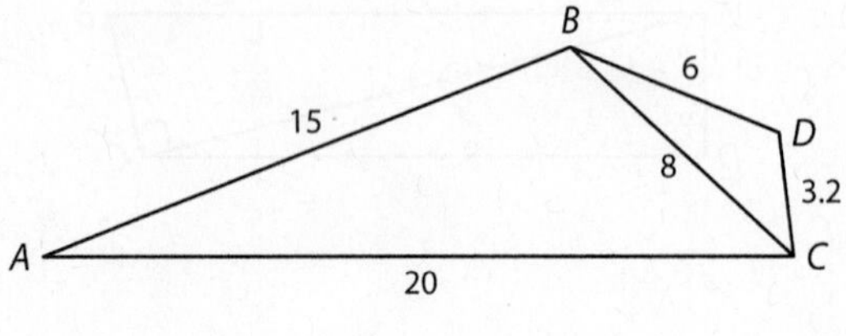

14.

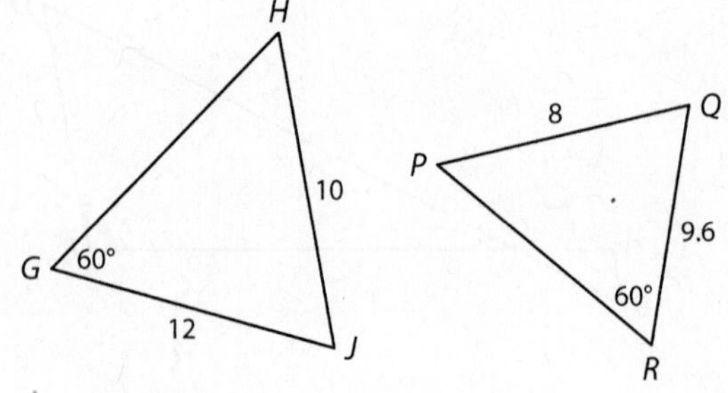

15. Explain the Error A student analyzes the two triangles shown below. Explain the error that the student makes.

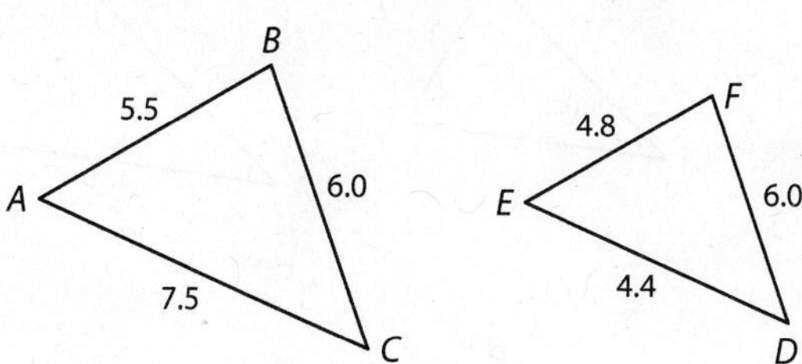

$\frac{AB}{EF} = \frac{5.5}{4.8} = 1.15$, and $\frac{BC}{DF} = \frac{6}{6} = 1$

Because the two ratios are not equal, the two triangles are not similar.

16. Algebra Find all possible values of x for which these two triangles are similar.

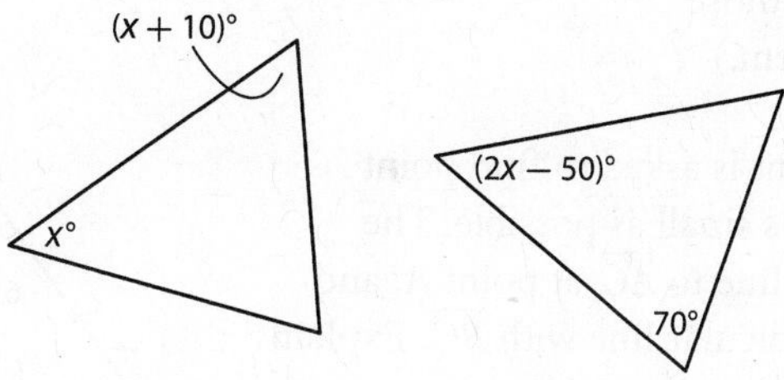

17. Multi-Step Identify two similar triangles in the figure, and explain why they are similar. Then find AB.

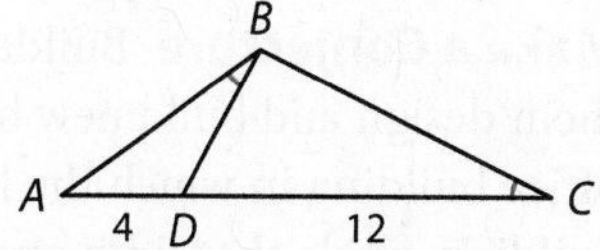

18. The picture shows a person taking a pinhole photograph of himself. Light entering the opening reflects his image on the wall, forming similar triangles. What is the height of the image to the nearest inch?

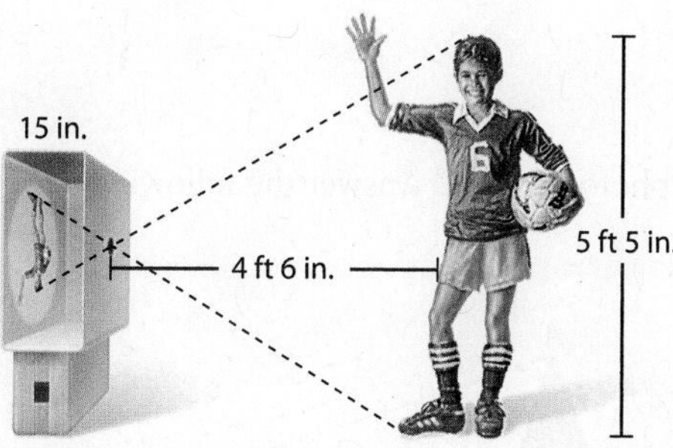

H.O.T. Focus on Higher Order Thinking

19. Analyze Relationships Prove the SAS Triangle Similarity Theorem.

Given: $\frac{XY}{AB} = \frac{XZ}{AC}$ and $\angle A \cong \angle X$.

Prove: $\triangle ABC \sim \triangle XYZ$

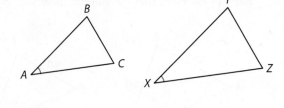

20. Analyze Relationships Prove the SSS Triangle Similarity Theorem.

Given: $\frac{XY}{AB} = \frac{XZ}{AC} = \frac{YZ}{BC}$

Prove: $\triangle ABC \sim \triangle XYZ$

(Hint: The main steps of the proof are similar to those of the proof of the AA Triangle Similarity Theorem.)

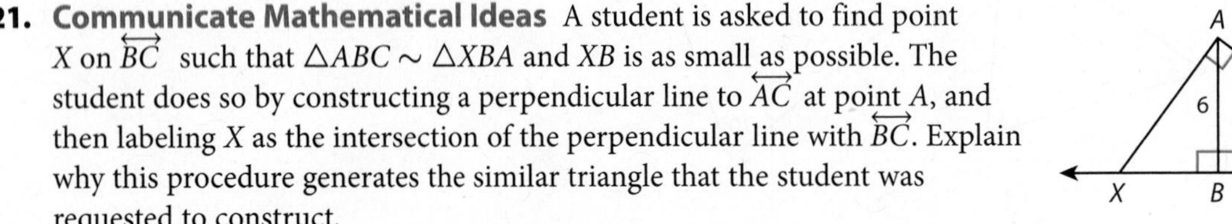

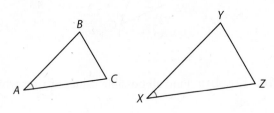

21. Communicate Mathematical Ideas A student is asked to find point X on $\overleftrightarrow{BC}$ such that $\triangle ABC \sim \triangle XBA$ and XB is as small as possible. The student does so by constructing a perpendicular line to $\overleftrightarrow{AC}$ at point A, and then labeling X as the intersection of the perpendicular line with $\overleftrightarrow{BC}$. Explain why this procedure generates the similar triangle that the student was requested to construct.

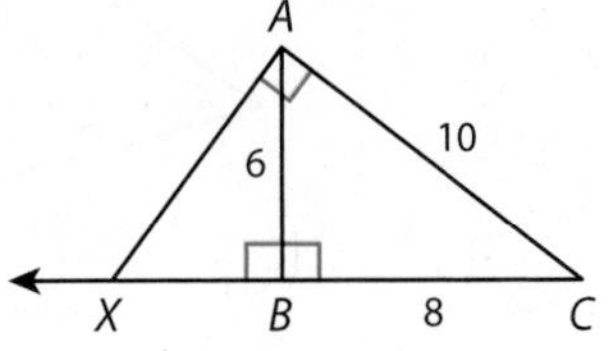

22. Make a Conjecture Builders and architects use scale models to help them design and build new buildings. An architecture student builds a model of an office building in which the height of the model is $\frac{1}{400}$ of the height of the actual building, while the width and length of the model are each $\frac{1}{200}$ of the corresponding dimensions of the actual building. The model includes several triangles. Describe how a triangle in this model could be similar to the corresponding triangle in the actual building, then describe how a triangle in this model might not be similar to the corresponding triangle in the actual building. Use a similarity theorem to support each answer.

Lesson Performance Task

The figure shows a camera obscura and the object being "photographed." Answer the following questions about the figure:

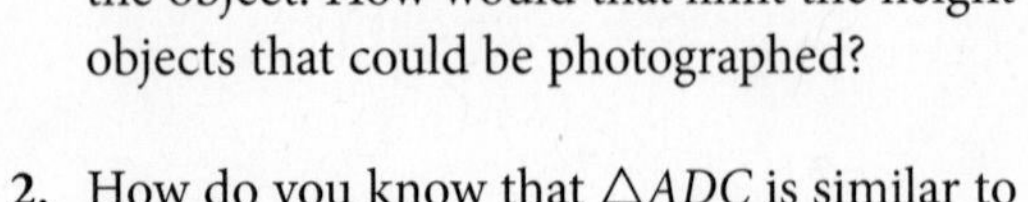

1. Explain how the image of the object would be affected if the camera were moved closer to the object. How would that limit the height of objects that could be photographed?

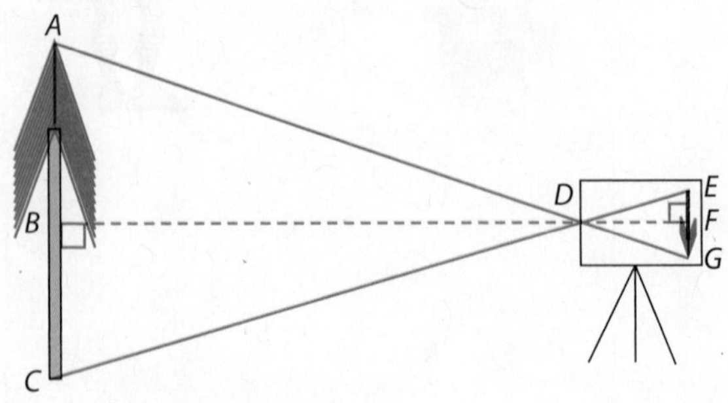

2. How do you know that $\triangle ADC$ is similar to $\triangle GDE$?

3. Write a proportion you could use to find the height of the pine tree.

4. $DF = 12$ in., $EG = 8$ in., $BD = 96$ ft. How tall is the pine tree?

STUDY GUIDE REVIEW

Similarity and Transformations

MODULE 11

Essential Question: How can you use similarity and transformations to solve real-world problems?

Key Vocabulary

center of dilation *(centro de dilatación)*

dilation *(dilatación)*

scale factor *(factor de escala)*

Side-Side-Side Similarity *(Similitud Lado -Lado -Lado)*

Side-Angle-Side Similarity *(Similitud Lado-Ángulo-Lado)*

similar *(semejantes)*

similarity transformation *(transformación de semejanza)*

KEY EXAMPLE *(Lesson 11.1)*

Determine the center of dilation and the scale factor of the dilation.

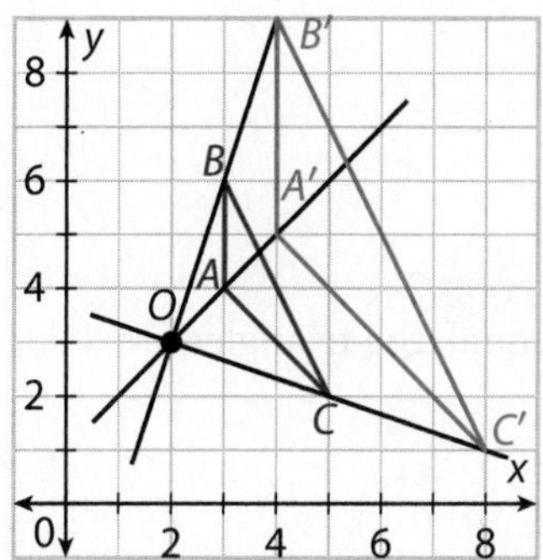

Draw a line through A and A'. Draw a line through B and B'. Draw a line through C and C'.

The three lines intersect at point $O(2, 3)$.

Find the distance from point O to points A and A'.

$d_A = \sqrt{(2-3)^2 + (3-4)^2} = \sqrt{2}$ — Find the distance to point ***A***.

$d_{A'} = \sqrt{(2-4)^2 + (3-5)^2} = 2\sqrt{2}$ — Find the distance to point ***A***′.

The distance from point O to point A' is twice the distance from point O to point A. The scale factor of dilation is 2 to 1.

KEY EXAMPLE *(Lesson 11.3)*

$\triangle ABCD$ maps to $\triangle EFGH$ by a similarity transformation. Write a proportion that contains $\overline{BC}$ and $\overline{EH}$. Then list any angles that are congruent to $\angle D$ or $\angle E$.

Corresponding sides of similar figures are proportional.

$\overline{BC} \cong \overline{FG}$ and $\overline{EH} \cong \overline{AD}$, so $\frac{BC}{FG} = \frac{AD}{EH}$.

Corresponding angles of similar figures are congruent.

$\angle D \cong \angle H$ and $\angle E \cong \angle A$.

KEY EXAMPLE (Lesson 11.4)

Determine whether $\triangle ABC$ and $\triangle DEF$ are similar. If so, justify by SSS Similarity or SAS Similarity.

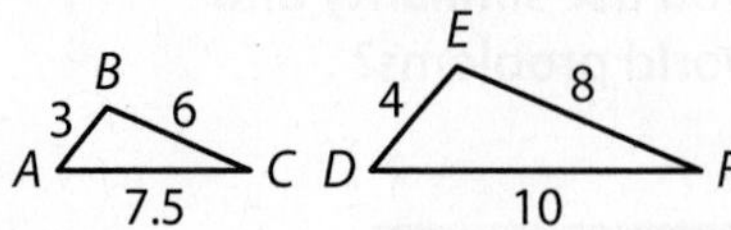

Check that the ratios of the lengths of corresponding sides are equal.

$\frac{3}{4}$

$\frac{6}{8} = \frac{3}{4}$

$\frac{7.5}{10} = \frac{3}{4}$

Since all the ratios of the lengths of corresponding sides are equal, the triangles are similar by SSS Similarity.

EXERCISES

Determine the following for the dilation. (Lesson 11.1)

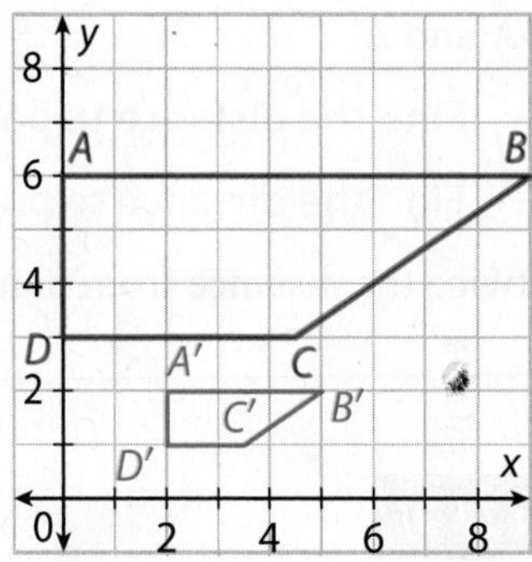

1. center ___?___

2. scale factor ___?___

Determine whether the two figures are similar using similarity transformations.
(Lesson 11.2)

3. $\triangle ABC$ to $\triangle DEF$ ______________

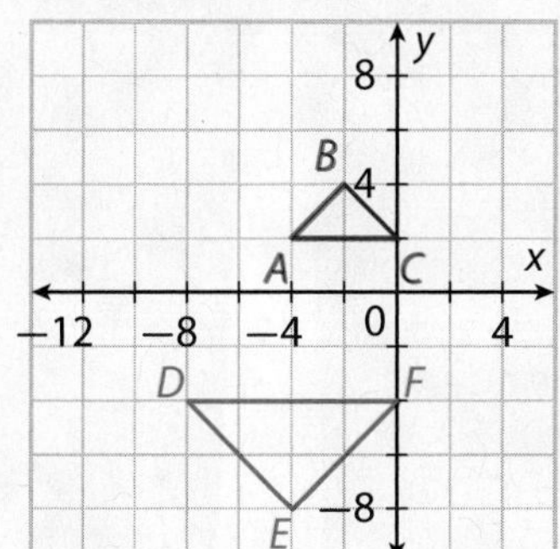

4. $\triangle ABCD$ to $\triangle EFGH$ ______________

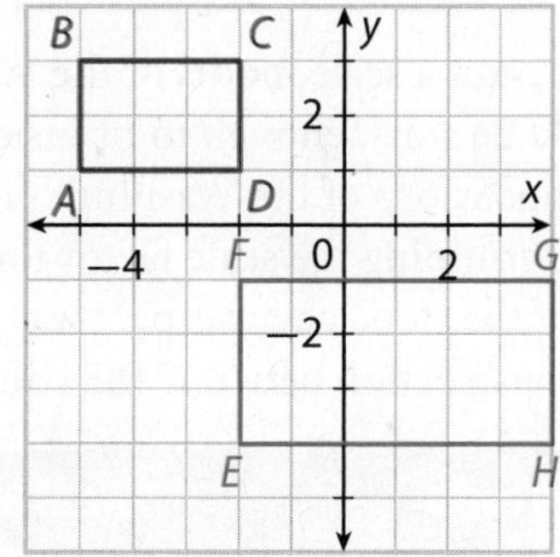

$\triangle ABC$ maps to $\triangle DEF$ by a similarity transformation. *(Lesson 11.3)*

5. Write a proportion that contains AB and EF.

6. Write a proportion that contains BC and DF.

7. List any angles that are congruent to $\angle A$ or $\angle E$.

Determine whether $\triangle ABC$ and $\triangle DEF$ are similar. If so, justify by SSS or *SAS*.
(Lesson 11.4)

8.

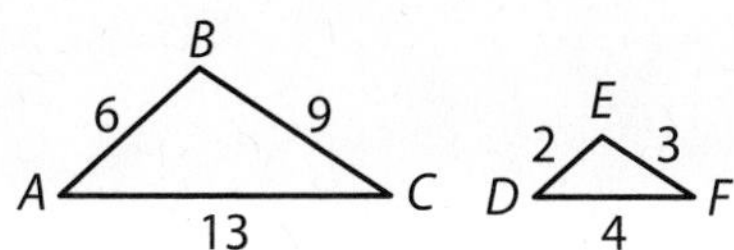

9.

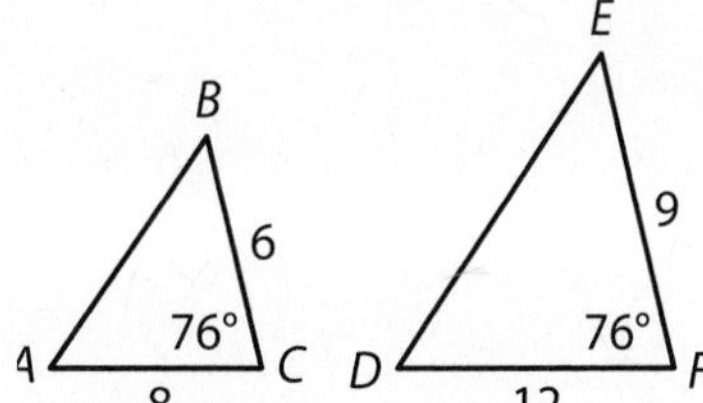

MODULE PERFORMANCE TASK

Designing a Model of the Washington Monument

Your challenge is to design a scale model of the Washington Monument that would be small enough to fit inside your classroom. Here are some key dimensions of the Washington Monument for you to consider in determining the scale factor for your model. (Note that the color of the stone changes part way up the monument because of a halt in construction between 1854 and 1877.)

Key Dimension	Measurement
Total height	555 ft 5 in.
Height to top of trapezoidal side	500 ft
Width at base	55 ft 1 in.
Width at top of trapezoidal side	34 ft 5 in.
Height at which stone color changes	151 ft

What scale factor will you use for your model? What are the key dimensions of your model?

Begin by making some notes in the space below about your strategy for designing the model. Then complete the task. Present your plan using diagrams, words, and/or numbers.

Ready to Go On?

11.1–11.4 Similarity and Transformations

- Online Homework
- Hints and Help
- Extra Practice

Answer each problem about the image. *(Lesson 11.1)*

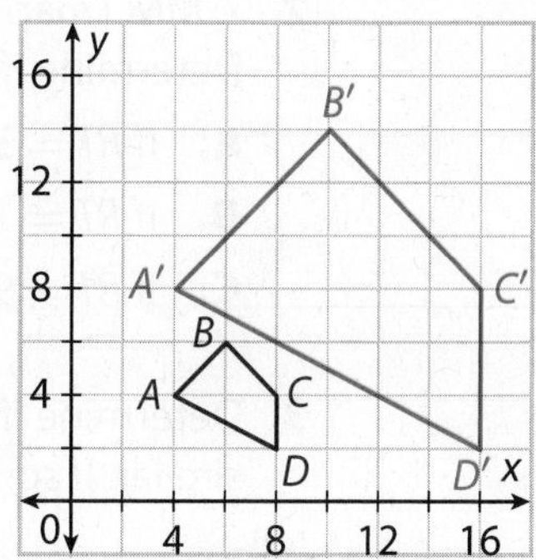

1. Are the two shapes similar?

2. Find the scale factor k.

3. Find the center of dilation.

4. Compare k to the ratio $\frac{\text{area } \triangle A'D'C'}{\text{area } \triangle ADC}$.

Determine which of the following transformations are dilations. *(Lesson 11.1)*

5. $(x, y) \rightarrow (4x, 4y)$

6. $(x, y) \rightarrow (-x, 3y)$

7. $(x, y) \rightarrow (x - 2, y - 2)$

8. $(x, y) \rightarrow \left(\frac{1}{3}x, \frac{1}{3}y\right)$

Find the missing length. *(Lesson 11.3)*

9. $\triangle XYZ$ maps to $\triangle MNO$ with the transformation $(x, y) \rightarrow (7x, 7y)$. If $XY = 3$, what is the length of MN?

Find the appropriate statements about the triangles. *(Lesson 11.4)*

10. $\triangle ABC$ is similar to $\triangle RTS$. Write a proportion that contains AC and RT. Also write the angle congruence statements that must be true.

ESSENTIAL QUESTION

11. How can you determine whether a shape is similar to another shape?

MODULE 11
MIXED REVIEW

Assessment Readiness

1. Consider each transformation. Does the transformation preserve distance? Write Yes or No for A–C.
   A. Dilations
   B. Reflections
   C. Rotations

2. $\triangle MNO$ maps to $\triangle RST$ with the transformation $(x, y) \rightarrow \left(\frac{1}{3}x, \frac{1}{3}y\right)$. Determine if each statement is True or False.
   A. If $RT = 3$, $MO = 9$.
   B. If $RT = 12$, $MO = 4$.
   C. If $RT = 9$, $MO = 27$.

3. Determine if the following pair of triangles are similar. If so, explain how. Note that $\overline{AC} \parallel \overline{BD}$.

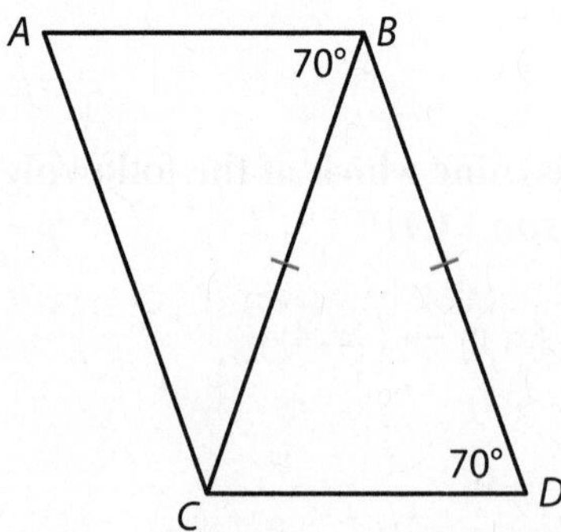

4. If $\triangle ABC$ is similar to $\triangle XYZ$ and $\triangle YZX$, what special type of triangle is $\triangle ABC$? Justify your reasoning.

Using Similar Triangles

MODULE 12

Essential Question: How can you use similar triangles to solve real-world problems?

REAL WORLD VIDEO
Check out how properties of similar triangles can be used to determine real-world areas of geographic regions like the Bermuda Triangle.

MODULE PERFORMANCE TASK PREVIEW

How Large Is the Bermuda Triangle?

In this module, you will be asked to determine the area of the Bermuda Triangle from a map. How can indirect measurement and the properties of similar triangles help you find the answer? Let's get started on solving this "mystery" of the Bermuda Triangle!

Are YOU Ready?

Complete these exercises to review skills you will need for this module.

Personal Math Trainer

- Online Homework
- Hints and Help
- Extra Practice

Scale Factor and Scale Drawings

Example 1 Determine the length of the side $\overline{A'B'}$ given $AB = 4$, $BC = 3$, and $B'C' = 6$.

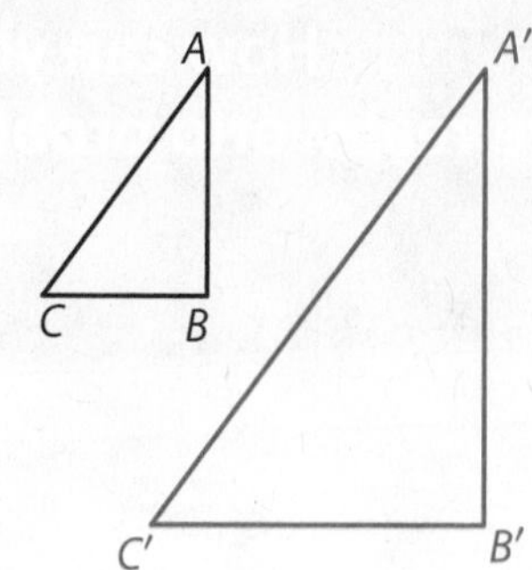

The image of $\triangle ABC$ is created as a result of a scale drawing, so the transformation is a dilation.

$2BC = B'C'$, so $2AB = A'B'$.

$A'B' = 2(4) = 8$

Give the side length in $\triangle RST$.

1. ST, given $RT = 5$, $R'T' = 15$, and $S'T' = 18$

Similar Figures

Example 2 The figures $PQRS$ and $KLMN$ are similar. Determine the angle in figure $KLMN$ that is congruent to $\angle Q$ and find its measure if $m\angle Q = 45°$.

$\angle Q \cong \angle L$ — Corresponding angles of similar figures are congruent.

$m\angle Q = m\angle L = 45°$ — Definition of congruency of angle.

Give each angle measure.

2. $m\angle A$, given $\triangle ABC \cong \triangle DEF$ and $m\angle D = 67°$

3. $m\angle E$, given $\triangle PQR \cong \triangle DEF$, $m\angle R = 13°$, and $m\angle D = 67°$

The Pythagorean Theorem

Example 3 A right triangle $\triangle ABC$ has side lengths $AB = 3$ and $BC = 4$. Find the length of the hypotenuse $\overline{AC}$.

$\triangle ABC$ is a right triangle, so the Pythagorean Theorem can be used.

$AC = \sqrt{(AB)^2 + (BC)^2}$ — Write the Pythagorean Theorem.

$AC = \sqrt{3^2 + 4^2} = \sqrt{9 + 16}$ — Substitute and simplify.

$AC = 5$ — Simplify.

Find the side length for each right triangle.

4. DE, given $DF = 5$, $EF = 12$, and $\overline{DE}$ is the hypotenuse

5. BC, given $AB = 15$, $AC = 17$, and $\overline{AC}$ is the hypotenuse

12.1 Triangle Proportionality Theorem

Resource Locker

Essential Question: When a line parallel to one side of a triangle intersects the other two sides, how does it divide those sides?

Explore Constructing Similar Triangles

In the following activity you will see one way to construct a triangle similar to a given triangle.

(A) Draw a triangle on a separate sheet of paper. Label it ABC as shown.

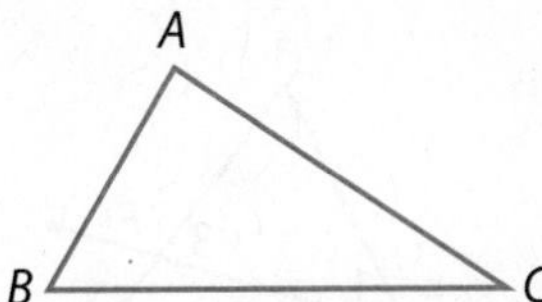

(B) Select a point on $\overline{AB}$. Label it E.

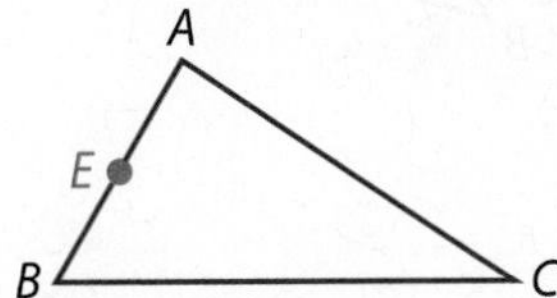

(C) Construct an angle with vertex E that is congruent to $\angle B$. Label the point where the side of the angle you constructed intersects $\overline{AC}$ as F.

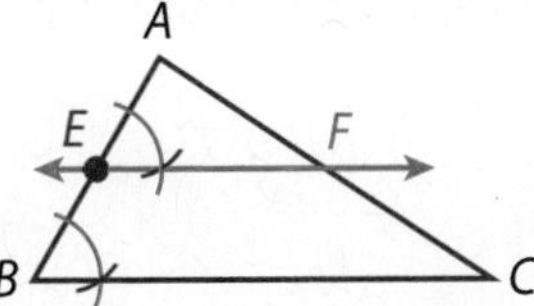

(D) Why are $\overleftrightarrow{EF}$ and $\overline{BC}$ parallel?

(E) Use a ruler to measure $\overline{AE}$, $\overline{EB}$, $\overline{AF}$, and $\overline{FC}$. Then compare the ratios $\frac{AE}{EB}$ and $\frac{AF}{FC}$.

Reflect

1. **Discussion** How can you show that $\triangle AEF \sim \triangle ABC$? Explain.
2. What do you know about the ratios $\frac{AE}{AB}$ and $\frac{AF}{AC}$? Explain.
3. **Make a Conjecture** Use your answer to Step E to make a conjecture about the line segments produced when a line parallel to one side of a triangle intersects the other two sides.

Explain 1 Proving the Triangle Proportionality Theorem

As you saw in the Explore, when a line parallel to one side of a triangle intersects the other two sides of the triangle, the lengths of the segments are proportional.

Triangle Proportionality Theorem

Theorem	Hypothesis	Conclusion
If a line parallel to a side of a triangle intersects the other two sides, then it divides those sides proportionally.	A, E, F, B, C $\overline{EF} \parallel \overline{BC}$	$\frac{AE}{EB} = \frac{AF}{FC}$

Example 1 Prove the Triangle Proportionality Theorem

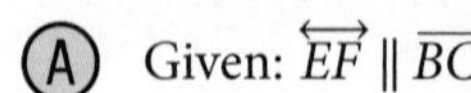

Ⓐ Given: $\overleftrightarrow{EF} \parallel \overline{BC}$

Prove: $\frac{AE}{EB} = \frac{AF}{FC}$

Step 1 Show that $\triangle AEF \sim \triangle ABC$.

Because $\overleftrightarrow{EF} \parallel \overline{BC}$, you can conclude that $\angle 1 \cong \angle 2$ and $\angle 3 \cong \angle 4$ by the Corresponding Angles Theorem.

So, $\triangle AEF \sim \triangle ABC$ by the AA Similarity Theorem.

Step 2 Use the fact that corresponding sides of similar triangles are proportional to prove that $\frac{AE}{EB} = \frac{AF}{FC}$.

$\frac{AB}{AE} = \frac{AC}{AF}$	Corresponding sides are proportional.
$\frac{AE + EB}{AE} = \frac{AF + FC}{AF}$	Segment Addition Postulate
$1 + \frac{EB}{AB} = 1 + \frac{FC}{AF}$	Use the property that $\frac{a+b}{c} = \frac{a}{c} + \frac{b}{c}$.
$\frac{EB}{AE} = \frac{FC}{AF}$	Subtract 1 from both sides.
$\frac{AE}{EB} = \frac{AF}{FC}$	Take the reciprocal of both sides.

Reflect

4. Explain how you conclude that $\triangle AEF \sim \triangle ABC$ without using $\angle 3$ and $\angle 4$.

Explain 2 Applying the Triangle Proportionality Theorem

Example 2 **Find the length of each segment.**

(A) $\overline{CY}$

It is given that $\overline{XY} \parallel \overline{BC}$ so $\frac{AX}{XB} = \frac{AY}{YC}$ by the Triangle Proportionality Theorem.

Substitute 9 for AX, 4 for XB, and 10 for AY.

Then solve for CY.

$$\frac{9}{4} = \frac{10}{CY}$$

Take the reciprocal of both sides.

$$\frac{4}{9} = \frac{CY}{10}$$

Next, multiply both sides by 10.

$$10\left(\frac{4}{9}\right) = \left(\frac{CY}{10}\right)10 \quad \rightarrow \quad \frac{40}{9} = CY, \text{ or } 4\frac{4}{9} = CY$$

 Find PN.

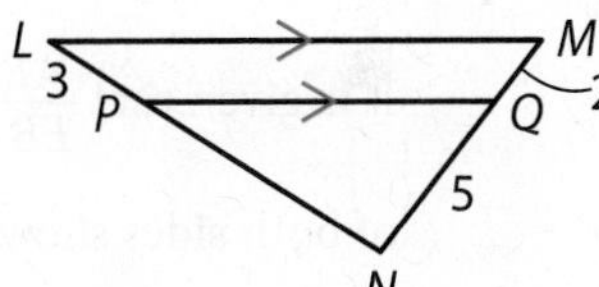

It is given that $\overline{PQ} \parallel \overline{LM}$, so $\frac{NQ}{QM} = \frac{NP}{PL}$ by the Triangle Proportionality Theorem.

Substitute 5 for NQ, 2 for QM, and 3 for PL.

$$\frac{5}{2} = \frac{NP}{3}$$

Multiply both sides by 3: $3\left(\frac{5}{2}\right) = 3\left(\frac{NP}{3}\right) \rightarrow \frac{15}{2} \text{ or } 7\frac{1}{2} = NP$

Your Turn

Find the length of each segment.

5. $\overline{DG}$

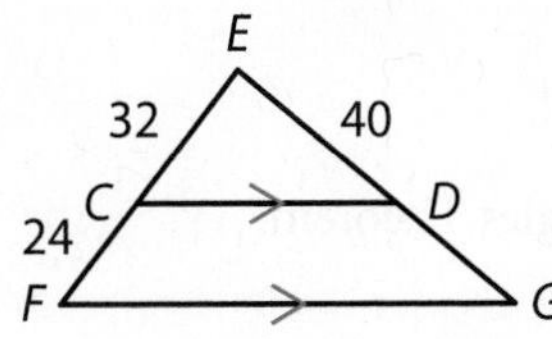

6. $\overline{RN}$

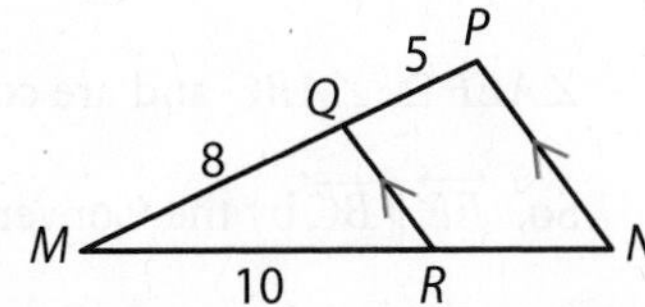

Explain 3 Proving the Converse of the Triangle Proportionality Theorem

The converse of the Triangle Proportionality Theorem is also true.

Converse of the Triangle Proportionality Theorem		
Theorem	**Hypothesis**	**Conclusion**
If a line divides two sides of a triangle proportionally, then it is parallel to the third side.	$\frac{AE}{EB} = \frac{AF}{FC}$	$\overleftrightarrow{EF} \parallel \overline{BC}$

Example 3 Prove the Converse of the Triangle Proportionality Theorem

Given: $\frac{AE}{EB} = \frac{AF}{FC}$

Prove: $\overleftrightarrow{EF} \parallel \overline{BC}$

Step 1 Show that $\triangle AEF \sim \triangle ABC$.

It is given that $\frac{AE}{EB} = \frac{AF}{FC}$, and taking the reciprocal of both sides shows that $\frac{EB}{AE} = \frac{FC}{AF}$. Now add 1 to both sides by adding $\frac{AE}{AE}$ to the left side and $\frac{AF}{AF}$ to the right side.

This gives $\frac{AE}{AE} + \frac{EB}{AE} = \frac{AF}{AF} + \frac{FC}{AF}$.

Adding and using the Segment Addition Postulate gives $\frac{AB}{AE} = \frac{AC}{AF}$.

Since $\angle A \cong \angle A$, $\triangle AEF \sim \triangle ABC$ by the SAS Similarity Theorem.

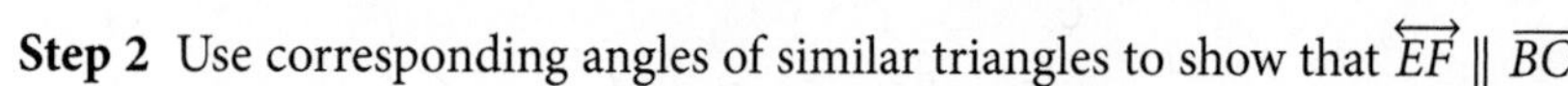

Step 2 Use corresponding angles of similar triangles to show that $\overleftrightarrow{EF} \parallel \overline{BC}$.

$\angle AEF \cong \angle ABC$ and are corresponding angles.

So, $\overleftrightarrow{EF} \parallel \overline{BC}$ by the Converse of the Corresponding Angles Theorem.

Reflect

7. **Critique Reasoning** A student states that $\overline{UV}$ must be parallel to $\overline{ST}$. Do you agree? Why or why not?

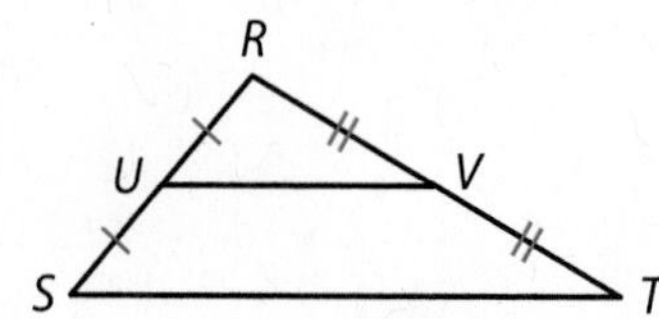

Explain 4 Applying the Converse of the Triangle Proportionality Theorem

You can use the Converse of the Triangle Proportionality Theorem to verify that a line is parallel to a side of a triangle.

Example 4 **Verify that the line segments are parallel.**

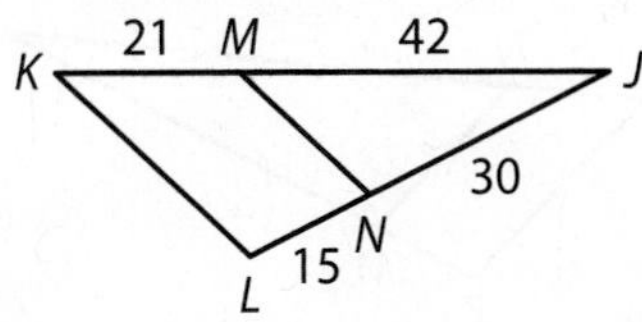

(A) $\overline{MN}$ and $\overline{KL}$

$\frac{JM}{MK} = \frac{42}{21} = 2$ $\frac{JN}{NL} = \frac{30}{15} = 2$

Since $\frac{JM}{MK} = \frac{JN}{NL}$, $\overline{MN} \parallel \overline{KL}$ by the Converse of the Triangle Proportionality Theorem.

(B) $\overline{DE}$ and $\overline{AB}$ (Given that $AC = 36$ cm, and $BC = 27$ cm)

$AD = AC - DC = 36 - 20 = 16$

$BE = BC - EC = 27 - 15 = 12$

$\frac{CD}{DA} = \frac{20}{16} = \frac{5}{4}$ $\frac{CE}{EB} = \frac{15}{12} = \frac{5}{4}$

Since $\frac{CD}{DA} = \frac{CE}{EB}$, $\overline{DE} \parallel \overline{AB}$ by the Converse of the Triangle Proportionality Theorem.

Reflect

8. **Communicate Mathematical Ideas** In $\triangle ABC$, in the example, what is the value of $\frac{AB}{DE}$? Explain how you know.

Your Turn

9. Verify that $\overline{TU}$ and $\overline{RS}$ are parallel.

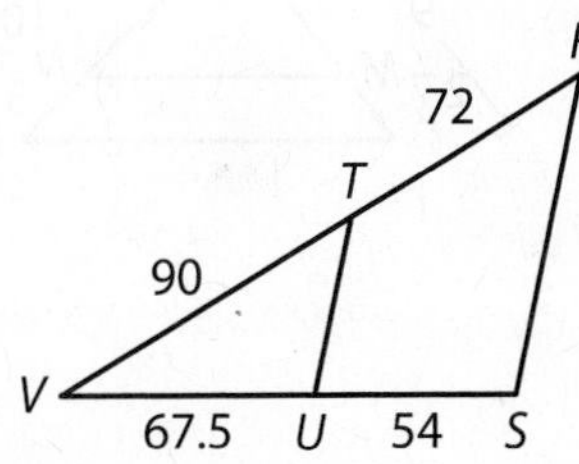

Elaborate

10. In $\triangle ABC$, $\overline{XY} \parallel \overline{BC}$. Use what you know about similarity and proportionality to identify as many different proportions as possible.

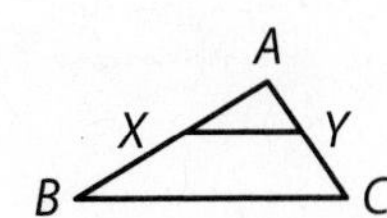

11. **Discussion** What theorems, properties, or strategies are common to the proof of the Triangle Proportionality Theorem and the proof of Converse of the Triangle Proportionality Theorem?

12. **Essential Question Check-In** Suppose a line parallel to side $\overline{BC}$ of $\triangle ABC$ intersects sides $\overline{AB}$ and $\overline{AC}$ at points X and Y, respectively, and $\frac{AX}{XB} = 1$. What do you know about X and Y? Explain.

Evaluate: Homework and Practice

- Online Homework
- Hints and Help
- Extra Practice

1. Copy the triangle ABC that you drew for the Explore activity. Construct a line $\overleftrightarrow{FG}$ parallel to $\overline{AB}$ using the same method you used in the Explore activity.

2. $\overline{ZY} \| \overleftrightarrow{MN}$. Write a paragraph proof to show that $\frac{XM}{MZ} = \frac{XN}{NY}$.

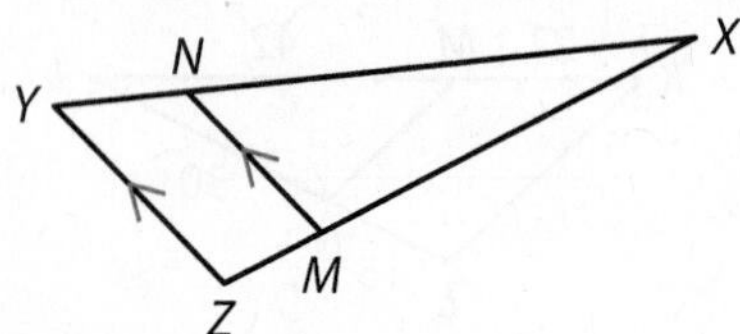

Find the length of each segment.

3. $\overline{KL}$

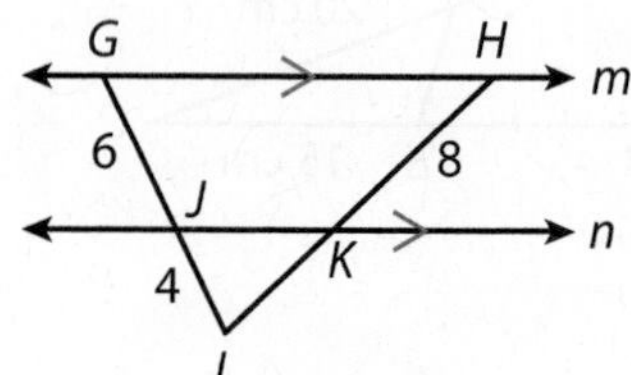

4. $\overline{XZ}$

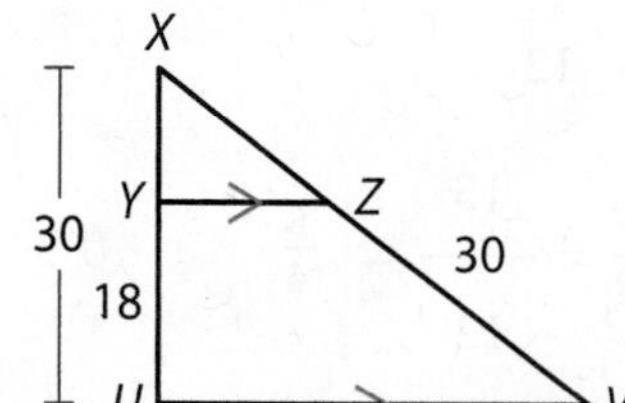

5. $\overline{VM}$

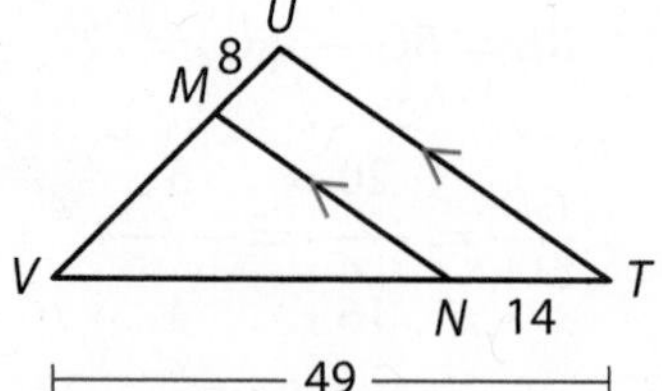

Verify that the given segments are parallel.

6. $\overline{AB}$ and $\overline{CD}$

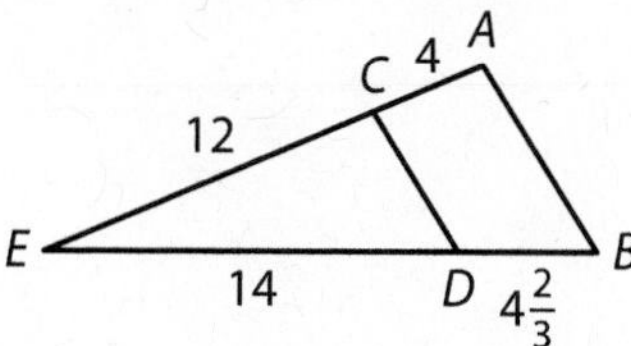

7. $\overline{MN}$ and $\overline{QR}$

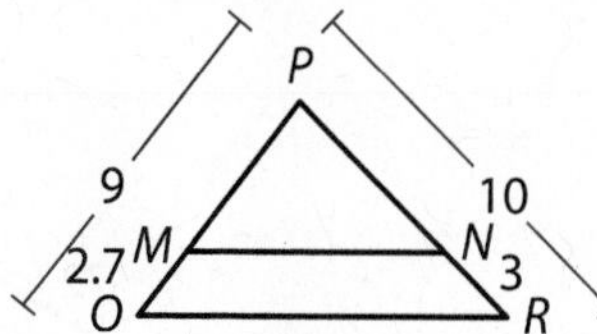

8. $\overline{WX}$ and $\overline{DE}$

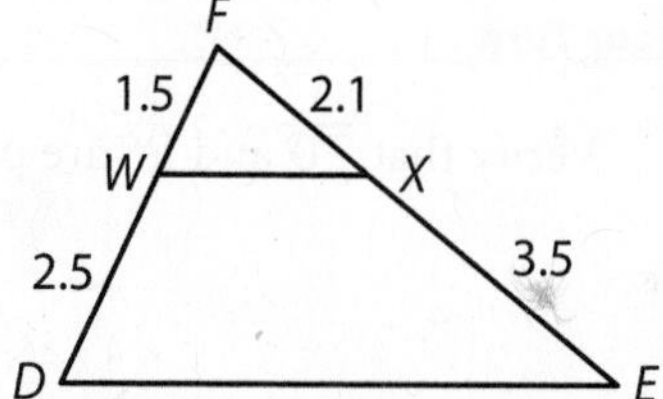

9. Use the Converse of the Triangle Proportionality Theorem to identify parallel lines in the figure.

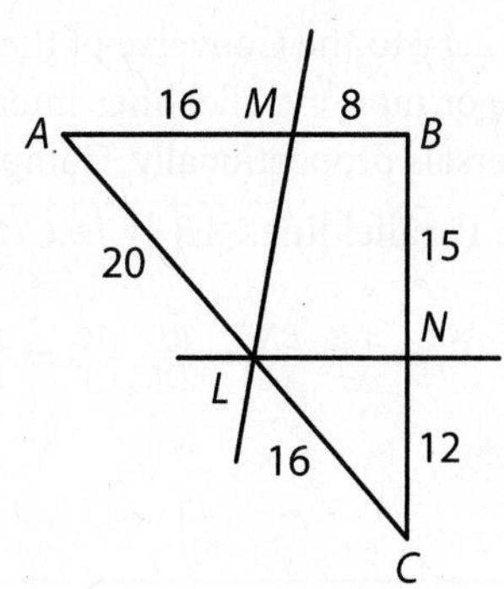

10. On the map, 1st Street and 2nd Street are parallel. What is the distance from City Hall to 2nd Street along Cedar Road?

11. On the map, 5th Avenue, 6th Avenue, and 7th Avenue are parallel. What is the length of Main Street between 5th Avenue and 6th Avenue?

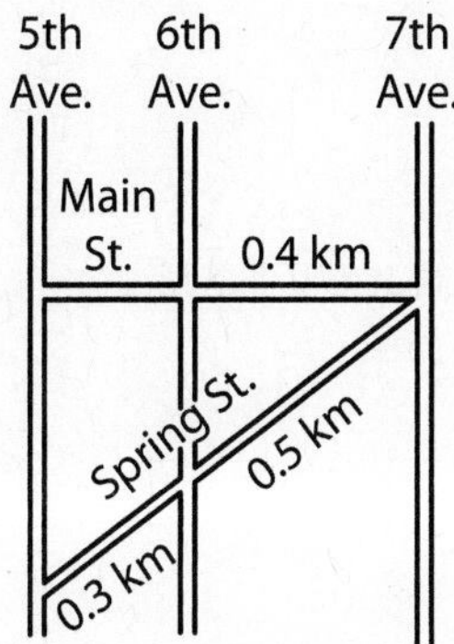

12. **Multi-Step** The storage unit has horizontal siding that is parallel to the base.

a. Find *LM*.

b. Find *GM*.

c. Find *MN* to the nearest tenth of a foot.

d. **Make a Conjecture** Write the ratios $\frac{LM}{MN}$ and $\frac{HJ}{JK}$ as decimals to the nearest hundredth and compare them. Make a conjecture about the relationship between parallel lines $\overleftrightarrow{LD}$, $\overleftrightarrow{ME}$, and $\overleftrightarrow{NF}$ and transversals $\overleftrightarrow{GN}$ and $\overleftrightarrow{GK}$.

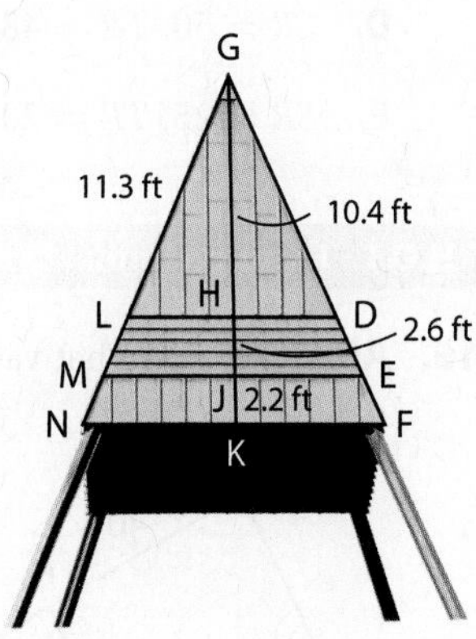

13. A corollary to the Converse of the Triangle Proportionality Theorem states that if three or more parallel lines intersect two transversals, then they divide the transversals proportionally. Complete the proof of the corollary.

Given: Parallel lines $\overleftrightarrow{AB} \parallel \overleftrightarrow{CD}$, $\overleftrightarrow{CD} \parallel \overleftrightarrow{EF}$

Prove: $\frac{AC}{CE} = \frac{BX}{XE}$, $\frac{BX}{XE} = \frac{BD}{DF}$, $\frac{AC}{CE} = \frac{BD}{DF}$

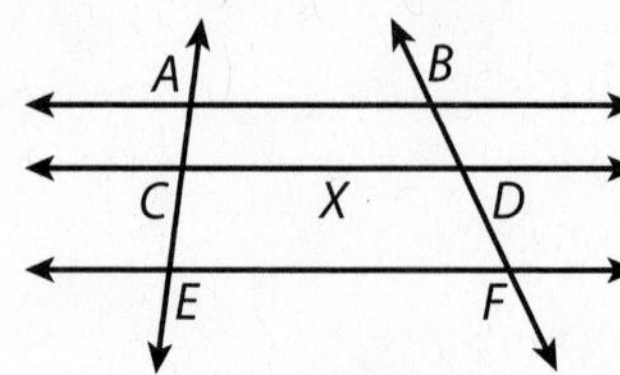

Statements	Reasons
1. $\overleftrightarrow{AB} \parallel \overleftrightarrow{CD}$, $\overleftrightarrow{CD} \parallel \overleftrightarrow{AF}$	1. Given
2. Draw $\overleftrightarrow{EB}$ intersecting $\overleftrightarrow{CD}$ at X.	2. Two points __?__
3. $\frac{AC}{CE} = \frac{BX}{XE}$	3. __?__
4. $\frac{BX}{XE} = \frac{BD}{DF}$	4. __?__
5. $\frac{AC}{CE} = \frac{BD}{DF}$	5. __?__ Property of Equality

14. Suppose that $LM = 24$. Use the Triangle Proportionality Theorem to find PM.

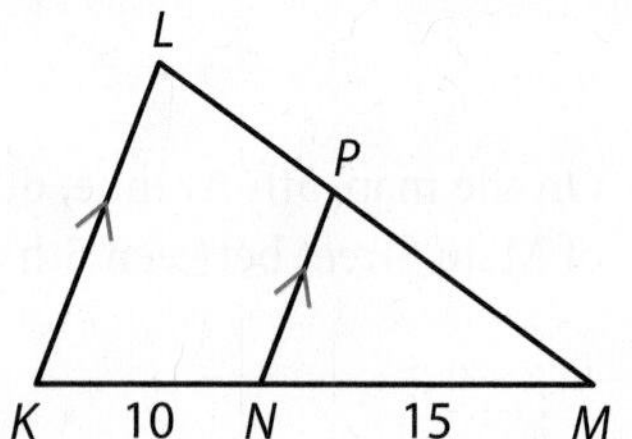

15. Which of the given measures allow you to conclude that $\overline{UV} \parallel \overline{ST}$? Select all that apply.

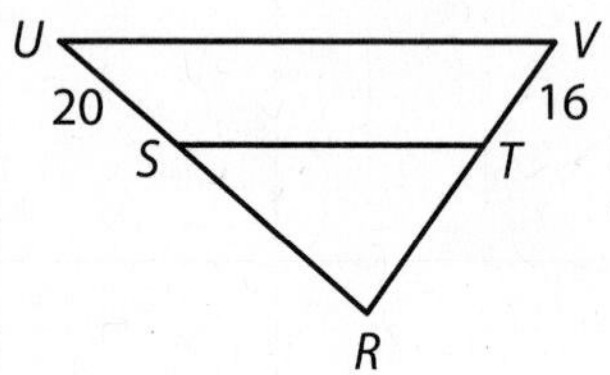

A. $SR = 12$, $TR = 9$

B. $SR = 16$, $TR = 20$

C. $SR = 35$, $TR = 28$

D. $SR = 50$, $TR = 48$

E. $SR = 25$, $TR = 20$

H.O.T. Focus on Higher Order Thinking

16. Algebra For what value of x is $\overline{GF} \parallel \overline{HJ}$?

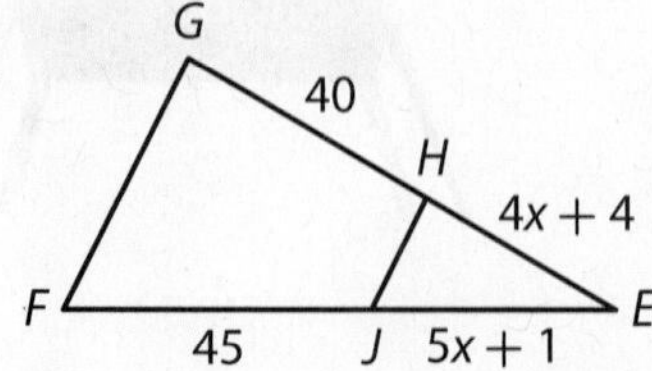

17. Communicate Mathematical Ideas John used $\triangle ABC$ to write a proof of the Centroid Theorem. He began by drawing medians $\overline{AK}$ and $\overline{CL}$, intersecting at Z. Next he drew midsegments $\overline{LM}$ and $\overline{NP}$, both parallel to median $\overline{AK}$.

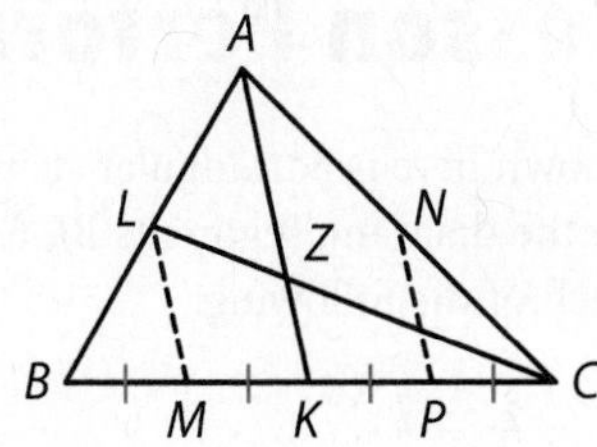

Given: $\triangle ABC$ with medians $\overline{AK}$ and $\overline{CL}$, and midsegments $\overline{LM}$ and $\overline{NP}$

Prove: Z is located $\frac{2}{3}$ of the distance from each vertex of $\triangle ABC$ to the midpoint of the opposite side.

a. Complete each statement to justify the first part of John's proof.

By the definition of [?], $MK = \frac{1}{2}BK$. By the definition of [?], $BK = KC$. So, by [?], $MK = \frac{1}{2}KC$, or $\frac{KC}{MK} = 2$.

Consider $\triangle LMC$. $\overline{LM} \parallel \overline{AK}$ (and therefore $\overline{LM} \parallel \overline{ZK}$), so $\frac{ZC}{LZ} = \frac{KC}{MK}$ by the [?] Theorem, and $ZC = 2LZ$. Because $LC = 3LZ$, $\frac{ZC}{LC} = \frac{2LZ}{3LZ} = \frac{2}{3}$, and Z is located $\frac{2}{3}$ of the distance from vertex C of $\triangle ABC$ to the midpoint of the opposite side.

b. Explain how John can complete his proof.

18. Persevere in Problem Solving Given $\triangle ABC$ with $FC = 5$, you want to find BF. First, find the value that y must have for the Triangle Proportionality Theorem to apply. Then describe more than one way to find BF, and find BF.

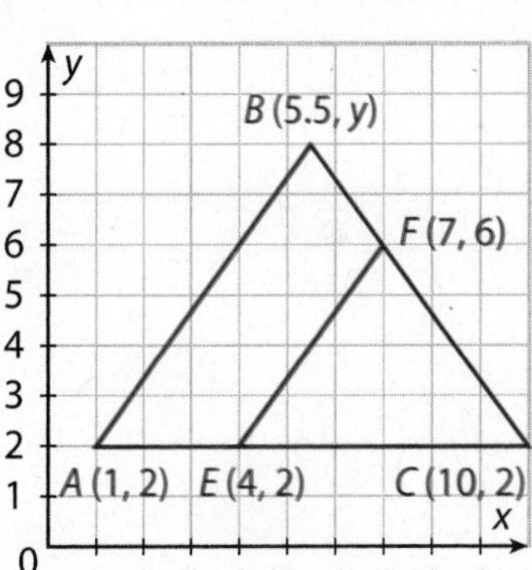

Lesson Performance Task

Shown here is a triangular striped sail, together with some of its dimensions. In the diagram, segments *BJ*, *CI*, and *DH* are all parallel to segment *EG*. Find each of the following:

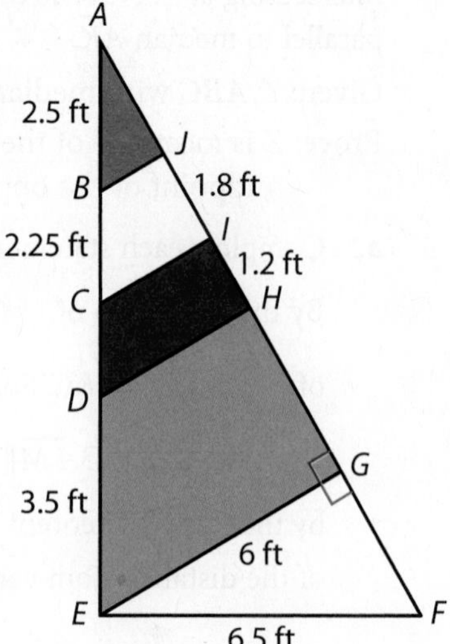

1. AJ
2. CD
3. HG
4. GF
5. the perimeter of $\triangle AEF$
6. the area of $\triangle AEF$
7. the number of sails you could make for $10,000 if the sail material costs $30 per square yardv

12.2 Subdividing a Segment in a Given Ratio

Resource Locker

Essential Question: How do you find the point on a directed line segment that partitions the given segment in a given ratio?

Partitioning a Segment in a One-Dimensional Coordinate System

It takes just one number to specify an exact location on a number line. For this reason, a number line is sometimes called a one-dimensional coordinate system. The mile markers on a straight stretch of a highway turn that part of the highway into a one-dimensional coordinate system.

On a straight highway, the exit for Arthur Avenue is at mile marker 14. The exit for Collingwood Road is at mile marker 44. The state highway administration plans to put an exit for Briar Street at a point that is $\frac{2}{3}$ of the distance from Arthur Avenue to Collingwood Road. Follow these steps to determine where the new exit should be placed.

(A) Draw a number line from 10 to 50 marked in units of 1. Mark Arthur Avenue (point A) and Collingwood Road (point C) on the number line.

(B) What is the distance from Arthur Avenue to Collingwood Road? Explain.

(C) How far will the Briar Street exit be from Arthur Avenue? Explain.

(D) What is the mile marker number for the Briar Street exit? Why?

(E) Plot and label the Briar Street exit (point B) on the number line.

(F) The highway administration also plans to put an exit for Dakota Lane at a point that divides the highway from Arthur Avenue to Collingwood Road in a ratio of 2 to 3. What is the mile marker number for Dakota Lane? Why? (*Hint*: Let the distance from Arthur Avenue to Dakota Lane be $2x$ and let the distance from Dakota Lane to Collingwood Road be $3x$.)

(G) Plot and label the Dakota Lane exit (point D) on the number line.

Reflect

1. How can you tell that the location at which you plotted point B is reasonable?
2. Would your answer in Step F be different if the exit for Dakota Lane divided the highway from Arthur Avenue to Collingwood Road in a ratio of 3 to 2? Explain.

Explain 1 Partitioning a Segment in a Two-Dimensional Coordinate System

A *directed line segment* is a segment between two points A and B with a specified direction, from A to B or from B to A. To partition a directed line segment is to divide it into two segments with a given ratio.

Example 1 **Find the coordinates of the point P that divides the directed line segment from A to B in the given ratio.**

(A) $A(-8, -7), B(8, 5)$; 3 to 1

Step 1 Write a ratio that expresses the distance of point P along the segment from A to B.

Point P is $\frac{3}{3+1} = \frac{3}{4}$ of the distance from A to B.

Step 2 Find the run and the rise of the directed line segment.

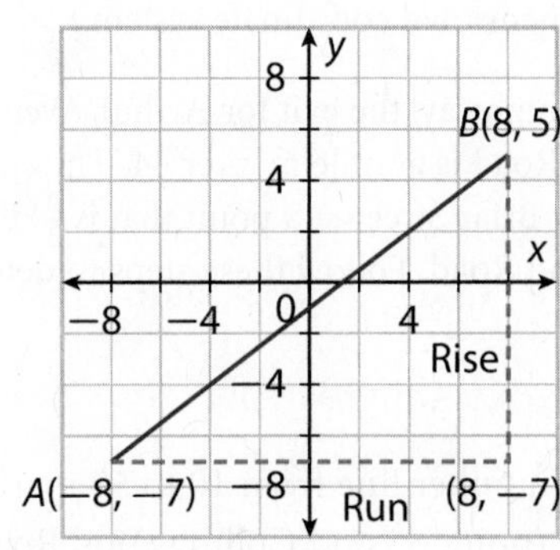

$\text{run} = 8 - (-8) = 16$

$\text{rise} = 5 - (-7) = 12$

Step 3 Point P is $\frac{3}{4}$ of the distance from point A to point B, so find $\frac{3}{4}$ of both the rise and the run.

$\frac{3}{4}$ of run $= \frac{3}{4}(16) = 12$ $\qquad$ $\frac{3}{4}$ of rise $= \frac{3}{4}(12) = 9$

Step 4 To find the coordinates of point P, add the values from Step 3 to the coordinates of point A.

x-coordinate of point $P = -8 + 12 = 4$

y-coordinate of point $P = -7 + 9 = 2$

The coordinates of point P are $(4, 2)$.

(B) $A(-4, 4), B(2, 1)$; 1 to 2

Step 1 Write a ratio that expresses the distance of point P along the segment from A to B.

Point P is $\dfrac{\boxed{1}}{\boxed{1} + \boxed{2}} = \dfrac{\boxed{1}}{\boxed{3}}$ of the distance from A to B.

Step 2 Graph the directed line segment. Find the run and the rise of the directed line segment.

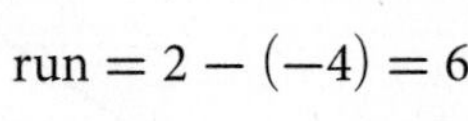

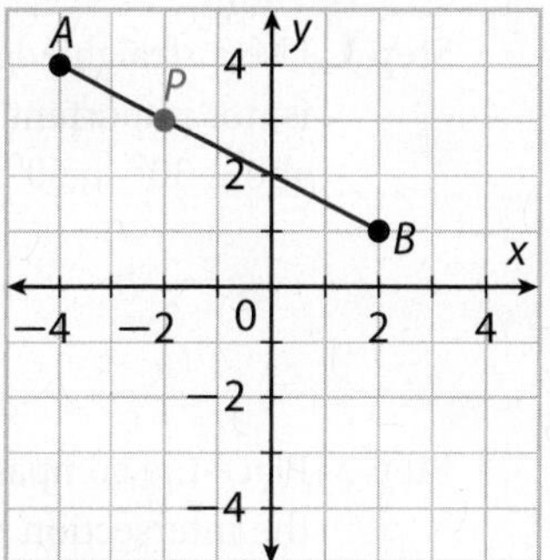

rise $= \boxed{1} - \boxed{4} = \boxed{-3}$

Step 3 Point P is $\dfrac{\boxed{1}}{\boxed{3}}$ of the distance from point A to point B.

$\dfrac{\boxed{1}}{\boxed{3}}$ of run $= \dfrac{\boxed{1}}{\boxed{3}}(6) = \boxed{2}$ $\qquad$ $\dfrac{\boxed{1}}{\boxed{3}}$ of rise $= \dfrac{\boxed{1}}{\boxed{3}}\left(\boxed{-3}\right) = \boxed{-1}$

Step 4 To find the coordinates of point P, add the values from Step 3 to the coordinates of point A.

x-coordinate of point $P = -4 + \boxed{2} = \boxed{-2}$ $\qquad$ y-coordinate of point $P = 4 + \boxed{-1} = \boxed{3}$

The coordinates of point P are $\left(\boxed{-2}, \boxed{3}\right)$. Plot point P on the above graph.

Reflect

3. In Part A, show how you can use the Distance Formula to check that point P partitions the directed line segment in the correct ratio.

4. **Discussion** What can you conclude about a point that partitions a segment in the ratio 1 to 1? How can you find the coordinates of such a point?

Your Turn

Find the coordinates of the point P that divides the directed line segment from A to B in the given ratio.

5. $A(-6, 5), B(2, -3)$; 5 to 3

6. $A(4, 2), B(-6, -13)$; 3 to 2

Explain 2 Constructing a Partition of a Segment

Example 2 **Given the directed line segment from *A* to *B*, construct the point *P* that divides the segment in the given ratio from *A* to *B*.**

(A) 2 to 1

Step 1 Use a straightedge to draw $\overrightarrow{AC}$. The exact measure of the angle is not important, but the construction is easiest for angles from about 30° to 60°.

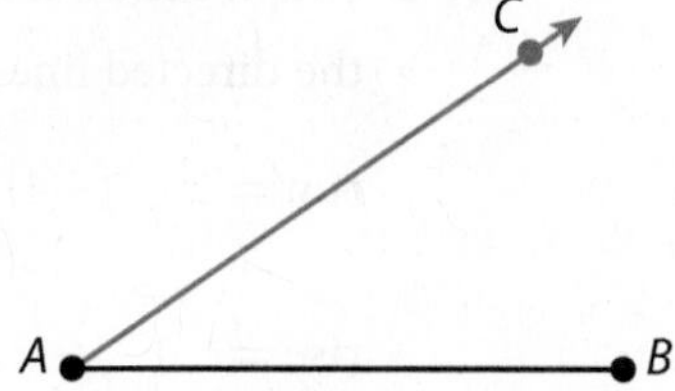

Step 2 Place the compass point on *A* and draw an arc through $\overrightarrow{AC}$. Label the intersection *D*. Using the same compass setting, draw an arc centered on *D* and label the intersection *E*. Using the same compass setting, draw an arc centered on *E* and label the intersection *F*.

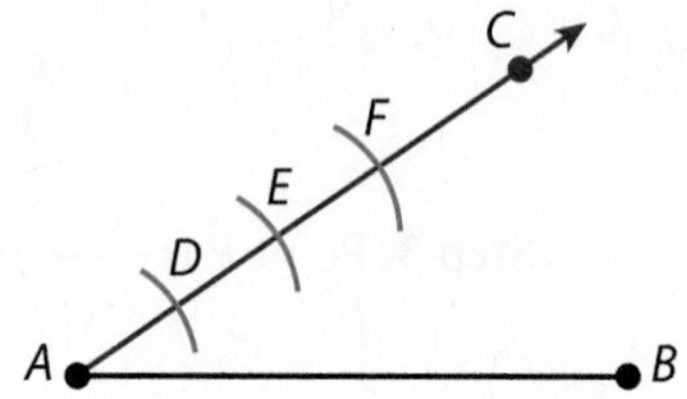

Step 3 Use the straightedge to connect points *B* and *F*. Construct an angle congruent to ∠*AFB* with *D* as its vertex. Construct an angle congruent to ∠*AFB* with *E* as its vertex.

Step 4 The construction partitions $\overline{AB}$ into 3 equal parts. Label point *P* atthe point that divides the segment in the ratio 2 to 1 from *A* to *B*.

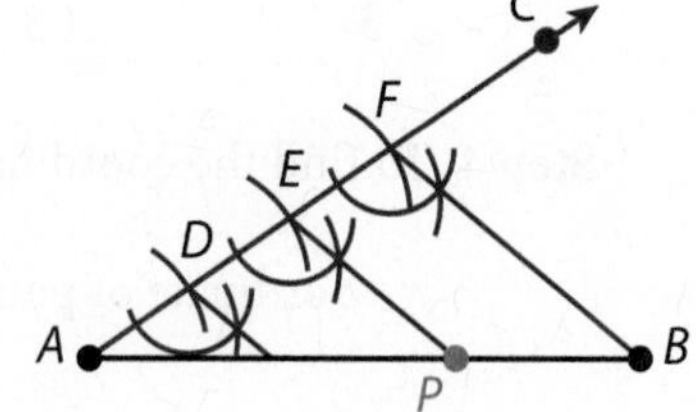

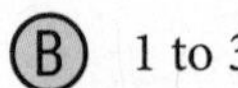

(B) 1 to 3

Step 1 Use a straightedge to draw $\overrightarrow{AC}$.

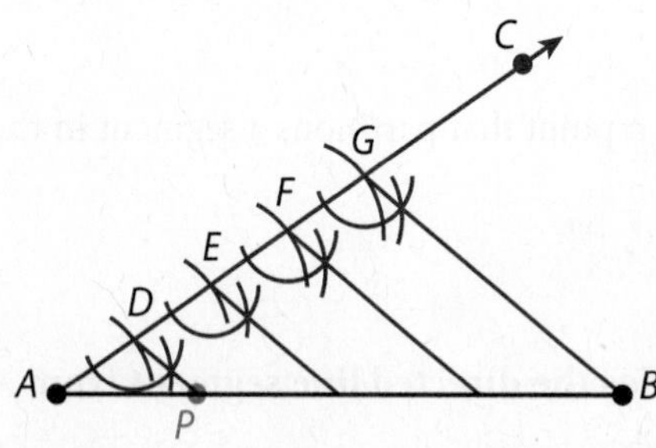

Step 2 Place the compass point on *A* and draw an arc through $\overrightarrow{AC}$. Label the intersection *D*. Using the same compass setting, draw an arc centered on *D* and label the intersection *E*. Using the same compass setting, draw an arc centered on *E* and label the intersection *F*. Using the same compass setting, draw an arc centered on *F* and label the intersection *G*.

Step 3 Use the straightedge to connect points *B* and *G*. Construct angles congruent to ∠*AGB* with *D*, *E*, and *F* as the vertices.

Step 4 The construction partitions $\overline{AB}$ into 4 equal parts. Label point *P* at the point that divides the segment in the ratio 1 to 3 from *A* to *B*.

Reflect

7. In Part A, why is $\overline{EP}$ is parallel to $\overline{FB}$?
8. How can you use the Triangle Proportionality Theorem to explain why this construction method works?

Your Turn

Copy the directed line segment from *A* to *B*. Then construct the point *P* that divides the segment in the given ratio from *A* to *B*.

9. 1 to 2

10. 3 to 2

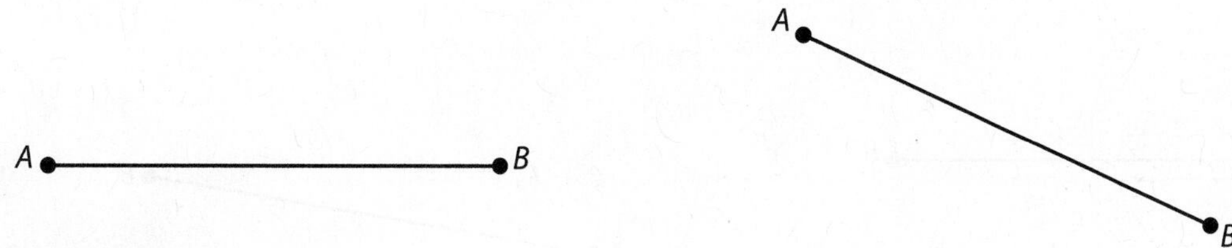

Elaborate

11. How is a one-dimensional coordinate system similar to a two-dimensional coordinate system? How is it different?
12. Is finding a point that is $\frac{4}{5}$ of the distance from point *A* to point *B* the same as finding a point that divides $\overline{AB}$ in the ratio 4 to 5? Explain.
13. **Essential Question Check-In** What are some different ways to divide a segment in the ratio 2 to 1?

Evaluate: Homework and Practice

- Online Homework
- Hints and Help
- Extra Practice

A choreographer uses a number line to position dancers for a ballet. Dancers *A* and *B* have coordinates 5 and 23, respectively. In Exercises 1–4, find the coordinate for each of the following dancers based on the given locations.

1. Dancer *C* stands at a point that is $\frac{5}{6}$ of the distance from Dancer *A* to Dancer *B*.
2. Dancer *D* stands at a point that is $\frac{1}{3}$ of the distance from Dancer *A* to Dancer *B*.
3. Dancer *E* stands at a point that divides the line segment from Dancer *A* to Dancer *B* in a ratio of 2 to 1.
4. Dancer *F* stands at a point that divides the line segment from Dancer *A* to Dancer *B* in a ratio of 1 to 5.

Find the coordinates of the point *P* that divides the directed line segment from *A* to *B* in the given ratio.

5. $A(-3, -2)$, $B(12, 3)$; 3 to 2

6. $A(-1, 5)$, $B(7, -3)$; 7 to 1

7. $A(-1, 4)$, $(B-9, 0)$; 1 to 3

8. $A(7, -3)$, $B(-7, 4)$; 3 to 4

Copy the directed line segment from *A* to *B*. Then construct the point *P* that divides the segment in the given ratio from *A* to *B*.

9. 3 to 1

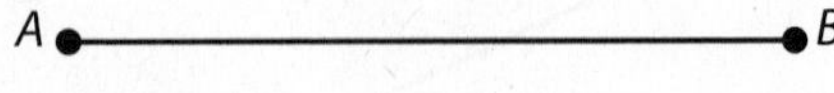

10. 2 to 3

A
B

11. 1 to 4

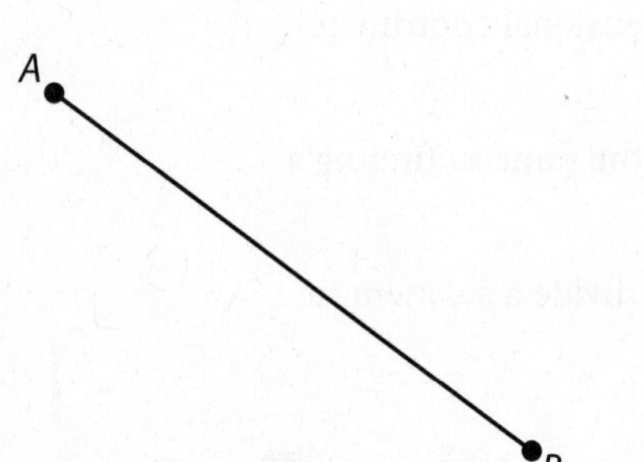

12. 4 to 1

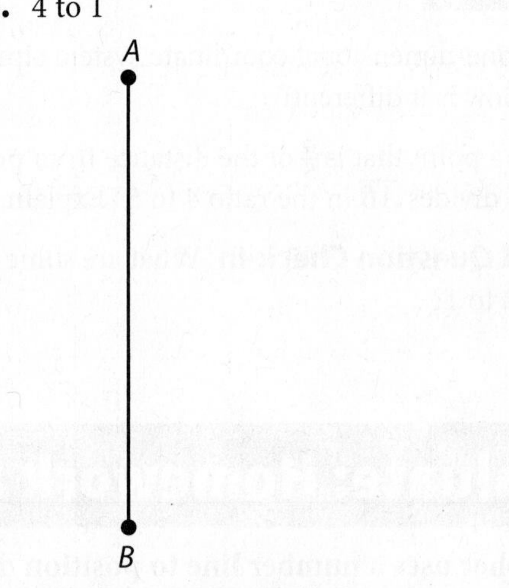

Find the coordinate of the point *P* that divides each directed line segment in the given ratio.

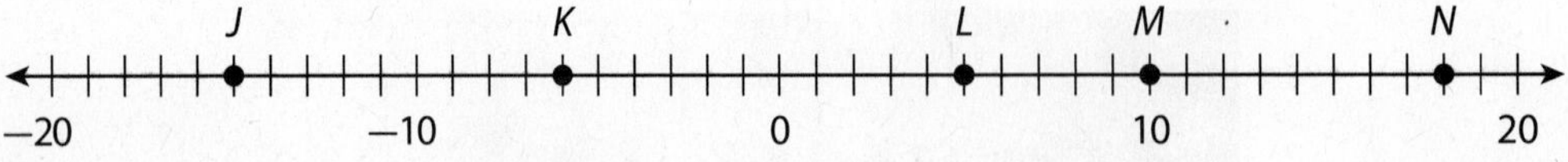

13. from *J* to *M*; 1 to 9

14. from *K* to *L*; 1 to 1

15. from *N* to *K*; 3 to 5

16. from *K* to *J*; 7 to 11

17. **Communicate Mathematical Ideas** Leon constructed a point *P* that divides the directed segment from *A* to *B* in the ratio 2 to 1. Chelsea constructed a point *Q* that divides the directed segment from *B* to *A* in the ratio 1 to 2. How are points *P* and *Q* related? Explain.

18. City planners use a number line to place landmarks along a new street. Each unit of the number line represents 100 feet. A fountain F is located at coordinate -3 and a plaza P is located at coordinate 21. The city planners place two benches along the street at points that divide the segment from F to P in the ratios 1 to 2 and 3 to 1. What is the distance between the benches?

19. The course for a marathon includes a straight segment from city hall to the main library. The planning committee wants to put water stations along this part of the course so that the stations divide the segment into three equal parts. Find the coordinates of the points at the which the water stations should be placed.

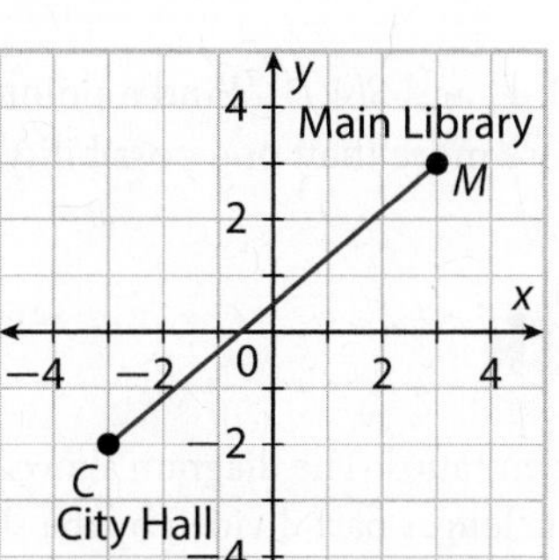

20. **Multi-Step** Carlos is driving on a straight section of highway from Ashford to Lincoln. Ashford is at mile marker 433 and Lincoln is at mile marker 553. A rest stop is located along the highway $\frac{2}{3}$ of the distance from Ashford to Lincoln. Assuming Carlos drives at a constant rate of 60 miles per hour, how long will it take him to drive from Ashford to the rest stop?

21. The directed segment from J to K is shown in the figure.

Points divide the segment from J to K in the each of the following ratios. Which points have integer coordinates? Determine all that apply.

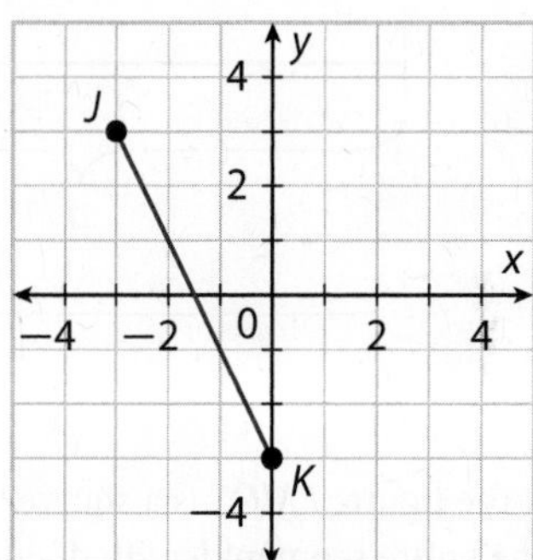

A. 1 to 1

B. 2 to 1

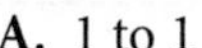

C. 2 to 3

D. 1 to 3

E. 1 to 2

H.O.T. Focus on Higher Order Thinking

22. **Critique Reasoning** Jeffrey was given a directed line segment and was asked to use a compass and straightedge to construct the point that divides the segment in the ratio 4 to 2. He said he would have to draw a ray and then construct 6 congruent segments along the ray. Tamara said it is not necessary to construct 6 congruent segments along the ray. Do you agree? If so, explain Tamara's shortcut. If not, explain why not.

23. Explain the Error Point A has coordinate -9 and point B has coordinate 9. A student was asked to find the coordinate of the point P that is $\frac{2}{3}$ of the distance from A to B. The student said the coordinate of point P is -3.

a. Without doing any calculations, how can you tell that the student made an error?

b. What error do you think the student made?

24. Analyze Relationships Point P divides the directed segment from A to B in the ratio 3 to 2. The coordinates of point A are $(-4, -2)$ and the coordinates of point P are $(2, 1)$. Find the coordinates of point B.

25. Critical Thinking $\overline{RS}$ passes through $R(-3, 1)$ and $S(4, 3)$. Find a point P on $\overline{RS}$ such that the ratio of RP to SP is 5 to 4. Is there more than one possibility? Explain.

Lesson Performance Task

In this lesson you will subdivide line segments in given ratios. The diagram shows a line segment divided into two parts in such a way that the longer part divided by the shorter part equals the entire length divided by the longer part:

$$\frac{a}{b} = \frac{a+b}{a}$$

Each of these ratios is called the Golden Ratio. To find the point on a line segment that divides the segment this way, study this figure:

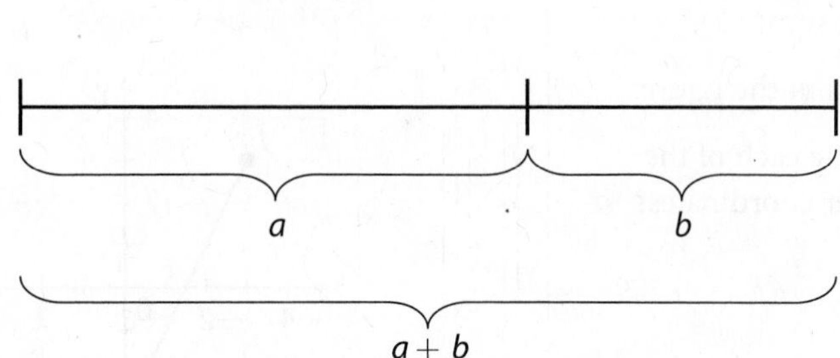

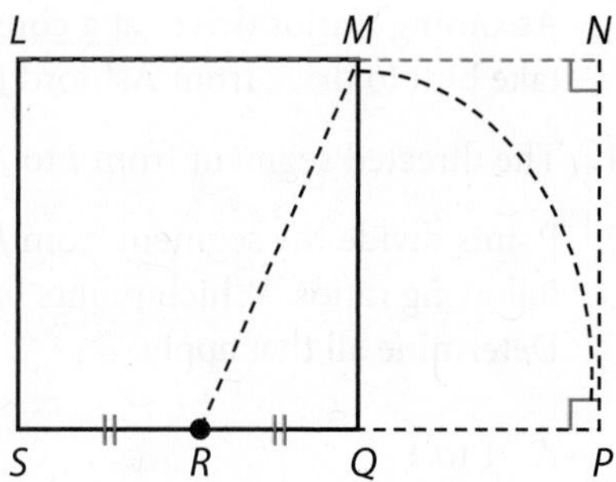

In the figure, $LMQS$ is a square. $\frac{LN}{LM}$ equals the Golden Ratio (the entire segment length divided by the longer part).

1. Describe how, starting with line segment $\overline{LM}$, you can find the location of point N.

2. Letting LM equal 1, find $\frac{LN}{LM} = \frac{LN}{1} = LN$, the Golden Ratio. Describe your method.

12.3 Using Proportional Relationships

Resource Locker

Essential Question: How can you use similar triangles to solve problems?

Explore Exploring Indirect Measurement

In this Explore, you will consider how to find heights, lengths, or distances that are too great to be measured directly, that is, with measuring tools like rulers. **Indirect measurement** involves using the properties of similar triangles to measure such heights or distances.

(A) During the day sunlight creates shadows, as shown in the figure below. The dashed segment represents the ray of sunlight. What kind of triangle is formed by the flagpole, its shadow, and the ray of sunlight?

(B) Suppose the sun is shining, and you are standing near a flagpole, but out of its shadow. You will cast a shadow as well. You can assume that the rays of the sun are parallel. What do you know about the two triangles formed? Explain your reasoning.

(C) In the diagram, what heights or lengths do you already know?

(D) What heights or lengths can be measured directly?

Reflect

1. How could you use similar triangles to measure the height of the flagpole indirectly?

Explain 1 Finding an Unknown Height

Example 1 **Find the indicated dimension using the measurements shown in the figure and the properties of similar triangles.**

(A) In order to find the height of a palm tree, you measure the tree's shadow and, at the same time of day, you measure the shadow cast by a meter stick that you hold at a right angle to the ground. Find the height h of the tree.

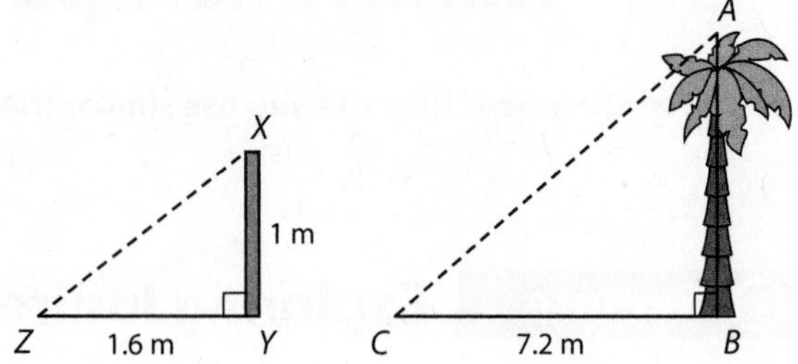

Because $\overline{ZX} \parallel \overline{CA}$, $\angle Z \cong \angle C$. All right angles are congruent, so $\angle Y \cong \angle B$. So $\triangle XYZ \cong \triangle ABC$.

Set up proportion. $\frac{AB}{XY} = \frac{BC}{YZ}$

Substitute. $\frac{h}{7.2} = \frac{1}{1.6}$

Multiply each side by 7.2. $h = 7.2\left(\frac{1}{1.6}\right)$

Simplify. $h = 4.5$

The tree is 4.5 meters high.

(B) Sid is 72 inches tall. To measure a flagpole, Sid stands near the flag. Sid's friend Miranda measures the lengths of Sid's shadow and the flagpole's shadow. Find the height h of the flagpole.

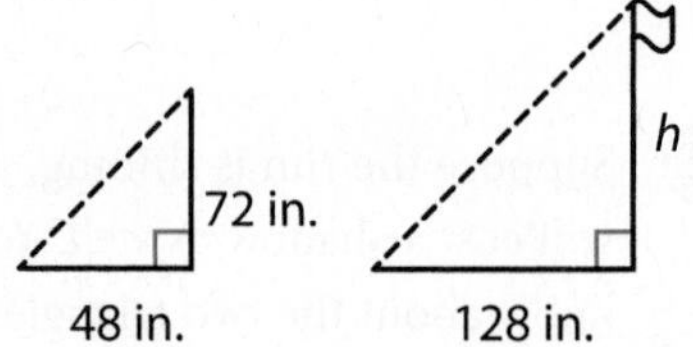

The triangles are similar by the AA Triangle Similarity Theorem.

Set up proportion. $\frac{\text{flagpole's height}}{\text{person's height}} = \frac{\text{flagpole's shadow}}{\text{person's shadow}}$

Substitute. $\frac{h}{72} = \frac{\boxed{128}}{48}$

Multiply each side by 72. $h = 72\left(\frac{\boxed{128}}{48}\right)$

Simplify. $x = \boxed{192}$

The flagpole is 192 inches tall.

Reflect

2. In the tree example, how can you check that your answer is reasonable?

Your Turn

3. Liam is 6 feet tall. To find the height of a tree, he measures his shadow and the tree's shadow. The measurements of the two shadows are shown. Find the height h of the tree.

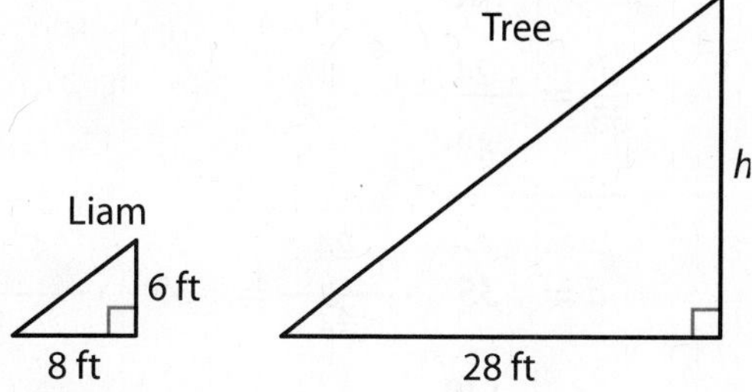

Explain 2 Finding an Unknown Distance

In real-world situations, you may not be able to measure an object directly because there is a physical barrier separating you from the object. You can use similar triangles in these situations as well.

Example 2 **Explain how to use the information in the figure to find the indicated distance.**

(A) A hiker wants to find the distance d across a canyon. She locates points as described.

1. She identifies a landmark at X. She places a marker (Y) directly across the canyon from X.
2. At Y, she turns 90° away from X and walks 400 feet in a straight line. She places a marker (Z) at this location.
3. She continues walking another 600 feet, and places a marker (W) at this location.
4. She turns 90° away from the canyon and walks until the marker Z aligns with X. She places a marker (V) at this location and measures $\overline{WV}$.

$\angle VWZ \cong \angle XYZ$ (All right angles are congruent) and $\angle VZW \cong \angle XZY$ (Vertical angles are congruent). So, $\triangle VWZ \sim \triangle XYZ$ by the AA Triangle Similarity Theorem.

$\frac{XY}{VW} = \frac{YZ}{WZ}$, So $\frac{d}{327} = \frac{400}{600}$, or $\frac{d}{327} = \frac{2}{3}$

Then $d = 327\left(\frac{2}{3}\right) = 218$.

The distance across the canyon is 218 feet.

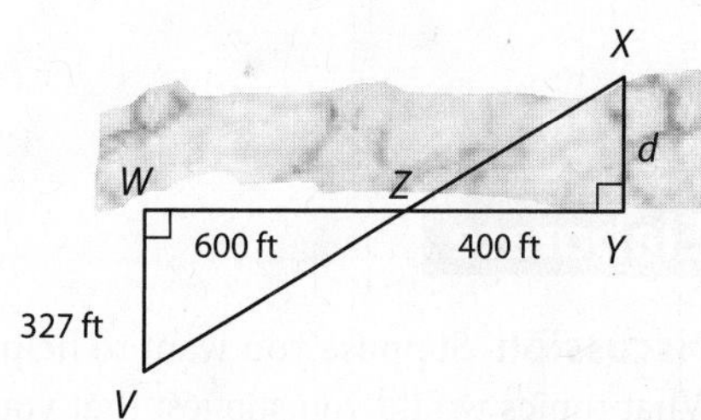

(B) To find the distance d across the gorge, a student identifies points as shown in the figure. Find d.

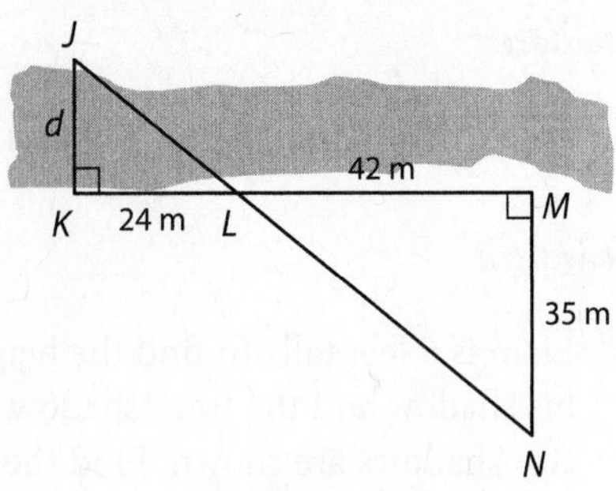

$\triangle JKL \sim \triangle NML$ by the AA Triangle Similarity Theorem

$$\frac{JK}{NM} = \frac{KL}{\boxed{ML}}$$

$$\frac{d}{35} = \frac{24}{\boxed{42}}$$

$$d = \boxed{35} \cdot \frac{24}{42} = \boxed{35} \cdot \frac{\boxed{4}}{7}$$

$$d = \frac{\boxed{140}}{7}$$

$$d = \boxed{20}$$

The distance across the gorge is 20 meters.

Reflect

4. In the example, why is $\angle JLK \cong \angle NLM$?

Your Turn

5. To find the distance d across a stream, Levi located points as shown in the figure. Use the given information to find d.

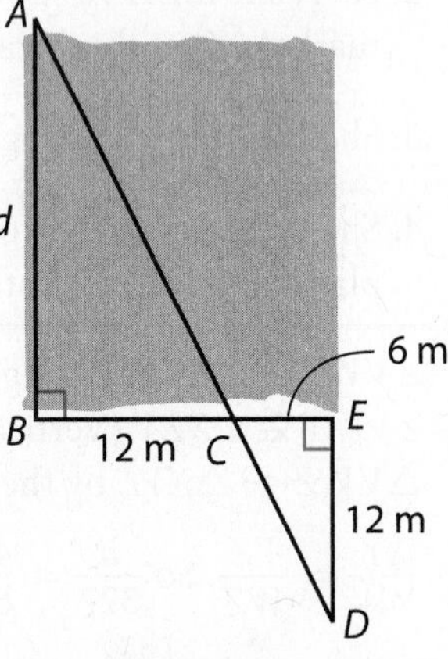

Elaborate

6. Discussion Suppose you want to help a friend prepare for solving indirect measurement problems. What topics would you suggest that your friend review?

7. Essential Question Check-In You are given a figure including triangles that represent a real-world situation. What is the first step you should take to find an unknown measurement?

Evaluate: Homework and Practice

- Online Homework
- Hints and Help
- Extra Practice

1. Finding distances using similar triangles is called ___?___.

Use similar triangles $\triangle ABC$ and $\triangle XYZ$ to find the missing height h.

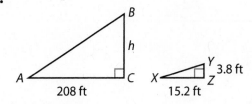

2.

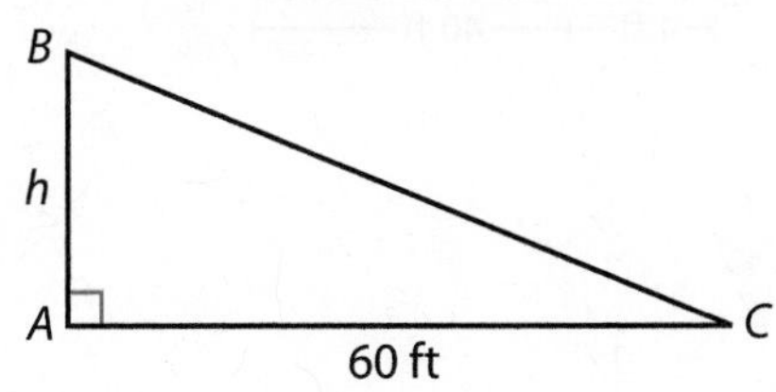

3.

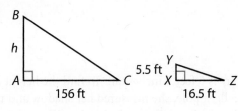

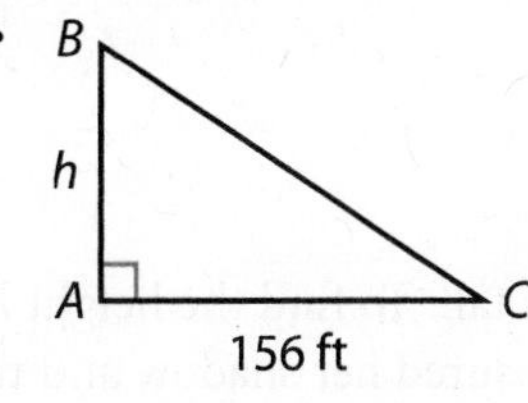

4.

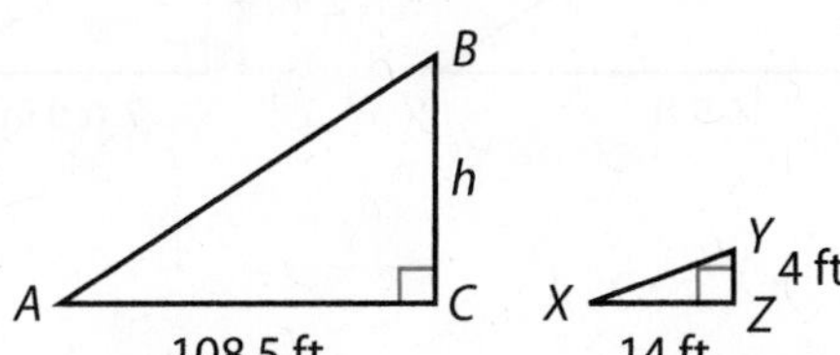

5.

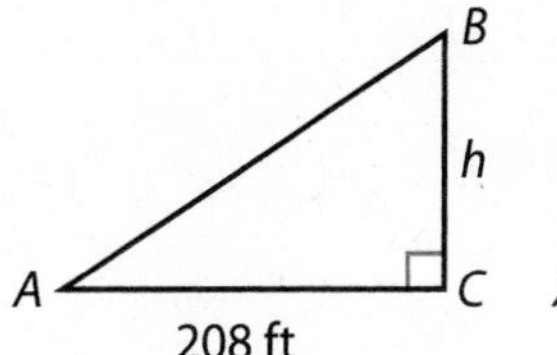

Use similar triangles $\triangle EFG$ and $\triangle IHG$ to find the missing distance d.

6.

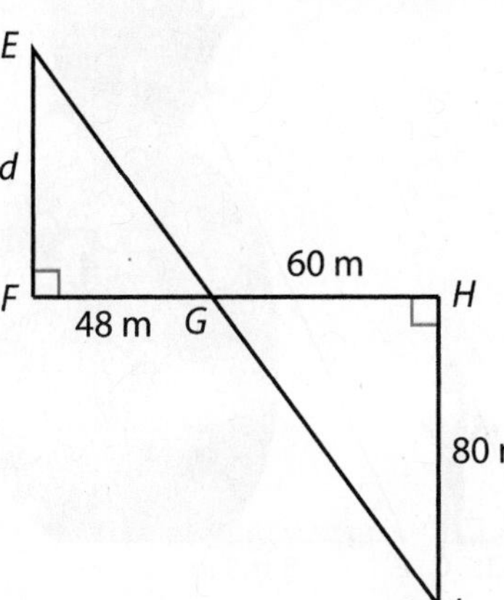

7.

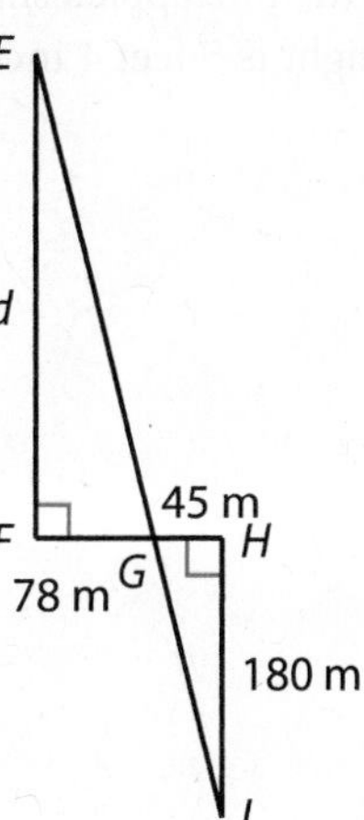

8.

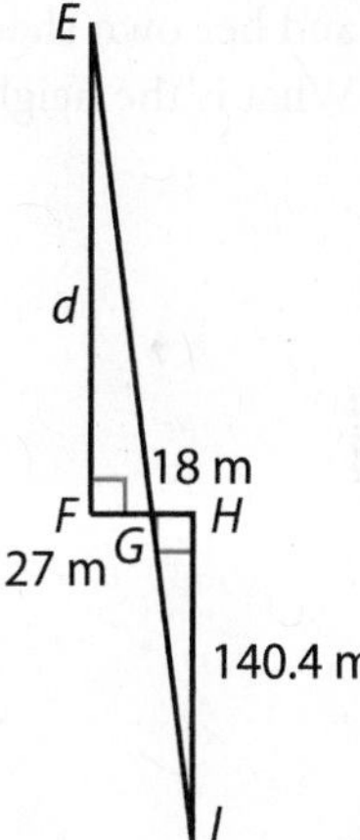

9.

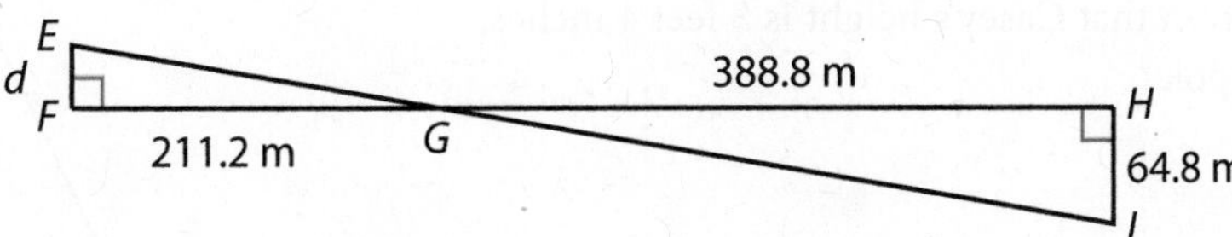

10. To find the height h of a dinosaur in a museum, Amir placed a mirror on the ground 40 feet from its base. Then he stepped back 4 feet so that he could see the top of the dinosaur in the mirror. Amir's eyes were approximately 5 feet 6 inches above the ground. What is the height of the dinosaur?

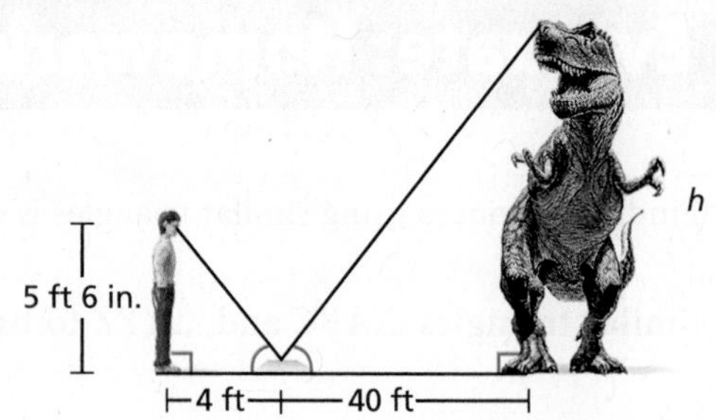

11. Jenny is 5 feet 2 inches tall. To find the height h of a light pole, she measured her shadow and the pole's shadow. What is the height of the pole?

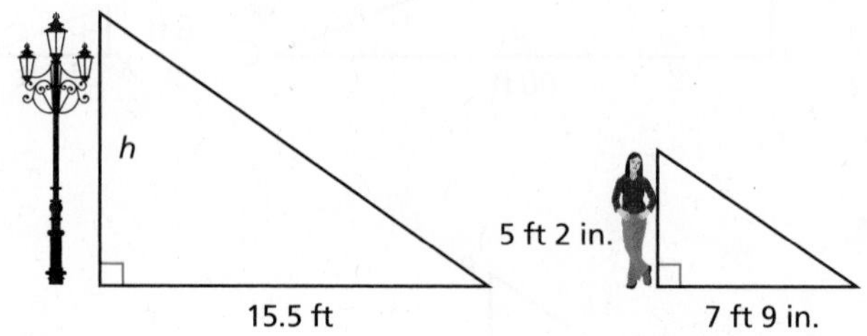

12. A student wanted to find the height h of a statue of a pineapple in Nambour, Australia. She measured the pineapple's shadow and her own shadow. The student's height is 5 feet 4 inches. What is the height of the pineapple?

13. To find the height h of a flagpole, Casey measured her own shadow and the flagpole's shadow. Given that Casey's height is 5 feet 4 inches, what is the height of the flagpole?

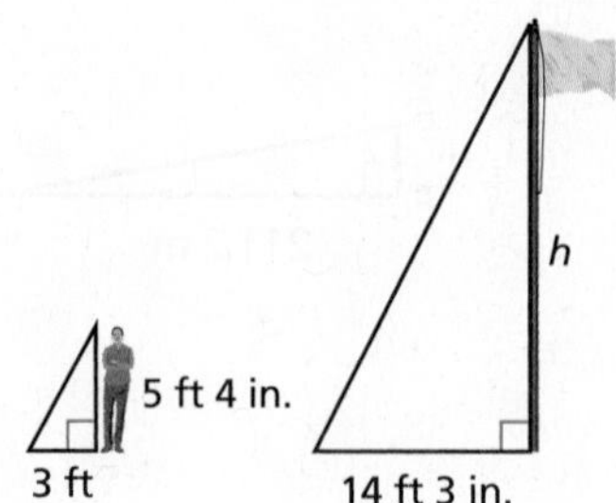

A city is planning an outdoor concert for an Independence Day celebration. To hold speakers and lights, a crew of technicians sets up a scaffold with two platforms by the stage. The first platform is 8 feet 2 inches off the ground. The second platform is 7 feet 6 inches above the first platform. The shadow of the first platform stretches 6 feet 3 inches across the ground.

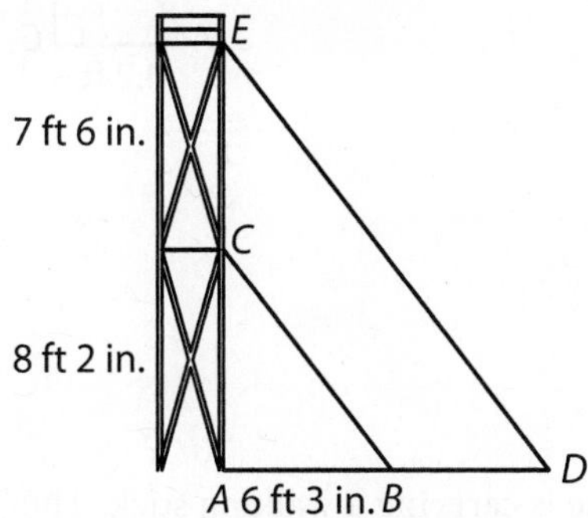

14. Explain why $\triangle ABC$ is similar to $\triangle ADE$. (*Hint*: rays of light are parallel.)

15. Find the length of the shadow of the second platform in feet and inches to the nearest inch.

16. A technician is 5 feet 8 inches tall. The technician is standing on top of the second platform. Find the length *s* of the shadow that is cast by the scaffold and the technician to the nearest inch.

17. To find the distance *XY* across a lake, you locate points as shown in the figure. Explain how to use this information to find *XY*.

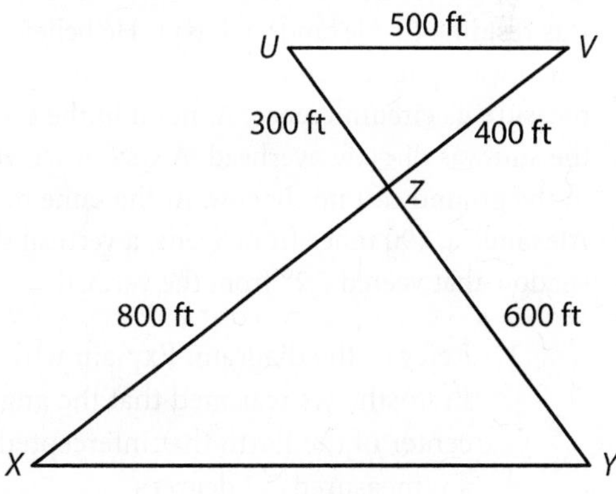

18. In order to find the height of a cliff, you stand at the bottom of the cliff, walk 60 feet from the base, and place a mirror on the ground. Then you face the cliff and step back 5 feet so that can see the top of the cliff in the mirror. Assuming your eyes are 6 feet above the ground, explain how to use this information to find the height of the cliff. (The angles marked congruent are congruent because of the nature of the reflection of light in a mirror.)

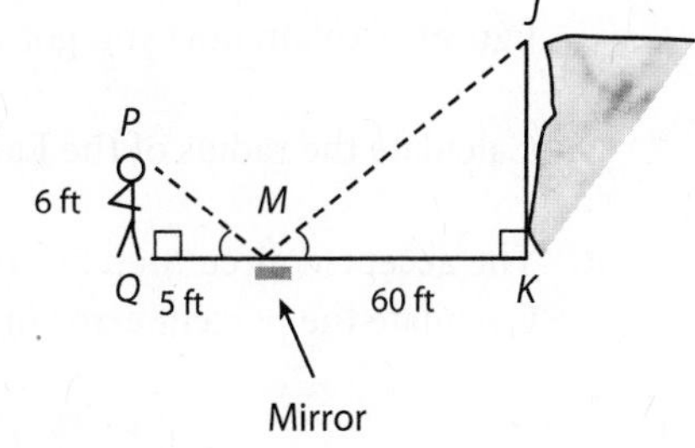

19. To find the height of a tree, Adrian measures the tree's shadow and then his shadow. Which proportion could Adrian use to find the height of the tree? Determine all that apply.

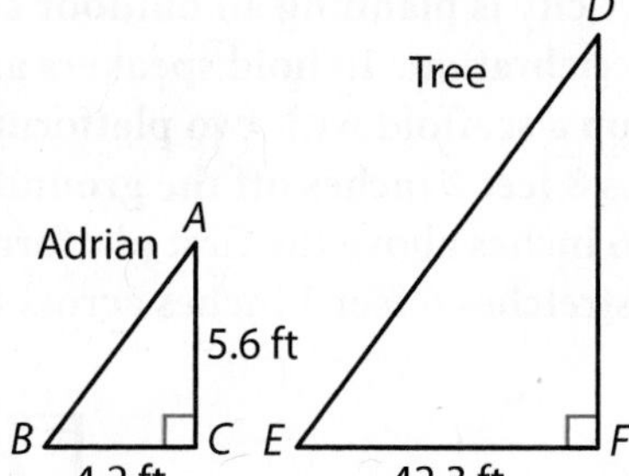

A. $\frac{AC}{DF} = \frac{BC}{EF}$

B. $\frac{DF}{AC} = \frac{EF}{BC}$

C. $\frac{AB}{DF} = \frac{BC}{EF}$

D. $\frac{DF}{BC} = \frac{EF}{AC}$

E. $\frac{BC}{EF} = \frac{AC}{DF}$

H.O.T. Focus on Higher Order Thinking

20. **Critique Reasoning** Jesse and Kyle are hiking. Jesse is carrying a walking stick. They spot a tall tree and use the walking stick as a vertical marker to create similar triangles and measure the tree indirectly. Later in the day they come upon a rock formation. They measure the rock formation's shadow and again want to use similar triangles to measure its height indirectly. Kyle wants to use the shadow length they measured earlier for the stick. Jesse says they should measure it again. Who do you think is right?

21. **Error Analysis** Andy wants to find the distance d across a river. He located points as shown in the figure and then used similar triangles to find that $d = 220.5$ feet. How can you tell without calculating that he must be wrong? Tell what you think he did wrong and correct his error.

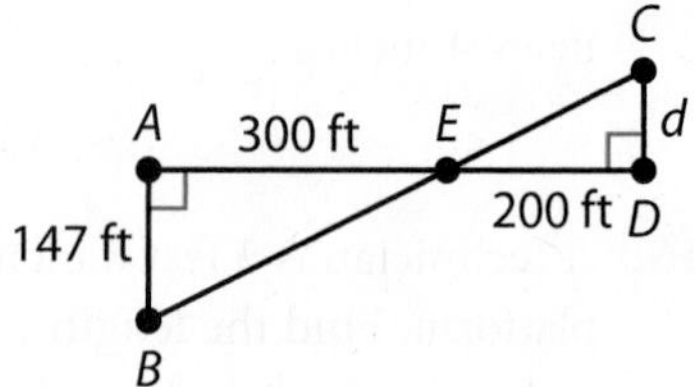

Lesson Performance Task

Around 240 B.C., the Greek astronomer Eratosthenes was residing in Alexandria, Egypt. He believed that the Earth was spherical and conceived of an experiment to measure its circumference. At noon in the town of Syene, the sun was directly overhead. A stick stuck vertically in the ground cast no shadow. At the same moment in Alexandria, 490 miles from Syene, a vertical stick cast a shadow that veered 7.2° from the vertical.

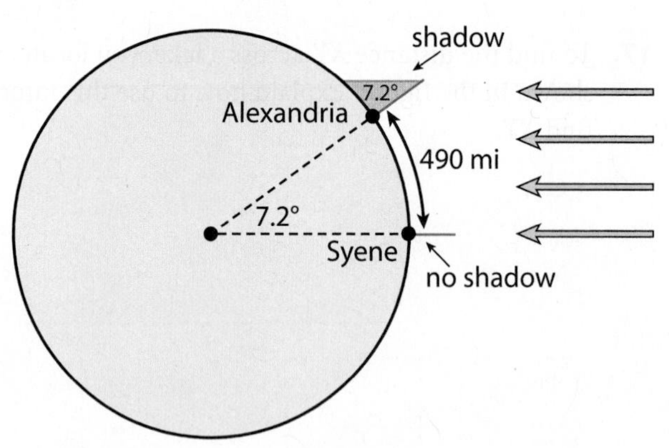

1. Refer to the diagram. Explain why Eratosthenes reasoned that the angle at the center of the Earth that intercepted a 490-mile arc measured 7.2 degrees.

2. Calculate the circumference of the Earth using Eratosthenes's figures. Explain how you got your answer.

3. Calculate the radius of the Earth using Eratosthenes's figures.

4. The accepted circumference of the Earth today is 24,901 miles. Calculate the percent error in Eratosthenes's calculations.

12.4 Similarity in Right Triangles

Resource Locker

Essential Question: How does the altitude to the hypotenuse of a right triangle help you use similar right triangles to solve problems?

Explore Identifying Similarity in Right Triangles

(A) Make two copies of the right triangle on a piece of paper and cut them out.

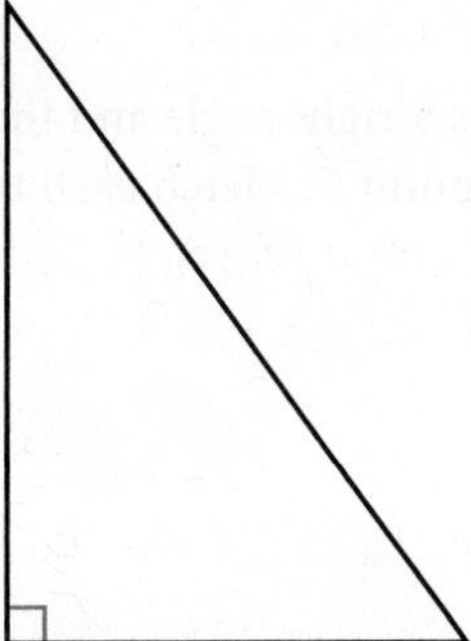

(B) Choose one of the triangles. Fold the paper to find the altitude to the hypotenuse.

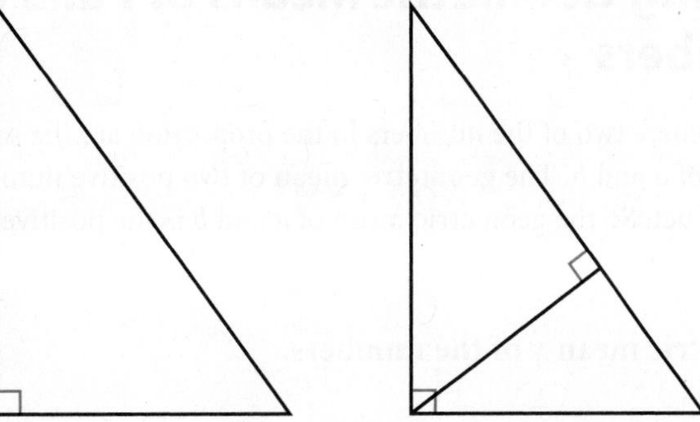

(C) Cut the second triangle along the altitude. Label the triangles as shown.

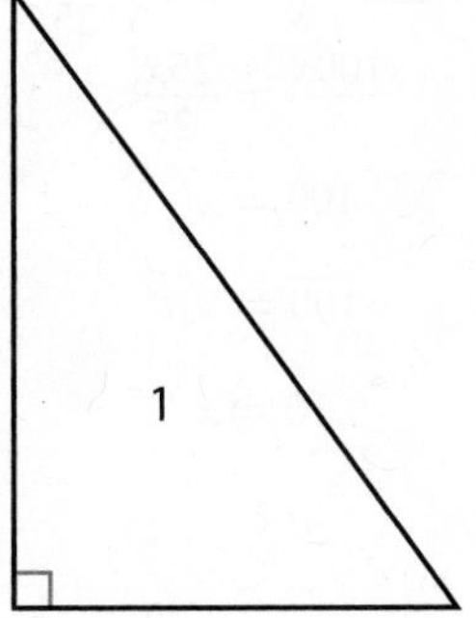

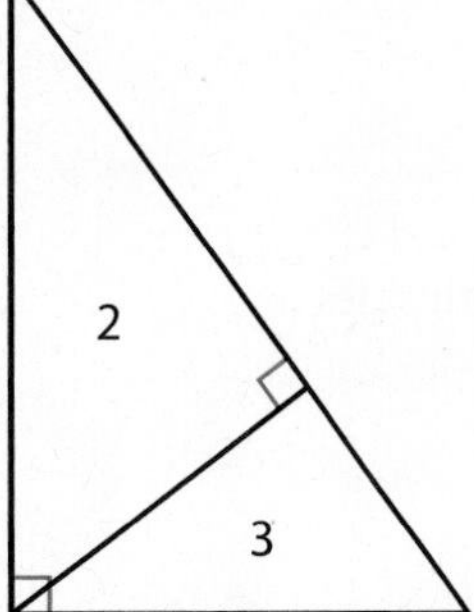

(D) Place triangle 2 on top of triangle 1. What do you notice about the angles?

(E) What is true of triangles 1 and 2? How do you know?

(F) Repeat Steps 1 and 2 for triangles 1 and 3. Does the same relationship hold true for triangles 1 and 3?

Reflect

1. How are the hypotenuses of the triangles 2 and 3 related to triangle 1?
2. What is the relationship between triangles 2 and 3? Explain.
3. When you draw the altitude to the hypotenuse of a right triangle, what kinds of figures are produced?
4. Suppose you draw $\triangle ABC$ such that $\angle B$ is a right angle and the altitude to the hypotenuse intersects hypotenuse $\overline{AC}$ at point P. Match each triangle to a similar triangle. Explain your reasoning.

A. $\triangle ABC$	a. _?_ $\triangle PAB$
B. $\triangle PBC$	b. _?_ $\triangle CAB$
C. $\triangle BAP$	c. _?_ $\triangle BPC$

 Explain 1 Finding Geometric Means of Pairs of Numbers

Consider the proportion $\frac{a}{x} = \frac{x}{b}$ where two of the numbers in the proportion are the same. The number x is the *geometric mean* of a and b. The **geometric mean** of two positive numbers is the positive square root of their product. So the geometric mean of a and b is the positive number x such that $x = \sqrt{ab}$ or $x^2 = ab$.

Example 1 **Find the geometric mean x of the numbers.**

(A) 4 and 25

Write proportion.	$\frac{4}{x} = \frac{x}{25}$
Multiply both sides by the product of the denominators.	$25x \cdot \frac{4}{x} = 25x \cdot \frac{x}{25}$
Multiply.	$\frac{100x}{x} = \frac{25x^2}{25}$
Simplify.	$100 = x^2$
Take the square root of both sides.	$\sqrt{100} = \sqrt{x^2}$
Simplify.	$10 = x$

(B) 9 and 20

Write proportion. $\frac{\boxed{9}}{x} = \frac{x}{20}$

Multiply both sides by the product of the denominators. $20x \cdot \frac{\boxed{9}}{x} = 20x \cdot \frac{x}{20}$

Multiply. $\frac{\boxed{180}x}{x} = \frac{20x^2}{20}$

Simplify. $\boxed{180} = x^2$

Take the square root of both sides. $\sqrt{\boxed{180}} = \sqrt{x^2}$

Simplify. $\boxed{6\sqrt{5}} = x$

Reflect

5. How can you show that if positive numbers a and b are such that $\frac{a}{x} = \frac{x}{b}$, then $x = \sqrt{ab}$?

Your Turn

Find the geometric mean of the numbers. If necessary, give the answer in simplest radical form.

6. 6 and 24

7. 5 and 12

Explain 2 Proving the Geometric Means Theorems

In the Explore activity, you discovered a theorem about right triangles and similarity.

The altitude to the hypotenuse of a right triangle forms two triangles that are similar to each other and to the original triangle.

That theorem leads to two additional theorems about right triangles. Both of the theorems involve geometric means.

Geometric Means Theorems		
Theorem	**Example**	**Diagram**
The length of the altitude to the hypotenuse of a right triangle is the geometric mean of the lengths of the segments of the hypotenuse.	$h^2 = xy$ or $h = \sqrt{xy}$	x, c, y, a, h, b
The length of a leg of a right triangle is the geometric mean of the lengths of the hypotenuse and the segment of the hypotenuse adjacent to that leg.	$a^2 = xc$ or $a = \sqrt{xc}$ $b^2 = yc$ or $b = \sqrt{yc}$	

Example 2 **Prove the first Geometric Means Theorem.**

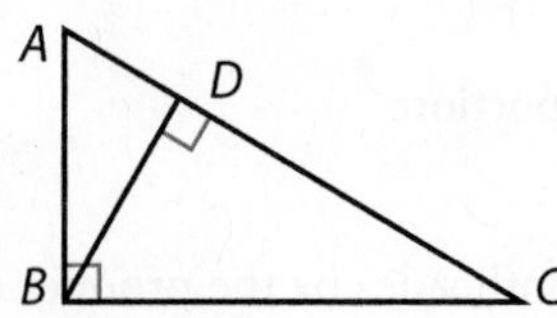

Given: Right triangle ABC with altitude $\overline{BD}$

Prove: $\frac{CD}{BD} = \frac{BD}{AD}$

Statements	Reasons
1. $\triangle ABC$ with altitude $\overline{BD}$	1. Given
2. $\triangle CBD \sim \triangle BAD$	2. The altitude to the hypotenuse of a right triangle forms two triangles that are similar to the original triangle and to each other.
3. $\frac{CD}{BD} = \frac{BD}{AD}$	3. Corresponding sides of similar triangles are proportional.

Reflect

8. Discussion How can you prove the second Geometric Means Theorem?

Explain 3 Using the Geometric Means Theorems

You can use the Geometric Means Theorems to find unknown segment lengths in a right triangle.

Example 3 **Find the indicated value.**

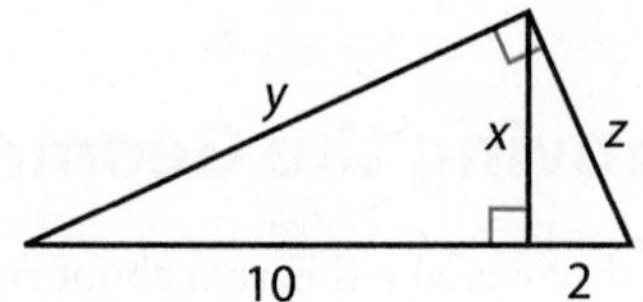

 x

Write proportion. $\frac{2}{x} = \frac{x}{10}$

Multiply both sides by the product of the denominators. $10x \cdot \frac{2}{x} = 10x \cdot \frac{x}{10}$

Multiply. $\frac{20x}{x} = \frac{10x^2}{10}$

Simplify. $20 = x^2$

Take the square root of both sides. $\sqrt{20} = \sqrt{x^2}$

Simplify. $2\sqrt{5} = x$

(B) y

Write proportion. $\frac{10}{y} = \frac{y}{12}$

Multiply both sides by the product of the denominators. $\boxed{12y}\,\frac{10}{y} = \boxed{12y}\,\frac{y}{12}$

Multiply. $\frac{\boxed{120y}}{y} = \frac{\boxed{12y^2}}{12}$

Simplify. $\boxed{120} = \boxed{y^2}$

Take the square root of both sides. $\sqrt{\boxed{120}} = \sqrt{\boxed{y^2}}$

Simplify. $\boxed{2\sqrt{30}} = y$

Reflect

9. Discussion How can you check your answers?

Your Turn

10. Find x.

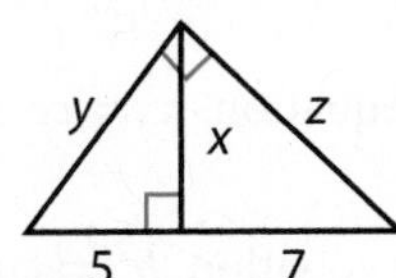

Explain 4 Proving the Pythagorean Theorem using Similarity

You have used the Pythagorean Theorem in earlier courses as well as in this one. There are many, many proofs of the Pythagorean Theorem. You will prove it now using similar right triangles.

The Pythagorean Theorem

In a right triangle, the square of the sum of the lengths of the legs is equal to the square of the length of the hypotenuse.

Example 4 **Complete the proof of the Pythagorean Theorem.**

Given: Right $\triangle ABC$

Prove: $a^2 + b^2 = c^2$

Part 1

Draw the altitude to the hypotenuse.
Label the point of intersection X.

$\angle BXC \cong \angle BCA$ because all right angles are congruent.

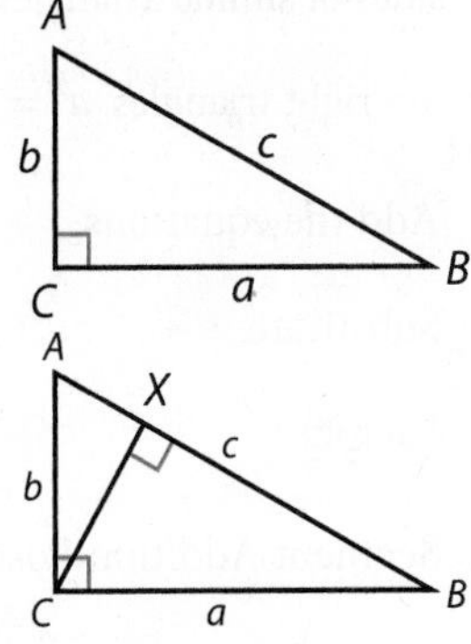

$\angle B \cong \angle B$ by the Reflexive Property of Congruence.

So, $\triangle BXC \sim \triangle BCA$ by the AA Triangle Similarity Theorem

$\angle AXC \cong \angle ACB$ because all right angles are congruent.

$\angle A \cong \angle A$ by the Reflexive Property of Congruence.

So, $\triangle AXC \sim \triangle ACB$ by the AA Triangle Similarity Theorem

Part 2

Let the lengths of the segments of the hypotenuse be d and e, as shown in the figure.

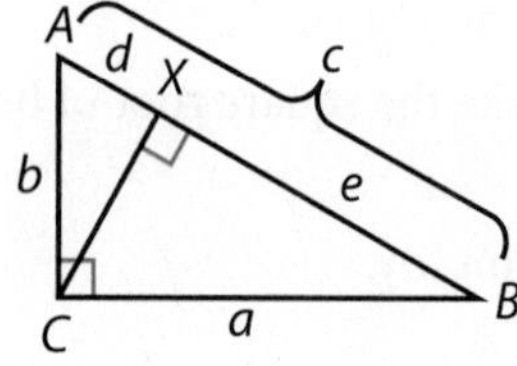

Use the fact that corresponding sides of similar triangles are proportional to write two proportions.

Proportion 1: $\triangle BXC \sim \triangle BCA$, so $\frac{a}{c} = \frac{\boxed{e}}{a}$.

Proportion 2: $\triangle AXC \sim \triangle ACB$, so $\frac{b}{c} = \frac{\boxed{d}}{b}$.

Part 3

Now perform some algebra to complete the proof as follows.

Multiply both sides of Proportion1 by ac. Write the resulting equation. $a^2 = ce$

Multiply both sides of Proportion12 by bc. Write the resulting equation. $b^2 = cd$

Adding the two resulting equations give this: $a^2 + b^2 = ce + cd$

Factor the right side of the equation: $a^2 + b^2 = c(e + d)$

Finally, use the fact that $e + d = c$ by the Segment Addition Postulate to rewrite the equation as $a^2 + b^2 = c^2$.

Reflect

11. Error Analysis A student used the figure in Part 2 of the example, and wrote the following incorrect proof of the Pythagorean Theorem. Critique the student's proof. $\triangle BXC \sim \triangle BCA$ and $\triangle BCA \sim \triangle CXA$, so $\triangle BXC \sim \triangle CXA$ by transitivity of similarity. Let $CX = f$. Since corresponding sides of similar triangles are proportional, $\frac{e}{f} = \frac{f}{d}$ and $f^2 = ed$. Because $\triangle BXC \sim \triangle CXA$ and they are right triangles, $a^2 = e^2 + f^2$ and $b^2 = f^2 + d^2$.

Add the equations.	$a^2 + b^2 = e^2 + 2f^2 + d^2$
Substitute.	$= e^2 + 2ed + d^2$
Factor.	$= (e + d)^2$
Segment Addition Postulate	$= c^2$

Elaborate

12. How would you explain to a friend how to find the geometric mean of two numbers?

13. $\triangle XYZ$ is an isosceles right triangle and the right angle is $\angle Y$. Suppose the altitude to hypotenuse $\overline{XZ}$ intersects $\overline{XZ}$ at point P. Describe the relationships among triangles $\triangle XYZ$, $\triangle YPZ$ and $\triangle XPY$.

14. Can two different pairs of numbers have the same geometric mean? If so, give an example. If not, explain why not.

15. **Essential Question Check-In** How is the altitude to the hypotenuse of a right triangle related to the segments of the hypotenuse it creates?

Evaluate: Homework and Practice

- Online Homework
- Hints and Help
- Extra Practice

Write a similarity statement comparing the three triangles to each diagram.

1.

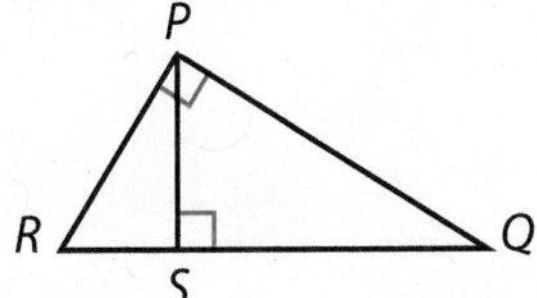

2.

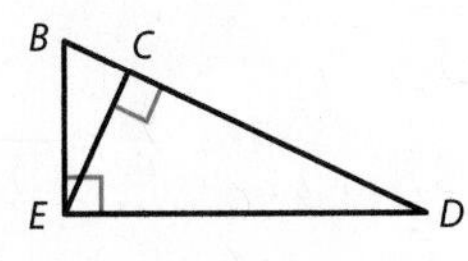

3.

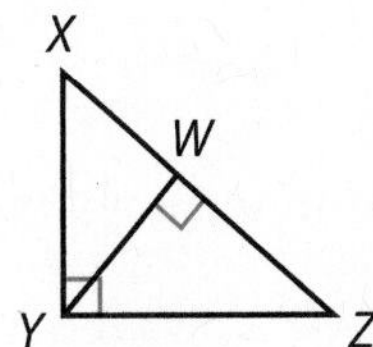

Find the geometric mean x of each pair of numbers. If necessary, give the answer in simplest radical form.

4. 5 and 20

5. 3 and 12

6. 8 and 13

7. 3.5 and 20

8. 1.5 and 84

9. $\frac{2}{3}$ and $\frac{27}{40}$

For Exercises 10–12, find x, y, and z.

10.

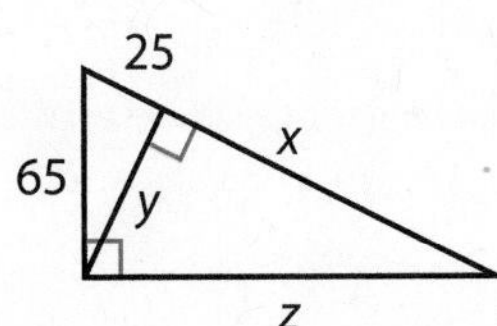

11.

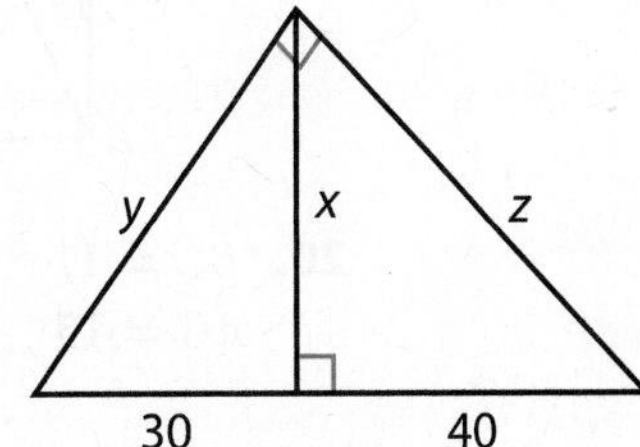

12.

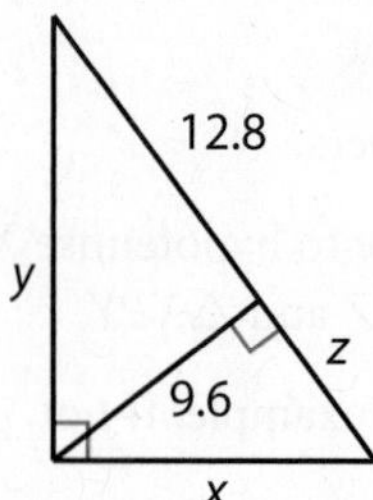

Use the diagram to complete each equation.

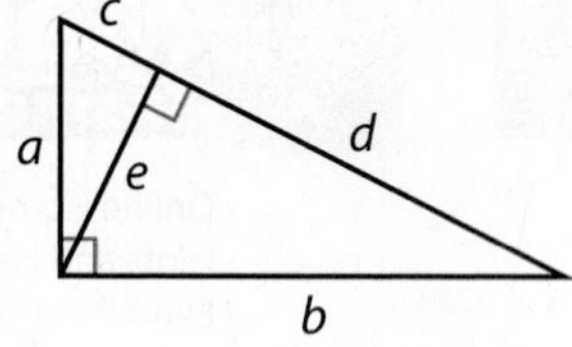

13. $\frac{c}{e} = \frac{?}{d}$

14. $\frac{c}{a} = \frac{a}{?}$

15. $\frac{c+d}{b} = \frac{b}{?}$

16. $\frac{d}{?} = \frac{e}{c}$

17. $c(c+d) = \ ?$

18. $?^2 = cd$

Find the length of the altitude to the hypotenuse under the given conditions.

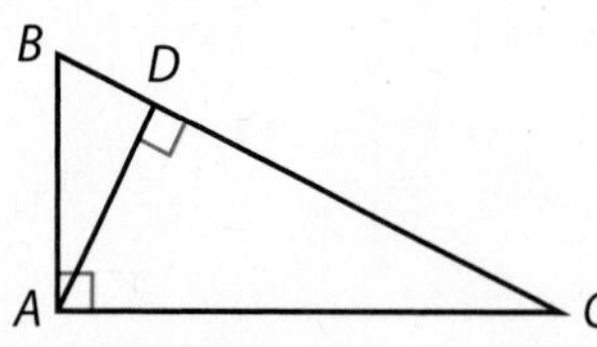

19. $BC = 5$
$AC = 4$

20. $BC = 17$
$AC = 15$

21. $BC = 13$
$AC = 12$

22. **Communicate Mathematical Ideas** The area of a rectangle with a length of ℓ and a width of w has the same area as a square. Show that the side length of the square is the geometric mean of the length and width of the rectangle.

H.O.T. Focus on Higher Order Thinking

23. Algebra An 8-inch-long altitude of a right triangle divides the hypotenuse into two segments. One segment is 4 times as long as the other. What are the lengths of the segments of the hypotenuse?

24. Error Analysis Cecile and Amelia both found a value for EF in $\triangle DEF$. Both students work are shown. Which student's solution is correct? What mistake did the other student make?

Cecile: $\frac{12}{EF} = \frac{EF}{8}$

So $EF^2 = 12(8) = 96$.

Then $EF = \sqrt{96} = 4\sqrt{6}$.

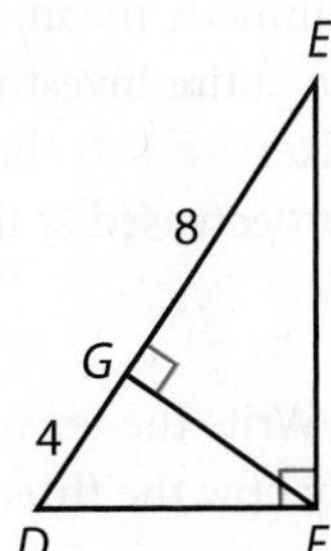

Amelia: $\frac{8}{EF} = \frac{EF}{4}$

So $EF^2 = 8(4) = 32$.

Then $EF = \sqrt{32} = 4\sqrt{2}$.

Lesson Performance Task

In the example at the beginning of the lesson, a \$100 investment grew for one year at the rate of 50%, to \$150, then fell for one year at the rate of 50%, to \$75. The arithmetic mean of +50% and −50%, which is 0%, was not a good predictor of the change, for it predicted the investment would still be worth \$100 after two years, not \$75.

1. Find the geometric mean of $1 + 50\%$ and $1 - 50\%$. (Each 1 represents the fact that at the beginning of each year, an investment is worth 100% of itself.) Round to the nearest thousandth.

2. It is the geometric mean, not the arithmetic mean, that tells you what the interest rate would have had to have been over an entire investment period to achieve the end result. You can use your answer to Exercise 1 to check this claim. Find the value of a \$100 investment after it increased or decreased at the rate you found in Exercise 1 for two years. Show your work.

3. Copy the right triangle shown here. Write the terms "Year 1 Rate", "Year 2 Rate", and "Average Rate" to show geometrically how the three investment rates relate to each other.

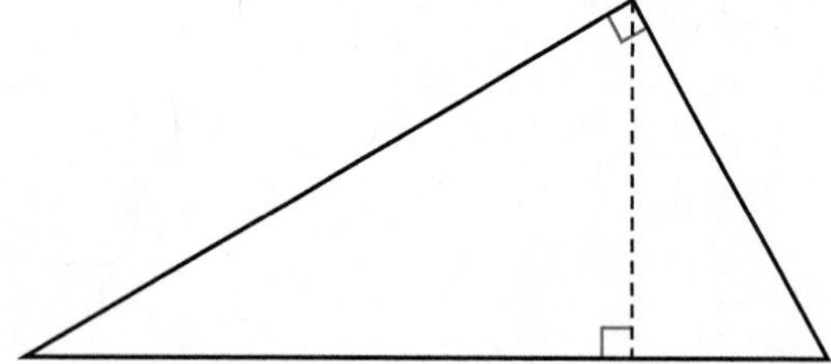

4. The geometric mean of n numbers is the nth root of the product of the numbers. Find what the interest rate would have had to have been over 4 years to achieve the result of a \$100 investment that grew 20% in Year 1 and 30% in Year 2, then lost 20% in Year 3 and 30% in Year 4. Show your work. Round your answer to the nearest tenth of a percent.

STUDY GUIDE REVIEW

Using Similar Triangles

MODULE 12

Essential Question: How can you use similar triangles to solve real-world problems?

Key Vocabulary
indirect measurement *(medición indirecta)*
geometric mean *(media geométrica)*

KEY EXAMPLE *(Lesson 12.1)*

Find the missing length x.

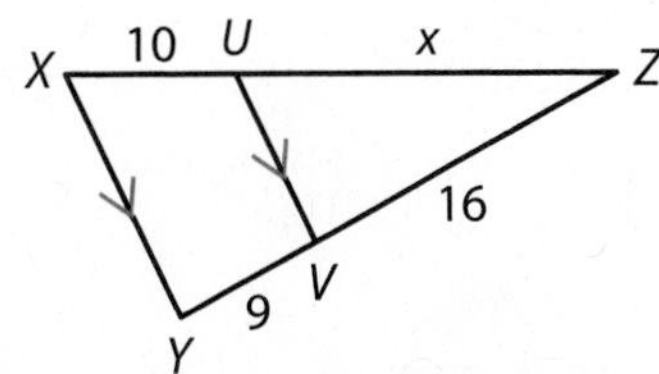

$\frac{ZU}{UX} = \frac{ZV}{VY}$ Write a proportion.

$\frac{x}{10} = \frac{16}{9}$ Substitute.

$x = \left(\frac{16}{9}\right)(10)$ Multiply both sides by 10.

$x \approx 17.8$ Simplify.

KEY EXAMPLE *(Lesson 12.2)*

Given the directed line segment from A to B, construct the point P that divides the segment in the ratio 2 to 3 from A to B.

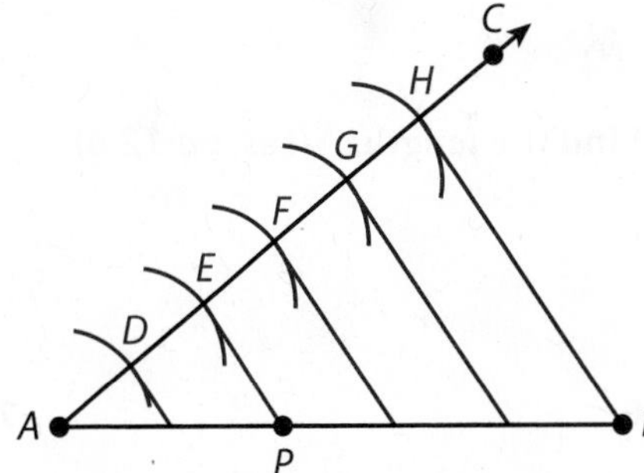

Use a straightedge to draw $\overrightarrow{AC}$.

Place a compass on point A and draw an arc through $\overrightarrow{AC}$. Label the intersection D. Continue this for intersections D through H.

Use a straightedge to connect points B and H.

Construct angles congruent to $\angle AHB$ with points D through G.

$\overline{AB}$ is partitioned into five equal parts. Label point P at the point that divides the segment in the ratio 2 to 3 from A to B.

KEY EXAMPLE *(Lesson 12.3)*

A 5.8-foot-tall man is standing next to a basketball hoop that casts an 11.2-foot shadow. The man's shadow is 6.5 feet long. How tall is the basketball hoop?

Let x be the height of the basketball hoop.

$\frac{x}{11.2} = \frac{5.8}{6.5}$ Write a proportion.

$x = \left(\frac{5.8}{6.5}\right)(11.2)$ Multiply both sides by 11.2.

$x \approx 10$

EXERCISES

Find the missing lengths. *(Lesson 12.1)*

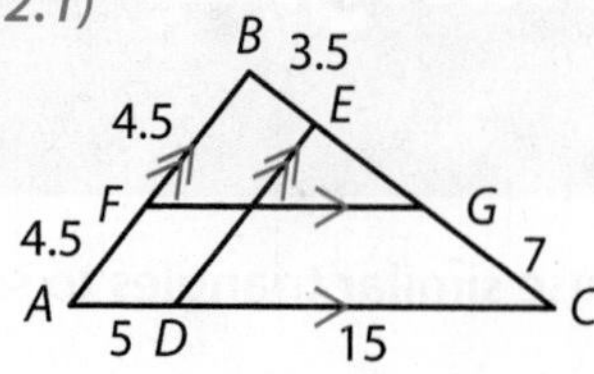

1. $BG =$

2. $CE =$

Copy the directed line segment from A to B. Construct the point P that divides the segment in the ratio 3 to 1 from A to B. *(Lesson 12.2)*

3.

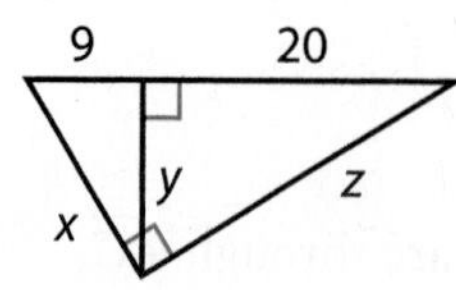

Find the unknown length. *(Lesson 12.3)*

4. A 5.9-foot-tall-man stands near a 12-foot statue. The man places a mirror on the ground a certain distance from the base of the statue, and then stands another 7 feet from the mirror to see the top of the statue in it. How far is the mirror from the base of the statue?

5. A 45-foot flagpole casts a 22-foot shadow. At the same time of day, a woman casts a 2.7-foot shadow. How tall is the woman?

Find the lengths. *(Lesson 12.4)*

9 20

y z x

6. x

7. y

8. z

MODULE PERFORMANCE TASK

How Large Is the Bermuda Triangle?

The boundaries of the Bermuda Triangle are not well defined, but the region is often represented as a triangle with vertices at Miami, Florida; San Juan, Puerto Rico; and Hamilton, Bermuda. The distance between Miami and San Juan is about 1,034 miles. What is the approximate area of this region? One tool that you may find helpful in solving this problem is the similar triangle shown here with angle measures labeled.

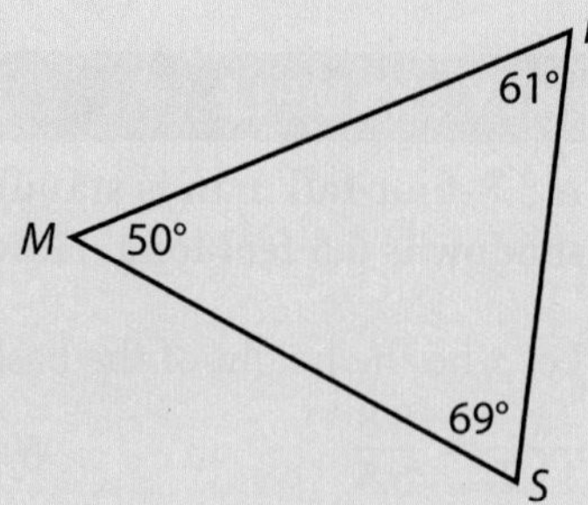

Be sure to record all your data and assumptions. Then use graphs, diagrams, words, or numbers to explain how you reached your conclusion.

Ready to Go On?

12.1–12.4 Using Similar Triangles

- Online Homework
- Hints and Help
- Extra Practice

Find the missing lengths. *(Lesson 12.1)*

1.

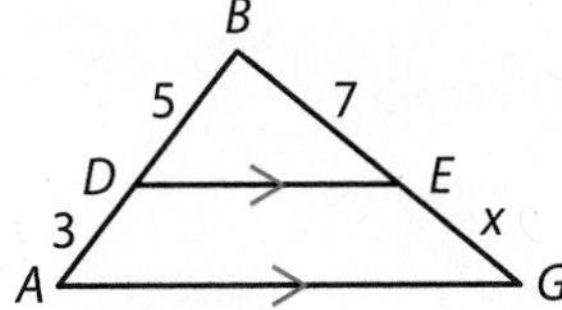

2.

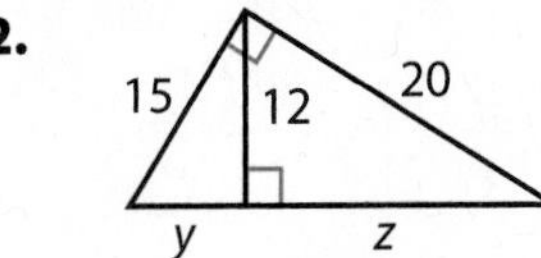

Copy the directed line segment from *A* to *B*. Construct the point *P* that divides the segment in the given ratio from *A* to *B*. *(Lesson 12.2)*

3. 3 to 4

Find the missing height. *(Lesson 12.3)*

4. The height of a street light is 25 feet. It casts a 12-foot shadow. At the same time, a man standing next to the street light casts a 3-foot shadow. How tall is the man?

ESSENTIAL QUESTION

5. How can you use similar triangles to find the missing parts of a triangle?

MODULE 12
MIXED REVIEW

Assessment Readiness

SELECTED RESPONSE

1. $\triangle XYZ$ is given by the points $X(-1, -1)$, $Y(3, 5)$, and $Z(5, 1)$. Consider each of the points below. Is each point a vertex of the image under the transformation $(x, y) \rightarrow (x + 3, y - 2) \rightarrow \left(\frac{1}{2}x, y\right) \rightarrow (y, -x)$?

Write Yes or No for A–C.

A. $X'''(-3, -1)$
B. $Y'''(3, -3)$
C. $Z'''(-1, -4)$

2. Which of the following statements are true about the triangle at the right? Determine if each statement is True or False.

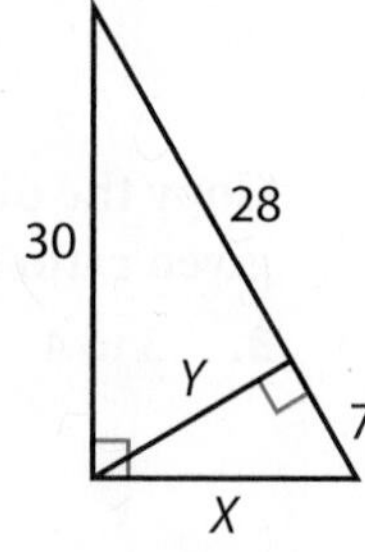

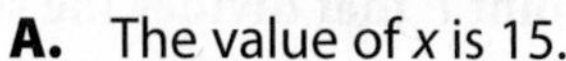

A. The value of x is 15.

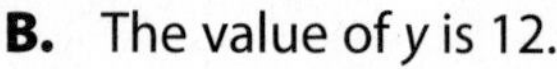

B. The value of y is 12.
C. The value of y is 16.

3. $\triangle ABC$ is given by the points $A(-1, 2)$, $B(2, 5)$, and $C(4, -1)$. What is the point $\left(\frac{1}{2}, \frac{5}{2}\right)$? Explain what this means.

4. Copy the directed segment from A to B. Construct the point P that divides the segment in the ratio 1 to 5 from A to B. Explain your process and how it relates to similar triangles.

UNIT 4 MIXED REVIEW

Assessment Readiness

- Online Homework
- Hints and Help
- Extra Practice

1. Determine whether the statements are true.

Determine if each statement is True or False.

A. Dilations preserve angle measure.

B. Dilations preserve distance.

C. Dilations preserve collinearity.

D. Dilations preserve orientation.

2. Was the given transformation used to map *ABCD* to *QRST*?

Tell whether each statement is correct.

A. Reflection across the *y*-axis

B. Reflection across the *x*-axis

C. Dilation

D. Translation

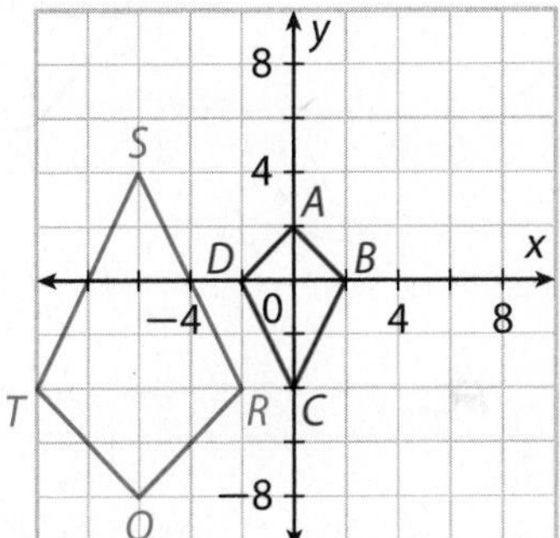

3. The vertices of quadrilateral *JKLM* are $J(-2, 0)$, $K(-1, 2)$, $L(1, 3)$, and $M(0, 1)$. Can you use slopes and/or the distance formula to prove each statement?

Write Yes or No for A–C.

A. Quadrilateral *JKLM* is a parallelogram.

B. Quadrilateral *JKLM* is a rhombus.

C. Quadrilateral *JKLM* is a rectangle.

4. Will the transformation produce similar figures?

Write Yes or No for each statement.

A. $(x, y) \rightarrow (x - 5, y + 5) \rightarrow (-x, -y) \rightarrow (3x, 3y)$

B. $(x, y) \rightarrow (3x, y + 5) \rightarrow (x, 3y) \rightarrow (x - 1, y - 1)$

C. $(x, y) \rightarrow (x, y + 5) \rightarrow (2x, y) \rightarrow (x + 5, y)$

5. Is *ABC* similar to *DEF*? Write Yes or No for each set of vertices.

A. $A(-1, -3), B(1, 3), C(3, -5)$
$D(2, -6), E(3, 0), F(6, -8)$

B. $A(-1, -3), B(1, 3), C(3, -5)$
$D(-5, -1), E(-4, 2), F(-3, -2)$

C. $A(-1, -3), B(1, 3), C(3, -5)$
$D(-2, -2), E(2, 4), F(2, -4)$

6. Are the triangles similar? Write Yes or No for each pair of figures.

A.

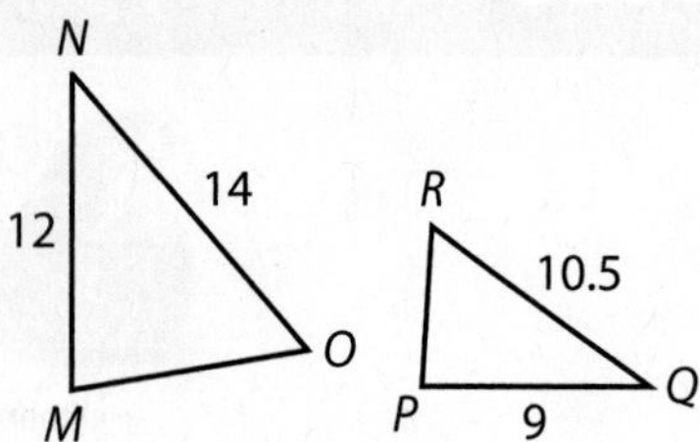

B.

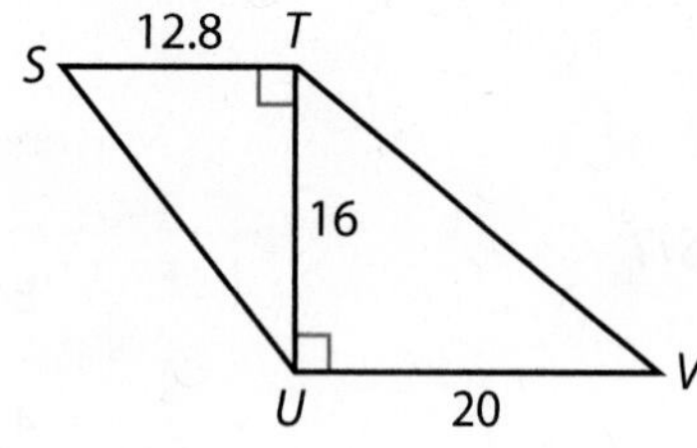

C.

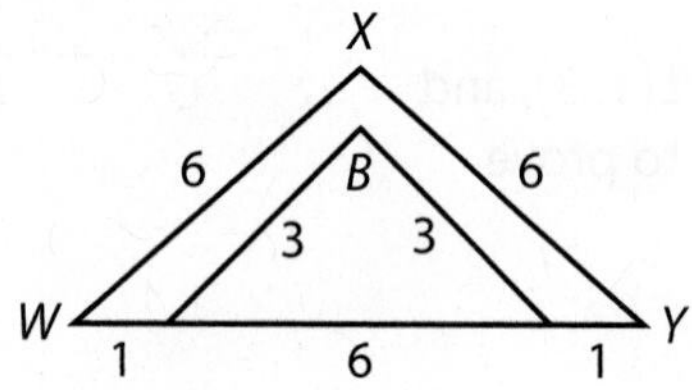

7. Find the missing side lengths *PQ*, *PR*, and *TU*.

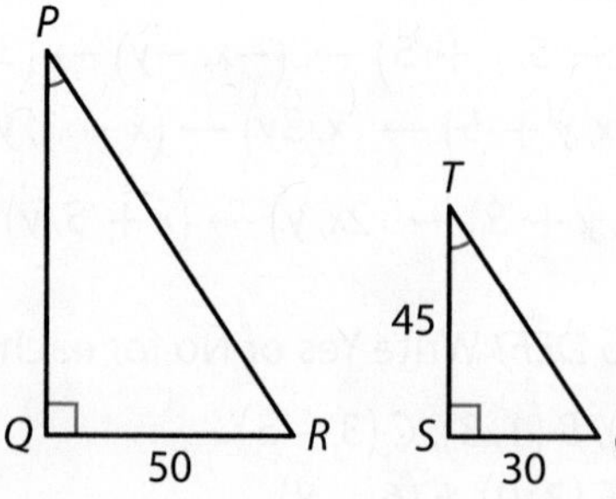

Performance Tasks

★ **8.** The map shows that A Street and B Street are parallel. Find the distance on 6th Ave between A Street and the library. Explain any theorems that come into play here.

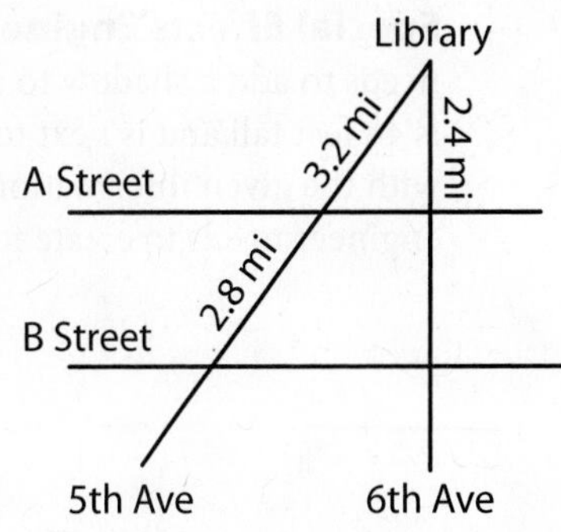

★★ **9.** A city has a walkway between the middle school and the library that can be represented in the image given. The city decides it wants to place three trash cans, equally spaced along the walkway, to help reduce any littering. Find the coordinates of the points at which the trash cans should be placed, and then plot them on the graph.

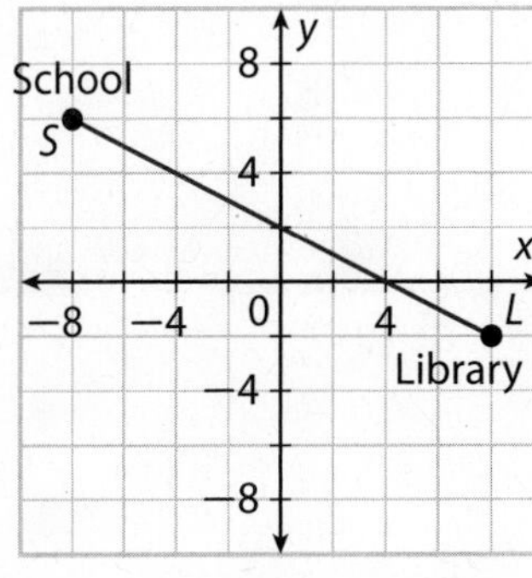

★★★**10.** A person playing table tennis can be represented by the image shown, where A is the point where the person hits the ball with the paddle, at a vertical distance of 152.25 cm from the floor. The height of the table is 76 cm and the net is 15.25 cm tall. Determine the path of the ball.

MATH IN CAREERS

Special Effects Engineers A special effects engineer is helping create a movie and needs to add a shadow to a tall totem pole that is next to a 6-foot-tall man. The totem pole is 48 feet tall and is next to the man, who has a shadow that is 2.5 feet long. Create an image with the given information and then use the image to find the length of the shadow that the engineer needs to create for the totem pole.

UNIT 5

Trigonometry

MODULE 13

Trigonometry with Right Triangles

MODULE 14

Trigonometry with All Triangles

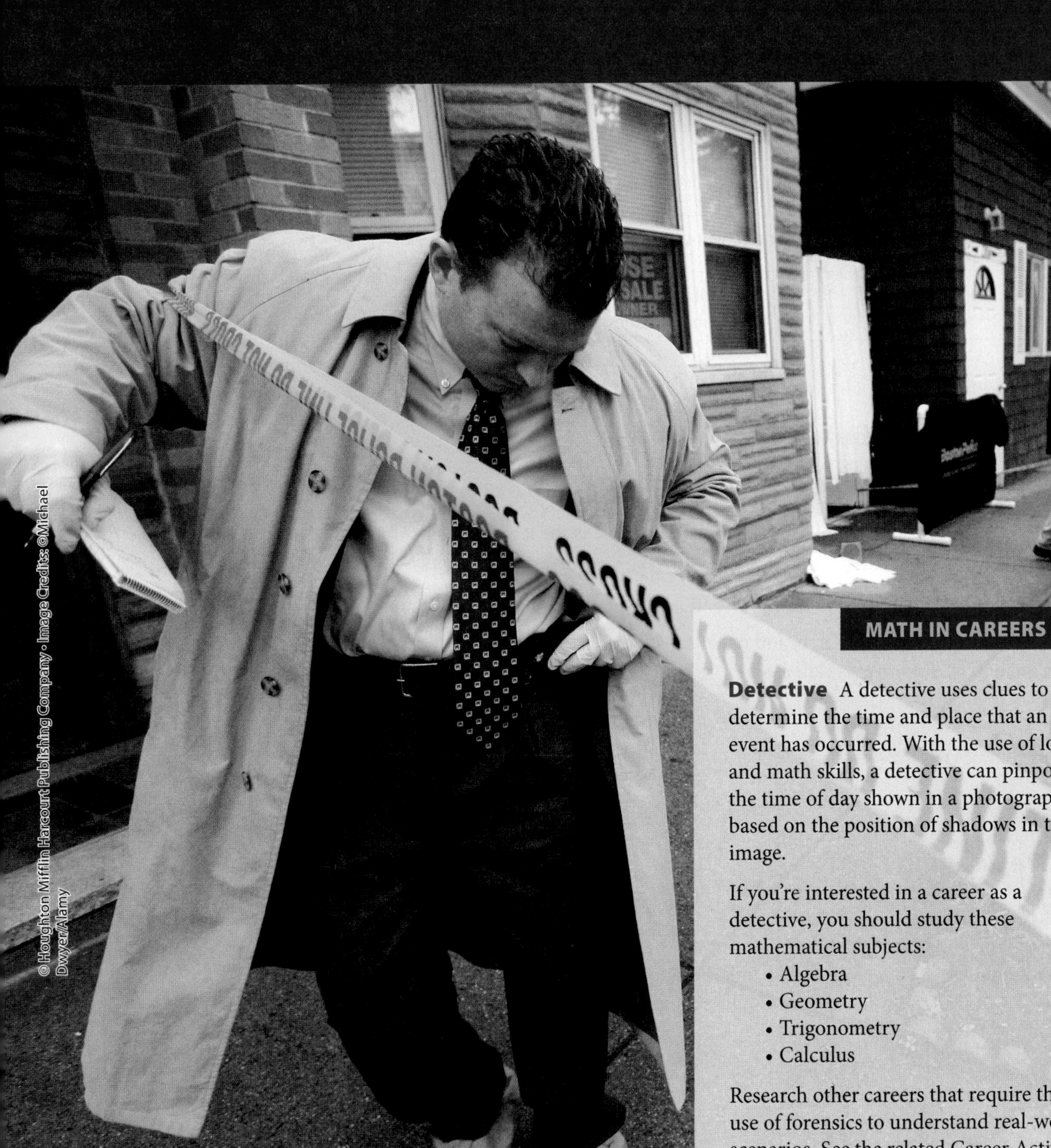

MATH IN CAREERS

Detective A detective uses clues to determine the time and place that an event has occurred. With the use of logic and math skills, a detective can pinpoint the time of day shown in a photograph, based on the position of shadows in the image.

If you're interested in a career as a detective, you should study these mathematical subjects:

- Algebra
- Geometry
- Trigonometry
- Calculus

Research other careers that require the use of forensics to understand real-world scenarios. See the related Career Activity at the end of this unit.

Visualize Vocabulary

Use the review words to complete the chart.

Term	Description
a. ?	A triangle with a right angle
b. ?	An angle whose measure is 90°
c. ?	The longest side of a right triangle
d. ?	The shorter sides of a right triangle
e. ?	Angles whose measures sum to 90°
f. ?	Angles whose measures sum to 180°
g. ?	A representation of the relative sizes of two or more values

Review Words

- ✔ complementary angles *(ángulos complementarios)*
- ✔ hypotenuse *(hipotenusa)*
- ✔ legs *(catetos)*
- ✔ ratio *(razón)*
- ✔ right angle *(ángulo recto)*
- ✔ right triangle *(triángulo rectángulo)*
- ✔ supplementary angles *(ángulos suplementarios)*

Preview Words

adjacent *(adyacente)*
cosine *(coseno)*
inverse trigonometric ratios *(razónes trigonométricas inversas)*
opposite *(opuesto)*
Pythagorean triple *(terna pitagórica)*
sine *(seno)*
tangent *(tangente)*
trigonometric ratio
razón trigonométrica

Understand Vocabulary

Complete the sentences using the preview words.

1. In a right triangle, the side __?__ to an acute angle is the leg that forms one side of the angle.

2. Sine, cosine, and tangent are examples of __?__.

3. A set of positive integers a, b, and c that satisfy the equation $a^2 + b^2 = c^2$ is called a(n) __?__.

Active Reading

Booklet Create a booklet at the start of the unit. During discussions of the material in class, write vocabulary that you know toward the front, vocabulary that you recognize but are unsure of toward the middle, and vocabulary that you do not know toward the back. Use the booklet as a tool for studying the vocabulary.

Trigonometry with Right Triangles

MODULE 13

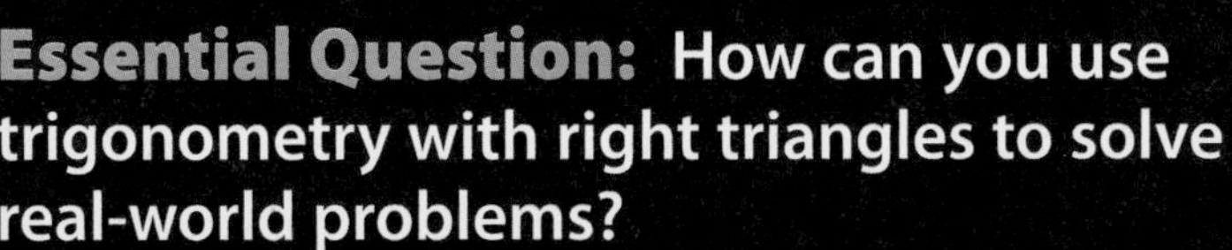

Essential Question: How can you use trigonometry with right triangles to solve real-world problems?

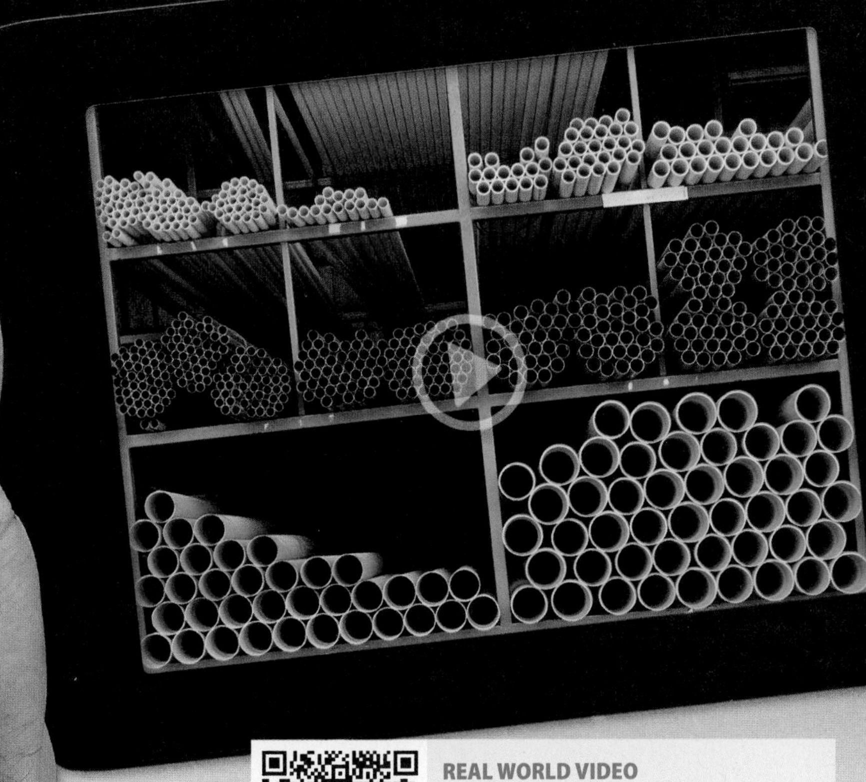

REAL WORLD VIDEO
Check out how right triangle trigonometry is used in real-world warehouses to minimize the space needed for items being shipped or stored.

MODULE PERFORMANCE TASK PREVIEW

How Much Shorter Are Staggered Pipe Stacks?

In this module, you will investigate how much space can be saved by stacking pipes in a staggered pattern rather than directly on top of each other. How can trigonometry help you find the answer to this problem? Get prepared to discover the "staggering" results!

Are YOU Ready?

Complete these exercises to review skills you will need for this module.

Personal Math Trainer

- Online Homework
- Hints and Help
- Extra Practice

Angle Relationships

Example 1 Find the angle complementary to the given angle. 75°

$x + 75° = 90°$ Write as an equation.

$x = 90° - 75°$ Solve for x.

$x = 15°$

Find the complementary angle.

1. 20°

2. 35°

3. 67°

Find the supplementary angle.

4. 80°

5. 65°

6. 34°

Find the remaining angle or angles for $\triangle ABC$.

7. $m\angle A = 50°$, $m\angle B = 40°$

8. $m\angle A = 60°$, $m\angle C = 20°$

9. $m\angle B = 70°$ and $\angle A \cong \angle C$

10. $\angle A \cong \angle B \cong \angle C$

11. $m\angle B = 30°$ and $m\angle A = \frac{1}{2}m\angle C$

12. $\triangle ABC$ is similar to $\triangle DEF$ and $m\angle D = 70°$ and $m\angle F = 50°$

13. $\triangle ABC$ is similar to $\triangle PQR$ and $m\angle R = 50°$ and $\angle P \cong \angle Q$

14. $m\angle A = 45°$ and $m\angle B = m\angle C$

15. $m\angle B = 105°$ and $m\angle A = 2 \cdot m\angle C$

16. $m\angle A = 5°$ and $m\angle B = 9 \cdot m\angle C$

13.1 Tangent Ratio

Essential Question: How do you find the tangent ratio for an acute angle?

Explore Investigating a Ratio in a Right Triangle

In a given a right triangle, $\triangle ABC$, with a right angle at vertex C, there are three sides. The side adjacent to $\angle A$ is the leg that forms one side of $\angle A$. The side opposite $\angle A$ is the leg that does not form a side of $\angle A$. The side that connects the adjacent and opposite legs is the hypotenuse.

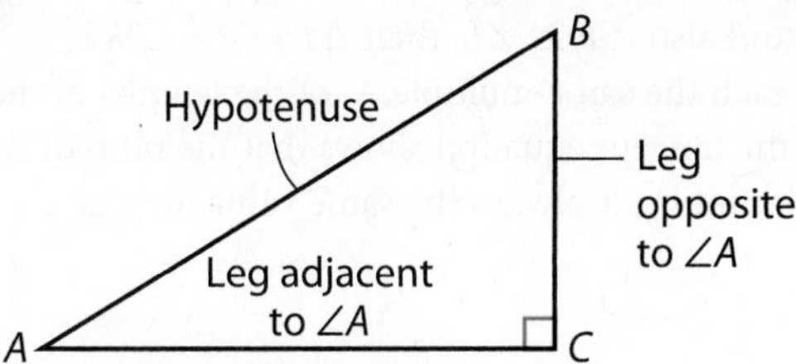

(A) In $\triangle DEF$, the legs opposite and adjacent to $\angle D$ are labeled. Measure the lengths of the legs in centimeters and record their values.

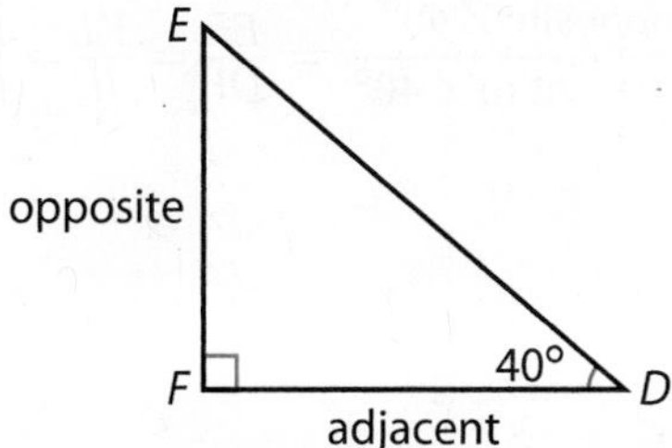

(B) What is the ratio of the opposite leg length to the adjacent leg length, rounded to the nearest hundredth?

$\frac{EF}{DF} \approx$?

(C) Using a protractor and ruler, draw right triangle $\triangle JKL$ with a right angle at vertex L and $\angle J = 40°$ so that $\triangle JKL \sim \triangle DEF$. Label the opposite and adjacent legs to $\angle J$ and include their measurements.

(D) What is the ratio of the opposite leg length to the adjacent leg length, rounded to the nearest hundredth?

$\frac{KL}{JL} \approx$?

Reflect

1. **Discussion** Compare your work with that of other students. Do all the triangles have the same angles? Do they all have the same side lengths? Do they all have the same leg ratios? Summarize your findings.

2. If you repeated Steps A–D with a right triangle having a 30° angle, how would your results be similar? How would they be different?

Explain 1 Finding the Tangent of an Angle

The ratio you calculated in the Explore section is called the *tangent* of an angle. The **tangent** of acute angle A, written tan $\angle A$, is defined as follows:

$$\tan A = \frac{\text{length of leg opposite } \angle A}{\text{length of leg adjacent to } \angle A}$$

You can use what you know about similarity to show why the tangent of an angle is constant. By the AA Similarity Theorem, given $\angle D \cong \angle J$ and also $\angle F \cong \angle L$, then $\triangle DEF \sim \triangle JKL$. This means the lengths of the sides of $\triangle JKL$ are each the same multiple, k, of the lengths of the corresponding sides of $\triangle DEF$. Substituting into the tangent equation shows that the ratio of the length of the opposite leg to the length of the adjacent leg is always the same value for a given acute angle.

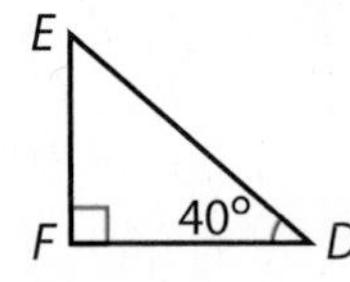

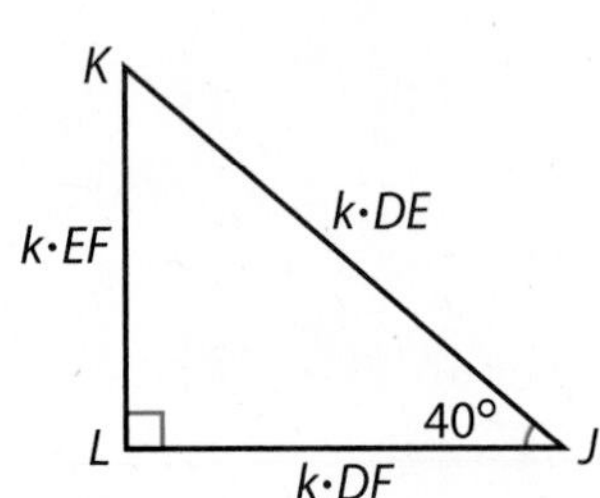

tangent defined for specified angle $\triangle DEF$ $\triangle JKL$

$$\tan 40° = \frac{\text{leg opposite } \angle 40°}{\text{leg adjacent to } \angle 40°} = \frac{EF}{DF} = \frac{KL}{JL} = \frac{k \cdot EF}{k \cdot DF} = \frac{EF}{DF}$$

Example 1 **Find the tangent of each specified angle. Write each ratio as a fraction and as a decimal rounded to the nearest hundredth.**

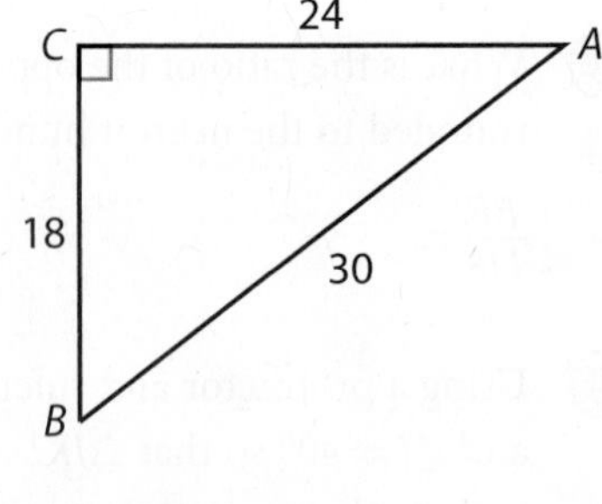

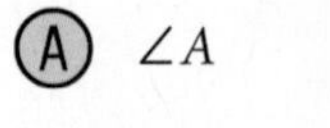

(A) $\angle A$

$$\tan A = \frac{\text{length of leg opposite } \angle A}{\text{length of leg adjacent to } \angle A} = \frac{18}{24} = \frac{3}{4} = 0.75$$

(B) $\angle B$

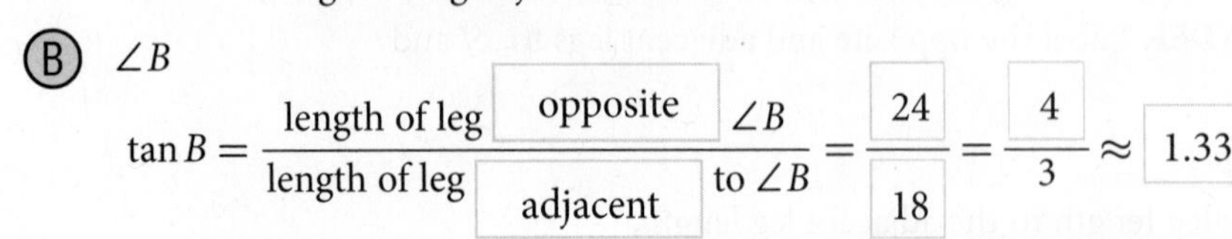

$$\tan B = \frac{\text{length of leg } \boxed{\text{opposite}} \ \angle B}{\text{length of leg } \boxed{\text{adjacent}} \text{ to } \angle B} = \frac{\boxed{24}}{\boxed{18}} = \frac{\boxed{4}}{3} \approx \boxed{1.33}$$

Reflect

3. What is the relationship between the ratios for tan A and tan B? Do you believe this relationship will be true for acute angles in other right triangles? Explain.

4. Why does it not make sense to ask for the value of tan L?

Your Turn

Find the tangent of each specified angle. Write each ratio as a fraction and as a decimal rounded to the nearest hundredth.

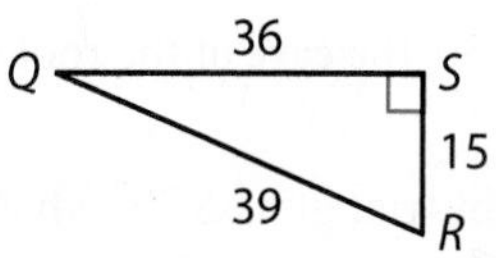

5. $\angle Q$

6. $\angle R$

Explain 2 Finding a Side Length using Tangent

When you know the length of a leg of a right triangle and the measure of one of the acute angles, you can use the tangent to find the length of the other leg. This is especially useful in real-world problems.

Example 2 **Apply the tangent ratio to find unknown lengths.**

(A) In order to meet safety guidelines, a roof contractor determines that she must place the base of her ladder 6 feet away from the house, making an angle of 76° with the ground. To the nearest tenth of a foot, how far above the ground is the eave of the roof?

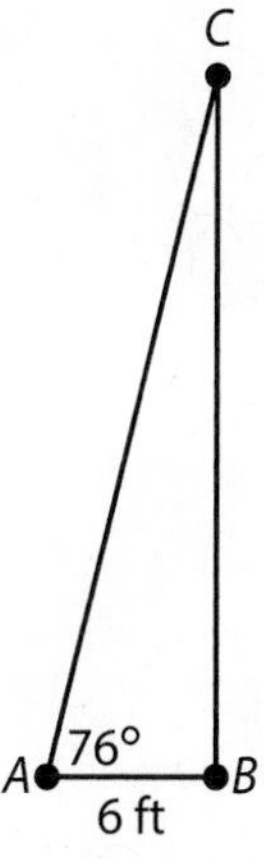

Step 1 Write a tangent ratio that involves the unknown length.

$$\tan A = \frac{\text{length of leg opposite } \angle A}{\text{length of leg adjacent to } \angle A} = \frac{BC}{BA}$$

Step 2 Identify the given values and substitute into the tangent equation.

Given: $BA = 6$ ft and $m\angle A = 76°$

Substitute: $\tan 76° = \frac{BC}{6}$

Step 3 Solve for the unknown leg length. Be sure the calculator is in degree mode and do not round until the final step of the solution.

Multiply each side by 6. $6 \cdot \tan 76° = \frac{6}{1} \cdot \frac{BC}{6}$

Use a calculator to find tan 76°. $6 \cdot \tan 76° = BC$

Substitute this value in for tan 76°. $6(4.010780934) = BC$

Multiply. Round to the nearest tenth. $24.1 \approx BC$

So, the eave of the roof is about 24.1 feet above the ground.

(B) For right triangle $\triangle STU$, what is the length of the leg adjacent to $\angle S$?

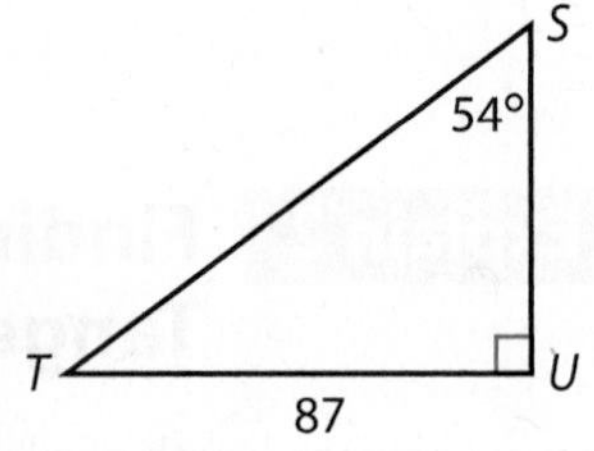

Step 1 Write a tangent ratio that involves the unknown length.

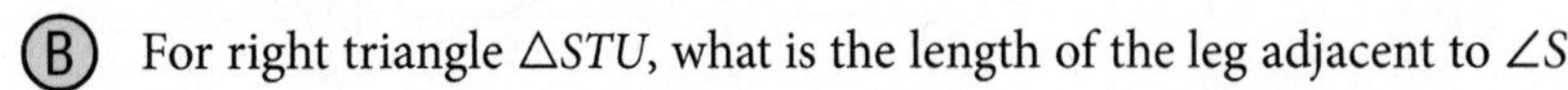

$$\tan S = \frac{\text{length of leg opposite } \angle S}{\text{length of leg adjacent to } \angle S} = \frac{TU}{SU}$$

Step 2 Identify the given values and substitute into the tangent equation.

Given: $TU = 87$ and $m\angle S = 54°$

Substitute: $\tan 54° = \frac{87}{SU}$

Step 3 Solve for the unknown leg length.

Multiply both sides by *SU*, then divide both sides by 54°. $SU = \frac{87}{\tan 54°}$

Use a calculator to find 54° and substitute. $SU \approx \frac{87}{1.37638192}$

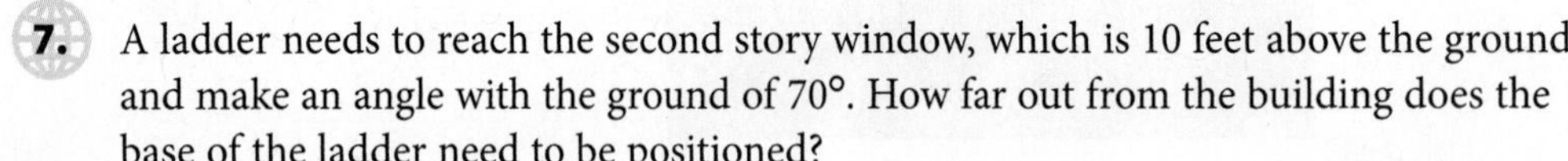

Divide. Round to the nearest tenth. $SU \approx 63.2$

Your Turn

7. A ladder needs to reach the second story window, which is 10 feet above the ground, and make an angle with the ground of 70°. How far out from the building does the base of the ladder need to be positioned?

Explain 3 Finding an Angle Measure using Tangent

In the previous section you used a given angle measure and leg measure with the tangent ratio to solve for an unknown leg. What if you are given the leg measures and want to find the measures of the acute angles? If you know the tan A, read as "tangent of $\angle A$," then you can use the **$\tan^{-1} A$**, read as "**inverse tangent of $\angle A$**," to find $m\angle A$. So, given an acute angle $\angle A$, if $\tan A = x$, then $\tan^{-1} x = m\angle A$.

Example 3 **Find the measure of the indicated angle. Round to the nearest degree.**

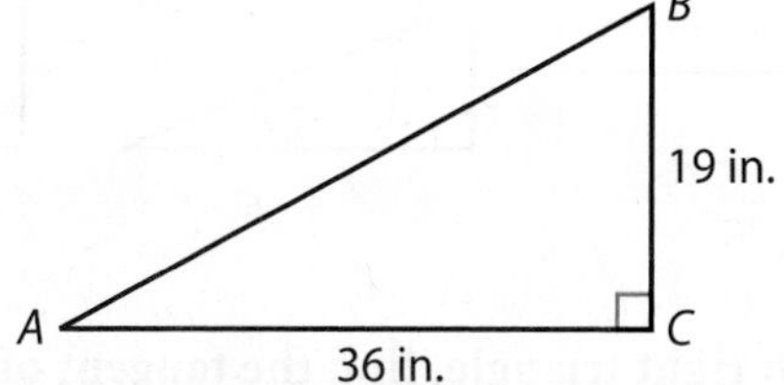

(A) What is $m\angle A$?

Step 1 Write the tangent ratio for $\angle A$ using the known values.	Step 2 Write the inverse tangent equation.	Step 3 Evaluate using a calculator and round as indicated.
$\tan A = \frac{19}{36}$	$\tan^{-1} \frac{19}{36} = m\angle A$	$m\angle A \approx 27.82409638 \approx 28°$

(B) What is $m\angle B$?

Step 1 Write the tangent ratio for $\angle B$ using the known values.	Step 2 Write the inverse tangent equation.	Step 3 Evaluate using a calculator and round as indicated.
$\tan B = \frac{36}{19}$	$\tan^{-1} \frac{36}{19} = m\angle B$	$m\angle B \approx 62.17590362° \approx 62°$

Your Turn

8. Find $m\angle J$.

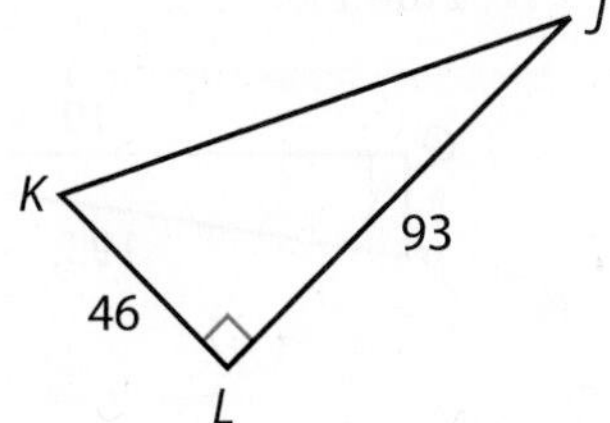

Elaborate

9. Explain how to identify the opposite and adjacent legs of a given acute angle.

10. Discussion How does tan A change as $m\angle A$ increases? Explain the basis for the identified relationship.

11. Essential Question Check-In Compare and contrast the use of the tangent and inverse tangent ratios for solving problems.

Evaluate: Homework and Practice

- Online Homework
- Hints and Help
- Extra Practice

1. In each triangle, measure the length of the adjacent side and the opposite side of the 22° angle. Then calculate and compare the ratios.

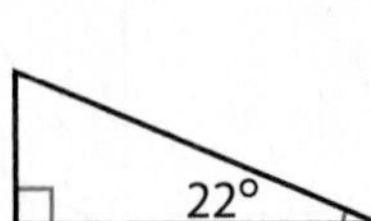

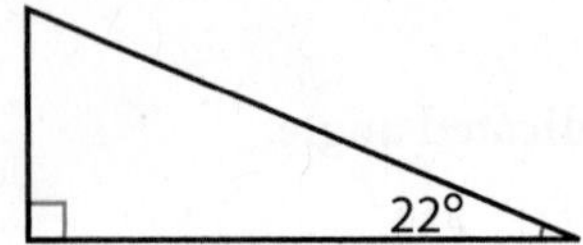

In each right triangle, find the tangent of each angle that is not the right angle.

2.

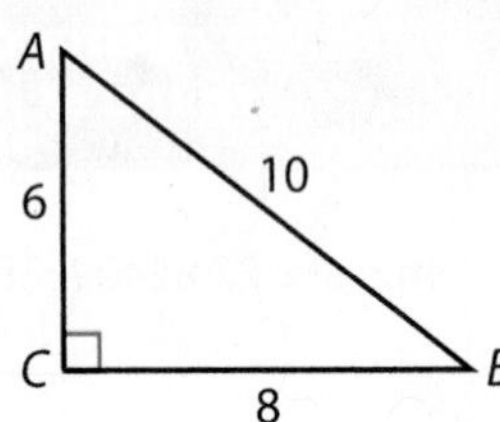

3.

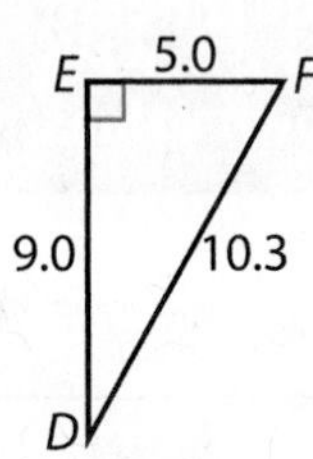

4.

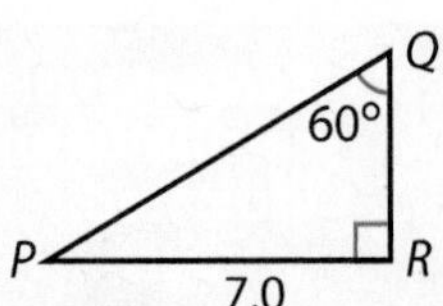

5.

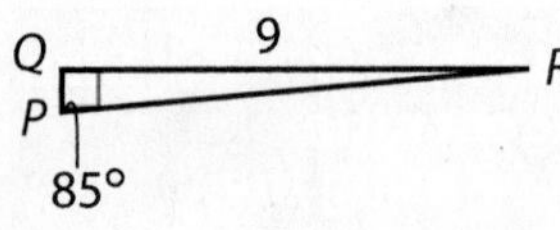

Let $\triangle ABC$ be a right triangle, with $m\angle C = 90°$. Given the tangent of one of the complementary angles of the triangle, find the tangent of the other angle.

6. $\tan \angle A = 1.25$

7. $\tan \angle B = 0.50$

8. $\tan \angle B = 1.0$

Use the tangent to find the unknown side length.

9. Find *QR*.

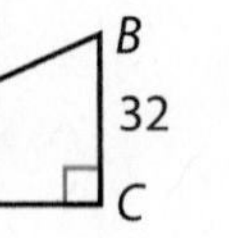

10. Find *AC*.

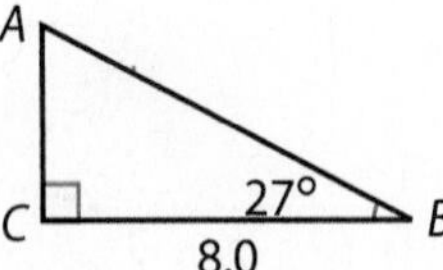

11. Find *PQ*.

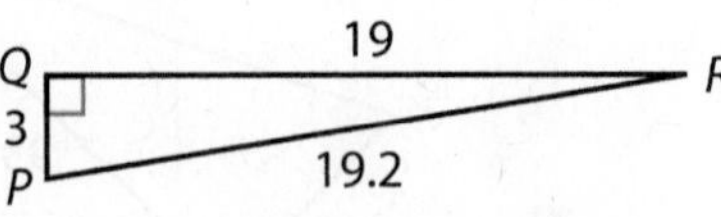

12. Find *DE*.

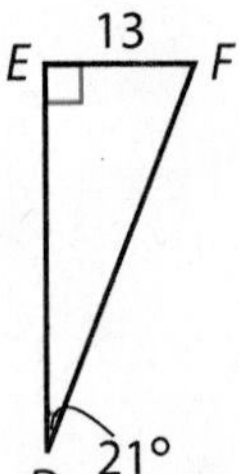

13. Find *AB*.

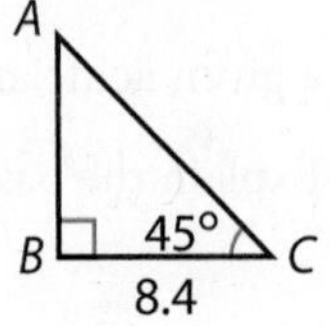

14. Find *PR*.

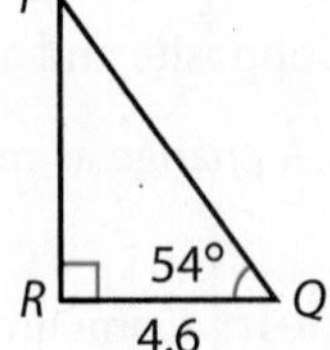

Find the measure of the angle specified for each triangle. Use the inverse tangent ($\tan^{-1}$) function of your calculator. Round your answer to the nearest degree.

15. Find $\angle A$.

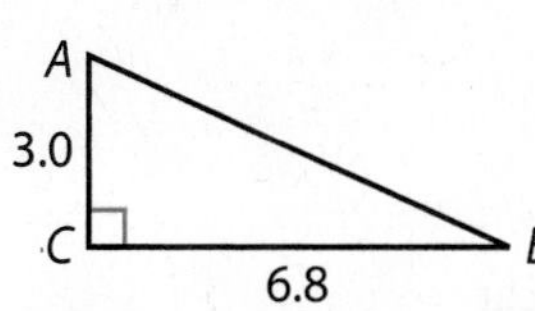

16. Find $\angle R$.

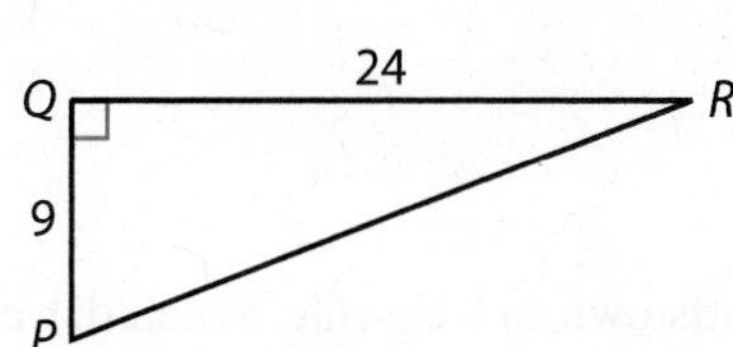

17. Find $\angle B$.

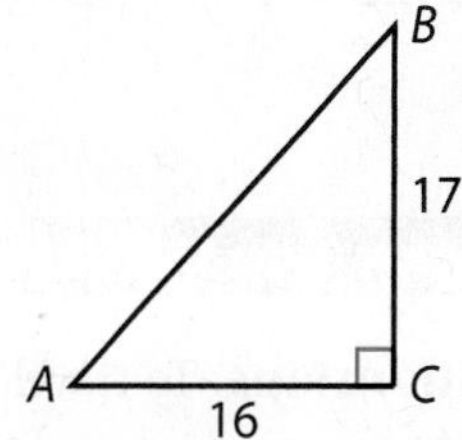

Write an equation using either tan or $\tan^{-1}$ to express the measure of the angle or side. Then solve the equation.

18. Find BC.

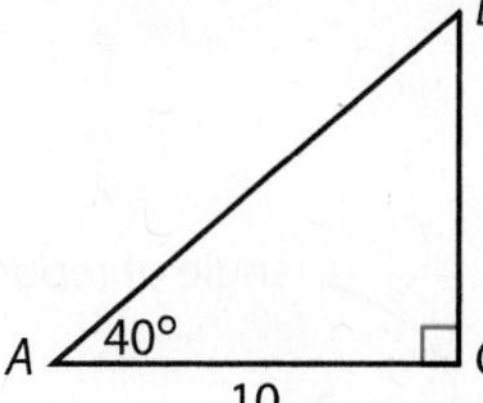

19. Find PQ.

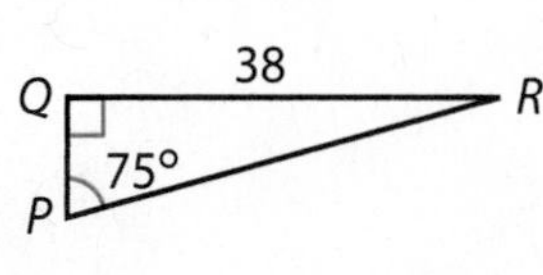

20. Find $\angle A$ and $\angle C$.

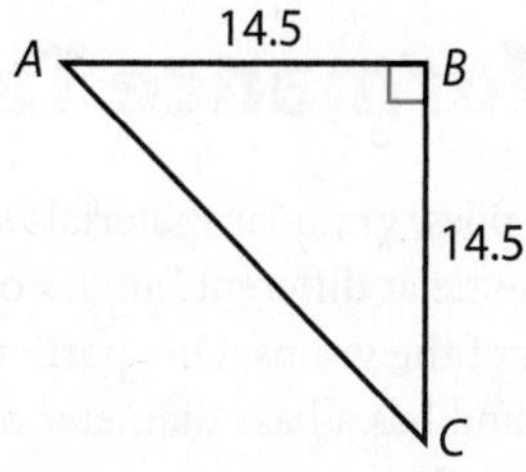

21. Multi-Step Find the measure of angle D. Show your work.

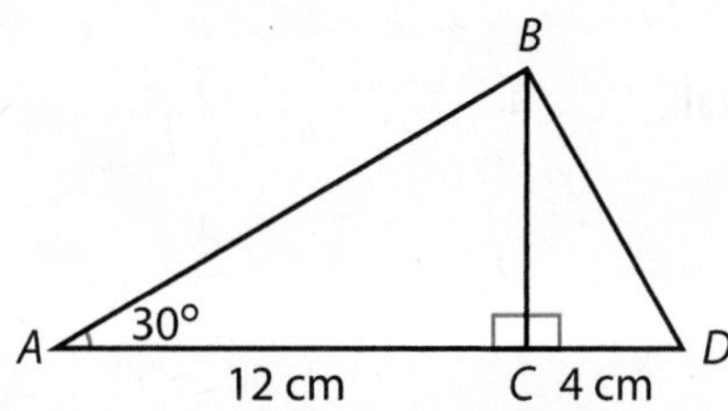

22. Engineering A client wants to build a ramp that carries people to a height of 1.4 meters, as shown in the diagram. What additional information is necessary to identify the measure of angle a, the angle the ramp forms with the horizontal? After the additional measurement is made, describe how to find the measure of the angle.

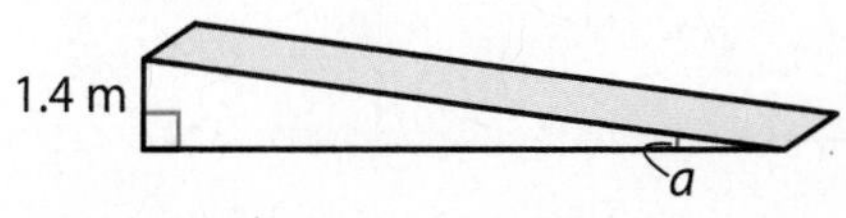

23. Explain the Error A student uses the triangle shown to calculate a. Find and explain the student's error.

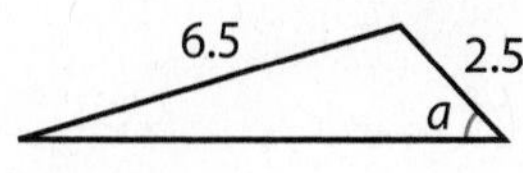

$$a = \tan^{-1}\left(\frac{6.5}{2.5}\right) = \tan^{-1}(2.6)$$

$$a = 69.0°$$

24. When $m\angle A + m\angle B = 90°$, what relationship is formed by tan $\angle A$ and tan $\angle B$? Determine all that apply.

A. $\tan\angle A = \frac{1}{\tan B}$

B. $\tan\angle A + \tan\angle B = 1$

C. $(\tan\angle A)(\tan\angle B) = 1$

D. $(\tan\angle A)(\tan\angle B) = -1$

H.O.T. Focus on Higher Order Thinking

25. Analyze Relationships To travel from Pottstown to Cogsville, a man drives his car 83 miles due east on one road, and then 15 miles due north on another road. Describe the path that a bird could fly in a straight line from Pottstown to Cogsville. What angle does the line make with the two roads that the man used?

26. Critical Thinking A right triangle has only one 90° angle. Both of its other angles have measures greater than 0° and less than 90°. Why is it useful to define the tangent of 90° to equal 1, and the tangent of 0° to equal 0?

Lesson Performance Task

When they form conical piles, granular materials such as salt, gravel, and sand settle at different "angles of repose," depending on the shapes of the grains. One particular 13-foot tall cone of dry sand has a base diameter of 38.6 feet.

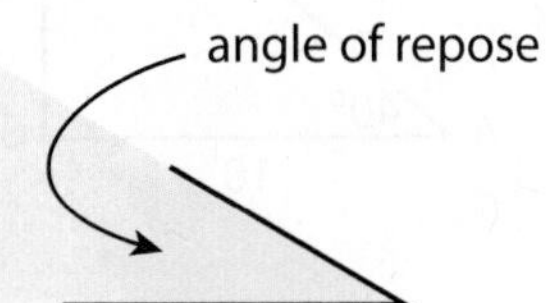

1. To the nearest tenth of a degree, what is the angle of repose of this type of dry sand?

2. A different conical pile of the same type of sand is 10 feet tall. What is the diameter of the cone's base?

3. Henley Landscaping Supply sells a type of sand with a 30° angle of repose for $32 per cubic yard. Find the cost of an 11-foot-tall cone of this type of sand. Show your work.

13.2 Sine and Cosine Ratios

Resource Locker

Essential Question: How can you use the sine and cosine ratios, and their inverses, in calculations involving right triangles?

Explore Investigating Ratios in a Right Triangle

You can use geometry software or an online tool to explore ratios of side lengths in right triangles.

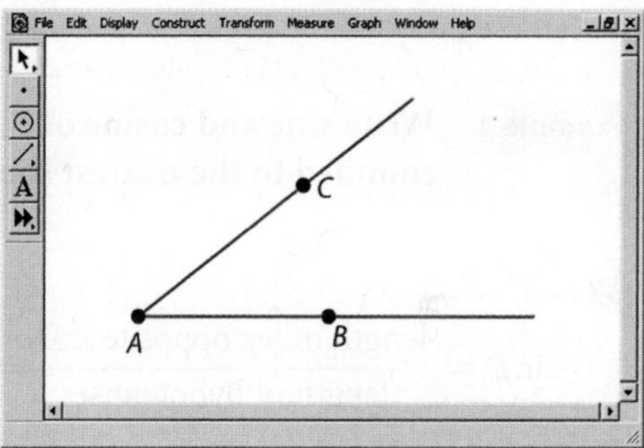

(A) Construct three points A, B, and C. Construct rays $\overrightarrow{AB}$ and $\overrightarrow{AC}$. Move C so that $\angle A$ is acute.

(B) Construct point D on $\overline{AC}$. Construct a line through D perpendicular to $\overline{AB}$. Construct point E as the intersection of the perpendicular line and $\overline{AB}$.

(C) Measure $\angle A$. Measure the side lengths DE, AE, and AD of $\triangle ADE$.

(D) Calculate the ratios $\frac{DE}{AD}$ and $\frac{AE}{AD}$.

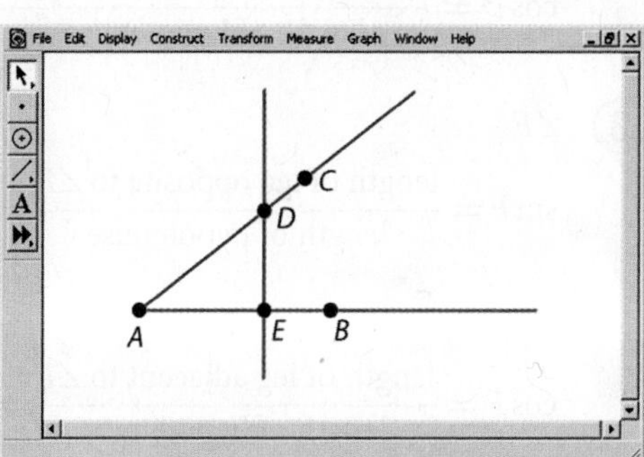

Reflect

1. Drag D along $\overrightarrow{AC}$. What happens to $m\angle A$ as D moves along $\overrightarrow{AC}$? What postulate or theorem guarantees that the different triangles formed are similar to each other?

2. As you move D along $\overrightarrow{AC}$, what happens to the values of the ratios $\frac{DE}{AD}$ and $\frac{AE}{AD}$? Use the properties of similar triangles to explain this result.

3. Move C. What happens to $m\angle A$? With a new value of $m\angle A$, note the values of the two ratios. What happens to the ratios if you drag D along $\overrightarrow{AC}$?

Explain 1 Finding the Sine and Cosine of an Angle

Trigonometric Ratios

A **trigonometric ratio** is a ratio of two sides of a right triangle. You have already seen one trigonometric ratio, the tangent. There are two additional trigonometric ratios, the sine and the cosine, that involve the hypotenuse of a right triangle.

The **sine** of $\angle A$, written $\sin A$, is defined as follows:

$$\sin A = \frac{\text{length of leg opposite } \angle A}{\text{length of hypotenuse}} = \frac{BC}{AB}$$

The **cosine** of $\angle A$, written $\cos A$, is defined as follows:

$$\cos A = \frac{\text{length of leg adjacent to } \angle A}{\text{length of hypotenuse}} = \frac{AC}{AB}$$

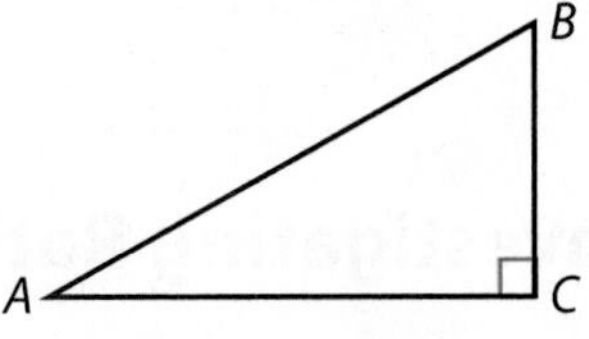

You can use these definitions to calculate trigonometric ratios.

Example 1 **Write sine and cosine of each angle as a fraction and as a decimal rounded to the nearest thousandth.**

$$\sin D = \frac{\text{length of leg opposite } \angle D}{\text{length of hypotenuse}} = \frac{EF}{DF} = \frac{8}{17} \approx 0.471$$

$$\cos D = \frac{\text{length of leg adjacent to } \angle D}{\text{length of hypotenuse}} = \frac{DE}{DF} = \frac{15}{17} \approx 0.882$$

$$\sin F = \frac{\text{length of leg opposite to } \angle F}{\text{length of hypotenuse}} = \frac{DE}{DF} = \frac{15}{17} \approx 0.882$$

$$\cos F = \frac{\text{length of leg adjacent to } \angle F}{\text{length of hypotenuse}} = \frac{8}{17} \approx 0.471$$

Reflect

4. What do you notice about the sines and cosines you found? Do you think this relationship will be true for any pair of acute angles in a right triangle? Explain.

5. In a right triangle $\triangle PQR$ with $PR = 5$, $QR = 3$, and $m\angle Q = 90°$, what are the values of $\sin P$ and $\cos P$?

Explain 2 Using Complementary Angles

The acute angles of a right triangle are complementary. Their trigonometric ratios are related to each other as shown in the following relationship.

Trigonometric Ratios of Complementary Angles

If $\angle A$ and $\angle B$ are the acute angles in a right triangle, then $\sin A = \cos B$ and $\cos A = \sin B$.

Therefore, if θ ("theta") is the measure of an acute angle, then $\sin\theta = \cos(90° - \theta)$ and $\cos\theta = \sin(90° - \theta)$.

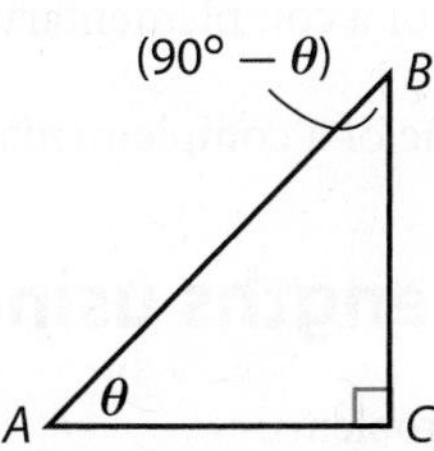

You can use these relationships to write equivalent expressions.

Example 2 **Write each trigonometric expression.**

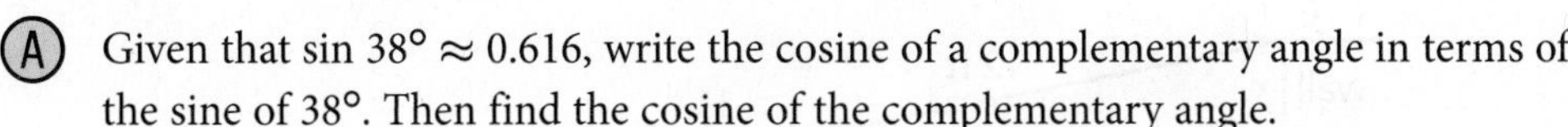

(A) Given that $\sin 38° \approx 0.616$, write the cosine of a complementary angle in terms of the sine of 38°. Then find the cosine of the complementary angle.

Use an expression relating trigonometric ratios of complementary angles.

$$\sin\theta = \cos(90° - \theta)$$

Substitute 38 into both sides.	$\sin 38° = \cos(90° - 38°)$
Simplify.	$\sin 38° = \cos 52°$
Substitute for sin 38°.	$0.616 \approx \cos 52°$

So, the cosine of the complementary angle is about 0.616.

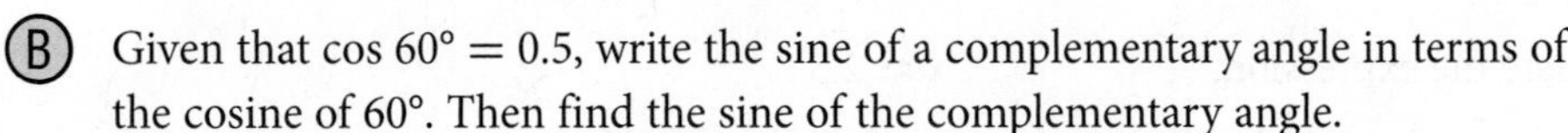

(B) Given that $\cos 60° = 0.5$, write the sine of a complementary angle in terms of the cosine of 60°. Then find the sine of the complementary angle.

Use an expression relating trigonometric ratios of complementary angles.

$$\cos\theta = \sin(90° - \theta)$$

Substitute 60 into both sides.	$\cos 60° = \sin(90° - 60°)$
Simplify the right side.	$\cos 60° = \sin 30°$
Substitute for the cosine of 60°.	$0.5 = \sin 30°$

So, the sine of the complementary angle is 0.5.

Reflect

6. What can you conclude about the sine and cosine of 45°? Explain.

7. **Discussion** Is it possible for the sine or cosine of an acute angle to equal 1? Explain.

Your Turn

Write each trigonometric expression.

8. Given that $\cos 73° \approx 0.292$, write the sine of a complementary angle.

9. Given that $\sin 45° \approx 0.707$, write the cosine of a complementary angle.

Explain 3 Finding Side Lengths using Sine and Cosine

You can use sine and cosine to solve real-world problems.

Example 3 **A 12-ft ramp is installed alongside some steps to provide wheelchair access to a library. The ramp makes an angle of 11° with the ground. Find each dimension, to the nearest tenth of a foot.**

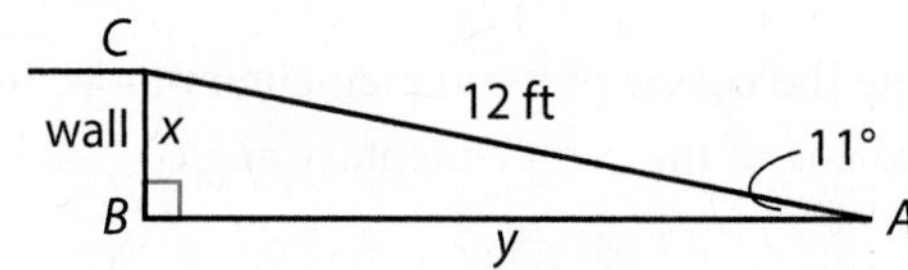

(A) Find the height x of the wall.

Use the definition of sine. $\sin A = \dfrac{\text{length of leg opposite } \angle A}{\text{length of hypotenuse}} = \dfrac{AB}{AC}$

Substitute 11° for A, x for BC, and 12 for AC. $\sin 11° = \dfrac{x}{12}$

Multiply both sides by 12. $12 \sin 11° = x$

Use a calculator to evaluate the expression. $x \approx 2.3$

So, the height of the wall is about 2.3 feet.

(B) Find the distance y that the ramp extends in front of the wall.

Use the definition of cosine. $\cos A = \dfrac{\text{length of leg adjacent to } \angle A}{\text{length of hypotenuse}} = \dfrac{AB}{AC}$

Substitute 11 ° for A, y for AB, and 12 for AC. $\cos 11° = \dfrac{y}{12}$

Multiply both sides by 12. $12 \cos 11° = y$

Use a calculator to evaluate the expression. $y \approx 11.8$

So, the ramp extends in front of the wall about 11.8 feet.

Reflect

10. Could you find the height of the wall using the cosine? Explain.

Your Turn

11. Suppose a new regulation states that the maximum angle of a ramp for wheelchairs is 8°. At least how long must the new ramp be? Round to the nearest tenth of a foot.

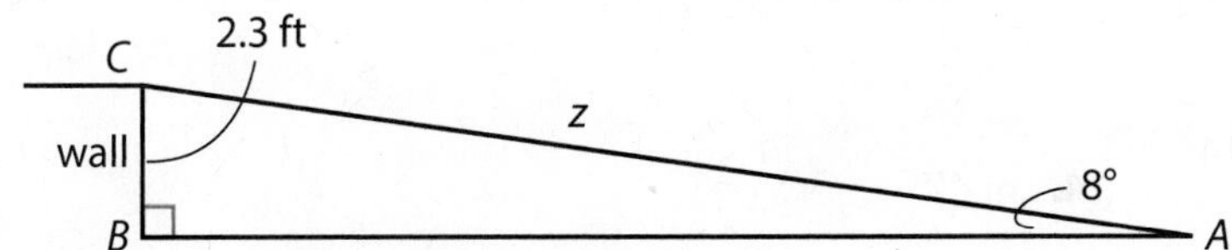

Explain 4 Finding Angle Measures using Sine and Cosine

In the triangle, $\sin A = \frac{5}{10} = \frac{1}{2}$. However, you already know that $\sin 30° = \frac{1}{2}$. So you can conclude that $m\angle A = 30°$, and write $\sin^{-1}\left(\frac{1}{2}\right) = 30°$.

Extending this idea, the **inverse trigonometric ratios** for sine and cosine are defined as follows:

Given an acute angle, $\angle A$,

- if $\sin A = x$, then $\sin^{-1} x = m\angle A$, read as "inverse sine of x"
- if $\cos A = x$, then $\cos^{-1} x = m\angle A$, read as "inverse cosine of x"

You can use a calculator to evaluate inverse trigonometric expressions.

Example 4 **Find the acute angle measures in $\triangle PQR$, to the nearest degree.**

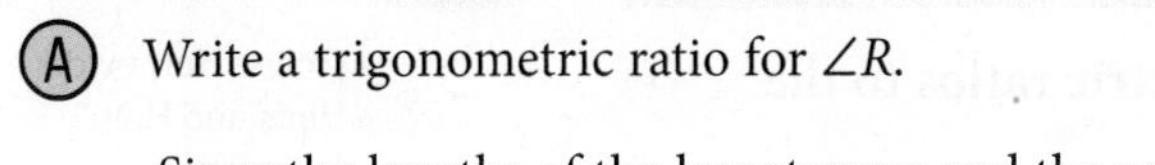

(A) Write a trigonometric ratio for $\angle R$.

Since the lengths of the hypotenuse and the opposite leg are given,

use the sine ratio. $\sin R = \frac{PQ}{PR}$

Substitute 7 for PQ and 13 for PR. $\sin R = \frac{7}{13}$

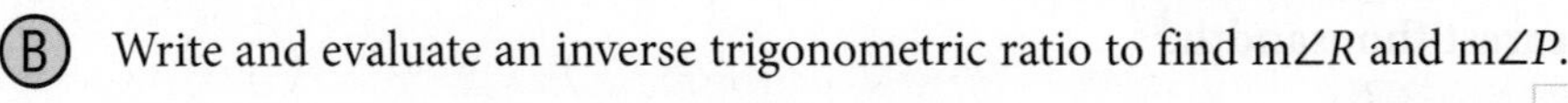

(B) Write and evaluate an inverse trigonometric ratio to find $m\angle R$ and $m\angle P$.

Start with the trigonometric ratio for $\angle R$. $\sin R = \frac{7}{13}$

Use the definition of the inverse sine ratio. $m\angle R = \sin^{-1} \frac{7}{13}$

Use a calculator to evaluate the inverse sine ratio. $m\angle R = 33°$

Write a cosine ratio for $\angle P$. $\cos P = \frac{PQ}{PR}$

Substitute 7 for PQ and 13 for PR. $\cos P = \frac{7}{13}$

Use the definition of the inverse cosine ratio. $m\angle P = \cos^{-1} \frac{7}{13}$

Use a calculator to evaluate the inverse cosine ratio. $m\angle P = 57°$

Reflect

12. How else could you have determined $m\angle P$?

Your Turn

Find the acute angle measures in $\triangle XYZ$, to the nearest degree.

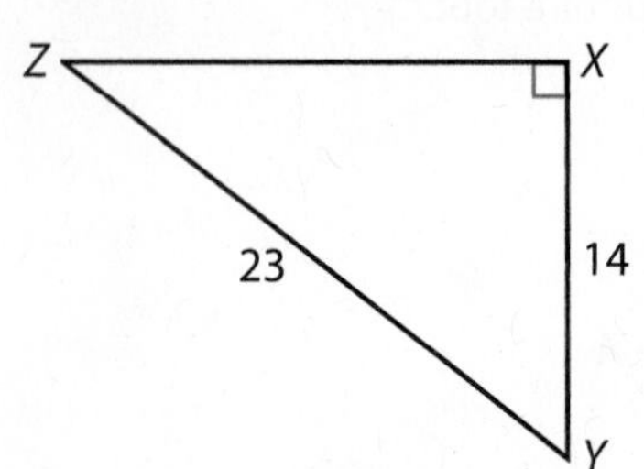

13. $m\angle Y$

14. $m\angle Z$

Elaborate

15. How are the sine and cosine ratios for an acute angle of a right triangle defined?

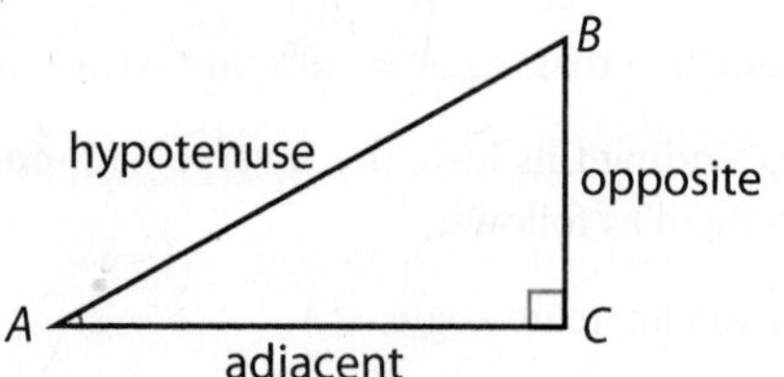

16. How are the inverse sine and cosine ratios for an acute angle of a right triangle defined?

17. **Essential Question Check-In** How do you find an unknown angle measure in a right triangle?

Evaluate: Homework and Practice

- Online Homework
- Hints and Help
- Extra Practice

Write each trigonometric expression. Round trigonometric ratios to the nearest thousandth.

1. Given that $\sin 60° \approx 0.866$, write the cosine of a complementary angle.

2. Given that $\cos 26° \approx 0.899$, write the sine of a complementary angle.

Write each trigonometric ratio as a fraction and as a decimal, rounded (if necessary) to the nearest thousandth.

3. $\sin A$

4. $\cos A$

5. $\cos B$

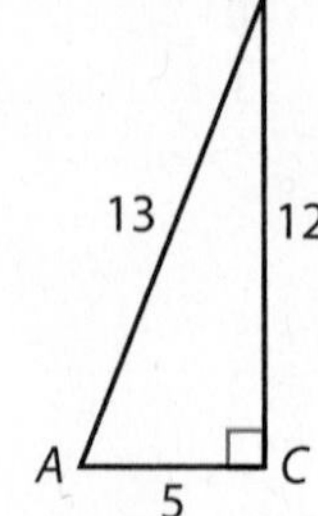

6. sin D

7. cos F

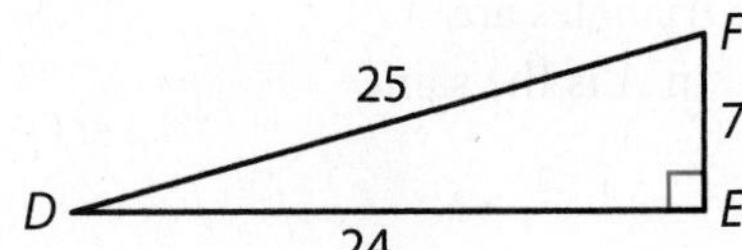

8. sin F

Find the unknown length x in each right triangle, to the nearest tenth.

9.

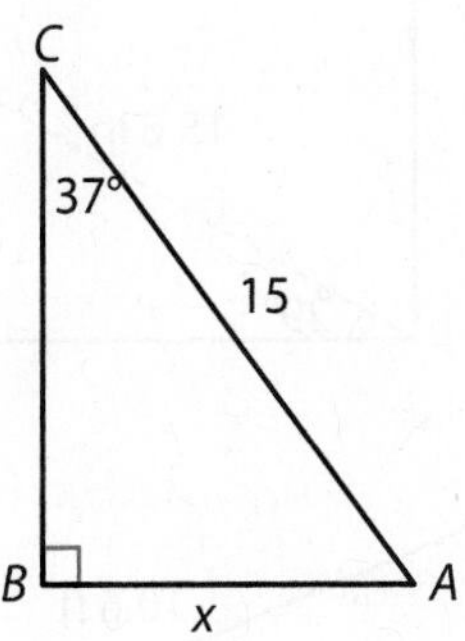

10.

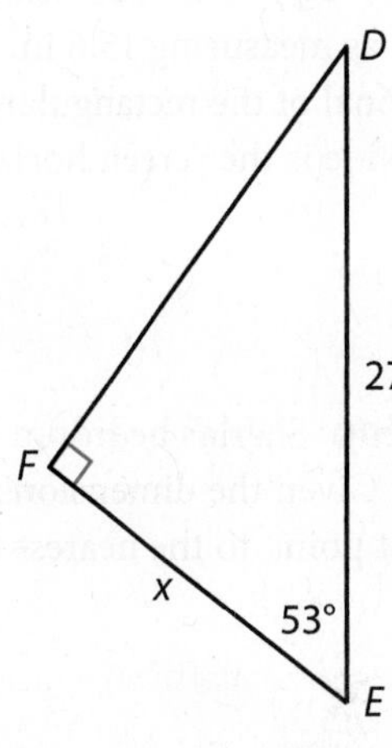

11.

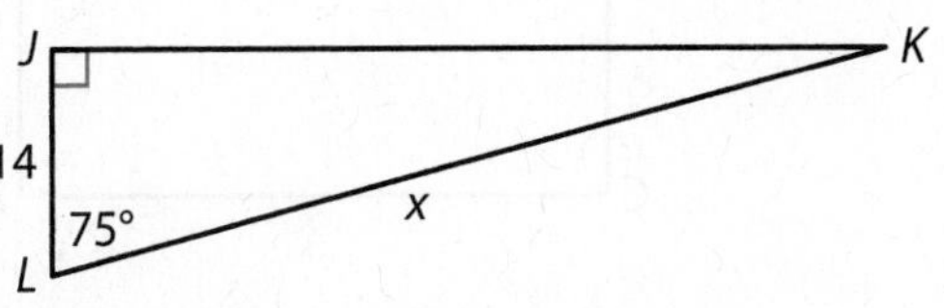

12.

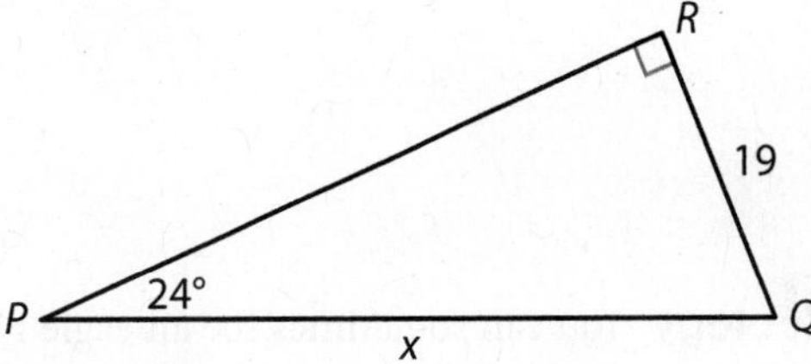

Find each acute angle measure, to the nearest degree.

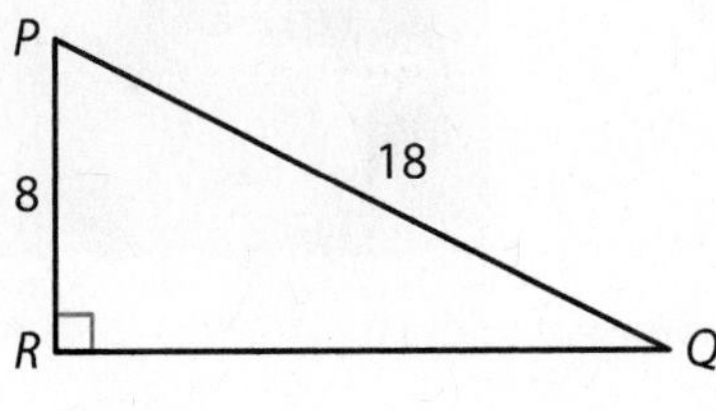

11
V
W
15
U

13. $m\angle P$

14. $m\angle Q$

15. $m\angle U$

16. $m\angle W$

17. Use the property that corresponding sides of similar triangles are proportional to explain why the trigonometric ratio sin A is the same when calculated in $\triangle ADE$ as in $\triangle ABC$.

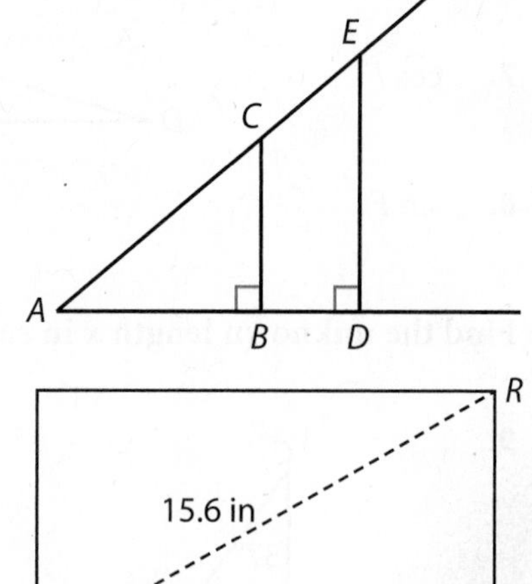

18. Technology The specifications for a laptop computer describe its screen as measuring 15.6 in. However, this is actually the length of a diagonal of the rectangular screen, as represented in the figure. How wide is the screen horizontally, to the nearest tenth of an inch?

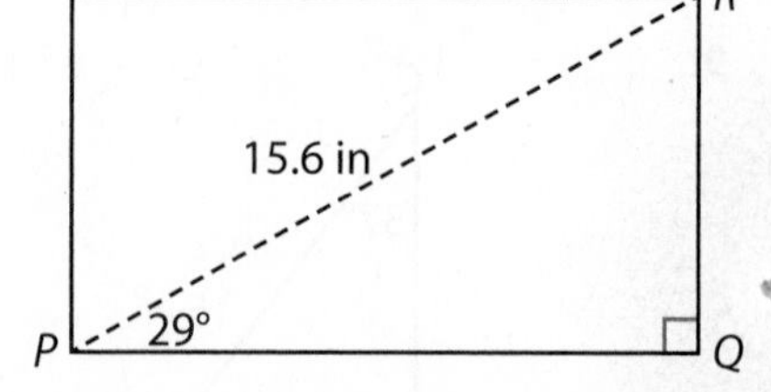

19. Building Sharla's bedroom is directly under the roof of her house. Given the dimensions shown, how high is the ceiling at its highest point, to the nearest tenth of a foot?

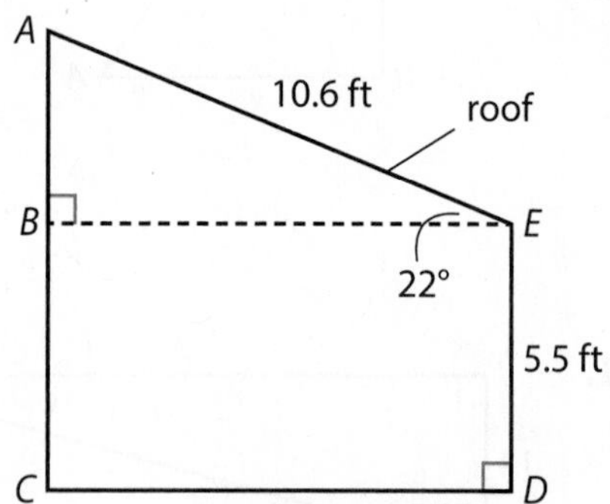

20. Zoology You can sometimes see an eagle gliding with its wings flexed in a characteristic double-vee shape. Each wing can be modeled as two right triangles as shown in the figure. Find the measure of the angle in the middle of the wing, $\angle DHG$ to the nearest degree.

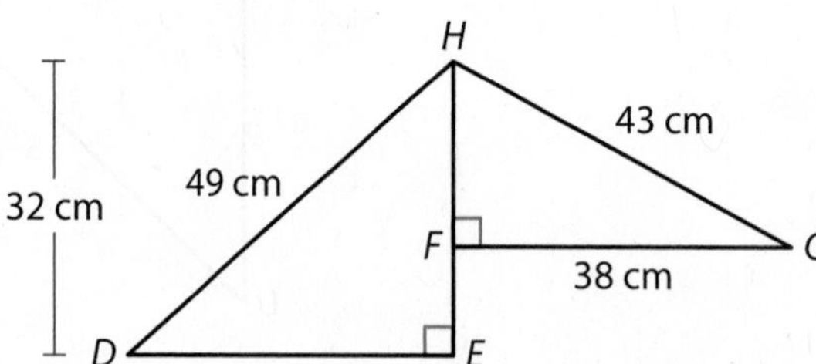

21. Algebra Find a pair of acute angles that satisfy the equation $\sin(3x + 9) = \cos(x + 5)$. Check that your answers make sense.

22. Multi-Step Reginald is planning to fence his back yard. Every side of the yard except for the side along the house is to be fenced, and fencing costs \$3.50/yd. How much will the fencing cost?

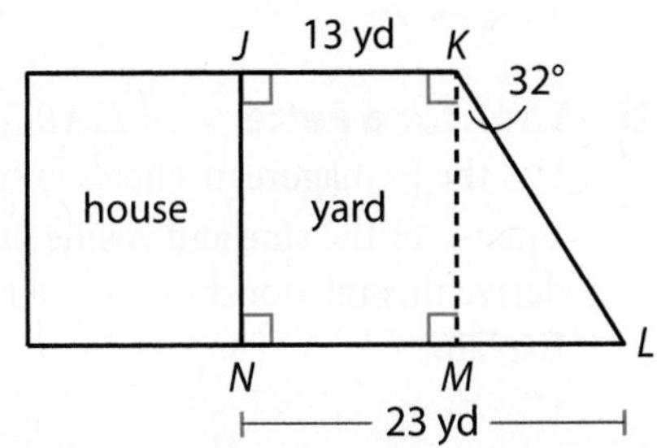

23. Architecture The sides of One World Trade Center in New York City form eight isosceles triangles, four of which are 200 ft long at their base BC. The length AC of each sloping side is approximately 1185 ft.

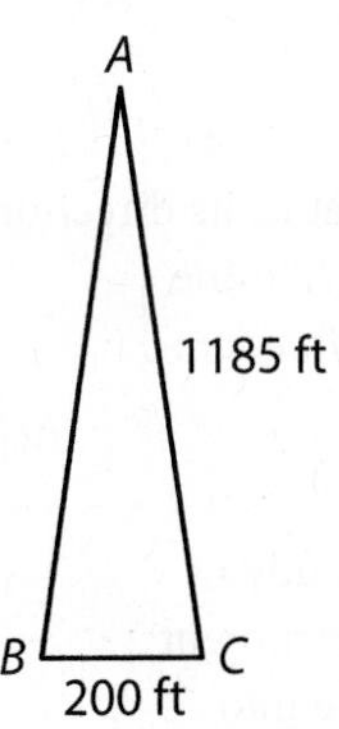

Find the measure of the apex angle BAC of each isosceles triangle, to the nearest tenth of a degree. (*Hint:* Use the midpoint D of $\overline{BC}$ to create two right triangles.)

H.O.T. Focus on Higher Order Thinking

24. Explain the Error Melissa has calculated the length of $\overline{XZ}$ in $\triangle XYZ$. Explain why Melissa's answer must be incorrect, and identify and correct her error.

Melissa's solution:

$\cos X = \dfrac{XZ}{XY}$

$XZ = \dfrac{XY}{\cos X}$

$XZ = 27 \cos 42° \approx 20.1$

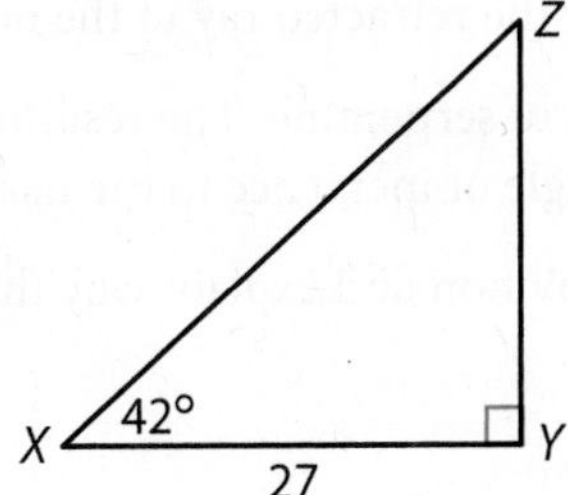

25. Communicate Mathematical Ideas Explain why the sine and cosine of an acute angle are always between 0 and 1.

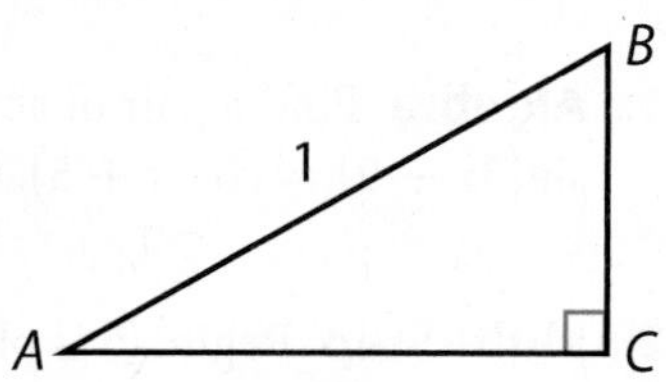

26. Look for a Pattern In $\triangle ABC$, the hypotenuse $\overline{AB}$ has a length of 1. Use the Pythagorean Theorem to explore the relationship between the squares of the sine and cosine of $\angle A$, written $\sin^2 A$ and $\cos^2 A$. Could you derive this relationship using a right triangle without any lengths specified? Explain.

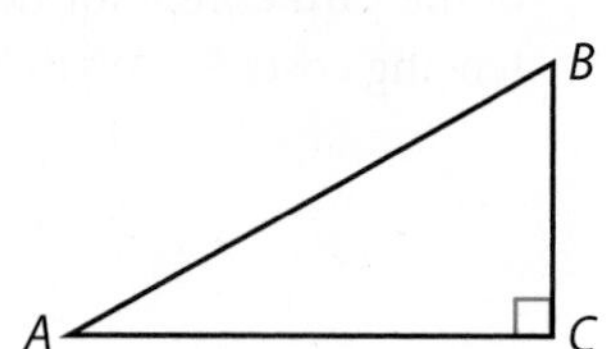

27. Justify Reasoning Use the Triangle Proportionality Theorem to explain why the trigonometric ratio cos *A* is the same when calculated in $\triangle ADE$ as in $\triangle ABC$.

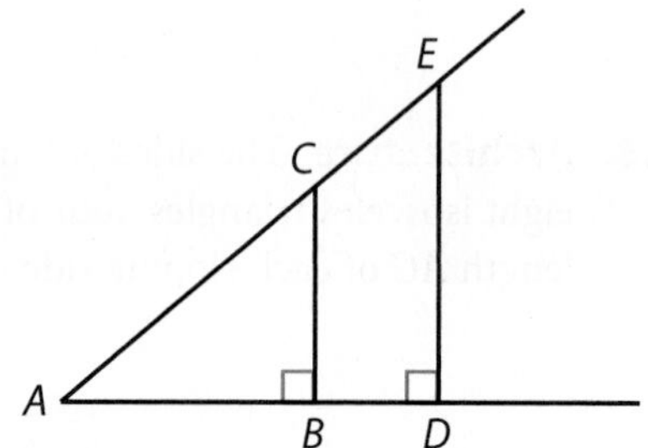

Lesson Performance Task

As light passes from a vacuum into another medium, it is *refracted*—that is, its direction changes. The ratio of the sine of the angle of the incoming *incident* ray, *I*, to the sine of the angle of the outgoing *refracted* ray, *r*, is called the *index of refraction*:

$n = \frac{\sin I}{\sin r}$. where n is the index of refraction.

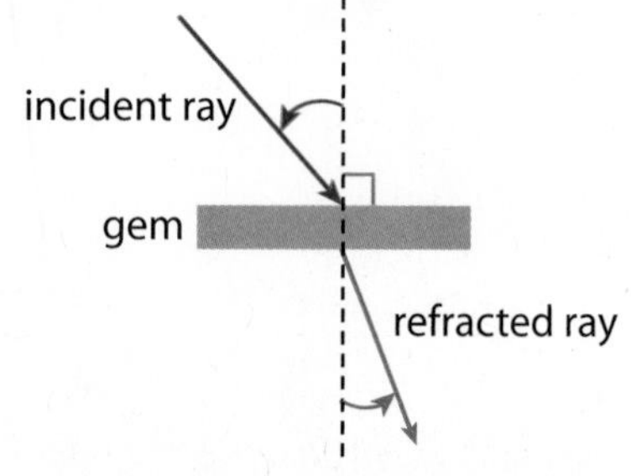

This relationship is important in many fields, including gemology, the study of precious stones. A gemologist can place an unidentified gem into an instrument called a refractometer, direct an incident ray of light at a particular angle into the stone, measure the angle of the refracted ray, and calculate the index of refraction. Because the indices of refraction of thousands of gems are known, the gemologist can then identify the gem.

1. Identify the gem, given these angles obtained from a refractometer:

a. $I = 71°, r = 29°$

b. $I = 51°, r = 34°$

c. $I = 45°, r = 17°$

2. A thin slice of sapphire is placed in a refractometer. The angle of the incident ray is 56°. Find the angle of the refracted ray to the nearest degree.

3. An incident ray of light struck a slice of serpentine. The resulting angle of refraction measured 21°. Find the angle of incidence to the nearest degree.

4. Describe the error(s) in a student's solution and explain why they were error(s):

$$n = \frac{\sin I}{\sin r} = \frac{\sin 51°}{\sin 34°} = \frac{51°}{34°} = 1.5 \rightarrow \text{coral}$$

Gem	Index of Refraction
Hematite	2.94
Diamond	2.42
Zircon	1.95
Azurite	1.85
Sapphire	1.77
Tourmaline	1.62
Serpentine	1.56
Coral	1.49
Opal	1.39

13.3 Special Right Triangles

Essential Question: What do you know about the side lengths and the trigonometric ratios in special right triangles?

Explore 1 Investigating an Isosceles Right Triangle

Discover relationships that always apply in an isosceles right triangle.

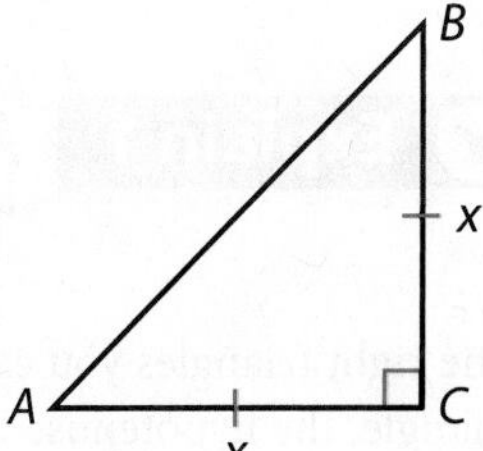

(A) The figure shows an isosceles right triangle. Identify the base angles, and use the fact that they are complementary to write an equation relating their measures.

(B) Use the Isosceles Triangle Theorem to write a different equation relating the base angle measures.

(C) What must the measures of the base angles be? Why?

(D) Use the Pythagorean Theorem to find the length of the hypotenuse in terms of the length of each leg, x.

Reflect

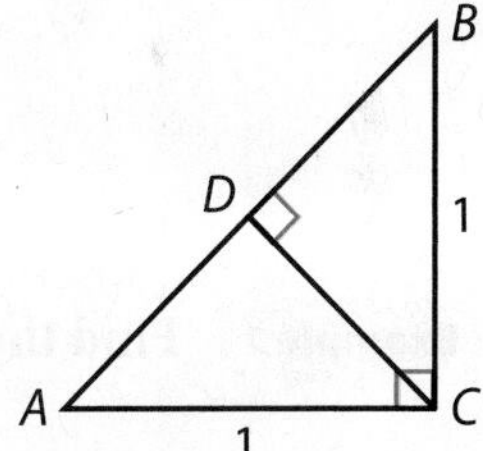

1. Is it true that if you know one side length of an isosceles right triangle, then you know all the side lengths? Explain.
2. **What if?** Suppose you draw the perpendicular from C to $\overline{AB}$. Explain how to find the length of $\overline{CD}$.

Explore 2 Investigating Another Special Right Triangle

Discover relationships that always apply in a right triangle formed as half of an equilateral triangle.

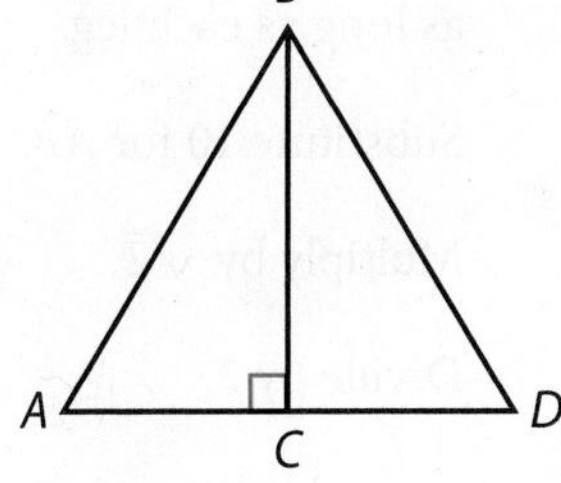

(A) $\triangle ABD$ is an equilateral triangle and $\overline{BC}$ is a perpendicular from B to $\overline{AD}$. Determine all three angle measures in $\triangle ABC$.

(B) Explain why $\triangle ABC \cong \triangle DBC$.

(C) Let the length of $\overline{AC}$ be x. What is the length of $\overline{AB}$, and why?

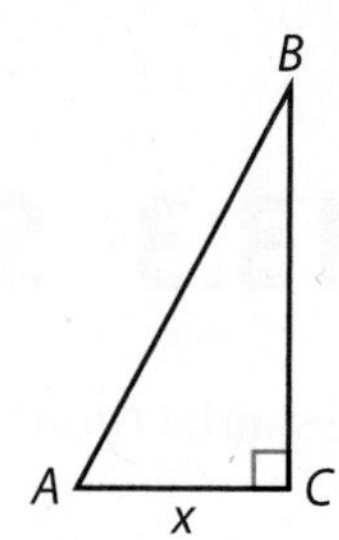

(D) Using the Pythagorean Theorem, find the length of $\overline{BC}$.

Reflect

3. What is the numerical ratio of the side lengths in a right triangle with acute angles that measure 30° and 60°? Explain.

4. **Explain the Error** A student has drawn a right triangle with a 60° angle and a hypotenuse of 6. He has labeled the other side lengths as shown. Explain how you can tell at a glance that he has made an error and how to correct it.

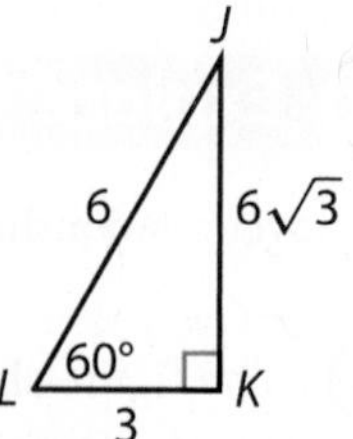

Explain 1 Applying Relationships in Special Right Triangles

The right triangles you explored are sometimes called 45°—45°—90° and 30°—60°—90° triangles. In a 45°—45°—90° triangle, the hypotenuse is $\sqrt{2}$ times as long as each leg. In a 30°—60°—90° triangle, the hypotenuse is twice as long as the shorter leg and the longer leg is $\sqrt{3}$ times as long as the shorter leg. You can use these relationships to find side lengths in these special types of right triangles.

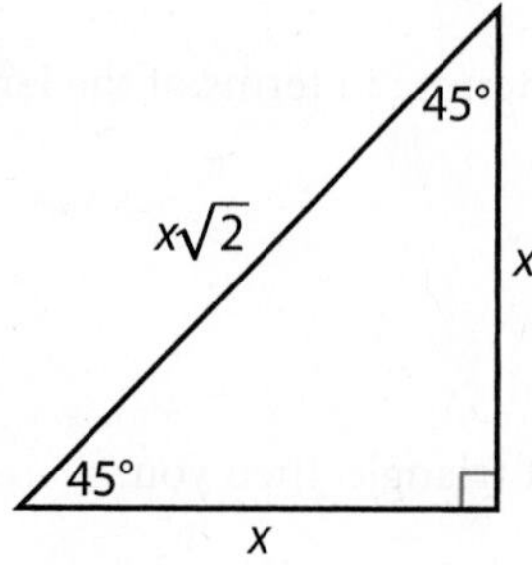

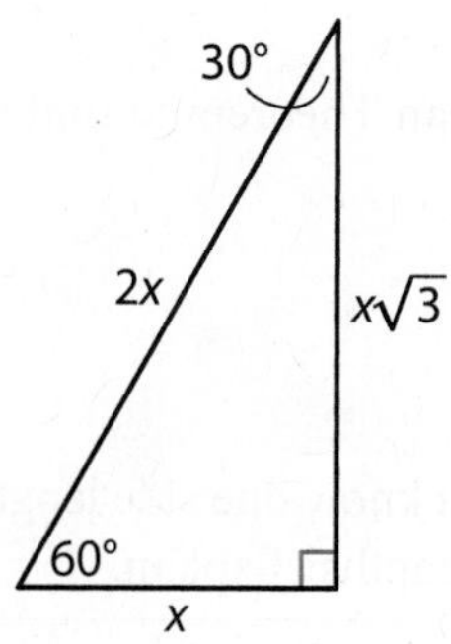

Example 1 **Find the unknown side lengths in each right triangle.**

(A) Find the unknown side lengths in $\triangle ABC$.

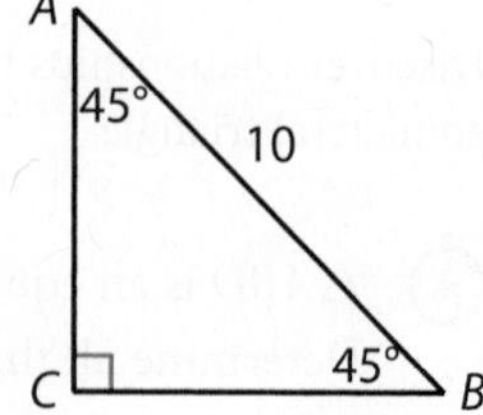

The hypotenuse is $\sqrt{2}$ times as long as each leg. $AB = AC\sqrt{2} = BC\sqrt{2}$

Substitute 10 for AB. $10 = AC\sqrt{2} = BC\sqrt{2}$

Multiply by $\sqrt{2}$. $10\sqrt{2} = 2AC = 2BC$

Divide by 2. $5\sqrt{2} = AC = BC$

(B) In right $\triangle DEF$, $m\angle D = 30°$ and $m\angle E = 60°$. The shorter leg measures $5\sqrt{3}$. Find the remaining side lengths.

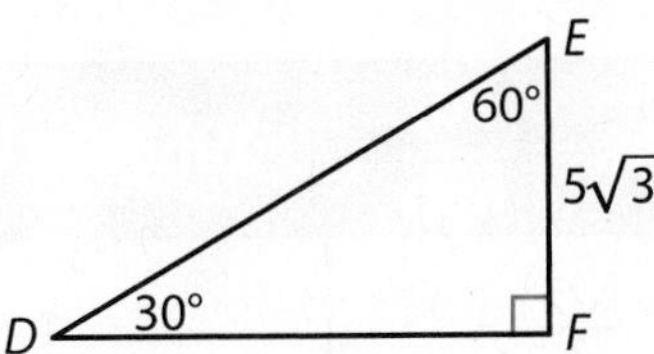

The hypotenuse is twice as long as the shorter leg.	$DE = 2\ \boxed{EF}$
Substitute $\boxed{5\sqrt{3}}$ for $\boxed{EF}$.	$DE = 2\left(\boxed{5\sqrt{3}}\right)$
Simplify.	$DE = \boxed{10\sqrt{3}}$
The longer leg is $\sqrt{3}$ times as long as the shorter leg.	$\boxed{DF} = \boxed{EF}\sqrt{3}$
Substitute $\boxed{5\sqrt{3}}$ for $\boxed{EF}$.	$\boxed{DF} = \boxed{5\sqrt{3}}\sqrt{3}$
Simplify.	$\boxed{DF} = \boxed{15}$

Your Turn

Find the unknown side lengths in each right triangle.

5.

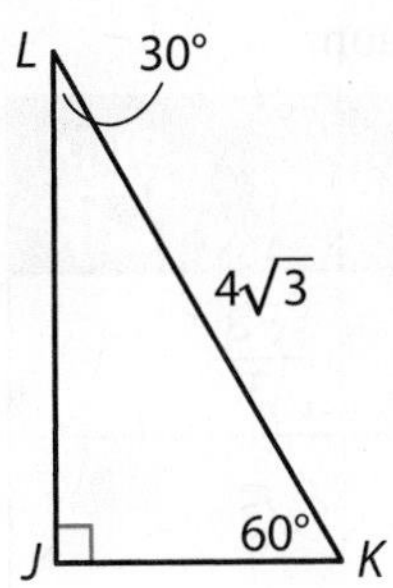

6.

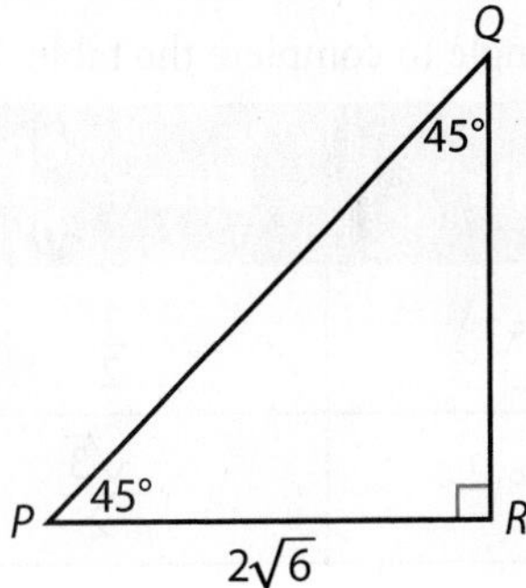

 Explain 2 Trigonometric Ratios of Special Right Triangles

You can use the relationships you found in special right triangles to find trigonometric ratios for the angles 45°, 30°, and 60°.

Example 2 **For each triangle, find the unknown side lengths and trigonometric ratios for the angles.**

(A) **A 45°–45°–90° triangle with a leg length of 1**

Step 1

Since the lengths of the sides opposite the 45° angles are congruent, they are both 1. The length of the hypotenuse is $\sqrt{2}$ times as long as each leg, so it is $1(\sqrt{2})$, or $\sqrt{2}$.

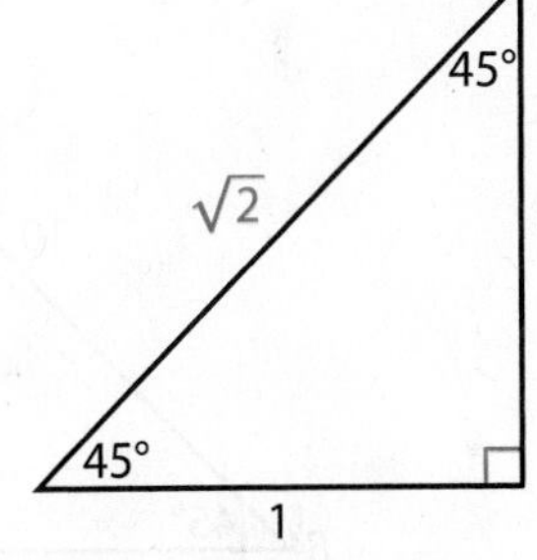

Step 2

Use the triangle to find the trigonometric ratios for 45°. Write each ratio as a simplified fraction.

Angle	Sine $= \frac{\text{opp}}{\text{hyp}}$	Cosine $= \frac{\text{adj}}{\text{hyp}}$	Tangent $= \frac{\text{opp}}{\text{adj}}$
45°	$\frac{\sqrt{2}}{2}$	$\frac{\sqrt{2}}{2}$	1

Ⓑ **A 30°—60°—90° triangle with a shorter leg of 1**

Step 1

The hypotenuse is twice as long as the shorter leg, so the length of the hypotenuse is 2.

The longer leg is $\sqrt{3}$ times as long as the shorter leg, so the length of the longer leg is $\sqrt{3}$.

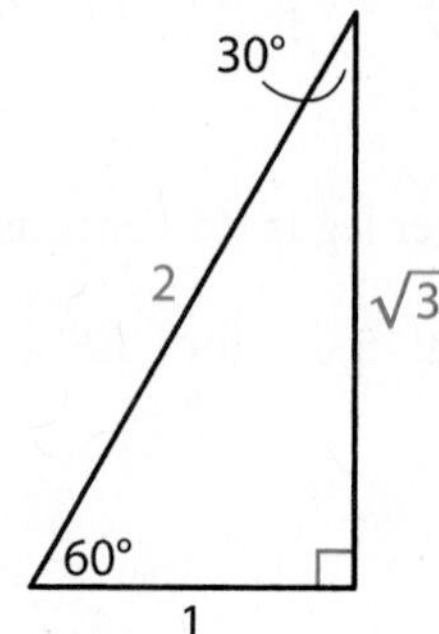

Step 2

Use the triangle to complete the table. Write each ratio as a simplified fraction.

Angle	Sine $= \frac{\text{opp}}{\text{hyp}}$	Cosine $= \frac{\text{adj}}{\text{hyp}}$	Tangent $= \frac{\text{opp}}{\text{adj}}$
30°	$\frac{1}{2}$	$\frac{\sqrt{3}}{2}$	$\frac{\sqrt{3}}{3}$
60°	$\frac{\sqrt{3}}{2}$	$\frac{1}{2}$	$\sqrt{3}$

Reflect

7. Write any patterns or relationships you see in the tables in Part A and Part B as equations. Why do these patterns or relationships make sense?

8. For which acute angle measure θ, is $\tan\theta$ less than 1? equal to 1? greater than 1?

Your Turn

Find the unknown side lengths and trigonometric ratios for the 45° angles.

9.

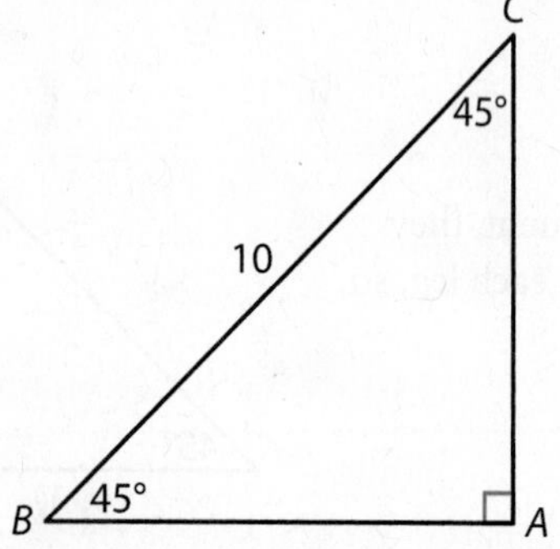

Explain 3 Investigating Pythagorean Triples

Pythagorean Triples

A **Pythagorean triple** is a set of positive integers a, b, and c that satisfy the equation $a^2 + b^2 = c^2$. This means that a, b, and c are the legs and hypotenuse of a right triangle. Right triangles that have non-integer sides will not form Pythagorean triples.

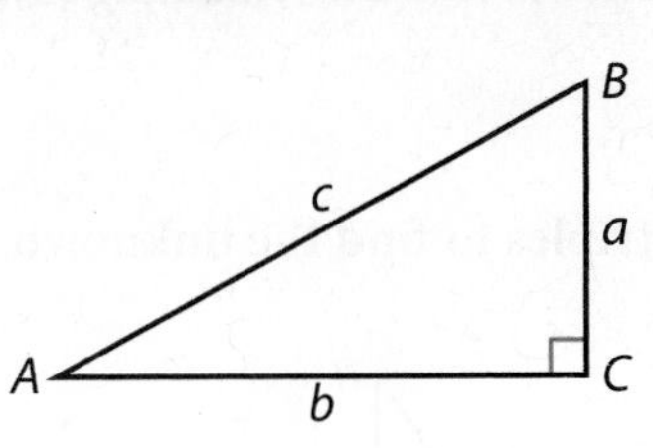

Examples of Pythagorean triples include 3, 4, and 5; 5, 12, and 13; 7, 24, and 25; and 8, 15, and 17.

Example 3 **Use Pythagorean triples to find side lengths in right triangles.**

(A) Verify that the side lengths 3, 4, and 5; 5, 12, and 13; 7, 24, and 25; and 8, 15, and 17 are Pythagorean triples.

$3^2 + 4^2 = 9 + 16 = 25 = 5^2$ ✓ $\quad$ $5^2 + 12^2 = 25 + 144 = 169 = 13^2$ ✓

$7^2 + 24^2 = 49 + 576 = 625 = 25^2$ ✓ $\quad$ $8^2 + 15^2 = 64 + 225 = 289 = 17^2$ ✓

The numbers in Step A are not the only Pythagorean triples. In the following steps you will discover that multiples of known Pythagorean triples are also Pythagorean triples.

(B) In right triangles DEF and JKL, a, b, and c form a Pythagorean triple, and k is a positive integer greater than 1. Explain how the two triangles are related.

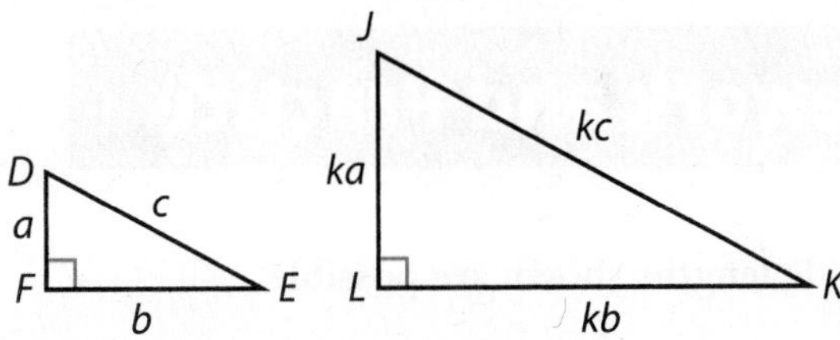

$\triangle DEF$ is similar to $\triangle JKL$ by the Side-Side-Side (SSS) Triangle Similarity Theorem because the corresponding sides are proportional. Complete the ratios to verify Side-Side-Side (SSS) Triangle Similarity.

$a : b : c = ka : kb : kc$

(C) You can use the Pythagorean Theorem to compare the lengths of the sides of $\triangle JKL$. What must be true of the set of numbers ka, kb, and kc?

$$(ka^2) + (kb^2) = k^2a^2 + k^2b^2$$

$$= k^2(a^2 + b^2)$$

$$= k^2(c^2) = (kc)^2$$

The set of numbers ka, kb, and kc form a Pythagorean triple.

Reflect

10. Suppose you are given a right triangle with two side lengths. What would have to be true for you to use a Pythagorean triple to find the remaining side length?

Your Turn

Use Pythagorean triples to find the unknown side length.

11.

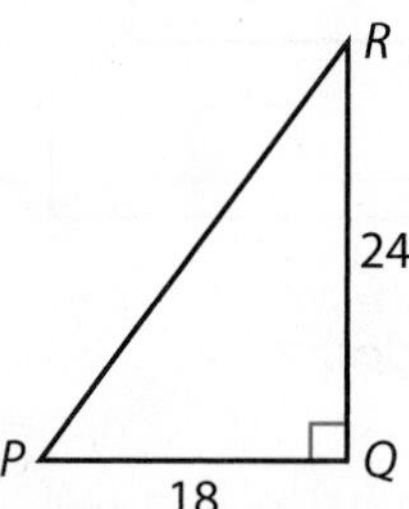

12. In $\triangle XYZ$, the hypotenuse $\overline{XY}$ has length 68, and the shorter leg $\overline{XZ}$ has length 32.

Elaborate

13. Describe the type of problems involving special right triangles you can solve.

14. How can you use Pythagorean triples to solve right triangles?

15. **Discussion** How many Pythagorean triples are there?

16. **Essential Question Check-In** What is the ratio of the length of the hypotenuse to the length of the shorter leg in any 30°-60°-90° triangle?

Evaluate: Homework and Practice

- Online Homework
- Hints and Help
- Extra Practice

For each triangle, state whether the side lengths shown are possible. Explain why or why not.

1.

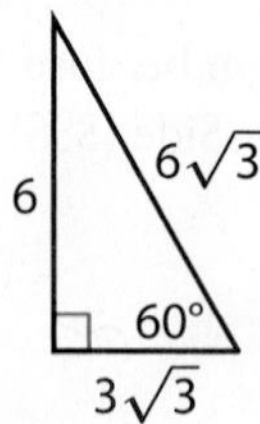

2.

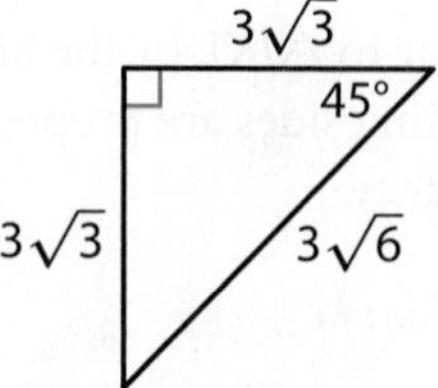

3.

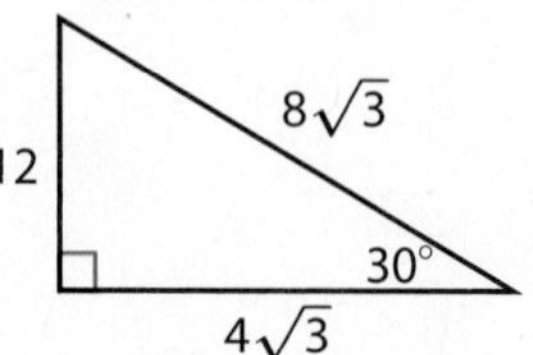

4.

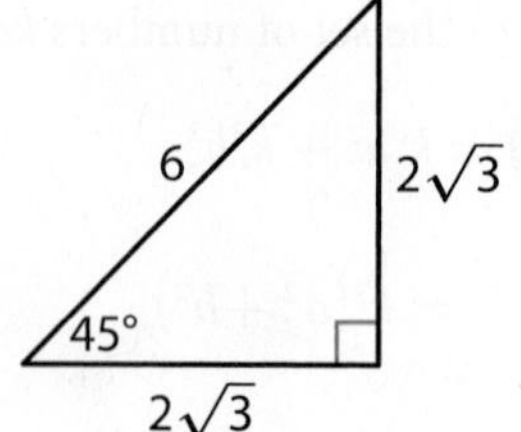

Find the unknown side lengths in each right triangle.

5.

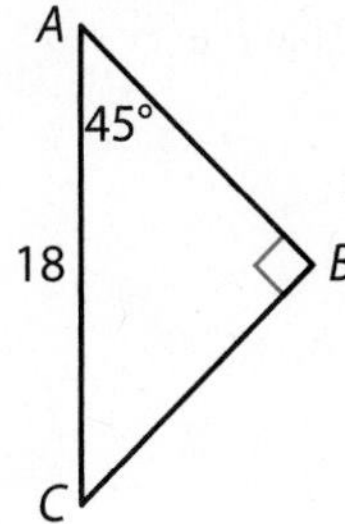

6.

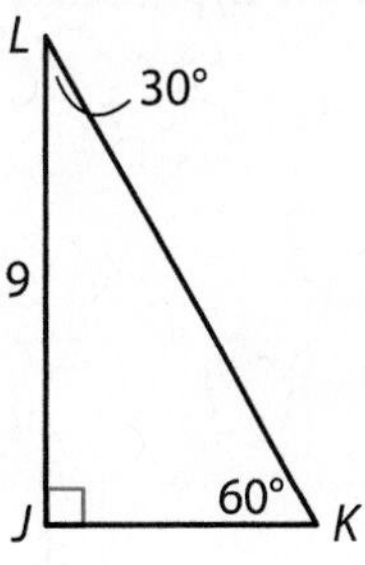

7. Right triangle UVW has acute angles U measuring 30° and W measuring 60°. Hypotenuse $\overline{UW}$ measures 12. (You may want to draw the triangle in your answer.)

8. Right triangle PQR has acute angles P and Q measuring 45°. Leg $\overline{PR}$ measures $5\sqrt{10}$. (You may want to draw the triangle in your answer.)

Use trigonometric ratios to solve each right triangle.

9.

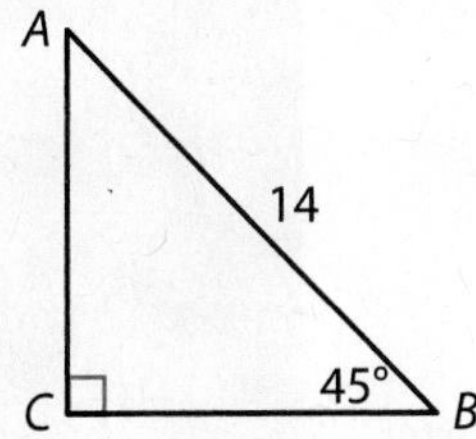

10.

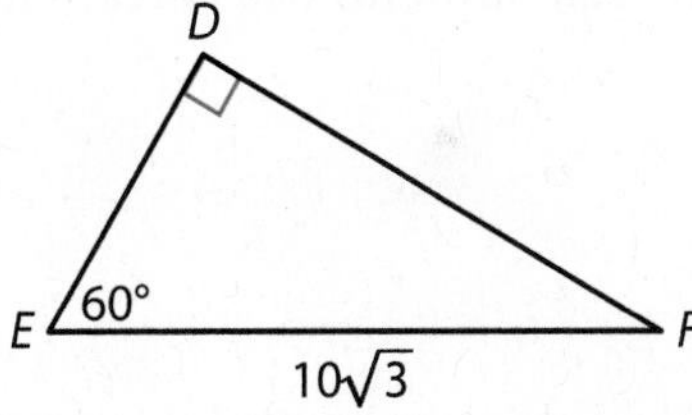

11. Right $\triangle KLM$ with $m\angle J = 45°$, leg $JK = 4\sqrt{3}$

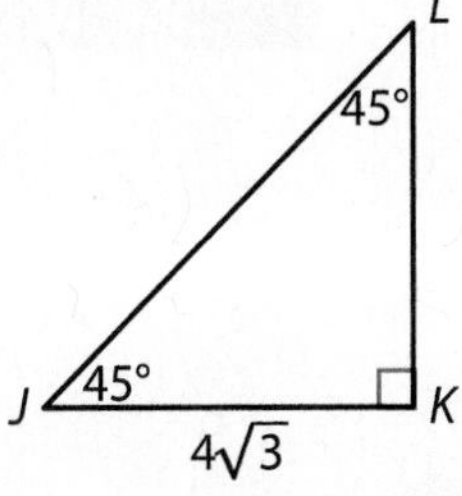

12. Right $\triangle PQR$ with $m\angle Q = 30°$, leg $QR = 15$

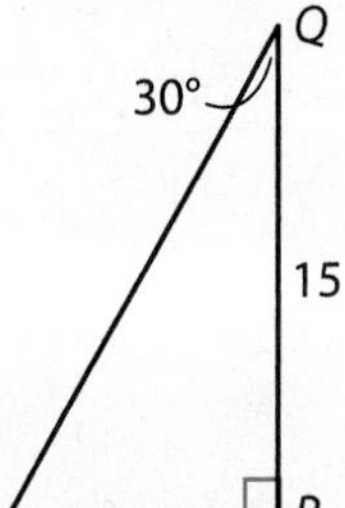

For each right triangle, find the unknown side length using a Pythagorean triple. If it is not possible, state why.

13.

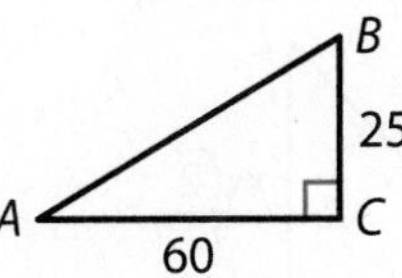

14.

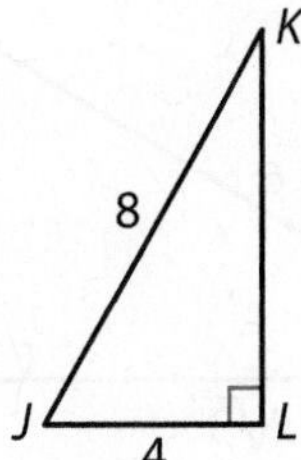

15. In right $\triangle PQR$, the legs have lengths $PQ = 9$ and $QR = 21$.

16. In right $\triangle XYZ$, the hypotenuse $\overline{XY}$ has length 35, and the shorter leg $\overline{YZ}$ has length 21.

17. Solve for x.

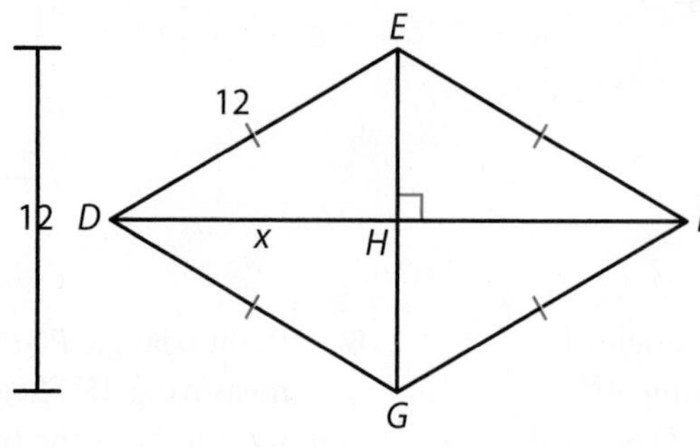

18. Represent Real-World Problems A baseball "diamond" actually forms a square, each side measuring 30 yards. How far, to the nearest yard, must the third baseman throw the ball to reach first base?

19. In a right triangle, the longer leg is exactly $\sqrt{3}$ times the length of the shorter leg. Use the inverse tangent trigonometric ratio to prove that the acute angles of the triangle measure 30° and 60°.

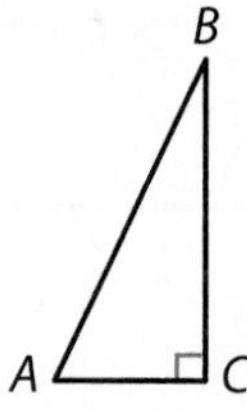

Algebra Find the value of x in each right triangle.

20.

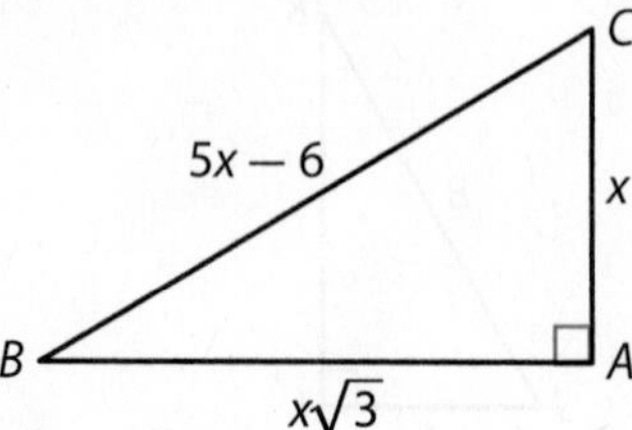

21.

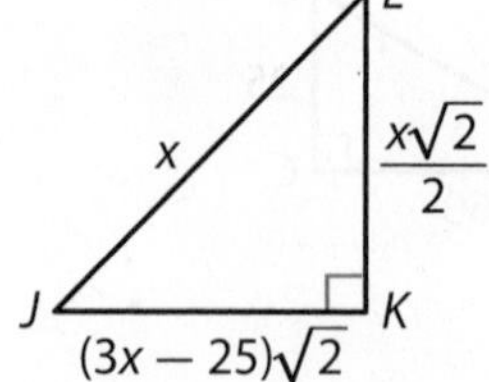

22. Explain the Error Charlene is trying to find the unknown sides of a right triangle with a 30° acute angle, whose hypotenuse measures $12\sqrt{2}$. Identify, explain, and correct Charlene's error.

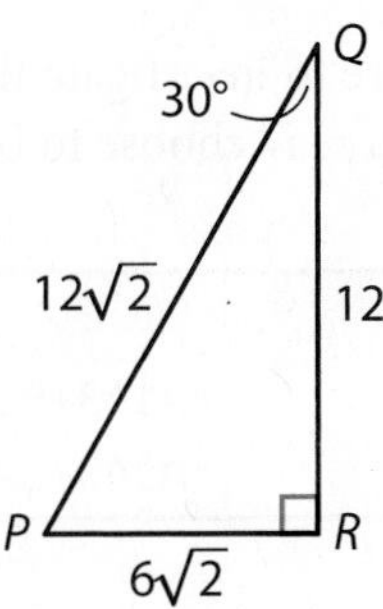

23. Represent Real-World Problems Honeycomb blinds form a string of almost-regular hexagons when viewed end-on. Approximately how much material, to the nearest ten square centimeters, is needed for each 3.2-cm deep cell of a honeycomb blind that is 125 cm wide? (*Hint: Draw a picture.* A regular hexagon can be divided into 6 equilateral triangles.)

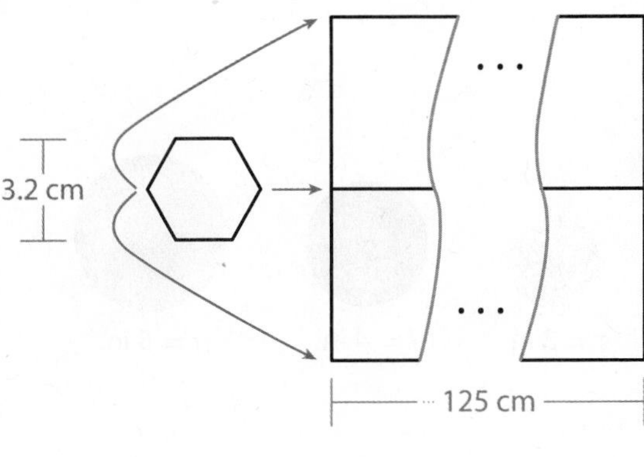

24. Which of these pairs of numbers are two out of three integer-valued side lengths of a right triangle? (*Hint:* for positive integers *a*, *b*, *c*, and *k*, *ka*, *kb*, and *kc* are side lengths of a right triangle if and only if *a*, *b*, and *c* are side lengths of a right triangle.) Write true or false for each pair.

A. 15, 18

B. 15, 30

C. 15, 51

D. 16, 20

E. 16, 24

H.O.T. Focus on Higher Order Thinking

25. **Communicate Mathematical Ideas** Is it possible for the three side lengths of a right triangle to be odd integers? Explain.

26. **Make a Conjecture** Use spreadsheet software to investigate this question: are there sets of positive integers a, b, and c such that $a^3 + b^3 = c^3$? You may choose to begin with these formulas:

	A	B	C	D
1	1	=A1+1	=A1^3+B1^3	=C1^(1/3)
2	=A1	=B1+1	=A2^3+B2^3	=C2^(1/3)

Lesson Performance Task

Kate and her dog are longtime flying disc players. Kate has decided to start a small business making circles of soft material that dogs can catch without injuring their teeth. Since she also likes math, she's decided to see whether she can apply Pythagorean principles to her designs. She used the Pythagorean triple 3-4-5 for the dimensions of her first three designs.

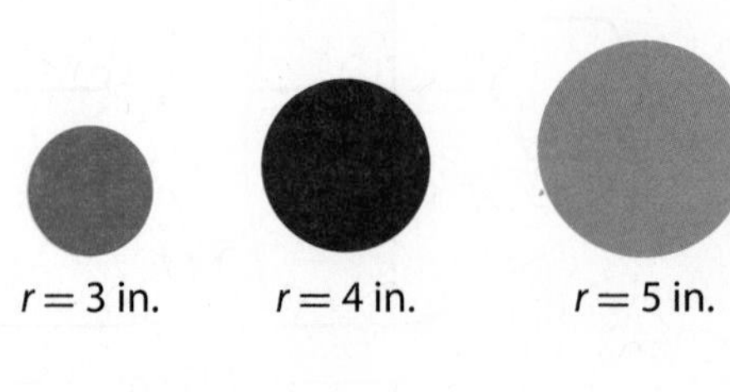

1. Is it true that the (small area) + (medium area) = (large area)? Explain.

2. If the circles had radii based on the Pythagorean triple 5—12—13, would the above equation be true? Explain.

3. Three of Kate's circles have radii of a, b, and c, where a, b, and c form a Pythagorean triple $(a^2 + b^2 = c^2)$. Show that the sum of the areas of the small and medium circles equals the area of the large circle.

4. Kate has decided to go into the beach ball business. Sticking to her Pythagorean principles, she starts with three spherical beach balls—a small ball with radius 3 in., a medium ball with radius 4 in., and a large ball with radius 5 in. Is it true that (small volume) + (medium volume) = (large volume)? Show your work.

5. Explain the discrepancy between your results in Exercises 3 and 4.

13.4 Problem Solving with Trigonometry

Essential Question: How can you solve a right triangle?

Explore Deriving an Area Formula

You can use trigonometry to find the area of a triangle without knowing its height.

(A) Suppose you draw an altitude $\overline{AD}$ to side $\overline{BC}$ of $\triangle ABC$. Then write an equation using a trigonometric ratio in terms of $\angle C$, the height h of $\triangle ABC$, and the length of one of its sides.

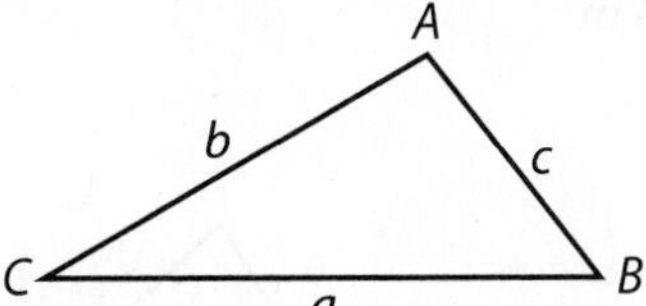

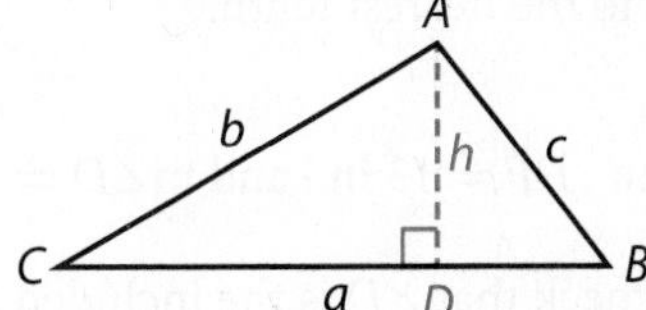

(B) Solve your equation from Step A for h.

(C) Complete this formula for the area of $\triangle ABC$ in terms of h and another of its side lengths: Area $= \frac{1}{2}$?

(D) Substitute your expression for h from Step B into your formula from Step C.

Reflect

1. Does the area formula you found work if $\angle C$ is a right angle? Explain.
2. Suppose you used a trigonometric ratio in terms of $\angle B$, h, and a different side length. How would this change your findings? What does this tell you about the choice of sides and included angle?

Explain 1 Using the Area Formula

Area Formula for a Triangle in Terms of its Side Lengths

The area of $\triangle ABC$ with sides a, b, and c can be found using the lengths of two of its sides and the sine of the included angle: Area $= \frac{1}{2}bc \sin A$, Area $= \frac{1}{2}ac \sin B$, or Area $= \frac{1}{2} ab \sin C$.

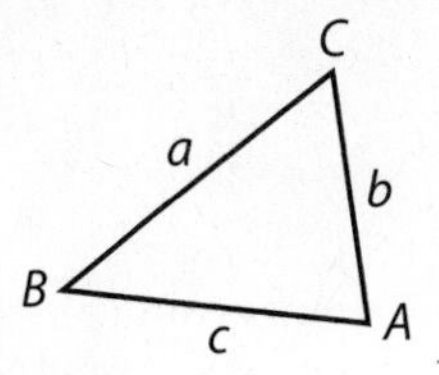

You can use any form of the area formula to find the area of a triangle, given two side lengths and the measure of the included angle.

Example 1 **Find the area of each triangle to the nearest tenth.**

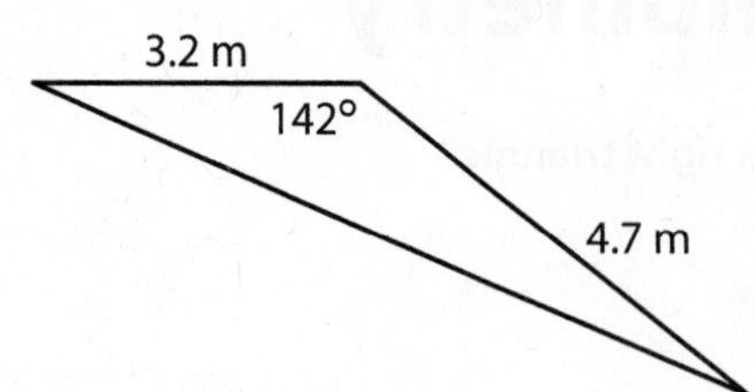

Let the known side lengths be a and b. $a = 3.2$ m and $b = 4.7$ m

Let the known angle be $\angle C$. $m\angle C = 142°$

Substitute in the formula Area $= \frac{1}{2}ab \sin C$. Area $= \frac{1}{2}(3.2)(4.7)\sin 142°$

Evaluate, rounding to the nearest tenth. Area $\approx 4.6 \text{ m}^2$

In $\triangle DEF$, $DE = 9$ in., $DF = 13$ in., and $m\angle D = 57°$.

Sketch $\triangle DEF$ and check that $\angle D$ is the included angle.

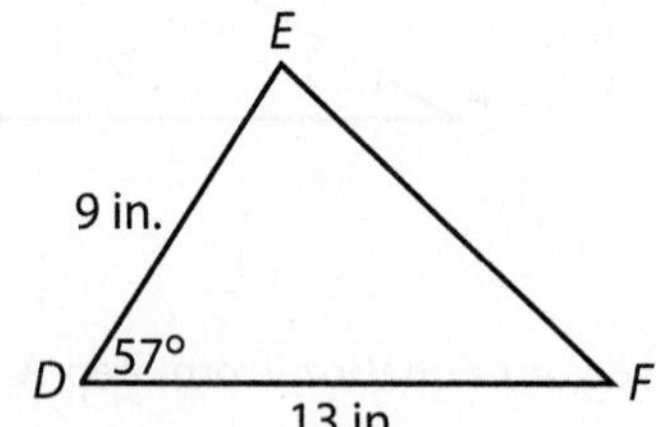

Write the area formula in terms of $\triangle DEF$. Area $= \frac{1}{2}(DE)(DF)\sin D$

Substitute in the area formula. Area $= \frac{1}{2}(9)(13)\sin 57°$

Evaluate, rounding to the nearest tenth. Area $\approx$ 49.1 in.^{2}

Your Turn

Find the area of each triangle to the nearest tenth.

3.

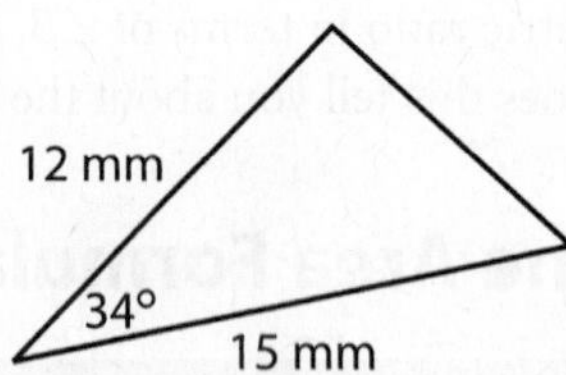

4. In $\triangle PQR$, $PQ = 3$ cm, $QR = 6$ cm, and $m\angle Q = 108°$.

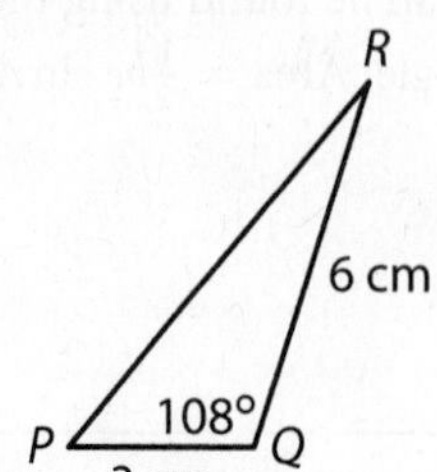

Explain 2 Solving a Right Triangle

Solving a right triangle means finding the lengths of all its sides and the measures of all its angles. To solve a right triangle you need to know two side lengths or one side length and an acute angle measure. Based on the given information, choose among trigonometric ratios, inverse trigonometric ratios, and the Pythagorean Theorem to help you solve the right triangle.

A shelf extends perpendicularly 7 in. from a wall. You want to place a 9-in. brace under the shelf, as shown. To the nearest tenth of an inch, how far below the shelf will the brace be attached to the wall? To the nearest degree, what angle will the brace make with the shelf and with the wall?

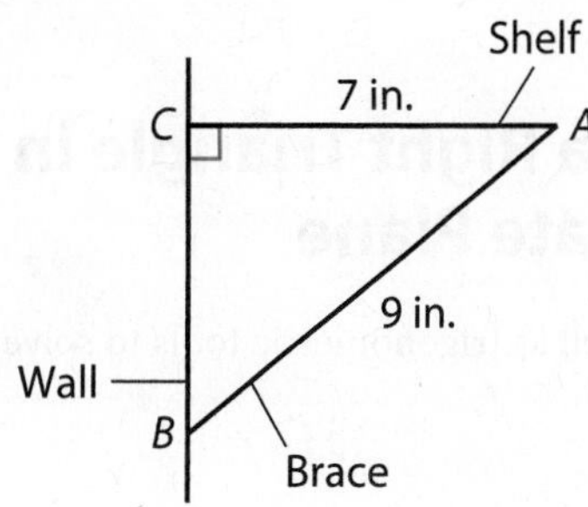

(A) Find *BC*.

Use the Pythagorean Theorem to find the length of the third side. $AC^2 + BC^2 = AB^2$

Substitute 7 for *AC* and 9 for *AB*. $7^2 + BC^2 = 9^2$

Find the squares. $49 + BC^2 = 81$

Subtract 49 from both sides. $BC^2 = 32$

Find the square root and root. $BC \approx 5.7$

(B) Find m∠*A* and m∠*B*.

Use an inverse trigonometric ratio to find m∠*A*. You know the lengths of the adjacent side and the hypotenuse, so use the cosine ratio.

Write a cosine ratio for ∠*A*. $\cos A = \boxed{\frac{7}{9}}$

Write an inverse cosine ratio. $m\angle A = \cos^{-1}\left(\boxed{\frac{7}{9}}\right)$

Evaluate the inverse cosine ratio and round. $m\angle A \approx \boxed{39}°$

∠ $\boxed{A}$ and ∠*B* are complementary. $m\angle \boxed{A} + m\angle B = 90°$

Substitute $\boxed{39}$° for m∠ $\boxed{A}$. $\boxed{39}° + m\angle B \approx 90°$

Subtract $\boxed{39}$° from both sides. $m\angle B \approx \boxed{51}°$

Reflect

5. Is it possible to find m∠*B* before you find m∠*A*? Explain.

Your Turn

A building casts a 33-m shadow when the Sun is at an angle of 27° to the vertical. How tall is the building, to the nearest meter? How far is it from the top of the building to the tip of the shadow? What angle does a ray from the Sun along the edge of the shadow make with the ground?

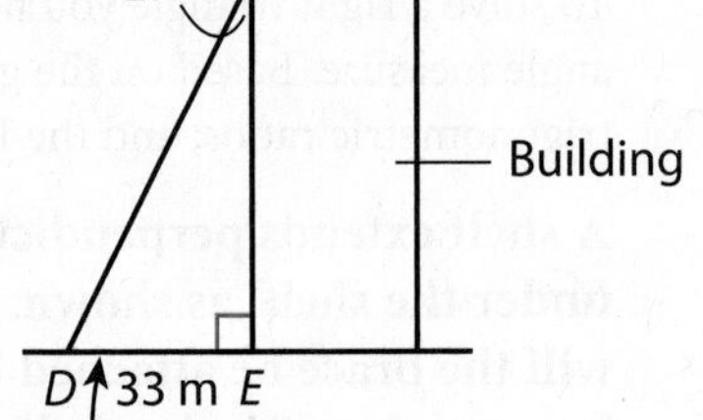

6. Use a trigonometric ratio to find the distance *EF*.

7. Use another trigonometric ratio to find the distance *DF*.

8. Use the fact that acute angles of a right triangle are complementary to find m∠*D*.

Explain 3 Solving a Right Triangle in the Coordinate Plane

You can use the distance formula as well as trigonometric tools to solve right triangles in the coordinate plane.

Example 3 **Solve each triangle.**

(A) Triangle *ABC* has vertices $A(-3, 3)$, $B(-3, -1)$, and $C(4, -1)$. Find the side lengths to the nearest hundredth and the angle measures to the nearest degree.

Plot points *A*, *B*, and *C*, and draw $\triangle ABC$.

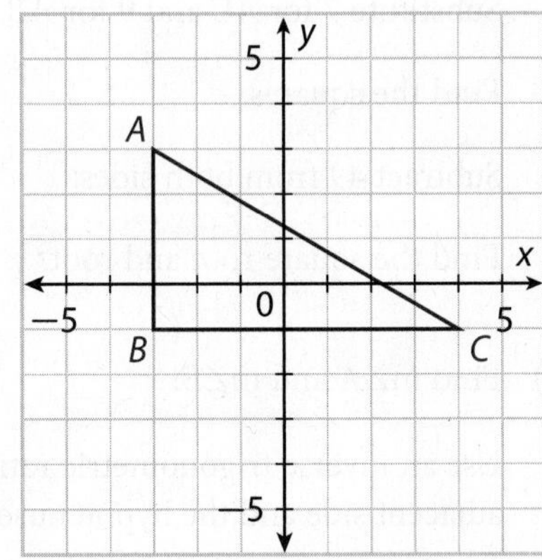

Find the side lengths: $AB = 4$, $BC = 7$

Use the distance formula to find the length of $\overline{AC}$.

$$AC = \sqrt{(4-(-3))^2 + (-1-3)^2} = \sqrt{65} \approx 8.06$$

Find the angle measures: $\overline{AB} \perp \overline{BC}$, so $m\angle B = 90°$.

Use an inverse tangent ratio to find

$$m\angle C = \tan^{-1}\left(\frac{AB}{BC}\right) = \tan^{-1}\left(\frac{4}{7}\right) \approx 30°.$$

$\angle A$ and $\angle C$ are complementary, so $m\angle A \approx 90° - 30° = 60°$.

Ⓑ Triangle *DEF* has vertices $D(-4, 3)$, $E(3, 4)$, and $F(0, 0)$. Find the side lengths to the nearest hundredth and the angle measures to the nearest degree.

Plot points *D*, *E*, and *F*, and draw $\triangle DEF$.

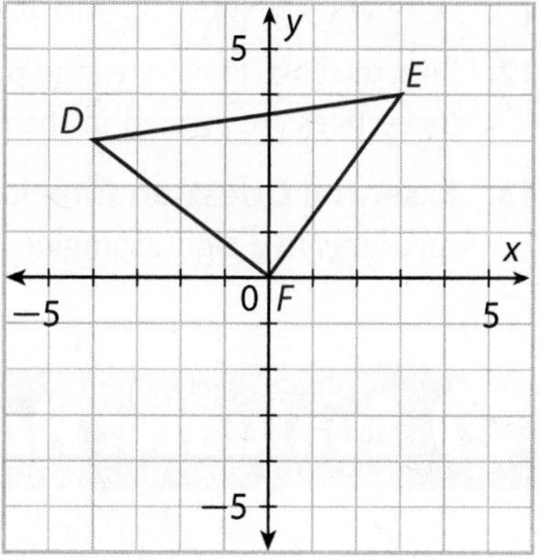

$\angle F$ appears to be a right angle. To check, find the slope

of $\overline{DF}$: $\dfrac{0 - 3}{0 - (-4)} = \dfrac{-3}{4} = -\dfrac{3}{4}$;

slope of $\overline{EF}$: $\dfrac{0 - 4}{0 - 3} = \dfrac{-4}{-3} = \dfrac{4}{3}$;

so $m\angle F = 90°$.

Find the side lengths using the distance formula:

$$DE = \sqrt{\left(3 - (-4)\right)^2 + \left(4 - 3\right)^2} = \sqrt{50} = 5\sqrt{2} \approx 7.07,$$

$$DF = \sqrt{\left(0 - (-4)\right)^2 + \left(0 - 3\right)^2} = \sqrt{25} = 5,$$

$$EF = \sqrt{\left(0 - 3\right)^2 + \left(0 - 4\right)^2} = \sqrt{25} = 5$$

Use an inverse sine ratio to find $m\angle D$.

$$m\angle D = \sin^{-1}\left(\frac{EF}{DE}\right) = \sin^{-1}\left(\frac{5}{5\sqrt{2}}\right) = 45°$$

$\angle D$ and $\angle E$ are complementary, so $m\angle E = 90° - 45° = 45°$.

Reflect

9. How does the given information determine which inverse trigonometric ratio you should use to determine an acute angle measure?

Your Turn

10. Triangle *JKL* has vertices $J(3, 5)$, $K(-3, 2)$, and $L(5, 1)$. Find the side lengths to the nearest hundredth and the angle measures to the nearest degree.

Elaborate

11. Would you use the area formula you determined in this lesson for a right triangle? Explain.

12. **Discussion** How does the process of solving a right triangle change when its vertices are located in the coordinate plane?

13. **Essential Question Check-In** How do you find the unknown angle measures in a right triangle?

Evaluate: Homework and Practice

- Online Homework
- Hints and Help
- Extra Practice

Find the area of each triangle to the nearest tenth.

1.

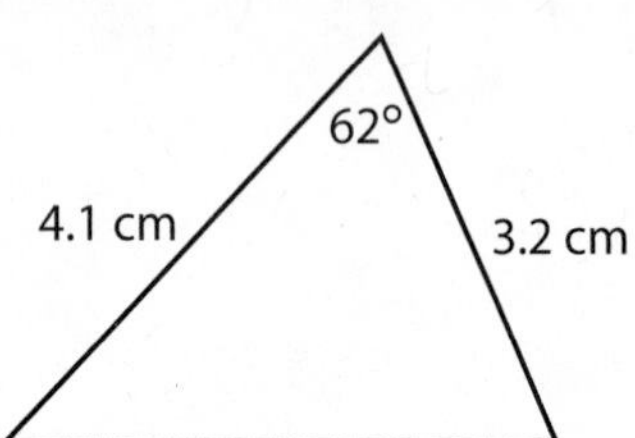

2. In $\triangle PQR$, $PR = 23$ mm, $QR = 39$ mm, and $m\angle R = 163°$.

Solve each right triangle. Round lengths to the nearest tenth and angles to the nearest degree.

3.

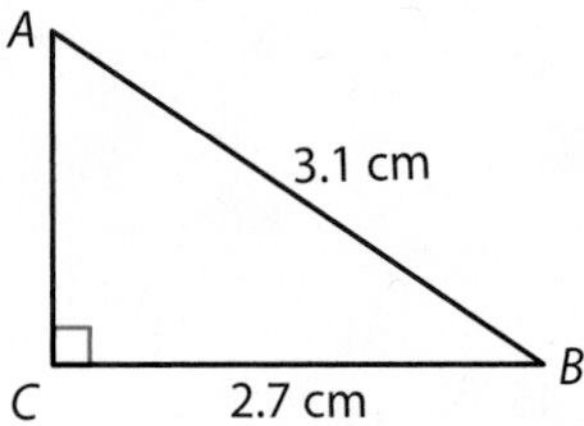

4.

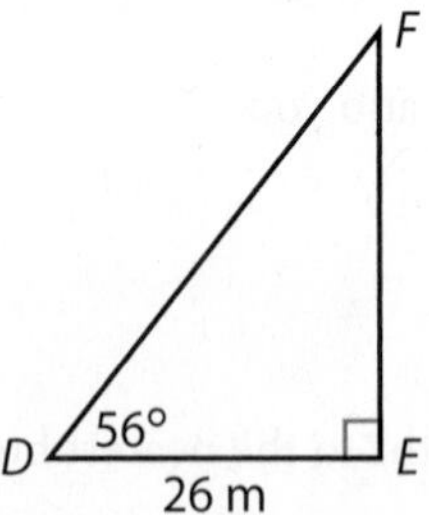

5. Right $\triangle PQR$ with $\overline{PQ} \perp \overline{PR}$, $QR = 47$ mm, and $m\angle Q = 52°$

Solve each triangle. Find the side lengths to the nearest hundredth and the angle measures to the nearest degree.

6. Triangle ABC with vertices $A(-4, 4)$, $B(3, 4)$, and $C(3, -2)$

7. Triangle JKL with vertices $J(-3, 1)$, $K(-1, 4)$, and $L(6, -5)$

8. Triangle PQR with vertices $P(5, 5)$, $Q(-5, 3)$, and $R(-4, -2)$

9. **Surveying** A plot of land is in the shape of a triangle, as shown. Find the area of the plot, to the nearest hundred square yards.

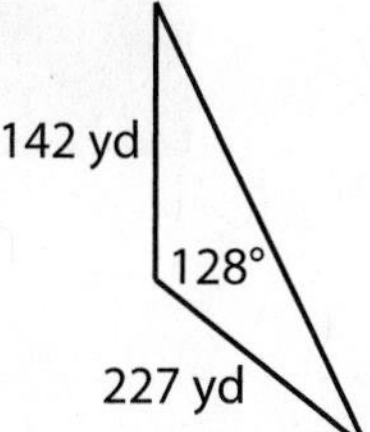

10. **History** A drawbridge at the entrance to an ancient castle is raised and lowered by a pair of chains. The figure represents the drawbridge when flat. Find the height of the suspension point of the chain, to the nearest tenth of a meter, and the measures of the acute angles the chain makes with the wall and the drawbridge, to the nearest degree.

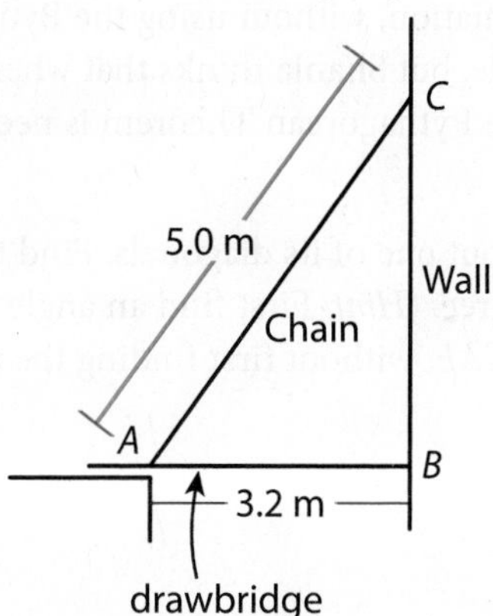

11. **Building** For safety, the angle a wheelchair ramp makes with the horizontal should be no more than 3.5°. What is the maximum height of a ramp of length 30 ft? What distance along the ground would this ramp cover? Round to the nearest tenth of a foot.

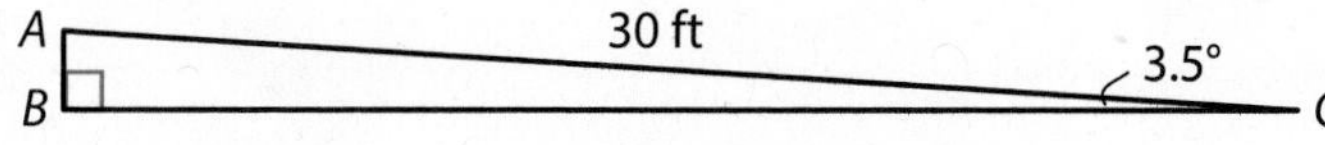

12. Multi-Step The figure shows an origami crane as well as a stage of its construction. The area of each wing is shown by the shaded part of the figure, which is symmetric about its vertical center line. Use the information in the figure to find the total wing area of the crane, to the nearest tenth of a square inch.

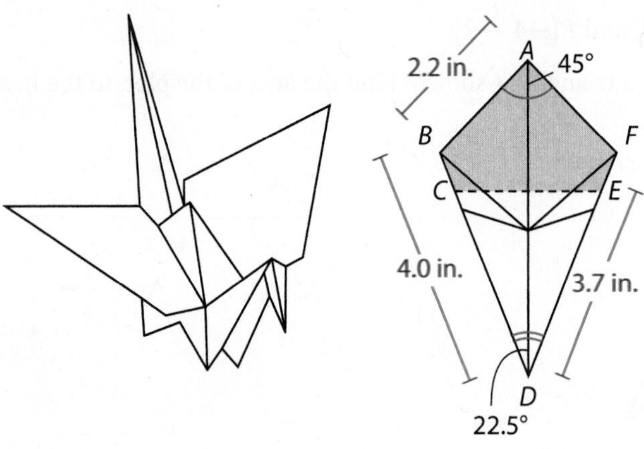

13. Right triangle $\triangle XYZ$ has vertices $X(1, 4)$ and $Y(2, -3)$. The vertex Z has positive integer coordinates, and $XZ = 5$. Find the coordinates of Z and solve $\triangle XYZ$; give exact answers.

14. Critique Reasoning Shania and Pedro are discussing whether it is always possible to solve a right triangle, given enough information, without using the Pythagorean Theorem. Pedro says that it is always possible, but Shania thinks that when two side lengths and no angle measures are given, the Pythagorean Theorem is needed. Who is correct, and why?

15. Design The logo shown is symmetrical about one of its diagonals. Find the angle measures in $\triangle CAE$, to the nearest degree. (*Hint:* First find an angle in $\triangle ABC$, $\triangle CDE$ or $\triangle AEF$) Then, find the area of $\triangle CAE$, without first finding the areas of the other triangles.

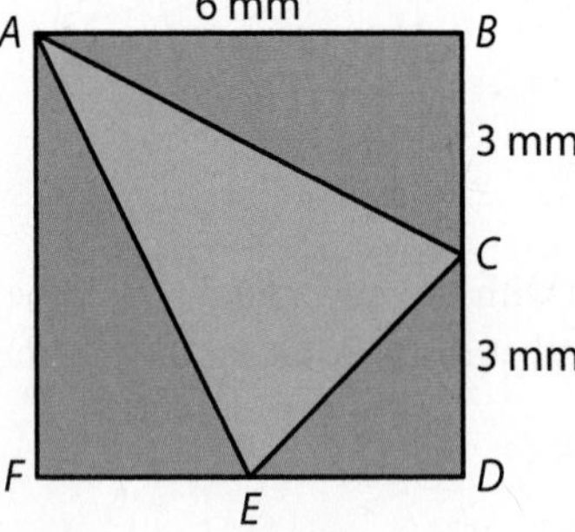

16. Use the area formula for obtuse $\angle B$ in the diagram to show that if an acute angle and an obtuse angle are supplementary, then their sines are equal.

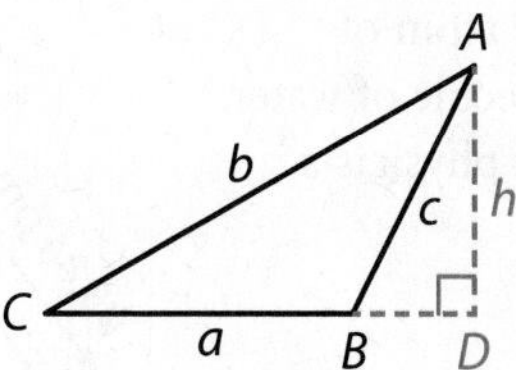

H.O.T. Focus on Higher Order Thinking

17. **Communicate Mathematical Ideas** The HL Congruence Theorem states that for right triangles ABC and DEF such that $\angle A$ and $\angle D$ are right angles, $\overline{BC} \cong \overline{EF}$, and $\overline{AB} \cong \overline{DE}$, $\triangle ABC \cong \triangle DEF$.

Explain, without formal proof, how solving a right triangle with given leg lengths, or with a given side length and acute angle measure, shows that right triangles with both legs congruent, or with corresponding sides and angles congruent, must be congruent.

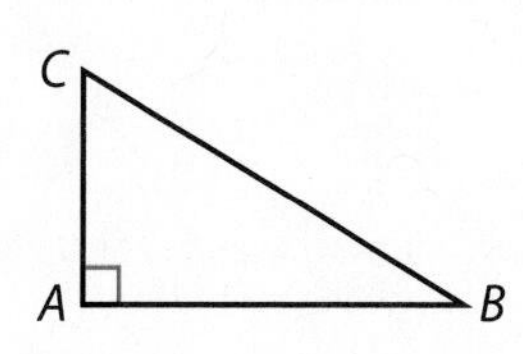

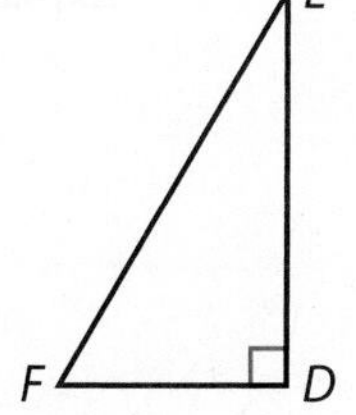

18. **Persevere in Problem Solving** Find the perimeter and area of $\triangle ABC$, as exact numbers. Then, find the measures of all the angles to the nearest degree.

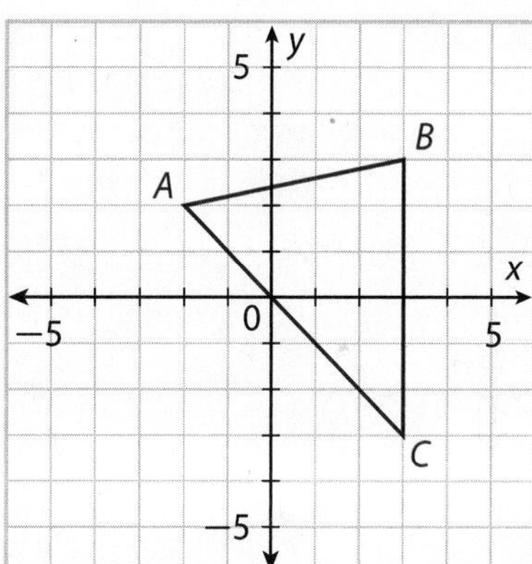

19. **Analyze Relationships** Find the area of the triangle using two different formulas, and deduce an expression for $\sin 2\theta$.

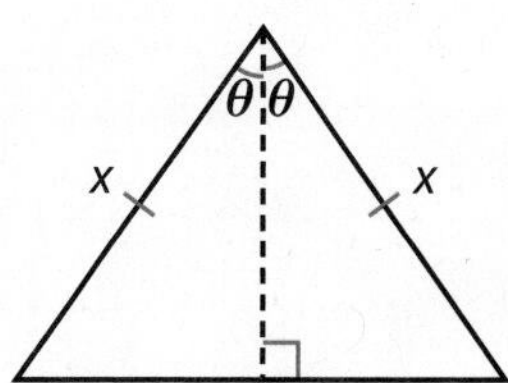

Lesson Performance Task

Every molecule of water contains two atoms of hydrogen and one atom of oxygen. The drawing shows how the atoms are arranged in a molecule of water, along with the incredibly precise dimensions of the molecule that physicists have been able to determine. (1 pm = 1 picometer = 10^{-12}m)

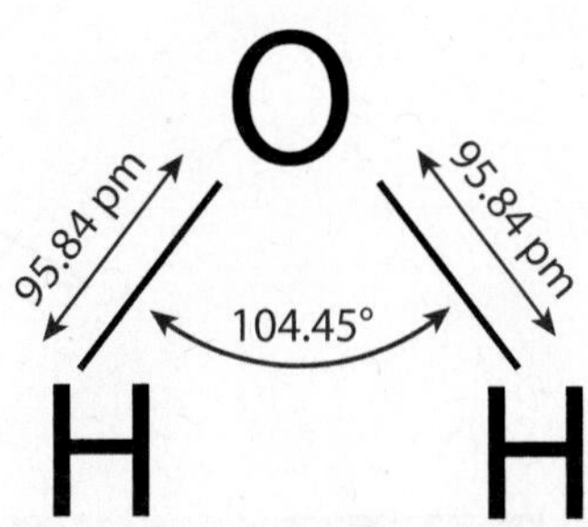

1. Draw and label a triangle with the dimensions shown.

2. Find the area of the triangle in square centimeters. Show your work.

3. Find the distance between the hydrogen atoms in centimeters. Explain your method.

Trigonometry with Right Triangles

Essential Question: How can you use trigonometry with right triangles to solve real-world problems?

Key Vocabulary
- adjacent *(adyacente)*
- opposite *(opuesto)*
- tangent *(tangente)*
- $tan^{-1} A$ *($tan^{-1} A$)* inverse tangent of $\angle A$ *(tangente inversa de $\angle A$)*
- trigonometric ratio *(proporción trigonométrica)*
- sine *(seno)*
- cosine *(coseno)*
- inverse trigonometric ratios *(proporción inversa trigonométrica)*
- Pythagorean triple *(terna pitagórica)*

KEY EXAMPLE *(Lesson 13.1)*

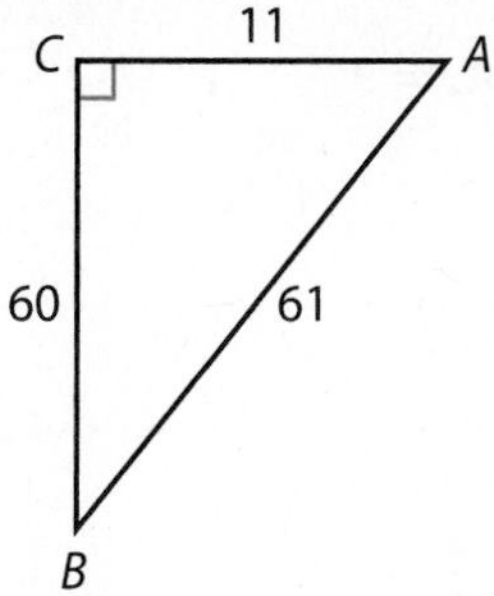

Find the tangent of angle A.

$\tan A = \dfrac{\text{length of leg opposite } \angle A}{\text{length of leg adjacent to } \angle A}$ Definition of tangent

$\tan A = \dfrac{60}{11} \approx 5.45$ Substitute and simplify

KEY EXAMPLE *(Lesson 13.2)*

Find the sine and cosine of angle A.

$\sin A = \dfrac{\text{length of leg opposite } \angle A}{\text{length of hypotenuse}}$ Definition of sine

$\sin A = \dfrac{60}{61} \approx .98$ Simplify.

$\cos A = \dfrac{\text{length of leg adjacent to } \angle A}{\text{length of hypotenuse}}$ Definition of cosine

$\cos A = \dfrac{11}{61} \approx .18$ Simplify.

KEY EXAMPLE *(Lesson 13.3)*

Given an isosceles right triangle *DEF* with m$\angle F = 90°$ and $DE = 7$, find the length of the other two sides.

$DE = DF\sqrt{2}$ Apply the relationship of 45°-45°-90° triangles.

$7 = DF\sqrt{2}$ Substitute.

$\dfrac{7}{\sqrt{2}} = DF$ Simplify.

$DF = EF = \dfrac{7}{\sqrt{2}} = \dfrac{7\sqrt{2}}{2}$ Apply properties of isosceles triangles.

EXERCISES

Given a right triangle $\triangle XYZ$ where $\angle Z$ is a right angle, $XY = 53$, $YZ = 28$, and $XZ = 45$, find the following rounded to the nearest hundredth. *(Lessons 13.1, 13.2)*

1. $\sin X$ **2.** $\cos X$ **3.** $\tan X$

Find the lengths of the other two sides of the following triangle. Find exact answers in order of least to greatest. *(Lesson 13.3)*

4. 30°—60°—90° triangle with a hypotenuse of length 14

Find the area of the following triangle, rounded to the nearest tenth. *(Lesson 13.4)*

5. triangle $\triangle ABC$, where $m\angle C = 127°$, $AC = 5$, and $BC = 9$

MODULE PERFORMANCE TASK

How Much Shorter Are Staggered Pipe Stacks?

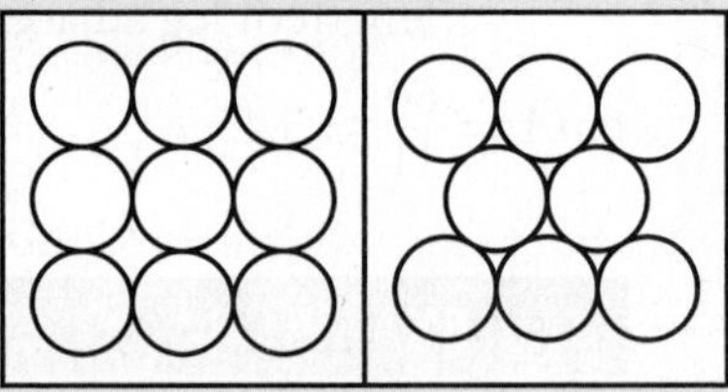

How much space can be saved by stacking pipe in a staggered pattern? The illustration shows you the difference between layers of pipe stacked directly on top of each other (left) and in a staggered pattern (right). Suppose you have pipes that are 2 inches in diameter. How much shorter will a staggered stack of 10 layers be than a non-staggered stack with the same number of layers? In general, how much shorter are n layers of staggered pipe?

Start by listing how you plan to tackle the problem. Then complete the task. Be sure to write down all your data and assumptions. Then use numbers, graphs, diagrams, or algebraic equations to explain how you reached your conclusion.

Ready to Go On?

13.1–13.4 Trigonometry with Right Triangles

- Online Homework
- Hints and Help
- Extra Practice

Solve the problem. *(Lesson 13.1)*

1. A painter is placing a ladder to reach the third story window, which is 20 feet above the ground and makes an angle with the ground of 70°. How far out from the building does the base of the ladder need to be positioned?

2. Given the value of $\cos 30° = \frac{\sqrt{3}}{2}$, write the sine of a complementary angle. Use an expression relating trigonometric ratios of complementary angles. *(Lesson 13.2)*

Find the area of the regular polygon. *(Lesson 13.3)*

3. What is the area of a regular hexagon with a distance from its center to a vertex of 1 cm? (Hint: A regular hexagon can be divided into six equilateral triangles.)

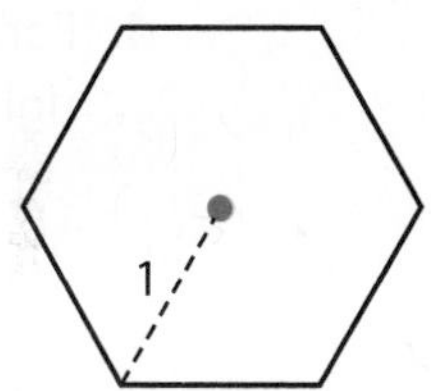

ESSENTIAL QUESTION

4. How would you go about finding the area of a regular pentagon given the distance from its center to the vertices?

MODULE 13
MIXED REVIEW

Assessment Readiness

1. Julia is standing 2 feet away from a lamppost. She casts a shadow of 5 feet and the light makes a 20° angle relative to the ground from the top of her shadow. Consider each expression. Does the expression give you the height of the lamppost?

   Write Yes or No for A–C.

   A. 7 sin 20°

   B. 7 tan 20°

   C. 7 tan 70°

2. A right triangle has two sides with lengths 10 and 10. Determine if each statement is True or False.

   A. The triangle has two angles that measure 45° each.

   B. The triangle is equilateral.

   C. The length of the third side is $10\sqrt{2}$.

3. The measure of $\angle 1$ is 125° and the measure of $\angle 2$ is 55°. State two different relationships that can be used to prove $m\angle 3 = 125°$.

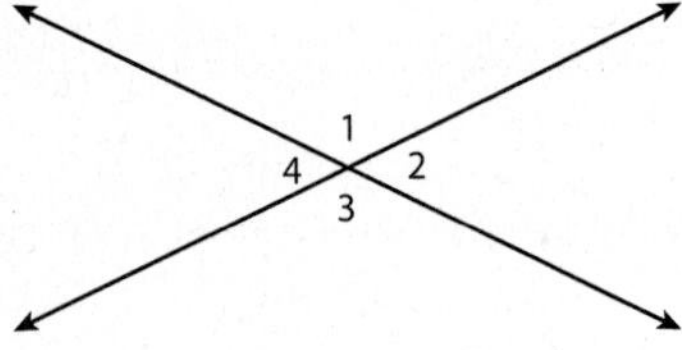

4. For the rhombus, specify how to find its area using the four congruent right triangles with variable angle θ.

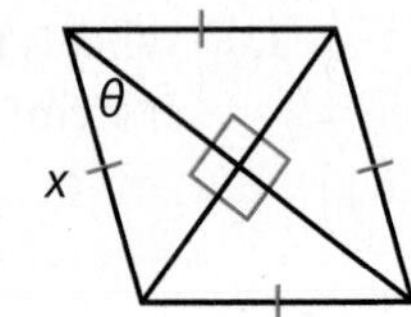

Trigonometry with All Triangles

MODULE 14

Essential Question: How can you use triangle trigonometry to solve real-world problems?

REAL WORLD VIDEO
Air traffic controllers must understand trigonometry and other mathematics to make rapid judgments about the positions of aircraft and the distances between them.

MODULE PERFORMANCE TASK PREVIEW

Controlling the Air

You've probably seen photos of air traffic controllers studying green-tinted screens covered with blinking blips. Their job is to analyze the positions of every plane in the airspace near the airport and see to it that the planes land safely. In this module, you'll learn to solve triangles of the type air traffic controllers encounter. Then you'll apply what you've learned to find the distance between two planes approaching an airport.

Are YOU Ready?

Complete these exercises to review skills you will need for this module.

- Online Homework
- Hints and Help
- Extra Practice

Similar Triangles

Example 1 In $\triangle PRK$, $PK = 34$, $RK = 50$, and $m\angle K = 74°$. Why is this triangle similar to $\triangle ABC$? What is the similarity statement?

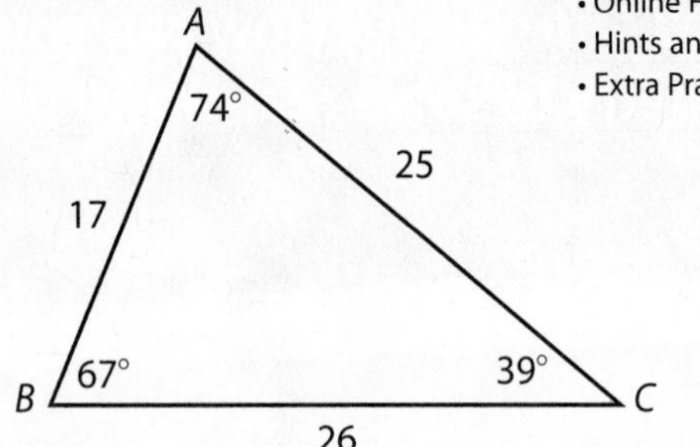

$PK = 34 = 2AB$ (Side),

$m\angle K = 74° = m\angle A$ (Angle),

and $RK = 50 = 2AC$ (Side).

So, $\triangle ABC \sim \triangle KPR$ by $SAS\triangle\sim$.

Complete each similarity statement and name the theorem that supports it.

1. Given: In $\triangle MNT$, $MN = 8.5$, $TM = 13$, and $TN = 12.5$.

$\triangle ABC \sim$ __?__ by __?__

2. Given: In $\triangle ZQE$, $m\angle E = 67°$, $ZQ = 4$, and $m\angle Q = 39°$.

$\triangle ABC \sim$ __?__ by __?__

Proportional Relationships

Example 2 Given: $\triangle PQR \sim \triangle NCL$, $PQ = 15$, $QR = 12$, $PR = 18$, and $CL = 15$. What is NL?

$\frac{CL}{QR} = \frac{NL}{PR}$ Write a proportion.

$\frac{15}{12} = \frac{NL}{18}$ Substitute.

$NL = 22.5$ Solve.

Solve, given that $\triangle RST \sim \triangle FGH$, $RT = 9$, $ST = 6$, $FG = 7.5$, and $FH = 13.5$.

3. Find RS.

4. Find GH.

Multi-Step Equations

Example 3 Solve $4x + 15 = 1$ for x.

$4x + 15 - 15 = 1 - 15$ Subtract 15 from both sides.

$4x = -14$ Combine like terms.

$x = -3.5$ Divide.

Solve each equation.

5. $2r - 5 = -9$

6. $\frac{4m - 5}{3} = -7$

7. $9.9 - 4.2k = 3k - 0.9$

14.1 Law of Sines

Resource Locker

Essential Question: How can you use trigonometric ratios to find side lengths and angle measures of non-right triangles?

Explore Use an Area Formula to Derive the Law of Sines

Recall that the area of a triangle can be found using the sine of one of the angles.

$\text{Area} = \frac{1}{2}b \cdot c \cdot \sin(A)$

You can write variations of this formula using different angles and sides from the same triangle.

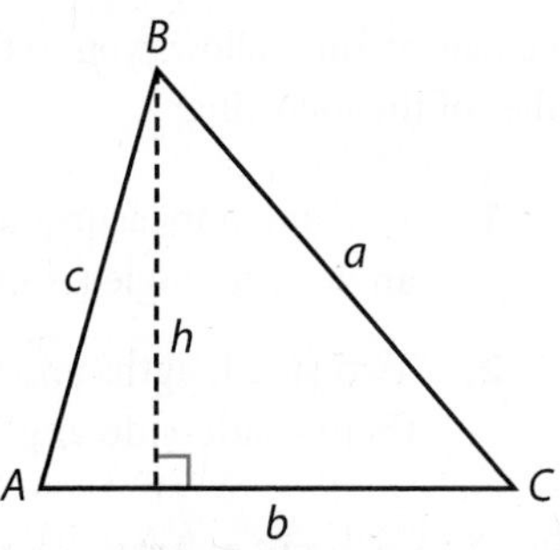

(A) Rewrite the area formula using side length a as the base of the triangle and $\angle C$.

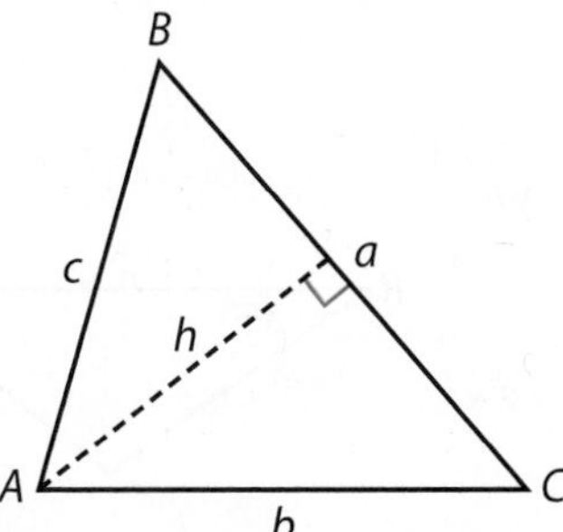

(B) Rewrite the area formula using side length c as the base of the triangle and $\angle B$.

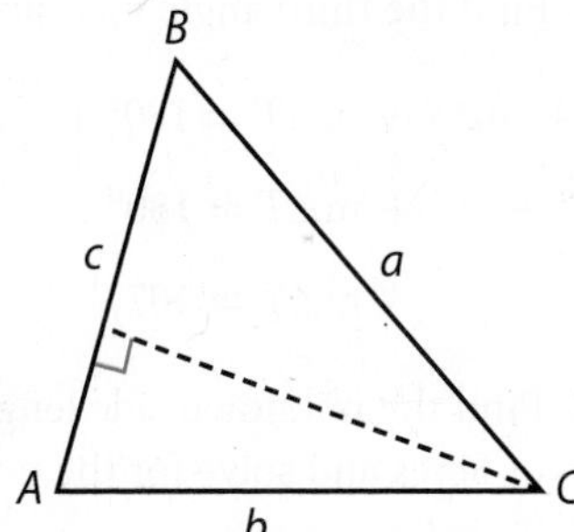

(C) What do all three formulas have in common?

(D) Why is this statement true?

$\frac{1}{2}b \cdot c \cdot \sin(A) = \frac{1}{2}a \cdot b \cdot \sin(C) = \frac{1}{2}c \cdot a \cdot \sin(B)$

(E) Multiply each area by the expression $\frac{2}{abc}$. Write an equivalent statement.

Reflect

1. In the case of a right triangle, where $\angle C$ is the right angle, what happens to the area formula?

2. **Discussion** In all three cases of the area formula you explored, what is the relationship between the angle and the two side lengths in the area formula?

Explain 1 Applying the Law of Sines

The results of the Explore activity are summarized in the Law of Sines.

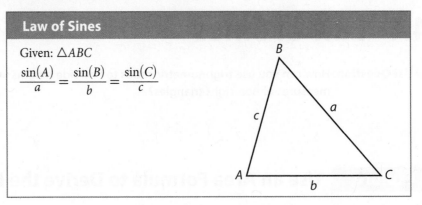

Law of Sines

Given: $\triangle ABC$

$$\frac{\sin(A)}{a} = \frac{\sin(B)}{b} = \frac{\sin(C)}{c}$$

The Law of Sines allows you to find the unknown measures for a given triangle, as long as you know either of the following:

1. Two angle measures and any side length—angle-angle-side (AAS) or angle-side-angle (ASA) information
2. Two side lengths and the measure of an angle that is not between them—side-side-angle (SSA) information

Example 1 **Find all the unknown measures using the given triangle. Round to the nearest tenth.**

(A) **Step 1** Find the third angle measure.

$m\angle R + m\angle S + m\angle T = 180°$	Triangle Sum Theorem
$35° + 38° + m\angle T = 180°$	Substitute the known angle measures.
$m\angle T = 107°$	Solve for the measure of $\angle T$.

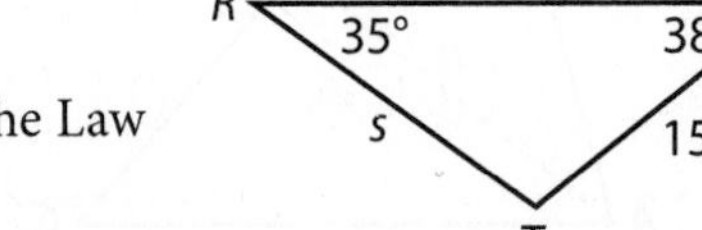

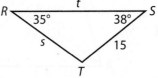

Step 2 Find the unknown side lengths. Set up proportions using the Law of Sines and solve for the unknown.

$\frac{\sin(T)}{t} = \frac{\sin(R)}{r}$	Law of Sines	$\frac{\sin(S)}{s} = \frac{\sin(R)}{r}$
$\frac{\sin(107°)}{t} = \frac{\sin(35°)}{15}$	Substitute.	$\frac{\sin(38°)}{s} = \frac{\sin(35°)}{15}$
$t = \frac{15 \cdot \sin(107°)}{\sin(35°)}$	Solve for the unknown.	$s = \frac{15 \cdot (\sin 38°)}{\sin(35°)}$
$t \approx 25$	Evaluate.	$s \approx 16.1$

(B) **Step 1** Find the third angle measure.

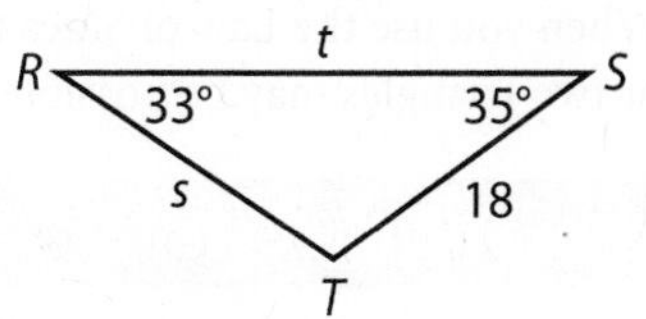

$m\angle R + m\angle S + m\angle T = 180°$	Triangle Sum Theorem
$33° + 35° + m\angle T = 180°$	Substitute the known angle measures.
$m\angle T = 112°$	Solve for the measure of ∠T.

Step 2 Find the unknown side lengths. Set up proportions using the Law of Sines and solve for the unknown.

$\frac{\sin(T)}{t} = \frac{\sin(R)}{r}$	Law of Sines	$\frac{\sin(S)}{s} = \frac{\sin(R)}{r}$
$\frac{\sin(112°)}{t} = \frac{\sin(33°)}{18}$	Substitute.	$\frac{\sin(35°)}{s} = \frac{\sin(33°)}{18}$
$t = \frac{18 \cdot \sin(112°)}{\sin(33°)}$	Solve for the unknown.	$s = \frac{18 \cdot \sin(35°)}{\sin(33°)}$
$t \approx 30.6$	Evaluate.	$s \approx 19.0$

Reflect

3. Suppose that you are given $m\angle A$. To find c, what other measures do you need to know?

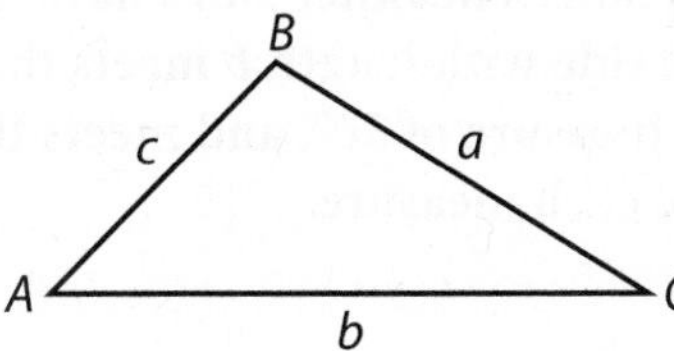

Your Turn

Find all the unknown measures using the given triangle. Round to the nearest tenth.

4.

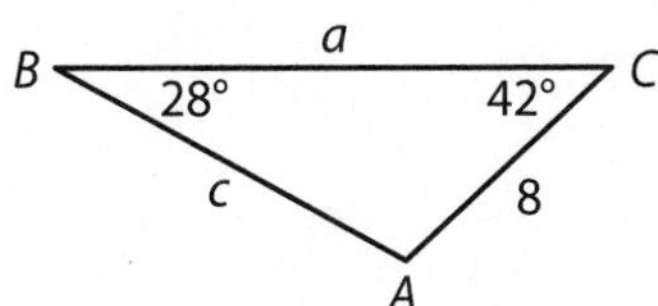

5.

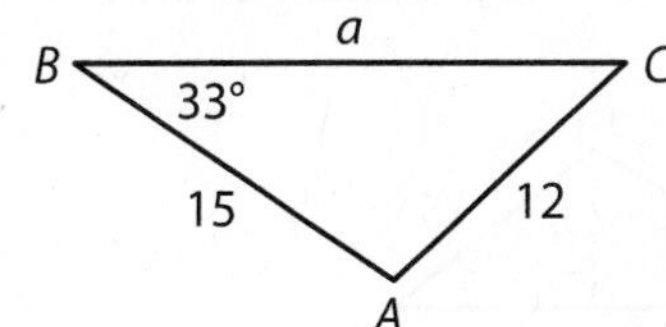

Explain 2 Evaluating Triangles When SSA is Known Information

When you use the Law of Sines to solve a triangle for which you know side-side-angle (SSA) information, zero, one, or two triangles may be possible. For this reason, SSA is called the ambiguous case.

Ambiguous Case

Given a, b, and $m\angle A$.

$\angle A$ is acute.		$\angle A$ is right or obtuse.
$a < h$ No triangle	$a = h$ One triangle	$a \leq b$ No triangle
$h < a < b$ Two triangles	$a \geq b$ One triangle	$a > b$ One triangle

Example 2 **Design** **Each triangular wing of a model airplane has one side that joins the wing to the airplane. The other sides have lengths $b = 18$ in. and $a = 15$ in. The side with length b meets the airplane at an angle A with a measure of 30°, and meets the side with length a at point C. Find each measure.**

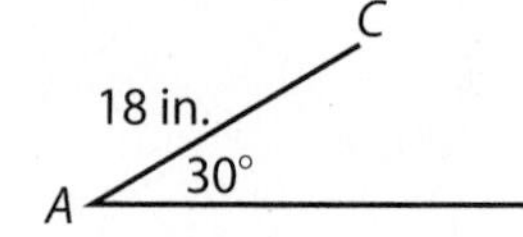

(A) Find $m\angle B$.

Step 1 Determine the number of possible triangles. Find h.

$\sin(30°) = \frac{h}{18}$, so $h = 18 \cdot \sin(30°) = 9$

Because $h < a < b$, two triangles are possible.

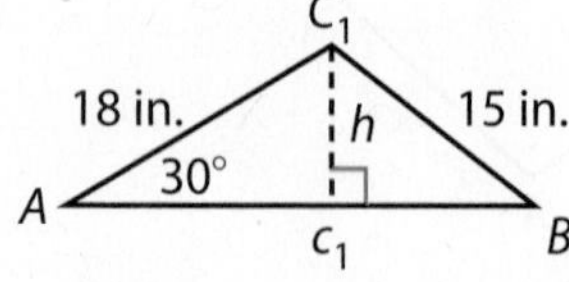

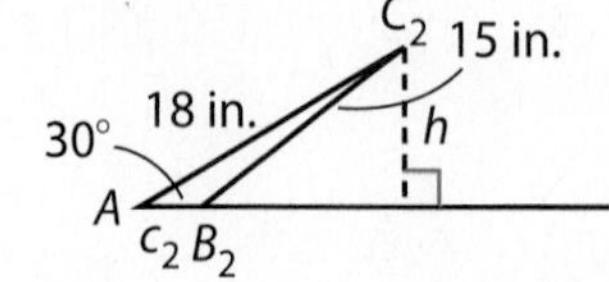

Step 2 Determine $m\angle B_1$ and $m\angle B_2$.

$$\frac{\sin(A)}{a} = \frac{\sin(B)}{b} \quad \text{Law of Sines}$$

$$\frac{\sin(30°)}{15} = \frac{\sin(B)}{18} \quad \text{Substitute.}$$

$$\sin(B) = \frac{18 \cdot \sin(30°)}{15} \quad \text{Solve for } \sin(B).$$

Let $\angle B_1$ be the acute angle with the given sine, and let $\angle B_2$ be the obtuse angle. Use the inverse sine function on your calculator to determine the measures of the angles.

$$m\angle B_1 = \sin^{-1}\left(\frac{18 \cdot \sin(30°)}{15}\right) \approx 36.9° \text{ and } m\angle B_2 = 180° - 36.9° = 143.1°$$

(B) Determine $m\angle C$ and length c.

Solve for $m\angle C_1$.

$$\boxed{36.9}° + 30° + m\angle C_1 = 180°$$

$$m\angle C_1 = \boxed{113.1}°$$

Solve for $m\angle C_2$.

$$\boxed{143.1}° + 30° + m\angle C_2 = 180°$$

$$m\angle C_2 = \boxed{6.9}°$$

Law of Sines

$$\frac{\sin(A)}{a} = \frac{\sin(C_1)}{c_1} \qquad \frac{\sin(A)}{a} = \frac{\sin(C_2)}{c_2}$$

Substitute.

$$\frac{\sin(\boxed{30}°)}{\boxed{15}} = \frac{\sin(\boxed{113.1}°)}{c_1} \qquad \frac{\sin(\boxed{30}°)}{\boxed{15}} = \frac{\sin(\boxed{6.9}°)}{c_2}$$

Solve for the unknown.

$$c_1 = \frac{\boxed{15} \cdot \sin(\boxed{113.1}°)}{\sin(\boxed{30}°)} \qquad c_2 = \frac{\boxed{15} \cdot \sin(\boxed{6.9}°)}{\sin(\boxed{30}°)}$$

Evaluate.

$$c_1 \approx \boxed{27.6} \text{ in.} \qquad c_2 \approx \boxed{3.6} \text{ in.}$$

Your Turn

In Exercises 6 and 7, suppose that for the model airplane in the Example, $a = 21$ in., $b = 18$ in., and $m\angle A = 25°$.

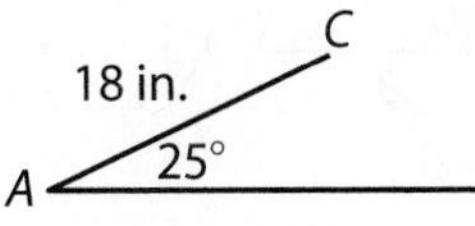

6. How many triangles are possible with this configuration? Explain.

7. Find the unknown measurements. Round to the nearest tenth.

Elaborate

8. If the base angles of a triangle are congruent, use the Law of Sines to show the triangle is isosceles.

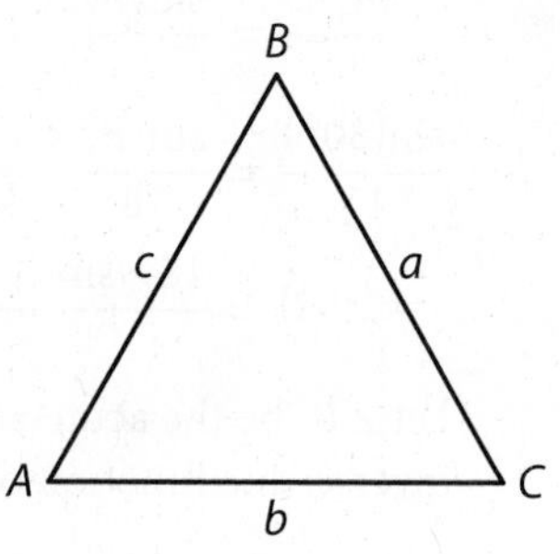

9. Show that when $h = a$, $\angle C$ is a right angle.

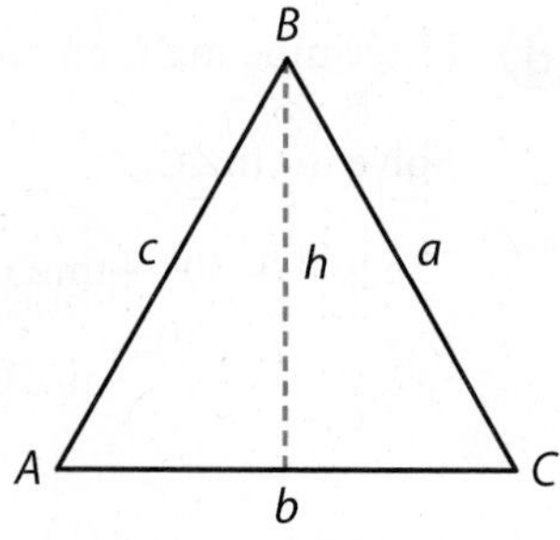

10. **Essential Question Check-In** Given the measures of $\triangle ABC$, describe a method for finding any of the altitudes of the triangle.

Evaluate: Homework and Practice

- Online Homework
- Hints and Help
- Extra Practice

Find the area of each triangle. Round to the nearest tenth.

1.

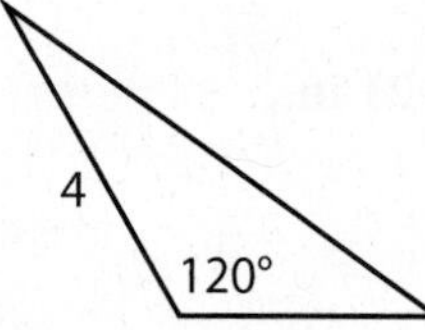

2.

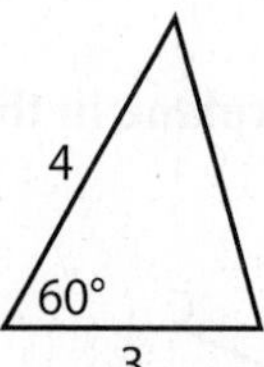

3.

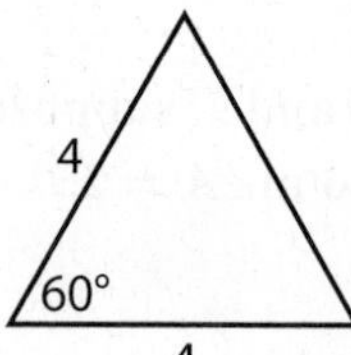

4.

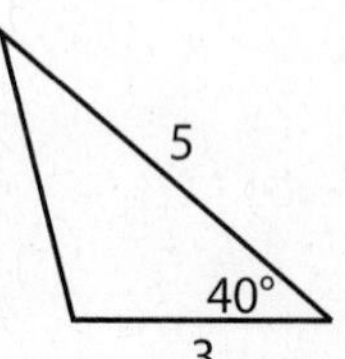

5.

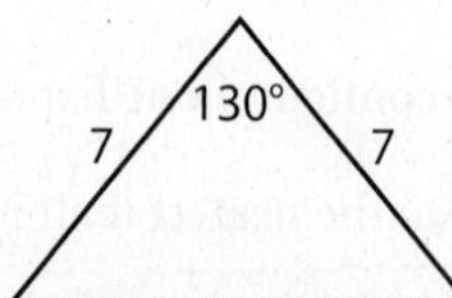

6.

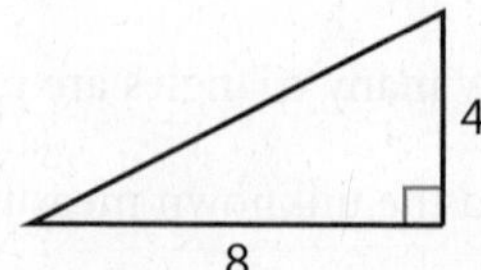

7. What is the area of an isosceles triangle with congruent side lengths x and included angle θ?

8. What is the area of an equilateral triangle of side length x?

Find all the unknown measurements using the Law of Sines.

9.

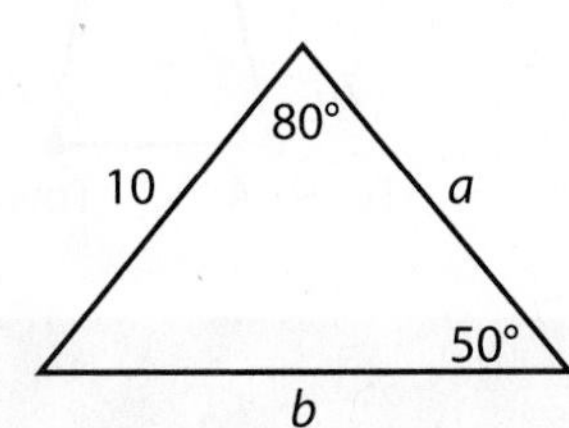

10.

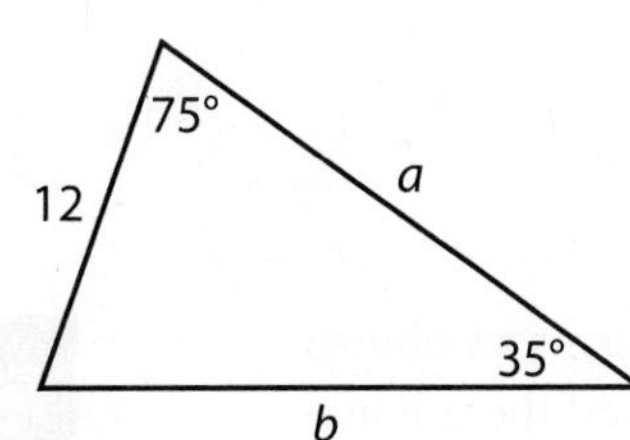

11.

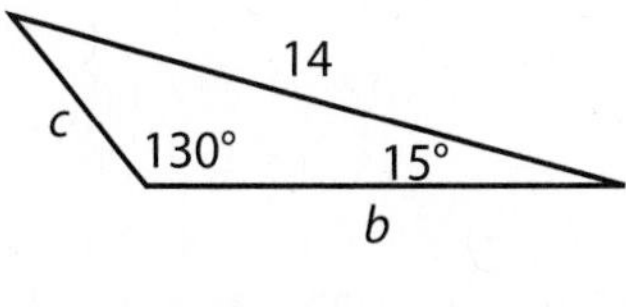

12.

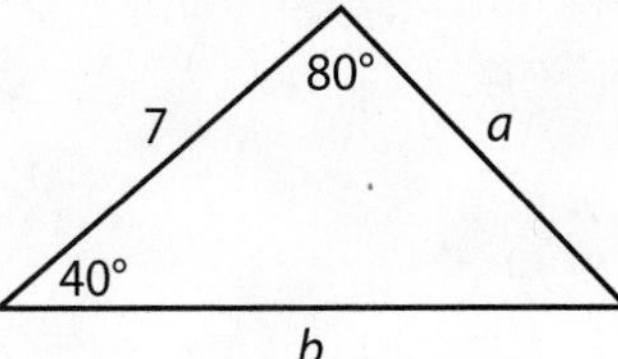

13.

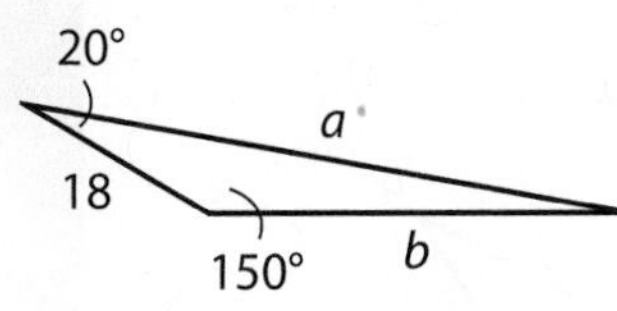

14.

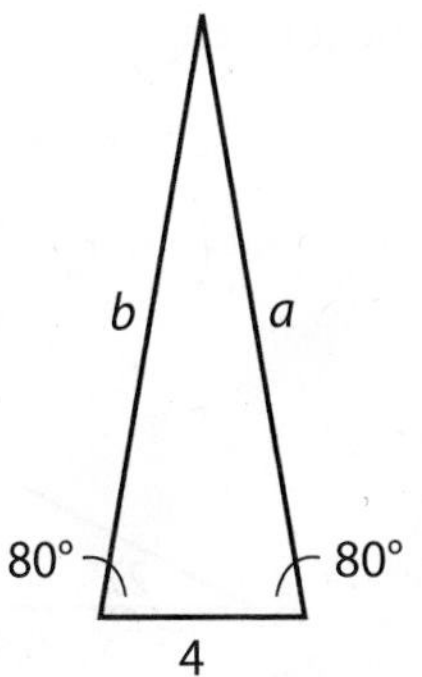

Design **A model airplane designer wants to design wings of the given dimensions. Determine the number of different triangles that can be formed. Then find all the unknown measurements. Round values to the nearest tenth.**

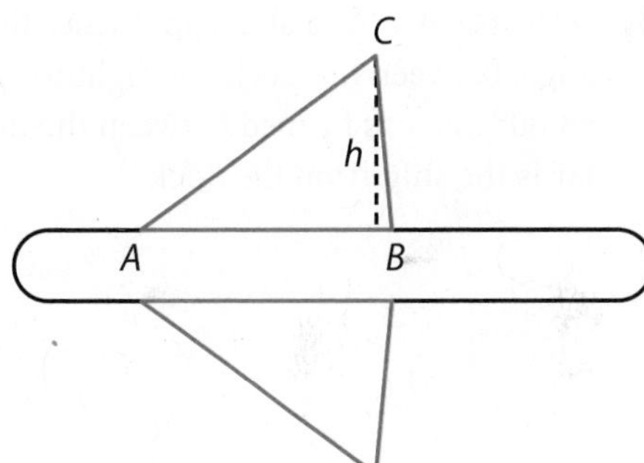

15. $a = 7$ m, $b = 9$ m, $m\angle A = 55°$

16. $a = 12$ m, $b = 4$ m, $m\angle A = 120°$

17. $a = 9$ m, $b = 10$ m, $m\angle A = 35°$

18. $a = 7$ m, $b = 5$ m, $m\angle A = 45°$

19. **Space Travel** Two radio towers that are 50 miles apart track a satellite in orbit. The first tower's signal makes a 76° angle between the ground and satellite. The second tower forms an 80.5° angle.

a. How far is the satellite from each tower?

b. How could you determine how far above Earth the satellite is? What is the satellite's altitude?

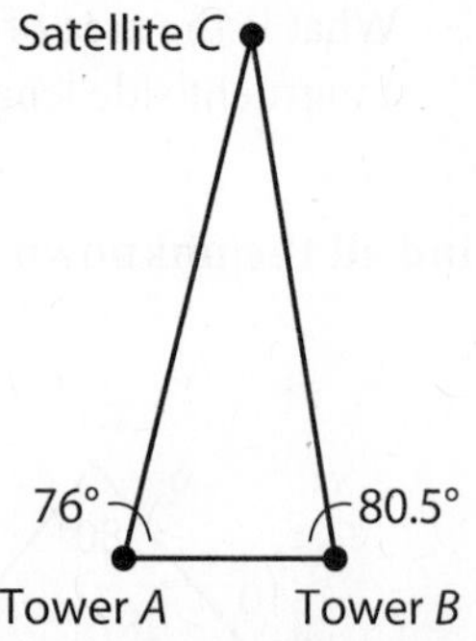

20. **Biology** The dorsal fin of a shark forms an obtuse triangle with these measurements. Find the missing measurements and determine if another triangle can be formed.

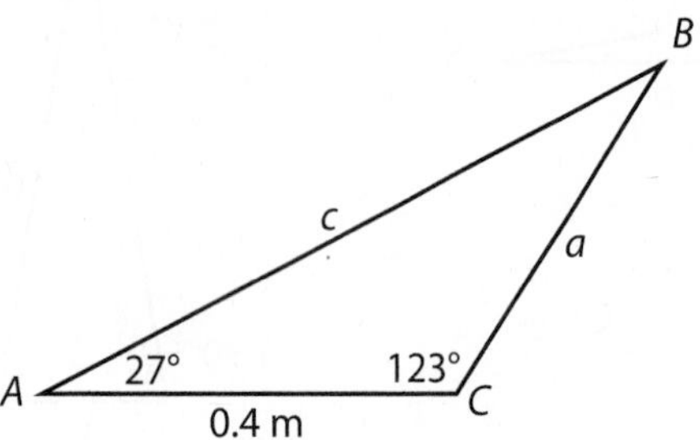

21. **Navigation** As a ship approaches the dock, it forms a 70° angle between the dock and lighthouse. At the lighthouse, an 80° angle is formed between the dock and the ship. How far is the ship from the dock?

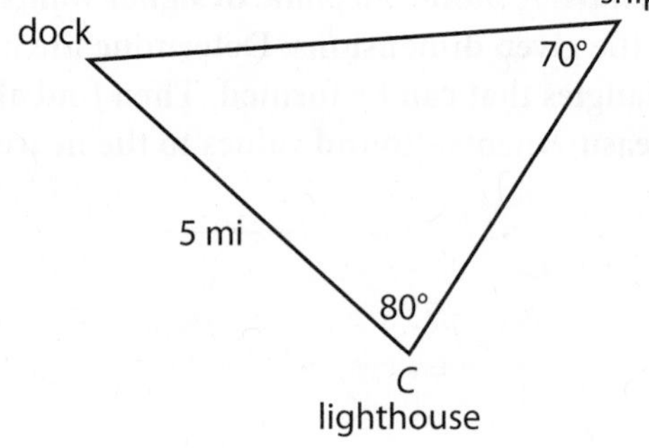

22. For the given triangle, match each altitude with its equivalent expression.

A. h_1 a. ___?___ $a \cdot \sin(B)$

B. h_2 b. ___?___ $c \cdot \sin(A)$

C. h_3 c. ___?___ $b \cdot \sin(C)$

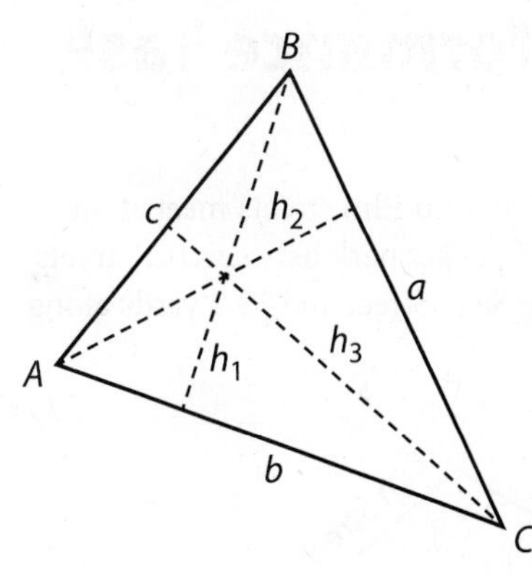

H.O.T. Focus on Higher Order Thinking

Use the diagram, in which $\triangle ABC \sim \triangle DEF$.

23. To find the missing measurements for either triangle using the Law of Sines, what must you do first?

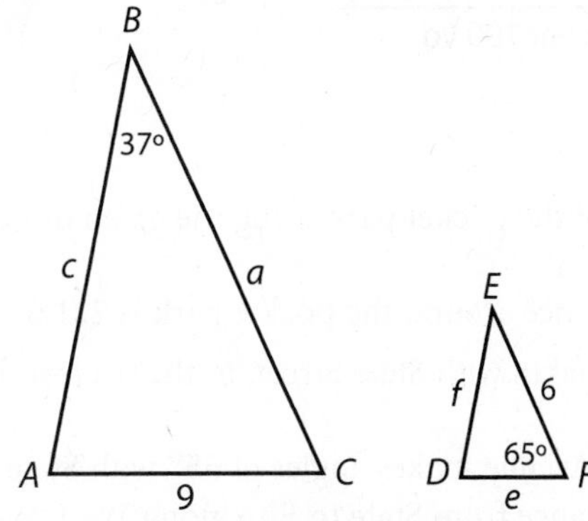

24. Find the missing measurements for $\triangle ABC$.

25. Find the missing measurements for $\triangle DEF$.

26. **Surveying** Two surveyors are at the same altitude and are 10 miles apart on opposite sides of a mountain. They each measure the angle relative to the ground and the top of the mountain. Use the given diagram to indirectly measure the height of the mountain.

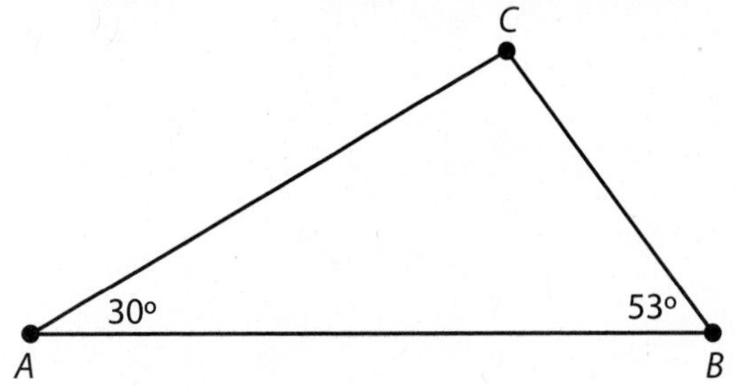

Lesson Performance Task

In the middle of town, State and Elm streets meet at an angle of 40°. A triangular pocket park between the streets stretches 100 yards along State Street and 53.2 yards along Elm Street.

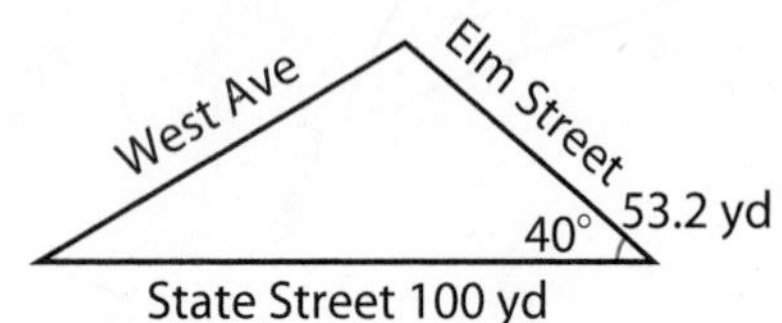

a. Find the area of the pocket park using the given dimensions.

b. If the total distance around the pocket park is 221.6 yards, find $\angle S$, the angle that West Avenue makes with State Street, to the nearest degree.

c. Suppose West Avenue makes angles of 55° with State Street and 80° with Elm Street. The distance from State to Elm along West Avenue is 40 yards. Find the distance from West Avenue to Elm Street along State Street.

14.2 Law of Cosines

Essential Question: How can you use the Law of Cosines to find measures of any triangle?

Resource Locker

Explore Deriving the Law of Cosines

You learned to solve triangle problems by using the Law of Sines. However, the Law of Sines cannot be used to solve triangles for which side-angle-side (SAS) or side-side-side (SSS) information is given. Instead, you must use the Law of Cosines.

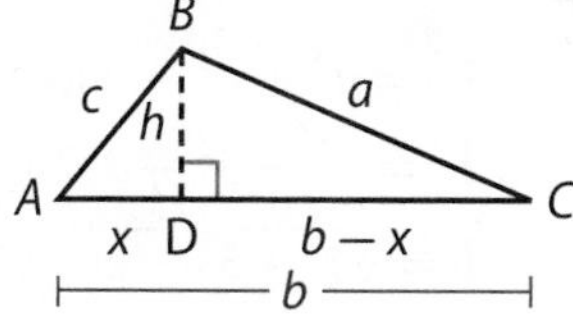

To derive the Law of Cosines, draw $\triangle ABC$ with altitude $\overline{BD}$. If x represents the length of $\overline{AD}$, the length of $\overline{DC}$ is $b - x$.

(A) Use the Pythagorean Theorem to write a relationship for the side lengths of $\triangle BCD$ and for the side lengths of $\triangle ABD$.

(B) Notice that c^2 is equal to a sum of terms in the equation for a^2. Substitute c^2 for those terms.

(C) In $\triangle ABD$, $\cos A = \frac{x}{c}$. Solve for x. Then substitute into the equation you wrote for a^2.

$\cos A = \frac{x}{c}$, or $x =$ [?].

$a^2 = b^2 -$ [?] $+ c^2$

Reflect

1. The equation you wrote in Step C is the Law of Cosines, which is usually written as $a^2 = b^2 + c^2 - 2bc\cos A$. Write formulas using $\cos B$ or $\cos C$ to describe the same relationships in this triangle.

Explain 1 Using the Law of Cosines

To find the missing side length of a right triangle, you can use the Pythagorean Theorem. To find a missing side length of a general triangle, you can use the Law of Cosines.

Law of Cosines

For $\triangle ABC$, the Law of Cosines states that

$a^2 = b^2 + c^2 - 2bc\cos A$

$b^2 = a^2 + c^2 - 2ac\cos B$

$c^2 = a^2 + b^2 - 2ab\cos C$

When performing multi-step calculations, you need to be aware of *round-off error*. This error is the difference between the exact value of a number and a rounded form of the number. For instance, the difference between $\frac{1}{3}$ and the rounded form 0.3 is 0.03333..., which is the round-off error. When a rounded result from one step of a calculation is used in a subsequent step, round-off errors can accumulate, making the result from the subsequent step no longer be the correct rounded value of the exact result for that step. One way to avoid accumulating round-off errors is to carry more decimal places than you need for the first step's rounded result into the subsequent step. A result from one step used in another step is a called an *intermediate result*.

Example 1 **Solve $\triangle ABC$. Round intermediate results to 3 decimal places and final answers to 1 decimal place.**

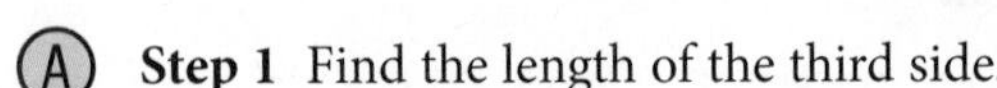

Ⓐ **Step 1** Find the length of the third side.

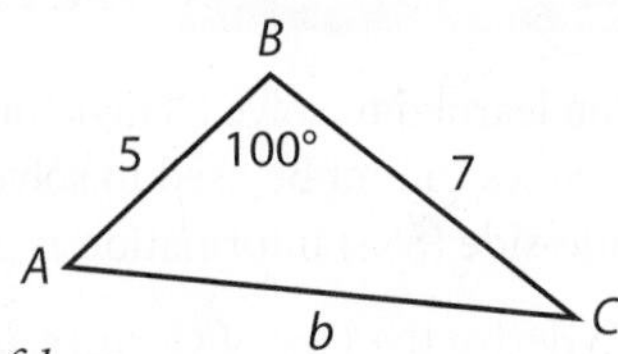

$b^2 = a^2 + c^2 - 2ac\cos B$ Law of Cosines

$b^2 = 7^2 + 5^2 - 2(7)(5)\cos 100°$ Substitute.

$b = \sqrt{7^2 + 5^2 - 2(7)(5)\cos 100°} \approx 9.282 \approx 9.3$ Solve for a positive value of *b*.

Step 2 Find an angle measure.

$\frac{\sin A}{a} = \frac{\sin B}{b}$ Law of Sines

$\frac{\sin A}{7} = \frac{\sin 100°}{9.282}$ Substitute using the more accurate approximation of *b*.

$\sin A = \frac{7\sin 100°}{9.282}$ Solve for $\sin A$.

$m\angle A = \sin^{-1}\left(\frac{7\sin 100°}{9.282}\right) \approx 47.961° \approx 48.0°$ Solve for $m\angle A$.

Step 3 Find the third angle measure.

$47.961° + 100° + m\angle C = 180°$

$m\angle C = 32.039° \approx 32.0°$

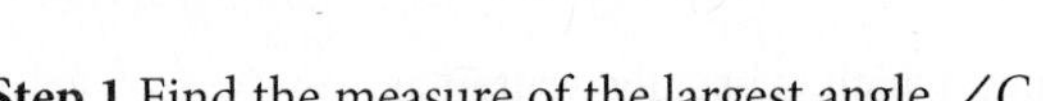

Ⓑ **Step 1** Find the measure of the largest angle, $\angle C$.

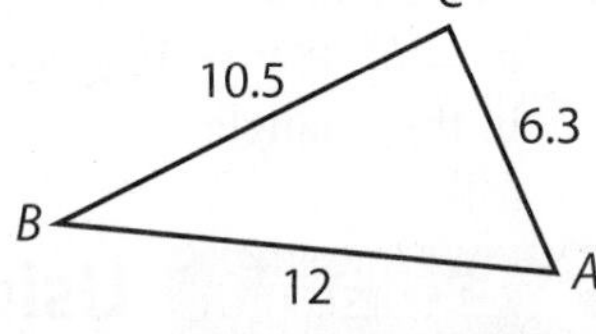

$c^2 = a^2 + b^2 - 2ab\cos C$ Law of Cosines

$12^2 = 10.5^2 + 6.3^2 - 2(10.5)(6.3)\cos C$ Substitute.

$m\angle C = \cos^{-1}\left(\frac{10.5^5 + 6.3^2 - 12^2}{2(10.5)(6.3)}\right) \approx 87.427° \approx 87.4°$ Solve for $m\angle C$.

Step 2 Find another angle measure.

$b^2 = a^2 + c^2 - 2ac\cos B$ Law of Cosines

$6.3^2 = 10.5^2 + 12^2 - 2(10.5)(12)\cos B$ Substitute.

$m\angle B = \cos^{-1}\left(\frac{10.5^5 + 12^2 - 6.3^2}{2(10.5)(12)}\right) \approx 31.633° \approx 31.6°$ Solve for $m\angle B$.

Step 3 Find the third angle measure.

$m\angle A + 31.633° + 87.427° = 180°$ Triangle Sum Theorem

$m\angle A = 60.940 \approx 60.9°$ Solve for $m\angle A$.

Reflect

2. Suppose a student used the Law of Sines to solve this triangle. Determine whether the measurements are correct. Explain.

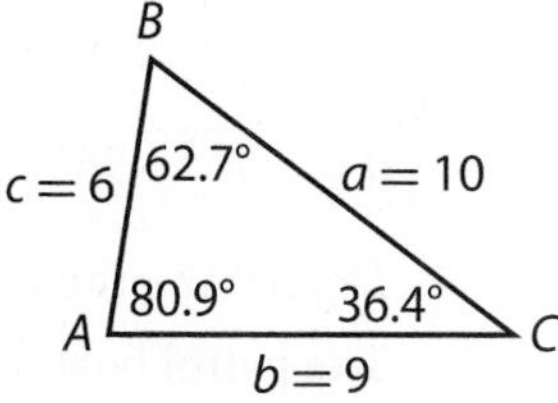

Your Turn

Solve $\triangle ABC$. Round intermediate results to 3 decimal places and final answers to 1 decimal place.

3. $b = 23$, $c = 18$, $m\angle A = 173°$

4. $a = 35$, $b = 42$, $c = 50.3$

Explain 2 Problem Solving Using the Law of Cosines

You now know many triangle relationships that you can use to solve real-world problems.

Example 2

A coast guard patrol boat and a fishing boat leave a dock at the same time at the courses shown. The patrol boat travels at a speed of 12 nautical miles per hour (12 knots), and the fishing boat travels at a speed of 5 knots. After 3 hours, the fishing boat sends a distress signal picked up by the patrol boat. If the fishing boat does not drift, how long will it take the patrol boat to reach it at a speed of 12 knots?

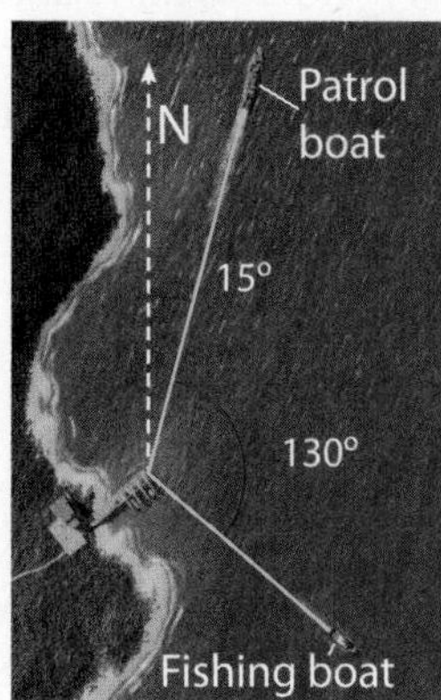

Step 1 Understand the Problem

The answer will be the number of hours that the patrol boat needs to reach the fishing boat.

List the important information:

- The patrol boat's speed is 12 knots. Its direction is 15° east of north.
- The fishing boat's speed is 5 knots. Its direction is 130° east of north.
- The boats travel for 3 hours before the distress call is given.

Step 2 Make a Plan

Determine the angle between the boats' courses and the distance that each boat travels in 3 hours. Use this information to draw and label a diagram.

Then use the Law of Cosines to find the distance d between the boats at the time of the distress call. Finally, determine how long it will take the patrol boat to travel this distance.

Step 3 Draw and Label a Diagram

- The angle between the boats' courses is $130° - 15° = 115°$. In 3 hours, the patrol boat travels $3(12) = 36$ nautical miles and the fishing boat travels $3(5) = 15$ nautical miles.

- Find the distance d between the boats.

$d^2 = p^2 + f^2 - 2pf\cos D$ Law of Cosines

$d^2 = 15^2 + 36^2 - 2(15)(36)\cos 115°$ Substitute.

$d = \sqrt{15^2 + 36^2 - 2(15)(36)\cos 115°} \approx 44.468$ Solve for the positive value of d.

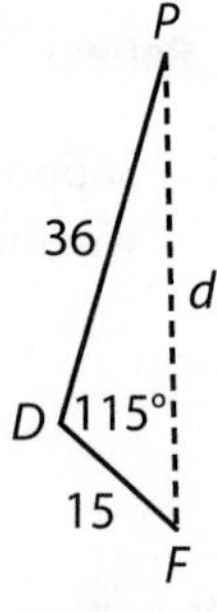

- Determine the number of hours.

The patrol boat must travel about 44.468 nautical miles to reach the fishing boat. At a speed of 12 nautical miles per hour, it will take the patrol boat $\frac{44.468}{12} \approx 3.7$ hours to reach the fishing boat.

Step 4 Look Back

To reach the fishing boat, the patrol boat will have to travel a greater distance than it did during the first 3 hours of its trip. Therefore, it makes sense that it will take the patrol boat longer than 3 hours to reach the fishing boat. An answer of 3.7 hours seems reasonable.

Your Turn

5. If Lucas hikes at an average of 2.5 miles per hour, how long will it take him to travel from the cave to the waterfall? Round intermediate results to 3 decimal places and the final answer to the nearest tenth of an hour.

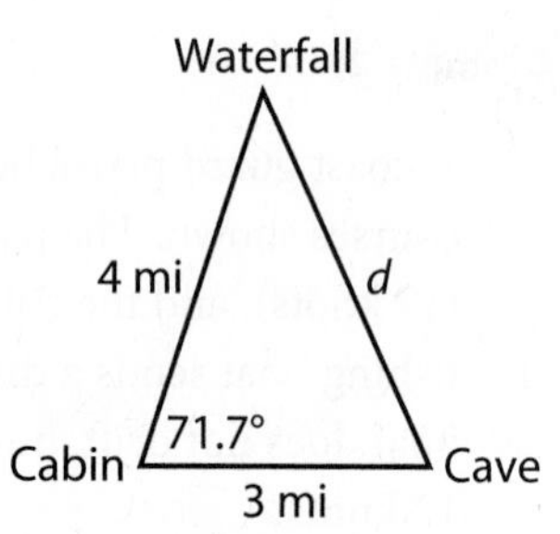

6. A pilot is flying from Houston to Oklahoma City. To avoid a thunderstorm, the pilot flies 28° off of the direct route for a distance of 175 miles. He then makes a turn and flies straight on to Oklahoma City. To the nearest mile, how much farther than the direct route was the route taken by the pilot? Round intermediate results to 3 decimal places.

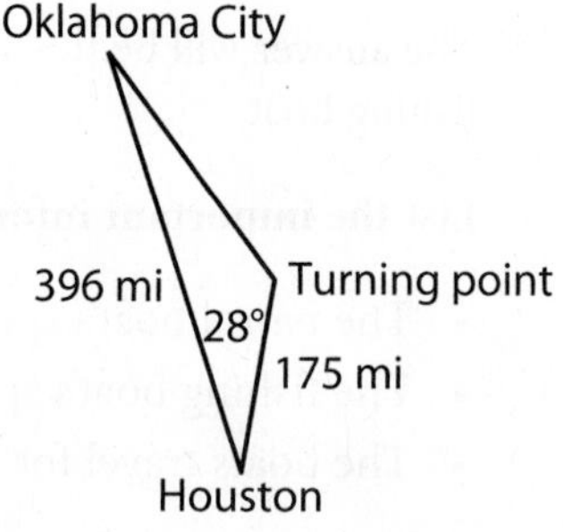

Elaborate

7. Explain why you cannot solve a triangle if you are given only angle-angle-angle information.

8. When using the Law of Cosines, $a^2 = b^2 + c^2 - 2bc\cos A$, you can take the square root of both sides to find the value of a. Explain why the negative square root is not used when considering the answer.

9. **Essential Question Check-In** Copy and complete the graphic organizer. List the types of triangles that can be solved by using each law. Consider the following types of triangles: ASA, AAS, SAS, SSA, and SSS.

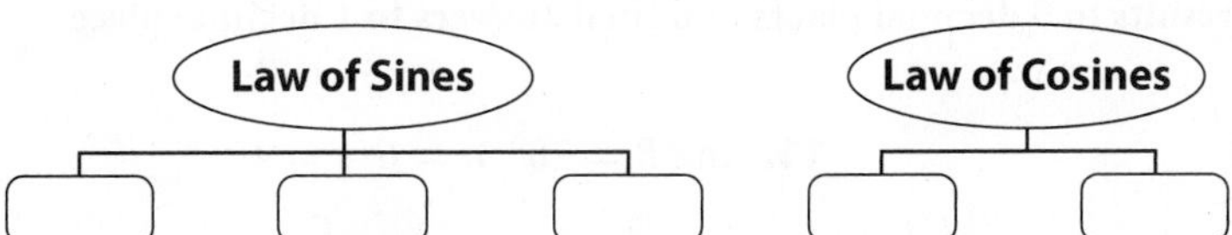

Evaluate: Homework and Practice

- Online Homework
- Hints and Help
- Extra Practice

Draw and label the diagram you would use to derive the given form of the Law of Cosines.

1. $b^2 = a^2 + c^2 - 2ac\cos B$

2. $c^2 = a^2 + b^2 - 2ab\cos C$

3. What information do you need to be able to use the Law of Cosines to solve a triangle?

Solve each triangle. Round intermediate results to 3 decimal places and final answers to 1 decimal place.

4.

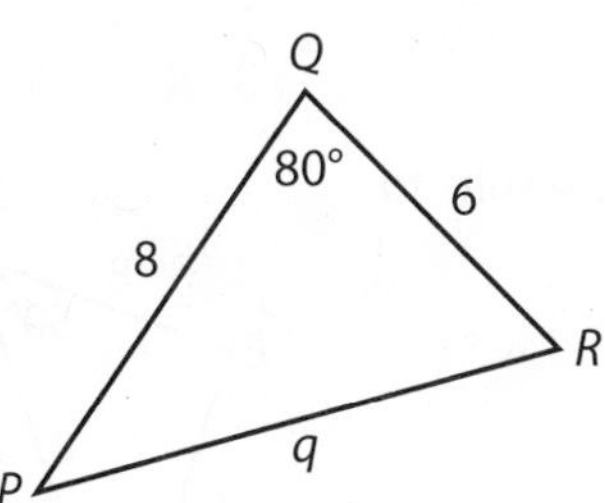

5.

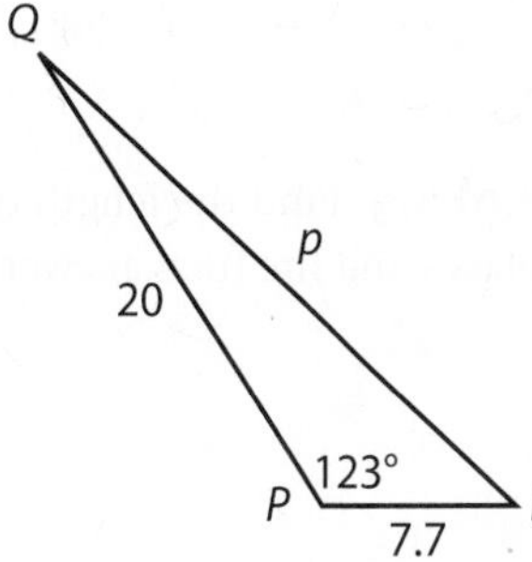

6.

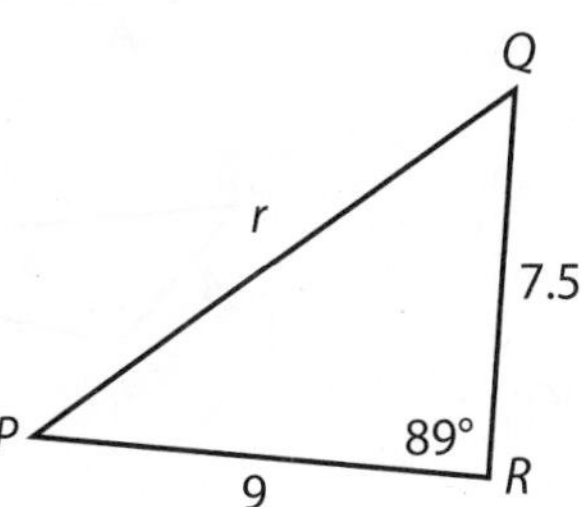

7.

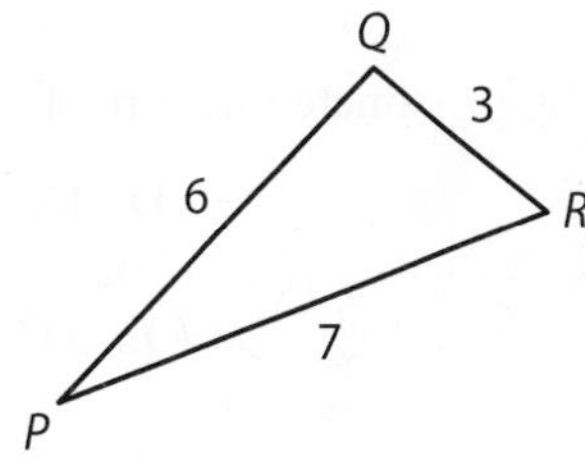

8.

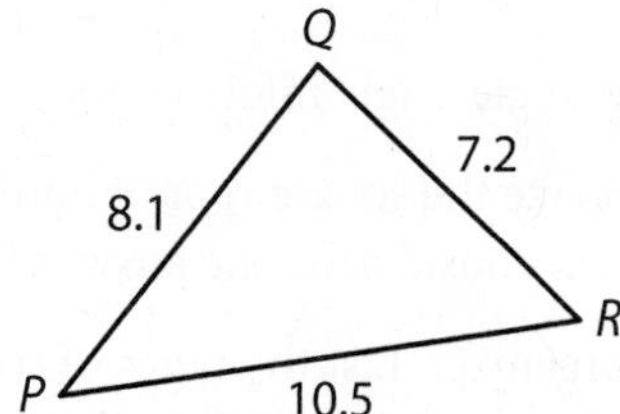

9.

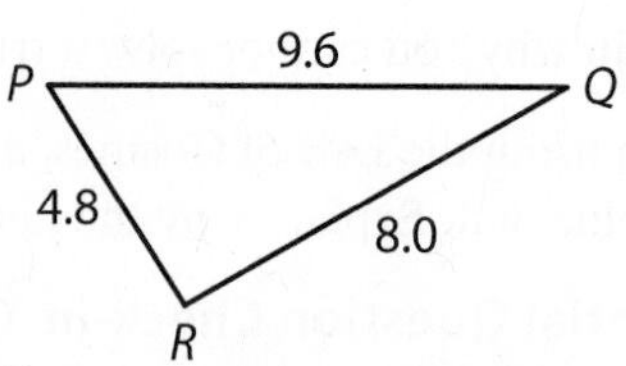

Solve $\triangle ABC$. Round intermediate results to 3 decimal places and final answers to 1 decimal place.

10. $m\angle A = 120°, b = 16, c = 20$

11. $m\angle B = 78°, a = 6, c = 4$

12. $m\angle C = 96°, a = 13, b = 9$

13. $a = 14, b = 9, c = 10$

14. $a = 5, b = 8, c = 6$

15. $a = 30, b = 26, c = 35$

16. A triangular hiking trail is being planned. At an average walking speed of 2 m/s, how many minutes will it take a hiker to make a complete circuit around the trail? Round intermediate results to 3 decimal places and the final answer to the nearest minute.

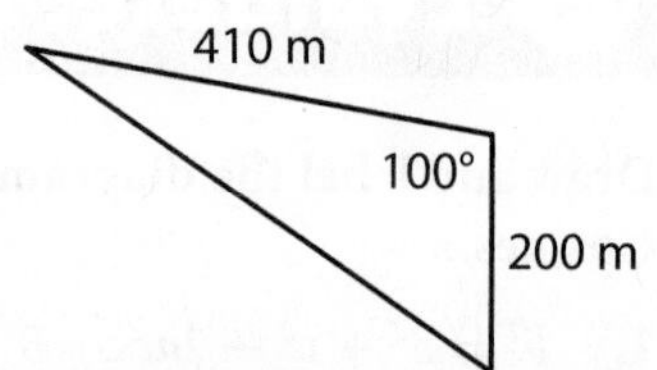

17. An ecologist is studying a pair of zebras fitted with radio-transmitter collars. One zebra is 1.4 miles from the ecologist, and the other is 3.5 miles from the ecologist. To the nearest tenth of a mile, how far apart are the two zebras? Round intermediate results to 3 decimal places.

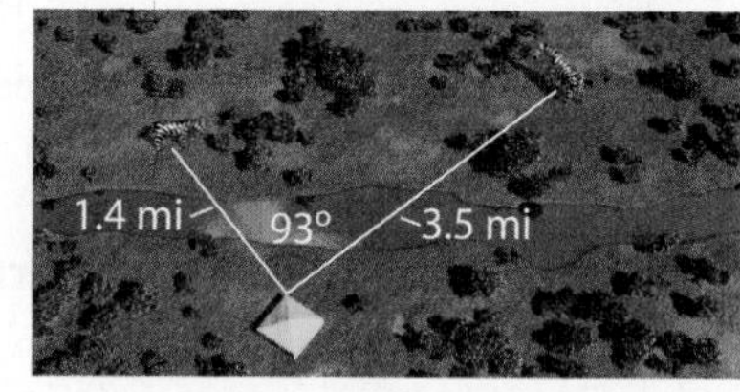

18. **Critical Thinking** Find the length of $\overline{AE}$. Round intermediate results to 3 decimal places and the final answer to 1 decimal place.

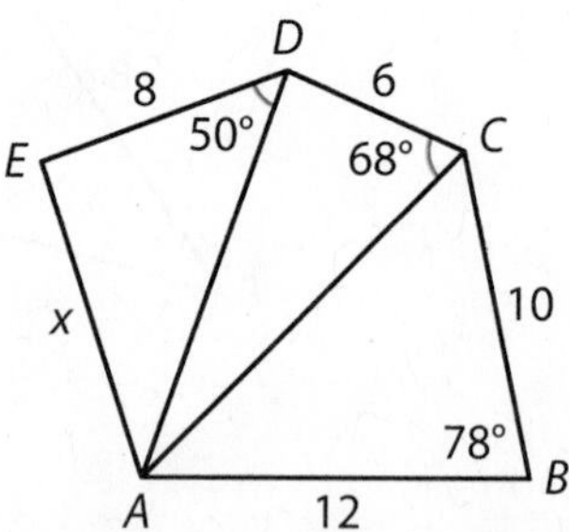

19. Which is the approximate measure of $\angle K$ in the triangle shown?

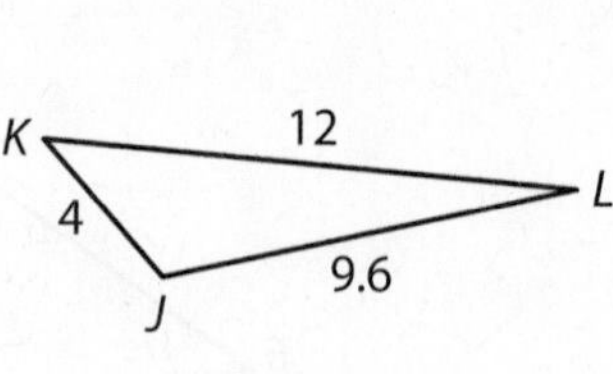

A. −30°

B. −45°

C. 30°

D. 45°

E. 54°

F. 60°

20. Critical Thinking Use the Law of Cosines to explain why $c^2 = a^2 + b^2$ for $\triangle ABC$, where $\angle C$ is a right angle.

21. A graphic artist is asked to draw a triangular logo with sides measuring 15 cm, 18 cm, and 20 cm. If she draws the triangle correctly, what will be the measures of its angles to the nearest degree? Round intermediate results to 3 decimal places.

H.O.T. Focus on Higher Order Thinking

In Exercises 22 and 23, round intermediate results to 3 decimal places and the final anwer to 1 decimal place.

22. Represent Real-World Problem Two performers hang by their knees from trapezes, as shown.

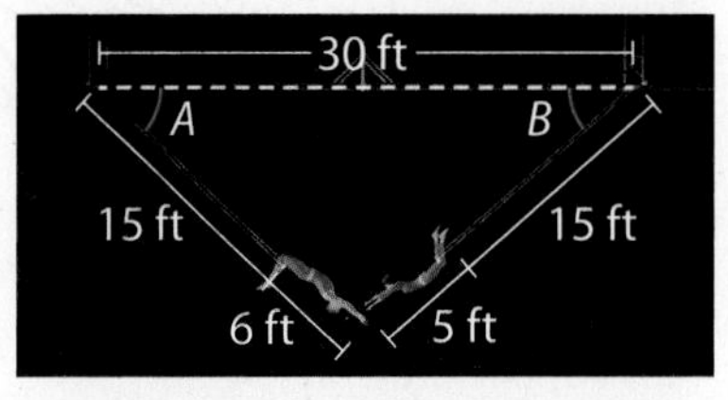

a. To the nearest degree, what acute angles A and B must the ropes of each trapeze make with the horizontal if the performer on the left is to grab the wrists of the performer on the right and pull her away from her trapeze?

b. Later, the performer on the left grabs the trapeze of the performer on the right and lets go of his trapeze. To the nearest degree, what angles A and B must the ropes of each trapeze make with the horizontal for this trick to work?

23. Barrington Crater in Arizona was produced by the impact of a meteorite. Based on the measurements shown, what is the diameter d of Barrington Crater to the nearest tenth of a kilometer?

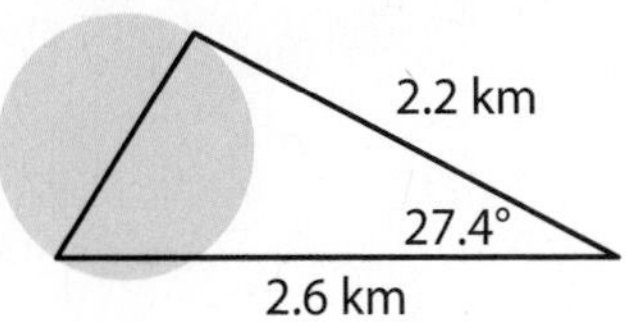

24. Analyze Relationships What are the angle measures of an isosceles triangle whose base is half as long as its congruent legs? Round to the nearest tenth.

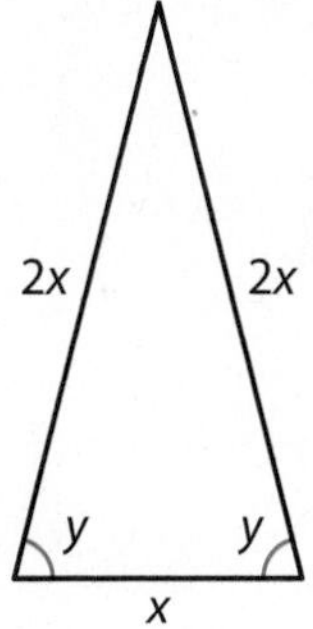

25. Explain the Error Abby uses the Law of Cosines to find m$\angle A$ when $a = 2$, $b = 3$, $c = 5$. The answer she gets is 0°. Did she make an error? Explain.

Lesson Performance Task

Standing on a small bluff overlooking a local pond, Clay wants to calculate the width of the pond.

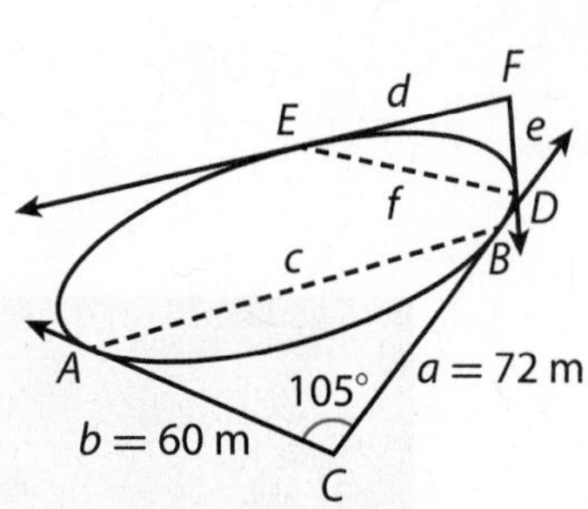

a. From point *C*, Clay walks the distances *CA* and *CB*. Then he measures the angle between these line segments. What is the distance to the nearest meter from *A* to *B*?

b. From another point *F*, Clay measures 20 meters to *D* and 50 meters to *E*. Reece says that last summer this area dried out so much that he could walk the 49 meters from *D* to *E*. What is the measure of $\angle F$?

c. Reece tells Clay that when the area defined by $\triangle DEF$ dries out, it becomes covered with native grasses and plants. What is the area of this section?

STUDY GUIDE REVIEW

Trigonometry with All Triangles

MODULE 14

Essential Question: How can you use triangle trigonometry to solve real-world problems?

Key Vocabulary
cosine *(coseno)*
sine *(seno)*
trigonometric ratio *(razón trigonométrica)*

KEY EXAMPLE (Lesson 14.1)

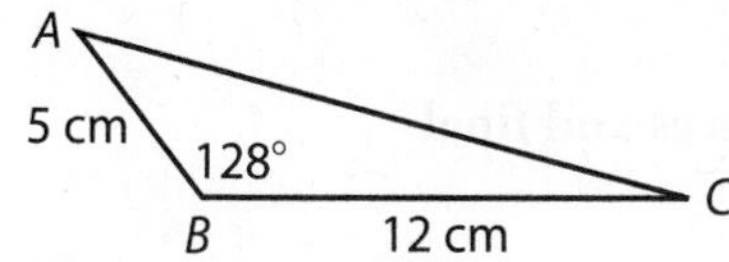

Find the area of the triangle. Round to the nearest tenth.

$\text{area} = \frac{1}{2}ac \sin B$ — *Write the area formula.*

$= \frac{1}{2}(5)(12)\sin 128°$ — *Substitute the known values.*

≈ 23.6 — *Use a calculator to evaluate the expression.*

The area of the triangle is about 23.6 cm^2.

KEY EXAMPLE (Lesson 14.1)

Solve the triangle. Round to the nearest tenth.

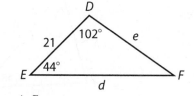

$m\angle F = 180° - (102° + 44°) = 34°$ — *Triangle Sum Theorem*

$\frac{\sin D}{d} = \frac{\sin F}{f}$ — *Law of Sines* — $\frac{\sin E}{e} = \frac{\sin F}{f}$

$\frac{\sin 102°}{d} = \frac{\sin 34°}{21}$ — *Substitute.* — $\frac{\sin 44°}{e} = \frac{\sin 34°}{21}$

$d = \frac{21 \sin 102°}{\sin 34°} \approx 36.7$ — *Solve for d and e.* — $e = \frac{21 \sin 44°}{\sin 34°} \approx 26.1$

KEY EXAMPLE (Lesson 14.2)

Find a. Round to the nearest tenth.

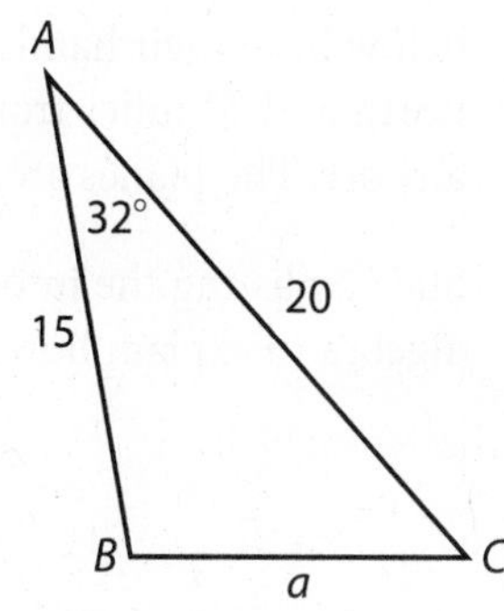

$a^2 = b^2 + c^2 - 2bc\cos A$ — *Law of Cosines*

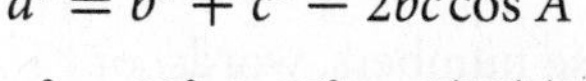

$a^2 = 20^2 + 15^2 - 2(20)(15)\cos 32°$ — *Substitute.*

$a = \sqrt{20^2 + 15^2 - 2(20)(15)\cos 32°}$ — *Take square root.*

$a \approx 10.778 \approx 10.8$ — *Use a calculator to solve for the positive value of a.*

EXERCISES

Find the area of each triangle. Round to the nearest tenth. *(Lesson 14.1)*

1.

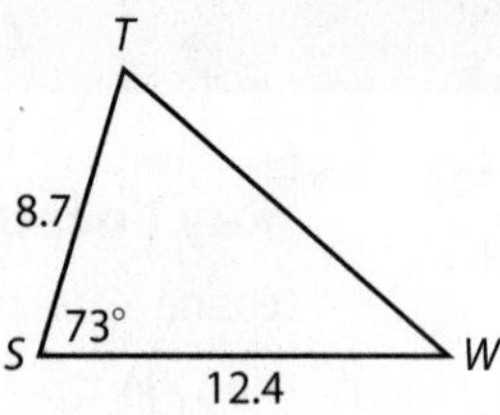

E
14
46°
F
T
10

Solve each triangle. Round intermediate results to 3 decimal places and final answers to 1 decimal place. *(Lessons 14.1 and 14.2)*

2.

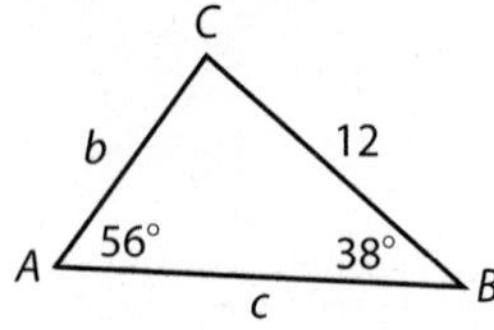

3.

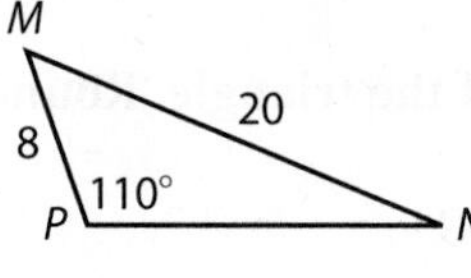

4.

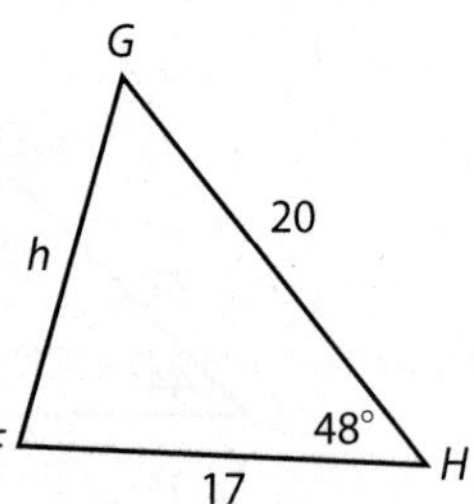

5.

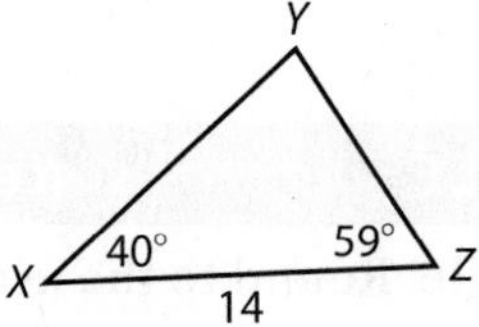

MODULE PERFORMANCE TASK

Controlling the Air

It's a busy day in the airspace above Metropolitan Airport and the traffic controllers in the tower below have their hands full. Right now there's a passenger jet that's located at a bearing of 45° east of north and 22 miles from the airport. A private plane is located 34° east of north and 14 miles from the airport. The planes are at the same altitude. How far apart are they?

Start by listing the information you will need to solve the problem. Then use numbers, words, or algebra to explain how you reached your conclusion.

Ready to Go On?

14.1–14.2 Trigonometry with All Triangles

- Online Homework
- Hints and Help
- Extra Practice

Solve. Round intermediate results to 3 decimal places and final answers to 1 decimal place.

1. The sides of a triangle measure 31 inches, 23 inches, and 17 inches. What is the area of the triangle?

2. The sides of a triangle measure 11 centimeters, 13 centimeters, and 15 centimeters. What are the measures of the angles of the triangles?

3. A triangle has two sides measuring 10 inches and 16 inches. The angle opposite the 16-inch side measures 70.3°. Solve the triangle.

4. One of the base angles of an isosceles triangle measures 72°. The base of the triangle measures 11 centimeters. What is the perimeter of the triangle?

5. Tony is standing at sea level. From his location, the angle of elevation of the top of Blue Mountain is 23°. Staying at sea level, he walks 200 yards toward the mountain. The angle of elevation of the top is now 27°. Find the height of Blue Mountain.

ESSENTIAL QUESTION

6. How can you use trigonometric ratios to find a side length in a non-right triangle?

Assessment Readiness

1. You know the two legs of a right triangle. You also know the measure of one of the acute angles of the triangle. Could you use the given law or theorem to find the length of the hypotenuse? Write Yes or No for A–C.
   A. Law of Sines
   B. Law of Cosines
   C. Pythagorean Theorem

2. Consider each statement about finding the measurements of triangles. Determine if each statement is True or False.
   A. If you know the measures of the three angles of a triangle, you can find the lengths of the sides.
   B. If you know the lengths of the three sides of a triangle, you can find the measures of the angles.
   C. If you know the measures of the two sides of a triangle and the measure of an angle not included between the two sides, you can solve the triangle.

3. In the figure, *O* is the center of the circle and *G* and *H* are points on the circle. What is the circumference of the circle? Round your answer to the nearest tenth. Explain how you found the answer.

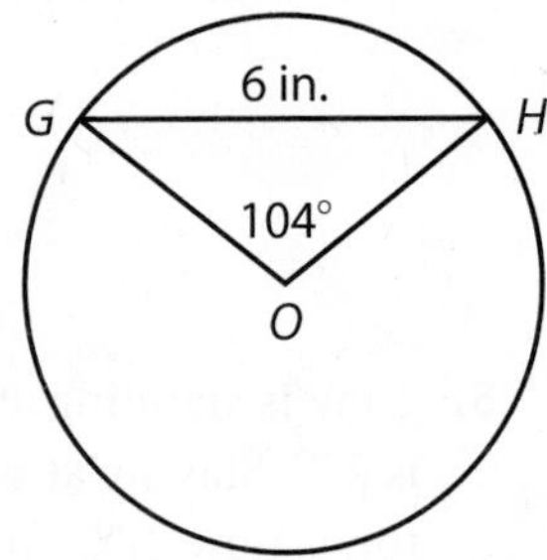

4. In solving triangle *ABC*, Dawn found that the cosine of $\angle B$ and the sine of $\angle A$ were both negative. What conclusions can she draw about her solution? Why?

UNIT 5 MIXED REVIEW

Assessment Readiness

- Online Homework
- Hints and Help
- Extra Practice

1. Given $\triangle JKL$ where $\angle K$ is a right angle, determine which measurements will result in the measure of $\angle J$ being greater than 45°.

Write Yes or No for each pair of sides.

A. $KL = 27, JK = 23$

B. $KL = 15, JK = 32$

C. $KL = 10, JK = 10$

2. Using the image provided, which of the following equations could be used to find x?

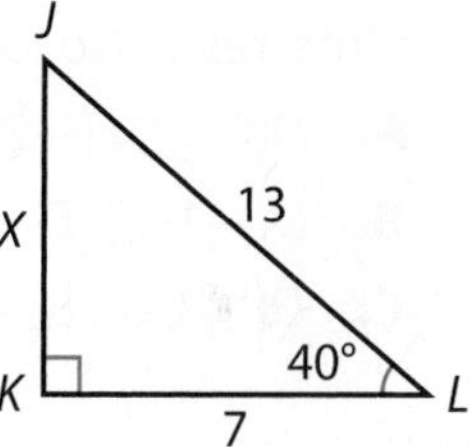

Write Yes or No for each equation.

A. $\sin 40 = \frac{x}{13}$

B. $\tan 40 = \frac{x}{7}$

C. $\cos 40 = \frac{13}{x}$

3. Which of the following statements are true?

Determine if each statement is True or False.

A. When given an angle and the opposite leg, you should use cosine to find the measure of the adjacent leg.

B. The values of sine and cosine are always between 0 and 1.

C. Use the inverse sine ratio when you know the length of the leg opposite the required angle and the length of the hypotenuse.

4. The following points are graphed on the coordinate plane: $A(-3, 5)$, $B(3, 3)$, and $C(4, 1)$. Does the given point make $ABCD$ a trapezoid?

Write Yes or No for ordered pairs A–C.

A. $D(-3, 3)$

B. $D(-1, 1)$

C. $D(-4, 4)$

5. Determine if each statement is True or False.

A. $\sin 90° = \cos 90° = \frac{1}{2}$

B. $\sin 45° = \cos 45° = \frac{\sqrt{2}}{2}$

C. $\sin 60° = \cos 30° = \frac{\sqrt{3}}{2}$

D. $\tan \theta < 1$ for $\theta \leq 45°$

6. Do the numbers form a Pythagorean triple?
Write Yes or No for each set of numbers.

A. 3, 4, and 5

B. 11, 12, and 13

C. 9, 24, and 25

7. Is $\triangle DEF$ a right triangle?
Write Yes or No for each set of points.

A. $D(0, 2)$, $E(-2, 5)$, $F(5, 5)$

B. $D(-1, 0)$, $E(-1, -7)$, $F(0, 3)$

C. $D(-8, 8)$, $E(-10, -2)$, $F(0, -4)$

8. The plans for a new house include a wall with two triangular windows, $\triangle ABC$ and $\triangle A'B'C'$. The vertices of $\triangle ABC$ are $A(-4, 1)$, $B(-1, 1)$, and $C(-1, 5)$. The vertices of $\triangle A'B'C'$ are $A'(-1, -5)$, $B'(-1, -2)$, and $C'(-5, -2)$. The architect wants to give a sequence of rigid motions that maps $\triangle ABC$ to $\triangle A'B'C'$. Provide verbal descriptions and algebraic rules for the appropriate sequence of rigid motions.

9. Find the side lengths to the nearest hundredth and the angle measures to the nearest degree.

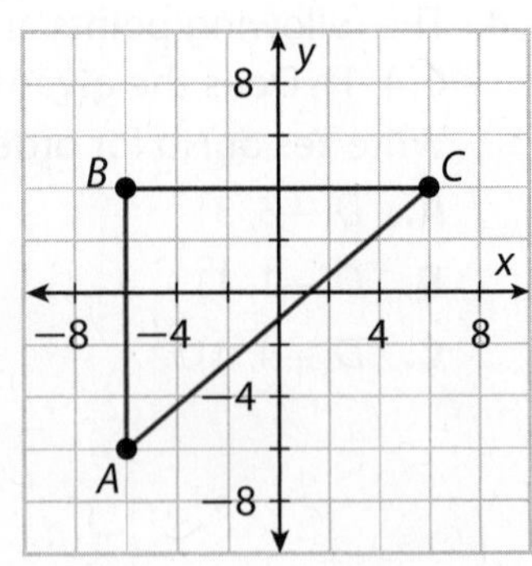

Performance Tasks

★**10.** A painter is using a ladder to help reach the top of a house. If the house is 12 feet tall and the angle of the ladder needs to be at an angle of at least 60° and no greater than 75° to be safe, how far away should the painter place the ladder from the house? Show your work.

★★**11.** Gerta and Jeremy are talking on their two-way hand-held radios, which have a range of 35 miles. Gerta is sitting in her car on the side of the road as Jeremy drives past. He continues along the straight road for 28 miles, and then makes a right turn onto a straight road, turning through an angle of 100°. How many miles can Jeremy drive along this second road until he is out of range of Gerta's radio? Show your work.

★★★**12.** Sam is planning to fence his backyard. Every side of the yard except for the side along the house is to be fenced, and fencing costs \$3/yd and can only be bought in whole yards. (Note that $m\angle NPM = 28°$, and the side of his yard opposite the house measures 35 yd.) How much will the fencing cost? Explain how you found your answer.

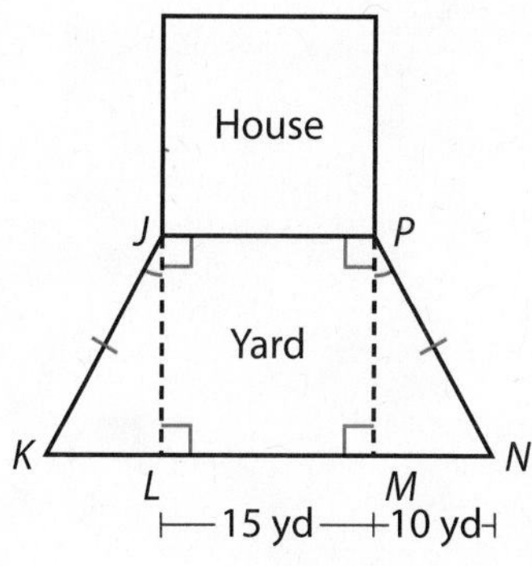

MATH IN CAREERS

A detective knows what time of day it is based on the angle at which the sun is hitting a man. Suppose a detective is looking at a photograph of a 6-foot-tall man with a shadow that is 3.5 feet long. Find the angle at which the sun was hitting the ground.

UNIT 6

Properties of Circles

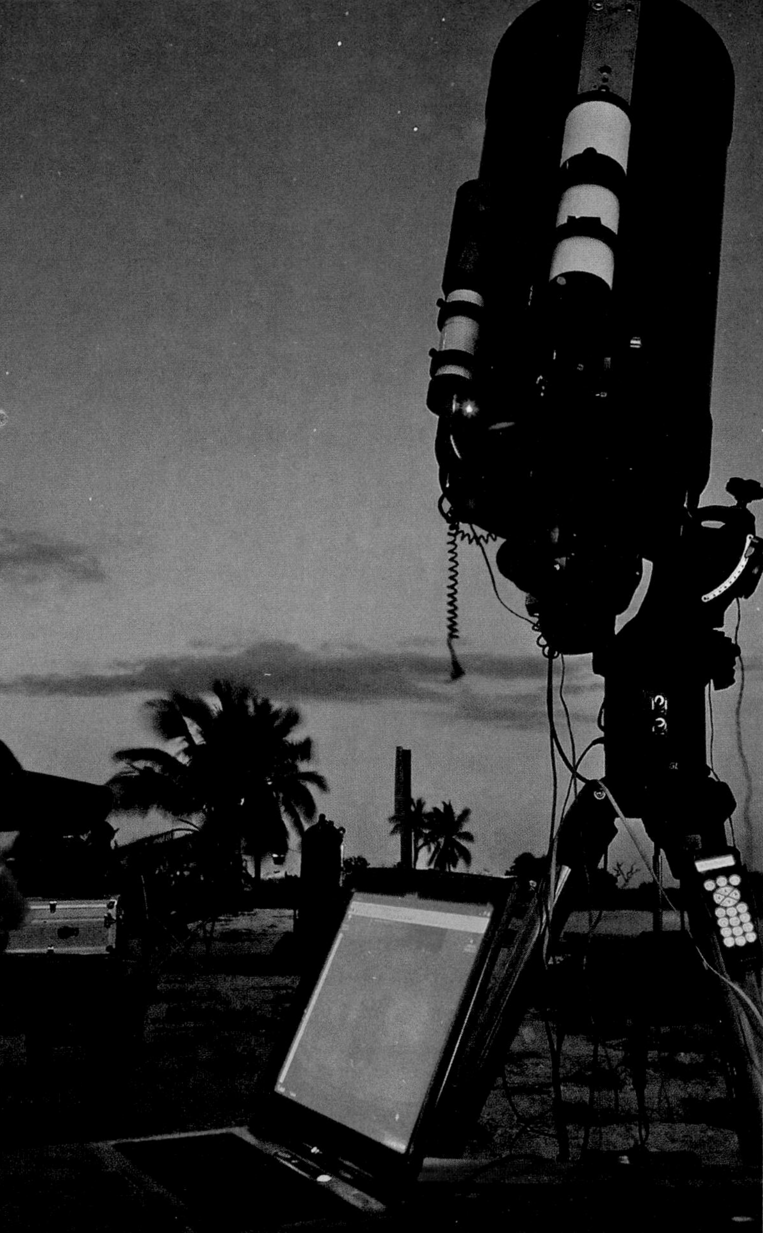

MATH IN CAREERS

Astronomer An astronomer uses advanced technology and mathematics to study outer space. Astronomers apply mathematics to study the positions, movement, and energy of celestial objects.

If you're interested in a career as an astronomer, you should study these mathematical subjects:

- Algebra
- Geometry
- Trigonometry
- Calculus

Research other careers that require the use of physics to understand real-world scenarios. See the related Career Activity at the end of this unit.

Review Words

✔ area *(área)*

✔ circumference *(circunferencia)*

✔ diameter *(diámetro)*

✔ perpendicular *(perpendicular)*

✔ radius *(radio)*

✔ vertical angles *(ángulos verticales)*

Preview Words

adjacent arcs *(arcos adyacentes)*

arc *(arco)*

arc length *(longitud de arco)*

central angle *(ángulo central)*

chord *(acorde)*

circumscribed *(circunscrito)*

inscribed angle *(ángulo apuntado)*

point of tangency *(punto de tangencia)*

radian measure *(radianes)*

secant *(secante)*

sector *(sector)*

semicircle *(semicírculo)*

tangent *(tangente)*

Visualize Vocabulary

Use the ✔ words to complete the sequence diagram.

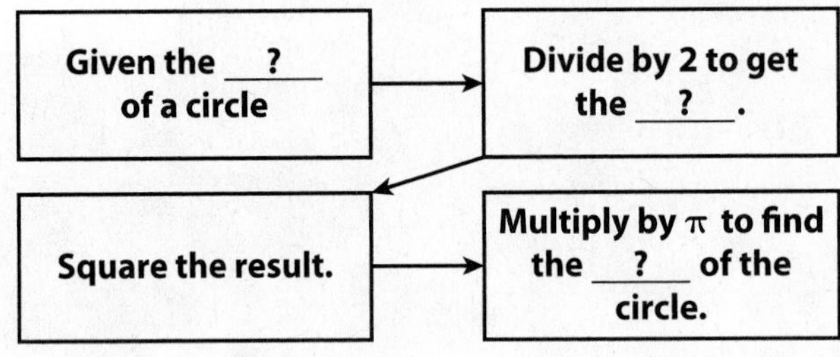
Given the ? of a circle
Divide by 2 to get the ? .
Square the result.
Multiply by π to find the ? of the circle.

Understand Vocabulary

Complete the sentences using the preview words.

1. An angle with a vertex on a circle formed by two rays that intersect other points on the circle is called a(n) __?__.

2. A radius of a circle is perpendicular to a tangent line at __?__.

3. A __?__ of a circle is a line segment with both endpoints on the circle.

Active Reading

Four-Corner Fold Create a Four-Corner Fold with flaps for segments, angles, arcs, and sectors. Add relevant vocabulary terms while reading the modules. Emphasize using the written words when discussing these topics with teachers and classmates.

Angles and Segments in Circles

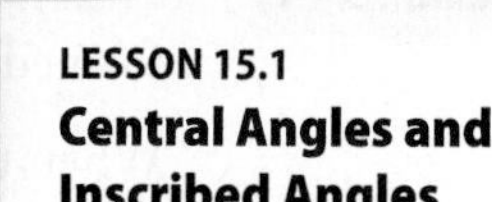

Essential Question: How can you use angles and segments in circles to solve real-world problems?

REAL WORLD VIDEO
Check out how package designers make use of the mathematics of angles and segments to design efficient and attractive packages and containers.

MODULE PERFORMANCE TASK PREVIEW

How Many Marbles Will Fit?

In this module, you will be challenged to determine the size of the largest marble that can fit into a triangular package. How can an understanding of segment and angle relationships in circles help you to solve this problem? Don't "lose your marbles" before you get a chance to find out!

Are YOU Ready?

Complete these exercises to review skills you will need for this module.

Personal Math Trainer

- Online Homework
- Hints and Help
- Extra Practice

Angle Relationships

Example 1 Find $m\angle ABD$ given that $m\angle CBE = 40°$ and the angles are formed by the intersection of the lines $\overleftrightarrow{AC}$ and $\overleftrightarrow{DE}$ at point m.

When two lines intersect, they form two pairs of vertical angles at their intersection. Note that $\angle ABD$ and $\angle CBE$ are vertical angles and $\angle DBC$ and $\angle ABE$ are vertical angles.

$\angle ABD \cong \angle CBE$ — Theorem: Vertical Angles are Congruent

$m\angle ABD = m\angle CBE = 40°$ — Definition of congruence of angles

Find the measure of the complementary or supplementary angle.

1. Complementary to 40°

2. Complementary to 67°

3. Supplementary to 80°

4. Supplementary to 65°

Use the figure to find the angles or their measures, assuming $\overleftrightarrow{CD}$ is parallel to $\overleftrightarrow{EF}$.

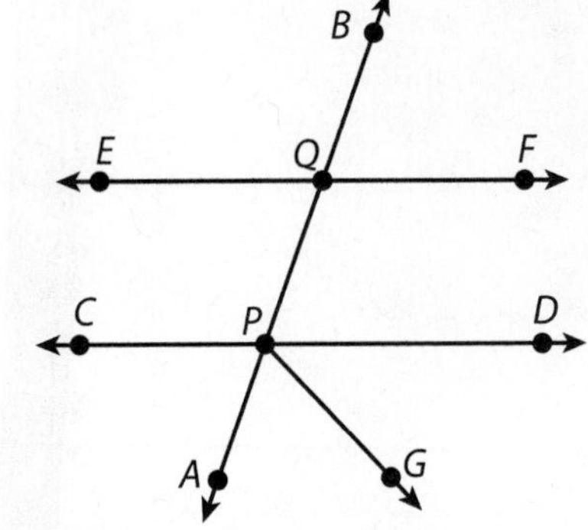

5. All angles congruent to $\angle APD$

6. $m\angle BPD$ when $m\angle BQE = 165°$

7. $m\angle APG$ when $m\angle DPG = 55°$ and $m\angle BPC = 110°$

8. All angles congruent to $\angle GPC$

Determine whether the lines $\overleftrightarrow{CD}$ and $\overleftrightarrow{EF}$ in the above figure are parallel for the given angle measures.

9. $m\angle BPG = 135°$, $m\angle GPC = 95°$, and $m\angle BQF = 110°$

10. $m\angle BPD = 35°$, $m\angle APG = 115°$, and $m\angle EQA = 35°$

15.1 Central Angles and Inscribed Angles

Resource Locker

Essential Question: How can you determine the measures of central angles and inscribed angles of a circle?

Explore — Investigating Central Angles and Inscribed Angles

A **chord** is a segment whose endpoints lie on a circle.

A **central angle** is an angle with measure less than or equal to 180° whose vertex lies at the center of a circle.

An **inscribed angle** is an angle whose vertex lies on a circle and whose sides contain chords of the circle.

The diagram shows two examples of an inscribed angle and the corresponding central angle.

Chords
$\overline{AB}$ and $\overline{BD}$
Central Angle
$\angle ACD$
Inscribed Angle
$\angle ABD$

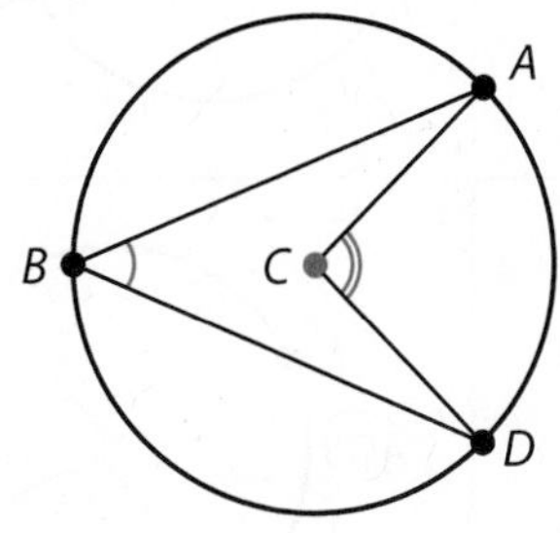

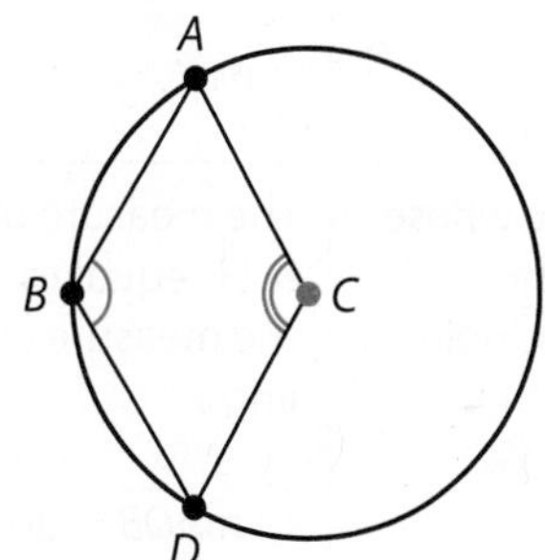

(A) Use a compass to draw a circle. Label the center C.

(B) Use a straightedge to draw an acute inscribed angle on your circle from Step A. Label the angle as $\angle DEF$.

(C) Use a straightedge to draw the corresponding central angle, $\angle DCF$.

(D) Use a protractor to measure the inscribed angle and the central angle. Record the measure of the inscribed angle, the measure of the central angle, and 360° minus the measure of the central angle. List your results in a table.

Angle Measure	Circle C	Circle 2	Circle 3	Circle 4	Circle 5	Circle 6	Circle 7
$m\angle DEF$	?	?	?	?	?	?	?
$m\angle DCF$	?	?	?	?	?	?	?
$360° - m\angle DCF$	?	?	?	?	?	?	?

(E) Repeat Steps A-D six more times. Examine a variety of inscribed angles (two more acute, one right, and three obtuse). Record your results in the table in Step D.

Reflect

1. Examine the values in the first and second rows of the table. Is there a mathematical relationship that exists for some or all of the values? Make a conjecture that summarizes your observation.
2. Examine the values in the first and third rows of the table. Is there a mathematical relationship that exists for some or all of the values? Make a conjecture that summarizes your observation.

Explain 1 Understanding Arcs and Arc Measure

An **arc** is a continuous portion of a circle consisting of two points (called the endpoints of the arc) and all the points on the circle between them.

Arc	Measure	Figure
A **minor arc** is an arc whose points are on or in the interior of a corresponding central angle.	The measure of a minor arc is equal to the measure of the central angle. $m\widehat{AB} = m\angle ACB$	A, $\widehat{AB}$, C, B
A **major arc** is an arc whose points are on or in the exterior of a corresponding central angle.	The measure of a major arc is equal to 360° minus the measure of the central angle. $m\widehat{ADB} = 360° - m\angle ACB$	A, D, $\widehat{ADB}$, C, B
A **semicircle** is an arc whose endpoints are the endpoints of a diameter.	The measure of a semicircle is 180°.	$\widehat{ADB}$, A, D, C, B

Adjacent arcs are arcs of the same circle that intersect in exactly one point. $\widehat{DE}$ and $\widehat{EF}$ are adjacent arcs.

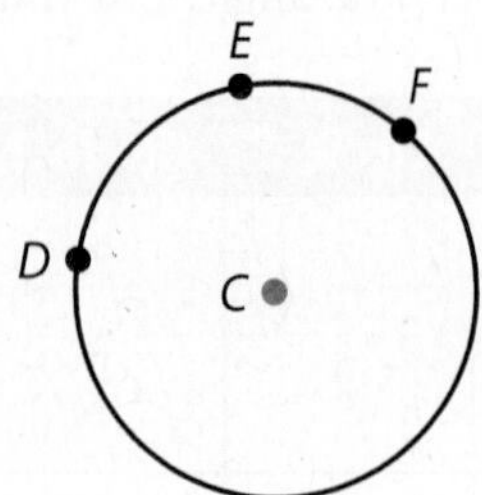

Arc Addition Postulate

The measure of an arc formed by two adjacent arcs is the sum of the measures of the two arcs.

$m\widehat{ADB} = m\widehat{AD} + m\widehat{DB}$

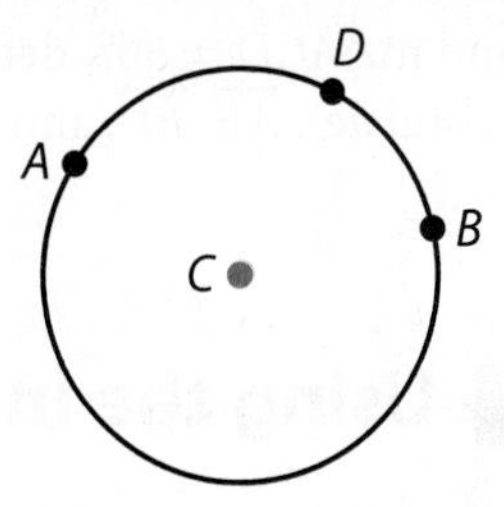

Example 1

(A) If $m\angle BCD = 18°$ and $m\widehat{EF} = 33°$, determine $m\widehat{ABD}$ using the appropriate theorems and postulates. $\overleftrightarrow{AF}$ and $\overleftrightarrow{BE}$ intersect at Point C.

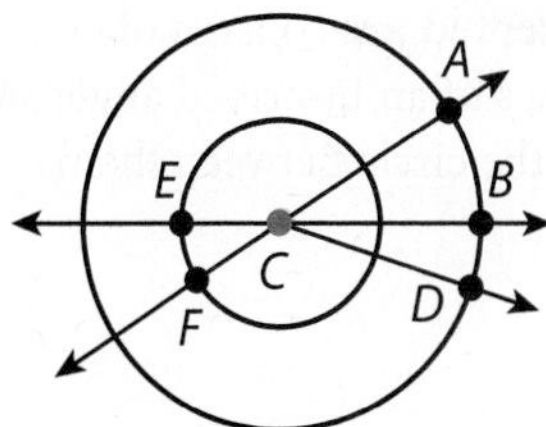

If $m\widehat{EF} = 33°$, then $m\angle ECF = 33°$. If $m\angle ECF = 33°$, then $m\angle ACB = 33°$ by the Vertical Angles Theorem. If $m\angle ACB = 33°$ and $m\angle BCD = 18°$, then $m\widehat{AB} = 33°$ and $m\widehat{BD} = 18°$. By the Arc Addition Postulate, $m\widehat{ABD} = m\widehat{AB} + m\widehat{BD}$, and so $m\widehat{ABD} = 51°$.

(B) If $m\widehat{JK} = 27°$, determine $m\widehat{NP}$ using the appropriate theorems and postulates. $\overleftrightarrow{MK}$ and $\overleftrightarrow{NJ}$ intersect at Point C.

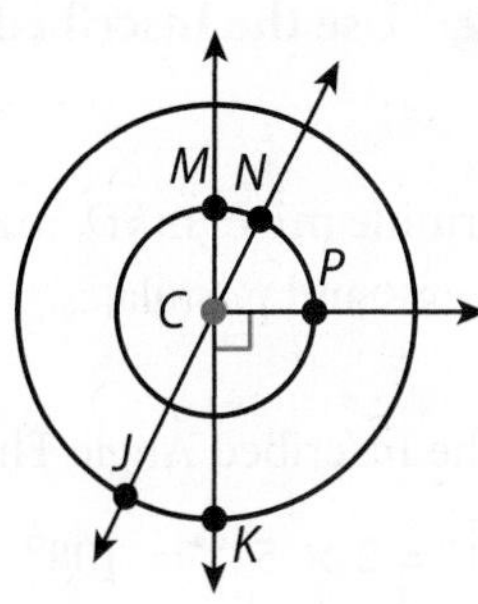

If $m\widehat{JK} = 27°$, then $m\angle JCK = 27°$. If $m\angle JCK = 27°$, then

$m\angle$ [MCN] $= 27°$ by the Vertical Angles Theorem.

If $m\angle MCN = 27°$ and $m\angle MCP =$ [90]°, then $m\widehat{MN} = 27°$

and $m\widehat{MNP} =$ [90]°. By the Arc Addition Postulate,

$m\widehat{MNP} = m\widehat{MN} + m\widehat{NP}$, and so $m\widehat{NP} = m$ [$\widehat{MNP}$] $- m\widehat{MN} =$ [63]°

Reflect

3. The minute hand of a clock sweeps out an arc as time moves forward. From 3:10 p.m. to 3:30 p.m., what is the measure of this arc? Explain your reasoning.

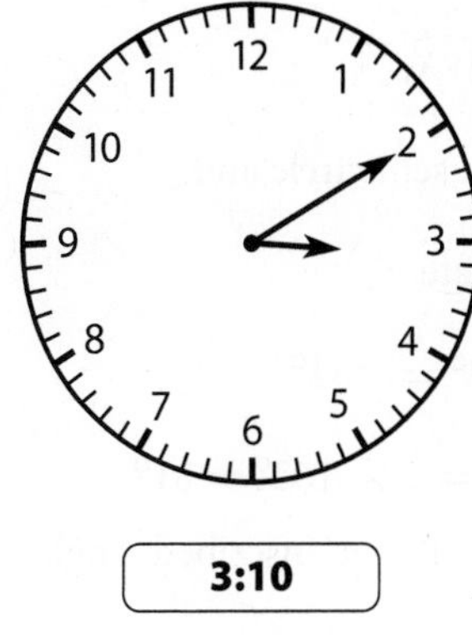

3:10

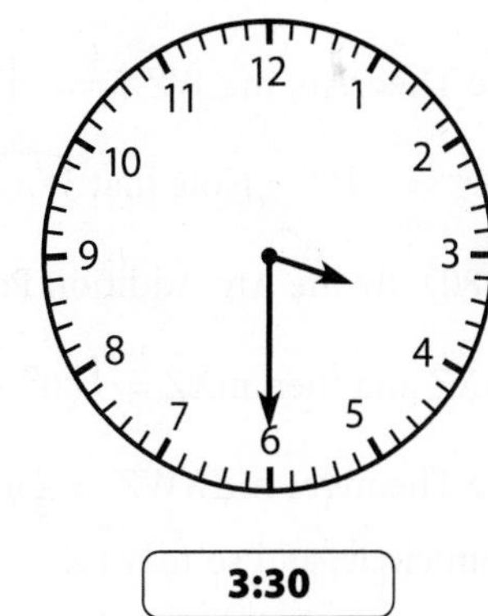

3:30

Your Turn

4. If $m\widehat{EF} = 45°$ and $m\angle ACD = 56°$, determine $m\widehat{BD}$ using the appropriate theorems and postulates. $\overleftrightarrow{AE}$, $\overleftrightarrow{BF}$, and $\overleftrightarrow{DC}$ intersect at Point C.

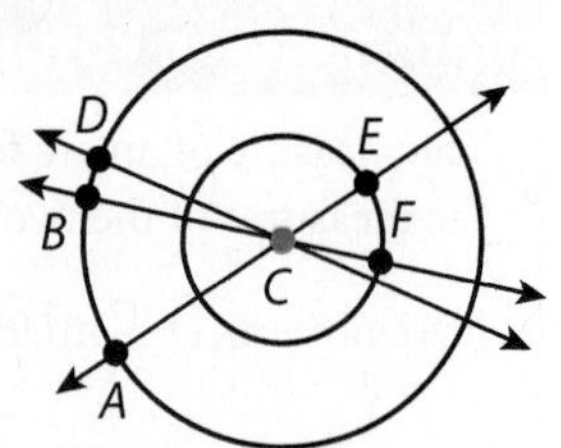

Explain 2 Using the Inscribed Angle Theorem

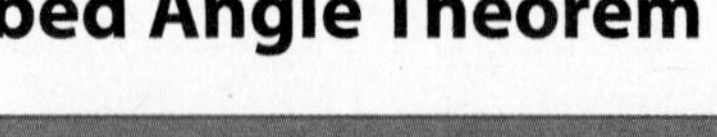

In the Explore you looked at the relationship between central angles and inscribed angles. Those results, combined with the definitions of arc measure, lead to the following theorem about inscribed angles and their *intercepted arcs*. An **intercepted arc** consists of endpoints that lie on the sides of an inscribed angle and all the points of the circle between them.

Inscribed Angle Theorem

The measure of an inscribed angle is equal to half the measure of its intercepted arc.

$$m\angle ADB = \frac{1}{2}m\widehat{AB}$$

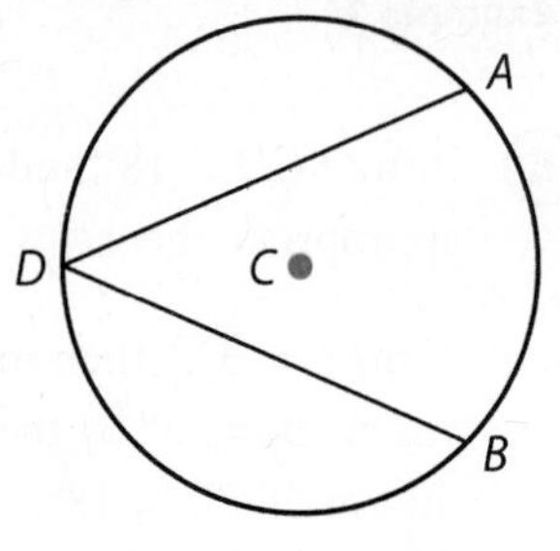

Example 2 **Use the Inscribed Angle Theorem to find inscribed angle measures.**

Ⓐ Determine $m\widehat{DE}$, $m\widehat{BD}$, $m\angle DAB$, and $m\angle ADE$ using the appropriate theorems and postulates.

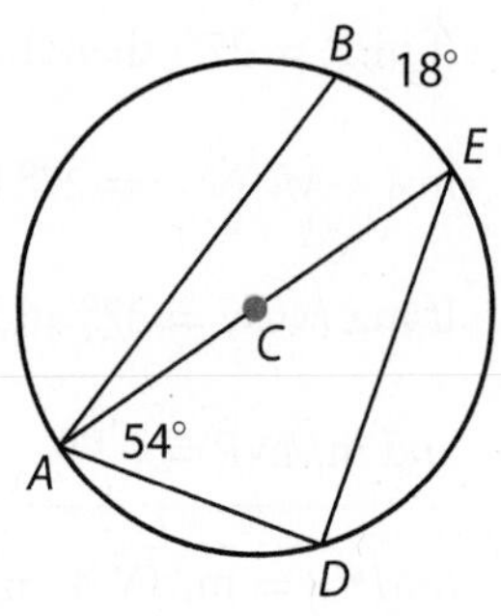

By the Inscribed Angle Theorem, $m\angle DAE = \frac{1}{2}m\widehat{DE}$, and so $m\widehat{DE} = 2 \times 54° = 108°$. By the Arc Addition Postulate, $m\widehat{BD} = m\widehat{BE} + m\widehat{ED} = 18° + 108° = 126°$. By the Inscribed Angle Theorem, $m\angle DAB = \frac{1}{2}m\widehat{BD} = \frac{1}{2} \times 126° = 63°$. Note that $\widehat{ABE}$ is a semicircle, and so $m\widehat{ABE} = 180°$. By the Inscribed Angle Theorem, $m\angle ADE = \frac{1}{2}m\widehat{ABE} = \frac{1}{2} \times 180° = 90°$.

Ⓑ Determine $m\widehat{WX}$, $m\widehat{XZ}$, $m\angle XWZ$, and $m\angle WXZ$ using the appropriate theorems and postulates.

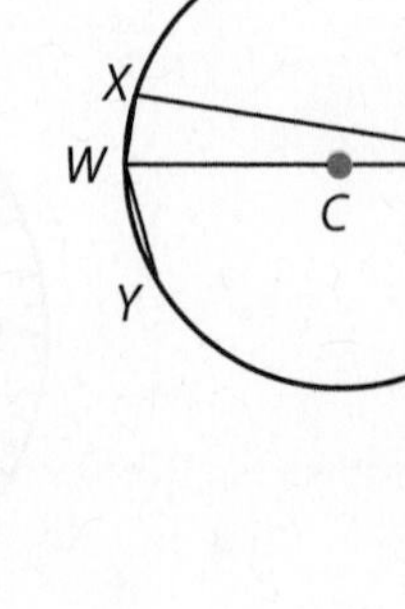

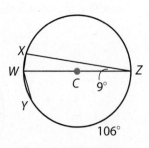

By the Inscribed Angle Theorem, $m\angle WZX = \boxed{\frac{1}{2}}\ m\widehat{WX}$,

and so $m\widehat{WX} = 2 \times 9° = \boxed{18°}$. Note that $\widehat{WXZ}$ is a semicircle and,

therefore, $m\widehat{WXZ} = 180°$. By the Arc Addition Postulate,

$m\widehat{WXZ} = m\widehat{WX} + m\widehat{XZ}$ and then $m\widehat{XZ} = 180° - 18° = \boxed{162°}$

By the Inscribed Angle Theorem, $m\angle XWZ = \frac{1}{2}m\widehat{XZ} = \frac{1}{2} \times 162° = 81°$. Note that $\widehat{WYZ}$ is a semicircle, and so $m\widehat{WYZ} = 180°$. By the Inscribed Angle Theorem, $m\angle WXZ = \frac{1}{2}m\widehat{WYZ} = \frac{1}{2} \times 180° = 90°$.

Reflect

5. **Discussion** Explain an alternative method for determining $m\angle\widehat{XZ}$ in Example 2B.

6. **Justify Reasoning** How does the measure of $\angle ABD$ compare to the measure of $\angle ACD$? Explain your reasoning.

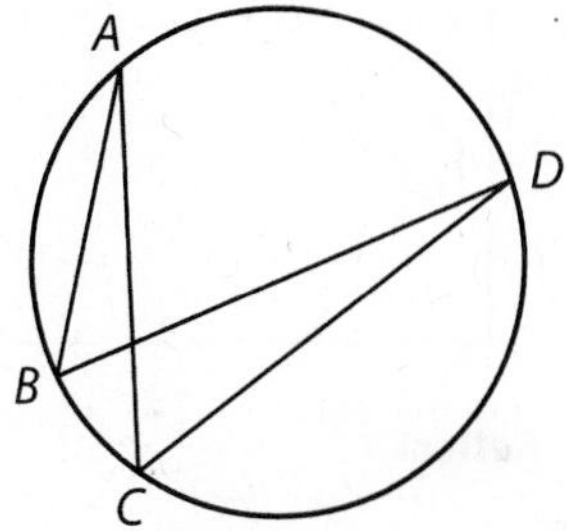

Your Turn

7. If $m\angle EDF = 15°$, determine $m\angle ABE$ using the appropriate theorems and postulates.

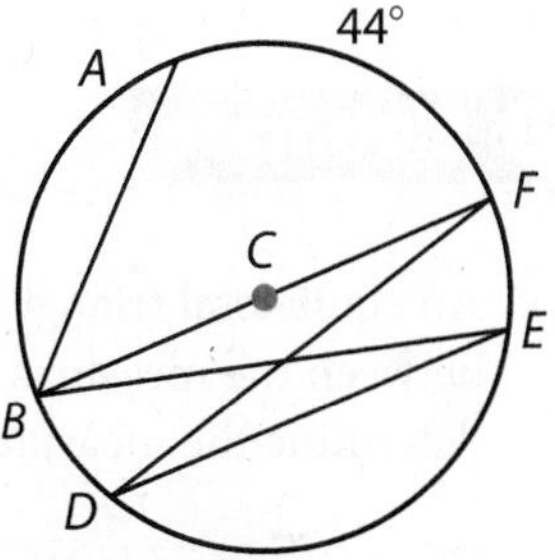

Explain 3 Investigating Inscribed Angles on Diameters

You can examine angles that are inscribed in a semicircle.

Example 3 **Construct and analyze an angle inscribed in a semicircle.**

(A) Use a compass to draw a circle with center *C*. Use a straightedge to draw a diameter of the circle. Label the diameter $\overline{DF}$.

(B) Use a straightedge to draw an inscribed angle $\angle DEF$ on your circle from Step A whose sides contain the endpoints of the diameter.

(C) Use a protractor to determine the measure of $\angle DEF$ (to the nearest degree). Copy the table and record the results in the table.

Angle Measure	Circle C	Circle 2	Circle 3	Circle 4
$m\angle DEF$	?	?	?	?

(D) Repeat the process three more times. Make sure to vary the size of the circle, and the location of the vertex of the inscribed angle. Record the results in the table in Part C.

(E) Examine the results, and make a conjecture about the measure of an angle inscribed in a semicircle.

(F) How can does the Inscribed Angle Theorem justify your conjecture?

Inscribed Angle of a Diameter Theorem

The endpoints of a diameter lie on an inscribed angle if and only if the inscribed angle is a right angle.

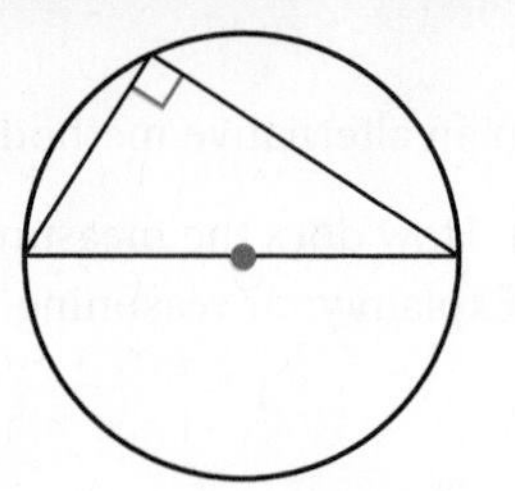

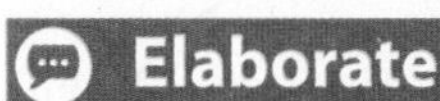

8. A right angle is inscribed in a circle. If the endpoints of its intercepted arc are connected by a segment, must the segment pass through the center of the circle?

Elaborate

9. An equilateral triangle is inscribed in a circle. How does the relationship between the measures of the inscribed angles and intercepted arcs help determine the measure of each angle of the triangle?

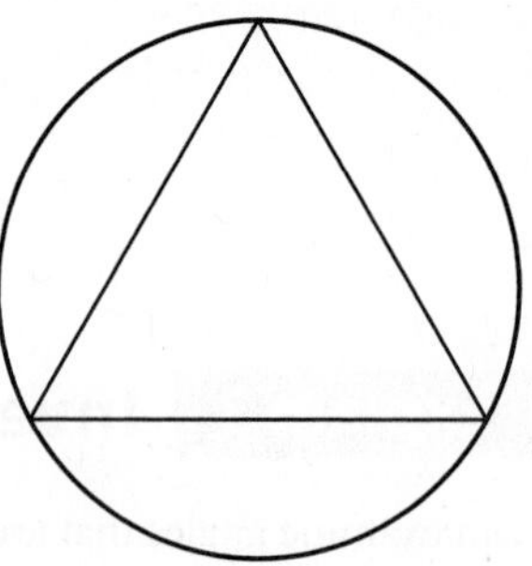

10. **Essential Question Check-In** What is the relationship between inscribed angles and central angles in a circle?

Evaluate: Homework and Practice

- Online Homework
- Hints and Help
- Extra Practice

Identify the chord(s), inscribed angle(s), and central angle(s) in the figure. The center of the circles in Exercises 1, 2, and 4 is *C*.

1.

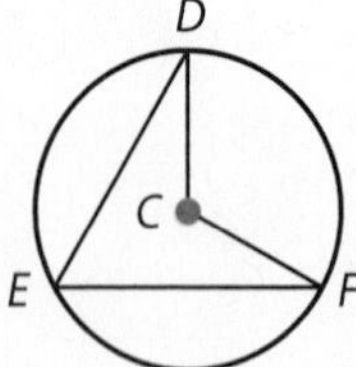

2.

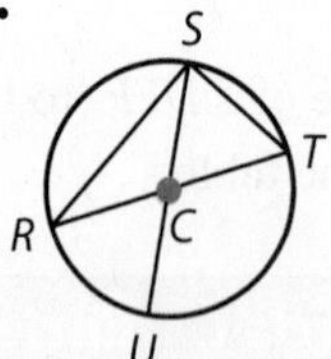

3.

4.

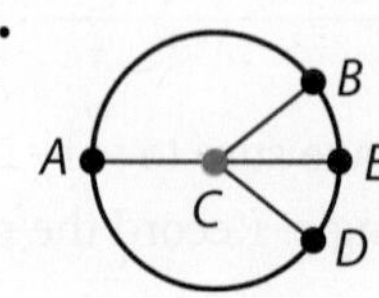

In circle C, $m\widehat{DE} = 84°$. Find each measure.

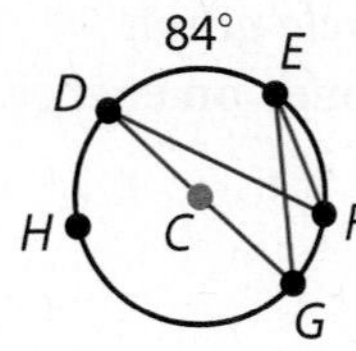

5. $m\angle DGE$

6. $m\angle EFD$

The center of the circle is A. Find each measure using the appropriate theorems and postulates.

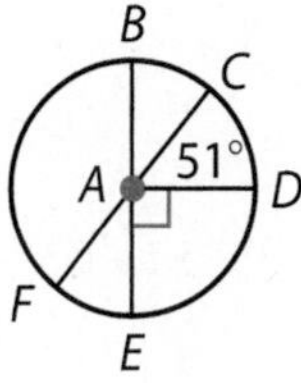

7. $m\widehat{CE}$

8. $m\widehat{DF}$

9. $m\widehat{BEC}$

Find each measure using the appropriate theorems and postulates. $m\widehat{AC} = 116°$

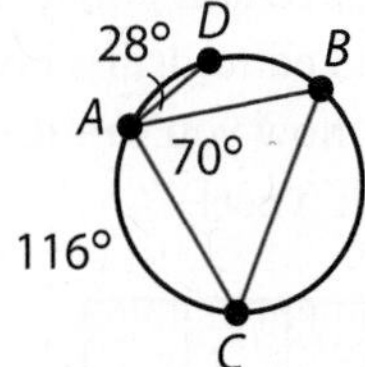

10. $m\widehat{BC}$

11. $m\widehat{AD}$

The center of the circle is C. Find each measure using the appropriate theorems and postulates. $m\widehat{LM} = 70°$ and $m\widehat{NP} = 60°$.

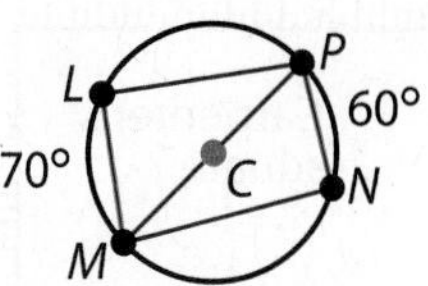

12. $m\angle MNP$

13. $m\angle LMN$

The center of the circle is O. Find each arc or angle measure using the appropriate theorems and postulates.

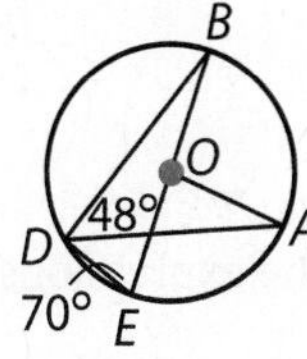

14. $m\angle BDE$

15. $m\widehat{ABD}$

16. $m\widehat{ED}$

17. $m\angle DBE$

Represent Real-World Problems **The circle graph shows how a typical household spends money on energy. Use the graph to find the measure of each arc.**

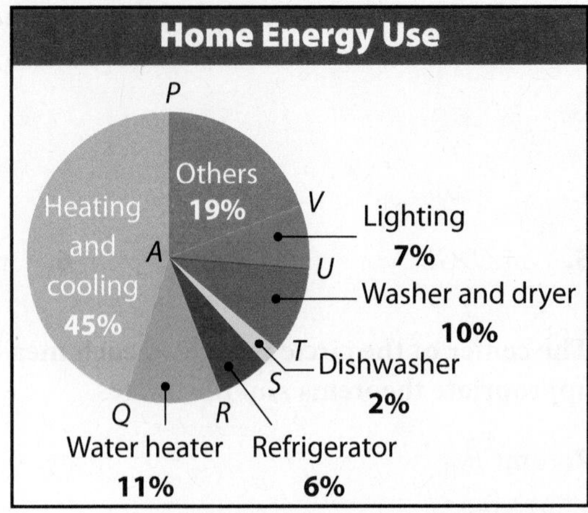

18. $m\widehat{PQ}$

19. $m\widehat{UPT}$

20. **Communicate Mathematical Ideas** A carpenter's square is a tool that is used to draw right angles. Suppose you are building a toy car and you have four small circles of wood that will serve as the wheels. You need to drill a hole in the center of each wheel for the axle. Explain how you can use the carpenter's square to find the center of each wheel.

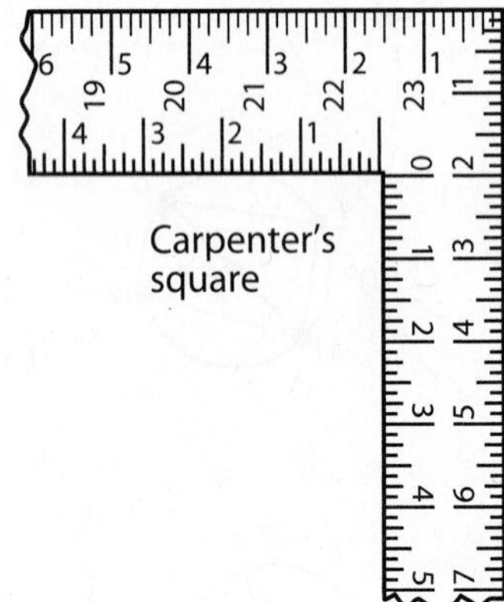

21. Choose the expressions that are equivalent to $m\angle AOB$.

A. $\frac{1}{2}m\angle ACB$

B. $m\angle ACB$

C. $2m\angle ACB$

D. $m\widehat{AB}$

E. $m\angle DOE$

F. $m\angle DFE$

G. $2m\angle DFE$

H. $m\widehat{DE}$

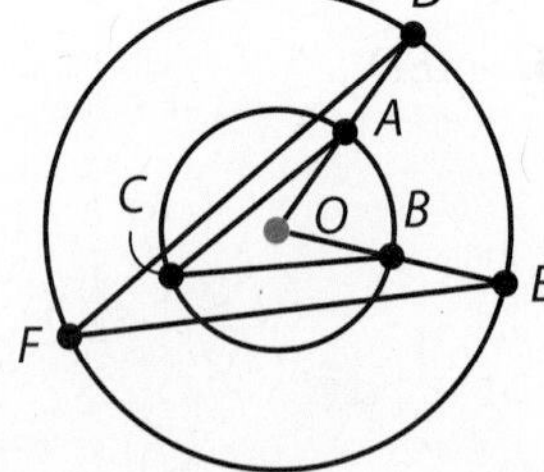

22. Analyze Relationships Copy the diagram. Draw arrows to connect the concepts shown in the boxes. Then explain how the terms shown in the concept map are related.

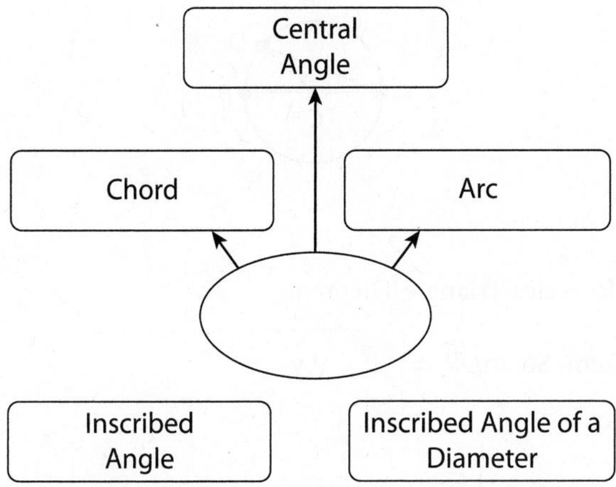

23. In circle E, the measures of $\angle DEC$, $\angle CEB$, and $\angle BEA$ are in the ratio 3:4:5. Find $m\overset{\frown}{AC}$.

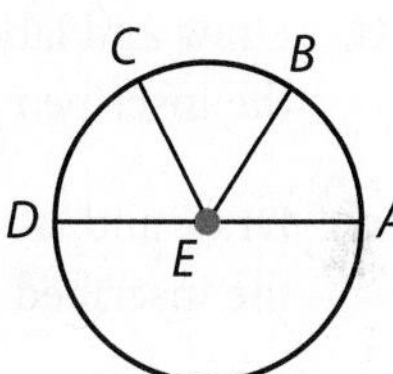

H.O.T. Focus on Higher Order Thinking

24. Explain the Error The center of the circle is G. Below is a student's work to find the value of x. Explain the error and find the correct value of x.

$\overline{AD}$ is a diameter, so $m\overset{\frown}{ACD} = 180°$.

Since $m\overset{\frown}{ACD} = m\overset{\frown}{AB} + m\overset{\frown}{BC} + m\overset{\frown}{CD}$, $m\overset{\frown}{AB} + m\overset{\frown}{BC} + m\overset{\frown}{CD} = 180°$.

$5x + 90 + 15x = 180$

$20x = 90$

$x = 4.5$

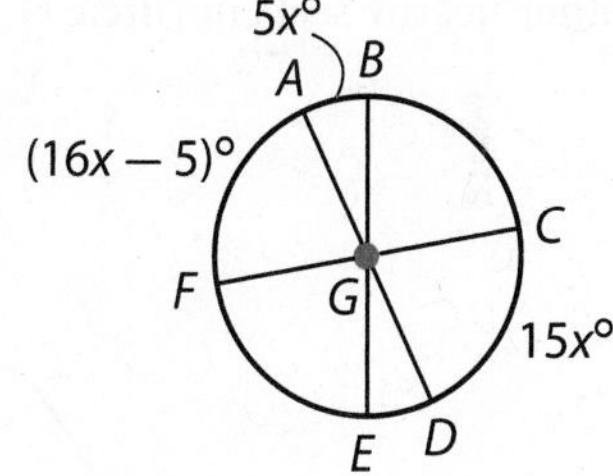

25. Multi-Step An inscribed angle with a diameter as a side has measure $x°$. If the ratio of $m\overset{\frown}{AD}$ to $m\overset{\frown}{DB}$ is 1:4, what is $m\overset{\frown}{DB}$?

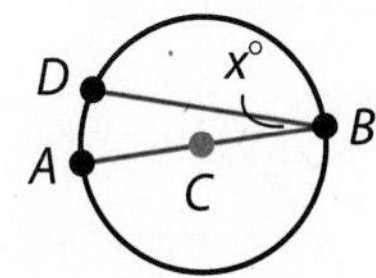

26. Justify Reasoning To prove the Inscribed Angle Theorem you need to prove three cases. In Case 1, the center of the circle is on a side of the inscribed angle. In Case 2, the center the circle is in the interior of the inscribed angle. In Case 3, the center the circle is in the exterior of the inscribed angle.

a. Complete the proof for Case 1 to show that $m\angle DAB = \frac{1}{2} m\widehat{DB}$.

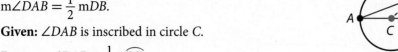

Given: $\angle DAB$ is inscribed in circle C.

Prove: $m\angle DAB = \frac{1}{2} m\widehat{DB}$

Proof: Let $m\angle A = x°$. Draw $\overline{DC}$.

$\triangle ADC$ is __?__. So $m\angle A = m\angle$? by the Isosceles Triangle Theorem.

Then ? $= 2x°$ by the Exterior Angle Theorem. So, $m\widehat{DB} =$? by the definition of the measure of an arc of a circle.

Since $m\widehat{DB} =$? and $m\angle DAB =$? , $m\angle DAB = \frac{1}{2}\widehat{DB}$.

b. Draw and label a diagram for Case 2. Then use a paragraph proof to prove that the inscribed angle is one-half the intercepted arc.

c. Draw and label a diagram for Case 3. Then use a paragraph proof to prove that the inscribed angle is one-half the intercepted arc.

Lesson Performance Task

Diana arrives late at the theater for a play. Her ticket entitles her to sit anywhere in Circle G. She had hoped to sit in Seat *D*, which she thought would give her the widest viewing angle of the stage. But Seat *D* is taken, as are all the other nearby seats in Circle G. The seating chart for the theater is shown.

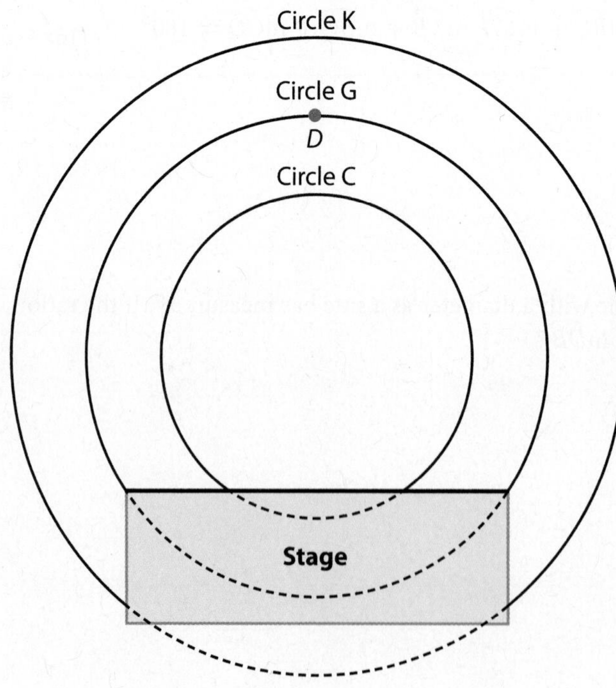

Identify two other spots where Diana can sit that will give her the same viewing angle she would have had in Seat *D*. Explain how you know how your points would provide the same viewing angle, and support your claim by showing the viewing angles on the drawing.

15.2 Angles in Inscribed Quadrilaterals

Resource Locker

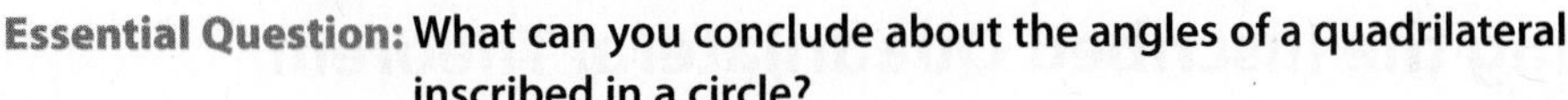

Essential Question: What can you conclude about the angles of a quadrilateral inscribed in a circle?

Explore — Investigating Inscribed Quadrilaterals

There is a relationship among the angles of a quadrilateral that is inscribed in a circle. You can use a protractor and compass to explore the angle measures of a quadrilateral inscribed in a circle.

(A) Measure the four angles of quadrilateral *ABCD* and record their values to the nearest degree.

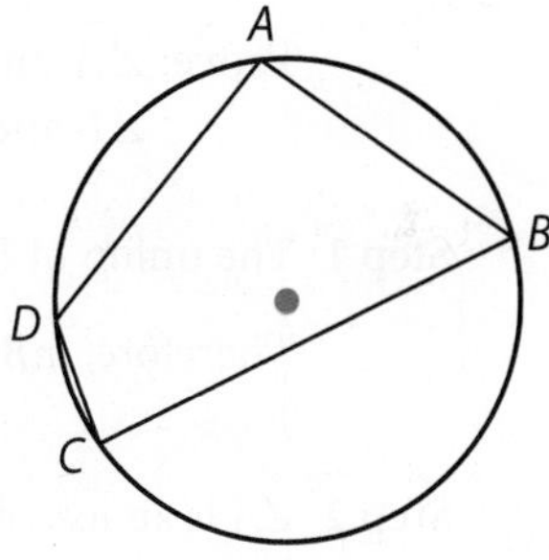

(B) Find the sums of the indicated angles.

$m\angle DAB + m\angle ABC =$? ° $m\angle ABC + m\angle BCD =$? °

$m\angle DAB + m\angle BCD =$? ° $m\angle ABC + m\angle CDA =$? °

$m\angle DAB + m\angle CDA =$? ° $m\angle BCD + m\angle CDA =$? °

(C) Use a compass to draw a circle with a diameter greater than the circle in Step A. Plot points *E*, *F*, *G*, and *H* consecutively around the circumference of the circle so that the center of the circle is not inside quadrilateral *EFGH*. Use a straightedge to connect each pair of consecutive points to draw quadrilateral *EFGH*.

(D) Measure the four angles of *EFGH* to the nearest degree and record their values.

(E) Find the sums of the indicated angles.

$m\angle HEF + m\angle EFG =$? ° $m\angle EFG + m\angle FGH =$? °

$m\angle HEF + m\angle FGH =$? ° $m\angle EFG + m\angle GHE =$? °

$m\angle HEF + m\angle GHE =$? ° $m\angle FGH + m\angle GHE =$? °

Reflect

1. **Discussion** Compare your work with that of other students. What conclusions can you make about the angles of a quadrilateral inscribed in a circle?
2. Based on your observations, does it matter if the center of the circle is inside or outside the inscribed quadrilateral for the relationship between the angles to hold? Explain.

Explain 1 Proving the Inscribed Quadrilateral Theorem

The result from the Explore can be formalized in the Inscribed Quadrilateral Theorem.

Inscribed Quadrilateral Theorem
If a quadrilateral is inscribed in a circle, then its opposite angles are supplementary.

Example 1 **Prove the Inscribed Quadrilateral Theorem.**

Given: Quadrilateral $ABCD$ is inscribed in circle O.

Prove: $\angle A$ and $\angle C$ are supplementary.
$\angle B$ and $\angle D$ are supplementary.

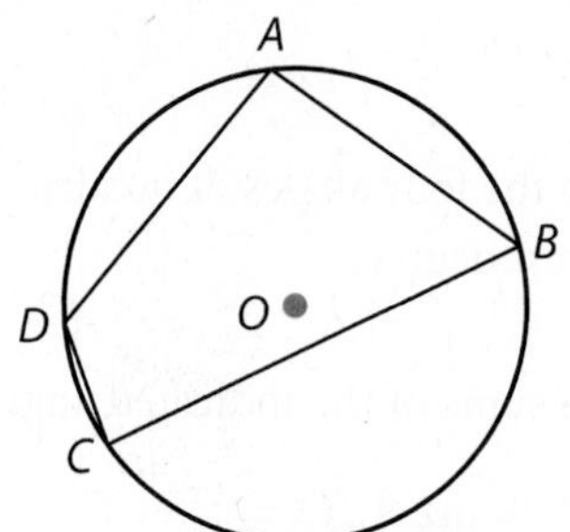

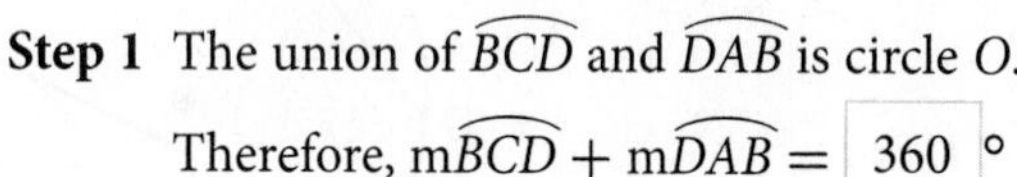

Step 1 The union of $\overparen{BCD}$ and $\overparen{DAB}$ is circle O.

Therefore, $m\overparen{BCD} + m\overparen{DAB} =$ 360 °

Step 2 $\angle A$ is an inscribed angle and its intercepted arc is $\overparen{BCD}$.

$\angle$ C is an inscribed angle and its intercepted arc is $\overparen{DAB}$.

By the Inscribed Angle Theorem, $m\angle A = \frac{1}{2} m\overparen{BCD}$ and

$m\angle C = \frac{1}{2} m\overparen{DAB}$.

Step 3 So, $m\angle A + m\angle C = \frac{1}{2}m\overparen{BCD} + \frac{1}{2}m\overparen{DAB}$ Substitution Property of Equality

$= \frac{1}{2}\left(m\overparen{BCD} + m\overparen{DAB}\right)$ Distributive Property

$= \frac{1}{2}(360°)$ Substitution Property of Equality

$= 180°$ Simplify.

So, $\angle A$ and $\angle C$ are supplementary, by the definition of supplementary. Similar reasoning shows that $\angle B$ and $\angle D$ are also supplementary.

The converse of the Inscribed Quadrilateral Theorem is also true. That is, if the opposite angles of a quadrilateral are supplementary, it can be inscribed in a circle. Taken together, these statements can be stated as the following biconditional statement. A quadrilateral can be inscribed in a circle *if and only if* its opposite angles are supplementary.

Reflect

3. What must be true about a parallelogram that is inscribed in a circle? Explain.

4. Quadrilateral $PQRS$ is inscribed in a circle and $m\angle P = 57°$. Is it possible to find the measure of some or all of the other angles? Explain.

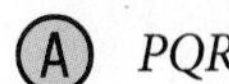

Explain 2 Applying the Inscribed Quadrilateral Theorem

Example 2 **Find the angle measures of each inscribed quadrilateral.**

(A) $PQRS$

Find the value of y.

$m\angle P + m\angle R = 180°$	$PQRS$ is inscribed in a circle.
$(5y + 3) + (15y + 17) = 180$	Substitute.
$20y + 20 = 180$	Simplify.
$y = 8$	Solve for y.

Find the measure of each angle.

$m\angle P = 5(8) + 3 = 43°$	Substitute the value of y into each angle expression and evaluate.
$m\angle R = 15(8) + 17 = 137°$	
$m\angle Q = 8^2 + 53 = 117°$	
$m\angle S + m\angle Q = 180°$	Definition of supplementary
$m\angle S + 117° = 180°$	Substitute.
$m\angle S = 63°$	Subtract 117 from both sides.

So, $m\angle P = 43°$, $m\angle R = 137°$, $m\angle Q = 117°$, and $m\angle S = 63°$.

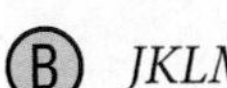

(B) $JKLM$

Find the value of x.

$m\angle J + m\angle \boxed{L} = \boxed{180}°$	$JKLM$ is inscribed in a circle.
$(\boxed{39} + \boxed{7x}) + (\boxed{6x} - \boxed{15}) = \boxed{180}$	Substitute.
$\boxed{13}x + \boxed{24} = \boxed{180}$	Simplify.
$\boxed{13}x = \boxed{156}$	Subtract 24 from both sides.
$x = \boxed{12}$	Divide both sides by 13.

Find the measure of each angle.

$m\angle J = 39 + 7\left(12\right) = 123°$ — Substitute the value of x into each angle expression and evaluate.

$m\angle L = 6\left(12\right) - 15 = 57°$

$m\angle K = \dfrac{20\left(12\right)}{3} = 80°$

$m\angle M + m\angle K = 180°$ — Definition of supplementary

$m\angle M + 80° = 180°$ — Substitute.

$m\angle M = 100°$ — Subtract 80 from both sides.

So, $m\angle J = 123°$, $m\angle L = 57°$, $m\angle K = 80°$, and $m\angle M = 100°$.

Your Turn

5. Find the measure of each angle of inscribed quadrilateral *TUVW*.

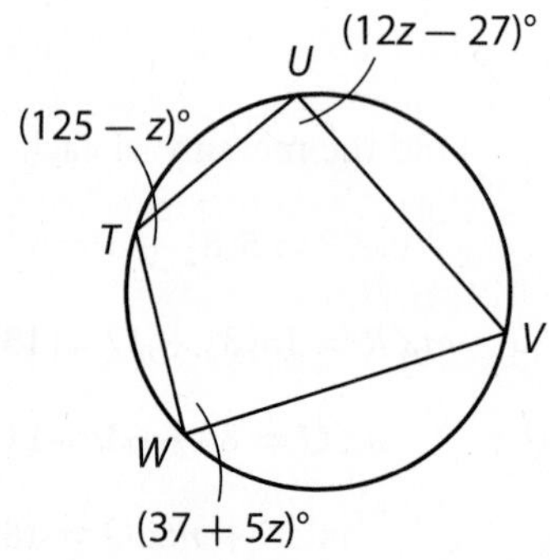

Explain 3 Constructing an Inscribed Square

Many designs are based on a square inscribed in a circle. Follow the steps to construct rectangle *ACBD* inscribed in a circle. Then show *ACBD* is a square.

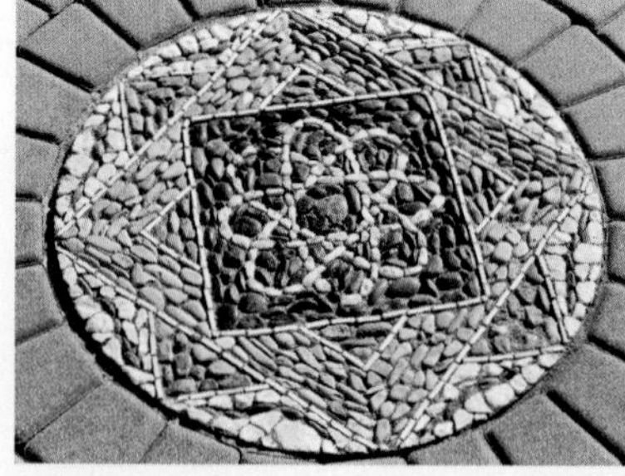

Example 3 **Construct an inscribed square.**

Step 1 Use your compass to draw a circle. Mark the center, *O*. Draw diameter $\overline{AB}$ using a straightedge.

Step 2 Use your compass to construct the perpendicular bisector of $\overline{AB}$. Label the points where the bisector intersects the circle as *C* and *D*. See Step 1 answer.

Step 3 Use your straightedge to draw $\overline{AC}$, $\overline{CB}$, $\overline{BD}$, and $\overline{DA}$. See Step 1 answer.

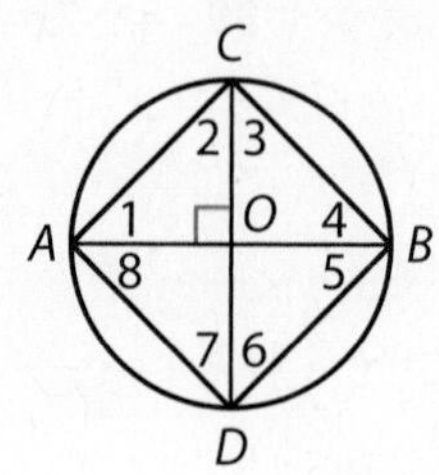

Step 4 To show that *ACBD* is a square, you need to show that it has 4 congruent sides and 4 right angles.

Step 5 Complete the two-column proof to prove that *ACBD* has four congruent sides.

Statements	Reasons
$\overline{OA} \cong \overline{OC} \cong \overline{OB} \cong \overline{OD}$	Radii of the circle *O*
$m\angle AOC = m\angle COB = m\angle BOD = m\angle DOA = 90°$	$\overline{CD}$ is the perpendicular bisector of $\overline{AB}$.
$\triangle AOC \cong \triangle COB \cong \triangle BOD \cong \triangle DOA$	SAS
$\overline{AC} \cong \overline{CB} \cong \overline{BD} \cong \overline{DA}$	CPCTC

Use the diagram to complete the paragraph proof in Steps 6 and 7 that *ACBD* has four right angles.

Step 6 Since $\triangle AOC \cong \triangle COB$, then $\angle 1 \cong \angle 3$ by CPCTC. By reasoning similar to that in the previous proof, it can be shown that $\triangle BOC \cong \triangle COB$. Therefore, by the Transitive Property of Congruence, $\triangle AOC \cong \triangle BOC$, and $\angle 1 \cong \angle 4$ by CPCTC. Also by the Transitive Property of Congruence, $\angle 3 \cong \angle 4$. Similar arguments show that $\angle 1 \cong \angle 2$, $\angle 5 \cong \angle 6$, and $\angle 7 \cong \angle 8$.

Step 7 The sum of all the angle measures in a triangle is 180°, so $m\angle 1 + m\angle 2 + m\angle AOC = 180°$. Since $m\angle AOC = 90°$, $m\angle 1 + m\angle 2 + 90° = 180°$. This means that $m\angle 1 + m\angle 2 = 90°$. Since $m\angle 1 = m\angle 2$, it can be concluded that $m\angle 1 = m\angle 2 = 45°$. By similar reasoning, it is shown that the measure of each of the congruent numbered angles is 45°. Therefore, the measure of each of the four angles of quadrilateral *ACBD* is the sum of the measures of two of the adjacent numbered angles, which is 90°.

Reflect

6. How could reflections be used to construct an inscribed square?

Your Turn

7. Copy the quilt block pattern. Finish the pattern by inscribing a square in the circle. Shade in your square.

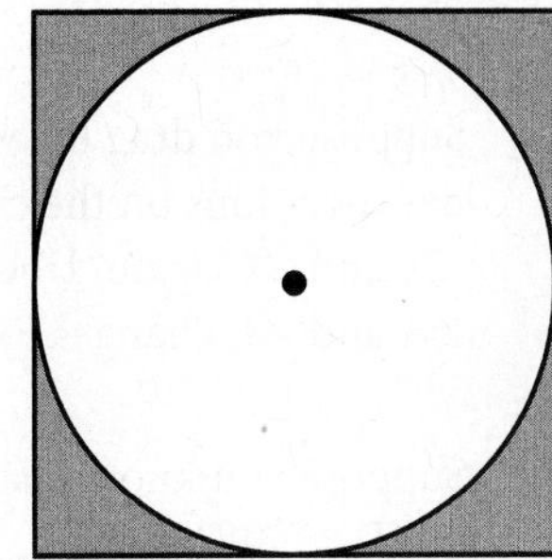

Elaborate

8. Critique Reasoning Marcus said he thought some information was missing from one of his homework problems because it was impossible to answer the question based on the given information. The question and his work are shown. Critique Marcus's work and reasoning.

Homework Problem

Find the measures of the angles of quadrialatral *ABCD*, which can be inscribed in a circle.

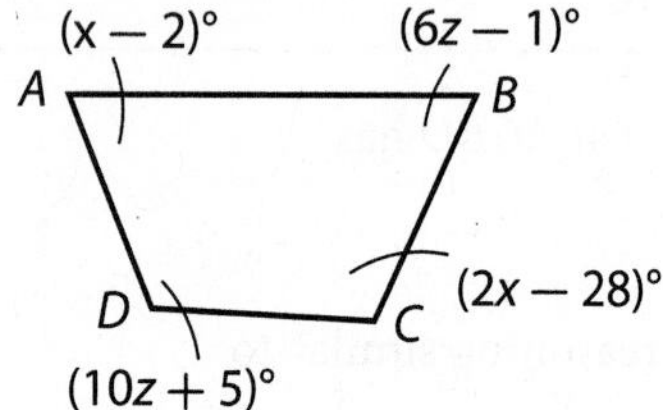

Marcus's Work

$$x - 2 + 6z - 1 + 2x - 28 + 10z + 5 = 360$$
$$3x + 16z - 26 = 360$$
$$3x + 16z = 386$$

Cannot solve for two different variables!

9. What must be true about a rhombus that is inscribed in a circle? Explain.

10. Essential Question Check-In Can all types of quadrilaterals be inscribed in a circle? Explain.

Evaluate: Homework and Practice

- Online Homework
- Hints and Help
- Extra Practice

You use geometry software to inscribe quadrilaterals *ABCD* and *GHIJ* in a circle as shown in the figures. You then measure the angle at each vertex.

Use the figure for Exercises 1–2.

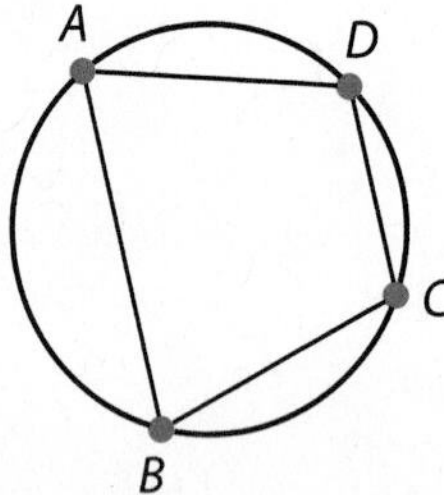

Use the figure for Exercises 3–4.

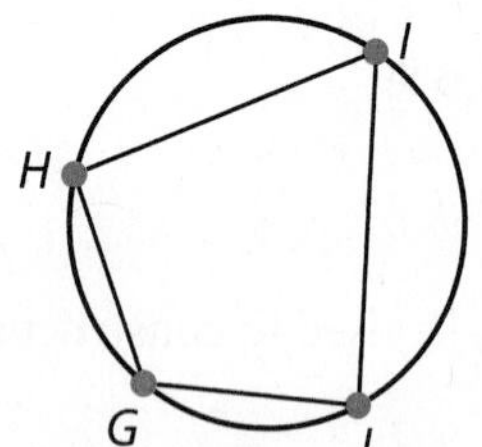

1. Suppose you drag the vertices of $\angle A$ and $\angle C$ to new positions on the circle and then measure $\angle A$ and $\angle C$ again. Does the relationship between $\angle A$ and $\angle C$ change? Explain.

2. Suppose you know that $m\angle B$ is 74°. Is $m\angle D = 74°$? Explain.

3. Suppose $m\angle HIJ = 65°$ and that $m\angle H = m\angle J$. Can you find the measures of all the angles? Explain.

4. Justify Reasoning You have found that $m\angle H = m\angle J$, but then you drag the vertex of $\angle G$ so that $m\angle H$ changes. Is the statement $m\angle H = m\angle J$ still true? Justify your reasoning.

Use the figure for Exercices 5–6. Find each measure using the appropriate theorems and postulates.

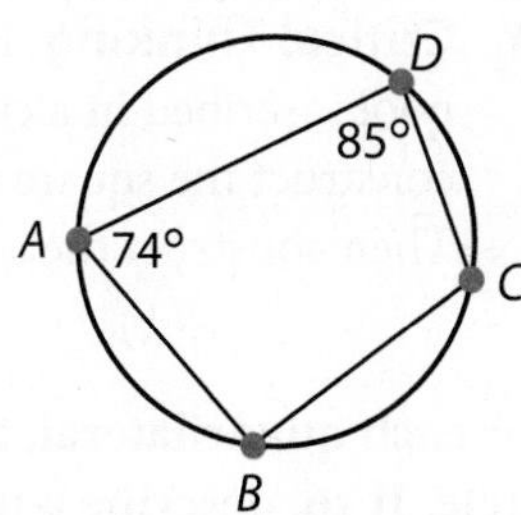

5. $m\angle B$

6. $m\widehat{DAB}$

7. $GHIJ$ is a quadrilateral. If $m\angle HIJ + m\angle HGJ = 180°$ and $m\angle H + m\angle J = 180°$, could the points G, H, I, and J points of a circle? Explain.

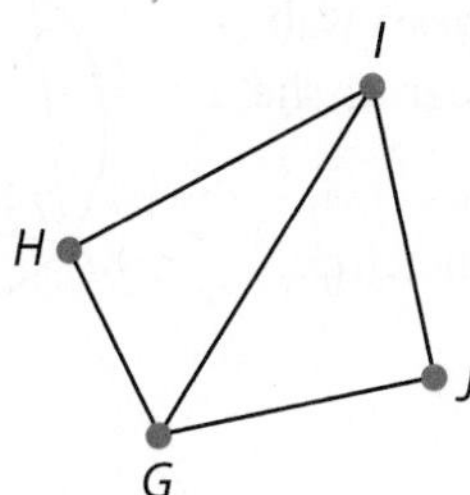

8. $LMNP$ is a quadrilateral inscribed in a circle. If $m\angle L = m\angle N$, is $\overline{MP}$ a diameter of the circle? Explain.

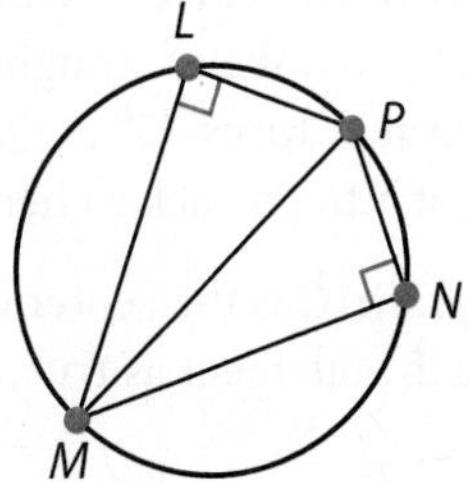

9. Rafael was asked to construct a square inscribed in a circle. He drew a circle and a diameter of the circle. Describe how to complete his construction. Then, complete the construction.

Multi-Step Find the angle measures of each inscribed quadrilateral.

10.

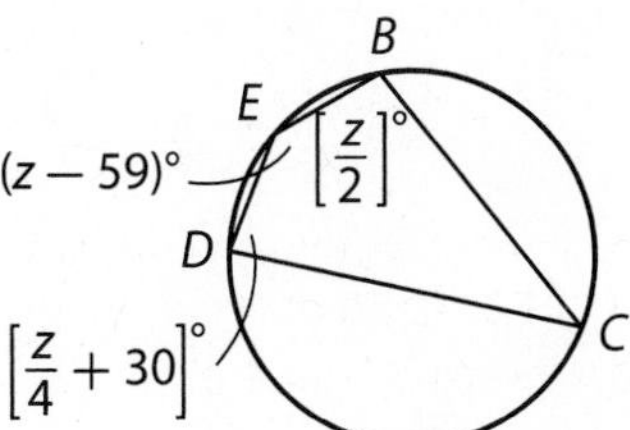

11.

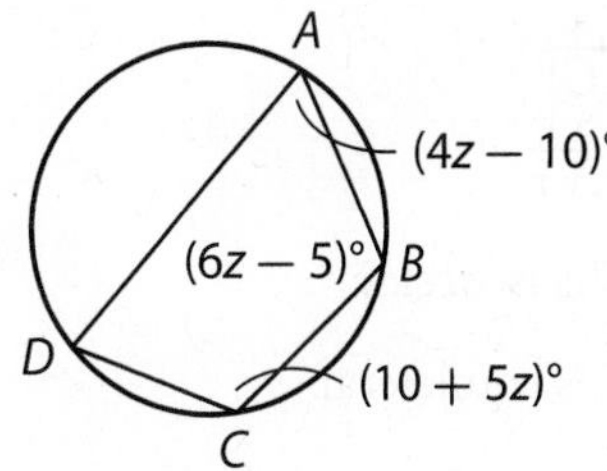

12.

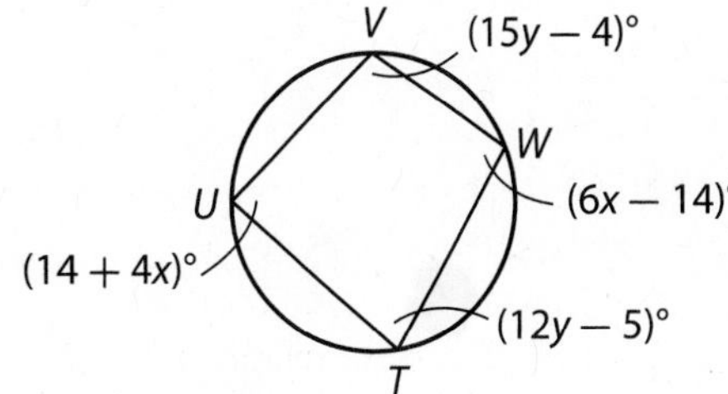

13.

14. **Critical Thinking** Haruki is designing a fountain that consists of a square pool inscribed in a circular base represented by circle O. He wants to construct the square so that one of its vertices is point X. Copy the figure. Then construct the square and explain your method.

For each quadrilateral, tell whether it can be inscribed in a circle. If so, describe a method for doing so using a compass and straightedge. If not, explain why not.

15. a parallelogram that is not a rectangle

16. a kite with two right angles

17. **Represent Real-World Problems** Lisa has not yet learned how to stop on ice skates, so she just skates straight across the circular rink until she reaches a wall. If she starts at P, turns 75° at Q, and turns 100° at R, find how many degrees she must turn at S to go back to her starting point.

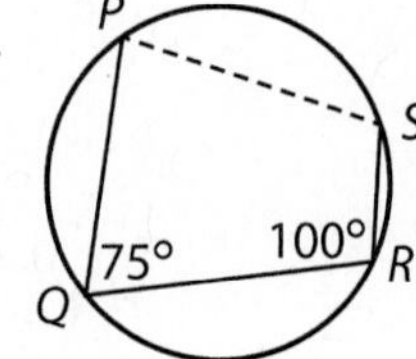

18. In the diagram, C is the center of the circle and $\angle YXZ$ is inscribed in the circle. Classify each statement as true, false, or cannot be determined..

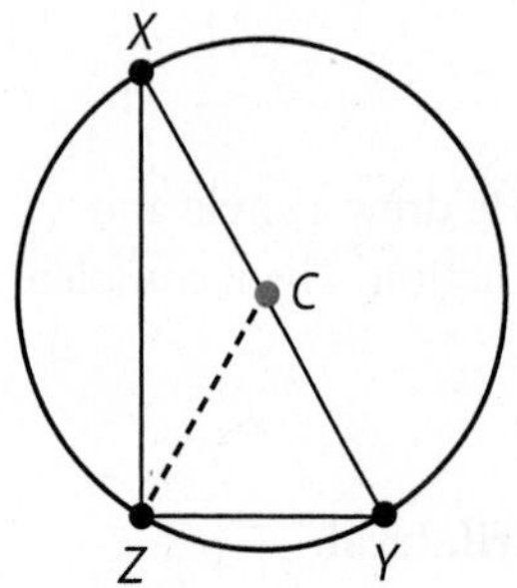

a. $\overline{CX} \cong \overline{CY}$

b. $\overline{CZ} \cong \overline{XY}$

c. $\triangle CXZ$ is isosceles.

d. $\triangle CYZ$ is equilateral.

e. $\overline{XY}$ is a diameter of circle C.

H.O.T. Focus on Higher Order Thinking

19. Multi-Step In the diagram, $m\widehat{JKL} = 198°$ and $m\widehat{KLM} = 216°$. Find the measures of the angles of quadrilateral *JKLM*.

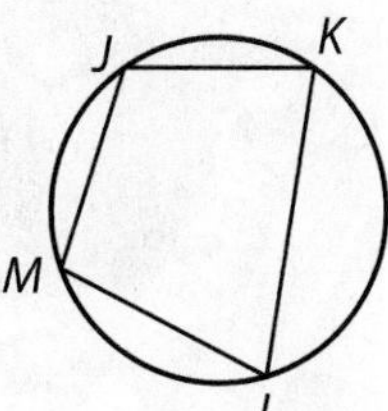

20. Critical Thinking Explain how you can construct a regular octagon inscribed in a circle.

21. Represent Real-World Problems A patio tile design is constructed from a square inscribed in a circle. The circle has radius $5\sqrt{2}$ feet.

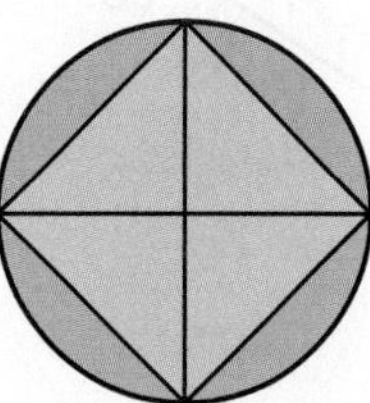

a. Find the area of the square.

b. Find the area of the shaded region outside the square.

Lesson Performance Task

Here are some facts about the baseball field shown here:

- *ABCD* is the baseball "diamond," a square measuring 90 feet on a side.
- Points *A*, *B*, *E*, *H* are collinear.
- The distance from third base (Point *B*) to the left field fence (Point *E*) equals the distance from first base (point *D*) to the right field fence (Point *G*).

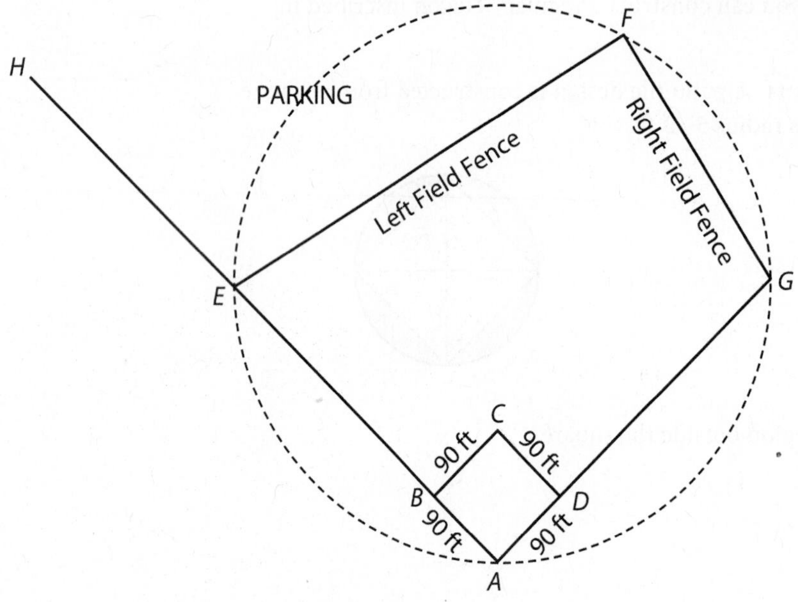

a. Is $\overset{\frown}{EA}$ congruent to $\overset{\frown}{AG}$? Explain why or why not.

b. Find m∠*F*. Explain your reasoning.

c. Identify an angle congruent to ∠*HEF*. Explain your reasoning.

15.3 Tangents and Circumscribed Angles

Essential Question: What are the key theorems about tangents to a circle?

Explore Investigating the Tangent-Radius Theorem

A **tangent** is a line in the same plane as a circle that intersects the circle in exactly one point. The point where a tangent and a circle intersect is the **point of tangency**.

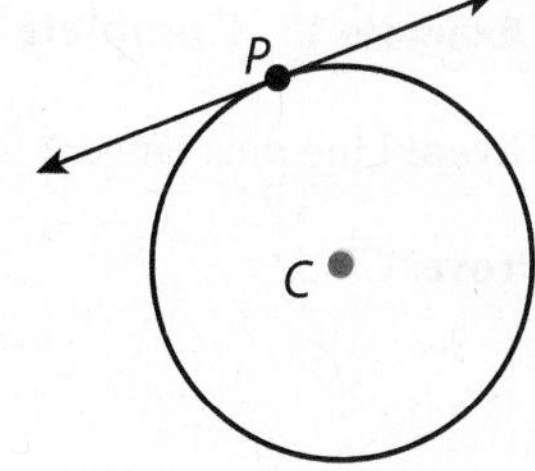

In the figure, the line is tangent to circle C, and point P is the point of tangency. You can use a compass and straightedge to construct a circle and a line tangent to it.

(A) Use a compass to draw a circle. Label the center C.

(B) Mark a point P on the circle. Using a straightedge, draw a tangent to the circle through point P. Mark a point Q at a different position on the tangent line.

(C) Use a straightedge to draw the radius $\overline{CP}$.

(D) Use a protractor to measure $\angle CPQ$. Record the result. Repeat the process two more times. Make sure to vary the size of the circle and the location of the point of tangency.

Reflect

1. **Make a Conjecture** Examine your results. Make a conjecture about the relationship between a tangent line and the radius to the point of tangency.
2. **Discussion** Describe any possible inaccuracies related to the tools you used in this Explore.

Explain 1 Proving the Tangent-Radius Theorem

The Explore illustrates the Tangent-Radius Theorem.

Tangent-Radius Theorem

If a line is tangent to a circle, then it is perpendicular to a radius drawn to the point of tangency.

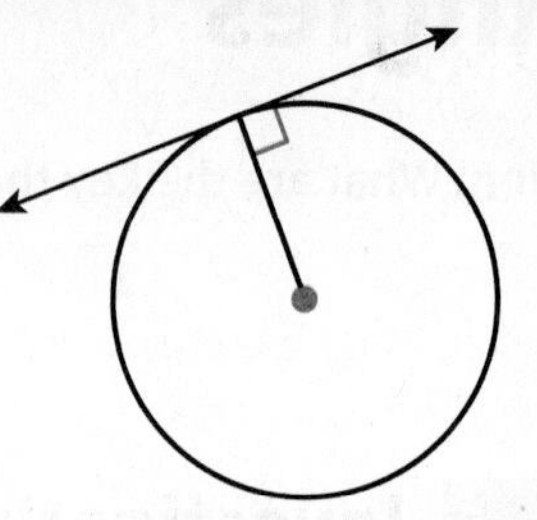

Example 1 **Complete the proof of the Tangent–Radius Theorem.**

Given: Line m is tangent to circle C at point P.

Prove: $\overline{CP} \perp m$

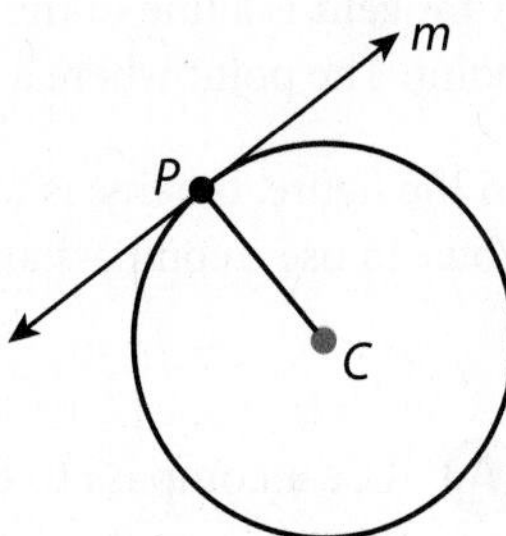

(A) Use an indirect proof. Assume that $\overline{CP}$ is not perpendicular to line m. There must be a point Q on line m such that $\overline{CQ} \perp m$.

If $\overline{CQ} \perp m$, then $\triangle CQP$ is a right triangle, and $CP > CQ$ because $\overline{CP}$ is the hypotenuse of the right triangle.

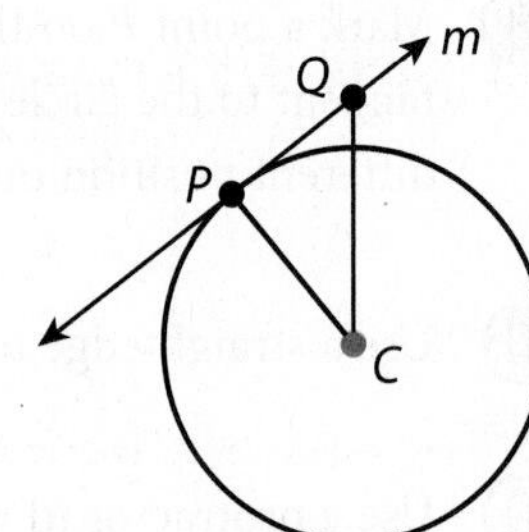

(B) Since line m is a tangent line, it can intersect circle C at only point P, and all other points of line m are in the exterior of the circle.

(C) This means point Q is in the exterior of the circle. You can conclude that $CP < CQ$ because $\overline{CP}$ is a radius of circle C.

(D) This contradicts the initial assumption that a point Q exists such that $\overline{CQ} \perp m$, because that meant that $CP > CQ$. Therefore, the assumption is false and $\overline{CP}$ must be perpendicular to line m.

Reflect

3. Both lines in the figure are tangent to the circle, and $\overline{AB}$ is a diameter. What can you conclude about the tangent lines?

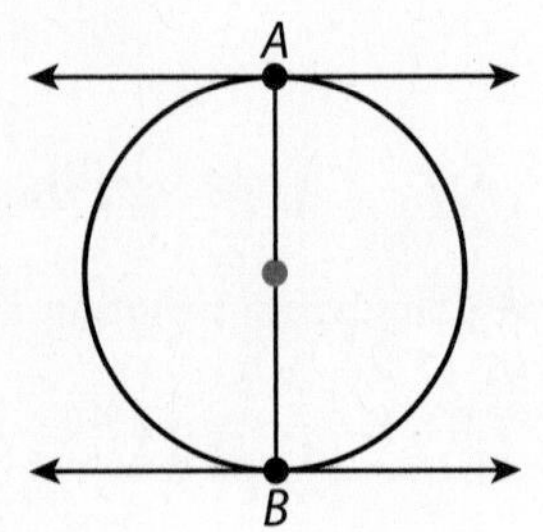

The converse of the Tangent-Radius Theorem is also true. You will be asked to prove this theorem as an exercise.

Converse of the Tangent-Radius Theorem

If a line is perpendicular to a radius of a circle at a point on the circle, then it is tangent to the circle at that point on the circle.

Explain 2 Constructing Tangents to a Circle

From a point outside a circle, two tangent lines can be drawn to the circle.

Example 2 **Use the steps to construct two tangent lines from a point outside a circle.**

(A) Use a compass to draw a circle. Label the center C.

(B) Mark a point X outside the circle and use a straightedge to draw $\overline{CX}$.

(C) Use a compass and straightedge to construct the midpoint of $\overline{CX}$ and label the midpoint M.

(D) Use a compass to construct a circle with center M and radius CM.

(E) Label the points of intersection of circle C and circle M as A and B. Use a straightedge to draw $\overleftrightarrow{XA}$ and $\overleftrightarrow{XB}$. Both lines are tangent to circle C.

Reflect

4. How can you justify that $\overleftrightarrow{XA}$ (or $\overleftrightarrow{XB}$) is a tangent line? (Hint: Draw $\overline{CA}$ on your diagram.)

5. Draw $\overline{CA}$ and $\overline{CB}$ on your diagram. Consider quadrilateral $CAXB$. State any conclusions you can reach about the measures of the angles of quadrilateral $CAXB$.

Explain 3 Proving the Circumscribed Angle Theorem

A **circumscribed angle** is an angle formed by two rays from a common endpoint that are tangent to a circle.

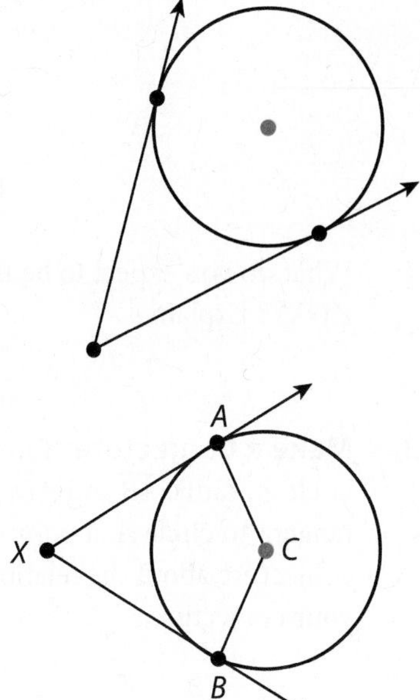

Circumscribed Angle Theorem

A circumscribed angle of a circle and its associated central angle are supplementary.

Example 3 **Prove the Circumscribed Angle Theorem.**

Given: $\angle AXB$ is a circumscribed angle of circle C.

Prove: $\angle AXB$ and $\angle ACB$ are supplementary.

Since $\angle AXB$ is a circumscribed angle of circle C, $\overline{XA}$ and $\overline{XB}$ are tangents to the circle. Therefore, $\angle XAC$ and $\angle XBC$ are right angles by the Tangent-Radius Theorem.

In quadrilateral $XACB$, the sum of the measures of its four angles is 360°.

Since $m\angle XAC + m\angle XBC =$ 180°, this means $m\angle AXB + m\angle ACB = 360° - 180° =$ 180°.

So, $\angle AXB$ and $\angle ACB$ are supplementary by the definition of supplementary angles.

Reflect

6. Is it possible for quadrilateral $AXBC$ to be a parallelogram? If so, what type of parallelogram must it be? If not, why not?

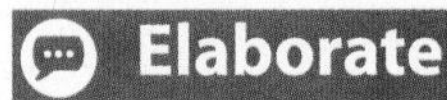

Elaborate

7. $\overrightarrow{KM}$ and $\overrightarrow{KN}$ are tangent to circle C. Explain how to show that $\overline{KM} \cong \overline{KN}$, using congruent triangles.

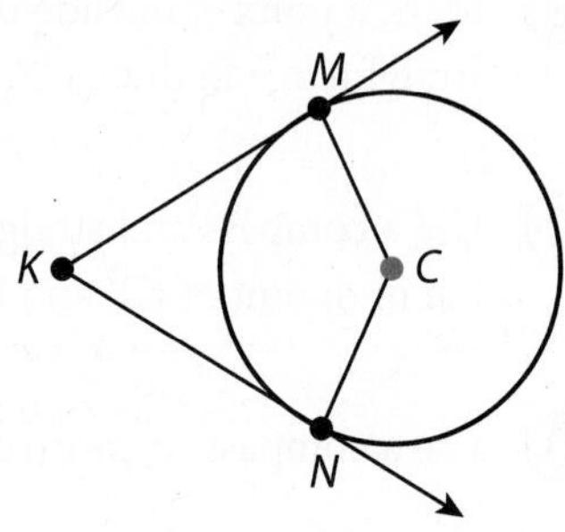

8. **Essential Question Check-In** What are the key theorems regarding tangent lines to a circle?

Evaluate: Homework and Practice

- Online Homework
- Hints and Help
- Extra Practice

Use the figure for Exercises 1–2. You use geometry software to construct a tangent to circle O at point X on the circle, as shown in the diagram.

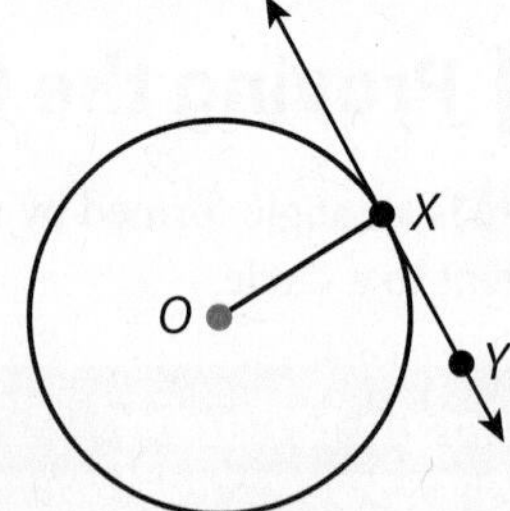

1. What do you expect to be the measure of $\angle OXY$? Explain.

2. Suppose you drag point X so that is in a different position on the circle. Does the measure of $\angle OXY$ change? Explain.

3. **Make a Conjecture** You use geometry software to construct circle A, radii $\overline{AB}$ and $\overline{AD}$, and lines m and n which are tangent to circle A at points D and B, respectively. Make a conjecture about the relationship of the two tangents. Explain your conjecture.

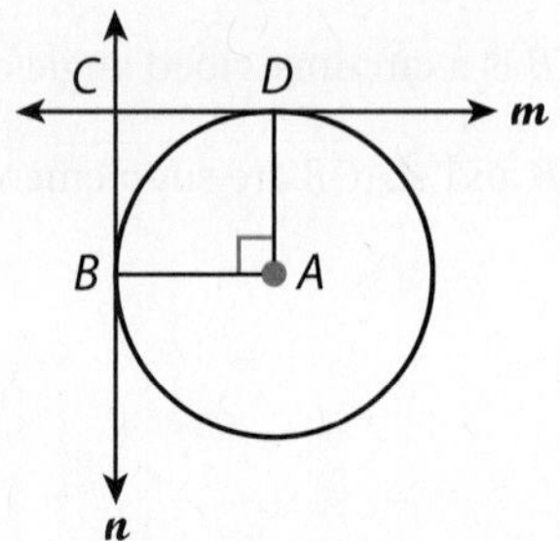

4. In the figure, $\overline{RQ}$ is tangent to circle P at point Q. What is $m\angle PRQ$? Explain your reasoning.

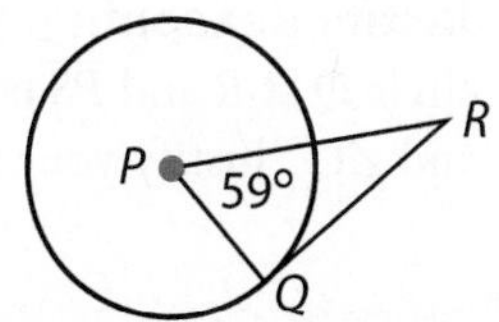

5. **Represent Real-World Problems** The International Space Station orbits Earth at an altitude of about 240 miles. In the diagram, the Space Station is at point E. The radius of Earth is approximately 3960 miles. To the nearest ten miles, what is EH, the distance from the space station to the horizon?

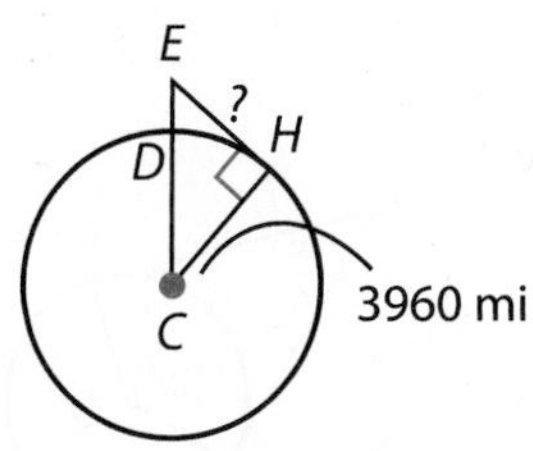

Multi-Step Find the length of each radius. Identify the point of tangency, and write the equation of the tangent line at that point.

6.

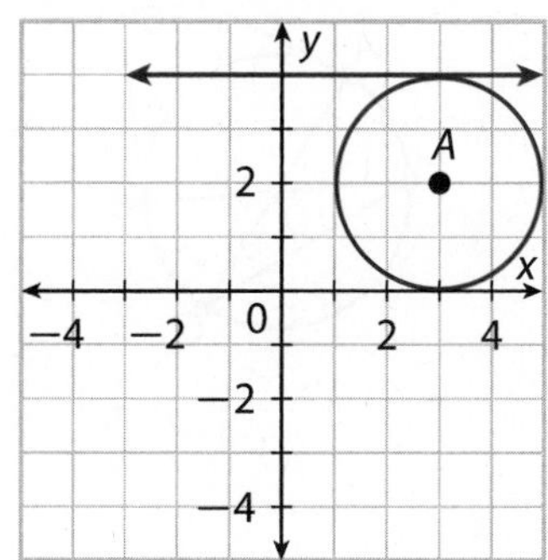

7.

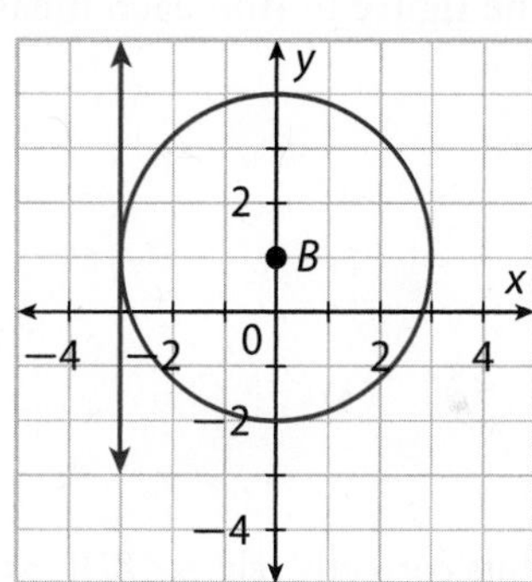

8. In the figure, $QS = 5$, $RT = 12$, and $\overleftrightarrow{RT}$ is tangent to radius $\overline{QR}$ with the point of tangency at R. Find QT.

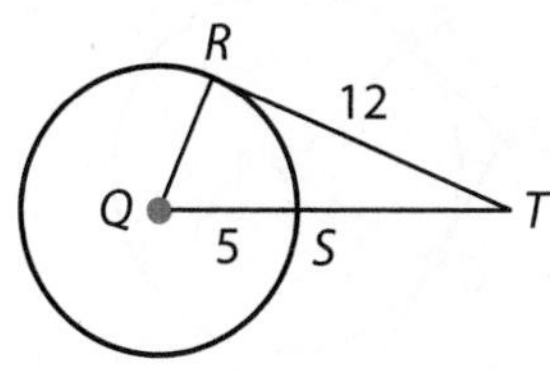

The segments in each figure are tangent to the circle at the points shown. Find each length.

9.

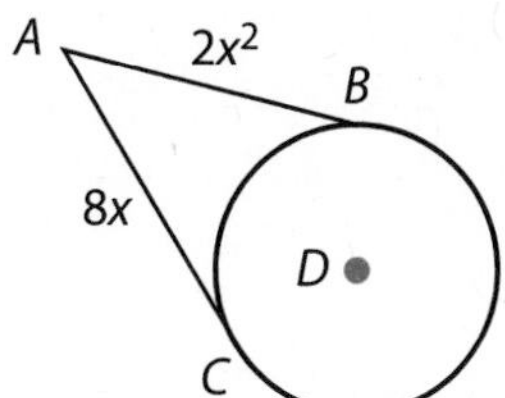

10.

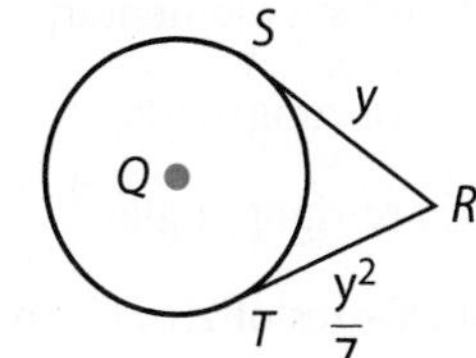

11. Justify Reasoning Suppose you construct a figure with $\overline{PR}$ tangent to circle Q at R and $\overline{PS}$ tangent to circle Q at S. Make a conjecture about $\angle P$ and $\angle Q$. Justify your reasoning.

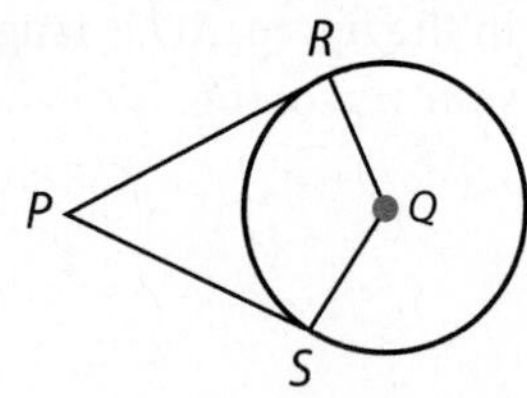

12. $\overline{PR}$ is tangent to circle Q at R and $\overline{PS}$ is tangent to circle Q at S. Find $m\angle Q$.

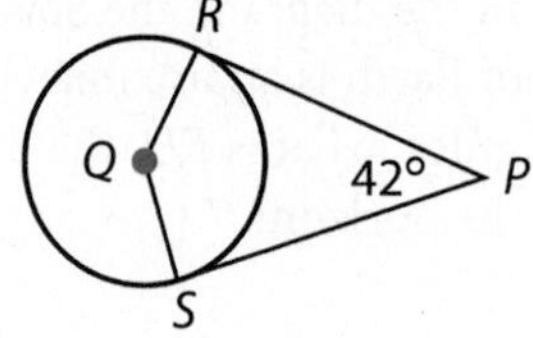

13. $\overline{PR}$ is tangent to circle Q at R and $\overline{PS}$ is tangent to circle Q at S. Find $m\angle P$.

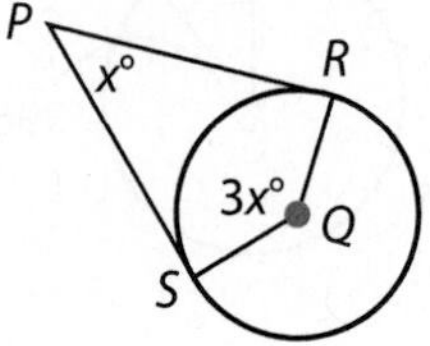

$\overline{PA}$ is tangent to circle O at A and $\overline{PB}$ is tangent to circle O at B, and $m\angle P = 56°$. Use the figure to find each measure.

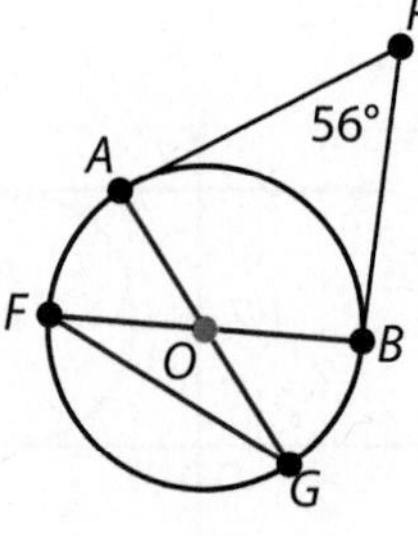

14. $m\angle AOB$

15. $m\angle OGF$

16. Which statements correctly relate $\angle BDC$ and $\angle BAC$?

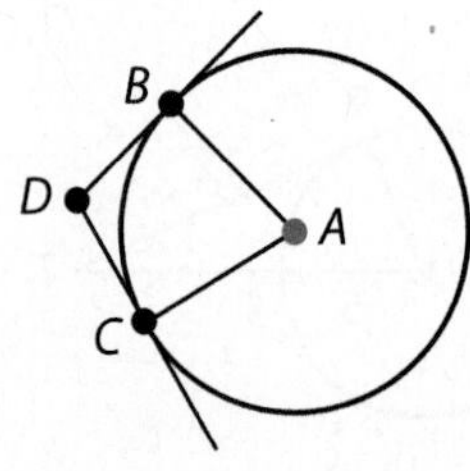

A. $\angle BDC$ and $\angle BAC$ are complementary.

B. $\angle BDC$ and $\angle BAC$ are supplementary.

C. $\angle BDC$ and $\angle BAC$ are congruent.

D. $\angle BDC$ and $\angle BAC$ are right angles.

E. The sum of the measures of $\angle BDC$ and $\angle BAC$ is 180°.

F. It is impossible to determine a relationship between $\angle BDC$ and $\angle BAC$.

17. Critical Thinking Given a circle with diameter $\overline{BC}$, is it possible to construct tangents to B and C from an external point X? If so, make a construction. If not, explain why it is not possible.

$\overrightarrow{KJ}$ is tangent to circle C at J, $\overrightarrow{KL}$ is tangent to circle C at L, and $m\widehat{ML} = 138°$.

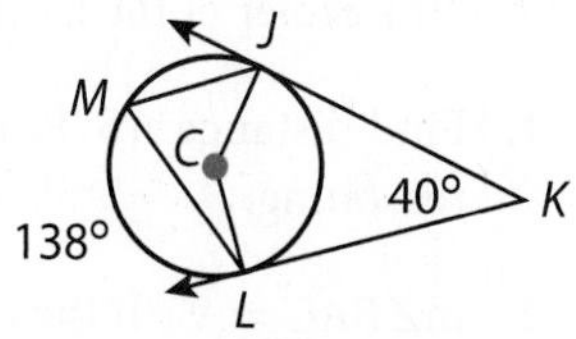

18. Find $m\angle M$.

19. Find $m\widehat{MJ}$.

H.O.T. Focus on Higher Order Thinking

20. Justify Reasoning Prove the converse of the Tangent-Radius Theorem.
Given: Line m is in the plane of circle C, P is a point of circle C, and $\overline{CP} \perp m$
Prove: m is tangent to circle C at P.

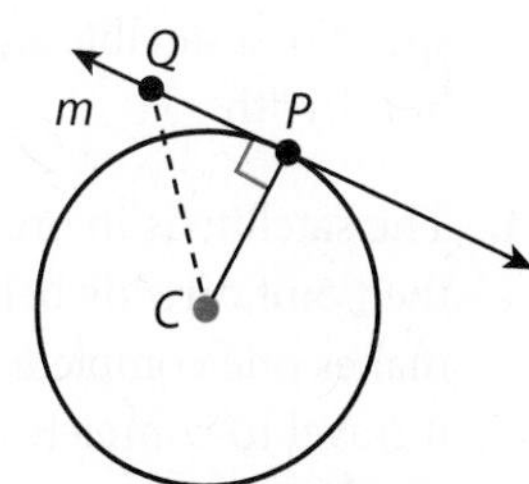

21. Draw Conclusions A grapic designer created a preliminary sketch for a company logo. In the figure, $\overleftrightarrow{BC}$ and $\overleftrightarrow{CD}$ are tangent to circle A and $BC > BA$. What type of quadrilateral is figure $ABCD$ that she created? Explain.

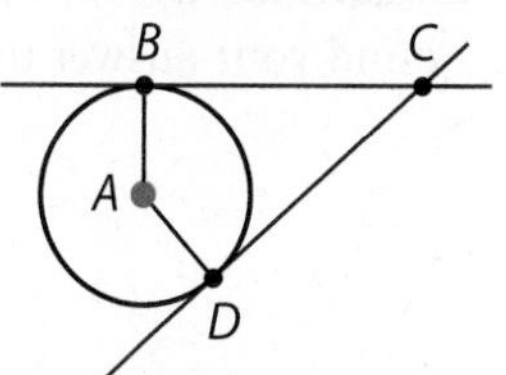

22. Explain the Error In the given figure, $\overleftrightarrow{QP}$ and $\overleftrightarrow{QR}$ are tangents. A student was asked to find $m\angle PSR$. Critique the student's work and correct any errors.

Since $\angle PQR$ is a circumscribed angle, $\angle PQR$ and $\angle PCR$ are supplementary. So $m\angle PCR = 110°$. Since $\angle PSR \cong \angle PCR$, $m\angle PSR = 110°$.

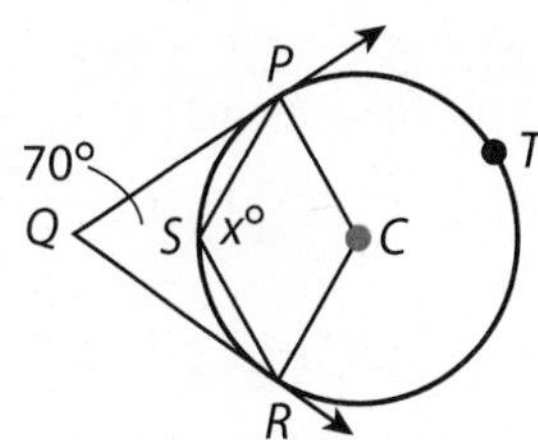

23. Copy circle O and points B and C. Construct a triangle that is circumscribed around the circle.

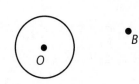

Lesson Performance Task

A communications satellite is in a synchronous orbit 22,000 miles above Earth's surface. Points B and D in the figure are points of tangency of the satellite signal with the Earth. They represent the greatest distance from the satellite at which the signal can be received directly. Point C is the center of the Earth.

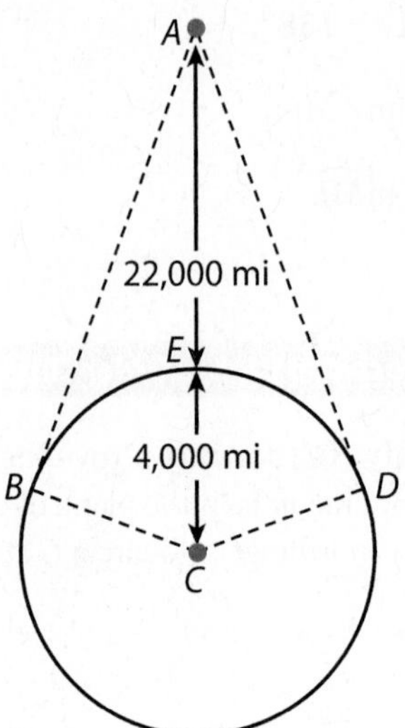

1. Find distance AB. Round to the nearest mile. Explain your reasoning.

2. $m\angle BAC = 9°$. If the circumference of the circle represents the Earth's equator, what percent of the Earth's equator is within range of the satellite's signal? Explain your reasoning.

3. How much longer does it take a satellite signal to reach point B than it takes to reach point E? Use 186,000 mi/sec as the speed of a satellite signal. Round your answer to the nearest hundredth.

4. The satellite is in orbit above the Earth's equator. Along with the point directly below it on the Earth's surface, the satellite makes one complete revolution every 24 hours. How fast must it travel to complete a revolution in that time? You can use the formula $C = 2\pi r$ to find the circumference of the orbit. Round your answer to the nearest whole number.

15.4 Segment Relationships in Circles

Essential Question: What are the relationships between the segments in circles?

Resource Locker

Explore Exploring Segment Length Relationships in Circles

Any segment connecting two points on a circle is a chord. In some cases, two chords drawn inside the same circle will intersect, creating four segments. In the following activity, you will look for a pattern in how these segments are related and form a conjecture.

(A) Using geometry software or a compass and straightedge, construct circle A with two chords $\overline{CD}$ and $\overline{EF}$ that intersect inside the circle. Label the intersection point G.

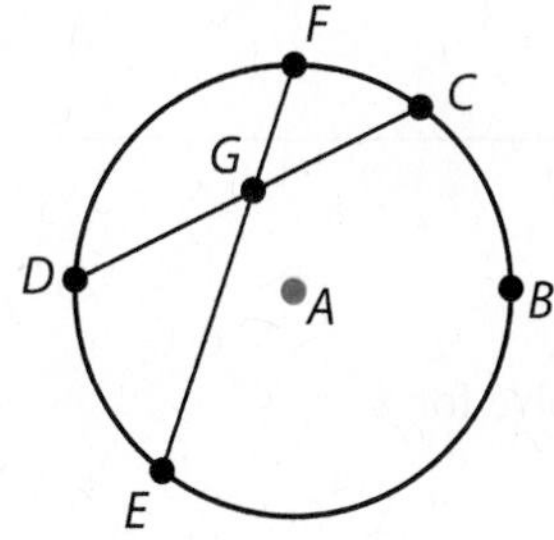

(B) Repeat your construction with two more circles. Vary the size of the circles and where you put the intersecting chords inside them.

(C) Copy the table, insert the lengths of the segments measured to the nearest millimeter, and calculate their products.

	DG	GC	EG	GF	$DG \cdot GC$	$EG \cdot GF$
Circle 1	?	?	?	?	?	?
Circle 2	?	?	?	?	?	?
Circle 3	?	?	?	?	?	?

(D) Look for a pattern among the measurements and calculations of the segments. From the table, it appears that ? will always equal ?.

Reflect

1. **Discussion** Compare your results with those of your classmates. What do you notice?
2. What conjecture can you make about the products of the segments of two chords that intersect inside a circle?

Explain 1 Applying the Chord-Chord Product Theorem

In the Explore, you discovered a pattern in the relationship between the parts of two chords that intersect inside a circle. In this Example, you will apply the following theorem to solve problems.

Chord-Chord Product Theorem

If two chords intersect inside a circle, then the products of the lengths of the segments of the chords are equal.

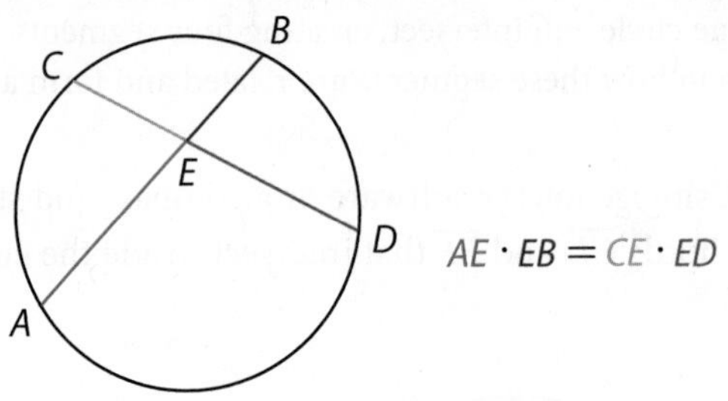

Example 1 **Find the value of x and the length of each chord.**

(A) Set up an equation according to the Chord-Chord Product Theorem and solve for x.

$CE \cdot ED = AE \cdot EB$

$6(2) = 3(x)$

$12 = 3x$

$4 = x$

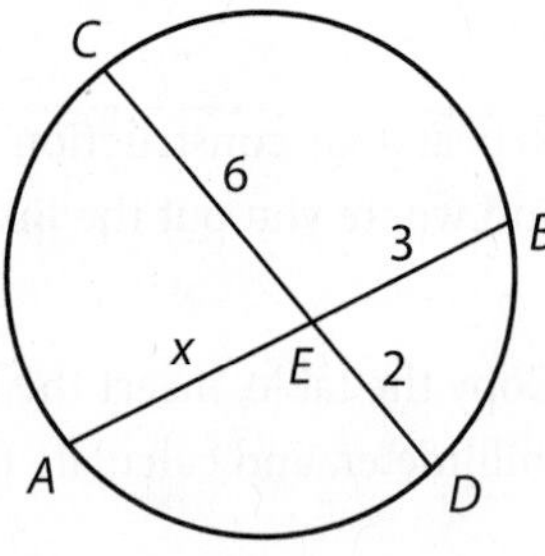

Add the segment lengths to find the length of each chord.

$CD = CE + ED = 6 + 2 = 8$

$AB = AE + EB = 4 + 3 = 7$

(B) Set up an equation according to the Chord-Chord Product Theorem and solve for x:

$HG \cdot GJ = KG \cdot GI$

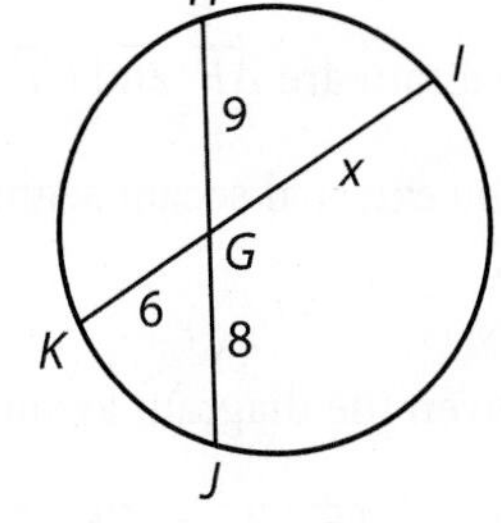

$9(8) = 6(x)$

$72 = 6x$

$12 = x$

Add the segment lengths together to find the lengths of each chord:

$HJ = HG + GJ = 9 + 8 = 17$

$KI = KG + GI = 6 + 12 = 18$

Your Turn

3. Given $AD = 12$. Find the value of x and the length of each chord.

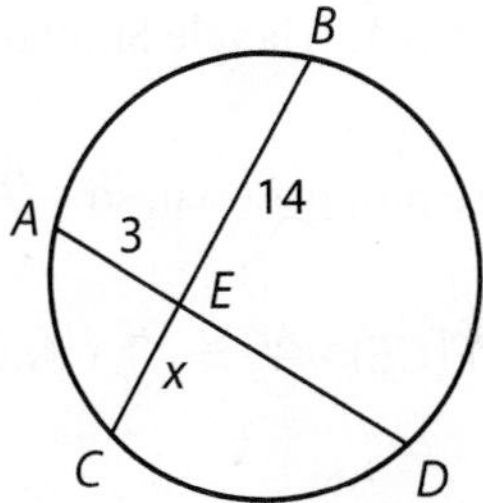

Explain 2 Proving the Secant-Secant Product Theorem

A **secant** is any line that intersects a circle at exactly two points. A **secant segment** is part of a secant line with at least one point on the circle. A secant segment that lies in the exterior of the circle with one point on the circle is called an **external secant segment**. Secant segments drawn from the same point in the exterior of a circle maintain a certain relationship that can be stated as a theorem.

Secant-Secant Product Theorem

If two secants intersect in the exterior of a circle, then the product of the lengths of one secant segment and its external segment equals the product of the lengths of the other secant segment and its external segment.

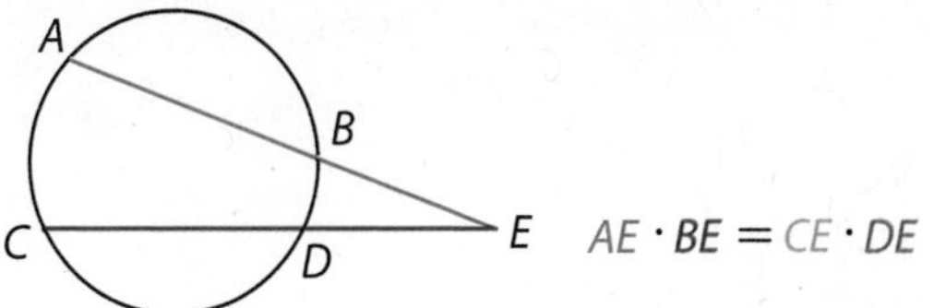

Example 2 **Use similar triangles to prove the Secant-Secant Product Theorem.**

Step 1 Identify the segments in the diagram. The whole secant segments in this diagram are $\overline{AE}$ and $\overline{CE}$.

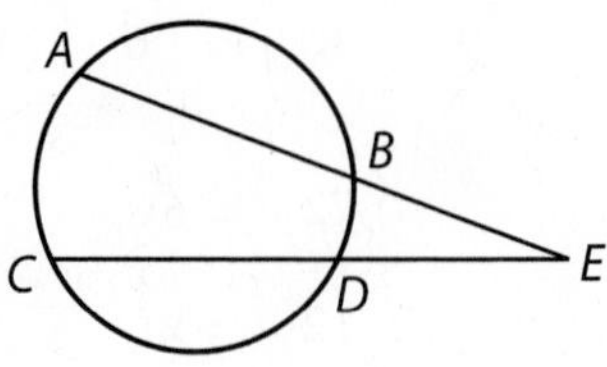

The external secant segments in this diagram are $\overline{BE}$ and $\overline{DE}$.

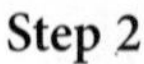

Step 2

Given the diagram as shown, prove that $AE \cdot BE = CE \cdot DE$.

Prove: $AE \cdot BE = CE \cdot DE$

Proof: Draw auxiliary line segments $\overline{AD}$ and $\overline{CB}$. $\angle EAD$ and $\angle ECB$ both intercept $\widehat{BD}$, so $\angle$ EAD $\cong \angle$ ECB. $\angle E \cong \angle E$ by the Reflexive Property. Thus, $\triangle EAD \sim \triangle ECB$ by the AA Triangle Similarity Theorem. Therefore, corresponding sides are proportional, so $\frac{AE}{CE} = \frac{DE}{BE}$. By the Multiplication Property of Equality, $BE(CE) \cdot \frac{AE}{CE} = \frac{DE}{BE} \cdot BE(CE)$, and thus $AE \cdot BE = CE \cdot DE$.

Reflect

4. Rewrite the Secant-Secant Theorem in your own words. Use a diagram or shortcut notation to help you remember what it means.

5. **Discussion**: Suppose that two secants are drawn so that they intersect on the circle. Can you determine anything about the lengths of the segments formed? Explain.

Explain 3 Applying the Secant-Secant Product Theorem

You can use the Secant-Secant Product Theorem to find unknown measures of secants and secant segments by setting up an equation.

Example 3 **Find the value of x and the length of each secant segment.**

Ⓐ Set up an equation according to the Secant-Secant Product Theorem and solve for x.

$AC \cdot AB = AE \cdot AD$

$(5 + x)(5) = (12)(6)$

$5x + 25 = 72$

$5x = 47$

$x = 9.4$

Add the segments together to find the lengths of each secant segment.

$AC = 5 + 9.4 = 14.4$; $AE = 6 + 6 = 12$

Ⓑ Set up an equation according to the Secant-Secant Product Theorem and solve for x.

$UP \cdot TP = SP \cdot RP$

$(x + 7)(7) = (14)(6)$

$7x + 49 = 84$

$7x = 35$

$x = 5$

Add the segments together to find the lengths of each secant segment.

$UP = 7 + 5 = 12$; $SP = 8 + 6 = 14$

Your Turn

Find the value of x and the length of each secant segment.

6.

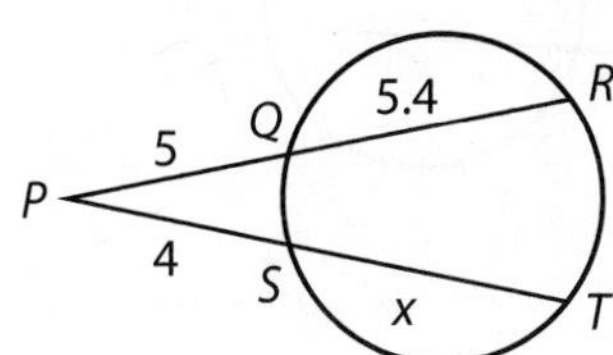

7.

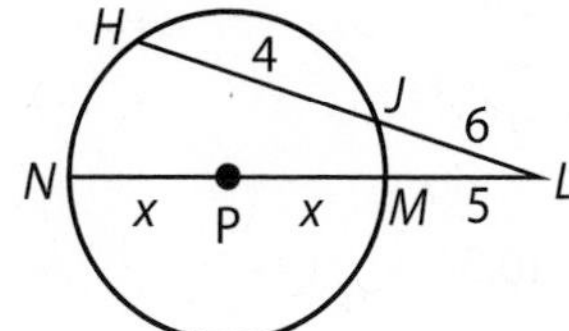

Explain 4 Applying the Secant-Tangent Product Theorem

A similar theorem applies when both a secant segment and tangent segment are drawn to a circle from the same exterior point. A **tangent segment** is a segment of a tangent line with exactly one endpoint on the circle.

Secant-Tangent Product Theorem

If a secant and a tangent intersect in the exterior of a circle, then the product of the lengths of the secant segment and its external segment equals the length of the tangent segment squared.

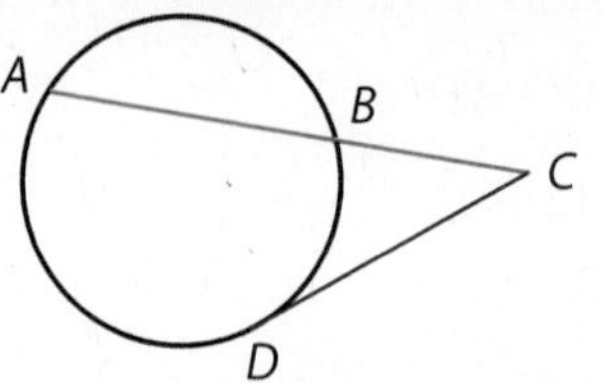

$AC \cdot BC = DC^2$

Example 4 **Find the value of x.**

(A) Given the diameter of the Earth as 8,000 miles, a satellite's orbit is 6,400 miles above the Earth. Its range, shown by $\overline{SP}$, is a tangent segment.

Set up an equation according to the Secant-Tangent Product Theorem and solve for x:

$$SA \cdot SE = SP^2$$

$$(8000 + 6400)(6400) = x^2$$

$$(14400)(6400) = x^2$$

$$92{,}160{,}000 = x^2$$

$$\pm 9600 = x$$

Since distance must be positive, the value of x must be 9600 miles.

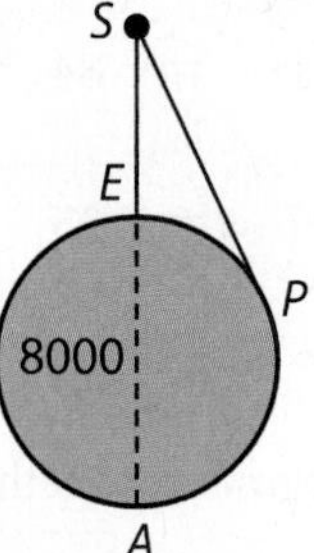

(B) Set up an equation according to the Secant-Tangent Product Theorem and solve for x:

$$BD \cdot BC = BA^2$$

$$(x + 2)(2) = 5^2$$

$$2x + 4 = 25$$

$$2x = 21$$

$$x = 10.5$$

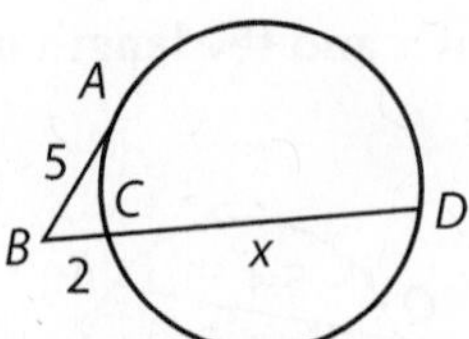

Reflect

8. Compare and contrast the Secant-Secant Product Theorem with the Secant-Tangent Product Theorem.

Your Turn

Find the value of *x*.

9. On a bird-watching trip, you travel along a path tangent to a circular pond to a lookout station that faces a hawk's nest. Given the measurements in the diagram on your bird-watching map, how far is the nest from the lookout station?

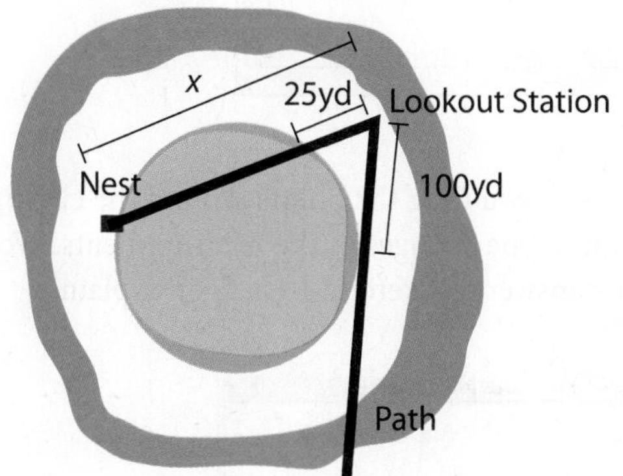

10.

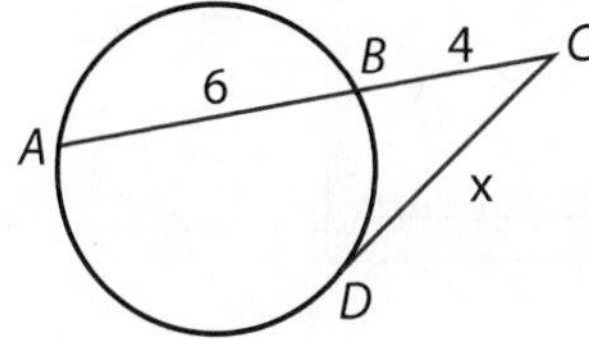

Elaborate

11. How is solving for *y* in the following diagram different from Example 3?

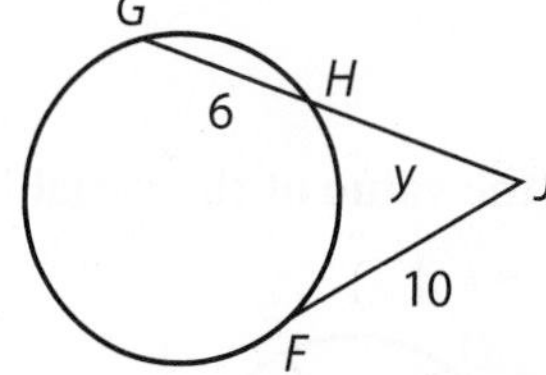

12. A circle is constructed with two secant segments that intersect outside the circle. If both external secant segments are equal, is it reasonable to conclude that both secant segments are equal? Explain.

13. **Essential Question Check-In** How are the theorems in this lesson related?

Evaluate: Homework and Practice

- Online Homework
- Hints and Help
- Extra Practice

Use the figure for Exercises 1–2.

Suppose you use geometry software to construct two chords $\overline{RS}$ and $\overline{TU}$ that intersect inside a circle at V.

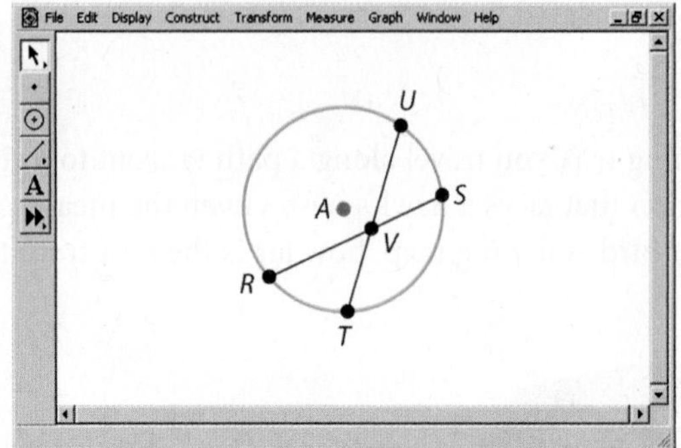

1. If you measured $\overline{RV}$, $\overline{VS}$, $\overline{TV}$, and $\overline{VU}$, what would be true about the relationship between their lengths?

2. Suppose you drag the points around the circle and examine the changes in the measurements. Would your answer to Exercise 1 change? Explain.

Use the figure for Exercises 3–4.

Suppose you use geometry software to construct two secants $\overleftrightarrow{DC}$ and $\overleftrightarrow{BE}$ that intersect outside a circle at F.

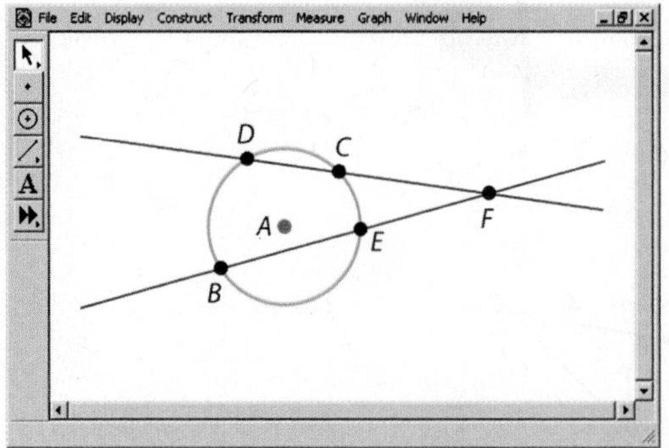

3. If you measured $\overline{DF}$, $\overline{CF}$, $\overline{BF}$, and $\overline{EF}$, what would be true about the relationship between their lengths?

4. Suppose you drag F and examine the changes in the measurements. Would your answer to Exercise 3 change? Explain.

Find the value of the variable and the length of each chord.

5.

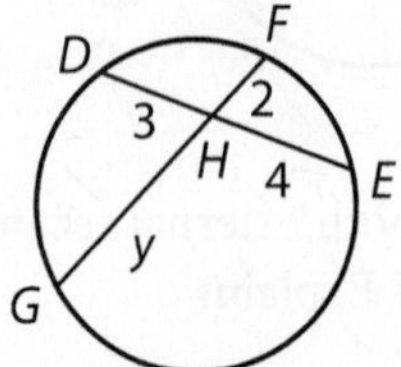

6.

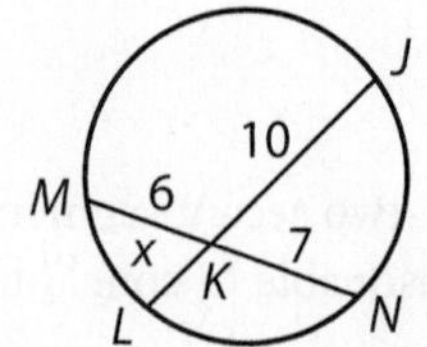

7. M is the midpoint of $\overline{PQ}$, The diameter of circle O is 13 in. and $RM = 4$ in.

a. Find PM.

b. Find PQ.

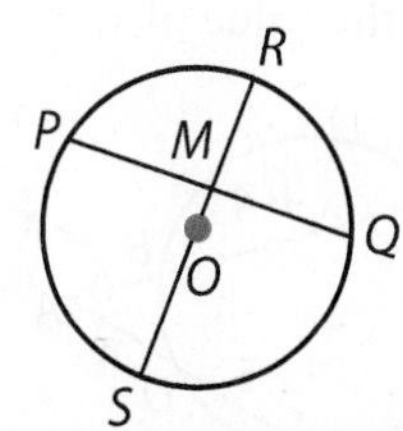

8. Representing a Real-World Problem A broken pottery shard found at archaeological dig has a curved edge. Find the diameter of the original plate. (Use the fact that the diameter $\overline{PR}$ is the perpendicular bisector of chord $\overline{AB}$.)

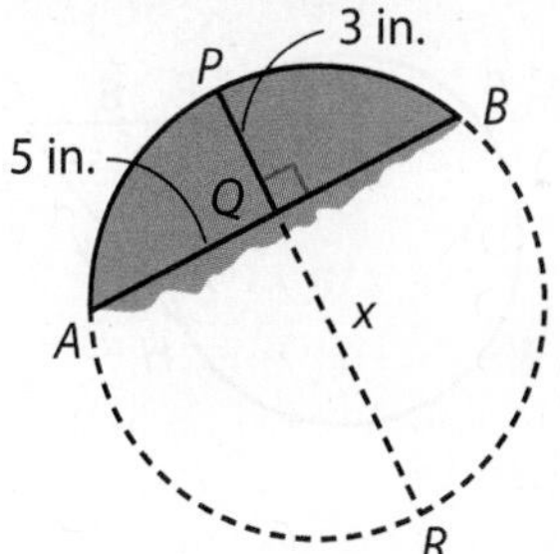

9. Critique Reasoning A student drew a circle and two secant segments. He concluded that if $\overline{PQ} \cong \overline{PS}$, then $\overline{QR} \cong \overline{ST}$. Do you agree with the student's conclusion? Why or why not?

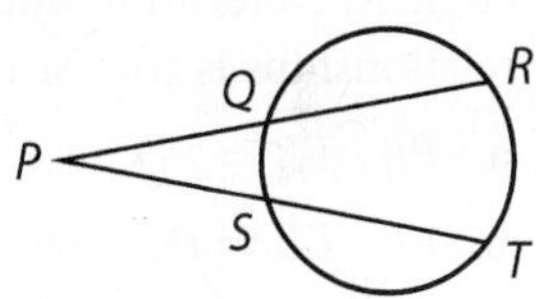

Find the value of the variable and the length of each secant segment.

10.

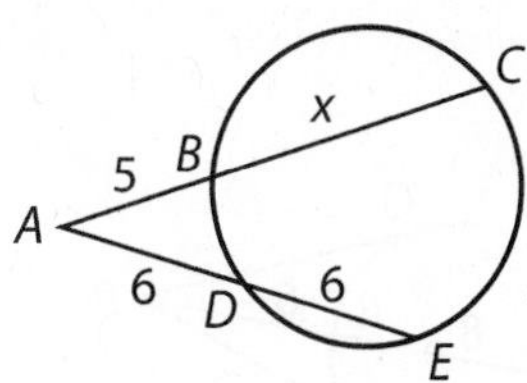

11.

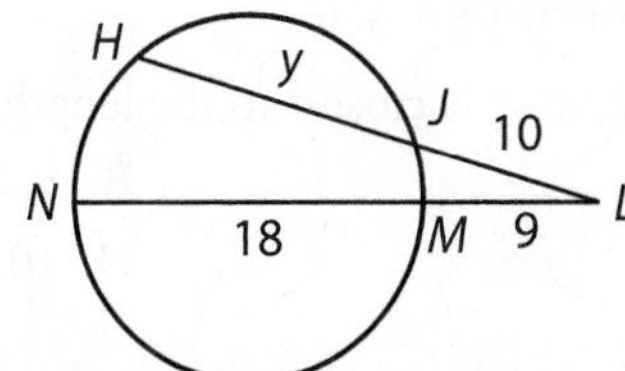

12. Find the value of x.

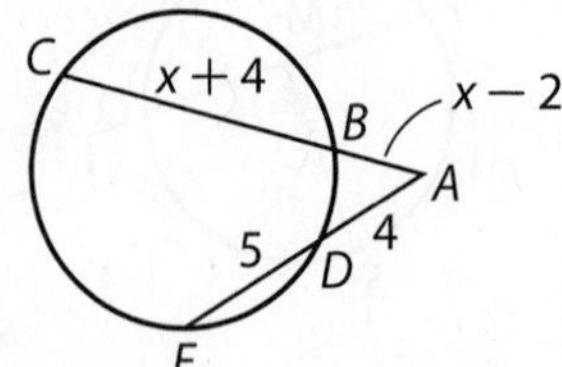

Find the value of the variable.

13.

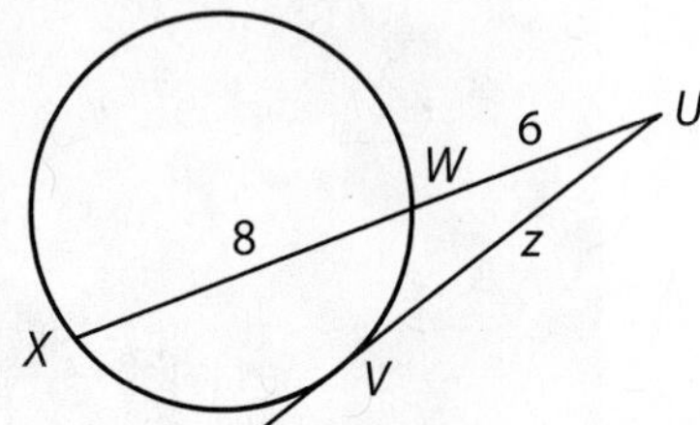

14.

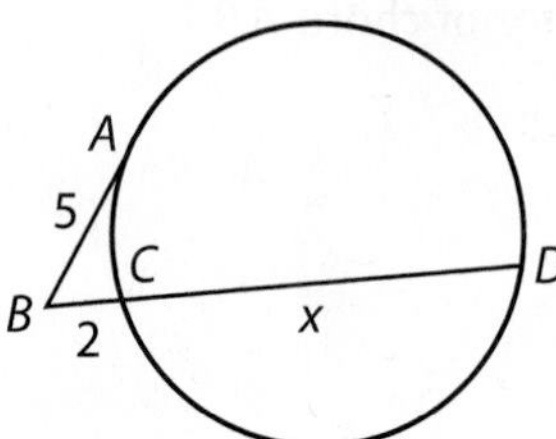

15.

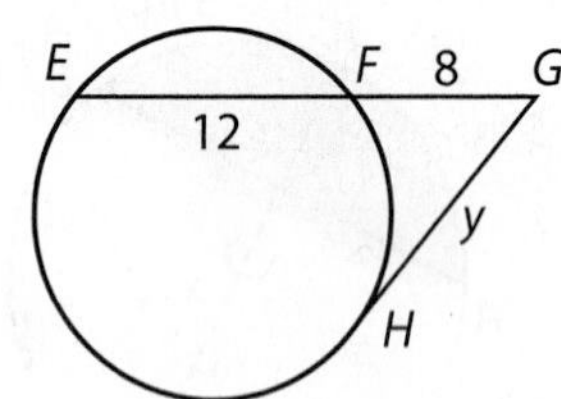

16. Tangent $\overleftrightarrow{PF}$ and secants $\overleftrightarrow{PD}$ and $\overleftrightarrow{PB}$ are drawn to circle A. Determine whether each of the following relationships is true or false. .

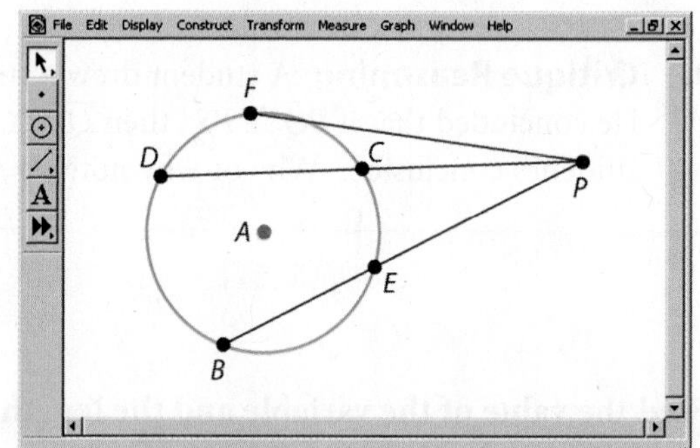

a. $PB \cdot EB = PD \cdot DC$

b. $PE \cdot EB = PC \cdot DC$

c. $PB \cdot PE = PF^2$

d. $PB \cdot DC = PD \cdot EB$

e. $PB \cdot PE = PD \cdot PC$

f. $PB \cdot PE = PF \cdot PC$

17. Which of these is closest to the length of tangent segment $\overline{PQ}$?

A. 6.9 B. 9.2

C. 9.9 D. 10.6

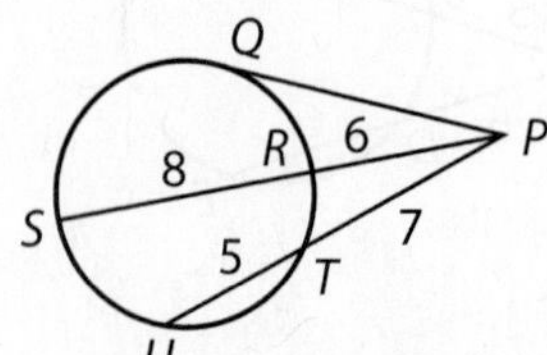

18. Explain the Error Below is a student's work to find the value of x. Explain the error and find the correct value of x.

$AB \cdot BC = DC^2$

$6(4) = x^2$

$x^2 = 24$

$x = \pm\sqrt{24} = \pm 2\sqrt{6}$

19. Represent Real-World Problems Molokini is a small, crescent-shaped island $2\frac{1}{2}$ miles from the Maui, Hawaii, coast. It is all that remains of an extinct volcano. To approximate the diameter of the mouth of the volcano, a geologist used a diagram like the one shown. The geologist assumed that the mouth of the volcano was a circle. What was the approximate diameter of the volcano's mouth to the nearest ten feet?

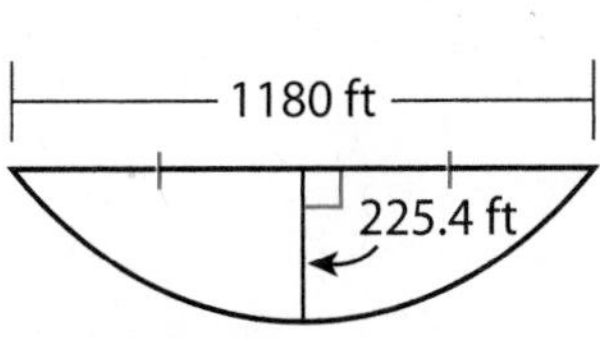

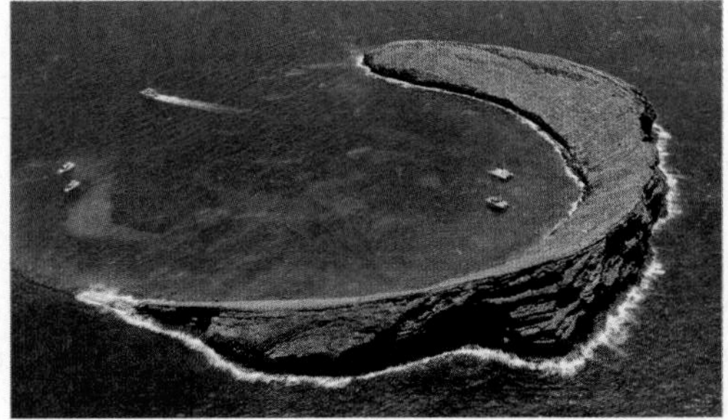

20. Multi-step Find the value of both variables in the figure.

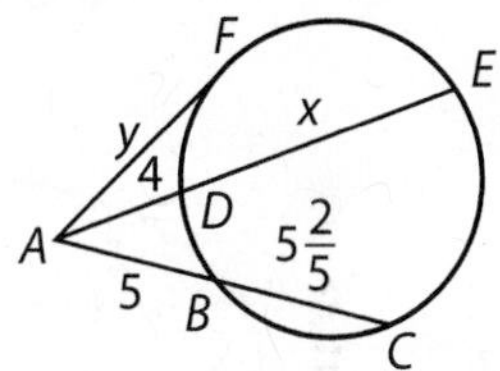

21. $\overline{KL}$ is a tangent segment of circle N and $\overline{KM}$ and $\overline{LM}$ are secants of the circle. Find the value of x.

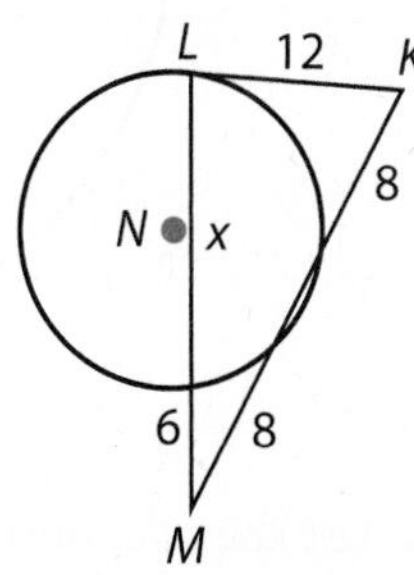

H.O.T. Focus on Higher Order Thinking

22. Justify Reasoning Prove the Chord-Chord Product Theorem

Given: Chords $\overline{AB}$ and $\overline{CD}$ intersect at point E.

Prove: $AE \cdot EB = CE \cdot ED$ (*Hint*: Draw $\overline{AC}$ and $\overline{BD}$.)

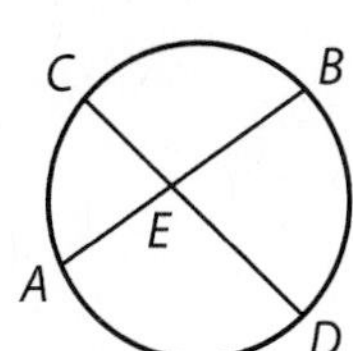

23. Justify Reasoning $\overline{PQ}$ is a tangent segment of a circle with radius 4 in. Q lies on the circle, and $PQ = 6$ in. Make a sketch and find the distance from P to the circle. Round to the nearest tenth of an inch. Explain your reasoning.

24. Justify Reasoning The circle in the diagram has radius c. Use this diagram and the Chord-Chord Product Theorem to prove the Pythagorean Theorem.

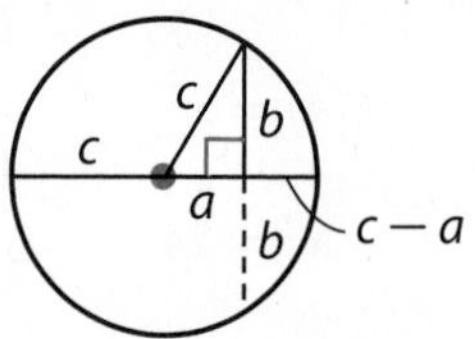

25. Critical Thinking The radius of circle A is 4. $CD = 4$, and $\overline{CB}$ is a tangent segment. Describe two different methods you can use to find BC.

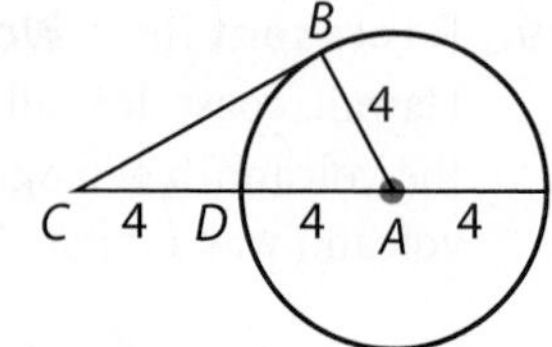

Lesson Performance Task

The figure shows the basic design of a Wankel rotary engine. The triangle is equilateral, with sides measuring 10 inches. An arc on each side of the triangle has as its center the vertex on the opposite side of the triangle. In the figure, the arc ADB is an arc of a circle with its center at C.

a. Use the sketch of the engine. What is the measure of each arc along the side of the triangle?

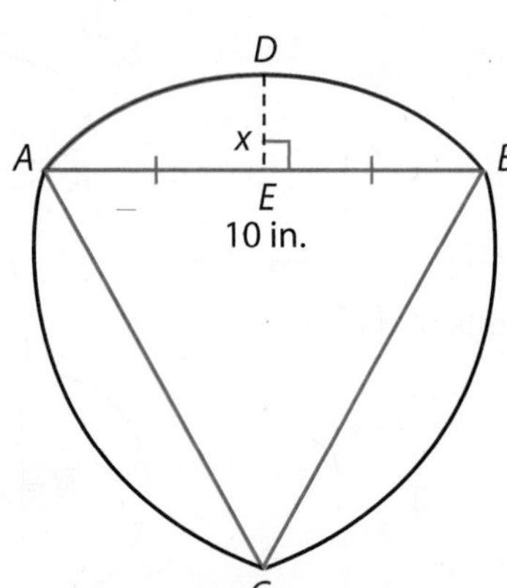

b. Use the relationships in an equilateral triangle to find the value of x. Explain.

c. Use the Chord-Chord Product Theorem to find the value of x. Explain.

15.5 Angle Relationships in Circles

Essential Question: What are the relationships between angles formed by lines that intersect a circle?

Explore Exploring Angle Measures in Circles

The sundial is one of many instruments that use angles created in circles for practical applications, such as telling time.

In this lesson, you will observe the relationships between angles created by various line segments and their intercepted arcs.

(A) Using geometry software, construct a circle with two secants $\overleftrightarrow{CD}$ and $\overleftrightarrow{EF}$ that intersect inside the circle at G, as shown in the figure.

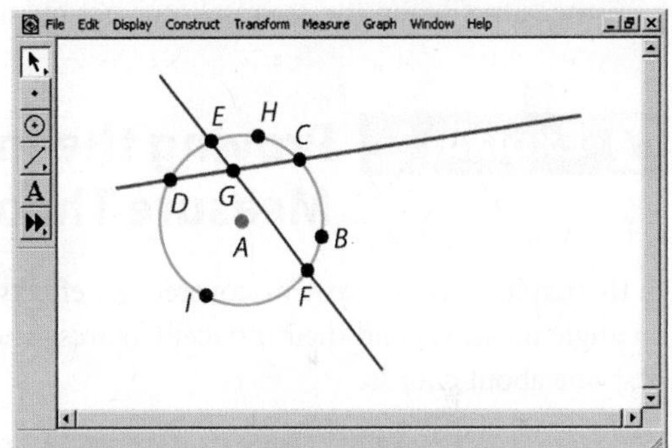

(B) Create two new points H and I that are on the circle as shown. These will be used to measure the arcs. Hide B if desired.

(C) Measure $\angle DGF$ formed by the secant lines, and measure $\overset{\frown}{CHE}$ and $\overset{\frown}{DIF}$. Copy the table and record the angle and arc measurements in the first column.

$m\angle DGF$	?	?	?	?	?	?
$m\overset{\frown}{CHE}$	?	?	?	?	?	?
$m\overset{\frown}{DIF}$	?	?	?	?	?	?
Sum of Arc Measures	?	?	?	?	?	?

(D) Drag F around the circle and record the changes in measures in the table in Part C. Try to create acute, right, and obtuse angles. Be sure to keep H between C and E and I between D and F for accurate arc measurement. Move them if necessary.

Reflect

1. Can you make a conjecture about the relationship between the angle measure and the two arc measures?

2. Using the same circle you created in step A, drag points around the circle so that the intersection is outside the circle, as shown. Measure $\angle FGC$ formed by the secant lines and measure $\overset{\frown}{CIF}$ and $\overset{\frown}{DHE}$. Drag points around the circle and observe the changes in measures. Copy the table and record some of your measurements.

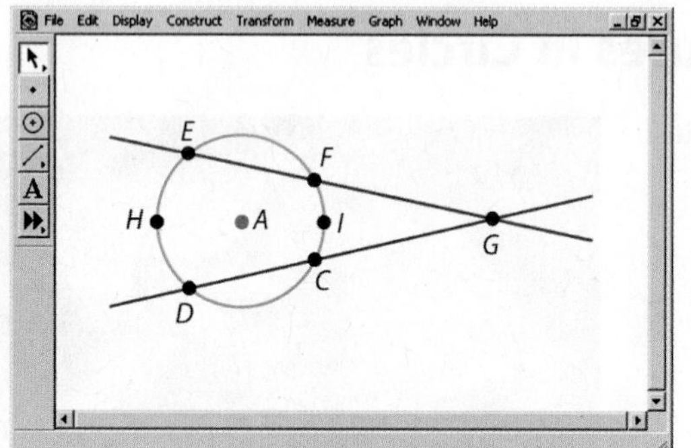

$m\angle FGC$	?	?	?
$m\overset{\frown}{CIF}$	?	?	?
$m\overset{\frown}{DHE}$	?	?	?
Difference of Arc Measures	?	?	?

What is similar and different about the relationships between the angle measure and the arc measures when the secants intersect outside the circle?

Explain 1 Proving the Intersecting Chords Angle Measure Theorem

In the Explore section, you discovered the effects that line segments, such as chords and secants, have on angle measures and their intercepted arcs. These relationships can be stated as theorems, with the first one about chords.

The Intersecting Chords Angle Measure Theorem

If two secants or chords intersect in the interior of a circle, then the measure of each angle formed is half the sum of the measures of its intercepted arcs.

Chords $\overline{AD}$ and $\overline{BC}$ intersect at E.

$m\angle 1 = \frac{1}{2}\left(m\overset{\frown}{AB} + m\overset{\frown}{CD}\right)$

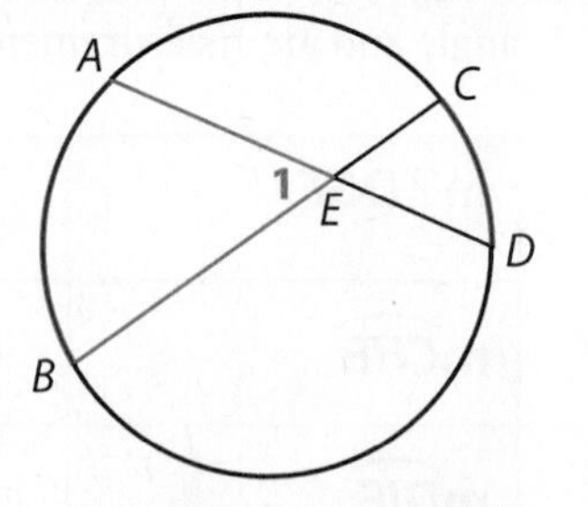

Example 1 **Prove the Intersecting Chords Angle Measure Theorem**

Given: $\overline{AD}$ and $\overline{BC}$ intersect at E.

Prove: $m\angle 1 = \frac{1}{2}\left(m\overset{\frown}{AB} + m\overset{\frown}{CD}\right)$

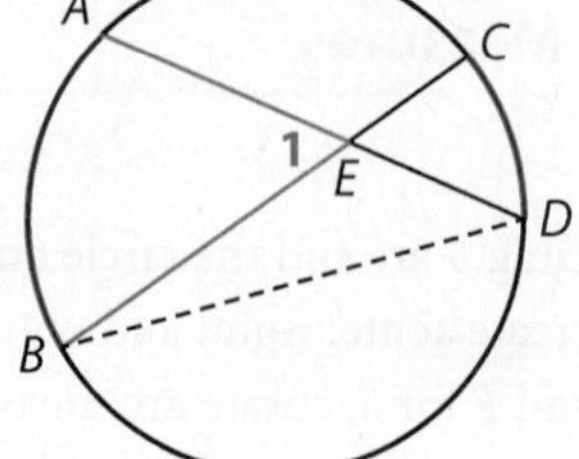

Statements	Reasons
1. $\overline{AD}$ and $\overline{BC}$ intersect at E.	1. Given
2. Draw $\overline{BD}$.	2. Through any two points, there is exactly one line.
3. $m\angle 1 = m\angle EDB + m\angle EBD$	3. Exterior Angle Theorem
4. $m\angle EDB = \frac{1}{2} m\widehat{AB}$, $m\angle EBD = \frac{1}{2} m\widehat{CD}$	4. Inscribed Angle Theorem
5. $m\angle 1 = \frac{1}{2} m\widehat{AB} + \frac{1}{2} m\widehat{CD}$	5. Substitution Property
6. $m\angle 1 = \frac{1}{2}\left(m\widehat{AB} + m\widehat{CD}\right)$	6. Distributive Property

Reflect

3. **Discusssion** Explain how an auxiliary segment and the Exterior Angle Theorem are used in the proof of the Intersecting Chords Angle Measure Theorem.

Your Turn

Find each unknown measure.

4. $m\angle MPK$

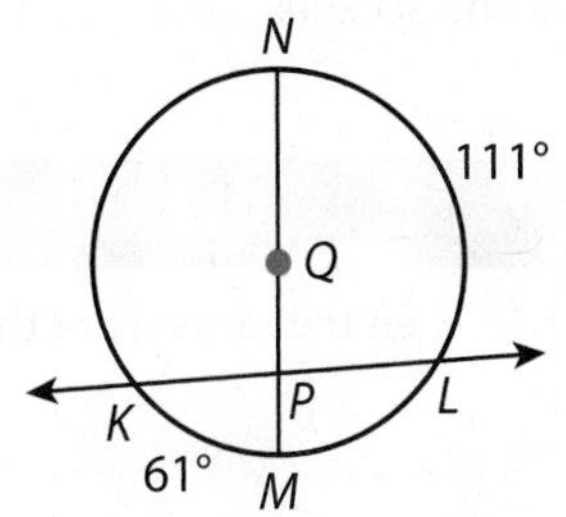

5. $m\widehat{PR}$

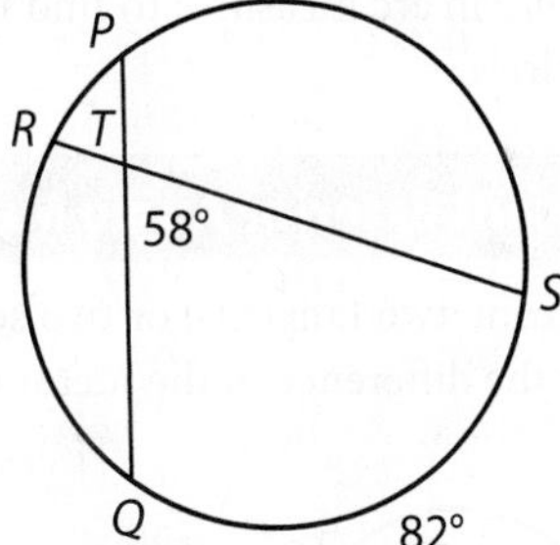

Explain 2 Applying the Tangent-Secant Interior Angle Measure Theorem

The angle and arc formed by a tangent and secant intersecting *on* a circle also have a special relationship.

The Tangent-Secant Interior Angle Measure Theorem

If a tangent and a secant (or a chord) intersect on a circle at the point of tangency, then the measure of the angle formed is half the measure of its intercepted arc.

Tangent $\overrightarrow{BC}$ and secant $\overrightarrow{BA}$ intersect at B.

$$m\angle ABC = \frac{1}{2} m\widehat{AB}$$

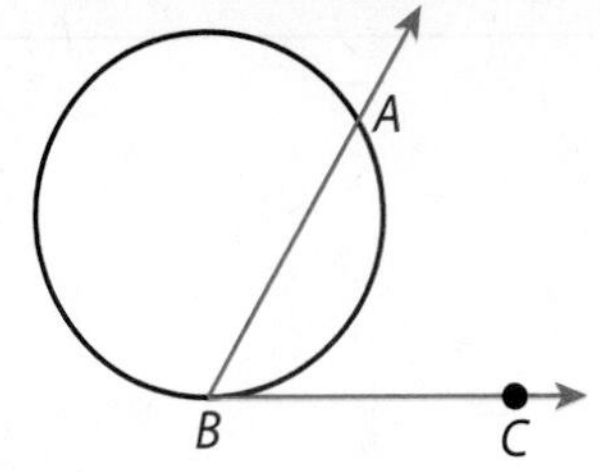

Example 2 **Find each unknown measure.**

Ⓐ $m\angle BCD$

$$m\angle BCD = \frac{1}{2}m\overset{\frown}{BC}$$
$$= \frac{1}{2}(142°)$$
$$= 71°$$

Ⓑ $m\overset{\frown}{ABC}$

$$m\angle ACD = \frac{1}{2}\left(m\overset{\frown}{ABC}\right)$$
$$\boxed{90°} = \frac{1}{2}\left(m\overset{\frown}{ABC}\right)$$
$$\boxed{180°} = m\overset{\frown}{ABC}$$

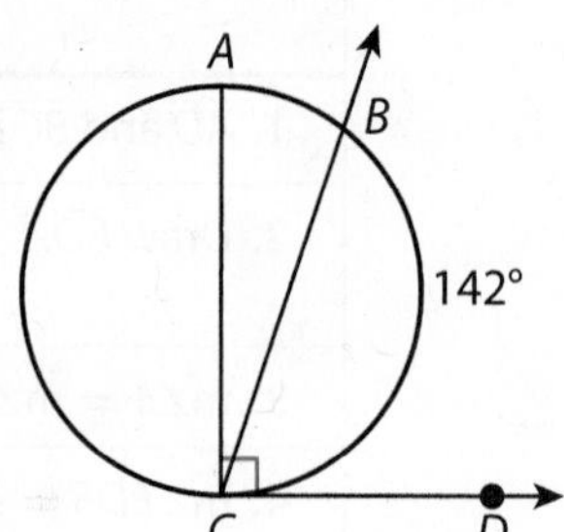

Your Turn

Find the measure.

6. $m\overset{\frown}{PN}$

7. $m\angle MNP$

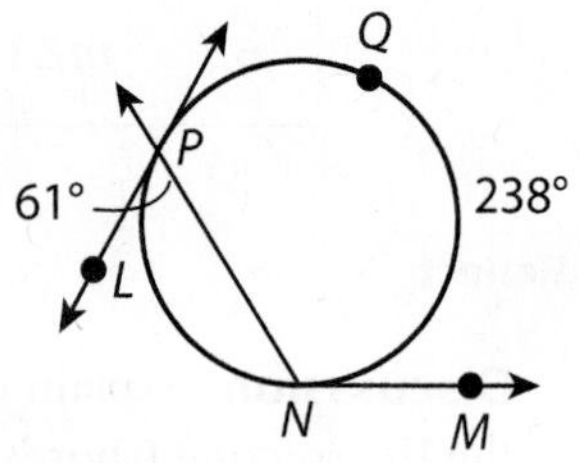

Explain 3 Applying the Tangent-Secant Exterior Angle Measure Theorem

You can use the *difference* in arc measures to find measures of angles formed by tangents and secants intersecting *outside* a circle.

The Tangent-Secant Exterior Angle Measure Theorem

If a tangent and a secant, two tangents, or two secants intersect in the exterior of a circle, then the measure of the angle formed is half the difference of the measures of its intercepted arcs.

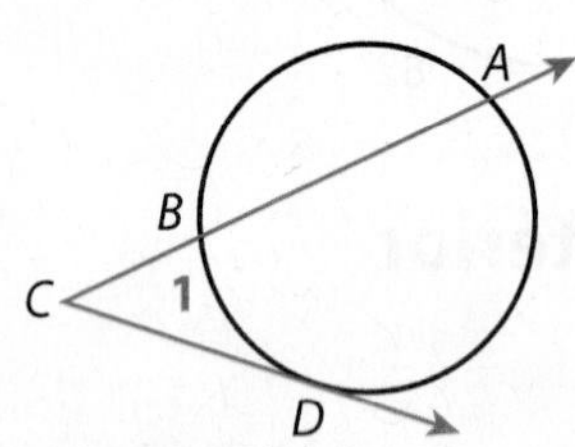

$$m\angle 1 = \frac{1}{2}\left(m\overset{\frown}{AD} - m\overset{\frown}{BD}\right)$$

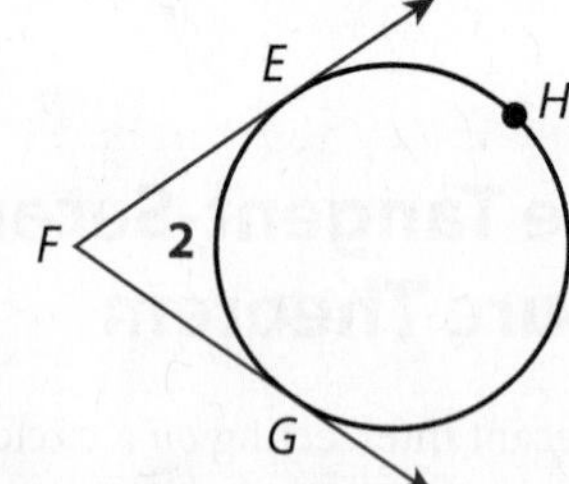

$$m\angle 2 = \frac{1}{2}\left(m\overset{\frown}{EHG} - m\overset{\frown}{EG}\right)$$

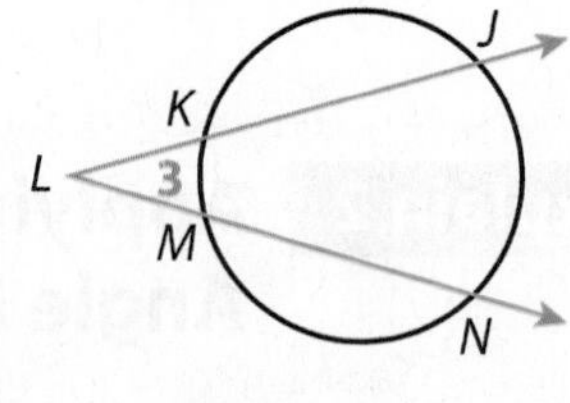

$$m\angle 3 = \frac{1}{2}\left(m\overset{\frown}{JN} - m\overset{\frown}{KM}\right)$$

Example 3 **Find the value of x.**

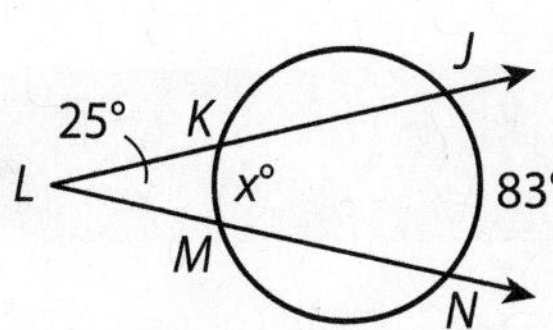

$$m\angle L = \frac{1}{2}\left(m\widehat{JN} - m\widehat{KM}\right)$$

$$25° = \frac{1}{2}(83° - x°)$$

$$50 = 83 - x$$

$$-33 = -x$$

$$33 = x$$

(B)

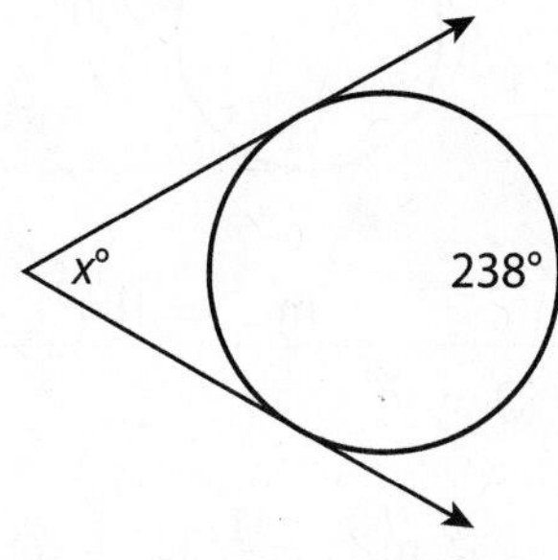

$$x° = \frac{1}{2}\left(238° - \left(360° - \boxed{238°}\right)\right)$$

$$x = \frac{1}{2}\left(238 - \boxed{122}\right)$$

$$x = \frac{1}{2}\left(\boxed{116}\right)$$

$$x = \boxed{58}$$

Your Turn

Find the value of x.

8.

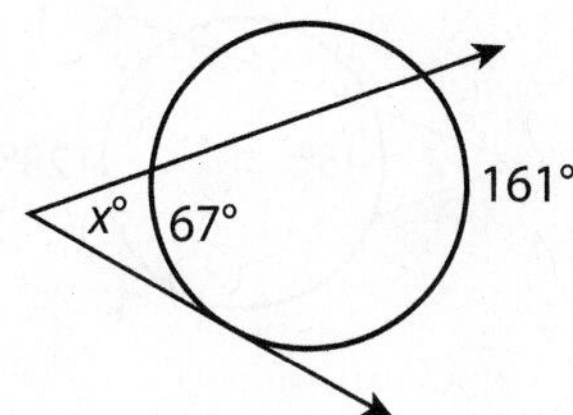

9. The superior oblique and inferior oblique are two muscles that help control eye movement. They intersect behind the eye to create an angle, as shown. If $m\widehat{AEB} = 225°$, what is $m\angle ACB$?

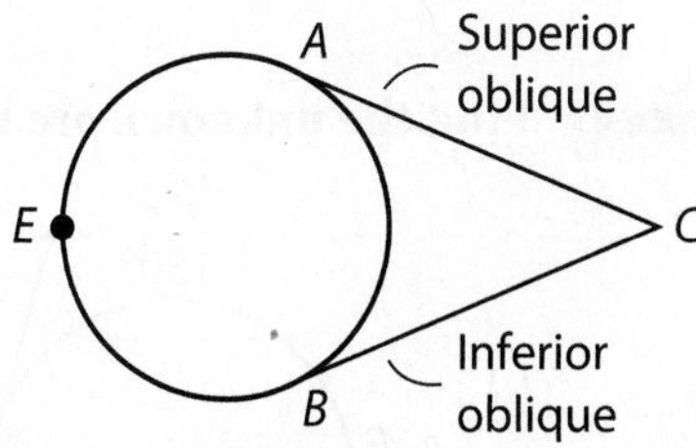

Explain 4 Understanding Angle Relationships in Circles

You can summarize angle relationships in circles by looking at where the vertex of the angle lies: on the circle, inside the circle, or outside the circle.

Angle Relationships in Circles		
Vertex of the Angle	**Measure of Angle**	**Diagrams**
On a circle	Half the measure of its intercepted arc	120°; $m\angle 1 = 60°$ 200°; $m\angle 2 = 100°$
Inside a circle	Half the sum of the measures of its intercepted arcs	44°, 86°; $m\angle 1 = \frac{1}{2}(44° + 86°)$ $= 65°$
Outside a circle	Half the difference of the measures of its intercepted arcs	78°, 202°; $m\angle 1 = \frac{1}{2}(202° - 78°)$ $= 62°$ 45°, 125°; $m\angle 2 = \frac{1}{2}(125° - 45°)$ $= 40°$

Example 4 Find the unknown arc measures.

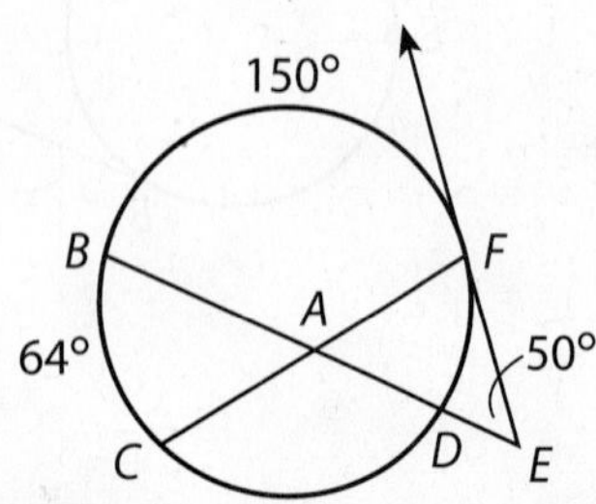

Ⓐ Find m$\widehat{FD}$.

$$m\angle E = \frac{1}{2}\left(m\widehat{BF} - m\widehat{FD}\right)$$
$$50° = \frac{1}{2}\left(150° - m\widehat{FD}\right)$$
$$100° = \left(50° - m\widehat{FD}\right)$$
$$-50° = -m\widehat{FD}$$
$$50° = m\widehat{FD}$$

Ⓑ Find $m\widehat{CD}$.

$$m\widehat{CD} = \boxed{360°} - \left(m\widehat{BC} + m\widehat{BF} + m\widehat{FD}\right)$$
$$= \boxed{360°} - \left(64° + \boxed{150°} + \boxed{50°}\right)$$
$$= \boxed{360°} - \boxed{264°}$$
$$= \boxed{96°}$$

Your Turn

10. Find m$\widehat{KN}$.

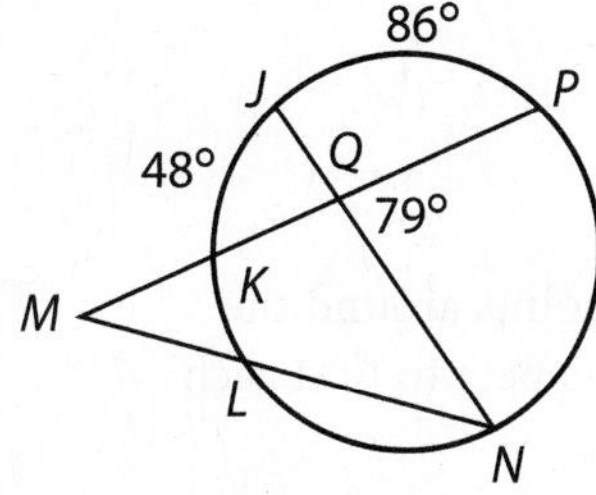

Elaborate

11. Copy and complete the graphic organizer that shows the relationship between the angle measurement and the location of its vertex.

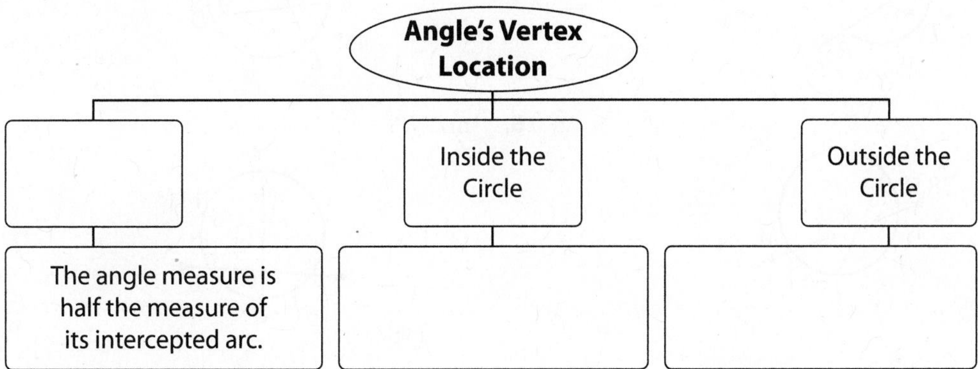

12. **Essential Question Check-In** What is similar about all the relationships between angle measures and their intercepted arcs?

Evaluate: Homework and Practice

- Online Homework
- Hints and Help
- Extra Practice

Use the figure for Exercises 1–2.

Suppose you use geometry software to construct a secant $\overleftrightarrow{CE}$ and tangent $\overleftrightarrow{CD}$ that intersect on a circle at point *C*.

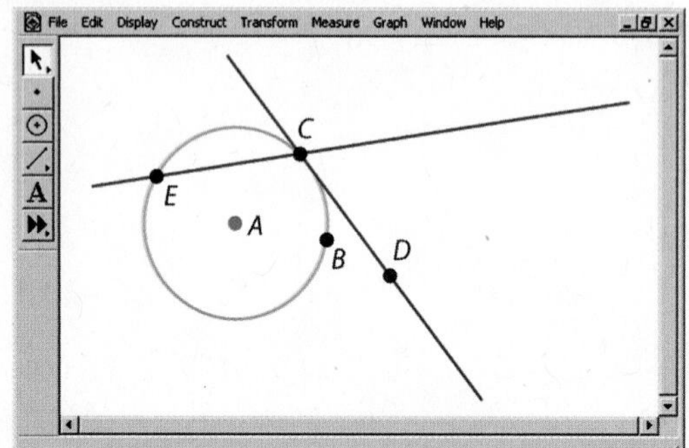

1. Suppose you measure $\angle DCE$ and you measure $\overset{\frown}{CBE}$. Then you drag the points around the circle and measure the angle and arc three more times. What would you expect to find each time? Which theorem from the lesson would you be demonstrating?

2. When the measure of the intercepted arc is 180°, what is the measure of the angle? What does that tell you about the secant?

Find each measure.

3. $m\angle QPR$

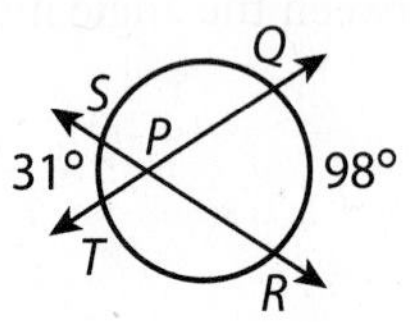

4. $m\angle ABC$

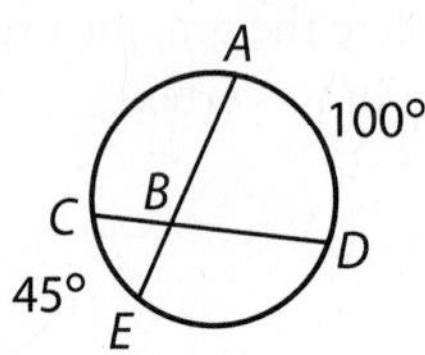

5. $m\angle MKJ$

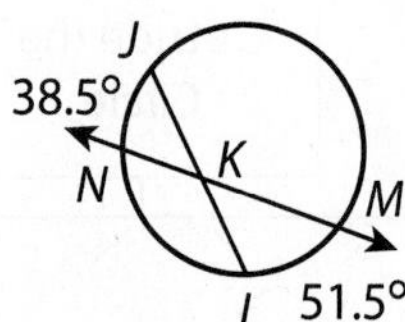

6. $m\angle NPK$

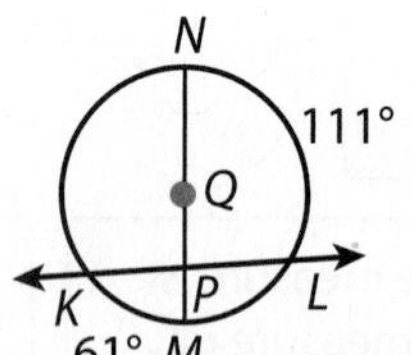

Find each measure. Use the figure for Exercises 7–8.

7. $m\angle BCD$

8. $m\angle ABC$

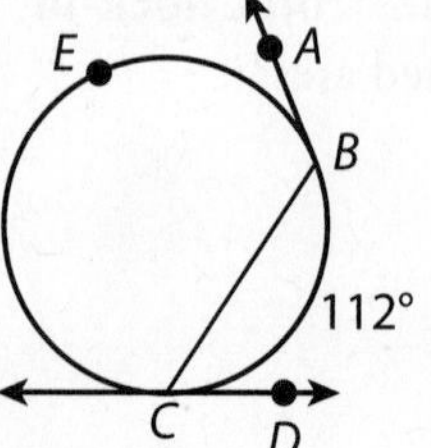

Find each measure. Use the figure for Exercises 9–10.

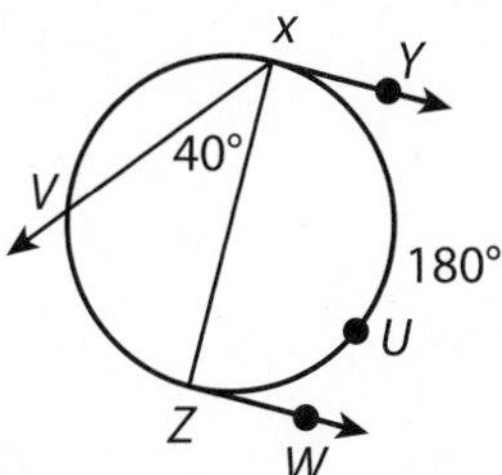

9. $m\angle XZW$

10. $m\angle YXZ$

Find the value of *x*.

11.

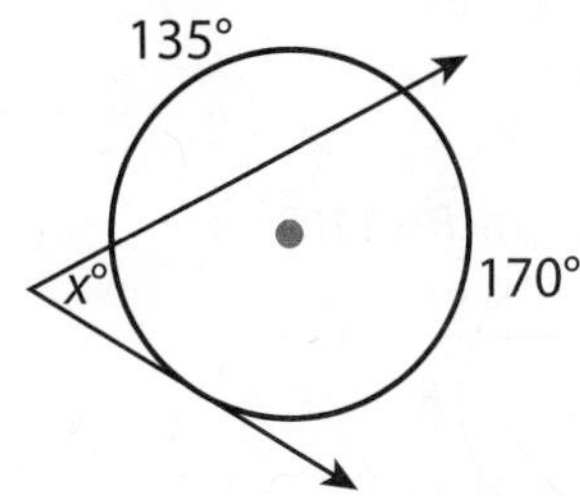

12.

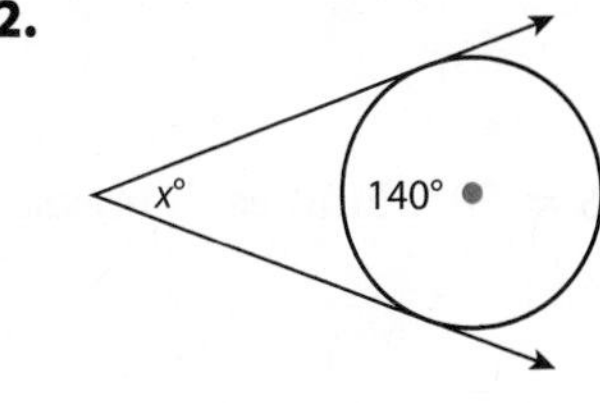

13.

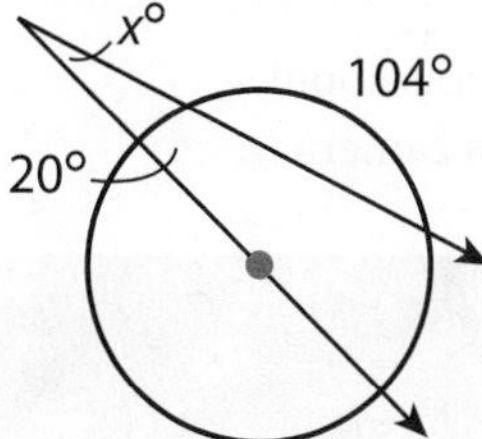

14. Represent Real-World Problems Stonehenge is a circular arrangement of massive stones near Salisbury, England. A viewer at V observes the monument from a point where two of the stones A and B are aligned with stones at the endpoints of a diameter of the circular shape. Given that $m\overset{\frown}{AB} = 48°$, what is $m\angle AVB$?

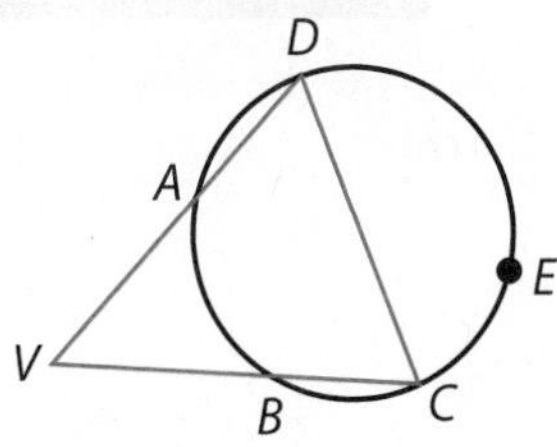

15. **Multi-Step** Find each measure.

a. Find m$\widehat{PN}$.

b. Use your answer to part a to find m$\widehat{KN}$.

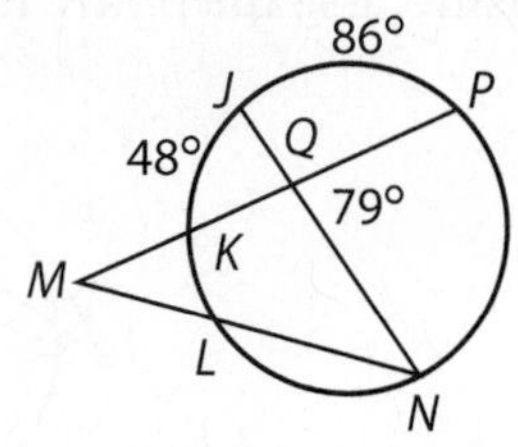

16. **Multi-Step** Find each measure.

a. Find m$\widehat{DE}$.

b. Use your answer to part a to find m∠F.

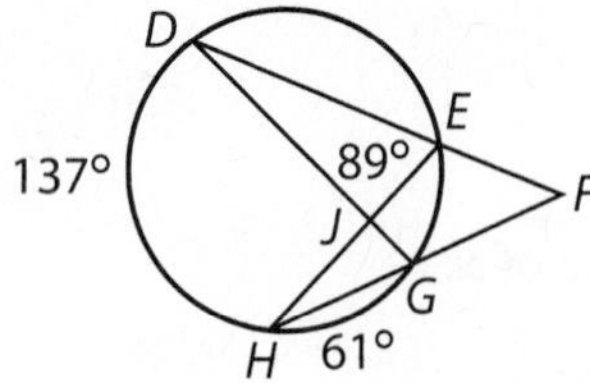

$\overleftrightarrow{MS} \parallel \overleftrightarrow{PQ}$ **and m∠PNS = 50°. Find each measure.**

17. m$\widehat{PR}$

18. m$\widehat{LP}$

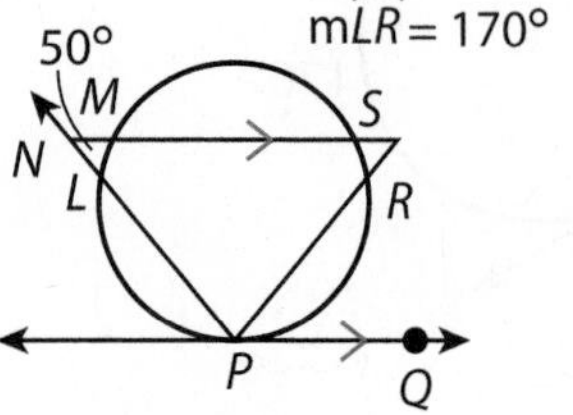

19. **Represent Real-World Problems** A satellite orbits Mars. When it reaches S it is about 12,000 km above the planet. What is $x°$, the measure of the arc that is visible to a camera in the satellite?

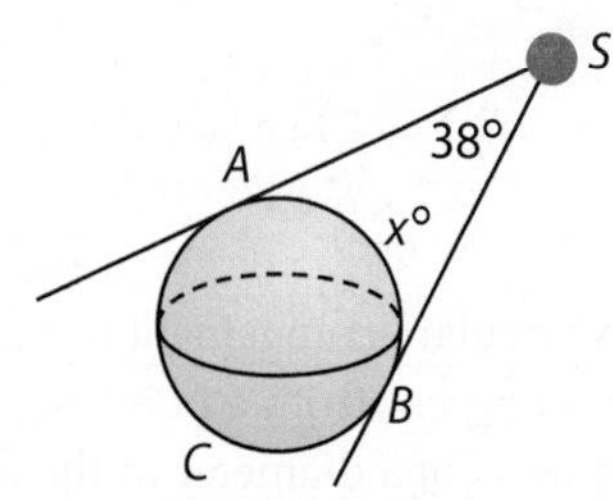

20. Use the circle with center J. Match each angle or arc on the left with its measure on the right. Indicate a match by writing the letter for the angle or arc on the line in front of the corresponding measure.

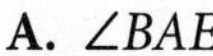

A. $\angle BAE$	**a.** ___?___	41°
B. $\angle ACD$	**b.** ___?___	180°
C. $\overset{\frown}{AF}$	**c.** ___?___	101°
D. $\angle AED$	**d.** ___?___	90°
E. $\overset{\frown}{ADE}$	**e.** ___?___	60°

21. Use the Plan for Proof to write a proof for one case of the Tangent-Secant Exterior Angle Measure Theorem.

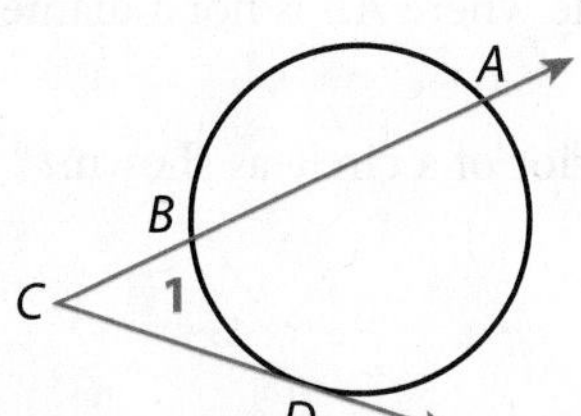

Given: Tangent $\overrightarrow{CD}$ and secant $\overrightarrow{CA}$

Prove: $m\angle ACD = \frac{1}{2}\left(m\overset{\frown}{AD} - m\overset{\frown}{BD}\right)$

Plan: Draw auxiliary line segment $\overline{BD}$. Use the Exterior Angle Theorem to show that $m\angle ACD = m\angle ABD - m\angle BDC$. Then use the Inscribed Angle Theorem and the Tangent-Secant Interior Angle Measure Theorem.

22. Justify Reasoning Write a proof that the figure shown is a square.
Given: $\overline{YZ}$ and $\overline{WZ}$ are tangent to circle X, $m\overset{\frown}{WY} = 90°$

Prove: $WXYZ$ is a square.

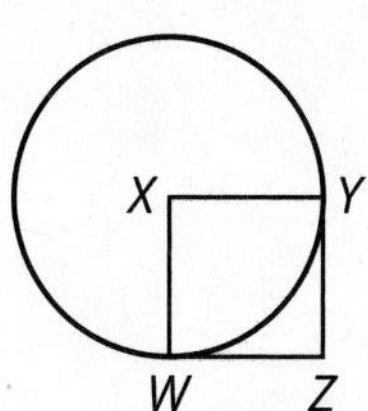

H.O.T. Focus on Higher Order Thinking

23. Justify Reasoning Prove the Tangent-Secant Interior Angle Theorem.

Given: Tangent $\overrightarrow{BC}$ and secant $\overrightarrow{BA}$

Prove: $m\angle ABC = \frac{1}{2}m\overset{\frown}{AB}$

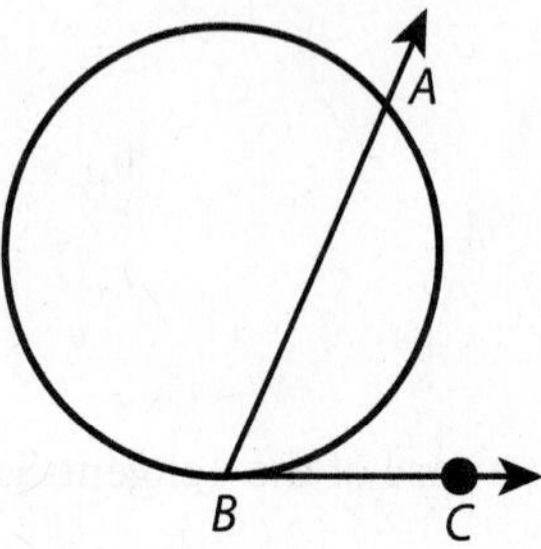

$\left(Hint\text{: Consider two cases, one where } \overline{AB} \text{ is a diameter and one where } \overline{AB} \text{ is not a diameter.}\right)$

24. Critical Thinking Suppose two secants intersect in the exterior of a circle as shown. Which is greater, $m\angle 1$ or $m\angle 2$? Justify your answer.

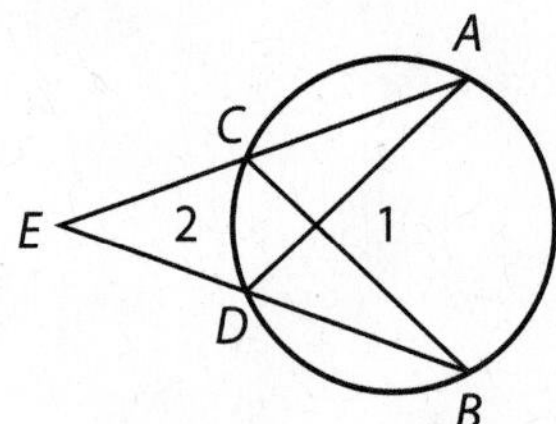

Lesson Performance Task

The diameter of the Moon is about 2160 miles. From Earth, the portion of the Moon's surface that an observer can see is from a circumscribed angle of approximately 0.5°.

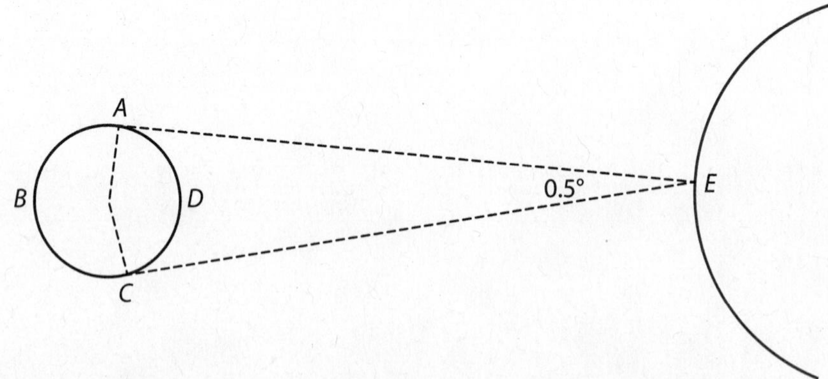

a. Find the measure of $\overset{\frown}{ADC}$. Explain how you found the measure.

b. What fraction of the circumference of the Moon is represented by $\overset{\frown}{ADC}$?

c. Find the length of $\overset{\frown}{ADC}$. You can use the formula $C = 2\pi r$ to find the circumference of the Moon.

STUDY GUIDE REVIEW

Angles and Segments in Circles

MODULE 15

Essential Question: How can you use angles and segments in circles to solve real-world problems?

Key Vocabulary

chord *(cuerda)*
central angle *(ángulo central)*
inscribed angle *(ángulo inscrito)*
arc *(arco)*
minor arc *(arco menor)*
major arc *(arco principal)*
semicircle *(semicirculo)*
adjacent arcs *(arcos adyacentes)*
Inscribed Angle Theorem *(teorema del ángulo inscrito)*
Inscribed Quadrilateral Theorem *(teorema del ángulo inscrito)*
tangent *(tangent)*
point of tangency *(punto de tangencia)*
Tangent-Radius Theorem *(teorema de la tangente-radio)*
Chord-Chord Product Theorem *(teorema del producto de la cuerda de la cuerda)*
secant *(secante)*
secant segment *(segmente secante)*
external secant segment *(segmento externo secante)*
Secant-Secant Theorem *(Teorema de la secante-secante)*
tangent segment *(segmento tangente)*
Intersecting Chords Angle Measure Theorem *(teorema de medida de ángulo de intersección acordes)*
Tangent-Secant Interior Angle Measure Theorem *(teorema de la medida de ángulo interior tangente-secante)*
Tangent-Secant Exterior Angle Measure Theorem *(teorema de la medida de ángulo exterior tangente-secante)*

KEY EXAMPLE (Lesson 15.1)

Determine $m\widehat{DE}$, $m\widehat{BD}$, $m\widehat{DAB}$, and $m\angle ADE$.

B 18° E C A 54° D

Since chord AE passes through the center of the circle at C, the chord AE is a diameter of the circle. $\widehat{ABE}$ is then a semicircle, and $m\widehat{ABE} = 180°$.

But $m\angle ADE = \frac{1}{2}m\widehat{ABE} = 90°$. ΔADE is a right triangle with $m\angle AED = 36°$.

Also, $m\angle DAE = \frac{1}{2}m\widehat{DE}$, which implies that $m\widehat{DE} = 2m\angle DAE = 108°$. Since $m\widehat{BD} = m\widehat{BE} + m\widehat{DE}$, $m\widehat{BD} = 18° + 108° = 126°$. Finally, $m\angle DAB = \frac{1}{2}m\widehat{BD} = 63°$.

KEY EXAMPLE (Lesson 15.2)

Determine the angles J, K, L, and M in the given quadrilateral.

J $(40 + 8x)°$ $\left(\frac{20x}{3}\right)°$ K M L $(5x - 16)°$

$(40 + 8x) + (5x - 16) = 180.$
$24 + 13x = 180.$
$13x = 156.\ x = 12.$

$m\angle J = 40 + 8x = 40 + 8(12)$
$= 136°$

$m\angle L = 5x - 16 = 5(12) - 16$
$= 60 - 16 = 44°$

$m\angle K = \dfrac{20(12)}{4} = 60°.\ m\angle M + m\angle K = 180°.$
$m\angle M = 180° - 60° = 120°$

KEY EXAMPLE *(Lesson 15.3)*

Two tangent lines are drawn to a circle from point K intersecting the circle at points M and N. If $m\widehat{MPN} = 210°$, what is $m\angle MKN$?

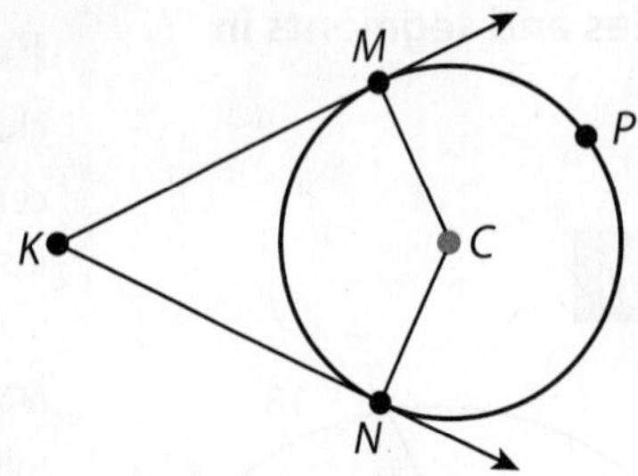

If $m\widehat{MPN} = 210°$, then $m\widehat{MN} = 360° - 210° = 150°$.

$m\angle MKN = \frac{1}{2}\left(m\widehat{MPN} - m\widehat{MN}\right)$

$m\angle MKN = \frac{1}{2}(210° - 150°) = \frac{1}{2}(60°) = 30°$

KEY EXAMPLE *(Lesson 15.4)*

A tangent and a secant are drawn to a circle from the external point B. The point of tangency is at point A, and the secant intersects the circle at points C and D. Find x.

From the Secant-Tangent Product Theorem, we can say that $BD \cdot BC = AB^2$. So $(2 + x) \cdot 2 = 8^2$.

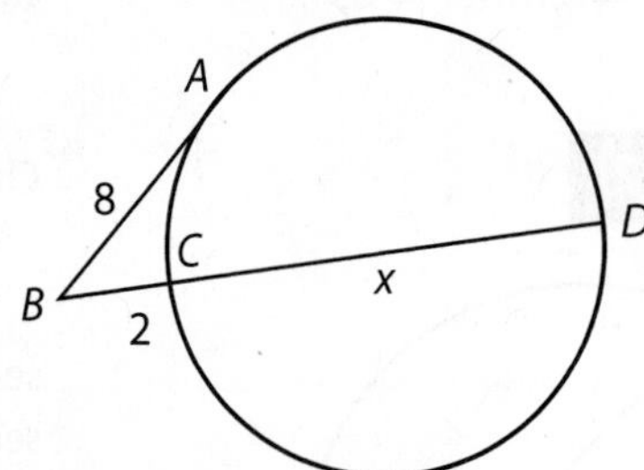

So $4 + 2x = 64$. $2x = 60$ and $x = 30$.

KEY EXAMPLE *(Lesson 15.5)*

Two chords intersect the interior of a circle at point T. Find $m\widehat{PR}$.

By the Intersecting Chords Angle Measure Theorem we can say the following:

$m\angle QTS = \frac{1}{2}\left(m\widehat{QS} + m\widehat{PR}\right)$

$60° = \frac{1}{2}\left(80° + m\widehat{PR}\right)$

$120° = \left(80° + m\widehat{PR}\right)$

$120° - 80° = m\widehat{PR}$

$40° = m\widehat{PR}$

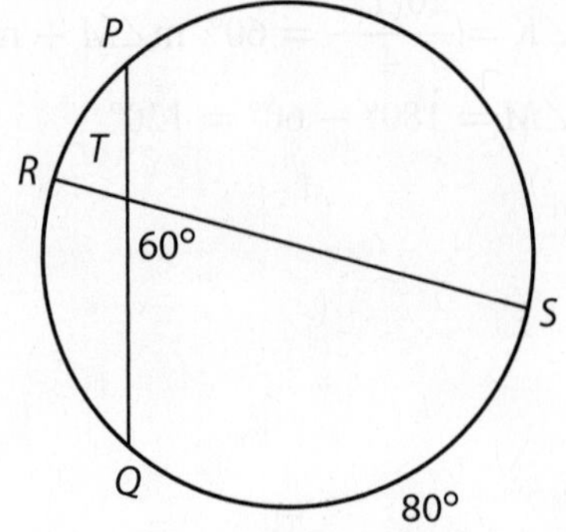

EXERCISES

Use the Inscribed Angle Theorem. *(Lesson 15.1)*

1. Find the measure of the intercepted arc for an inscribed angle of 50°.

Use the Inscribed Quadrilateral Theorem. *(Lesson 15.2)*

2. If one angle of a quadrilateral inscribed in a circle is 50°, what is the measure of its opposite angle?

Use the Circumscribed Angle Theorem. *(Lesson 15.3)*

3. Two tangents are drawn from an external point A to a circle. If one of the intercepted arcs on the circle is 120°, what must be the measure of the other intercepted arc?

Use the Chord-Chord Product Theorem. *(Lesson 15.4)*

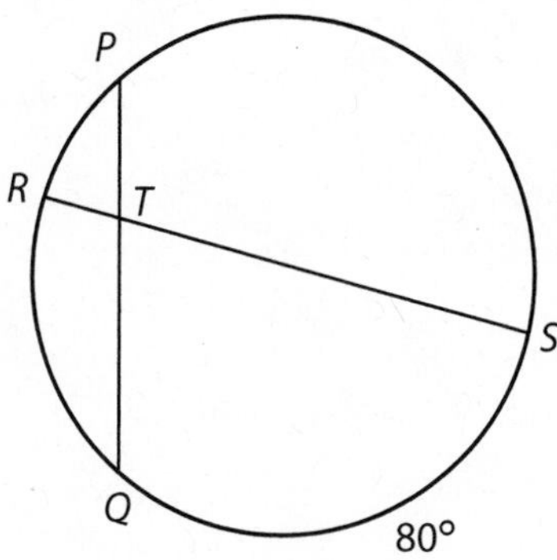

4. Given $RT = 2$, $TS = 6$, and $PT = 3$. Find TQ

Use the Tangent-Secant Exterior Angle Measure Theorem. *(Lesson 15.5)*

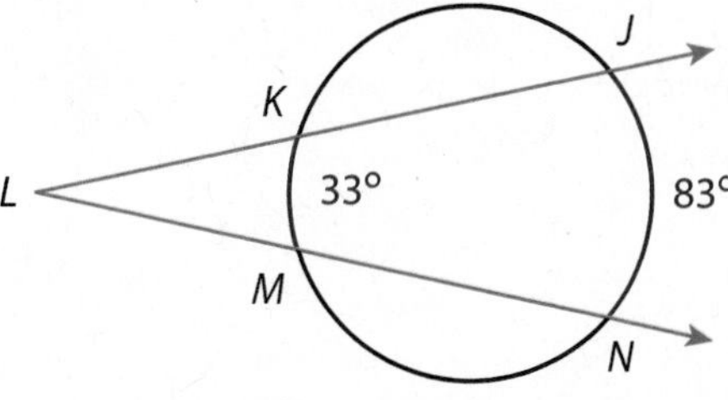

5. Find $m\angle L$ in the diagram given the $m\widehat{KM}$ and $m\widehat{JN}$.

MODULE PERFORMANCE TASK

How Many Marbles Will Fit?

Consider a package of marbles in the shape of a triangular prism. The cross-section of the package is an equilateral triangle with a side length of 1.5 inches, and the length of the package is 10 inches. What is the diameter of the largest marble that will fit inside the package? How many such marbles can fit within the package?

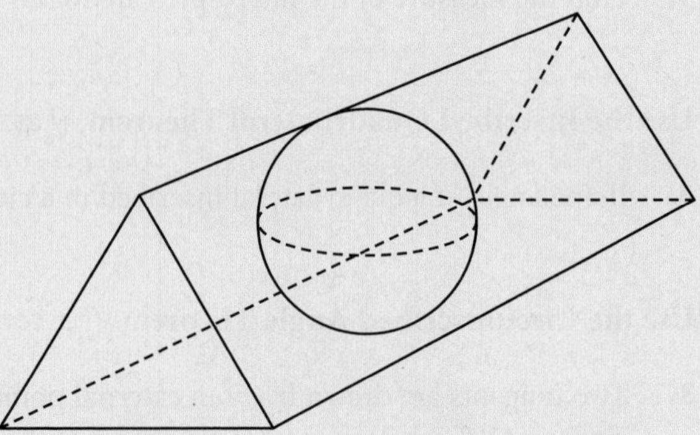

Start by listing how you plan to tackle the problem. Then complete the task. Be sure to write down all your data and assumptions. Then use words, numbers, diagrams, or algebra to explain how you reached your conclusion.

Ready to Go On?

15.1–15.5 Angles and Segments in Circles

- Online Homework
- Hints and Help
- Extra Practice

1. If $m\angle BCD = 20°$ and $m\widehat{EF} = 34°$, determine $m\widehat{ABD}$ using the appropriate theorems and postulates. *(Lesson 15.1)*

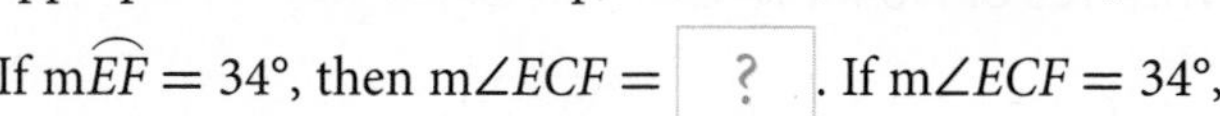
If $m\widehat{EF} = 34°$, then $m\angle ECF =$? . If $m\angle ECF = 34°$,

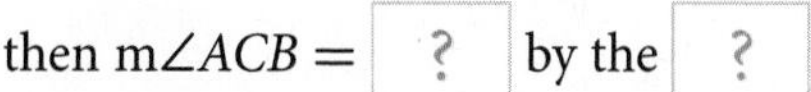
then $m\angle ACB =$? by the ?

Theorem. If $m\angle ACB = 34°$ and $m\angle BCD = 20°$, then

$m\widehat{AB} =$? and ? . By the ? , $m\widehat{ABD} = m\widehat{AB} + m\widehat{BD}$,

and so $m\widehat{ABD} =$? .

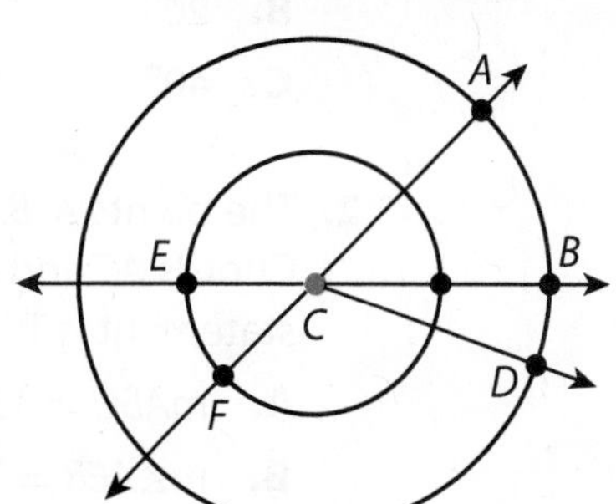

2. Find the measures of each angle in the inscribed quadrilateral. *(Lesson 15.2)*

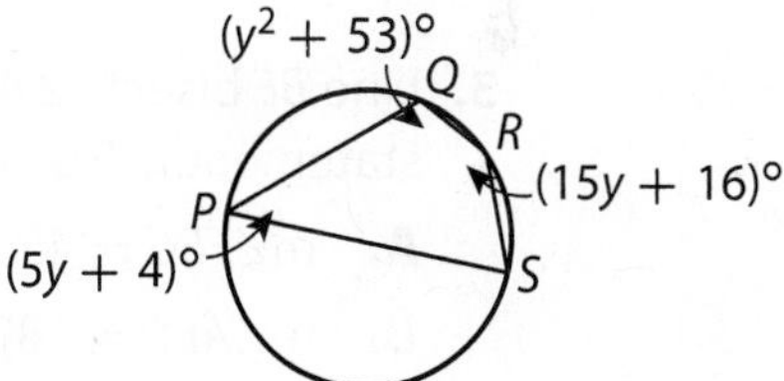

Fill in the proper conclusions based on known theorems and relationships. *(Lesson 15.5)*

3. Use the given figure, where $\overline{KM}$ and $\overline{KN}$ are tangent to the circle at M and N respectively.

a. What angles are right angles?

b. Suppose that $m\angle MKN = 80°$. What is $m\angle MCN$?

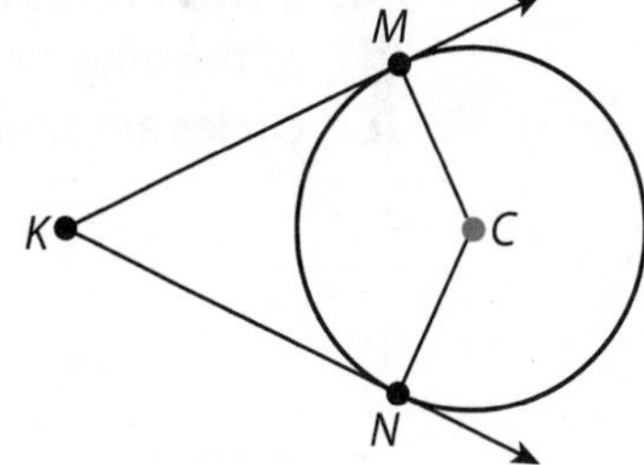

ESSENTIAL QUESTION

4. What are the major theorems that allow you to determine the relationships between angles formed by lines that intersect a circle?

MODULE 15
MIXED REVIEW

Assessment Readiness

SELECTED RESPONSE

1. An angle of 20° is inscribed in a circle. Could the given value be the measure of the arc intercepted by this angle? Write Yes or No for A–C.
   A. 10°
   B. 20°
   C. 40°

2. The points *A, B, C,* and *D* are taken in order on the circumference of a circle. Chords *AC* and *BD* intersect at point *E*. $m\widehat{AB} = 76°$ and $m\widehat{CD} = 80°$. Determine if each statement is True or False.
   A. $m\widehat{ABC} = 156°$
   B. $m\angle AEB = 78°$
   C. $m\angle AED = 72°$

3. Line *BF* bisects $\angle ABC$, $m\angle ABF = 6x°$, and $m\angle FBC = (2x + 60)°$. Determine if each statement is True or False.
   A. $m\angle FBC = 45°$
   B. $m\angle ABC = 180°$
   C. $\angle ABF$ is a right angle.

4. If two chords intersect inside a circle, then what do you know about the products of the lengths of the segments of the chords? How can you determine whether two circles are similar?

5. $\triangle ABC$ is inscribed in a circle such that vertices *A* and *B* lie on a diameter of the circle. If the length of the diameter of the circle is 13 and the length of chord *BC* is 5, find side *AC*.

Arc Length and Sector Area

Essential Question: How can the arc length and sector area of a circle be used to solve real-world problems?

REAL WORLD VIDEO
Check out how you can use sector areas to help you order wisely the next time you're buying pizza.

MODULE PERFORMANCE TASK PREVIEW

What's the Better Deal on Pizza?

In this module, you will use geometry to figure out which pizza order gets you more pizza for your money. How can calculating sector area help you to solve this problem? Let's find out.

Are YOU Ready?

Complete these exercises to review skills you will need for this module.

- Online Homework
- Hints and Help
- Extra Practice

Area of a Circle

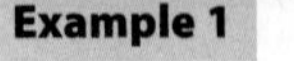

Example 1 Find the area of a circle with radius equal to 5.

$A = \pi r^2$ Write the equation for the area of a circle of radius r.

$A = \pi(5)^2$ Substitute the radius.

$A = 25\pi$ Simplify.

Find each area.

1. A circle with radius 3

2. A circle with radius 6

3. A circle with radius 2π

4. A circle with radius $\frac{5}{\pi}$

Circumference

Example 2 Find the circumference of a circle with radius equal to 6.

$C = 2\pi r$ Write the equation for the circumference of a circle with radius r.

$C = 2\pi(6)$ Substitute the radius.

$C = 12\pi$ Simplify.

Find each circumference.

5. A circle with radius 4

6. A circle with radius 3π

7. A circle with diameter 2

8. A circle with diameter $\frac{6}{\pi}$

Quadratic Functions

Example 3 Write x in terms of y. $10yx^2 = 60$

$10yx^2 = 60$ Write the equation.

$yx^2 = 6$ Divide both sides by 10.

$x^2 = \frac{6}{y}$ Divide both sides by y.

$x = \sqrt{\frac{6}{y}}, x = -\sqrt{\frac{6}{y}}$ Find the square root and its negative.

Solve each equation for x.

9. $4x^2 + 8x + 4 = 100$

10. $5y^2x^2 = 125$

16.1 Justifying Circumference and Area of a Circle

Resource Locker

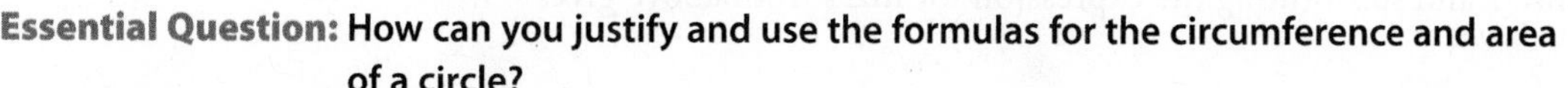

Essential Question: How can you justify and use the formulas for the circumference and area of a circle?

Explore Justifying the Circumference Formula

To find the circumference of a given circle, consider a regular polygon that is inscribed in the circle. As you increase the number of sides of the polygon, the perimeter of the polygon gets closer to the circumference of the circle.

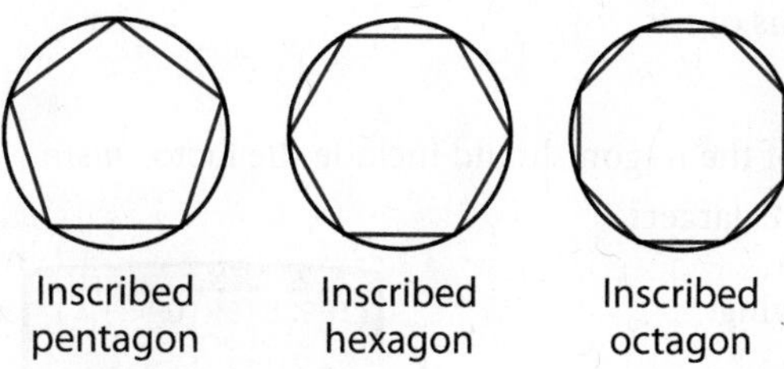

Let circle O be a circle with center O and radius r. Inscribe a regular n–gon in circle O and draw radii from O to the vertices of the n-gon.

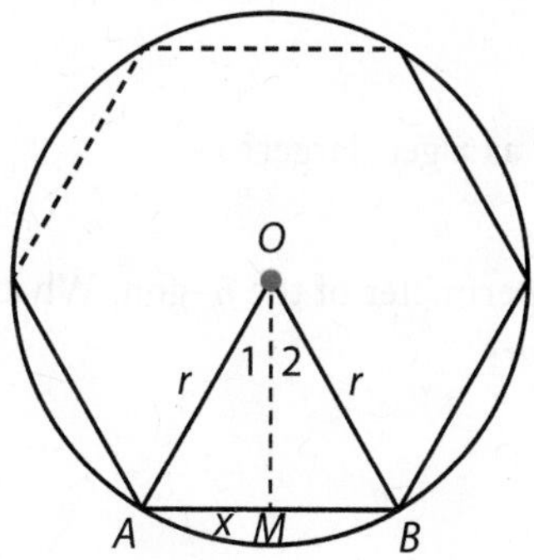

Let $\overline{AB}$ be one side of the n-gon. Draw $\overline{OM}$, the segment from O to the midpoint of $\overline{AB}$.

(A) Then $\triangle AOM \cong \triangle BOM$ by ? .

(B) So, $\angle 1 \cong \angle 2$ by ? .

(C) There are n triangles, all congruent to $\triangle AOB$, that surround point O and fill the n-gon.

Therefore, $m\angle AOB =$? and $m\angle 1 =$? .

(D) Since $\angle OMA \cong \angle OMB$ by CPCTC, and $\angle OMA$ and $\angle OMB$ form a linear pair, these angles are supplementary and must have measures of 90°. So $\triangle AOM$ and $\triangle BOM$ are right triangles.

In $\triangle AOM$, $\sin\angle 1 = \dfrac{\text{length of opposite leg}}{\text{length of hypotenuse}} = \dfrac{x}{r}$.

So, $x = r \sin\angle 1$ and substituting the expression for $m\angle 1$ from above gives

$x = r \sin$? .

(E) Now express the perimeter of the n-gon in terms of r.

The length of $\overline{AB}$ is $2x$, because ? .

This means the perimeter of the n-gon in terms of x is ? .

Substitute the expression for x found in Step D.

The perimeter of the n-gon in terms of r is ? .

(F) Your expression for the perimeter of the n-gon should include the factor $n \sin\left(\frac{180°}{n}\right)$. What happens to this factor as n gets larger?

Use your calculator to do the following.

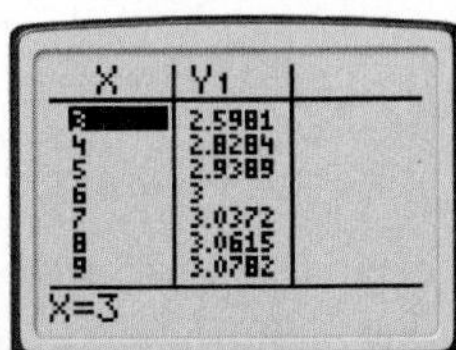

- Enter the expression $x \sin\left(\frac{180}{x}\right)$ as Y_1.
- Go to the Table Setup menu and enter the values shown.
- View a table for the function.
- Use arrow keys to scroll down.

What happens to the value of $x \sin\left(\frac{180°}{x}\right)$ as x gets larger?

(G) Look at the expression you wrote for the perimeter of the n-gon. What happens to the value of this expression, as n gets larger?

Reflect

1. When n is very large, does the perimeter of the n-gon ever equal the circumference of the circle? Why or why not?
2. How does the above argument justify the formula $C = 2\pi r$?

Explain 1 Applying the Circumference Formula

Example 1 **Find the circumference indicated.**

Ⓐ A Ferris wheel has a diameter of 40 feet. What is its circumference? Use 3.14 for π.

Diameter $= 2r$

$40 = 2r$

$20 = r$

Use the formula $C = 2\pi r$ to find the circumference.

$C = 2\pi r$

$C = 2\pi(20)$

$C = 2(3.14)(20)$

$C \approx 125.6$

The circumference is about 125.6 feet.

Ⓑ A pottery wheel has a diameter of 2 feet. What is its circumference? Use 3.14 for π.

The diameter is 2 feet, so the radius in inches is $r =$ 12.

$C = 2\pi r$

$C =$ 2 · 3.14 · 12

$C \approx$ 75.36 in.

The circumference is about 75.36 inches.

Reflect

3. **Discussion** Suppose you double the radius of a circle. How does the circumference of this larger circle compare with the circumference of the smaller circle? Explain.

Your Turn

4. The circumference of a tree is 20 feet. What is its diameter? Round to the nearest tenth of a foot. Use 3.14 for π.

5. The circumference of a circular fountain is 32 feet. What is its diameter? Round to the nearest tenth of a foot. Use 3.14 for π.

Explain 2 Justifying the Area Formula

To find the area of a given circle, consider a regular polygon that is inscribed in the circle. As you increase the number of sides of the polygon, the area of the polygon gets closer to the area of the circle.

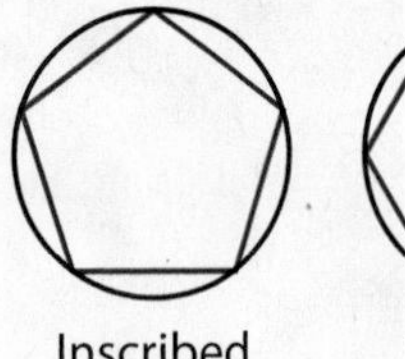

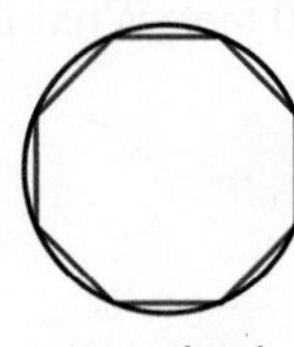

Inscribed pentagon | Inscribed hexagon | Inscribed octagon

Let circle O be a circle with center O and radius r. Inscribe a regular n–gon in circle O and draw radii from O to the vertices of the n-gon.

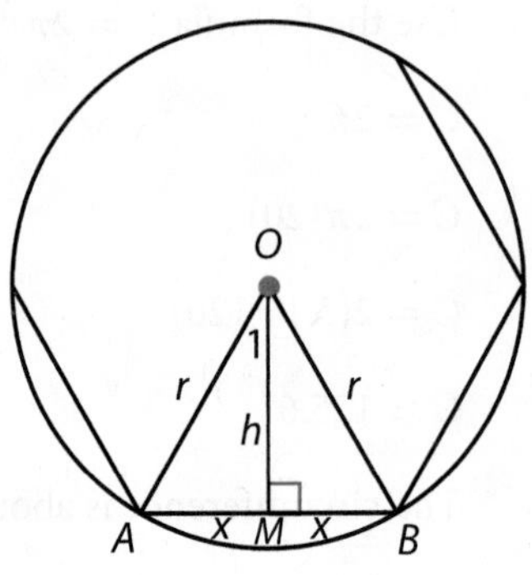

Let $\overline{AB}$ be one side of the n–gon. Draw $\overline{OM}$, the segment from O to the midpoint of $\overline{AB}$.

We know that $\overline{OM}$ is perpendicular to $\overline{AB}$ because triangle AOM is congruent to triangle BOM.

Let the length of $\overline{OM}$ be h.

Example 2 **Justify the formula for the area of a circle.**

(A) There are n triangles, all congruent to $\triangle AOB$, that surround point O and fill the n-gon.

Therefore, the measure of $\angle AOB$ is $\frac{360°}{n}$, and the measure of $\angle 1$ is $\frac{180°}{n}$.

We know that $x = r\sin\left(\frac{180°}{n}\right)$. Write a similar expression for h: $h = r\cos\left(\frac{180°}{n}\right)$

(B) The area of $\triangle AOB$ is $\frac{1}{2}(2x)(h) = xh = r\sin\left(\frac{180°}{n}\right)h$.

Substitute your value for h to get area $\triangle AOB = r^2\sin\left(\frac{180°}{n}\right)\cos\left(\frac{180°}{n}\right)$.

(C) There are n of these triangles, so the area of the n-gon is $nr^2\sin\left(\frac{180°}{n}\right)\cos\left(\frac{180°}{n}\right)$.

(D) Your expression for the area of the n–gon includes the factor $n\sin\left(\frac{180°}{n}\right)\cos\left(\frac{180°}{n}\right)$. What happens to this expression as n gets larger?

Use your graphing calculator to do the following.

- Enter the expression $x\sin\left(\frac{180°}{x}\right)\cos\left(\frac{180°}{x}\right)$ as Y_1.
- View a table for the function.
- Use arrow keys to scroll down.

What happens to the value of $x\sin\left(\frac{180°}{x}\right)\cos\left(\frac{180°}{x}\right)$ as x gets larger? The value gets closer to π.

(E) Look at the expression you wrote for the area of the n–gon. What happens to the value of this expression as n gets larger? The expression gets closer to πr^2.

Reflect

6. When n is very large, does the area of the n-gon ever equal the area of the circle? Why or why not?

7. How does the above argument justify the formula $A = \pi r^2$?

Explain 3 Applying the Area Formula

Example 3 **Find the area indicated.**

Ⓐ A rectangular piece of cloth is 3 ft by 6 ft. What is the area of the largest circle that can be cut from the cloth? Round the nearest square inch.

The diameter of the largest circle is 3 feet, or 36 inches. The radius of the circle is 18 inches.

$A = \pi r^2$

$A = \pi(18)^2$

$A = 324\pi$

$A \approx 1{,}017.9 \text{ in}^2$

So, the area is about 1,018 square inches.

Ⓑ A slice of a circular pizza measures 9 inches in length. What is the area of the entire pizza? Use 3.14 for π.

The 9-in. side of the pizza is also the length of the radius of the circle. So, $r = \boxed{9}$.

$A = \pi r^2$

$A = \pi \boxed{9}^2$

$A = \boxed{81}\ \pi \approx \boxed{254.34}$

To the nearest square inch, the area of the pizza is 255 in^2.

Reflect

8. Suppose the slice of pizza represents $\frac{1}{6}$ of the whole pizza. Does this affect your answer to Example 3B? What additional information can you determine with this fact?

Your Turn

9. A circular swimming pool has a diameter of 18 feet. To the nearest square foot, what is the smallest amount of material needed to cover the surface of the pool? Use 3.14 for π.

Elaborate

10. If the radius of a circle is doubled, is the area doubled? Explain.

11. **Essential Question Check-In** How do you justify and use the formula for the circumference of a circle?

Evaluate: Homework and Practice

- Online Homework
- Hints and Help
- Extra Practice

1. Which inscribed figure has a perimeter closer to the circumference of a circle, a regular polygon with 20 sides or a regular polygon with 40 sides? Explain.

Find the circumference of each circle with the given radius or diameter. Round to the nearest tenth. Use 3.14 for π.

2. $r = 9$ cm

3. $r = 24$ in.

4. $d = 14.2$ mm

5. A basketball rim has a radius of 9 inches. Find the circumference of the rim. Round to the nearest tenth. Use 3.14 for π.

6. The diameter of a circular swimming pool is 12 feet. Find its circumference. Use 3.14 for π.

7. The diameter of the U.S. Capitol Building's dome is 96 feet at its widest point. Find its circumference. Use 3.14 for π.

Find the area of each circle with the given radius or diameter. Use 3.14 for π.

8. $r = 7$ yd

9. $d = 5$ m

10. $d = 16$ ft

11. A drum has a diameter of 10 inches. Find the area of the top of the drum. Use 3.14 for π.

12. The circumference of a quarter is about 76 mm. What is the area? Round to the nearest tenth.

Algebra Find the area of the circle with the given circumference C. Use 3.14 for π.

13. $C = 31.4$ ft

14. $C = 21.98$ ft

15. $C = 69.08$ ft

16. A Ferris wheel has a diameter of 56 ft. How far will a rider travel during a 4-minute ride if the wheel rotates once every 20 seconds?
Use $\frac{22}{7}$ for π.

17. A giant water lily pad is shaped like a circle with a diameter of up to 5 feet. Find the circumference and area of the pad. Round to the nearest tenth.

18. A pizza parlor offers pizzas with diameters of 8 in., 10 in., and 12 in. Find the area of each size pizza. Round to the nearest tenth. If the pizzas cost \$9, \$12, and \$18 respectively, which is the better buy?

19. **Critical Thinking** Which do you think would seat more people, a 4 ft by 6 ft rectangular table or a circular table with a diameter of 6 ft? How many people would you sit at each table? Explain your reasoning.

20. You can estimate a tree's age in years by using the formula $a = \frac{r}{w}$, where r is the tree's radius without bark and w is the average thickness of the tree's rings. The circumference of a white oak tree is 100 inches. The bark is 0.5 in. thick, and the average thickness of a ring is 0.2 in. Estimate the tree's age and the area enclosed by the outer circumference of the widest ring.

21. **Multi-Step** A circular track for a model train has a diameter of 8.5 feet. The train moves around the track at a constant speed of 0.7 ft/s.

a. To the nearest foot, how far does the train travel when it goes completely around the track 10 times?

b. To the nearest minute, how long does it take the train to go completely around the track 10 times?

22. The Parthenon is a Greek temple dating to about 445 BCE. The temple features 46 Doric columns, which are roughly cylindrical. The circumference of each column at the base is about 5.65 meters. What is the approximate diameter of each column? Round to the nearest tenth.

23. **Explain the Error** A circle has a circumference of 2π in. Which calculation of the area is incorrect? Explain.

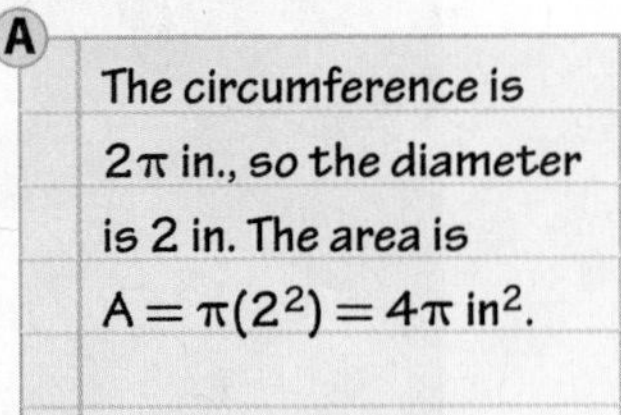

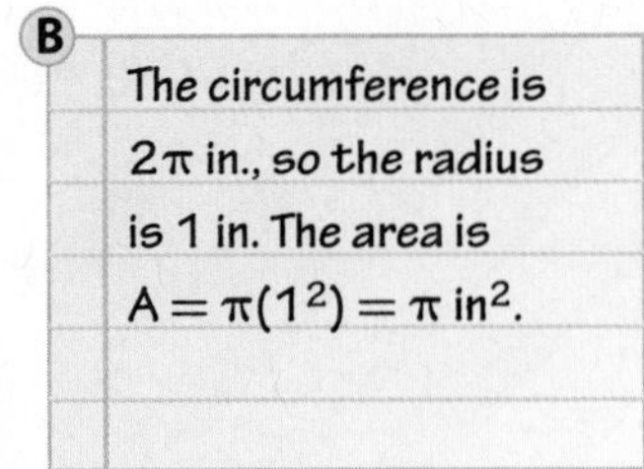

B
The circumference is
2π in., so the radius
is 1 in. The area is
A = π(1²) = π in².

24. **Write About It** The center of each circle in the figure lies on the number line. Describe the relationship between the circumference of the largest circle and the circumferences of the four smaller circles.

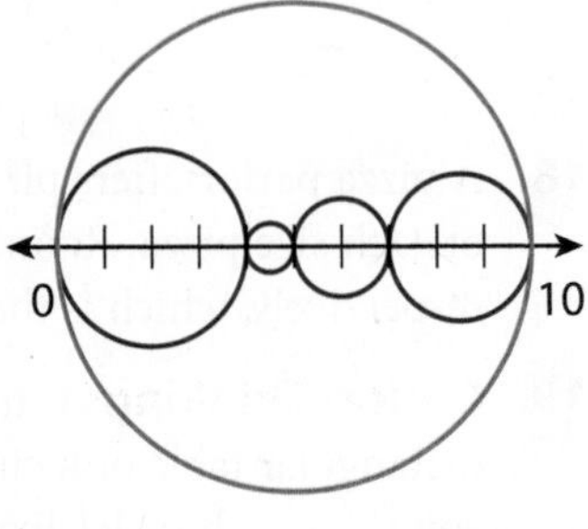

25. Find the diameter of a data storage disk with an area 113.1 cm^2.

26. Which of the following ratios can be derived from the formula for the circumference of a circle? Determine all that apply.

A. $\frac{C}{d}$

B. $\frac{C}{2r}$

C. $\frac{C}{\pi}$

D. $\frac{C}{2\pi}$

E. $\frac{C}{2c}$

27. A meteorologist measured the eyes of hurricanes to be 15 to 20 miles in diameter during one season. What is the range of areas of the land underneath the eyes of the hurricanes?

28. A circle with a 6 in. diameter is stamped out of a rectangular piece of metal as shown. Find the area of the remaining piece of metal. Use 3.14 for π.

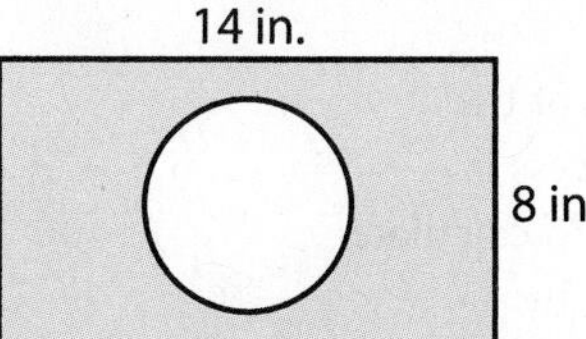

H.O.T. Focus on Higher Order Thinking

29. Critique Reasoning A standard bicycle wheel has a diameter of 26 inches. A student claims that during a one-mile bike ride the wheel makes more than 1000 complete revolutions. Do you agree or disagree? Explain. (*Hint:* 1 mile = 5280 feet)

30. Algebra A graphic artist created a company logo from two tangent circles whose diameters are in the ratio 3:2. What percent of the total logo is the area of the region outside of the smaller circle?

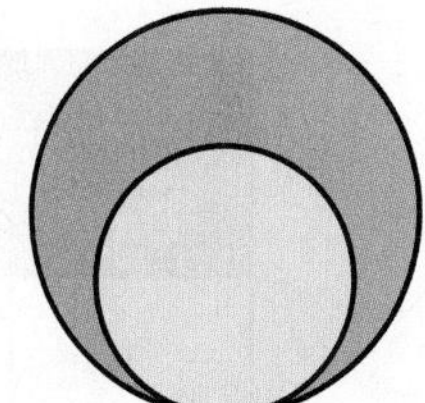

31. Communicate Mathematical Ideas In the figure, $\overline{AB}$ is a diameter of circle C, D is the midpoint of $\overline{AC}$, and E is the midpoint of $\overline{AD}$. How does the circumference of circle E compare to the circumference of circle C? Explain.

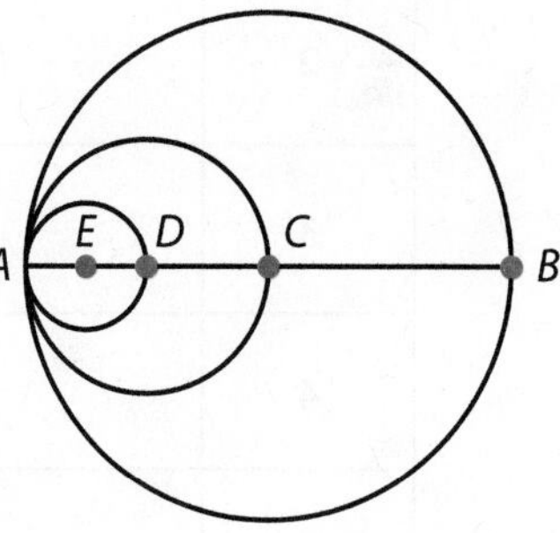

32. Critical Thinking Evelyn divides the circle and rearranges the pieces to make a shape that resembles a parallelogram.

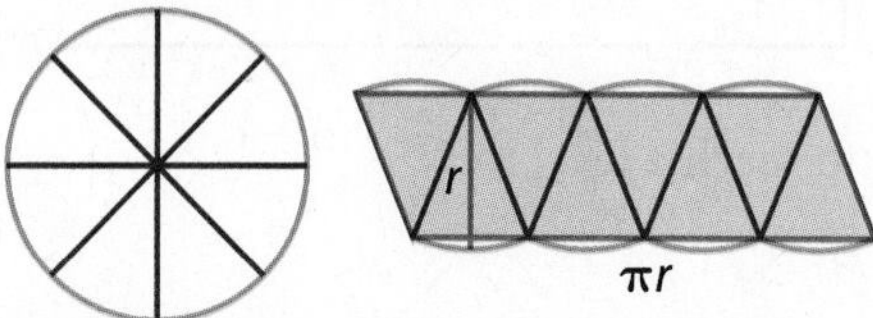

She then divides the circle into more pieces and rearranges them into a shape that resembles a parallelogram. She thinks that the area of the new parallelogram will be closer to the area of a circle. Is she correct? Explain.

Lesson Performance Task

In the lesson, you saw that the more wedges into which you divide a circle, the more closely each wedge resembles a triangle, and the closer to the area of a circle the area of the reassembled wedges becomes. In the branch of mathematics called calculus, this process is called finding a *limit.* Even though you can't cut a circle into millions of tiny wedges to calculate the actual area of the circle, you can see what the area is going to be long before that, by spotting a pattern. You can apply this method in many ways, some of them unexpected.

Mac is a race walker. He is training for a race. He has decided that in the weeks leading up to the race, he'll work up to a level where he is walking 20 kilometers a day. His plan is to walk 10 kilometers the first day of training and increase the distance he walks each day until he reaches his goal.

1. Copy and complete the table for Mac's first 6 days of training.

Day	Increase in distance walked from the day before (in kilometers)	Total distance walked that day (in kilometers)
1	10	10
2	5	10 + 5 = ?
3	2.5	? + 5 = ?
4	?	? + ? = ?
5	?	? + ? = ?
6	?	? + ? = ?

2. Describe your results in relation to Mac's plan to reach a level where he walks 20 kilometers a day.

3. Suppose Mac continues his training plan. Will Mac ever reach his goal?

16.2 Arc Length and Radian Measure

Resource Locker

Essential Question: How do you find the length of an arc?

Explore Deriving the Formula for Arc Length

An **arc** is an unbroken part of a circle consisting of two points called the endpoints and all the points on the circle between them. **Arc length** is understood to be the distance along a circular arc measured in linear units (such as feet or centimeters). You can use proportional reasoning to find arc length.

Find the arc length of $\overset{\frown}{AB}$. Express your answer in terms of π and rounded to the nearest tenth.

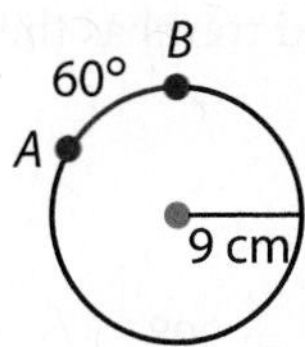

(A) First find the circumference of the circle.

$C = 2\pi r$ Substitute the radius, 9, for r.

$C =$?

(B) The entire circle has 360°. Therefore, the arc's length is $\frac{60}{360}$ or $\frac{1}{6}$ of the circumference.

Arc length of $\overset{\frown}{AB} = \frac{1}{6} \cdot$? Arc length is $\frac{1}{6}$ of the circumference.

$=$? Multiply.

$\approx$? Use a calculator to evaluate. Then round.

So, the arc length of $\overset{\frown}{AB}$ is ? or ? .

Reflect

1. How could you use the reasoning process you used above to find the length of an arc of the circle that measures $m°$?

Explain 1 Applying the Formula for Arc Length

You were able to find an arc length using concepts of circumference. Using the same reasoning results in the formula for finding arc length.

Arc Length

The arc length, s, of an arc with measure $m°$ and radius r is given by the formula $s = \frac{m}{360} \cdot 2\pi r$.

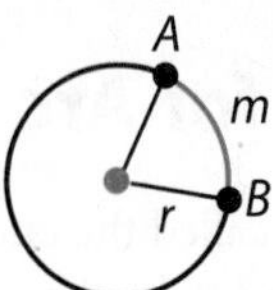

Example 1 Find the arc length.

Ⓐ On a clock face, the minute hand of a clock is 10 inches long. To the nearest tenth of an inch, how far does the tip of the minute hand travel as the time progresses from 12:00 to 12:15?

The minute hand moves 15 minutes.

$\frac{15 \text{ minutes}}{60 \text{ minutes}} = \frac{1}{4}$ so the central angle formed is $\frac{1}{4} \cdot 360° = 90°$.

$s = \frac{m}{360} \cdot 2\pi r$ Use the formula for arc length.

$= \frac{90}{360} \cdot 2\pi(10)$ Substitute 10 for r and 90 for m.

$= 5\pi$ Simplify.

≈ 15.7 in. Simplify.

Ⓑ The minute hand of a clock is 6 inches long. To the nearest tenth of an inch, how far does the tip of the minute hand travel as the time progresses from 12:00 to 12:30?

The minute hand moves 30 minutes.

$\frac{30 \text{ minutes}}{60 \text{ minutes}} = \boxed{\frac{1}{2}}$, so the central angle formed is $\frac{1}{2} \cdot \boxed{360°} = \boxed{180°}$.

$s = \frac{m}{360} \cdot \underline{2\pi r}$ Use the formula for arc length.

$= \frac{\boxed{180}}{360} \cdot 2\pi\left(\boxed{6}\right)$ Substitute 6 for r and 180 for m.

$= \boxed{6\pi}$ Simplify.

$\approx \boxed{18.8}$ in. Simplify.

The length of the arc is $\boxed{18.8}$ inches.

Reflect

2. **Discussion** Why does the formula represent the length of an arc of a circle?

Your Turn

3. The minute hand of a clock is 8 inches long. To the nearest tenth of an inch, how far does the tip of the minute hand travel as the time progresses from 12:00 to 12:45?

Explain 2 Investigating Arc Lengths in Concentric Circles

Consider a set of concentric circles with center O and radius 1, 2, and 3, and so on. The central angle shown in the figure is a right angle and it cuts off arcs that measure 90°.

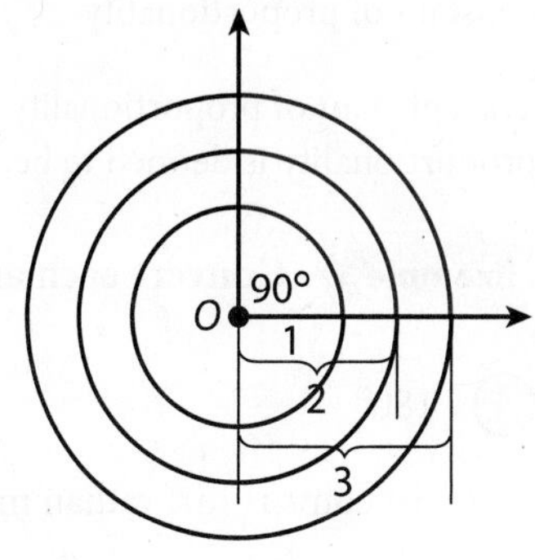

Example 2 **Find and graph arc lengths for different radii.**

(A) For each value of the radius r listed in the table below, find the corresponding arc length. Write the length in terms of π and rounded to the nearest hundredth.

For example, when $r = 1$, the arc length is $\frac{90}{360} \cdot 2\pi(1) = \frac{1}{2}\pi \approx 1.57$.

Radius r	1	2	3	4	5
Arc length s in terms of π	$\frac{1}{2}\pi$	π	$\frac{3}{2}\pi$	2π	$\frac{5}{2}\pi$
Arc length s to the nearest hundredth	1.57	3.14	4.71	6.28	7.85

(B) Plot the ordered pairs from the table on a coordinate plane.

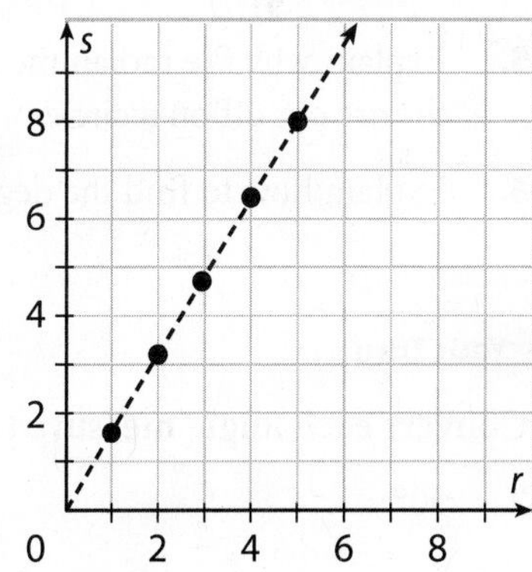

What do you notice about the points?
The points lie on a straight line through the origin.

What type of relationship is the relationship between arc length and radius?
The relationship is proportional (direct variation).

What is the constant of proportionality for this relationship?
The constant of proportionality is $\frac{1}{2}\pi$.

Reflect

4. What happens to the arc length when you double the radius? How is this connected to the idea that all circles are similar?

Explain 3 Converting Radian Measure

As you discovered in Explain 2, when the central angle is fixed at $m°$, the length of the arc cut off by a central angle is proportional to (or varies directly with) the radius. In fact, you can see that the formula for arc length is a proportional relationship when m is fixed.

$$s = \underbrace{\frac{m}{360} \cdot 2\pi}_{} r$$

constant of proportionality

The constant of proportionality for the proportional relationship is $\frac{m}{360} \cdot 2\pi$. This constant of proportionality is defined to be the **radian measure** of the angle.

Example 3 **Convert each angle measure to radian measure.**

(A) 180°

To convert to a radian measure, let $m = 180$ in the expression $\frac{m}{360} \cdot 2\pi$.

$180° = \frac{180}{360} \cdot 2\pi$ Substitute 180 for m.

$= \pi$ radians Simplify.

(B) 60°

To convert to a radian measure, let $m = 60$ in the expression $\frac{m}{360} \cdot 2\pi$.

$60° = \frac{60}{360} \cdot 2\pi$ Substitute 60 for m.

$= \frac{\pi}{3}$ radians Simplify.

Reflect

5. Explain why the radian measure for an angle $m°$ is sometimes defined as the length of the arc cut off on a circle of radius 1 by a central angle of $m°$.

6. Explain how to find the degree measure of an angle whose radian measure is $\frac{\pi}{4}$.

Your Turn

Convert each angle measure to radian measure.

7. 90°

8. 45°

Elaborate

9. You know that 360° is the degree measure that corresponds to a full circle. What is the radian measure that corresponds to a full circle?

10. Suppose you are given that the measure in radians of an arc of a circle with radius r is θ. How can you find the length of the arc in radians?

11. **Essential Question Check-In** What two pieces of information do you need to calculate arc length?

Evaluate: Homework and Practice

- Online Homework
- Hints and Help
- Extra Practice

Use the formula, $s = \frac{m}{360} \cdot 2\pi r$, to answer the questions.

1. What part of the circle does the expression $2\pi r$ represent?
2. What part of the circle does $\frac{m}{360}$ represent?
3. What part of the circle does the expression $2r$ represent?
4. **Critical Thinking** Suppose an arc were intercepted by a central angle measuring 15°. The diameter of the circle is 9 cm. Can both of these values be substituted into the arc length formula? Explain.

Find the arc length of $\widehat{AB}$ to the nearest tenth.

5.

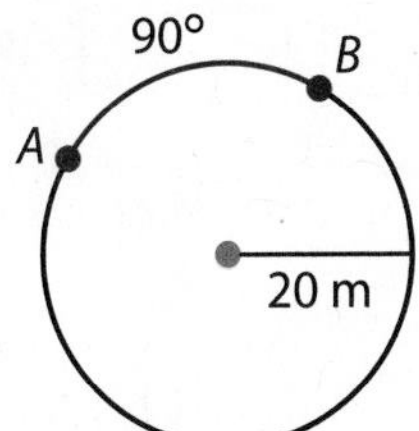

6.

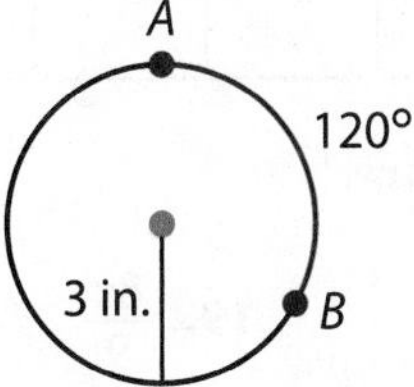

7.

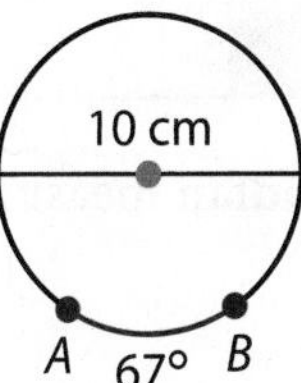

8. The minute hand of a clock is 5 inches long. To the nearest tenth of an inch, how far does the tip of the minute hand travel as the time progresses from 12:00 to 12:25?
9. The circles are concentric. Find the length of the intercepted arc in the larger circle.

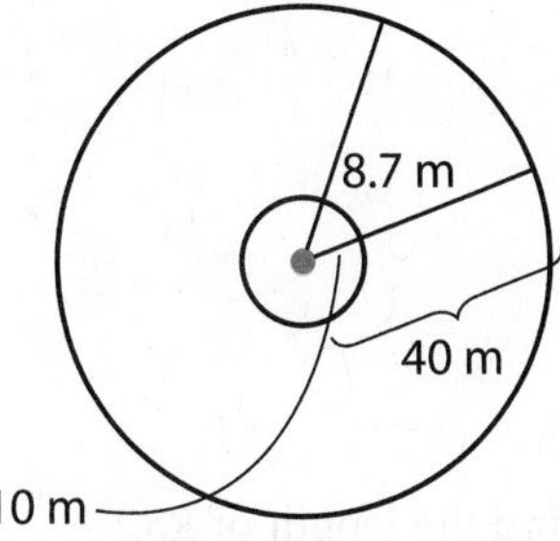

10. The circles are concentric. Find the length of $\widehat{PQ}$

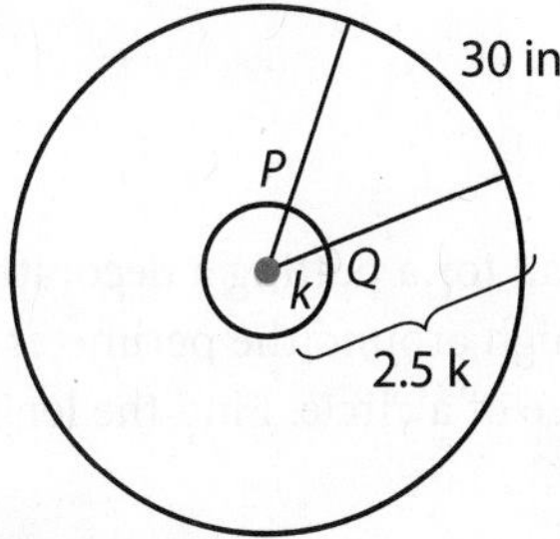

11. Two arcs of concentric circles are intercepted by the same central angle. The resulting arc length of the arc of the larger circle is 16 m and the radius of the larger circle is 12 m. The radius of the smaller circle is 7.5 m. Find the length of the corresponding arc of the smaller circle.
12. Two arcs of concentric circles are intercepted by the same central angle. The resulting arc length of the arc of the smaller circle is 36 ft and its radius is 30 ft. The radius of the larger circle is 45 ft. Find the length of the corresponding arc of the larger circle.

Convert each angle measure to radian measure.

13. 40° **14.** 80°

15. 100° **16.** 12°

17. It is convenient to know the radian measure for benchmark angles such as 0°, 30°, 45°, and so on. Copy and complete the table by finding the radian measure for each of the given benchmark angles.

Benchmark Angles									
Degree Measure	0°	30°	45°	60°	90°	120°	135°	150°	180°
Radian Measure	?	?	?	?	?	?	?	?	?

Convert each radian measure to degree measure.

18. $\frac{5\pi}{8}$ **19.** $\frac{8\pi}{9}$

20. In the diagram, $\overline{WY}$, and $\overline{XZ}$ are diameters of $\odot T$, and $WY = XZ = 6$. If $m\widehat{XY} = 140°$, what is the length of $\widehat{YZ}$? Determine all that apply.

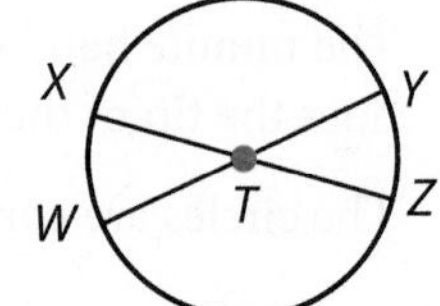

A. $\frac{4\pi}{6}$

B. $\frac{4\pi}{3}$

C. $\frac{2}{3}\pi$

D. 4π

E. 6π

21. Algebra The length of $\widehat{TS}$ is 12 in. Find the length of $\widehat{RS}$.

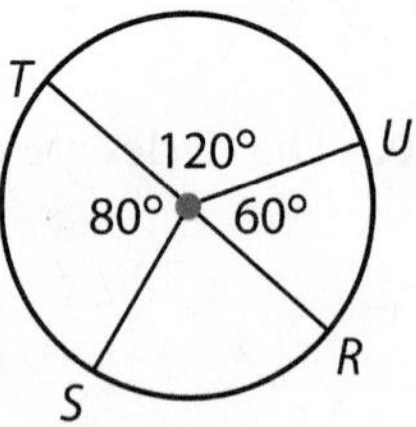

22. Multi-Step The diagram shows the plan for a putting a decorative trim around a corner desk. The trim will be 4-inch high around the perimeter of the desk. The curve is one quarter of the circumference of a circle. Find the length of trim needed to the nearest half foot.

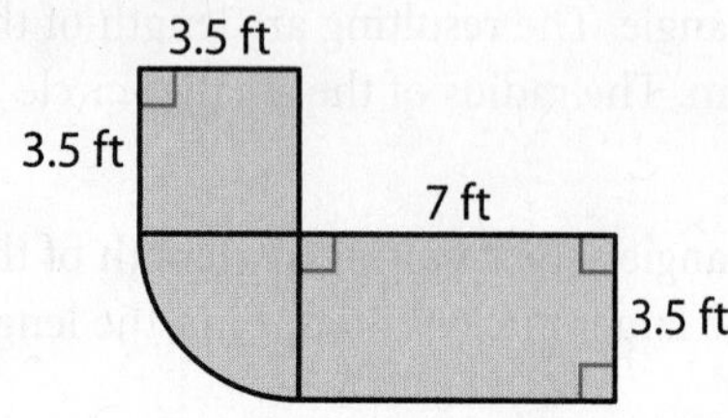

23. Explain the Error A student was asked to find the arc length of $\overset{\frown}{PQ}$. The student's work is shown. Explain the student's error and give the correct arc length.

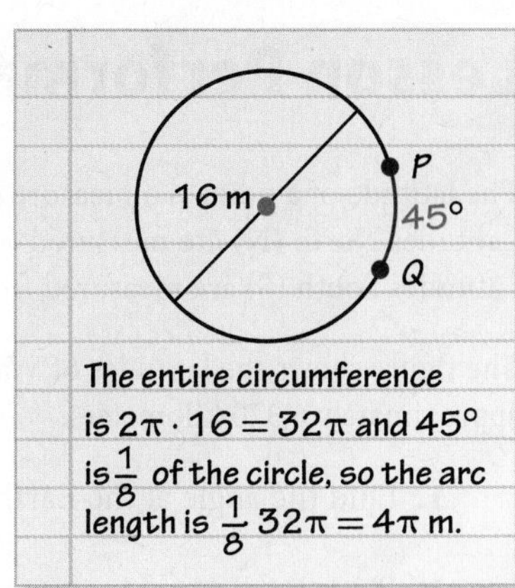

16 m
P
45°
Q
The entire circumference is $2\pi \cdot 16 = 32\pi$ and 45° is $\frac{1}{8}$ of the circle, so the arc length is $\frac{1}{8}\,32\pi = 4\pi$ m.

H.O.T. Focus on Higher Order Thinking

24. Critique Reasoning A friend tells you two arcs from different circles have the same arc length if their central angles are equal. Is your friend correct? Explain your reasoning.

25. Multi-Step A carpenter is making a tray to fit between two circular pillars in the shape of the shaded area as shown. She is using a jigsaw to cut along the edge of the tray. What is the length of the cut encompassing the tray? Round to the nearest half foot.

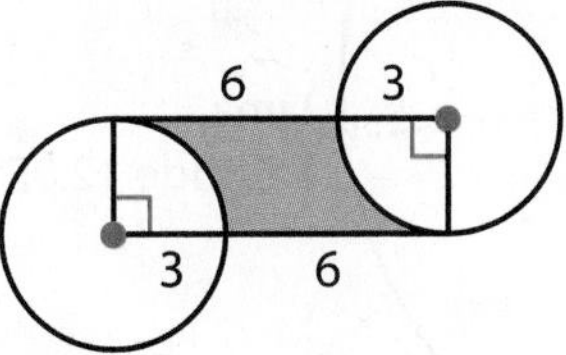

26. Critical Thinking The pedals of a penny-farthing Bicycle are directly connected to the front wheel.

a. Suppose a penny-farthing bicycle has a front wheel with a diameter of 5 ft. To the nearest tenth of a foot, how far does the bike move when you turn the pedals through an angle of 90°?

b. Through what angle should you turn the pedals in order to move forward by a distance of 4.5 ft? Round to the nearest degree.

Lesson Performance Task

The latitude of a point is a measure of its position north or south on the Earth's surface. Latitudes North (N) are measured from 0° N at the equator to 90° N at the North Pole. Latitudes South (S) are measured from 0° S at the equator to 90° S at the South Pole.

The figure shows the latitudes of Washington, D.C. and Lima, Peru. The radius of the Earth is approximately 6,370 kilometers.

1. Find the angle at the Earth's center between radii drawn to Washington and Lima.

2. Find the distance between Washington and Lima. Show your work.

3. A point's longitude is a measure of its position east or west on the Earth's surface. In order for your calculation of the distance between Washington and Lima to be accurate, what must be true about the longitudes of the two cities?

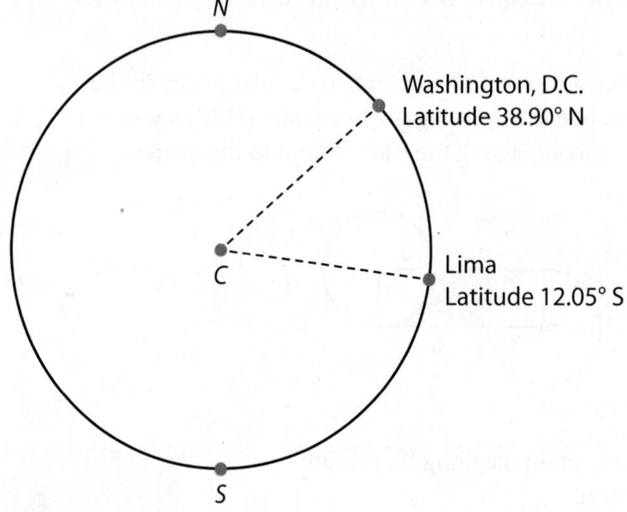

16.3 Sector Area

Essential Question: How do you find the area of a sector of a circle?

Explore Derive the Formula for the Area of a Sector

A **sector** of a circle is a region bounded by two radii and their intercepted arc. A sector is named by the endpoints of the arc and the center of the circle. For example, the figure shows sector POQ.

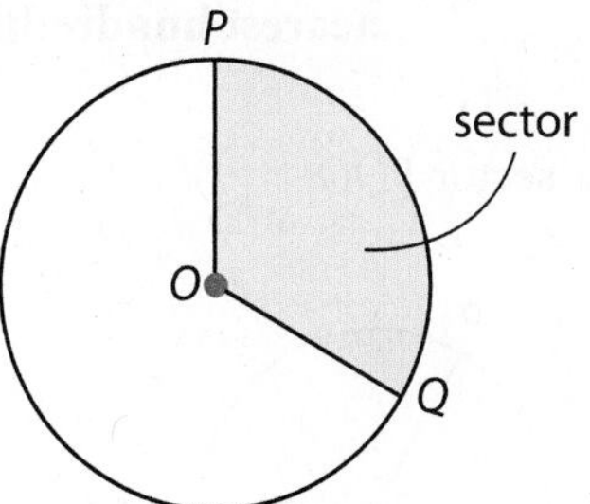

In the same way that you used proportional reasoning to find the length of an arc, you can use proportional reasoning to find the area of a sector.

Find the area of sector AOB. Express your answer in terms of π and rounded to the nearest tenth.

(A) First find the area of the circle.

$A = \pi r^2 = \pi(\ ?\ )^2$

$= \ ?$

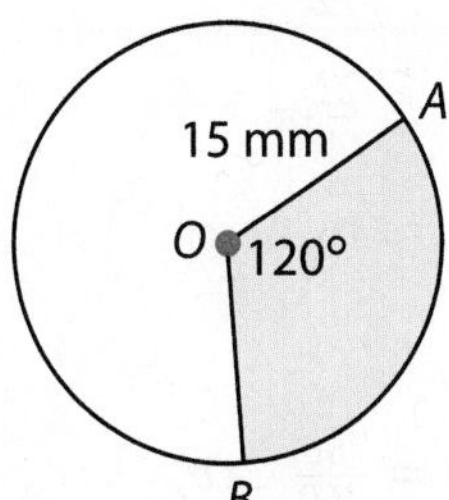

(B) The entire circle is 360°, but $\angle AOB$ measures 120°. Therefore, the sector's area is $\frac{120}{360}$ or $\frac{1}{3}$ of the circle's area.

Area of sector $AOB = \frac{1}{3} \cdot \ ?$ The area is $\frac{1}{3}$ of the circle's area.

$= \ ?$ Simplify.

$= \ ?$ Use a calculator to evaluate. Then round.

So, the area of sector AOB is ? or ?.

Reflect

1. How could you use the above process to find the area of a sector of the circle whose central angle measures $m°$?

2. **Make a Conjecture** What do you think is the formula for the area of a sector with a central angle of $m°$ and radius r?

Explain 1 Using the Formula for the Area of a Sector

The proportional reasoning process you used in the Explore can be generalized. Given a sector with a central angle of $m°$ and radius r, the area of the entire circle is πr^2 and the area of the sector is $\frac{m}{360}$ times the circle's area. This gives the following formula.

Area of a Sector

The area A of a sector with a central angle of $m°$ of a circle with radius r is given by $A = \frac{m}{360} \cdot \pi r^2$

Example 1 **Find the area of each sector, as a multiple of π and to the nearest hundredth.**

(A) sector POQ

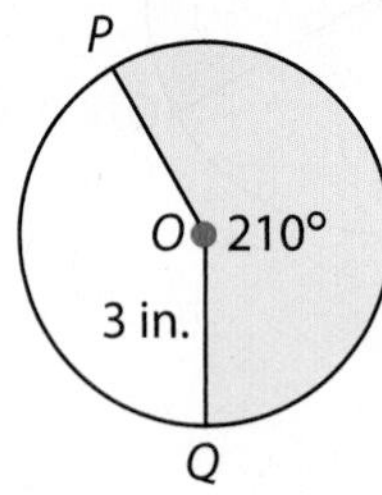

$$A = \frac{m}{360} \cdot \pi r^2$$
$$= \frac{210}{360} \cdot \pi(3)^2$$
$$= \frac{7}{12} \cdot 9\pi$$
$$= \frac{21}{4}\pi$$
$$\approx 16.49 \text{ in}^2$$

(B) sector HGJ

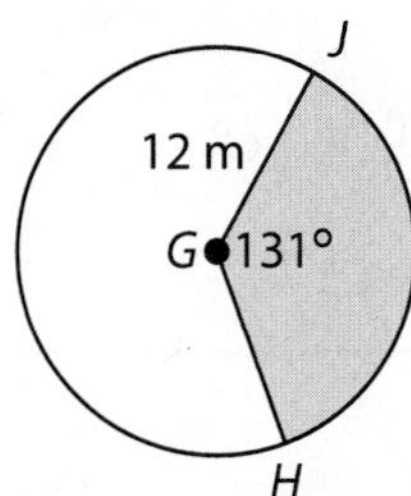

$$A = \frac{m}{360} \cdot \pi r^2$$
$$= \frac{131}{360} \cdot \pi\left(12\right)^2$$
$$= \frac{131}{360} \cdot 144\pi$$
$$= 52.4\pi$$
$$\approx 164.62 \text{ m}^2$$

Reflect

3. **Discussion** Your friend said that the value of $m°$ in the formula for the area of a sector can never be larger than 360°. Do you agree or disagree? Explain your reasoning.

Your Turn

Find the area of each sector, as a multiple of π and to the nearest hundredth.

4. sector AOB

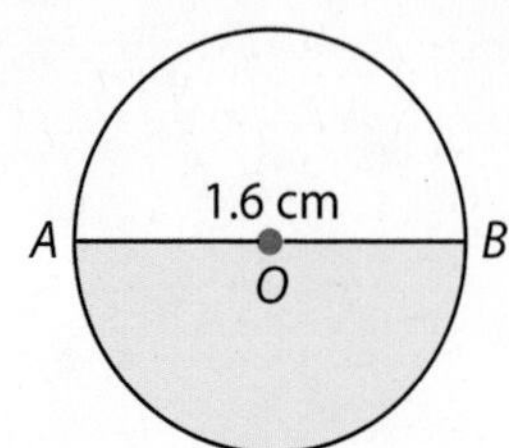

5. sector POQ

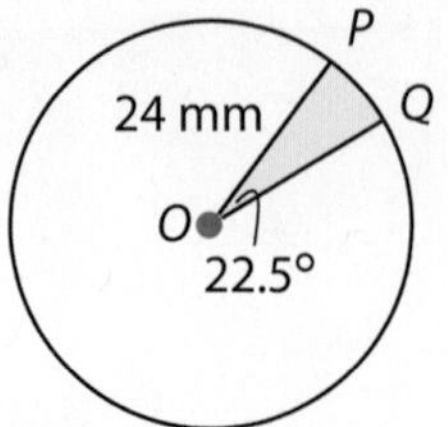

Explain 2 Applying the Formula for the Area of a Sector

You can apply the formula for the area of a sector to real-world problems.

Example 2 **Find each area.**

(A) A beam from a lighthouse is visible for a distance of 3 mi. To the nearest square mile, what is the area covered by the beam as it sweeps in an arc of 150°?

$$A = \frac{m}{360} \cdot \pi r^2$$
$$= \frac{150}{360} \cdot \pi(3)^2$$
$$= \frac{5}{12} \cdot 9\pi$$
$$= 3.75\pi$$
$$\approx 12 \text{ mi}^2$$

(B) A circular plot with a 180-foot diameter is watered by a spray irrigation system. To the nearest square foot, what is the area that is watered as the sprinkler rotates through an angle of 50°?

$d = 180$ ft, so $r = 90$ ft

$$A = \frac{m}{360} \cdot \pi r^2$$
$$= \frac{\boxed{50}}{360} \cdot \pi\left(\boxed{90}\right)^2$$
$$= \boxed{\frac{5}{36}} \cdot \boxed{1800}\,\pi$$
$$= \boxed{1125}\,\pi$$
$$\approx \boxed{3534} \text{ ft}^2$$

Your Turn

6. To the nearest square foot, what is the area watered in Example 2B as the sprinkler rotates through a semicircle?

Elaborate

7. **Discussion** When can you use proportional reasoning to find the area of a sector without knowing or finding its central angle? Explain your reasoning by giving an example.

8. **Essential Question Check-In** What information do you need to find the area of a sector?

Evaluate: Homework and Practice

Personal Math Trainer

- Online Homework
- Hints and Help
- Extra Practice

1. The region within a circle that is bounded by two radii and an arc is called a.
2. Suppose you know the area of a circle and the measure of the central angle of a sector of the circle. Describe the process of finding the area of the sector.
3. What is the formula for the area of a circle? Define all variables in the formula.
4. If the angle of a sector measures 45°, what fraction of the circle is the sector?

Find the area of sector *AOB*. Express your answer in terms of π and rounded to the nearest tenth.

5.

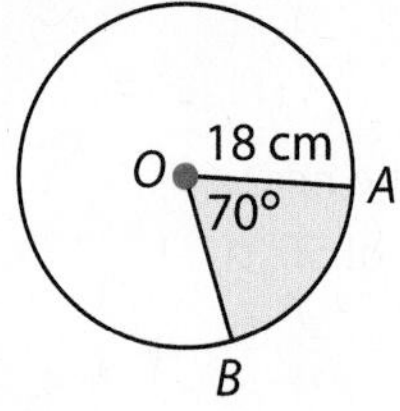

6.

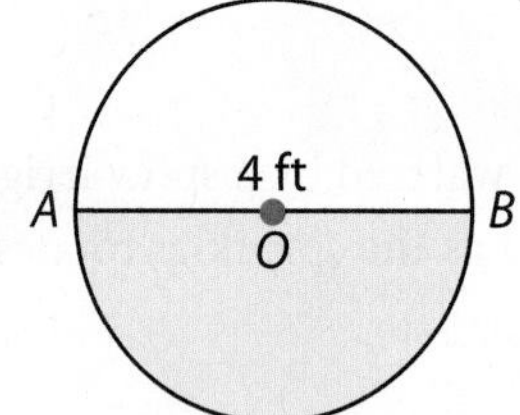

7.

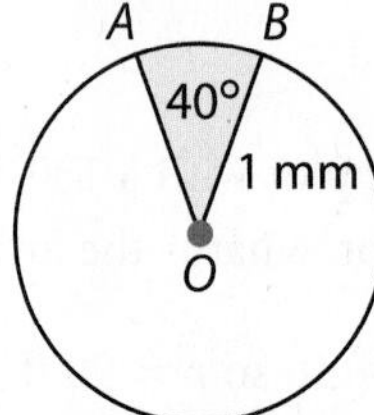

8.

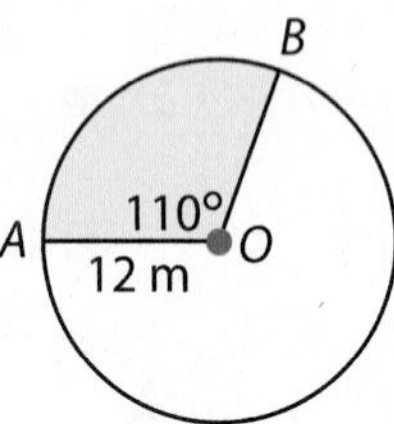

9.

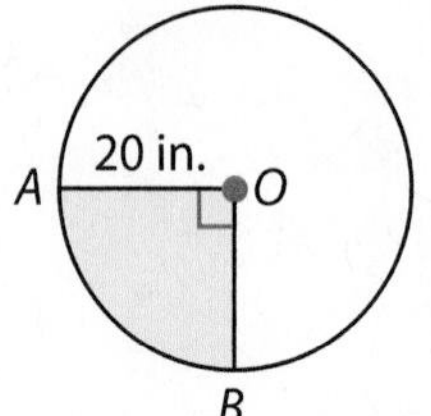

10.

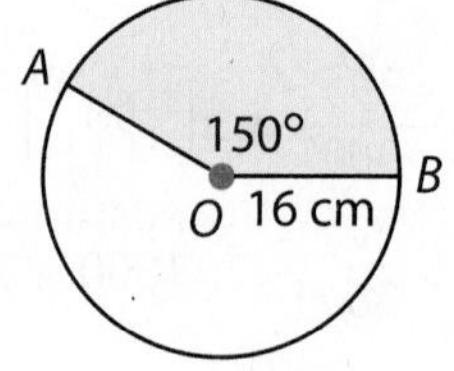

11. A round pizza is cut into congruent sectors. If the angle measure of the pizza slice is 20°, how many pieces are in the whole pizza?
12. The area of a piece of pie in the shape of a sector is 7.1 in^2. The angle of the sector is 40°.
    - **a.** What is the area of the entire pie?
    - **b.** What is the diameter of the pie?
13. A *lunette* is a semicircular window that is sometimes placed above a doorway or above a rectangular window. The diameter of the lunette is 40 inches. To the nearest square inch, what is the area of the lunette?

Find the area of each sector. Give your answer in terms of π and rounded to the nearest hundredth.

14. sector PQR

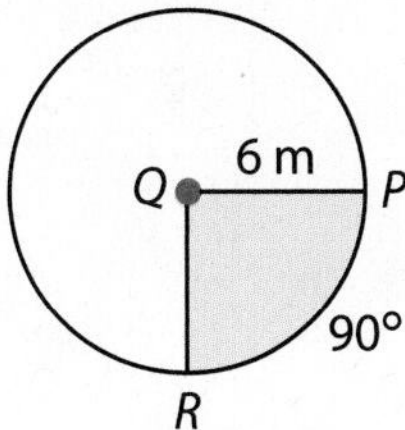

15. sector JKL

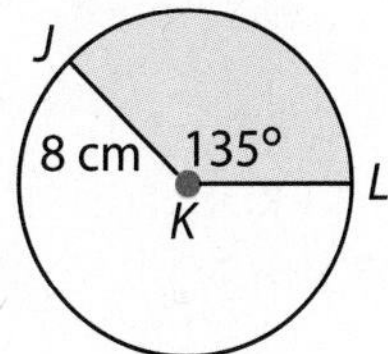

16. sector ABC

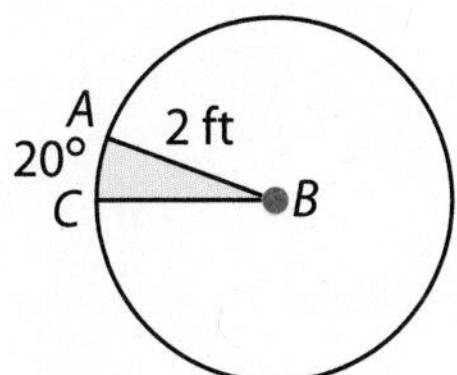

17. sector RST

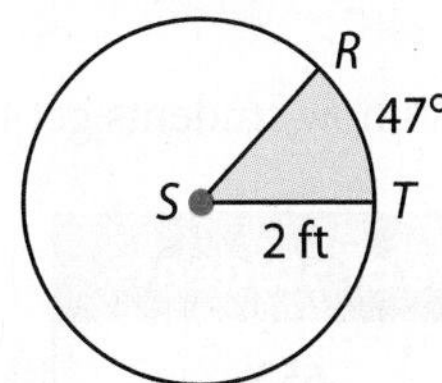

18. The beam from a lighthouse is visible for a distance of 15 mi. To the nearest square mile, what is the area covered by the beam as it sweeps in an arc of 270°?

19. The radius of circle O is 6 mm. The area of sector AOB is $\frac{9}{2}\pi$ mm². Explain how to find m$\angle AOB$.

The Artisan Pizza Co sells take-out pizza in two shapes: an "individual" 6-in. square slice and a circular "party" wheel with an 18 in. diameter. The party wheel is cut into 8 slices/sectors for the customer. An individual square slice costs \$2.95 and the entire party wheel costs \$15.95.

20. Which is larger, the square slice or one sector of the wheel?

21. Which option is the better value, buying 8 square slices or buying the party wheel?

22. Greek mathematicians studied the *salinon*, a figure bounded by four semicircles. What is the area of this salinon to the nearest tenth of a square inch?

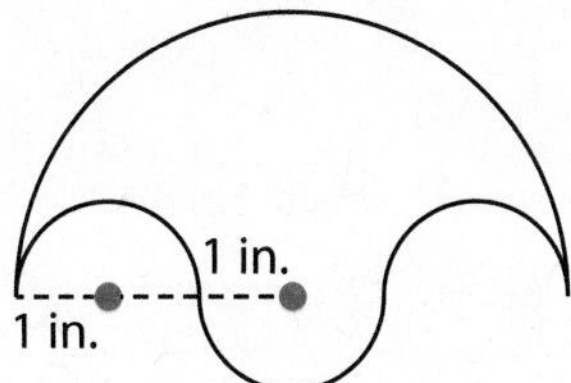

23. Which of the following express the measure of the angle of a sector, m, as a ratio between the area of the sector and the radius of the circle?

A. $\frac{360\pi}{Ar^2}$

B. $\frac{360\,A}{\pi r^2}$

C. $360r^2 \cdot \frac{A}{\pi}$

D. $\frac{A\pi r^2}{360}$

E. $\frac{Ar^2}{360\pi}$

F. $360A \cdot \frac{1}{\pi r^2}$

24. Algebra The table shows how students get to school.

Methods	% of Students
Bus	65%
Walk	25%
Other	10%

a. Explain why a circle graph is appropriate for the data.

b. Use a proportion to find the measure of the central angle for each sector. Then use a protractor and a compass to draw the circle graph.

c. Find the area of each sector. Use a radius of 2 inches.

Multi-Step **A *segment of a circle* is a region bounded by an arc and its chord. Find the area of each segment to the nearest hundredth.**

area of segment = area of sector − area of triangle

25.

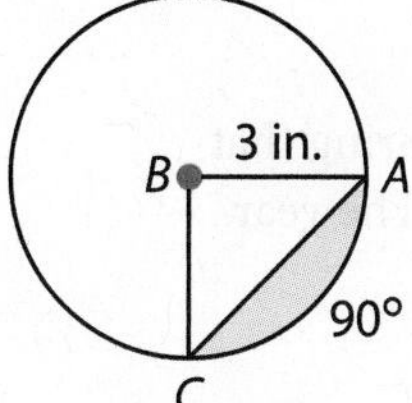

26.

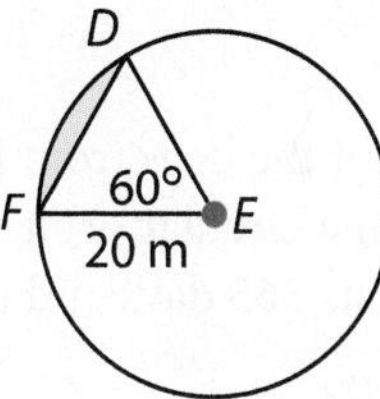

H.O.T. Focus on Higher Order Thinking

27. Critique Reasoning A student claims that when you double the radius of a sector while keeping the measure of the central angle constant, you double the area of the sector. Do you agree or disagree? Explain.

28. Multi-Step The exclamation point (!) on a billboard consists of a circle sector and circle. The radius of the sector is 9 ft, and the radius of the circle is 1.5 ft. The angle of the sector is 24°. What is the total area of the exclamation point on the billboard? Round to the nearest tenth.

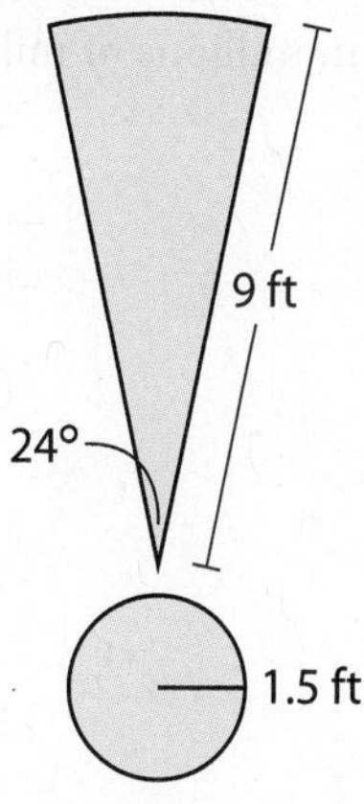

29. Analyze Relationships Compare finding arc length to finding the area of a sector. Name any common and different processes.

30. Critique Reasoning Melody says that she needs only to know the length of an arc and radius of a circle to find the area of the corresponding sector. If arc length is L and sector area is A, then $A = \frac{2L}{r}$. Is she correct? Justify your answer.

Lesson Performance Task

The planets orbit the Sun not in circles but in ellipses, which are "flattened" circles. The Earth's orbit, however, isn't flattened much. Its greatest distance from the Sun, 94.5 million miles, differs from its least distance, 91.4 million miles, by only about 3%.

To answer the following questions, make the following assumptions:

a. Summer includes all of the days from June 21 through September 21. During that time Earth travels in a circular orbit with a radius of 94.5 million miles. A year lasts 365 days.

b. Winter includes all of the days from December 21 through March 20. During that time Earth travels in a circular orbit with a radius of 91.4 million miles. The year you will consider lasts 365 days and is not a leap year.

Solve. Show your work. Use 3.14 for π.

1. Find the distances that the Earth travels in summer and in winter. Give your answers in millions of miles rounded to the nearest tenth.

2. Find the Earth's average rate of speed in summer and in winter. Give your answers in millions of miles per day rounded to the nearest hundredth.

3. Find the areas of the sectors that the Earth traverses in summer and in winter. Give your answers in millions of miles squared rounded to the nearest tenth.

Arc Length and Sector Area

Essential Question: How can the arc length and sector area of a circle be used to solve a real-world problem? How are they related?

KEY EXAMPLE *(Lesson 16.1)*

The circumference of a tire is 90 inches. What is its radius? Round to the nearest inch.

$C = 2\pi r$	Write the circumference formula.
$90 = 2\pi r$	Substitute the circumference.
$\frac{90}{2\pi} = r$	Simplify.
$14 \text{ in} \approx r$	Substitute 3.14 for π to approximate the solution.

KEY EXAMPLE *(Lesson 16.2)*

Find the arc length of an arc that measures 150° in a circle with a radius of 8 meters. Give your answer in terms of π.

$A = \frac{m}{360} \cdot 2\pi r$	Write the arc length formula.
$A = \frac{150}{360} \cdot 2\pi 8$	Substitute the angle measure and radius.
$A = \frac{20}{3}\pi$	Simplify.

KEY EXAMPLE *(Lesson 16.3)*

A sandwich shop sells sandwiches on two types of bread: a 9-inch square flatbread and a round roll with a 4-inch radius. Which type of bread is larger?

$A = s^2$	Write the area of a square.
$A = (9 \text{ in})^2$	Substitute the side length of the flatbread.
$A = 81 \text{ in}^2$	Simplify.
$A = \pi r^2$	Write the area of a circle.
$A = \pi(4)^2 \text{ in}^2$	Substitute the radius of the roll.
$A = 16\pi \text{ in}^2$	Simplify.
$A \approx 50.24 \text{ in}^2$	Substitute 3.14 for π to approximate the solution.

The flatbread is larger than the roll.

EXERCISES

Find the radius of the circle with the given circumference. *(Lesson 16.1)*

1. $C = 15$ in

2. $C = \pi$ cm

Find the arc length given the angle measure and radius of the circle. Give your answer in terms of π. *(Lesson 16.2)*

3. $m = 180°$, $r = 4$ inches

Apply the formula for the area of a sector to solve the real-world problem. *(Lesson 16.3)*

4. A paper airplane can be made out of two different pieces of paper: a circular piece 10 inches wide and a square piece 11 inches wide. Which piece of paper will provide the greater area for flight?

MODULE PERFORMANCE TASK

What's the Better Deal on Pizza?

You are ordering pizza and you have two choices: a slice of pizza from a large pizza with a diameter of 22 inches or an entire personal-size pizza that has a diameter of 6 inches. The slice costs $4.95, and the smaller pizza costs $3.75. Assuming that the large pizza is cut into 8 slices, will you get more pizza for your money by buying one slice of the larger pizza or by buying the personal-size pizza?

Be sure to write down all of your assumptions and data. Then use words, diagrams, numbers, or geometry to explain how you came to your conclusion.

16.1–16.3 Arc Length and Sector Area

- Online Homework
- Hints and Help
- Extra Practice

Apply the appropriate area formula. *(Lesson 16.1)*

1. At a campground, the area of a rectangular fire pit is 5 feet by 4 feet. What is the area of the largest circular fire than can be made in this fire pit? Round to the nearest square inch.

Find the arc length. Give your answer in terms of π and round to the nearest hundredth. *(Lesson 16.2)*

2. $\overset{\frown}{AB}$

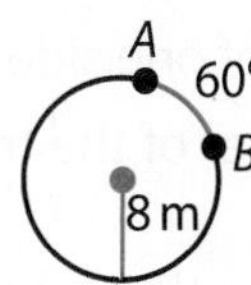

Apply the formula for the area of a sector to solve the real-world problem. *(Lesson 16.3)*

3. A Mexican restaurant sells quesadillas in two sizes: a "large" 10–inch round quesadilla and a "small" 6–inch round quesadilla. Which is larger, half of the 10-inch quesadilla or the entire 6-inch quesadilla?

ESSENTIAL QUESTION

4. What is the relationship between the arc length and sector area of a circle?

MODULE 16
MIXED REVIEW

Assessment Readiness

SELECTED RESPONSE

1. Consider each equation. Does it show a true relationship between degree measure and radian measure? Write Yes or No for A–C.

A. $\frac{5\pi}{12}$ radians $= 75°$

B. $\frac{\pi}{2}$ radians $= 180°$

C. $\frac{\pi}{3}$ radians $= 60°$

2. Consider a circle with a radius of 2 meters that has a central angle of 90°. Determine if each statement is True or False.

A. The arc measure is 90°.

B. The circumference and the area of this circle, taking away the units, are equal.

C. The arc length is π meters.

3. $\triangle ABC$ is an equilateral triangle, $AB = 3x + 27$, and $BC = 5x - 9$. Determine if each statement is True or False.

A. $x = 18$

B. The length of one side of the triangle is 162 units.

C. The perimeter of the triangle is 243 units.

4. Write an equation that represents the circumference of a circle with a radius of 6 feet. What is the diameter of the circle?

5. Given the sector area, how can the radius be determined? From the radius, how can the arc length be determined?

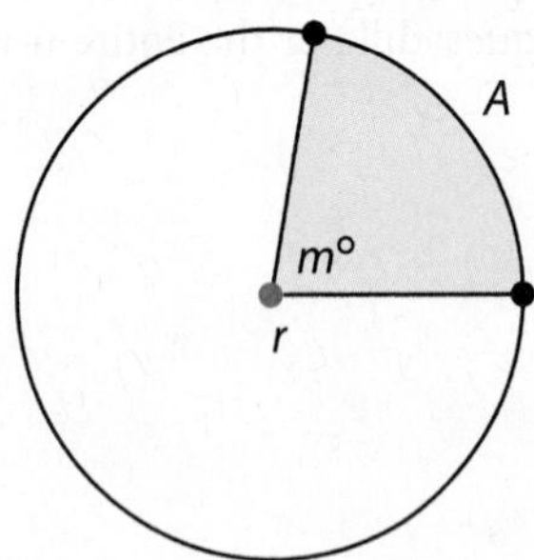

Equations of Circles and Parabolas

MODULE 17

Essential Question: How can you use equations of circles and parabolas to solve real-world problems?

REAL WORLD VIDEO
Check out some of the mathematics involved in the flight of rescue helicopters, such as this H-65 helicopter flown by the United States Coast Guard.

MODULE PERFORMANCE TASK PREVIEW

Rescue at Sea

One of the critical functions of the United States Coast Guard is carrying out search and rescue missions at sea. Teams of H-65 helicopters, each carrying two pilots, a flight mechanic, and a rescue swimmer, conduct coordinated sweeps over huge areas of ocean in search of the missing craft. The mathematics involved in executing such missions is complex, but you'll learn some of the basics in this module. Then you'll plan an ocean rescue of your own.

Are YOU Ready?

Complete these exercises to review skills you will need for this module.

- Online Homework
- Hints and Help
- Extra Practice

Circumference

Example 1 The center of a circle is $(-4, 1)$, and a point on the circle is $(1, -11)$. Find the circumference of the circle to the nearest tenth.

The circumference formula is $C = 2\pi r$.

$r = \sqrt{(-4-1)^2 + (1-(-11))^2} = 13$ Use the distance formula.

$C = 2\pi(13)$ Substitute.

$C = 26\pi$, or about 81.7. Simplify.

The center and a point on a circle are given. Find the circumference to the nearest tenth.

1. center: $(5, -5)$ point on the circle: $(25, 10)$

2. center: $(-12, -20)$ point on the circle: $(3, -12)$

3. center: $(8, 8)$ point on the circle: $(-2, 1)$

Characteristics of Quadratic Functions

Example 2 The vertex of a quadratic function is at $(2, 5)$ and one of the x-intercepts is at $(-1, 0)$. Find the other x-intercept.

The missing x-intercept is of the form $(x, 0)$. The midpoint between the two x-intercepts lies on the axis of symmetry, which passes through the vertex of the parabola. The x-value of the vertex is 2, so the axis of symmetry is $x = 2$, and the midpoint between the intercepts is $(2, 0)$. Therefore, 2 is the mean of the x-values of the intercepts: $2 = \frac{x + (-1)}{2}$, so $x = 5$. The missing x-intercept is $(5, 0)$.

The vertex and one x-intercept are given. Find the other x-intercept.

4. $(-3, 4), (6, 0)$

5. $(8, 1), (7, 0)$

6. $(-9\ -1), (-4, 0)$

17.1 Equation of a Circle

Essential Question: How can you write the equation of a circle if you know its radius and the coordinates of its center?

Explore — Deriving the Equation of a Circle

You have already worked with circles in several earlier lessons. Now you will investigate circles in a coordinate plane and learn how to write an equation of a circle.

We can define a **circle** as the set of all points in the coordinate plane that are a fixed distance r from the center (h, k).

Consider the circle in a coordinate plane that has its center at $C(h, k)$ and that has radius r.

(A) Let P be any point on the circle and let the coordinates of P be (x, y).

Create a right triangle by drawing a horizontal line through C and a vertical line through P, as shown.

What are the coordinates of point A? [?] Explain how you found the coordinates of A.

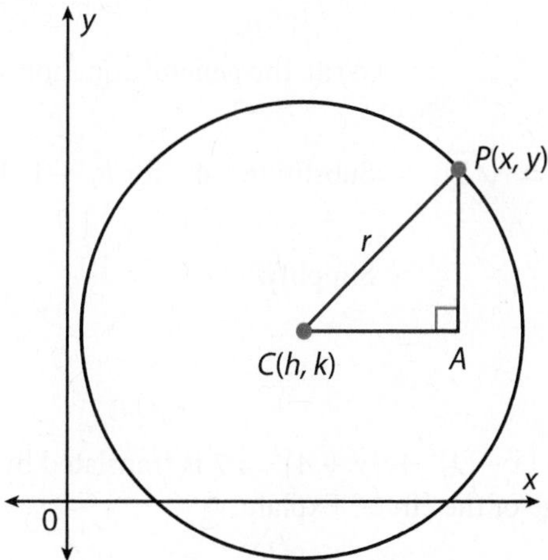

(B) Use absolute value to write expressions for the lengths of the legs of $\triangle CAP$.

$CA =$ [?]; $PA =$ [?]

(C) Use the Pythagorean Theorem to write a relationship among the side lengths of $\triangle CAP$.

[?] + [?] = [?]

Reflect

1. Compare your work with that of other students. Then, write an equation for the circle with center $C(h, k)$ and radius r.
2. Why do you need absolute values when you write expressions for the lengths of the legs in Step B, but not when you write the relationship among the side lengths in Step C?
3. Suppose a circle has its center at the origin. What is the equation of the circle in this case?

Explain 1 Writing the Equation of a Circle

You can write the equation of a circle given its center and radius.

Equation of a Circle

The equation of a circle with center (h, k) and radius r is $(x - h)^2 + (y - k)^2 = r^2$.

Example 1 **Write the equation of the circle with the given center and radius.**

(A) Center: $(-2, 5)$; radius: 3

$(x - h)^2 + (y - k)^2 = r^2$	Write the general equation of a circle.
$(x - (-2))^2 + (y - 5)^2 = 3^2$	Substitute -2 for h, 5 for k, and 3 for r.
$(x + 2)^2 + (y - 5)^2 = 9$	Simplify.

(B) Center: $(4, -1)$; radius: $\sqrt{5}$

$(x - h)^2 + (y - k)^2 = r^2$	Write the general equation of a circle.
$(x - (\boxed{4}))^2 + (y - (\boxed{-1}))^2 = \boxed{\sqrt{5}}^2$	Substitute $\boxed{4}$ for h, $\boxed{-1}$ for k, and $\boxed{\sqrt{5}}$ for r.
$(x \boxed{-4})^2 + (y \boxed{+1})^2 = \boxed{5}$	Simplify.

Reflect

4. Suppose the circle with equation $(x - 2)^2 + (y + 4)^2 = 7$ is translated by $(x, y) \rightarrow (x + 3, y - 1)$. What is the equation of the image of the circle? Explain.

Your Turn

Write the equation of the circle with the given center and radius.

5. Center: $(4, 3)$; radius: 4
6. Center: $(-1, -1)$; radius: $\sqrt{3}$

Explain 2 Finding the Center and Radius of a Circle

Sometimes you may find an equation of a circle in a different form. In that case, you may need to rewrite the equation to determine the circle's center and radius. You can use the process of completing the square to do so.

Example 2 **Find the center and radius of the circle with the given equation. Then graph the circle.**

(A) $x^2 - 4x + y^2 + 2y = 20$

Step 1 Complete the square twice to write the equation in the form $(x - h)^2 + (y - k)^2 = r^2$.

$x^2 - 4x + (\ )^2 + y^2 + 2y + (\ )^2 = 20 + (\ )^2$	Set up to complete the square.
$x^2 - 4x + \left(\frac{-4}{2}\right)^2 + y^2 + 2y + \left(\frac{2}{2}\right)^2 = 20 + \left(\frac{-4}{2}\right)^2 + \left(\frac{2}{2}\right)^2$	Add $\left(\frac{-4}{2}\right)^2$ and $\left(\frac{2}{2}\right)^2$ to both sides.
$x^2 - 4x + 4 + y^2 + 2y + 1 = 20 + 5$	Simplify.
$(x - 2)^2 + (y + 1)^2 = 25$	Factor.

Step 2 Identify h, k, and r to determine the center and radius.

$h = 2 \qquad k = -1 \qquad r = \sqrt{25} = 5$

So, the center is $(2, -1)$ and the radius is 5.

Step 3 Graph the circle.

- Locate the center of the circle.
- Place the point of your compass at the center
- Open the compass to the radius.
- Use the compass to draw the circle.

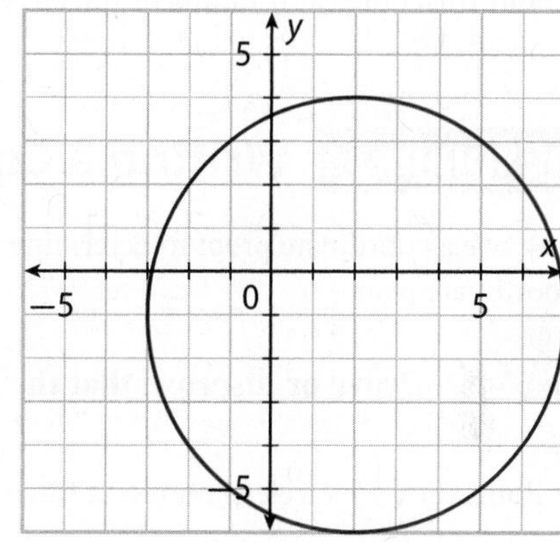

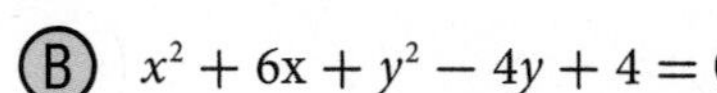

(B) $x^2 + 6x + y^2 - 4y + 4 = 0$

Step 1 Complete the square twice to write the equation in the form $(x - h)^2 + (y - k)^2 = r^2$.

$x^2 + 6x + y^2 - 4y = -4$	Subtract 4 from both sides.
$x^2 + 6x + \left(\boxed{\frac{6}{2}}\right)^2 + y^2 - 4y + \left(\boxed{\frac{-4}{2}}\right)^2 = -4 + \left(\boxed{\frac{6}{2}}\right)^2 + \left(\boxed{\frac{-4}{2}}\right)^2$	Add $\left(\boxed{\frac{6}{2}}\right)^2$ and $\left(\boxed{\frac{-4}{2}}\right)^2$ to both sides.
$x^2 + 6x + \boxed{9} + y^2 - 4y + \boxed{4} = -4 + \boxed{13}$	Simplify.
$\left(x \boxed{+3}\right)^2 + \left(y \boxed{-2}\right)^2 = \boxed{9}$	Factor.

Step 2 Identify h, k, and r to determine the center and radius.

$h = \boxed{-3}$ $k = \boxed{2}$ $r = \sqrt{\boxed{9}} = \boxed{3}$

So, the center is $\left(\boxed{-3}, \boxed{2}\right)$ and the radius is $\boxed{3}$.

Step 3 Graph the circle.

- Locate the center of the circle.
- Place the point of your compass at the center
- Open the compass to the radius.
- Use the compass to draw the circle.

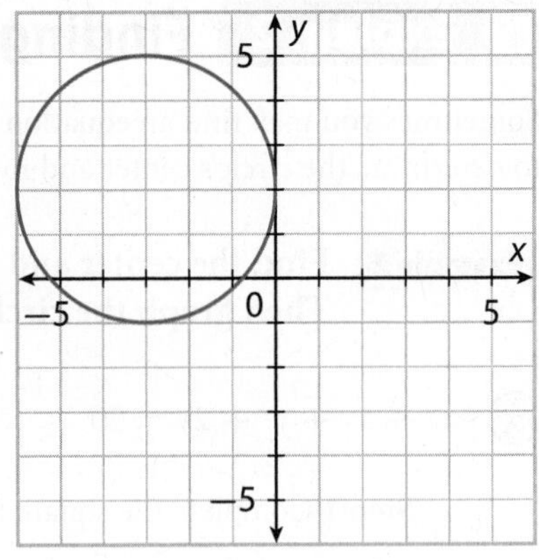

Reflect

7. How can you check your graph by testing specific points from the graph in the original equation? Give an example.

Your Turn

8. Find the center and radius of the circle with the equation. $x^2 + 2x + y^2 - 8y + 13 = 0$. Then graph the circle.

9. Find the center and radius of the circle with the equation $x^2 + y^2 + 4y = 5$. Then graph the circle.

Explain 3 Writing a Coordinate Proof

You can use a coordinate proof to determine whether or not a given point lies on a given circle in the coordinate plane.

Example 3 **Prove or disprove that the given point lies on the given circle.**

Ⓐ Point $(3, \sqrt{7})$, circle centered at the origin and containing the point $(-4, 0)$

Step 1 Plot a point at the origin and at $(-4, 0)$. Use these to help you draw the circle centered at the origin that contains $(-4, 0)$.

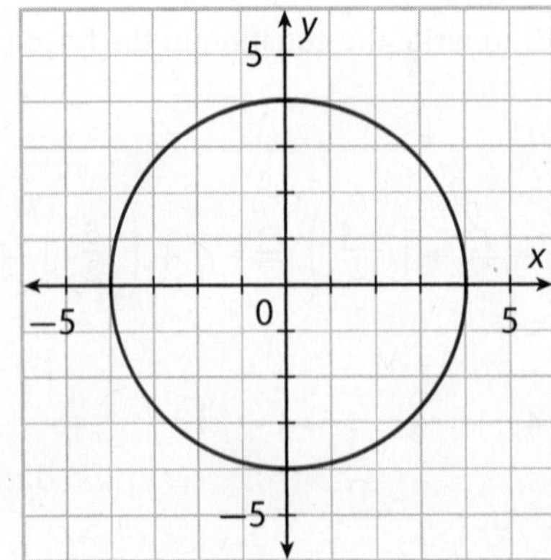

Step 2 Determine the radius: $r = 4$

Step 3 Use the radius and the coordinates of the center to write the equation of the circle.

$(x-h)^2 + (y-k)^2 = r^2$	Write the equation of the circle.
$(x-0)^2 + (y-0)^2 = (4)^2$	Substitute 0 for h, 0 for k, and 4 for r.
$x^2 + y^2 = 16$	Simplify.

Step 4 Substitute the x- and y-coordinates of the point $(3, \sqrt{7})$ in the equation of the circle to check whether they satisfy the equation of the circle.

$(3)^2 + (\sqrt{7})^2 \stackrel{?}{=} 16$	Substitute 3 for x and $\sqrt{7}$ for y.
$9 + 7 = 16$	Simplify.

So, the point $(3,\sqrt{7})$ lies on the circle because the point's x- and y-coordinates satisfy the equation of the circle.

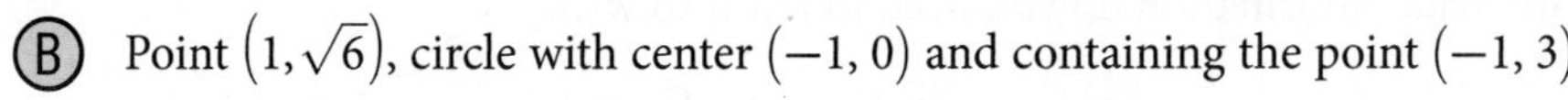

(B) Point $(1, \sqrt{6})$, circle with center $(-1, 0)$ and containing the point $(-1, 3)$

Step 1 Plot a point at $(-1, 0)$ and at $(-1, 3)$.

Draw the circle centered at $(-1, 0)$ that contains $(-1, 3)$.

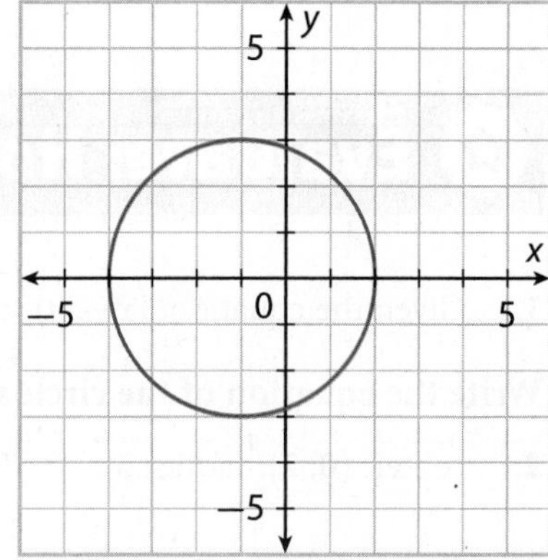

Step 2 Determine the radius: $r = 3$

Step 3 Use the radius and the coordinates of the center to write the equation of the circle.

$(x-h)^2 + (y-k)^2 = r^2$	Write the equation of the circle.
$(x-(-1))^2 + (y-(0))^2 = (3)^2$	Substitute -1 for h, 0 for k, and 3 for r.
$(x+1)^2 + y^2 = 9$	Simplify.

Step 4 Substitute the x- and y-coordinates of the point $(1, \sqrt{6})$ in the equation of the circle to check whether they satisfy the equation of the circle.

$(1+1)^2 + (\sqrt{6})^2 \stackrel{?}{=} 9$	Substitute 1 for x and $\sqrt{6}$ for y.
$4 + 6 \neq 9$	Simplify.

So the point $(1, \sqrt{6})$ does not lie on the circle because the x- and y-coordinates of the point do not satisfy the equation of the circle.

Reflect

10. How do you know that the radius of the circle in Example 3A is 4?

11. Name another point with noninteger coordinates that lies on the circle in Example 3A. Explain.

Your Turn

Prove or disprove that the given point lies on the given circle.

12. Point $(\sqrt{18}, -4)$, circle centered at the origin and containing the point $(6, 0)$

13. Point $(4, -4)$, circle with center $(1, 0)$ and containing the point $(1, 5)$

Elaborate

14. Discussion How is the distance formula related to the equation of a circle?

15. Essential Question Check-In What information do you need to know to write the equation of a circle?

Evaluate: Homework and Practice

- Online Homework
- Hints and Help
- Extra Practice

1. Given the equation, $(x - h)^2 = (y - k)^2 = r^2$, what are the coordinates of the center?

Write the equation of the circle with the given center and radius.

2. center: $(0, 2)$; radius: 5

3. center: $(-1, 3)$; radius 8

4. center: $(-4, -5)$; radius $\sqrt{2}$

5. center: $(9, 0)$; radius $\sqrt{3}$

Find the center and radius of the circle with the given equation. Then graph the circle.

6. $x^2 + y^2 = 16$

7. $x^2 - 6x + y^2 + 8y + 16 = 0$

8. $x^2 - 2x + y^2 + 4y - 4 = 0$

9. $x^2 - 6x + y^2 - 6y + 14 = 0$

10. Prove or disprove that the point $(1, \sqrt{3})$ lies on the circle that is centered at the origin and contains the point $(0, 2)$.

11. Prove or disprove that the point $(2, \sqrt{3})$ lies on the circle that is centered at the origin and contains the point $(-3, 0)$.

12. Prove or disprove that the circle with equation $x^2 - 4x + y^2 = -3$ intersects the y-axis.

13. Prove or disprove that the circle with equation $x^2 + y^2 - 10y = -16$ intersects the x-axis.

14. The center of a circle is $(0, -8)$. The radius is 9. What is the equation of the circle? Determine all that apply.

A. $x^2 + (y + 8)^2 = 3$

B. $x^2 + (y + 8)^2 = 9$

C. $x^2 + (y + 8)^2 = 81$

D. $x^2 + y^2 + 16y = 17$

E. $x^2 + y^2 + 16y = -55$

Algebra **Write the equation of each circle.**

15.

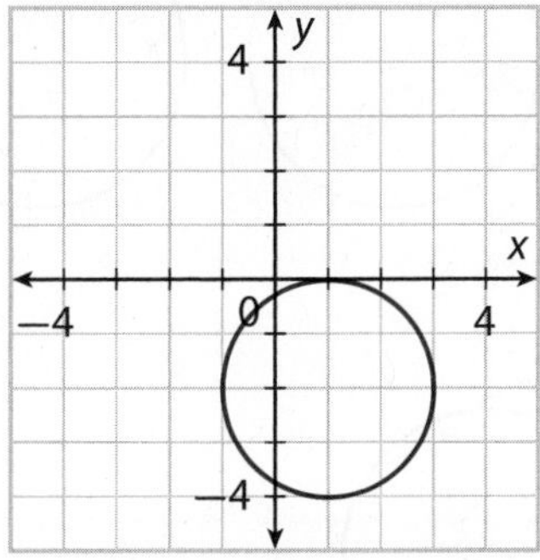

16.

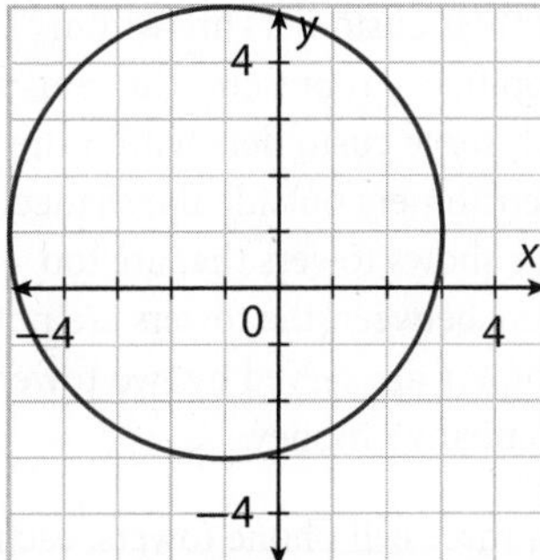

17. Prove or disprove that the circle with equation $x^2 + 4x + y^2 - 4y = 0$ contains the point $(0, 4)$.

18. The point $(2, n)$ lies on the circle whose equation is $(x - 3)^2 + (y + 2)^2 = 26$. Find the value of n.

Determine whether each statement is true or false. If false, explain why.

19. The circle $x^2 + y^2 = 7$ has radius 7.

20. The circle $(x - 2)^2 + (y + 3)^2 = 9$ passes through the point $(-1, -3)$.

21. The center of the circle $(x - 6)^2 + (y + 4)^2 = 1$ lies in the second quadrant.

22. The circle $(x + 1)^2 + (y - 4)^2 = 4$ intersects the y-axis.

23. The equation of the circle centered at the origin with diameter 6 is $x^2 + y^2 = 36$.

H.O.T. Focus on Higher Order Thinking

24. **Multi-Step** Carousels can be found in many different settings, from amusement parks to city plazas. Suppose that the center of a carousel is at the origin and that one of the animals on the circumference of the carousel has coordinates $(24, 32)$.

a. If one unit of the coordinate plane equals 1 foot, what is the diameter of the carousel?

b. As the carousel turns, the animals follow a circular path. Write the equation of this circle.

25. **Critical Thinking** The diameter of a circle has endpoints $(-6, 4)$ and $(0, 2)$.

  a. Write an equation for the circle in standard form.

  b. Prove or disprove that the point $(0, 4)$ lies on the circle.

26. **Communicate Mathematical Ideas** Can a unique circle be constructed from three nonlinear points? Explain.

Lesson Performance Task

Cell phone towers are expensive to build, so phone companies try to build as few towers as possible, while still ensuring that all of their customers are within range of a tower. The top figure represents the ranges of three towers that each serve customers within the shaded areas but leave customers outside the shaded areas. The bottom figure shows towers that are too close together. Customers between the towers are not left out, but many customers are served by two towers, a waste of the phone company's money.

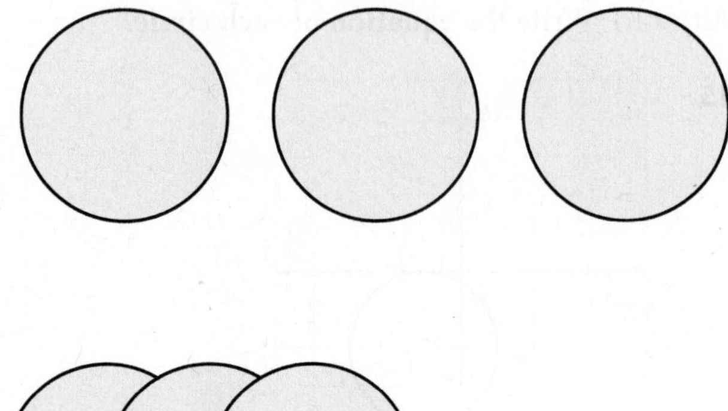

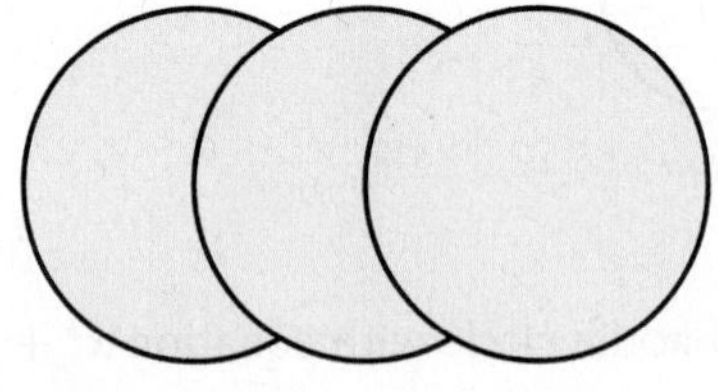

On a coordinate grid of three cell phone towers, each unit represents 1 mile. The graph of the range of Tower A has the equation $x^2 + y^2 = 36$. Tower B is 10 miles west of Tower A. Tower C is 10 miles east of Tower A.

1. Graph the ranges of the three towers. (All three have the same range.)

2. Write the equations of the ranges of Tower B and Tower C.

3. Estimate the area of the overlap between Tower A and Tower B.

4. A new tower with a range of 8 miles is being built 5 miles west and 11 miles north of Tower A. Write the equation of the range of the new tower.

17.2 Equation of a Parabola

Resource Locker

Essential Question: How do you write the equation of a parabola that opens up or down given its focus and directrix?

Explore 1 Identify Points That Are Equidistant From a Point and a Line

Remember that the distance from a point to a line is the length of the perpendicular segment from the point to the line. In the figure, the distance from point A to line ℓ is AB.

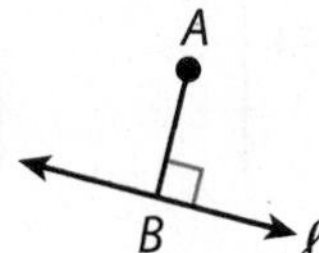

You will use the idea of the distance from a point to a line below.

On a coordinate grid, draw the line $y = -3$ and label it line ℓ. Plot the point (0, 3) and label it point R. Now follow these instructions.

(A) Choose a point on line ℓ. Plot point Q at this location.

(B) Using a straightedge, draw a perpendicular to ℓ that passes through point Q. Label this line m.

(C) Use the straightedge to draw $\overline{RQ}$. Then use a compass and straightedge to construct the perpendicular bisector of $\overline{RQ}$.

(D) Plot a point X where the perpendicular bisector intersects the line m.

(E) Write the approximate coordinates of point X.

(F) Repeat Steps A–D to plot multiple points. You may want to work together with other students, plotting all of your points on each of your graphs.

Reflect

The figure shows the construction of point Q, along with several other points constructed using the same method.

1. Explain why point X is equidistant from point R and line ℓ.

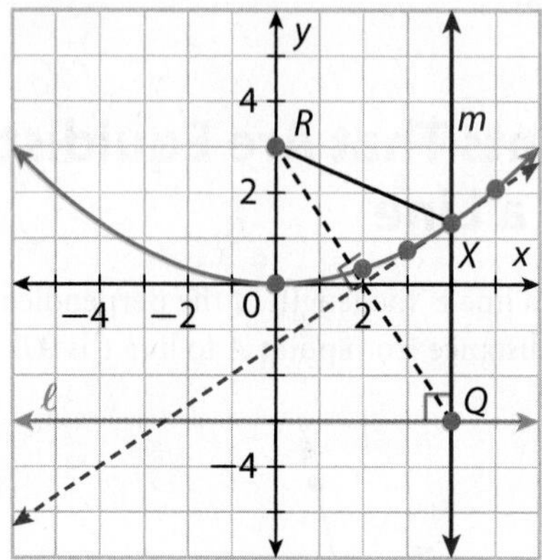

2. What do you notice about the points you plotted?

Explore 2 Deriving the Equation of a Parabola

A **parabola** is the set of all points P in a plane that are equidistant from a given point, called the **focus**, and a given line, called the **directrix**. The **vertex** of a parabola is the midpoint of the segment, perpendicular to the directrix, that connects the focus and the directrix.

For the parabola shown, the vertex is at the origin.

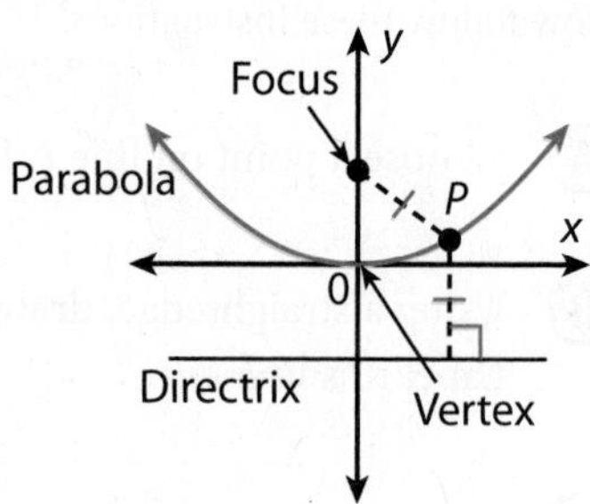

To derive the general equation of a parabola, you can use the definition of a parabola, the distance formula, and the idea that the distance from a point to a line is the length of the perpendicular segment from the point to the line.

Ⓐ Let the focus of the parabola be $F(0, p)$ and let the directrix be the line $y = -p$. Let P be a point on the parabola with coordinates (x, y).

Ⓑ Let Q be the point of intersection of the perpendicular from P and the directrix. Then the coordinates of Q are ? .

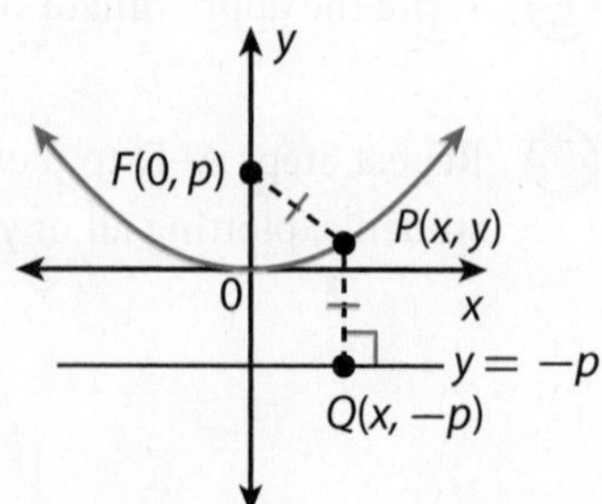

(C) By the definition of a parabola, $FP = QP$.

By the distance formula, $FP = \sqrt{(x-0)^2 + (y-p)^2} = \sqrt{x^2 + (y-p)^2}$ and
$QP = \sqrt{(x-x)^2 + \left(y-(-p)\right)^2} = \sqrt{0 + (y+p)^2} = |y+p|$.

Set FP equal to QP.	$\boxed{?} = \lvert y+p \rvert$
Square both sides.	$x^2 + \boxed{?} = \lvert y+p \rvert^2$
Expand the squared terms.	$x^2 + y^2 - \boxed{?} + p^2 = y^2 + \boxed{?} + p^2$
Subtract y^2 and p^2 from both sides.	$\boxed{?} = \boxed{?}$
Add $2py$ to both sides.	$x^2 = \boxed{?}$
Solve for y.	$\frac{1}{\boxed{?}} x^2 = y$

Reflect

3. Explain how the value of p determines whether the parabola opens up or down.

4. Explain why the origin $(0, 0)$ is always a point on a parabola with focus $F(0, p)$ and directrix $y = -p$.

Explain 1 Writing an Equation of a Parabola with Vertex at the Origin

You can use the focus and directrix of a parabola to write an equation of the parabola with vertex at the origin.

Example 1 **Write the equation of the parabola with the given focus and directrix. Then graph the parabola.**

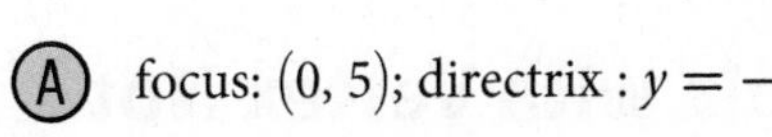

(A) focus: $(0, 5)$; directrix : $y = -5$

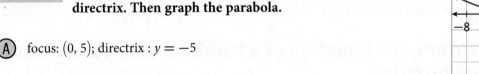

- The focus of the parabola is $(0, p)$, so $p = 5$.

  The general equation of a parabola is $y = \frac{1}{4p} x^2$.

  So, the equation of this parabola is $y = \frac{1}{4(5)} x^2$ or $y = \frac{1}{20} x^2$.

- To graph the parabola, complete the table of values. Then plot points and draw the curve.

x	y
−10	5
−5	1.25
0	0
5	1.25
10	5

(B) Write the equation of the parabola with focus $(0, -4)$ and directrix $y = 4$.

- The focus of the parabola is $(0, p)$, so $p = -4$.

  The general equation of a parabola is $y = \frac{1}{4p}x^2$.

  So, the equation of this parabola is $y = -\frac{1}{16}x^2$.

- To graph the parabola, complete the table of values. Then plot points and draw the curve.

x	y
−4	−1
−2	−0.25
0	0
2	−0.25
4	−1

Reflect

5. Describe any symmetry in your graph from Example 1B. Why does this make sense based on the parabola's equation?

Your Turn

Write the equation of the parabola with the given focus and directrix. Then graph the parabola.

6. Parabola with focus $(0, -1)$ and directrix $y = 1$.

Explain 2 Writing the Equation of a Parabola with Vertex Not at the Origin

The vertex of a parabola may not be at the origin. But given the focus and directrix of a parabola, you can find the coordinates of the vertex and write an equation of the parabola.

A parabola with vertex (h, k) that opens up or down has equation $(x - h)^2 = 4p(y - k)$ where $|p|$ is the distance from the vertex to the focus.

Example 2 **Write the equation of the parabola with the given focus and directrix. Then graph the parabola.**

 focus: $(3, 5)$, directrix: $y = -3$

- Draw the focus and the directrix on the graph.
- Draw a segment perpendicular to the directrix from the focus.
- Find the midpoint of the segment. The segment is 8 units long, so the vertex is 4 units below the focus. Then $p = 4$, and the coordinates of the vertex are $(3, 1)$.

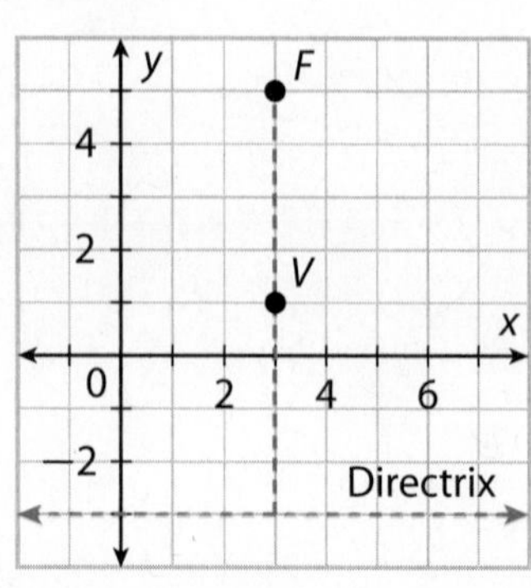

- Since the formula for a parabola is $(x - h)^2 = 4p(y - k)$, the equation of the parabola is $(x - 3)^2 = 16(y - 1)$.
- To graph the parabola, complete the table of values. Round to the nearest tenth if necessary. Then plot the points and draw the curve.

x	y
−1	2
1	1.3
2	1.1
3	1
4	1.1
6	1.6
7	2

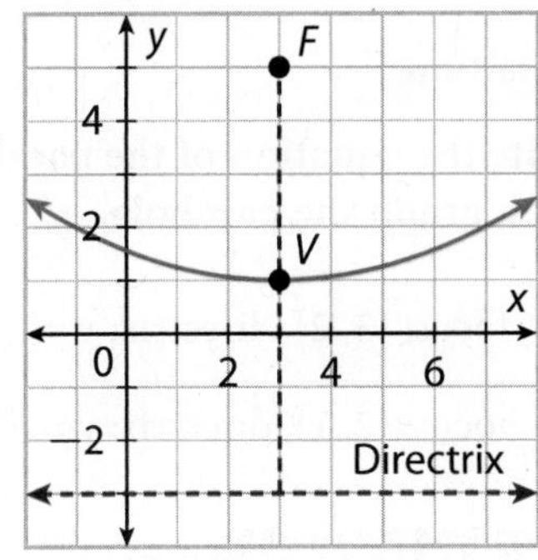

(B) focus: $(-1, 4)$; directrix: $y = 6$

- Draw the focus and the directrix on the graph.
- Draw a segment perpendicular to the directrix through the focus.
- Find the midpoint of the segment. The segment is 2 units long, so the vertex is 1 unit above the focus. The coordinates of the vertex are $(-1, 5)$. The parabola opens down so $p = -1$.
- Since the formula for a parabola is $(x - h)^2 = 4p(y - k)$, the equation of the parabola is $(x - (-1))^2 = -4\,(y - 5)$.
- To graph the parabola, complete the table of values. Round to the nearest tenth if necessary. Then plot the points and draw the curve.

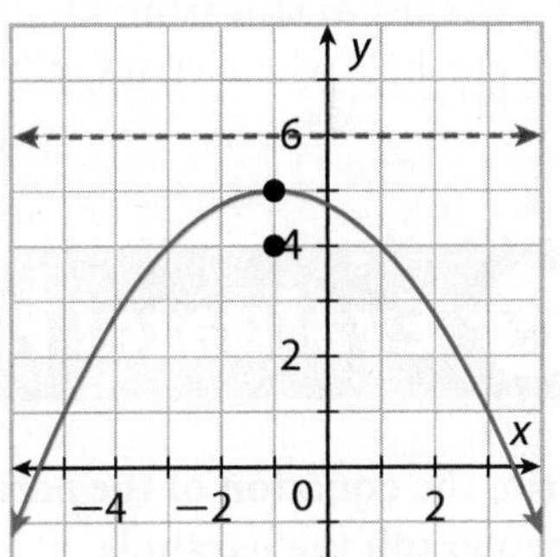

x	y
−4	2.8
−3	4
−2	4.8
−1	5
0	4.8
1	4
2	2.8

Reflect

7. **Discussion** Without calculating, how can you determine by considering the focus and directrix of a parabola whether the parabola opens up or down?

Your Turn

Write the equation of the parabola with the given focus and directrix. Then graph the parabola.

8. focus: $(3, 2)$, directrix: $y = -4$

9. focus: $(2, 1)$, directrix: $y = 9$

Elaborate

10. What does the sign of p in the equation of a parabola tell you about the parabola?

11. Explain how to choose appropriate x-values when completing a table of values given the equation of a parabola.

12. **Essential Question Check-In** How is an equation for the general parabola related to the equation for a parabola with a vertex of (0, 0)?

Evaluate: Homework and Practice

- Online Homework
- Hints and Help
- Extra Practice

Write the equation of the parabola with the given focus and directrix. Then graph the parabola.

1. focus: $(0, 2)$; directrix: $y = -2$
2. focus: $(0, -3)$; directrix: $y = 3$
3. focus: $(0, -5)$; directrix: $y = 5$
4. focus: $(0, 4)$; directrix: $y = -4$

Find the directrix and focus of a parabola with the given equation.

5. $y = -\frac{1}{24}x^2$
6. $y = 2x^2$
7. $y = -\frac{1}{2}x^2$
8. $y = \frac{1}{40}x^2$

Write the equation of the parabola with the given focus and directrix. Then graph the parabola.

9. focus: $(2, 3)$; directrix: $y = 7$
10. focus: $(-3, 2)$; directrix: $y = -4$
11. focus: $(4, 2)$; directrix: $y = -8$
12. focus: $(-3, 8)$; directrix: $y = 9$

Find the focus and directrix of a parabola with the given equation.

13. $(x+2)^2 = 16(y+1)$

14. $(x-4)^2 = 40(y-4)$

15. $-(x+5)^2 = y + 3.25$

16. $(x-3)^2 = -24(y+4)$

17. **Make a Conjecture** Complete the table by writing the equation of each parabola. Then use a calculator to graph the equations in the same window to help you make a conjecture: What happens to the graph of a parabola as the focus and directrix move apart?

Focus	(0, 1)	(0, 2)	(0, 3)	(0, 4)
Directrix	$y = -1$	$y = -2$	$y = -3$	$y = -4$
Equation				

18. Find the length of the line segment that is parallel to the directrix of a parabola, that passes through the focus, and that has endpoints on the parabola. Explain your reasoning.

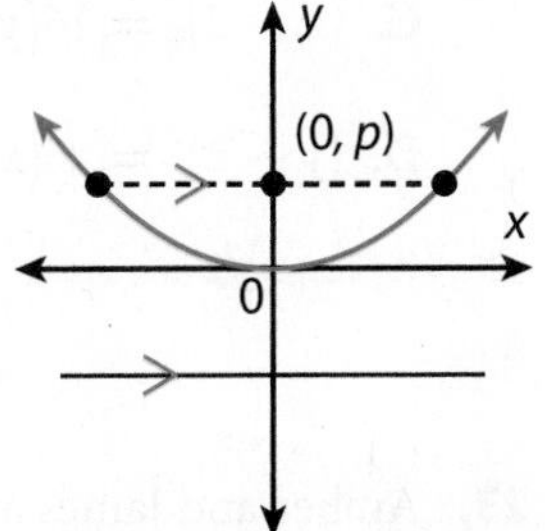

19. **Represent Real-World Problems** The light from the lamp shown has parabolic cross sections. Write an equation for a cross section of the lamp if the bulb is 6 inches from the vertex and the vertex is placed at the origin. (Hint: The bulb of the lamp is the focus of the parabola.)

20. At a bungee-jumping contest, Gavin makes a jump that can be modeled by the equation $(x-6)^2 = 12(y-4)$ with dimensions in feet.

   a. Which point on the path identifies the lowest point that Gavin reached? What are the coordinates of this point? How close to the ground was he?

   b. **Analyze Relationships** Nicole makes a similar jump that can be modeled by the equation $(x-2)^2 = 8(y-8.5)$. How close to the ground did Nicole get? Did Nicole get closer to the ground than Gavin? If so, by how much?

H.O.T. Focus on Higher Order Thinking

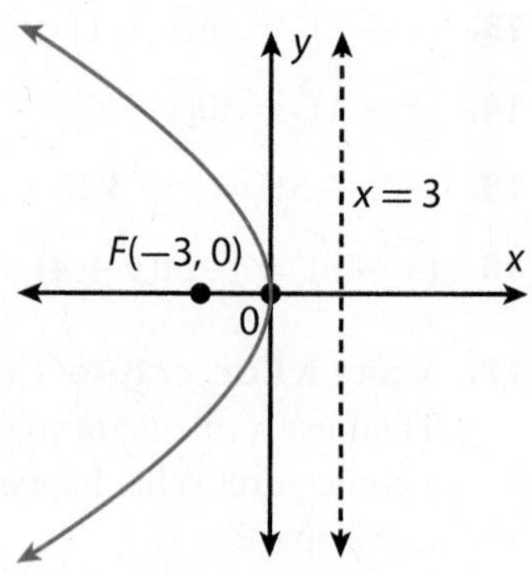

21. **Critical Thinking** Some parabolas open to the left or right rather than up or down. For such parabolas, if $p > 0$, the parabola opens to the right. If $p < 0$, the parabola opens to the left. What is the value of p for the parabola shown? Explain your reasoning.

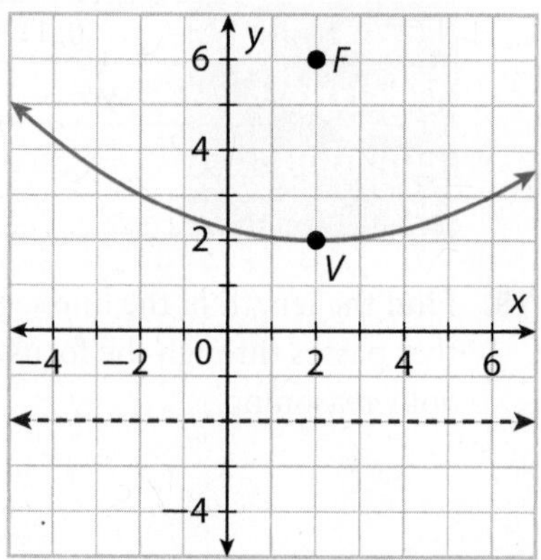

22. **Critical Thinking** Which equation represents the parabola shown?

    A. $(x - 2)^2 = -16(y - 2)$

    B. $(y - 2)^2 = -16(x - 2)$

    C. $(x - 2)^2 = 16(y - 2)$

    D. $(y - 2)^2 = 16(x - 2)$

23. Amber and James are lying on the ground, each tossing a ball into the air, and catching it. The paths of the balls can be represented by the following equations, with the x-values representing the horizontal distances traveled thrown and the y-values representing the heights of the balls, both measured in feet.

    Amber: $-20(x - 15)^2 = y - 11.25$ James: $-24(x - 12)^2 = y - 6$

    a. What are the bounds of the equations for the physical situation? Explain.

    b. Whose ball went higher? Which traveled the farthest horizontal distance? Justify your answers.

Lesson Performance Task

Suppose a park wants to build a new half-pipe structure for the skateboarders. To make sure all parts of the ramp are supported, the inside of the ramp needs to be equidistant from a focus point, which is at a height of 3 feet. Find the equation of the half-pipe and sketch it, along with the focus point and the directrix. Would the ramp get steeper or flatten out if the focus point height were at a height of 4 feet? Explain.

STUDY GUIDE REVIEW

Equations of Circles and Parabolas

MODULE 17

Essential Question: How can you use equations of circles and parabolas to solve real-world problems?

Key Vocabulary

circle *(círculo)*

parabola *(parábola)*

focus *(foco)*

directrix *(directriz)*

KEY EXAMPLE *(Lesson 17.1)*

Find the center and radius of the circle with the equation $x^2 + 2x + y^2 - 6y = 6$.

$x^2 + 2x + (\ )^2 + y^2 - 6y + (\ )^2 = 6 + (\ )^2$ Set up to complete the square.

$x^2 + 2x + \left(\frac{2}{2}\right)^2 + y^2 - 6y + \left(\frac{-6}{2}\right)^2 = 6 + \left(\frac{2}{2}\right)^2 + \left(\frac{-6}{2}\right)^2$ Add $\left(\frac{2}{2}\right)^2$ and $\left(\frac{-6}{2}\right)^2$ to both sides.

$x^2 + 2x + 1 + y^2 - 6y + 9 = 6 + 10$ Simplify.

$(x + 1)^2 + (y - 3)^2 = 16$ Factor.

$h = -1, k = 3, r = \sqrt{16} = 4$ Identify h, k, and r to determine the center and radius.

The center is $(-1, 3)$ and the radius is 4.

KEY EXAMPLE *(Lesson 17.2)*

Find the focus and directrix of the parabola with the equation $y = -\frac{1}{12}x^2$.

$h = 0, k = 0, p = -3$ Use the general equation $y - k = \frac{1}{4p}(x - h)^2$ to identify h, k, and p.

focus: $(0, -3)$ The vertex is at $(0, 0)$, so the focus is at $(0, p)$.

directrix: $y = 3$ The vertex is at $(0, 0)$, so the directrix is $y = -p$.

KEY EXAMPLE *(Lesson 17.2)*

Find the equation of the parabola with focus $(1, 6)$ and directrix $y = 2$.

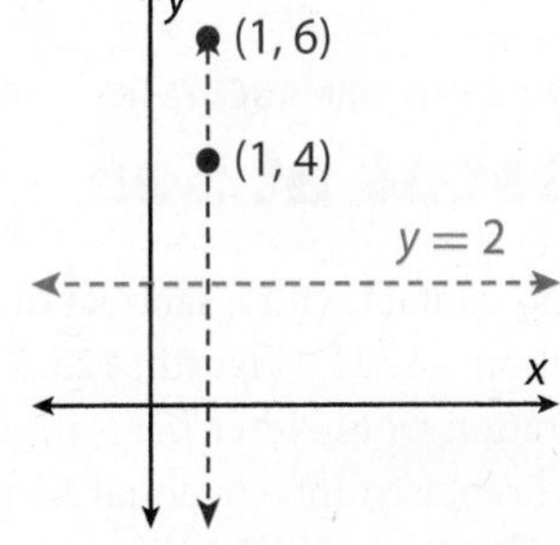

vertex: $(1, 4)$ The vertex is the midpoint of the line through the focus and perpendicular to the directrix.

$h = 1, k = 4, p = 2$ Identify h, k, and p.

$y - 4 = \frac{1}{8}(x - 1)^2$ Substitute h, k, and p in the general equation $y - k = \frac{1}{4p}(x - h)^2$

The equation of the parabola is $y - 4 = \frac{1}{8}(x - 1)^2$.

EXERCISES

Find the center and radius of the circle with the given equation. *(Lesson 17.1)*

1. $(x - 3)^2 + (y + 5)^2 = 49$

2. $(x + 8.5)^2 + y^2 = 75$

3. $x^2 + 6x + y^2 - 2y = 15$

4. $x^2 - 18x + y^2 - 18y + 53 = 0$

Find the focus, vertex, and directrix of the parabola with the given equation. *(Lesson 17.2)*

5. $y = \frac{1}{32}x^2$

6. $y + 3 = -\frac{1}{2}(x + 5)^2$

Find the equation of the parabola with the given focus and directrix. *(Lesson 17.2)*

7. focus $(-2, 3)$; directrix $y = -5$

8. focus $(5, -4)$; directrix $y = 8$

MODULE PERFORMANCE TASK

Rescue at Sea

Radio contact with a sailboat off the coast of California has been lost. The craft's last known position was 35.5° North, 123.7° West. The Coast Guard is mounting a search-and-rescue operation from either Los Angeles International Airport (LAX), located at 33.9° N, 118.4° W; San Francisco International Airport (SFO), located at 37.8° N, 122.4° W; or both. The Coast Guard will use H-65 helicopters with ranges of approximately 290 nautical miles.

Should helicopters be flown from LAX, SFO, or both?

Start by listing the information you will need to solve the problem. Then work on the task. Use numbers, words, or algebra to explain how you reached your conclusion.

Ready to Go On?

17.1–17.2 Equation of Circles and Parabolas

- Online Homework
- Hints and Help
- Extra Practice

Solve. Round answers to the nearest tenth. *(Lessons 17.1, 17.2)*

1. Find the center and radius of the circle $x^2 + 4x + y^2 - 2y - 4 = 0$.

2. Find the focus, vertex, and directrix of the parabola with the equation $y = (x - 8)^2 - 6$

3. A circle has its center at $(-2, 4)$ and a radius of $5\sqrt{2}$. Does the point $(3, -1)$ lie on the circle? Explain.

4. Does the graph of the parabola $y = -\frac{1}{100}x^2$ open upward or downward? Explain.

5. A new cellular phone tower services all phones within a 17 mile radius. Doreen lives 15 miles east and 8 miles south of the tower. Is she within the area serviced by the tower? Explain. *(Lesson 17.2)*

ESSENTIAL QUESTION

6. What information about a circle and a parabola do you need in order to draw their graphs on the coordinate plane?

MODULE 17
MIXED REVIEW

Assessment Readiness

1. The graph of the equation $x^2 + 6x + y^2 - 16y = -9$ is a circle. Determine if each statement is True or False.

A. The center of the circle is $(3, -8)$.

B. The circle is tangent to the x-axis.

C. The circle has a radius of 64.

2. Consider the graph of the parabola $y = x^2 + 4$. Write Yes or No for A–C.

A. The vertex is $(0, 4)$

B. The parabola opens upward.

C. The directrix is $y = -4.25$.

3. An engineer drew the graph of a new tire on a coordinate plane. The equation of the tire was $x^2 + y^2 - 26y = 0$. How many feet will the tire roll in 100 complete revolutions? Explain.

4. Find the points of intersection of the circle $x^2 + y^2 = 25$ and the parabola $y = x^2 - 5$. Explain how you found the points.

UNIT 6 MIXED REVIEW

Assessment Readiness

- Online Homework
- Hints and Help
- Extra Practice

1. Write whether each arc is a minor arc, a major arc, or a semicircle.

A. $\overset{\frown}{AB}$

B. $\overset{\frown}{ABE}$

C. $\overset{\frown}{ADB}$

2. Quadrilateral *ABCD* is inscribed in a circle with angle measures $m\angle A = (11x - 8)°$, $m\angle B = (3x^2 + 1)°$, $m\angle C = (15x + 32)°$, and $m\angle D = (2x^2 - 1)°$. Are each of the following measures of the quadrilateral's angles? Write yes or no for each statement.

A. $m\angle A = 135°$

B. $m\angle B = 109°$

C. $m\angle C = 227°$

D. $m\angle D = 71°$

3. ΔABC and ΔDEF are congruent.

Write if each statement is True or False.

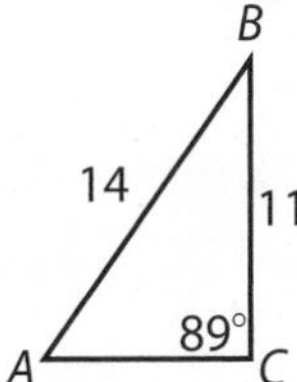

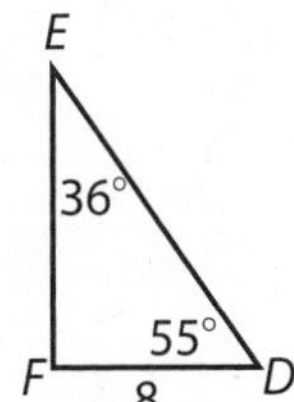

A. $m\angle F = 91°$

B. $m\angle A = 55°$

C. $EF = 11$

4. Determine whether the vertex of $\angle 1$ is on the circle, inside the circle, or outside the circle given its measure and the measure of its intercepted arc(s).

A. $m\angle 1 = 59°$, $m\overset{\frown}{AB} = 86°$, $m\overset{\frown}{CD} = 32°$

B. $m\angle 1 = 43°$, $m\overset{\frown}{AB} = 86°$

C. $m\angle 1 = 27°$, $m\overset{\frown}{AB} = 86°$, $m\overset{\frown}{CD} = 32°$

5. Are each of the following lengths of chords in the circle?
Write yes or no for each statement.

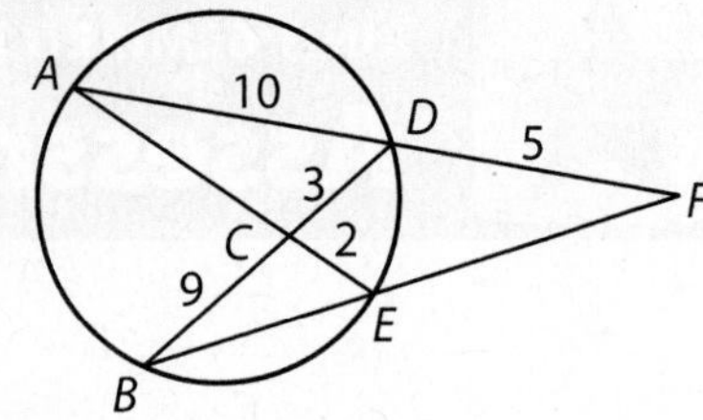

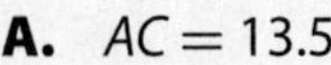

A. $AC = 13.5$

B. $EF = 7.1$

C. $BF = 2.9$

6. Are each of the following lengths of the segments in the triangle?
Write yes or no for each statement.

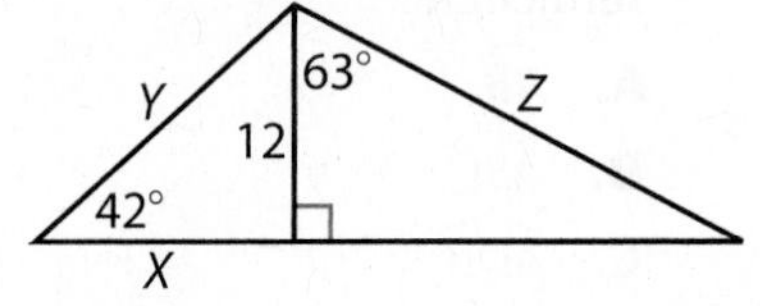

A. $x = 13.3$

B. $y = 16.1$

C. $z = 13.5$

7. Given that $\triangle ABC$ is a right triangle, determine if it is a special right triangle.
Write yes or no for each statement.

A. $AC = BC = 3\sqrt{2}$ and $AB = 6$

B. $AC = BC = 5\sqrt{2}$ and $AB = 10$

C. $m\angle A = 30°$

8. Renee is designing a logo for an airline. She starts by making a figure with angle measures as shown. She measures $\overline{AB}$ and finds that the length of the segment is 5 inches. Can she determine the length of $\overline{DB}$ without measuring? If so, explain how. If not, explain why not.

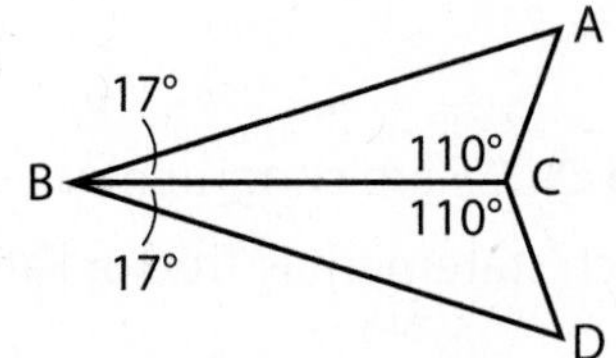

9. A car tire has a diameter of 21.3 inches. What are the circumference and the area of the tire?

Performance Tasks

★**10.** A city planner is designing a bridge to cross a circular lake in the park. There will be two footpaths, both tangent to the lake, that connect to each side of the bridge. At what angles do the footpaths connect with the bridge?

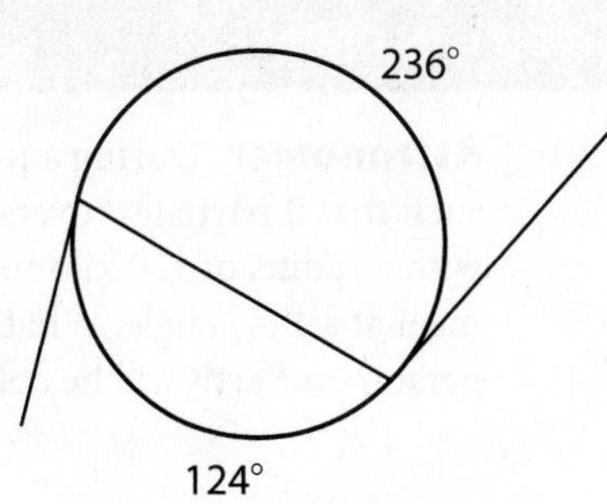

★★**11.** Nestor cuts a cake with a 12-inch diameter. One of the pieces he cuts has a central angle of 24°. What is the area of the slice of cake? What fraction of the entire cake is this? Explain.

★★★**12.** Jeanine's swimming pool has a diameter of 27 feet. Surrounding the pool is a deck that extends 5 feet from the edges of the pool. Jeanine wants to paint the deck and then put a fence around it. Paint costs $0.85 per square foot and fencing costs $8.25 per foot. How much will it cost Jeanine to paint the deck and add fencing? Explain how you found your answer.

MATH IN CAREERS

Astronomer During a partial solar eclipse, the moon aligns with the sun and Earth such that it partially covers the sun from view on a circular area on Earth's surface with a radius of 130 kilometers (km). The lines tangent to both the moon and this area meet at a 144° angle. What is the measure and length of the arc on the area in which a person on Earth will be able to witness a partial eclipse?

UNIT 7

Measurement and Modeling in Two and Three Dimensions

MATH IN CAREERS

Model Maker Model kits often contain detailed parts made of etched metal. The model designers need to visualize the shapes and surfaces of the finished 3-D parts to create patterns for etching and folding the metal.

If you're interested in a career as a model maker, you should study these mathematical subjects:

- Algebra
- Geometry
- Trigonometry
- Calculus

Research other careers that require the use of engineering to understand real-world scenarios. See the related Career Activity at the end of this unit.

Visualize Vocabulary

Copy and complete the chart. Use four of the ✔ words and draw an example of each.

Object	Example
?	?
?	?
?	?
?	?

Review Words

✔ area (*área*)
✔ composite figure (*figura compuesta*)
✔ cone (*cono*)
✔ cylinder (*cilindro*)
✔ pyramid (*pirámide*)
✔ sphere (*esfera*)
✔ volume (*volume*)

Preview Words

apothem (*apotema*)
cross section (*sección transversal*)
great circle (*gran círculo*)
net (*neto*)
oblique cylinder (*cilindro oblicuo*)
oblique prism (*prisma oblicuo*)
regular pyramid (*pirámide regular*)
right cone (*cono recto*)
right cylinder (*cilindro recto*)
right prism (*prisma recto*)
surface area (*área de la superficie*)

Understand Vocabulary

Complete the sentences using the preview words.

1. A(n) __?__ is the region of a plane that intersects a solid figure.

2. A cross section of a sphere with the same radius as the sphere is called a __?__.

3. The __?__ of a right prism is a two-dimensional image containing six rectangles.

Active Reading

Pyramid Create a pyramid and organize the adjectives used to describe different objects—right, regular, oblique—on each of its faces. When listening to descriptions of objects, look for these words and associate them with the object that follows.

Volume Formulas

MODULE 18

Essential Question: How can you use volume formulas to solve real-world problems?

REAL WORLD VIDEO
Check out how volume formulas can be used to find the volumes of real-world objects, including sinkholes.

MODULE PERFORMANCE TASK PREVIEW

How Big Is That Sinkhole?

In 2010, a giant sinkhole opened up in a neighborhood in Guatemala and swallowed up the three-story building that stood above it. In this module, you will choose and apply an appropriate formula to determine the volume of this giant sinkhole.

Complete these exercises to review skills you will need for this module.

Personal Math Trainer
- Online Homework
- Hints and Help
- Extra Practice

Area of a Circle

Example 1 Find the area of a circle with radius equal to 5.

$A = \pi r^2$ Write the equation for the area of a circle of radius r.

$A = \pi(5)^2$ Substitute the radius.

$A = 25\pi$ Simplify.

Find each area.

1. A circle with radius 4

2. A circle with radius 6

3. A circle with radius 3π

4. A circle with radius $\frac{2}{\pi}$

Volume Properties

Example 2 Find the number of cubes that are 1 cm^3 in size that fit into a cube of size 1 m^3.

Notice that the base has a length and width of 1 m or 100 cm, so its area is 1 m^2 or 10,000 cm^2.

The 1 m^3 cube is 1 m or 100 cm high, so multiply the area of the base by the height to find the volume of 1,000,000 cm^3.

Find the volume.

5. The volume of a 1 km^3 body of water in m^3

6. The volume of a 1 ft^3 box in $in.^3$

Volume of Rectangular Prisms

Example 3 Find the volume of a rectangular prism with height 4 cm, length 3 cm, and width 5 cm.

$V = Bh$ Write the equation for the volume of a rectangular prism.

$V = (3)(5)(4)$ The volume of a rectangular prism is the area of the base times the height.

$V = 60\ cm^3$ Simplify.

Find each volume.

7. A rectangular prism with length 3 m, width 4 m, and height 7 m

8. A rectangular prism with length 2 cm, width 5 cm, and height 12 cm

18.1 Volume of Prisms and Cylinders

Essential Question: How do the formulas for the volume of a prism and cylinder relate to area formulas that you already know?

Explore Developing a Basic Volume Formula

The volume of a three-dimensional figure is the number of nonoverlapping cubic units contained in the interior of the figure. This prism is made up of 8 cubes, each with a volume of 1 cubic centimeter, so it has a volume of 8 cubic centimeters. You can use this idea to develop volume formulas.

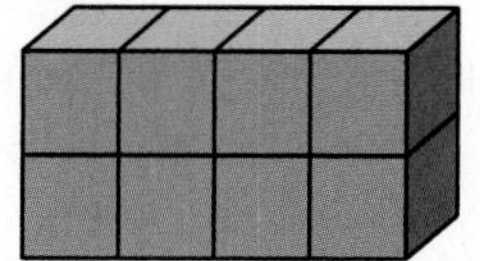

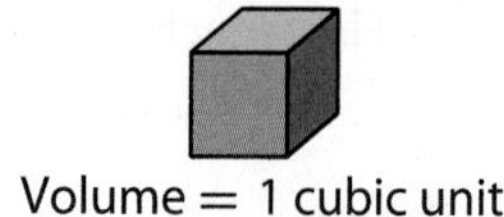

In this activity you'll explore how to develop a volume formula for a right prism and a right cylinder.

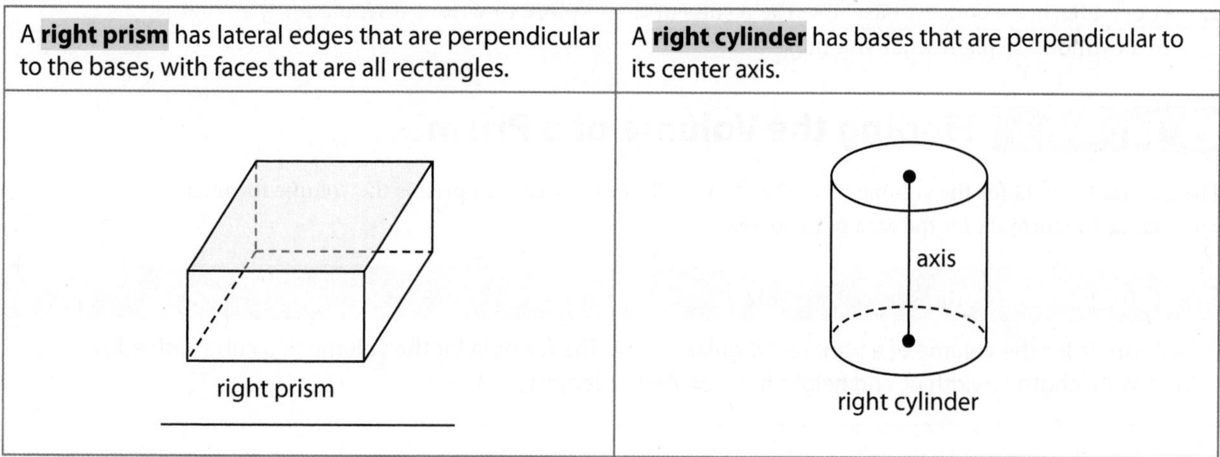

A **right prism** has lateral edges that are perpendicular to the bases, with faces that are all rectangles.	A **right cylinder** has bases that are perpendicular to its center axis.
right prism	axis right cylinder

(A) On a sheet of paper draw a quadrilateral shape. Make sure the sides aren't parallel. Assume the figure has an area of B square units.

(B) Use it as the base for a prism. Take a block of Styrofoam and cut to the shape of the base. Assume the prism has a height of 1 unit.

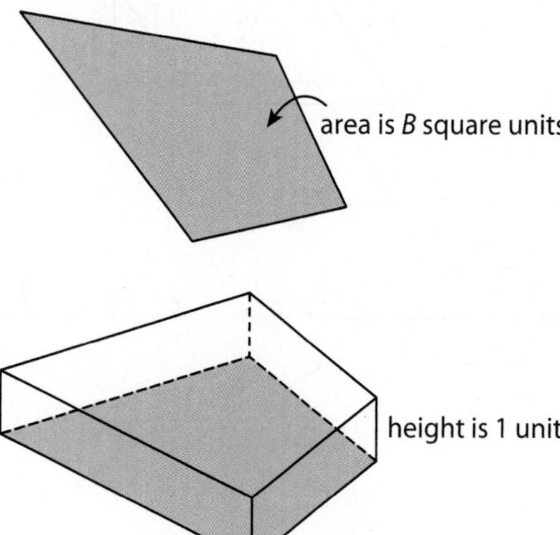

How would changing the area of the base change the volume of the prism?

(C) If the base has an area of B square units, how many cubic units does the prism contain?

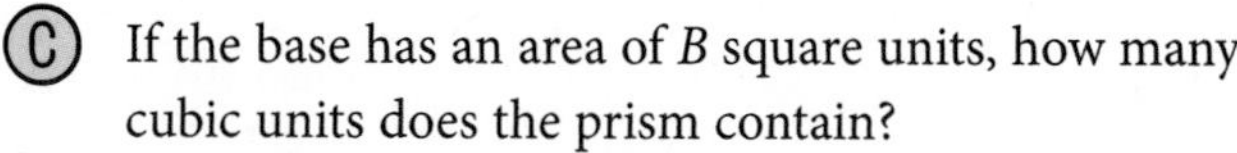

Ⓓ Now use the base to build a prism with a height of h units.

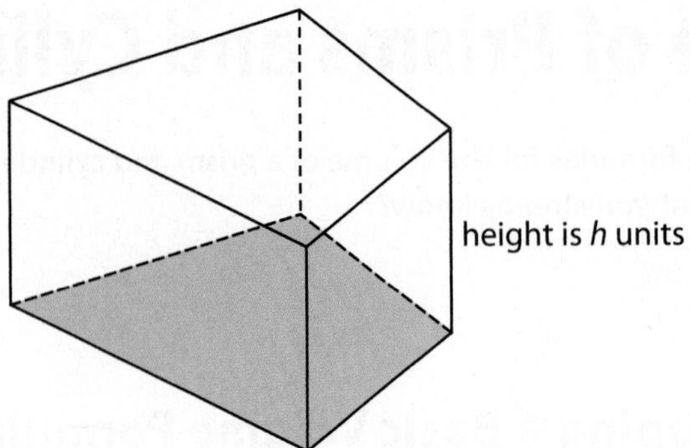

How much greater is the volume of this prism compared to the one with a height of 1?

Reflect

1. Suppose the base of the prism was a rectangle of sides l and w. Write a formula for the volume of the prism using l, w, and h.

2. A cylinder has a circular base. Use the results of the Explore to write a formula for the volume of a cylinder. Explain what you did.

Explain 1 Finding the Volume of a Prism

The general formula for the volume of a prism is $V = B \cdot h$. With certain prisms the volume formula can include the formula for the area of the base.

Volume of a Prism	
The formula for the volume of a right rectangular prism with length ℓ, width w, and height h is $V = \ell wh$.	The formula for the volume of a cube with edge length s is $V = s^3$.
h, ℓ, w	s, s, s

Example 1 **Use volume formulas to solve real world problems.**

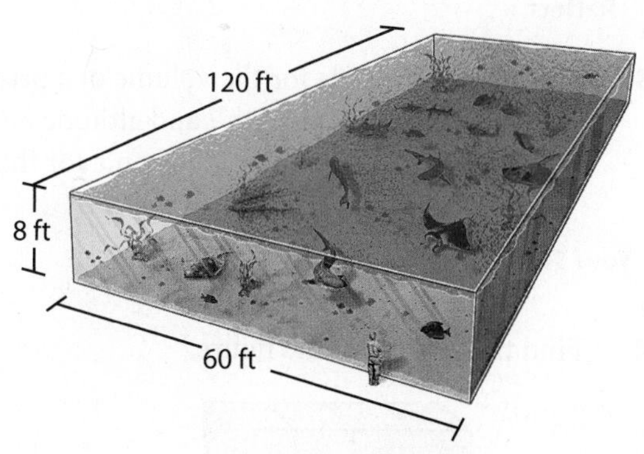

(A) A shark and ray tank at the aquarium has the dimensions shown. Estimate the volume of water in gallons. Use the conversion 1 gallon = 0.134 ft^3.

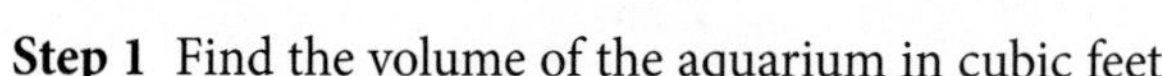

Step 1 Find the volume of the aquarium in cubic feet.

$$V = \ell wh = (120)(60)(8) = 57{,}600 \text{ ft}^3$$

Step 2 Use the conversion factor $\frac{1 \text{ gallon}}{0.134 \text{ ft}^3}$ to estimate the volume of the aquarium in gallons.

$$57{,}600 \text{ ft}^3 \cdot \frac{1 \text{ gallon}}{0.134 \text{ ft}^3} \approx 429{,}851 \text{ gallons} \qquad \frac{1 \text{ gallon}}{0.134 \text{ ft}^3} = 1$$

Step 3 Use the conversion factor $\frac{1 \text{ gallon}}{8.33 \text{ pounds}}$ to estimate the weight of the water.

$$429{,}851 \text{ gallons} \cdot \frac{8.33 \text{ pounds}}{1 \text{ gallon}} \approx 3{,}580{,}659 \text{ pounds} \qquad \frac{8.33 \text{ pounds}}{1 \text{ gallon}} = 1$$

The aquarium holds about 429,851 gallons. The water in the aquarium weighs about 3,580,659 pounds.

(B) **Chemistry** Ice takes up more volume than water. This cubic container is filled to the brim with ice. Estimate the volume of water once the ice melts.

3 cm

Density of ice: 0.9167 g/cm^3 Density of water: 1 g/cm^3

Step 1 Find the volume of the cube of ice.

$$V = s^3 = \boxed{3}^3 = \boxed{27} \text{ cm}^3$$

Step 2 Convert the volume to mass using the conversion factor $\boxed{0.9167} \frac{\text{g}}{\text{cm}^3}$.

$$\boxed{27} \text{ cm}^3 \cdot \boxed{0.9167} \frac{\text{g}}{\text{cm}^3} \approx \boxed{24.8} \text{ g}$$

Step 3 Use the mass of ice to find the volume of water. Use the conversion factor $\boxed{1\frac{\text{cm}^3}{\text{g}}}$.

$$24.8 \text{ g} \cdot \boxed{1\frac{\text{cm}^3}{\text{g}}} \approx \boxed{24.8} \text{ cm}^3$$

Reflect

3. The general formula for the volume of a prism is $V = B \cdot h$. Suppose the base of a prism is a parallelogram of length l and altitude h. Use H as the variable to represent the height of the prism. Write a volume formula for this prism.

Your Turn

4. Find the volume of the figure.

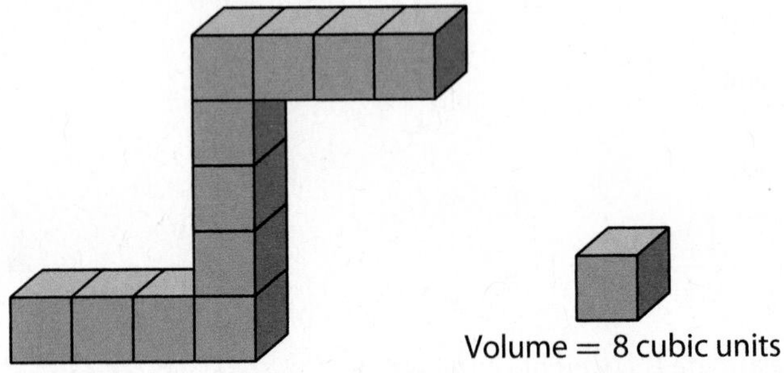
Volume = 8 cubic units

5. Find the volume of the figure.

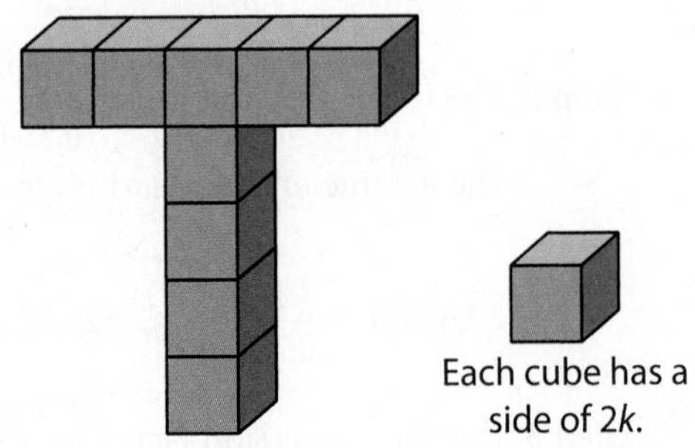
Each cube has a side of 2k.

Explain 2 Finding the Volume of a Cylinder

You can also find the volume of prisms and cylinders whose edges are not perpendicular to the base.

Oblique Prism	Oblique Cylinder
An **oblique prism** is a prism that has at least one non-rectangular lateral face.	An **oblique cylinder** is a cylinder whose axis is not perpendicular to the bases.
h	h

Cavalieri's Principle

If two solids have the same height and the same cross-sectional area at every level, then the two solids have the same volume.

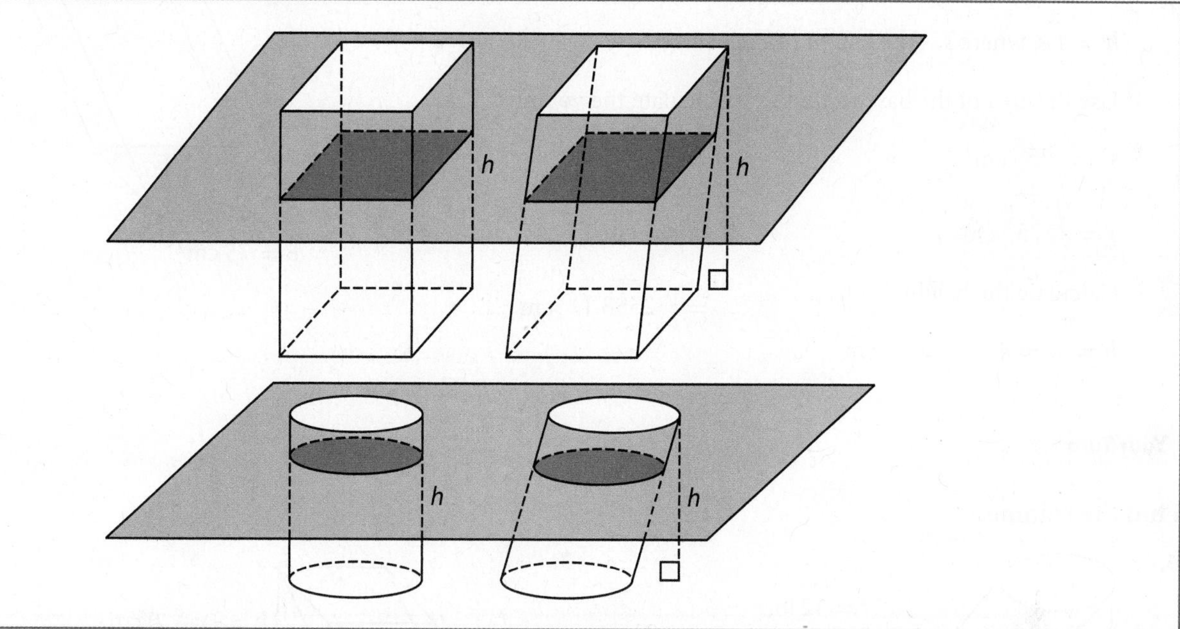

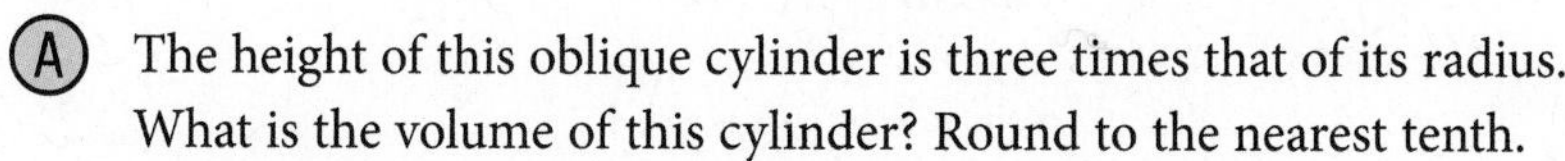
Example 2 **To find the volume of an oblique cylinder or oblique prism, use Cavalieri's Principle to find the volume of a comparable right cylinder or prism.**

Ⓐ The height of this oblique cylinder is three times that of its radius. What is the volume of this cylinder? Round to the nearest tenth.

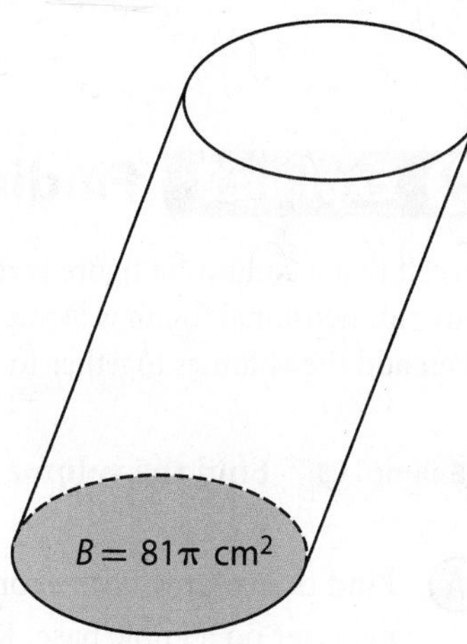

Use Cavalieri's Principle to find the volume of a comparable right cylinder.

Represent the height of the oblique cylinder: $h = 3r$

Use the area of the base to find r: $\pi r^2 = 81\pi$ cm^2, so $r = 9$.

Calculate the height: $h = 3r = 27$ cm

Calculate the volume: $V = Bh = (81\pi)27 \approx 6870.7$

The volume is about 6870.7 cubic centimeters.

(B) The height of this oblique square-based prism is four times that of side length of the base. What is the volume of this prism? Round to the nearest tenth.

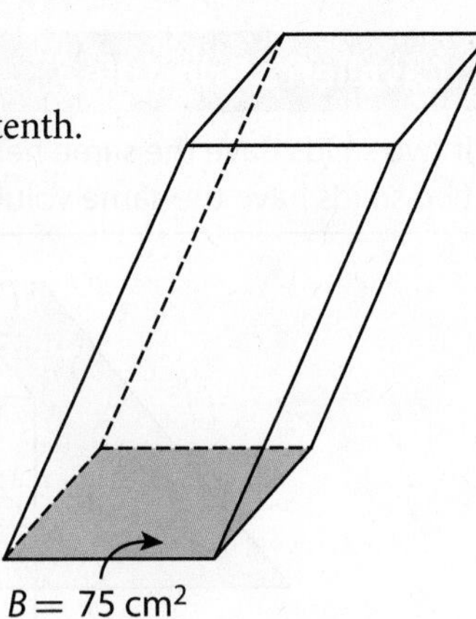

Calculate the height of the oblique prism:

$h = 4\ s$, where s is the length of the square base.

Use the area of the base to find s.

$s^2 = \boxed{75}$ cm^2

$s = \sqrt{\boxed{75}}$ cm

Calculate the height.

$h = 4s = 4\ \boxed{\sqrt{75}}$ cm

Calculate the volume.

$V = Bh$

$= (75 \text{ cm}^2)\left(\boxed{4\sqrt{75}} \text{ cm}\right)$

$= \boxed{2598.1}$ cm^3

Your Turn

Find the volume.

6.

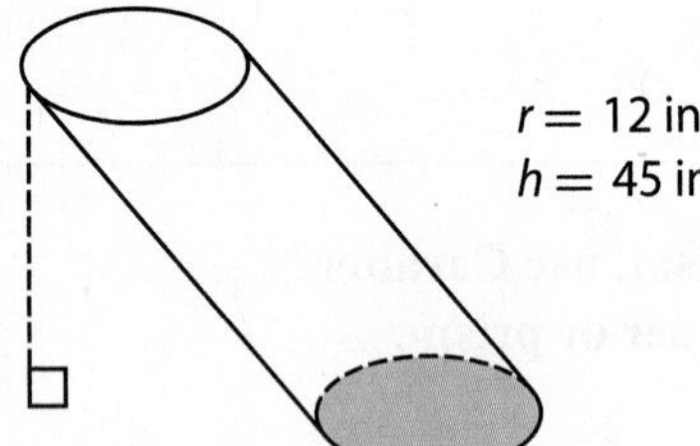

7.

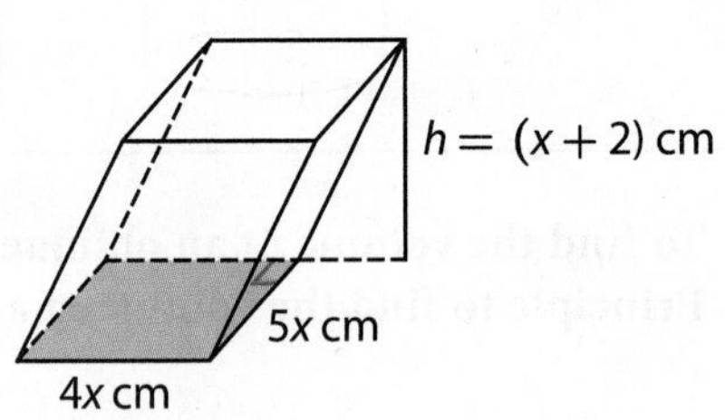

Explain 3 Finding the Volume of a Composite Figure

Recall that a composite figure is made up of simple shapes that combine to create a more complex shape. A composite three-dimensional figure is formed from prisms and cylinders. You can find the volume of each separate figure and then add the volumes together to find the volume of the composite figure.

Example 3 **Find the volume of each composite figure.**

(A) Find the volume of the composite figure, which is an oblique cylinder on a cubic base. Round to the nearest tenth.

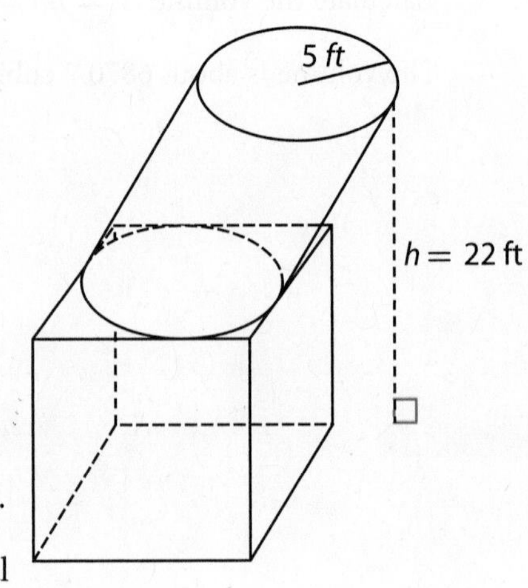

The base area of the cylinder is $B = \pi r^2 = \pi(5)^2 = 25\pi$ ft^2.

The cube has side lengths equal to the diameter of the cylinder's circular base: $s = 10$.

The height of the cylinder is $h = 22 - 10 = 12$ ft.

The volume of the cube is $V = s^3 = 10^3 = 1000$ ft^3.

The volume of the cylinder is $V = Bh = (25\pi \text{ ft}^2)(12 \text{ ft}) \approx 942.5$ ft^3.

The total volume of the composite figure is the sum of the individual volumes.

$V = 1000 \text{ ft}^3 + 942.5 \text{ ft}^3 = 1942.5 \text{ ft}^3$

Ⓑ This periscope is made up of two congruent cylinders and two congruent triangular prisms, each of which is a cube cut in half along one of its diagonals. The height of each cylinder is 6 times the length of the radius. Use the measurements provided to estimate the volume of this composite figure. Round to the nearest tenth.

$B = 36\pi \text{ in}^2$

Use the area of the base to find the radius. $B = \pi r^2$

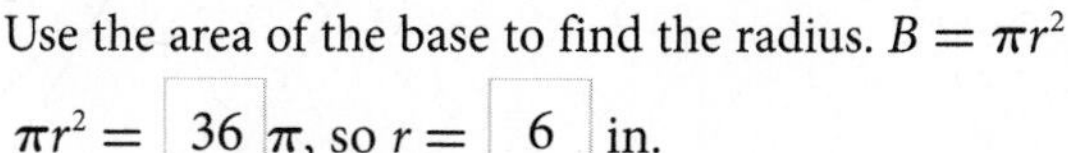

$\pi r^2 =$ 36 π, so $r =$ 6 in.

Calculate the height of each cylinder:

$h = 6r = 6 \cdot$ 6 $=$ 36 in.

The faces of the triangular prism that intersect the cylinders are congruent squares. The side length s of each square is the same as the diameter of the circle.

$s = d = 2 \cdot$ 6 $=$ 12 in.

The two triangular prisms form a cube. What is the volume of this cube?

$V = s^3 =$ 12^3 $=$ 1728 in^3

Find the volume of the two cylinders: $V = 2 \cdot 36\pi \cdot$ 36 $=$ 2592π in^3

The total volume of the composite figure is the sum of the individual volumes.

$V =$ 1728 $\text{in}^3 +$ 2592π $\text{in}^3 \approx$ 9871.0 in^3

Reflect

8. A pipe consists of two concentric cylinders, with the inner cylinder hollowed out. Describe how you could calculate the volume of the solid pipe. Write a formula for the volume.

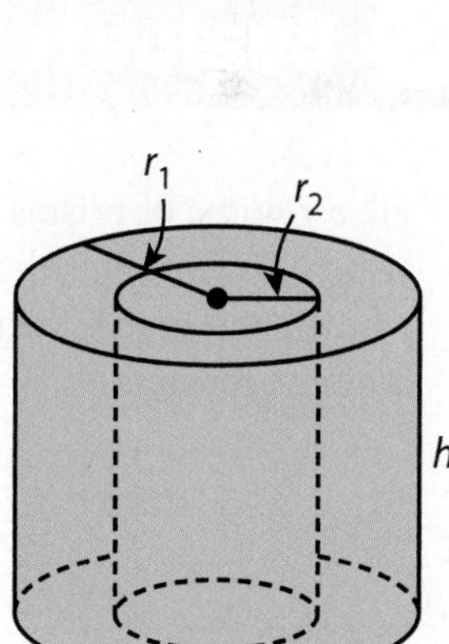

Your Turn

9. This robotic arm is made up of two cylinders with equal volume and two triangular prisms for a hand. The volume of each prism is $\frac{1}{2}r \times \frac{1}{3}r \times 2r$, where r is the radius of the cylinder's base. What fraction of the total volume does the hand take up?

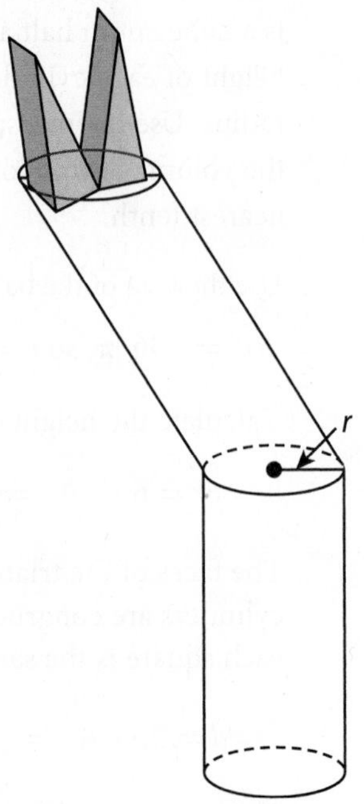

Elaborate

10. If an oblique cylinder and a right cylinder have the same height but not the same volume, what can you conclude about the cylinders?

11. A right square prism and a right cylinder have the same height and volume. What can you conclude about the radius of the cylinder and side lengths of the square base?

12. **Essential Question Check-In** How does the formula for the area of a circle relate to the formula for the volume of a cylinder?

Evaluate: Homework and Practice

- Online Homework
- Hints and Help
- Extra Practice

1. The volume of prisms and cylinders can be represented with Bh, where B represents the area of the base. Identify the type of figure shown and match the prism or cylinder with the appropriate volume formula.

A. __?__ $V = (\pi r^2)h$ B. __?__ $V = \left(\frac{1}{2}bh\right)h$ C. __?__ $V = \ell wh$

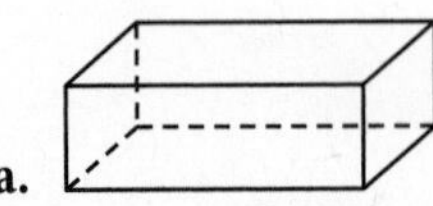

a.

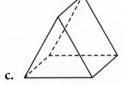

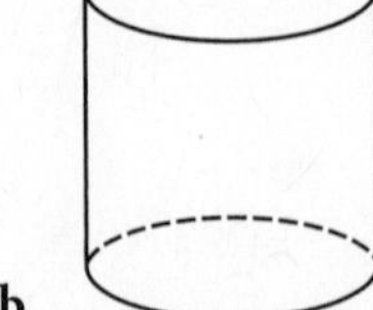

b.

c.

Find the volume of each prism or cylinder. Round to the nearest hundredth.

2.

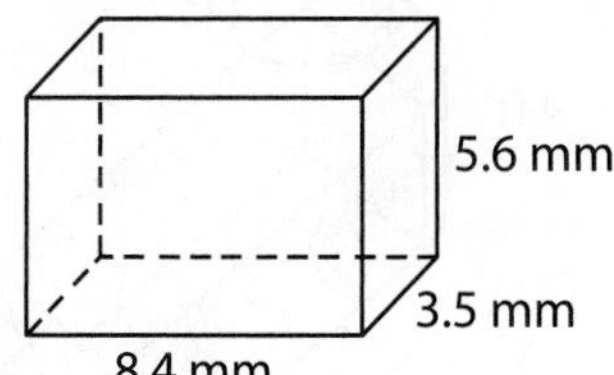

3.

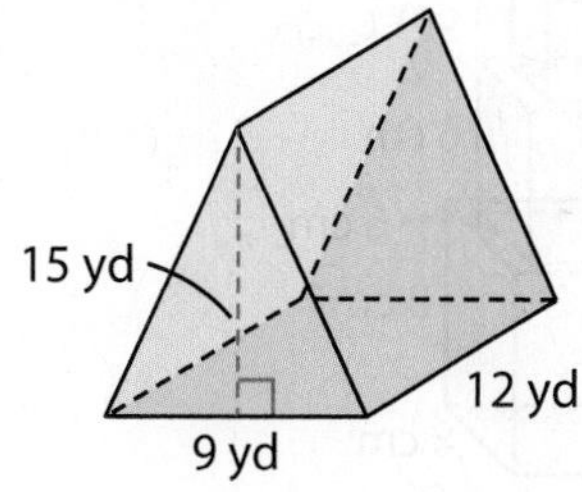

4. The area of the hexagonal base is $\left(\frac{54}{\tan 30°}\right)$ m^2. Its height is 8 m.

5. The area of the pentagonal base is $\left(\frac{125}{\tan 36°}\right)$ m^2. Its height is 15 m.

6.

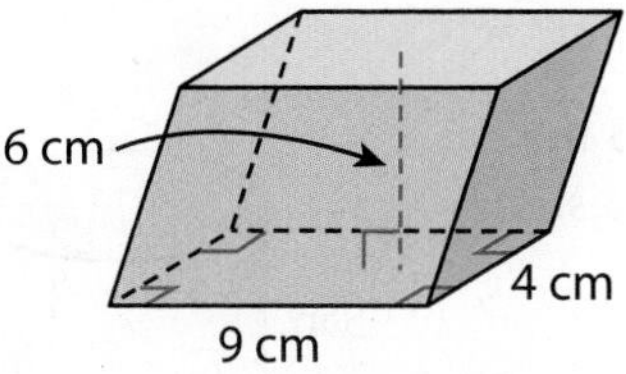

7.

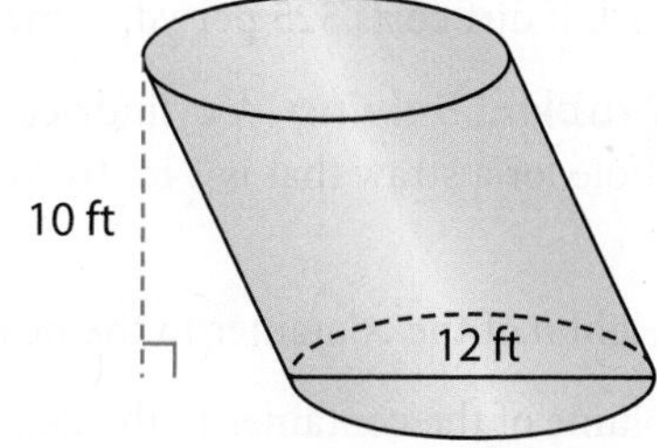

8. **Multi-Step** A vase in the shape of an oblique cylinder has the dimensions shown. What is the volume of the vase in liters? Round to the nearest tenth. (*Hint:* Use the right triangle in the cylinder to find its height.)

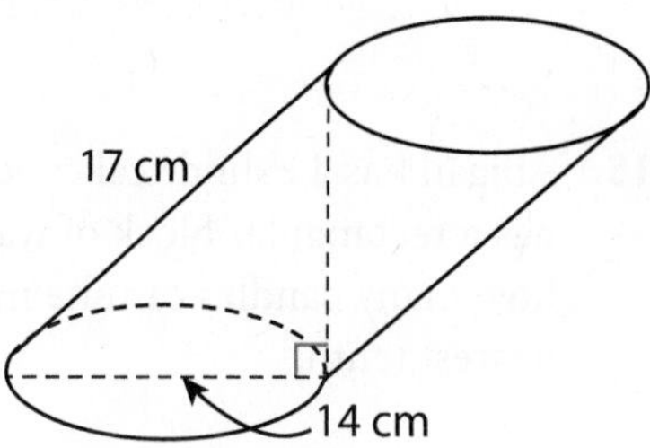

Find the volume of each composite figure. Round to the nearest tenth.

9.

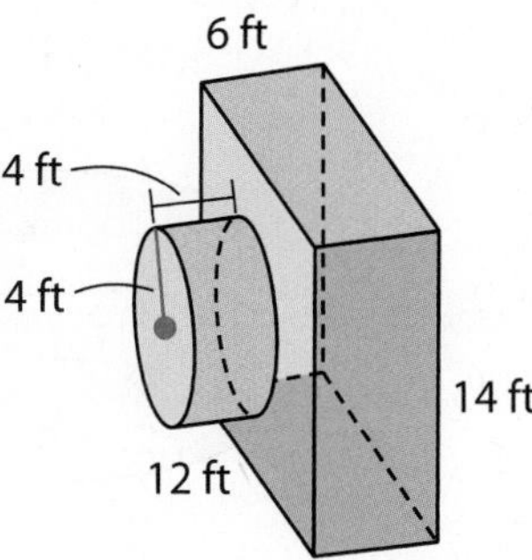

10.

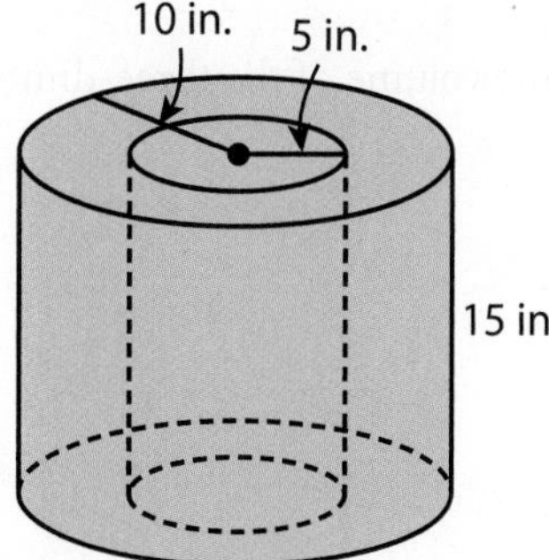

11.

12. The two figures on each end combine to form a right cylinder.

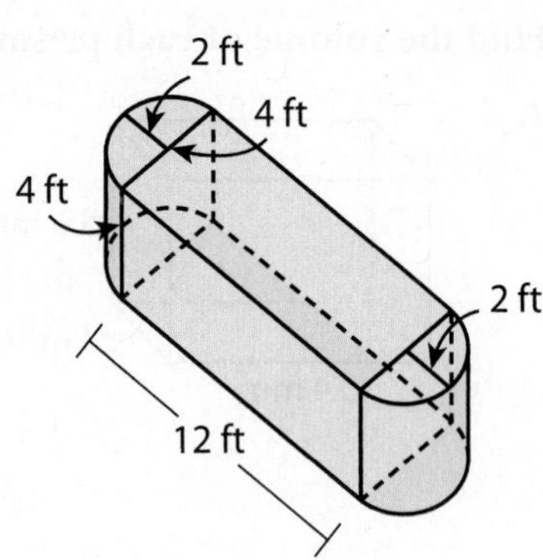

13. Colin is buying dirt to fill a garden bed that is a 9 ft by 16 ft rectangle. If he wants to fill it to a depth of 4 in., how many cubic yards of dirt does he need? Round to the nearest cubic yard. If dirt costs \$25 per yd^3, how much will the project cost?

14. Persevere in Problem Solving A cylindrical juice container with a 3 in. diameter has a hole for a straw that is 1 in. from the side. Up to 5 in. of a straw can be inserted.

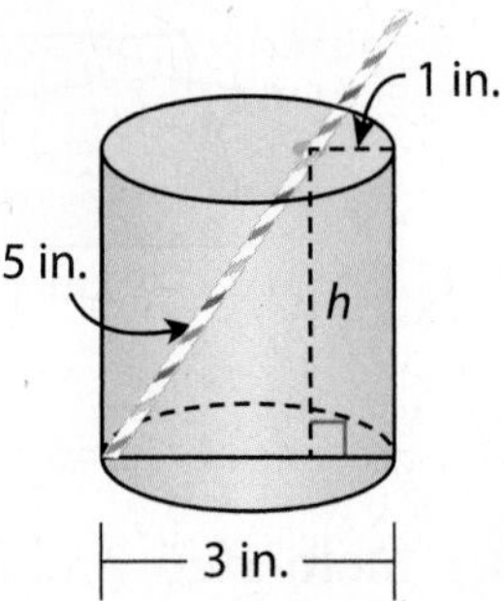

a. Find the height h of the container to the nearest tenth.

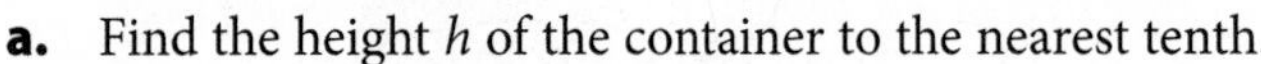

b. Find the volume of the container to the nearest tenth.

c. How many ounces of juice does the container hold? (*Hint*: 1 in$^3 \approx 0.55$ oz)

15. Abigail has a cylindrical candle mold with the dimensions shown. If Abigail has a rectangular block of wax measuring 15 cm by 12 cm by 18 cm, about how many candles can she make after melting the block of wax? Round to the nearest tenth.

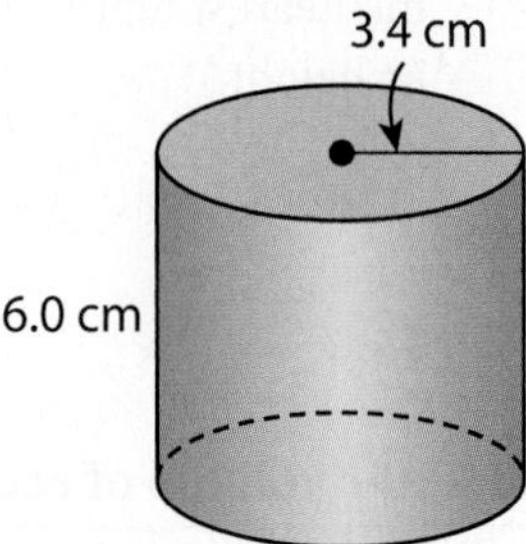

16. Algebra Find the volume of the three-dimensional figure in terms of x.

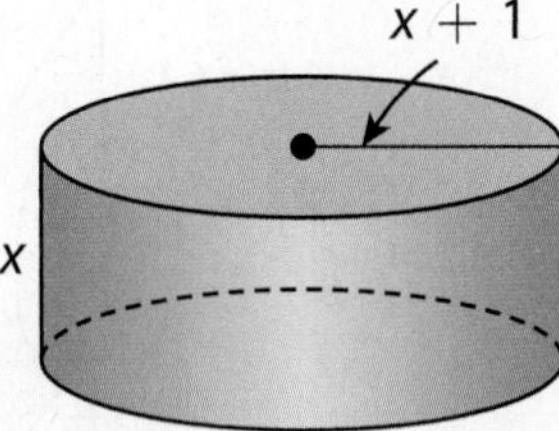

17. One cup is equal to 14.4375 in^3. If a 1-cup measuring cylinder has a radius of 2 in., what is its height? If the radius is 1.5 in., what is its height? Round to the nearest tenth.

18. Make a Prediction A cake is a cylinder with a diameter of 10 in. and a height of 3 in. For a party, a coin has been mixed into the batter and baked inside the cake. The person who gets the piece with the coin wins a prize.

a. Find the volume of the cake. Round to the nearest tenth.

b. Keka gets a piece of cake that is a right rectangular prism with a 3 in. by 1 in. base. What is the probability that the coin is in her piece? Round to the nearest hundredth.

H.O.T. Focus on Higher Order Thinking

19. Multi-Step What is the volume of the three-dimensional object with the dimensions shown in the three views?

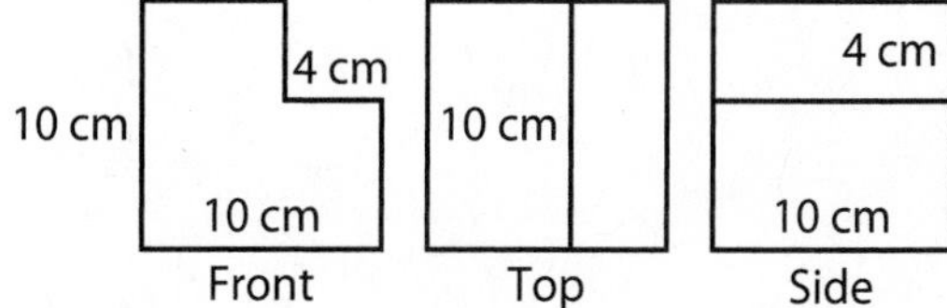

20. Draw Conclusions You can use *displacement* to find the volume of an irregular object, such as a stone. Suppose a 2 foot by 1 foot tank is filled with water to a depth of 8 in. A stone is placed in the tank so that it is completely covered, causing the water level to rise by 2 in. Find the volume of the stone.

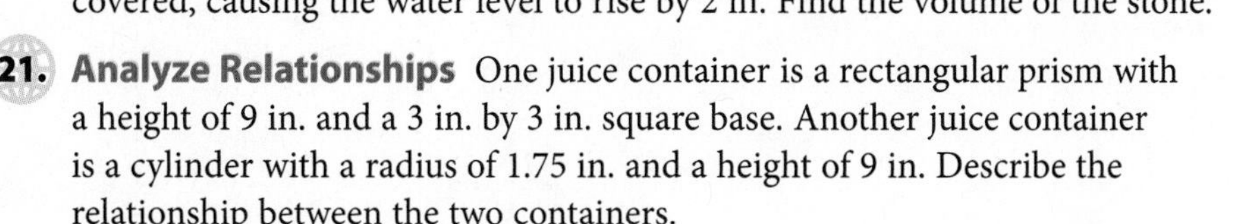

21. Analyze Relationships One juice container is a rectangular prism with a height of 9 in. and a 3 in. by 3 in. square base. Another juice container is a cylinder with a radius of 1.75 in. and a height of 9 in. Describe the relationship between the two containers.

Lesson Performance Task

A full roll of paper towels is a cylinder with a diameter of 6 inches and a hollow inner cylinder with a diameter of 2 inches.

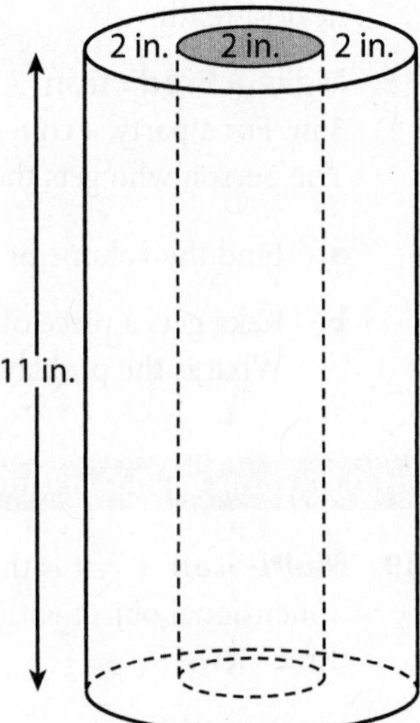

1. Find the volume of the paper on the roll. Explain your method.

2. Each sheet of paper on the roll measures 11 inches by 11 inches by $\frac{1}{32}$ inch. Find the volume of one sheet. Explain how you found the volume.

3. How many sheets of paper are on the roll? Explain.

18.2 Volume of Pyramids

Essential Question: How do you find the volume of a pyramid?

Resource Locker

Explore Developing a Volume Formula

As shown at the left below, $\overline{AB}$ has length b, and C is any point on line ℓ parallel to $\overline{AB}$. The distance between the line containing $\overline{AB}$ and line ℓ is h. No matter where C is located on line ℓ, the area of the resulting $\triangle ABC$ is always a constant equal to $\frac{1}{2}bh$. Similarly, given a polygon and a plane R that is parallel to the plane containing the polygon, suppose you choose a point on R and create a pyramid with the chosen point as the vertex and the polygon as the base. Both the base area and the height of the pyramid remain constant as you vary the location of the vertex on R, so it is reasonable to assume that the volume of the pyramid remains constant.

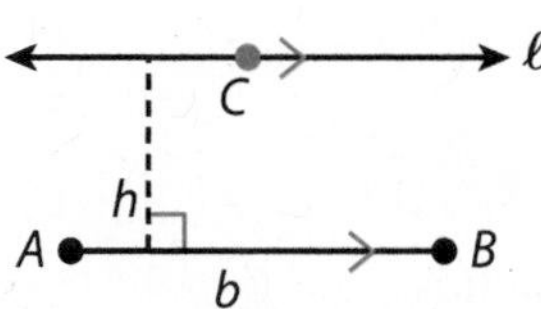

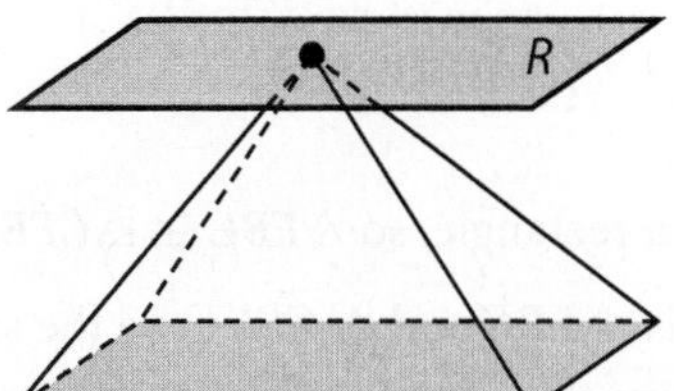

Postulate

Pyramids that have equal base areas and equal heights have equal volumes.

Consider a triangular pyramid with vertex A directly over vertex D of the base BCD. This triangular pyramid A-BCD can be thought of as part of a triangular prism with $\triangle EFA \cong \triangle BCD$. Let the area of the base be B and let $AD = h$.

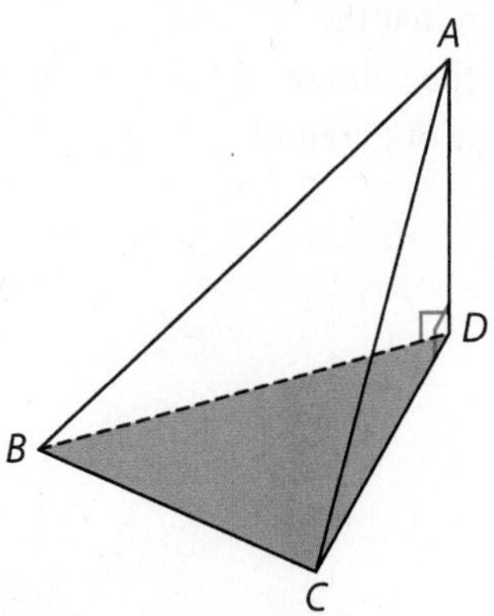

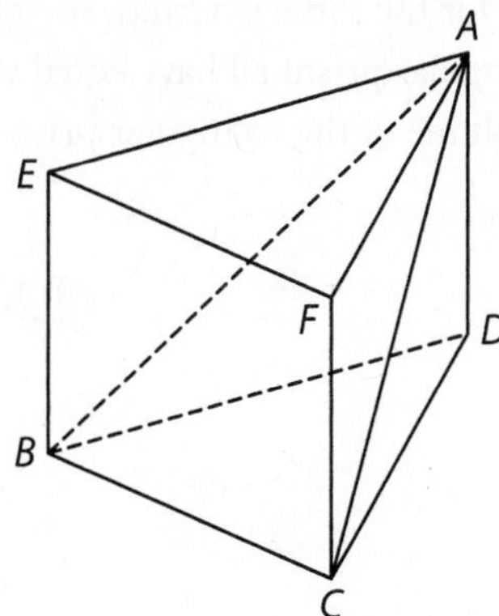

(A) What is the volume of the triangular prism in terms of b and h?

(B) Draw $\overline{EC}$ on one face of the triangular prism. Consider the three pyramids: *A-BCD*, *A-EBC*, and *A-CFE*. Explain why the sum of the volumes of these three pyramids is equal to the volume of the prism.

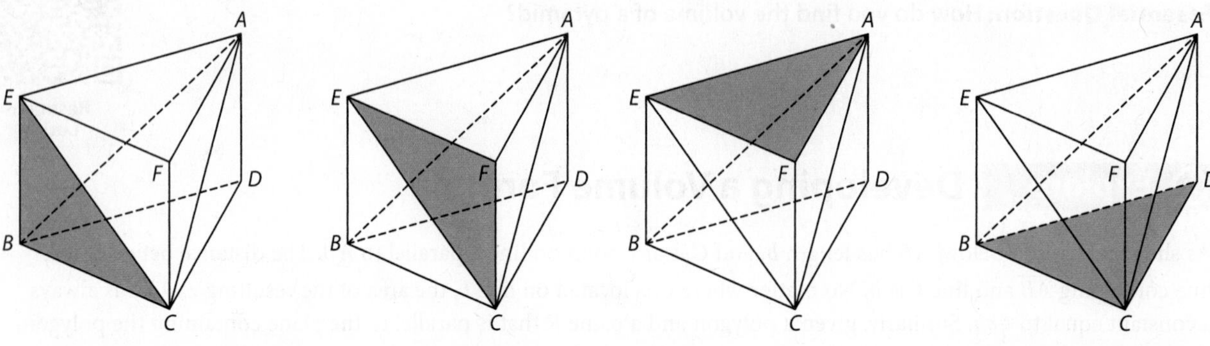

(C) $\overline{EC}$ is the diagonal of a rectangle, so $\triangle EBC \cong \triangle CFE$.

Explain why pyramids *A-EBC* and *A-CFE* have the same volume. Explain why pyramids *C-EFA* and *A-BCD* have the same volume.

(D) *A-CFE* and *C-EFA* are two names for the same pyramid, so you now have shown that the three pyramids that form the triangular prism all have equal volume. Compare the volume of the pyramid *A-BCD* and the volume of the triangular prism. Write the volume of pyramid *A-BCD* in terms of *B* and *h*.

Reflect

1. Explain how you know that the three pyramids that form that triangular prism all have the same volume.

Explain 1 Finding the Volume of a Pyramid

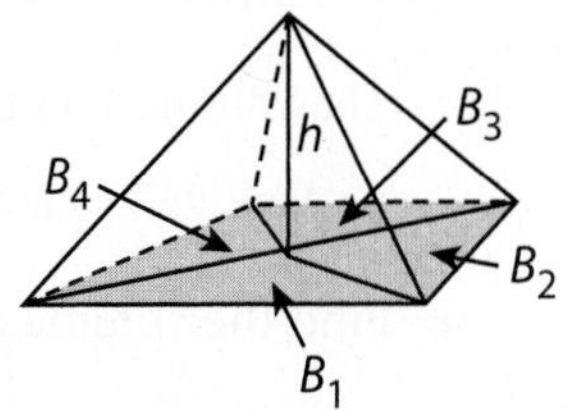

In the Explore, you showed that the volume of a "wedge pyramid" having its vertex directly over one of the vertices of the base is one-third the product of the base area and the height. Now consider a general pyramid. As shown in the figure, a pyramid can be partitioned into nonoverlapping wedge pyramids by drawing a perpendicular from the vertex to the base. The volume V of the given pyramid is the sum of the volumes of the wedge pyramids.

That is, $V = \frac{1}{3}B_1h + \frac{1}{3}B_2h + \frac{1}{3}B_3h + \frac{1}{3}B_4h.$

Using the distributive property, this may be rewritten as $V = \frac{1}{3}h\left(B_1 + B_2 + B_3 + B_4\right)$.

Notice that $B_1 + B_2 + B_3 + B_4 = B$, where B is the base area of the given pyramid.

So, $V = \frac{1}{3}Bh$.

The above argument provides an informal justification for the following result.

Volume of a Pyramid

The volume V of a pyramid with base area B and height h is given by $V = \frac{1}{3}Bh$.

Example 1 **Solve a volume problem.**

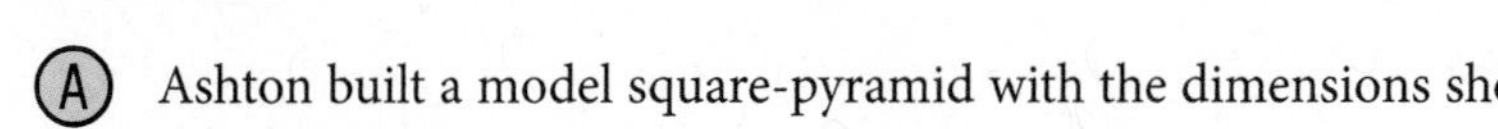

(A) Ashton built a model square-pyramid with the dimensions shown. What is the volume of the pyramid?

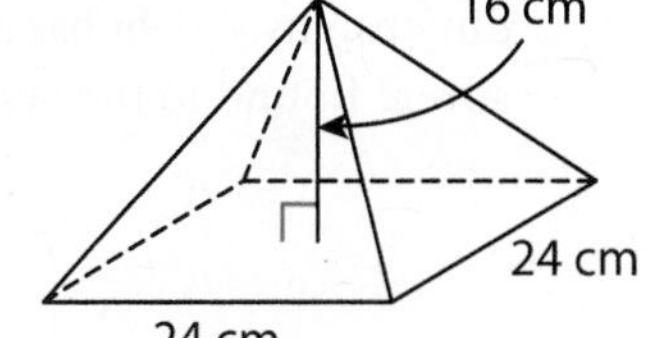

The pyramid is composed of wooden blocks that are in the shape of cubes. A block has the dimensions 4 cm by 4 by 4 cm. How many wooden blocks did Ashton use to build the pyramid?

- Find the volume of the pyramid.

  The area of the base B is the area of the square with sides of length 24 cm. So, $B = 576\text{ cm}^2$.

  The volume V of the pyramid is $\frac{1}{3}Bh = \frac{1}{3} \cdot 576 \cdot 16$.

  So $V = 3072\text{ cm}^3$.

- Find the volume of an average block.

  The volume of a cube is given by the formula $V = s^3$. So the volume W of a wooden block is 64 cm^3.

- Find the approximate number of wooden blocks in the pyramid, divide V by W. So the number of blocks that Ashton used is 48.

(B) The Great Pyramid in Giza, Egypt, is approximately a square pyramid with the dimensions shown. The pyramid is composed of stone blocks that are rectangular prisms. An average block has dimensions 1.3 m by 1.3 m by 0.7 m. Approximately how many stone blocks were used to build the pyramid? Round to the nearest hundred thousand.

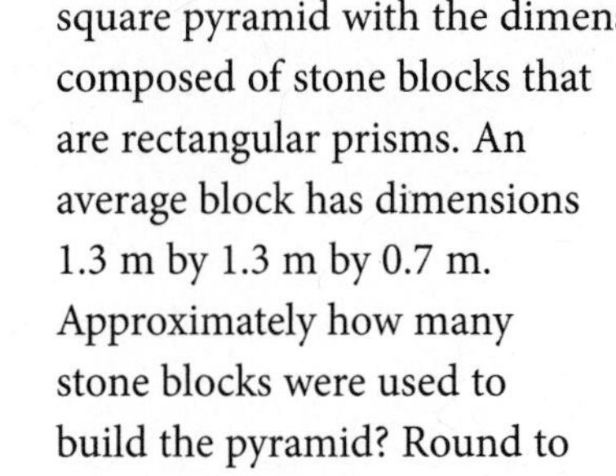

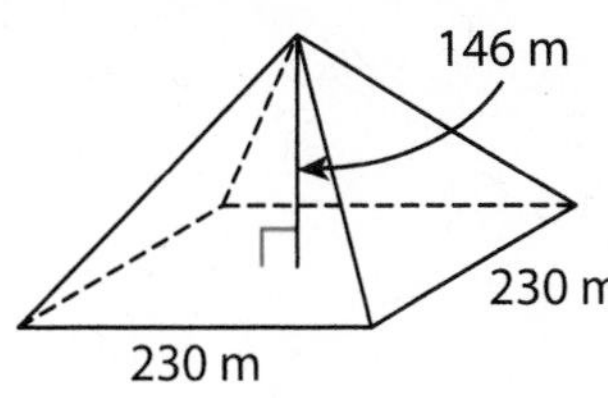

- Find the volume of the pyramid.

  The area of the base B is the area of the square with sides of length 230 m. So, $B = 52{,}900\ \text{m}^2$.

  The volume V of the pyramid is $\frac{1}{3}Bh = \frac{1}{3} \cdot 52{,}900 \cdot 146$.

  So $V \approx 25{,}744{,}666.67\ \text{m}^3$.

- Find the volume of an average block.

  The volume of a rectangular prism is given by the formula $V = lwh$. So the volume W of an average block is $1.183\ \text{m}^3$.

- Find the approximate number of stone blocks in the pyramid, divide V by W. So the approximate number of blocks is 2,200,000.

Reflect

2. What aspects of the model in Part B may lead to inaccuracies in your estimate?

3. Suppose you are told that the average height of a stone block 0.69 m rather than 0.7 m. Would the increase or decrease your estimate of the total number of blocks in the pyramid? Explain.

Your Turn

4. A piece of pure silver in the shape of a rectangular pyramid with the dimensions shown has a mass of 19.7 grams. What is the density of silver? Round to the nearest tenth. (Hint: $density = \frac{mass}{volume}$.)

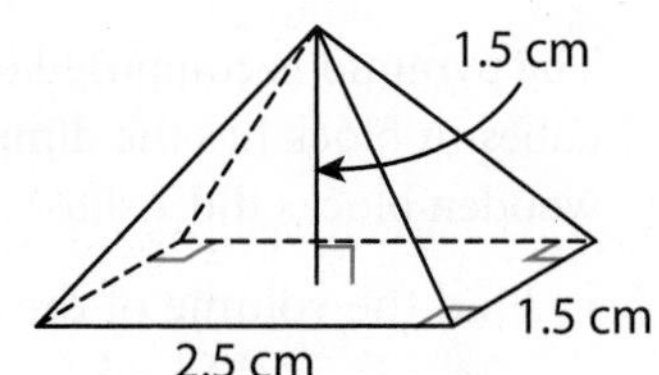

Explain 2 Finding the Volume of a Composite Figure

You can add or subtract to find the volume of composite figures.

Example 2 **Find the volume of the composite figure formed by a pyramid removed from a prism. Round to the nearest tenth.**

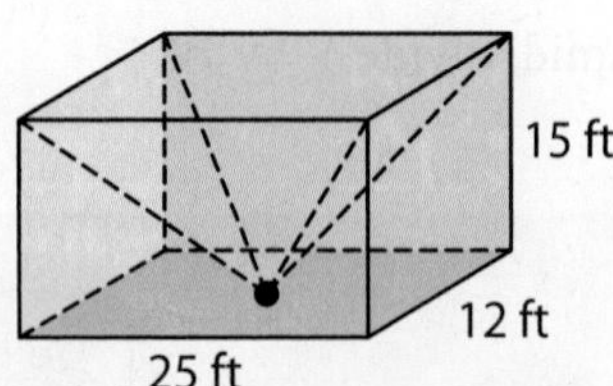

- Find the volume of the prism.

  $V = lwh = (25)(12)(15) = 4500\ \text{ft}^3$

- Find the volume of pyramid.

  Area of base: $B = (25)(12) = 300\ \text{ft}^2$

  Volume of pyramid: $V = \frac{1}{3}(300)(15) = 1500\ \text{ft}^3$

- Subtract the volume of the pyramid from volume of the prism to find the volume of the composite figure.

  $4500 - 1500 = 3000$

  So the volume of the composite figure is $3000\ \text{ft}^3$.

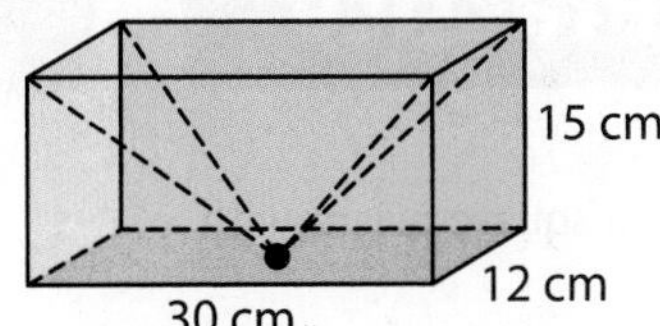

- Find the volume of the prism.

  $V = lwh = (30)(12)(15) = (5400)\ \text{cm}^3$

- Find the volume of the pyramid.

  Area of base: $B = (30)(12) = 360\ \text{cm}^2$

  Volume of pyramid: $V = \frac{1}{3}(360)(15) = (1800)\ \text{cm}^3$

- Subtract volume of pyramid from volume of prism to find volume of composite figure.

  $5400 - 1800 = 3600$

  So the volume of the composite figure is $3600\ \text{cm}^3$.

Your Turn

Find the volume of the composite figure. Round to the nearest tenth.

5. The composite figure is formed from two pyramids. The base of each pyramid is a square with a side length of 6 inches and each pyramid has a height of 8 inches.

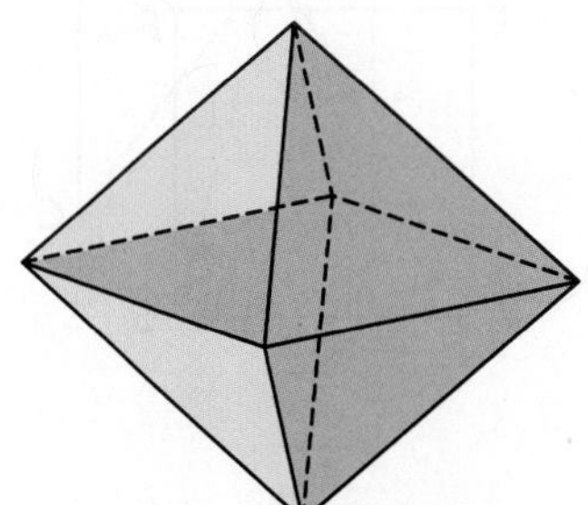

6. The composite figure is formed by a rectangular prism with two square pyramids on top of it.

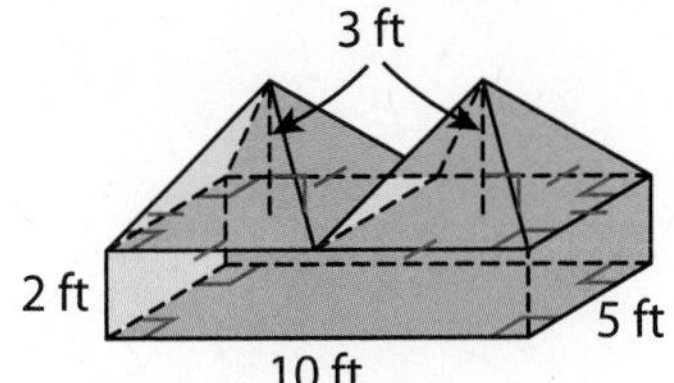

Elaborate

7. Explain how the volume of a pyramid is related to the volume of a prism with the same base and height.

8. If the length and width of a rectangular pyramid are doubled and the height stays the same, how does the volume of the pyramid change? Explain.

9. **Essential Question Check-In** How do you calculate the volume of a pyramid?

Evaluate: Homework and Practice

- Online Homework
- Hints and Help
- Extra Practice

1. Compare the volume of a square pyramid to the volume of a square prism with the same base and height as the pyramid.

2. Which of the following equations could describe a square pyramid? Determine all that apply.

   A. $3Vh = B$

   B. $V = \frac{1}{3}\ell wB$

   C. $w = \frac{3V}{\ell h}$

   D. $\frac{V}{B} = \frac{h}{3}$

   E. $V = \frac{w^2h}{3}$

   F. $\frac{1}{3} = VBh$

3. **Justify Reasoning** As shown in the figure, polyhedron *ABCDEFGH* is a cube and *P* is any point on face *EFGH*. Compare the volume of the pyramid *PABCD* and the volume of the cube. Demonstrate how you came to your answer.

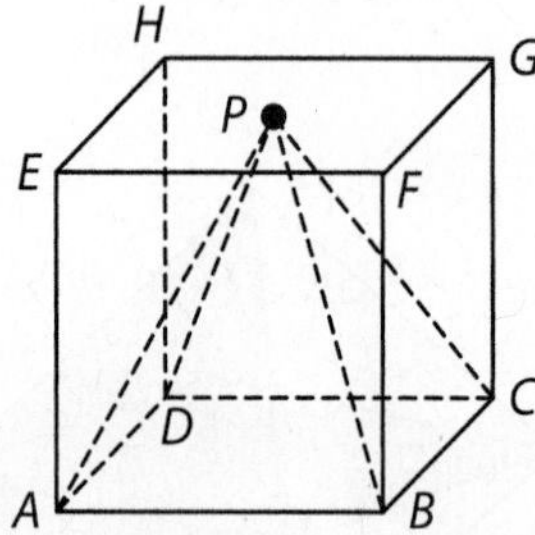

Find the volume of the pyramid. Round your answer to the nearest tenth.

4.

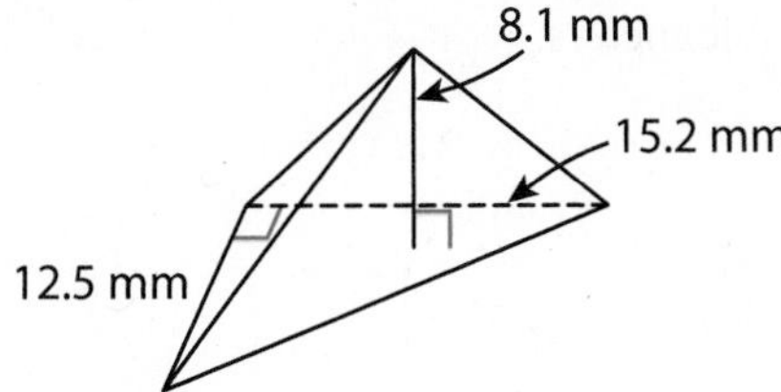

5.

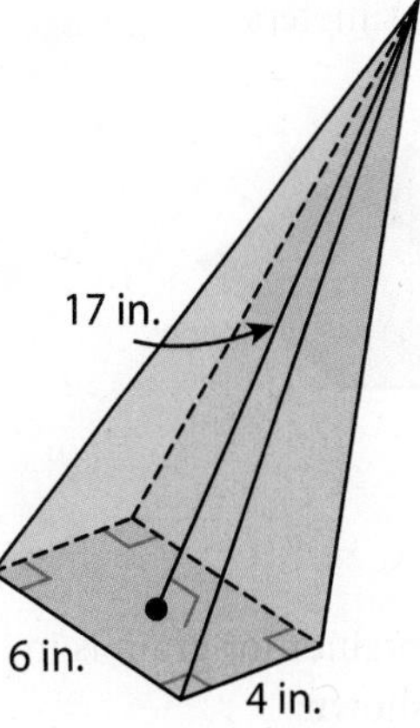

6. Find the volume of a hexagonal pyramid with a base area of 25 ft^2 and a height of 9 ft.

7. The area of the base of a hexagonal pyramid is $\frac{24}{\tan 30°}$ cm^2. Find its volume.

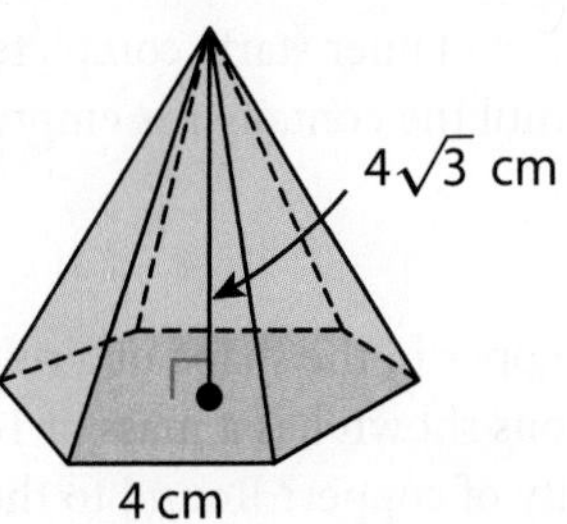

Find the volume of the composite figure. Round to the nearest tenth.

8.

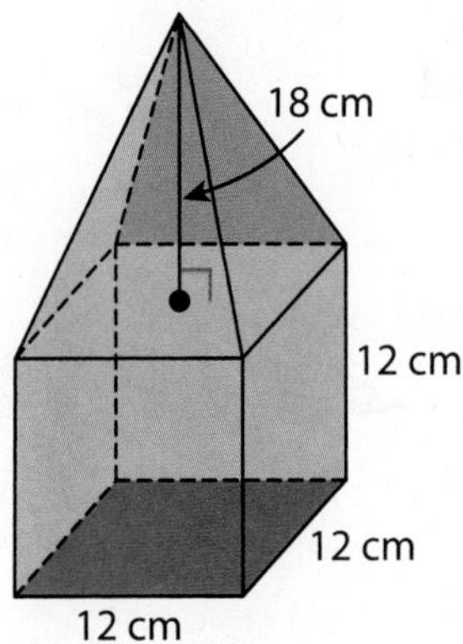

9.

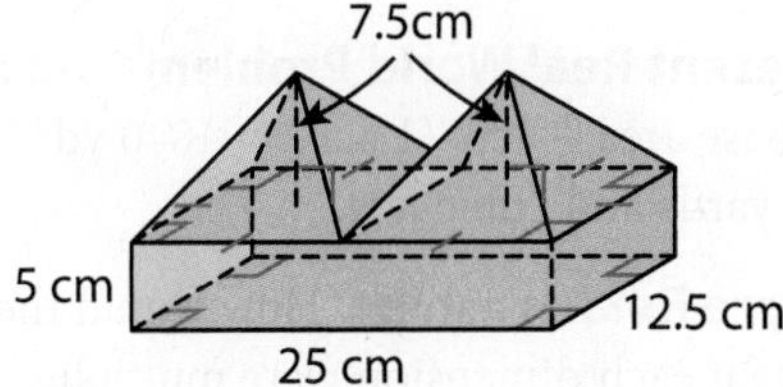

10. Given a square pyramid with a height of 21 ft and a volume of 3969 cubic feet, find the length of one side of the square base. Round to the nearest tenth.

11. Consider a pyramid with height 10 feet and a square base with side length of 7 feet. How does the volume of the pyramid change if the base stays the same and the height is doubled?

12. Algebra Find the value of x if the volume of the pyramid shown is 200 cubic centimeters.

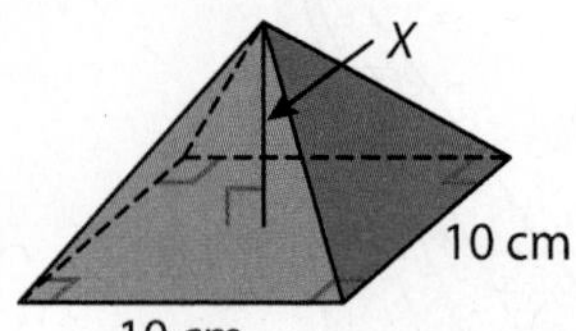

13. Find the height of a rectangular pyramid with length 3 meters, width 8 meters, and volume 112 cubic meters.

14. A storage container for grain is in the shape of a square pyramid with the dimensions shown.

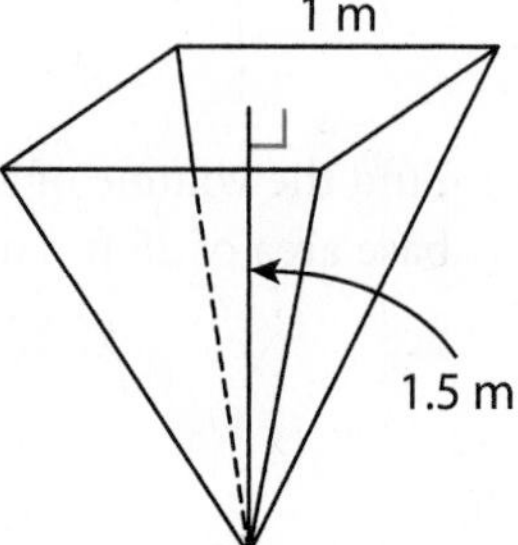

a. What is the volume of the container in cubic centimeters?

b. Grain leaks from the container at a rate of 4 cubic centimeters per second. Assuming the container starts completely full, about how many hours does it take until the container is empty?

15. A piece of pure copper in the shape of a rectangular pyramid with the dimensions shown has a mass of 16.76 grams. What is the density of copper? Round to the nearest hundredth. (Hint: $density = \frac{mass}{volume}$.)

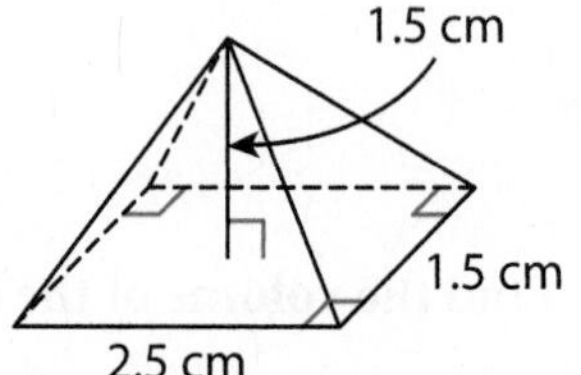

16. Represent Real World Problems An art gallery is a 6 story square pyramid with base area $\frac{1}{2}$ acre (1 acre $= 4840\ \text{yd}^2$, 1 story ≈ 10 ft). Estimate the volume in cubic yards and cubic feet.

17. Analyze Relationships How would the volume of the pyramid shown change if each dimension were multiplied by 6? Explain how you found your answer.

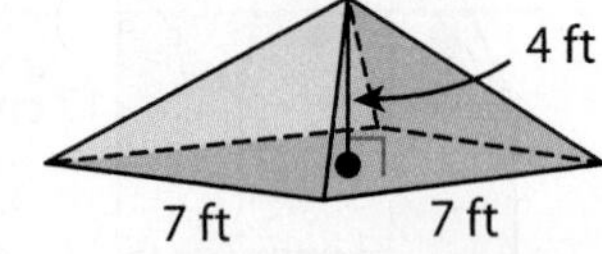

18. **Geology** A crystal is cut into a shape formed by two square pyramids joined at the base. Each pyramid has a base edge length of 5.7 mm and a height of 3 mm. What is the volume of the crystal to the nearest cubic millimeter?

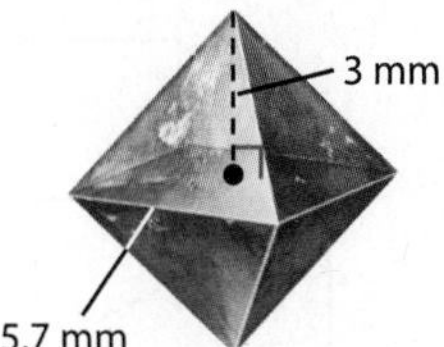

19. A roof that encloses an attic is a square pyramid with a base edge length of 45 feet and a height of 5 yards. What is the volume of the attic in cubic feet? In cubic yards?

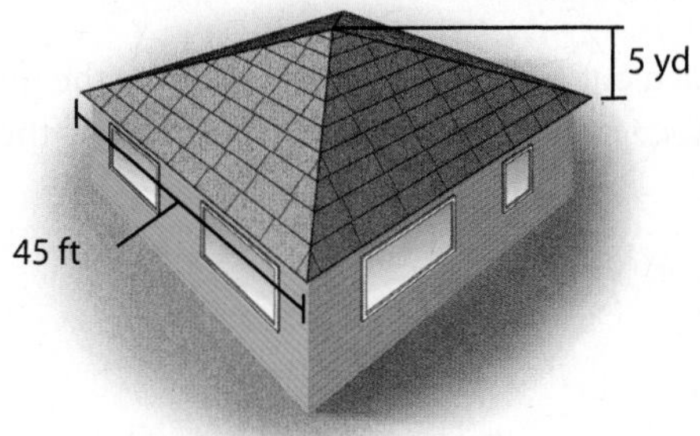

H.O.T. Focus on Higher Order Thinking

20. **Explain the Error** Describe and correct the error in finding the volume of the pyramid.

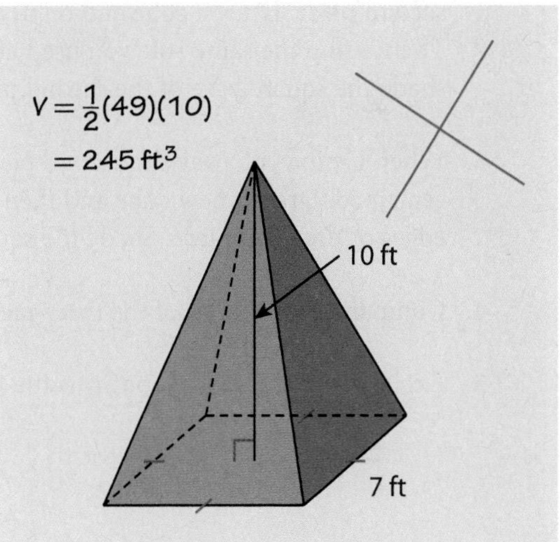

21. **Communicate Mathematical Ideas** A pyramid has a square base and a height of 5 ft. The volume of the pyramid is 60 ft^3. Explain how to find the length of a side of the pyramid's base.

22. **Critical Thinking** A rectangular pyramid has a base length of 2, a base width of x, and a height of $3x$. Its volume is 512 cm^3. What is the area of the base?

Lesson Performance Task

Genna is making a puzzle using a wooden cube. She's going to cut the cube into three pieces. The figure below shows the lines along which she plans to cut away the first piece. The result will be a piece with four triangular sides and a square side (shaded).

1. Each cut Genna makes will begin at the upper left corner of the cube. Write a rule describing where she drew the lines for the first piece.

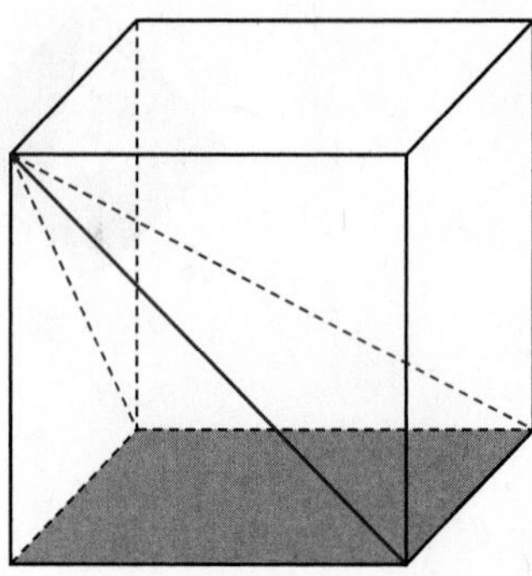

2. The figure below shows two of the lines along which Genna will cut the second piece. Draw a cube and on it, draw the two lines Genna drew. Then, using the same rule you used above, draw the third line and shade the square base of the second piece.

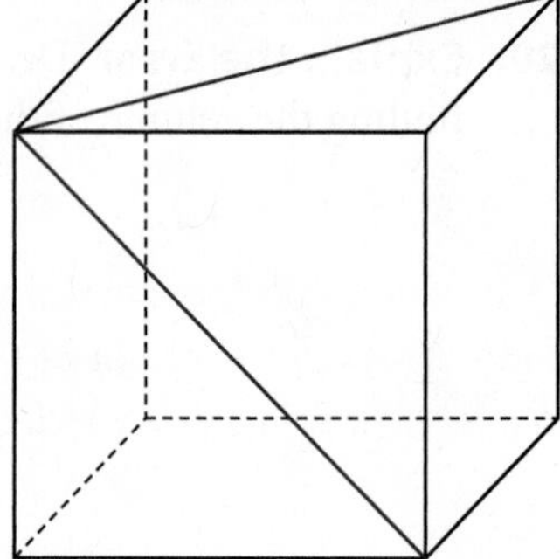

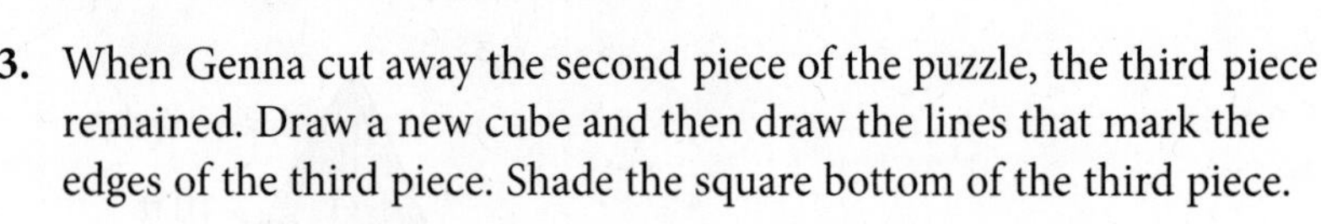

3. When Genna cut away the second piece of the puzzle, the third piece remained. Draw a new cube and then draw the lines that mark the edges of the third piece. Shade the square bottom of the third piece.

4. Compare the volumes of the three pieces. Explain your reasoning.

5. Explain how the model confirms the formula for the volume of a pyramid.

18.3 Volume of Cones

Essential Question: How do you calculate the volumes of composite figures that include cones?

Resource Locker

Explore Developing a Volume Formula

You can approximate the volume of a cone by finding the volumes of inscribed pyramids.

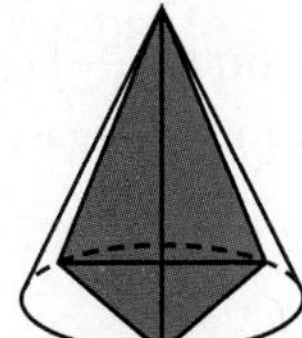
Base of inscribed pyramid has 3 sides

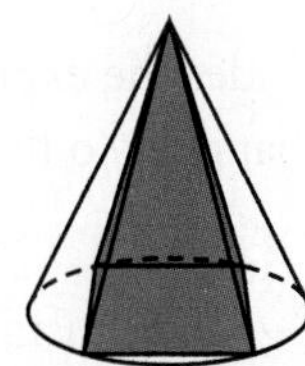
Base of inscribed pyramid has 4 sides

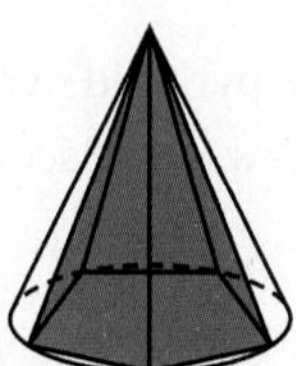
Base of inscribed pyramid has 5 sides

(A) The base of a pyramid is inscribed in the circular base of the cone and is a regular n-gon. Let O be the center of the cone's base, let r be the radius of the cone, and let h be the height of the cone. Draw radii from O to the vertices of the n-gon.

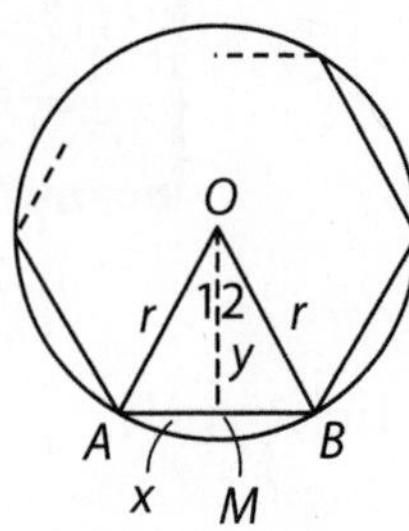

Construct segment $\overline{OM}$ from O to the midpoint M of $\overline{AB}$. How can you prove that $\triangle AOM \cong \triangle BOM$?

(B) How is $\angle 1 \cong \angle 2$?

(C) How many triangles congruent to $\triangle AOB$ surround point O to make up the n-gon that is the base of the pyramid? How can this be used to find the angle measures of $\triangle AOM$ and $\triangle BOM$?

(D) In $\triangle AOM$, $\sin \angle 1 = \frac{x}{r}$, so $x = r\sin \angle 1$. In $\triangle AOM$, $\cos \angle 1 = \frac{y}{r}$, so $y = r\cos \angle 1$. Since $\angle 1$ has a known value, rewrite x and y using substitution.

Ⓔ To write an expression for the area of the base of the pyramid, first write an expression for the area of $\triangle AOB$.

$$\text{Area of } \triangle AOB = \frac{1}{2} \cdot \textit{base} \cdot \textit{height}$$
$$= \frac{1}{2} \cdot 2x \cdot y$$
$$= xy$$

What is the area of $\triangle AOB$, substituting the new values for x and y? What is the area of the n triangles that make up the base of the pyramid?

Ⓕ Use the area of the base of the pyramid to find an equation for the volume of the pyramid.

Ⓖ Your expression for the pyramid's volume includes the expression $n \sin\left(\frac{180°}{n}\right) \cos\left(\frac{180°}{n}\right)$. Use a calculator, as follows, to discover what happens to this expression as n gets larger and larger.

- Enter the expression $n \sin\left(\frac{180°}{n}\right) \cos\left(\frac{180°}{n}\right)$ as Y_1, using x for n.
- Go to the Table Setup menu and enter the values shown.
- View a table for the function and scroll down.

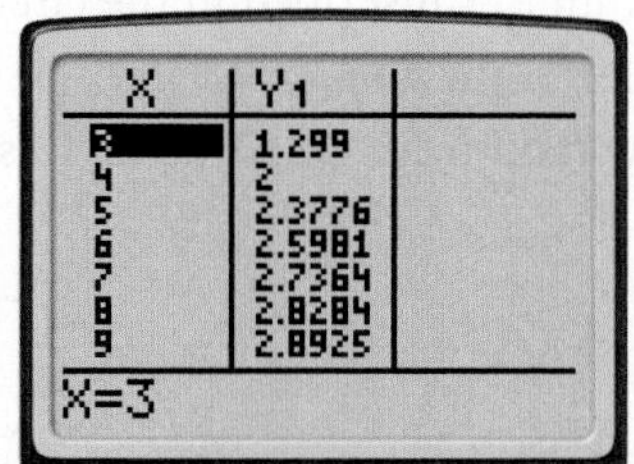

What happens to the expression as n gets very large?

Ⓗ If $n \sin\left(\frac{180°}{n}\right) \cos\left(\frac{180°}{n}\right)$ gets closer to π as n becomes greater, what happens to the entire expression for the volume of the inscribed pyramid? How is the area of the circle related to the expression for the base?

Reflect

1. How is the formula for the volume of a cone related to the formula for the volume of a pyramid?

Explain 1 Finding the Volume of a Cone

The volume relationship for cones that you found in the Explore can be stated as the following formula.

Volume of a Cone

The volume of a cone with base radius r and base area $B = \pi r^2$ and height h is given by $V = \frac{1}{3}Bh$ or by $V = \frac{1}{3}\pi r^2 h$.

You can use a formula for the volume of a cone to solve problems involving volume and capacity.

Example 1 **The figure represents a conical paper cup. How many fluid ounces of liquid can the cup hold? Round to the nearest tenth. (*Hint*: 1 in^3 ≈ 0.554 fl oz.)**

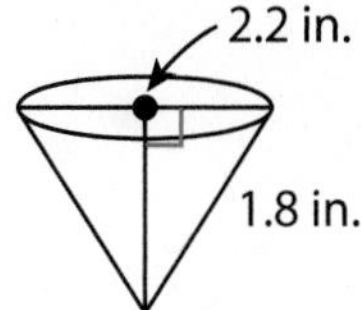

(A) Find the radius and height of the cone to the nearest hundredth.

The radius is half of the diameter, so $r = \frac{1}{2}(2.2 \text{ in.}) = 1.1$ in.

To find the height of the cone, use the Pythagorean Theorem:

$$r^2 + h^2 = (1.8)^2$$

$$(1.1)^2 + h^2 = (1.8)^2$$

$$1.21 + h^2 = 3.24$$

$$h^2 = 2.03, \text{ so } h \approx 1.42 \text{ in.}$$

(B) Find the volume of the cone in cubic inches.

$$V = \frac{1}{3}\pi r^2 h \approx \frac{1}{3}\pi\left(\boxed{1.1}\right)^2\left(\boxed{1.42}\right) \approx \boxed{1.80} \text{ in}^3$$

(C) Find the capacity of the cone to the nearest tenth of a fluid ounce.

$$\boxed{1.80} \text{ in}^3 \approx \boxed{1.80} \text{ in}^3 \times \frac{0.554 \text{ fl oz}}{1 \text{ in}^3} \approx \boxed{1.00} \text{ fl oz}$$

Your Turn

Right after Cindy buys a frozen yogurt cone, her friend Maria calls her, and they talk for so long that the frozen yogurt melts before Cindy can eat it. The cone has a slant height of 3.9 in. and a diameter of 2.4 in. If the frozen yogurt has the same volume before and after melting, and when melted just fills the cone, how much frozen yogurt did Cindy have before she talked to Maria, to the nearest tenth of a fluid ounce?

2. Find the radius. Then use the Pythagorean Theorem to find the height of the cone.

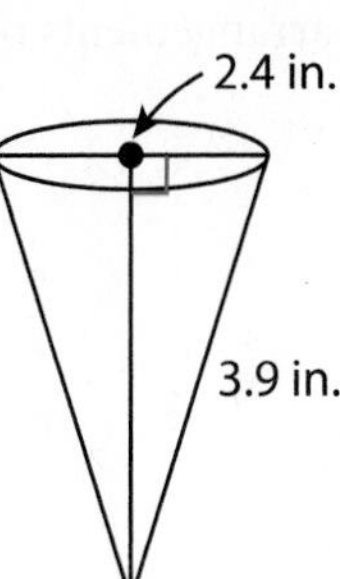

3. Find the volume of the cone in cubic inches.

4. Find the capacity of the cone to the nearest fluid ounce.

Explain 2 Finding the Volume of a Composite Figure

You can find the volume of a composite figure using appropriate volume formulas for the different parts of the figure.

Example 2 **Find the volume of the composite figure. Round to the nearest cubic millimeter.**

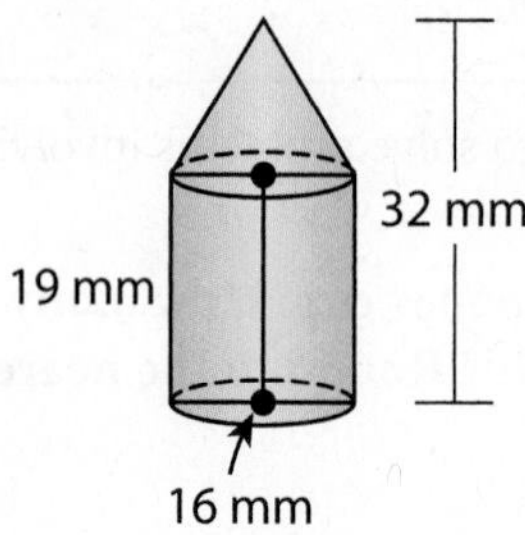

(A) Find the volume of the cylinder.

First, find the radius: $r = \frac{1}{2}(16 \text{ mm}) = 8 \text{ mm}$

$V = \pi r^2 h = \pi(8)^2(19) = 3{,}820.176 \ldots \text{ mm}^3$

(B) Find the volume of the cone.

The height of the cone is $h =$ 32 mm $-$ 19 mm $=$ 13 mm.

It has the same radius as the cylinder, $r =$ 8 mm.

$V = \frac{1}{3}\pi r^2 h = \frac{1}{3}\pi\left(8\right)^2\left(13\right) \approx 871.268 \text{ mm}^3$

(C) Find the total volume.

Total volume = volume of cylinder + volume of cone

$= 3{,}820.177 \text{ mm}^3 + 871.268 \text{ mm}^3$

$\approx 4{,}691 \text{ mm}^3$

Reflect

5. **Discussion** A composite figure is formed from a cone and a cylinder with the same base radius, and its volume can be calculated by multiplying the volume of the cylinder by a rational number, $\frac{a}{b}$. What arrangements of the cylinder and cone could explain this?

Your Turn

Making a cone-shaped hole in the top of a cylinder forms a composite figure, so that the apex of the cone is at the base of the cylinder. Find the volume of the figure, to the nearest tenth.

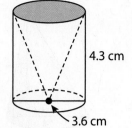

4.3 cm

3.6 cm

6. Find the volume of the cylinder.

7. Find the volume of the figure.

Elaborate

8. Could you use a circumscribed regular n-gon as the base of a pyramid to derive the formula for the volume of a cone? Explain.

9. **Essential Question Check-In** How do you calculate the volumes of composite figures that include cones?

Evaluate: Homework and Practice

- Online Homework
- Hints and Help
- Extra Practice

1. **Interpret the Answer** Katherine is using a cone to fill a cylinder with sand. If the radii and height are equal on both objects, and Katherine fills the cone to the very top, how many cones will it take to fill the cylinder with sand? Explain your answer.

Find the volume of the cone. Round the answer to the nearest tenth.

2.

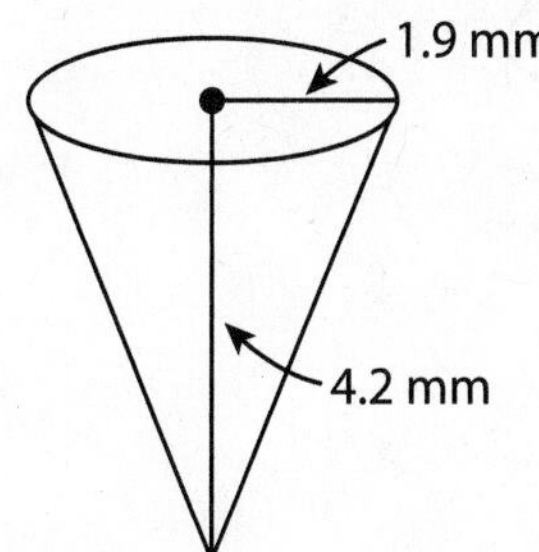

3.

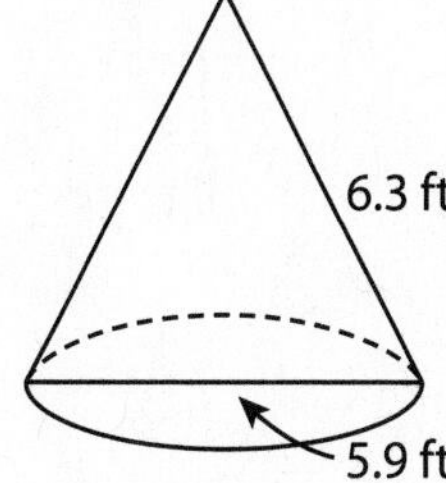

4.

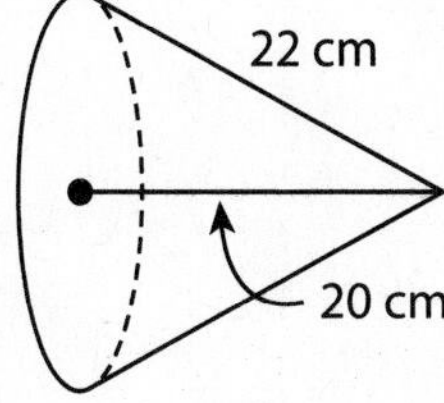

Find the volume of the cone. Leave the answer in terms of π.

5.

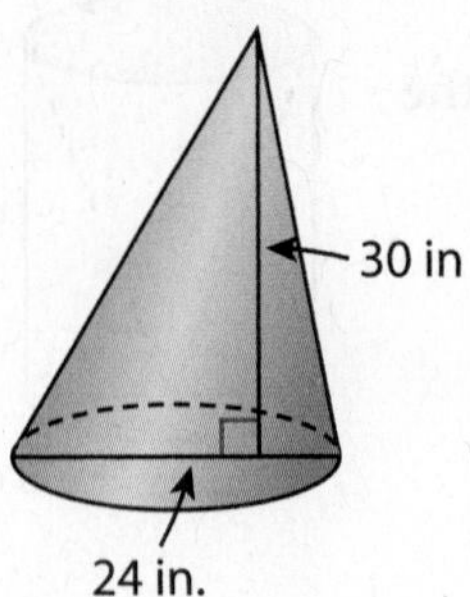

6.

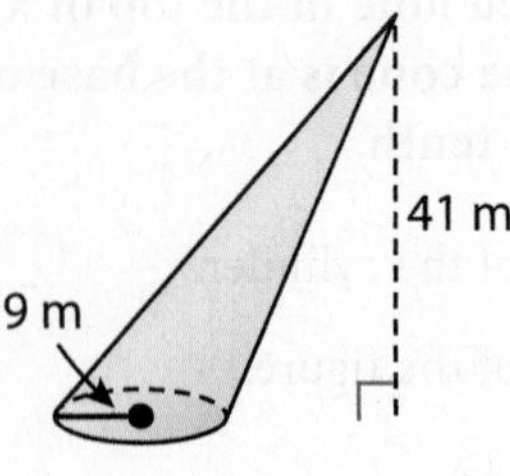

Find the volume of the composite figures. Round the answer to the nearest tenth.

7.

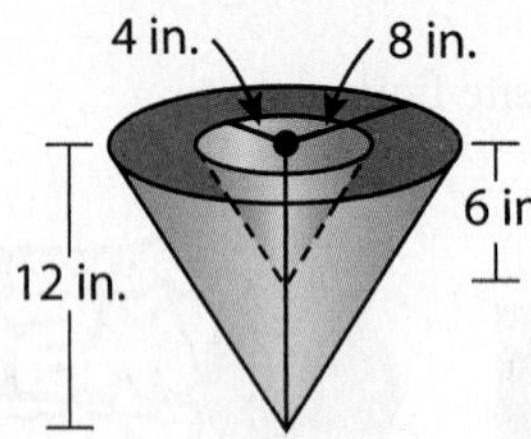

8.

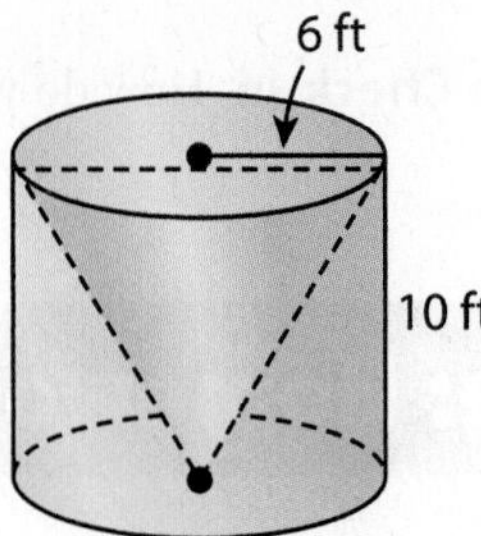

9.

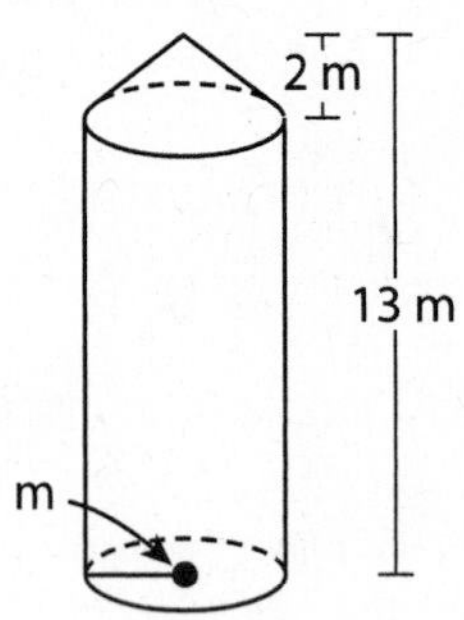

10.

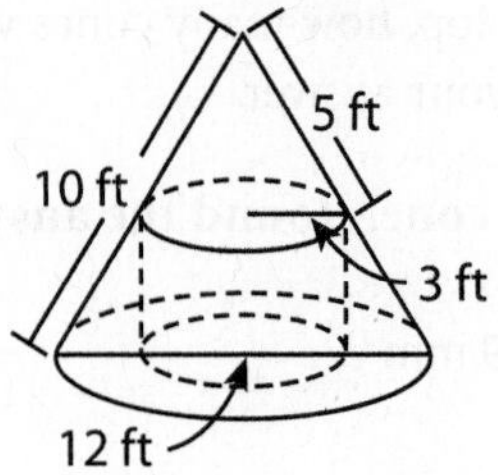

11. Match the dimensions of each cone with its volume.

A. radius 3 units, height 7 units

B. diameter 5 units, height 2 units

C. radius 28 units, slant height 53 units

D. diameter 24 units, slant height 13 units.

a. __?__ $\frac{25\pi}{6}$ units^3

b. __?__ 240π units^3

c. __?__ $11{,}760\pi$ units^3

d. __?__ 21π units^3

12. The roof of a grain silo is in the shape of a cone. The inside radius is 20 feet, and the roof is 10 feet tall. Below the cone is a cylinder 30 feet tall, with the same radius.

a. What is the volume of the silo?

b. If one cubic foot of wheat is approximately 48 pounds, and the farmer's crop consists of approximately 2 million pounds of wheat, will all of the wheat fit in the silo?

13. A cone has a volume of 18π in^3. Which are possible dimensions of the cone? Determine all that apply.

A. diameter 1 in., height 18 in.

B. diameter 6 in., height 6 in.

C. diameter 3 in., height 6 in.

D. diameter 6 in., height 3 in.

E. diameter 4 in., height 13.5 in.

F. diameter 13.5 in., height 4 in.

14. The figure shows a water tank that consists of a cylinder and a cone. How many gallons of water does the tank hold? Round to the nearest gallon. (Hint: 1 ft^3 = 7.48 gal)

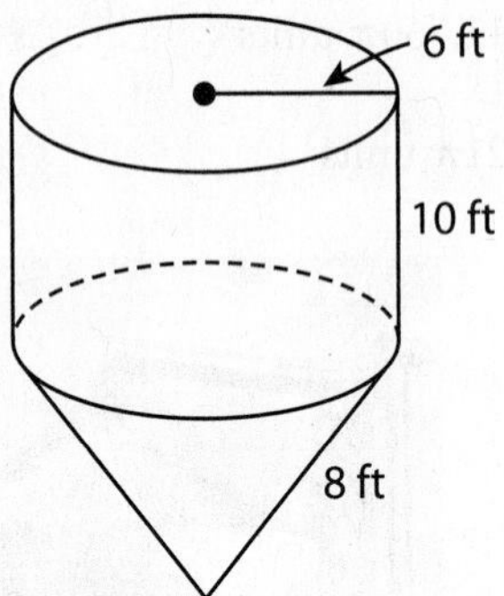

15. Roland is using a special machine to cut cones out of cylindrical pieces of wood. The machine is set to cut out two congruent cones from each piece of wood, leaving no gap in between the vertices of the cones. What is the volume of material left over after two cones are cut out?

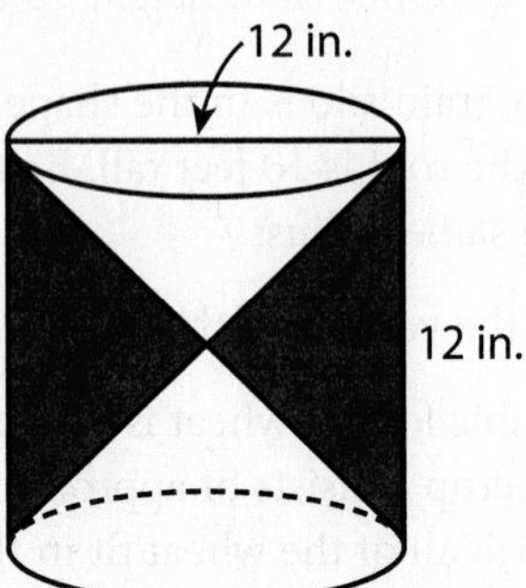

16. Algebra Develop an expression that could be used to solve for the volume of this solid for any value of x.

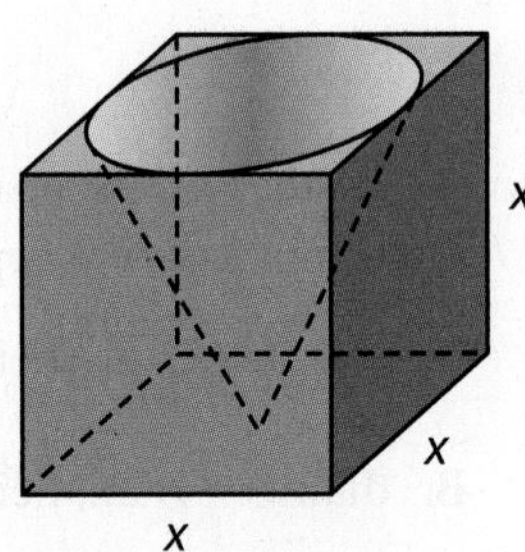

17. Persevere in Problem Solving A juice stand sells smoothies in cone-shaped cups that are 8 in. tall. The regular size has a 4 in. diameter. The jumbo size has an 8 in. diameter.

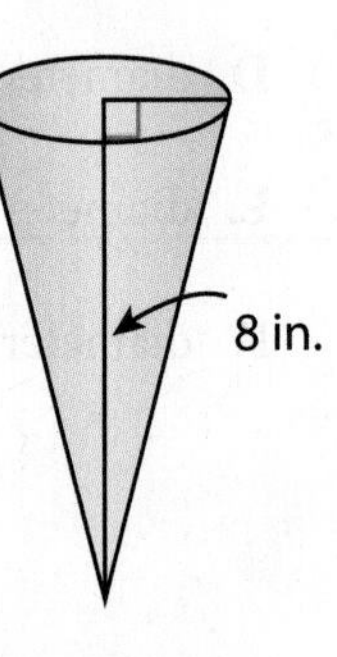

a. Find the volume of the regular size to the nearest tenth.

b. Find the volume of the jumbo size to the nearest tenth.

c. The regular size costs $1.25. What would be a reasonable price for the jumbo size? Explain your reasoning.

18. Find the volume of a cone with base area 36π ft^2 and a height equal to twice the radius.

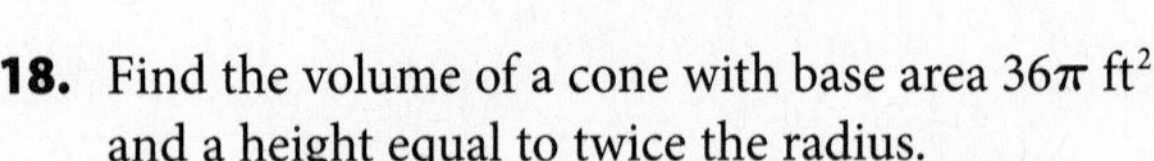

19. Find the base circumference of a cone with height 5 cm and volume 125π cm^3.

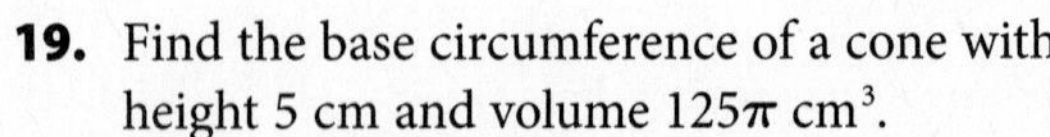

H.O.T. Focus on Higher Order Thinking

20. Analyze Relationships Popcorn is available in two cups: a square pyramid or a cone, as shown. The price of each cup of popcorn is the same. Which cup is the better deal? Explain.

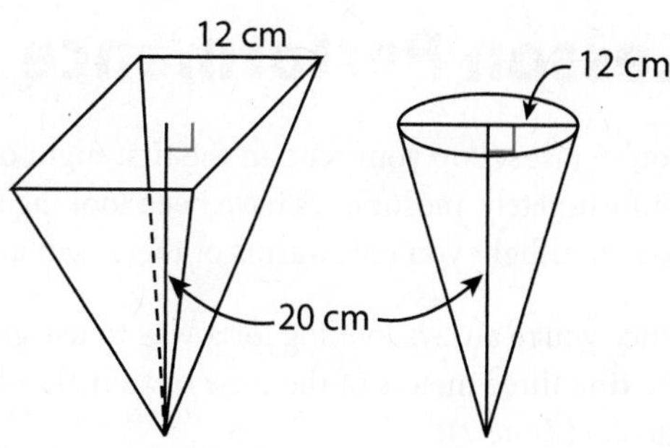

21. Make a Conjecture A cylinder has a radius of 5 in. and a height of 3 in. Without calculating the volumes, find the height of a cone with the same base and the same volume as the cylinder. Explain your reasoning.

22. Analyze Relationships A sculptor removes a cone from a cylindrical block of wood so that the vertex of the cone is the center of the cylinder's base, as shown. Explain how the volume of the remaining solid compares with the volume of the original cylindrical block of wood.

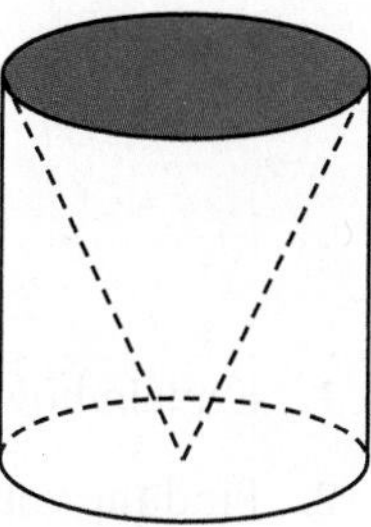

23. Explain the Error Which volume is incorrect? Explain the error.

(A)

$V = \frac{1}{3}(8^2\pi)(17)$

$= \frac{1088\pi}{3}$ cm³

(B)

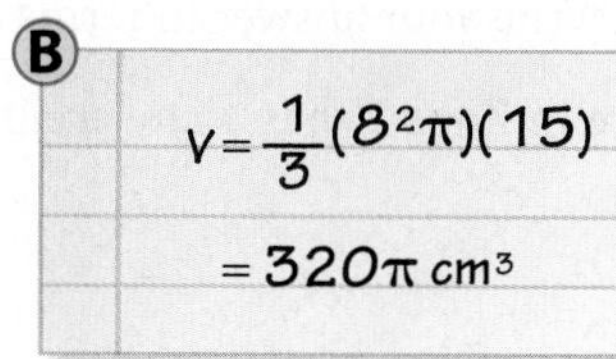

$V = \frac{1}{3}(8^2\pi)(15)$

$= 320\pi$ cm³

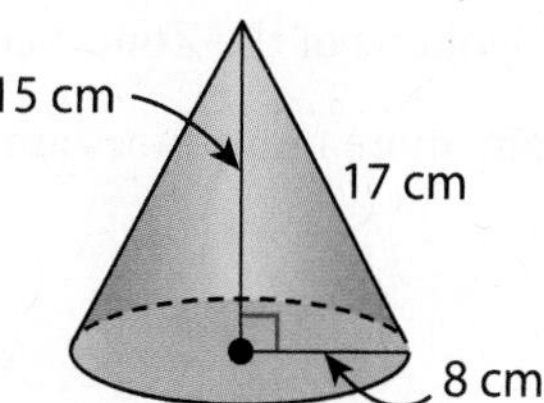

Lesson Performance Task

You've just set up your tent on the first night of a camping trip that you've been looking forward to for a long time. Unfortunately, mosquitoes have been looking forward to your arrival even more than you have. When you turn on your flashlight you see swarms of them—an average of 800 mosquitoes per square meter, in fact.

Since you're always looking for a way to use geometry, you decide to solve a problem: How many mosquitoes are in the first three meters of the cone of your flashlight (Zone 1 in the diagram), and how many are in the second three meters (Zone 2)?

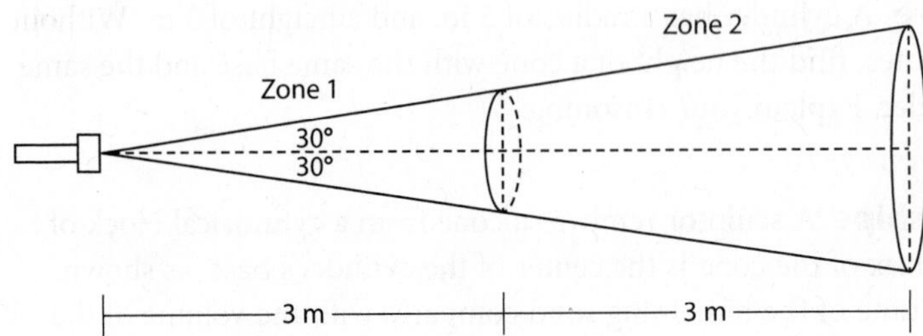

1. Explain how you can find the volume of the Zone 1 cone.
2. Find the volume of the Zone 1 cone. Write your answer in terms of π.
3. Explain how you can find the volume of the Zone 2 cone.
4. Find the volume of the Zone 2 cone. Write your answer in terms of π.
5. How many more mosquitoes are there in Zone 2 than there are in Zone 1? Use 3.14 for π.

18.4 Volume of Spheres

Essential Question: **How can you use the formula for the volume of a sphere to calculate the volumes of composite figures?**

Resource Locker

Explore Developing a Volume Formula

To find the volume of a sphere, compare one of its hemispheres to a cylinder of the same height and radius from which a cone has been removed.

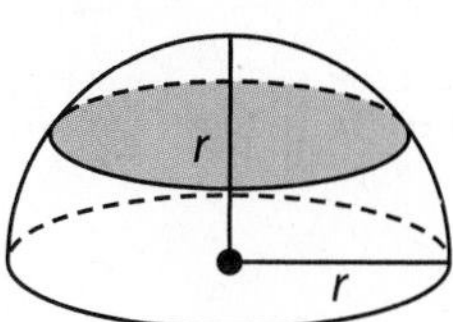

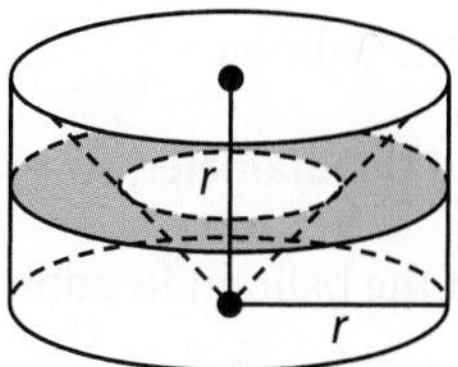

(A) The region of a plane that intersects a solid figure is called a **cross section**. To show that cross sections have the same area at every level, use the Pythagorean Theorem to find a relationship between r, x, and R.

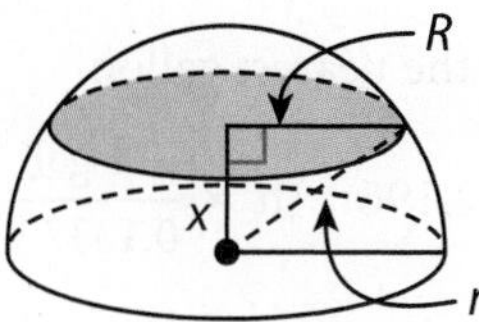

(B) A cross section of the cylinder with the cone removed is a ring.

To find the area of the ring, find the area of the outer circle and of the inner circle. Then subtract the area of the inner circle from the outer circle.

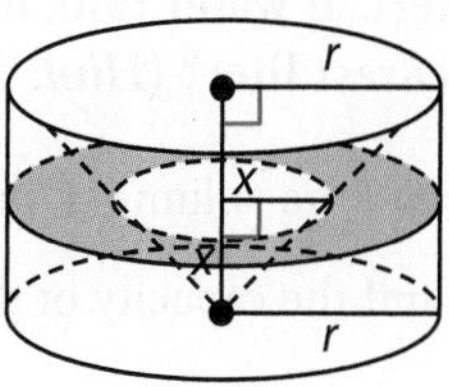

(C) Find an expression for the volume of the cylinder with the cone removed.

(D) Use Cavalieri's principle to deduce the volume of a sphere with radius r.

Reflect

1. How do you know that the height h of the cylinder with the cone removed is equal to the radius r?

2. What happens to the cross-sectional areas when $x = 0$? when $x = r$?

Explain 1 Finding the Volume of a Sphere

The relationship you discovered in the Explore can be stated as a volume formula.

Volume of a Sphere

The volume of a sphere with radius r is given by $V = \frac{4}{3}\pi r^3$.

You can use a formula for the volume of a sphere to solve problems involving volume and capacity.

Example 1 **The figure represents a spherical helium-filled balloon. This tourist attraction allows up to 28 passengers at a time to ride in a gondola suspended underneath the balloon, as it cruises at an altitude of 500 ft. How much helium, to the nearest hundred gallons, does the balloon hold? Round to the nearest tenth. (*Hint:* 1 gal ≈ 0.1337 ft³)**

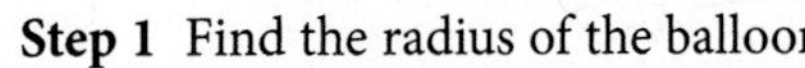

Step 1 Find the radius of the balloon.

The radius is half of the diameter, so $r = \frac{1}{2}(72 \text{ ft}) = 36$ ft.

Step 2 Find the volume of the balloon in cubic feet.

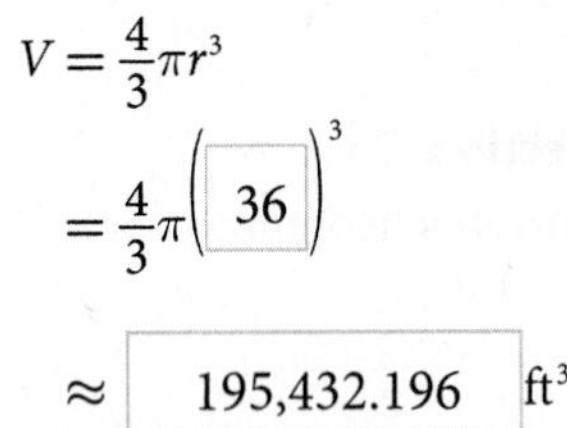

$$V = \frac{4}{3}\pi r^3$$

$$= \frac{4}{3}\pi\left(\boxed{36}\right)^3$$

$$\approx \boxed{195{,}432.196} \text{ ft}^3$$

Step 3 Find the capacity of the balloon to the nearest gallon.

$$\boxed{195{,}432.196} \text{ ft}^3 \approx \boxed{195{,}432.196} \text{ ft}^3 \times \frac{1 \text{ gal}}{0.1337 \text{ ft}^3} \approx \boxed{1{,}462{,}000} \text{ gal}$$

Your Turn

A spherical water tank has a diameter of 27 m. How much water can the tank hold, to the nearest liter? (*Hint:* 1,000 L = 1 m³)

3. Find the volume of the tank in cubic meters.

4. Find the capacity of the tank to the nearest liter.

Explain 2 Finding the Volume of a Composite Figure

You can find the volume of a composite figure using appropriate volume formulas for the different parts of the figure.

Example 2 **Find the volume of the composite figure. Round to the nearest cubic centimeter.**

Step 1 Find the volume of the hemisphere.

Step 2 Find the height of the cone.

$h^2 + \left(5\right)^2 = \left(13\right)^2$

$h^2 + 25 = 169$

$h^2 = 144$

$h = 12$

Step 3 Find the volume of the cone.

The cone has the same radius as the hemisphere, $r = 5$ cm.

$V = \frac{1}{3}\pi r^2 h$

$= \frac{1}{3}\pi\left(5\right)^2\left(12\right)$

$= 314.159$ cm^3

Step 4 Find the total volume.

Total volume = volume of hemisphere + volume of cone

$= 261.799$ cm^3 + 314.159 cm^3

≈ 576 cm^3

Reflect

5. Is it possible to create a figure by taking a cone and removing from it a hemisphere with the same radius?

Your Turn

6. A composite figure is a cylinder with a hemispherical hole in the top. The bottom of the hemisphere is tangent to the base of the cylinder. Find the volume of the figure, to the nearest tenth.

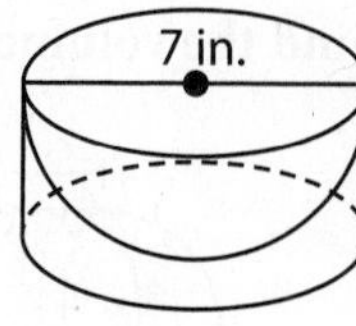

Elaborate

7. **Discussion** Could you use an inscribed prism to derive the volume of a hemisphere? Why or why not? Are there any other ways you could approximate a hemisphere, and what problems would you encounter in finding its volume?

8. **Essential Question Check-In** A gumball is in the shape of a sphere, with a spherical hole in the center. How might you calculate the volume of the gumball? What measurements are needed?

Evaluate: Homework and Practice

- Online Homework
- Hints and Help
- Extra Practice

1. **Analyze Relationships** Use the diagram of a sphere inscribed in a cylinder to describe the relationship between the volume of a sphere and the volume of a cylinder.

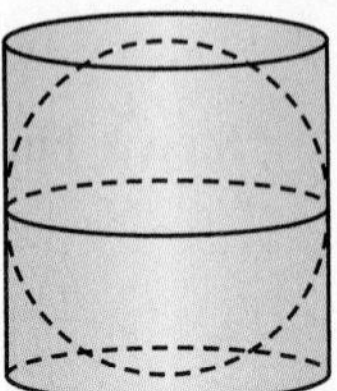

Find the volume of the sphere. Round the answer to the nearest tenth.

2. 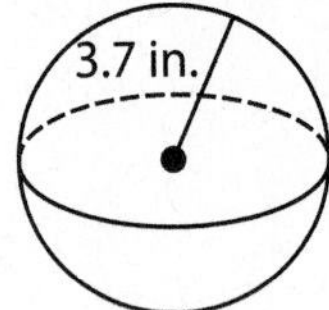

3. 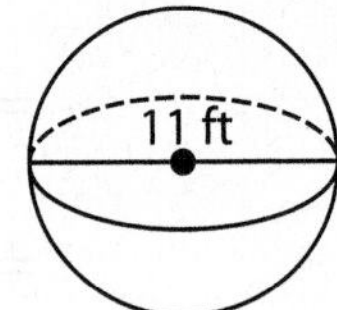

4. 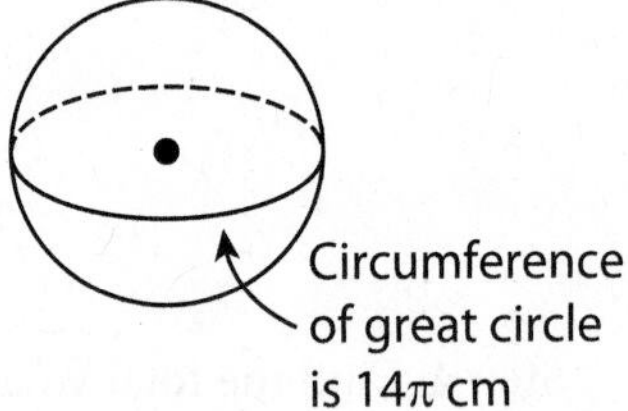

Find the volume of the sphere. Leave the answer in terms of π.

5. 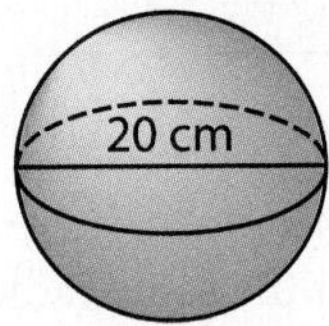

6. 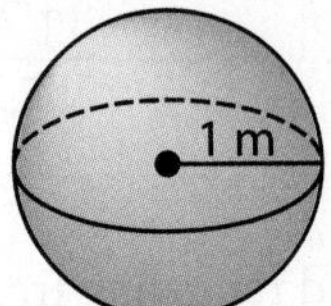

7. 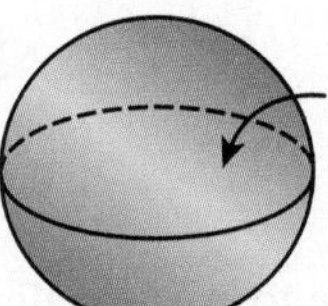

Find the volume of the composite figure. Leave the answer in terms of π.

8. 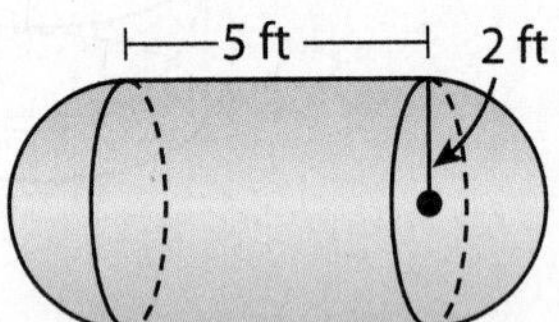

9. 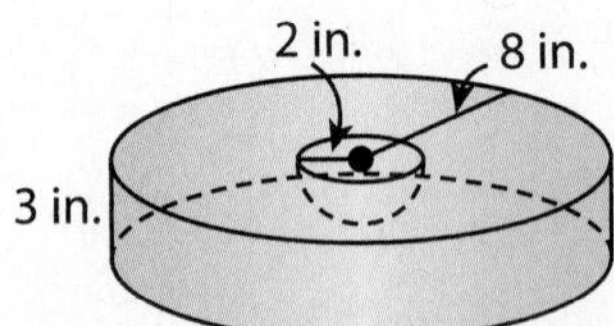

Find the volume of the composite figure. Round the answer to the nearest tenth.

10.

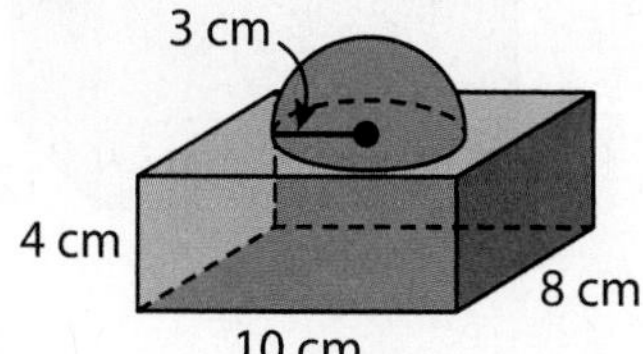

11.

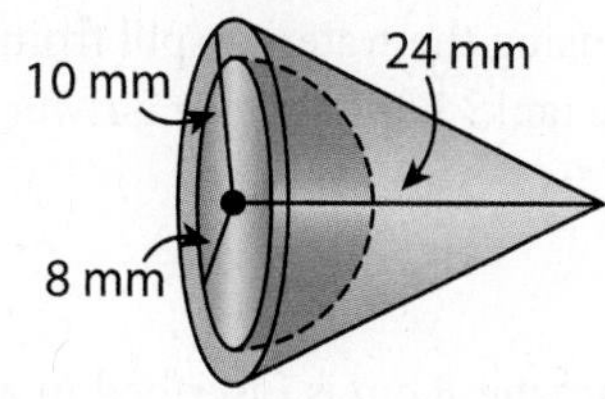

12. **Analyze Relationships** Approximately how many times as great is the volume of a grapefruit with diameter 10 cm as the volume of a lime with diameter 5 cm?

13. A bead is formed by drilling a cylindrical hole with a 2-mm diameter through a sphere with an 8-mm diameter. Estimate the volume of the bead to the nearest whole.

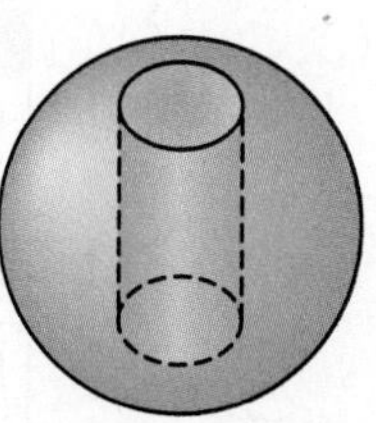

14. **Algebra** Write an expression representing the volume of the composite figure formed by a hemisphere with radius r and a cube with side length $2r$.

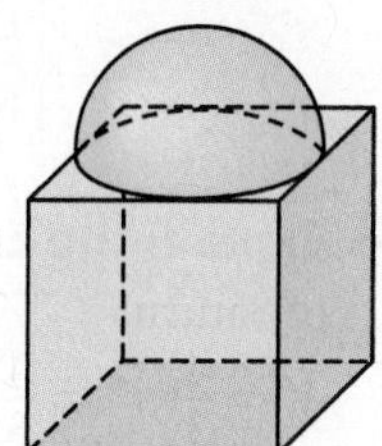

15. One gallon of propane yields approximately 91,500 BTU. About how many BTUs does the spherical storage tank shown provide? Round to the nearest million BTUs. (*Hint:* $1 \text{ ft}^3 \approx 7.48$ gal)

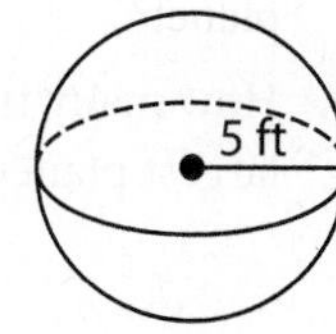

16. The aquarium shown is a rectangular prism that is filled with water. You drop a spherical ball with a diameter of 6 inches into the aquarium. The ball sinks, causing the water to spill from the tank. How much water is left in the tank? Express your answer to the nearest tenth. (*Hint:* 1 in.$^3 \approx$ 0.00433 gal)

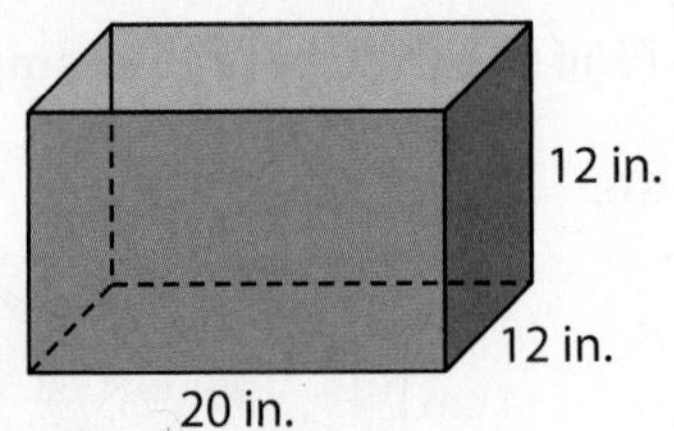

17. A sphere with diameter 8 cm is inscribed in a cube. Find the ratio of the volume of the cube to the volume of the sphere.

A. $\frac{6}{\pi}$

B. $\frac{2}{3\pi}$

C. $\frac{3\pi}{4}$

D. $\frac{3\pi}{2}$

For Exercises 18–20, use the table. Round each volume to the nearest billion π.

Planet	Diameter (mi)
Mercury	3,032
Venus	7,521
Earth	7,926
Mars	4,222
Jupiter	88,846
Saturn	74,898
Uranus	31,763
Neptune	30,775

18. Explain the Error Margaret used the mathematics shown to find the volume of Saturn.

$V = \frac{4}{3}\pi r^2 = \frac{4}{3}\pi(74{,}898)^2 \approx \frac{4}{3}\pi(6{,}000{,}000{,}000) \approx 8{,}000{,}000{,}000\pi$

Explain the two errors Margaret made, then give the correct answer.

19. The sum of the volumes of Venus and Mars is about equal to the volume of which planet?

20. How many times as great as the volume of the smallest planet is the volume of the largest planet? Round to the nearest thousand.

H.O.T. Focus on Higher Order Thinking

21. Make a Conjecture The *bathysphere* was an early version of a submarine, invented in the 1930s. The inside diameter of the bathysphere was 54 inches, and the steel used to make the sphere was 1.5 inches thick. It had three 8-inch diameter windows. Estimate the volume of steel used to make the bathysphere.

22. Explain the Error A student solved the problem shown. Explain the student's error and give the correct answer to the problem.

A spherical gasoline tank has a radius of 0.5 ft. When filled, the tank provides 446,483 BTU. How many BTUs does one gallon of gasoline yield? Round to the nearest thousand BTUs and use the fact that 1 $\text{ft}^3 \approx 7.48$ gal.

> The volume of the tank is $\frac{4}{3}\pi r^3 = \frac{4}{3}\pi(0.5)^3$ ft^3. Multiplying by 7.48 shows that this is approximately 3.92 gal. So the number of BTUs in one gallon of gasoline is approximately $446{,}483 \times 3.92 \approx 1{,}750{,}000$ BTU.

23. Persevere in Problem Solving The top of a gumball machine is an 18 in. sphere. The machine holds a maximum of 3300 gumballs, which leaves about 43% of the space in the machine empty. Estimate the diameter of each gumball.

Lesson Performance Task

For his science project, Bizbo has decided to build a scale model of the solar system. He starts with a grapefruit with a radius of 2 inches to represent Earth. His "Earth" weighs 0.5 pounds.

	Radius (mi)	Distance from Sun (mi)
Earth	4×10^3	9.3×10^7
Neptune	1.5×10^4	2.8×10^9
Sun	4.3×10^5	

Find each of the following for Bizbo's model. Use the rounded figures in the table. Round your answers to two significant figures. Use 3.14 for π.

1. the scale of Bizbo's model: 1 inch = __?__ miles
2. Earth's distance from the Sun, in inches and in miles
3. Neptune's distance from the Sun, in inches and in miles
4. the Sun's volume, in cubic inches and cubic feet
5. the Sun's weight, in pounds and in tons (Note: the Sun's density is 0.26 times the Earth's density.)

Volume Formulas

Essential Question: How can you use volume formulas to solve real-world problems?

Key Vocabulary

right prism *(prisma recto)*
right cylinder *(cilindro recto)*
oblique prism *(prisma oblicuo)*
oblique cylinder *(cilindro oblicuo)*
cross section *(sección transversal)*

KEY EXAMPLE *(Lesson 18.1)*

Find the volume of a cylinder with a base radius of 3 centimeters and a height of 5 centimeters. Write an exact answer.

$V = \pi r^2 h$ Write the formula for the volume of a cylinder.

$= \pi(3)^2(5)$ Substitute.

$= 45\pi \text{ cm}^3$ Simplify.

KEY EXAMPLE *(Lesson 18.2)*

Find the volume of a square pyramid with a base side length of 12 inches and a height of 7 inches.

$V = \frac{1}{3}Bh$ Write the formula for the volume of a pyramid.

$= \frac{1}{3}(12)^2(7)$ Substitute.

$= 336 \text{ in}^3$ Simplify.

KEY EXAMPLE *(Lesson 18.3)*

Find the volume of a cone with a base diameter of 16 feet and a height of 18 feet. Write an exact answer.

$r = \frac{1}{2}(16 \text{ ft})$ Find the radius.

$= 8 \text{ ft}$ Simplify.

$V = \frac{1}{3}\pi r^2 h$ Write the formula for the volume of a cone.

$= \frac{1}{3}\pi(8)^2(18)$ Substitute.

$= 384\pi \text{ ft}^3$ Simplify.

KEY EXAMPLE *(Lesson 18.4)*

Find the volume of a sphere with a radius of 30 miles. Write an exact answer.

$V = \frac{4}{3}\pi r^3$ Write the formula for the volume of a sphere.

$= \frac{4}{3}\pi(30)^3$ Substitute.

$= 36{,}000\pi \text{ mi}^3$ Simplify.

EXERCISES

Find the volume of each figure. Write an exact answer. *(Lessons 18.1–18.4)*

1.

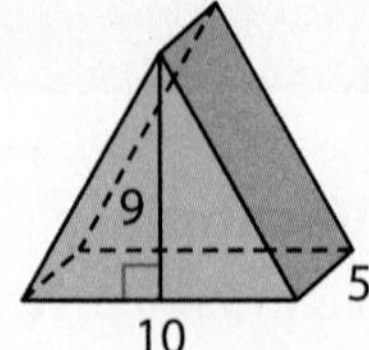

2.

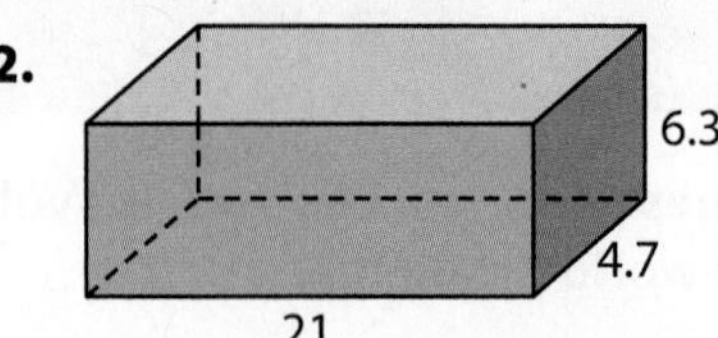

3.

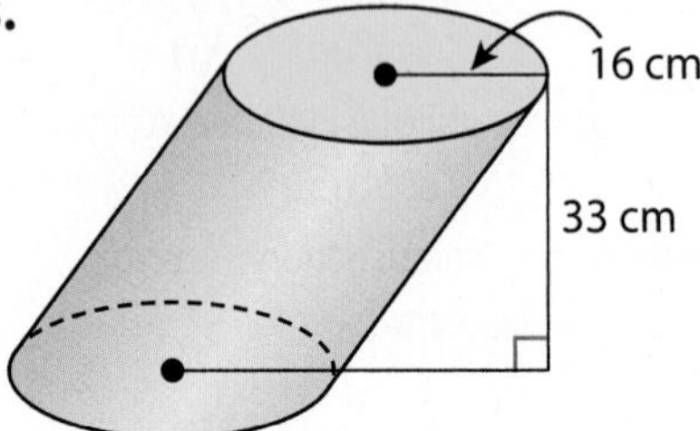

4.

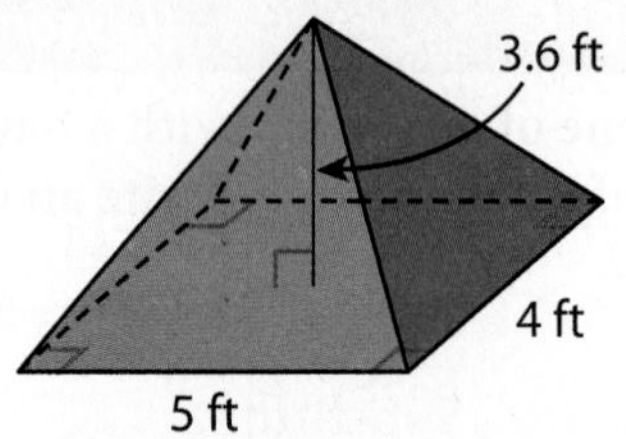

5.

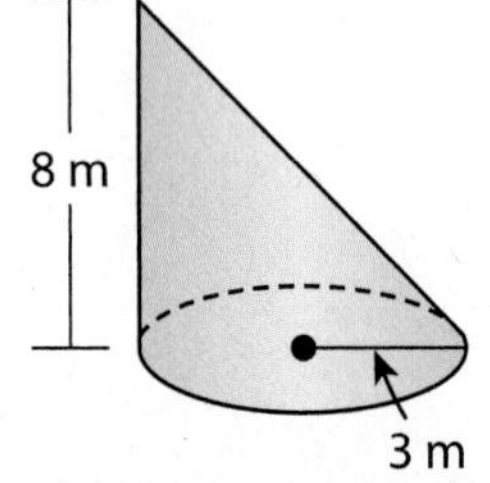

6.

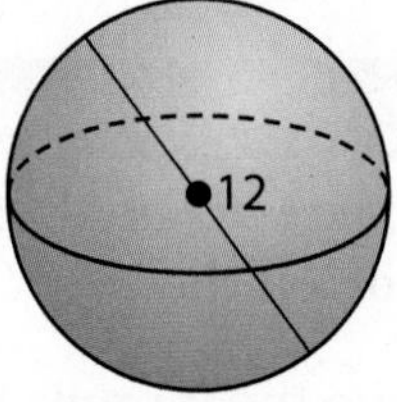

7.

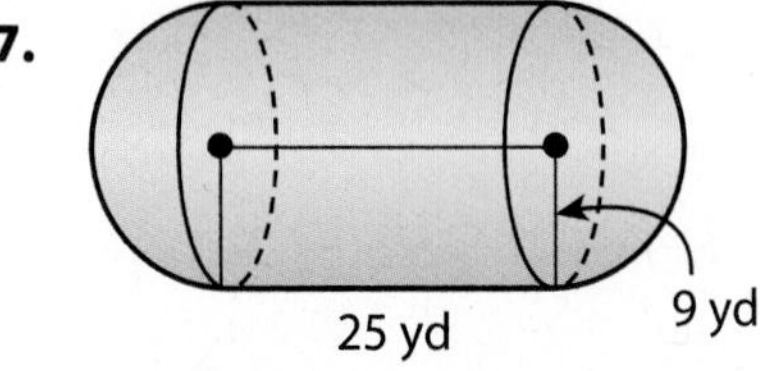

MODULE PERFORMANCE TASK

How Big Is That Sinkhole?

In 2010 an enormous sinkhole suddenly appeared in the middle of a Guatemalan neighborhood and swallowed a three-story building above it. The sinkhole has an estimated depth of about 100 feet.

How much material is needed to fill the sinkhole? Determine what information is needed to answer the question. Do you think your estimate is more likely to be too high or too low?

What are some material options for filling the sinkhole, and how much would they cost? Which material do you think would be the best choice?

Ready to Go On?

18.1–18.4 Volume Formulas

- Online Homework
- Hints and Help
- Extra Practice

Find the volume of the figure. *(Lessons 18.1–18.4)*

1. An oblique cylinder next to a cube.

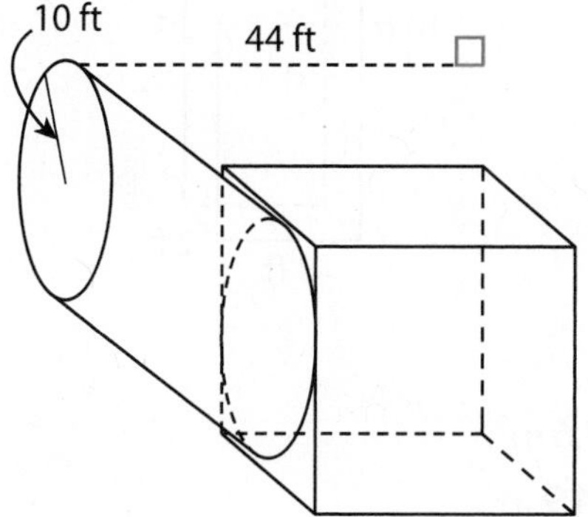

2. A prism of volume 3 with a pyramid of the same height cut out.

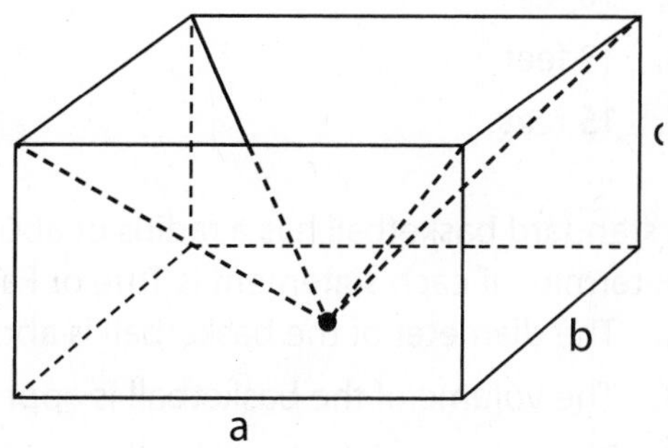

3. A cone with a square pyramid of the same height cut out. The pyramid has height l, and its square base has area l^2.

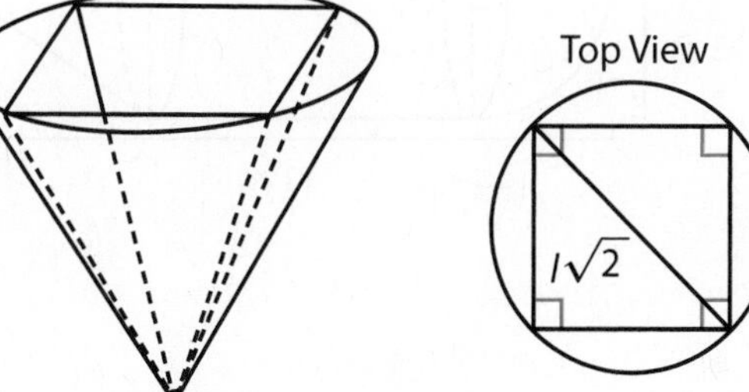

4. A cube with sides of length s with the biggest sphere that fits in it cut out.

ESSENTIAL QUESTION

5. How would you find the volume of an ice-cream cone with ice cream in it? What measurements would you need?

MODULE 18
MIXED REVIEW

Assessment Readiness

1. A simplified model of a particular monument is a rectangular pyramid placed on top of a rectangular prism, as shown. The volume of the monument is 66 cubic feet. Determine whether the given measurement could be the height of the monument.
Write Yes or No for A–C.

A. 10 feet

B. 13 feet

C. 15 feet

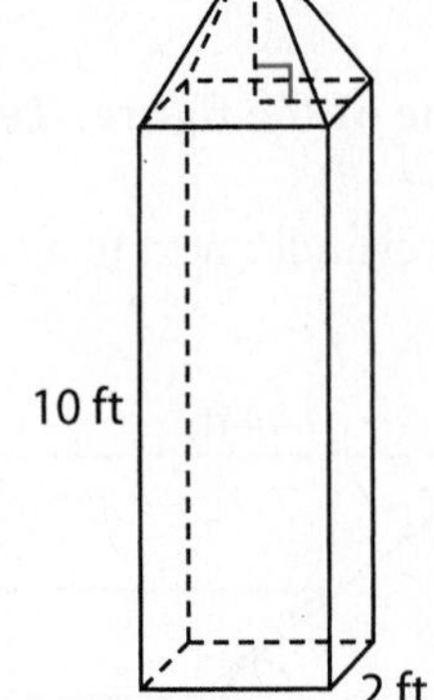

2. A standard basketball has a radius of about 4.7 inches. Determine if each statement is True or False.

A. The diameter of the basketball is about 25 inches.

B. The volume of the basketball is approximately 277.6 in^3.

C. The volume of the basketball is approximately 434.9 in^3.

3. A triangle has a side of length 8, a second side of length 17, and a third side of length *x*. Find the range of possible values for *x*.

4. Find the approximate volume of the figure at right, composed of a cone, a cylinder, and a hemisphere. Explain how you found the values needed to compute the volume.

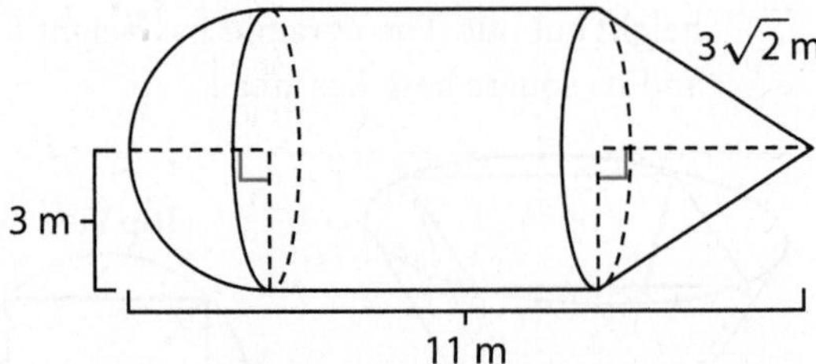

Visualizing Solids

MODULE 19

Essential Question: How can visualizing solids help you to solve real-world problems?

REAL WORLD VIDEO
Check out how visualization of solids and surface area can be used to determine critical dimensions of the Space Shuttle and other spacecraft.

MODULE PERFORMANCE TASK PREVIEW

How Much Does the Paint on the Space Shuttle Weigh?

At some point, NASA stopped painting the fuel tanks for the Space Shuttle because of the extra weight it added. In this module, you will be challenged to use surface area to come up with an estimate for the weight of that paint. Let's start the countdown!

Are YOU Ready?

Complete these exercises to review skills you will need for this module.

- Online Homework
- Hints and Help
- Extra Practice

Cross Sections

Example 1 What is the cross section of a plane that passes through (but not tangent to) a sphere?

No matter how or where the plane passes, the cross section will always be a circle with radius less than or equal to the radius of the sphere.

Find the cross section of the following.

1. A plane passing through a cylinder parallel to the bases.

Volume

Example 2 Find the exact volume of a right cylinder with a radius 9 and height 5.

$V = Bh$ Volume of a cylinder

$B = \pi r^2$ Area of base equals the area of a circle.

$B = \pi(9)^2 = 81\pi$ Substitute and solve.

$V = (81\pi)(5) = 405\pi$ Substitute and solve to find the volume.

Find the volume of the following. Give exact values.

2. A sphere with radius 6

3. A pyramid whose base is a square with a base having sides of length 17 and whose height is 9

Surface Area

Example 3 Given a cube with a side of length 5, find the surface area.

Since the surface area of a cube is 6 squares of equal area, find the area of one face of the cube and then multiply by 6.

$A = s^2$ Area of a square

$A = (5)^2 = 25$ Substitute and solve.

$SA = 25 \cdot 6 = 150$ Multiply by 6, the number of faces of a cube.

Find the surface area of a cube with the following side lengths.

4. 7

5. 10

19.1 Cross Sections and Solids of Rotation

Resource Locker

Essential Question: What tools can you use to visualize solid figures accurately?

Explore Exploring Nets

A **net** is a diagram of the surfaces of a three-dimensional figure that can be folded to form the three-dimensional figure. To identify a three-dimensional figure from a net, look at the number of faces and the shape of each face.

(A) Complete each row of the table. Express the circumference of the cylinder as a multiple of π.

Type of Solid	Example	Faces	Net
	1.5 m 2 m 4 m		4 m 1.5 m 2 m 1.5 m 2 m
triangular prism		a pair of congruent triangles and 3 rectangles	
		a rectangle and 2 pairs of congruent isosceles triangles	11 cm 6 cm
cylinder	7 ft 12 ft		

Reflect

1. **Discussion** Is there more than one way to draw a net for a solid? Are there rules for how the faces of a solid are joined to create a net for it?

Explain 1 Identifying Cross Sections

Recall that a *cross section* is a region of a plane that intersects a solid figure. Cross sections of three-dimensional figures sometimes turn out to be simple figures such as triangles, rectangles, or circles.

Example 1 **Describe the cross section of each figure. Compare the dimensions of the cross section to those of the figure.**

Ⓐ The bases of the cylinder are congruent circles.

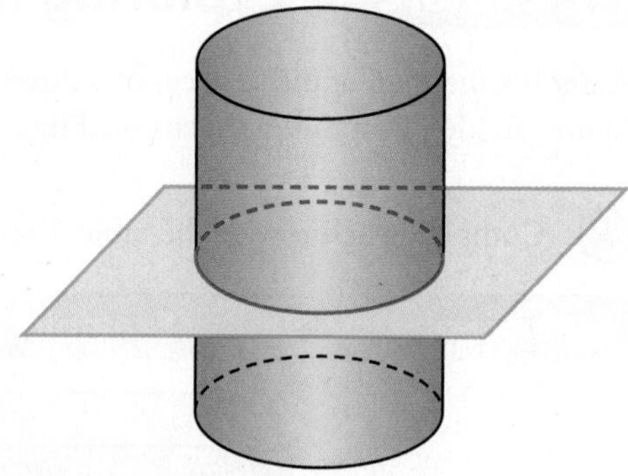

The cross section is formed by a plane that is parallel to the bases of the cylinder. Any cross section of a cylinder made by a plane parallel to the bases will have the same shape as the bases.

Therefore, the cross section is a circle with the same radius or diameter as the bases.

Ⓑ The lateral surface of the cone curves in the horizontal direction, but not the vertical direction. Therefore the two sides of the cross section along this surface are straight line segments with equal lengths.

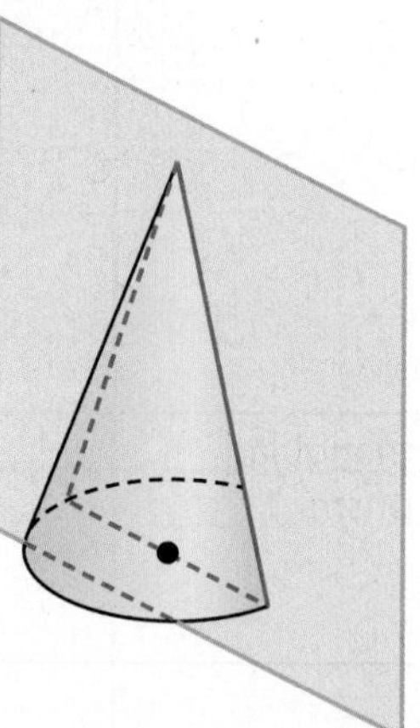

The third side is a diameter of the base of the cone. Therefore, the cross section is a(n) [isosceles] triangle. Its base is the [diameter] of the cone and its leg length is the [slant] height of the cone.

Reflect

2. A plane intersects a sphere. Make a conjecture about the resulting cross section.

Your Turn

Describe the cross section of the figure. Compare the dimensions of the cross section to those of the figure.

3.

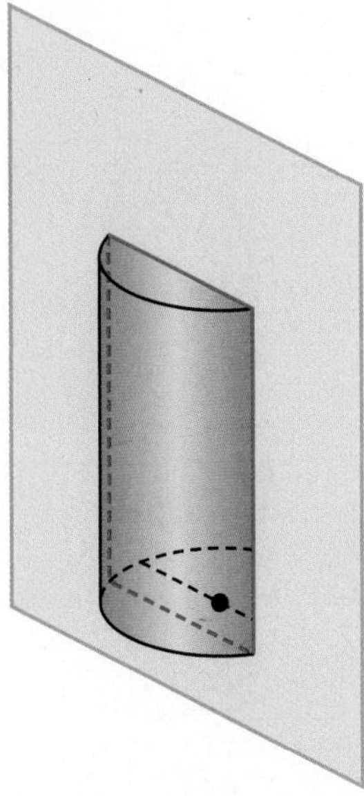

Explain 2 Generating Three-Dimensional Figures

You can generate a three-dimensional figure by rotating a two-dimensional figure around an appropriate axis.

Example 2 **Describe and then sketch the figure that is generated by each rotation in three-dimensional space.**

(A) A right triangle rotated around a line containing one of its legs

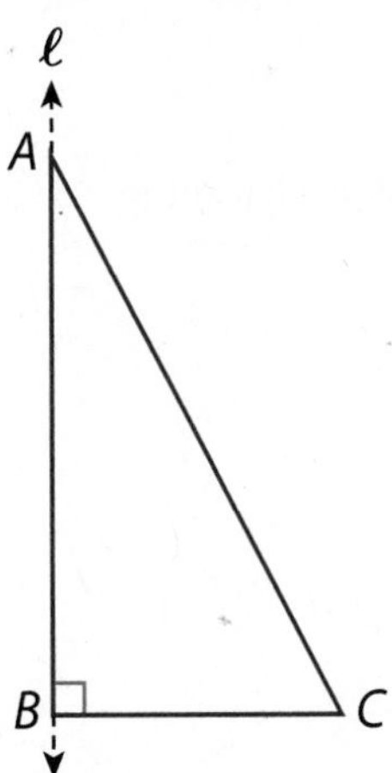

Leg $\overline{BC}$ is perpendicular to ℓ, so vertex C traces out a circle as it rotates about ℓ, and therefore $\overline{BC}$ traces out a circular base. The hypotenuse, $\overline{AC}$, traces out the curving surface of the cone whose base is formed by $\overline{BC}$. The figure formed by the rotation is a cone.

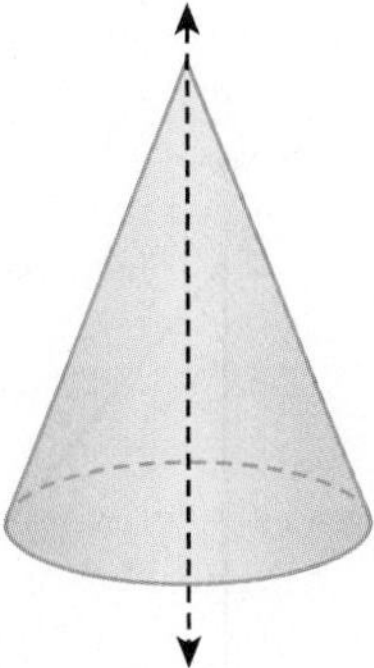

Ⓑ A rectangle rotated around a line containing one of its sides

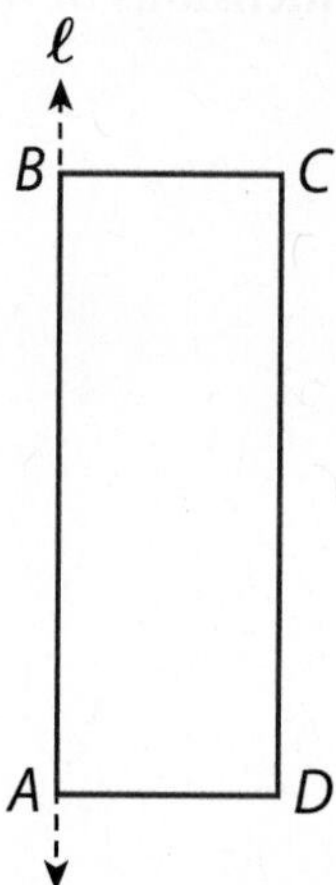

Sides $\overline{BC}$ and $\overline{AD}$ are both perpendicular to ℓ, so they each trace out congruent circles with common radius $BC = AD$. Side $\overline{CD}$ is parallel to ℓ, so it traces out a surface formed by moving a line at a constant distance from ℓ. The figure formed by the rotation is a cylinder.

Reflect

4. **Discussion** What principles can you identify for generating a solid by rotation of a two-dimensional figure?

Your Turn

Describe and then sketch the figure that is generated by each rotation in three-dimensional space.

5. A trapezoid with two adjacent acute angles rotated around a line containing the side adjacent to these angles

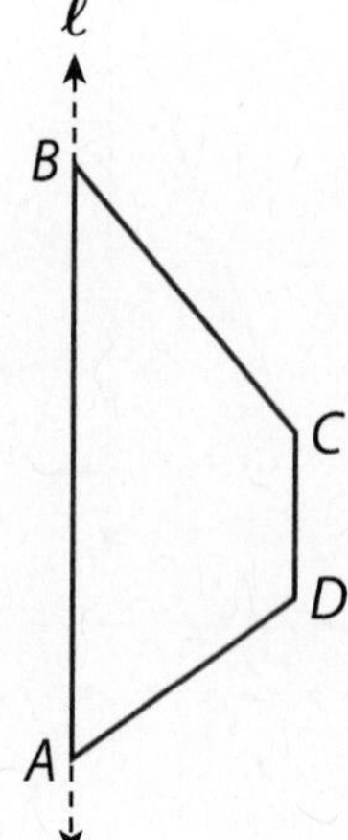

6. A semicircle rotated around a line containing its diameter

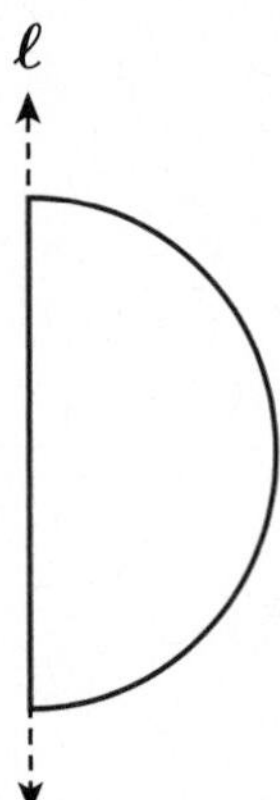

Elaborate

7. **Discussion** If a solid has been generated by rotating a plane figure around an axis, will the solid always have cross-sections that are circles? Will it always have cross sections that are not circles? Explain.

8. **Essential Question Check-In** What tools can you use to visualize solid figures? Explain how each tool is helpful.

Evaluate: Homework and Practice

- Online Homework
- Hints and Help
- Extra Practice

1. Which of the figures is not a net for a cube? Explain.

a.

c.

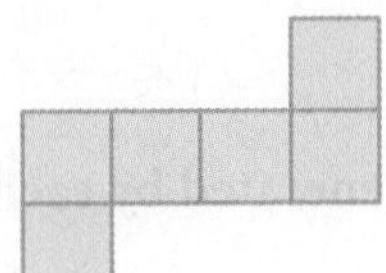

b.

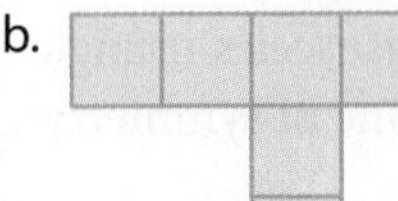

d.

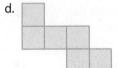

Describe the three-dimensional figure that can be made from the given net.

2.

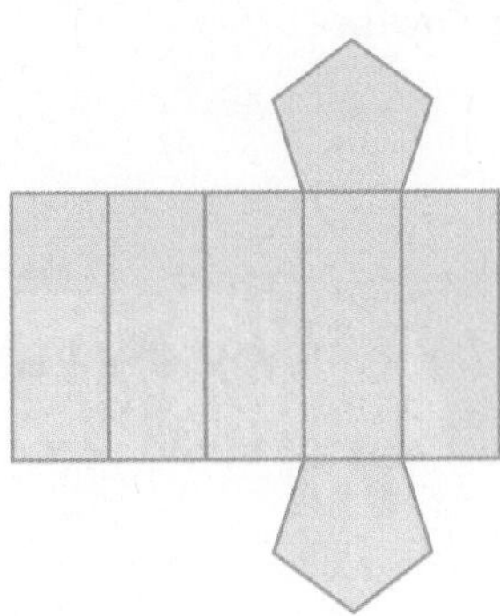

3.

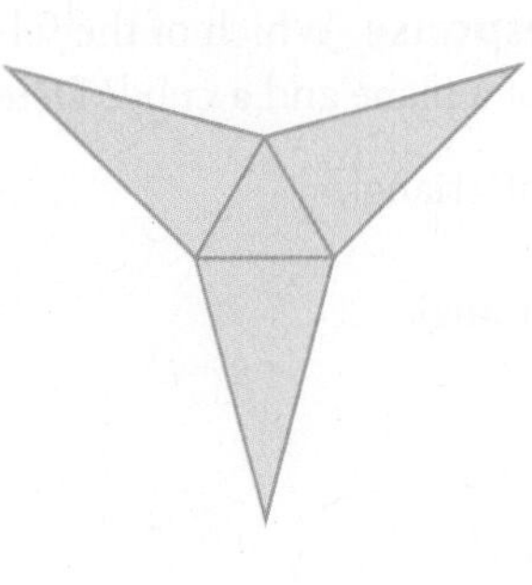

Describe the cross-section.

4.

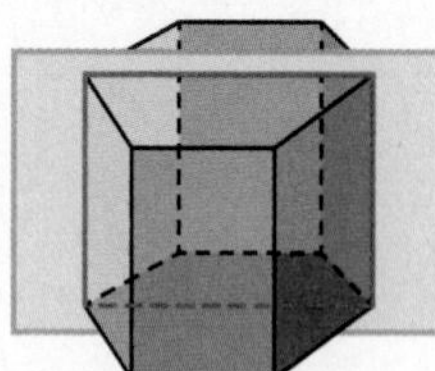

5.

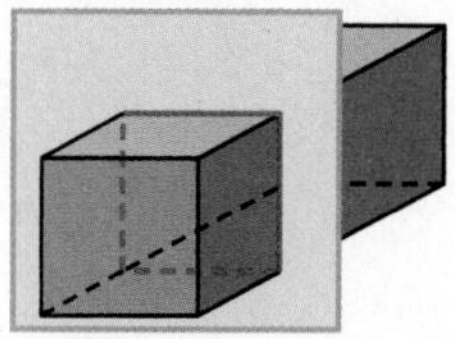

6.

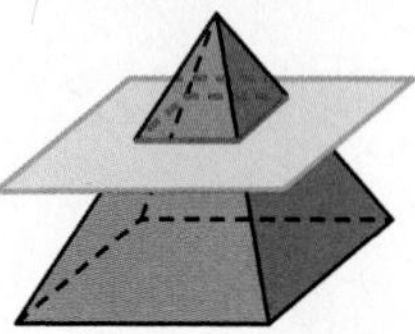

7.

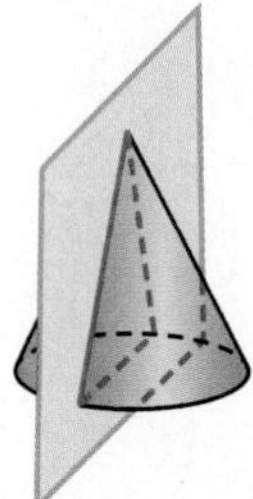

8.

9.

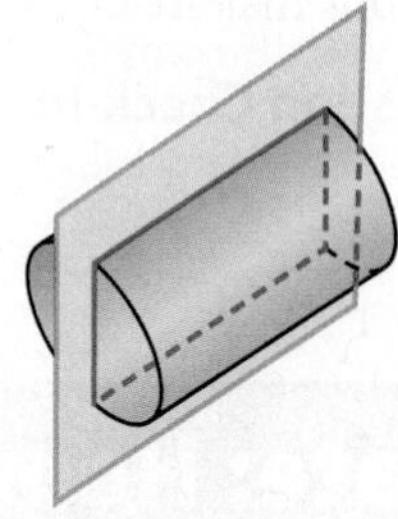

10. Describe the cross section formed by the intersection of a cone and a plane parallel to the base of the cone.

11. Describe the cross section formed by the intersection of a sphere and a plane that passes through the center of the sphere.

Sketch and describe the figure that is generated by each rotation in three-dimensional space.

12. Rotate a semicircle around a line through the endpoints of the semicircle.

13. Rotate an isosceles triangle around the triangle's line of symmetry.

14. Rotate an isosceles right triangle around a line that contains the triangle's hypotenuse

15. Rotate a line segment around a line that is perpendicular to the segment that passes through an endpoint to the segment.

16. Multiple Response Which of the following shapes could be formed by the intersection of a plane and a cube? Determine all that apply.

A. Equilateral Triangle

B. Scalene Triangle

C. Square

D. Rectangle

E. Circle

17. A student claims that if you dilate the net for a cube using a scale factor of 2, the surface area of the resulting cube is multiplied by 4 and the volume is multiplied by 8. Does this claim make sense?

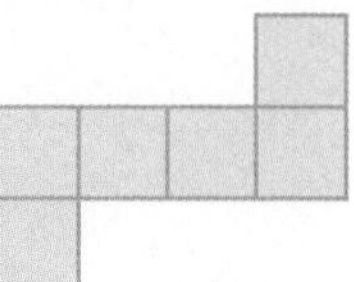

18. **Find the Error** A regular hexagonal prism is intersected by a plane as shown. Which cross section is incorrect? Explain.

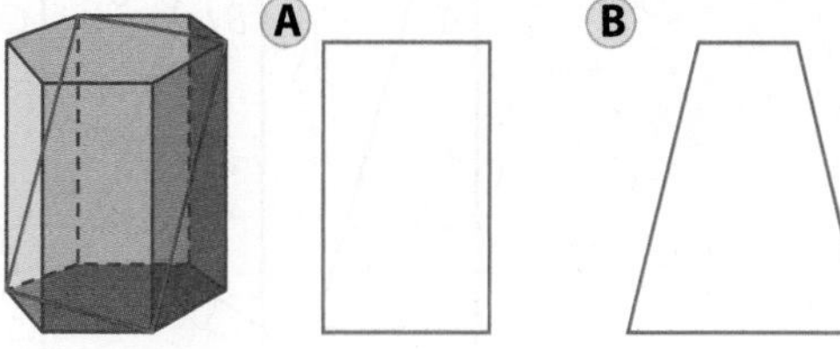

H.O.T. Focus on Higher Order Thinking

19. **Architecture** An architect is drawing plans for a building that is a hexagonal prism. Describe how the architect could draw a cutaway of the building that shows a cross section in the shape of a hexagon, and a cross section in the shape of a rectangle.

20. **Draw Conclusions** Is it possible for a cross section of a cube to be an octagon? Explain.

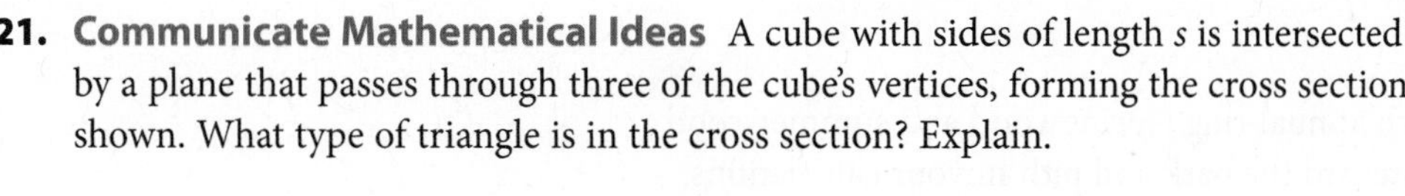

21. **Communicate Mathematical Ideas** A cube with sides of length s is intersected by a plane that passes through three of the cube's vertices, forming the cross section shown. What type of triangle is in the cross section? Explain.

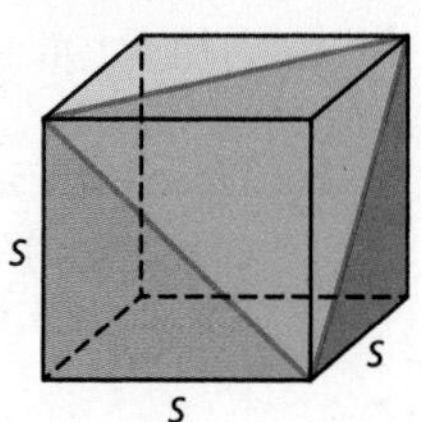

22. The three triangles all have the same area because each base and each height are congruent. Make and test a conjecture about the volume of the solids generated by rotating these triangles around the base.

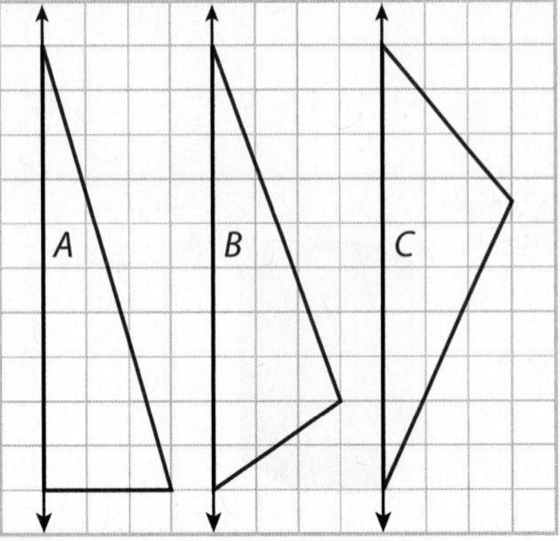

Lesson Performance Task

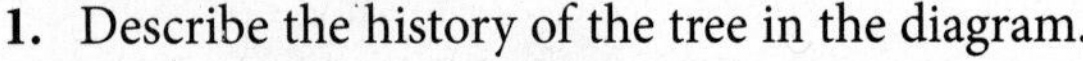

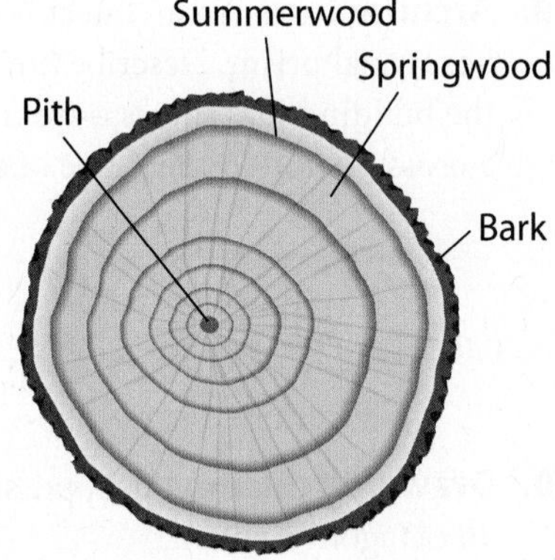

Each year of its life, a tree grows a new ring just under the outside bark. The new ring consists of two parts, light-colored *springwood,* when the tree grows the fastest, and a darker-colored *summerwood,* when growth slows. When conditions are good and there is lots of sun and rain, the new ring is thicker than the rings formed when there is drought or excessive cold. At the center of the tree is a dark circle called *pith* that is not connected to the age of the tree.

1. Describe the history of the tree in the diagram.

2. The redwood trees of coastal California are the tallest living things on earth. One redwood is 350 feet tall, 20 feet in diameter at its base, and around 2000 years old. Assume that the lower 50 feet of the tree form a cylinder 20 feet in diameter and that all of the rings grew at the same rate.

a. What is the total volume of wood in the 50-foot section? Use 3.14 for π.

b. How wide is each annual ring (springwood and summerwood combined)? Disregard the bark and pith in your calculations. Show your work. Write your answer in inches.

19.2 Surface Area of Prisms and Cylinders

Essential Question: How can you find the surface area of a prism or cylinder?

Explore Developing a Surface Area Formula

Surface area is the total area of all the faces and curved surfaces of a three-dimensional figure. The *lateral area* of a prism is the sum of the areas of the lateral faces.

(A) Consider the right prism shown here and the net for the right prism. Find the length (*h*, *a*, *b*, or *c*) of each indicated edge of the net.

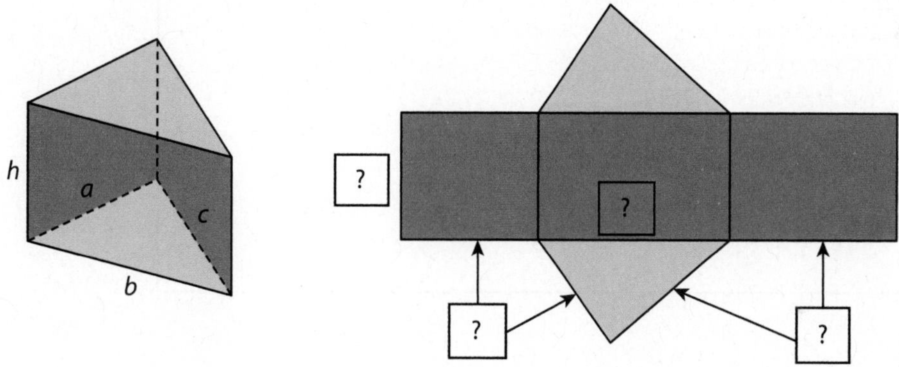

(B) In the net, what type of figure is formed by the lateral faces of the prism?

(C) Write an expression for the length of the base of the rectangle.

(D) How is the base of the rectangle related to the perimeter of the base of the prism?

(E) The lateral area L of the prism is the area of the rectangle. Write a formula for L in terms of h, a, b, and c.

(F) Write the formula for L in terms of P, where P is the perimeter of the base of the prism.

(G) Let B be the area of the base of the prism. Write a formula for the surface area S of the prism in terms of B and L. Then write the formula in terms of B, P, and h.

Reflect

1. Explain why the net of the lateral surface of any right prism will always be a rectangle.
2. Suppose a rectangular prism has length ℓ, width w, and height h, as shown. Explain how you can write a formula for the surface area of the prism in terms of ℓ, w, and h.

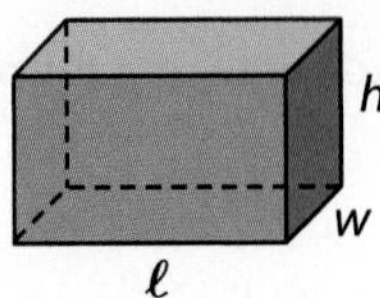

Explain 1 Finding the Surface Area of a Prism

Lateral Area and Surface Area of Right Prisms

The lateral area of a right prism with height h and base perimeter P is $L = Ph$.

The surface area of a right prism with lateral area L and base area B is $S = L + 2B$, or $S = Ph + 2B$.

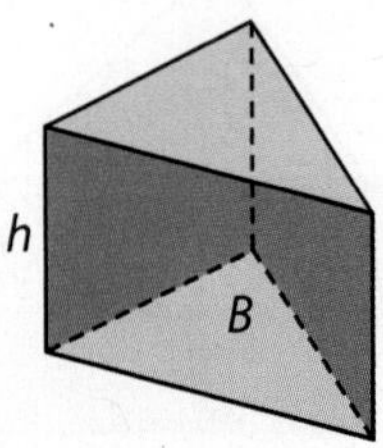

Example 1 **Each gift box is a right prism. Find the total amount of paper needed to wrap each box, not counting overlap.**

 **Step 1** Find the lateral area.

Lateral area formula	$L = Ph$
$P = 2(8) + 2(6) = 28$ cm	$= 28(12)$
Multiply.	$= 336 \text{ cm}^2$

Step 2 Find the surface area.

Surface area formula	$S = L + 2B$
Substitute the lateral area.	$= 336 + 2(6)(8)$
Simplify.	$= 432 \text{ cm}^2$

12 cm
6 cm
8 cm

(B) **Step 1** Find the length c of the hypotenuse of the base.

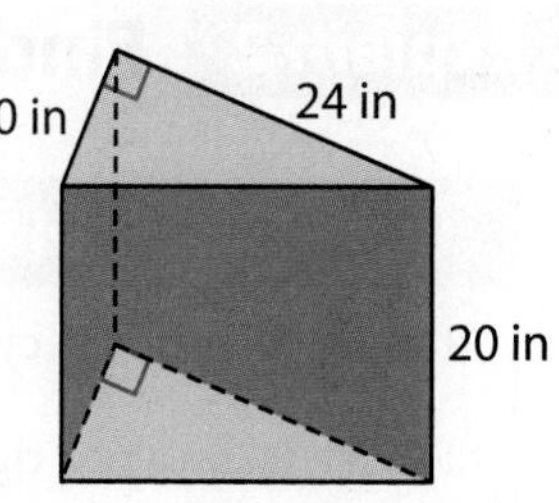

Pythagorean Theorem $c^2 = a^2 + b^2$

Substitute. $= 10^2 + 24^2$

Simplify. $= 676$

Take the square root of each side. $c = 26$

Step 2 Find the lateral area.

Lateral area formula $L = Ph$

Substitute. $= 60(20)$

Multiply. $= 1200 \text{ in}^2$

Step 3 Find the surface area.

Surface area formula $S = L + 2B$

Substitute. $= 1200 + 2 \cdot \frac{1}{2} 24 \cdot 10$

Simplify. $= 1440 \text{ in}^2$

Reflect

3. A gift box is a rectangular prism with length 9.8 cm, width 10.2 cm, and height 9.7 cm. Explain how to estimate the amount of paper needed to wrap the box, not counting overlap.

Your Turn

Each gift box is a right prism. Find the total amount of paper needed to wrap each box, not counting overlap.

4.

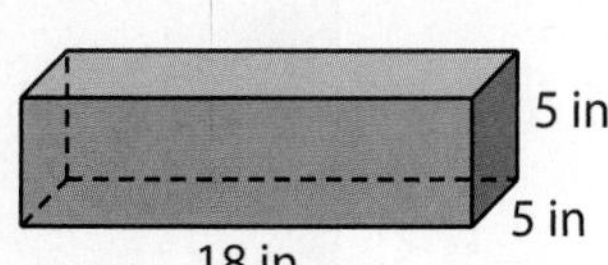

5.

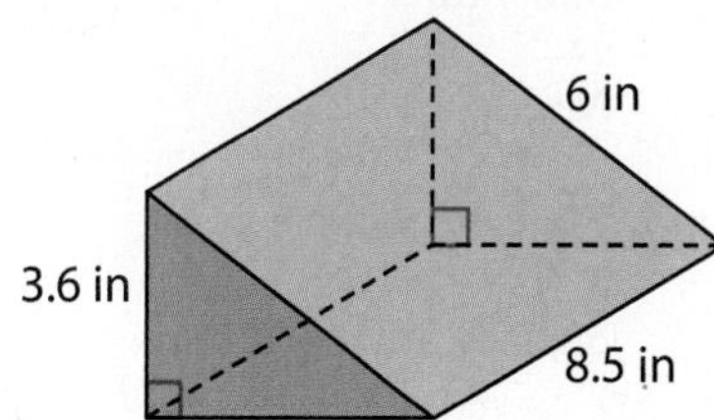

Explain 2 Finding the Surface Area of a Cylinder

Lateral Area and Surface Area of Right Cylinders

The *lateral area* of a cylinder is the area of the curved surface that connects the two bases.

The lateral area of a right cylinder with radius r and height h is $L = 2\pi rh$.

The surface area of a right cylinder with lateral area L and base area B is $S = L + 2B$, or $S = 2\pi rh + 2\pi r^2$.

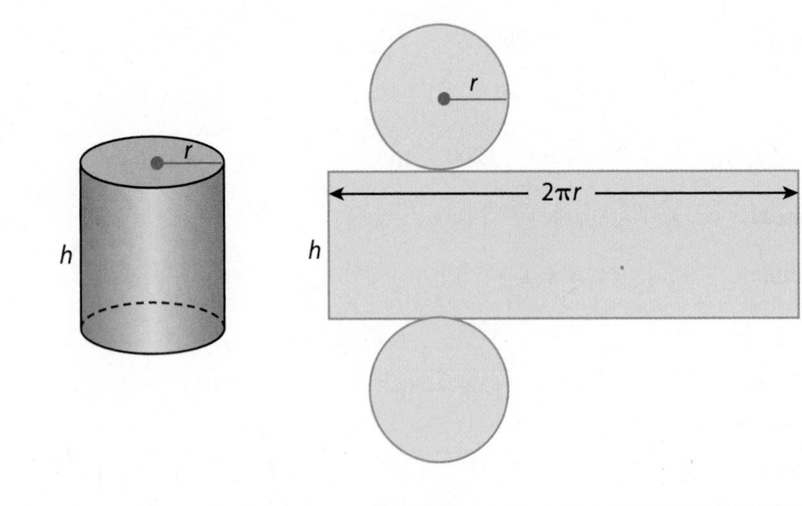

Example 2 **Each aluminum can is a right cylinder. Find the amount of paper needed for the can's label and the total amount of aluminum needed to make the can. Round to the nearest tenth.**

(A) **Step 1** Find the lateral area.

Lateral area formula	$L = 2\pi rh$
Substitute.	$L = 2\pi(3)(9)$
Multiply.	$= 54\pi \text{ cm}^2$

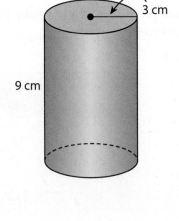

Step 2 Find the surface area.

Surface area formula	$S = L + 2\pi r^2$
Substitute the lateral area and radius.	$= 54\pi + 2\pi(3)^2$
Simplify.	$= 72\pi \text{ cm}^2$

3 cm

9 cm

Step 3 Use a calculator and round to the nearest tenth.

The amount of paper needed for the label is the lateral area, $54\pi \approx 169.6 \text{ cm}^2$.

The amount of aluminum needed for the can is the surface area, $72\pi \approx 226.2 \text{ cm}^2$.

(B) **Step 1** Find the lateral area.

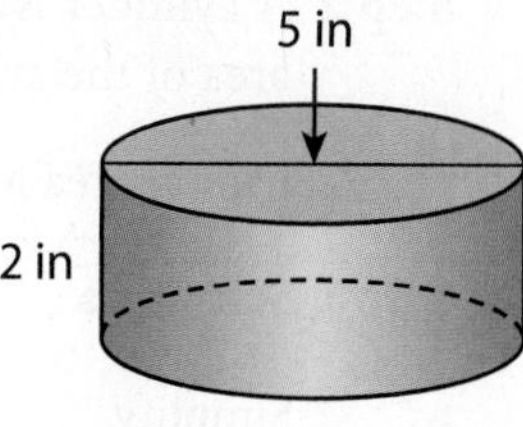

Lateral area formula $L = 2\pi rh$

Substitute; the radius is half the diameter. $= 2\pi(\boxed{2.5})(\boxed{2})$

Multiply. $= \boxed{10}\ \pi \text{ in}^2$

Step 2 Find the surface area.

Surface area formula $S = L + 2\pi r^2$

Substitute the lateral area and radius. $= \boxed{10}\ \pi + 2\pi(\boxed{2.5})^2$

Simplify. $= \boxed{22.5}\ \pi \text{ in}^2$

Step 3 Use a calculator and round to the nearest tenth.

The amount of paper needed for the label is the lateral area, $\boxed{10}\ \pi \approx \boxed{31.4}$ in^2.

The amount of aluminum needed for the can is the surface area, $\boxed{22.5}\ \pi \approx \boxed{70.7}$ in^2.

Reflect

6. In these problems, why is it best to round only in the final step of the solution?

Your Turn

Each aluminum can is a right cylinder. Find the amount of paper needed for the can's label and the total amount of aluminum needed to make the can. Round to the nearest tenth.

7.

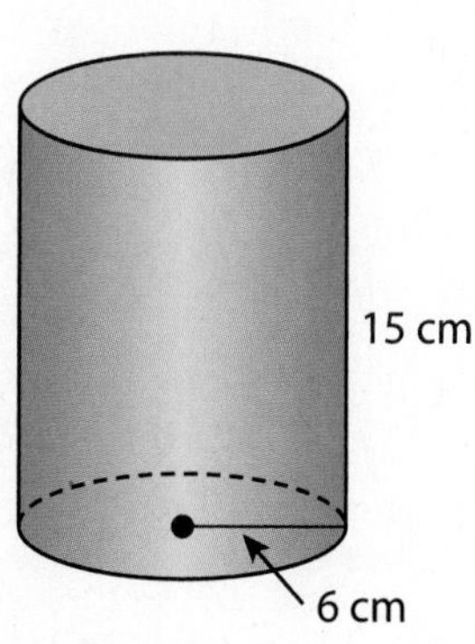

8.

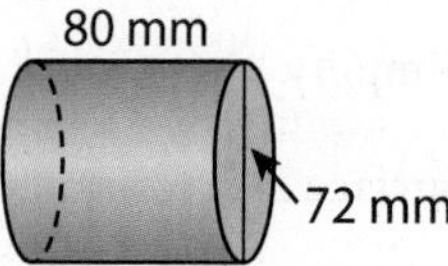

 Explain 3 Finding the Surface Area of a Composite Figure

Example 3 **Find the surface area of each composite figure. Round to the nearest tenth.**

(A) **Step 1** Find the surface area of the right rectangular prism.

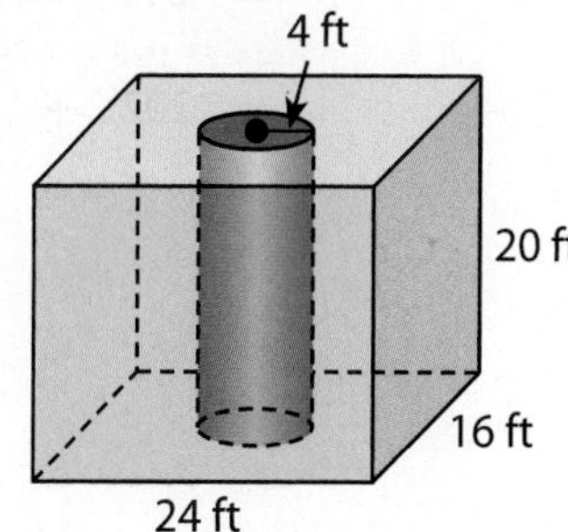

Surface area formula $S = Ph + 2B$

Substitute. $= 80(20) + 2(24)(16)$

Simplify. $= 2368 \text{ ft}^2$

Step 2 A cylinder is removed from the prism. Find the lateral area of the cylinder and the area of its bases.

Lateral area formula	$L = 2\pi rh$
Substitute.	$= 2\pi(4)(20)$
Simplify.	$= 160\pi\ \text{ft}^2$
Base area formula	$B = \pi r^2$
Substitute.	$= \pi(4)^2$
Simplify.	$= 16\pi\ \text{ft}^2$

Step 3 Find the surface area of the composite figure. The surface area is the sum of the areas of all surfaces on the exterior of the figure.

$S =$ (prism surface area) + (cylinder lateral area) − (cylinder base areas)

$= 2368 + 160\pi - 2(16\pi)$

$= 2368 + 128\pi \approx 2770.1\ \text{ft}^2$

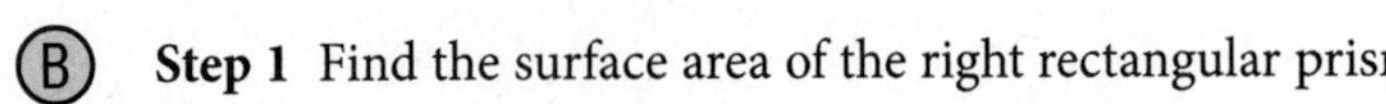

(B) **Step 1** Find the surface area of the right rectangular prism.

Surface area formula	$S = Ph + 2B$
Substitute.	$= 26(5) + 2(9)(4)$
Simplify.	$= 202\ \text{cm}^2$

Step 2 Find the surface area of the cylinder.

Lateral area formula	$L = 2\pi rh$
Substitute.	$= 2\pi(2)(3)$
Simplify.	$= 12\pi\ \text{cm}^2$
Surface area formula	$S = L + 2\pi r^2$
Substitute.	$= 12\pi + 2\pi(2)^2$
Simplify.	$= 20\pi\ \text{cm}^2$

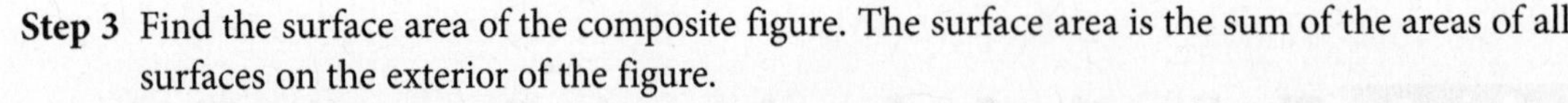

Step 3 Find the surface area of the composite figure. The surface area is the sum of the areas of all surfaces on the exterior of the figure.

$S =$ (prism surface area) + (cylinder surface area) − 2(area of one cylinder base)

$= 202 + 20\pi - 2\pi(2)^2$

$= 202 + 12\pi \approx 239.7\ \text{cm}^2$

Reflect

9. **Discussion** A student said the answer in Part A must be incorrect since a part of the rectangular prism is removed, yet the surface area of the composite figure is greater than the surface area of the rectangular prism. Do you agree with the student? Explain.

Your Turn

Find the surface area of each composite figure. Round to the nearest tenth.

10.

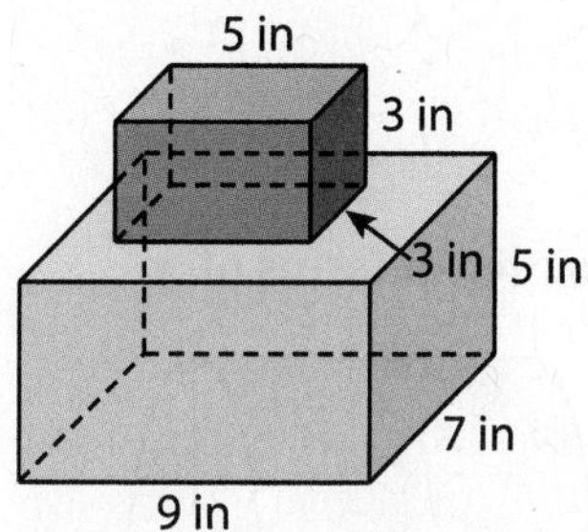

11.

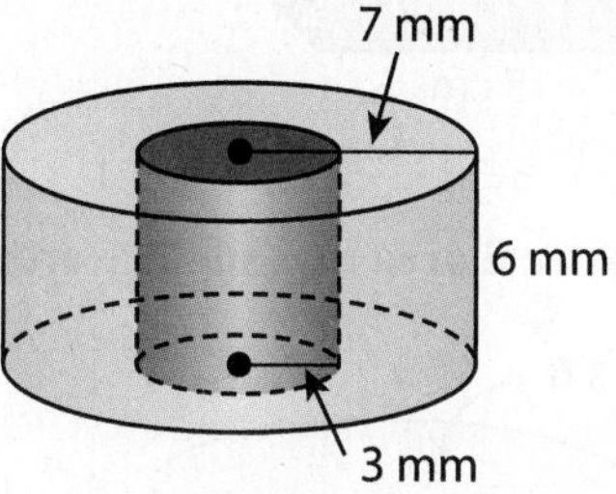

Elaborate

12. Can the surface area of a cylinder ever be less than the lateral area of the cylinder? Explain.

13. Is it possible to find the surface area of a cylinder if you know the height and the circumference of the base? Explain.

14. **Essential Question Check-In** How is finding the surface area of a right prism similar to finding the surface area of a right cylinder?

Evaluate: Homework and Practice

- Online Homework
- Hints and Help
- Extra Practice

Find the lateral area and surface area of each prism.

1.

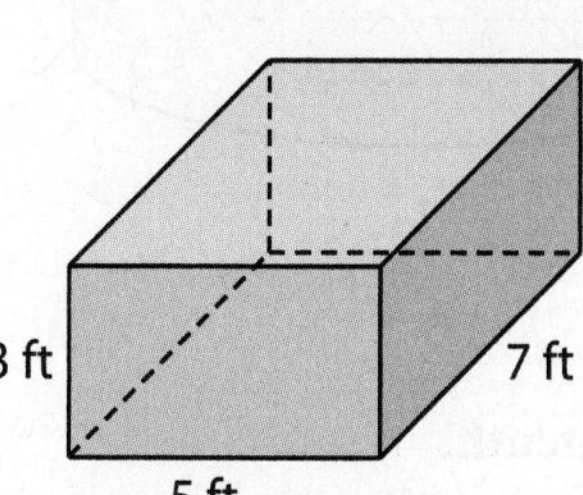

2.

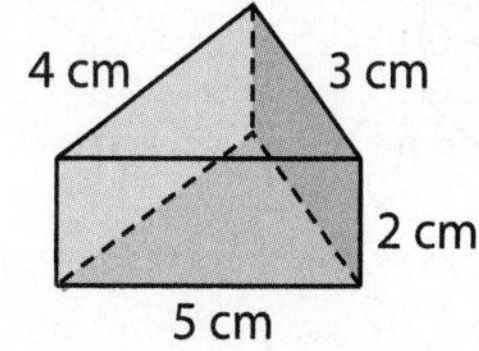

3.

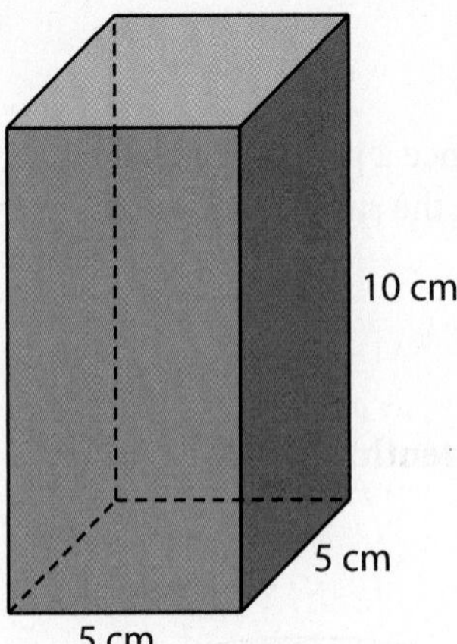

4.

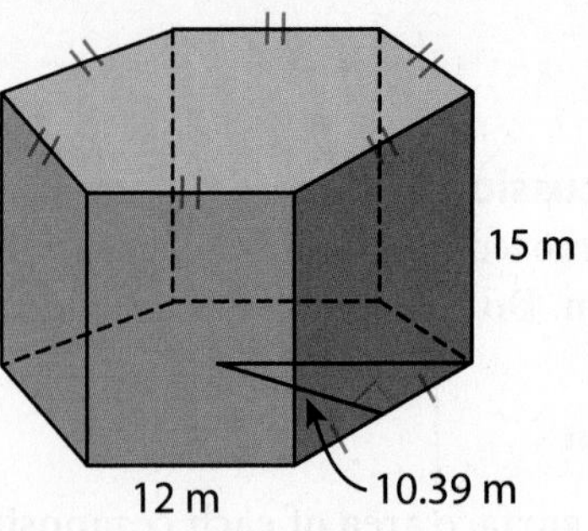

Find the lateral area and surface area of the cylinder. Leave your answer in terms of π.

5.

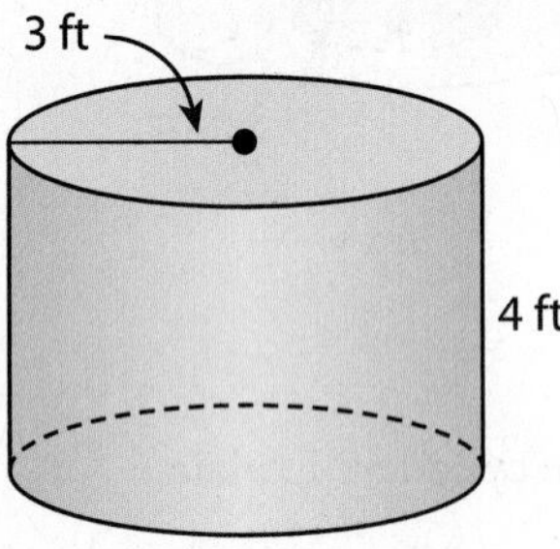

6.

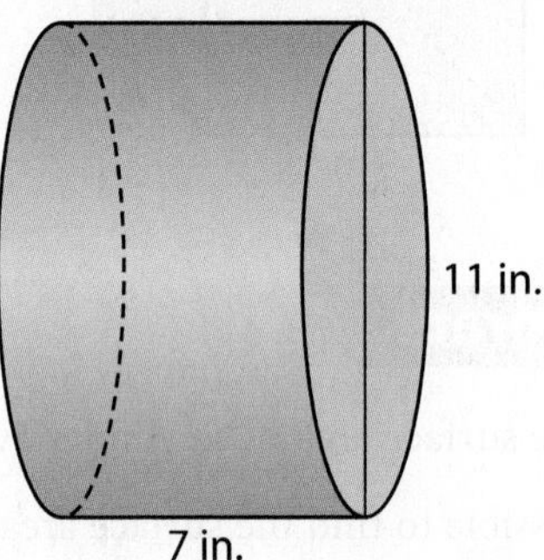

Find the total surface area of the composite figure. Round to the nearest tenth.

7.

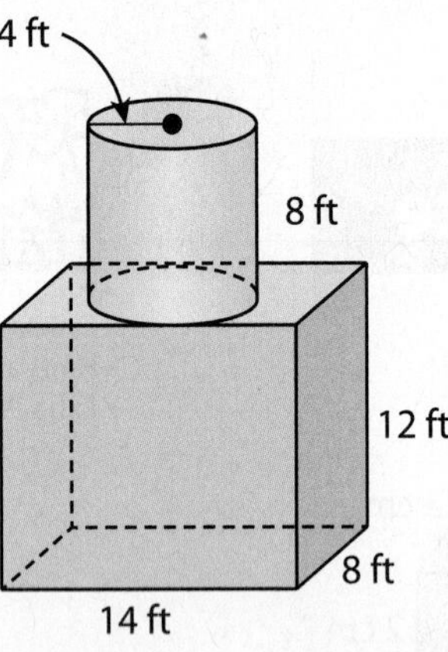

8.

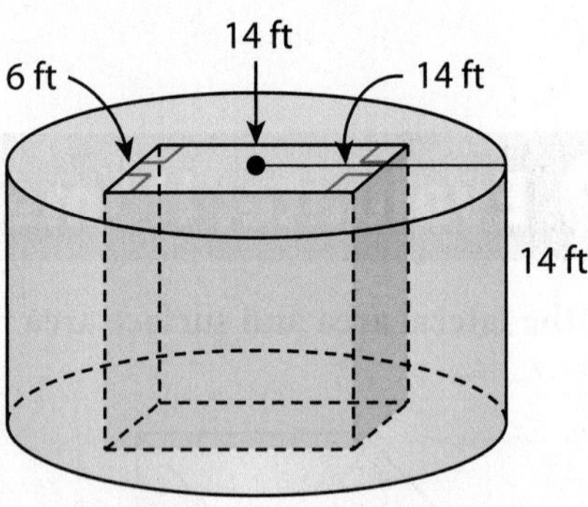

Find the total surface area of the composite figure. Round to the nearest tenth.

9.

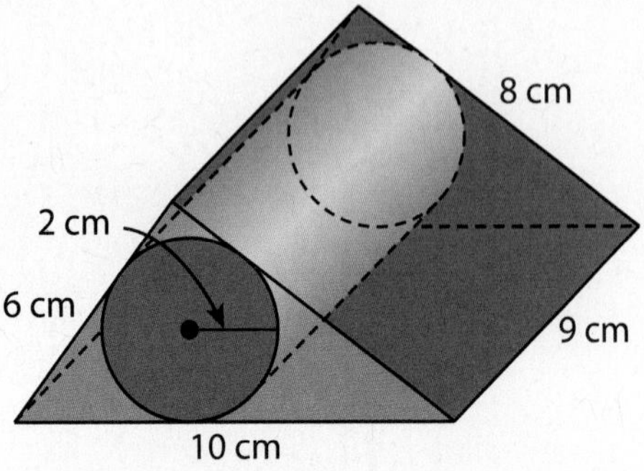

10.

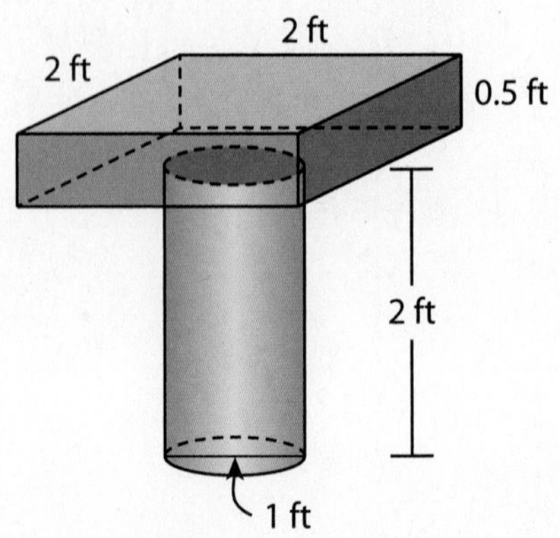

11. The greater the lateral area of a florescent light bulb, the more light the bulb produces. One cylindrical light bulb is 16 inches long with a 1-inch radius. Another cylindrical bulb is 23 inches long with a $\frac{3}{4}$-inch radius. Which bulb will produce more light?

12. Find the lateral and surface area of a cube with edge length 9 inches.

13. Find the lateral and surface area of a cylinder with base area 64π m^2 and a height 3 meters less than the radius.

14. **Biology** Plant cells are shaped approximately like a right rectangular prism. Each cell absorbs oxygen and nutrients through its surface. Which cell can be expected to absorb at a greater rate? (*Hint:* 1 μm = 1 micrometer = 0.000001 meter)

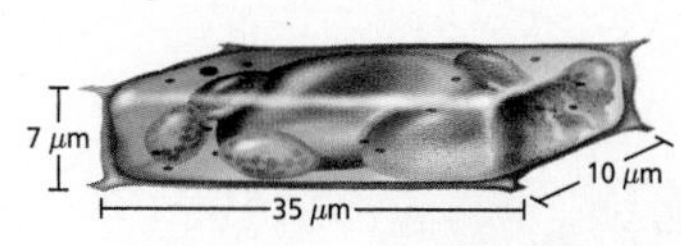

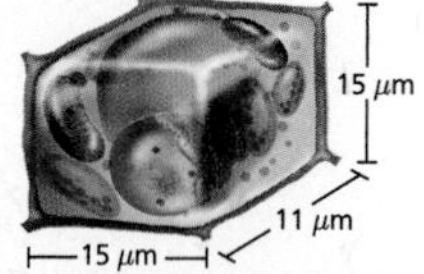

15. Find the height of a right cylinder with surface area 160π ft^2 and radius 5 ft.

16. Find the height of a right rectangular prism with surface area 286 m^2, length 10 m, and width 8 m.

17. **Represent Real-World Problems** If one gallon of paint covers 250 square feet, how many gallons of paint will be needed to cover the shed, not including the roof? If a gallon of paint costs $25, about how much will it cost to paint the walls of the shed?

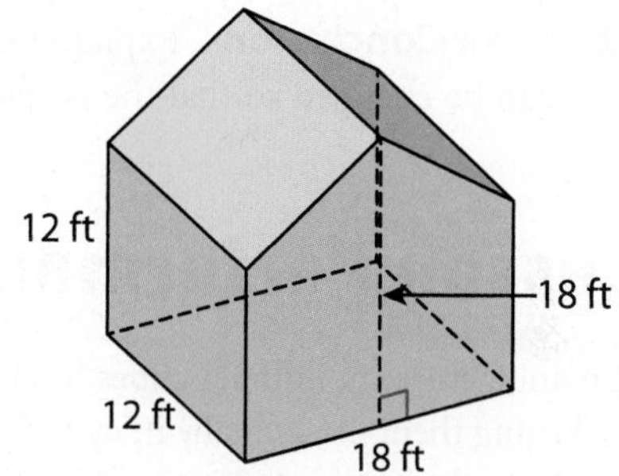

18. Match the surface area with the appropriate coin in the table.

Coin	Diameter (mm)	Thickness (mm)	Surface Area (mm^2)
Penny	19.05	1.55	
Nickel	21.21	1.95	
Dime	17.91	1.35	
Quarter	24.26	1.75	

A. 836.58

B. 579.82

C. 662.81

D. 1057.86

19. **Algebra** The lateral area of a right rectangular prism is 144 cm^2. Its length is three times its width, and its height is twice its width. Find its surface area.

20. A cylinder has a radius of 8 cm and a height of 3 cm. Find the height of another cylinder that has a radius of 4 cm and the same surface area as the first cylinder.

H.O.T. Focus on Higher Order Thinking

21. **Analyze Relationships** Ingrid is building a shelter to protect her plants from freezing. She is planning to stretch plastic sheeting over the top and the ends of the frame. Assume that the triangles in the frame on the left are equilateral. Which of the frames shown will require more plastic? Explain how finding the surface area of these figures is different from finding the lateral surface area of a figure.

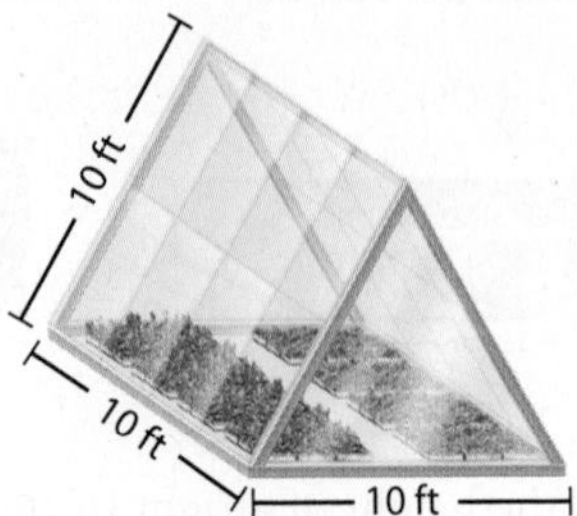

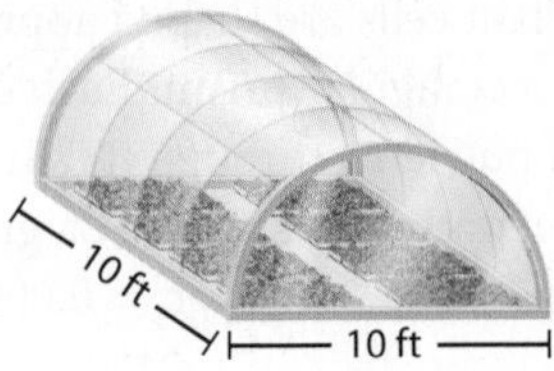

22. **Draw Conclusions** Explain how the edge lengths of a rectangular prism can be changed so that the surface area is multiplied by 9.

Lesson Performance Task

A manufacturer of number cubes has the bright idea of packaging them individually in cylindrical boxes. Each number cube measures 2 inches on a side.

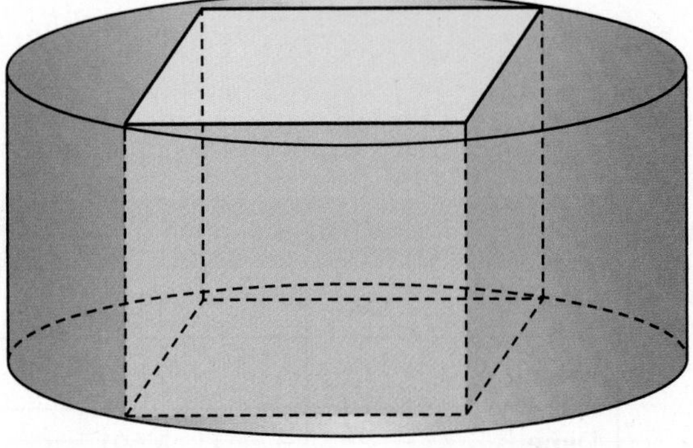

1. What is the surface area of each cube?

2. What is the surface area of the cylindrical box? Assume the cube fits snugly in the box and that the box includes a top. Use 3.14 for π.

19.3 Surface Area of Pyramids and Cones

Resource Locker

Essential Question: How is the formula for the lateral area of a regular pyramid similar to the formula for the lateral area of a right cone?

Explore Developing a Surface Area Formula

The base of a **regular pyramid** is a regular polygon, and the lateral faces are congruent isosceles triangles.

(A) The lateral faces of a regular pyramid can be arranged to cover half of a rectangle whose height is equal to the slant height of the pyramid. Find the length (s or l) of each indicated edge of the net.

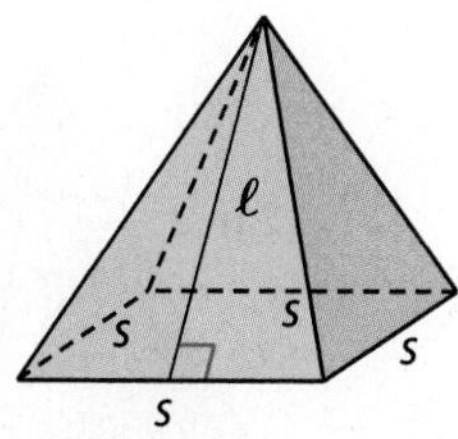

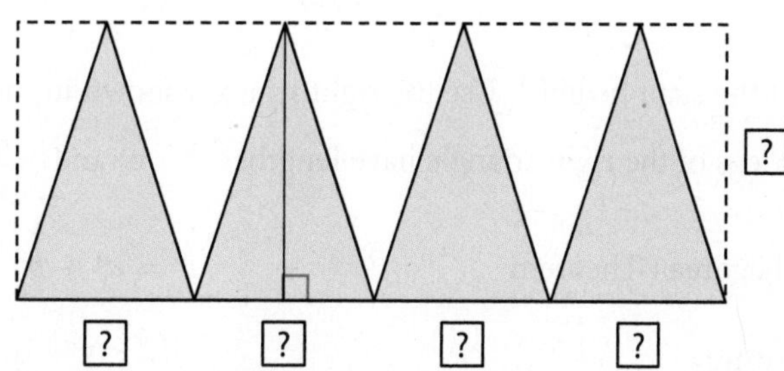

(B) Write an expression for the length of the rectangle in terms of s.

(C) How does the length of the rectangle compare to P, the perimeter of the base of the pyramid?

(D) Write an expression for the area of the rectangle in terms of P and ℓ.

(E) Write a formula for the lateral area L of the pyramid. (*Hint*: Use the fact that the lateral faces of the pyramid cover half of the rectangle.)

(F) Let B be the base area of the pyramid. Write a formula for the surface area S of the pyramid in terms of B and L. Then write the formula in terms of B, P, and ℓ.

Reflect

1. **Discussion** The pyramid in the above figure has a square base. Do your formulas only hold for square pyramids or do they hold for other pyramids as well? Explain.

Explain 1 Finding the Surface Area of a Pyramid

Lateral Area and Surface Area of a Regular Pyramid

The lateral area of a regular pyramid with perimeter P and slant height ℓ is $L = \frac{1}{2}P\ell$.

The surface area of a regular pyramid with lateral area L and base area B is $S = L + B$, or $S = \frac{1}{2}P\ell + B$.

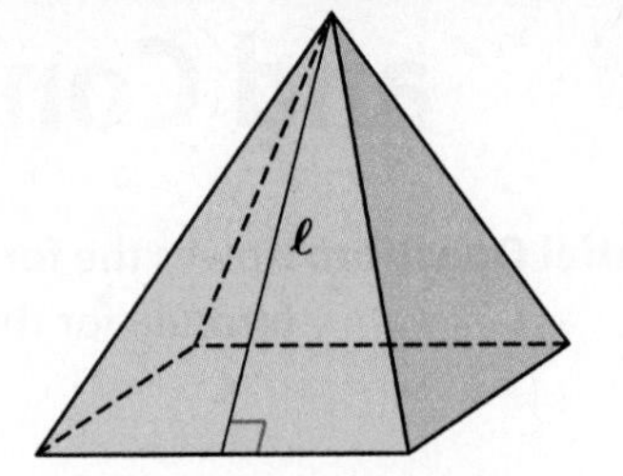

Example 1 **Find the lateral area and surface area of each regular pyramid.**

(A) **Step 1** Find the lateral area.

Lateral area formula	$L = \frac{1}{2}P\ell$
$P = 4(5) = 20$ in.	$= \frac{1}{2}(20)(9)$
Multiply.	$= 90 \text{ in}^2$

Step 2 Find the surface area.

Surface area formula	$S = L + B$
Substitute the lateral area; $B = 5^2 = 25$ in.	$= 90 + 25$
Add.	$= 115 \text{ in}^2$

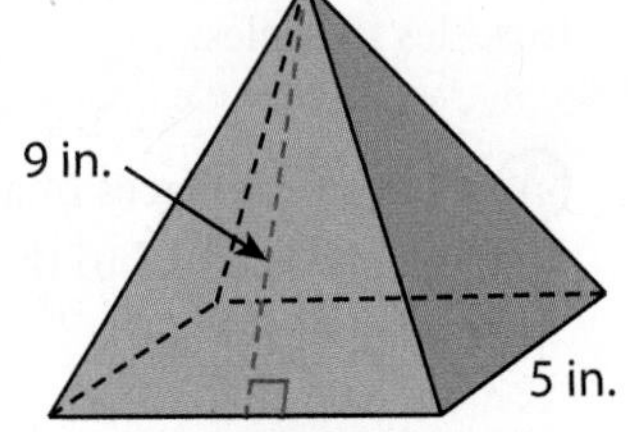

(B) **Step 1** Find the slant height ℓ. Use the right triangle shown in the figure.

The legs of the right triangle have lengths 5 m and 12 m.

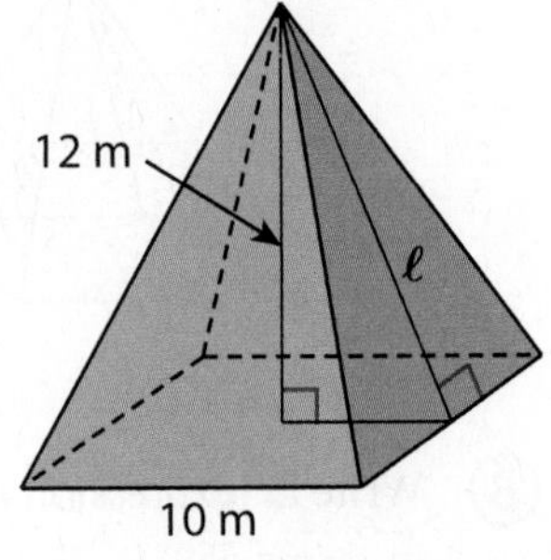

Pythagorean Theorem	$\ell^2 = a^2 + b^2$
Substitute.	$= 5^2 + 12^2$
Simplify.	$= 169$
Take the square root of each side.	$\ell = 13$

Step 2 Find the lateral area.

Lateral area formula	$L = \frac{1}{2}P\ell$
Substitute.	$= \frac{1}{2}(40)(13)$
Multiply.	$= 260 \text{ m}^2$

Step 3 Find the surface area.

Surface area formula	$S = L + B$
Substitute.	$= 260 + 10^2$
Simplify.	$= 360 \text{ m}^2$

Reflect

2. Can you use the formula $L = \frac{1}{2}P\ell$ to find the lateral area of a pyramid whose base is a scalene triangle? If so, describe the dimensions that you need to know. If not, explain why not.

Your Turn

Find the lateral area and surface area of each regular pyramid. Round to the nearest tenth, if necessary.

3.

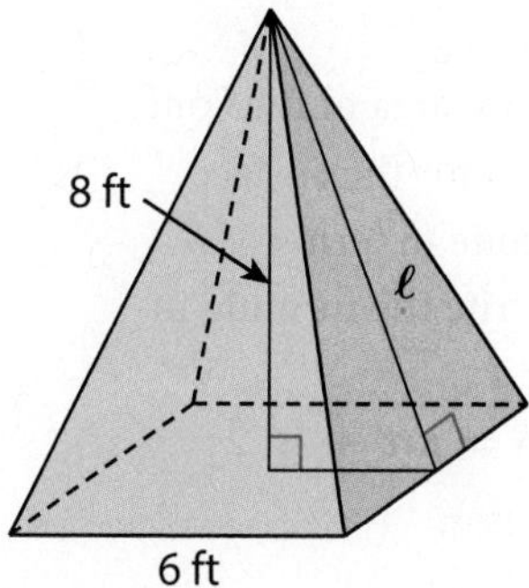

4.

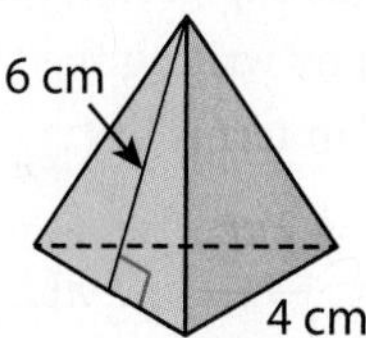

Explain 2 Developing Another Surface Area Formula

The axis of a cone is a segment with endpoints at the vertex and the center of the base. A **right cone** is a cone whose axis is perpendicular to the base.

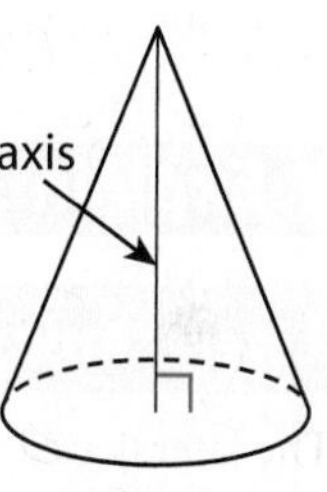

Right Cone

Example 2 **Justify a formula for the surface area of a cone.**

(A) A net for a right cone consists of a circle and a sector of a circle, as shown. Identify the missing dimensions.

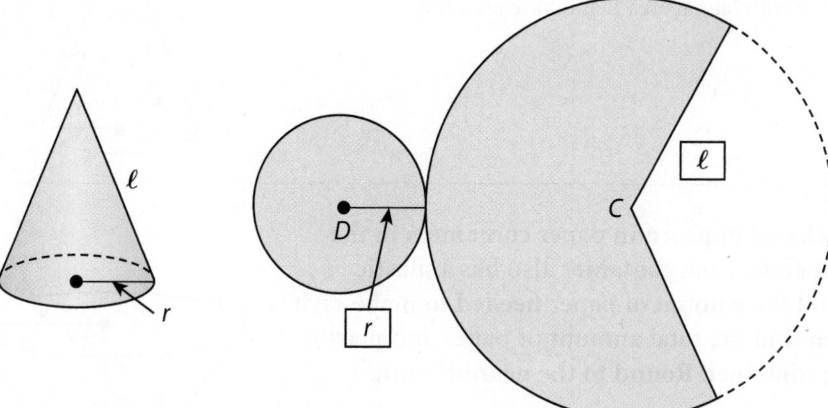

(B) Consider the shaded sector in the net. Complete the proportion.

$$\frac{\text{Area of sector}}{\text{Area of } \odot C} = \frac{\text{Arc length of sector}}{\text{Circumference of } \odot C}$$

(C) Multiply both sides of the proportion by the area of $\odot$ C. Complete the equation.

$$\text{Area of sector} = \frac{\text{Arc length of sector}}{\text{Circumference of } \odot C} \cdot \text{Area of } \odot C$$

(D) The arc length of the sector is equal to the circumference of $\odot D$. Therefore, the arc length of the sector equals $2\pi r$. Complete the equation by substituting this expression for the arc length of the sector and by writing the circumference and area of $\odot C$ in terms of ℓ.

Area of sector $= \dfrac{2\pi r}{2\pi \ell} \cdot \pi \ell^2$

(E) Simplify the right side of the equation as much as possible.

Area of sector $= \pi r \ell$

(F) The area of the sector in Step E is the lateral area L of the cone. Complete the formula.

$L = \pi r \ell$

(G) Let B be the base area of the cone. Write a formula for the surface area S of the cone in terms of B and L. Then write the formula in terms of r and ℓ.

$S = L + B$; $S = \pi r \ell + \pi r\ 2$

Reflect

5. In Step D, why is the arc length of the sector equal to the circumference of $\odot D$?

Explain 3 Finding the Surface Area of a Cone

Lateral Area and Surface Area of a Right Cone

The lateral area of a right cone with radius r and slant height ℓ is $L = \pi r \ell$.

The surface area of a right cone with lateral area L and base area B is $S = L + B$, or $S = \pi r \ell + \pi r^2$.

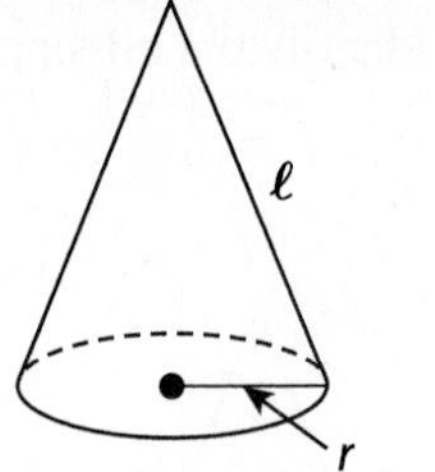

Example 3 **A company packages popcorn in paper containers in the shape of a right cone. Each container also has a plastic circular lid. Find the amount of paper needed to make each container. Then find the total amount of paper and plastic needed for the container. Round to the nearest tenth.**

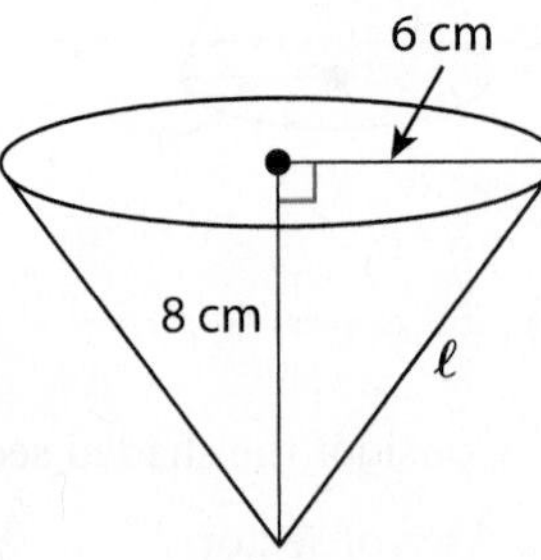

(A) **Step 1** Find the slant height.

Pythagorean Theorem	$\ell^2 = 6^2 + 8^2$
Simplify.	$= 100$
Take the square root of each side.	$\ell = 10$

Step 2 Find the lateral area.

Lateral area formula	$L = \pi r \ell$
Substitute.	$= \pi(6)(10)$
Multiply.	$= 60\pi \text{ cm}^2$

Step 3 Find the surface area.

Surface area formula	$S = L + \pi r^2$
Substitute.	$= 60\pi + \pi(6)^2$
Simplify.	$= 96\pi \text{ cm}^2$

Step 4 Use a calculator and round to the nearest tenth.

The amount of paper needed for the container is the lateral area, $60\pi \approx 188.5 \text{ cm}^2$. The amount of paper and plastic needed for the container is the surface area, $96\pi \approx 301.6 \text{ cm}^2$.

(B) **Step 1** Find the radius.

Pythagorean Theorem	$25^2 = r^2 + 24^2$
Simplify.	$625 = r^2 + 576$
Subtract 576 from each side.	$49 = r^2$
Take the square root of each side.	$7 = r$

Step 2 Find the lateral area. $L = \pi r \ell$

Substitute and simplify. $= \pi(7)(25) = 175\pi \text{ cm}^2$

Step 3 Find the surface area. $S = L + \pi r^2$

Substitute and simplify. $= 175\pi + \pi(7)^2 = 224\pi \text{ cm}^2$

Step 4 Use a calculator and round to the nearest tenth.

The amount of paper needed for the container is the lateral area, $175\pi \approx 549.8 \text{ cm}^2$.

The amount of paper and plastic needed for the container is $224\pi \approx 703.7 \text{ cm}^2$.

Reflect

6. Two right cones have the same radius. A student said that the cone with the greater slant height must have the greater lateral area. Do you agree? Explain.

Your Turn

A company makes candles in the shape of a right cone. The lateral surface of each candle is covered with paper for shipping and each candle also has a plastic circular base. Find the amount of paper needed to cover the lateral surface of each candle. Then find the total amount of paper and plastic needed. Round to the nearest tenth.

7.

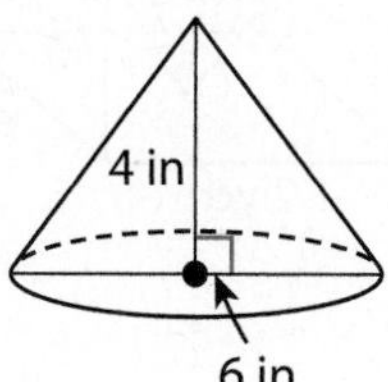

8.

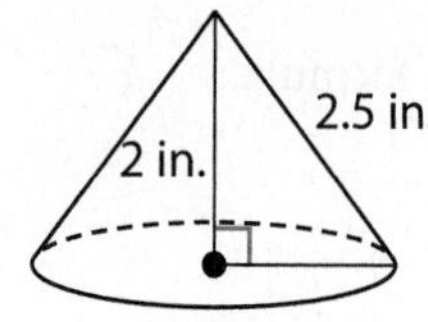

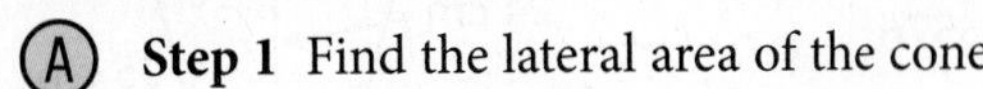

Explain 4 Finding the Surface Area of a Composite Figure

Example 4 **Find the surface area of each composite figure. Round to the nearest tenth.**

(A) **Step 1** Find the lateral area of the cone.

28 cm
90 cm
45 cm

The height of the cone is $90 - 45 = 45$ cm.

By the Pythagorean Theorem, $\ell = \sqrt{28^2 + 45^2} = 53$ cm.

Lateral area formula	$L = \pi r \ell$
Substitute.	$= \pi(28)(53)$
Simplify.	$= 1484\pi \text{ cm}^2$

Step 2 Find the lateral area of the cylinder.

Lateral area	$L = 2\pi rh$
Substitute.	$= 2\pi(28)(45)$
Simplify.	$= 2520\pi \text{ cm}^2$

Step 3 Find the area of the base of the cylinder.

Area of circle	$B = \pi r^2$
Substitute.	$= \pi(28)^2$
Simplify.	$= 784\pi \text{ cm}^2$

Step 4 Find the surface area of the composite figure.

$S =$ (cone lateral area) + (cylinder lateral area) + (base area)

$= 1484\pi + 2520\pi + 784\pi$

$= 4788\pi \approx 15,041.9 \text{ cm}^2$

(B) **Step 1** Find the slant height of the pyramid.

By the Pythagorean Theorem, $\ell = \sqrt{1^2 + 2^2} = \sqrt{5}$ yd.

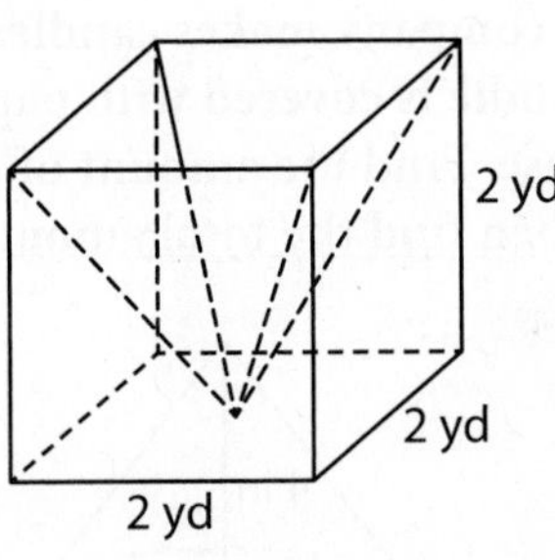

Step 2 Find the lateral area of the pyramid.

Lateral area formula	$L = \frac{1}{2}P\ell$
Substitute.	$= \frac{1}{2}(8)(\sqrt{5})$
Simplify.	$= 4\sqrt{5} \text{ yd}^2$

Step 3 Find the lateral area of the rectangular prism.

Lateral area formula	$L = Ph$
Substitute.	$= (8)(2)$
Simplify.	$= 16 \text{ yd}^2$

Step 4 Find the surface area of the composite figure.

$S =$ (pyramid lateral area) + (prism lateral area) + (base area)

$= 4\sqrt{5} + 16 + 4$

$= 20 + 4\sqrt{5} \approx 28.9 \text{ yd}^2$

Reflect

9. How can you check that your answer in Part B is reasonable?

Your Turn

Find the surface area of each composite figure. Round to the nearest tenth.

10.

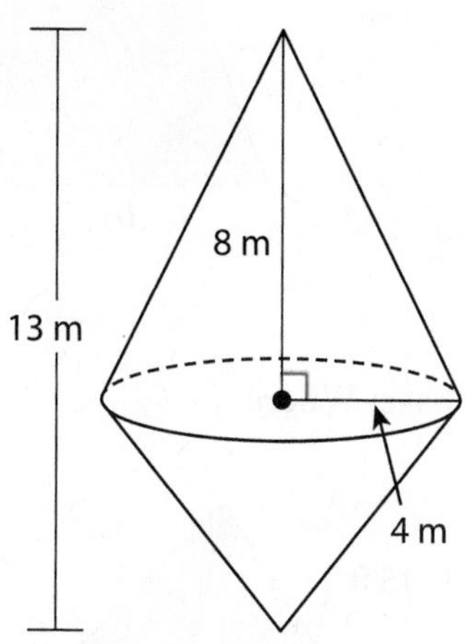

11.

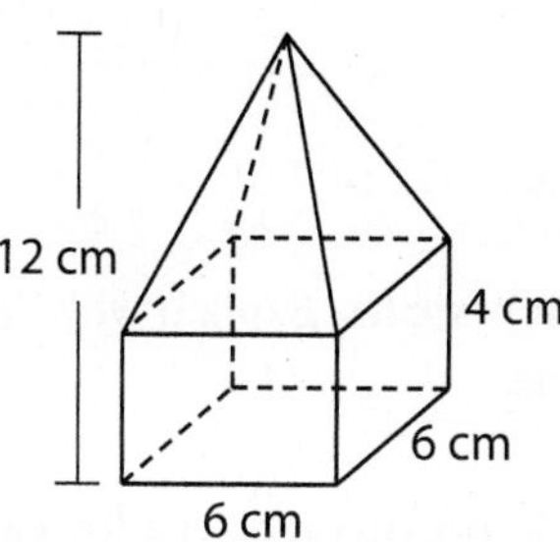

Elaborate

12. A regular pyramid has a base that is an equilateral triangle with sides 16 inches long. Is it possible to determine the surface area of the pyramid? If not, what additional information do you need?

13. Explain how to estimate the lateral area of a right cone with radius 5 cm and slant height 6 cm. Is your estimate an underestimate or overestimate? Explain.

14. **Essential Question Check-In** How is the formula for the lateral area of a regular pyramid similar to the formula for the lateral area of a right cone?

Evaluate: Homework and Practice

- Online Homework
- Hints and Help
- Extra Practice

1. **Multiple Response** Which expression represents the surface area of the regular square pyramid shown? Determine all that apply.

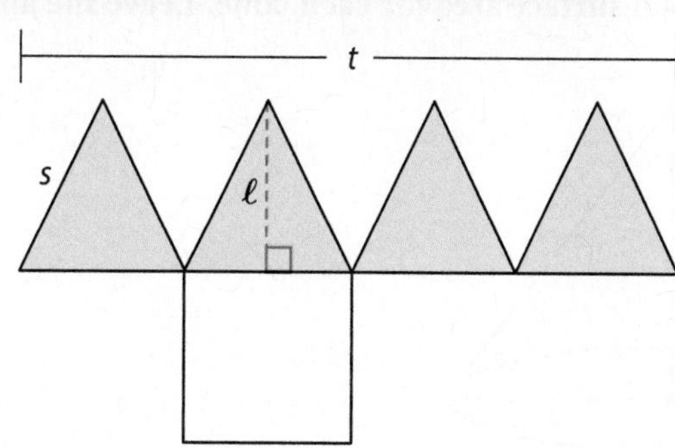

A. $\frac{t^2}{16} + \frac{ts}{2}$ **B.** $\frac{t^2}{16}$ **C.** $\frac{t^2}{4} + t\ell + \frac{t\ell}{2}$ **D.** $\frac{t}{2}\left(\frac{t}{8} + \ell\right)$ **E.** $\frac{t}{2}\left(\frac{t}{8} + s\right)$

2. **Justify Reasoning** A frustum of a pyramid is a part of the pyramid with two parallel bases. The lateral faces of the frustum are trapezoids. Use the area formula for a trapezoid to derive a formula for the lateral area of a frustum of a regular square pyramid with base edge lengths b_1 and b_2 and slant height ℓ. Show all of your steps.

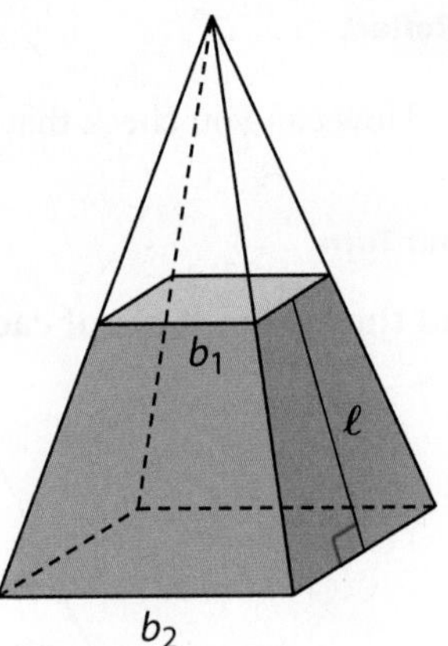

3. **Draw Conclusions** Explain why slant height is not defined for an oblique cone.

Find the lateral and surface area for each pyramid with a regular base. Where necessary, round to the nearest tenth.

4.

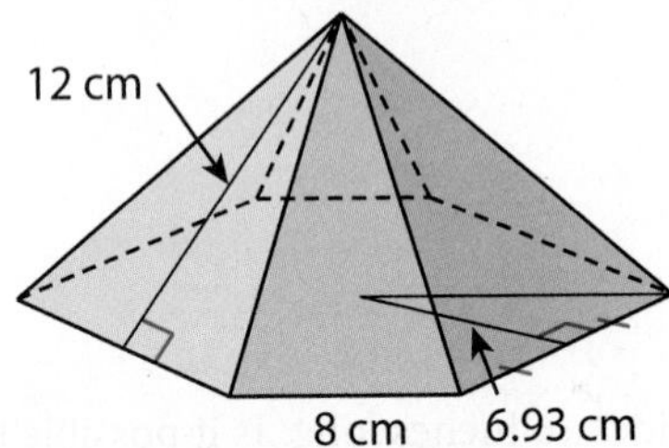

5.

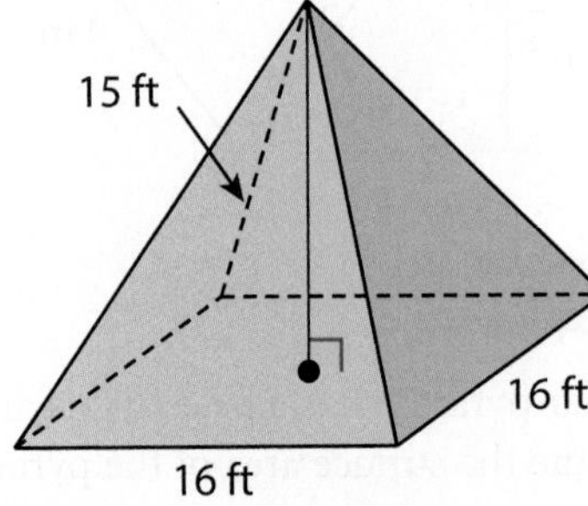

6.

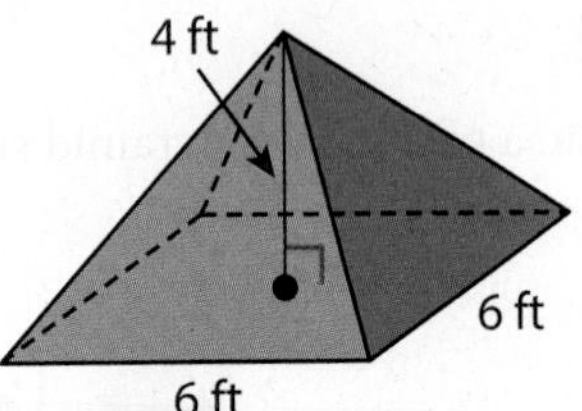

7.

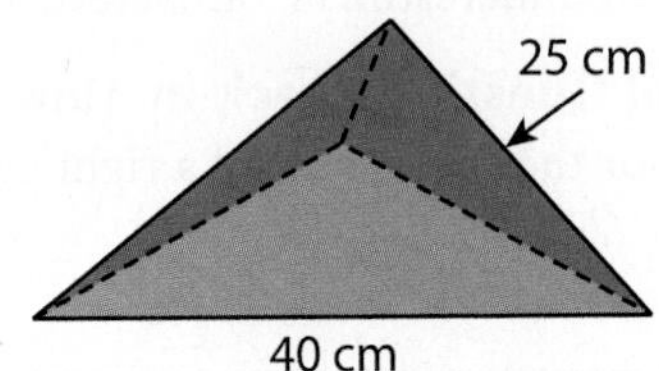

Find the lateral and total surface area for each cone. Leave the answer in terms of π.

8.

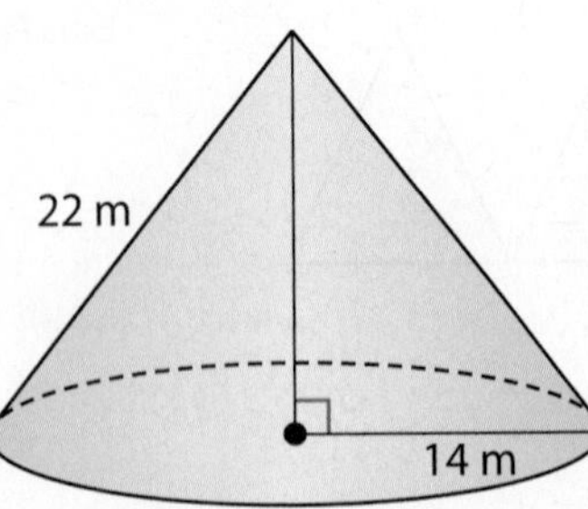

9.

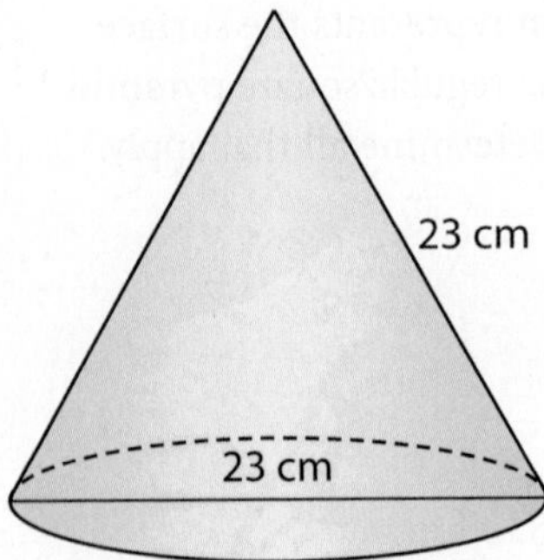

10.

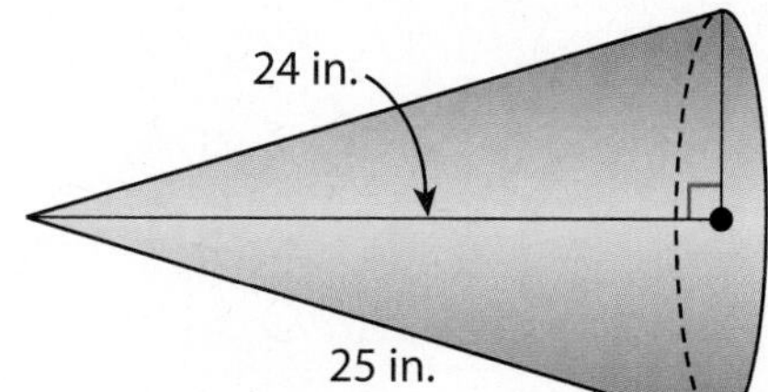

11.

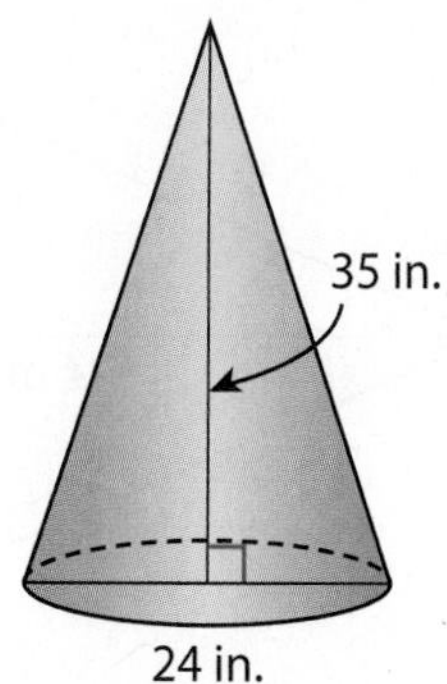

Find the surface area for the composite shape. Where appropriate, leave in terms of π. When necessary, round to nearest tenth.

12.

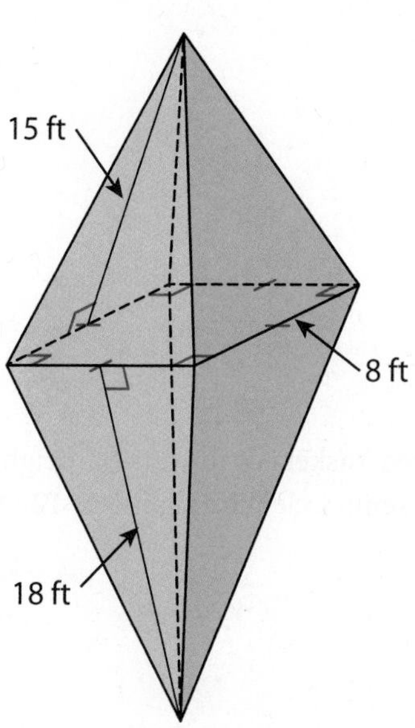

13.

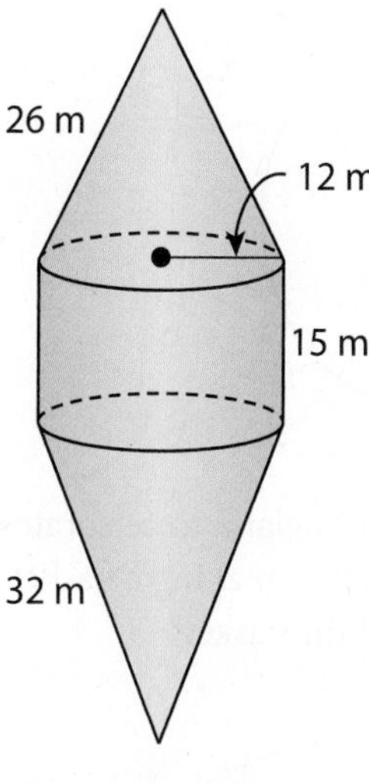

14.

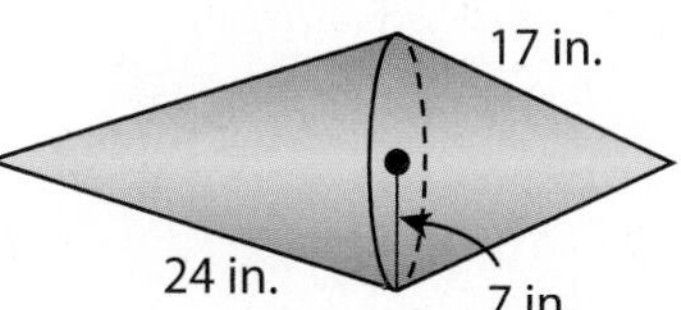

15.

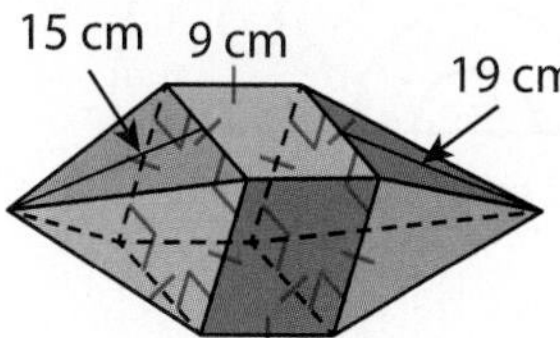

16.

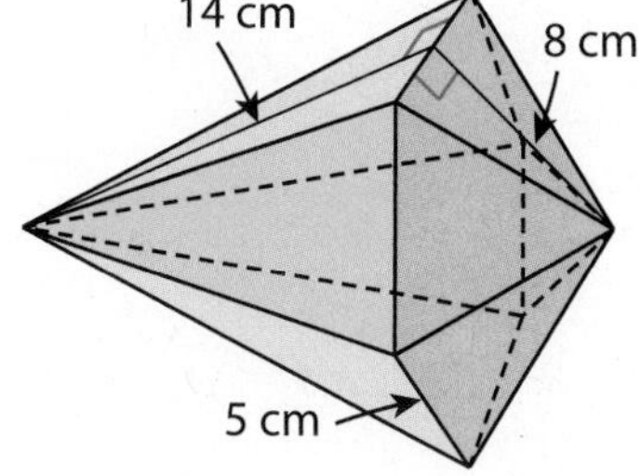

17.

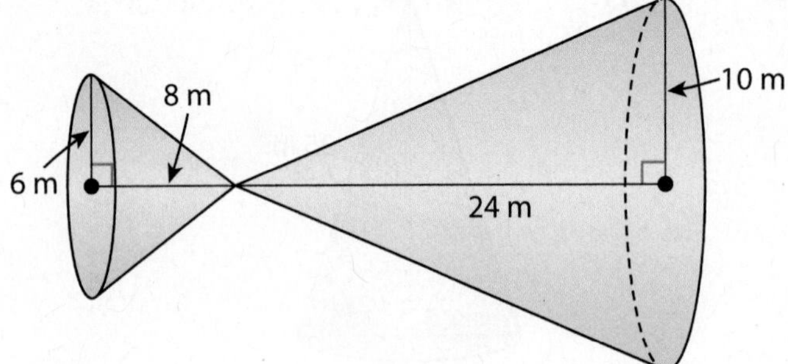

18. Anna is making a birthday hat from a pattern that is $\frac{3}{4}$ of a circle of colored paper. If Anna's head is 7 inches in diameter, will the hat fit her? Explain.

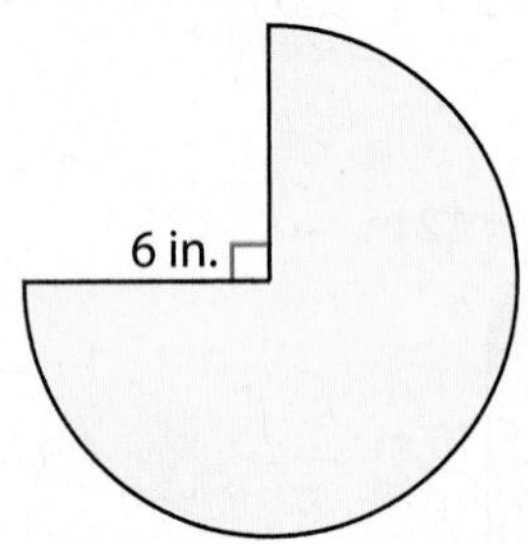

19. It is a tradition in England to celebrate May 1st by hanging cone-shaped baskets of flowers on neighbors' door handles. Addy is making a basket from a piece of paper that is a semicircle with diameter 12 in. What is the diameter of the basket?

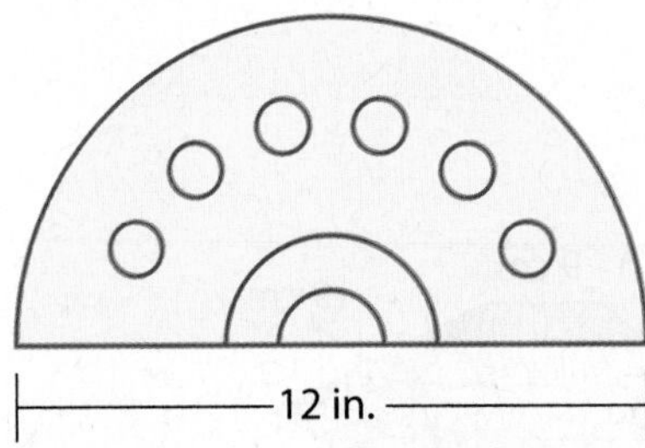

20. Match the figure with the correct surface area. Indicate a match by writing a letter for the correct surface area in the final column for each shape.

Shape	Base Area	Slant Height	Surface Area
Regular square pyramid	36 cm^2	5 cm	
Regular triangular pyramid	$\sqrt{3}\text{ cm}^2$	$\sqrt{3}$ cm	
Right cone	$16\pi\text{ cm}^2$	7 cm	
Right cone	$\pi\text{ cm}^2$	2 cm	

A. 9.4 cm^2

B. 6.9 cm^2

C. 96 cm^2

D. 138.2 cm^2

21. The Pyramid Arena in Memphis, Tennessee, is a square pyramid with base edge lengths of 200 yd and a height of 32 stories. Estimate the area of the glass on the sides of the pyramid. (*Hint:* 1 story $\approx$ 10 ft)

22. A juice container is a regular square pyramid with the dimensions shown.

a. Find the surface area of the container to the nearest tenth.

b. The manufacturer decides to make a container in the shape of a right cone that requires the same amount of material. The base diameter must be 9 cm. Find the slant height of the container to the nearest tenth.

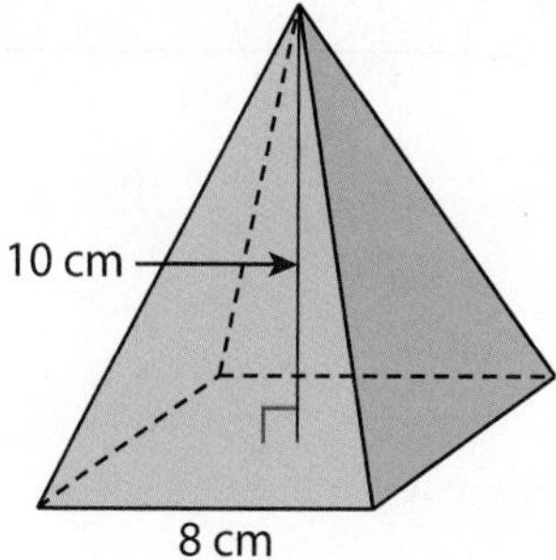

23. Persevere in Problem Solving A *frustum* of a cone is a part of the cone with two parallel bases. The height of the frustum of the cone that is shown is half the height of the original cone.

a. Find the surface area of the original cone.

b. Find the lateral area of the top of the cone.

c. Find the area of the top base of the frustum.

d. Use your results from parts a, b, and c to find the surface area of the frustum of the cone.

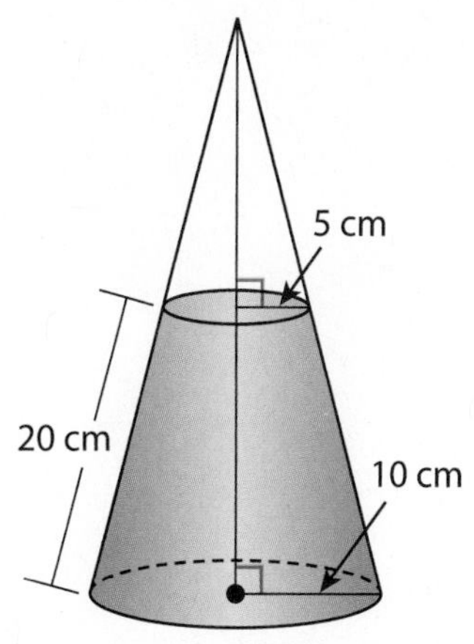

H.O.T. Focus on Higher Order Thinking

24. **Communicate Mathematical Ideas** Explain how you would find the volume of a cone, given the radius and the surface area.

25. **Draw Conclusions** Explain why the slant height of a regular square pyramid must be greater than half the base edge length.

Lesson Performance Task

The pyramid in the figure is built in two levels.

$AC = 200$ feet

You have a summer job as an intern archaeologist. The archaeologists you are working with need to apply a liquid microbial biofilm inhibitor to the pyramid to prevent bacterial degradation of the stones and have asked you to calculate the volume of inhibitor needed for the job. You find that you need 36,000 gallons of inhibitor for the top level. How many gallons will you need for the bottom level? (Keep in mind that you won't be treating the square bases of the levels.) Explain how you found the answer.

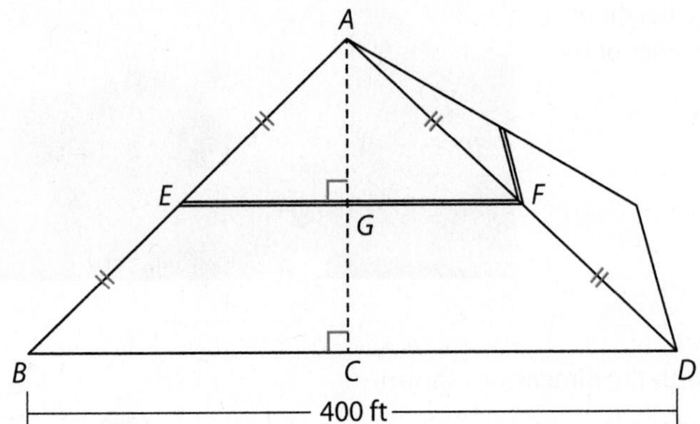

19.4 Surface Area of Spheres

Resource Locker

Essential Question: How can you use the formula for the surface area of a sphere to calculate the surface areas of composite figures?

Explore Developing a Surface Area Formula

You can derive the formula for the surface area of a sphere with radius r by imagining that it is filled with a large number of pyramids, whose apexes all meet at the center of the sphere and whose bases rest against the sphere's surface. It does not matter exactly what shape each base is, as long as all the bases have the same area, B, and they are not too far from regular polygons in shape. The figure shows a sphere with the first three pyramids inscribed.

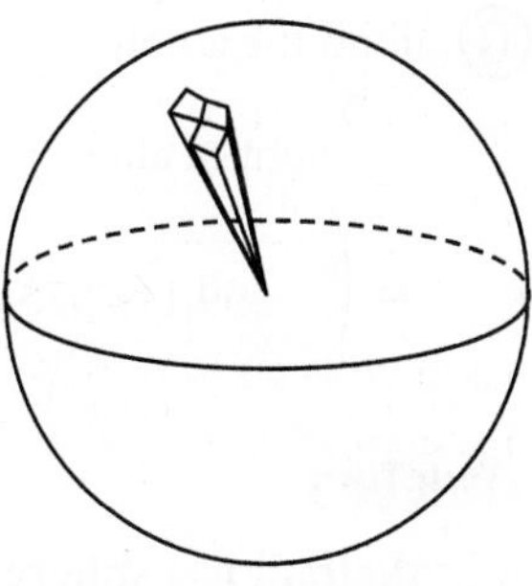

(A) What is the approximate volume of each pyramid?

(B) Express the approximate volume of the sphere in terms of the n pyramids.

(C) Use the formula for the volume of a sphere to write an approximate equation that can be solved for B, and solve it.

(D) Write an approximate expression for the sphere's surface area S in terms of the pyramid bases.

(E) Substitute your expression for the base area B of each pyramid from step C into your expression from step D. This gives you an approximate expression for the surface area S that does not involve the pyramids.

Reflect

1. As n gets larger and larger, what do you think will happen to the closeness of the approximations in steps A, B, C, and E? Explain.

2. As a conjecture, write the formula for the surface area S of a sphere with radius r.

Explain 1 Finding the Surface Area of a Sphere

Surface Area of a Sphere
The surface area of a sphere with radius r is given by $S = 4\pi r^2$.

You can use a formula for the surface area of a sphere to solve real-world problems.

Example 1 **A spherical water tank is 21.5 ft in diameter. The corrosion-resistant alloy skin of the tank is $\frac{1}{8}$ in thick. How much alloy is used to make the tank, to the nearest cubic inch?**

(A) Find the radius of the tank in inches.

The radius of the tank is $\frac{1}{2}(21.5 \text{ ft}) = 10.75 \text{ ft} \times \frac{12 \text{ in.}}{1 \text{ ft}} = 129 \text{ in.}$

(B) Find the surface area of the tank.

$S = 4\pi r^2 = 4\pi\left(\boxed{129}\right)^2 = \boxed{209{,}116.973}\ldots \text{ in}^2$

(C) Find the amount of alloy, to the nearest cubic inch.

Amount of alloy = surface area × thickness

$= \left(\boxed{209{,}116.973}\ldots \text{ in}^2\right) \times \left(\boxed{\frac{1}{8}} \text{ in.}\right) \approx \boxed{26{,}140} \text{ in}^3$

Your Turn

A basketball is a sphere 29.5 in. in circumference. A baseball is a sphere of circumference 9.0 in. How much material is needed to make each ball, and how does the ratio of these amounts compare to the ratio of the circumferences?

3. How much material is needed to make a basketball, to the nearest tenth of a square inch?

4. How much material is needed to make a baseball, to the nearest tenth?

5. Compare the ratio of the amounts of material to the ratio of the circumferences. What do you notice?

Explain 2 Finding the Surface Area of a Composite Figure

You can find the surface area of a composite figure using appropriate formulas for the areas of the different surfaces of the figure.

Example 2 **Find the surface area of the composite figure, in terms of π and to the nearest tenth.**

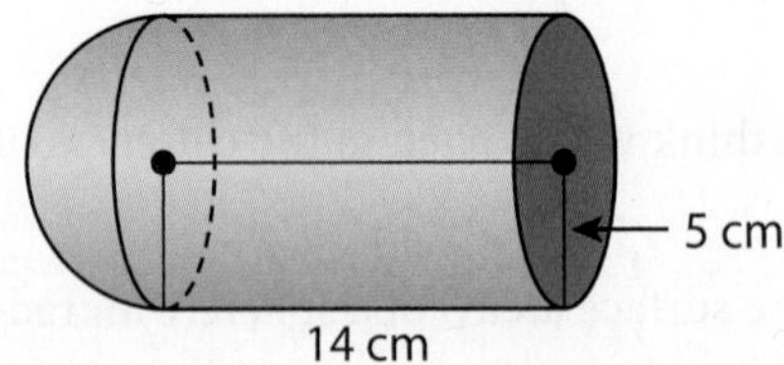

(A) Find the area of the base of the cylinder.

$A_1 = \pi r^2 = \pi(5)^2 = 25\pi \text{ cm}^2$

(B) Find the area of the curved surface of the cylinder.

$A_2 = 2\pi rh = 2\pi\left(\boxed{5}\right)\left(\boxed{14}\right) = \boxed{140}\ \pi \text{ cm}^2$

Ⓒ Find the surface area of the hemisphere.

$A_3 = \frac{1}{2}(4\pi r^2) = 2\pi\left(\boxed{5} \right)^2 = \boxed{50}\ \pi\ \text{cm}^2$

Ⓓ Find the surface area of the composite figure.

$S = A_1 + A_2 + A_3$

$= \boxed{25}\ \pi\ \text{cm}^2 + \boxed{140}\ \pi\ \text{cm}^2 + \boxed{50}\ \pi\ \text{cm}^2$

$= \boxed{215}\ \pi\ \text{cm}^2 \approx \boxed{675.4}\ \text{cm}^2$

Reflect

6. Discussion Could you have used the formula for the surface area of a cylinder? Explain.

Your Turn

Find the surface area of the composite figure, in terms of π and to the nearest tenth.

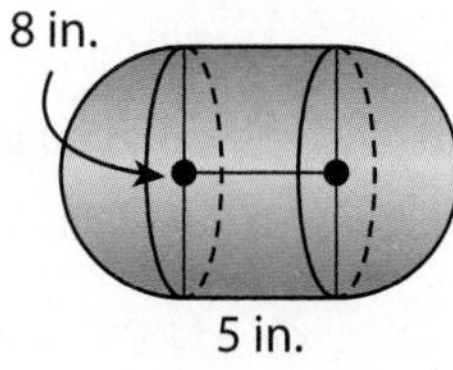

7. Find the lateral area of the cylinder.

8. Find the surface area of each hemisphere.

9. Find the surface area of the composite figure.

Elaborate

10. How does deriving the formula for the surface area of a sphere depend on knowing the formula for its volume?

11. Essential Question Check-In How can you use the formula for the surface area of a sphere to calculate the surface areas of composite figures?

Evaluate: Homework and Practice

- Online Homework
- Hints and Help
- Extra Practice

1. Using your knowledge of surface area and area, create a formula that will work to find the total surface area of the closed hemisphere for any value of *r*.

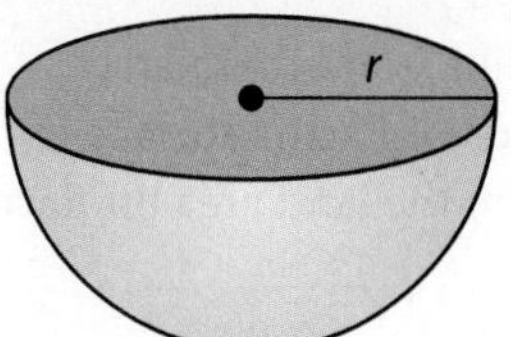

Find the surface area of the sphere. Leave the answer in terms of π.

2.

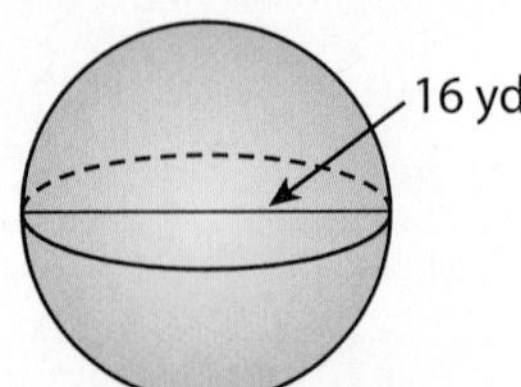

3.

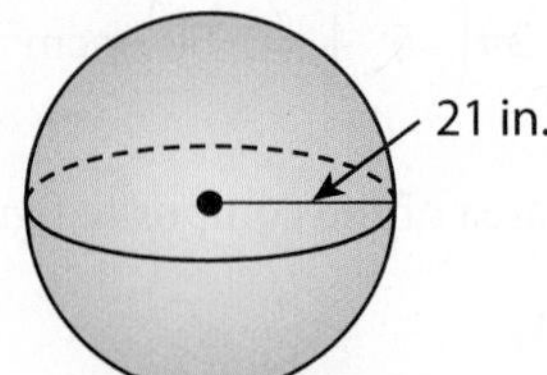

4.

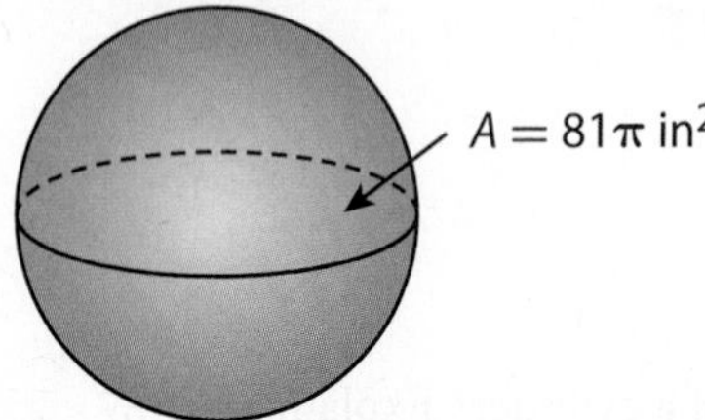

5.

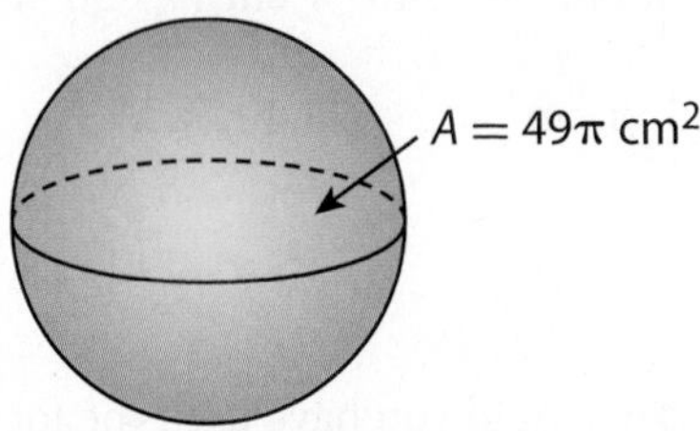

Find the surface area of the composite figure. Leave the answer in terms of π.

6.

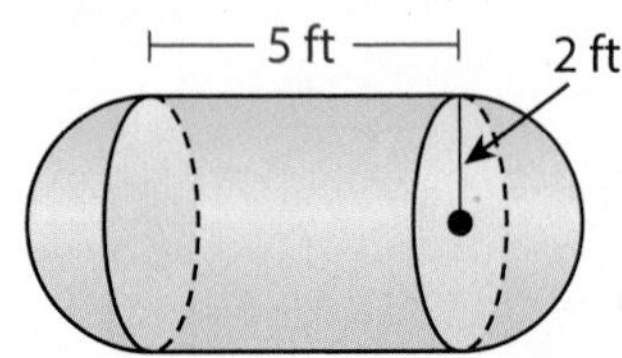

7.

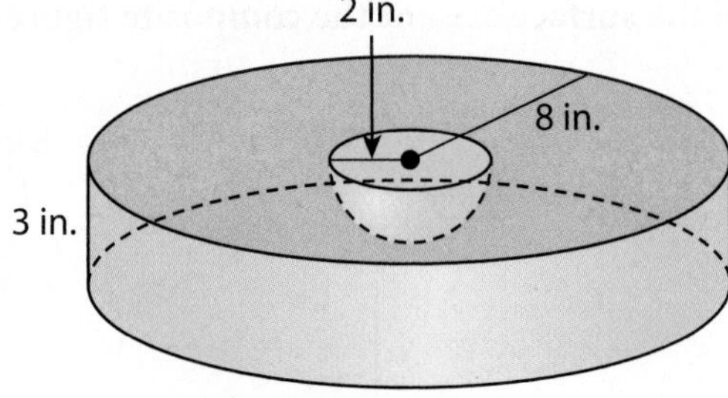

8.

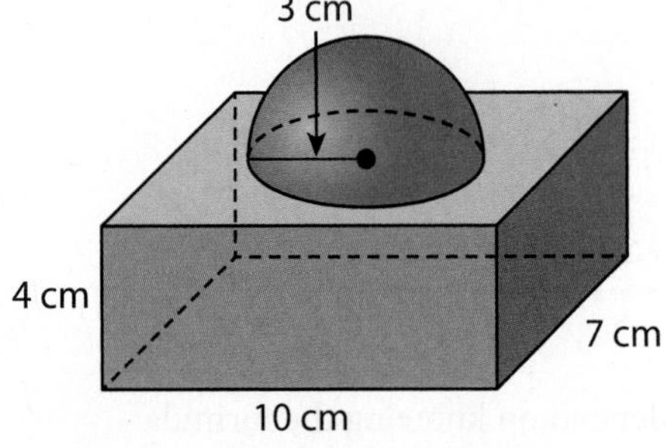

9.

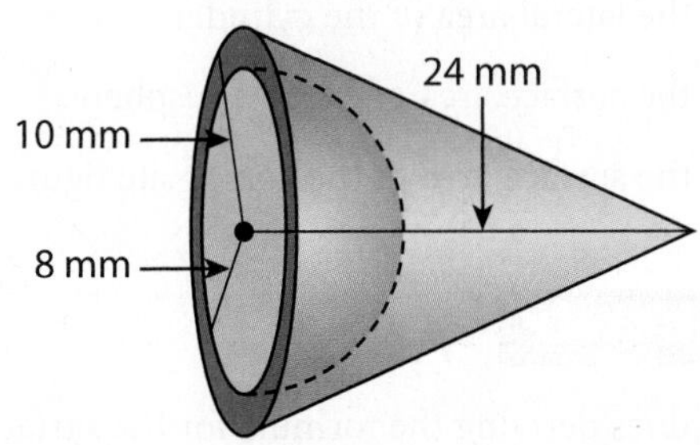

10. Find the surface area of the closed hemisphere.

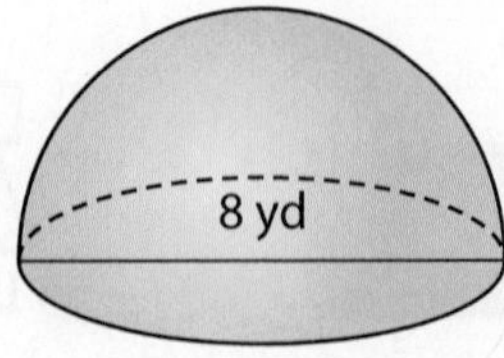

11. Find the circumference of the sphere with a surface area of 60π in^2. Leave the answer in terms of π.

12. **Geography** Earth's radius is approximately 4000 mi. About two-thirds of Earth's surface is covered by water. Estimate the land area on Earth.

13. A baseball has a radius of approximately 1.5 inches. Estimate the amount of leather used to cover the baseball. Leave the answer in terms of π.

14. Which of the following expressions represents the ratio of the surface area of a cylinder to the surface area of a sphere with the same radius, r?

A. $\frac{1}{2} + \frac{h}{r}$

B. $\frac{\pi + h}{r^2}$

C. $\frac{h}{4\pi}$

D. $\frac{r + h}{4r}$

E. $\frac{r + h}{2r}$

15. Explain the Error Susana solved for the surface area of the sphere using the following method:

$$S = \frac{4}{3}\pi r^2$$
$$= \frac{4}{3}\pi(10)^2$$
$$= \frac{4}{3}\pi 100$$
$$= \frac{400}{3}\pi \text{ m}^2$$

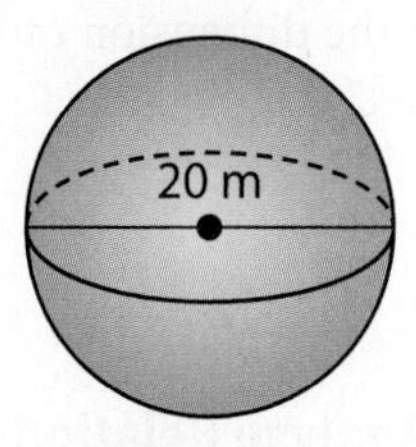

Find her error, and explain how to fix it.

16. Use the table to answer the question.

a. Which is greater, the sum of the surface areas of Uranus and Neptune or the surface area of Saturn?

b. About how many times as great is the surface area of Earth as the surface area of Mars?

Planet	Diameter (mi)
Mercury	3,032
Venus	7,521
Earth	7,926
Mars	4,222
Jupiter	88,846
Saturn	74,898
Uranus	31,763
Neptune	30,775

17. A globe has a volume of 288π in^3. What is the surface area of the globe? Give your answer in terms of π.

18. A bead is formed by drilling a cylindrical hole, with a 2 mm diameter, through a sphere with an 8 mm diameter. Estimate the surface area of the bead.

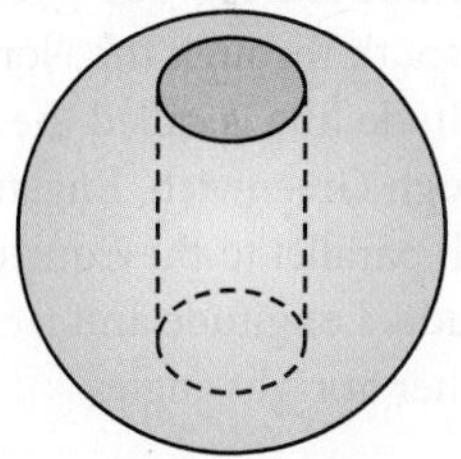

19. The size of a cultured pearl is typically indicated by its diameter in mm. About how many times as great is the surface area of the 9 mm pearl as the surface area of the 6 mm pearl?

20. The diameter of an orange is 10 cm and the diameter of a lime is 5 cm. About how many times as great is the surface area of a half of the orange as the surface area of a half of the lime?

21. A hemisphere has a surface area of 972π cm^2. If the radius is multiplied by $\frac{1}{3}$, what will be the surface area of the new hemisphere?

H.O.T. Focus on Higher Order Thinking

22. **Communicate Mathematical Ideas** Describe the effect on the surface area if the dimension on the sphere is doubled.

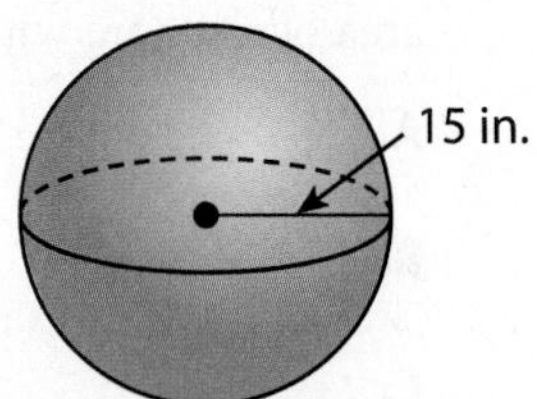

23. **Analyze Relationships** What is the relationship between the surface area of the sphere and the lateral area of the cylinder?

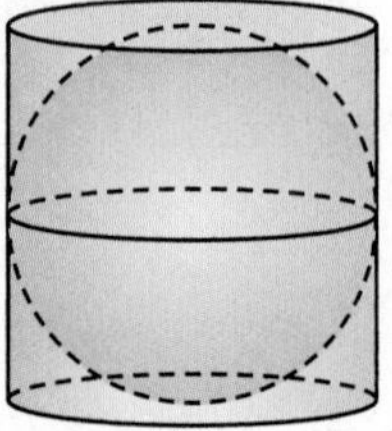

24. **Persevere in Problem Solving** A company sells orange juice in spherical containers that look like oranges. Each container has a surface area of approximately 50.3 in^2.

    a. What is the volume of the container? Round to the nearest tenth.

    b. The company decides to increase the radius of the container by 10%. What is the surface area of the new container?

25. **Draw Conclusions** Suppose a sphere and a cube have equal surface areas. Using r for the radius of the sphere and s for the side of a cube, write an equation to show the relationship between r and s.

Lesson Performance Task

Locations on Earth are measured in relation to longitude and latitude lines. Longitude lines run north and south through the North and South poles. The 0° longitude line is called the Prime Meridian and runs through Greenwich, England. Latitude lines circle the Earth parallel to the Equator, which is designated 0° latitude. Longitude and latitude lines intersect one another at right angles.

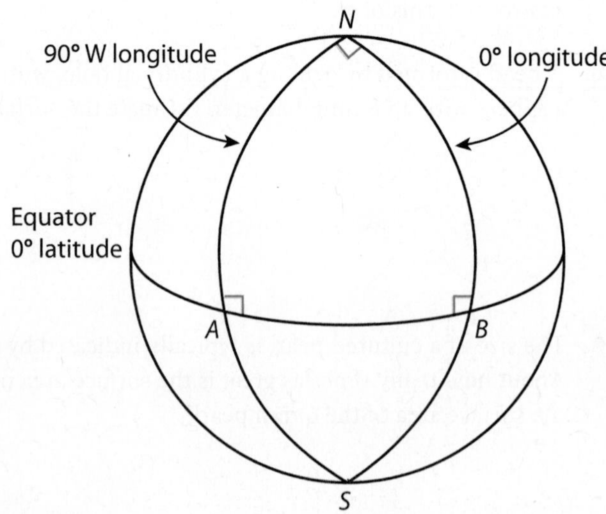

1. Triangle ABN is formed by the Equator and two lines of longitude. It is called a spherical triangle. Describe the ways that it is similar to a plane triangle and the ways that it differs.

2. Find the area of spherical triangle ABN. Explain how you found the area. Use 7912 miles as the diameter of the Earth. Use 3.14 for π.

Visualizing Solids

Essential Question: How can you use visualizing solids to solve real-world problems?

Key Vocabulary

net *(red)*

surface area *(área de la superficie)*

regular pyramid *(pirámide regular)*

right cone *(cono recto)*

KEY EXAMPLE (Lesson 19.1)

Describe the cross section formed when a plane cuts through the center of a sphere. Compare the dimensions of the cross section to those of the figure.

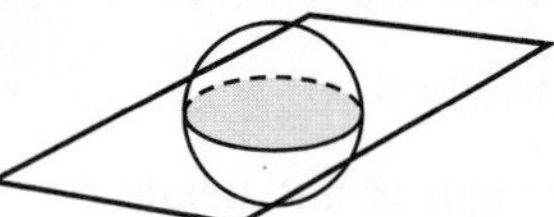

Since the sphere and the plane are both rotationally symmetric about the perpendicular axis, the cross section is also rotationally symmetric and is therefore a circle. Since it passes through the sphere's widest part, the circle's radius is equal to the radius of the sphere.

KEY EXAMPLE (Lesson 19.2)

Find the surface area of a right prism with length of 10, width of 5, and height of 4.

$L = Ph$	Apply the lateral area formula.
$L = (2 \cdot 10 + 2 \cdot 5)4 = 120$	Substitute and solve.
$S = L + 2B$	Apply the surface area formula.
$S = 120 + 2 \cdot 10 \cdot 5 = 220$	Substitute and solve.

KEY EXAMPLE (Lesson 19.3)

Find the surface area of a right cone with radius 12 and height 16.

$l^2 = 12^2 + 16^2$	Use the Pythagorean Theorem to find the slant height.
$l = 20$	Solve.
$L = \pi r l$	Find the lateral area.
$L = \pi(12)(20) = 240\pi$	Substitute and multiply.
$S = L + \pi r^2$	Find the surface area.
$S = 240\pi + \pi(12)^2 = 384\pi$	Substitute and solve.

KEY EXAMPLE (Lesson 19.4)

Find the surface area of a sphere with radius 14.

$S = 4\pi r^2$	Use the formula for surface area of a sphere.
$S = 4\pi(14)^2 = 784\pi$	Substitute and solve.

EXERCISES

Determine if it is possible to form the following shapes by rotating a two-dimensional shape around the *y*-axis. If so, state the shape needed to do so. *(Lesson 19.1)*

1. sphere
2. right prism
3. cylinder

Find the exact surface area of the following shapes. *(Lessons 19.2 , 19.3, 19.4)*

4. right prism with length 3, width 4, and height 5
5. cylinder with radius 8 and height 3
6. regular pyramid with side length 12 and height 8
7. right cone with diameter 8 and height 3
8. sphere with radius 8
9. hemisphere with radius 9

MODULE PERFORMANCE TASK

How Much Does the Paint on a Space Shuttle Weigh?

NASA used to paint the fuel tanks for the Space Shuttle with white latex paint, but they decided to stop painting them because of the extra weight that the paint added. Just how much could that paint weigh?

The photo gives you a good sense of the shape of the fuel tank. According to NASA, the tank has a height of 153.8 feet and a diameter of 27.6 feet. Use one or more of the formulas you have learned to find the surface area of the tank. Then use your calculation to come up with your best estimate of the weight of the paint required to cover the fuel tank.

Start by listing any additional information you will need to solve the problem. Then complete the task. Be sure to write down all of your assumptions and data. Use tables, diagrams, words, or numbers to explain how you came to your conclusion.

Ready to Go On?

19.1–19.4 Visualizing Solids

- Online Homework
- Hints and Help
- Extra Practice

State the figure obtained when rotating the figure about an axis along its largest side, and find the exact surface area of the resulting figure.

1. A rectangle with length 18 and width 14. *(Lesson 19.1)*

Find the exact surface area of the composite figure. *(Lessons 19.2, 19.3, 19.4)*

2.

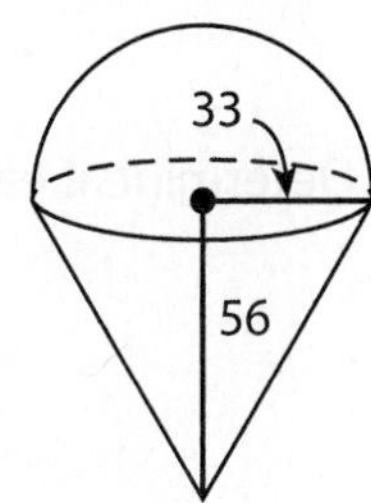

ESSENTIAL QUESTION

3. When finding the surface area of a composite figure, why is it often necessary to subtract sides common to each individual shape?

MODULE 19
MIXED REVIEW

Assessment Readiness

1. A rectangular prism has a surface area of 922 square units. Consider each set of dimensions. Could these be the dimensions of the right prism?
Write Yes or No for A–C.

A. length $= 23$, width $= 7$, height $= 10$

B. length $= 17$, width $= 8$, height $= 13$

C. length $= 10$, width $= 9$, height $= 12$

2. A sphere has a radius of 27. Determine if each statement is True or False.

A. The surface area of the sphere is 729π square units.

B. The volume of the sphere is $26{,}244\pi$ cubic units.

C. The surface area of the sphere is 2916π square units.

3. $\triangle ABC$ maps to $\triangle DEF$ with the transformation $(x, y) \rightarrow \left(\frac{1}{4}x, \frac{1}{4}y\right)$. Determine if each statement is True or False.

A. If $BC = 8$, $EF = 2$.

B. If $BC = 4$, $EF = 16$.

C. If $BC = 20$, $EF = 5$.

4. What solid is formed when rotating a square about a horizontal or vertical axis through the center of the square? Does this solid have a square for a base? Does this solid have a square for a cross-section?

5. Draw the net of a right cylinder with a radius of 2 and a height of 6, and then explain if this answer is the only possible net for this cylinder.

Modeling and Problem Solving

MODULE 20

Essential Question: How can you use modeling to solve real-world problems?

REAL WORLD VIDEO
Check out how GPS coordinates can be used to calculate the area of a region of the Earth's surface.

MODULE PERFORMANCE TASK PREVIEW

Population Density

It's easy to find the population density of a region once you know the population and the area. What's not always so easy is counting the population (New York City, 8,336,697 in 2012) and calculating the area (New York City, 302.64 square miles). Of course, there are some regions whose populations are much smaller than that of New York City and whose areas are easier to calculate. You'll find the population density of one of them after you complete this module.

Are YOU Ready?

Complete these exercises to review skills you will need for this module.

- Online Homework
- Hints and Help
- Extra Practice

Scale Factor and Scale Drawings

Example 1 The width on an architectural plan for a rectangular room is 8 cm. The actual room will be 12 ft wide and 18 ft long. How long is the length of the room on the plan?

$$\frac{\text{plan width}}{\text{actual width}} = \frac{\text{plan length}}{\text{actual length}} \rightarrow \frac{8}{12} = \frac{x}{18}$$

$$x = \frac{18 \cdot 8}{12} = 12$$ Multiply and simplify.

The plan length is 12 cm.

Find the missing length for a rectangular room.

1. plan length: 4 in.
actual width: 28 ft
actual length: 32 ft
Find the plan width.

2. plan width: 6 in.
plan length: 8 in.
actual length: 24 yd
Find the actual width.

3. plan width: 2.4 cm
plan length: 9 cm
actual width: 3.6 m
Find the actual length.

Volume

Example 2 The volume of a cylinder is 42 cm^3. Its height is 3.5 cm. Find the diameter of the cylinder.

$V = \pi r^2 h$ Write the formula.

$42 = \pi r^2(3.5)$ Substitute.

$r^2 = \frac{42}{3.5\pi} = \frac{12}{\pi}$ Solve for r^2.

$r \approx 1.954$ Solve for r to the nearest thousandth.

$2r \approx 3.91$ Find the diameter.

The diameter of the cylinder is about 3.91 cm.

Find the missing measure of the cylinder to the nearest hundredth.

4. diameter: 7 ft
height: 2 ft
Find the volume.

5. radius: 10 in.
volume: 490 in^3
Find the height.

6. diameter: 1.2 m
volume: 4.8 m^3
Find the height.

20.1 Scale Factor

Essential Question: How does multiplying one or more of the dimensions of a figure affect its attributes?

Explore — Exploring Effects of Changing Dimensions on Perimeter and Area

Changes made to the dimensions of a figure can affect the perimeter and the area.

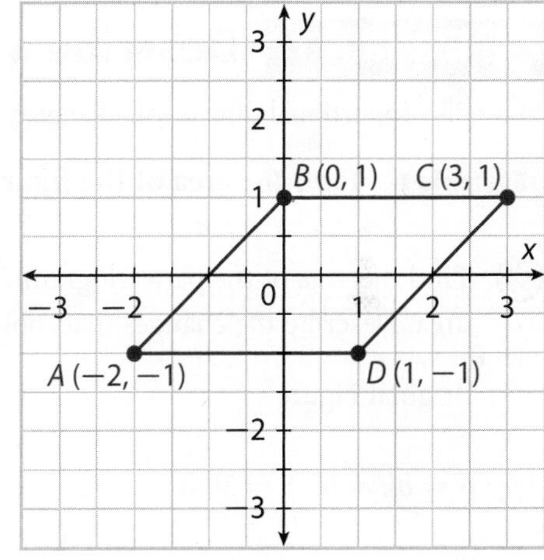

Use the figure to investigate how changing one or more dimensions of the figure affect its perimeter and area.

(A) Apply the transformation $(x, y) \to (3x, y)$. Find the perimeter and the area.

Original Dimensions	Dimensions after $(x, y) \to (3x, y)$
$P = 6 + 4\sqrt{2}$	$P =$?
$A = 6$	$A =$?

(B) Apply the transformation $(x, y) \to (x, 3y)$. Find the perimeter and the area.

Original Dimensions	Dimensions after $(x, y) \to (x, 3y)$
$P = 6 + 4\sqrt{2}$	$P =$?
$A = 6$	$A =$?

(C) Apply the transformation $(x, y) \rightarrow (3x, 3y)$. Find the perimeter and the area.

Original Dimensions	Dimensions after $(x, y) \rightarrow (3x, 3y)$
$P = 6 + 4\sqrt{2}$	$P =$?
$A = 6$	$A =$?

Reflect

1. Describe the changes that occurred in Steps A and B. Did the perimeter or area change by a constant factor?
2. Describe the changes that occurred in Step C. Did the perimeter or area change by a constant factor?

Explain 1 Describe a Non-Proportional Dimension Change

In a non-proportional dimension change, you do not use the same factor to change each dimension of a figure.

Example 1 **Find the area of the figure.**

(A) Find the area of the parallelogram. Then multiply the length by 2 and determine the new area. Describe the changes that took place.

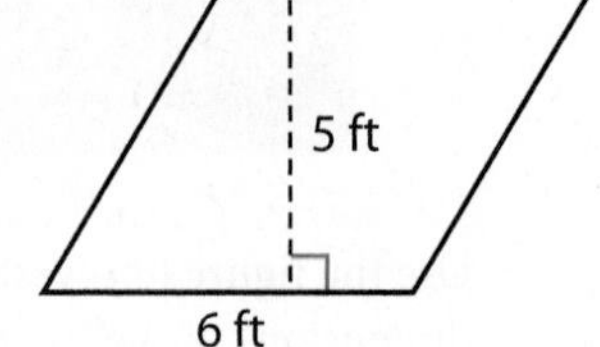

Original Figure

$A = bh = 6 \cdot 5 = 30 \text{ ft}^2$

Transformed Figure

$A = bh = 12 \cdot 5 = 60 \text{ ft}^2$

When the length of the parallelogram changes by a factor of 2, the area changes by a factor of 2.

(B) Find the area of the trapezoid. Then multiply the height by 0.5 and determine the new area. Describe the changes that took place.

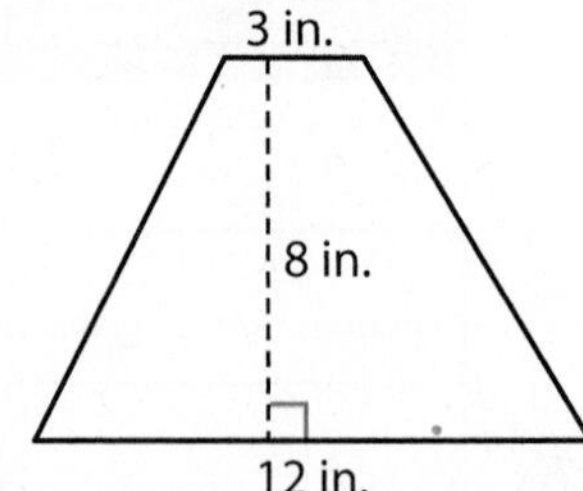

Original Figure $A = \frac{1}{2}(b_1 + b_2)h =$ $\frac{1}{2}(3 + 12)8 = 60$

Transformed Figure $A = \frac{1}{2}(b_1 + b_2)h =$ $\frac{1}{2}(3 + 12)4 = 30$

When the height of the trapezoid changes by a factor of 0.5, the area of the trapezoid changes by a factor of 0.5.

Reflect

3. **Discussion** When a non-proportional change is applied to the dimensions of a figure, does the perimeter change in a predictable way?

Your Turn

4. Find the area of a triangle with vertices $(-5, -2)$, $(-5, 7)$, and $(3, 1)$. Then apply the transformation $(x, y) \rightarrow (x, 4y)$ and determine the new area. Describe the changes that took place.

5. Find the area of the figure. Then multiply the width by 5 and determine the new area. Describe the changes that took place.

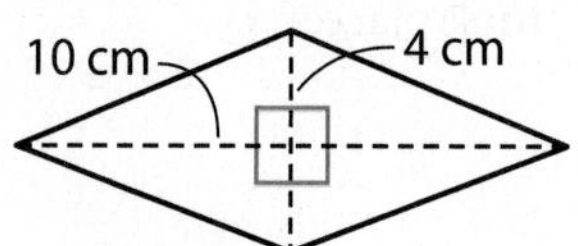

Explain 2 Describe a Proportional Dimension Change

In a proportional dimension change, you use the same factor to change each dimension of a figure.

Example 2 **Find the area and perimeter of a circle.**

Ⓐ Find the circumference and area of the circle. Then multiply the radius by 3 and find the new circumference and area. Describe the changes that took place.

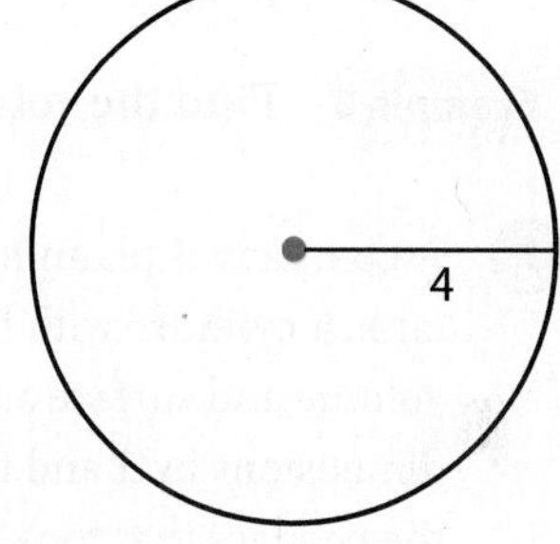

Original Figure $C = 2\pi(4) = 8\pi$

$A = \pi(4)^2 = 16\pi$

Transformed Figure $C = 2\pi(12) = 24\pi$

$A = \pi(12)^2 = 144\pi$

The circumference changes by a factor of 3, and the area changes by a factor of 9 or 3^2.

Ⓑ Find the perimeter and area of the figure. Then multiply the length and height by $\frac{1}{3}$ and find the new perimeter and area. Describe the changes that took place.

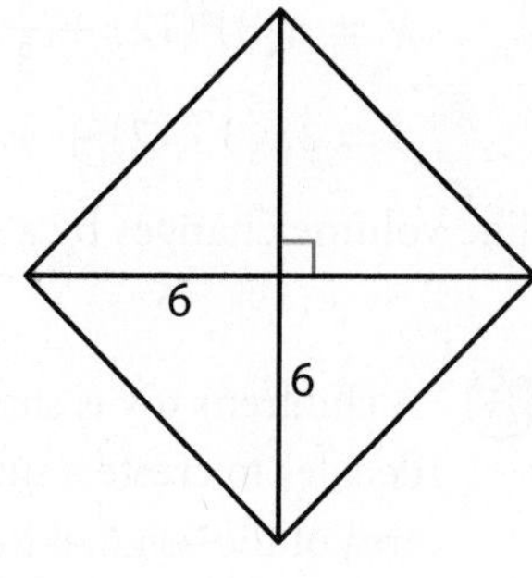

Original Figure	Transformed Figure
$P = 4(6\sqrt{2}) = 24\sqrt{2}$	$P = 4(2\sqrt{2}) = 8\sqrt{2}$
$A = \frac{1}{2}d_1d_2 = \frac{1}{2}(12 \cdot 12) = 72$	$A = \frac{1}{2}d_1d_2 = \frac{1}{2}(4 \cdot 4) = 8$

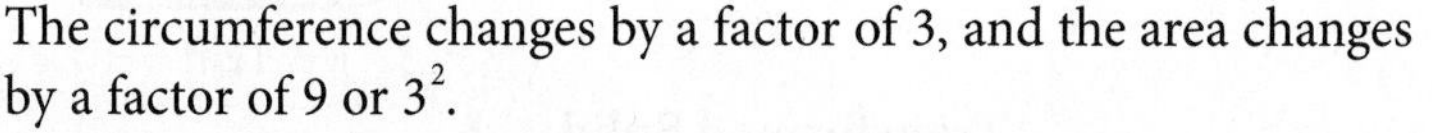

The perimeter changes by a factor of $\frac{1}{3}$, and the area changes by a factor of $\frac{1}{9}$ or $\frac{1}{3^2}$.

Reflect

6. Describe the effect on perimeter (or circumference) and area when the dimensions of a figure are changed proportionally.

Effects of Changing Dimensions Proportionally		
Change in Dimensions	**Perimeter or Circumference**	**Area**
All dimensions multiplied by a		

Your Turn

7. Find the circumference and area of the circle. Then multiply the radius by 0.25 and find the new circumference and area. Describe the changes that took place.

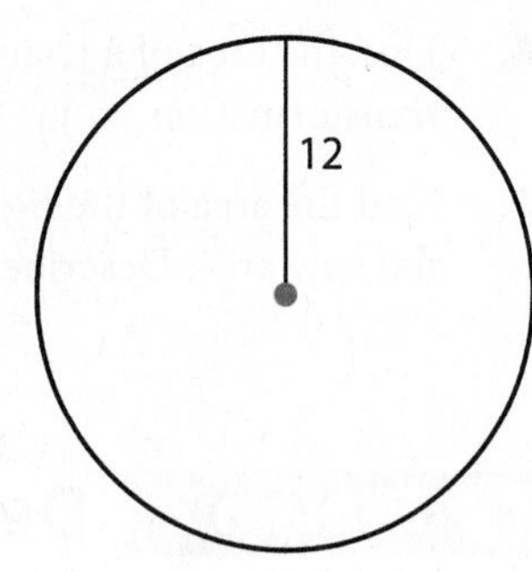

Explain 3 Describe a Proportional Dimension Change for a Solid

In a proportional dimension change to a solid, you use the same factor to change each dimension of a figure.

Example 3 **Find the volume of the composite solid.**

(A) A company is planning to create a similar version of this storage tank, a cylinder with hemispherical caps at each end. Find the volume and surface area of the original tank. Then multiply all the dimensions by 2 and find the new volume and surface area. Describe the changes that took place.

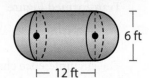

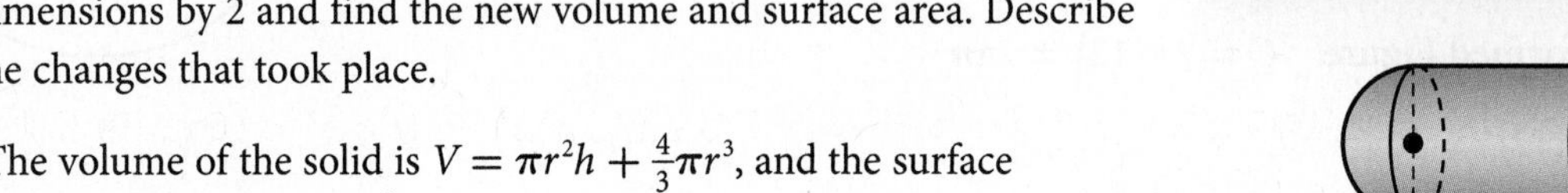

The volume of the solid is $V = \pi r^2 h + \frac{4}{3}\pi r^3$, and the surface area is $S = 2\pi rh + 4\pi r^2$.

6 ft

12 ft

Original Solid

$V = \pi(3)^2(12) + \frac{4}{3}\pi(3)^3 = 144\pi$ cu. ft.

$S = 2\pi(3 \cdot 12) + 4\pi(3)^2 = 108\pi$ sq. ft.

Transformed Solid

$V = \pi(6)^2(24) + \frac{4}{3}\pi(6)^3 = 1152\pi$ cu. ft.

$S = 2\pi(6 \cdot 24) + 4\pi(6)^2 = 432\pi$ sq. ft.

The volume changes by a factor of 8, and the surface area changes by a factor of 4.

(B) A children's toy is shaped like a hemisphere with a conical top. A company decides to create a smaller version of the toy. Find the volume and surface area of the original toy. Then multiply all dimensions by $\frac{2}{3}$ and find the new volume and surface area. Describe the changes that took place.

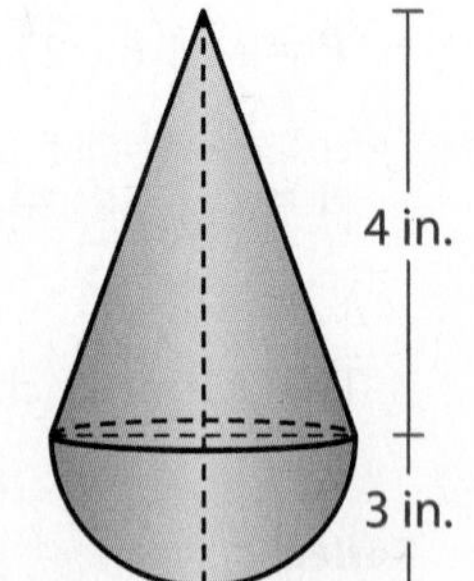

The volume of the solid is $V = \frac{1}{3}\pi r^2 h + \frac{2}{3}\pi r^3$,

and the surface area is $S = \pi r\sqrt{r^2 + h^2} + 2\pi r^2$.

Original Solid

$V =$ $\frac{1}{3}\pi(3)^2 4 + \frac{2}{3}\pi(3)^3 = 30\pi$ cu. in.

$S =$ $\pi(3)\sqrt{3^2 + 4^2} + 2\pi(3)^2 = 33\pi$ sq. in.

Transformed Solid

$V =$ $\frac{1}{3}\pi(2)^2\left(\frac{8}{3}\right) + \frac{2}{3}\pi(2)^3 = \frac{80}{9}\pi$ cu. in.

$S =$ $\pi(2)\sqrt{(2)^2 + \left(\frac{8}{3}\right)^2} + 2\pi(2)^2 = \frac{44}{3}\pi$ sq. in.

The volume changes by a factor of $\frac{8}{27}$, and the surface area changes by a factor of $\frac{4}{9}$.

Reflect

8. Describe the effect on surface area and volume when the dimensions of a figure are changed proportionally.

Effects of Changing Dimensions Proportionally		
Change in Dimensions	**Surface Area**	**Volume**
All dimensions multiplied by a		

Your Turn

9. A farmer has made a scale model of a new grain silo. Find the volume and surface area of the model. Use the scale ratio 1 : 36 to find the volume and surface area of the silo. Compare the volumes and surface areas relative to the scale ratio. Be consistent with units of measurement.

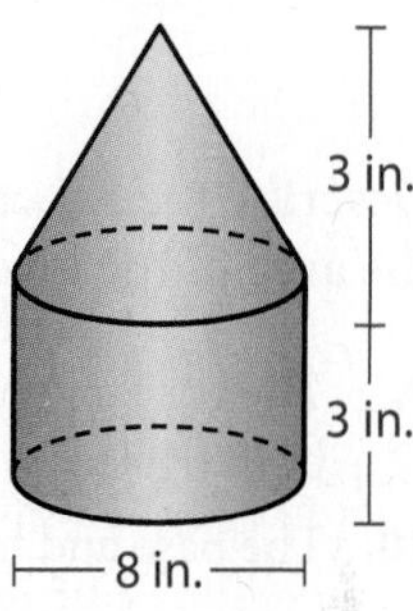

Elaborate

10. Two square pyramids are similar. If the ratio of a pair of corresponding edges is $a : b$, what is the ratio of their volumes? What is the ratio of their surface areas?

11. **Essential Question Check-In** How is a non-proportional dimension change different from a proportional dimension change?

Evaluate: Homework and Practice

- Online Homework
- Hints and Help
- Extra Practice

A trapezoid has the vertices (0, 0), (4, 0), (4, 4), and (−3, 4).

1. Describe the effect on the area if only the x-coordinates of the vertices are multiplied by $\frac{1}{2}$.

2. Describe the effect on the area if only the y-coordinates of the vertices are multiplied by $\frac{1}{2}$.

3. Describe the effect on the area if both the x- and y-coordinates of the vertices are multiplied by $\frac{1}{2}$.

4. Describe the effect on the area if the x-coordinates are multiplied by 2 and y-coordinates are multiplied by $\frac{1}{2}$.

Describe the effect of the change on the area of the given figure.

5. The height of the triangle is doubled.

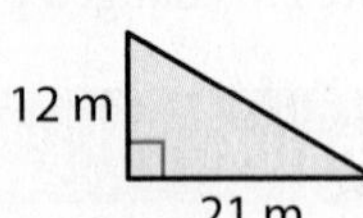

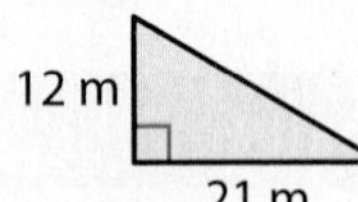

6. The height of a trapezoid with base lengths 12 cm and 8 cm and height 5 cm is multiplied by $\frac{1}{3}$.

7. The base of the parallelogram is multiplied by $\frac{2}{3}$.

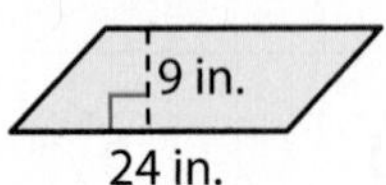

8. **Communicate Mathematical Ideas** A triangle has vertices (1, 5), (2, 3), and (−1, −6). Find the effect that multiplying the height of the triangle by 4 has on the area of the triangle, without doing any calculations. Explain.

Describe the effect of each change on the perimeter or circumference and the area of the given figure.

9. The base and height of an isosceles triangle with base 12 in. and height 6 in. are both tripled.

10. The base and height of the rectangle are both multiplied by $\frac{1}{2}$.

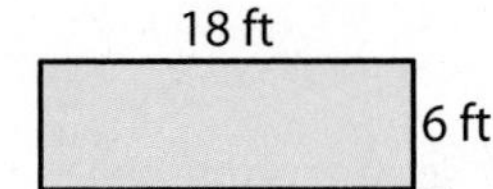

11. The dimensions are multiplied by 5.

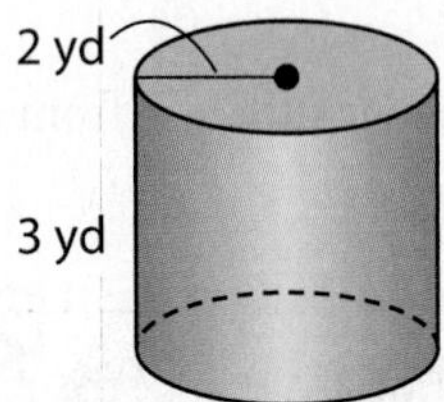

12. The dimensions are multiplied by $\frac{3}{5}$.

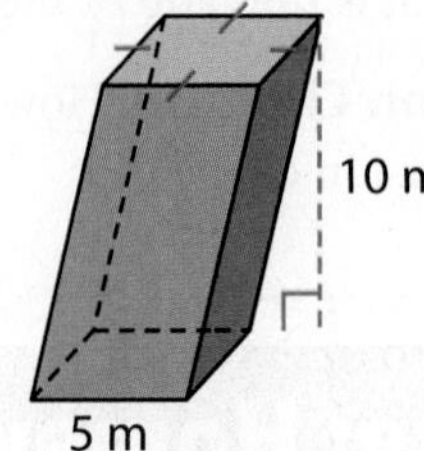

13. For each change, state whether the change is non-proportional or proportional.

    A. The height of a triangle is doubled.

    B. All sides of a square are quadrupled.

    C. The length of a rectangle is multiplied by $\frac{3}{4}$.

    D. The height of a triangular prism is tripled.

    E. The radius of a sphere is multiplied by $\sqrt{5}$.

14. Tina and Kleu built rectangular play areas for their dogs. The play area for Tina's dog is 1.5 times as long and 1.5 times as wide as the play area for Kleu's dog. If the play area for Kleu's dog is 60 square feet, how big is the play area for Tina's dog?

15. A map has the scale 1 inch = 10 miles. On the map, the area of Big Bend National Park in Texas is about 12.5 square inches. Estimate the actual area of the park in acres. (*Hint:* 1 square mile = 640 acres)

16. A restaurant has a weekly ad in a local newspaper that is 2 inches wide and 4 inches high and costs $36.75 per week. The cost of each ad is based on its area. If the owner of the restaurant decided to double the width and height of the ad, how much will the new ad cost?

17. Suppose the dimensions of a triangle with a perimeter of 18 inches are doubled. Find the perimeter of the new triangle in inches.

A rectangular prism has vertices (0, 0, 0), (0, 3, 0), (7, 0, 0), (7, 3, 0), (0, 0, 6), (0, 3, 6), (7, 0, 6) and (7, 3, 6).

18. Suppose all the dimensions are tripled. Find the new vertices.

19. Find the effect of the change on the volume of the prism.

20. How would the effect of the change be different if only the height had been tripled?

21. **Analyze Relationships** How could you change the dimensions of a parallelogram to increase the area by a factor of 5 if the parallelogram does not have to be similar to the original parallelogram? if the parallelogram does have to be similar to the original parallelogram?

H.O.T. Focus on Higher Order Thinking

22. **Algebra** A square has a side length of $(2x + 5)$ cm.

 a. If the side length is mulitplied by 5, what is the area of the new square?

 b. Use your answer to part (a) to find the area of the original square without using the area formula. Justify your answer.

23. **Algebra** A circle has a diameter of 6 in. If the circumference is multiplied by $(x + 3)$, what is the area of the new circle? Justify your answer.

24. **Communicate Mathematical Ideas** The dimensions of a prism with volume V and surface area S are multiplied by a scale factor of k to form a similar prism. Make a conjecture about the ratio of the surface area of the new prism to its volume. Test your conjecture using a cube with an edge length of 1 and a scale factor of 2.

Lesson Performance Task

On a computer screen, lengths and widths are measured not in inches or millimeters but in **pixels**. A pixel is the smallest visual element that a computer is capable of processing. A common size for a large computer screen is 1024 × 768 pixels. (Widths rather than heights are conventionally listed first.) For the following, assume you're working on a 1024 × 768 screen.

1. You have a photo measuring 640 × 300 pixels and you want to enlarge it proportionally so that it is as wide as the computer screen. Find the measurements of the photo after it has been scaled up. Explain how you found the answer.

1024 pixels

768 pixels

2. a. Explain why you can't enlarge the photo proportionally so that it is as tall as the computer screen.

   b. Why can't you correct the difficulty in (a) by scaling the width of the photo by a factor of $1024 \div 640$ and the height by a factor of $768 \div 300$?

3. You have some square photos and you would like to fill the screen with them, so there is no overlap and there are no gaps between photos. Find the dimensions of the largest such photos you can use (all of them the same size), and find the number of photos. Explain your reasoning.

20.2 Modeling and Density

Essential Question: How can you model real-world situations involving density?

Resource Locker

Explore Comparing Density

Density is the amount of matter that an object has in a given unit of volume. The density of an object is calculated by dividing its mass by its volume.

$$\text{density} = \frac{\text{mass}}{\text{volume}}$$

Density can be used to help distinguish between similar materials, like identifying different types of wood.

Data about two approximately cylindrical wood logs is shown in the table. Determine which wood is denser.

Type of wood	Diameter (cm)	Height (cm)	Mass (kg)
Douglas fir	6	17	254
American redwood	8	12	271

(A) Make a prediction, based on the data but without calculating, about which wood is denser. Describe your reasoning

(B) Determine the volume of each log.

(C) Determine the density of each log. Identify the denser wood.

Reflect

1. What do your results tell you about the two types of wood?

Explain 1 Calculating a Population Density

You can define density in other situations that involve area or volume besides mass per unit volume. For example, the population density of a region, or the population per unit area, can be found by using the density formula.

Example 1 **Find the approximate population density.**

(A) Burlington, Vermont has an area of about 160 km² and a population of 109,000 people. What is the approximate population density of Burlington?

$$\text{Population density} = \frac{\text{population}}{\text{area}} = \frac{109{,}000}{160} \approx 681 \text{ persons/km}^2$$

(B) The state of Vermont has a population of 626,000. Vermont's territory can be modeled as a trapezoid, as shown in the figure. Each unit on the coordinate grid represents one mile. Find the approximate population density of Vermont.

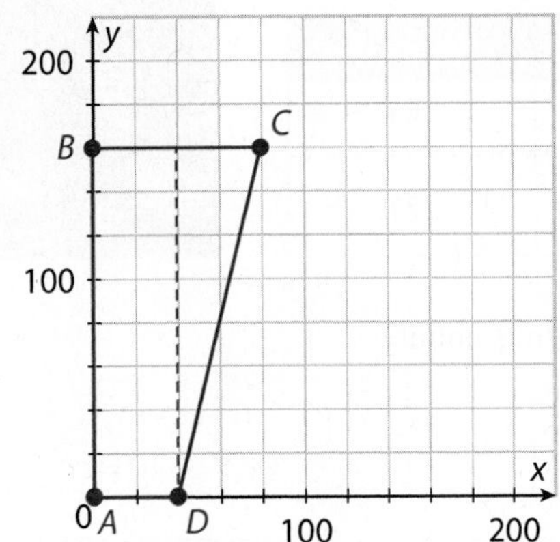

$$\text{Area} = \frac{1}{2}(b_1+b_2)h = \frac{1}{2}\left(40 + \boxed{80}\right)\left(\boxed{160}\right) = \boxed{9600} \text{ mi}^2$$

$$\text{Population density} = \frac{\text{population}}{\text{area}} = \frac{\boxed{626{,}000}}{\boxed{9600}} \approx \boxed{65} \text{ persons/mi}^2$$

Reflect

2. **Discussion** The actual area of Vermont is 9,620 mi². Is your approximation an overestimate or underestimate? Explain.

3. How would the population density of Vermont change if its given population doubled by 2100? Why?

4. **Critique Reasoning** Marya claims that Burlington is about 10 times more densely populated than the state average. Is she correct? Explain your reasoning.

Your Turn

5. Chicago has a population of about 2,715,000. Its territory can be modeled as a parallelogram, as shown in the figure. Each unit on the coordinate grid represents one mile. Find the approximate population density of Chicago.

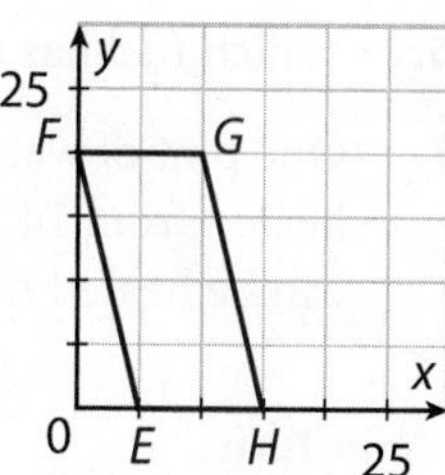

Explain 2 Calculating Measures of Energy

A British thermal unit (BTU), a unit of energy, is approximately the amount of energy needed to increase the temperature of one pound of water by one degree Fahrenheit. The energy content of a fuel may be measured in BTUs per unit of volume.

Example 2 **A spherical tank is filled with a gas and it has the dimensions shown. Find the number of BTUs produced by one cubic foot of the gas. Round to the nearest BTU.**

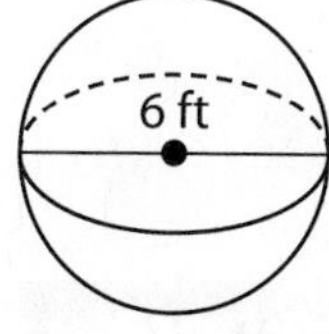

(A) When the tank is filled with natural gas, it provides 116,151 BTUs.

Find the volume of the spherical tank.

$r = \frac{1}{2}(6 \text{ ft}) = 3 \text{ ft}$

$V = \frac{4}{3}\pi r^3 = \frac{4}{3}\pi(3)^3 = 36\pi \text{ ft}^3$

Divide to find the number of BTUs in one cubic foot of natural gas.

$\frac{\text{BTUs}}{1 \text{ ft}^3} = \frac{\text{BTUs in tank}}{\text{volume of tank}}$

$= \frac{116{,}151 \text{ BTUs}}{36\pi \text{ ft}^3}$

$\approx 1{,}027 \text{ BTUs}$

(B) When the tank is filled with kerosene, it provides about 114,206,000 BTUs.

The volume of the tank is 36π ft³.

$\frac{\text{BTUs}}{1 \text{ ft}^3} = \frac{\text{BTUs in tank}}{\text{volume of tank}}$

$= \frac{\boxed{114{,}206{,}000} \text{ BTUs}}{\boxed{36\pi} \text{ ft}^3}$

$\approx \boxed{1{,}009{,}803} \text{ BTUs}$

Reflect

6. Which fuel has a higher energy density?
7. One pint of water weighs approximately one pound. How many pints of water can be heated from 74°F to 75°F by one cubic foot of natural gas? How many pints of water can be heated from 75°F to 85°F by one cubic foot of natural gas?

Your Turn

8. A cylindrical tank has the dimensions shown. How many BTUs will the tank provide when filled with natural gas?

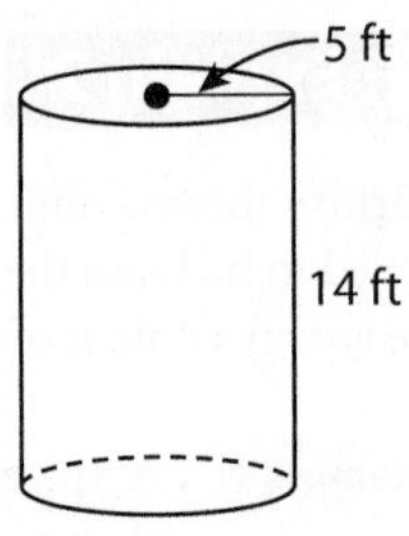

Elaborate

9. Pressure is defined in terms of force per unit area. Is pressure an example of a density?
10. **Essential Question Check-In** Describe the general concept of *density* and give two real-world examples.

Personal Math Trainer

- Online Homework
- Hints and Help
- Extra Practice

Evaluate: Homework and Practice

Determine which is denser.

1. Cylindrical logs of wood

Type of wood	Diameter (ft)	Height (ft)	Mass (lb)
Aspen	3.6	4.5	1,195
Juniper	3.0	6.0	1,487

2. Cylindrical bars of alloy

Alloy	Radius (cm)	Height (cm)	Mass (g)
Nichrome	3.9	27.2	10,800
Mild steel	4.6	18.8	9,840

3. Spherical tanks of liquefied gases

Liquefied Gas	Radius (m)	Mass (kg)
Oxygen (O_2), at −186°C	0.8	2477
Hydrogen (H_2), at −256°C	1.2	514

4. Colorado has a population of 5,268,367. Its territory can be modeled by a rectangle approximately 280 mi by 380 mi. Find the approximate population density of Colorado.

5. Tennessee has a population of 6,495,978. Its territory can be modeled by a trapezoid, as shown in the figure. Each unit on the coordinate grid represents one mile. Find the approximate population density of Tennessee.

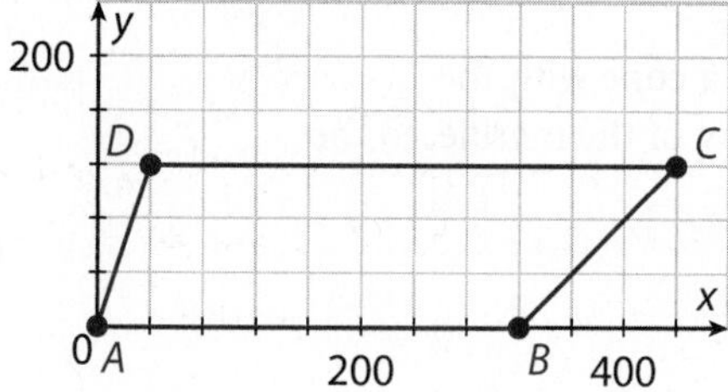

6. New Hampshire has a population of 1,323,459. Its territory can be modeled by a triangle, as shown in the figure. Each unit on the coordinate grid represents one mile. Find the approximate population density of New Hampshire.

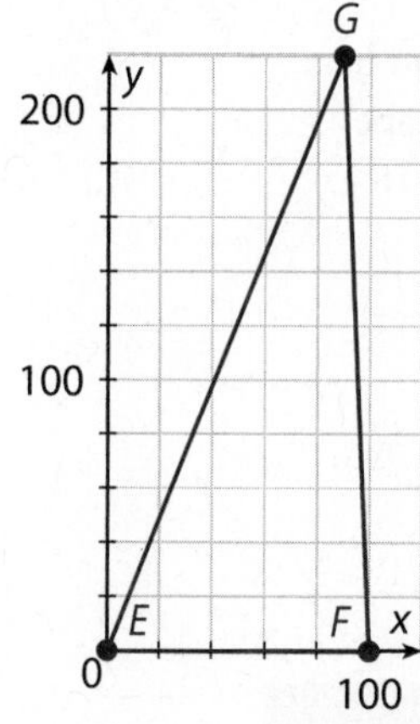

7. A spherical gas tank has a 10 foot diameter. When filled with propane, it provides 358,000,000 BTUs. How many BTUs does 1 cubic foot of propane yield? Round to the nearest thousand.

8. Ethan has collected information about the energy content of various fuels. Order the fuels by their energy density from greatest to least. (1 barrel = 42 gallons; 1 gallon = 8 pints)

Fuel	Heat Content
Jet fuel	5,670,000 BTUs/barrel
Gasoline	160,937 BTUs/gallon
Home fuel	138,690 BTUs/gallon
Propane	11,417 BTUs/pint

9. A fuel tank has a volume of 32 gallons. When filled with biodiesel, it provides 4,000,000 BTUs. How many BTUs does 1 gallon of biodiesel yield?

10. A piece of marble has been machine-carved into the shape of a cone with the dimensions shown. It has a mass of 169 kg. What is the density of the marble, to the nearest kilogram per cubic meter?

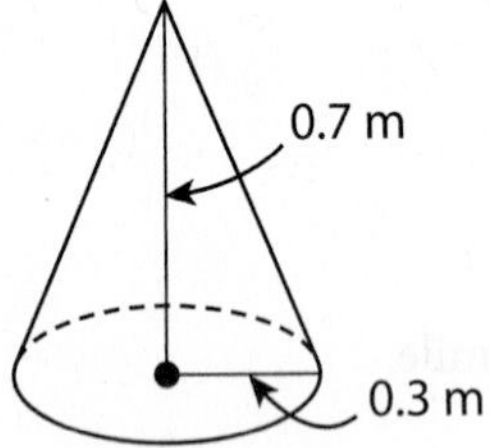

11. **Metallurgy** The purity of gold is measured in carats. 24-carat gold is pure gold, and has a density of 19.3 g/cm^3. 18-carat gold is often used for jewelry because it holds its shape better than pure gold. An 18-carat gold ring, which is 75% pure gold, has a mass of 18 g. What volume of pure gold was used to make the ring, to the nearest hundredth?

12. **Agriculture** The maximum grain yield for corn is achieved by planting at a density of 38,000 plants per acre. A farmer wants to maximize the yield for the field represented on the coordinate grid. Each unit on the coordinate grid represents one foot. How many corn plants, to the nearest thousand, does the farmer need? (*Hint:* 1 acre = 43,560 ft^2)

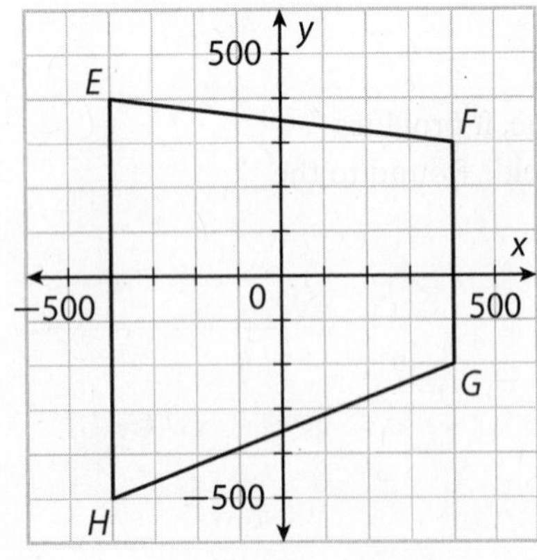

13. The density of water at 4°C is 1000 kg/m^3. A cubic meter of water, when frozen to −20°C, has a volume of 1.0065 m^3. What is the density of ice at this temperature, to the nearest tenth?

14. Space A launch vehicle is designed to carry up to 35 tons of payload into orbit. When fully fueled, it will contain 1,216,000 kg of liquid oxygen (LO_2) at a density of 1155 kg/m^3 and 102,000 kg of liquid hydrogen (LH_2) at a density of 71 kg/m^3. What is the total volume of liquefied gases carried by the launch vehicle, to the nearest tenth?

15. Manila, Philippines, has one of the highest population densities in the world with 111,002 people/mi^2. Manila's total population is 1,652,171. How large is Manilla, to the nearest tenth of a square mile?

16. Multistep A building has apartments on 67 floors and each floor measures 110 feet by 85 feet. Currently, 2340 people live in the building. Find the population density of the building to the nearest person per square mile, in terms of the area occupied by the building at street level. Also find the population density of the building in terms of its total floor area. (*Hint*: 1 mi^2 = 27,878,400 ft^2)

17. The caloric density of foods is a useful tool when comparing calorie counts. The table shows typical serving sizes for several foods and the number of calories per serving. Complete the fourth column, rounding to the nearest calorie per 100 grams. Then rank the foods from the lowest caloric density to the highest.

Food	Grams (g)	Calories (Cal)	Cal per 100 g
1 cubic inch cheddar cheese	17	69	
1 large hard boiled egg	50	78	
1 medium apple	138	72	
1.5 ounces raisins	43	129	

H.O.T. Focus on Higher Order Thinking

18. Analyze Relationships The graph shows the relationship between mass and volume for pure silver. Use the graph to determine the density of pure silver to the nearest tenth and explain your method.

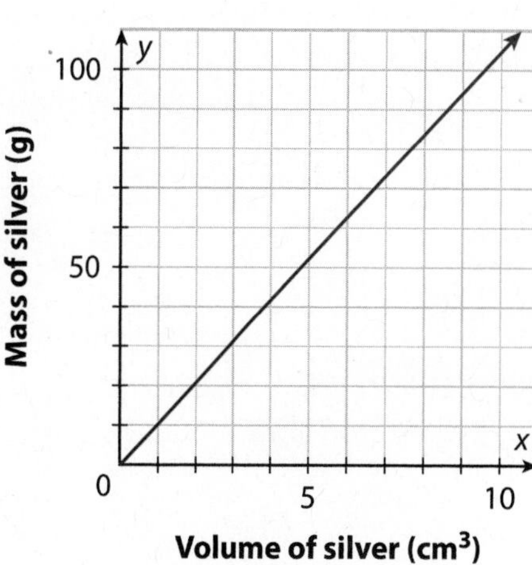

19. Communicate Mathematical Ideas According to Archimedes' Principle, an object placed in water will experience an upward force equal to the weight of water the object displaces. It is this upward force that causes objects less dense than water to float. For example, a cork floats when it is displacing a weight of water exactly equal to its own weight. When placed in water, what percent of a cork's volume will remain above the surface? Explain your answer.

	Density
Cork	0.24 g/cm^3
Water	1.00 g/cm^3

Lesson Performance Task

A regular pyramid made of pure gold with the dimensions shown has a mass of 160.5 grams. Find the density of gold. Round to the nearest tenth. If the dimensions of the pyramid doubled, what would change about the mass and density?

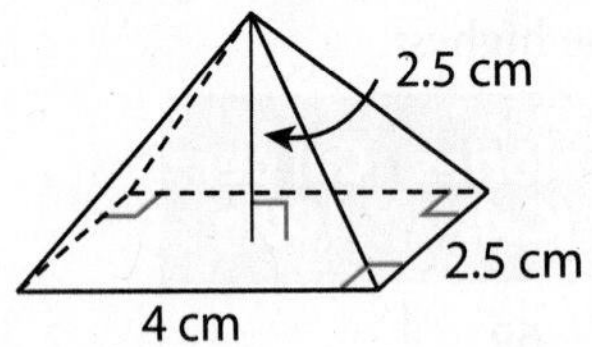

20.3 Problem Solving with Constraints

Essential Question: How can you model situations to meet real-world constraints?

Explore Maximizing Volume

Real-world problems often involve constraints. For example, for a given surface area, a sphere maximizes volume, but this is not usually the best shape for a package design.

Suppose you want to build a storage box from a rectangular piece of plywood that measures 4 ft by 8 ft. You must use six pieces, for the top, bottom, and sides of the box, and you can only make cuts perpendicular to the edges of the plywood. Given these constraints, what design appears to give the maximum possible volume for the box?

(A) Consider the top, bottom, front, and back of the box. Which dimensions must these rectangular pieces have in common?

(B) Sketch two possible sets of cuts of the plywood. You do not have to use all the plywood in your design. Label your sketch with all the dimension information you have, using variable expressions if necessary.

(C) Calculate the volume of the resulting box for each of your designs.

(D) Which design is better? Do you think one of your designs provides the greatest possible volume given the constraints of the problem?

Reflect

1. How effective is this design in maximizing the volume? Explain.
2. **Discussion** Compare results with others in your class. What seems to be a good strategy?

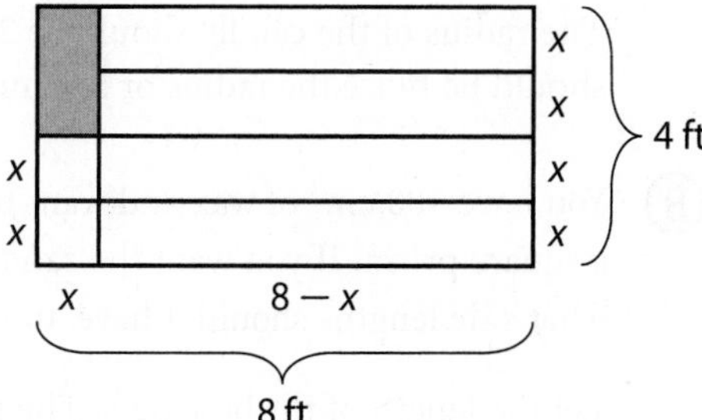

Explain 1 Determining Dimensions Given a Volume

Volume formulas are useful for solving problems where the constraint is to use a given volume of material for a given shape. For instance, suppose you want to make a cylindrical candle using a given amount of wax. You can use the formula for the volume of a cylinder to determine the candle's dimensions.

Example 1 **Determine the necessary dimensions.**

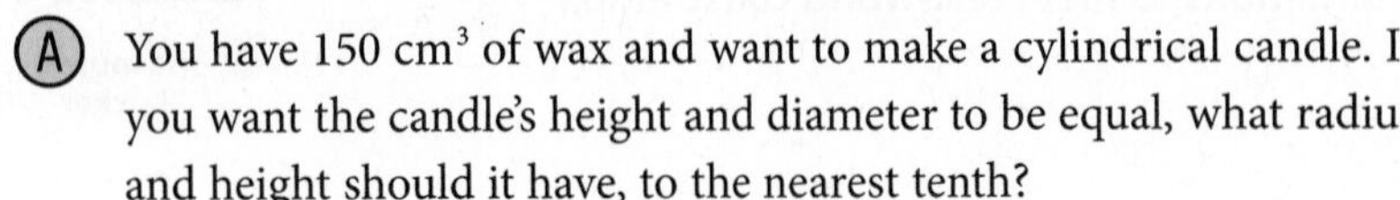

(A) You have 150 cm^3 of wax and want to make a cylindrical candle. If you want the candle's height and diameter to be equal, what radius and height should it have, to the nearest tenth?

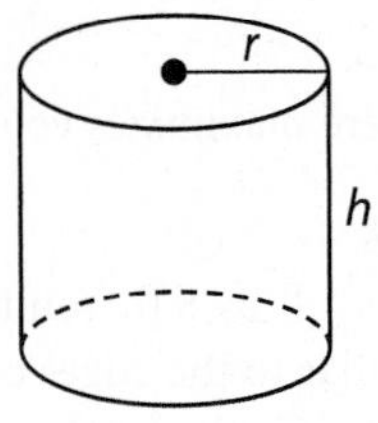

The diameter of the candle is $2r$. The height is equal to the diameter, so $h = 2r$.

The candle's volume is:	$V = \pi r^2 h$
Substitute $2r$ for h:	$V = \pi r^2(2r)$
Simplify:	$V = 2\pi r^3$
Substitute the given volume of wax:	$150 = 2\pi r^3$
Solve for r^3.	$r^3 = \frac{150}{2\pi} \approx 23.9$

Use a graphing calculator to graph each side of the equation as a separate function.

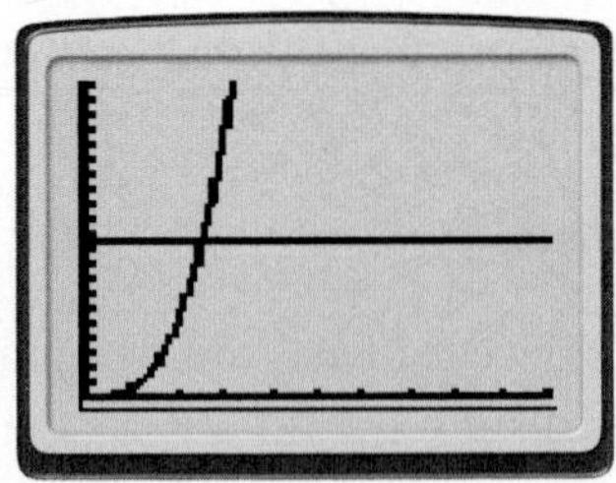

Graph $y = r^3$ and $y = 23.9$. The coordinates of the intersection are $(2.879..., 23.9)$.

The radius of the candle should be 2.9 cm. The height of the candle should be twice the radius or 5.8 cm.

(B) You have 300 cm^3 of wax and want to make a candle in the shape of a square prism. If you want the candle to be twice as tall as it is wide, what side lengths should it have, to the nearest tenth?

Let the length of the base be b. The height h is twice the base or $2b$.

The candle's volume is:	$V = b^2 h$
Substitute $2b$ for h:	$V = b^2(2b)$
Simplify:	$V = 2b^3$
Substitute the given volume of wax:	$300 = 2b^3$
Solve for b^3.	$b^3 = 150$

Graph $y = b^3$ and $y = 150$. The coordinates of the intersection are (5.31, 150).

The side lengths of the square base of the candle should be 5.3 cm. The height of the candle should be twice the base or 10.6 cm.

Reflect

3. How can you check that your answer to Example 1B is reasonable?

Your Turn

4. You want to make a conical candle using 15 in^3 of wax. If the candle's height is twice its diameter, what radius and height should it have, to the nearest tenth?

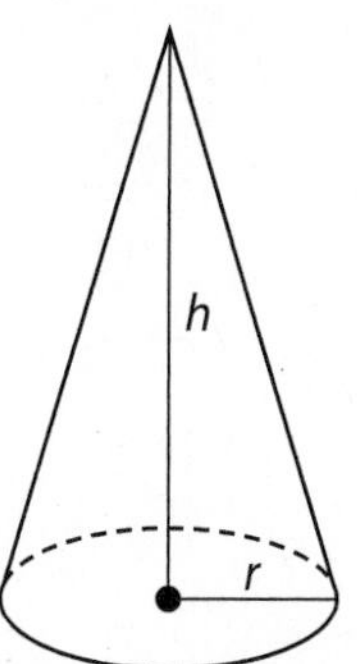

5. You have an octagonal candle mold that has a base that is three inches across and has side length 1.2 inches. If you use this mold to make a candle using 50 in^3 of wax, how tall will the candle be?

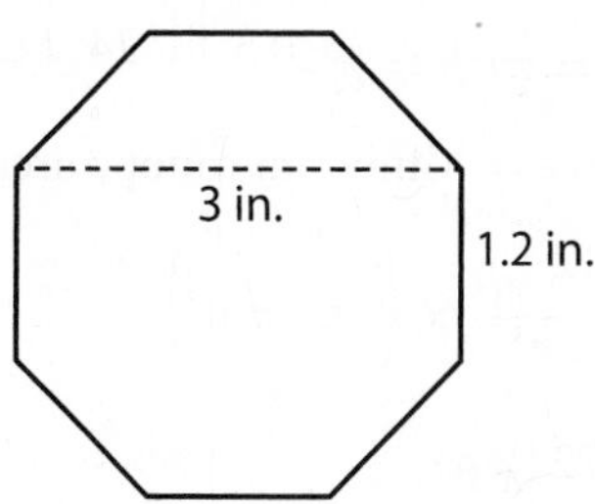

Explain 2 Modeling to Meet Constraints

A full-grown tree needs to have a minimum size canopy to photosynthesize enough sugar to feed the tree's bulk. This constraint can be modeled by relating the tree's canopy surface area to the volume of its trunk. By making some simplifying assumptions, you can explore this relationship.

Example 2 **What is the minimum radius for the described tree, to the nearest foot?**

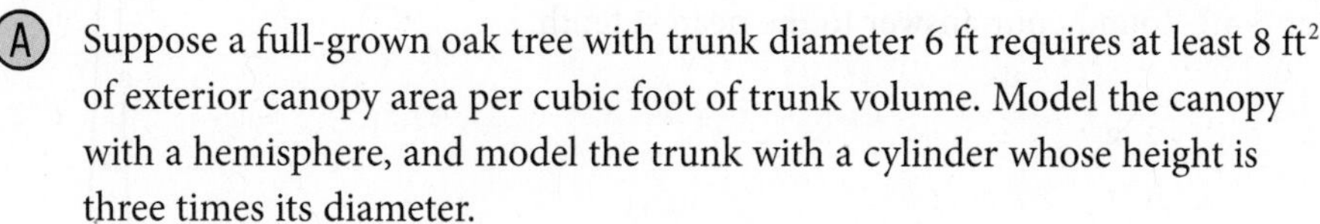

(A) Suppose a full-grown oak tree with trunk diameter 6 ft requires at least 8 ft^2 of exterior canopy area per cubic foot of trunk volume. Model the canopy with a hemisphere, and model the trunk with a cylinder whose height is three times its diameter.

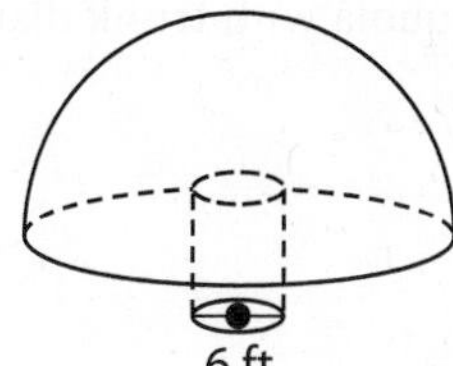

Find the volume of the trunk.

Radius of trunk $= \frac{1}{2}(6 \text{ ft}) = 3$ ft   Height of trunk $= 3(6 \text{ ft}) = 18$ ft

Volume of trunk $= \pi r^2 h = \pi(3)^2(18) = 162\pi$ ft^3

Find the minimum exterior canopy area for this size of trunk.

Minimum exterior canopy area $= \frac{8 \text{ ft}^2}{1 \text{ ft}^3} \times \left(162\pi \text{ ft}^3\right) = 1{,}296\pi$ ft^2

Write an expression for the curved surface area of a hemisphere with radius r.

Surface area $= \frac{1}{2}(4\pi r^2) = 2\pi r^2$

Write an equation that shows the relation between the surface area and the canopy area.

Surface area = Minimum canopy area

$$2\pi r^2 = 1{,}296\pi$$

$$r^2 = \frac{1{,}296\pi}{2\pi} = 648 \qquad r = \sqrt{648} \approx 25\text{ft}$$

The minimum radius of canopy required for this oak tree is 25 feet.

Ⓑ Suppose a growing oak tree with trunk diameter 12 inches requires at least 12 ft² of exterior canopy area per cubic foot of trunk volume. Model the canopy with a hemisphere, and model the trunk with a cylinder whose height is 24 times its diameter.

radius of trunk = $\boxed{0.5}$ ft height of trunk = $\boxed{24(1\text{ ft}) = 24\text{ ft}}$

Volume of trunk $= \pi r^2 h = \pi\left(\boxed{0.5}\right)^2\left(\boxed{24}\right) = \boxed{6}\ \pi\text{ ft}^3$

Curved surface area = Minimum canopy area

$$\frac{1}{2}(4\pi r^2) = \frac{\boxed{12}\text{ ft}^2}{1\text{ ft}^3} \times \left(\boxed{6}\ \pi\text{ ft}^3\right)$$

$$2\pi r^2 = \boxed{72}\ \pi\text{ ft}^2$$

$$r^2 = \frac{\boxed{72\pi\text{ ft}^2}}{\boxed{2\pi}} = \boxed{36} \qquad r = \boxed{\sqrt{36}} = \boxed{6\text{ ft}}$$

The minimum radius of canopy required for this oak tree is 6 feet.

Reflect

6. **Discussion** How could you use this model to make decisions about planting trees?

Your Turn

7. Assume a mature sequoia tree requires at least 0.6 m² of exterior canopy area per cubic meter of trunk volume. Also assume that the canopy can be modeled by a cone whose slant height is 4 times its radius, and that the trunk of the tree can be modeled by a cone whose height is 12 times its diameter. The formula for the lateral surface area of a cone is $A = \pi(\text{radius})(\text{slant height})$. What is the minimum base radius of canopy required for a sequoia with trunk diameter 5 m? Round your answer to the nearest tenth.

Elaborate

8. What is the role of a constraint in solving a real-world problem?

9. **Essential Question Check-In** How can you model situations to meet real-world constraints?

Evaluate: Homework and Practice

Personal Math Trainer

- Online Homework
- Hints and Help
- Extra Practice

Find the volume of each design for a box built from a piece of plywood measuring 60 cm by 180 cm.

1.

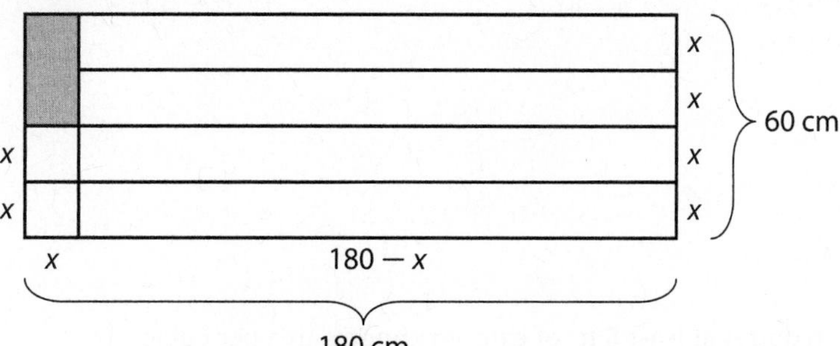

2.

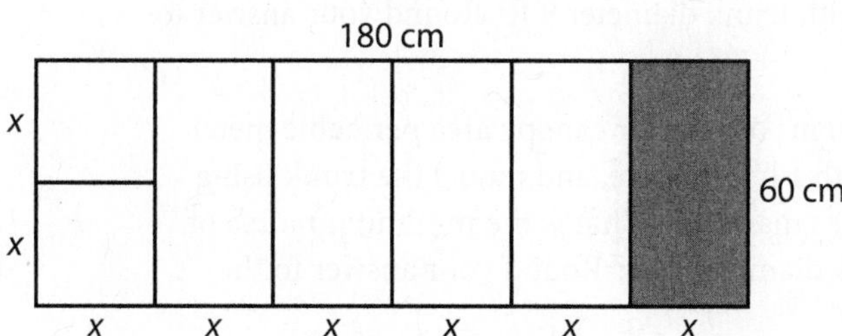

3.

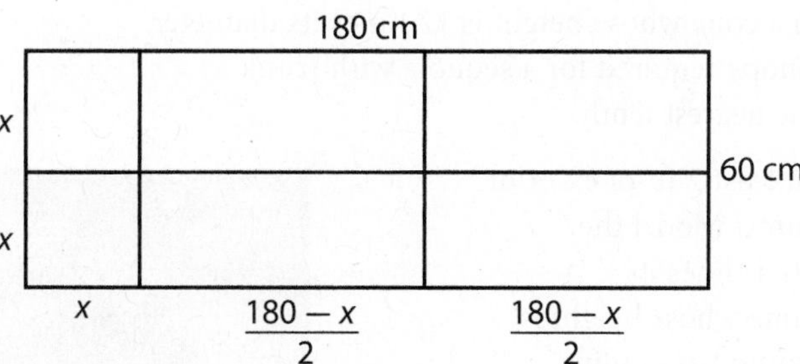

4.

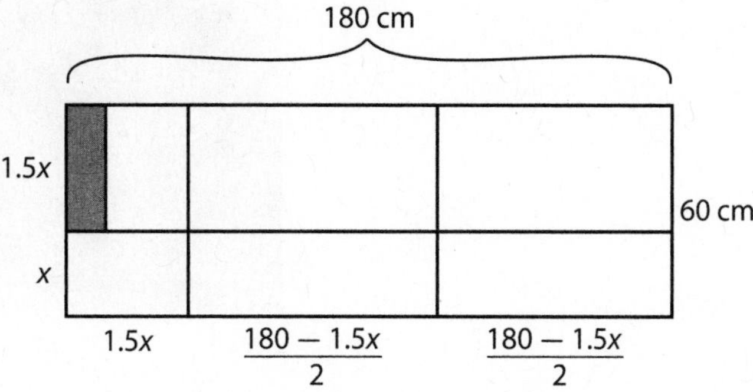

5. A cylindrical candle is to be made from 18 in^3 of wax. If the candle's height is twice its diameter, what radius and height should it have, to the nearest tenth?

6. A conical candle is to be made from 240 cm^3 of wax. If the candle's height is three times its diameter, what radius and height should it have, to the nearest tenth?

7. The design specifications for a coffee mug state that it should be cylindrical, with height 1.5 times its diameter, and with a capacity of 450 mL when filled to the brim. What interior radius and height should the coffee mug have, to the nearest tenth of a centimeter? (*Hint:* 1 mL = 1 cm^3)

8. A bob for a pendulum clock will be a cone of equal height and diameter, made from 3 in^3 of metal. What radius and height should the bob have, to the nearest tenth?

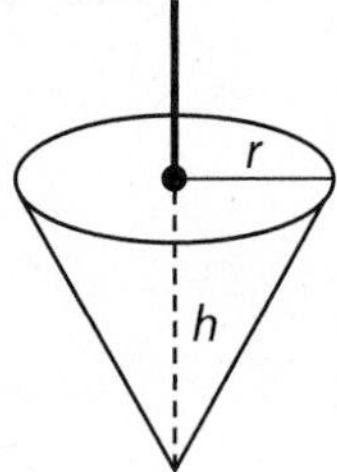

9. Assume a full-grown oak tree requires at least 8 ft^2 of exterior canopy area per cubic foot of trunk volume. Model the canopy with a hemisphere, and model the trunk using a cylinder whose height is three times its diameter. What is the minimum radius of canopy required for an oak with trunk diameter 9 ft? Round your answer to the nearest foot.

10. A mature beech tree requires at least 20 m^2 of exterior canopy area per cubic meter of trunk volume. Model the canopy with a hemisphere, and model the trunk using a cylinder whose height is three times its diameter. What is the minimum radius of canopy required for a beech with trunk diameter 2 m? Round your answer to the nearest foot.

11. Assume a mature sequoia tree requires at least 0.6 m^2 of exterior canopy area per cubic meter of trunk volume. Model the canopy with a cone whose slant height is 4 times its radius. Model the trunk with a cone whose height is 12 times its diameter. What is the minimum base radius of canopy required for a sequoia with trunk diameter 8 m? Round your answer to the nearest tenth.

12. Assume a mature Douglas fir requires at least 2 ft^2 of exterior canopy area per cubic foot of trunk volume. Model the canopy with a cone whose slant height is 4 times its diameter, and model the trunk with a cone whose height is 12 times its diameter. What is the minimum base radius of canopy required for a Douglas fir with trunk diameter 4 ft? Round your answer to the nearest tenth.

13. None of the designs in Questions 1–4 actually maximize the volume of a box made from a 60 cm by 180 cm plywood sheet. Find a design that does maximize the volume. (*Hint:* Use two variables, x and y, for the dimensions of the two side pieces.)

14. Jack is planning to build an aquarium in the shape of a rectangular prism. He wants the base to measure 90 cm by 40 cm. The maximum safe weight this type of aquarium can support is 150 kg. Given that the density of water is 0.001 kg/cm^3 and that Jack estimates he will have 5 kg of rocks, sand, and fish to put in the aquarium, what is the aquarium's maximum height, to the nearest centimeter?

15. Rita is making a box from a 2 ft by 5 ft piece of plywood. The box does not need a top, so only five pieces are needed. Suggest two designs to maximize the volume of the box. Check your designs by calculating the volume.

16. **Multi-step** A propane tank is designed in the shape of a cylinder with two hemispherical ends. The cylinder's height is twice its diameter, and the tank's capacity is 1,000 gal. What is the radius of the tank, to the nearest tenth of a foot? (*Hint:* 1 ft^3 = 7.48 gal)

17. A cylindrical space station is 5 m in diameter and 12 m long, and it requires 0.2 m^2 of solar panels per cubic meter of volume to provide power. If it has two sets of rectangular solar panels, each 2 m wide, how long should each set of panels be? Round your answer to the nearest tenth.

18. Create a design to make a cylinder, including both circular ends, from a sheet of metal that measures 150 cm by 60 cm. Calculate the volume of your design, to the nearest thousand cubic centimeters.

19. A roll of aluminum foil is 15 in. wide. It has an interior diameter of 1.2 in. and an exterior diameter of 1.6 in. If the foil is 0.001 in. thick, what length of foil is rolled up, to the nearest foot? (*Hint:* Start by finding the volume of a 1-ft length of foil 15 in. wide.)

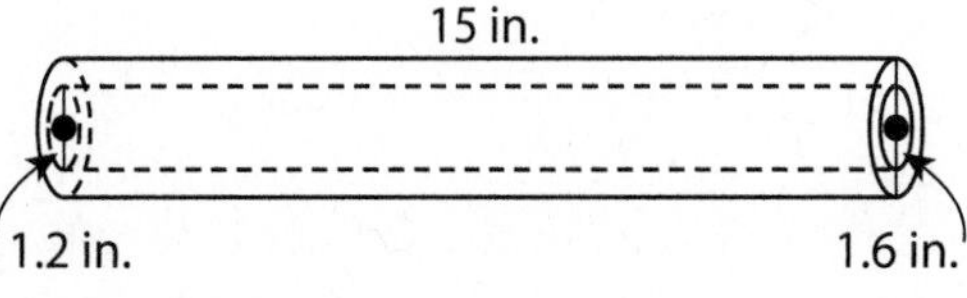

20. Assume a full-grown oak tree requires at least 8 ft^2 of exterior canopy area per cubic foot of trunk volume. Model the canopy with a hemisphere. Model the trunk with a cylinder whose height is three times its diameter. Develop a formula for the minimum radius R of canopy required for an oak with trunk radius r, in feet.

H.O.T. Focus on Higher Order Thinking

21. What If? An animal's weight is proportional to its volume. The strength in its legs to support its weight is proportional to their cross-sectional area. Imagine magnifying a mouse to the size of an elephant. If its length is multiplied by 50, and its density and proportions stay the same, what are the multipliers for its weight and the cross-sectional areas for its legs? Would a mouse this size be able to support itself?

22. Multi-step A stopper will be the shape of the frustum of a cone. The height of the complete cone would be 8 times its base diameter, but the stopper's height is to be only twice the larger base diameter. The stopper is to be made from 10 cm^3 of silicone. What should the stopper's base radius R, base radius r, and height be, to the nearest tenth?

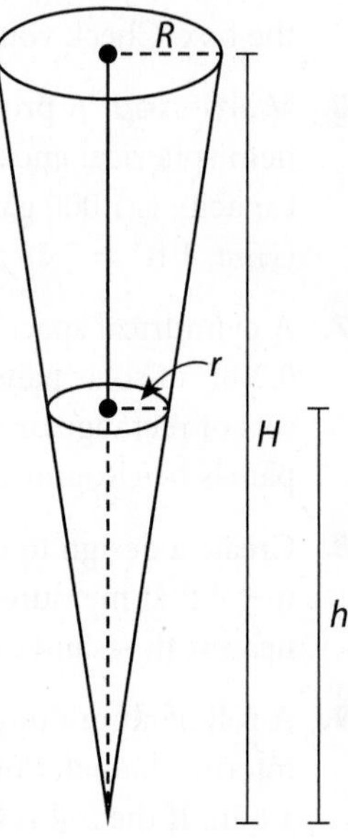

23. Look for a Pattern An aluminum soda can holds 12 fl oz. Investigate the least amount of aluminum needed to make the can: Use the given volume to find a formula for the can's height h in terms of its radius r, substitute into a formula for the can's surface area, and use trial values to determine the values of r and h, to the nearest tenth of an inch, that minimize the can's surface area. (*Hint*: 1 fl oz = 1.73 in^3)

24. Persevere in Problem Solving People have a wide variety of body plans, from endomorphic (short and stocky) to ectormorphic (tall and slender). These body plans represent adaptations to cold or hot climates from earlier in human history. A higher surface area to volume ratio allows body heat to be shed more easily in a hot climate, while a lower ratio helps to retain body heat in very cold conditions. Complete the table. Find the ratio of surface area to volume for each body plan. How much greater is the ratio for the ectomorphic body plan than for the endomorphic one? (For each cylindrical form, count only one circular base in addition to the curved surface.)

Endomorphic body plan			
Part of Body	**Form and Dimensions**	**Volume**	**Exterior Surface Area**
Head	sphere, $d = 6$ in.		
Torso	cylinder, $d = 15$ in., $h = 30$ in.		
Arms	cylinder, $d = 3$ in., $h = 24$ in.		
Legs	cylinder, $d = 6$ in., $h = 28$ in.		
Whole body			

Ectomorphic body plan			
Part of Body	**Form and Dimensions**	**Volume**	**Exterior Surface Area**
Head	sphere, $d = 6$ in.		
Torso	cylinder, $d = 10$ in., $h = 32$ in.		
Arms	cylinder, $d = 2$ in., $h = 34$ in.		
Legs	cylinder, $d = 4$ in., $h = 36$ in.		
Whole body			

Lesson Performance Task

In trying to disguise a gift, Henry decides to put a box of blocks into a cylindrical box. The set of blocks is a cube that measures 4 inches on each side. About how much extra wrapping paper will Henry use as a result of this decision?

Modeling and Problem Solving

Essential Question: How can you use modeling to solve real-world problems?

Key Vocabulary
density *(densidad)*
scale factor *(factor de escala)*

KEY EXAMPLE *(Lesson 20.1)*

Find the surface area and volume of a rectangular prism-shaped box measuring 6 inches by 8 inches by 12 inches. Then multiply the dimensions by 2 and find the new surface area and volume. Describe the changes that took place.

$2(6 \times 8) + 2(6 \times 12) + 2(8 \times 12) = 96 + 144 + 192$
$= 432 \text{ in}^2$ — Find the original surface area.

$6 \times 8 \times 12 = 576 \text{ in}^3$ — Find the original volume.

$2(12 \times 16) + 2(12 \times 24) + 2(16 \times 24) = 384 + 576 + 768$
$= 1{,}728 \text{ in}^2$ — Find the new surface area.

$12 \times 16 \times 24 = 4608 \text{ in}^3$ — Find the new volume

$\frac{1728}{432} = 4$ Compare the surface areas. $\frac{4608}{576} = 8$ Compare the volumes.

The surface area is multiplied by 4. The volume is multiplied by 8.

KEY EXAMPLE *(Lesson 20.2)*

Logan County, Kansas, has a population of 2,784. Its border can be modeled by a rectangle with vertices $A(-18, 15)$, $B(18, 15)$, $C(18, -15)$, and $D(-18, -15)$, where each unit on the coordinate plane represents 1 mile. Find the approximate population density of Logan County. Round to the nearest tenth.

$18 - (-18) = 36$ mi — The width of Logan County is the difference of the *x*-coordinates.

$15 - (-15) = 30$ mi — The height of Logan County is the difference of the *y*-coordinates.

$36 \times 30 = 1080 \text{ mi}^2$ — area = length × width

$\frac{2784}{1080} \approx 2.6$ — Population density $= \frac{\text{population}}{\text{area}}$

The population density is about 2.6 persons per square mile.

KEY EXAMPLE *(Lesson 20.3)*

The height of a filing cabinet is 1.5 times the width. The depth is twice the width. The volume of the cabinet is 12,288 in³. What are the cabinet's dimensions?

$\text{Volume} = l \times w \times h$ — Write the formula for the volume.

$12{,}288 = x \times 1.5x \times 2x$ — Substitute for the volume, width, height, and depth.

$x = \sqrt[3]{4096}$ — Simplify.

$x = 16$ — Evaluate the cube root.

Width: 16 inches. Height: $1.5 \times 16 = 24$ inches. Depth: $2 \times 16 = 32$ inches.

EXERCISES

1. One side of a rhombus measures 12 inches. Two angles measure 60°. Find the perimeter and area of the rhombus. Then multiply the side lengths by 3. Find the new perimeter and area. Describe the changes that took place. *(Lesson 20.1)*

2. A box of cereal measures 2.25 inches by 7.5 inches by 10 inches. The box contains 16 ounces of cereal. Find the cereal density, to the nearest thousandth. *(Lesson 20.2)*

3. The height and diameter of a cylindrical water tank are equal. The tank has a volume of 1200 cubic feet. Find the height of the tank to the nearest tenth. *(Lesson 20.3)*

MODULE PERFORMANCE TASK

Population Density

Unlike most geographical regions, the Canadian province of Saskatchewan has a shape that is almost exactly a regular geometric figure. That figure is an isosceles trapezoid. Here are the lengths of the province's four borders:

North: 277 miles South: 390 miles East: 761 miles West: 761 miles

- Saskatchewan's population in the 2011 census was 1,033,381. What was its population density?
- Saskatchewan is divided into 18 census divisions. Division 18, which makes up the northern half of the province (actually 49.3% of the area), has a population of 36,557. How does the population density of Division 18 compare with that of the southern half of the province?

Start by listing the information you will need to solve the problem. Then complete the task. Use numbers, words, or algebra to explain how you reached your conclusion.

Ready to Go On?

20.1–20.3 Modeling and Problem Solving

- Online Homework
- Hints and Help
- Extra Practice

Solve. Round answers to the nearest tenth. *(Lessons 20.1, 20.2, 20.3)*

1. A circle containing the point $(4, -2)$ has its center at $(1, 2)$. Describe the changes in the circumference and area of the circle if the radius is multiplied by 2.

2. Seven hundred people are gathered in a trapezoidal park with bases measuring 60 yards and 80 yards and a height of 50 yards.

a. Find the population density of the park.

b. Find the population density if the bases and height are halved.

3. An aquarium in the shape of a rectangular prism has a bottom, no top, two square sides, and two sides the same height as the square sides but twice their length. The total area of the five sides is 1800 in^2. Find the volume of the aquarium. Explain your reasoning.

4. A triangle has base b and height h. The base is doubled. Describe how the height must change so that the area remains the same. Explain your reasoning.

ESSENTIAL QUESTION

5. How can you use mathematics to model real-world situations?

MODULE 20
MIXED REVIEW

Assessment Readiness

1. The dimensions of a cube are tripled. Determine if each statement is True or False.

A. The perimeter of each face is tripled.

B. The surface area of the cube is multiplied by 6.

C. The volume of the cube is multiplied by 27.

2. A solid figure has a volume of 300 cubic centimeters. The radius and the height of the figure are equal. Write Yes or No for A–C.

A. The figure could be a cylinder with a radius of $\sqrt{\frac{300}{\pi}}$.

B. The figure could be a cone with a radius of $\sqrt[3]{\frac{900}{\pi}}$.

C. The figure could be a cylinder with a height of $\sqrt[3]{\frac{300}{\pi}}$.

3. A 4-square-mile community of prairie dogs in South Dakota has a total population of 12,000. Over a 3-year period, the total population increases at an average rate of 2% per year. Describe the change in the population density, assuming the total area of the community remains unchanged.

4. A city park in the shape of a right triangle has an area of $450\sqrt{3}$ square yards. One leg of the triangle measures half the length of the hypotenuse. What are the dimensions of the park? Explain your reasoning.

- Online Homework
- Hints and Help
- Extra Practice

1. Consider each congruence theorem below.
Can you use the theorem to determine whether $\triangle ABC \cong \triangle ABD$?

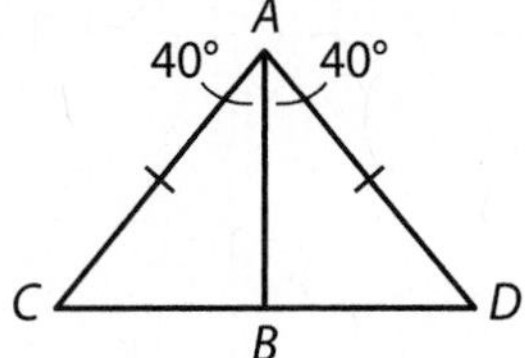

Write Yes or No for A–C.

A. ASA Triangle Congruence Theorem

B. SAS Triangle Congruence Theorem

C. SSS Triangle Congruence Theorem

2. For each pyramid, determine whether the statement regarding its volume is True or False.

A. A rectangular pyramid with $\ell = 3$ m, $w = 4$ m, $h = 7$ m has volume 84 m^3.

B. A triangular pyramid with base $B = 14$ ft^2 and $h = 5$ ft has volume 60 ft^2.

C. A pyramid with the same base and height of a prism has less volume.

3. For each shape, determine whether the statement regarding its volume is True or False.

A. A cone with base radius $r = 5$ in. and $h = 12$ in. has volume 100π in^3.

B. A sphere with radius $r = \frac{6}{\pi}$ m has volume $\frac{8}{\pi^2}$ m^3.

C. A sphere is composed of multiple cones with the same radius.

4. DeMarcus draws $\triangle ABC$. Then he translates it along the vector $\langle -4, -3 \rangle$, rotates it 180°, and reflects it across the x-axis.

Determine if each statement is True or False.

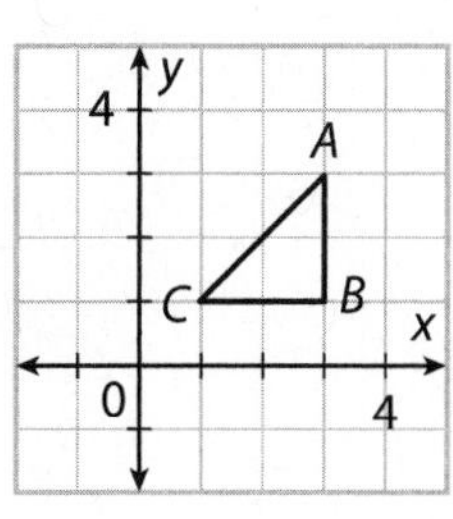

A. The final image of $\triangle ABC$ is in Quadrant IV.

B. The final image of $\triangle ABC$ is a right triangle.

C. DeMarcus will get the same result if he performs the reflection followed by the translation and rotation.

5. Determine whether each statement regarding surface area is True or False.

A. The surface area of a cone is the sum of the areas of a circle and sector of a circle.

B. The surface area of a sphere is greater than a cube's surface area with $s = r$.

C. A composite figure's surface area is the sum of each individual figure's surface area.

6. Can each of the shapes below be expressed as a composite figure of equilateral triangles? Write Yes or No for each shape.

A. A pyramid

B. A hexagon

C. A pentagon

7. The figure shows a composite figure formed by two right triangles, a square, and a circle. Determine whether the probability of throwing a dart into each shape is correct, assuming that the dart will always land in one of the shapes. Determine if each statement is True or False.

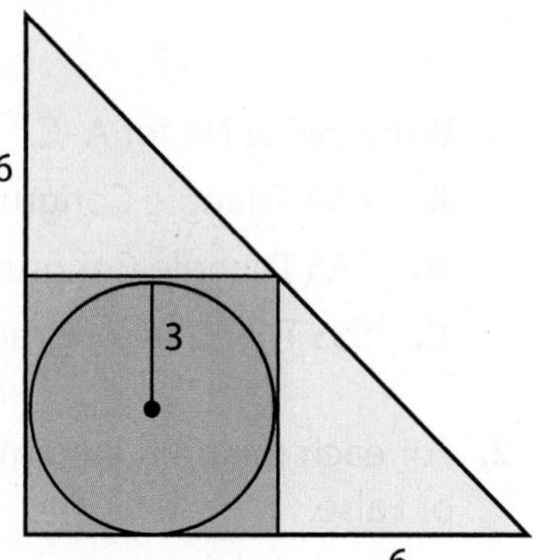

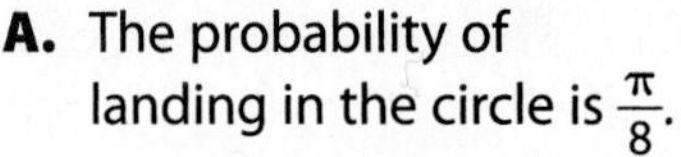

A. The probability of landing in the circle is $\frac{\pi}{8}$.

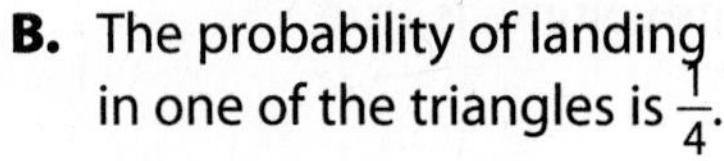

B. The probability of landing in one of the triangles is $\frac{1}{4}$.

C. The probability of landing in the square is $\frac{1}{2}$.

8. A cube is dilated by a factor of 4. By what factor does its volume increase? Explain your reasoning.

9. The perimeter of $\triangle PQR$ is 44 cm, and $\triangle PQR \sim \triangle WXY$. If $PQ = 12$ and $XY + WY = 24$, what is the perimeter of WXY?

Performance Tasks

★**10.** A scientist wants to compare the densities of two cylinders, but one is twice as high and has a diameter two times as long as the other. How should the scientist compare the two densities of the cylinders if he doesn't know the volume of the larger cylinder? If the volume of the smaller cylinder is 30 cm^3, what is the volume of the larger cylinder?

★★**11.** You are trying to pack in preparation for a trip and need to fit a collection of children's toys in a box. Each individual toy is a composite figure of four cubes, and all of the toys are shown in the figure. Arrange the toys in an orderly fashion so that they will fit in the smallest box possible. Draw the arrangement. What is the volume of the box if each of the cubes have side lengths of 10 cm?

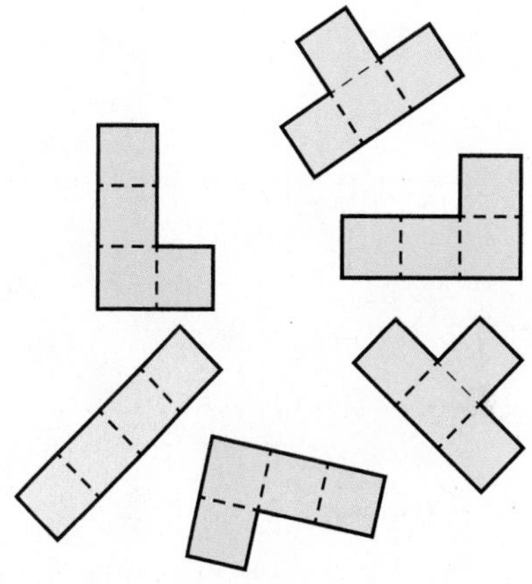

★★★**12.** A carpenter has a wooden cone with a slant height of 16 inches and a diameter of 12 inches. The vertex of the cone is directly above the center of its base. He measures halfway down the slant height and makes a cut parallel to the base. He now has a truncated cone and a cone half the height of the original.

A. He expected the two parts to weigh about the same, but they don't. Which is heavier? Why?

B. Find the ratio of the weight of the small cone to that of the truncated cone. Show your work.

MATH IN CAREERS

Model Maker A model maker wants to create a scale model of a sphere with a volume of 1000 m^3. The model should have a volume of 1000 cm^3. What scale factor should the model maker use? If a triangle drawn on the model has three right angles, what is its area?

UNIT 8

Probability

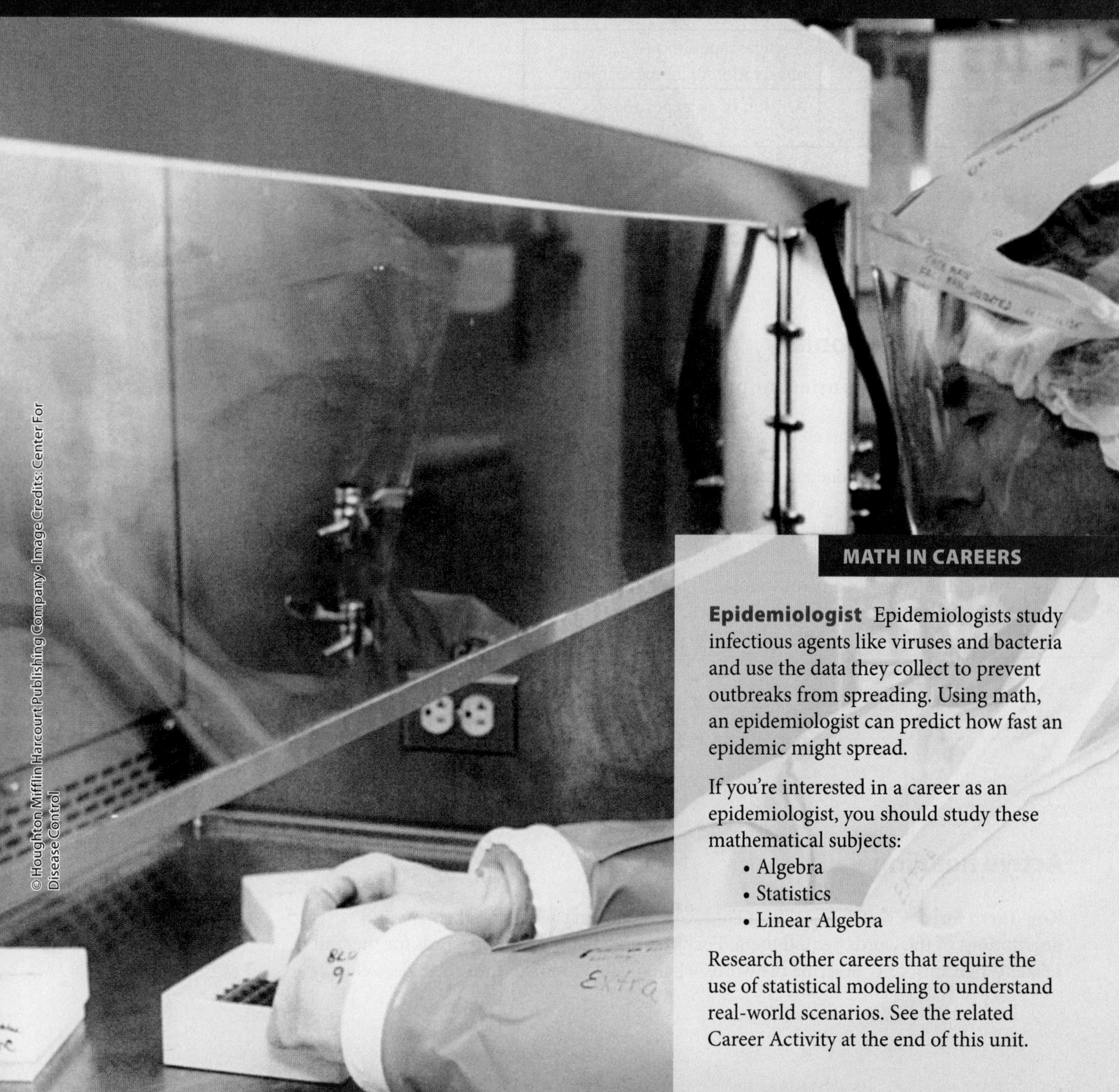

MATH IN CAREERS

Epidemiologist Epidemiologists study infectious agents like viruses and bacteria and use the data they collect to prevent outbreaks from spreading. Using math, an epidemiologist can predict how fast an epidemic might spread.

If you're interested in a career as an epidemiologist, you should study these mathematical subjects:

- Algebra
- Statistics
- Linear Algebra

Research other careers that require the use of statistical modeling to understand real-world scenarios. See the related Career Activity at the end of this unit.

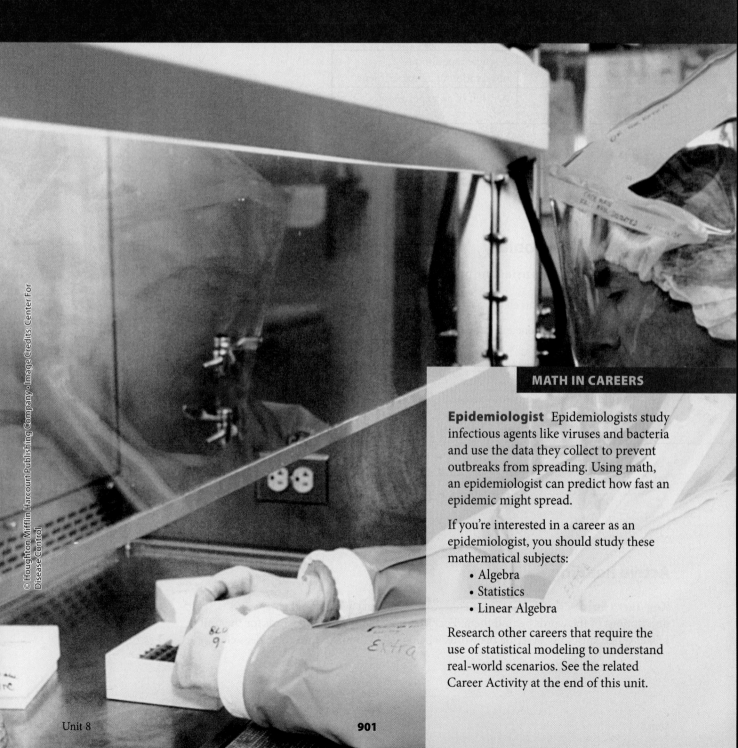

Visualize Vocabulary

Match the √ words to their descriptions to complete the chart.

Word	Description
	The measure of how likely an event is to occur
	All possible outcomes of an experiment
	Any set of outcomes
	A single repetition or observation of an experiment
	A result of an experiment

Vocabulary

Review Words

✔ event (*evento*)
✔ outcome (*resultado*)
✔ probability (*probabilidad*)
✔ sample space (*muestra de espacio*)
✔ trial (*prueba*)

Preview Words

combination (*combinación*)
complement (*complementar*)
conditional probability (*probabilidad condicional*)
dependent events (*eventos dependientes*)
element (*elemento*)
empty set (*conjunto vacío*)
factorial (*factorial*)
independent events (*eventos independientes*)
intersection (*intersección*)
permutation (*permutación*)
set (*conjunto*)
subset (*subconjunto*)
union (*unión*)

Understand Vocabulary

Complete the sentences using the preview words.

1. The __?__ contains no elements.

2. If the occurrence of one event does not affect the occurrence of another event, then the events are called __?__.

3. A(n) __?__ is a group of objects in a particular order.

4. To find the __?__ of a positive integer, find the product of the number and all of the positive integers less than the number.

Active Reading

Key-Term Fold Create a Key-Term Fold with vocabulary words on the flaps and descriptions of the words behind them. Focus on how the vocabulary words for the unit relate. When speaking, describe the words when needed to make sure your ideas clear.

Introduction to Probability

MODULE 21

Essential Question: How can you use probability to solve real-world problems?

REAL WORLD VIDEO
Check out how principles of statistics and probability are used to derive and interpret baseball players' statistics.

MODULE PERFORMANCE TASK PREVIEW

Baseball Probability

In this module, you will use concepts of probability to determine the chances of various outcomes for a baseball player at bat. To successfully complete this task, you'll need to calculate a theoretical probability for a real-world situation. Batter up!

Are YOU Ready?

Complete these exercises to review skills you will need for this module.

- Online Homework
- Hints and Help
- Extra Practice

Probability of Simple Events

Example 1 Find the probability of rolling a 4 when using a normal six-sided die with each side having equal probability.

Each of the six faces has equal probability, so the probability of any face being rolled is $\frac{1}{6}$.

There is only one face with a four on it, so the probability of rolling a four is also $\frac{1}{6}$.

Find each probability.

1. The probability of flipping a coin and getting a heads, given that the probability of getting a tails is the same, and there is no chance that the coin lands on its side

2. The probability of drawing a jack of hearts from a 52-card deck given the deck is properly shuffled

3. The probability of any particular day being Sunday

Probability of Compound Events

Example 2 Find the probability of drawing a red card or a black card when the probability of either is $\frac{1}{4}$ and you only draw one card.

Only one card is drawn and either card has a $\frac{1}{4}$ probability, so the probability of drawing one or the other is the sum of their probabilities.

Probability of drawing a red card or black card $\frac{1}{4} + \frac{1}{4} = \frac{1}{2}$.

Find each probability.

4. The probability of rolling a twelve-sided die and getting a 4 or a 6 given the probability of getting a 4 is $\frac{1}{12}$ and is equal to the probability of getting a 6

5. The probability of pulling a red or a blue marble from a jar given the probability of drawing a red marble is $\frac{1}{4}$ and the probability of pulling a blue marble is $\frac{1}{2}$ and you only pull one marble

21.1 Probability and Set Theory

Essential Question: How are sets and their relationships used to calculate probabilities?

Resource Locker

Explore Working with Sets

A **set** is a collection of distinct objects. Each object in a set is called an **element** of the set. A set is often denoted by writing the elements in braces.

The set with no elements is the **empty set**, denoted by ∅ or { }.

The set of all elements under consideration is the **universal set**, denoted by U.

Identifying the number of elements in a set is important for calculating probabilities.

(A) Use set notation to identify each set described in the table and identify the number of elements in each set.

Set	Set Notation	Number of Elements in the Set
Set A is the set of prime numbers less than 10.	$A = \{2, 3, ?, 7\}$	$n(A) = 4$
Set B is the set of even natural numbers less than 10.	$B = \{?, ?, ?, ?\}$	$n(B) = ?$
Set C is the set of natural numbers less than 10 that are multiples of 4.	$? = \{4, ?\}$	$n(C) = ?$
The universal set is all natural numbers less than 10.	$U = ?$	$?(?) = 9$

The following table identifies terms used to describe relationships among sets. Use sets A, B, C, and U from the previous table. Copy the Example column of the table. Then draw Venn diagrams in each of the four empty cells of your Example column by completing Steps B–I.

Term	Notation	Venn Diagram	Example
Set C is a **subset** of set B if every element of C is also an element of B.	$C \subset B$	U B C	?
The **intersection** of sets A and B is the set of all elements that are in both A *and* B.	$A \cap B$	U A B $A \cap B$ is the double-shaded region.	?
The **union** of sets A and B is the set of all elements that are in A *or* B.	$A \cup B$	U A B $A \cup B$ is the entire shaded region.	?
The **complement** of set A is the set of all elements in the universal set U that are *not* in A.	A^c or $\sim A$	U A A^c is the shaded region.	?

(B) Since C is a subset of B, every element of set C, which consists of the numbers ? and ?, is located not only in oval C, but also within oval B. Set B includes the elements of C as well as the additional elements ? and ?, which are located in oval B outside of oval C. The universal set includes the elements of sets B and C as well as the additional elements ?, ?, ?, ?, and ?, which are located in region U outside of ovals B and C.

(C) In the top cell of your Example column, draw the corresponding Venn diagram that includes the elements of B, C, and U.

(D) To determine the intersection of A and B, first define the elements of set A and set B separately, then identify all the elements found in both sets A and B.

$A = \{?, ?, ?, ?\}$

$B = \{?, ?, ?, ?\}$

$A \cap B = \{?\}$

Ⓔ In the second cell of your Example column, draw the Venn diagram for $A \cap B$ that includes the elements of A, B, and U and the double-shaded intersection region.

Ⓕ To determine the union of sets A and B, identify all the elements found in either set A or set B by combining all the elements of the two sets into the union set.

$A \cup B = \{ ?, ?, ?, ?, ?, ?, ? \}$

Ⓖ In the third cell of your Example column, draw the Venn diagram for $A \cup B$ that includes the elements of A, B, and U and the shaded union region.

Ⓗ To determine the complement of set A, first identify the elements of set A and universal set U separately, then identify all the elements in the universal set that are *not* in set A.

$A = \{ ?, ?, ?, ? \}$

$U = \{ ?, ?, ?, ?, ?, ?, ?, ?, ? \}$

$A^C = \{ ?, ?, ?, ?, ? \}$

Ⓘ In the bottom cell of your Example column, draw the Venn diagram for A^c that includes the elements of A and U and the shaded region that represents the complement of A.

Reflect

1. **Draw Conclusions** Do sets always have an intersection that is not the empty set? Provide an example to support your conclusion.

Explain 1 Calculating Theoretical Probabilities

A *probability experiment* is an activity involving chance. Each repetition of the experiment is called a *trial* and each possible result of the experiment is termed an *outcome*. A set of outcomes is known as an *event*, and the set of all possible outcomes is called the *sample space*.

Probability measures how likely an event is to occur. An event that is impossible has a probability of 0, while an event that is certain has a probability of 1. All other events have a probability between 0 and 1. When all the outcomes of a probability experiment are equally likely, the **theoretical probability** of an event A in the sample space S is given by

$$P(A) = \frac{\text{number of outcomes in the event}}{\text{number of outcomes in the sample space}} = \frac{n(A)}{n(S)}.$$

Example 1 **Calculate $P(A)$, $P(A \cup B)$, $P(A \cap B)$, and $P(A^C)$ for each situation.**

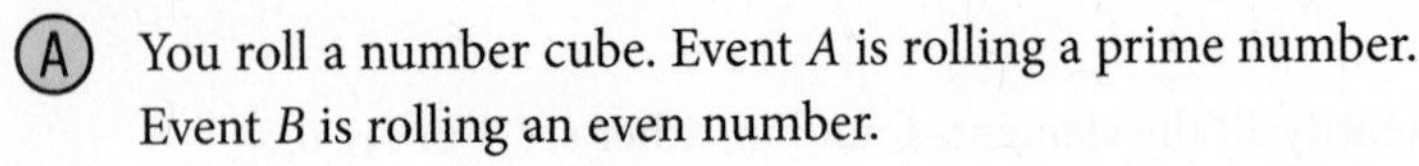

Ⓐ You roll a number cube. Event A is rolling a prime number. Event B is rolling an even number.

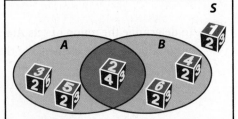

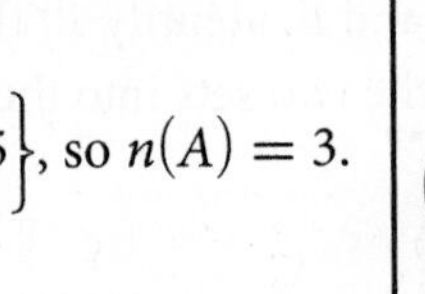

$S = \{1, 2, 3, 4, 5, 6\}$, so $n(S) = 6$. $A = \{2, 3, 5\}$, so $n(A) = 3$.

So, $P(A) = \dfrac{n(A)}{n(S)} = \dfrac{3}{6} = \dfrac{1}{2}$.

$A \cup B = \{2, 3, 4, 5, 6\}$, so $n(A \cup B) = 5$. So, $P(A \cup B) = \dfrac{n(A \cup B)}{n(S)} = \dfrac{5}{6}$.

$A \cap B = \{2\}$, so $n(A \cap B) = 1$. So, $P(A \cap B) = \dfrac{n(A \cap B)}{n(S)} = \dfrac{1}{6}$.

$A^C = \{1, 4, 6\}$, so $n(A^C) = 3$. So, $P(A^C) = \dfrac{n(A^C)}{n(S)} = \dfrac{3}{6} = \dfrac{1}{2}$.

Ⓑ Your grocery basket contains one bag of each of the following items: oranges, green apples, green grapes, green broccoli, white cauliflower, orange carrots, and green spinach. You are getting ready to transfer your items from your cart to the conveyer belt for check-out. Event A is picking a bag containing a vegetable first. Event B is picking a bag containing a green food first. All bags have an equal chance of being picked first.

Order of objects in sets may vary.

$S = \{\text{orange, apple, grape, broccoli, cauliflower, carrot, spinach}\}$, so $n(S) = 7$.

$A = \{\text{broccoli, cauliflower, carrot, spinach}\}$, so $n(A) = 4$. So $P(A) = \dfrac{n(A)}{n(S)} = \dfrac{4}{7}$.

$A \cup B = \{\text{broccoli, cauliflower, carrot, spinach, apple, grape}\}$, so $n(A \cup B) = 6$.

$P(A \cup B) = \dfrac{n(A \cup B)}{n(S)} = \dfrac{6}{7}$

$A \cap B = \{\text{carrot, spinach}\}$, so $n(A \cap B) = 2$

$P(A \cap B) = \dfrac{n(A \cap B)}{n(S)} = \dfrac{2}{7}$

$P(A^c) = \dfrac{n(A^c)}{n(S)} = \dfrac{3}{7}$

Reflect

2. **Discussion** In Example 1B, which is greater, $P(A \cup B)$ or $P(A \cap B)$? Do you think this result is true in general? Explain.

Your Turn

The numbers 1 through 30 are written on slips of paper that are then placed in a hat. Students draw a slip to determine the order in which they will give an oral report. Event A is being one of the first 10 students to give their report. Event B is picking a multiple of 6. If you pick first, calculate each of the indicated probabilities.

3. $P(A)$
4. $P(A \cup B)$
5. $P(A \cap B)$
6. $P(A^c)$

Explain 2 Using the Complement of an Event

You may have noticed in the previous examples that the probability of an event occurring and the probability of the event not occurring (i.e., the probability of the complement of the event) have a sum of 1. This relationship can be useful when it is more convenient to calculate the probability of the complement of an event than it is to calculate the probability of the event.

Probabilities of an Event and Its Complement	
$P(A) + P(A^c) = 1$	The sum of the probability of an event and the probability of its complement is 1.
$P(A) = 1 - P(A^c)$	The probability of an event is 1 minus the probability of its complement.
$P(A^c) = 1 - P(A)$	The probability of the complement of an event is 1 minus the probability of the event.

Example 2 **Use the complement to calculate the indicated probabilities.**

(A) You roll a blue number cube and a white number cube at the same time. What is the probability that you do not roll doubles?

Step 1 **Define the events.** Let A be that you do not roll doubles and A^c that you do roll doubles.

Step 2 **Make a diagram.** A two-way table is one helpful way to identify all the possible outcomes in the sample space.

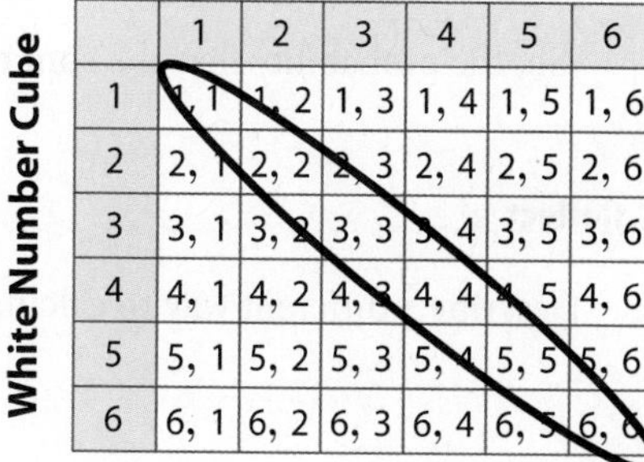

Blue Number Cube (columns) / **White Number Cube** (rows)

	1	2	3	4	5	6
1	1, 1	1, 2	1, 3	1, 4	1, 5	1, 6
2	2, 1	2, 2	2, 3	2, 4	2, 5	2, 6
3	3, 1	3, 2	3, 3	3, 4	3, 5	3, 6
4	4, 1	4, 2	4, 3	4, 4	4, 5	4, 6
5	5, 1	5, 2	5, 3	5, 4	5, 5	5, 6
6	6, 1	6, 2	6, 3	6, 4	6, 5	6, 6

Step 3 Determine $P(A^c)$. Since there are fewer outcomes for rolling doubles, it is more convenient to determine the probability of rolling doubles, which is $P(A^c)$. To determine $n(A^c)$, draw a loop around the outcomes in the table that correspond to A^c and then calculate $P(A^c)$.

$$P(A^c) = \frac{n(A^c)}{n(S)} = \frac{6}{36} = \frac{1}{6}$$

Step 4 Determine $P(A)$. Use the relationship between the probability of an event and itsvcomplement to determine $P(A)$.

$$P(A) = 1 - P(A^c) = 1 - \frac{1}{6} = \frac{5}{6}$$

So, the probability of not rolling doubles is $\frac{5}{6}$.

(B) One pile of cards contains the numbers 2 through 6 in red hearts. A second pile of cards contains the numbers 4 through 8 in black spades. Each pile of cards has been randomly shuffled. If one card from each pile is chosen at the same time, what is the probability that the sum will be less than 12?

Step 1 Define the events. Let A be the event that the sum is less than 12 and A^c be the event that the sum is not less than 12.

Step 2 Make a diagram. Complete the table to show all the outcomes in the sample space.

	Red Hearts ♥				
Black Spades ♠	2	3	4	5	6
4	4+2	4+3	4+4	4+5	4+6
5	5+2	5+3	5+4	5+5	5+6
6	6+2	6+3	6+4	6+5	6+6
7	7+2	7+3	7+4	7+5	7+6
8	8+2	8+3	8+4	8+5	8+6

Step 3 Determine $P(A^c)$. Circle the outcomes in the table that correspond to A^c, then determine $P(A^c)$.

$$P(A^c) = \frac{n(A^c)}{n(S)} = \frac{6}{25}$$

Step 4 Determine $P(A)$. Use the relationship between the probability of an event and its complement to determine $P(A^c)$.

$$P(A) = 1 - P(A^c) = 1 - \frac{6}{25} = \frac{19}{25}$$

So, the probability that the sum of the two cards is less than 12 is $\frac{19}{25}$.

Reflect

7. Describe a different way to calculate the probability that the sum of the two cards will be less than 12.

Your Turn

One bag of marbles contains two red, one yellow, one green, and one blue marble. Another bag contains one marble of each of the same four colors. One marble from each bag is chosen at the same time. Use the complement to calculate the indicated probabilities.

8. Probability of selecting two different colors

9. Probability of not selecting a yellow marble

Elaborate

10. Can a subset of A contain elements of A^C? Why or why not?

11. For any set A, what does $A \cap \emptyset$ equal? What does $A \cup \emptyset$ equal? Explain.

12. **Essential Question Check-In** How do the terms *set*, *element*, and *universal set* correlate to the terms used to calculate theoretical probability?

Evaluate: Homework and Practice

- Online Homework
- Hints and Help
- Extra Practice

Set A is the set of factors of 12, set B is the set of even natural numbers less than 13, set C is the set of odd natural numbers less than 13, and set D is the set of even natural numbers less than 7. The universal set for these questions is the set of natural numbers less than 13.

So, $A = \{1, 2, 3, 4, 6, 12\}$, $B = \{2, 4, 6, 8, 10, 12\}$, $C = \{1, 3, 5, 7, 9, 11\}$, $D = \{2, 4, 6\}$, and $U = \{1, 2, 3, 4, 5, 6, 7, 8, 9, 10, 11, 12\}$.

Answer each question.

1. Is $D \subset A$? Explain why or why not.

2. Is $B \subset A$? Explain why or why not.

3. What is $A \cap B$?

4. What is $A \cap C$?

5. What is $A \cup B$?

6. What is $A \cup C$?

7. What is A^C?

8. What is B^C?

You have a set of 10 cards numbered 1 to 10. You choose a card at random. Event A is choosing a number less than 7. Event B is choosing an odd number. Calculate the probability.

9. $P(A)$

10. $P(B)$

11. $P(A \cup B)$

12. $P(A \cap B)$

13. $P(A^C)$

14. $P(B^C)$

Use the complement of the event to find the probability.

15. You roll a 6-sided number cube. What is the probability that you do not roll a 2?

16. You choose a card at random from a standard deck of cards. What is the probability that you do not choose a red king?

17. You spin the spinner shown. The spinner is divided into 12 equal sectors. What is the probability of not spinning a 2?

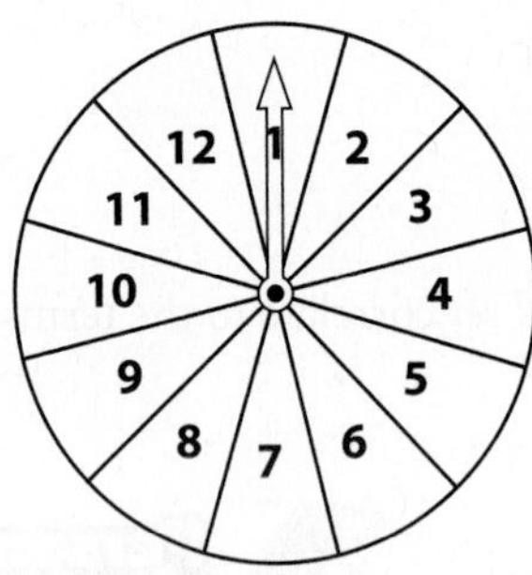

18. A bag contains 2 red, 5 blue, and 3 green balls. A ball is chosen at random. What is the probability of not choosing a red ball?

19. Cards numbered 1–12 are placed in a bag. A card is chosen at random. What is the probability of not choosing a number less than 5?

20. Slips of paper numbered 1–20 are folded and placed into a hat, and then a slip of paper is drawn at random. What is the probability the slip drawn has a number which is not a multiple of 4 or 5?

21. You are going to roll two number cubes, a white number cube and a red number cube, and find the sum of the two numbers that come up.

    a. What is the probability that the sum will be 6?

    b. What is the probability that the sum will not be 6?

22. You have cards with the letters A, B, C, D, E, F, G, H, I, J, K, L, M, N, O, P. Event U is choosing the cards A, B, C or D. Event V is choosing a vowel. Event W is choosing a letter in the word "APPLE". Find $P(U \cap V \cap W)$.

A standard deck of cards has 13 cards (2, 3, 4, 5, 6, 7, 8, 9, 10, jack, queen, king, ace) in each of 4 suits (hearts, clubs, diamonds, spades). The hearts and diamonds cards are red. The clubs and spades cards are black. Answer each question.

23. You choose a card from a standard deck of cards at random. What is the probability that you do not choose an ace? Explain.

24. You choose a card from a standard deck of cards at random. What is the probability that you do not choose a club? Explain.

25. You choose a card from a standard deck of cards at random. Event A is choosing a red card. Event B is choosing an even number. Event C is choosing a black card. Find $P(A \cap B \cap C)$. Explain.

26. You are selecting a card at random from a standard deck of cards. Match each event with the correct probability.

A. __?__ Picking a card that is both red and a heart. **a.** $\frac{1}{52}$

B. __?__ Picking a card that is both a heart and an ace. **b.** $\frac{1}{4}$

C. __?__ Picking a card that is not both a heart and an ace. **c.** $\frac{51}{52}$

H.O.T. Focus on Higher Order Thinking

27. Critique Reasoning A bag contains white tiles, black tiles, and gray tiles. Someone is going to choose a tile at random. $P(W)$, the probability of choosing a white tile, is $\frac{1}{4}$. A student claims that the probability of choosing a black tile, $P(B)$, is $\frac{3}{4}$ since $P(B) = 1 - P(W) = 1 - \frac{1}{4} = \frac{3}{4}$. Do you agree? Explain.

28. Communicate Mathematical Ideas A bag contains 5 red marbles and 10 blue marbles. You are going to choose a marble at random. Event A is choosing a red marble. Event B is choosing a blue marble. What is $P(A \cap B)$? Explain.

29. Critical Thinking Jeffery states that for a sample space S where all outcomes are equally likely, $0 \leq P(A) \leq 1$ for any subset A of S. Create an argument that will justify his statement or state a counterexample.

Lesson Performance Task

For the sets you've worked with in this lesson, membership in a set is binary: Either something belongs to the set or it doesn't. For instance, 5 is an element of the set of odd numbers, but 6 isn't.

In 1965, Lofti Zadeh developed the idea of "fuzzy" sets to deal with sets for which membership is not binary. He defined a *degree* of membership that can vary from 0 to 1. For instance, a membership function $m_L(w)$ for the set L of large dogs where the degree of membership m is determined by the weight w of a dog might be defined as follows:

- A dog is a full member of the set L if it weighs 80 pounds or more. This can be written as $m_L(w) = 1$ for $w \geq 80$.
- A dog is not a member of the set L if it weighs 60 pounds or less. This can be written as $m_L(w) = 0$ for $w \leq 60$.
- A dog is a partial member of the set L if it weighs between 60 and 80 pounds. This can be written as $0 < m_L(w) < 1$ for $60 < w < 80$.

The "large dogs" portion of the graph shown displays the membership criteria listed above. Note that the graph shows only values of $m(w)$ that are positive.

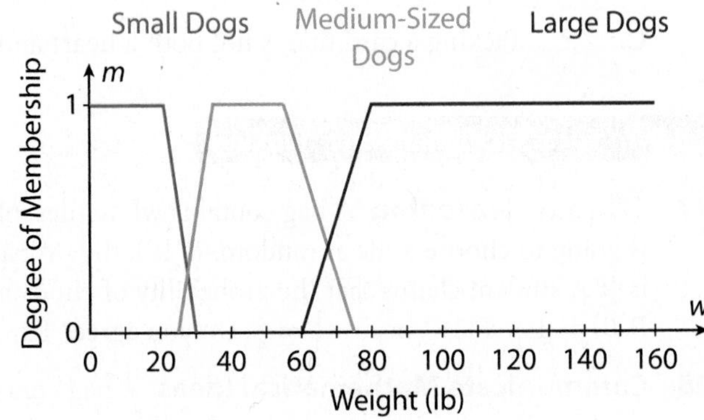

1. Using the graph, give the approximate weights for which a dog is considered a full member, a partial member, and not a member of the set S of small dogs.

2. The union of two "fuzzy" sets A and B is given by the membership rule $m_{A \cup B}(x) = \text{maximum}\big(m_A(x), m_B(x)\big)$. So, for a dog of a given size, the degree of its membership in the set of small or medium-sized dogs $(S \cup M)$ is the greater of its degree of membership in the set of small dogs and its degree of membership in the set of medium-sized dogs.

The intersection of A and B is given by the membership rule $m_{A \cap B}(x) = \text{minimum}\big(m_A(x), m_B(x)\big)$. So, for a dog of a given size, the degree of its membership in the set of dogs that are both small and medium-sized $(S \cap M)$ is the lesser of its degree of membership in the set of small dogs and its degree of membership in the set of medium-sized dogs.

Using the graph above and letting S be the set of small dogs, M be the set of medium-sized dogs, and L be the set of large dogs, draw the graph of each set.

a. $S \cup M$

b. $M \cap L$

21.2 Permutations and Probability

Essential Question: When are permutations useful in calculating probability?

Resource Locker

Explore Finding the Number of Permutations

A **permutation** is a selection of objects from a group in which order is important. For example, there are 6 permutations of the letters A, B, and C.

ABC	ACB	BAC	BCA	CAB	CBA

You can find the number of permutations with the **Fundamental Counting Principle**.

Fundamental Counting Principle

If there are n items and a_1 ways to choose the first item, a_2 ways to select the second item after the first item has been chosen, and so on, there are $a_1 \times a_2 \times \ldots \times a_n$ ways to choose n items.

There are 7 members in a club. Each year the club elects a president, a vice president, and a treasurer.

(A) What is the number of permutations of all 7 members of the club?

There are ? different ways to make the first selection.

Once the first person has been chosen, there are ? different ways to make the second selection.

Once the first two people have been chosen, there are ? different ways to make the third selection.

Continuing this pattern, there are ? permutations of all the members of the club.

(B) The club is holding elections for a president, a vice president, and a treasurer. How many different ways can these positions be filled?

There are ? different ways the position of president can be filled.

Once the president has been chosen, there are ? different ways the position of vice president can be filled. Once the president and vice president have been chosen, there are ? different ways the position of treasurer can be filled.

So, there are ? different ways that the positions can be filled.

(C) What is the number of permutations of the members of the club who were not elected as officers?

After the officers have been elected, there are ? members remaining. So there are ? different ways to make the first selection.

Once the first person has been chosen, there are ? different ways to make the second selection.

Continuing this pattern, there are ? permutations of the unelected members of the club.

(D) Divide the number of permutations of all the members by the number of permutations of the unelected members.

There are ? permutations of all the members of the club.

There are ? permutations of the unelected members of the club.

The quotient of these two values is ? .

Reflect

1. How does the answer to Step D compare to the answer to Step B?
2. **Discussion** Explain the effect of dividing the total number of permutations by the number of permutations of items not selected.

Explain 1 Finding a Probability Using Permutations

The results of the Explore can be generalized to give a formula for permutations. To do so, it is helpful to use *factorials.* For a positive integer *n*, ***n* factorial,** written $n!$, is defined as follows.

$$n! = n \times (n-1) \times (n-2) \times \ldots \times 3 \times 2 \times 1$$

That is, $n!$ is the product of n and all the positive integers less than n. Note that $0!$ is defined to be 1.

In the Explore, the number of permutations of the 7 objects taken 3 at a time is

$$7 \times 6 \times 5 = \frac{7 \times 6 \times 5 \times \cancel{4} \times \cancel{3} \times \cancel{2} \times \cancel{1}}{\cancel{4} \times \cancel{3} \times \cancel{2} \times \cancel{1}} = \frac{7!}{4!} = \frac{7!}{(7-3)!}$$

This can be generalized as follows.

Permutations

The number of permutations of n objects taken r at a time is given by ${}_nP_r = \frac{n!}{(n-r)!}$.

Example 1 Use permutations to find the probabilities.

(A) A research laboratory requires a four-digit security code to gain access to the facility. A security code can contain any of the digits 0, 1, 2, 3, 4, 5, 6, 7, 8, and 9, but no digit is repeated. What is the probability that a scientist is randomly assigned a code with the digits 1, 2, 3, and 4 in any order?

The sample space S consists of permutations of 4 digits selected from 10 digits.

$$n(S) = {}_{10}P_4 = \frac{10!}{(10-4)!} = \frac{10!}{6!} = 5040$$

Event A consists of permutations of a security code with the digits 1, 2, 3, and 4.

$$n(A) = {}_4P_4 = \frac{4!}{(4-4)!} = \frac{4!}{0!} = 24$$

The probability of getting a security code with the digits 1, 2, 3, and 4 is

$$P(A) = \frac{n(A)}{n(S)} = \frac{24}{5040} = \frac{1}{210}.$$

(B) A certain motorcycle license plate consists of 5 digits that are randomly selected. No digit is repeated. What is the probability of getting a license plate consisting of all even digits?
The sample space S consists of permutations of 5 digits selected from 10 digits.

$$n(S) = {}_{10}P_{5} = \frac{10!}{5!} = 30,240$$

Event A consists of permutations of a license plate with all even digits.

$$n(A) = {}_{5}P_{5} = \frac{5!}{0!} = 120$$

The probability of getting a license plate with all even digits is

$$P(A) = \frac{n(A)}{n(S)} = \frac{120}{30,240} = \frac{1}{252}.$$

Your Turn

There are 8 finalists in the 100-meter dash at the Olympic Games. Suppose 3 of the finalists are from the United States, and that all finalists are equally likely to win.

3. What is the probability that the United States will win all 3 medals in this event?

4. What is the probability that the United States will win no medals in this event?

Explain 2 Finding the Number of Permutations with Repetition

Up to this point, the problems have focused on finding the permutations of distinct objects. If some of the objects are repeated, this will reduce the number of permutations that are distinguishable.

For example, here are the permutations of the letters A, B, and C.

ABC	ACB	BAC	BCA	CAB	CBA

Next, here are the permutations of the letters M, O, and M. Bold type is used to show the different positions of the repeated letter.

MOM	MO**M**	**M**MO	M**M**O	O**M**M	OM**M**

Shown without the bold type, here are the permutations of the letters M, O, and M.

MOM	MOM	MMO	MMO	OMM	OMM

Notice that since the letter M is repeated, there are only 3 distinguishable permutations of the letters. This can be generalized with a formula for permutations with repetition.

Permutations with Repetition

The number of different permutations of n objects where one object repeats a times, a second object repeats b times, and so on is

$$\frac{n!}{a! \times b! \times ...}$$

Example 2 **Find the number of permutations.**

(A) How many different permutations are there of the letters in the word ARKANSAS?

There are 8 letters in the word, and there are 3 A's and 2 S's, so the number of permutations of the letters in ARKANSAS is $\frac{8!}{3!2!} = 3360$.

(B) One of the zip codes for Anchorage, Alaska, is 99522. How many permutations are there of the numbers in this zip code?

There are 5 digits in the zip code, and there are 2 nines, and 2 twos in the zip code, so the number of permutations of the zip code is

$$\frac{\boxed{5!}}{\boxed{2!2!}} = \boxed{30}.$$

Your Turn

5. How many different permutations can be formed using all the letters in MISSISSIPPI?

6. One of the standard telephone numbers for directory assistance is 555–1212. How many different permutations of this telephone number are possible?

Explain 3 Finding a Probability Using Permutations with Repetition

Permutations with repetition can be used to find probablilities.

Example 3 **The school jazz band has 4 boys and 4 girls, and they are randomly lined up for a yearbook photo.**

(A) Find the probability of getting an alternating boy-girl arrangement.

The sample space S consists of permutations of 8 objects, with 4 boys and 4 girls.

$n(S)\ \frac{8!}{4!4!} = 70$

Event A consists of permutations that alternate boy-girl or girl-boy. The possible permutations are BGBGBGBG and GBGBGBGB.

$n(A) = 2$

The probability of getting an alternating boy-girl arrangement is $P(A) = \frac{n(A)}{n(S)} = \frac{2}{70} = \frac{1}{35}$.

(B) Find the probability of getting all of the boys grouped together.

The sample space S consists of permutations of 8 students, with 4 boys and 4 girls.

$$n(S) = \frac{\boxed{8!}}{\boxed{4!4!}} = \boxed{70}$$

Event A consists of permutations with all 4 boys in a row. The possible permutations are BBBBGGGG, GBBBBGGG, GGBBBBGG, GGGBBBBG, and GGGGBBBB

$$n(A) = \boxed{5}$$

The probability of getting all the boys grouped together is $P(A) = \frac{n(A)}{n(S)} = \frac{\boxed{5}}{\boxed{70}} = \frac{\boxed{1}}{\boxed{14}}$.

Your Turn

7. There are 2 mystery books, 2 romance books, and 2 poetry books to be randomly placed on a shelf. What is the probability that the mystery books are next to each other, the romance books are next to each other, and the poetry books are next to each other?

8. What is the probability that a random arrangement of the letters in the word APPLE will have the two P's next to each other?

Elaborate

9. If ${}_nP_a = {}_nP_b$, what is the relationship between a and b? Explain your answer.

10. It was observed that there are 6 permutations of the letters A, B, and C. They are ABC, ACB, BAC, BCA, CAB, and CBA. If the conditions are changed so that the order of selection does not matter, what happens to these 6 different groups?

11. **Essential Question Check-In** How do you determine whether choosing a group of objects involves permutations?

Evaluate: Homework and Practice

- Online Homework
- Hints and Help
- Extra Practice

1. An MP3 player has a playlist with 12 songs. You select the shuffle option, which plays each song in a random order without repetition, for the playlist. In how many different orders can the songs be played?

2. There are 10 runners in a race. Medals are awarded for 1st, 2nd, and 3rd place. In how many different ways can the medals be awarded?

3. There are 9 players on a baseball team. In how many different ways can the coach choose players for first base, second base, third base, and shortstop?

4. A bag contains 9 tiles, each with a different number from 1 to 9. You choose a tile without looking, put it aside, choose a second tile without looking, put it aside, then choose a third tile without looking. What is the probability that you choose tiles with the numbers 1, 2, and 3 in that order?

5. There are 11 students on a committee. To decide which 3 of these students will attend a conference, 3 names are chosen at random by pulling names one at a time from a hat. What is the probability that Sarah, Jamal, and Mai are chosen in any order?

6. A clerk has 4 different letters that need to go in 4 different envelopes. The clerk places one letter in each envelope at random. What is the probability that all 4 letters are placed in the correct envelopes?

7. A swim coach randomly selects 3 swimmers from a team of 8 to swim in a heat. What is the probability that she will choose the three strongest swimmers?

8. How many different sequences of letters can be formed using all the letters in ENVELOPE?

9. Yolanda has 3 each of red, blue, and green marbles. How many possible ways can the 9 marbles be arranged in a row?

10. Jane has 16 cards. Ten of the cards look exactly the same and have the number 1 on them. The other 6 cards look exactly the same and have the number 2 on them. Jane is going to make a row containing all 16 cards. How many different ways can she order the row?

11. Ramon has 10 cards, each with one number on it. The numbers are 1, 2, 3, 4, 4, 6, 6, 6, 6, 6. Ramon is going to make a row containing all 10 cards. How many different ways can he order the row?

12. A grocer has 5 apples and 5 oranges for a window display. The grocer makes a row of the 10 pieces of fruit by choosing one piece of fruit at random, making it the first piece in the row, choosing a second piece of fruit at random, making it the second piece in the row, and so on. What is the probability that the grocer arranges the fruits in alternating order? (Assume that the apples are not distinguishable and that the oranges are not distinguishable.)

13. The letters G, E, O, M, E, T, R, Y are on 8 tiles in a bag, one letter on each tile. If you select tiles randomly from the bag and place them in a row from left to right, what is the probability the tiles will spell out GEOMETRY?

14. There are 11 boys and 10 girls in a classroom. A teacher chooses a student at random and puts that student at the head of a line, chooses a second student at random and makes that student second in the line, and so on, until all 21 students are in the line. What is the probability that the teacher puts them in a line alternating boys and girls, where no two of the same gender stand together?

15. There are 4 female and 4 male kittens are sleeping together in a row. Assuming that the arrangement is a random arrangement, what is the probability that all the female kittens are together, and all the male kittens are together?

16. If a ski club with 12 members votes to choose 3 group leaders, what is the probability that Marsha, Kevin, and Nicola will be chosen in any order for President, Treasurer, and Secretary?

17. There are 7 books numbered 1–7 on the summer reading list. Peter randomly chooses 2 books. What is the probability that Peter chooses books numbered 1 and 2, in either order?

18. On an exam, students are asked to list 5 historical events in the order in which they occurred. A student randomly orders the events. What is the probability that the student chooses the correct order?

19. A fan makes 6 posters to hold up at a basketball game. Each poster has a letter of the word TIGERS. Six friends sit next to each other in a row. The posters are distributed at random. What is the probability that TIGERS is spelled correctly when the friends hold up the posters?

20. The 10 letter tiles S, A, C, D, E, E, M, I, I, and O are in a bag. What is the probability that the letters S-A-M-E will be drawn from the bag at random, in that order?

21. If three cards are drawn at random from a standard deck of 52 cards, what is the probability that they will all be 7s? (There are four 7s in a standard deck of 52 cards.)

22. A shop classroom has ten desks in a row. If there are 6 students in shop class and they choose their desks at random, what is the probability they will sit in the first six desks?

23. Match each event with its probability. All orders are chosen randomly.

A. There are 15 floats that will be in a town parade. Event *A*: The mascot float is chosen to be first and the football team float is chosen to be second.

a. ___?___ $\frac{1}{1365}$

B. Beth is one of 10 students performing in a school talent show. Event *B*: Beth is chosen to be the fifth performer and her best friend is chosen to be fourth.

b. ___?___ $\frac{1}{210}$

C. Sylvester is in a music competition with 14 other musicians. Event *C*: Sylvester is chosen to be last, and his two best friends are chosen to be first and second.

c. ___?___ $\frac{1}{90}$

H.O.T. Focus on Higher Order Thinking

24. **Explain the Error** Describe and correct the error in evaluating the expression.

$$_5P_3 = \frac{5!}{3!} = \frac{5 \times 4 \times 3!}{3!} = 20$$

25. **Make a Conjecture** If you are going to draw four cards from a deck of cards, does drawing four aces from the deck have the same probability as drawing four 3s? Explain.

26. **Communicate Mathematical Ideas** Nolan has Algebra, Biology, and World History homework. Assume that he chooses the order that he does his homework at random. Explain how to find the probability of his doing his Algebra homework first.

27. Explain the Error A student solved the problem shown. The student's work is also shown. Explain the error and provide the correct answer.

A bag contains 6 tiles with the letters A, B, C, D, E, and F, one letter on each tile. You choose 4 tiles one at a time without looking and line them up from left to right as you choose them. What is the probability that your tiles spell BEAD?

Let S be the sample space and let A be the event that the tiles spell BEAD.

$$n(S) = {}_6P_4 = \frac{6!}{(6-4)!} = \frac{6!}{2!} = 360$$

$$n(A) = {}_4P_4 = \frac{4!}{(4-4)!} = \frac{4!}{0!} = 24$$

$$P(A) = \frac{n(A)}{n(S)} = \frac{24}{360} = \frac{1}{5}$$

Lesson Performance Task

How many different ways can a blue card, a red card, and a green card be arranged? The diagram shows that the answer is six.

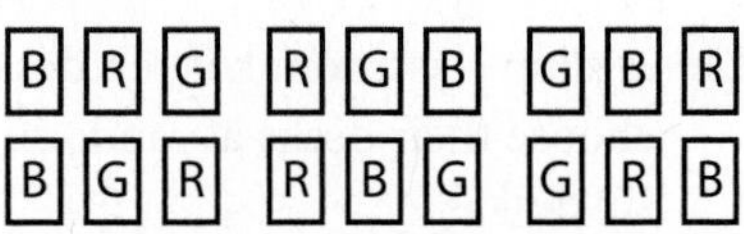

1. Now solve this problem: What is the least number of colors needed to color the pattern shown here, so that no two squares with a common boundary have the same color? Draw a sketch to show your answer.

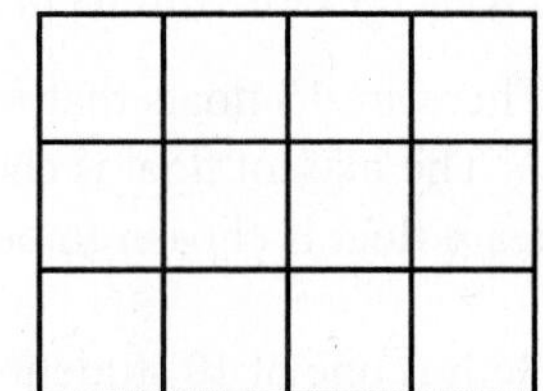

2. Now try this one. Again, find the least number of colors needed to color the pattern so that no two regions with a common boundary have the same color. Draw a sketch to show your answer.

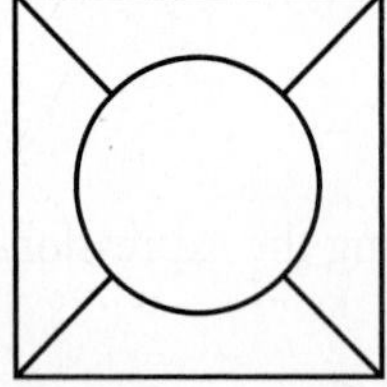

3. In 1974, Kenneth Appel and Wolfgang Haken solved a problem that had confounded mathematicians for more than a century. They proved that no matter how complex a map is, it can be colored in a maximum of four colors, so that no two regions with a common boundary have the same color. Sketch the figure shown here. Can you color it in four colors? Can you color it in three colors?

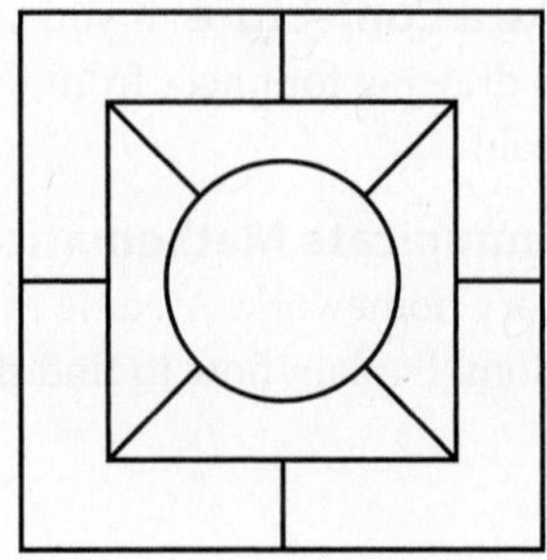

21.3 Combinations and Probability

Essential Question: What is the difference between a permutation and a combination?

Resource Locker

Explore Finding the Number of Combinations

A **combination** is a selection of objects from a group in which order is unimportant. For example, if 3 letters are chosen from the group of letters A, B, C, and D, there are 4 different combinations.

ABC	ABD	ACD	BCD

A restaurant has 8 different appetizers on the menu, as shown in the table. They also offer an appetizer sampler, which contains any 3 of the appetizers served on a single plate. How many different appetizer samplers can be created? The order in which the appetizers are selected does not matter.

Appetizers	
Nachos	Chicken Wings
Chicken Quesadilla	Vegetarian Egg Rolls
Potato Skins	Soft Pretzels
Beef Chili	Guacamole Dip

(A) Find the number appetizer samplers that are possible if the order of selection does matter. This is the number of permutations of 8 objects taken 3 at a time.

$${}_8P_3 = \frac{?}{(? - ?)!} = \frac{?}{?} = ?$$

(B) Find the number of different ways to select a particular group of appetizers. This is the number of permutations of 3 objects.

$${}_3P_3 = \frac{?}{(? - ?)!} = \frac{?}{?} = ?$$

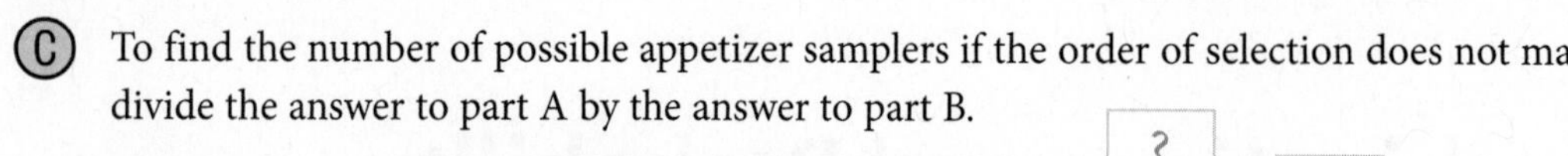

(C) To find the number of possible appetizer samplers if the order of selection does not matter, divide the answer to part A by the answer to part B.

So the number of appetizer samplers that can be created is $\frac{?}{?} = ?$.

Reflect

1. Explain why the answer to Part A was divided by the answer to Part B.
2. On Mondays and Tuesdays, the restaurant offers an appetizer sampler that contains any 4 of the appetizers listed. How many different appetizer samplers can be created?
3. In general, are there more ways or fewer ways to select objects when the order does not matter? Why?

Explain 1 Finding a Probability Using Combinations

The results of the Explore can be generalized to give a formula for combinations. In the Explore, the number of combinations of the 8 objects taken 3 at a time is

$$_8P_3 \div {_3P_3} = \frac{8!}{(8-3)!} \div \frac{3!}{(3-3)!} = \frac{8!}{(8-3)!} \cdot \frac{0!}{3!} = \frac{8!}{(8-3)!} \cdot \frac{1}{3!} = \frac{8!}{3!(8-3)!}$$

This can be generalized as follows.

Combinations
The number of combinations of n objects taken r at a time is given by $$_nC_r = \frac{n!}{r!(n-r)!}$$

Example 1 **Find each probability.**

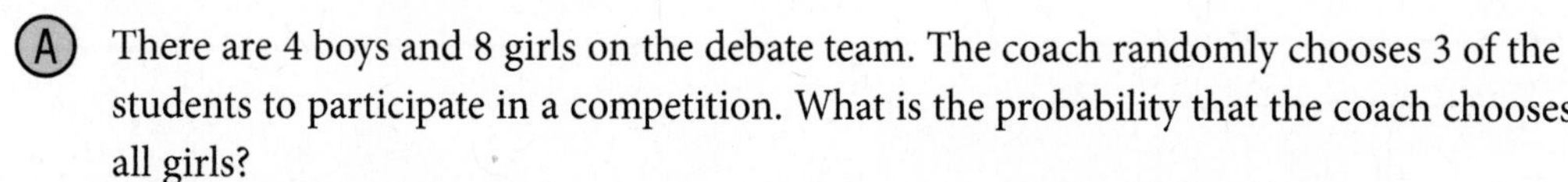

(A) There are 4 boys and 8 girls on the debate team. The coach randomly chooses 3 of the students to participate in a competition. What is the probability that the coach chooses all girls?

The sample space S consists of combinations of 3 students taken from the group of 12 students.

$n(S) = {_{12}C_3} = \frac{12!}{3!9!} = 220$

Event A consists of combinations of 3 girls taken from the set of 8 girls.

$n(A) = {_8C_3} = \frac{8!}{3!5!} = 56$

The probability that the coach chooses all girls is $P(A) = \frac{n(A)}{n(S)} = \frac{56}{220} = \frac{14}{55}$.

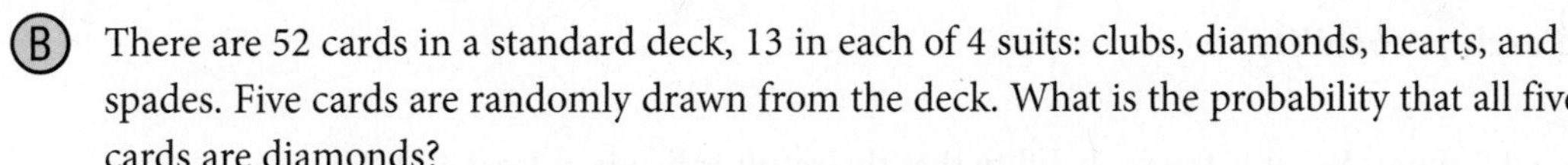

Ⓑ There are 52 cards in a standard deck, 13 in each of 4 suits: clubs, diamonds, hearts, and spades. Five cards are randomly drawn from the deck. What is the probability that all five cards are diamonds?

The sample space S consists of combinations of 5 cards drawn from 52 cards.

$$n(S) = {}_{52}C_{5} = \frac{52!}{5!47!} = 2{,}598{,}960$$

Event A consists of combinations of 5 cards drawn from the 13 diamonds.

$$n(A) = {}_{13}C_{5} = \frac{13!}{5!8!} = 1287$$

The probability of randomly selecting 5 cards that are diamonds is

$$P(A) = \frac{n(A)}{n(S)} = \frac{1287}{2{,}598{,}960} = \frac{33}{66,640}.$$

Your Turn

4. A coin is tossed 4 times. What is the probability of getting exactly 3 heads?

5. A standard deck of cards is divided in half, with the red cards (diamonds and hearts) separated from the black cards (spades and clubs). Four cards are randomly drawn from the red half. What is the probability they are all diamonds?

Explain 2 Finding a Probability Using Combinations and Addition

Sometimes, counting problems involve the phrases "at least" or "at most." For these problems, combinations must be added.

For example, suppose a coin is flipped 3 times. The coin could show heads 0, 1, 2, or 3 times. To find the number of combinations with at least 2 heads, add the number of combinations with 2 heads and the number of combinations with 3 heads $\left({}_3C_2 + {}_3C_3\right)$.

Example 2 **Find each probability.**

 A coin is flipped 5 times. What is the probability that the result is heads at least 4 of the 5 times?

The number of outcomes in the sample space S can be found by using the Fundamental Counting Principle since each flip can result in heads or tails.

$$n(S) = 2 \cdot 2 \cdot 2 \cdot 2 \cdot 2 = 2^5 = 32$$

Let A be the event that the coin shows heads at least 4 times. This is the sum of 2 events, the coin showing heads 4 times and the coin showing heads 5 times. Find the sum of the combinations with 4 heads from 5 coins and with 5 heads from 5 coins.

$$n(A) = {}_5C_4 + {}_5C_5 = \frac{5!}{4!1!} + \frac{5!}{5!0!} = 5 + 1 = 6$$

The probability that the coin shows at least 4 heads is $P(A) = \frac{n(A)}{n(S)} = \frac{6}{32} = \frac{3}{16}$.

 Three number cubes number cubes are rolled and the result is recorded. What is the probability that at least 2 of the number cubes show 6?

The number of outcomes in the sample space S can be found by using the Fundamental Counting Principle since each roll can result in 1, 2, 3, 4, 5, or 6.

$$n(S) = 6^3 = 216$$

Let A be the event that at least 2 number cubes show 6. This is the sum of 2 events, 2 number cubes showing 6 or 3 number cubes showing 6. The event of getting 6 on 2 number cubes occurs 5 times since there are 5 possibilities for the other number cube.

$$n(A) = 5 \cdot {}_3C_2 + {}_3C_3 = 5 \cdot \frac{3!}{2!1!} + \frac{3!}{3!0!} = 15 + 1 = 16$$

The probability of getting a 6 at least twice in 3 rolls is $P(A) = \frac{n(A)}{n(S)} = \frac{16}{216} = \frac{2}{27}$.

Your Turn

6. A math department has a large database of true-false questions, half of which are true and half of which are false, that are used to create future exams. A new test is created by randomly selecting 6 questions from the database. What is the probability the new test contains at most 2 questions where the correct answer is "true"?

7. There are equally many boys and girls in the senior class. If 5 seniors are randomly selected to form the student council, what is the probability the council will contain at least 3 girls?

Elaborate

8. **Discussion** A coin is flipped 5 times, and the result of heads or tails is recorded. To find the probability of getting tails at least once, the events of 1, 2, 3, 4, or 5 tails can be added together. Is there a faster way to calculate this probability?

9. If ${}_nC_a = {}_nC_b$, what is the relationship between a and b? Explain your answer.

10. **Essential Question Check-In** How do you determine whether choosing a group of objects involves combinations?

Evaluate: Homework and Practice

- Online Homework
- Hints and Help
- Extra Practice

1. A cat has a litter of 6 kittens. You plan to adopt 2 of the kittens. In how many ways can you choose 2 of the kittens from the litter?

2. An amusement park has 11 roller coasters. In how many ways can you choose 4 of the roller coasters to ride during your visit to the park?

3. Four students from 30-member math club will be selected to organize a fundraiser. How many groups of 4 students are possible?

4. A school has 5 Spanish teachers and 4 French teachers. The school's principal randomly chooses 2 of the teachers to attend a conference. What is the probability that the principal chooses 2 Spanish teachers?

5. There are 6 fiction books and 8 nonfiction books on a reading list. Your teacher randomly assigns you 4 books to read over the summer. What is the probability that you are assigned all nonfiction books?

6. A bag contains 26 tiles, each with a different letter of the alphabet written on it. You choose 3 tiles from the bag without looking. What is the probability that you choose the tiles with the letters A, B, and C?

7. You are randomly assigned a password consisting of 6 different characters chosen from the digits 0 to 9 and the letters A to Z. As a percent, what is the probability that you are assigned a password consisting of only letters? Round your answer to the nearest tenth of a percent.

8. A bouquet of 6 flowers is made up by randomly choosing between roses and carnations. What is the probability the bouquet will have at most 2 roses?

9. A bag of fruit contains 10 pieces of fruit, chosen randomly from bins of apples and oranges. What is the probability the bag contains at least 6 oranges?

10. You flip a coin 10 times. What is the probability that you get at most 3 heads?

11. You flip a coin 8 times. What is the probability you will get at least 5 heads?

12. You flip a coin 5 times. What is the probability that every result will be tails?

13. There are 12 balloons in a bag: 3 each of blue, green, red, and yellow. Three balloons are chosen at random. Find the probability that all 3 balloons are green.

14. There are 6 female and 3 male kittens at an adoption center. Four kittens are chosen at random. What is the probability that all 4 kittens are female?

There are 21 students in your class. The teacher wants to send 4 students to the library each day. The teacher will choose the students to go to the library at random each day for the first four days from the list of students who have not already gone. Answer each question.

15. What is the probability you will be chosen to go on the first day?

16. If you have not yet been chosen to go on days 1–3, what is the probability you will be chosen to go on the fourth day?

17. Your teacher chooses 2 students at random to represent your homeroom. The homeroom has a total of 30 students, including your best friend. What is the probability that you and your best friend are chosen?

There are 12 peaches and 8 bananas in a fruit basket. You get a snack for yourself and three of your friends by choosing four of the pieces of fruit at random. Answer each question.

18. What is the probability that all 4 are peaches?

19. What is the probability that all 4 are bananas?

20. There are 30 students in your class. Your science teacher will choose 5 students at random to create a group to do a project. Find the probability that you and your 2 best friends in the science class will be chosen to be in the group.

21. On a television game show, 9 members of the studio audience are randomly selected to be eligible contestants.

a. Six of the 9 eligible contestants are randomly chosen to play a game on the stage. How many combinations of 6 players from the group of eligible contestants are possible?

b. You and your two friends are part of the group of 9 eligible contestants. What is the probability that all three of you are chosen to play the game on stage? Explain how you found your answer.

22. Determine whether you should use permutations or combinations to find the number of possibilities in each of the following situations.

a. Selecting a group of 5 people from a group of 8 people

b. Finding the number of combinations for a combination lock

c. Awarding first and second place ribbons in a contest

d. Choosing 3 books to read in any order from a list of 7 books

H.O.T. Focus on Higher Order Thinking

23. Communicate Mathematical Ideas Using the letters *A*, *B*, and *C*, explain the difference between a permutation and a combination.

24. Draw Conclusions Calculate ${}_{10}C_6$ and ${}_{10}C_4$.

a. What do you notice about these values? Explain why this makes sense.

b. Use your observations to help you state a generalization about combinations.

25. Justify Reasoning Use the formula for combinations to make a generalization about ${}_nC_n$. Explain why this makes sense.

26. Explain the Error Describe and correct the error in evaluating ${}_9C_4$.

$${}_9C_4 = \frac{9!}{(9-4)!} = \frac{9!}{5!} = 3024$$

Lesson Performance Task

1. In the 2012 elections, there were six candidates for the United States Senate in Vermont. In how many different orders, from first through sixth, could the candidates have finished?

2. The winner of the Vermont Senatorial election received 208,253 votes, 71.1% of the total votes cast. The candidate coming in second received 24.8% of the vote. How many votes did the second-place candidate receive? Round to the nearest ten.

3. Following the 2012 election there were 53 Democratic, 45 Republican, and 2 Independent senators in Congress.

   a. How many committees of 5 Democratic senators could be formed?

   b. How many committees of 48 Democratic senators could be formed?

   c. Explain how a clever person who knew nothing about combinations could guess the answer to (b) if the person knew the answer to (a).

4. Following the election, a newspaper printed a circle graph showing the make-up of the Senate. How many degrees were allotted to the sector representing Democrats, how many to Republicans, and how many to Independents?

21.4 Mutually Exclusive and Overlapping Events

Essential Question: How are probabilities affected when events are mutually exclusive or overlapping?

Resource Locker

Explore 1 Finding the Probability of Mutually Exclusive Events

Two events are **mutually exclusive events** if they cannot both occur in the same trial of an experiment. For example, if you flip a coin it cannot land heads up and tails up in the same trial. Therefore, the events are mutually exclusive.

A number dodecahedron has 12 sides numbered 1 through 12. What is the probability that you roll the cube and the result is an even number or a 7?

(A) Let A be the event that you roll an even number. Let B be the event that you roll a 7. Let S be the sample space.

Copy and complete the Venn diagram by writing all outcomes in the sample space in the appropriate region.

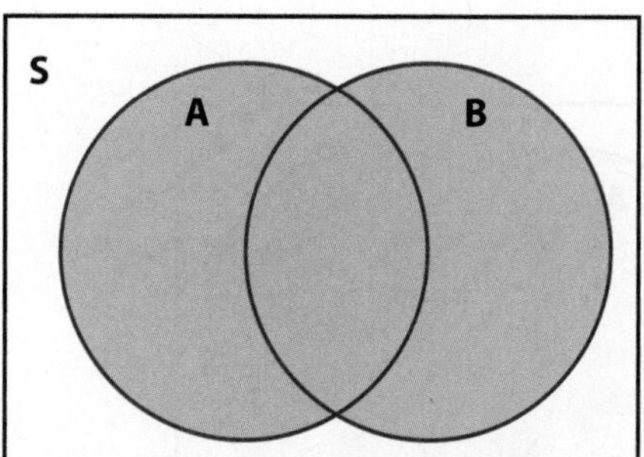

(B) Calculate $P(A)$.

$$P(A) = \frac{?}{?} = \frac{?}{?}$$

(C) Calculate $P(B)$.

$$P(B) = \frac{?}{?}$$

(D) Calculate $P(A \text{ or } B)$.

$n(S) = ?$

$n(A \text{ or } B) = n(A) + n(B)$

$= ? + ? = ?$

So, $P(A \text{ or } B) = \frac{n(A \text{ or } B)}{n(S)} = \frac{?}{?}$.

(E) Calculate $P(A) + P(B)$. Compare the answer to Step D.

$$P(A) + P(B) = \frac{?}{?} + \frac{?}{?} = \frac{?}{?}$$

$P(A) + P(B)$? $P(A \text{ or } B)$.

Reflect

1. **Discussion** How would you describe mutually exclusive events to another student in your own words? How could you use a Venn diagram to assist in your explanation?

2. Look back over the steps. What can you conjecture about the probability of the union of events that are mutually exclusive?

Explore 2 Finding the Probability of Overlapping Events

The process used in the previous Explore can be generalized to give the formula for the probability of mutually exclusive events.

Mutually Exclusive Events

If A and B are mutually exclusive events, then $P(A \text{ or } B) = P(A) + P(B)$.

Two events are **overlapping events** (or inclusive events) if they have one or more outcomes in common.

What is the probability that you roll a number dodecahedron and the result is an even number or a number greater than 7?

(A) Let A be the event that you roll an even number. Let B be the event that you roll a number greater than 7. Let S be the sample space.

Copy and complete the Venn diagram by writing all outcomes in the sample space in the appropriate region.

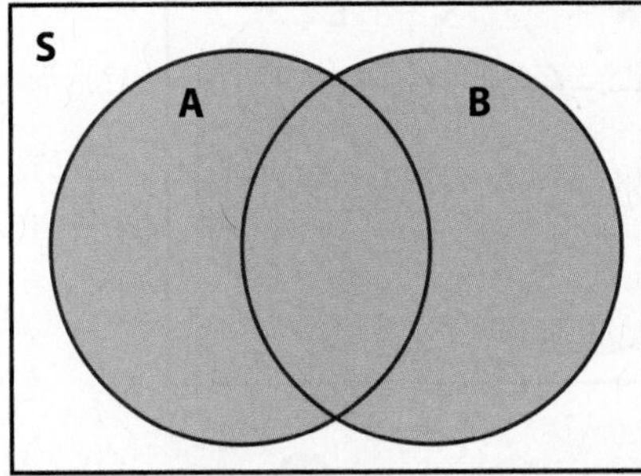

(B) Calculate $P(A)$.

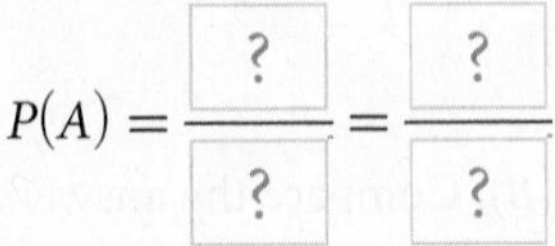

$P(A) = \frac{?}{?} = \frac{?}{?}$

(C) Calculate $P(B)$.

$P(B) = \frac{?}{?}$

(D) Calculate $P(A \text{ and } B)$.

$P(A \text{ and } B) = \frac{?}{?} = \frac{?}{?}$

(E) Use the Venn diagram to find $P(A \text{ or } B)$.

$P(A \text{ or } B) = \frac{?}{?} = \frac{?}{?}$

(F) Now, use $P(A)$, $P(B)$, and $P(A \text{ and } B)$ to calculate $P(A \text{ or } B)$.

$P(A) = \boxed{?}$ $\quad P(B) = \boxed{?}$ $\quad P(A \text{ and } B) = \boxed{?}$

$P(A) + P(B) - P(A \text{ and } B) = \boxed{?} + \boxed{?} - \boxed{?} = \boxed{?}$

Reflect

3. Why must you subtract $P(A \text{ and } B)$ from $P(A) + P(B)$ to determine $P(A \text{ or } B)$?

4. Look back over the steps. What can you conjecture about the probability of the union of two events that are overlapping?

Explain 1 Finding a Probability From a Two-Way Table of Data

The previous Explore leads to the following rule.

The Addition Rule

$P(A \text{ or } B) = P(A) + P(B) - P(A \text{ and } B)$

Example 1 **Use the given two-way tables to determine the probabilities.**

(A) $P(\text{senior or girl})$

	Freshman	Sophomore	Junior	Senior	TOTAL
Boy	98	104	100	94	396
Girl	102	106	96	108	412
Total	200	210	196	202	808

To determine $P(\text{senior or girl})$, first calculate $P(\text{senior})$, $P(\text{girl})$, and $P(\text{senior and girl})$.

$P(\text{senior}) = \frac{202}{808} = \frac{1}{4}$; $P(\text{girl}) = \frac{412}{808} = \frac{103}{202}$ $\quad P(\text{senior and girl}) = \frac{108}{808} = \frac{27}{202}$

Use the addition rule to determine $P(\text{senior or girl})$.

$$P(\text{senior or girl}) = P(\text{senior}) + P(\text{girl}) - P(\text{senior and girl})$$
$$= \frac{1}{4} + \frac{103}{202} - \frac{27}{202}$$
$$= \frac{253}{404}$$

Therefore, the probability that a student is a senior or a girl is $\frac{253}{404}$.

(B) $P\left((\text{domestic or late})^c\right)$

	Late	On Time	Total
Domestic Flights	12	108	120
International Flights	6	54	60
Total	18	162	180

To determine $P\left((\text{domestic or late})^c\right)$, first calculate $P(\text{domestic or late})$.

$P(\text{domestic}) = \frac{120}{180} = \frac{2}{3}$; $P(\text{late}) = \frac{18}{180} = \frac{1}{10}$; $P(\text{domestic and late}) = \frac{12}{180} = \frac{1}{15}$

Use the addition rule to determine $P(\text{domestic or late})$.

$P(\text{domestic or late}) = P(\text{domestic}) + P(\text{late}) - P(\text{domestic and late})$

$$= \frac{2}{3} + \frac{1}{10} - \frac{1}{15} = \frac{7}{10}$$

Therefore, $P\left((\text{domestic or late})^c\right) = 1 - P(\text{domestic or late})$

$$= 1 - \frac{7}{10}$$

$$= \frac{3}{10}$$

Your Turn

5. Use the table to determine $P(\text{headache or no medicine})$.

	Took Medicine	No Medicine	TOTAL
Headache	12	15	27
No Headache	48	25	73
TOTAL	60	40	100

Elaborate

6. Give an example of mutually exclusive events and an example of overlapping events.

7. **Essential Question Check-In** How do you determine the probability of mutually exclusive events and overlapping events?

Evaluate: Homework and Practice

- Online Homework
- Hints and Help
- Extra Practice

1. A bag contains 3 blue marbles, 5 red marbles, and 4 green marbles. You choose one without looking. What is the probability that it is red or green?

2. A number icosahedron has 20 sides numbered 1 through 20. What is the probability that the result of a roll is a number less than 4 or greater than 11?

3. A bag contains 26 tiles, each with a different letter of the alphabet written on it. You choose a tile without looking. What is the probability that you choose a vowel (a, e, i, o, or u) or a letter in the word GEOMETRY?

4. **Persevere in Problem Solving** You roll two number cubes at the same time. Each cube has sides numbered 1 through 6. What is the probability that the sum of the numbers rolled is even or greater than 9? (*Hint:* Create and fill out a probability chart.)

The table shows the data for car insurance quotes for 125 drivers made by an insurance company in one week.

	Teen	Adult (20 or over)	Total
0 accidents	15	53	68
1 accident	4	32	36
2+ accidents	9	12	21
Total	28	97	125

You randomly choose one of the drivers. Find the probability of each event.

5. The driver is an adult.

6. The driver is a teen with 0 or 1 accident.

7. The driver is a teen.

8. The driver has 2+ accidents.

9. The driver is a teen and has 2+ accidents.

10. The driver is a teen or a driver with 2+ accidents.

Use the following information for Exercises 11–16. The table shown shows the results of a customer satisfaction survey for a cellular service provider, by location of the customer. In the survey, customers were asked whether they would recommend a plan with the provider to a friend.

	Arlington	Towson	Parkville	Total
Yes	40	35	41	116
No	18	10	6	34
Total	58	45	47	150

One of the customers that was surveyed was chosen at random. Find the probability of each event.

11. The customer was from Towson and said No.

12. The customer was from Parkville.

13. The customer said Yes.

14. The customer was from Parkville and said Yes.

15. The customer was from Parkville or said Yes.

16. Explain why you cannot use the rule $P(A \text{ or } B) = P(A) + P(B)$ in Exercise 15.

Use the following information for Exercises 17–21. Roberto is the owner of a car dealership. He is assessing the success rate of his top three salespeople in order to offer one of them a promotion. Over two months, for each attempted sale, he records whether the salesperson made a successful sale or not. The results are shown in the chart.

	Successful	Unsuccessful	Total
Becky	6	6	12
Raul	4	5	9
Darrell	6	9	15
Total	16	20	36

Roberto randomly chooses one of the attempted sales.

17. Find the probability that the sale was one of Becky's or Raul's successful sales.

18. Find the probability that the sale was one of the unsuccessful sales or one of Raul's successful sales.

19. Find the probability that the sale was one of Darrell's unsuccessful sales or one of Raul's unsuccessful sales.

20. Find the probability that the sale was an unsuccessful sale or one of Becky's attempted sales.

21. Find the probability that the sale was a successful sale or one of Raul's attempted sales.

22. You are going to draw one card at random from a standard deck of cards. A standard deck of cards has 13 cards (2, 3, 4, 5, 6, 7, 8, 9, 10, jack, queen, king, ace) in each of 4 suits (hearts, clubs, diamonds, spades). The hearts and diamonds cards are red. The clubs and spades cards are black. Which of the following have a probability of less than $\frac{1}{4}$? Choose all that apply.

a. Drawing a card that is a spade and an ace

b. Drawing a card that is a club or an ace

c. Drawing a card that is a face card or a club

d. Drawing a card that is black and a heart

e. Drawing a red card and a number card from 2–9

H.O.T. Focus on Higher Order Thinking

23. Draw Conclusions A survey of 1108 employees at a software company finds that 621 employees take a bus to work and 445 employees take a train to work. Some employees take both a bus and a train, and 321 employees take only a train. To the nearest percent, find the probability that a randomly chosen employee takes a bus or a train to work. Explain.

24. Communicate Mathematical Ideas Explain how to use a Venn diagram to find the probability of randomly choosing a multiple of 3 or a multiple of 4 from the set of numbers from 1 to 25. Then find the probability.

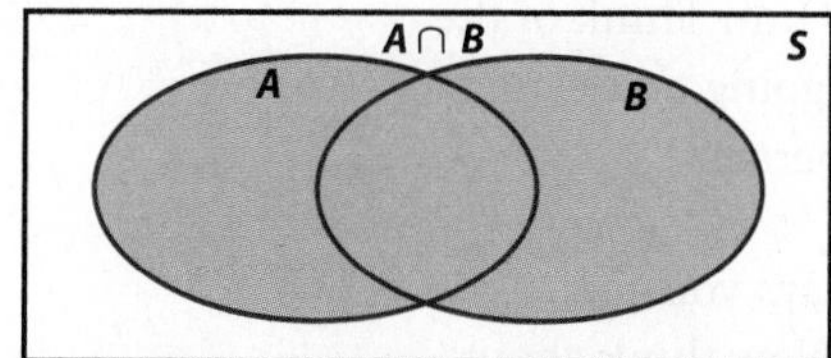

25. Explain the Error Sanderson attempted to find the probability of randomly choosing a 10 or a diamond from a standard deck of playing cards. He used the following logic:

Let S be the sample space, A be the event that the card is a 10, and B be the event that the card is a diamond.

There are 52 cards in the deck, so $n(S) = 52$.

There are four 10s in the deck, so $n(A) = 4$.

There are 13 diamonds in the deck, so $n(B) = 13$.

One 10 is a diamond, so $n(A \cap B) = 1$.

$$P(A \cup B) = \frac{n(A \cup B)}{n(S)} = \frac{n(A) \cdot n(B) - n(A \cap B)}{n(S)} = \frac{4 \cdot 13 - 1}{52} = \frac{51}{52}$$

Describe and correct Sanderson's mistake.

Lesson Performance Task

What is the smallest number of randomly chosen people that are needed in order for there to be a better than 50% probability that at least two of them will have the same birthday? The astonishing answer is 23. Follow these steps to find why.

1. Can a person have a birthday on two different days? Use the vocabulary of this lesson to explain your answer.

Looking for the probability that two or more people in a group of 23 have matching birthdays is a challenge. Maybe there is one match but maybe there are five matches or seven or fourteen. A much easier way is to look for the probability that there are *no* matches in a group of 23. In other words, all 23 have different birthdays. Then use that number to find the answer.

2. There are 365 days in a non-leap year.

a. Write an expression for the number of ways you can assign different birthdays to 23 people. (Hint: Think of the people as standing in a line, and you are going to assign a different number from 1 to 365 to each person.)

b. Write an expression for the number of ways you can assign any birthday to 23 people. (Hint: Now think about assigning any number from 1 to 365 to each of 23 people.)

c. How can you use your answers to (a) and (b) to find the probability that no people in a group of 23 have the same birthday? Use a calculator to find the probability to the nearest ten-thousandth.

d. What is the probability that at least two people in a group of 23 have the same birthday? Explain your reasoning.

Introduction to Probability

Essential Question: How can you use probability to solve real-world problems?

Key Vocabulary

set *(conjunto, juego)*
element *(elemento)*
empty set *(conjunto vacío)*
universal set *(conjunto universal)*
subset *(subconjunto)*
intersection *(intersección)*
union *(unión)*
complement *(complemento)*
theoretical probability *(probabilidad teórica)*
permutation *(permutación)*
Fundamental Counting Principle *(principio fundamental de conteo)*
factorial *(factorial)*
combination *(combinación)*

KEY EXAMPLE *(Lesson 21.1)*

When rolling two fair number cubes, what is the probability that the sum of the two cubes will not be even or prime?

The sum of two number cubes can be any integer from 2 through 12. Of these, the only possible sum that is not even or prime is 9. There are 36 possible outcomes for rolling two number cubes. Of these, the only ones that sum to 9 are (3, 6), (6, 3), (4, 5), and (5, 4). So, $P(\text{sum is not even or prime}) = \frac{4}{36} = \frac{1}{9}$.

KEY EXAMPLE *(Lesson 21.2)*

Ten marbles are placed in a jar. Of the 10 marbles, 3 are blue, 2 are red, 3 are green, 1 is orange, and 1 is yellow. The 10 marbles are randomly placed in a line. What is the probability that all marbles of the same color are next to each other?

Marbles of the same color are indistinguishable objects. The sample space S consists of permutations of 10 objects, with 3 of one type, 3 of another type, and 2 of a third type.

$$n(S) = \frac{10!}{3!3!2!} = 50{,}400$$

Event A consists of permutations that have all marbles of the same color next to each other, so it is the number of ways of ordering the 5 colors.

$$n(A) = 5! = 120$$

The probability that all marbles of the same color are next to each other is

$$P(A) = \frac{n(A)}{n(S)} = \frac{120}{50{,}400} = \frac{1}{420}.$$

KEY EXAMPLE *(Lesson 21.3)*

A class of 15 boys and 15 girls is putting together a random group of 3 students to do classroom chores. What is the probability that at least 2 of the students are boys?

The sample space S consists of combinations of three student groups.

$$n(S) = \frac{30!}{3!27!} = 4060$$

Event A consists of combinations that have 2 boys or 3 boys in the group. The event of getting 2 boys in the group occurs 15 times, once for each individual girl in the class.

$$n(A) = 15 \cdot {}_{15}C_2 + {}_{15}C_3 = 15 \cdot \frac{15!}{2!13!} + \frac{15!}{3!12!} = 2030$$

The probability that there will be at least 2 boys in the group is $P(A) = \frac{n(A)}{n(S)} = \frac{2030}{4060} = \frac{1}{2}$.

EXERCISES

Use the sets below to find the indicated set for problems 1–4. *(Lesson 21.1)*

$U = \{1, 2, 3, 4, 5, 6, 7, 8, 9\}$

$A = \{1, 3, 5, 7, 9\}$

$B = \{2, 4, 6, 8\}$

$C = \{1, 2, 4, 5, 7, 9\}$

1. $A \cup C$

2. $B \cap C$

3. A^C

4. $A \cap B$

5. A computer password can use all digits (0–9) and all letters (*a*–*z*) that are case sensitive (upper and lower). How many different permutations of 5-figure passwords are there if there is no repeated input? *(Lesson 21.2)*

6. Brandon is rolling a 10-sided number cube 5 times. What is the probability that he will roll at least two 7s? *(Lesson 21.3)*

Determine if the given events are mutually exclusive. If not, explain why. *(Lesson 21.4)*

7. Rolling a 3 or a 4 on a regular number cube

8. Drawing a queen or a red card from a standard deck of 52 cards

9. Flipping a coin and having it land on heads or tails

10. Rolling an even number or a prime number on a number cube

MODULE PERFORMANCE TASK

Baseball Probability

A baseball player will be batting three times during today's game. So far this season, the player has gotten an average of 1 hit in every 3 times at bat. Based on this data, what is the probability that the player will get exactly one hit in today's game? Is that outcome more or less likely than getting no hits?

Start by making notes about your plan for solving the problem. Then use words, numbers, or diagrams to explain how your reached your conclusions.

Ready to Go On?

21.1–21.4 Introduction to Probability

- Online Homework
- Hints and Help
- Extra Practice

Find the probabilities. *(Lessons 21.3, 21.4)*

1. Twenty-six tiles with the letters A through Z are placed face down on a table and mixed. (For the purpose of this exercise assume that the letter Y is a vowel.) Five tiles are drawn in order. Compute the probability that only consonants are selected.

2. The two-way table shows the results of a poll in a certain country that asked voters, sorted by political party, whether they supported or opposed a proposed government initiative. Find the given probabilities.

	Party A	Party B	Other Party	No Party	Total
Support	97	68	8	19	192
Oppose	32	81	16	11	140
Undecided	9	23	10	26	68
Total	138	172	34	56	400

a. $P(\text{no party or undecided})$

b. $P\left((\text{party A or support})^c\right)$

ESSENTIAL QUESTION

3. A teacher is assigning 32 presentation topics to 9 students at random. Each student will get 3 topics, and no topic will be repeated. Somil is very interested in 5 topics. What is the probability that Somil will be assigned at least one of his preferred topics? Explain how you arrived at your answer.

MODULE 21
MIXED REVIEW

Assessment Readiness

1. Jonah is arranging books on a shelf. The order of the books matters to him. There are 336 ways he can arrange the books. Write Yes or No for A–C.

A. He might be arranging 3 books from a selection of 8 different books.

B. He might be arranging 4 books from a selection of 8 different books.

C. He might be arranging 5 books from a selection of 8 different books.

2. Decide whether the probability of tossing the given sum with two dice is $\frac{5}{36}$. Write Yes or No for A–C.

A. A sum of 6

B. A sum of 7

C. A sum of 8

3. Let H be the event that a coin flip lands with heads showing, and let T be the event that a flip lands with tails showing. (Note that $P(H) = P(T) = 0.5$.) What is the probability that you will get heads at least once if you flip the coin ten times? Explain your reasoning.

4. There are 8 girls and 6 boys on the student council. How many committees of 3 girls and 2 boys can be formed? Show your work.

Conditional Probability and Independence of Events

MODULE 22

Essential Question: How can you use conditional probability and independence of events to solve real-world problems?

REAL WORLD VIDEO
Check out how principles of conditional probability are used to understand the chances of events in playing cards.

MODULE PERFORMANCE TASK PREVIEW
Playing Cards

In this module, you will use concepts of conditional probability to determine the chance of drawing a hand of cards with a certain property. To successfully complete this task, you'll need to master these skills:

- Distinguish between independent and dependent events.
- Apply the conditional probability formula to a real-world situation.
- Use the Multiplication Rule appropriately.

Complete these exercises to review skills you will need for this module.

Personal Math Trainer

- Online Homework
- Hints and Help
- Extra Practice

Probability of Compound Events

Example 1

Find the probability of rolling a pair of six-sided dice and the sum of their faces being even or equal to 3.

Three is not even, so the two probabilities are mutually exclusive. The probability is equal to the sums of the probabilities of rolling an even sum or rolling a sum of 3.

Probability of rolling an even sum $= \frac{18}{36}$ — Count the number of outcomes for the first event.

Probability of rolling a sum of 3 $= \frac{2}{36}$ — Count the number of outcomes for the second event.

Probability of rolling an even sum or a sum of 3 $= \frac{18}{36} + \frac{2}{36} = \frac{20}{36} = \frac{5}{9}$

Find each probability.

1. The probability of rolling two dice at the same time and getting a 4 with either die or the sum of the dice is 6.

2. The probability of rolling two dice at the same time and getting a 4 with either die and the sum of the dice is 6.

3. The probability of pulling red or blue marbles (or both) from a jar of only red and blue marbles when you pull out two marbles given that pulling red and pulling blue are equally likely events.

4. The probability of pulling a red marble and a blue marble from a jar of only red and blue marbles when you pull out two marbles given that pulling red and pulling blue are equally likely events.

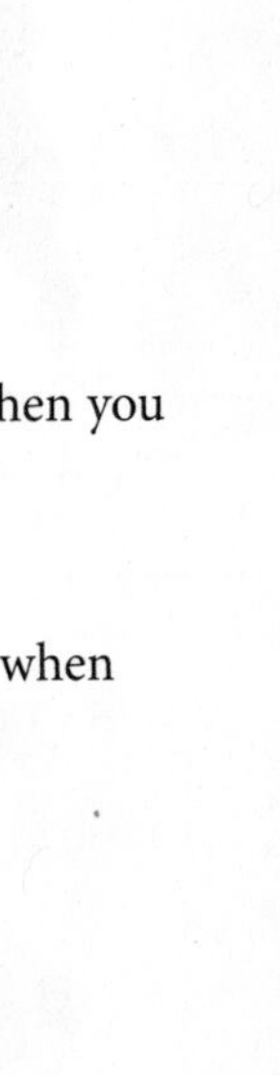

5. The probability of flipping a coin three times and getting exactly two heads or at least one tails given the probability of getting a heads is $\frac{1}{2}$ and the probability of getting a tails is $\frac{1}{2}$.

6. The probability of flipping a coin three times and getting exactly two heads and at least one tails given the probability of getting a heads is $\frac{1}{2}$ and the probability of getting a tails is $\frac{1}{2}$.

7. The probability of flipping a coin three times and getting at least two heads or at least one tails given the probability of getting a heads is $\frac{1}{2}$ and the probability of getting a tails is $\frac{1}{2}$.

22.1 Conditional Probability

Resource Locker

Essential Question: How do you calculate a conditional probability?

Explore 1 Finding Conditional Probabilities from a Two-Way Frequency Table

The probability that event A occurs given that event B has already occurred is called the **conditional probability** of A given B and is written $P(A \mid B)$.

One hundred migraine headache sufferers participated in a study of a new medicine. Some were given the new medicine, and others were not. After one week, participants were asked if they had experienced a headache during the week. The two-way frequency table shows the results.

	Took medicine	No medicine	Total
Headache	11	13	24
No headache	54	22	76
Total	65	35	100

Let event A be the event that a participant did not get a headache. Let event B be the event that a participant took the medicine.

(A) To the nearest percent, what is the probability that a participant who took the medicine did not get a headache?

? participants took the medicine.

Of these, ? did not get a headache.

So, $P(A \mid B) = \frac{?}{?} \approx$? %.

(B) To the nearest percent, what is the probability that a participant who did not get a headache took the medicine?

? participants did not get a headache.

Of these, ? took the medicine.

So, $P(B \mid A) = \frac{?}{?} \approx$? %.

(C) Let $n(A)$ be the number of participants who did not get a headache, $n(B)$ be the number of participants who took the medicine, and $n(A \cap B)$ be the number of participants who took the medicine and did not get a headache.

$n(A) =$? $n(B) =$? $n(A \cap B) =$?

Express $P(A \mid B)$ and $P(B \mid A)$ in terms of $n(A)$, $n(B)$, and $n(A \cap B)$.

$P(A \mid B) = \frac{?}{?}$ $P(B \mid A) = \frac{?}{?}$

Reflect

1. For the question "What is the probability that a participant who did not get a headache took the medicine?", what event is assumed to have already occurred?

2. In general, does it appear that $P(A \mid B) = P(B \mid A)$? Why or why not?

Explore 2 Finding Conditional Probabilities from a Two-Way Relative Frequency Table

You can develop a formula for $P(A \mid B)$ that uses relative frequencies (which are probabilities) rather than frequencies (which are counts).

	Took medicine	No medicine	Total
Headache	11	13	24
No headache	54	22	76
Total	65	35	100

(A) To obtain relative frequencies, divide every number in the table by 100, the total number of participants in the study.

	Took medicine	No medicine	Total
Headache	?	?	?
No headache	?	?	?
Total	?	?	1

(B) Recall that event A is the event that a participant did not get a headache and that event B is the event that a participant took the medicine. Use the relative frequency table from Step A to find $P(A)$, $P(B)$, and $P(A \cap B)$.

(C) In the first Explore, you found the conditional probabilities $P(A \mid B) \approx 83\%$ and $P(B \mid A) \approx 71\%$ by using the frequencies in the two-way frequency table. Use the relative frequencies from the table in Step A to find the equivalent conditional probabilities.

$$P(A \mid B) = \frac{P(A \cap B)}{P(B)} = \frac{?}{?} \approx ?\ \% \qquad P(B \mid A) = \frac{P(A \cap B)}{P(A)} = \frac{?}{?} \approx ?\ \%$$

(D) Generalize the results by using $n(S)$ as the number of elements in the sample space (in this case, the number of participants in the study). For instance, you can write $P(A) = \frac{n(A)}{n(S)}$. Write each of the following probabilities in a similar way.

$$P(B) = \frac{?}{?} \qquad P(A \cap B) = \frac{?}{?} \qquad P(A \mid B) = \frac{\dfrac{n(A \cap B)}{?}}{\dfrac{n(B)}{?}} = \frac{P(A \cap B)}{?}$$

Reflect

3. Why are the two forms of $P(A \cap B)$, $\frac{n(A \cap B)}{n(B)}$ and $\frac{P(A \cap B)}{P(B)}$, equivalent?

4. What is a formula for $P(B \mid A)$ that involves probabilities rather than counts? How do you obtain this formula from the fact that $P(B \mid A) = \frac{n(A \cap B)}{n(A)}$?

Explain 1 Using the Conditional Probability Formula

In the previous Explore, you discovered the following formula for conditional probability.

Conditional Probability

The conditional probability of A given B (that is, the probability that event A occurs given that event B occurs) is as follows:

$$P(A \mid B) = \frac{P(A \cap B)}{P(B)}$$

Example 1 **Find the specified probability.**

(A) For a standard deck of playing cards, find the probability that a red card randomly drawn from the deck is a jack.

Step 1 Find $P(R)$, the probability that a red card is drawn from the deck.

There are 26 red cards in the deck of 52 cards, so $P(R) = \frac{26}{52}$.

Step 2 Find $P(J \cap R)$, the probability that a red jack is drawn from the deck.

There are 2 red jacks in the deck, so $P(J \cap R) = \frac{2}{52}$.

Step 3 Substitute the probabilities from Steps 1 and 2 into the formula for conditional probability.

$$P(J \mid R) = \frac{P(J \cap R)}{P(R)} = \frac{\frac{2}{52}}{\frac{26}{52}}$$

Step 4 Simplify the result.

$$P(J \mid R) = \frac{\frac{2}{52} \cdot 52}{\frac{26}{52} \cdot 52} = \frac{2}{26} = \frac{1}{13}$$

(B) For a standard deck of playing cards, find the probability that a jack randomly drawn from the deck is a red card.

Step 1 Find $P(J)$, the probability that a jack is drawn from the deck.

There are 4 jacks in the deck of 52 cards, so $P(J) = \frac{4}{52}$.

Step 2 Find $P(J \cap R)$, the probability that a red jack is drawn from the deck.

There are 2 red jacks in the deck, so $P(J \cap R) = \frac{2}{52}$.

Step 3 Substitute the probabilities from Steps 1 and 2 into the formula for conditional probability.

$$P(R \mid J) = \frac{P(J \cap R)}{P(J)} = \frac{\frac{2}{52}}{\frac{4}{52}}$$

Step 4 Simplify the result.

$$P(R \mid J) = \frac{\frac{2}{52} \cdot 52}{\frac{4}{52} \cdot 52} = \frac{2}{4} = \frac{1}{2}$$

Your Turn

5. For a standard deck of playing cards, find the probability that a face card randomly drawn from the deck is a king. (The ace is *not* a face card.)

6. For a standard deck of playing cards, find the probability that a queen randomly drawn from the deck is a diamond.

Elaborate

7. When calculating a conditional probability from a two-way table, explain why it doesn't matter whether the table gives frequencies or relative frequencies.

8. **Discussion** Is it possible to have $P(B \mid A) = P(A \mid B)$ for some events A and B? What conditions would need to exist?

9. **Essential Question Check-In** In a two-way frequency table, suppose event A represents a row of the table and event B represents a column of the table. Describe how to find the conditional probability $P(A \mid B)$ using the frequencies in the table.

Evaluate: Homework and Practice

- Online Homework
- Hints and Help
- Extra Practice

In order to study the relationship between the amount of sleep a student gets and his or her school performance, a researcher collected data from 120 students. The two-way frequency table shows the number of students who passed and failed an exam and the number of students who got more or less than 6 hours of sleep the night before. Use the table to answer the questions in Exercises 1–3.

	Passed exam	Failed exam	Total
Less than 6 hours of sleep	12	10	22
More than 6 hours of sleep	90	8	98
Total	102	18	120

1. To the nearest percent, what is the probability that a student who failed the exam got less than 6 hours of sleep?

2. To the nearest percent, what is the probability that a student who got less than 6 hours of sleep failed the exam?

3. To the nearest percent, what is the probability that a student got less than 6 hours of sleep and failed the exam?

4. You have a standard deck of playing cards from which you randomly select a card. Event D is getting a diamond, and event F is getting a face card (a jack, queen, or king).

   Show that $P(D|F) = \dfrac{n(D \cap F)}{n(F)}$ and $P(D|F) = \dfrac{P(D \cap F)}{P(F)}$ are equal.

The table shows data in the previous table as relative frequencies (rounded to the nearest thousandth when necessary). Use the table for Exercises 5–7.

	Passed exam	Failed exam	Total
Less than 6 hours of sleep	0.100	0.083	0.183
More than 6 hours of sleep	0.750	0.067	0.817
Total	0.850	0.150	1.000

5. To the nearest percent, what is the probability that a student who passed the exam got more than 6 hours of sleep?

6. To the nearest percent, what is the probability that a student who got more than 6 hours of sleep passed the exam?

7. Which is greater, the probability that a student who got less than 6 hours of sleep passed the exam or the probability that a student who got more than 6 hours of sleep failed the exam? Explain.

You randomly draw a card from a standard deck of playing cards. Let A be the event that the card is an ace, let B be the event that the card is black, and let C be the event that the card is a club. Find the specified probability as a fraction.

8. $P(A|B)$

9. $P(B|A)$

10. $P(A|C)$

11. $P(C|A)$

12. $P(B|C)$

13. $P(C|B)$

14. A botanist studied the effect of a new fertilizer by choosing 100 orchids and giving 70% of these plants the fertilizer. Of the plants that got the fertilizer, 40% produced flowers within a month. Of the plants that did not get the fertilizer, 10% produced flowers within a month.

a. Use the given information to complete the two-way frequency table.

	Received fertilizer	Did not receive fertilizer	Total
Did not flower in one month	?	?	?
Flowered in one month	?	?	?
Total	?	?	?

b. To the nearest percent, what is the probability that an orchid that produced flowers got fertilizer?

c. To the nearest percent, what is the probability that an orchid that got fertilizer produced flowers?

15. At a school fair, a box contains 24 yellow balls and 76 red balls. One-fourth of the balls of each color are labeled "Win a prize." Match each description of a probability with its value as a percent.

A. The probability that a randomly selected ball labeled "Win a prize" is yellow

B. The probability that a randomly selected ball labeled "Win a prize" is red

C. The probability that a randomly selected ball is labeled "Win a prize" and is red

D. The probability that a randomly selected yellow ball is labeled "Win a prize"

a. ___?___ 76%

b. ___?___ 25%

c. ___?___ 24%

d. ___?___ 19%

16. A teacher gave her students two tests. If 45% of the students passed both tests and 60% passed the first test, what is the probability that a student who passed the first test also passed the second?

17. You randomly select two marbles, one at a time, from a pouch containing blue and green marbles. The probability of selecting a blue marble on the first draw and a green marble on the second draw is 25%, and the probability of selecting a blue marble on the first draw is 56%. To the nearest percent, what is the probability of selecting a green marble on the second draw, given that the first marble was blue?

You roll two number cubes, one red and one blue. The table shows the probabilities for events based on whether or not a 1 is rolled on each number cube. Use the table to find the specified conditional probability, expressed as a fraction. Then show that the conditional probability is correct by listing the possible outcomes as ordered pairs of the form (number on red cube, number on blue cube) and identifying the successful outcomes.

	Rolling a 1 on the red cube	Not rolling a 1 on the red cube	Total
Rolling a 1 on the blue cube	$\frac{1}{36}$	$\frac{5}{36}$	$\frac{1}{6}$
Not rolling a 1 on the blue cube	$\frac{5}{36}$	$\frac{25}{36}$	$\frac{5}{6}$
Total	$\frac{1}{6}$	$\frac{5}{6}$	1

18. P(not rolling a 1 on the blue cube | rolling a 1 on the red cube)

19. P(not rolling a 1 on the blue cube | not rolling a 1 on the red cube)

20. The table shows the results of a quality-control study at a computer factory.

	Shipped	Not shipped	Total
Defective	3	7	10
Not defective	89	1	90
Total	92	8	100

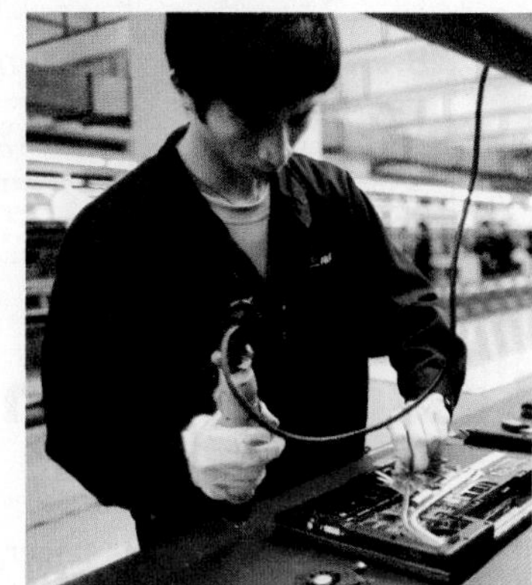

a. To the nearest tenth of a percent, what is the probability that a shipped computer is not defective?

b. To the nearest tenth of a percent, what is the probability that a defective computer is shipped?

H.O.T. Focus on Higher Order Thinking

21. Analyze Relationships In the Venn diagram, the circles representing events A and B divide the sample space S into four regions: the overlap of the circles, the part of A not in the overlap, the part of B not in the overlap, and the part of S not in A or B. Suppose that the area of each region is proportional to the number of outcomes that fall within the region. Which conditional probability is greater: $P(A|B)$ or $P(B|A)$? Explain.

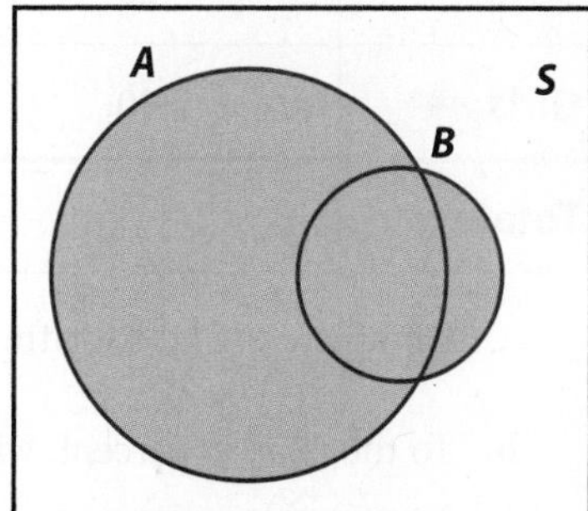

22. **Explain the Error** A student was asked to use the table shown to find the probability, to nearest percent, that a participant in a study of a new medicine for migraine headaches did not take the medicine, given that the participant reported no headaches.

	Took medicine	No medicine	Total
Headache	11	13	24
No headache	54	22	76
Total	65	35	100

The student made the following calculation.
$P(\text{no medicine} \mid \text{no headache}) = \frac{22}{35} \approx 0.63 = 63\%$
Explain the student's error, and find the correct probability.

23. **Communicate Mathematical Ideas** Explain how a conditional probability based on a two-way frequency table effectively reduces it to a one-way table. In your explanation, refer to the two-way table shown, which lists frequencies for events *A*, *B*, and their complements. Highlight the part of the table that supports your explanation.

	A	Not *A*	Total
B	$n(A \cap B)$	$n(\text{not } A \cap B)$	$n(B)$
Not *B*	$n(A \cap \text{not } B)$	$n(\text{not } A \cap \text{not } B)$	$n(\text{not } B)$
Total	$n(A)$	$n(\text{not } A)$	$n(S)$

Lesson Performance Task

The two-way frequency table gives the results of a survey that asked students this question: Which of these would you most like to meet: a famous singer, a movie star, or a sports star?

	Famous singer	Movie star	Sports star	Total
Boys	20	15	55	?
Girls	40	50	20	?
Total	?	?	?	?

a. Complete the table by finding the row totals, column totals, and grand total.

b. To the nearest percent, what is the probability that a student who chose "movie star" is a girl?

c. To the nearest percent, what is the probability that a student who chose "famous singer" is a boy?

d. To the nearest percent, what is the probability that a boy chose "sports star"?

e. To the nearest percent, what is the probability that a girl chose "famous singer"?

f. To the nearest percent, what is the probability that a student who chose either "famous singer" or "movie star" is a boy?

g. To the nearest percent, what is the probability that a girl did not choose "sports star"?

22.2 Independent Events

Essential Question: What does it mean for two events to be independent?

Resource Locker

Explore Understanding the Independence of Events

Suppose you flip a coin and roll a number cube. You would expect the probability of getting heads on the coin to be $\frac{1}{2}$ regardless of what number you get from rolling the number cube. Likewise, you would expect the probability of rolling a 3 on the number cube to be $\frac{1}{6}$ regardless of whether of the coin flip results in heads or tails.

When the occurrence of one event has no effect on the occurrence of another event, the two events are called **independent events**.

(A) A jar contains 15 red marbles and 17 yellow marbles. You randomly draw a marble from the jar. Let R be the event that you get a red marble, and let Y be the event that you get a yellow marble.

Since the jar has a total of ? marbles, $P(R) = \frac{?}{?}$ and $P(Y) = \frac{?}{?}$.

(B) Suppose the first marble you draw is a red marble, and you put that marble back in the jar before randomly drawing a second marble. Find $P(Y|R)$, the probability that you get a yellow marble on the second draw after getting a red marble on the first draw. Explain your reasoning.

Since the jar still has a total of ? marbles and ? of them are yellow, $P(Y|R) = \frac{?}{?}$.

(C) Suppose you *don't* put the red marble back in the jar before randomly drawing a second marble. Find $P(Y|R)$, the probability that you get a yellow marble on the second draw after getting a red marble on the first draw. Explain your reasoning.

Since the jar now has a total of ? marbles and ? of them are yellow, $P(Y|R) = \frac{?}{?}$.

Reflect

1. In one case you replaced the first marble before drawing the second, and in the other case you didn't. For which case was $P(Y|R)$ equal to $P(Y)$? Why?
2. In which of the two cases would you say the events of getting a red marble on the first draw and getting a yellow marble on the second draw are independent? What is true about $P(Y|R)$ and $P(Y)$ in this case?

Explain 1 Determining if Events are Independent

To determine the independence of two events A and B, you can check to see whether $P(A|B) = P(A)$ since the occurrence of event A is unaffected by the occurrence of event B if and only if the events are independent.

Example 1 **The two-way frequency table gives data about 180 randomly selected flights that arrive at an airport. Use the table to answer the question.**

	Late Arrival	On Time	Total
Domestic Flights	12	108	120
International Flights	6	54	60
Total	18	162	180

(A) Is the event that a flight is on time independent of the event that a flight is domestic?

Let O be the event that a flight is on time. Let D be the event that a flight is domestic. Find $P(O)$ and $P(O|D)$. To find $P(O)$, note that the total number of flights is 180, and of those flights, there are 162 on-time flights. So, $P(O) = \frac{162}{180} = 90\%$.

To find $P(O|D)$, note that there are 120 domestic flights, and of those flights, there are 108 on-time flights.

So, $P(O|D), = \frac{108}{120} = 90\%$.

Since $P(O|D) = P(O)$, the event that a flight is on time is independent of the event that a flight is domestic.

(B) Is the event that a flight is international independent of the event that a flight arrives late?

Let I be the event that a flight is international. Let L be the event that a flight arrives late. Find $P(I)$ and $P(I|L)$. To find $P(I)$, note that the total number of flights is 180, and of those

flights, there are 60 international flights. So, $P(I) = \frac{60}{180} = 33\frac{1}{3}\%$.

To find $P(I|L)$, note that there are 18 flights that arrive late, and of those flights, there are 6

international flights. So, $P(I|L) = \frac{6}{18} = 33\frac{1}{3}\%$.

Since $P(I|L)$ $=$ $P(I)$, the event that a flight is international is independent of the event that a flight arrives late.

Your Turn

The two-way frequency table gives data about 200 randomly selected apartments in a city. Use the table to answer the question.

	1 Bedroom	2+ Bedrooms	Total
Single Occupant	64	12	76
Multiple Occupants	26	98	124
Total	90	110	200

3. Is the event that an apartment has a single occupant independent of the event that an apartment has 1 bedroom?

4. Is the event that an apartment has 2 or more bedrooms independent of the event that an apartment has multiple occupants?

Explain 2 Finding the Probability of Independent Events

From the definition of conditional probability you know that $P(A|B) = \frac{P(A \cap B)}{P(B)}$ for any events A and B. If those events happen to be independent, you can replace $P(A|B)$ with $P(A)$ and get $P(A) = \frac{P(A \cap B)}{P(B)}$. Solving the last equation for $P(A \cap B)$ gives the following result.

Probability of Independent Events

Events A and B are independent if and only if $P(A \cap B) = P(A) \cdot P(B)$.

Example 2 **Find the specified probability.**

(A) Recall the jar with 15 red marbles and 17 yellow marbles from the Explore. Suppose you randomly draw one marble from the jar. After you put that marble back in the jar, you randomly draw a second marble. What is the probability that you draw a yellow marble first and a red marble second?

Let Y be the event of drawing a yellow marble first. Let R be the event of drawing a red marble second. Then $P(Y) = \frac{17}{32}$ and, because the first marble drawn is replaced before the second marble is drawn, $P(R|Y) = P(R) = \frac{15}{32}$. Since the events are independent, you can multiply their probabilities: $P(Y \cap R) = P(Y) \cdot P(R) = \frac{17}{32} \cdot \frac{15}{32} = \frac{255}{1024} \approx 25\%$.

(B) You spin the spinner shown two times. What is the probability that the spinner stops on an even number on the first spin, followed by an odd number on the second spin?

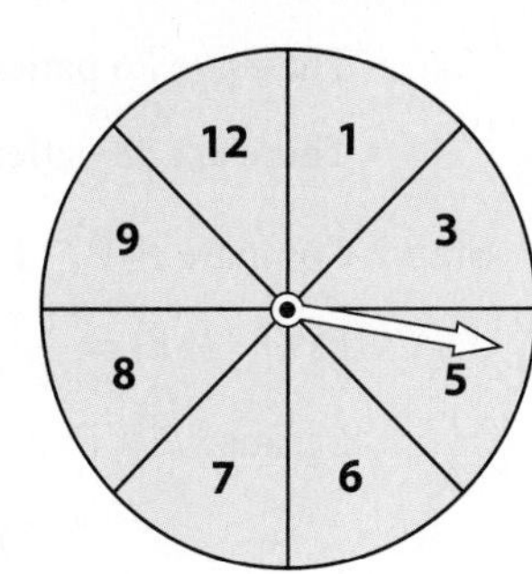

Let E be the event of getting an even number on the first spin. Let O be the event of getting an odd number on the second spin. Then $P(E) = \frac{3}{8}$ and, because the first spin has no effect on the second spin, $P(O|E) = P(O) = \frac{5}{8}$. Since the events are independent, you can multiply their probabilities:

$P(E \cap O) = P(E) \cdot P(O) = \frac{3}{8} \cdot \frac{5}{8} = \frac{15}{64} \approx 23$ %.

Reflect

5. In Part B, what is the probability that the spinner stops on an odd number on the first spin, followed by an even number on the second spin? What do you observe? What does this tell you?

Your Turn

6. You spin a spinner with 4 red sections, 3 blue sections, 2 green sections, and 1 yellow section. If all the sections are of equal size, what is the probability that the spinner stops on green first and blue second?

7. A number cube has the numbers 3, 5, 6, 8, 10, and 12 on its faces. You roll the number cube twice. What is the probability that you roll an odd number on both rolls?

Explain 3 Showing That Events Are Independent

So far, you have used the formula $P(A \cap B) = P(A) \cdot P(B)$ when you knew that events A and B are independent. You can also use the formula to determine whether two events are independent.

Example 3 **Determine if the events are independent.**

(A) The two-way frequency table shows data for 120 randomly selected patients who have the same doctor. Determine whether a patient who takes vitamins and a patient who exercises regularly are independent events.

	Takes Vitamins	No Vitamins	Total
Regular Exercise	48	28	76
No regular Exercise	12	32	44
Total	60	60	120

Let V be the event that a patient takes vitamins. Let E be the event that a patient exercises regularly.

Step 1 Find $P(V)$, $P(E)$, and $P(V \cap E)$. The total number of patients is 120.

There are 60 patients who take vitamins, so $P(V) = \frac{60}{120} = \frac{1}{2}$.

There are 76 patients who exercise regularly, so $P(B) = \frac{76}{120} = \frac{19}{30}$.

There are 48 patients who take vitamins and exercise regularly, so $P(V \cap E) = \frac{48}{120} = 40\%$.

Step 2 Compare $P(V \cap E)$ and $P(V) \cdot P(E)$.

$P(V) \cdot P(E) = \frac{1}{2} \cdot \frac{19}{30} = \frac{19}{60} \approx 32\%$

Because $P(V \cap E) \neq P(V) \cdot P(E)$, the events are not independent.

(B) The two-way frequency table shows data for 60 randomly selected children at an elementary school. Determine whether a child who knows how to ride a bike and a child who knows how to swim are independent events.

	Knows how to Ride a Bike	Doesn't Know how to Ride a Bike	Total
Knows how to Swim	30	10	40
Doesn't Know how to Swim	15	5	20
Total	45	15	60

Let B be the event a child knows how to ride a bike. Let S be the event that a child knows how to swim.

Step 1 Find $P(B)$, $P(S)$, and $P(B \cap S)$. The total number of children is 60.

There are 45 children who know how to ride a bike, so $P(B) = \frac{45}{60} = \frac{3}{4}$.

There are 40 children who know how to swim, so $P(S) = \frac{40}{60} = \frac{2}{3}$.

There are 30 children who know how to ride a bike and swim, so $P(B \cap S) = \frac{30}{60} = \frac{1}{2}$.

Step 2 Compare $P(B \cap S)$ and $P(B) \cdot P(S)$.

$$P(B) \cdot P(S) = \frac{3}{4} \cdot \frac{2}{3} = \frac{1}{2}$$

Because $P(B \cap S)$ $=$ $P(B) \cdot P(S)$, the events are independent.

Your Turn

8. A farmer wants to know if an insecticide is effective in preventing small insects called aphids from damaging tomato plants. The farmer experiments with 80 plants and records the results in the two-way frequency table. Determine whether a plant that was sprayed with insecticide and a plant that has aphids are independent events.

	Has Aphids	No Aphids	Total
Sprayed with Insecticide	12	40	52
Not Sprayed with Insecticide	14	14	28
Total	26	54	80

9. A student wants to know if right-handed people are more or less likely to play a musical instrument than left-handed people. The student collects data from 250 people, as shown in the two-way frequency table. Determine whether being right-handed and playing a musical instrument are independent events.

	Right-Handed	Left-Handed	Total
Plays a Musical Instrument	44	6	50
Does not Play a Musical Instrument	176	24	200
Total	220	30	250

Elaborate

10. What are the ways that you can show that two events A and B are independent?

11. How can you find the probability that two independent events A and B both occur?

12. **Essential Question Check-In** Give an example of two independent events and explain why they are independent.

Evaluate: Homework and Practice

- Online Homework
- Hints and Help
- Extra Practice

1. A bag contains 12 red and 8 blue chips. Two chips are separately drawn at random from the bag.

a. Suppose that a single chip is drawn at random from the bag. Find the probability that the chip is red and the probability that the chip is blue.

b. Suppose that two chips are separately drawn at random from the bag and that the first chip is returned to the bag before the second chip is drawn. Find the probability that the second chip drawn is blue given the first chip drawn was red.

c. Suppose that two chips are separately drawn at random from the bag and that the first chip is not returned to the bag before the second chip is drawn. Find the probability that the second chip drawn is blue given the first chip drawn was red.

d. In which situation—the first chip is returned to the bag or not returned to the bag—are the events that the first chip is red and the second chip is blue independent? Explain.

2. Identify whether the events are independent or not independent.

a. Flip a coin twice and get tails both times.

b. Roll a number cube and get 1 on the first roll and 6 on the second.

c. Draw an ace from a shuffled deck, put the card back and reshuffle the deck, and then draw an 8.

d. Rotate a bingo cage and draw the ball labeled B-4, set it aside, and then rotate the cage again and draw the ball labled N-38.

Answer the question using the fact that $P(A|B) = P(A)$ only when events A and B are independent.

3. The two-way frequency table shows data for 80 randomly selected people who live in a metropolitan area. Is the event that a person prefers public transportation independent of the event that a person lives in the city?

	Prefers to Drive	Prefers Public Transportation	Total
Lives in the City	12	24	36
Lives in the Suburbs	33	11	44
Total	45	35	80

4. The two-way frequency table shows data for 120 randomly selected people who take vacations. Is the event that a person prefers vacationing out of state independent of the event that a person is a woman?

	Prefers Vacationing Out of State	Prefers Vacationing in State	Total
Men	48	32	80
Women	24	16	40
Total	72	48	120

A jar contains marbles of various colors as listed in the table. Suppose you randomly draw one marble from the jar. After you put that marble back in the jar, you randomly draw a second marble. Use this information to answer the question, giving a probability as a percent and rounding to the nearest tenth of percent when necessary.

Color of Marble	Number of Marbles
Red	20
Yellow	18
Green	12
Blue	10

5. What is the probability that you draw a blue marble first and a red marble second?

6. What is the probability that you draw a yellow marble first and a green marble second?

7. What is the probability that you draw a yellow marble both times?

8. What color marble for the first draw and what color marble for the second draw have the greatest probability of occurring together? What is that probability?

You spin the spinner shown two times. Each section of the spinner is the same size. Use this information to answer the question, giving a probability as a percent and rounding to the nearest tenth of a percent when necessary.

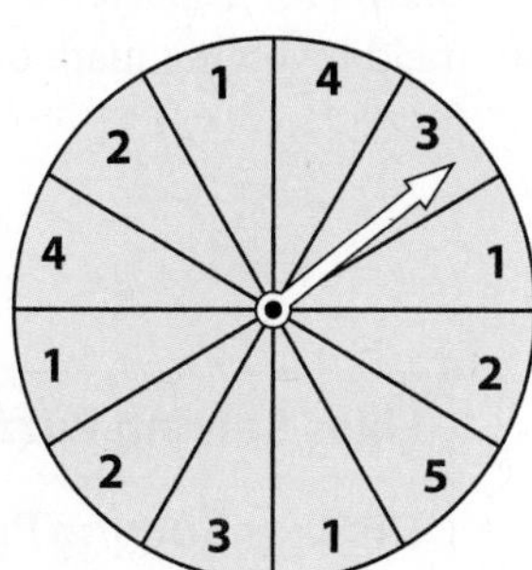

9. What is the probability that the spinner stops on 1 first and 2 second?

10. What is the probability that the spinner stops on 4 first and 3 second?

11. What is the probability that the spinner stops on an odd number first and an even number second?

12. What first number and what second number have the least probability of occurring together? What is that probability?

13. Find the probability of getting heads on every toss of a coin when the coin is tossed 3 times.

14. You are randomly choosing cards, one at a time and with replacement, from a standard deck of cards. Find the probability that you choose an ace, then a red card, and then a face card. (Remember that face cards are jacks, queens, and kings.)

Determine whether the given events are independent using the fact that $P(A \cap B) = P(A) \cdot P(B)$ only when events A and B are independent.

15. The manager of a produce stand wants to find out whether there is a connection between people who buy fresh vegetables and people who buy fresh fruit. The manager collects data on 200 randomly chosen shoppers, as shown in the two-way frequency table. Determine whether buying fresh vegetables and buying fresh fruit are independent events.

	Bought Vegetables	No Vegetables	Total
Bought Fruit	56	20	76
No Fruit	49	75	124
Total	105	95	200

16. The owner of a bookstore collects data about the reading preferences of 60 randomly chosen customers, as shown in the two-way frequency table. Determine whether being a female and preferring fiction are independent events.

	Prefers Fiction	Prefers Nonfiction	Total
Female	15	10	25
Male	21	14	35
Total	36	24	60

17. The psychology department at a college collects data about whether there is a relationship between a student's intended career and the student's like or dislike for solving puzzles. The two-way frequency table shows the collected data for 80 randomly chosen students. Determine whether planning for a career in a field involving math or science and a like for solving puzzles are independent events.

	Plans a Career in a Math/Science Field	Plans a Career in a Non-Math/Science Field	Total
Likes Solving Puzzles	35	15	50
Dislikes Solving Puzzles	9	21	30
Total	44	36	80

18. A local television station surveys some of its viewers to determine the primary reason they watch the station. The two-way frequency table gives the survey data. Determine whether a viewer is a man and a viewer primarily watches the station for entertainment are independent events.

	Primarily Watches for Information (News, Weather, Sports)	Primarily Watches for Entertainment (Comedies, Dramas)	Total
Men	28	12	40
Women	35	15	50
Total	63	27	90

19. Using what you know about independent events, complete the two-way frequency table in such a way that any event from a column will be independent of any event from a row. Give an example using the table to demonstrate the independence of two events.

	Women	Men	Total
Prefers Writing with a Pen	?	?	100
Prefers Writing with a Pencil	?	?	50
Total	60	90	150

H.O.T. Focus on Higher Order Thinking

20. Make a Prediction A box contains 100 balloons. The balloons come in two colors: 80 are yellow and 20 are green. The balloons are also either marked or unmarked: 50 are marked "Happy Birthday!" and 50 are not. A balloon is randomly chosen from the box. How many yellow "Happy Birthday!" balloons must be in the box if the event that a balloon is yellow and the event that a balloon is marked "Happy Birthday!" are independent? Explain.

21. Construct Arguments Given that events A and B are independent, prove that the complement of event A, A^c, is also independent of event B.

22. Multi-Step The two-way frequency table shows two events, A and B, and their complements, A^c and B^c. Let $P(A) = a$ and $P(B) = b$. Using a, b, and the grand total T, form the products listed in the table to find the number of elements in $A \cap B$, $A \cap B^c$, $A^c \cap B$, and $A^c \cap B^c$.

	A	A^c	Total
B	abT	$(1-a)bT$	?
B^c	$a(1-b)T$	$(1-a)(1-b)T$	?
Total	?	?	T

a. Find the table's missing row and column totals in simplest form.

b. Show that events A and B are independent using the fact that $P(A \mid B) = P(A)$ only when events A and B are independent.

c. Show that events A and B^c are independent.

d. Show that events A^c and B are independent.

e. Show that events A^c and B^c are independent.

Lesson Performance Task

Before the mid-1800s, little was known about the way that plants pass along characteristics such as color and height to their offspring. From painstaking observations of garden peas, the Austrian monk Gregor Mendel discovered the basic laws of heredity. The table shows the results of three of Mendel's experiments. In each experiment, he looked at a particular characteristic of garden peas by planting seeds exclusively of one type.

Characteristic	Type Planted	Results in Second Generation
Flower color	100% violet	705 violet, 224 white
Seed texture	100% round	5474 round, 1850 wrinkled
Seed color	100% yellow	6022 yellow, 2011 green

1. Suppose you plant garden peas with violet flowers and round, yellow seeds. Estimate the probability of obtaining second-generation plants with violet flowers, the probability of obtaining second-generation plants with round seeds, and the probability of obtaining second-generation plants with yellow seeds. Explain how you made your estimates.

Mendel saw that certain traits, such as violet flowers and round seeds, seemed stronger than others, such white flowers and wrinkled seeds. He called the stronger traits "dominant" and the weaker traits "recessive." Both traits can be carried in the genes of a plant, because a gene consists of two *alleles*, one received from the mother and one from the father. (For plants, the "father" is the plant from which the pollen comes, and the "mother" is the plant whose pistil receives the pollen.) When at least one of the alleles has the dominant trait, the plant exhibits the dominant trait. Only when both alleles have the recessive trait does the plant exhibit the recessive trait.

You can use a 2×2 Punnett square, like the one shown, to see the results of crossing the genes of two parent plants. In this Punnett square, V represents the dominant flower color violet and v represents the recessive flower color white. If each parent's genes contain both V and v alleles, the offspring may receive, independently and with equal probability, either a V allele or a v allele from each parent.

	V	v
V	VV	Vv
v	vV	vv

2. After planting a first generation of plants exhibiting only dominant traits, Mendel observed that the second generation consisted of plants with a ratio of about 3:1 dominant-to-recessive traits. Does the Punnett square support or refute Mendel's observation? Explain.

3. Draw a 4×4 Punnett square for finding the results of crossing two violet-flower-and-round-seed parent plants. Let V and R represent the dominant traits violet flowers and round seeds, respectively. Let v and r represent the recessive traits white flowers and wrinkled seeds, respectively. Each column heading and row heading of your Punnett square should contain a two-letter combination of V or v and R or r. Each cell of your Punnett square will then contain four letters. Use the Punnett square to find the probability that a second-generation plant will have white flowers and round seeds. Explain your reasoning.

22.3 Dependent Events

Essential Question: How do you find the probability of dependent events?

Resource Locker

Explore — Finding a Way to Calculate the Probability of Dependent Events

You know two tests for the independence of events A and B:

1. If $P(A|B) = P(A)$, then A and B are independent.
2. If $P(A \cap B) = P(A) \cdot P(B)$, then A and B are independent.

Two events that fail either of these tests are **dependent events** because the occurrence of one event affects the occurrence of the other event.

(A) The two-way frequency table shows the results of a survey of 100 people who regularly walk for exercise. Let O be the event that a person prefers walking outdoors. Let M be the event that a person is male. Find $P(O)$, $P(M)$, and $P(O \cap M)$ as fractions. Then determine whether events O and M are independent or dependent.

	Prefers walking outdoors	Prefers walking on a treadmill	Total
Male	40	10	50
Female	20	30	50
Total	60	40	100

(B) Calculate the conditional probabilities $P(O|M)$ and $P(M|O)$.

$$P(O|M) = \frac{n(O \cap M)}{n(M)} = \frac{?}{?} = \frac{?}{5}$$

$$P(M|O) = \frac{n(O \cap M)}{n(O)} = \frac{?}{?} = \frac{?}{3}$$

Ⓒ Complete the multiplication table using the fractions for $P(O)$ and $P(M)$ from Step A and the fractions for $P(O|M)$ and $P(M|O)$ from Step B.

×	$P(O)$	$P(M)$
$P(O\|M)$	?	?
$P(M\|O)$	?	?

Ⓓ Do any of the four products in Step C equal $P(O \cap M)$, calculated in Step A? If so, which of the four products?

Reflect

1. In a previous lesson you learned the conditional probability formula $P(B|A) = \frac{P(A \cap B)}{P(A)}$. How does this formula explain the results you obtained in Step D?

2. Let F be the event that a person is female. Let T be the event that a person prefers walking on a treadmill. Write two formulas you can use to calculate $P(F \cap T)$. Use either one to find the value of $P(F \cap T)$, and then confirm the result by finding $P(F \cap T)$ directly from the two-way frequency table.

Explain 1 Finding the Probability of Two Dependent Events

You can use the Multiplication Rule to find the probability of dependent events.

Multiplication Rule

$P(A \cap B) = P(A) \cdot P(B|A)$ where $P(B|A)$ is the conditional probability of event B, given that event A has occurred.

Example 1 **There are 5 tiles with the letters A, B, C, D, and E in a bag. You choose a tile without looking, put it aside, and then choose another tile without looking. Use the Multiplication Rule to find the specified probability, writing it as a fraction.**

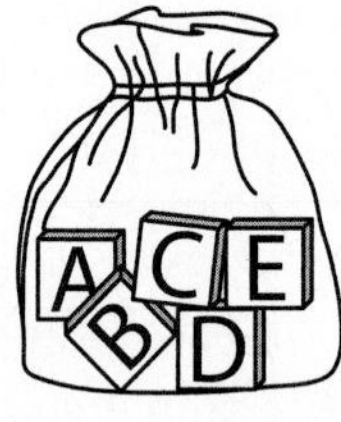

Ⓐ Find the probability that you choose a vowel followed by a consonant.

Let V be the event that the first tile is a vowel. Let C be the event that the second tile is a consonant. Of the 5 tiles, there are 2 vowels, so $P(V) = \frac{2}{5}$.

Of the 4 remaining tiles, there are 3 consonants, so $P(C|V) = \frac{3}{4}$.

By the Multiplication Rule, $P(V \cap C) = P(V) \cdot P(V|C) = \frac{2}{5} \cdot \frac{3}{4} = \frac{6}{20} = \frac{3}{10}$.

Ⓑ Find the probability that you choose a vowel followed by another vowel.

Let $V1$ be the event that the first tile is a vowel. Let $V2$ be the event that the second tile is also a vowel. Of the 5 tiles, there are 2 vowels, so $P(V1) = \frac{2}{5}$.

Of the 4 remaining tiles, there is 1 vowel, so $P(V2|V1) = \frac{\boxed{1}}{4}$.

By the Multiplication Rule, $P(V1 \cap V2) = P(V1) \cdot P(V2|V1) = \frac{\boxed{2}}{5} \cdot \frac{\boxed{1}}{4} = \frac{\boxed{2}}{20} = \frac{\boxed{1}}{10}$.

Your Turn

A bag holds 4 white marbles and 2 blue marbles. You choose a marble without looking, put it aside, and choose another marble without looking. Use the Multiplication Rule to find the specified probability, writing it as a fraction.

3. Find the probability that you choose a white marble followed by a blue marble.

4. Find the probability that you choose a white marble followed by another white marble.

Explain 2 Finding the Probability of Three or More Dependent Events

You can extend the Multiplication Rule to three or more events. For instance, for three events *A*, *B*, and *C*, the rule becomes $P(A \cap B \cap C) = P(A) \cdot P(B|A) \cdot P(C|A \cap B)$.

Example 2 **You have a key ring with 7 different keys. You're attempting to unlock a door in the dark, so you try keys one at a time and keep track of which ones you try.**

(A) Find the probability that the third key you try is the right one.

Let *W*1 be the event that the first key you try is wrong. Let *W*2 be the event that the second key you try is also wrong. Let *R* be the event that the third key you try is right.

On the first try, there are 6 wrong keys among the 7 keys, so $P(W1) = \frac{6}{7}$.

On the second try, there are 5 wrong keys among the 6 remaining keys, so $P(W2|W1) = \frac{5}{6}$.

On the third try, there is 1 right key among the 5 remaining keys, so $P(R|W2 \cap W1) = \frac{1}{5}$.

By the Multiplication Rule, $P(W1 \cap W2 \cap R) = P(W1) \cdot P(W2|W1) \cdot P(R|W1 \cap W2) = \frac{6}{7} \cdot \frac{5}{6} \cdot \frac{1}{5} = \frac{1}{7}$.

(B) Find the probability that one of the first three keys you try is right.

There are two ways to approach this problem:

1. You can break the problem into three cases: (1) the first key you try is right; (2) the first key is wrong, but the second key is right; and (3) the first two keys are wrong, but the third key is right.

2. You can use the complement: The complement of the event that one of the first three keys is right is the event that *none* of the first three keys is right.

Use the second approach.

Let *W*1, *W*2, and *W*3 be the events that the first, second, and third keys, respectively, are wrong.

From Part A, you already know that $P(W1) = \frac{\boxed{6}}{7}$ and $P(W2|W1) = \frac{\boxed{5}}{6}$.

On the third try, there are 4 wrong keys among the 5 remaining keys, so $P(W3|W2 \cap W1) = \frac{\boxed{4}}{5}$.

By the Multiplication Rule,

$$P(W1 \cap W2 \cap W3) = P(W1) \cdot P(W2|W1) \cdot P(W3|W1 \cap W2) = \frac{6}{7} \cdot \frac{5}{6} \cdot \frac{4}{5} = \frac{4}{7}$$

The event $W1 \cap W2 \cap W3$ is the complement of the one you want. So, the probability that one of the first three keys you try is right is $1 - P(W1 \cap W2 \cap W3) = 1 - \frac{4}{7} = \frac{3}{7}$.

Reflect

5. In Part B, show that the first approach to solving the problem gives the same result.

6. In Part A, suppose you don't keep track of the keys as you try them. How does the probability change? Explain.

Your Turn

Three people are standing in line at a car rental agency at an airport. Each person is willing to take whatever rental car is offered. The agency has 4 white cars and 2 silver ones available and offers them to customers on a random basis.

7. Find the probability that all three customers get white cars.

8. Find the probability that two of the customers get the silver cars and one gets a white car.

Elaborate

9. When are two events dependent?

10. Suppose you are given a bag with 3 blue marbles and 2 red marbles, and you are asked to find the probability of drawing 2 blue marbles by drawing one marble at a time and not replacing the first marble drawn. Why does not replacing the first marble make these events dependent? What would make these events independent? Explain.

11. **Essential Question Check-In** According to the Multiplication Rule, when finding $P(A \cap B)$ for dependent events A and B, you multiply $P(A)$ by what?

Evaluate: Homework and Practice

- Online Homework
- Hints and Help
- Extra Practice

1. Town officials are considering a property tax increase to finance the building of a new school. The two-way frequency table shows the results of a survey of 110 town residents.

	Supports a property tax increase	Does not support a property tax increase	Total
Lives in a household with children	50	20	70
Lives in a household without children	10	30	40
Total	60	50	110

a. Let C be the event that a person lives in a household with children. Let S be the event that a person supports a property tax increase. Are the events C and S independent or dependent? Explain.

b. Find $P(C|S)$ and $P(S|C)$. Which of these two conditional probabilities can you multiply with $P(C)$ to get $P(C \cap S)$? Which of the two can you multiply with $P(S)$ to get $P(C \cap S)$?

2. A mall surveyed 120 shoppers to find out whether they typically wait for a sale to get a better price or make purchases on the spur of the moment regardless of price. The two-way frequency table shows the results of the survey.

	Waits for a Sale	Buys on Impulse	Total
Woman	40	10	50
Man	50	20	70
Total	90	30	120

a. Let W be the event that a shopper is a woman. Let S be the event that a shopper typically waits for a sale. Are the events W and S independent or dependent? Explain.

b. Find $P(W|S)$ and $P(S|W)$. Which of these two conditional probabilities can you multiply with $P(W)$ to get $P(W \cap S)$? Which of the two can you multiply with $P(S)$ to get $P(W \cap S)$?

There are 4 green, 10 red, and 6 yellow marbles in a bag. Each time you randomly choose a marble, you put it aside before choosing another marble at random. Use the Multiplication Rule to find the specified probability, writing it as a fraction.

3. Find the probability that you choose a red marble followed by a yellow marble.

4. Find the probabilty that you choose one yellow marble followed by another yellow marble.

5. Find the probability that you choose a red marble, followed by a yellow marble, followed by a green marble.

6. Find the probability that you choose three red marbles.

The table shows the sums that are possible when you roll two number cubes and add the numbers. Use this information to answer the questions.

+	1	2	3	4	5	6
1	2	3	4	5	6	7
2	3	4	5	6	7	8
3	4	5	6	7	8	9
4	5	6	7	8	9	10
5	6	7	8	9	10	11
6	7	8	9	10	11	12

7. Let A be the event that you roll a 2 on the number cube represented by the row labeled 2. Let B be the event that the sum of the numbers on the cubes is 7.

a. Are these events independent or dependent? Explain.

b. What is $P(A \cap B)$?

8. Let A be the event that you roll a 3 on the number cube represented by the row labeled 3. Let B be the event that the sum of the numbers on the cubes is 5.

a. Are these events independent or dependent? Explain.

b. What is $P(A \cap B)$?

9. A cooler contains 6 bottles of apple juice and 8 bottles of grape juice. You choose a bottle without looking, put it aside, and then choose another bottle without looking. Match each situation with its probability. More than one situation can have the same probability.

A. Choose apple juice and then grape juice. **a.** ___?___ $\frac{4}{13}$

B. Choose apple juice and then apple juice. **b.** ___?___ $\frac{24}{91}$

C. Choose grape juice and then apple juice. **c.** ___?___ $\frac{15}{91}$

D. Choose grape juice and then grape juice.

10. Jorge plays all tracks on a playlist with no repeats. The playlist he's listening to has 12 songs, 4 of which are his favorites.

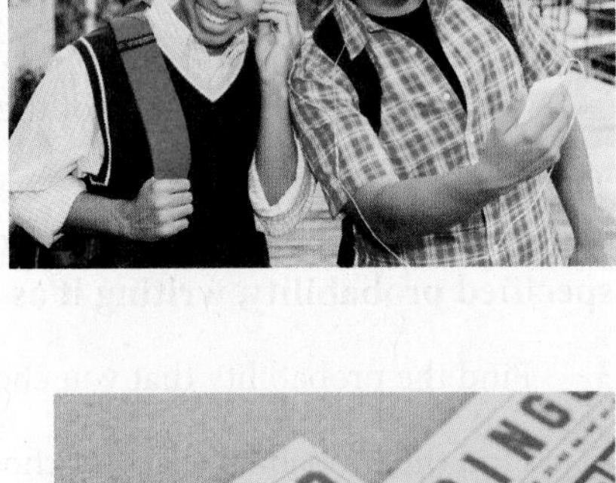

a. What is the probability that the first song played is one of his favorites, but the next two songs are not?

b. What is the probability that the first three songs played are all his favorites?

c. Jorge can also play the tracks on his playlist in a random order with repeats possible. If he does this, how does your answer to part b change? Explain why.

11. You are playing a game of bingo with friends. In this game, balls are labeled with one of the letters of the word BINGO and a number. Some of these letter-number combinations are written on a bingo card in a 5 × 5 array, and as balls are randomly drawn and announced, players mark their cards if the ball's letter-number combination appears on the cards. The first player to complete a row, column, or diagonal on a card says "Bingo!" and wins the game. In the game you're playing, there are 20 balls left. To complete a row on your card, you need N-32 called. To complete a column, you need G-51 called. To complete a diagonal, you need B-6 called.

a. What is the probability that the next two balls drawn do not have a letter-number combination you need, but the third ball does?

b. What is the probability that none of the letter-number combinations you need is called from the next three balls?

H.O.T. Focus on Higher Order Thinking

12. You are talking with 3 friends, and the conversation turns to birthdays.

a. What is the probability that no two people in your group were born in the same month?

b. Is the probability that at least two people in your group were born in the same month greater or less than $\frac{1}{2}$? Explain.

c. How many people in a group would it take for the probability that at least two people were born in the same month to be greater than $\frac{1}{2}$? Explain.

13. Construct Arguments Show how to extend the Multiplication Rule to three events *A*, *B*, and *C*.

14. Make a Prediction A bag contains the same number of red marbles and blue marbles. You choose a marble without looking, put it aside, and then choose another marble. Is there a greater-than-50% chance or a less-than-50% chance that you choose two marbles with different colors? Explain.

Lesson Performance Task

To prepare for an accuracy landing competition, a team of skydivers has laid out targets in a large open field. During practice sessions, team members attempt to land inside a target.

Two rectangular targets are shown on each field. Assuming a skydiver lands at random in the field, find the probabilities that the skydiver lands inside the specified target(s).

1. Calculate the probabilities using the targets shown here.

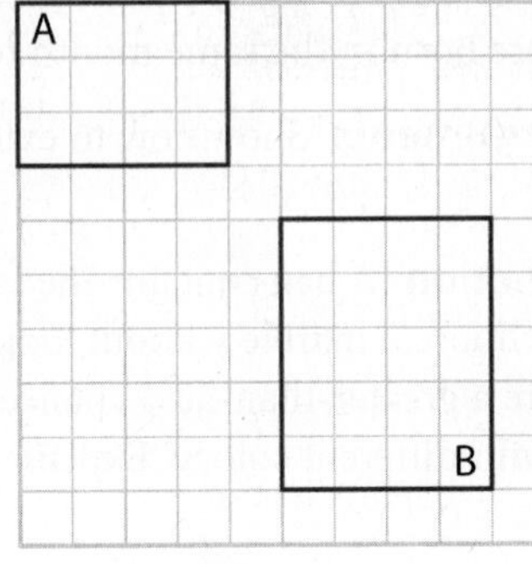

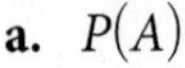

a. $P(A)$

b. $P(B)$

c. $P(A \cap B)$

d. $P(A \cup B)$

e. $P(A|B)$

f. $P(B|A)$

2. Calculate the probabilities using the targets shown here.

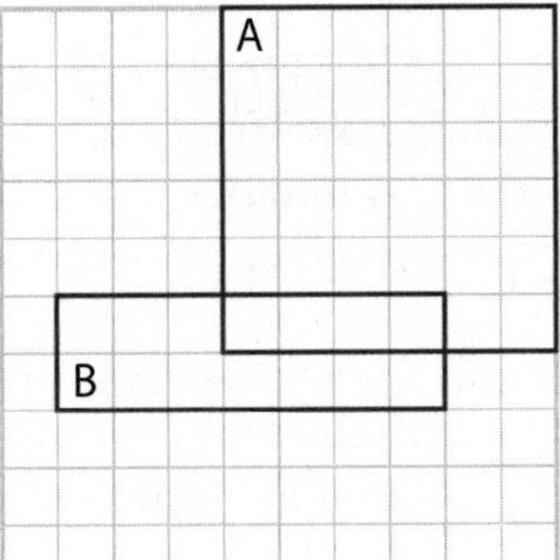

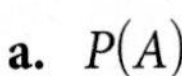

a. $P(A)$

b. $P(B)$

c. $P(A \cap B)$

d. $P(A \cup B)$

e. $P(A|B)$

f. $P(B|A)$

3. Calculate the probabilities using the targets shown here.

a. $P(A)$

b. $P(B)$

c. $P(A \cap B)$

d. $P(A \cup B)$

e. $P(A|B)$

f. $P(B|A)$

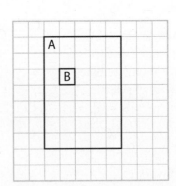

Conditional Probability and Independence of Events

Essential Question: How can you use conditional probability and independence of events to solve real-world problems?

Key Vocabulary
conditional probability
(probabilidad condicional)
independent events
(eventos independientes)
dependent events
(eventos dependientes)

KEY EXAMPLE *(Lesson 22.1)*

Find the probability that a black card drawn from the deck is a queen. (The deck is a standard one of 52 cards.)

The deck has 52 cards and 26 of them are black, so the probability of drawing a black card is $P(B) = \frac{26}{52}$.

There are 2 black queens in the deck, so the probability of drawing one of them from the deck is $P(Q \cap B) = \frac{2}{52} = \frac{1}{26}$.

Using the formula for conditional probability, $P(Q \mid B) = \frac{P(Q \cap B)}{P(B)} = \frac{\frac{2}{52}}{\frac{26}{52}} = \frac{1}{13}$.

KEY EXAMPLE *(Lesson 22.2)*

Jim rolled a set of two number cubes. If these are standard 6-sided number cubes, what is the probability of obtaining 12? (That means the values of the top faces add up to 12.)

The only way to get 12 is for both of the top sides of the number cubes to be 6. The events of obtaining 6s are independent. Each of these events has the probability of $\frac{1}{6}$ (1 out of 6 options), so the probability of getting 12 is $\frac{1}{6} \cdot \frac{1}{6} = \frac{1}{36}$ by the multiplication rule.

KEY EXAMPLE *(Lesson 22.3*

What is the probability of selecting 2 blue marbles out of a jar of 20, half of them blue? How did you obtain it?

Let event A be selecting a blue marble on the first pick. Let event B be selecting a blue marble on the second one. The first marble is not replaced, so these are dependent events. Of the 20 marbles, half of them are blue, so $P(A) = \frac{1}{2}$. Of the remaining 19 marbles, 9 of them are blue, so the probability of selecting one is $P(B) = \frac{9}{19}$. Thus, the probability of selecting 2 blue marbles is $P(A \text{ and } B) = \frac{1}{2} \cdot \frac{9}{19} = \frac{9}{38}$, using the multiplication rule.

Exercises

Determine the conditional probability. *(Lesson 22.1)*

1. What is the probability that a diamond that is drawn from the deck is a queen?

2. What is the probability that a queen drawn is a diamond?

Show that the following situation refers to independent events. *(Lesson 22.2)*

3. Isabelle believes that right- and left-footed soccer players are equally likely to score goals. She collected data from 260 players from a local soccer league. Using the following two-way frequency table, show that being right-footed and scoring goals are independent events.

	Right-Footed	Left-Footed	Total
Has scored a goal	39	13	52
Has not scored a goal	156	52	208
TOTAL	195	65	260

Identify whether a situation involves independent or dependent events. *(Lesson 22.3)*

4. Jim has 2 blue, 2 green, and 2 black socks in his drawer. He picks out 2 socks, one after the other. Determine the probability of him getting a matching pair of blue socks.

MODULE PERFORMANCE TASK

Drawing Aces

You have a standard deck of 52 playing cards. You pick three cards in a row without replacement. What is the probability that all three are aces?

Now you replace the three cards, shuffle, and pick four cards in a row without replacement. What is the probability that none are aces?

Begin by making notes about your plan for approaching this problem. Then complete the task using words, numbers, or diagrams to explain how you reached your conclusions.

22.1–22.3 Conditional Probability and Independence of Events

- Online Homework
- Hints and Help
- Extra Practice

Compute the requested probability and explain how you obtained it.

1. A farmer wants to know if a particular fertilizer can cause blackberry shrubs to produce fruit early. Using the following two-way table, compute the probability of a plant producing fruit early without receiving fertilizer. *(Lesson 22.1)*

	Early Fruit	No Fruit	Total
Received fertilizer	37	3	40
Did not receive fertilizer	19	21	40
TOTAL	56	24	80

2. Lisa flipped the same coin twice. Determine the probability of the coin landing on tails on the second try. *(Lesson 22.2)*

3. Lisa flipped the same coin three times. What is the probability she obtained all tails? *(Lesson 22.2)*

ESSENTIAL QUESTION

4. A jar contains 12 pennies, 5 nickels, and 18 quarters. You select 2 coins at random, one after the other. Does selecting a nickel affect the probability of selecting another nickel? Does not selecting a dime affect the probability of selecting a nickel? Describe how you would find the probability of selecting 2 nickels.

MODULE 22
MIXED REVIEW

Assessment Readiness

1. Are the events independent? Write Yes or No for A–C.

A. Picking a penny and a marble out of a jar of pennies and marbles.

B. Drawing cards from a deck to form a 4-card hand.

C. Rolling a 3 on a fair number cbe and flipping tails on a fair coin.

2. Of the boys running for School President, 2 are juniors and 3 are seniors. Of the girls who are running, 4 are juniors and 1 is a senior. Decide whether the situation has a probability of $\frac{2}{5}$. Write Yes or No for A–C.

A. A girl wins.

B. A candidate who is a boy is a junior.

C. A candidate who is a junior is a boy.

3. You shuffle a standard deck of playing cards and deal one card. What is the probability that you deal an ace or a club? Explain your reasoning.

4. Claude has 2 jars of marbles. Each jar has 10 blue marbles and 10 green marbles. He selects 2 marbles from each jar. What is the probability they are all blue? Explain your reasoning.

Probability and Decision Making

MODULE 23

Essential Question: How can you use probability to solve real-world problems?

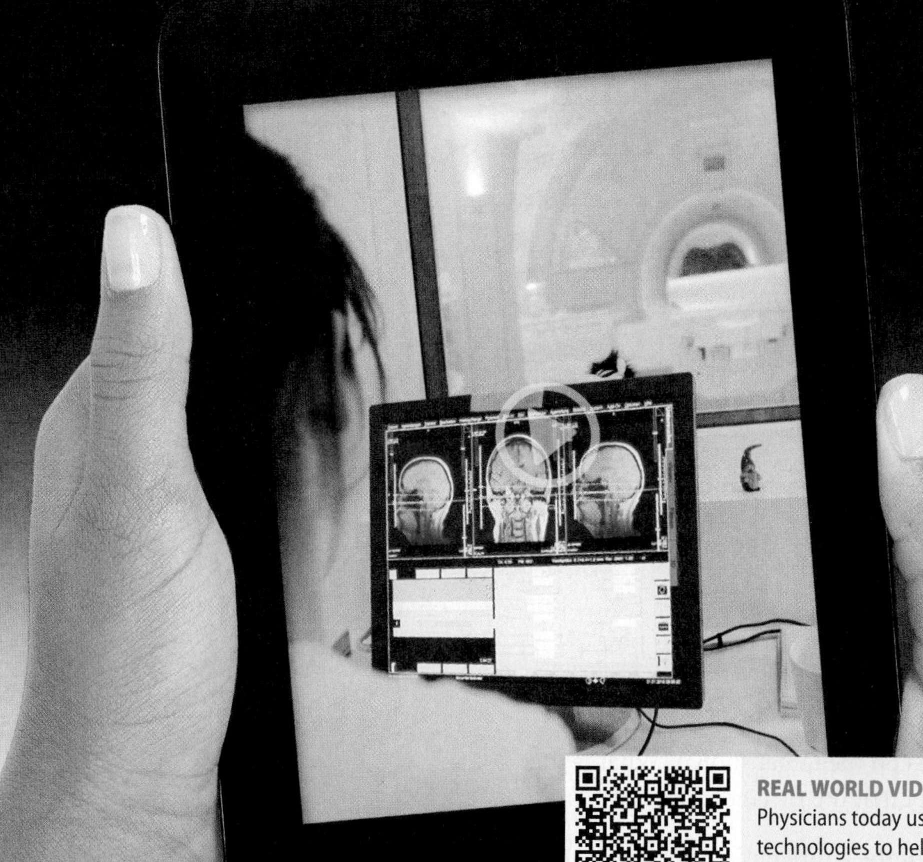

REAL WORLD VIDEO
Physicians today use many sophisticated tests and technologies to help diagnose illnesses, but they must still consider probability in their diagnoses and decisions about treatment.

MODULE PERFORMANCE TASK PREVIEW

What's the Diagnosis?

The science of medicine has come a long way since surgeries were performed by the neighborhood barber and leeches were used to treat just about every ailment. Nevertheless, modern medicine isn't perfect, and widely used tests for diagnosing illnesses aren't always 100 percent accurate. In this module, you'll learn how probability can be used to measure the reliability of tests and then use what you learned to evaluate decisions about a diagnosis.

Are YOU Ready?

Complete these exercises to review skills you will need for this module.

- Online Homework
- Hints and Help
- Extra Practice

Probability of Simple Events

Example 1 Two 6-sided conventional number cubes are tossed. What is the probability that their sum is greater than 8?

+	**1**	**2**	**3**	**4**	**5**	**6**
1	2	3	4	5	6	7
2	3	4	5	6	7	8
3	4	5	6	7	8	9
4	5	6	7	8	9	10
5	6	7	8	9	10	11
6	7	8	9	10	11	12

There are 10 values greater than 8 and a total number of 36 values.

$$\frac{\text{number of favorable outcomes}}{\text{total number of outcomes}} = \frac{10}{36} = \frac{5}{18}$$

The probability that the sum of the two number cubes is greater than 8 is $\frac{5}{18}$.

Two number cubes are tossed. Find each probability.

1. The sum is prime.

2. The product is prime.

3. The product is a perfect square.

Making Predictions with Probability

Example 2 A fly lands on the target shown. What is the probability that the fly landed on red?

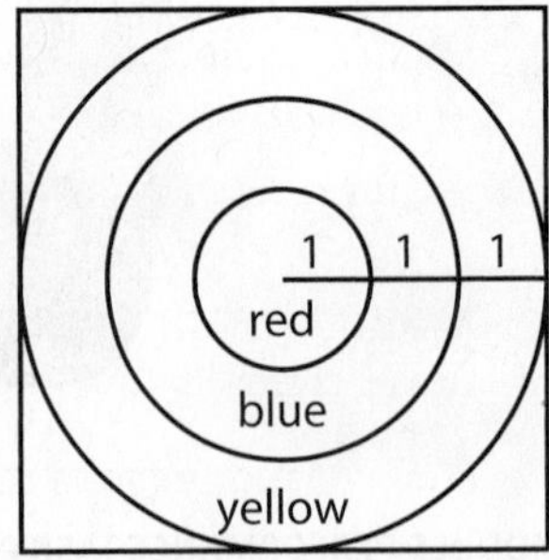

The area of the entire target is 6^2, or 36 units^2.

Red area is: $A = \pi r^2 = \pi(1)^2 = \pi$.

$$\frac{\text{number of favorable outcomes}}{\text{total number of outcomes}} = \frac{\pi}{36} \approx 8.7\%$$

Use the target to find the percent probability, to the nearest tenth.

4. Blue

5. Yellow or red

6. Not within a circle

23.1 Using Probability to Make Fair Decisions

Resource Locker

Essential Question: How can you use probability to help you make fair decisions?

Explore Using Probabilities When Drawing at Random

You are sharing a veggie supreme pizza with friends. There is one slice left and you and a friend both want it. Both of you have already had two slices. What is a fair way to solve this problem?

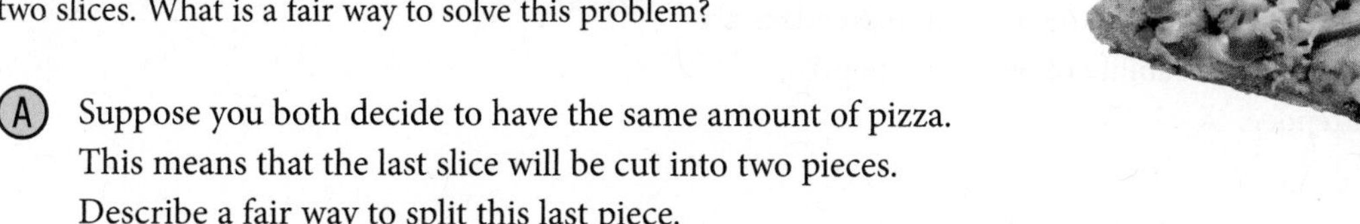

(A) Suppose you both decide to have the same amount of pizza. This means that the last slice will be cut into two pieces. Describe a fair way to split this last piece.

(B) Suppose instead you decide that one of you will get the whole slice. Complete the table so that the result of each option gives a fair chance for each of you to get the last slice. Why do each of these possibilities give a fair chance?

Option	Result (you get last slice)	Result (friend gets last slice)
Flip a coin	Heads	?
Roll a standard die	?	1, 3, 5
Play Rock, Paper, Scissors	You win.	You ? .
Draw lots using two straws of different lengths	?	Short straw

Reflect

1. Suppose, when down to the last piece, you tell your friend, “I will cut the last piece, and I will choose which piece you get.” Why is this method unfair?

2. Your friend suggests that you shoot free throws to decide who gets the last piece. Use probability to explain why this might not be a fair way to decide.

Explain 1 Awarding a Prize to a Random Winner

Suppose you have to decide how to award a prize to a person at an event. You might want every person attending to have the same chance of winning, or you might want people to do something to improve their chance of winning. How can you award the prize fairly?

Example 1 **Explain whether each method of awarding a prize is fair.**

(A) The sponsor of an event wants to award a door prize to one attendee. Each person in attendance is given a ticket with a unique number on it. All of the numbers are placed in a bowl, and one is drawn at random. The person with the matching number wins the prize.

The method of awarding a door prize is fair. Each number has the same chance of being chosen, so each attendee has an equal probability of winning the prize. If n attendees are at the event, then the probability of winning the prize is $\frac{1}{n}$ for each attendee.

(B) A fundraiser includes a raffle in which half of the money collected goes to a charity, and the other half goes to one winner. Tickets are sold for $5 each. Copies of all the tickets are placed in a box, and one ticket is drawn at random. The person with the matching ticket wins the raffle.

The method of choosing a raffle winner is fair because each ticket has an equal probability of being drawn.

Reflect

3. In Example 1B, the probability may not be the same for each person to win the raffle. Explain why the method is still fair.

Your Turn

4. Each month, a company wants to award a special parking space to an employee at random. Describe a fair way to do this. Include a way to ensure that a person doesn't win a second time before each employee has won once.

Explain 2 Solving Real-World Problems Fairly

You can use a random number generator to choose a winner of a prize.

Example 2 **Use a problem solving plan.**

A class of 24 students sold 65 magazine subscriptions to raise money for a trip. As an incentive to participate, you will award a prize to one student in the class. Describe a method of awarding the prize fairly. Use probabilities to explain why your method is fair for the students listed.

Student	Subscriptions Sold
Miri	5
Liam	2
Madison	0

Analyze Information

Identify the important information.

- There are 24 students.
- They sold 65 magazine subscriptions.
- There is one prize, so there will be one winner.

Formulate a Plan

To be fair, students who sold more subscriptions should have a better chance of winning the prize than the students who sold fewer.

Find a method of assigning and choosing chances to win so that the chance of winning is proportional to the number of subscriptions sold.

Solve

The class sold 65 subscriptions, so assign the numbers 1–65 to the students. Each student gets as many numbers as the number of subscriptions he or she sold.

Student	Subscriptions Sold	Numbers Assigned	Probability of Winning
Miri	5	1–5	$\frac{5}{65} \approx$ 0.077
Liam	2	6, 7	$\frac{2}{65} \approx$ 0.031
Madison	0	none	$\frac{0}{65} =$ 0

Then use a calculator to find a random integer from 1 to 65. If the result is 7, then Liam wins the prize.

Justify and Evaluate

This method seems fair because it gives everyone who sold subscriptions a chance of winning. You could award a prize to the student who sold the most subscriptions, but this might not be possible if multiple students all sold the same number, and it might not seem fair if some students have better access to buyers than others.

Reflect

5. A student suggests that it would be better to assign the numbers to students randomly rather than in numerical order. Would doing this affect the probability of winning?

6. A charity is giving a movie ticket for every 10 coats donated. Jacob collected 8 coats, Ben collected 6, and Ryan and Zak each collected 3. They decide to donate the coats together so that they will get 2 movie tickets. Describe how to use a random number generator to decide which 2 boys get a ticket.

Explain 3 Solving the Problem of Points

The decision-making situation that you will apply in this example is based on the "Problem of Points" that was studied by the French mathematicians Blaise Pascal and Pierre de Fermat in the 17th century. Their work on the problem launched the branch of mathematics now known as probability.

Example 3 **Two students, Lee and Rory, find a box containing 100 baseball cards. To determine who should get the cards, they decide to play a game with the rules shown.**

Game Rules
• One of the students repeatedly tosses a coin.
• When the coin lands heads up, Lee gets a point.
• When the coin lands tails up, Rory gets a point.
• The first student to reach 20 points wins the game and gets the baseball cards.

As Lee and Rory are playing the game they are interrupted and are unable to continue. How should the 100 baseball cards be divided between the students given that the game was interrupted at the described moment?

 When they are interrupted, Lee has 19 points and Rory has 17 points.

At most, 3 coin tosses would have been needed for someone to win the game.

Make a list of all possible results using H for heads and T for tails. Circle or box the outcomes in which Lee wins the game.

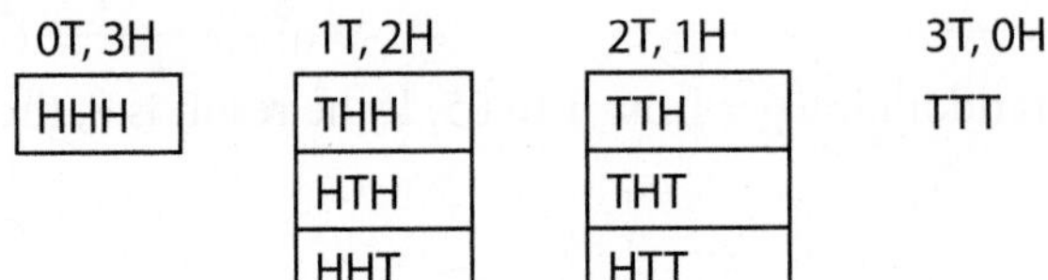

0T, 3H	1T, 2H	2T, 1H	3T, 0H
HHH	THH	TTH	TTT
	HTH	THT	
	HHT	HTT	

There are 8 possible results. Lee wins in 7 of them and Rory wins in 1 of them.

The probability of Lee winning is $\frac{7}{8}$, so he should get $\frac{7}{8}$ of the cards which is 87.5 cards. The probability of Rory winning is $\frac{1}{8}$, so he should get $\frac{1}{8}$ of the cards which is 12.5 cards. Rather than split a card into two, they might decide to flip a coin for that card or to let Lee have it because he was more likely to win it.

(B) When they are interrupted, Lee has 18 points and Rory has 17 points.

At most, four more coin tosses would have been needed.

List all possible results. Circle or box the outcomes in which Lee wins.

0T, 4H	1T, 3H	2T, 2H	3T, 1H	4T, 0H
HHHH	THHH	TTHH	TTTH	TTTT
	HTHH	THTH	TTHT	
	HHTH	THHT	THTT	
	HHHT	HTTH	HTTT	
		HTHT		
		HHTT		

There are 16 possible results. Lee wins in 11 of them and Rory wins in 5 of them.

The probability of Lee winning is $\frac{11}{16}$, so he should get 69 of the 100 cards.

The probability of Rory winning is $\frac{5}{16}$, so he should get 31 of the 100 cards.

Reflect

7. **Discussion** A student suggests that a better way to divide the cards in Example 3B would be to split the cards based on the number of points earned so far. Which method do you think is better?

Your Turn

8. Describe a situation where the game is interrupted, resulting in the cards needing to be divided evenly between the two players.

Elaborate

9. **Discussion** In the situation described in the Explore, suppose you like the crust and your friend does not. Is there a fair way to cut the slice of pizza that might not result in two equal size pieces?

10. How would the solution to Example 2 need to change if there were two prizes to award? Assume that you do not want one student to win both prizes.

11. **Essential Question Check-In** Describe a way to use probability to make a fair choice of a raffle winner.

☆ Evaluate: Homework and Practice

Personal Math Trainer

- Online Homework
- Hints and Help
- Extra Practice

1. You and a friend split the cost of a package of five passes to a climbing gym. Describe a way that you could fairly decide who gets to use the fifth pass.

2. In addition to prizes for first, second, and third place, the organizers of a race have a prize that they want each participant to have an equal chance of winning. Describe a fair method of choosing a winner for this prize.

Decide whether each method is a fair way to choose a winner if each person should have an equal chance of winning. Explain your answer by evaluating each probability.

3. Roll a standard die. Meri wins if the result is less than 3. Riley wins if the result is greater than 3.

4. Draw a card from a standard deck of cards. Meri wins if the card is red. Riley wins if the card is black.

5. Flip a coin. Meri wins if it lands heads. Riley wins if it lands tails.

6. Meri and Riley both jump as high as they can. Whoever jumps higher wins.

7. Roll a standard die. Meri wins if the result is even. Riley wins if the result is odd.

8. Draw a stone from a box that contains 5 black stones and 4 white stones. Meri wins if the stone is black. Riley wins if the stone is white.

9. A chess club has received a chess set to give to one of its members. The club decides that everyone should have a chance of winning the set based on how many games they have won this season. Describe a fair method to decide who wins the set. Find the probability that each member will win it.

Member	Games Won	Probability of Winning	Member	Games Won	Probability of Winning
Kayla	30	?	Hailey	12	?
Noah	23	?	Gabe	12	?
Ava	18	?	Concour	5	?

10. Owen, Diego, and Cody often play a game during lunch. When they can't finish, they calculate the probability that each will win given the current state of the game and assign partial wins. Today, when they had to stop, it would have taken at most 56 more moves for one of them to win. Owen would have won 23 of the moves, Diego would have won 18 of them, and Cody would have won 15. To 2 decimal places, how should they assign partial wins?

Represent Real-World Problems **Twenty students, including Paige, volunteer to work at the school banquet. Each volunteer worked at least 1 hour. Paige worked 4 hours. The students worked a total of 45 hours. The organizers would like to award a prize to 1 of the volunteers.**

11. Describe a process for awarding the prize so that each volunteer has an equal chance of winning. Find the probability of Paige winning.

12. Describe a process for awarding the prize so that each volunteer's chance of winning is proportional to how many hours the volunteer worked. Find the probability of Paige winning.

There are 10,000 seats available in a sports stadium. Each seat has a package beneath it, and 20 of the seats have an additional prize winning package with a family pass for the entire season.

13. Is this method of choosing a winner for the family passes fair?

14. What is the probability of winning a family pass if you attend the game?

15. What is the probability of not winning a family pass if you attend the game?

A teacher tells students, "For each puzzle problem you complete, I will assign you a prize entry." In all, 10 students complete 53 puzzle problems. Leon completed 7. To award the prize, the teacher sets a calculator to generate a random integer from 1 to 53. Leon is assigned 18 to 24 as "winners".

16. What is the probability that a specific number is chosen?

17. What is the probability that one of Leon's numbers will be chosen?

18. What is the probability that one of Leon's numbers will not be chosen?

19. Is this fair to Leon according to the original instructions? Explain.

H.O.T. Focus on Higher Order Thinking

20. **Make a Conjecture** Two teams are playing a game against one another in class to earn 10 extra points on an assignment. The teacher said that the points will be split fairly between the two teams, depending on the results of the game. If Team A earned 1300 points, and Team B earned 2200 points, describe one way the teacher could split up the 10 extra points. Explain.

21. **Persevere in Problem Solving** Alexa and Sofia are at a yard sale, and they find a box of 20 collectible toys that they both want. They can't agree about who saw it first, so they flip a coin until Alexa gets 10 heads or Sofia gets 10 tails. When Alexa has 3 heads and Sofia has 6 tails, they decide to divide the toys proportionally based on the probability each has of winning under the original rules. How should they divide the toys?

Lesson Performance Task

Three games are described below. For each game, tell whether it is fair (all players are equally likely to win) or unfair (one player has an advantage). Explain how you reached your decision, being sure to discuss how probability entered into your decision.

1. You and your friend each toss a quarter. If two heads turn up, you win. If a head and a tail turn up, your friend wins. If two tails turn up, you play again.

2. You and your friend each roll a die. If the sum of the numbers is odd, you get 1 point. If the sum is even, your friend gets 1 point.

3. You and your friend each roll a die. If the product of the numbers is odd, you get 1 point. If the product is even, your friend gets 1 point.

23.2 Analyzing Decisions

Essential Question: How can conditional probability help you make real-world decisions?

Resource Locker

Explore Analyzing a Decision Using Probability

Suppose scientists have developed a test that can be used at birth to determine whether a baby is right-handed or left-handed. The test uses a drop of the baby's saliva and instantly gives the result. The test has been in development, long enough for the scientists to track the babies as they grow into toddlers and to see whether their test is accurate. About 10% of babies turn out to be left-handed.

The scientists have learned that when children are left-handed, the test correctly identifies them as left-handed 92% of the time. Also when children are right-handed, the test correctly identifies them as right-handed 95% of the time.

(A) In the first year on the market, the test is used on 1,000,000 babies. Complete the table starting with the Totals. Then use the given information to determine the expected number in each category.

	Tests Left-handed	Tests Right-handed	Total
Truly Left-handed	?	?	?
Truly Right-handed	?	?	?
Total	?	?	?

(B) What is the probability that a baby who tests left-handed actually is left-handed?

(C) What is the probability that a baby who tests right-handed actually is right-handed?

Reflect

1. Is the test a good test of right-handedness?
2. A baby is tested, and the test shows the baby will be left-handed. The parents decide to buy a left-handed baseball glove for the baby. Is this a reasonable decision?
3. **Discussion** Describe two ways in which the test can become a more reliable indicator of left-handedness.

Explore 2 Deriving Bayes' Theorem

You can generalize your results so that they are applicable to other situations in which you want to analyze decisions. Now, you will derive a formula known as Bayes' Theorem.

(A) Complete the steps to derive Bayes' Theorem.

Write the formula for $P(B|A)$. ?

Solve for $P(A \text{ and } B)$. ?

Write the formula for $P(A|B)$. ?

Substitute the expression for $P(A \text{ and } B)$. ?

(B) Explain how you can use a table giving the number of results for each case to find $P(B)$.

	B	B^c	Total
A	n	p	$n+p$
A^c	m	q	$m+q$
Total	$n+m$	$p+q$	$n+m+p+q$

(C) Explain how you can use the tree diagram to find $P(B)$.

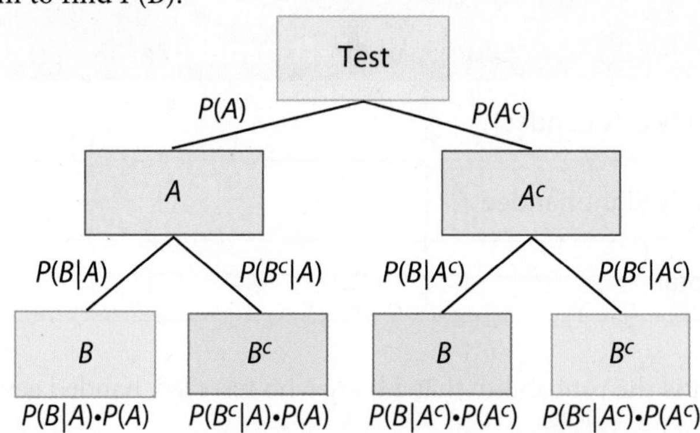

(D) Use your result from Step C to rewrite your final expression from Step A to get another form of Bayes' Theorem.

Reflect

4. Explain in words what each expression means in the context of Explore 1.

$P(A)$ is the probability of actually being left-handed.

$P(B)$ is the probability of testing left-handed.

$P(A|B)$ is ___?___

$P(B|A)$ is ___?___

5. Use Bayes' Theorem to calculate the probability that a baby actually is left-handed, given that the baby tests left-handed. Explain what this probability means.

Explain 1 Using Bayes' Theorem

Bayes' Theorem is a useful tool when you need to analyze decisions.

Bayes' Theorem

Given two events A and B with $P(B) \neq 0$, $P(A|B) = \frac{P(B|A) \cdot P(A)}{P(B)}$.

Another form is $P(A|B) = \frac{P(B|A) \cdot P(A)}{P(B|A) \cdot P(A) + P(B|A^c) \cdot P(A^c)}$.

Example 1 **Suppose Walter operates an order-filling machine that has an error rate of 0.5%. He installs a new order-filling machine that has an error rate of only 0.1%. The new machine takes over 80% of the order-filling tasks.**

(A) One day, Walter gets a call from a customer complaining that her order wasn't filled properly. Walter blames the problem on the old machine. Was he correct in doing so?

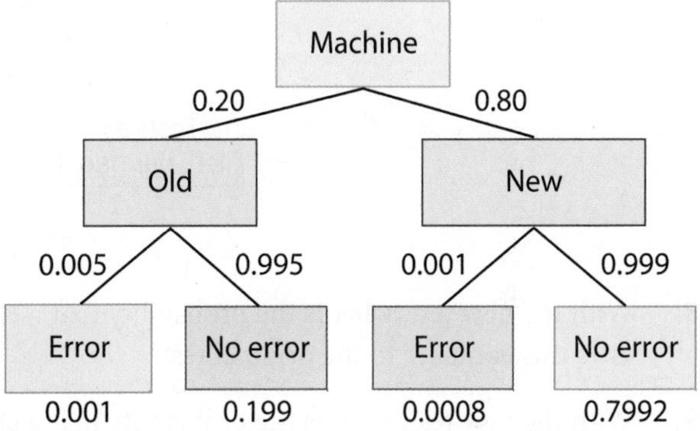

First, find the probability that the order was filled by the old machine given that there was an error in filling the order, $P(\text{old} \mid \text{error})$.

$$P(\text{old}|\text{error}) = \frac{P(\text{error}|\text{old}) \cdot P(\text{old})}{P(\text{error})}$$

$$= \frac{0.005 \cdot (0.20)}{0.001 + 0.0008} = \frac{0.001}{0.0018} = \frac{5}{9} \approx 0.56$$

Given that there is a mistake, the probability is about 56% that the old machine filled the order. The probability that the new machine filled the order is 1 − 0.56 = 0.44 = 44%. The old machine is only slightly more likely than the new machine to have filled the order. Walter shouldn't blame the old machine.

(B) Walter needs to increase capacity for filling orders, so he increases the number of orders being filled by the old machine to 30% of the total orders. What percent of errors in filled orders are made by the old machine? Is Walter unreasonably increasing the risk of shipping incorrectly filled orders?

Find the probability that the order was filled by the old machine given that there is an error in filling the package, P(old | error).

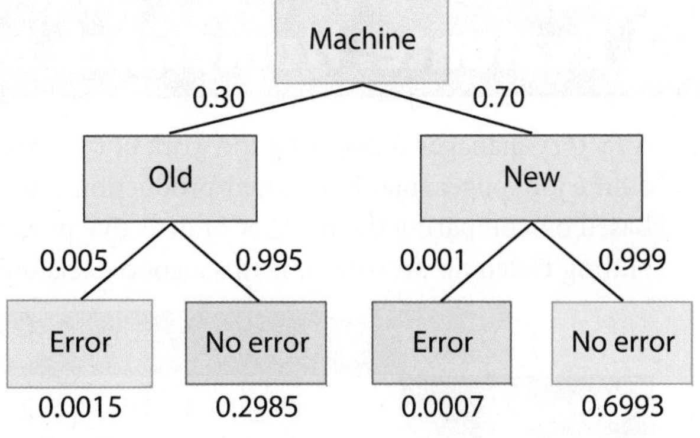

Use Bayes' Theorem.

$$P(A|B) = \frac{P(B|A) \cdot P(A)}{P(B)} \quad \frac{0.005(0.30)}{0.0015 + 0.0007}$$

$$= \frac{0.0015}{0.0022} = \frac{15}{22} \approx 0.68$$

Describe the result of making this change.

Given that there is a mistake, the probability is about 68% that the old machine filled the package. Making this change increases the number of errors by 4 orders for every 10,000 orders. This seems like a worthwhile risk.

Reflect

6. The old machine fills so few orders. How can it be responsible for more than half of the errors?

Your Turn

In the situation described in the Explore, suppose the scientists have changed the test so that now it correctly identifies left-handed children 100% of the time, and still correctly identifies right-handed children 95% of the time.

7. Complete the tree diagram.

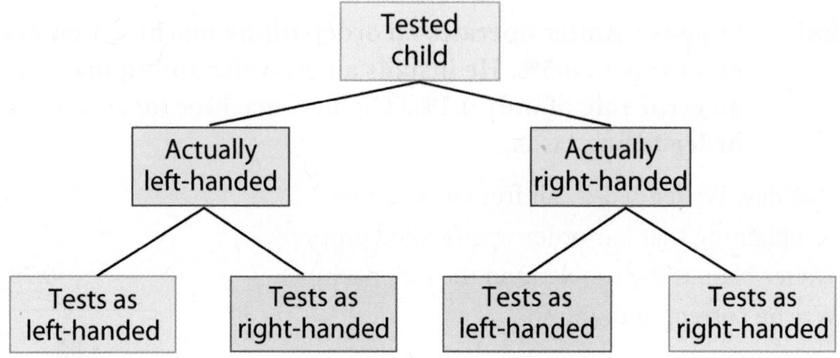

8. With the new test, what is the probability that a child who tests as left-handed will be left-handed? How does this compare to the original test?

9. With the new test, what is the probability that a child who tests as right-handed will be left-handed? How does this compare to the original test?

Elaborate

10. **Discussion** Compare the probabilities you found in the Explore and Your Turn 8 and 9. Why did the percent of babies who test as right-handed and are actually left-handed increase?

11. **Essential Question Check-In** How can you use probability to help you analyze decisions?

Evaluate: Homework and Practice

• Online Homework
• Hints and Help
• Extra Practice

1. A factory manager is assessing the work of two assembly-line workers. Helen has been on the job longer than Kyle. Their production rates for the last month are in the table. Based on comparing the number of defective products, the manager is considering putting Helen on probation. Is this a good decision? Why or why not?

	Helen	Kyle	Total
Defective	50	20	70
Not defective	965	350	1,315
Total	1,015	370	1,385

2. **Multiple Step** A reporter asked 150 voters if they plan to vote in favor of a new library and a new arena. The table shows the results. If you are given that a voter plans to vote ***no*** to the new arena, what is the probability that the voter also plans to vote no to the new library?

		Library		
		Yes	No	**Total**
Arena	Yes	21	30	51
	No	57	42	99
	Total	78	72	**150**

3. You want to hand out coupons for a local restaurant to students who live off campus at a rural college with a population of 10,000 students. You know that 10% of the students live off campus and that 98% of those students ride a bike. Also, 62% of the students who live on campus do not have a bike. You decide to give a coupon to any student you see who is riding a bike. Complete the table. Then explain whether this a good decision.

	bike	**no bike**	**Total**
on campus	?	?	?
off campus	?	?	?
Total	?	?	?

4. A test for a virus correctly identifies someone who has the virus (by returning a positive result) 99% of the time. The test correctly identifies someone who does not have the virus (by returning a negative result) 99% of the time. It is known that 0.5% of the population has the virus. A doctor decides to treat anyone who tests positive for the virus. Complete the two-way table assuming a total population of 1,000,000 people have been tested. Is this a good decision?

	Tests Positive	**Tests Negative**	**Total**
Virus	?	?	?
No virus	?	?	?
Total	?	?	1,000,000

5. It is known that 2% of the population has a certain allergy. A test correctly identifies people who have the allergy 98% of the time. The test correctly identifies people who do not have the allergy 95% of the time. A website recommends that anyone who tests positive for the allergy should begin taking medication. Complete the two-way table. Do you think this is a good recommendation? Why or why not?

	Test Positive	**Test Negative**	**Total**
?	?	?	?
?	?	?	?
Total	?	?	10,000

6. Use the tree diagram shown.

a. Find $P(B|A^c) \cdot P(A^c)$.

b. Find $P(B)$.

c. Use Bayes Theorem to find $P(A^c|B)$.

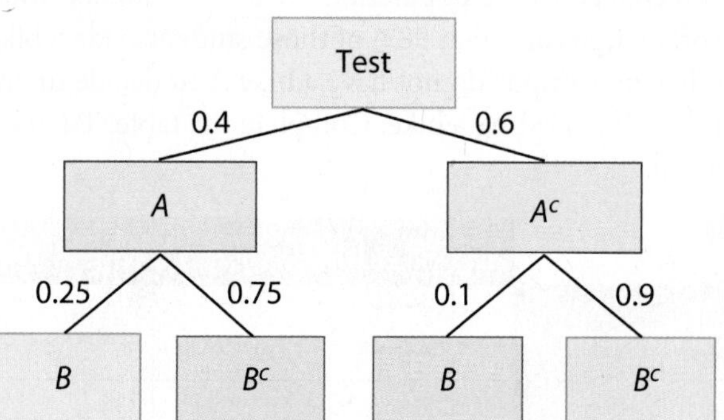

7. The probabilities of drawing lemons and limes from a bag are shown in the tree diagram. Find the probability of drawing the two pieces of fruit randomly from the bag.

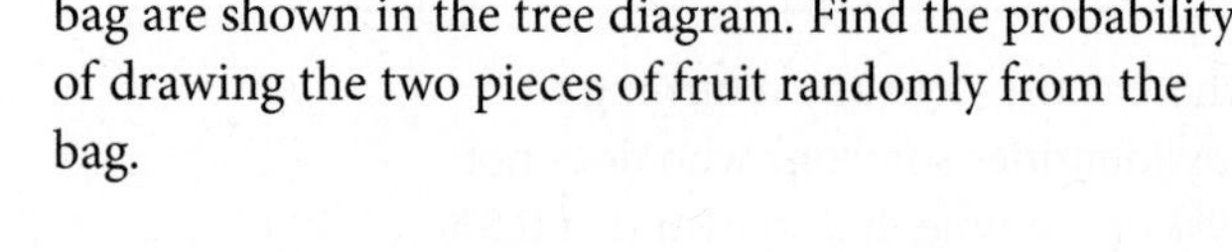

a. two lemons

b. two limes

c. lime, then lemon

d. lemon, then lime

8. **Multiple Step** A school principal plans a school picnic for June 2. A few days before the event, the weather forecast predicts rain for June 2, so the principal decides to cancel the picnic. Consider the following information.

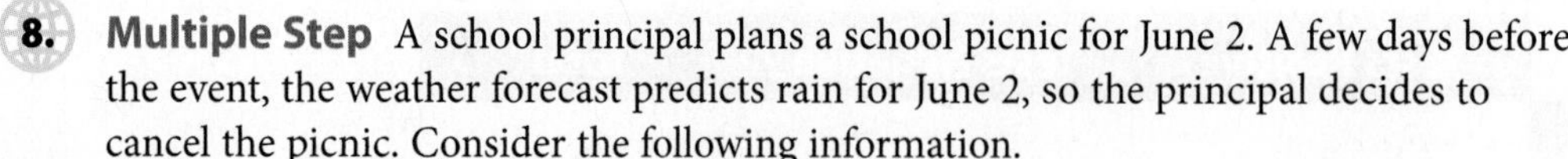

- In the school's town, the probability that it rains on any day in June is 3%.
- When it rains, the forecast correctly predicts rain 90% of the time.
- When it does not rain, the forecast incorrectly predicts rain 5% of the time.

a. Find $P(\text{prediction of rain} \mid \text{rains})$ and $P(\text{rains})$.

b. Complete the tree diagram, and find P(Prediction of rain).

c. Find P(rains| prediction of rain).

d. Is the decision to cancel the picnic reasonable?

Days in June

Rain | Does not rain

Rain predicted | No rain predicted | Rain predicted | No rain predicted

9. Pamela has collected data on the number of students in the sophomore class who play a sport or play a musical instrument. She has learned the following.

- 42.5% of all students in her school play a musical instrument.
- 20% of those who play a musical instrument also play a sport.
- 40% of those who play no instrument also play no sport.

Complete the tree diagram. Would it be reasonable to conclude that a student who doesn't play a sport plays a musical instrument?

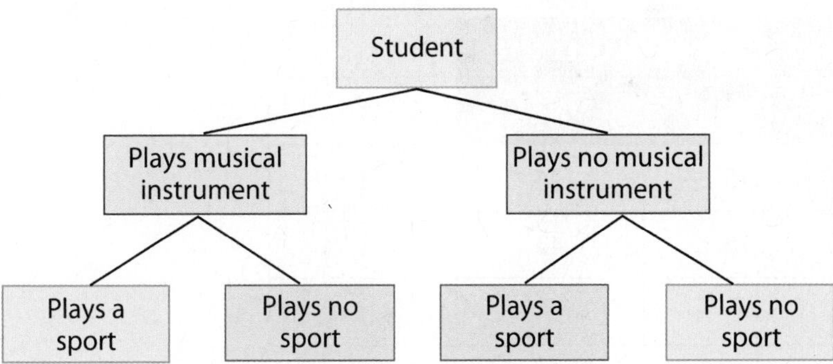

10. **Interpret the Answer** Company X supplies 35% of the phones to an electronics store and Company Y supplies the remainder. The manager of the store knows that 25% of the phones in the last shipment from Company X were defective, while only 5% of the phones from Company Y were defective. The manager chooses a phone at random and finds that it is defective. The manager decides that the phone must have come from Company X. Do you think this is a reasonable conclusion? Why or why not?

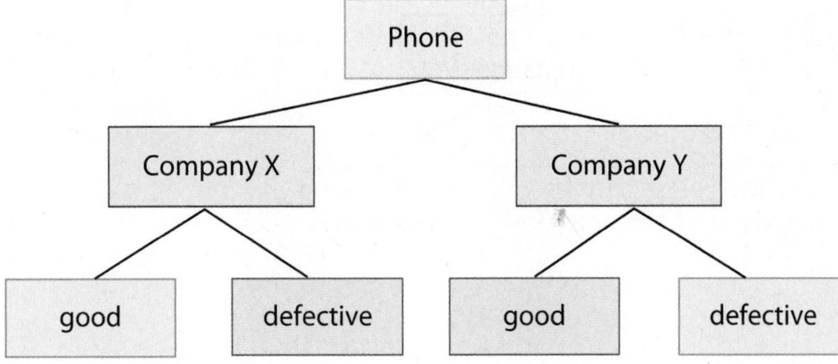

11. Suppose that strep throat affects 2% of the population and a test to detect it produces an accurate result 99% of the time. Create a tree diagram and use Bayes, Theorem to find the probability that someone who tests positive actually has strep throat.

12. A hand-made quilt is first prize in a fund-raiser raffle. The table shows information about all the ticket buyers. Given that the winner of the quilt is a man, what is the probability that he resides in Sharonville?

	Men	Women	Total
Forestview	35	45	80
Sharonville	15	25	40
?	?	?	?

13. Recall that the Multiplication Rule says the $P(A \cap B) = P(A) \cdot P(B \mid A)$. If you switch the order of events A and B, then the rule becomes $P(B \cap A) = P(B) \cdot P(A \mid B)$. Use the Multiplication Rule and the fact that $P(B \cap A) = P(A \cap B)$ to prove Bayes' Theorem. (*Hint*: Divide each side by $P(B)$.)

14. **Sociology** A sociologist collected data on the types of pets in 100 randomly selected households. Suppose you want to offer a service to households that own both a cat and a dog. Based on the data in the table, would it be more effective to hand information to people walking dogs or to people buying cat food?

		Owns a Cat		
		Yes	No	?
Owns a Dog	Yes	15	24	?
	No	18	43	?
	?	?	?	?

15. **Interpret the Answer** It is known that 1% of all mice in a laboratory have a genetic mutation. A test for the mutation correctly identifies mice that have the mutation 98% of the time. The test correctly identifies mice that do not have the mutation 96% of the time. A lab assistant tests a mouse and finds that the mouse tests positive for the mutation. The lab assistant decides that the mouse must have the mutation. Is this a good decision? Complete the tree diagram and explain your answer.

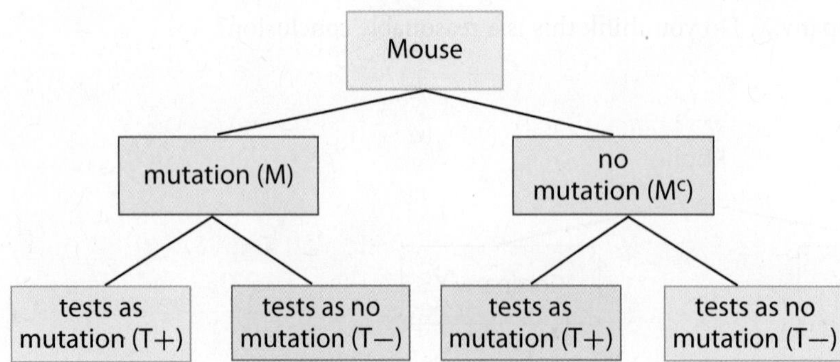

16. Interpret the Answer It is known that 96% of all dogs do not get trained. One professional trainer claims that 54% of trained dogs will sit on one of the first four commands and that no other dogs will sit on command. A condominium community wants to impose a restriction on dogs that are not trained. They want each dog owner to show that his or her dog will sit on one of the first four commands. Assuming that the professional trainer's claim is correct, is this a fair way to identify dogs that have not been trained? Explain.

17. Multiple Steps Tomas has a choice of three possible routes to work. On each day, he randomly selects a route and keeps track of whether he is late. Based on this 40-day trial, which route makes Tomas least likely to be late for work?

	Late	Not Late
Route A	IIII	卌 卌
Route B	III	卌 II
Route C	IIII	卌 卌 II

H.O.T. Focus on Higher Order Thinking

18. Critique Reasoning When Elisabeth saw this tree diagram, she said that the calculations must be incorrect. Do you agree? Justify your answer.

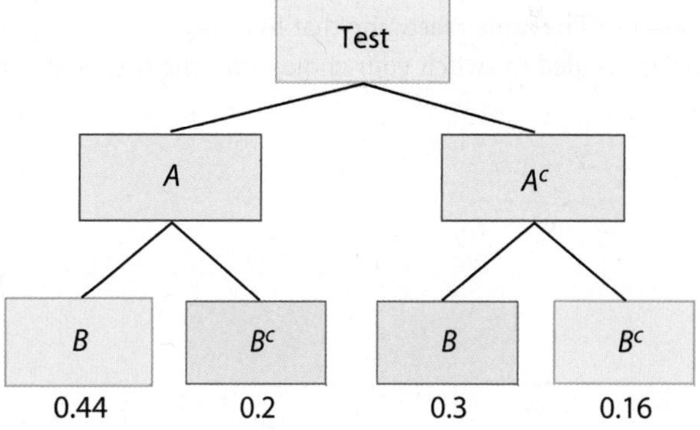

19. Multiple Representations The Venn diagram shows how many of the first 100 customers of a new bakery bought either bread or cookies, both, or neither. Taryn claims that the data indicate that a customer who bought cookies is more likely to have bought bread than a customer who bought bread is likely to have bought cookies. Is she correct?

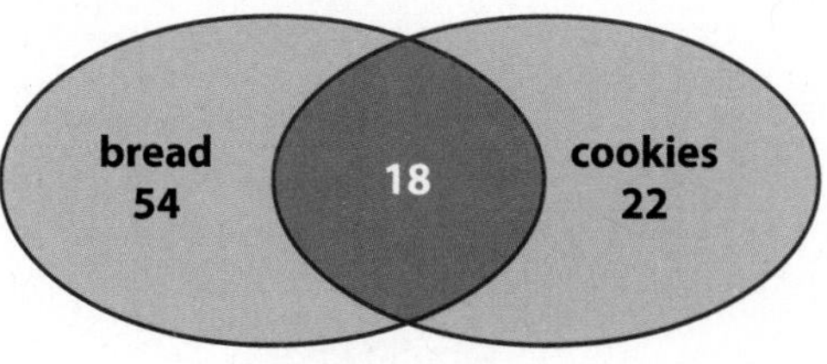

20. Persevere in Problem Solving At one high school, the probability that a student is absent today, given that the student was absent yesterday, is 0.12. The probability that a student is absent today, given that the student was present yesterday, is 0.05. The probability that a student was absent yesterday is 0.1. A teacher forgot to take attendance in several classes yesterday, so he assumed that attendance in his class today is the same as yesterday. If there were 40 students in these classes, how many errors would you expect by doing this?

Lesson Performance Task

You're a contestant on a TV quiz show. Before you are three doors. Behind two of the doors, there's a goat. Behind one of the doors, there's a new car. You are asked to pick a door. After you make your choice, the quizmaster opens one of the doors you *didn't* choose, revealing a goat.

Door 1

Door 2

Door 3

Now there are only two doors. You can stick with your original choice or you can switch to the one remaining door. Should you switch?

Intuition tells most people that, with two doors left, there's a 50% probability that they're right and a 50% probability that they're wrong. They conclude that it doesn't matter whether they switch or not.

Does it? Using Bayes' Theorem, it can be shown mathematically that you're much better off switching! You can reach the same conclusion using logical thinking skills. Assume that the car is behind Door #1. (The same reasoning that follows can be applied if the car is behind one of the other doors.) You've decided to switch your choice after the first goat is revealed. There are three possibilities.

STUDY GUIDE REVIEW

Probability and Decision Making

MODULE 23

Essential Question: How can you use probability to solve real-world problems?

KEY EXAMPLE *(Lesson 23.1)*

Determine whether the method of awarding a prize is fair. Explain.

A festival has a baked goods fundraising raffle in which tickets are drawn for winners. The tickets are sold for \$2 each, and the purchaser of the ticket places his or her name on the ticket before placing the ticket into a fishbowl on a table. There are 20 cakes for prizes. A ticket is drawn at random from the fishbowl for each cake.

The method of awarding the prize is fair. This is because each ticket has an equal probability of being drawn. For each of n tickets bought, that ticket has a $\frac{1}{n}$ chance of being drawn. The more tickets someone buys, the better chance they have of winning a cake.

KEY EXAMPLE *(Lesson 23.2)*

Suppose Rhonda's Block Warehouse operates a block-making machine that has an error rate of 0.7%. Then Rhonda installs a new block-making machine that has an error rate of only 0.3%. The new machine takes over 75% of the block-making tasks. One day, Rhonda gets a call from a customer complaining that his block is not made properly. Rhonda blames the problem on the old machine. Was she correct in doing so?

Find Event A, Event B, $P(A|B)$, $P(B)$, and $P(A)$.

Event A is the error making the block, Event B is that the old machine made the block, $P(A|B)$ is the error rate of the old machine (0.007), $P(B)$ is the probability the old machine made the block (0.25), and $P(A)$ is $0.75 \cdot 0.003 + 0.25 \cdot 0.007 = 0.004$.

$$P(B|A) = \frac{P(A|B)P(B)}{P(A)}$$ Bayes' Theorem

$$P(\text{old machine}|\text{bad block}) = \frac{0.007 \cdot 0.25}{0.004}$$ Substitute known probabilities

$$P(\text{old machine}|\text{bad block}) = 0.4375 = 43.75\%$$

Given that the probability that a bad block is made by the old machine is less than 50%, Rhonda should not blame the old machine for the bad block.

EXERCISES

Determine whether the method of awarding a prize is fair. Explain. If it is not fair, describe a way that would be fair. *(Lesson 23.1)*

1. A teacher gives a ticket to each student who earns a 90 or above on any homework assignment. At the end of each week, the teacher draws from the ticket jar and gives the winning student a free homework pass for the next week.

Determine whether the method of awarding a prize is fair. Explain. If it is not fair, describe a way that would be fair. *(Lesson 23.2)*

2. If each machine is used 50% of the time, and a face card is the next card drawn, what is the probability the new machine drew the card?

MODULE PERFORMANCE TASK

What's the Diagnosis?

Lenny works in a factory that makes cleaning products. Lately he has been suffering from headaches. He asks his doctor if the chemicals used in the factory might be responsible for his headaches. The doctor performs a blood test that is routinely used to diagnose the kind of illness Lenny is concerned about.

Use the following facts to gauge the probability that Lenny has the illness if he tests positive:

1. The test has a reliability rate of 85 percent.
2. The test has a false positive rate of 8 percent.
3. The illness affects 3 percent of people who are Lenny's age and who work in conditions similar to those he works in.

Start by listing the information you will need to solve the problem. Then complete the task. Use numbers, words, or algebra to explain how you reached your conclusion.

Ready to Go On?

23.1–23.2 Probability and Decision Making

- Online Homework
- Hints and Help
- Extra Practice

Determine whether the method of awarding a prize is fair. Explain briefly. *(Lesson 23.1)*

1. Prize to every 500th customer

2. Ticket to every customer; drawing

3. Choose number 1–10; draw number

4. Ticket to all cars; two to red cars

Rodney's Repair Service has a lug nut tightening machine that works well 89% of the time. They got a new machine that works well 98% of the time. Each machine is used 50% of the time. Use Bayes' Theorem to find each probability. *(Lesson 23.2)*

5. new machine malfunctioned

6. old machine malfunctioned

7. old machine worked well

8. new machine worked well

ESSENTIAL QUESTION

9. How can probability and decision making help the organizer of a raffle?

MODULE 23
MIXED REVIEW

Assessment Readiness

1. Consider the situation. Is the method of awarding the prize fair? Write Yes or No for A–C.

A. Ticket for every $10 spent

B. Coupon every 10 guests

C. Entry for every mile driven

2. Consider the situation of having four tiles in a bag spelling M–A–T–H drawn randomly without replacement. Determine if each statement is True or False.

A. There is one way to draw all 4 tiles from the bag, if order doesn't matter.

B. There are six ways to draw 2 tiles from the bag, if order matters.

C. There are twenty four ways to draw 3 tiles from the bag if order matters.

3. The band class has two trumpet players. Of the two, the first trumpet player plays a wrong note 4% of the time, and the second trumpet player plays a wrong note 9% of the time. If one song has the first trumpet player playing 75% of the song, and the second trumpet player playing the rest, use Bayes' Theorem to find the probability that a wrong note was played by the second trumpet. Explain whether your answer makes sense.

4. Given a triangle with a side of length 11 and another side of length 6, find the range of possible values for x, the length of the third side. Explain your reasoning.

- Online Homework
- Hints and Help
- Extra Practice

1. Figure *ABCDE* is similar to figure *LMNOP*. Determine if each statement is True or False.

A. $\frac{BC}{AE} = \frac{MN}{OP}$

B. $\frac{AB}{DE} = \frac{LM}{OP}$

C. $\frac{BD}{AE} = \frac{MN}{LP}$

2. The transformation $(x, y) \rightarrow (x - 2, y + 1)$ is applied to $\triangle XYZ$. Determine if each statement is True or False.

A. The area of $\triangle X'Y'Z'$ is the same as the area of $\triangle XYZ$.

B. The distance from X to X' is equal to the distance from Z to Z'.

C. The transformation is a rotation.

3. Does each scenario describe independent events? Write Yes or No for each situation.

A. Drawing two cards from a standard deck of cards that are both aces

B. Rolling a fair number cube twice and getting 6 on both rolls

C. Rolling a 3 on a fair number cube and flipping tails on a fair coin

4. Each student in a class has been assigned at random to draw a parallelogram, a rectangle, a rhombus, or a square. Write True or False for each statement about the likelihood that a student will draw a parallelogram.

A. It is unlikely because the probability is less than 0.5.

B. It is likely because the probability is between 0.5 and 0.75.

C. It is impossible for it not to happen because the probability is 1.

5. The events A and B are independent. Determine if each statement is True or False.

A. $P(A \mid B) = P(B \mid A)$

B. $P(A \text{ and } B) = P(B)P(A)$

C. $P(A) = P(B)$

6. Vera needs to place 15 student volunteers at a local fire station. Five students will wash fire trucks, 7 will be assigned to paint, and 3 will be assigned to wash windows. What is the number of possible job assignments expressed using factorials and as a simplified number?

7. The table below shows the number of days that a meteorologist predicted it would be sunny and the number of days it was sunny. Based on the data in the table, what is the conditional probability that it will be sunny on a day when the meteorologist predicts it will be sunny? Show your work.

	Sunny	Not Sunny	Total
Predicts Sunny	570	20	590
Does Not Predict Sunny	63	347	410
Total	633	367	1000

8. Complete the two-way table below. Then find the fraction of red cards in a standard 52-card deck that have a number on them and find the fraction of numbered cards that are red.

	Red	Black	Total
Number	?	?	?
No Number	?	?	?
Total	?	?	?

Performance Tasks

★ **9.** Sixteen cards numbered 1 through 16 are placed face down, and Stephanie chooses one at random. What is the probability that the number on Stephanie's card is less than 5 or greater than 10? Show your work.

★★**10.** Students in 4 different classes are surveyed about their favorite movie type. What is the probability that a randomly selected student in class B prefers comedies? What is the probability that a randomly selected student who prefers comedies is in class B? Explain why the two probabilities are not the same. Show your work.

	A	B	C	D
Action	12	9	8	11
Comedy	13	11	15	4
Drama	6	11	7	18

★★★**11.** A Chinese restaurant has a buffet that includes ice cream for dessert. The table shows the selections made last week.

	Chocolate	Vanilla	Strawberry
Cone	24	18	12
Dish	12	21	15

A. Which flavor is the most popular? Which serving method? Is the combination of the most popular flavor and serving method the most popular dessert choice overall? Explain.

B. Which of the following is more likely? Explain.

- A customer chooses vanilla, given that the customer chose a cone.
- A customer chooses a cone, given that the customer chose vanilla.

C. A class of 24 students gets the buffet for lunch. If all the students get ice cream, about how many will get a cone or vanilla? Explain.

MATH IN CAREERS

Epidemiologist An epidemiologist is aiding in the treatment of a community plagued by two different infectious agents, X and Z. Each infectious agent must be treated differently with a new treatment if the patient has been infected by both agents. The community has a total population of 15,000 people, where 5% are not affected by either agent and 60% are afflicted by the X infection. 39% of the population is afflicted by X but not by Z. Unfortunately, the treatment for the X infection fails 35% of the time. The same incident happened to 10 other communities with similar results as the first. What is the probability that people will be healthy? have the X affliction? have the Z affliction? have both afflictions?

Focus on Careers

The following Focus on Career pages can be used after you have completed each unit in the book. Each feature shows how mathematics is used in some career.

UNIT 1

Transformations and Congruence

Mathematics and Architecture

Every architectural project begins with a *grid geometry plan*, an overall scheme that shows how a building, such as a sports stadium, will be laid out and supported structurally. More advanced plans containing the details the contractor needs to start building the structure follow. In the final drawings, the architect precisely spells out all of the building's elements and features. Knowledge of mathematics, especially geometry, is essential for determining how three-dimensional spaces work in order to fit the elements inside the building without wasting space.

Symmetry is a basic element that an architect uses when designing a stadium. If you draw a vertical line through the middle of a stadium's front façade, chances are that the left half is a mirror image of the right half. This symmetry also extends to elements within the stadium, such as concession stands and rest rooms. This cuts down on design time and makes the stadium easier to build.

The stadium in the figure is divided into four quadrants. After designing Quadrant A, the architects can generate Quadrants B and D by reflecting Quadrant A over the horizontal and vertical axes shown in the diagram. Quadrant C is created by reflecting Quadrant A over both axes, one after the other. Alternately, Quadrant C can be created by a 180° rotation of Quadrant A about the origin. Once this is done, the entire building is composed.

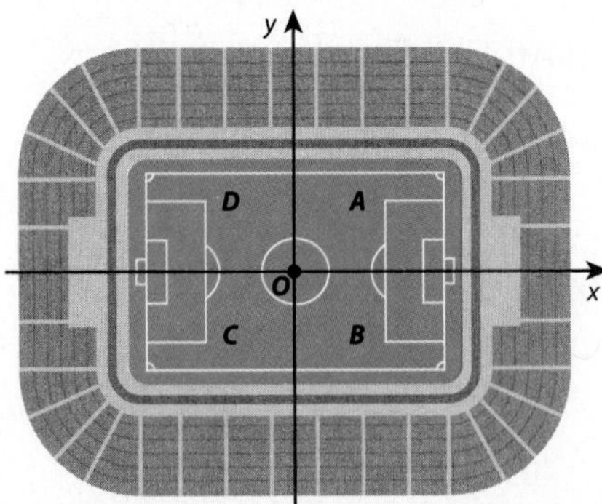

Building elements, such as a section of stairway, can be reproduced on paper via a process called *translation*, which involves reflecting the set of stairs twice over two parallel lines. This double reflection results in a new stairway identical to the original appearing in another position in the drawing. This process enables architects to use the same set of stairs in their designs and then translate it to various locations in the building.

Exercises

The diagram below shows the entrance to a stadium in Charlotte, North Carolina.

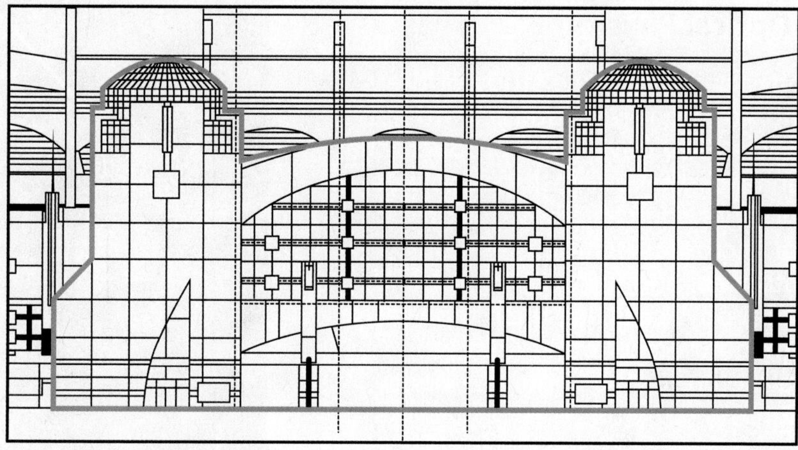

1. **a.** Trace the items outlined in green on a piece of paper. Fold your paper to locate the line of symmetry for the stadium entrance. Describe its location.

b. The towers on each side of the entrance are chambers for stairwells. Which parts of one tower have reflection symmetry? Which parts do not?

Suppose you are creating a drawing of a football field, such as the one shown, using a drawing application on a computer. The application allows you to copy sections of your drawing and to reflect, translate, and rotate them to create new sections.

2. **a.** In what way might you use translation when creating your drawing?

b. In what way might you use reflection when creating your drawing?

c. In what way might you use rotation when creating your drawing?

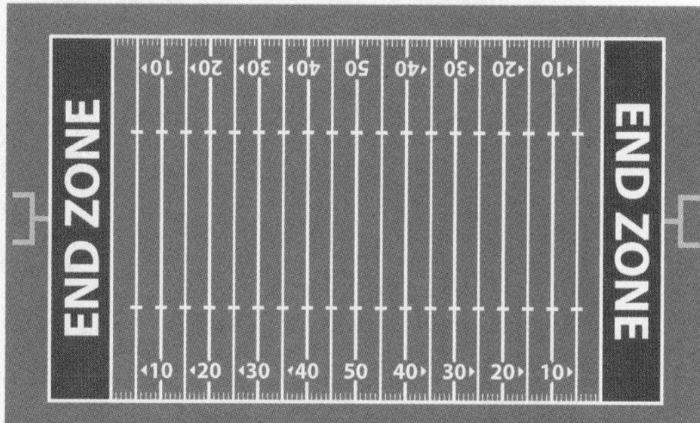

UNIT 2

Lines, Angles, and Triangles

Mathematics and Optical Physics

The field of optical physics involves the study of the properties of light and how light rays interact with matter. Optical physicists have developed products that reflect light rays to enhance the luminosity of objects, such as road signs and light sources. They design surfaces covered with microscopic structures—tiny bumps, ridges, indentations, and furrows—that bend and reflect light. Optical physicists use their knowledge of geometry to determine the angle that light is reflected off a microstructure or the angle it is bent when it passes through the structure.

A road sign appears brightly lit because of a special film designed by optical physicists that is applied to the front surface of the sign. The back of the film contains about 7000 tiny pyramids per square inch. The base of each pyramid is an isosceles triangle. All of these triangles are congruent. The light passes through the film and reflects inside the pyramids on the back. The pyramids are designed to reflect the light from the headlights back to the driver, no matter where the car is. This allows drivers to see the signs from any position on the road.

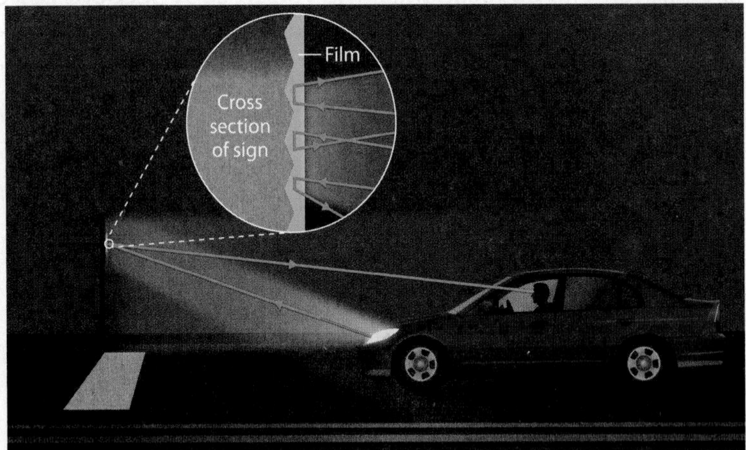

As optical physicists work to improve the film, they need to understand the geometric relationships between the surfaces of these microstructures and the location of the light source illuminating them. To achieve the desired effects, the precise shape, angle, and position of these structures must be designed carefully.

Exercises

Optical physicists design surfaces made up of millions of tiny microstructures. The reflective film used on road signs, described on the preceding page, is one example. The back of the film has thousands of tiny pyramids with congruent bases on it. The figures below show a magnified view of a portion of the back of the film and a single pyramid.

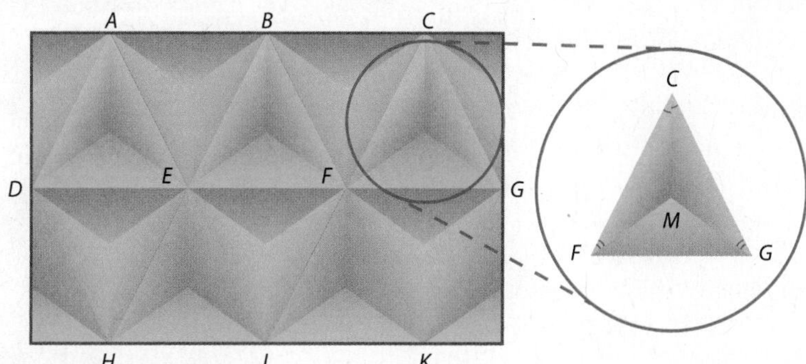

1. **a.** It appears that $\triangle AEB \cong$ ________.

b. How many triangles with labeled vertices appear to be congruent to $\triangle AEB$?

c. Can you identify another, larger pair of triangles with labeled vertices that appear to be congruent?

2. **a.** Prove that $\triangle FCM \cong \triangle GCM$.

b. Explain how you can conclude that $\triangle FCG$ is isosceles.

c. Name another isosceles triangle in the pyramid on the right. Explain how you know that it is isosceles.

Optical physicists have also designed the microstructures found in light pipes. Light pipes are smooth on the inside and grooved on the outside. This design allows light entering at one end to travel down the pipe, while allowing some of the light to leak out along the way. Light pipes are used in many diverse applications, such as in electronic devices and skylights. The surface of one such light pipe is shown below.

3. **a.** What is the meaning of the single and double line segments in the figure?

b. A mold is used to make tiny parallel ridges on the outside of the pipe. The ridges and mold fit together as shown. What postulate can you use to explain why $\triangle ABC \cong \triangle DEF$?

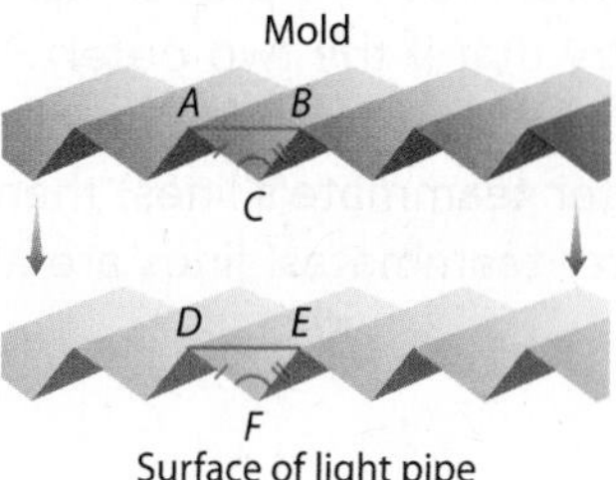

UNIT 3

Quadrilaterals and Coordinate Proof

Mathematics and Kite Design

Kites can be made in an amazing array of shapes and sizes, including animals like birds and dragons, as long as the shape of the kite is balanced. Despite the variety of possible forms, the typical kite design is a diamond shape. However, squares, rectangles, triangles, and even hexagons are sometimes used. In competitions, kites are judged for aesthetics, structural integrity, craftsmanship, and most importantly, flight characteristics. A kite must be stable in the air and fly at a good angle, the higher the better. These are the primary concerns of a good kite designer. In order for a kite to be stable and balanced, the designer must use his knowledge of geometry.

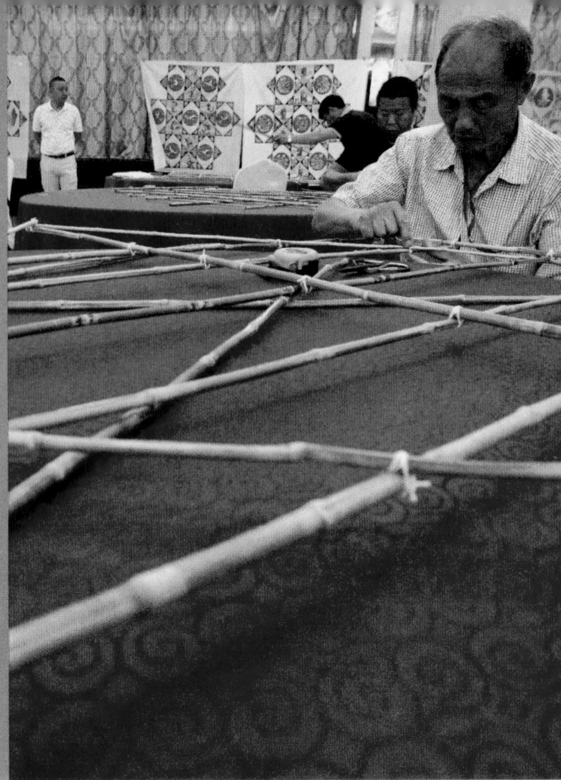

A kite with just a single string attached is called a single-line kite. The angle at which a conventional, single-line kite will fly, which determines the height of the kite, depends on the shape of the kite and the wind speed. Two kites of the exact same shape will fly at the same angle and their lines will be parallel. This means that if two people are flying identical kites, they can stand very close together and their lines will not get tangled.

Dual-line stunt kites are guided by two lines that run parallel from the kite flyer's hands to the bridle point, where they attach to the kite. By using two lines instead of just one, an expert can make his kite perform "tricks" in the air, such as flips and loops. One of the most exciting events in an exhibition takes place when the members of a four-person team stand side by side while performing synchronized precision maneuvers in the sky using dual-line kites. The kites are flipping and looping in unison, which requires that the lines of all four kites remain parallel throughout the maneuvers.

In events where the members of a three-person team perform their synchronized maneuvers while standing side by side, the teammates on the left and right each focus on keeping their kite's lines parallel with the lines of the teammate in the middle. It can be proven using geometry that if the two outer teammates' lines are each parallel to the center teammate's lines, then the two outer teammates' lines are also parallel.

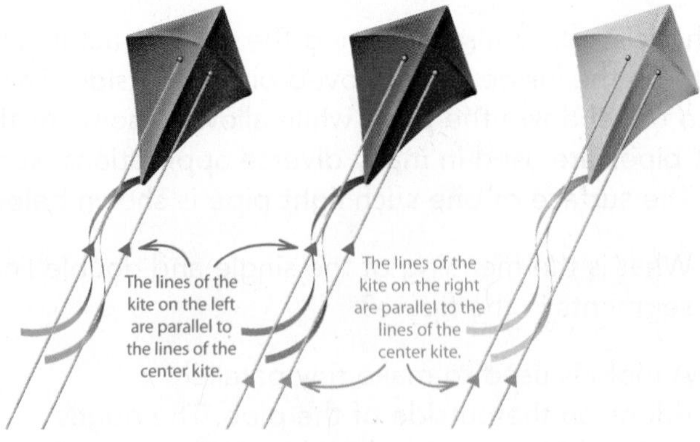
The lines of the kite on the left are parallel to the lines of the center kite.
The lines of the kite on the right are parallel to the lines of the center kite.

Exercises

In a team formation exhibition, three kites might be flown side by side such that the dual lines on the left and right kites are parallel to the lines of the center kite.

Suppose the lines to the kite on the right were not parallel to the lines to the kite in the center. How would the lines to the kite on the right be related to the lines to the kite on the left?

A kite designed in the shape of a regular hexagon is modeled by the figure. The fabric of the kite is supported by six hollow sticks that are joined at the center of the kite and extend to the six vertices of the hexagon.

a. $\overleftrightarrow{PS}$ is a transversal of $\overleftrightarrow{UP}$ and $\overleftrightarrow{SR}$. Name another pair of lines that have $\overleftrightarrow{PS}$ for a transversal.

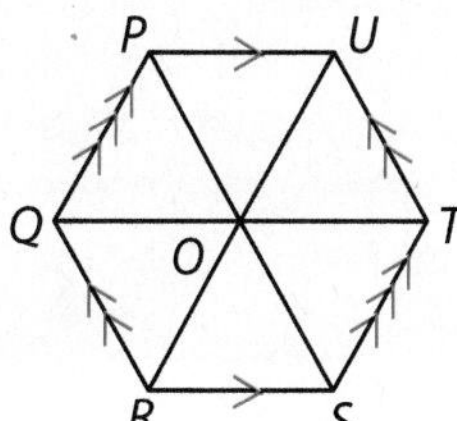

b. Name a pair of angles on the kite that the Alternate Interior Angles Theorem guarantees are congruent.

c. Copy the hexagon. Extend $\overline{QR}$ and $\overline{UT}$ into lines. Label two new points on each line beyond the endpoints of the segment. Name two angles that are supplementary by the Same-Side Interior Angles Theorem.

d. $\overline{PS}$ is parallel to $\overline{UT}$, and $\overline{QT}$ is parallel to $\overline{RS}$. Identify two different types of quadrilaterals contained within the hexagon. Give an example of each.

A kite is designed with the following geometry: It is primarily rectangular in shape, with four flaps extending outward from both of its vertical sides and three flaps extending outward from both of its horizontal sides. All of the flaps are identical quadrilaterals. There are eight cross-supports across the back of the kite and six vertical supports.

a. If all of the cross-supports are perpendicular to one vertical support, what do you know about all of the cross-supports? Explain.

b. Each of the flaps of the kite is a quadrilateral as shown in the figure. If $m\angle ABC = 60°$ and $m\angle BCD = 120°$, what do you know about $\overline{AB}$ and $\overline{CD}$? Explain how you know.

A B D C

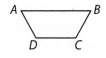

c. Based on your answer to part (b), what type of quadrilateral is $ABCD$?

d. If you know that $\overline{AB}$ is parallel to one of the cross-supports, what can you conclude about $\overline{CD}$? Explain.

UNIT 4

Similarity

Mathematics and Set Design

Actors certainly play a very important role in a theater production, but one cannot overlook the importance of the set. While some modern plays place the actors on a nearly empty stage, a well-designed set serves to set the mood and draw the audience deeper into the actors' performance. While a set designer faces many challenges, establishing the appropriate mood is perhaps the biggest. By carefully choosing props, backdrops, and lighting, the designer influences the actors' and audience's emotions. Set design is really about subtly using the relationship between the actors and the space around them to create the desired impression. When done correctly, the set makes the action on stage seem real to both the actors and the audience.

The set designer begins by reading the play, developing some initial ideas, and then conferring with the director. After forming a rough plan, the designer performs some mental calculations to ensure that the pieces of a set he or she envisions will fit together on the stage. After checking the calculations, the set designer will usually have a *scale model* of the set built. This model helps the designer understand and improve the plan for the stage. A good set designer will include miniature people in order to check the proportions of the design relative to the actors. The scale model also allows the designer to determine if everyone in the audience will be able to see the whole stage. Finally, the scale model is used to guarantee that all of the pieces of the set really do fit together.

Each piece in the model is similar, in a geometric sense, to its corresponding piece of the full-scale stage set. This means that the lengths all change by the same factor between the model and the stage set, but the angles do not change. The *scale* of the model indicates how the lengths will change between the model and the stage set. A scale of 1 : 48 is common for the scale models in set design; this means that 0.25 inch in the model corresponds to 12 inches, or 1 foot, in the finished stage set.

After constructing the model and making any necessary modifications, the set designer creates a blueprint for the craftsmen to use while building the set. The blueprint might use a scale of 1 : 24, so that 0.5 inch in the blueprint corresponds to 1 foot in the actual set. The dimensions of the scale models and in the blueprints are typically rounded to the nearest sixteenth of an inch, mainly because measurements for the plans are often made using a standard ruler. For example, consider an actual set dimension of 5 feet 8 inches, or 68 inches. Using a 1 : 48 scale, this dimension on a scale model would be $1\frac{5}{12}$ inches. Since standard rulers are not marked in twelfths of an inch, the dimension of the scale model would be rounded to $1\frac{7}{16}$ inches.

Exercises

Set designers may provide the set builders with both a scale model and a set of blueprints for a stage set. Suppose the final dimensions of a particular set are 34 feet 6 inches wide by 12 feet 10 inches tall.

1. **a.** If the blueprint drawing of the stage set is $17\frac{1}{4}$ inches by $6\frac{7}{16}$ inches, what is the scale of the drawing?

   b. The scale of the model stage is 1 : 48. What are the dimensions of the scale model, to the nearest sixteenth of an inch?

When designing a set, the designer has to consider the amount of space available. The set builder uses the designer's model and scale drawings to estimate the amount of material needed to build the set. Relationships between similar figures can help the builder make decisions about area and materials.

2. **a.** Suppose a stage set is rectangular, with a width of $21\frac{1}{2}$ feet. The scale drawing of the set shows the set as a rectangle that is $5\frac{3}{8}$ inches wide by $7\frac{3}{8}$ inches long. What is the ratio of a side length of the rectangle in the scale drawing to the corresponding side length in the stage set?

   b. What is the length of the set, in feet?

   c. Find the perimeters of the two rectangles from part (a). What is the ratio of the perimeters?

   d. What is the ratio of the two areas of the rectangles in part (a)?

   e. The scale drawing of the set described in part (a) includes a bed that measures $1\frac{3}{8}$ inches wide by $1\frac{3}{4}$ inches long. What are these dimensions of the bed in the stage set? Explain your reasoning.

The stage set for a particular play includes an outdoor, snowy winter scene. A model of the stage was built using a scale of 1 : 36. The snow depth on the model stage is $\frac{1}{4}$ inch.

3. **a.** What is the depth of the snow on the set?

   b. If a volume of 6 cubic inches of artificial snow is required for the scale model, what volume of artificial snow is required for the stage set? Give your answer in both cubic inches and cubic feet.

UNIT 5

Trigonometry

Mathematics and Solar Energy

Solar energy is an alternative, renewable energy source. The energy contained in sunlight is converted to electricity by the photovoltaic cells in solar panels. In most residential installations, the panels are mounted on the roof of the home. As of summer 2016, more than one million homes in the United States have solar panels. Some estimates indicate that nearly 40% of the country's energy requirement could be supplied by rooftop solar panels on existing, suitable rooftops.

Solar panels can be utilized anywhere there is sufficient sunlight. Solar panel installations need to be performed by electricians familiar with the specific requirements of the panels. The electricians use trigonometry in order to optimize both the size and placement of the panels, as well as ensuring that the supporting hardware is placed properly. Solar panels are mounted at an angle that maximizes their exposure to sunlight. The angle depends on the latitude where the building is located and also varies with the season and even with the time of day. In order to produce the maximum amount of electricity for a given location, panels would need to be motorized so their angle could change over time. However, this feature is expensive and the cost essentially offsets the net value of the energy produced by a small group of panels.

Most residential panels are installed at a fixed angle that is typically the optimal angle for the sun's position at "solar noon" (halfway between sunrise and sunset) during the months when the owner wants to achieve the best performance from the system. For example, in the southwestern United States, solar panels are usually mounted at a 55° angle measured from the horizontal.

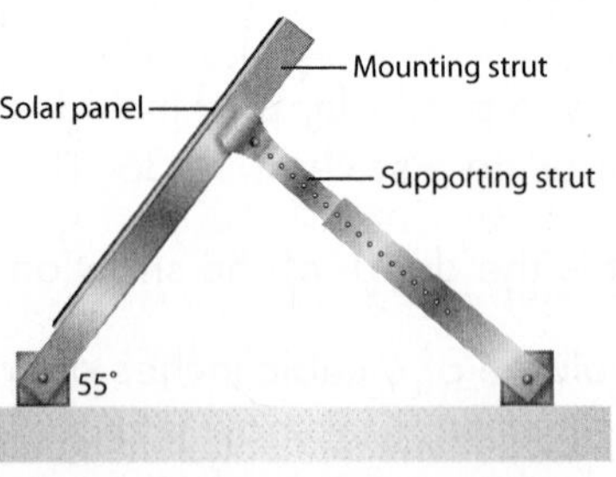

Rooftops in the southwest are often flat, so a solar panel, its supports, and the roof form a triangle that allows an electrician to use basic trigonometry to determine the proper installation. However, roofs in New England, for example, are typically sloped to account for snow load. So electricians there must use more advanced trigonometry to determine the sizes of the mounting and support struts once the angle of the solar panels has been determined for a sloped-roof installation.

Exercises

One type of solar panel contains solar cells that are approximately equiangular octagons with the dimensions shown. Each octagon can be thought of as a square with its corners removed.

1. a. What type of triangles must the corners be if the octagon is equiangular? Explain your reasoning.

   b. Use your answer to part (a) to find the side length of the square, rounded to the nearest tenth.

   c. Find the area of the square and of one of the triangular corners, rounded to the nearest tenth if necessary.

   d. Use your answers to part (c) to estimate the area of each solar cell.

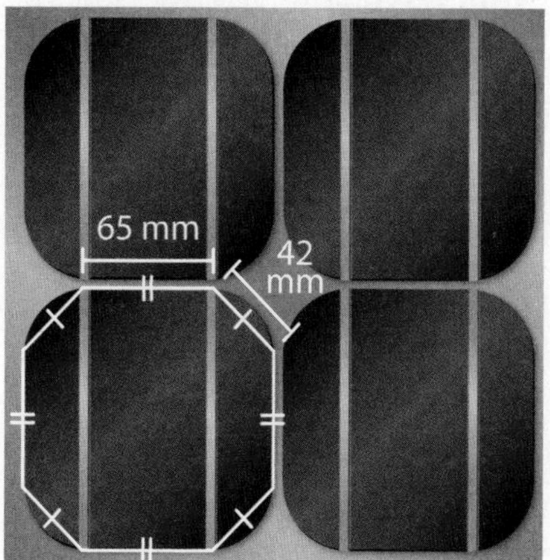

A special structure like the one shown below might be used to support a solar panel. In the diagram, AC and AB are permanently set to be 43 inches and 66 inches, respectively. The measure of $\angle A$ can be changed by adjusting the length s of the support strut.

2. For a home with a flat roof in the southwestern United States, the exposure to sunlight is maximized when $m\angle A = 55°$. Round all answers to the nearest tenth.

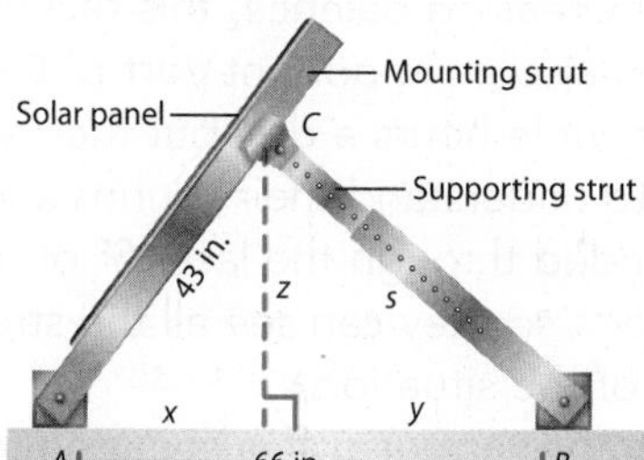

   a. What should the value of z be in order for $\angle A$ to measure 55°?

   b. Use your answer to part (a) and the Pythagorean Theorem to find the values of x and y.

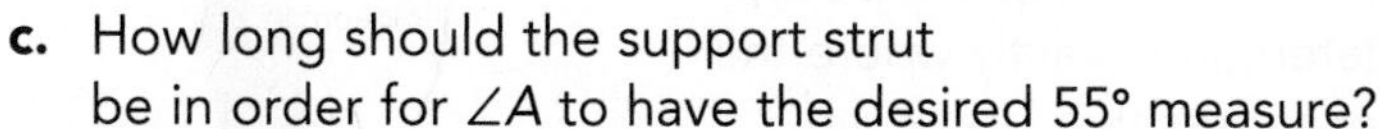

   c. How long should the support strut be in order for $\angle A$ to have the desired 55° measure?

3. Repeat parts (a)–(c) of Exercise 2 for $m\angle A = 35°$.

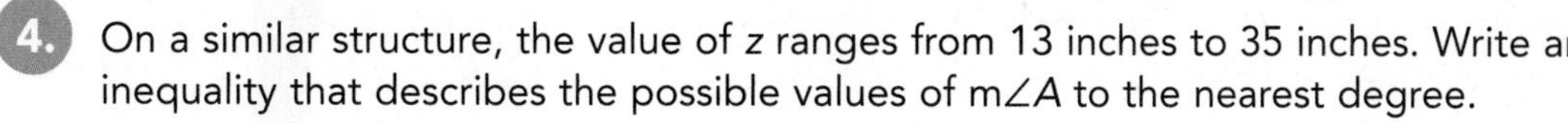

4. On a similar structure, the value of z ranges from 13 inches to 35 inches. Write an inequality that describes the possible values of $m\angle A$ to the nearest degree.

UNIT 6

Properties of Circles

Mathematics and Athletic Training

Athletic trainers and physical therapists work with athletes to help them perform at their best. Much of what is done during training or rehabilitation relates to the range of motion of joints like the shoulder, hip, or knee. A joint's range of motion is the geometric arc through which it can move. One of the first things a trainer does when evaluating an athlete is to measure these arcs to determine whether the athlete has a normal range of motion. The trainer then recommends exercises, such as leg extensions or leg curls, which strengthen the injured body part while keeping it within an appropriate arc of motion.

In addition to limiting range of motion, injuries can affect an athlete's sense of balance. To improve balance, a trainer might use a technique in which the athlete lies on top of a ball and tries to balance him or herself. The size of the ball affects how difficult it is to balance. In addition to increasing balance, this technique also increases muscle strength.

Education is also an important part of the rehabilitation process. Athletes may work with a trainer for a couple hours a day, but they are then on their own for the rest of the day. The athletes need to understand their injuries and why, for instance, their knee hurts so much when it is extended through the last 45° of motion. Trainers show the athletes an anatomical model of the joint so they can see all the stresses on the joint and understand the physics and geometry of the situation.

An injury to the rotator cuff is common for swimmers, tennis players, baseball pitchers, and volleyball players. This injury makes it painful for them to rotate their arm through an arc between 130° and 150° (where 0° corresponds to the arm positioned at rest by the side of the body and the motion is outward in front of the body). The athletic trainer performs tests to determine exactly where the painful zone is and then recommends exercises that break the shoulder motion down into smaller arcs. These exercises avoid the restricted zone, preventing further injury to the athlete.

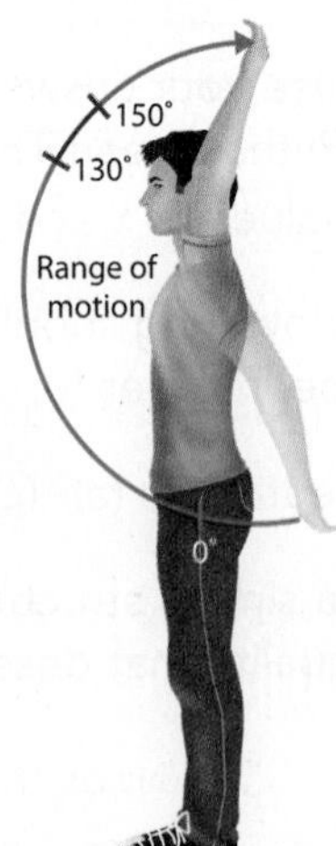

Exercises

A physical therapist may measure range of motion to make a diagnosis or treatment plan. Range of motion is the arc through which a part of the body can move. The arc through which the shoulder can move measured from the vertical (arms at sides), with motion in the forward, upward direction, is called the shoulder flexion. The arc measured from the vertical with its motion in the backward, upward direction is called the shoulder extension.

1. **a.** A total arc of about 225° for shoulder flexion and extension combined is common in healthy adults. The measure of the arc for shoulder flexion alone that is commonly found in healthy adults is about 180°. What is the measure of the arc for shoulder extension that a physical therapist would expect to find in a healthy adult?

b. Injuries to the rotator cuff often result in painful motion when the arm is rotated through an arc between 130° and 150°. Convert 130° and 150° to radian measure. Express your answers as multiples of π.

A physical therapist may have a client use a tilt board as a way to improve balance and flexibility. A cross section of a tilt board shows that the bottom is an arc of a circle.

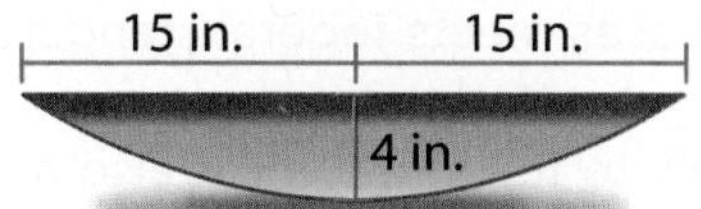

2. **a.** Imagine that the cross section is part of a circle. Use the Pythagorean theorem to find the radius of the circle to the nearest inch.

b. Use trigonometry to find the measure of the central angle that intercepts the arc of the tilt board.

c. What is the cross-sectional area of the tilt board shown in the figure? Round to the nearest square inch.

d. What is the arc length of the bottom surface of the tilt board? Round to the nearest tenth inch.

e. What is the maximum angle that the flat surface of the tilt board can make with the ground while a person is standing on it? Explain your reasoning.

To help rehabilitate a hamstring injury, an athletic trainer may have an athlete ride a stationary bicycle. A certain stationary bike has a wheel with diameter 18 inches.

3. An athlete rides the bike for 15 minutes at a pedaling rate of 60 revolutions per minute (rpm). If this pedaling rate corresponds to a 120 rpm wheel rate, what is the equivalent distance that the athlete has ridden, to the nearest tenth of a mile?

UNIT 7

Measurement and Modeling in Two and Three Dimensions

Mathematics and Urban Planning

Urban planners work with cities and towns to decide how to make changes to buildings, streets, and sidewalks. One thing they must consider is compliance with the Americans with Disabilities Act (ADA). Title III of the ADA requires that all new construction in public facilities be accessible to individuals with disabilities and that any modifications made to existing structures must bring the portion modified into compliance if possible. In addition, any barriers to services within existing facilities must be removed if the removal can be readily achieved.

As cities and towns improve their infrastructure, urban planners must make sure that there are a certain number of parking spaces set aside for drivers or passengers with disabilities and that the area in and around these spaces meets federal standards. Wheelchair ramps providing access to buildings with elevated entrances as well as "curb cuts" that smoothly transition from a raised sidewalk to the street must also meet federal standards. The incline of these ramps cannot exceed a specified angle; if a ramp is too steep, most people would not be able to make their way up. In addition, there must be a flat section whenever a ramp changes direction or after the length of a ramp has reached a specific number of feet. The flat sections serve as rest points for users and also to ensure that if someone were to fall, the person would not fall very far.

In order to ensure compliance with Title III, urban planners must measure and calculate geometric quantities such as slope, area, and volume as part of their work. For instance, regulations specify the minimum width and length of each rectangular parking space for people with disabilities. The total area of a parking lot that is to be dedicated to accessible parking must be determined during the planning phase.

Wheelchair ramps are frequently made of concrete, and the volume of concrete needed must be determined in advance. The ramp itself is often prism-shaped, and its volume can therefore be found using the formula for the volume V of a prism,

$$V = Bh$$

where B is the area of the base and h is the height of the prism. In terms of the ramp, h is the width of the ramp and B is the area of the side of the ramp.

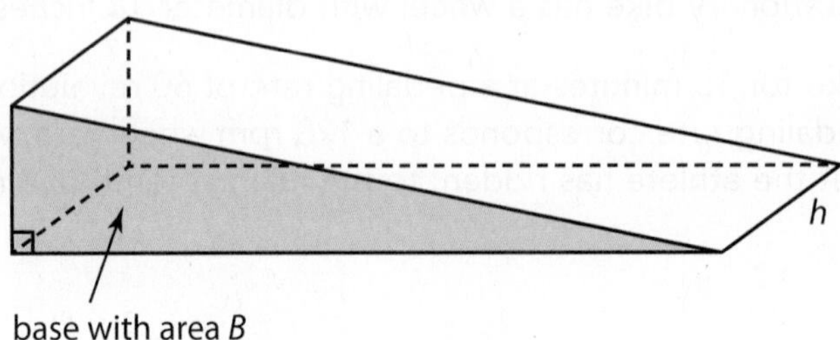

Exercises

By regulation, each accessible parking space for people with disabilities must be a rectangle 8 feet wide and 20 feet long. Amendments to the ADA now require that in large parking areas a specified number of accessible spaces must be van-accessible spaces. Each van-accessible parking space must be 11 feet wide by 20 feet long.

1. **a.** What is the area of one accessible parking space? One van-accessible parking space?

   b. There must be 5 feet between accessible spaces. Find the minimum area covered by four spaces that are next to each other if one of them is a van-accessible space.

   c. How many accessible parking spaces will fit in an area that is 35 feet wide?

Wheelchair ramps are built to meet certain requirements. If they are too steep or too narrow, they can be dangerous. A ramp must be at least 3 feet wide and extend at least 12 inches horizontally for every inch it rises vertically. Some ramps are wooden, but they can also be made of concrete. The shape of a concrete ramp is usually a prism.

2. **a.** How long must a ramp be in order to reach an entrance that is $2\frac{1}{4}$ feet above the ground?

   b. Find the amount of concrete needed to make the ramp described in part (a). Assume the ramp is 3 feet wide and that it is solid concrete.

   c. If the cost of concrete is \$100 per cubic yard, estimate the minimum cost of the concrete needed to build the ramp described in part (a). Round your answer to the nearest \$10.

3. Find the amount of concrete needed to make the ramp structure shown below.

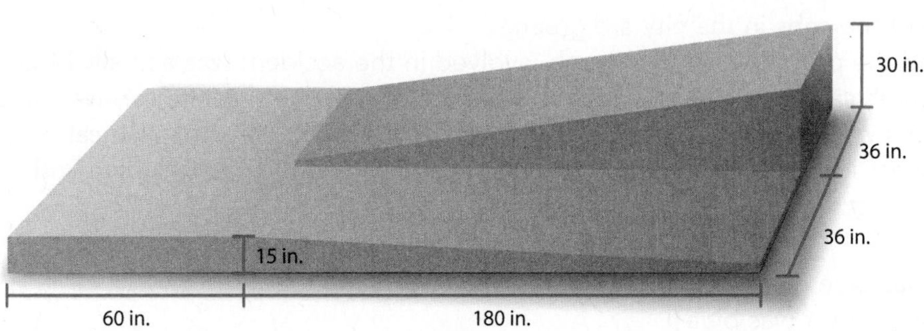

UNIT 8

Probability

Mathematics and Law

The role of an attorney in a jury trial is to convince the jury members of the defendant's innocence or guilt. Which of these depends, of course, on whether the attorney represents the defendant or is part of the prosecution. Evidence involving statistical information can be difficult for jury members to fully understand. Attorneys must strive to ensure that jurors understand how to correctly interpret statistical evidence based on probability.

Here is a situation in which jurors might misunderstand probability-based evidence if further guidance is not given during the trial. This example is sometimes called the *juror's fallacy*. The mathematics applies Bayes' Theorem, though you need not know the theorem to understand the result. Suppose you are a juror in a civil case involving a nighttime hit-and-run accident by a taxicab in your city. You are told the following:

- Of the cabs in your city, 85% are green and 15% are blue.
- A witness has identified the cab as blue.
- In reenactments of the accident, the witness correctly identified the color of the cab 80% of the time.

Given this information, jurors are likely to believe that the probability of the cab being blue is 80%, or at least very close to 80%. This belief does not properly take into account the fact that 85% of the cabs in the city are green.

In order to find the probability that the cab involved in the accident was actually blue given that the witness says it was blue, you must take the probability that the cab was blue and that the witness was correct and divide by the sum of the probability that the cab was green but the witness identified it as blue and the probability that the cab was blue and the witness was correct.

$$P\begin{pmatrix}\text{cab was blue given the}\\ \text{witness says it was blue}\end{pmatrix} = \frac{P(\text{blue and identified as blue})}{P\begin{pmatrix}\text{green and}\\ \text{identified as blue}\end{pmatrix} + P\begin{pmatrix}\text{blue and}\\ \text{identified as blue}\end{pmatrix}}$$

$$= \frac{(0.15)(0.80)}{(0.85)(0.20) + (0.15)(0.80)} = \frac{0.12}{0.29} \approx 0.414$$

So, the actual probability that the cab involved in the accident was blue, given the witness's statement, is only about 41%. Attorneys—in this case, those representing the blue-cab company and its driver—must be sure that the jurors understand the effect that all of the statistical data have on any potential outcomes.

Exercises

Suppose a six-member jury is comprised of three men and three women and that the probability that any given jury member thinks the defendant is guilty is 50%.

1. **a.** Find the probability that all of the jurors believe the defendant to be guilty.

   b. Find the probability that exactly three of the jurors believe the defendant to be guilty.

   c. Find the probability that two of the men and one of the women believe the defendant to be guilty.

In United States courts, the jury members for a civil or criminal trial are chosen from a pool of potential jurors selected at random from among the eligible members of the community. Potential jurors are questioned and may be dismissed by the judge *for cause* at the request of either lawyer or by *peremptory challenge* by either lawyer, until the number of jurors required for the trial has been selected.

2. **a.** Suppose that twenty prospective jurors have arrived at a courthouse for jury selection for an upcoming trial. Assume that each person has an equally likely chance of being selected to serve on the twelve-member jury. Find the probability that the person who arrived first will be selected for the jury.

   b. For the situation described in part (a), find the probability that the first three potential jurors to arrive at the courthouse are selected for the jury.

Suppose residents downstream from a chemical plant had the water in the stream tested for the presence of a certain contaminant. The test is known to have both a sensitivity and a specificity of 99%, meaning that 99 out of every 100 samples of contaminated water will test positive for the contaminant, while 1 out of every 100 samples of clean water will test positive for the contaminant. The single test result of the stream water was positive for the contaminant. The residents have sued the corporation, and their attorneys argue in court that the 99% accuracy rate of the test is more than sufficient reason for the jury to find the corporation guilty of contaminating the water.

3. **a.** What important statistical piece of information have the prosecuting attorneys not told the jurors?

   b. If the probability of leakage of the contaminant into the water from the plant by any means is 0.05%, what is the likelihood that the water was actually contaminated by the chemical plant?

   c. Pose this problem to five people who are not taking a probability class. Ask each of them to give an estimate of the likelihood (as a percent) that the water was contaminated and that the contamination came from the plant. Comment on your results.

UNIT 1 Selected Answers

MODULE 1

Lesson 1.1 Segment Length and Midpoints

Your Turn

6\.

8\. $JK = LM = \sqrt{13}$. Therefore, $\overline{JK}$ and $\overline{LM}$ have the same length.

10\. Measure each of the segments formed by the bisector. The two segments should each have a length that is half as long as the given segment.

11\. M is the origin, since the x- and y-coordinates are both 0.

12\. M lies in Quadrant IV, since the x-coordinate is positive and the y-coordinate is negative.

Evaluate

1\. line segment; defined term

3\. ray; defined term

5\.

9\. $AB \neq BC$, so $\overline{AB}$ and $\overline{BC}$ do not have the same length.

11\. $AB = CD = \sqrt{29}$. Therefore, $\overline{AB}$ and $\overline{CD}$ have the same length.

13\. M lies in Quadrant I, since the x- and y-coordinates are both positive.

15\. Both midpoints have the same coordinates, so the segments have the same midpoint.

17\. $\overrightarrow{DE}$ (or $\overrightarrow{DF}$) and $\overrightarrow{EF}$

19\.

21\.

23\. 30 mi

25\. approximately 104 meters

27\. Answer: B, D

29\. (4, −1)

UNIT 1 Selected Answers

MODULE 1

Lesson 1.2 Angle Measures and Angle Bisectors

Your Turn

4\. $\angle AEB$, $\angle BEA$

5\.

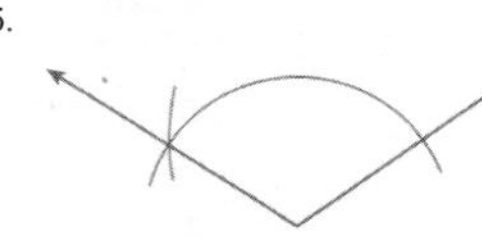

7\. 40°

8\. 105°

10\.

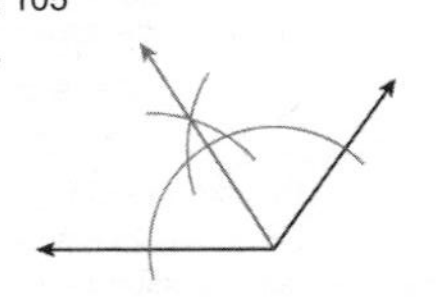

11\.

Evaluate

1\.

3\.

5\.

7\. $\angle L$, $\angle GLJ$, $\angle JLG$, and $\angle 2$

9\.

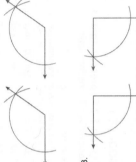

11\. 172°

13\.

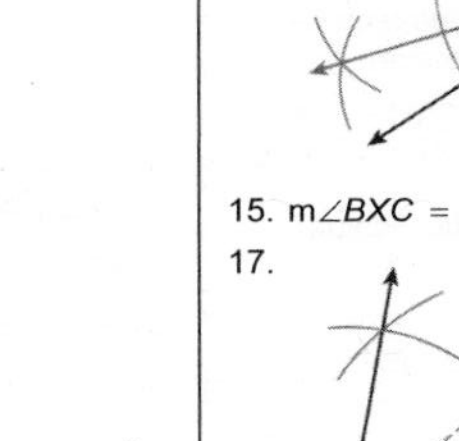

15\. $m\angle BXC = 30°$

17\.

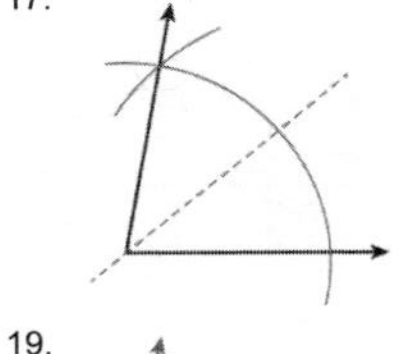

19\.

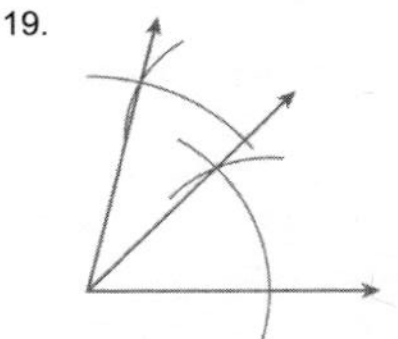

21\. $y = 5.5$

23\. $m\angle ADB = 29°$ and $m\angle BDC = 61°$

25. A. No
    B. Yes
    C. Yes
    D. No
    E. No
27. Yes; the construction still works. In this case, the construction produces two right angles since each has half the measure of a straight angle (180°).
29. Construct the bisector of the given angle. Then construct the bisector of one of the angles that was formed.

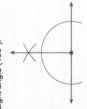

UNIT 1 Selected Answers

MODULE 1

Lesson 1.3 Representing and Describing Transformations

Your Turn

5. The transformation is a rotation of 180° around the origin $(x, y) \to (-x, -y)$.

   $DE = D'E' = 6$ $m\angle D = m\angle D' = 90°$

   $EF = E'F' = \sqrt{45}$ $m\angle E = m\angle E' = 27°$

   $DF = D'F' = 3$ $m\angle F = m\angle F' = 63°$

   The transformation preserves length and angle measure.
6. The transformation is a translation $(x, y) \to (x + 1, y - 2)$.

   $ST = S'T' = 5$ $m\angle S = m\angle S' = 76°$

   $TU = T'U' = \sqrt{32}$ $m\angle T = m\angle T' = 45°$

   $SU = S'U' = \sqrt{17}$ $m\angle U = m\angle U' = 59°$

   The transformation preserves length and angle measure.
8. $(x, y) \to (1.5x, 1.5y)$

   $AB = 2$

   $A'B' = 3$

   Since $AB \neq A'B'$, the transformation is not a rigid motion.
9. $(x, y) \to \left(\frac{1}{2}x, 3y\right)$

   $RS = \sqrt{37}$

   $R'S' = \sqrt{18}$

   Since $RS \neq R'S'$, the transformation is not a rigid motion.

Evaluate

1. 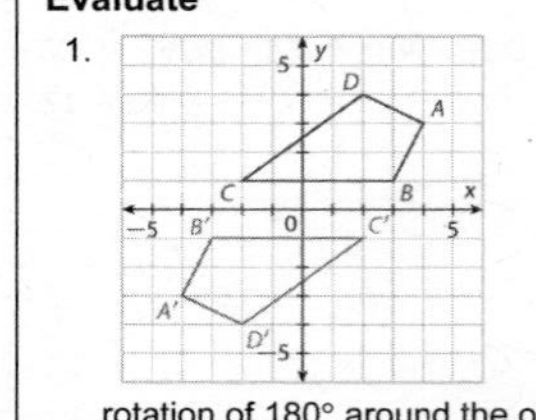

   rotation of 180° around the origin
3. 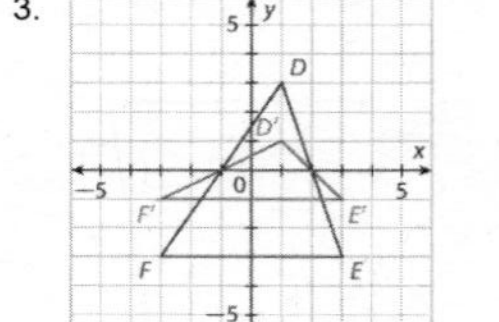

   vertical compression by a factor of $\frac{1}{3}$
5. $(x, y) \to (y, -x)$; rotation of 90° clockwise around the origin.

   The transformation preserves length and angle measure.
7. $(x, y) \to \left(\frac{1}{2}x, \frac{1}{2}y\right)$

   Since $AB \neq A'B'$, the transformation is not a rigid motion.
9. 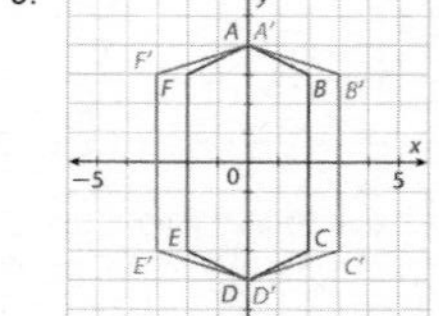

   $(x, y) \to (1.5x, y)$

11. a. Segment HK is a horizontal segment that is 8 units long.
    b. The image of segment HK is a vertical segment that is 8 units long.
    c. The image of segment HK is a horizontal segment that is 16 units long.
    d. Possible answer: $(x, y) \to (-y, x)$ is rigid, because it does not change the length of the segment. $(x, y) \to (2x, y)$ is not rigid because it doubles the length of the segment. The transformation given by $(x, y) \to (-y, x)$ switches the segment from horizontal to vertical, while $(x, y) \to (2x, y)$ does not.

13. The x-coordinate does not change. The y-coordinate has a constant added to it (for a translation up) or subtracted from it (translation down). The coordinate notation has the form $(x, y) \to (x, y + b)$, where b is a real number, $b \neq 0$.

15. Since $QR \neq Q'R'$, the transformation is not a rigid motion.

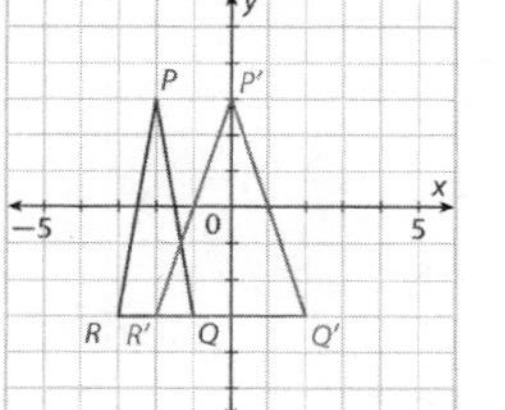

17. The transformation is a horizontal stretch by a factor of 3, so it preserves the length of vertical segments but not the length of horizontal or diagonal segments. In order to be a rigid motion, the transformation must preserve all lengths, so this transformation is not a rigid motion.

19. The transformation maps all points to the origin, so the image of any figure under this transformation is a single point, (0, 0). The transformation is not a rigid motion because all line segments are mapped to a point, so the length of the segment is not preserved.

UNIT 1 Selected Answers

MODULE 1

Lesson 1.4 Reasoning and Proof

Your Turn

3. If an animal is a zebra, then it belongs to the genus *Equus*.
4. If the bill gets two-thirds of the vote in the Senate, then it will pass.
5. $3 - 4x = -5$

   $-4x = -8$ Subtraction Property of Equality

   $x = 2$ Division Property of Equality

6. Multiplication Property of Equality

   Symmetric Property of Equality

   Substitution Property of Equality

   Transitive Property of Equality

8. $m\angle LMN = 120°$

Evaluate

1. The conclusion is based on observing three numbers.
3. The conclusion is based on two observations.
5. Counterexample: 2; if $x = 2$, then $x + 1 = 3$, which is a prime number.
7. When I draw three points that are noncollinear, I can draw a single plane through all three points, so they are coplanar after all.

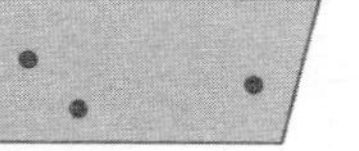

9. The number 14 is an even number.
11. There is exactly one plane containing points W, X, and Y.
13. Hypothesis: the ball is red.
    Conclusion: it will bounce higher.
15. Hypothesis: the light does not come on.
    Conclusion: the circuit is broken.
17. Use the Segment Addition Postulate; $9 = x$
19. Because $\overline{SV}$ is an angle bisector of $\angle RST$, $m\angle RSV = m\angle VST$. Use this fact and the Angle Addition Postulate; $12 = x$
21. Possible answer: P, R, and T
23. When two planes cross, they intersect each other at an infinite number of points, i.e., in a line.
25. A line can be in more than one plane.
27. Four coplanar lines can intersect in up to 6 points.

Up to four planes can be determined by 4 noncollinear points.

UNIT 1 Selected Answers

MODULE 2

Lesson 2.1 Translations

Your Turn

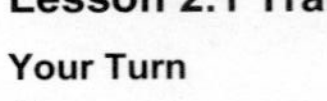

4.

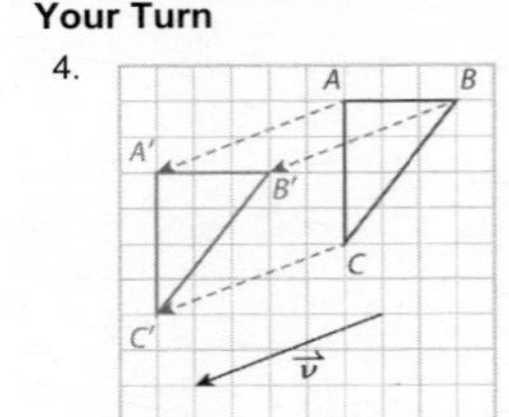

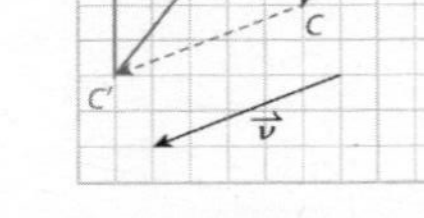

5.

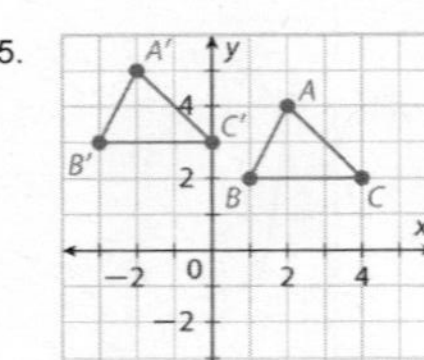

6.

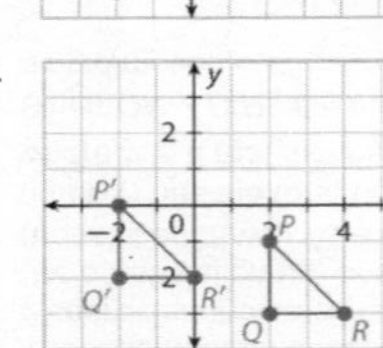

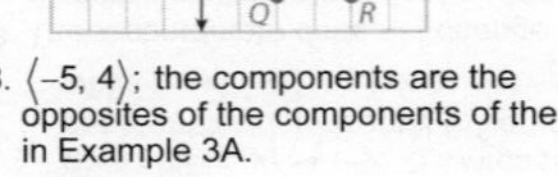

8. $\langle -5, 4\rangle$; the components are the opposites of the components of the vector in Example 3A.

Evaluate

1.

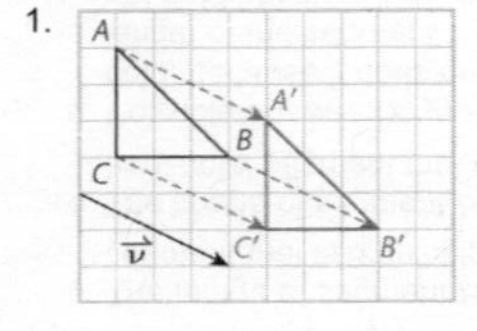

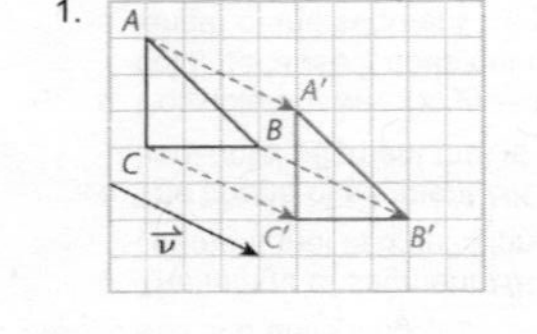

3.

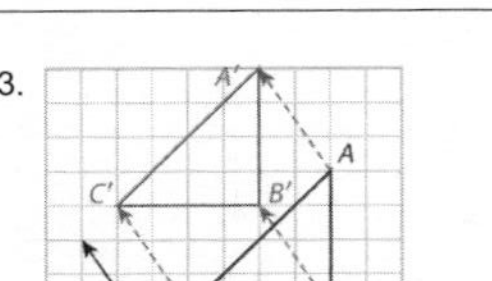

5.

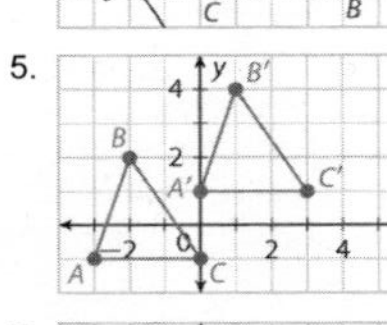

7.

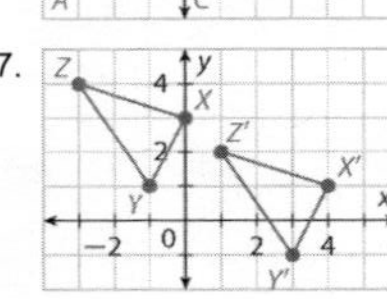

9. $\overline{GH}$, $\langle 5, -2\rangle$

11. Emma: Quadrant I; Tony: Quadrant III

13. $\langle 2, -5\rangle$

15. Possible answer: He drew vectors from *A* to *A*′ and from *B* to *B*′ that were not parallel to or the same length as $\vec{v}$. The correct vectors should each point 3 units right and 3 units down.

17. $y = 2x - 3$; (2, 1)

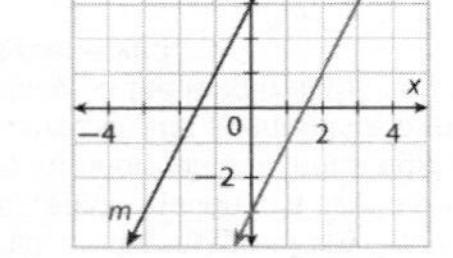

19. $\langle 4, -6\rangle$

21. (0, 2); (1, 3); (2, 2); (1, 1); Possible answer: I used a table to find the coordinates of the second polygon. Then I made a new table, using the coordinates from the second polygon to find the coordinates of the third polygon.

UNIT 1 Selected Answers

MODULE 2

Lesson 2.2 Reflections

Your Turn

5.

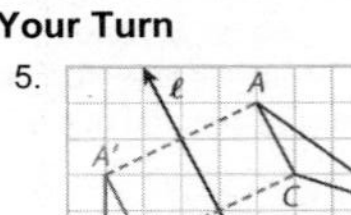

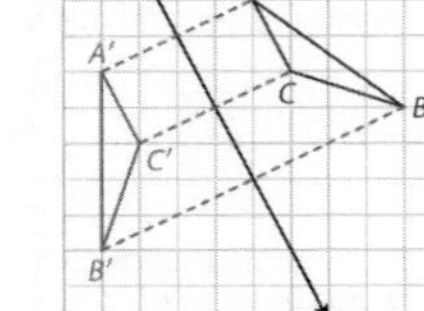

6.

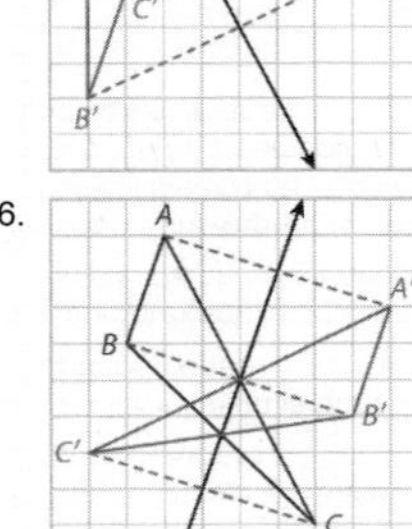

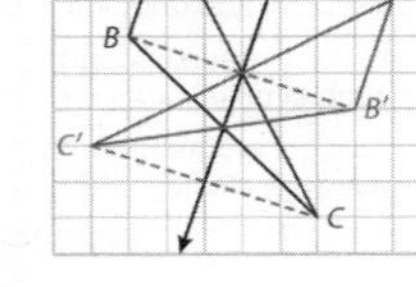

9.

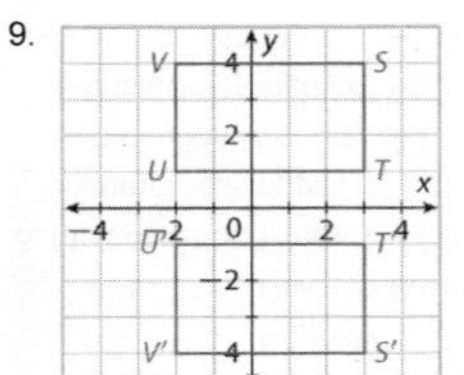

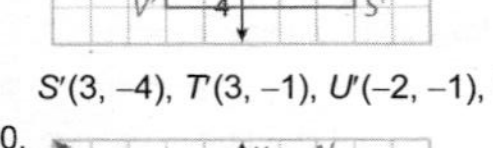

$S'(3, -4)$, $T'(3, -1)$, $U'(-2, -1)$, $V'(-2, -4)$

10.

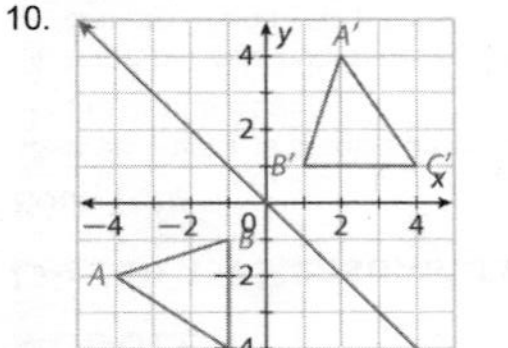

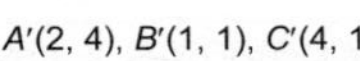

$A'(2, 4)$, $B'(1, 1)$, $C'(4, 1)$

12.

midpoints: $\overline{AA'}$: (1, 1);
$\overline{BB'}$: (2, 2);
$\overline{CC'}$: (−2, −2)

13.

midpoints: $\overline{AA'}$: (5, 5);
$\overline{BB'}$: (1, 3);
$\overline{CC'}$: (3, 4)

15. (−1, −1)

Evaluate

1.

3.

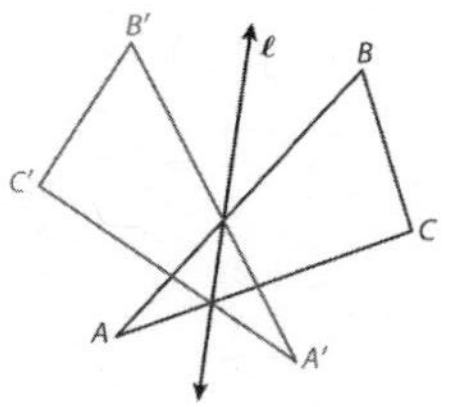

5.

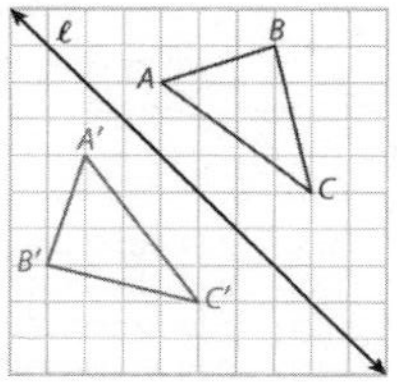

7.

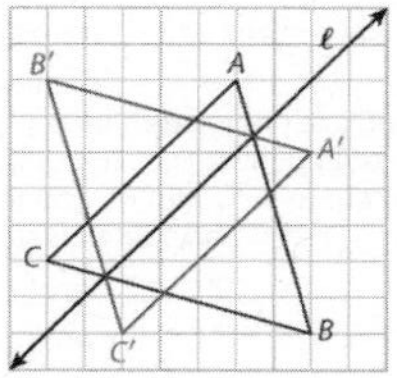

9.

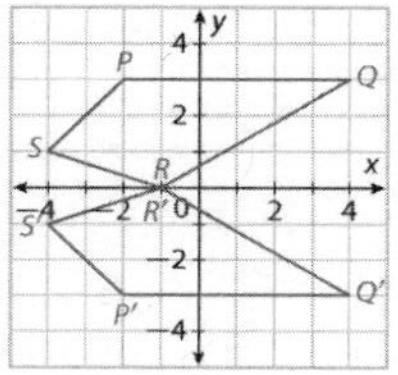

11.

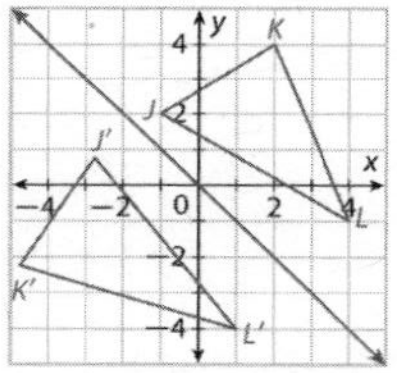

13.

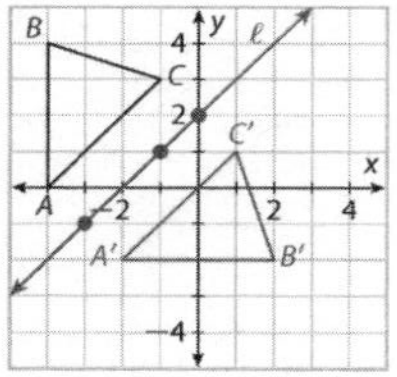

15.

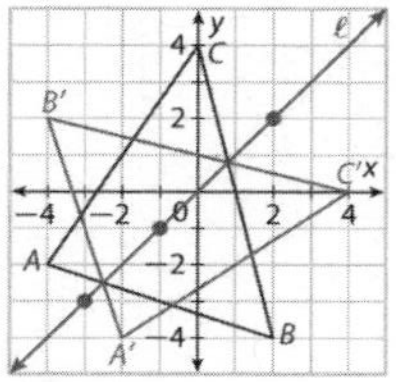

17. (0, 2)

19. $JM = 14$

21. When the tab key is pressed twice, the logo is reflected into Quadrant III and then reflected back to its original position in Quadrant II. So after the tab key is pressed 24 times, the logo is in its original position. When the tab key is pressed for the 25th time, the logo is reflected across the *x*-axis into Quadrant III.

23. No; the translation would move rectangle *PQRS* into the same position as rectangle *P′Q′R′S′*, but the corresponding vertices would not be in the same locations.

25. No; line ℓ is not perpendicular to $\overline{MM'}$, $\overline{NN'}$, and $\overline{PP'}$ so it cannot be the line of reflection. There is a translation required in addition to a reflection to map $\triangle MNP$ to $\triangle M'N'P'$.

27. Yes; points *X* and *Y* are fixed under the reflection, so they must lie on the line of reflection. Since two points determine a line, the line of reflection is $\overline{XY}$.

UNIT 1 Selected Answers

MODULE 2

Lesson 2.3 Rotations

Your Turn

4.

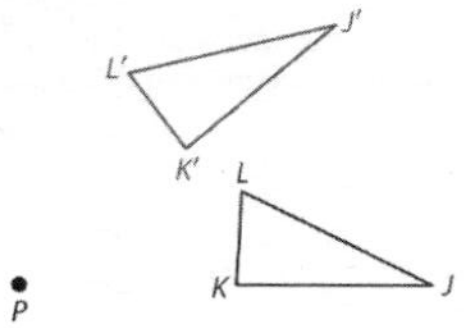

5.

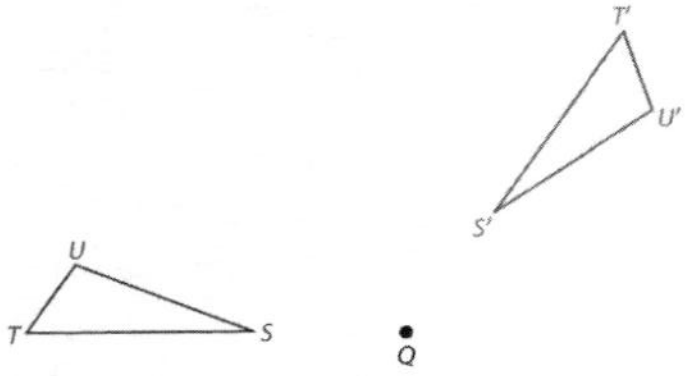

7.

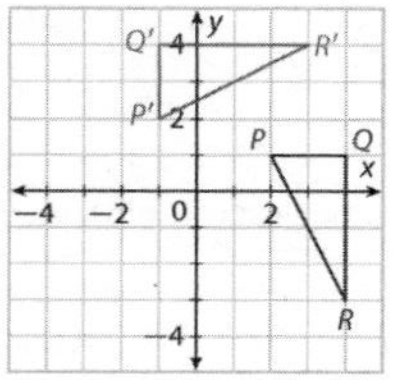

8.

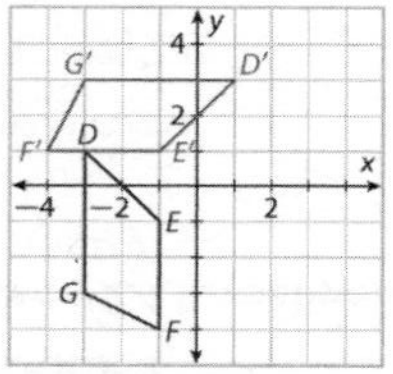

11. The transformation is a 70° clockwise rotation.

Evaluate

1. $\angle SPS'$, $\angle TPT'$, and $\angle UPU'$; all three angles measure 115°.

3.

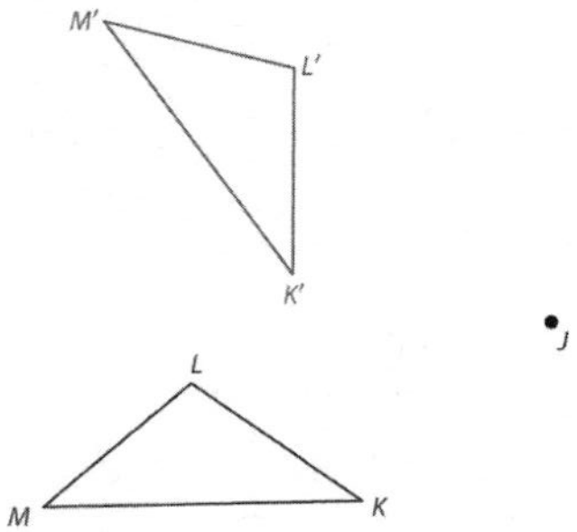

5.

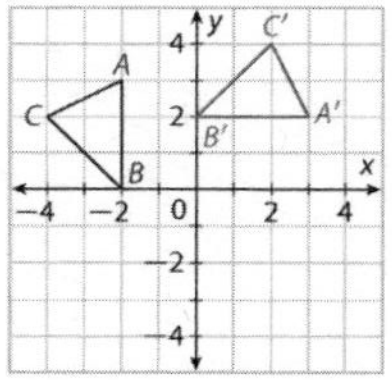

7.

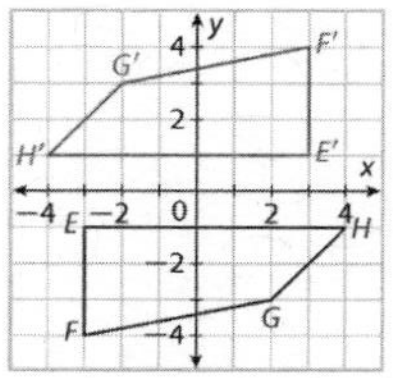

9. The rotation is 50° counterclockwise.

11. The rule is $(x, y) \rightarrow (-x, -y)$ and the transformation is a rotation of 180°.

13. No; according to the definition of a rotation, every point and its image must be the same distance from *P*, and that is not the case in the given figure.

15.

$M(-4, 2)$
$N(-1, 2)$
$P(-1, 4)$

17. 18°

19. Possible answer: Starting with triangle 1, rotate clockwise 60° around the vertex at the center of the hexagon. Repeat the process using each successive image as a preimage.

21. a. False
b. True
c. True

23. Possible answer: $\triangle A'B'C'$ should be rotated so that B' is at the top of the figure. After correctly locating the image of point A, Kevin translated the figure rather than rotating it.

25. The remainder after dividing n by 4 defines a pattern for the table.
A remainder of 0 → QI
A remainder of 1 → QII
A remainder of 2 → QIII
A remainder of 3 → QIV

UNIT 1 Selected Answers

MODULE 2

Lesson 2.4 Investigating Symmetry

Your Turn

6. line, rotational
4
90°, 180°, 270°

7. line
1
none

8. rotational
0
72°, 144°, 216° and 288°

9. none
0
none

Evaluate

1. 1

3. 1

5. 45°, 90°, 135°, 180°, 225°, 270°, 315°

7. rotational symmetry

9. *EDCBAF*

11. *DCBAFE*

13. Possible answers are shown.

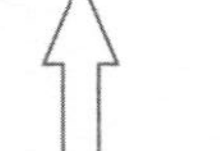

15. Both have two perpendicular lines of symmetry, and both have 180° rotational symmetry.

UNIT 1 Selected Answers

MODULE 3

Lesson 3.1 Sequences of Transformations

Your Turn

7.

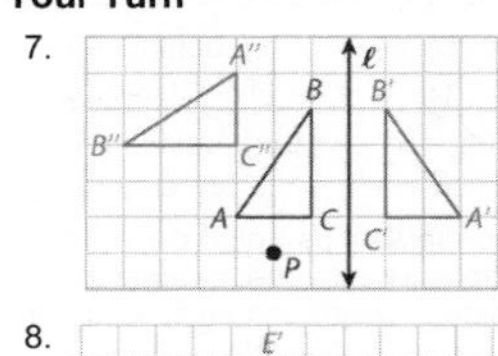

8.

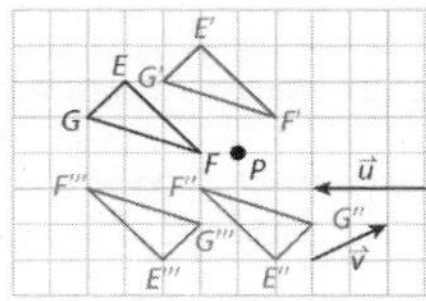

11.

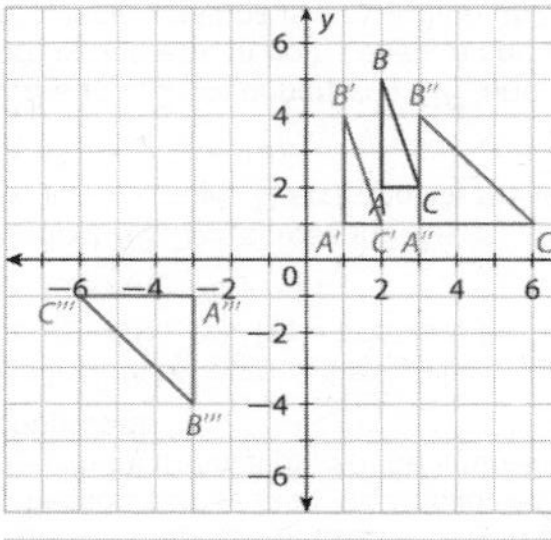

12.

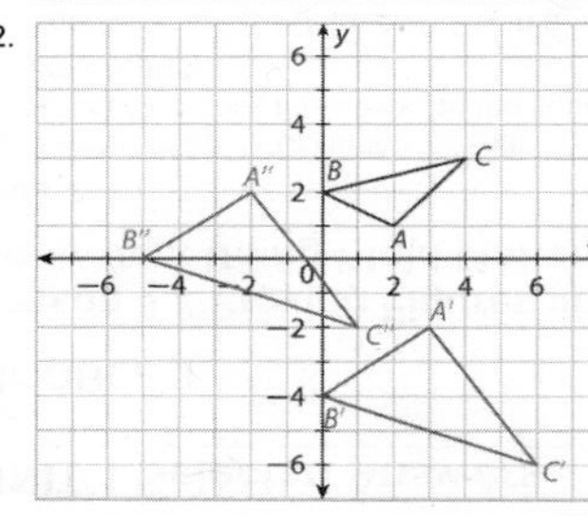

13. The reflection across the y-axis will move the rectangle from the right of the y-axis to the left of it. Due to the symmetry of the rectangle, it will appear to have been translated left 6 units. Then, translating along the vector $\langle 5, 4\rangle$ will move the rectangle right 5 units and up 4 units. This will bring the rectangle fully into Quadrant I. The final result will be a rectangle that is the same shape and size as the preimage that has moved to sit on the x-axis in Quadrant I, closer to the y-axis than the preimage.

14. A horizontal stretch will pull points U and T away from the y-axis, making the triangle longer in the left-to-right direction. The translation along the vector $\langle 2, 1\rangle$ will move the stretched triangle 2 units right and 1 unit up, which will move the triangle closer to the origin with one vertex on the x-axis and another across the y-axis. The final image will not be the same shape or size as the preimage.

Evaluate

1.

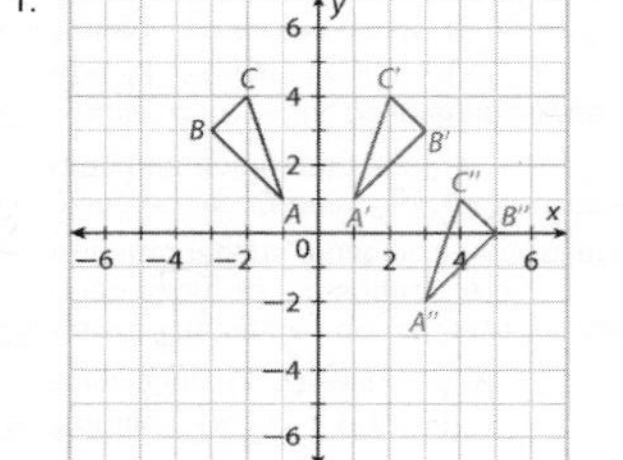

3.

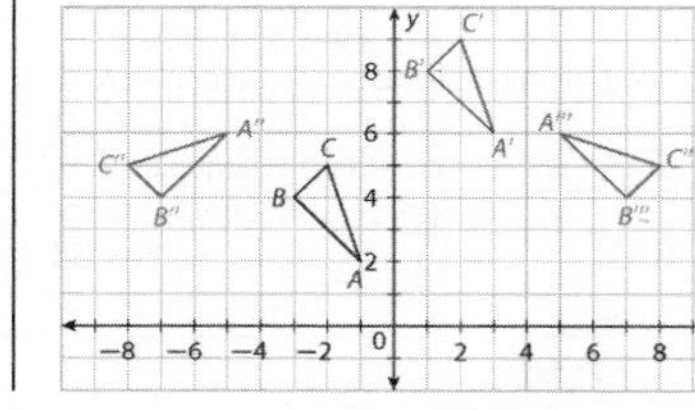

5. 7.

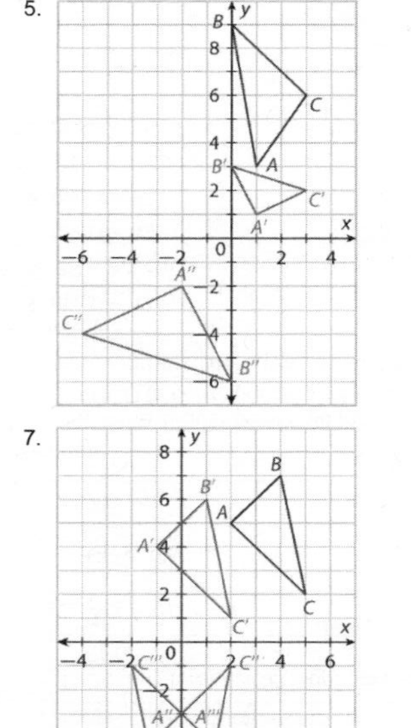

Possible answer: The translation moves the figure down one unit and left three units, mapping A' to the left of the y-axis and C' closer to the origin. The reflection first will map $A''B''C''$ below the x-axis and change the orientation. The second reflection will map the figure mostly into Quadrant III, with A''' in Quadrant IV, and again change the orientation. The final image is the same size, shape, and orientation as the preimage.

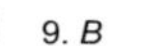

9. *B*
11. *F*
13. sometimes
15. sometimes
17. sometimes
19. a. Yes
    b. Yes
    c. No
    d. Yes
21. Possible answer: Reflect $\triangle ABC$ across the y-axis and then translate it down 7 units.

    $(x, y) \rightarrow (-x, y - 7)$
23. The order of these two reflections does not matter. The resulting image is the same for a reflection in the y-axis followed by a reflection in the x-axis as for a reflection in the x-axis followed by a reflection in the y-axis.

UNIT 1 Selected Answers

MODULE 3

Lesson 3.2 Proving Figures are Congruent Using Rigid Motions

Your Turn

2. You can map *ABCD* to *WXYZ* with a reflection across the *x*-axis, so the figures are congruent.
3. You can map ΔJKL to ΔXYZ with a reflection across the *y*-axis, followed by a horizontal translation, so the figures are congruent.
5. Reflect *JKLM* across the *x*-axis: $(x, y) \rightarrow (x, -y)$. Then translate the image: $(x, y) \rightarrow (x - 4, y - 2)$.
6. Reflect *ABCDE* across the *y*-axis: $(x, y) \rightarrow (-x, y)$. Then translate the image: $(x, y) \rightarrow (x, y - 10)$.
7. $\angle B$ and $\angle C$ are congruent. $\overline{EF}$ and $\overline{GH}$ are congruent. In both cases, a sequence of transformations is a reflection and a translation.

Evaluate

1. $(x, y) \rightarrow (x, -y)$; translation: $(x, y) \rightarrow (x + 8, y)$
3. The figures are congruent. translation: $(x, y) \rightarrow (x - 2, y - 7)$.
5. There is no sequence of rigid transformations that will map one figure onto the other, so they are not congruent.
7. rotation: $(x, y) \rightarrow (-x, -y)$; translation: $(x, y) \rightarrow (x + 2, y + 6)$
9. rotation: $(x, y) \rightarrow (-x, -y)$; translation: $(x, y) \rightarrow (x - 2, y)$
11. $\angle A$, $\angle B$ and $\angle C$ are all congruent. The sequence of transformations is a reflection and a translation.
13. None of the segments are congruent. There is no rigid transformation that maps one of them to another.
15. Yes. reflection: $(x, y) \rightarrow (x, -y)$ translation: $(x, y) \rightarrow (x - 4, y)$
17. No. There are no transformations to map ΔKLM to ΔWXY.
19. reflection: $(x, y) \rightarrow (-x, y)$; translation: $(x, y) \rightarrow (x, y + 6)$
21. Rotation: $(x, y) \rightarrow (-x, -y)$; translation: $(x, y) \rightarrow (x - 4, y)$
23. False. The figures do not have the same orientation, so the sequence of transformations must include a reflection.
25. None are congruent. No rigid motions map one angle onto another.
27. Rotate ΔLMN 90° counterclockwise about the origin: $(x, y) \rightarrow (-y, x)$. Reflect across the *y*-axis: $(x, y) \rightarrow (-x, y)$. Translate: $(x, y) \rightarrow (x - 3, y - 13)$.
29. rotation: $(x, y) \rightarrow (y, -x)$; reflection: $(x, y) \rightarrow (-x, y)$; translation: $(x, y) \rightarrow (x + 2, y - 9)$
31. The petals can be mapped onto each other by a reflection, which is a rigid transformation.
33. Both students are correct.
35. Yes; by the definition of congruence, there is a sequence of rigid motions that maps ΔABC onto ΔDEF and another that maps ΔDEF onto ΔGHJ. The first sequence followed by the second sequence maps ΔABC onto ΔGHJ, so the triangles are congruent.

UNIT 1 Selected Answers

MODULE 3

Lesson 3.3 Corresponding Parts of Congruent Figures Are Congruent

Your Turn

4. $SU = 43$ ft.
5. $m\angle S = 38°$.
6. $LM = 35$ cm
7. $m\angle H = 98°$
8.

Statements	Reasons
1. $\Delta SVT \cong \Delta SWT$	1. Given
2. $\angle VST \cong \angle WST$	2. Corresponding parts of congruent figures are congruent.
3. $\overline{ST}$ bisects $\angle VSW$.	3. Definition of angle bisector.

9.

Statements	Reasons
1. Quadrilateral *ABCD* ≅ quadrilateral *EFGH*	1. Given
2. $\overline{AD} \cong \overline{CD}$	2. Given
3. $\overline{CD} \cong \overline{GH}$	3. Corresponding parts of congruent figures are congruent.
4. $\overline{AD} \cong \overline{GH}$	4. Transitive Property of Congruence

Evaluate

1. The same sequence of rigid motions that maps *ABCD* to *WXYZ* also maps sides and angles of *ABCD* to corresponding sides and angles of *WXYZ*. Therefore, those sides and angles are congruent: $\overline{AB} \cong \overline{WX}$, $\overline{BC} \cong \overline{XY}$, $\overline{CD} \cong \overline{YZ}$, $\overline{AD} \cong \overline{WZ}$, $\angle A \cong \angle W$, $\angle B \cong \angle X$, $\angle C \cong \angle Y$, $\angle D \cong \angle Z$.
3. $m\angle D = 43°$
5. $PS = 2.1$ cm
7. $m\angle U = 62°$
9. $m\angle D = 92°$
11. $\angle U$
13. $m\angle G = m\angle S$

15.

Statements	Reasons
1. $\Delta ABC \cong \Delta DEF$	1. Given
2. $\angle BAC \cong \angle DAC$	2. Corr. parts of ≅ fig. are ≅
3. $\angle BCA \cong \angle DCA$	3. Corr. parts of ≅ fig. are ≅
4. $\overline{AC}$ bisects $\angle BAD$ and $\overline{AC}$ bisects $\angle BCD$.	4. Definition of angle bisector

17. $m\angle D = 28°$
19. 1700 ft.
21. 92 ft.
23. a. True
   b. False
   c. False
   d. False
   e. True
25. The student incorrectly identified corresponding sides. Since $\Delta GHJ \cong \Delta RST$, $\overline{GH} \cong \overline{RS}$. $5x - 2 = 4x + 3 \rightarrow x = 5$; $GH = 5(5) - 2 = 23$ m.
27. Yes;

Statements	Reasons
1. $\Delta PQR \cong \Delta SQR$	1. Given
2. $\overline{RP} \cong \overline{RS}$	2. Corr parts of ≅ figs. are ≅
3. $\overline{RS} \cong \overline{RT}$	3. Given
4. $\overline{RP} \cong \overline{RT}$	4. Transitive Property
5. R is the midpoint of $\overline{PT}$	5. Definition of midpoint

UNIT 2 Selected Answers

MODULE 4

Lesson 4.1 Angles Formed by Intersecting Lines

Your Turn

6. $18 = x$
7. $10 = x$
   The measure of each angle is 13°.
9. The measure of the angle is 45°.
   The measure of its complement is 45°.
10. The measure of the angle is 120°.
   The measure of its supplement is 60°.

Evaluate

1. A. Vertical
   B. Neither
   C. Linear Pair
   D. Linear Pair
   E. Vertical
   F. Neither
3. 130°
5. $m\angle 2 = 47.5°$
   $m\angle 3 = 42.5°$
   $m\angle 4 = 42.5°$
7. False. Vertical angles do not share a common side.
9. True
11. The measure of the angle is 45°, the measure of its complement is 45°, and the measure of its supplement is 135°.
13. Plan for Proof: If $\angle ABC \cong \angle DEF$, then $m\angle ABC = m\angle DEF$.
   The measure of the complement of $\angle ABC = 90° - m\angle ABC$.
   The measure of the complement of $\angle DEF = 90° - m\angle DEF$.
   Since $m\angle ABC = m\angle DEF$, the measure of the complement of $\angle DEF = 90° - m\angle ABC$.
   Therefore, the measure of the complement of $\angle ABC$ = the measure of the complements of $\angle DEF$.
   The measures of the complements of the angles are equal, so the complements of the angles are congruent.
15. 2. supplement
   3. Definition of the supplement of an angle.
   4. $m\angle ABC = m\angle DEF$
   5. Equality
   6. Substitution Property of Equality
   7. $\angle DEF$
17. In the diagram of intersecting lines, $\angle 2$ and $\angle 4$ are vertical angles. Also, $\angle 2$ and $\angle 3$ are a linear pair and $\angle 3$ and $\angle 4$ are a linear pair. By the Linear Pair Theorem, $\angle 2$ and $\angle 3$ are supplementary and $\angle 3$ and $\angle 4$ are supplementary. Then $m\angle 2 + m\angle 3 = 180°$ and $m\angle 3 + m\angle 4 = 180°$ by the definition of supplementary angles. By the Transitive Property of Equality, $m\angle 2 + m\angle 3 = m\angle 3 + m\angle 4$. Using the Subtraction Property of Equality, $m\angle 2 = m\angle 4$. So, $\angle 2 \cong \angle 4$ by the definition of congruence.
19. Yes; 90°: the measure of its complement is 0°, and the measure of its supplement is 90°, so $0° + 90° = 90°$.

UNIT 2 Selected Answers

MODULE 4

Lesson 4.2 Transversals and Parallel Lines

Your Turn

7. $x = 10$, $y = 3$; the Corresponding Angles Theorem and the Alternate Interior Angles Theorem.

Evaluate

1. A. C
   B. A
   C. D
   D. B
3. m∠5 = 98°
5. m∠5 = 122°
7. m∠1 = 109°
9. m∠10 = 69°
11. m∠7 = 118°
13. m∠14 = 66°
15. $y = 40$
    $x = 15$
17. $y = 15$
19.

Statements	Reasons
1. $p \parallel q$	1. Given
2. m∠3 = m∠5	2. Alternate Interior Angles Theorem
3. m∠1 = m∠3	3. Vertical Angles Theorem
4. m∠1 = m∠5	4. Substitution Property of Equality

21. A possible diagram is shown, with two nonparallel lines cut by a transversal. I can measure the angles in my drawing with a protractor as a counterexample. ∠4 and ∠5 are alternate interior angles, but m∠4 = 90° and m∠5 = 130°, so the measures are not the same when the lines are not parallel.
23. B

UNIT 2 Selected Answers

MODULE 4

Lesson 4.3 Proving Lines are Parallel

Your Turn

4. m∠1 = 120° and m∠2 = 120°. They are congruent alternate interior angles. The lines are parallel because of the Converse of the Alternate Interior Angles Theorem.
5. m∠1 = 120° and m∠2 = 60°. The angles are supplementary. The lines are parallel because of the Converse of the Same-Side Interior Angles Postulate.
7.

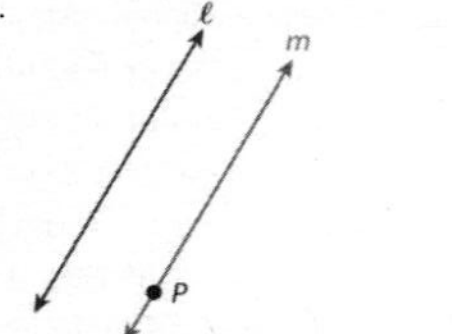

8. Same side interior angles; by the Converse of the Same Side Interior Angles Postulate.
9. Corresponding angles; by the Converse of the Corresponding Angles Theorem.

Evaluate

1. lines ℓ and m are parallel; 5.
   If ∠1 ≅ ∠5, then lines ℓ and m are parallel.
3. lines ℓ and m are parallel; 4.
   If ∠4 ≅ ∠6, then lines ℓ and m are parallel.
5. ∠7 ≅ ∠3; Converse of the Corresponding Angles Theorem
7. m∠4 = 65° and m∠5 = 115°, so m∠4 + m∠5 = 180°. Yes, the lines are parallel by the Converse of the Same-Side Interior Angles Postulate.
9. When $x = 25$, $x + 25 = 2x = 50$; the alternate interior angles are congruent and the horizontal parts of the letter Z are parallel.
11. $x = 28$
13. m ←•P→

15.

Statements	Reasons
1. lines ℓ and m are cut by a transversal; ∠1 ≅ ∠2	1. Given
2. m∠1 = m∠2	2. Definition of congruence
3. ∠2 and ∠3 are supplementary.	3. Linear Pair Theorem
4. m∠2 + m∠3 = 180°	4. Definition of supplementary angles
5. m∠1 + m∠3 = 180°	5. Substitution Property of Equality
6. ∠1 and ∠3 are supplementary.	6. Definition of supplementary angles
7. ℓ ∥ m	7. Converse of Same-Side Interior Angles Postulate

UNIT 2 Selected Answers

MODULE 4

Lesson 4.4 Perpendicular Lines

Your Turn

4. $DC = 20$ cm
5. $BC = 25$ cm
7. $AC = 16$ in.
9. $m\angle 4 = 40°$

Evaluate

1. Fold line ℓ onto itself so that the crease passes through point P. The crease is the required perpendicular line.
3. The midpoint of the segment is the point on the perpendicular bisector that is closest to the endpoints of the segment.
5. $PC = 5$ cm
7. 8 cm
9. 52°
11. 90°
13. 180°
15. $x = 45$; $y = 5$.
17. The valve pistons are lines that are perpendicular to the same line (the lead pipe), so they form right angles with the same line. By the corresponding angles theorem, all the congruent right angles mean the valve pistons are parallel to each other.
19. are both obtuse
    90°
    the definition of obtuse angles
    180°
    $m\angle 1 + m\angle 2 = 180°$
    false
    $\angle 1$ and $\angle 2$ cannot both be obtuse

UNIT 2 Selected Answers

MODULE 4

Lesson 4.5 Equations of Parallel and Perpendicular Lines

Your Turn

4. $y = -x + 7.5$
5. $y = \frac{3}{2}x + 6$
7. $y = -\frac{2}{3}x + 1$
8. $y = \frac{1}{4}x$

Evaluate

1. $\frac{4}{5}$
3. $\frac{1}{4}$
5. $y = -3x + 27$
7. $y = 5x - 3$
9. $y = 3x - 36$
11. The top line slope is $\frac{3}{4}$. The bottom line slope is $\frac{2}{3}$. The lines do not have the same slope, so they are not parallel.
13. $y = \frac{1}{2}x - \frac{1}{2}$
15. $y = -2x + 17$
17. a. $y = x + 30$
    b. $y = -x + 30$
    c. They are perpendicular.
19. a. Neither
    b. Perpendicular
    c. Perpendicular
    d. Parallel
    e. Perpendicular
21. He should have said “two nonvertical lines” because vertical lines have undefined slope. should have had a negative sign on one of his expressions for slope because the slopes of perpendicular lines have a product of –1.

UNIT 2 Selected Answers

MODULE 5

Lesson 5.1 Exploring What Makes Triangles Congruent

Your Turn

4. $\triangle RST \cong \triangle UVW$, because all six pairs of corresponding parts are congruent.
5. $m\angle B \neq m\angle E$ and $m\angle D \neq m\angle G$. The triangles are not congruent because some pairs of the corresponding angles are not congruent.
7. $x = 26$
8. $y = 5$

Evaluate

1. Possible answer: counterclockwise rotation about point M by $m\angle QMN$ followed by a reflection across $\overline{MQ}$.
3. $\triangle ABC \cong \triangle DEF$ because all six pairs of corresponding parts are congruent.
5. $JK \neq MN$. Not congruent; there aren't six pairs of congruent corresponding parts.
7. $z = 1.6$
9. $w = 27$
11. $\overline{LM}$ is not congruent to $\overline{QR}$. So, the triangles are not congruent.
13. The triangles have six pairs of congruent corresponding parts, and are congruent by the converse of CPCTC.
15. $7 = x$

    $y = 37$
17. Never true
19. Sometimes true
21. a. Not congruent

    b. Congruent

    c. Congruent

    d. Not congruent

    e. Congruent
23. No; $\overline{LN} \cong \overline{LN}$ by the Reflexive Property of Congruence. Therefore, the triangles are congruent.

UNIT 2 Selected Answers

MODULE 5

Lesson 5.2 ASA Triangle Congruence

Your Turn

5. $\triangle ADB \cong \triangle ADC$ by the ASA Triangle Congruence Theorem.
6. None of the angles in $\triangle PQR$ has a measure of 67°. So, $\triangle PQR$ is not congruent to $\triangle STU$.
8.

Statements	Reasons
1. $\angle JLM \cong \angle KML$	1. Given
2. $\angle JML \cong \angle KLM$	2. Given
3. $\overline{LM} \cong \overline{LM}$	3. Reflexive Property of Congruence
4. $\triangle JML \cong \triangle KLM$	4. ASA Triangle Congruence Theorem

9.

Statements	Reasons
1. $\angle S$ and $\angle U$ are right angles.	1. Given
2. $\angle S \cong \angle U$	2. All right angles are congruent.
3. $\overline{RV}$ bisects $\overline{SU}$	3. Given
4. $\overline{ST} \cong \overline{UT}$	4. Definition of bisector
5. $\angle RTS \cong \angle VTU$	5. Vertical angles are congruent.
6. $\triangle RST \cong \triangle VUT$	6. ASA Triangle Congruence Theorem

Evaluate

1. a.

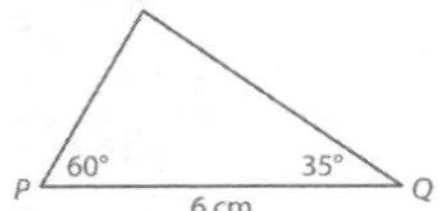

   b. Yes; the triangles are congruent by ASA. Therefore, there is a sequence of rigid motions that will map my triangle onto Natasha's triangle.
3. $\triangle JKL \cong \triangle MNP$ by ASA.
5. None of the angles in $\triangle STU$ has a measure of 34°. So, $\triangle STU$ is not congruent to $\triangle PQR$.
7. Given

   $\angle CBA \cong \angle DBA$

   $\overline{AB} \cong \overline{AB}$

   ASA Triangle Congruence Theorem

9.

Statements	Reasons
1. $\angle H \cong \angle J$	1. Given
2. G is the midpoint of $\overline{HJ}$.	2. Given
3. $\overline{HG} \cong \overline{JG}$	3. Definition of midpoint
4. $\overline{FG}$ is perpendicular to $\overline{HJ}$.	4. Given
5. $\angle FGH$ and $\angle FGJ$ are right angles.	5. Definition of perpendicular
6. $\angle FGH \cong \angle FGJ$	6. All right angles are congruent.
7. $\triangle FGH \cong \triangle FGJ$	7. ASA Triangle Congruence Theorem

11. a. Translate $\overline{LM}$ to $\overline{WX}$, then reflect $\triangle LMN$ across $\overline{WX}$.

b. Since $\angle L \cong \angle W$ and $\angle M \cong \angle X$, the images of $\overrightarrow{LN}$ and $\overrightarrow{MN}$ lie on $\overrightarrow{WY}$, and $\overrightarrow{XY}$, respectively. The image of N must lie on both rays, so the image is the intersection point Y.

13.

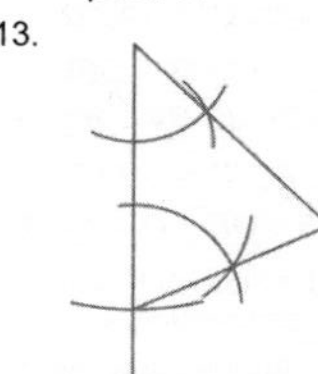

15.

Statements	Reasons
1. $\angle A \cong \angle E$	1. Given
2. C is the midpoint of $\overline{AE}$.	2. Given
3. $\overline{AC} \cong \overline{EC}$	3. Definition of midpoint
4. $\angle ACB \cong \angle ECD$	4. Vertical angles are congruent.
5. $\triangle ACB \cong \triangle ECD$	5. ASA Triangle Congruence Theorem
6. $\overline{AB} \cong \overline{ED}$	6. CPCTC

17. In each sign, the side that is 36 in. long is the included side between two 60° angles. Therefore, by the ASA Triangle Congruence Theorem, the signs are congruent.

19. $\angle B$ and $\angle D$ are both right angles, so $\angle B \cong \angle D$; $CB = CD$, so $\overline{CB} \cong \overline{CD}$; $\angle ACB$ and $\angle ECD$ are vertical angles, so $\angle ACB \cong \angle ECD$. Therefore, $\triangle ACB \cong \triangle ECD$ by the ASA Triangle Congruence Theorem. Since corresponding parts of congruent triangles are congruent, $\overline{AB} \cong \overline{ED}$, so $AB = ED$. Mariela can find the distance AB across the canyon by measuring the distance ED.

21. Possible sketch:

23. No; the quadrilaterals in the figure meet the conditions of the proposed ASAS Congruence Theorem, but they are not congruent. Therefore, the quadrilaterals serve as a counterexample to show that there is no such theorem.

UNIT 2 Selected Answers

MODULE 5

Lesson 5.3 SAS Triangle Congruence

Your Turn

3. $\overline{DE} \cong \overline{GH}$, $\overline{DF} \cong \overline{GJ}$, $\angle D \cong \angle G$, because corresponding parts have the same measure. $\triangle EDF \cong \triangle HGJ$ by the SAS Triangle Congruence Theorem.
4. Possible answer: You are given that $\overline{AB} \cong \overline{AD}$ and $\angle 1 \cong \angle 2$. You also know that $\overline{AC} \cong \overline{AC}$ by the reflexive property. Two sides and the included angle of $\triangle BAC$ are congruent to two sides and the included angle of $\triangle DAC$. The triangles are congruent by the SAS Triangle Congruence Theorem.

Evaluate

1. No; she can map $\overline{AC}$ to $\overline{DF}$ by a reflection across $\overline{DE}$, but C will map to F only if $AC = DF$.
3. $\overline{AB} \cong \overline{DB}$, $\overline{BC} \cong \overline{BC}$, and $\angle ABC \cong \angle DBC$, $\triangle ABC \cong \triangle DBC$ by SAS.
5. $\overline{AB} \cong \overline{AB}$, $\overline{CB} \cong \overline{DB}$, $\angle ABC \cong \angle ABD$ $\triangle ABC \cong \triangle ABD$ by SAS.
7. $\triangle ABC \cong \triangle DEF$ by SAS when x is 7.
9. You are given that $\overline{BD} \cong \overline{FD}$ and $\overline{CD} \cong \overline{ED}$. You also know that $\angle D \cong \angle D$ by the reflexive property. Two sides and the included angle of $\triangle BDE$ are congruent to two sides and the included angle of $\triangle FDC$. The triangles are congruent by the SAS Triangle Congruence Theorem. So, by CPCTC, the braces $\overline{BE}$ and $\overline{FC}$ and are also congruent.
11. a. Measure $\overline{AB}$ and $\overline{BD}$; so he can confirm that a pair of sides and their included angles are congruent.

    b. Measure $\angle ACB$ and $\angle DCB$; so he can confirm that a pair of angles and their included sides are congruent.

13. a. Each triangle has side lengths of 2 and 6 and an included right angle. By SAS they are congruent.

    b. Possible answer: Reflect the triangle across the y-axis. Next translate it 1 unit to the left. Then translate it 6 units down.

15. Yes; since the opposite sides of a rectangle are congruent and the included angles between the sides are right angles, the two triangles are congruent by the SAS Theorem.

UNIT 2 Selected Answers

MODULE 5

Lesson 5.4 SSS Triangle Congruence

Your Turn

4. $\overline{AB} \cong \overline{AD}$ and $\overline{CB} \cong \overline{CD}$, so A is equidistant from B and D, and C is equidistant from B and D. By the converse of the Perpendicular Bisector Theorem, $\overline{AC}$ is the perpendicular bisector of $\overline{BD}$. By the definition of a reflection, point D is the image of point B reflected across $\overline{AC}$. The reflection also maps $\overline{AC}$ onto $\overline{AC}$, so $\triangle ABC \cong \triangle ADC$.
5. The corresponding sides $\overline{MN}$ and $\overline{QR}$ are not congruent. Therefore, the triangles are not congruent.
6. It is given that $\overline{GK} \cong \overline{GL}$ and $\overline{JK} \cong \overline{JL}$, and $\overline{GJ} \cong \overline{GJ}$ by the Reflexive Property.
7. ASA. $x = 3$; $y = 8$

Evaluate

1.

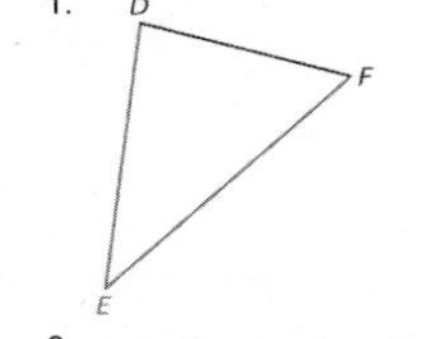

3.

11 cm, 3 cm, 12 cm   11 cm, 12 cm, 3 cm

5. Possible answer: A translation along $\overline{AD}$, and then a counterclockwise rotation about D so that $\overline{AB}$ coincides with $\overline{DE}$.
7. Possible answer: A translation along $\overline{CF}$, and then a counterclockwise rotation about F so that $\overline{CA}$ coincides with $\overline{FD}$.
9. $\overline{DF}$ is the perpendicular bisector of $\overline{EG}$. This shows that E maps to G by a reflection across $\overline{DF}$.
11. Not congruent
13. Not congruent
15. $x = 4$, $y = 4$; ASA
17. no solution
19. $x = 6$, $y = -15$
21. Possible solution: $x = 8$, $y = 8$
23. A. not sufficient; B. sufficient; C. not sufficient; D. sufficient; E. sufficient; F. sufficient
25. No; At least one pair of sides must be congruent. For example, two triangles that have three 60 degree angles may not have at least one pair of congruent corresponding sides, such as a triangle with side lengths of 4 inches and another triangle with side lengths of 8 inches.
27.

Statements	Reasons
1. $\angle BFC \cong \angle ECF$, $\angle BCF \cong \angle EFC$	1. Given
2. $\overline{FC} \cong \overline{FC}$	2. Reflexive Property of Congruence
3. $\triangle BFC \cong \triangle ECF$	3. ASA Triangle Congruence Theorem
4. $\overline{FB} \cong \overline{CE}$	4. CPCTC
5. $\overline{AB} \cong \overline{DE}$, $\overline{AF} \cong \overline{DC}$	5. Given
6. $\triangle ABF \cong \triangle DEC$	6. SSS Triangle Congruence Theorem

MODULE 6

Lesson 6.1 Justifying Constructions

Your Turn

8. You need to add an extra step to say that because $\overline{PQ}$ is the perpedicular bisector of $\overline{MN}$, the point of intersection will be the midpoint of $\overline{MN}$ by the definition of midpoint.
9. First construct a perpendicular bisector of a segment. This creates 90° angles. Choose one of the angles to bisect. This will construct two 45° angles.

Evaluate

1. She should adjust the angle of the reflective device until the image of line ℓ coincides with line ℓ. Then she should draw a line along the edge of the reflective device. This is the required line.
3. 1. BC, BD
   2. Converse of the Perpendicular Bisector Theorem
   3. Converse of the Perpendicular Bisector Theorem
   4. $\overline{CD}$
   5. $\overline{CD}$ bisects $\overline{AB}$; perpendicular bisector
5. They are congruent.
7. They are congruent.
9. They are congruent.
11. Line m is a transversal of lines ℓ and n. Angles 1 and 2 are congruent corresponding angles, because angle 2 is a constructed copy of angle 1. By the Converse of the Corresponding Angles Postulate, $\ell \parallel n$.
13. 30°
15. Fold the paper so that the segment's endpoints coincide. The fold line is the segment's perpendicular bisector, so any three points on the fold line will be equidistant from the endpoints.
17. Fold the circle so that one half coincides with the other. The crease is a diameter. Then fold the diameter onto itself to make another crease that is the perpendicular bisector of the diameter. The two creases determine the four vertices of the square on the circle.
19. a. B; AB; P; T
    b. $\overline{AP} \cong \overline{BT}$; $\overline{AB} \cong \overline{PT}$
    c. Draw $\overline{PB}$. $\overline{PB} \cong \overline{PB}$ by the Reflexive Property of Congruence. $\triangle PAB \cong \triangle BTP$ by SSS, and therefore $\triangle ABP \cong \triangle TPB$ by CPCTC. So by the Alternate Interior Angles Theorem, $\overline{PT} \parallel \overline{AB}$.
23.

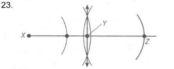

MODULE 6

Lesson 6.2 AAS Triangle Congruence

Your Turn

5. Because $\overline{BC}$ is parallel to $\overline{EF}$, this means that $\angle ACB$ is congruent to $\angle DFE$, using the Corresponding Angles Theorem. Since $\angle ABC$ is congruent to $\angle DEF$ and $\overline{AC}$ is congruent to $\overline{DF}$, then two angles and two non-included sides are congruent. This means that $\triangle ABC$ is congruent to $\triangle DEF$ using the AAS Triangle Congruence Theorem.
7. It is given that $\angle A \cong \angle D$ and $\angle B \cong \angle E$.

$$BC = \sqrt{(-5-(-1))^2 + (5-2)^2} = \sqrt{16+9} = 5$$

$$EF = \sqrt{(1-5)^2 + (2-(-1))^2} = \sqrt{16+9} = 5$$

Sides BC and EF are equal. Therefore, because two angles and a non-included side are congruent, $\triangle ABC \cong \triangle DEF$ by the AAS Theorem.

8. It is given that $\angle A \cong \angle D$ and $\angle B \cong \angle E$.

$$AC = \sqrt{(-4-(-1))^2 + (0-2)^2} = \sqrt{9+4} = \sqrt{13}$$

$$DF = \sqrt{(2-5)^2 + (-3-(-1))^2} = \sqrt{9+4} = \sqrt{13}$$

Sides AC and DF are equal. Therefore, because two angles and a non-included side are congruent, $\triangle ABC \cong \triangle DEF$ by the AAS Theorem.

Evaluate

1. Congruent, by AAS Congruence.
3. Congruent, by ASA Congruence.
5. Cannot be determined.
7. $\overline{AB} \cong \overline{DE}$, or $\overline{BC} \cong \overline{EF}$
9. $\overline{AB} \cong \overline{DE}$, $\overline{AB} \cong \overline{DF}$, $\overline{AC} \cong \overline{DE}$, or $\overline{AC} \cong \overline{DF}$
11. $\overline{AB} \cong \overline{DE}$, or $\overline{BC} \cong \overline{DC}$
13. 1. Reflexive Property of Congruence;
    3. $\angle ACB \cong \angle ACD$; 4. $\angle B \cong \angle D$;
    5. AAS Triangle Congruence Theorem
15. Congruent; $AB = DE = 4$; $BC = DF = 2$; $AC = EF = 4.47$
17. Not congruent. Segments $\overline{AB}$ and $\overline{DF}$ are corresponding, but they have different lengths $(AB = 4, DF = 5)$.
19. Not congruent. Segments $\overline{AC}$ and $\overline{EF}$ are corresponding, but they have different lengths $(AC = 9, EF = 10)$.
21. A; B; D
23. They are not necessarily congruent.
25. The two triangles cannot be congruent.
27. Yes, the sum of the $\angle$ measures in each triangle must be 180°, which makes it possible to solve for x and y. The value of x is 15, and the value of y is 12. Each triangle has angles measuring 82°, 68°, and 30°. $\overline{VU} \cong \overline{VU}$ by the Reflexive Property of Congruence. So $\triangle VSU \cong \triangle VTU$ by ASA or AAS.

UNIT 2 Selected Answers

MODULE 6

Lesson 6.3 HL Triangle Congruence

Your Turn

3. Yes. ΔVWX and ΔYXW are right triangles that share hypotenuse $\overline{WX}$ • $\overline{WX} \cong \overline{WX}$ by the Reflexive Property of Congruence. It is given that $\overline{WV} \cong \overline{XY}$, therefore $\Delta VWX \cong \Delta YXW$ by the HL Triangle Congruence Theorem.
5. It is given that and $\angle CAB$ and $\angle DBA$ are right angles and $\overline{AD} \cong \overline{BC}$. $\overline{AB} \cong \overline{AB}$ by the Reflexive Property of Congruence. Then $\Delta ABC \cong \Delta BAD$ by the HL Triangle Congruence Property.

Evaluate

1. No.
3. No.
5. Yes.
7.

Statements	Reasons
1. $\angle FGH$ and $\angle JHK$ are right angles.	1. Given
2. H is the midpoint of $\overline{GK}$.	2. Given
3. $\overline{GH} \cong \overline{HK}$	3. Definition of midpoint
4. $\overline{FH} \cong \overline{JK}$	4. Given
5. $\Delta FGH \cong \Delta JHK$	5. HL Triangle Congruence Theorem

9.

Statements	Reasons
1. $\angle ADC$ and $\angle BDC$ are right angles.	1. Given
2. $\overline{AC} \cong \overline{BC}$	2. Given
3. $\overline{DC} \cong \overline{DC}$	3. Reflexive Property of Congruence
4. $\Delta ADC \cong \Delta BDC$	4. HL Triangle Congruence Theorem
5. $\overline{AD} \cong \overline{BD}$	5. Corresponding parts of congruent triangles are congruent.

11. $x = 11$.
13. $x = 10$.
15. By the Distance Formula,

$AB = \sqrt{(0-(-3))^2 + (3-4)^2} = \sqrt{10}$,

$DE = \sqrt{(1-0)^2 + (-3-0)^2} = \sqrt{10}$,

$BC = \sqrt{(-4-0)^2 + (1-3)^2} = \sqrt{20}$,

and $EF = \sqrt{(4-0)^2 + (-2-0)^2} = \sqrt{20}$.

Therefore, $\overline{AB} \cong \overline{DE}$ and $\overline{BC} \cong \overline{EF}$. By the Slope Formula,

slope of $\overline{AB} = \frac{3-4}{0-(-3)} = -\frac{1}{3}$, slope of $\overline{AC} = \frac{1-4}{-4-(-3)} = 3$,

slope of $\overline{DE} = \frac{0-(-3)}{0-1} = -3$, slope of $\overline{DF} = \frac{-2-(-3)}{4-1} = \frac{1}{3}$.

Since $\left(\text{slope of } \overline{AB}\right) \cdot \left(\text{slope of } \overline{AC}\right) = -1$, $\overline{AB} \perp \overline{AC}$ and $\angle A$ is a right angle.

Since $\left(\text{slope of } \overline{DE}\right) \cdot \left(\text{slope of } \overline{DF}\right) = -1$, $\overline{DE} \perp \overline{DF}$ and $\angle D$ is a right angle.

So, $\Delta ABC \cong \Delta DEF$ by the HL Triangle Congruence Theorem.

17. a. No; there is not enough information to use any of the triangle congruence theorems.
    b. Yes; $\Delta KJL \cong \Delta MJL$ by the HL Triangle Congruence Theorem since $\overline{KJ} \cong \overline{MJ}$ and $\overline{JL} \cong \overline{JL}$.
19. The perimeter of ΔPQR is 16 ft.
21. Yes. Let the remaining leg of the first triangle have a length of x inches. Then by the Pythagorean Theorem, $x^2 + 10^2 = 26^2$. So, $x^2 = 576$, and $x = 24$. Therefore, the hypotenuse and a leg of the first right triangle are congruent to the hypotenuse and a leg of the second right triangle, so the triangles are congruent by the HL Triangle Congruence Theorem.
23. There is an LL Triangle Congruence Theorem.

Statements	Reasons
1. $\angle A$ and $\angle D$ are right angles.	1. Given
2. $\angle A \cong \angle D$	2. All right angles are congruent.
3. $\overline{AB} \cong \overline{DE}$	3. Given
4. $\overline{AC} \cong \overline{DF}$	4. Given
5. $\Delta ABC \cong \Delta DEF$	5. SAS Triangle Congruence Theorem

UNIT 2 Selected Answers

MODULE 7

Lesson 7.1 Interior and Exterior Angles

Your Turn

6. Each unknown angle measure is 135°.
7. 87°
8. 68° and 136°
11. 100°
12. 37°

Evaluate

1. They must be complementary.
3. 1980°
5. 103°
7. 146°
9. 120°
11. $w = 136$
13. 59°
15. A. A; B. B; C. D; D. E; E. C
17. 135°
19. 1440°

    144°; 36°
21. $x = 20°$; $y = 45°$; $z = 115°$
23. A regular hexagon; if the construction continues and the sides are kept congruent, the polygon will include six 120° angles and six congruent sides, so it is a regular hexagon.
25. 360°; 360°; 72°, 72°(5) = 360°; 720°, 60°, 60°(6) = 360°

    It appears from the table that the sum of the measures of the exterior angles of any polygon is always 360°.
27. By the Triangle Sum Theorem, $m\angle L + m\angle M + m\angle N = 180°$ and $m\angle R + m\angle S + m\angle T = 180°$. Since each set of angle measures total 180°, they are equal using the substitution property of equality. So, $m\angle L + m\angle M + m\angle N = m\angle R + m\angle S + m\angle T$. Since $\angle L \cong \angle R$ and $\angle M \cong \angle S$, then $m\angle L = m\angle R$ and $m\angle M = m\angle S$ by the definition of congruence. Subtracting equals from both sides gives $m\angle N = m\angle T$. Then $\angle N \cong \angle T$ by the definition of congruence.
29.

Number of Sides, n	3	4	5	6	7	8
Number of Diagonals, d	0	2	5	9	14	20

The number of diagonals increases by 2, then 3, 4, 5, etc. A formula relating n and d is $d = \frac{n(n-3)}{2}$.

UNIT 2 Selected Answers

MODULE 7

Lesson 7.2 Isosceles and Equilateral Triangles

Your Turn

5. 51°
6. 15 cm

Evaluate

1.

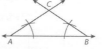

$\angle CAB \cong \angle CBA$, so opposite sides $\overline{CA}$ a nd $\overline{CB}$ are congruent. Therefore, it is an isosceles triangle.

3.

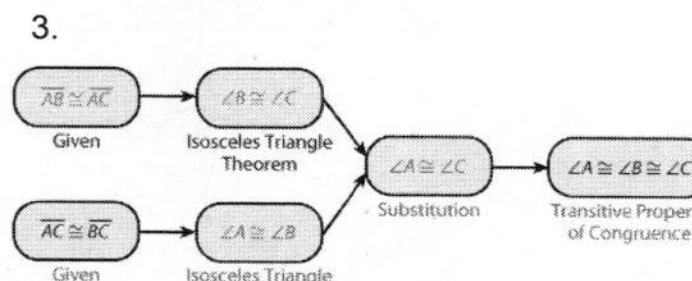

5. 76°
7. 57°
9. $KL = 33$
11. $BC = \frac{2}{13}$
13. $x°$ will equal 112°
15. By the Angle Addition Postulate, $m\angle ATB = 80° - 40° = 40°$. $m\angle BAT = 40°$ by Alt. Int. ∠ Thm. $\angle ATB \cong \angle BAT$ by the definition of congruence and $\overline{BA} \cong \overline{BT}$ by the Converse of the Isosceles Triangle Theorem. Then $BA = BT = 2.4$ mi.
17. 48°
19.

1. M is the midpoint of $\overline{BC}$.	1. Given
2. $\overline{BM} \cong \overline{CM}$	2. Definition of midpoint
3. $\overline{AB} \cong \overline{AC}$	3. Given
4. $\overline{AM} \cong \overline{AM}$	4. Reflexive Property of Congruence
5. $\triangle AMB \cong \triangle AMC$	5. SSS Triangle Congruence Theorem
6. $\angle B \cong \angle C$	6. CPCTC

21. Triangles ABD and CBD are congruent by ASA.
23.

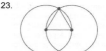

    The three line segments drawn are radii, which have the same length in both circles, since the circles are the same size. Therefore, all of the line segments are congruent and form the three sides of an equilateral triangle.

UNIT 2 Selected Answers

MODULE 7

Lesson 7.3 Triangle Inequalities

Your Turn

6. No; $12 + 4 \not> 17$
7. Yes; $24 + 8 > 30$, $8 + 30 > 24$, and $24 + 30 > 8$
9. $7 < x < 35$
10. $9 < x < 27$
11. $m\angle A, m\angle B, m\angle C$
12. $m\angle B, m\angle C, m\angle A$
13. CB, AC, AB
14. AC, BC, AB

Evaluate

1. No
3. No
5. No
7. Yes
9. $5 < x < 11$
11. $5.3 < x < 49.9$
13. $m\angle A, m\angle B, m\angle C$
15. $m\angle P, m\angle R, m\angle Q$
17. DE, EF, DF
19. PR, PQ, QR
21. The safest route is to avoid sailing between the islands at X and Y.
23. The towers at Q and R are closest together.
25. $AB + BC > x$

    $AB + x > BC$

    $x > BC - AB$

    $BC + x > AB$

    $x > AB - BC$

    Since $AB > BC$, $BC - AB < 0$, so the second inequality is not relevant. Combining the first and last inequalities gives $AB - BC < x < AB + BC$.

    The constructions show that AC approaches but is always greater than $AB - BC$, and that AC approaches but is always less than $AB + BC$.
27. B, C, D
29. Write two equations, $AD^2 + CD^2 = AC^2$ and $BD^2 + CD^2 = BC^2$. Equating expressions for CD^2, $AC^2 - AD^2 = BC^2 - BD^2$ and therefore $AC^2 - BC^2 = AD^2 - BD^2$. Since the right side is positive, so is the left side, which leads to $BC < AC$.

UNIT 2 Selected Answers

MODULE 8

Lesson 8.1 Perpendicular Bisectors of Triangles

Your Turn

5. $ZJ = 65$
6. $GM = 60$

   $ZG = 65$
8. 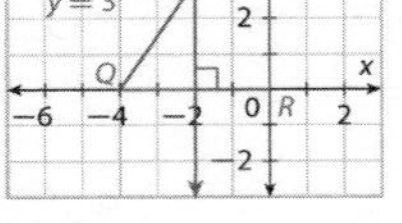

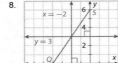

   $(-2, 3)$
9. 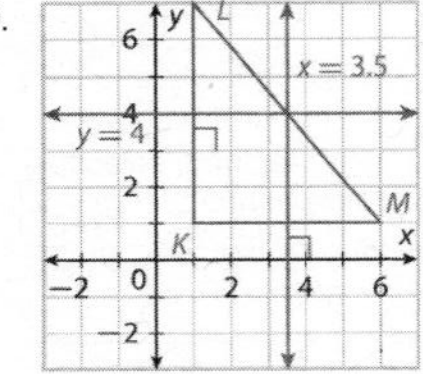

   $(3.5, 4)$

Evaluate

1. 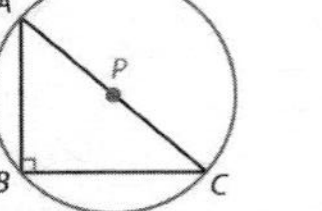

3.
5. $ZC = 85$

   $AC = 154$
7. $BC = 136$
9. 1. Given; 2. Given; 3. PB; 4. PB; 5. PB PC; Transitive Property of Equality
11. $(-2.5, 3.5)$
13. Let the three towns be vertices of a triangle. By the Circumcenter Theorem, the circumcenter of the triangle is equidistant from the vertices. Trace the outline of the lake. Draw the triangle formed by the towns. To find the circumcenter, find the perpendicular bisectors of each side. The position of the boat is the circumcenter, F.
15. a. To find AB, note that $\overline{DB}$ is a leg of right triangle $\triangle ZBD$ and $\overline{ZB}$ is the hypotenuse. Use the Pythagorean Theorem to find DB and multiply by 2 because D is the midpoint of $\overline{AB}$. To find AC, use the same method, noting first that $ZC = ZB$ because C is the circumcenter of ABC. Also, $\overline{ZF}$ is a leg of right triangle $\triangle ZCF$ and $\overline{ZC}$ is the hypotenuse.

    b. $AB = 210$; $AC = 288$

    c. No; the only information given about isosceles $\triangle ZBC$ is the length of two sides, which is insufficient for finding BC

MODULE 8

Lesson 8.2 Angle Bisectors of Triangles

Your Turn

4. $QS = 14.7$
5. $m\angle KJM = 58°$
8. *19.2*
9. $m\angle PQX = 52°$

Evaluate

1. Use the compass to measure both perpendicular segments from *P* to the sides of $\angle A$
3. $m\angle LKM = 31.5°$
5. $m\angle HFJ = 90°$
7.

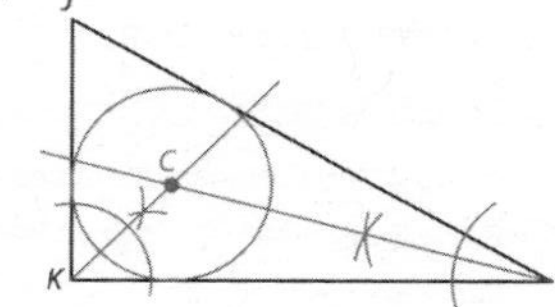

9. $m\angle FED = 46°$
11. $m\angle RTJ = 55°$
13. $VY = 17$
15. $m\angle GDF = 39°$
17. 1. Given; 2. Definition of perpendicular; 3. Reflexive Property of Congruence; 4. HL Triangle Congruence Theorem; 5. Corresponding parts of congruent triangles are congruent.; 6. $\overline{YV}$ bisects $\angle XYZ$; 8. Definition of angle bisector
19. Fillmore Street, Polk Street, Buchanan Street

Draw the bisectors of two angles of the triangular park. The monument should be at the intersection of the bisectors. This point is the incenter of the triangle. By the Incenter Theorem, it is equidistant from the sides of the triangle.

21. a. False b. True c. False d. True e. False
23. The circle will not necessarily pass through the points where the angle bisectors intersect the sides of the triangle. Instead, the student should have used *S* as the center of the circle and made a circle that just touches the three sides of the triangle.

MODULE 8

Lesson 8.3 Medians and Altitudes of Triangles

Your Turn

6. 12 units; $SP = 12$; $PW = 6$
8. The centroid is located 7 feet above the ground along *AD*, or 14 feet below point *A*.
9. $S(4, 5)$
10. $S(0, 4)$
13. $(-2, -3)$
15. $(4, -1)$

Evaluate

1. D, E, F, P
3. No; no matter how you change the shape of $\triangle ABC$, the point at which the medians intersect is always in the interior of the triangle.
5. $24 = FH$;
7. $GX = 13.5$
9. $KY = 3.6$ in
11. a. $x = 11$; b. $y = 5$; c. $BP = 10$; d. $BD = 15$; e. $CP = 18$; f. $PE = 9$
13. $(5, -0.5)$
15. $x = 5$
17. $(5, 3)$
19.

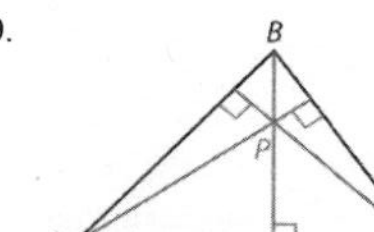

21.

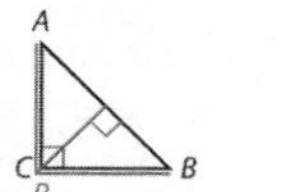

23. The coordinates of the orthocenter are (2, 2).
25. The coordinates of the orthocenter are (8, 0).
27. Yes. The orthocenter is *B*.
29. As the triangle is stretched to the right, the centroid moves to the right along a horizontal line. The orthocenter remains at *C*, the origin.

UNIT 2 Selected Answers

MODULE 8

Lesson 8.4 Midsegments of Triangles

Your Turn

4.

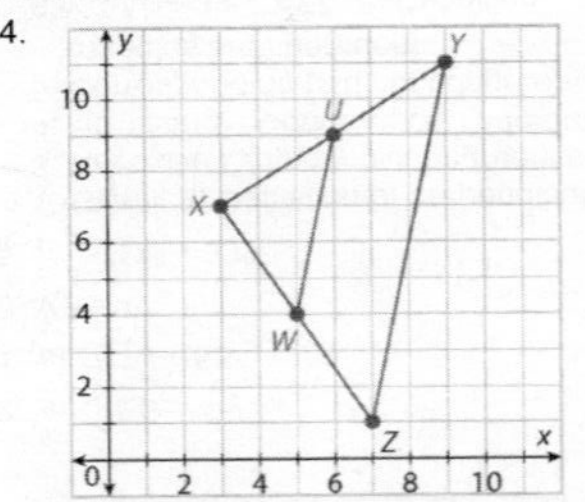

slope of $\overline{UW} = 5$; slope of $\overline{YZ} = 5$; Since the slopes are the same, $\overline{UW} \parallel \overline{YZ}$.

$UW = \sqrt{26}$; $YZ = 2\sqrt{26}$; So $UW = \frac{1}{2}$ YZ.

6. $JL = 78$; $PM = 47.5$; $m\angle MLK = 105°$

Evaluate

1. Drawings will vary. Students should conclude that the midsegment is half the length of the third side.
3. The slope of $\overline{XY}$ and $\overline{GH}$ is undefined, so the lines are parallel. The length of $\overline{XY}$ is 3 and the length of $\overline{GH}$ is 6, so $XY = \frac{1}{2}GH$.
5. The slope of $\overline{JK}$ and $\overline{BA}$ is 0, so the lines are parallel. The length of $\overline{JK}$ is $\frac{5}{2}$ and the length of $\overline{BA}$ is 5, so $JK = \frac{1}{2}BA$.
7. 7.9
9. 68°
11. $n = 4$
13. $n = 6$
15. a. True b. False c. True d. False e. False f. True
17. An equilateral triangle with sides 4 units long
19. No. If $\overline{AC}$ is 36 feet long, $\overline{DE}$ is 18 feet long. Because he needs to insert two crossbars, he needs 2 × 18, or 36, feet of timber. He needs 4 more feet.
21. Possible answer: First construct a triangle with a straightedge. Next use the compass to find the midpoint of two sides of the triangle. Finally, connect the two midpoints to create a midsegment parallel to the third side.
23. $\triangle QXY \cong \triangle XPZ \cong \triangle YZR \cong \triangle ZYX$; area of $\triangle XYZ \cong \frac{1}{4}$ area of $\triangle PQR$

UNIT 3 Selected Answers

MODULE 9

Lesson 9.1 Properties of Parallelograms

Your Turn

8. $QR = 20$
9. $PR = 28$

Evaluate

1. Possible answer: He can use the ruler to draw $\overline{JL}$ and $\overline{KM}$, label their intersection as point N, and use the ruler to find that $JN = LN$ and $KN = MN$. His conjecture would be that the diagonals of a parallelogram bisect each other.
3. $ABCD$ is a parallelogram.

   $\overline{AB} \parallel \overline{DC}, \overline{AD} \parallel \overline{BC}$; Draw $\overline{DB}$.

   $\angle ADB \cong \angle CBD$, $\angle ABD \cong \angle CDB$; $\overline{DB} \cong \overline{DB}$

   $\triangle ABD \cong \triangle CDB$

   $\overline{AB} \cong \overline{CB}$ and $\overline{AD} \cong \overline{CB}$
5. 1. $ABCD$ is a parallelogram
   2. $\overline{AB} \parallel \overline{DC}$
   3. $\angle ABE \cong \angle CDE$, $\angle BAE \cong \angle DCE$
   4. $\overline{AB} \cong \overline{DC}$
   5. $\triangle ABE \cong \triangle CDE$
   6. $\overline{AE} \cong \overline{CE}$ and $\overline{BE} \cong \overline{DE}$

   1. Given
   2. Definition of parallelogram
   3. Alt. Int. Angles Thm.
   4. Opposite sides of a parallelogram are congruent
   5. ASA Triangle Cong. Thm.
   6. CPCTC
7. 80
9. 23
11. The diag. of $PRQS$ bisect each other, so $QT = ST = 18$.
13. Opp. angles of $PRQS$ are congruent, so $m\angle SPQ \cong m\angle QRS = 110°$.
15. 1. $PSTV$ is a parallelogram
    2. $\angle STV \cong \angle P$
    3. $\overline{PQ} \cong \overline{RQ}$
    4. $\triangle PQR$ is isosceles
    5. $\angle P \cong \angle R$
    6. $\angle STV \cong \angle R$

    1. Given
    2. Opp. angles of a ▱ are congruent
    3. Given
    4. Definition of isosceles triangle
    5. Isosceles Triangle Theorem
    6. Transitive Property of Congruence
17. Sometimes; opposite sides of a parallelogram are congruent, but consecutive sides, such as $\overline{RS}$ and $\overline{ST}$, may or may not be congruent.
19. Always; opposite sides of a parallelogram are congruent.
21. Never; diagonals of a parallelogram bisect each other.
23. a. $\angle 3$, $\angle 6$, $\angle 8$;

    b. $\angle 1$ is supplementary to $\angle 2$, $\angle 4$, $\angle 5$, and $\angle 7$.
25. The side lengths of the tile are 6 inches and 8.5 inches.
27. $y = 2x$

UNIT 3 Selected Answers

MODULE 9

Lesson 9.2 Conditions for Parallelograms

Your Turn

6. $PQ = 16.8$

   $RS = 16.8$

   $m\angle Q = 74°$

   $m\angle R = 106°$

   So, $PQ = RS$. Also, $\overline{PQ} \parallel \overline{RS}$ since same-side interior angles are supplementary. *PQRS* is a parallelogram since a pair of opposite sides are parallel and congruent.

7. $JN = 14$

   $LN = 14$

   $KN = 22$

   $MN = 22$

   So $JN = LN$ and $KN = MN$. *JKLM* is a parallelogram since the diagonals bisect each other.

Evaluate

1. Draw $\overline{DB}$

   $\overline{AB} \cong \overline{CD}$ $\quad \overline{AD} \cong \overline{CB}$ $\quad \overline{DB} \cong \overline{DB}$

   $\Delta ABD \cong \Delta CDB$

   $\angle ADB \cong \angle CBD$, $\angle ABD \cong \angle CDB$

   $\overline{AB} \parallel \overline{DC}$, $\overline{AD} \parallel \overline{BC}$

   ABCD is a parallelogram.

3. Possible answer: It is given that $\overline{AE} \cong \overline{CE}$ and $\overline{DE} \cong \overline{BE}$. Since vertical angles are congruent, $\angle AEB \cong \angle CED$ and $\angle AED \cong \angle CEB$. Therefore, $\Delta AEB \cong \Delta CED$ and $\Delta AED \cong \Delta CEB$ by the SAS Triangle Congruence Theorem. Since corresponding parts of congruent triangles are congruent, $\overline{AB} \cong \overline{CD}$ and $\overline{AD} \cong \overline{CB}$. So, *ABCD* is a parallelogram because if both pairs of opposite sides of a quadrilateral are congruent, then the quadrilateral is a parallelogram.

5. $JK = 27$

   $LM = 27$

   $KL = 13$

   $MJ = 13$

   So, $JK = LM$ and $KL = MJ$. *JKLM* is a parallelogram.

7. No. One pair of opposite sides are parallel. A different pair of opposite sides are congruent.

9. Yes. A pair of alternate interior angles are congruent, so a pair of opposite sides are parallel. The same pair of opposite sides are congruent by SAS and CPCTC.

11. Yes. The 73° angle is supplementary to both of the 107° angles. This shows that both pairs of opposite sides are parallel by the Converse of the Same-Side Interior Angles Postulate.

13. He should draw $\overline{KL}$. $\overline{KL}$ is a midsegment of ΔPQR because it connects the midpoints of two sides of the triangle.

    $\overline{KL}$ is parallel to $\overline{PQ}$ and $\overline{KL} = \frac{1}{2}PQ$ by the Triangle Midsegment Theorem.

15. No. The figure shows a counterexample. The diagonals are congruent, but the quadrilateral does not have two pairs of parallel opposite sides, so it is not a parallelogram.

17. 1. Draw $\overline{DB}$
    2. $\overline{AB} \cong \overline{CD}$
    3. $\overline{AB} \parallel \overline{CD}$
    4. $\angle ABD \cong \angle CDB$
    5. $\overline{DB} \cong \overline{DB}$
    6. $\Delta ABD \cong \Delta CDB$
    7. $\overline{AD} \cong \overline{CB}$
    8. *ABCD* is a parallelogram.

    1. Through any two points, there is exactly one line.
    2. Given
    3. Given
    4. Alternate Interior Angles Theorem
    5. Reflexive Property of Congruence
    6. SAS Triangle Congruence Theorem
    7. CPCTC
    8. If both pairs of opposite sides of a quadrilateral are congruent, then the quadrilateral is a parallelogram.

19. Possible answer: The student used an invalid reason in Step 7. The student should also show that $\overline{AD} \cong \overline{CB}$. This is true because $\angle 1 \cong \angle 2$ and these are alternate interior angles. Then the student can conclude that *ABCD* is a parallelogram because a pair of opposite sides are both parallel and congruent.

21. Possible answer: When you draw $\overline{AC}$, you form ΔDAC and ΔBAC. $\overline{LM}$ is a midsegment of ΔDAC, so $\overline{LM} \parallel \overline{AC}$ and $LM = \frac{1}{2}AC$. $\overline{JK}$ is a midsegment of ΔBAC, so $\overline{JK} \parallel \overline{AC}$ and $JK = \frac{1}{2}AC$.

    This shows that $\overline{LM} \parallel \overline{JK}$ and $LM = JK$, so $\overline{LM} \parallel \overline{JK}$. A pair of opposite sides of *JKLM* are both parallel and congruent, so *JKLM* is a parallelogram.

MODULE 9

Lesson 9.3 Properties of Rectangles, Rhombuses, and Squares

Your Turn

5. 12.5 cm
6. 21.25 cm
9. Since *JKLM* is a rhombus, $\overline{JM} \cong \overline{LM}$ and $\overline{JK} \cong \overline{LK}$. $\overline{MK} \cong \overline{MK}$ by the Reflexive Property of Congruence. So, $\triangle MJK \cong \triangle MLK$ by the SSS Triangle Congruence Theorem. Therefore, $\angle JMK \cong \angle LMK$ and $\angle JKM \cong \angle LKM$ by CPCTC, so $\overline{MK}$ bisects $\angle JML$ and $\angle JKL$. A similar argument shows that $\overline{JL}$ bisects $\angle MJK$ and $\angle MLK$.
10. $m\angle VYX = 73°$
11. $m\angle XYZ = 36.5°$
12. By definition, a rhombus is a quadrilateral with four congruent sides. Since a square is also a quadrilateral that has four congruent sides, then a square is a rhombus.
13. Possible answer: All four angles of a square are right angles. All right angles are congruent. Any quadrilateral with both pairs of opposite angles congruent is a parallelogram, so a square is a parallelogram.

Evaluate

1. parallelogram
   all right angles are congruent
   it is a quadrilateral that has congruent opposite angles
   opposite sides of a parallelogram are congruent
   $\overline{DC} \cong \overline{DC}$
   $\angle D \cong \angle C$
   congruent
   SAS Triangle Congruence Theorem
   $\overline{AC} \cong \overline{BD}$
3. $BD - AC = 0$
5. 48 in.
7. $m\angle 1 = 29°$, $m\angle 2 = 61°$, $m\angle 3 = 90°$, $m\angle 4 = 29°$, and $m\angle 5 = 90°$.
9. $32\frac{1}{3}$
11. $m\angle 1 = 126°$, $m\angle 2 = 27°$, $m\angle 3 = 27°$, $m\angle 4 = 126°$, and $m\angle 5 = 27°$.
13. A. always; B. sometimes; C. always; D. sometimes; E. sometimes
15. You cannot use a theorem that assumes the quadrilateral is a parallelogram to justify the final statement because you do not know that *JKLM* is a parallelogram. That is what you are trying to prove. Instead, use the converse, which states that if both pairs of opposite sides of a quadrilateral are congruent, then the quadrilateral is a parallelogram. So therefore, *JKLM* is a parallelogram.
17. 25.3 feet
19. a. • Both pairs of opposite sides are parallel.
   • Both pairs of opposite sides are congruent.
   • Both pairs of opposite angles are congruent.
   • One angle is supplementary to both of its consecutive angles.
   • The diagonals bisect each other.
   b. • The diagonals are congruent.
   c. • The diagonals are perpendicular.
   • Each diagonal bisects a pair of opposite angles.
21. 180° rotation around its center; reflectional symmetry across a line that contains the midpoints of opposite sides (two lines)
23. A square has the reflectional properties of both a rhombus that is not a square and a rectangle that is not a square. Because squares have all angles congruent and all sides congruent, as opposed to only all sides congruent (rhombuses) or only all angles congruent (rectangles), a square has 90° rotational symmetry.

MODULE 9

Lesson 9.4 Conditions for Rectangles, Rhombuses, and Squares

Your Turn

4. Yes; the figure is a parallelogram because of congruent opposite sides, and it is a rectangle because it is a parallelogram with congruent diagonals.
5. No; by the Angle Addition Postulate, $m\angle FEH = 45° + 50° = 95°$, so $\angle FEH$ is not a right angle and *EFGH* is not a rectangle.
6. It is given that $\overline{JK} \cong \overline{KL}$. Because opposite sides of a parallelogram are congruent, $\overline{KL} \cong \overline{MJ}$ and $\overline{JK} \cong \overline{LM}$. By substituting the sides $\overline{JK}$ for $\overline{KL}$ and visa versa, $\overline{JK} \cong \overline{MJ}$ and $\overline{KL} \cong \overline{LM}$. So, $\overline{JK} \cong \overline{KL} \cong \overline{LM} \cong \overline{MJ}$, making *JKLM* a rhombus.
8. The conclusion is not valid. You must also first be given that ABCD is a parallelogram.

Evaluate

1. Square; because the diagonals are congruent, it is a rectangle and because the diagonals are perpendicular, it is a rhombus. A figure that is both a rectangle and a rhombus must be a square.
3. No information is known about its sides or angles, so it may not be a parallelogram. So, it cannot be determined if it is a rectangle
5. Rhombus
7. You need to know that *JKLM* is a parallelogram.
9. The conclusion is valid.
11. 6.5
13. parallelogram, rhombus, rectangle, square
15. parallelogram, rhombus
17. Since both pairs of opposite sides are congruent, *PQRS* is a parallelogram. Since *PZ*, *QZ*, *RZ*, and *SZ* are all equal lengths, $PZ + RZ = QZ + SZ$. So $\overline{QS} \cong \overline{PR}$ Since the diagonals are congruent, *PQRS* is a rectangle.
19. parallelogram
    rhombus
21. $\angle ABC$ is a right angle. And since $\overline{DE} \perp \overline{EF}$, $\angle DEF$ is a right angle. By the Hypotenuse-Leg (HL) Triangle Congruence Theorem, $\triangle ABC \cong \triangle DEF$. By CPCTC, $\overline{BC} \cong \overline{EF}$. Since the opposite sides of *EBCF* are parallel and congruent, it is a parallelogram. Since $\overline{BE} \perp \overline{EF}$, then $\angle BEF$ is a right angle, which makes *EBCF* a rectangle.

UNIT 3 Selected Answers

MODULE 9

Lesson 9.5 Properties and Conditions for Kites and Trapezoids

Your Turn

4. 86°
7. $\overline{BC} \cong \overline{AD}$; Parallel Postulate; $\overline{BA}$; $\overline{CE}$
   $\angle CED$; $\angle D$
   $\angle CED \cong \angle D$; $\overline{CD}$
   $ABCE$; opposite sides
   $\overline{CE}$; $\overline{CD}$
   $ABCD$; isosceles trapezoid
8. $m\angle R = 103°$
9. $y = 4$
10. 12.6

Evaluate

1. $m\angle ABE = 62°$
3. $m\angle ABC = 95°$
5. $\angle CDA$
   $\overline{AD} \cong \overline{AD}$
   CPCTC
7. $MN = 11.2$
9. $m\angle E = 43°$
11. $XY = 15.6$
13. $XY = 11.5$
15. A. kite; B. kite; C. trapezoid; D. kite; E. trapezoid
17. 1. $JKLN$ is a parallelogram. (Given); 2. $\overline{KL} \cong \overline{NJ}$ (Opposite sides of a parallelogram are congruent.); 3. $JKMN$ is an isosceles trapezoid. (Given); 4. $\overline{NJ} \cong \overline{MK}$ (Definition of isosceles trapezoid); 5. $\overline{KL} \cong \overline{KM}$ (Transitive Property of Congruence); 6. ΔKLM is an isosceles triangle. (Definition of isosceles triangle)
19. 14
21. $m\angle A = 90°$; $m\angle C = 45°$
    $m\angle B = m\angle D = 112.5°$
23. Terrence mistakenly reasoned that $\angle ABC \cong \angle ADC$; only one pair of opposite angles in a kite are congruent, and they are adjacent to the bisected diagonal, not the bisecting diagonal. To find $m\angle ABC$: Since $\angle BAE$ and $\angle ABE$ are complementary, $m\angle ABE$ can be found by $90° - 66° = 24°$. Then, since $\Delta AEB \cong \Delta CEB$ so that $\angle ABE \cong \angle CBE$, $m\angle ABC$ is twice $m\angle ABE$, or $2(24°) = 48°$.
25. Rhombuses and kites both have pairs of congruent consecutive sides, but in a rhombus, this is because all four sides are congruent. In a kite, two distinct pairs of consecutive sides are congruent. The diagonals of both types of quadrilaterals are perpendicular. In a kite, exactly one diagonal is bisected by the other, while in a rhombus, each diagonal bisects the other. Finally, in a kite, exactly one pair of opposite angles are congruent, while both pairs of opposite angles of a rhombus are congruent.

UNIT 3 Selected Answers

MODULE 10

Lesson 10.1 Slope and Parallel Lines

Your Turn

4. slope of $\overline{JK} = -\frac{1}{3}$
   slope of $\overline{LM} = -\frac{1}{3}$
   slopes are the same, so $\overline{JK}$ is parallel to $\overline{LM}$
   Quadrilateral $JKLM$ is a trapezoid because it is a quadrilateral with exactly one pair of parallel sides.
5. slope of $\overline{AB} = \frac{3}{2}$
   slope of $\overline{BC} = -2$
   slope of $\overline{CD} = \frac{3}{2}$
   slope of $\overline{DA} = -2$
   Quadrilateral $ABCD$ is a parallelogram because both pairs of opposite sides are parallel.
7. (4, 0)
8. (−3, −1)

Evaluate

1. She should use the fact that corresponding parts of congruent triangles are congruent to show that $KL = ST$, which will allow her to conclude that $\frac{KL}{JL} = \frac{ST}{RT}$.
3. slope of $\overline{KL} = 1$
   slope of $\overline{LM} = -\frac{1}{2}$
   slope of $\overline{MN} = 1$
   slope of $\overline{NK} = -\frac{1}{2}$
   Quadrilateral $KLMN$ is a parallelogram because both pairs of opposite sides are parallel.
5. U is at (2, 2)
   Check: slope of $\overline{TU} = \frac{1}{3}$
   slope of $\overline{SV} = \frac{1}{3}$
7. slope of $\overline{FG}$ is 0
   slope of $\overline{GH} = -\frac{3}{2}$
   slope of $\overline{HJ}$ is 0
   slope of $\overline{JF} = -3$
   Slope of $\overline{FG} = \overline{HJ}$, so $\overline{FG}$ is parallel to $\overline{HJ}$.
   Slope of $\overline{GH} \neq \overline{JF}$, so $\overline{GH}$ is not parallel to $\overline{JF}$.
   The quadrilateral has only one pair of parallel sides, so it is a trapezoid but not a parallelogram.
9. Sometimes
11. Always
13. Neither
15. Trapezoid
17. $p = 5$
    $q = 9$
19. $w = 1$
    $z = 3$
21. No; since the slopes of $\overline{RU}$ and $\overline{ST}$ are undefined, these two segments are vertical. Since all vertical lines are parallel, this means a pair of sides of the quadrilateral are parallel, and therefore the quadrilateral is a trapezoid.
23. $y = \frac{1}{2}x + 3$

25. The slope of $\overline{QP}$ should be $\frac{3-(-3)}{0-3}=-2$.

The slope of $\overline{QR}=-\frac{1}{3}$ and the slope of $\overline{RS}=\frac{3}{2}$. No sides of *PQRS* are parallel, so *PQRS* is not a trapezoid.

27. Possible answer: Plot the points *A*(–4, 2), *B*(2, 4), *C*(4, 0), *D*(0, –2).

midpoint of $\overline{AB}=M(-1, 3)$; midpoint of $\overline{BC}=N(3, 2)$; midpoint of $\overline{CD}=P(2, -1)$; midpoint of $\overline{DA}=Q(-2, 0)$;

slope of $\overline{MN}=-\frac{1}{4}$; slope of $\overline{NP}=3$;

slope of $\overline{PQ}=-\frac{1}{4}$; slope of $\overline{QM}=3$.

Since opposite sides are parallel, *MNPQ* is a parallelogram. This is true when starting with any set of four points. Conjecture: The quadrilateral formed by connecting the midpoints of consecutive sides of a quadrilateral is a parallelogram.

UNIT 3 Selected Answers

MODULE 10

Lesson 10.2 Slope and Perpendicular Lines

Your Turn

5. slope of $\overline{DE}=-\frac{2}{3}$

slope of $\overline{EF}=\frac{3}{2}$

slope of $\overline{FG}=-\frac{2}{3}$

slope of $\overline{GD}=\frac{3}{2}$

Consecutive sides are perpendicular since the product of the slopes is –1. Quadrilateral *DEFG* is a rectangle because it is a quadrilateral with four right angles.

7. The quadrilateral is a parallelogram since both pairs of opposite sides are parallel.

Evaluate

1. a. $-\frac{a}{b}$

b. $\frac{b}{a}$

c. The product of the slopes of the lines is $-\frac{a}{b}\cdot\frac{b}{a}=-1$.

3. slope of $\overline{KL}$ = slope of $\overline{MN}=-\frac{2}{3}$;

slope of $\overline{LM}=\frac{3}{2}$; slope of $\overline{NK}=-5$;

$\overline{KL}\perp\overline{LM}$ and $\overline{LM}\perp\overline{MN}$.

KLMN is a trapezoid with two right angles because a pair of opposite sides are parallel and two pairs of consecutive sides are perpendicular.

5. The quadrilateral is a parallelogram since both pairs of opposite sides are parallel.

7. slope of $\overline{KL}=\frac{4-2}{-1-(-4)}=\frac{2}{3}$;

slope of $\overline{LM}=-\frac{1}{4}$; slope of $\overline{MN}=\frac{2}{3}$;

slope of $\overline{NK}=-3$; A pair of opposite sides do not have the same slope, so these sides are not parallel. Therefore, *KLMN* is not a parallelogram.

9. Always

11. Never

13. Never

15. *PQ* = *RS* = 10.5 and *QR* = *SP* = 31.5

17. *PQ* = *RS* = 6 and *QR* = *SP* = 36

19. $y=-\frac{1}{2}x-2$

21. The coordinates of *C* are (0, –4). The coordinates of *D* are (–4, –2).

UNIT 3 Selected Answers

MODULE 10

Lesson 10.3 Coordinate Proof Using Distance with Segments and Triangles

Your Turn

5. Possible answer: Let the coordinates of the vertices be $A(0, 4)$, $B(0, 0)$, and $C(2, 0)$.
   area of $\Delta ABC = 4$ units^2
   The coordinates of D, the midpoint of $\overline{AC}$, are (1, 2).
   area of $\Delta DBC = 2$ units^2
   The area of ΔDBC is one half the area of ΔABC.
6. Possible answer: Let the coordinates of the vertices be $A(0, 8)$, $B(0, 0)$, and $C(8, 0)$ area of $\Delta ABC = 32$ units^2.
   The coordinates of D, the midpoint of $\overline{AC}$, are (4, 4).
   area of $\Delta DBC = 16$ units^2
   The area of ΔDBC is one half the area of ΔABC.
10. By the Distance Formula, $AB = \sqrt{17}$, $BC = \sqrt{5}$, $AC = \sqrt{34}$, $DE = \sqrt{17}$, $EF = \sqrt{5}$, $DF = \sqrt{34}$. So, $\overline{AB} \cong \overline{DE}$, $\overline{BC} \cong \overline{EF}$, and $\overline{AC} \cong \overline{DF}$. Therefore, $\Delta ABC \cong \Delta DEF$ by the SSS Triangle Congruence Theorem and $\angle BCA \cong \angle EFD$ since corresponding parts of congruent triangles are congruent.
11. By the Midpoint Formula, the coordinates of M are $M\left(\frac{-3+(-1)}{2}, \frac{5+(-1)}{2}\right) =$
    $M(-2, 2)$ and the coordinates of N are $N\left(\frac{4+2}{2}, \frac{5+(-1)}{2}\right) = N(3, 2)$.
    By the Distance Formula, $PQ = \sqrt{40}$, $QN = 5$, $PN = \sqrt{45}$, $RS = \sqrt{40}$, $SM = 5$, $RM = \sqrt{45}$.
    So, $\overline{PQ} \cong \overline{RS}$, $\overline{QN} \cong \overline{SM}$, and $\overline{PN} \cong \overline{RM}$. Therefore, $\Delta PQN \cong \Delta RSM$ by the SSS Triangle Congruence Theorem and $\angle PQN \cong \angle RSM$ since corresponding parts of congruent triangles are congruent.

Evaluate

1. The coordinates of point R are $R(x_1, y_2)$.
   $PR = y_2 - y_1$ and $RQ = x_2 - x_1$
   ΔPQR is a right triangle with hypotenuse $\overline{PQ}$, $PQ^2 = RQ^2 + PR^2$
   By substitution, $PQ^2 = (x_2 - x_1)^2 + (y_2 - y_1)^2$
   $= \sqrt{(x_2 - x_1)^2 + (y_2 - y_1)^2}$.
3. By the Midpoint Formula, the coordinates of X, Y, and Z are as follows.
   $X\left(\frac{2a+0}{2}, \frac{2b+0}{2}\right) = X(a, b)$,
   $Y\left(\frac{2a+4a}{2}, \frac{2b+0}{2}\right) = Y(3a, b)$,
   $Z\left(\frac{0+4a}{2}, \frac{0+0}{2}\right) = Z(2a, 0)$
   By the Distance Formula,
   $XZ = \sqrt{(2a - a^2) + (0 - b^2)} = \sqrt{a^2 + b^2}$ and
   $YZ = \sqrt{(2a - 3a^2) + (0 - b^2)} = \sqrt{a^2 + b^2}$.
   Since $XZ = YZ$, $\overline{XZ} \cong \overline{YZ}$ and ΔXYZ is isosceles.
5. Assign coordinates as shown in the figure. By the Midpoint Formula, the coordinates of M and N are as follows.
   $M\left(\frac{0+2a}{2}, \frac{0+2b}{2}\right) = M(a, b)$;
   $N\left(\frac{2a+4a}{2}, \frac{2b+0}{2}\right) = N(3a, b)$
   By the Distance Formula,
   $MC = \sqrt{(4a - a)^2 + (0 - b)^2} = \sqrt{9a^2 + b^2}$

and $NB = \sqrt{(0 - 3a)^2 + (0 - b)^2} = \sqrt{9a^2 + b^2}$,
so $MC = NB$ and $\overline{MC} \cong \overline{NB}$.

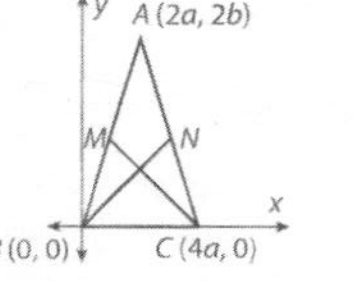

7. No; these coordinates result in a triangle that is a right triangle, so the proof would not hold for triangles in general.
9. $DE = \sqrt{37}$, $EF = \sqrt{8}$, $DF = \sqrt{17}$,
   $ST = \sqrt{37}$, $TU = \sqrt{8}$, $SU = \sqrt{17}$.
   So, $\overline{DE} \cong \overline{ST}$, $\overline{EF} \cong \overline{TU}$, and $\overline{DF} \cong \overline{SU}$. Therefore, $\Delta DEF \cong \Delta STU$ by the SSS Triangle Congruence Theorem and $\angle FDE \cong \angle UST$ since corresponding parts of congruent triangles are congruent.
11. The coordinates of U are U
    $\left(\frac{-1+3}{2}, \frac{4+0}{2}\right) = U(1, 2)$ and the coordinates of V are
    $V\left(\frac{3+(-1)}{2}, \frac{-6+(-2)}{2}\right) = V(1, -4)$.
    $JK = \sqrt{32}$, $KV = \sqrt{20}$, $JV = \sqrt{68}$,
    $PQ = \sqrt{32}$, $QU = \sqrt{20}$, $PU = \sqrt{68}$.
    So, $\overline{JK} \cong \overline{PQ}$, $\overline{KV} \cong \overline{QU}$, and $\overline{JV} \cong \overline{PU}$. Therefore, $\Delta JKV \cong \Delta PQU$ by the SSS Triangle Congruence Theorem and $\angle KVJ \cong \angle QUP$ since corresponding parts of congruent triangles are congruent.
13. $JK = \sqrt{17}$, $KL = \sqrt{34}$, and $JL = \sqrt{17}$.
    Since $\overline{JK}$ and $\overline{JL}$ have the same length, $\overline{JK} \cong \overline{JL}$, and therefore the triangle is isosceles.
15. The distance between the ships is
    $AB \approx 128$ nautical miles.
    $AP \approx 64$ nautical miles and
    $BP \approx 64$ nautical miles.
    Since $AP = BP = \frac{1}{2}AB$,
    P is the midpoint of $\overline{AB}$.
17. The perimeter of is ΔJKL twice the perimeter of ΔMNP.
19. The proof is incorrect because the assigned coordinates do not result in a general right triangle. For a general right triangle, the coordinates of R should be (a, b).
21. Possible answer: (0, 0), (0, 2s) and (2s, 0). This results in an easier coordinate proof since there are no negative coordinates and more of the coordinates are 0. If the proof does not involve midpoints, and even easier choice is (0, 0), (0, s), and (s, 0).

UNIT 3 Selected Answers

MODULE 10

Lesson 10.4 Coordinate Proof Using Distance with Quadrilaterals

Your Turn

4. Possible answer:

$AB = \sqrt{(8-3)^2 + (2-2)^2} = 5;$

$DC = \sqrt{(5-0)^2 + (0-0)^2} = 5$

$AD = \sqrt{(3-0)^2 + (2-0)^2} = \sqrt{13};$

$BC = \sqrt{(8-5)^2 + (2-0)^2} = \sqrt{13}$

Since the opposite sides have the same lengths, *ABCD* is a parallelogram.

5. Midpoint of $\overline{DB}$: $\left(\frac{0+8}{2}, \frac{0+2}{2}\right) = (4, 1)$

Midpoint of $\overline{AC}$: $\left(\frac{3+5}{2}, \frac{2+0}{2}\right) = (4, 1)$

Since the diagonals share a midpoint, they bisect each other.

7. $WX = \sqrt{(4-0)^2 + (3-0)^2} = \sqrt{25} = 5$

$XY = \sqrt{(9-4)^2 + (3-3)^2} = \sqrt{25} = 5$

$YZ = \sqrt{(5-9)^2 + (0-3)^2} = \sqrt{25} = 5$

$ZW = \sqrt{(0-5)^2 + (0-0)^2} = \sqrt{25} = 5$

Since all four sides have the same length, *WXYZ* is a rhombus.

8. Slope of $\overline{WY} = \frac{3-0}{9-0} = \frac{1}{3}$

Slope of $\overline{XZ} = \frac{0-3}{5-4} = \frac{-3}{1}$

(Slope of $\overline{WY}$) (Slope of $\overline{XZ}$) = $\frac{1}{3} \cdot \frac{-3}{1} = -1$

So, $\overline{WY}$ is perpendicular to $\overline{XZ}$.

9. The diagonals are congruent; *KLMN* is a rectangle.

The diagonals are perpendicular; *KLMN* is a rhombus.

Since *KLMN* is both a rectangle and a rhombus, it is also a square.

10. The diagonals are not congruent. So *PQRS* is not a rectangle, and thus not a square.

The diagonals are perpendicular, so *PQRS* is a rhombus.

Evaluate

1. A

3. Slope of $\overline{AB} = \frac{-5}{2}$; Slope of $\overline{BC} = \frac{2}{5}$;

Slope of $\overline{DC}$ $\frac{-5}{2}$; Slope of $\overline{DA} = \frac{2}{5}$

The slopes of opposite sides are equal.

This means that opposite sides are parallel, so *ABCD* is a parallelogram.

5. In Evaluate 3 we proved that *ABCD* is a parallelogram.

Slope of $\overline{AC} = \frac{7}{3}$; Slope of $\overline{DB} = \frac{-3}{7}$

Since $\left(\frac{7}{3}\right)\left(\frac{-3}{7}\right) = -1$, the diagonals are perpendicular. So, *ABCD* is a rhombus.

7. $WY = \sqrt{(-2-5)^2 + (5-0)^2} = \sqrt{74}$

$XZ = \sqrt{(-2-5)^2 + (0-5)^2} = \sqrt{74}$

So the diagonals are congruent.

9. midpoint of

$\overline{WY} = \left(\frac{-2+5}{2}, \frac{5+0}{2}\right) = \left(\frac{3}{2}, \frac{5}{2}\right)$

midpoint of $\overline{XZ}$ =

$\left(\frac{5+(-2)}{2}, \frac{5+0}{2}\right) = \left(\frac{3}{2}, \frac{5}{2}\right)$

Since they share a midpoint, the diagonals bisect each other.

11. The diagonals are perpendicular. *ABCD* is a rhombus.

The lengths of the diagonals are equal. *ABCD* is a rectangle. Since *ABCD* is both a rhombus and a rectangle, it is also a square.

13. *C* must be (–5, 4)

15. *D* is at (–4, –2)

17. $BD = 38$ in.

$CE = 24$ in.

$BE \approx 36.88$ in.

19. Possible answer: To know that the reflecting pool is a parallelogram, the congruent sides must be opposite each other. If this is true, then knowing that one angle in the pool is a right angle or that the diagonals are congruent proves that the pool is a rectangle.

21. Midpoint of $\overline{AB} = (10, 50)$

Since *P* is the midpoint of $\overline{AB}$ it lies on $\overline{AB}$. Therefore, points *A*, *B*, and *P* are collinear and the port and the two cruise ships are in a line.

23. Point *C* is at (3.1).

Point *D* is at (–6, –3.5).

25. Slope of $\overline{OQ} = \frac{(a+b)-0}{(a+b)-0} = \frac{a+b}{a+b} = 1;$

Slope of $\overline{PR} = \frac{a-b}{b-a} = \frac{a-b}{-1(a-b)} = -1$

Because the product of the slopes is –1, the diagonals are perpendicular.

UNIT 3 Selected Answers

MODULE 10

Lesson 10.5 Perimeter and Area on the Coordinate Plane

Your Turn

4. Area of $JKLM = 15$
6. 34 units^2
7. 32 units^2
8. area of wastage: 0.625 in^2

Evaluate

1. 14.8 units
3. 19.6 units
5. 34 units^2
7. 32 units^2
9. 27.5 units^2
11. cost of fencing: $1493.90
13. B, C, and D
15. 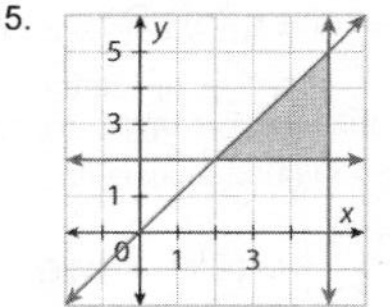

$P \approx 10.2$ units

$A = 4.5$ units^2

17. $JK = \sqrt{18} = 3\sqrt{2}$; $KL = \sqrt{45} = 3\sqrt{5}$;

$LM = \sqrt{45} = 3\sqrt{5}$; $JM = \sqrt{18} = 3\sqrt{2}$

So $\overline{JK} \cong \overline{JM} \ncong \overline{KL} \cong \overline{LM}$, and therefore $JKLM$ is a kite.

$A = 27$ units^2

19. Since $ABCD$ is a kite, $\overline{AD} \cong \overline{AB}$ and $\overline{CD} \cong \overline{CB}$. The kite can then be divided into two triangles with the same base.

Therefore, $\overline{AE}$ is an altitude for $\triangle ABD$ with base $\overline{BD}$, and $\overline{CE}$ is an altitude for $\triangle CBD$ with base $\overline{BD}$.

area of $\triangle ABD$: $A = \frac{1}{2}(BD)(AE)$;

area of $\triangle CBD$: $A = \frac{1}{2}(BD)(CE)$

area of $ABCD$: $A = \frac{1}{2}(BD)(AE) + \frac{1}{2}(BD)$

$(CE) = \frac{1}{2}(BD)(AE + CE) = \frac{1}{2}(BD)(AC)$

UNIT 4 Selected Answers

MODULE 11

Lesson 11.1 Dilations

Your Turn

5. It is a dilation. The scale factor is $\frac{3}{2}$.
6. This is not a dilation.
8.

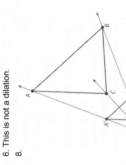

1 to 3.

Evaluate

1. The ratios of the lengths of the corresponding sides are equal.
3. No, this is not a dilation.
5. (c)
7. 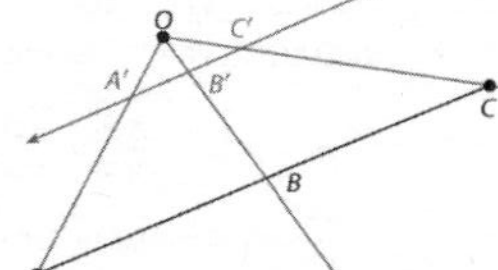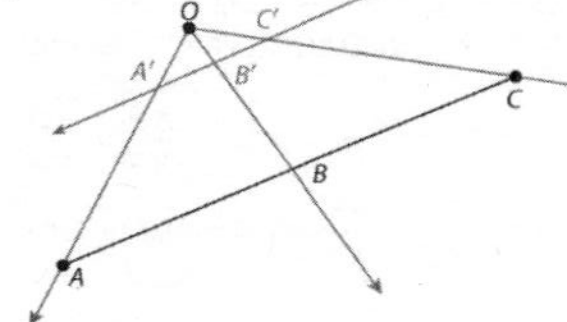

9.

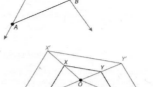

11. Rigid motions preserve angle measure, betweenness, and collinearity. Dilations preserve all of these except distance.
13. It is a dilation $\frac{1}{2}$.
15. 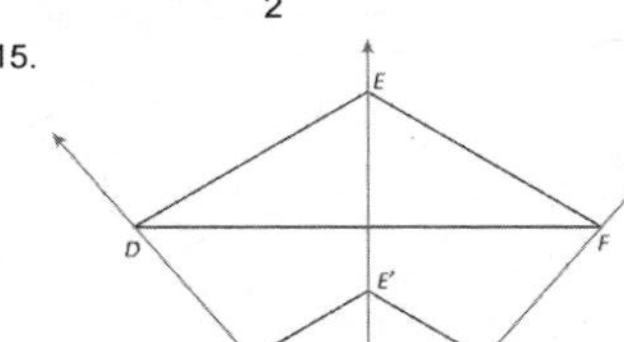

1 to 2.

17. 3 to 1.
19. 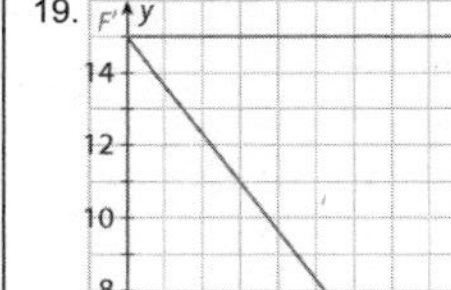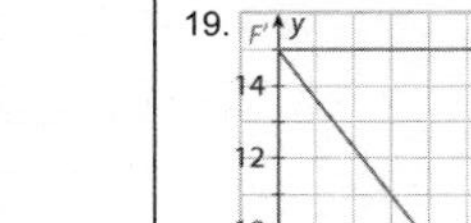

a. Perimeter is 12 units, Area is 6 square units

b. Perimeter is 36 units, Area is 54 square units

c. $\frac{\text{perimeter}}{\text{perimeter}} = \frac{3}{1} = \text{scale factor}$

$\frac{\text{area}}{\text{area}} = \frac{9}{1} = \text{scale factor squared}$

UNIT 4 Selected Answers

MODULE 11

Lesson 11.2 Proving Figures are Similar Using Transformations

Your Turn

3. Yes
4. No, the angles are different.
5. Yes
8. Reflection: $(x, y) \to (-x, y)$

   Dilation: $(x, y) \to \left(\frac{1}{3}x, \frac{1}{3}y\right)$

9. Rotation: $(x, y) \to (-x, -y)$

   Dilation: $(x, y) \to \left(\frac{3}{2}x, \frac{3}{2}y\right)$

   Translation: (x, y) $(x - 3, y + 1.5)$

10. Translate *JKLMN* right 7 units so that *J* maps to *V*.

    Reflect *JKLMN* across $\overline{JN}$.

    Dilate *JKLMN* with center *J* and scale factor $\frac{1}{2}$.

Evaluate

1. *EFGH* can be mapped onto *ABCD* with a dilation of 4 with center at the origin.
3. *JKLMN* is similar to *JPQRS*.
5. Reflection: $(x, y) \to (-x, y)$

   Translation: $(x, y) \to (x, y - 6)$

7. Reflection: $(x, y) \to (-x, y)$

   Dilation: $(x, y) \to \left(\frac{1}{2}x, \frac{1}{2}y\right)$

9. Reflection: $(x, y) \to (x, -y)$

   Dilation: $(x, y) \to (3x, 3y)$

   Translation: $(x, y) \to (x + 1, y - 2)$

11. Step A: Dilate *ABCD* with center of dilation *A* and scale factor $\frac{y}{x}$, producing square *A′B′C′D′*. Square *ABCD* has four sides of length *x*. Square *A′B′C′D′* will have four sides of length $\frac{y}{x}(x) = y$. These are the same side lengths as *EFGH*. The angles are all 90° in each square, so *A′B′C′D′* is congruent to *EFGH*.

    Step B: Translate *A′B′C′D′* with a translation along the vector $\overline{A'E}$, producing *A″B″C″D″*. Through this translation, *A″* is mapped to *E*. It may be true that *B″* is mapped to *F*, *C″* is mapped to *G*, and *D″* is mapped to *H*. If not, rotate *A″B″C″D″* about *E* so *that B‴ is mapped to F*. Then, *C‴* lands on *G* and *D‴* lands on *H*.

13. Step A: Dilate $\triangle ABC$ with center of dilation *B* and scale factor $K = \frac{x}{a}$, producing $\triangle A'B'C'$. After the dilation $\triangle A'B'C'$ will have sides of length $B'C' = ka = \frac{x}{a}(a) = x$,

    $A'C' = kb = \frac{x}{a}(b) = \frac{bx}{a}$, and

    $A'B' = kc = \frac{x}{a}(c) = \frac{cx}{a}$. These are the same side lengths of $\triangle XYZ$. By SSS Triangle Congruence, $\triangle A'B'C'$ is congruent to $\triangle XYZ$.

    Step B: Translate $\triangle A'B'C'$ along the vector $\overline{B'Y}$, producing $\triangle A''B''C''$. Through this translation, *B″* is mapped to *Y*. It may be true that *A″* and *C″* are mapped to *X* and *Z*. If not, rotate $\triangle A''B''C''$ about *Y* so that *B‴* is mapped to *Y*. Then, *C‴* is mapped to *Z*.

15. Since the base and the height of the triangles are equal, no dilation has occurred. The triangles are 180° rotations of each other around the center of the rectangle (where the diagonals intersect). The triangles are similar to each other.

17. 180 in., or 15 ft

19. D

21. Step A: Rearrange $\frac{AX}{BX} = \frac{DX}{CX}$ into $\frac{AX}{DX} = \frac{BX}{CX}$. Let $K = \frac{AX}{DX}$.

    Step B: Rotate $\triangle DXC$ 180° around point X so that $\angle DXC$ coincides with $\angle AXB$.

    Step C: Dilate $\angle DXC$ by a factor of k about the center X. This dilation moves the point *D* to *A*, since $k(DX) = AX$, and moves *C* to *B*, since $k(CX) = BX$. Since the dilation is through point X and dilations take line segments to line segments, $\triangle DXC$ is mapped to $\triangle AXB$. So $\triangle DXC$ is similar to $\triangle AXB$.

23. Step A: Draw the bisector of $\angle AXC$.

    Step B: Reflect $\triangle CXD$ across the angle bisector. This maps $\overline{XC}$ to $\overline{XA}$. Since reflections preserve angles, it also maps $\overline{XD}$ onto $\overline{XB}$. Since $\triangle XCD \cong \triangle XAB$, the image of $\overline{CD}$ is parallel to $\overline{AB}$.

    Step C: Dilate $\triangle XCD$ about point *X*. This moves the new point C to A. Since $\overline{AB}$ is parallel to $\overline{CD}$, the new $\overline{CD}$, moves to $\overline{AB}$. Therefore, the new point *D* is mapped to *B* and $\triangle XCD$ is mapped to $\triangle XAB$. So $\triangle XCD$ is similar to $\triangle XAB$.

UNIT 4 Selected Answers

MODULE 11

Lesson 11.3 Corresponding Parts of Similar Figures

Your Turn

5. The similarity transformation is $(x, y) \to (1.5x, 1.5y)$.
6. No
8. $12 = x$
9. $y = 1.4$

Evaluate

1. Yes; yes; yes
3. No; no; no
5. $\frac{BC}{NK} = \frac{CD}{KL}$
7. $\angle X \cong \angle X$, $\angle Y \cong \angle V$, and $\angle Z \cong \angle W$
9. $\frac{1}{5}$
11. $XZ = 42$
13. $YZ = n^2 - 4n + 4$
15. $x = 7$
17. $a = 2$; $b = 3$
19. Yes, corresponding angles are congruent. The ratio of corresponding sides is constant.
21. $x \to 48x$
23. Possible answer: $(x, y) \to (2x, 2y) \to (x + 14, y - 8)$ or $(x, y) \to (x + 7, y - 4) \to (2x, 2y)$
25. The statement is false. A rectangle measuring 5 units by 2 units is not similar to a rectangle measuring 4 units by 3 units.
27. The statement is false.

UNIT 4 Selected Answers

MODULE 11

Lesson 11.4 AA Similarity of Triangles

Your Turn

6. $AB = 10$ feet
7. $PQ = 11$
10. The two triangles cannot be proven similar. Although the two given sides are in proportion, there is not a pair of included congruent angles.
11. By the Pythagorean Theorem, $NO = 6$ and $GH = 4$, so $\frac{HJ}{NO} = \frac{GH}{MN} = \frac{GJ}{MO} = \frac{1}{2}$. $\triangle MNO \sim \triangle GHI$ by the SSS Triangle Similarity Theorem

Evaluate

1. $\frac{4.5}{3} = \frac{3}{2}$ or 1.5

   $\frac{2.1}{1.4} = \frac{3}{2}$ or 1.5

   $\frac{3.9}{2.6} = \frac{3}{2}$ or 1.5
3. By the AA Triangle Similarity Theorem, $\triangle ABC \sim \triangle DEF$.
5. $\triangle ABC \sim \triangle EDC$ by the AA Triangle Similarity Theorem.
7. The triangles are similar by the AA Triangle Similarity Theorem. It is not possible to find the indicated length.
9. The triangles are similar by AA Similarity. $QR = 0.96$
11. The ratios are not equal, so the two triangles are not similar.
13. $\triangle ABC \sim \triangle BDC$ by SSS Similarity.
15. The student did not compare corresponding sides of the two triangles. $\overline{AB}$ is the shortest side of $\triangle ABC$, so its corresponding side is $\overline{DE}$ the shortest side of $\triangle DEF$. The ratios $\frac{AB}{DE}$, $\frac{BC}{EF}$ and $\frac{AC}{DF}$ are equal, so the triangles are similar by SSS Similarity.
17. $\triangle ABD \sim \triangle ACB$ by the AA Triangle Similarity Theorem. $AB = 8$
19. Apply a dilation to $\triangle ABC$ with scale factor $k = \frac{XY}{AB}$ and let the image of $\triangle ABC$ be $\triangle A'B'C'$. Then $\angle A' \cong \angle A$. It is given that $\angle A \cong \angle X$, so by transitivity $\angle A' \cong \angle X$. Also $A'B' = k \cdot AB = \frac{XY}{AB} \cdot AB = XY$ and $A'C' = k \cdot AC = \frac{XY}{AB} \cdot AC = \frac{XZ}{AC} \cdot AC = XZ$. Therefore, $\triangle A'B'C \cong \triangle XYZ$ by SAS Congruence. So a sequence of rigid motions maps $\triangle A'B'C$ to $\triangle XYZ$. The dilation followed by this sequence of rigid motions shows that there is a sequence of similarity transformations that maps $\triangle ABC$ to $\triangle XYZ$. So $\triangle ABC \sim \triangle XYZ$.
21. Possible Answer: For XB to be as small as possible, it should correspond to the shortest side of $\triangle ABC$, which is $\overline{AB}$. Thus, X corresponds to A.

UNIT 4 Selected Answers

MODULE 12

Lesson 12.1 Triangle Proportionality Theorem

Your Turn

5. $40\left(\frac{24}{32}\right) = DG$; $DG = \frac{960}{32} = 30$
6. $RN = 6\frac{1}{4}$
9. $\frac{VT}{TR} = \frac{90}{72} = \frac{5}{4}$, $\frac{VU}{US} = \frac{67.5}{54} = \frac{135}{108} = \frac{5}{4}$
   $\frac{VT}{TR} = \frac{VU}{US}$, so $\overline{RS} \parallel \overline{TU}$.

Evaluate

3. $5\frac{1}{3}$
5. 20
7. $\overline{MN} \parallel \overline{QR}$
9. $\overline{LN} \parallel \overline{AB}$
11. 0.24 kilometer
13. Determine a line
    Triangle Proportionality Theorem
    Triangle Proportionality Theorem
    Transitive
15. C and E
17. a. midsegment
    median
    substitution
    Triangle Proportionality
    b. Can repeat the same process twice to show that Z is also located $\frac{2}{3}$ of the distance from vertices A and B of ΔABC to the midpoints of their opposite sides.

UNIT 4 Selected Answers

MODULE 12

Lesson 12.2 Subdividing a Segment in a Given Ratio

Your Turn

5. (–1, 0)
6. (–2, –7)
9.

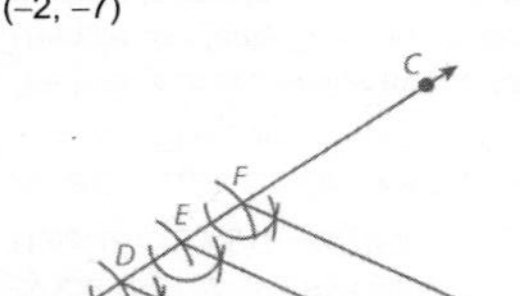
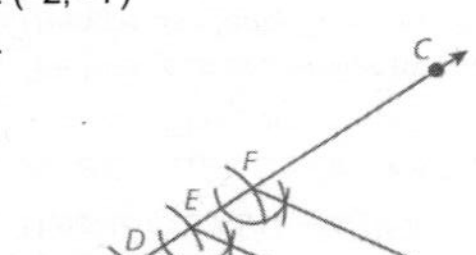

10.

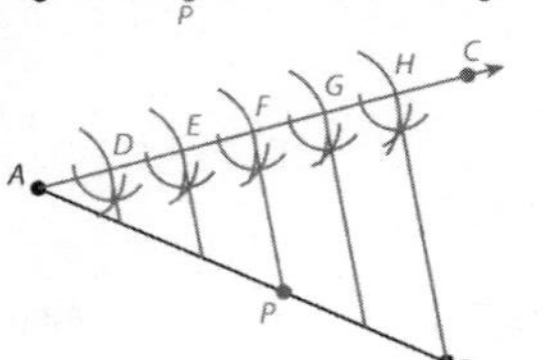

Evaluate

1. 20
3. 17
5. (6, 1)
7. (–3, 3)

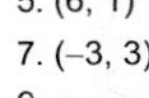

9.

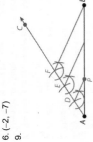

11. [figure]

13. –12.5
15. 9
17. Points P and Q are the same point.
    Sample explanation: Point P is $\frac{2}{3}$ of the distance from A to B. Point Q is $\frac{1}{3}$ of the distance from B to A. This means the points lie at the same location along the line segment.
19. $\left(-1, -\frac{1}{3}\right)$ and $\left(1, 1\frac{1}{3}\right)$
21. B
    E
23. Point P must be closer to point B than to point A, so the coordinate of point P should be positive.
    Sample answer: The student found the coordinate of the point that is $\frac{2}{3}$ of the distance from B to A.
25. If point P is on $\overline{RS}$, $\left(\frac{8}{9}, 2\frac{1}{9}\right)$. There is also a point P, not on $\overline{RS}$, that lies beyond point S (32, 11).

UNIT 4 Selected Answers

MODULE 12

Lesson 12.3 Using Proportional Relationships

Your Turn

3. The tree is 21 feet tall.
5. 24 meters

Evaluate

1. Indirect measurement
3. 52 ft
5. 52
7. 312 meters
9. 35.2 meters
11. $10\frac{1}{3}$ feet, or 10 feet 4 inches
13. 304 inches or 25 feet 4 inches
15. 69 inches or 5 feet 9 inches
17. $\triangle XYZ \sim \triangle VUZ$ by the SAS Similarity Criterion, so $\frac{XY}{VU} = \frac{XZ}{VZ}$. Then $\frac{XY}{500} = \frac{800}{400}$, so $XY = 1{,}000$ ft.
19. A
    B
    E
21. $\overline{AB}$ is the shortest side of right $\triangle ABE$, so corresponding side $\overline{DC}$ of $\triangle DCE$ must be shorter than $\overline{DE}$, that is, $DE < 200$. The triangles are similar, but Andy must have used the wrong proportion. The correct proportion is $\frac{d}{147} = \frac{200}{300}$, so $d = 147\left(\frac{200}{300}\right) = 98$. The distance across the river is 98 ft.

UNIT 4 Selected Answers

MODULE 12

Lesson 12.4 Similarity in Right Triangles

Your Turn

6. 12
7. $2\sqrt{15}$
10. $\sqrt{35}$

Evaluate

1. $\triangle PQR \sim \triangle SPR \sim \triangle SQP$
3. $\triangle XYZ \sim \triangle XWY \sim \triangle YWZ$
5. 6
7. $\sqrt{70}$
9. $\frac{3\sqrt{5}}{10}$
11. $x = 20\sqrt{3}$
    $y = 10\sqrt{21}$
    $z = 20\sqrt{7}$
13. *e*
15. *d*
17. *a*
19. 2.4
21. ≈ 4.62
23. 4 inches and 16 inches

UNIT 5 Selected Answers

MODULE 13

Lesson 13.1 Tangent Ratio

Your Turn

5. $\frac{5}{12} \approx 0.42$
6. $\frac{12}{5} = 2.4$
7. 3.6 ft
8. 26°

Evaluate

1. 0.40
   0.40; The ratios are the same.
3. $\tan\angle F = 1.8$
   $\tan\angle D = 0.56$
5. $\tan\angle R = 0.16$
   $\tan\angle P = 6.33$
7. $\tan\angle A = 2.0$
9. $QR = 4.0$
11. $PQ = 0.79$
13. $AB = 8.4$
15. $m\angle A = 66°$
17. $m\angle B = 43°$
19. $PQ = \frac{38}{\tan 75°} = 10.2$
21. 60°
23. The student's calculations are correct only if the triangle is a right triangle.
25. 10.2° with the first road and 79.8° with the second road.

UNIT 5 Selected Answers

MODULE 13

Lesson 13.2 Sine and Cosine Ratios

Your Turn

8. $\sin 17° \approx 0.292$
9. $\cos 45° \approx 0.707$
11. ≈ 16.5
13. $m\angle Y \approx 53°$
14. $m\angle Z \approx 37°$

Evaluate

1. $0.866 \approx \cos 30°$
3. $\frac{12}{13} \approx 0.923$
5. $\frac{12}{13} \approx 0.923$
7. $\frac{7}{25} \approx 0.28$
9. $9.0 \approx x$
11. ≈ 54.1
13. $\approx 64°$
15. $\approx 47°$
17. $\angle A \cong \angle A$ and $\angle ABC \cong \angle ADE$, since both are right angles.
    By AA~, $\triangle ABC \sim \triangle ADE$, so corresponding sides are proportional:
    $\frac{AC}{AE} = \frac{BC}{DE} \Rightarrow AC = \frac{(BC)(AE)}{DE} \Rightarrow \frac{AC}{BC} = \frac{AE}{DE}$
    These ratios determine sin *A*, and since they are equal, sin *A* is the same when calculated in either right triangle.
19. 9.5 ft
21. 66° and 24°
    Check: $66° + 24° = 90°$
23. So $m\angle BAC = 2m\angle BAD$
    $= 2\sin^{-1}\left(\frac{100}{1185}\right) \approx 9.7°$
25. $0 < BC < AB \Rightarrow \frac{0}{AB} < \frac{BC}{AB} < \frac{AB}{AB} \Rightarrow 0$
    $< \sin A < 1$
    The same argument shows that $0 < \cos A < 1$.
27. Two segments ⊥ to the same line are ∥ to each other, so $\overline{BC} \parallel \overline{DE}$. By the Triangle Proportionality Theorem, $\overline{BC}$ divides sides $\overline{AD}$ and $\overline{AE}$ of $\triangle ADE$ proportionally:
    $\frac{BD}{AB} = \frac{CE}{AC} \Rightarrow 1 + \frac{BD}{AB} = 1 + \frac{CE}{AC} \Rightarrow \frac{AB + BD}{AB}$
    $= \frac{AC + CE}{AC} \Rightarrow \frac{AD}{AB} = \frac{AE}{AC} \Rightarrow \frac{AD}{AE} = \frac{AB}{AC}$
    These ratios determine cos *A*, and since they are equal, cos *A* is the same when calculated in either triangle.

UNIT 5 Selected Answers

MODULE 13

Lesson 13.3 Special Right Triangles

Your Turn

5. $2\sqrt{3} = JK$

   $JL = 6$

6. $PR = 2\sqrt{6}$

   $PQ = 4\sqrt{3}$

9. $AB = 5\sqrt{2}$

   $AC = 5\sqrt{2}$

   $\sin 45° = \cos 45° = \frac{5\sqrt{2}}{10} = \frac{\sqrt{2}}{2}$

   $\tan 45° = 1$

11. $PR = 30$
12. $YZ = 60$

Evaluate

1. No; $3\sqrt{3} : 6 : 6\sqrt{3} \neq 1 : \sqrt{3} : 2$
3. Yes; $4\sqrt{3} : 12 : 8\sqrt{3} = 1 : \sqrt{3} : 2$
5. $9\sqrt{2} = AB = BC$
7. $UV = 6\sqrt{3}$

   $6 = VW$

9. $7\sqrt{2} = AC$ $\quad 7\sqrt{2} = BC$
11. $JL = 4\sqrt{6}$ $\quad KL = 4\sqrt{3}$
13. $AB = 65$
15. Not possible: $9^2 + 21^2 = 522$; 522 is not a perfect square.
17. $x = 6\sqrt{3}$
19. Given: $BC = AC\sqrt{3}$. Since $\tan A = \frac{BC}{AC}$, use an inverse tangent ratio:

   $\tan A = \frac{BC}{AC} = \frac{AC\sqrt{3}}{AC} = \sqrt{3}$

   $m\angle A = \tan^{-1}\sqrt{3} = 60°$

   $\angle A$ and $\angle B$ are complementary, so $m\angle B = 90° - m\angle A = 90° - 60° = 30°$.

21. $10 = x$
23. $\approx 4{,}160\ cm^2$
25. No; if the two shorter side lengths are odd, then their squares are odd, because the square of an odd number is always odd. But the sum of their squares is even, because the sum of two odd numbers is always even. Therefore the sum of the squares of the two shorter side lengths cannot itself be the square of an odd number.

UNIT 5 Selected Answers

MODULE 13

Lesson 13.4 Problem Solving with Trigonometry

Your Turn

3. $\approx 50.3\ mm^2$
4. $\approx 8.6\ cm^2$
6. ≈ 65 m
7. ≈ 73 m
8. 63°
10. $JK \approx 6.71$; $JL \approx 4.47$; $KL \approx 8.06$

   $m\angle J = 90°$.

   $m\angle K \approx 34°$.

   $m\angle L \approx 66°$

Evaluate

1. $\approx 5.8\ cm^2$
3. $AC \approx 1.5$ cm

   $m\angle A \approx 61°$

   $m\angle B \approx 29°$

5. $m\angle R = 38°$

   37.0 mm $\approx PR$ $\quad$ 28.9 mm $\approx PQ$

7. $m\angle J = 90°$; $JK \approx 3.6$; $JL \approx 10.8$; $KL \approx 11.4$; $m\angle L \approx 18°$; $m\angle K \approx 72°$
9. $\approx 12{,}700\ yd^2$
11. 1.8 ft $\approx AB$ $\quad$ 29.9 ft $\approx BC$
13. $Z(5, 1)$

   $m\angle Z = 90°$

   $XY = 5\sqrt{2}$, $XZ = 5$, $YZ = 5$

   $m\angle X = m\angle Y = 45°$.

15. $m\angle CAE \approx 37°$; $m\angle AEC \approx 27°$; $m\angle ACE \approx 27°$

   Area $\approx 13.5\ mm^2$

17. Suppose $\overline{AB} \cong \overline{DE}$ and $\overline{AC} \cong \overline{DF}$. Solving either of these right triangles determines the length of the hypotenuse in the same way, e.g., using the Pythagorean Theorem, so $BC = EF$ and therefore, by SSS ≅, $\triangle ABC \cong \triangle DEF$.

   Suppose $\angle B \cong \angle E$. The given corresponding side lengths allow the unknown sides to be calculated in the same way using trigonometric ratios, so that all corresponding side lengths are equal and therefore all corresponding sides are congruent. Again, by SSS ≅, $\triangle ABC \cong \triangle DEF$.

19. $\sin 2\theta = 2\sin\theta\cos\theta$

UNIT 5 Selected Answers

MODULE 14

Lesson 14.1 Law of Sines

Your Turn

4. ≈ 11.4
5. ≈ 21.4
6. Only one triangle; $\angle A$ is acute and $a > b$.
7. $m\angle B \approx 21.2°$; $m\angle C = 133.8°$; $c \approx 35.9$ in.

Evaluate

1. ≈ 5.2
3. ≈ 6.9
5. ≈ 18.8
7. $\frac{x^2}{2}\sin(\theta)$
9. $m\angle A = 50°$; $a = 10$; $b \approx 12.9$
11. $m\angle B = 35°$; $b \approx 10.5$; $c \approx 4.7$
13. $m\angle C = 10°$; $a \approx 51.8$; $b \approx 35.5$
15. No triangles are possible.
17. There are two triangles.
   $m\angle B \approx 39.6°$; $m\angle C = 105.4°$; $c \approx 15.1$ m
   Second triangle
   $m\angle B \approx 140.4°$; $m\angle C = 4.6°$; $c \approx 1.3$ m
19. a. ≈ 123.7 mi
   b. Possible answer: Calculate the area using the sine formula. Use the value of the area to solve for h using the other form of the area formula.
   ≈ 120 mi
21. ≈ 5.2 mi
23. Transfer corresponding angle measures from each triangle to the other.
25. $f \approx 2.1$; $e \approx 3.7$

UNIT 5 Selected Answers

MODULE 14

Lesson 14.2 Law of Cosines

Your Turn

3. $a \approx 40.9$; $m\angle B \approx 3.9°$; $m\angle C = 3.1°$
4. $m\angle A \approx 43.4°$; $m\angle B \approx 55.6°$; $m\angle C = 81.0°$
5. ≈ 1.7 hours
6. about 34 miles greater than the direct route

Evaluate

1. 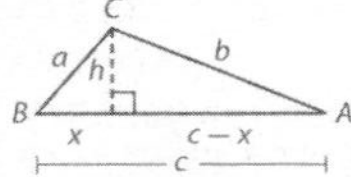

3. You need two side lengths and the angle measure for the unknown side, or you need all three side lengths.
5. $p \approx 25.0$; $m\angle R \approx 42.1°$; $m\angle Q \approx 14.9°$
7. $m\angle P \approx 25.2°$; $m\angle R \approx 58.4°$; $m\angle Q \approx 96.4°$
9. $m\angle R \approx 93.8°$; $m\angle Q \approx 29.9°$; $m\angle P = 56.3°$
11. $b \approx 6.5$; $m\angle A \approx 64.9°$; $m\angle C = 37.1°$
13. $m\angle A \approx 94.8°$; $m\angle B \approx 39.8°$;
   $m\angle C = 45.4°$
15. $m\angle A \approx 56.6°$; $m\angle B \approx 46.4°$; $m\angle C = 77.0°$
17. 3.8 miles
19. D. 45°
21. $m\angle A \approx 45°$; $m\angle B \approx 60°$; $m\angle C \approx 74°$
23. 1.2 km
25. Abby did not make an error. The three lengths cannot form a triangle because $a + b = c$.

UNIT 6 Selected Answers

MODULE 15

Lesson 15.1 Central Angles and Inscribed Angles

Your Turn

4. $m\widehat{BD} = 11°$
7. $m\angle ABE = 37°$

Evaluate

1. $\overline{DE}$, $\overline{EF}$; $\angle DEF$; $\angle DCF$
3. $\overline{DF}$, $\overline{DG}$, $\overline{EF}$, $\overline{EG}$; $\angle DGE$, $\angle DFE$, $\angle FDG$, $\angle FEG$; none
5. 42°
7. 141°
9. 321°
11. 48°
13. 85°
15. 236°
17. 20°
19. 324°
21. C, D, E, G, H
23. 135°
25. 144°

UNIT 6 Selected Answers

MODULE 15

Lesson 15.2 Angles in Inscribed Quadrilaterals

Your Turn

7.

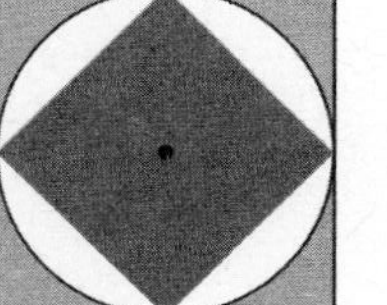

Evaluate

1. No. $\angle A$ and $\angle C$ are still supplementary. Opposite angles of an inscribed quadrilateral are always supplementary.
3. Yes; $m\angle HGJ = 115°$; $\angle H$ and $\angle J$ measure 90°
5. 95°
7. Yes. Since the opposite angles of quadrilateral *GHIJ* are supplementary, the quadrilateral can be inscribed in a circle.
9.

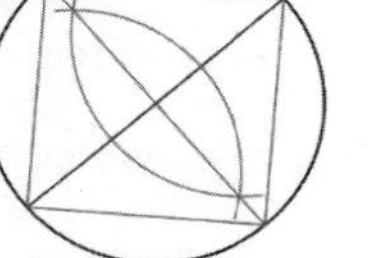

Construct the perpendicular bisector of the diameter. Connect the points where the perpendicular bisector and the diameter intersect the circle.

11. $m\angle A = 70°$; $m\angle B = 115°$; $m\angle C = 110°$; $m\angle D = 65°$
13. $m\angle V = 101°$; $m\angle T = 79°$; $m\angle U = 86°$; $m\angle W = 94°$
15. Cannot be inscribed in a circle.
17. 105°
19. $m\angle M = 99°$; $m\angle J = 108°$; $m\angle K = 81°$; $m\angle L = 72°$.
21. a. 100 square feet
    b. $(50\pi - 100)$ square feet

UNIT 6 Selected Answers

MODULE 15

Lesson 15.3 Tangents and Circumscribed Angles

Evaluate

1. 90°
3. The tangents are perpendicular.
5. approximately 1400 mi
7. 3 units
   (−3, 1)
   $x = -3$
9. $AC = 32$
   $AB = 32$
11. $\angle P$ and $\angle Q$ are supplementary angles.
13. $m\angle P = 45°$
15. 28°
17. It is not possible.
19. $m\overset{\frown}{MJ} = 82$
21. *ABCD* is a kite.
23. From point *B*, construct two tangents to circle *O*. From point *C*, construct two tangents to circle *O*. Label the point of intersection of the tangent from *B* and the tangent from *C* as point *D*. Triangle *DEB* is circumscribed about circle *O*.
    (Also, triangle *FEC* is circumscribed about circle *O*.)

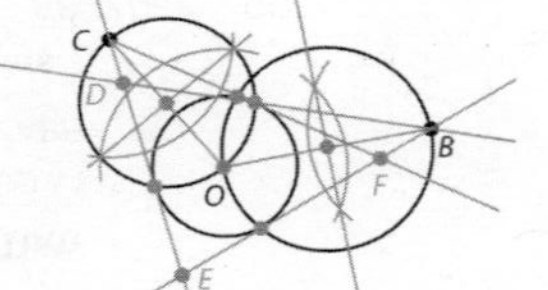

UNIT 6 Selected Answers

MODULE 15

Lesson 15.4 Segment Relationships in Circles

Your Turn

3. $1.93 \approx x$
   $CB \approx 15.93$
   $AD = 12$ (given)
6. $x = 9$
   $PT = 13$; $PR = 10.4$
7. $x = 3.5$
   HL = 10; NL = 12
9. 400 yards

Evaluate

1. The product of the lengths of the segments on one chord will equal the product of the lengths of the segments on the other chord: $RV \cdot VS = TV \cdot VU$.
3. $DF \cdot CF = BF \cdot EF$
5. $y = 6$. $DE = 7$; $FG = 8$.
7. a. $PM = 6$ in.
   b. $PQ = 12$ in.
9. I agree.
11. $y = 14.3$; $HL = 24.3$; $NL = 27$
13. $z = 2\sqrt{21}$
15. $y = 4\sqrt{10}$
17. B
19. 1770 feet
21. $x = 18$
23. about 3.2 in
25. Method 1: By the Secant-Tangent Product Theorem, $BC^2 = 12 \cdot 4$ and so $BC = \sqrt{48} = 4\sqrt{3}$.
    Method 2: Because a line tangent to a circle is a line ⊥ to the radius, $\angle ABC$ is a right angle. By the Pythagorean Theorem, $BC^2 + 4^2 = 8^2$. Thus $BC^2 = 64 - 16 = 48$ and $BC = \sqrt{48} = 4\sqrt{3}$.

UNIT 6 Selected Answers

MODULE 15

Lesson 15.5 Angle Relationships in Circles

Your Turn

4. 86°
5. 34°
6. 122°
7. 119°
8. 47
9. 45°
10. 116°

Evaluate

1. The measure of the angle will be half the measure of its intercepted arc; the Tangent-Secant Interior Angle Theorem.
3. 64.5°
5. 135°
7. 56°
9. 90°
11. 57.5°
13. 18°
15. a. 110°
    b. 116°
17. 90°
19. 142°
21. Since though any two points, there exists exactly one line, then $\overline{BD}$ can be drawn. By the Exterior Angle Theorem, $m\angle ABD = m\angle ACD + m\angle BDC$, so $m\angle ACD = m\angle ABD - m\angle BDC$. $m\angle ABD = \frac{1}{2}m\widehat{AD}$ by the Inscribed Angle Theorem, and $m\angle BCD = \frac{1}{2}m\widehat{BD}$ because the measure of an angle formed by a tangent and a secant intersecting on a circle at the point of tangency is half the measure of the intercepted arc. By subst., $m\angle ACD = \frac{1}{2}m\widehat{AD} - \frac{1}{2}m\widehat{BD}$. Thus by the Distributive Property, $m\angle ACD = \frac{1}{2}\left(m\widehat{AD} - m\widehat{BD}\right)$.
23. Case 1: Assume $\overline{AB}$ is a diameter of the circle. Then $m\widehat{AB} = 180°$, and $\angle ABC$ is a right angle, because a diameter is perpendicular to a tangent at the point of tangency. Thus $m\angle ABC = \frac{1}{2}m\widehat{AB}$.

    Case 2: Assume $\overline{AB}$ is not a diameter of the circle. Let X be the center of the circle and draw radii $\overline{XA}$ and $\overline{XB}$. Since they are radii, $\overline{XA} \cong \overline{XB}$ so $\triangle AXB$ is isosceles. Thus $\angle XAB \cong \angle XBA$, and $2m\angle XBA + m\angle AXB = 180°$. This means that $m\angle XBA = 90° - \frac{1}{2}m\angle AXB$. Because a line tangent to a circle is perpendicular to the radius at the point of tangency, $\angle XBC$ is a right angle, so $m\angle XBA + m\angle ABC = 90°$ or $m\angle ABC = 90° - m\angle XBA$. By substitution, $m\angle ABC = 90° - \left(90° - \frac{1}{2}m\angle AXB\right)$.

    Simplifying gives $m\angle ABC = \frac{1}{2}m\angle AXB$.

    $m\angle AXB = m\widehat{AB}$ because $\angle AXB$ is a central angle. Thus $m\angle ABC = \frac{1}{2}m\widehat{AB}$.

UNIT 6 Selected Answers

MODULE 16

Lesson 16.1 Justifying Circumference and Area of a Circle

Your Turn

4. about 6.4 feet
5. about 10.2 feet
9. 254 ft^2

Evaluate

1. A regular polygon with 40 sides.
3. ≈ 150.7 cm
5. ≈ 56.5 in.
7. ≈ 301.4 ft
9. 19.625 m^2
11. 78.5 in^2.
13. $5 = r$; $A = \pi(5)^2 \approx 78.5$ ft^2
15. $11 = r$; $A = \pi(11)^2 \approx 379.9$ ft^2
17. $C \approx 15.7$ ft.
    $A \approx 19.6$ ft^2
19. Possible answer: The circular table would fit at least as many people as the rectangular table. At the rectangular table, 2 people would fit at each of the 4 ft sides and 3 people would fit at each of the 6 ft sides, for a total of 10 people. Each person would have 2 ft of space. The circumference of the circular table is $C = \pi d = \pi(6) \approx 18.8$ ft. If 11 people sat at the circular table, each person would have $\frac{18.8}{11} \approx 1.7$ ft, or about 1 ft 8 in. of space.
21. a. 267 ft
    b. ≈ 6 min
23. The calculation shown in A is incorrect because the diameter, instead of the radius, is used to find the area.
25. about 12 cm
27. The range of areas is about 177 square miles to about 314 square miles.
29. Disagree; the total distance is 5280 • 12 = 63,360 inches and the number of revolutions equals the total distance divided by the circumference, which is $\frac{63,360}{26\pi} \approx 775.7$ revolutions.
31. The circumference of circle E is $\frac{1}{4}$ the circumference of circle C because the radius of circle E is $\frac{1}{4}$ the radius of circle C.

UNIT 6 Selected Answers

MODULE 16

Lesson 16.2 Arc Length and Radian Measure

Your Turn

3. ≈ 37.7 in.
7. $\frac{\pi}{2}$ radians
8. $\frac{\pi}{4}$ radians

Evaluate

1. The circumference of the circle.
3. The diameter of the circle.
5. ≈ 31.4 m
7. ≈ 5.8 cm
9. 34.8 m
11. 10 m
13. $\frac{2}{9}\pi$
15. $\frac{5\pi}{9}$
17. For 0°: 0
    For 30°: $\frac{\pi}{6}$
    For 45°: $\frac{\pi}{4}$
    For 60°: $\frac{\pi}{3}$
    For 90°: $\frac{\pi}{2}$
    For 120°: $\frac{2\pi}{3}$
    For 135°: $\frac{3\pi}{4}$
    For 150°: $\frac{5\pi}{6}$
    For 180°: π
19. 160°
21. 15 in.
23. The student used the diameter instead of the radius in the circumference formula. 2π m.
25. ≈ 21.5 ft

UNIT 6 Selected Answers

MODULE 16

Lesson 16.3 Sector Area

Your Turn

4. $\approx 0.32\pi$
   ≈ 1.01 cm^2
5. $= 36\pi$
   ≈ 113.10 mm^2
6. ≈ 12, 723 ft^2

Evaluate

1. sector
3. $A = \pi r^2$, where A represents the area and r represents the length of the radius.
5. $A = 63\pi \approx 197.7$ cm^2
7. $A = \frac{\pi}{9} \approx 0.3$ mm^2
9. $A = 100\pi \approx 314.2$ in^2
11. 18 pieces
13. ≈ 628.3 in^2
15. $= 24\pi$
    ≈ 75.40 cm^2
17. $= \frac{47}{90}\pi$
    ≈ 1.64 ft^2
19. Let $m\angle AOB = x°$, then $\frac{x}{360} \cdot \pi(6)^2 = \frac{9}{2}\pi$. Solving for x shows that $m\angle AOB = 45°$.
21. Buying a party wheel is the better value.
23. B, F
25. 2.57 in^2
27. Disagree; the original area is $\frac{m}{360} \cdot \pi r^2$ and the new area is $\frac{m}{360} \cdot \pi(2r)^2$ or $4 \cdot \frac{m}{360} \cdot \pi r^2$, so the area becomes 4 times greater.
29. Arc length requires using the circumference of the circle, whereas area requires the circle's area. In each, the central angle is used to find the fraction of the circumference or area of the circle.

UNIT 6 Selected Answers

MODULE 17

Lesson 17.1 Equation of a Circle

Your Turn

5. $(x-4)^2 + (y-3)^2 = 16$
6. $(x+1)^2 + (y+1)^2 = 3$
8. Center: (–1, 4), radius: 2

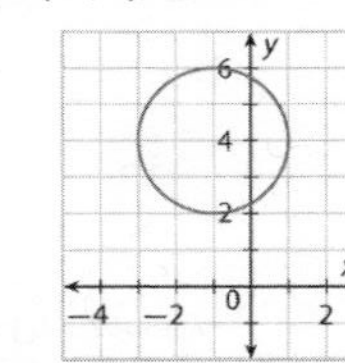

9. Center (0, –2), radius 3

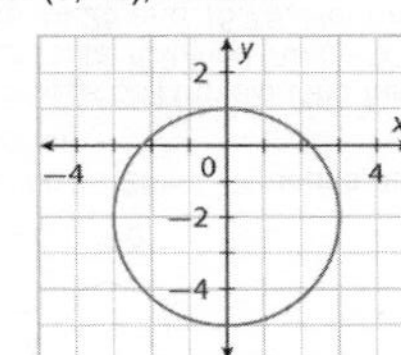

12. The point $(\sqrt{18}, -4)$ does not lie on the circle because the point's x- and y-coordinates do not satisfy the equation of the circle.
13. The point (4, –4) lies on the circle because the point's x- and y-coordinates satisfy the equation of the circle.

Evaluate

1. (h, k)
3. $(x+1)^2 + (y-3)^2 = 64$
5. $(x-9)^2 + y^2 = 3$
7. center: (3, –4); radius: 3

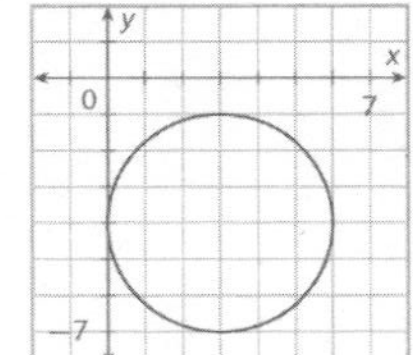

9. center: (3, 3); radius: 2

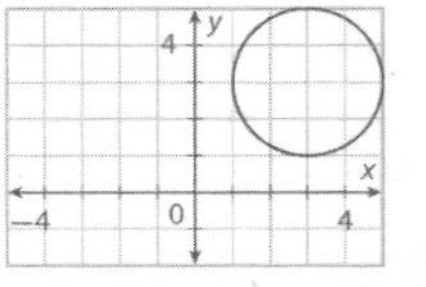

11. The point $(2, \sqrt{3})$ does not lie on the circle because its x- and y-coordinates do not satisfy the equation:
$2^2 + (\sqrt{3})^2 = 4 + 3 = 7 \neq 9$.
13. The graph of the circle intersects the x-axis at both (3, 0) and (–3, 0).
15. $(x-1)^2 + (y+2)^2 = 4$
17. The point does lie on the equation because its x- and y coordinates satisfy the equation: $0^2 + 4(0) + 4^2 - 4(4) = 0$
19. False; $r = \sqrt{7}$
21. False; the center is (6, –4), which is in the fourth quadrant.
23. False; the equation is $x^2 + y^2 = 3^2 = 9$
25. a. $(x+3)^2 + (y-3)^2 = 10$
b. It does lie on the circle because $x = 0$ and $y = 4$ satisfies the equation $(x+3)^2 + (y-3)^2 = 10$

UNIT 6 Selected Answers

MODULE 17

Lesson 17.2 Equation of a Parabola

Your Turn

6. $y = -\frac{1}{4}x^2$

8. $(x-3)^2 = 12(y-(-1))$ or $(x-3)^2 = 12(y+1)$

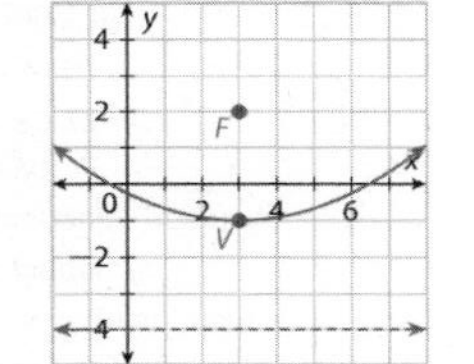

9. $(x-2)^2 = -16(y-5)$

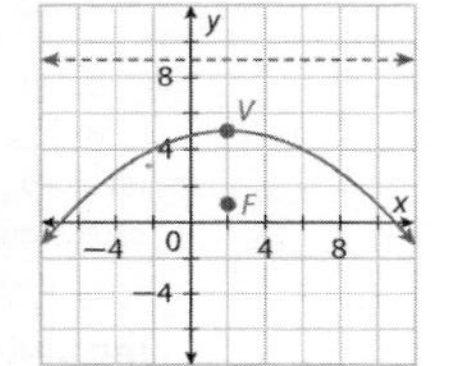

Evaluate

1. $\frac{1}{4(2)}x^2 = \frac{1}{8}x^2$

3. $\frac{1}{4(-5)}x^2 = -\frac{1}{20}x^2$

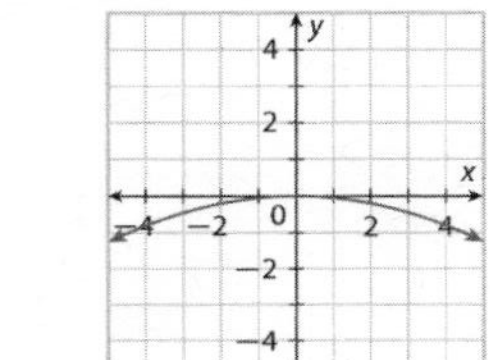

5. Focus: (0, –6); directrix is $y = 6$.
7. Focus: $\left(0, -\frac{1}{2}\right)$; directrix is $y = \frac{1}{2}$.

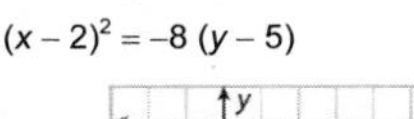

9. $(x-2)^2 = -8(y-5)$

11. equation of parabola: $(x - 4)^2 = 20(y + 3)$

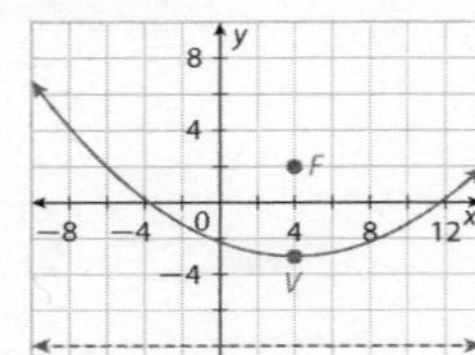

13. Focus is (−2, 3) and directrix is $y = -5$.

15. Focus is (−5, −3.5) and directrix is $y = -3$.

17. $y = \frac{1}{4}x^2$; $y = \frac{1}{8}x^2$; $y = \frac{1}{12}x^2$; $y = \frac{1}{16}x^2$

    As the focus and directrix move apart, the parabola is vertically compressed.

19. $y = \frac{1}{24}x^2$

21. −3

23. a. $x \geq 0, y \geq 0$

    b. Since $11.25 > 6$, Amber's ball went higher.

    Amber's ball traveled the farthest horizontal distance. Amber's *x*-intercepts are 14.25 and 15.75. Her ball traveled 1.5 feet horizontally. James's *x*-intercepts are 11.5 and 12.5. His ball traveled 1 foot horizontally.

UNIT 7 Selected Answers

MODULE 18

Lesson 18.1 Volume of Prisms and Cylinders

Your Turn

4. 88 cubic units
5. $72k^3$ cubic units
6. 20,357.5 in.^{3}
7. $20x^2(x + 2)$ cm^3
9. $\frac{r}{3\pi h + r}$

Evaluate

1. A. rectangular prism; C
   B. cylinder; A
   C. triangular prism; B
3. 810 yd^3
5. ≈ 2580.72 m^3
7. ≈ 1130.97 ft^3
9. ≈ 1209.1 ft^3
11. 792 cm^3
13. ≈ 2 yd^3; \$50
15. ≈ 14.9
    Because 0.9 of a candle would not make an entire candle, 14 candles.
17. 2 in. radius $h \approx 1.1$ in.
    1.5 in. radius $h \approx 2.0$ in.
19. $V = 840$ cm^3
21. The cylinder's volume is greater than the rectangular prism's volume by 5.6 in^3.

UNIT 7 Selected Answers

MODULE 18

Lesson 18.2 Volume of Pyramids

Your Turn

4. $D = 10.5$
5. 192 in^3
6. 150 ft^2

Evaluate

1. The volume of the square pyramid is $\frac{1}{3}$ the volume of the square prism.
3. The volume of *PABCD* is $\frac{1}{3}$ the volume of the cube.
5. 136 in^3
7. 96 cm^3
9. 2343.8 cm^3
11. The volume doubles.
13. $h = 14$ m
15. $\approx 10.5 \frac{g}{cm^3}$
17. The volume would be 216 times larger; dividing the volume of the enlarged pyramid by the volume of the original pyramid gives 216.
19. 10, 125 ft^3

    375 ft^3
21. Let s be the length of a side of the pyramid's base. Then the area of the base is s^2, and $\frac{1}{3}s^2(5) = 60$. Solving shows that $s = 6$ ft.

UNIT 7 Selected Answers

MODULE 18

Lesson 18.3 Volume of Cones

Your Turn

2. $r = 1.2$ in.

   $h \approx 3.710$ in.
3. ≈ 5.596 in^3
4. ≈ 3.1 fl oz
6. 43.769 cm^3
7. ≈ 29.2 cm^3

Evaluate

1. It will take three cones to fill the cylinder with sand. Because the volume formula for a cylinder is $V = \pi r^2 h$, and the volume formula for a cone is $V = \frac{1}{3}\pi r^2 h$, the volume of a cone is $\frac{1}{3}$ the volume of the cylinder.
3. ≈ 51.0 ft^3
5. 1440π in^3
7. ≈ 703.7 in^3
9. ≈ 42.9 m^3
11. A. B

    B. D

    C. C

    D. A
13. B; E
15. 904.8 in^3
17. a. ≈ 33.5 in^3

    b. ≈ 134.0 in^3

    c. $5; the large size holds 4 times as much.
19. $10\pi\sqrt{3}$ cm
21. $h = 9$ in.
23. The calculation show in A is incorrect because it uses the slant height of the cone instead of the height.

UNIT 7 Selected Answers

MODULE 18

Lesson 18.4 Volume of Spheres

Your Turn

3. 10,305.9947... m^3
4. $\approx$ 10,305,995 L
6. $\approx$ 44.9 in^3

Evaluate

1. The volume of the cylinder is 1.5 times the volume of the sphere.
3. 696.9 ft^3
5. $1333.\overline{3}\pi$ cm^3
7. 972π in^3
9. $\frac{560\pi}{3}$ in^3
11. $\approx$ 1441 mm^3
13. 243 mm^3
15. $\approx$ 358,000,000 BTU
17. A
19. Volume of Venus + Volume of Mars = Volume of Earth
21. 14,294 in^3
23. approximately 1 in.

UNIT 7 Selected Answers

MODULE 19

Lesson 19.1 Cross Sections and Solids of Rotation

Your Turn

3. The cross section is a rectangle. Its base is smaller than the diameter of the cylinder, and its height is the same as the cylinder's.
5. A composite of two cones with a cylinder in between.

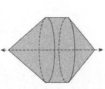

6. a sphere

Evaluate

1. Figure B
3. triangular pyramid
5. square
7. (isosceles) triangle
9. rectangle
11. circle
13. cone

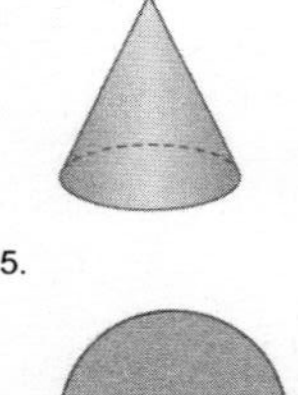

15. disc (circle and its interior)
17. Yes
19. For a hexagon, cut parallel to the ground; for a rectangle, cut perpendicular to the ground.
21. Equilateral triangle; each side of the triangle has length $s\sqrt{2}$.

UNIT 7 Selected Answers

MODULE 19

Lesson 19.2 Surface Area of Prisms and Cylinders

Your Turn

4. 410 in^2
5. 139.68 in^2
7. paper needed ≈ 565.5 cm^2
   aluminum needed ≈ 791.7 cm^2
8. paper needed ≈ 18,095.6 mm^2
   aluminum needed ≈ 26,238.6 mm^2
10. 344 in^2
11. ≈ 628.3 mm^2

Evaluate

1. $L = 72$ ft^2
   $S = 142$ ft^2
3. $L = 200$ cm^2
   $S = 250$ cm^2
5. $L = 24\pi$ ft^2
   $S = 42\pi$ ft^2
7. $S \approx$ 953.1 ft^2
9. $S \approx$ 352.0 cm^2
11. The 23 inch bulb will produce more light.
13. $L = 80\pi$ m^2
    $S = 208\pi$ m^2
15. $h = 11$ ft
17. 4 gallons; $100
19. 198 cm^2
21. The triangular-prism-shaped frame will take more plastic.

UNIT 7 Selected Answers

MODULE 19

Lesson 19.3 Surface Area of Pyramids and Cones

Your Turn

3. lateral area ≈ 102.5 ft^2
   surface area ≈ 138.5 ft^2
4. lateral area = 36 cm^2
   surface area ≈ 42.9 cm^2
7. paper: ≈ 47.1 in^2
   paper and plastic: ≈ 75.4 in^2
8. paper: ≈ 11.8 in^2
   paper and plastic: ≈ 18.8 in^2
10. ≈ 192.9 m^2
11. ≈ 234.5 m^2

Evaluate

1. B; D
3. In an oblique cone, the distance from a point on the edge of the base to the vertex is not the same point for each point on the base.
5. $L = 544$ ft^2; $S = 800$ ft^2
7. $L = 900$ cm^2; $S \approx 1592.8$ cm^2
9. $L = 2564.5\pi$ cm^2; $S = 2696.75\pi$ cm^2
11. $L = 444\pi$ in^2; $S = 588\pi$ in^2
13. $S = 1056\pi$ m^2
15. $L = 324$ cm^2, $S = 936$ cm^2
17. $S = 456\pi$ m^2
19. $d = 6$ in.
21. Possible Answer: 528, 000 ft^2
23. a. 500π cm^2; b. 100π cm^2; c. 25π cm^2;
    d. 425π cm^2
25. A triangle is formed with 2 vertices at the midpoints of opposite sides of the square base and the third vertex at the vertex of the pyramid. The side lengths of the triangle are ℓ, ℓ, and s, the edge length of the base. By the Triangle Inequality Theorem, $\ell + \ell > s$, so $2\ell > s$. Therefore $\ell > \frac{1}{2}s$.

UNIT 7 Selected Answers

MODULE 19

Lesson 19.4 Surface Area of Spheres

Your Turn

3. $\approx 277.0 \text{ in}^2$
4. $\approx 25.8 \text{ in}^2$
5. ratio of amounts of material ≈ 10.736
   ratio of circumferences = 3.277
   square of ratio of circumferences = 10.743
   $\approx$ ratio of amounts of material
7. $40\pi \text{ in}^2$
8. $32\pi \text{ in}^2$
9. $\approx 326.7 \text{ in}^2$

Evaluate

1. $3\pi r^2$
3. $1764\pi \text{ in}^2$
5. $196\pi \text{ cm}^2$
7. $180\pi \text{ in}^2$
9. $\approx 1332.0 \text{ mm}^2$
11. $2\pi\sqrt{15}$ in.
13. $9\pi \text{ in}^2$
15. Susana used $\frac{4}{3}$, which is part of the volume formula, not the surface area formula. The surface area formula is $4\pi r^2$.
17. $144\pi \text{ in}^2$
19. About twice as great.
21. $S = 108\pi \text{ cm}^2$
23. The surface area of the sphere is equal to the lateral area of the cylinder.
25. $s = 2r \cdot \sqrt{\frac{\pi}{6}}$, or $s \approx 1.4r$

UNIT 7 Selected Answers

MODULE 20

Lesson 20.1 Scale Factor

Your Turn

4. Possible answer: The original area is 36. After the transformation the area is 144. When the base length changes by a factor of 4, the area changes by a factor of 4.
5. Original area is 20. After the transformation the area is 100. When the width changes by a factor of 5, the area changes by a factor of 5.
7. Possible answer: The original circumference is 24π, the original area is 144π. After the transformation, the circumference is 6π, and the area is 9π. The circumference changes by a factor of 0.25, and the area changes by a factor of $(0.25)^2$.
9. For the model, the volume is 64π cu. in., and the surface area is 60π sq. in. For the silo, the volume is 2985984π cu. in. and the surface area is 77760π sq. in. The volume changes by a factor of 36^3, and the surface area changes by a factor of 36^2.

Evaluate

1. The area is multiplied by $\frac{1}{2}$.
3. The area is multiplied by $\frac{1}{4}$.
5. The area is doubled.
7. The area is multiplied by $\frac{2}{3}$.
9. The perimeter is tripled. The area is multiplied by 9.
11. Volume is multiplied by 125.
13. A. non-proportional; B. proportional; C. non-proportional; D. non-proportional; E. proportional
15. $\approx$ 800,000 acres
17. 36 in.
19. The volume is multiplied by 27.
21. Multiply the base or height by 5; Multiply the base and height by $\sqrt{5}$.
23. The area of the new circle is $A = (9\pi x^2 + 54\pi x + 81\pi) \text{ in.}^2$

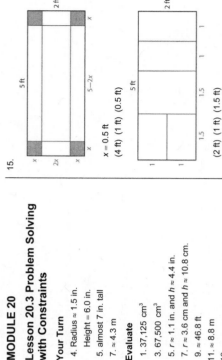

UNIT 7 Selected Answers

MODULE 20

Lesson 20.2 Modeling and Density

Your Turn

5. ≈ 13,600 persons/mi^2
8. ≈ 1,129,245

Evaluate

1. Juniper is denser than Aspen.
3. Liquid oxygen is denser than liquid hydrogen.
5. 150 persons/mi^2
7. ≈ 684,000 BTUs
9. 125,000 BTUs
11. ≈ 0.70 cm^3
13. ≈ 993.5 kg/m^3
15. ≈ 14.9 mi^2
17. 406, 4; 156, 2; 52, 1; 300, 3
19. 76% of the cork's volume, will remain above the surface.

UNIT 7 Selected Answers

MODULE 20

Lesson 20.3 Problem Solving with Constraints

Your Turn

4. Radius ≈ 1.5 in.
   Height = 6.0 in.
5. almost 7 in. tall
7. ≈ 4.3 m

Evaluate

1. 37,125 cm^3
3. 67,500 cm^3
5. $r \approx 1.1$ in. and $h \approx 4.4$ in.
7. $r \approx 3.6$ cm and $h \approx 10.8$ cm.
9. ≈ 46.8 ft
11. ≈ 8.8 m
13.

180 cm; 60 cm; x; x; y; x; y; x; y

$x = 30$ cm
$y = 40$ cm
(60 cm) (40 cm) (30 cm)

15.

5 ft; x; 2x; x; 2 ft; x; 5−2x; x

$x = 0.5$ ft
(4 ft) (1 ft) (0.5 ft)

5 ft; 1; 1; 2 ft; 1.5; 1.5; 1; 1

(2 ft) (1 ft) (1.5 ft)

17. ≈ 11.8 m
19. ≈ 73 ft
21. Weight multiplier = 125,000
    Cross-section multiplier = 2,500
    No, because the ratio of leg cross-section to weight has been reduced by a factor of $\frac{1}{50}$.
23. $\frac{20.76}{\pi r^2} = h$
    $r \approx 1.5$ in. and $h \approx 3.0$ in.

UNIT 8 Selected Answers

MODULE 21

Lesson 21.1 Probability and Set Theory

Your Turn

3. $\frac{1}{3}$
4. $\frac{14}{30}$
5. $\frac{1}{30}$
6. $\frac{2}{3}$
8. $\frac{3}{4}$
9. $\frac{3}{5}$

Evaluate

1. Yes, because every element of *D* is also an element of *A*.
3. {2, 4, 6, 12}
5. {1, 2, 3, 4, 6, 8, 10, 12}
7. {5, 7, 9, 10, 11}
9. $\frac{3}{5}$
11. $\frac{4}{5}$
13. $\frac{2}{5}$
15. $\frac{5}{6}$
17. $\frac{11}{12}$
19. $\frac{2}{3}$
21. a. $\frac{5}{36}$
    b. $\frac{31}{36}$
23. $\frac{12}{13}$
25. 0
27. No; choosing a black tile is not the complement of choosing a white tile since the bag also contains gray tiles.
29. Assume *A* is a subset of *S*. Then $0 \le n(A) \le n(S)$. For example, if *S* has 10 elements, the number of elements of *A* is greater than or equal to 0 and less than or equal to 10. No subset of *S* can have fewer than 0 elements or more than 10 elements. So $0 \le \frac{n(A)}{n(S)} \le 1$. When all the outcomes are equally likely, $P(A) = \frac{n(A)}{n(S)}$. Therefore $0 \le P(A) \le 1$.

UNIT 8 Selected Answers

MODULE 21

Lesson 21.2 Permutations and Probability

Your Turn

3. $\frac{1}{56}$
4. $\frac{5}{28}$
5. 34,650
6. 210
7. $\frac{1}{15}$
8. $\frac{2}{5}$

Evaluate

1. 479,001,600 different orders
3. 3024 ways
5. $\frac{1}{165}$
7. $\frac{1}{56}$
9. 1680
11. 15,120
13. $\frac{1}{20,160}$
15. $\frac{1}{35}$
17. $\frac{1}{21}$
19. $\frac{1}{720}$
21. $\frac{1}{5525}$
23. A. C
    B. A
    C. B
25. Yes
27. $n(A)$ should be 1 since the tiles must appear in the order B-E-A-D. The correct probability is $\frac{1}{360}$.

UNIT 8 Selected Answers

MODULE 21

Lesson 21.3 Combinations and Probability

Your Turn

4. $\frac{1}{4}$
5. $\frac{11}{230}$
6. $\frac{11}{32}$
7. $\frac{1}{2}$

Evaluate

1. 15 ways
3. 27,405 groups
5. $\frac{10}{143}$
7. ≈ 11.8%
9. $\frac{193}{512}$
11. $\frac{93}{256}$
13. $\frac{1}{220}$
15. $\frac{4}{21}$
17. $\frac{1}{435}$
19. $\frac{14}{969}$
21. a. 84
    b. $\frac{5}{21}$
23. In permutations, order matters. In combinations, order does not matter. In a permutation of *A*, *B*, and *C*, *ABC* is different from *CBA*, so they would be counted as two different permutations. In a combination, *ABC* is the same as *CBA*, and would not be counted again.
    a. 210; 210
    b. ${}_{10}C_6 = {}_{10}C_4 = 210$
    c. In general, ${}_nC_r = {}_cC_{n-r}$.
25. ${}_nC_n = 1$

UNIT 8 Selected Answers

MODULE 21

Lesson 21.4 Mutually Exclusive and Overlapping Events

Your Turn

5. $\frac{13}{25}$

Evaluate

1. $\frac{3}{4}$
3. $\frac{5}{13}$
5. $\frac{97}{125}$
7. $\frac{28}{125}$
9. $\frac{9}{125}$
11. $\frac{1}{15}$
13. $\frac{58}{75}$
15. $\frac{61}{75}$
17. $\frac{5}{18}$
19. $\frac{7}{18}$
21. $\frac{7}{12}$
23. 85%
25. When finding $n(A \cup B)$, $n(A)$ should be added to $n(B)$, not multiplied.
    $\frac{4}{13}$

UNIT 8 Selected Answers

MODULE 22

Lesson 22.1 Conditional Probability

Your Turn

5. $\frac{1}{3}$

6. $\frac{1}{4}$

Evaluate

1. $\approx 56\%$

3. $\approx 8\%$

5. $\approx 88\%$

7. $P(Pa|L)$; $\approx 55\%$, and $P(F|M)$ $\approx 8\%$, so the probability that a student who got less than 6 hours of sleep passed the exam is greater.

9. $\frac{1}{2}$

11. $\frac{1}{4}$

13. $\frac{1}{2}$

15. A. B
    B. D
    C. A
    D. C

17. 45%

19. $\frac{5}{6}$

    Given that not rolling a 1 on the red number cube has occurred, there are 30 possible outcomes:
    (2, 1), (2, 2), (2, 3), (2, 4), (2, 5), (2, 6), (3, 1), (3, 2), (3, 4), (3, 5), (3, 6), (4, 1), (4, 2), (4, 3), (4, 4), (4, 5), (4, 6), (5, 1), (5, 2), (5, 3), (5, 4), (5, 5), (5, 6), (6, 1), (6, 2), (6, 3), (6, 4), (6, 5), and (6, 6).
    all but 5 outcomes—(2, 1), (3, 1), (4, 1), (5, 1), and (6, 1)—are successful

21. $P(A|B) > \frac{1}{2} > P(B|A)$

23. $n(A \cap B)$; $n(\text{not } A \cap B)$; $n(B)$

    The conditional probability $P(A|B) = \frac{n(A \cap B)}{n(B)}$ restricts the discussion to event B because that event is assumed to have occurred. The numbers used to calculate $P(A|B)$ both come from the highlighted row in the table: $n(A \cap B)$ is the number of outcomes in event B that are also in event A, while $n(B)$ is the number of all outcomes in event B. The rest of the table is irrelevant.

UNIT 8 Selected Answers

MODULE 22

Lesson 22.2 Independent Events

Your Turn

3. The events are not independent.
4. The events are not independent.
6. 6%
7. $\approx 11\%$
8. The events are not independent.
9. The events are independent.

Evaluate

1. a. $P(R) = \frac{3}{5}$ and $P(B) = \frac{2}{5}$

   b. $\frac{2}{5}$

   c. $\frac{8}{19}$

   d. Events R and B are independent when the first chip is returned to the bag because $P(B|R) = P(B)$ in that case

3. The events are not independent.

5. $\approx 5.6\%$

7. $= 9\%$

9. $\approx 8.3\%$

11. $\approx 24.3\%$

13. $\frac{1}{8}$

15. The events are not independent.

17. The events are not independent.

19. 40; 60
    20; 30
    Sample answer: Let W be the event that a person is a woman. Let Pe be the event that a person prefers writing with a pen.
    $P(W) = \frac{60}{150} = \frac{2}{5}$, $P(Pe) = \frac{100}{150} = \frac{2}{5}$, and
    $P(W) \cdot P(Pe) = \frac{2}{5} \cdot \frac{2}{3} = \frac{4}{15}$. Since
    $P(W \cap Pe) = \frac{40}{150} = \frac{4}{15}$ and
    $P(W \cap Pe) = P(W) \cdot P(Pe)$, the events are independent.

21. $P(A^c|B) = 1 - P(A|B)$ Definition of complementary events
    $= 1 - P(A)$ Definition of independent events
    $= P(A^c)$ Definition of complementary events
    So, events A^c and B are also independent.

UNIT 8 Selected Answers

MODULE 22

Lesson 22.3 Dependent Events

Your Turn

3. $\frac{4}{15}$
4. $\frac{2}{5}$
7. $\frac{1}{5}$
8. $\frac{1}{5}$

Evaluate

1. a. The events C and S are dependent.
   b. $P(C|S) = \frac{5}{6}$ and $P(S|C) = \frac{5}{7}$.
   Multiplying $P(C)$ and $P(S|C)$ gives $P(C \cap S)$.
   Multiplying $P(S)$ and $P(C|S)$ gives $P(C \cap S)$.
3. $\frac{3}{19}$
5. $\frac{2}{57}$
7. Events A and B are independent.
9. a. D
   b. A, C
   c. B
11. a. $\frac{34}{285}$
    b. $\frac{34}{57}$
13. $P(A \cap B \cap C) = P((A \cap B) \cap C)$ Group events A and B as one event.
    $= P(A \cap B) \cdot P(C|A \cap B)$ Apply the Multiplication Rule to $A \cap B$ and C.
    $= P(A) \cdot P(B|A) \cdot P(C|A \cap B)$ Apply the Multiplication Rule to A and B.

UNIT 8 Selected Answers

MODULE 23

Lesson 23.1 Using Probability to Make Fair Decisions

Your Turn

4. Possible answer: Choose an employee's name at random from a list of all employees. Each month, remove the previous winners from the list. Once every employee has won once, begin again with the list of all employees.
8. Possible answer: If the game is interrupted when the players are tied, they each have a probability of winning equal to $\frac{1}{2}$.

Evaluate

1. Possible answer: You could split the cost of a sixth pass to the climbing gym so that you each get a third visit for half of the price of an additional pass. Or you could toss a coin and the winner gets the fifth pass. Tossing a coin gives each of you a 50% (or equal) chance of winning the last pass.
3. Not fair; $P(\text{Meri wins}) = \frac{1}{3}$; $P(\text{Riley wins}) = \frac{1}{2}$
5. Fair; $P(\text{Meri wins}) = \frac{1}{2}$; $P(\text{Riley wins}) = \frac{1}{2}$
7. Fair; $P(\text{Meri wins}) = \frac{1}{2}$; $P(\text{Riley wins}) = \frac{1}{2}$
9. 0.30; 0.12
   0.23; 0.12
   0.18; 0.05
   Find the total number of games won: $30 + 23 + 18 + 12 + 12 + 5 = 100$. Assign numbers from 1–100 to the members so each has as many numbers assigned as the number of games won. Then use a random number generator to choose an integer from 1 to 100.
11. Possible answer: Write the names on slips of paper, but for each hour that a student worked, write his or her name on an extra slip. Then draw a slip at random. The probability of Paige winning is 4 out of 45, or about 0.089.
13. $\frac{1}{500}$
15. $\approx 1.89\%$
17. $\approx 86.79\%$
19. Possible answer: Team A should receive 3.7 points. Team B should receive 6.3 points.

UNIT 8 Selected Answers

MODULE 23

Lesson 23.2 Analyzing Decisions

Your Turn

7.

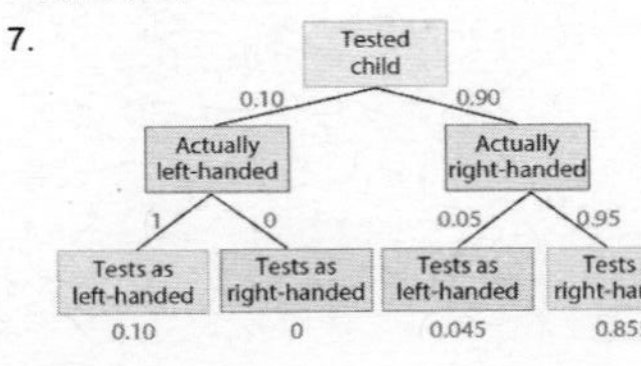

8. 69%

The probability of the test being correct in this case increases about 2%.

9. 31%

The probability of the test being correct in this case increases about 30%.

Evaluate

1. No; Of the 1,015 products that Helen completed, 50 were defective, which is about 4.9%. Of the 370 products that Kyle completed, 20 were defective, which is about 5.5%.

3. 9,000(0.38) = 3,420

1,000(0.98) = 980

4,400

9,000(0.62) = 5,580

1,000(0.02) = 20

5,600

10,000(0.90) = 9,000

10,000(0.10) = 1,000

10,000

Only 22% of the coupons will go to the intended target of students living off campus. Therefore, this is not a good decision.

5. Allergy 196; 4; 200

No allergy 490; 9,310; 9,800

686; 9,314

No; Only 196 people out of the 686 who tested positive actually have the allergy. This is about 29% of those who test positive.

7. $\frac{1}{3}$; 0

$\frac{1}{3}$; $\frac{2}{3}$

9.

Student
0.425
0.575
Plays musical instrument
Plays no musical instrument
0.2
0.8
0.6
0.4
Plays a sport
Plays no sport
Plays a sport
Plays no sport
0.085
0.340
0.345
0.230

It would not be reasonable to assume that this is true.

11.

Person
0.02
0.98
has strep (S)
does not have strep(S^c)
0.99
0.01
0.01
0.99
tests positive (+)
tests negative (−)
tests positive (+)
tests negative (−)
0.0198
0.0002
0.0098
0.9702

About 67%

Glossary/Glosario

A

ENGLISH	SPANISH	EXAMPLES
acute angle An angle that measures greater than 0° and less than 90°.	**ángulo agudo** Ángulo que mide más de 0° y menos de 90°.	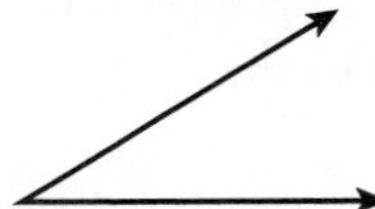
acute triangle A triangle with three acute angles.	**triángulo acutángulo** Triángulo con tres ángulos agudos.	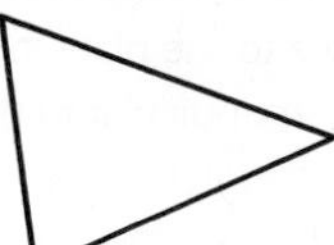
adjacent angles Two angles in the same plane with a common vertex and a common side, but no common interior points.	**ángulos adyacentes** Dos ángulos en el mismo plano que tienen un vértice y un lado común pero no comparten puntos internos.	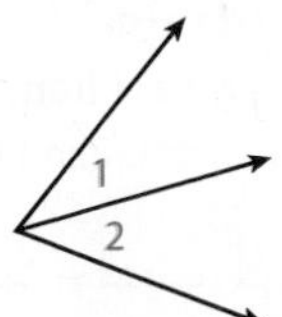 ∠1 and ∠2 are adjacent angles.
adjacent arcs Two arcs of the same circle that intersect at exactly one point.	**arcos adyacentes** Dos arcos del mismo círculo que se cruzan en un punto exacto.	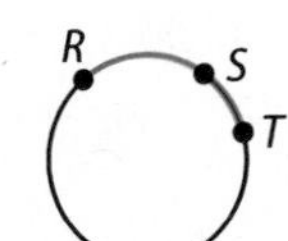 $\widehat{RS}$ and $\widehat{ST}$ are adjacent arcs.
alternate exterior angles For two lines intersected by a transversal, a pair of angles that lie on opposite sides of the transversal and outside the other two lines.	**ángulos alternos externos** Dadas dos líneas cortadas por una transversal, par de ángulos no adyacentes ubicados en los lados opuestos de la transversal y fuera de las otras dos líneas.	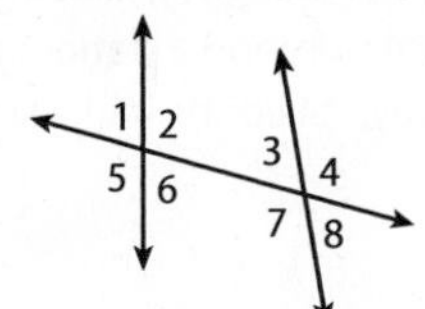 ∠4 and ∠5 are alternate exterior angles.
alternate interior angles For two lines intersected by a transversal, a pair of nonadjacent angles that lie on opposite sides of the transversal and between the other two lines.	**ángulos alternos internos** Dadas dos líneas cortadas por una transversal, par de ángulos no adyacentes ubicados en los lados opuestos de la transversal y entre las otras dos líneas.	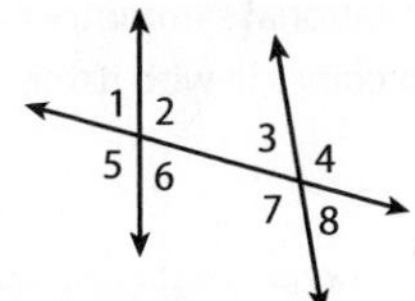 ∠3 and ∠6 are alternate interior angles.
altitude of a cone A segment from the vertex to the plane of the base that is perpendicular to the plane of the base.	**altura de un cono** Segmento que se extiende desde el vértice hasta el plano de la base y es perpendicular al plano de la base.	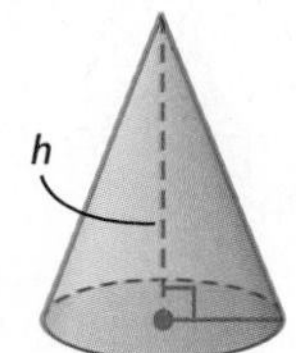

Glossary/Glosario

ENGLISH	SPANISH	EXAMPLES
altitude of a cylinder A segment with its endpoints on the planes of the bases that is perpendicular to the planes of the bases.	**altura de un cilindro** Segmento con sus extremos en los planos de las bases que es perpendicular a los planos de las bases.	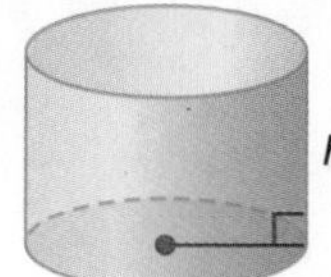 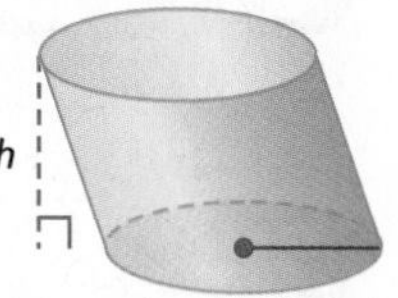
altitude of a prism A segment with its endpoints on the planes of the bases that is perpendicular to the planes of the bases.	**altura de un prisma** Segmento con sus extremos en los planos de las bases que es perpendicular a los planos de las bases.	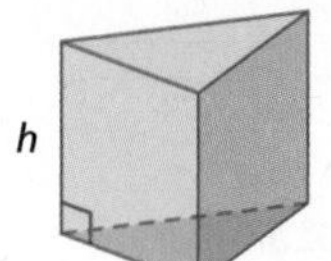 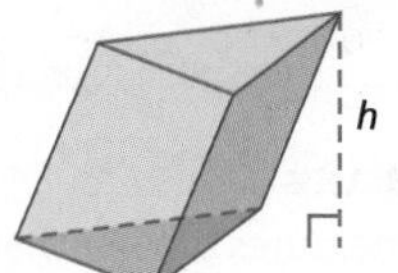
altitude of a pyramid A segment from the vertex to the plane of the base that is perpendicular to the plane of the base.	**altura de una pirámide** Segmento que se extiende desde el vértice hasta el plano de la base y es perpendicular al plano de la base.	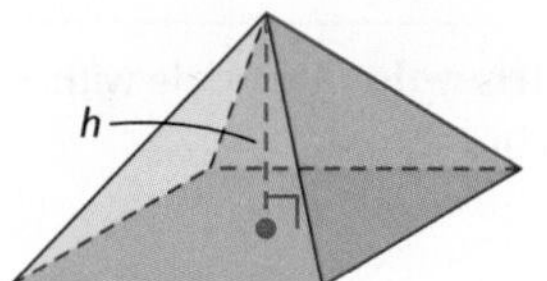
altitude of a triangle A perpendicular segment from a vertex to the line containing the opposite side.	**altura de un triángulo** Segmento perpendicular que se extiende desde un vértice hasta la línea que forma el lado opuesto.	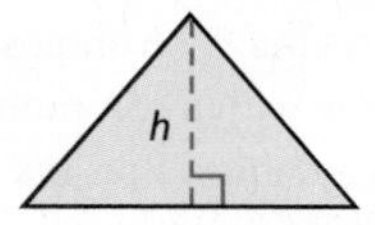
angle bisector A ray that divides an angle into two congruent angles.	**bisectriz de un ángulo** Rayo que divide un ángulo en dos ángulos congruentes.	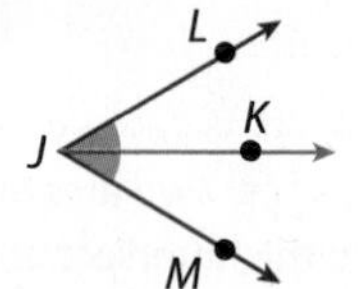 $\overrightarrow{JK}$ is an angle bisector of $\angle LJM$.
angle of rotation An angle formed by a rotating ray, called the terminal side, and a stationary reference ray, called the initial side.	**ángulo de rotación** Ángulo formado por un rayo rotativo, denominado lado terminal, y un rayo de referencia estático, denominado lado inicial.	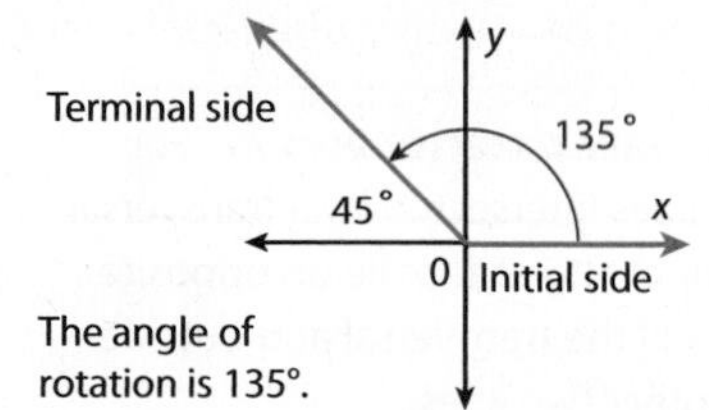
angle of rotational symmetry The smallest angle through which a figure with rotational symmetry can be rotated to coincide with itself.	**ángulo de simetría de rotación** El ángulo más pequeño alrededor del cual se puede rotar una figura con simetría de rotación para que coincida consigo misma.	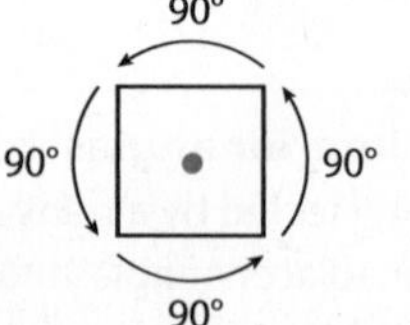
apothem The perpendicular distance from the center of a regular polygon to a side of the polygon.	**apotema** Distancia perpendicular desde el centro de un polígono regular hasta un lado del polígono.	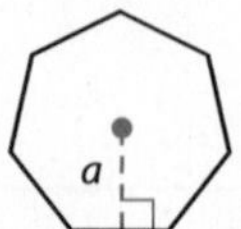

ENGLISH	SPANISH	EXAMPLES
arc An unbroken part of a circle consisting of two points on the circle, called the endpoints, and all the points on the circle between them.	**arco** Parte continua de una circunferencia formada por dos puntos de la circunferencia denominados extremos y todos los puntos de la circunferencia comprendidos entre éstos.	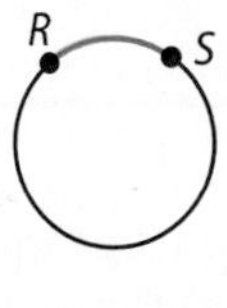
arc length The distance along an arc measured in linear units.	**longitud de arco** Distancia a lo largo de un arco medida en unidades lineales.	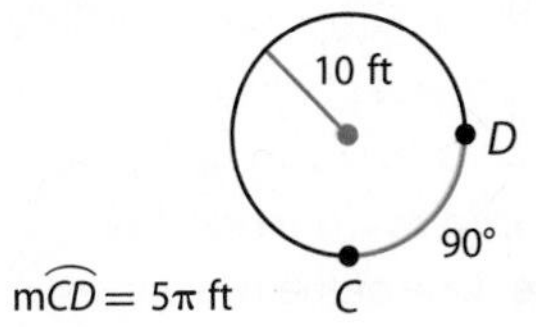 $m\widehat{CD} = 5\pi$ ft
arc marks Marks used on a figure to indicate congruent angles.	**marcas de arco** Marcas utilizadas en una figura para indicar ángulos congruentes.	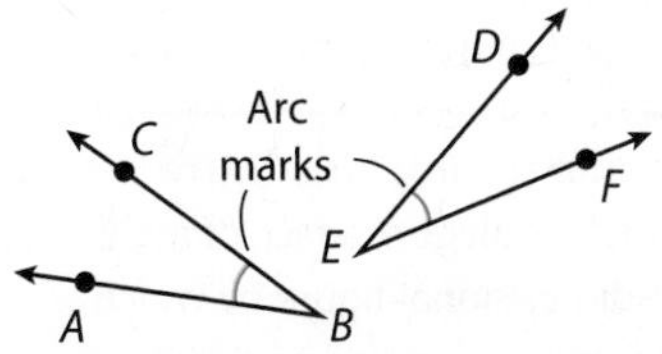
auxiliary line A line drawn in a figure to aid in a proof.	**línea auxiliar** Línea dibujada en una figura como ayuda en una demostración.	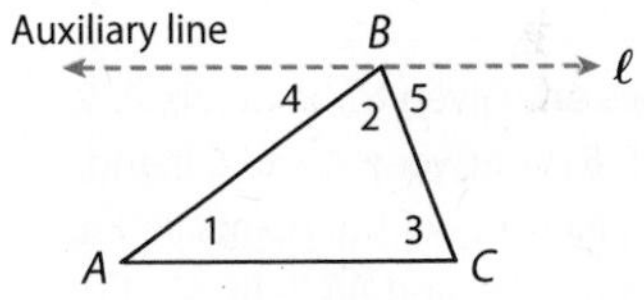
axiom *See* postulate.	**axioma** *Ver* postulado.	
axis of a cone The segment with endpoints at the vertex and the center of the base.	**eje de un cono** Segmento cuyos extremos se encuentran en el vértice y en el centro de la base.	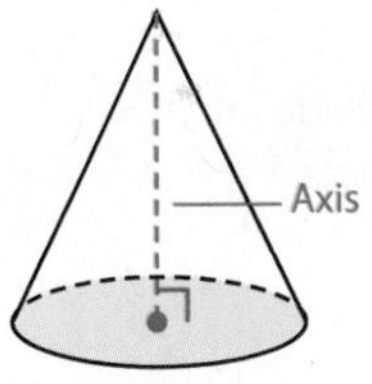
axis of a cylinder The segment with endpoints at the centers of the two bases.	**eje de un cilindro** Segmentos cuyos extremos se encuentran en los centros de las dos bases.	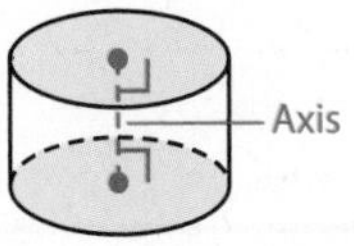
axis of symmetry A line that divides a plane figure or a graph into two congruent reflected halves.	**eje de simetría** Línea que divide una figura plana o una gráfica en dos mitades reflejadas congruentes.	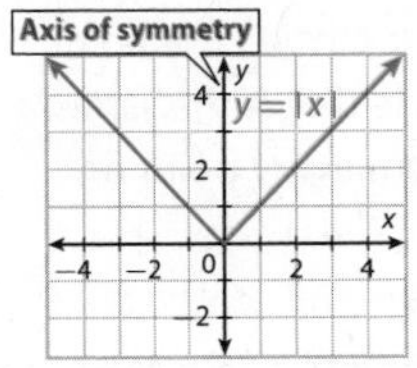

ENGLISH	SPANISH	EXAMPLES

B

base angle of a trapezoid One of a pair of consecutive angles whose common side is a base of the trapezoid.

ángulo base de un trapecio Uno de los dos ángulos consecutivos cuyo lado en común es la base del trapecio.

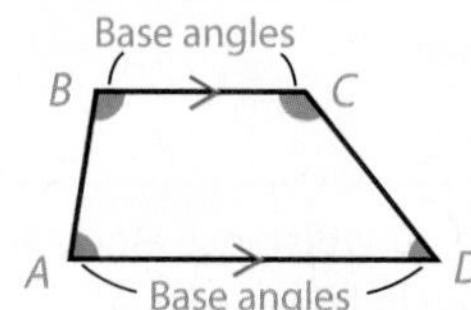

base angle of an isosceles triangle One of the two angles that have the base of the triangle as a side.

ángulo base de un triángulo isósceles Uno de los dos ángulos que tienen como lado la base del triángulo.

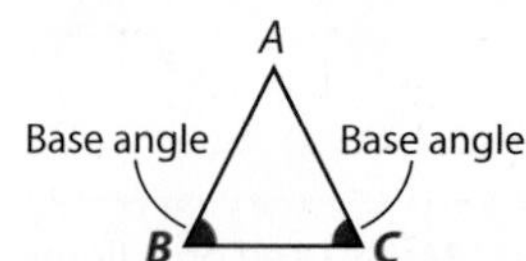

base of a geometric figure A side of a polygon; a face of a three-dimensional figure by which the figure is measured or classified.

base de una figura geométrica Lado de un polígono; cara de una figura tridimensional por la cual se mide o clasifica la figura.

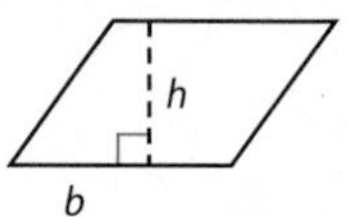

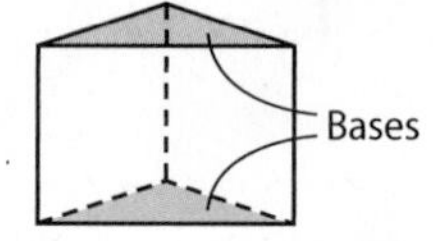

between Given three points A, B, and C, B is between A and C if and only if all three of the points lie on the same line, and $AB + BC = AC$.

entre Dados tres puntos A, B y C, B está entre A y C si y sólo si los tres puntos se encuentran en la misma línea y $AB + BC = AC$.

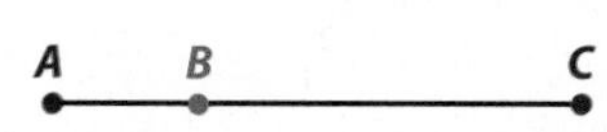

biconditional statement A statement that can be written in the form "*p* if and only if *q*."

enunciado bicondicional Enunciado que puede expresarse en la forma "*p* si y sólo si *q*".

A figure is a triangle if and only if it is a three-sided polygon.

bisect To divide into two congruent parts.

trazar una bisectriz Dividir en dos partes congruentes.

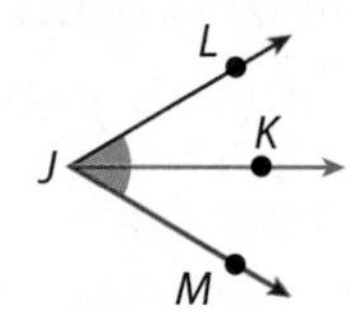

$\overrightarrow{JK}$ bisects $\angle LJM$.

C

center of a circle The point inside a circle that is the same distance from every point on the circle.

centro de un círculo Punto dentro de un círculo que se encuentra a la misma distancia de todos los puntos del círculo.

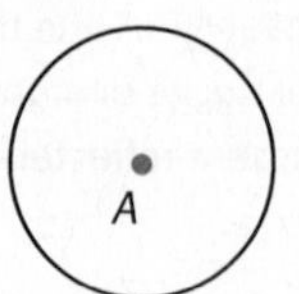

center of dilation The intersection of the lines that connect each point of the image with the corresponding point of the preimage.

centro de dilatación Intersección de las líneas que conectan cada punto de la imagen con el punto correspondiente de la imagen original.

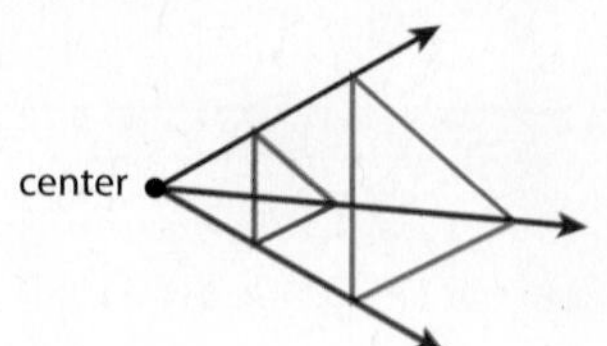

ENGLISH	SPANISH	EXAMPLES
center of rotation The point around which a figure is rotated.	**centro de rotación** Punto alrededor del cual rota una figura.	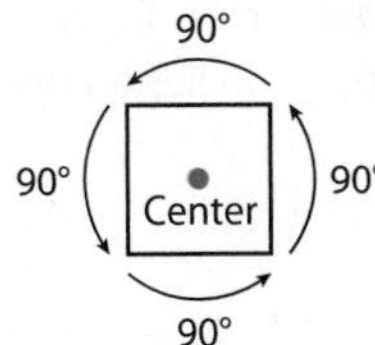
central angle of a circle An angle with measure less than or equal to 180°whose vertex is the center of a circle.	**ángulo central de un círculo** Ángulo con medida inferior o igual a 180°cuyo vértice es el centro de un círculo.	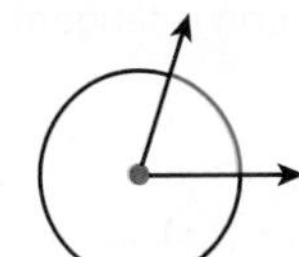
centroid of a triangle The point of concurrency of the three medians of a triangle. Also known as the *center of gravity*.	**centroide de un triángulo** Punto donde se encuentran las tres medianas de un triángulo. También conocido como *centro de gravedad*.	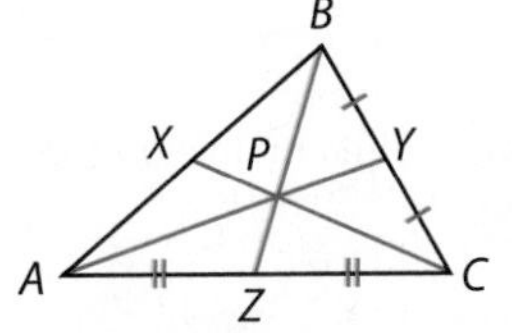 The centroid is *P*.
chord A segment whose endpoints lie on a circle.	**cuerda** Segmento cuyos extremos se encuentran en un círculo.	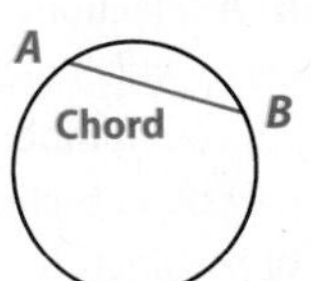
circle The set of points in a plane that are a fixed distance from a given point called the center of the circle.	**círculo** Conjunto de puntos en un plano que se encuentran a una distancia fija de un punto determinado denominado centro del círculo.	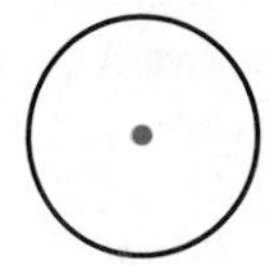
circumcenter of a triangle The point of concurrency of the three perpendicular bisectors of a triangle.	**circuncentro de un triángulo** Punto donde se cortan las tres mediatrices de un triángulo.	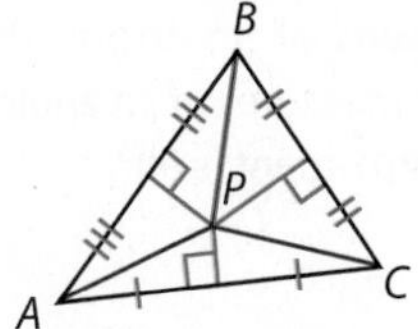 The circumcenter is *P*.
circumcircle *See* circumscribed circle.	**circuncírculo** *Véase* círculo circunscrito.	
circumference The distance around the circle.	**circunferencia** Distancia alrededor del círculo.	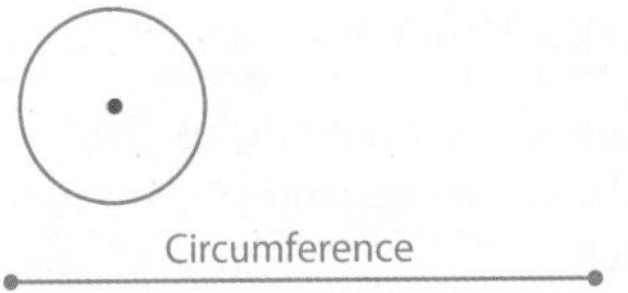
circumscribed angle An angle formed by two rays from a common endpoint that are tangent to a circle	**ángulo circunscrito** Ángulo formado por dos semirrectas tangentes a un círculo que parten desde un extremo común.	

ENGLISH	SPANISH	EXAMPLES
circumscribed circle Every vertex of the polygon lies on the circle.	**círculo circunscrito** Todos los vértices del polígono se encuentran sobre el círculo.	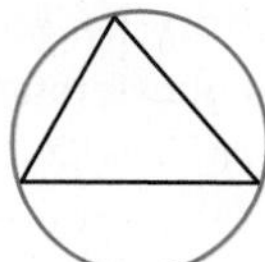
circumscribed polygon Each side of the polygon is tangent to the circle.	**polígono circunscrito** Todos los lados del polígono son tangentes al círculo.	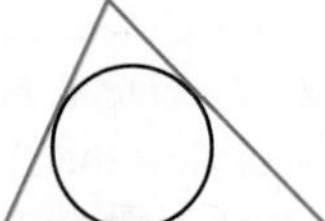
coincide To correspond exactly; to be identical.	**coincidir** Corresponder exactamente, ser idéntico.	
collinear Points that lie on the same line.	**colineal** Puntos que se encuentran sobre la misma línea.	 *K*,*L*, and *M* are collinear points.
combination A selection of a group of objects in which order is *not* important. The number of combinations of *r* objects chosen from a group of *n* objects is denoted ${}_nC_r$.	**combinación** Selección de un grupo de objetos en la cual el orden *no* es importante. El número de combinaciones de *r* objetos elegidos de un grupo de *n* objetos se expresa así: ${}_nC_r$.	For 4 objects *A*, *B*, *C*, and *D*, there are ${}_4C_2 = 6$ different combinations of 2 objects: *AB*, *AC*, *AD*, *BC*, *BD*, *CD*.
common tangent A line that is tangent to two circles.	**tangente común** Línea que es tangente a dos círculos.	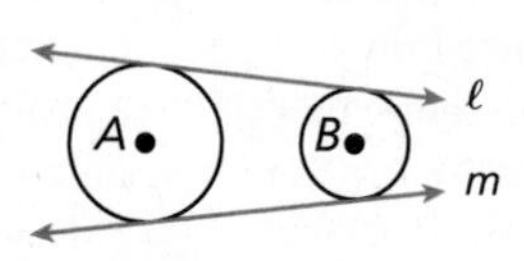 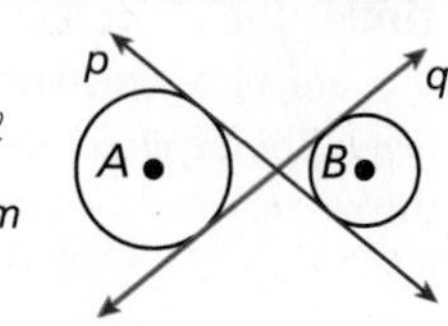
complement of an angle The sum of the measures of an angle and its complement is 90°.	**complemento de un ángulo** La suma de las medidas de un ángulo y su complemento es 90°.	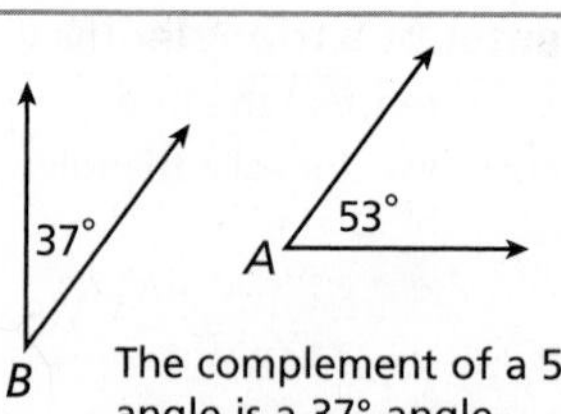 The complement of a 53° angle is a 37° angle.
complement of an event All outcomes in the sample space that are not in an event *E*, denoted $\overline{E}$.	**complemento de un suceso** Todos los resultados en el espacio muestral que no están en el suceso *E* y se expresan $\overline{E}$.	In the experiment of rolling a number cube, the complement of rolling a 3 is rolling a 1, 2, 4, 5, or 6.
complementary angles Two angles whose measures have a sum of 90°.	**ángulos complementarios** Dos ángulos cuyas medidas suman 90°.	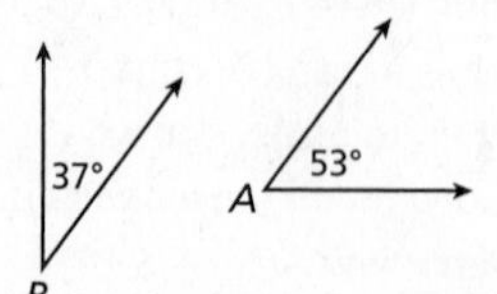

ENGLISH	SPANISH	EXAMPLES
component form The form of a vector that lists the vertical and horizontal change from the initial point to the terminal point.	**forma de componente** Forma de un vector que muestra el cambio horizontal y vertical desde el punto inicial hasta el punto terminal.	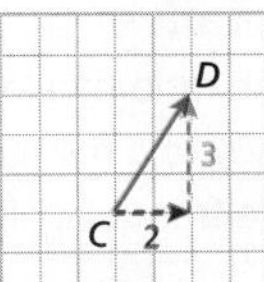 The component form of $\overrightarrow{CD}$ is $\langle 2, 3 \rangle$.
composite figure A plane figure made up of triangles, rectangles, trapezoids, circles, and other simple shapes, or a three-dimensional figure made up of prisms, cones, pyramids, cylinders, and other simple three-dimensional figures.	**figura compuesta** Figura plana compuesta por triángulos, rectángulos, trapecios, círculos y otras figuras simples, o figura tridimensional compuesta por prismas, conos, pirámides, cilindros y otras figuras tridimensionales simples.	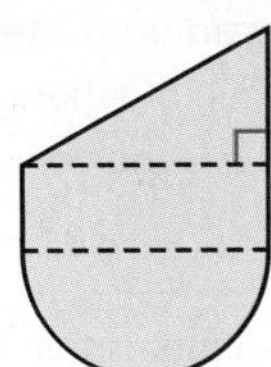
composition of transformations One transformation followed by another transformation.	**composición de transformaciones** Una transformación seguida de otra transformación.	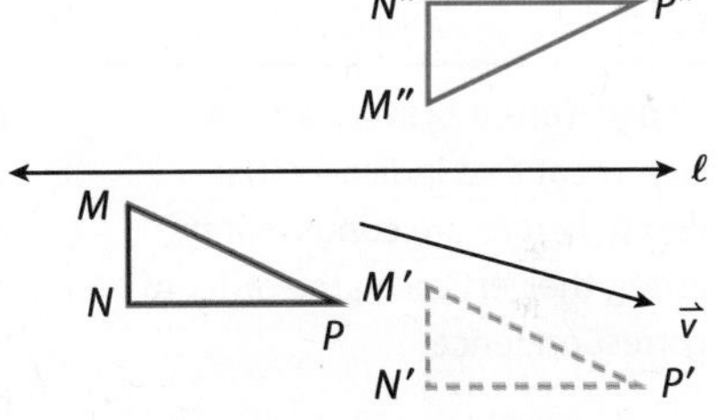
compound event An event made up of two or more simple events.	**suceso compuesto** Suceso formado por dos o más sucesos simples.	In the experiment of tossing a coin and rolling a number cube, the event of the coin landing heads and the number cube landing on 3.
concave polygon A polygon in which a diagonal can be drawn such that part of the diagonal contains points in the exterior of the polygon.	**polígono cóncavo** Polígono en el cual se puede trazar una diagonal tal que parte de la diagonal contiene puntos ubicados fuera del polígono.	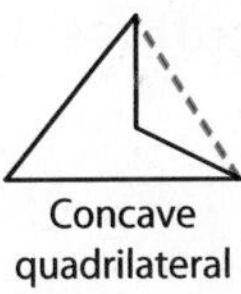 Concave quadrilateral
conclusion The part of a conditional statement following the word *then.*	**conclusión** Parte de un enunciado condicional que sigue a la palabra *entonces*.	If $x + 1 = 5$, then $\underbrace{x = 4}_{\text{Conclusion}}$.
concurrent Three or more lines that intersect at one point.	**concurrente** Tres o más líneas que se cortan en un punto.	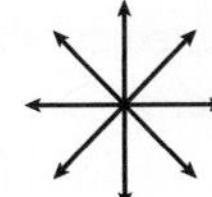
conditional probability The probability of event B, given that event A has already occurred or is certain to occur, denoted $P(B \mid A)$; used to find probability of dependent events.	**probabilidad condicional** Probabilidad del suceso B, dado que el suceso A ya ha ocurrido o es seguro que ocurrirá, expresada como $P(B \mid A)$; se utiliza para calcular la probabilidad de sucesos dependientes.	

Glossary/Glosario

ENGLISH	SPANISH	EXAMPLES
conditional relative frequency The ratio of a joint relative frequency to a related marginal relative frequency in a two-way table.	**frecuencia relativa condicional** Razón de una frecuencia relativa conjunta a una frecuencia relativa marginal en una tabla de doble entrada.	
conditional statement A statement that can be written in the form "if *p*, then *q*," where *p* is the hypothesis and *q* is the conclusion.	**enunciado condicional** Enunciado que se puede expresar como "si *p*, entonces *q*", donde *p* es la hipótesis y *q* es la conclusión.	If $\underbrace{x+1=5}_{\text{Hypothesis}}$, then $\underbrace{x=4}_{\text{Conclusion}}$.
cone A three-dimensional figure with a circular base and a curved lateral surface that connects the base to a point called the vertex.	**cono** Figura tridimensional con una base circular y una superficie lateral curva que conecta la base con un punto denominado vértice.	
congruence statement A statement that indicates that two polygons are congruent by listing the vertices in the order of correspondence.	**enunciado de congruencia** Enunciado que indica que dos polígonos son congruentes enumerando los vértices en orden de correspondencia.	K W H L Y X $\triangle HKL \cong \triangle YWX$
congruence transformation *See* isometry.	**transformación de congruencia** *Ver* isometría.	
congruent Having the same size and shape, denoted by ≅.	**congruente** Que tiene el mismo tamaño y la misma forma, expresado por ≅.	Q R P S $\overline{PQ} \cong \overline{SR}$
congruent polygons Two polygons whose corresponding sides and angles are congruent.	**polígonos congruentes** Dos polígonos cuyos lados y ángulos correspondientes son congruentes.	P Q S R Z W Y X
conjecture A statement that is believed to be true.	**conjetura** Enunciado que se supone verdadero.	A sequence begins with the terms 2, 4, 6, 8, 10. A reasonable conjecture is that the next term in the sequence is 12.
consecutive interior angles *See* same-side interior angles.	**ángulos internos consecutivos** *Ver* ángulos internos del mismo lado.	
contrapositive The statement formed by both exchanging and negating the hypothesis and conclusion of a conditional statement.	**contrarrecíproco** Enunciado que se forma al intercambiar y negar la hipótesis y la conclusión de un enunciado condicional.	Statement: If $n+1=3$, then $n=2$. Contrapositive: If $n \neq 2$, then $n+1 \neq 3$.

ENGLISH	SPANISH	EXAMPLES
converse The statement formed by exchanging the hypothesis and conclusion of a conditional statement.	**recíproco** Enunciado que se forma intercambiando la hipótesis y la conclusión de un enunciado condicional.	Statement: If $n + 1 = 3$, then $n = 2$. Converse: If $n = 2$, then $n + 1 = 3$.
convex polygon A polygon in which no diagonal contains points in the exterior of the polygon.	**polígono convexo** Polígono en el cual ninguna diagonal contiene puntos fuera del polígono.	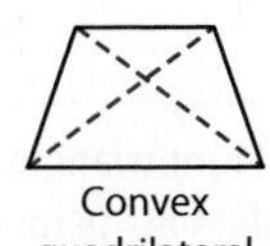 Convex quadrilateral
coordinate A number used to identify the location of a point. On a number line, one coordinate is used. On a coordinate plane, two coordinates are used, called the *x*-coordinate and the *y*-coordinate. In space, three coordinates are used, called the *x*-coordinate, the *y*-coordinate, and the *z*-coordinate.	**coordenada** Número utilizado para identificar la ubicación de un punto. En una recta numérica se utiliza una coordenada. En un plano cartesiano se utilizan dos coordenadas, denominadas coordenada *x* y coordenada *y*. En el espacio se utilizan tres coordenadas, denominadas coordenada *x*, coordenada *y* y coordenada *z*.	 The coordinate of point *A* is 3. 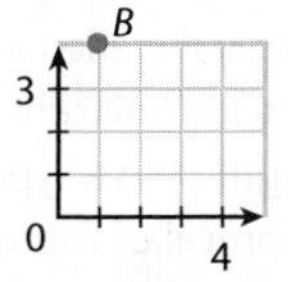 The coordinates of point *B* are (1, 4).
coordinate proof A style of proof that uses coordinate geometry and algebra.	**prueba de coordenadas** Tipo de demostración que utiliza geometría de coordenadas y álgebra.	
coplanar Points that lie in the same plane.	**coplanar** Puntos que se encuentran en el mismo plano.	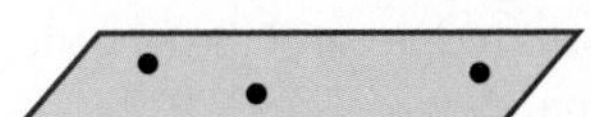
corollary A theorem whose proof follows directly from another theorem.	**corolario** Teorema cuya demostración proviene directamente de otro teorema.	
corresponding angles of lines intersected by a transversal For two lines intersected by a transversal, a pair of angles that lie on the same side of the transversal and on the same sides of the other two lines.	**ángulos correspondientes de líneas cortadas por una transversal** Dadas dos líneas cortadas por una transversal, el par de ángulos ubicados en el mismo lado de la transversal y en los mismos lados de las otras dos líneas.	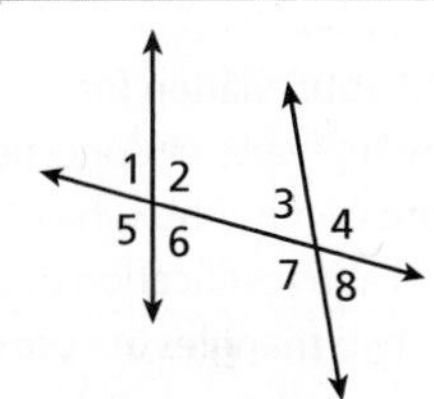 ∠1 and ∠3 are corresponding.
corresponding angles of polygons Angles in the same position in two different polygons that have the same number of angles.	**ángulos correspondientes de los polígonos** Ángulos que tienen la misma posición en dos polígonos diferentes que tienen el mismo número de ángulos.	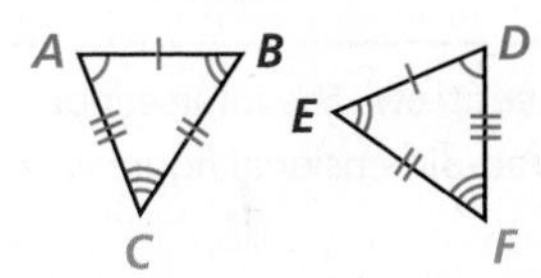 ∠*A* and ∠*D* are corresponding angles.

Glossary/Glosario

ENGLISH	SPANISH	EXAMPLES
corresponding sides of polygons Sides in the same position in two different polygons that have the same number of sides.	**lados correspondientes de los polígonos** Lados que tienen la misma posición en dos polígonos diferentes que tienen el mismo número de lados.	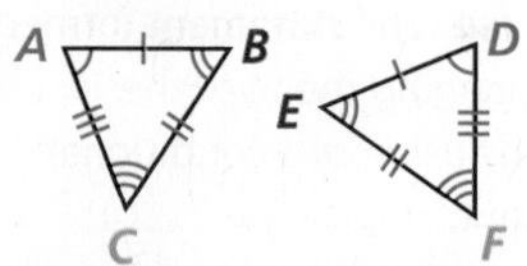 $\overline{AB}$ and $\overline{DE}$ are corresponding sides.
cosecant In a right triangle, the cosecant of angle *A* is the ratio of the length of the hypotenuse to the length of the side opposite *A*. It is the reciprocal of the sine function.	**cosecante** En un triángulo rectángulo, la cosecante del ángulo *A* es la razón entre la longitud de la hipotenusa y la longitud del cateto opuesto a *A*. Es la inversa de la función seno.	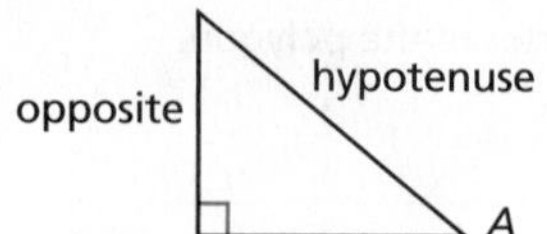 $\csc A = \frac{\text{hypotenuse}}{\text{opposite}} = \frac{1}{\sin A}$
cosine In a right triangle, the cosine of angle *A* is the ratio of the length of the leg adjacent to angle *A* to the length of the hypotenuse. It is the reciprocal of the secant function.	**coseno** En un triángulo rectángulo, el coseno del ángulo *A* es la razón entre la longitud del cateto adyacente al ángulo *A* y la longitud de la hipotenusa. Es la inversa de la función secante.	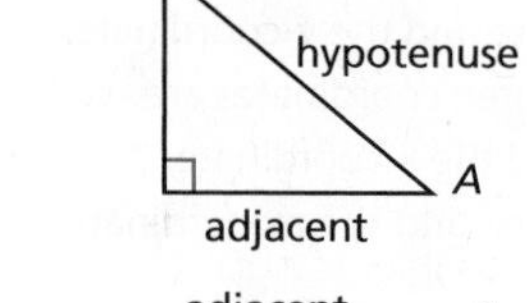 $\cos A = \frac{\text{adjacent}}{\text{hypotenuse}} = \frac{1}{\sec A}$
cotangent In a right triangle, the cotangent of angle A is the ratio of the length of the side adjacent to *A* to the length of the side opposite *A*. It is the reciprocal of the tangent function.	**cotangente** En un triángulo rectángulo, la cotangente del ángulo *A* es la razón entre la longitud del cateto adyacente a *A* y la longitud del cateto opuesto a *A*. Es la inversa de la función tangente.	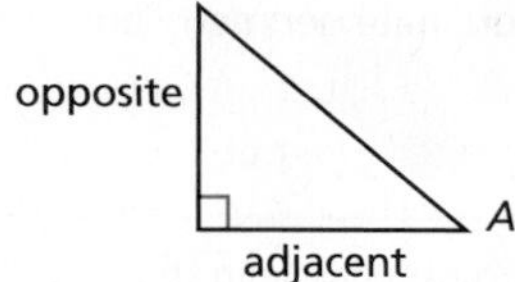 $\cot A = \frac{\text{adjacent}}{\text{opposite}} = \frac{1}{\tan A}$
counterexample An example that proves that a conjecture or statement is false.	**contraejemplo** Ejemplo que demuestra que una conjetura o enunciado es falso.	
CPCTC An abbreviation for "Corresponding Parts of Congruent Triangles are Congruent," which can be used as a justification in a proof after two triangles are proven congruent.	**PCTCC** Abreviatura que significa "Las partes correspondientes de los triángulos congruentes son congruentes", que se puede utilizar para justificar una demostración después de demostrar que dos triángulos son congruentes (CPCTC, por sus siglas en inglés).	
cross section The intersection of a three-dimensional figure and a plane.	**sección transversal** Intersección de una figura tridimensional y un plano.	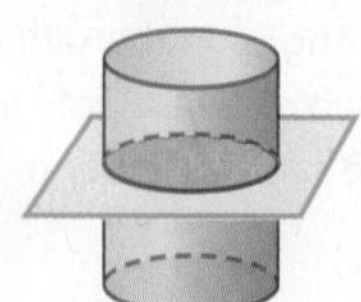

ENGLISH	SPANISH	EXAMPLES
cube A prism with six square faces.	**cubo** Prisma con seis caras cuadradas.	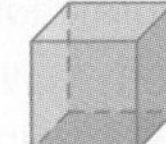
cylinder A three-dimensional figure with two parallel congruent circular bases and a curved lateral surface that connects the bases.	**cilindro** Figura tridimensional con dos bases circulares congruentes y paralelas y una superficie lateral curva que conecta las bases.	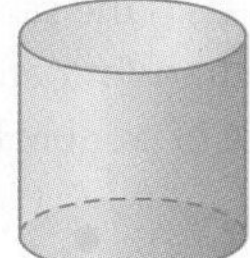

D

ENGLISH	SPANISH	EXAMPLES
decagon A ten-sided polygon.	**decágono** Polígono de diez lados.	
deductive reasoning The process of using logic to draw conclusions.	**razonamiento deductivo** Proceso en el que se utiliza la lógica para sacar conclusiones.	
definition A statement that describes a mathematical object and can be written as a true biconditional statement.	**definición** Enunciado que describe un objeto matemático y se puede expresar como un enunciado bicondicional verdadero.	
degree A unit of angle measure; one degree is $\frac{1}{360}$ of a circle.	**grado** Unidad de medida de los ángulos; un grado es $\frac{1}{360}$ de un círculo.	
density The amount of matter that an object has in a given unit of volume. The density of an object is calculated by dividing its mass by its volume.	**densidad** La cantidad de materia que tiene un objeto en una unidad de volumen determinada. La densidad de un objeto se calcula dividiendo su masa entre su volumen.	$\text{density} = \frac{\text{mass}}{\text{volume}}$
dependent events Events for which the occurrence or nonoccurrence of one event affects the probability of the other event.	**sucesos dependientes** Dos sucesos son dependientes si el hecho de que uno de ellos se cumpla o no afecta la probabilidad del otro.	From a bag containing 3 red marbles and 2 blue marbles, drawing a red marble, and then drawing a blue marble without replacing the first marble.
diagonal of a polygon A segment connecting two nonconsecutive vertices of a polygon.	**diagonal de un polígono** Segmento que conecta dos vértices no consecutivos de un polígono.	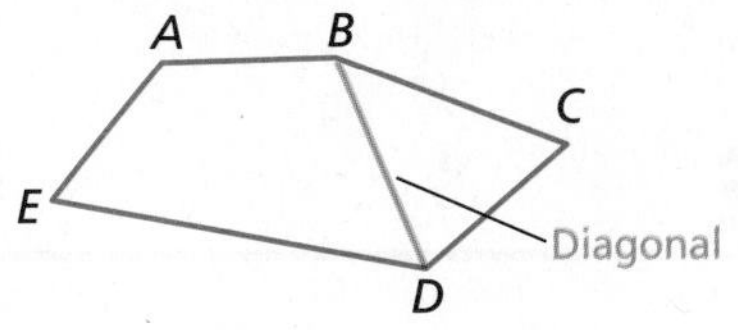
diameter A segment that has endpoints on the circle and that passes through the center of the circle; also the length of that segment.	**diámetro** Segmento que atraviesa el centro de un círculo y cuyos extremos están sobre la circunferencia; longitud de dicho segmento.	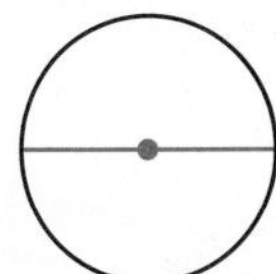

ENGLISH	SPANISH	EXAMPLES
dilation A transformation in which the lines connecting every point *P* with its preimage *P′* all intersect at a point *C* known as the center of dilation, and $\frac{CP'}{CP}$ is the same for every point *P*; a transformation that changes the size of a figure but not its shape.	**dilatación** Transformación en la cual las líneas que conectan cada punto *P* con su imagen original *P′* se cruzan en un punto *C* conocido como centro de dilatación, y $\frac{CP'}{CP}$ es igual para cada punto *P*; transformación que cambia el tamaño de una figura pero no su forma.	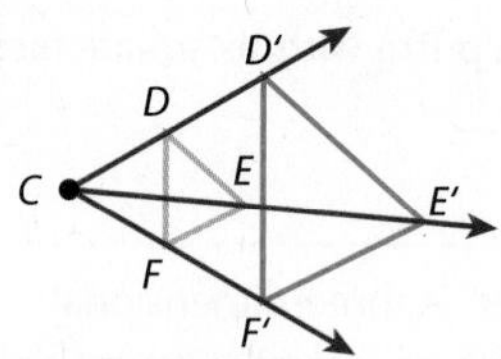
directed line segment A segment between two points *A* and *B* with a specified direction, from *A* to *B* or from *B* to *A*.	**segmento de una línea con dirección** Un segmento entro dos puntos con una dirección especificada.	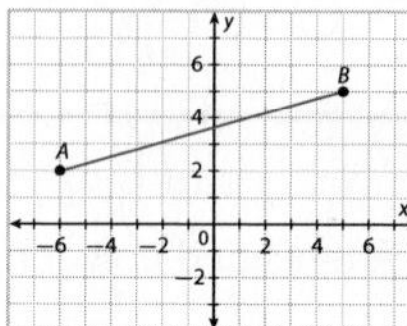
direction of a vector The orientation of a vector, which is determined by the angle the vector makes with a horizontal line.	**dirección de un vector** Orientación de un vector, determinada por el ángulo que forma el vector con una línea horizontal.	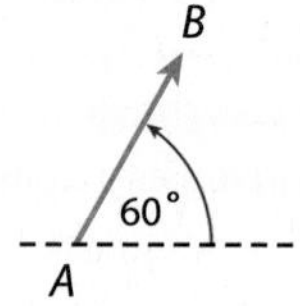
directrix A fixed line used to define a *parabola*. Every point on the parabola is equidistant from the directrix and a fixed point called the *focus*.	**directriz** Línea fija utilizada para definir una *parábola*. Cada punto de la parábola es equidistante de la directriz y de un punto fijo denominado *foco*.	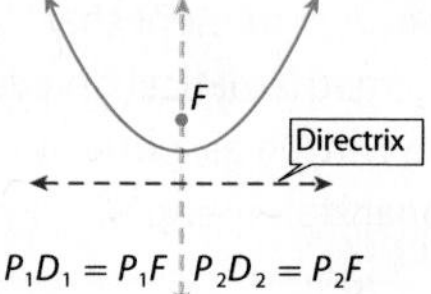
distance between two points The absolute value of the difference of the coordinates of the points.	**distancia entre dos puntos** Valor absoluto de la diferencia entre las coordenadas de los puntos.	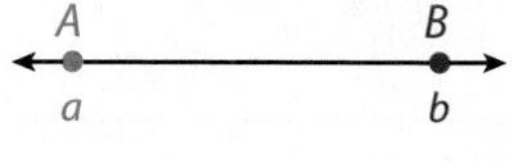 $AB = \lvert a - b \rvert = \lvert b - a \rvert$
distance from a point to a line The length of the perpendicular segment from the point to the line.	**distancia desde un punto hasta una línea** Longitud del segmento perpendicular desde el punto hasta la línea.	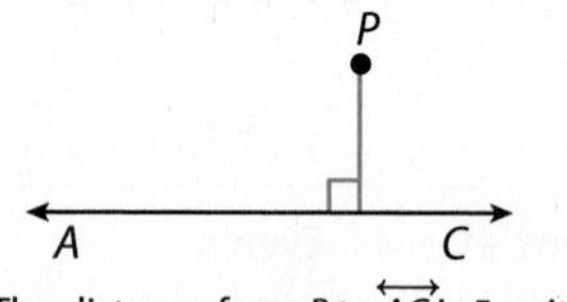 The distance from *P* to $\overleftrightarrow{AC}$ is 5 units.
dodecagon A 12-sided polygon.	**dodecágono** Polígono de 12 lados.	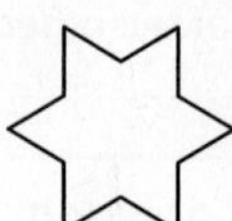

E

element of a set An item in a set.	**elemento de un conjunto** Componente de un conjunto.	4 is an element of the set of even numbers. $4 \in \{\text{even numbers}\}$

Glossary/Glosario

ENGLISH	SPANISH	EXAMPLES
empty set A set with no elements.	**conjunto vacío** Conjunto sin elementos.	The solution set of $\lvert \boldsymbol{x} \rvert < 0$ is the empty set, $\{\,\}$, or $\varnothing$.
endpoint A point at an end of a segment or the starting point of a ray.	**extremo** Punto en el final de un segmento o punto de inicio de un rayo.	A B D
enlargement A dilation with a scale factor greater than 1. In an enlargement, the image is larger than the preimage.	**agrandamiento** Dilatación con un factor de escala mayor que 1. En un agrandamiento, la imagen es más grande que la imagen original.	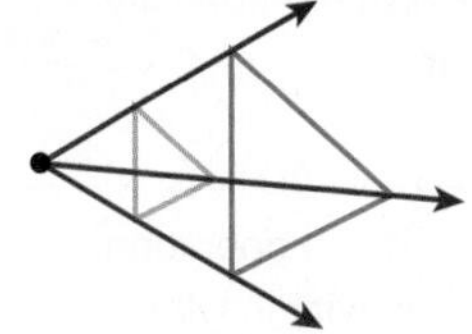
equally likely outcomes Outcomes are equally likely if they have the same probability of occurring. If an experiment has n equally likely outcomes, then the probability of each outcome is $\frac{1}{n}$.	**resultados igualmente probables** Los resultados son igualmente probables si tienen la misma probabilidad de ocurrir. Si un experimento tiene n resultados igualmente probables, entonces la probabilidad de cada resultado es $\frac{1}{n}$.	If a coin is tossed, and heads and tails are equally likely, then $P(\text{heads}) = P(\text{tails}) = \frac{1}{2}$.
equiangular polygon A polygon in which all angles are congruent.	**polígono equiangular** Polígono cuyos ángulos son todos congruentes.	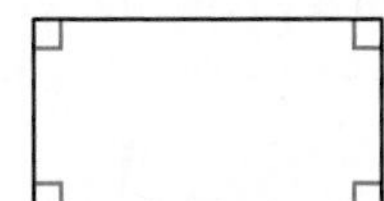
equiangular triangle A triangle with three congruent angles.	**triángulo equiangular** Triángulo con tres ángulos congruentes.	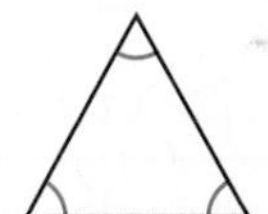
equidistant The same distance from two or more objects.	**equidistante** Igual distancia de dos o más objetos.	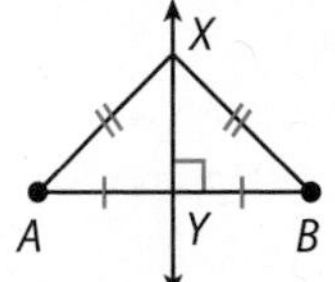 X is equidistant from A and B.
equilateral polygon A polygon in which all sides are congruent.	**polígono equilátero** Polígono cuyos lados son todos congruentes.	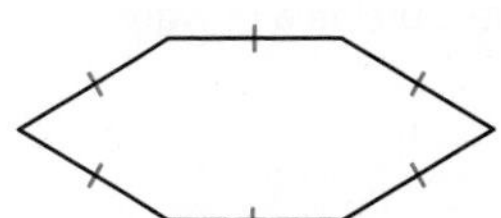
equilateral triangle A triangle with three congruent sides.	**triángulo equilátero** Triángulo con tres lados congruentes.	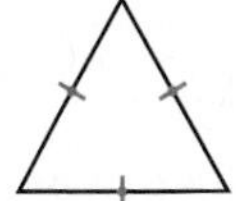

ENGLISH	SPANISH	EXAMPLES
Euclidean geometry The system of geometry described by Euclid. In particular, the system of Euclidean geometry satisfies the Parallel Postulate, which states that there is exactly one line through a given point parallel to a given line.	**geometría euclidiana** Sistema geométrico desarrollado por Euclides. Específicamente, el sistema de la geometría euclidiana cumple con el postulado de las paralelas, que establece que por un punto dado se puede trazar una única línea paralela a una línea dada.	
event An outcome or set of outcomes in a probability experiment.	**suceso** Resultado o conjunto de resultados en un experimento de probabilidad.	In the experiement of rolling a number cube, the event "an odd number" consists of the outcomes 1, 3, 5.
experiment An operation, process, or activity in which outcomes can be used to estimate probability.	**experimento** Una operación, proceso o actividad en la que se usan los resultados para estimar una probabilidad.	Tossing a coin 10 times and noting the number of heads.
experimental probability The ratio of the number of times an event occurs to the number of trials, or times, that an activity is performed.	**probabilidad experimental** Razón entre la cantidad de veces que ocurre un suceso y la cantidad de pruebas, o veces, que se realiza una actividad.	Kendra made 6 of 10 free throws. The experimental probability that she will make her next free throw is $P\left(\text{free throw}\right) = \frac{\text{number made}}{\text{number attempted}} = \frac{6}{10}$.
exterior of a circle The set of all points outside a circle.	**exterior de un círculo** Conjunto de todos los puntos que se encuentran fuera de un círculo.	Exterior
exterior of an angle The set of all points outside an angle.	**exterior de un ángulo** Conjunto de todos los puntos que se encuentran fuera de un ángulo.	Exterior
exterior of a polygon The set of all points outside a polygon.	**exterior de un polígono** Conjunto de todos los puntos que se encuentran fuera de un polígono.	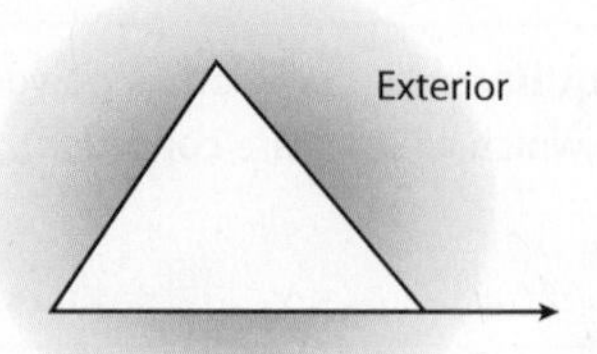
exterior angle of a polygon An angle formed by one side of a polygon and the extension of an adjacent side.	**ángulo externo de un polígono** Ángulo formado por un lado de un polígono y la prolongación del lado adyacente.	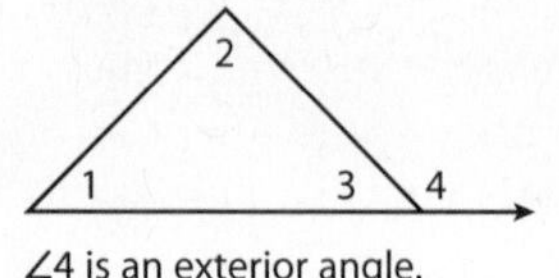 $\angle 4$ is an exterior angle.

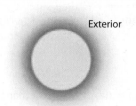

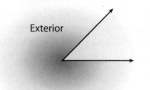

ENGLISH	SPANISH	EXAMPLES
external secant segment A segment of a secant that lies in the exterior of the circle with one endpoint on the circle.	**segmento secante externo** Segmento de una secante que se encuentra en el exterior del círculo y tiene un extremo sobre el círculo.	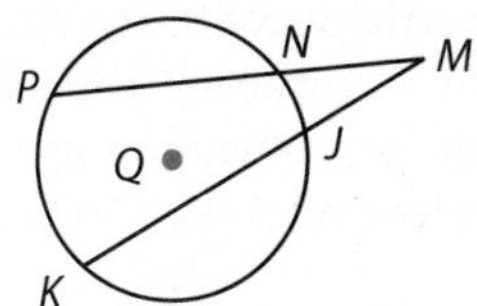 $\overline{NM}$ is an external secant segment.

F

factorial If n is a positive integer, then n factorial, written $n!$, is $n \cdot (n-1) \cdot (n-2) \cdot \ldots \cdot 2 \cdot 1$. The factorial of 0 is defined to be 1.	**factorial** Si n es un entero positivo, entonces el factorial de n, expresado como $n!$, es $n \cdot (n-1) \cdot (n-2) \cdot \ldots \cdot 2 \cdot 1$. Por definición, el factorial de 0 será 1.	$7! = 7 \cdot 6 \cdot 5 \cdot 4 \cdot 3 \cdot 2 \cdot 1 = 5040$ $0! = 1$
fair When all outcomes of an experiment are equally likely.	**justo** Cuando todos los resultados de un experimento son igualmente probables.	When tossing a fair coin, heads and tails are equally likely. Each has a probability of $\frac{1}{2}$.
favorable outcome The occurrence of one of several possible outcomes of a specified event or probability experiment.	**resultado favorable** Cuando se produce uno de varios resultados posibles de un suceso específico o experimento de probabilidad.	In the experiment of rolling an odd number on a number cube, the favorable outcomes are 1, 3, and 5.
focus (pl. foci) of a parabola A fixed point F used with a *directrix* to define a *parabola*.	**foco de una parábola** Punto fijo F utilizado con una *directriz* para definir una *parábola*.	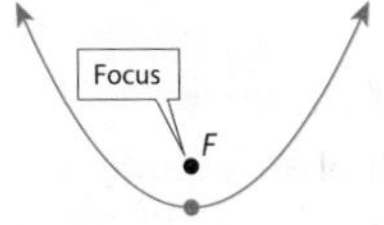
Fundamental Counting Principle For n items, if there are m_1 ways to choose a first item, m_2 ways to choose a second item after the first item has been chosen, and so on, then there are $m_1 \cdot m_2 \cdot \ldots \cdot m_n$ ways to choose n items.	**Principio fundamental deconteo** Dados n elementos, si existen m_1 formas de elegir un primer elemento, m_2 formas de elegir un segundo elemento después de haber elegido el primero, y así sucesivamente, entonces existen $m_1 \cdot m_2 \cdot \ldots \cdot m_n$ formas de elegir n elementos.	If there are 4 colors of shirts, 3 colors of pants, and 2 colors of shoes, then there are $4 \cdot 3 \cdot 2 = 24$ possible outfits.

G

geometric mean For positive numbers a and b, the positive number x such that $\frac{a}{x} = \frac{x}{b}$. In a geometric sequence, a term that comes between two given nonconsecutive terms of the sequence.	**media geométrica** Dados los números positivos a y b, el número positivo x tal que $\frac{a}{x} = \frac{x}{b}$. En una sucesión geométrica, un término que está entre dos términos no consecutivos dados de la sucesión.	$\frac{a}{x} = \frac{x}{b}$ $x^2 = ab$ $x = \sqrt{ab}$

ENGLISH	SPANISH	EXAMPLES
geometric probability A form of theoretical probability determined by a ratio of geometric measures such as lengths, areas, or volumes.	**probabilidad geométrica** Una forma de la probabilidad teórica determinada por una razón de medidas geométricas, como longitud, área o volumen.	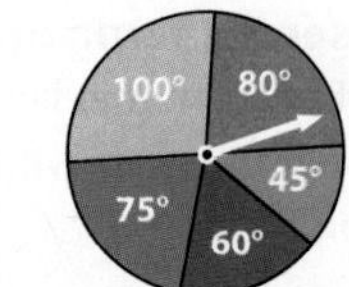 The probability of the pointer landing on 80° is $\frac{2}{9}$.
glide reflection A composition of a translation and a reflection across a line parallel to the translation vector.	**deslizamiento con inversión** Composición de una traslación y una reflexión sobre una línea paralela al vector de traslación.	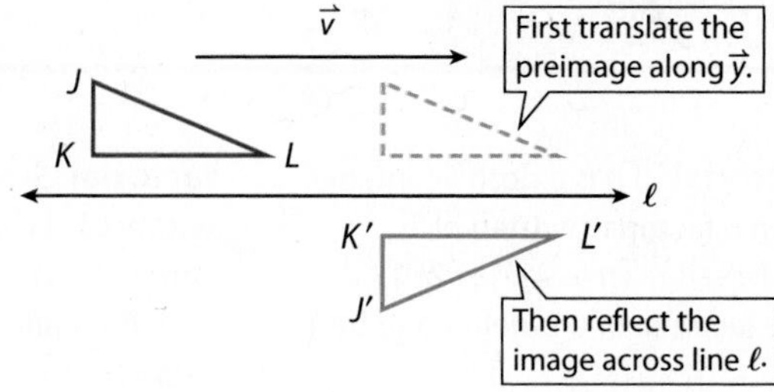
great circle A circle on a sphere that divides the sphere into two hemispheres.	**círculo máximo** En una esfera, círculo que divide la esfera en dos hemisferios.	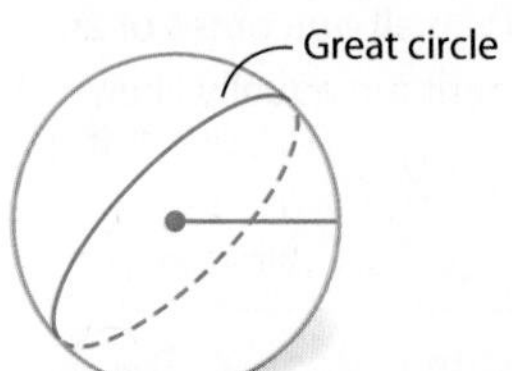

H

height of a figure The length of an altitude of the figure.	**altura de una figura** Longitud de la altura de la figura.	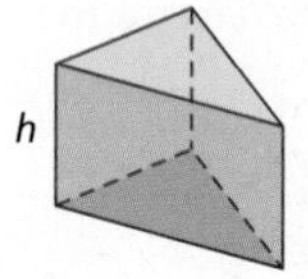 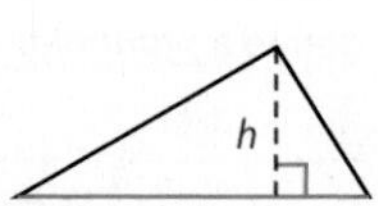
hemisphere Half of a sphere.	**hemisferio** Mitad de una esfera.	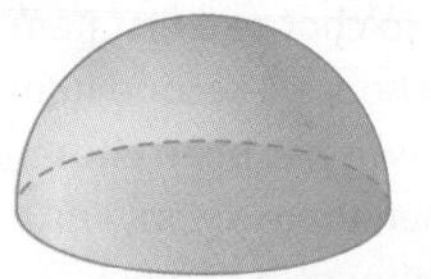
heptagon A seven-sided polygon.	**heptágono** Polígono de siete lados.	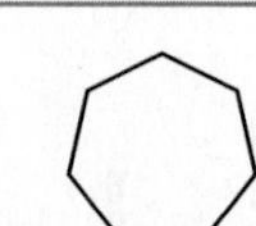
hexagon A six-sided polygon.	**hexágono** Polígono de seis lados.	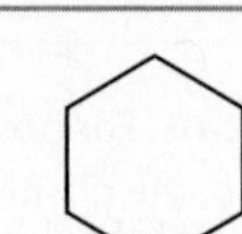
hypotenuse The side opposite the right angle in a right triangle.	**hipotenusa** Lado opuesto al ángulo recto de un triángulo rectángulo.	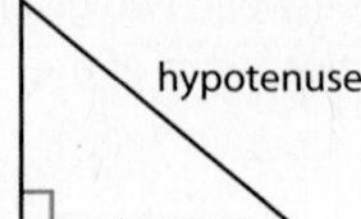

ENGLISH	SPANISH	EXAMPLES
hypothesis The part of a conditional statement following the word *if*.	**hipótesis** La parte de un enunciado condicional que sigue a la palabra *si*.	If $x + 1 = 5$, then $x = 4$. Hypothesis

I

ENGLISH	SPANISH	EXAMPLES
identity An equation that is true for all values of the variables.	**identidad** Ecuación verdadera para todos los valores de las variables.	$3 = 3$ $2(x - 1) = 2x - 2$
image A shape that results from a transformation of a figure known as the preimage.	**imagen** Forma resultante de la transformación de una figura conocida como imagen original.	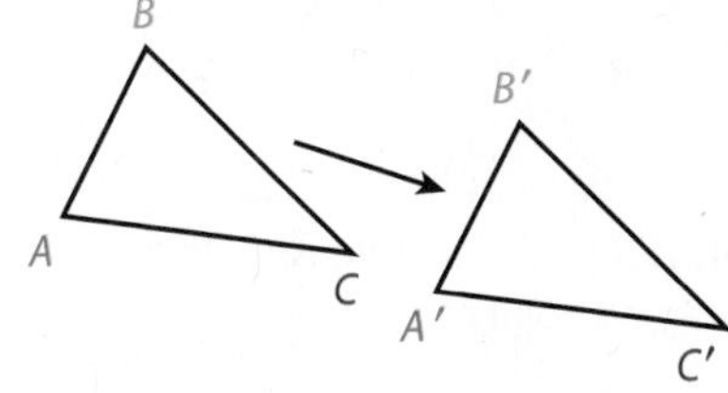
incenter of a triangle The point of concurrency of the three angle bisectors of a triangle.	**incentro de un triángulo** Punto donde se encuentran las tres bisectrices de los ángulos de un triángulo.	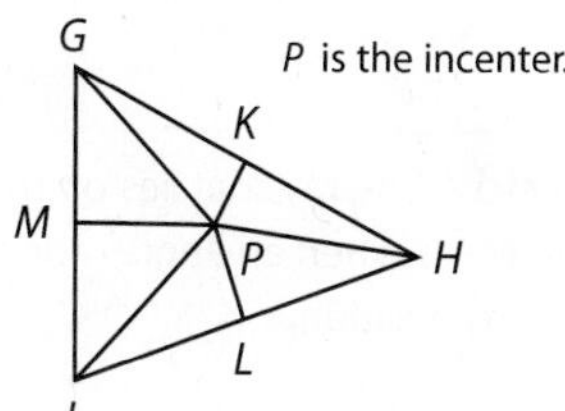P is the incenter.
incircle *See* inscribed circle.	**incírculo** *Véase* círculo inscrito.	
included angle The angle formed by two adjacent sides of a polygon.	**ángulo incluido** Ángulo formado por dos lados adyacentes de un polígono.	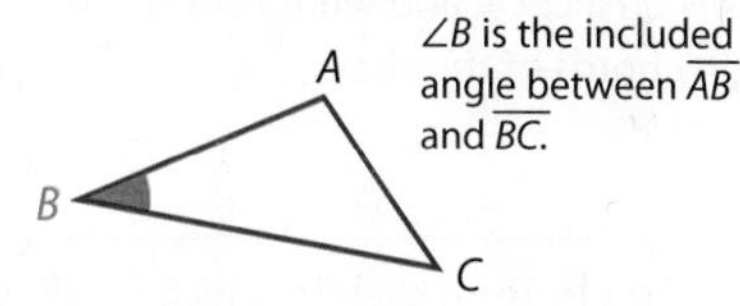$\angle B$ is the included angle between $\overline{AB}$ and $\overline{BC}$.
included side The common side of two consecutive angles of a polygon.	**lado incluido** Lado común de dos ángulos consecutivos de un polígono.	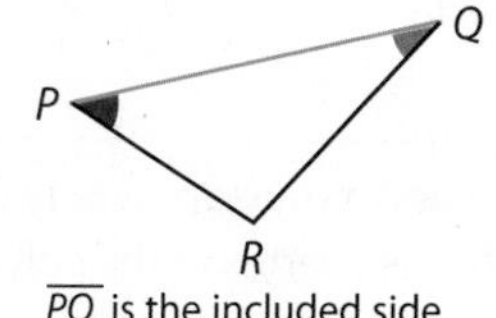$\overline{PQ}$ is the included side between $\angle P$ and $\angle Q$.
independent events Events for which the occurrence or nonoccurrence of one event does not affect the probability of the other event.	**sucesos independientes** Dos sucesos son independientes si el hecho de que se produzca o no uno de ellos no afecta la probabilidad del otro suceso.	From a bag containing 3 red marbles and 2 blue marbles, drawing a red marble, replacing it, and then drawing a blue marble.
indirect measurement A method of measurement that uses formulas, similar figures, and/or proportions.	**medición indirecta** Método para medir objetos mediante fórmulas, figuras semejantes y/o proporciones.	

ENGLISH	SPANISH	EXAMPLES
indirect proof A proof in which the statement to be proved is assumed to be false and a contradiction is shown.	**demostración indirecta** Prueba en la que se supone que el enunciado a demostrar es falso y se muestra una contradicción.	
indirect reasoning *See* indirect proof.	**razonamiento indirecto** *Ver* demostración indirecta.	
inductive reasoning The process of reasoning that a rule or statement is true because specific cases are true.	**razonamiento inductivo** Proceso de razonamiento por el que se determina que una regla o enunciado son verdaderos porque ciertos casos específicos son verdaderos.	
initial point of a vector The starting point of a vector.	**punto inicial de un vector** Punto donde comienza un vector.	A, B, $\vec{v}$, Initial point
initial side The ray that lies on the positive *x*-axis when an angle is drawn in standard position.	**lado inicial** Rayo que se encuentra sobre el eje *x* positivo cuando se traza un ángulo en posición estándar.	y, x, 135°, 45°, 0, Initial side
inscribed angle An angle whose vertex is on a circle and whose sides contain chords of the circle.	**ángulo inscrito** Ángulo cuyo vértice se encuentra sobre un círculo y cuyos lados contienen cuerdas del círculo.	D, E, F
inscribed circle A circle in which each side of the polygon is tangent to the circle.	**círculo inscrito** Círculo en el que cada lado del polígono es tangente al círculo.	
inscribed polygon A polygon in which every vertex of the polygon lies on the circle.	**polígono inscrito** Polígono cuyos vértices se encuentran sobre el círculo.	
intercepted arc An arc that consists of endpoints that lie on the sides of an inscribed angle and all the points of the circle between the endpoints.	**arco abarcado** Arco cuyos extremos se encuentran en los lados de un ángulo inscrito y consta de todos los puntos del círculo ubicados entre dichos extremos.	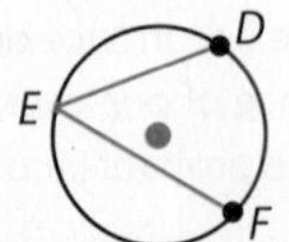 $\overset{\frown}{DF}$ is the intercepted arc.

ENGLISH	SPANISH	EXAMPLES
interior angle An angle formed by two sides of a polygon with a common vertex.	**ángulo interno** Ángulo formado por dos lados de un polígono con un vértice común.	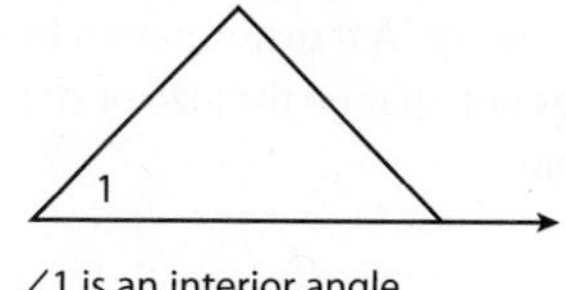 $\angle 1$ is an interior angle.
interior of a circle The set of all points inside a circle.	**interior de un círculo** Conjunto de todos los puntos que se encuentran dentro de un círculo.	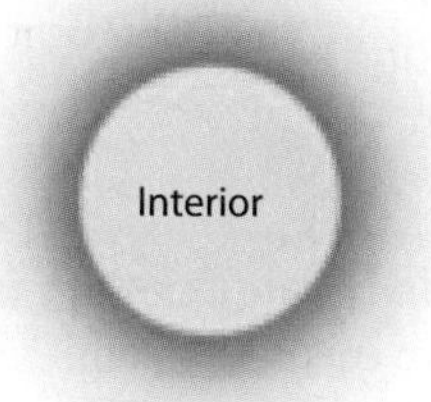
interior of an angle The set of all points between the sides of an angle.	**interior de un ángulo** Conjunto de todos los puntos entre los lados de un ángulo.	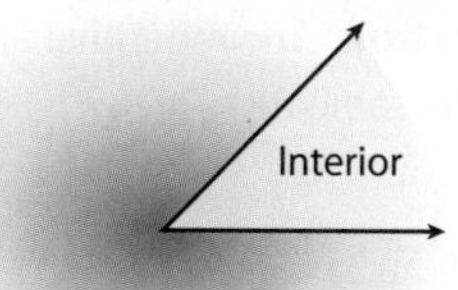
interior of a polygon The set of all points inside a polygon.	**interior de un polígono** Conjunto de todos los puntos que se encuentran dentro de un polígono.	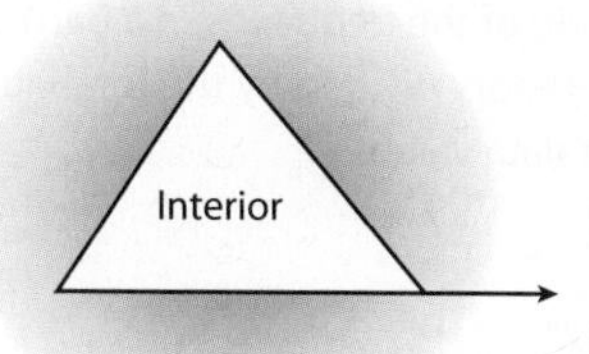
inverse The statement formed by negating the hypothesis and conclusion of a conditional statement.	**inverso** Enunciado formado al negar la hipótesis y la conclusión de un enunciado condicional.	Statement: If $n + 1 = 3$, then $n = 2$. Inverse: If $n + 1 \neq 3$, then $n \neq 2$.
inverse cosine The measure of an angle whose cosine ratio is known.	**coseno inverso** Medida de un ángulo cuya razón coseno es conocida.	If $\cos A = x$, then $\cos^{-1} x = m\angle A$.
inverse sine The measure of an angle whose sine ratio is known.	**seno inverso** Medida de un ángulo cuya razón seno es conocida.	If $\sin A = x$, then $\sin^{-1} x = m\angle A$.
inverse tangent The measure of an angle whose tangent ratio is known.	**tangente inversa** Medida de un ángulo cuya razón tangente es conocida.	If $\tan A = x$, then $\tan^{-1} x = m\angle A$.
irregular polygon A polygon that is not regular.	**polígono irregular** Polígono que no es regular.	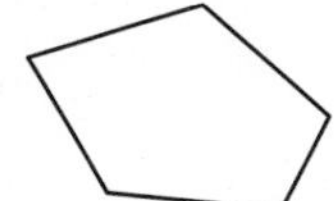

ENGLISH	SPANISH	EXAMPLES
isometry A transformation that does not change the size or shape of a figure.	**isometría** Transformación que no cambia el tamaño ni la forma de una figura.	Reflections, translations, and rotations are all examples of isometries.
isosceles trapezoid A trapezoid in which the legs are congruent but not parallel.	**trapecio isósceles** Trapecio cuyos lados no paralelos son congruentes.	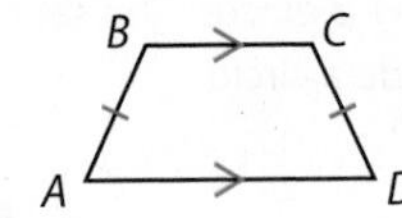
isosceles triangle A triangle with at least two congruent sides.	**triángulo isósceles** Triángulo que tiene al menos dos lados congruentes.	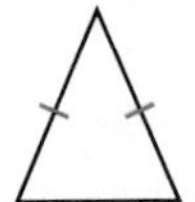
iteration The repetitive application of the same rule.	**iteración** Aplicación repetitiva de la misma regla.v	  

J

ENGLISH	SPANISH	EXAMPLES
joint relative frequency The ratio of the frequency in a particular category divided by the total number of data values.	**frecuencia relativa conjunta** La razón de la frecuencia en una determinada categoría dividida entre el número total de valores.	

ENGLISH	SPANISH	EXAMPLES
kite A quadrilateral with exactly two pairs of congruent consecutive sides.	**cometa o papalote** Cuadrilátero con exactamente dos pares de lados congruentes consecutivos.	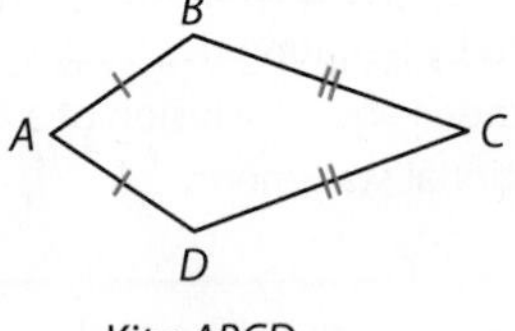 Kite *ABCD*

L

ENGLISH	SPANISH	EXAMPLES
lateral area The sum of the areas of the lateral faces of a prism or pyramid, or the area of the lateral surface of a cylinder or cone.	**área lateral** Suma de las áreas de las caras laterales de un prisma o pirámide, o área de la superficie lateral de un cilindro o cono.	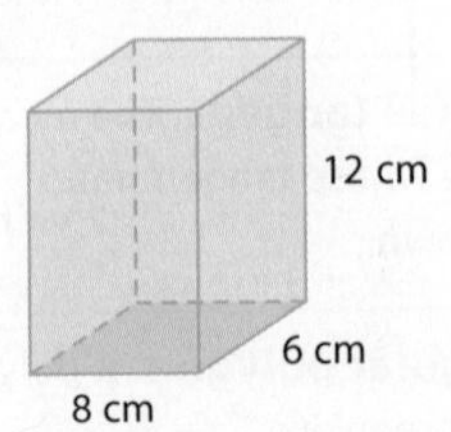 Lateral area $= 4(6)(12) = 288\text{mc}^2$

ENGLISH	SPANISH	EXAMPLES
lateral edge An edge of a prism or pyramid that is not an edge of a base.	**arista lateral** Arista de un prisma o pirámide que no es la arista de una base.	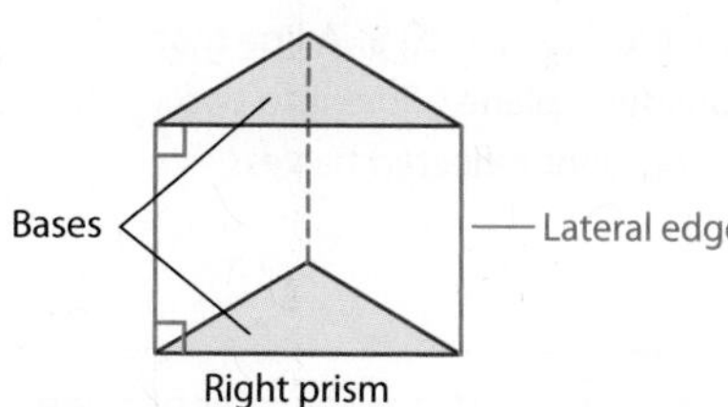
lateral face A face of a prism or a pyramid that is not a base.	**cara lateral** Cara de un prisma o pirámide que no es la base.	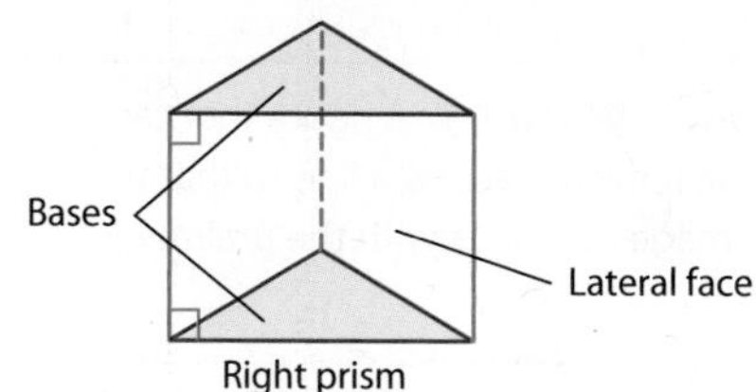
lateral surface The curved surface of a cylinder or cone.	**superficie lateral** Superficie curva de un cilindro o cono.	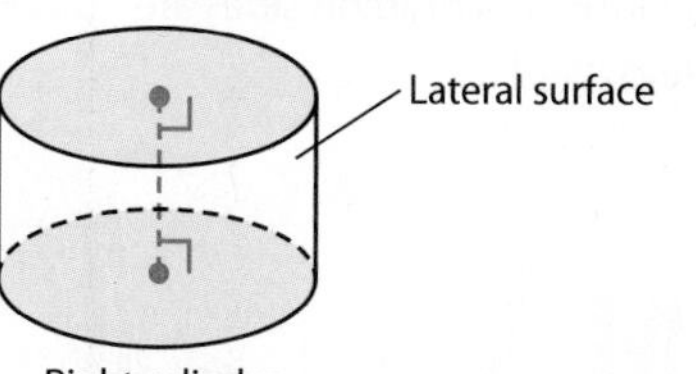
leg of a right triangle One of the two sides of the right triangle that form the right angle.	**cateto de un triángulo rectángulo** Uno de los dos lados de un triángulo rectángulo que forman el ángulo recto.	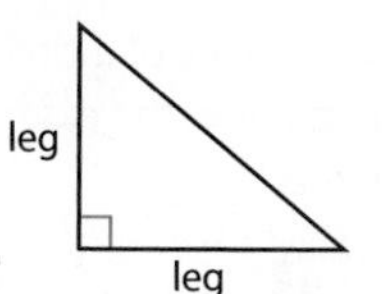
leg of an isosceles triangle One of the two congruent sides of the isosceles triangle.	**cateto de un triángulo isósceles** Uno de los dos lados congruentes del triángulo isósceles.	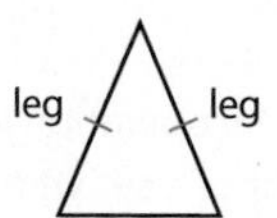
legs of a trapezoid The sides of the trapezoid that are not the bases.	**catetos de un trapecio** Los lados del trapecio que no son las bases.	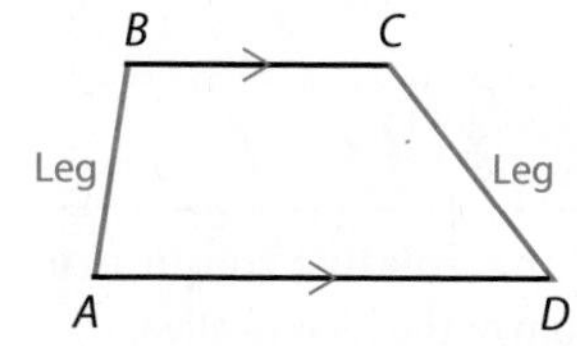
length The distance between the two endpoints of a segment.	**longitud** Distancia entre los dos extremos de un segmento.	A B a b $AB = \|a - b\| = \|b - a\|$
line An undefined term in geometry, a line is a straight path that has no thickness and extends forever.	**línea** Término indefinido en geometría; una línea es un trazo recto que no tiene grosor y se extiende infinitamente.	

ENGLISH	SPANISH	EXAMPLES
line of symmetry A line that divides a plane figure into two congruent reflected halves.	**eje de simetría** Línea que divide una figura plana en dos mitades reflejas congruentes.	
line segment *See* segment of a line.	**segmento** *Véase* segmento de recta.	
line symmetry A figure that can be reflected across a line so that the image coincides with the preimage.	**simetría axial** Figura que puede reflejarse sobre una línea de forma tal que la imagen coincida con la imagen original.	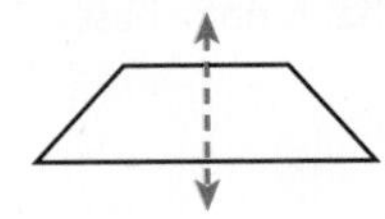
linear pair A pair of adjacent angles whose noncommon sides are opposite rays.	**par lineal** Par de ángulos adyacentes cuyos lados no comunes son rayos opuestos.	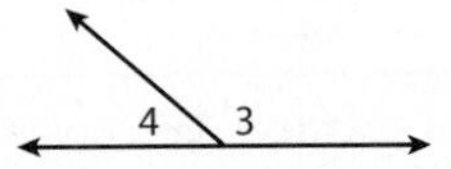 ∠3 and ∠4 form a linear pair.

M

ENGLISH	SPANISH	EXAMPLES
major arc An arc of a circle whose points are on or in the exterior of a central angle.	**arco mayor** Arco de un círculo cuyos puntos están sobre un ángulo central o en su exterior.	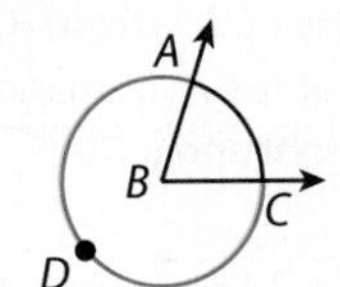 $\overset{\frown}{ADC}$ is a major arc of the circle.
mapping An operation that matches each element of a set with another element, its image, in the same set.	**correspondencia** Operación que establece una correlación entre cada elemento de un conjunto con otro elemento, su imagen, en el mismo conjunto.	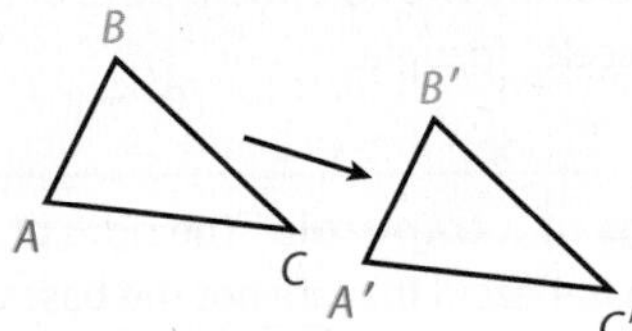
marginal relative frequency The sum of the joint relative frequencies in a row or column of a two-way table.	**frecuencia relativa marginal** La suma de las frecuencias relativas conjuntas en una fila o columna de una tabla de doble entrada.	
measure of an angle Angles are measured in degrees. A degree is $\frac{1}{360}$ of a complete circle.	**medida de un ángulo** Los ángulos se miden en grados. Un grado es $\frac{1}{360}$ de un círculo completo.	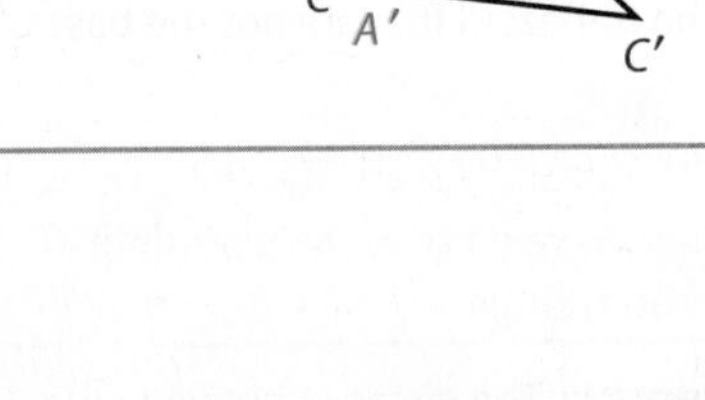 $m\angle M = 26.8°$

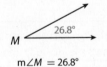

ENGLISH	SPANISH	EXAMPLES
measure of a major arc The difference of 360° and the measure of the associated minor arc.	**medida de un arco mayor** Diferencia entre 360° y la medida del arco menor asociado.	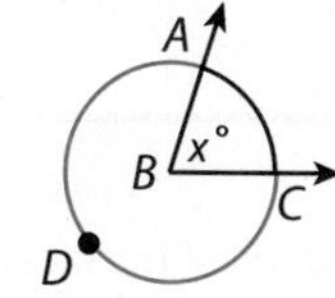 $m\widehat{ADC} = 360° - x°$
measure of a minor arc The measure of its central angle.	**medida de un arco menor** Medida de su ángulo central.	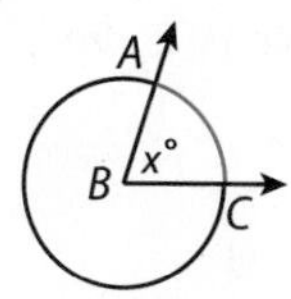 $m\widehat{AC} = x°$
median of a triangle A segment whose endpoints are a vertex of the triangle and the midpoint of the opposite side.	**mediana de un triángulo** Segmento cuyos extremos son un vértice del triángulo y el punto medio del lado opuesto.	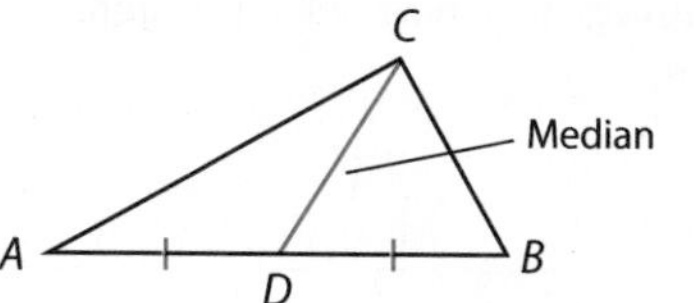
midpoint The point that divides a segment into two congruent segments.	**punto medio** Punto que divide un segmento en dos segmentos congruentes.	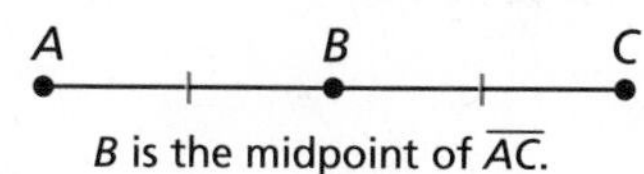 B is the midpoint of $\overline{AC}$.
midsegment of a trapezoid The segment whose endpoints are the midpoints of the legs of the trapezoid.	**segmento medio de un trapecio** Segmento cuyos extremos son los puntos medios de los catetos del trapecio.	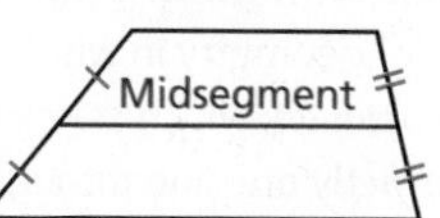
midsegment of a triangle A segment that joins the midpoints of two sides of the triangle.	**segmento medio de un triángulo** Segmento que une los puntos medios de dos lados del triángulo.	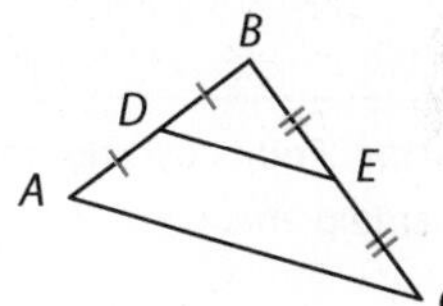
minor arc An arc of a circle whose points are on or in the interior of a central angle.	**arco menor** Arco de un círculo cuyos puntos están sobre un ángulo central o en su interior.	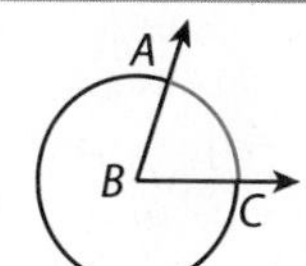 $\widehat{AC}$ is a minor arc of the circle.
mutually exclusive events Two events are mutually exclusive if they cannot both occur in the same trial of an experiment.	**sucesos mutuamente excluyentes** Dos sucesos son mutuamente excluyentes si ambos no pueden ocurrir en la misma prueba de un experimento.	In the experiment of rolling a number cube, rolling a 3 and rolling an even number are mutually exclusive events.

Glossary/Glosario

ENGLISH	SPANISH	EXAMPLES

N

net A diagram of the faces of a three-dimensional figure arranged in such a way that the diagram can be folded to form the three-dimensional figure.

plantilla Diagrama de las caras de una figura tridimensional que se puede plegar para formar la figura tridimensional.

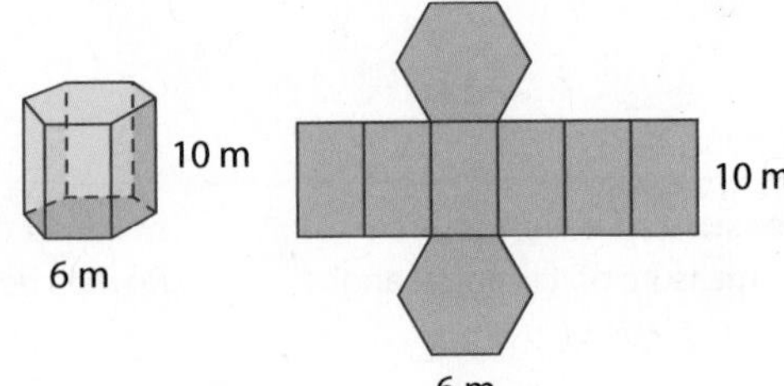

***n*-gon** An *n*-sided polygon.

***n*-ágono** Polígono de *n* lados.

nonagon A nine-sided polygon.

nonágono Polígono de nueve lados.

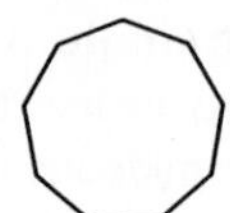

noncollinear Points that do not lie on the same line.

no colineal Puntos que no se encuentran sobre la misma línea.

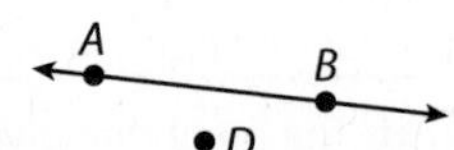

Points *A*,*B*, and *D* are not collinear.

non-Euclidean geometry A system of geometry in which the Parallel Postulate, which states that there is exactly one line through a given point parallel to a given line, does not hold.

geometría no euclidiana Sistema de geometría en el cual no se cumple el postulado de las paralelas, que establece que por un punto dado se puede trazar una única línea paralela a una línea dada.

In spherical geometry, there are no parallel lines. The sum of the angles in a triangle is always greater than 180°.

noncoplanar Points that do not lie on the same plane.

no coplanar Puntos que no se encuentran en el mismo plano.

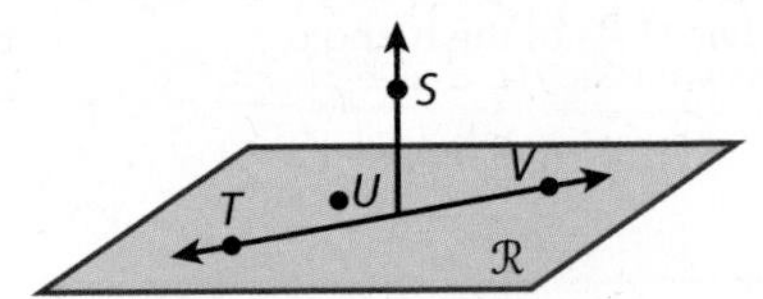

T, *U*, *V*, and *S* are not coplanar.

O

oblique cone A cone whose axis is not perpendicular to the base.

cono oblicuo Cono cuyo eje no es perpendicular a la base.

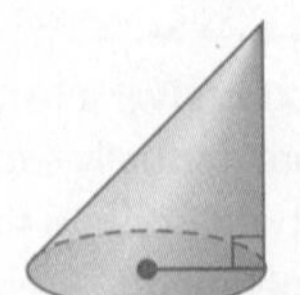

oblique cylinder A cylinder whose axis is not perpendicular to the bases.

cilindro oblicuo Cilindro cuyo eje no es perpendicular a las bases.

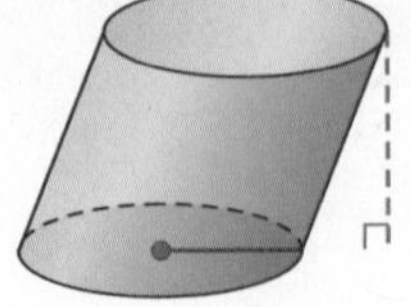

ENGLISH	SPANISH	EXAMPLES
oblique prism A prism that has at least one nonrectangular lateral face.	**prisma oblicuo** Prisma que tiene por lo menos una cara lateral no rectangular.	
obtuse angle An angle that measures greater than 90° and less than 180°.	**ángulo obtuso** Ángulo que mide más de 90° y menos de 180°.	
obtuse triangle A triangle with one obtuse angle.	**triángulo obtusángulo** Triángulo con un ángulo obtuso.	
octagon An eight-sided polygon.	**octágono** Polígono de ocho lados.	
opposite rays Two rays that have a common endpoint and form a line.	**rayos opuestos** Dos rayos que tienen un extremo común y forman una línea.	F E G $\overrightarrow{EF}$ and $\overrightarrow{EG}$ are opposite rays.
order of rotational symmetry The number of times a figure with rotational symmetry coincides with itself as it rotates 360°.	**orden de simetría de rotación** Cantidad de veces que una figura con simetría de rotación coincide consigo misma cuando rota 360°.	90° 90° 90° 90° Order of rotational symmetry: 4
orthocenter of a triangle The point of concurrency of the three altitudes of a triangle.	**ortocentro de un triángulo** Punto de intersección de las tres alturas de un triángulo.	*P* is the orthocenter. *P*
outcome A possible result of a probability experiment.	**resultado** Resultado posible de un experimento de probabilidad.	In the experiment of rolling a number cube, the possible outcomes are 1, 2, 3, 4, 5, and 6.
overlapping events Events that have one or more outcomes in common. Also called inclusive events.	**sucesos superpuestos** Sucesos que tienen uno o más resultados en común. También se denominan sucesos inclusivos.	Rolling an even number and rolling a prime number on a number cube are overlapping events because they both contain the outcome rolling a 2.

ENGLISH	SPANISH	EXAMPLES

P

parabola The shape of the graph of a quadratic function. Also, the set of points equidistant from a point F, called the focus, and a line d, called the *directrix*.

parábola Forma de la gráfica de una función cuadrática. También, conjunto de puntos equidistantes de un punto F, denominado *foco*, y una línea d, denominada *directriz*.

Focus
Directrix

parallel lines Lines in the same plane that do not intersect.

líneas paralelas Líneas rectas en el mismo plano que no se cruzan.

$r \parallel s$

parallel planes Planes that do not intersect.

planos paralelos Planos que no se cruzan.

Plane AEF and plane CGH are parallel planes.

parallelogram A quadrilateral with two pairs of parallel sides.

paralelogramo Cuadrilátero con dos pares de lados paralelos.

pentagon A five-sided polygon.

diagrama Polígono de cinco lados.

perimeter The sum of the side lengths of a closed plane figure.

perímetro Suma de las longitudes de los lados de una figura plana cerrada.

18 ft
6ft

Perimeter $= 18 + 6 + 18 + 6 = 48$ ft

permutation An arrangement of a group of objects in which order is important. The number of permutations of r objects from a group of n objects is denoted ${}_nP_r$.

permutación Arreglo de un grupo de objetos en el cual el orden es importante. El número de permutaciones de r objetos de un grupo de n objetos se expresa ${}_nP_r$.

For 4 objects A, B, C, and D, there are ${}_4P_2 = 12$ different permutations of 2 objects: AB, AC, AD, BC, BD, CD, BA, CA, DA, CB, DB, and DC.

perpendicular Intersecting to form 90° angles, denoted by $\perp$.

perpendicular Que se cruza para formar ángulos de 90°, expresado por $\perp$.

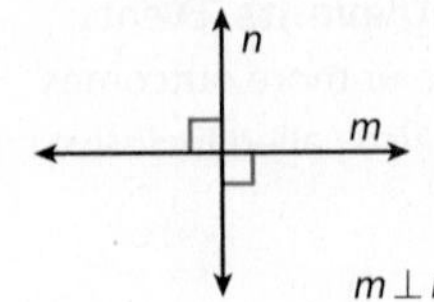

$m \perp n$

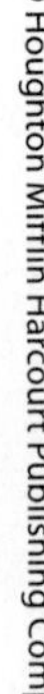

ENGLISH	SPANISH	EXAMPLES
perpendicular bisector of a segment A line perpendicular to a segment at the segment's midpoint.	**mediatriz de un segmento** Línea perpendicular a un segmento en el punto medio del segmento.	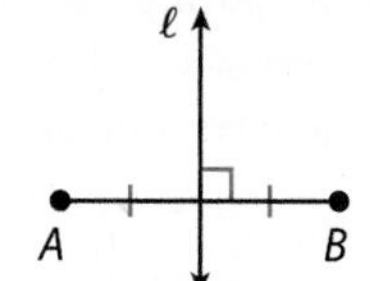 ℓ is the perpendicular bisector of $\overline{AB}$.
perpendicular lines Lines that intersect at 90° angles.	**líneas perpendiculares** Líneas que se cruzan en ángulos de 90°.	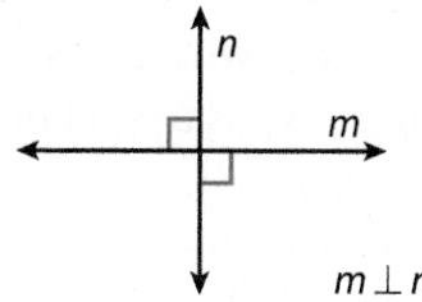
pi The ratio of the circumference of a circle to its diameter, denoted by the Greek letter π (pi). The value of π is irrational, often approximated by 3.14 or $\frac{22}{7}$.	**pi** Razón entre la circunferencia de un círculo y su diámetro, expresado por la letra griega π (pi). El valor de π es irracional y por lo general se aproxima a 3.14 ó $\frac{22}{7}$.	If a circle has a diameter of 5 inches and a circumference of C inches, then $\frac{C}{5} = \pi$, or $C = 5\pi$ inches, or about 15.7 inches.
plane An undefined term in geometry, it is a flat surface that has no thickness and extends forever.	**plano** Término indefinido en geometría; un plano es una superficie plana que no tiene grosor y se extiende infinitamente.	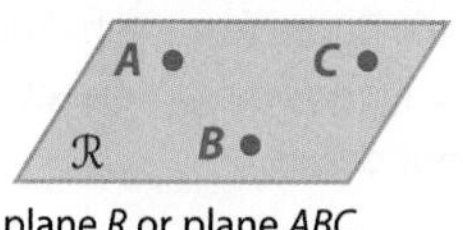 plane *R* or plane *ABC*
plane symmetry A three-dimensional figure that can be divided into two congruent reflected halves by a plane has plane symmetry.	**simetría de plano** Una figura tridimensional que se puede dividir en dos mitades congruentes reflejadas por un plano tiene simetría de plano.	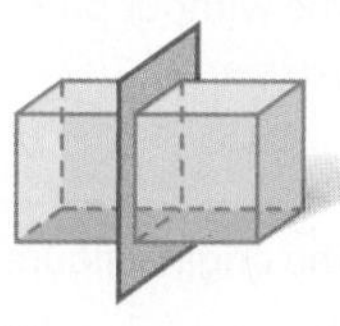 Plane symmetry
Platonic solid One of the five regular polyhedra: a tetrahedron, a cube, an octahedron, a dodecahedron, or an icosahedron.	**sólido platónico** Uno de los cinco poliedros regulares: tetraedro, cubo, octaedro, dodecaedro o icosaedro.	
point An undefined term in geometry, it names a location and has no size.	**punto** Término indefinido de la geometría que denomina una ubicación y no tiene tamaño.	*P* • point *P*
point of concurrency A point where three or more lines coincide.	**punto de concurrencia** Punto donde se cruzan tres o más líneas.	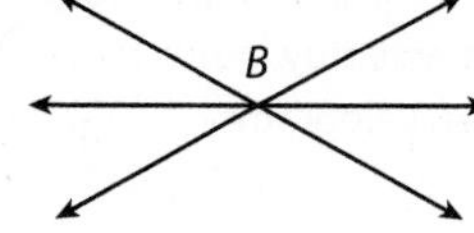

Glossary/Glosario

ENGLISH	SPANISH	EXAMPLES
point of tangency The point of intersection of a circle or sphere with a tangent line or plane.	**punto de tangencia** Punto de intersección de un círculo o esfera con una línea o plano tangente.	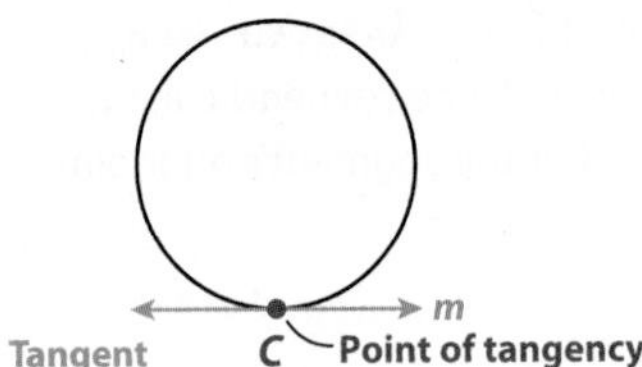
point-slope form $y - y_1 = m(x - x_1)$, where m is the slope and (x_1, y_1) is a point on the line.	**forma de punto y pendiente** $(y - y_1) = m(x - x_1)$, donde m es la pendiente y (x_1, y_1)es un punto en la línea.	
polygon A closed plane figure formed by three or more segments such that each segment intersects exactly two other segments only at their endpoints and no two segments with a common endpoint are collinear. 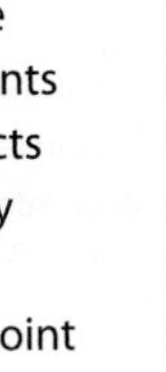	**polígono** Figura plana cerrada formada por tres o más segmentos tal que cada segmento se cruza únicamente con otros dos segmentos sólo en sus extremos y ningún segmento con un extremo común a otro es colineal con éste.	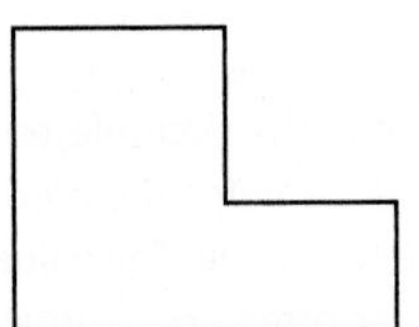
polyhedron A closed three-dimensional figure formed by four or more polygons that intersect only at their edges.	**poliedro** Figura tridimensional cerrada formada por cuatro o más polígonos que se cruzan sólo en sus aristas.	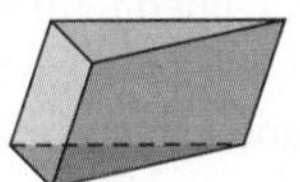
postulate A statement that is accepted as true without proof. Also called an *axiom*.	**postulado** Enunciado que se acepta como verdadero sin demostración. También denominado *axioma*.	
preimage The original figure in a transformation.	**imagen original** Figura original en una transformación.	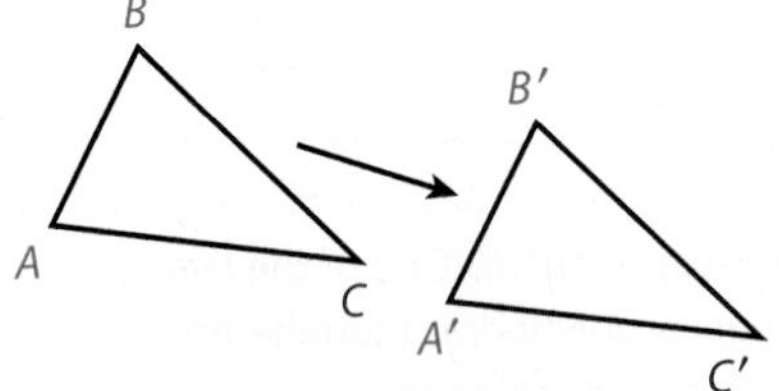
primes Symbols used to label the image in a transformation.	**apóstrofos** Símbolos utilizados para identificar la imagen en una transformación.	A′B′C′
prism A polyhedron formed by two parallel congruent polygonal bases connected by lateral faces that are parallelograms.	**prisma** Poliedro formado por dos bases poligonales congruentes y paralelas conectadas por caras laterales que son paralelogramos.	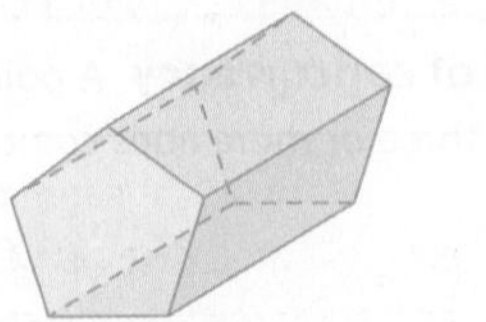
probability A number from 0 to 1 (or 0% to 100%) that is the measure of how likely an event is to occur.	**probabilidad** Número entre 0 y 1 (o entre 0% y 100%) que describe cuán probable es que ocurra un suceso.	A bag contains 3 red marbles and 4 blue marbles. The probability of randomly choosing a red marble is $\frac{3}{7}$.

Glossary/Glosario

ENGLISH	SPANISH	EXAMPLES
proof An argument that uses logic to show that a conclusion is true.	**demostración** Argumento que se vale de la lógica para probar que una conclusión es verdadera.	
proof by contradiction *See* indirect proof.	**demostración por contradicción** *Ver* demostración indirecta.	
pyramid A polyhedron formed by a polygonal base and triangular lateral faces that meet at a common vertex.	**pirámide** Poliedro formado por una base poligonal y caras laterales triangulares que se encuentran en un vértice común.	
Pythagorean triple A set of three nonzero whole numbers a, b, and c such that $a^2 + b^2 = c^2$.	**Tripleta de Pitágoras** Conjunto de tres números cabales distintos de cero a, b y c tal que $a^2 + b^2 = c^2$.	$\{3, 4, 5\}$ $3^2 + 4^2 = 5^2$

Q

ENGLISH	SPANISH	EXAMPLES
quadrilateral A four-sided polygon.	**cuadrilátero** Polígono de cuatro lados.	

R

ENGLISH	SPANISH	EXAMPLES
radial symmetry *See* rotational symmetry.	**simetría radial** *Ver* simetría de rotación.	
radian A unit of angle measure based on arc length. In a circle of radius r, if a central angle has a measure of 1 radian, then the length of the intercepted arc is r units. 2π radians $= 360°$ 1 radian $\approx 57°$	**radián** Unidad de medida de un ángulo basada en la longitud del arco. En un círculo de radio r, si un ángulo central mide 1 radián, entonces la longitud del arco abarcado es r unidades. 2π radians $= 360°$ 1 radian $\approx 57°$	r r O $\theta = 1$ radian
radius of a circle A segment whose endpoints are the center of a circle and a point on the circle; the distance from the center of a circle to any point on the circle.	**radio de un círculo** Segmento cuyos extremos son el centro y un punto de la circunferencia; distancia desde el centro de un círculo hasta cualquier punto de la circunferencia.	Radius
radius of a sphere A segment whose endpoints are the center of a sphere and any point on the sphere; the distance from the center of a sphere to any point on the sphere.	**radio de una esfera** Segmento cuyos extremos son el centro de una esfera y cualquier punto sobre la esfera; distancia desde el centro de una esfera hasta cualquier punto sobre la esfera.	r

Glossary/Glosario

ENGLISH	SPANISH	EXAMPLES
ray A part of a line that starts at an endpoint and extends forever in one direction.	**rayo** Parte de una línea que comienza en un extremo y se extiende infinitamente en una dirección.	
rectangle A quadrilateral with four right angles.	**rectángulo** Cuadrilátero con cuatro ángulos rectos.	
reduction A dilation with a scale factor greater than 0 but less than 1. In a reduction, the image is smaller than the preimage.	**reducción** Dilatación con un factor de escala mayor que 0 pero menor que 1. En una reducción, la imagen es más pequeña que la imagen original.	
reflection A transformation across a line, called the line of reflection, such that the line of reflection is the perpendicular bisector of each segment joining each point and its image.	**reflexión** Transformación sobre una línea, denominada la línea de reflexión. La línea de reflexión es la mediatriz de cada segmento que une un punto con su imagen.	
reflection symmetry *See* line symmetry.	**simetría de reflexión** *Ver* simetría axial.	
regular polygon A polygon that is both equilateral and equiangular.	**polígono regular** Polígono equilátero de ángulos iguales.	
regular polyhedron A polyhedron in which all faces are congruent regular polygons and the same number of faces meet at each vertex. *See also* Platonic solid.	**poliedro regular** Poliedro cuyas caras son todas polígonos regulares congruentes y en el que el mismo número de caras se encuentran en cada vértice. *Ver también* sólido platónico.	
regular pyramid A pyramid whose base is a regular polygon and whose lateral faces are congruent isosceles triangles.	**pirámide regular** Pirámide cuya base es un polígono regular y cuyas caras laterales son triángulos isósceles congruentes.	
remote interior angle An interior angle of a polygon that is not adjacent to the exterior angle.	**ángulo interno remoto** Ángulo interno de un polígono que no es adyacente al ángulo externo.	The remote interior angles of $\angle 4$ are $\angle 1$ and $\angle 2$.

ENGLISH	SPANISH	EXAMPLES
rhombus A quadrilateral with four congruent sides.	**rombo** Cuadrilátero con cuatro lados congruentes.	
right angle An angle that measures 90°.	**ángulo recto** Ángulo que mide 90°.	
right cone A cone whose axis is perpendicular to its base.	**cono recto** Cono cuyo eje es perpendicular a su base.	Axis
right cylinder A cylinder whose axis is perpendicular to its bases.	**cilindro recto** Cilindro cuyo eje es perpendicular a sus bases.	Axis
right prism A prism whose lateral faces are all rectangles.	**prisma recto** Prisma cuyas caras laterales son todas rectángulos.	
right triangle A triangle with one right angle.	**triángulo rectángulo** Triángulo con un ángulo recto.	
rigid motion *See* isometry.	**movimiento rígido** *Ver* isometría.	
rigid transformation A transformation that does not change the size or shape of a figure.	**transformación rígida** Transformación que no cambia el tamaño o la forma de una figura.	
rise The difference in the *y*-values of two points on a line.	**distancia vertical** Diferencia entre los valores de *y* de dos puntos de una línea.	For the points $(3, -1)$ and $(6, 5)$, the rise is $5 - (-1) = 6$.
rotation A transformation about a point *P*, also known as the center of rotation, such that each point and its image are the same distance from *P*. All of the angles with vertex *P* formed by a point and its image are congruent.	**rotación** Transformación sobre un punto *P*, también conocido como el centro de rotación, tal que cada punto y su imagen estén a la misma distancia de *P*. Todos los ángulos con vértice *P* formados por un punto y su imagen son congruentes.	F′ E′ G′ D′ G F P D E

Glossary/Glosario

ENGLISH	SPANISH	EXAMPLES
rotational symmetry A figure that can be rotated about a point by an angle less than 360° so that the image coincides with the preimage has rotational symmetry.	**simetría de rotación** Una figura que puede rotarse alrededor de un punto en un ángulo menor de 360° de forma tal que la imagen coincide con la imagen original tiene simetría de rotación.	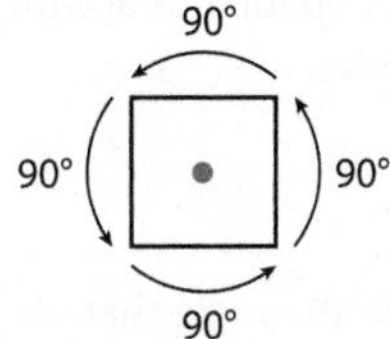 Order of rotational symmetry: 4
run The difference in the x-values of two points on a line.	**distancia horizontal** Diferencia entre los valores de x de dos puntos de una línea.	For the points $(3, -1)$ and $(6, 5)$, the run is $6 - 3 = 3$.

S

ENGLISH	SPANISH	EXAMPLES
same-side interior angles For two lines intersected by a transversal, a pair of angles that lie on the same side of the transversal and between the two lines.	**ángulos internos del mismo lado** Dadas dos líneas cortadas por una transversal, el par de ángulos ubicados en el mismo lado de la transversal y entre las dos líneas.	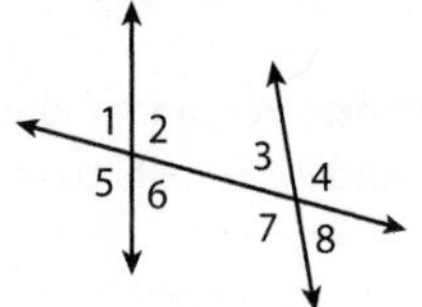 $\angle 2$ and $\angle 3$ are same-side interior angles.
sample space The set of all possible outcomes of a probability experiment.	**espacio muestral** Conjunto de todos los resultados posibles de un experimento de probabilidad.	In the experiment of rolling a number cube, the sample space is $\{1, 2, 3, 4, 5, 6\}$.
scale The ratio between two corresponding measurements.	**escala** Razón entre dos medidas correspondientes.	1 cm : 5 mi
scale drawing A drawing that uses a scale to represent an object as smaller or larger than the actual object.	**dibujo a escala** Dibujo que utiliza una escala para representar un objeto como más pequeño o más grande que el objeto original.	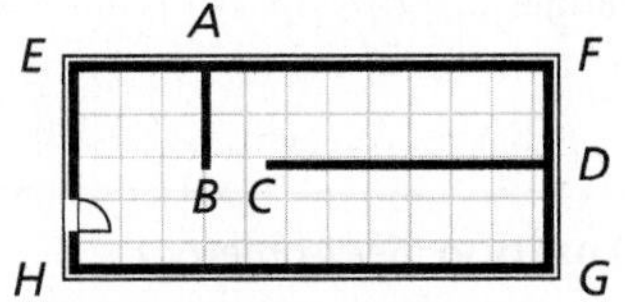 A blueprint is an example of a scale drawing.
scale factor The multiplier used on each dimension to change one figure into a similar figure.	**factor de escala** El multiplicador utilizado en cada dimensión para transformar una figura en una figura semejante.	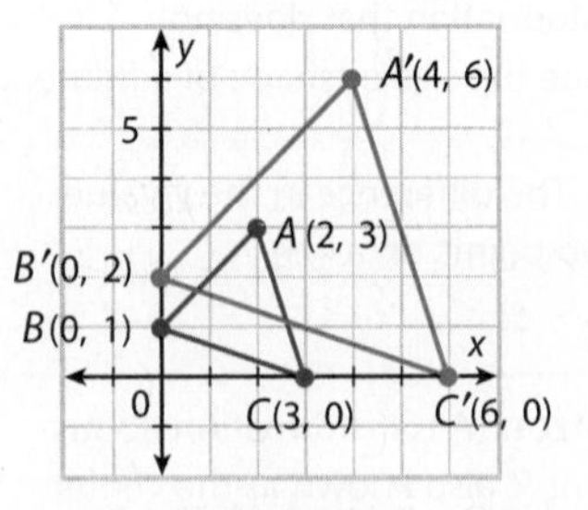 Scale factor: 2
scale model A three-dimensional model that uses a scale to represent an object as smaller or larger than the actual object.	**modelo a escala** Modelo tridimensional que utiliza una escala para representar un objeto como más pequeño o más grande que el objeto real.	

ENGLISH	SPANISH	EXAMPLES
scalene triangle A triangle with no congruent sides.	**triángulo escaleno** Triángulo sin lados congruentes.	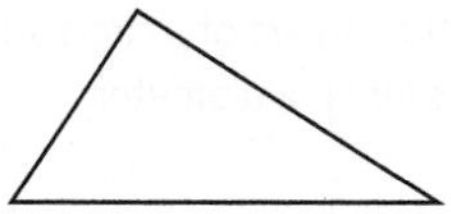
secant of a circle A line that intersects a circle at two points.	**secante de un círculo** Línea que corta un círculo en dos puntos.	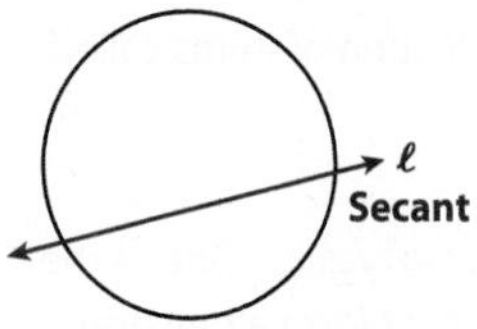 ℓ Secant
secant of an angle In a right triangle, the ratio of the length of the hypotenuse to the length of the side adjacent to angle *A*. It is the reciprocal of the cosine function.	**secante de un ángulo** En un triángulo rectángulo, la razón entre la longitud de la hipotenusa y la longitud del cateto adyacente al ángulo *A*. Es la inversa de la función coseno.	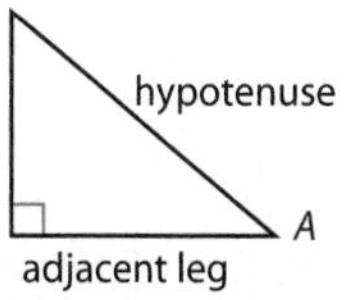 hypotenuse, adjacent leg, *A*; $\sec A = \frac{\text{hypotenuse}}{\text{adjacent}} = \frac{1}{\cos A}$
secant segment A segment of a secant with at least one endpoint on the circle.	**segmento secante** Segmento de una secante que tiene al menos un extremo sobre el círculo.	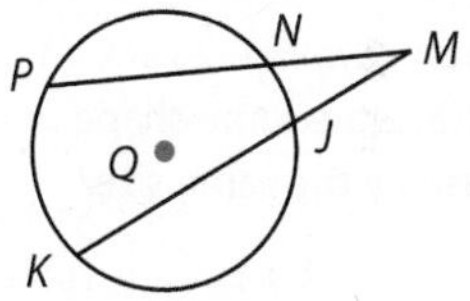 *P*, *N*, *M*, *J*, *Q*, *K*; $\overline{NM}$ is an external secant segment. $\overline{JK}$ is an internal secant segment.
sector of a circle A region inside a circle bounded by two radii of the circle and their intercepted arc.	**sector de un círculo** Región dentro de un círculo delimitado por dos radios del círculo y por su arco abarcado.	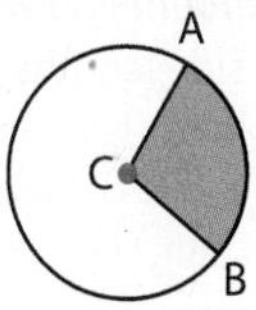 A, C, B
segment bisector A line, ray, or segment that divides a segment into two congruent segments.	**bisectriz de un segmento** Línea, rayo o segmento que divide un segmento en dos segmentos congruentes.	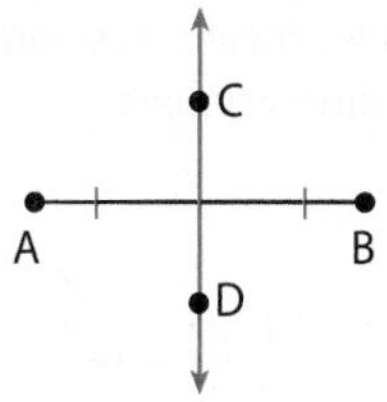 C, A, B, D
segment of a circle A region inside a circle bounded by a chord and an arc.	**segmento de un círculo** Región dentro de un círculo delimitada por una cuerda y un arco.	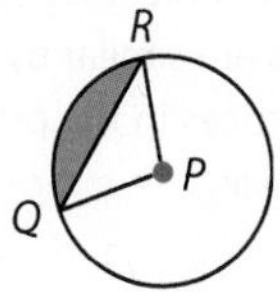 *R*, *P*, *Q*
segment of a line A part of a line consisting of two endpoints and all points between them.	**segmento de una línea** Parte de una línea que consiste en dos extremos y todos los puntos entre éstos.	 A, B

ENGLISH	SPANISH	EXAMPLES

semicircle An arc of a circle whose endpoints lie on a diameter.

semicírculo Arco de un círculo cuyos extremos se encuentran sobre un diámetro.

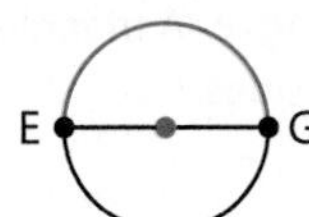

---

set A collection of items called elements.

conjunto Grupo de componentes denominados elementos.

$\{1, 2, 3\}$

---

side of a polygon One of the segments that form a polygon.

lado de un polígono Uno de los segmentos que forman un polígono.

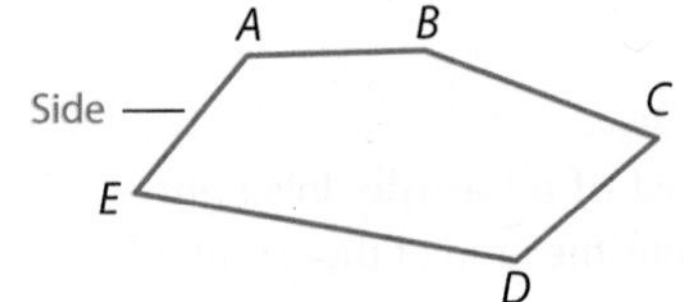

---

side of an angle One of the two rays that form an angle.

lado de un ángulo Uno de los dos rayos que forman un ángulo.

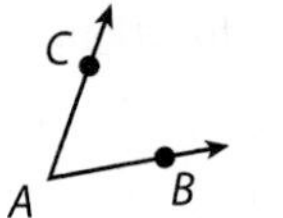

$\overrightarrow{AC}$ and $\overrightarrow{AB}$ are sides of $\angle CAB$.

---

similar Two figures are similar if they have the same shape but not necessarily the same size.

semejantes Dos figuras con la misma forma pero no necesariamente del mismo tamaño.

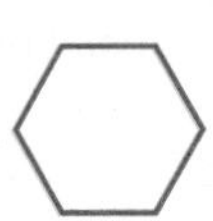 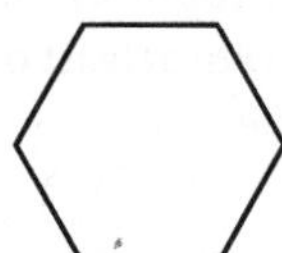

---

similar polygons Two polygons whose corresponding angles are congruent and whose corresponding side lengths are proportional.

polígonos semejantes Dos polígonos cuyos ángulos correspondientes son congruentes y cuyos lados correspondientes tienen longitudes proporcionales.

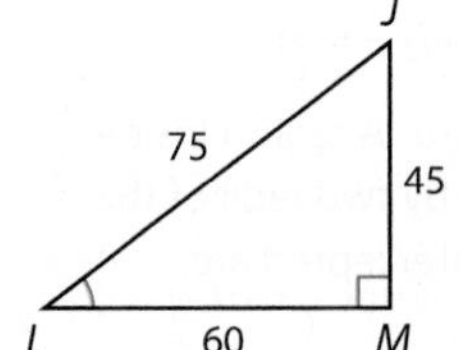

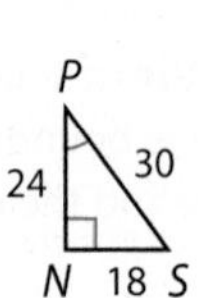

---

similarity ratio The ratio of two corresponding linear measurements in a pair of similar figures.

razón de semejanza Razón de dos medidas lineales correspondientes en un par de figuras semejantes.

Similarity ratio: $\frac{3.5}{2.1} = \frac{5}{3}$

---

similarity statement A statement that indicates that two polygons are similar by listing the vertices in the order of correspondence.

enunciado de semejanza Enunciado que indica que dos polígonos son semejantes enumerando los vértices en orden de correspondencia.

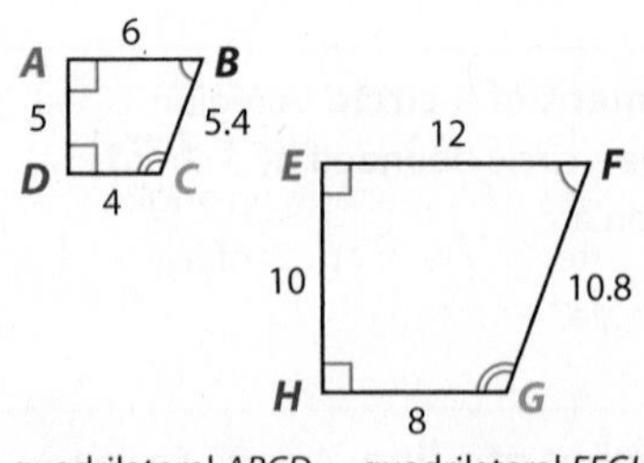

quadrilateral $ABCD \sim$ quadrilateral $EFGH$

---

similarity transformation A transformation that produces similar figures.

transformación de semejanza Una transformación que resulta en figuras semejantes.

Dilations are similarity transformations.

ENGLISH	SPANISH	EXAMPLES
simple event An event consisting of only one outcome.	**suceso simple** Suceso que contiene sólo un resultado.	In the experiment of rolling a number cube, the event consisting of the outcome 3 is a simple event.
sine In a right triangle, the ratio of the length of the leg opposite $\angle A$ to the length of the hypotenuse.	**seno** En un triángulo rectángulo, razón entre la longitud del cateto opuesto a $\angle A$ y la longitud de la hipotenusa.	opposite, hypotenuse, A $\sin A = \frac{\text{opposite}}{\text{hypotenuse}}$
skew lines Lines that are not coplanar.	**líneas oblicuas** Líneas que no son coplanares.	A, B, E, F, C, D, G, H $\overleftrightarrow{AE}$ and $\overleftrightarrow{CD}$ are skew lines.
slide *See* translation.	**deslizamiento** *Ver* traslación.	
slope A measure of the steepness of a line. If (x_1, y_1) and (x_2, y_2) are any two points on the line, the slope of the line, known as m, is represented by the equation $m = \frac{y_2 - y_1}{x_2 - x_1}$.	**pendiente** Medida de la inclinación de una línea. Dados dos puntos (x_1, y_1) y (x_2, y_2) en una línea, la pendiente de la línea, denominada m, se representa con la ecuación $m = \frac{y_2 - y_1}{x_2 - x_1}$.	
slope-intercept form The slope-intercept form of a linear equation is $y = mx + b$, where m is the slope and b is the y-intercept.	**forma de pendiente-intersección** La forma de pendiente-intersección de una ecuación lineal es $y = mx + b$, donde m es la pendiente y b es la intersección con el eje y.	$y = -2x + 4$ The slope is -2. The y-intercept is 4.
solid A three-dimensional figure.	**cuerpo geométrico** Figura tridimensional.	
solving a triangle Using given measures to find unknown angle measures or side lengths of a triangle.	**resolución de un triángulo** Utilizar medidas dadas para hallar las medidas desconocidas de los ángulos o las longitudes de los lados de un triángulo.	
special right triangle A 45°—45°—90° triangle or a 30°—60°—90° triangle.	**triángulo rectángulo especial** Triángulo de 45°—45°—90° o triángulo de 30°—60°—90°.	A, B, C, 2s, 60°, s, 30°, $s\sqrt{3}$ B, A, C, $\ell\sqrt{2}$, 45°, ℓ, 45°, ℓ

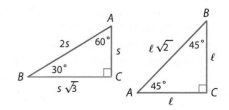

Glossary/Glosario

ENGLISH	SPANISH	EXAMPLES
sphere The set of points in space that are a fixed distance from a given point called the center of the sphere.	**esfera** Conjunto de puntos en el espacio que se encuentran a una distancia fija de un punto determinado denominado centro de la esfera.	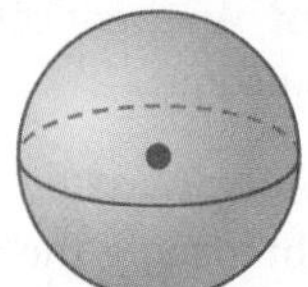
square A quadrilateral with four congruent sides and four right angles.	**cuadrado** Cuadrilátero con cuatro lados congruentes y cuatro ángulos rectos.	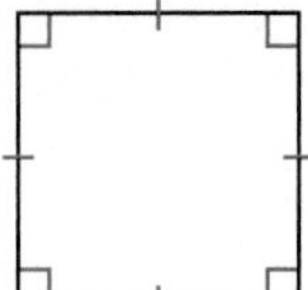
straight angle A 180° angle.	**ángulo llano** Ángulo que mide 180°.	
subset A set that is contained entirely within another set. Set B is a subset of set A if every element of B is contained in A, denoted $B \subset A$.	**subconjunto** Conjunto que se encuentra dentro de otro conjunto. El conjunto *B* es un subconjunto del conjunto *A* si todos los elementos de *B* son elementos de *A*; se expresa $B \subset A$.	The set of integers is a subset of the set of rational numbers.
supplementary angles Two angles whose measures have a sum of 180°.	**ángulos suplementarios** Dos ángulos cuyas medidas suman 180°.	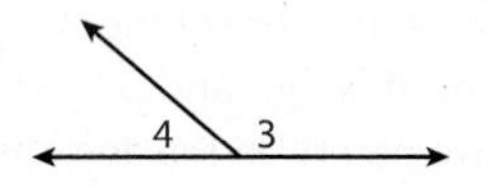 $\angle 3$ and $\angle 4$ are supplementary angles.
surface area The total area of all faces and curved surfaces of a three-dimensional figure.	**área total** Área total de todas las caras y superficies curvas de una figura tridimensional.	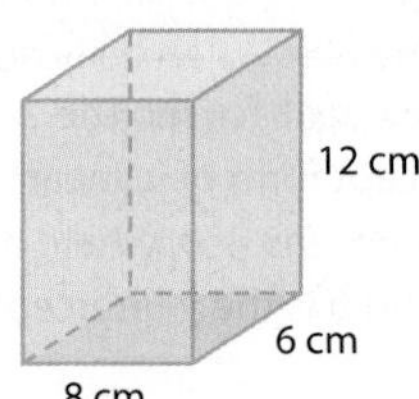 Surface area $= 2(8)(12) + 2(8)(6) + 2(12)(6) = 432 \text{ cm}^2$
symmetry In the transformation of a figure such that the image coincides with the preimage, the image and preimage have symmetry.	**simetría** En la transformación de una figura tal que la imagen coincide con la imagen original, la imagen y la imagen original tienen simetría.	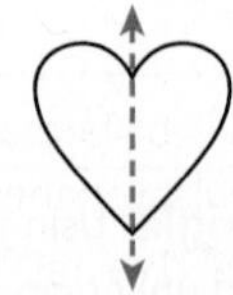
symmetry about an axis In the transformation of a figure such that there is a line about which a three-dimensional figure can be rotated by an angle greater than 0° and less than 360° so that the image coincides with the preimage, the image and preimage have symmetry about an axis.	**simetría axial** En la transformación de una figura tal que existe una línea sobre la cual se puede rotar una figura tridimensional a un ángulo mayor que 0° y menor que 360° de forma que la imagen coincida con la imagen original, la imagen y la imagen original tienen simetría axial.	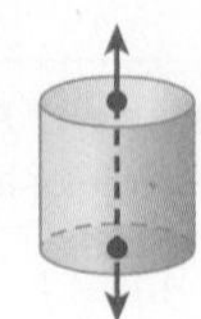

ENGLISH	SPANISH	EXAMPLES

T

tangent circles Two coplanar circles that intersect at exactly one point. If one circle is contained inside the other, they are *internally tangent*. If not, they are *externally tangent*.

círculos tangentes Dos círculos coplanares que se cruzan únicamente en un punto. Si un círculo contiene a otro, son *tangentes internamente*. De lo contrario, son *tangentes externamente*.

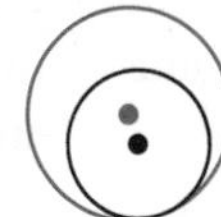

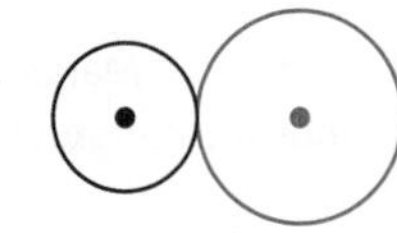

tangent of an angle In a right triangle, the ratio of the length of the leg opposite $\angle A$ to the length of the leg adjacent to $\angle A$.

tangente de un ángulo En un triángulo rectángulo, razón entre la longitud del cateto opuesto a $\angle A$ y la longitud del cateto adyacente a $\angle A$.

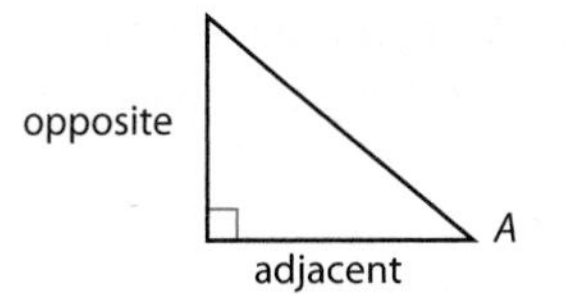

$$\tan A = \frac{\text{opposite}}{\text{adjacent}}$$

tangent segment A segment of a tangent with one endpoint on the circle.

segmento tangente Segmento de una tangente con un extremo en el círculo.

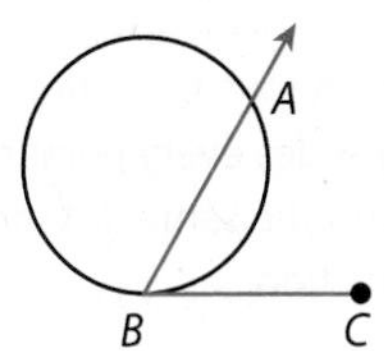

$\overline{BC}$ is a tangent segment.

tangent of a circle A line that is in the same plane as a circle and intersects the circle at exactly one point.

tangente de un círculo Línea que se encuentra en el mismo plano que un círculo y lo cruza únicamente en un punto.

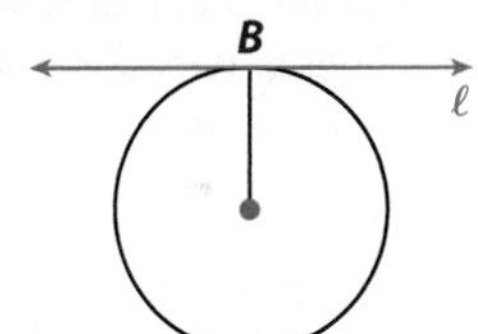

terminal point of a vector The endpoint of a vector.

punto terminal de un vector Extremo de un vector.

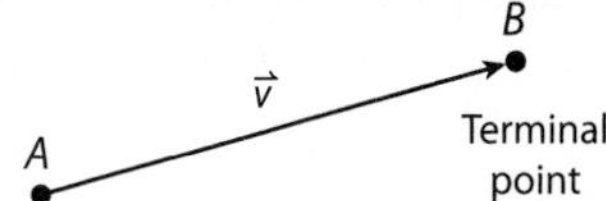

tetrahedron A polyhedron with four faces. A regular tetrahedron has equilateral triangles as faces, with three faces meeting at each vertex.

tetraedro Poliedro con cuatro caras. Las caras de un tetraedro regular son triángulos equiláteros y cada vértice es compartido por tres caras.

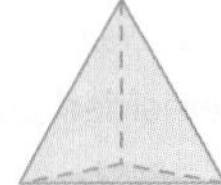

theorem A statement that has been proven.

teorema Enunciado que ha sido demostrado.

ENGLISH	SPANISH	EXAMPLES
theoretical probability The ratio of the number of equally likely outcomes in an event to the total number of possible outcomes.	**probabilidad teórica** Razón entre el número de resultados igualmente probables de un suceso y el número total de resultados posibles.	In the experiment of rolling a number cube, the theoretical probability of rolling an odd number is $\frac{3}{6} = \frac{1}{2}$.
tick marks Marks used on a figure to indicate congruent segments.	**marcas "|"** Marcas utilizadas en una figura para indicar segmentos congruentes.	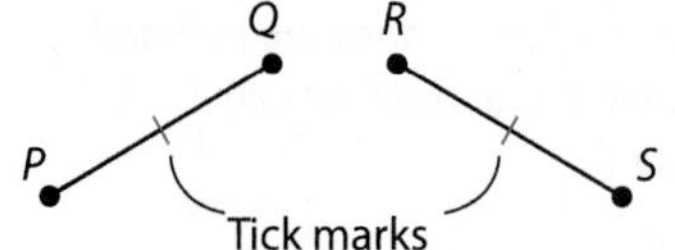
transformation A change in the position, size, or shape of a figure or graph.	**transformación** Cambio en la posición, tamaño o forma de una figura o gráfica.	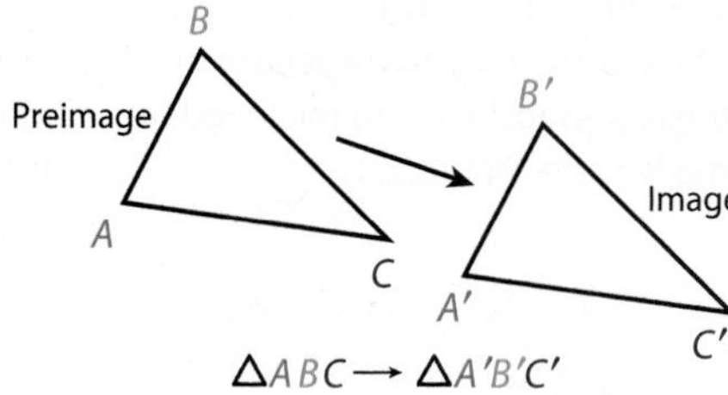
translation A transformation that shifts or slides every point of a figure or graph the same distance in the same direction.	**traslación** Transformación en la que todos los puntos de una figura o gráfica se mueven la misma distancia en la misma dirección.	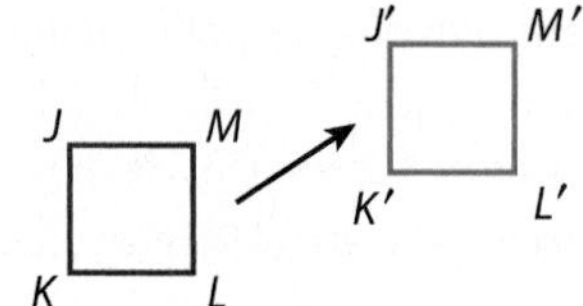
transversal A line that intersects two coplanar lines at two different points.	**transversal** Línea que corta dos líneas coplanares en dos puntos diferentes.	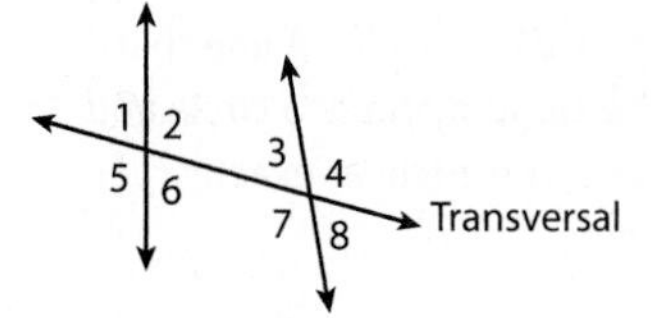
trapezoid A quadrilateral with at least one pair of parallel sides.	**trapecio** Cuadrilátero con al menos un par de lados paralelos.	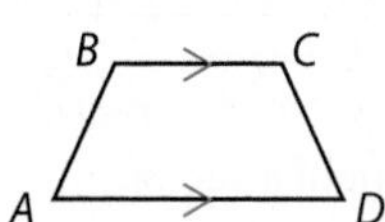
trial In probability, a single repetition or observation of an experiment.	**prueba** En probabilidad, una sola repetición u observación de un experimento.	In the experiment of rolling a number cube, each roll is one trial.
triangle A three-sided polygon.	**triángulo** Polígono de tres lados.	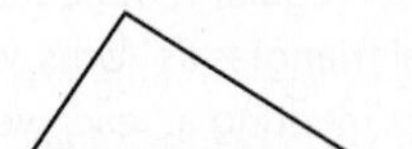
triangle rigidity A property of triangles that states that if the side lengths of a triangle are fixed, the triangle can have only one shape.	**rigidez del triángulo** Propiedad de los triángulos que establece que, si las longitudes de los lados de un triángulo son fijas, el triángulo puede tener sólo una forma.	

ENGLISH	SPANISH	EXAMPLES
trigonometric ratio A ratio of two sides of a right triangle.	**razón trigonométrica** Razón entre dos lados de un triángulo rectángulo.	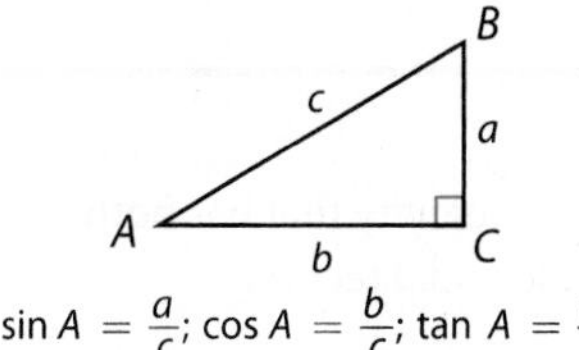 $\sin A = \frac{a}{c}$; $\cos A = \frac{b}{c}$; $\tan A = \frac{a}{b}$
trigonometry The study of the measurement of triangles and of trigonometric functions and their applications.	**trigonometría** Estudio de la medición de los triángulos y de las funciones trigonométricas y sus aplicaciones.	
trisect To divide into three equal parts.	**trisecar** Dividir en tres partes iguales.	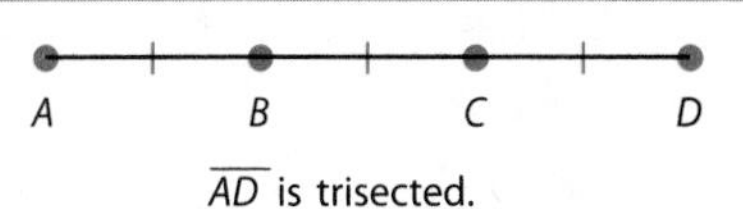 $\overline{AD}$ is trisected.
truth table A table that lists all possible combinations of truth values for a statement and its components.	**tabla de verdad** Tabla en la que se enumeran todas las combinaciones posibles de valores de verdad para un enunciado y sus componentes.	
truth value A statement can have a truth value of true (T) or false (F).	**valor de verdad** Un enunciado puede tener un valor de verdad verdadero (V) o falso (F).	

U

ENGLISH	SPANISH	EXAMPLES
undefined term A basic figure that is not defined in terms of other figures. The undefined terms in geometry are point, line, and plane.	**término indefinido** Figura básica que no está definida en función de otras figuras. Los términos indefinidos en geometría son el punto, la línea y el plano.	
union The union of two sets is the set of all elements that are in either set, denoted by ∪.	**unión** La unión de dos conjuntos es el conjunto de todos los elementos que se encuentran en ambos conjuntos, expresado por ∪.	$A = \{1, 2, 3, 4\}$ $B = \{1, 3, 5, 7, 9\}$ $A \cup B = \{1, 2, 3, 4, 5, 7, 9\}$
universal set The set of all elements in a particular context.	**conjunto universal** Conjunto de todos los elementos de un contexto determinado.	

Glossary/Glosario

ENGLISH	SPANISH	EXAMPLES

V

vector A quantity that has both magnitude and direction.

vector Cantidad que tiene magnitud y dirección.

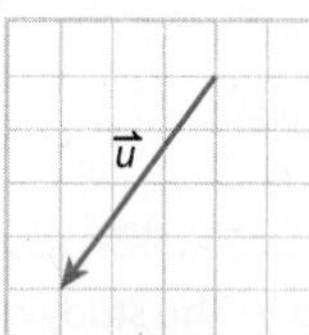

Venn diagram A diagram used to show relationships between sets.

diagrama de Venn Diagrama utilizado para mostrar la relación entre conjuntos.

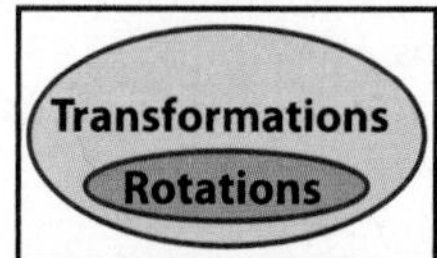

vertex angle of an isosceles triangle The angle formed by the legs of an isosceles triangle.

ángulo del vértice de un triángulo isósceles Ángulo formado por los catetos de un triángulo isósceles.

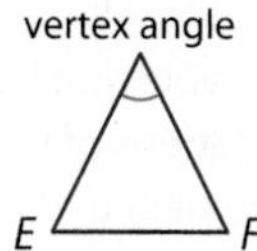

vertex of a cone The point opposite the base of the cone.

vértice de un cono Punto opuesto a la base del cono.

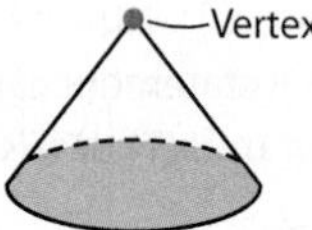

vertex of a parabola The highest or lowest point on the parabola.

vértice de una parábola Punto más alto o más bajo de una parábola.

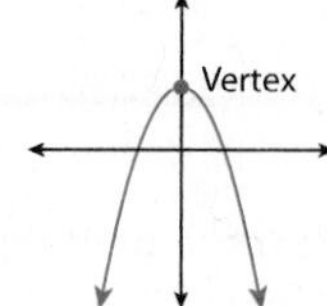

vertex of a polygon The intersection of two sides of the polygon.

vértice de un polígono La intersección de dos lados del polígono.

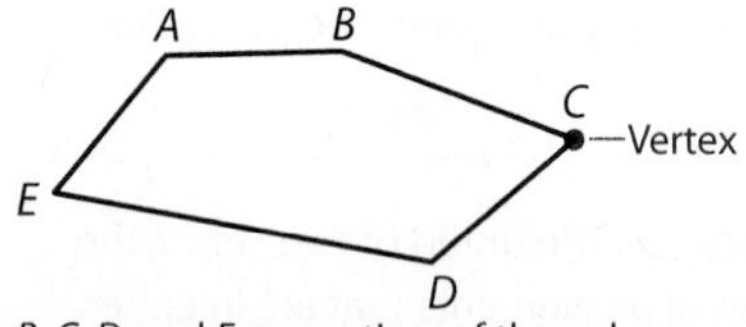

A, *B*, *C*, *D*, and *E* are vertices of the polygon.

vertex of a pyramid The point opposite the base of the pyramid.

vértice de una pirámide Punto opuesto a la base de la pirámide.

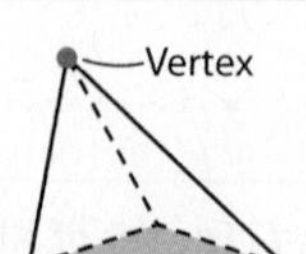

vertex of a three-dimensional figure The point that is the intersection of three or more faces of the figure.

vértice de una figura tridimensional Punto que representa la intersección de tres o más caras de la figura.

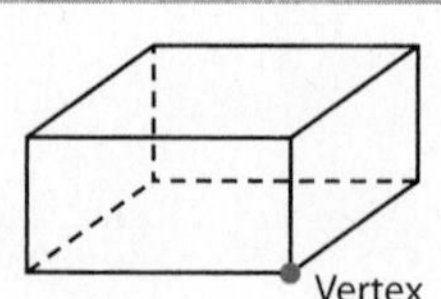

ENGLISH	SPANISH	EXAMPLES
vertex of a triangle The intersection of two sides of the triangle.	**vértice de un triángulo** Intersección de dos lados del triángulo.	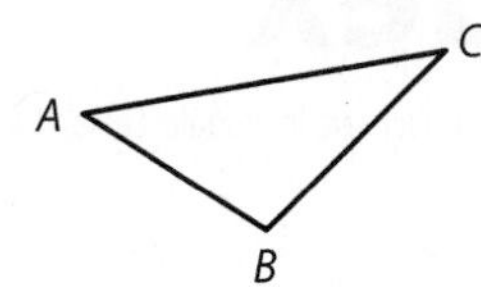 *A*, *B*, and *C* are vertices of $\triangle ABC$.
vertex of an angle The common endpoint of the sides of the angle.	**vértice de un ángulo** Extremo común de los lados del ángulo.	*A* is the vertex of $\angle CAB$.
vertical angles The nonadjacent angles formed by two intersecting lines.	**ángulos opuestos por el vértice** Ángulos no adyacentes formados por dos rectas que se cruzan.	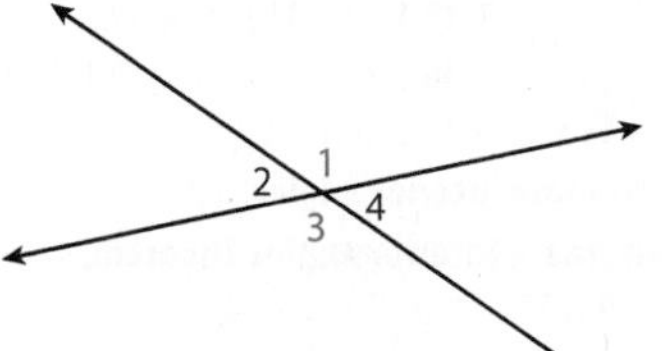 $\angle 1$ and $\angle 3$ are vertical angles. $\angle 2$ and $\angle 4$ are vertical angles.
volume The number of nonoverlapping unit cubes of a given size that will exactly fill the interior of a three-dimensional figure.	**volumen** Cantidad de cubos unitarios no superpuestos de un determinado tamaño que llenan exactamente el interior de una figura tridimensional.	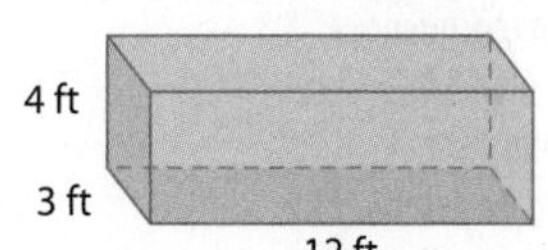 Volume $= (3)(4)(12) = 144 \text{ ft}^3$

***x*-axis** The horizontal axis in a coordinate plane.	**eje *x*** Eje horizontal en un plano cartesiano.	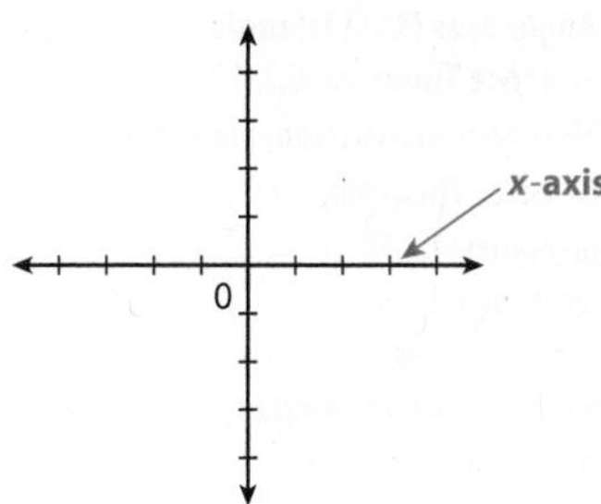

Y

***y*-axis** The vertical axis in a coordinate plane.	**eje *y*** Eje vertical en un plano cartesiano.	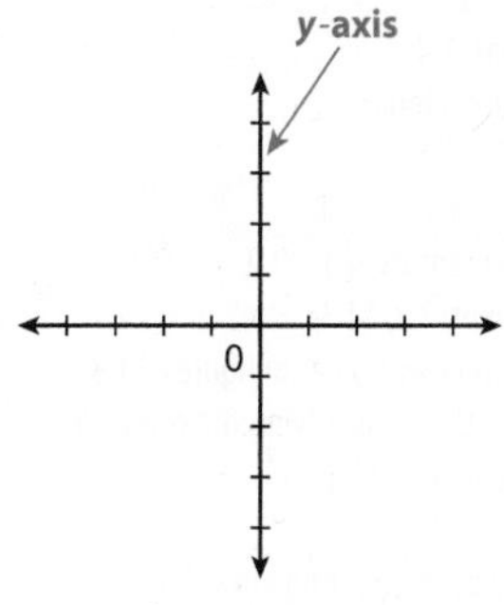

Index

Index locator numbers are in Module. Lesson form. For example, 2.1 indicates Module 2, Lesson 1 as listed in the Table of Contents.

D

E

F

Index

G

H

I

K

L

M

Q

R

S

T

U

V

Z

Index

Table of Measures

LENGTH

1 inch = 2.54 centimeters
1 meter = 39.37 inches
1 mile = 5,280 feet
1 mile = 1760 yards
1 mile = 1.609 kilometers
1 kilometer = 0.62 mile

MASS/WEIGHT

1 pound = 16 ounces
1 pound = 0.454 kilograms
1 kilogram = 2.2 pounds
1 ton = 2000 pounds

CAPACITY

1 cup = 8 fluid ounces
1 pint = 2 cups
1 quart = 2 pints
1 gallon = 4 quarts
1 gallon = 3.785 liters
1 liter = 0.264 gallons
1 liter = 1000 cubic centimeters

Symbols

$\neq$	is not equal to
$\approx$	is approximately equal to
10^2	ten squared; ten to the second power
$2.\overline{6}$	repeating decimal 2.66666...
$\lvert -4 \rvert$	the absolute value of negative 4
$\sqrt{}$	square root
π	pi: (about 3.14)
$\perp$	is perpendicular to
$\parallel$	is parallel to
$\overleftrightarrow{AB}$	line AB
$\overrightarrow{AB}$	ray AB
$\overline{AB}$	line segment AB
$m\angle A$	measure of $\angle A$

Formulas

Triangle	$A = \frac{1}{2}bh$
Parallelogram	$A = bh$
Circle	$A = \pi r^2$
Circle	$C = \pi d$ or $C = 2\pi r$
General Prisms	$V = Bh$
Cylinder	$V = \pi r^2 h$
Sphere	$V = \frac{4}{3}\pi r^3$
Cone	$V = \frac{1}{3}\pi r^2 h$
Pyramid	$V = \frac{1}{3}Bh$

Pythagorean Theorem	$a^2 + b^2 = c^2$
Quadratic Formula	$x = \frac{-b \pm \sqrt{b^2 - 4ac}}{2a}$
Arithmetic Sequence	$a_n = a_1 + (n - 1)d$
Geometric Sequence	$a_n = a_1 r^{n-1}$
Geometric Series	$S_n = \frac{a_1 - a_1 r^n}{1 - r}$ where $r \neq 1$
Radians	$1\ radian = \frac{180}{\pi}\ degrees$
Degrees	$1\ degree = \frac{\pi}{180}\ radians$
Exponential Growth/Decay	$A = A_0 e^{k(t - t_0)} + B_0$